The N.E.B. is
recommended by
archbishop Stewart

Rom 3.23
JERA 17; 9
Rom 6:23

Heb 9:27

Rom 2: 1
? 2 Peter 3:12
 Acts 17:30
 Rom 10:17
 John 1:12
[John 5:13
 John 14:15
 Math 10:32
Galatians 5: 22,23 Fruit of the
spirit.

THE NEW
ENGLISH BIBLE

WITH THE APOCRYPHA
OXFORD STUDY EDITION

THE BIBLE
A NEW ENGLISH TRANSLATION

Directed by Representatives of

THE BAPTIST UNION OF GREAT BRITAIN AND IRELAND

THE CHURCH OF ENGLAND

THE CHURCH OF SCOTLAND

THE COUNCIL OF CHURCHES FOR WALES

THE IRISH COUNCIL OF CHURCHES

THE LONDON YEARLY MEETING OF
THE SOCIETY OF FRIENDS

THE METHODIST CHURCH OF GREAT BRITAIN

THE ROMAN CATHOLIC CHURCH IN
ENGLAND AND WALES

THE ROMAN CATHOLIC CHURCH IN IRELAND

THE ROMAN CATHOLIC CHURCH
IN SCOTLAND

THE UNITED REFORMED CHURCH

THE BRITISH AND FOREIGN BIBLE SOCIETY

THE NATIONAL BIBLE SOCIETY OF SCOTLAND

The publication of the books of the Apocrypha in this translation prepared under the auspices of the Joint Committee on the New Translation of the Bible does not imply that the bodies represented on the Joint Committee hold a common opinion upon the canonical status of these books.

THE NEW ENGLISH BIBLE

WITH THE APOCRYPHA
OXFORD STUDY EDITION

SAMUEL SANDMEL
GENERAL EDITOR

M. JACK SUGGS
NEW TESTAMENT EDITOR

ARNOLD J. TKACIK
APOCRYPHA EDITOR

Introductions, Annotations, Cross-References

Special Articles, Maps, and Indexes

NEW YORK   OXFORD UNIVERSITY PRESS
1976

Library of Congress Catalogue Card Number: 75-32364

PRINTED IN THE UNITED STATES OF AMERICA

CONTENTS

CONTENTS

THE OLD TESTAMENT

THE APOCRYPHA

THE NEW TESTAMENT

SPECIAL ARTICLES

THE EDITORS' PREFACE

The New English Bible is distinctive for its clarity and readability. But more than that, a concern for accuracy in rendering the Hebrew and Greek languages into our tongue has resulted in an achievement rare in translations—the retention of the tone and feeling of the original writings.

Yet there are matters that call for explanation. The introductions and annotations, dealing with the literary, historical, theological, geographical, and archaeological aspects of the text, and the cross-references from one passage to another, provide the reader with ready information that should heighten his appreciation and understanding of the Scriptures.

Both in brevity and in deliberate avoidance of the highly personal viewpoint, the explanations here differ from those found in what is usually called a commentary. There is a splendid array of just such penetrating commentaries available to the student and scholar, but these often reflect special theories or dispositions of the authors. Such characteristics do not occur in this edition, or at least not as a central point. Rather, the explanations bear on findings of recent decades, as provided in published studies of the text, the biblical languages, and biblical archaeology.

Special articles by competent scholars in the field of biblical knowledge yield further data to enhance the reading and study of the Bible.

In our times the scholarly study of the Bible cuts across sectarian lines; hence, both the editors and the contributors represent a diversity of religious persuasions and traditions.

PAUL J. ACHTEMEIER
Union Theological Seminary
Richmond, Virginia
Acts of the Apostles,
1 and 2 Timothy, Titus

LLOYD R. BAILEY
The Divinity School
Duke University
Durham, North Carolina
Genesis, Exodus, Leviticus,
Numbers, Deuteronomy,
Introduction to the Pentateuch

ALBERT BAUMGARTEN
McMaster University
Hamilton, Ontario, Canada
Wisdom of Solomon

WILLIAM BEARDSLEE
Emory University
Atlanta, Georgia
Ecclesiasticus

SHELDON H. BLANK
Hebrew Union College–Jewish Institute
of Religion, Cincinnati, Ohio
Jeremiah

MYLES M. BOURKE
Corpus Christi Church
New York City
Ephesians, Philippians, Colossians,
1 and 2 Thessalonians, Philemon

D. PETER BURROWS
Episcopal Diocese of Western New York
Buffalo, New York

and the late

RICHARD V. BERGREN, JR.
Alfred University
Alfred, New York
Select Index to People, Places, and
Themes in the Bible

JAMES L. CRENSHAW
The Divinity School
Vanderbilt University
Nashville, Tennessee
Job, Proverbs, Ecclesiastes

EDWARD J. CROWLEY
Department of Theology
University of Windsor
Windsor, Ontario, Canada
Joshua, Judges, Ruth, Esther

JOHN J. DREESE
Holy Spirit Church
Columbus, Ohio
A Sketch of the History and Geography of the Lands of the Bible

DEMETRIUS DUMM, O.S.B.
St. Vincent Seminary
Latrobe, Pennsylvania
Tobit, Judith, Rest of Esther

LOREN R. FISHER
School of Theology
Claremont, California
The Psalms

VICTOR P. FURNISH
Perkins School of Theology
Southern Methodist University
Dallas, Texas
Hebrews, James, 1 and 2 Peter, Jude

EDWIN M. GOOD
Stanford University
Stanford, California
The Twelve Prophets

PAUL HAMMER
Colgate Rochester Divinity School/
Bexley Hall/Crozer Theological Seminary
Rochester, New York
Revelation

RICHARD A. HENSHAW
Colgate Rochester Divinity School/
Bexley Hall/Crozer Theological Seminary
Rochester, New York
Song of Songs, Lamentations, Daniel

JOHN C. HURD
Faculty of Divinity
Trinity College
Toronto, Ontario, Canada
Romans, 1 and 2 Corinthians, Galatians

LEANDER E. KECK
Candler School of Theology
Emory University
Atlanta, Georgia
Literary Forms of the Bible
(with Gene M. Tucker)

NEIL J. McELENEY, C.S.P.
Saint Patrick's Seminary
Menlo Park, California
1 and 2 Maccabees

SAMUEL SANDMEL
Hebrew Union College-Jewish Institute
of Religion, Cincinnati, Ohio
Reading the Bible (with M. Jack
Suggs and Arnold J. Tkacik)

DAVID M. STANLEY, S.J.
Regis College
Willowdale, Ontario, Canada
The Gospel of John; 1, 2, and 3 John

CARROLL STUHLMUELLER, C.P.
Catholic Theological Union at Chicago
St. John's University
New York City
Letter of Jeremiah, Baruch

M. JACK SUGGS
Brite Divinity School
Texas Christian University
Fort Worth, Texas
Matthew, Mark, Luke

ARNOLD J. TKACIK, O.S.B.
St. Benedict's College
Atchison, Kansas
*Ezekiel, The Place of the
Apocrypha, Reckoning Time*

GENE M. TUCKER
Candler School of Theology
Emory University
Atlanta, Georgia
Literary Forms of the Bible (with
Leander E. Keck), *Isaiah*

DAVID B. WEISBERG
Hebrew Union College-Jewish Institute
of Religion, Cincinnati, Ohio
Ezra, Nehemiah, 1 Esdras

JAY A. WILCOXEN
The Divinity School
University of Chicago
Chicago, Illinois
*1 and 2 Samuel, 1 and 2 Kings,
1 and 2 Chronicles*

CLYDE M. WOODS
Freed-Hardeman College
Henderson, Tennessee
*2 Esdras, Song of the Three, Daniel
and Susanna, Daniel, Bel and the
Snake, Prayer of Manasseh*

The editors have followed the British spelling (such as labour) only where Scripture is cited (in the introductions, in the annotations, and in the special articles); the American spelling (e.g. labor) is used elsewhere. Also, the editors utilized capitalization for Temple and Law, but retained THE NEW ENGLISH BIBLE usage of temple and law in citations of the biblical text.

The Bishop of Worcester, Massachusetts, the Most Reverend Bernard J. Flanagan, has graciously given THE NEW ENGLISH BIBLE: OXFORD STUDY EDITION, his *imprimatur*. The editors and the publisher are also grateful for the advice and help of the Reverend William Van Etten Casey, S.J., College of the Holy Cross, Worcester, Massachusetts.

PREFACE
TO THE NEW ENGLISH BIBLE

In May 1946 the General Assembly of the Church of Scotland received an overture from the Presbytery of Stirling and Dunblane, where it had been initiated by the Reverend G. S. Hendry, recommending that a translation of the Bible be made in the language of the present day, inasmuch as the language of the Authorized Version, already archaic when it was made, had now become even more definitely archaic and less generally understood. The General Assembly resolved to make an approach to other Churches, and, as a result, delegates of the Church of England, the Church of Scotland, and the Methodist, Baptist, and Congregational Churches met in conference in October. They recommended that the work should be undertaken; that a completely new translation should be made, rather than a revision, such as had earlier been contemplated by the University Presses of Oxford and Cambridge; and that the translators should be free to employ a contemporary idiom rather than reproduce the traditional 'biblical' English.

In January 1947 a second conference, held like the first in the Central Hall, Westminster, included representatives of the University Presses. At the request of this conference, the Churches named above appointed representatives to form the Joint Committee on the New Translation of the Bible. This Committee met for the first time in July of the same year. By January 1948, when its third meeting was held, invitations to be represented had been sent to the Presbyterian Church of England, the Society of Friends, the Churches in Wales, the Churches in Ireland, the British and Foreign Bible Society, and the National Bible Society of Scotland: these invitations were accepted. At a much later stage the hierarchies of the Roman Catholic Church in England and Scotland accepted an invitation to appoint representatives, and these attended as observers.

The Joint Committee provided for the actual work of translation from the original tongues by appointing three panels, to deal, respectively, with the Old Testament, the Apocrypha, and the New Testament. Their members were scholars drawn from various British universities, whom the Committee believed to be representative of competent biblical scholarship at the present time. Apprehending, however, that sound scholarship does not necessarily carry with it a delicate sense of English style, the Committee appointed a fourth panel, of trusted literary advisers, to whom all the work of the translating panels was to be submitted for scrutiny. It should be said that denominational considerations played no part in the appointment of the panels.

The Joint Committee issued general directions to the panels, in pursuance of the aims which the enterprise had in view. The translating panels adopted the following procedure. An individual was invited to submit a draft translation of a particular book, or group of books. Normally he would be a member of the panel concerned. Very occasionally a draft translation was invited from a scholar outside the panel, who was known to have worked specially on the book in question. The draft was circulated in typescript to members of the panel for their consideration. They then met together and discussed the draft round a table, verse by verse, sentence by sentence. Each member brought his view about the meaning of the original to the judgement of his fellows, and discussion went on until they reached a common mind. There are passages where, in the present state of our knowledge, no one could say with certainty which of two (or even more) possible meanings is intended. In such cases, after careful discussion, alternative meanings have been recorded in footnotes, but only where they seemed of sufficient importance. There is probably no member of a panel who has not found himself obliged to give up, perhaps with lingering regret, a cherished view about the meaning of this or that difficult passage, but in the end the panel accepted corporate responsibility for the interpretation set forth in the translation adopted.

The resultant draft was now remitted to the panel of literary advisers. They scrutinized it, once again, verse by verse, sentence by sentence, and took pains to secure, as best they could, the tone and level of language appropriate to the different kinds of writing to be found in the Bible, whether narrative, familiar discourse, argument, law, rhetoric or poetry. The translation thus amended was returned to the translating panel, who examined it to make sure that the meaning intended had not been in any way misunderstood. Passages of peculiar difficulty might on occasion pass repeatedly between the panels. The final form of the version was reached by agreement between the translators concerned and the literary advisers. It was then ready for submission to the Joint Committee.

Since January 1948 the Joint Committee has met regularly twice a year in the Jerusalem Chamber, Westminster Abbey, with four exceptions during 1954–5 when the Langham Room in the precincts of the Abbey was kindly made available. At these meetings the Committee has received reports on the progress of the work from the Conveners of the four panels, and its members have had in their hands typescripts of the books so far translated and revised. They have made such comments and given such advice or decisions as they judged to be necessary, and from time to time they have met members of the panels in conference.

Of the original members of the panels most have happily been able to stay with the work all through, though some have been lost, through death or otherwise, and their places have been filled by fresh appointments.

The Committee has warmly appreciated the courteous hospitality of the Dean of Westminster and of the Trustees of the Central Hall. We owe a great debt to the support and the experienced counsel of the University Presses of Oxford and Cambridge. We recognize gratefully the service rendered to the enterprise by the Reverend Dr. G. S. Hendry and the Reverend Professor J. K. S. Reid, who have successively held the office of Secretary to the Committee. To those who have borne special responsibility, as Chairmen of the Joint Committee, we owe more than could readily be told. Dr. J. W. Hunkin, Bishop of Truro, our first Chairman, brought to the work an exuberant vigour and initiative without which the formidable project might hardly have got off the ground at all. On his lamented death in 1950 he was succeeded by Dr. A. T. P. Williams, then Bishop of Durham and subsequently Bishop of Winchester, who for eighteen years guided our enterprise with judicious wisdom, tact, and benign firmness, but who to our sorrow died when the end of the task was in sight. To both of these we would put on record the gratitude of the Committee and of all engaged in the enterprise.

If we embarked on mentioning the names of those who have served on the various committees and panels, the list would be a long one; and if we mentioned some and not others, the selection would be an invidious one. There are, nevertheless, three names the omission of which would be utterly wrong. As Vice-Chairman and Director, Dr. C. H. Dodd has from start to finish given outstanding leadership and guidance to the project, bringing to the work scholarship, sensitivity, and an ever watchful eye. Professor Sir Godfrey Driver, Joint Director since 1965, has also brought to the work a wealth of knowledge and wisdom; to his enthusiasm, tenacity of purpose, and unflagging devotion the whole enterprise is greatly indebted. Professor W. D. McHardy, Deputy Director since 1968, has made an invaluable contribution particularly, but by no means exclusively, in the sphere of the Apocrypha. It is right that the names of these three scholars should always be associated with The New English Bible. Our debt to them is incalculably great.

DONALD EBOR
Chairman of the Joint Committee

Since publication of THE NEW ENGLISH BIBLE *The Roman Catholic Church in England and Wales, The Roman Catholic Church in Ireland, and The Roman Catholic Church in Scotland joined as sponsors. In addition, since the above Preface was written The Congregational Church in England and Wales and The Presbyterian Church of England have united under the name of The United Reformed Church.*

The Names and Order of
the Books of the Bible

THE OLD TESTAMENT

THE APOCRYPHA

THE NEW TESTAMENT

Abbreviations of the Books of the Bible
in Alphabetical Order

		PAGE			PAGE
Acts NT	Acts of the Apostles	141	*Jn.* NT	John	108
Amos OT	Amos	982	*1 Jn.* NT	1 John	302
Bar. Apoc.	Baruch	176	*2 Jn.* NT	2 John	307
1 Chr. OT	1 Chronicles	418	*3 Jn.* NT	3 John	308
2 Chr. OT	2 Chronicles	451	*Job* OT	Job	529
Col. NT	Colossians	249	*Joel* OT	Joel	977
1 Cor. NT	1 Corinthians	201	*Jonah* OT	Jonah	994
2 Cor. NT	2 Corinthians	218	*Josh.* OT	Joshua	223
Dan. OT	Daniel	945	*Jude* NT	Jude	309
Dan. & Bel. Apoc.	Daniel, Bel, and the Snake	191	*Judg.* OT	Judges	250
Dan. & Su. Apoc.	Daniel and Susanna	188	*1 Kgs.* OT	1 Kings	349
			2 Kgs. OT	2 Kings	385
Deut. OT	Deuteronomy	181	*Lam.* OT	Lamentations	878
Eccles. OT	Ecclesiastes	708	*Let. Jer.* Apoc.	A Letter of Jeremiah	182
Ecclus. Apoc.	Ecclesiasticus or the Wisdom of Jesus Son of Sirach	115	*Lev.* OT	Leviticus	100
			Lk. NT	Luke	67
Eph. NT	Ephesians	237	*1 Macc.* Apoc.	1 Maccabees	195
1 Esd. Apoc.	1 Esdras	1	*2 Macc.* Apoc.	2 Maccabees	232
2 Esd. Apoc.	2 Esdras	19	*Mal.* OT	Malachi	1030
Esther OT	Esther	520	*Mic.* OT	Micah	997
Exod. OT	Exodus	55	*Mk.* NT	Mark	42
Ezek. OT	Ezekiel	886	*Mt.* NT	Matthew	3
Ezra OT	Ezra	490	*Nahum* OT	Nahum	1005
Gal. NT	Galatians	230	*Neh.* OT	Nehemiah	503
Gen. OT	Genesis	1	*Num.* OT	Numbers	135
Hab. OT	Habakkuk	1009	*Obad.* OT	Obadiah	992
Hag. OT	Haggai	1017	*1 Pet.* NT	1 Peter	294
Heb. NT	Hebrews	276	*2 Pet.* NT	2 Peter	299
Hos. OT	Hosea	964	*Phil.* NT	Philippians	243
Isa. OT	Isaiah	724	*Philem.* NT	Philemon	274
Jas. NT	James	289	*Pr. M.* Apoc.	The Prayer of Manasseh	193
Jdt. Apoc.	Judith	67			
Jer. OT	Jeremiah	805	*Prov.* OT	Proverbs	675

Miscellaneous Abbreviations

Ant.	Josephus, Flavius (37-95 A.D.), *Antiquities of the Jews:* a history and also a paraphrase of the Old Testament by the Jewish writer
Apoc.	Apocrypha
Aram.	Aramaic (text or word)
B.J.	*The Jewish War:* a history of the background and course of the Judeo-Roman War of 63-70 by Josephus
ch(s).	chapter(s)
cp.	compare
Gk.	Greek
Heb.	Hebrew (text or word)
Lat.	Latin version
lit.	literally
mng.	meaning
MS(S).	manuscript(s)
MT	Massoretic Text: Hebrew of the Old Testament in the form transmitted by Jews
n(n).	note(s)
NT	New Testament
om.	omit(s)
OT	Old Testament
Pesh.	Peshitta: version of Scripture in the Syriac language
poss.	possible
prob.	probable
Sam.	Samaritan: version of the Hebrew Scriptures preserved by the Samaritans
rdg.	reading
Sept.	Septuagint: Greek version of the Old Testament
Syr.	The language, kindred to Aramaic, in which the Peshitta version occurs. Other Syriac portions of Scripture have been preserved
Tfn.	translators' footnote(s)
Tg.	Targum: Aramaic version of the Old Testament preserved by Jews
Vg.	Vulgate: Latin version, from older or Latin rendering, of the Old Testament
v(v).	verse(s)
Vs(s)	Version(s)
Or	indicates an alternative interpretation
[...]	In the text itself square brackets are used to indicate words that are probably late additions to the Hebrew text

THE NEW
ENGLISH BIBLE

THE OLD TESTAMENT
OXFORD STUDY EDITION

CONTENTS

INTRODUCTION
TO THE OLD TESTAMENT

The Old Testament as here translated consists of a body of literature spread over a period extending from the twelfth to the second century B.C.; this literature is written in classical Hebrew, except some brief portions which are in Aramaic, a cognate or sister language (Ezra 4.8–6.18 and 7.12–26, Jeremiah 10.11, Daniel 2.4–7.28). No manuscripts of the Old Testament from the earlier part of this period have been preserved; indeed much of it must have been handed down by oral tradition from generation to generation. The impetus to collect, edit and make copies of the national literature may well have come from the disaster of 587/6 B.C., when the Babylonians captured and burnt Jerusalem and carried off many of its inhabitants into exile.

The earliest known Hebrew manuscripts containing any parts of the Old Testament are among the Scrolls (commonly called the Dead Sea Scrolls) found in caves at Qumran near the north-western end of the Dead Sea; they may be dated in the last two centuries B.C., though some may be a little earlier and others somewhat later. They include two copies of Isaiah, one complete and another badly damaged, a commentary containing most of the text of the first two chapters of Habakkuk, and fragments of every other Old Testament book, except Esther. The text which they present is to a large extent identical with that in our Hebrew Bibles.

In the second century A.D. or even earlier the Rabbis, the Jewish religious leaders, compiled a text from such manuscripts as had survived the destruction of Jerusalem in A.D. 70, and on this basis was established the traditional or Massoretic text, so called from the Hebrew word *massorah* 'tradition'. This text incorporated the mistakes of generations of copyists, and, in spite of the care bestowed on it, many errors of later copyists also found their way into it. The earliest surviving manuscripts of this text date from the ninth to eleventh centuries A.D.; and it is this text, as printed in R. Kittel's *Biblia Hebraica* (3rd edition, 1937), which has been used for the present translation.

The traditional text was originally written only in consonants, but in order to preserve what they regarded as the correct pronunciation of the words the Rabbis added vowel-signs to the text. Of the various systems of vowel-signs which were devised, that developed at Tiberias in the fifth to sixth centuries A.D. ultimately prevailed and is still used in our printed Bibles. The vowels are here represented by means of strokes and dots added to the consonantal text, and this method of vocalization made it possible for the Rabbis to indicate variant readings which they preferred, without meddling with the consonants: they put in the margin of their manuscript the consonants of the reading which they wished to adopt and added the vowel-signs of this reading to the consonants in the text which they were rejecting. The reader knew that he was to pronounce the consonants in the margin with the vowels in the text.

One variation of this convention is of special importance, inasmuch as it affects the divine name. This personal proper name, written with the consonants *YHWH*, was considered too sacred to be uttered; so the vowels for the words 'my Lord' or 'God' were added to the consonants *YHWH*, and the reader was warned by these vowels that he must substitute other consonants. This change having to be made so frequently, the Rabbis did not consider it necessary to put the consonants of the new reading in the margin. In course of time the true pronunciation of the divine name, probably *Yahweh*, passed into oblivion, and *YHWH* was read with the intruded vowels, the vowels of an entirely different word, namely 'my Lord' or 'God'. In late medieval times this mispronunciation became current as *Jehova*, and it was taken over as *Jehovah* by the Reformers in Protestant Bibles. The present translators have retained this incorrect but customary form in the text of passages where the name is explained with a note on its pronunciation (e.g. Exodus 3.15) and in four place-names of which it forms a constituent element; elsewhere they have followed ancient translators in substituting 'LORD' or 'GOD', printed as here in capital letters, for the Hebrew name.

So much for the text of the Hebrew Old Testament as it lies before us; but it is certain that this does not always represent what was originally written. The translator must often go behind the traditional text to discover the writer's meaning. For this purpose he may have recourse first to the Scrolls; but these cover only a very small part of the Old Testament writings. Secondly he may have recourse to the Samaritan Pentateuch, which, though extant only in late manuscripts, the earliest being dated about the eleventh century A.D., may be somewhat earlier than the Scrolls and represents the text of the five books of the Law (Genesis to Deuteronomy) which the Samaritans took with them when they seceded from Judaism. It differs from the traditional Hebrew text in a considerable number of small and mostly unimportant points.

For further help the translator may turn to the ancient versions. Of these the earliest is the Old Testament in Greek, designed to meet the needs of Greek-speaking Jews in Egypt in the third and second centuries B.C. According to tradition the Pentateuch was translated by seventy-two elders, six from each of the twelve tribes of Israel, and so the Greek version of the Old Testament came to be called the Septuagint, from the Latin *septuaginta* 'seventy'. Clearly it is the work of a number of translators of unequal skill; their rendering is now literal, now paraphrastic, and now interpretative. Not infrequently it contains absurd mistranslations. Yet it is valuable for the recovery of the original Hebrew, because it is based on an underlying Hebrew text older than the Massoretic, and it often preserves the correct reading in passages where our Hebrew manuscripts are manifestly in error, or the true interpretation where this has been obscured in the traditional text. Its defects, however, were patent, and early in the Christian era several scholars, Aquila, Symmachus and Theodotion, tried to improve on it; other scholars produced fresh recensions of it, among which the text associated with the name of Lucian is commonly included.

The Greek-speaking Christians adopted the Septuagint as their Scriptures, but with the spread of Christianity across the Mediterranean world there arose in time the need for a Latin translation. This, the Old Latin version, made from the Septuagint by unknown translators, was so unsatisfactory that towards the end of the fourth century Jerome produced a new translation. In the books with which we are here concerned he worked directly from the Hebrew text, and he had the help of Jewish scholars. His translation is idiomatic and forceful, and is specially helpful in recovering the form and sense of the Hebrew text. Jerome's new version is commonly called the Vulgate; it may be noted, however, that the Vulgate Psalter is not his translation from the Hebrew, but an earlier revision he had made of the Old Latin Psalms.

As the knowledge of Hebrew died out among the Jews, the reading of the Scriptures in the synagogue had to be followed by a translation of the passages into Aramaic, the language which had supplanted Hebrew. Such renderings, known as Targums (Aramaic *targum*, 'translation'), tended to become traditional and stereotyped and finally were written down. Some of them contain pre-Christian material. There are Targums to every book of the Old Testament except Daniel, Ezra, and Nehemiah, but only one, on the Pentateuch, is a straightforward translation.

Between the first and third centuries A.D. a Syriac translation, known as the Peshitta (i.e. 'simple') Version, was made; some parts of it are more literal than others, and, though it agrees in the main with the Hebrew text, it bears traces of the influence of the Septuagint. Other versions in various languages appeared between the third and thirteenth centuries A.D., but they are of little value for the recovery and interpretation of the Hebrew text.

In spite of this wealth of ancient versions, and even when the earliest known form of the text has been established, many obscurities still remain in the Hebrew Scriptures. The classical Hebrew vocabulary as known today is small, with the consequence that the meaning of an unusually large number of words is uncertain or unknown. In such cases recourse may be had to the cognate languages. Already medieval scholars had begun to use the Arabic language for this purpose, and in later centuries Syriac and Ethiopic also were used. In more recent times scholars have had access to the vast literature in Babylonian, Assyrian, and kindred dialects which has been preserved on cuneiform tablets. Archaeology, too, has at times been helpful in clearing up an obscurity in the Hebrew text. But in the last resort, the translator may have to arrive at the sense of a word from the context alone, or he may even have to emend what is demonstrably faulty; such corrections of the text, except when only the vowels are affected, are recorded in the notes of the present translation.

The paragraphs in this translation are a modified form of those in the Authorized and Revised Versions, and the present translators have added headings to the main sections into which the text falls. Sometimes, for what seemed sufficient reasons, the order of the verses has been changed, as will be seen from the verse-numbering. Occasionally passages have been brought together if a common refrain or other evidence shows that they have been wrongly separated; such changes are recorded in the notes.

The headings of the Psalms, consisting partly of musical instructions, of which the meanings have mostly been lost, and partly of historical notices, deduced (sometimes incorrectly) from the individual Psalms, have been omitted; they are almost certainly not original. On the other hand, the designations of the speakers in the Song of Songs, though absent from the Hebrew text, have been introduced, with occasional corrections, from two manuscripts of the Septuagint.

A major difficulty in translating the Old Testament lies in the difference of time and place. Palestine differs greatly from the Western world in its physical aspects, in its plants, birds and beasts, its arts and crafts, as it did also in its social, administrative and religious, institutions, so that no English words exist to represent much about which the Old Testament speaks. The modern translator then must be content to use paraphrase or even to transliterate certain Hebrew words. The present translators have transliterated the Hebrew words for technical terms, where verbal exactness has seemed essential, while in other passages they have allowed themselves a paraphrase to bring out the general sense, where no technical problem requiring particularization is involved; but they have adopted such devices as rarely as possible.

Finally, the translators have endeavoured to avoid anachronisms and expressions reminiscent of foreign idioms. They have tried to keep their language as close to current usage as possible, while avoiding words and phrases likely soon to become obsolete. They have made every effort not only to make sense but also to offer renderings that will meet the needs of readers with no special knowledge of the background of the Old Testament.

G. R. D.

xxii

The Pentateuch

The Pentateuch (literally, the "five scrolls"; popularly, the Five Books of Moses) is the final edition of the traditions about her early history which Israel considered important for her self-identity. It contains the following themes: the summoning of the patriarchs to form an obedient community, made necessary by mankind's previous rebellions (Gen.); the deliverance from Egyptian bondage and the grateful acceptance of the LORD's covenant (Exod. and Lev.); the preservation of Israel despite her generation-long rebellion in the Wilderness (Num.); and warnings about ingratitude during the affluent life in the "promised land" (Deut.).

The earliest summary of the traditions may have been little more than a sentence (as in 1 Sam.12.8) or paragraph (Josh.24.2–10), formulated soon after the settlement in Canaan (thirteenth century B.C.) for recital in the cult.

It was perhaps during the reign of Solomon (tenth century B.C.) that many of the local cultic recitations, histories, songs, and law codes were first gathered and edited into a sustained account (the earliest skeleton underlying Gen. 1 Kgs. ch. 2). Its purpose was to suggest that the Israelite Kingdom was the fulfillment of the ancient promises to the patriarchs. Modern scholars call this work "J," because it uses for the deity the name Jehovah (Heb. *Yahweh*), and was produced by Judean theologians; they believe that it was soon supplemented by other ancient traditions preserved in Ephraim, and called "E" because the divine term *Elohim* is used.

When Judah was threatened religiously from within and militarily from without (eighth–seventh centuries), the old traditions were expanded and interpreted in contemporary terms ("D"). D is contained primarily in the book of Deuteronomy.

The destruction of Jerusalem (587 B.C.) and the necessity to live under Babylonian and Persian domination (sixth–fifth centuries) produced a final stage of collection and reflection upon the ancient traditions, generally called the Priestly Code ("P"). The P Code itself seems composite and a result of growth, containing a somewhat older Priestly section (Lev. chs. 17–26) known as the "Holiness Code." While J–E went beyond Genesis–Deuteronomy, and extended through Joshua–1 Kings ch. 2, the Priests effected a division between Genesis–Deuteronomy and the ensuing material. As a result of this separation, the Pentateuch emerged as an entity.

Accordingly, the Pentateuch, beginning in oral stages, grew with the generations. The product of communal insight and authorship, with new reflections placed beside older ones, the Pentateuch reached its present written form after the Babylonian Exile.

Since it was Moses who relayed God's word to Israel at Sinai, later generations spoke of "the law of Moses" (2 Chr.30.16). Later, when the entirety of Genesis–Deuteronomy was called "the Law" (Preface to Ecclus.), it became an accepted conclusion that he had recorded this totality (Jn.1.45).

Translators' Footnotes

The footnotes in this edition of the Old Testament serve (a) to give cross-references to parallel passages, chiefly in the historical books, (b) to indicate where verses or parts of verses have been transposed, (c) to give the meaning of proper names where it appears to be reflected in the context, (d) to give an alternative interpretation where the Hebrew is capable of such, and (e) to indicate places where the translators have adopted what seemed to them the most probable correction of the text where the Hebrew and the ancient versions cannot be convincingly translated as they stand.

Unless otherwise indicated by its wording, a note refers to the single word against which the reference is placed.

Marginal Numbers

The conventional verse divisions in the Old Testament are based on those in Hebrew manuscripts. Nevertheless any system of division into numbered verses is foreign to the spirit of this translation, which is intended to convey the meaning in natural English—the prose in paragraphs, the poetic passages in lines corresponding to the structure of the Hebrew.

For purposes of reference, and of comparison with other translations, verse numbers are placed in the margin opposite the line in which the first word belonging to the verse in question appears. Sometimes, however, successive verses are combined in a continuous translation, so that the precise point where a new verse begins cannot be fixed; in these cases the verse numbers, joined by a hyphen, are placed at the point where the passage begins.

GENESIS

GENESIS, meaning "beginning," contains two major parts: the primeval history (chs. 1–11), which tells how man's self-assertion brought the world to the brink of destruction; and the history of the patriarchs (chs. 12–50), which relates how the LORD, in an awesome and inexplicable act of grace, chose the clan of Abraham as the instrument for the rehabilitation of mankind. Yet for a variety of reasons, whether perceptible or hidden, the divine promise was not immediately realized. Even the existence of the next generation (i.e. Israel herself) was often uncertain. And as Genesis concludes, the clan has been delivered from famine through divine providence, only to become enslaved in Egypt.

When succeeding generations heard this part of their story freshly interpreted in light of new experiences (see Introduction to the Pentateuch), they understood that the crises of the present were not unique and were enabled to hope that the ancient promise would yet be realized.

The patriarchal material differs from the account of primeval time in that it can be placed within the context of the known history of the Ancient Near East (2000–1500 B.C.).

The creation of the world

1 IN THE BEGINNING OF CREATION, WHEN
2 God made heaven and earth,ᵃ the earth was without form and void, with darkness over the face of the abyss, and a mighty wind that sweptᵇ over the
3 surface of the waters. God said, 'Let
4 there be light', and there was light; and God saw that the light was good, and
5 he separated light from darkness. He called the light day, and the darkness night. So evening came, and morning came, the first day.
6 God said, 'Let there be a vault between the waters, to separate water
7 from water.' So God made the vault, and separated the water under the vault from the water above it, and so it was;
8 and God called the vault heaven. Evening came, and morning came, a second day.
9 God said, 'Let the waters under heaven be gathered into one place, so that dry land may appear'; and so it
10 was. God called the dry land earth, and the gathering of the waters he called seas; and God saw that it was good.
11 Then God said, 'Let the earth produce fresh growth, let there be on the earth plants bearing seed, fruit-trees bearing

fruit each with seed according to its kind.' So it was; the earth yielded fresh 12 growth, plants bearing seed according to their kind and trees bearing fruit each with seed according to its kind; and God saw that it was good. Evening 13 came, and morning came, a third day.
God said, 'Let there be lights in the 14 vault of heaven to separate day from night, and let them serve as signs both for festivals and for seasons and years. Let them also shine in the vault of 15 heaven to give light on earth.' So it was; God made the two great lights, the 16 greater to govern the day and the lesser to govern the night; and with them he made the stars. God put these lights in 17 the vault of heaven to give light on earth, to govern day and night, and to 18 separate light from darkness; and God saw that it was good. Evening came, 19 and morning came, a fourth day.
God said, 'Let the waters teem with 20 countless living creatures, and let birds fly above the earth across the vault of heaven.' God then created the great 21 sea-monsters and all living creatures that move and swarm in the waters, according to their kind, and every kind

ᵃ Or In the beginning God created heaven and earth.
ᵇ Or and the spirit of God hovering.

1.1–2.4: The creation account, composed by priests. Order evolves from chaos by divine command, followed by God's resting, in example, on the Sabbath. 1: That *creation* arose out of nothing—that is, not out of materials at hand—became the usual understanding of this verse; see 2 Macc.7.28. 2: *Abyss:* in Ancient Near Eastern thought, the sea, personified as a dragon, fathered the great sea serpents. *Wind:* in non-Hebrew epics, the wind-god was the creator. Here, however, sea and wind are portrayed as creations, subject to God. 5: *Evening . . . morning:* day began at sundown and hence the order given here. 6: *Vault:* a solid dome (Job 37.18), retaining the upper waters whence the rains come (Gen.7.11–12). 14: *Lights:* Israel's neighbors regarded the celestial bodies as deities (see Deut.4.19). Here, they are mere results of God's creation. 20: *Living creatures:* hence, the worship of animals as gods, by Israel's neigh-

of bird; and God saw that it was good.
22 So he blessed them and said, 'Be fruitful and increase, fill the waters of the seas; and let the birds increase on land.'
23 Evening came, and morning came, a fifth day.
24 God said, 'Let the earth bring forth living creatures, according to their kind: cattle, reptiles, and wild animals, all according to their kind.' So it was;
25 God made wild animals, cattle, and all reptiles, each according to its kind; and
26 he saw that it was good. Then God said, 'Let us make man in our image and likeness to rule the fish in the sea, the birds of heaven, the cattle, all wild animals on earth, and all reptiles that
27 crawl upon the earth.' So God created man in his own image; in the image of God he created him; male and female
28 he created them. God blessed them and said to them, 'Be fruitful and increase, fill the earth and subdue it, rule over the fish in the sea, the birds of heaven, and every living thing that moves upon the
29 earth.' God also said, 'I give you all plants that bear seed everywhere on earth, and every tree bearing fruit which yields seed: they shall be yours for food.
30 All green plants I give for food to the wild animals, to all the birds of heaven, and to all reptiles on earth, every living
31 creature.' So it was; and God saw all that he had made, and it was very good. Evening came, and morning came, a sixth day.
2 Thus heaven and earth were completed with all their mighty throng. On
2 the sixth day God completed all the work he had been doing, and on the seventh day he ceased from all his work. God blessed the seventh day and 3 made it holy, because on that day he ceased from all the work he had set himself to do.

This is the story of the making of 4 heaven and earth when they were created.

The beginnings of history

WHEN THE LORD GOD MADE EARTH AND 5 heaven, there was neither shrub nor plant growing wild upon the earth, because the LORD God had sent no rain on the earth; nor was there any man to till the ground. A flood*c* used to rise 6 out of the earth and water all the surface of the ground. Then the LORD 7 God formed a man*d* from the dust of the ground*e* and breathed into his nostrils the breath of life. Thus the man became a living creature. Then the 8 LORD God planted a garden in Eden away to the east, and there he put the man whom he had formed. The LORD 9 God made trees spring from the ground, all trees pleasant to look at and good for food; and in the middle of the garden he set the tree of life and the tree of the knowledge of good and evil.

There was a river flowing from Eden 10 to water the garden, and when it left the garden it branched into four streams. The name of the first is 11 Pishon, that is the river which encircles all the land of Havilah, where the gold*f* is. The gold*f* of that land is good; 12 bdellium*g* and cornelians are also to be

c Or mist.   *d Heb.* adam.   *e Heb.* adamah.
f Or frankincense.   *g Or* gum resin.

---

bors, was foolish. **26:** The plural *us* (3.22; 11.7) may be a majestic plural, or else refer to the minor divine beings thought to surround God, like courtiers of a human king (1 Kgs.22.19–22; Job 1.6). *Image:* most often used to denote a physical thing, its meaning here is not precisely stated. **28:** To *subdue* the earth is to be free from nature's tyranny and from idolizing mere objects.

2.5–3.24: A second account of primeval time. This account is generally regarded as more ancient than 1.1–2.4. Man does not accept the limits placed on his existence and disrupts God's intended harmony. **5:** *LORD God:* a compound designation (Introduction, p. xx) largely confined to this section. **6:** *Flood:* the earth was thought to be suspended upon the abyss (Ps. 24.2), which could break through with great force (Gen.7.11). **7:** *Dust:* an idea derived from the observation of bones in the tomb. A pun is present, linking man and earth; see Tfn. *d* and *e*. *Living creature:* not a duality of "body" and "soul" (a Greek idea), but rather a unity animated by God's creative act. The animals are also designated by the same term for "living" (1.20, 24). **8:** *Eden:* originally not a place name, it means "plain," "steppe," and is equivalent to "delight." In ancient polytheism, the idea that the gods inhabit a fertile *garden* is widely attested; most often it lies in the east where the life-giving sun rises. **9:** *Tree of life:* the notion that immortality could be attained by eating a magic plant is found elsewhere, also, in antiquity. **13:** *Cush:* the

13 found there. The name of the second river is Gihon; this is the one which
14 encircles all the land of Cush. The name of the third is Tigris; this is the river which runs east of Asshur. The fourth river is the Euphrates.
15 The LORD God took the man and put him in the garden of Eden to till it and
16 care for it. He told the man, 'You may
17 eat from every tree in the garden, but not from the tree of the knowledge of good and evil; for on the day that you
18 eat from it, you will certainly die.' Then the LORD God said, 'It is not good for the man to be alone. I will provide a
19 partner for him.' So God formed out of the ground all the wild animals and all the birds of heaven. He brought them to the man to see what he would call them, and whatever the man called each living creature, that was its name.
20 Thus the man gave names to all cattle, to the birds of heaven, and to every wild animal; but for the man himself
21 no partner had yet been found. And so the LORD God put the man into a trance, and while he slept, he took one of his ribs and closed the flesh over the
22 place. The LORD God then built up the rib, which he had taken out of the man, into a woman. He brought her to the
23 man, and the man said:

> 'Now this, at last—
> bone from my bones,
> flesh from my flesh!—
> this shall be called woman,[h]
> for from man[i] was this taken.'

24 That is why a man leaves his father and mother and is united to his wife, and
25 the two become one flesh. Now they were both naked, the man and his wife, but they had no feeling of shame towards one another.

THE SERPENT WAS MORE CRAFTY THAN **3** any wild creature that the LORD God had made. He said to the woman, 'Is it true that God has forbidden you to eat from any tree in the garden?' The 2 woman answered the serpent, 'We may eat the fruit of any tree in the garden, except for the tree in the 3 middle of the garden; God has forbidden us either to eat or to touch the fruit of that; if we do, we shall die.' The serpent said, 'Of course you will 4 not die. God knows that as soon as you 5 eat it, your eyes will be opened and you will be like gods[j] knowing both good and evil.' When the woman saw 6 that the fruit of the tree was good to eat, and that it was pleasing to the eye and tempting to contemplate, she took some and ate it. She also gave her husband some and he ate it. Then the 7 eyes of both of them were opened and they discovered that they were naked; so they stitched fig-leaves together and made themselves loincloths.

The man and his wife heard the 8 sound of the LORD God walking in the garden at the time of the evening breeze and hid from the LORD God among the trees of the garden. But the LORD 9 God called to the man and said to him, 'Where are you?' He replied, 'I heard 10 the sound as you were walking in the garden, and I was afraid because I was naked, and I hid myself.' God answered, 11 'Who told you that you were naked? Have you eaten from the tree which I forbade you?' The man said, 'The 12 woman you gave me for a companion, she gave me fruit from the tree and I ate it.' Then the LORD God said to the 13 woman, 'What is this that you have done?' The woman said, 'The serpent

h Heb. ishshah.
i Heb. ish.
j Or God.

land of the Kassites, to the east, in Mesopotamia. **14:** The headwaters of the *Tigris* and *Euphrates* were sacred to the Assyrians. The other two of the four "original" rivers are unknown. **17:** *On the day that:* idiomatic for "when." *Certainly die:* become mortal. **22:** The selection of the *rib* may be the result of borrowing a pun from the ancient Sumerians; the same word means both "rib" and "to make alive" in Sumerian (see 3.20). **24:** A folk explanation is given for the origin of the sexual urge. **3.1:** *Serpent:* an ancient extrabiblical story tells how a serpent stole the plant which would have given immortality to man. It was believed that when the snake shed his skin, he was rejuvenated. *Crafty:* there is a pun in the Hebrew words for *crafty* and *naked*. *Had made:* a phrase deliberately used to show that he was only one among God's many creatures. The idea of the serpent as a primeval adversary of God, indeed, the Devil, arose much later (see Wis.2.24); so too the fixing of blame on the *woman* arose at a much later time (Ecclus.25.24). **7:** *Naked:* not intrinsically shameful, nakedness became so as the result of

14 tricked me, and I ate.' Then the LORD God said to the serpent:

'Because you have done this you are accursed
more than all cattle and all wild creatures.
On your belly you shall crawl, and dust you shall eat
all the days of your life.
15 I will put enmity between you and the woman,
between your brood and hers.
They shall strike at your head, and you shall strike at their heel.'

16 To the woman he said:

'I will increase your labour and your groaning,
and in labour you shall bear children.
You shall be eager[k] for your husband, and he shall be your master.'

17 And to the man he said:

'Because you have listened to your wife
and have eaten from the tree which I forbade you,
accursed shall be the ground on your account.
With labour you shall win your food from it
all the days of your life.
18 It will grow thorns and thistles for you,
none but wild plants for you to eat.
19 You shall gain your bread by the sweat of your brow
until you return to the ground;
for from it you were taken.
Dust you are, to dust you shall return.'

20 The man called his wife Eve[l]

because she was the mother of all who live. The LORD God made tunics of 21 skins for Adam and his wife and clothed them. He said, 'The man has become 22 like one of us, knowing good and evil, what if he now reaches out his hand and takes fruit from the tree of life also, eats it and lives for ever?' So the LORD 23 God drove him out of the garden of Eden to till the ground from which he had been taken. He cast him out, and 24 to the east of the garden of Eden he stationed the cherubim and a sword whirling and flashing to guard the way to the tree of life.

The man lay with his wife Eve, and 4 she conceived and gave birth to Cain. She said, 'With the help of the LORD I have brought a man into being.' Afterwards she had another child, his 2 brother Abel. Abel was a shepherd and Cain a tiller of the soil. The day came 3 when Cain brought some of the produce of the soil as a gift to the LORD; and Abel brought some of the first-born 4 of his flock, the fat portions of them.[m] The LORD received Abel and his gift with favour; but Cain and his gift he 5 did not receive. Cain was very angry and his face fell. Then the LORD said 6 to Cain, 'Why are you so angry and cast down?

If you do well, you are accepted;[n] 7
if not, sin is a demon crouching at the door.
It shall be eager for you, and you will be mastered by it.'[o]

Cain said to his brother Abel, 'Let us 8 go into the open country.' While they were there, Cain attacked his brother

k *Or* feel an urge.   l *That is* Life.
m *Or* some of the first-born, that is the sucklings, of his flock.
n *Or* you hold your head up.
o *Or* but you must master it.

---

man's sin and alienation from God. **14–19**: A series of originally independent folk explanations is woven together: Why is mankind hostile to serpents? Why is childbirth painful? Why is woman's social position subordinate? Why must man work? These explanations serve in context to show that the world as now encountered is of man's making rather than remaining the divine ideal. **20**: *Eve:* see 2.22 n. **21**: *Adam:* the word "man" occurs here for the first time without the definite article, becoming a name (see 2.7, Tfn. *d*). **22**: *Us:* see 1.26 n. **24**: *Cherubim:* winged semidivine creatures, half-human and half-lion (Ezek.41.19), often the guardians of sacred areas (1 Kgs.8.6–7).
    4.1–26: The first offspring. Cain and Abel may personify a culture conflict between the settled farmer and the seminomadic shepherd. *Cain:* "smith," "metallurgist." *Abel:* "herdsman." **4–5**: The preference for Abel's offering reflects the view of the deity's full freedom (see

4

9 Abel and murdered him. Then the LORD
said to Cain, 'Where is your brother
Abel?' Cain answered, 'I do not know.
10 Am I my brother's keeper?' The LORD
said, 'What have you done? Hark!
your brother's blood that has been shed
is crying out to me from the ground.
11 Now you are accursed, and banished
from[p] the ground which has opened
its mouth wide to receive your brother's
12 blood, which you have shed. When you
till the ground, it will no longer yield
you its wealth. You shall be a vagrant
13 and a wanderer on earth.' Cain said to
the LORD, 'My punishment is heavier
14 than I can bear; thou hast driven me
today from the ground, and I must hide
myself from thy presence. I shall be a
vagrant and a wanderer on earth, and
15 anyone who meets me can kill me.' The
LORD answered him, 'No: if anyone
kills Cain, Cain shall be avenged
sevenfold.' So the LORD put a mark on
Cain, in order that anyone meeting
16 him should not kill him. Then Cain
went out from the LORD's presence and
settled in the land of Nod[q][r] to the east
of Eden.

17 Then Cain lay with his wife; and she
conceived and bore Enoch. Cain was
then building a city, which he named
18 Enoch after his son. Enoch begot Irad;
Irad begot Mehujael; Mehujael begot Methushael; Methushael begot
Lamech.
19 Lamech married two wives, one
named Adah and the other Zillah.
20 Adah bore Jabal who was the ancestor
21 of herdsmen who live in tents; and his
brother's name was Jubal; he was the
ancestor of those who play the harp and
22 pipe. Zillah, the other wife, bore
Tubal-cain, the master of all copper-
smiths and blacksmiths, and Tubal-

cain's sister was Naamah. Lamech 23
said to his wives:

'Adah and Zillah, listen to me;
wives of Lamech, mark what I say:
I kill a man for wounding me,
a young man for a blow.
Cain may be avenged seven times, 24
but Lamech seventy-seven.'

Adam lay with his wife again. She 25
bore a son, and named him Seth,[s] 'for',
she said, 'God has granted me another
son in place of Abel, because Cain
killed him.' Seth too had a son, whom 26
he named Enosh. At that time men
began to invoke the LORD[t] by name.

THIS IS THE RECORD OF THE DESCENDANTS **5**
of Adam. On the day when God created
man he made him in the likeness of
God. He created them male and female, 2
and on the day when he created them,
he blessed them and called them man.
Adam was one hundred and thirty 3
years old when he begot a son in his
likeness and image, and named him
Seth. After the birth of Seth he lived 4
eight hundred years, and had other
sons and daughters. He lived nine 5
hundred and thirty years, and then he
died.

Seth was one hundred and five years 6
old when he begot Enosh. After the 7
birth of Enosh he lived eight hundred
and seven years, and had other sons
and daughters. He lived nine hundred 8
and twelve years, and then he died.

[p] and banished from: *or* more than (*cp.* 3. 17).
[q] *That is* Wandering.
[r] and settled . . . Nod: *or* and he lived as a wanderer in
the land.
[s] *That is* Granted.
[t] *This represents the Hebrew consonants* YHWH,
probably pronounced Yahweh, *but traditionally read as*
Jehovah.

Exod.33.19). **10:** *Blood* was regarded as the seat of the life-force (see Deut.12.23–24). **14:**
Anyone: this passage presupposes an established society; possibly this account was once independent of 2.5–3.24 and only after the two accounts were joined were Cain and Abel regarded
as the offspring of Adam and Eve (v. 1). **15:** *Mark:* devotees of deities wore distinctive emblems.
Cain is designated here as a ward of the LORD. **17:** *Wife:* her mention is a surprise, for whence
did she come? Perhaps we have here a fragment of a once independent tradition; see v. 14 n.
19–22: The development of human culture is depicted. **23–24:** An ancient boast is used to
illustrate the growing pride and callousness of mankind. **26:** *Enosh* is another word for "man."
This is possibly a fragment of a once separate, primitive genealogy. *At that time:* the worship
of the LORD by some groups within Israel began much later (see Exod.3.13–15; 6.3 n.).
5.1–32: Adam's descendants. In form and content this section is a self-contained unit, related
to 1.1–2.4, inserted here to bridge a narrative gap between earliest creation and the later deluge
(7.1ff.). **4:** *Eight hundred:* Ancient Near Eastern peoples attributed great longevity to their remote ancestors. The biblical writers steadily decrease man's life span, symbolizing the con-

9ᵘ   Enosh was ninety years old when he
10 begot Kenan. After the birth of Kenan
he lived eight hundred and fifteen
years, and had other sons and
11 daughters. He lived nine hundred and
five years, and then he died.
12   Kenan was seventy years old when he
13 begot Mahalalel. After the birth of
Mahalalel he lived eight hundred
and forty years, and had other sons and
14 daughters. He lived nine hundred and
ten years, and then he died.
15   Mahalalel was sixty-five years old
16 when he begot Jared. After the birth
of Jared he lived eight hundred and
thirty years, and had other sons and
17 daughters. He lived eight hundred and
ninety-five years, and then he died.
18   Jared was one hundred and sixty-
two years old when he begot Enoch.
19 After the birth of Enoch he lived eight
hundred years, and had other sons and
20 daughters. He lived nine hundred and
sixty-two years, and then he died.
21   Enoch was sixty-five years old when
22 he begot Methuselah. After the birth
of Methuselah, Enoch walked with
God for three hundred years, and had
23 other sons and daughters. He lived
three hundred and sixty-five years.
24 Having walked with God, Enoch was
seen no more, because God had taken
him away.
25   Methuselah was one hundred and
eighty-seven years old when he begot
26 Lamech. After the birth of Lamech he
lived for seven hundred and eighty-
two years, and had other sons and
27 daughters. He lived nine hundred and
sixty-nine years, and then he died.
28   Lamech was one hundred and
eighty-two years old when he begot a
29 son. He named him Noah, saying, 'This
boy will bring us relief from our work,
and from the hard labour that has come

upon us because of the LORD's curse
upon the ground.' After the birth of 30
Noah, he lived for five hundred and
ninety-five years, and had other sons
and daughters. Lamech lived seven 31
hundred and seventy-seven years, and
then he died. Noah was five hundred 32
years old when he begot Shem, Ham
and Japheth.

The flood and the tower of Babel

WHEN MANKIND BEGAN TO INCREASE 6
and to spread all over the earth and
daughters were born to them, the sons 2
of the gods saw that the daughters of
men were beautiful; so they took for
themselves such women as they chose.
But the LORD said, 'My life-giving 3
spirit shall not remain in man for ever;
he for his part is mortal flesh: he shall
live for a hundred and twenty years.'
In those days,ᵛ when the sons of the 4
gods had intercourse with the daughters
of men and got children by them, the
Nephilimʷ were on earth. They were the
heroes of old, men of renown.
When the LORD saw that man had 5
done much evil on earth and that his
thoughts and inclinations were always
evil, he was sorry that he had made man 6
on earth, and he was grieved at heart.
He said, 'This race of men whom I have 7
created, I will wipe them off the face of
the earth—man and beast, reptiles and
birds. I am sorry that I ever made
them.' But Noah had won the LORD's 8
favour.
This is the story of Noah. Noah was 9
a righteous man, the one blameless
man of his time; he walked with God.

u *Verses 9–32: cp. 1 Chr. 1. 2–4.*
v *Prob. rdg.; Heb. adds* and also afterwards (*cp. Num. 13. 33*).
w *Or* giants.

sequences of man's sin. **29:** *Relief:* by folk etymology, the name "Noah" is derived from the verb "to rest." Perhaps his cultivation of the vineyard and his wine making (9.20) are alluded to.
6.1–4: The birth of the Nephilim is an ancient fragment, a folk explanation for a race of giants. It is used here to illustrate man's growing wickedness, to explain the decreasing life span, and to set the stage for the deluge. **1:** *Sons of the gods:* a term of Canaanite origin for members of the pantheon ("assembly of the gods"). Later these were viewed as fallen angels (Jude 6–7). **3:** *Mortal:* in ancient belief, sexual contact between gods and men transmitted the qualities of the former. Here, however, man has overstepped his bounds as creature, so that divine correction is needed; compare 11.1–9. *A hundred and twenty years:* a round number (Num.7.86; 1 Kgs. 9.14; 10.10); see 5.4 n.
6.5–8.22: The great deluge. God's judgment takes the form of a punishing flood, while his grace takes the form of preserving a remnant through whom a new beginning can take place.

10 He had three sons, Shem, Ham and
11 Japheth. Now God saw that the whole
world was corrupt^x and full of violence.
12 In his sight the world had become
corrupted, for all men had lived
13 corrupt lives on earth. God said to
Noah, 'The loathsomeness^y of all
mankind has become plain to me, for
through them the earth is full of
violence. I intend to destroy them, and
14 the earth with them. Make yourself an
ark with ribs of cypress; cover it with
reeds and coat it inside and out with
15 pitch. This is to be its plan: the length
of the ark shall be three hundred
cubits, its breadth fifty cubits, and its
16 height thirty cubits. You shall make a
roof for the ark, giving it a fall of one
cubit when complete; and put a door
in the side of the ark, and build three
17 decks, upper, middle, and lower. I
intend to bring the waters of the flood
over the earth to destroy every human
being under heaven that has the spirit
of life; everything on earth shall perish.
18 But with you I will make a covenant,
and you shall go into the ark, you and
your sons, your wife and your sons'
19 wives with you. And you shall bring
living creatures of every kind into the
ark to keep them alive with you, two
of each kind, a male and a female;
20 two of every kind of bird, beast, and
reptile, shall come to you to be kept
21 alive. See that you take and store every
kind of food that can be eaten; this
shall be food for you and for them.'
22 Exactly as God had commanded him,
so Noah did.
7 The LORD said to Noah, 'Go into
the ark, you and all your household;
for I have seen that you alone are
righteous before me in this generation.
2 Take with you seven pairs, male and
female, of all beasts that are ritually
clean, and one pair, male and female,
3 of all beasts that are not clean; also
seven pairs, male and female, of every
bird—to ensure that life continues on
4 earth. In seven days' time I will send

rain over the earth for forty days and
forty nights, and I will wipe off the
face of the earth every living thing that
I have made.' Noah did all that the 5
LORD had commanded him. He was 6
six hundred years old when the waters
of the flood came upon the earth.

And so, to escape the waters of the 7
flood, Noah went into the ark with his
sons, his wife, and his sons' wives. And 8–9
into the ark with Noah went one pair,
male and female, of all beasts, clean
and unclean, of birds and of everything
that crawls on the ground, two by two,
as God had commanded. Towards the 10
end of seven days the waters of the
flood came upon the earth. In the year 11
when Noah was six hundred years old,
on the seventeenth day of the second
month, on that very day, all the springs
of the great abyss broke through, the
windows of the sky were opened, and 12
rain fell on the earth for forty days and
forty nights. On that very day Noah 13
entered the ark with his sons, Shem,
Ham and Japheth, his own wife, and
his three sons' wives. Wild animals of 14
every kind, cattle of every kind, reptiles
of every kind that move upon the
ground, and birds of every kind—all 15
came to Noah in the ark, two by two
of all creatures that had life in them.
Those which came were one male and 16
one female of all living things; they
came in as God had commanded
Noah, and the LORD closed the door
on him. The flood continued upon the 17
earth for forty days, and the waters
swelled and lifted up the ark so that it
rose high above the ground. They 18
swelled and increased over the earth,
and the ark floated on the surface of the
waters. More and more the waters 19
increased over the earth until they
covered all the high mountains everywhere under heaven. The waters in- 20
creased and the mountains were
covered to a depth of fifteen cubits.
Every living creature that moves on 21

x Or ripe for destruction.   *y Or* end.

The story was adapted from the Babylonian Gilgamesh Epic, itself possibly the "explanation"
of a local but catastrophic flood in the Tigris-Euphrates Valley. **9–22:** The story was transmitted
in several versions; on being combined in the text as we now have it, some duplication and
divergence have ensued. **15:** *Cubits:* see Appendix, p. 1035. **7.2:** *Seven:* a round number
(21.28; Num.28.11). **4:** *Forty:* another round number (Exod.16.35; 2 Sam.5.4; Jonah 3.4).
11: *Springs:* 2.6 n. *Windows:* 1.6 n. The earth was threatened with a return to the pre-creation

7

earth perished, birds, cattle, wild animals, all reptiles, and all mankind. 22 Everything died that had the breath of life in its nostrils, everything on dry 23 land. God wiped out every living thing that existed on earth, man and beast, reptile and bird; they were all wiped out over the whole earth, and only Noah and his company in the ark survived.

24 When the waters had increased over the earth for a hundred and fifty days, 8 God thought of Noah and all the wild animals and the cattle with him in the ark, and he made a wind pass over the earth, and the waters began to subside. 2 The springs of the abyss were stopped up, and so were the windows of the sky; the downpour from the skies was 3 checked. The water gradually receded from the earth, and by the end of a hundred and fifty days it had disap- 4 peared. On the seventeenth day of the seventh month the ark grounded on a 5 mountain in Ararat. The water con- tinued to recede until the tenth month, and on the first day of the tenth month the tops of the mountains could be seen.

6 After forty days Noah opened the trap-door that he had made in the 7 ark, and released a raven to see whether the water had subsided, but the bird continued flying to and fro until the water on the earth had dried 8 up. Noah waited for seven days,[z] and then he released a dove from the ark to see whether the water on the earth 9 had subsided further. But the dove found no place where she could settle, and so she came back to him in the ark, because there was water over the whole surface of the earth. Noah stretched out his hand, caught her and took 10 her into the ark. He waited another seven days and again released the dove 11 from the ark. She came back to him towards evening with a newly plucked olive leaf in her beak. Then Noah knew for certain that the water on the earth

had subsided still further. He waited 12 yet another seven days and released the dove, but she never came back. And so it came about that, on the first 13 day of the first month of his six hundred and first year, the water had dried up on the earth, and Noah removed the hatch and looked out of the ark. The surface of the ground was dry.

By the twenty-seventh day of the 14 second month the whole earth was dry. And God said to Noah, 'Come 15,16 out of the ark, you and your wife, your sons and their wives. Bring out 17 every living creature that is with you, live things of every kind, bird and beast and every reptile that moves on the ground, and let them swarm over the earth and be fruitful and increase there.' So Noah came out with his sons, his 18 wife, and his sons' wives. Every wild 19 animal, all cattle, every bird, and every reptile that moves on the ground, came out of the ark by families. Then Noah 20 built an altar to the LORD. He took ritually clean beasts and birds of every kind, and offered whole-offerings on the altar. When the LORD smelt the 21 soothing odour, he said within himself, 'Never again will I curse the ground because of man, however evil his inclinations may be from his youth upwards. I will never again kill every living creature, as I have just done.

While the earth lasts   22
seedtime and harvest, cold and heat,
summer and winter, day and night,
shall never cease.'

GOD BLESSED NOAH AND HIS SONS AND 9 said to them, 'Be fruitful and increase, and fill the earth. The fear and dread 2 of you shall fall upon all wild animals on earth, on all birds of heaven, on everything that moves upon the ground and all fish in the sea; they are given into your hands. Every creature that 3

z Noah . . . days: *prob. rdg., cp. verse 10; Heb. om.*

chaos (1.2). **24:** *One hundred and fifty days:* this precise number may reflect an effort to bind the events to a liturgical calendar. **8.4:** *Ararat* was in upper Mesopotamia, an area from which some of Israel's ancestors migrated (11.27–12.5). **21:** *Again:* the earth had been cursed earlier (3.17–19). God's mercy will no longer depend upon man's response.
   9.1–17: The covenant with Noah. 1: The blessing given at creation (1.28) is renewed. **3–4:** Man's eating of meat is sanctioned but possibly regarded as undesirable (see 1.29–30). *Blood:*

lives and moves shall be food for you: I give you them all, as once I gave you all

4 green plants. But you must not eat the flesh with the life, which is the blood,

5 still in it. And further, for your life-blood I will demand satisfaction; from every animal I will require it, and from a man also I will require satisfaction for the death of his fellow-man.

6 He that sheds the blood of a man,
  for that man his blood shall be shed;
  for in the image of God
  has God made man.

7 But you must be fruitful and increase, swarm throughout the earth and rule[a] over it.'

8 God spoke to Noah and to his sons
9 with him: 'I now make my covenant with you and with your descendants
10 after you, and with every living creature that is with you, all birds and cattle, all the wild animals with you on earth, all that have come out of
11 the ark. I will make my covenant with you: never again shall all living creatures be destroyed by the waters of the flood, never again shall there be a flood to lay waste the earth.'
12 God said, 'This is the sign of the covenant which I establish between myself and you and every living creature with you, to endless generations:

13 My bow I set in the cloud,
  sign of the covenant
  between myself and earth.
14 When I cloud the sky over the earth,
  the bow shall be seen in the cloud.

15 Then will I remember the covenant which I have made between myself and you and living things of every

kind. Never again shall the waters

16 become a flood to destroy all living creatures. The bow shall be in the cloud; when I see it, it will remind me of the everlasting covenant between God and living things on earth of every

17 kind.' God said to Noah, 'This is the sign of the covenant which I make between myself and all that lives on earth.'

18 The sons of Noah who came out of the ark were Shem, Ham and Japheth;

19 Ham was the father of Canaan. These three were the sons of Noah, and their descendants spread over the whole earth.

20 Noah, a man of the soil, began the

21 planting of vineyards. He drank some of the wine, became drunk and lay

22 naked inside his tent. When Ham, father of Canaan, saw his father naked,

23 he told his two brothers outside. So Shem and Japheth took a cloak, put it on their shoulders and walked back-wards, and so covered their father's naked body; their faces were turned the other way, so that they did not see

24 their father naked. When Noah woke from his drunken sleep, he learnt what

25 his youngest son had done to him, and said:

  'Cursed be Canaan,
    slave of slaves
    shall he be to his brothers.'

26 And he continued:

  'Bless, O LORD,
    the tents of Shem;[b]
    may Canaan be his slave.

27 May God extend[c] Japheth's bounds,

---

a *Prob. rdg., cp. 1. 28; Heb.* increase.
b Bless . . . Shem: *prob. rdg.; Heb.* Blessed is the LORD the God of Shem.　　c *Heb.* japht.

---

see 4.10 n. **6:** The violence of the preceding age is restrained by law basic to the creation (1.26) and enforced by punishment; the passage explains the origin of blood revenge, but without approving it. **8–9:** The covenant was made with all mankind (vv. 18–19); other covenants were with individuals or the Hebrew people. **13:** In ancient mythology the [rain]*bow* was a weapon of the deity (Hab.3.9). Folk explanation regarded it as a sign of divine victory. Here it is re-interpreted as divine reassurance to man.

9.18–27: The curse upon Canaan. 20: The origin of *wine* making is attributed to Noah (5.29 n.). The story likely is an attack on the Canaanite farming life-style (see 4.1–26 n.). **25:** The story makes its point by shifting the blame from Ham to Canaan, the ancestor whose name signified his descendants; see 10.6 n. **26:** *Shem* is the eponymous ("name-giving") ancestor of the Semites, including Israel (10.21–25; 11.18–26); the verse attempts to explain the later conquest of Canaan (see Josh.–Judg.) in theological terms. The sexual liberties of the later Canaanites offended the Israelites (see 19.5 n.; Lev.18.3, 6–30). **27.** *Japheth:* the ancestor of peoples from

let him dwell in the tents of Shem,
may Canaan be their slave.'

28 After the flood Noah lived for three
29 hundred and fifty years, and he was
nine hundred and fifty years old when
he died.

10 These are the descendants of the sons
of Noah, Shem, Ham and Japheth, the
sons born to them after the flood.
2[d] The sons of Japheth: Gomer, Magog,
Madai, Javan,[e] Tubal, Meshech and
3 Tiras. The sons of Gomer: Ashkenaz,
4 Riphath and Togarmah. The sons of
Javan: Elishah, Tarshish, Kittim[f] and
5 Rodanim. From these the peoples of
the coasts and islands separated into
their own countries, each with their
own language, family by family, nation
by nation.
6[g] The sons of Ham: Cush, Mizraim,[h]
7 Put and Canaan. The sons of Cush:
Seba, Havilah, Sabtah, Raamah and
Sabtecha. The sons of Raamah: Sheba
8 and Dedan. Cush was the father of
Nimrod, who began to show himself a
9 man of might on earth; and he was a
mighty hunter before the LORD, as the
saying goes, 'Like Nimrod, a mighty
10 hunter before the LORD.' His kingdom
in the beginning consisted of Babel,
Erech, and Accad, all of them in the
11 land of Shinar. From that land he
migrated to Asshur and built Nineveh,
12 Rehoboth-Ir, Calah, and Resen, a
great city between Nineveh and Calah.
13[i] From Mizraim sprang the Lydians,
Anamites, Lehabites, Naphtuhites,
14 Pathrusites, Casluhites, and the Caphtorites, from whom the Philistines were
descended.
15 Canaan was the father of Sidon, who
16 was his eldest son, and Heth,[j] the
Jesubites, the Amorites, the Girga-

shites, the Hivites, the Arkites, the 17
Sinites, the Arvadites, the Zemarites, 18
and the Hamathites. Later the
Canaanites spread, and then the 19
Canaanite border ran from Sidon
towards Gerar all the way to Gaza;
then all the way to Sodom and
Gomorrah, Admah and Zeboyim as
far as Lasha. These were the sons of 20
Ham, by families and languages with
their countries and nations.

Sons were born also to Shem, elder 21
brother of Japheth, the ancestor of all
the sons of Eber. The sons of Shem: 22[k]
Elam, Asshur, Arphaxad, Lud[l] and
Aram. The sons of Aram: Uz, Hul, 23
Gether and Mash. Arphaxad was the 24
father of Shelah, and Shelah the father
of Eber. Eber had two sons: one was 25
named Peleg,[m] because in his time the
earth was divided; and his brother's
name was Joktan. Joktan was the 26
father of Almodad, Sheleph, Hazarmoth, Jerah, Hadoram, Uzal, Diklah, 27
Obal, Abimael, Sheba, Ophir, Havilah 28,29
and Jobab. All these were sons of
Joktan. They lived in the eastern hill- 30
country, from Mesha all the way to
Sephar. These were the sons of Shem, 31
by families and languages with their
countries and nations.

These were the families of the sons of 32
Noah according to their genealogies,
nation by nation; and from them came
the separate nations on earth after the
flood.

ONCE UPON A TIME ALL THE WORLD **11**
spoke a single language and used the
same[n] words. As men journeyed in the 2

d Verses 2–4: cp. 1 Chr. 1. 5–7.   e Or Greece.
f Or Tarshish of the Kittians.
g Verses 6–8; cp. 1. 8–10.   h Or Egypt.
i Verses 13–18: cp. 1. Chr. 1. 11–16.   j Or the Hittites.
k Verses 22–29: cp. 1 Chr. 1. 17–23.   l Or the Lydians.
m That is Division.   n Or used few.

the Aegean Sea; among these were the Philistines who settled in Palestine during the thirteenth
century.
  10.1–32: The "Table of the Nations." This chapter is a composite work, the latest editing of
which intends it as a continuation of 5.32. By means of eponymous ("name-giving") ancestors,
it shows the spread of mankind after the deluge. Ch. 11 offers a different explanation for the
spread and diversity of mankind. **6:** *Ham:* the Egyptian political orbit; Canaan was under
Egyptian control, about 1500–1200 B.C. *Cush:* sometimes this term denotes Ethiopia, as here,
or else the land of the Kassites (v. 8; 2.13 n.). **21:** *Eber* is an eponymous ("name-giving")
ancestor of the *'ibrim,* "the Hebrews." This designation was used by the local population for
waves of invaders and migrants around 1500–1200 B.C. Israelites understood the term as a
designation of a people, namely, of themselves (14.13 n.).
  11.1–9: The tower of Babel. An ancient story explaining the origin of diverse languages
of mankind; here, it is another illustration of man's refusal to accept limitations (2.5–3.24 n.;
6.3 n.). It sets the stage for the true climax of chs. 1–11, namely, the divine choice of Abram

3 east, they came upon a plain in the land of Shinar and settled there. They said to one another, 'Come, let us make bricks and bake them hard'; they used bricks for stone and bitumen for 4 mortar. 'Come,' they said, 'let us build ourselves a city and a tower with its top in the heavens, and make a name for ourselves; or we shall be dispersed 5 all over the earth.' Then the LORD came down to see the city and tower 6 which mortal men had built, and he said, 'Here they are, one people with a single language, and now they have started to do this; henceforward nothing they have a mind to do will be 7 beyond their reach. Come, let us go down there and confuse their speech, so that they will not understand what 8 they say to one another.' So the LORD dispersed them from there all over the earth, and they left off building the 9 city. That is why it is called Babel,*o* because the LORD there made a babble of the language of all the world; from that place the LORD scattered men all over the face of the earth.

10*p* This is the table of the descendants of Shem. Shem was a hundred years old when he begot Arphaxad, two years 11 after the flood. After the birth of Arphaxad he lived five hundred years, and had other sons and daughters. 12 Arphaxad was thirty-five years old 13 when he begot Shelah. After the birth of Shelah he lived four hundred and three years, and had other sons and daughters. 14 Shelah was thirty years old when he 15 begot Eber. After the birth of Eber he lived four hundred and three years, and had other sons and daughters. 16 Eber was thirty-four years old when 17 he begot Peleg. After the birth of Peleg he lived four hundred and thirty years, and had other sons and daughters.

18 Peleg was thirty years old when he 19 begot Reu. After the birth of Reu he lived two hundred and nine years, and had other sons and daughters.

20 Reu was thirty-two years old when he begot Serug. After the birth of Serug 21 he lived two hundred and seven years, and had other sons and daughters.

22 Serug was thirty years old when he 23 begot Nahor. After the birth of Nahor he lived two hundred years, and had other sons and daughters.

24 Nahor was twenty-nine years old when he begot Terah. After the birth of 25 Terah he lived a hundred and nineteen years, and had other sons and daughters.

26 Terah was seventy years old when he begot Abram, Nahor and Haran.

27 This is the table of the descendants of Terah. Terah was the father of Abram, Nahor and Haran. Haran was the 28 father of Lot. Haran died in the presence of his father in the land of his birth, Ur of the Chaldees. Abram and 29 Nahor married wives; Abram's wife was called Sarai, and Nahor's Milcah. She was Haran's daughter; and he was also the father of Milcah and of Iscah. 30 Sarai was barren; she had no child. 31 Terah took his son Abram, his grandson Lot the son of Haran, and his daughter-in-law Sarai Abram's wife, and they set out from Ur of the Chaldees for the land of Canaan. But when they reached Harran, they settled there. 32 Terah was two hundred and five years old when he died in Harran.

Abraham and Isaac

THE LORD SAID TO ABRAM, 'LEAVE YOUR **12** own country, your kinsmen, and your father's house, and go to a country

o That is Babylon.
p Verses 10–26: cp. 1 Chr. 1. 24–27.

(12.1ff.). **2:** *Shinar:* Sumeria (see 10.10). **4:** *Tower:* the center of the Mesopotamian city was a complex of buildings including a pyramidal temple, extending upward toward a "gate" in the heavens through which the gods came down to reveal themselves. **8:** Probably the observation of vast temple ruins elicited this theological explanation by those to whom this culture was alien. **9:** *Babel:* this term, which for the Babylonians meant "the gate of the gods," is punned on through the verb *balal,* "to confuse," "make babble."
  11.10–32: Abram's genealogy. This material connects the deluge and the call of Israel's ancestor. Its insertion at this point heightens the effect of God's gracious but unexplained election of Abraham. **20–27:** Several of the names are personified cities. **28:** *Chaldees:* here the name is an anachronism; Chaldeans did not occupy lower Mesopotamia until much later.
  12.1–9: The call of Abram. His migration may have been part of a population movement

2 that I will show you. I will make you into a great nation, I will bless you and make your name so great that it shall be used in blessings!

3 Those that bless you I will bless,
  those that curse you, I will execrate.
  All the families on earth
  will pray to be blessed as you are blessed.'

4 And so Abram set out as the LORD had bidden him, and Lot went with him. Abram was seventy-five years old when 5 he left Harran. He took his wife Sarai, his nephew Lot, all the property they had collected, and all the dependants they had acquired in Harran, and they started on their journey to Canaan. 6 When they arrived, Abram passed through the country to the sanctuary at Shechem, the terebinth-tree of Moreh. At that time the Canaanites lived in this 7 land. There the LORD appeared to Abram and said, 'I give this land to your descendants.' So Abram built an altar there to the LORD who had ap-8 peared to him. Thence he went on to the hill-country east of Bethel and pitched his tent between Bethel on the west and Ai on the east. There he built an altar to the LORD and invoked the 9 LORD by name. Thus Abram journeyed by stages towards the Negeb.

10 There came a famine in the land, so severe that Abram went down to Egypt 11 to live there for a while. When he was approaching Egypt, he said to his wife Sarai, 'I know very well that you are a 12 beautiful woman, and that when the Egyptians see you, they will say, "She is his wife"; then they will kill me but 13 let you live. Tell them that you are my sister, so that all may go well with me because of you and my life may be 14 spared on your account.' When Abram arrived in Egypt, the Egyptians saw that she was indeed very beautiful. Pharaoh's courtiers saw her and praised 15 her to Pharaoh, and she was taken into Pharaoh's household. He treated 16 Abram well because of her, and Abram came to possess sheep and cattle and asses, male and female slaves, she-asses, and camels. But the LORD struck 17 Pharaoh and his household with grave diseases on account of Abram's wife Sarai. Pharaoh summoned Abram and 18 said to him, 'Why have you treated me like this? Why did you not tell me that 19 she is your wife? Why did you say that she was your sister, so that I took her as a wife? Here she is: take her and be gone.' Then Pharaoh gave his men 20 orders, and they sent Abram away with his wife and all that he had.

Abram went up from Egypt into the 13 Negeb, he and his wife and all that he had, and Lot went with him. Abram 2 was now very rich in cattle and in silver and gold. From the Negeb he journeyed 3 by stages to Bethel, to the place between Bethel and Ai where he had pitched his tent in the beginning, where 4 he had set up an altar on the first occasion and had invoked the LORD by name. Now Lot was travelling with 5 Abram, and he too possessed sheep and cattle and tents. The land could 6 not support them both together; for their livestock were so numerous that they could not settle in the same district, and there were quarrels between 7 Abram's herdsmen and Lot's. The Canaanites and the Perizzites were then living in the land. So Abram said to 8 Lot, 'Let there be no quarrelling between us, between my herdsmen and yours; for we are close kinsmen. The 9 whole country is there in front of you; let us part company. If you go left, I will go right; if you go right, I will go

(known to modern scholars) in the early second millennium B.C. **3**: A traditional interpretation is: "Through you all the families of the earth will be blessed." The call of Abram marks a culmination of the deity's efforts to restore the harmony of creation. **7**: *Altar*: the account attributes to Israel's ancestor the founding of an ancient Canaanite sanctuary. **9**: *Negeb*: "south," the barren area between Beersheba and the Gulf of Aqabah.

12.10–13.1: Abram in Egypt. God's promise to Abram (vv. 2–3) encounters its first challenge. Abram is here found wanting, for he is willing to sacrifice the future ancestress of Israel for self-security. But God's grace does not depend upon human worthiness, so that Sarai is preserved anyway. That the incident is repeated in 20.1–18; 26.6–11 reflects the bringing together of independent traditions in the editorial growth of the Pentateuch.

13.2–18: Abram and Lot. 4: *First occasion*: 12.8. **11:** *Chose*: through human freedom, God's

10 left.' Lot looked up and saw how well-watered the whole Plain of the Jordan was; all the way to Zoar it was like the Garden of the LORD, like the land of Egypt. This was before the LORD had 11 destroyed Sodom and Gomorrah. So Lot chose all the Plain of the Jordan and took the road on the east side. Thus 12 they parted company. Abram settled in the land of Canaan; but Lot settled among the cities of the Plain and 13 pitched his tents near Sodom. Now the men of Sodom were wicked, great sinners against the LORD.

14 After Lot and Abram had parted, the LORD said to Abram, 'Raise your eyes and look into the distance from the place where you are, north and south, 15 east and west. All the land you can see I will give to you and to your descen-16 dants for ever. I will make your descendants countless as the dust of the earth; if anyone could count the dust upon the ground, then he could count 17 your descendants. Now go through the length and breadth of the land, for I 18 give it to you.' So Abram moved his tent and settled by the terebinths of Mamre at Hebron; and there he built an altar to the LORD.

14 IT WAS IN THE TIME OF AMRAPHEL KING of Shinar, Arioch king of Ellasar, Kedorlaomer king of Elam, and Tidal 2 king of Goyim. They went to war against Bera king of Sodom, Birsha king of Gomorrah, Shinab king of Admah, Shemeber king of Zeboyim, and the king of Bela, that is Zoar. 3 These kings joined forces in the valley of Siddim, which is now the Dead Sea. 4 They had been subject to Kedorlaomer for twelve years, but in the thirteenth 5 year they rebelled. Then in the four-teenth year Kedorlaomer and his confederate kings came and defeated the Rephaim in Ashteroth-karnaim, the Zuzim in Ham, the Emim in 6 Shaveh-kiriathaim, and the Horites in

the hill-country from Seir^q as far as El-paran on the edge of the wilderness. On their way back they came to En-7 mishpat, which is now Kadesh, and laid waste all the country of the Amalekites and also that of the Amorites who lived in Hazazon-tamar. Then the kings of Sodom, Gomorrah, 8 Admah, Zeboyim, and Bela, which is now Zoar, marched out and drew up their forces against them in the valley of Siddim, against Kedorlaomer king of 9 Elam, Tidal king of Goyim, Amraphel king of Shinar, and Arioch king of Ellasar, four kings against five. Now 10 the valley of Siddim was full of bitumen pits; and when the kings of Sodom and Gomorrah fled, they fell into them, but the rest escaped to the hill-country. The 11 four kings captured all the flocks and herds of Sodom and Gomorrah and all their provisions, and went away. They 12 also carried off Lot, Abram's nephew, who was living in Sodom, and with him his flocks and herds. But a fugitive came 13 and told Abram the Hebrew, who at that time was dwelling by the terebinths of Mamre the Amorite. This Mamre was the brother of Eshcol and Aner, who were allies of Abram. When 14 Abram heard that his kinsman had been taken prisoner, he mustered his retainers, men born in his household, three hundred and eighteen of them, and pursued as far as Dan. Abram and 15 his followers surrounded the enemy by night, attacked them and pursued them as far as Hobah, north of Damascus; he then brought back all the flocks and 16 herds and also his kinsman Lot with his flocks and herds, together with the women and the other captives. On his 17 return from this defeat of Kedorlaomer and his confederate kings, the king of Sodom came out to meet him in the valley of Shaveh, which is now the King's Valley.

q Prob. rdg.; Heb. in their hill-country, Seir.

---

promise of the land (12.7) begins to be fulfilled; i.e. by Lot's choice, the land of the promise was left to Abram. **18:** *Terebinth:* the exact species of tree is uncertain.

   14.1–24: The defeat of the four eastern kings. Style and content indicate a one-time independent tradition. Its function may be to suggest that the Canaanite cult at Jerusalem, later assimilated and legitimized by David (2 Sam. chs. 6 and 24), had long previously been legitimized by Abram. **1–2:** Some of the personal names are attested in extrabiblical materials from the early second millennium B.C. This supports the basic historical reliability of the account, although a specific date cannot be assigned. **13:** *Hebrew:* "migrant"; see 10.21 n. This passage may have

18 Then Melchizedek king of Salem brought food and wine. He was priest 19 of God Most High, and he pronounced this blessing on Abram:

'Blessed be Abram
by God Most High,
creator^r of heaven and earth.
20 And blessed be God Most High,
who has delivered your enemies into
your power.'

Abram gave him a tithe of all the booty. 21 The king of Sodom said to Abram, 'Give me the people, and you can take 22 the property'; but Abram said to the king of Sodom, 'I lift my hand and swear by the LORD, God Most High, 23 creator of heaven and earth: not a thread of a shoe-string will I accept of anything that is yours. You shall never 24 say, "I made Abram rich." I will accept nothing but what the young men have eaten and the share of the men who went with me. Aner, Eshcol, and Mamre shall have their share.'

15 AFTER THIS THE WORD OF THE LORD came to Abram in a vision. He said, 'Do not be afraid, Abram, I am giving you a 2 very great reward.'^s Abram replied, 'Lord GOD, what canst thou give me? I have no standing among men, for the heir to my household is Eliezer of 3 Damascus.' Abram continued, 'Thou hast given me no children, and so my heir must be a slave born in my house.' 4 Then came the word of the LORD to him: 'This man shall not be your heir; your heir shall be a child of your own 5 body.' He took Abram outside and said, 'Look up into the sky, and count the stars if you can. So many', he said, 'shall your descendants be.'

Abram put his faith in the LORD, 6 and the LORD counted that faith to him as righteousness; he said to him, 'I am 7 the LORD who brought you out from Ur of the Chaldees to give you this land to occupy.' Abram said, 'O Lord 8 GOD, how can I be sure that I shall occupy it?' The LORD answered, 'Bring 9 me a heifer three years old, a she-goat three years old, a ram three years old, a turtle-dove, and a fledgling.' He 10 brought him all these, halved the animals down the middle and placed each piece opposite its corresponding piece, but he did not halve the birds. When the birds of prey swooped down 11 on the carcasses, Abram scared them away. Then, as the sun was going 12 down, a trance came over Abram and great fear came upon him. The LORD 13 said to Abram, 'Know this for certain, that your descendants will be aliens living in a land that is not theirs; they will be slaves, and will be held in oppression there for four hundred years. But I will punish that nation 14 whose slaves they are, and after that they shall come out with great possessions. You yourself shall join your 15 fathers in peace and be buried in a good old age; and the fourth generation 16 shall return here, for the Amorites will not be ripe for punishment till then.' The sun went down and it was dusk, 17 and there appeared a smoking brazier and a flaming torch passing between

r *Or* owner.
s I am giving . . . reward: *or* I am your shield, your very great reward.

played a role in giving the term its "ethnic" meaning. **18:** *Salem:* a variant name for Jerusalem (Ps.76.2). *God Most High:* a divine name, attested in antiquity in both this and the shorter form, "the Most High" (Isa.14.14; Ps.9.2). Here the Most High is identified with the LORD (Yahweh) of Israel (v. 22).

15.1–21: The covenant with Abram. 2–3: The Nuzi Texts (from Mesopotamia, about fourteenth century B.C.) stipulate that a *slave* can be adopted in case of childlessness. **7:** A separate tradition now begins, concerned with the promise of land (12.7). The covenant ceremony has parallels in the Mari Texts from Mesopotamia, eighteenth century B.C. By means of it, the LORD replaces Abram's human associates (14.13); Abram has rejected the gifts of the king of Sodom (14.22–24). **10:** The covenanting parties walked between the sliced parts of the animals, swearing to keep the stipulations lest they likewise be dismembered; see Jer.34.18, and compare, obliquely, 1 Sam.11.7 and Judg.19.29–30. **12:** Dreams were often regarded as the medium of divine revelation (20.3–7; Mt.2.19–23). **13–14:** The period of oppression in Egypt is given as an illustration of how the "promise" may be delayed, and serves to exhort future generations to maintain their faith. **16:** The *punishment* was to be the conquest of the Amorites, who were Canaanites, in the time of Joshua. **17:** *Torch:* the presence of the deity is often symbolized by fire (Exod.3.2; 13.21; 19.18). **18:** The boundaries given generally conform to those of the Davidic period (2 Sam.8.1–12; 1 Kgs.4.21; 8.65), this an indication of the date at which this

18 the divided pieces. That very day the LORD made a covenant with Abram, and he said, 'To your descendants I give this land from the River of Egypt to the Great River, the river Euphrates, 19 the territory of the Kenites, Kenizzites, 20 Kadmonites, Hittites, Perizzites, Reph-21 aim, Amorites, Canaanites, Girgashites, Hivites, and Jebusites.'

16 Abram's wife Sarai had borne him no children. Now she had an Egyptian 2 slave-girl whose name was Hagar, and she said to Abram, 'You see that the LORD has not allowed me to bear a child. Take my slave-girl; perhaps I shall found a family through her.' Abram agreed to what his wife said; 3 so Sarai, Abram's wife, brought her slave-girl, Hagar the Egyptian, and gave her to her husband Abram as a wife.[t] When this happened Abram had 4 been in Canaan for ten years. He lay with Hagar and she conceived; and when she knew that she was with child, 5 she despised her mistress. Sarai said to Abram, 'I have been wronged and you must answer for it. It was I who gave my slave-girl into your arms, but since she has known that she is with child, she has despised me. May the LORD see justice done between you 6 and me.' Abram replied to Sarai, 'Your slave-girl is in your hands; deal with her as you will.' So Sarai ill-treated her and she ran away.

7 The angel of the LORD found her by a spring of water in the wilderness 8 on the way to Shur, and he said, 'Hagar, Sarai's slave-girl, where have you come from and where are you going?' She answered, 'I am running 9 away from Sarai my mistress.' The angel of the LORD said to her, 'Go back to your mistress and submit to her ill-treatment.' The angel also said, 'I will 10 make your descendants too many to be counted.' And the angel of the LORD 11 said to her:

'You are with child and will bear a son.

You shall name him Ishmael,[u] because the LORD has heard of your ill-treatment.

He shall be a man like the wild ass, 12 his hand against every man and every man's hand against him; and he shall live at odds with[v] all his kinsmen.'

She called the LORD who was speaking 13 to her by the name El-Roi,[w] for she said, 'Have I indeed seen God and still live[x] after that vision?' That is why 14 men call the well Beer-lahai-roi;[y] it lies between Kadesh and Bered. Hagar 15 bore Abram a son, and he named the child she bore him Ishmael. Abram 16 was eighty-six years old when Hagar bore Ishmael.

When Abram was ninety-nine years 17 old, the LORD appeared to him and said, 'I am God Almighty. Live always in my presence and be perfect, so that 2 I may set my covenant between myself and you and multiply your descendants.' Abram threw himself down on his face, 3 and God spoke with him and said, 'I 4 make this covenant, and I make it with you: you shall be the father of a host of nations. Your name shall no longer be 5

t Or concubine. u That is God heard.
v Or live to the east of . . .
w That is God of a vision.
x God and still live: prob. rdg.; Heb. hither.
y That is the Well of the Living One of Vision.

---

material was gathered. 21: *Jebusites:* an ancient designation for the inhabitants of Jerusalem (2 Sam.5.6).

16.1–16: The birth of Ishmael. 1: The gap between promise and realization (see Introduction) is here reflected for a didactic ("teaching") purpose. **2:** The Nuzi Texts (15.2–3 n.) stipulate that a barren wife must provide her husband with a slave woman in order to insure his posterity (see 30.3,9). **4–5:** Ancient law codes provide for punishment if a pregnant female slave claimed equality with her mistress. **6–14:** Sarai has exceeded the limit of justice, and the God of Israel, ever concerned with the oppressed (Exod.3.7–10), comes to Hagar's aid. **7:** *Angel:* a messenger of the divine council (1.26 n.). Depicted in human form, angels usually mediate between the deity and man. They both symbolize and mitigate the extreme loftiness of the deity. But sometimes "angel" is used as a manifestation of the deity himself, as here (v. 13). **12:** Ishmael is regarded as the ancestor of the Bedouin. **13–14:** *El-Roi* is an epithet, or name, of the deity of this sacred spring; the writer identifies him with Israel's God (14.18 n.).

17.1–27: Second account of the covenant with Abram. In contrast to the earlier tradition (ch. 15), this late, Priestly account stresses the eternal nature of the covenant. **1:** *God Almighty:* lit. "the God of the Mountain(s)," an epithet possibly brought from Mesopotamia. It is here

Abram,[z] your name shall be Abraham,[a] for I make you father of a host of
6 nations. I will make you exceedingly fruitful; I will make nations out of you, and kings shall spring from you.
7 I will fulfil my covenant between myself and you and your descendants after you, generation after generation, an everlasting covenant, to be your God, yours and your descendants' after
8 you. As an everlasting possession I will give you and your descendants after you the land in which you now are aliens, all the land of Canaan, and I will be God to your descendants.'
9 God said to Abraham, 'For your part, you must keep my covenant, you and your descendants after you,
10 generation by generation. This is how you shall keep my covenant between myself and you and your descendants after you; circumcise yourselves, every
11 male among you. You shall circumcise the flesh of your foreskin, and it shall be the sign of the covenant between us.
12 Every male among you in every generation shall be circumcised on the eighth day, both those born in your house and any foreigner, not of your blood but
13 bought with your money. Circumcise both those born in your house and those bought with your money; thus shall my covenant be marked in your
14 flesh as an everlasting covenant. Every uncircumcised male, everyone who has not had the flesh of his foreskin circumcised, shall be cut off from the kin of his father. He has broken my covenant.'
15 God said to Abraham, 'As for Sarai your wife; you shall call her not Sarai,[b]
16 but Sarah.[c] I will bless her and give you a son by her. I will bless her and she shall be the mother of nations; the kings of many people shall spring from
17 her.' Abraham threw himself down on his face; he laughed and said to

himself, 'Can a son be born to a man who is a hundred years old? Can Sarah bear a son when she is ninety?'
18 He said to God, 'If only Ishmael might live under thy special care!' But
19 God replied, 'No. Your wife Sarah shall bear you a son, and you shall call him Isaac.[d] With him I will fulfil my covenant, an everlasting covenant with his descendants after him. I have heard
20 your prayer for Ishmael. I have blessed him and will make him fruitful. I will multiply his descendants; he shall be father of twelve princes, and I will raise a great nation from him. But my cove-
21 nant I will fulfil with Isaac, whom Sarah will bear to you at this season next year.' When he had finished talking with
22 Abraham, God ascended and left him.

23 Then Abraham took Ishmael his son, everyone who had been born in his household and everyone bought with money, every male in his household, and he circumcised them that very same day in the flesh of their foreskins as God had told him to do.
24 Abraham was ninety-nine years old when he circumcised the flesh of his
25 foreskin. Ishmael was thirteen years old when he was circumcised in the flesh of his foreskin. Both Abraham and
26 Ishmael were circumcised on the same day, and all the men of his household,
27 born in the house or bought with money from foreigners, were circumcised with him.

THE LORD APPEARED TO ABRAHAM BY **18** the terebinths of Mamre. As Abraham was sitting at the opening of his tent
2 in the heat of the day, he looked up and saw three men standing in front of him. When he saw them, he ran from the opening of his tent to meet them
3 and bowed low to the ground. 'Sirs,'

z *That is* High Father.   a *That is* Father of a Multitude.
b *That is* Mockery.   c *That is* Princess.
d *That is* He laughed.

---

applied to the God of Israel (see Exod. 6.2–3). **5:** A person entering a new relationship or achieving a new status may receive an appropriate new name. Compare 32.28. Abram and Abraham are probably dialectical variants of the same name. **9–14:** Circumcision is an ancient rite; by it the writer seeks to give Israel a new sense of tradition and focus for identity, as the external *sign* of membership in the eternal covenant community. The Noachian covenant (9.9–17), which comes from the same tradition, was with all mankind; the Abrahamic covenant is limited to Abraham's descendants. **15:** Again, the names are dialectical variants. **19:** *Isaac:* explanations of the name are also given in 18.12 and 21.6, which are part of older traditions. The meaning is joy, in that the parent rejoices at the newborn child.

    18.1–33: Abraham intercedes for Sodom. 2: Abraham addresses his visitors sometimes in the

he said, 'if I have deserved your favour, do not pass by my humble self without 4 a visit. Let me send for some water so that you may wash your feet and rest 5 under a tree; and let me fetch a little food so that you may refresh yourselves. Afterwards you may continue the journey which has brought you my way.' They said, 'Do by all means as 6 you say.' So Abraham hurried into the tent to Sarah and said, 'Take three measures of flour quickly, knead it 7 and make some cakes.' Then Abraham ran to the cattle, chose a fine tender calf and gave it to a servant, who 8 hurriedly prepared it. He took curds and milk and the calf he had prepared, set it before them, and waited on them himself under the tree while they ate. 9 They asked him where Sarah his wife was, and he said, 'There, in the tent.' 10 The stranger said, 'About this time next year I will be sure to come back to you, and Sarah your wife shall have a son.' Now Sarah was listening at the opening of the tent, and he was close 11 beside it. Both Abraham and Sarah had grown very old, and Sarah was 12 past the age of child-bearing. So Sarah laughed to herself and said, 'I am past bearing children now that I am out of my time, and my husband is old.' 13 The LORD said to Abraham, 'Why did Sarah laugh and say, "Shall I indeed 14 bear a child when I am old?" Is anything impossible for the LORD? In due season I will come back to you, about this time next year, and Sarah shall 15 have a son.' Sarah lied because she was frightened, and denied that she had laughed; but he said, 'Yes, you did laugh.'

16   The men set out and looked down towards Sodom, and Abraham went with them to start them on their way. 17 The LORD thought to himself, 'Shall I conceal from Abraham what I intend 18 to do? He will become a great and powerful nation, and all nations on

earth will pray to be blessed as he is blessed. I have taken care of him on 19 purpose that he may charge his sons and family after him to conform to the way of the LORD and to do what is right and just; thus I shall fulfil all that I have promised for him.' So the LORD 20 said, 'There is a great outcry over Sodom and Gomorrah; their sin is very grave. I must go down and see whether 21 their deeds warrant the outcry which has reached me. I am resolved to know the truth.' When the men turned and 22 went towards Sodom, Abraham remained standing before the LORD. Abraham drew near him and said, 23 'Wilt thou really sweep away good and bad together? Suppose there are fifty 24 good men in the city; wilt thou really sweep it away, and not pardon the place because of the fifty good men? Far be 25 it from thee to do this—to kill good and bad together; for then the good would suffer with the bad. Far be it from thee. Shall not the judge of all the earth do what is just?' The LORD said, 'If I find 26 in the city of Sodom fifty good men, I will pardon the whole place for their sake.' Abraham replied, 'May I pre- 27 sume to speak to the Lord, dust and ashes that I am: suppose there are five 28 short of the fifty good men? Wilt thou destroy the whole city for a mere five men?' He said, 'If I find forty-five there I will not destroy it.' Abraham spoke 29 again, 'Suppose forty can be found there?'; and he said, 'For the sake of the forty I will not do it.' Then 30 Abraham said, 'Please do not be angry, O Lord, if I speak again: suppose thirty can be found there?' He answered, 'If I find thirty there I will not do it.' Abraham continued, 'May 31 I presume to speak to the Lord: suppose twenty can be found there?' He replied, 'For the sake of the twenty I will not destroy it.' Abraham said, 32 'I pray thee not to be angry, O Lord, if I speak just once more: suppose ten

singular, sometimes in the plural, and the responses likewise shift in number. **11–12:** This tradition shows no knowledge of the similar one immediately before it (17.15–22); it abstains from explaining the name of the child as due to Sarah's laughter. **21:** The human qualities, including the lack of knowledge attributed to the deity, reflect a sophisticated dramatic literary style, and by no means a primitive stage of religious development. **23–33:** A basic Ancient Near Eastern belief held that the wickedness of the few contaminated the entire community and rendered it liable to punishment. This account, applying the principle in reverse, marks a major development in Israel's religious thought. See 19.4 n.

can be found there?' He said, 'For the sake of the ten I will not destroy it.'

33 When the LORD had finished talking with Abraham, he left him, and Abraham returned home.

19 The two angels came to Sodom in the evening, and Lot was sitting in the gateway of the city. When he saw them he rose to meet them and bowed low

2 with his face to the ground. He said, 'I pray you, sirs, turn aside to my humble home, spend the night there and wash your feet; you can rise early and continue your journey.' 'No,' they answered, 'we will spend the night in the

3 street.' But Lot was so insistent that they did turn aside and enter his house. He prepared a meal for them, baking unleavened cakes, and they ate them.

4 Before they lay down to sleep, the men of Sodom, both young and old, surrounded the house—everyone without

5 exception. They called to Lot and asked him where the men were who had entered his house that night. 'Bring them out,' they shouted, 'so that we can have intercourse with them.'

6 Lot went out into the doorway to

7 them, closed the door behind him and said, 'No, my friends, do not be so

8 wicked. Look, I have two daughters, both virgins; let me bring them out to you, and you can do what you like with them; but do not touch these men, because they have come under the

9 shelter of my roof.' They said, 'Out of our way! This man has come and settled here as an alien, and does he now take it upon himself to judge us? We will treat you worse than them.' They crowded in on the man Lot and pressed close to smash in the door.

10 But the two men inside reached out, pulled Lot in, and closed the door.

11 Then they struck the men in the doorway with blindness, both small and great, so that they could not find the door.

12 The two men said to Lot, 'Have you anyone else here, sons-in-law, sons, or daughters, or any who belong to you in the city? Get them out of this place,

13 because we are going to destroy it. The outcry against it has been so great that the LORD has sent us to destroy it.' So

14 Lot went out and spoke to his intended sons-in-law.[e] He said, 'Be quick and leave this place; the LORD is going to destroy the city.' But they did not take him seriously.

15 As soon as it was dawn, the angels urged Lot to go, saying, 'Be quick, take your wife and your two daughters who are here, or you will be swept away when the city is punished.' When

16 he lingered, they took him by the hand, with his wife and his daughters, and, because the LORD had spared him, led him on until he was outside the city.

17 When they had brought them out, they said, 'Flee for your lives; do not look back and do not stop anywhere in the Plain. Flee to the hills or you will be swept away.' Lot replied, 'No, sirs. You

18,19 have shown your servant favour and you have added to your unfailing care for me by saving my life, but I cannot escape to the hills; I shall be overtaken

20 by the disaster, and die. Look, here is a town, only a small place, near enough for me to reach quickly. Let me escape to it—it is very small—and save my

21 life.' He said to him, 'I grant your request: I will not overthrow this town

22 you speak of. But flee there quickly, because I can do nothing until you are there.' That is why the place was

23 called Zoar.[f] The sun had risen over the

24 land as Lot entered Zoar; and then the LORD rained down fire and brimstone from the skies on Sodom and

25 Gomorrah. He overthrew those cities and destroyed all the Plain, with everyone living there and everything growing

e Or his sons-in-law, who had married his daughters.
f That is Small.

19.1–29: The destruction of Sodom and Gomorrah. This is a theological explanation of the ancient destruction of cities on the south shore of the Dead Sea; in Gen.14.2, the cities number five. **4:** The entire population (see 18.23–33 n.), is here depicted as surrounding Lot's house. **5:** The intent is to illustrate the sexual excesses of the Canaanites, warning Israel not to participate in them; see 9.26 n. From the episode comes the term "sodomy." **6–8:** In traditional fashion, Lot places the welfare of his guests above all else. Once a guest has eaten in the house, the Near Eastern host must guarantee his safety. See Judg.19.16–24. **24:** *Brimstone:* sulphur, a flammable element found in the area. **26:** *Pillar:* a folk explanation for an oddly shaped column in the area, one of which is still today associated with Lot's wife.

26 in the ground. But Lot's wife, behind him, looked back, and she turned into a pillar of salt.

27 Next morning Abraham rose early and went to the place where he had 28 stood in the presence of the LORD. He looked down towards Sodom and Gomorrah and all the wide extent of the Plain, and there he saw thick smoke rising high from the earth like the 29 smoke of a lime-kiln. Thus, when God destroyed the cities of the Plain, he thought of Abraham and rescued Lot from the disaster, the overthrow of the cities where he had been living.

30 Lot went up from Zoar and settled in the hill-country with his two daughters, because he was afraid to stay in Zoar; he lived with his two 31 daughters in a cave. The elder daughter said to the younger, 'Our father is old and there is not a man in the country 32 to come to us in the usual way. Come now, let us make our father drink wine and then lie with him and in this way keep the family alive through our 33 father.' So that night they gave him wine to drink, and the elder daughter came and lay with him, and he did not know when she lay down and when 34 she got up. Next day the elder said to the younger, 'Last night I lay with my father. Let us give him wine to drink again tonight; then you go in and lie with him. So we shall keep the 35 family alive through our father.' So they gave their father wine to drink again that night, and the younger daughter went and lay with him, and he did not know when she lay down and 36 when she got up. In this way both Lot's daughters came to be with child by their 37 father. The elder daughter bore a son and called him Moab; he was the 38 ancestor of the present Moabites. The younger also bore a son, whom she called Ben-ammi; he was the ancestor of the present Ammonites.

20 ABRAHAM JOURNEYED BY STAGES FROM there into the Negeb, and settled between Kadesh and Shur, living as an alien in Gerar. He said that Sarah his 2 wife was his sister, and Abimelech king of Gerar sent and took her. But God 3 came to Abimelech in a dream by night and said, 'You shall die because of this woman whom you have taken. She is a married woman.' Now Abimelech 4 had not gone near her; and he said, 'Lord, wilt thou destroy an innocent people? Did he not tell me himself that 5 she was his sister, and she herself said that he was her brother. It was with a clear conscience and in all innocence that I did this.' God said to him in the 6 dream, 'Yes: I know that you acted with a clear conscience. Moreover, it was I who held you back from committing a sin against me: that is why I did not let you touch her. Send back 7 the man's wife now; he is a prophet, and he will intercede on your behalf, and you shall live. But if you do not send her back, I tell you that you are doomed to die, you and all that is yours.' So Abimelech rose early in the 8 morning, summoned all his servants and told them the whole story; the men were terrified. Abimelech then 9 summoned Abraham and said to him, 'Why have you treated us like this? What harm have I done to you that you should bring this great sin on me and my kingdom? You have done a thing that ought not to be done.' And 10 he asked Abraham, 'What was your purpose in doing this?' Abraham 11 answered, 'I said to myself, There can be no fear of God in this place, and they will kill me for the sake of my wife. She is in fact my sister, she is 12 my father's daughter though not by the same mother; and she became my wife. When God set me wandering 13 from my father's house, I said to her, "There is a duty towards me which you must loyally fulfil: wherever we go, you must say that I am your brother."' Then Abimelech took sheep and cattle, 14

<hr>

19.30–38: The origin of the Moabites and Ammonites. The previous episode leads to this story of the unflattering origin of the two traditional enemies of Israel.

　　20.1–18: Abraham and Sarah at Gerar. God continues to deliver the ancestress of Israel, so that the promise can be realized (see 12.10–13.1 n.). **1:** *From there:* Mamre (18.1; 19.27); 19.30–38 seem to have been added intrusively. **12:** Marriage to a half-sister (2 Sam.13.13) was later forbidden (Lev.18.11). The Nuzi Texts (15.2–3 n.) mention that one's wife may be legally

and male and female slaves, gave them to Abraham, and returned his wife 15 Sarah to him. Abimelech said, 'My country lies before you; settle wherever 16 you please.' To Sarah he said, 'I have given your brother a thousand pieces of silver, so that your own people may turn a blind eye on it all, and you will 17 be completely vindicated.' Then Abraham interceded with God, and God healed Abimelech, his wife, and his 18 slave-girls, and they bore children; for the LORD had made every woman in Abimelech's household barren on account of Abraham's wife Sarah.

21 The LORD showed favour to Sarah as he had promised, and made good 2 what he had said about her. She conceived and bore a son to Abraham for his old age, at the time which God 3 had appointed. The son whom Sarah bore to him, Abraham named Isaac.*g* 4 When Isaac was eight days old Abraham circumcised him, as God had 5 commanded. Abraham was a hundred years old when his son Isaac was born. 6 Sarah said, 'God has given me good reason to laugh, and everybody who 7 hears will laugh with me.' She said, 'Whoever would have told Abraham that Sarah would suckle children? Yet I have borne him a son for his old age.' 8 The boy grew and was weaned, and on the day of his weaning Abraham gave a 9 feast. Sarah saw the son whom Hagar the Egyptian had borne to Abraham 10 laughing at him, and she said to Abraham, 'Drive out this slave-girl and her son; I will not have this slave-girl's son sharing the inheritance with my 11 son Isaac.' Abraham was vexed at this 12 on his son Ishmael's account, but God said to him, 'Do not be vexed on account of the boy and the slave-girl. Do what Sarah says, because you shall 13 have descendants through Isaac. I will make a great nation of the slave-girl's

son too, because he is your own child.' Abraham rose early in the morning, 14 took some food and a waterskin full of water and gave it to Hagar; he set the child on her shoulder and sent her away, and she went and wandered in the wilderness of Beersheba. When the 15 water in the skin was finished, she thrust the child under a bush, and went 16 and sat down some way off, about two bowshots away, for she said, 'How can I watch the child die?' So she sat some way off, weeping bitterly. God heard 17 the child crying, and the*h* angel of God called from heaven to Hagar, 'What is the matter, Hagar? Do not be afraid: God has heard the child crying where you laid him. Get to your feet, lift 18 the child up and hold him in your arms, because I will make of him a great nation.' Then God opened her eyes and 19 she saw a well full of water; she went to it, filled her waterskin and gave the child a drink. God was with the child, 20-21 and he grew up and lived in the wilderness of Paran. He became an archer, and his mother found him a wife from Egypt.

Now about that time Abimelech, 22 with Phicol the commander of his army, addressed Abraham in these terms: 'God is with you in all that you do. Now swear an oath to me in the 23 name of God, that you will not break faith with me, my offspring, or my descendants. As I have kept faith with you, so shall you keep faith with me and with the country where you have come to live as an alien.' Abraham said, 'I 24 swear.' It happened that Abraham had 25 a complaint against Abimelech about a well which Abimelech's men had seized. Abimelech said, 'I do not know 26 who did this. You never told me, and I have heard nothing about it till now.' So Abraham took sheep and cattle and 27

g That is He laughed.   *h Or* an.

adopted as a sister. **18**: Only in the final verse is the LORD identified with the deity of the story (see 14.18 n.; 16.13 n.; 17.1 n.).

21.1–7: The birth of Isaac. The extraordinary miracle of Israel's emergence and survival continues to be emphasized.

21.8–21: The expulsion of Ishmael. The account may be a variant of 16.1–12. **10**: Ancient Near Eastern law stipulated that the offspring of a slave wife could either inherit with the children of the free woman or be set free. Sarah demands the latter option. **17**: *God has heard:* a pun on the name Ishmael; see 16.11 and Tfn. *u* there.

21.22–34: Abraham's dispute with Abimelech. The patriarch obtains property rights in the vicinity of Beersheba, where the origin of an ancient sanctuary is attributed to him (see 12.7 n.).

gave them to Abimelech; and the two 28 of them made a pact. Abraham set 29 seven ewe-lambs apart, and when Abimelech asked him why he had set 30 these lambs apart, he said, 'Accept these from me in token that I dug this 31 well.' Therefore that place was called Beersheba,[i] because there the two of 32 them swore an oath. When they had made the pact at Beersheba, Abimelech and Phicol the commander of his army returned at once to the country of the 33 Philistines, and Abraham planted a strip of ground[j] at Beersheba. There he invoked the LORD, the everlasting God, 34 by name, and he lived as an alien in the country of the Philistines for many a year.

22 THE TIME CAME WHEN GOD PUT ABRAHAM to the test. 'Abraham', he called, and 2 Abraham replied, 'Here I am.' God said, 'Take your son Isaac, your only son, whom you love, and go to the land of Moriah. There you shall offer him as a sacrifice on one of the hills which I will 3 show you.' So Abraham rose early in the morning and saddled his ass, and he took with him two of his men and his son Isaac; and he split the firewood for the sacrifice, and set out for the 4 place of which God had spoken. On the third day Abraham looked up and 5 saw the place in the distance. He said to his men, 'Stay here with the ass while I and the boy go over there; and when we have worshipped we will 6 come back to you.' So Abraham took the wood for the sacrifice and laid it on his son Isaac's shoulder; he himself carried the fire and the knife, and the 7 two of them went on together. Isaac said to Abraham, 'Father', and he answered, 'What is it, my son?' Isaac said, 'Here are the fire and the wood, but where is the young beast for the 8 sacrifice?' Abraham answered, 'God will provide himself with a young beast

for a sacrifice, my son.' And the two of them went on together and came to the 9 place of which God had spoken. There Abraham built an altar and arranged the wood. He bound his son Isaac and laid him on the altar on top of the wood. Then he stretched out his hand 10 and took the knife to kill his son; but 11 the angel of the LORD called to him from heaven, 'Abraham, Abraham.' He answered, 'Here I am.' The angel 12 of the LORD said, 'Do not raise your hand against the boy; do not touch him. Now I know that you are a God-fearing man. You have not withheld from me your son, your only son.' Abraham looked up, and there he saw 13 a ram caught by its horns in a thicket. So he went and took the ram and offered it as a sacrifice instead of his son. Abraham named that place Je- 14 hovah-jireh;[k] and to this day the saying is: 'In the mountain of the LORD it was provided.' Then the angel of the 15 LORD called from heaven a second time to Abraham, 'This is the word of the 16 LORD: By my own self I swear: inasmuch as you have done this and have not withheld your son, your only son, I will bless you abundantly and greatly 17 multiply your descendants until they are as numerous as the stars in the sky and the grains of sand on the sea-shore. Your descendants shall possess the cities of their enemies. All nations on 18 earth shall pray to be blessed as your descendants are blessed, and this because you have obeyed me.'

Abraham went back to his men, and 19 together they returned to Beersheba; and there Abraham remained.

After this Abraham was told, 'Milcah 20 has borne sons to your brother Nahor: Uz his first-born, then his brother Buz, 21 and Kemuel father of Aram, and 22 Kesed, Hazo, Pildash, Jidlaph and

i That is Well of Seven *and* Well of an Oath.
j Or planted a tamarisk.
k That is the LORD will provide.

31: Two explanations for the name of the place have been combined; see Tfn. *i.* **32:** *Philistines:* an anachronism, for they settled in Palestine only later; see 9.27 n. **33:** *The everlasting God:* an ancient epithet, probably from the pre-Israelite cult at Beersheba, is here applied to the LORD.
 22.1–19: The testing of Abraham. At the very moment when the future of Israel seems finally established (21.1–7), it receives its most serious challenge, namely, can Israel continue to keep its identity despite adverse circumstance? **2:** The earliest form of this story may have been directed against child *sacrifice*, proposing that the deity desires the substitution of animals. **14:** *Jehovah:* see Introduction, p. xx.
 22.20–24: Abraham's Aramaean relatives. A league of twelve tribes paralleling the descendants

23 Bethuel; and a daughter, Rebecca, has been born to Bethuel.' These eight Milcah bore to Abraham's brother
24 Nahor. His concubine, whose name was Reumah, also bore him sons: Tebah, Gaham, Tahash and Maacah.

23 Sarah lived for a hundred and
2 twenty-seven years, and died in Kiriath-arba, which is Hebron, in Canaan. Abraham went in to mourn over Sarah
3 and to weep for her. At last he rose and left the presence of the dead. He said
4 to the Hittites, 'I am an alien and a settler among you. Give me land enough for a burial-place, so that I can
5 give my dead proper burial.' The
6 Hittites answered Abraham, 'Do, pray, listen to what we have to say, sir. You are a mighty prince among us. Bury your dead in the best grave we have. There is not one of us who will deny you his grave or hinder you from
7 burying your dead.' Abraham stood up and then bowed low to the Hittites,
8 the people of that country. He said to them, 'If you are willing to let me give my dead proper burial, then listen to me and speak for me to Ephron son of
9 Zohar, asking him to give me the cave that belongs to him at Machpelah, at the far end of his land. Let him give it to me for the full price, so that I may take possession of it as a burial-place
10 within your territory.' Ephron the Hittite was sitting with the others, and he gave Abraham this answer in the hearing of everyone as they came into
11 the city gate: 'No, sir; hear what I have to say. I will make you a gift of the land and I will also give you the cave which is on it. In the presence of all my kinsmen I give it to you; so bury your
12 dead.' Abraham bowed low before the
13 people of the country and said to Ephron in their hearing, 'If you really mean it—but do listen to me! I give you the price of the land: take it and I
14 will bury my dead there.' And Ephron
15 answered, 'Do listen to me, sir: the land is worth four hundred shekels of silver. But what is that between you and me? There you may bury your dead.' Abraham came to an agreement 16 with him and weighed out the amount that Ephron had named in the hearing of the Hittites, four hundred shekels of the standard recognized by merchants. Thus the plot of land belonging 17 to Ephron at Machpelah to the east of Mamre, the plot, the cave that is on it, every tree on the plot, within the whole area, became the legal possession of 18 Abraham, in the presence of all the Hittites as they came into the city gate. After this Abraham buried his wife 19 Sarah in the cave on the plot of land at Machpelah to the east of Mamre, which is Hebron, in Canaan. Thus the 20 plot and the cave on it became Abraham's possession as a burial-place, by purchase from the Hittites.

By THIS TIME ABRAHAM HAD BECOME A **24** very old man, and the LORD had blessed him in all that he did. Abraham 2 said to his servant, who had been long in his service and was in charge of all his possessions, 'Put your hand under my thigh: I want you to swear by the 3 LORD, the God of heaven and earth, that you will not take a wife for my son from the women of the Canaanites in whose land I dwell; you must go to my 4 own country and to my own kindred to find a wife for my son Isaac.' The 5 servant said to him, 'What if the woman is unwilling to come with me to this country? Must I in that event take your son back to the land from which you came?' Abraham said to 6 him, 'On no account are you to take my son back there. The LORD the God 7 of heaven who took me from my father's house and the land of my birth, the LORD who swore to me that he would give this land to my descendants—he will send his angel before you, and from there you shall take a

---

of Ishmael (25.13–15) and Jacob (29.31–30.24; 35.16–20,23–26) is presented. The list here differs from the Aramaean genealogy in 10.23.
    23.1–20: The tomb of the patriarchs. 3: The *Hittites*, originally from Asia Minor, were part of the pre-Israelite population of Canaan (10.15, Tfn. *j*). **11–18:** This marks another development in the patriarchal claim to the land (see 21.22–34 n.).
    24.1–67: The marriage of Isaac. 2: The *thigh* may be a euphemism for the male organ. The significance of the act, accompanying the most solemn of oaths (see 47.29), is not clear. **3:** The fear is not that of the mixing of people but of religious deterioration; see Exod. 34.15–16;

8 wife for my son. If the woman is un-willing to come with you, then you will be released from your oath to me; but you must not take my son back there.'
9 So the servant put his hand under his master Abraham's thigh and swore an oath in those terms.
10   The servant took ten camels from his master's herds, and also all kinds of gifts from his master; he set out for Aram-naharaim[1] and arrived at the
11 city where Nahor lived. Towards evening, the time when the women come out to draw water, he made the camels kneel down by the well outside
12 the city. He said, 'O LORD God of my master Abraham, give me good fortune this day; keep faith with my master
13 Abraham. Here I stand by the spring, and the women of the city are coming
14 out to draw water. Let it be like this: I shall say to a girl, "Please lower your jar so that I may drink"; and if she answers, "Drink, and I will water your camels also", that will be the girl whom thou dost intend for thy servant Isaac. In this way I shall know that thou hast kept faith with my master.'
15   Before he had finished praying silently, he saw Rebecca coming out with her water-jug on her shoulder. She was the daughter of Bethuel son of Milcah, the wife of Abraham's brother
16 Nahor. The girl was very beautiful, a virgin, who had had no intercourse with a man. She went down to the spring, filled her jar and came up again.
17 Abraham's servant hurried to meet her and said, 'Give me a sip of water from
18 your jar.' 'Drink, sir', she answered, and at once lowered her jar on to her
19 hand to let him drink. When she had finished giving him a drink, she said, 'Now I will draw water for your camels
20 until they have had enough.' So she quickly emptied her jar into the water-trough, hurried again to the well to draw water and watered all the camels.
21 The man was watching quietly to see whether or not the LORD had made his
22 journey successful. When the camels had finished drinking, the man took a gold nose-ring weighing half a shekel,

and two bracelets for her wrists weighing ten shekels, also of gold, and 23 said, 'Tell me, please, whose daughter you are. Is there room in your father's house for us to spend the night?' She 24 answered, 'I am the daughter of Bethuel, the son of Nahor and Milcah; and we have plenty of straw and fodder 25 and also room for you to spend the night.' So the man bowed down and 26 prostrated himself to the LORD. He 27 said, 'Blessed be the LORD the God of my master Abraham, who has not failed to keep faith and truth with my master; for I have been guided by the LORD to the house of my master's kinsman.'
    The girl ran to her mother's house 28 and told them what had happened. Now Rebecca had a brother named 29-30 Laban; and, when he saw the nose-ring, and also the bracelets on his sister's wrists, and heard his sister Rebecca tell what the man had said to her, he ran out to the man at the spring. When he came to him and found him still standing there by the camels, he 31 said, 'Come in, sir, whom the LORD has blessed. Why stay outside? I have prepared the house, and there is room for the camels.' So he brought the man 32 into the house, unloaded the camels and provided straw and fodder for them, and water for him and all his men to wash their feet. Food was set before 33 him, but he said, 'I will not eat until I have delivered my message.' Laban said, 'Let us hear it.' He answered, 'I am 34 the servant of Abraham. The LORD has 35 greatly blessed my master, and he has become a man of power. The LORD has given him flocks and herds, silver and gold, male and female slaves, camels and asses. My master's wife 36 Sarah in her old age bore him a son, to whom he has given all that he has. So 37 my master made me swear an oath, saying, "You shall not take a wife for my son from the women of the Canaanites in whose land I dwell; but 38 you shall go to my father's house and to my family to find a wife for him."
1 That is Aram of Two Rivers.

Deut. 7.3–4. **10**: *Aram-naharaim*: central Mesopotamia. **14**: It was a common ancient assumption that the deity would reveal his will through such possible incidents; see 1 Sam.14.6–10; Judg.

39 So I said to my master, "What if the
40 woman will not come with me?" He
answered, "The LORD, in whose presence I have lived, will send his angel
with you and will make your journey
successful. You shall take a wife for my
son from my family and from my
41 father's house; then you shall be
released from the charge I have laid
upon you. But if, when you come to my
family, they will not give her to you,
you shall still be released from the
42 charge." So I came to the spring today,
and I said, "O LORD God of my
master Abraham, if thou wilt make my
43 journey successful, let it be like this.
Here I stand by the spring. When a
young woman comes out to draw
water, I shall say to her, 'Give me a
44 little water to drink from your jar.' If
she answers, 'Yes, do drink, and I will
draw water for your camels as well', she
is the woman whom the LORD intends
45 for my master's son." Before I had
finished praying silently, I saw Rebecca
coming out with her water-jar on her
shoulder. She went down to the spring
and drew some water, and I said to her,
46 "Please give me a drink." She quickly
lowered her jar from her shoulder and
said, "Drink; and I will water your
camels as well." So I drank, and she
47 also gave my camels water. I asked her
whose daughter she was, and she said,
"I am the daughter of Bethuel, the son
of Nahor and Milcah." Then I put the
ring in her nose and the bracelets on
48 her wrists, and I bowed low and
prostrated myself before the LORD. I
blessed the LORD the God of my master
Abraham, who had led me by the right
road to take my master's niece for his
49 son. Now tell me if you will keep faith
and truth with my master. If not, say
so, and I will turn elsewhere.'
50 Laban and Bethuel answered, 'This
is from the LORD; we can say nothing
51 for or against. Here is Rebecca herself;
take her and go. She shall be the wife
of your master's son, as the LORD has
52 decreed.' When Abraham's servant
heard what they said, he prostrated
himself on the ground before the LORD.

Then he brought out gold and silver 53
ornaments, and robes, and gave them
to Rebecca, and he gave costly gifts to
her brother and her mother. He and 54
his men then ate and drank and spent
the night there. When they rose in the
morning, he said, 'Give me leave to go
back to my master.' Her brother and 55
her mother said, 'Let the girl stay with
us for a few days, say ten days, and
then she shall go.' But he said to them, 56
'Do not detain me, for the LORD has
granted me success. Give me leave to
return to my master.' They said, 'Let 57
us call the girl and see what she says.'
They called Rebecca and asked her if 58
she would go with the man, and she
said, 'Yes, I will go.' So they let their 59
sister Rebecca and her nurse go with
Abraham's servant and his men. They 60
blessed Rebecca and said to her:

'You are our sister, may you be the
  mother of myriads;
may your sons possess the cities of
  their enemies.'

Then Rebecca and her companions 61
mounted their camels at once and
followed the man. So the servant took
Rebecca and went his way.

Isaac meanwhile had moved on as 62
far as Beer-lahai-roi and was living in
the Negeb. One evening when he had 63
gone out into the open country hoping
to meet them,[m] he looked up and saw
camels approaching. When Rebecca 64
raised her eyes and saw Isaac, she
slipped hastily from her camel, saying 65
to the servant, 'Who is that man walking across the open towards us?' The servant answered, 'It is my master.' So she
took her veil and covered herself. The
servant related to Isaac all that had hap- 66
pened. Isaac conducted her into the 67
tent[n] and took her as his wife. So she
became his wife, and he loved her and
was consoled for the death of his mother.

ABRAHAM MARRIED ANOTHER WIFE, 25[o]
whose name was Keturah. She bore 2

m hoping . . . them: *or* to relieve himself.
n *Prob. rdg.; Heb. adds* Sarah his mother.
o *Verses 1–4: cp. 1 Chr. 1. 32, 33.*

6.36–37. 57–58: Nuzi Texts (see 15.2–3 n.) show that the consent of the girl was necessary among
the people of this area. 62: *Beer-lahai-roi:* see 16.13–14 n.; see there Tfn. *y.*
25.1–18: The death of Abraham. 1–6: This section may be out of place, for Abraham in 24.1

him Zimran, Jokshan, Medan, Midian,
3 Ishbak and Shuah. Jokshan became
the father of Sheba and Dedan. The
sons of Dedan were Asshurim, Letush-
4 im and Leummin, and the sons of
Midian were Ephah, Epher, Enoch,
Abida and Eldaah. All these were
descendants of Keturah.
5   Abraham had given all that he had
6 to Isaac; and he had already in his
lifetime given presents to the sons of
his concubines, and had sent them away
eastwards, to a land of the east, out of
7 his son Isaac's way. Abraham had
lived for a hundred and seventy-five
8 years when he breathed his last. He
died at a good old age, after a very long
life, and was gathered to his father's
9 kin. His sons, Isaac and Ishmael, buried
him in the cave at Machpelah, on the
land of Ephron son of Zohar the
10 Hittite, east of Mamre, the plot which
Abraham had bought from the Hittites.
There Abraham was buried with his
11 wife Sarah. After the death of Abraham, God blessed his son Isaac, who
settled close by Beer-lahai-roi.
12   This is the table of the descendants
of Abraham's son Ishmael, whom
Hagar the Egyptian, Sarah's slave-girl,
13p bore to him. These are the names of the
sons of Ishmael named in order of their
birth: Nebaioth, Ishmael's eldest son,
14 then Kedar, Adbeel, Mibsam, Mishma,
15 Dumah, Massa, Hadad, Teman, Jetur,
16 Naphish and Kedemah. These are the
sons of Ishmael, after whom their
hamlets and encampments were named,
twelve princes according to their tribal
17 groups. Ishmael had lived for a hundred
and thirty-seven years when he breathed
his last. So he died and was gathered
18 to his father's kin. Ishmael's sons
inhabited the land from Havilah to
Shur, which is east of Egypt on the
way to Asshur, having settled to the
east of his brothers.

THIS IS THE TABLE OF THE DESCENDANTS 19
of Abraham's son Isaac. Isaac's father
was Abraham. When Isaac was forty 20
years old he married Rebecca the
daughter of Bethuel the Aramaean
from Paddan-aram and the sister of
Laban the Aramaean. Isaac appealed 21
to the LORD on behalf of his wife
because she was barren; the LORD
yielded to his entreaty, and Rebecca
conceived. The children pressed hard 22
on each other in her womb, and she
said, 'If this is how it is with me, what
does it mean?' So she went to seek
guidance of the LORD. The LORD said 23
to her:

'Two nations in your womb,
  two peoples, going their own ways
    from birth!
  One shall be stronger than the other;
  the older shall be servant to the
    younger.'

When her time had come, there were 24
indeed twins in her womb. The first 25
came out red, hairy all over like a hair-
cloak, and they named him Esau.*q*
Immediately afterwards his brother 26
was born with his hand grasping
Esau's heel, and they called him Jacob.*r*
Isaac was sixty years old when they
were born. The boys grew up; and 27
Esau became skilful in hunting, a man
of the open plains, but Jacob led a
settled life and stayed among the tents.
Isaac favoured Esau because he kept 28
him supplied with venison, but Rebecca
favoured Jacob. One day Jacob pre- 29
pared a broth and when Esau came in
from the country, exhausted, he said to 30
Jacob, 'I am exhausted; let me swallow
some of that red broth': this is why he
was called Edom.*s* Jacob said, 'Not till 31

p Verses 13–16: cp. 1 Chr. 1. 29–31.
q That is Covering.
r That is He caught by the heel.
s That is Red.

is already a very old man, and in 25.8 seems to be on his deathbed. **9–10:** *Machpelah:* see
23.8–20. **16:** The *sons* number *twelve*; see 22.20–24 n.
   25.19–34: The third patriarch and the rivalry between Jacob (Israel) and Esau (Edom).
20: *Paddan-aram:* a variant of Aram-naharaim; see 24.10 n. **21:** The repetition of the barrenness
motif is another means of emphasizing the difficulties Israel would encounter in realizing the
divine promise. **23:** The firstborn had exclusive rights of inheritance, and hence an unexpected
reversal is here proposed. **25:** The Heb. word for *red* (*admoni*) is a play on Edom (v. 30), as
hairy (*se'ar*) is on Seir (32.3). **26:** *Jacob* is explained by folk etymology. The name may actually
have meant "Let (God) protect." **27:** The two typify the ways of life of the peoples whom they
represent. **30:** In actuality, the name Edom may derive from the characteristic redness of the

you sell me your rights as the first-
32 born.' Esau replied, 'I am at death's
door; what use is my birthright to me?'
33 Jacob said, 'Not till you swear!'; so he
swore an oath and sold his birthright
34 to Jacob. Then Jacob gave Esau bread
and the lentil broth, and he ate and
drank and went away without more
ado. Thus Esau showed how little he
valued his birthright.

26 There came a famine in the land—
not the earlier famine in Abraham's
time—and Isaac went to Abimelech the
2 Philistine king at Gerar. The LORD
appeared to Isaac and said, 'Do not
go down to Egypt, but stay in this
3 country as I bid you. Stay in this
country and I will be with you and bless
you, for to you and to your descendants
I will give all these lands. Thus shall I
fulfil the oath which I swore to your
4 father Abraham. I will make your
descendants as many as the stars in the
sky; I will give them all these lands, and
all the nations of the earth will pray to
5 be blessed as they are blessed—all
because Abraham obeyed me and kept
my charge, my commandments, my
6 statutes, and my laws.' So Isaac lived
in Gerar.
7 When the men of the place asked
him about his wife, he told them that
she was his sister; he was afraid to say
that Rebecca was his wife, in case they
killed him because of her; for she was
8 very beautiful. When they had been
there for some considerable time,
Abimelech the Philistine king looked
down from his window and saw Isaac
and his wife Rebecca laughing to-
9 gether. He summoned Isaac and said,
'So she is your wife, is she? What made
you say she was your sister?' Isaac
answered, 'I thought I should be killed
10 because of her.' Abimelech said, 'Why
have you treated us like this? One of
the people might easily have gone to
bed with your wife, and then you would
have made us liable to retribution.'
11 So Abimelech warned all the people,

threatening that whoever touched this
man or his wife would be put to death.
Isaac sowed seed in that land, and 12
that year he reaped a hundredfold,
and the LORD blessed him. He became 13
more and more powerful, until he was
very powerful indeed. He had flocks 14
and herds and many slaves, so that the
Philistines were envious of him. They 15
had stopped up all the wells dug by the
slaves in the days of Isaac's father
Abraham, and filled them with earth.
Isaac dug them again, all those wells 18
dug in his father Abraham's time, and
stopped up by the Philistines after his
death, and he called them by the names
which his father had given them.
Then Abimelech said to him, 'Go 16
away from here; you are too strong for
us.' So Isaac left that place and en- 17
camped in the valley of Gerar, and
stayed there. Then Isaac's slaves dug 19*t*
in the valley and found a spring of
running water, but the shepherds of 20
Gerar quarrelled with Isaac's shepherds, claiming the water as theirs. He
called the well Esek,*u* because they
made difficulties for him. His men then 21
dug another well, but the others
quarrelled with him over that also, so
he called it Sitnah.*v* He moved on from 22
there and dug another well, but there
was no quarrel over that one, so he
called it Rehoboth,*w* saying, 'Now the
LORD has given us plenty of room and
we shall be fruitful in the land.'
Isaac went up country from there to 23
Beersheba. That same night the LORD 24
appeared to him there and said, 'I am
the God of your father Abraham. Fear
nothing, for I am with you. I will bless
you and give you many descendants
for the sake of Abraham my servant.'
So Isaac built an altar there and in- 25
voked the LORD by name. Then he
pitched his tent there, and there also
his slaves dug a well. Abimelech came 26
to him from Gerar with Ahuzzath his

t Verse 18 transposed to follow 15.　u That is Difficulty.
v That is Enmity.　　*w That is* Plenty of room.

---

soil of the area. **31:** Specifically, the *birthright* included a double share of the inheritance (Deut.
21.15–17). **33:** The intent is to explain how, in the mystery of God's providence, Israel flourished
while their close kinsmen, the Edomites, did not. The latter, subdued by David (2 Sam. 8.13–14),
were apparently securely established in their area before Israel (Num. 20.14–21; compare
Gen.36.31).
　26.1–33: Isaac at Gerar. 1: *Earlier famine.* 12.10. **7–11:** Again, the ancestress is rescued, and

friend and Phicol the commander of
27 his army. Isaac said to them, 'Why
have you come here? You hate me and
28 you sent me away.' They answered,
'We have seen plainly that the LORD is
with you, so we thought, "Let the two
of us put each other to the oath and
29 make a treaty that will bind us." We
have not attacked you, we have done
you nothing but good, and we let you
go away peaceably. Swear that you will
do us no harm, now that the LORD has
30 blessed you.' So Isaac gave a feast and
31 they ate and drank. They rose early in
the morning and exchanged oaths.
Then Isaac bade them farewell, and
32 they parted from him in peace. The
same day Isaac's slaves came and told
him about a well that they had dug:
33 'We have found water', they said. He
named the well Shibah.*x* This is why
the city is called Beersheba*y* to this day.
34   When Esau was forty years old he
married Judith daughter of Beeri the
Hittite, and Basemath daughter of Elon
35 the Hittite; this was a bitter grief to
Isaac and Rebecca.

Jacob and Esau

27 WHEN ISAAC GREW OLD AND HIS EYES
became so dim that he could not see, he
called his elder son Esau and said to
him, 'My son', and he answered, 'Here I
2 am.' Isaac said, 'Listen now: I am old
3 and I do not know when I may die. Take
your hunting gear, your quiver and
your bow, and go out into the country
4 and get me some venison. Then make
me a savoury dish of the kind I like,
and bring it to me to eat so that I may
5 give you my blessing before I die.' Now
Rebecca was listening as Isaac talked
to his son Esau. When Esau went off
into the country to find some venison
6 and bring it home, she said to her son
Jacob, 'I heard your father talking to
7 your brother Esau, and he said, "Bring
me some venison and make it into a
savoury dish so that I may eat it and
bless you in the presence of the LORD
8 before I die." Listen to me, my son,

and do what I tell you. Go to the flock 9
and pick me out two fine young kids,
and I will make them into a savoury
dish for your father, of the kind he likes.
Then take them in to your father, and 10
he will eat them so that he may bless
you before he dies.' Jacob said to 11
his mother Rebecca, 'But my brother
Esau is a hairy man, and my skin is
smooth. Suppose my father feels me, 12
he will know I am tricking him and I
shall bring a curse upon myself instead
of a blessing.' His mother answered 13
him, 'Let the curse fall on me, my son,
but do as I say; go and bring me the
kids.' So Jacob fetched them and 14
brought them to his mother, who made
them into a savoury dish of the kind
that his father liked. Then Rebecca 15
took her elder son's clothes, Esau's best
clothes which she kept by her in the
house, and put them on her younger
son Jacob. She put the goatskins on 16
his hands and on the smooth nape of
his neck; and she handed her son 17
Jacob the savoury dish and the bread
she had made. He came to his father
and said, 'Father.' He answered, 'Yes, 18
my son; who are you?' Jacob answered 19
his father, 'I am Esau, your elder son. I
have done as you told me. Come, sit up
and eat some of my venison, so that
you may give me your blessing.' Isaac 20
said to his son, 'What is this that you
found so quickly?', and Jacob answered,
'It is what the LORD your God put in
my way.' Isaac then said to Jacob, 21
'Come close and let me feel you, my
son, to see whether you are really my
son Esau.' When Jacob came close to 22
his father, Isaac felt him and said, 'The
voice is Jacob's voice, but the hands
are the hands of Esau.' He did not 23
recognize him because his hands were
hairy like Esau's, and that is why he
blessed him. He said, 'Are you really 24
my son Esau?', and he answered, 'Yes.'
Then Isaac said, 'Bring me some of 25
your venison to eat, my son, so that I
may give you my blessing.' Then Jacob
brought it to him, and he ate it; he
brought wine also, and he drank it.

x That is Oath.   *y That is* Well of an Oath.

---

the promise is kept alive; see 12.10–13.1 n. **28–31:** The promise of 12.3 is further realized in that
the patriarchal claim to the land is widened. **33:** *Shibah:* there is a duplicate tradition in 21.31.
    27.1–45: Jacob obtains his father's blessing. 4: Deathbed blessings play an important role in

26 Then his father Isaac said to him,
27 'Come near, my son, and kiss me.' So
he came near and kissed him, and
when Isaac smelt the smell of his
clothes, he blessed him and said:

'Ah! The smell of my son is like the
　　smell of open country
　　blessed by the LORD.
28 God give you dew from heaven
　　and the richness of the earth,
　　corn and new wine in plenty!
29 Peoples shall serve you,
　　nations bow down to you.
　　Be lord over your brothers;
　　may your mother's sons bow down to
　　　you.
　　A curse upon those who curse you;
　　a blessing on those who bless you!'

30 Isaac finished blessing Jacob; and
Jacob had scarcely left his father
Isaac's presence, when his brother Esau
31 came in from his hunting. He too made
a savoury dish and brought it to his
father. He said, 'Come, father, and eat
some of my venison, so that you may
32 give me your blessing.' His father Isaac
said, 'Who are you?' He said, 'I am
33 Esau, your elder son.' Then Isaac became greatly agitated[z] and said, 'Then
who was it that hunted and brought me
venison? I ate it all before you came in
and I blessed him, and the blessing will
34 stand.' When Esau heard what his
father said, he gave a loud and bitter
35 cry and said, 'Bless me too, father.' But
Isaac said, 'Your brother came treacherously and took away your blessing.'
36 Esau said, 'He is rightly called Jacob.[a]
This is the second time he has supplanted me. He took away my right as
the first-born and now he has taken
away my blessing. Have you kept back
37 any blessing for me?' Isaac answered,
'I have made him lord over you, and I
have given him all his brothers as
slaves. I have bestowed upon him corn
and new wine for his sustenance. What
is there left that I can do for you, my
38 son?' Esau asked his father, 'Had you

then only one blessing, father? Bless
me too, my father.' And Esau cried
bitterly. Then his father Isaac answered: 39

'Your dwelling shall be far from the
　　richness of the earth,
　　far from the dew of heaven above.
　　By your sword shall you live, 40
　　and you shall serve your brother;
　　but the time will come when you
　　　grow restive
　　and break off his yoke from your
　　　neck.'

Esau bore a grudge against Jacob 41
because of the blessing which his father
had given him, and he said to himself,
'The time of mourning for my father
will soon be here; then I will kill my
brother Jacob.' When Rebecca was 42
told what her elder son Esau was
saying, she called her younger son
Jacob, and she said to him, 'Esau your
brother is threatening to kill you. Now, 43
my son, listen to me. Slip away at once
to my brother Laban in Harran. Stay 44
with him for a while until your brother's
anger cools. When it has subsided and 45
he forgets what you have done to him,
I will send and fetch you back. Why
should I lose you both in one day?'

Rebecca said to Isaac, 'I am weary to 46
death of Hittite women! If Jacob
marries a Hittite woman like those who
live here, my life will not be worth
living.' Isaac called Jacob, blessed him **28**
and gave him instructions. He said,
'You must not marry one of these
women of Canaan. Go at once to the 2
house of Bethuel, your mother's father,
in Paddan-aram, and there find a wife,
one of the daughters of Laban, your
mother's brother. God Almighty bless 3
you, make you fruitful and increase
your descendants until they become a
host of nations. May he bestow on you 4
and your offspring the blessing of
Abraham, and may you thus possess
the country where you are now living,
the land which God gave to Abraham!'

z Or incensed.　a That is He supplanted.

---

the literature of ancient Israel (48.10–20; 49.1–27). **33–35:** Blessing or curse, once uttered,
could not be revoked. **40:** During the Solomonic period (1 Kgs.11.14–25), Edom revolted
against Israelite domination.
　27.46–28.22: Jacob's flight and dream at Bethel. The origin of this ancient Canaanite sanctuary
is in this section traced to Israel's ancestor, Jacob (12.7 n.; 21.22–34 n.). **28.1–2:** See 24.3 n.

5 So Isaac sent Jacob away, and he went to Paddan-aram to Laban, son of Bethuel the Aramaean, and brother to Rebecca the mother of Jacob and Esau.
6 Esau discovered that Isaac had given Jacob his blessing and had sent him away to Paddan-aram to find a wife there; and that when he blessed him he had forbidden him to marry a woman
7 of Canaan, and that Jacob had obeyed his father and mother and gone to
8 Paddan-aram. Then Esau, seeing that his father disliked the women of
9 Canaan, went to Ishmael, and, in addition to his other wives, he married Mahalath sister of Nebaioth and daughter of Abraham's son Ishmael.
10 Jacob set out from Beersheba and
11 went on his way towards Harran. He came to a certain place and stopped there for the night, because the sun had set; and, taking one of the stones there, he made it a pillow for his head
12 and lay down to sleep. He dreamt that he saw a ladder, which rested on the ground with its top reaching to heaven, and angels of God were going up and
13 down upon it. The LORD was standing beside him[b] and said, 'I am the LORD, the God of your father Abraham and the God of Isaac. This land on which you are lying I will give to you and your
14 descendants. They shall be countless as the dust upon the earth, and you shall spread far and wide, to north and south, to east and west. All the families of the earth shall pray to be blessed as
15 you and your descendants are blessed. I will be with you, and I will protect you wherever you go and will bring you back to this land; for I will not leave you until I have done all that I
16 have promised.' Jacob woke from his sleep and said, 'Truly the LORD is in
17 this place, and I did not know it.' Then he was afraid and said, 'How fearsome is this place! This is no other than the house of God, this is the gate

of heaven.' Jacob rose early in the 18 morning, took the stone on which he had laid his head, set it up as a sacred pillar and poured oil on the top of it. He named that place Beth-El;[c] but the 19 earlier name of the city was Luz.

Thereupon Jacob made this vow: 'If 20 God will be with me, if he will protect me on my journey and give me food to eat and clothes to wear, and I come 21 back safely to my father's house, then the LORD shall be my God, and this 22 stone which I have set up as a sacred pillar shall be a house of God. And of all that thou givest me, I will without fail allot a tenth part to thee.'

JACOB CONTINUED HIS JOURNEY AND 29 came to the land of the eastern tribes. There he saw a well in the open country 2 and three flocks of sheep lying beside it, because the flocks were watered from that well. Over its mouth was a huge stone, and all the herdsmen used to 3 gather there and roll it off the mouth of the well and water the flocks; then they would put it back in its place over the well. Jacob said to them, 'Where are 4 you from, my friends?' 'We are from Harran,' they replied. He asked them 5 if they knew Laban the grandson of Nahor. They answered, 'Yes, we do.' 'Is he well?' Jacob asked; and they 6 answered 'Yes, he is well, and here is his daughter Rachel coming with the flock.' Jacob said, 'The sun is still high, 7 and the time for folding the sheep has not yet come. Water the flocks and then go and graze them.' But they 8 replied, 'We cannot, until all the herdsmen have gathered together and the stone is rolled away from the mouth of the well; then we can water our flocks.' While he was talking to them, Rachel 9 came up with her father's flock, for she was a shepherdess. When Jacob 10 saw Rachel, the daughter of Laban his

b Or on it or by it.   c That is House of God.

12: In ancient belief, deities revealed themselves by dream at sacred sites (see 1 Sam.3.1–14). Mesopotamians described their temple towers in similar terms; see 11.4 n. **13:** The LORD is here identified both as the traditional deity of the site and as the deity of the patriarchs (see Exod. 3.15). **18:** The pouring of oil on an object or person conferred extraordinary, often sacred, status. **19:** *Beth-El,* the name of an ancient Canaanite deity (Jer.48.13), is likely the actual source of the place name, rather than the folk etymology given here.
   29.1–31.55: Jacob at Harran. 1: *Eastern tribes:* a general designation for Mesopotamia. **7:** *Folding:* gathering together in preparation for the night. **8:** Bedouin custom demanded that all rightful parties be present when the well was opened, so that the water would be

mother's brother, with Laban's flock, he stepped forward, rolled the stone off the mouth of the well and watered 11 Laban's sheep. He kissed Rachel, and 12 was moved to tears. He told her that he was her father's kinsman and Rebecca's son; so she ran and told her 13 father. When Laban heard the news of his sister's son Jacob, he ran to meet him, embraced him, kissed him warmly and welcomed him to his home. Jacob 14 told Laban everything, and Laban said, 'Yes, you are my own flesh and blood.' So Jacob stayed with him for a whole month.

15   Laban said to Jacob, 'Why should you work for me for nothing simply because you are my kinsman? Tell me 16 what your wages ought to be.' Now Laban had two daughters: the elder was called Leah, and the younger 17 Rachel. Leah was dull-eyed, but Rachel 18 was graceful and beautiful. Jacob had fallen in love with Rachel and he said, 'I will work seven years for your 19 younger daughter Rachel.' Laban replied, 'It is better that I should give her to you than to anyone else; stay with 20 me.' So Jacob worked seven years for Rachel, and they seemed like a few 21 days because he loved her. Then Jacob said to Laban, 'I have served my time. Give me my wife so that we may 22 sleep together.' So Laban gathered all the men of the place together and gave 23 a feast. In the evening he took his daughter Leah and brought her to 24 Jacob, and Jacob slept with her. At the same time Laban gave his slave-25 girl Zilpah to his daughter Leah. But when morning came, Jacob saw that it was Leah and said to Laban, 'What have you done to me? Did I not work for Rachel? Why have you deceived 26 me?' Laban answered, 'In our country it is not right to give the younger sister 27 in marriage before the elder. Go through with the seven days' feast for the elder, and the younger shall be given you in return for a further seven years' 28 work.' Jacob agreed, and completed the seven days for Leah.

Then Laban gave Jacob his daughter Rachel as wife; and he gave his slave-29 girl Bilhah to serve his daughter Rachel. Jacob slept with Rachel also; 30 he loved her rather than Leah, and he worked for Laban for a further seven years. When the LORD saw that Leah 31 was not loved, he granted her a child; but Rachel was childless. Leah con-32 ceived and bore a son; and she called him Reuben,*d* for she said, 'The LORD has seen my humiliation; now my husband will love me.' Again she 33 conceived and bore a son and said, 'The LORD, hearing that I am not loved, has given me this child also'; and she called him Simeon.*e* She conceived 34 again and bore a son; and she said, 'Now that I have borne him three sons my husband and I will surely be united.' So she called him Levi.*f* Once more she 35 conceived and bore a son; and she said, 'Now I will praise the LORD'; therefore she named him Judah.*g* Then for a while she bore no more children.

When Rachel found that she bore **30** Jacob no children, she became jealous of her sister and said to Jacob, 'Give me sons, or I shall die.' Jacob said 2 angrily to Rachel, 'Can I take the place of God, who has denied you children?' She said, 'Here is my slave-girl Bilhah. 3 Lie with her, so that she may bear sons to be laid upon my knees, and through her I too may build up a family.' So she 4 gave him her slave-girl Bilhah as a wife, and Jacob lay with her. Bilhah con-5 ceived and bore Jacob a son. Then 6 Rachel said, 'God has given judgement for me; he has indeed heard me and given me a son', so she named him Dan.*h* Rachel's slave-girl Bilhah again 7 conceived and bore Jacob another son. Rachel said, 'I have played a fine trick 8 on my sister, and it has succeeded'; so she named him Naphtali.*i* When Leah 9 found that she was bearing no more children, she took her slave-girl Zilpah and gave her to Jacob as a wife, and 10 Zilpah bore Jacob a son. Leah said, 11 'Good fortune has come', and she

d That is See, a son.   *e That is* Hearing.
f That is Union.   *g That is* Praise.
h That is He has given judgement.   *i That is* Trickery.

distributed fairly. **23**: Likely, the deception was possible because of a veil (24. 65). **29.31–30.24**: The fourth generation of the Hebrews emerged in the form of twelve tribes, indeed as a league of them; see 22.20–24 n. Each name is explained by folk etymology involving a word play

12 named him Gad.*ʲ* Zilpah, Leah's slave-
13 girl, bore Jacob another son, and Leah said, 'Happiness has come, for young women will call me happy.' So she named him Asher.*ᵏ*
14 In the time of wheat-harvest Reuben went out and found some mandrakes in the open country and brought them to his mother Leah. Then Rachel asked Leah for some of her son's mandrakes,
15 but Leah said, 'Is it so small a thing to have taken away my husband, that you should take my son's mandrakes as well?' But Rachel said, 'Very well, let him sleep with you tonight in exchange
16 for your son's mandrakes.' So when Jacob came in from the country in the evening, Leah went out to meet him and said, 'You are to sleep with me tonight; I have hired you with my son's mandrakes.' That night he slept with her,
17 and God heard Leah's prayer, and she
18 conceived and bore a fifth son. Leah said, 'God has rewarded me, because I gave my slave-girl to my husband.'
19 So she named him Issachar.*ˡ* Leah again
20 conceived and bore a sixth son. She said, 'God has endowed me with a noble dowry. Now my husband will treat me in princely style, because I have borne him six sons.' So she named him
21 Zebulun.*ᵐ* Later she bore a daughter
22 and named her Dinah. Then God thought of Rachel; he heard her
23 prayer and gave her a child; so she conceived and bore a son and said, 'God has taken away my humiliation.'
24 She named him Joseph,*ⁿ* saying, 'May the LORD add another son!'
25 When Rachel had given birth to Joseph, Jacob said to Laban, 'Let me go, for I wish to return to my own home
26 and country. Give me my wives and my children for whom I have served you, and I will go; for you know what
27 service I have done for you.' Laban said to him, 'Let me have my say, if you please. I have become prosperous and the LORD has blessed me for your sake.
28 So now tell me what I owe you in wages,
29 and I will give it you.' Jacob answered, 'You must know how I have served

you, and how your herds have pros-
30 pered under my care. You had only a few when I came, but now they have increased beyond measure, and the LORD brought blessings to you wher-ever I went. But is it not time for me
31 to provide for my family?' Laban said, 'Then what shall I give you?', but Jacob answered, 'Give me nothing; I will mind your flocks*ᵒ* as before, if you
32 will do what I suggest. Today I will go over your flocks and pick out from them every black lamb, and all the brindled and the spotted goats, and
33 they shall be my wages. This is a fair offer, and it will be to my own disad-vantage later on, when we come to settling my wages: every goat amongst mine that is not spotted or brindled and every lamb that is not black will
34 have been stolen.' Laban said, 'Agreed;
35 let it be as you have said.' But that day he removed the he-goats that were striped and brindled and all the spotted and brindled she-goats, all that had any white on them, and every ram that was black, and he handed them over
36 to his own sons. Then he put a distance of three days' journey between himself and Jacob, while Jacob was left tending those of Laban's flocks that remained.
37 Thereupon Jacob took fresh rods of white poplar, almond, and plane tree, and peeled off strips of bark, exposing
38 the white of the rods. Then he fixed the peeled rods upright in the troughs at the watering-places where the flocks came to drink; they faced the she-goats that were on heat when they came to
39 drink. They felt a longing for the rods and they gave birth to young that were
40 striped and spotted and brindled. As for the rams, Jacob divided them, and let the ewes run only with such of the rams in Laban's flock as were striped and black; and thus he bred separate flocks for himself, which he did not add
41 to Laban's sheep. As for the goats, whenever the more vigorous were on

j That is Good Fortune.   *k That is* Happy.
l That is Reward.   *m That is* Prince.
n The name may mean either He takes away *or* May he add.   *o Prob. rdg.; Heb. adds* I will watch.

(Tfn. *d–n*). **30.14:** In antiquity these plants were widely regarded as "aphrodisiacs," that is, they stimulated passion. The word in Hebrew resembles the Hebrew word for "love." **27:** *For your sake:* an echo of the promise in 12.3. **32:** Since sheep in the area are usually white and goats are usually black, Laban quickly agreed to a deal so obviously to his advantage. **39:** Many

heat, he put the rods in front of them at the troughs so that they would long 42 for the rods; he did not put them there for the weaker goats. Thus the weaker came to be Laban's and the stronger 43 Jacob's. So Jacob increased in wealth more and more until he possessed great flocks, male and female slaves, camels, and asses.

31 JACOB LEARNT THAT LABAN'S SONS WERE saying, 'Jacob has taken everything that was our father's, and all his wealth has come from our father's property.' 2 He also noticed that Laban was not so well disposed to him as he had once 3 been. Then the LORD said to Jacob, 'Go back to the land of your fathers and to 4 your kindred. I will be with you.' So Jacob sent to fetch Rachel and Leah to 5 his flocks out in the country and said to them, 'I see that your father is not as well disposed to me as once he was; yet the God of my father has been with 6 me. You know how I have served your 7 father to the best of my power, but he has cheated me and changed my wages ten times over. Yet God did not let 8 him do me any harm. If Laban said, "The spotted ones shall be your wages", then all the flock bore spotted young; and if he said, "The striped ones shall be your wages", then all the flock bore 9 striped young. God has taken away your father's property and has given it 10 to me. In the season when the flocks were on heat, I had a dream: I looked up and saw that the he-goats mounting the flock were striped and spotted and 11 dappled. The angel of God said to me in my dream, "Jacob", and I replied, 12 "Here I am", and he said, "Look up and see: all the he-goats mounting the flock are striped and spotted and dappled. I have seen all that Laban is 13 doing to you. I am the God who appeared to you at Bethel where you anointed a sacred pillar and where you made your vow. Now leave this country at once and return to the land of your 14 birth."' Rachel and Leah answered him,

'We no longer have any part or lot in our father's house. Does he not look 15 on us as foreigners, now that he has sold us and spent on himself the whole of the money paid for us? But all the 16 wealth which God has saved from our father's clutches is ours and our children's. Now do everything that God has said.' Jacob at once set his sons and 17 his wives on camels, and drove off all 18 the herds and livestock which he had acquired in Paddan-aram, to go to his father Isaac in Canaan.

When Laban the Aramaean had gone 19 to shear his sheep, Rachel stole her father's household gods, and Jacob 20 deceived Laban, keeping his departure secret. So Jacob ran away with all that 21 he had, crossed the River and made for the hill-country of Gilead. Three days 22 later, when Laban heard that Jacob had run away, he took his kinsmen 23 with him, pursued Jacob for seven days and caught up with him in the hill-country of Gilead. But God came to 24 Laban in a dream by night and said to him, 'Be careful to say nothing to Jacob, either good or bad.'

When Laban overtook him, Jacob 25 had pitched his tent in the hill-country of Gilead, and Laban pitched his in the company of his kinsmen in the same hill-country. Laban said to Jacob, 26 'What have you done? You have deceived me and carried off my daughters as though they were captives taken in war. Why did you slip away secretly 27 without telling me? I would have set you on your way with songs and the music of tambourines and harps. You 28 did not even let me kiss my daughters and their children. In this you were at fault. It is in my power to do you an 29 injury, but yesterday the God of your father spoke to me; he told me to be careful to say nothing to you, either good or bad. I know that you went 30 away because you were homesick and pining for your father's house, but why did you steal my gods?'

Jacob answered, 'I was afraid; I 31

---

people, ancient and modern, have believed that a fetus can be affected by the visual impressions of the mother. **31.14–16:** Ancient law, such as the Hurrian, provided for part of the bride payment to be reserved for the woman herself. **19:** Possession of the *household gods* insured the right of inheritance; hence, Rachel may have sought compensation for the loss of the bride payment. **21:** *The River:* Euphrates. **35:** The ancient, humorous story now becomes a sarcastic

thought you would take your daughters 32 from me by force. Whoever is found in possession of your gods shall die for it. Let our kinsmen here be witnesses: point out anything I have that is yours, and take it back.' Jacob did not know 33 that Rachel had stolen the gods. So Laban went into Jacob's tent and Leah's tent and that of the two slave-girls, but he found nothing. When he came out of Leah's tent he went into 34 Rachel's. Now she had taken the household gods and put them in the camel-bag and was sitting on them. Laban went through everything in the 35 tent and found nothing. Rachel said to her father, 'Do not take it amiss, sir, that I cannot rise in your presence: the common lot of woman is upon me.' So for all his search Laban did not find his household gods.

36 Jacob was angry, and he expostulated with Laban, exclaiming, 'What have I done wrong? What is my offence, that you have come after me in hot pursuit 37 and gone through all my possessions? Have you found anything belonging to your household? If so, set it here in front of my kinsmen and yours, and let them judge between the two of us. 38 In all the twenty years I have been with you, your ewes and she-goats have never miscarried; I have not eaten the 39 rams of your flocks; I have never brought to you the body of any animal mangled by wild beasts, but I bore the loss myself; you claimed compensation from me for anything stolen by day or 40 by night. This was the way of it: by day the heat consumed me and the frost by 41 night, and sleep deserted me. For twenty years I have been in your household. I worked for you fourteen years to win your two daughters and six years for your flocks, and you changed 42 my wages ten times over. If the God of my father, the God of Abraham and the Fear of Isaac, had not been with me, you would have sent me away empty-handed. But God saw my labour and my hardships, and last night he rebuked you.'

Laban answered Jacob, 'The daugh- 43 ters are my daughters, the children are my children, the flocks are my flocks, all that you see is mine. But as for my daughters, what can I do today about them and the children they have borne? Come now, we will make an agreement, 44 you and I, and let it stand as a witness between us.' So Jacob chose a great 45 stone and set it upright as a sacred pillar. Then he told his kinsmen to 46 gather stones, and they took them and built a cairn, and there beside the cairn they ate together. Laban called it 47 Jegar-sahadutha,*p* and Jacob called it Gal-ed.*q* Laban said, 'This cairn is 48 witness today between you and me.' For this reason it was named Gal-ed; it was also named Mizpah,*r* for Laban 49 said, 'May the LORD watch between you and me, when we are parted from each other's sight. If you ill-treat my 50 daughters or take other wives beside them when no one is there to see, then God be witness between us.' Laban said 51 further to Jacob, 'Here is this cairn, and here the pillar which I have set up between us. This cairn is witness and the 52 pillar is witness: I for my part will not pass beyond this cairn to your side, and you for your part shall not pass beyond this cairn and this pillar to my side to do an injury, otherwise the 53 God of Abraham and the God of Nahor will judge between us.' And Jacob swore this oath in the name of the Fear of Isaac his father. He 54 slaughtered an animal for sacrifice, there in the hill-country, and summoned his kinsmen to the feast. So they ate together and spent the night there.

Laban rose early in the morning, 55 kissed his daughters and their children, blessed them and went home again. Then Jacob continued his journey and **32** was met by angels of God. When he 2 saw them, Jacob said, 'This is the company of God', and he called that place Mahanaim.*s*

p Aramaic for Cairn of Witness.
q Hebrew for Cairn of Witness.
r That is Watch-tower.   *s That is* Two Companies.

---

attack on idolatry; the "gods" have been stolen, hidden, and soiled by menstrual blood (see Lev.15.19–20). **39:** *Mangled:* on responsibility in such cases, see Exod. 22.10–13. **42:** *Fear:* an unusual divine name. **43:** The custom of Laban's homeland is reflected, by which the husband moves into the wife's household. **46:** *Cairn:* a heap of stones.
32.1–33.20: Jacob's return and reconciliation with Esau. 1: *Angels of God:* see Ps.91.11.

3 Jacob sent messengers on ahead to his brother Esau to the district of Seir 4 in the Edomite country, and this is what he told them to say to Esau, 'My lord, your servant Jacob says, I have been living with Laban and have stayed 5 there till now. I have oxen, asses, and sheep, and male and female slaves, and I have sent to tell you this, my lord, so 6 that I may win your favour.' The messengers returned to Jacob and said, 'We met your brother Esau already on the way to meet you with four hundred 7 men.' Jacob, much afraid and distressed, divided the people with him, as well as the sheep, cattle, and camels, 8 into two companies, thinking that, if Esau should come upon one company and destroy it, the other company 9 would survive. Jacob said, 'O God of my father Abraham, God of my father Isaac, O LORD at whose bidding I came back to my own country and to my kindred, and who didst promise me 10 prosperity, I am not worthy of all the true and steadfast love which thou hast shown to me thy servant. When I crossed the Jordan, I had nothing but the staff in my hand; now I have two 11 companies. Save me, I pray, from my brother Esau, for I am afraid that he may come and destroy me, sparing 12 neither mother nor child. But thou didst say, I will prosper you and will make your descendants like the sand of the sea, which is beyond all counting.' 13 Jacob spent that night there; and as a present for his brother Esau he chose 14 from the herds he had with him two hundred she-goats, twenty he-goats, two hundred ewes and twenty rams, 15 thirty milch-camels with their young, forty cows and ten young bulls, twenty 16 she-asses and ten he-asses. He put each herd separately into the care of a servant and said to each, 'Go on ahead of me, and leave gaps between the 17 herds.' Then he gave these instructions to the first: 'When my brother Esau meets you and asks you to whom you belong and where you are going and

who owns these beasts you are driving, you are to say, "They belong to your 18 servant Jacob; he sends them as a present to my lord Esau, and he is behind us." ' He gave the same in- 19 structions to the second, to the third, and all the drovers, telling them to say the same thing to Esau when they met him. And they were to add, 'Your 20 servant Jacob is behind us'; for he thought, 'I will appease him with the present that I have sent on ahead, and afterwards, when I come into his presence, he will perhaps receive me kindly.' So Jacob's present went on 21 ahead of him, but he himself spent that night at Mahaneh.

During the night Jacob rose, took 22 his two wives, his two slave-girls, and his eleven sons, and crossed the ford of Jabbok. He took them and sent them 23 across the gorge with all that he had. So Jacob was left alone, and a man 24 wrestled with him there till*t* daybreak. When the man saw that he could not 25 throw Jacob, he struck him in the hollow of his thigh, so that Jacob's hip was dislocated as they wrestled. The 26 man said, 'Let me go, for day is breaking', but Jacob replied, 'I will not let you go unless you bless me.' He 27 said to Jacob, 'What is your name?', and he answered, 'Jacob.' The man 28 said, 'Your name shall no longer be Jacob, but Israel,*u* because you strove with God and with men, and prevailed.' Jacob said, 'Tell me, I pray, your name.' 29 He replied, 'Why do you ask my name?', but he gave him his blessing there. Jacob called the place Peniel,*v* 30 'because', he said, 'I have seen God face to face and my life is spared.' The 31 sun rose as Jacob passed through Penuel, limping because of his hip. This is why the Israelites to this day do 32 not eat the sinew of the nerve that runs in the hollow of the thigh; for the man had struck Jacob on that nerve in the hollow of the thigh.

t Or at.
u That is God strove.
v That is Face of God (*elsewhere* Penuel).

9: *God of my father Abraham:* see 31.42. 20: compare Prov. 21.14. 24–26: In keeping with much ancient folklore, the phantom visitor vanished with the sunrise. He may have been, in the earliest circulation of the story, either a border guardian or the "spirit" of the river. In context, his "blessing" helps to authenticate Jacob's right to the land. 27–32: Folk explanations are given for the names *Israel* and *Peniel/Penuel*, and also for a food taboo (v.32), mentioned only here.

33 Jacob raised his eyes and saw Esau coming towards him with four hundred men; so he divided the children between Leah and Rachel and the two slave-girls. 2 He put the slave-girls with their children in front, Leah with her children next, and Rachel with Joseph last. 3 He then went on ahead of them, bowing low to the ground seven times 4 as he approached his brother. Esau ran to meet him and embraced him; he threw his arms round him and kissed him, and they wept. 5 When Esau looked up and saw the women and children, he said, 'Who are these with you?' Jacob replied, 'The children whom God has graciously given to your 6 servant.' The slave-girls came near, each with her children, and they bowed 7 low. Then Leah with her children came near and bowed low, and afterwards Joseph and Rachel came near and 8 bowed low also. Esau said, 'What was all that company of yours that I met?' And he answered, 'It was meant to win 9 favour with you, my lord.' Esau answered, 'I have more than enough. 10 Keep what is yours, my brother.' But Jacob said, 'On no account: if I have won your favour, then, I pray, accept this gift from me; for, you see, I come into your presence as into that of a god, 11 and you receive me favourably. Accept this gift which I bring you; for God has been gracious to me, and I have all I want.' So he urged him, and he accepted it. 12 Then Esau said, 'Let us set out, and 13 I will go at your pace.' But Jacob answered him, 'You must know, my lord, that the children are small; the flocks and herds are suckling their young and I am concerned for them, and if the men overdrive them for a 14 single day, all my beasts will die. I beg you, my lord, to go on ahead, and I will go by easy stages at the pace of the children and of the livestock that I am driving, until I come to my lord in

Seir.' Esau said, 'Let me detail some of 15 my own men to escort you,' but he replied, 'Why should my lord be so kind to me?' That day Esau turned 16 back towards Seir, but Jacob set out 17 for Succoth; and there he built himself a house and made shelters for his cattle. Therefore he named that place Succoth.*w*

On his journey from Paddan-aram, 18 Jacob came safely to the city of Shechem in Canaan and pitched his tent to the east of it. The strip of 19 country where he had pitched his tent he bought from the sons of Hamor father of Shechem for a hundred sheep.*x* There he set up an altar and 20 called it El-Elohey-Israel.*y*

DINAH, THE DAUGHTER WHOM LEAH HAD **34** borne to Jacob, went out to visit the women of the country, and Shechem, 2 son of Hamor the Hivite the local prince, saw her; he took her, lay with her and dishonoured her. But he re- 3 mained true to Jacob's daughter Dinah; he loved the girl and comforted her. So 4 Shechem said to his father Hamor, 'Get me this girl for a wife.' When 5 Jacob heard that Shechem had violated his daughter Dinah, his sons were with the herds in the open country, so he said nothing until they came home. Meanwhile Shechem's father Hamor 6 came out to Jacob to discuss it with him. When Jacob's sons came in from 7 the country and heard, they were grieved and angry, because in lying with Jacob's daughter he had done what the Israelites held to be an outrage, an intolerable thing. Hamor appealed to 8 them in these terms: 'My son Shechem is in love with this girl; I beg you to let him have her as his wife. Let us ally 9 ourselves in marriage; you shall give us your daughters, and you shall take ours in exchange. You must settle 10

w That is Shelters.
x Or pieces of money (*cp. Josh. 24. 32; Job 42. 11*).
y That is God the God of Israel.

On a new name, see 17.5 n. **33.20:** *El* was the chief god of the Canaanites, apparently worshiped at Shechem before the introduction of the cult of the LORD.

34.1–31: The rape of Dinah. This is an ancient, once independent account of relations between the tribes of Simeon and Levi and their Canaanite neighbors, the tribes being represented by eponymous ("name-giving") ancestors. The episode is mentioned in 49.5–7, as the basis for the decline of these tribes in the tribal confederation. Simeon goes unmentioned in the list of tribes given in Deut. ch. 33, a passage from a later time.

among us. The country is open to you; make your home in it, move about freely and acquire land of your own.'

11 And Shechem said to the girl's father and brothers, 'I am eager to win your favour and I will give whatever you

12 ask. Fix the bride-price and the gift as high as you like, and I will give whatever you ask; but you must give me the girl in marriage.'

13 Jacob's sons gave a dishonest reply to Shechem and his father Hamor, laying a trap for them because Shechem

14 had violated their sister Dinah: 'We cannot do this,' they said; 'we cannot give our sister to a man who is un-

15 circumcised; for we look on that as a disgrace. There is one condition on which we will consent: if you will follow our example and have every male

16 among you circumcised, we will give you our daughters and take yours for ourselves. Then we can live among you, and we shall all become one people.

17 But if you refuse to listen to us and be circumcised, we will take the girl and

18 go away.' Their proposal pleased

19 Hamor and his son Shechem; and the young man, who was held in respect above anyone in his father's house, did not hesitate to do what they had said, because his heart was taken by Jacob's daughter.

20 So Hamor and Shechem went back to the city gate and addressed their

21 fellow-citizens: 'These men are friendly to us; let them live in our country and move freely in it. The land has room enough for them. Let us marry their

22 daughters and give them ours. But these men will agree to live with us and become one people on this one condition only: every male among us must

23 be circumcised as they have been. Will not their herds, their livestock, and all their chattels then be ours? We need only consent to their condition, and

24 then they are free to live with us.' All the able-bodied men agreed with Hamor and Shechem, and every single one of them was circumcised, every

25 able-bodied male. Then two days later, while they were still in great pain,

Jacob's two sons Simeon and Levi, full brothers to Dinah, armed themselves with swords, boldly entered the city

26 and killed every male. They cut down Hamor and his son Shechem and took Dinah from Shechem's house and went

27 off with her. Then Jacob's other sons came in over the dead bodies and plundered the city, to avenge their

28 sister's dishonour. They seized flocks, cattle, asses, and everything, both inside the city and outside in the open

29 country; they also carried off all their possessions, their dependants, and their women, and plundered everything in the houses.

30 Jacob said to Simeon and Levi, 'You have brought trouble on me, you have made my name stink among the people of the country, the Canaanites and the Perizzites. My numbers are few; if they muster against me and attack me, I shall be destroyed, I and my household

31 with me.' They answered, 'Is our sister to be treated as a common whore?'

35 GOD SAID TO JACOB, 'GO UP TO BETHEL and settle there; build an altar there to the God who appeared to you when you were running away from your

2 brother Esau.' So Jacob said to his household and to all who were with him, 'Rid yourselves of the foreign gods which you have among you, purify yourselves, and see your clothes are

3 mended.*z* We are going to Bethel, so that I can set up an altar there to the God who answered me in the day of my distress, and who has been with me all

4 the way that I have come.' So they handed over to Jacob all the foreign gods in their possession and the rings from their ears, and he buried them under the terebinth-tree near Shechem.

5 Then they set out, and the cities round about were panic-stricken, and the inhabitants dared not pursue the sons of

6 Jacob. Jacob and all the people with him came to Luz, that is Bethel, in

7 Canaan. There he built an altar, and he called the place El-bethel, because it was there that God had revealed him-

z Or change your clothes.

35.1–15: Variant traditions about the founding of Bethel. Given Jacob's prior visit (28.18–19) and the importance of the place in Israel's religious heritage, some duplication and even misplacement have resulted. **2:** A change of garment was a necessary part of ceremonial purification

self to him when he was running away
8 from his brother. Rebecca's nurse
Deborah died and was buried under
the oak below Bethel, and he named it
Allon-bakuth.[a]
9 God appeared again to Jacob when
he came back from Paddan-aram and
10 blessed him. God said to him:

'Jacob is your name,
but your name shall no longer be
Jacob:
Israel shall be your name.'

11 So he named him Israel. And God said
to him:

'I am God Almighty.
Be fruitful and increase as a nation;
a host of nations shall come from
you,
and kings shall spring from your
body.
12 The land which I gave to Abraham
and Isaac I give to you;
and to your descendants after you I
give this land.'

13,14 God then left him, and Jacob erected a
sacred pillar in the place where God
had spoken with him, a pillar of stone,
and he offered a drink-offering over it
15 and poured oil on it. Jacob called the
place where God had spoken with him
Bethel.
16 They set out from Bethel, and when
there was still some distance to go to
Ephrathah, Rachel was in labour and
17 her pains were severe. While her pains
were upon her, the midwife said, 'Do
not be afraid, this is another son for
18 you.' Then with her last breath, as
she was dying, she named him Ben-
oni,[b] but his father called him Ben-
19 jamin.[c] So Rachel died and was buried
by the side of the road to Ephrathah,

that is Bethlehem. Jacob set up a sacred 20
pillar over her grave; it is known to
this day as the Pillar of Rachel's
Grave. Then Israel journeyed on and 21
pitched his tent on the other side of
Migdal-eder. While Israel was living in 22
that district, Reuben went and lay with
his father's concubine Bilhah, and
Israel came to hear of it.
The sons of Jacob were twelve. The 23
sons of Leah: Jacob's first-born
Reuben, then Simeon, Levi, Judah,
Issachar and Zebulun. The sons of 24
Rachel: Joseph and Benjamin. The 25
sons of Rachel's slave-girl Bilhah: Dan
and Naphtali. The sons of Leah's 26
slave-girl Zilpah: Gad and Asher.
These were Jacob's sons, born to him
in Paddan-aram. Jacob came to his 27
father Isaac at Mamre by Kiriath-arba,
that is Hebron, where Abraham and
Isaac had dwelt. Isaac had lived for a 28
hundred and eighty years when he
breathed his last. He died and was 29
gathered to his father's kin at a very
great age, and his sons Esau and Jacob
buried him.

THIS IS THE TABLE OF THE DESCENDANTS 36
of Esau: that is Edom. Esau took 2
Canaanite women in marriage, Adah
daughter of Elon the Hittite and
Oholibamah daughter of Anah son of
Zibeon the Horite,[d] and Basemath, 3
Ishmael's daughter, sister of Nebaioth.
Adah bore Eliphaz to Esau; Ba- 4[e]
semath bore Reuel, and Oholibamah 5
bore Jeush, Jalam and Korah. These
were Esau's sons, born to him in
Canaan. Esau took his wives, his sons 6
and daughters and everyone in his
household, his herds, his cattle, and all
the chattels that he had acquired in

a *That is* Oak of Weeping.
b *That is* Son of my ill luck.
c *That is* Son of good luck *or* Son of the right hand.
d *Prob. rdg. (cp. verses* 20, 21); *Heb.* Hivite.
e *Verses* 4, 5, 9–13: *cp.* 1 Chr. 1. 35–37.

(Exod. 19.10). **9–10:** A variant version of 32.24–28. **11–12:** An extension to Jacob of the promise
to Abraham and Isaac. It might have been better placed after Jacob's return from Harran and
his new name. **13–15:** A variant of 28.16–19.
   35.16–22: The birth of Benjamin. The name (see end of Tfn. *c*) likely refers to a geographical
location south (i.e. "right") of Ephraim. **22:** An incomplete fragment, it explains the tribe's later
loss of prestige (49.3–4) and of numbers (Deut. 33.6).
   35.23–29: The death of Isaac. In 27.1, Isaac was already an old man at the point of death;
this passage reflects an independent tradition.
   36.1–43: The genealogy of Esau. Relations between Israel and Edom were usually better than
between most neighbors in the area; the Edomites are never accused of idolatry. Perhaps that
is why this non-Israelite material was preserved. **2:** This verse differs from a similar tradition in

Canaan, and went to the district of Seir out of the way of his brother Jacob, because they had so much stock that they could not live together; the land where they were staying could not support them because of their herds. [8] So Esau lived in the hill-country of Seir. Esau is Edom.

[9] This is the table of the descendants of Esau father of the Edomites in the hill-country of Seir.

[10] These are the names of the sons of Esau: Eliphaz was the son of Esau's wife Adah. Reuel was the son of Esau's [11] wife Basemath. The sons of Eliphaz were Teman, Omar, Zepho, Gatam [12] and Kenaz. Timna was concubine to Esau's son Eliphaz, and she bore Amalek to him. These are the descen- [13] dants of Esau's wife Adah. These are the sons of Reuel: Nahath, Zerah, Shammah and Mizzah. These were the descendants of Esau's wife Basemath. [14] These were the sons of Esau's wife Oholibamah daughter of Anah son of Zibeon. She bore him Jeush, Jalam and Korah.

[15] These are the chiefs descended from Esau. The sons of Esau's eldest son Eliphaz: chief Teman, chief Omar, [16] chief Zepho, chief Kenaz, chief Korah, chief Gatam, chief Amalek. These are the chiefs descended from Eliphaz in Edom. These are the descendants of Adah.

[17] These are the sons of Esau's son Reuel: chief Nahath, chief Zerah, chief Shammah, chief Mizzah. These are the chiefs descended from Reuel in Edom. These are the descendants of Esau's wife Basemath.

[18] These are the sons of Esau's wife Oholibamah: chief Jeush, chief Jalam, chief Korah. These are the chiefs born to Oholibamah daughter of Anah wife of Esau.

[19] These are the sons of Esau, that is Edom, and these are their chiefs.

[20]*f* These are the sons of Seir the Horite, the original inhabitants of the land: [21] Lotan, Shobal, Zibeon, Anah, Dishon, Ezer and Dishan. These are the chiefs of the Horites, the sons of Seir in Edom.

The sons of Lotan were Hori and [22] Hemam, and Lotan had a sister named Timna.

These are the sons of Shobal: Alvan, [23] Manahath, Ebal, Shepho and Onam.

These are the sons of Zibeon: Aiah [24] and Anah. This is the Anah who found some mules in the wilderness while he was tending the asses of his father Zibeon. These are the children of Anah: [25] Dishon and Oholibamah daughter of Anah.

These are the children of Dishon: [26] Hemdan, Eshban, Ithran and Cheran. These are the sons of Ezer: Bilhan, [27] Zavan and Akan. These are the sons of [28] Dishan: Uz and Aran.

These are the chiefs descended from [29] the Horites: chief Lotan, chief Shobal, chief Zibeon, chief Anah, chief Dishon, [30] chief Ezer, chief Dishan. These are the chiefs that were descended from the Horites according to their clans in the district of Seir.

These are the kings who ruled over [31]*g* Edom before there were kings in Israel: Bela son of Beor became king in Edom, [32] and his city was named Dinhabah; when he died, he was succeeded by [33] Jobab son of Zerah of Bozrah. When [34] Jobab died, he was succeeded by Husham of Teman. When Husham [35] died, he was succeeded by Hadad son of Bedad, who defeated Midian in Moabite country. His city was named Avith. When Hadad died, he was [36] succeeded by Samlah of Masrekah. When Samlah died, he was succeeded [37] by Saul of Rehoboth on the River. When Saul died, he was succeeded by [38] Baal-hanan son of Akbor. When Baal- [39] hanan died, he was succeeded by Hadar.*h* His city was named Pau; his wife's name was Mehetabel daughter of Matred a woman of Me-zahab.*i*

These are the names of the chiefs [40] descended from Esau, according to their families, their places, by name: chief Timna, chief Alvah, chief Jetheth, chief Oholibamah, chief Elah, chief [41]

f Verses 20–28: cp. 1 Chr. 1. 38–42.
g Verses 31–43: cp. 1 Chr. 1. 43–54.
h Or Hadad; cp. 1 Chr. 1. 50.
i Or daughter of Mezahab.

26.34 and 28.9. **10:** The list is drawn from different sources and repeats matters given in other verses; see v. 4. **31:** See 25.33 n.

42 Pinon, chief Kenaz, chief Teman,
43 chief Mibzar, chief Magdiel, and chief
Iram: all chiefs of Edom according to
their settlements in the land which they
possessed. (Esau is the father of the
Edomites.)

Joseph in Egypt

37 SO JACOB LIVED IN CANAAN, THE COUN-
try in which his father had settled. And
2 this is the story of the descendants of
Jacob.

When Joseph was a boy of seventeen,
he used to accompany his brothers, the
sons of Bilhah and Zilpah, his father's
wives, when they were in charge of the
flock; and he brought their father a bad
3 report of them. Now Israel loved
Joseph more than any other of his sons,
because he was a child of his old age,
and he made him a long, sleeved robe.
4 When his brothers saw that their father
loved him more than any of them, they
hated him and could not say a kind
word to him.
5 Joseph had a dream; and when he
told it to his brothers, they hated him
6 still more. He said to them, 'Listen to
7 this dream I have had. We were in the
field binding sheaves, and my sheaf
rose on end and stood upright, and your
sheaves gathered round and bowed low
8 before my sheaf.' His brothers answered
him, 'Do you think you will one day be
a king and lord it over us?' and they
hated him still more because of his
9 dreams and what he said. He had
another dream, which he told to his
father and his brothers. He said,
'Listen: I have had another dream. The
sun and moon and eleven stars were
10 bowing down to me.' When he told it
to his father and his brothers, his father
took him to task: 'What is this dream
of yours?' he said. 'Must we come and
bow low to the ground before you, I
and your mother and your brothers?'

His brothers were jealous of him, but 11
his father did not forget.

Joseph's brothers went to mind their 12
father's flocks in Shechem. Israel said 13
to him, 'Your brothers are minding the
flocks in Shechem; come, I will send
you to them,' and he said, 'I am ready.'
He said to him, 'Go and see if all is well 14
with your brothers and the sheep, and
bring me back word.' So he sent off
Joseph from the vale of Hebron and he
came to Shechem. A man met him 15
wandering in the open country and
asked him what he was looking for. He 16
replied, 'I am looking for my brothers.
Tell me, please, where they are minding
the flocks.' The man said, 'They have 17
gone away from here; I heard them
speak of going to Dothan.' So Joseph
followed his brothers and he found them
in Dothan. They saw him in the dis- 18
tance, and before he reached them,
they plotted to kill him. They said to 19
each other, 'Here comes that dreamer.
Now is our chance; let us kill him and 20
throw him into one of these pits and
say that a wild beast has devoured him.
Then we shall see what will come of his
dreams.' When Reuben heard, he came 21
to his rescue, urging them not to take
his life. 'Let us have no bloodshed', he 22
said. 'Throw him into this pit in the
wilderness, but do him no bodily harm.'
He meant to save him from them so as
to restore him to his father. When 23
Joseph came up to his brothers, they
stripped him of the long, sleeved robe
which he was wearing, took him and 24
threw him into the pit. The pit was
empty and had no water in it.

Then they sat down to eat some food 25
and, looking up, they saw an Ishmaelite
caravan coming in from Gilead on the
way down to Egypt, with camels
carrying gum tragacanth and balm
and myrrh. Judah said to his brothers, 26
'What shall we gain by killing our
brother and concealing his death? Why 27
not sell him to the Ishmaelites? Let us

37.1–36: Joseph is sold into Egypt. This material sets the stage for the Egyptian bondage, and
hence for their deliverance and realization of the divine promise (12.1–3). Chs. 37, 39–47, 50
constitute a single literary unit, although composed out of earlier independent elements. Chs.
48–49 are later additions. Ch. 38 is an extraneous fragment. **7:** *Bowed low:* his future status in
Egypt is foreshadowed (42.6; 50.18). **9:** *Eleven stars:* the zodiac is possibly meant, since the
number of constellations in it agrees with that of the members of the tribal league. **18–30:**
Variations from Reuben to Judah, and from Ishmaelites to Midianites, suggest that diverse

do him no harm, for he is our brother, our own flesh and blood'; and his **28** brothers agreed with him. Meanwhile some Midianite merchants passed by and drew Joseph up out of the pit. They sold him for twenty pieces of silver to the Ishmaelites, and they **29** brought Joseph to Egypt. When Reuben went back to the pit, Joseph was not **30** there. He rent his clothes and went back to his brothers and said, 'The boy is not there. Where can I go?'

31 Joseph's brothers took his robe, killed a goat and dipped it in the goat's **32** blood. Then they tore the robe, the long, sleeved robe, brought it to their father and said, 'Look what we have found. Do you recognize it? Is this your son's **33** robe or not?' Jacob did recognize it, and he replied, 'It is my son's robe. A wild beast has devoured him. Joseph **34** has been torn to pieces.' Jacob rent his clothes, put on sackcloth and mourned **35** his son for a long time. His sons and daughters all tried to comfort him, but he refused to be comforted. He said, 'I will go to my grave mourning for my son.' Thus Joseph's father wept for **36** him. Meanwhile the Midianites had sold Joseph in Egypt to Potiphar, one of Pharaoh's eunuchs, the captain of the guard.*j*

38 ABOUT THAT TIME JUDAH LEFT HIS brothers and went south and pitched his tent in company with an Adul- **2** lamite named Hirah. There he saw Bathshua the daughter of a Canaanite **3** and married her. He slept with her, and she conceived and bore a son, whom **4** she called Er. She conceived again and bore a son whom she called Onan. **5** Once more she conceived and bore a son whom she called Shelah, and she ceased to bear children*k* when she had **6** given birth to him. Judah found a wife for his eldest son Er; her name was **7** Tamar. But Judah's eldest son Er was wicked in the LORD'S sight, and the LORD took his life. Then Judah told **8** Onan to sleep with his brother's wife, to do his duty as the husband's brother and raise up issue for his brother. But Onan knew that the issue **9** would not be his; so whenever he slept with his brother's wife, he spilled his seed on the ground so as not to raise up issue for his brother. What he did was **10** wicked in the LORD'S sight, and the LORD took his life. Judah said to his **11** daughter-in-law Tamar, 'Remain as a widow in your father's house until my son Shelah grows up'; for he was afraid that he too would die like his brothers. So Tamar went and stayed in her father's house.

Time passed, and Judah's wife **12** Bathshua died. When he had fininished mourning, he and his friend Hirah the Adullamite went up to Timnath at sheep-shearing. When Tamar was told **13** that her father-in-law was on his way to shear his sheep at Timnath, she took **14** off her widow's weeds, veiled her face, perfumed herself and sat where the road forks in two directions on the way to Timnath. She did this because she knew that Shelah had grown up and she had not been given to him as a wife. When Judah saw her, he thought **15** she was a prostitute, although she had veiled her face. He turned to her where **16** she sat by the roadside and said, 'Let me lie with you,' not knowing that she was his daughter-in-law. She said 'What will you give me to lie with me?' He **17** answered, 'I will send you a kid from my flock,' but she said, 'Will you give me a pledge until you send it?' He **18** asked what pledge he should give her, and she replied, 'Your seal and its cord, and the staff which you hold in your hand.' So he gave them to her and lay with her, and she conceived. She then **19** rose and went home, took off her veil

j Or executioner. *k* ceased ... children: *or* was at Kezib.

accounts have been combined. **36:** *Eunuch:* the basic meaning of the Heb. word seems to be "official," and this might include emasculated guards of the harem. In either case, marriage was permissible (see 39.7, where Potiphar's wife is mentioned).
38.1–30: Judah and Tamar. After the tribe of Judah rose to prominence as the tribe of king David, its traditions received special preservation. The account here interrupts the flow of the Joseph narrative. When the latter resumes (ch. 39) Judah is still a member of his father's household. **7:** In the absence of alternatives, divine causation was assumed. **8:** *Duty:* levirate ("brother-in-law") marriage (Deut. 25.5–10), to insure the perpetuity of family name and property. **10:** The offense was in the unwillingness of Onan to insure posterity for the deceased.

and resumed her widow's weeds.
20 Judah sent the kid by his friend the
Adullamite in order to recover the
pledge from the woman, but he could
21 not find her. He asked the men of that
place, 'Where is that temple-prostitute,
the one who was sitting where the road
forks?', but they answered, 'There is no
22 temple-prostitute here.' So he went
back to Judah and told him that he had
not found her and that the men of the
place had said there was no such
23 prostitute there. Judah said, 'Let her
keep my pledge, or we shall get a bad
name. I did send a kid, but you could
24 not find her.' About three months later
Judah was told that his daughter-in-
law Tamar had behaved like a common
prostitute and through her wanton
conduct was with child. Judah said,
'Bring her out so that she may be
25 burnt.' But when she was brought out,
she sent to her father-in-law and said,
'The father of my child is the man to
whom these things belong. See if you
recognize whose they are, the engraving
on the seal, the pattern of the cord, and
26 the staff.' Judah recognized them and
said, 'She is more in the right than I am,
because I did not give her to my son
Shelah.' He did not have intercourse
27 with her again. When her time was
come, there were twins in her womb,
28 and while she was in labour one of
them put out a hand. The midwife took
a scarlet thread and fastened it round
the wrist, saying, 'This one appeared
29 first.' No sooner had he drawn back
his hand, than his brother came out
and the midwife said, 'What! you have
broken out first!' So he was named
30 Perez.*l* Soon afterwards his brother
was born with the scarlet thread on his
wrist, and he was named Zerah.*m*

39 WHEN JOSEPH WAS TAKEN DOWN TO
Egypt, he was bought by Potiphar, one
of Pharaoh's eunuchs, the captain of
the guard, an Egyptian. Potiphar

bought him from the Ishmaelites who
had brought him there. The LORD was 2
with Joseph and he prospered. He
lived in the house of his Egyptian
master, who saw that the LORD was 3
with him and was giving him success in
all that he undertook. Thus Joseph 4
found favour with his master, and he
became his personal servant. Indeed,
his master put him in charge of his
household and entrusted him with all
that he had. From the time that he put 5
him in charge of his household and all
his property, the LORD blessed the
Egyptian's household for Joseph's sake.
The blessing of the LORD was on all that
was his in house and field. He left 6
everything he possessed in Joseph's
care, and concerned himself with nothing but the food he ate.

Now Joseph was handsome and
good-looking, and a time came when 7
his master's wife took notice of him
and said, 'Come and lie with me.' But 8
he refused and said to her, 'Think of
my master. He does not know as much
as I do about his own house, and he has
entrusted me with all he has. He has 9
given me authority in this house
second only to his own, and has withheld nothing from me except you,
because you are his wife. How can I do
anything so wicked, and sin against
God?' She kept asking Joseph day 10
after day, but he refused to lie with her
and be in her company. One day he 11
came into the house as usual to do his
work, when none of the men of the
household were there indoors. She 12
caught him by his cloak, saying, 'Come
and lie with me', but he left the cloak
in her hands and ran out of the house.
When she saw that he had left his cloak 13
in her hands and had run out of the
house, she called out to the men of the 14
household, 'Look at this! My husband
has brought in a Hebrew to make a
mockery of us. He came in here to lie

l That is Breaking out.   *m That is* Redness.

14: *Weeds:* mourning garments. 21: Hirah, to preserve Judah from embarrassment, suggests
that the woman he seeks is not a common whore (v. 15) but one respected in the Canaanite
worship. On sacred prostitutes, see 1 Kgs.14.24; 2 Kgs.23.7; Hos.4.13–14. 26: Since no brother
was alive to carry out the levirate ("brother-in-law") obligation, the father-in-law might have
done so, and hence Tamar acted quite legally. 28: On the importance of determining the first-
born, see 25.31 n.
    39.1–23: Joseph's temptation and imprisonment. The account follows on 37.36. The story has
a very close Egyptian parallel, "The Story of the Two Brothers."

with me, but I gave a loud scream.
15 When he heard me scream and call out,
he left his cloak in my hand and ran
16 off.' She kept his cloak with her until
17 his master came home, and then she
repeated her tale. She said, 'That
Hebrew slave whom you brought in to
make a mockery of me, has been here
18 with me. But when I screamed for help
and called out, he left his cloak in my
19 hands and ran off.' When Joseph's
master heard his wife's story of what his
slave had done to her, he was furious.
20 He took Joseph and put him in the
Round Tower, where the king's prisoners were kept; and there he stayed in
21 the Round Tower. But the LORD was
with Joseph and kept faith with him,
so that he won the favour of the gover-
22 nor of the Round Tower. He put
Joseph in charge of all the prisoners in
23 the tower and of all their work. He
ceased to concern himself with anything entrusted to Joseph, because the
LORD was with Joseph and gave him
success in everything.

40 It happened later that the king's
butler and his baker offended their
2 master the king of Egypt. Pharaoh was
angry with these two eunuchs, the
3 chief butler and the chief baker, and he
put them in custody in the house of the
captain of the guard, in the Round
Tower where Joseph was imprisoned.
4 The captain of the guard appointed
Joseph as their attendant, and he
5 waited on them. One night, when they
had been in prison for some time, they
both had dreams, each needing its own
interpretation—the king of Egypt's
butler and his baker who were im-
6 prisoned in the Round Tower. When
Joseph came to them in the morning,
7 he saw that they looked dejected. So
he asked these eunuchs, who were in
custody with him in his master's house,
why they were so downcast that day.
8 They replied, 'We have each had a
dream and there is no one to interpret
it for us.' Joseph said to them, 'Does
not interpretation belong to God? Tell
9 me your dreams.' So the chief butler
told Joseph his dream: 'In my dream',

he said, 'there was a vine in front of me.
On the vine there were three branches, 10
and as soon as it budded, it blossomed
and its clusters ripened into grapes.
Now I had Pharaoh's cup in my hand, 11
and I plucked the grapes, crushed them
into Pharaoh's cup and put the cup
into Pharaoh's hand.' Joseph said to 12
him, 'This is the interpretation. The
three branches are three days: within 13
three days Pharaoh will raise you and
restore you to your post, and then you
will put the cup into Pharaoh's hand as
you used to do when you were his
butler. But when things go well with 14
you, if you think of me, keep faith with
me and bring my case to Pharaoh's
notice and help me to get out of this
house. By force I was carried off[n] from 15
the land of the Hebrews, and I have
done nothing here to deserve being put
in this dungeon.'

When the chief baker saw that 16
Joseph had given a favourable interpretation, he said to him, 'I too had a
dream, and in my dream there were
three baskets of white bread on my
head. In the top basket there was every 17
kind of food which the baker prepares
for Pharaoh, and the birds were eating
out of the top basket on my head.'
Joseph answered, 'This is the inter- 18
pretation. The three baskets are three
days: within three days Pharaoh will 19
raise you and hang you up on a tree,
and the birds of the air will eat your
flesh.'

The third day was Pharaoh's birth- 20
day and he gave a feast for all his
servants. He raised the chief butler and
the chief baker in the presence of his
court. He restored the chief butler to 21
his post, and the butler put the cup
into Pharaoh's hand; but he hanged the 22
chief baker. All went as Joseph had
said in interpreting the dreams for
them. Even so the chief butler did not 23
remember Joseph, but forgot him.

Nearly two years later Pharaoh had a **41**
dream: he was standing by the Nile,
and there came up from the river seven 2

n Or stolen.

40.1–23: **The dreams of Pharaoh's servants. 19:** *Will raise you:* the expression is the same as
in v. 13, but here it is given a gruesome turn.
41.1–57: **Pharaoh's dreams,** which provide the opportunity for Joseph to become an Egyptian

cows, sleek and fat, and they grazed on
3 the reeds. After them seven other cows
came up from the river, gaunt and lean,
and stood on the river-bank beside
4 the first cows. The cows that were
gaunt and lean devoured the cows that
were sleek and fat. Then Pharaoh woke
5 up. He fell asleep again and had a
second dream: he saw seven ears of
corn, full and ripe, growing on one
6 stalk. Growing up after them were
seven other ears, thin and shrivelled by
7 the east wind. The thin ears swallowed
up the ears that were full and ripe. Then
Pharaoh woke up and knew that it was
8 a dream. When morning came, Pharaoh
was troubled in mind; so he summoned
all the magicians and sages of Egypt.
He told them his dreams, but there was
no one who could interpret them for
9 him. Then Pharaoh's chief butler spoke
up and said, 'It is time for me to recall
10 my faults. Once Pharaoh was angry
with his servants, and he imprisoned
me and the chief baker in the house of
11 the captain of the guard. One night we
both had dreams, each needing its own
12 interpretation. We had with us a young
Hebrew, a slave of the captain of the
guard, and we told him our dreams and
he interpreted them for us, giving each
man's dream its own interpretation.
13 Each dream came true as it had been
interpreted to us: I was restored to my
position, and he was hanged.'
14 Pharaoh thereupon sent for Joseph,
and they hurriedly brought him out of
the dungeon. He shaved and changed
his clothes, and came in to Pharaoh.
15 Pharaoh said to him, 'I have had a
dream, and no one can interpret it to
me. I have heard it said that you can
understand and interpret dreams.'
16 Joseph answered, 'Not I, but God, will
17 answer for Pharaoh's welfare.' Then
Pharaoh said to Joseph, 'In my dream I
was standing on the bank of the Nile,
18 and there came up from the river seven
cows, fat and sleek, and they grazed on
19 the reeds. After them seven other cows
came up that were poor, very gaunt and
lean; I have never seen such gaunt
20 creatures in all Egypt. These lean,

gaunt cows devoured the first cows, the
21 fat ones. They were swallowed up, but
no one could have guessed that they
were in the bellies of the others, which
looked as gaunt as before. Then I woke
22 up. After I had fallen asleep again, I
saw in a dream seven ears of corn, full
23 and ripe, growing on one stalk. Growing up after them were seven other ears,
shrivelled, thin, and blighted by the
24 east wind. The thin ears swallowed up
the seven ripe ears. When I told all this
to the magicians, no one could explain
it to me.'
25 Joseph said to Pharaoh, 'Pharaoh's
dreams are one dream. God has told
26 Pharaoh what he is going to do. The
seven good cows are seven years, and
the seven good ears of corn are seven
27 years. It is all one dream. The seven
lean and gaunt cows that came up after
them are seven years, and the empty
ears of corn blighted by the east wind
28 will be seven years of famine. It is as I
have said to Pharaoh: God has let
Pharaoh see what he is going to do
29 There are to be seven years of great
30 plenty throughout the land. After
them will come seven years of famine;
all the years of plenty in Egypt will be
forgotten, and the famine will ruin the
31 country. The good years will not be
remembered in the land because of the
famine that follows; for it will be very
32 severe. The doubling of Pharaoh's
dream means that God is already
resolved to do this, and he will very
33 soon put it into effect. Pharaoh should
now look for a shrewd and intelligent
man, and put him in charge of the
34 country. This is what Pharaoh should
do: appoint controllers over the land,
and take one fifth of the produce of
Egypt during the seven years of plenty.
35 They should collect all this food produced in the good years that are coming
and put the corn under Pharaoh's control in store in the cities, and keep it
36 under guard. This food will be a reserve
for the country against the seven years
of famine which will come upon Egypt.
Thus the country will not be devastated
by the famine.'

official. **6:** *East wind:* a seasonal wind (*hamsin*) from the desert which destroys the vegetation
(Ps.103.15–16; Ezek.17.10; 19.12). **8:** The scorn here of the Egyptian magicians becomes more

37 The plan pleased Pharaoh and all his
38 courtiers, and he said to them, 'Can we
find a man like this man, one who has
39 the spirit of a god*o* in him?' He said to
Joseph, 'Since a god*p* has made all this
known to you, there is no one so
40 shrewd and intelligent as you. You shall
be in charge of my household, and all
my people will depend on your every
word. Only my royal throne shall make
41 me greater than you.' Pharaoh said to
Joseph, 'I hereby give you authority
42 over the whole land of Egypt.' He took
off his signet-ring and put it on Joseph's
finger, he had him dressed in fine linen,
and hung a gold chain round his neck.
43 He mounted him in his viceroy's
chariot and men cried 'Make way!'
before him. Thus Pharaoh made him
44 ruler over all Egypt and said to him, 'I
am the Pharaoh. Without your consent
no man shall lift hand or foot through-
45 out Egypt.' Pharaoh named him Zaphe-
nath-paneah, and he gave him as wife
Asenath the daughter of Potiphera
priest of On. And Joseph's authority
extended over the whole of Egypt.
46 Joseph was thirty years old when he
entered the service of Pharaoh king of
Egypt. When he took his leave of the
king, he made a tour of inspection
47 through the country. During the seven
years of plenty there were abundant
48 harvests, and Joseph gathered all the
food produced in Egypt during those
years and stored it in the cities, putting
in each the food from the surrounding
49 country. He stored the grain in huge
quantities; it was like the sand of the
sea, so much that he stopped measuring:
it was beyond all measure.
50 Before the years of famine came, two
sons were born to Joseph by Asenath
the daughter of Potiphera priest of On.
51 He named the elder Manasseh,*q* 'for,'
he said, 'God has caused me to forget
all my troubles and my father's family.'
52 He named the second Ephraim,*r* 'for,'
he said, 'God has made me fruitful in
53 the land of my hardships.' When the
seven years of plenty in Egypt came to
54 an end, seven years of famine began, as

Joseph had foretold. There was famine
in every country, but throughout Egypt
there was bread. So when the famine 55
spread through all Egypt, the people
appealed to Pharaoh for bread, and he
ordered them to go to Joseph and do
as he told them. In every region there 56
was famine, and Joseph opened all the
granaries and sold corn to the Egyptians, for the famine was severe. The 57
whole world came to Egypt to buy corn
from Joseph, so severe was the famine
everywhere.

WHEN JACOB SAW THAT THERE WAS CORN **42**
in Egypt, he said to his sons, 'Why do
you stand staring at each other? I have 2
heard that there is corn in Egypt. Go
down and buy some so that we may
keep ourselves alive and not starve.'
So Joseph's brothers, ten of them, went 3
down to buy grain from Egypt, but 4
Jacob did not let Joseph's brother
Benjamin go with them, for fear that he
might come to harm.
So the sons of Israel came down with 5
everyone else to buy corn, because of
the famine in Canaan. Now Joseph was 6
governor of all Egypt, and it was he
who sold the corn to all the people of
the land. Joseph's brothers came and
bowed to the ground before him, and 7
when he saw his brothers, he recognized
them but pretended not to know them
and spoke harshly to them. 'Where do
you come from?' he asked. 'From
Canaan,' they answered, 'to buy food.'
Although Joseph had recognized his 8
brothers, they did not recognize him.
He remembered also the dreams he had 9
had about them; so he said to them,
'You are spies; you have come to spy
out the weak points in our defences.'
They answered, 'No, sir: your servants 10
have come to buy food. We are all sons 11
of one man. Your humble servants are
honest men, we are not spies.' 'No,' he 12
insisted, 'it is to spy out our weaknesses
that you have come.' They answered 13
him, 'Sir, there are twelve of us, all

o Or of God.   p Or God.
q That is Causing to forget.   r That is Fruit.

---

fully developed in the account of the ten plagues (Exod. chs. 7–12). **42:** The *ring* would give
Pharaoh's authority to Joseph, since it could be used to stamp the Pharaoh's "signature."
45: *Potiphera* is apparently a fuller form of Potiphar (37.36), but is a different person.
42.1 38: Joseph's brothers travel to Egypt. 6: *Bowed:* thus fulfilling Joseph's dream (37.5–11).

brothers, sons of one man in Canaan. The youngest is still with our father,

14 and one has disappeared.' But Joseph said again to them, 'No, as I said

15 before, you are spies. This is how you shall be put to the proof: unless your youngest brother comes here, by the life of Pharaoh, you shall not leave this

16 place. Send one of your number to bring your brother; the rest will be kept in prison. Thus your story will be tested, and we shall see whether you are telling the truth. If not, then, by the life of

17 Pharaoh, you must be spies.' So he kept them in prison for three days.

18 On the third day Joseph said to the brothers, 'Do what I say and your lives will be spared; for I am a God-fearing

19 man: if you are honest men, your brother there shall be kept in prison, and the rest of you shall take corn for

20 your hungry households and bring your youngest brother to me; thus your words will be proved true, and you will not die.'[s]

21 They said to one another, 'No doubt we deserve to be punished because of our brother, whose suffering we saw; for when he pleaded with us we refused to listen. That is why these sufferings

22 have come upon us.' But Reuben said, 'Did I not tell you not to do the boy a wrong? But you would not listen, and his blood is on our heads, and we must

23 pay.' They did not know that Joseph understood, because he had used an

24 interpreter. Joseph turned away from them and wept. Then, turning back, he played a trick on them. First he took Simeon and bound him before their

25 eyes; then he gave orders to fill their bags with grain, to return each man's silver, putting it in his sack, and to give them supplies for the journey. All this

26 was done; and they loaded the corn on

27 to their asses and went away. When they stopped for the night, one of them opened his sack to give fodder to his ass, and there he saw his silver at the

28 top of the pack. He said to his brothers, 'My silver has been returned to me, and here it is in my pack.' Bewildered and trembling, they said to each other,

'What is this that God has done to us?'

29 When they came to their father Jacob in Canaan, they told him all that

30 had happened to them. They said, 'The man who is lord of the country spoke harshly to us and made out that we

31 were spies. We said to him, "We are

32 honest men, we are not spies. There are twelve of us, all brothers, sons of one father. One has disappeared, and the youngest is with our father in Canaan."

33 This man, the lord of the country, said to us, "This is how I shall find out if you are honest men. Leave one of your brothers with me, take food for your hungry households and go.

34 Bring your youngest brother to me, and I shall know that you are not spies, but honest men. Then I will restore your brother to you, and you can move about the country freely."' But on

35 emptying their sacks, each of them found his silver inside, and when they and their father saw the bundles of

36 silver, they were afraid. Their father Jacob said to them, 'You have robbed me of my children. Joseph has disappeared; Simeon has disappeared; and now you are taking Benjamin. Every-

37 thing is against me.' Reuben said to his father, 'You may kill both my sons if I do not bring him back to you. Put him in my charge, and I shall bring

38 him back.' But Jacob said, 'My son shall not go with you, for his brother is dead and he alone is left. If he comes to any harm on the journey, you will bring down my grey hairs in sorrow to the grave.'

43 The famine was still severe in the

2 country. When they had used up the corn they had brought from Egypt, their father said to them, 'Go back and buy a little more corn for us to eat.'

3 But Judah replied, 'The man plainly warned us that we must not go into his presence unless our brother was with

4 us. If you let our brother go with us, we will go down and buy food for you.

5 But if you will not let him, we will not go; for the man said to us, "You shall not come into my presence, unless

s Prob. rdg.; Heb. adds and they did so.

15: Joseph's purpose is to discomfit his half-brothers (see v. 21) by demanding to see Benjamin, his only full brother.

43.1–34: The second journey to Egypt. Jacob reluctantly lets Benjamin accompany his brothers.

6 your brother is with you." ' Israel said,
'Why have you treated me so badly?
Why did you tell the man that you had
7 yet another brother?' They answered,
'He questioned us closely about ourselves and our family: "Is your father
still alive?" he asked, "Have you a
brother?", and we answered his questions. How could we possibly know that
he would tell us to bring our brother to
8 Egypt?' Judah said to his father Israel,
'Send the boy with me; then we can
start at once. By doing this we shall
save our lives, ours, yours, and our
dependants', and none of us will starve.
9 I will go surety for him and you may
hold me responsible. If I do not bring
him back and restore him to you, you
10 shall hold me guilty all my life. If we
had not wasted all this time, by now
we could have gone back twice over.'
11 Their father Israel said to them, 'If it
must be so, then do this: take in your
baggage, as a gift for the man, some of
the produce for which our country is
famous: a little balsam, a little honey,
gum tragacanth, myrrh, pistachio nuts,
12 and almonds. Take double the amount
of silver and restore what was returned
to you in your packs; perhaps it was a
13 mistake. Take your brother with you
14 and go straight back to the man. May
God Almighty make him kindly disposed to you, and may he send back
the one whom you left behind, and
Benjamin too. As for me, if I am be-
15 reaved, then I am bereaved.' So they
took the gift and double the amount of
silver, and with Benjamin they started
at once for Egypt, where they presented
themselves to Joseph.
16 When Joseph saw Benjamin with
them, he said to his steward, 'Bring
these men indoors, kill a beast and
make dinner ready, for they will eat
17 with me at noon.' He did as Joseph told
him and brought the men into the
18 house. When they came in they were
afraid, for they thought, 'We have been
brought in here because of that affair of
the silver which was replaced in our
packs the first time. He means to trump
up some charge against us and victimize

us, seize our asses and make us his
slaves.' So they approached Joseph's 19
steward and spoke to him at the door
of the house. They said, 'Please listen, 20
my lord. After our first visit to buy
food, when we reached the place where 21
we were to spend the night, we opened
our packs and each of us found his
silver in full weight at the top of his
pack. We have brought it back with us,
and have added other silver to buy 22
food. We do not know who put the
silver in our packs.' He answered, 'Set 23
your minds at rest; do not be afraid. It
was your God, the God of your father,
who hid treasure for you in your packs.
I did receive the silver.' Then he
brought Simeon out to them.
The steward brought them into 24
Joseph's house and gave them water to
wash their feet, and provided fodder
for their asses. They had their gifts 25
ready when Joseph arrived at noon, for
they had heard that they were to eat
there. When Joseph came into the 26
house, they presented him with the gifts
which they had brought, bowing to the
ground before him. He asked them how 27
they were and said, 'Is your father well,
the old man of whom you spoke? Is he
still alive?' They answered, 'Yes, my 28
lord, our father is still alive and well.'
And they bowed low and prostrated
themselves. Joseph looked and saw his 29
own mother's son, his brother Benjamin, and asked, 'Is this your youngest
brother, of whom you told me?', and
to Benjamin he said, 'May God be
gracious to you, my son!' Joseph was 30
overcome; his feelings for his brother
mastered him, and he was near to tears.
So he went into the inner room and
wept. Then he washed his face and 31
came out; and, holding back his
feelings, he ordered the meal to be
served. They served him by himself, 32
and the brothers by themselves, and
the Egyptians who were at dinner were
also served separately; for Egyptians
hold it an abomination to eat with
Hebrews. The brothers were seated in 33
his presence, the eldest first according
to his age and so on down to the

8–10: Judah is here the spokesman; it was Reuben in 42.37. See 37.18–30 n. 26–28: *Bowed:*
42.6 n. 32: *Hebrews:* 10.21 n.

youngest: they looked at one another in
21 astonishment. Joseph sent them each a
portion from what was before him, but
Benjamin's was five times larger than
any of the other portions. Thus they
drank with him and all grew merry.

44 Joseph gave his steward this order:
'Fill the men's packs with as much food
as they can carry and put each man's
2 silver at the top of his pack. And put my
goblet, my silver goblet, at the top of
the youngest brother's pack with the
silver for the corn.' He did as Joseph
3 said. At daybreak the brothers were
allowed to take their asses and go on
4 their journey; but before they had gone
very far from the city, Joseph said to
his steward, 'Go after those men at
once, and when you catch up with
them, say, "Why have you repaid good
5 with evil? Why have you stolen the
silver goblet? It is the one from which
my lord drinks, and which he uses for
divination. You have done a wicked
6 thing." ' When he caught up with them,
7 he repeated all this to them, but they
replied, 'My lord, how can you say
such things? No, sir, God forbid that
8 we should do any such thing! You
remember the silver we found at the
top of our packs? We brought it back
to you from Canaan. Why should we
steal silver or gold from your master's
9 house? If any one of us is found with
the goblet, he shall die; and, what is
more, my lord, we will all become your
10 slaves.' He said, 'Very well, then; I
accept what you say. The man in whose
possession it is found shall be my slave,
11 but the rest of you shall go free.' Each
man quickly lowered his pack to the
12 ground and opened it. The steward
searched them, beginning with the
eldest and finishing with the youngest,
and the goblet was found in Benjamin's
pack.
13 At this they rent their clothes; then
each man loaded his ass and they
14 returned to the city. Joseph was still in
the house when Judah and his brothers
came in. They threw themselves on the
15 ground before him, and Joseph said,
'What have you done? You might have

known that a man like myself would
practise divination.' Judah said, 'What 16
shall we say, my lord? What can we say
to prove our innocence? God has found
out our sin. Here we are, my lord, ready
to be made your slaves, we ourselves as
well as the one who was found with the
goblet.' Joseph answered, 'God forbid 17
that I should do such a thing! The one
who was found with the goblet shall
become my slave, but the rest of you
can go home to your father in peace.'

Then Judah went up to him and said, 18
'Please listen, my lord. Let me say a
word to your lordship, I beg. Do not
be angry with me, for you are as great
as Pharaoh. You, my lord, asked us 19
whether we had a father or a brother.
We answered, "We have an aged 20
father, and he has a young son born in
his old age; this boy's full brother is
dead and he alone is left of his mother's
children, he alone, and his father loves
him." Your lordship answered, "Bring 21
him down to me so that I may set eyes
on him." We told you, my lord, that 22
the boy could not leave his father, and
that his father would die if he left
him. But you answered, "Unless your 23
youngest brother comes here with you,
you shall not enter my presence again."
We went back to your servant our 24
father, and told him what your lordship
had said. When our father told us to 25
go and buy food, we answered, "We 26
cannot go down; for without our
youngest brother we cannot enter the
man's presence; but if our brother is
with us, we will go." Our father, my 27
lord, then said to us, "You know that
my wife bore me two sons. One left me, 28
and I said, 'He must have been torn to
pieces.' I have not seen him to this day.
If you take this one from me as well, 29
and he comes to any harm, then you
will bring down my grey hairs in
trouble to the grave." Now, my lord, 30
when I return to my father without the
boy—and remember, his life is bound
up with the boy's—what will happen is 31
this: he will see that the boy is not with
us and will die, and your servants will
have brought down our father's grey

44.1–34: Joseph further discomfits his brothers. 15: He implies that the theft was discovered
through *divination*. **17:** Joseph wants to see if his brothers will, as previously, sell one of their
own into slavery.

32 hairs in sorrow to the grave. Indeed, my lord, it was I who went surety for the boy to my father. I said, "If I do not bring him back to you, then you 33 shall hold me guilty all my life." Now, my lord, let me remain in place of the boy as your lordship's slave, and let 34 him go with his brothers. How can I return to my father without the boy? I could not bear to see the misery which my father would suffer.'

45 Joseph could no longer control his feelings in front of his attendants, and he called out, 'Let everyone leave my presence.' So there was nobody present when Joseph made himself known to 2 his brothers, but so loudly did he weep that the Egyptians and Pharaoh's 3 household heard him. Joseph said to his brothers, 'I am Joseph; can my father be still alive?' His brothers were so dumbfounded at finding themselves face to face with Joseph that they could 4 not answer. Then Joseph said to his brothers, 'Come closer', and so they came close. He said, 'I am your brother Joseph whom you sold into Egypt. 5 Now do not be distressed or take it amiss that you sold me into slavery here; it was God who sent me ahead of 6 you to save men's lives. For there have now been two years of famine in the country, and there will be another five years with neither ploughing nor 7 harvest. God sent me ahead of you to ensure that you will have descendants on earth, and to preserve you all, a 8 great band of survivors. So it was not you who sent me here, but God, and he has made me a father[t] to Pharaoh, and lord over all his household and 9 ruler of all Egypt. Make haste and go back to my father and give him this message from his son Joseph: "God has made me lord of all Egypt. Come 10 down to me; do not delay. You shall live in the land of Goshen and be near me, you, your sons and your grandsons, your flocks and herds and all that you 11 have. I will take care of you there, you and your household and all that you have, and see that you are not reduced

to poverty; there are still five years of famine to come." You can see for 12 yourselves, and so can my brother Benjamin, that it is Joseph himself who is speaking to you. Tell my father of all 13 the honour which I enjoy in Egypt, tell him all you have seen, and make haste to bring him down here.' Then he 14 threw his arms round his brother Benjamin and wept, and Benjamin too embraced him weeping. He kissed all 15 his brothers and wept over them, and afterwards his brothers talked with him.

When the report that Joseph's 16 brothers had come reached Pharaoh's house, he and all his courtiers were pleased. Pharaoh said to Joseph, 'Say 17 to your brothers: "This is what you are to do. Load your beasts and go to Canaan. Fetch your father and your 18 households and bring them to me. I will give you the best that there is in Egypt, and you shall enjoy the fat of the land." You shall also tell them: 19 "Take wagons from Egypt for your dependants and your wives and fetch your father and come. Have no regrets 20 at leaving your possessions, for all the best that there is in Egypt is yours."' The sons of Israel did as they were told, 21 and Joseph gave them wagons, according to Pharaoh's orders, and food for the journey. He provided each of 22 them with a change of clothing, but to Benjamin he gave three hundred pieces of silver and five changes of clothing. Moreover he sent his father ten asses 23 carrying the best that there was in Egypt, and ten she-asses loaded with grain, bread, and provisions for his journey. So he dismissed his brothers, 24 telling them not to quarrel among themselves on the road, and they set out. Thus they went up from Egypt and 25 came to their father Jacob in Canaan. There they gave him the news that 26 Joseph was still alive and that he was ruler of all Egypt. He was stunned and could not believe it, but they told him 27 all that Joseph had said; and when he

t Or counsellor.

45.1–28: Joseph discloses his identity. 5–8: A central teaching of the Joseph story now unfolds: despite the evil intent of the brothers, God has worked to insure the realization of his promise. Thus, ultimate judgment cannot be passed upon momentarily unfavorable events. **16–20:** Ancient Egyptian sources relate the arrival of Asiatic nomads by such means.

saw the wagons which Joseph had sent to take him away, his spirit revived,

28 Israel said, 'It is enough. Joseph my son is still alive; I will go and see him before I die.'

46 SO ISRAEL SET OUT WITH ALL THAT HE had and came to Beersheba where he offered sacrifices to the God of his
2 father Isaac. God said to Israel in a vision by night, 'Jacob, Jacob', and he
3 answered, 'I am here.' God said, 'I am God, the God of your father. Do not be afraid to go down to Egypt, for
4 there I will make you a great nation. I will go down with you to Egypt, and I myself will bring you back again without fail; and Joseph shall close your
5 eyes.' So Jacob set out from Beersheba. Israel's sons conveyed their father Jacob, their dependants, and their wives in the wagons which Pharaoh had sent
6 to carry them. They took the herds and the stock which they had acquired in Canaan and came to Egypt, Jacob and
7 all his descendants with him, his sons and their sons, his daughters and his sons' daughters: he brought all his descendants to Egypt.

8[u] These are the names of the Israelites who entered Egypt: Jacob and his sons, as follows: Reuben, Jacob's eldest son.
9 The sons of Reuben: Enoch, Pallu,
10 Hezron and Carmi. The sons of Simeon: Jemuel, Jamin, Ohad, Jachin, Zohar, and Saul, who was the son of a
11 Canaanite woman. The sons of Levi:
12 Gershon, Kohath and Merari. The sons of Judah: Er, Onan, Shelah, Perez and Zerah; of these Er and Onan died in Canaan. The sons of Perez were
13 Hezron and Hamul. The sons of Issachar: Tola, Pua, Iob and Shimron. The
14 sons of Zebulun: Sered, Elon and
15 Jahleel. These are the sons of Leah whom she bore to Jacob in Paddanaram, and there was also his daughter Dinah. His sons and daughters numbered thirty-three in all.
16 The sons of Gad: Ziphion, Haggi, Shuni, Ezbon, Eri, Arodi and Areli.
17 The sons of Asher: Imnah, Ishvah,

Ishvi, Beriah, and their sister Serah. The sons of Beriah: Heber and Mal-
18 chiel. These are the descendants of Zilpah whom Laban gave to his daughter Leah; sixteen in all, born to Jacob.

19 The sons of Jacob's wife Rachel:
20 Joseph and Benjamin. Manasseh and Ephraim were born to Joseph in Egypt. Asenath daughter of Potiphera
21 priest of On bore them to him. The sons of Benjamin: Bela, Becher and Ashbel; and the sons of Bela: Gera, Naaman, Ehi, Rosh, Muppim, Huppim
22 and Ard. These are the descendants of Rachel; fourteen in all, born to Jacob.

23,24 The son[v] of Dan, Hushim. The sons of Naphtali: Jahzeel, Guni, Jezer and
25 Shillem. These are the descendants of Bilhah whom Laban gave to his daughter Rachel; seven in all, born to Jacob.

26 The persons belonging to Jacob who came to Egypt, all his direct descendants, not counting the wives of his
27 sons, were sixty-six in all. Two sons were born to Joseph in Egypt. Thus the house of Jacob numbered seventy when it entered Egypt.

28 Judah was sent ahead that he might appear before Joseph in Goshen, and
29 so they entered Goshen. Joseph had his chariot made ready and went up to meet his father Israel in Goshen. When they met, he threw his arms round him and wept, and embraced him for a long
30 time, weeping. Israel said to Joseph, 'I have seen your face again, and you are still alive. Now I am ready to die.'
31 Joseph said to his brothers and to his father's household, 'I will go and tell Pharaoh; I will say to him, "My brothers and my father's household who were in Canaan have come to
32 me."' Now his brothers were shepherds, men with their own flocks and herds, and they had brought them with them, their flocks and herds and all that they
33 possessed. So Joseph said, 'When Pharaoh summons you and asks you

u Verses 8–25: cp. Exod. 6.14–16; Num. 26.5–50; 1 Chr. 4. 1, 24; 5. 3; 6. 1; 7. 1, 6, 13, 30; 8. 1–5.
v Prob. rdg.; Heb. sons.

46.1–47.12: Jacob and his family settle in Egypt. The stage is now set for the subsequent enslavement and deliverance. **4:** *You:* here the "you" is the corporate Israel, not the single patriarch himself, for Jacob died in Egypt (49.33–50.3). **27:** *Seventy:* usually a round number (Exod.15.27; 24.1; 2 Sam.24.15; for other such numbers see 7.2 n.; 7.4 n.). The previous list (vv. 8–25) has

34 what your occupation is, you must say, "My lord, we have been herdsmen all our lives, as our fathers were before us." You must say this if you are to settle in the land of Goshen, because all shepherds are an abomination to the Egyptians.'

47 Joseph came and told Pharaoh, 'My father and my brothers have arrived from Canaan, with their flocks and their cattle and all that they have, and 2 they are now in Goshen.' Then he chose five of his brothers and presented 3 them to Pharaoh, who asked them what their occupation was, and they answered, 'My lord, we are shepherds, 4 we and our fathers before us, and we have come to stay in this land; for there is no pasture in Canaan for our sheep, because the famine there is so severe. We beg you, my lord, to let us settle 5 now in Goshen.' Pharaoh said to Joseph, 'So your father and your 6 brothers have come to you. The land of Egypt is yours; settle them in the best part of it. Let them live in Goshen, and if you know of any capable men among them, make them chief herdsmen over my cattle.'

7 Then Joseph brought his father in and presented him to Pharaoh, and Jacob gave Pharaoh his blessing. 8, 9 Pharaoh asked Jacob his age, and he answered, 'The years of my earthly sojourn are one hundred and thirty; hard years they have been and few, not equal to the years that my fathers lived 10 in their time.' Jacob then blessed Pharaoh and went out from his 11 presence. So Joseph settled his father and his brothers, and gave them lands in Egypt, in the best part of the country, in the district of Rameses, as Pharaoh 12 had ordered. He supported his father, his brothers, and all his father's household with all the food they needed.

13 There was no bread in the whole country, so very severe was the famine, and Egypt and Canaan were laid low 14 by it. Joseph collected all the silver in Egypt and Canaan in return for the corn which the people bought, and deposited it in Pharaoh's treasury. When all the silver in Egypt and Canaan 15 had been used up, the Egyptians came to Joseph and said, 'Give us bread, or we shall die before your eyes. Our silver is all spent.' Joseph said, 'If your 16 silver is spent, give me your herds and I will give you bread in return.' So they 17 brought their herds to Joseph, who gave them bread in exchange for their horses, their flocks of sheep and herds of cattle, and their asses. He maintained them that year with bread in exchange for their herds. The year came to an 18 end, and the following year they came to him again and said, 'My lord, we cannot conceal it from you: our silver is all gone and our herds of cattle are yours. Nothing is left for your lordship but our bodies and our lands. Why 19 should we perish before your eyes, we and our land as well? Take us and our land in payment for bread, and we and our land alike will be in bondage to Pharaoh. Give us seed-corn to keep us alive, or we shall die and our land will become desert.' So Joseph bought all 20 the land in Egypt for Pharaoh, because the Egyptians sold all their fields, so severe was the famine; the land became Pharaoh's. As for the people, 21 Pharaoh set them to work as slaves from one end of the territory of Egypt to the other. But Joseph did not buy 22 the land which belonged to the priests; they had a fixed allowance from Pharaoh and lived on this, so that they had no need to sell their land.

Joseph said to the people, 'Listen; I 23 have today bought you and your land for Pharaoh. Here is seed-corn for you. Sow the land, and give one fifth of the 24 crop to Pharaoh. Four fifths shall be yours to provide seed for your fields and food for yourselves, your households, and your dependants.' The 25 people said, 'You have saved our lives. If it please your lordship, we will be

---

undergone several adjustments and harmonizations. **47.9:** *One hundred and thirty:* Abraham lived to one hundred and seventy-five (25.7), Isaac to one hundred and eighty (35.28); see 5.4 n. **11:** *District of Rameses:* a synonym for Goshen (45.10), it is also the name of a city built by Hebrew slaves (see Exod.1.11).

47.13–26: Joseph's economic policies. The story may reflect the actual affairs in Egypt (such as the Pharaoh's property rights at a given age) at the beginning of the New Kingdom.

26 Pharaoh's slaves.' Joseph established it as a law in Egypt that one fifth should belong to Pharaoh, and this is still in force. It was only the priests' land that did not pass into Pharaoh's hands.

27 Thus Israel settled in Egypt, in Goshen; there they acquired land, and were fruitful and increased greatly.
28 Jacob stayed in Egypt for seventeen years and lived to be a hundred and
29 forty-seven years old. When the time of his death drew near, he summoned his son Joseph and said to him, 'If I may now claim this favour from you, put your hand under my thigh and swear by the LORD that you will deal loyally and truly with me and not bury me in
30 Egypt. When I die like my forefathers, you shall carry me from Egypt and bury me in their grave.' He answered,
31 'I will do as you say'; but Jacob said, 'Swear it.' So he swore the oath, and Israel sank down over the end of the bed.

48 The time came when Joseph was told that his father was ill, so he took with him his two sons, Manasseh and
2 Ephraim. Jacob heard that his son Joseph was coming to him, and he summoned his strength and sat up on
3 the bed. Jacob said to Joseph, 'God Almighty appeared to me at Luz in
4 Canaan and blessed me. He said to me, "I will make you fruitful and increase your descendants until they become a host of nations. I will give this land to your descendants after you
5 as a perpetual possession." Now, your two sons, who were born to you in Egypt before I came here, shall be counted as my sons; Ephraim and Manasseh shall be mine as Reuben and
6 Simeon are. Any children born to you after them shall be counted as yours, but in respect of their tribal territory they shall be reckoned under their elder
7 brothers' names. As I was coming from Paddan-aram I was bereaved of Rachel your mother on the way, in Canaan,

whilst there was still some distance to go to Ephrath, and I buried her there by the road to Ephrath, that is Bethlehem.'

When Israel saw Joseph's sons, he 8 said, 'Who are these?' Joseph replied 9 to his father, 'They are my sons whom God has given me here.' Israel said, 'Bring them to me, I beg you, so that I may take them on my knees.'*w* Now 10 Israel's eyes were dim with age, and he could not see; so Joseph brought the boys close to his father, and he kissed them and embraced them. He said to 11 Joseph, 'I had not expected to see your face again, and now God has granted me to see your sons also.' Joseph took 12 them from his father's knees and bowed to the ground. Then he took the two of 13 them, Ephraim on his right at Israel's left and Manasseh on his left at Israel's right, and brought them close to him. Israel stretched out his right 14 hand and laid it on Ephraim's head, although he was the younger, and, crossing his hands, laid his left hand on Manasseh's head; but Manasseh was the elder. He blessed Joseph and said: 15

'The God in whose presence my
      forefathers lived,
my forefathers Abraham and Isaac,
the God who has been my shepherd
      all my life until this day,
the angel who ransomed me from all 16
      misfortune,
may he bless these boys;
they shall be called by my name,
and by that of my forefathers,
      Abraham and Isaac;
may they grow into a great people
      on earth.'

When Joseph saw that his father was 17 laying his right hand on Ephraim's head, he was displeased; so he took hold of his father's hand to move it from Ephraim's head to Manasseh's.

w Or may bless them.

47.27–48.22: Jacob's blessing of Ephraim and Manasseh. 29: *Thigh:* see 24.2 n. **48.5:** *My sons:* the account seems to suggest that these two tribes were not among the early members of the league of twelve tribes specified in 49.1–27, but later came to be included (see Deut.33.17). The prose account here is younger than the poem in ch. 49. The fading away of Simeon (see 34.1–31 n.) kept the total number at twelve. **9:** *On my knees:* a formal part of an adoption procedure. **14:** *Elder:* preceded in military prominence (see Num.26.28–37 n.). **17–19:** The later emergence of Ephraim to a position of great power in Israel is explained. It was, like events both before

18 He said, 'That is not right, my father. This is the elder; lay your right hand on
19 his head.' But his father refused; he said, 'I know, my son, I know. He too shall become a people; he too shall become great, but his younger brother shall be greater than he, and his descendants shall be a whole nation in
20 themselves.' That day he blessed them and said:

'When a blessing is pronounced in Israel,
men shall use your names and say,
God make you like Ephraim and Manasseh',

thus setting Ephraim before Manasseh.
21 Then Israel said to Joseph, 'I am dying. God will be with you and will bring
22 you back to the land of your fathers. I give you one ridge of land more than your brothers: I took it from the Amorites with my sword and my bow.'

49 JACOB SUMMONED HIS SONS AND SAID, 'Come near, and I will tell you what will happen to you in days to come.

2 Gather round me and listen, you
       sons of Jacob;
    listen to Israel your father.
3 Reuben, you are my first-born,
    my strength and the first fruit of
       my vigour,
    excelling in pride, excelling in might,
4 turbulent as a flood, you shall not
       excel;
    because you climbed into your
       father's bed;
    then you defiled his concubine's
       couch.
5 Simeon and Levi are brothers,
    their spades became weapons of
       violence.

My soul shall not enter their   6
    council,
my heart shall not join their
    company;
for in their anger they killed men,
wantonly they hamstrung oxen.
A curse be on their anger because it   7
    was fierce;
a curse on their wrath because it was
    ruthless!
I will scatter them in Jacob,
I will disperse them in Israel.
Judah, your brothers shall praise   8
    you,
your hand is on the neck of your
    enemies.
Your father's sons shall do you
    homage.
Judah, you lion's whelp,   9
you have returned from the kill,
    my son,
and crouch and stretch like a lion;
and, like a lion,[x] who dare rouse
    you?
The sceptre shall not pass from   10
    Judah,
nor the staff from his descendants,
so long as tribute is brought to him
and the obedience of the nations is
    his.
To the vine he tethers his ass,   11
and the colt of his ass to the red
    vine;
he washes his cloak in wine,
his robes in the blood of grapes.
Darker than wine are his eyes,   12
his teeth whiter than milk.
Zebulun dwells by the sea-shore,   13
his shore is a haven for ships,
and his frontier rests on Sidon.
Issachar, a gelded ass   14
lying down in the cattle-pens,
saw that a settled home was good   15
and that the land was pleasant,

x Or lioness.

and after, a manifestation of God's mysterious freedom. **20:** The blessing seems to be another version of that in vv. 15–16. **21:** *Bring you back:* see Exod.13.19. **22:** *Ridge:* in Heb., *sh'chem;* there is a pun here on the place name Shechem. There may be some historical allusion, an obscure one, which is at variance with the peaceful settlement suggested in 33.18–20.
    49.1–27: The "Blessing of Jacob." The patriarch portrays the character and destiny of the tribes, these represented by their ancestors. **3–4:** A leading tribe in the early period, *Reuben* had acted indecisively (Judg.5.15–16) and dwindled in numbers (Deut.33.6). See 35.22 n. **5–7:** On their attack against Shechem, here alluded to, see 34.1–31 n. *Simeon* was later absorbed into the tribe of Judah while the *Levites* assumed a religious status, losing their political character (Deut.10.8–9). **8–12:** The passage seems to allude to the reign of David; this provides a clue to the date of the composition of the chapter, which, however, uses earlier material. **14–15:** The writer utilizes a folk etymology, whereby *Issachar* means "hired man," in order to explain the

so he bent his back to the burden
and submitted to perpetual forced
labour.

16 Dan—how insignificant his people,
lowly as any tribe in Israel![y]

17 Let Dan be a viper on the road,
a horned snake on the path,
who bites the horse's fetlock
so that the rider tumbles backwards.

18 For thy salvation I wait in hope,
O LORD.

19 Gad is raided by raiders,
and he raids them from the rear.

20 Asher shall have rich food as daily
fare,
and provide dishes fit for a king.

21 Naphtali is a spreading terebinth
putting forth lovely boughs.

22 Joseph is a fruitful tree[z] by a spring
with branches climbing over the wall.

23 The archers savagely attacked him,
they shot at him and pressed him
hard,

24 but their bow was splintered by the
Eternal
and the sinews of their arms were
torn apart
by the power of the Strong One of
Jacob,
by the name of the Shepherd[a] of
Israel,

25 by the God of your father—so may
he help you,
by God Almighty—so may he bless
you
with the blessings of heaven above,
the blessings of the deep that lurks
below.
The blessings of breast and womb

26 and the blessings of your father
are stronger
than the blessings of the everlasting
pools[b]
and the bounty of the eternal hills.
They shall be on the head of
Joseph,

on the brow of the prince among[c]
his brothers.

27 Benjamin is a ravening wolf:
in the morning he devours the
prey,
in the evening he snatches a share
of the spoil.'

28 These, then, are the twelve tribes of
Israel, and this is what their father
Jacob said to them, when he blessed
them each in turn. He gave them his 29 last charge and said, 'I shall soon be
gathered to my father's kin; bury me
with my forefathers in the cave on the
plot of land which belonged to Ephron
the Hittite, that is the cave on the plot 30 of land at Machpelah east of Mamre
in Canaan, the field which Abraham
bought from Ephron the Hittite for
a burial-place. There Abraham was 31 buried with his wife Sarah; there Isaac
and his wife Rebecca were buried; and
there I buried Leah. The land and the 32 cave on it were bought from the
Hittites.' When Jacob had finished 33 giving his last charge to his sons, he
drew his feet up on to the bed, breathed
his last, and was gathered to his father's
kin.

50 Then Joseph threw himself upon his
father, weeping and kissing his face. 2 He ordered the physicians in his service to embalm his father Israel, and 3 they did so, finishing the task in forty
days, which was the usual time for
embalming. The Egyptians mourned
him for seventy days; and then, when 4 the days of mourning for Israel were
over, Joseph approached members of
Pharaoh's household and said, 'If I can
count on your goodwill, then speak for
me to Pharaoh; tell him that my 5 father made me take an oath, saying,

[y] *Or* Dan shall judge his people as one of the tribes of
Israel.
[z] *Or* a fruitful ben-tree.
[a] *Prob. rdg.; Heb. adds* stone.
[b] *Or* hills.   [c] the prince among: *or* the one cursed by.

---

tribe's subordination, possibly to Canaanites. The animal is a domesticated beast. **16–17:** The
Heb. word for "shall judge" (Tfn. *y*), *yadin*, involves a play on the tribal name. **18:** Possibly an
invocation, used when the material was read in public. **19:** Situated east of the Jordan River,
Gad was often subject to raids from the east by desert tribes. **20:** The fertile Mediterranean coast
north of Carmel is meant (see Deut.33.24). **21:** *Naphtali* was situated in the beautiful territory
around Lake Tiberias. **22:** *Joseph:* this tradition is relatively early, since Ephraim and Manasseh
have not yet emerged as significant political entities (see 48.5 n.). **25:** *Deep:* see 2.6 n.
49.28–50.26: The deaths of Jacob and Joseph. 50.3: *Forty:* 7.4 n. *Seventy:* other sources say
that the Egyptians mourned their kings for seventy-two days. Because of Joseph's position, his

"I am dying. Bury me in the grave that I bought*d* for myself in Canaan." Ask him to let me go up and bury my father, and afterwards I will return.'
6 Pharaoh answered, 'Go and bury your father, as he has made you swear to do.'
7 So Joseph went to bury his father, accompanied by all Pharaoh's courtiers, the elders of his household, and all
8 the elders of Egypt, together with all Joseph's own household, his brothers, and his father's household; only their dependants, with the flocks and herds,
9 were left in Goshen. He took with him chariots and horsemen; they were a
10 very great company. When they came to the threshing-floor of Atad beside the river Jordan, they raised a loud and bitter lament; and there Joseph observed seven days' mourning for his
11 father. When the Canaanites who lived there saw this mourning at the threshing-floor of Atad, they said, 'How bitterly the Egyptians are mourning!'; accordingly they named the place beside the Jordan Abel-mizraim.*e*
12 Thus Jacob's sons did what he had
13 told them to do. They took him to Canaan and buried him in the cave on the plot of land at Machpelah, the land which Abraham had bought as a burial-place from Ephron the Hittite,
14 to the east of Mamre. Then, after he had buried his father, Joseph returned to Egypt with his brothers and all who had gone up with him.
15 When their father was dead Joseph's brothers were afraid and said, 'What if Joseph should bear a grudge against us and pay us out for all the harm that we

did to him?' They therefore approached 16 Joseph with these words: 'In his last words to us before he died, your father gave us this message for you: "I ask 17 you to forgive your brothers' crime and wickedness; I know they did you harm." So now forgive our crime, we beg; for we are servants of your father's God.' When they said this to him, Joseph wept. His brothers also wept*f* 18 and prostrated themselves before him; they said, 'You see, we are your slaves.' But Joseph said to them, 'Do not be 19 afraid. Am I in the place of God? You 20 meant to do me harm; but God meant to bring good out of it by preserving the lives of many people, as we see to-day. Do not be afraid. I will provide 21 for you and your dependants.' Thus he comforted them and set their minds at rest.

Joseph remained in Egypt, he and 22 his father's household. He lived there to be a hundred and ten years old and 23 saw Ephraim's children to the third generation; he also recognized as his the children of Manasseh's son Machir. He said to his brothers, 'I am dying; 24 but God will not fail to come to your aid and take you from here to the land which he promised on oath to Abraham, Isaac and Jacob.' He made the 25 sons of Israel take an oath, saying, 'When God thus comes to your aid, you must take my bones with you from here.' So Joseph died at the age of a 26 hundred and ten. He was embalmed and laid in a coffin in Egypt.

d Or dug.
e That is Mourning (*or* Meadow) of Egypt.
f Prob. rdg.; Heb. came.

father is given a royal funeral. **10–11:** *Atad:* an unknown location, seemingly not Machpelah of vv. 12–13 (see ch. 23). **18:** *Prostrated:* the story concludes by hearkening back to a motif presented at its beginning (37.5–11). **20:** *God meant:* see 45.5–8 n. **23:** *Recognized as his:* lit. "were born upon the knees of Joseph." This adoption procedure (see 48.9 n.) signifies the admission of the clans of Machir (Judg.5.14; Num.32.39–40) into the Israelite confederation.

EXODUS

The migration of Jacob's family to Egypt, undertaken with high expectation and understood as an act of God's grace (Gen. chs. 37–50), becomes the occasion for bondage to the Pharaoh. The promise (Gen.12.1–3; 15.1–21; 17.1–8) now seemed but a delusion. Yet, the day arrived when Israel escaped and survived in the Wilderness. At a sacred mountain she reflected upon the meaning of God's past redemption, and pledged to become a community obedient only to the LORD's will. (The account was handed down in several versions, which were then combined into the present form; see Introduction to the Pentateuch). When subsequent generations heard the stirring story, they found parallels to the disappointments of their times, and also hope for the future.

The book has two major parts: chs. 1–18, relating the oppression, the manner of deliverance and the arrival at the sacred mountain under the leadership of Moses; and chs. 19–40, giving various accounts of the covenant regulations by means of which the community was to govern her life and worship.

Literary and archaeological evidence points to the period of the Nineteenth Egyptian Dynasty (about 1300 B.C.) as the most likely setting for the events.

Israel enslaved in Egypt

1 THESE ARE THE NAMES OF THE Israelites who entered Egypt with Jacob, each with his household: 2 Reuben, Simeon, Levi and Judah; 3,4 Issachar, Zebulun and Benjamin; Dan 5 and Naphtali, Gad and Asher. There were seventy of them all told, all direct descendants of Jacob. Joseph was already in Egypt.

6 In course of time Joseph died, he and all his brothers and that whole 7 generation. Now the Israelites were fruitful and prolific; they increased in numbers and became very powerful,[a] so that the country was overrun by 8 them. Then a new king ascended the throne of Egypt, one who knew noth- 9 ing of Joseph. He said to his people, 'These Israelites have become too many 10 and too strong for us. We must take precautions to see that they do not increase any further; or we shall find that, if war breaks out, they will join the enemy and fight against us, and they will become masters of the country.' 11 So they were made to work in gangs with officers set over them, to break their spirit with heavy labour. This is how Pharaoh's store-cities, Pithom 12 and Rameses, were built. But the more harshly they were treated, the more their numbers increased beyond all bounds, until the Egyptians came to loathe the sight of them. So they treat- 13 ed their Israelite slaves with ruthless severity, and made life bitter for them 14 with cruel servitude, setting them to work on clay and brick-making, and all sorts of work in the fields. In short they made ruthless use of them as slaves in every kind of hard labour.

Then the king of Egypt spoke to the 15 Hebrew midwives, whose names were Shiphrah and Puah. 'When you are 16 attending the Hebrew women in child-birth', he told them, 'watch as the child is delivered and if it is a boy, kill him; if it is a girl, let her live.' But they were 17 God-fearing women. They did not do what the king of Egypt had told them to do, but let the boys live. So he sum- 18 moned those Hebrew midwives and asked them why they had done this and let the boys live. They told Pharaoh 19 that Hebrew women were not like Egyptian women. When they were in labour they gave birth before the mid-wife could get to them. So God made 20 the midwives prosper, and the people increased in numbers and in strength. God gave the midwives homes and 21 families of their own, because they feared him. Pharaoh then ordered all 22

a Or numerous.

1.1–22: The bondage in Egypt begins. 5: *Seventy:* a round number (Gen.46.27 n.). 7: *Were fruitful:* in keeping with the divine command at creation (Gen.1.28) and with the promise to Abraham (Gen.15.5; 17.5–6). 8: The *new king* may be a member of the Nineteenth Dynasty, which came to power between 1320 and 1310 B.C. 10: The new dynasty, hoping to recover an Asiatic empire, regarded the alien Hebrews (Gen.10.21 n.) along its border as a security risk (compare Gen.42.9–12).

55

his people to throw every new-born Hebrew boy into the Nile, but to let the girls live.

2 A descendant of Levi married a Levite woman who conceived and bore a son. When she saw what a fine child he was, she hid him for three months, but she could conceal him no longer. So she got a rush basket for him, made it watertight with clay and tar, laid him in it, and put it among the reeds by the bank of the Nile. The child's sister took her stand at a distance to see what would happen to him. Pharaoh's daughter came down to bathe in the river, while her ladies-in-waiting walked along the bank. She noticed the basket among the reeds and sent her slave-girl for it. She took it from her and when she opened it, she saw the child. It was crying, and she was filled with pity for it. 'Why,' she said, 'it is a little Hebrew boy.' Thereupon the sister said to Pharaoh's daughter, 'Shall I go and fetch one of the Hebrew women as a wet-nurse to suckle the child for you?' Pharaoh's daughter told her to go; so the girl went and called the baby's mother. Then Pharaoh's daughter said to her, 'Here is the child, suckle him for me, and I will pay you for it myself.' So the woman took the child and suckled him. When the child was old enough, she brought him to Pharaoh's daughter, who adopted him and called him Moses,[b] 'because', she said, 'I drew[c] him out of the water.'

11 ONE DAY WHEN MOSES WAS GROWN UP, he went out to his own kinsmen and saw them at their heavy labour. He saw an Egyptian strike one of his fellow-12 Hebrews. He looked this way and that, and, seeing there was no one about, he struck the Egyptian down and hid his body in the sand. When he went out 13 next day, two Hebrews were fighting together. He asked the man who was in the wrong, 'Why are you striking him?' 'Who set you up as an officer and judge 14 over us?' the man replied. 'Do you mean to murder me as you murdered the Egyptian?' Moses was alarmed. 'The thing must have become known', he said to himself. When Pharaoh 15 heard of it, he tried to put Moses to death, but Moses made good his escape and settled in the land of Midian.

Now the priest of Midian had seven 16 daughters. One day as Moses sat by a well, they came to draw water and filled the troughs to water their father's sheep. Some shepherds came and drove 17 them away; but Moses got up, took the girls' part and watered their sheep himself. When the girls came back to their 18 father Reuel, he asked, 'How is it that you are back so quickly today?' 'An 19 Egyptian rescued us from the shepherds', they answered; 'and he even drew the water for us and watered the sheep.' 'But where is he then?' he said 20 to his daughters. 'Why did you leave him behind? Go and invite him to eat with us.' So it came about that Moses 21 agreed to live with the man, and he gave Moses his daughter Zipporah in marriage. She bore him a son, and 22 Moses called him Gershom, 'because', he said, 'I have become an alien[d] living in a foreign land.'

YEARS PASSED, AND THE KING OF EGYPT 23 died, but the Israelites still groaned in slavery. They cried out, and their appeal for rescue from their slavery rose up to God. He heard their groaning 24 and remembered his covenant with Abraham, Isaac and Jacob; he saw the 25

b Heb. Mosheh.　　*c Heb. verb* mashah.　　*d Heb.* ger.

2.1–10: **The birth of Moses. 3:** The theme of the exposed child who is rescued and rises to a position of fame is attested elsewhere in the ancient world. Quite similar is the legend of Sargon, king of Akkad (about 2300 B.C.), who was rescued from a bitumen-sealed rush basket. **4:** *Sister:* Miriam (Num.26.59). **7–10:** God uses Pharaoh's evil design to prepare for the deliverance of Israel. For a similar theme, see Gen.45.5–8 n. **10:** A folk explanation for the child's name is given, in keeping with the details of the story. In reality, *Moses* is an Egyptian name meaning "has begotten a child." It may have been joined, originally, with the name of an Egyptian deity (as in Ra-moses, i.e. Rameses of 1.11).

2.11–22: **Moses flees to Midian. 16:** *Seven:* see Gen.7.2 n. **18:** *Father:* see Judg.1.16.

2.23–4.17: **The call of Moses. 23:** The *king* may be Seti I, the founder of the Nineteenth Dynasty (1.8 n.), who ruled about fifteen years. The oppressive building programs were continued by his successors, notably Rameses II. **24:** *Covenant:* Gen.12.1–3; 26.1–5; 28.13–15.

plight of Israel, and he took heed of it.

3 Moses was minding the flock of his father-in-law Jethro, priest of Midian. He led the flock along the side of the wilderness and came to Horeb, the 2 mountain of God. There the angel of the LORD appeared to him in the flame of a burning bush. Moses noticed that, although the bush was on fire, it was 3 not being burnt up; so he said to himself, 'I must go across to see this wonderful sight. Why does not the bush 4 burn away?' When the LORD saw that Moses had turned aside to look, he called to him out of the bush, 'Moses, Moses.' And Moses answered, 'Yes, 5 I am here.' God said, 'Come no nearer; take off your sandals; the place where 6 you are standing is holy ground.' Then he said, 'I am the God of your forefathers, the God of Abraham, the God of Isaac, the God of Jacob.' Moses covered his face, for he was afraid to gaze on God.

7 The LORD said, 'I have indeed seen the misery of my people in Egypt. I have heard their outcry against their slave-masters. I have taken heed of their 8 sufferings, and have come down to rescue them from the power of Egypt, and to bring them up out of that country into a fine, broad land; it is a land flowing with milk and honey, the home of Canaanites, Hittites, Amorites, 9 Perizzites, Hivites, and Jebusites. The outcry of the Israelites has now reached me; yes, I have seen the brutality of the 10 Egyptians towards them. Come now; I will send you to Pharaoh and you shall bring my people Israel out of 11 Egypt.' 'But who am I', Moses said to God, 'that I should go to Pharaoh, and

that I should bring the Israelites out of Egypt?' God answered, 'I am*e* with you. 12 This shall be the proof that it is I who have sent you: when you have brought the people out of Egypt, you shall all worship God here on this mountain.'

Then Moses said to God, 'If I go to 13 the Israelites and tell them that the God of their forefathers has sent me to them, and they ask me his name, what shall I say?' God answered, 'I AM; that 14 is who I am.*f* Tell them that I AM has sent you to them.' And God said fur- 15 ther, 'You must tell the Israelites this, that it is JEHOVAH*g* the God of their forefathers, the God of Abraham, the God of Isaac, the God of Jacob, who has sent you to them. This is my name for ever; this is my title in every generation. Go and assemble the elders of 16 Israel and tell them that JEHOVAH the God of their forefathers, the God of Abraham, Isaac and Jacob, has appeared to you and has said, "I have indeed turned my eyes towards you; I have marked all that has been done to 17 you in Egypt, and I am resolved to bring you up out of your misery in Egypt, into the country of the Canaanites, Hittites, Amorites, Perizzites, Hivites, and Jebusites, a land flowing with milk and honey." They will listen to 18 you, and then you and the elders of Israel must go to the king of Egypt. Tell him, "It has happened that the LORD the God of the Hebrews met us. So now give us leave to go a three days' journey into the wilderness to offer sacrifice to the LORD our God." I know well that 19

e Or I will be; *Heb.* ehyeh.
f I AM . . . I am: *or* I will be what I will be.
g The Hebrew consonants are YHWH, *probably pronounced* Yahweh, *but traditionally read* Jehovah.

3.1: *Horeb* seems to be a local Midianite shrine, and hence the alien Moses is unaware of its sacred nature (v. 5). It is later to be the site of the giving of the Law (18.5–20.21) and is called Sinai in another version of the tradition (19.1–2). Its location is unknown, but post-Christian tradition placed it in the Sinai Peninsula. **2:** *Flame:* on fire as a symbol for the divine presence, see Gen.15.17 n. **5:** The removal of *sandals* before entering a sacred place was an ancient custom (Josh.5.15), continued by Muslims until the present. **6:** *The God of your forefathers* is an ancient designation for the deity of one's ancestors (Gen.26.24; 49.25). Here, the patriarchal god is identified with Yahweh, the LORD. **8:** *Milk and honey* were basic food for the semi-nomadic Israelites, and hence the term describes the desirability of the land to them. **12:** *I am:* by folk explanation the divine name (Yahweh) is derived from the verb "to be." Thus, Israel understood the very essence of the deity to be expressed by his name. Actually, the form *YHWH* (v. 15, Tfn. *g*) would be third person ("he is"), but since the deity is depicted as explaining his own name in the first person, the explanation becomes "I am." See also 6.3. **14–15:** The meaning of the divine name (v. 12) is repeated and expanded. God's freedom from and control of history are denoted by the phrase, "I will be what I will be" (Tfn. *f*). For another paraphrase, which also expresses the divine freedom, see 33.19. **18:** *Three:* a commonly used round number

the king of Egypt will not give you
20 leave unless he is compelled. I shall
then stretch out my hand and assail the
Egyptians with all the miracles I shall
work among them. After that he will
21 send you away. Further, I will bring
this people into such favour with the
Egyptians that, when you go, you will
22 not go empty-handed. Every woman
shall ask her neighbour or any woman
who lives in her house for jewellery of
silver and gold and for clothing. Load
your sons and daughters with them,
and plunder Egypt.'

4   Moses answered, 'But they will never
believe me or listen to me; they will
say, "The LORD did not appear to
2 you." ' The LORD said, 'What have you
there in your hand?' 'A staff', Moses
3 answered. The LORD said, 'Throw it on
the ground.' Moses threw it down and
it turned into a snake. He ran away
4 from it, but the LORD said, 'Put your
hand out and seize it by the tail.' He
did so and gripped it firmly, and it
turned back into a staff in his hand.
5 'This is to convince the people that the
LORD the God of their forefathers, the
God of Abraham, the God of Isaac,
the God of Jacob, has appeared to
6 you.' Then the LORD said, 'Put your
hand inside the fold of your cloak.'
He did so, and when he drew it out the
7 skin was diseased, white as snow. The
LORD said, 'Put it back again', and he
did so. When he drew it out this time
it was as healthy as the rest of his body.
8 'Now,' said the LORD, 'if they do not
believe you and do not accept the evidence of the first sign, they may accept
9 the evidence of the second. But if they
are not convinced even by these two
signs, and will not accept what you say,
then fetch some water from the Nile
and pour it out on the dry ground, and
the water you take from the Nile will
turn to blood on the ground.'
10   But Moses said, 'O LORD, I have
never been a man of ready speech, never

in my life, not even now that thou hast
spoken to me; I am slow and hesitant
of speech.' The LORD said to him, 11
'Who is it that gives man speech? Who
makes him dumb or deaf? Who makes
him clear-sighted or blind? Is it not I,
the LORD? Go now; I will help your 12
speech and tell you what to say.' But 13
Moses still protested, 'No, Lord, send
whom thou wilt.' At this the LORD grew 14
angry with Moses and said, 'Have you
not a brother, Aaron the Levite? He,
I know, will do all the speaking. He is
already on his way out to meet you, and
he will be glad indeed to see you. You 15
shall speak to him and put the words
in his mouth; I will help both of you to
speak and tell you both what to do. He 16
will do all the speaking to the people
for you, he will be the mouthpiece, and
you will be the god he speaks for. But 17
take this staff, for with it you are to
work the signs.'

At length Moses went back to Jethro 18
his father-in-law and said, 'Let me
return to my kinsfolk in Egypt and see
if they are still alive.' Jethro told him
to go and wished him well.

THE LORD SPOKE TO MOSES IN MIDIAN 19
and said to him, 'Go back to Egypt, for
all those who wished to kill you are
dead.' So Moses took his wife and 20
children, mounted them on an ass and
set out for Egypt with the staff of God
in his hand. The LORD said to Moses, 21
'While you are on your way back to
Egypt, keep in mind all the portents I
have given you power to show. You
shall display these before Pharaoh, but
I will make him obstinate and he will
not let the people go. Then tell Phar- 22
aoh that these are the words of the
LORD: "Israel is my first-born son. I 23
have told you to let my son go, so that
he may worship me. You have refused
to let him go, so I will kill your first-
born son." '
During the journey, while they were 24

(Gen.30.36; 40.13; Exod.2.2). **21–22:** See 11.2–3; 12.35–36. **4.1–9:** God supplies Moses with
three signs of authentication. Israelite tradition presents Moses as able to compete with and
triumph over the magicians of Egypt (see 7.11; 8.16–19; 9.10–11).
    4.18–31: Moses returns to Egypt. 20: *The staff of God:* see 4.17. **21:** Since, in ancient Israelite
belief, a human being could hardly defy the divine will, Pharaoh's reluctance must ultimately
be a part of Yahweh's plan. **22:** *First-born son:* an alternative way of expressing the election
of Abraham (Gen.11.10–32 n.). **24–26:** This obscure passage seems to be a fragment of a
once independent tradition about how a divine being, perhaps the god of the Midianite clan,

encamped for the night, the LORD met 25 Moses, meaning to kill him, but Zipporah picked up a sharp flint, cut off her son's foreskin, and touched him with it, saying, 'You are my blood-26 bridegroom.' So the LORD let Moses alone. Then she said,[h] 'Blood-bridegroom by circumcision.'

27 Meanwhile the LORD had ordered Aaron to go and meet Moses in the wilderness. Aaron went and met him at the mountain of God, and he kissed 28 him. Then Moses told Aaron everything, the words the LORD had sent him to say and the signs he had commanded 29 him to perform. Moses and Aaron went and assembled all the elders of 30 Israel. Aaron told them everything that the LORD had said to Moses; he performed the signs before the people, 31 and they were convinced. They heard that the LORD had shown his concern for the Israelites and seen their misery; and they bowed themselves to the ground in worship.

5 After this, Moses and Aaron came to Pharaoh and said, 'These are the words of the LORD the God of Israel: "Let my people go so that they may keep my pilgrim-feast in the wilderness."'
2 'Who is the LORD,' asked Pharaoh, 'that I should obey him and let Israel go? I care nothing for the LORD: and 3 I tell you I will not let Israel go.' They replied, 'It has happened that the God of the Hebrews met us. So let us go three days' journey into the wilderness to offer sacrifice to the LORD our God, or else he will attack us with pestilence 4 or sword.' But the king of Egypt said, 'Moses and Aaron, what do you mean by distracting the people from their 5 work? Back to your labours! Your people already outnumber the native Egyptians; yet you would have them stop working!'
6 That very day Pharaoh ordered the people's overseers and their foremen

not to supply the people with the straw 7 used in making bricks, as they had done hitherto. 'Let them go and collect their own straw, but see that they produce 8 the same tally of bricks as before. On no account reduce it. They are a lazy people, and that is why they are clamouring to go and offer sacrifice to their god. Keep the men hard at work; let 9 them attend to that and take no notice of a pack of lies.' The overseers and 10 foremen went out and said to the people, 'Pharaoh's orders are that no more straw is to be supplied. Go and 11 get it for yourselves wherever you can find it; but there will be no reduction in your daily task.' So the people scat- 12 tered all over Egypt to gather stubble for straw, while the overseers kept 13 urging them on, bidding them complete, day after day, the same quantity as when straw was supplied. Then the 14 Israelite foremen were flogged because they were held responsible by Pharaoh's overseers, who asked them, 'Why did you not complete the usual number of bricks yesterday or today?' So the 15 foremen came and appealed to Pharaoh: 'Why do you treat your servants like this?' they said. 'We are given no 16 straw, yet they keep on telling us to make bricks. Here are we being flogged, but it is your people's fault.' But Phar- 17 aoh replied, 'You are lazy, you are lazy. That is why you talk about going to offer sacrifice to the LORD. Now go; 18 get on with your work. You will be given no straw, but you must produce the tally of bricks.' When they were 19 told that they must not let the daily tally of bricks fall short, the Israelite foremen saw that they were in trouble. As they came out from Pharaoh's 20 presence they found Moses and Aaron waiting to meet them, and said, 'May 21 this bring the LORD's judgement down upon you: you have made us stink in

[h] *Or* Therefore women say.

sought the life of Moses' child because he was uncircumcised. Zipporah performs the rite, proclaiming that the child is now a *blood*-bridegroom (perhaps an initiated member of the religious community). The name "Moses" does not occur in the MT; only because the passage appears in its present context is it he who appears to be threatened.
　5.1–6.1: The first audience with Pharaoh. 1: *Pilgrim-feast:* see 3.18. **2:** The gods of powerless foreigners (Hebrews) command little respect from the Pharaoh, who is himself deified in Egyptian religion. **7:** Chopped *straw* was added to the wet clay to facilitate drying and bonding. **9:** The request to observe the festival is regarded as a pretext to leave the country permanently.

the nostrils of Pharaoh and his subjects; you have put a sword in their hands to kill us.'

22 Moses went back to the LORD, and said, 'Why, O LORD, hast thou brought misfortune on this people? And why
23 didst thou ever send me? Since I first went to Pharaoh to speak in thy name he has heaped misfortune on thy people and thou hast done nothing at all to
6 rescue them.' The LORD answered, 'Now you shall see what I will do to Pharaoh. In the end Pharaoh will let them go with a strong hand, nay, will drive them from his country with an outstretched arm.'
2 God spoke to Moses and said, 'I am
3 the LORD. I appeared to Abraham, Isaac, and Jacob as God Almighty. But I did not let myself be known to
4 them by my name JEHOVAH.[i] Moreover, I made a covenant with them to give them Canaan, the land where they
5 settled for a time as foreigners. And now I have heard the groaning of the Israelites, enslaved by the Egyptians, and I have called my covenant to mind.
6 Say therefore to the Israelites, "I am the LORD. I will release you from your labours in Egypt. I will rescue you from slavery there. I will redeem you with arm outstretched and with mighty
7 acts of judgement. I will adopt you as my people, and I will become your God. You shall know that I, the LORD, am your God, the God who releases
8 you from your labours in Egypt. I will lead you to the land which I swore with uplifted hand to give to Abraham, to Isaac and to Jacob. I will give it you for your possession. I am the LORD." '
9 Moses repeated these words to the Israelites, but they did not listen to him; they had become impatient because of their cruel slavery.
10 Then the LORD spoke to Moses and
11 said, 'Go and tell Pharaoh king of

Egypt to set the Israelites free to leave his country.' Moses made answer in 12 the presence of the LORD, 'If the Israelites do not listen to me, how will Pharaoh listen to such a halting speaker as I am?'

Thus the LORD spoke to Moses and 13 Aaron and gave them their commission to the Israelites and to Pharaoh, namely that they should bring the Israelites out of Egypt.

THESE WERE THE HEADS OF FATHERS' 14[j] families:

Sons of Reuben, Israel's eldest son: Enoch, Pallu, Hezron and Carmi; these were the families of Reuben.

Sons of Simeon: Jemuel, Jamin, 15 Ohad, Jachin, Zohar, and Saul, who was the son of a Canaanite woman; these were the families of Simeon.

These were the names of the sons of 16 Levi in order of seniority: Gershon, Kohath and Merari. Levi lived to be a hundred and thirty-seven.

Sons of Gershon, family by family: 17 Libni and Shimei.

Sons of Kohath: Amram, Izhar, 18 Hebron and Uzziel. Kohath lived to be a hundred and thirty-three.

Sons of Merari: Mahli and Mushi. 19

These were the families of Levi in order of seniority. Amram married his 20 father's sister Jochebed, and she bore him Aaron and Moses. Amram lived to be a hundred and thirty-seven.

Sons of Izhar: Korah, Nepheg and 21 Zichri.

Sons of Uzziel: Mishael, Elzaphan 22 and Sithri.

Aaron married Elisheba, who was 23 the daughter of Amminadab and the sister of Nahshon, and she bore him Nadab, Abihu, Eleazar and Ithamar.

Sons of Korah: Assir, Elkanah and Ab- 24

i See note on 3. 15.
j Verses 14–16: cp. Gen. 46. 8–11; Num. 26. 5, 6, 12, 13.

6.2–7.7: An alternative account of Moses' commission (compare 3.1–4.17), editorially placed so that it now serves as a reaffirmation of his call after Pharaoh's negative response. **3:** *God Almighty:* see Gen.17.1 n.; 49.25. According to some modern interpreters, the Israelite twelve-tribal league (Gen.29.31–30.24 n.) arose only after the conquest of Canaan, and included clans, escaped from Egypt, who previously had not worshiped Yahweh (3.14–15 n.), and other clans who traced their worship of him back to primeval time (Gen.4.26). Later, all Israel accepted the Exod. tradition as her own (1.1–5) and identified Yahweh with her former deities (3.12 n.). **7:** *My people . . . your God:* the essence of the covenant relationship. **13–27:** There is an alternate account of the commission of Moses in vv. 13,26–27; this brief account reflects almost nothing of the elaborate narrative in the preceding and ensuing chapters. The genealogy (vv. 14–25),

iasaph; these were the Korahite families. 26 Eleazar son of Aaron married one of the daughters of Putiel, and she bore him Phinehas. These were the heads of the Levite families, family by family.

26 It was this Aaron, together with Moses, to whom the LORD said, 'Bring the Israelites out of Egypt, mustered 27 in their tribal hosts.' These were the men who told Pharaoh king of Egypt to let the Israelites leave Egypt. It was this same Moses and Aaron.

28 WHEN THE LORD SPOKE TO MOSES IN 29 Egypt he said, 'I am the LORD. Tell Pharaoh king of Egypt all that I say to 30 you.' Moses made answer in the presence of the LORD, 'I am a halting speaker; how will Pharaoh listen to 7 me?' The LORD answered Moses, 'See now, I have made you like a god for Pharaoh, with your brother Aaron as 2 your spokesman. You must tell your brother Aaron all I bid you say, and he will tell Pharaoh, and Pharaoh will let the Israelites go out of his country; 3 but I will make him stubborn. Then will I show sign after sign and portent 4 after portent in the land of Egypt. But Pharaoh will not listen to you, so I will assert my power in Egypt, and with mighty acts of judgement I will bring my people, the Israelites, out of Egypt 5 in their tribal hosts. When I put forth my power against the Egyptians and bring the Israelites out from them, then Egypt will know that I am the 6 LORD.' So Moses and Aaron did exactly as the LORD had commanded. 7 At the time when they spoke to Pharaoh, Moses was eighty years old and Aaron eighty-three.

8 The LORD said to Moses and Aaron, 9 'If Pharaoh demands some portent from you, then you, Moses, must say to Aaron, "Take your staff and throw it down in front of Pharaoh, and it will turn into a serpent."' When Moses 10 and Aaron came to Pharaoh, they did as the LORD had told them. Aaron threw down his staff in front of Pharaoh and his courtiers, and it turned into a serpent. At this, Pharaoh sum- 11 moned the wise men and the sorcerers, and the Egyptian magicians too did 12 the same thing by their spells. Every man threw his staff down, and each staff turned into a serpent; but Aaron's staff swallowed up theirs. Pharaoh, 13 however, was obstinate; as the LORD had foretold, he would not listen to Moses and Aaron.

Then the LORD said to Moses, 14 'Pharaoh is obdurate: he has refused to set the people free. Go to him in the 15 morning on his way out to the river. Stand and wait on the bank of the Nile to meet him, and take with you the staff that turned into a snake. Say this 16 to him: "The LORD the God of the Hebrews sent me to bid you let his people go in order to worship him in the wilderness. So far you have not listened to his words; so now the LORD 17 says, 'By this you shall know that I am the LORD.' With this rod that I have in my hand, I shall now strike the water in the Nile and it will be changed into blood. The fish will die and the 18 river will stink, and the Egyptians will be unable to drink water from the Nile."' The LORD then told Moses to 19 say to Aaron, 'Take your staff and stretch your hand out over the waters

---

which seems pointed toward emphasizing the role of Aaron and his relation to Moses, was apparently once independent and self-contained. **7.3:** *Stubborn:* see 4.21 n.

7.8–13: An alternative account of the first audience with Pharaoh, varying considerably in detail from 5.1–6.1. The miracles used to authenticate Moses to the people of Israel (4.1–9) are here understood as the means of his authentication to Pharaoh. As it now stands, the passage serves as introduction to the account of the even greater miracles (the ten plagues). It took its final shape when the Aaronite priesthood ruled Israel, and hence it enhances the role of Aaron.

7.14–11.10: The ten plagues. This section, inspired by and meant to serve as a preface for Israel's miraculous departure from Egypt (chs. 12–15), presents dramatic episodes in which Pharaoh alternately agrees and refuses to let Israel realize her destiny, typifying the reversals which Israel would experience throughout her history and encouraging the belief that the promise to the patriarchs will ultimately be realized. Although each plague may rest upon a natural phenomenon enhanced through cultic recitation, the literary purpose here is to ridicule the deities of Egypt as forces of nature under Yahweh's control.

7.14–25: The first plague is directed against the deified Nile upon which all life in Egypt depends. Its annual inundation replenishes (and fertilizes) the soil. **17:** Pharaoh has professed

of Egypt, its rivers and its streams, and over every pool and cistern, to turn them into blood. There shall be blood throughout the whole of Egypt, blood even in their wooden bowls and jars of 20 stone.' So Moses and Aaron did as the LORD had commanded. He lifted up his staff and struck the water of the Nile in the sight of Pharaoh and his courtiers, and all the water was changed into 21 blood. The fish died and the river stank, and the Egyptians could not drink water from the Nile. There was blood 22 everywhere in Egypt. But the Egyptian magicians did the same thing by their spells; and still Pharaoh remained obstinate, as the LORD had foretold, and did not listen to Moses and Aaron. 23 He turned away, went into his house and dismissed the matter from his 24 mind. Then the Egyptians all dug for drinking water round about the river, because they could not drink from the 25 waters of the Nile itself. This lasted for seven days from the time when the LORD struck the Nile.

8   The LORD then told Moses to go into Pharaoh's presence and say to him, 'These are the words of the LORD: "Let my people go in order to worship 2 me. If you refuse to let them go, I will plague the whole of your territory with 3 frogs. The Nile shall swarm with them. They shall come up from the river into your house, into your bedroom and on to your bed, into the houses of your courtiers and your people, into your 4 ovens and your kneading-troughs. The frogs shall clamber over you, your 5 people, and your courtiers." ' Then the LORD told Moses to say to Aaron, 'Take your staff in your hand and stretch it out over the rivers, streams, and pools, to bring up frogs upon the 6 land of Egypt.' So Aaron stretched out his hand over the waters of Egypt, and the frogs came up and covered all the 7 land. The magicians did the same thing

by their spells: they too brought up frogs upon the land of Egypt. Then 8 Pharaoh summoned Moses and Aaron. 'Pray to the LORD', he said, 'to take the frogs away from me and my people, and I will let the people go to sacrifice to the LORD.' Moses said, 'Of your 9 royal favour, appoint a time when I may intercede for you and your courtiers and people, so that you and your houses may be rid of the frogs, and none be left except in the Nile.' 'To- 10 morrow', Pharaoh said. 'It shall be as you say,' replied Moses, 'so that you may know there is no one like our God, the LORD. The frogs shall depart from 11 you, from your houses, your courtiers, and your people: none shall be left except in the Nile.' Moses and Aaron 12 left Pharaoh's presence, and Moses appealed to the LORD to remove the frogs which he had brought on Pharaoh. The LORD did as Moses had 13 asked, and in house and courtyard and in the open the frogs all perished. They 14 piled them into countless heaps and the land stank; but when Pharaoh 15 found that he was given relief he became obdurate; as the LORD had foretold, he did not listen to Moses and Aaron.

The LORD then told Moses to say to 16 Aaron, 'Stretch out your staff and strike the dust on the ground, and it will turn into maggots throughout the land of Egypt', and they obeyed. 17 Aaron stretched out his staff and struck the dust, and it turned into maggots on man and beast. All the dust turned into maggots throughout the land of Egypt. The magicians tried to 18 produce maggots in the same way by their spells, but they failed. The maggots were everywhere, on man and beast. 'It is the finger of God', said the 19 magicians to Pharaoh, but Pharaoh remained obstinate; as the LORD had foretold, he did not listen to them.

no such knowledge in 5.2. **19**: On Aaron's role, see 7.8–13 n. **22**: The feat of the magicians is an embellishment meant to heighten the contest between Yahweh and the gods of Egypt.
8.1–15: The second plague is directed against the frog-goddess Heqet. It follows naturally upon the first, since the mud of the Nile's overflow could serve as a breeding place. **8**: Thus Pharaoh indirectly acknowledges Yahweh's existence for the first time.
8.16–19: The third plague follows naturally from the previous plague, since vermin could breed in the decaying carcasses of the frogs. **18**: The failure of the magicians heightens the drama and leads us toward Yahweh's ultimate victory. **19**: The *finger* or "hand" of God is an Ancient Near Eastern idiom for a manifestation of divine power (Ps.8.3; Lk.11.20).

20 The LORD told Moses to rise early in the morning and stand in Pharaoh's path as he went out to the river and to say to him, 'These are the words of the LORD: "Let my people go in order to 21 worship me. If you do not let my people go, I will send swarms of flies upon you, your courtiers, your people, and your houses. The houses of the Egyptians shall be filled with the swarms and so shall all the land they live in, 22 but on that day I will make an exception of Goshen, the land where my people live: there shall be no swarms there. Thus you shall know that I, the 23 LORD, am here in the land. I will make a distinction between my people and yours. Tomorrow this sign shall ap- 24 pear."' The LORD did this; dense swarms of flies infested Pharaoh's house and those of his courtiers; throughout Egypt the land was threat- 25 ened with ruin by the swarms. Pharaoh summoned Moses and Aaron and said to them, 'Go and sacrifice to 26 your God, but in this country'. 'That we cannot do', replied Moses, 'because the victim we shall sacrifice to the LORD our God is an abomination to the Egyptians. If the Egyptians see us offer such an animal, will they not stone us 27 to death? We must go a three days' journey into the wilderness to sacrifice to the LORD our God, as he commands 28 us.' 'I will let you go,' said Pharaoh, 'and you shall sacrifice to your God in the wilderness; only do not go far. 29 Now intercede for me.' Moses answered, 'As soon as I leave you I will intercede with the LORD. Tomorrow the swarms will depart from Pharaoh, his courtiers, and his people. Only let not Pharaoh trifle any more with the people by preventing them from going 30 to sacrifice to the LORD.' Then Moses left Pharaoh and interceded with the 31 LORD. The LORD did as Moses had said; he removed the swarms from Pharaoh, his courtiers, and his people; not one was left. But once again Phar- 32 aoh became obdurate and did not let the people go.

The LORD said to Moses, 'Go into 9 Pharaoh's presence and say to him, "These are the words of the LORD the God of the Hebrews: 'Let my people go in order to worship me.' If you 2 refuse to let them go and still keep your hold on them, the LORD will strike your 3 grazing herds, your horses and asses, your camels, cattle, and sheep with a terrible pestilence. But the LORD will 4 make a distinction between Israel's herds and those of the Egyptians. Of all that belong to Israel not a single one shall die."' The LORD fixed a time 5 and said, 'Tomorrow I will do this throughout the land.' The next day the 6 LORD struck. All the herds of Egypt died, but from the herds of the Israelites not one single beast died. Pharaoh 7 inquired and was told that not a beast from the herds of Israel had died; and yet he remained obdurate and did not let the people go.

The LORD said to Moses and Aaron, 8 'Take handfuls of soot from a kiln. Moses shall toss it into the air in Pharaoh's sight, and it will turn into 9 a fine dust over the whole of Egypt. All over Egypt it will become festering boils on man and beast.' They took the 10 soot from the kiln and stood before Pharaoh. Moses tossed it into the air and it produced festering boils on man and beast. The magicians were no 11 match for Moses because of the boils, which attacked them and all the Egyptians. But the LORD made Pharaoh 12 obstinate; as the LORD had foretold to Moses, he did not listen to Moses and Aaron.

The LORD then told Moses to rise 13 early in the morning, present himself

---

8.20–32: **The fourth plague** is the mature larvae of the previous plague. 22: The exemption of Goshen demonstrates that the plagues are not natural catastrophes, and heightens the drama. 26–27: Whether the *abomination* represents an unstated Egyptian taboo, or whether it is a literary embellishment for dramatic effect, is unclear. Compare Gen.43.32; 46.34. 28: For Pharaoh's suspicions of Moses' true intent, see 5.9 n.

9.1–7: **The fifth plague** is directed, in part, against the bovine-deities Hathor and Apis. It may be connected with the previous plague as a disease spread by flies. 4: *Distinction:* see 8.22 n.

9.8–12: **The sixth plague.** This account may be a variant of the previous one. In any case, this plague does not seem to have been immediately consecutive; beasts presumably killed by the fifth plague are here afflicted as if anew.

before Pharaoh, and say to him, 'These are the words of the LORD the God of the Hebrews: "Let my people go in 14 order to worship me. This time I will strike home with all my plagues against you, your courtiers, and your people, so that you may know that there is none 15 like me in all the earth. By now I could have stretched out my hand, and struck you and your people with pestilence, and you would have vanished from the 16 earth. I have let you live only to show you my power and to spread my fame 17 throughout the land. Since you still obstruct my people and will not let 18 them go, tomorrow at this time I will send a violent hailstorm, such as has never been in Egypt from its first be-19 ginnings until now. Send now and bring your herds under cover, and everything you have out in the open field. If anything, whether man or beast, which happens to be in the open, is not brought in, the hail will fall on 20 it, and it will die." ' Those of Pharaoh's subjects who feared the word of the LORD hurried their slaves and cattle 21 into their houses. But those who did not take to heart the word of the LORD left their slaves and cattle in the open. 22 The LORD said to Moses, 'Stretch out your hand towards the sky to bring down hail on the whole land of Egypt, on man and beast and every growing 23 thing throughout the land.' Moses stretched out his staff towards the sky, and the LORD sent thunder and hail, with fire flashing down to the ground. The LORD rained down hail on the land 24 of Egypt, hail and fiery flashes through the hail, so heavy that there had been nothing like it in all Egypt from the time that Egypt became a nation. 25 Throughout Egypt the hail struck everything in the fields, both man and beast; it beat down every growing 26 thing and shattered every tree. Only in the land of Goshen, where the Israelites lived, was there no hail.

Pharaoh sent and summoned Moses 27 and Aaron. 'This time I have sinned', he said; 'the LORD is in the right; I and my people are in the wrong. Intercede 28 with the LORD, for we can bear no more of this thunder and hail. I will let you go; you need wait no longer.' Moses 29 said, 'When I leave the city I will spread out my hands in prayer to the LORD. The thunder shall cease, and there shall be no more hail, so that you may know that the earth is the LORD's. But 30 you and your subjects—I know that you do not yet fear the LORD God.' (The flax and barley were destroyed 31 because the barley was in the ear and the flax in bud, but the wheat and 32 spelt were not destroyed because they come later.) Moses left Pharaoh's 33 presence, went out of the city and lifted up his hands to the LORD in prayer: the thunder and hail ceased, and no more rain fell. When Pharaoh saw 34 that the downpour, the hail, and the thunder had ceased, he sinned again, he and his courtiers, and became obdurate. So Pharaoh remained obsti-35 nate; as the LORD had foretold through Moses, he did not let the people go.

Then the LORD said to Moses, 'Go 10 into Pharaoh's presence. I have made him and his courtiers obdurate, so that I may show these my signs among them, and so that you can tell your 2 children and grandchildren the story: how I made sport of the Egyptians, and what signs I showed among them. Thus you will know that I am the LORD.' Moses and Aaron went in to 3 Pharaoh and said to him, 'These are the words of the LORD the God of the Hebrews: "How long will you refuse to humble yourself before me? Let my people go in order to worship me. If 4

9.13–35: The seventh plague. 15–16: An explanation for the persistence of the oppression is offered, meant to comfort later Israel in similar circumstances. **19:** That *herds* abound, despite the fifth plague (see 9.8–12 n.), suggests that we do not have a unified chronicle of consecutive historical events. **20:** Elements of the Egyptian people begin to acknowledge Yahweh's lordship, emphasizing Pharaoh's stubbornness and setting the stage for the climactic plague. **27:** The narrative is advanced by the initial confession of failure by Pharaoh. **31–32:** This comment, perhaps editorial, explains how, in the following plague, there was something left for the locusts to devour.

10.1–20: The eighth plague. Swarms of locusts were known and feared throughout the Ancient Near East.

you refuse to let my people go, tomorrow I will bring locusts into your coun-
5 try. They shall cover the face of the land so that it cannot be seen. They shall eat up the last remnant left you by the hail. They shall devour every tree that grows in your country-side.
6 Your houses and your courtiers' houses, every house in Egypt, shall be full of them; your fathers never saw the like nor their fathers before them; such a thing has not happened from their time until now." ' He turned and left
7 Pharaoh's presence. Pharaoh's courtiers said to him, 'How long must we be caught in this man's toils? Let their menfolk go and worship the LORD their God. Do you not know by now that
8 Egypt is ruined?' So Moses and Aaron were brought back to Pharaoh, and he said to them, 'You may go and worship the LORD your God; but who exactly
9 is to go?' 'All,' said Moses, 'young and old, boys and girls, sheep and cattle; for we have to keep the LORD's pilgrim-
10 feast.' Pharaoh replied, 'Very well then; take your dependants with you when you go; and the LORD be with you. But beware, there is trouble in
11 store for you. No, your menfolk may go and worship the LORD, for that is all you asked.' So they were driven out from Pharaoh's presence.
12 Then the LORD said to Moses, 'Stretch out your hand over Egypt so that the locusts may come and invade the land and devour all the vegetation in it, everything the hail has left.'
13 Moses stretched out his staff over the land of Egypt, and the LORD sent a wind roaring in from the east all that day and all that night. When morning came, the east wind had brought the
14 locusts. They invaded the whole land of Egypt, and settled on all its territory in swarms so dense that the like of them had never been seen before, nor
15 ever will be again. They covered the surface of the whole land till it was black with them. They devoured all the vegetation and all the fruit of the trees that the hail had spared. There was no green left on tree or plant throughout all Egypt. Pharaoh hastily 16 summoned Moses and Aaron. 'I have sinned against the LORD your God and against you', he said. 'Forgive my sin, 17 I pray, just this once. Intercede with the LORD your God and beg him only to remove this deadly plague from me.' Moses left Pharaoh and interceded 18 with the LORD. The LORD changed the 19 wind into a westerly gale, which carried the locusts away and swept them into the Red Sea.*k* There was not a single locust left in all the territory of Egypt. But the LORD made Pharaoh obstinate, 20 and he did not let the Israelites go.

Then the LORD said to Moses, 21 'Stretch out your hand towards the sky so that there may be darkness over the land of Egypt, darkness that can be felt.' Moses stretched out his hand 22 towards the sky, and it became pitch dark throughout the land of Egypt for three days. Men could not see one 23 another; for three days no one stirred from where he was. But there was no darkness wherever the Israelites lived. Pharaoh summoned Moses. 'Go', he 24 said, 'and worship the LORD. Your dependants may go with you; but your flocks and herds must be left with us.' But Moses said, 'No, you must your-25 self supply us with animals for sacrifice and whole-offering to the LORD our God; and our own flocks must go with 26 us too—not a hoof must be left behind. We may need animals from our own flocks to worship the LORD our God; we ourselves cannot tell until we are there how we are to worship the LORD.' The LORD made Pharaoh obstinate, 27 and he refused to let them go. 'Out! 28 Pester me no more!' he said to Moses. 'Take care you do not see my face again, for on the day you do, you die.' 'You are right,' said Moses; 'I shall 29 never see your face again.'

k Or the Sea of Reeds.

10.21–29: The ninth plague is possibly directed against the sun-god. **21:** *A darkness that can be felt* adequately describes a "*hamsin*," a hot, dust-laden wind from the desert, covering the land with an eerie gloom during which breathing becomes difficult. But that there was no darkness where the Israelites dwelled (v. 23) suggests something supernatural. **28:** With Pharaoh's threat, on the day you see my face again *you die*, it is obvious that the plagues are not endless; rather their climax is now at hand.

11 Then the LORD said to Moses, 'One last plague I will bring upon Pharaoh and Egypt. After that he will let you go; he will send you packing, as a man dis-**2** misses a rejected bride. Let the people be told that men and women alike should ask their neighbours for jewell-**3** ery of silver and gold.' The LORD made the Egyptians well-disposed towards them, and, moreover, Moses was a very great man in Egypt in the eyes of Pharaoh's courtiers and of the people. **4** Moses then said, 'These are the words of the LORD: "At midnight I will go out among the Egyptians. **5** Every first-born creature in the land of Egypt shall die: the first-born of Pharaoh who sits on his throne, the first-born of the slave-girl at the hand-mill, and all the first-born of the cattle. **6** All Egypt will send up a great cry of anguish, a cry the like of which has never been heard before, nor ever will **7** be again. But among all Israel not a dog's tongue shall be so much as scratched, no man or beast be hurt." Thus you shall know that the LORD does make a distinction between Egypt **8** and Israel. Then all these courtiers of yours will come down to me, prostrate themselves and cry, "Go away, you and all the people who follow at your heels." After that I will go away.' Then Moses left Pharaoh's presence hot with anger.

9 The LORD said to Moses, 'Pharaoh will not listen to you; I will therefore show still more portents in the land of **10** Egypt.' All these portents had Moses and Aaron shown in the presence of Pharaoh, and yet the LORD made him obstinate, and he did not let the Israelites leave the country.

The institution of the Passover

THE LORD SAID TO MOSES AND AARON IN **12** Egypt: This month is for you the first of **2** months; you shall make it the first month of the year. Speak to the whole **3** community of Israel and say to them: On the tenth day of this month let each man take a lamb or a kid for his family, one for each household, but if a house-**4** hold is too small for one lamb or one kid, then the man and his nearest neighbour may take one between them. They shall share the cost, taking into account both the number of persons and the amount each of them eats. Your lamb or kid must be without **5** blemish, a yearling male. You may take equally a sheep or a goat. You must **6** have it in safe keeping until the fourteenth day of this month, and then all the assembled community of Israel shall slaughter the victim between dusk and dark. They must take some of the **7** blood and smear it on the two door-posts and on the lintel of every house in which they eat the lamb. On that **8** night they shall eat the flesh roast on the fire; they shall eat it with un-leavened cakes and bitter herbs. You **9** are not to eat any of it raw or even boiled in water, but roasted, head, shins, and entrails. You shall not leave **10** any of it till morning; if anything is left over until morning, it must be destroyed by fire.

This is the way in which you must eat **11** it: you shall have your belt fastened, your sandals on your feet and your staff in your hand, and you must eat in urgent haste. It is the LORD's Passover. On that night I shall pass through the **12** land of Egypt and kill every first-born

---

11.1–10: The announcement of a final plague. 8: Up to this point, the context suggests that Moses' speech is to the Hebrews. Here, however, the Pharaoh is addressed, despite 10.28. Apparently, we have a second account of the final confrontation between the two leaders. **10:** Probably an editorial summary of the plague accounts, not a direct continuation of 11.1–9.
  12.1–27: Preparation for the Passover. 2: *The first month of the year* is reckoned as at Passover time, the month of Nisan (March–April), in keeping with the late, postexilic calendar. Thus, vv. 1–20 belong to a late stage of the tradition; in the preexilic calendar, the new year began in autumn (23.16 n.; 34.22). **3–6:** This annual sacrifice of a lamb or a goat at the coming of spring may have had its origins in a pre-Mosaic shepherds' festival, meant both to insure fertility and to preserve the newborn lambs during the nomadic pasturing. Indeed, it may have been this traditional festival which Moses demanded that the people be allowed to observe (5.1; 10.9). **11–13:** The origin of the old festival is now connected with Israel's history: the people must be ready to move, not to new pasture, but to the realization of God's promise in the land of Canaan. The name *Passover*, whose original meaning is uncertain, is now connected with the impending deliverance from Egypt. **12:** *Against all the gods of Egypt:* see 7.14–11.10 n.

of man and beast. Thus will I execute judgement, I the LORD, against all the
13 gods of Egypt. And as for you, the blood will be a sign on the houses in which you are: when I see the blood I will pass over[l] you; the mortal blow shall not touch you, when I strike the land of Egypt.

14 You shall keep this day as a day of remembrance, and make it a pilgrim-feast, a festival of the LORD; you shall keep it generation after generation as
15 a rule for all time. For seven days you shall eat unleavened cakes. On the very first day you shall rid your houses of leaven; from the first day to the seventh anyone who eats leavened bread shall
16 be outlawed from Israel. On the first day there shall be a sacred assembly and on the seventh day there shall be a sacred assembly: on these days no work shall be done, except what must be done to provide food for everyone;
17 and that will be allowed. You shall observe these commandments because this was the very day on which I brought you out of Egypt in your tribal hosts. You shall observe this day from generation to generation as a rule for all time.
18 You shall eat unleavened cakes in the first month from the evening which begins the fourteenth day until the evening which begins the twenty-first
19 day. For seven days no leaven may be found in your houses, for anyone who eats anything fermented shall be outlawed from the community of Israel,
20 be he foreigner or native. You must eat nothing fermented. Wherever you live you must eat your cakes unleavened.

21 Moses summoned all the elders of Israel and said to them, 'Go at once and get sheep for your families and
22 slaughter the Passover. Then take a bunch of marjoram,[m] dip it in the blood in the basin[n] and smear some blood from the basin[o] on the lintel and the two door-posts. Nobody may go out through the door of his house till

morning. The LORD will go through 23 Egypt and strike it, but when he sees the blood on the lintel and the two door-posts, he will pass over that door and will not let the destroyer enter your houses to strike you. You shall keep 24 this as a rule for you and your children for all time. When you enter the land 25 which the LORD will give you as he promised, you shall observe this rite. Then, when your children ask you, 26 "What is the meaning of this rite?" you 27 shall say, "It is the LORD's Passover, for he passed over the houses of the Israelites in Egypt when he struck the Egyptians but spared our houses." ' The people bowed down and prostrated themselves.

The Israelites went and did all that 28 the LORD had commanded Moses and Aaron; and by midnight the LORD had 29 struck down every first-born in Egypt, from the first-born of Pharaoh on his throne to the first-born of the captive in the dungeon, and the first-born of cattle. Before night was over Pharaoh 30 rose, he and all his courtiers and all the Egyptians, and a great cry of anguish went up, because not a house in Egypt was without its dead. Pharaoh sum- 31 moned Moses and Aaron while it was still night and said, 'Up with you! Be off, and leave my people, you and your Israelites. Go and worship the LORD, as you ask; take your sheep and cattle, 32 and go; and ask God's blessing on me also.' The Egyptians urged on the 33 people and hurried them out of the country, 'or else', they said, 'we shall all be dead.' The people picked up their 34 dough before it was leavened, wrapped their kneading-troughs in their cloaks, and slung them on their shoulders. Meanwhile the Israelites had done as 35 Moses had told them, asking the Egyptians for jewellery of silver and gold and for clothing. As the LORD had 36

l Or stand guard over.   *m Or* hyssop.
n Or on the threshold.   *o Or* from the threshold.

15: The festival of *unleavened cakes*, probably an ancient Canaanite agricultural rite to celebrate the barley harvest, is here joined to the pastoral Passover festival and is connected in origin with Israel's impending departure. The absence of leaven, originally prohibited because it was considered ritually impure, is now attributed to the need for haste. **22:** *Marjoram:* an aromatic plant often used for ritual purposes (Lev.14.4; Num.19.6). **23:** The *destroyer*, the death-demon of the old shepherds' festival, is reinterpreted as an agent of the LORD.
12.28–36: The tenth plague, continuing the account of 11.1–10.

made the Egyptians well-disposed towards them, they let them have what they asked; in this way they plundered the Egyptians.

The exodus from Egypt

37 THE ISRAELITES SET OUT FROM RAMESES on the way to Succoth, about six hundred thousand men on foot, not count-
38 ing dependants. And with them too went a large company of every kind, and cattle in great numbers, both flocks
39 and herds. The dough they had brought from Egypt they baked into unleavened cakes, because there was no leaven; for they had been driven out of Egypt and allowed no time even to get food ready for themselves.
40 The Israelites had been settled in Egypt for four hundred and thirty
41 years. At the end of four hundred and thirty years, on this very day, all the tribes of the LORD came out of Egypt.
42 This was a night of vigil as the LORD waited to bring them out of Egypt. It is the LORD's night; all Israelites keep their vigil generation after generation.
43 The LORD said to Moses and Aaron: These are the rules for the Passover.
44 No foreigner may partake of it; any bought slave may eat it if you have
45 circumcised him; no stranger or hired
46 man may eat it. Each lamb must be eaten inside the one house, and you must not take any of the flesh outside the house. You must not break a single
47 bone of it. The whole community of
48 Israel shall keep this feast. If there are aliens living with you and they are to keep the Passover to the LORD, every male of them must be circumcised, and then he can take part; he shall rank as native-born. No one who is uncircum-
49 cised may eat of it. The same law shall apply both to the native-born and to the alien who is living among you.
50 The Israelites did all that the LORD had commanded Moses and Aaron;
51 and on this very day the LORD brought the Israelites out of Egypt mustered in their tribal hosts.

13 The LORD spoke to Moses and said,
2 'Every first-born, the first birth of every womb among the Israelites, you must dedicate to me, both man and beast; it is mine.'
3 Then Moses said to the people, 'Remember this day, the day on which you have come out of Egypt, the land of slavery, because the LORD by the strength of his hand has brought you out. No leaven may be eaten this day,
4 for today, in the month of Abib, is the
5 day of your exodus; and when the LORD has brought you into the country of the Canaanites, Hittites, Amorites, Hivites, and Jebusites, the land which he swore to your forefathers to give you, a land flowing with milk and honey, then you must observe this rite
6 in this same month. For seven days you shall eat unleavened cakes, and on the seventh day there shall be a pilgrim-
7 feast of the LORD. Only unleavened cakes shall be eaten during the seven days; nothing fermented and no leaven shall be seen throughout your territory.
8 On that day you shall tell your son, "This commemorates what the LORD did for me when I came out of Egypt."
9 You shall have the record of it as a sign upon your hand, and upon your forehead as a reminder, to make sure that the law of the LORD is always on your lips, because the LORD with a strong

---

12.37–13.22: **Israel moves to the border of Egypt. 37:** *Rameses:* one of the store-cities which the Hebrews had built (1.11). *Six hundred thousand:* for how the figure was derived, see Num. 1.17–46. **40:** *Four hundred and thirty:* this length of stay differs from Gen.15.13 (four hundred years) and from Gen.15.16 (four generations; compare 6.16–20, which lists only four generations between Jacob and Moses.) **43–49:** Supplementary regulations about the Passover, related to 12.1–27. The mention of *bought slave, hired man,* and *native-born* presupposes social conditions after the later settlement in the agricultural setting of Canaan. **13.1–16:** Additional Passover regulations, not directly related to those in ch. 12. **2:** The *first-born* of animals must be sacrificed to Yahweh in thanks and in recognition of his lordship; so too, the first yield of the harvest (Deut.26.1–2). For the exclusion of humans, see v. 13. **4:** *Abib:* the name of the month during which Passover fell according to the preexilic calendar (contrast 12.2 n.). This way of dating suggests a relatively early age for the formulation of this unit of material. **8:** *Me...I:* when the story of Yahweh's deliverance is related annually in the cult, it becomes a personal and contemporary experience. **9:** *Sign:* an old practice of placing a mark on the hand or an amulet

10 hand brought you out of Egypt. This is a rule, and you shall keep it at the appointed time from year to year.

11 'When the LORD has brought you into the land of the Canaanites as he swore to you and to your forefathers,

12 and given it to you, you shall surrender to the LORD the first birth of every womb; and of all first-born offspring of your cattle the males belong to the

13 LORD. Every first-born male ass you may redeem with a kid or lamb, but if you do not redeem it, you must break its neck. Every first-born among your

14 sons you must redeem. When in time to come your son asks you what this means, you shall say to him, "By the strength of his hand the LORD brought us out of Egypt, out of the land of

15 slavery. When Pharaoh proved stubborn and refused to let us go, the LORD killed all the first-born in Egypt both man and beast. That is why I sacrifice to the LORD the first birth of every womb if it is a male and redeem every

16 first-born of my sons. You shall have the record of it as a sign upon your hand, and upon your forehead as a phylactery, because by the strength of his hand the LORD brought us out of Egypt." '

17 Now WHEN PHARAOH LET THE PEOPLE go, God did not guide them by the road towards the Philistines, although that was the shortest; for he said, 'The people may change their minds when they see war before them, and turn

18 back to Egypt.' So God made them go round by way of the wilderness towards the Red Sea; and the fifth genera-

tion of Israelites departed from Egypt.

19 Moses took the bones of Joseph with him, because Joseph had exacted an oath from the Israelites: 'Some day', he said, 'God will show his care for you, and then, as you go, you must take my bones with you.'

20 They set out from Succoth and encamped at Etham on the edge of the

21 wilderness. And all the time the LORD went before them, by day a pillar of cloud to guide them on their journey, by night a pillar of fire to give them light, so that they could travel night

22 and day. The pillar of cloud never left its place in front of the people by day, nor the pillar of fire by night.

14 The LORD spoke to Moses and said,

2 'Speak to the Israelites: they are to turn back and encamp before Pi-hahiroth,*p* between Migdol and the sea to the east of Baal-zephon; your camp shall be

3 opposite, by the sea. Pharaoh will then think that the Israelites are finding themselves in difficult country, and are

4 hemmed in by the wilderness. I will make Pharaoh obstinate, and he will pursue them, so that I may win glory for myself at the expense of Pharaoh and all his army; and the Egyptians shall know that I am the LORD.' The Israelites did as they were bidden.

5 When the king of Egypt was told that the Israelites had slipped away, he and his courtiers changed their minds completely, and said, 'What have we done? We have let our Israelite slaves go free!'

6 So Pharaoh put horses to his chariot,

7 and took his troops with him. He took

p Or where the desert tracks begin.

on the forehead as a sign of tribal membership is reinterpreted as a reminder of Yahweh's deliverance from Egypt. Compare Gen.4.15 n.; Deut.6.6–8. **13:** Human sacrifice, particularly of the firstborn, was practiced in the Ancient Near East (Deut.12.31; 1 Kgs.16.34; 2 Kgs.16.3), but Israel was commanded to substitute an animal. See Gen.22.2 n. **14–15:** The explanation of the ancient practice of substitution is here based on the events of the Passover in an attempt to make the prohibition more authoritative. **16:** *Phylactery:* a small leather case containing a verse of Scripture, worn originally as a reminder of one's identity (v. 9 n.). **17:** *Philistines:* Gen.9.27 n.; the main route to Canaan, here avoided, was along the seacoast, and would have been guarded by garrisons of Egyptian troops. **18:** *Red Sea:* lit. "Sea of Reeds," and hence a shallow papyrus marsh on the border of Egypt. The Red Sea is the name of the Gulf of Elath, much further east. **19:** See Gen.50.25. **21:** It is uncertain whether the *cloud* and *fire* derive from ordinary practices in travel (such as the ancient custom of carrying a burning brazier at the head of a caravan) or are, instead, symbols of the divine presence (Gen.15.17 n.); the latter seems preferable, for the intent is to suggest the supernatural. The Canaanites personified the clouds on the fringes of a storm as minor deities (messengers) who announced the impending arrival of the storm-god.

14.1–31: The deliverance at the sea. At the moment when the LORD's promise of deliverance

six hundred picked chariots and all the other chariots of Egypt, with a com-
8 mander in each. Then Pharaoh king of Egypt, made obstinate by the LORD, pursued the Israelites as they marched
9 defiantly away. The Egyptians, all Pharaoh's chariots and horses, cavalry and infantry, pursued them and over-took them encamped beside the sea by Pi-hahiroth to the east of Baal-zephon.
10 Pharaoh was almost upon them when the Israelites looked up and saw the Egyptians close behind. In their terror they clamoured to the LORD for help
11 and said to Moses, 'Were there no graves in Egypt, that you should have brought us here to die in the wilder-ness? See what you have done to us by
12 bringing us out of Egypt! Is not this just what we meant when we said in Egypt, "Leave us alone; let us be slaves to the Egyptians"? We would rather be slaves to the Egyptians than die here
13 in the wilderness.' 'Have no fear,' Moses answered; 'stand firm and see the deliverance that the LORD will bring you this day; for as sure as you see the Egyptians now, you will never see
14 them again. The LORD will fight for you; so hold your peace.'
15   The LORD said to Moses, 'What is the meaning of this clamour? Tell the
16 Israelites to strike camp. And you shall raise high your staff, stretch out your hand over the sea and cleave it in two, so that the Israelites can pass through
17 the sea on dry ground. For my part I will make the Egyptians obstinate and they will come after you; thus will I win glory for myself at the expense of Pharaoh and his army, chariots and
18 cavalry all together. The Egyptians will know that I am the LORD when I win glory for myself at the expense of their Pharaoh, his chariots and cavalry.'
19   The angel of God, who had kept in front of the Israelites, moved away to the rear. The pillar of cloud moved from the front and took its place be-hind them and so came between the 20 Egyptians and the Israelites. And the cloud brought on darkness and early nightfall, so that contact was lost throughout the night.

Then Moses stretched out his hand 21 over the sea, and the LORD drove the sea away all night with a strong east wind and turned the sea-bed into dry land. The waters were torn apart, and 22 the Israelites went through the sea on the dry ground, while the waters made a wall for them to right and to left. The Egyptians went in pursuit of them 23 far into the sea, all Pharaoh's horse, his chariots, and his cavalry. In the 24 morning watch the LORD looked down on the Egyptian army through the pillar of fire and cloud, and he threw them into a panic. He clogged their 25 chariot wheels and made them lumber along heavily, so that the Egyptians said, 'It is the LORD fighting for Israel against Egypt; let us flee.' Then the 26 LORD said to Moses, 'Stretch out your hand over the sea, and let the water flow back over the Egyptians, their chariots and their cavalry.' So Moses 27 stretched out his hand over the sea, and at daybreak the water returned to its accustomed place; but the Egyp-tians were in flight as it advanced, and the LORD swept them out into the sea. The water flowed back and covered all 28 Pharaoh's army, the chariots and the cavalry, which had pressed the pursuit into the sea. Not one man was left alive. Meanwhile the Israelites had 29 passed along the dry ground through the sea, with the water making a wall for them to right and to left. That day 30 the LORD saved Israel from the power of Egypt, and the Israelites saw the Egyptians lying dead on the sea-shore. When Israel saw the great power which 31 the LORD had put forth against Egypt, all the people feared the LORD, and they put their faith in him and in Moses his servant.

(3.7–8) is about to be realized, Pharaoh attempts to reassert his power. For a somewhat similar challenge to Israel's faith, see Gen.22.1–19 n. **12:** Compare 5.20–21. **13–14:** Israel is exhorted to believe that, even in her darkest hour, the promise will yet be realized. **19:** *Angel of God* and *pillar of cloud* are used as synonyms. See 13.21 n. **21–29:** The story may be based upon natural phenomena, and enhanced through ages of recital: the *east wind* (v. 21) drives back the waters of the shallow marsh (13.18 n.), but later generations ascribed this to direct divine intervention, as in v.30.

15 Then Moses and the Israelites sang this song to the LORD:

I will sing to the LORD, for he has risen up in triumph;
the horse and his rider he has hurled into the sea.
2 The LORD is my refuge and my defence,
he has shown himself my deliverer.
He is my God, and I will glorify him;
he is my father's God, and I will exalt him.
3 The LORD is a warrior: the LORD is his name.
4 The chariots of Pharaoh and his army
he has cast into the sea;
the flower of his officers
are engulfed in the Red Sea.
5 The watery abyss has covered them,
they sank into the depths like a stone.
6 Thy right hand, O LORD, is majestic in strength:
thy right hand, O LORD, shattered the enemy.
7 In the fullness of thy triumph
thou didst cast the rebels down:
thou didst let loose thy fury;
it consumed them like chaff.
8 At the blast of thy anger the sea piled up:
the waters stood up like a bank:
out at sea the great deep congealed.
9 The enemy said, 'I will pursue, I will overtake;
I will divide the spoil,
I will glut my appetite upon them;
I will draw my sword,
I will rid myself of them.'
10 Thou didst blow with thy blast; the sea covered them.
They sank like lead in the swelling waves.
11 Who is like thee, O LORD, among the gods*q*?
Who is like thee, majestic in holiness,
worthy of awe and praise, who workest wonders?

Thou didst stretch out thy right 12
hand,
earth engulfed them.
In thy constant love thou hast led 13
the people
whom thou didst ransom:
thou hast guided them by thy strength
to thy holy dwelling-place.
Nations heard and trembled; 14
agony seized the dwellers in Philistia.
Then the chieftains of Edom were 15
dismayed,
trembling seized the leaders of Moab,
all the inhabitants of Canaan were in turmoil;
terror and dread fell upon them: 16
through the might of thy arm they stayed stone-still,
while thy people passed, O LORD,
while the people whom thou madest thy own*r* passed by.
Thou broughtest them in and didst 17
plant them
in the mount that is thy possession,
the dwelling-place, O LORD, of thy own making,
the sanctuary, O LORD, which thy own hands prepared.
The LORD shall reign for ever and 18
for ever.

For Pharaoh's horse, both chariots 19
and cavalry, went into the sea, and the LORD brought back the waters over them, but Israel had passed through the sea on dry ground. And Miriam the 20 prophetess, Aaron's sister, took up her tambourine, and all the women followed her, dancing to the sound of tambourines; and Miriam sang them 21 this refrain:

Sing to the LORD, for he has risen up in triumph;
the horse and his rider he has hurled into the sea.

q Or in might.
r madest thy own: or didst create.

15.1–21: Songs of victory, attributed to Moses (vv. 1–18) and Miriam (v. 21). These two extremely old hymns, possibly used in an ancient liturgy memorializing the deliverance, are depicted as originating immediately after the event. **11:** *Among the gods:* see Gen.1.26 n. **13–18:** The allusions seem to assume Israel's settlement in Canaan, and to mark the age when this part of the hymn was composed.

22 MOSES LED ISRAEL FROM THE RED SEA out into the wilderness of Shur. For three days they travelled through the 23 wilderness without finding water. They came to Marah, but could not drink the Marah water because it was bitter; that is why the place was called Marah. 24 The people complained to Moses and 25 asked, 'What are we to drink?' Moses cried to the LORD, and the LORD showed him a log which he threw into the water, and then the water became sweet.

It was there that the LORD laid down a precept and rule of life; there he put 26 them to the test. He said, 'If only you will obey the LORD your God, if you will do what is right in his eyes, if you will listen to his commands and keep all his statutes, then I will never bring upon you any of the sufferings which I brought on the Egyptians; for I the LORD am your healer.'

27 They came to Elim, where there were twelve springs and seventy palm-trees, and there they encamped beside the water.

16 The whole community of the Israelites set out from Elim and came into the wilderness of Sin, which lies between Elim and Sinai. This was on the fifteenth day of the second month after they had left Egypt.

2 The Israelites complained to Moses 3 and Aaron in the wilderness and said, 'If only we had died at the LORD's hand in Egypt, where we sat round the flesh-pots and had plenty of bread to eat! But you have brought us out into this wilderness to let this whole assembly 4 starve to death.' The LORD said to Moses, 'I will rain down bread from heaven for you. Each day the people shall go out and gather a day's supply, so that I can put them to the test and see whether they will follow my in-structions or not. But on the sixth day, 5 when they prepare what they bring in, it shall be twice as much as they have gathered on other days.' Moses and 6 Aaron then said to all the Israelites, 'In the evening you will know that it was the LORD who brought you out of Egypt, and in the morning you will see 7 the glory of the LORD, because he has heeded your complaints against him; it is not against us that you bring your complaints; we are nothing.' 'You 8 shall know this', Moses said, 'when the LORD, in answer to your complaints, gives you flesh to eat in the evening, and in the morning bread in plenty. What are we? It is against the LORD that you bring your complaints, and not against us.'

Moses told Aaron to say to the 9 whole community of Israel, 'Come into the presence of the LORD, for he has heeded your complaints.' While Aaron 10 was speaking to the community of the Israelites, they looked towards the wilderness, and there was the glory of the LORD appearing in the cloud. The 11 LORD spoke to Moses and said, 'I have 12 heard the complaints of the Israelites. Say to them, "Between dusk and dark you will have flesh to eat and in the morning bread in plenty. You shall know that I the LORD am your God."'

That evening a flock of quails flew in 13 and settled all over the camp, and in the morning a fall of dew lay all around it. When the dew was gone, there in the 14 wilderness, fine flakes appeared, fine as hoar-frost on the ground. When the 15 Israelites saw it, they said to one an-other, 'What is that?',*s* because they did not know what it was. Moses said to them, 'That is the bread which the

s Heb. man-hu (*cp. verse 31*).

15.22–17.7: Complaints in the Wilderness. Common to Israel's history are moments of exhilaration followed by challenges and despair (compare 7.14–11.10 n.; 14.1–31 n.). **25:** The idea that water may be made drinkable by casting pieces of wood into it is elsewhere attested in antiquity. **16.1:** The precise chronology reflects the concern of later generations. Here the motive is to bind the events of the Exodus to a liturgical calendar. See Gen.7.24 n. **4:** The *test* is to determine whether Israel is willing to continue into the Wilderness, with food available only on a daily basis. **5:** The double portion for the Sabbath is to make labor on that day unnecessary. **6–8:** Here, the blessings of *bread* (manna) and *flesh* (quail) are both given, whereas in another version (Num.11.4–34) the quail is provided only when the people grow tired of the manna. **10:** *Glory:* radiance, a light, like fire (Gen.15.17 n.), serves as a symbol of the divine presence. **14–15:** The *bread* (manna) may be the "honey-dew" secretion of the tamarisk tree which drops to the ground and solidifies during the cool of the night. It is still gathered

16 LORD has given you to eat. This is the command the LORD has given: "Each of you is to gather as much as he can eat: let every man take an omer a head
17 for every person in his tent." ' The Israelites did this, and they gathered,
18 some more, some less, but when they measured it by the omer, those who had gathered more had not too much, and those who had gathered less had not too little. Each had just as much as he
19 could eat. Moses said, 'No one may
20 keep any of it till morning.' Some, however, did not listen to Moses; they kept part of it till morning, and it became full of maggots and stank, and
21 Moses was angry with them. Each morning every man gathered as much as he could eat, and when the sun grew
22 hot, it melted away. On the sixth day they gathered twice as much food, two omers each. All the chiefs of the community came and told Moses. 'This',
23 he answered, 'is what the LORD has said: "Tomorrow is a day of sacred rest, a sabbath holy to the LORD." So bake what you want to bake now, and boil what you want to boil; put aside what remains over and keep it safe till
24 morning.' So they put it aside till morning as Moses had commanded, and it did not stink, nor did maggots appear
25 in it. 'Eat it today,' said Moses, 'because today is a sabbath of the LORD.
26 Today you will find none outside. For six days you may gather it, but on the seventh day, the sabbath, there will be none.'
27 Some of the people did go out to gather it on the seventh day, but they
28 found none. The LORD said to Moses, 'How long will you refuse to obey my
29 commands and instructions? The LORD has given you the sabbath, and so he gives you two days' food every sixth day. Let each man stay where he is; no one may stir from his home on the
30 seventh day.' And the people kept the sabbath on the seventh day.
31 Israel called the food manna; it was white, like coriander seed, and it tasted like a wafer made with honey.

32 'This', said Moses, 'is the command which the LORD has given: "Take a full omer of it to be kept for future generations, so that they may see the bread with which I fed you in the wilderness when I brought you out of Egypt." '
33 So Moses said to Aaron, 'Take a jar and fill it with an omer of manna, and store it in the presence of the LORD to be kept for future generations.' Aaron
34 did as the LORD had commanded Moses, and stored it before the Testi-
35 mony for safe keeping. The Israelites ate the manna for forty years until they came to a land where they could settle; they ate it until they came to the
36 border of Canaan. (An omer is one tenth of an ephah.)

17 The whole community of Israel set out from the wilderness of Sin and travelled by stages as the LORD told them. They encamped at Rephidim, where there was no water for the people to drink, and a dispute arose between
2 them and Moses. When they said, 'Give us water to drink', Moses said, 'Why do you dispute with me? Why do you challenge the LORD?' There
3 the people became so thirsty that they raised an outcry against Moses: 'Why have you brought us out of Egypt with our children and our herds to let us
4 all die of thirst?' Moses cried to the LORD, 'What shall I do with these people? In a moment they will be
5 stoning me.' The LORD answered, 'Go forward ahead of the people; take with you some of the elders of Israel and the staff with which you struck the Nile,
6 and go. You will find me waiting for you there, by a rock in Horeb. Strike the rock; water will pour out of it, and the people shall drink.' Moses did this
7 in the sight of the elders of Israel. He named the place Massah[t] and Meribah,[u] because the Israelites had disputed with him and challenged the

t That is Challenge.   *u That is* Dispute.

---

today by inhabitants of the area. **18:** *Omer:* see p. 1035. **31:** *Manna:* the original meaning of the term cannot be ascertained; the tradition here supplies a folk explanation (v. 15). Elsewhere (Ps.78.25) it is called "the bread of angels." **34:** A movable sanctuary, sometimes called the *Testimony*, seemingly housed a record of God's actions and requirements. See 25.16 n. **35:** *Forty:* see Gen.7.4 n. **17.6:** *Horeb:* announced as the goal of the journey in 3.12. **7:** Despite the previous evidence of God's guidance, Israel's trust vanished at the first difficulty.

LORD with their question, 'Is the LORD in our midst or not?'

8 The Amalekites came and attacked 9 Israel at Rephidim. Moses said to Joshua, 'Pick your men, and march out tomorrow to fight for us against Amalek; and I will take my stand on the hill-top with the staff of God in my 10 hand.' Joshua carried out his orders and fought against Amalek while Moses, Aaron and Hur climbed to the 11 top of the hill. Whenever Moses raised his hands Israel had the advantage, and when he lowered his hands Amalek 12 had the advantage. But when his arms grew heavy they took a stone and put it under him and, as he sat, Aaron and Hur held up his hands, one on each side, so that his hands remained steady 13 till sunset. Thus Joshua defeated Amalek and put its people to the sword.

14 The LORD said to Moses, 'Record this in writing, and tell it to Joshua in these words: "I am resolved to blot out all memory of Amalek from under 15 heaven."' Moses built an altar, and 16 named it Jehovah-nissi and said, 'My oath upon it: the LORD is at war with Amalek generation after generation.'

18 JETHRO PRIEST OF MIDIAN, FATHER-IN-law of Moses, heard all that God had done for Moses and Israel his people, and how the LORD had brought Israel 2 out of Egypt. When Moses had dismissed his wife Zipporah, Jethro his 3 father-in-law had received her and her two sons. The name of the one was Gershom, 'for', said Moses, 'I have become an alien[v] living in a foreign 4 land'; the other's name was Eliezer,[w] 'for', he said, 'the God of my father was my help and saved me from Pharaoh's sword.'

5 Jethro, Moses' father-in-law, now came to him with his sons and his wife, to the wilderness where he was en-camped at the mountain of God. Moses 6 was told, 'Here is Jethro, your father-in-law, coming to you with your wife and her two sons.' Moses went out to 7 meet his father-in-law, bowed low to him and kissed him, and they greeted one another. When they came into the tent Moses told him all that the LORD 8 had done to Pharaoh and to Egypt for Israel's sake, and about all their hard-ships on the journey, and how the LORD had saved them. Jethro rejoiced at all 9 the good the LORD had done for Israel in saving them from the power of Egypt. He said, 'Blessed be the LORD 10 who has saved you from the power of Egypt and of Pharaoh. Now I know 11 that the LORD is the greatest of all gods, because he has delivered the people from the power of the Egyptians who dealt so arrogantly with them.' Jethro, 12 Moses' father-in-law, brought a whole-offering and sacrifices for God; and Aaron and all the elders of Israel came and shared the meal with Jethro in the presence of God.

The next day Moses took his seat to 13 settle disputes among the people, and they were standing round him from morning till evening. When Jethro saw 14 all that he was doing for the people, he said, 'What are you doing for all these people? Why do you sit alone with all of them standing round you from morning till evening?' 'The people 15 come to me', Moses answered, 'to seek God's guidance. Whenever there is a 16 dispute among them, they come to me, and I decide between man and man. I declare the statutes and laws of God.' But his father-in-law said to Moses, 17 'This is not the best way to do it. You 18 will only wear yourself out and wear

[v] *Cp. 2. 22.*   [w] *That is* God my help.

17.8–16: War with the Amalekites. A once-independent story, its function here is to explain and justify the continued animosity between Israel and a strong desert-dwelling tribe from the vicinity of Kadesh (Num.24.20; Deut.25.17–19; 1 Sam.15.2–3; 1 Chr.4.43). **9:** *Joshua's* sudden appearance here suggests that this story once belonged in another context. **15:** *Jehovah-nissi:* for this pronunciation of the divine name, see Introduction, p. xx. The place name means "Yahweh is my banner," a name given in celebration of a victory there.

18.1–27: Israel arrives at the sacred mountain. 1: *Jethro:* in 2.16–21, the name of the priest of Midian is Reuel. **2:** Moses may have left his family in Midian on leaving for Egypt. **5:** *Mountain of God:* Horeb (3.1), thus fulfilling the sign given to Moses (3.12). **13–26:** The judicial system of Israel is traced back to Mosaic authority. To limit the power of civil courts ("officers over units": v. 25), the ultimate decision remains in the hands of religious leadership (Moses).

out all the people who are here. The task is too heavy for you; you cannot 19 do it by yourself. Now listen to me: take my advice, and God be with you. It is for you to be the people's representative before God, and bring their 20 disputes to him. You must instruct them in the statutes and laws, and teach them how they must behave and 21 what they must do. But you must yourself search for capable, God-fearing men among all the people, honest and incorruptible men, and appoint them over the people as officers over units of a thousand, of a hundred, of fifty or 22 of ten. They shall sit as a permanent court for the people; they must refer difficult cases to you but decide simple cases themselves. In this way your burden will be lightened, and they will 23 share it with you. If you do this, God will give you strength, and you will be able to go on. And, moreover, this whole people will here and now regain 24 peace and harmony.' Moses listened to his father-in-law and did all he had 25 suggested. He chose capable men from all Israel and appointed them leaders of the people, officers over units of a thousand, of a hundred, of fifty or of 26 ten. They sat as a permanent court, bringing the difficult cases to Moses but deciding simple cases themselves. 27 Moses set his father-in-law on his way, and he went back to his own country.

Israel at Mount Sinai

19 IN THE THIRD MONTH AFTER ISRAEL HAD left Egypt,*x* they came to the wilderness 2 of Sinai. They set out from Rephidim and entered the wilderness of Sinai, where they encamped, pitching their 3 tents opposite the mountain. Moses

went up the mountain of God, and the LORD called to him from the mountain and said, 'Speak thus to the house of Jacob, and tell this to the sons of Israel: You have seen with your own 4 eyes what I did to Egypt, and how I have carried you on eagles' wings and brought you here to me. If only you will 5 now listen to me and keep my covenant, then out of all peoples you shall become my special possession; for the whole earth is mine. You shall be my 6 kingdom of priests, my holy nation. These are the words you shall speak to the Israelites.'

Moses came and summoned the 7 elders of the people and set before them all these commands which the LORD had laid upon him. The people 8 all answered together, 'Whatever the LORD has said we will do.' Moses brought this answer back to the LORD. The LORD said to Moses, 'I am now 9 coming to you in a thick cloud, so that I may speak to you in the hearing of the people, and their faith in you may never fail.' Moses told the LORD what the people had said, and the LORD said 10 to him, 'Go to the people and hallow them today and tomorrow and make them wash their clothes. They must be 11 ready by the third day, because on the third day the LORD will descend upon Mount Sinai in the sight of all the people. You must put barriers round 12 the mountain and say, "Take care not to go up the mountain or even to touch the edge of it." Any man who touches the mountain must be put to death. No hand shall touch him;*y* he shall be 13 stoned or shot dead:*z* neither man nor beast may live. But when the ram's horn sounds, they may go up the

x Prob. rdg.; Heb. adds on this day.
y Or it.
z Or hurled to his death.

19.1–25: Moses prepares the people to enter into covenant with Yahweh. 1: *Sinai:* see 3.1 n. **2:** This version of the conclusion of Israel's wandering omits the meeting with Jethro (18.1–12) as the initial event at the sacred mountain. **3:** The idea that gods dwell upon or reveal themselves upon high mountains is attested throughout the ancient world. Yahweh was believed to dwell in heaven and to come down to the mountain top (v. 20) to meet with Moses. **9:** The association of a *cloud* with the divine presence may have originated in the observation of mists surrounding the tops of high mountains (see v. 3 n.) or may have been borrowed from Canaanite mythology (see 13.21 n.). Here, the cloud serves to obscure God from mortal eyes (see 33.20 for a reason why) and to avoid the impression that he exists in bodily form (Deut.4.11–12). **10:** A change of clothing was a regular prescription for preparation for rituals (Gen.35.2). **12–13:** The place at which the deity reveals himself is holy (Gen.28.16–17; Exod.3.5), and holiness was regarded as a mysterious energy transmittable by touch (Lev.6.25–27), which is sometimes fatal to man

14 mountain.' Moses came down from the mountain to the people. He hallowed them and they washed their 15 clothes. He said to the people, 'Be ready by the third day; do not go near 16 a woman.' On the third day, when morning came, there were peals of thunder and flashes of lightning, dense cloud on the mountain and a loud trumpet blast; the people in the camp were all terrified.

17   Moses brought the people out from the camp to meet God, and they took their stand at the foot of the mountain. 18 Mount Sinai was all smoking because the LORD had come down upon it in fire; the smoke went up like the smoke of a kiln; all the people were terrified, 19 and the sound of the trumpet grew ever louder. Whenever Moses spoke, God answered him in a peal of thunder.*a* 20 The LORD came down upon the top of Mount Sinai and summoned Moses to the mountain-top, and Moses went 21 up. The LORD said to Moses, 'Go down; warn the people solemnly that they must not force their way through to the LORD to see him, or many of 22 them will perish. Even the priests, who have access to the LORD, must hallow themselves, for fear that the LORD may 23 break out against them.' Moses answered the LORD, 'The people cannot come up Mount Sinai, because thou thyself didst solemnly warn us to set a barrier to the mountain and so to keep 24 it holy.' The LORD therefore said to him, 'Go down; then come up and bring Aaron with you, but let neither priests nor people force their way up to the LORD, for fear that he may break 25 out against them.' So Moses went down to the people and spoke to them.

God spoke, and these were his words: 20
I am the LORD your God who 2 brought you out of Egypt, out of the land of slavery.

You shall have no other god*b* to set 3 against me.

You shall not make a carved image 4 for yourself nor the likeness of anything in the heavens above, or on the earth below, or in the waters under the earth.

You shall not bow down to them or 5 worship*c* them; for I, the LORD your God, am a jealous god. I punish the children for the sins of the fathers to the third and fourth generations of those who hate me. But I keep faith 6 with thousands, with*d* those who love me and keep my commandments.

You shall not make wrong use of the 7 name of the LORD your God: the LORD will not leave unpunished the man who misuses his name.

Remember to keep the sabbath day 8 holy. You have six days to labour and 9 do all your work. But the seventh day 10 is a sabbath of the LORD your God; that day you shall not do any work, you, your son or your daughter, your slave or your slave-girl, your cattle or the alien within your gates; for in six 11 days the LORD made heaven and earth, the sea, and all that is in them, and on the seventh day he rested. Therefore the LORD blessed the sabbath day and declared it holy.

Honour your father and your moth- 12 er, that you may live long in the land which the LORD your GOD is giving you.

You shall not commit murder.   13
You shall not commit adultery.   14

a in . . . thunder: *or* by voice.   *b Or* gods.
c Or or be led to worship.
d with . . . with: *or* for a thousand generations with . . .

(2 Sam.6.6–7). **15:** The prohibition against sexual intercourse in the context of divine worship may be an attempt to distinguish the cult of the LORD from that of the gods of Canaan; see Lev.15.16–18 n. **16:** The sounding of the *trumpet* was the means of summoning the people to an assembly (Ps.81.3).

   20.1–21: The Ten Commandments are the basic requirements if Israel is to enter into covenant with the LORD and become his "holy nation" (19.6). In adopting them to regulate her internal affairs, she renounces all other loyalties, divine or human. Other versions in various stages of expansion are recorded (34.14–26; Deut.5.6–21). **2:** As in recorded secular alliances of the time, a great king recited his gracious deeds on behalf of formerly oppressed peoples, inviting them to respond with gratitude and to formalize the relationship. **4:** The prohibition is not against all plastic art, but only the use of such items in the cult of the LORD, since they tend to reduce the LORD of all the world (19.5) to a physical object (Isa.44.9–17). **5:** Inherited guilt, a common assumption in the ancient world, was rejected by some biblical writers (Jer.31.29–30; Ezek. 18.19–20) though it continued to hold sway with the populace (Jn.9.1–2). **7:** Lev.19.12 specifies one such *wrong use of the name:* in a false oath. **13:** That *murder* does not include capital

15 You shall not steal.

16 You shall not give false evidence against your neighbour.

17 You shall not covet your neighbour's house; you shall not covet your neighbour's wife, his slave, his slave-girl, his ox, his ass, or anything that belongs to him.

18 When all the people saw how it thundered and the lightning flashed, when they heard the trumpet sound and saw the mountain smoking, they trembled and stood at a distance.

19 'Speak to us yourself,' they said to Moses, 'and we will listen; but if God

20 speaks to us we shall die.' Moses answered, 'Do not be afraid. God has come only to test you, so that the fear of him may remain with you and keep

21 you from sin.' So the people stood at a distance, while Moses approached the dark cloud where God was.

22 THE LORD SAID TO MOSES, SAY THIS TO the Israelites: You know now that I

23 have spoken to you from heaven. You shall not make gods of silver to be worshipped as well as me, nor shall you

24 make yourselves gods of gold. You shall make an altar of earth for me, and you shall sacrifice on it both your whole-offerings and your shared-offerings, your sheep and your cattle. Wherever I cause my name to be invoked, I

25 will come to you and bless you. If you make an altar of stones for me, you must not build it of hewn stones, for if you use a chisel on it, you will pro-

26 fane it. You must not mount up to my altar by steps, in case your private parts be exposed on it.

These are the laws you shall set **21** before them:

2 When you buy a Hebrew slave, he shall be your slave for six years, but in the seventh year he shall go free and pay nothing.

3 If he comes to you alone, he shall go away alone; but if he is married, his wife shall go away with him.

4 If his master gives him a wife, and she bears him sons or daughters, the woman and her children shall belong to her master, and the man shall go

5 away alone. But if the slave should say, 'I love my master, my wife, and my

6 children; I will not go free', then his master shall bring him to God: he shall bring him to the door or the door-post, and his master shall pierce his ear with an awl, and the man shall be his slave for life.

7 When a man sells his daughter into slavery, she shall not go free as a male

8 slave may. If her master has not had intercourse with her and she does not please him, he shall let her be ransomed. He has treated her unfairly and therefore has no right to sell her to

9 strangers. If he assigns her to his son, he shall allow her the rights of a daugh-

10 ter. If he takes another woman, he shall not deprive the first of meat, clothes,

11 and conjugal rights. If he does not provide her with these three things, she shall go free without any payment.

12 Whoever strikes another man and

13 kills him shall be put to death. But if he did not act with intent, but they met by act of God, the slayer may flee to a place which I will appoint for you. But

14 if a man has the presumption to kill

---

punishment or killing in war is suggested by 21.12–17 and Deut.20.10–18. **18–21:** This section, a logical continuation of 19.25, is the bridge between the Commandments and the loosely related material which follows.

20.22–22.23: The Book of the Covenant: See 24.7. Several earlier collections are recognizable by topical similarity and similar structure. Portions presuppose settled agrarian life, suggesting secular legislation operative in the land of Canaan, or even borrowed from the Canaanites. Israel, however, came to regard the legislation as an extension of the covenant requirements (20.2–17) and hence given at Sinai.

20.22–26: Cultic regulations. 24: This verse seems to sanction a variety of sanctuaries, in contrast to limitations encountered elsewhere, e.g. Deut.12.5. **25:** The altars of the LORD must remain distinct from those of the gods of Canaan. **26:** *Private parts:* see Gen.19.5 n.

21.1–22.17: Social and economic regulations. These rules are introduced by "when" or "if," and represent an origin different from those in 22.18–23.13. **2:** *Hebrew:* see Gen.10.21 n. Contrast Deut.15.12, where the term has become synonymous with "Israelite." **6:** This extremely old law may be a relic of belief in household gods (Gen.31.19) who dwell at the *door-post*. **7:** The rights of the female slave are equated with those of the male in Deut.15.12, a passage from a later period. This passage is one of many which are protective of women. **13:** See Num.35.9–12.

another by treachery, you shall take him even from my altar to be put to death.

13 Whoever strikes his father or mother shall be put to death.

16 Whoever kidnaps a man shall be put to death, whether he has sold him, or the man is found in his possession.

17 Whoever reviles his father or mother shall be put to death.

18 When men quarrel and one hits another with a stone or with a spade,[e] and the man is not killed but takes to 19 his bed; if he recovers so as to walk about outside with a stick, then the one who struck him has no liability, except that he shall pay for loss of time and shall see that he is cured.

20 When a man strikes his slave or his slave-girl with a stick and the slave dies 21 on the spot, he must be punished. But he shall not be punished if the slave survives for one day or two, because he is worth money to his master.

22 When, in the course of a brawl, a man knocks against a pregnant woman so that she has a miscarriage but suffers no further hurt, then the offender must pay whatever fine the woman's husband demands after assessment.

23 Wherever hurt is done, you shall give 24 life for life, eye for eye, tooth for tooth, 25 hand for hand, foot for foot, burn for burn, bruise for bruise, wound for wound.

26 When a man strikes his slave or slave-girl in the eye and destroys it, he shall let the slave go free in compensa- 27 tion for the eye. When he knocks out the tooth of a slave or a slave-girl, he shall let the slave go free in compensation for the tooth.

28 When an ox gores a man or a woman to death, the ox shall be stoned, and its flesh may not be eaten; the owner of the ox shall be free from 29 liability. If, however, the ox has for some time past been a vicious animal, and the owner has been duly warned but has not kept it under control, and the ox kills a man or a woman, then the ox shall be stoned, and the owner 30 shall be put to death as well. If, however, the penalty is commuted for a

money payment, he shall pay in redemption of his life whatever is imposed upon him. If the ox gores a son 31 or a daughter, the same rule shall apply. If the ox gores a slave or slave- 32 girl, its owner shall pay thirty shekels of silver to their master, and the ox shall be stoned.

When a man removes the cover of a 33 well[f] or digs a well[f] and leaves it uncovered, then if an ox or an ass falls into it, the owner of the well shall make 34 good the loss. He shall repay the owner of the beast in silver, and the dead beast shall be his.

When one man's ox butts another's 35 and kills it, they shall sell the live ox, share the price and also share the dead beast. But if it is known that the ox has 36 for some time past been vicious and the owner has not kept it under control, he shall make good the loss, ox for ox, but the dead beast is his.

When a man steals an ox or a sheep **22** and slaughters or sells it, he shall repay five beasts for the ox and four sheep for the sheep. He shall pay in full; if he 2-4[g] has no means, he shall be sold to pay for the theft. But if the animal is found alive in his possession, be it ox, ass, or sheep, he shall repay two.

If a burglar is caught in the act and is fatally injured, it is not murder; but if he breaks in after sunrise and is fatally injured, then it is murder.

When a man burns off a field or a 5 vineyard and lets the fire spread so that it burns another man's field,[h] he shall make restitution from his own field according to the yield expected; and if the whole field is laid waste, he shall make restitution from the best part of his own field or vineyard.

When a fire starts and spreads to a 6 heap of brushwood, so that sheaves, or standing corn, or a whole field is destroyed, he who started the fire shall make full restitution.

When one man gives another silver 7 or chattels for safe keeping, and they are stolen from that man's house, the

e *Or* fist.   f *Or* cistern.
g *Verses 2–4 rearranged thus: 3b, 4, 2, 3a.*
h *Or* When a man uses his field or vineyard for grazing, and lets his beast loose, and it feeds in another man's field.

17: *Reviles:* a curse was expected; see Gen.27.33–35 n.; Num.26.6. 23–25: The punishment

thief, if he is found, shall restore two-
8 fold. But if the thief is not found, the
owner of the house shall appear before
God, to make a declaration that he has
not touched his neighbour's property.
9 In every case of law-breaking involving
an ox, an ass, or a sheep, a cloak, or
any lost property which may be claimed,
each party shall bring his case before
God; he whom God declares to be in
the wrong shall restore twofold to his
neighbour.
10   When a man gives an ass, an ox, a
sheep or any beast into his neighbour's
keeping, and it dies or is injured or is
11 carried off, there being no witness, the
neighbour shall swear by the LORD
that he has not touched the man's
property. The owner shall accept this,
12 and no restitution shall be made. If it
has been stolen from him, he shall make
13 restitution to the owner. If it has been
mauled by a wild beast, he shall bring
it in as evidence; he shall not make
restitution for what has been mauled.
14   When a man borrows a beast from
his neighbour and it is injured or dies
while its owner is not with it, the bor-
15 rower shall make full restitution; but
if the owner is with it, the borrower
shall not make restitution. If it was
hired, only the hire shall be due.
16   When a man seduces a virgin who is
not yet betrothed, he shall pay the
17 bride-price for her to be his wife. If her
father refuses to give her to him, the
seducer shall pay in silver a sum equal
to the bride-price for virgins.
18   You shall not allow a witch to live.
19   Whoever has unnatural connection
with a beast shall be put to death.
20   Whoever sacrifices to any god but
the LORD shall be put to death under
solemn ban.
21   You shall not wrong an alien, or be
hard upon him; you were yourselves
22 aliens in Egypt. You shall not ill-treat
23 any widow or fatherless child. If you
do, be sure that I will listen if they
24 appeal to me; my anger will be roused
and I will kill you with the sword;

your own wives shall become widows
and your children fatherless.
    If you advance money to any poor 25
man amongst my people, you shall not
act like a money-lender: you must not
exact interest in advance from him.
    If you take your neighbour's cloak 26
in pawn, you shall return it to him by
sunset, because it is his only covering. 27
It is the cloak in which he wraps his
body; in what else can he sleep? If he
appeals to me, I will listen, for I am full
of compassion.
    You shall not revile God, nor curse 28
a chief of your own people.
    You shall not hold back the first of 29
your harvest, whether corn or wine.
You shall give me your first-born sons.
You shall do the same with your oxen 30
and your sheep. They shall stay with
the mother for seven days; on the
eighth day you shall give them to me.
    You shall be holy to me: you shall 31
not eat the flesh of anything in the open
country killed by beasts, but you shall
throw it to the dogs.
    You shall not spread a baseless **23**
rumour. You shall not make common
cause with a wicked man by giving
malicious evidence.
    You shall not be led into wrong- 2
doing by the majority, nor, when you
give evidence in a lawsuit, shall you side
with the majority to pervert justice; nor 3
shall you favour the poor man in his
suit.
    When you come upon your enemy's 4
ox or ass straying, you shall take it back
to him. When you see the ass of some- 5
one who hates you lying helpless under
its load, however unwilling you may be
to help it, you must give him a hand
with it.
    You shall not deprive the poor man 6
of justice in his suit. Avoid all lies, and 7
do not cause the death of the innocent
and the guiltless; for I the LORD will
never acquit the guilty. You shall not 8
accept a bribe, for bribery makes the
discerning man blind and the just man
give a crooked answer.

---

must not exceed the crime and must be equitably applied (Lev.24.19–22). **22.8:** *Before God:*
at the sanctuary, where the priests will decide the case (1 Kgs.8.31).
    22.18–23.13: Social and economic regulations, introduced by "You shall not"; see 21.1–22.17 n.
20: *Ban:* compare Deut.13.12–16 and see Josh.6.17. **23:** *I will listen:* see 3.7–10. **29–30:** See
13.2 n. **31:** Such food was forbidden because it was impossible to remove the blood from it

9 You shall not oppress the alien, for you know how it feels to be an alien; you were aliens yourselves in Egypt.

10 For six years you may sow your land 11 and gather its produce; but in the seventh year you shall let it lie fallow and leave it alone. It shall provide food for the poor of your people, and what they leave the wild animals may eat. You shall do likewise with your vineyard and your olive-grove.

12 For six days you may do your work, but on the seventh day you shall abstain from work, so that your ox and your ass may rest, and your home-born slave and the alien may refresh themselves.

13 Be attentive to every word of mine. You shall not invoke other gods: your lips shall not speak their names.

14 Three times a year you shall keep a 15 pilgrim-feast to me. You shall celebrate the pilgrim-feast of Unleavened Bread for seven days; you shall eat unleavened cakes as I have commanded you, at the appointed time in the month of Abib, for in that month you came out of Egypt.

No one shall come into my presence 16 empty-handed. You shall celebrate the pilgrim-feast of Harvest, with the firstfruits of your work in sowing the land, and the pilgrim-feast of Ingathering at the end*i* of the year, when you bring in the fruits of all your work on the land.

17 These three times a year shall all your males come into the presence of the Lord GOD.

18 You shall not offer the blood of my sacrifice at the same time as anything leavened.

The fat of my festal offering shall not remain overnight till morning.

19 You shall bring the choicest firstfruits of your soil to the house of the LORD your God.

You shall not boil a kid in its mother's milk.

And now I send an angel before you 20 to guard you on your way and to bring you to the place I have prepared. Take 21 heed of him and listen to his voice. Do not defy him; he will not pardon your rebelliousness, for my authority rests in him. If you will only listen to his 22 voice and do all I tell you, then I will be an enemy to your enemies, and I will harass those who harass you. My 23 angel will go before you and bring you to the Amorites, the Hittites, the Perizzites, the Canaanites, the Hivites, and the Jebusites, and I will make an end of them. You are not to bow down to 24 their gods, nor worship them, nor observe their rites, but you shall tear down all their images and smash their sacred pillars. Worship the LORD your 25 God, and he will bless your bread and your water. I will take away all sickness out of your midst. None shall mis- 26 carry or be barren in your land. I will grant you a full span of life.

I will send my terror before you and 27 throw into confusion all the peoples whom you find in your path. I will make all your enemies turn their backs. I will spread panic before you to drive 28 out in front of you the Hivites, the Canaanites and the Hittites. I will not 29 drive them out all in one year, or the land would become waste and the wild beasts too many for you. I will drive them 30 out little by little until your numbers have grown enough to take possession of the whole country. I will estab- 31 lish your frontiers from the Red Sea

i Or beginning.

(Lev.17.13–15; see Gen.4.10 n.). **23.9:** This repeats 22.21; such repetitions suggest that materials have been compiled from diverse sources.
   23.14–19: Cultic regulations. 15: Since there is no mention of Passover, this section may reflect a time before the *Feast of Unleavened Bread* and Passover were joined; see 12.15 n. **16:** The *pilgrim-feast of Harvest,* also called the pilgrim-feast of Weeks (34.22), came fifty days after Passover (Lev.23.16; hence its Greek name, "Pentecost"); it celebrated the wheat harvest. The *Ingathering,* also called Booths and Tabernacles, celebrated the harvest of grapes and olives which, in the preexilic calendar, ended the year; on the postexilic calendar, see 12.2 n. **19:** *Boil a kid in its mother's milk:* a Canaanite ritual, here forbidden to Israel.
   23.20–33: Instructions for the entry into Canaan. While this section presupposes that the giving of the Law is now complete and Israel is ready to depart from the sacred mountain, much more legislation appears in the ensuing chapters. This suggests that several old traditions have been combined, but with little regard for precise sequence. **20:** *Angel:* compare the previous

to the sea of the Philistines, and from the wilderness to the River. I will give the inhabitants of the country into your power, and you shall drive them out 32 before you. You shall make no coven- 33 ant with them and their gods. They shall not stay in your land for fear they make you sin against me; for then you would worship their gods, and in this way you would be ensnared.

24 THEN HE SAID TO MOSES, 'COME UP TO the LORD, you and Aaron, Nadab and Abihu, and seventy of the elders of Israel. While you are still at a distance, 2 you are to bow down; and then Moses shall approach the LORD by himself, but not the others. The people may not go up with him at all.'

3 Moses came and told the people all the words of the LORD, all his laws. The whole people answered with one voice and said, 'We will do all that the LORD 4 has told us.' Moses wrote down all the words of the LORD. He rose early in the morning and built an altar at the foot of the mountain, and put up twelve sacred pillars, one for each of the twelve 5 tribes of Israel. He then sent the young men of Israel and they sacrificed bulls to the LORD as whole-offerings and 6 shared-offerings. Moses took half the blood and put it in basins and the other 7 half he flung against*j* the altar. Then he took the book of the covenant and read it aloud for all the people to hear. They said, 'We will obey, and do all 8 that the LORD has said.' Moses then took the blood and flung it over the people, saying, 'This is the blood of the covenant which the LORD has made

with you on the terms of this book.'

Moses went up with Aaron, Nadab 9 and Abihu, and seventy of the elders of Israel, and they saw*k* the God of 10 Israel. Under his feet there was, as it were, a pavement of sapphire,*l* clear blue as the very heavens; but the LORD 11 did not stretch out his hand towards the leaders of Israel. They stayed there before God;*m* they ate and they drank. The LORD said to Moses, 'Come 12 up to me on the mountain, stay there and let me give you the tablets of stone, the law and the commandment, which I have written down that you may teach them.' Moses arose with Joshua 13 his assistant and went up the mountain of God; he said to the elders, 'Wait for 14 us here until we come back to you. You have Aaron and Hur; if anyone has a dispute, let him go to them.' So Moses 15 went up the mountain and a cloud covered it. The glory of the LORD rested 16 upon Mount Sinai, and the cloud covered the mountain for six days; on the seventh day he called to Moses out of the cloud. The glory of the LORD 17 looked to the Israelites like a devouring fire on the mountain-top. Moses en- 18 tered the cloud and went up the mountain; there he stayed forty days and forty nights.

THE LORD SPOKE TO MOSES AND SAID: **25** Tell the Israelites to set aside a con- 2 tribution for me; you shall accept whatever contribution each man shall freely offer. This is what you shall accept: 3

j Or upon.   *k Or* they were afraid of ...
l Or lapis lazuli.   *m Or* They saw God; and ...

---

symbol of divine leadership in the Wilderness (13.21 n.). **31:** *Red Sea:* here, the gulf of Elath (see 13.18 n.). *River:* the Euphrates; see Gen.15.18 n.
24.1–11: Israel accepts the covenant obligations. Two old traditions have been combined. In vv. 3–8 the ceremony takes place at the foot of the mountain, with all the people participating; in vv. 1–2,9–11, it takes place on the mountain in the presence only of the leaders. **1:** The abrupt mention of *Nadab and Abihu* emphasizes the fragmentary nature of this account and suggests that it once belonged to another context (compare 17.9 n.). **3:** The *words:* Ten Commandments (see 20.1–21 n.); the *laws* are the regulations of 20.22–23.33. **6–8:** The *altar* represents the deity. **10:** Back of this account lies the older notion that a high mountain could reach into the heavens (Gen.11.4 n.), into the domain of the deity. This idea, though present in passing clues, was superseded in the developing thought. **11:** *Stretch out his hand:* to slay. But contrast 33.20. *Ate and drank:* a meal formalized a covenant; see Gen.31.54.
24.12–18: Moses prepares to receive the tablets of stone, upon which the Ten Commandments are written. Chronologically, this segment of tradition should come before ch. 20. **18:** *Forty:* on the number, see Gen.7.4 n. This verse prepares for ch. 32, which once followed immediately.
25.1–31.17: The sanctuary and its personnel. This material, inserted during the last (priestly) stage of tradition collection and information, ascribes the cultic practices of the postexilic

4 gold, silver, copper; violet, purple, and
scarlet yarn; fine linen and goats' hair,
5 tanned rams' skins, porpoise[n]-hides,
6 and acacia-wood; oil for the lamp,
balsam for the anointing oil and for
7 the fragrant incense; cornelian and
other stones ready for setting in the
8 ephod and the breast-piece.[o] Make me
a sanctuary, and I will dwell among
9 them. Make it exactly according to the
design I show you, the design for the
Tabernacle and for all its furniture.
This is how you must make it:

10 Make an Ark, a chest of acacia-
wood, two and a half cubits long, one
cubit and a half wide, and one cubit
11 and a half high. Overlay it with pure
gold both inside and out, and put a
12 band of gold all round it. Cast four
gold rings for it, and fasten them to its
13 four feet, two rings on each side. Make
poles of acacia-wood and plate them
14 with gold, and insert the poles in the
rings at the sides of the Ark to lift it.
15 The poles shall remain in the rings of
16 the Ark and never be removed. Put
into the Ark the Tokens of the Coven-
17 ant,[p] which I shall give you. Make a
cover of pure gold, two and a half
cubits long and one cubit and a half
18 wide. Make two gold cherubim of
beaten work at the ends of the cover,
19 one at each end; make each cherub of
20 one piece with the cover. They shall be
made with wings outspread and pointing upwards, and shall screen the cover
with their wings. They shall be face to
face, looking inwards over the cover.
21 Put the cover above the Ark, and put
into the Ark the Tokens that I shall
22 give you. It is there that I shall meet
you, and from above the cover, between
the two cherubim over the Ark of the
Tokens, I shall deliver to you all my
commands for the Israelites.
23 Make a table of acacia-wood, two

cubits long, one cubit wide, and one
cubit and a half high. Overlay it with 24
pure gold, and put a band of gold all
round it. Make a rim round it a hand's 25
breadth wide, and a gold band round
the rim. Make four gold rings for the 26
table, and put the rings at the four
corners by the legs. The rings, which 27
are to receive the poles for carrying the
table, must be adjacent to the rim.
Make the poles of acacia-wood and 28
plate them with gold; they are to be
used for carrying the table. Make its 29
dishes and saucers, and its flagons and
bowls from which drink-offerings may
be poured: make them of pure gold.
Put the Bread of the Presence[q] on the 30
table, to be always before me.

Make a lamp-stand of pure gold. 31
The lamp-stand, stem and branches,
shall be of beaten work, its cups, both
calyxes and petals, shall be of one piece
with it. There are to be six branches 32
springing from its sides; three branches
of the lamp-stand shall spring from the
one side and three branches from the
other side. There shall be three cups 33
shaped like almond blossoms, with
calyx and petals, on the first branch,
three cups shaped like almond blossoms, with calyx and petals, on the
next branch, and similarly for all six
branches springing from the lamp-
stand. On the main stem of the lamp- 34
stand there are to be four cups shaped
like almond blossoms, with calyx and
petals, and there shall be calyxes of one 35
piece with it under the six branches
which spring from the lamp-stand, a
single calyx under each pair of branches. The calyxes and the branches are 36
to be of one piece with it, all a single
piece of beaten work of pure gold.

n *Strictly* sea-cow.   o *Or* pouch.
p Tokens of the Covenant: *or* Testimony.
q *Or* Shewbread.

---

period to the Sinai period. The wealth (and technology) required for such a structure as described would have been an intolerable strain during the Wilderness period.
   25.1–40: Furnishings for the Tabernacle. 7: *Ephod:* here a garment; see 28.6–12; 1 Sam.2.18.
8: The abiding presence of the deity, who was formerly thought to dwell in heaven and to
reveal himself especially upon sacred mountains (3.1; 19.3 n.), is symbolized through the
erection of the portable sanctuary. **10:** The *Ark:* a portable wooden chest. *Cubit:* see
p. 1035. **16:** The *Tokens of the Covenant* included a copy of the Ten Commandments (31.18;
Deut.10.1–5) and relics of the LORD's acts of salvation (e.g. as in 16.32–34); see Tfn. *p.* **18:**
Cherubim: see Gen.3.24 n. **22:** It is in the presence of the Tokens (v. 16 n.), as Israel reflects
upon the LORD's requirements and his gracious acts (20.2 n.), that his commands will be
communicated to her. **30:** *Bread:* see Lev. 24.5–9. **40:** Ancient Near Eastern temples and their

37 Make seven lamps for this and mount them to shed light over the space in
38 front of it. Its tongs and firepans shall
39 be of pure gold. The lamp-stand and all these fittings shall be made from
40 one talent of pure gold. See that you work to the design which you were shown on the mountain.

26 Make the Tabernacle of ten hangings of finely woven linen, and violet, purple, and scarlet yarn, with cherubim worked on them, all made by a
2 seamster. The length of each hanging shall be twenty-eight cubits and the breadth four cubits; all are to be of the
3 same size. Five of the hangings shall be joined together, and similarly the
4 other five. Make violet loops along the edge of the last hanging in each set,
5 fifty for each set; they must be opposite
6 one another. Make fifty gold fasteners, join the hangings one to another with them, and the Tabernacle will be a single whole.

7 Make hangings of goats' hair, eleven in all, to form a tent over the Taber-
8 nacle; each hanging is to be thirty cubits long and four wide; all eleven
9 are to be of the same size. Join five of the hangings together, and similarly the other six; then fold the sixth hang-
10 ing double at the front of the tent. Make fifty loops on the edge of the last hanging in the first set and make fifty loops on the joining edge of the second set.
11 Make fifty bronze[r] fasteners, insert them into the loops and join up the
12 tent to make it a single whole. The additional length of the tent hanging[s] is to fall over the back of the Taber-
13 nacle. On each side there will be an additional cubit in the length of the tent hangings; this shall fall over the two sides of the Tabernacle to cover it.
14 Make for the tent a cover of tanned rams' skins and an outer covering of porpoise-hides.
15 Make for the Tabernacle planks of acacia-wood as uprights, each plank 16 ten cubits long and a cubit and a half wide, and two tenons for each plank 17 joined to each other. You shall do the same for all the planks of the Tabernacle. Arrange the planks thus: twenty 18 planks for the south side, facing southwards, with forty silver sockets under 19 them, two sockets under each plank for its two tenons; and for the second 20 or northern side of the Tabernacle, twenty planks, with forty silver sockets, 21 two under each plank. Make six planks 22 for the far end of the Tabernacle on the west. Make two planks for the 23 corners of the Tabernacle at the far end; at the bottom they shall be alike, 24 and at the top, both alike, they shall fit into a single ring. Do the same for both of them; they shall be for the two corners. There shall be eight planks 25 with their silver sockets, sixteen sockets in all, two sockets under each plank severally.

Make bars of acacia-wood: five for 26 the planks on the one side of the Tabernacle, five for the planks on the 27 other side and five for the planks on the far end of the Tabernacle on the west. The middle bar is to run along 28 from end to end half-way up the planks. Overlay the planks with gold, make 29 rings of gold on them to hold the bars, and plate the bars with gold. Set up the 30 Tabernacle according to the design you were shown on the mountain.

Make a Veil of finely woven linen 31 and violet, purple, and scarlet yarn, with cherubim worked on it, all made by a seamster. Fasten it with hooks of 32 gold to four posts of acacia-wood overlaid with gold, standing in four silver sockets. Hang the Veil below the 33 fasteners and bring the Ark of the Tokens inside the Veil. Thus the Veil

r Or copper and so throughout the description of the Tabernacle.
s Prob. rdg.; Heb. adds half the hanging which remains over.

---

furnishings were believed to be based upon celestial models rather than human design (compare the developed idea in Rev.21.2).

26.1–37: The design of the Tabernacle. Two conceptions of the portable sanctuary are here combined: the Tent of the Presence (33.7–10; Num.11.16–17), which is seemingly simple and unadorned, and the ornate Tabernacle. In v. 7 the two are so combined that the former covers the latter. Although the Tabernacle and its adornments are presented as forerunners of the Temple in Jerusalem, it is more likely that the temples of Solomon (1 Kgs. ch. 6) or Zerubbabel (Hag. ch. 1) provided the priestly author with his view of the structure and adornments of the Tabernacle. See 25.1–31.17 n. **33:** *Holy Place:* the outer shrine, containing incense altar

will make a clear separation for you between the Holy Place and the Holy
34 of Holies. Place the cover over the Ark of the Tokens in the Holy of Holies.
35 Put the table outside the Veil and the lamp-stand at the south side of the Tabernacle, opposite the table which
36 you shall put at the north side. For the entrance of the tent make a screen of finely woven linen, embroidered with
37 violet, purple, and scarlet. Make five posts of acacia-wood for the screen and overlay them with gold; make golden hooks for them and cast five bronze sockets for them.

27 Make the altar of acacia-wood; it shall be square, five cubits long by five cubits broad and three cubits high.
2 Let its horns at the four corners be of one piece with it, and overlay it with
3 bronze. Make for it pots to take away the fat and the ashes, with shovels, tossing bowls, forks, and firepans, all
4 of bronze. Make a grating for it of bronze network, and fit four bronze rings on the network at its four corners.
5 Put it below the ledge of the altar, so that the network comes half-way up the
6 altar. Make poles of acacia-wood for the altar and overlay them with bronze.
7 They shall be inserted in the rings at
8 both sides of the altar to carry it. Leave the altar a hollow shell. As you were shown on the mountain, so shall it be made.
9 Make the court of the Tabernacle. For the one side, the south side facing southwards, the court shall have hangings of finely woven linen a hundred
10 cubits long, with twenty posts and twenty sockets of bronze; the hooks and bands on the posts shall be of
11 silver. Similarly all along the north side there shall be hangings a hundred cubits long, with twenty posts and twenty sockets of bronze; the hooks and bands
12 on the posts shall be of silver. For the breadth of the court, on the west side, there shall be hangings fifty cubits long,

with ten posts and ten sockets. On the 13 east side, towards the sunrise, which was fifty cubits, hangings shall extend 14 fifteen cubits from one corner, with three posts and three sockets, and 15 hangings shall extend fifteen cubits from the other corner, with three posts and three sockets. At the gateway of 16 the court, there shall be a screen twenty cubits long of finely woven linen embroidered with violet, purple, and scarlet, with four posts and four sockets. The posts all round the court shall 17 have bands of silver, with hooks of silver, and sockets of bronze. The 18 length of the court shall be a hundred cubits, and the breadth fifty, and the height five cubits, with finely woven linen and bronze sockets throughout. All the equipment needed for serving 19 the Tabernacle, all its pegs and those of the court, shall be of bronze.

You yourself are to command the 20 Israelites to bring you pure oil of pounded olives ready for the regular mounting of the lamp. In the Tent of 21 the Presence*t* outside the Veil that hides the Tokens, Aaron and his sons shall keep the lamp in trim from dusk to dawn before the LORD. This is a rule binding on their descendants among the Israelites for all time.

You yourself are to summon to your **28** presence your brother Aaron and his sons out of all the Israelites to serve as my priests: Aaron and his sons Nadab and Abihu, Eleazar and Ithamar. For 2 your brother Aaron make sacred vestments, to give him dignity and grandeur. Tell all the craftsmen whom I 3 have endowed with skill to make the vestments for the consecration of Aaron as my priest. These are the vest- 4 ments they shall make: a breast-piece, an ephod, a mantle, a chequered tunic, a turban, and a sash. They shall make sacred vestments for Aaron your brother and his sons to wear when they

t Or Tent of Meeting.

(30.1–6), lamp-stand, and table. *Holy of Holies:* the inner shrine containing the Ark. See 1 Kgs. 6.14–17.

27.1–21: The court of the Tabernacle. 1: The *altar*, for animals, was the main object in the court. **2:** *Horns:* elevations at each corner, creating a shallow depression atop the altar onto which the sacrifice was placed. The horns were regarded as especially sacred (29.12; 1 Kgs.1.50). **20:** The *lamp* was located inside the Tabernacle (25.31–40).

28.1–43: Instructions for making the priestly garments. 9–12: *Sons of Israel:* the tribal names.

5 serve as my priests, using gold; violet, purple, and scarlet yarn; and fine linen.
6 The ephod shall be made of gold, and with violet, purple, and scarlet yarn, and with finely woven linen
7 worked by a seamster. It shall have two shoulder-pieces joined back and front.
8 The waist-band on it shall be of the same workmanship and material as the fabric of the ephod, and shall be of gold, with violet, purple, and scarlet
9 yarn, and finely woven linen. You shall take two cornelians and engrave on them the names of the sons of Israel:
10 six of their names on the one stone, and the six other names on the second,
11 all in order of seniority. With the skill of a craftsman, a seal-cutter, you shall engrave the two stones with the names of the sons of Israel; you shall set them
12 in gold rosettes, and fasten them on the shoulders of the ephod, as reminders of the sons of Israel. Aaron shall bear their names on his two shoulders as a reminder before the LORD.
13,14 Make gold rosettes and two chains of pure gold worked into the form of ropes, and fix them on the rosettes.
15 Make the breast-piece of judgement; it shall be made, like the ephod, by a seamster in gold, with violet, purple, and scarlet yarn, and finely woven
16 linen. It shall be a square folded, a span
17 long and a span wide. Set in it four rows of precious stones: the first row, sardin, chrysolite and green felspar;
18 the second row, purple garnet, lapis
19 lazuli and jade; the third row, tur-
20 quoise, agate and jasper; the fourth row, topaz, cornelian and green jasper,
21 all set in gold rosettes. The stones shall correspond to the twelve sons of Israel name by name; each stone shall bear the name of one of the twelve tribes engraved as on a seal.
22 Make for the breast-piece chains of
23 pure gold worked into a rope. Make two gold rings, and fix them on the two upper corners of the breast-piece.
24 Fasten the two gold ropes to the two rings at those corners of the breast-
25 piece, and the other ends of the ropes to the two rosettes, thus binding the breast-piece to the shoulder-pieces on
26 the front of the ephod. Make two gold rings and put them at the two lower corners of the breast-piece on the inner
27 side next to the ephod. Make two gold rings and fix them on the two shoulder-pieces of the ephod, low down in front, along its seam above the waist-band of
28 the ephod. Then the breast-piece shall be bound by its rings to the rings of the ephod with violet braid, just above the waist-band of the ephod, so that the breast-piece will not be detached from the ephod. Thus, when Aaron
29 enters the Holy Place, he shall carry over his heart in the breast-piece of judgement the names of the sons of Israel, as a constant reminder before the LORD.
30 Finally, put the Urim and the Thummim into the breast-piece of judgement, and they will be over Aaron's heart when he enters the presence of the LORD. So shall Aaron bear these symbols of judgement upon the sons of Israel over his heart constantly before the LORD.
31 Make the mantle of the ephod a
32 single piece of violet stuff. There shall be a hole for the head in the middle of it. All round the hole there shall be a hem of woven work, with an oversewn
33 edge, so that it cannot be torn. All round its skirts make pomegranates of violet, purple, and scarlet stuff, with
34 golden bells between them, a golden bell and a pomegranate alternately the whole way round the skirts of the
35 mantle. Aaron shall wear it when he ministers, and the sound of it shall be heard when he enters the Holy Place before the LORD and when he comes out; and so he shall not die.
36 Make a rosette of pure gold and engrave on it as on a seal, 'Holy to the
37 LORD'.*u* Fasten it on a violet braid and set it on the very front of the turban.
38 It shall be on Aaron's forehead; he has to bear the blame for shortcomings in

u as ... LORD: or 'JEHOVAH' *as on a seal in sacred characters.*

15: The *breast-piece of judgement* contained *the Urim and Thummim* (v. 30), the two sacred lots by which the priests could determine the divine will (compare 1 Sam.14.38–42). **33–35:** *Bells:* their purpose is uncertain, but possibly derived from an ancient practice of ringing bells to frighten away demons.

the rites with which the Israelites offer their sacred gifts, and the rosette shall be always on his forehead so that they may be acceptable to the LORD.

39 Make the chequered tunic and the turban of fine linen, but the sash of
40 embroidered work. For Aaron's sons make tunics and sashes; and make tall head-dresses to give them dignity and
41 grandeur. With these invest your brother Aaron and his sons, anoint them, install them and consecrate them; so shall they serve me as priests.
42 Make for them linen drawers reaching to the thighs to cover their private
43 parts; and Aaron and his sons shall wear them when they enter the Tent of the Presence or approach the altar to minister in the Holy Place. Thus they will not incur guilt and die. This is a rule binding on him and his descendants for all time.

29 In consecrating them to be my priests this is the rite to be observed. Take a young bull and two rams with-
2 out blemish. Take unleavened loaves, unleavened cakes mixed with oil, and unleavened wafers smeared with oil,
3 all made of wheaten flour; put them in a single basket and bring them in it. Bring also the bull and the two rams.
4 Bring Aaron and his sons to the entrance of the Tent of the Presence, and
5 wash them with water. Take the vestments and invest Aaron with the tunic, the mantle of the ephod, the ephod itself and the breast-piece, and fasten the ephod to him with its waist-band.
6 Set the turban on his head, and the symbol of holy dedication on the tur-
7 ban. Take the anointing oil, pour it on
8 his head and anoint him. Then bring his sons forward, invest them with tunics,
9 gird them with the sashes and tie their tall head-dresses on them. They shall hold the priesthood by a rule binding for all time.

Next you shall install Aaron and his
10 sons. Bring the bull to the front of the Tent of the Presence, and they shall lay
11 their hands on its head. Slaughter the bull before the LORD at the entrance
12 to the Tent of the Presence. Take some of its blood, and put it with your finger on the horns of the altar. Pour all the
13 rest of it at the base of the altar. Then take the fat covering the entrails, the long lobe of the liver, and the two kidneys with the fat upon them, and
14 burn it on the altar; but the flesh of the bull, and its skin and offal, you shall destroy by fire outside the camp. It is a sin-offering.

15 Take one of the rams, and Aaron and his sons shall lay their hands on its
16 head. Then slaughter it, take its blood and fling it against the sides of the altar.
17 Cut the ram up; wash its entrails and its shins, lay them with the pieces and
18 the head, and burn the whole ram on the altar: it is a whole-offering to the LORD; it is a soothing odour, a food-offering to the LORD.

19 Take the second ram, and let Aaron and his sons lay their hands on its head.
20 Then slaughter it, take some of its blood, and put it on the lobes of the right ears of Aaron and his sons, and on their right thumbs and big toes. Fling the rest of the blood against the
21 sides of the altar. Take some of the blood which is on the altar and some of the anointing oil, and sprinkle it on Aaron and his vestments, and on his sons and their vestments. So shall he and his vestments, and his sons and
22 their vestments become holy. Take the fat from the ram, the fat-tail, the fat covering the entrails, the long lobe of the liver, the two kidneys with the fat upon them, and the right leg: for it is a
23 ram of installation. Take also one round loaf of bread, one cake cooked with oil, and one wafer from the

---

29.1–46: Instructions for the installation of the priests. The passage ascribes the origin of the Aaronite priesthood to the Mosaic period (see 25.1–31.17 n.). However, in early Israelite history, eligibility for serving as a priest was not confined to a tribe, or to a clan within a tribe (see Judg. ch. 17). As history unfolded, the Levites came to be recognized as the priestly tribe (Deut.33.8–11). Later (namely in the postexilic period) a subgroup, supposedly descended from Aaron, a Levite, became the only priests. **4:** The *Tent of the Presence:* see 26.1–37 n. **10:** By touching the sacrificial victim, the worshiper identified with it. **12:** *Blood,* the life-force (Gen.9.4), was sacred to God. The blood was to be used to add to the sense of communion with the deity which the sacrifice brought about. **18:** *Soothing odour:* an idiom meaning "acceptable sacrifice" (Gen.8.21). In earlier polytheistic times, the gods were believed

basket of unleavened bread that is
24 before the LORD. Set all these on the
hands of Aaron and of his sons and
present them as a special gift before
25 the LORD. Then take them out of their
hands, and burn them on the altar with
the whole-offering for a soothing odour
to the LORD: it is a food-offering to the
26 LORD. Take the breast of Aaron's ram
of installation, present it as a special
gift before the LORD, and it shall be
your perquisite.
27 Hallow the breast of the special gift
and the leg of the contribution, that
which is presented and that which is set
aside from the ram of installation, that
which is for Aaron and that which is
28 for his sons; and they shall belong to
Aaron and his sons, by a rule binding
for all time, as a gift from the Israelites,
for it is a contribution, set aside from
their shared-offerings, their contribution to the LORD.
29 Aaron's sacred vestments shall be
kept for the anointing and installation
30 of his sons after him. The priest appointed in his stead from among his
sons, the one who enters[v] the Tent of
the Presence to minister in the Holy
Place, shall wear them for seven days.
31 Take the ram of installation, and
32 boil its flesh in a sacred place; Aaron
and his sons shall eat the ram's flesh
and the bread left in the basket, at the
entrance to the Tent of the Presence.
33 They shall eat the things with which
expiation was made at their installation
and their consecration. No unqualified
person may eat them, for they are holy.
34 If any of the flesh of the installation,
or any of the bread, is left over till
morning, you shall destroy it by fire;
it shall not be eaten, for it is holy.
35 Do this with Aaron and his sons as
I have commanded you, spending seven
days over their installation.
36 Offer a bull daily, a sin-offering as
expiation for sin; offer the sin-offering
on the altar when you make expiation
for it, and consecrate it by anointing.

For seven days you shall make expia- 37
tion for the altar, and consecrate it,
and it shall be most holy. Whatever
touches the altar shall be forfeit as
sacred.
This is what you shall offer on the 38
altar: two yearling rams regularly every
day. You shall offer the one ram at 39
dawn, and the second between dusk
and dark, a tenth of an ephah of flour 40
mixed with a quarter of a hin of pure
oil of pounded olives, and a drink-
offering of a quarter of a hin of wine
for the first ram. You shall offer the 41
second ram between dusk and dark,
and with it the same grain-offering and
drink-offering as at dawn, for a soothing odour: it is a food-offering to the
LORD, a regular whole-offering in every 42
generation; you shall make the offering
at the entrance to the Tent of the Presence before the LORD, where I meet
you and speak to you. I shall meet the 43
Israelites there, and the place will be
hallowed by my glory. I shall hallow 44
the Tent of the Presence and the altar;
and Aaron and his sons I shall consecrate to serve me as priests. I shall 45
dwell in the midst of the Israelites, I
shall become their God, and by my 46
dwelling among them they will know
that I am the LORD their God who
brought them out of Egypt. I am the
LORD their God.
Make an altar on which to burn **30**
incense; make it of acacia-wood. It 2
shall be a square, a cubit long by a cubit
broad and two cubits high; the horns of
one piece with it. Overlay it with pure 3
gold, the top, the sides all round, and
the horns; and put round it a band of
gold. Make pairs of gold rings for it; 4
put them under the band at the two
corners on both sides to receive the
poles by which it is to be carried. Make 5
the poles of acacia-wood and overlay
them with gold. Put it before the Veil 6
in front of the Ark of the Tokens where
I will meet you. On it Aaron shall burn 7

[v] *Or* when he enters.

---

attracted by the smell. **26:** *Perquisite:* a gift equivalent to wages, or beyond the stipulated wage.
The officiating priest was to receive an agreed portion of the sacrifice; see Lev.7.31–36; Deut.
18.3. An abuse is related in 1 Sam.2.12–17. **27–28:** In subsequent times portions of some
sacrifices were to be preserved perpetually for Aaron's descendants. **36–42:** The daily sacrificial
ritual of the postexilic Temple is here ascribed to the period of Aaron's consecration.
30.1–10: The construction of the incense altar. The *altar* for *incense* was part of the furnishings

fragrant incense; every morning when he tends the lamps he shall burn the
8 incense, and when he mounts the lamps between dusk and dark, he shall burn the incense; so there shall be a regular burning of incense before the LORD for
9 all time. You shall not offer on it any unauthorized incense, nor any whole-offering or grain-offering; and you shall not pour a drink-offering over it.
10 Aaron shall make expiation with blood on its horns once a year; with blood from the sin-offering of the yearly Expiation[w] he shall do this for all time. It is most holy to the LORD.
11 The LORD spoke to Moses and said:
12 When you number the Israelites for the purpose of registration, each man shall give a ransom for his life to the LORD, to avert plague among them
13 during the registration. As each man crosses over to those already counted he shall give half a shekel by the sacred standard (twenty gerahs to the shekel)
14 as a contribution to the LORD. Everyone from twenty years old and upwards who has crossed over to those already counted shall give a contribution to
15 the LORD. The rich man shall give no more than the half-shekel, and the poor man shall give no less, when you give the contribution to the LORD to make
16 expiation for your lives. The money received from the Israelites for expiation you shall apply to the service of the Tent of the Presence. The expiation for your lives shall be a reminder of the Israelites to the LORD.
17 The LORD spoke to Moses and said:
18 Make a bronze basin for ablution with its stand of bronze; put it between the Tent of the Presence and the altar, and
19 fill it with water with which Aaron and his sons shall wash their hands and
20 feet. When they enter the Tent of the Presence they shall wash with water,

lest they die. So also when they approach the altar to minister, to burn a food-offering to the LORD, they shall 21 wash their hands and feet, lest they die. It shall be a rule for all time binding on him and his descendants in every generation.

The LORD spoke to Moses and said: 22 You yourself shall take spices as fol- 23 lows: five hundred shekels of sticks of myrrh, half that amount (two hundred and fifty shekels) of fragrant cinnamon, two hundred and fifty shekels of aromatic cane, five hundred shekels of 24 cassia by the sacred standard, and a hin of olive oil. From these prepare 25 sacred anointing oil, a perfume compounded by the perfumer's art. This shall be the sacred anointing oil. Anoint with it the Tent of the Presence 26 and the Ark of the Tokens, the table 27 and all its vessels, the lamp-stand and its fittings, the altar of incense, the altar 28 of whole-offering and all its vessels, the basin and its stand. You shall con- 29 secrate them, and they shall be most holy; whatever touches them shall be forfeit as sacred. Anoint Aaron and his 30 sons, and consecrate them to be my priests. Speak to the Israelites and say: 31 This shall be the holy anointing oil for my service in every generation. It shall 32 not be used for anointing the human body, and you must not prepare any oil like it after the same prescription. It is holy, and you shall treat it as holy. The man who compounds perfume like 33 it, or who puts any of it on any unqualified person, shall be cut off from his father's kin.

The LORD said to Moses, Take 34 fragrant spices: gum resin,[x] aromatic shell, galbanum; add pure frankincense to the spices in equal proportions. Make it into incense, perfume 35

w Or Atonement.   *x Or* mastic.

---

of the outer shrine (v. 6; 26.33 n.). This section logically belongs with 25.1–40. **10:** The *yearly Expiation:* the Day of Atonement; see Lev. ch. 16.

30.11–16: The financial support of the cult. The census for military and financial purposes, introduced possibly under the monarchy, was considered offensive to God (2 Sam.24.10). The tax paid by the worshiper was a *ransom* (v. 12) to protect him from the offense to the deity. **13:** *Shekel:* see p. 1035.

30.17–21: The basin for ritual washing. The *basin* stood in the Tabernacle court. This section logically belongs with 27.1–21. Compare the Sea in Solomon's temple, 1 Kgs.7.23–26.

30.22–38: Formulas for the sacred oil and incense. 23: *Myrrh:* a fragrant resin. **24:** *Cassia:* an aromatic bark. *Hin:* see p. 1035. **34:** *Aromatic shell:* derived from a mollusk found in the Red Sea. *Galbanum . . . frankincense:* resinous (vegetable) gums.

made by the perfumer's craft, salted
36 and pure, a holy thing. Pound some of
it into fine powder, and put it in front
of the Tokens in the Tent of the
Presence, where I shall meet you; you
37 shall treat it as most holy. The incense
prepared according to this prescription
you shall not make for your own use.
You shall treat it as holy to the LORD.
38 The man who makes any like it for his
own pleasure shall be cut off from his
father's kin.

31 THE LORD SPOKE TO MOSES AND SAID,
2 Mark this: I have specially chosen
Bezalel son of Uri, son of Hur, of the
3 tribe of Judah. I have filled him with
divine spirit, making him skilful and
4 ingenious, expert in every craft, and a
master of design, whether in gold,
5 silver, copper, or cutting stones to be
set, or carving wood, for workmanship
6 of every kind. Further, I have appointed Aholiab*y* son of Ahisamach of the
tribe of Dan to help him, and I have
endowed every skilled craftsman with
the skill which he has. They shall make
everything that I have commanded
7 you: the Tent of the Presence, the Ark
for the Tokens, the cover over it, and all
8 the furnishings of the tent; the table
and its vessels, the pure lamp-stand
and all its fittings, the altar of incense,
9 the altar of whole-offering and all its
10 vessels, the basin and its stand; the
stitched vestments, that is the sacred
vestments for Aaron the priest and the
vestments for his sons when they
11 minister as priests, the anointing oil
and the fragrant incense for the Holy
Place. They shall carry out all I have
commanded you.
12 The LORD spoke to Moses and said,
13 Speak to the Israelites, you yourself,
and say to them: Above all you shall
observe my sabbaths, for the sabbath
is a sign between me and you in every

generation that you may know that I
am the LORD who hallows you. You 14
shall keep the sabbath, because it is a
holy day for you. If anyone profanes it
he must be put to death. Anyone who
does work on it shall be cut off from
his father's kin. Work may be done on 15
six days, but on the seventh day there
is a sabbath of sacred rest, holy to the
LORD. Whoever does work on the sab- 16
bath day must be put to death. The
Israelites shall keep the sabbath, they
shall keep it in every generation as a
covenant for ever. It is a sign for ever 17
between me and the Israelites, for in
six days the LORD made the heavens
and the earth, but on the seventh day
he ceased work and refreshed himself.
When he had finished speaking with 18
Moses on Mount Sinai, the LORD gave
him the two tablets of the Tokens, tablets of stone written with the finger of
God.

WHEN THE PEOPLE SAW THAT MOSES WAS 32
so long in coming down from the
mountain, they confronted Aaron and
said to him, 'Come, make us gods to go
ahead of us. As for this fellow Moses,
who brought us up from Egypt, we do
not know what has become of him.'
Aaron answered them, 'Strip the gold 2
rings from the ears of your wives and
daughters, and bring them to me.' So 3
all the people stripped themselves of
their gold earrings and brought them
to Aaron. He took them out of their 4
hands, cast the metal in a mould, and
made it into the image of a bull-calf.
'These', he said, 'are your gods, O
Israel, that brought you up from
Egypt.' Then Aaron was afraid and 5
built an altar in front of it and issued
this proclamation, 'Tomorrow there is
to be a pilgrim-feast to the LORD.' Next 6
day the people rose early, offered whole-

y Or Oholiab.

31.1–11: The appointment of craftsmen.

31.12–17: The Sabbath, the sign of the covenant. This strong emphasis on the Sabbath
observance may reflect the exilic period when the great pilgrim festivals (23.14–17) could not
be kept; if so, its intent was to give the community a deeper sense of corporate identity.

31.18–32.35: The breach of the covenant. The ancient narrative strand, last met in 24.18,
is resumed here. Aaron is seriously involved in the idolatrous incident of the golden calf; the
effect of the intervening priestly material (25.1–31.17) centering on him softens the account of
the sin. 32.1: *So long:* forty days (24.18). Despite earlier enthusiasm for the covenant (24.7),
Israel's faith in the LORD wavers at the delay. *Gods:* the Heb. noun is plural in form, but has a
singular meaning (as in Gen.1.1) throughout the chapter. 4: The *bull-calf* was to serve as a

offerings, and brought shared-offerings. After this they sat down to eat and drink and then gave themselves up to 7 revelry. But the LORD said to Moses, 'Go down at once, for your people, the people you brought up from Egypt, 8 have done a disgraceful thing; so quickly have they turned aside from the way I commanded them. They have made themselves an image of a bull-calf, they have prostrated themselves before it, sacrificed to it and said, "These are your gods, O Israel, that 9 brought you up from Egypt." ' So the LORD said to Moses, 'I have considered this people, and I see that they 10 are a stubborn people. Now, let me alone to vent my anger upon them, so that I may put an end to them and make a great nation spring from you.' 11 But Moses set himself to placate the LORD his God: 'O LORD', he said, 'why shouldst thou vent thy anger upon thy people, whom thou didst bring out of Egypt with great power and a strong 12 hand? Why let the Egyptians say, "So he meant evil when he took them out, to kill them in the mountains and wipe them off the face of the earth"? Turn from thy anger, and think better of the evil thou dost intend against thy people. 13 Remember Abraham, Isaac and Israel, thy servants, to whom thou didst swear by thy own self: "I will make your posterity countless as the stars in the sky, and all this land, of which I have spoken, I will give to them, and they 14 shall possess it for ever." ' So the LORD relented, and spared his people the evil with which he had threatened them.

15   Moses turned and went down the mountain with the two tablets of the Tokens in his hands, inscribed on both sides; on the front and on the back 16 they were inscribed. The tablets were the handiwork of God, and the writing was God's writing, engraved on the 17 tablets. Joshua, hearing the uproar the people were making, said to Moses, 'Listen! There is fighting in the camp.' 18 Moses replied,

'This is not the clamour of warriors, nor the clamour of a defeated
        people;
it is the sound of singing that I hear.'

As he approached the camp, Moses saw 19 the bull-calf and the dancing, and he was angry; he flung the tablets down, and they were shattered to pieces at the foot of the mountain. Then he took 20 the calf they had made and burnt it; he ground it to powder, sprinkled it on water, and made the Israelites drink it. He demanded of Aaron, 'What did this 21 people do to you that you should have brought such great guilt upon them?' Aaron replied, 'Do not be angry, sir. 22 The people were deeply troubled; that you well know. And they said to me, 23 "Make us gods to go ahead of us, because, as for this fellow Moses, who brought us up from Egypt, we do not know what has become of him." So I 24 said to them, "Those of you who have any gold, strip it off." They gave it me, I threw it in the fire, and out came this bull-calf.' Moses saw that the people 25 were out of control and that Aaron had laid them open to the secret malice of their enemies. He took his place at 26 the gate of the camp and said, 'Who is on the LORD's side? Come here to me'; and the Levites all rallied to him. He 27 said to them, 'These are the words of the LORD the God of Israel: "Arm yourselves, each of you, with his sword. Go through the camp from gate to gate and back again. Each of you kill his brother, his friend, his neighbour." ' The Levites obeyed, and about three 28 thousand of the people died that day. Moses then said, 'Today you have con- 29 secrated yourselves to the LORD completely, because you have turned each against his own son and his own brother and so have this day brought a blessing upon yourselves.'

The next day Moses said to the 30 people, 'You have committed a great sin. I shall now go up to the LORD; perhaps I may be able to secure pardon

---

visible symbol of the presence of the deity. See 1 Kgs.12.28 n. **9–14:** God continues to accept Israel, not because of her merits, but as another manifestation of his mysterious grace. **19:** Moses' action symbolizes the state of the covenant at that moment. **21–24:** This may be a priestly attempt to bring out the role of the people and thus minimize Aaron's guilt. **26–29:** The Levites here earn recognition as the LORD's priests by demonstrating a loyalty higher than

31 for your sin.' So Moses returned to the LORD and said, 'O hear me! This people has committed a great sin: they have
32 made themselves gods of gold. If thou wilt forgive them, forgive. But if not, blot out my name, I pray, from thy
33 book which thou hast written.' The LORD answered Moses, 'It is the man who has sinned against me that I will
34 blot out from my book. But go now, lead the people to the place which I have told you of. My angel shall go ahead of you, but a day will come when
35 I shall punish them for their sin.' And the LORD smote the people for worshipping the bull-calf which Aaron had made.

33 THE LORD SPOKE TO MOSES: 'COME, GO up from here, you and the people you have brought up from Egypt, to the land which I swore to Abraham, Isaac, and Jacob that I would give to their
2 posterity. I will send an angel ahead of you, and will drive out the Canaanites, the Amorites and the Hittites and the Perizzites, the Hivites and the Jebusites.
3 I will bring you to a land flowing with milk and honey, but I will not journey in your company, for fear that I annihilate you on the way; for you are a
4 stubborn people.' When the people heard this harsh sentence they went about like mourners, and no man put
5 on his ornaments. The LORD said to Moses, 'Tell the Israelites, "You are a stubborn people: at any moment, if I journey in your company, I may annihilate you. Put away your ornaments now, and I will determine what
6 to do to you." ' And so the Israelites stripped off their ornaments, and wore them no more from Mount Horeb onwards.
7 Moses used to take a[z] tent and pitch it at a distance outside the camp. He called it the Tent of the Presence, and everyone who sought the LORD would

go out to the Tent of the Presence out-
8 side the camp. Whenever Moses went out to the tent, all the people would rise and stand, each at the entrance to his tent, and follow Moses with their
9 eyes until he entered the tent. When Moses entered it, the pillar of cloud came down, and stayed at the entrance to the tent while the LORD spoke with
10 Moses. As soon as the people saw the pillar of cloud standing at the entrance to the tent, they would all prostrate themselves, every man at the entrance
11 to his tent. The LORD would speak with Moses face to face, as one man speaks to another. Then Moses would return to the camp, but his young assistant, Joshua son of Nun, never moved from inside the tent.
12 Moses said to the LORD, 'Thou bidst me lead this people up, but thou hast not told me whom thou wilt send with me. Thou hast said to me, "I know you by name, and, further, you have found
13 favour with me." If I have indeed won thy favour, then teach me to know thy way, so that I can know thee and continue in favour with thee, for this
14 nation is thy own people.' The LORD answered, 'I will go with you in person
15 and set your mind at rest.' Moses said to him, 'Indeed if thou dost not go in person, do not send us up from here;
16 for how can it ever be known that I and thy people have found favour with thee, except by thy going with us? So shall we be distinct, I and thy people,
17 from all the peoples on earth.' The LORD said to Moses, 'I will do this thing that you have asked, because you have found favour with me, and I know you by name.'
18 And Moses prayed, 'Show me thy glory.' The LORD answered, 'I will
19 make all my goodness[a] pass before you, and I will pronounce in your hearing the Name JEHOVAH.[b] I will be

z Or the. a Or character. b See note on 3. 15.

---

that to family and people. **33:** *My book:* see Mal.3.16. The allusion is to a belief of a record of man's merits or trespasses, kept in heaven; late Judaism embroidered this theme.

33.1–23: Israel prepares to leave the sacred mountain. Another tradition has already been related; see 23.20–33 n. The inclusion of various ancient traditions about Sinai (24.1–32.35) creates a sense of some delay. **7–11:** This seems an old tradition, originally independent, about the *Tent of the Presence* (29.4; see 26.1–37 n.). Why the material was placed in this particular context is not clear. **19:** *JEHOVAH:* see 3.12 n.; 3.15 Tfn. *g.* It is only because the LORD is *gracious* and compassionate that he will continue with Israel despite her disobedience in the episode of the calf (ch. 32).

gracious to whom I will be gracious, and I will have compassion on whom
20 I will have compassion.' But he added, 'My face you cannot see, for no mortal
21 man may see me and live.' The LORD said, 'Here is a place beside me. Take
22 your stand on the rock and when my glory passes by, I will put you in a crevice of the rock and cover you with
23 my hand until I have passed by. Then I will take away my hand, and you shall see my back, but my face shall not be seen.'

34 The LORD said to Moses, 'Cut two stone tablets like the first, and I will write on the tablets the words which were on the first tablets, which you
2 broke in pieces. Be ready by morning. Then in the morning go up Mount Sinai; stand and wait for me there on
3 the top. No man shall go up with you, no man shall even be seen anywhere on the mountain, nor shall flocks or herds graze within sight of that moun-
4 tain.' So Moses cut two stone tablets like the first, and he rose early in the morning and went up Mount Sinai as the LORD had commanded him, taking the two stone tablets in his hands.
5 And the LORD came down in the cloud and took his place beside him and pro-
6 nounced the Name JEHOVAH. Then the LORD passed in front of him and called aloud, 'JEHOVAH, the LORD, a god com-passionate and gracious, long-suffering,
7 ever constant and true, maintaining constancy to thousands, forgiving in-iquity, rebellion, and sin, and not sweeping the guilty clean away; but one who punishes sons and grandsons to the third and fourth generation for
8 the iniquity of their fathers!' Moses made haste, bowed to the ground and
9 prostrated himself. He said, 'If I have indeed won thy favour, O Lord, then may the Lord go in our company. However stubborn a people they are, forgive our iniquity and our sin and take us as thy own possession.'

The LORD said, Here and now I make 10 a covenant. In full view of all your people I will do such miracles as have never been performed in all the world or in any nation. All the surrounding peoples shall see the work of the LORD, for fearful is that which I will do for you.*c* Observe all I command you this 11 day; and I for my part will drive out before you the Amorites and the Canaanites and the Hittites and the Perizzites and the Hivites and the Jebusites. Be careful not to make a 12 covenant with the natives of the land against which you are going, or they will prove a snare in your midst. No: 13 you shall demolish their altars, smash their sacred pillars and cut down their sacred poles. You shall not prostrate 14 yourselves to any other god. For the LORD's name is the Jealous God, and a jealous god he is. Be careful not to make 15 a covenant with the natives of the land, or, when they go wantonly after their gods and sacrifice to them, you may be invited, any one of you, to partake of their sacrifices, and marry your sons 16 to their daughters, and when their daughters go wantonly after their gods, they may lead your sons astray too.

You shall not make yourselves gods 17 of cast metal.

You shall observe the pilgrim-feast 18 of Unleavened Bread: for seven days, as I have commanded you, you shall eat unleavened cakes at the appointed time, in the month of Abib, because in the month of Abib you went out from Egypt.

Every first birth of the womb belongs 19 to me, and the males of all your herds, both cattle and sheep. You may buy 20 back the first birth of an ass by giving a sheep instead, but if you do not buy it, you must break its neck. You shall buy back all the first-born of your sons,

---

c for fearful . . . for you: *or* (for he is to be feared) which I will do for you.

34.1–35: The renewal of the covenant. The episodes of the shattering of the tablets (32.19) and of Moses' request for a theophany or "divine self-manifestation" (33.18–23) provide the narrator with an opportunity to relate still other ancient Sinaitic traditions, including a (some-what different) list of Ten Commandments (vv. 14–26; see 20.1–21 n.), under the theme of a covenant renewal. Israel's departure is again apparently delayed. **6–7:** This seems to be an extremely ancient cultic confession, and it is repeated many times (Num.14.18; Neh.9.17; Ps 103.8; Joel 2.13; Jonah 4.2). **13:** *Sacred pillars* and *poles* were a central feature of Canaanite shrines, symbolizing the presence of the fertility gods Baal and Asherah. **14–26:** The covenant

and no one shall come into my presence empty handed.

21 For six days you shall work, but on
the seventh day you shall cease work:
even at ploughing time and harvest you
shall cease work.

22 You shall observe the pilgrim-feast of
Weeks, the firstfruits of the wheat harvest, and the pilgrim-feast of Ingather-
23 ing at the turn of the year. Three times
a year all your males shall come into
the presence of the Lord, the LORD the
24 God of Israel; for after I have driven
out the nations before you and extended your frontiers, there will be no
danger from covetous neighbours when
you go up these three times to enter the
presence of the LORD your God.

25 You shall not offer the blood of my
sacrifice at the same time as anything
leavened, nor shall any portion of the
victim of the pilgrim-feast of Passover
remain overnight till morning.

26 You shall bring the choicest firstfruits of your soil to the house of the
LORD your God.

You shall not boil a kid in its
mother's milk.

27 The LORD said to Moses, 'Write
these words down, because the covenant I make with you and with Israel is
28 in these words.' So Moses stayed there
with the LORD forty days and forty
nights, neither eating nor drinking,
and wrote down the words of the
covenant, the Ten Words,[d] on the
29 tablets. At length Moses came down
from Mount Sinai with the two stone
tablets of the Tokens in his hands, and
when he descended, he did not know
that the skin of his face shone because
he had been speaking with the LORD.
30 When Aaron and the Israelites saw how
the skin of Moses' face shone, they
31 were afraid to approach him. He called
out to them, and Aaron and all the
chiefs in the congregation turned to-

wards him. Moses spoke to them, and 32
afterwards all the Israelites drew near.
He gave them all the commands with
which the LORD had charged him on
Mount Sinai, and finished what he had 33
to say.

Then Moses put a veil over his face,
and whenever he went in before the 34
LORD to speak with him, he removed
the veil until he came out. Then he
would go out and tell the Israelites all
the commands he had received. When- 35
ever the skin of Moses' face shone in
the sight of the Israelites, he would put
the veil back over his face until he went
in again to speak with the LORD.

MOSES CALLED THE WHOLE COMMUNITY 35
of Israelites together and thus addressed them: These are the LORD's
commands to you: On six days you 2
may work, but the seventh you are to
keep as a sabbath of sacred rest, holy
to the LORD. Whoever works on that
day shall be put to death. You are not 3
even to light your fire at home on the
sabbath day.

These words Moses spoke to all the 4
community of Israelites: This is the
command the LORD has given: Each of 5
you set aside a contribution to the
LORD. Let all who wish, bring a contribution to the LORD: gold, silver,
copper; violet, purple, and scarlet yarn; 6
fine linen and goats' hair; tanned rams' 7
skins, porpoise-hides, and acacia-
wood; oil for the lamp, perfume for the 8
anointing oil and for the fragrant
incense; cornelians and other stones 9
ready for setting in the ephod and the
breast-piece. Let every craftsman 10
among you come and make everything
the LORD has commanded. The Taber- 11
nacle, its tent and covering, fasteners,

d Or Ten Commandments.

---

regulations, paralleled in 20.3–6, 8–11; 22.29–30; 23.14–19. **29:** God's "glory," which Moses
has requested to see (33.18,22), is ofttimes described as a visible radiance (16.10). Because
of the unique revelation accorded Moses, his face is now said to "shine." Vg. mistranslated
"Moses' face had horns" (hence Michelangelo's horned Moses); the mistranslation arises from
the fact that Heb. *qeren* means both "ray of light" and "horn" and may be related to the
way ancient priests were sometimes depicted with a horned headpiece which symbolized their
semidivine status.

35.1–40.38: The erection of the Tabernacle. The priestly narrative now continues from 31.17,
showing how the instructions which began in 25.1 were carried out.

35.4–36.7: The obtaining of finances and craftsmen. 4–29: This is an expansion of 25.1–9.

12 planks, bars, posts, and sockets, the Ark and its poles, the cover and the
13 Veil of the screen, the table, its poles, and all its vessels, and the Bread of the
14 Presence, the lamp-stand for the light,
15 its fittings, lamps and the lamp oil; the altar of incense and its poles, the anointing oil, the fragrant incense, and the screen for the entrance of the
16 Tabernacle, the altar of whole-offering, its bronze grating, poles, and all appurtenances, the basin and its stand;
17 the hangings of the court, its posts and sockets, and the screen for the gateway
18 of the court; the pegs of the Taber-
19 nacle and court and their cords, the stitched vestments for ministering in the Holy Place, that is the sacred vestments for Aaron the priest and the vestments for his sons when they minister as priests.
20   The whole community of the Israelites went out from Moses' presence,
21 and everyone who was so minded brought of his own free will a contribution to the LORD for the making of the Tent of the Presence and all its service,
22 and for the sacred vestments. Men and women alike came and freely brought clasps, earrings, finger-rings, and pendants, gold ornaments of every kind, every one of them presenting a special
23 gift of gold to the LORD. And every man brought what he possessed of violet, purple, and scarlet yarn, fine linen and goats' hair, tanned rams' skins and
24 porpoise-hides. Every man, setting aside a contribution of silver or copper, brought it as a contribution to the LORD, and all who had acacia-wood suitable for any part of the work
25 brought it. Every woman with the skill spun and brought the violet, purple,
26 and scarlet yarn, and fine linen. All the women whose skill moved them spun
27 the goats' hair. The chiefs brought cornelians and other stones ready for setting in the ephod and the breast-piece,
28 the perfume and oil for the light, for the anointing oil, and for the fragrant in-
29 cense. Every Israelite man and woman who was minded to bring offerings to the LORD for all the work which he had commanded through Moses did so freely.

30   Moses said to the Israelites, 'Mark this: the LORD has specially chosen Bezalel son of Uri, son of Hur, of the
31 tribe of Judah. He has filled him with divine spirit, making him skilful and
32 ingenious, expert in every craft, and a master of design, whether in gold,
33 silver, and copper, or cutting precious stones for setting, or carving wood, in
34 every kind of design. He has inspired both him and Aholiab son of Ahisamach of the tribe of Dan to instruct
35 workers and designers of every kind, engravers, seamsters, embroiderers in violet, purple, and scarlet yarn and fine linen, and weavers, fully endowing them with skill to execute all kinds of work. Bezalel and Aholiab shall work **36** exactly as the LORD has commanded, and so also shall every craftsman whom the LORD has made skilful and ingenious in these matters, to know how to execute every kind of work for the service of the sanctuary.'

2   Moses summoned Bezalel, Aholiab, and every craftsman to whom the LORD had given skill and who was willing, to
3 come forward and set to work. They received from Moses every contribution which the Israelites had brought for the work of the service of the sanctuary, but the people still brought freewill
4 offerings morning after morning, so that the craftsmen at work on the sanctuary left what they were doing,
5 every one of them, and came to Moses and said, 'The people are bringing much more than we need for doing the work which the LORD has commanded.'
6 So Moses sent word round the camp that no man or woman should prepare anything more as a contribution for the sanctuary. So the people stopped
7 bringing gifts; what was there already was more than enough for all the work they had to do.
8   Then all the craftsmen among the workers made the Tabernacle of ten hangings of finely woven linen, and violet, purple, and scarlet yarn, with cherubim worked on them, all made
9 by a seamster. The length of each hanging was twenty-eight cubits and the breadth four cubits, all of the same

---

35.30–36.7: See 31.1–11. **36.8–39.43**: Execution of the Tabernacle designs. **8–38**: See 26.1–37.

10 size. They joined five of the hangings together, and similarly the other five.
11 They made violet loops on the outer edge of the one set of hangings and they did the same for the outer edge of
12 the other set of hangings. They made fifty loops for each hanging; they made also fifty loops for the end hanging in the second set, the loops being oppo-
13 site each other. They made fifty gold fasteners, with which they joined the hangings one to another, and the Tabernacle became a single whole.
14 They made hangings of goats' hair, eleven in all, to form a tent over the
15 Tabernacle; each hanging was thirty cubits long and four cubits wide, all
16 eleven of the same size. They joined five of the hangings together, and
17 similarly the other six. They made fifty loops on the edge of the outer hanging in the first set and fifty loops on the
18 joining edge of the second set, and fifty bronze fasteners to join up the tent and
19 make it a single whole. They made for the tent a cover of tanned rams' skins and an outer covering of porpoise-hides.
20 They made for the Tabernacle planks
21 of acacia-wood as uprights, each plank ten cubits long and a cubit and a half
22 wide, and two tenons for each plank joined to each other. They did the same for all the planks of the Tabernacle.
23 They arranged the planks thus: twenty planks for the south side, facing south-
24 wards, with forty silver sockets under them, two sockets under each plank
25 for its two tenons; and for the second or northern side of the Tabernacle
26 twenty planks with forty silver sockets,
27 two under each plank. They made six planks for the far end of the Taber-
28 nacle on the west. They made two planks for the corners of the Taber-
29 nacle at the far end; at the bottom they were alike, and at the top, both alike, they fitted into a single ring. They did the same for both of them at the two
30 corners. There were eight planks with their silver sockets, sixteen sockets in all, two sockets under each plank.
31 They made bars of acacia-wood: five for the planks on the one side of

the Tabernacle, five bars for the planks 32 on the second side of the Tabernacle, and five bars for the planks on the far end of the Tabernacle on the west. They made the middle bar to run along 33 from end to end half-way up the frames. They overlaid the frames with 34 gold, made rings of gold on them to hold the bars and plated the bars with gold.

They made the Veil of finely woven 35 linen and violet, purple, and scarlet yarn, with cherubim worked on it, all made by a seamster. And they made 36 for it four posts of acacia-wood over-laid with gold, with gold hooks, and cast four silver sockets for them. For 37 the entrance of the tent a screen of finely woven linen was made, em-broidered with violet, purple, and scarlet, and five posts of acacia-wood 38 with their hooks. They overlaid the tops of the posts and the bands round them with gold; the five sockets for them were of bronze.

Bezalel then made the Ark, a chest **37** of acacia-wood, two and a half cubits long, one cubit and a half wide, and one cubit and a half high. He overlaid 2 it with pure gold, both inside and out, and put a band of gold all round it. He 3 cast four gold rings to be on its four feet, two rings on each side of it. He 4 made poles of acacia-wood and plated them with gold, and inserted the poles 5 in the rings at the sides of the Ark to lift it. He made a cover of pure gold, 6 two and a half cubits long and one cubit and a half wide. He made two 7 gold cherubim of beaten work at the ends of the cover, one at each end; he 8 made each cherub of one piece with the cover. They had wings outspread and 9 pointing upwards, screening the cover with their wings; they stood face to face, looking inwards over the cover.

He made the table of acacia-wood, 10 two cubits long, one cubit wide, and one cubit and a half high. He overlaid 11 it with pure gold and put a band of gold all round it. He made a rim round 12 it a hand's breadth wide, and a gold band round the rim. He cast four gold 13 rings for it, and put the rings at the

37.1–9: See 25.10–22. **10–16:** See 25.23–30; here, too, execution follows the instructions

14 four corners by the four legs. The rings, which were to receive the poles for carrying the table, were close to the
15 rim. These carrying poles he made of acacia-wood and plated them with
16 gold. He made the vessels for the table, its dishes and saucers, and its flagons and bowls from which drink-offerings were to be poured; he made them of pure gold.

17 He made the lamp-stand of pure gold. The lamp-stand, stem, and branches, were of beaten work, its cups, both calyxes and petals, were of one
18 piece with it. There were six branches springing from its sides; three branches of the lamp-stand sprang from one side and three branches from the other
19 side. There were three cups shaped like almond blossoms, with calyx and petals, on the first branch, three cups shaped like almond blossoms, with calyx and petals, on the next branch, and similarly for all six branches
20 springing from the lamp-stand. On the main stem of the lamp-stand there were four cups shaped like almond blos-
21 soms, with calyx and petals, and there were calyxes of one piece with it under the six branches which sprang from the lamp-stand, a single calyx under
22 each pair of branches. The calyxes and the branches were of one piece with it, all a single piece of beaten work of pure
23 gold. He made its seven lamps, its
24 tongs and firepans of pure gold. The lamp-stand and all these fittings were made from one talent of pure gold.

25 He made the altar of incense of acacia-wood, square, a cubit long by a cubit broad and two cubits high, the
26 horns of one piece with it. He overlaid it with pure gold, the top, the sides all round, and the horns, and he put
27 round it a band of gold. He made pairs of gold rings for it; he put them under the band at the two corners on both sides to receive the poles by which it
28 was to be carried. He made the poles of acacia-wood and overlaid them with gold.
29 He prepared the sacred anointing oil and the fragrant incense, pure,

compounded by the perfumer's art.

He made the altar of whole-offering **38** of acacia-wood, square, five cubits long by five cubits broad and three cubits high. Its horns at the four corners were 2 of one piece with it, and he overlaid it with bronze. He made all the vessels 3 for the altar, its pots, shovels, tossing bowls, forks, and firepans, all of bronze. He made for the altar a grating 4 of bronze network under the ledge, coming half-way up. He cast four rings 5 for the four corners of the bronze grating to receive the poles, and he 6 made the poles of acacia-wood and overlaid them with bronze. He inserted 7 the poles in the rings at the sides of the altar to carry it. He left the altar a hollow shell.

The basin and its stand of bronze 8 he made out of the bronze mirrors of the women who were on duty at the entrance to the Tent of the Presence.

He made the court. For the south 9 side facing southwards the hangings of the court were of finely woven linen a hundred cubits long, with twenty posts 10 and twenty sockets of bronze; the hooks and bands on the posts were of silver. Along the north side there were 11 hangings of a hundred cubits, with twenty posts and twenty sockets of bronze; the hooks and bands on the posts were of silver. On the west side 12 there were hangings fifty cubits long, with ten posts and ten sockets; the hooks and bands on the posts were of silver. On the east side, towards the 13 sunrise, fifty cubits, there were hang- 14-15 ings on either side of the gateway of the court; they extended fifteen cubits to one corner, with their three posts and their three sockets, and fifteen cubits to the second corner, with their three posts and their three sockets. The hangings 16 of the court all round were of finely woven linen. The sockets for the posts 17 were of bronze, the hooks and bands on the posts of silver, the tops of them overlaid with silver, and all the posts of the court were bound with silver. The screen at the gateway of the court 18 was of finely woven linen, embroidered

---

previously given. **17–24**: See 25.31–40. **25–28**: See 30.1–10. **29**: See 30.22–38. **38:1–7**: See 27.1–8. **8**: See 30.17–21. **9–20**: See 27.9–19; there is no deviation here from the instructions given there.

with violet, purple, and scarlet, twenty cubits long and five cubits high to cor respond to the hangings of the court, 19 with four posts and four sockets of bronze, their hooks of silver, and the tops of them and their bands overlaid 20 with silver. All the pegs for the Tabernacle and those for the court were of bronze.

21 These were the appointments of the Tabernacle, that is the Tabernacle of the Tokens which was assigned by Moses to the charge of the Levites under Ithamar son of Aaron the priest. 22 Bezalel son of Uri, son of Hur, of the tribe of Judah made everything the 23 LORD had commanded Moses. He was assisted by Aholiab son of Ahisamach of the tribe of Dan, an engraver, a seamster, and an embroiderer in fine linen with violet, purple, and scarlet yarn.

24 The gold of the special gift used for the work of the sanctuary amounted in all to twenty-nine talents seven hundred and thirty shekels, by the sacred 25 standard. The silver contributed by the community when registered was one hundred talents one thousand seven hundred and seventy-five shekels, by the sacred standard.

26 This amounted to a beka a head, that is half a shekel by the sacred standard, for every man from twenty years old and upwards, who had been registered, a total of six hundred and three thousand five hundred and fifty 27 men. The hundred talents of silver were for casting the sockets for the sanctuary and for the Veil, a hundred sockets to a hundred talents, a talent to a socket. 28 With the one thousand seven hundred and seventy-five shekels he made hooks for the posts, overlaid the tops of the 29 posts and put bands round them. The bronze of the special gift came to seventy talents two thousand four 30 hundred shekels; with this he made sockets for the entrance to the Tent of the Presence, the bronze altar and its bronze grating, all the vessels for the 31 altar, the sockets all round the court, the sockets for the posts at the gate-way of the court, all the pegs for the Tabernacle, and the pegs all round the court.

They used violet, purple, and scarlet **39** yarn in making the stitched vestments for ministering in the sanctuary and in making the sacred vestments for Aaron, as the LORD had commanded Moses.

They made the ephod of gold, with 2 violet, purple, and scarlet yarn, and finely woven linen. The gold was beaten 3 into thin plates, cut and twisted into braid to be worked in by a seamster with the violet, purple, and scarlet yarn, and fine linen. They made shoulder- 4 pieces for it, joined back and front. The waist-band on it was of the same 5 workmanship and material as the fabric of the ephod; it was gold, with violet, purple, and scarlet yarn, and finely woven linen, as the LORD commanded Moses.

They prepared the cornelians, fixed 6 in gold rosettes, engraved by the art of a seal-cutter with the names of the sons of Israel, and fastened them on the 7 shoulders of the ephod as reminders of the sons of Israel, as the LORD had commanded Moses.

They made the breast-piece; it was 8 worked like the ephod by a seamster, in gold, with violet, purple, and scarlet yarn, and finely woven linen. They 9 made the breast-piece square, folded, a span long and a span wide. They set 10 in it four rows of precious stones: the first row, sardin, chrysolite and green felspar; the second row, purple garnet, 11 lapis lazuli and jade; the third row, 12 turquoise, agate and jasper; the fourth 13 row, topaz, cornelian and green jasper, all set in gold rosettes. The stones cor- 14 responded to the twelve sons of Israel, name by name, each bearing the name of one of the twelve tribes engraved as on a seal. They made for the breast- 15 piece twisted cords of pure gold worked into a rope. They made two gold ros- 16 ettes and two gold rings, and they fixed the two rings on the two corners of the breast-piece. They fastened the two 17 gold ropes to the two rings at those corners of the breast-piece, and the 18

A single court is presumed; some temples often had two courts. **21:** *Tokens:* see 25.16 (Tfn. *p*) and 16.34 n. The *appointments* probably included a copy of the Ten Commandments kept in the Ark. **26:** The figure is the same as that in the census recorded in Num.1.46. **39.1–31:** See 28.1–43.

other ends of the two ropes to the two rosettes, thus binding them to the shoulder-pieces on the front of the 19 ephod. They made two gold rings and put them at the two corners of the breast-piece on the inner side next to 20 the ephod. They made two gold rings and fixed them on the two shoulder-pieces of the ephod, low down and in front, close to its seam above the waist-21 band on the ephod. They bound the breast-piece by its rings to the rings of the ephod with a violet braid, just above the waist-band on the ephod, so that the breast-piece would not become detached from the ephod; so the LORD 22 had commanded Moses. They made the mantle of the ephod a single piece of 23 woven violet stuff, with a hole in the middle of it which had a hem round it, with an oversewn edge so that it could 24 not be torn. All round its skirts they made pomegranates of violet, purple, and scarlet stuff, and finely woven 25 linen. They made bells of pure gold and put them all round the skirts of the 26 mantle between the pomegranates, a bell and a pomegranate alternately the whole way round the skirts of the mantle, to be worn when ministering, as the LORD commanded Moses.

27 They made the tunics of fine linen, woven work, for Aaron and his sons, 28 the turban of fine linen, the tall head-dresses and their bands all of fine linen, 29 the drawers of finely woven linen, and the sash of finely woven linen, embroidered in violet, purple, and scarlet, as the LORD had commanded Moses.

30 They made a rosette of pure gold as the symbol of their holy dedication and inscribed on it as the engraving on a 31 seal, 'Holy to the LORD',*e* and they fastened on it a violet braid to fix it on the turban at the top, as the LORD had commanded Moses.

32 Thus all the work of the Tabernacle of the Tent of the Presence was completed, and the Israelites did everything exactly as the LORD had com-33 manded Moses. They brought the Tabernacle to Moses, the tent and all its furnishings, its fasteners, planks,

bars, posts and sockets, the covering 34 of tanned rams' skins and the outer covering of porpoise-hides, the Veil of the screen, the Ark of the Tokens and 35 its poles, the cover, the table and its 36 vessels, and the Bread of the Presence, the pure lamp-stand with its lamps in a 37 row and all its fittings, and the lamp oil, the gold altar, the anointing oil, the 38 fragrant incense, and the screen at the entrance of the tent, the bronze altar, 39 the bronze grating attached to it, its poles and all its furnishings, the basin 40 and its stand, the hangings of the court, its posts and sockets, the screen for the gateway of the court, its cords and pegs, and all the equipment for the service of the Tabernacle for the Tent of the Presence, the stitched vestments for minis-41 tering in the sanctuary, that is the sacred vestments for Aaron the priest and the vestments for his sons when they minister as priests. As the LORD 42 had commanded Moses, so the Israelites carried out the whole work. Moses 43 inspected all the work, and saw that they had carried it out according to the command of the LORD; and he blessed them.

THE LORD SPOKE TO MOSES AND SAID: **40** On the first day of the first month you 2 shall set up the Tabernacle, the Tent of the Presence. You shall put the Ark 3 of the Tokens in it and screen the Ark with the Veil. You shall bring in the 4 table and lay it; then you shall bring in the lamp-stand and mount its lamps. You shall then set the gold altar of 5 incense in front of the Ark of the Tokens and put the screen of the entrance of the Tabernacle in place. You 6 shall put the altar of whole-offering in front of the entrance of the Tabernacle, the Tent of the Presence. You shall put 7 the basin between the Tent of the Presence and the altar and put water in it. You shall set up the court all 8 round and put in place the screen of the gateway of the court. You shall take 9 the anointing oil and anoint the Taber-

e on it . . . LORD: *or* 'JEHOVAH' on it in sacred characters as engraved on a seal.

32–43: A summary of the completed work. **43:** *Inspected:* to be sure of precise workmanship.
40.1–38: The erection of the Tabernacle. 1: For the purpose of the chronological references,

nacle and everything in it; thus you shall consecrate it and all its furnish-
10 ings, and it shall be holy. You shall anoint the altar of whole-offering and all its vessels; thus shall you consecrate
11 it, and it shall be most holy. You shall anoint the basin and its stand and con-
12 secrate it. You shall bring Aaron and his sons to the entrance of the Tent of the Presence and wash them with the
13 water. Then you shall clothe Aaron with the sacred vestments, anoint him and consecrate him; so shall he be my
14 priest. You shall then bring forward
15 his sons, clothe them in tunics, anoint them as you anointed their father, and they shall be my priests. Their anoint-ing shall inaugurate a hereditary priesthood for all time.
16   Exactly as the LORD had commanded
17 him, so Moses did. In the first month of the second year, on the first day of that month, the Tabernacle was set up.
18   Moses set up the Tabernacle. He put the sockets in place, inserted the planks, fixed the crossbars and set up the posts.
19 He spread the tent over the Tabernacle and fixed the covering of the tent above it, as the LORD had commanded him.
20 He took the Tokens and put them in the Ark, inserted the poles in the Ark, and put the cover over the top of
21 the Ark. He brought the Ark into the Tabernacle, set up the Veil of the screen and so screened the Ark of the Tokens, as the LORD had commanded
22 him. He put the table in the Tent of the Presence on the north side of the
23 Tabernacle outside the Veil and ar-ranged bread on it before the LORD,
24 as the LORD had commanded him. He set the lamp-stand in the Tent of the

Presence opposite the table at the south side of the Tabernacle and mounted the 25 lamps before the LORD, as the LORD had commanded him. He set up the 26 gold altar in the Tent of the Presence in front of the Veil and burnt fragrant 27 incense on it, as the LORD had com-manded him. He set up the screen at 28 the entrance of the Tabernacle, fixed 29 the altar of whole-offering at the en-trance of the Tabernacle, the Tent of the Presence, and offered on it whole-offerings and grain-offerings, as the LORD had commanded him. He set up 30 the basin between the Tent of the Presence and the altar and put water there for washing, and Moses and 31 Aaron and his sons used to wash their hands and feet when they entered the 32 Tent of the Presence or approached the altar, as the LORD had commanded Moses. He set up the court all round 33 the Tabernacle and the altar, and put a screen at the gateway of the court.

Thus Moses completed the work, and the cloud covered the Tent of the 34 Presence, and the glory of the LORD filled the Tabernacle. Moses was un- 35 able to enter the Tent of the Presence, because the cloud had settled on it and the glory of the LORD filled the Taber-nacle. At every stage of their journey, 36 when the cloud lifted from the Taber-nacle, the Israelites broke camp; but 37 if the cloud did not lift from the Taber-nacle, they did not break camp until the day it lifted. For the cloud of the 38 LORD hovered over the Tabernacle by day, and there was fire in the cloud by night, and the Israelites could see it at every stage of their journey.

---

see 16.1. n. **34:** *Cloud:* see 14.19; 19.9 n. *Glory:* see 34.29 n. **35:** See also 1 Kgs.8.10–11. **38:** See 13.21–22.

LEVITICUS

This segment of Israel's tradition is part of a larger priestly account of the origins of the sanctuary, its personnel and rituals, which begins in Exodus chs. 25–31, 35–40 and continues into Numbers chs. 1–10 (see Introduction to the Pentateuch). Despite the probability that the account assumed its present form early in the postexilic age, it contains many units and even collections of material handed down from a much earlier time.

The title, Leviticus, supplied in the Greek and Latin translations, arose from the emphasis upon the duties of the tribe of Levi as priests. The concerns of the book, however, are much wider than the title suggests, and may be classified as follows: (1) guidelines for laymen bringing offerings of animals or grain (chs. 1–7); (2) the installation of the Aaronite priests (chs. 8–10); (3) legislation concerning uncleanness (chs. 11–15); (4) the annual Day of Atonement (ch. 16); (5) the exhortation to be a holy people (chs. 17–26, the section being called the "Holiness Code"); (6) regulations for the fulfillment of religious vows (ch. 27).

During the postexilic age, an impoverished, harassed Israel lived under the domination of the Persian Empire. Her identity as a monarchical political state no longer secure or adequate, she sought to recover her ancient identity as a worshiping community ruled by the LORD. Accordingly, Leviticus stresses the antiquity of the Aaronite priestly leadership and of the attendant rituals. In a time of uncertainty about Israel's election and of a tendency to assimilate to the culture of her neighbors, Leviticus placed great stress on the uniqueness of Israel's socio-economic legislation and encouraged the observance of even the smallest details of the cultic regulations. In contrast to the unrestrained social and economic abuses of the late monarchic and exilic periods, it reasserted the ancient prohibition against absolute human domination of persons and physical property. Thus, in spite of the failures of the past and the hardships of the present, Israel could once again recover her identity as a "holy people" in whose midst the LORD dwelled.

Laws concerning offerings and sacrifices

1 THE LORD SUMMONED MOSES AND spoke to him from the Tent of the 2 Presence, and said, Say this to the Israelites: When any man among you presents an animal as an offering to the LORD, the offering may be presented either from the herd or from the flock. 3 If his offering is a whole-offering from the cattle, he shall present a male without blemish; he shall present it at the entrance to the Tent of the Presence before the LORD so as to secure acceptance for himself. 4 He shall lay his hand on the head of the victim and it will be accepted on his behalf[a] to make expiation for him. 5 He shall slaughter the bull before the LORD, and the Aaronite priests shall present the blood and fling it against the altar all round at the entrance of the Tent of the Presence. 6 He shall then flay the victim and cut it up. The sons of Aaron the priest 7 shall kindle a fire on the altar and arrange wood on the fire. The Aaronite 8 priests shall arrange the pieces, including the head and the suet, on the wood on the altar-fire, the entrails and shins 9 shall be washed in water, and the priest shall burn it all on the altar as a whole-offering, a food-offering of soothing odour to the LORD.

If the man's whole-offering is from 10 the flock, either from the rams or from the goats, he shall present a male without blemish. He shall slaughter it before 11 the LORD at the north side of the altar, and the Aaronite priests shall fling the blood against the altar all round. He 12 shall cut it up, and the priest shall arrange the pieces, together with the head and the suet, on the wood on the altar-fire, the entrails and shins shall be 13 washed in water, and the priest shall present and burn it all on the altar: it

a Or by him (the LORD).

1.1–17: The whole offering of an animal by fire (also called a "holocaust" or "burnt offering"). 1: Moses: the transmitter of these sacrificial regulations assigned their origin to the LORD at Sinai. Tent of the Presence: see Exod.26.1–37 n. 2: When: these are not requirements for specific occasions, but voluntary offerings by individuals. 4: Originally an offering of praise and gratitude, this ancient sacrifice was increasingly used as a rite of expiation, by means of which atonement with God was effected. 5: Aaronite priests: see Exod.29.1 46 n. Against the altar: see Exod.29.12 n. 9: The shins are washed to remove dirt and dung (compare Exod.29.14),

is a whole-offering, a food-offering of soothing odour to the LORD.

14 If a man's offering to the LORD is a whole-offering of birds, he shall present turtle-doves or young pigeons as
15 his offering. The priest shall present it at the altar, and shall wrench off the head and burn it on the altar; and the blood shall be drained out against
16 the side of the altar. He shall take away the crop and its contents in one piece, and throw it to the east side of the altar
17 where the ashes are. He shall tear it by its wings without severing them completely, and shall burn it on the altar, on top of the wood of the altar-fire: it is a whole-offering, a food-offering of soothing odour to the LORD.

2 When any person presents a grain-offering to the LORD, his offering shall be of flour. He shall pour oil on it and
2 add frankincense to it. He shall bring it to the Aaronite priests, one of whom shall scoop up a handful of the flour and oil with all the frankincense. The priest shall burn this as a token on the altar, a food-offering of soothing odour
3 to the LORD. The remainder of the grain-offering belongs to Aaron and his sons: it is most sacred, it is taken from the food-offerings of the LORD.
4 When you present as a grain-offering something baked in an oven, it shall consist of unleavened cakes of flour mixed with oil and unleavened wafers
5 smeared with oil. If your offering is a grain-offering cooked on a griddle, it shall be an unleavened cake of flour
6 mixed with oil. Crumble it in pieces and pour oil on it. This is a grain-offering.
7 If your offering is a grain-offering cooked in a pan, it shall be made of
8 flour with oil. Bring an offering made up in this way to the LORD and present

it to the priest, who shall bring it to the altar; then he shall set aside part of 9 the grain-offering as a token and burn it on the altar, a food-offering of soothing odour to the LORD. The remainder 10 of the grain-offering belongs to Aaron and his sons: it is most sacred, it is taken from the food-offerings of the LORD.

No grain-offering which you present 11 to the LORD shall be made of anything that ferments; you shall not burn any leaven or any honey as a food-offering to the LORD. As for your offering of 12 firstfruits, you shall present them to the LORD, but they shall not be offered up at the altar as a soothing odour. Every 13 offering of yours which is a grain-offering shall be salted; you shall not fail to put the salt of your covenant with God on your grain-offering. Salt shall accompany all offerings.

If you present to the LORD a grain- 14 offering of first-ripe grain, you must present fresh corn roasted, crushed meal from fully ripened corn. You shall 15 add oil to it and put frankincense upon it. This is a grain-offering. The priest 16 shall burn as its token some of the crushed meal, some of the oil, and all the frankincense as a food-offering to the LORD.

If a man's offering is a shared-offer- 3 ing from the cattle, male or female, he shall present it without blemish before the LORD. He shall lay his hand on the 2 head of the victim and slaughter it at the entrance to the Tent of the Presence. The Aaronite priests shall fling the blood against the altar all round. One of them shall present part of the 3 shared-offering as a food-offering to the LORD: he shall remove the fat covering the entrails and all the fat

impediments to sacrifices. *Soothing odour*: see Exod.29.18 n. **14–17:** The poor, unable to afford cattle or sheep, are given this equally acceptable option.

2.1–16: Grain offerings by fire as a gift to God. Three types are mentioned: flour (vv.1–3), cakes (vv. 4–10), or roasted meal (vv. 14–16). **2:** *Oil:* of the olive. *Frankincense:* see Exod. 30.34 n. **3:** *Most sacred:* hence to be eaten by the priests only, in the sanctuary area (compare 6.25–26). **11:** *Honey*, like *leaven*, caused fermentation, which was regarded as ritually impure. **12:** *Firstfruits:* see Deut.26.1–11. **13:** *Salt* symbolized sharing. Possibly, too, its purifying (2 Kgs.2.21) and preserving properties made it desirable for the meal which sealed a covenant (Num.18.19). **14:** *Corn:* barley or wheat.

3.1–17: The shared-offering for deity, priests and worshipers. Only the preparation of the victim is dealt with here (see also 7.11–36). **1:** *Male or female:* for the whole-offering only a male was permitted. **3:** Since *part* is offered *to the LORD*, the ritual departs from that of the whole-offering because the priests and worshipers share in the "meal." *Fat*, considered a source of great vitality and delicacy, was, like blood (17.10–16), to be reserved for the deity

4 upon the entrails, the two kidneys with the fat on them beside the haunches, and the long lobe of the liver with the

5 kidneys. The Aaronites shall burn it on the altar on top of the whole-offering which is upon the wood on the fire, a food-offering of soothing odour to the LORD.

6 If a man's offering as a shared-offering to the LORD is from the flock, male or female, he shall present it

7 without blemish. If he is presenting a ram as his offering, he shall present it

8 before the LORD, lay his hand on the head of the victim and slaughter it in front of the Tent of the Presence. The Aaronites shall then fling its blood

9 against the altar all round. He shall present part of the shared-offering as a food-offering to the LORD; he shall remove its fat, the entire fat-tail cut off close by the spine, the fat covering the entrails and all the fat upon the en-

10 trails, the two kidneys with the fat on them beside the haunches, and the long

11 lobe of the liver with the kidneys. The priest shall burn it at the altar, as food offered to the LORD.

12 If the man's offering is a goat, he

13 shall present it before the LORD, lay his hand on its head and slaughter it in front of the Tent of the Presence. The Aaronites shall then fling its blood

14 against the altar all round. He shall present part of the victim as a food-offering to the LORD; he shall remove the fat covering the entrails and all the

15 fat upon the entrails, the two kidneys with the fat on them beside the haunches and the long lobe of the liver with

16 the kidneys. The priest shall burn this at the altar, as a food-offering of soothing odour. All fat belongs to the LORD.

17 This is a rule for all time from genera-

tion to generation wherever you live: you shall not eat any fat or any blood.

4 THE LORD SPOKE TO MOSES AND SAID,
2 Say this to the Israelites: These are the rules for any man who inadvertently transgresses any of the commandments of the LORD and does anything pro-hibited by them:

3 If the anointed priest sins so as to bring guilt on the people, for the sin he has committed he shall present to the LORD a young bull without blemish as

4 a sin-offering. He shall bring the bull to the entrance of the Tent of the Pres-ence before the LORD, lay his hand on its head and slaughter it before the

5 LORD. The anointed priest shall then take some of its blood and bring it to

6 the Tent of the Presence. He shall dip his finger in the blood and sprinkle some of the blood in front of the sacred

7 Veil seven times before the LORD. The priest shall then put some of the blood before the LORD in the Tent of the Pres-ence on the horns of the altar where fragrant incense is burnt, and he shall pour the rest of the bull's blood at the base of the altar of whole-offering at the entrance of the Tent of the Pres-

8 ence. He shall set aside all the fat from the bull of the sin-offering; he shall set aside the fat covering the entrails and

9 all the fat upon the entrails, the two kidneys with the fat on them beside the haunches, and the long lobe of the liver

10 with the kidneys. It shall be set aside as the fat from the ox at the shared-offering is set aside. The priest shall burn the pieces of fat on the altar of

11 whole-offering. But the skin of the bull and all its flesh, including head and

12 shins, its entrails and offal, the whole of it, he shall take away outside the

---

alone (vv. 16–17). **5:** The whole-offering, made afresh each day (6.9), would already be on the altar when the shared-offering was being prepared.

4.1–5.13: The sin-offering for inadvertent transgression. For deliberate sin, see Num.15.30.
3: *To bring guilt:* compare Gen.18.23–33 n. Since *the priest* represents the entire community before God and vice versa, any sin on his part contaminates the people and excludes his offering an atoning sacrifice in their behalf. *A young bull:* the most expensive sacrificial animal. **5–6:** Unlike the previously mentioned rituals, part of this more serious sacrifice is offered *in the Tent.* Sins of the *whole community* were regarded as equally as grave as those of priests (vv. 13–21), whereas those of individuals were less serious (vv. 22–35). **6:** *Veil:* see Exod.26.31–33. **7:** *Horns:* see Exod.27.2 n. *Altar . . . incense:* see Exod.30.1–10. *Blood:* the locus of the life-force and forbidden for human consumption, blood was especially effective in expiation (17.10–12; Heb.9.22). **11–12:** Although part of other sacrifices was reserved for the priests (2.10; 7.14; Exod.29.27–28 n.), they could not eat of one offered in their own behalf (compare 6.29–30).

camp to a place ritually clean, where the ash-heap is, and destroy it on a wood-fire on top of the ash-heap.

13 If the whole community of Israel sins inadvertently and the matter is not known to the assembly, if they do what is forbidden in any commandment of 14 the LORD and so incur guilt, then, when the sin they have committed is notified to them, the assembly shall present a young bull as a sin-offering and shall bring it in front of the Tent of the Pres-15 ence. The elders of the community shall lay their hands on the victim's head before the LORD, and it shall be 16 slaughtered before the LORD. The anointed priest shall then bring some of the blood to the Tent of the Pres-17 ence, dip his finger in it and sprinkle it in front of the Veil seven times before 18 the LORD. He shall put some of the blood on the horns of the altar before the LORD in the Tent of the Presence and pour all the rest at the base of the altar of whole-offering at the entrance 19 of the Tent of the Presence. He shall then set aside all the fat from the bull 20 and burn it on the altar. He shall deal with this bull as he deals with the bull of the sin-offering, and in this way the priest shall make expiation for their 21 guilt and they shall be forgiven. He shall take the bull outside the camp and burn it as the other bull was burnt. This is a sin-offering for the assembly. 22 When a man of standing sins by doing inadvertently what is forbidden in any commandment of the LORD his 23 God, thereby incurring guilt, and the sin he has committed is made known to him, he shall bring as his offering a 24 he-goat without blemish. He shall lay his hand on the goat's head and shall slaughter it before the LORD in the place where the whole-offering is 25 slaughtered. It is a sin-offering. The priest shall then take some of the blood of the victim with his finger and put it on the horns of the altar of whole-offering. He shall pour out the rest of the blood at the base of the altar of 26 whole-offering. He shall burn all the

fat at the altar in the same way as the fat of the shared-offering. Thus the priest shall make expiation for that man's sin, and it shall be forgiven him.

27 If any person among the common people sins inadvertently and does what is forbidden in any command-ment of the LORD, thereby incurring 28 guilt, and the sin he has committed is made known to him, he shall bring as his offering for the sin which he has committed a she-goat without blemish. 29 He shall lay his hand on the head of the victim and slaughter it in the place where the whole-offering is slaughtered. 30 The priest shall then take some of its blood with his finger and put it on the horns of the altar of whole-offering. 31 All the rest of the blood he shall pour at the base of the altar. He shall remove all its fat as the fat of the shared-offer-ing is removed, and the priest shall burn it on the altar as a soothing odour to the LORD. So the priest shall make expiation for that person's guilt, and it shall be forgiven him.

32 If the man brings a sheep as his offering for sin, it shall be a ewe with-33 out blemish. He shall lay his hand on the head of the victim and slaughter it as a sin-offering in the place where 34 the whole-offering is slaughtered. The priest shall then take some of the blood of the victim with his finger and put it on the horns of the altar of whole-offering. All the rest of the blood he shall pour out at the base of the altar. 35 He shall remove all the fat, as the fat of the sheep is removed from the shared-offering. The priest shall burn the pieces of fat at the altar on top of the food-offerings to the LORD, and shall make expiation for the sin that the man has committed, and it shall be forgiven him.

5 IF A PERSON HEARS A SOLEMN ADJURA-tion to give evidence as a witness to something he has seen or heard and does not declare what he knows, he commits a sin and must accept re-sponsibility.

13–21: Community-wide sin also requires that the inner altar be purified with sacrificial blood. **22–35:** For those less serious individual offenses there is permission to use cheaper sacrificial animals (vv. 23,28,32), to conduct the rite at the outer altar only (v. 25), and to omit the burning of the nonfat portions which are to go to the priest (6.26). **5.1–4:** An appendix

2 If a person touches anything unclean, such as the dead body of an unclean animal, whether wild or domestic, or of 3 an unclean reptile, or if he touches anything unclean in a man, whatever that uncleanness may be, and it is concealed by him although he is aware of it, he 4 shall incur guilt. Or if a person rashly utters an oath to do something evil or good, in any matter in which such a man may swear a rash oath, and it is concealed by him although he is aware of it, he shall in either case incur guilt. 5 Whenever a man incurs guilt in any of these cases and confesses how he has 6 sinned therein, he shall bring to the LORD, as his penalty for the sin that he has committed, a female of the flock, either a ewe or a she-goat, as a sin-offering, and the priest shall make expiation for him on account of his sin which he has committed, and he shall be pardoned.

7 But if he cannot afford as much as a young animal, he shall bring to the LORD for the sin he has committed two turtle-doves or two young pigeons, one for a sin-offering and the other for a 8 whole-offering. He shall bring them to the priest, and present first the one intended for the sin-offering. He shall wrench its head back without severing 9 it. He shall sprinkle some of the blood of the victim against the side of the altar, and what is left of the blood shall be drained out at the base of the altar: 10 it is a sin-offering. He shall deal with the second bird as a whole-offering according to custom, and the priest shall make expiation for the sin the man has committed, and it shall be forgiven him.

11 If the man cannot afford two turtle-doves or two young pigeons, for his sin he shall bring as his offering a tenth of an ephah of flour, as a sin-offering. He shall add no oil to it nor put frankincense on it, because it is a sin-offer-

ing. He shall bring it to the priest, who 12 shall scoop up a handful from it as a token and burn it on the altar on the food-offerings to the LORD: it is a sin-offering. The priest shall make expia- 13 tion for the sin the man has committed in any one of these cases, and it shall be forgiven him. The remainder belongs to the priest, as with the grain-offering.

The LORD spoke to Moses and said: 14 When any person commits an offence 15 by inadvertently defaulting in dues sacred to the LORD, he shall bring as his guilt-offering to the LORD a ram without blemish from the flock, the value to be determined by you in silver shekels according to the sacred standard, for a guilt-offering; he shall make 16 good his default in sacred dues, adding one fifth. He shall give it to the priest, who shall make expiation for his sin with the ram of the guilt-offering, and it shall be forgiven him.

If and when any person sins un- 17 wittingly and does what is forbidden by any commandment of the LORD, thereby incurring guilt, he must accept responsibility. He shall bring to the 18 priest as a guilt-offering a ram without blemish from the flock, valued by you, and the priest shall make expiation for the error into which he has unwittingly fallen, and it shall be forgiven him. It is 19 a guilt-offering; he has been guilty of an offence against the LORD.

The LORD spoke to Moses and said: 6 When any person sins and commits 2 a grievous fault against the LORD, whether he lies to a fellow-countryman about a deposit or contract, or a theft, or wrongs him by extortion, or finds 3 lost property and then lies about it, and swears a false oath in regard to any sin of this sort that he commits—if he 4 does this, thereby incurring guilt, he shall restore what he has stolen or gained by extortion, or the deposit left with him or the lost property which he

---

illustrating situations for which a sin-offering is required. **2–3:** For details concerning *uncleanness*, see chs. 11–15. **7–13:** Less expensive but equally acceptable sin-offerings are listed (see 1.14–17 n.). **11:** *Ephah:* see p. 1035.
    5.14–6.7: The guilt-offering, a special designation for the sin-offering when it must be accompanied by reparation to an offended party. **15:** *Sacred standard:* see p. 1035. **6.1–7:** Whereas the previous section has been concerned with offenses strictly against the deity, here the focus is offenses against one's fellowman. Only when the latter has been satisfied may one then bring a guilt-offering to the deity.

5 found, or anything at all concerning which he swore a false oath. He shall make full restitution, adding one fifth to it, and give it back to the aggrieved party on the day when he offers his 6 guilt-offering. He shall bring to the LORD as his guilt-offering a ram without blemish from the flock, valued by 7 you, as a guilt-offering. The priest shall make expiation for his guilt before the LORD, and he shall be forgiven for any act which has brought guilt upon him.

8 THE LORD SPOKE TO MOSES AND SAID, 9 Give this command to Aaron and his sons: This is the law of the whole-offering. The whole-offering shall remain on the altar-hearth all night till morning, and the altar-fire shall be kept 10 burning there. Then the priest, having donned his linen robe and put on linen drawers to cover himself, shall remove the ashes to which the fire reduces the whole-offering on the altar and put 11 them beside the altar. He shall then change into other garments and take the ashes outside the camp to a ritually 12 clean place. The fire shall be kept burning on the altar; it shall never go out. Every morning the priest shall have fresh wood burning thereon, arrange the whole-offering on it, and on top burn the fat from the shared-13 offerings. Fire shall always be kept burning on the altar; it shall not go out. 14 This is the law of the grain-offering. The Aaronites shall present it before 15 the LORD in front of the altar. The priest shall set aside a handful of the flour from it, with the oil of the grain-offering, and all the frankincense on it. He shall burn this token of it on the altar as a soothing odour to the LORD. 16 The remainder Aaron and his sons shall eat. It shall be eaten in the form of unleavened cakes and in a holy place.

They shall eat it in the court of the Tent of the Presence. It shall not be baked 17 with leaven. I have allotted this to them as their share of my food-offerings. Like the sin-offering and the guilt-offering, it is most sacred. Any male 18 descendant of Aaron may eat it, as a due from the food-offerings to the LORD, for generation after generation for all time. Whatever touches them is to be forfeit as sacred.

The LORD spoke to Moses and said: 19 This is the offering which Aaron and 20 his sons shall present to the LORD:*b* one tenth of an ephah of flour, the usual grain-offering, half of it in the morning and half in the evening. It shall be 21 cooked with oil on a griddle; you shall bring it well-mixed, and so present it crumbled in small pieces as a grain-offering, a soothing odour to the LORD. The anointed priest in the line of 22 Aaron shall offer it. This is a rule binding for all time. It shall be burnt in sacrifice to the LORD as a complete offering. Every grain-offering of a 23 priest shall be a complete offering; it shall not be eaten.

The LORD spoke to Moses and said, 24 Speak to Aaron and his sons in these 25 words: This is the law of the sin-offering. The sin-offering shall be slaughtered before the LORD in the place where the whole-offering is slaughtered; it is most sacred. The priest who offici-26 ates shall eat of the flesh; it shall be eaten in a sacred place, in the court of the Tent of the Presence. Whatever 27 touches its flesh is to be forfeit as sacred. If any of the blood is splashed on a garment, that shall be washed in a sacred place. An earthenware vessel 28 in which the sin-offering is boiled shall be smashed. If it has been boiled in a

b Prob. rdg.; Heb. adds on the day when he is anointed.

6.8–7.38: The role of the Aaronite priests in the sacrifices previously mentioned (1.1–6.7). To this point, the directions are primarily for the layman who has brought the animal (see 1.2 n.); here the directions are for the priests. **9:** A *whole-offering* for the entire people is to be offered twice daily and to consist of a ram (Exod.29.38–39; Num.28.3–4). In the preexilic period it was required but once daily (2 Kgs.16.15). **12–13:** The undying *fire on the altar* symbolizes Israel's unceasing obedience to the will of the LORD. **14:** *Grain-offering:* the layman's voluntary sacrifice (2.1–16). **16:** Since the priests share in a portion of this offering made to God, it must be eaten *in the court,* not in a profane area (compare v. 11; 2.3 n.). **19–23:** This special *grain-offering* by the priests must, unlike the previous one, be burned entirely. See 4.11–12 n. **27–28:** Holiness, regarded almost like a fluid substance, and transmitted by contact (see Exod. 19.12–13 n.), must be washed from a garment, scoured from a copper vessel, and released from

copper vessel, that shall be scoured and
29 rinsed with water. Any male of priestly
family may eat of this offering; it is
30 most sacred. If, however, part of the
blood is brought to the Tent of the
Presence to make expiation in the holy
place, the sin-offering shall not be
eaten; it shall be destroyed by fire.

7 This is the law of the guilt-offering:
2 it is most sacred. The guilt-offering
shall be slaughtered in the place where
the whole-offering is slaughtered, and
its blood shall be flung against the altar
3 all round. The priest shall set aside and
present all the fat from it: the fat-tail
4 and the fat covering the entrails, the
two kidneys with the fat on them beside
the haunches, and the long lobe of the
5 liver with the kidneys. The priest shall
burn these pieces on the altar as a food-
offering to the LORD; it is a guilt-
6 offering. Any male of priestly family
may eat it. It shall be eaten in a sacred
7 place; it is most sacred. There is one
law for both sin-offering and guilt-
offering: they shall belong to the priest
who performs the rite of expiation.
8 The skin of any man's whole-offering
shall belong to the priest who presents
9 it. Every grain-offering baked in an
oven and everything that is cooked in
a pan or on a griddle shall belong to
10 the priest who presents it. Every grain-
offering, whether mixed with oil or dry,
shall be shared equally among all the
Aaronites.

11 This is the law of the shared-offering
12 presented to the LORD. If a man presents it as a thank-offering, then, in
addition to the thank-offering, he shall
present unleavened cakes mixed with
oil, wafers of unleavened flour smeared
with oil, and well-mixed flour and flat
13 cakes mixed with oil. He shall present
flat cakes of leavened bread in addition
14 to his shared thank-offering. One part

of every offering he shall present as a
contribution for the LORD: it shall
belong to the priest who flings the
blood of the shared-offering against
the altar. The flesh shall be eaten on 15
the day of its presentation; none of it
shall be put aside till morning.

If a man's sacrifice is a votive offer- 16
ing or a freewill offering, it may be
eaten on the day it is presented or on
the next day. Any flesh left over on the 17
third day shall be destroyed by fire. If 18
any flesh of his shared-offering is eaten
on the third day, the man who has presented it shall not be accepted. It will
not be counted to his credit, it shall be
reckoned as tainted and the person
who eats any of it shall accept responsibility. No flesh which comes into 19
contact with anything unclean shall be
eaten; it shall be destroyed by fire.

The flesh may be eaten by anyone
who is clean, but the person who, while 20
unclean, eats flesh from a shared-
offering presented to the LORD shall
be cut off from his father's kin. When 21
any person is contaminated by contact
with anything unclean, be it man,
beast, or reptile, and then eats any of
the flesh from the shared-offerings presented to the LORD, that person shall
be cut off from his father's kin.

The LORD spoke to Moses and said, 22
Speak to the Israelites in these words: 23
You shall not eat the fat of any ox,
sheep, or goat. The fat of an animal 24
that has died a natural death or has
been mauled by wild beasts may be put
to any other use, but you shall not eat
it. Every man who eats fat from a beast 25
of which he has presented any part as a
food-offering to the LORD shall be cut
off from his father's kin.

You shall eat none of the blood, 26
whether of bird or of beast, wherever
you may live. Every person who eats 27

a porous vessel by smashing it. **30:** The distinction here is between the sin-offering for priest
or community (4.3–21) and that for individuals (4.22–35). See 4.5–6 n.; 4.22–35 n. **7.1–10:** The
ritual for the *guilt-offering*, omitted in 5.14–6.7 because of its similarity to the preceding sin-
offering, is here outlined. Since it is prescribed for individuals only, the blood is not applied
to the incense-altar and hence the meat is available for consumption by the priests (6.30 n.).
11–19: Various occasions for a *shared-offering* (3.1–17) are mentioned, with minor accompanying procedures. **16:** *A votive offering:* one vowed to the deity if he would grant a special request;
see ch. 27. *A freewill offering:* presented without special reason or occasion. **20:** *Eaten by
anyone:* that is, except for the portions reserved for the priests (vv. 31–36). *Clean . . . unclean:*
for the relevant rules, see chs. 11–15. **21:** It is unclear here whether *cut off* means execution
by the community or death by divine causation; compare 20.1–8. **24:** *Fat:* see 3.3 n. *Mauled:*

any of the blood shall be cut off from his father's kin.

28 The LORD spoke to Moses and said,
29 Speak to the Israelites in these words: Whoever comes to present a shared-offering shall set aside part of it as an
30 offering to the LORD. With his own hands he shall bring the food-offerings to the LORD. He shall also bring the fat together with the breast which is to be presented as a special gift before the
31 LORD; the priest shall burn the fat on the altar, but the breast shall belong
32 to Aaron and his descendants. You shall give the right hind-leg of your shared-offerings as a contribution for
33 the priest; it shall be the perquisite of the Aaronite who presents the blood
34 and the fat of the shared-offering. I have taken from the Israelites the breast of the special gift and the leg of the contribution made out of the shared offerings, and have given them as a due from the Israelites to Aaron the priest and his descendants for all time.
35 This is the portion prescribed for Aaron and his descendants out of the LORD's food-offerings, appointed on the day when they were presented as
36 priests to the LORD; and on the day when they were anointed, the LORD commanded that these prescribed portions should be given to them by the Israelites. This is a rule binding on their descendants for all time.
37 This, then, is the law of the whole-offering, the grain-offering, the sin-offering, the guilt-offering, the installation-offerings, and the shared-offerings,
38 with which the LORD charged Moses on Mount Sinai on the day when he commanded the Israelites to present their offerings to the LORD in the wilderness of Sinai.

The hallowing and installation of the priests

THE LORD SPOKE TO MOSES AND SAID, 8 'Take Aaron and his sons with him, 2 the vestments, the anointing oil, the ox for a sin-offering, the two rams, and the basket of unleavened cakes, and as- 3 semble all the community at the entrance to the Tent of the Presence.' Moses did as the LORD had command- 4 ed him, and the community assembled at the entrance to the Tent of the Presence. He told the community that this 5 was what the LORD had commanded. He presented Aaron and his sons and 6 washed them in water. He invested 7 Aaron with the tunic, girded him with the sash, robed him with the mantle, put the ephod on him, tied it with its waist-band and fastened the ephod to him with the band. He put the breast- 8 piece[c] on him and set the Urim and Thummim in it. He then put the turban 9 upon his head and set the gold rosette as a symbol of holy dedication on the front of the turban, as the LORD had commanded him. Moses then took the 10 anointing oil, anointed the Tabernacle and all that was within it and con- secrated them. He sprinkled some of 11 the oil seven times on the altar, anoint- ing the altar, all its vessels, the basin and its stand, to consecrate them. He 12 poured some of the anointing oil on Aaron's head and so consecrated him. Moses then brought the sons of Aaron 13 forward, invested them with tunics, girded them with sashes and tied their tall head-dresses on them, as the LORD had commanded him.

He then brought up the ox for the 14 sin-offering; Aaron and his sons laid

[c] *Or* pouch.

see Exod.22.31 n. **28–36:** This is a supplement to vv. 11–21, specifying or expanding the priestly share of the sacrificial meat. **35–38:** The obligation to support the priesthood in the specified ways is integrated into the very foundation of the cult at Sinai (see 1.1 n.; compare Exod. 29.36–42 n.).

8.1–36: The installation of the Aaronite priesthood, following the instructions of Exod.29.1–46 (see also Exod.40.12–15). The instructions for the sanctuary and its personnel are given in Exod.25.1–31.17 and the carrying out in Exod.35.1–40.38. The delay in the installation of the priesthood (despite the wording of Exod.40.16) is logical: the cultic activity can only begin when the Tabernacle is completed. Accordingly, the instructions for sacrifice (Lev. chs. 1–7) interrupt the flow of the narrative. **1:** *Aaron:* for the development of the priesthood, see Exod. 29.1–46 n. **2:** The *vestments* are described in Exod. ch. 28. *Anointing oil:* see Exod.30.22–33 for the formula. *Ox . . . rams . . . unleavened cakes:* Exod.29.1–2. **6:** *Washed them in water:* see Exod.29.4; compare Exod.30.17–21 for the more general ritual. **7:** *Ephod:* see Exod.28.6–12. **8:** *Urim and Thummim:* see Exod.28.15 n. **10–11:** The instructions for anointing the furniture

15 their hands on its head, and he slaughtered it. Moses took some of the blood and put it with his finger on the horns round the altar. Thus he purified the altar, and when he had poured out the rest of the blood at the base of the altar, he consecrated it by making
16 expiation for it. He took all the fat upon the entrails, the long lobe of the liver, and the two kidneys with their
17 fat, and burnt them on the altar, but the ox, its skin, its flesh, and its offal, he destroyed by fire outside the camp, as the LORD had commanded him.
18   Moses then brought forward the ram of the whole-offering; Aaron and his sons laid their hands on the ram's
19 head, and he slaughtered it. Moses flung its blood against the altar all
20 round. He cut the ram up and burnt
21 the head, the pieces, and the suet. He washed the entrails and the shins in water and burnt the whole on the altar. This was a whole-offering, a food-offering of soothing odour to the LORD, as the LORD had commanded Moses.
22   Moses then brought forward the second ram, the ram for the installation of priests. Aaron and his sons laid
23 their hands upon its head, and he slaughtered it. Moses took some of its blood and put it on the lobe of Aaron's right ear, on his right thumb, and on
24 the big toe of his right foot. He then brought forward the sons of Aaron, put some of the blood on the lobes of their right ears, on their right thumbs, and on the big toes of their right feet. He flung the rest of the blood against the
25 altar all round; he took the fat, the fat-tail, the fat covering the entrails, the long lobe of the liver, the two kidneys
26 with their fat, and the right leg. Then from the basket of unleavened cakes before the LORD he took one unleavened cake, one cake of bread made with oil, and one wafer, and laid them on

the fatty parts and the right leg. He put 27 the whole on the hands of Aaron and of his sons, and he presented it as a special gift before the LORD. He took 28 it from their hands and burnt it on the altar on top of the whole-offering. This was an installation-offering, it was a food-offering of soothing odour to the LORD.
    Moses then took the breast and 29 presented it as a special gift before the LORD; it was his portion of the ram of installation, as the LORD had commanded him. He took some of the 30 anointing oil and some of the blood on the altar and sprinkled it on Aaron and his vestments, and on his sons and their vestments with him. Thus he consecrated Aaron and his vestments, and with him his sons and their vestments.
    Moses said to Aaron and his sons, 31 'Boil the flesh of the ram at the entrance to the Tent of the Presence, and eat it there, together with the bread in the installation-basket, in accordance with the command: "Aaron and his sons shall eat it." The remainder of the 32 flesh and bread you shall destroy by fire. You shall not leave the entrance 33 to the Tent of the Presence for seven days, until the day which completes the period of your installation, for it lasts seven days. What was done this day 34 followed the LORD's command to make expiation for you. You shall stay at the 35 entrance to the Tent of the Presence day and night for seven days, keeping vigil to the LORD, so that you do not die, for so I was commanded.'
    Aaron and his sons did everything 36 that the LORD had commanded through Moses.
    On the eighth day Moses summoned 9 Aaron and his sons and the Israelite elders. He said to Aaron, 'Take for 2 yourself a bull-calf for a sin-offering and a ram for a whole-offering, both

and vessels of the Tabernacle are contained in Exod.30.26–29; 40.9–11. **15:** *Purified the altar:* for the instructions, see Exod.29.36–37; for the reason, see Lev.4.5–6 n.; 4.13–21 n. **22:** The *ram of the installation* is a shared-offering (3.1–17; 7.11–36), and hence consumed by God (v. 28), by Moses as the officiating priest (v. 29), and by the Aaronites as the community (v. 31). **23:** *Ear ... thumb ... toe:* the significance of this act is unsure (compare 14.14,17,25,28), but the parts chosen may be extremities representative of the whole man. **24:** The *blood,* put on the priests' bodies and the *altar* (representing the deity: see Exod.29.12 n.), expresses the special relationship between the priesthood and the LORD. **30:** *Sprinkled ... his vestments:* see Exod. 29.21.
    9.1–24: The priests assume their sacrificial duties, which have been described in 6.8–7.38. **1:** *The eighth day:* at the conclusion of the installation (8.33–35). **5–6:** The function of the

without blemish, and present them
3 before the LORD. Then bid the Israelites take a he-goat for a sin-offering, a
calf and a lamb, both yearlings without
4 blemish, for a whole-offering, and a
bull and a ram for shared-offerings to
be sacrificed before the LORD, together
with a grain-offering mixed with oil.
This day the LORD will appear to you.'
5 They brought what Moses had commanded to the front of the Tent of the
Presence, and all the community approached and stood before the LORD.
6 Moses said, 'This is what the LORD has
commanded you to do, so that the glory
7 of the LORD may appear to you. Come
near to the altar,' he said to Aaron;
'prepare your sin-offering and your
whole-offering and make expiation for
yourself and for your household. Then
prepare the offering of the people and
make expiation for them, as the LORD
has commanded.'
8 So Aaron came near to the altar and
slaughtered the calf, which was his sin-
9 offering. The sons of Aaron presented
the blood to him, and he dipped his
finger in the blood and put it on the
horns of the altar. The rest of the blood
he poured out at the base of the altar.
10 Part of the sin-offering, the fat, the
kidneys, and the long lobe of the liver,
he burnt on the altar as the LORD had
11 commanded Moses, but the flesh and
the skin he destroyed by fire outside the
12 camp. Then he slaughtered the whole-
offering; his sons handed him the blood,
and he flung it against the altar all
13 round. They handed him the pieces of
the whole-offering and the head, and
14 he burnt them on the altar. He washed
the entrails and the shins and burnt
them on the altar, on top of the whole-
offering.
15 He then brought forward the offering

of the people. He took the he-goat, the
people's sin-offering, slaughtered it and
performed the rite of the sin-offering
as he had previously done for himself.
He presented the whole-offering and 16
prepared it in the manner prescribed.
He brought forward the grain-offering, 17
took a handful of it and burnt it on the
altar, in addition to the morning
whole-offering. He slaughtered the bull 18
and the ram, the shared-offerings of the
people. His sons handed him the blood,
and he flung it against the altar all
round. But the fatty parts of the bull, 19
the fat-tail of the ram, the fat covering
the entrails, and the two kidneys
with the fat upon them, and the long
lobe of the liver, all this fat they first 20
put on the breasts of the animals and
then burnt it on the altar. Aaron 21
presented the breasts and the right leg
as a special gift before the LORD, as
Moses had commanded.

Then Aaron lifted up his hands to- 22
wards the people and pronounced the
blessing over them. He came down
from performing the rites of the sin-
offering, the whole-offering, and the
shared-offerings. Moses and Aaron 23
entered the Tent of the Presence, and
when they came out, they blessed the
people, and the glory of the LORD
appeared to all the people. Fire came 24
out from before the LORD and consumed the whole-offering and the fatty
parts on the altar. All the people saw,
and they shouted and fell on their
faces.

Now NADAB AND ABIHU, SONS OF 10
Aaron, took their firepans, put fire in
them, threw incense on the fire and
presented before the LORD illicit fire
which he had not commanded. Fire 2
came out from before the LORD and

---

sacrificial ritual is to bring about an awareness of the divine presence. **8–11:** Aaron begins with
a sin-offering for priests (4.3–12), following that already offered by Moses (8.14–17), so that
he will be sinless when he ministers before the congregation (compare 4.3 n.). **15:** The sacrificial
animal differs from that of 4.13–21, and this suggests that the practice changed from time to
time. **22:** *The blessing:* Num.6.22–27. *Came down:* from the altar. **23:** *Glory:* Exod.16.10 n.
   10.1–20: Ritual deviation and its consequences. It is in part through precise ritual that postexilic Israel maintained her identity and distinctiveness, and a specific episode is here cited in
order to encourage strict obedience (vv. 1–7). This then presented a suitable occasion for the
transmitters of the traditions to append related warnings (vv. 8–20). **1:** *Nadab and Abihu* were
the oldest of Aaron's sons who once played an important role in Israel's traditions (see Exod.
6.23 and 24.1–10). What exactly is meant by *illicit fire* is unclear, although the plain lesson of
the incident is to warn against unauthorized ritual acts. **2:** The story may perhaps be based
on a struggle for power between different priestly groups (compare Num. ch. 16; see Exod.

destroyed them; and so they died in
3 the presence of the LORD. Then Moses
said to Aaron, 'This is what the LORD
meant when he said: Among those who
approach me, I must be treated as holy;
in the presence of all the people I must
be given honour.' Aaron was dumb-
4 founded. Moses sent for Mishael and
Elzaphan, the sons of Aaron's uncle
Uzziel, and said to them, 'Come and
carry your cousins outside the camp
5 away from the holy place.' They came
and carried them away in their tunics
outside the camp, as Moses had told
6 them. Moses then said to Aaron and
to his sons Eleazar and Ithamar, 'You
shall not leave your hair dishevelled or
tear your clothes in mourning, lest you
die and the LORD be angry with the
whole community. Your kinsmen, all
the house of Israel, shall weep for the
destruction by fire which the LORD has
7 kindled. You shall not leave the entrance to the Tent of the Presence lest
you die, because the LORD's anointing
oil is on you.' They did as Moses had
said.

8 THE LORD SPOKE TO AARON AND SAID:
9 You and your sons with you shall not
drink wine or strong drink when you
are to enter the Tent of the Presence,
lest you die. This is a rule binding on
10 your descendants for all time, to make
a distinction between sacred and pro-
11 fane, between clean and unclean, and
to teach the Israelites all the decrees
which the LORD has spoken to them
through Moses.
12   Moses said to Aaron and his surviving sons Eleazar and Ithamar, 'Take

what is left over of the grain-offering
out of the food-offerings of the LORD,
and eat it without leaven beside the
altar; it is most sacred. You shall eat it 13
in a sacred place; it is your due and that
of your sons out of the LORD's food-
offerings, for so I was commanded.
You shall eat the breast of the special 14
gift and the leg of the contribution in
a clean place, you and your sons and
daughters; for they have been given
to you and your children as your due
out of the shared-offerings of the
Israelites. The leg of the contribution 15
and the breast of the special gift shall
be brought, along with the food-offerings of fat, to be presented as a special
gift before the LORD, and it shall belong to you and your children together,
a due for all time; for so the LORD has
commanded.'
    Moses made searching inquiry about 16
the goat of the sin-offering and found
that it had been burnt. He was angry
with Eleazar and Ithamar, Aaron's surviving sons, and said, 'Why did you not 17
eat the sin-offering in the sacred place?
It is most sacred. It was given to you
to take away the guilt of the community by making expiation for them
before the LORD. If the blood is not 18
brought within the sacred precincts,
you shall eat the sin-offering there as I
was commanded.' But Aaron replied 19
to Moses, 'See, they have today presented their sin-offering and their
whole-offering before the LORD, and
this is what has befallen me; if I eat a
sin-offering today, will it be right in the
eyes of the LORD?' When Moses heard 20
this, he deemed it right.

29.1–46 n.), which resulted in a defeat for the descendants of these two men, so that the priesthood descended through the next oldest son, Eleazar (Num.20.25–28). **3**: *Those who approach
me:* the priests. **4**: *Outside the camp:* where the sacrificial remains were burned and the altar
ashes deposited (4.12). **6**: *Hair . . . clothes:* these funeral actions were forbidden to the chief
priest; see 21.10–11. **7**: To prevent contamination, the priest must remain within the temple-
complex (21.12; for the consequences, see 4.3 n.). **9**: The warning against alcoholic beverage
may rest upon two bases: to ensure the ability to observe the fine details of the ritual (compare
Isa.28.7–8), and to avoid the cultic practices of Israel's neighbors. It also probably reflects
the persistence of the antialcohol ethic of eastern nomads, an ethic that disappeared among
laymen as Israel emerged as an agricultural society. **12–13**: See 6.16–18. **14–15**: See 7.28–34.
16–20: On the sacrificial animal (v. 16), see 9.15 n. According to 4.13–21, the blood should
have been sprinkled inside the sanctuary and applied to the incense-altar there. This Aaron
apparently failed to do (9.15; compare 9.8–9), applying the blood rather to the sacrificial altar
in the court. Thus the meat should have been eaten by the priests (6.25–30). A discrepancy in
such precise and central material (10.1–20 n.) called for explanation, and those who collected
the priestly materials saw in the Nadab and Abihu episode the opportunity to provide Aaron
with an excuse which would not create a precedent for future deviations. Since Aaron shared

Laws of purification and atonement

11 THE LORD SPOKE TO MOSES AND AARON
2 and said, Speak to the Israelites in these words: Of all animals on land these are the creatures you may eat:
3 you may eat any animal which has a parted foot or a cloven hoof and also
4 chews the cud; those which have only a cloven hoof or only chew the cud you may not eat. These are: the camel, because it chews the cud but has not a cloven hoof; you shall regard it as
5 unclean; the rock-badger,*d* because it chews the cud but has not a parted foot; you shall regard it as unclean;
6 the hare, because it chews the cud but has not a parted foot; you shall regard
7 it as unclean; the pig, because it has a parted foot and a cloven hoof but does not chew the cud; you shall regard it
8 as unclean. You shall not eat their flesh or even touch their dead bodies; you shall regard them as unclean.

9 Of creatures that live in water these you may eat: all those that have fins and scales, whether in salt water or
10 fresh; but all that have neither fins nor scales, whether in salt or fresh water, including both small creatures in shoals and larger creatures, you shall regard
11 as vermin. They shall be vermin to you; you shall not eat their flesh, and their dead bodies you shall treat as those of
12 vermin. Every creature in the water that has neither fins nor scales shall be vermin to you.

13 These are the birds you shall regard as vermin, and for this reason they shall not be eaten: the griffon-vulture,*e* the black vulture, and the bearded vul-
14 ture;*f* the kite and every kind of falcon;
15,16 every kind of crow,*g* the desert-owl, the short-eared owl, the long-eared owl,

17 and every kind of hawk; the tawny owl, the fisher-owl, and the screech-
18 owl; the little owl, the horned owl, the
19 osprey, the stork,*h* every kind of cormorant, the hoopoe, and the bat.

20 All teeming winged creatures that go on four legs shall be vermin to you,
21 except those which have legs jointed above their feet for leaping on the
22 ground. Of these you may eat every kind of great locust, every kind of long-headed locust, every kind of green locust, and every kind of desert-locust.
23 Every other teeming winged creature that has four legs you shall regard as
24 vermin; you would make yourselves unclean with them: whoever*i* touches their dead bodies shall be unclean till
25 evening. Whoever picks up their dead bodies shall wash his clothes but remain unclean till evening.

26 You shall regard as unclean every animal which has a parted foot but has not a cloven hoof and does not chew the cud: whoever*i* touches them shall
27 be unclean. You shall regard as unclean all four-footed wild animals that go on flat paws; whoever*i* touches their dead bodies shall be unclean till even-
28 ing. Whoever takes up their dead bodies shall wash his clothes but remain unclean till evening. You shall regard them as unclean.

29 You shall regard these as unclean among creatures that teem on the ground: the mole-rat,*j* the jerboa, and
30 every kind of thorn-tailed lizard; the gecko, the sand-gecko, the wall-gecko, the great lizard, and the chameleon.
31 You shall regard these as unclean among teeming creatures; whoever*i* touches them when they are dead shall

d Or rock-rabbit.   *e Or* eagle.   *f Or* ossifrage.
g Or raven.   *h Or* heron.   *i Or* whatever.   *j Or* weasel.

in his sons' guilt (compare 4.3 n.), it would be inappropriate for him to consume a sin-offering (compare 4.11–12 n.). However, the occasion for the excuse creates a chronological difficulty: the erroneous sin-offering occurred before the sins of Aaron's sons!
  11.1–47: Clean and unclean animals. The priestly theologians believed that God had intended for man to be vegetarian (Gen.1.29), but had approved the eating of meat from the time of Noah onward (Gen.9.3–4). But now Israel's distinctiveness as a "holy nation" (vv. 43–45; Exod.19.6) is enforced and a focus for identity provided, by severely restricting the creatures which she might consume. This would be especially important during the exilic (Dan. ch. 1) and postexilic periods (compare Exod.31.12–17 n.), although it is here suggested that the origins of the prohibition lie in the Mosaic Age (see Exod.25.1–31.17 n.). A similar but shorter account is found in Deut.14.3–21. **3:** The original basis for this distinction is obscure: it may perhaps be related to the sacredness of the animals to the deities of Israel's neighbors (see Exod.23.19 n.). **5–6:** The *rock-badger* and the *hare* do not really chew the cud, but only appear to do so. **24–25:** Uncleanness, like holiness (6.27–28 n.), can be transferred from one object

32 be unclean till evening. Anything on which any of them falls when they are dead shall be unclean, any article of wood or garment or skin or sacking, any article in regular use; it shall be plunged into water but shall remain unclean till evening, when it shall be 33 clean. If any of these falls into an earthenware vessel, its contents shall be unclean and it shall be smashed. 34 Any food on which water from such a vessel is poured shall be unclean, and any drink in such a vessel shall be un-35 clean. Anything on which the dead body of such a creature falls shall be unclean; an oven or a stove shall be broken, for they are unclean and you 36 shall treat them as such; but a spring or a cistern where water collects shall remain clean, though whatever[k] touches the dead body shall be un-37 clean. When any of their dead bodies falls on seed intended for sowing, it 38 remains clean; but if the seed has been soaked in water and any dead body falls on it, you shall treat it as unclean. 39 When any animal allowed as food dies, all that touch the carcass shall be 40 unclean till evening. Whoever eats any of the carcass shall wash his clothes but remain unclean till evening; whoever takes up the carcass shall wash his clothes and be unclean till evening. 41 All creatures that teem on the ground are vermin; they shall not be eaten. 42 All creatures that teem on the ground, crawl on their bellies, go on all fours or have many legs, you shall not eat, because they are vermin which con-43 taminate. You shall not contaminate yourselves through any teeming creature. You shall not defile yourselves with them and make yourselves un-44 clean by them. For I am the LORD your God; you shall make yourselves holy

and keep yourselves holy, because I am holy. You shall not defile yourselves with any teeming creature that creeps on the ground. I am the LORD who 45 brought you up from Egypt to become your God. You shall keep yourselves holy, because I am holy.

This, then, is the law concerning 46 beast and bird, every living creature that swims in the water and every living creature that teems on the land. It is to 47 make a distinction between the unclean and the clean, between living creatures that may be eaten and living creatures that may not be eaten.

The LORD spoke to Moses and said, 12 Speak to the Israelites in these words: 2 When a woman conceives and bears a male child, she shall be unclean for seven days, as in the period of her impurity through menstruation. On 3 the eighth day, the child shall have the flesh of his foreskin circumcised. The 4 woman shall wait for thirty-three days because her blood requires purification; she shall touch nothing that is holy, and shall not enter the sanctuary till her days of purification are completed. If 5 she bears a female child, she shall be unclean for fourteen days as for her menstruation and shall wait for sixty-six days because her blood requires purification. When her days of purifi- 6 cation are completed for a son or a daughter, she shall bring a yearling ram for a whole-offering and a young pigeon or a turtle-dove for a sin-offering to the priest at the entrance to the Tent of the Presence. He shall present it before 7 the LORD and make expiation for her, and she shall be clean from the issue of her blood. This is the law for the woman who bears a child, whether male or female. If she cannot afford a 8

k Or whoever.

to another. **33:** *Smashed:* compare 6.28. **36:** Basic sources of water (*spring* or *cistern*) were, like *seed* (v. 37), exempt because of their value to the community. **38:** The reason for the exclusion of *soaked* seed is not made clear, but it may have been that "uncleanness" could then permeate it more thoroughly.

12.1–8: Uncleanness from childbirth. The mysterious power at work in childbirth was regarded with awe throughout the ancient world. The "uncleanness" was ritual rather than literal or hygienic. **2:** *Menstruation:* see 15.19–24. **4:** On the frequent use of the number forty (thirty-three plus the seven of v. 2), see Gen.7.4 n. *Purification:* the loss of blood marked an imperfection, a blemish, and hence cultic unacceptability (compare the sacrifices "without blemish": 1.3,10; and the limitations of priests with bodily blemishes: 21.16–23). **5:** The longer delay after the birth of a daughter may reflect the view that girls were considered less desirable than sons. **6:** On the need for a sin-offering, compare 4.1–5.13 n.

ram, she shall bring two little-doves or two young pigeons, one for a whole-offering and the other for a sin-offering. The priest shall make expiation for her and she shall be clean.

13 The LORD spoke to Moses and 2 Aaron and said: When any man has a discoloration on the skin of his body, a pustule or inflammation, and it may develop into the sores of a malignant skin-disease, he shall be brought to the priest, either to Aaron or to one of his 3 sons. The priest shall examine the sore on the skin; if the hairs on the sore have turned white and it appears to be deeper than the skin, it shall be considered the sore of a malignant skin-disease, and the priest, after examination, shall pronounce him ritually unclean. 4 But if the inflammation on his skin is white and seems no deeper than the skin, and the hairs have not turned white, the priest shall isolate the af-5 fected person for seven days. If, when he examines him on the seventh day, the sore remains as it was and has not spread in the skin, he shall keep him in 6 isolation for another seven days. When the priest examines him again on the seventh day, if the sore has faded and has not spread in the skin, the priest shall pronounce him ritually clean. It is only a scab; the man shall wash his 7 clothes and so be clean. But if the scab spreads on the skin after he has been to the priest to be pronounced ritually clean, the man shall show himself a 8 second time to the priest. The priest shall examine him again, and if it continues to spread, he shall pronounce him ritually unclean; it is a malignant skin-disease.

9 When anyone has the sores of a malignant skin-disease, he shall be 10 brought to the priest, and the priest shall examine him. If there is a white mark on the skin, turning the hairs white, and an ulceration appears in the 11 mark, it is a chronic skin-disease on the body, and the priest shall pronounce him ritually unclean; there is no need for isolation because he is unclean 12 already. If the skin-disease breaks out and covers the affected person from head to foot as far as the priest can see, the priest shall examine him, and if he 13 finds the condition spread all over the body, he shall pronounce him ritually clean. It has all gone white; he is clean. But from the moment when raw flesh 14 appears, the man shall be considered unclean. When the priest sees it, he 15 shall pronounce him unclean. Raw flesh is to be considered unclean; it is a malignant skin-disease. On the other 16 hand, when the raw flesh heals and turns white, the man shall go to the priest, who shall examine him, and if 17 the sores have gone white, he shall pronounce him clean. He is ritually clean.

When a fester appears on the skin 18 and heals up, but is followed by a 19 white mark or reddish-white inflammation on the site of the fester, the man shall show himself to the priest. The priest shall examine him; if it 20 seems to be beneath the skin and the hairs have turned white, the priest shall pronounce him ritually unclean. It is a malignant skin-disease which has broken out on the site of the fester. But if the priest on examination finds 21 that it has no white hairs, is not beneath the skin and has faded, he shall isolate him for seven days. If the affec-22 tion has spread at all in the skin, then the priest shall pronounce him unclean; for it is a malignant skin-disease. But 23 if the inflammation is no worse and has not spread, it is only the scar of the fester, and the priest shall pronounce him ritually clean.

Again, in the case of a burn on the 24 skin, if the raw spot left by the burn becomes a reddish-white or white inflammation, the priest shall examine it. 25 If the hairs on the inflammation have turned white and it is deeper than the skin, it is a malignant skin-disease which has broken out at the site of the burn. The priest shall pronounce the man ritually unclean; it is a malignant skin-disease. But if the priest on ex-26 amination finds that there is no white hair on the inflammation and it is not

13.1–46; 14.1–32: Uncleanness from skin disease. Illness, when it produced marked imperfection, rendered the person cultically "unclean" (see 12.4 n.). **4–5:** The *isolation* was to prevent the inadvertent transfer of cultic impurity (see 11.24–25 n.) by one's touching of the impure.

beneath the skin and has faded, he shall keep him in isolation for seven days.

27 When the priest examines him on the seventh day, if the inflammation has spread at all in the skin, the priest shall pronounce him unclean; it is a malig-

28 nant skin-disease. But if the inflammation is no worse, has not spread and has faded, it is only a mark from the burn. The priest shall pronounce him ritually clean because it is the scar of the burn.

29 When a man, or woman, has a sore

30 on the head or chin, the priest shall examine it; and if it seems deeper than the skin and the hair is yellow and sparse, the priest shall pronounce him ritually unclean; it is a scurf, a malignant skin-disease of the head or chin.

31 But when the priest sees the sore, if it appears to be no deeper than the skin and yet there is no yellow hair on the place, the priest shall isolate the af-

32 fected person for seven days. He shall examine the sore on the seventh day: if the scurf has not spread and there are no yellow hairs on it and it seems

33 no deeper than the skin, the man shall get himself shaved except for the scurfy part, and the priest shall keep him in

34 isolation for another seven days. The priest shall examine it again on the seventh day, and if the scurf has not spread on the skin and appears to be no deeper than the skin, the priest shall pronounce him clean. The man shall wash his clothes and so be ritually

35 clean. But if the scurf spreads at all in the skin after the man has been pro-

36 nounced clean, the priest shall examine him again. If it has spread in the skin, the priest need not even look for yellow

37 hair; the man is unclean. If, however, the scurf remains as it was but black hair has begun to grow on it, it has healed. The man is ritually clean and the priest shall pronounce him so.

38 When a man, or woman, has inflamed patches on the skin and they

39 are white, the priest shall examine them. If they are white and fading, it is dull-white leprosy that has broken out on the skin. The man is ritually clean.

40 When a man's hair falls out from his head, he is bald behind but not ritually

41 unclean. If the hair falls out from the front of the scalp, he is bald on the forehead but clean. But if on the bald 42 patch behind or on the forehead there is a reddish-white sore, it is a malignant skin-disease breaking out on those parts. The priest shall examine him, 43 and if the discoloured sore on the bald patch behind or on the forehead is reddish-white, similar in appearance to a malignant skin-disease on the body, the man is suffering from such a 44 disease; he is ritually unclean and the priest must not fail to pronounce him so. The symptoms are in this case on his head.

One who suffers from a malignant 45 skin-disease shall wear his clothes torn, leave his hair dishevelled, conceal his upper lip, and cry, 'Unclean, unclean.' So long as the sore persists, he shall 46 be considered ritually unclean. The man is unclean: he shall live apart and must stay outside the settlement.

When there is a stain of mould, 47 whether in a garment of wool or linen, or in the warp or weft of linen or wool, 48 or in a skin or anything made of skin; if the stain is greenish or reddish in the 49 garment or skin, or in the warp or weft, or in anything made of skin, it is a stain of mould which must be shown to the priest. The priest shall examine it and 50 put the stained material aside for seven days. On the seventh day he shall ex- 51 amine it again. If the stain has spread in the garment, warp, weft, or skin, whatever the use of the skin, the stain is a rotting mould: it is ritually unclean. He shall burn the garment or the 52 warp or weft, whether wool or linen, or anything of skin which is stained; because it is a rotting mould, it must be destroyed by fire. But if the priest 53 sees that the stain has not spread in the garment, warp or weft, or anything made of skin, he shall give orders for 54 the stained material to be washed, and then he shall put it aside for another seven days. After it has been washed 55 the priest shall examine the stain; if it has not changed its appearance, although it has not spread, it is unclean and you shall destroy it by fire, whether the rot is on the right side or the wrong. If the priest examines it and finds the 56 stain faded after being washed, he shall tear it out of the garment, skin, warp,

57 or weft. If, however, the stain reappears in the garment, warp or weft, or in anything of skin, it is breaking out afresh and you shall destroy by fire **58** whatever is stained. If you wash the garment, warp, weft, or anything of skin and the stain disappears, it shall be washed a second time and then it shall be ritually clean. **59** This is the law concerning stain of mould in a garment of wool or linen, in warp or weft, or in anything made of skin; by it they shall be pronounced clean or unclean.

14 THE LORD SPOKE TO MOSES AND SAID: **2** This is the law concerning a man suffering from a malignant skin-disease. On the day when he is to be cleansed **3** he shall be brought to the priest. The priest shall go outside the camp and examine him. If the man is healed of **4** his disease, then the priest shall order two clean small birds to be brought alive for the man who is to be cleansed, together with cedar-wood, scarlet **5** thread, and marjoram.*l* He shall order one of the birds to be killed over an earthenware bowl containing fresh **6** water. He shall then take the living bird and the cedar-wood, scarlet thread, and marjoram and dip them and the living bird in the blood of the bird that has been killed over the fresh water. **7** He shall sprinkle the blood seven times on the man who is to be cleansed from his skin-disease and so cleanse him; the living bird he shall release to fly away **8** over the open country. The man to be cleansed shall wash his clothes, shave off all his hair, bathe in water and so be ritually clean. He may then enter the camp but must stay outside his tent for **9** seven days. On the seventh day he shall shave off all the hair on his head, his beard, and his eyebrows, and then shave the rest of his hair, wash his clothes and bathe in water; then he shall be ritually clean.

10 On the eighth day he shall bring two yearling rams and one yearling ewe, all three without blemish, a grain-offering of three tenths of an ephah of flour mixed with oil, and one log of oil. The **11** officiating priest shall place the man to be cleansed and his offerings before the LORD at the entrance to the Tent of the Presence. He shall then take one **12** of the rams and offer it with the log of oil as a guilt-offering, presenting them as a special gift before the LORD. The **13** ram shall be slaughtered where the sin-offerings and the whole-offerings are slaughtered, within the sacred precincts, because the guilt-offering, like the sin-offering, belongs to the priest. It is most sacred. The priest shall then take some **14** of the blood of the guilt-offering and put it on the lobe of the right ear of the man to be cleansed and on his right thumb and the big toe of his right foot. He shall next take the log of oil and **15** pour some of it on the palm of his own left hand, dip his right forefinger into **16** the oil on his left palm and sprinkle some of it with his finger seven times before the LORD. He shall then put **17** some of the oil remaining on his palm on the lobe of the right ear of the man to be cleansed, on his right thumb and on the big toe of his right foot, on top of the blood of the guilt-offering. The **18** remainder of the oil on the priest's palm shall be put upon the head of the man to be cleansed, and thus the priest shall make expiation for him before the LORD. The priest shall then perform **19** the sin-offering and make expiation for the uncleanness of the man who is to be cleansed. After this he shall slaughter the whole-offering and offer **20** it and the grain-offering on the altar. Thus the priest shall make expiation for him, and then he shall be clean.

21 If the man is poor and cannot afford these offerings, he shall bring one young ram as a guilt-offering to be a

l Or hyssop.

14.2: *Cleansed:* The ritual is not for healing (since that is here assumed), but for the removal of impurity (vv. 3–20) for reentry into the community. **4:** The color *scarlet* was regarded as effective in the exorcism of demons. *Marjoram:* see Exod.12.22 n. **5–7:** On the effectiveness of *blood* as a cleansing agent, see 4.7 n. The flight of the *living bird* symbolizes the man's freedom from impurity, his uncleanness perhaps having been transferred to it (compare 16.20–22). **8:** *Wash...shave...bathe:* thus cleansing all places to which the impurity might cling. **10:** *Ephah; log:* see p. 1035. **12:** *Guilt-offering:* see 5.14–6.7. **13:** *To the priest:* 6.29; 10.16–18. **14–17:** See 8.23 n. **19:** *The sin-offering:* the ewe (4.32–35). **20:** *The whole-offering:* the second special gift making expiation for him, and a grain-offering of a tenth of an ephah of flour mixed with oil, and a 22 log of oil, also two turtle-doves or two young pigeons, whichever he can afford, one for a sin-offering and the 23 other for a whole-offering. He shall bring them to the priest for his cleansing on the eighth day, at the entrance to the Tent of the Presence before the 24 LORD. The priest shall take the ram for the guilt-offering and the log of oil, and shall present them as a special gift 25 before the LORD. The ram for the guilt-offering shall then be slaughtered, and the priest shall take some of the blood of the guilt-offering, and put it on the lobe of the right ear of the man to be cleansed and on his right thumb and 26 on the big toe of his right foot. He shall pour some of the oil on the palm of his 27 own left hand and sprinkle some of it with his right forefinger seven times 28 before the LORD. He shall then put some of the oil remaining on his palm on the lobe of the right ear of the man to be cleansed, and on his right thumb and on the big toe of his right foot exactly where the blood of the guilt-29 offering was put. The remainder of the oil on the priest's palm shall be put upon the head of the man to be cleansed to make expiation for him before the 30 LORD. Of the birds which the man has been able to afford, turtle-doves or young pigeons, whichever it may be, 31 the priest shall deal with one as a sin-offering and with the other as a whole-offering and shall make the grain-offering with them. Thus the priest shall make expiation before the LORD for the 32 man who is to be cleansed. This is the law for the man with a malignant skin-disease who cannot afford the regular offering for his cleansing.

33 The LORD spoke to Moses and 34 Aaron and said: When you have entered the land of Canaan which I give you to occupy, if I inflict a fungous infection upon a house in the land you 35 have occupied, its owner shall come and report to the priest that there ap-pears to him to be a patch of infection in his house. The priest shall order the 36 house to be cleared before he goes in to examine the infection, or everything in it will become unclean. After this the priest shall go in to inspect the house. If on inspection he finds the 37 patch on the walls consists of greenish or reddish depressions, apparently going deeper than the surface, he shall 38 go out of the house and, standing at the entrance, shall put it in quarantine for seven days. On the seventh day he 39 shall come back and inspect the house, and if the patch has spread in the walls, he shall order the infected stones to be 40 pulled out and thrown away outside the city in an unclean place. He shall 41 then have the house scraped inside throughout, and all the daub[m] they have scraped off shall be tipped outside the city in an unclean place. They shall 42 take fresh stones to replace the others and replaster the house with fresh daub.

If the infection reappears in the 43 house and spreads after the stones have been pulled out and the house scraped and redaubed, the priest shall 44 come and inspect it. If the infection has spread in the house, it is a corrosive growth; the house is unclean. The 45 house shall be demolished, stones, timber, and daub, and it shall all be taken away outside the city to an unclean place. Anyone who has entered the 46 house during the time it has been in quarantine shall be unclean till evening. Anyone who has slept or eaten a 47 meal in the house shall wash his clothes. But if, when the priest goes 48 into the house and inspects it, he finds that the infection has not spread after the redaubing, then he shall pronounce the house ritually clean, because the infection has been cured.

In order to rid the house of impurity, 49 he shall take two small birds, cedar-wood, scarlet thread, and marjoram. He shall kill one of the birds over an 50 earthenware bowl containing fresh

m Or mud.

ram (1.10–13). **21–32:** Regulations allowing less valuable animals are given in 1.14–17 (whole-offering) and 5.7–13 (sin-offering).
  13.47–59; 14.33–53: Uncleanness in fabric or buildings. *Mould* (13.47) or *fungous infection* (14.34), like fermentation (2.11 n.), are corruptions not to be introduced into the cultic sphere.

51 water. He shall then take the cedar-wood, marjoram, and scarlet thread, together with the living bird, dip them in the blood of the bird that has been killed and in the fresh water, and 52 sprinkle the house seven times. Thus he shall purify the house, using the blood of the bird, the fresh water, the living bird, the cedar-wood, the mar-53 joram, and the scarlet thread. He shall set the living bird free outside the city to fly away over the open country, and make expiation for the house; and then it shall be clean.

54 This is the law for all malignant skin-55 diseases, and for scurf, for mould in 56 clothes and fungus in houses, for a discoloration of the skin, scab, and in-57 flammation, to declare when these are pronounced unclean and when clean. This is the law for skin-disease, mould, and fungus.

15 THE LORD SPOKE TO MOSES AND AARON 2 and said, Speak to the Israelites and say to them: When any man has a discharge from his body, the discharge is 3 ritually unclean. This is the law concerning the uncleanness due to his discharge whether it continues or has been stopped; in either case he is unclean.

4 Every bed on which the man with a discharge lies down shall be ritually unclean, and everything on which he 5 sits shall be unclean. Any man who touches the bed shall wash his clothes, bathe in water and remain unclean till 6 evening. Whoever sits on anything on which the man with a discharge has sat shall wash his clothes, bathe in water and remain unclean till evening. 7 Whoever touches the body of the man with a discharge shall wash his clothes, bathe in water and remain unclean till 8 evening. If the man spits on one who is ritually clean, the latter shall wash his clothes, bathe in water and remain 9 unclean till evening. Everything on

which the man sits when riding shall be unclean. Whoever touches anything 10 that has been under him shall be unclean till evening, and whoever handles such things shall wash his clothes, bathe in water and remain unclean till evening. Anyone whom the man with 11 a discharge touches without having rinsed his hands in water shall wash his clothes, bathe in water and remain unclean till evening. Any earthenware 12 bowl touched by the man shall be smashed, and every wooden bowl shall be rinsed with water.

When the man is cleansed from his 13 discharge, he shall reckon seven days to his cleansing, wash his clothes, bathe his body in fresh water and be ritually clean. On the eighth day he shall ob-14 tain two turtle-doves or two young pigeons and, coming before the LORD at the entrance to the Tent of the Presence, shall give them to the priest. The priest shall deal with one as a sin-15 offering and the other as a whole-offering, and shall make for him before the LORD the expiation required by the discharge.

When a man has emitted semen, he 16 shall bathe his whole body in water and be unclean till evening. Every piece 17 of clothing or skin on which there is any semen shall be washed and remain unclean till evening. This applies also 18 to the woman with whom a man has had intercourse; they shall both bathe themselves in water and remain unclean till evening.

When a woman has a discharge of 19 blood, her impurity shall last for seven days; anyone who touches her shall be unclean till evening. Everything on 20 which she lies or sits during her impurity shall be unclean. Anyone who 21 touches her bed shall wash his clothes, bathe in water and remain unclean till evening. Whoever touches anything on 22 which she sits shall wash his clothes, bathe in water and remain unclean till

---

15.1–33: Uncleanness from genital discharge. 2: *Body:* possibly a polite term for the sex organ (see Ezek.23.20 where the same Heb. word is translated "member"). The condition referred to is likely gonorrhea. **16–18:** The intent is to effect a complete separation between sexual activity and cult worship; the unclean person could not approach the sanctuary. This separation is in sharp contrast to some forms of religious expression among ancient peoples, for whom fertility rites were not uncommon. Compare Gen.19.5 n.; 20.26; Exod.28.42–43. **19–24:** Regulations concerning menstruation.

23 evening. If he is on the bed or seat where she is sitting, by touching it he 24 shall become unclean till evening. If a man goes so far as to have intercourse with her and any of her discharge gets on to him, then he shall be unclean for seven days, and every bed on which he lies down shall be unclean.

25 When a woman has a prolonged discharge of blood not at the time of her menstruation, or when her discharge continues beyond the period of menstruation, her impurity shall last all the time of her discharge; she shall be unclean as during the period of her men- 26 struation. Any bed on which she lies during the time of her discharge shall be like that which she used during menstruation, and everything on which she sits shall be unclean as in her men- 27 strual uncleanness. Every person who touches them shall be unclean; he shall wash his clothes, bathe in water and 28 remain unclean till evening. If she is cleansed from her discharge, she shall reckon seven days and after that she 29 shall be ritually clean. On the eighth day she shall obtain two turtle-doves or two young pigeons and bring them 30 to the priest at the entrance to the Tent of the Presence. The priest shall deal with one as a sin-offering and with the other as a whole-offering, and make for her before the LORD the expiation required by her unclean discharge.

31 In this way you shall warn the Israelites against uncleanness, in order that they may not bring uncleanness upon the Tabernacle where I dwell among them, and so die.

32 This is the law for the man who has a discharge, or who has an emission of 33 semen and is thereby unclean, and for the woman who is suffering her men-

struation—for everyone, male or female, who has a discharge, and for the man who has intercourse with a woman who is unclean.

THE LORD SPOKE TO MOSES AFTER THE **16** death of Aaron's two sons, who died when they offered illicit fire before the LORD. He said to him: Tell your 2 brother Aaron that he must not enter the sanctuary within the Veil, in front of the cover over the Ark, except at the appointed time, on pain of death; for I appear in the cloud above the cover. When Aaron enters the sanctuary, this 3 is what he shall do. He shall bring a young bull for a sin-offering and a ram for a whole-offering. He shall wear a 4 sacred linen tunic and linen drawers to cover himself, and he shall put a linen sash round his waist and wind a linen turban round his head; all these are sacred vestments, and he shall bathe in water before putting them on. He shall 5 take from the community of the Israelites two he-goats for a sin-offering and a ram for a whole-offering. He shall 6 present the bull as a sin-offering and make expiation for himself and his household. Then he shall take the two 7 he-goats and set them before the LORD at the entrance to the Tent of the Presence. He shall cast lots over the two 8 goats, one to be for the LORD and the other for the Precipice.[n] He shall pre- 9 sent the goat on which the lot for the LORD has fallen and deal with it as a sin-offering; but the goat on which the 10 lot for the Precipice has fallen shall be made to stand alive before the LORD, for expiation to be made over it before it is driven away into the wilderness to the Precipice.

n Or for Azazel.

16.1–34: The annual purification ritual purges the sanctuary and forgives the community of the accumulated transgressions which voluntary sin-offerings (4.1–5.13) have not covered. The origin of this regular ritual (v. 29) of the postexilic period is ascribed to the Mosaic age (compare Exod.20.22–23.33 n.; 25.1–31.17 n.; Lev.1.1 n.). The combination of the sins of Nadab and Abihu (10.1–7) plus the presence of their corpses in the sanctuary (v. 1; compare ch. 21) created the need for a special ritual of purification. This section logically follows ch. 10, and the insertion of the laws on uncleanness (chs. 11–15) has served to heighten the need for a regular ritual such as that here described. **2:** Only on this occasion does the sacrifice take the priest *within the veil;* previously mentioned sin-offerings took place either at the sacrificial altar in the Tabernacle court (Exod.27.1 n.) or at the incense-altar in the outer part of the structure (Exod.26.33 n.). See 4.6,17,25,30. *Ark:* see Exod.25.10 n. *Appointed time:* see vv. 29–30. *Death:* see Exod.33.20. *Cloud:* see Exod.19.9 n. **5:** *He-goats:* see 9.15 n. **8:** *Precipice:* see Tfn. *n.* Azazel was possibly the name of a demon who, in earlier times, was thought to be exorcised from the community. **9:** *Lot:* see Exod.28.15 n. **11:** *For himself:* see 9.8–11 n. **14:** *Eastwards:*

11 Aaron shall present his bull as a sin-offering, making expiation for himself and his household, and then slaughter 12 the bull as a sin-offering. He shall take a firepan full of glowing embers from the altar before the LORD, and two handfuls of powdered fragrant incense, 13 and bring them within the Veil. He shall put the incense on the fire before the LORD, and the cloud of incense will hide the cover over the Tokens so that 14 he shall not die. He shall take some of the bull's blood and sprinkle it with his finger both on the surface of the cover, eastwards, and seven times in front of the cover.

15 He shall then slaughter the people's goat as a sin-offering, bring its blood within the Veil and do with its blood as he did with the bull's blood, sprinkling 16 it on the cover and in front of it. He shall make for the sanctuary the expiation required by the ritual uncleanness of the Israelites and their acts of rebellion, that is by all their sins; and he shall do the same for the Tent of the Presence, which dwells among them in 17 the midst of all their uncleanness. No other man shall be within the Tent of the Presence from the time when he enters the sanctuary to make expiation until he comes out, and he shall make expiation for himself, his household, and the whole assembly of Israel.

18 He shall then come out to the altar which is before the LORD and make expiation for it. He shall take some of the bull's blood and some of the goat's 19 blood and put it all over the horns of the altar; he shall sprinkle some of the blood on the altar with his finger seven times. So he shall purify it from all the uncleanness of the Israelites and hallow it.

20 When Aaron has finished making expiation for the sanctuary, for the Tent of the Presence, and for the altar, he shall bring forward the live goat.

He shall lay both his hands on its head 21 and confess over it all the iniquities of the Israelites and all their acts of rebellion, that is all their sins; he shall lay them on the head of the goat and send it away into the wilderness in charge of a man who is waiting ready. The 22 goat shall carry all their iniquities upon itself into some barren waste and the man shall let it go, there in the wilderness.

Aaron shall then enter the Tent of 23 the Presence, take off the linen clothes which he had put on when he entered the sanctuary, and leave them there. He shall bathe in water in a conse- 24 crated place and put on his vestments; then he shall go out and perform his own whole-offering and that of the people, thus making expiation for himself and for the people. He shall burn 25 the fat of the sin-offering upon the altar. The man who drove the goat 26 away to the Precipice shall wash his clothes and bathe in water, and not till then may he enter the camp. The two 27 sin-offerings, the bull and the goat, the blood of which was brought within the Veil to make expiation in the sanctuary, shall be taken outside the camp and destroyed by fire—skin, flesh, and offal. The man who burns them shall 28 wash his clothes and bathe in water, and not till then may he enter the camp.

This shall become a rule binding on 29 you for all time. On the tenth day of the seventh month you shall mortify yourselves; you shall do no work, whether native Israelite or alien settler, because on this day expiation shall be 30 made on your behalf to cleanse you, and so make you clean before the LORD from all your sins. This is a sab- 31 bath of sacred rest for you, and you shall mortify yourselves; it is a rule binding for all time. Expiation shall be 32 made by the priest duly anointed and installed to serve in succession to his

---

the direction of the desert (Wilderness: v. 21), where demons were thought to dwell. **16:** *For the sanctuary:* see 4.13–21 n. **20–22:** The idea of transferring sin to animals is found in many societies. Here, the action may only symbolize the community's freedom from sin. Compare 14.5–7 n. **27:** *Destroyed by fire:* in keeping with the requirements of 4.12,21. **29:** The *tenth day* is near the autumnal equinox, which marked the new year in the older preexilic solar calendar (Ezek.40.1; see Exod.12.2 n.). In 23.27 and 25.9 it is called "the Day of Atonement." Throughout the ancient world, the days of the equinox were marked by rites of mortification (v. 29), purgation (v. 30), and renewal.

father; he shall put on the sacred linen
33 clothes and shall make expiation for
the holy sanctuary, the Tent of the
Presence, and the altar, on behalf of
the priests and the whole assembly of
34 the people. This shall become a rule
binding on you for all time, to make
for the Israelites once a year the expiation required by all their sins.

And Moses carried out the LORD's
commands.

The law of holiness

17 THE LORD SPOKE TO MOSES AND SAID,
2 Speak to Aaron, his sons, and all
the Israelites in these words: This is
3 what the LORD has commanded. Any
Israelite who slaughters an ox, a sheep,
or a goat, either inside or outside the
4 camp, and does not bring it to the
entrance of the Tent of the Presence to
present it as an offering to the LORD
before the Tabernacle of the LORD shall
be held guilty of bloodshed: that man
has shed blood and shall be cut off
5 from his people. The purpose is that
the Israelites should bring to the LORD
the animals which they slaughter in the
open country; they shall bring them to
the priest at the entrance to the Tent of
the Presence and sacrifice them as
shared-offerings to the LORD. The
6 priest shall fling the blood against the
altar of the LORD at the entrance to the
Tent of the Presence, and burn the fat
7 as a soothing odour to the LORD. They
shall no longer sacrifice their slaughtered beasts to the demons*o* whom they

wantonly follow. This shall be a rule
binding on them and their descendants
for all time.

8 You shall say to them: Any Israelite
or alien settled in Israel who offers a
9 whole-offering or a sacrifice and does
not bring it to the entrance of the Tent
of the Presence to sacrifice it to the
LORD shall be cut off from his father's
kin.

10 If any Israelite or alien settled in
Israel eats any blood, I will set my face
against the eater, and cut him off from
11 his people, because the life of a creature is the blood, and I appoint it to
make expiation on the altar for yourselves: it is the blood, that is the life,
12 that makes expiation. Therefore I have
told the Israelites that neither you, nor
any alien settled among you, shall eat
blood.

13 Any Israelite or alien settled in
Israel who hunts beasts or birds that
may lawfully be eaten shall drain out
14 the blood and cover it with earth, because the life of every living creature is
the blood, and I have forbidden the
Israelites to eat the blood of any creature, because the life of every creature
is its blood: every man who eats it shall
be cut off.

15 Every person, native or alien, who
eats that which has died a natural death
or has been mauled by wild beasts shall
wash his clothes and bathe in water,
and remain ritually unclean till eve-
16 ning; then he shall be clean. If he
does not wash his clothes and bathe
his body, he must accept responsibility.

o Or satyrs.

17.1–26.46: The Law of Holiness, by means of which Israel is to be holy because God is holy
(19.2; 20.7–8). This collection of regulations and exhortations, once independent, serves here
to stress the obligations of the community, rather than those of the priests. The section gets its
name, Holiness Code, from the repeated refrain, "You shall be holy."
17.1–16: Regulations concerning the slaughter of animals. 3: *Slaughters:* the animals are here
intended for food. **4:** Contrast the regulations in Deut.12.15,20–21, written earlier, which
exempted food animals from this requirement. The Holiness Code envisages proximity to
Jerusalem, while Deut. supposes possible residence in places far distant from it. *Cut off:* see
7.21 n. **5:** *Bring to the LORD:* i.e. to the Temple in Jerusalem. This mandate reflects a time directly
before or shortly after the Babylonian Exile (see Introduction), when there was a Judean
community, but small and confined to the immediate environs of Jerusalem. **7:** According to
2 Kgs.23.8, a cult of *demons* was widespread in Judah before the Babylonian Exile. The need
to exterminate it seemed sufficient justification for the requirement in vv. 3–6. **8:** *Aliens* were
increasingly common in Judah during the Babylonian Exile and shortly thereafter. **10:** *Blood:*
see also Deut.12.23–25. **11:** *Expiation:* see 4.7 n., and for the rites involved, 4.1–6.7; ch. 16.
13: *Beasts or birds:* nonsacrificial animals. *Lawfully be eaten:* see ch. 11. Every meal involving
meat thus became an opportunity for Israel to remember her special identity, a task which
became increasingly difficult during the exilic and postexilic periods (see Introduction to Lev.
and 11.1–47 n.).

18 THE LORD SPOKE TO MOSES AND SAID,
2 Speak to the Israelites in these words:
3 I am the LORD your God. You shall not
do as they do in Egypt where you once
dwelt, nor shall you do as they do in the
land of Canaan to which I am bringing
you; you shall not conform to their in-
4 stitutions. You must keep my laws and
conform to my institutions without
5 fail: I am the LORD your God. You
shall observe my institutions and my
laws: the man who keeps them shall
have life through them. I am the LORD.
6 No man shall approach a blood-
relation for intercourse. I am the
7 LORD. You shall not bring shame on
your father by intercourse with your
mother: she is your mother; you shall
8 not bring shame upon her. You shall
not have intercourse with your father's
wife: that is to bring shame upon your
9 father. You shall not have intercourse
with your sister, your father's daughter, or your mother's daughter, whether
brought up in the family or in
another home; you shall not bring
10 shame upon them. You shall not have
intercourse with your son's daughter
or your daughter's daughter: that is to
11 bring shame upon yourself. You shall
not have intercourse with a daughter
of your father's wife, begotten by your
father: she is your sister, and you shall
12 not bring shame upon her. You shall
not have intercourse with your father's
sister: she is a blood-relation of your
13 father. You shall not have intercourse
with your mother's sister: she is a
14 blood-relation of your mother. You
shall not bring shame upon your
father's brother by approaching his
15 wife: she is your aunt. You shall not
have intercourse with your daughter-
in-law: she is your son's wife; you
16 shall not bring shame upon her. You
shall not have intercourse with your
brother's wife: that is to bring shame

upon him. You shall not have inter- 17
course with both a woman and her
daughter, nor shall you take her son's
daughter or her daughter's daughter to
have intercourse with them: they are
her blood-relations, and such conduct
is lewdness. You shall not take a 18
woman who is your wife's sister to
make her a rival-wife, and to have
intercourse with her during her sister's
lifetime.

You shall not approach a woman to 19
have intercourse with her during her
period of menstruation. You shall not 20
have sexual intercourse with the wife
of your fellow-countryman and so
make yourself unclean with her. You 21
shall not surrender any of your children
to Molech and thus profane the name
of your God: I am the LORD. You shall 22
not lie with a man as with a woman:
that is an abomination. You shall not 23
have sexual intercourse with any beast
to make yourself unclean with it, nor
shall a woman submit herself to intercourse with a beast: that is a violation
of nature. You shall not make your- 24
selves unclean in any of these ways;
for in these ways the heathen, whom I
am driving out before you, made themselves unclean. This is how the land 25
became unclean, and I punished it for
its iniquity so that it spewed out its
inhabitants. You, unlike them, shall 26
keep my laws and my rules: none of
you, whether natives or aliens settled
among you, shall do any of these
abominable things. The people who 27
were there before you did these abominable things and the land became unclean. So the land will not spew you out 28
for making it unclean as it spewed them
out; for anyone who does any of these 29
abominable things shall be cut off from
his people. Observe my charge, there- 30
fore, and follow none of the abominable
institutions customary before your

18.1–30: Prohibited sexual relations. 2: *I am the* LORD *your God:* the introductory words
of the covenant ceremony (Exod.20.2), calling to mind the LORD's gracious deeds for Israel, and
Israel's need of obedience. **3:** On Canaanite sexual practices, see Gen.19.5 n. **11:** Marriage to a
half-sister was previously allowable (Gen.20.12 n.). **12:** Marriage to an aunt was apparently
acceptable at an earlier time. Indeed, Moses and Aaron were the product of such a union
(Exod.6.20). **16:** *Brother's wife:* while he is alive. After his death, however, such a marriage
could become an obligation (Deut.25.5–10 n.). **18:** Marriage to women who were sisters was
allowable at an earlier time (Gen.29.1–30). **21:** The Ammonite god was offered child sacrifices
by fire (Jer.32.35). **25–29:** That Israel has already settled in Canaan seems clearly presupposed.
Compare Exod.20.22–23.33 n.

time; do not make yourselves unclean with them. I am the LORD your God.

19 THE LORD SPOKE TO MOSES AND SAID,
2 Speak to all the community of the Israelites in these words: You shall be holy, because I, the LORD your God,
3 am holy. You shall revere, every man of you, his mother and his father. You shall keep my sabbaths. I am the LORD
4 your God. Do not resort to idols; you shall not make gods of cast metal for yourselves. I am the LORD your God.
5 When you sacrifice a shared-offering to the LORD, you shall slaughter it so as
6 to win acceptance for yourselves. It must be eaten on the day of your sacrifice or the next day. Whatever is left over till the third day shall be destroyed
7 by fire; it is tainted, and if any of it is eaten on the third day, it will not be
8 acceptable. He who eats it must accept responsibility, because he has profaned the holy-gift to the LORD: that person shall be cut off from his father's kin.
9 When you reap the harvest of your land, you shall not reap right into the edges of your field; neither shall you
10 glean the loose ears of your crop; you shall not completely strip your vineyard nor glean the fallen grapes. You shall leave them for the poor and the alien. I am the LORD your God.
11 You shall not steal; you shall not cheat or deceive a fellow-countryman.
12 You shall not swear in my name with intent to deceive and thus profane the name of your God. I am the LORD.
13 You shall not oppress your neighbour, nor rob him. You shall not keep back a hired man's wages till next morning.
14 You shall not treat the deaf with contempt, nor put an obstruction in the way of the blind. You shall fear your God. I am the LORD.

15 You shall not pervert justice, either by favouring the poor or by subservience to the great. You shall judge your fellow-countryman with strict justice.
16 You shall not go about spreading slander among your father's kin, nor take sides against your neighbour on a
17 capital charge. I am the LORD. You shall not nurse hatred against your brother. You shall reprove your fellow-countryman frankly and so you will
18 have no share in his guilt.*p* You shall not seek revenge, or cherish anger towards your kinsfolk; you shall love your neighbour as a man like yourself. I am the LORD.
19 You shall keep my rules. You shall not allow two different kinds of beast to mate together. You shall not plant your field with two kinds of seed. You shall not put on a garment woven with two kinds of yarn.
20 When a man has intercourse with a slave-girl who has been assigned to another man and neither ransomed nor given her freedom, inquiry shall be made. They shall not be put to death, because she has not been freed. The
21 man shall bring his guilt-offering, a ram, to the LORD to the entrance of the Tent of the Presence, and with it the
22 priest shall make expiation for him before the LORD for his sin, and he shall be forgiven the sin he has committed.
23 When you enter the land, and plant any kind of tree for food, you shall treat it as bearing forbidden fruit. For three years it shall be forbidden and
24 may not be eaten. In the fourth year all its fruit shall be a holy-gift to the LORD, and this releases it for use. In the fifth
25 year you may eat its fruit, and thus the yield it gives you shall be increased. I am the LORD your God.

p Or and for that you will incur no blame.

19.1–37: **Diverse social and cultic regulations,** possibly constructed around a version of part of the Ten Commandments (vv. 3–4,11–12; see Exod.20.1–21 n.). The importance of these guidelines is emphasized by the repeated remark, "I am the LORD" (18.2 n.). **2:** There is stressed here the theme for man's obedience: his imitation of God's holiness. **6:** See 7.16–18. **18:** See Mk.12.28–31. This love is to be extended to the alien as well (vv. 33–34). See Lk.10.29–37. **19:** Fabric made of the *two kinds of yarn* was reserved for the sanctuary (Exod.26.1) and the garments of the Aaronite priest (Exod.28.5–6). **20:** *Assigned:* chosen for marriage. **21:** Since a *guilt-offering* would be accompanied by compensation for damages (see 6.1–7), the law is concerned not only with the sin of illicit intercourse but also with the damages to the owner who could not sell her as a virgin. **23–25:** The purpose behind this legislation is obscure; perhaps the Canaanites regarded the *tree* as a new creation of the fertility gods. Here, it is enjoined simply as the demand of the LORD, although the language of MT in v. 23 (lit. "you will leave its foreskin, namely its fruit, uncircumcised") draws on the analogy of the male child who can

26 You shall not eat meat with the blood in it. You shall not practise 27 divination or soothsaying. You shall not round off your hair from side to side, and you shall not shave the edge 28 of your beards. You shall not gash yourselves in mourning for the dead; you shall not tattoo yourselves. I am the LORD.

29 Do not prostitute your daughter and so make her a whore; thus the land shall not play the prostitute and be full 30 of lewdness. You shall keep my sabbaths, and revere my sanctuary. I am the LORD.

31 Do not resort to ghosts and spirits, nor make yourselves unclean by seeking them out. I am the LORD your God.

32 You shall rise in the presence of grey hairs, give honour to the aged, and fear God. I am the LORD.

33 When an alien settles with you in your land, you shall not oppress him. 34 He shall be treated as a native born among you, and you shall love him as a man like yourself, because you were aliens in Egypt. I am the LORD your God.

35 You shall not pervert justice in measurement of length, weight, or quantity. 36 You shall have true scales, true weights, true measures dry and liquid. I am the LORD your God who brought you out 37 of Egypt. You shall observe all my rules and laws and carry them out. I am the LORD.

20 The LORD spoke to Moses and said, 2 Say to the Israelites: Any Israelite or alien settled in Israel who gives any of his children to Molech shall be put to death: the common people shall stone 3 him. I, for my part, set my face against that man and cut him off from his people, because he has given a child of his to Molech, thus making my sanctuary unclean and profaning my holy name. If the common people connive 4 at it when a man has given a child of his to Molech and do not put him to death, I will set my face against man 5 and family, and both him and all who follow him in his wanton following after Molech,*q* I will cut off from their people.

I will set my face against the man 6 who wantonly resorts to ghosts and spirits, and I will cut that person off 7 from his people. Hallow yourselves and 7 be holy, because I the LORD your God am holy. You shall keep my rules and 8 obey them: I am the LORD who hallows you.

When any man reviles his father and 9 his mother, he shall be put to death. He has reviled his father and his mother; his blood shall be on his own head. If a man commits adultery with 10 his neighbour's wife, both adulterer and adulteress shall be put to death. The man who has intercourse with his 11 father's wife has brought shame on his father. They shall both be put to death; their blood shall be on their own heads. If a man has intercourse with his 12 daughter-in-law, they shall both be put to death. Their deed is a violation of nature; their blood shall be on their own heads. If a man has intercourse 13 with a man as with a woman, they both commit an abomination. They shall be put to death; their blood shall be on their own heads. If a man takes both 14 a woman and her mother, that is lewdness. Both he and they shall be burnt; thus there shall be no lewdness in your midst. A man who has sexual 15 intercourse with any beast shall be put to death, and you shall kill the beast. If a woman approaches any animal to 16

q Or in his lusting after human sacrifice.

only be dedicated after circumcision. **26:** *Divination or soothsaying:* methods of determining the divine will, practiced in the cults of Israel's neighbors. **27–28:** These actions are possibly forbidden because of their role in the cult of Canaanite gods. **29:** Sacred, rather than ordinary, prostitution is meant. See Gen.38.21 n. **31:** The dead were supposed to have knowledge of the future. See 1 Sam. ch. 28.

20.1–27: Transgressions punishable by death. The subject matter is essentially that of ch. 18, but now with penalties attached. Perhaps the two chapters were once independent, self-contained units. **2:** *Molech:* see 18.21 n. **3:** *Cut him off:* see 7.21 n. *Sanctuary unclean:* compare 4.13–21 n. **10–16:** The community is to apply the death penalty for these sexual offenses, as opposed to those in vv. 17–21 where retribution is seemingly left to the deity. Since these relationships (in vv. 17–21) had been practiced in an earlier age (18.11–12 nn., 18.18 n.), their prohibition was likely regarded as unenforceable.

have intercourse with it, you shall kill both woman and beast. They shall be put to death; their blood shall be on 17 their own heads. If a man takes his sister, his father's daughter or his mother's daughter, and they see one another naked, it is a scandalous disgrace. They shall be cut off in the presence of their people. The man has had intercourse with his sister and he shall 18 accept responsibility. If a man lies with a woman during her monthly period and brings shame upon her, he has exposed her discharge and she has uncovered the source of her discharge; they shall both be cut off from their 19 people. You shall not have intercourse with your mother's sister or your father's sister: it is the exposure of a blood-relation. They shall accept re- 20 sponsibility. A man who has intercourse with his uncle's wife has brought shame upon his uncle. They shall accept responsibility for their sin and shall be proscribed and put to death. 21 If a man takes his brother's wife, it is impurity. He has brought shame upon his brother; they shall be proscribed.

22   You shall keep all my rules and my laws and carry them out, that the land into which I am bringing you to live 23 may not spew you out. You shall not conform to the institutions of the nations whom I am driving out before you: they did all these things and I 24 abhorred them, and I told you that you should occupy their land, and I would give you possession of it, a land flowing with milk and honey. I am the LORD your God: I have made a clear separation between you and the na- 25 tions, and you shall make a clear separation between clean beasts and unclean beasts and between unclean and clean birds. You shall not make yourselves vile through beast or bird or anything that creeps on the ground, for I have made a clear separation between them and you, declaring them 26 unclean. You shall be holy to me, because I the LORD am holy. I have made a clear separation between you and the heathen, that you may belong to me.

Any man or woman among you who 27 calls up ghosts or spirits shall be put to death. The people shall stone them; their blood shall be on their own heads.

THE LORD SAID TO MOSES, SAY TO THE 21 priests, the sons of Aaron: A priest shall not render himself unclean for the death of any of his kin except for a near 2 blood-relation, that is for mother, father, son, daughter, brother, or full 3 sister who is unmarried and a virgin; nor shall he make himself unclean for 4 any married woman[r] among his father's kin, and so profane himself.

Priests shall not make bald patches 5 on their heads as a sign of mourning, nor cut the edges of their beards, nor gash their bodies. They shall be holy to 6 their God, and they shall not profane the name of their God, because they present the food-offerings of the LORD, the food of their God, and they shall be holy. A priest shall not marry a 7 prostitute or a girl who has lost her virginity, nor shall he marry a woman divorced from her husband; for he is holy to his God. You shall keep him 8 holy because he presents the food of your God; you shall regard him as holy because I the LORD, I who hallow them, am holy. When a priest's daughter pro- 9 fanes herself by becoming a prostitute, she profanes her father. She shall be burnt to death.

The high priest, the one among his 10 fellows who has had the anointing oil poured on his head and has been consecrated to wear the vestments, shall neither leave his hair dishevelled nor tear his clothes. He shall not enter the 11 place where any man's dead body lies; not even for his father or his mother shall he render himself unclean. He 12 shall not go out of the sanctuary for fear that he dishonour the sanctuary of his God, because the consecration of the anointing oil of his God is upon him. I am the LORD. He shall marry a 13 woman who is still a virgin. He shall 14 not marry a widow, a divorced woman, a woman who has lost her virginity, or

r for any married woman: prob. rdg.; Heb. husband.

21.1–24: The preservation of priestly sanctity. On the importance of this, see 4.3 n. **1:** *Render himself unclean:* by participating in the funeral rites (see Num.19.11–19). **5:** See 19.27–28 n. **10–12:** See 10.6 n.; 10.7 n. **16–23:** Compare 12.4 n.; 13.1–46 n.

15 a prostitute, but only a virgin from his father's kin; he shall not dishonour his descendants among his father's kin, for I am the LORD who hallows him.

16 The LORD spoke to Moses and said, 17 Speak to Aaron in these words: No man among your descendants for all time who has any physical defect shall come and present the food of his God. 18 No man with a defect shall come, whether a blind man, a lame man, a 19 man stunted or overgrown, a man de-20 formed in foot or hand, or with mis-shapen brows or a film over his eye or a discharge from it, a man who has a scab or eruption or has had a testicle 21 ruptured. No descendant of Aaron the priest who has any defect in his body shall approach to present the food-offerings of the LORD; because he has a defect he shall not approach to pre-22 sent the food of his God. He may eat the bread of God both from the holy-gifts and from the holiest of holy-gifts, 23 but he shall not come up to the Veil nor approach the altar, because he has a defect in his body. Thus he shall not profane my sanctuaries, because I am the LORD who hallows them.

24 Thus did Moses speak to Aaron and his sons and to all the Israelites.

22 The LORD spoke to Moses and said, 2 Tell Aaron and his sons that they must be careful in the handling of the holy-gifts of the Israelites which they hallow to me, lest they profane my holy name. 3 I am the LORD. Say to them: Any man of your descent for all time who while unclean approaches the holy-gifts which the Israelites hallow to the LORD shall be cut off from my presence. I 4 am the LORD. No man descended from Aaron who suffers from a malignant skin-disease, or has a discharge, shall eat of the holy-gifts until he is cleansed. A man who touches anything which makes him unclean or who has an 5 emission of semen, a man who touches any vermin which makes him unclean or any human being who makes him 6 unclean: any person who touches such a thing shall be unclean till sunset and

unless he washes his body shall not eat of the holy-gifts. When the sun 7 goes down, he shall be clean, and after that he may eat from the holy-gifts, because they are his food. He shall not 8 eat an animal that has died a natural death or has been mauled by wild beasts, thereby making himself un-clean. I am the LORD. The priests shall 9 observe my charge, lest they make themselves guilty and die for profaning my name. I am the LORD who hallows them. No unqualified person may eat 10 any holy-gift; nor may a stranger lodg-ing with a priest or a hired man eat a holy-gift. A slave bought by a priest with 11 his own money may do so, and slaves born in his household may also share his food. When a priest's daughter mar-12 ries an unqualified person, she shall not eat any of the contributions of holy-gifts; but if she is widowed or divorced 13 and is childless and comes back to her father's house as in her childhood, she shall share her father's food. No un-qualified person may eat any of it.

When a man inadvertently eats a 14 holy-gift, he shall make good the holy-gift to the priest, adding a fifth to its value. The priests shall not profane the 15 holy-gifts of the Israelites which they set aside for the LORD; they shall not 16 let men eat their holy-gifts and so incur guilt and its penalty, because I am the LORD who hallows them.

The LORD spoke to Moses and said, 17 Speak to Aaron and his sons and to all 18 the Israelites in these words: When any man of the house of Israel or any alien in Israel presents, whether in fulfilment of a vow or for a freewill offering, such an offering as is presented to the LORD for a whole-offering so as to win ac-19 ceptance for yourselves, it shall be a male without defect, of cattle, sheep, or goats. You shall not present any-20 thing which is defective, because it will not be acceptable on your behalf. When a man presents a shared-offering 21 to the LORD, whether cattle or sheep, to fulfil a special[s] vow or as a freewill

s fulfil a special: or discharge a . . .

22.1–33: Preservation of the sanctity of sacrificial gifts. These rules concern those who may consume the parts of the sacrifice reserved for priests (2.3; 5.13; 6.16–18,29–30; 7.6–10). **3:** *Unclean:* as defined by the regulations in chs. 11–15. **10:** *Unqualified person:* a nonpriest. **16:** The priest is forbidden to give or sell the sacrificial food to the unsuspecting layman and

offering, if it is to be acceptable it must be perfect; there shall be no defect in 22 it. You shall present to the LORD nothing blind, disabled, mutilated, with running sore, scab, or eruption, nor set any such creature on the altar as a food-23 offering to the LORD. If a bull or a sheep is overgrown or stunted, you may make of it a freewill offering, but it will not be acceptable in fulfilment of a vow. 24 If its testicles have been crushed or bruised, torn or cut, you shall not present it to the LORD; this is forbidden in your land. 25 You shall not procure any such creature from a foreigner and present it as food for your God. Their deformity is inherent in them, a permanent defect, and they will not be acceptable on your behalf. 26 The LORD spoke to Moses and said: 27 When a calf, a lamb, or a kid is born, it must not be taken from its mother for seven days. From the eighth day onwards it will be acceptable when offered as a food-offering to the LORD. 28 You shall not slaughter a cow or sheep 29 at the same time as its young. When you make a thank-offering to the LORD, you shall sacrifice it so as to win ac-30 ceptance for yourselves; it shall be eaten that same day, and none be left till morning. I am the LORD. 31 You shall observe my commandments and perform them. I am the 32 LORD. You shall not profane my holy name; I will be hallowed among the Israelites. I am the LORD who hallows 33 you, who brought you out of Egypt to become your God. I am the LORD.

23 THE LORD SPOKE TO MOSES AND SAID, 2 Speak to the Israelites in these words: These are the appointed seasons of the LORD, and you shall proclaim them as sacred assemblies; these are my ap-3 pointed seasons. On six days work may be done, but every seventh day is a sabbath of sacred rest, a day of sacred assembly, on which you shall do no work. Wherever you live, it is the LORD's sabbath.

These are the appointed seasons of 4 the LORD, the sacred assemblies which you shall proclaim in their appointed order. In the first month on the four- 5 teenth day between dusk and dark is the LORD's Passover. On the fifteenth 6 day of this month begins the LORD's pilgrim-feast of Unleavened Bread; for seven days you shall eat unleavened cakes. On the first day there shall be a 7 sacred assembly; you shall not do your daily work. For seven days you shall 8 present your food-offerings to the LORD. On the seventh day also there shall be a sacred assembly; you shall not do your daily work.

The LORD spoke to Moses and said, 9 Speak to the Israelites in these words: 10 When you enter the land which I give you, and you reap its harvest, you shall bring the first sheaf of your harvest to the priest. He shall present the sheaf 11 as a special gift before the LORD on*t* the day after the sabbath, so as to gain acceptance for yourselves. On the day 12 you present the sheaf, you shall prepare a perfect yearling ram for a whole-offering to the LORD, with the proper 13 grain-offering, two tenths of an ephah of flour mixed with oil, as a food-offering to the LORD, of soothing odour, and also with the proper drink-offering, a quarter of a hin of wine. You shall eat neither bread, nor grain, 14 parched or fully ripened, during that day, the day on which you bring your God his offering; this is a rule binding on your descendants for all time wherever you live.

From the day after the sabbath, the 15 day on which you bring your sheaf as a special gift, you shall count seven full weeks. The day after the seventh sab- 16 bath will make fifty days, and then you shall present to the LORD a grain-

t Or from.

---

then collect a fine from him (v. 15). **26–27:** Compare 19.23–25 n. **28:** Such may have been a Canaanite cult practice. **29–30:** See 7.11–15. **31–33:** See 18.2 n.

23.1–44: The calendar of the sacred days. 2: The entire community is addressed, since it is the obligation of every individual to observe the sacred occasions. **4:** *Assemblies:* festivals requiring pilgrimage to the sanctuary. See Deut.16.16. **5:** *Passover:* see Exod.12.1–27 and the notes. **6:** *Unleavened bread:* Exod.12.15 n. **9:** This second introduction suggests that a once independent regulation about Passover has been joined to the context. **10:** The *first sheaf* was of barley, which ripened in April. **16:** *Fifty days* (Gk. "Pentecost"): see Exod.23.16 n. This

17 offering from the new crop. You shall bring from your homes two loaves as a special gift; they shall contain two tenths of an ephah of flour and shall be baked with leaven. They are the
18 LORD's firstfruits. In addition to the bread you shall present seven perfect yearling sheep, one young bull, and two rams. They shall be a whole-offering to the LORD with the proper grain-offering and the proper drink-offering, a food-offering of soothing
19 odour to the LORD. You shall also prepare one he-goat for a sin-offering and two yearling sheep for a shared-
20 offering, and the priest shall present them in addition to the bread of the first-fruits as a special gift before the LORD. They shall be a holy-gift to
21 the LORD for the priest. On that same day you shall proclaim a sacred assembly for yourselves; you shall not do your daily work. This is a rule binding on your descendants for all time wherever you live.
22 When you reap the harvest in your land, you shall not reap right into the edges of your field, neither shall you glean the fallen ears. You shall leave them for the poor and for the alien. I am the LORD your God.
23 The LORD spoke to Moses and said,
24 Speak to the Israelites in these words: In the seventh month you shall keep the first day as a sacred rest, a day of remembrance and acclamation, a day
25 of sacred assembly. You shall not do your daily work; you shall present a food-offering to the LORD.
26 The LORD spoke to Moses and said:
27 Further, the tenth day of this seventh month is the Day of Atonement. There shall be a sacred assembly; you shall mortify yourselves and present a food-
28 offering to the LORD. On that same day you shall do no work because it is a day of expiation, to make expiation for you
29 before the LORD your God. Therefore every person who does not mortify himself on that day shall be cut off
30 from his father's kin. I will extirpate any person who does any work on that

31 day. You shall do no work; it is a rule binding on your descendants for all time wherever you live. It is for you a
32 sabbath of sacred rest, and you shall mortify yourselves. From the evening of the ninth day to the following evening you shall keep your sabbath-rest.
33 The LORD spoke to Moses and said,
34 Speak to the Israelites in these words: On the fifteenth day of this seventh month the LORD's pilgrim-feast of Tabernacles[u] begins, and it lasts for
35 seven days. On the first day there shall be a sacred assembly; you shall not do your daily work. For seven days you
36 shall present a food-offering to the LORD; and on the eighth day there shall be a sacred assembly, and you shall present a food-offering to the LORD. It is the closing ceremony; you shall not do your daily work.
37 These are the appointed seasons of the LORD which you shall proclaim as sacred assemblies for presenting food-offerings to the LORD, whole-offerings and grain offerings, shared-offerings and drink-offerings, each on its day,
38 besides the LORD's sabbaths and all your gifts, your vows, and your freewill offerings to the LORD.
39 Further, from the fifteenth day of the seventh month, when the harvest has been gathered, you shall keep the LORD's pilgrim-feast for seven days. The first day is a sacred rest and so is
40 the eighth day. On the first day you shall take the fruit of citrus-trees, palm fronds, and leafy branches, and willows[v] from the riverside, and you shall rejoice before the LORD your God for
41 seven days. You shall keep this as a pilgrim-feast in the LORD's honour for seven days every year. It is a rule binding for all time on your descendants; in the seventh month you shall hold
42 this pilgrim-feast. You shall live in arbours for seven days, all who are native Israelites, so that your de-
43 scendants may be reminded how I made the Israelites live in arbours when

u Or Booths *or* Arbours.
v Or poplars.

---

observance was of the wheat harvest in May or June. **22:** See 19.9–10. **23:** See v. 9 n. **24–25:** The new year day. It varies in biblical calendars, at times in the fall, and at times in the spring (see Exod.12.2 n.). **26–32:** The ritual is outlined in ch. 16. **34:** *Tabernacles:* see Exod.23.16 n. **43:** An old Canaanite agricultural festival is here connected with the LORD's gracious deliverance

I brought them out of Egypt. I am the LORD your God.

44 Thus Moses announced to the Israelites the appointed seasons of the LORD.

24 THE LORD SPOKE TO MOSES AND SAID:
2 Command the Israelites to take pure oil of pounded olives ready for the regular
3 mounting of the lamp outside the Veil of the Tokens in the Tent of the Presence. Aaron shall keep the lamp in trim regularly from dusk to dawn before the LORD: this is a rule binding
4 on your descendants for all time. The lamps on the lamp-stand, ritually clean, shall be regularly kept in trim by him before the LORD.

5 You shall take flour and bake it into twelve loaves, two tenths of an ephah
6 to each. You shall arrange them in two rows, six to a row on the table,
7 ritually clean, before the LORD. You shall sprinkle pure frankincense on the rows, and this shall be a token of the bread, offered to the LORD as a food-
8 offering. Sabbath after sabbath he shall arrange it regularly before the LORD as a gift from the Israelites. This is a
9 covenant for ever; it is the privilege of Aaron and his sons, and they shall eat the bread in a holy place, because it is the holiest of holy-gifts. It is his due out of the food-offerings of the LORD for all time.

10-11 Now there was in the Israelite camp a man whose mother was an Israelite and his father an Egyptian; his mother's name was Shelomith daughter of Dibri of the tribe of Dan; and he went out and became involved in a brawl with an Israelite of pure descent.

He uttered the Holy Name in blasphemy, so they brought him to Moses;
12 and they kept him in custody until the LORD's will should be clearly made known to them.

13 The LORD spoke to Moses and said,
14 Take the man who blasphemed out of the camp. Everyone who heard him shall put a hand[w] on his head, and then all the community shall stone him to death.
15 You shall say to the Israelites: When any man whatever blasphemes his God, he shall accept responsibility for his sin.
16 Whoever utters the Name of the LORD shall be put to death: all the community shall stone him; alien or native, if he utters the Name, he shall be put to death.

17 When one man strikes another and kills him, he shall be put to death.
18 Whoever strikes a beast and kills it shall make restitution, life for life.
19 When one man injures and disfigures his fellow-countryman, it shall be done to him as he has done;
20 fracture for fracture, eye for eye, tooth for tooth; the injury and disfigurement that he has inflicted upon another shall in turn be inflicted upon him.

21 Whoever strikes a beast and kills it shall make restitution, but whoever strikes a man and kills him shall be put to death.
22 You shall have one penalty for alien and native alike. For I am the LORD your God.

23 Thus did Moses speak to the Israelites, and they took the man who blasphemed out of the camp and stoned him to death. The Israelites did as the LORD had commanded Moses.

w Or their hands.

of Israel: the harvester's temporary shelter imitates the dwellings in the Wilderness (compare Exod.12.11–13 n., 15 n.). Thus, that great event was to be "relived" annually (compare Exod.13.8 n.).

24.1–9: Regulations concerning the sanctuary. This belongs topically with the instructions to the priests found in chs. 21–22; the concern with the calendar (ch. 23) resumes in ch. 25. Ch. 24 is possibly a priestly addition to the Holiness Code (see 17.1–26.46 n.). **3:** *From dusk to dawn:* a change from earlier practice in which the lamp did not burn to dawn (1 Sam.3.4). **5:** *Twelve:* one for each of the twelve tribes of Israel. **7:** *Token:* and hence to be burned at the weekly renewal of the bread (compare 2.1–3). Topically, vv. 5–9 belong with the instructions for the priests in 6.14–23.

24.10–16: An instance of contempt for God (blasphemy). The intent is not only to provide legislation through a precedent-setting case, but also to recall how the alien was protected under law, and his near equality to the native (16.29; 17.8–16; 19.33–34). **11:** *Blasphemy* was cursing God, or showing contempt for him by word or action (see Num.15.30–31; compare Isa.36.18–20; 37.6). Blasphemy is extended in v. 16 to the mere pronunciation of the divine name, Yahweh. **13–15:** Compare Deut.17.2–7.

24.17–22: The law of retaliation, topically related to vv. 10–16 by the theme of capital punishment and equality under the law. **19–20:** See Exod.21.23–25 n.

25 THE LORD SPOKE TO MOSES ON MOUNT
2 Sinai and said, Speak to the Israelites
in these words: When you enter the
land which I give you, the land shall
3 keep sabbaths to the LORD. For six
years you may sow your fields and for
six years prune your vineyards and
4 gather the harvest, but in the seventh
year the land shall keep a sabbath of
sacred rest, a sabbath to the LORD. You
shall not sow your field nor prune your
5 vineyard. You shall not harvest the
crop that grows from fallen grain, nor
gather in the grapes from the unpruned
vines. It shall be a year of sacred rest for
6 the land. Yet what the land itself produces in the sabbath year shall be food
for you, for your male and female
slaves, for your hired man, and for the
7 stranger lodging under your roof, for
your cattle and for the wild animals in
your country. Everything it produces
may be used for food.

8   You shall count seven sabbaths of
years, that is seven times seven years,
9 forty-nine years, and in the seventh
month on the tenth day of the month,
on the Day of Atonement, you shall
send the ram's horn round. You shall
send it through all your land to sound
10 a blast, and so you shall hallow the
fiftieth year and proclaim liberation
in the land for all its inhabitants. You
shall make this your year of jubilee.
Every man of you shall return to his
patrimony, every man to his family.
11 The fiftieth year shall be your jubilee.
You shall not sow, and you shall not
harvest the self-sown crop, nor shall
you gather in the grapes from the un-
12 pruned vines, because it is a jubilee,

to be kept holy by you. You shall eat
the produce direct from the land.

In this year of jubilee you shall re- 13
turn, every one of you, to his patrimony. When you sell or buy land 14
amongst yourselves, neither party shall
drive a hard bargain. You shall pay 15
your fellow-countryman according to
the number of years since the jubilee,
and he shall sell to you according to
the number of annual crops. The more 16
years there are to run, the higher the
price, the fewer the years, the lower,
because he is selling you a series of
crops. You must not victimize one 17
another, but you shall fear your God,
because I am the LORD your God.
Observe my statutes, keep my judge- 18
ments and carry them out; and you
shall live in the land in security. The 19
land shall yield its harvest; you shall
eat your fill and live there secure. If 20
you ask what you are to eat during the
seventh year, seeing that you will
neither sow nor gather the harvest, I 21
will ordain my blessing for you in the
sixth year and the land shall produce a
crop to carry over three years. When 22
you sow in the eighth year, you will
still be eating from the earlier crop;
you shall eat the old until the new crop
is gathered in the ninth year.

No land shall be sold outright, be- 23
cause the land is mine, and you are
coming into it as aliens and settlers.
Throughout the whole land of your 24
patrimony, you shall allow land which
has been sold to be redeemed.

When one of you is reduced to pov- 25
erty and sells part of his patrimony,
his next-of-kin who has the duty of

25.1–55: The sabbatical and Jubilee years. The former celebration (vv. 2–7) symbolizes the
LORD's ultimate ownership of the land; the latter (vv. 8–34) attempts to prevent the growth of
economic classes. **1:** That this legislation is allocated to *Sinai*, rather than to the Tent of the
Presence (1.1 and subsequent chapter headings), suggests not only its original independence of
the present context but also its importance in the opinion of those who transmitted it. The
legislation assumes the settlement of Israel in Canaan and subsequent economic abuses. **4:** The
application of the *sacred rest* notion to the *sabbath* of the *land* introduces a dimension absent
from the form of the regulation given in Exod.23.10–11. **6:** Permission for the owner to benefit
from the land also differs from Exod.23.10–11 and may be a concession to economic necessity
or to the impossibility of strict enforcement. **8–12:** A brief summary of the Jubilee regulation.
9: *Day of Atonement:* see 16.29 n. *Ram's horn:* in Heb. *yobhel*, whence the English word
"jubilee." The horn was blown to announce the celebration (compare Exod.19.16 n.). **10:** "Sale"
or "lease" of land was not in perpetuity; rather, land was to return to the original owner at
the Jubilee. This is expanded in vv. 23–28. **15–16:** In addition to area and fertility, the value
of land to be leased depended on the duration of the contract, the maximum being until the
next Jubilee. **23:** The LORD had given the land to Israel through no merit of her own (Deut.
9.1–6) and hence it is not hers to use for unrestrained personal gain. Man is only an *alien,*

redemption shall come and redeem
26 what his kinsman has sold. When a
man has no such next-of-kin and himself becomes able to afford its re-
27 demption, he shall take into account
the years since the sale and pay the
purchaser the balance up to the
jubilee. Then he may return to his
28 patrimony. But if the man cannot
afford to buy back the property, it shall
remain in the hands of the purchaser
till the year of jubilee. It shall then
revert to the original owner, and he
shall return to his patrimony.
29 When a man sells a dwelling-house
in a walled town, he shall retain the
right of redemption till the end of the
year of the sale; for a time he shall
30 have the right of redemption. If it is not
redeemed before a full year is out, the
house in the walled town shall vest in
perpetuity in the buyer and his descendants; it shall not revert at the
31 jubilee. Houses in unwalled hamlets
shall be treated as property in the open
country: the right of redemption shall
hold good, and in any case the house
32 shall revert at the jubilee. Levites shall
have the perpetual right to redeem
houses of their own patrimony in
33 towns belonging to them. If one of the
Levites does not redeem his house in
such a town, then it shall still revert to
him at the jubilee, because the houses
in Levite towns are their patrimony in
34 Israel. The common land surrounding
their towns shall not be sold, because
it is their property in perpetuity.
35 When your brother-Israelite is reduced to poverty and cannot support
himself in the community, you shall
assist him as you would an alien or a
stranger, and he shall live with you.
36 You shall not charge him interest on a
loan, either by deducting it in advance
from the capital sum, or by adding it
on repayment. You shall fear your
God, and your brother shall live with

37 you; you shall not deduct interest when
advancing him money nor add interest
to the payment due for food supplied
on credit. I am the LORD your God
38 who brought you out of Egypt to give
you the land of Canaan and to become
your God.
39 When your brother is reduced to
poverty and sells himself to you, you
shall not use him to work for you as a
40 slave. His status shall be that of a hired
man or a stranger lodging with you;
he shall work for you until the year of
41 jubilee. He shall then leave your service, with his children, and go back to
his family and to his ancestral prop-
42 erty: because they are my slaves
whom I brought out of Egypt, they
43 shall not be sold as slaves are sold. You
shall not drive him with ruthless
severity, but you shall fear your God.
44 Such slaves as you have, male or
female, shall come from the nations
round about you; from them you may
45 buy slaves. You may also buy the children of those who have settled and
lodge with you and such of their family
as are born in the land. These may be-
46 come your property, and you may
leave them to your sons after you; you
may use them as slaves permanently.
But your fellow-Israelites you shall not
drive with ruthless severity.
47 When an alien or a stranger living
with you becomes rich, and your
brother becomes poor and sells himself
to the alien or stranger or to a member
48 of some alien family, he shall have the
right of redemption after he has sold
himself. One of his brothers may re-
49 deem him, or his uncle, his cousin, or
any blood-relation of his family, or, if
he can afford it, he may redeem him-
50 self. He and his purchaser together
shall reckon from the year when he sold
himself to the year of jubilee, and the
price shall be adjusted to the number
of years. His period of service with his

dependent upon the LORD's land. **29–31:** City property is exempted from the law of redemption.
32–34: The Levites, having no tribal territory of their own (Num.18.20–24; 35.1–8; Deut.
10.8–9; see Gen.34.1–31 n.), must be protected from dispossession more rigidly than the
general population. **38:** Just as the LORD aided the landless, alien Hebrews in Egypt, so must
they respond to the needs of those around them. See 18.2 n.; Deut.5.12–15. **42–43:** Members
of the community are, like land (v. 23 n.), the possession of the LORD. **44–46:** There are striking
differences between the legislation here and that of Exod.21.1–11 (see especially Exod.21.2 n.).
47–48: On the status of aliens under Israelite law, see 24.10–16 n.

owner shall be reckoned at the rate of a
51 hired man. If there are still many years
to run to the year of jubilee, he must
repay for his redemption a propor-
tionate amount of the sum for which
52 he sold himself; if there are few, he shall
53 reckon and repay accordingly. He shall
have the status of a labourer hired from
year to year, and you shall not let him
be driven with ruthless severity by his
54 owner. If the man is not redeemed in
the intervening years, he and his children shall be released in the year of
55 jubilee; for it is to me that the Israelites
are slaves, my slaves whom I brought
out of Egypt. I am the LORD your God.

26 YOU SHALL NOT MAKE IDOLS FOR YOUR-
selves; you shall not erect a carved
image or a sacred pillar; you shall not
put a figured stone on your land to
prostrate yourselves upon, because I
2 am the LORD your God. You shall
keep my sabbaths and revere my sanctuary. I am the LORD.
3 　If you conform to my statutes, if you
observe my commandments and carry
4 them out, I will give you rain at the
proper time; the land shall yield its
produce and the trees of the country-
5 side their fruit. Threshing shall last till
vintage and vintage till sowing; you
shall eat your fill and live secure in
6 your land. I will give peace in the land,
and you shall lie down to sleep with no
one to terrify you. I will rid your land
of dangerous beasts and it shall not be
7 ravaged by war. You shall put your enemies to flight and they shall fall in
8 battle before you. Five of you shall
pursue a hundred and a hundred of you
ten thousand; so shall your enemies fall
9 in battle before you. I will look upon
you with favour, I will make you fruitful and increase your numbers: I will
give my covenant with you its full
10 effect. Your old harvest shall last you
in store until you have to clear out the

old to make room for the new. I will 11
establish my Tabernacle among you
and will not spurn you. I will walk to 12
and fro among you; I will become your
God and you shall become my people.
I am the LORD your God who brought 13
you out of Egypt and let you be their
slaves no longer; I broke the bars of
your yoke and enabled you to walk
upright.
　But if you do not listen to me, if you 14
fail to keep all these commandments
of mine, if you reject my statutes, if 15
you spurn my judgements, and do not
obey all my commandments, but break
my covenant, then be sure that this is 16
what I will do: I will bring upon you
sudden terror, wasting disease, recurrent fever, and plagues that dim the
sight and cause the appetite to fail.
You shall sow your seed to no purpose,
for your enemies shall eat the crop. I 17
will set my face against you, and you
shall be routed by your enemies. Those
that hate you shall hound you on until
you run when there is no pursuit.
　If after all this you do not listen to 18
me, I will go on to punish you seven
times over for your sins. I will break 19
down your stubborn pride. I will make
the sky above you like iron and the
earth beneath you like bronze. Your 20
strength shall be spent in vain; your
land shall not yield its produce nor the
trees of the land their fruit.
　If you still defy me and refuse to 21
listen, I will multiply your calamities
seven times, as your sins deserve. I will 22
send wild beasts among you; they shall
tear your children from you, destroy
your cattle and bring your numbers
low; and your roads shall be deserted.
If after all this you have not learnt 23
discipline but still defy me, I in turn 24
will defy you and scourge you seven
times over for your sins. I will bring 25
war in vengeance upon you, vengeance
irrevocable under covenant; you shall

26.1–46: The consequence of obedience or disobedience. This conclusion of the Holiness
Code (see 17.1–26.46 n.) is patterned after Ancient Near Eastern contracts which conclude
with a list of curses against those who disregard their stipulations. **1–2:** This appears to be
either an isolated fragment or the conclusion of ch. 25. **9:** *Covenant:* see Exod.20.1–21 n.; Gen.
chs. 15 and 17. **11–13:** A summary of the fundamental goal of the foregoing legislation. See
9.5–6 n. **18:** The LORD uses only that amount of discipline necessary to accomplish his task.
On progressive intensification, see Amos 4.6–12. **21–39:** See 26.1–46 n. While the language, in
keeping with this form of document, seems extreme, it may, in part, be based upon the obser-

be herded into your cities, I will send pestilence among you, and you shall 26 be given over to the enemy. I will cut short your daily bread until ten women can bake your bread in a single oven; they shall dole it out by weight, and though you eat, you shall not be satisfied.

27 If in spite of this you do not listen to 28 me and still defy me, I will defy you in anger, and I myself will punish you 29 seven times over for your sins. Instead of meat you shall eat your sons and 30 your daughters. I will destroy your hill-shrines and demolish your incense-altars. I will pile your rotting carcasses on the rotting logs[x] that were your idols, 31 and I will spurn you. I will make your cities desolate and destroy your sanctuaries; the soothing odour of your 32 offerings I will not accept. I will destroy your land, and the enemies who occupy 33 it shall be appalled. I will scatter you among the heathen, and I will pursue you with the naked sword; your land shall be desolate and your cities heaps 34 of rubble. Then, all the time that it lies desolate, while you are in exile in the land of your enemies, your land shall 35 enjoy its sabbaths to the full. All the time of its desolation it shall have the sabbath rest which it did not have when 36 you lived there. And I will make those of you who are left in the land of your enemies so ridden with fear that, when a leaf flutters behind them in the wind, they shall run as if it were the sword behind them; they shall fall with no 37 one in pursuit. Though no one pursues them they shall stumble over one another, as if the sword were behind them, and there shall be no stand made 38 against the enemy. You shall meet your end among the heathen, and your enemies' land shall swallow you up. 39 Those who are left shall pine away in an enemy land under their own iniquities; and with their fathers' iniquities upon them too, they shall pine away as they did.

40 But though they confess their in-

iquity, their own and their fathers', their treachery, and even their defiance 41 of me, I will defy them in my turn and carry them off into their enemies' land. Yet if then their stubborn spirit is broken and they accept their punishment in full, I will remember my cov- 42 enant with Jacob and my covenant with Isaac, yes, and my covenant with Abraham, and I will remember the land. The land shall be rid of its people 43 and enjoy in full its sabbaths while it lies desolate, and they shall pay in full the penalty because they rejected my judgements and spurned my statutes. Yet even then, in their enemies' land, 44 I shall not have rejected nor spurned them, bringing them to an end and so breaking my covenant with them, because I am the LORD their God. I 45 will remember on their behalf the covenant with the men of former times whom I brought out of Egypt in full sight of all the nations, that I might be their God. I am the LORD.

These are the statutes, the judge- 46 ments, and the laws which the LORD established between himself and the Israelites on Mount Sinai through Moses.

THE LORD SPOKE TO MOSES AND SAID, 27 Speak to the Israelites in these words: 2 When a man makes a special[y] vow to the LORD which requires your valuation of living persons, a male between 3 twenty and sixty years old shall be valued at fifty silver shekels, that is shekels by the sacred standard. If it is a 4 female, she shall be valued at thirty shekels. If the person is between five 5 years old and twenty, the valuation shall be twenty shekels for a male and ten for a female. If the person is be- 6 tween a month and five years old, the valuation shall be five shekels for a male and three for a female. If the person is 7 over sixty and a male, the valuation shall be fifteen shekels, but if a female,

[x] rotting logs: *or* effigies.
[y] makes a special: *or* discharges a . . .

vation of the results of warfare among Israel's neighbors. **30:** *Rotting logs:* a sarcastic allusion to idols. **46:** *Sinai:* see 25.1 n.
   27.1–34: The fulfillment of religious vows. In return for success (Judg.11.29–31) or recovery from misfortune (Ps.66.13–15), a person would make *a special vow* of a sacrifice or donation to the sanctuary. **2:** *Valuation:* persons dedicated to perform minor cultic services (compare

8 ten shekels. If the man is too poor to pay the amount of your valuation, the person shall be set before the priest, and the priest shall value him according to the sum which the man who makes the vow can afford: the priest shall make the valuation.

9 If the vow concerns a beast such as may be offered as an offering to the LORD, then every gift shall be holy to

10 the LORD. He shall not change it for another, or substitute good for bad or bad for good. But if a substitution is in fact made of one beast for another, then both the original beast and its substitute shall be holy to the LORD.

11 If the vow concerns any unclean beast such as may not be offered as an offering to the LORD, then the animal shall

12 be brought before the priest, and he shall value it whether good or bad. The

13 priest's valuation shall be decisive; in case of redemption the payment shall be increased by one fifth.

14 When a man dedicates his house as holy to the LORD, the priest shall value it whether good or bad, and the priest's

15 valuation shall be decisive. If the donor redeems his house, he shall pay the amount of the valuation increased by one fifth, and the house shall be his.

16 If a man dedicates to the LORD part of his ancestral land, you shall value it according to the amount of seed-corn it can carry, at the rate of fifty shekels

17 of silver for a homer of barley seed. If he dedicates his land from the year of jubilee, it shall stand at your valuation;

18 but if he dedicates it after the year of jubilee, the priest shall estimate the price in silver according to the number of years remaining till the next year of jubilee, and this shall be deducted from

19 your valuation. If the man who dedi-

cates his field should redeem it, he shall pay the amount of your valuation in silver, increased by one fifth, and it

20 shall be his. If he does not redeem it but sells the land to another man, it

21 shall no longer be redeemable; when the land reverts at the year of jubilee, it shall be like land that has been devoted, holy to the LORD. It shall belong to the priest as his patrimony.

22 If a man dedicates to the LORD land which he has bought, land which is not

23 part of his ancestral land, the priest shall estimate the amount of the value for the period until the year of jubilee, and the man shall give the amount fixed as at that day; it is holy to the

24 LORD. At the year of jubilee the land shall revert to the man from whom he

25 bought it, whose patrimony it is. Every valuation you make shall be made by the sacred standard (twenty gerahs to the shekel).

26 Notwithstanding, no man may dedicate to the LORD the first-born of a beast which in any case has to be offered as a first-born, whether an ox

27 or a sheep. It is the LORD's. If it is any unclean beast, he may redeem it at your valuation and shall add one fifth; but if it is not redeemed, it shall be sold at

28 your valuation. Notwithstanding, nothing which a man devotes to the LORD irredeemably from his own property, whether man or beast or ancestral land, may be sold or redeemed. Everything so devoted is most holy to the LORD.

29 No human being thus devoted may be redeemed, but he shall be put to death.

30 Every tithe on land, whether from grain or from the fruit of a tree, belongs to the LORD; it is holy to LORD. If a man wishes to redeem any

31 of his tithe, he shall pay its value in-

---

1 Sam.1.11,21–28) could be released through a payment of money. **11:** The *unclean beast*, since it cannot be sacrificed, may be redeemed by the person who vowed it, but only at the expense of a penalty. **16:** The value of the land depends upon its productivity (the annual yield of barley). *Homer:* see p. 1035. **17–19:** Priests, like laymen (25.8–34), cannot gain permanent possession of another man's land and thus impoverish him, even though the man has vowed it to the LORD. He may redeem it, at a penalty, or receive it back at the Jubilee. This is in contrast to other Ancient Near Eastern religions which allowed the temples to accumulate vast estates. **20–21:** If the man seeks to disregard his vow to the LORD by selling his property to another, he forfeits the right of the Jubilee. **25:** *Gerahs:* see p. 1035. **26:** *First-born:* one cannot vow to the LORD that which already belongs to him (Exod.13.11–13). **27:** *Unclean beast:* compare Exod.13.13 for the case of a male ass. Here, however, the beast may be kept by the sanctuary for sale. "Clean" first-born could not be redeemed (Num.18.17). **30:** The *tithe*, used to support the priesthood (Num.18.21,24; compare Lev.25.32–34 n.) and the poor (Deut.26.12), cannot be a vowed donation, for it is already an obligation. **31:** *Redeem any of his tithe:* the opportunity is here

32 creased by one fifth. Every tenth creature that passes under the counting rod
shall be holy to the LORD; this applies
33 to all tithes of cattle and sheep. There
shall be no inquiry whether it is good
or bad, and no substitution. If any

substitution is made, then both the
tithe-animal and its substitute shall be
forfeit as holy; it shall not be redeemed.

These are the commandments which 34
the LORD gave Moses for the Israelites
on Mount Sinai.

---

provided to pay in money rather than in kind. **32–33:** *Cattle and sheep:* these tithes are regarded
as "devoted" to the LORD, and whatever was devoted (see v. 28) could not be "redeemed," that
is, cash could not be substituted. (What was "devoted" was deemed as thereafter unsuitable
for normal human use.) Moreover, the actual tenth animal was to be given; probably the intent
was to prevent the gift of a sickly or emaciated animal rather than a healthy one. **32:** *Counting
rod:* compare Jer.33.13 for the method of counting the flock.

NUMBERS

This segment of Israel's early story is known in the Hebrew Bible as "In the Wilderness" (a phrase occurring in the initial verse), a title more characteristic of the whole book than is "Numbers." The latter, found in the Greek and Latin translations, is derived from the various censuses and the general arithmetical precision which characterize the work.

The book may be topically divided as follows: (1) preparation for departure from the sacred mountain, Sinai (1.1–10.10); (2) the journey to the oasis at Kadesh where, according to the priestly chronology, most of the "forty years" (33.38) in the Wilderness were spent (10.11–12.16; compare 13.26); (3) the stay at Kadesh (13.1–20.21); (4) an abortive attempt to enter Canaan from the south (14.39–45; 21.1–3); (5) the detour around Edom through Transjordan to the eastern border of Canaan (20.22–36.13). With the departure from Sinai, the place of divine revelation shifts from the mountain to the movable Tent of the Presence.

The theme is repeated that the community was willing to shun its destiny through exchanging the perils of the Wilderness journey for a return to the supposed safety of Egypt. Yet Israel was preserved by the grace of God in order that the ancient promise to the patriarchs (see Introduction to the Pentateuch) would be realized.

Israel in the wilderness of Sinai

1 ON THE FIRST DAY OF THE SECOND month in the second year after the Israelites came out of Egypt, the LORD spoke to Moses at the Tent of the Presence in the wilderness of Sinai in 2 these words: 'Number the whole community of Israel by families in the father's line, recording the name of every 3 male person aged twenty years and upwards fit for military service. You and Aaron are to make a detailed list of 4 them by their tribal hosts, and you shall have to assist you one head of family 5 from each tribe. These are their names:

6 of Reuben, Elizur son of Shedeur;
6 of Simeon, Shelumiel son of Zurishaddai;
7 of Judah, Nahshon son of Amminadab;
8 of Issachar, Nethaneel son of Zuar;
9 of Zebulun, Eliab son of Helon;
10 of Joseph: of Ephraim, Elishama son of Ammihud;
of Manasseh, Gamaliel son of Pedahzur;
11 of Benjamin, Abidan son of Gideoni;
12 of Dan, Ahiezer son of Ammishaddai;
13 of Asher, Pagiel son of Ocran;
14 of Gad, Eliasaph son of Reuel;
15 of Naphtali, Ahira son of Enan.'

These were the conveners of the whole 16 community, chiefs of their fathers' tribes and heads of Israelite clans. So 17 Moses and Aaron took these men who had been indicated by name. They 18 summoned the whole community on the first day of the second month, and they registered their descent by families in the father's line, recording every male person aged twenty years and upwards, as the LORD had told Moses 19 to do. Thus it was that he drew up the detailed lists in the wilderness of Sinai:

The tribal list of Reuben, Israel's 20 eldest son, by families in the father's line, with the name of every male person aged twenty years and upwards fit for service, the number in the list 21 of the tribe of Reuben being forty-six thousand five hundred.

The tribal list of Simeon, by families 22 in the father's line, with the name of every male person aged twenty years and upwards fit for service, the number 23 in the list of the tribe of Simeon being fifty-nine thousand three hundred.

The tribal list of Gad, by families in 24 the father's line, with the names of all men aged twenty years and upwards fit for service, the number in the list of 25

1.1–54: A census of the tribes. In anticipation of departure from Sinai (10.11) and of armed opposition to the Canaanites (chs. 13–14), a survey of military potential is conducted. **1:** *Second month:* one month since the construction of the Tabernacle (Exod.40.2); on the priestly chronology, see Gen.7.24 n. **5–15:** Although Israel as a league of twelve tribes took shape only after the conquest of Canaan (Exod.6.3 n.), here each tribe is represented as part of a united Israel in the Wilderness. On the omission of Levi, see vv. 47–49 n. **6:** *Simeon:* see Gen.34.1–31 n. **10:** *Joseph* is subdivided (Gen.48.5 n.) in order to keep the total number of tribes at twelve (compare Gen.22.20–24 n.). **20–46:** A preserved ancient census, possibly taken well after the conquest of Canaan (Exod.30.11–16 n.), is here presented as conducted at Sinai, for the

the tribe of Gad being forty-five thousand six hundred and fifty.

26 The tribal list of Judah, by families in the father's line, with the names of all men aged twenty years and upwards

27 fit for service, the number in the list of the tribe of Judah being seventy-four thousand six hundred.

28 The tribal list of Issachar, by families in the father's line, with the names of all men aged twenty years and upwards

29 fit for service, the number in the list of the tribe of Issachar being fifty-four thousand four hundred.

30 The tribal list of Zebulun, by families in the father's line, with the names of all men aged twenty years and upwards

31 fit for service, the number in the list of the tribe of Zebulun being fifty-seven thousand four hundred.

32 The tribal lists of Joseph: that of Ephraim, by families in the father's line, with the names of all men aged twenty

33 years and upwards fit for service, the number in the list of the tribe of Ephraim being forty thousand five hundred; that of Manasseh, by families in

34 the father's line, with the names of all men aged twenty years and upwards

35 fit for service, the number in the list of the tribe of Manasseh being thirty-two thousand two hundred.

36 The tribal list of Benjamin, by families in the father's line, with the names of all men aged twenty years and up-

37 wards fit for service, the number in the list of the tribe of Benjamin being thirty-five thousand four hundred.

38 The tribal list of Dan, by families in the father's line, with the names of all men aged twenty years and upwards

39 fit for service, the number in the list of the tribe of Dan being sixty-two thousand seven hundred.

40 The tribal list of Asher, by families in the father's line, with the names of all men aged twenty years and upwards

41 fit for service, the number in the list of the tribe of Asher being forty-one thousand five hundred.

42 The tribal list of Naphtali, by families in the father's line, with the names of all men aged twenty years and upwards fit for service, the number in

43 the list of the tribe of Naphtali being fifty-three thousand four hundred.

44 These were the numbers recorded in the detailed lists by Moses and Aaron and the twelve chiefs of Israel, each representing one tribe and being the head of a family. The total number

45 of Israelites aged twenty years and upwards fit for service, recorded in the lists of fathers' families, was six hundred

46 and three thousand five hundred and fifty. A list of the Levites by their

47 fathers' families was not made.

48 The LORD spoke to Moses and said,

49 'You shall not record the total number of the Levites or make a detailed list of them among the Israelites. You

50 shall put the Levites in charge of the Tabernacle of the Tokens, with its equipment and everything in it. They shall carry the Tabernacle and all its equipment; they alone shall be its attendants and shall pitch their tents round it. The Levites shall take the

51 Tabernacle down when it is due to move and shall put it up when it halts; any unqualified person who comes near it shall be put to death. All other

52 Israelites shall pitch their tents, each tribal host in its proper camp and under its own standard. But the Levites shall

53 encamp round the Tabernacle of the Tokens, so that divine wrath may not follow the whole community of Israel; the Tabernacle of the Tokens shall be in their keeping.'

54 The Israelites did exactly as the LORD had told Moses to do.

2 The LORD spoke to Moses and Aaron

2 and said, 'The Israelites shall encamp each under his own standard by the emblems of his father's family; they shall pitch their tents round the Tent of the Presence, facing it.

3 'In front of it, on the east, the division of Judah shall be stationed under

---

Wilderness could scarcely have supported this aggregate (v. 46) of persons for a sustained period (33.38). **47–49**: Contrast 3.14–39, where a census for nonmilitary purposes is taken. On the lack of *a list* . . ., see Gen.49.5–7 n. **50–53**: On the duties of the Levites, see ch. 3.
2.1–34: The arrangement of the tribes for encampment or march. The model for this conception may possibly have been encampments around the sanctuary at one of the pilgrimage festivals (Deut.16.16). **3**: The preferential position assigned to *Judah* may reflect its eminence in later

the standard of its camp by tribal hosts. The chief of Judah shall be 4 Nahshon son of Amminadab. His host, with its members as detailed, numbers seventy-four thousand six hundred 5 men. Next to Judah the tribe of Issachar shall be stationed. Its chief shall be 6 Nethaneel son of Zuar; his host, with its members as detailed, numbers fifty-7 four thousand four hundred. Then the tribe of Zebulun: its chief shall be 8 Eliab son of Helon: his host, with its members as detailed, numbers fifty-9 seven thousand four hundred. The number listed in the camp of Judah, by hosts, is one hundred and eighty-six thousand four hundred. They shall be the first to march.

10 'To the south the division of Reuben shall be stationed under the standard of its camp by tribal hosts. The chief of Reuben shall be Elizur son of She-11 deur; his host, with its members as detailed, numbers forty-six thousand 12 five hundred. Next to him the tribe of Simeon shall be stationed. Its chief shall be Shelumiel son of Zurishaddai; 13 his host, with its members as detailed, numbers fifty-nine thousand three 14 hundred. Then the tribe of Gad: its chief shall be Eliasaph son of Reuel; 15 his host, with its members as detailed, numbers forty-five thousand six hun-16 dred and fifty. The number listed in the camp of Reuben, by hosts, is one hundred and fifty-one thousand four hundred and fifty. They shall be the second to march.

17 'When the Tent of the Presence moves, the camp of the Levites shall keep its station in the centre of the other camps; they shall all move in the order of their encamping, each man in his proper place under his standard.

18 'To the west the division of Ephraim shall be stationed under the standard of its camp by tribal hosts. The chief of Ephraim shall be Elishama son of Ammihud; his host, with its members 19 as detailed, numbers forty thousand five hundred. Next to him the tribe of 20 Manasseh shall be stationed. Its chief shall be Gamaliel son of Pedahzur; his 21 host, with its members as detailed, numbers thirty-two thousand two hun-dred. Then the tribe of Benjamin: its 22 chief shall be Abidan son of Gideoni; his host, with its members as detailed, 23 numbers thirty-five thousand four hundred. The number listed in the 24 camp of Ephraim, by hosts, is one hundred and eight thousand one hun-dred. They shall be the third to march.

'To the north the division of Dan 25 shall be stationed under the standard of its camp by tribal hosts. The chief of Dan shall be Ahiezer son of Am-mishaddai; his host, with its members 26 as detailed, numbers sixty-two thousand seven hundred. Next to him the tribe of 27 Asher shall be stationed. Its chief shall be Pagiel son of Ocran; his host, with 28 its members as detailed, numbers forty-one thousand five hundred. Then the 29 tribe of Naphtali: its chief shall be Ahira son of Enan; his host, with its members 30 as detailed, numbers fifty-three thous-and four hundred. The number listed 31 in the camp of Dan is a hundred and fifty-seven thousand six hundred. They shall march, under their standards, last.'

These were the Israelites listed by 32 their fathers' families. The total number in the camp, recorded by tribal hosts, was six hundred and three thousand five hundred and fifty.

The Levites were not included in the 33 detailed lists with their fellow-Israelites, for so the LORD had commanded Moses. The Israelites did exactly as the 34 LORD had commanded Moses, pitching and breaking camp standard by stan-dard, each man according to his family in his father's line.

---

times (compare Gen.38.1–30 n.), especially its survival after other tribes had been overrun and exiled by the Assyrians in 721 B.C. *Nahshon:* his name is found in the list in 1.5–15. **4:** The numbers throughout this chapter conform with those in 1.20–47. **17:** The central position of the *Tent* reflected its importance as well as insured its protection. In an old version of the tradition (Exod.33.7–11), it was located outside the encampment. **18:** On the position of *Ephraim* and Manasseh (v. 20), contrast the preferential place of Judah (v. 3 n.). Ephraim was the seat of the "apostate" cult of the golden calves (1 Kgs.12.25–33) and Manasseh contained the capital city (Samaria) from which the "evil" kings of the northern tribes reigned (2 Kgs. 17.5–17). In the postexilic period, the Samaritans were regarded as racially impure by the priestly leadership of Judah (see 2 Kgs.17.24).

3 THESE WERE THE DESCENDANTS OF
Aaron and Moses at the time when the
LORD spoke to Moses on Mount Sinai.
2 The names of the sons of Aaron were
Nadab the eldest, Abihu, Eleazar and
3 Ithamar. These were the names of
Aaron's sons, the anointed priests who
had been installed in the priestly office.
4 Nadab and Abihu fell dead before the
LORD because they had presented illicit
fire before the LORD in the wilderness
of Sinai. They left no sons; Eleazar and
Ithamar continued to perform the
priestly office in their father's presence.
5 The LORD spoke to Moses and said,
6 'Bring forward the tribe of Levi and
appoint them to serve Aaron the priest
7 and to minister to him. They shall be in
attendance on him and on the whole
community before the Tent of the Presence, undertaking the service of the
8 Tabernacle. They shall be in charge of
all the equipment in the Tent of the
Presence, and be in attendance on the
Israelites, undertaking the service of
9 the Tabernacle. You shall assign the
Levites to Aaron and his sons as
especially dedicated to him out of all
10 the Israelites. To Aaron and his line
you shall commit the priestly office
and they shall perform its duties; any
unqualified person who intrudes upon
it shall be put to death.'
11 The LORD spoke to Moses and said,
12 'I take the Levites for myself out of all
the Israelites as a substitute for the
eldest male child of every woman; the
13 Levites shall be mine. For every eldest
child, if a boy, became mine when I
destroyed all the eldest sons in Egypt.
So I have consecrated to myself all the

first-born in Israel, both man and beast.
They shall be mine. I am the LORD.'
The LORD spoke to Moses in the 14
wilderness of Sinai and said, 'Make a 15
detailed list of all the Levites by their
families in the father's line, every male
from the age of one month and
upwards.'
Moses made a detailed list of them in 16
accordance with the command given
him by the LORD. Now these were the 17
names of the sons of Levi:

Gershon, Kohath and Merari.
Descendants of Gershon, by families: 18
Libni and Shimei.
Descendants of Kohath, by families: 19
Amram, Izhar, Hebron and Uzziel.
Descendants of Merari, by families: 20
Mahli and Mushi.

These were the families of Levi, by
fathers' families:
Gershon: the family of Libni and 21
the family of Shimei. These were the
families of Gershon, and the number of 22
males in their list as detailed, from the
age of one month and upwards, was
seven thousand five hundred. The 23
families of Gershon were stationed on
the west, behind the Tabernacle. Their 24
chief was Eliasaph son of Lael, and in 25
the service of the Tent of the Presence
they were in charge of the Tabernacle
and its coverings, of the screen at the
entrance to the Tent of the Presence,
the hangings of the court, the screen 26
at the entrance to the court all round the
Tabernacle and the altar, and of all else
needed for its maintenance.
Kohath: the family of Amram, the 27

3.1–51: The appointment and enumeration of the Levites. 4: See Lev.10.1–7 and the notes.
6: *To serve Aaron:* The differentiation between Aaron's family and the rest of the Levites arose
historically in the postexilic period; here the priestly (Aaronite) writers ascribe it as commanded
at Sinai. See Exod.29.1–46 n. **10:** *Be put to death:* the warning about the unqualified persons
who may be put to death is directed to Levitical groups who might become dissatisfied with the
custodial duties here assigned to them, especially so since other ancient traditions know nothing
of exclusive eminence for the family of Aaron (Deut.33.8–11). For a controversy over this
eminence, see ch. 16. **11–13:** This positive view of the Levites, seemingly old, is here placed in a
context of subordination to the Aaronites. See also vv. 40–51 and the repetition in 8.15–19.
12: Regulations concerning the *eldest male* are found in Exod.13.2,11–15 but there it is
suggested that an animal *substitute* is in order (Exod.13.13 n.). **13:** *When I destroyed:* see
Exod.13.14–15 n. **15:** Those below the age of *one month* are possibly excluded because of a
high infant mortality rate. On the reason for the census, see vv. 40–48. **17–20:** See also Exod.
6.16–19. This division of Levi is functional, providing for a group for each of the four sides
of the Tabernacle (vv. 23,29,35,38). The Aaronites (v. 38) make a fifth group. See also 26.58.
23: The reason for the unfavorable position given the descendants of *Gershon* is obscure
(compare 2.18 n.). See Judg.18.30–31, the idolatrous service instituted by the sons of Jonathan

family of Izhar, the family of Hebron, the family of Uzziel. These were the
20 families of Kohath, and the number of males, from the age of one month and upwards, was eight thousand six hundred. They were the guardians of the
29 holy things. The families of Kohath were stationed on the south, at the side
30 of the Tabernacle. Their chief was
31 Elizaphan son of Uzziel; they were in charge of the Ark, the table, the lampstands and the altars, together with the sacred vessels used in their service, and the screen with everything needed for its
32 maintenance. The chief over all the chiefs of the Levites was Eleazar son of Aaron the priest, who was appointed overseer of those in charge of the sanctuary.
33 Merari: the family of Mahli, the family of Mushi. These were the families
34 of Merari, and the number of males in their list as detailed from the age of one month and upwards was six thousand
35 two hundred. Their chief was Zuriel son of Abihail; they were stationed on the north, at the side of the Tabernacle.
36 The Merarites were in charge of the planks, bars, posts, and sockets of the Tabernacle, together with its vessels and all the equipment needed for its main-
37 tenance, the posts, sockets, pegs, and cords of the surrounding court.
38 In front of the Tabernacle on the east, Moses was stationed, with Aaron and his sons, in front of the Tent of the Presence eastwards. They were in charge of the sanctuary on behalf of the Israelites; any unqualified person who came near would be put to death.
39 The number of Levites recorded by Moses on the detailed list by families at the command of the LORD was twenty-two thousand males aged one month and upwards.
40 The LORD said to Moses, 'Make a detailed list of all the male first-born in

Israel aged one month and upwards, and count the number of persons. You 41 shall reserve the Levites for me—I am the LORD—in substitution for the eldest sons of the Israelites, and in the same way the Levites' cattle in substitution for the first-born cattle of the Israelites.' As the LORD had told him to do, Moses 42 made a list of all the eldest sons of the Israelites, and the total number of 43 first-born males recorded by name in the register, aged one month and upwards, was twenty-two thousand two hundred and seventy-three.

The LORD spoke to Moses and said, 44 'Take the Levites as a substitute for all 45 the eldest sons in Israel and the cattle of the Levites as a substitute for their cattle. The Levites shall be mine. I am the LORD. The eldest sons in Israel will 46 outnumber the Levites by two hundred amd seventy-three. This remainder must 47 be ransomed, and you shall accept five shekels for each of them, taking the sacred shekel and reckoning twenty gerahs to the shekel; you shall give the 48 money with which they are ransomed to Aaron and his sons.'

Moses took the money paid as ran- 49 som for those who remained over when the substitution of Levites was complete. The amount received was 50 one thousand three hundred and sixty-five shekels of silver by the sacred standard. In accordance with what the 51 LORD had said, he gave the money to Aaron and his sons, doing what the LORD had told him to do.

The LORD spoke to Moses and **4** Aaron and said, 'Among the Levites, 2 make a count of the descendants of Kohath between the ages of thirty and 3 fifty, by families in the father's line, comprising everyone who comes to take duty in the service of the Tent of the Presence.

'This is the service to be rendered 4

(son of Gershom), a group possibly to be identified with Gershonites. **29:** The descendants of *Kohath* are given charge of *the holy things* because they are the nearest relatives of the Aaronites (Exod.6.18, 20). **32:** *Eleazar:* see Lev.10.2 n. **39:** For a possible origin of this census figure, compare 1.20–46 n. The numbers given in vv. 22, 28, 34 actually total 22,300. In v. 46, the excess of firstborn sons in Israel over Levites is derived from this figure. **40–48:** See vv. 11–13 n., 12 n. **41:** The substitution of the Levites' cattle is elsewhere unattested, and was not always practiced (18.17). **49–51:** Financial support of the cult rests on Mosaic authority. **50:** *Shekels:* see p. 1035.

4.1–49: An alternative account of the assignment of Levitical duties, particularly in relation to preparation of the Tent for travel. **2:** On the priority of *Kohath*, see 3.29 n. **3:** The minimum

by the Kohathites in the Tent of the 5 Presence; it is most sacred. When the camp is due to move, Aaron and his sons shall come and take down the Veil of the screen and cover the Ark of the 6 Tokens with it; over this they shall put a covering of porpoise-hide[a] and over that again a violet cloth all of one piece; they shall then put its poles in place. 7 Over the Table of the Presence they shall spread a violet cloth and lay on it the dishes, saucers, and flagons, and the bowls for drink-offerings; the Bread regularly presented shall also lie upon 8 it; then they shall spread over them a scarlet cloth and over that a covering of porpoise-hide, and put the poles in 9 place. They shall take a violet cloth and cover the lamp-stand, its lamps, tongs, firepans, and all the containers for the 10 oil used in its service; they shall put it with all its equipment in a sheet of 11 porpoise-hide slung from a pole. Over the gold altar they shall spread a violet cloth, cover it with a porpoise-hide covering, and put its poles in place. 12 They shall take all the articles used for the service of the sanctuary, put them on a violet cloth, cover them with a porpoise-hide covering, and sling them 13 from a pole. They shall clear the altar of the fat and ashes, spread a purple 14 cloth over it, and then lay on it all the equipment used in its service, the firepans, forks, shovels, tossing-bowls, and all the equipment of the altar, spread a covering of porpoise-hide 15 over it and put the poles in place. Once Aaron and his sons have finished covering the sanctuary and all the sacred equipment, when the camp is due to move, the Kohathites shall come to carry it; they must not touch it on pain of death. All these things are the load to be carried by the Kohathites, the things connected with the Tent of 16 the Presence. Eleazar son of Aaron the priest shall have charge of the lamp-oil,

the fragrant incense, the regular grain-offering, and the anointing oil, with the general oversight of the whole Tabernacle and its contents, the sanctuary and its equipment.'

The LORD spoke to Moses and 17 Aaron and said, 'You must not let 18 the families of Kohath be extirpated, and lost to the tribe of Levi. If they are 19 to live and not die when they approach the most holy things, this is what you must do: Aaron and his sons shall come and set each man to his appointed task and to his load, and the Kohathites 20 themselves shall not enter to cast even a passing glance on the sanctuary, on pain of death.'

The LORD spoke to Moses and said, 21 'Number the Gershonites by families 22 in the father's line. Make a detailed 23 list of all those between the ages of thirty and fifty who come on duty to perform service in the Tent of the Presence.

'This is the service to be rendered by 24 the Gershonite families, comprising their general duty and their loads. They shall carry the hangings of the 25 Tabernacle, the Tent of the Presence, its covering, that is the covering of porpoise-hide which is over it, the screen at the entrance to the Tent of the Presence, the hangings of the court, 26 the screen at the entrance to the court surrounding the Tabernacle and the altar, their cords and all the equipment for their service; and they shall perform all the tasks connected with them. These are the acts of service they shall render. All the service of the Gershonites, their 27 loads and their other duties, shall be directed by Aaron and his sons; you shall assign them the loads for which they shall be responsible. This is the 28 service assigned to the Gershonite families in connection with the Tent of

---

a Strictly hide of sea-cow.

age for service varied from time to time (8.24). **5:** *Veil:* see Exod.26.31–35. *Ark:* see Exod. 25.10 n. *Tokens:* see Exod.25.16 n. **7:** *Bread:* Exod.25.30; Lev.24.5–9. **9:** *Lamp-stand:* see Exod.25.31–40. **11:** *Gold altar:* for incense (see Exod.30.1–10). **13:** *The altar:* for whole offerings (Lev.1.1–17), located in the court (Exod.27.1–8). **15:** It is only after the Aaronites have packed the furniture of the sanctuary and insulated it from touch and view with bags of skin that their nearest relatives (3.29 n.) are allowed to approach it. **17–20:** The repeated warnings against the Kohathites' approaching the sacred objects (v. 15; compare 3.10,38) possibly reflect an obscure power struggle within the priesthood (compare Lev.10.2 n. and Exod.32.26–29 n.); this section anticipates the challenge in ch. 16. **25:** *Hangings:* see Exod.26.1–6. *Tent:* see Exod.

the Presence; Ithamar son of Aaron shall be in charge of them

29 'You shall make a detailed list of the Merarites by families in the father's 30 line, all those between the ages of thirty and fifty, who come on duty to perform service in the Tent of the Presence. 31 'These are the loads for which they shall be responsible in virtue of their service in the Tent of the Presence: the planks of the Tabernacle with its bars, 32 posts, and sockets, the posts of the surrounding court with their sockets, pegs, and cords, and all that is needed for the maintenance of them; you shall assign to each man by name the load 33 for which he is responsible. These are the duties of the Merarite families in virtue of their service in the Tent of the Presence. Ithamar son of Aaron the priest shall be in charge of them.'

34 Moses and Aaron and the chiefs of the community made a detailed list of the Kohathites by families in the 35 father's line, taking all between the ages of thirty and fifty who came on duty to perform service in the Tent of the 36 Presence. The number recorded by families in the detailed lists was two thousand seven hundred and fifty. 37 This was the total number in the detailed lists of the Kohathite families who did duty in the Tent of the Presence; they were recorded by Moses and Aaron as the LORD had told them to do through Moses.

38-39 The Gershonites between the ages of thirty and fifty, who came on duty for service in the Tent of the Presence, were recorded in detailed lists by fam- 40 ilies in the father's line. Their number, by families in the father's line, was two 41 thousand six hundred and thirty. This was the total recorded in the lists of the Gershonite families who came on duty in the Tent of the Presence, and were recorded by Moses and Aaron as the LORD had told them to do.

42-43 The families of Merari, between the

ages of thirty and fifty, who came on duty to perform service in the Tent of the Presence, were recorded in detailed lists by families in the father's line. Their number by families was three 44 thousand two hundred. These were 45 recorded in the Merarite families by Moses and Aaron as the LORD had told them to do through Moses.

Thus Moses and Aaron and the chiefs 46 of Israel made a detailed list of all the Levites by families in the father's line, between the ages of thirty and fifty 47 years; these were all who came to perform their various duties and carry their loads in the service of the Tent of the Presence. Their number was eight 48 thousand five hundred and eighty. They 49 were recorded one by one by Moses at the command of the LORD, according to their general duty and the loads they carried.[b] For so the LORD had told Moses to do.

THE LORD SPOKE TO MOSES AND SAID: 5 Command the Israelites to expel from 2 the camp everyone who suffers from a malignant skin-disease or a discharge, and everyone ritually unclean from contact with a corpse. You shall put 3 them outside the camp, both male and female, so that they will not defile your camps in which I dwell among you. The Israelites did this: they put them 4 outside the camp. As the LORD had said when he spoke to Moses, so the Israelites did.

The LORD spoke to Moses and said, 5 Say to the Israelites: When anyone, 6 man or woman, wrongs another and thereby breaks faith with the LORD, that person has incurred guilt which demands reparation. He shall confess 7 the sin he has committed, make restitution in full with the addition of one fifth, and give it to the man to whom compensation is due. If there is no next- 8 of-kin to whom compensation can be

---

b *Prob. rdg.; Heb. adds* and his registered ones.

26.1–37 n. **31:** *Planks:* see Exod.26.15–30. **48:** For a possible origin of this figure, compare 1.20–46 n.

    5.1–6.27: An appendix of unrelated regulations, most of which clarify prior legislation. The Sinai narrative is nearing its completion: the writers here assemble all remaining material understood to have had its origin there. **2:** *Skin-disease:* see Lev.13.1–46. *Discharge:* see Lev.15.1–33. *Contact with a corpse:* 19.11–22; compare Lev.21.1–12. **3:** *Put them outside:* although earlier legislation commanded the unclean to "stay outside" (Lev.13.46), it made no provision for their failure to do so. *Defile:* see Lev.11.24–25 n. **5–8:** Lev.6.1–7 does not cover

paid, the compensation payable in that case shall be the LORD's, for the use of the priest, in addition to the ram of expiation with which the priest makes expiation for him.

9 Every contribution made by way of holy-gift which the Israelites bring to 10 the priest shall be the priest's. The priest shall have the holy-gifts which a man gives; whatever is given to him shall be his.

11 The LORD spoke to Moses and said, 12 Speak to the Israelites in these words: When a married woman goes astray, is 13 unfaithful to her husband, and has sexual intercourse with another man, and this happens without the husband's knowledge, and the crime is undetected, because, though she has been defiled, there is no direct evidence against her and she was not caught in 14 the act, but when in such a case a fit of jealousy comes over the husband which causes him to suspect his wife, she being in fact defiled; or when, on the other hand, a fit of jealousy comes over a husband which causes him to suspect his wife, when she is not in fact defiled; 15 then in either case, the husband shall bring his wife to the priest together with the prescribed offering for her, a tenth of an ephah of barley meal. He shall not pour oil on it nor put frankincense on it, because it is a grain-offering for jealousy, a grain-offering of protestation 16 conveying an imputation of guilt. The priest shall bring her forward and set 17 her before the LORD. He shall take clean*c* water in an earthenware vessel, and shall take dust from the floor of the Tabernacle and add it to the water. 18 He shall set the woman before the LORD, uncover her head, and place the grain-offering of protestation in her hands; it is a grain-offering for jealousy. The priest shall hold in his own hand the water of contention which brings 19 out the truth. He shall then put the woman on oath and say to her, 'If no

man has had intercourse with you, if you have not gone astray and let yourself become defiled while owing obedience to your husband, then may your innocence be established by the water of contention which brings out the truth. But if, while owing him obedience, 20 you have gone astray and let yourself become defiled, if any man other than your husband has had intercourse with you' (the priest shall here put the 21 woman on oath with an adjuration, and shall continue), 'may the LORD make an example of you among your people in adjurations and in swearing of oaths by bringing upon you miscarriage and untimely birth; and this water 22 that brings out the truth shall enter your body, bringing upon you miscarriage and untimely birth.' The woman shall respond, 'Amen, Amen.' The priest shall write these curses on a 23 scroll and wash them off into the water of contention; he shall make the woman 24 drink the water that brings out the truth, and the water shall enter her body. The priest shall take the grain- 25 offering for jealousy from the woman's hand, present it as a special gift before the LORD, and offer it at the altar. He shall 26 take a handful from the grain-offering by way of token, and burn it at the altar; after this he shall make the woman drink the water. If she has let herself 27 become defiled and has been unfaithful to her husband, then when the priest makes her drink the water that brings out the truth and the water has entered her body, she will suffer a miscarriage or untimely birth, and her name will become an example in adjuration among her kin. But if the woman has 28 not let herself become defiled and is pure, then her innocence is established and she will bear her child.

Such is the law for cases of jealousy, 29 where a woman, owing obedience to her husband, goes astray and lets herself

c Or holy.

the case of the man who is not present to receive damages for injury to his property. Even if he has no next-of-kin, the guilty person cannot escape his obligation: payment must be made to the sanctuary. **11–31:** Lev.20.10 presupposes the presence of witnesses with evidence to prove adultery and justify the death penalty. Here, in the absence of such evidence, a divine indication of guilt or innocence was sought through "trial by ordeal" (vv. 16–28). Such "ordeals" were widely practiced in the ancient world. **15:** See Lev.5.11. **17:** *Dust from the ... Tabernacle:* a holy ingredient, meant to enhance respect for the oath to be taken (vv. 19–22). **18:** *Uncover her head:*

142

30 become defiled, or where a fit of jealousy comes over a man which causes him to suspect his wife. He shall set her before the LORD, and the priest shall deal with her as this law prescribes. 31 No guilt will attach to the husband, but the woman shall bear the penalty of her guilt.

6 The LORD spoke to Moses and said, 2 Speak to the Israelites in these words: When anyone, man or woman, makes a special*d* vow dedicating himself to the 3 LORD as a Nazirite,*e* he shall abstain from wine and strong drink. These he shall not drink, nor anything made from the juice of grapes; nor shall he 4 eat grapes, fresh or dried. During the whole term of his vow he shall eat nothing that comes from the vine, nothing 5 whatever, shoot or berry. During the whole term of his vow no razor shall touch his head; he shall let his hair grow long and plait it until he has completed the term of his dedication: he shall keep himself holy to the LORD. 6 During the whole term of his vow he 7 shall not go near a corpse, not even when his father or mother, brother or sister, dies; he shall not make himself ritually unclean for them, because the Nazirite vow to his God is on his head. 8 He shall keep himself holy to the LORD during the whole term of his Nazirite vow.

9 If someone suddenly falls dead by his side touching him and thereby making his hair, which has been dedicated, ritually unclean, he shall shave his head seven days later, on the day appointed 10 for his ritual cleansing. On the eighth day he shall bring two turtle-doves or two young pigeons to the priest at the entrance to the Tent of the Presence. 11 The priest shall offer one as a sin-offering and the other as a whole-offering and shall make expiation for him for the sin he has incurred through contact with the dead body; and he shall consecrate his head afresh on that 12 day. The man shall re-dedicate himself to the LORD for the term of his vow and bring a yearling ram as a guilt-

offering. The previous period shall not be reckoned, because the hair which he dedicated became unclean.

The law for the Nazirite, when the 13 term of his dedication is completed, shall be this. He shall be brought to the entrance to the Tent of the Presence and shall present his offering to the 14 LORD: one yearling ram without blemish as a whole-offering, one yearling ewe without blemish as a sin-offering, one ram without blemish as a shared-offering, and a basket of cakes made 15 of flour mixed with oil, and of wafers smeared with oil, both unleavened, together with the proper grain-offerings and drink-offerings. The priest 16 shall present all these before the LORD and offer the man's sin-offering and whole-offering; the ram he shall offer 17 as a shared-offering to the LORD, together with the basket of unleavened cakes and the proper grain-offering and drink-offering. The Nazirite shall 18 shave his head at the entrance to the Tent of the Presence, take the hair which had been dedicated and put it on the fire where the shared-offering is burning. The priest shall take the 19 shoulder of the ram, after boiling it, and take also one unleavened cake from the basket and one unleavened wafer, and put them on the palms of the Nazirite's hands, his hair which had been dedicated having been shaved. The priest shall then present them as a 20 special gift before the LORD; these, together with the breast of the special gift and the leg of the contribution, are holy and belong to the priest. When this has been done, the Nazirite is again free to drink wine.

Such is the law for the Nazirite who 21 has made his vow. Such is the offering he must make to the LORD for his dedication, apart from anything else that he can afford. He must carry out his vow in full according to the law governing his dedication.

d makes a special: or performs a . . .
e That is separated one or dedicated one.

a custom otherwise connected with mourning (Lev.10.6). **6.3:** *Wine* may have been avoided because it could induce drunkenness, unbecoming in a holy man; see also Lev.2.11 n.; 10.9 n. **5:** See, for example, Judg.13.5 and 16.15–19. **6–7:** Compare Lev.21.1–12. **9:** The elapse of *seven days* is normal (19.11). **10:** The sacrificial animals correspond to those required in some

22 The LORD spoke to Moses and said,
23 Speak to Aaron and his sons in these words: These are the words with which you shall bless the Israelites:

24 The LORD bless you and watch over you;
25 the LORD make his face shine upon*f* you and be gracious to you;
26 the LORD look kindly on you and give you peace.

27 They shall pronounce my name over the Israelites, and I will bless them.

7 ON THE DAY THAT MOSES COMPLETED THE setting up of the Tabernacle, he anointed and consecrated it; he also anointed and consecrated its equipment, and the
2 altar and its vessels. The chief men of Israel, heads of families—that is the chiefs of the tribes, who had assisted in preparing the detailed lists—came for-
3 ward and brought their offering before the LORD, six covered wagons and twelve oxen, one wagon from every two chiefs and from each one an ox.*g* These they brought forward before the Taber-
4 nacle; and the LORD spoke to Moses
5 and said, 'Accept these from them: they shall be used for the service of the Tent of the Presence. Assign them to the Levites as their several duties require.'
6 So Moses accepted the wagons and oxen and assigned them to the Levites.
7 He gave two wagons and four oxen to the Gershonites as required for their
8 service; four wagons and eight oxen to the Merarites as required for their service, in charge of Ithamar the son of
9 Aaron the priest. He gave none to the Kohathites because the service laid upon them was that of the holy things: these they had to carry themselves on their shoulders.
10 When the altar was anointed, the

chiefs brought their gift for its dedication and presented their offering before it. The LORD said to Moses, 'Let the 11 chiefs present their offering for the dedication of the altar one by one, on consecutive days.'

The chief who presented his offering 12 on the first day was Nahshon son of Amminadab of the tribe of Judah. His 13 offering was one silver dish weighing a hundred and thirty shekels by the sacred standard and one silver tossing-bowl weighing seventy, both full of flour mixed with oil as a grain-offering; one saucer weighing ten gold shekels, 14 full of incense; one young bull, one full- 15 grown ram, and one yearling ram, as a whole-offering; one he-goat as a sin- 16 offering; and two bulls, five full-grown 17 rams, five he-goats, and five yearling rams, as a shared-offering. This was the offering of Nahshon son of Amminadab.

On the second day Nethaneel son of 18 Zuar, chief of Issachar, brought his offering. He brought one silver dish 19 weighing a hundred and thirty shekels by the sacred standard and one silver tossing-bowl weighing seventy, both full of flour mixed with oil as a grain-offering; one saucer weighing ten gold 20 shekels, full of incense; one young bull, 21 one full-grown ram, and one yearling ram, as a whole-offering; one he-goat 22 as a sin-offering; and two bulls, five 23 full-grown rams, five he-goats, and five yearling rams, as a shared-offering. This was the offering of Nethaneel son of Zuar.

On the third day the chief of the 24 Zebulunites, Eliab son of Helon, came. His offering was one silver dish weigh- 25 ing a hundred and thirty shekels by the sacred standard and one silver tossing-bowl weighing seventy, both full of flour mixed with oil as a grain-offering;

f Or to.   *g Or* a bull.

---

other cases of recovery from uncleanness (Lev.12.8 and 14.22). **22–26:** This blessing was likely part of the regular Temple service (see Lev.9.22). **25:** *Make his face shine* is alternatively expressed in v. 26 as *look kindly on*. See Pss.31.16 and 80.3.

7.1–89: Offerings of the tribal leaders at the consecration of the Tabernacle. Topically, this once independent unit belongs with Exod. ch. 40 which describes the completion of the sanctuary. The narrative in Lev. chs. 8–9, where the sacrificial ritual was initiated, does not reflect it; in the priestly chronology (see 1.1 n.), a month has now passed. The placement here is logical: this unit presupposes rules for laymen bringing sacrifices (Lev. chs. 1–7) and the presence of Aaronites (Lev. chs. 8–9) and Levites (Num. ch. 3) to receive the offerings. **2:** *Detailed lists:* the census of ch. 1. **9:** *Holy things:* see 4.1–15. **11:** *Consecutive days.* the length and detail

26 one saucer weighing ten gold shekels,
27 full of incense; one young bull, one full-grown ram, and one yearling ram,
28 as a whole-offering; one he-goat as a
29 sin-offering; and two bulls, five full-grown rams, five he-goats, and five yearling rams, as a shared offering. This was the offering of Eliab son of Helon.

30 On the fourth day the chief of the Reubenites, Elizur son of Shedeur,
31 came. His offering was one silver dish weighing a hundred and thirty shekels by the sacred standard and one silver tossing-bowl weighing seventy, both full of flour mixed with oil as a grain-
32 offering; one saucer weighing ten gold
33 shekels, full of incense; one young bull, one full-grown ram, and one yearling
34 ram, as a whole-offering; one he-goat
35 as a sin-offering; and two bulls, five full-grown rams, five he-goats, and five yearling rams, as a shared-offering. This was the offering of Elizur son of Shedeur.

36 On the fifth day the chief of the Simeonites, Shelumiel son of Zuri-
37 shaddai, came. His offering was one silver dish weighing a hundred and thirty shekels by the sacred standard and one silver tossing-bowl weighing seventy, both full of flour mixed with
38 oil as a grain-offering; one saucer weighing ten gold shekels, full of in-
39 cense; one young bull, one full-grown ram, and one yearling ram, as a whole-
40 offering; one he-goat as a sin-offering;
41 and two bulls, five full-grown rams, five he-goats, and five yearling rams, as a shared-offering. This was the offering of Shelumiel son of Zurishad-dai.

42 On the sixth day the chief of the Gadites, Eliasaph son of Reuel, came.
43 His offering was one silver dish weighing a hundred and thirty shekels by the sacred standard and one silver tossing-bowl weighing seventy, both full of flour mixed with oil as a grain-offering;
44 one saucer weighing ten gold shekels,
45 full of incense; one young bull, one full-grown ram, and one yearling ram, as a
46 whole-offering; one he-goat as a sin-
47 offering; and two bulls, five full-grown rams, five he-goats, and five yearling rams, as a shared offering. This was the offering of Eliasaph son of Reuel.

48 On the seventh day the chief of the
49 Ephraimites, Elishama son of Ammi-hud, came. His offering was one silver dish weighing a hundred and thirty shekels by the sacred standard and one silver tossing-bowl weighing seventy, both full of flour mixed with oil as a grain-offering; one saucer weighing ten
50 gold shekels, full of incense; one young
51 bull, one full-grown ram, and one yearling ram, as a whole-offering; one
52 he-goat as a sin-offering; and two bulls,
53 five full-grown rams, five he-goats, and five yearling rams, as a shared-offering. This was the offering of Elishama son of Ammihud.

54 On the eighth day the chief of the Manassites, Gamaliel son of Pedahzur,
55 came. His offering was one silver dish weighing a hundred and thirty shekels by the sacred standard and one silver tossing-bowl weighing seventy, both full of flour mixed with oil as a grain-offering; one saucer weighing ten gold
56 shekels, full of incense; one young bull,
57 one full-grown ram, and one yearling ram, as a whole-offering; one he-goat
58 as a sin-offering; and two bulls, five
59 full-grown rams, five he-goats, and five yearling rams, as a shared-offering. This was the offering of Gamaliel son of Pedahzur.

60 On the ninth day the chief of the Benjamites, Abidan son of Gideoni,
61 came. His offering was one silver dish weighing a hundred and thirty shekels by the sacred standard and one silver tossing-bowl weighing seventy, both full of flour mixed with oil as a grain-offering; one saucer weighing ten gold
62 shekels, full of incense; one young bull,
63 one full-grown ram, and one yearling ram, as a whole-offering; one he-goat
64 as a sin-offering; and two bulls, five
65 full-grown rams, five he-goats, and five yearling rams, as a shared-offering. This was the offering of Abidan son of Gideoni.

66 On the tenth day the chief of the Danites, Ahiezer son of Ammishaddai,
67 came. His offering was one silver dish

---

of the narrative which follows (12–83) suggest the importance of financial support for the cult,

Israel in the wilderness of Sinai

weighing a hundred and thirty shekels by the sacred standard and one silver tossing-bowl weighing seventy, both full of flour mixed with oil as a grain-offering; 68 one saucer weighing ten gold 69 shekels, full of incense; one young bull, one full-grown ram, and one yearling 70 ram, as a whole-offering; one he-goat 71 as a sin-offering; and two bulls, five full-grown rams, five he-goats, and five yearling rams, as a shared-offering. This was the offering of Ahiezer son of Ammishaddai.

72 On the eleventh day the chief of the Asherites, Pagiel son of Ocran, came. 73 His offering was one silver dish weighing a hundred and thirty shekels by the sacred standard and one silver tossing-bowl weighing seventy, both full of flour mixed with oil as a grain-offering; 74 one saucer weighing ten gold shekels, 75 full of incense; one young bull, one full-grown ram, and one yearling ram, 76 as a whole-offering; one he-goat as a 77 sin-offering; and two bulls, five full-grown rams, five he-goats, and five yearling rams, as a shared-offering. This was the offering of Pagiel son of Ocran.

78 On the twelfth day the chief of the Naphtalites, Ahira son of Enan, came. 79 His offering was one silver dish weighing a hundred and thirty shekels by the sacred standard and one silver tossing-bowl weighing seventy, both full of flour mixed with oil as a grain-offering; 80 one saucer weighing ten gold shekels, 81 full of incense; one young bull, one full-grown ram, and one yearling ram, 82 as a whole-offering; one he-goat as a 83 sin-offering; and two bulls, five full-grown rams, five he-goats, and five yearling rams, as a shared-offering. This was the offering of Ahira son of Enan.

84 This was the gift from the chiefs of Israel for the dedication of the altar when it was anointed: twelve silver dishes, twelve silver tossing-bowls, and 85 twelve golden saucers; each silver dish weighed a hundred and thirty shekels, each silver tossing-bowl seventy shekels. The total weight of the silver vessels was two thousand four hundred shekels by the sacred standard. There 86 were twelve golden saucers full of incense, ten shekels each by the sacred standard: the total weight of the gold of the saucers was a hundred and twenty shekels. The number of beasts 87 for the whole-offering was twelve bulls, twelve full-grown rams, and twelve yearling rams, with the prescribed grain-offerings, and twelve he-goats for the sin-offering. The number of 88 beasts for the shared-offering was twenty-four bulls, sixty full-grown rams, sixty he-goats, and sixty yearling rams. This was the gift for the dedication of the altar when it was anointed. And when Moses entered the Tent of 89 the Presence to speak with God, he heard the Voice speaking from above the cover over the Ark of the Tokens from between the two cherubim: the Voice spoke to him.

The LORD spoke to Moses and said, **8** 'Speak to Aaron in these words: "When 2 you mount the seven lamps, see that they shed their light forwards in front of the lamp-stand."' Aaron did this: 3 he mounted the lamps, so as to shed light forwards in front of the lamp-stand, as the LORD had instructed Moses. The lamp-stand was made of 4 beaten-work in gold, as well as the stem and the petals. Moses made it to match the pattern which the LORD had shown him.

The LORD spoke to Moses and said: 5 Take the Levites apart from the rest of 6 the Israelites and cleanse them ritually. This is what you shall do to cleanse 7 them. Sprinkle lustral water over them; they shall then shave their whole bodies, wash their clothes, and so be cleansed. Next, they shall take a young 8 bull as a whole-offering[h] with its prescribed grain-offering, flour mixed with

h as a whole-offering: prob. rdg.; Heb. om.

---

and encourage imitation of the generosity of the tribal leaders. **89:** This appears to be a fragment with no relation to its present context. See Exod.25.22.

8.1–9.14: Another collection of miscellaneous materials (see 5.1–6.27 n. for the reason). **1–4:** Belonging topically with Exod.25.31–40 and 37.17–24, this section specifies the orientation of the lamps. **5–26:** The consecration of the Levites. The material of ch. 3 is enlarged as the story moves from appointment to installation. The procedure is similar to that for the Aaronites in

oil; and you shall take a second young
9 bull as a sin-offering. Bring the Levites
before the Tent of the Presence and
call the whole community of Israelites
10 together. Bring the Levites before the
LORD, and let the Israelites lay their
11 hands on their heads. Aaron shall
present the Levites before the LORD as
a special gift from the Israelites, and
they shall be dedicated to the service
12 of the LORD. The Levites shall lay their
hands on the heads of the bulls; one
bull shall be offered as a sin-offering
and the other as a whole-offering to the
LORD, to make expiation for the
13 Levites. Then you shall set the Levites
before Aaron and his sons, presenting
14 them to the LORD as a special gift. You
shall thus separate the Levites from
the rest of the Israelites, and they shall
be mine.

15 After this, the Levites shall enter the
Tent of the Presence to serve in it,
ritually cleansed and presented as a
16 special gift; for they are given and
dedicated to me, out of all the Israelites. I have accepted them as mine in
place of all that comes first from the
womb, every first child among the
17 Israelites; for every first-born male
creature, man or beast, among the
Israelites is mine. On the day when I
struck down every first-born creature
in Egypt, I hallowed all the first-born of
18 the Israelites to myself, and I have
19 accepted the Levites in their place. I
have given the Levites to Aaron and his
sons, dedicated among the Israelites to
perform the service of the Israelites in
the Tent of the Presence and to make
expiation for them, and then no calamity will befall them when they come
close to the sanctuary.
20 Moses and Aaron and the whole
community of Israelites carried out all
the commands the LORD had given to
Moses for the dedication of the Levites.
21 The Levites purified themselves of sin
and washed their clothes, and Aaron

presented them as a special gift before
the LORD and made expiation for them,
to cleanse them. Then at last they went 22
in to perform their service in the Tent
of the Presence, before Aaron and his
sons. Thus the commands the LORD
had given to Moses concerning the
Levites were all carried out.

The LORD spoke to Moses and said: 23
Touching the Levites: they shall begin 24
their active work in the service of the
Tent of the Presence at the age of
twenty-five. At the age of fifty a Levite 25
shall retire from regular service and
shall serve no longer. He may continue 26
to assist his colleagues in attendance in
the Tent of the Presence but shall perform no regular service. This is how
you shall arrange the attendance of the
Levites.

In the first month of the second year 9
after they came out of Egypt, the LORD
spoke to Moses in the wilderness of
Sinai and said, 'Let the Israelites pre- 2
pare the Passover at the time appointed
for it. This shall be between dusk and 3
dark on the fourteenth day of this
month, and you shall keep it at this
appointed time, observing every rule
and custom proper to it.' So Moses 4
told the Israelites to prepare the Passover, and they prepared it on the four- 5
teenth day of the first month, between
dusk and dark, in the wilderness of
Sinai. The Israelites did exactly as the
LORD had instructed Moses.

It happened that some men were 6
ritually unclean through contact with
a corpse and so could not keep the
Passover on the right day. They came
before Moses and Aaron that same day
and said, 'We are unclean through 7
contact with a corpse. Must we therefore be debarred from presenting the
LORD's offering at its appointed time
with the rest of the Israelites?' Moses 8
answered, 'Wait, and let me hear what
commands the LORD has for you.'

The LORD spoke to Moses and said, 9

Lev. ch. 8. 7: *Shave... wash:* see Lev.14.8 n. 10: *Lay their hands:* thus the Levites become an
offering brought by the people, a variation upon the theme that they are a substitute for the
firstborn (vv. 16–18; 3.11–13). 13: *Before Aaron:* see 3.6 n. 24: *Touching:* concerning. *Twenty-
five:* see 4.3 n. 9.1–14: Provision for a delayed Passover celebration. 1: *First month:* chronologically, this material, like ch. 7, belongs before 1.1 which is dated to the second month.
2–3: See Exod.12.1–10. 6: For seven days after *contact with a corpse,* a person could not
approach the Tabernacle (19.11–22). 6–8: The tension between the laws of uncleanness and
the command for each person to observe the Passover (Exod.12.3) is resolved by a precedent

10 Tell the Israelites: If any one of you or of your descendants is ritually unclean through contact with a corpse, or if he is away on a long journey, he shall keep a Passover to the LORD none the 11 less. But in that case he shall prepare the victim in the second month, between dusk and dark on the fourteenth day. It shall be eaten with unleavened 12 cakes and bitter herbs; nothing shall be left over till morning, and no bone of it shall be broken. The Passover shall be 13 kept exactly as the law prescribes. The man who, being ritually clean and not absent on a journey, neglects to keep the Passover, shall be cut off from his father's kin, because he has not presented the LORD's offering at its appointed time. That man shall accept responsibility for his sin.

14 When an alien is settled among you, he also shall keep the Passover to the LORD, observing every rule and custom proper to it. The same law is binding on you all, alien and native alike.

The journey from Sinai to Edom

15 ON THE DAY WHEN THEY SET UP THE Tabernacle, that is the Tent of the Tokens, cloud covered it, and in the evening a brightness like fire appeared 16 over it till morning. So it continued: the cloud covered it by day and a 17 brightness like fire by night. Whenever the cloud lifted from the tent, the Israelites struck camp, and at the place where the cloud settled, there they 18 pitched their camp. At the command of the LORD they struck camp, and at the command of the LORD they encamped again, and continued in camp as long as the cloud rested over the 19 Tabernacle. When the cloud stayed long over the Tabernacle, the Israelites remained in attendance on the LORD 20 and did not move on; and it was the same when the cloud continued over the Tabernacle only a few days: at the command of the LORD they remained in camp, and at the command of the LORD they struck camp. There were 21 also times when the cloud continued only from evening till morning, and in the morning, when the cloud lifted, they moved on. Whether by day or by night, they moved as soon as the cloud lifted. Whether it was for a day or two, 22 for a month or a year, whenever the cloud stayed long over the Tabernacle, the Israelites remained where they were and did not move on; they did so only when the cloud lifted. At the command 23 of the LORD they encamped, and at his command they struck camp. At the LORD's command, given through Moses, they remained in attendance on the LORD.

The LORD spoke to Moses and said: 10 Make two trumpets of beaten silver and 2 use them for summoning the community and for breaking camp. When 3 both are sounded, the whole community shall muster before you at the entrance to the Tent of the Presence. If a single trumpet is sounded, the 4 chiefs who are heads of the Israelite clans shall muster. When you give the 5 signal for a shout, those encamped on the east side are to move off. When the 6 signal is given for a second shout those encamped to the south are to move off. A signal to shout is the signal to move off. When you convene the assembly, 7 you shall sound a trumpet but not raise a shout. This sounding of the trumpets 8 is the duty of the Aaronite priests and shall be a rule binding for all time on your descendants.

When you go into battle against an 9 invader and you are hard pressed by him, you shall raise a cheer when the trumpets sound, and this will serve as a reminder of you before the LORD your God and you will be delivered from your enemies. On your festal days 10 and at your appointed seasons and on the first day of every month, you shall sound the trumpets over your whole-

---

placed in the time of Moses. **10:** *Away:* a possibility not covered by previous legislation. For similar extensions or liberalizations, indicative of the flexibility with which later generations viewed their laws, see 5.3 n., 5–8 n., 11–31 n. **13:** *Cut off:* see Lev.7.21 n. **14:** See Exod.12.43–49.
9.15–10.36: Preparation and departure from Sinai. The narrative has reached this point twice previously (see Exod.23.20–33 n. and 33.1–23 n., plus Exod.34.1–35 n.): it resumes from Exod.40.38. **16:** *Cloud...fire:* see Exod.13.21 n. **10.13–27:** The order of the march follows the

offerings and your shared-offerings, and the trumpets shall be a reminder on your behalf before the LORD your God. I am the LORD your God.

11 In the second year, on the twentieth day of the second month, the cloud lifted from the Tabernacle of the 12 Tokens, and the Israelites moved by stages from the wilderness of Sinai, until the cloud came to rest in the wil-13 derness of Paran. The first time that they broke camp at the command of the 14 LORD given through Moses, the standard of the division of Judah moved off first with its tribal hosts: the host of Judah under Nahshon son of Am-15 minadab, the host of Issachar under 16 Nethaneel son of Zuar, and the host of Zebulun under Eliab son of Helon. 17 Then the Tabernacle was taken down, and its bearers, the sons of Gershon and Merari, moved off.

18 Secondly, the standard of the division of Reuben moved off with its tribal hosts: the host of Reuben under Elizur 19 son of Shedeur, the host of Simeon under Shelumiel son of Zurishaddai, 20 and the host of Gad under Eliasaph 21 son of Reuel. The Kohathites, the bearers of the holy things, moved off next, and on their arrival found the Tabernacle set up.

22 Thirdly, the standard of the division of Ephraim moved off with its tribal hosts: the host of Ephraim under 23 Elishama son of Ammihud, the host of Manasseh under Gamaliel son of 24 Pedahzur, and the host of Benjamin under Abidan son of Gideoni.

25 Lastly, the standard of the division of Dan, the rearguard of all the divisions, moved off with its tribal hosts: the host of Dan under Ahiezer son of 26 Ammishaddai, the host of Asher under 27 Pagiel son of Ocran, and the host of Naphtali under Ahira son of Enan.

28 This was the order of march for the Israelites, mustered in their hosts, and in this order they broke camp.

29 And Moses said to Hobab son of

Reuel the Midianite, his brother-in-law, 'We are setting out for the place which the LORD promised to give us. Come with us, and we will deal generously with you, for the LORD has given an assurance of good fortune for Israel.' But he replied, 'No, I will not; 30 I would rather go to my own country and my own people.' Moses said, 'Do 31 not desert us, I beg you; for you know where we ought to camp in the wilderness, and you will be our guide. If you 32 will go with us, then all the good fortune with which the LORD favours us we will share with you.'

Then they moved off from the 33 mountain of the LORD and journeyed for three days, and the Ark of the Covenant of the LORD kept a day's journey ahead of them to find them a place to rest. The cloud of the LORD 34 hung over them by day when they moved camp. Whenever the Ark began 35 to move, Moses said,

'Up, Lord, and may thy enemies be scattered
and those that hate thee flee before thee.'

When it halted, he said, 36

'Rest, LORD of the countless thousands of Israel.'

There came a time when the people 11 complained to the LORD of their hardships. When he heard, he became angry and fire from the LORD broke out among them, and was raging at one end of the camp, when the people appealed 2 to Moses. He interceded with the LORD, and the fire died down. Then they 3 named that place Taberah,[i] because the fire of the LORD had burned among them there.

Now there was a mixed company of 4 strangers who had joined the Israelites. These people began to be greedy for

i *That is* Burning.

prescription of 2.3–31 and the responsibilities follow that of 4.1–33. **29:** The tradition here, different from later priestly versions, continues from Exod.34.35. *Reuel:* see Exod.18.1 n.
11.1–34: Rebellion in the Wilderness. Despite Israel's certainty of God's presence and graciousness in granting the covenant (Exod. chs. 20–24) and in renewing it (Exod. ch. 34), doubts and complaints nevertheless arose at the first new difficulty. **1:** On *fire* as a means or symbol of divine punishment, see Lev.10.1–2. **4:** *Strangers:* see Exod.12.38; *greedy:* see Ps.78.18.

better things, and the Israelites themselves wept once again and cried, 'Will
5 no one give us meat? Think of it! In
Egypt we had fish for the asking, cucumbers and water-melons, leeks and
6 onions and garlic. Now our throats are
parched; there is nothing wherever we
7 look except this manna.' (The manna
looked like coriander seed, the colour
8 of gum resin. The people went about
collecting it, ground it up in hand-mills
or pounded it in mortars, then boiled it
in the pot and made it into cakes. It
9 tasted like butter-cakes. When dew fell
on the camp at night, the manna fell
10 with it.) Moses heard the people wailing, all of them in their families at the
opening of their tents. Then the LORD
became very angry, and Moses was
11 troubled. He said to the LORD, 'Why
hast thou brought trouble on thy servant? How have I displeased the LORD
that I am burdened with the care of this
12 whole people? Am I their mother?
Have I brought them into the world,
and am I called upon to carry them in
my bosom, like a nurse with her babies,
to the land promised by thee on oath
13 to their fathers? Where am I to find
meat to give them all? They pester me
with their wailing and their "Give us
14 meat to eat." This whole people is a
burden too heavy for me; I cannot
15 carry it alone. If that is thy purpose for
me, then kill me outright. But if I have
won thy favour let me suffer this
trouble at thy hands*ʲ* no longer.'
16   The LORD answered Moses, 'Assemble seventy elders from Israel, men
known to you as elders and officers in
the community; bring them to me at the
Tent of the Presence, and there let them
17 take their stand with you. I will come
down and speak with you there. I will
take back part of that same spirit which
has been conferred on you and confer
it on them, and they will share with
you the burden of taking care for the

people; then you will not have to bear
it alone. And to the people you shall 18
say this: "Hallow yourselves in readiness for tomorrow; you shall have
meat to eat. You wailed in the LORD's
hearing; you said, 'Will no one give us
meat? In Egypt we lived well.' The
LORD will give you meat and you shall
eat it. Not for one day only, nor for 19
two days, nor five, nor ten, nor twenty,
but for a whole month you shall eat it 20
until it comes out at your nostrils and
makes you sick; because you have
rejected the LORD who dwells in your
midst, wailing in his presence and saying, 'Why did we ever come out of
Egypt?'"'

Moses replied, 'Here am I with six 21
hundred thousand men on the march
around me, and thou dost promise
them meat to eat for a whole month.
How can the sheep and oxen be 22
slaughtered that would be enough for
them? If all the fish in the sea could be
caught, would they be enough?' The 23
LORD said to Moses, 'Is there a limit to
the power of the LORD? You will see
this very day whether or not my words
come true.'

Moses came out and told the people 24
what the LORD had said. He assembled
seventy men from the elders of the
people and stationed them round
the Tent. Then the LORD descended in 25
the cloud and spoke to him. He took
back part of that same spirit which he
had conferred on Moses and conferred
it on the seventy elders; as the spirit
alighted on them, they fell into a
prophetic ecstasy, for the first and only
time.

Now two men named Eldad and 26
Medad, who had been enrolled with
the seventy, were left behind in the
camp. But, though they had not gone
out to the Tent, the spirit alighted on

*ʲ this trouble ... hands: prob. original rdg., altered in
Heb. to my trouble.*

6: *Manna:* see Exod.16.14–15,31 nn. In another version, placed after the escape from Egypt
(Exod. ch. 16), manna and meat (quails) are the LORD's response to a single demand for food.
In its present setting, however, the story depicts Israel as increasingly inappreciative: the quails
are granted only when the manna is declared insufficient. See Exod.16.6–8 n. **14–17, 24b–30**:
The intensification of the rebellion provides the opportunity for introduction of a new theme:
the sharing of Moses' responsibility as leader. The elders, who must have exercised tribal
leadership since antiquity, are here said to derive their power from and to remain under the
authority of the community's religious leadership. Compare Exod.18.13–26 n. **16**: *Seventy*: as in
Exod.24.1; see Gen.46.27 n. **18–24a, 31–34**: Continuation of the food tradition. **26**: *Out to the*

them none the less, and they fell into
27 an ecstasy there in the camp. A young
man ran and told Moses that Eldad and
Medad were in an ecstasy in the camp,
28 whereupon Joshua son of Nun, who
had served with Moses since he was a
boy, broke in, 'My lord Moses, stop
29 them!' But Moses said to him, 'Are
you jealous on my account? I wish that
all the LORD's people were prophets
and that the LORD would confer his
30 spirit on them all!' And Moses rejoined
the camp with the elders of Israel.
31   Then a wind from the LORD sprang
up; it drove quails in from the west,
and they were flying all round the camp
for the distance of a day's journey,
32 three feet above the ground. The people
were busy gathering quails all that day,
all night, and all next day, and even the
man who got least gathered ten homers.
They spread them out to dry all about
33 the camp. But the meat was scarcely
between their teeth, and they had not
so much as bitten it, when the LORD's
anger broke out against the people and
he struck them with a deadly plague.
34 That place was called Kibroth-hattaavah[k] because there they buried the
people who had been greedy for meat.
35   From Kibroth-hattaavah the Israelites went on to Hazeroth, and while
12 they were at Hazeroth, Miriam and
Aaron began to speak against Moses.
They blamed him for his Cushite wife
(for he had married a Cushite woman),
2 and they said, 'Is Moses the only one
with[l] whom the LORD has spoken?
Has he not spoken with[l] us as well?'
3 Moses was in fact a man of great
humility, the most humble man on
4 earth. But the LORD heard them and
suddenly he said to Moses, Aaron and
Miriam, 'Go out all three of you to the
Tent of the Presence.' So the three went
5 out, and the LORD descended in a
pillar of cloud; he stood at the entrance

to the tent and summoned Aaron and
Miriam. The two of them went for-
ward, and he said,   6

'Listen to my words.
If he[m] were your prophet and
    nothing more,
I would make myself known to him
    in a vision,
I would speak with him in a dream.
But my servant Moses is not such a   7
    prophet;
he alone is faithful[n] of all my
    household.
With him I speak face to face,   8
openly and not in riddles.
He shall see the very form of the
    LORD.
How do you dare speak against my
    servant Moses?'

    Thus the anger of the LORD was   9
roused against them, and he left them;
and as the cloud moved from the tent,   10
there was Miriam, her skin diseased
and white as snow. Aaron turned towards her and saw her skin diseased.
Then he said to Moses, 'Pray, my lord, 11
do not make us pay the penalty of sin,
foolish and wicked though we have
been. Let her not be like something   12
still-born, whose flesh is half eaten
away when it comes from the womb.'
So Moses cried, 'Not this, O LORD!   13
Heal her, I pray.' The LORD replied,   14
'Suppose her father had spat in her face,
would she not have to remain in disgrace for seven days? Let her be kept for
seven days in confinement outside the
camp and then be brought back.' So
Miriam was kept outside for seven days,
and the people did not strike camp   15
until she was brought back. After this
they set out from Hazeroth and pitched 16
camp in the wilderness of Paran.

k That is the Graves of Greed.   *l* Or by.
m Prob. rdg.; Heb. the LORD.   *n* Or to be trusted.

Tent: see 2.17 n. for various traditions as to its location. **27–30:** *Prophets*, deriving their
inspiration directly from God, were a challenge to all established forms of religious authority.
Here, the later prophetic movement is traced back to Moses and receives sanction from his
blessing. **31:** *Quails:* see Exod.16.6–8 n. **32:** *Homer:* see p. 1035.
    11.35–12.16: A challenge to Moses' authority. 12.1: *Cushite:* possibly another designation for
Midianite (Hab.3.7), and hence Zipporah (Exod.2.16–22). Compare 25.6–18; 31.1–18. For other
possibilities, see Gen.10.6 n. **2:** *With us:* Miriam is called a "prophetess" and recognized as
a leader in Exod.15.20. **8:** *Face to face:* Exod.33.11. *Form:* Exod.33.18–23. **14:** Spit is mentioned
as causing uncleanness in Lev.15.8. *Seven days:* the prescribed period following recovery from
skin disease (Lev.14.8–9). **16:** The itinerary does not accord with 10.12.

13 THE LORD SPOKE TO MOSES AND SAID, 'Send men out to explore the land of Canaan which I am giving to the Israelites; from each of their fathers' tribes send one man, and let him be a man of high rank.' So Moses sent them from the wilderness of Paran at the command of the LORD, all of them leading men among the Israelites. These were their names:

from the tribe of Reuben, Shammua son of Zaccur;
from the tribe of Simeon, Shaphat son of Hori;
from the tribe of Judah, Caleb son of Jephunneh;
from the tribe of Issachar, Igal son of Joseph;
from the tribe of Ephraim, Hoshea son of Nun;
from the tribe of Benjamin, Palti son of Raphu;
from the tribe of Zebulun, Gaddiel son of Sodi;
from the tribe of Joseph (that is from the tribe of Manasseh), Gaddi son of Susi;
from the tribe of Dan, Ammiel son of Gemalli;
from the tribe of Asher, Sethur son of Michael;
from the tribe of Naphtali, Nahbi son of Vophsi;
from the tribe of Gad, Geuel son of Machi.

These are the names of the men whom Moses sent to explore the land. But Moses called the son of Nun Joshua, not Hoshea.

When Moses sent them to explore the land of Canaan, he said to them, 'Make your way up by the Negeb, and go on into the hill-country. See what the land is like, and whether the people who live there are strong or weak, few or many. See whether it is easy or difficult country in which they live, and whether the cities in which they live are weakly defended or well fortified; is the land fertile or barren, and does it grow trees or not? Go boldly in and take some of its fruit.' It was the season when the first grapes were ripe.

They went up and explored the country from the wilderness of Zin as far as Rehob by Lebo-hamath. They went up by the Negeb and came to Hebron, where Ahiman, Sheshai and Talmai, the descendants of Anak,*o* were living. (Hebron was built seven years before Zoan in Egypt.) They came to the gorge of Eshcol,*p* and there they cut a branch with a single bunch of grapes, and they carried it on a pole two at a time; they also picked pomegranates and figs. It was from the bunch of grapes which the Israelites cut there that that place was named the gorge of Eshcol. After forty days they returned from exploring the country, and came back to Moses and Aaron and the whole community of Israelites at Kadesh in the wilderness of Paran. They made their report to them and to the* whole community, and showed them the fruit of the country. And this was the story they told Moses: 'We made our way into the land to which you sent us. It is flowing with milk and honey, and here is the fruit it grows; but its inhabitants are sturdy, and the cities are very strongly fortified; indeed, we saw there the descendants of Anak. We also saw the Amalekites who live in the Negeb, Hittites, Jebusites, and Amorites who live in the hill-country, and the Canaanites who live by the sea and along the Jordan.'

Then Caleb called for silence before Moses and said, 'Let us go up at once and occupy the country; we are well able to conquer it.' But the men who

o descendants of Anak: or tall men.
p Eshcol: that is Bunch of Grapes.

13.1–33: Spying out the land of Canaan. With this account, the theme of the conquest of the promised land begins to rise, to reach its climax in the Book of Josh. Various memories have here been combined, with duplications and variations. **16:** *Joshua, not Hoshea:* the two names, however, come from the same Heb. verb. Hoshea means "save"; Joshua, "the LORD saves." "Jesus" is a much later form of Joshua. **21:** *Lebo-hamath:* this tradition, at variance with a shallow exploration in v. 22, may be based on the northern boundaries of the Solomonic kingdom (1 Kgs.8.65). Compare Gen.15.18 n. **25:** *Forty days:* see Gen. 7.4 n. **26:** *Kadesh:* the setting for the events until 20.22, forty years later (14.32–33). **33:** *Nephilim:* see Gen.6.1–4 n.

had gone with him said, 'No, we cannot
attack these people; they are stronger
than we are.' Thus their report to the
Israelites about the land which they had
explored was discouraging: 'The country we explored', they said, 'will swallow up any who go to live in it. All the
people we saw there are men of gigantic
33 size. When we set eyes on the Nephilim*q* (the sons of Anak*r* belong to the
Nephilim) we felt no bigger than grass-
hoppers; and that is how we looked to
them.'

14 Then the whole Israelite community
cried out in dismay; all night long they
2 wept. One and all they made complaints against Moses and Aaron: 'If
only we had died in Egypt or in the
wilderness!' they said. 'Far happier if
3 we had! Why should the LORD bring us
to this land, to die in battle and leave
our wives and our dependants to become the spoils of war? To go back to
4 Egypt would be better than this.' And
they began to talk of choosing someone to lead them back,
5 Then Moses and Aaron flung themselves on the ground before the
assembled community of the Israelites,
6 and two of those who had explored the
land, Joshua son of Nun and Caleb son
7 of Jephunneh, rent their clothes and
addressed the whole community: 'The
country we penetrated and explored',
8 they said, 'is very good land indeed. If
the LORD is pleased with us, he will
bring us into this land which flows with
9 milk and honey, and give it to us. But
you must not rebel against the LORD.
You need not fear the people of the
land; for there we shall find food. They
have lost the protection that they had:
the LORD is with us. You have nothing
10 to fear from them.' But by way of
answer the assembled Israelites threatened to stone them, when suddenly the
glory of the LORD appeared to them all
in the Tent of the Presence.
11 Then the LORD said to Moses, 'How
much longer will this people treat me
with contempt? How much longer will

they refuse to trust me in spite of all
the signs I have shown among them? I 12
will strike them with pestilence. I will
deny them their heritage, and you and
your descendants I will make into a
nation greater and more numerous
than they.' But Moses answered the 13
LORD, 'What if the Egyptians hear of
it? It was thou who didst bring this
people out of Egypt by thy strength.
What if they tell the inhabitants of this 14
land? They too have heard of thee,
LORD, that thou art with this people,
and art seen face to face, that thy cloud
stays over them, and thou goest before
them in a pillar of cloud by day and in a
pillar of fire by night. If then thou dost 15
put them all to death at one blow, the
nations who have heard these tales of
thee will say, "The LORD could not 16
bring this people into the land which
he promised them by oath; and so he
destroyed them in the wilderness."

'Now let the LORD's might be shown 17
in its greatness, true to thy proclamation of thyself "The LORD, long- 18
suffering, ever constant, who forgives
iniquity and rebellion, and punishes
sons to the third and fourth generation
for the iniquity of their fathers, though
he does not sweep them clean away."
Thou hast borne with this people from 19
Egypt all the way here; forgive their
iniquity, I beseech thee, as befits thy
great and constant love.'

The LORD said, 'Your prayer is 20
answered; I pardon them. But as I live, 21
in very truth the glory of the LORD shall
fill the earth. Not one of all those who 22-23
have seen my glory and the signs which
I wrought in Egypt and in the wilderness shall see the country which I promised on oath to their fathers. Ten
times they have challenged me and not
obeyed my voice. None of those who
have flouted me shall see this land. But 24-25
my servant Caleb showed a different
spirit: he followed me with his whole
heart. Because of this, I will bring him

q Or giants.
r sons of Anak: *or* tall men.

14.1–45: Israel's response to the report of the spies. The theme of "rebellion" (11.1–34;
Exod.15.22–17.7) here reaches a climax with a theological explanation for "forty" years of
wandering in the Wilderness. The combination of variant traditions evident in ch. 13 continues
in ch. 14. **18:** See Exod.34.6–7 n. The LORD's sovereignty is evident in graciousness as well as in
power. **25:** *Vale:* the coastal plain. *Turn back:* from direct entry from the south, and detour to

into the land in which he has already set foot, the territory of the Amalekites and the Canaanites who dwell in the Vale, and put his descendants in possession of it. Tomorrow you must turn back and set out for the wilderness by way of the Red Sea.'[s]

26 The LORD spoke to Moses and Aaron 27 and said, 'How long must I tolerate[t] the complaints of this wicked community? I have heard the Israelites 28 making complaints against me. Tell them that this is the very word of the LORD: As I live, I will bring home to you the words I have heard you utter. 29 Here in this wilderness your bones shall lie, every man of you on the register from twenty years old and upwards, because you have made these complaints 30 against me. Not one of you shall enter the land which I swore with uplifted hand should be your home, except only Caleb son of Jephunneh and Joshua 31 son of Nun. As for your dependants, those dependants who, you said, would become the spoils of war, I will bring them in to the land you have rejected, 32 and they shall enjoy it. But as for the rest of you, your bones shall lie in this 33 wilderness; your sons shall be wanderers in the wilderness forty years, paying the penalty of your wanton disloyalty till the last man of you dies 34 there. Forty days you spent exploring the country, and forty years you shall spend—a year for each day—paying the penalty of your iniquities. You shall know what it means to have me against 35 you.[u] I, the LORD, have spoken. This I swear to do to all this wicked community who have combined against me. There shall be an end of them here in this wilderness; here they shall die.' 36 But the men whom Moses had sent to explore the land, and who came back and by their report set all the community complaining against him, died 37 of the plague before the LORD; they died of the plague because they had made a bad report. Of those who went 38 to explore the land, Joshua son of Nun and Caleb son of Jephunneh alone remained alive.

When Moses reported the LORD's 39 words to all the Israelites, the people were plunged in grief. They set out early 40 next morning and made for the heights of the hill-country, saying, 'Look, we are on our way up to the place the LORD spoke of. We admit that we have been wrong.' But Moses replied, 'Must 41 you persist in disobeying the LORD's command? No good will come of this. Go no further; you will not have the 42 LORD with you, and your enemies will defeat you. For in front of you are the 43 Amalekites and Canaanites, and you will die by the sword, because you have ceased to follow the LORD, and he will no longer be with you.' But they went 44 recklessly on their way towards the heights of the hill-country, though neither the Ark of the Covenant of the LORD nor Moses moved with them out of the camp; and the Amalekites and 45 Canaanites from those hills came down and fell upon them, and crushed them at Hormah.

THE LORD SPOKE TO MOSES AND SAID, **15** Speak to the Israelites in these words: 2 When you enter the land where you are to live, the land I am giving you, you 3 will make food-offerings to the LORD; they may be whole-offerings or any sacrifice made in fulfilment of a special[v] vow or by way of freewill offering or at one of the appointed seasons. When you thus make an offering of soothing odour from herd or flock to the LORD, the man who offers, in presenting it, 4 shall add a grain-offering of a tenth of an ephah of flour mixed with a quarter of a hin of oil. You shall also add to the 5 whole-offering or shared-offering a

s Or the Sea of Reeds.
t must I tolerate: *prob. rdg.; Heb.* for.
u Or to thwart me.
v in fulfilment of a special: *or* to discharge a . . .

the east by way of Elath (*the Red Sea*: Exod.13.18 n.). See 21.4. Part of the group disregarded this directive (vv. 39–45). **26–38:** This is an alternative version of vv. 11–25.

15.1–41: A collection of miscellaneous cultic regulations. It possibly was placed here, rather than with the Sinai legislation, because it was to be operative after the conquest of Canaan (v. 2), and that theme makes its appearance only in chs. 13–14. Possibly, though, it was placed here because the episode of vv. 32–36 occurred in the Wilderness. **1–16:** Grain and wine, products common in Canaan as opposed to the Wilderness, must then accompany the previously specified animal sacrifice (Lev. chs. 1–7). **4:** *Ephah; hin:* see p. 1035. **5:** *Lamb;* see 28.3, 7, 14.

quarter of a hin of wine as a drink-offering with each lamb sacrificed.

6 If the animal is a ram, the grain-offering shall be two tenths of an ephah of flour mixed with a third of a hin of

7 oil, and the wine for the drink-offering shall be a third of a hin; in this way you will make an offering of soothing odour to the LORD.

8 When you offer to the LORD a young bull, whether as a whole-offering or as a sacrifice to fulfil a special*w* vow, or as

9 a shared-offering, you shall add a grain-offering of three tenths of an ephah of flour mixed with half a hin of

10 oil, and for the drink-offering, half a hin of wine; the whole will thus be a food-offering of soothing odour to the

11 LORD. This is what must be done in each case, for every bull or ram, lamb

12 or kid, whatever the number of each

13 that you vow. Every native Israelite shall observe these rules in each case when he offers a food-offering of soothing odour to the LORD.

14 When an alien residing with you or permanently settled among you offers a food-offering of soothing odour to

15 the LORD, he shall do as you do. There is one and the same rule for you and for the resident alien, a rule binding for all time on your descendants; you and the alien are alike before the LORD.

16 There shall be one law and one custom for you and for the alien residing with you.

17 The LORD spoke to Moses and said,

18 Speak to the Israelites in these words: After you have entered the land into

19 which I am bringing you, whenever you eat the bread of the country, you shall set aside a contribution for the LORD.

20 You shall set aside a cake made of your first kneading of dough, as you set aside the contribution from the thresh-

21 ing-floor. You must give a contribution to the LORD from your first kneading of dough; this rule is binding on your descendants.

22 When through inadvertence you omit to carry out any of these commands which the LORD gave to Moses

—any command whatever that the 23 LORD gave you through Moses on that first day and thereafter and made binding on your descendants—if it be done 24 inadvertently, unnoticed by the community, then the whole community shall offer one young bull as a whole-offering, a soothing odour to the LORD, with its proper grain-offering and drink-offering according to custom; and they shall add one he-goat as a sin-offering. The priest shall make expia- 25 tion for the whole community of Israelites, and they shall be forgiven. The omission was inadvertent; and they have brought their offering, a food-offering to the LORD; they have made their sin-offering before the LORD for their inadvertence; the whole com- 26 munity of Israelites and the aliens residing among you shall be forgiven. The inadvertence was shared by the whole people.

If any individual sins inadvertently, 27 he shall present a yearling she-goat as a sin-offering, and the priest shall make 28 expiation before the LORD for the said individual, and he shall be forgiven. For anyone who sins inadvertently, 29 there shall be one law for all, whether native Israelite or resident alien. But 30 the person who sins presumptuously, native or alien, insults the LORD. He shall be cut off from his people, because 31 he has brought the word of the LORD into contempt and violated his command. That person shall be wholly cut off; the guilt shall be on his head alone.

During the time that the Israelites 32 were in the wilderness, a man was found gathering sticks on the sabbath day. Those who had caught him in the 33 act brought him to Moses and Aaron and all the community, and they kept 34 him in custody, because it was not clearly known what was to be done with him. The LORD said to Moses, 35 'The man must be put to death; he must be stoned by all the community outside the camp.' So they took him 36 outside the camp and all stoned him

w fulfil a special: or discharge a . . .

14: *Alien:* see Lev.24.10–16 n. 17–21: This seems to be an extension of Lev.23.9–14 and Deut. 26.1–4, which required an offering of cakes in addition to the first sheaf. 22–31: The expanded requirements of vv. 1–16 are here applied to the sin-offering (Lev.4.1–5.13). 22–29: Expiation in the case of sin by *inadvertence.* 32–36: The law about "presumptuous" sin (vv. 30–31) is

to death, as the LORD had commanded Moses,

37 The LORD spoke to Moses and said,
38 Speak to the Israelites in these words: You must make tassels like flowers on the corners of your garments, you and your children's children. Into this tassel
39 you shall work a violet thread, and whenever you see this in the tassel, you shall remember all the LORD's commands and obey them, and not go your own wanton ways, led astray by your
40 own eyes and hearts. This token is to ensure that you remember all my commands and obey them, and keep yourselves holy, consecrated to your God.
41 I am the LORD your God who brought you out of Egypt to become your God. I am the LORD your God.

16 NOW KORAH SON OF IZHAR, SON OF Kohath, son of Levi, with the Reubenites Dathan and Abiram sons of Eliab
2 and On son of Peleth, challenged the authority of Moses. With them in their revolt were two hundred and fifty Israelites, all men of rank in the community, conveners of assembly and men
3 of good standing. They confronted Moses and Aaron and said to them, 'You take too much upon yourselves. Every member of the community is holy and the LORD is among them all. Why do you set yourselves up above
4 the assembly of the LORD?' When Moses heard this, he prostrated him-
5 self, and he said to Korah and all his company, 'Tomorrow morning the LORD shall declare who is his, who is holy and may present offerings to him. The man whom the LORD chooses shall
6 present them. This is what you must do, you, Korah, and all your company:
7 you must take censers and put fire in them, and then place incense on them before the LORD tomorrow. The man whom the LORD then chooses is the man who is holy. You take too much upon yourselves, you sons of Levi.'

Moses said to Korah, 'Now listen, 8 you sons of Levi. Is it not enough for 9 you that the God of Israel has set you apart from the community of Israel, bringing you near him to maintain the service of the Tabernacle of the LORD and to stand before the community as their ministers? He has brought you 10 near him and your brother Levites with you; now you seek the priesthood as well. That is why you and all your com- 11 pany have combined together against the LORD. What is Aaron that you should make these complaints against him?'

Moses sent to fetch Dathan and 12 Abiram sons of Eliab, but they answered, 'We are not coming. Is it a 13 small thing that you have brought us away from a land flowing with milk and honey to let us die in the wilderness? Must you also set yourself up as prince over us? What is more, you have 14 not brought us into a land flowing with milk and honey, nor have you given us fields and vineyards to inherit. Do you think you can hoodwink men like us? We are not coming.' This answer made 15 Moses very angry, and he said to the LORD, 'Take no notice of their murmuring. I have not taken from them so much as a single ass; I have done no wrong to any of them.'

Moses said to Korah, 'Present your- 16 selves before the LORD tomorrow, you and all your company, you and they and Aaron. Each man of you is to take 17 his censer and put incense on it. Then you shall present them before the LORD with their two hundred and fifty censers, and you and Aaron shall also bring your censers.' So each man took 18 his censer and put fire in it and placed incense on it; Moses and Aaron took their stand at the entrance to the Tent of the Presence, and Korah gathered 19 his whole company together and faced them at the entrance to the Tent of the Presence.

Then the glory of the LORD appeared

---

concretely illustrated. **37–40:** An ancient custom of dress (*tassels*) is here reinterpreted as a reminder of religious identity. Compare Gen.17.9–14 n. **41:** See Lev.18.2 n.

    16.1–17.13 The Wilderness revolt. Two different accounts are seen blended together. One is between factions of Levites (3.6 n.; compare Lev.10.2 n.); this account is anticipated in previous warnings (3.10 n.), especially those directed against the descendants of Kohath (4.17–20 n.). The other account is non-Levite. Possibly the older, non-Levite revolt by Dathan and Abiram (compare Deut.11.6; Ps.106.16–18) is here expanded by the priestly writers so as to include the Levite Korah as a rebel (vv. 1a,2b 11,16–24,27a,32b,35–50). **15:** Compare

20 to the whole community. And the LORD spoke to Moses and Aaron and said,
21 'Stand apart from this company, so that I may make an end of them in a
22 single instant.' But they prostrated themselves and said, 'O God, God of the spirits of all mankind, if one man sins, wilt thou be angry with the whole
23 community?' But the LORD said to
24 Moses, 'Tell them to stand back from the dwellings of Korah, Dathan and Abiram.'

25 So Moses rose and went to Dathan and Abiram, and the elders of Israel
26 followed him. He said to the whole community, 'Stand well away from the tents of these wicked men; touch nothing of theirs, or you will be swept
27 away because of all their sins.' So they moved away from the places occupied by Korah, Dathan and Abiram. Now Dathan and Abiram, holding themselves erect, had come out to the entrance of their tents with their wives,
28 their sons, and their dependants. Then Moses said, 'This shall prove to you that it is the LORD who sent me to do all these things, and it was not my own
29 heart that prompted me. If these men die a natural death and share the common fate of man, then the LORD has
30 not sent me; but if the LORD makes a great chasm, and the ground opens its mouth and swallows them and all that is theirs, and they go down alive to Sheol, then you will know that these men have held the LORD in contempt.'
31 Hardly had Moses spoken when the
32 ground beneath them split; the earth opened its mouth and swallowed them and their homes—all the followers of
33 Korah and all their property. They went down alive into Sheol with all that they had; the earth closed over them, and they vanished from the assembly.
34 At their cries all the Israelites round them fled, shouting, 'Look to yourselves! the earth will swallow us up.'
35 Meanwhile fire had come out from the LORD and burnt up the two hundred and fifty men who were presenting the incense.
36 Then the LORD spoke to Moses and

said, 'Bid Eleazar son of Aaron the 37 priest set aside the censers from the burnt remains, and scatter the fire from them far and wide, because they are holy. And the censers of these men 38 who sinned at the cost of their lives you shall make into beaten plates to cover the altar; they are holy, because they have been presented before the LORD. Let them be a sign to the Israelites.' So 39 Eleazar the priest took the bronze*x* censers which the victims of the fire had presented, and they were beaten into plates to make a covering for the altar, as a reminder to the Israelites 40 that no person unqualified, not descended from Aaron, should come forward to burn incense before the LORD, or his fate would be that of Korah and his company. All this was done as the LORD commanded Eleazar through Moses.

Next day all the community of the 41 Israelites raised complaints against Moses and Aaron and taxed them with causing the death of some of the LORD's people. As they gathered 42 against Moses and Aaron, they turned towards the Tent of the Presence and saw that the cloud covered it, and the glory of the LORD appeared. Moses and 43 Aaron came to the front of the Tent of the Presence, and the LORD spoke to 44 Moses and Aaron and said, 'Stand well 45 clear of this community, so that in a single instant I may make an end of them.' Then they prostrated themselves, and Moses said to Aaron, 'Take 46 your censer, put fire from the altar in it, set incense on it, and go with it quickly to the assembled community to make expiation for them. Wrath has gone forth already from the presence of the LORD. The plague has begun.' So Aaron took his censer, as Moses 47 had said, ran into the midst of the assembly and found that the plague had begun among the people. He put incense on the censer and made expiation for the people, standing between the 48 dead and the living, and the plague stopped. Fourteen thousand seven 49 hundred died of it, in addition to those

x *Or* copper.

1 Sam.12.3. **30**: *Sheol:* the underworld, domain of the dead. **37**: *Set aside:* compare Lev.10.4 n. **39–40**: But see Exod.27.2 and 38.2, according to which the *altar plates* were attached earlier at Sinai. (See Exod.25.1–31.17 n.) **41–50**: The larger community is warned never to assist the

who had died for the offence of Korah.
50 When Aaron came back to Moses at the entrance to the Tent of the Presence, the plague had stopped.

17 The LORD spoke to Moses and said,
2 'Speak to the Israelites and tell them to give you a staff for each tribe, one from every tribal chief, twelve in all, and
3 write each man's name on his staff. On Levi's staff write the name of Aaron, for there shall be one staff for each
4 head of a tribe. You shall put them all in the Tent of the Presence before the
5 Tokens, where I meet you, and the staff of the man I choose shall sprout. I will rid myself of the complaints of these Israelites, who keep on complaining against you.'
6 Moses thereupon spoke to the Israelites, and each of their chiefs handed him a staff, each of them one for his tribe, twelve in all, and Aaron's staff
7 among them. Moses put them before
8 the LORD in the Tent of the Tokens, and next day when he entered the tent, he found that Aaron's staff, the staff for the tribe of Levi, had sprouted. Indeed, it had sprouted, blossomed, and pro-
9 duced ripe almonds. Moses then brought out the staffs from before the LORD and showed them to all the Israelites; they saw for themselves, and
10 each man took his own staff. The LORD said to Moses, 'Put back Aaron's staff in front of the Tokens to be kept as a warning to all rebels, so that you may rid me once and for all of their complaints, and then they shall not die.'
11 Moses did this; as the LORD had commanded him, so he did.
12 The Israelites said to Moses, 'This is the end of us! We perish, one and all!
13 Every single person who goes near the Tabernacle of the LORD dies. Is this to be our final end?'

18 THE LORD SAID TO AARON: YOU AND your sons, together with the members of your father's tribe, shall be fully answerable for the sanctuary. You and your sons alone shall be answerable for your priestly office; but you shall ad- 2 mit your kinsmen of Levi, your father's tribe, to be attached to you and assist you while you and your sons are before the Tent of the Tokens. They shall be 3 in attendance on you and fulfil all the duties of the Tent, but shall not go near the holy vessels and the altar, or they will die and you with them. They shall 4 be attached to you and be responsible for the maintenance of the Tent of the Presence in every detail; no unqualified person shall come near you. You your- 5 selves shall be responsible for the sanctuary and the altar, so that wrath may no more fall on the Israelites. I have 6 myself taken the Levites your kinsmen out of all the Israelites as a gift for you, given to the LORD for the maintenance of the Tent of the Presence. But only 7 you and your sons may fulfil the duties of your priestly office that concern the altar or lie within the Veil. This duty is yours; I bestow on you this gift of priestly service. The unqualified person who intrudes on it shall be put to death.

The LORD said to Aaron: I, the 8 LORD, commit to your control the contributions made to me, that is all the holy-gifts of the Israelites. I give them to you and to your sons for your allotted portion due to you in perpetuity. Out of the most holy gifts kept 9 back from the altar-fire this part shall belong to you: every offering, whether grain-offering, sin-offering, or guilt-offering, rendered to me as a most holy gift, belongs to you and to your sons. You shall eat it as befits most holy 10 gifts; every male may eat it. You shall regard it as holy.

This also is yours: the contribution 11 from all such of their gifts as are presented as special gifts by the Israelites. I give them to you and to your sons and

---

Levites in their aspiration for the priesthood, and informed that only Aaron's expiatory activity can prevent catastrophe. **17.1–11:** In a final attempt to secure recognition for the Aaronite priesthood, God chooses Aaron's *staff* from among those of the tribes. Levites other than the descendants of Aaron are here ignored. The motif of a flowering rod as a sign of divine election is found in many parts of the world. **12–13:** These verses fit more logically after 16.34. They now form a conclusion to the entire passage, 16.1–17.11.
18.1–32: The duties and rights of the priests and Levites. The catastrophes of chs. 16–17, caused by neglect and violation of guidelines for the Levites, provided an appropriate setting for the repetition and expansion of material previously related. **1–7:** See 3.5–10. **8–10:** For the kinds

daughters with you as a due in perpetuity. Every person in your household who is ritually clean may eat them.

12 I give you all the choicest of the oil, the choicest of the new wine and the corn, the firstfruits which are given to

13 the LORD. The first-ripe fruits of all produce in the land which are brought to the LORD shall be yours. Everyone in your household who is clean may eat them.

14 Everything in Israel which has been devoted to God shall be yours.

15 All the first-born of man or beast which are brought to the LORD shall be yours. Notwithstanding, you must accept payment in redemption of any first-born of man and of unclean

16 beasts: at the end of one month you shall redeem it at the fixed price of five shekels of silver by the sacred standard

17 (twenty gerahs to the shekel). You must not, however, allow the redemption of the first-born of a cow, sheep, or goat; they are holy. You shall fling their blood against the altar and burn their fat in sacrifice as a food-offering

18 of soothing odour to the LORD; their flesh shall be yours, as are the breast of the special gift and the right leg.

19 All the contributions from holy-gifts, which the Israelites set aside for the LORD, I give to you and to your sons and daughters with you as a due in perpetuity. This is a perpetual covenant of salt before the LORD with you and your descendants also.

20 The LORD said to Aaron: You shall have no patrimony in the land of Israel, no holding among them; I am your holding in Israel, I am your patrimony.

21 To the Levites I give every tithe in Israel to be their patrimony, in return for the service they render in maintaining the Tent of the Presence. In order

22 that the Israelites may not henceforth approach the Tent and thus incur the penalty of death, the Levites alone shall

23 perform the service of the Tent, and they shall accept the full responsibility for it. This rule is binding on your descendants for all time. They shall have no patrimony among the Israelites, because I give them as their patri-

24 mony the tithe which the Israelites set aside as a contribution to the LORD. Therefore I say to them: You shall have no patrimony among the Israelites.

25 The LORD spoke to Moses and said,

26 Speak to the Levites in these words: When you receive from the Israelites the tithe which I give you from them as your patrimony, you shall set aside from it the contribution to the LORD, a

27 tithe of the tithe. Your contribution shall count for you as if it were corn from the threshing-floor and juice from

28 the vat. In this way you too shall set aside the contribution due to the LORD out of all tithes which you receive from the Israelites and shall give the LORD's

29 contribution to Aaron the priest. Out of all the gifts you receive you shall set aside the contribution due to the LORD; and the gift which you hallow[y] must be taken from the choicest of them.

30 You shall say to the Levites: When you have set aside the choicest part of your portion, the remainder shall count for you as the produce of the threshing-floor and the winepress, and you may

31 eat it anywhere, you and your households. It is your payment for service in the Tent of the Presence. When you

32 have set aside its choicest part, you will incur no penalty in respect of it, and you will not be profaning the holy-gifts of the Israelites; so you will not die.

19 THE LORD SPOKE TO MOSES AND AARON

2 and said: This is a law and a statute which the LORD has ordained. Tell the

y you hallow: prob. rdg.; Heb. obscure.

---

of offerings, see Lev. chs. 1–7. **12–13**: On the offering of *firstfruits*, see 15.17–21 n. **15**: See Exod.13.11–13 for the redemption of the firstborn. **16**: Compare 3.44–48. **17**: Compare Lev. 27.9–10,26–27. **18**: See Lev.7.28–36. **19**: *Covenant of salt*: see Lev.2.13 n. **21**: *Tithe*: see Lev. 27.30–33. In older legislation (Deut.26.12–13), the Levites were not the sole recipients. **24**: See Lev.25.32–34 n.

19.1–22: Purification after contact with a corpse. This ritual is related here, rather than with the other regulations regarding uncleanness (Lev. chs. 11–15), possibly because of the large number of fatalities reported in chs. 16–17. **2**: *Red*: compare Lev.14.4 n. **3**: *East*: see Lev.

Israelites to bring you a red cow without blemish or defect, which has never
3 borne the yoke. You shall give it to Eleazar the priest, and it shall be taken outside the camp and slaughtered[z] to
4 the east of it. Eleazar the priest shall take some of the blood on his finger and sprinkle it seven times towards the
5 front of the Tent of the Presence. The cow shall be burnt in his sight, skin, flesh, and blood, together with the offal.
6 The priest shall then take cedar-wood, marjoram, and scarlet thread, and throw them into the heart of the fire in
7 which the cow is burning. He shall wash his clothes and bathe his body in water; after which he may enter the camp, but he remains ritually unclean
8 till sunset. The man who burnt the cow shall wash his clothes and bathe his body in water, but he also remains
9 unclean till sunset. Then a man who is clean shall collect the ashes of the cow and deposit them outside the camp in a clean place. They shall be reserved for use by the Israelite community in the water of ritual purification; for the
10 cow is a sin-offering. The man who collected the ashes of the cow shall wash his clothes, but he remains unclean till sunset. This rule shall be binding for all time on the Israelites and on the alien who is living with them.
11 Whoever touches a corpse shall be
12 ritually unclean for seven days. He shall get himself purified with the water of ritual purification on the third day and on the seventh day, and then he shall be clean. If he is not purified both on the third day and on the seventh, he
13 shall not be clean. Everyone who touches a corpse, that is the body of a man who has died, and does not purify himself, defiles the Tabernacle of the LORD. That person shall be cut off from Israel. The water of purification has not been flung over him; he remains unclean, and his impurity is still upon him.

When a man dies in a tent, this is the 14 law: everyone who goes into the tent and everyone who was inside the tent shall be ritually unclean for seven days, and every open vessel which has no 15 covering tied over it shall also be unclean. In the open, anyone who 16 touches a man killed with a weapon or one who has died naturally, or who touches a human bone or a grave, shall be unclean for seven days. For such 17 uncleanness, they shall take some of the ash from the burnt mass of the sin-offering and add fresh water to it in a vessel. Then a man who is clean shall 18 take marjoram, dip it in the water, and sprinkle the tent with all the vessels in it and all the people who were there, or the man who has touched a human bone, a corpse (whether the man was killed or died naturally), or a grave. The man 19 who is clean shall sprinkle the unclean man on the third day and on the seventh; on the seventh day he shall purify him; then the man shall wash his clothes and bathe in water, and at sunset he shall be clean. If a man who 20 is unclean does not get himself purified, that person shall be cut off from the assembly, because he has defiled the sanctuary of the LORD. The water of purification has not been flung over him: he is unclean. This rule shall be 21 binding on you for all time. The man who sprinkles the water of purification shall also wash his clothes, and whoever touches the water shall be unclean till sunset. Whatever the unclean man 22 touches shall be unclean, and any person who touches that shall be unclean till sunset.

IN THE FIRST MONTH THE WHOLE **20** community of Israel reached the wilderness of Zin and stayed some time at Kadesh; there Miriam died and was buried.

z Or he shall take it outside the camp and slaughter it . . .

16.14 n. **5:** The burning of the *skin, blood,* and *offal* is here unique; contrast Lev.1.3–9. **6:** *Cedar-wood, marjoram, and scarlet thread* are also used in the ritual of purification after recovery from skin-disease (Lev.14.1–9). **7:** *Wash . . . bathe:* see Lev.14.8 n. **13:** *Cut off:* see Lev.7.21 n. **15:** The uncleanness of an *open vessel* may have originated from the fear that the demon which caused the death or disease might have taken refuge in the vessel.
    20.1–13: The demand for water at Meribah. Exod.17.1–7 places this event, in slightly different form, before the arrival at Sinai. **1:** This account was once independent of the present context,

2 There was no water for the community; so they gathered against Moses
3 and Aaron. The people disputed with Moses and said, 'If only we had perished when our brothers perished in the
4 presence of the LORD! Why have you brought the assembly of the LORD into this wilderness for us and our beasts to
5 die here? Why did you fetch us up from Egypt to bring us to this vile place, where nothing will grow, neither corn nor figs, vines nor pomegranates? There is not even any water to drink.'
6 Moses and Aaron came forward in front of the assembly to the entrance of the Tent of the Presence. There they fell prostrate, and the glory of the LORD appeared to them.

7 The LORD spoke to Moses and said,
8 'Take a*ᵃ* staff, and then with Aaron your brother assemble all the community, and, in front of them all, speak to the rock and it will yield its water. Thus you will produce water for the community out of the rock, for them
9 and their beasts to drink.' Moses left the presence of the LORD with the
10 staff, as he had commanded him. Then he and Aaron gathered the assembly together in front of the rock, and he said to them, 'Listen to me, you rebels. Must we get water out of this rock for
11 you?' Moses raised his hand and struck the rock twice with his staff. Water gushed out in abundance and
12 they all drank, men and beasts. But the LORD said to Moses and Aaron, 'You did not trust me so far as to uphold my holiness in the sight of the Israelites; therefore you shall not lead this assembly into the land which I promised to
13 give them.' Such were the waters of Meribah,*ᵇ* where the people disputed with the LORD and through which his holiness was upheld.

FROM KADESH MOSES SENT ENVOYS TO 14 the king of Edom: 'This is a message from your brother Israel. You know all the hardships we have encountered, how our fathers went down to Egypt, 15 and we lived there for many years. The Egyptians ill-treated us and our fathers before us, and we cried to the LORD 16 for help. He listened to us and sent an angel, and he brought us out of Egypt; and now we are here at Kadesh, a town on your frontier. Grant us passage 17 through your country. We will not trespass on field or vineyard, or drink from your wells. We will keep to the king's highway; we will not turn off to right or left until we have crossed your territory.' But the Edomites answered, 18 'You shall not cross our land. If you do, we will march out and attack you in force.' The Israelites said, 'But we will 19 keep to the main road. If we and our flocks drink your water, we will pay you for it; we will simply cross your land on foot.' But the Edomites said, 20 'No, you shall not', and took the field against them with a large army in full strength. Thus the Edomites refused to 21 allow Israel to cross their frontier, and Israel went a different way to avoid a conflict.

The whole community of Israel set 22 out from Kadesh and came to Mount Hor. At Mount Hor, near the frontier 23 of Edom, the LORD said to Moses and Aaron, 'Aaron shall be gathered to his 24 father's kin. He shall not enter the land which I promised to give the Israelites, because over the waters of Meribah you rebelled against my command. Take Aaron and his son Eleazar, and go 25 up Mount Hor. Strip Aaron of his robes 26

a Or the.   *b* That is Dispute.

for in 13.26, the people have already arrived at Kadesh. The precise year is here missing, but the context requires that it be toward the end of the "forty" years of wandering (see 13.26 n.). **12:** The reason given for the LORD's anger is not clear. It may have been because Moses, by acting himself, high-handedly, thereby impedes a miracle dependent on divine grace. See also Deut.32.48–52. The episode reflects the knowledge of later generations that Joshua, not Moses, led Israel into Canaan, for Moses had died before the conquest. See Deut.1.37. The account is placed here because of Aaron's death in vv. 22–29.

20.14–29: Preparation and departure from Kadesh. 14: A detour through *Edom* was necessary because an attempt at direct entry had failed (14.39–45). *Brother:* see Gen.25.24–30. **17:** The *king's highway* was the main route from Elath (14.25 n.) northward to Syria. **24:** *Gathered to his father's kin* is a common biblical idiom for death, reflecting the ancient practice of a burial in a family tomb (Gen.49.29–33).

and invest Eleazar his son with them, for Aaron shall be taken from you: he
27 shall die there.' Moses did as the LORD had commanded him: they went up Mount Hor in sight of the whole
28 community, and Moses stripped Aaron of his robes and invested his son Eleazar with them. There Aaron died on the mountain-top, and Moses and Eleazar came down from the moun-
29 tain. So the whole community saw that Aaron had died, and all Israel mourned him for thirty days.

21 When the Canaanite king of Arad who lived in the Negeb heard that the Israelites were coming by way of Atharim, he attacked them and took
2 some of them prisoners. Israel thereupon made a vow to the LORD and said, 'If thou wilt deliver this people into my power, I will destroy their cities.'
3 The LORD listened to Israel and delivered the Canaanites into their power. Israel destroyed them and their cities and called the place Hormah.*c*
4 Then they left Mount Hor by way of the Red Sea to march round the flank of Edom. But on the way they grew
5 impatient and spoke against God and Moses. 'Why have you brought us up from Egypt', they said, 'to die in the desert where there is neither food nor water? We are heartily sick of this
6 miserable fare.' Then the LORD sent poisonous snakes among the people, and they bit the Israelites so that many
7 of them died. The people came to Moses and said, 'We sinned when we spoke against the LORD and you. Plead with the LORD to rid us of the snakes.' Moses therefore pleaded with the LORD for the
8 people; and the LORD told Moses to make a serpent*d* of bronze and erect it as a standard, so that anyone who had been bitten could look at it and
9 recover. So Moses made a bronze serpent and erected it as a standard, so that when a snake had bitten a man,

he could look at the bronze serpent and recover.

10 The Israelites went on and en-
11 camped at Oboth. They moved on from Oboth and encamped at Iye-abarim in the wilderness on the eastern frontier
12 of Moab. From there they moved and encamped by the gorge of the Zared.
13 They moved on from the Zared and encamped by the farther side of the Arnon in the wilderness which extends into Amorite territory, for the Arnon was the Moabite frontier; it lies
14 between Moab and the Amorites. That is why the Book of the Wars of the LORD speaks of Vaheb*e* in Suphah and the gorges:

15 Arnon and the watershed of the gorges
that falls away towards the dwellings at Ar
and slopes towards the frontier of Moab.

16 From there they moved on to Beer:*f* this is the water-hole where the LORD said to Moses, 'Gather the people together and I will give them water.'
17 It was then that Israel sang this song:

Well up, spring water! Greet it with song,
18 the spring unearthed by the princes, laid open by the leaders of the people with sceptre and with mace,
a gift from the wilderness.

19 And they proceeded from Beer*g* to Nahaliel, and from Nahaliel to Bamoth;
20 then from Bamoth to the valley in the Moabite country below the summit of Pisgah overlooking the desert.
21 Then Israel sent envoys to the
22 Amorite king Sihon and said, 'Grant

c That is Destruction.　　　*d Or* snake.
e Name meaning Watershed.
f Name meaning Water-hole.
g Prob. rdg.; Heb. from a gift.

21.1–35: From the border of Edom to the plains of Moab. 1–3: This seems to be an originally independent unit, interrupting the continuity between 20.29 and 21.4. It tells how Israel later avenged the defeat at Hormah (14.39–45), and suggests that it happened just before the detour around Edom. Judg.1.16–17, however, places the event at a later time. **4–9:** An idol in the Temple at Jerusalem (2 Kgs.18.4) was later traced back to this episode. Unlike previous protests because of lack of food or water (chs. 11,20; Exod.15.22–17.1), this protest brings no relief. **13:** *Amorites:* an alternative name for the Canaanites. **14–15:** *The Book of the Wars of the LORD* has not been preserved beyond this quotation. **17–18:** Since the custom of music and dance at the clearing of a well is widely attested in the Near East, this likely was a traditional chant

us passage through your country. We will not trespass on field or vineyard, nor will we drink from your wells. We will travel by the king's highway till we have crossed your territory.'
23 But Sihon would not grant Israel passage through his territory; he mustered all his people and came out against Israel in the wilderness. He advanced
24 as far as Jahaz and attacked Israel, but Israel put them to the sword, giving no quarter, and occupied their land from the Arnon to the Jabbok, the territory of the Ammonites, where the country
25 became difficult. So Israel took all these Amorite cities and settled in them, that is in Heshbon and all its dependent
26 villages. Heshbon was the capital of the Amorite king Sihon, who had fought against the former king of Moab and taken from him all his territory as far
27 as the Arnon. Therefore the bards say:

Come to Heshbon, come!
　Let us see the city of Sihon rebuilt
　　and restored!
28 For fire blazed out from Heshbon,
　and flames from Sihon's city.
　It devoured Ar of Moab,
　and swept the high ground at Arnon
　　head.

29 　Woe to you, Moab;
　it is the end of you, you people of
　　Kemosh.
　He has made his sons fugitives
　and his daughters the prisoners of
　　Sihon the Amorite king.
30 From Heshbon to Dibon their very
　　embers are burnt out
　and they are extinct,
　while the fire spreads onward to
　　Medeba.

31 Thus Israel occupied the territory of the Amorites.
32 Moses then sent men to explore Jazer; the Israelites captured it together with its dependent villages and drove out the Amorites living there. Then 33 they turned and advanced along the road to Bashan. Og king of Bashan, with all his people, took the field against them at Edrei. The LORD said to 34 Moses, 'Do not be afraid of him. I have delivered him into your hands, with all his people and his land. Deal with him as you dealt with Sihon the Amorite king who lived in Heshbon.' So they put him to the sword with his 35 sons and all his people, until there was no survivor left, and they occupied his land.

Israel in the plains of Moab

THE ISRAELITES WENT FORWARD AND **22** encamped in the lowlands of Moab on the farther side of the Jordan from Jericho.
　Balak son of Zippor saw what Israel 2 had done to the Amorites, and Moab 3 was in terror of the people because there were so many of them. The Moabites were sick with fear at the sight of them; and they said to the elders 4 of Midian, 'This horde will soon lick up everything round us as a bull crops the spring grass.' Balak son of Zippor was at that time king of Moab. He 5 sent a deputation to summon Balaam son of Beor, who was at Pethor by the Euphrates in the land of the Amavites, with this message, 'Look, an entire nation has come out of Egypt; they cover the face of the country and are settling at my very door. Come at once 6 and lay a curse on them, because they are too many for me; then I may be able to defeat them and drive them from the country. I know that those whom you bless are blessed, and those whom you curse are cursed.'
　The elders of Moab and Midian took 7

---

for such an occasion. **27–30:** An Amorite victory ballad is cited, in order to enhance the subsequent victory of Israel. *Kemosh* (v. 29) was the chief god of the Moabites (1 Kgs.11.33). **33–35:** See Deut.3.1–7.
　22.1–40: Balaam is summoned to curse Israel. 6: *Lay a curse:* see Exod.21.17 n. The use of professional cursers, regarded as having special rapport with the deity, is well attested from antiquity. **7–20:** This is one version of the next phase of the story, the other being vv. 21–35. According to the first, Balaam consults the LORD and is forbidden (vv. 7–14), then allowed (vv. 15–20), to accept Balak's invitation. According to the second, he does not consult the LORD and learns of his opposition only after an angel has threatened his life. He is then allowed to proceed. **7:** *Augury* is the so-called science of determining the divine will through omens.

the fees for augury with them, and they came to Balaam and told him what

8 Balak had said. 'Spend this night here,' he said, 'and I will give you whatever answer the LORD gives to me.' So the Moabite chiefs stayed with Balaam.

9 God came to Balaam and asked him,
10 'Who are these men with you?' Balaam replied, 'Balak son of Zippor king of Moab has sent them to me and he says,
11 "Look, a people newly come out of Egypt is covering the face of the country. Come at once and denounce them for me; then I may be able to fight
12 them and drive them away."' God said to Balaam, 'You are not to go with them or curse the people, because they
13 are to be blessed.'ʰ So Balaam rose in the morning and said to Balak's chiefs, 'Go back to your own country; the LORD has refused to let me go with you.'
14 Then the Moabite chiefs took their leave and went back to Balak, and told him that Balaam had refused to come
15 with them; whereupon Balak sent a second and larger embassy of higher
16 rank than the first. They came to Balaam and told him, 'This is the message from Balak son of Zippor: "Let nothing stand in the way of your
17 coming. I will confer great honour upon you; I will do whatever you ask me. But you must come and denounce
18 this people for me."' Balaam gave this answer to Balak's messengers: 'Even if Balak were to give me all the silver and gold in his house, I could not disobey the command of the LORD my God in
19 anything, small or great. But stay here for this night, as the others did, that I may learn what more the LORD has to
20 say to me.' During the night God came to Balaam and said to him, 'If these men have come to summon you, then rise and go with them, but do only what
21 I tell you.' So in the morning Balaam rose, saddled his ass and went with the Moabite chiefs.

22 But God was angry because Balaam was going, and as he came riding on his ass, accompanied by his two servants, the angel of the LORD took his
23 stand in the road to bar his way. When the ass saw the angel standing in the road with his sword drawn, she turned off the road into the fields, and Balaam beat the ass to bring her back on to the road. Then the angel of the LORD 24 stood where the road ran through a hollow, with fenced vineyards on either side. The ass saw the angel and, crushing 25 herself against the wall, crushed Balaam's foot against it, and he beat her again. The angel of the LORD moved 26 on further and stood in a narrow place where there was no room to turn either to right or left. When the ass saw the 27 angel, she lay down under Balaam. At that Balaam lost his temper and beat the ass with his stick. The LORD then made 28 the ass speak, and she said to Balaam, 'What have I done? This is the third time you have beaten me.' Balaam 29 answered the ass, 'You have been making a fool of me. If I had had a sword here, I should have killed you on the spot.' But the ass answered, 'Am I 30 not still the ass which you have ridden all your life? Have I ever taken such a liberty with you before?' He said, 'No.' Then the LORD opened Balaam's eyes: 31 he saw the angel of the LORD standing in the road with his sword drawn, and he bowed down and fell flat on his face before him. The angel said to him, 32 'What do you mean by beating your ass three times like this? I came out to bar your way but you made straight for me, and three times your ass saw me 33 and turned aside. If she had not turned aside, I should by now have killed you and spared her.' Balaam replied to the 34 angel of the LORD, 'I have done wrong. I did not know that you stood in the road confronting me. But now, if my journey displeases you, I am ready to go back.' The angel of the LORD said to 35 Balaam, 'Go on with these men; but say only what I tell you.' So Balaam went on with Balak's chiefs.

When Balak heard that Balaam was 36 coming, he came out to meet him as far as Ar of Moab by the Arnon on his frontier. Balak said to Balaam, 'Did I 37 not send time and again to summon

ʰ *Or* are blessed.

15–17: Balak's insistence is ironic in view of the final result of Balaam's services: he is unknowingly arranging his own defeat. 21–35: See vv. 7–20 n.

you? Why did you not come? Did you think that I could not do you honour?' 38 Balaam replied, 'I have come, as you see. But now that I am here, what power have I of myself to say anything? Whatever the word God puts into my 39 mouth, that is what I will say.' So Balaam went with Balak till they came to 40 Kiriath-huzoth, and Balak slaughtered cattle and sheep and sent them to Balaam and to the chiefs who were with him.

41 In the morning Balak took Balaam and led him up to the Heights of Baal, from where he could see the full extent 23 of the Israelite host. Then Balaam said to Balak, 'Build me here seven altars and prepare for me seven bulls and 2 seven rams.' Balak did as he asked and offered a bull and a ram on each 3-4 altar. Then he said to him, 'I have prepared the seven altars, and I have offered the bull and the ram on each altar.' Balaam said to Balak, 'Take your stand beside your sacrifice, and let me go off by myself. It may happen that the LORD will meet me. Whatever he reveals to me, I will tell you.' So he 5 went forthwith, and God met him. The LORD put words into Balaam's mouth and said, 'Go back to Balak, and speak 6 as I tell you.' So he went back, and found Balak standing by his sacrifice, and with him all the Moabite chiefs. 7 And Balaam uttered his oracle:

From Aram,[i] from the mountains of the east,
Balak king of Moab has brought me:
'Come, lay a curse for me on Jacob,
come, execrate Israel.'
8 How can I denounce whom God has not denounced?
How can I execrate whom the LORD has not execrated?
9 From the rocky heights I see them,
I watch them from the rounded hills.
I see a people that dwells alone,
that has not made itself one with the nations.

Who can count the host[j] of Jacob 10
or number the hordes[k] of Israel?
Let me die as men die who are righteous,
grant that my end may be as theirs!

Then Balak said to Balaam, 'What is 11 this you have done? I sent for you to denounce my enemies, and what you have done is to bless them.' But he 12 replied, 'Must I not keep to the words that the LORD puts into my mouth?'

Balak then said to him, 'Come with 13 me now to another place from which you will see them, though not the full extent of them; you will not see them all. Denounce them for me from there.' So he took him to the Field of the 14 Watchers[l] on the summit of Pisgah, where he built seven altars and offered a bull and a ram on each altar. Balaam said to Balak, 'Take your stand 15 beside your sacrifice, and I will meet God over there.' The LORD met Balaam 16 and put words into his mouth, and said, 'Go back to Balak, and speak as I tell you.' So he went back, and 17 found him standing beside his sacrifice, with the Moabite chiefs. Balak asked what the LORD had said, and Balaam 18 uttered his oracle:

Up, Balak, and listen:
hear what I am charged to say, son of Zippor.
God is not a mortal that he should 19 lie,
not a man that he should change his mind.[m]
Has he not spoken, and will he not make it good?
What he has proclaimed, he will surely fulfil.
I have received command to bless; 20
I will bless and I cannot gainsay it.
He has discovered no iniquity in 21 Jacob

i Or Syria. j Or dust.
k Or quarter or sands. l Or Field of Zophim.
m Or feel regret.

22.41–24.25: The oracles of Balaam. 23.1–2: Balaam may have desired the sacrifices in order to examine the markings of the livers for omens (compare Ezek.21.21). **3–5:** Balaam looks for omens which will reveal the divine will. **9:** Israel's distinctiveness is emphasized in much of the legislation contained in Exod.-Num. **10:** *Hordes:* thus fulfilling the promise to the patriarchs (Gen.15.5). Since it is obvious from their numbers that God has blessed Israel, Balaam concludes that he must do likewise (v. 8). **14:** *Watchers:* the term is sometimes used in the Ancient Near East for observers of astrological omens. **19:** *Change his mind:* from that of the first oracle.

165

and has seen no mischief in Israel.[n]
The LORD their God is with them,
acclaimed among them as king.[o]

22 What its curving horns are to the
    wild ox,
God is to them, who brought them
    out of Egypt.

23 Surely there is no divination in[p]
    Jacob,
and no augury in[p] Israel;
now is the time to say of Jacob
and of Israel, 'See what God has
    wrought!'

24 Behold a people rearing up like a
    lioness,
rampant like a lion;
he will not couch till he devours the
    prey
and drinks the blood of the slain.

25 Then Balak said to Balaam, 'You will
26 not denounce them; then at least do
not bless them'; and he answered,
27 'Did I not warn you that I must do all
the LORD tells me?' Balak replied,
'Come, let me take you to another place;
perhaps God will be pleased to let you
denounce them for me from there.'
28 So he took Balaam to the summit
29 of Peor overlooking Jeshimon, and
Balaam told him to build seven altars
for him there and prepare seven bulls
30 and seven rams. Balak did as Balaam
had said, and he offered a bull and a
ram on each altar.

24 But now that Balaam knew that the
LORD wished him to bless Israel, he
did not go and resort to divination as
before. He turned towards the desert;
2 and as he looked, he saw Israel encamped tribe by tribe. The spirit of God
3 came upon him, and he uttered his
oracle:

The very word of Balaam son of
    Beor,
the very word of the man whose
    sight is clear,
4 the very word of him who hears the
    words of God,
who with staring eyes sees in a trance
the vision from the Almighty:
5 how goodly are your tents, O Jacob,

your dwelling-places, Israel,
like long rows of palms,   6
like gardens by a river,
like lign-aloes planted by the LORD,
like cedars beside the water!
The water in his vessels shall   7
    overflow,
and his seed shall be like great waters
so that his king may be taller than
    Agag,
and his kingdom lifted high.
What its curving horns are to the   8
    wild ox,
God is to him, who brought him out
    of Egypt;
he shall devour his adversaries the
    nations,
crunch their bones, and smash their
    limbs in pieces.
When he reclines he couches like a lion,   9
like a lioness, and no one dares
    rouse him.
Blessed be they that bless you,
and they that curse you be accursed!

At that Balak was very angry with 10
Balaam, beat his hands together and
said, 'I summoned you to denounce
my enemies, and three times you have
persisted in blessing them. Off with 11
you to your own place! I promised to
confer great honour upon you, but now
the LORD has kept this honour from
you.' Balaam answered, 'But I told 12
your own messengers whom you sent:
"If Balak gives me all the silver and 13
gold in his house, I cannot disobey the
command of the LORD by doing anything of my own will, good or bad.
What the LORD speaks to me, that is
what I will say." Now I am going to 14
my own people; but first, I will warn
you what this people will do to yours
in the days to come.' So he uttered his 15
oracle:

The very word of Balaam son of
    Beor,
the very word of the man whose
    sight is clear,

---

n Or None can discover calamity in Jacob nor see trouble
in Israel.
o Or royal care is bestowed on them.   *p Or* against.

23: The techniques which Balak desires are ineffective against Israel. **27:** Balak's increasing
desperation continues to add to his ultimate defeat (22.15–17 n.). **24.4:** *Almighty:* see Gen.17.1 n.
7: *Agag:* if this is the king of the Amalekites of Saul's time (1 Sam.15.8), this part of the blessing

16 the very word of him who hears the
　　words of God,
who shares the knowledge of the
　　Most High,
who with staring eyes sees in a
　　trance
the vision from the Almighty:

17　I see him, but not now;
I behold him, but not near:
a star shall come forth out of Jacob,
a comet arise from Israel.
He shall smite the squadrons*q* of
　　Moab,
and beat down all the sons of strife.

18　Edom shall be his by conquest
and Seir, his enemy, shall be his.
Israel shall do valiant deeds;

19　Jacob shall trample them down,
the last survivor from Ar shall he
　　destroy.

20 He saw Amalek and uttered his
oracle:

First of all the nations was Amalek,
but his end shall be utter destruction.

21 He saw the Kenites and uttered his
oracle:

Your refuge, though it seems secure,
your nest, though set on the
　　mountain crag,

22　is doomed to burning, O Cain.
How long must you dwell there in
　　my sight?

23 He uttered his oracle:

Ah, who are these assembling in the
　　north,

24 invaders from the region of Kittim?

They will lay waste Assyria; they will
　　lay Eber waste:
he too shall perish utterly.

Then Balaam arose and returned home, 25
and Balak also went on his way.

WHEN THE ISRAELITES WERE IN SHITTIM, **25**
the people began to have intercourse
with Moabite women, who invited 2
them to the sacrifices offered to their
gods; and they ate the sacrificial food
and prostrated themselves before the
gods of Moab. The Israelites joined 3
in the worship of the Baal of Peor, and
the LORD was angry with them. He said 4
to Moses, 'Take all the leaders of the
people and hurl them down to their
death before the LORD in the full light
of day, that the fury of his anger may
turn away from Israel.' So Moses said 5
to the judges of Israel, 'Put to death,
each one of you, those of his tribe
who have joined in the worship of the
Baal of Peor.'
　　One of the Israelites brought a 6
Midianite woman into his family in
open defiance of Moses and all the
community of Israel, while they were
weeping by the entrance of the Tent of
the Presence. Phinehas son of Eleazar, 7
son of Aaron the priest, saw him. He
stepped out from the crowd and took
up a spear, and he went into the inner 8
room after the Israelite and transfixed
the two of them, the Israelite and
the woman, pinning them together.
Thus the plague which had attacked the
Israelites was brought to a stop; but 9
twenty-four thousand had already died.

q Or heads.

---

was composed much later than the time of Balaam. **16:** *Most high:* see Gen.14.18 n. **17–19:**
The Davidic conquest of Moab and Edom (2 Sam.8.2,13–14) seems referred to; this may be an
indication of the period of authorship of this oracle (compare v. 7 n.). **20:** See Exod.17.8–16 n.
This may also refer to the time of Saul (1 Sam. ch. 15) or David (1 Sam. ch. 30). **21–22:** On the
Kenites, see Judg.1.16 n. In Heb. Kenite is *qēni; nest* (Heb. *qēn*) is a pun on *qēni*, and on the
name Cain (Heb. *qayyin*). The smith (see Gen.4.1–26 n.) will himself be smelted. **23–24:** The
text is obscure at every point. *Kittim* is Cyprus (see Gen.10.4).
　　25.1–18: Apostasy to the Moabite gods. Israel's rebellion against the LORD (11.1–34; ch. 14;
20.1–13; Exod.14.10–14; 15.22–17.7) continues even after survival in the Wilderness and arrival
at the border of the promised land. That it occurs again just after the blessing of Balaam (chs.
23–24) is meant as ironic. **2:** The charge is religious disloyalty, not sexual immorality, although
in the fertility cults of Canaan sexual activity was part of the ritual. Compare Gen.24.3 n.
Sacrificial food: see Lev.3.3 n. and 7.20 n.; 1 Cor. ch. 8. **3:** *Baal:* see Exod.34.13 n. *Peor:* a
place (23.28). **4:** The *leaders* are responsible for the activity. **5:** This seems to be an alternative
account of the punishment. **6:** Another story may begin here, since the topic switches from
Moabite women to Midianite ones. **8:** *Inner room:* that part of the sanctuary where the fertility

10 The LORD spoke to Moses and said,
11 'Phinehas son of Eleazar, son of Aaron the priest, has turned my wrath away from the Israelites; he displayed among them the same jealous anger that moved me, and therefore in my jealousy I did
12 not exterminate the Israelites. Tell him that I hereby grant him my covenant of
13 security of tenure. He and his descendants after him shall enjoy the priesthood under a covenant for all time, because he showed his zeal for his God and made expiation for the Israelites.'
14 The name of the Israelite struck down with the Midianite woman was Zimri son of Salu, a chief in a Simeonite
15 family, and the Midianite woman's name was Cozbi daughter of Zur, who was the head of a group of fathers' families in Midian.

16 The LORD spoke to Moses and said,
17-18 'Make the Midianites suffer as they made you suffer with their crafty tricks, and strike them down; their craftiness was your undoing at Peor and in the affair of Cozbi their sister, the daughter of a Midianite chief, who was struck down at the time of the plague that followed Peor.'

19 26 1 AFTER THE PLAGUE THE LORD SAID TO Moses and Eleazar the priest, son of
2 Aaron, 'Number the whole community of Israel by fathers' families, recording everyone in Israel aged twenty years and upwards fit for military service.'
3 Moses and Eleazar collected them in the lowlands of Moab by the Jordan
4 near Jericho,*r* all who were twenty years of age and upwards, as the LORD had commanded Moses.

These were the Israelites who came out of Egypt:
5*s* Reubenites (Reuben was Israel's eldest son): Enoch, the Enochite family;
6 Pallu, the Palluite family; Hezron, the

Hezronite family; Carmi, the Carmite family. These were the Reubenite fam- 7 ilies; the number in their detailed list was forty-three thousand seven hundred and thirty. Son of Pallu: Eliab. Sons of 8,9 Eliab: Nemuel, Dathan and Abiram. These were the same Dathan and Abiram, conveners of the community, who defied Moses and Aaron and joined the company of Korah in defying the LORD. Then the earth opened its mouth 10 and swallowed them up with Korah, and so their company died, while fire burnt up the two hundred and fifty men, and they became a warning sign. The Korahites, however, did not die. 11

Simeonites, by their families: Nemuel, 12 the Nemuelite family; Jamin, the Jaminite family; Jachin, the Jachinite family; Zerah, the Zarhite family; Saul, 13 the Saulite family. These were the 14 Simeonite families; the number in their detailed list was twenty-two thousand two hundred.

Gadites, by their families: Zephon, 15 the Zephonite family; Haggi, the Haggite family; Shuni, the Shunite family; Ozni, the Oznite family; Eri, the Erite 16 family; Arod, the Arodite family; Areli, 17 the Arelite family. These were the 18 Gadite families; the number in their detailed list was forty thousand five hundred.

The sons of Judah were Er, Onan, 19 Shelah, Perez and Zerah; Er and Onan died in Canaan. Judahites, by their 20 families: Shelah, the Shelanite family; Perez, the Perezite family; Zerah, the Zarhite family. Perezites: Hezron, the 21 Hezronite family; Hamul, the Hamulite family. These were the families of 22 Judah; the number in their detailed list was seventy-six thousand five hundred.

r Prob. rdg.; Heb. adds saying.
s Verses 5–50: cp. Gen. 46. 8–25; Exod. 6. 14, 15; 1 Chr. chs. 4–8.

ritual was celebrated. That the plague has not been mentioned previously supports the possibility that a new unit began in v. 6. **13:** Phinehas is specifically granted the priesthood for zealous deeds (compare Exod.32.26–29), though he was entitled to this through his descent from Aaron (Exod.6.25), to whose descendants the office was promised forever (Exod.29.9). **16–18:** These verses, possibly the latest part of the chapter, shift the blame from the Israelites (vv. 1–5) to the Midianites (vv. 6–15) and anticipate the events of ch. 31.
   26.1–65: The second census, taken in anticipation of the invasion of the promised land. It seeks to show that, despite the hardships of the Wilderness and the deaths from divine punishment (11.1–3,33–34; 14.44–45; 16.1–35,46–50; 21.1–3,6), the population remained constant. For a possible origin of the census, see 1.20–46 n. **7:** Contrast 1.21. Reuben evidently continued to decline in number. See the prayer in Deut.33.6. **9:** *Dathan and Abiram:* see 16.1–40. **14:** On

23 Issacharites, by their families: Tola, the Tolaite family; Pua, the Puite
24 family; Jashub, the Jashubite family;
25 Shimron, the Shimronite family. These were the families of Issachar; the number in their detailed list was sixty-four thousand three hundred.
26 Zebulunites, by their families: Sered, the Sardite family; Elon, the Elonite family; Jahleel, the Jahleelite family.
27 These were the Zebulunite families; the number in their detailed list was sixty thousand five hundred.
28 Josephites, by their families:
29 Manasseh and Ephraim. Manassites: Machir, the Machirite family. Machir was the father of Gilead: Gilead, the
30 Gileadite family. Gileadites: Jeezer, the Jeezerite family; Helek, the Helek-
31 ite family; Asriel, the Asrielite family;
32 Shechem, the Shechemite family; Shemida, the Shemidaite family; Hepher,
33 the Hepherite family. Zelophehad son of Hepher had no sons, only daughters; their names were Mahlah, Noah,
34 Hoglah, Milcah and Tirzah. These were the families of Manasseh; the number in their detailed list was fifty-two thousand seven hundred.
35 Ephraimites, by their families: Shuthelah, the Shuthalhite family; Becher, the Bachrite family; Tahan, the
36 Tahanite family. Shuthalhites: Eran,
37 the Eranite family. These were the Ephraimite families; the number in their detailed list was thirty-two thousand five hundred. These were the Josephites, by families.
38 Benjamites, by their families: Bela, the Belaite family; Ashbel, the Ashbelite family; Ahiram, the Ahiramite
39 family; Shupham, the Shuphamite family; Hupham, the Huphamite family.
40 Belaites: Ard and Naaman. Ard, the Ardite family; Naaman, the Naamite
41 family. These were the Benjamite families; the number in their detailed list was forty-five thousand six hundred.
42 Danites, by their families: Shuham, the Shuhamite family. These were the

43 families of Dan by their families; the number in the detailed list of the Shuhamite family was sixty-four thousand four hundred.
44 Asherites, by their families: Imna, the Imnite family; Ishvi, the Ishvite family;
45 Beriah, the Beriite family. Beriite families: Heber, the Heberite family;
46 Malchiel, the Malchielite family. The daughter of Asher was named Serah.
47 These were the Asherite families; the number in their detailed list was fifty-three thousand four hundred.
48 Naphtalites, by their families: Jahzeel, the Jahzeelite family; Guni, the Gunite family; Jezer, the Jezerite
49 family; Shillem, the Shillemite family.
50 These were the Naphtalite families by their families; the number in their detailed list was forty-five thousand four hundred.
51 The total in the Israelite lists was six hundred and one thousand seven hundred and thirty.
52 The LORD spoke to Moses and said,
53 'The land shall be apportioned among these tribes according to the number of names recorded. To the larger group
54 you shall give a larger property and to the smaller a smaller; a property shall be given to each in proportion to its
55 size as shown in the detailed lists. The land, however, shall be apportioned by lot; the lots shall be cast for the properties by families in the father's
56 line. Properties shall be apportioned by lot between the larger families and the smaller.'
57 The detailed lists of Levi, by families: Gershon, the Gershonite family; Kohath, the Kohathite family; Merari, the Merarite family.
58 These were the families of Levi: the Libnite, Hebronite, Mahlite, Mushite, and Korahite families.
59 Kohath was the father of Amram; Amram's wife was named Jochebed daughter of Levi, born to him in Egypt.
60 She bore to Amram Aaron, Moses, and their sister Miriam. Aaron's sons were

---

Simeon's drastic decline, compare Gen.49.5–7 n. **28–37:** Manasseh is listed first, in keeping with the order of birth given in Gen.41.50–52. This reflects tribal and military prominence (Gen.48.14 n.) which was later reversed (Gen.48.17–19 n.), in keeping with the order of 1.32–35. (Accordingly, the present census may be older than that of ch. 1.) **55–56:** Since *lots* were thought to reveal the divine will (see Exod.28.15 n.), such apportionment confessed the LORD's sovereignty over the land (compare Lev.25.1–55 n., 23 n.). **57–62:** See 3.14–39.

Nadab, Abihu, Eleazar and Ithamar.
61 Nadab and Abihu died because they presented illicit fire before the LORD.
62 In the detailed lists of Levi the number of males, aged one month and upwards, was twenty-three thousand. They were recorded separately from the other Israelites because no property was allotted to them among the Israelites
63 These were the detailed lists prepared by Moses and Eleazar the priest when they numbered the Israelites in the lowlands of Moab by the Jordan near
64 Jericho. Among them there was not a single one of the Israelites whom Moses and Aaron the priest had recorded in
65 the wilderness of Sinai; for the LORD had said they should all die in the wilderness. None of them was still living except Caleb son of Jephunneh and Joshua son of Nun.

27 A claim was presented by the daughters of Zelophehad son of Hepher, son of Gilead, son of Machir, son of Manasseh, son of Joseph. Their names were Mahlah, Noah, Hoglah,
2 Milcah and Tirzah. They appeared at the entrance of the Tent of the Presence before Moses, Eleazar the priest, the chiefs, and all the community, and
3 spoke as follows: 'Our father died in the wilderness. He was not among the company of Korah which combined together against the LORD; he died for
4 his own sin and left no sons. Is it right that, because he had no son, our father's name should disappear from his family? Give us our property on the same footing as our father's brothers.'
5 So Moses brought their case before
6 the LORD, and the LORD spoke to Moses
7 and said, 'The claim of the daughters of Zelophehad is good. You must allow them to inherit on the same footing as their father's brothers. Let their father's
8 patrimony pass to them. Then say this to the Israelites: "When a man dies leaving no son, his patrimony shall pass

to his daughter. If he has no daughter, 9
you shall give it to his brothers. If he 10
has no brothers, you shall give it to his father's brothers. If his father had no 11
brothers, then you shall give possession to the nearest survivor in his family, and he shall inherit. This shall be a legal precedent for the Israelites, as the LORD has commanded Moses."'
The LORD said to Moses, 'Go up this 12
mountain, Mount Abarim, and look out over the land which I have given to the Israelites. Then, when you have 13
looked out over it, you shall be gathered to your father's kin like your brother Aaron; for you and Aaron 14
disobeyed my command when the community disputed with me in the wilderness of Zin: you did not uphold my holiness before them at the waters.' These were the waters of Meribah-by-Kadesh in the wilderness of Zin.
Then Moses said, 'Let the LORD, the 15,16
God of the spirits of all mankind, appoint a man over the community to go 17
out and come in at their head, to lead them out and bring them home, so that the community of the LORD may not be like sheep without a shepherd.' The 18
LORD answered Moses, 'Take Joshua son of Nun, a man endowed with spirit; lay your hand on him and set 19
him before Eleazar the priest and all the community. Give him his commission in their presence, and delegate some of 20
your authority to him, so that all the community of the Israelites may obey him. He must appear before Eleazar 21
the priest, who will obtain a decision for him by consulting the Urim before the LORD; at his word they shall go out and shall come home, both Joshua and the whole community of the Israelites.'
Moses did as the LORD had com- 22
manded him. He took Joshua, presented him to Eleazar the priest and the whole community, laid his hands on him and 23
gave him his commission, as the LORD had instructed him.

27.1–11: Women's right to receive property in the promised land. This precedent-setting case is anticipated in 26.33 and clarified in ch. 36. Similar concern for preserving family property is expressed in Lev. ch. 25; 1 Kgs.21.1–3.
27.12–23: Moses' successor is appointed. 13: See 20.22–29. **14:** See 20.1–13. **17:** *Go out and come in:* at the head of the army. **19–21:** In the postexilic community, the priesthood retained ultimate authority over military affairs (see Introduction to Lev.); thus Joshua *must appear before Eleazar . . . who will obtain a decision. Urim:* see Exod.28.15 n.

28 THE LORD SPOKE TO MOSES AND SAID,
2 Give this command to the Israelites.
See that you present my offerings, the
food for the food-offering of soothing
odour, to me at the appointed time.
3 Tell them: This is the food-offering
which you shall present to the LORD:
the regular daily whole-offering of two
4 yearling rams without blemish. One
you shall sacrifice in the morning and
the second between dusk and dark.
5 The grain-offering shall be a tenth of
an ephah of flour mixed with a quarter
6 of a hin of oil of pounded olives. (This
was the regular whole-offering made at
Mount Sinai, a soothing odour, a food-
7 offering to the LORD.) The wine for the
proper drink-offering shall be a quarter
of a hin to each ram; you are to pour
out this strong drink in the holy place
8 as an offering to the LORD. You shall
sacrifice the second ram between dusk
and dark, with the same grain-offering
as at the morning sacrifice and with the
proper drink-offering; it is a food-
offering of soothing odour to the
LORD.
9 For the sabbath day: two yearling
rams without blemish, a grain-offering
of two tenths of an ephah of flour
mixed with oil, and the proper drink-
10 offering. This whole-offering, presented
every sabbath, is in addition to the
regular whole-offering and the proper
drink-offering.
11 On the first day of every month you
shall present a whole-offering to the
LORD, consisting of two young bulls,
one ram and seven yearling rams with-
12 out blemish. The grain-offering shall
be three tenths of flour mixed with oil
for each bull, two tenths of flour mixed
13 with oil for the full-grown ram, and one
tenth of flour mixed with oil for each
young ram. This is a whole-offering, a
food-offering of soothing odour to the
14 LORD. The proper drink-offering shall
be half a hin of wine for each bull, a
third for the full-grown ram and a

quarter for each young ram. This is the
whole-offering to be made, month by
month, throughout the year. Further, 15
one he-goat shall be sacrificed as a sin
offering to the LORD, in addition to the
regular whole-offering and the proper
drink-offering.
The Passover of the LORD shall be 16
held on the fourteenth day of the first
month, and on the fifteenth day there 17
shall be a pilgrim-feast; for seven days
you must eat only unleavened cakes.
On the first day there shall be a sacred 18
assembly; you shall not do your daily
work. As a food-offering, a whole- 19
offering to the LORD, you shall present
two young bulls, one ram, and seven
yearling rams, all without blemish.
You shall offer the proper grain-offer- 20
ings of flour mixed with oil, three tenths
for each bull, two tenths for the ram,
and one tenth for each of the seven 21
young rams; and as a sin-offering, 22
one he-goat to make expiation for you.
All these you shall offer in addition to 23
the morning whole-offering, which is
the regular sacrifice. You shall repeat 24
this daily till the seventh day, presenting
food as a food-offering of soothing
odour to the LORD, in addition to the
regular whole-offering and the proper
drink-offering. On the seventh day 25
there shall be a sacred assembly; you
shall not do your daily work.
On the day of Firstfruits, when you 26
bring to the LORD your grain-offering
from the new crop at your Feast of
Weeks, there shall be a sacred assembly;
you shall not do your daily work. You 27
shall bring a whole-offering as a soothing odour to the LORD: two young
bulls, one full-grown ram, and seven
yearling rams. The proper grain-offering 28
shall be of flour mixed with oil, three
tenths for each bull, two tenths for the
one ram, and a tenth for each of the 29
seven young rams, and there shall be 30
one he-goat as a sin-offering to make
expiation for you; they shall all be 31

28.1–29.40: The sacrificial calendar. This is a summary of all the sacrifices to be made by
the community and is an expansion of Lev. ch. 23 (and of Ezek.45.18–46.15). (For offerings by
individuals, see 29.39 and Lev. chs. 1–7.) The definitive statement on the subject, it is placed
just after the note of Moses' impending death (27.12–23). **2:** *Soothing odour:* see Exod.29.18 n.
3–8: See Exod.29.38–42; Lev.6.8–13. **9–10:** Ezek.46.4–5 differs considerably. **11–15:** The
lunar calendar, with these sacrifices at the new moon, was dominant in postexilic times. Compare
10.10; Isa.1.14; Amos 8.5. **16–26:** See Exod.12.1–27; 13.3–10; Lev. 23.5–8. **26–31:** See Exod.

without blemish. All these you shall offer in addition to the regular whole-offering with the proper grain-offering and drink-offering.

29 On the first day of the seventh month there shall be a sacred assembly; you shall not do your daily work. It shall 2 be a day of acclamation. You shall sacrifice a whole-offering as a soothing odour to the LORD: one young bull, one full-grown ram, and seven yearling 3 rams, without blemish. Their proper grain-offering shall be of flour mixed with oil, three tenths for the bull, two 4 tenths for the one ram, and one tenth 5 for each of the seven young rams, and there shall be one he-goat as a sin-6 offering to make expiation for you. This is in addition to the monthly whole-offering and the regular whole-offering with their proper grain-offerings and drink-offerings according to custom; it is a food-offering of soothing odour to the LORD.

7 On the tenth day of this seventh month there shall be a sacred assembly, and you shall mortify yourselves; you 8 shall not do any work. You shall bring a whole-offering to the LORD as a sooth-ing odour: one young bull, one full-grown ram, and seven yearling rams; 9 they shall all be without blemish. The proper grain-offering shall be of flour mixed with oil, three tenths for the bull, 10 two tenths for the one ram, and one tenth for each of the seven young 11 rams, and there shall be one he-goat as a sin-offering, in addition to the expiatory sin-offering and the regular whole-offering, with the proper grain-offering and drink-offering.

12 On the fifteenth day of the seventh month there shall be a sacred assembly. You shall not do your daily work, but shall keep a pilgrim-feast to the LORD 13 for seven days. As a whole-offering, a food-offering of soothing odour to the LORD, you shall bring thirteen young bulls, two full-grown rams, and fourteen yearling rams; they shall all be 14 without blemish. The proper grain-offer-ing shall be of flour mixed with oil, three tenths for each of the thirteen bulls, two

tenths for each of the two rams, and one tenth for each of the fourteen young 15 rams, and there shall be one he-goat as 16 a sin-offering, in addition to the regular whole-offering with the proper grain-offering and drink-offering.

On the second day: twelve young 17 bulls, two full-grown rams, and four-teen yearling rams, without blemish, together with the proper grain-offerings 18 and drink-offerings for bulls, full-grown rams, and young rams, as prescribed according to their number, and there 19 shall be one he-goat as a sin-offering, in addition to the regular whole-offering with the proper grain-offering and drink-offering.

On the third day: eleven bulls, two 20 full-grown rams, and fourteen yearling rams, without blemish, together with 21 the proper grain-offerings and drink-offerings for bulls, full-grown rams, and young rams, as prescribed according to their number, and there shall be one 22 he-goat as a sin-offering, in addition to the regular whole-offering, with the proper grain-offering and drink-offering.

On the fourth day: ten bulls, two 23 full-grown rams, and fourteen yearling rams, without blemish, together with 24 the proper grain-offerings and drink-offerings for bulls, full-grown rams, and young rams, as prescribed accord-ing to their number, and there shall be 25 one he-goat as a sin-offering, in addition to the regular whole-offering with the proper grain-offering and drink-offering.

On the fifth day: nine bulls, two 26 full-grown rams, and fourteen yearling rams, without blemish, together with 27 the proper grain-offerings and drink-offerings for bulls, full-grown rams, and young rams, as prescribed accord-ing to their number, and there shall be 28 one he-goat as a sin-offering, in addi-tion to the regular whole-offering with the proper grain-offering and drink-offering.

On the sixth day: eight bulls, two 29 full-grown rams, and fourteen yearling rams, without blemish, together with 30

23.16; 34.22; Lev.23.15–21. **29.1–6:** This day is called the "new year" in the calendar in Lev. ch. 23 (see Lev.23.24–25 n.). **7–11:** The Day of Atonement (see Lev. ch. 16; 23.26–32). **12–38:** The Feast of Ingathering (see Exod.23.16; Lev.23.34–36).

the proper grain-offerings and drink-offerings for bulls, full-grown rams, and young rams, as prescribed according to
31 their number, and there shall be one he-goat as a sin-offering, in addition to the regular whole-offering with the proper grain-offering and drink-offering.

32 On the seventh day: seven bulls, two full-grown rams, and fourteen
33 yearling rams, without blemish, together with the proper grain-offerings and drink-offerings for bulls, full-grown rams, and young rams, as prescribed
34 according to their number, and there shall be one he-goat as a sin-offering, in addition to the regular whole-offering with the proper grain-offering and drink-offering.

35 The eighth day you shall keep as a closing ceremony; you shall not do
36 your daily work. As a whole-offering, a food-offering of soothing odour to the LORD, you shall bring one bull, one full-grown ram, and seven yearling rams,
37 without blemish, together with the proper grain-offerings and drink-offerings for bulls, full-grown rams, and young rams, as prescribed according
38 to their number, and there shall be one he-goat as a sin-offering, in addition to the regular whole-offering with the proper grain-offering and drink-offering.

39 These are the sacrifices which you shall offer to the LORD at the appointed seasons, in addition to the votive offerings, the freewill offerings, the whole-offerings, the grain-offerings, the drink-offerings, and the shared-offerings.

40 Moses told the Israelites exactly what the LORD had commanded him.

30 THEN MOSES SPOKE TO THE HEADS OF the Israelite tribes and said, This is the
2 LORD's command: When a man makes a vow to the LORD or swears an oath and so puts himself under a binding obligation, he must not break his word. Every word he has spoken, he must
3 make good. When a woman, still young

and living in her father's house, makes a vow to the LORD or puts herself under a binding obligation, if her 4 father hears of it and keeps silence, then any such vow or obligation shall be valid. But if her father disallows it 5 when he hears of it, none of her vows or obligations shall be valid; the LORD will absolve her, because her father has disallowed it. If the woman is married 6 when she is under a vow or a binding obligation rashly uttered, then if her 7 husband hears of it and keeps silence when he hears, her vow or obligation by which she has bound herself shall be valid. If, however, her husband 8 disallows it when he hears of it and repudiates the vow which she has taken upon herself or the rash utterance with which she has bound herself, then the LORD will absolve her. Every vow by 9 which a widow or a divorced woman has bound herself shall be valid. But 10 if it is in her husband's house that a woman makes a vow or puts herself under a binding obligation by an oath, and her husband, hearing of it, keeps 11 silence and does not disallow it, then every vow and obligation under which she has put herself shall be valid; but 12 if her husband clearly repudiates them when he hears of them, then nothing that she has uttered, whether vow or obligation, shall be valid. Her husband has repudiated them, and the LORD will absolve her.

The husband can confirm or 13 repudiate any vow or oath by which a woman binds herself to mortification. If he maintains silence day after day, 14 he thereby confirms every vow or obligation under which she has put herself: he confirms them, because he kept silence at the time when he heard them. If he repudiates them some time after 15 he has heard them, he shall be responsible for her default.

Such are the decrees which the LORD 16 gave to Moses concerning a husband and his wife and a father and his daughter, still young and living in her father's house.

30.1–16: Vows taken by women. Israel's cultic obligations were mandatory only on adult males (Exod.10.7–11; 23.17), but women might volunteer to undertake sacrificial obligations within the limits specified. For other regulations concerning vows, see 6.1–21; Lev. ch. 27; Deut.23.21–23. **2:** On observing such vows, see Eccles.5.4–5. **13:** *Mortification:* fasting.

31 THE LORD SPOKE TO MOSES AND SAID, 2 'You are to exact vengeance for Israel on the Midianites and then you will be gathered to your father's kin.'

3 Then Moses spoke to the people in these words: 'Let some men among you be drafted for active service. They shall fall upon Midian and exact ven- 4 geance in the LORD's name. You shall send out a thousand men from each of 5 the tribes of Israel.' So the men were called up from the clans of Israel, a thousand from each tribe, twelve thousand in all, drafted for active 6 service. Moses sent out this force, a thousand from each tribe, with Phinehas son of Eleazar the priest, who was in charge of the holy vessels and of the trumpets to give the signal for the 7 battle-cry. They made war on Midian as the LORD had commanded Moses, 8 and slew all the men. In addition to those slain in battle they killed the kings of Midian—Evi, Rekem, Zur, Hur, and Reba, the five kings of Midian—and they put to death also 9 Balaam son of Beor. The Israelites took captive the Midianite women and their dependants, and carried off all their beasts, their flocks, and their 10 property. They burnt all their cities, in which they had settled, and all their 11 encampments. They took all the spoil 12 and plunder, both man and beast, and brought them—captives, plunder, and spoil—to Moses and Eleazar the priest and to all the community of the Israelites, to the camp in the lowlands of Moab by the Jordan at Jericho. 13 Moses and Eleazar the priest and all the leaders of the community went to 14 meet them outside the camp. Moses spoke angrily to the officers of the army, the commanders of units of a thousand and of a hundred, who were 15 returning from the campaign: 'Have you spared all the women?' he said. 16 'Remember, it was they who, on Balaam's departure, set about seduc-

ing the Israelites into disloyalty to the LORD that day at Peor, so that the plague struck the community of the LORD. Now kill every male dependant, 17 and kill every woman who has had intercourse with a man, but spare for 18 yourselves every woman among them who has not had intercourse. You 19 yourselves, every one of you who has taken life and every one who has touched the dead, must remain outside the camp for seven days. Purify your- selves and your captives on the third day and on the seventh day, and purify 20 also every piece of clothing, every ar- ticle made of skin, everything woven of goat's hair, and everything made of wood.'

Eleazar the priest said to the soldiers 21 returning from battle, 'This is a law and statute which the LORD has ordained through Moses. Anything 22–23 which will stand fire, whether gold, silver, copper, iron, tin, or lead, you shall pass through fire and then it will be clean. Other things shall be purified by the water of ritual purification; whatever cannot stand fire shall be passed through the water. On the 24 seventh day you shall wash your clothes, and then be clean; after this you may re-enter the camp.'

The LORD spoke to Moses and said, 25 'Count all that has been captured, 26 man or beast, you and Eleazar the priest and the heads of families in the community, and divide it equally be- 27 tween the fighting men who went on the campaign and the whole com- munity. You shall levy a tax for the 28 LORD: from the combatants it shall be one out of every five hundred, whether men, cattle, asses, or sheep, to be taken 29 out of their share and given to Eleazar the priest as a contribution for the LORD. Out of the share of the Israelites 30 it shall be one out of every fifty taken, whether man or beast, cattle, asses, or sheep, to be given to the Levites who

---

31.1–54: Vengeance against the Midianites. The chapter is a sequel to 25.16–18 and illustrates the rules for "holy" war. For another instance, see 1 Sam.15.2–33, and for a statement of guidance, see Deut.13.12–17. **6:** Phinehas serves here as priest both because of his valor in the previous episode (25.7–13) and because the high priest (Eleazar) must avoid contact with corpses (Lev.21.10–12). **8:** Why Balaam should have been in the Midianite camp (contrast 24.25) or been blamed for the incident at Shittim (ch. 25) is unclear. He is viewed negatively also in 2 Pet.2.15 16; Jude 11; Rev.2.14. **19–20:** See ch. 19 for the obligatory ritual of purifica- tion. **21–24:** The various items of booty must likewise be purified (see 19.14–18; Lev.11.24–25 n.);

are in charge of the LORD's Tabernacle.'

31 Moses and Eleazar the priest did as the LORD had commanded Moses.

32 These were the spoils, over and above the plunder taken by the fighting men: six hundred and seventy-five thousand

33 sheep, seventy-two thousand cattle,

34,35 sixty-one thousand asses; and of persons, thirty-two thousand girls who had had no intercourse with a man.

36 The half-share of those who took part in the campaign was thus three hundred and thirty-seven thousand

37 five hundred sheep, the tax for the LORD from these being six hundred and

38 seventy-five; thirty-six thousand cattle,

39 the tax being seventy-two; thirty thousand five hundred asses, the tax

40 being sixty-one; and sixteen thousand

41 persons, the tax being thirty-two. Moses gave Eleazar the priest the tax levied for the LORD, as the LORD had commanded him.

42–43 The share of the community, being the half-share for the Israelites which Moses divided off from that of the combatants, was three hundred and thirty-seven thousand five hundred

44,45 sheep, thirty-six thousand cattle, thirty

46 thousand five hundred asses, and

47 sixteen thousand persons. Moses took one out of every fifty, whether man or beast, from the half-share of the Israelites, and gave it to the Levites who were in charge of the LORD's Tabernacle, as the LORD had commanded him.

48 Then the officers who had commanded the forces on the campaign, the commanders of units of a thousand

49 and of a hundred, came to Moses and said to him, 'Sir, we have checked the roll of the fighting men who were under our command, and not one of them is

50 missing. So we have brought the gold ornaments, the armlets, bracelets, finger-rings, earrings, and pendants that each man has found, to offer them before the LORD as a ransom for our lives.'

51 Moses and Eleazar the priest received this gold from the commanders of units of a thousand and of a hundred, all of

52 it craftsman's work, and the gold thus levied as a contribution to the LORD weighed sixteen thousand seven hun-

53 dred and fifty shekels; for every man in the army had taken plunder. So Moses

54 and Eleazar the priest received the gold from the commanders of units of a thousand and of a hundred, and brought it to the Tent of the Presence that the LORD might remember Israel.

32 Now the Reubenites and the Gadites had large and very numerous flocks, and when they saw that the land of Jazer and Gilead was good grazing

2 country, they came and said to Moses and Eleazar the priest and to the leaders

3 of the community, 'Ataroth, Dibon, Jazer, Nimrah, Heshbon, Elealeh, Se-

4 bam, Nebo, and Beon, the region which the LORD has subdued before the advance of the Israelite community, is grazing country, and our flocks are our

5 livelihood. If', they said, 'we have found favour with you, sir, then let this country be given to us as our possession, and do not make us cross the Jordan.'

6 Moses replied to the Gadites and the Reubenites, 'Are your kinsmen to go

7 into battle while you stay here? How dare you discourage the Israelites from crossing over to the land which the

8 LORD has given them? This is what your fathers did when I sent them out from Kadesh-barnea to view the land.

9 They went up as far as the gorge of Eshcol and viewed the land, and on their return so discouraged the Israelites that they would not enter the land

10 which the LORD had given them. The LORD became angry that day, and he

11 solemnly swore: "Because they have not followed me with their whole heart, none of the men who came out of Egypt, from twenty years old and upwards, shall see the land which I promised on oath to Abraham, Isaac

12 and Jacob." This meant all except

---

fire as the means of doing so has not been specified previously. **50:** A *ransom* was needed because taking a census, even of men returning from battle, was offensive to God (see Exod.30.11–16 n.).
32.1–42: The distribution of the territory east of the Jordan. Possibly the story was preserved in order to encourage future generations east of the Jordan to participate in the military actions of the larger whole. (For an instance of such failure to do so, see Judg.5.15–17.) The episode is reviewed in Deut.3.12–20 and the boundaries involved are outlined in Josh.13.8–32. **8–13:** See

Caleb son of Jephunneh the Kenizzite and Joshua son of Nun, who followed the LORD with their whole heart.
13 The LORD became angry with Israel, and he made them wander in the wilderness for forty years until that whole generation was dead which had done
14 what was wrong in his eyes. And now you are following in your fathers' footsteps, a fresh brood of sinful men to fire the LORD's anger once more against
15 Israel; for if you refuse to follow him, he will again abandon this whole people in the wilderness and you will be the cause of their destruction.'
16 Presently they came forward with this offer: 'We will build folds for our sheep here and towns for our depen-
17 dants. Then we can be drafted as a fighting force to go at the head of the Israelites until we have brought them to the lands that will be theirs. Meanwhile our dependants can live in the walled towns, safe from the people of the
18 country. We will not return until every Israelite is settled in possession of his
19 patrimony; we will claim no share of the land with them over the Jordan and beyond, because our patrimony has already been allotted to us east of the
20 Jordan.' Moses answered, 'If you stand by your promise, if in the presence of the LORD you are drafted for battle,
21 and the whole draft crosses the Jordan in front of the LORD and remains there until the LORD has driven out his
22 enemies, and the land falls before him, then you may come back and be quit of your obligation to the LORD and to Israel; and this land shall be your possession in the sight of the LORD.
23 But I warn you, if you fail to do all this, you will have sinned against the LORD, and your sin will find you out.
24 So build towns for your dependants and folds for your sheep; but carry out your promise.'
25 The Gadites and Reubenites answered Moses, 'Sir, we are your servants
26 and will do as you command. Our dependants and wives, our flocks and all our beasts shall remain here in the cities of Gilead; but we, all who have 27 been drafted for active service with the LORD, will cross the river and fight, according to your command.'

Accordingly Moses gave these in- 28 structions to Eleazar the priest and Joshua son of Nun and to the heads of the families in the Israelite tribes: 'If 29 the Gadites and Reubenites, all who have been drafted for battle before the LORD, cross the Jordan with you, and if the land falls into your hands, then you shall give them Gilead for their possession. But if, thus drafted, they 30 fail to cross with you, then they shall acquire land alongside you in Canaan.' The Gadites and Reubenites said in 31 response, 'Sir, the LORD has spoken, and we will obey. Once we have been 32 drafted, we will cross over before the LORD into Canaan; then we shall have our patrimony here beyond the Jordan.'

So to the Gadites, the Reubenites, 33 and half the tribe of Manasseh son of Joseph, Moses gave the kingdoms of Sihon king of the Amorites and Og king of Bashan, the whole land with its towns and the country round them. The Gadites built Dibon, Ataroth, 34 Aroer, Atroth-shophan, Jazer, Jogbe- 35 hah, Beth-nimrah, and Beth-haran, all 36 of them walled towns with folds for their sheep. The Reubenites built Hesh- 37 bon, Elealeh, Kiriathaim, Nebo, Baal- 38 meon (whose name was changed), and Sibmah; these were the names they gave to the towns they built. The sons of 39 Machir son of Manasseh invaded Gilead, took it and drove out the Amorite inhabitants; Moses then as- 40 signed Gilead to Machir son of Manasseh, and he made his home there. Jair son of Manasseh attacked 41 and took the tent-villages of Ham*t* and called them Havvoth-jair.*u* Nobah at- 42 tacked and took Kenath and its villages and gave it his own name, Nobah.

t Prob. rdg.; Heb. their tent-villages.
u That is Tent-villages of Jair.

chs. 13–14. **33:** *Half the tribe:* for the settlement of the remainder west of the Jordan, see Josh.17.1–6.
33.1–49: A review of Israel's itinerary from Egypt to the lowlands of Moab. It has been shaped so as to contain forty stages before the mountains overlooking the promised land are reached (v. 47), in keeping with the forty years in the Wilderness (14.32–33). Relics of older sources

33 THESE ARE THE STAGES IN THE JOURNEY of the Israelites, when they were led by Moses and Aaron in their tribal hosts 2 out of Egypt. Moses recorded their starting-points stage by stage as the LORD commanded him. These are their stages from one starting-point to the next:

3 The Israelites left Rameses on the fifteenth day of the first month, the day after the Passover; they marched out defiantly in full view of all the Egyptians, 4 while the Egyptians were burying all the first-born struck down by the LORD as a judgement on their gods.

5 The Israelites left Rameses and encamped at Succoth.

6 They left Succoth and encamped at Etham on the edge of the wilderness.

7 They left Etham, turned back near Pi-hahiroth*v* on the east of Baal-zephon, and encamped before Migdol.

8 They left Pi-hahiroth, passed through the Sea into the wilderness, marched for three days through the wilderness of Etham, and encamped at Marah.

9 They left Marah and came to Elim, where there were twelve springs of water and seventy palm-trees, and encamped there.

10 They left Elim and encamped by the Red Sea.

11 They left the Red Sea and encamped in the wilderness of Sin.

12 They left the wilderness of Sin and encamped at Dophkah.

13 They left Dophkah and encamped at Alush.

14 They left Alush and encamped at Rephidim, where there was no water for the people to drink.

15 They left Rephidim and encamped in the wilderness of Sinai.

16 They left the wilderness of Sinai and encamped at Kibroth-hattaavah.

17 They left Kibroth-hattaavah and encamped at Hazeroth.

18 They left Hazeroth and encamped at Rithmah.

19 They left Rithmah and encamped at Rimmon-parez.

20 They left Rimmon-parez and encamped at Libnah.

21 They left Libnah and encamped at Rissah.

22 They left Rissah and encamped at Kehelathah.

23 They left Kehelathah and encamped at Mount Shapher.

24 They left Mount Shapher and encamped at Haradah.

25 They left Haradah and encamped at Makheloth.

26 They left Makheloth and encamped at Tahath.

27 They left Tahath and encamped at Tarah.

28 They left Tarah and encamped at Mithcah.

29 They left Mithcah and encamped at Hashmonah.

30 They left Hashmonah and encamped at Moseroth.

31 They left Moseroth and encamped at Bene-jaakan.

32 They left Bene-jaakan and encamped at Hor-haggidgad.

33 They left Hor-haggidgad and encamped at Jotbathah.

34 They left Jotbathah and encamped at Ebronah.*w*

35 They left Ebronah and encamped at Ezion-geber.

36 They left Ezion-geber and encamped in the wilderness of Zin, that is of Kadesh.

37 They left Kadesh and encamped on Mount Hor on the frontier of Edom.

38 Aaron the priest went up Mount Hor at the command of the LORD and there he died, on the first day of the fifth month in the fortieth year after the Israelites came out of Egypt; he was a 39 hundred and twenty-three years old when he died there.

40 The Canaanite king of Arad, who lived in the Canaanite Negeb, heard that the Israelites were coming.

41 They left Mount Hor and encamped at Zalmonah.

42 They left Zalmonah and encamped at Punon.

43 They left Punon and encamped at Oboth.

v See Exod. 14. 2.
w Or Abronah.

have been used, as is evident from several omissions from and additions to the basic account in Exod.–Num. **5–15**: See Exod.12.37–19.2. **16–36**: See 10.11–20.1. **37–49**: See 20.22–22.1.

44 They left Oboth and encamped at Iye-abarim on the frontier of Moab.

45 They left Iyim and encamped at Dibon-gad.

46 They left Dibon-gad and encamped at Almon-diblathaim.

47 They left Almon-diblathaim and encamped in the mountains of Abarim east of Nebo.

48 They left the mountains of Abarim and encamped in the lowlands of Moab

49 by the Jordan near Jericho. Their camp beside the Jordan extended from Beth-jeshimoth to Abel-shittim in the

50 lowlands of Moab. In the lowlands of Moab by the Jordan near Jericho the

51 LORD spoke to Moses and said, Speak to the Israelites in these words: You will soon be crossing the Jordan to enter

52 Canaan. You must drive out all its inhabitants as you advance, destroy all their carved figures and their images of cast metal, and lay their hill-shrines in

53 ruins. You must take possession of the land and settle there, for to you I have

54 given the land to occupy. You must divide it by lot among your families, each taking its own territory, the large family a large territory and the small family a small. It shall be assigned to them according to the fall of the lot, each tribe and family taking its own

55 territory. If you do not drive out the inhabitants of the land as you advance, any whom you leave in possession will become like a barbed hook in your eye and a thorn in your side. They shall continually dispute your possession of

56 the land, and what I meant to do to them I will do to you.

34 The LORD spoke to Moses and said,

2 Give these instructions to the Israelites: Soon you will be entering Canaan. This is the land assigned to you as a perpetual patrimony, the land of Canaan thus

3 defined by its frontiers. Your southern border shall start from the wilderness of Zin, where it marches with Edom, and run southwards from the end of the

4 Dead Sea on its eastern side. It shall then turn from the south up the ascent of Akrabbim and pass by Zin, and its

southern limit shall be Kadesh-barnea. It shall proceed by Hazar-addar to Azmon and from Azmon turn towards 5 the Torrent of Egypt, and its limit shall be the sea. Your western frontier shall 6 be the Great Sea and the seaboard; this shall be your frontier to the west. This shall be your northern frontier: you 7 shall draw a line from the Great Sea to Mount Hor and from Mount Hor to 8 Lebo-hamath, and the limit of the frontier shall be Zedad. From there it 9 shall run to Ziphron, and its limit shall be Hazar-enan; this shall be your frontier to the north. To the east you shall 10 draw a line from Hazar-enan to Shepham; it shall run down from 11 Shepham to Riblah east of Ain, continuing until it strikes the ridge east of the sea of Kinnereth. The frontier shall 12 then run down to the Jordan and its limit shall be the Dead Sea. The land defined by these frontiers shall be your land.

Moses gave these instructions to the 13 Israelites: This is the land which you shall assign by lot, each taking your own territory; it is the land which the LORD has ordered to be given to nine tribes and a half tribe. For the 14 Reubenites, the Gadites, and the half tribe of Manasseh have already occupied their territories, family by family. These two and a half tribes have re- 15 ceived their territory here beyond the Jordan, east to Jericho, towards the sunrise.

The LORD spoke to Moses and said, 16 These are the men who shall assign the 17 land for you: Eleazar the priest and Joshua son of Nun. You shall also take 18 one chief from each tribe to assign the land. These are their names: 19

from the tribe of Judah: Caleb son of Jephunneh;

from the tribe of Simeon: Samuel 20 son of Ammihud;

from the tribe of Benjamin: Elidad 21 son of Kislon;

from the tribe of Dan: the chief 22 Bukki son of Jogli;

from the Josephites: from Manasseh, 23

33.50–34.29: Directions for the distribution of territory west of the Jordan. **54:** *Lot:* see 26.55–56 n. for the reason. **55–56:** For a slightly different reason for expelling the Canaanites, see Deut.7.1–6. **34.8:** *Lebo-hamath:* see 13.21 n. **14-15:** See ch. 32. **19-28:** The order is roughly that of the geographical position of the tribes from south to north after the conquest, under

24 the chief Hanniel son of Ephod; and from Ephraim, the chief Kemuel son of Shiphtan;

25 from Zebulun: the chief Elizaphan son of Parnach;

26 from Issachar: the chief Paltiel son of Azzan;

27 from Asher: the chief Ahihud son of Shelomi;

28 from Naphtali: the chief Pedahel son of Ammihud.

29 These were the men whom the LORD appointed to assign the territories in the land of Canaan.

35 THE LORD SPOKE TO MOSES IN THE lowlands of Moab by the Jordan near 2 Jericho and said: Tell the Israelites to set aside towns in their patrimony as homes for the Levites, and give them also the common land surrounding the 3 towns. They shall live in the towns, and keep their beasts, their herds, and all their livestock on the common land. 4 The land of the towns which you give the Levites shall extend from the centre of the town outwards for a thousand 5 cubits in each direction. Starting from the town the eastern boundary shall measure two thousand cubits, the southern two thousand, the western two thousand, and the northern two thousand, with the town in the centre. They shall have this as the common land adjoining their towns. 6 When you give the Levites their towns, six of them shall be cities of refuge, in which the homicide may take sanctuary; and you shall give them 7 forty-two other towns. The total number of towns to be given to the Levites, each with its common land, is forty-8 eight. When you set aside these towns out of the territory of the Israelites, you shall allot more from the larger tribe and less from the smaller; each tribe shall give towns to the Levites in proportion to the patrimony assigned to it.

The LORD spoke to Moses and said, 9 Speak to the Israelites in these words: 10 You are crossing the Jordan to the land of Canaan. You shall designate 11 certain cities to be places of refuge, in which the homicide who has killed a man by accident may take sanctuary. These cities shall be places of refuge 12 from the vengeance of the dead man's next-of-kin, so that the homicide shall not be put to death without standing his trial before the community. The 13 cities appointed as places of refuge shall be six in number, three east of the Jor- 14 dan and three in Canaan. These six 15 cities shall be places of refuge, so that any man who has taken life inadvertently, whether he be Israelite, resident alien, or temporary settler, may take sanctuary in one of them.

If the man strikes his victim with 16 anything made of iron and he dies, then he is a murderer: the murderer must be put to death. If a man has a stone in 17 his hand capable of causing death and strikes another man and he dies, he is a murderer: the murderer must be put to death. If a man has a wooden thing in 18 his hand capable of causing death, and strikes another man and he dies, he is a murderer: the murderer must be put to death. The dead man's next-of-kin shall 19 put the murderer to death; he shall put him to death because he had attacked his victim. If the homicide sets upon a 20 man openly of malice aforethought or aims a missile at him of set purpose and he dies, or if in enmity he falls 21 upon him with his bare hands and he dies, then the assailant must be put to death; he is a murderer. His next-of-kin shall put the murderer to death because he had attacked his victim.

If he attacks a man on the spur of 22 the moment, not being his enemy, or hurls a missile at him not of set pur- pose, or if without looking he throws a 23 stone capable of causing death and it hits a man, then if the man dies, pro-

Joshua, thus reflecting the date of its composition; however, Judah unexpectedly appears before Simeon (see 2.3 n.; Gen.34.1–31 n.).

35.1–34: Levitical cities and cities of refuge. 2–8: The *Levites*, having been set aside for special duties at the sanctuary, are not given a separate allotment of territory (Deut.10.8–9). In compensation, they receive tithes (Num.18.21–24), spoils of war (31.30), special rights at the Jubilee (Lev.25.32–34), and now cities scattered throughout the tribes. See Josh. ch. 21; 1 Chr. 6.54–81. For another perspective on the decline of the tribe of Levi, see Gen.34.1–31 n. **11:** *Places of refuge:* see Exod.21.13; Deut.19.1–13; Josh. ch. 20. **12:** *From the vengeance:*

vided he was not the man's enemy and was not harming him of set purpose, the community shall judge between the striker and the next-of-kin according to these rules. The community shall protect the homicide from the vengeance of the kinsman and take him back to the city of refuge where he had taken sanctuary. He must stay there till the death of the duly anointed high priest. If the homicide ever goes beyond the boundaries of the city where he has taken sanctuary, and the next-of-kin finds him outside and kills him, then the next-of-kin shall not be guilty of murder. The homicide must remain in the city of refuge till the death of the high priest; after the death of the high priest he may go back to his property. These shall be legal precedents for you for all time wherever you live.

The homicide shall be put to death as a murderer only on the testimony of witnesses; the testimony of a single witness shall not be enough to bring him to his death. You shall not accept payment for the life of a homicide guilty of a capital offence; he must be put to death. You shall not accept a payment from a man who has taken sanctuary in a city of refuge, allowing him to go back before the death of the high priest and live at large. You shall not defile your land by bloodshed. Blood defiles the land, and expiation cannot be made on behalf of the land for blood shed on it except by the blood of the man that shed it. You shall not make the land which you inhabit unclean, the land in which I dwell; for I, the LORD, dwell among the Israelites.

36 THE HEADS OF THE FATHERS' FAMILIES of Gilead son of Machir, son of Manasseh, one of the families of the sons of Joseph, approached Moses and the chiefs, heads of families in Israel, and addressed them. 'Sir,' they said, 'the LORD commanded you to distribute the land by lot to the Israelites, and you were also commanded to give the patrimony of our brother Zelophehad to his daughters. Now if any of them shall be married to a husband from another Israelite tribe, her patrimony will be lost to the patrimony of our fathers and be added to that of the tribe into which she is married, and so part of our allotted patrimony will be lost. Then, when the jubilee year comes round in Israel, her patrimony would be added to the patrimony of the tribe into which she is married, and it would be permanently lost to the patrimony of our fathers' tribe.'

So Moses, instructed by the LORD, gave the Israelites this ruling: 'The tribe of the sons of Joseph is right. This is the LORD's command for the daughters of Zelophehad: They may marry whom they please, but only within a family of their father's tribe. No patrimony in Israel shall pass from tribe to tribe, but every Israelite shall retain his father's patrimony. Any woman of an Israelite tribe who is an heiress may marry a man from any family in her father's tribe. Thus the Israelites shall retain each one the patrimony of his forefathers. No patrimony shall pass from one tribe to another, but every tribe in Israel shall retain its own patrimony.'

The daughters of Zelophehad acted in accordance with the LORD's command to Moses; Mahlah, Tirzah, Hoglah, Milcah and Noah, the daughters of Zelophehad, married sons of their father's brothers. They married within the families of the sons of Manasseh son of Joseph, and their patrimony remained with the tribe of their father's family.

These are the commandments and the decrees which the LORD issued to the Israelites through Moses in the lowlands of Moab by the Jordan near Jericho.

---

see Josh.20.3. **24:** *Community shall judge:* see v. 12. **28:** Perhaps now the *high priest*, functioning as the monarch in the postexilic community (see Introduction to Lev.), could grant amnesty to all such homicides at the beginning of his rule; or perhaps such amnesty was automatic. **31:** This is in contrast to some Ancient Near Eastern codes.
36.1–13: An appendix on women's right to receive property. The basic legislation is contained in 27.1–11. **4:** It is difficult to understand precisely how the Jubilee legislation (Lev. ch. 25) applies. **13:** The concluding statement refers back to chs. 22–36.

DEUTERONOMY

Deuteronomy means "second law," a name appropriate because chs. 12–26 repeat much of the legislation found in Exodus–Leviticus–Numbers. In Deuteronomy Moses speaks in the first person in three addresses (1.6–4.40; 5.1–28.68; and 29.1–30.20) given in the plains of Moab, as his farewell to his people. Chapters 31–34 resume in the third person the narrative found at the end of Numbers.

The first address is a review of the Wilderness experience as the basis for exhorting Israel to fidelity in its forthcoming invasion of Canaan. The tone of the legal section is hortatory rather than legislative. The climactic third address (chs. 29–30), in the renewal of the covenant, joins the beckoning future to the record of God's gracious action in the past.

Within the repetition of the laws, a theme recurs that there is to be only one valid sanctuary, this in order for Israel to avoid contamination by the paganism lurking in a multiplicity of local shrines. Since the early nineteenth century, modern scholarship has associated this theme, and hence the book of Deuteronomy, with the religious reformation in 621 of King Josiah (2 Kgs. chs. 22–23), by which the Temple of Jerusalem became the only legitimate shrine. The writing of Deuteronomy is attributed to the age of Josiah, though older traditions are embodied and later materials apparently added (see Introduction to the Pentateuch). The exhortation seems addressed specifically to the kingdom of Judah so as to enable it to escape the fate of conquest and exile suffered by the kingdom of Israel which fell to Assyria in 721 B.C.

Deuteronomy speaks not only to the people assembled before Moses just prior to his death, but to all future generations.

Primary charge of Moses to the people

1 THESE ARE THE WORDS THAT MOSES spoke to all Israel in Transjordan, in the wilderness, that is to say in the Arabah opposite Suph, between Paran on the one side and Tophel, Laban, Hazeroth, and Dizahab on the **2** other. (The journey from Horeb through the hill-country of Seir to Kadesh-barnea takes eleven days.) **3-4** On the first day of the eleventh month of the fortieth year, after the defeat of Sihon king of the Amorites who ruled in Heshbon, and the defeat at Edrei of Og king of Bashan who ruled in Ashtaroth, Moses repeated to the Israelites all the commands that the **5** LORD had given him for them. It was in Transjordan, in Moab, that Moses resolved to promulgate this law. These **6** were his words: The LORD our God spoke to us at Horeb and said, 'You have stayed on this mountain long **7** enough; go now, make for the hill-country of the Amorites, and pass on to all their neighbours in the Arabah, in the hill-country, in the Shephelah, in the Negeb, and on the coast, in short, all Canaan and the Lebanon as far as the great river, the Euphrates. I have laid **8** the land open before you; go in and occupy it, the land which the LORD swore to give to your forefathers Abraham, Isaac and Jacob, and to their descendants after them.'

At that time I said to you, 'You are a **9** burden too heavy for me to carry unaided. The LORD your God has in- **10** creased you so that today you are as numerous as the stars in the sky. May **11** the LORD the God of your fathers increase your number a thousand times and may he bless you as he promised. How can I bear unaided the heavy **12** burden you are to me, and put up with your complaints? Choose men of wis- **13** dom, understanding, and repute for each of your tribes, and I will set them in authority over you.' Your answer **14** was, 'What you have told us to do is right.' So I took men of **15** wisdom and repute and set them in authority over you, some as commanders over units of a thousand, of a hundred, of fifty or of ten, and others

---

1.1–3.29: A review of Israel's journey from Horeb (Sinai) to the plains of Moab. See 4.44–49 n. The LORD's graciousness, despite repeated rebellion, is stressed in order to instruct future generations. **1.1–5:** The setting of Moses' final addresses. **2:** *Kadesh-barnea:* Kadesh (Num.20.1). **3:** *Eleventh month:* see Gen.7.24 n. **4:** See Num.21.21–24. **5:** *This law:* chs. 12–26, which contain both a review of previous legislation and much that is new. See 5.22–31 n. **6–7:** See Exod.33.1–2. *Amorites:* see Num.21.13 n. *Euphrates:* see Gen.15.18 n. **8:** *Forefathers:* Gen.12.1–3; 15.12–21; 26.1–5; 28.10–15. **9–18:** Elements of Num.11.14–17 (in vv. 9–12) and Exod.18.13–27 (in vv.

16 as officers, for each of your tribes. And at that time I gave your judges this command: 'You are to hear the cases that arise among your kinsmen and judge fairly between man and man, whether fellow-countryman or resident 17 alien. You must be impartial and listen to high and low alike: have no fear of man, for judgement belongs to God. If any case is too difficult for you, bring 18 it before me and I will hear it.' At the same time I instructed you in all these duties.

19 Then we set out from Horeb, in obedience to the orders of the LORD our God, and marched through that vast and terrible wilderness, as you found it to be, on the way to the hill-country of the Amorites; and so we 20 came to Kadesh-barnea. Then I said to you, 'You have reached the hill-country of the Amorites which the LORD our 21 God is giving us. The LORD your God has indeed now laid the land open before you. Go forward and occupy it in fulfilment of the promise which the LORD the God of your fathers made you; do not be discouraged or afraid.' 22 But you all came to me and said, 'Let us send men ahead to spy out the country and report back to us about the route we should take and the cities we 23 shall find.' I approved this plan and picked twelve of you, one from each 24 tribe. They set out and made their way up into the hill-country as far as the gorge of Eshcol, which they explored. 25 They took samples of the fruit of the country and brought them back to us, and made their report: 'It is a rich land that the LORD our God is giving us.'

26 But you refused to go up and rebelled against the command of the 27 LORD your God. You muttered treason in your tents and said, 'It was because the LORD hated us that he brought us out of Egypt to hand us over to the 28 Amorites to be wiped out. What shall we find up there? Our kinsmen have discouraged us by their report of a people bigger and taller than we are, and of great cities with fortifications towering to the sky. And they told us they saw there the descendants of the Anakim.'[a]

29 Then I said to you, 'You must not 30 dread them nor be afraid of them. The LORD your God who goes at your head will fight for you and he will do again what you saw him do for you in 31 Egypt and in the wilderness. You saw there how the LORD your God carried you all the way to this place, as a father 32 carries his son.' In spite of this you did not trust the LORD your God, who 33 went ahead on the journey to find a place for your camp. He went in fire by night to show you the way you should take, and in a cloud by day.

34 When the LORD heard your complaints, he was indignant and solemnly 35 swore: 'Not one of these men, this wicked generation, shall see the rich land which I swore to give your fore-fathers, except Caleb son of Jephun-36 neh. He shall see it, and to him and his descendants I will give the land on which he has set foot, because he followed the LORD with his whole 37 heart.' On your account the LORD was angry with me also and said, 'You 38 yourself shall never enter it, but Joshua son of Nun, who is in attendance on you, shall enter it. Encourage him, for he shall put Israel in possession of that 39 land. Your dependants who, you thought, would become spoils of war, and your children who do not yet know good and evil, they shall enter; I will give it to them, and they shall occupy 40 it. You must turn back and set out for the wilderness by way of the Red Sea.'[b]

41 You answered me, 'We have sinned against the LORD; we will now go up and attack just as the LORD our God commanded us.' And each of you fastened on his weapons, thinking it an easy thing to invade the hill-country. 42 But the LORD said to me, 'Tell them not to go up and not to fight; for I will not be with them, and their enemies will

a the descendants . . . Anakim: *or* the tall men.
b *Or* the Sea of Reeds.

13–17) have been combined. **19**: See Num.10.11–13.26; 20.1. **20–46**: See Num.13.1–14.45. Here, rather than the LORD (Num.13.1–2), it is the people who request spies (v. 22); this is indicative of their lack of faith. **28**: *Towering*: built atop hills for defensive purposes. **30**: See Exod.14.13–14. **33**: See Exod.13.21 n. **37**: *On your account*: compare Num.25.4 n.; contrast

43 defeat them.' And I told you this, but you did not listen; you rebelled against the LORD's command and defiantly 44 went up to the hill-country. The Amorites living in the hills came out against you and like bees they chased you; they 45 crushed you at Hormah in Seir. Then you came back and wept before the LORD, but he would not hear you or 46 listen to you. That is why you remained in Kadesh as long as you did.

2 So we turned and set out for the wilderness by way of the Red Sea as the LORD had told me we must do, and we spent many days marching round the 2 hill-country of Seir. Then the LORD 3 said to me, 'You have been long enough marching round these hills; 4 turn towards the north. And give the people this charge: "You are about to go through the territory of your kinsmen the descendants of Esau who live in Seir. Although they are afraid of you, 5 be on your guard and do not provoke them; for I shall not give you any of their land, not so much as a foot's-breadth: I have given the hill-country 6 of Seir to Esau as a possession. You may purchase food from them for silver, and eat it, and you may buy[c] 7 water to drink." ' The LORD your God has blessed you in everything you have undertaken; he has watched your journey through this great wilderness; these forty years the LORD your God has been with you and you have gone short 8 of nothing. So we went on past our kinsmen, the descendants of Esau who live in Seir, and along the road of the Arabah which comes from Elath and Ezion-geber, and we turned and followed the road to the wilderness of 9 Moab. There the LORD said to me, 'Do not harass the Moabites nor provoke them to battle, for I will not give you any of their land as a possession. I have given Ar to the descendants of Lot as a 10 possession.' (The Emim once lived there—a great and numerous people, 11 as tall as the Anakim. The Rephaim also were reckoned as Anakim; but the Moabites called them Emim. The 12 Horites lived in Seir at one time, but the descendants of Esau occupied their territory: they destroyed them as they advanced and then settled in the land instead of them, just as Israel did in their own territory which the LORD gave them.) 'Come now, cross the 13 gorge of the Zared.' So we went across. The journey from Kadesh-barnea to 14 the crossing of the Zared took us thirty-eight years, until the whole generation of fighting men had passed away as the LORD had sworn that they would. The LORD's hand was raised 15 against them, and he rooted them out of the camp to the last man.

When the last of the fighting men 16 among the people had died, the LORD 17 spoke to me, 'Today', he said, 'you are 18 to cross by Ar[d] which lies on the frontier of Moab, and when you reach the 19 territory of the Ammonites, you must not harass them or provoke them to battle, for I will not give you any Ammonite land as a possession; I have assigned it to the descendants of Lot.' (This also is reckoned as the territory of 20 the Rephaim, who lived there at one time; but the Ammonites called them Zamzummim. They were a great and 21 numerous people, as tall as the Anakim, but the LORD destroyed them as the Ammonites advanced and occupied their territory instead of them, just as 22 he had done for the descendants of Esau who lived in Seir. As they advanced, he destroyed the Horites so that they occupied their territory and took possession instead of them: so it is to this day. It was Caphtorites from 23 Caphtor who destroyed the Avvim who lived in the hamlets near Gaza, and settled in the land instead of them.) 'Come, set out on your journey and 24 cross the gorge of the Arnon, for I have put Sihon the Amorite, king of Heshbon, and his territory into your hands. Begin to occupy it and provoke him to battle. Today I will begin to put the 25

c Or dig for.   *d by Ar: or* the gully.

Num.20.12 n. **2.1–25**: From Kadesh to the Amorite border (Num.20.14–21.15). **1**: *Way of the Red Sea*: see Num.14.25 n. **4**: *Go through*: contrast Num.20.14–21. **7**: *Short of nothing*: contrast Num. chs. 11; 20. **9**: The *Moabites* and Ammonites (v. 19) were relatives of Israel (Gen.19.30–38; 11.27). **14**: *Thirty-eight*: this is a different tradition from v. 7, which places this span of time at Kadesh (see Num.13.26 n.). **23**: *Caphtor*: Crete (or possibly Asia Minor); the

fear and dread of you upon all the peoples under heaven; if they so much as hear a rumour of you, they will quake and tremble before you.'

26 Then I sent messengers from the wilderness of Kedemoth to Sihon king of Heshbon with these peaceful over-
27 tures: 'Grant us passage through your country by the highway: we will keep to the highway, trespassing neither to
28 right nor to left, and we will pay you the full price for the food we eat and
29 the water we drink. The descendants of Esau who live in Seir granted us passage, and so did the Moabites who live in Ar. We will simply pass through your land on foot, until we cross the Jordan to the land which the LORD our
30 God is giving us.' But Sihon king of Heshbon refused to grant us passage; for the LORD your God had made him stubborn and obstinate, in order that he and his land might become subject to
31 you, as it still is. So the LORD said to me, 'Come, I have begun to deliver Sihon and his territory into your hands.
32 Begin now to occupy his land.' Then Sihon with all his people came out to
33 meet us in battle at Jahaz, and the LORD our God delivered him into our hands; we killed him with his sons and all his
34 people. We captured all his cities at that time and put to death everyone in the cities, men, women, and depen-
35 dants; we left no survivor. We took the cattle as booty and plundered the cities
36 we captured. From Aroer on the edge of the gorge of the Arnon and the level land of the gorge, as far as Gilead, no city walls were too lofty for us; the LORD our God laid them all open to us.
37 But you avoided the territory of the Ammonites, both the parts along the gorge of the Jabbok and their cities in the hills, thus fulfilling all that the LORD our God had commanded.

3 Next we turned and advanced along the road to Bashan. Og king of Bashan, with all his people, came out against
2 us at Edrei. The LORD said to me, 'Do not be afraid of him, for I have delivered him into your hands, with all his people and his land. Deal with him

as you dealt with Sihon the king of the Amorites who lived in Heshbon.' So 3 the LORD our God also delivered Og king of Bashan into our hands, with all his people. We slaughtered them and left no survivor, and at the same time 4 we captured all his cities; there was not a single town that we did not take from them. In all we took sixty cities, the whole region of Argob, the kingdom of Og in Bashan; all these were fortified 5 cities with high walls, gates, and bars, apart from a great many open settlements. Thus we put to death all the 6 men, women, and dependants in every city, as we did to Sihon king of Heshbon. All the cattle and the spoil from 7 the cities we took as booty for ourselves.

At that time we took from these two 8 Amorite kings in Transjordan the territory that runs from the gorge of the Arnon to Mount Hermon (the moun- 9 tain that the Sidonians call Sirion and the Amorites Senir), all the cities of the 10 tableland, and the whole of Gilead and Bashan as far as Salcah and Edrei, cities in the kingdom of Og in Bashan. (Only Og king of Bashan remained as 11 the sole survivor of the Rephaim. His sarcophagus of basalt*e* was nearly fourteen feet long and six feet wide, and it may still be seen in the Ammonite city of Rabbah.)

At that time, when we occupied this 12 territory, I assigned to the Reubenites and Gadites the land beyond Aroer on the gorge of the Arnon and half the hill-country of Gilead with its towns. The rest of Gilead and the whole of 13 Bashan the kingdom of Og, all the region of Argob, I assigned to half the tribe of Manasseh. (All Bashan used to be called the land of the Rephaim. Jair son of Manasseh took all the 14 region of Argob as far as the Geshurite and Maacathite border. There are tent-villages in Bashan still called by his name, Havvoth-jair.*f*) To Machir I 15 assigned Gilead, and to the Reubenites 16 and the Gadites I assigned land from Gilead to the gorge of the Arnon, that

e Or iron.　　f That is Tent-villages of Jair.

Philistine invasion is meant (Amos 9.7; Gen. 9.27 n.). **2.26–3.11:** Victory over the Amorites (Num.21.21–35). **30:** *Made him stubborn:* see Exod.4.21 n. **35:** *No survivor:* on "holy" war, see 20.1–20. **3.11:** *Sarcophagus:* such stone coffins were widely used in the area. **12–20:** Dis-

is to the middle of the gorge; and its territory ran[gh] to the gorge of the Jab-
17 bok, the Ammonite frontier, and included the Arabah, with the Jordan and adjacent land, from Kinnereth to the Sea of the Arabah, that is the Dead Sea, below the watershed of Pisgah on
18 the east. At that time I gave you this command: 'The LORD your God has given you this land to occupy; let all your fighting men be drafted and cross at the head of their fellow-Israelites.
19 Only your wives and dependants and your livestock—I know you have much livestock—shall stay in the towns I have
20 given you. This you shall do until the LORD gives your kinsmen security as he has given it to you, and until they too occupy the land which the LORD your God is giving them on the other side of the Jordan; then you may return to the possession which I have given you, every man to his own.'
21 At that time also I gave Joshua this charge: 'You have seen with your own eyes all that the LORD your God has done to these two kings; he will do the same to all the kingdoms into which
22 you will cross over. Do not be afraid of them, for the LORD your God himself will fight for you.'
23 At that same time I pleaded with the
24 LORD, 'O Lord GOD, thou hast begun to show to thy servant thy greatness and thy strong hand: what god is there in heaven or on earth who can match thy
25 works and mighty deeds? Let me cross over and see that rich land which lies beyond the Jordan, and the fine hill-
26 country and the Lebanon.' But because of you the LORD brushed me aside and would not listen. 'Enough!' he an-
27 swered. 'Say no more about this. Go to the top of Pisgah and look west and north, south and east; look well at what you see, for you shall not cross
28 this river Jordan. Give Joshua his commission, encourage him and

strengthen him; for he will lead this people across, and he will put them in possession of the land you see before you.'
29 So we remained in the valley opposite Beth-peor.

4 NOW, ISRAEL, LISTEN TO THE STATUTES and laws which I am teaching you, and obey them; then you will live, and go in and occupy the land which the LORD the God of your fathers is giving you.
2 You must not add anything to my charge, nor take anything away from it. You must carry out all the commandments of the LORD your God which I lay upon you.
3 You saw with your own eyes what the LORD did at Baal-peor; the LORD your God destroyed among you every man who went over to the Baal of
4 Peor, but you who held fast to the
5 LORD your God are all alive today. I have taught you statutes and laws, as the LORD my God commanded me; these you must duly keep when you
6 enter the land and occupy it. You must observe them carefully, and thereby you will display your wisdom and understanding to other peoples. When they hear about these statutes, they will say, 'What a wise and understanding
7 people this great nation is!' What great nation has a god[i] close at hand as the LORD our God is close to us whenever
8 we call to him? What great nation is there whose statutes and laws are just, as is all this law which I am setting
9 before you today? But take good care: be on the watch not to forget the things that you have seen with your own eyes, and do not let them pass from your minds as long as you live, but teach them to your sons and to your sons'
10 sons. You must never forget that day

g *that is . . . ran: or* including the bed of the gorge and the adjacent strip of land . . .
h *and its territory ran: prob. rdg.; Heb.* and territory and . . .
i *Or* gods.

---

tribution of the Amorite territory (Num. ch. 32). **21–28:** Moses' successor (see 31.1–29 n.). **26:** *Because of you:* see 1.37 n. **27:** See 34.1–4.
   4.1–43: An exhortation to obey the law after the settlement in Canaan. **1:** *Now . . . listen:* the LORD's previous gracious acts should motivate obedience. Compare Exod.20.2 n.; Lev.18.2 n. **2:** The prohibition against altering the wording follows Ancient Near Eastern legislative custom and is motivated by fear that the new situation in Canaan would lead to deviation. **3:** An illustration of the consequences of disobedience, taken from Num. ch. 25. **8:** *Today:* on possible liturgical reenactment of the past, see 5.1–3 n.; Exod.13.8 n. **10–11:** See Exod.19.10–19. *Fire:*

when you stood before the LORD your God at Horeb, and the LORD said to me, 'Assemble the people before me; I will make them hear my words and they shall learn to fear me all their lives on earth, and they shall teach their sons 11 to do so.' Then you came near and stood at the foot of the mountain. The mountain was ablaze with fire to the very skies: there was darkness, cloud, 12 and thick mist. When the LORD spoke to you from the fire you heard a voice speaking, but you saw no figure; there 13 was only a voice. He announced the terms of his covenant to you, bidding you observe the Ten Words,*j* and he 14 wrote them on two tablets of stone. At that time the LORD charged me to teach you statutes and laws which you should observe in the land into which you are passing to occupy it.

15 On the day when the LORD spoke to you out of the fire on Horeb, you saw no figure of any kind; so take good care 16 not to fall into the degrading practice of making figures carved in relief, in the 17 form of a man or a woman, or of any animal on earth or bird that flies in the 18 air, or of any reptile on the ground or 19 fish in the waters under the earth. Nor must you raise your eyes to the heavens and look up to the sun, the moon, and the stars, all the host of heaven, and be led on to bow down to them and worship them; the LORD your God assigned these for the worship of*k* the various 20 peoples under heaven. But you are the people whom the LORD brought out of Egypt, from the smelting-furnace, and took for his own possession, as you are 21 to this day. The LORD was angry with me on your account and swore that I should not cross the Jordan nor enter the rich land which the LORD your God is giving you for your possession. 22 I shall die in this country; I shall not cross the Jordan, but you are about to 23 cross and occupy that rich land. Be careful not to forget the covenant which the LORD your God made with you, and do not make yourselves a carved figure of anything which the LORD your God has forbidden. For the LORD your 24 God is a devouring fire, a jealous god.

When you have children and grand- 25 children and grow old in the land, if you then fall into the degrading practice of making any kind of carved figure, doing what is wrong in the eyes of the LORD your God and provoking him to anger, I summon heaven and 26 earth to witness against you this day: you will soon vanish from the land which you are to occupy after crossing the Jordan. You will not live long in it; you will be swept away. The LORD will 27 disperse you among the peoples, and you will be left few in number among the nations to which the LORD will lead you. There you will worship gods 28 made by human hands out of wood and stone, gods that can neither see nor hear, neither eat nor smell. But if 29 from there you seek the LORD your God, you will find him, if indeed you search with all your heart and soul. When you are in distress and all these 30 things come upon you, you will in days to come turn back to the LORD your God and obey him. The LORD your 31 God is a merciful god; he will never fail you nor destroy you, nor will he forget the covenant guaranteed by oath with your forefathers.

Search into days gone by, long before 32 your time, beginning at the day when God created man on earth; search from one end of heaven to the other, and ask if any deed as mighty as this has been seen or heard. Did any people ever 33 hear the voice of God speaking out of the fire, as you heard it, and remain alive? Or did ever a god attempt to 34 come and take a nation for himself

j Or Ten Commandments.
k assigned . . . worship of: *or* created these for.

---

compare Gen.15.17 n. *Darkness:* compare Exod.19.9 n. *Cloud:* see Exod.19.9 n.; compare Exod.13.21 n. **12:** *No figure:* the LORD's self-revelation, which Israel regarded as the center of her faith, is cited in support of Exod.20.4. To the Canaanites, idols were an indispensable part of worship. **13:** *Covenant:* see Exod.20.1–21 n. **15–16:** On the reason for the prohibition, see Exod.20.4 n. **17–19:** Compare Gen.1.14 n., 20 n., 28 n. **21:** See 1.37 n. **26:** *Summon heaven and earth:* This is very old covenant (legal) terminology, originating in a polytheistic environment, and surviving in later times. The gods of those domains served as witnesses to an agreement between parties, and their testimony was invoked in case of violation (Deut.30.19 n.; 31.28; see Isa.1.2; Mic.6.1–2). **32–33:** See Exod.20.18–21. **32:** See 28.64; 32.7. **34:** See Exod. chs. 1–15.

away from another nation, with a challenge, and with signs, portents, and wars, with a strong hand and an outstretched arm, and with great deeds of terror, as the LORD your God did for you in Egypt in the sight of you all? 35 You have had sure proof that the LORD 36 is God; there is no other. From heaven he let you hear his voice for your instruction, and on earth he let you see his great fire, and out of the fire you 37 heard his words. Because he loved your fathers and chose their children after them, he in his own person brought you out of Egypt by his great strength, 38 so that he might drive out before you nations greater and more powerful than you and bring you in to give you their land in possession as it is today. 39 This day, then, be sure and take to heart that the LORD is God in heaven above and on earth below; there is no other. 40 You shall keep his statutes and his commandments which I give you today; then all will be well with you and with your children after you, and you will live long in the land which the LORD your God is giving you for all time.

41 Then Moses set apart three cities in 42 the east, in Transjordan, to be places of refuge for the homicide who kills a man without intent, with no previous enmity between them. If he takes sanctuary in one of these cities his life shall be safe. 43 The cities were: Bezer-in-the-Wilderness on the tableland for the Reubenites, Ramoth in Gilead for the Gadites, and Golan in Bashan for the Manassites.

44 This is the law which Moses laid 45 down for the Israelites. These are the precepts, the statutes, and the laws which Moses proclaimed to the Israelites, when they came out of Egypt

and were in Transjordan in the valley 46 opposite Beth-peor in the land of Sihon king of the Amorities who lived in Heshbon. Moses and the Israelites had defeated him when they came out of Egypt and had occupied his territory 47 and the territory of Og king of Bashan, the two Amorite kings in the east, in Transjordan. The territory ran from 48 Aroer on the gorge of the Arnon to Mount Sirion, that is Hermon; and all 49 the Arabah on the east, in Transjordan, as far as the Sea of the Arabah below the watershed of Pisgah.

Moses summoned all Israel and said 5 to them: Listen, O Israel, to the statutes and the laws which I proclaim in your hearing today. Learn them and be careful to observe them. The LORD our God 2 made a covenant with us at Horeb. It 3 was not with our forefathers that the LORD made this covenant, but with us, all of us who are alive and are here this day. The LORD spoke with you face to 4 face on the mountain out of the fire. I 5 stood between the LORD and you at that time to report the words of the LORD; for you were afraid of the fire and did not go up the mountain. And the LORD said:

I am the LORD your God who 6 brought you out of Egypt, out of the land of slavery.

You shall have no other god[*l*] to set 7 against me.

You shall not make a carved image 8 for yourself nor the likeness of anything in the heavens above, or on the earth below, or in the waters under the earth.

You shall not bow down to them or 9 worship[*m*] them; for I, the LORD your God, am a jealous god. I punish the children for the sins of the fathers to

[*l*] Or gods.   [*m*] Or or be led to worship . . .

37: Here, for the first time, the LORD's election of Israel is explained as the result of love (see 7.7–8). It should evoke a responding love which results in obedience (6.5). **41–43:** A once independent fragment whose relationship to the present context is not clear. *Places of refuge:* compare 19.1–13; Num.35.9–34.

4.44–49: An older historical preface. At one stage in the collection and writing of materials attributed to Moses in the plains of Moab, this section may have been the opening. At a later stage, these verses provided the setting for 4.1–43; the brief historical review of vv. 46b–49 was expanded into 2.24–3.17, which was preceded by an account summarizing the journey from Sinai (Horeb) onward (1.6–2.23); thereafter a new introduction (1.1–5) was written.

5.1–31: A review of the covenant at Sinai. 1–3: Israel's past acceptance of the covenant obligations is to turn out to be of no consequence unless the covenant becomes the contemporary experience of the present generation. The passage may be part of a liturgy by means of which the relationship was regularly renewed. See 31.9–13; Josh.24.1–28. **6–21:** This version of the Ten Commandments (see Exod.20.1–21 n.) is substantially that of Exod.20.2–17, except for the

the third and fourth generations of
10 those who hate me. But I keep faith
with thousands, with[n] those who love
me and keep my commandments.

11 You shall not make wrong use of the
name of the LORD your God; the LORD
will not leave unpunished the man who
misuses his name.

12 Keep the sabbath day holy as the
13 LORD your God commanded you. You
have six days to labour and do all your
14 work. But the seventh day is a sabbath
of the LORD your God; that day you
shall not do any work, neither you,
your son or your daughter, your slave
or your slave-girl, your ox, your ass, or
any of your cattle, nor the alien within
your gates, so that your slaves and
15 slave-girls may rest as you do. Remember that you were slaves in Egypt and
the LORD your God brought you out
with a strong hand and an outstretched
arm, and for that reason the LORD your
God commanded you to keep the
sabbath day.

16 Honour your father and your
mother, as the LORD your God commanded you, so that you may live long,
and that it may be well with you in the
land which the LORD your God is giving
you.

17 You shall not commit murder.
18 You shall not commit adultery.
19 You shall not steal.
20 You shall not give false evidence
against your neighbour.
21 You shall not covet your neighbour's wife; you shall not set your
heart on your neighbour's house, his
land, his slave, his slave-girl, his ox, his
ass, or on anything that belongs to him.

22 These Commandments the LORD
spoke in a great voice to your whole
assembly on the mountain out of the
fire, the cloud, and the thick mist; then
he said no more. He wrote them on
two tablets of stone and gave them to
23 me. When you heard the voice out of
the darkness, while the mountain was

ablaze with fire, all the heads of your
tribes and the elders came to me and 24
said, 'The LORD our God has shown us
his glory and his greatness, and we have
heard his voice out of the fire: today
we have seen that God may speak with
men and they may still live. Why 25
should we now risk death? for this
great fire will devour us. If we hear the
voice of the LORD our God again, we
shall die. Is there any mortal man who 26
has heard the voice of the living God
speaking out of the fire, as we have,
and has lived? You shall go near and 27
listen to all that the LORD our God says,
and report to us all that the LORD our
God has said to you; we will listen and
obey.'

When the LORD heard these words 28
which you spoke to me, he said, 'I have
heard what this people has said to you;
every word they have spoken is right.
Would that they always had such a 29
heart to fear me and to observe all my
commandments, so that all might be
well with them and their children for
ever! Go, and tell them to return to 30
their tents, but you yourself stand here 31
beside me, and I will set forth to you all
the commandments, the statutes and
laws which you shall teach them to
observe in the land which I am giving
them to occupy.'

You shall be careful to do as the 32
LORD your God has commanded you;
do not turn from it to right or to left.
You must conform to all the LORD your 33
God commands you, if you would live
and prosper and remain long in the
land you are to occupy.

These are the commandments, stat- **6**
utes, and laws which the LORD your
God commanded me to teach you to
observe in the land into which you are
passing to occupy it, a land flowing
with milk and honey, so that you may 2
fear the LORD your God and keep all
his statutes and commandments which

n with . . . with: or for a thousand generations with . . .

added motivation for Sabbath observance. **22–31:** The purpose in the prefatory verses (4.44–49)
and the review (5.1–33) here become specific: the fear exhibited by the people (Exod.20.18–21)
necessitated that Moses act as mediator. Thus, some of the legislation received while he was
alone atop the mountain has not yet been conveyed to the people; now the laws for the new life
in Canaan are to be disclosed.
  5.32–11.32: Exhortations and warnings to revere the law after the settlement in Canaan.
  6.1–25: Fidelity to the one LORD. Much of the chapter may be viewed as an elaboration of the
first commandment (5.7). **1:** *Commandments* is singular in MT, and possibly refers to vv. 4–5.

I am giving you, both you, your sons, and your descendants all your lives, and
3 so that you may live long. If you listen, O Israel, and are careful to observe them, you will prosper and increase greatly as the LORD the God of your fathers promised you.

4 Hear, O Israel, the LORD[o] is our God,
5 one LORD, and you must love the LORD your God with all your heart and soul
6 and strength. These commandments which I give you this day are to be kept
7 in your heart; you shall repeat them to your sons, and speak of them indoors and out of doors, when you lie down
8 and when you rise. Bind them as a sign on the hand and wear them as a
9 phylactery on the forehead; write them up on the door-posts of your houses and on your gates.

10 The LORD your God will bring you into the land which he swore to your forefathers Abraham, Isaac and Jacob that he would give you, a land of great and fine cities which you did not build,
11 houses full of good things which you did not provide, rock-hewn cisterns which you did not hew, and vineyards and olive-groves which you did not
12 plant. When you eat your fill there, be careful not to forget the LORD who brought you out of Egypt, out of the
13 land of slavery. You shall fear the LORD your God, serve him alone and
14 take your oaths in his name. You must not follow other gods, gods of the
15 nations that are around you; if you do, the LORD your God who is in your midst will be angry with you, and he will sweep you away off the face of the earth, for the LORD your God is a jealous god.

16 You must not challenge the LORD your God as you challenged him at

Massah.[p] You must diligently keep the 17 commandments of the LORD your God as well as the precepts and statutes which he gave you. You must do what 18 is right and good in the LORD's eyes so that all may go well with you, and you may enter and occupy the rich land which the LORD promised by oath to your forefathers; then you shall drive 19 out all your enemies before you, as the LORD promised.

When your son asks you in time to 20 come, 'What is the meaning of the precepts, statutes, and laws which the LORD our God gave you?', you shall 21 say to him, 'We were Pharaoh's slaves in Egypt, and the LORD brought us out of Egypt with his strong hand, sending 22 great disasters, signs, and portents against the Egyptians and against Pharaoh and all his family, as we saw for ourselves. But he led us out from 23 there to bring us into the land and give it to us as he had promised to our forefathers. The LORD commanded us to 24 observe all these statutes and to fear the LORD our God; it will be for our own good at all times, and he will continue to preserve our lives. It will be counted 25 to our credit if we keep all these commandments in the sight of the LORD our God, as he has bidden us.'

WHEN THE LORD YOUR GOD BRINGS YOU 7 into the land which you are entering to occupy and drives out many nations before you—Hittites, Girgashites, Amorites, Canaanites, Perizzites, Hivites, and Jebusites, seven nations more numerous and powerful than you— when the LORD your God delivers them 2 into your power and you defeat them, you must put them to death. You must

o See note on Exod. 3. 15.　　*p That is* Challenge.

The specific *statutes and laws* are delayed until ch. 12. **2:** *Milk and honey:* see Exod.3.8 n. **4–9:** These verses are a standard preface to private and public prayer in the Jewish tradition. They are called the Shema, from the initial word which means "Hear!" The Shema is virtually a Jewish "creed." **4–5:** These verses are described as the greatest commandment in Mk. 12.28–34. **4:** *One LORD:* the only God (4.35,39; Isa.45.18). **5:** *Heart:* intellect, will. *Soul:* self, total being. Compare Gen.2.7 n. *Strength:* determination. See 4.37 n. **8:** *Sign:* see Exod.13.9 n. *Phylactery:* see Exod.13.16 n. **10–15:** This theme, central to the entire book, is expanded in ch. 8. **16:** *Massah:* see Exod.17.2–7. To *challenge the LORD* means to require his granting of material blessings as a prerequisite for worshiping him. **20–25:** These verses may be part of the ancient Passover liturgy (Exod.12.26–27 and 13.8–9; compare Exod.15.1–21 n.).

7.1–26: The inhabitants of Canaan. The reason for the injunctions in the chapter is given in v. 4. Compare Exod. 20.1–21 n. **2:** *Put them to death:* on rules for "holy" war, see 20.1–20. Those who gathered the Deuteronomic traditions believed that the kingdom of Israel had suffered defeat through succumbing to Canaanite influence (compare 2 Kgs.17.1–23). The

not make a treaty with them or spare them. You must not intermarry with them, neither giving your daughters to their sons nor taking their daughters 4 for your sons; if you do, they will draw your sons away from the LORD*q* and make them worship other gods. Then the LORD will be angry with you and 5 will quickly destroy you. But this is what you must do to them: pull down their altars, break their sacred pillars, hack down their sacred poles and 6 destroy their idols by fire, for you are a people holy to the LORD your God; the LORD your God chose you out of all nations on earth to be his special possession.

7 It was not because you were more numerous than any other nation that the LORD cared for you and chose you, for you were the smallest of all nations; 8 it was because the LORD loved you and stood by his oath to your forefathers, that he brought you out with his strong hand and redeemed you from the land of slavery, from the power of Pharaoh 9 king of Egypt. Know then that the LORD your God is God, the faithful God; with those who love him and keep his commandments he keeps covenant and faith for a thousand gen-10 erations, but those who defy him and show their hatred for him he repays with destruction: he will not be slow to requite any who so hate him.

11 You are to observe these commandments, statutes, and laws which I give you this day, and keep them.

12 If you listen to these laws and are careful to observe them, then the LORD your God will observe the sworn covenant he made with your forefathers 13 and will keep faith with you. He will love you, bless you and cause you to increase. He will bless the fruit of your body and the fruit of your land, your corn and new wine and oil, the offspring of your herds, and of your lambing flocks, in the land which he swore to your forefathers to give you.

14 You shall be blessed above every other nation; neither among your people nor among your cattle shall there be im-15 potent male or barren female. The LORD will take away all sickness from you; he will not bring upon you any of the foul diseases of Egypt which you know so well, but will bring them upon 16 all your enemies. You shall devour all the nations which the LORD your God is giving over to you. Spare none of them, and do not worship their gods; that is the snare which awaits you.

17 You may say to yourselves, 'These nations outnumber us, how can we 18 drive them out?' But you need have no fear of them; only remember what the LORD your God did to Pharaoh and to 19 the whole of Egypt, the great challenge which you yourselves witnessed, the signs and portents, the strong hand and the outstretched arm by which the LORD your God brought you out. He will deal thus with all the nations of whom you are afraid. He will also 20 spread panic among them until all who are left or have gone into hiding perish 21 before you. Be in no dread of them, for the LORD your God is in your midst, a 22 great and terrible god. He will drive out these nations before you little by little. You will not be able to exterminate them quickly, for fear the wild beasts become too numerous for you. The 23 LORD your God will deliver these nations over to you and will throw them into great panic in the hour of their destruction. He will put their 24 kings into your hands, and you shall wipe out their name from under heaven. When you destroy them, no man will be able to withstand you. Their idols 25 you shall destroy by fire; you must not covet the silver and gold on them and take it for yourselves, or you will be ensnared by it; for these things are abominable to the LORD your God. You must not introduce any abomin-26 able idol into your houses and thus

q Prob. rdg.; Heb. me.

---

measures described here are meant to protect the kingdom of Judah from a similar catastrophe. *Not make a treaty:* this is in marked contrast to earlier attitudes (Gen.21.22–32 and 26.26–31). **5:** *Pillars; poles:* see Exod.34.13 n. **9–10:** See Exod.34.6–7 n. **12:** *Forefathers:* see 1.8 n. **13–14:** The emphasis upon the LORD as the source of material blessings is a polemic against the Canaanite gods of fertility. See Hos.2.2–13 for a classic prophetic stance of the type reflected in Deut. **26:** *Ban:* the state of being accursed (see Exod.22.20 n.).

bring yourselves under solemn ban along with it. You shall hold it loathsome and abominable, for it is forbidden under the ban.

8 You must carefully observe everything that I command you this day so that you may live and increase and may enter and occupy the land which the LORD promised to your forefathers 2 upon oath. You must remember all that road by which the LORD your God has led you these forty years in the wilderness to humble you, to test you and to discover whether or no it was in your 3 heart to keep his commandments. He humbled you and made you hungry; then he fed you on manna which neither you nor your fathers had known before, to teach you that man cannot live on bread alone but lives by every word that comes from the mouth of the 4 LORD. The clothes on your backs did not wear out nor did your feet swell all 5 these forty years. Take this lesson to heart: that the LORD your God was disciplining you as a father disciplines 6 his son; and keep the commandments of the LORD your God, conforming to 7 his ways and fearing him. For the LORD your God is bringing you to a rich land, a land of streams, of springs and underground waters gushing out in hill and 8 valley, a land of wheat and barley, of vines, fig-trees, and pomegranates, a 9 land of olives, oil, and honey. It is a land where you will never live in poverty nor want for anything, a land whose stones are iron-ore and from 10 whose hills you will dig copper. You will have plenty to eat and will bless the LORD your God for the rich land that he has given you.

11 Take care not to forget the LORD your God and do not fail to keep his commandments, laws, and statutes 12 which I give you this day. When you have plenty to eat and live in fine houses of your own building, when 13 your herds and flocks increase, and your silver and gold and all your possessions increase too, do not become 14 proud and forget the LORD your God who brought you out of Egypt, out of the land of slavery; he led you through 15 the vast and terrible wilderness infested with poisonous snakes and scorpions, a thirsty, waterless land, where he caused water to flow from the hard rock; he fed you in the wilderness on 16 manna which your fathers did not know, to humble you and test you, and in the end to make you prosper. Nor 17 must you say to yourselves, 'My own strength and energy have gained me this wealth', but remember the LORD 18 your God; it is he that gives you strength to become prosperous, so fulfilling the covenant guaranteed by oath with your forefathers, as he is doing now.

If you forget the LORD your God 19 and adhere to other gods, worshipping them and bowing down to them, I give you a solemn warning this day that you will certainly be destroyed. You will be 20 destroyed because of your disobedience to the LORD your God, as surely as were the nations whom the LORD destroyed at your coming.

Listen, O Israel; this day you will 9 cross the Jordan to occupy the territory of nations greater and more powerful than you, and great cities with walls towering to the sky. They are great and 2 tall people, the descendants of the Anakim, of whom you know, for you have heard it said, 'Who can withstand the sons of Anak?' Know then this day 3 that it is the LORD your God himself who goes at your head as a devouring fire; he will subdue them and destroy them at your approach; you shall drive them out and overwhelm them, as he promised you.

8.1–20: Injunction for life in the promised land. The lesson learned through hardship, that "man cannot live on bread alone" (v. 3), must not be forgotten amidst the abundance of Canaan. **2:** The hardships of the *wilderness*, against which Israel rebelled and was punished (see Num. 25.1–18 n.), are reinterpreted as discipline in preparation for life in "a rich land" (v. 7). **3:** *Manna:* see Num.11.6 n. It was given, not alone to satisfy physical hunger, but to remind man of his dependence upon God. **4:** This tradition is not found outside Deut. **15:** *Snakes:* see Num.21.4–9. *Rock:* see Num.20.2–11.

9.1–10.11: The basis for the granting of the land. It was the wickedness of the Canaanites that led to their displacement, not the merit of Israel. Indeed, the latter would have been entirely destroyed in the Wilderness were it not for the intercession of Moses. **2:** *Anakim:* see 1.28;

4 When the LORD your God drives them out before you, do not say to yourselves, 'It is because of my own merit that the LORD has brought me in 5 to occupy this land.' It is not because of your merit or your integrity that you are entering their land to occupy it; it is because of the wickedness of these nations that the LORD your God is driving them out before you, and to fulfil the promise which the LORD made to your forefathers, Abraham, Isaac and Jacob.

6 Know then that it is not because of any merit of yours that the LORD your God is giving you this rich land to occupy; indeed, you are a stubborn 7 people. Remember and never forget, how you angered the LORD your God in the wilderness: from the day when you left Egypt until you came to this 8 place you have defied the LORD. In Horeb you roused the LORD's anger, and the LORD in his wrath was on the 9 point of destroying you. When I went up the mountain to receive the tablets of stone, the tablets of the covenant which the LORD made with you, I remained on the mountain forty days and forty nights without food or drink. 10 Then the LORD gave me the two tablets of stone written with the finger of God, and upon them were all the words the LORD spoke to you out of the fire, upon the mountain on the day of the 11 assembly. At the end of forty days and forty nights the LORD gave me the two tablets of stone, the tablets of the 12 covenant, and said to me, 'Make haste down from the mountain because your people whom you brought out of Egypt have done a disgraceful thing. They have already turned aside from the way which I told them to follow and have cast for themselves an image of metal.' 13 Then the LORD said to me, 'I have considered this people and I find them 14 a stubborn people. Let me be, and I will destroy them and blot out their name from under heaven; and of you alone I will make a nation more power-

ful and numerous than they.' So I 15 turned and went down the mountain, and it was ablaze; and I had the two tablets of the covenant in my hands. When I saw that you had sinned against 16 the LORD your God and had cast for yourselves an image of a bull-calf, and had already turned aside from the way the LORD had told you to follow, I took 17 the two tablets and flung them down and shattered them in the sight of you all. Then once again I lay prostrate 18 before the LORD, forty days and forty nights without food or drink, on account of all the sins that you had committed, and because you had done what was wrong in the eyes of the LORD and provoked him to anger. I dreaded 19 the LORD's anger and his wrath which threatened to destroy you; and once again the LORD listened to me. The 20 LORD was greatly incensed with Aaron also and would have killed him; so I prayed for him as well at that same time. I took the calf, that sinful thing 21 that you had made, and burnt it and pounded it, grinding it until it was as fine as dust; then I flung its dust into the torrent that flowed down the mountain. You also roused the LORD's anger 22 at Taberah, and at Massah, and at Kibroth-hattaavah. Again, when the 23 LORD sent you from Kadesh-barnea with orders to advance and occupy the land which he was giving you, you defied the LORD your God and did not trust him or obey him. You were defiant 24 from the day that the LORD first knew you. Forty days and forty nights I lay 25 prostrate before the LORD because he had threatened to destroy you, and I 26 prayed to the LORD and said, 'O Lord GOD, do not destroy thy people, thy own possession, whom thou didst redeem by thy great power and bring out of Egypt by thy strong hand. Remember thy servants, Abraham, Isaac and 27 Jacob, and overlook the stubbornness of this people, their wickedness and their sin; otherwise the people in the 28 land out of which thou didst lead us

---

Num.13.22,27–28. **9:** See Exod.24.12–18. **11–21:** See Exod. ch. 32. **20:** The prayer for Aaron is not recorded in Exod. ch. 32. **21:** *Into the torrent:* contrast Exod.32.20. **22–24:** These verses interrupt the context and logically belong before the post-Sinai itinerary in 10.6–7. They heighten the need for the intercessory prayer which follows. **22:** *Taberah:* Num.11.1–3. *Massah:* Exod. 17.1–7; compare Num.20.2–13. *Kibroth-hattaavah:* Num.11.4–34. **23:** See Num. chs. 13–14.

will say, "It is because the LORD was not able to bring them into the land which he promised them and because he hated them, that he has led them out 29 to kill them in the wilderness." But they are thy people, thy own possession, whom thou didst bring out by thy great strength and by thy outstretched arm.'

10 AT THAT TIME THE LORD SAID TO ME, 'Cut two tablets of stone like the first, and make also a wooden chest, an Ark. 2 Come to me on the mountain, and I will write on the tablets the words that were on the first tablets which you broke in pieces, and you shall put them 3 into the Ark.' So I made the Ark of acacia-wood and cut two tablets of stone like the first, and went up the mountain taking the tablets with me. 4 Then in the same writing as before, the LORD wrote down the Ten Words*r* which he had spoken to you out of the fire, upon the mountain on the day of the assembly, and the LORD gave them 5 to me. I turned and came down the mountain, and I put the tablets in the Ark that I had made, as the LORD had commanded me, and there they have remained ever since.

6*s*　(The Israelites journeyed by stages from Beeroth-bene-jaakan to Moserah. There Aaron died and was buried; and his son Eleazar succeeded him in the 7 priesthood. From there they came to Gudgodah and from Gudgodah to 8 Jotbathah, a land of many ravines. At that time the LORD set apart the tribe of Levi to carry the Ark of the Covenant of the LORD, to attend on the LORD and minister to him, and to give the blessing in his name, as they have 9 done to this day. That is why the

Levites have no holding or patrimony with their kinsmen; the LORD is their patrimony, as he promised them.)

I stayed on the mountain forty days 10 and forty nights, as I did before, and once again the LORD listened to me; he consented not to destroy you. The LORD 11 said to me, 'Set out now at the head of the people so that they may enter and occupy the land which I swore to give to their forefathers.'

What then, O Israel, does the LORD 12 your God ask of you? Only to fear the LORD your God, to conform to all his ways, to love him and to serve him with all your heart and soul. This you will 13 do by keeping the commandments of the LORD and his statutes which I give you this day for your good. To the 14 LORD your God belong heaven itself, the highest heaven, the earth and everything in it; yet the LORD cared for 15 your forefathers in his love for them and chose their descendants after them. Out of all nations you were his chosen people as you are this day. So now you 16 must circumcise the foreskin of your hearts and not be stubborn any more, for the LORD your God is God of gods 17 and Lord of lords, the great, mighty, and terrible God. He is no respecter of persons and is not to be bribed; he 18 secures justice for widows and orphans, and loves the alien who lives among you, giving him food and clothing. You too must love the alien, for you 19 once lived as aliens in Egypt. You must 20 fear the LORD your God, serve him, hold fast to him and take your oaths in his name. He is your praise, your God 21 who has done for you these great and

r Or Ten Commandments.
s Verses 6, 7: cp. Num. 33. 31, 32.

25–29: This prayer is prior to the breaking of the tablets in Exod.32.11–13. **10.1–11:** The renewal of the covenant. The theme of Israel's unworthiness to inherit the land is resumed only in vv. 10–11. **1:** See Exod.34.1, which contains no mention of the Ark. **6–7:** Since these verses, like 9.22–24, cover the itinerary after the departure from Sinai (Num.33.16,30–33), they logically belong after v. 11. They may allude to examples of Israel's unworthiness which have not been preserved in the OT. Placed here, they emphasize that Israel would not have entered the land but for the prayers of Moses (vv. 10–11). *Beeroth-bene-jaakan:* the Bene-jaakan of Num. 33.30–31, where the order is reversed. Aaron died on Mount Hor according to Num.20.22–29; 33.37–39. *Gudgodah:* possibly the (Hor-hag)gidgad of Num.33.32. **8–9:** This event should follow 9.29, according to Exod.32.26–29. The point that the Levites did not share in Aaron's sin is emphasized by their being set apart after his death. **10:** The narrative resumes from v. 5.
　　10.12–11.32: A final exhortation to future obedience. 12: *What then* refers to the conclusions to be drawn from the historical review (9.7–10.11). Compare 4.1 n.; Mic.6.4–8. The answer is summarized in a single sentence, repeating 6.4–5 (see 6.1 n.). **12–13:** One keeps the commandments not for fear or desire of reward, but as an expression of love and gratitude. **16:** *Circumcise*

terrible things which you have seen with your own eyes. When your forefathers 22 went down into Egypt they were only seventy strong, but now the LORD your God has made you countless as the stars in the sky.

11 You shall love the LORD your God and keep for all time the charge he laid upon you, the statutes, the laws, and the commandments. This day you know 2 the discipline of the LORD, though your children who have neither known nor experienced it do not; you know his greatness, his strong hand and out-stretched arm, the signs he worked and 3 his acts in Egypt against Pharaoh the king and his country, and all that he 4 did to the Egyptian army, its horses and chariots, when he caused the waters of the Red Sea to flow over them as they pursued you. In this way the LORD destroyed them, and so things remain to this day. You know what he did for 5 you in the wilderness as you journeyed to this place, and what he did to 6 Dathan and Abiram sons of Eliab, son of Reuben, when the earth opened its mouth and swallowed them in the sight of all Israel, together with their households and their tents and every living thing in their company. With 7 your own eyes you have seen the mighty work that the LORD did.

You shall observe all that I com- 8 mand you this day, so that you may have strength to enter and occupy the land into which you are crossing, and 9 so that you may live long in the land which the LORD swore to your fore-fathers to give them and their descen-dants, a land flowing with milk and honey. The land which you are entering 10 to occupy is not like the land of Egypt from which you have come, where, after sowing your seed, you irrigated it by foot like a vegetable garden. But the 11 land into which you are crossing to occupy is a land of mountains and valleys watered by the rain of heaven. It is a land which the LORD your God 12 tends[t] and on which his eye rests from

year's end to year's end. If you pay 13 heed to the commandments which I give you this day, and love the LORD your God and serve him with all your heart and soul, then I will send rain 14 for your land in season, both autumn and spring rains, and you will gather your corn and new wine and oil, and I 15 will provide pasture in the fields for your cattle: you shall eat your fill. Take 16 good care not to be led astray in your hearts nor to turn aside and serve other gods and prostrate yourselves to them, or the LORD will become angry with 17 you: he will shut up the skies and there will be no rain, your ground will not yield its harvest, and you will soon vanish from the rich land which the LORD is giving you. You shall take 18 these words of mine to heart and keep them in mind; you shall bind them as a sign on the hand and wear them as a phylactery on the forehead. Teach 19 them to your children, and speak of them indoors and out of doors, when you lie down and when you rise. Write 20 them up on the door-posts of your houses and on your gates. Then you 21 will live long, you and your children, in the land which the LORD swore to your forefathers to give them, for as long as the heavens are above the earth.

If you diligently keep all these com- 22 mandments that I now charge you to observe, by loving the LORD your God, by conforming to his ways and by hold-ing fast to him, the LORD will drive out 23 all these nations before you and you shall occupy the territory of nations greater and more powerful than you. Every place where you set the soles of 24 your feet shall be yours. Your borders shall run from the wilderness to[u] the Lebanon and from the River, the river Euphrates, to the western sea. No man 25 will be able to withstand you; the LORD your God will put the fear and dread of

t which . . . tends: or whose soil the LORD your God has made firm.
u Prob. rdg.; Heb. and.

. . . your hearts: see Jer.4.3–4 n. **22:** *Seventy:* see Exod.1.5 n. **11.2:** *This day:* see 5.1–3 n. *Discipline:* see 8.5; Lev.26.18 n. **6:** *Dathan and Abiram:* see Num.16.1–17.13 n.; note here the absence of mention of Korah. **17:** If Israel worships the gods of Canaan (idolizes material property), nature will fail and demonstrate their powerlessness (see 8.1–20 n.). **18–21:** See 6.6–9. **24:** *Your borders:* for the LORD's covenant with Abraham, see Gen.15.18 and note there.

you upon the whole land on which you
26 set foot, as he promised you. Understand that this day I offer you the
27 choice of a blessing and a curse. The blessing will come if you listen to the commandments of the LORD your God
28 which I give you this day, and the curse if you do not listen to the commandments of the LORD your God but turn aside from the way that I command you this day and follow other gods whom you do not know.
29 When the LORD your God brings you into the land which you are entering to occupy, there on Mount Gerizim you shall pronounce the blessing and on
30 Mount Ebal the curse. (These mountains are on the other side of the Jordan, close to Gilgal beside the terebinth of Moreh, beyond the road to the west which lies in the territory of
31 the Canaanites of the Arabah.) You are about to cross the Jordan to enter and occupy the land which the LORD your God is giving you; you shall occupy it
32 and settle in it, and you shall be careful to observe all the statutes and laws which I set before you this day.

God's laws delivered by Moses

12 THESE ARE THE STATUTES AND LAWS that you shall be careful to observe in the land which the LORD the God of your fathers is giving you to occupy as
2 long as you live on earth. You shall demolish all the sanctuaries where the nations whose place you are taking worship their gods, on mountain-tops and hills and under every spreading
3 tree. You shall pull down their altars and break their sacred pillars, burn their sacred poles and hack down the idols of their gods and thus blot out the name of them from that place.
4 You shall not follow such practices in the worship of the LORD your God,
5 but you shall resort to the place which the LORD your God will choose out of all your tribes to receive his Name that it may dwell there. There you shall
6 come and bring your whole-offerings and sacrifices, your tithes and contributions, your vows and freewill offerings, and the first-born of your herds and
7 flocks. There you shall eat before the LORD your God; so you shall find joy in whatever you undertake, you and your families, because the LORD your God has blessed you.
8 You shall not act as we act here today, each of us doing what he
9 pleases, for till now you have not reached the place of rest, the patrimony which the LORD your God is giving you.
10 You shall cross the Jordan and settle in the land which the LORD your God allots you as your patrimony; he will grant you peace from all your enemies on every side, and you will live in
11 security. Then you shall bring everything that I command you to the place which the LORD your God will choose as a dwelling for his Name—your whole-offerings and sacrifices, your tithes and contributions, and all the choice gifts that you have vowed to the
12 LORD. You shall rejoice before the LORD your God with your sons and daughters, your male and female slaves, and the Levites who live in your settlements because they have no holding or patrimony among you.
13 See that you do not offer your whole-
14 offerings in any place at random, but offer them only at the place which the LORD will choose in one of your tribes,

---

26–28: Examples of *blessing* and *curse* are given in vv. 16–17, 22–25; on their place in the covenant ceremony, see Lev.26.1–46 n. **29:** See 27.11–28.68.
  12.1–32: The one legitimate sanctuary. The command for centralization of worship, presented under three aspects (vv. 2–7,8–12,13–28), was intended to prevent the Canaanite influence and practices at local shrines (vv. 29–31). **1:** Here begin the laws, continuing to 26.15. See 1.5 n. **2–3:** See ch. 7. **4:** Israel's uniqueness is enhanced in the sanctuary. Compare Exod.20.25 n.; 23.19 n.; 28.42–43; Lev.15.16–18 n. **5:** *The place:* Jerusalem. Prior to 621 B.C. (see Introduction), worship had been conducted throughout the land without criticism (Josh.18.1; 24.1,26; 1 Sam.1.3; 10.8; see Deut.27.5 n.). Although the LORD is present in the sanctuary where his *Name* is invoked, he is not bound to the sanctuary as gods of many temples in the ancient world were limited by their "dwellings." **6:** For the various kinds of *offerings,* see Lev. chs. 1–7; *vows,* Lev. ch. 27; *tithes,* Num.18.21–32. **12:** *Levites:* see Num.35.1–8. **13–28:** In earlier periods, every slaughter of an animal was a religious act, to be performed at the local sanctuary. With centralization, a distinction is drawn between sacrifice and slaughter for food. The distinction,

and there you must do all I command
15 you. On the other hand, you may
freely kill for food in all your settlements, as the LORD your God blesses
you. Clean and unclean alike may eat it,
as they would eat the meat of gazelle
16 or buck. But on no account must you
eat the blood; pour it out on the
17 ground like water. In all your settlements you may not eat any of the tithe
of your corn and new wine and oil, or
any of the first-born of your cattle and
sheep, or any of the gifts that you vow,
or any of your freewill offerings and
18 contributions; but you shall eat it before the LORD your God in the place
that the LORD your God will choose—
you, your sons and daughters, your
male and female slaves, and the
Levites in your settlements; so you shall
find joy before the LORD your God in
19 all that you undertake. Be careful not
to neglect the Levites in your land as
long as you live.
20   When the LORD your God extends
your boundaries, as he has promised
you, and you say to yourselves, 'I
would like to eat meat', because you
have a craving for it, then you may
21 freely eat it. If the place that the LORD
your God will choose to receive his
Name is far away, then you may
slaughter a beast from the herds or
flocks which the LORD has given you
and freely eat it in your own settlements
22 as I command you. You may eat it as
you would the meat of gazelle or buck;
both clean and unclean alike may eat
23 it. But you must strictly refrain from
eating the blood, because the blood is
the life; you must not eat the life with
24 the flesh. You must not eat it, you must
pour it out on the ground like water.
25 If you do not eat it, all will be well with
you and your children after you; for
you will be doing what is right in the
26 eyes of the LORD. But such holy-gifts as
you may have and the gifts you have
vowed, you must bring to the place

which the LORD will choose. You must 27
present your whole-offerings, both the
flesh and the blood, on the altar of the
LORD your God; but of your shared-
offerings you shall eat the flesh, while
the blood is to be poured on the altar
of the LORD your God. See that you 28
listen and do all that I command you,
and then it will go well with you and
your children after you for ever; for
you will be doing what is good and right
in the eyes of the LORD your God.
When the LORD your God exterm- 29
inates, as you advance, the nations
whose country you are entering to
occupy, you shall take their place and
settle in their land. After they have 30
been destroyed, take care that you are
not ensnared into their ways. Do not
inquire about their gods and say, 'How
do these nations worship their gods? I
too will do the same.' You must not do 31
for the LORD your God what they do,
for all that they do for their gods is
hateful and abominable to the LORD.
As sacrifices for their gods they even
burn their sons and their daughters.
See that you observe everything I 32
command you: you must not add anything to it, nor take anything away
from it.
When a prophet or dreamer appears **13**
among you and offers you a sign or a
portent and calls on you to follow 2
other gods whom you have not known
and worship them, even if the sign or
portent should come true, do not listen 3
to the words of that prophet or that
dreamer. God is testing you through
him to discover whether you love the
LORD your God with all your heart and
soul. You must follow the LORD your 4
God and fear him; you must keep his
commandments and obey him, serve
him and hold fast to him. That prophet 5
or that dreamer shall be put to death,
for he has preached rebellion against
the LORD your God who brought you
out of Egypt and redeemed you from

---

however, is absent from the priestly code, which came at a later time (Lev.17.4,5 nn.). **15:** An
unclean person, however, could not participate in a sacrifice (compare Lev. 7.20–21; Num.18.11).
For the rules governing uncleanness, see Lev. chs. 11–15; Num. ch. 19. **16:** *Blood:* see Lev.
17.10–12. **31:** *Burn their sons:* see Exod.13.13 n.; Lev.18.21 n.
    13.1–18: The treatment of enticers to apostasy. For a reason behind such extreme measures,
see 7.2 n. **1:** Throughout the ancient world dreams were regarded as a medium of divine
communication (Gen.15.12 n.; 41.25; Num.12.6). **3:** *Testing:* a divine action continuing from

that land of slavery; he has tried to lead you astray from the path which the LORD your God commanded you to take. You must rid yourselves of this wickedness.

6 If your brother, your father's son or your mother's son, or your son or daughter, or the wife of your bosom or your dearest friend should entice you secretly to go and worship other gods—gods whom neither you nor 7 your fathers have known, gods of the people round about you, near or far, at 8 one end of the land or the other—then you shall not consent or listen. You shall have no pity on him, you shall not 9 spare him nor shield him, you shall put him to death; your own hand shall be the first to be raised against him and 10 then all the people shall follow. You shall stone him to death, because he tried to lead you astray from the LORD your God who brought you out of 11 Egypt, out of the land of slavery. All Israel shall hear of it and be afraid; never again will anything as wicked as this be done among you.

12-13 When you hear that miscreants have appeared in any of the cities which the LORD your God is giving you to occupy, and have led its inhabitants astray by calling on them to serve other gods 14 whom you have not known, then you shall investigate the matter carefully. If, after diligent examination, the report proves to be true and it is shown that this abominable thing has been done 15 among you, you shall put the inhabitants of that city to the sword; you shall lay the city under solemn ban 16 together with everything in it. You shall gather all its goods into the square and burn both city and goods as a complete offering to the LORD your God; and it shall remain a mound of 17 ruins, never to be rebuilt. Let nothing out of all that has been laid under the ban be found in your possession, so that the LORD may turn from his anger and

show you compassion; and in his compassion he will increase you as he swore to your forefathers, provided 18 that you obey the LORD your God and keep all his commandments which I give you this day, doing only what is right in the eyes of the LORD your God.

YOU ARE THE SONS OF THE LORD YOUR 14 God: you shall not gash yourselves nor shave your forelocks in mourning for the dead. You are a people holy to the 2 LORD your God, and the LORD has chosen you out of all peoples on earth to be his special possession.

You shall not eat any abominable 3 thing. These are the animals you may 4 eat: ox, sheep, goat, buck, gazelle, roe- 5 buck, wild-goat, white-rumped deer, long-horned antelope, and rock-goat. You may eat any animal which has a 6 parted foot or a cloven hoof and also chews the cud; those which only chew 7 the cud or only have a parted or cloven hoof you may not eat. These are: the camel, the hare, and the rock-badger,*v* because they chew the cud but do not have cloven hoofs; you shall regard them as unclean; and the pig, because 8 it has a cloven hoof but does not chew the cud, you shall regard as unclean. You shall not eat their flesh or even touch their dead carcasses. Of creatures 9 that live in water you may eat all those that have fins and scales, but you may 10 not eat any that have neither fins nor scales; you shall regard them as unclean. You may eat all clean birds. 11 These are the birds you may not eat: 12 the griffon-vulture,*w* the black vulture, the bearded vulture,*x* the kite, every 13 kind of falcon, every kind of crow,*y* 14 the desert-owl, the short-eared owl, 15 the long-eared owl, every kind of hawk, the tawny owl, the screech-owl, 16 the little owl, the horned owl, the 17 osprey, the fisher-owl, the stork,*z* every 18

v Or rock-rabbit.   *w Or* eagle.   *x Or* ossifrage.
y Or raven.   *z Or* heron.

---

the Wilderness experience (8.2). **6–11:** No loyalty may be placed ahead of that which belongs to the LORD. See 7.1–26 n.; compare Mt.10.34–39.
14.1–21: Restrictions on mourning custom and diet. This was intended to stress Israel's uniqueness and to prevent participation in the cult of the Canaanite gods. **1:** Possibly these rites were connected with the worship of the dead (26.14; Num.19.1–22 n.) or of the fertility gods who were thought to "die" and "arise" with the cycle of vegetation. Compare Ezek.8.14; Zech.12.11. **3–20:** See Lev.11.1–23; see also Lev.11.1–47 n. on eating clean and unclean animals.

kind of cormorant, the hoopoe, and the bat.

19 All teeming winged creatures you shall regard as unclean; they may not 20 be eaten. You may eat every clean insect.

21 You shall not eat anything that has died a natural death. You shall give it to the aliens who live in your settlements, and they may eat it, or you may sell it to a foreigner; for you are a people holy to the LORD your God.

You shall not boil a kid in its mother's milk.

22 Year by year you shall set aside a tithe of all the produce of your seed, of everything that grows on the land. 23 You shall eat it in the presence of the LORD your God in the place which he will choose as a dwelling for his Name —the tithe of your corn and new wine and oil, and the first-born of your cattle and sheep, so that for all time you may learn to fear the LORD your 24 God. When the LORD your God has blessed you with prosperity, and the place which he will choose to receive his Name is far from you and the journey too great for you to be able to carry 25 your tithe, then you may exchange it for silver. You shall tie up the silver and take it with you to the place which 26 the LORD your God will choose. There you shall spend it as you will on cattle or sheep, wine or strong drink, or whatever you desire; you shall consume it there with rejoicing, both you and your family, in the presence of the 27 LORD your God. You must not neglect the Levites who live in your settlements; for they have no holding or patrimony among you.

28 At the end of every third year you shall bring out all the tithe of your produce for that year and leave it in 29 your settlements so that the Levites, who have no holding or patrimony among you, and the aliens, orphans, and widows in your settlements may

come and eat their fill. If you do this the LORD your God will bless you in everything to which you set your hand.

At the end of every seventh year you 15 shall make a remission of debts. This is 2 how the remission shall be made: everyone who holds a pledge shall remit the pledge of anyone indebted to him. He shall not press a fellow-countryman for repayment, for the LORD's year of remission has been declared.[a] You may 3 press foreigners; but if it is a fellow-countryman that holds anything of yours, you must remit all claim upon it. There will never be any poor among 4-5 you if only you obey the LORD your God by carefully keeping these commandments which I lay upon you this day; for the LORD your God will bless you with great prosperity in the land which he is giving you to occupy as your patrimony. When the LORD your 6 God blesses you, as he promised, you will lend to men of many nations, but you yourselves will not borrow; you will rule many nations, but they will not rule you.

When one of your fellow-country- 7 men in any of your settlements in the land which the LORD your God is giving you becomes poor, do not be hard-hearted or close-fisted with your countryman in his need. Be open- 8 handed towards him and lend him on pledge as much as he needs. See that 9 you do not harbour iniquitous thoughts when you find that the seventh year, the year of remission, is near, and look askance at your needy countryman and give him nothing. If you do, he will appeal to the LORD against you, and you will be found guilty of sin. Give 10 freely to him and do not begrudge him your bounty, because it is for this very bounty that the LORD your God will bless you in everything that you do or undertake. The poor will always be 11 with you in the land, and for that reason

a Or has come.

21: *A natural death:* see Lev.17.15; compare Exod.22.31 n. On boiling a *kid*, see Exod.23.19 n.
14.22–29: Tithing and centralization. 23–27: One intent was to deprive local sanctuaries of support. **28–29:** Since it was not possible for all of the abundance of Levites to serve at the central sanctuary (18.6–8), many continued to live throughout the land (Num.35.1–8) and to receive tithes like the poor.
15.1–23: The sabbatical year. The rest granted the land every seventh year in acknowledgment of the LORD's ownership (Lev.25.2–7) or for the use of the poor (Exod.23.10–11) must now be accompanied by a cancellation of debts. Compare the termination of sale or lease of property at

I command you to be open-handed with your countrymen, both poor and distressed, in your own land.

12 When a fellow-Hebrew, man or woman, sells himself to you as a slave, he shall serve you for six years and in the seventh year you shall set him free. 13 But when you set him free, do not let 14 him go empty-handed. Give to him lavishly from your flock, from your threshing-floor and your wine-press. Be generous to him, because the LORD 18 your God has blessed you. Do not take it amiss when you have to set him free, for his six years' service to you has been worth twice[b] the wage of a hired man. Then the LORD your God will 15 bless you in everything you do. Remember that you were slaves in Egypt and the LORD your God redeemed you; that is why I am giving you this command today.

16 If, however, a slave is content to be with you and says, 'I will not leave you, 17 I love you and your family', then you shall take an awl and pierce through his ear to the door, and he will be your slave for life. You shall treat a slave-girl in the same way.

19[c] You shall dedicate to the LORD your God every male first-born of your herds and flocks. You shall not plough with the first-born of your cattle, nor shall you shear the first-born of your sheep. 20 Year by year you and your family shall eat them in the presence of the LORD your God, in the place which the LORD 21 will choose. If any animal is defective, if it is lame or blind, or has any other serious defect, you must not sacrifice it 22 to the LORD your God. Eat it in your settlements; both clean and unclean alike may eat it as they would the meat

of gazelle or buck. But you must not 23 eat the blood; pour it out on the ground like water.

OBSERVE THE MONTH OF ABIB AND KEEP 16 the Passover to the LORD your God, for it was in that month that the LORD your God brought you out of Egypt by night. You shall slaughter a lamb, a 2 kid, or a calf as a Passover victim to the LORD your God in the place which he will choose as a dwelling for his Name. You shall eat nothing leavened with it. 3 For seven days you shall eat unleavened cakes, the bread of affliction. In urgent haste you came out of Egypt, and thus as long as you live you shall commemorate the day of your coming out of Egypt. No leaven shall be seen in all 4 your territory for seven days, nor shall any of the flesh which you have slaughtered in the evening of the first day remain overnight till morning. You 5 may not slaughter the Passover victim in any of the settlements which the LORD your God is giving you, but only 6 in the place which he will choose as a dwelling for his Name; you shall slaughter the Passover victim in the evening as the sun goes down, the time of your coming out of Egypt. You shall 7 boil it and eat it in the place which the LORD your God will choose, and then next morning you shall turn and go to your tents. For six days you shall eat 8 unleavened cakes, and on the seventh day there shall be a closing ceremony in honour of the LORD your God; you shall do no work.

Seven weeks shall be counted: start 9

b *worth twice:* or *equivalent to.*
c *Verse 18 transposed to follow verse 14.*

the Jubilee (Lev.25.8–34). **12:** While a foreigner might be enslaved for six years (Exod.21.2), a fellow Israelite could only be reduced to a "hired man" until the Jubilee (Lev.25.39–40). In understanding the word "Hebrew" here to mean "Israelite"—at times it does not; see Gen. 10.21 n.; Exod.21.2 n.—the term of service as a hired man is reduced from a maximum of fifty years to six. *Woman:* see Exod.21.7 n. **13–14:** This was not required by an earlier law (Exod.21.1–4). **17:** *To the door:* see Exod.21.6 n. **19:** *First-born:* see Exod.13.2 n. **20:** *Year by year:* the centralization of worship and hence great distance from Jerusalem made sacrifice on the eighth day (Exod.22.30) impractical. **21:** *Defective:* see Lev. 12.4 n.

16.1–17: The annual pilgrim-feasts, hereafter to be celebrated only at the central sanctuary. Formerly, with the exception of Passover (which was kept in the home: Exod.12.21–27), they had been observed at the local shrines. Other special days which do not require the bringing of offerings, such as the New Year and the Day of Atonement (Lev.23.23–32; Num.29.1–11), are not mentioned here. **1:** *Abib:* see Exod.13.4 n. *Passover:* see Exod.12.1–27; 13.1–16. **2:** *Calf:* a general term for an animal allowed for sacrifice at the sanctuary. In Exod.12.3–5 only "lamb" and "kid" are specified. **3:** *Unleavened cakes:* see Exod.12.15 n. **9–12:** *The Feast of Weeks:*

counting the seven weeks from the time when the sickle is put to the standing 10 corn; then you shall keep the pilgrim-feast of Weeks to the LORD your God and offer a freewill offering in proportion to the blessing that the LORD your 11 God has given you. You shall rejoice before the LORD your God, with your sons and daughters, your male and female slaves, the Levites who live in your settlements, and the aliens, orphans, and widows among you. You shall rejoice in the place which the LORD your God will choose as a dwell-12 ing for his Name and remember that you were slaves in Egypt. You shall keep and observe all these statutes.

13 You shall keep the pilgrim-feast of Tabernacles[d] for seven days, when you bring in the produce from your thresh-14 ing-floor and winepress. You shall rejoice in your feast, with your sons and daughters, your male and female slaves, the Levites, aliens, orphans, and widows who live in your settlements. 15 For seven days you shall keep this feast to the LORD your God in the place which he will choose, when the LORD your God gives you his blessing in all your harvest and in all your work; you shall keep the feast with joy.

16 Three times a year all your males shall come into the presence of the LORD your God in the place which he will choose: at the pilgrim-feasts of Unleavened Bread, of Weeks, and of Tabernacles. No one shall come into the presence of the LORD empty-handed. 17 Each of you shall bring such a gift as he can in proportion to the blessing which the LORD your God has given you.

18 You shall appoint for yourselves judges and officers, tribe by tribe, in every settlement which the LORD your God is giving you, and they shall dis-19 pense true justice to the people. You shall not pervert the course of justice or show favour, nor shall you accept a bribe; for bribery makes the wise man blind and the just man give a crooked answer. Justice, and justice alone, you 20 shall pursue, so that you may live and occupy the land which the LORD your God is giving you.

You shall not plant any kind of tree 21 as a sacred pole beside the altar of the LORD your God which you shall build. You shall not set up a sacred pillar, 22 for the LORD your God hates them.

You shall not sacrifice to the LORD **17** your God a bull or sheep that has any defect or serious blemish, for that would be abominable to the LORD your God.

If so be that, in any one of the settle-2 ments which the LORD your God is giving you, a man or woman is found among you who does what is wrong in the eyes of the LORD your God, by breaking his covenant and going to 3 worship other gods and prostrating himself before them or before the sun and moon and all the host of heaven—a thing that I have forbidden—then, if 4 it is reported to you or you hear of it, make thorough inquiry. If the report proves to be true, and it is shown that this abominable thing has been done in Israel, then bring the man or woman 5 who has done this wicked deed to the city gate and stone him to death. Sen-6 tence of death shall be carried out on the testimony of two or of three witnesses: no one shall be put to death on the testimony of a single witness. The 7 first stones shall be thrown by the witnesses and then all the people shall follow; thus you shall rid yourselves of this wickedness.

When the issue in any lawsuit is 8 beyond your competence, whether it be a case of blood against blood, plea against plea, or blow against blow, that is disputed in your courts, then go up without delay to the place which the LORD your God will choose. There you 9

d *Or* Booths *or* Arbours.

---

see Exod.23.16 n.; Lev.23.15–21. **13–15:** *The Feast of Tabernacles:* see Exod.23.16 n.; Lev.23.33–35,39–43.
  16.18–17.13: Centralization of the judicial system. 18: Guidance for the local courts. **21–22:** *Pole; pillar:* see Exod.34.13 n. The verses belong topically with 12.30–31. **17.1:** *Blemish:* see Lev.12.4 n. **2–5:** See ch. 13 for similar instances; for the reason, see 7.2 n. **6:** So also 19.15; Num.35.30. For a procedure in the absence of witnesses, see Num.5.11–31. **8–13:** The ultimate authority in case of litigation (1.17; see Exod.18.13–26 n.).

must go to the levitical priests or to the judge then in office; seek their guidance, and they will pronounce the 10 sentence. You shall act on the pronouncement which they make from the place which the LORD will choose. See that you carry out all their instructions. 11 Act on the instruction which they give you, or on the precedent that they cite; do not swerve from what they tell you, 12 either to right or to left. Anyone who presumes to reject the decision either of the priest who ministers there to the LORD your God, or of the judge, shall die; thus you will rid Israel of wickedness. 13 Then all the people will hear of it and be afraid, and will never again show such presumption.

14 When you come into the land which the LORD your God is giving you, and occupy it and settle in it, and you then say, 'Let us appoint over us a king, as 15 all the surrounding nations do', you shall appoint as king the man whom the LORD your God will choose. You shall appoint over you a man of your own race; you must not appoint a foreigner, one who is not of your own 16 race. He shall not acquire many horses, nor, to add to his horses, shall he cause the people to go back to Egypt, for this is what the LORD said to you, 'You shall never go back that way.' 17 He shall not acquire many wives and so be led astray; nor shall he acquire great quantities of silver and gold for himself. 18 When he has ascended the throne of the kingdom, he shall make a copy of this law in a book at the dictation 19 of the levitical priests. He shall keep it by him and read from it all his life, so

that he may learn to fear the LORD his God and keep all the words of this law and observe these statutes. In this way 20 he shall not become prouder than his fellow-countrymen, nor shall he turn from these commandments to right or to left; then he and his sons will reign long over his kingdom in Israel.

The levitical priests, the whole tribe 18 of Levi, shall have no holding or patrimony in Israel; they shall eat the food-offerings of the LORD, their patrimony. They shall have no patri- 2 mony among their fellow-countrymen; the LORD is their patrimony, as he promised them.

This shall be the customary due of 3 the priests from those of the people who offer sacrifice, whether a bull or a sheep: the shoulders, the cheeks, and the stomach shall be given to the priest. You shall give him also the firstfruits 4 of your corn and new wine and oil, and the first fleeces at the shearing of your flocks. For it was he whom the LORD 5 your God chose from all your tribes to attend on the LORD and to minister in the name of the LORD, both he and his sons for all time.

When a Levite comes from any 6 settlement in Israel where he may be lodging to the place which the LORD will choose, if he comes in the eagerness of his heart and ministers in the 7 name of the LORD his God, like all his fellow-Levites who attend on the LORD there, he shall have an equal share of 8 food with them, besides what he may inherit from his father's family.

When you come into the land which 9 the LORD your God is giving you, do

17.14–20: Regulations concerning kingship. This office had been established during the eleventh century, accompanied by both positive and negative attitudes (1 Sam. chs. 8–12; see also Judg.8.22–23; 9.1–21). The point here is that the role of the king must not be patterned after those of the surrounding nations. **15:** *God will choose:* legitimate kings are to be approved and anointed by the LORD's spokesmen, as were Saul (1 Sam. chs. 9–10) and David (1 Sam. chs. 15–16). See Hos.8.4. *Foreigner:* possibly an allusion to Queen Jezebel (a Phoenician from the city of Sidon, 1 Kgs.16.31), who violated the customs of Israel by introducing the worship of her foreign god (1 Kgs. chs. 18–19; 21). **16–17:** The economic and military policies of Solomon (1 Kgs.10.26–29), as well as his many marriages to foreign women (1 Kgs.11.1–8), may be alluded to here. **18:** *This law:* namely, chs. 12–26.
18.1–8: Support for the centralized priesthood. For the early history of the tribe of Levi, see Gen.34.1–31 n.; for their rise to the priestly office, see Exod.32.26–29 n. Here, the entire tribe serves as priests, but in the postexilic period the descendants of Aaron received special designation (Num.16.1–17.13 n.). **3–5:** See Num.35.2–8 n. **6:** *Any settlement:* local sanctuary (14.28–29 n.). Those Levites unable or unwilling to transfer to the central shrine (2 Kgs.23.8–9) remained in their cities (12.18–19; 14.27,29) or moved to the cities set aside for them (Num. 35.1–8).
18.9–22: The office of prophet. 9–13: Various Canaanite ways of seeking the divine will are

not learn to imitate the abominable
10 customs of those other nations. Let no
one be found among you who makes
his son or daughter pass through fire,
no augur or soothsayer or diviner or
11 sorcerer, no one who casts spells or
traffics with ghosts and spirits, and no
12 necromancer. Those who do these
things are abominable to the LORD,
and it is because of these abominable
practices that the LORD your God is
13 driving them out before you. You shall
be whole-hearted in your service of the
LORD your God.

14 These nations whose place you are
taking listen to soothsayers and augurs,
but the LORD your God does not per-
15 mit you to do this. The LORD your God
will raise up a prophet from among you
like myself, and you shall listen to him.
16 All this follows from your request to the
LORD your God on Horeb on the day
of the assembly. There you said, 'Let
us not hear again the voice of the LORD
our God, nor see this great fire again,
17 or we shall die.' Then the LORD said to
18 me, 'What they have said is right. I will
raise up for them a prophet like you,
one of their own race, and I will put
my words into his mouth. He shall con-
19 vey all my commands to them, and if
anyone does not listen to the words
which he will speak in my name I will
20 require satisfaction from him. But the
prophet who presumes to utter in my
name what I have not commanded
him or who speaks in the name of
21 other gods—that prophet shall die.' If
you ask yourselves, 'How shall we
recognize a word that the LORD has not
22 uttered?', this is the answer: When the
word spoken by the prophet in the
name of the LORD is not fulfilled and
does not come true, it is not a word
spoken by the LORD. The prophet has

spoken presumptuously; do not hold
him in awe.

WHEN THE LORD YOUR GOD EXTERM- **19**
inates the nations whose land he is
giving you, and you take their place
and settle in their cities and houses,
you shall set apart three cities in the 2
land which he is giving you to occupy.
Divide into three districts the territory 3
which the LORD your God is giving you
as patrimony, and determine where
each city shall lie. These shall be places
in which homicides may take sanctuary.
This is the kind of homicide who 4
may take sanctuary there and save his
life: the man who strikes another without intent and with no previous enmity
between them; for instance, the man 5
who goes into a wood with his mate to
fell trees, and, when cutting a tree, he
relaxes his grip on the axe,*f* the head
glances off the tree, hits the other man
and kills him. The homicide may take
sanctuary in any one of these cities, and
his life shall be safe. Otherwise, when 6
the dead man's next-of-kin who had
the duty of vengeance pursued him in
the heat of passion, he might overtake
him if the distance were great, and take
his life, although the homicide was not
liable to the death-penalty because there
had been no previous enmity on his
part. That is why I command you to set 7
apart three cities.
If the LORD your God extends your 8
boundaries, as he swore to your forefathers, and gives you the whole land
which he promised to them, because 9
you keep all the commandments that I
am laying down today and carry them
out by loving the LORD your God and

e Or it.
f when . . . axe: or as he swings the axe to cut a tree.

contrasted with the LORD's initiative in speaking through a prophet (vv. 14–19). **10:** *Pass through fire:* see Lev.18.21 n.; 2 Kgs.16.3; 21.6. *Augur:* see Num.22.7 n. *Soothsayer:* see Lev.19.26 n. **11:** *Necromancer:* one who consults the dead for oracles (see Lev.19.31 n.). **15:** On the origin of the prophetic office in Moses' time, see Num.11.27–30 n. **16:** *You said:* see Exod.20.18–21. **17–18:** The people's fear of God is interpreted as a permanent state and hence the office of mediator (5.22–31 n.) is necessary in every succeeding age. For the development in much later times of the idea of a prophet like Moses, see Jn.6.14 n.; 7.40. Acts 3.17–24 applies the passage to Jesus. **20:** See 13.1–5. **21–22:** History is to be the final judge of the truth of uttered prophecies. On "false prophets" see Jer. ch. 28 and 1 Kgs.22.1–28.
19.1–13: Cities of refuge for the accidental homicide. They must be conveniently located throughout the land, since the local altars which served the purpose (Exod.21.14; 1 Kgs.1.50–53) were to be closed (ch. 12). See also Num.35.9–34.

by conforming to his ways for all time, then you shall add three more cities of
10 refuge to these three. Let no innocent blood be shed in the land which the LORD your God is giving you as your patrimony, or blood-guilt will fall on you.

11 When one man is the enemy of another, and he lies in wait for him, attacks him and strikes him a blow so that he dies, and then takes sanctuary
12 in one of these cities, the elders of his own city shall send to fetch him; they shall hand him over to the next-of-kin,
13 and he shall die. You shall show him no mercy, but shall rid Israel of the guilt of innocent blood; then all will be well with you.

14 Do not move your neighbour's boundary stone, fixed by the men of former times in the patrimony which you shall occupy in the land the LORD your God gives you for your possession.

15 A single witness may not give evidence against a man in the matter of any crime or sin which he commits: a charge must be established on the evidence of two or of three witnesses.

16 When a malicious witness comes forward to give false evidence against a
17 man, and the two disputants stand before the LORD, before the priests and
18 the judges then in office, if, after careful examination by the judges, he be proved to be a false witness giving false
19 evidence against his fellow, you shall treat him as he intended to treat his fellow, and thus rid yourselves of this
20 wickedness. The rest of the people when they hear of it will be afraid: never again will anything as wicked as this be
21 done among you. You shall show no mercy: life for life, eye for eye, tooth for tooth, hand for hand, foot for foot.

20 WHEN YOU TAKE THE FIELD AGAINST AN enemy and are faced by horses and chariots and an army greater than yours, do not be afraid of them; for the LORD your God, who brought you out
2 of Egypt, will be with you. When you are about to join battle, the priest shall
3 come forward and address the army in these words: 'Hear, O Israel, this day you are joining battle with the enemy; do not lose heart, or be afraid, or give
4 way to panic in face of them; for the LORD your God will go with you to fight your enemy for you and give you
5 the victory.' Then the officers shall address the army in these words: 'Any man who has built a new house and has not dedicated it shall go back to his house; or he may die in battle and
6 another man dedicate it. Any man who has planted a vineyard and has not begun to use it shall go back home; or he may die in battle and another man
7 use it. Any man who has pledged himself to take a woman in marriage and has not taken her shall go back home; or he may die in battle and another
8 man take her.' The officers shall further address the army: 'Any man who is afraid and has lost heart shall go back home; or his comrades will be discouraged as he is.' When these officers
9 have finished addressing the army, commanders shall be appointed to lead it.

10 When you advance on a city to
11 attack it, make an offer of peace. If the city accepts the offer and opens its gates to you, then all the people in it shall be put to forced labour and shall serve
12 you. If it does not make peace with you but offers battle, you shall besiege
13 it, and the LORD your God will deliver it into your hands. You shall put all its
14 males to the sword, but you may take the women, the dependants, and the cattle for yourselves, and plunder everything else in the city. You may enjoy the use of the spoil of your enemies which the LORD your God
15 gives you. That is what you shall do to cities at a great distance, as opposed to those which belong to nations near at

19.14–21: Boundary markers and witnesses. This is related topically to the previous section by the mention of districts (v. 3) and boundaries (v. 8). **14:** On the preservation of ancestral property, see Num.27.1–11 n. **15:** See 17.6 n. **16:** The giving of *false evidence* is forbidden in Exod.20.16, but no penalty is given there. **21:** See Exod.21.23–25 n.
20.1–20: Rules for warfare. 5–7: The reluctance of such individuals to participate enthusiastically would, like fear (v. 8), infect the other troops. **6:** A *vineyard* could not be harvested until the fifth year (Lev.19.23–25). **7:** The exemption of the newlywed was for one year (24.5). **10–15:** Procedure for remote cities which offer little danger of cultic contamination. For an

16 hand. In the cities of these nations whose land the LORD your God is giving you as a patrimony, you shall not 17 leave any creature alive. You shall annihilate them—Hittites, Amorites, Canaanites, Perizzites, Hivites, Jebusites—as the LORD your God com- 18 manded you, so that they may not teach you to imitate all the abominable things that they have done for their gods and so cause you to sin against the LORD your God.

19 When you are at war, and lay siege to a city for a long time in order to take it, do not destroy its trees by taking the axe to them, for they provide you with food; you shall not cut them down. The trees of the field are not men that 20 you should besiege them. But you may destroy or cut down any trees that you know do not yield food, and use them in siege-works against the city that is at war with you, until it falls.

21 When a dead body is found lying in open country, in the land which the LORD your God is giving you to occupy, and it is not known who struck the 2 blow, your elders and your judges shall come out and measure the distance to the surrounding towns to find which is 3 nearest. The elders of that town shall take a heifer that has never been 4 mated*g* or worn a yoke, and bring it down to a ravine where there is a stream that never runs dry and the ground is never tilled or sown, and there in the 5 ravine they shall break its neck. The priests, the sons of Levi, shall then come forward; for the LORD your God has chosen them to minister to him and to bless in the name of the LORD, and their voice shall be decisive in all cases of

dispute and assault. Then all the elders 6 of the town nearest to the dead body shall wash their hands over the heifer whose neck has been broken in the ravine. They shall solemnly declare: 7 'Our hands did not shed this blood, nor did we witness the bloodshed. Accept expiation, O LORD, for thy 8 people Israel whom thou hast redeemed, and do not let the guilt of innocent blood rest upon thy people Israel: let this bloodshed be expiated on their behalf.' Thus, by doing what 9 is right in the eyes of the LORD, you shall rid yourselves of the guilt of innocent blood.

When you wage war against your 10 enemy and the LORD your God delivers them into your hands and you take some of them captive, then if you see a 11 comely woman among the captives and take a liking to her, you may marry her. You shall bring her into your house, 12 where she shall shave her head, pare her nails, and discard the clothes which 13 she had when captured. Then she shall stay in your house and mourn for her father and mother for a full month. After that you may have intercourse with her; you shall be her husband and she your wife. But if you no longer find 14 her pleasing, let her go free. You must not sell her, nor treat her harshly, since you have had your will with her.

When a man has two wives, one 15 loved and the other unloved, if they both bear him sons, and the son of the unloved wife is the elder, then, when the 16 day comes for him to divide his property among his sons, he shall not treat the son of the loved wife as his first-

g Prob. rdg.; Heb. put to work.

---

illustration, see Num. ch. 31. **16–18:** Procedure for nearby cities (7.1–5). For an illustration, see Josh.6.15–27.

21.1–25.19: A collection of civil laws unrelated to centralization.

21.1–9: Expiation for an unsolved murder. Topically, the unit belongs with 19.1–13. Since the blood of the murderer is not available for expiation (Num.35.33) and the land is hence polluted, an animal substitute is used. The removal of guilt is symbolized by the washing of hands and by the blood being carried away by the stream (compare Lev. 14.5–7 n.). The earliest form of this ritual may have been a Canaanite sacrifice to the gods of the underworld (compare Num.19.1–22 n.). **4:** *Ravine:* a traditional place of sacrifice to underworld deities (2 Chr.33.6; Isa.57.5–6). *Streams* were thought to flow up from the underworld source; the Canaanites personified these as divine judges. Hence, springs were often the sites of sanctuaries where legal disputes were resolved. *Never tilled:* barren ground was once thought to be the domain of demons. **7–9:** The ritual act is largely only a formality, and is made effective by prayer to the LORD.

21.10–22.12: Miscellaneous laws. 10–14: This belongs topically with 20.1–20. **18–21:** Execution of an incorrigible son. The complaint must be lodged by both parents and evaluated by legal

born in contempt of his true first-born, the son of the unloved wife. He shall recognize the rights of his first-born, the son of the unloved wife, and give him a double share of all that he possesses; for he was the firstfruits of his manhood, and the right of the first-born is his.

18 When a man has a son who is disobedient and out of control, and will not obey his father or his mother, or pay attention when they punish him, 19 then his father and mother shall take hold of him and bring him out to the elders of the town, at the town gate. 20 They shall say to the elders of the town, 'This son of ours is disobedient and out of control; he will not obey us, 21 he is a wastrel and a drunkard.' Then all the men of the town shall stone him to death, and you will thereby rid yourselves of this wickedness. All Israel will hear of it and be afraid.

22 When a man is convicted of a capital offence and is put to death, you shall 23 hang him on a gibbet; but his body shall not remain on the gibbet overnight; you shall bury it on the same day, for a hanged man is offensive*h* in the sight of God. You shall not pollute the land which the LORD your God is giving you as your patrimony.

22 WHEN YOU SEE A FELLOW-COUNTRY-man's ox or sheep straying, do not 2 ignore it but take it back to him. If the owner is not a near neighbour and you do not know who he is, take the animal into your own house and keep it with you until he claims it, and then give it 3 back to him. Do the same with his ass or his cloak or anything else that your fellow-countryman has lost, if you find it. You may not ignore it.

4 When you see your fellow-countryman's ass or ox lying on the road, do not ignore it; you must help him to lift it to its feet again.

5 No woman shall wear an article of man's clothing, nor shall a man put on woman's dress; for those who do these

things are abominable to the LORD your God.

When you come across a bird's nest 6 by the road, in a tree or on the ground, with fledglings or eggs in it and the mother-bird on the nest, do not take both mother and young. Let the 7 mother-bird go free, and take only the young; then you will prosper and live long.

When you build a new house, put a 8 parapet along the roof, or you will bring the guilt of bloodshed on your house if anyone should fall from it.

You shall not sow your vineyard with 9 a second crop, or the full yield will be forfeit, both the yield of the seed you sow and the fruit of the vineyard.

You shall not plough with an ox and 10 an ass yoked together.

You shall not wear clothes woven 11 with two kinds of yarn, wool and flax together.

You shall make twisted tassels on the 12 four corners of your cloaks which you wrap round you.

When a man takes a wife and after 13 having intercourse with her turns against her and brings trumped-up 14 charges against her, giving her a bad name and saying, 'I took this woman and slept with her and did not find proof of virginity in her', then the girl's 15 father and mother shall take the proof of her virginity to the elders of the town, at the town gate. The girl's 16 father shall say to the elders, 'I gave my daughter in marriage to this man, and he has turned against her. He has 17 trumped up a charge and said, "I have not found proofs of virginity in your daughter." Here are the proofs.' They shall then spread the garment before the elders of the town. The elders shall 18 take the man and punish him: they 19 shall fine him a hundred pieces of silver because he has given a bad name to a virgin of Israel, and hand them to the girl's father. She shall be his wife: he is not free to divorce her all his life

h Or accursed.

authorities. **22.1–4:** See Exod.23.4–5. **5:** The effect of the regulation was to prevent Israelites from attending Canaanite worship where priests and worshipers wore the dress of the opposite sex. **9–11:** The origin of these prohibitions is obscure. *A second crop:* compare Lev.25.4 n., 23 n. *Two kinds of yarn:* see Lev.19.19 n. **12:** *Tassels:* see Num.15.37–40.
    22.13–30: Sexual relations. 15: *Proof:* a bloodstained sheet. **19:** On *divorce*, compare 24.1–4.

20 long. If, on the other hand, the accusation is true and no proof of the girl's
21 virginity is found, then they shall bring her out to the door of her father's house and the men of her town shall stone her to death. She has committed an outrage in Israel by playing the prostitute in her father's house: you shall rid yourselves of this wickedness.

22 When a man is discovered lying with a married woman, they shall both die, the woman as well as the man who lay with her: you shall rid Israel of this wickedness.

23 When a virgin is pledged in marriage
24 to a man and another man comes upon her in the town and lies with her, you shall bring both of them out to the gate of that town and stone them to death; the girl because, although in the town, she did not cry for help, and the man because he dishonoured another man's
25 wife: you shall rid yourselves of this wickedness. If the man comes upon such a girl in the country and rapes her, then the man alone shall die be-
26 cause he lay with her. You shall do nothing to the girl, she has done nothing worthy of death: this deed is like that of a man who attacks another and
27 murders him, for the man came upon her in the country and, though the girl cried for help, there was no one to rescue her.

28 When a man comes upon a virgin who is not pledged in marriage and forces her to lie with him, and they are
29 discovered, then the man who lies with her shall give the girl's father fifty pieces of silver, and she shall be his wife because he has dishonoured her. He is not free to divorce her all his life long.

30 A man shall not take his father's

wife: he shall not bring shame on his father.

23 No man whose testicles have been crushed or whose organ has been severed shall become a member of the assembly of the LORD.

2 No descendant of an irregular union, even down to the tenth generation, shall become a member of the assembly of the LORD.

3 No Ammonite or Moabite, even down to the tenth generation, shall become a member of the assembly of the LORD. They shall never become members of the assembly of the LORD,
4 because they did not meet you with food and water on your way out of Egypt, and because they hired Balaam son of Beor from Pethor in Aram-naharaim[i] to revile you. The LORD
5 your God refused to listen to Balaam and turned his denunciation into a blessing, because the LORD your God loved you. You shall never seek their
6 welfare or their good all your life long.

7 You shall not regard an Edomite as an abomination, for he is your own kin; nor an Egyptian, for you were aliens in his land. The third generation of
8 children born to them may become members of the assembly of the LORD.

9 When you are encamped against an enemy, you shall be careful to avoid any foulness. When one of your
10 number is unclean because of an emission of seed at night, he must go outside the camp; he may not come within it.
11 Towards evening he shall wash himself in water, and at sunset he may come
12 back into the camp. You shall have a sign outside the camp showing where
13 you can withdraw. With your equip-

i That is Aram of Two Rivers.

22: See Lev.20.10. The Ten Commandments (Exod.20.14) do not specify a penalty. 23–27: The violation is more against one's neighbor than against the girl, as the next regulation makes clear. 28–29: See Exod.22.16–17. 30: See 27.20; Lev.18.8; 20.11.

23.1–14: **Exclusion from the community worship.** Since the initial categories are sexual, this unit logically follows the previous one. 1: For more general regulations concerning imperfection, see Lev.12.4 n.; 13.1–46 n. 2: *Irregular union:* possibly those described in Lev.18.6–18. 3–6: The basis for exclusion shifts from sexual irregularities to ancestry and historical events. Recurring warfare with Ammonites and Moabites lies behind this prohibition. 4: Num. chs. 21–24 do not mention Ammonite participation in the Balaam episode. 7: *Brother:* Gen.25.24–26. That the Edomites are here accepted, despite their one-time hostility to Israel (see Num.20.14–21), suggests that this passage is very late in origin, reflecting a time when the age-old hostilities had ceased. The basis for the view of the Egyptians here is unknown. 9–14: These supplements to the rules for "holy" warfare (20.1–20) are included here because they deal with temporary disqualification from the sacred assembly. 10–11: See Lev.15.16–17.

ment you will have a trowel, and when you squat outside, you shall scrape a hole with it and then turn and cover 14 your excrement. For the LORD your God goes about in your camp, to keep you safe and to hand over your enemies as you advance, and your camp must be kept holy for fear that he should see something indecent and go with you no further.

15 You shall not surrender to his master a slave who has taken refuge with you. 16 Let him stay with you anywhere he chooses in any one of your settlements, wherever suits him best; you shall not force him.

17 No Israelite woman shall become a temple-prostitute, and no Israelite man shall prostitute himself in this way. 18 You shall not allow a common prostitute's fee, or the pay of a male prostitute, to be brought into the house of the LORD your God in fulfilment of any vow, for both of them are abominable to the LORD your God.

19 You shall not charge interest on anything you lend to a fellow-countryman, money or food or anything else on 20 which interest can be charged. You may charge interest on a loan to a foreigner but not on a loan to a fellow-countryman, for then the LORD your God will bless you in all you undertake in the land which you are entering to occupy.

21 When you make a vow to the LORD your God, do not put off its fulfilment; otherwise the LORD your God will require satisfaction of you and you will 22 be guilty of sin. If you choose not to make a vow, you will not be guilty of 23 sin; but if you voluntarily make a vow to the LORD your God, mind what you say and do what you have promised.

24 When you go into another man's vineyard, you may eat as many grapes as you wish to satisfy your hunger, but you may not put any into your basket. 25 When you go into another man's standing corn, you may pluck ears to rub in your hands, but you may not put a sickle to his standing corn.

24 When a man has married a wife, but she does not win his favour because he finds something shameful in her, and he writes her a note of divorce, gives it to her and dismisses her; and suppose 2 after leaving his house she goes off to become the wife of another man, and 3 this next husband turns against her and writes her a note of divorce which he gives her and dismisses her, or dies after making her his wife—then in that 4 case her first husband who dismissed her is not free to take her back to be his wife again after she has become for him unclean. This is abominable to the LORD; you must not bring sin upon the land which the LORD your God is giving you as your patrimony.

5 When a man is newly married, he shall not be liable for military service or any other public duty. He shall remain at home exempt from service for one year and enjoy the wife he has taken.

6 No man shall take millstones, or even the upper one alone, in pledge; that would be taking a life in pledge.

7 When a man is found to have kidnapped a fellow-countryman, an Israelite, and to have treated him harshly and sold him, he shall die: you shall rid yourselves of this wickedness.

8 Be careful how you act in all cases of malignant skin-disease; be careful to observe all that the levitical priests tell you; I gave them my commands which you must obey. Remember what the 9 LORD your God did to Miriam, on your way out of Egypt.

10 When you make a loan to another man, do not enter his house to take a pledge from him. Wait outside, and the 11 man whose creditor you are shall bring the pledge out to you. If he is a poor 12 man, you shall not sleep in the cloak he has pledged. Give it back to him at 13 sunset so that he may sleep in it and

---

23.15–25.19: Miscellaneous laws. 15–16: In contrast, other Ancient Near Eastern codes provided the death penalty for harboring a fugitive slave. **17–18:** See Gen.38.21 n. **19–20:** See Exod.22.25; Lev.25.35–38. **21–23:** See Lev. ch. 27; Num. ch. 30. **24–25:** See 24.19–22. *Rub in your hands:* to remove the husks before eating. See Mt.12.1. **24.1–4:** The intent is to prevent impulsive divorce. **1:** *Shameful:* probably not adultery, which carried the death penalty (22.22). **5:** See 20.5–7; Exod.19.15 n. **6:** *Millstones:* used to grind grain, the dietary staple. **7:** See Exod.21.16. **8:** See Lev. chs. 13–14. **9:** See Num. ch. 12. **12–13:** The regulation made loans

bless you; then it will be counted to your credit in the sight of the LORD your God.

14 You shall not keep back the wages of a man who is poor and needy, whether a fellow-countryman or an alien living in your country in one of 15 your settlements. Pay him his wages on the same day before sunset, for he is poor and his heart is set on them: he may appeal to the LORD against you, and you will be guilty of sin.

16 Fathers shall not be put to death for their children, nor children for their fathers; a man shall be put to death only for his own sin.

17 You shall not deprive aliens and orphans of justice nor take a widow's 18 cloak in pledge. Remember that you were slaves in Egypt and the LORD your God redeemed you from there; that is why I command you to do this.

19 When you reap the harvest in your field and forget a swathe, do not go back to pick it up; it shall be left for the alien, the orphan, and the widow, in order that the LORD your God may bless you in all that you undertake.

20 When you beat your olive-trees, do not strip them afterwards; what is left shall be for the alien, the orphan, and the widow.

21 When you gather the grapes from your vineyard, do not glean afterwards; what is left shall be for the alien, the 22 orphan, and the widow. Remember that you were slaves in Egypt; that is why I command you to do this.

25 When two men go to law and present themselves for judgement, the judges shall try the case; they shall acquit the 2 innocent and condemn the guilty. If the guilty man is sentenced to be flogged, the judge shall cause him to lie down and be beaten in his presence; the number of strokes shall correspond 3 to the gravity of the offence. They may give him forty strokes, but not more; otherwise, if they go further and exceed this number, your fellow-countryman will have been publicly degraded.

You shall not muzzle an ox while it 4 is treading out the corn.

When brothers live together and one 5 of them dies without leaving a son, his widow shall not marry outside the family. Her husband's brother shall have intercourse with her; he shall take her in marriage and do his duty by her as her husband's brother. The 6 first son she bears shall perpetuate the dead brother's name so that it may not be blotted out from Israel. But if the 7 man is unwilling to take his brother's wife, she shall go to the elders at the town gate and say, 'My husband's brother refuses to perpetuate his brother's name in Israel; he will not do his duty by me.' At this the elders of the 8 town shall summon him and reason with him. If he still stands his ground and says, 'I will not take her', his 9 brother's widow shall go up to him in the presence of the elders; she shall pull his sandal off his foot and spit in his face and declare: 'Thus we requite the man who will not build up his brother's family.' His family shall be known in 10 Israel as the House of the Unsandalled Man.

When two men are fighting and the 11 wife of one of them comes near to drag her husband clear of his opponent, if she puts out her hand and catches hold of the man's genitals, you shall cut off 12 her hand and show her no mercy.

You shall not have unequal weights 13 in your bag, one heavy, the other light. You shall not have unequal measures 14 in your house, one large, the other small. You shall have true and correct 15 weights and true and correct measures, so that you may live long in the land which the LORD your God is giving

available to those least able to provide surety. **14–15:** See Lev.19.13; Jer.22.13. **16:** Inherited guilt (5.9–10) must not be punished by human agents (for instances to the contrary, see Josh. 7.24–26; 2 Sam.21.1–9). On the rejection of inherited guilt, see Exod.20.5 n. **19–22:** See Lev. 19.9–10; 23.22; for related legislation, see Exod.23.10–11. **20:** See also 10.18; 14.29. **25.2:** The presence of the *judge* assures that punishment is not exceeded. **4:** For similar concern for animals, see 5.14; 22.4,6–7; Exod.23.11. **5–10:** The *duty* of levirate marriage (from the Latin *levir*, "brother-in-law") was adopted not only to preserve the family name, but to keep the property intact (compare Num.27.1–11 n.). See Gen.38.8,10,26 nn.; Ruth 4.1–13 and notes. **11–12:** The wish to avoid causing an inability to beget offspring links this unit topically with the previous one. **13–16:** See Lev.19.35–36. **17–19:** See Exod.17.8–16 n.

16 you. All who commit these offences, all who deal dishonestly, are abominable to the LORD.

17 Remember what the Amalekites did
18 to you on your way out of Egypt, how they met you on the road when you were faint and weary and cut off your rear, which was lagging behind exhausted: they showed no fear of God.
19 When the LORD your God gives you peace from your enemies on every side, in the land which he is giving you to occupy as your patrimony, you shall not fail to blot out the memory of the Amalekites from under heaven.

26 WHEN YOU COME INTO THE LAND WHICH the LORD your God is giving you to occupy as your patrimony and settle in
2 it, you shall take the firstfruits of all the produce of the soil, which you gather in from the land which the LORD your God is giving you, and put them in a basket. Then you shall go to the place which the LORD your God will choose
3 as a dwelling for his Name and come to the priest, whoever he shall be in those days. You shall say to him, 'I declare this day to the LORD your God that I have entered the land which the LORD swore to our forefathers to give us.'
4 The priest shall take the basket from your hand and set it down before the
5 altar of the LORD your God. Then you shall solemnly recite before the LORD your God: 'My father was a homeless*j* Aramaean who went down to Egypt with a small company and lived there until they became a great, powerful, and
6 numerous nation. But the Egyptians illtreated us, humiliated us and imposed
7 cruel slavery upon us. Then we cried to the LORD the God of our fathers for help, and he listened to us and saw our humiliation, our hardship and distress;

and so the LORD brought us out of 8 Egypt with a strong hand and outstretched arm, with terrifying deeds, and with signs and portents. He 9 brought us to this place and gave us this land, a land flowing with milk and honey. And now I have brought the 10 firstfruits of the soil which thou, O LORD, hast given me.' You shall then set the basket before the LORD your God and bow down in worship before him. You shall all rejoice, you and the 11 Levites and the aliens living among you, for all the good things which the LORD your God has given to you and to your family.

When you have finished taking a 12 tithe of your produce in the third year, the tithe-year, you shall give it to the Levites and to the aliens, the orphans, and the widows. They shall eat it in your settlements and be well fed. Then 13 you shall declare before the LORD your God: 'I have rid my house of the tithe that was holy to thee and given it to the Levites, to the aliens, the orphans, and the widows, according to all the commandments which thou didst lay upon me. I have not broken or forgotten any of thy commandments. I have not eaten 14 any of the tithe while in mourning, nor have I rid myself of it for unclean purposes, nor offered any of it to*k* the dead. I have obeyed the LORD my God: I have done all that thou didst command me. Look down from heaven, 15 thy holy dwelling-place, and bless thy people Israel and the ground which thou hast given to us as thou didst swear to our forefathers, a land flowing with milk and honey.'

This day the LORD your God com- 16 mands you to keep these statutes and

j Or wandering.
k Or for.

26.1–15: Liturgies for the bringing of firstfruits and tithes. 2: *Firstfruits* were offered at the pilgrim-feasts (16.1–17) of Unleavened Bread (Lev.23.6–14), Weeks (16.9–12; Num.28.26–31), and Tabernacles–Ingathering (16.13–15; Exod.23.16). *The place:* Jerusalem; see 12.5 n. **5–10:** An ancient liturgical summary of Israel's history. **5:** *Father:* Jacob. **6:** *Us:* see 5.1–3 n.; Exod.13.8 n. **10:** *And now:* see 4.1 n. **12–15:** See 14.28–29. **14:** *While in mourning:* that is, while "unclean" from contact with the corpse (Num.19.11–16) and able to transfer "uncleanness" to the sacred tithe (Hag.2.12–13; Lev.11.24–25 n.). *To the dead:* see 14.1 n.; 21.1–9 n.

26.16–30.20: Ratification of the covenant in Moab. The covenant stipulations given (Exod. ch. 20) and received (Exod. ch. 24) at Sinai are viewed as extended to the end of the Wilderness period. The present generation now accepts the expansions (29.1) and is urged to renew its dedication regularly thereafter (31.9–13).

26.16–19: A fragment of the covenant renewal ceremony. The section is a part of a larger liturgy connected with covenant renewal. It included the recitation of the LORD's demands

laws: be careful to observe them with all your heart and soul. You have 17 recognized the LORD this day as your God; you are to conform to his ways, to keep his statutes, his commandments, and his laws, and to obey him. 18 The LORD has recognized you this day as his special possession, as he promised you, and to keep his commandments; 19 he will raise you high above all the nations which he has made, to bring him praise and fame and glory, and to be a people holy to the LORD your God, according to his promise.

Concluding charge of Moses to the people

27 MOSES, WITH THE ELDERS OF ISRAEL, gave the people this charge: 'Keep all the commandments that I lay upon you 2 this day. On the day that you cross the Jordan to the land which the LORD your God is giving you, you shall set up great stones and plaster them over. 3 You shall inscribe on them all the words of this law, when you have crossed over to enter the land which the LORD your God is giving you, a land flowing with milk and honey, as the LORD the God of your fathers promised 4 you. When you have crossed the Jordan you shall set up these stones on Mount Ebal, as I command you this 5 day, and cover them with plaster. You shall build an altar there to the LORD your God: it shall be an altar of stones on which you shall use no tool of iron. 6 You shall build the altar of the LORD your God with blocks of undressed stone, and you shall offer whole-offerings upon it to the LORD your God. You shall slaughter shared- 7 offerings and eat them there, and rejoice before the LORD your God. You shall inscribe on the stones all the 8 words of this law, engraving them with care.'

Moses and the levitical priests spoke 9 to all Israel, 'Be silent, Israel, and listen; this day you have become a people belonging to the LORD your God. Obey the LORD your God, and observe 10 his commandments and statutes which I lay upon you this day.'

That day Moses gave the people this 11 command: 'Those who shall stand for 12 the blessing of the people on Mount Gerizim when you have crossed the Jordan are these: Simeon, Levi, Judah, Issachar, Joseph, and Benjamin. Those 13 who shall stand on Mount Ebal for the curse are these: Reuben, Gad, Asher, Zebulun, Dan, and Naphtali.'

The Levites, in the hearing of all 14 Israel, shall intone these words:

'A curse upon the man who carves 15 an idol or casts an image, anything abominable to the LORD that craftsmen make, and sets it up in secret': the people shall all respond and say, 'Amen.'

'A curse upon him who slights his 16 father or his mother': the people shall all say, 'Amen.'

'A curse upon him who moves his 17 neighbour's boundary stone': the people shall all say, 'Amen.'

'A curse upon him who misdirects a 18 blind man': the people shall all say, 'Amen.'

'A curse upon him who withholds 19 justice from the alien, the orphan, and

---

(v. 16; chs. 12–26), the acceptance of him as the only God (v. 17; 6.1–25), and his promise that Israel will remain as his people (vv. 18–19), as a prelude to the close (28.68) of the second of Moses' three addresses. On the terminology involved, see Exod.6.7 n.
  27.1–28.68: Provision for the renewal of the covenant at Shechem, an event anticipated in 11.29–32 and found in Josh.8.30–35. Josh. ch. 24 may be intended as an example for the regular observance of the ceremony at Shechem. **4:** *Mount Ebal:* opposite Mount Gerizim (v. 12) and near Shechem. **5:** *Altar:* perhaps this may have been the earliest location of the central sanctuary demanded in ch. 12. If so, after the Assyrian conquest in 721 B.C., the "chosen" place was understood as not here, but Jerusalem (12.5 n.). **6:** *Undressed stone:* see Exod.20.25 n. **9–10:** These verses interrupt the ceremony prescribed for Shechem and continue the account of covenant renewal in Moab (26.16–19), resumed again in 29.1. **11–13:** The ceremony of blessing and cursing. Their content is amplified in ch. 28. For their role in contracts, see Lev.26.1–46 n.; Deut.11.26–28 n. **14–26:** An ancient list of twelve brief curses. Since most of them are directed against violations of covenant stipulations, they have been added to the present ceremony. They are announced by Levites rather than the six tribes of v. 13. **15:** See 5.8; compare 12.1–4. **16:** Compare 5.16; 21.18–21. **17:** See 19.14. **18:** See Lev.19.14. **19:** See 24.17. **20:** See 22.30.

the widow': the people shall all say, 'Amen.'

20 'A curse upon him who lies with his father's wife, for he brings shame upon his father': the people shall all say, 'Amen.'

21 'A curse upon him who lies with any animal': the people shall all say, 'Amen.'

22 'A curse upon him who lies with his sister, his father's daughter or his mother's daughter': the people shall all say, 'Amen.'

23 'A curse upon him who lies with his wife's mother': the people shall all say, 'Amen.'

24 'A curse upon him who strikes another man in secret': the people shall all say, 'Amen.'

25 'A curse upon him who takes reward to kill a man with whom he has no feud': the people shall all say, 'Amen.'

26 'A curse upon any man who does not fulfil this law by doing all that it prescribes': the people shall all say, 'Amen.'

28 IF YOU WILL OBEY THE LORD YOUR GOD by diligently observing all his commandments which I lay upon you this day, then the LORD your God will raise you high above all nations of the 2 earth, and all these blessings shall come to you and light upon you, because you obey the LORD your God:

3 A blessing on you in the city; a blessing on you in the country.

4 A blessing on the fruit of your body, the fruit of your land and of your cattle, the offspring of your herds and of your lambing flocks.

5 A blessing on your basket and your kneading-trough.

6 A blessing on you as you come in; and a blessing on you as you go out.

7 May the LORD deliver up the enemies who attack you and let them be put to rout before you. Though they come out against you by one way, they shall flee before you by seven ways.

8 May the LORD grant you a blessing

in your granaries and in all your labours, may the LORD your God bless you in the land which he is giving you.

The LORD will set you up as his own 9 holy people, as he swore to you, if you keep the commandments of the LORD your God and conform to his ways. Then all people on earth shall see that 10 the LORD has named you as his very own, and they shall go in fear of you. The LORD will make you prosper 11 greatly in the fruit of your body and of your cattle, and in the fruit of the ground in the land which he swore to your forefathers to give you. May the 12 LORD open the heavens for you, his rich treasure house, to give rain upon your land at the proper time and bless everything to which you turn your hand. You shall lend to many nations, but you shall not borrow; the LORD will 13 make you the head and not the tail: you shall be always at the top and never at the bottom, when you listen to the commandments of the LORD your God, which I give you this day to keep and to fulfil. You shall turn neither to 14 the right nor to the left from all the things which I command you this day nor shall you follow after and worship other gods.

BUT IF YOU DO NOT OBEY THE LORD 15 your God by diligently observing all his commandments and statutes which I lay upon you this day, then all these maledictions shall come to you and light upon you:

A curse upon you in the city; a curse 16 upon you in the country.

A curse upon your basket and your 17 kneading-trough.

A curse upon the fruit of your body, 18 the fruit of your land, the offspring of your herds and of your lambing flocks.

A curse upon you as you come in; 19 and a curse upon you as you go out.

May the LORD send upon you starva- 20 tion, burning thirst, and dysentery,[l] whatever you are about, until you are

l Or cursing, confusion, and rebuke.

21: See Exod.22.19. **22–23:** See 23.2 n. **24:** See 5.17; 21.1–9. **28.1:** The ceremony continues from 27.13. **3–6:** Six blessings are given, in agreement with the number of tribes in 27.12. They emphasize that the LORD is the source of fertility of flock and soil, rather than the Canaanite gods (see 7.13–14 n.). **7–14:** Amplification of the blessings. **7:** *Seven ways:* compare Lev.26.18 n. **16–19:** Six curses that are the reverse of the blessings. **20–46:** Amplification of the curses.

destroyed and quickly perish for your evil doings, because you have forsaken me.

21 May the LORD cause pestilence to haunt you until he has exterminated you out of the land which you are 22 entering to occupy; may the LORD afflict you with wasting disease and recurrent fever, ague and eruptions; with drought, black blight and red; and may these plague you until you perish. 23 May the skies above you be bronze, 24 and the earth beneath you iron. May the LORD turn the rain upon your country into fine sand, and may dust come down upon you from the sky until you are blotted out.

25 May the LORD put you to rout before the enemy. Though you go out against them by one way, you shall flee before them by seven ways. May you be repugnant to all the kingdoms on 26 earth. May your bodies become food for the birds of the air and the wild beasts, with no man to scare them away.

27 May the LORD strike you with Egyptian boils and with tumours, scabs, and itches, for which you will find no 28 cure. May the LORD strike you with madness, blindness, and bewilderment; 29 so that you will grope about in broad daylight, just as a blind man gropes in darkness, and you will fail to find your way. You will also be oppressed and robbed, day in, day out, with no one to 30 save you. A woman will be pledged to you, but another shall ravish her; you will build a house but not live in it; you will plant a vineyard but not enjoy 31 its fruit. Your ox will be slaughtered before your eyes, but you will not eat any of it; and before your eyes your ass will be stolen and will not come back to you; your sheep will be given to the enemy, and there will be no one to 32 recover them. Your sons and daughters will be given to another people while you look on; your eyes will strain after them all day long, and you will be 33 powerless. A nation whom you do not know shall eat the fruit of your land and all your toil, and your lot will be noth-ing but brutal oppression. The sights 34 you see will drive you mad. May the 35 LORD strike you on knee and leg with malignant boils for which you will find no cure; they will spread from the sole of your foot to the crown of your head. May the LORD give you up, you 36 and the king whom you have appointed, to a nation whom neither you nor your fathers have known, and there you will worship other gods, gods of wood and stone. You will be- 37 come a horror, a byword, and an object-lesson to all the peoples amongst whom the LORD disperses you.

You will carry out seed for your fields 38 in plenty, but you will harvest little; for the locusts will devour it. You will 39 plant vineyards and cultivate them, but you will not drink the wine or gather the grapes; for the grub will eat them. You will have olive-trees all over your 40 territory, but you will not anoint yourselves with their oil; for your olives will drop off. You will bear sons 41 and daughters, but they will not remain yours because they will be taken into captivity. All your trees and the 42 fruit of the ground will be infested with the mole-cricket. The alien who lives 43 with you will raise himself higher and higher, and you will sink lower and lower. He will lend to you but you will 44 not lend to him: he will be the head and you the tail.

All these maledictions will come 45 upon you; they will pursue you and overtake you until you are destroyed because you did not obey the LORD your God by keeping the commandments and statutes which he gave you. They shall be a sign and a portent to 46 you and your descendants for ever, because you did not serve the LORD 47 your God with joy and with a glad heart for all your blessings. Then in 48 hunger and thirst, in nakedness and extreme want, you shall serve your enemies whom the LORD will send against you, and they will put a yoke of iron on your neck when they have subdued you. May the LORD raise 49 against you a nation from afar, from

22: Seven afflictions (Lev.26.18 n.). 27: The plague once directed toward the Egyptians (Exod. 9.8–12) would now strike Israel. 30: Contrast 20.5–7. 47–68: An expansion of the curses, possibly alluding to the fate of the kingdom of Israel in 721 B.C., when the Assyrians destroyed

the other end of the earth, who will swoop upon you like a vulture, a nation whose language you will not under-
50 stand, a nation of grim aspect with no reverence for age and no pity for the
51 young. They will devour the young of your cattle and the fruit of your land, when you have been subdued. They will leave you neither corn, nor new wine nor oil, neither the offspring of your herds nor of your lambing flocks,
52 until you are annihilated. They will besiege you in all your cities until they bring down your lofty impregnable walls, those city walls throughout your land in which you trust. They will besiege you within all your cities, throughout the land which the LORD your God
53 has given you. Then you will eat your own children, the flesh of your sons and daughters whom the LORD your God has given you, because of the dire straits to which you will be reduced
54 when your enemy besieges you. The pampered, delicate man will not share with his brother, or the wife of his bosom, or his own remaining children,
55 any of the meat which he is eating, the flesh of his own children. He is left with nothing else because of the dire straits to which you will be reduced when your enemy besieges you within your
56 cities. The pampered, delicate woman, the woman who has never even tried to put a foot to the ground, so delicate and pampered she is, will not share with her own husband or her son or her
57 daughter the afterbirth which she expels, or any boy or girl that she may bear. She will herself eat them secretly in her extreme want, because of the dire straits to which you will be reduced when your enemy besieges you within your cities.
58 If you do not observe and fulfil all the law written down in this book, if you do not revere this honoured and dreaded name, this name 'the LORD[m]
59 your God', then the LORD will strike you and your descendants with unimaginable plagues, malignant and persistent, and with sickness, per-

sistent and severe. He will bring upon 60 you once again all the diseases of Egypt which you dread, and they will cling to you. The LORD will bring upon 61 you sickness and plague of every kind not written down in this book of the law, until you are destroyed. Then you 62 who were countless as the stars in the sky will be left few in number, because you did not obey the LORD your God. Just as the LORD took delight in you, 63 prospering and increasing you, so now it will be his delight to destroy and exterminate you, and you will be uprooted from the land which you are entering to occupy. The LORD will 64 scatter you among all peoples from one end of the earth to the other, and there you will worship other gods whom neither you have known nor your forefathers, gods of wood and stone. Among those nations you will find no 65 peace, no rest for the sole of your foot. Then the LORD will give you an unquiet mind, dim eyes, and failing appetite. Your life will hang continually 66 in suspense, fear will beset you night and day, and you will find no security all your life long. Every morning you 67 will say, 'Would God it were evening!', and every evening, 'Would God it were morning!', for the fear that lives in your heart and the sights that you see. The LORD will bring you sorrowing 68 back to Egypt by that very road of which I said to you, 'You shall not see that road again'; and there you will offer to sell yourselves to your enemies as slaves and slave-girls, but there will be no buyer.

These are the words of the covenant 29 which the LORD commanded Moses to make with the Israelites in Moab, in addition to the covenant which he made with them on Horeb.

MOSES SUMMONED ALL THE ISRAELITES 2 and said to them: 'You have seen with your own eyes all that the LORD did in Egypt to Pharaoh, to all his

m See note on Exod. 3. 15.

the country and took most of its population into captivity (2 Kgs.17.1–6). **62:** *Few in number:* a reversal of the promise to Abraham (Gen.15.5). **68:** *Of which I said:* compare 17.16.
29.1–30.20: The third address of Moses. 1: *The covenant* is a renewal of the Sinai covenant. For its conditions, see 28.1,15,63; 30.1,5,7,9. **2–8:** Recitation of previous history (for the reason,

3 servants, and to the whole land, the great challenge which you yourselves witnessed, those great signs and por-
4 tents, but to this day the LORD has not given you a mind to learn, or eyes to
5 see, or ears to hear. I led you for forty years in the wilderness; your clothes did not wear out on you, nor did your sandals wear out and fall off your feet;
6 you ate no bread and drank no wine or strong drink, in order that you might learn that I am the LORD your God.
7 You came to this place where Sihon king of Heshbon and Og king of Bashan came to attack us, and we de-
8 feated them. We took their land and gave as patrimony to the Reubenites, the Gadites, and half the tribe of
9 Manasseh. You shall observe the provisions of this covenant and keep them so that you may be successful in all you do.
10 'You all stand here today before the LORD your God, tribal chiefs, elders,
11 and officers, all the men of Israel, with your dependants, your wives, the aliens who live in your camp—all of them, from those who chop wood to those
12 who draw water—and you are ready to accept the oath and enter into the covenant which the LORD your God is
13 making with you today. The covenant is to constitute you his people this day, and he will be your God, as he promised you and as he swore to your fore-
14 fathers, Abraham, Isaac and Jacob. It is not with you alone that I am making
15 this covenant and this oath, but with all those who stand here with us today before the LORD our God and also with those who are not here with us today.
16 For you know how we lived in Egypt and how we and you, as we passed
17 through the nations, saw their loathsome idols and the false gods they had, the gods of wood and stone, of
18 silver and gold. If there should be among you a man or woman, family or tribe, who is moved today to turn from the LORD our God and to go worshipping the gods of those nations —if there is among you such a root from which springs gall and worm-

wood, then when he hears the terms of 19 this oath, he may inwardly flatter himself and think, "All will be well with me even if I follow the promptings of my stubborn heart"; but this will bring everything to ruin. The LORD will not 20 be willing to forgive him; for then his anger and resentment will overwhelm this man, and the denunciations prescribed in this book will fall heavily on him, and the LORD will blot out his name from under heaven. The LORD 21 will single him out from all the tribes of Israel for disaster to fall upon him, according to the oath required by the covenant and prescribed in this book of the law.

'The next generation, your sons who 22 follow you and the foreigners who come from distant countries, will see the plagues of this land and the ulcers which the LORD has brought upon its people, the whole land burnt up with 23 brimstone and salt, so that it cannot be sown, or yield herb or green plant. It will be as desolate as were Sodom and Gomorrah, Admah and Zeboyim, when the LORD overthrew them in his anger and rage. Then they, and all the 24 nations with them, will ask, "Why has the LORD so afflicted this land? Why has there been this great outburst of wrath?" The answer will be: "Because 25 they forsook the covenant of the LORD the God of their fathers which he made with them when he brought them out of Egypt. They began to worship 26 other gods and to bow down to them, gods whom they had not known and whom the LORD had not assigned to them. The anger of the LORD was 27 roused against that land, so that he brought upon it all the maledictions written in this book. The LORD up- 28 rooted them from their soil in anger, in wrath and great fury, and banished them to another land, where they are to this day."

'There are things hidden, and they 29 belong to the LORD our God, but what is revealed belongs to us and our children for ever; it is for us to observe all that is prescribed in this law.

---

see 4.1 n.). **5:** See 8.4; 2.7. **7–8:** A summary of 2.26–3.17. **9:** Chs. 12–26. **13:** *His people; your god:* 26.17–18; Exod.6.7 n. *Forefathers: see* 1.8 n. **15:** *Today:* see 5.1–3 n. **18:** *Wormwood:* a bitter drug. **23:** *Brimstone:* sulphur. *Admah and Zeboyim:* see Gen.10.19. **26:** *Assigned:* see 32.8–9 n.

30 'When these things have befallen you, the blessing and the curse of which I have offered you the choice, if you and your sons take them to heart there in all the countries to which the LORD 2 your God has banished you, if you turn back to him and obey him heart and soul in all that I command you 3 this day, then the LORD your God will show you compassion and restore your fortunes. He will gather you again from all the countries to which he has 4 scattered you. Even though he were to banish you to the four corners of the world, the LORD your God will gather you from there, from there he will 5 fetch you home. The LORD your God will bring you into the land which your forefathers occupied, and you will occupy it again; then he will bring you prosperity and make you more num- 6 erous than your forefathers were. The LORD your God will circumcise[n] your hearts and the hearts of your descendants, so that you will love him with all your heart and soul and you will live. 7 Then the LORD your God will turn all these denunciations against your enemies and the foes who persecute 8 you. You will then again obey the LORD and keep all his commandments 9–10 which I give you this day. The LORD your God will make you more than prosperous in all that you do, in the fruit of your body and of your cattle and in the fruits of the earth; for, when you obey the LORD your God by keeping his commandments and statutes, as they are written in this book of the law, and when you turn back to the LORD your God with all your heart and soul, he will again rejoice over you and be good to you, as he rejoiced over your forefathers.

11 'The commandment that I lay on you this day is not too difficult for you, 12 it is not too remote. It is not in heaven, that you should say, "Who will go up

to heaven for us to fetch it and tell it to us, so that we can keep it?" Nor is it 13 beyond the sea, that you should say, "Who will cross the sea for us to fetch it and tell it to us, so that we can keep it?" It is a thing very near to you, upon 14 your lips and in your heart ready to be kept.

'Today I offer you the choice of life 15 and good, or death and evil. If you 16 obey the commandments of the LORD your God which I give you this day, by loving the LORD your God, by conforming to his ways and by keeping his commandments, statutes, and laws, then you will live and increase, and the LORD your God will bless you in the land which you are entering to occupy. But if your heart turns away and you 17 do not listen and you are led on to bow down to other gods and worship them, I tell you this day that you will perish; 18 you will not live long in the land which you will enter to occupy after crossing the Jordan. I summon heaven and 19 earth to witness against you this day: I offer you the choice of life or death, blessing or curse. Choose life and then you and your descendants will live; love the LORD your God, obey him 20 and hold fast to him: that is life for you and length of days in the land which the LORD swore to give to your forefathers, Abraham, Isaac and Jacob.'

Moses finished speaking these words **31** to all Israel, and then he said, 'I am 2 now a hundred and twenty years old, and I can no longer move about as I please; and the LORD has told me that I may not cross the Jordan. The LORD 3 your God will cross over at your head and destroy these nations before your advance, and you shall occupy their lands; and, as he directed, Joshua will lead you across. The LORD will do to 4 these nations as he did to Sihon and Og, kings of the Amorites, and to their

n Or incline.

30.1–10: Exile and return. An expansion of 4.29–31, possibly written either during the Exile of Israel (721 B.C.: see 28.47–68 n.) or Judah (587 B.C.) in order to encourage those whose situation then appeared hopeless (see 26.5–10 n.). **15–18:** The passage gives the precise blessing and curse pronounced after the acceptance of the covenant (as in 27.11–28.68; see 27.11–13 n.). **19:** The summoning of witnesses closes the covenant ceremony (4.26 n.).
   31.1–29: The appointment of Moses' successor (vv. 1–8, 14–23; compare Num.27.12–23) alternates with the provisions for writing, preserving, and reciting the law (vv. 9–13,24–27). **2:** *Hundred and twenty:* eighty (Exod.7.7) plus the forty in the Wilderness (2.7). *I may not cross:* see 1.37 n. **3:** *At your head and destroy:* see 9.3. *As he directed:* 3.23–28. **4:** See Num.21.21–35.

5 lands; he will destroy them. The LORD will deliver them into your power, and you shall do to them as I commanded 6 you. Be strong, be resolute; you must not dread them or be afraid, for the LORD your God himself goes with you; he will not fail you or forsake you.'

7 Moses summoned Joshua and said to him in the presence of all Israel, 'Be strong, be resolute; for it is you who are to lead this people into the land which the LORD swore to give their forefathers, and you are to bring them 8 into possession of it. The LORD himself goes at your head; he will be with you; he will not fail you or forsake you. Do not be discouraged or afraid.'

9 Moses wrote down this law and gave it to the priests, the sons of Levi, who carried the Ark of the Covenant of the LORD, and to all the elders of Israel. 10 Moses gave them this command: 'At the end of every seven years, at the appointed time for the year of remission, at the pilgrim-feast of Taber- 11 nacles, when all Israel comes to enter the presence of the LORD your God in the place which he will choose, you shall read this law publicly in the hear- 12 ing of all Israel. Assemble the people, men, women, and dependants, together with the aliens who live in your settlements, so that they may listen, and learn to fear the LORD your God and observe 13 all these laws with care. Their children, too, who do not know them, shall hear them, and learn to fear the LORD your God all their lives in the land which you will occupy after crossing the Jordan.'

Joshua appointed successor to Moses

14 THE LORD SAID TO MOSES, 'THE TIME OF your death is drawing near; call Joshua, and then come and stand in the Tent of the Presence so that I may give him his commission.' So Moses and Joshua went and took their stand in the Tent of the Presence; and the LORD 15 appeared in the tent in a pillar of cloud, and the pillar of cloud stood at the entrance of the tent.

The LORD said to Moses, 'You are 16 about to die like your forefathers, and this people, when they come into the land and live among foreigners, will go wantonly after their gods; they will abandon me and break the covenant which I have made with them. Then 17 my anger will be roused against them, and I will abandon them and hide my face from them. They will be an easy prey, and many terrible disasters will come upon them. They will say on that day, "These disasters have come because our God is not among us." On 18 that day I will hide my face because of all the evil they have done in turning to other gods.

'Now write down this rule of life[o] 19 and teach it to the Israelites; make them repeat it, so that it may be on record against them. When I have 20 brought them into the land which I swore to give to their forefathers, a land flowing with milk and honey, and they have plenty to eat and grow fat, they will turn to other gods and worship them, they will spurn me and break my covenant; and many calam- 21 ities and disasters will follow. Then this rule of life will confront them as a record, for it will not be forgotten by their descendants. For even before I bring them into the land which I swore to give them, I know which way their thoughts incline already.'

That day Moses wrote down this rule 22 of life and taught it to the Israelites. The LORD[p] gave Joshua son of Nun 23 his commission in these words: 'Be strong, be resolute; for you shall bring the Israelites into the land which I swore to give them, and I will be with you.'

o rule of life: or song.   p Prob. rdg.; Heb. He.

10: *Year of remission:* see 15.1–18. *Tabernacles:* see 16.13–15 n. **11–13:** Provision for public reading was a regular part of Ancient Near Eastern treaties (covenants), and the festival would be the occasion for renewal (27.1–28.68 n.) **14–15:** These verses are conceptually and linguistically related to Exod.33.7–11; Num.11.16–17, 24–25. **16–22:** These verses intrude; they anticipate ch.32, the "Song of Moses" (v. 19, Tfn. *o*), which may have been sung as part of the covenant renewal ceremony. Thus the Song, like the "book of the law" (vv. 24–27), would serve as a "witness" to God's graciousness in the past and as a challenge to Israel's life in the future.

24 When Moses had finished writing down these laws in a book, from be-
25 ginning to end, he gave this command to the Levites who carried the Ark of
26 the Covenant of the LORD: 'Take this book of the law and put it beside the Ark of the Covenant of the LORD your
27 God to be a witness against you. For I know how defiant and stubborn you are; even during my lifetime you have defied the LORD; how much more, then, will you do so when I am dead?
28 Assemble all the elders of your tribes and your officers; I will say all these things in their hearing and will sum-mon heaven and earth to witness
29 against them. For I know that after my death you will take to degrading practices and turn aside from the way which I told you to follow, and in days to come disaster will come upon you, because you are doing what is wrong in the eyes of the LORD and so provoking him to anger.'

Two historical poems

30 MOSES RECITED THIS SONG FROM beginning to end in the hearing of the whole assembly of Israel:

32 Give ear to what I say, O heavens, earth, listen to my words;
2 my teaching shall fall like drops of rain,
my words shall distil like dew, like fine rain upon the grass and like the showers on young plants.

3 When I call aloud the name of the LORD,*q*
you shall respond, 'Great is our God,
4 the creator*r* whose work is perfect, and all his ways are just,
a faithful god, who does no wrong, righteous and true is He!'

Perverse and crooked generation   5
whose faults have proved you no children of his,
is this how you repay the LORD,   6
you brutish and stupid people?
Is he not your father who formed you?
Did he not make you and establish you?
Remember the days of old,   7
think of the generations long ago;
ask your father to recount it
and your elders to tell you the tale.

When the Most High parcelled out   8
the nations,
when he dispersed all mankind,
he laid down the boundaries of every people
according to the number of the sons of God;
but the LORD's share was his own   9
people,
Jacob was his allotted portion.
He found him in a desert land,   10
in a waste and howling void.
He protected and trained him,
he guarded him as the apple of his eye,
as an eagle watches over its nest,   11
hovers above its young,
spreads its pinions and takes them up,
and carries them upon its wings.
The LORD alone led him,   12
no alien god at his side.
He made him ride on the heights of   13
the earth
and fed him on the harvest of the fields;
he satisfied him with honey from the crags
and oil from the flinty rock,
curds from the cattle, milk from the   14
ewes,
the fat of lambs' kidneys,

q Or the name JEHOVAH.   *r Or* rock.

23: This verse is a sequel to vv.14–15. **26:** *Beside the Ark:* symbolizing its authority and making it accessible for public reading (vv. 10–11). Compare 10.1–5. **28:** *Witness:* see 30.19 n.
  31.30–32.47: The "Song of Moses." See 31.16–22 n. The song is linked to the previous chapter by the summoning of heaven and earth (31.28 and 32.1). In reality, it is an appended psalm, perhaps older than Deut. itself. **32.1–4:** **Invocation.** **5–6:** **An accusation of ingratitude** (see 4.1 n.). **7:** **A call to consider the past.**
  32.8–14: **Recitation of the LORD's gracious deeds.** **8–9:** *The sons of God* are minor figures in the divine council (Gen.1.26 n.) to whom *the Most High* has assigned governorship of the nations, retaining Israel for himself. **10:** This may be part of a tradition that Israel became the LORD's people in the Wilderness (see also Hos.9.10), against the dominant view, e.g. Gen. ch. 12.

of rams, the breed of Bashan, and of
    goats,
with the finest flour of wheat;
and he drank wine from the blood
    of the grape.

15 Jacob ate and was well fed,
Jeshurun grew fat and unruly,*s*
he grew fat, he grew bloated and
    sleek.
He forsook God who made him
and dishonoured the Rock of his
    salvation.

16 They roused his jealousy with
    foreign gods
and provoked him with abominable
    practices.

17 They sacrificed to foreign demons
    that are no gods,
gods who were strangers to them;
they took up with new gods from
    their neighbours,
gods whom your fathers did not
    acknowledge.

18 You forsook the creator*t* who begot
    you
and cared nothing for God who
    brought you to birth.

19 The LORD saw and spurned them;
his own sons and daughters
    provoked him.

20 'I will hide my face from them,' he
    said;
'let me see what their end will be,
for they are a mutinous generation,
sons who are not to be trusted.

21 They roused my jealousy with a god
    of no account,
with their false gods they provoked
    me;
so I will rouse their jealousy with a
    people of no account,
with a brutish nation I will provoke
    them.

22 For fire is kindled by my anger,
it burns to the depths of Sheol;
it devours earth and its harvest

and sets fire to the very roots of the
    mountains.
23 I will heap on them one disaster
    after another,
I will use up all my arrows on them;
24 pangs of hunger, ravages of plague,
and bitter pestilence.
I will harry them with the fangs of
    wild beasts
and the poison of creatures that
    crawl in the dust.
25 The sword will make orphans in the
    streets
and widows in their own homes;
it will take toll of young man and
    maid,
of babes in arms and old men.
26 I had resolved to strike them down
and to destroy all memory of them,
27 but I feared that I should be
    provoked by their foes,
that their enemies would take the
    credit
and say, "It was not the LORD,
it was we who raised the hand that
    did this."'

28 They are a nation that lacks good
    counsel,
devoid of understanding.
29 If only they had the wisdom to
    understand this
and give thought to their end!
30 How could one man pursue a
    thousand of them,
how could two put ten thousand to
    flight,
if their Rock had not sold them to
    their enemies,
if the LORD had not handed them
    over?
31 For the enemy have no Rock like
    ours,
in themselves they are mere fools.
32 Their vines are vines of Sodom,

s Or and kicked.   t Or rock.

15–18: Israel's ungrateful response. **15:** *Jeshurun:* an occasional, ancient name for Israel (33.5.26).
    32.19–47: God's judgment. 19: The historical event to which *spurned them* refers is uncertain; the allusion is meant as a warning for future generations. **22:** *Sheol:* Num.16.30 n. Destruction of the *harvest* demonstrates the powerlessness of the gods of fertility (7.13–14 n.; 8.1–10 n.). In all, seven evils are enumerated (28.22 n.). **26–35:** God's reflections upon his judgment. It cannot be a final one, lest Israel's neighbors misunderstand the cause. When Israel is restored, God's sovereignty over both punishment and deliverance will be evident. The passage 30.1–10, however, demands repentance as the prerequisite for restoration. **27:** Compare Isa.10.12–15. **28:** *They:* the enemies who have defeated Israel. **30:** *One man:* of the enemy. *Thousand:* of Israel. That such a small force defeated Israel indicates that it was God's will. *Rock:* a common Ancient Near Eastern divine title denoting permanence. **31:** The speaker shifts from God to

218

grown on the terraces of Gomorrah;
their grapes are poisonous,
the clusters bitter to the taste.

33 Their wine is the venom of serpents,
the cruel poison of asps;

34 all this I have in reserve,
sealed up in my storehouses

35 till the day of punishment and
vengeance,
till the moment when they slip and
fall;
for the day of their downfall is near,
their doom is fast approaching.

36 The LORD will give his people justice
and have compassion on his
servants;
for he will see that their strength is
gone:
alone, or defended by his clan, no
one is left.

37 He will say, 'Where are your gods,
the rock in which you sought
shelter,

38 the gods who ate the fat of your
sacrifices
and drank the wine of your drink-
offerings?
Let them rise to help you!
Let them give you shelter!

39 See now that I, I am He,
and there is no god beside me:
I put to death and I keep alive,
I wound and I heal;
there is no rescue from my grasp.

40 I lift my hand to heaven
and swear: As I live for ever,

41 when I have whetted my flashing
sword,
when I have set my hand to
judgement,
then I will punish my adversaries
and take vengeance on my enemies.

42 I will make my arrows drunk with
blood,
my sword shall devour flesh,
blood of slain and captives,
the heads of the enemy princes.'

43 Rejoice with him, you heavens,
bow down, all you gods, before him;

for he will avenge the blood of his
sons
and take vengeance on his adversaries;
he will punish those who hate him
and make expiation for his people's
land.

This is the song that Moses came and 44
recited in the hearing of the people, he
and Joshua son of Nun.

Moses finished speaking to all Israel, 45
and then he said, 'Take to heart all 46
these warnings which I solemnly give
you this day: command your children
to be careful to observe all the words of
this law. For you they are no empty 47
words; they are your very life, and by
them you shall live long in the land
which you are to occupy after crossing
the Jordan.'

That same day the LORD spoke to 48
Moses and said, 'Go up this mount 49
Abarim, Mount Nebo in Moab, to the
east of Jericho, and look out over the
land of Canaan that I am giving to the
Israelites for their possession. On this 50
mountain you shall die and be gathered to your father's kin, just as
Aaron your brother died on Mount
Hor and was gathered to his father's
kin. This is because both of you were 51
unfaithful to me at the waters of
Meribah-by-Kadesh in the wilderness
of Zin, when you did not uphold my
holiness among the Israelites. You shall 52
see the land from a distance but you
may not enter the land I am giving to
the Israelites.'

THIS IS THE BLESSING THAT MOSES THE 33
man of God pronounced upon the
Israelites before his death:

The LORD came from Sinai 2
and shone forth from Seir.
He showed himself from Mount Paran,
and with him were myriads of holy
ones[u]

---

u and with . . . holy ones: *prob. rdg.; Heb.* and he came
from myriads of holiness.

---

the congregation. **36–42:** The renunciation of foreign gods and the anticipation of deliverance.
43: Closing hymn of praise. **45–47:** The insertion of the "Song of Moses" seems to sever these
verses from the context in 31.29.
　　32.48–52: Moses prepares for his death. For related materials, see 3.23–28; Num.20.1–13.
　　33.1–29: The "Blessing of Moses," a second psalm appended to Deut. (see 31.30–32.47 n.).
1: *Pronounced before his death:* see Gen.27.4 n., 33–35 n. for deathbed blessing or curse.

streaming along at his right hand.
3 Truly he loves his people
and blesses his saints.[v]
They sit at his feet
and receive his instruction,
4 the law which Moses laid upon us,
as a possession for the assembly of
Jacob.
5 Then a king arose[w] in Jeshurun,
when the chiefs of the people were
assembled
together with all the tribes of Israel.

6 Of Reuben he said:[x]

May Reuben live and not die out,
but may he be few in number.

7 And of Judah he said this:

Hear, O LORD, the cry of Judah
and join him to his people,
thou whose hands fight for him,
who art his helper against his foes.

8 Of Levi he said:

Thou didst give thy Thummim to
Levi,
thy Urim to thy loyal servant
whom thou didst prove at Massah,
for whom thou didst plead at the
waters of Meribah,
9 who said of his parents, I do not
know them,
who did not acknowledge his
brothers,
nor recognize his children.
They observe thy word
and keep thy covenant;
10 they teach thy precepts to Jacob,
thy law to Israel.
They offer thee the smoke of
sacrifice
and offerings on thy altar.
11 Bless all his powers,[y] O LORD,
and accept the work of his hands.
Strike his adversaries hip and thigh,
and may his enemies rise no more.

12 Of Benjamin he said:

The LORD's beloved dwells in
security,
the High God[z] shields him all the
day long,
and he dwells under his protection.

13 Of Joseph he said:

The LORD's blessing is on his land
with precious fruit watered from
heaven above
and from the deep that lurks below,
14 with precious fruit ripened by the
sun,
precious fruit, the produce of the
months,
15 with all good things from the
ancient mountains,
the precious fruit of the everlasting
hills,
16 the precious fruits of earth and all
its store,
by the favour of him who dwells in
the burning bush.
This shall rest[a] upon the head of
Joseph,
on the brow of him who was prince
among[b] his brothers.
17 In majesty he shall be like a first-
born ox,
his horns those of a wild ox
with which he will gore nations
and drive[c] them to the ends of earth.
Such will be the myriads of
Ephraim,
and such the thousands of Manasseh.

18 Of Zebulun he said:

Rejoice, Zebulun, when you sally
forth,

v Or holy ones.
w Or Then there was a king . . .
x Of Reuben he said: prob. rdg.; Heb. om.
y Or skill.
z the High God: prob. rdg.; Heb. upon him.
a Prob. rdg.; cp. Gen. 49. 26; Heb. has an unintelligible form.
b him . . . among: or the one cursed by.
c and drive: prob. rdg.; Heb. together.

5: *Jeshurun:* see 32.15 n. **6:** On the decline of *Reuben* as a tribal power (*May Reuben live . . . but . . . be few in number*), see Gen.49.3–4 n.; Num.26.7 n. That Simeon is not mentioned at all suggests that it had ceased to exist as a tribe and hence the present passage was composed later than the "Blessing of Jacob" (see Gen.49.5–7 n.). **8:** *Levi:* see 18.1–8 n. for references to the development of the tribe and priesthood. *Thummim; Urim:* see Exod.28.15 n. *Massah; Meribah:* for the loyalty of the Levites see Exod.32.25–29. The Massah-Meribah incidents lack specific mention of the Levites. **12:** *High God:* see Gen.14.18 n. **16:** *Burning bush:* see Exod.3.2.

rejoice in your tents, Issachar.

10 They shall summon nations to the
    mountain,
there they will offer true sacrifices,
for they shall suck the abundance of
    the seas
and draw out*d* the hidden wealth of
    the sand.

20 Of Gad he said:

Blessed be Gad, in his wide domain;
he couches like a lion
tearing an arm or a scalp.

21 He chose the best for himself,
for to him was allotted a ruler's
    portion,
when the chiefs of the people were
    assembled together.
He did what the LORD deemed right,
observing his ordinances for Israel.

22 Of Dan he said:

Dan is a lion's cub
springing out from Bashan.

23 Of Naphtali he said:

Naphtali is richly favoured
and full of the blessings of the LORD;
his patrimony stretches to the sea and
    southward.

24 Of Asher he said:

Asher is most blest of sons,
may he be the favourite among*e* his
    brothers
and bathe his feet in oil.

25 May your bolts be of iron and
    bronze,
and your strength last as long as you
    live.

26 There is none like the God of
    Jeshurun
who rides the heavens to your help,
riding the clouds in his glory,

who humbled the gods of old   27
and subdued*f* the ancient powers;
who drove out the enemy before you
and gave the word to destroy.
Israel lives in security,   28
the tribes of Jacob by themselves,
in a land of corn and wine*g*
where the skies drip with dew.
Happy are you, people of Israel,   29
    peerless, set free;
the LORD is the shield that guards
    you,
the Blessed One is your glorious
    sword.
Your enemies come cringing to you,
and you shall trample their bodies
    under foot.

The death of Moses

THEN MOSES WENT UP FROM THE LOW-   **34**
lands of Moab to Mount Nebo, to the
top of Pisgah, eastwards from Jericho,
and the LORD showed him the whole
land. Gilead as far as Dan, the whole of 2
Naphtali; the territory of Ephraim and
Manasseh, and all Judah as far as the
western sea; the Negeb and the Plain; 3
the valley of Jericho, the Vale of Palm
Trees, as far as Zoar. The LORD said to 4
him, 'This is the land which I swore to
Abraham, Isaac and Jacob that I would
give to their descendants. I have let you
see it with your own eyes, but you shall
not cross over into it.'
    There in the land of Moab Moses the 5
servant of the LORD died, as the LORD
had said. He was buried in a valley in 6
Moab opposite Beth-peor, but to this
day no one knows his burial-place.
Moses was a hundred and twenty years 7
old when he died; his sight was not
dimmed nor had his vigour failed. The 8
Israelites wept for Moses in the lowlands of Moab for thirty days; then the

d draw out: prob. rdg.; Heb. obscure.
e Or of.
f Prob. rdg.; Heb. under.
g Or new wine.

17: *Ephraim; Manasseh:* see Gen.49.22 n. **19:** *Mountain:* possibly Mount Tabor (Judg.4.12–14;
Hos.5.1). **20:** *Tearing an arm:* see Gen.49.19 n. **23:** *Sea:* of Galilee.
   34.1–12: The death of Moses, which resumes the narrative from 32.52. Vv. 1–6 may once have
concluded the account of the division of the territory east of the Jordan (Num. ch. 32) and have
become separated from it by the later insertion of other traditions. **1:** *Nebo:* (32.49); *Pisgah*
(3.27): either variant traditions have been combined, or *Pisgah* is the very peak of *Nebo*.
4: See Gen.12.7; 28.13. **5:** See 32.50; Josh.1.1–2. **7:** *A hundred and twenty years:* see 31.2 n.

time of mourning for Moses was
9 ended. And Joshua son of Nun was
filled with the spirit of wisdom, for
Moses had laid his hands on him, and
the Israelites listened to him and did
what the LORD had commanded Moses.
10 There has never yet risen in Israel a
prophet like Moses, whom the LORD

knew face to face: remember all the 11
signs and portents which the LORD sent
him to show in Egypt to Pharaoh and
all his servants and the whole land;
remember the strong hand of Moses 12
and the terrible deeds which he did in
the sight of all Israel.

9: See 31.7–8, 14–15,23. 10: *Face to face:* See Exod.33.11 and Num.12.6–8. While on the surface
the meaning is that Moses was able to see the invisible Deity, it is likely that this is not the intent;
the intent, rather, is to speak of the unique stature of Moses. The thought that a Moses could
see the Deity is a relic of early times, before the view matured that the Deity is invisible.

THE BOOK OF
JOSHUA

This book, the story of the conquest of Canaan, follows on the wanderings in the Wilderness. Modern criticism considers Joshua to be part of a unique and extensive history, a writing that carried on the account of the Wilderness period in Deuteronomy and that included Joshua, Judges, Samuel, and Kings; the entirety is known as the "Deuteronomic history." Joshua begins with the crossing of the Jordan River and the destruction of Jericho (chs. 1–6). The conquest of the south through battles and alliances is next described (chs. 7–10). A final battle at Hazor in the north completes the conquest (ch. 11). After a short summary of Joshua's triumphs (ch. 12), the account deals with the division of the land among the tribes (chs. 13–22). The final two chapters present Joshua's farewell discourse, the covenant ceremony at Shechem, and the death of Joshua (chs. 23–24). God is pictured as closely involved in the events; he is a God of Battles, whose power is clearly manifested in the conquest.

Comparison with the Book of Judges indicates that the story of the conquest in Joshua is very much idealized and that the conquest was, in fact, quite complicated and much less decisive and less complete (see 13.1–6 and 17.12–18) than the book repeatedly suggests.

Israel's entry into the promised land

1 AFTER THE DEATH OF MOSES THE servant of the LORD, the LORD said to Joshua son of Nun, his 2 assistant, 'My servant Moses is dead; now it is for you to cross the Jordan, you and this whole people of Israel, to the land which I am giving them. 3 Every place where you set foot is yours: I have given it to you, as I promised 4 Moses. From the desert and the Lebanon to the great river, the river Euphrates, and across all the Hittite country westwards to the Great Sea,*a* 5 all this shall be your land. No one will ever be able to stand against you: as I was with Moses, so will I be with you; I will not fail you or forsake you. 6 Be strong, be resolute; it is you who are to put this people in possession of the land which I swore to give to their 7 fathers. Only be strong and resolute; observe diligently all the law which my servant Moses has given you.

You must not turn from it to right or left, if you would prosper wherever you go. This book of the law must 8 ever be on your lips; you must keep it in mind day and night so that you may diligently observe all that is written in it. Then you will prosper and be successful in all that you do. This is 9 my command: be strong, be resolute; do not be fearful or dismayed, for the LORD your God is with you wherever you go.' Then Joshua told the officers 10 to pass through the camp and give this 11 order to the people: 'Get food ready to take with you; for within three days you will be crossing the Jordan to occupy the country which the LORD your God is giving you to possess.' To the Reubenites, the Gadites, and 12 the half tribe of Manasseh, Joshua said, 'Remember the command which 13 Moses the servant of the LORD gave you when he said, "The LORD your God will grant you security here and will

a Or the Mediterranean Sea.

1.1–12.24: Israel's entry into the promised land.

1.1–9: The command to conquer the land. The invasion of Canaan came *after the death of Moses:* he had been forbidden to lead it (Num.20.12). *Joshua* was from the tribe of Ephraim (Num.13.8,16). 2: *Jordan:* this river was the eastern boundary of Canaan. 4: The extent of the promised land (see Gen.15.18; Deut.1.7) is here: the *desert* to the south; the *Lebanon* mountains to the northwest; *the river Euphrates* to the east; *the Hittite country,* northern Syria, at one time part of the Hittite empire; *westwards to the Great Sea,* the Mediterranean. This extent exceeds considerably the boundaries indicated by chs. 13–19 and Judg.20.1. 7–8: *This book of the law* refers to the Book of Deut., which teaches that fidelity to the law brings prosperity (see Deut. ch. 6).

1.10–18: Preparations for the invasion. 12: *The Reubenites, the Gadites, and the half tribe of Manasseh* were Transjordanian tribes (see Num. ch. 32 and 32.1–42 n.), who would return home after the conquest (v. 15). The conquest, according to the Book of Joshua, is the work of the entire people; in Judg. it is the work of isolated tribes.

14 give you this territory." Your wives and dependants and your herds may stay east of the Jordan in the territory which Moses has given you, but for yourselves, all the warriors among you must cross over as a fighting force at the head of your kinsmen. You must
15 help them, until the LORD grants them security like you and they too take possession of the land which the LORD your God is giving them. You may then return to the land which is your own possession, the territory which Moses the servant of the LORD has given you east of the Jordan.'
16 They answered Joshua, 'Whatever you tell us, we will do; wherever you
17 send us, we will go. As we obeyed Moses, so will we obey you; and may the LORD your God be with you as he
18 was with Moses! Whoever rebels against your authority, and fails to carry out all your orders, shall be put to death. Only be strong and resolute.'

2 Joshua son of Nun sent two spies out from Shittim secretly with orders to reconnoitre the country. The two men came to Jericho and went to the house of a prostitute named Rahab, and spent
2 the night there. It was reported to the king of Jericho that some Israelites had arrived that night to explore the
3 country. So the king sent to Rahab and said, 'Bring out the men who have come to you and are now in your house; they are here to explore the
4 whole country.' The woman, who had taken the two men and hidden them,[b] replied, 'Yes, the men did come to me, but I did not know where they
5 came from; and when it was time to shut the gate at nightfall, they had gone. I do not know where they were going, but if you hurry after them, you will
6 catch them up.' In fact, she had taken them up on to the roof and concealed them among the stalks of flax which she
7 had laid out there in rows. The messengers went in pursuit of them down the road to the fords of the Jordan, and the gate was closed as soon as they had gone out. The men had not yet 8 settled down, when Rahab came up to them on the roof and said to them, 'I 9 know that the LORD has given this land to you, that terror of you has descended upon us all, and that because of you the whole country is panic-stricken. For we have heard how the LORD dried 10 up the water of the Red Sea[c] before you when you came out of Egypt, and what you did to Sihon and Og, the two Amorite kings beyond the Jordan, whom you put to death. When we heard 11 this, our courage failed us; your coming has left no spirit in any of us; for the LORD your God is God in heaven above and on earth below. Swear to me now by the LORD that you 12 will keep faith with my family, as I have kept faith with you. Give me a token of good faith; promise that you 13 will spare the lives of my father and mother, my brothers and sisters and all who belong to them, and save us from death.' The men replied, 'Our lives for 14 yours, so long as you do not betray our business. When the LORD gives us the country, we will deal honestly and faithfully by you.' She then let them 15 down through an opening by a rope; for the house where she lived was on an angle of the wall. 'Take to the hills,' 16 she said, 'or the pursuers will come upon you. Hide yourselves there for three days until they come back, and then go on your way.' The men warned 17 her that they would be released from the oath she had made them take unless 18 she did what they told her. 'When we enter the land,' they said, 'you must fasten this strand of scarlet cord in the opening through which you have lowered us, and get everybody together here in the house, your father and mother, your brothers and all your family. If anybody goes out of doors 19

b Prob. rdg.; Heb. him.　　c Or the Sea of Reeds.

2.1–24: The spies at Jericho and Rahab. Since Rahab was a prostitute, visitors to her could fail to arouse attention. **1:** *Shittim:* the Israelite camp, in the lowlands of Moab just east of the Jordan (Num.33.49). *Jericho* was the main city in the lower Jordan valley and guarded the westward way to the central highlands. Archaeologists have not yet succeeded in finding any definite remains of the Jericho of Joshua's time. **10:** *Sihon and Og:* see Num.21.21–35. **11:** Rahab's profession of faith has a Deuteronomic ring to it; see Deut.4.39. Heb.11.31 emphasizes Rahab's faith; Jas.2.25, her works. **17–21:** These verses are considered by some to be a fragment from a separate tradition. **18:** The *scarlet cord* is not mentioned after v. 21.

into the street, his blood shall be on his own head; we shall be quit of the oath. But if a hand is laid on anyone who stays indoors with you, his blood 20 shall be on our heads. Remember too that, if you betray our business, then we shall be quit of the oath you have 21 made us take.' She replied, 'It shall be as you say', and sent them away. They set off, and she fastened the strand of scarlet cord in the opening. 22 The men made their way into the hills and stayed there three days until the pursuers returned. They had searched all along the road, but had not found 23 them.*d* The two men then turned and came down from the hills, crossed the river and returned to Joshua son of Nun. They told him all that had 24 happened to them and said to him, 'The LORD has put the whole country into our hands, and now all its people are panic-stricken at our approach.'

3 Joshua rose early in the morning, and he and all the Israelites set out from Shittim and came to the Jordan, where they encamped before crossing 2 the river. At the end of three days the 3 officers passed through the camp, and gave this order to the people: 'When you see the Ark of the Covenant of the LORD your God being carried forward by the levitical priests, then you too shall leave your positions and set out. 4 Follow it, but do not go close to it; keep some distance behind, about a thousand yards. This will show you the way you are to go, for you have not 5 travelled this way before.' Joshua then said to the people, 'Hallow yourselves, for tomorrow the LORD will do 6 a great miracle among you.' To the priests he said, 'Lift up the Ark of the Covenant and pass in front of the people.' So they lifted up the Ark of

the Covenant and went in front of the people. Then the LORD said to 7 Joshua, 'Today I will begin to make you stand high in the eyes of all Israel, and they shall know that I will be with you as I was with Moses. Give orders 8 to the priests who carry the Ark of the Covenant, and tell them that when they come to the edge of the waters of the Jordan, they are to take their stand in the river.'

Then Joshua said to the Israelites, 9 'Come here and listen to the words of the LORD your God. By this you shall 10 know that the living God is among you and that he will drive out before you the Canaanites, the Hittites, the Hivites, the Perizzites, the Girgashites, the Amorites, and the Jebusites: the 11 Ark of the Covenant of the LORD,*e* the lord of all the earth, is to cross Jordan at your head. Choose twelve 12 men from the tribes of Israel, one man from each tribe. When the priests 13 carrying the Ark of the LORD, the lord of all the earth, set foot in the waters of the Jordan, then the waters of the Jordan will be cut off; the water coming down from upstream will stand piled up like a bank.' So the people set out from 14 their tents to cross the Jordan, with the priests in front of them carrying the Ark of the Covenant. Now the Jordan is in 15 full flood in all its reaches throughout the time of harvest. When the priests reached the Jordan and dipped their feet in the water at the edge, the water 16 coming down from upstream was brought to a standstill; it piled up like a bank for a long way back, as far as Adam, a town near Zarethan. The waters coming down to the Sea of the

d three days ... found them: *or* three days while the pursuers scoured the land and searched all along the road, but did not find them.
e of the LORD: prob. rdg., cp. verse 17; Heb. om.

3.1–17: The crossing of the Jordan. In 3.1–5.12 there is a deliberate general parallelism with the account of the crossing of the Red Sea in Exod. **3:** *The Ark of the Covenant* was a sign of the presence of God (Exod.25.8,10 nn.); it was carried into battle as a war palladium, a "safeguard" (see Num.10.35–36; 1 Sam.4.3–22). *Levitical priests:* see Num.3.6–10. **4:** *Keep some distance behind:* to show reverence to the Ark and to the presence of God; see 2 Sam.6.6–7. **5:** *Hallow yourselves:* refers to a ritual purification before a religious ceremony; see Exod. 19.10,15. **10:** On these peoples, see Deut.7.1; Gen.10.15–20. **13:** *Piled up like a bank* recalls Exod.14.22; see 4.23. Some scholars regard this incident as a ceremony commemorating the crossing of the Red Sea. **15:** *Throughout the time of harvest:* in the spring, the melting snow of Mount Hermon brings the *Jordan* to full flood. **16:** *Adam* is about eighteen miles north of Jericho; *Zarethan* is about twelve miles farther north. *Arabah:* the extensive geological depression in which the Jordan and the Dead Sea, and areas further south, were situated. It is often rendered "desert."

Arabah, the Dead Sea, were completely cut off, and the people crossed over
17 opposite Jericho. The priests carrying the Ark of the Covenant of the LORD stood firm on the dry bed in the middle of the Jordan; and all Israel passed over on dry ground until the whole nation had crossed the river.

4 WHEN THE WHOLE NATION HAD FIN- ished crossing the Jordan, the LORD
2 said to Joshua, 'Take twelve men from
3 the people, one from each tribe, and order them to lift up twelve stones from this place, out of the middle of the Jordan, where the feet of the priests stood firm. They are to carry them across and set them down in the
4 camp where you spend the night.' Josh- ua summoned the twelve men whom he had chosen out of the Israelites,
5 one man from each tribe, and said to them, 'Cross over in front of the Ark of the LORD your God as far as the middle of the Jordan, and let each of you take a stone and hoist it on his shoulder, one for each of the tribes
6 of Israel. These stones are to stand as a memorial among you; and in days to come, when your children ask you
7 what these stones mean, you shall tell them how the waters of the Jordan were cut off before the Ark of the Covenant of the LORD when it crossed the Jordan. Thus these stones will always be a reminder to the Israelites.'
8 The Israelites did as Joshua had commanded: they lifted up twelve stones from the middle of the Jordan, as the LORD had instructed Joshua, one for each of the tribes of Israel, carried them across to the camp and set them down there.
9 Joshua set up twelve stones in the middle of the Jordan at the place where the priests stood who carried the Ark of the Covenant, and there
10 they are to this day. The priests carrying the Ark remained standing in the middle of the Jordan until every command

which the LORD had told Joshua to give to the people was fulfilled, and the people had made good speed across.
11 When all the people had finished cross- ing, then the Ark of the LORD crossed,
12 and the priests with it.*f* At the head of the Israelites, there crossed over the Reubenites, the Gadites, and the half tribe of Manasseh, as a fighting force, as Moses had told them to do;
13 about forty thousand strong, drafted for active service, they crossed over to the lowlands of Jericho in the presence of the LORD to do battle.
14 That day the LORD made Joshua stand very high in the eyes of all Israel, and the people revered him, as they had revered Moses all his life.
15,16 The LORD said to Joshua, 'Com- mand the priests carrying the Ark of the Tokens to come up from the
17 Jordan.' So Joshua commanded the priests to come up from the Jordan;
18 and when the priests carrying the Ark of the Covenant of the LORD came up from the river-bed, they had no sooner set foot on dry land than the waters of the Jordan came back to their place and filled up all its reaches
19 as before. On the tenth day of the first month the people came up out of the Jordan and camped in Gilgal in the
20 district east of Jericho, and there Joshua set up the twelve stones which they had taken from the Jordan. He
21 said to the Israelites, 'In days to come, when your descendants ask their
22 fathers what these stones mean, you shall explain that the Jordan was dry
23 when Israel crossed over, and that the LORD your God dried up the waters of the Jordan in front of you until you had gone across, just as the LORD your God did at the Red Sea when he dried it up for us until we had
24 crossed. Thus all people on earth will know how strong is the hand of the LORD; and thus they will stand in awe of the LORD your God for ever.'

f Prob. rdg.; Heb. adds before the people.

4.1–5.1: **Twelve memorial stones.** There are traces of two traditions: one speaks of twelve stones to be set up at Gilgal (4.1–8), the other of twelve stones set up in the Jordan (9–13). **12:** The Transjordanian tribes crossed first. **19:** *The first month* was Abib (March–April), later called Nisan (Exod.12.2 n.). *Gilgal* was somewhere near Jericho; later it became an important sanctuary in the tribe of Benjamin (see 1 Sam.11.15; 2 Sam.19.15,40). Amos (4.4; 5.5) and Hos. (4.15; 9.15; 12.11) spoke against the worship there.

5 When all the Amorite kings to the west of Jordan and all the Canaanite kings by the sea-coast heard that the LORD had dried up the waters before the advance of the Israelites until they had crossed, their courage melted away and there was no more spirit left in them for fear of the Israelites.

2 At that time the LORD said to Joshua, 'Make knives of flint, seat yourself, and make Israel a circumcised people 3 again.' Joshua thereupon made knives of flint and circumcised the Israelites 4 at Gibeath-haaraloth.*g* This is why Joshua circumcised them: all the males who came out of Egypt, all the fighting men, had died in the wilderness on the 5 journey from Egypt. The people who came out of Egypt had all been circumcised, but not those who had been born in the wilderness during 6 the journey. For the Israelites travelled in the wilderness for forty years, until the whole nation, all the fighting men among them, had passed away, all who came out of Egypt and had disobeyed the voice of the LORD. The LORD swore that he would not allow any of these to see the land which he had sworn to their fathers to give us, a land 7 flowing with milk and honey. So it was their sons, whom he had raised up in their place, that Joshua circumcised; they were uncircumcised because they had not been circumcised on the 8 journey. When the circumcision of the whole nation was complete, they stayed where they were in camp until they 9 had recovered. The LORD then said to Joshua, 'Today I have rolled away from you the reproaches of the Egyp-

tians.' Therefore the place is called Gilgal*h* to this very day.

The Israelites encamped in Gilgal, 10 and at sunset on the fourteenth day of the month they kept the Passover in the lowlands of Jericho. On the day 11 after the Passover, they ate their unleavened cakes and parched grain, and that day it was the produce of the country. It was from that day, when 12 they first ate the produce of the country, that the manna ceased. The Israelites received no more manna; and that year they ate what had grown in the land of Canaan.

When Joshua came near Jericho he 13 looked up and saw a man standing in front of him with a drawn sword in his hand. Joshua went up to him and said, 'Are you for us or for our enemies?' And the man said to him, 'I am here as 14 captain of the army of the LORD.' Joshua fell down before him, face to the ground, and said, 'What have you to say to your servant, my lord?' The 15 captain of the LORD's army said to him, 'Take off your sandals; the place where you are standing is holy'; and Joshua did so.

JERICHO WAS BOLTED AND BARRED **6** against the Israelites; no one went out, no one came in. The LORD said to 2 Joshua, 'Look, I have delivered Jericho and her king*i* into your hands. You 3 shall march round the city with all your fighting men, making the circuit of it once, for six days running. Seven priests 4 shall go in front of the Ark carrying

g *That is* the Hill of Foreskins.
h *That is* Rolling Stones.
i *Prob. rdg.; Heb. adds* the fighting men.

5.2–9: Circumcision of Israelites at Gilgal. Circumcision was primitively a rite of initiation for marriage and for admission into full membership in the community; in the later traditions of Israel it became a sign of God's covenant relationship with his people (Gen.17.9–14 n.); it took on its full importance with the Babylonian Exile. **2:** *Knives of flint:* used because religious ceremonies tend to preserve ancient ways of doing things; the Israelites were already familiar with the use of metal. *A circumcised people again:* see vv. 4–7. **3:** *Gibeath-haaraloth* means "the hill of the foreskins." **6:** *Until the whole nation, all the fighting men, had passed away:* see Num.14.20–38. **9:** *Reproaches:* the allusion is unclear; possibly the reproaches were for being uncircumcised. The Heb. contains a pun, *Gilgal* and *rolled away*. The meaning of Gilgal is "circle" (of stones), a circle recalling a wheel which can roll.

5.10–12: Passover at Gilgal. 10: The first Passover in Canaan. **12:** On *manna* see Exod. ch. 16 and notes.

5.13–15: A theophany. Joshua meets *the captain of the army of the LORD* (compare Num.22.22; 2 Kgs.6.17). The story is fragmentary, for a sequel seems expected, but is not given (compare Exod.3.5–12).

6.1–27: The capture of Jericho. The divine mandate was for the Israelites to march around the city once a day for six days, carrying the Ark and blowing trumpets. On the seventh day the procession moved around the city seven times; then, the shout of the Israelites was enough to

seven trumpets made from rams' horns. On the seventh day you shall march round the city seven times and the priests shall blow their trumpets. 5 At the blast of the rams' horns, when you hear the trumpet sound, the whole army shall raise a great shout; the wall of the city will collapse and the army shall advance, every man straight 6 ahead.' So Joshua son of Nun summoned the priests and gave them their orders: 'Take up the Ark of the Covenant; let seven priests with seven trumpets of ram's horn go in front of 7 the Ark of the LORD.' Then he said to the army, 'March on and make the circuit of the city, and let the men drafted from the two and a half tribes go in front of the Ark of the LORD.' 8 When Joshua had spoken to the army, the seven priests carrying the seven trumpets of ram's horn before the LORD passed on and blew the trumpets, with the Ark of the Covenant of the 9 LORD following them. The drafted men marched in front of the priests who blew the trumpets, and the rearguard followed the Ark, the trumpets sound- 10 ing as they marched. But Joshua ordered the army not to shout, or to raise their voices or utter a word, till the day came when he would tell them to shout; then they were to give a loud 11 shout. Thus he caused the Ark of the LORD to go round the city, making the circuit of it once, and then they went back to the camp and spent the night 12 there. Joshua rose early in the morning and the priests took up the Ark of the 13 LORD. The seven priests carrying the seven trumpets of ram's horn went marching in front of the Ark of the LORD, blowing the trumpets as they went, with the drafted men in front of them and the rearguard following the Ark of the LORD, the trumpets 14 sounding as they marched. They marched round the city once on the second day and returned to the camp; 15 this they did for six days. But on the seventh day they rose at dawn and marched seven times round the city in the same way; that was the only day on which they marched round seven times. The seventh time the priests blew 16 the trumpets and Joshua said to the army, 'Shout! The LORD has given you the city. The city shall be under 17 solemn ban: everything in it belongs to the LORD. No one is to be spared except the prostitute Rahab and everyone who is with her in the house, because she hid the men whom we sent. And you 18 must beware of coveting anything that is forbidden under the ban; you must take none of it for yourselves; this would put the Israelite camp itself under the ban and bring trouble on it. All the 19 silver and gold, all the vessels of copper and iron, shall be holy; they belong to the LORD and they must go into the LORD's treasury.' So they blew 20 the trumpets, and when the army heard the trumpet sound, they raised a great shout, and down fell the walls. The army advanced on the city, every man straight ahead, and took it. Under the 21 ban they destroyed everything in the city; they put everyone to the sword, men and women, young and old, and also cattle, sheep, and asses.

But the two men who had been sent 22 out as spies were told by Joshua to go into the prostitute's house and bring out her and all who belonged to her, as they had sworn to do. So the young 23 men went and brought out Rahab, her father and mother, her brothers and all who belonged to her. They brought out the whole family and left them outside the Israelite camp. They 24 then set fire to the city and everything in it, except that they deposited the silver and gold and the vessels of copper and iron in the treasury of the LORD's house. Thus Joshua spared the lives 25 of Rahab the prostitute, her household and all who belonged to her, because she had hidden the men whom Joshua had sent to Jericho as spies;

---

overthrow the walls; on Jericho see 2.1 n. **4:** *Seven*, often a sacred number, occurs repeatedly in this chapter. **5:** The *shout* is part of the ritual of the Ark (see Num.10.5–9; 1 Sam.4.5; 2 Sam. 6.15). **17:** *Solemn ban* is a technical term meaning that the city and all that is in it is to be offered as a holocaust to God (see v. 21); no booty is allowed to be taken (but see 8.2) and any deviation would be a sacrilege to be severely punished (see v. 18; 7.1; 1 Sam.15.14–23); the only exception is mentioned in vv. 19 and 24. **24:** *The* LORD'*s house* is an anachronism, since

she and her family settled permanently
26 among the Israelites. It was then that
Joshua laid this curse on Jericho:

May the LORD's curse light on the
    man who comes forward
to rebuild this city of Jericho:
the laying of its foundations shall
    cost him his eldest son,
the setting up of its gates shall cost
    him his youngest.

27   Thus the LORD was with Joshua,
and his fame spread throughout the
country.
7   But the Israelites defied the ban:
Achan son of Carmi, son of Zabdi,
son of Zerah, of the tribe of Judah,
took some of the forbidden things, and
the LORD was angry with the Israelites.
2   Joshua sent men from Jericho with
orders to go up to Ai, near Beth-aven,
east of Bethel, and see how the land
lay; so the men went up and explored
3 Ai. They returned to Joshua and
reported that there was no need for the
whole army to move: 'Let some two
or three thousand men go forward to
attack Ai. Do not make the whole army
toil up there; the population is small.'
4 And so about three thousand men
went up, but they turned tail before the
5 men of Ai, who killed some thirty-six
of them; they chased them all the
way from the gate to the Quarries*j* and
killed them on the pass. At this the
courage of the people melted and
6 flowed away like water. Joshua and the
elders of Israel rent their clothes and
flung themselves face downwards to the
ground; they lay before the Ark of the
LORD till evening and threw dust on
7 their heads. Joshua said, 'Alas, O
Lord GOD, why didst thou bring this
people across the Jordan only to hand
us over to the Amorites to be destroyed? If only we had been content

to settle on the other side of the
Jordan! I beseech thee, O Lord; what 8
can I say, now that Israel has been
routed by the enemy? When the 9
Canaanites and all the natives of the
country hear of this, they will come
swarming around us and wipe us off
the face of the earth. What wilt thou
do then for the honour of thy great
name?'
    The LORD said to Joshua, 'Stand 10
up; why lie prostrate on your face?
Israel has sinned: they have broken 11
the covenant which I laid upon them,
by taking forbidden things for themselves. They have stolen them, and
concealed it by mingling them with
their own possessions. That is why 12
the Israelites cannot stand against their
enemies: they are put to flight because
they have brought themselves under
the ban. Unless they destroy every
single thing among them that is forbidden under the ban, I will be with
them no longer. Stand up; you must 13
hallow the people; tell them they must
hallow themselves for tomorrow. Tell
them, These are the words of the
LORD the God of Israel: You have forbidden things among you, Israel; you
cannot stand against your enemies
until you have rid yourselves of them.
In the morning come forward tribe by 14
tribe, and the tribe which the LORD
chooses shall come forward clan by
clan; the clan which the LORD chooses
shall come forward family by family;
and the family which the LORD chooses
shall come forward man by man.
The man who is chosen as the har- 15
bourer of forbidden things shall be
burnt, he and all that is his, because he
has broken the covenant of the LORD
and committed outrage in Israel.'
Early in the morning Joshua rose and 16
brought Israel forward tribe by tribe,
j Or to Shebarim.

the Temple did not yet exist. **26:** The fulfillment of this curse is narrated in 1 Kgs.16.34.
    7.1–26: The setback at Ai. 1: This verse foreshadows the narrative in vv. 6–21. **2:** *Ai* was in
the central highlands northwest of Jericho. Archaeology indicates that it was in ruins (for
Ai means "ruin") in Joshua's time, yet these ruins could have served as an outpost for Bethel
(MT adds Bethel in 8.17). Many scholars think that there was behind this story a battle for the
important site, *Bethel*, and not for Ai; the Book of Joshua, otherwise, has no account of the
capture of Bethel (but see Judg.1.22–26). *Beth-aven* means "house of wickedness," referring to
Bethel in Hos.4.15 (see Amos 5.5); some regard *near Beth-aven* as a gloss. **11:** That *Israel has
sinned* because one man (see v. 1) has trespassed reflects the ancient unitary view of society.
14: *The LORD chooses:* probably by the casting of lots; on sacred lots see Exod.28.15 n.; 1 Sam.

and the tribe of Judah was chosen.
17 He brought forward the clans of
Judah, and the clan of Zerah was
chosen; then the clan of Zerah family
by family, and the family of Zabdi
18 was chosen. He brought that family
forward man by man, and Achan son
of Carmi, son of Zabdi, son of Zerah,
of the tribe of Judah, was chosen.
19 Then Joshua said to Achan, 'My son,
give honour to the LORD the God of
Israel and make your confession to
him: tell me what you have done,
20 hide nothing from me.' Achan answered
Joshua, 'I confess, I have sinned against
the LORD the God of Israel. This is what
21 I did: among the booty I caught sight
of a fine mantle from Shinar, two
hundred shekels of silver, and a bar
of gold weighing fifty shekels. I
coveted them and I took them. You
will find them hidden in the ground
inside my tent, with the silver under-
22 neath.' So Joshua sent messengers,
who ran to the tent, and there was the
stuff*k* hidden in the tent with the
23 silver underneath. They took the
things from the tent, brought them
to Joshua and all the Israelites, and
24 spread them out before the LORD. Then
Joshua took Achan son of Zerah, with
the silver, the mantle, and the bar of
gold, together with his sons and his
daughters, his oxen, his asses, and his
sheep, his tent, and everything he had,
and he and all Israel brought them up
25 to the Vale of Achor.*l* Joshua said,
'What trouble you have brought on us!
Now the LORD will bring trouble on
you.' Then all the Israelites stoned
26 him to death; and they raised a great
pile of stones over him, which remains
to this day. So the LORD's anger was
abated. That is why to this day that place
is called the Vale of Achor.

8 THE LORD SAID TO JOSHUA, 'DO NOT
be fearful or dismayed; take the whole

army and attack Ai. I deliver the king
of Ai into your hands, him and his
people, his city and his country. Deal 2
with Ai and her king as you dealt with
Jericho and her king; but you may
keep for yourselves the cattle and any
other spoil that you may take. Set an
ambush for the city to the west of it.'
So Joshua and all the army prepared 3
for the assault on Ai. He chose thirty
thousand fighting men and dispatched
them by night, with these orders: 'Lie 4
in ambush to the west of the city, not
far from it, and all of you hold yourselves in readiness. I myself will 5
approach the city with the rest of the
army, and when the enemy come out to
meet us as they did last time, we shall
take to flight before them. Then they 6
will come out and pursue us until we
have drawn them away from the city,
thinking that we have taken to flight
as we did last time. While we are in
flight, come out from your ambush 7
and occupy the city; the LORD your God
will deliver it into your hands. When 8
you have taken it, set it on fire. Thus
you will do what the LORD commands. These are your orders.' So 9
Joshua sent them off, and they went
to the place of ambush and waited
between Bethel and Ai to the west of
Ai, while Joshua spent the night with
the army.

Early in the morning Joshua rose, 10
mustered the army and marched
against Ai, he himself and the elders
of Israel at its head. All the armed 11
forces with him marched on until
they came within sight of the city. They
encamped north of Ai, with the valley
between them and the city; but Joshua 12
took some five thousand men and
set them in ambush between Bethel
and Ai to the west of the city.*m* When 14

k Or the mantle.
l That is Trouble.
m So Sept.; Heb. adds (13) So the army pitched camp to
the north of the city, and the rearguard to the west,
while Joshua went that night into the valley.

14.40–42. **24–25:** The unitary concept of society required that Achan and all he had be purged
from Israel (see Num.16.16–35). *Achor:* a pun, for it is from the same root as the Heb. word
trouble (see Hos.2.15). **26:** *A great pile of stones* marked the burial places of criminals (see 8.29;
10.27; 2 Sam.18.17). *To this day:* a fixed formula in stories told to explain curious surviving
facts, names, and institutions (see 4.9; 8.28–29; 9.27; 10.27).
  8.1–29: Victory at Ai. Israel, now free from Achan's guilt, easily captures and destroys Ai
by a clever stratagem. **9:** *Bethel,* later one of the chief shrines of the Northern Kingdom (1 Kgs.
12.28–30; see also Gen.28.10–22), is about one and one-quarter miles northwest of Ai; see 7.2 n.
12: *Five thousand:* thirty thousand is the figure in v. 3. **13:** See Tfn. *m.* **15:** *Towards the wilder-*

the king of Ai saw them, he and the citizens rose with all speed that morning and marched out to do battle against Israel; he did not know that there was an ambush set for him 15 to the west of the city. Joshua and all the Israelites made as if they were routed by them and fled towards the 16 wilderness, and all the people in the city were called out in pursuit. So they pursued Joshua and were drawn away 17 from the city. Not a man was left in Ai; they had all gone out in pursuit of the Israelites and during the pursuit had left the city undefended.

18   Then the LORD said to Joshua, 'Point towards Ai with the dagger you are holding, for I will deliver the city into your hands.' So Joshua pointed with his 19 dagger towards Ai. At his signal, the men in ambush rose quickly from their places and, entering the city at a run, took it and promptly set fire to it. 20 The men of Ai looked back and saw the smoke from the city already going up to the sky; they were powerless to make their escape in any direction, and the Israelites who had feigned flight towards the wilderness turned on their 21 pursuers. For when Joshua and all the Israelites saw that the ambush had seized the city and that smoke was already going up from it, they turned and fell upon the men of Ai. 22 Those who had come out to meet the Israelites were now hemmed in with Israelites on both sides of them, and the Israelites cut them down until there was not a single survivor, nor 23 had any escaped. The king of Ai was taken alive and brought to Joshua. 24 When the Israelites had cut down to the last man all the citizens of Ai who were in the open country or in the wilderness to which they had pursued them, and the massacre was complete, they all turned back to Ai and put it 25 to the sword. The number who were killed that day, men and women, was

twelve thousand, the whole population of Ai. Joshua held out his dagger and 26 did not draw back his hand until he had put to death all who lived in Ai; but the Israelites kept for themselves the 27 cattle and any other spoil that they took, following the word of the LORD spoken to Joshua. So Joshua burnt Ai to the 28 ground, and left it the desolate ruined mound it remains to this day. He hanged 29 the king of Ai on a tree and left him there till sunset; and when the sun had set, he gave the order and they cut him down and flung down his body at the entrance of the city gate. Over the body they raised a great pile of stones, which is there to this day.

At that time Joshua built an altar 30 to the LORD the God of Israel on Mount Ebal. The altar was of blocks 31 of undressed stone on which no tool of iron had been used, following the commands given to the Israelites by Moses the servant of the LORD, as is described in the book of the law of Moses. At the altar they offered whole-offerings to the LORD, and slaughtered share-offerings. There in 32 the presence of the Israelites he engraved on blocks[n] of stone a copy of the law of Moses. And all Israel, 33 elders, officers, and judges, took their stand on either side of the Ark, facing the levitical priests who carried the Ark of the Covenant of the LORD— all Israel, native and alien alike. Half of them stood facing Mount Gerizim and half facing Mount Ebal, to fulfil the command of Moses the servant of the LORD that the blessing should be pronounced first. Then Joshua 34 recited the whole of the blessing and the cursing word by word, as they are written in the book of the law. There 35 was not a single word of all that Moses had commanded which he did not read aloud before the whole congregation of Israel, including the

n Or on the blocks.

---

ness: eastward. **18:** *Point towards Ai with the dagger:* this is obviously not an ordinary signal (see v. 26) but a symbolic gesture (see Exod.17.8–13; 2 Kgs.13.14–19).
    8.30–35: Mount Ebal: the building of an altar and reading of the Law. These verses interrupt the story of the conquest and probably are not in their original position here (see ch. 24 for events in the same area). Josh. here carries out the prescriptions of Deut.27.4–13 (see also Deut.11.29–30). The events take place just west of Shechem, about twenty miles north of Ai, with Mount Ebal to the north and Mount Gerizim (v. 33) to the south.

women and dependants and the aliens resident in their company.

9 When the news of these happenings reached all the kings west of the Jordan, in the hill-country, the Shephelah, and all the coast of the Great Sea running up to the Lebanon, the kings of the Hittites, Amorites, Canaanites, 2 Perizzites, Hivites, and Jebusites agreed to join forces and fight against Joshua and Israel.

3 When the inhabitants of Gibeon heard how Joshua had dealt with 4 Jericho and Ai, they adopted a ruse of their own. They went and disguised themselves, with old sacking for their asses, old wine-skins split and 5 mended, old and patched sandals for their feet, old clothing to wear, and by way of provisions nothing but dry and 6 mouldy bread. They came to Joshua in the camp at Gilgal and said to him and the Israelites, 'We have come from a distant country to ask 7 you now to grant us a treaty.' The Israelites said to the Hivites, 'But maybe you live in our neighbourhood: if so, how can we grant you a treaty?' 8 They said to Joshua, 'We are your slaves.' Joshua asked them who they were and where they came from. 9 'Sir,' they replied, 'our country is very far away, and we have come because of the renown of the LORD your God. We have heard of his fame, of all that 10 he did to Egypt, and to the two Amorite kings east of the Jordan, Sihon king of Heshbon and Og king of Bashan who lived at Ashtaroth. 11 Our elders and all the people of our country told us to take provisions for the journey and come to meet you, and say, "We are your slaves; please 12 grant us a treaty." Look at our bread; it was hot from the oven when we packed it at home on the day we came 13 away. Now it is dry and mouldy. Look at the wine-skins; they were new when

we filled them, and now they are all split; look at our clothes and our sandals, worn out by the long jour- ney.' The chief men of the com- 14 munity accepted some of their provis- ions and did not at first seek guidance from the LORD. So Joshua received 15 them peaceably and granted them a treaty, promising to spare their lives, and the chiefs pledged their faith to them on oath.

Within three days of granting them 16 the treaty, the Israelites learnt that they were in fact neighbours and lived near by. So the Israelites set out 17 and on the third day they reached their cities; these were Gibeon, Kephi- rah, Beeroth, and Kiriath-jearim. The 18 Israelites did not slaughter them, because of the oath which the chief men of the community had sworn to them by the LORD the God of Israel, but the people were all indignant with their chiefs. The chiefs all replied to 19 the assembled people, 'But we swore an oath to them by the LORD the God of Israel; we cannot touch them now. What we will do is this: we will spare 20 their lives so that the oath which we swore to them may bring no harm upon us. But though their lives must be 21 spared, they shall be set to chop wood and draw water for the community.' The people agreed to do as their chiefs had said. Joshua summoned the 22 Gibeonites and said, 'Why did you play this trick on us? You told us that you live a long way off, when you are near neighbours. There is a curse upon 23 you for this: for all time you shall pro- vide us with slaves, to chop wood and draw water for the house of my God.' They answered Joshua. 'We were told, 24 sir, that the LORD your God had commanded Moses his servant to give you the whole country and to exterm- inate all its inhabitants; so because of you we were in terror of our lives, and

---

9.1–27: The stratagem of the Gibeonites. 1: The victories at Jericho and Ai lead to a coalition against Israel. 3–15: *The inhabitants of Gibeon* gained a treaty by pretending to be from *a distant country;* in Deut.20.10–18, Israel was permitted to make peace only with those who lived at a great distance; those near at hand were to be annihilated. *Gibeon* is modern El-Jib, about seven miles southwest of Ai; but the Gibeonites also dwelt in three neighboring cities (v. 17). 7: The Gibeonites are called *Hivites* (see 11.19); they were possibly an isolated non-Canaanite group. Their towns are listed in v. 17. 10: *Sihon and Og:* Num.21.21–35. 14: Sharing in the *provisions* would constitute a treaty. 20: An *oath* once made, even in error, could not be broken. 21: The Gibeonites were to perform menial services at the temple (see 1 Kgs.9.20–21;

25 that is why we did this. We are in your power: do with us whatever you think
26 right and proper.' What he did was this: he saved them from death at the hands of the Israelites, and they did not
27 kill them; but thenceforward he set them to chop wood and draw water for the community and for the altar of the LORD. And to this day they do it at the place which the LORD chose.

10 When Adoni-zedek king of Jerusalem heard that Joshua had captured Ai and destroyed it (for Joshua had dealt with Ai and her king as he had dealt with Jericho and her king), and that the inhabitants of Gibeon had made their peace with Israel and were living
2 among them, he was greatly alarmed; for Gibeon was a large place, like a royal city: it was larger than Ai, and
3 its men were all good fighters. So Adoni-zedek king of Jerusalem sent to Hoham king of Hebron, Piram king of Jarmuth, Japhia king of Lachish, and Debir king of Eglon, and said,
4 'Come up and help me, and we will attack the Gibeonites, because they have made their peace with Joshua and
5 the Israelites.' So the five Amorite kings, the kings of Jerusalem, Hebron, Jarmuth, Lachish, and Eglon, joined forces and advanced to take up their positions for the attack on Gibeon.
6 But the men of Gibeon sent this message to Joshua in the camp at Gilgal: 'We are your slaves, do not abandon us, come quickly to our relief. All the Amorite kings in the hill-country have joined forces against us;
7 come and help us.' So Joshua went up from Gilgal with all his forces and all
8 his fighting men. The LORD said to Joshua, 'Do not be afraid of them; I have delivered them into your hands,

and not a man will be able to stand against you.' Joshua came upon them 9 suddenly, after marching all night from Gilgal. The LORD threw them into con- 10 fusion before the Israelites, and Joshua defeated them utterly in Gibeon; he pursued them down the pass of Beth-horon and kept up the slaughter as far as Azekah and Makkedah. As they 11 were fleeing from Israel down the pass, the LORD hurled great hailstones at them out of the sky all the way to Azekah: more died from the hailstones than the Israelites slew by the sword.

On that day when the LORD de- 12 livered the Amorites into the hands of Israel, Joshua spoke with the LORD, and he said in the presence of Israel:

Stand still, O Sun, in Gibeon;
stand, Moon, in the Vale of Aijalon.

So the sun stood still and the moon 13 halted until a nation had taken vengeance on its enemies, as indeed is written in the Book of Jashar.*o* The sun stayed in mid heaven and made no haste to set for almost a whole day. Never before or since has there been 14 such a day as this day on which the LORD listened to the voice of a man; for the LORD fought for Israel. So 15 Joshua and all the Israelites returned to the camp at Gilgal.

The five kings fled and hid themselves 16 in a cave at Makkedah, and Joshua 17 was told that they had been found hidden in this cave. Joshua replied, 18 'Roll some great stones to the mouth of the cave and post men there to keep watch over the kings. But you must 19 not stay; keep up the pursuit, attack your enemies from the rear and do not

o Or the Book of the Upright.

Ezek.44.4–8 n.). **27:** *The place . . . chose:* a conventional allusion to Jerusalem in Deut. (e.g. 12.5) and related books.
    10.1–27: Israel's victory over the five kings. Joshua comes to the rescue of the Gibeonites when they are attacked by a coalition of five Amorite cities; the Israelite capture of Jericho and Ai impelled that coalition. **3:** *Hebron:* twenty miles south of Jerusalem. The other three places are about fifteen to thirty-five miles southwest of Jerusalem. **10:** *The pass of Beth-horon* led westward to the coastal plain. **11:** *More died from the hailstones than the Israelites slew* is the writer's way of expressing his belief that the victories were miracles accomplished by God's intervention rather than by military skill. **12:** *Aijalon* is about ten miles west of Gibeon. **13:** *Jashar:* "upright." *The Book of Jashar* was an ancient collection of Heb. poetry now lost (compare 2 Sam.1.18). The poetic imagery of *Stand still, O Sun . . .* is repeated literally in the prose to glorify the LORD, and Joshua too. **16–27:** The fugitive kings are captured, humiliated, and killed; their bodies were then returned to the caves in which they had hidden.

let them reach their cities; the LORD your God has delivered them into your
20 hands.' When Joshua and the Israelites had finished the work of slaughter and all had been put to the sword except a few survivors who escaped
21 and entered the fortified cities—the whole army rejoined Joshua at Makkedah in peace; not a man of the Israelites suffered so much as a scratch
22 on his tongue. Then Joshua said, 'Open the mouth of the cave, and bring me
23 out those five kings.' They did so; they brought the five kings out of the cave, the kings of Jerusalem, Hebron, Jar-
24 muth, Lachish, and Eglon. When they had brought them to Joshua, he summoned all the Israelites and said to the commanders of the troops who had served with him, 'Come forward and put your feet on the necks of these kings.' So they came forward and put
25 their feet on their necks. Joshua said to them, 'Do not be fearful or dismayed; be strong and resolute; for the LORD will do this to every enemy you
26 fight against.' And he struck down the kings and slew them; then he hung their bodies on five trees, where they
27 remained hanging till evening. At sunset, on Joshua's orders they took them down from the trees and threw them into the cave in which they had hidden; they piled great stones against its mouth, and there the stones are to this day.*p*
28 On that same day, Joshua captured Makkedah and put both king and people to the sword, destroying both them and every living thing in the city. He left no survivor, and he dealt with the king of Makkedah as he had
29 dealt with the king of Jericho. Then Joshua and all the Israelites marched on from Makkedah to Libnah and
30 attacked it. The LORD delivered the city and its king to the Israelites, and they put its people and every living thing in it to the sword; they left no survivor there, and dealt with its king as they had dealt with the king
31 of Jericho. From Libnah Joshua and all

the Israelites marched on to Lachish, took up their positions and attacked it. The LORD delivered Lachish into 32 their hands; they took it on the second day and put every living thing in it to the sword, as they had done at Libnah.

Meanwhile Horam king of Gezer 33 had advanced to the relief of Lachish; but Joshua struck them down, both king and people, and not a man of them survived. Then Joshua and all the 34 Israelites marched on from Lachish to Eglon, took up their positions and attacked it; that same day they 35 captured it and put its inhabitants to the sword, destroying every living thing in it as they had done at Lachish. From Eglon Joshua and all the 36 Israelites advanced to Hebron and attacked it. They captured it and put its 37 king to the sword together with every living thing in it and in all its villages; as at Eglon, he left no survivor, destroying it and every living thing in it. Then Joshua and all the Israelites 38 wheeled round towards Debir and attacked it. They captured the city 39 with its king, and all its villages, put them to the sword and destroyed every living thing; they left no survivor. They dealt with Debir and its king as they had dealt with Hebron and with Libnah and its king.

So Joshua massacred the population 40 of the whole region—the hill-country, the Negeb, the Shephelah, the watersheds—and all their kings. He left no survivor, destroying everything that drew breath, as the LORD the God of Israel had commanded. Joshua carried 41 the slaughter from Kadesh-barnea to Gaza, over the whole land of Goshen and as far as Gibeon. All these kings 42 he captured at the same time, and their country with them, for the LORD the God of Israel fought for Israel. And Joshua returned with all the 43 Israelites to the camp at Gilgal.

When Jabin king of Hazor heard of 11 all this, he sent to Jobab king of Madon, to the kings of Shimron and

p and there . . . day: or on this very day.

10.28–43: Summary of Joshua's conquests in the south. After the defeat of the five kings, Israel had no difficulty in conquering the whole of southern Palestine (but see 13.1–6).
11.1–23: The conquest of the north. When the northern Canaanite rulers, hearing of Israel's victories in the south, unite to oppose her, they are overwhelmingly defeated. **1:** *Hazor* was one

2 Akshaph, to the northern kings in the hill-country, in the Arabah opposite Kinnereth, in the Shephelah, and in the district of Dor on the west, 3 the Canaanites to the east and the west, the Amorites, Hittites, Perizzites, and Jebusites in the hill-country, and the Hivites below Hermon in the 4 land of Mizpah. They took the field with all their forces, a great horde countless as the grains of sand on the sea-shore, among them a great number 5 of horses and chariots. All these kings made common cause, and came and encamped at the waters of Merom to 6 fight against Israel. The LORD said to Joshua, 'Do not be afraid of them, for at this time tomorrow I shall deliver them to Israel all dead men; you shall hamstring their horses and burn their 7 chariots.' So Joshua and his army surprised them by the waters of 8 Merom and fell upon them. The LORD delivered them into the hands of Israel; they struck them down and pursued them as far as Greater Sidon, Misrephoth on the west, and the Vale of Mizpah on the east. They struck them down until not a man was 9 left alive. Joshua dealt with them as the LORD had commanded: he hamstrung their horses and burnt their chariots.

10   At this point Joshua turned his forces against Hazor, formerly the head of all these kingdoms. He captured the city and put its king to death with the 11 sword. They killed every living thing in it and wiped them all out; they spared nothing that drew breath, and 12 Hazor itself they destroyed by fire. So Joshua captured these kings and their cities and put them to the sword, destroying them all, as Moses the servant 13 of the LORD had commanded. The cities whose ruined mounds are still standing were not burnt by the Israel-

ites; it was Hazor alone that Joshua burnt. The Israelites plundered all these 14 cities and kept for themselves the cattle and any other spoil they took; but they put every living soul to the sword until they had destroyed every one; they did not leave alive any one that drew breath. The LORD laid his com- 15 mands on his servant Moses, and Moses laid these same commands on Joshua, and Joshua carried them out. Not one of the commands laid on Moses by the LORD did he leave unfulfilled.

And so Joshua took the whole 16 country, the hill-country, all the Negeb, all the land of Goshen, the Shephelah, the Arabah, and the Israelite hill-country with the adjoining lowlands. His conquests extended from the bare 17 mountain which leads up to Seir as far as Baal-gad in the Vale of Lebanon under Mount Hermon. He took prisoner all their kings, struck them down and put them to death. It was a long 18 war that he fought against all these kingdoms. Except for the Hivites who 19 lived in Gibeon, not one of their cities came to terms with the Israelites; all were taken by storm. It was the 20 LORD's purpose that they should offer an obstinate resistance to the Israelites in battle, and that thus they should be annihilated without mercy and utterly destroyed,*q* as the LORD had commanded Moses.

It was then that Joshua proceeded to 21 wipe out the Anakim from the hill-country, from Hebron, Debir, Anab, all the hill-country of Judah and all the hill-country of Israel, destroying both them and their cities. No Anakim were 22 left in the land taken by the Israelites; they survived only in Gaza, Gath, and Ashdod.

q offer . . . destroyed: or obstinately engage the Israelites in battle so that they should annihilate them without mercy, only that he might destroy them . . .

---

of the largest cities of Galilee. Excavations have shown its importance in antiquity, and confirm a capture of the city at about the period of time indicated in this narrative. The other three places in this verse are all between the Sea of Galilee and the Mediterranean. **2:** *Arabah:* see 3.16 n. *Kinnereth:* the ancient name for the Sea of Galilee. *Shephelah:* the low hill country immediately east of the Mediterranean plain. *Dor:* on the coast, west of Megiddo. *Hivites:* see 9.7 n. **5:** *The waters of Merom:* probably the brook which flows from Merom (modern Meiron) into the Sea of Galilee at its northwest corner. **8:** *Sidon:* the great Phoenician seaport to the north of Palestine. *Misrephoth:* on the Mediterranean coast, west of Hazor. *Mizpah:* see v. 3. **16–20:** A summary of the victories in the south and the north. **17:** *Seir:* a synonym for Edom. **20:** *The LORD's purpose:* see Deut.7.2–6; 20.16–18. **21:** *Anakim* were reputed to be men of gigantic size (see Num.13.33; Deut.2.10–11). In Josh. they seem to be an aristocracy in

23 Thus Joshua took the whole country, fulfilling all the commands that the LORD had laid on Moses; he assigned it as Israel's patrimony, allotting to each tribe its share; and the land was at peace.

12 These are the names of the kings of the land whom the Israelites slew, and whose territory they occupied beyond the Jordan towards the sunrise from the gorge of the Arnon as far as Mount Hermon and all the Arabah 2 on the east. Sihon the Amorite king who lived in Heshbon: his rule extended from Aroer, which is on the edge of the gorge of the Arnon, along the middle of the gorge and over half Gilead as far as the gorge of the Jabbok, the 3 Ammonite frontier; along the Arabah as far as the eastern side of the Sea of Kinnereth and as far as the eastern side of the Sea of the Arabah, the Dead Sea, by the road to Beth-jeshimoth and from Teman under the 4 watershed of Pisgah. Og king of Bashan, one of the survivors of the Rephaim, who lived in Ashtaroth and 5 Edrei: he ruled over Mount Hermon, Salcah, all Bashan as far as the Geshurite and Maacathite borders, and half Gilead as far as the boundary of 6 Sihon king of Heshbon. Moses the servant of the LORD put them to death, he and the Israelites, and he gave their land to the Reubenites, the Gadites, and half the tribe of Manasseh, as their possession.

7 These are the names of the kings whom Joshua and the Israelites put to death beyond the Jordan to the west, from Baal-gad in the Vale of Lebanon as far as the bare mountain that leads up to Seir. Joshua gave their land to the Israelite tribes to be their possession according to their allotted shares,

in the hill-country, the Shephelah, the 8 Arabah, the watersheds, the wilder-ness, and the Negeb; lands of the Hittites, Amorites, Canaanites, Periz-zites, Hivites, and Jebusites. The king of 9 Jericho; the king of Ai which is beside Bethel; the king of Jerusalem; 10 the king of Hebron; the king of 11 Jarmuth; the king of Lachish; the 12 king of Eglon; the king of Gezer; the 13 king of Debir; the king of Geder; the 14 king of Hormah; the king of Arad; the king of Libnah; the king of Adul- 15 lam; the king of Makkedah; the king 16 of Bethel; the king of Tappuah; the 17 king of Hepher; the king of Aphek; 18 the king of Aphek*r*-in-Sharon; the 19 king of Madon; the king of Hazor; the king of Shimron-meron; the king of 20 Akshaph; the king of Taanach; the 21 king of Megiddo; the king of Kedesh; 22 the king of Jokneam-in-Carmel; the 23 king of Dor in the district of Dor; the king of Gaiam-in-Galilee; the king of 24 Tirzah: thirty-one kings in all, one of each town.

*The division of the land among
the tribes*

BY THIS TIME JOSHUA HAD BECOME **13** very old, and the LORD said to him, 'You are now a very old man, and much of the country remains to be occupied. The country which remains 2 is this: all the districts of the Philistines and all the Geshurite country (this is 3 reckoned as Canaanite territory from Shihor to the east of Egypt as far north as Ekron; and it belongs to the five lords of the Philistines, those of Gaza, Ashdod, Ashkelon, Gath, and Ekron);

r of Aphek: *prob. rdg.; Heb. om.*

---

the hill country around Hebron and in the coastal towns; in 14.12–15 and 15.13–15 Caleb, not Joshua, is their conqueror. **23:** Nothing remained to be done but to divide the land among the tribes.
12.1–24: Summary of Israel's victories. 1–6: Moses' victories in Transjordan (see Deut. 2.26–3.11). **6:** On the land of the Transjordan tribes, see Deut.3.12–17. **7–24:** Joshua's conquests west of the Jordan. Some of these names were not mentioned previously. The "kings" were merely local chieftains.
13.1–33: The beginning of the distribution of the land. The distribution continues through ch. 18. **2–7:** These territories were still unconquered, even though ideally they were to be part of Israel according to 1.4 and Num.34.1–12. **2:** *The Philistines* came from Caphtor (Deut. 2.23 n.). They settled on the coast of Palestine (which gets its name from them) shortly after 1200 B.C.; their five districts are listed in v. 3. Not Semites, they did not practice circumcision. They were mortal enemies of Israel for over 200 years. *Geshurite country:* south of the Philistine

all the districts of the Avvim on the
4 south; all the Canaanite country from
the low-lying land which belongs to the
Sidonians as far as Aphek, the Amorite
5 frontier; the land of the Gebalites and
all the Lebanon to the east from Baal-
gad under Mount Hermon as far as
6 Lebo-hamath. I will drive out in favour
of the Israelites all the inhabitants
of the hill-country from the Lebanon
as far as Misrephoth on the west, and
all the Sidonians. In the mean time
you are to allot all this to the Israelites
for their patrimony, as I have com-
7 manded you. Distribute this land now
to the nine tribes and half the tribe of
8 Manasseh for their patrimony.' For half
the tribe of Manasseh and[s] with them
the Reubenites and the Gadites had
each taken their patrimony which
Moses gave them east of the Jordan,
as Moses the servant of the LORD had
9 ordained. It started from Aroer which
is by the edge of the gorge of the
Arnon, and the level land half-way
along the gorge, and included all the
tableland from Medeba as far as Dibon;
10 all the cities of Sihon, the Amorite
king who ruled in Heshbon, as far as
11 the Ammonite frontier; and it also
included Gilead and the Geshurite
Maacathite territory, and all Mount
Hermon and the whole of Bashan as
12 far as Salcah, all the kingdom of Og
which he ruled from both Ashtaroth
and Edrei in Bashan. He was a survivor
of the remnant of the Rephaim, but
Moses put them both to death and occu-
13 pied their lands. But the Israelites did
not drive out the Geshurites and the
Maacathites; the Geshurites and the
Maacathites live among the Israelites
14 to this day. The tribe of Levi, however, received no patrimony; the LORD
the God of Israel is their patrimony,
as he promised them.
15 So Moses allotted territory to the
tribe of the Reubenites family by
16 family. Their territory started from

Aroer which is by the edge of the
gorge of the Arnon, and the level land
half-way along the gorge, and included all the tableland as far as Medeba; Heshbon and all its cities on the 17
tableland, Dibon, Bamoth-baal, Beth-
baal-meon, Jahaz, Kedemoth, Me- 18
phaath, Kiriathaim, Sibmah, Zereth- 19
shahar on the hill in the Vale, Beth- 20
peor, the watershed of Pisgah, and
Beth-jeshimoth, all the cities of the 21
tableland, all the kingdom of Sihon
the Amorite king who ruled in Heshbon, whom Moses put to death together
with the princes of Midian, Evi, Rekem,
Zur, Hur, and Reba, the vassals of
Sihon who dwelt in the country. Ba- 22
laam son of Beor, who practised augury,
was among those whom the Israelites
put to the sword. The boundary of the 23
Reubenites was the Jordan and the
adjacent land: this is the patrimony
of the Reubenites family by family,
both the cities and their hamlets.
Moses allotted territory to the Gad- 24
ites family by family. Their territory 25
was Jazer, all the cities of Gilead and
half the Ammonite country as far as
Aroer which is east of Rabbah. It 26
reached from Heshbon as far as
Ramoth-mizpeh and Betonim, and
from Mahanaim as far as the boundary
of Lo-debar; it included in the valley 27
Beth-haram, Beth-nimrah, Succoth,
and Zaphon, the rest of the kingdom
of Sihon king of Heshbon. The boundary was the Jordan and the adjacent
land as far as the end of the Sea of
Kinnereth east of the Jordan. This is 28
the patrimony of the Gadites family
by family, both the cities and their
hamlets.
Moses allotted territory to the half 29
tribe of Manasseh: it was for half the
tribe of the Manassites family by
family. Their territory ran from 30
Mahanaim and included all Bashan,
all the kingdom of Og king of Bashan

s For half ... Manasseh and: prob. rdg.; Heb. om.

cities; see 1 Sam.27.7–8. **3:** *Avvim* lived around Gaza. **4–6:** This is unconquered territory on
the northern edges of Palestine. **7:** This is done in chs. 14–19. **8–32:** The land east of the Jordan
is allotted to Reuben, Gad, and half of Manasseh; see Num. ch. 32 and Deut.3.12–17. The
boundaries of Reuben and Gad were pushed back when the Ammonite and Moabite kingdoms
developed. The origins of the half-tribe of Manasseh are obscure. **13:** That *the Israelites did
not drive out the Geshurites* ... is the first of several passages (14.6–13; 15.13–19,63; 16.10;
17.12–18; Judg.1.19,21,27–35) derived from an ancient source, which indicate that the conquest
was less complete than the late editor of Joshua usually states. **14:** *Levi:* see ch. 21.

and all Havvoth-jair in Bashan—sixty
31 cities. Half Gilead, and Ashtaroth and
Edrei the royal cities of Og in Bashan,
belong to the sons of Machir son of
Manasseh on behalf of half the
Machirites family by family.
32 These are the territories which
Moses allotted to the tribes as their
patrimonies in the lowlands of Moab
33 east of the Jordan. But to the tribe of
Levi he gave no patrimony: the LORD
the God of Israel is their patrimony,
as he promised them.

14 Now follow the possessions which
the Israelites acquired in the land of
Canaan, as Eleazar the priest, Joshua
son of Nun, and the heads of the
families of the Israelite tribes allotted
2 them. They were assigned by lot,
following the LORD's command given
through Moses, to the nine and a half
3 tribes. To two and a half tribes
Moses had given patrimonies beyond
the Jordan; but he gave none to the
4 Levites as he did to the others. The
tribe of Joseph formed the two tribes
of Manasseh and Ephraim. The
Levites were given no share in the land,
only cities to dwell in, with their
common land for flocks and herds.
5 So the Israelites, following the LORD's
command given to Moses, assigned the
land.
6 Now the tribe of Judah had come
to Joshua in Gilgal, and Caleb son of
Jephunneh the Kenizzite said to him,
'You remember what the LORD said to
Moses the man of God concerning you
7 and me at Kadesh-barnea. I was forty
years old when Moses the servant of the
LORD sent me from there to explore
the land, and I brought back an
8 honest report. The others who went
with me discouraged the people, but I
loyally carried out the purpose of the
9 LORD my God. Moses swore an oath

that day and said, "The land on which
you have set foot shall be your patrimony and your sons' after you as a
possession for ever; for you have
loyally carried out the purpose of the
LORD my God." Well, the LORD has 10
spared my life as he promised; it is now
forty-five years since he made this
promise to Moses, at the time when
Israel was journeying in the wilderness. Today I am eighty-five years old.
I am still as strong as I was on the day 11
when Moses sent me out; I am as fit
now for war as I was then and am ready
to take the field again. Give me today 12
this hill-country which the LORD then
promised me. You heard on that day
that the Anakim were there and their
cities were large and well fortified.
Perhaps the LORD will be with me and
I shall dispossess them as he promised.' Joshua blessed Caleb and gave 13
him Hebron for his patrimony, and 14
that is why Hebron remains to this day
in the patrimony of Caleb son of
Jephunneh the Kenizzite. It is because
he loyally carried out the purpose of
the LORD the God of Israel. Formerly 15
the name of Hebron was Kiriath-arba.
This Arba was the chief man of the
Anakim. And the land was at peace.

This is the territory allotted to the **15**
tribe of the sons of Judah family by
family. It started from the Edomite
frontier at the wilderness of Zin and ran
as far as the Negeb at its southern end,
and it had a common border with the 2
Negeb at the end of the Dead Sea,
where an inlet of water bends towards
the Negeb. It continued from the south 3
by the ascent of Akrabbim, passed by
Zin, went up from the south of Kadesh-
barnea, passed by Hezron, went on to
Addar and turned round to Karka.
It then passed along to Azmon, reached 4
the Torrent of Egypt, and its limit was

14.1–5: General introduction to the allotment of land.
   14.6–15: Hebron assigned to Caleb. Caleb in Num.13.6; 34.19 is of the tribe of Judah, but is
here and in Num.32.12 a Kenizzite, therefore a non-Israelite (see v. 14; Gen.15.19); he receives
land *within the tribe of Judah* as Moses had promised (see Num.14.24) because he "showed a
different spirit" than the others sent to explore the land (Num.13.30; 14.6–9). Some scholars
think that Caleb and some other non-Israelite elements had penetrated Canaan from the south
along with some elements of Judah and Simeon; this opinion is based on a comparison of
Judg.1.16–17 and Num.21.3 as well as Judg.1.9–15 and Josh.15.13–19.
   15.1–63: The territory allotted to Judah. In this and the following sections the boundaries
of each tribe are described as they existed before the rise of the monarchy. 1–12: These are the
boundaries of Judah. vv. 2–4, the southern, from the Dead Sea to the Mediterranean; vv. 5–11,

the sea. This was their southern boundary.

5 The eastern boundary is the Dead Sea as far as the mouth of the Jordan and the adjacent land northwards from the inlet of the sea, at the mouth of the 6 Jordan. The boundary goes up to Beth-hoglah; it passes north of Beth-arabah and thence to the stone of 7 Bohan son of Reuben, thence to Debir from the Vale of Achor, and then turns north to the districts[t] in front of the ascent of Adummim south of the gorge. The boundary then passes the waters of En-shemesh and the limit 8 there is En-rogel. It then goes up by the Valley of Ben-hinnom to the southern slope of the Jebusites (that is Jerusalem). Thence it goes up to the top of the hill which faces the Valley of Hinnom on the west; this is at the northern end 9 of the Vale of Rephaim. The boundary then bends round from the top of the hill to the spring of the waters of Nephtoah, runs round to the cities of Mount Ephron and round to Baalah, 10 that is Kiriath-jearim. It then continues westwards from Baalah to Mount Seir, passes on to the north side of the slope of Mount Jearim, that is Kesalon, down to Beth-shemesh and on to 11 Timnah. The boundary then goes north to the slope of Ekron, bends round to Shikkeron, crosses to Mount Baalah and reaches Jabneel; its limit 12 is the sea. The western boundary is the Great Sea and the land adjacent. This is the whole circuit of the boundary of the tribe of Judah family by family. 13 Caleb son of Jephunneh received his share of the land within the tribe of Judah as the LORD had said to Joshua. It was Kiriath-arba, that is Hebron. This Arba was the ancestor of 14 the Anakim. Caleb drove out the three Anakim: these were Sheshai, Ahiman and Talmai, descendants of Anak. 15 From there he attacked the inhabitants of Debir; the name of Debir was 16 formerly Kiriath-sepher. Caleb announced that whoever should attack Kiriath-sepher and capture it would receive his daughter Achsah in

marriage. Othniel, son of Caleb's 17 brother Kenaz, captured it, and Caleb gave him his daughter Achsah. When 18 she came to him, he incited her to ask her father for a piece of land. As she sat on the ass, she made a noise, and Caleb asked her, 'What did you mean by that?' She replied, 'I want a favour 19 from you. You have put me in this dry Negeb; you must give me pools of water as well.' So Caleb gave her the upper pool and the lower pool.

This is the patrimony of the tribe 20 of the sons of Judah family by family. These are the cities belonging to the 21 tribe of Judah, the full count. By the Edomite frontier in the Negeb: Kabzeel, Eder, Jagur, Kinah, Dimonah, 22 Ararah,[u] Kedesh, Hazor, Ithnan, Ziph, 23,24 Telem, Bealoth, Hazor-hadattah, 25 Kerioth-hezron, Amam, Shema, Mola-26 dah, Hazar-gaddah, Heshmon, Beth-27 pelet, Hazar-shual, Beersheba and its 28 villages, Baalah, Iyim, Ezem, Eltolad, 29,30 Kesil, Hormah, Ziklag, Madmannah, 31 Sansannah, Lebaoth, Shilhim, Ain, 32 and Rimmon: in all, twenty-nine cities with their hamlets.

In the Shephelah: Eshtaol, Zorah, 33 Ashnah, Zanoah, En-gannim, Tap-34 puah, Enam, Jarmuth, Adullam, Socoh, 35 Azekah, Shaaraim, Adithaim, Gederah, 36 namely both parts of Gederah: four-teen cities with their hamlets. Zenan, 37 Hadashah, Migdal-gad, Dilan, Miz-38 peh, Joktheel, Lachish, Bozkath, Eg-39 lon, Cabbon, Lahmas, Kithlish, Geder-40,41 oth, Beth-dagon, Naamah, and Mak-kedah: sixteen cities with their ham-lets. Libnah, Ether, Ashan, Jiphtah, 42,43 Ashnah, Nezib, Keilah, Achzib, and 44 Mareshah: nine cities with their ham-lets. Ekron, with its villages and 45 hamlets, and from Ekron westwards, 46 all the cities near Ashdod and their hamlets. Ashdod with its villages and 47 hamlets, Gaza with its villages and hamlets as far as the Torrent of Egypt and the Great Sea and the land adjacent.

t Prob. rdg., cp. 18. 17; Heb. to Gilgal.
u Prob. rdg.; Heb. Adadah.

the eastern, the Dead Sea; and the northern, from the mouth of the Jordan to the Mediterranean, passing just south of Jerusalem; v. 12, the western, the Mediterranean. **13–19:** Another reference to Caleb (compare 14.6–15); vv. 14–19 are almost identical with Judg.1.11–15. **20–63:** A list of

48 In the hill-country: Shamir, Jattir,
49 Socoh, Dannah, Kiriath-sannah, that
50 is Debir, Anab, Eshtemoh, Anim,
51 Goshen, Holon, and Giloh: eleven
52 cities in all with their hamlets. Arab,
53 Dumah, Eshan, Janim, Beth-tappuah,
54 Aphek,ᵛ Humtah, Kiriath-arba, that is
Hebron, and Zior: nine cities in all
55 with their hamlets. Maon, Carmel,
56 Ziph, Juttah, Jezreel, Jokdeam, Za-
57 noah, Cain, Gibeah, and Timnah: ten
58 cities in all with their hamlets. Halhul,
59 Beth-zur, Gedor, Maarath, Beth-
anoth, and Eltekon: six cities in all
with their hamlets. Tekoa, Ephrathah,
that is Bethlehem, Peor, Etam, Culom,
Tatam, Sores, Carem, Gallim, Baither,
and Manach: eleven cities in all with
60 their hamlets. Kiriath-baal, that is
Kiriath-jearim, and Rabbah: two cities
with their hamlets.
61 In the wilderness: Beth-arabah,
62 Middin, Secacah, Nibshan, Ir-melach,
and En-gedi: six cities with their
hamlets.
63 At Jerusalem, the men of Judah
were unable to drive out the Jebusites
who lived there, and to this day
Jebusites and men of Judah live
together in Jerusalem.

16 This is the lot that fell to the sons
of Joseph: the boundary runs from
the Jordan at Jericho, east of the waters
of Jericho by the wilderness, and goes up
from Jericho into the hill-country to
2 Bethel. It runs on from Bethel to Luz
and crosses the Archite border at
3 Ataroth.ʷ Westwards it descends to the
boundary of the Japhletites as far as the
boundary of Lower Beth-horon and
4 Gezer; its limit is the sea. Here Manasseh and Ephraim the sons of Joseph
received their patrimony.
5 This was the boundary of the
Ephraimites family by family: their
eastern boundary ran from Ataroth-
6 addar up to Upper Beth-horon. It
continued westwards to Michmethath
on the north, going round by the

east of Taanath-shiloh and passing by
it on the east of Janoah. It descends 7
from Janoah to Ataroth and Naarath,
touches Jericho and continues to the
Jordan, and from Tappuah it goes 8
westwards by the gorge of Kanah; and
its limit is the sea. This is the patrimony of the tribe of Ephraim family
by family. There were also cities re- 9
served for the Ephraimites within the
patrimony of the Manassites, each of
these cities with its hamlets. They did 10
not however drive out the Canaanites
who dwelt in Gezer; the Canaanites
have lived among the Ephraimites to
the present day but have been subject
to forced labour in perpetuity.
This is the territory allotted to the **17**
tribe of Manasseh, Joseph's eldest
son. Machir was Manasseh's eldest
son and father of Gilead, a fighting
man; Gilead and Bashan were allotted
to him.
The rest of the Manassites family by 2
family were the sons of Abiezer, the
sons of Helek, the sons of Asriel, the
sons of Shechem, the sons of Hepher,
and the sons of Shemida; these were
the male offspring of Manasseh son
of Joseph family by family.
Zelophehad son of Hepher, son of 3
Gilead, son of Machir, son of Manasseh, had no sons but only daughters:
their names were Mahlah, Noah,
Hoglah, Milcah and Tirzah. They 4
presented themselves before Eleazar
the priest and Joshua son of Nun,
and before the chiefs, and they said,
'The LORD commanded Moses to
allow us to inherit on the same footing
as our kinsmen.' They were therefore
given a patrimony on the same footing
as their father's brothers according to
the commandment of the LORD.
There fell to Manasseh's lot ten 5
shares, apart from the country of
Gilead and Bashan beyond the Jordan,
because Manasseh's daughters had 6

ᵛ *Or* Aphekah.   ʷ Ataroth-addar *in 16. 5; 18. 13.*

Judah's towns by districts. Many think this list was taken from an official register of the subdivisions of the kingdom of Judah, either after the division of Judah and Israel in 922 B.C., or
perhaps in the time of Josiah (626–609). 63: See 2 Sam.5.6–9.
    16.1–17.18: The territory allotted to the Joseph tribes. The two tribes of Ephraim and Ma-
nasseh receive the central highlands. 1–4: The southern boundary ran roughly from the Jordan
at Jericho to Bethel, then slightly south toward Gezer and on to the Mediterranean. 5–10: The
boundaries of Ephraim were south of Manasseh, but some Ephraimite cities were within Manasseh (v. 9). 17.1 6: Arrangements for Manasseh. 2: The rest of the Manassites: those not

received a patrimony on the same footing as his sons. The country of Gilead belonged to the rest of Manas- 7 seh's sons. The boundary of Manasseh reached from Asher as far as Mich-methath, which is to the east of Shechem, and thence southwards 8 towards Jashub by*x* En-tappuah. The territory of Tappuah belonged to Manasseh, but Tappuah itself was on the border of Manasseh and belonged 9 to Ephraim. The boundary then followed the gorge of Kanah to the south of the gorge (these cities*y* belong to Ephraim, although they lie among the cities of Manasseh), the boundary of Manasseh being on the north of the 10 gorge; its limit was the sea. The southern side belonged to Ephraim and the northern to Manasseh, and their boundary was the sea. They marched with Asher on the north and 11 Issachar on the east. But in Issachar and Asher, Manasseh possessed Beth-shean and its villages, Ibleam and its villages, the inhabitants of Dor and its villages, the inhabitants of En-dor and its villages, the inhabitants of Taanach and its villages, and the inhabitants of Megiddo and its villages. (The third is 12 the district of Dor.*z*) The Manassites were unable to occupy these cities; the Canaanites maintained their hold 13 on that part of the country. When the Israelites grew stronger, they put the Canaanites to forced labour, but they did not drive them out.

14 The sons of Joseph appealed to Joshua and said, 'Why have you given us only one lot and one share as our patrimony? We are a numerous people; so far the LORD has blessed 15 us.' Joshua replied, 'If you are so numerous, go up into the forest in the territory of the Perizzites and the Rephaim and clear it for yourselves. You are their near neighbours*a* in the 16 hill-country of Ephraim.' The sons of Joseph said, 'The hill-country is not enough for us; besides, all the Canaan-

ites have chariots of iron, those who inhabit the valley beside Beth-shean and its villages and also those in the Vale of Jezreel.' Joshua replied to the 17 tribes of Joseph, that is Ephraim and Manasseh: 'You are a numerous people with great resources. You shall not have one lot only. The hill-country 18 is yours. It is forest land; clear it and it shall be yours to its furthest limits. The Canaanites may be powerful and equipped with chariots of iron, but you will be able to drive them out.'

THE WHOLE COMMUNITY OF THE ISRAEL- 18 ites met together at Shiloh and estab-lished the Tent of the Presence there. The country now lay subdued at their feet, but there remained seven tribes 2 among the Israelites who had not yet taken possession of the patrimonies which would fall to them. Joshua 3 therefore said to them, 'How much longer will you neglect to take posses-sion of the land which the LORD the God of your fathers has given you? Appoint three men from each tribe 4 whom I may send out to travel through the whole country. They shall make a register showing the patrimony suitable for each tribe, and come back to me, and then it can be shared out among 5 you in seven portions. Judah shall retain his boundary in the south, and the house of Joseph their boundary in the north. You shall register the land in 6 seven portions, bring the lists here, and I will cast lots for you in the presence of the LORD our God. Levi 7 has no share among you, because his share is the priesthood of the LORD; and Gad, Reuben, and the half tribe of Manasseh have each taken posses-sion of their patrimony east of the Jordan, which Moses the servant of the LORD gave them.' So the men set out 8 on their journeys. Joshua ordered the

x Jashub by: *prob. rdg.; Heb.* the inhabitants of.
y these cities: *prob. rdg.; Heb. obscure.*
z The third . . . Dor: *prob. rdg.; Heb.* The three districts.
a You are . . . neighbours: *prob. rdg.; Heb. obscure.*

---

already settled east of the Jordan (vv. 1, 5–6; 13.29–31). **7–13:** The boundaries of Manasseh. **11–13:** These verses closely parallel Judg.1.27–28. **16–18:** The Joseph tribes ask for and receive a double portion.

18.1–19.51: The territory of the seven other tribes. 1–10: Preparations for the further division of the land. **1:** *Shiloh,* in Ephraim, ten miles north of Bethel, was the new religious center, replacing Gilgal; see 19.51; 21.2; 22.9,12; Judg.18.31; 1 Sam.1.3; 4.3–4. *Tent of the Presence:*

emissaries to survey the country: 'Go through the whole country,' he said, 'survey it and return to me, and I will cast lots for you here before the LORD 9 in Shiloh.' So the men went and passed through the country; they registered it on a scroll, city by city, in seven portions, and came to Joshua 10 in the camp at Shiloh. Joshua cast lots for them in Shiloh before the LORD, and distributed the land there to the Israelites in their proper shares.

11 This is the lot which fell to the tribe of the Benjamites family by family. The territory allotted to them lay between the territory of Judah and 12 Joseph. Their boundary at its northern corner starts from the Jordan; it goes up the slope on the north side of Jericho, continuing westwards into the hill-country, and its limit there is 13 the wilderness of Beth-aven. From there it runs on to Luz, to the southern slope of Luz, that is Bethel, and down to Ataroth-addar over the hill-country 14 south of Lower Beth-horon. The boundary then bends round at the west corner southwards from the hill-country above Beth-horon, and its limit is Kiriath-baal, that is Kiriath-jearim, a city of Judah. This is the 15 western side. The southern side starts from the edge of Kiriath-jearim and ends[b] at the spring of the waters of 16 Nephtoah. It goes down to the edge of the hill to the east of the Valley of Ben-hinnom, north of the Vale of Rephaim, down the Valley of Hinnom, to the southern slope of the Jebusites 17 and so to En-rogel. It then bends round north and comes out at En-shemesh, goes on to the districts in front of the ascent of Adummim and thence down to the Stone of Bohan 18 son of Reuben. It passes to the northern side of the slope facing the Arabah 19 and goes down to the Arabah, passing the northern slope of Beth-hoglah, and its limit is the northern inlet of the Dead Sea, at the southern mouth of the Jordan. This forms the southern boun-

dary. The Jordan is the boundary on 20 the east side. This is the patrimony of the Benjamites, the complete circuit of their boundaries family by family. The cities belonging to the tribe of 21 the Benjamites family by family are: Jericho, Beth-hoglah, Emek-keziz, Beth- 22 arabah, Zemaraim, Bethel, Avvim, 23 Parah, Ophrah, Kephar-ammoni, Oph- 24 ni, and Geba: twelve cities in all with their hamlets. Gibeon, Ramah, Be- 25 eroth, Mizpah, Kephirah, Mozah, Re- 26,27 kem, Irpeel, Taralah, Zela, Eleph, 28 Jebus, that is Jerusalem, Gibeah, and Kiriath-jearim: fourteen cities in all with their hamlets. This is the patrimony of the Benjamites family by family.

The second lot cast was for Simeon, **19** the tribe of the Simeonites family by family. Their patrimony was included in that of Judah. For their patrimony 2 they had Beersheba,[c] Moladah, Hazar- 3 shual, Balah, Ezem, Eltolad, Bethul, 4 Hormah, Ziklag, Beth-marcaboth, 5 Hazar-susah, Beth-lebaoth, and Sharu- 6 hen: in all, thirteen cities and their hamlets. They had Ain, Rimmon, 7 Ether, and Ashan: four cities and their hamlets, all the hamlets round these 8 cities as far as Baalath-beer, Ramath-negeb. This was the patrimony of the tribe of Simeon family by family. The 9 patrimony of the Simeonites was part of the land allotted to the men of Judah, because their share was larger than they needed. The Simeonites therefore had their patrimony within the territory of Judah.

The third lot fell to the Zebulunites 10 family by family. The boundary of their patrimony extended to Shadud.[d] Their boundary went up westwards as 11 far as Maralah and touched Dabbe-sheth and the gorge east of Jokneam. It turned back from Shadud eastwards 12 towards the sunrise up to the border of Kisloth-tabor, on to Daberath and up to Japhia. From there it crossed 13 eastwards towards the sunrise to Gath-

b Prob. rdg.; Heb. adds westwards and ends . . .
c Prob. rdg., cp. 1 Chr. 4. 28; Heb. adds and Sheba.
d Prob. rdg.; Heb. Sarid *(similarly in verse 12).*

see Exod. 26.1–37 n.; 33.7–11 n. **11–28:** The territory of Benjamin, between Judah and Joseph. **19.1–9:** The territory of Simeon lay within Judah, because the Judahite *share was larger than they needed* (v. 9). Simeon had once been powerful (see Gen.34.1–31 n.; 49.5–7 n.); it seems secondary to Judah here and is not mentioned in the blessings of Deut. ch. 33. Some scholars believe it disappeared as a separate tribe. **10–18:** The territory of the Galilee tribes.

hepher, to Ittah-kazin, out to Rimmon,
14 and bent round[e] to Neah. The northern boundary went round to Hannathon, and its limits were the Valley of
15 Jiphtah-el, Kattath, Nahalal, Shimron, Idalah, and Bethlehem: twelve cities in
16 all with their hamlets. These cities and their hamlets were the patrimony of Zebulun family by family.
17 The fourth lot cast was for the sons
18 of Issachar family by family. Their boundary included Jezreel, Kesulloth,
19 Shunem, Hapharaim, Shion, Anahar-
20,21 ath, Rabbith, Kishion, Ebez, Remeth, En-gannim, En-haddah, and Beth-
22 pazzez. The boundary touched Tabor, Shahazumah, and Beth-shemesh, and its limit was the Jordan: sixteen cities
23 with their hamlets. This was the patrimony of the tribe of the sons of Issachar family by family, both cities and hamlets.
24 The fifth lot cast was for the tribe of the Asherites family by family.
25 Their boundary included Helkath,
26 Hali, Beten, Akshaph, Alammelech, Amad, and Mishal; it touched Carmel on the west and the swamp of Lib-
27 nath. It then turned back towards the east to Beth-dagon, touched Zebulun and the Valley of Jiphtah-el on the north at Beth-emek and Neiel, and reached Cabul on its northern side,
28 and Abdon, Rehob, Hammon, and
29 Kanah as far as Greater Sidon. The boundary turned at Ramah, going as far as the fortress city of Tyre, and then back again to Hosah, and its limits to the west were Mehalbeh, Achzib,
30 Acco,[f] Aphek, and Rehob: twenty-two cities in all with their hamlets.
31 This was the patrimony of the tribe of Asher family by family, these cities and their hamlets.
32 The sixth lot cast was for the sons of
33 Naphtali family by family. Their boundary started from Heleph and from Elon-bezaanannim and ran past Adami-nekeb and Jabneel as far as Lakkum, and its limit was the Jordan.
34 The boundary turned back westwards

to Aznoth-tabor and from there on to Hukok. It touched Zebulun on the south, Asher on the west, and the low-lying land by the Jordan on the east.
Their fortified cities were Ziddim, 35
Zer, Hammath, Rakkath, Kinnereth, Adamah, Ramah, Hazor, Kedesh, Ed- 36,37 rei, En-hazor, Iron, Migdal-el, Horem, 38 Beth-anath, and Beth-shemesh: nineteen cities with their hamlets. This was 39 the patrimony of the tribe of Naphtali family by family, both cities and hamlets.
The seventh lot cast was for the tribe 40 of the sons of Dan family by family. The boundary of their patrimony 41 was Zorah, Eshtaol, Ir-shemesh, Shaal- 42 abbin, Aijalon, Jithlah, Elon, Timnah, 43 Ekron, Eltekeh, Gibbethon, Baalath, 44 Jehud, Bene-berak, Gath-rimmon; and 45,46 on the west Jarkon was the boundary opposite Joppa. But the Danites, 47 when they lost this territory, marched against Leshem, attacked it and captured it. They put its people to the sword, occupied it and settled in it; and they renamed the place Dan after their ancestor Dan. This was the patrimony 48 of the tribe of the sons of Dan family by family, these cities and their hamlets.
So the Israelites finished allocating 49 the land and marking out its frontiers; and they gave Joshua son of Nun a patrimony within their territory. They 50 followed the commands of the LORD and gave him the city for which he asked, Timnath-serah in the hill-country of Ephraim, and he rebuilt the city and settled in it.
These are the patrimonies which 51 Eleazar the priest and Joshua son of Nun and the heads of families assigned by lot to the Israelite tribes at Shiloh before the LORD at the entrance of the Tent of the Presence. Thus they completed the distribution of the land.

e and bent round: *prob. rdg.*; *Heb.* which stretched.
f Mehalbeh . . . Acco: *prob. rdg.*; *Heb.* from the district of Achzib and Ummah.

10–16: *Zebulun.* **17–23**: *Issachar.* **24–31**: *Asher.* **32–39**: *Naphtali.* **40–48**: *Dan* never conquered these southern lands west of Benjamin (vv. 41–46); after being forced out, by the Amorites (Judg.1.34–35) or by the Philistines (Judg. chs. 13–16), they then emigrated north (v. 47) to Leshem (Laish); see Judg. 18.27. **49–51**: These verses conclude the distribution of land to the tribes.

20 THE LORD SPOKE TO JOSHUA AND COM-
2 manded him to say this to the Israelites:
'You must now appoint your cities of
refuge, of which I spoke to you
3 through Moses. They are to be places
where the homicide, the man who
kills another inadvertently without
intent, may take sanctuary. You shall
single them out as cities of refuge
from the vengeance of the dead man's
4 next-of-kin. When a man takes sanctuary in one of these cities, he shall
halt at the entrance of the city gate
and state his case in the hearing of the
elders of that city; if they admit him
into the city, they shall grant him a
place where he may live as one of
5 themselves. When the next-of-kin
comes in pursuit, they shall not surrender him: he struck down his fellow
without intent and had not previously
6 been at enmity with him. The homicide
may stay in that city until he stands
trial before the community. On the
death of the ruling high priest, he may
return to the city and home from
7 which he had fled.' They dedicated
Kedesh in Galilee in the hill-country
of Naphtali, Shechem in the hill-country
of Ephraim, and Kiriath-arba, that is
Hebron, in the hill-country of Judah.
8 Across the Jordan eastwards from
Jericho they appointed these cities:
from the tribe of Reuben, Bezer-in-
the-wilderness on the tableland, from
the tribe of Gad, Ramoth in Gilead,
and from the tribe of Manasseh, Golan
9 in Bashan. These were the appointed
cities where any Israelite or any alien
residing among them might take
sanctuary. They were intended for
any man who killed another inadvertently, to ensure that no one should
die at the hand of the next-of-kin until
he had stood his trial before the community.

The heads of the Levite families **21**
approached Eleazar the priest and
Joshua son of Nun and the heads of
the families of the tribes of Israel. They 2
came before them at Shiloh in the
land of Canaan and said, 'The LORD
gave his command through Moses that
we were to receive cities to live in,
together with the common land
belonging to them for our cattle.' The 3
Israelites therefore gave part of their
patrimony to the Levites, the following
cities with their common land, according to the command of the LORD.
This is the territory allotted to the 4
Kohathite family: those Levites who
were descended from Aaron the priest
received thirteen cities chosen by lot
from the tribes of Judah, Simeon,
and Benjamin; the rest of the Kohath- 5
ites were allotted family by family[g]
ten cities from the tribes of Ephraim,
Dan, and half Manasseh.
The Gershonites were allotted fam- 6
ily by family thirteen cities from the
tribes of Issachar, Asher, Naphtali,
and the half tribe of Manasseh in
Bashan.
The Merarites were allotted family 7
by family twelve cities from the tribes
of Reuben, Gad, and Zebulun.
So the Israelites gave the Levites 8
these cities with their common land,
allocating them by lot as the LORD had
commanded through Moses.
The Israelites designated the follow- 9
ing cities out of the tribes of Judah
and Simeon for those sons of Aaron 10
who were of the Kohathite families
of the Levites, because their lot came
out first. They gave them Kiriath-arba 11
(Arba was the father of Anak), that is
Hebron, in the hill-country of Judah,
and the common land round it, but 12

g family by family: *prob. rdg.; Heb.* from the families
(*similarly in verse 6*).

20.1–9: Cities of refuge. These are cities to which an accused murderer might flee until his
case was judged; see Exod.21.12–13; Num.35.12; Deut.4.41–43; 19.1–13. **3:** The dead man's
next-of-kin had the obligation of avenging his death; the word "next-of-kin" is translated
"avenger" or "vindicator" by some; it is "ransomer" when used of God in Isa.41.14, and
"guardian" in Prov.23.11. **4:** *The city gate* was the place where the *elders* of the city met;
business was also normally transacted there; see Ruth 4.1. The gate was not merely an entrance,
but also a building, often containing several rooms and more than one story.
    21.1–42: The cities allotted to the tribe of Levi. This tribe, because of its religious functions,
did not receive an allotment of territory; see 13.14,33; 18.7. It was given the six cities of refuge
of ch. 20 and forty-two others in all the tribes with rights to pasture land nearby; see Num.
35.1–34 n. The disapproval of Levi in Gen.49.5–7 does not seem to be reflected here.

they gave the open country near the city, and its hamlets, to Caleb son of Jephunneh as his patrimony.

13[h] To the sons of Aaron the priest they gave Hebron, a city of refuge for the 14 homicide, Libnah, Jattir, Eshtemoa, 15,16 Holon, Debir, Ashan,[i] Juttah, and Beth-shemesh, each with its common land: nine cities from these two tribes. 17 They also gave cities from the tribe 18 of Benjamin, Gibeon, Geba, Anathoth, and Almon, each with its common 19 land: four cities. The number of the cities with their common land given to the sons of Aaron the priest was thirteen.

20 The cities which the rest of the Kohathite families of the Levites received by lot were from the tribe of 21 Ephraim. They gave them Shechem, a city of refuge for the homicide, in the 22 hill-country of Ephraim, Gezer, Kib-zaim, and Beth-horon, each with its 23 common land: four cities. From the tribe of Dan, they gave them Eltekeh, 24 Gibbethon, Aijalon, and Gath-rimmon, each with its common land: four 25 cities. From the half tribe of Manasseh, they gave them Taanach and Gath-rimmon, each with its common land: 26 two cities. The number of the cities belonging to the rest of the Kohathite families with their common land was ten.

27 The Gershonite families of the Levites received, out of the share of the half tribe of Manasseh, Golan in Bashan, a city of refuge for the homicide, and Be-ashtaroth,[j] each with its 28 common land: two cities. From the tribe of Issachar they received Kishon, 29 Daberath, Jarmuth, and En-gannim, each with its common land: four 30 cities. From the tribe of Asher they 31 received Mishal, Abdon, Helkath, and Rehob, each with its common 32 land: four cities. From the tribe of Naphtali they received Kedesh in Galilee, a city of refuge for the homicide, Hammoth-dor, and Kartan, each with its common land: three cities. 33 The number of the cities of the Gershonite families with their common land was thirteen.

From the tribe of Zebulun the rest 34 of the Merarite families of the Levites received Jokneam, Kartah, Rimmon,[k] 35 and Nahalal, each with its common land: four cities. East of the Jordan at 36 Jericho, from the tribe of Reuben they were given Bezer-in-the-wilderness on the tableland, a city of refuge for the homicide, Jahaz, Kedemoth, and 37 Mephaath, each with its common land: four cities. From the tribe of Gad 38 they received Ramoth in Gilead, a city of refuge for the homicide, Mahanaim, Heshbon, and Jazer, each with its 39 common land: four cities in all. Twelve 40 cities in all fell by lot to the rest of the Merarite families of the Levites.

The cities of the Levites within the 41 Israelite patrimonies numbered forty-eight in all, with their common land. Each city had its common land round 42 it, and it was the same for all of them.

Thus the LORD gave Israel all the land 43 which he had sworn to give to their forefathers; they occupied it and settled in it. The LORD gave them security on 44 every side as he had sworn to their forefathers. Of all their enemies not a man could withstand them; the LORD delivered all their enemies into their hands. Not a word of the LORD's 45 promises to the house of Israel went unfulfilled; they all came true.

AT THAT TIME JOSHUA SUMMONED THE **22** Reubenites, the Gadites, and the half tribe of Manasseh, and said to them, 2 'You have observed all the commands of Moses the servant of the LORD, and you have obeyed me in all the commands that I too have laid upon you. All this time you have not deserted 3 your brothers; up to this day you have diligently observed the charge laid on you by the LORD your God. And now 4 that the LORD your God has given your brothers security as he promised them, you may turn now and go to your homes in your own land, the land which Moses the servant of the LORD gave you east of the Jordan.

h *Verses 13–39: cp. 1 Chr. 6. 57–81.*
i *Prob. rdg., cp. 1 Chr. 6. 59; Heb.* Ain.
j *Prob. rdg.; Heb.* Be-ashtarah.
k *Prob. rdg., cp. 19. 13; 1 Chr. 6. 77; Heb.* Dimnah.

21.43–22.34: The return of the Transjordan tribes. The conquest complete, the two and one-

5 But take good care to keep the commands and the law which Moses the servant of the LORD gave you: to love the LORD your God; to conform to his ways; to observe his commandments; to hold fast to him; to serve him with your whole heart and soul.'

6 Joshua blessed them and dismissed them; and they went to their homes.

7-8 He sent them home with his blessing, and with these words: 'Go to your homes richly laden, with great herds, with silver and gold, copper and iron, and with large stores of clothing. See that you share with your kinsmen the spoil you have taken from your enemies.'

Moses had given territory to one half of the tribe of Manasseh in Bashan, and Joshua gave territory to the other half west of the Jordan among their kinsmen.

9 So the Reubenites, the Gadites, and the half tribe of Manasseh left the rest of the Israelites and went from Shiloh in Canaan on their way into Gilead, the land which belonged to them according to the decree of the

10 LORD given through Moses. When these tribes came to Geliloth by the Jordan,[l] they built a great altar there

11 by the river for all to see. The Israelites heard that the Reubenites, the Gadites, and the half tribe of Manasseh had built the altar facing the land of Canaan, at Geliloth by the Jordan

12 opposite the Israelite side. When the news reached them, all the community of the Israelites assembled at Shiloh to advance against them with a display

13 of force. At the same time the Israelites sent Phinehas son of Eleazar the priest into the land of Gilead, to the Reubenites, the Gadites, and the half tribe of

14 Manasseh, and ten leading men with him, one from each of the tribes of Israel, each of them the head of a household among the clans of Israel.

15 They came to the Reubenites, the Gadites, and the half tribe of Manasseh in the land of Gilead, and remonstrated

16 with them in these words: 'We speak for the whole community of the LORD. What is this treachery you have committed against the God of Israel? Are you ceasing to follow the LORD and building your own altar this day in

17 defiance of the LORD? Remember our offence at Peor, for which a plague fell upon the community of the LORD; to this day we have not been purified

18 from it. Was that offence so slight that you dare cease to follow the LORD today? If you defy the LORD today, then tomorrow he will be angry with

19 the whole community of Israel. If the land you have taken is unclean, then cross over to the LORD's own land, where the Tabernacle of the LORD now rests, and take a share of it with us; but do not defy the LORD and involve us in your defiance by building an altar of your own apart from the altar of the

20 LORD our God. Remember the treachery of Achan son of Zerah, who defied the ban and the whole community of Israel suffered for it. He was not the only one who paid for that sin with his life.'

21 Then the Reubenites, the Gadites, and the half tribe of Manasseh remonstrated with the heads of the clans of

22 Israel: 'The LORD the God of gods, the LORD the God of gods, he knows, and Israel must know: if this had been an act of defiance or treachery against the LORD, you could not save

23 us today. If we had built ourselves an altar meaning to forsake the LORD, or had offered whole-offerings and grain-offerings upon it, or had presented shared-offerings, the LORD him-

24 self would exact punishment. The truth is that we have done this for fear that the day may come when your sons will say to ours, "What have you to do with

25 the LORD, the God of Israel? The LORD put the Jordan as a boundary between our sons and your sons. You have no share in the LORD, you men of Reuben and Gad." Thus your sons will prevent

l Prob. rdg.; Heb. adds which was in Canaan.

---

half tribes were free to go home (1.12–18). **22.12:** *Shiloh* was the place of the Ark of the Covenant and the Tent of the Presence and its adherents would be opposed to the multiplication of altars. **17:** *Offence at Peor:* Num.25.3–5. **20:** *Treachery of Achan:* see 7.1. **22–29:** The altar is considered only a memorial, *a witness* between the tribes on the two sides of the Jordan; see v. 34.

our sons from going in awe of the
26 LORD. So we resolved to set ourselves
to build an altar, not for whole offerings
27 and sacrifices, but as a witness between
us and you, and between our descendants after us. Thus we shall be able
to do service before the LORD, as we
do now, with our whole-offerings, our
sacrifices, and our shared-offerings;
and your sons will never be able to say
to our sons that they have no share in
28 the LORD. And we thought, if ever they
do say this to us and our descendants,
we will point to this copy of the altar
of the LORD which we have made, not
for whole-offerings and not for sacrifices, but as a witness between us and
29 you. God forbid that we should defy
the LORD and forsake him this day by
building another altar for whole-offerings, grain-offerings, and sacrifices, in
addition to the altar of the LORD our
God which stands in front of his Tabernacle.'
30   When Phinehas the priest and the
leaders of the community, the heads
of the Israelite clans, who were with
him, heard what the Reubenites, the
Gadites, and the Manassites said,
31 they were satisfied. Phinehas son of
Eleazar the priest said to the Reubenites, Gadites, and Manassites, 'We
know now that the LORD is in our midst
today; you have not acted treacherously against the LORD, and thus you
have preserved all Israel from punish-
32 ment at his hand.' Then Phinehas son
of Eleazar the priest and the leaders
left the Reubenites and the Gadites in
Gilead and reported to the Israelites in
33 Canaan. The Israelites were satisfied,
and they blessed God and thought no
more of attacking Reuben and Gad
34 and ravaging their land. The Reubenites and Gadites said, 'The altar is a
witness between us that the LORD is
God', and they named it 'Witness'.

Joshua's farewell and death

23 A LONG TIME HAD PASSED SINCE THE
LORD had given Israel security from all
the enemies who surrounded them,
and Joshua was now a very old man.
2 He summoned all Israel, their elders
and heads of families, their judges and
officers, and said to them, 'I have be-
3 come a very old man. You have seen
for yourselves all that the LORD our
God has done to these peoples for your
sake; it was the LORD God himself
4 who fought for you. I have allotted
you your patrimony tribe by tribe, the
land of all the peoples that I have
wiped out and of all these that remain
between the Jordan and the Great Sea
which lies towards the setting sun.
5 The LORD your God himself drove them
out for your sake; he drove them out
to make room for you, and you
occupied their land, as the LORD your
6 God had promised you. Be resolute
therefore: observe and perform everything written in the book of the law of
Moses, without swerving to right or to
7 left. You must not associate with the
peoples that are left among you; you
must not call upon their gods by name,
nor[m] swear by them nor prostrate
yourselves in worship before them.
8 You must hold fast to the LORD your
God as you have done down to this
9 day. For your sake the LORD has driven
out great and mighty nations; to this
day not a man of them has withstood
10 you. One of you can put to flight a
thousand, because the LORD your God
11 fights for you, as he promised. Be on
your guard then, love the LORD your
12 God, for[n] if you do turn away and
attach yourselves to the peoples that
still remain among you, and intermarry with them and associate with
13 them and they with you, then be sure
that the LORD will not continue to
drive those peoples out to make room
for you. They will be snares to entrap
you, whips for your backs and barbed
hooks in your eyes, until you vanish
from the good land which the LORD
14 your God has given you. And now I am
going the way of all mankind. You
know in your heart of hearts that nothing that the LORD your God has prom-

m you must not call . . . nor: *or* the name of their gods
shall not be your boast, nor must you . . .
n Be on . . . for: *or* Take very good care to love the LORD
your God, but . . .

23.1–16: Joshua's farewell and death. See Moses' farewell, Deut. ch. 31.

ised you has failed to come true, every
15 word of it. But the same LORD God who
has kept his word to you to such good
effect can equally bring every kind of
evil on you, until he has rooted you out
from this good land which he has
16 given you. If you break the covenant
which the LORD your God has prescribed and prostrate yourselves in
worship before other gods, then the
LORD will be angry with you and you
will quickly vanish from the good land
he has given you.'

24 Joshua assembled all the tribes of
Israel at Shechem. He summoned the
elders of Israel, the heads of families,
the judges and officers; and they pre-
2 sented themselves before God. Joshua
then said this to all the people: 'This
is the word of the LORD the God of
Israel: "Long ago your forefathers,
Terah and his sons Abraham and
Nahor, lived beside the Euphrates,
3 and they worshipped other gods. I
took your father Abraham from
beside the Euphrates and led him
through the length and breadth of
Canaan. I gave him many descendants:
4 I gave him Isaac, and to Isaac I gave
Jacob and Esau. I put Esau in possession of the hill-country of Seir, but
Jacob and his sons went down to
5 Egypt. I sent Moses and Aaron, and I
struck the Egyptians with plagues—
you know well what I did among them
—and after that I brought you out;
6 I brought your fathers out of Egypt
and you came to the Red Sea. The
Egyptians sent their chariots and cavalry to pursue your fathers to the sea.
7 But when they appealed to the LORD,
he put a screen of darkness between
you and the Egyptians, and brought the
sea down on them and it covered them;
you saw for yourselves what I did to
Egypt. For a long time you lived in the
8 wilderness. Then I brought you into
the land of the Amorites who lived east
of the Jordan; they fought against

you, but I delivered them into your
hands; you took possession of their
country and I destroyed them for your
sake. The king of Moab, Balak son of 9
Zippor, took the field against Israel.
He sent for Balaam son of Beor to lay
a curse on you, but I would not listen 10
to him. Instead of that he blessed you;
and so I saved you from the power of
Balak. Then you crossed the Jordan 11
and came to Jericho. The citizens of
Jericho fought against you,*o* but I
delivered them into your hands. I 12
spread panic before you, and it was
this, not your sword or your bow, that
drove out the two kings of the Amorites.
I gave you land on which you had 13
not laboured, cities which you had
never built; you have lived in those
cities and you eat the produce of vineyards and olive-groves which you did
not plant."

'Hold the LORD in awe then, and 14
worship him in loyalty and truth. Banish the gods whom your fathers worshipped beside the Euphrates and in
Egypt, and worship the LORD. But if 15
it does not please you to worship the
LORD, choose here and now whom
you will worship: the gods whom
your forefathers worshipped beside
the Euphrates, or the gods of the
Amorites in whose land you are
living. But I and my family, we will
worship the LORD.' The people an- 16
swered, 'God forbid that we should
forsake the LORD to worship other
gods, for it was the LORD our God who 17
brought us and our fathers up from
Egypt, that land of slavery; it was he
who displayed those great signs before
our eyes and guarded us on all our
wanderings among the many peoples
through whose lands we passed. The 18
LORD drove out before us the Amorites
and all the peoples who lived in that
country. We too will worship the

*o Prob. rdg.; Heb. adds Amorites, Perizzites, Canaanites,
Hittites, Girgashites, Hivites, and Jebusites.*

24.1–33: The covenant at Shechem. The generation born in the desert makes a covenant with
the LORD similar to the one which their fathers had entered into at Sinai; see Exod.24.1–11;
34.27–28; compare Josh.8.30–35. Some scholars think that involved here were clans related
to Israel who had not taken part in the Exodus events. **1:** *Shechem,* in the center of the country,
was ideally located for a gathering of the tribes; see 1 Kgs. ch. 12. Its religious history, too,
made it ideal for the making of a covenant: see Gen.12.6–7; 33.18–20. **2–13:** Joshua recalls the
LORD's interventions in favor of Israel; see Deut.6.21–23; 26.5–9. **14–24:** Israel pledges loyalty

19 LORD; he is our God.' Joshua answered the people, 'You cannot worship the LORD. He is a holy god, a jealous god, and he will not forgive your 20 rebellion and your sins. If you forsake the LORD and worship foreign gods, he will turn and bring adversity upon you and, although he once brought you prosperity, he will make an end 21 of you.' The people said to Joshua, 22 'No; we will worship the LORD.' He said to them, 'You are witnesses against yourselves that you have chosen the LORD and will worship him.' 'Yes,' 23 they answered, 'we are witnesses.' He said to them, 'Then here and now banish the foreign gods that are among you, and turn your hearts to the LORD 24 the God of Israel.' The people said to Joshua, 'The LORD our God we will worship and his voice we will obey.' 25 So Joshua made a covenant that day with*p* the people; he drew up a statute and an ordinance for them in Shechem 26 and wrote its terms in the book of the law of God. He took a great stone and set it up there under the terebinth*q* in 27 the sanctuary of the LORD, and said to all the people, 'This stone is a witness against us; for it has heard all the words which the LORD has spoken to us. If you renounce your God, it shall be a witness against you.' Then 28 Joshua dismissed the people, each man to his patrimony.

After these things, Joshua son of 29 Nun the servant of the LORD died; he was a hundred and ten years old. They buried him within the border of 30 his own patrimony in Timnath-serah in the hill-country of Ephraim to the north of Mount Gaash. Israel served 31 the LORD during the lifetime of Joshua and of the elders who outlived him and who well knew all that the LORD had done for Israel.

The bones of Joseph, which the 32 Israelites had brought up from Egypt, were buried in Shechem, in the plot of land which Jacob had bought from the sons of Hamor father of Shechem for a hundred sheep;*r* and they passed into the patrimony of the house of Joseph. Eleazar son of Aaron died 33 and was buried in the hill which had been given to Phinehas his son in the hill-country of Ephraim.

p Or for.
q Or pole.
r Or pieces of money (cp. Gen. 33. 19; Job 42. 11).

---

to the LORD. **25–28:** The covenant is established. **25:** The Canaanite god worshiped at Shechem was called Baal-Berith or El-Berith, "god of the covenant" (see Judg.9.4,46); hence the city had covenant associations for the Canaanites too. **26:** Sacred trees were often connected with ancient sanctuaries (Gen.12.6; 13.18; 35.4,8; Judg.9.6), as were stone pillars (Gen.28.18; Exod.24.4; Judg.9.6). **29–31:** Death and burial of Joshua. **30:** *Timnath-serah:* see 19.49–50. **32–33:** The burial of Joseph and Eleazar. *Brought up from Eygpt:* see Exod.13.19. *Which Jacob bought:* Gen.33.19.

THE BOOK OF
JUDGES

Whereas the Book of Joshua deals with the conquest of Canaan, Judges deals with the subsequent settlement. Largely an account of battles lasting through several generations before the country was securely in Israel's hands, Judges preserves traditions of various tribes and the exploits of their particular heroes, the "judges" (see 2.16 n.).

The opening section (1.1–2.5) describes the settlement of the tribes. It implies that much of Canaan was not yet subjugated, despite the view in Joshua of a complete conquest. The main part of the book, after a moralizing introduction (2.6–3.6), recalls the contribution of the individual judges who are given as a total of twelve, though long narratives are about only five: Ehud (3.12–30); Deborah (chs. 4–5); Gideon (chs. 6–8), ch. 9 treats his wicked son, Abimelech; Jephthah (10.6–12.7); and Samson (chs. 13–16). The other seven are to be found in 3.7–11, 31; 10.1–5; and 12.8–15. An appendix contains an account of the migration of Dan (chs. 17–18) and the trespass of the Benjaminites (chs. 19–21).

The final editor, in preserving these colorful stories, was concerned with the moral lesson that loyalty to God brings national success and disloyalty guarantees disaster. This is the theme also of Deuteronomy, especially Deut. ch. 28. Modern criticism considers Judges to be part of the "Deuteronomic history" (see Introduction to Josh.).

The conquest of Canaan completed

1 AFTER THE DEATH OF JOSHUA THE Israelites inquired of the LORD which tribe should attack the 2 Canaanites first. The LORD answered, 'Judah shall attack. I hereby deliver the 3 country into his power.' Judah said to his brother Simeon, 'Go forward with me into my allotted territory, and let us do battle with the Canaanites; then I in turn will go with you into your territory.' 4 So Simeon went with him; then Judah advanced to the attack, and the LORD delivered the Canaanites and Perizzites into their hands. They slaughtered ten 5 thousand of them at Bezek. There they came upon Adoni-bezek, engaged him in battle and defeated the Canaanites 6 and Perizzites. Adoni-bezek fled, but they pursued him, took him prisoner and cut off his thumbs and his great toes. 7 Adoni-bezek said, 'I once had seventy kings whose thumbs and great toes were cut off picking up the scraps from under my table. What I have done God has done to me.' He was brought to Jerusalem and died there.

The men of Judah made an assault 8 on Jerusalem and captured it, put its people to the sword and set fire to the city. Then they turned south to fight 9 the Canaanites of the hill-country, the Negeb, and the Shephelah. Judah at- 10 tacked the Canaanites in Hebron, formerly called Kiriath-arba, and defeated Sheshai, Ahiman and Talmai. From there they marched against the 11 inhabitants of Debir, formerly called Kiriath-sepher. Caleb said, 'Whoever 12 attacks Kiriath-sepher and captures it, to him I will give my daughter Achsah in marriage.' Othniel, son of Caleb's 13 younger brother Kenaz, captured it, and Caleb gave him his daughter Achsah. When she came to him, he incited 14

1.1–2.5: The conquest of Canaan completed. This historical prologue, considered by most scholars to be an ancient document, or derived from one, describes the arduous attempts at conquest by isolated tribes, with the native inhabitants being subjugated rather than exterminated; contrast Josh. chs. 10–11; see Josh.13.13 n. **1.1–21: The course of conquests.** Compare Josh. ch. 15. Many scholars hold that the ancient document (1.1–2.5 n.) has been shaped to enhance Judah, in which territory Jerusalem lay. **1:** After the death of Joshua is probably added so as to accord with Josh.24.29; it contradicts the ensuing narrative; see 2.6–8. They inquired of the LORD, probably by using sacred lots; see Exod.28.15 n. **3:** Simeon: see Josh.19.1–9 n. **4:** Perizzites: see Gen.13.7; Deut.7.1. The location of Bezek is uncertain. **5:** Adoni-bezek is possibly the same as the Adoni-zedek, king of Jerusalem, of Josh.10.1–3. **8:** Jerusalem is portrayed as captured at a later time by David in 2 Sam.5.6–9. **9:** Negeb: the southern desert. Shephelah: see Josh.11.2 n. **10:** Hebron: see Josh.10.36–37. According to v. 20 and Josh.14.6–15 and 15.13–14, it was given to the clan of Caleb. **11–15:** This story occurs also in Josh.15.15–19. **11:** Debir: probably the modern Tell Beit

her to ask her father for a piece of land. As she sat on the ass, she made a noise,

15 and Caleb said, 'What did you mean by that?' She replied, 'I want to ask a favour of you. You have put me in this dry Negeb; you must give me pools of water as well.' So Caleb gave her the upper pool and the lower pool.

16 The descendants of Moses' father-in-law, the Kenite, went up with the men of Judah from the Vale of Palm Trees to the wilderness of Judah which is in the Negeb of Arad and settled among

17 the Amalekites. Judah then accompanied his brother Simeon, attacked the Canaanites in Zephath and destroyed it; hence the city was called

18 Hormah.*a* Judah took Gaza, Ashkelon, and Ekron, and the territory of each.

19 The LORD was with Judah and they occupied the hill-country, but they could not drive out the inhabitants of the Vale because they had chariots of iron.

20 Hebron was given to Caleb as Moses had directed, and he drove out the

21 three sons of Anak. But the Benjamites did not drive out the Jebusites of Jerusalem; and the Jebusites have lived on in Jerusalem with the Benjamites till the present day.

22 The tribes of Joseph attacked Bethel,

23 and the LORD was with them. They sent spies to Bethel, formerly called Luz.

24 These spies saw a man coming out of the city and said to him, 'Show us how to enter the city, and we will see that

25 you come to no harm.' So he showed them how to enter, and they put the city to the sword, but let the man and

26 his family go free. He went into Hittite country, built a city and named it Luz, which is still its name today.

27 Manasseh did not drive out the inhabitants of Beth-shean with its villages, nor of Taanach, Dor, Ibleam, and Megiddo, with the villages of each of them; the Canaanites held their ground in that region. Later, when

28 Israel became strong, they put them to forced labour, but they never completely drove them out.

29 Ephraim did not drive out the Canaanites who lived in Gezer, but the Canaanites lived among them there.

30 Zebulun did not drive out the inhabitants of Kitron and Nahalol, but the Canaanites lived among them and were put to forced labour.

31 Asher did not drive out the inhabitants of Acco and Sidon, of Ahlab, Achzib, Helbah, Aphik and Rehob. Thus the

32 Asherites lived among the Canaanite inhabitants and did not drive them out.

33 Naphtali did not drive out the inhabitants of Beth-shemesh and of Beth-anath, but lived among the Canaanite inhabitants and put the inhabitants of Beth-shemesh and Beth-anath to forced labour.

34 The Amorites pressed the Danites back into the hill-country and did not allow them to come down into the Vale.

35 The Amorites held their ground in Mount Heres and in Aijalon and Shaalbim, but the tribes of Joseph increased their pressure on them until they reduced them to forced labour.

36 The boundary of the Edomites ran from the ascent of Akrabbim, upwards from Sela.

2 The angel of the LORD came up from Gilgal to Bokim, and said, 'I brought*b* you up out of Egypt and into

a That is Destruction. b Prob. rdg.; Heb. I will bring.

Mirsim, southwest of Hebron. **16:** The Kenites, a nomadic tribe, here mentioned as allies of Judah during the invasion of Canaan, settled among the Amalekites. Because of their aid to Israel, they are spared by Saul (1 Sam.15.6). *Amalekites:* see Exod.17.8 n. **17:** *Zephath:* a city in the Negeb; *Hormah* means "destruction." Some scholars think this reference is the same as the incident in Num.21.3. **18:** Gaza, Ashkelon, and Ekron are three of the five Philistine cities; see Josh.13.2 n. This account of their capture seems to anticipate 2 Sam.8.1; Sept., however, says specifically that Judah "did not" take them; the negative may have been omitted from the MT by a copyist. **19–21:** See Josh.13.13 n. **19:** The Philistines had a monopoly on iron; see 1 Sam.13.19–22.

1.22–29: Conquests of the Joseph tribes. See Josh. chs. 16–17 and 13.13 n. **22–26:** See Josh. 7.2 n.

1.30–35: The conquests of the Galilee area. See Josh. chs. 18–19 and 13.13 n. **36:** Boundary of Edom and Judah; see Num.34.3–5.

2.1–5: The moral reason for the delay in the conquest is Israel's infidelity. See Deut. ch. 28. In 1.28–35 the reason was the enemies' strength. **1:** *The angel:* the words that follow, *I brought you up out of Egypt*, indicate God himself, rather than an angel; see Gen.16.7 n. *Gilgal:* see Josh.4.19 n. *Bokim* is probably Bethel; the word means "weepers" (vv. 4–5).

the country which I vowed I would give to your forefathers. I said, I will never break my covenant with you,
2 and you in turn must make no covenant with the inhabitants of the country; you must pull down their altars. But you did not obey me, and look what
3 you have done! So I said, I will not drive them out before you; they will decoy you, and their gods will shut you fast
4 in the trap.' When the angel of the LORD said this to the Israelites, they all
5 wept and wailed, and so the place was called Bokim;[c] and they offered sacrifices there to the LORD.

Israel under the judges

6 JOSHUA DISMISSED THE PEOPLE, AND THE Israelites went off to occupy the country,
7 each man to his allotted portion. As long as Joshua was alive and the elders who survived him—everyone, that is, who had witnessed the whole great work which the LORD had done for Israel—the people worshipped the
8 LORD. At the age of a hundred and ten Joshua son of Nun, the servant of the
9 LORD, died, and they buried him within the border of his own property in Timnath-heres north of Mount Gaash
10 in the hill-country of Ephraim. Of that whole generation, all were gathered to their forefathers, and another generation followed who did not acknowledge the LORD and did not know what he
11 had done for Israel. Then the Israelites did what was wrong in the eyes of the LORD, and worshipped the Baalim.[d]
12 They forsook the LORD, their fathers' God who had brought them out of Egypt, and went after other gods, gods of the races among whom they lived; they bowed before them and provoked
13 the LORD to anger; they forsook the LORD and worshipped the Baal and
14 the Ashtaroth.[e] The LORD in his anger

made them the prey of bands of raiders and plunderers; he sold them to their enemies all around them, and they could no longer make a stand. Every 15 time they went out to battle the LORD brought disaster upon them, as he had said when he gave them his solemn warning, and they were in dire straits.

The LORD set judges over them, who 16 rescued them from the marauding bands. Yet they did not listen even to 17 these judges, but turned wantonly to worship other gods and bowed down before them; all too soon they abandoned the path of obedience to the LORD's commands which their forefathers had followed. They did not obey the LORD. Whenever the LORD set up 18 a judge over them, he was with that judge, and kept them safe from their enemies so long as he lived. The LORD would relent as often as he heard them groaning under oppression and ill-treatment. But as soon as the judge 19 was dead, they would relapse into deeper corruption than their forefathers and give their allegiance to other gods, worshipping them and bowing down before them. They gave up none of their evil practices and their wilful ways. And the LORD was angry with 20 Israel and said, 'This nation has broken the covenant which I laid upon their forefathers and has not obeyed me, and now, of all the nations which 21 Joshua left at his death, I will not drive out to make room for them one single man. By their means I will test Israel, 22 to see whether or not they will keep strictly to the way of the LORD as their forefathers did.' So the LORD left 23 those nations alone and made no haste to drive them out or give them into Joshua's hands.

These are the nations which the 3 LORD left as a means of testing all the

c *That is* Weepers.
d The Baalim *were Canaanite deities.*
e The Ashtaroth *were Canaanite deities.*

2.6–3.6: Second introduction. An editor explains the whole history of the age in terms of recurring cycles of prosperity, apostasy, punishment, repentance, and deliverance; "judges" are the deliverers who bring the people back from idolatry (vv. 16–18); deprived of judges the people relapse (v. 19). **8:** Joshua's death: see Josh.24.29. **11–13:** *Baalim:* male deities; *Ashtaroth*, female; see Tfn. *d* and *e.* **15:** *The LORD brought disaster upon them:* all is attributed to God; secondary causes are passed over. **16:** The *judges* were military heroes who defended and delivered the people from oppression and then continued to govern them; a divine impulse moves them (see 3.10). **22–23:** The native population is allowed to survive to *test* Israel's

Israelites who had not taken part in
2 the battles for Canaan, his purpose
being to teach succeeding generations
of Israel, or those at least who had not
learnt in former times, how to make
3 war. These were: the five lords of the
Philistines, all the Canaanites, the
Sidonians, and the Hivites who lived
in Mount Lebanon from Mount Baal-
4 hermon as far as Lebo-hamath. His
purpose also was to test whether the
Israelites would obey the commands
which the LORD had given to their fore-
5 fathers through Moses. Thus the
Israelites lived among the Canaanites,
the Hittites, the Amorites, the Perizzites, the Hivites, and the Jebusites.
6 They took their daughters in marriage
and gave their own daughters to their
sons; and they worshipped their gods.
7 The Israelites did what was wrong
in the eyes of the LORD; they forgot
the LORD their God and worshipped
8 the Baalim and the Asheroth.*f* The
LORD was angry with Israel and he sold
them to Cushan-rishathaim, king of
Aram-naharaim,*g* who kept them in
9 subjection for eight years. Then the
Israelites cried to the LORD for help
and he raised up a man to deliver them,
Othniel son of Caleb's younger
brother Kenaz, and he set them free.
10 The spirit of the LORD came upon
him and he became judge over Israel.
He took the field, and the LORD
delivered Cushan-rishathaim king of
Aram into his hands; Othniel was too
11 strong for him. Thus the land was at
peace for forty years until Othniel son
of Kenaz died.
12 Once again the Israelites did what
was wrong in the eyes of the LORD,
and because of this he roused Eglon
13 king of Moab against Israel. Eglon
mustered the Ammonites and the

Amalekites, advanced to attack Israel
and took possession of the Vale of
Palm Trees. The Israelites were subject 14
to Eglon king of Moab for eighteen
years. When they cried to the LORD 15
for help, he raised up a man to deliver
them, Ehud son of Gera the Benjamite,
who was left-handed. The Israelites sent
him to pay their tribute to Eglon king
of Moab. Ehud made himself a two- 16
edged sword, only fifteen inches long,
which he fastened on his right side
under his clothes, and he brought the 17
tribute to Eglon king of Moab. Eglon
was a very fat man. When Ehud had 18
finished presenting the tribute, he sent
on the men who had carried it, and he 19
himself turned back from the Carved
Stones at Gilgal. 'My lord king,' he
said, 'I have a word for you in private.'
Eglon called for silence and dismissed
all his attendants. Ehud then came up 20
to him as he sat in the roof-chamber
of his summer palace and said, 'I have
a word from God for you.' So Eglon
rose from his seat, and Ehud reached 21
with his left hand, drew the sword
from his right side and drove it into
his belly. The hilt went in after the 22
blade and the fat closed over the blade;
he did not draw the sword out but left
it protruding behind. Ehud went out to 23
the porch, shut the doors on him and
fastened them. When he had gone 24
away, Eglon's servants came and,
finding the doors fastened, they said,
'He must be relieving himself in the
closet of his summer palace.' They 25
waited until they were ashamed to
delay any longer, and still he did not
open the doors of the roof-chamber.
So they took the key and opened the
doors; and there was their master lying

f Plural of Asheroth, *the name of a Canaanite goddess.*
g That is Aram of Two Rivers.

loyalty to God; see 3.1–4. **3.3:** See Josh.13.2–6. **3.4:** See Deut.8.2; Judg.2.22. **5:** See Deut.7.1.
　　3.7–11: Othniel. The first judge is from Judah, a tribe of special interest to the author;
see 1.1–21 n. The story may be related to 1.12–13. **7:** *Asheroth* is the plural of Asherah,
the name of a goddess; see 2.11-13 n. **8:** *Sold:* see 2.15 n. *Cushan-rishathaim* is unknown
elsewhere. *Aram-naharaim,* "Aram of Two Rivers," is a name for Mesopotamia. The geographical improbability of an invasion from Mesopotamia leads some to conjecture that "Aram"
should be emended to the more probable "Edom." **10:** *The Spirit of the LORD came upon him:*
the judges were impelled or inspired as the prophets were. **11:** *Land had rest:* an editorial
formula frequent in Judg.
　　3.12–30: Ehud and delivery from the Moabites. 12: *Moab* was immediately east of the Dead
Sea, *Ammon* just north of Moab. *Amalek:* see Exod.17.8–16 n. **13:** *Vale of Palm Trees:* this is
usually considered to allude to Jericho; see 1.16. **19:** *Carved Stones at Gilgal:* see Josh.4.1–5.1 n.

26 on the floor dead. While they had been waiting, Ehud made his escape; he passed the Carved Stones and escaped 27 to Seirah. When he arrived there, he sounded the trumpet in the hill-country of Ephraim, and the Israelites came down from the hills with him at 28 their head. He said to them, 'Follow me, for the LORD has delivered your enemy the Moabites into your hands.' Down they came after him, and they seized the fords of the Jordan against the Moabites and allowed no man to 29 cross. They killed that day some ten thousand Moabites, all of them men of substance and all fighting men; not one 30 escaped. Thus Moab on that day became subject to Israel, and the land was at peace for eighty years.

31   After Ehud there was Shamgar of Beth-anath.[h] He killed six hundred Philistines with an ox-goad, and he too delivered Israel.

4   After Ehud's death the Israelites once again did what was wrong in the 2 eyes of the LORD, so he sold them to Jabin the Canaanite king, who ruled in Hazor. The commander of his forces was Sisera, who lived in Harosheth-3 of-the-Gentiles. The Israelites cried to the LORD for help, because Sisera had nine hundred chariots of iron and had oppressed Israel harshly for twenty 4 years. At that time Deborah wife of Lappidoth,[i] a prophetess, was judge 5 in Israel. It was her custom to sit beneath the Palm-tree of Deborah between Ramah and Bethel in the hill-country of Ephraim, and the Israelites 6 went up to her for justice. She sent for Barak son of Abinoam from Kedesh in Naphtali and said to him, 'These are the commands of the LORD the God of Israel: "Go and draw ten thousand men from Naphtali and Zebulun and

bring them with you to Mount Tabor, and I will draw Sisera, Jabin's com- 7 mander, to the Torrent of Kishon with his chariots and all his rabble, and there I will deliver them into your hands."' Barak answered her, 'If you 8 go with me, I will go; but if you will not go, neither will I.' 'Certainly I will 9 go with you,' she said, 'but this venture will bring you no glory, because the LORD will leave Sisera to fall into the hands of a woman.' So Deborah rose and went with Barak to Kedesh. Barak 10 summoned Zebulun and Naphtali to Kedesh and marched up with ten thousand men, and Deborah went with him.

Now Heber the Kenite had parted 11 company with the Kenites, the descendants of Hobab, Moses' brother-in-law, and he had pitched his tent at Elon-bezaanannim near Kedesh.

Word was brought to Sisera that 12 Barak son of Abinoam had gone up to Mount Tabor; so he summoned all his 13 chariots, nine hundred chariots of iron, and his troops, from Harosheth-of-the-Gentiles to the Torrent of Kishon. Then Deborah said to Barak, 'Up! 14 This day the LORD gives Sisera into your hands. Already the LORD has gone out to battle before you.' So Barak came charging down from Mount Tabor with ten thousand men at his back. The LORD put Sisera to rout with 15 all his chariots and his army before Barak's onslaught; but Sisera himself dismounted from his chariot and fled on foot. Barak pursued the chariots 16 and the army as far as Harosheth, and the whole army was put to the sword and perished; not a man was left alive. Meanwhile Sisera fled on foot to the 17 tent of Jael wife of Heber the Kenite,

h of Beth-anath: *or* son of Anath.
i wife of Lappidoth: *or* a spirited woman.

28: The Moabites had been occupying an area west of the Jordan. **29:** The massacre of the Moabites.
   3.31: Shamgar. This notably brief passage is to be found in some manuscripts after 16.31; Shamgar is mentioned in 5.6. The verse separates the stories of Ehud and Deborah, linked together in 4.1. The allusion here to the Philistines also points to a later period; see Josh.13.2 n.
   4.1–5.31: Deborah. The victory of Deborah and Barak over the Canaanites is told twice, in prose (ch. 4), and in poetry (ch. 5). Ch. 5 is by far older than ch. 4. **2:** *Jabin* is not mentioned in ch. 5; in Josh.11.1–5 he organizes a coalition against Joshua. *Hazor:* see Josh.11.1 n. *Harosheth-of-the-Gentiles* is tentatively identified with Tell Amr on the river Kishon; see v. 7 n. **3:** The *chariots of iron:* the Hebrews as yet were unskilled in working in iron (1.19 n.; Josh.17.16; 1 Sam.13.19–22) and lacked such chariots. **6:** *Naphtali* and *Zebulun* were two of the Galilean tribes; see 1.30,33. *Mount Tabor:* in Galilee north of the plain of Esdraelon. **7:** *Torrent of Kishon:* a stream flowing westward, north of Mount Carmel. **11:** *Kenite:* see 1.16 n.

because Jabin king of Hazor and the household of Heber the Kenite were

18 at peace. Jael came out to meet Sisera and said to him, 'Come in here, my lord, come in; do not be afraid.' So he went into the tent, and she covered him

19 with a rug. He said to her, 'Give me some water to drink; I am thirsty.' She opened a skin full of milk, gave him a drink and covered him up again.

20 He said to her, 'Stand at the tent door, and if anybody comes and asks if some-

21 one is here, say No.' But Jael, Heber's wife, took a tent-peg, picked up a hammer, crept up to him, and drove the peg into his skull as he lay sound asleep. His brains oozed out on the ground, his limbs twitched, and he

22 died. When Barak came up in pursuit of Sisera, Jael went out to meet him and said to him, 'Come, I will show you the man you are looking for.' He went in with her, and there was Sisera lying

23 dead with the tent-peg in his skull. That day God gave victory to the Israelites

24 over Jabin king of Canaan, and they pressed home their attacks upon that king of Canaan until they had made an end of him.

5 That day Deborah and Barak son of Abinoam sang this song:

2 For the leaders, the leaders[j] in Israel,
for the people who answered the call,
bless ye the LORD.

3 Hear me, you kings; princes, give ear;
I will sing, I will sing to the LORD.
I will raise a psalm to the LORD the God of Israel.

4 O LORD, at thy setting forth from Seir,
when thou camest marching out of the plains of Edom,
earth trembled; heaven quaked;
the clouds streamed down in torrents.

5 Mountains shook in fear before the LORD, the lord of Sinai,
before the LORD, the God of Israel.

In the days of Shamgar of Beth-anath,[k]   6
in the days of Jael, caravans plied no longer;
men who had followed the high roads went round by devious paths.
Champions there were none,   7
none left in Israel,
until I,[l] Deborah, arose,
arose, a mother in Israel.
They chose new gods,   8
they consorted with demons.[m]
Not a shield, not a lance was to be seen
in the forty thousand of Israel.
Be proud at heart, you marshals of   9
Israel;
you among the people that answered the call,
bless ye the LORD.
You that ride your tawny she-asses,   10
that sit on saddle-cloths,
and you that take the road afoot,
ponder this well.
Hark, the sound of the players   11
striking up
in the places where the women draw water!
It is the victories of the LORD that they commemorate there,
his triumphs as the champion of Israel.

Down to the gates came the LORD's people:
'Rouse, rouse yourself, Deborah,   12
rouse yourself, lead out the host.
Up, Barak! Take prisoners in plenty,
son of Abinoam.'
Then down marched the column[n]   13
and its chieftains,
the people of the LORD marched down[o] like warriors.
The men of Ephraim showed a brave   14
front in the vale,

j Or For those who had flowing locks.
k of Beth-anath: or son of Anath.   l Or you.
m Or satyrs.   n Prob. rdg.; Heb. survivor.
o Prob. rdg.; Heb. adds to me.

5.1–31: This song is the oldest surviving extended fragment of Heb. literature. At places the text is corrupt and almost unintelligible. **2:** *Leaders:* see Tfn. *j.* The unbinding of the hair was a war ritual. **4:** The LORD is pictured as coming *from Seir* and *Edom* to help his people; it is the route of the Exodus; note the reference to Sinai in v. 5. The *torrents* here and in v. 21 may refer to a rainstorm which enabled Israelite foot soldiers to overcome the chariots of 4.3,15. For Israel the storm (v. 21) manifested the presence of the LORD. **6:** *Caravans plied no longer:* it was a time of anarchy. **14:** *Machir:* part of the tribe of Manasseh, established in Gilead east of the Jordan; see Gen.50.23 and Josh.13.31. However, because Gilead took no part in this

crying, 'With you, Benjamin! Your
  clansmen are here!'
From Machir down came the
  marshals,
from Zebulun the bearers of the
  musterer's staff.
15 Issachar joined with Deborah in the
  uprising,*p*
Issachar stood by Barak;
down into the valley they rushed.
But Reuben, he was split into
  factions,
great were their heart-searchings.
16 What made you linger by the cattle-
  pens
to listen to the shrill calling of the
  shepherds?*q*
17 Gilead stayed beyond Jordan;
and Dan, why did he tarry by the
  ships?
Asher lingered by the sea-shore,
by its creeks he stayed.
18 The people of Zebulun risked their
  very lives,
so did Naphtali on the heights of the
  battlefield.
19 Kings came, they fought;
then fought the kings of Canaan
at Taanach by the waters of
  Megiddo;
no plunder of silver did they take.
20 The stars fought from heaven,
the stars in their courses fought
  against Sisera.
21 The Torrent of Kishon swept him
  away,
the Torrent barred his flight, the
  Torrent of Kishon;
march on in might, my soul!
22 Then hammered the hooves of his
  horses,
his chargers galloped, galloped away.
23 A curse on Meroz, said the angel
  of the LORD;
a curse, a curse on its inhabitants,

because they brought no help to the
  LORD,
no help to the LORD and the fighting
  men.
Blest above women be Jael,   24
the wife of Heber the Kenite;
blest above all women in the tents.
He asked for water: she gave him   25
  milk,
she offered him curds in a bowl fit
  for a chieftain.
She stretched out her hand for the   26
  tent-peg,
her right hand to hammer the
  weary.
With the hammer she struck Sisera,
she crushed his head;
she struck and his brains ebbed out.
At her feet he sank down, he fell,   27
  he lay;
at her feet he sank down and fell.
Where he sank down, there he fell,
  done to death.

The mother of Sisera peered through 28
  the lattice,
through the window she peered and
  shrilly cried,
'Why are his chariots so long
  coming?
Why is the clatter of his chariots so
  long delayed?'
The wisest of her princesses   29
  answered her,
yes, she found her own answer:
'They must be finding spoil, taking   30
  their shares,
a wench to each man, two wenches,
booty of dyed stuffs for Sisera,
booty of dyed stuffs,
dyed stuff, and striped, two lengths
  of striped stuff—
to grace the victor's neck.'

p in the uprising: prob. rdg.; Heb. my officers.
q Prob. rdg.; Heb. adds Reuben was split into factions,
great were their heart-searchings.

---

war (v. 17), some scholars think that here Machir is the part of Manasseh west of the Jordan.
15–17: The distant tribes of *Reuben, Gilead, Dan,* and *Asher* stayed at home. Judah, Simeon, and
Levi go unmentioned. *Gilead* may refer to the part of Manasseh east of the Jordan; see v. 14 n.
and Josh.13.29–32, or it may refer to the tribe of Gad; see Josh.13.24–28. *Dan* is already
conceived of as in the north and associated with Asher, although the migration from the south
is described only in ch. 18. **19:** *Taanach* and *Megiddo* guarded the passes through the Carmel
range. Some scholars think that the mention of *the waters of Megiddo* rather than the city
itself indicates that Megiddo was unoccupied at this time; using archaeological evidence they
then date the battle here about 1125 B.C. **21:** See v. 4 n. **23:** *Meroz* is probably a nearby town
which took no part in the battle. **24–27:** *Sisera* is here struck down apparently while standing;
see 4.17–22 where *Jael* killed him while he was asleep. **29–30:** The Canaanite women are ironically
pictured as waiting for the *spoil.*

31 So perish all thine enemies, O Lord;
but let all who love thee be like the
   sun rising in strength.

The land was at peace for forty years.

6 THE ISRAELITES DID WHAT WAS WRONG
in the eyes of the Lord and he delivered them into the hands of Midian
2 for seven years. The Midianites were
too strong for Israel, and the Israelites
were forced to find themselves hollow
places in the mountains, and caves
3 and strongholds. If the Israelites had
sown their seed, the Midianites and
the Amalekites and other eastern
tribes would come up and attack
4 Israel. They then pitched their camps
in the country and destroyed the
crops as far as the outskirts of Gaza,
leaving nothing to support life in
5 Israel, sheep or ox or ass. They came
up with their herds and their tents,
like a swarm of locusts; they and their
camels were past counting. They had
come into the land for its growing
6 crop,*r* and so the Israelites were
brought to destitution by the Midianites, and they cried to the Lord for
7 help. When the Israelites cried to the
Lord because of what they had suf-
8 fered from the Midianites, he sent them
a prophet who said to them, 'These
are the words of the Lord the God of
Israel: I brought you up from Egypt,
9 that land of slavery. I delivered you
from the Egyptians and from all
your oppressors. I drove them out
before you and gave you their lands.
10 I said to you, "I am the Lord your God:
do not stand in awe of the gods of the
Amorites in whose country you are
settling." But you did not listen to
me.'
11 Now the angel of the Lord came
and sat under the terebinth at Ophrah
which belonged to Joash the Abiez-
rite. His son Gideon was threshing
wheat in the winepress, so that he
might get it away quickly from the
Midianites. The angel of the Lord 12
showed himself to Gideon and said,
'You are a brave man, and the Lord
is with you.' Gideon said, 'But pray, 13
my lord, if the Lord really is with us,
why has all this happened to us?
What has become of all those wonderful deeds of his, of which we have
heard from our fathers, when they told
us how the Lord brought us out of
Egypt? But now the Lord has cast us
off and delivered us into the power of
the Midianites.' The Lord turned to 14
him and said, 'Go and use this strength
of yours to free Israel from the power
of the Midianites. It is I that send
you.' Gideon said, 'Pray, my lord, 15
how can I save Israel? Look at my
clan: it is the weakest in Manasseh,
and I am the least in my father's
family.' The Lord answered, 'I will be 16
with you, and you shall lay low all
Midian as one man.' He replied, 'If I 17
stand so well with you, give me a sign
that it is you who speak to me. Please 18
do not leave this place until I come
with my gift and lay it before you.'
He answered, 'I will stay until you
come back.' So Gideon went in, pre- 19
pared a kid and made an ephah of
flour into unleavened cakes. He put
the meat in a basket, poured the broth
into a pot and brought it out to him
under the terebinth. As he approached,
the angel of God said to him, 'Take the 20
meat and the cakes, and put them here
on the rock and pour out the broth',
and he did so. Then the angel of the 21
Lord reached out the staff in his hand
and touched the meat and the cakes
with the tip of it. Fire sprang up from
the rock and consumed the meat and
the cakes; and the angel of the Lord
was no more to be seen. Then Gideon 22
knew that it was the angel of the Lord
and said, 'Alas, Lord GOD! Then it is

r for its growing crop: or and laid it waste.

6.1–8.35: **Gideon and delivery from the Midianites,** a kindred people (Gen.25.1–6) who were
desert nomads. **3–4:** These nomadic raiders were pasturing their flocks on Israelite crops.
8: The appearance of a *prophet,* as here, is frequent in the Deuteronomic books, especially
Kgs. **10:** *You did not listen to me:* the Israelites had adopted the worship of the Baalim who,
the native *Amorites* thought, guaranteed good crops; see vv. 25–32 and 2.11–13. **11:** *The angel
of the Lord:* see 2.1 n. In v. 14 it is the Lord, not an angel, who speaks. *Terebinth* refers to a
sacred tree; see Gen.12.6. The location of *Ophrah* is not known beyond its being in Manasseh.

23 true: I have seen the angel of the LORD face to face.' But the LORD said to him, 'Peace be with you; do not 24 be afraid, you shall not die.' So Gideon built an altar there to the LORD and named it Jehovah-shalom.[s] It stands to this day at Ophrah-of-the-Abiezrites.

25 That night the LORD said to Gideon, 'Take a young bull of your father's, the yearling bull,[t] tear down the altar of Baal which belongs to your father and cut down the sacred pole which 26 stands beside[u] it. Then build an altar of the proper pattern[v] to the LORD your God on the top of this earthwork;[w] take the yearling bull and offer it as a whole-offering with the wood of the sacred pole that you cut 27 down.' So Gideon took ten of his servants and did as the LORD had told him. He was afraid of his father's family and his fellow-citizens, and so he 28 did it by night, and not by day. When the citizens rose early in the morning, they found the altar of Baal overturned and the sacred pole which had stood beside it cut down and the yearling bull offered up as a whole-offering 29 on the altar which he had built. They asked each other who had done it, and, after searching inquiries, were told that 30 it was Gideon son of Joash. So the citizens said to Joash, 'Bring out your son. He has overturned the altar of Baal and cut down the sacred pole 31 beside it, and he must die.' But as they crowded round him Joash retorted, 'Are you pleading Baal's cause then? Do you think that it is for you to save him? Whoever pleads his cause shall be put to death at dawn. If Baal is a god, and someone has torn down his altar, let him take up his own 32 cause.' That day Joash named Gideon Jerubbaal,[x] saying, 'Let Baal plead his

cause against this man, for he has torn down his altar.'

33 All the Midianites, the Amalekites, and the eastern tribes joined forces, crossed the river and camped in the 34 Vale of Jezreel. Then the spirit of the LORD took possession of Gideon; he sounded the trumpet and the Abiezrites 35 were called out to follow him. He sent messengers all through Manasseh; and they too were called out. He sent messengers to Asher, Zebulun, and Naphtali, and they came up to meet 36 the others. Gideon said to God, 'If thou wilt deliver Israel through me as 37 thou hast promised—now, look, I am putting a fleece of wool on the threshing-floor. If there is dew only on the fleece and all the ground is dry, then I shall be sure that thou wilt deliver Israel through me, as thou hast prom-38 ised.' And that is what happened. He rose early next day and wrung out the fleece, and he squeezed enough dew from it to fill a bowl with water. Gideon 39 then said to God, 'Do not be angry with me, but give me leave to speak once again. Let me, I pray thee, make one more test with the fleece. This time let the fleece alone be dry, and all the ground be covered with dew.' God let 40 it be so that night: the fleece alone was dry, and on all the ground there was dew.

7 Jerubbaal, that is Gideon, and all the people with him rose early and pitched camp at En-harod;[y] the Midianite camp was in the vale to the 2 north of the hill of Moreh. The LORD said to Gideon, 'The people with you are more than I need to deliver Midian

[s] *That is* the LORD is peace.
[t] the yearling bull: *prob. rdg.; Heb.* the second bull, seven years old.
[u] *Or* on.
[v] of ... pattern: *or* with the stones in rows.
[w] *Or* stronghold *or* refuge.
[x] *That is* Let Baal plead.   [y] *That is* Spring of Fright.

The Abiezrites were a small clan within Manasseh; see v. 15. 24: *Jehovah-shalom:* see Tfn. *s.* 25–32: Gideon destroys the altar of Baal. 25: *The sacred pole:* the object which symbolized the goddess Asherah; see 3.7 n. 32: This popular explanation of *Jerubbaal*, "*Let Baal plead*," is not the natural one; a person with this name, which really means "May Baal take action," would be a worshiper of Baal, not a foe. Other difficulties in the Gideon stories indicate that several different sources have not been perfectly fused; vv. 25–32 are unrelated to the context. 33–40: Gideon's military preparations. 33: *Vale of Jezreel* was at the eastern end of the valley of Esdraelon. 34: *The Spirit of the LORD:* compare 3.10 n. 36–40: The incident of the *fleece* is a sign additional to that of vv. 17–21.

    7.1–8.35: Gideon routs the Midianites. 1: *En-harod* was on the northern slopes of Mount Gilboa. It means "spring of fright"; see v. 3. *The hill of Moreh* was in the plain between Mount

into their hands: Israel will claim the glory for themselves and say that it is their own strength that has given them
3 the victory. Now make a proclamation for all the people to hear, that anyone who is scared or frightened is to leave Mount Galud[z] at once and go back home.' Twenty-two thousand of them went, and ten thousand were left.
4 The LORD then said to Gideon, 'There are still too many. Bring them down to the water, and I will separate them for you there. When I say to you, "This man shall go with you", he shall go; and if I say, "This man shall not go
5 with you", he shall not go.' So Gideon brought the people down to the water and the LORD said to him, 'Make every man who laps the water with his tongue like a dog stand on one side, and on the other every man who goes
6 down on his knees and drinks.' The number of those who lapped was three hundred, and all the rest went down on their knees to drink, putting
7 their hands to their mouths. The LORD said to Gideon, 'With the three hundred men who lapped I will save you and deliver Midian into your hands, and all the rest may go home.'
8 So Gideon sent all these Israelites home, but he kept the three hundred, and they took with them the jars[a] and the trumpets which the people had. The Midianite camp was below him in the vale.
9 That night the LORD said to him, 'Go down at once and attack the camp, for I have delivered it into your
10 hands. If you are afraid to do so, then
11 go down first with your servant Purah and listen to what they are saying. That will give you courage to go down and attack the camp.' So he and his servant Purah went down to the part of the camp where the fighting men
12 lay. Now the Midianites, the Amalekites, and the eastern tribes were so many that they lay there in the valley like a swarm of locusts; there was no counting their camels; in number they

were like grains of sand on the sea-
13 shore. When Gideon came close, there was a man telling his companion a dream. He said, 'I dreamt that I saw a hard, stale barley-cake rolling over and over through the Midianite camp; it came to a tent, hit it[b] and turned it upside down, and the
14 tent collapsed.' The other answered, 'Depend upon it, this is the sword of Gideon son of Joash the Israelite. God has delivered Midian and the whole
15 army into his hands.' When Gideon heard the story of the dream and its interpretation, he prostrated himself. Then he went back to the Israelite camp and said, 'Up! The LORD has delivered the camp of the Midianites
16 into your hands.' He divided the three hundred men into three companies,
17 and gave every man a trumpet and an empty jar with a torch inside it. Then he said to them, 'Watch me: when I come to the edge of the camp, do exactly
18 as I do. When I and my men blow our trumpets, you too all round the camp will blow your trumpets, and shout, "For the LORD and for Gideon!" '
19 Gideon and the hundred men who were with him reached the outskirts of the camp at the beginning of the middle watch; the sentries had just been posted. They blew their trumpets and
20 smashed their jars. The three companies all blew their trumpets and smashed their jars, then grasped the torches in their left hands and the trumpets in their right, and shouted, 'A sword for the LORD and for Gideon!'
21 Every man stood where he was, all round the camp, and the whole camp leapt up in a panic and fled. The three
22 hundred blew their trumpets, and throughout the camp the LORD set every man against his neighbour. The army fled as far as Beth-shittah in Zererah, as far as the ridge of Abelmeholah by Tabbath. The Israelites 23

z Prob. rdg.; Heb. Mount Gilead.
a Prob. rdg.; Heb. provisions.
b Prob. rdg.; Heb. adds and it fell.

Tabor and Mount Gilboa. **4–7:** The test as presented is a literary device; the number of Gideon's warriors is reduced in order to make clear that the victory belongs to the LORD. **8:** *The jars and the trumpets:* see vv. 16–22. Lighted torches are concealed in the jars. **10–15:** Another sign of victory for Gideon. **13–14:** The *barley-cake* symbolizes settled farmers, the *tent* the nomadic Midianites. **22:** *Bethshittah ... Tabbath:* all the places mentioned here are east of the Jordan.

from Naphtali and Asher and all Manasseh were called out and they
24 pursued the Midianites. Gideon sent men through all the hill-country of Ephraim with this message: 'Come down and cut off the Midianites. Hold the fords of the Jordan against them as far as Beth-barah.' So all the Ephraimites were called out and they held the fords of the Jordan as far as Beth-
25 barah. They captured the two Midianite princes, Oreb and Zeeb. Oreb they killed at the Rock of Oreb, and Zeeb by the Winepress of Zeeb, and they kept up the pursuit of the Midianites; afterwards they brought the heads of Oreb and Zeeb across the Jordan to Gideon.
8 The men of Ephraim said to Gideon, 'Why have you treated us like this? Why did you not summon us when you went to fight Midian?'; and they re-
2 proached him violently. But he said to them, 'What have I done compared with you? Are not Ephraim's gleanings better than the whole vintage of
3 Abiezer? God has delivered Oreb and Zeeb, the princes of Midian, into your hands. What have I done compared with you?' At these words of his, their anger died down.
4 Gideon came to the Jordan, and he and his three hundred men crossed over to continue the pursuit, weary
5 though they were. He said to the men of Succoth, 'Will you give these men of mine some bread, for they are weary, and I am pursuing Zebah and Zal-
6 munna, the kings of Midian?' But the chief men of Succoth replied, 'Are Zebah and Zalmunna already in your hands, that we should give your army
7 bread?' Gideon said, 'For that, when the LORD delivers Zebah and Zalmunna into my hands, I will thresh your bodies with desert thorns and
8 briars.' He went on from there to Penuel and made the same request; the men of Penuel answered like the men of Succoth. He said to the men of 9 Penuel, 'When I return safely, I will pull down your castle.'

Zebah and Zalmunna were in 10 Karkor with their army of fifteen thousand men. These were all that remained of the whole host of the eastern tribes; a hundred and twenty thousand armed men had fallen in battle. Gideon advanced along the track 11 used by the tent-dwellers east of Nobah and Jogbehah, and his attack caught the army when they were off their guard. Zebah and Zalmunna fled; but 12 he went in pursuit of these Midianite kings and captured them both; and their whole army melted away.

As Gideon son of Joash was re- 13 turning from the battle by the Ascent of Heres, he caught a young man from 14 Succoth. He questioned him, and one by one he numbered off the names of the rulers of Succoth and its elders, seventy-seven in all. Gideon then 15 came to the men of Succoth and said, 'Here are Zebah and Zalmunna, about whom you taunted me. "Are Zebah and Zalmunna", you said, "already in your hands, that we should give your weary men bread?"' Then 16 he took the elders of the city and he disciplined those men of Succoth with desert thorns and briars. He also 17 pulled down the castle of Penuel and put the men of the city to death. Then 18 he said to Zebah and Zalmunna, 'What of the men you killed in Tabor?' They answered, 'They were like you, every one had the look of a king's son.' 'They 19 were my brothers,' he said, 'my mother's sons. I swear by the LORD, if you had let them live I would not have killed you'; and he said to his eldest son 20 Jether, 'Up with you, and kill them.' But he was still only a lad, and did not

---

24–25: *Oreb* and *Zeeb* are captured and executed by the Ephraimites. The summons to Ephraim to hold *the fords of the Jordan*, after the Midianites had already fled across it, is another example of imperfectly fused accounts; see 6.32 n. **8.2–3:** Gideon placates the Ephraimites by assuring them that their *gleanings*, that is, their accomplishments, are more important and valuable than his own, the *vintage of Abiezer* (6.11 n.). This is probably a proverbial saying. **4–12:** Gideon asks for supplies, continues the pursuit of the Midianites, and kills their kings. *Zebah* and *Zalmunna*. This seems to be a somewhat different version of 7.24–8.3. **5–17:** The other places mentioned in this section were east of the Jordan. **10:** The numbers seem exaggerated. **18–19:** That Gideon's *brothers* had been killed at Mount Tabor by Midianites is not recorded in the account in ch. 6, nor is the personal motive given there. On

draw his sword, because he was afraid.
21 So Zebah and Zalmunna said, 'Rise up yourself and dispatch us, for you have a man's strength.' So Gideon rose and killed them both, and he took the crescents from the necks of their camels.
22 After this the Israelites said to Gideon, 'You have saved us from the Midianites; now you be our ruler, you and your son and your grandson.'
23 Gideon replied, 'I will not rule over you, nor shall my son; the LORD will
24 rule over you.' Then he said, 'I have a request to make: will every one of you give me the earrings from his booty?'—for the enemy wore golden earrings,
25 being Ishmaelites. They said, 'Of course, we will give them.' So a cloak was spread out and every man threw on to it the golden earrings from his booty.
26 The earrings for which he asked weighed seventeen hundred shekels of gold; this was in addition to the crescents and pendants and the purple cloaks worn by the Midianite kings, not counting the chains on the necks of their camels.
27 Gideon made it into an ephod and he set it up in his own city of Ophrah. All the Israelites turned wantonly to its worship, and it became a trap to catch Gideon and his household.
28 Thus the Midianites were subdued by the Israelites; they could no longer hold up their heads. For forty years the land was at peace, all the
29 lifetime of Gideon, that is Jerubbaal son of Joash; and he retired to his
30 own home. Gideon had seventy sons, his own offspring, for he had many
31 wives. He had a concubine who lived in Shechem, and she also bore him a son, whom he named Abimelech.
32 Gideon son of Joash died at a ripe old age and was buried in his father's grave
33 at Ophrah-of-the-Abiezrites. After his death, the Israelites again went wantonly to the worship of the Baalim and
34 made Baal-berith their god. They for-

got the LORD their God who had delivered them from their enemies on every side, and did not show to the 35 family of Jerubbaal, that is Gideon, the loyalty that was due to them for all the good he had done for Israel.

ABIMELECH SON OF JERUBBAAL WENT 9 to Shechem to his mother's brothers, and spoke with them and with all the clan of his mother's family. 'I beg 2 you,' he said, 'whisper a word in the ears of the chief citizens of Shechem. Ask them which is better for them: that seventy men, all the sons of Jerubbaal, should rule over them, or one man. Tell them to remember that I am their own flesh and blood.' So his 3 mother's brothers repeated all this to each of them on his behalf; and they were moved to come over to Abimelech's side, because, as they said, he was their brother. They gave him 4 seventy pieces of silver from the temple of Baal-berith, and with these he hired idle and reckless men, who followed him. He came to his father's 5 house in Ophrah and butchered his seventy brothers, the sons of Jerubbaal, on a single stone block, all but Jotham the youngest, who survived because he had hidden himself. Then 6 all the citizens of Shechem and all Beth-millo came together and made Abimelech king beside the old propped-up terebinth at Shechem.

When this was reported to Jotham, 7 he went and stood on the summit of Mount Gerizim. He cried at the top of his voice: 'Listen to me, you citizens of Shechem, and may God listen to you:

'Once upon a time the trees came to 8 anoint a king, and they said to the olive-tree: Be king over us. But the 9 olive-tree answered: What, leave my rich oil by which gods and men are honoured, to come and hold sway over the trees?

---

blood vengeance, see Josh.20.3. **21:** *Crescents:* ornaments, possibly amulets. **22–23:** Gideon refuses hereditary kingship. **24–27:** Here the *ephod* is some kind of image; elsewhere it is a sacred garment (Exod.25.7 n.). It brought disaster to Gideon's family. **28–35:** The section in part seems misplaced. Perhaps vv. 28–29, at least, belong after v. 23.
 9.1–57: Abimelech, son of Jerubbaal (Gideon). **1:** *Jerubbaal:* see 6.32 n. *Shechem:* see Josh. 24.1 n. It guarded the important highway between Mount Ebal and Mount Gerizim. **4:** *Baal-berith:* see Josh.24.25 n. **6:** *Beth-millo* probably refers to the fortified section of Shechem, the castle of vv. 46, 49. *Terebinth:* see Josh.24.26. **7–21:** Jotham denounces Abimelech. **8–15:** In

10 'So the trees said to the fig-tree:
Then will you come and be king over
11 us? But the fig-tree answered: What,
leave my good fruit and all its sweetness, to come and hold sway over the
trees?
12 'So the trees said to the vine: Then
will you come and be king over us?
13 But the vine answered: What, leave my
new wine which gladdens gods and
men, to come and hold sway over the
trees?
14 'Then all the trees said to the
thorn-bush: Will you then be king
15 over us? And the thorn said to the
trees: If you really mean to anoint me
as your king, then come under the
protection of my shadow; if not, fire
shall come out of the thorn and burn
up the cedars of Lebanon.'
16 Then Jotham said, 'Now, have you
acted fairly and honestly in making
Abimelech king? Have you done the
right thing by Jerubbaal and his
household? Have you given my father
17 his due—who fought for you, and
threw himself into the forefront of the
battle and delivered you from the
18 Midianites? Today you have risen
against my father's family, butchered
his seventy sons on a single stone
block, and made Abimelech, the son
of his slave-girl, king over the citizens
of Shechem because he is your brother.
19 In this day's work have you acted
fairly and honestly by Jerubbaal and
his family? If so, I wish you joy in
Abimelech and wish him joy in you!
20 If not, may fire come out of Abimelech
and burn up the citizens of Shechem
and all Beth-millo; may fire also come
out from the citizens of Shechem and
Beth-millo and burn up Abimelech.'
21 After which Jotham slipped away and
made his escape; he came to Beer, and
there he settled out of reach of his
brother Abimelech.
22 After Abimelech had been prince
23 over Israel for three years, God sent an
evil spirit to make a breach between
Abimelech and the citizens of She-
24 chem, and they played him false. This
was done on purpose, so that the

violent murder of the seventy sons of
Jerubbaal might recoil on their brother
Abimelech who did the murder and
on the citizens of Shechem who encouraged him to do it. The citizens of 25
Shechem set men to lie in wait for him
on the hill-tops, but they robbed all
who passed that way, and so the news
reached Abimelech.
Now Gaal son of Ebed came with 26
his kinsmen to Shechem, and the
citizens of Shechem transferred their
allegiance to him. They went out into 27
the country-side, picked the early grapes
in their vineyards, trod them in the
winepress and held festival. They
went into the temple of their god,
where they ate and drank and reviled
Abimelech. 'Who is Abimelech,' said 28
Gaal son of Ebed, 'and who are the
Shechemites, that we should be his
subjects? Have not this son of Jerubbaal and his lieutenant Zebul been
subjects of the men of Hamor the
father of Shechem? Why indeed should
we be subject to him? If only this 29
people were in my charge I should
know how to get rid of Abimelech!
I would say to him, "Get your men
together, and come out and fight."'
When Zebul the governor of the city 30
heard what Gaal son of Ebed said, he
was very angry. He resorted to a ruse 31
and sent messengers to Abimelech to
say, 'Gaal son of Ebed and his kinsmen have come to Shechem and are
turning the city against you. Get up 32
now in the night, you and the people
with you, and lie in wait in the open
country. Then be up in the morning 33
at sunrise, and advance rapidly against
the city. When he and his people come
out, do to him what the situation
demands.' So Abimelech and his people 34
rose in the night, and lay in wait to
attack Shechem, in four companies.
Gaal son of Ebed came out and stood 35
in the entrance of the city gate, and
Abimelech and his people rose from
their hiding-place. Gaal saw them and 36
said to Zebul, 'There are people coming
down from the tops of the hills', but
Zebul replied, 'What you see is the

---

this antimonarchic parable, the useless thorn-bush aspires to be king, but useful trees do not.
22–25: A quarrel between Abimelech and the Shechemites. **26–41**: Abimelech crushes Gaal's
rebellion. **28**: Abimelech lived at Arumah (v. 41); Shechem was governed by his deputy *Zebul*.

shadow of the hills, looking like men.'
37 Once more Gaal said, 'There are people
coming down from the central ridge
of the hills, and one company is
coming along the road of the Sooth-
38 sayers' Terebinth.' Then Zebul said
to him, 'Where are your brave words
now? You said, "Who is Abimelech
that we should be subject to him?"
Are not these the people you despised?
39 Go out and fight him.' Gaal led the
citizens of Shechem out and attacked
40 Abimelech, but Abimelech routed him
and he fled. The ground was strewn
with corpses all the way to the entrance
41 of the gate. Abimelech established
himself in Arumah, and Zebul drove
away Gaal and his kinsmen and allowed
them no place in Shechem.
42   Next day the people came out into
the open, and this was reported to
43 Abimelech. He on his side took his
supporters, divided them into three
companies and lay in wait in the open
country; and when he saw the people
coming out of the city, he rose and
44 attacked them. Abimelech and the
company with him advanced rapidly
and took up position at the entrance
of the city gate, while the other two
companies advanced against all those
who were in the open and struck them
45 down. Abimelech kept up the attack
on the city all that day and captured
it; he killed the people in it, pulled the
city down and sowed the site with salt.
46 When the occupants of the castle of
Shechem heard of this, they went into
the great hall*c* of the temple of El-
47 berith. It was reported to Abimelech
that all the occupants of the castle of
48 Shechem had collected together. So he
and his people went up Mount Zalmon
carrying axes; there he cut brushwood, and took it and hoisted it on his
shoulder. He said to his men, 'You
see what I am doing; be quick and do
49 the same.' So each man cut brushwood; then they followed Abimelech
and laid the brushwood against the
hall, and burnt it over their heads.

Thus all the occupants of the castle of
Shechem died, about a thousand men
and women.
      Abimelech then went to Thebez, 50
besieged it and took it. There was a 51
strong castle in the middle of the city,
and all the citizens, men and women,
took refuge there. They shut themselves
in and went on to the roof. Abimelech 52
came up to the castle and attacked it.
As he approached the entrance to the
castle to set fire to it, a woman threw 53
a millstone down on his head and
fractured his skull. He called hurriedly 54
to his young armour-bearer and said,
'Draw your sword and dispatch me, or
men will say of me: A woman killed
him.' So the young man ran him
through and he died. When the 55
Israelites saw that Abimelech was dead,
they all went back to their homes. It 56
was thus that God requited the crime
which Abimelech had committed
against his father by the murder of his
seventy brothers, and brought all the 57
wickedness of the men of Shechem
on their own heads. The curse of
Jotham son of Jerubbaal came home to
them.
      After Abimelech, Tola son of Pua, **10**
son of Dodo, a man of Issachar who
lived in Shamir in the hill-country of
Ephraim, came in his turn to deliver
Israel. He was judge over Israel for 2
twenty-three years, and when he died
he was buried in Shamir.
      After him came Jair the Gileadite; 3
he was judge over Israel for twenty-
two years. He had thirty sons, who rode 4
thirty asses; they had thirty towns in
the land of Gilead, which to this day
are called Havvoth-jair.*d* When Jair 5
died, he was buried in Kamon.
      Once more the Israelites did what 6
was wrong in the eyes of the LORD,
worshipping the Baalim and the
Ashtaroth, the deities of Aram and of
Sidon and of Moab, of the Ammonites
and of the Philistines. They forsook
the LORD and did not worship him.

c Or vault.   *d That is* Tent-villages of Jair.

42–49: Shechem destroyed. **45:** *Salt* would destroy fertility, implying total destruction.
      10.1–5: Two minor judges. 1: *Tola:* no more is known about him. **3–5:** No more is known
about *Jair*; he is mentioned, curiously enough, in Num.32.41, raising the problem of whether
he belonged to the age of Moses and Joshua, or the judges.
      10.6–12.7: Jephthah and delivery from the Ammonites. 10–16: Here it is the LORD himself,

7 The LORD was angry with Israel, and he sold them to the Philistines and the
8 Ammonites, who[e] for eighteen years harassed and oppressed the Israelites who lived beyond the Jordan in the
9 Amorite country in Gilead. Then the Ammonites crossed the Jordan to attack Judah, Benjamin, and Ephraim,
10 so that Israel was in great distress. The Israelites cried to the LORD for help and said, 'We have sinned against thee; we have forsaken our God and
11 worshipped the Baalim.' And the LORD said to the Israelites, 'The Egyptians, the Amorites, the Ammon-
12 ites, the Philistines; the Sidonians too and the Amalekites and the Midianites —all these oppressed you and you cried to me for help; and did not I deliver
13 you? But you forsook me and worshipped other gods; therefore I will
14 deliver you no more. Go and cry for help to the gods you have chosen, and let them save you in the day of your
15 distress.' But the Israelites said to the LORD, 'We have sinned. Deal with us as thou wilt; only save us this day, we
16 implore thee.' They banished the foreign gods and worshipped the LORD; and he could endure no longer to see the plight of Israel.
17 Then the Ammonites were called to arms, and they encamped in Gilead, while the Israelites assembled and en-
18 camped in Mizpah. The people of Gilead and their chief men said to one another, 'If any man will strike the first blow at the Ammonites, he shall be lord over the inhabitants of Gilead.'

11 Jephthah the Gileadite was a great warrior; he was the son of Gilead by
2 a prostitute. But Gilead had a wife who bore him several sons, and when they grew up they drove Jephthah away; they said to him, 'You have no inheritance in our father's house; you
3 are another woman's son.' So Jephthah, to escape his brothers, went away

and settled in the land of Tob, and swept up a number of idle men who followed him.

The time came when the Ammonites 4 made war on Israel, and when the 5 fighting began, the elders of Gilead went to fetch Jephthah from the land of Tob. They said to him, 'Come and be 6 our commander so that we can fight the Ammonites.' But Jephthah said to 7 the elders of Gilead, 'You drove me from my father's house in hatred. Why come to me now when you are in trouble?' 'It is because of that', they 8 replied, 'that we have turned to you now. Come with us and fight the Ammonites, and become lord over all the inhabitants of Gilead.' Jephthah 9 said to them, 'If you ask me back to fight the Ammonites and if the LORD delivers them into my hands, then I will be your lord.' The elders of Gilead 10 said again to Jephthah, 'We swear by the LORD, who shall be witness between us, that we will do what you say.' Jephthah then went with the elders of 11 Gilead, and the people made him their lord and commander. And at Mizpah, in the presence of the LORD, Jephthah repeated all that he had said.

Jephthah sent a mission to the king 12 of Ammon to ask what quarrel he had with them that made him invade their country. The king gave Jephthah's men 13 this answer: 'When the Israelites came up from Egypt, they took our land from the Arnon as far as the Jabbok and the Jordan. Give us back these lands in peace.' Jephthah sent a second 14 mission to the king of Ammon, and 15 they said, 'This is Jephthah's answer: Israel did not take either the Moabite country or the Ammonite country. When they came up from Egypt, the 16 Israelites passed through the wilderness to the Red Sea[f] and came to Kadesh.

e Prob. rdg.; Heb. adds in that year.
f Or the Sea of Reeds.

---

rather than a prophet, who rebukes the sinning Israelites. In 11–12, the allusions are broader than to the contents of Judges. MT has Maonites for Midianites. The Maonites may be the same as the Meunites of 2 Chr.20.1; 26.7. **10.17–11.11:** Jephthah, exiled by his own family, is summoned from Tob, in northeastern Gilead, to command the Israelite forces. **11.1:** *Gilead* is ordinarily a geographical name; it is possibly used here because the name of Jephthah's father was unknown. **3:** *Idle men:* probably brigands. **10:** The words recall Gen.31.49, and reflect a covenant between Jephthah and the elders. **11:** This *Mizpah* (there was one in Benjamin) was in Gilead, probably south of the Jabbok river. **12–28:** Negotiations with the king of Ammon fail.

17 They then sent envoys to the king of Edom asking him to grant them passage through his country, but the king of Edom would not hear of it. They sent also to the king of Moab, but he was not willing; so Israel re-

18 mained in Kadesh. They then passed through the wilderness, skirting Edom and Moab, and kept to the east of Moab. They encamped beside the Arnon, but they did not enter Moabite territory, because the Arnon is the

19 frontier of Moab. Israel then sent envoys to the king of the Amorites, Sihon king of Heshbon, asking him to give them free passage through his

20 country to their destination. But Sihon would not grant Israel free passage through his territory; he mustered all his people, encamped at

21 Jahaz and fought Israel. But the LORD the God of Israel delivered Sihon and all his people into the hands of Israel; they defeated them and occupied all the territory of the Amor-

22 ites in that region. They took all the Amorite territory from the Arnon to the Jabbok and from the wilderness

23 to the Jordan. The LORD the God of Israel drove out the Amorites for the benefit of his people Israel. And do you

24 now propose to take their place? It is for you to possess whatever Kemosh your god gives you; and all that the LORD our God gave us as we advanced

25 is ours. For that matter, are you any better than Balak son of Zippor, king of Moab? Did he ever quarrel with

26 Israel or attack them? For three hundred years Israelites have lived in Heshbon and its dependent villages, in Aroer and its villages, and in all the towns by the Arnon. Why did you not

27 oust*g* them during all that time? We have done you no wrong; it is you who are doing us wrong by attacking us. The LORD who is judge will judge this

day between the Israelites and the Ammonites.' But the king of the

28 Ammonites would not listen to the message which Jephthah had sent him.

29 Then the spirit of the LORD came upon Jephthah and he passed through Gilead and Manasseh, by Mizpeh of Gilead, and from Mizpeh over to the Ammonites. Jephthah made this vow

30 to the LORD: 'If thou wilt deliver the Ammonites into my hands, then the

31 first creature that comes out of the door of my house to meet me when I return from them in peace shall be the LORD's; I will offer that as a whole-offering.'

32 So Jephthah crossed over to attack the Ammonites, and the LORD delivered

33 them into his hands. He routed them with great slaughter all the way from Aroer to Minnith, taking twenty towns, and as far as Abel-keramim.

34 Thus Israel crushed Ammon. But when Jephthah came to his house in Mizpah, who should come out to meet him with tambourines and dances but his daughter, and she his only child; he had no

35 other, neither son nor daughter. When he saw her, he rent his clothes and said, 'Alas, my daughter, you have broken my heart, such trouble you have brought upon me. I have made a vow to the LORD and I cannot go back.'

36 She replied, 'Father, you have made a vow to the LORD; do to me what you have solemnly vowed, since the LORD has avenged you on the Ammonites,

37 your enemies. But, father, grant me this one favour. For two months let me be, that I may roam*h* the hills with my companions and mourn that I must

38 die a virgin.' 'Go', he said, and he let her depart for two months. She went with her companions and mourned her

39 virginity on the hills. At the end of two months she came back to her father,

g Or recover.
h Or that I may go down country to . . .

The passage echoes Num. chs. 20–24. **17:** See Num.20.14–21. **19–23:** See Num.21.21–31. **24:** A nation has a right to the land its god gives it. Usually *Kemosh* is god of the Moabites, Milcom (or Molech) god of the Ammonites; compare 1 Kgs.11.5,7. **25:** *Balak:* see Num. chs. 22–24. **26:** *Three hundred years:* the supposed time between Moses and Jephthah. The number is scarcely precise. **29–33:** Jephthah's vow. The point of the pathetic story is that man cannot play fast and loose with God as Jephthah had done in his oath. **29:** *The spirit:* see 3.10 n. **31:** *Creature:* a human being. See also 2 Kgs.3.27. The Israelites generally abhorred and ultimately prohibited human sacrifice (Lev.18.21; Gen.22.2 n.; Exod.13.13 n.); for an example of its practice, see 2 Kgs.21.6. **34–40:** Jephthah fulfills his vow. **37:** An Israelite woman could suffer no greater disgrace than to die unmarried and childless; she therefore mourns her virginity.

and he fulfilled the vow he had made; she died a virgin. It became a tradition
40 that the daughters of Israel should go year by year and commemorate the fate of Jephthah's daughter, four days in every year.

12 The Ephraimites mustered their forces and crossed over to Zaphon. They said to Jephthah, 'Why did you march against the Ammonites and not summon us to go with you? We will burn your house over your head.'
2 Jephthah answered, 'I and my people had a feud with the Ammonites, and had I appealed to you for help, you would not have saved us*i* from them.
3 When I saw that we were not to look for help from you, I took my life in my hands and marched against the Ammonites, and the LORD delivered them into my power. Why then do you attack
4 me today?' Jephthah then mustered all the men of Gilead and fought Ephraim,
5 and the Gileadites defeated them. The Gileadites seized the fords of the Jordan and held them against Ephraim. When any Ephraimite who had escaped begged leave to cross, the men of Gilead asked him, 'Are you an
6 Ephraimite?', and if he said, 'No', they would retort, 'Say Shibboleth.' He would say 'Sibboleth', and because he could not pronounce the word properly, they seized him and killed him at the fords of the Jordan. At that time forty-two thousand men of Ephraim lost their lives.
7 Jephthah was judge over Israel for six years; when he died he was buried
8 in his own city in Gilead. After him Ibzan of Bethlehem was judge over
9 Israel. He had thirty sons and thirty daughters. He gave away the thirty daughters in marriage and brought in thirty girls for his sons. He was judge

over Israel for seven years, and when he 10 died he was buried in Bethlehem.
After him Elon the Zebulunite was 11 judge over Israel for ten years. When he 12 died, he was buried in Aijalon in the land of Zebulun. Next Abdon son of 13 Hillel the Pirathonite was judge over Israel. He had forty sons and thirty 14 grandsons, who rode each on his own ass. He was judge over Israel for eight years; and when he died he was buried 15 in Pirathon in the land of Ephraim on the hill of the Amalekite.

Israel oppressed by the Philistines

ONCE MORE THE ISRAELITES DID WHAT 13 was wrong in the eyes of the LORD, and he delivered them into the hands of the Philistines for forty years.
There was a man from Zorah of the 2 tribe of Dan whose name was Manoah and whose wife was barren and childless. The angel of the LORD appeared to 3 her and said, 'You are barren and have no child, but you shall conceive and give birth to a son. Now you must 4 do as I say: be careful to drink no wine or strong drink, and to eat no forbidden food; you will conceive and 5 give birth to a son, and no razor shall touch his head, for the boy is to be a Nazirite consecrated to God from the day of his birth. He will strike the first blow to deliver Israel from the power of the Philistines.' The woman went 6 and told her husband; she said to him, 'A man of God came to me; his appearance was that of an*j* angel of God, most terrible to see. I did not ask him where he came from nor did he tell me his name. He said to me, "You 7 shall conceive and give birth to a son.

i and had I . . . saved us: *or* I did appeal to you for help, but you would not save us . . .
j Or the.

40: This mourning ceremony is not mentioned elsewhere. **12.1–7:** Jephthah's war with the Ephraimites; see also 8.1–3. **6:** *Shibboleth* means "ear of corn" or "flood water." The Ephraimites betrayed themselves by their inability to pronounce the "sh" sound.
12.8–15: Ibzan, Elon, and Abdon. These minor judges are otherwise unknown.
13.1–16.31: Israel oppressed by the Philistines. The emphasis is on Samson the man, rather than on tribal or national difficulties. Modern criticism considers these stories choice examples of early Israelite folklore. The tribe of *Dan* at this time lived in the southwest, near the Philistine plain; later they moved north (ch. 18). **1–25:** Samson's wondrous birth. The chapter seems a late composition, serving as a prologue to the ancient folktales which follow; it is kindred more with the ending, 16.28–31, than with the folktales. The account influences Lk. chs. 1–2. **1:** *Philistines:* see Josh.13.2 n. **2:** *Zorah* was about twelve miles west of Jerusalem. **3:** *Angel of the LORD:* see 2.1 n. **5:** A *Nazirite* was consecrated to God by these special vows, whether for a time or for life; compare Num.6.1–21. Samson is consecrated for life (v. 7). Since the folktales

From this time onwards drink no wine
or strong drink and eat no forbidden
food, for the boy is to be a Nazirite
consecrated to God from his birth to
8 the day of his death." ' Manoah prayed
to the LORD, 'If it please thee, O LORD,
let the man of God whom thou didst
send come again to tell us what we are
to do with the boy who is to be born.'
9 God heard Manoah's prayer, and the
angel of God came again to the
woman, who was sitting in the fields;
10 her husband was not with her. The
woman ran quickly and said to him,
'The man who came to me the other
11 day has appeared to me again.' Manoah
went with her at once and approached
the man and said, 'Was it you who
talked with my wife?' He said, 'Yes,
12 it was I.' 'Now when your words come
true,' Manoah said, 'what kind of boy
13 will he be and what will he do?' The
angel of the LORD answered him, 'Your
wife must be careful to do all that I
14 told her; she must not taste anything
that comes from the vine. She must
drink no wine or strong drink, and she
must eat no forbidden food. She must
15 do what I say.' Manoah said to the
angel of the LORD, 'May we urge you
to stay? Let us prepare a kid for you.'
16 The angel of the LORD replied, 'Though
you urge me to stay, I will not eat your
food; but prepare a whole-offering if
you will, and offer that to the LORD.'
Manoah did not perceive that he was
17 the angel of the LORD and said to him,
'What is your name? For we shall want
to honour you when your words come
18 true.' The angel of the LORD said to
him, 'How can you ask my name? It is
19 a name of wonder.' Manoah took a
kid with the proper grain-offering,
and offered it on the rock to the
LORD, to him whose works are full of
wonder. And while Manoah and his
20 wife were watching, the flame went up
from the altar towards heaven, and
the angel of the LORD went up in the

flame; and seeing this, Manoah and
his wife fell on their faces. The angel 21
of the LORD did not appear again to
Manoah and his wife; and Manoah
knew that he was the angel of the
LORD. He said to his wife, 'We are 22
doomed to die, we have seen God',[k]
but she replied, 'If the LORD had 23
wanted to kill us, he would not have
accepted a whole-offering and a grain-
offering at our hands; he would not
now have let us see and hear all this.'
The woman gave birth to a son and 24–25
named him Samson. The boy grew up
in Mahaneh-dan between Zorah and
Eshtaol, and the LORD blessed him,
and the spirit of the LORD began to drive
him hard.

Samson went down to Timnath, and **14**
there he saw a woman, one of the
Philistines. When he came back, he told 2
his father and mother that he had
seen a Philistine woman in Timnath
and asked them to get her for him as
his wife. His father and mother said to 3
him, 'Is there no woman among your
cousins or in all our own people? Must
you go and marry one of the uncircumcised Philistines?' But Samson
said to his father, 'Get her for me,
because she pleases me.' His father and 4
mother did not know that the LORD
was at work in this, seeking an
opportunity against the Philistines,
who at that time were masters of
Israel.

Samson[l] went down to Timnath 5
and, when he reached the vineyards
there, a young lion came at him
growling. The spirit of the LORD 6
suddenly seized him and, having no
weapon in his hand, he tore the lion
in pieces as if it were a kid. He did not
tell his parents what he had done. Then 7
he went down and spoke to the
woman, and she pleased him. After a 8
time he went down again to take her

k *Or* a god.
l *Prob. rdg.; Heb. adds* and his father and mother.

attributed Samson's strength to his hair, these stories were linked to the Nazirite vow. **13–14:**
Samson's mother must also observe special prohibitions, since he is consecrated even in the
womb. **17–18:** On the request to know the name, see Gen.32.29 and Exod.3.13. **22:** Compare
Exod.33.20–23. **25:** See 3.10 n.
  14.1–20: Samson's first wife. 1: *Timnah,* possibly at one time a Philistine town, was in Dan
(Josh.19.40) near the border of Judah (Josh.15.10). **3:** *Uncircumcised:* see Josh.13.2 n. **4:**
Masters of Israel: because of their higher level of material culture; see 1.19 n. **5–9:** Possibly
this passage should precede v. 1. **5–6:** The Asian *lion* was smaller than the African lion, but

to wife; he turned aside to look at the carcass of the lion, and he saw a 9 swarm of bees in it, and honey. He scraped the honey into his hands and went on, eating as he went. When he came to his father and mother, he gave them some and they ate it; but he did not tell them that he had scraped the 10 honey out of the lion's carcass. His father went down to see the woman, and Samson gave a feast there as the 11 custom of young men was. When the people saw him, they brought thirty 12 young men to be his escort. Samson said to them, 'Let me ask you a riddle. If you can guess it during the seven days of the feast, I will give you thirty lengths of linen and thirty 13 changes of clothing; but if you cannot guess the answer, then you shall give me thirty lengths of linen and thirty changes of clothing.' 'Tell us your 14 riddle,' they said; 'let us hear it.' So he said to them:

Out of the eater came something to eat;
out of the strong came something sweet.

At the end of three days they had 15 failed to guess the riddle. On the fourth day they said to Samson's wife, 'Coax your husband and make him tell you the riddle, or we shall burn you and your father's house. Did you invite 16 us here to beggar us?' So Samson's wife wept over him and said, 'You do not love me, you only hate me. You have asked my kinsfolk a riddle and you have not told it to me.' He said to her, 'I have not told it even to my father and mother; and am I to tell 17 you?' But she wept over him every day until the seven feast days were ended, and on the seventh day, because she pestered him, he told her, and she told 18 the riddle to her kinsfolk. So that same day the men of the city said to Samson before he entered the bridal chamber:*m*

What is sweeter than honey?
What is stronger than a lion?

and he replied, 'If you had not ploughed with my heifer, you would not have found out my riddle.' Then 19 the spirit of the LORD suddenly seized him. He went down to Ashkelon and there he killed thirty men, took their belts and gave their clothes to the men who had answered his riddle; but he was very angry and went off to his father's house. And Samson's wife was 20 given in marriage to the friend who had been his groomsman.

After a while, during the time of **15** wheat harvest, Samson went to visit his wife, taking a kid as a present for her. He said, 'I am going to my wife in our bridal chamber', but her father would not let him in. He said, 'I was 2 sure that you hated her, so I gave her in marriage to your groomsman. Her young sister is better than she—take her instead.' But Samson said, 'This 3 time I will settle my score with the Philistines; I will do them some real harm.' So he went and caught three 4 hundred jackals and got some torches; he tied the jackals tail to tail and fastened a torch between each pair of tails. He then set the torches alight and 5 turned the jackals loose in the standing corn of the Philistines. He burnt up standing corn and stooks as well, vineyards and olive groves. The Philistines 6 said, 'Who has done this?' They were told that it was Samson, because the Timnite, his father-in-law, had taken his wife and given her to his groomsman. So the Philistines came and burnt her and her father. Samson said, 'If 7 you do things like this, I swear I will be revenged upon you before I have done.' He smote them hip and thigh 8 with great slaughter; and after that he went down to live in a cave in the Rock of Etam.

The Philistines came up and pitched 9

m he entered . . . chamber: *prob. rdg.; Heb.* the sun went down.

Samson's feat is still impressive. **15–18:** The motif of a woman wheedling a secret from Samson appears again in 16.4–18. **19:** *Ashkelon:* see Josh.13.3.
    15.1–8: Samson's revenge. 8: *Hip and thigh* is a proverbial expression whose original significance is unknown.
    15.9–20: Samson's further revenge. 9: The location of *Lehi* is unknown; see 2 Sam.23.11. It

10 camp in Judah, and overran Lehi. The men of Judah said, 'Why have you attacked us?' They answered, 'We have come to take Samson prisoner and
11 serve him as he served us.' So three thousand men from Judah went down to the cave in the Rock of Etam. They said to Samson, 'Surely you know that the Philistines are our masters? Now see what you have brought upon us.' He answered, 'I only served them
12 as they had served me.' They said to him, 'We have come down to bind you and hand you over to the Philistines.' 'Then you must swear to me', he said, 'that you will not set upon me
13 yourselves.' They answered, 'No; we will only bind you and hand you over to them, we will not kill you.' So they bound him with two new ropes and brought him up from the cave in the
14 Rock. He came to Lehi, and when they met him, the Philistines shouted in triumph; but the spirit of the LORD suddenly seized him, the ropes on his arms became like burnt tow and his
15 bonds melted away. He found the jaw-bone of an ass, all raw, and picked it
16 up and slew a thousand men. He made this saying:

> With the jaw-bone of an ass[n] I have
>> flayed them like asses;[o]
> with the jaw-bone of an ass I have
>> slain a thousand men.

17 When he had said his say, he threw away the jaw-bone; and he called that
18 place Ramath-lehi.[p] He began to feel very thirsty and cried aloud to the LORD, 'Thou hast let me, thy servant, win this great victory, and must I now die of thirst and fall into the hands of
19 the uncircumcised?' God split open the Hollow of Lehi and water came out of it. Samson drank, his strength returned and he revived. This is why the spring in Lehi is called En-hakkore[q] to this day.
20 Samson was judge over Israel for twenty years in the days of the Philistines.

Samson went to Gaza, and there he 16 saw a prostitute and went in to spend the night with her. The people of 2 Gaza heard that Samson had come, and they surrounded him and lay in wait for him all that night at the city gate. During the night, however, they took no action, saying to themselves, 'When day breaks we shall kill him.' Samson lay in bed till midnight; and 3 when midnight came he rose, seized hold of the doors of the city gate and the two posts, pulled them out, bar and all, hoisted them on to his shoulders and carried them to the top of the hill east of Hebron.

After this Samson fell in love with a 4 woman named Delilah, who lived in the valley of Sorek. The lords of the 5 Philistines went up country to see her and said, 'Coax him and find out what gives him his great strength, and how we can master him, bind him and so hold him captive; then we will each give you eleven hundred pieces of silver.' So Delilah said to Samson, 6 'Tell me what gives you your great strength, and how you can be bound and held captive.' Samson replied, 7 'If they bind me with seven fresh bow-strings not yet dry, then I shall become as weak as any other man.' So the 8 lords of the Philistines brought her seven fresh bowstrings not yet dry, and she bound him with them. She had 9 men already hidden in the inner room, and she cried, 'The Philistines are upon you, Samson!' But he snapped the bowstrings as a strand of tow snaps when it feels the fire, and his strength was not tamed. Delilah said to Samson, 10 'I see you have made a fool of me and told me lies. Tell me this time how you can be bound.' He said to her, 11 'If you bind me tightly with new ropes that have never been used, then I shall become as weak as any other man.' So Delilah took new ropes and bound 12

n *ass: Heb.* hamor.
o *I have . . . asses: or* I have reddened them blood-red, *or* I have heaped them in heaps; *Heb.* hamor himmartim.
p *That is* Jaw-bone Hill.
q *That is* the Crier's Spring.

---

has the same spelling as the word for "jawbone" (vv.15–17). **14:** *Tow or flax.* **17:** *Ramath-lehi:* see Tfn. *p.* **19:** *En-hakkore:* see Tfn. *q.*
    16.1–3: Samson's escape. 1: *Gaza:* see Josh.13.3. **3:** *Hebron* was forty miles east of Gaza.
    16.4–22: Samson and Delilah. 4: *The valley of Sorek* led into the northern end of the Philistine

him with them. Then she cried, 'The Philistines are upon you, Samson!', while the men waited hidden in the inner room. He snapped the ropes off 13 his arms like pack-thread. Delilah said to him, 'You are still making a fool of me and have told me lies. Tell me: how can you be bound?' He said, 'Take the seven loose locks of my hair and weave them into the warp, and then drive them tight with the beater; and I shall become as weak as any other 14 man.' So she lulled him to sleep, wove the seven loose locks of his hair into the warp, and drove them tight with the beater, and cried, 'The Philistines are upon you, Samson!' He woke from sleep and pulled away the warp and the 15 loom with it.*r* She said to him, 'How can you say you love me when you do not confide in me? This is the third time you have made a fool of me and have not told me what gives you your 16 great strength.' She so pestered him with these words day after day, pressing him hard and wearying him to death, 17 that he told her his secret. 'No razor has touched my head,' he said, 'because I am a Nazirite, consecrated to God from the day of my birth. If my head were shaved, then my strength would leave me, and I should become as weak 18 as any other man.' Delilah saw that he had told her his secret; so she sent to the lords of the Philistines and said, 'Come up at once, he has told me his secret.' So the lords of the Philistines came up and brought the money 19 with them. She lulled him to sleep on her knees, summoned a man and he shaved the seven locks of his hair for her. She began to take him captive 20 and his strength left him. Then she cried, 'The Philistines are upon you, Samson!' He woke from his sleep and said, 'I will go out as usual and shake myself'; he did not know that the 21 LORD had left him. The Philistines seized him, gouged out his eyes and brought him down to Gaza. There they bound him with fetters of bronze, and he was set to grinding corn in the prison. But his hair, after it had been 22 shaved, began to grow again.

The lords of the Philistines assem- 23 bled together to offer a great sacrifice to their god Dagon and to rejoice before him. They said, 'Our god has delivered Samson our enemy into our hands.' The people, when they saw 24 him, praised their god, chanting:

Our god has delivered our enemy
    into our hands,
the scourge of our land who piled it
    with our dead.

When they grew merry, they said, 25 'Call Samson, and let him fight to make sport for us.' So they summoned Samson from prison and he made sport before them all. They stood him between the pillars, and Samson said 26 to the boy who held his hand, 'Put me where I can feel the pillars which support the temple, so that I may lean against them.' The temple was full of 27 men and women, and all the lords of the Philistines were there, and there were about three thousand men and women on the roof watching Samson as he fought. Samson called on the 28 LORD and said, 'Remember me, O Lord GOD, remember me: give me strength only this once, O God, and let me at one stroke be avenged on the Philistines for my two eyes.' He put 29 his arms round the two central pillars which supported the temple, his right arm round one and his left round the other, and braced himself and said, 30 'Let me die with the Philistines.' Then Samson leaned forward with all his might, and the temple fell on the lords and on all the people who were in it. So the dead whom he killed at his death were more than those he had killed in his life. His brothers and 31 all his father's family came down, carried him up to the grave of his father Manoah between Zorah and Eshtaol

r the warp ... with it: prob. rdg.; Heb. adds an unintelligible word.

plain. **13:** *Warp* and *beater* are weaving terms. **17:** See 13.5 n. **20:** LORD *had left him:* the Nazirite vow had been broken by the cutting of the hair.
    16.23–31: Samson's heroic death. 23: *Dagon:* Semitic grain deity, adopted by the Philistines; see 1 Sam.5.2–5.

and buried him there. He had been judge over Israel for twenty years.

Years of lawlessness

17 THERE WAS ONCE A MAN NAMED MICAH
2 from the hill-country of Ephraim. He said to his mother, 'You remember the eleven hundred pieces of silver which were taken from you, and how you called down a curse on the thief in my hearing? I have the money; I took it and now I will give it back to you.'*s*
3 His mother said, 'May the LORD bless you, my son.' So he gave the eleven hundred pieces of silver back to his mother, and she said, 'I now solemnly dedicate this money of mine to the LORD for the benefit of my son, to make
4 a carved idol and a cast image.' He returned the money to his mother, and she took two hundred pieces of silver and handed them to a silversmith, who made them into an idol and an image, which stood in Micah's house.
5 This man Micah had a shrine, and he made an ephod and teraphim*t* and installed one of his sons to be his
6 priest. In those days there was no king in Israel and every man did what
7 was right in his own eyes. Now there was a young man from Bethlehem in Judah, from the clan of Judah, a Levite named
8 Ben-gershom.*u* He had left the city of Bethlehem to go and find somewhere to live. On his way he came to Micah's house in the hill-country of Ephraim.
9 Micah said to him, 'Where have you come from?' He replied, 'I am a Levite from Bethlehem in Judah, and I am looking for somewhere to live.'
10 Micah said to him, 'Stay with me and be priest and father to me. I will give you ten pieces of silver a year, and pro-
11 vide you with food and clothes.' The

Levite agreed to stay with the man and was treated as one of his own sons.
Micah installed the Levite, and the 12 young man became his priest and a member of his household. Micah said, 13 'Now I know that the LORD will make me prosper, because I have a Levite for my priest.'

In those days there was no king in **18** Israel and the tribe of the Danites was looking for territory to occupy, because they had not so far come into possession of the territory allotted to them among the tribes of Israel. The Danites 2 therefore sent out five fighting men of their clan from Zorah and Eshtaol to prospect, with instructions to go and explore the land. They came to Micah's house in the hill-country of Ephraim and spent the night there. While they 3 were there, they recognized the speech of the young Levite; they turned there and then and said to him, 'Who brought you here? What are you doing? What is your business here?' He said, 'This 4 is all Micah's doing: he has hired me and I have become his priest.' They 5 said to him, 'Then inquire of God on our behalf whether our mission will be successful.' The priest replied, 'Go in 6 peace. Your mission is in the LORD's hands.' The five men went on their way 7 and came to Laish. There they found the inhabitants living a carefree life, in the same way as the Sidonians, a quiet, carefree folk, with no hereditary king to keep the country under his thumb.*v* They were a long way from the Sidonians, and had no contact with the Aramaeans. So the five men went back 8 to Zorah and Eshtaol, and when their

s and now . . . you: *transposed from verse 3.*
t Or household gods.
u named Ben-gershom: *prob. rdg., cp. 18. 30; Heb.* he lodged there.
v with no . . . thumb: *prob. rdg.; Heb.* and none humiliating anything in the land with inherited authority.

17.1–21.25: Years of lawlessness. The two tales in these chapters are not concerned with "judges"; they describe anarchy which the authors regard as necessitating the rise of the monarchy.
    17.1–18.31: The origin of the cult of Dan. 1–6: The laws forbidding images (Exod.20.4,23; 34.17) seem here unknown. **5:** *Ephod:* see 8.24–27 n. *Teraphim:* see Tfn. *t.* **6:** On this verse (compare 21.25) see 17.1–21.25 n. **7–13:** *Levite* here probably means a priest, not a member of a tribe; in v. 13, the word has a tribal meaning, unless the intention there is to explain that "levite" once meant "priest." **7:** *Bethlehem:* five miles south of Jerusalem.
    18.1–31: The migration of the Danites. The reason for the move northward by the tribe of Dan is not mentioned here; see 13.1–16.31 n. **5:** To *inquire of God:* probably by casting lots; see Josh.7.14 n. **7:** *Laish,* near the sources of the Jordan, was allied with *the Sidonians,* who were,

9 kinsmen asked their news, they said, 'Come and attack them. It is an excellent country that we have seen. Will you hang back and do nothing about it? Start off now and take possession 10 of the land. When you get there, you will find a people living a carefree life in a wide expanse of open country. God has delivered it into your hands, a place where there is no lack of anything on earth.'

11 And so six hundred armed men from the clan of the Danites set out 12 from Zorah and Eshtaol. They went up country and encamped in Kiriath-jearim in Judah: this is why that place to this day is called Mahaneh-dan;*w* 13 it lies west of Kiriath-jearim. From there they passed on to the hill-country of Ephraim and came to Micah's house. 14 The five men who had been to explore the country round Laish spoke up and said to their kinsmen, 'Do you know that in one of these houses there are now an ephod and teraphim, an idol and an image? Now consider what 15 you had best do.' So they turned aside to Micah's house and greeted him. 16 The six hundred armed Danites took their stand at the entrance of the gate, 17 and the five men who had gone to explore the country went indoors to take the idol and the image, ephod and teraphim, while the priest was standing at the entrance with the six hundred 18 armed men. The five men entered Micah's house and took the idol and the image, ephod and teraphim.*x* The priest asked them what they were 19 doing, but they said to him, 'Be quiet; not a word. Come with us and be our priest and father. Which is better, to be priest in the household of one man or to be priest to a whole tribe and 20 clan in Israel?' This pleased the priest; so he took the ephod and teraphim, the idol and the image, and joined the 21 company. They turned and went off, putting the dependants, the herds, and 22 the valuables in front. The Danites had gone some distance from Micah's

house, when his neighbours were called out in pursuit and caught up with them. They shouted after them, and the 23 Danites turned round and said to Micah, 'What is the matter with you? Why have you come after us?' He said, 24 'You have taken my gods which I made for myself, you have taken the priest, and you have gone off and left me nothing. How dare you say, "What is the matter with you?"' The Danites 25 said to him, 'Do not shout at us. We are desperate men and if we fall upon you it will be the death of yourself and your family.' With that the Danites 26 went on their way and Micah, seeing that they were too strong for him, turned and went home.

Thus they carried off the priest and 27 the things Micah had made for himself, and attacked Laish, whose people were quiet and carefree. They put them to the sword and set fire to their city. There was no one to save them, for the 28 city was a long way from Sidon and they had no contact with the Aramaeans,*y* although the city was in the vale near Beth-rehob. They rebuilt the city and settled in it, naming it Dan after 29 the name of their forefather Dan, a son of Israel; but its original name was Laish. The Danites set up the idol, 30 and Jonathan son of Gershom, son of Moses, and his sons were priests to the tribe of Dan until the people went into exile. (They set up for themselves 31 the idol which Micah had made, and it was there as long as the house of God was at Shiloh.)

IN THOSE DAYS WHEN NO KING RULED **19** in Israel, a Levite was living in the heart of the hill-country of Ephraim. He had taken himself a concubine from Bethlehem in Judah. In a fit of anger 2 she had left him and had gone to her father's house in Bethlehem in Judah. When she had been there four months,

w That is the Camp of Dan.
x Prob. rdg.; Heb. the idol of the ephod, and teraphim and image.
y Prob. rdg., cp. verse 7; Heb. men.

however, far away. **11–26:** The theft of Micah's priest and images. **12.** *Mahaneh-dan:* see Tfn. *w*. **30–31:** On the two great shrines of the later Northern Kingdom, see 1 Kgs.12.29. **30:** *Son of Moses:* the Heb. may also be read as Manasseh. The thrust of the verse is to give the priest's name for the first time.
19.1–21.25: The crime of the Benjaminites at Gibeah and the war against them. 1: *No king:*

3 her husband set out after her with his servant and two asses to appeal to her and bring her back. She brought him 4 in to the house of her father, who welcomed him when he saw him. His father-in-law, the girl's father, pressed him and he stayed with him three days, and they were well entertained during 5 their visit. On the fourth day, they rose early in the morning, and he prepared to leave, but the girl's father said to his son-in-law, 'Have something to 6 eat first, before you go.' So the two of them sat down and ate and drank together. The girl's father said to the man, 'Why not spend the night and 7 enjoy yourself?' When he rose to go, his father-in-law urged him to stay, and again he stayed for the night. 8 He rose early in the morning on the fifth day to depart, but the girl's father said, 'Have something to eat first.' So they lingered till late afternoon, eating 9 and drinking together. Then the man stood up to go with his concubine and servant, but his father-in-law said, 'See how the day wears on towards sunset. Spend the night here and enjoy yourself, and then rise early tomorrow 10 and set out for home.' But the man would not stay the night; he rose and left. He had reached a point opposite Jebus, that is Jerusalem, with his two 11 laden asses and his concubine, and when they were close to Jebus, the weather grew wild and stormy, and the young man said to his master, 'Come now, let us turn into this Jebusite 12 town and spend the night there.' But his master said to him, 'No, not into a strange town where the people are not 13 Israelites; let us go on to Gibeah. Come, we will go and find some other place, and spend the night in Gibeah or 14 Ramah.' So they went on until sunset overtook them; they were then near Gibeah which belongs to Benjamin. 15 They turned in to spend the night there, and went and sat down in the open street of the town; but nobody took them into his house for the night.

Meanwhile an old man was coming 16 home in the evening from his work in the fields. He was from the hill-country of Ephraim, but he lived in Gibeah, where the people were Benjamites. He looked up, saw the traveller in the 17 open street of the town, and asked him where he was going and where he came from. He answered, 'We are travelling 18 from Bethlehem in Judah to the heart of the hill-country of Ephraim. I come from there; I have been to Bethlehem in Judah and I am going home, but nobody has taken me into his house. I have straw and provender for the 19 asses, food and wine for myself, the girl, and the young man; we have all we need, sir.' The old man said, 'You 20 are welcome, I will supply all your wants; you must not spend the night in the street.' So he took him inside 21 and provided fodder for the asses; they washed their feet, and ate and drank. While they were enjoying themselves, 22 some of the worst scoundrels in the town surrounded the house, hurling themselves against the door and shouting to the old man who owned the house, 'Bring out the man who has gone into your house, for us to have intercourse with him.' The owner 23 of the house went outside to them and said, 'No, my friends, do nothing so wicked. This man is my guest; do not commit this outrage. Here is my 24 daughter, a virgin;*z* let me bring her*a* out to you. Rape her*a* and do to her*a* what you please; but you shall not commit such an outrage against this man.' But the men refused to listen 25 to him, so the Levite took hold of his concubine and thrust her outside for them. They assaulted her and abused her all night till the morning, and when dawn broke, they let her go. The 26 girl came at daybreak and fell down at the entrance of the man's house where her master was, and lay there until it was light. Her master rose in 27 the morning and opened the door of

z Prob. rdg.; Heb. adds and his concubine.
a Prob. rdg.; Heb. them.

see 17.1–21.25 n.; compare 17.6 and 21.25. **10–12:** *Jerusalem* was as yet unconquered by the Hebrews; contrast 1.8 but compare 2 Sam.5.6–9. (Extrabiblical sources always refer to it as Jerusalem, never as Jebus.) *Gibeah*, about five miles north of Jerusalem, was later the home of Saul (1 Sam.10.26). **22–26:** Compare Gen.19.4–9. Gibeah became proverbial as a place of

the house to set out on his journey, and there was his concubine lying at the door with her hands on the threshold.

28 He said to her, 'Get up and let us be off'; but there was no answer. So he lifted her on to his ass and set off for

29 home. When he arrived there, he picked up a knife, and he took hold of his concubine and cut her up limb by limb into twelve pieces; and he sent them through the length and breadth of

30 Israel. He told the men he sent with them to say to every Israelite, 'Has the like of this happened or been seen from the time the Israelites came up from Egypt till today? Consider this among yourselves and speak your minds.' So everyone who saw them said, 'No such thing has ever happened or been seen before.'

20 All the Israelites, the whole community from Dan to Beersheba and out of Gilead also, left their homes as one man and assembled before the

2 LORD at Mizpah. The leaders of the people and all the tribes of Israel presented themselves in the general assembly of the people of God, four hundred thousand foot-soldiers armed with

3 swords; and the Benjamites heard that the Israelites had gone up to Mizpah. The Israelites asked how this wicked

4 thing had come about, and the Levite, to whom the murdered woman belonged, answered, 'I and my concubine came to Gibeah in Benjamin to spend

5 the night there. The citizens of Gibeah rose against me that night and surrounded the house where I was, intending to kill me; and they raped my

6 concubine and she died. I took her and cut her in pieces, and sent them through the length and breadth of Israel, because of the filthy outrage

7 they had committed in Israel. Now it is for you, the whole of Israel, to say here and now what you think ought to be

8 done.' All the people rose to their feet as one man and said, 'Not one of us

shall go back to his tent, not one shall return home. This is what we will now 9 do to Gibeah. We will draw lots for the attack: and we will take ten men 10 out of every hundred in all the tribes of Israel, a hundred out of every thousand, and a thousand out of every ten thousand, to collect provisions from the people for those who have taken the field against Gibeah in Benjamin to avenge the outrage committed in Israel.' Thus all the Israelites 11 to a man were massed against the town.

The tribes of Israel sent men all 12 through the tribe of Benjamin saying, 'What is this wicked thing which has happened in your midst? Hand over 13 to us those scoundrels in Gibeah, and we will put them to death and purge Israel of this wickedness.' But the Benjamites refused to listen to their fellow-Israelites. They flocked from their cities 14 to Gibeah to go to war with the Israelites, and that day they mustered out of 15 their cities twenty-six thousand men armed with swords. There were also seven hundred picked men from Gibeah, left-handed men, who could sling a 16 stone and not miss by a hair's breadth. The Israelites, without Benjamin, num- 17 bered four hundred thousand men armed with swords, every one a fighting man. The Israelites at once moved on to 18 Bethel, and there they sought an oracle from God, asking, 'Which of us shall attack Benjamin first?', and the LORD's answer was, 'Judah shall attack first.' So the Israelites set out at dawn and 19 encamped opposite Gibeah. They ad- 20 vanced to do battle with Benjamin and drew up their forces before the town. The Benjamites made a sally from 21 Gibeah and left twenty-two thousand of Israel dead on the field that day. The Israelites went up to Bethel,[b] lam- 23[c]

b *to Bethel: prob. rdg., cp. verses 18, 26; Heb. om.*
c *Verses 22 and 23 transposed.*

shameful wickedness; see Hos.9.9; 10.9. **27–30:** The summons to vengeance. **29:** Compare 1 Sam.11.7.
   20.1–48: The tribes assemble against the Benjaminites. 1: *Dan to Beersheba:* that is, all Israel, from the extreme north to the extreme south. This *Mizpah* was on the northern border of Benjamin (see 11,11 n.). Some scholars believe the assembly (see v. 18) was at Bethel in Ephraim. **12–36a:** The Israelites suffer two setbacks, and then by a ruse defeat the Benjaminites. **17:** The numbers are greatly exaggerated. **18:** See Judg.18.30–31 n. On seeking *an oracle*, see 18.5 n.

ented before the LORD until evening and inquired whether they should again attack their brother Benjamin. 22 The LORD said, 'Yes, attack him.' Then the Israelites took fresh courage and again formed up on the same ground 24 as the first day. So the second day they 25 advanced against the Benjamites, who sallied out from Gibeah to meet them and laid another eighteen thousand 26 armed men low. The Israelites, the whole people, went back to Bethel, where they sat before the LORD lamenting and fasting until evening, and they offered whole-offerings and 27 shared-offerings before the LORD. In those days the Ark of the Covenant of 28 God was there, and Phinehas son of Eleazar, son of Aaron, served before the LORD.*d* The Israelites inquired of the LORD and said, 'Shall we again march out to battle against Benjamin our brother or shall we desist?' The LORD answered, 'Attack him: tomorrow I will deliver him into your hands.' 29 Israel then posted men in ambush all round Gibeah.

30 On the third day the Israelites advanced against the Benjamites and drew up their forces at Gibeah as they had 31 before; and the Benjamites sallied out to meet the army. They were drawn away from the town and began the attack as before by killing a few Israelites, about thirty,*e* on the highways which led across open country, one to Bethel and the other to Gibeah. 32 They thought they were defeating them once again, but the Israelites had planned a retreat to draw them away from the town out on to the highways. 33 Meanwhile the main body of Israelites left their positions and re-formed in Baal-tamar, while those in ambush, ten thousand picked men all told, burst out from their position in the neigh-34 bourhood of Gibeah and came in on the east of the town. There was soon heavy fighting; yet the Benjamites did not suspect the disaster that was 35 threatening them. So the LORD put Benjamin to flight before Israel, and on that day the Israelites killed twenty-

five thousand one hundred Benjamites, all armed men.

36 The men of Benjamin now saw that they had been defeated, for all that the Israelites, trusting in the ambush which they had set by Gibeah, had given way before them. The men in ambush 37 made a sudden dash on Gibeah, fell on the town from all sides and put all the inhabitants to the sword. The 38 agreed signal between the Israelites and those in ambush*f* was to be a column of smoke sent up from the town. The Israelites then faced about 39 in the battle; and Benjamin began to cut down the Israelites, killing about thirty of them,*g* in the belief that they were defeating them as they had done in the first encounter. As the column of 40 smoke began to go up from the town, the Benjamites looked back and thought the whole town was going up in flames. When the Israelites faced about, the 41 Benjamites saw that disaster had overtaken them and were seized with panic. They turned and fled before the 42 Israelites in the direction of the wilderness, but the fighting caught up with them and soon those from the town were among them, cutting them down. They hemmed in the Benjamites, pursu-43 ing them without respite,*h* and overtook them at a point to the east of Gibeah. Eighteen thousand of the Benjamites 44 fell, all of them fighting men. The 45 survivors turned and fled into the wilderness towards the Rock of Rimmon. The Israelites picked off the stragglers on the roads, five thousand of them, and chased them until they had cut down and killed two thousand more. Twenty-five thousand armed 46 men of Benjamin fell in battle that day, all fighting men. The six hundred 47 who survived turned and fled into the wilderness as far as the Rock of Rimmon, and there they remained for four months. The Israelites then turned 48 back to deal with the Benjamites, and put to the sword the people in the

d Or before the Ark.   e Or about thirty wounded men.
f Prob. rdg.; Heb. adds an unintelligible word.
g to cut . . . them: or to kill about thirty wounded men among the Israelites.
h without respite: or from Nohah.

27–28: Since only here in Judg. is the Ark mentioned, these verses are often regarded as a late insertion. *Phinehas:* see Num.25.6–13. **36b–48:** This is a second, fuller account of the ambush and victory of vv. 29–36.

towns and the cattle, every creature that they found; they also set fire to every town within their reach.

21 In Mizpah the Israelites had bound themselves by oath that none of them would marry his daughter to a Ben-² jamite. The people now came to Bethel and remained there in God's presence till sunset, raising their voices in loud ³ lamentation. They said, 'O LORD God of Israel, why has it happened in Israel that one tribe should this day be lost to ⁴ Israel?' Next day the people rose early, built an altar there and offered whole-⁵ offerings and shared-offerings. At that the Israelites asked themselves whether among all the tribes of Israel there was anyone who did not go up to the assembly before the LORD; for under the terms of the great oath anyone who had not gone up to the LORD at ⁶ Mizpah was to be put to death. And the Israelites felt remorse over their brother Benjamin, because, as they said, 'This day Israel has lost one ⁷ whole tribe.' So they asked, 'What shall we do for wives for those who are left? We have sworn to the LORD not to give any of our daughters to ⁸ them in marriage. Is there anyone in all the tribes of Israel who did not go up to the LORD at Mizpah? Now it happened that no one from Jabesh-gilead had come to the camp for the ⁹ assembly; so when they held a roll-call of the people, they found that no in-habitant of Jabesh-gilead was present. ¹⁰ Thereupon the community sent off twelve thousand fighting men with orders to go and put the inhabitants of Jabesh-gilead to the sword, men, ¹¹ women, and dependants. 'This is what you shall do,' they said: 'put to death every male person, and every woman who has had intercourse with a man, but spare any who are virgins.' This ¹² they did. Among the inhabitants of Jabesh-gilead they found four hundred young women who were virgins and had not had intercourse with a man, and they brought them to the camp at ¹³ Shiloh in Canaan. Then the whole com-munity sent messengers to the Benjam-ites at the Rock of Rimmon to parley with them, and peace was proclaimed. At this the Benhamites came back, and ¹⁴ were given those of the women of Jabesh-gilead who had been spared; but these were not enough.

The people were still full of remorse ¹⁵ over Benjamin because the LORD had made this gap in the tribes of Israel, and ¹⁶ the elders of the community said, 'What shall we do for wives for the rest? All the women in Benjamin have been massacred.' They said, 'Heirs there ¹⁷ must be for the remnant of Benjamin who have escaped! Then Israel will not see one of its tribes blotted out. We cannot give them our own daugh-¹⁸ ters in marriage because we have sworn that there shall be a curse on the man who gives a wife to a Benjamite.' Then ¹⁹ they bethought themselves of the pil-grimage in honour of the LORD, made every year to Shiloh, the place which lies to the north of Bethel, on the east side of the highway from Bethel to Shechem and to the south of Lebonah. They said to the Benjamites, 'Go and ²⁰ hide in the vineyards and keep watch. ²¹ When the girls of Shiloh come out to dance, sally out of the vineyards, and each of you seize one of them for his wife; then make your way home to the land of Benjamin. Then, if their fathers ²² or brothers come and complain to you, say to them, "Let us keep them with your approval, for none of us has captured a wife in battle. Had you offered them to us, the guilt would be yours."'

All this the Benjamites did. They ²³ carried off as many wives as they needed, snatching them as they danced; then they went their way and returned to their patrimony, rebuilt their cities and settled in them. The ²⁴ Israelites also dispersed by tribes and families, and every man went back to his own patrimony.

In those days there was no king in ²⁵ Israel and every man did what was right in his own eyes.

21.1–25: The rehabilitation of Benjamin. Two accounts (vv. 1–15 and 16–25) are blended. **5–15:** *Jabesh-gilead* was east of the Jordan. **12:** On the sparing of *virgins* in warfare, compare Num.31.17–18. **15–25:** No other biblical data are available about this festival which was perhaps the occasion of agricultural fertility rites. **19:** On *Shiloh* pilgrimages see 1 Sam.1.3,21.

RUTH

Ruth was a Moabite woman who, after the death of her Judean husband, chose to give up the security of her homeland to return to Judah with her mother-in-law, Naomi (ch. 1). There Ruth's loyalty and devotion to Naomi brought her to the notice of Boaz, a relative of her late husband. Boaz married Ruth (2.1–4.12), and through this marriage she became the great-grandmother of David (4.13–22).

The opening verse sets the story in the period of the Judges. Some scholars consider Ruth a postexilic literary creation, though perhaps based on an older tale; on this view, it was intended to counteract the harsh decrees of Ezra and Nehemiah against foreign wives (Ezra 10.1–5; Neh. 13.23–27). Others, however, date it much earlier, during the reigns of the first kings of Judah, before bitter enmity toward Moab had developed; furthermore, Davidic connections with Moab are indicated by 1 Sam.22.3–4, and it is argued that a foreign extraction would hardly have been attributed to David without any basis.

In the Hebrew Bible it is found in the Writings, in some MSS. in first place; it is placed after Judges in the Sept. and Vg. In the synagogue traditions, Ruth, one of the five Megilloth ("Scrolls"), is read in public at the Feast of Weeks ("Pentecost").

Naomi and Ruth

1 LONG AGO, IN THE TIME OF THE judges, there was a famine in the land, and a man from Bethlehem in Judah went to live in the Moabite country with his wife and his two 2 sons. The man's name was Elimelech, his wife's name was Naomi, and the names of his two sons Mahlon and Chilion. They were Ephrathites from Bethlehem in Judah. They arrived in the Moabite country and there they stayed. 3 Elimelech Naomi's husband died, so that she was left with her two sons. 4 These sons married Moabite women, one of whom was called Orpah and the other Ruth. They had lived there 5 about ten years, when both Mahlon and Chilion died, so that the woman was bereaved of her two sons as well 6 as of her husband. Thereupon she set out with her two daughters-in-law to return home, because she had heard while still in the Moabite country that the LORD had cared for his people and 7 given them food. So with her two daughters-in-law she left the place where she had been living, and took 8 the road home to Judah. Then Naomi said to her two daughters-in-law, 'Go

back, both of you, to your mothers' homes. May the LORD keep faith with you, as you have kept faith with the dead and with me; and may he grant 9 each of you security in the home of a new husband.' She kissed them and they wept aloud. Then they said to 10 her, 'We will return with you to your own people.' But Naomi said, 'Go 11 back, my daughters. Why should you go with me? Am I likely to bear any more sons to be husbands for you? Go back, my daughters, go. I am too 12 old to marry again. But even if I could say that I had hope of a child, if I were to marry this night and if I were to bear sons, would you then wait 13 until they grew up? Would you then refrain from marrying? No, no, my daughters, my lot is more bitter than yours, because the LORD has been against me.' At this they wept again. 14 Then Orpah kissed her mother-in-law and returned to her people, but Ruth clung to her.

'You see,' said Naomi, 'your sister- 15 in-law has gone back to her people and her gods;[a] go back with her.' 'Do not 16 urge me to go back and desert you', Ruth answered. 'Where you go, I will go, and where you stay, I will stay.

_a Or_ god.

1.1–22: Naomi and Ruth. 1–5: Introduction. 1: _Bethlehem in Judah_ distinguishes it from Bethlehem in the tribe of Zebulun (Josh.19.15). _Moab:_ east of the Dead Sea. In the late biblical period the Moabites were regarded as special enemies of the Israelites; see Deut.23.3–6 n. 2: _Ephrathites from Bethlehem:_ they belonged to a Judean clan settled in Bethlehem; see 1 Chr. 2.50–51. 6–18: Ruth chooses to return to Judah with Naomi. 8: _Your mothers' homes_ refers to the women's part of the dwelling; see S. of S.3.4. 11: _More sons to be husbands for you:_ according to levirate law; see Deut.25.5–10. 15–18: Orpah goes back to _her gods,_ the gods of Moab, or

277

Your people shall be my people, and
17 your God my God. Where you die, I
will die, and there I will be buried. I
swear a solemn oath before the LORD
your God: nothing but*b* death shall
18 divide us.' When Naomi saw that
Ruth was determined to go with her,
19 she said no more, and the two of them
went on until they came to Bethlehem.
When they arrived in Bethlehem, the
whole town was in great excitement
about them, and the women said,
20 'Can this be Naomi?' 'Do not call me
Naomi,'*c* she said, 'call me Mara,*d* for
it is a bitter lot that the Almighty has
21 sent me. I went away full, and the
LORD has brought me back empty. Why
do you call me Naomi? The LORD has
pronounced against me; the Almighty
22 has brought disaster on me.' This is
how Naomi's daughter-in-law, Ruth
the Moabitess, returned with her from
the Moabite country. The barley harvest
was beginning when they arrived in
Bethlehem.

Ruth and Boaz

2 Now NAOMI HAD A KINSMAN ON HER
husband's side, a well-to-do man of the
family of Elimelech; his name was
2 Boaz. Ruth the Moabitess said to
Naomi, 'May I go out to the cornfields and glean behind anyone who
will grant me that favour?' 'Yes, go,
3 my daughter', she replied. So Ruth
went gleaning in the fields behind the
reapers. As it happened, she was in
that strip of the fields which belonged
4 to Boaz of Elimelech's family, and
there was Boaz coming out from
Bethlehem. He greeted the reapers,
saying, 'The LORD be with you'; and
they replied, 'The LORD bless you.'
5 Then he asked his servant in charge

of the reapers, 'Whose girl is this?'
'She is a Moabite girl', the servant 6
answered, 'who has just come back
with Naomi from the Moabite country. She asked if she might glean and 7
gather among the swathes behind the
reapers. She came and has been on her
feet with hardly a moment's rest*e* from
daybreak till now.' Then Boaz said to 8
Ruth, 'Listen to me, my daughter:
do not go and glean in any other field,
and do not look any further, but keep
close to my girls. Watch where the 9
men reap, and follow the gleaners; I
have given them orders not to molest
you. If you are thirsty, go and drink
from the jars the men have filled.' She 10
fell prostrate before him and said, 'Why
are you so kind as to take notice of me
when I am only a foreigner?' Boaz 11
answered, 'They have told me all that
you have done for your mother-in-law
since your husband's death, how you
left your father and mother and the
land of your birth, and came to a
people you did not know before. The 12
LORD reward your deed; may the LORD
the God of Israel, under whose wings
you have come to take refuge, give you
all that you deserve.' 'Indeed, sir,' 13
she said, 'you have eased my mind
and spoken kindly to me; may I ask
you as a favour not to treat me only
as one of your slave-girls?'*f* When 14
meal-time came round, Boaz said to
her, 'Come here and have something
to eat, and dip your bread into the
sour wine.' So she sat beside the
reapers, and he passed her some roasted
grain. She ate all she wanted and still
had some left over. When she got up 15

b I swear . . . nothing but: *or* The LORD your God do so
  to me and more if . . .
c That is Pleasure.
d That is Bitter.
e Prob. rdg.; Heb. adds in the house.
f may I . . . slave-girls?: *or* if you please, treat me as one
  of your slave-girls.

---

to *her god* (Tfn. *a*), i.e. Kemosh, the chief god of Moab. Ruth chooses Israel and Israel's God.
However, Orpah is not being condemned here; there are no villains in the Book of Ruth. Though
the setting is in the time of the judges, the characters seem unmarked by the violent spirit
manifested in the Book of Judg. Vv. 16–17 are poetic prose, and reflect a meter found in Hebrew
poetry. **19–22:** Naomi and Ruth arrive in Bethlehem. **22:** *The barley harvest* usually began in
April.
  2.1–4.22: Ruth and Boaz. 1–3: While gleaning, Ruth happens to come to the field owned by
Boaz, a relative of her father-in-law Elimelech (1.2). **2:** Hebrew law allowed the poor to *glean*,
i.e. to pick up the grain left in the fields after the reapers had finished (Lev.19.9–10; Deut.
24.19–22). **4–7:** Ruth meets Boaz. **5:** In the Orient every woman belonged to someone: to father,
husband, brother, or master. **8–16:** The kindliness of Boaz. **15–16:** Boaz goes beyond the

to glean, Boaz gave the men orders. 'She', he said, 'may glean even among 16 the sheaves; do not scold her. Or you may even pull out some corn from the bundles and leave it for her to glean, without reproving her.'

17 So Ruth gleaned in the field till evening, and when she beat out what she had gleaned, it came to about a 18 bushel of barley. She took it up and went into the town, and her mother-in-law saw how much she had gleaned. Then Ruth brought out what she had saved from her meal and gave it to her. 19 Her mother-in-law asked her, 'Where did you glean today? Which way did you go? Blessings on the man who kindly took notice of you.' So she told her mother-in-law whom she had been working with. 'The man with whom I worked today', she said, 'is called 20 Boaz.' 'Blessings on him from the LORD', said Naomi. 'The LORD has kept faith with the living and the dead. For this man is related to us and 21 is our next-of-kin.' 'And what is more,' said Ruth the Moabitess, 'he told me to stay close to his men until they 22 had finished all his harvest.' 'It is best for you, my daughter,' Naomi answered, 'to go out with his girls; let no 23 one catch you in another field.' So she kept close to his girls, gleaning with them till the end of both barley and wheat harvests; but she lived with her mother-in-law.

3 One day Ruth's mother-in-law Naomi said to her, 'My daughter, I 2 want to see you happily settled. Now there is our kinsman Boaz; you were with his girls. Tonight he is winnowing 3 barley at his threshing-floor. Wash and anoint yourself, put on your cloak and go down to the threshing-floor, but do not make yourself known to the man until he has finished eating and 4 drinking. But when he lies down, take

note of the place where he lies. Then go in, turn back the covering at his feet and lie down. He will tell you what to do.' 'I will do whatever you tell 5 me', Ruth answered. So she went 6 down to the threshing-floor and did exactly as her mother-in-law had told her. When Boaz had eaten and drunk, 7 he felt at peace with the world and went to lie down at the far end of the heap of grain. She came in quietly, turned back the covering at his feet and lay down. About midnight something 8 disturbed the man as he slept; he turned over and, lo and behold, there was a woman lying at his feet. 'Who are you?' 9 he asked. 'I am your servant, Ruth', she replied. 'Now spread your skirt over your servant, because you are my next-of-kin.' He said, 'The LORD has 10 blessed you, my daughter. This last proof of your loyalty is greater than the first; you have not sought after any young man, rich or poor. Set your mind 11 at rest, my daughter. I will do whatever you ask; for, as the whole neighbourhood knows, you are a capable woman. Are you sure that I am the next-of- 12 kin? There is a kinsman even closer than I. Spend the night here and then 13 in the morning, if he is willing to act as your next-of-kin, well and good; but if he is not willing, I will do so; I swear it by the LORD. Now lie down till morning.' So she lay at his feet till 14 morning, but rose before one man could recognize another; and he said, 'It must not be known that a woman has been to the threshing-floor.' Then he 15 said, 'Bring me the cloak you have on, and hold it out.' So she held it out, and he put in six measures of barley and lifted it on her back, and she went to the town. When she came to her 16 mother-in-law, Naomi asked, 'How did things go with you, my daughter?' Ruth told her all that the man had

requirement of Hebrew law (see v. 2). **17–23:** Ruth relates her experiences to Naomi. **20:** The *next-of-kin*, a technical term, had certain rights and obligations: to restore the property which an impoverished kinsman had lost (Lev.25.25; see Ruth 4.3–4) and to marry the widow of a relative without male offspring (see 1.11–13; 4.5–6; Deut.25.5–10). It is also the term for a blood avenger (Num.35.12; 19.21). Boaz, however (3.12–13), is not the nearest next-of-kin. **23:** These *harvests* ended in June.

3.1–18. The threshing-floor incident. 1–5: Naomi's instructions. These relate to ordinary bridal customs. **6–13:** Carried out, Naomi's instructions win the assent of Boaz. **9:** To *spread* one's *skirt over* someone symbolizes marriage; compare Ezek.16.8. *Next-of-kin:* see 2.20 n. **14–18:** Boaz's concern for Ruth's good name.

17 done for her. 'He gave me these six measures of barley,' she said; 'he would not let me come home to my 18 mother-in-law empty-handed.' Naomi answered, 'Wait, my daughter, until you see what will come of it. He will not rest until he has settled the matter today.'

4 Now Boaz had gone up to the city gate, and was sitting there; and, after a time, the next-of-kin of whom he had spoken passed by. 'Here,' he cried, calling him by name, 'come and sit 2 down.' He came and sat down. Then Boaz stopped ten elders of the town, and asked them to sit there, and they 3 did so. Then he said to the next-of-kin, 'You will remember the strip of field that belonged to our brother Elimelech. Naomi has returned from the 4 Moabite country and is selling it. I promised to open the matter with you, to ask you to acquire it in the presence of those who sit here, in the presence of the elders of my people. If you are going to do your duty as next-of-kin, then do so, but if not, someone must do it. So tell me, and then I shall know; for I come after you as next-of-kin.' He answered, 'I will act as next-of-5 kin.' Then Boaz said, 'On the day when you acquire the field from Naomi, you also acquire Ruth the Moabitess, the dead man's wife, so as to perpetuate the name of the dead man with his 6 patrimony.' Thereupon the next-of-kin said, 'I cannot act myself, for I should risk losing my own patrimony. You must therefore do my duty as next-of-kin. I cannot act.'

7 Now in those old days, when property was redeemed or exchanged, it was the custom for a man to pull off his sandal and give it to the other party. This was the form of attestation in Israel. So the next-of-kin said to 8 Boaz, 'Acquire it for yourself', and pulled off his sandal. Then Boaz 9 declared to the elders and all the people, 'You are witnesses today that I have acquired from Naomi all that belonged to Elimelech and all that belonged to Mahlon and Chilion; and, further, that I have myself 10 acquired Ruth the Moabitess, wife of Mahlon, to be my wife, to perpetuate the name of the deceased with his patrimony, so that his name may not be missing among his kindred and at the gate of his native place. You are witnesses this day.' Then the elders 11 and all who were at the gate said, 'We are witnesses. May the LORD make this woman, who has come to your home, like Rachel and Leah, the two who built up the house of Israel. May you do great things in Ephrathah and keep a name alive in Bethlehem. May your house be like the house of 12 Perez, whom Tamar bore to Judah, through the offspring the LORD will give you by this girl.'

So Boaz took Ruth and made her 13 his wife. When they came together, the LORD caused her to conceive and she bore Boaz a son. Then the women said 14 to Naomi, 'Blessed be the LORD today, for he has not left you without a next-of-kin. May the dead man's name be kept alive in Israel. The child will 15 give you new life and cherish you in your old age; for your daughter-in-law

---

4.1–12: The nearer relative foregoes his right. 1: *The city gate:* the customary place for commerce and public transactions. **2:** *Ten elders* were to give a legal decision, as well as witness the settlement of business affairs. **3–4:** The *strip of field* is hitherto unmentioned. Compare 2.20 n. **5:** Boaz at first mentions only the field and not Ruth; a masterful storyteller is here keeping his audience in suspense about whether Ruth will become the wife of Boaz. Ruth is referred to as *the dead man's wife*, although it is Elimelech, and not his son, who has been mentioned in v. 3. **6:** *Risk:* the matter is not completely clear. The first *next-of-kin*, who is unnamed, is apparently afraid that to preserve another man's line could so bring it about that his property could go to a new son born to him, rather than to his older children. That is, he was ready to redeem the land, but not to enter into a next-of-kin marriage. **7–8:** The procedure is somewhat different from Deut.25.7–10. There the woman herself shows her contempt for the man unwilling to marry her; here the first next-of-kin is only publicly surrendering his right and obligation. The two passages possibly represent quite different stages in the development of Hebrew law, with Ruth an earlier one. **9–12:** Boaz assumes the obligations, both to the property and to Ruth. **11–12:** Like *Rachel and Leah;* see Gen.35.23–26. *Ephrathah:* another name for Bethlehem (1.2). *Perez:* see Gen.38.6–30. Tamar (Gen. ch. 38) was also involved in a levirate marriage. *Perez* is mentioned here as part of the tracing of the ancestry of David in the next verses.
    4.13–17: Naomi's new line. The climax of 4.11–17 is in the words *Jesse the father of David.*

who loves you, who has proved better to you than seven sons, has borne him.' 16 Naomi took the child and laid him in 17 her lap and became his nurse. Her neighbours gave him a name: 'Naomi has a son,' they said; 'we will call him Obed.' He was the father of Jesse, the father of David.

THIS IS THE GENEALOGY OF PEREZ: 18 Perez was the father of Hezron, Hezron of Ram, Ram of Amminadab, 19 Amminadab of Nahshon, Nahshon of 20 Salmon, Salmon of Boaz, Boaz of 21 Obed, Obed of Jesse, and Jesse of 22 David.

4.18–22: The genealogy from Perez. Some commentators regard this *genealogy* as a later addition to the Book of Ruth. Earlier concern was that Elimelech and Mahlon have an heir; here attention is directed to the line into which Boaz and David fitted. A genealogy, with similar names spelled differently, is found in 1 Chr.2.5,9–15. The genealogy here is not needed; its inclusion suggests a reflection of a view of its high importance. These genealogies are used in Mt.1.2–6; Lk.3.31–33. **18:** *Perez:* see 4.12; Gen.38.29.

THE FIRST BOOK OF
SAMUEL

In the ancient Greek Bible, the books of Samuel and Kings formed a single work (in four books) entitled "Concerning the Kingdoms," an arrangement and title appropriate for several reasons. First, Samuel appears only in parts of 1 Samuel; David is much more the hero of the total narrative. Second, the division in the Hebrew Bible between 2 Samuel and 1 Kings, ascribable only to the length, unduly separates the account of David's reign in 2 Samuel from the important narrative of the succession of his throne in 1 Kings 1.1–2.12. Third, the materials of Samuel and Kings are organized around the topic of kingship: how it came to be established in Israel (1 Sam. chs. 1–14); how the Davidic dynasty received divine sanction (1 Sam. ch. 15–2 Sam. ch. 7); and how the destiny of Israel in the land was shaped by the conduct of the subsequent kings, especially in relation to the Jerusalem Temple (1 Kgs. 1.1–2 Kgs. 25.30).

The establishment of David's dynasty (2 Sam. ch. 7) and the consecration of the Solomonic Temple (1 Kgs. 8.1–9.9) are the two subjects that give a unique content to the entire so-called "Deuteronomic history." This history begins in Deuteronomy, there as if stating a theme, and continues, in fidelity to the theme, through Joshua, Judges, and Samuel-Kings. A special viewpoint, appearing in Deuteronomy, expresses concern more with prophetic exhortation and judgment than with precision respecting laws (the latter marks the Priestly Code). The Deuteronomists stress fidelity to God, contending that to worship other gods, such as the Canaanite Baal, is to forsake him. At many junctures in Samuel-Kings, both named and anonymous prophets arise to pass judgment on the people, and especially on the rulers, in the light of the covenant obligations. In the Book of Deuteronomy, the view recurs that only one sanctuary was to be valid in the future; the Deuteronomic historians credit Solomon with building the valid sanctuary, and hence the welfare of Solomon's Temple is treated as of paramount importance after Solomon's time. Furthermore, since Israel is God's people by covenant, recurring attention is given to the covenant and, because of it, to Israel as God's unique people.

A variety of older sources were incorporated into the Deuteronomic history, sometimes untouched but sometimes retouched or rewritten by the Deuteronomic historians. Such older sources are particularly clear in Samuel: the Ark narrative in 1 Samuel chs. 4–6 and 2 Samuel ch. 6; the two conflicting strands concerning the origin of kingship in 1 Samuel chs. 8–14; the collection of stories about David's rise to kingship in 1 Samuel ch. 16–2 Samuel ch. 5; and the magnificent history of the succession to David's throne in 2 Samuel chs. 9–20; 1 Kings chs. 1–2. In addition to such longer sources, individual narratives (e.g. 1 Sam. 2.1–10) and early Deuteronomic speeches (e.g. 1 Sam. 12.6–15) were included. The events of 1 Samuel cover approximately the period 1050–1010 B.C. See also Introduction to 1 Kings.

The birth and call of Samuel

1 THERE WAS A MAN FROM RAMATH-aim, a Zuphite from the hill-country of Ephraim, named Elkanah son of Jeroham, son of Elihu, son of 2 Tohu, son of Zuph an Ephraimite; and he had two wives named Hannah and Peninnah. Peninnah had children, but Hannah was childless. This man used 3 to go up from his own town every year to worship and to offer sacrifice to the LORD of Hosts in Shiloh. There Eli's two sons, Hophni and Phinehas, were priests of the LORD. On the day 4 when Elkanah sacrificed, he gave several

---

1.1–4.1a: Samuel at Shiloh. This section establishes Samuel's legitimacy in Israel's history. Two themes are interwoven: the positive role of Samuel, and, negatively, the condemnation of the priestly family of Eli. Two narratives (Samuel's birth, ch. 1, and his first prophetic word, ch. 3), form the core of the section. Other materials are present to supplement the section which foreshadows Samuel's later activity as king maker.
1.1–28: Samuel's birth story. Birth stories are a response to curiosity about important historical figures, as may be seen in the cases of Moses (Exod.2.1–10), Samson (Judg.13.2–25), and Jesus (Mt.1.18–2.23; Lk. chs. 1–2). The barrenness of a favored wife is a repeated motif of such stories (Gen.18.1–15; 29.29–32; Judg.13.2–5; Lk.1.5–17). The birth story here is regarded by some as originally being about Saul rather than about Samuel; in v. 28 the Heb. word for *lent* is the same word as Saul, whose name is derived from the same Heb. roots in *asked* (1.20) and *lend* (1.28). **1:** *Ramathaim* is a variant of the Ramah mentioned as Samuel's home village at 1.19. **3:** *Lord of Hosts* occurs here for the first time in the OT; the "hosts"

shares of the meat to his wife Peninnah
5 with all her sons and daughters; but,
although he loved Hannah, he gave her
only one share, because the LORD had
6 not granted her children. Further,
Hannah's rival used to torment her and
humiliate her because she had no
7 children. Year after year this happened when they went up to the house
of the LORD; her rival used to torment
her. Once when she was in tears and
8 would not eat, her husband Elkanah
said to her, 'Hannah, why are you
crying and eating nothing? Why are
you so miserable? Am I not more to
9-10 you than ten sons?' After they had
finished eating and drinking at the
sacrifice at Shiloh, Hannah rose in deep
distress, and stood before the LORD
and prayed to him, weeping bitterly.
Meanwhile Eli the priest was sitting on
his seat beside the door of the temple
11 of the LORD. Hannah made a vow in
these words: 'O LORD of Hosts, if
thou wilt deign to take notice of my
trouble and remember me, if thou wilt
not forget me but grant me offspring,
then I will give the child to the LORD
for his whole life, and no razor shall
12 ever touch his head.' For a long time
she went on praying before the LORD,
13 while Eli watched her lips. Hannah was
praying silently; but, although her
voice could not be heard, her lips were
moving and Eli took her for a drunken
14 woman. He said to her, 'Enough of this
drunken behaviour! Go away till the
15 wine has worn off.' 'No, sir,' she
answered, 'I am a sober person, I have
drunk no wine or strong drink, and I
have been pouring out my heart before
16 the LORD. Do not think me so degraded sir; all this time I have been
speaking out of the fullness of my grief
17 and misery.' 'Go in peace,' said Eli,
'and may the God of Israel answer the
18 prayer you have made to him.' Hannah
said, 'May I be worthy of your kind-

ness.' And she went away and took
something to eat, no longer downcast. Next morning they were up early 19
and, after prostrating themselves
before the LORD, returned to their own
home at Ramah. Elkanah had intercourse with his wife Hannah, and the
LORD remembered her. She con- 20
ceived, and in due time bore a son,
whom she named Samuel, 'because',
she said, 'I asked the LORD for him.'
Elkanah, with his whole house- 21
hold, went up to make the annual
sacrifice to the LORD and to redeem
his vow. Hannah did not go with 22
them, but said to her husband, 'When
the child is weaned I will come up
with him to enter the presence of the
LORD, and he shall*a* stay there always.'
Her husband Elkanah said to her, 'Do 23
what you think best; stay at home until
you have weaned him. Only, may the
LORD indeed see your vow fulfilled.'
So the woman stayed and nursed her
son until she had weaned him; and 24
when she had weaned him, she took
him up with her. She took also a bull
three years old, an ephah of meal, and a
flagon of wine, and she brought him,
child as he was, into the house of the
LORD at Shiloh. They slaughtered the 25
bull, and brought the boy to Eli.
Hannah said to him, 'Sir, as sure as 26
you live, I am the woman who stood
near you here praying to the LORD.
It was this boy that I prayed for and the 27
LORD has given me what I asked.
What I asked I have received; and now 28
I lend him to the LORD; for his whole
life he is lent to the LORD.' And they
prostrated themselves there before the
LORD.
Then Hannah offered this prayer: **2**

My heart rejoices in the LORD,
in the LORD I now hold my head high;

*a come up ... he shall: or bring him up, and he shall
come into the presence of the LORD and ...*

---

may be either heavenly powers or the forces of the Israelites (see 17.45). This phrase apparently
arose in *Shiloh*, an important center before the monarchic period, but little is known about Shiloh
from the monarchy on (see Josh.18.1; Judg.21.19; 1 Kgs.11.29; 14.2; Jer.7.12; Ps.78.60). *Phinehas*, a name of Egyptian origin, was probably a descendant of the zealous priest of Num.25.6–15.
9–10: *Before the LORD* is a ritual position in front of the Temple. **11:** Not cutting the hair is a
mark of consecration to the LORD, combined in Nazirite vows with abstinence from wine
(see Num.6.1–21 and Judg.13.3–5). **20:** *Samuel* means "name of God"; curiously, the verse
explains the name "Saul"; see 1.1–28 n.
    2.1–10: The song of Hannah. Hannah's *prayer* is quite different from the idyllic narrative

my mouth is full of derision of my
    foes,
exultant because thou hast saved me.

2 There is none except thee,
    none so holy as the LORD,
    no rock like our God.

3 Cease your proud boasting,
    let no word of arrogance pass your
      lips;
    for the LORD is a god of all
      knowledge:
    he governs all that men do.

4 Strong men stand in mute[b] dismay
    but those who faltered put on new
      strength.

5 Those who had plenty sell
      themselves for a crust,
    and the hungry grow strong again.
    The barren woman has seven
      children,
    and the mother of many sons is left
      to languish.

6 The LORD kills and he gives life,
    he sends down to Sheol, he can
      bring the dead up again.

7 The LORD makes a man poor, he
      makes him rich,
    he brings down and he raises up.

8 He lifts the weak out of the dust
    and raises the poor from the
      dunghill;
    to give them a place among the
      great,
    to set them in seats of honour.

For the foundations of the earth
    are the LORD's,
he has built the world upon them.

9 He will guard the footsteps of his
    saints,
while the wicked sink into silence
    and gloom;

not by mere strength shall a man
    prevail.

10 Those that stand against the LORD
    will be terrified
    when the High God[c] thunders out
      of heaven.
    The LORD is judge even to the ends
      of the earth,
    he will give strength to his king
    and raise high the head of his
      anointed prince.

11 Then Elkanah went to Ramah with his household, but the boy remained behind in the service of the LORD under Eli the priest.

12 Now Eli's sons were scoundrels and had no regard for the LORD. 13 The custom of the priests in their dealings with the people was this: when a man offered a sacrifice, the priest's servant would come while the flesh was stewing and would thrust a three-pronged 14 fork into the cauldron or pan or kettle or pot; and the priest would take whatever the fork brought out. This should have been their practice whenever Israelites came to sacrifice at Shiloh; but now under Eli's sons, even before 15 the fat was burnt, the priest's servant came and said to the man who was sacrificing, 'Give me meat to roast for the priest; he will not accept what has been already stewed, only raw meat.' And if the man answered 'Let them 16 burn the fat first, and then take what you want', he said, 'No, give it to me now, or I will take it by force.' The 17 young men's sin was very great in the LORD's sight; for they brought the LORD's sacrifice into general contempt.

b in mute: *prob. rdg.; Heb. obscure.*
c the High God: *prob. rdg.; Heb. upon him.*

of ch. 1. The motifs of reversal of fortune (vv. 4–8) and the *barren woman* (v. 5) relate it to Hannah's story. A relatively old composition, it was incorporated into the Samuel story late in literary growth; see Introduction. **1:** The *I* is originally a king, recently victorious; the language, however, is quite stereotyped. **2:** *Rock* is a forceful metaphor common in poetic texts; see Deut.32.30. **6:** *Sheol* is the underworld, abode of the dead; compare Isa.14.9–11. **10:** The verse uses frequently found motifs to express the divine sanction of the king; see, in fuller form, 2 Sam.22.5–18. *High God:* a divine epithet, or name. It appears as "Most High" in 2 Sam.22.14 and, in a longer form, in Gen.14.18–19 and elsewhere. It derived from pre-Israelite traditions and eventually applied to Yahweh, the God of Israel. *Anointed:* see 10.1 n.

    2.11–36: Samuel and Eli's sons contrasted. A series of connective units precedes the second narrative of chs. 1–3. The positive theme of Samuel's future rise and the negative theme of the condemnation of Eli's sons alternate and culminate in the call of Samuel (ch. 3). **11,18–21:** The barren woman theme (1.1–28 n.) has its conclusion here, in the birth of other children. **12–17:** The sins of Eli's sons consist both in greed (v. 14) and in cultic violations (v. 16, although

18 Samuel continued in the service of the LORD, a mere boy with a linen
19 ephod fastened round him. Every year his mother made him a little cloak and took it to him when she went up with her husband to offer the annual
20 sacrifice. Eli would give his blessing to Elkanah and his wife and say, 'The LORD grant you children by this woman in place of the one for which you asked him.'*d* Then they went home again.
21 The LORD showed his care for Hannah, and she conceived and gave birth to three sons and two daughters; meanwhile the boy Samuel grew up in the presence of the LORD.
22 Eli, now a very old man, had heard how his sons were treating all the Israelites, and how they lay with the women who were serving at the entrance
23 to the Tent of the Presence. So he said to them, 'Why do you do such things? I hear from all the people how wickedly
24 you behave. Have done with it, my sons; for it is no good report that I hear spreading among the LORD's
25 people. If a man sins against another man, God will intervene; but if a man sins against the LORD, who can intercede for him?' For all this, they did not listen to their father's rebuke, for the
26 LORD meant that they should die. But the young Samuel, as he grew up, commended himself to the LORD and to men.
27 Now a man of God came to Eli and said, 'This is the word of the LORD: You know that I revealed myself to your forefather when he and his family were in Egypt in slavery in the house
28 of Pharaoh. You know that I chose him from all the tribes of Israel to be my priest, to mount the steps of my altar, to burn sacrifices and to carry*e*

the ephod before me; and that I assigned all the food-offerings of the Israelites to your family. Why then do 29 you show disrespect for my sacrifices and the offerings which I have ordained? What makes you resent them? Why do you honour your sons more than me by letting them batten on the choicest offerings of my people Israel? The LORD's word was, "I promise that 30 your house and your father's house shall serve before me for all time"; but now his word is, "I will have no such thing: I will honour those who honour me, and those who despise me shall meet with contempt. The time is 31 coming when I will lop off every limb of your own and of your father's family, so that no man in your house shall come to old age. You will even 32 resent*f* the prosperity I give to Israel; never again shall there be an old man in your house. If I allow any to survive 33 to serve my altar, his eyes will grow dim and his appetite fail, his issue will be weaklings and die off. The fate of 34 your two sons shall be a sign to you: Hophni and Phinehas shall both die on the same day. I will appoint for 35 myself a priest who will be faithful, who will do what I have in my mind and in my heart. I will establish his family to serve in perpetual succession before my anointed king. Any of your 36 family that still live will come and bow humbly before him to beg a fee, a piece of silver and a loaf, and will ask for a turn of priestly duty to earn a crust of bread."'

So the child Samuel was in the 3 LORD's service under his master Eli.

d for which ... him: *or* which you lent him.
e Or wear.
f You ... resent: *prob. rdg.; Heb. obscure.*

---

the details here are obscure). **18:** *Ephod:* see Exod.25.7 n. **22–26:** Eli here reproves his sons, in contrast to 3.13 where he is charged with laxity. **22:** *Serving:* the nature of the service of *the women* is not known, but probably reflects a sexual and perhaps fertility cult aspect of Canaanite and early Israelite religion. Such women may also be referred to in Exod.28.8. *Tent* is a traditional term, not taken literally, since it is clear that Shiloh had a temple as its sanctuary (ch. 3). **27–36:** An anonymous *man of God*, rather than Samuel, prophesies against Eli; this preserves 3.11–14 as the climax of the section. **27–28:** The *forefather* is presumably Aaron, to whose grandson Phinehas the promise was given; Num.25.13. **34–36:** This passage appears to have been written in the light of these subsequent events: (1) The deaths of Hophni and Phinehas in ch. 4; and (2) the Solomonic priestly establishment (see 1 Kgs.2.27). **3.1–4.1a: Samuel becomes a prophet.** Ch. 1 explains Samuel's priestly role. This narrative explains his prophetic role. The account of the wonder child (vv. 4–9) is lighthearted compared

Now in those days the word of the LORD was seldom heard, and no vision 2 was granted. But one night Eli, whose eyes were dim and his sight failing, was lying down in his usual place, 3 while Samuel slept in the temple of the LORD where the Ark of God was. Before the lamp of God had gone out, 4 the LORD called him, and Samuel 5 answered, 'Here I am', and ran to Eli saying, 'You called me: here I am.' 'No, I did not call you,' said Eli; 'lie down again.' So he went and lay 6 down. The LORD called Samuel again, and he got up and went to Eli. 'Here I am,' he said; 'surely you called me.' 'I did not call, my son,' he answered; 7 'lie down again.' Now Samuel had not yet come to know the LORD, and the word of the LORD had not been dis- 8 closed to him. When the LORD called him for the third time, he again went to Eli and said, 'Here I am; you did call me.' Then Eli understood that it was 9 the LORD calling the child; he told Samuel to go and lie down and said, 'If he calls again, say, "Speak, LORD; thy servant hears thee."' So Samuel went and lay down in his place.

10 The LORD came and stood there, and called, 'Samuel, Samuel', as before. Samuel answered, 'Speak; 11 thy servant hears thee.' The LORD said, 'Soon I shall do something in Israel which will ring in the ears of all who 12 hear it. When that day comes I will make good every word I have spoken against Eli and his family from begin- 13 ning to end. You are to*g* tell him that my judgement on his house shall stand

for ever because*h* he knew of his sons' blasphemies against God*i* and did not rebuke them. Therefore I have sworn 14 to the family of Eli that their abuse of sacrifices and offerings shall never be expiated.'

Samuel lay down till morning and 15 then opened the doors of the house of the LORD, but he was afraid to tell Eli about the vision. Eli called Samuel: 16 'Samuel, my son', he said; and he answered, 'Here I am.' Eli asked, 17 'What did the LORD say to you? Do not hide it from me. God forgive you if you hide one word of all that he said to you.' Then Samuel told him every- 18 thing and hid nothing. Eli said, 'The LORD must do what is good in his eyes.'

As Samuel grew up, the LORD was 19 with him, and none of his words went unfulfilled. From Dan to Beersheba, 20 all Israel recognized that Samuel was confirmed as a prophet of the LORD. So the LORD continued to appear in 21 Shiloh, because he had revealed himself there to Samuel.*j*

The struggle with the Philistines

SO SAMUEL'S WORD HAD AUTHORITY **4** throughout Israel. And the time came when the Philistines mustered for battle against Israel, and the Israelites went out to meet them. The Israelites encamped at Eben-ezer and the Philis-

g Prob. rdg.; Heb. I will.
h because: *prob. rdg.; Heb.* in guilt.
i against God: *prob. original reading, altered in Heb. to* to them.
j Prob. rdg.; Heb. adds according to the word of the LORD.

with the somber seriousness of the divine message (vv. 11–14). **3:** How and when the *Ark of God* came to be based at Shiloh is not known (but see Josh.18.1). **4:** *The lamp of God* was a regular feature of sanctuaries; see Exod.27.21; Lev.24.1–4; 1 Kgs.7.48–49. **4–9:** The artfulness of the story should not lead to regarding this as a primitive stage of the religion of Israel. **13:** This prophecy, not entirely compatible with 2.27–36, exhibits a view of Eli earlier than that in 2.22–25. **15–18:** Eli is here a tragic figure, in contrast to vv. 11–14.

4.1b–7.1: The Ark of the Lord and its movements. Chs. 1–3 prepare for ch. 4; however, Samuel does not appear in chs. 4–6, where the focus is on the Ark, that box-throne object upon which the Lord of Israel manifested his presence; see Exod.25.22; Num.7.89; 10.33–36; and Josh. chs. 3–4. The narrative of chs. 4–6 has a conclusion in 2 Sam. ch. 6, with the Ark finally brought to David's Jerusalem. The primary point of the total Ark story is that the LORD himself moved from Shiloh to Jerusalem; the narrative here is as mythical (that is, a story of the activities of a god) as any section in the historical books of the OT.

4.1b–22: The Philistine defeat of Israel. This chapter could be called "the departure of the Ark," since the LORD here permits the defeat of Israel and himself withdraws. This is the sequel toward which chs. 2–3 look.

4.1b–11: The battles. 1b: *The Philistines* were based in five main cities on the southwestern coastal plain of Palestine. The events reflected here occurred around 1050 B.C. and were part of a Philistine move to rule all of Palestine. The battle occurs at the base of a pass leading up

2 tines at Aphek. The Philistines drew up their lines facing the Israelites, and when they joined battle the Israelites were routed by the Philistines, who killed about four thousand men on the 3 field. When the army got back to the camp, the elders of Israel asked, 'Why did the LORD let us be routed today by the Philistines? Let us fetch the Ark of the Covenant of the LORD from Shiloh to go with us and deliver us from 4 the power of our enemies.' So the people sent to Shiloh and fetched the Ark of the Covenant of the LORD of Hosts, who is enthroned upon the cherubim; Eli's two sons, Hophni and Phinehas, were there with the 5 Ark. When the Ark came into the camp all the Israelites greeted it with a great shout, and the earth rang with 6 the shouting. The Philistines heard the noise and asked, 'What is this great shouting in the camp of the Hebrews?' When they knew that the Ark of the 7 LORD had come into the camp, they were afraid and cried, 'A god has come into the camp. We are lost! No such 8 thing has ever happened before. We are utterly lost! Who can deliver us from the power of these mighty gods? These are the very gods who broke the Egyptians and crushed them in the 9 wilderness. Courage, Philistines, and act like men, or you will become slaves to the Hebrews as they were 10 yours. Be men, and fight!' The Philistines then gave battle, and the Israelites were defeated and fled to their homes. It was a great defeat, and thirty thousand Israelite foot-soldiers per- 11 ished. The Ark of God was taken, and Eli's two sons, Hophni and Phinehas, were killed.

12   A Benjamite ran from the battle-

field and reached Shiloh on the same day, his clothes rent and dust on his head. When he arrived Eli was sitting 13 on a seat by the road to Mizpah, for he was deeply troubled about the Ark of God. The man entered the city with his news, and all the people cried out in horror. When Eli heard it, he asked, 14 'What does this uproar mean?' The man hurried to Eli and told him. Eli was 15 ninety-eight years old and sat staring with sightless eyes; so the man said 16 to him, 'I am the man who has just arrived from the battle; this very day I have escaped from the field.' Eli asked, 'What is the news, my son?' The 17 runner answered, 'The Israelites have fled from the Philistines; utter panic has struck the army; your two sons, Hophni and Phinehas, are killed, and the Ark of God is taken.' At the mention 18 of the Ark of God, Eli fell backwards from his seat by the gate and broke his neck, for he was old and heavy. So he died; he had been judge over Israel for forty years. His daughter- 19 in-law, the wife of Phinehas, was with child and near her time, and when she heard of the capture of the Ark and the deaths of her father-in-law and her husband, her labour suddenly began and she crouched down and was delivered. As she lay dying, the women 20 who attended her said, 'Do not be afraid; you have a son.' But she did not answer or heed what they said. Then 21 they named the boy Ichabod,*k* saying, 'Glory has departed from Israel' (in allusion to the capture of the Ark of God and the death of her father-in-law and her husband); 'Glory has departed 22 from Israel,' they said, 'because the Ark of God is taken.'

k That is No-glory.

to the hill country around Shiloh. **3:** Compare Josh.7.2–9. **4:** The throne character of the Ark is clear here. The LORD was understood to be seated invisibly between two winged creatures, the *cherubim*; compare Exod.25.10–22. **5–9:** This second Israelite effort, with the sacred object now with them, should have succeeded; instead the Ark's presence increases the dramatic tension. **6:** *Hebrews:* this term originally designated a social status rather than an ethnic group; (see 14.21 and Gen.14.13; 39.14; Exod.1.15–22). **8:** The Philistines are portrayed as garbling the Israelite sacred history.

  4.12–22: The fall of Eli's house. The prophecies in chs. 2.27–54 and 3.11–14 are here fulfilled. **12:** *Clothes rent and dust on his head* indicates mourning. **13:** *Seat* can also be translated "throne," which, if an elevated seat, could explain why Eli's fall breaks his neck in v. 18. **18:** *Judge over Israel* is a comment by a later writer bringing Eli into the system of judges presented by Deuteronomic historians; see 7.15; Judg.2.6–23. **21:** A popular etymology for the name *Ichabod* is based on the loss of the Ark. Though the Philistines captured and destroyed Shiloh at this time, some members of Eli's house escaped.

5 After the Philistines had captured the Ark of God, they brought it from 2 Eben-ezer to Ashdod; and there they carried it into the temple of Dagon 3 and set it beside Dagon himself. When the people of Ashdod rose next morning, there was Dagon fallen face downwards before the Ark of the LORD; so they took him and put him back in 4 his place. Next morning when they rose, Dagon had again fallen face downwards before the Ark of the LORD, with his head and his two hands lying broken off beside his platform; only Dagon's body re-5 mained on it. This is why from that day to this the priests of Dagon and all who enter the temple of Dagon at Ashdod do not set foot upon Dagon's platform.

6 Then the LORD laid a heavy hand upon the people of Ashdod; he threw them into distress and plagued them with tumours, and their territory swarmed with rats.[l] There was death and destruction all through the city. 7 When the men of Ashdod saw this, they said, 'The Ark of the God of Israel shall not stay here, for he has laid a heavy hand upon us and upon 8 Dagon our god.' So they sent and called all the Philistine princes together to ask what should be done with the Ark. They said, 'Let the Ark of the God of Israel be taken across to Gath.' 9 They took it there, and after its arrival the hand of the LORD caused great havoc in the city; he plagued everybody, high and low alike, with the tumours 10 which broke out. Then they sent the Ark of God on to Ekron. When the Ark reached Ekron, the people cried, 'They have brought the Ark of the God of Israel over to us, to kill us and 11 our families.' So they summoned all

the Philistine princes and said, 'Send the Ark of God of Israel away; let it go back to its own place, or it will be the death of us all.' There was death and destruction all through the city; for the hand of God lay heavy upon it. Even those who did not die were 12 plagued with tumours; the cry of the city went up to heaven.

When the Ark of the LORD had been 6 in their territory for seven months, the Philistines summoned the priests 2 and soothsayers and asked, 'What shall we do with the Ark of the LORD? Tell us how we ought to send it back to its own place.' They answered, 'If 3 you send the Ark of the God of Israel back, do not let it go without a gift, but send it back with a gift for him by way of indemnity; then you will be healed and restored to favour; there is no reason why his hand should not be lifted from you.' When they were 4 asked, 'What gift shall we send back to him?', they answered, 'Send five tumours modelled in gold and five gold rats, one for each of the Philistine princes, for the same plague afflicted all of you and your princes. Make 5 models of your tumours and of the rats which are ravaging the land, and give honour to the God of Israel; perhaps he will relax the pressure of his '
hand on you, on your god, and on your land. Why should you be stub-6 born like Pharaoh and the Egyptians? Remember how this god made sport of them until they let Israel go. Now 7 make a new wagon ready with two milch-cows which have never been yoked; harness the cows to the wagon, and take their calves from them and drive them back to their stalls. Then 8 take the Ark of the LORD and put it

l Or mice.

5.1–5: The LORD defeats Dagon. The action is presented realistically in terms of what the Philistines did and found, not in terms of what the gods did; it is nevertheless mythical (see 4.1b–7.1n.). **1:** *Ashdod* was one of the five Philistine cities; see 6.17. The others were Ashkelon, Ekron, Gath, and Gaza. **2:** *Dagon* was a god of grain worshiped in Palestine before the Philistines arrived (about 1200 B.C.) and adopted the worship of him.
5.6–12: The LORD plagues the Philistines. An epidemic of bubonic plague may lie behind this artistic presentation of the power of the God of Israel.
6.1–7.1: The Ark proceeds to Judah. 1–5: The golden *tumours* and *rats* represent sympathetic magic, i.e. ritual imitations of what is to be removed. **6:** The entire Ark story seems to reflect the influence of the account of the plagues on Egypt (Exod. chs. 7–11). **7–12:** This action shows that the LORD determined his own movements. Possibly old rituals for moving the Ark are reflected here. **7:** *A new wagon* was needed to avoid any contamination from previous use.

on the wagon, place in a casket, beside it, the gold offerings that you are sending to him as an indemnity,

9 and let it go where it will. Watch it: if it goes up towards its own territory to Beth-shemesh, then it is the LORD who has done us this great injury; but if not, then we shall know that his hand has not touched us, but we have been the victims of chance.'

10 The men did this. They took two milch-cows and harnessed them to a wagon, shutting up their calves in the

11 stall, and they placed the Ark of the LORD on the wagon together with the casket, the gold rats, and the models

12 of their haemorrhoids. Then the cows went straight in the direction of Beth-shemesh; they kept to the same road, lowing as they went and turning neither right nor left, while the Philistine princes followed them as far as

13 the territory of Beth-shemesh. Now the people of Beth-shemesh were harvesting their wheat in the Vale, and when they looked up and saw the Ark they

14 rejoiced at the sight of it. The wagon came to the farm of Joshua of Beth-shemesh and halted there. Close by stood a great stone; so they chopped up the wood of the wagon and offered the cows as a whole-offering to the

15 LORD. Then the Levites lifted down the Ark of the LORD and the casket containing the gold offerings, and laid them on the great stone; and the men of Beth-shemesh offered whole-offerings and shared-offerings that day to the

16 LORD. The five princes of the Philistines watched all this, and returned to Ekron the same day.

17 These golden haemorrhoids which the Philistines sent back as a gift of indemnity to the LORD were for Ashdod, Gaza, Ashkelon, Gath, and

18 Ekron, one for each city. The gold rats were for all the towns of the Philistines governed by the five princes, both fortified towns and open settlements. The great stone where they deposited the Ark of the LORD stands witness on the farm of Joshua of Beth-shemesh to this very day.

19 But the sons of Jeconiah did not rejoice with the rest of the men of Beth-shemesh when they welcomed the Ark of the LORD, and he struck down seventy of them. The people mourned because the LORD had struck

20 them so heavy a blow, and the men of Beth-shemesh said, 'No one is safe in the presence of the LORD, this holy God. To whom can we send it, to be

21 rid of him?' So they sent this message to the inhabitants of Kiriath-jearim: 'The Philistines have returned the Ark of the LORD; come down and take

7 charge of it.' Then the men of Kiriath-jearim came and took the Ark of the LORD away; they brought it into house of Abinadab on the hill and consecrated his son Eleazar as its custodian.

Samuel judge over Israel

2 SO FOR A LONG WHILE THE ARK WAS housed in Kiriath-jearim; and after some time, twenty years later, there was a movement throughout Israel to fol-

3 low the LORD. So Samuel addressed these words to the whole nation: 'If your return to the LORD is whole-hearted, banish the foreign gods and the Ashtaroth from your shrines; turn to the LORD with heart and mind, and worship him alone, and he will

4 deliver you from the Philistines.' The Israelites then banished the Baalim and the Ashtaroth, and worshipped the LORD alone.

5 Samuel summoned all Israel to an

9: *Beth-shemesh*, much further south than Shiloh and Eben-ezer, was situated in a pass leading up from Ekron toward Jerusalem. 13–18: A local sanctuary at Beth-shemesh is here reflected. The cows go directly to the *great stone*, and sacrifices are first offered to the LORD there. 15: This verse is a later correction to introduce *the Levites* as functionaries in accordance with subsequent practice. 17–18: *Golden haemorrhoids . . . rats:* the passage is old, as if the writer witnessed the events and saw these things. 6.19–7.1: This passage provides a transition from the end of the Philistine story (6.18) to the later movement of the Ark from Kiriath-jearim to Jerusalem (2 Sam. ch. 6).

7.2–17: **Samuel judges at Mizpah.** This passage portrays Samuel as a "judge," conforming to the schematic formula of the Deuteronomic authors; see 4.18n. 4: *Baalim* and *Ashtaroth* were cult objects representing the Canaanite fertility deities Baal and Astarte. 5: *Mizpah*, in the vicinity

assembly at Mizpah, so that he might intercede with the Lord for them. 6 When they had assembled there, they drew water and poured it out before the LORD and fasted all day, confessing that they had sinned against the LORD. It was at Mizpah that Samuel acted as judge over Israel.

7 When the Philistines heard that the Israelites had assembled at Mizpah, their princes marched against them. The Israelites heard that the Philistines were advancing, and they were afraid. 8 They said to Samuel, 'Do not cease to pray for us to the LORD our God to save us from the power of the Philis- 9 tines.' Thereupon Samuel took a sucking lamb, offered it up complete as a whole-offering and prayed aloud to the LORD on behalf of Israel; and the 10 LORD answered his prayer. As Samuel was offering the sacrifice and the Philistines were advancing to battle with the Israelites, the LORD thundered loud and long over the Philistines and threw them into confusion. They fled in panic before the Israelites, 11 who set out from Mizpah in pursuit and kept up the slaughter of the Philistines till they reached a point 12 below Beth-car. There Samuel took a stone and set it up as a monument between Mizpah and Jeshanah,[m] naming it Eben-ezer,[n] 'for to this point', 13 he said, 'the LORD has helped us.' Thus the Philistines were subdued and no longer encroached on the territory of Israel; and the hand of the LORD was

against them as long as Samuel lived. The cities they had captured were re- 11 stored to Israel, and from Ekron to Gath the borderland was freed from their control. Between Israel and the Amorites peace was maintained. Samuel 15 acted as judge in Israel as long as he lived, and every year went on circuit to 16 Bethel and Gilgal and Mizpah; he dispensed justice at all these places, returning always to Ramah. That was 17 his home and the place from which he governed Israel, and there he built an altar to the LORD.

Saul anointed king

WHEN SAMUEL GREW OLD, HE APPOINT- **8** ed his sons to be judges in Israel. The 2 eldest son was named Joel and the second Abiah; they acted as judges in Beersheba. His sons did not follow in 3 their father's footsteps but were intent on their own profit, taking bribes and perverting the course of justice. So all 4 the elders of Israel met, and came to Samuel at Ramah and said to him, 5 'You are now old and your sons do not follow in your footsteps; appoint us a king to govern us, like other nations.' But their request for a king to govern 6 them displeased Samuel, and he prayed to the LORD. The LORD answered 7 Samuel, 'Listen to the people and all that they are saying; they have not

m *Prob. rdg. (cp. 2 Chr. 13. 19); Heb.* the tooth.
n *That is* Stone of Help.

of Bethel, Gilgal, and Ramah (vv. 15–16), was in Benjaminite territory, considerably further south than Shiloh; this reflects the continued encroachment of the Philistines. **6:** Pouring out water (rather than wine) is not a common ritual in the OT. **7–10:** The notion that battles were won by divine intervention alone was a late view; see, e.g. 2 Chr.20.1–30. **13–14:** This period of peace conforms to the view of the Deuteronomic historians regarding the achievements of the judges; see Judg.2.18. **15–17:** This more modest view of Samuel is probably an accurate glimpse of him. Here he is based at Ramah, a local sanctuary, as is seen in ch. 9.

8.1–15.35: Israel becomes a kingdom. In chs. 1–7, Samuel was established as prophet, as judge, and as successor to the Shiloh priestly establishment, these achievements qualifying him to be king maker. Moreover, the LORD himself moved south from Shiloh to Judah. The scene is now set for kingship. Kingship is a topic with two parts: the question of the legitimacy of kingship itself (chs. 8–14); and the establishment of the house of David in place of the house of Saul (ch. 15–2 Sam. ch. 7).

8.1–22: The negative view of kingship. One strand of material (ch. 8; 10.17–27; ch. 12) regards human kingship as the rejection of the kingship of the LORD; this strand may be read as a single account without a gap. The positive strand begins in ch. 9. The negative, with some affinities with the Deuteronomic historians' views, is the later of the two strands, even though the basic attitude may go back to opposition to monarchy in principle in early Israel. **1:** *Judges* are not the military heroes of the Book of Judges, but only the men responsible for administering justice (see Exod.18.13–27 and 2 Chr.19.4–11). **2:** *Beersheba*, in southern Judah, was an important sanctuary; see Amos 5.5 and 8.14. **3:** *Taking bribes* was a recurrent problem; see Exod.23.6–8; Isa.5.22–23; Deut.16.19. **4:** *Ramah* is probably the city of Samuel's parents (see

rejected you, it is I whom they have rejected, I whom they will not have to 8 be their king. They are now doing to you just what they have done to me since I brought them up from Egypt: they have forsaken me and wor- 9 shipped other gods. Hear what they have to say now, but give them a solemn warning and tell them what sort 10 of king will govern them.' Samuel told the people who were asking him for a king all that the LORD had said to 11 him. 'This will be the sort of king who will govern you', he said. 'He will take your sons and make them serve in his chariots and with his cavalry, and will make them run before his chariot. 12 Some he will appoint officers over units of a thousand and units of fifty. Others will plough his fields and reap his harvest; others again will make weapons of war and equipment for 13 mounted troops. He will take your daughters for perfumers, cooks, and 14 confectioners, and will seize the best of your cornfields, vineyards, and olive-yards, and give them to his lackeys. 15 He will take a tenth of your grain and your vintage to give to his eunuchs 16 and lackeys. Your slaves, both men and women, and the best of your cattle and your asses he will seize and put 17 to his own use. He will take a tenth of your flocks, and you yourselves will 18 become his slaves. When that day comes, you will cry out against the king whom you have chosen; but it will be too late, the LORD will not answer 19 you.' The people refused to listen to Samuel; 'No,' they said, 'we will have 20 a king over us; then we shall be like other nations, with a king to govern us, to lead us out to war and fight our 21 battles.' So Samuel, when he had heard what the people said, told the LORD; 22 and he answered, 'Take them at their word and appoint them a king.' Samuel then dismissed all the men of Israel to their homes.

There was a man from the district of 9 Benjamin, whose name was Kish son of Abiel, son of Zeror, son of Bechor-ath, son of Aphiah a Benjamite. He was a man of substance, and had a son 2 named Saul, a young man in his prime; there was no better man among the Israelites than he. He was a head taller than any of his fellows.

One day some asses belonging to 3 Saul's father Kish had strayed, so he said to his son Saul, 'Take one of the servants with you, and go and look for the asses.' They crossed the hill- 4 country of Ephraim and went through the district of Shalisha but did not find them; they passed through the district of Shaalim but they were not there; they passed through the district of Benjamin but again did not find them. When they had entered the dis- 5 trict of Zuph, Saul said to the servant with him, 'Come, we ought to turn back, or my father will stop thinking about the asses and begin to worry about us.' The servant answered, 6 'There is a man of God in the city here, who has a great reputation, be-cause everything he says comes true. Suppose we go there; he may tell us something about this errand of ours.' Saul said, 'If we do go, what shall we 7 offer him? There is no food left in our packs and we have no present for the man of God, nothing at all.' The ser- 8 vant answered him again, 'Wait! I have here a quarter-shekel of silver. I can give that to the man, to tell us what we should do.' Saul said, 'Good! let 10[o] us go to him.' So they went to the city where the man of God was. (In days 9 gone by in Israel, when a man wished to consult God, he would say, 'Let us go to the seer.' For what is nowadays called a prophet used to be called a seer.) As they were going up the hill 11 to the city they met some girls coming

o Verses 9 and 10 transposed.

1.1 n.) and is Samuel's base from here on, especially in the strand favorable to kingship. **11–18:** This is mostly a portrayal of typical Ancient Near Eastern monarchy. The portrayal may be based on practices of Solomon which generated resentment as in 1 Kgs.12.4.
    9.1–10.16: The anointing of Saul. 2: The words *a young man* are suited to this hero story, but see 13.1 n. **4:** The *district(s)* mentioned here have not been identified in biblical geography. **5:** *Zuph:* see 1.1. **6:** *Everything he says comes true:* this repeats the substance of 3.19–21. **9:** The term *seer* was no longer used in the time of the writer, then a seer was *called a prophet.*

out to draw water and asked, 'Shall
12 we find the seer there?' 'Yes,' they said,
'the seer is ahead of you now; he has
just[p] arrived in the city because there
13 is a feast at the hill-shrine today. As
you enter the city you will meet him
before he goes up to the shrine to eat;
the people will not start until he
comes, for he has to bless the sacrifice
before the company can eat. Go up
now, and you will find him at once.'
14 So they went up to the city, and just
as they were going in, there was
Samuel coming towards them on his
way up to the shrine.
15   Now the day before Saul came, the
LORD had disclosed his intention to
16 Samuel in these words: 'At this same
time tomorrow I will send you a man
from the land of Benjamin. Anoint
him prince over my people Israel, and
then he shall deliver my people from the
Philistines. I have seen the sufferings
of my people and their cry has reached
17 my ears.' The moment Saul appeared
the LORD said to Samuel, 'Here is the
man of whom I spoke to you. This man
18 shall rule my people.' Saul came up to
Samuel in the gateway and said,
'Would you tell me where the seer
19 lives?' Samuel replied, 'I am the seer.
Go on ahead of me to the hill-shrine
and you shall eat with me today; in the
morning I will set you on your way,
after telling you what you have on your
20 mind. Trouble yourself no more about
the asses lost three days ago, for they
have been found. But what is it that
all Israel is wanting? It is you and your
21 ancestral house.' 'But I am a Benjamite,' said Saul, 'from the smallest of the
tribes of Israel, and my family is the
least important of all the families of
the tribe of Benjamin. Why do you say
22 this to me?' Samuel then brought Saul
and his servant into the dining-hall
and gave them a place at the head of
the company, which numbered about
23 thirty. Then he said to the cook, 'Bring

the portion that I gave you and told
you to put on one side.' So the cook 24
took up the whole haunch and leg and
put it before Saul; and Samuel said,
'Here is the portion of meat[q] kept for
you. Eat it: it has been reserved for
you at this feast to which I have invited the people.' So Saul dined with
Samuel that day, and when they came 25
down from the hill-shrine to the city a
bed was spread on the roof for Saul,
and he stayed there that night. At 26
dawn Samuel called to Saul on the roof,
'Get up, and I will set you on your
way.' When Saul rose, he and Samuel
went out together into the street. As 27
they came to the end of the town,
Samuel said to Saul, 'Tell the boy to go
on.' He did so, and then Samuel said,
'Stay here a moment, and I will tell
you the word of God.'

Samuel took a flask of oil and poured 10
it over Saul's head, and he kissed him
and said, 'The LORD anoints you prince
over his people Israel; you shall rule
the people of the LORD and deliver
them from the enemies round about
them. You shall have a sign that the
LORD has anointed you prince to
govern his inheritance: when you leave 2
me today, you will meet two men by
the tomb of Rachel at Zelzah in the
territory of Benjamin. They will tell
you that the asses you are looking for
have been found and that your father
is concerned for them no longer; he is
anxious about you and says again
and again, "What shall I do about
my son?" From there go across 3
country as far as the terebinth of
Tabor, where three men going up to
Bethel to worship God will meet you.
One of them will be carrying three kids,
the second three loaves, and the third a
flagon of wine. They will greet you and 4
will offer you two loaves, which you
will accept from them. Then when 5

p the seer . . . just: prob. rdg.; Heb. he is ahead of you,
  hurry now, for he has today . . .
q the portion of meat: prob. rdg.; Heb. what is left over.

12: *Hill-shrine:* high place. In early Israel no stigma applied to the local sanctuaries, but later
Israelite tradition condemned them without qualification; see 1 Kgs.3.2; 2 Kgs.12.3; 14.4.
15-16: Kingship here is a gracious benefit bestowed by the LORD. In the strand (see 8.1–22 n.)
favorable to kingship, *prince* is used rather than "king"; king is used in the negative strand
(10.1 and 13.14). ("King" in 10.16 translates the Heb. for "kingship.") **10.1:** *Anointing:* the rite
which raised a commoner to kingship in Israel. Saul and David were anointed in secret; compare 16.1–13. Later it was a more formal and public act; see 1 Kgs.1.32–40. **2:** *The tomb of*

you reach the Hill of God, where the Philistine governor[r] resides, you will meet a company of prophets coming down from the hill-shrine, led by lute, harp, fife, and drum, and filled with 6 prophetic rapture. Then the spirit of the LORD will suddenly take possession of you, and you too will be rapt like a prophet and become another man. 7 When these signs happen, do whatever the occasion demands; God will be with 8 you. You shall go down to Gilgal ahead of me, and I will come to you to sacrifice whole-offerings and shared-offerings. Wait seven days until I join you; then I will tell you what to do.' 9 As Saul turned to leave Samuel, God gave him a new heart. On that same 10 day all these signs happened. When they reached the Hill there was a company of prophets coming to meet him, and the spirit of God suddenly took possession of him, so that he too 11 was filled with prophetic rapture. When people who had known him previously saw that he was rapt like the prophets, they said to one another, 'What can have happened to the son of Kish? Is Saul also among the 12 prophets?' One of the men of that place said, 'And whose sons are they?' Hence the proverb, 'Is Saul also 13 among the prophets?' When the prophetic rapture had passed, he went 14 home.[s] Saul's uncle said to him and the boy, 'Where have you been?' Saul answered, 'To look for the asses, and when we could not find them, we went 15 to Samuel.' His uncle said, 'Tell me 16 what Samuel said.' 'He told us that the asses had been found', said Saul; but he did not repeat what Samuel had said about his being king.

17 Meanwhile Samuel summoned the Israelites to the LORD at Mizpah and 18 said to the people, 'This is the word of the LORD the God of Israel: I brought Israel up from Egypt; I delivered you from the Egyptians and from all the kingdoms that oppressed you; but 19 today you have rejected your God who saved you from all your misery and distress; you have said, "No, set up a king over us." Now therefore take up your positions before the LORD tribe by tribe and clan by clan.' Samuel 20 then presented all the tribes of Israel, and Benjamin was picked by lot. Then he 21 presented the tribe of Benjamin, family by family, and the family of Matri was picked. Then he presented the family of Matri, man by man, and Saul son of Kish was picked; but when they looked for him he could not be found. They 22 went on to ask the LORD, 'Will the man be coming back?' The LORD answered, 'There he is, hiding among the baggage.' So someone ran and 23 fetched him out, and as he took his stand among the people, he was a head taller than anyone else. Samuel said to 24 the people, 'Look at the man whom the LORD has chosen; there is no one like him in this whole nation.' They all acclaimed him, shouting, 'Long live the king!' Samuel then explained to the 25 people the nature of a king, and made a written record of it on a scroll which he deposited before the LORD; he then dismissed them to their homes. Saul too 26 went home to Gibeah, and with him went some fighting men whose hearts God had moved. But there were scoun- 27 drels who said, 'How can this fellow deliver us?' They thought nothing of him and brought him no gifts.

r Or garrison.
s Prob. rdg.; Heb. to the hill-shrine.

Rachel was especially associated with Benjamin; see Gen.35.16–20. **6–8:** Prophecy in early times was marked by a frantic dance which turned the prophet from what he ordinarily was into *another man.* Compare 19.23–24. **8:** This verse is an addition, preparing for the rupture between Samuel and Saul in 13.8–14. *Gilgal* seems to have had special importance for kingship (11.14–15; 13.7–14; 15.10–33; 2 Sam.19.15, 39–40), but why is not clear. **11–12:** In 19.19–24 the origin of the proverb about Saul is explained differently. **13:** *Saul's uncle* was probably Ner; see 14.50.
   10.17–27: Saul is acclaimed as king. Continuing the negative strand on kingship (see 8.1–22 n.) from ch. 8, the LORD here grudgingly provides the best man for kingship. **17:** *Mizpah* is the place of assembly in the negative strand, Gilgal in the positive. **20–21:** This method of divine selection is seen also in the Achan story in Josh. ch. 7. **22:** The verse is puzzling. Perhaps it is meant to stress Saul's passivity or modesty. **23–24:** Samuel's positive view here is surprising. **25:** This *scroll* apparently did more than repeat the substance of 8.11–18, but probably proceeded to put some limitations on the king's prerogatives.

11 About a month later Nahash the Ammonite attacked and besieged Jabesh-gilead. The men of Jabesh said to Nahash, 'Come to terms with us 2 and we will be your subjects.' Nahash answered them, 'On one condition only will I come to terms with you: that I gouge out your right eyes and 3 bring disgrace on Israel.' The elders of Jabesh-gilead then said, 'Give us seven days' respite to send messengers throughout Israel and then, if no one relieves us, we will surrender to you.' 4 When the messengers came to Gibeah, where Saul lived, and delivered their message, all the people broke into 5 lamentation. Saul was just coming from the field driving in the oxen, and asked why the people were lamenting; and they repeated what the men of Jabesh 6 had said. When Saul heard this, the spirit of God suddenly seized him. 7 In his anger he took a pair of oxen and cut them in pieces, and sent messengers with the pieces all through Israel to proclaim that the same would be done to the oxen of any man who did not follow Saul and Samuel into battle. The fear of the LORD fell upon the people and they came out, to a man. 8 Saul mustered them in Bezek; there were three hundred thousand men from Israel and thirty thousand from 9 Judah. He said to the men who brought the message, 'Tell the men of Jabesh-gilead, "Victory will be yours tomorrow by the time the sun is hot."' The men of Jabesh heard what the messengers reported and took 10 heart; and they said to Nahash, 'Tomorrow we will surrender to you, and then you may deal with us as you think fit.' Next day Saul drew up his 11 men in three columns; they forced their way right into the enemy camp during the morning watch and massacred the Ammonites while the day grew hot, after which the survivors scattered until no two men were left together.

Then the people said to Samuel, 12 'Who said that Saul should not reign over us? Hand the men over to us to be put to death.' But Saul said, 'No 13 man shall be put to death on a day when the LORD has won such a victory in Israel.' Samuel said to the people, 14 'Let us now go to Gilgal and there renew our allegiance to the kingdom.' So they all went to Gilgal and invested 15 Saul there as king in the presence of the LORD, sacrificing shared-offerings before the LORD; and Saul and all the Israelites celebrated the occasion with great joy.

THEN SAMUEL THUS ADDRESSED THE **12** assembled Israelites: 'I have listened to your request and installed a king to rule over you. And the king is now 2 your leader, while I am old and white-haired and my sons are with you; but I have been your leader ever since I was a child. Here I am. Lay your com- 3 plaints against me in the presence of the LORD and of his anointed king. Whose ox have I taken, whose ass have I taken? Whom have I wronged, whom have I oppressed? From whom have I taken a bribe, to turn a blind eye? Tell me, and I will make restitu- tion.' They answered, 'You have not 4 wronged us, you have not oppressed us; you have not taken anything from

---

11.1–15: Saul's victory over the Ammonites. In the positive strand (see 8.1–22 n.) on king-ship, this spectacular victory was the occasion for Saul's public establishment as king; see 10.7. **1:** Ammon, east of the Jordan, was the territory of the upper Jabbok River. *Jabesh-gilead* was a city on the lower Jabbok near the Jordan. The Ammonites were probably seeking to control the entirety of the Jabbok basin. **6:** *The spirit of God:* here it is not the ecstasy and frenzy as in 10.10–12; rather, it was the power to act with determination and effectiveness. **7:** The phrase *and Samuel* is probably a later addition to harmonize the different strands; Samuel is not a war leader elsewhere in the positive strand. **8:** *Bezek:* north of Shechem and west of the Jordan. **11:** *The morning watch:* the last third of the night. **14–16:** The people of Jabesh-gilead later show their gratitude to Saul (1 Sam.31.11–13). **14:** *Renew:* in the sense of a public proclamation.

12.1–25: Samuel's farewell address. The speech reviews past deeds of God for Israel and turns to the present situation, with the initiation of kingship. Views of late Deuteronomic writers are present, especially in the contention that the people have rejected the kingship of God by asking for a human king. See 8.1–22 n. **1:** Here it is the people who are held culpable for turning away from the LORD; by contrast, 1 and 2 Kgs. hold the kings responsible for infidelity

5 any man.' Samuel then said to them, 'This day the LORD is witness among you, his anointed king is witness, that you have found my hands empty.' They

6 said, 'He is witness.' Samuel said to the people, 'Yes, the LORD is witness, the LORD who gave you Moses and Aaron and brought your fathers out of Egypt.

7 Now stand up, and here in the presence of the LORD I will put the case against you and recite all the victories which he has won for you and for your fathers.

8 After Jacob and his sons had come down to Egypt and the Egyptians had made them suffer, your fathers cried to the LORD for help, and he sent Moses and Aaron, who brought them out of Egypt and settled them in this place.

9 But they forgot the LORD their God, and he abandoned them to Sisera, commander-in-chief of Jabin king of Hazor, to the Philistines, and to the king of Moab, and they had to fight against

10 them. Then your fathers cried to the LORD for help: "We have sinned, we have forsaken the LORD and we have worshipped the Baalim and the Ashtaroth. But now, if thou wilt deliver us from our enemies, we will worship

11 thee." So the LORD sent Jerubbaal and Barak, Jephthah and Samson, and delivered you from your enemies on every side; and you lived in peace and quiet.

12 'Then, when you saw Nahash king of the Ammonites coming against you, although the LORD your God was your king, you said to me, "No, let us have a

13 king to rule over us." Now, here is the king you asked for; you chose him, and the LORD has set a king over you.

14 If you will revere the LORD and give true and loyal service, if you do not rebel against his commands, and if you and the king who reigns over you are faithful to the LORD your God, well

and good; but if you do not obey the 15 LORD, and if you rebel against his commands, then he will set his face against you and against your king.

'Stand still, and see the great wonder 16 which the LORD will do before your eyes. It is now wheat harvest; when I 17 call upon the LORD and he sends thunder and rain, you will see and know how wicked it was in the LORD's eyes for you to ask for a king.' So Samuel 18 called upon the LORD and he sent thunder and rain that day; and all the people were in great fear of the LORD and of Samuel. They said to Samuel, 'Pray for 19 us your servants to the LORD your God, to save us from death; for we have added to all our other sins the great wickedness of asking for a king.' Samuel said to the people, 'Do not be 20 afraid; although you have been so wicked, do not give up the worship of the LORD, but serve him with all your heart. Give up the worship of false gods 21 which can neither help nor save, because they are false. For his name's 22 sake the LORD will not cast you off, because he has resolved to make you his own people. As for me, God forbid 23 that I should sin against the LORD and cease to pray for you. I will show you what is right and good: to revere the 24 LORD and worship him faithfully with all your heart. Consider what great things he has done for you; but if you 25 persist in wickedness, you shall be swept away, you and your king.'

Saul was fifty years*t* old when he be- **13** came king, and he reigned over Israel for twenty-two*u* years. He picked three 2 thousand men from Israel, two thousand to be with him in Michmash and the hill-country of Bethel and a thousand

t fifty years: *prob. rdg.; Heb.* a year.
u Prob. rdg.; Heb. two.

against the LORD. **7**: A recitation of the saving deeds of God for Israel is a part of other farewell addresses, e.g. Josh.24.2–13. **9–11**: *Sisera:* Judg. chs. 4–5. *Philistines:* Judg. chs. 13–16. *King of Moab:* Judg.3.12–30. *Jerubbaal:* Gideon, Judg. chs. 6–8. *Barak:* Judg. 4.6–5.11. *Samson:* Judg. chs. 13–16. **17–18**: *Wheat harvest* was in early summer when it never rained. **19–25**: The passage strikes a delicate balance between reproving the people and admitting a divine sanction for kingship in Israel. **22**: *For his name's sake:* a major motif in Israelite reflections; see Ezek. ch. 20; also Ps.23.3. **23**: Samuel is viewed as a renowned intercessor in Jer.15.1 and Ps.99.6–9.

13.1–14.46: Saul's victory over the Philistines. The action is now in the central hill country where the Philistines have virtually secured control. **1**: See Tfn. *t,u*. The Heb. text lacks numbers, due to faulty copying. Saul has grown children (14.1,49–50); it is reasonable to suppose he was between forty and *fifty*. **2**: *Michmash* was in central Benjaminite territory, as were most

to be with Jonathan in Gibeah of Benjamin; and he sent the rest of the people home.

3 Jonathan killed the Philistine governor[v] in Geba, and the news spread among the Philistines that the Hebrews were in revolt.[w] Saul sounded the trumpet all through the land; and when the Israelites all heard that Saul had killed a Philistine governor and that the name of Israel stank among the Philistines, they answered the call to arms and 5 came to join Saul at Gilgal.[x] The Philistines mustered to attack Israel; they had thirty thousand chariots and six thousand horse, with infantry as countless as sand on the sea-shore. They went up and camped at Michmash, to the 6 east of Beth-aven. The Israelites found themselves in sore straits, for the army was hard pressed, so they hid themselves in caves and holes and among 7 the rocks, in pits and cisterns. Some of them crossed the Jordan into the district of Gad and Gilead, but Saul remained at Gilgal, and all the people at 8 his back were in alarm.[y] He waited seven days for his meeting with Samuel, but Samuel did not come to Gilgal; so the people began to drift away from 9 Saul. He said therefore, 'Bring me the whole-offering and the shared-offerings', and he offered up the whole-10 offering. Saul had just finished the sacrifice, when Samuel arrived, and he 11 went out to greet him. Samuel said, 'What have you done?', and Saul answered, 'I saw that the people were drifting away from me, and you yourself had not come as you had promised, and the Philistines were assembling at 12 Michmash; and I thought, "The Philistines will now move against me at Gilgal, and I have not placated the LORD"; so I felt compelled to make 13 the whole-offering myself.' Samuel said to Saul, 'You have behaved foolishly. You have not kept the command laid on you by the LORD your God; if you

had, he would have established your dynasty over Israel for all time. But 14 now your line will not endure; the LORD will seek a man after his own heart, and will appoint him prince over his people, because you have not kept the LORD's command.'

Samuel left Gilgal without more ado 15 and went on his way. The rest of the people followed Saul, as he moved from Gilgal towards the enemy. At Gibeah of Benjamin he mustered the people who were with him; they were about six hundred men. Saul and his 16 son Jonathan and the men they had with them took up their quarters in Gibeah of Benjamin, while the Philistines were encamped in Michmash. Raiding parties went out from the 17 Philistine camp in three directions. One party turned towards Ophrah in the district of Shual, another towards 18 Beth-horon, and the third towards the range of hills overlooking the valley of Zeboim and the wilderness beyond.

No blacksmith was to be found in the 19 whole of Israel, for the Philistines were determined to prevent the Hebrews from making swords and spears. The 20 Israelites had to go down to the Philistines for their ploughshares, mattocks, axes, and sickles to be sharpened. The 21 charge was two-thirds of a shekel for ploughshares and mattocks, and one-third of a shekel for sharpening the axes and setting the goads.[z] So when 22 war broke out none of the followers of Saul and Jonathan had either sword or spear; only Saul and Jonathan carried arms.

Now the Philistines had posted a 23 force to hold the pass of Michmash; and one day Saul's son Jonathan said **14** to his armour-bearer, 'Come, let us go

v *Or* garrison.
w that . . . revolt: *prob. rdg.; Heb. has* saying, Let the Hebrews hear *after* through the land.
x they answered . . . Gilgal: *or* they were summoned to follow Saul to Gilgal.
y but Saul . . . in alarm: *or* but Saul was still at Gilgal, and all the army joined him there.
z one-third . . . the goads: *prob. rdg.; Heb. obscure.*

of the places named in this account. *Jonathan* was Saul's warrior son and later (18.1–4) David's bosom friend. *Gibeah* and *Geba* (v. 3) are at times interchanged in this passage. **3**: *Hebrews:* see 4.6 n. and 14.21. **4**: *Gilgal:* see 10.17 n. **5**: The numbers here, as often in OT narratives, are intended to give an impression of vastness rather than an exact count. *Chariots* would have been quite impractical in this terrain (14.4). **7b–15**: This section is a later addition; it is pro-David apologetic, and anti-Saul. Its condemnation of Saul (recurrent in such additions) is rather arbitrary. See 10.8. **19–22**: This period was the beginning of the Iron age. The Philistines had a monopoly on the new metal. **14.1**: *The armour-bearer* accompanied the heavily armored,

over to the Philistine post beyond that ridge', but he did not tell his father. 2 Saul, at the time, had his tent under the pomegranate-tree at Migron on the outskirts of Gibeah; and he had about 3 six hundred men with him. The ephod was carried by Ahijah son of Ahitub, Ichabod's brother, son of Phinehas son of Eli, the priest of the LORD at Shiloh. Nobody knew that Jonathan had gone. 4 On either side of the pass through which Jonathan tried to make his way over to the Philistine post stood two sharp columns of rock, called Bozez*a* 5 and Seneh;*b* one of them was on the north towards Michmash, and the other 6 on the south towards Geba. Jonathan said to his armour-bearer, 'Now we will visit the post of those uncircumcised rascals. Perhaps the LORD will take a hand in it, and if he will, nothing can stop him. He can bring us safe through, whether we are few or many.' 7 The young man answered, 'Do what you will, go forward; I am with you 8 whatever you do.' 'Good!' said Jonathan, 'we will cross over and let them 9 see us. If they say, "Stay where you are till we come to you", then we will stay where we are and not go up to them. 10 But if they say, "Come up to us", we will go up; this will be the sign that the LORD has put them into our power.' 11 So they showed themselves to the Philistines, and the Philistines said, 'Look! Hebrews coming out of the holes where they have been hiding!' 12 And they called across to Jonathan and the young man, 'Come up to us; we have something to show you.' Jonathan said to the young man, 'Come on, the LORD has put them into the power of 13 Israel.' Jonathan climbed up on hands and feet, and the young man followed him. The Philistines fell in front of

Jonathan, and the young man, coming behind him, dispatched them. In that 14 first attack Jonathan and his armour-bearer killed about twenty of them, like men cutting a furrow across a half-acre field. Terror spread through the 15 army in the field and through the whole people; the men at the post and the raiding parties were terrified; the very earth quaked, and there was panic.

Saul's men on the watch in Gibeah 16 of Benjamin saw the mob of Philistines surging to and fro in confusion; so he 17 ordered the people to call the roll and find out who was missing; and they called the roll and found that Jonathan and his armour-bearer were absent. Saul said to Ahijah, 'Bring forward the 18 ephod', for it was he who carried the ephod at that time before Israel. But 19 while Saul was still speaking, the confusion in the Philistine camp was increasing more and more, and he said to the priest, 'Hold your hand.' Then Saul 20 and all his men with shouting made for the battlefield, where they found the enemy fighting one another in complete disorder. The Hebrews who up to now 21 had been under the Philistines, and had been with them in camp, changed sides and joined the Israelites under Saul and Jonathan. All the Israelites in hiding in 22 the hill-country of Ephraim heard that the Philistines were in flight, and they also joined in and set off in hot pursuit. The LORD delivered Israel that day, and 23 the fighting passed on beyond Beth-aven.

Now the Israelites on that day had 24 been driven to exhaustion. Saul had adjured the people in these words: 'A curse be on the man who eats any food before nightfall until I have taken vengeance on my enemies.' So no one ate

a That is Shining.   *b That is* Bramble-bush.

---

elite warrior, as in the Homeric epics; see also ch. 17. **3:** This *ephod* is a box (see v. 41) containing lots, and not the linen garment, "cloak," in 2.18. *Ahijah's* lineage is given (probably by a later editor) so as to make his priestly descent clear. **6:** *Uncircumcised* was a term of reproach. Like their Semitic neighbors, the Israelites practiced circumcision, while the Philistines, deriving from Asia Minor and the Aegean, did not; compare Jer.9.25–26. **9–12:** Jonathan tests divine support for his enterprise; compare Gen.24.12–14; Judg.6.36–40. **14–15:** The panic that produces victory is not here ascribed simply to divine intervention, but to heroic and surprising action; contrast 7.10–11; see 7.7–10 n. **16–23:** Haste was required to take advantage of Jonathan's stroke. Consulting the oracle involved careful and time-consuming steps by the priest, and Saul (v. 19) sees that he cannot wait. **21:** In Scripture *Hebrews* has various meanings, ranging from merchants through an ethnic group related to, but separate from, the Israelites, and also the Israelites themselves. This verse suggests that not all Hebrews were Israelites. **24–30:** Abstinences

25 any food. Now there was honeycomb[c]
26 in the country-side; but when his men
came upon it, dripping with honey
though it was, not one of them put his
hand to his mouth for fear of the oath.
27 But Jonathan had not heard his father
lay this solemn prohibition on the
people, and he stretched out the stick
that was in his hand, dipped the end of
it in the honeycomb, put it to his mouth
28 and was refreshed. One of the people
said to him, 'Your father solemnly
forbade this; he said, "A curse on the
man who eats food today!" ' Now the
29 men were faint with hunger. Jonathan
said, 'My father has done the people
nothing but harm; see how I am refreshed by this mere taste of honey.
30 How much better if the people had
eaten today whatever they took from
their enemies by way of spoil! Then
there would indeed have been a great
slaughter of Philistines.'
31 They defeated the Philistines that
day, and pursued them from Michmash
to Aijalon. But the people were so faint
32 with hunger that they turned to plunder and seized sheep, cattle, and bullocks; they slaughtered them on the
bare ground, and ate the meat with
33 the blood in it. Someone told Saul
that the people were sinning against
the LORD by eating their meat with the
blood in it. 'This is treason!' cried Saul.
34 'Roll a great stone here at once.' He
then said, 'Go about among the people
and tell them to bring their oxen and
sheep, and let each man slaughter his
here and eat it; and so they will not
sin against the LORD by eating meat
with the blood in it.' So as night fell
each man came, driving his own ox,
35 and slaughtered it there. Thus Saul
came to build an altar to the LORD,
and this was the first altar to the LORD
that Saul built.
36 Saul said, 'Let us go down and make
a night attack on the Philistines and
harry them till daylight; we will not
spare a man of them.' The people
answered, 'Do what you think best',
but the priest said, 'Let us first consult
God.' So Saul inquired of God, 'Shall 37
I pursue the Philistines? Wilt thou put
them into Israel's power?'; but this
time he received no answer. So he said, 38
'Let all the leaders of the people come
forward and let us find out where the
sin lies this day. As the LORD lives, the 39
deliverer of Israel, even if it lies in my
son Jonathan, he shall die.' Not a soul
answered him. Then he said to the 40
Israelites, 'All of you stand on one side,
and I and my son Jonathan will stand
on the other.' The people answered,
'Do what you think best.' Saul said to 41
the LORD the God of Israel, 'Why hast
thou not answered thy servant today?
If this guilt lie in me or in my son
Jonathan, O LORD God of Israel, let
the lot be Urim; if it lie in thy people
Israel, let it be Thummim.' Jonathan
and Saul were taken, and the people
were cleared. Then Saul said, 'Cast 42
lots between me and my son Jonathan';
and Jonathan was taken. Saul said to 43
Jonathan, 'Tell me what you have
done.' Jonathan told him, 'True, I did
taste a little honey on the tip of my
stick. Here I am; I am ready to die.'
Then Saul swore a great oath that 44
Jonathan should die. But the people 45
said to Saul, 'Shall Jonathan die,
Jonathan who has won this great victory in Israel? God forbid! As the LORD
lives, not a hair of his head shall fall to
the ground, for he has been at work
with God today.' So the people ransomed Jonathan and he did not die.
Saul broke off the pursuit of the Philis- 46
tines because they had made their way
home.
When Saul had made his throne 47
secure in Israel, he fought against his
enemies on every side, the Moabites,
the Ammonites, the Edomites, the king

c Now ... honeycomb: *prob. rdg.; Heb.* All the land
went into the forest, and there was honey.

of various kinds were thought to enhance the sacred force of the soldiers; see 21.4–5. **31–35:**
Indulging in their plunder, the people ignore cult requirements, which Saul is very solicitous
to observe. **33:** On the *blood* in the *meat*, see Lev.19.26. **35:** It is assumed here, in contrast to
13.8–15, that *Saul* could exercise priestly functions. **36–46:** Night having come, Saul wished to
press the advantage against the Philistines. The inadvertent violation of the curse by Jonathan
prevented the proper divine approval. **45:** *Ransomed:* probably with an animal sacrifice.
    14.47–52: Summaries from Saul's reign. These lists indicate that Saul's reign was of some
length and had positive effect. There is no hint (as elsewhere) of condemnation of him.

of Zobah, and the Philistines; and wherever he turned he was successful.[d]

48 He displayed his strength by defeating the Amalekites and freeing Israel from hostile raids.

49 Saul's sons were: Jonathan, Ishyo and Malchishua. These were the names of his two daughters: Merab the elder

50 and Michal the younger. His wife was Ahinoam daughter of Ahimaaz, and his commander-in-chief was Abner son

51 of his uncle Ner; Kish, Saul's father, and Ner, Abner's father, were sons[e] of Abiel.

52 There was bitter warfare with the Philistines throughout Saul's lifetime; any strong man and any brave man that he found he took into his own service.

15 Samuel said to Saul, 'The LORD sent me to anoint you king over his people Israel. Now listen to the voice of the

2 LORD. This is the very word of the LORD of Hosts: "I am resolved to punish the Amalekites for what they did to Israel, how they attacked them

3 on their way up from Egypt." Go now and fall upon the Amalekites and destroy them, and put their property under ban. Spare no one; put them all to death, men and women, children and babes in arms, herds and flocks, camels

4 and asses.' Thereupon Saul called out the levy and mustered them in Telaim. There were two hundred thousand foot-soldiers and another ten thousand from

5 Judah.[f] He came to the Amalekite city and halted for a time in the gorge.

6 Meanwhile he sent word to the Kenites to leave the Amalekites and come down, 'or', he said, 'I shall destroy you as well as them; but you were friendly to Israel when they came up from Egypt.' So the Kenites left the Amalek-

7 ites. Then Saul cut the Amalekites to pieces, all the way from Havilah to

8 Shur on the borders of Egypt. Agag the king of the Amalekites he took alive, but he destroyed all the people, putting

9 them to the sword. Saul and his army spared Agag and the best of the sheep and cattle, the fat beasts and the lambs and everything worth keeping; they were unwilling to destroy them, but anything that was useless and of no value they destroyed.

10 Then the word of the LORD came to

11 Samuel: 'I repent of having made Saul king, for he has turned his back on me and has not obeyed my commands.' Samuel was angry; all night he cried

12 aloud to the LORD. Early next morning he went to meet Saul, but was told that he had gone to Carmel; Saul had set up a monument for himself there, and had then turned and gone down to

13 Gilgal. There Samuel found him, and Saul greeted him with the words, 'The LORD's blessing upon you! I have

14 obeyed the LORD's commands.' But Samuel said, 'What then is this bleating of sheep in my ears? Why do I hear

15 the lowing of cattle?' Saul answered, 'The people have taken them from the Amalekites. These are what they spared, the best of the sheep and cattle, to sacrifice to the LORD your God. The

16 rest we completely destroyed.' Samuel said to Saul, 'Let be, and I will tell you what the LORD said to me last night.'

17 'Tell me', said Saul. So Samuel went on, 'Time was when you thought little of yourself, but now you are head of the tribes of Israel, and the LORD has

18 anointed you king over Israel. The LORD sent you with strict instructions to destroy that wicked nation, the Amalekites; you were to fight against them until you had wiped them out.

19 Why then did you not obey the LORD? Why did you pounce upon the spoil and do what was wrong in the eyes of

d Or he found ample provision.
e Prob. rdg.; Heb. son.
f Prob. rdg.; Heb. ten thousand with the men of Judah.

15.1–35: Saul's final condemnation. This narrative is in some continuity with the negative strand in chs. 8, 10, and 12 (see 8.1–22 n.). Here, however, it is only Saul that is condemned, not kingship. As in the positive strand, however, Gilgal is the scene of the great decisions about kingship. **1–9:** Saul conducts a successful campaign against the Amalekites. **2:** *Amalekites:* see Exod.17.8–16. Saul's campaign did not end the old enmity; compare 2 Sam. ch. 30. **3:** The *ban,* making a battle an absolute, relentless struggle, was a powerful psychological force in holy war; see Josh. chs. 6–7. **4:** The numbers are impressionistic; see 13.5 n. *Judah* was a group of clans south of, and separated from, the central Israelite tribes. **5:** *The Amalekite city,* otherwise unknown, was far south of Judah. **6:** *Kenites:* see Judg.1.16. **11:** The OT does not view the LORD as governed by immutable plans; therefore, he could repent of a decision.

20 the LORD?' Saul answered Samuel, 'But I did obey the LORD; I went where the LORD sent me, and I have brought back Agag king of the Amalekites. The 21 rest of them I destroyed. Out of the spoil the people took sheep and oxen, the choicest of the animals laid under ban, to sacrifice to the LORD your God 22 at Gilgal.' Samuel then said:

Does the LORD desire offerings and
    sacrifices
as he desires obedience?
Obedience is better than sacrifice,
    and to listen to him than the fat of
    rams.
23 Defiance of him is sinful as
    witchcraft,
    yielding to men^g as evil as^h
    idolatry.^{i}
Because you have rejected the word
    of the LORD,
    the LORD has rejected you as king.

24   Saul said to Samuel, 'I have sinned. I have ignored the LORD's command and your orders: I was afraid of the 25 people and deferred to them. But now forgive my sin, I implore you, and come back with me, and I will make my sub-26 mission before the LORD.' Samuel answered, 'I will not come back with you; you have rejected the word of the LORD and therefore the LORD has rejected 27 you as king over Israel.' He turned to go, but Saul caught the edge of his 28 cloak and it tore. And Samuel said to him, 'The LORD has torn the kingdom of Israel from your hand today and will give it to another, a better man 29 than you. God who is the Splendour of Israel does not deceive or change his mind; he is not a man that he should 30 change his mind.' Saul said, 'I have sinned; but honour me this once before the elders of my people and before

Israel and come back with me, and I will make my submission to the LORD your God.' So Samuel went back with 31 Saul, and Saul made his submission to the LORD. Then Samuel said, 'Bring 32 Agag king of the Amalekites.' So Agag came to him with faltering step and said, 'Surely the bitterness of death has passed.' Samuel said, 'Your sword 33 has made women childless, and your mother of all women shall be childless too.' Then Samuel hewed Agag in pieces before the LORD at Gilgal.

Saul went to his own home at 34 Gibeah, and Samuel went to Ramah; and he never saw Saul again to his 35 dying day, but he mourned for him, because the LORD had repented of having made him king over Israel.

Saul and David

THE LORD SAID TO SAMUEL, 'HOW LONG 16 will you mourn for Saul because I have rejected him as king over Israel? Fill your horn with oil and take it with you; I am sending you to Jesse of Bethlehem; for I have chosen myself a king among his sons.' Samuel answered, 'How can 2 I go? Saul will hear of it and kill me.' 'Take a heifer with you,' said the LORD; 'say you have come to offer a sacrifice to the LORD, and invite Jesse to the 3 sacrifice; then I will let you know what you must do. You shall anoint for me the man whom I show you.' Samuel did 4 as the LORD had told him, and went to Bethlehem. The elders of the city came in haste to meet him, saying, 'Why have you come? Is all well?' 'All is well,' 5 said Samuel; 'I have come to sacrifice to the LORD. Hallow yourselves and come with me to the sacrifice.' He him-

g yielding to men: or arrogance or obstinacy.
h as evil as: prob. rdg.; Heb. evil and . . .
i Or household gods; Heb. teraphim.

Angry: compare Jer.20.7–9. **22:** This is a classic statement of the prophetic motif as opposed to the priestly. **29:** That God does not *change his mind* is not entirely right (see v. 11); here it means that the decision about Saul was final. **31:** Samuel keeps up appearances; this is consistent with the secrecy of the anointing of David, 16.1–13. **32–33:** The ban (v. 3 n.) demanded unrelieved violence.
   16.1–2 Sam. 5.25: David becomes king of Israel. In chs. 8–15 kingship was established as legitimate in Israel, but the house of Saul was rejected for that office. The rejection, however, was as yet only a divine decision and still to be worked out in events, as portrayed in 1 Sam. chs. 16–31; afterward David's rise is inevitable (2 Sam. chs. 1–5).
   16.1–17.58: The introduction of David. After the secret anointing of David, varying ways in which he was introduced to Saul's court are reported.

self hallowed Jesse and his sons and
6 invited them to the sacrifice also. They
came, and when Samuel saw Eliab he
thought, 'Here, before the LORD, is his
7 anointed king.' But the LORD said to
him, 'Take no account of it if he is
handsome and tall; I reject him. The
LORD does not see as man sees; men
judge by appearances but the LORD
8 judges by the heart.' Then Jesse called
Abinadab and made him pass before
Samuel, but he said, 'No, the LORD has
9 not chosen this one.' Then he presented
Shammah, and Samuel said, 'Nor has
10 the LORD chosen him.' Seven of his sons
Jesse presented to Samuel, but he said,
'The LORD has not chosen any of
11 these.' Then Samuel asked, 'Are these
all?' Jesse answered, 'There is still the
youngest, but he is looking after the
sheep.' Samuel said to Jesse, 'Send and
fetch him; we will not sit down until he
12 comes.' So he sent and fetched him. He
was handsome, with ruddy cheeks and
bright eyes.*j* The LORD said, 'Rise and
13 anoint him: this is the man.' Samuel
took the horn of oil and anointed him
in the presence of his brothers. Then
the spirit of the LORD came upon David
and was with him from that day onwards. And Samuel set out on his way
back to Ramah.
14   The spirit of the LORD had forsaken
Saul, and at times an evil spirit from
the LORD would seize him suddenly.
15 His servants said to him, 'You see, sir,
how an evil spirit from God seizes you;
16 why do you not command your servants here to go and find some man
who can play the harp?— then, when
an evil spirit from God comes on you,
17 he can play and you will recover.' Saul
said to his servants, 'Find me a man
who can play well and bring him to
18 me.' One of his attendants said, 'I have

seen a son of Jesse of Bethlehem who
can play; he is a brave man and a good
fighter, wise in speech and handsome,
and the LORD is with him.' Saul there- 19
fore sent messengers to Jesse and asked
him to send him his son David, who
was with the sheep. Jesse took a homer 20
of bread, a skin of wine, and a kid, and
sent them to Saul by his son David.
David came to Saul and entered his 21
service; and Saul loved him dearly,
and he became his armour-bearer. So 22
Saul sent word to Jesse: 'Let David
stay in my service, for I am pleased
with him.' And whenever a spirit from 23
God came upon Saul, David would
take his harp and play on it, so that
Saul found relief; he recovered and the
evil spirit left him alone.

The Philistines collected their forces **17**
for war and massed at Socoh in Judah;
they camped between Socoh and Azekah at Ephes-dammim. Saul and the 2
Israelites also massed, and camped in
the Vale of Elah. They drew up their
lines facing the Philistines, the Philis- 3
tines occupying a position on one hill
and the Israelites on another, with a
valley between them. A champion came 4
out from the Philistine camp, a man
named Goliath, from Gath; he was over
nine feet in height. He had a bronze 5
helmet on his head, and he wore plate-
armour of bronze, weighing five thous-
and shekels. On his legs were bronze 6
greaves, and one of his weapons was a
dagger of bronze. The shaft of his spear 7
was like a weaver's beam, and its head,
which was of iron, weighed six hundred
shekels; and his shield-bearer marched
ahead of him. The champion stood and 8
shouted to the ranks of Israel, 'Why do
you come out to do battle, you slaves
of Saul? I am the Philistine champion;

j and bright eyes: prob. rdg.; Heb. obscure.

16.1–13: The anointing of David. 8: *Jesse's* action indicates that those present for the sacrifice
understood the significance of the occasion. **11:** The selection of the least probable is a motif
also in the anointing of Saul in 9.21.
   16.14–23: David as harpist and warrior. Saul's ecstatic powers now take an *evil* turn, causing
periods of deep depression. **21:** A well-rounded courtier could be an accomplished musician
and also conduct himself expertly in battle. This narrative is inconsistent with parts of ch. 17
but stands here because of the close connection of the spirit of the LORD passing to David
(16.13) from Saul (16.14).
   17.1–58: David slays Goliath. This story assumes an entry by David into Saul's court quite
different from the preceding narrative, and it is not entirely consistent within itself. The story
is legendary, in the sense that it is intended to enhance the reputation of a famous figure;
in 2 Sam.21.19, the slaying of Goliath, ascribed by legend to David, was the deed of his warriors.
1–2: *Socoh, Azekah,* and the *Vale of Elah* were further south than any previous Philistine

9 choose your man to meet me. If he can kill me in fair fight, we will become your slaves; but if I prove too strong for him and kill him, you shall be our 10 slaves and serve us. Here and now I defy the ranks of Israel. Give me a man,' said the Philistine, 'and we will 11 fight it out.' When Saul and the Israelites heard what the Philistine said, they were shaken and dismayed.

12 David was the son of an Ephrathite[k] called Jesse, who had eight sons. By Saul's time he had become a feeble old 13 man, and his three eldest sons had followed Saul to the war. The eldest was called Eliab, the next Abinadab, and 14 the third Shammah; David was the youngest. The three eldest followed 15 Saul, while David used to go to Saul's camp and back to Bethlehem to mind his father's flocks.

16 Morning and evening for forty days the Philistine came forward and took 17 up his position. Then one day Jesse said to his son David, 'Take your brothers an ephah of this parched grain and these ten loaves of bread, and run with 18 them to the camp. These ten cream-cheeses are for you to take to the commanding officer. See if your brothers are well and bring back some token 19 from them.' Saul and the brothers and all the Israelites were in the Vale of 20 Elah, fighting the Philistines. Early next morning David left someone in charge of the sheep, set out on his errand and went as Jesse had told him. He reached the lines just as the army was going out to take up position and 21 was raising the war-cry. The Israelites and the Philistines drew up their ranks 22 opposite each other. David left his things in charge of the quartermaster, ran to the line and went up to his 23 brothers to greet them. While he was talking to them the Philistine champion, Goliath, came out from the Philistine ranks and issued his challenge in the same words as before; and 24 David heard him. When the Israelites saw the man they ran from him in fear. 25 'Look at this man who comes out day after day to defy Israel', they said. 'The king is to give a rich reward to the man who kills him; he will give him his daughter in marriage too and will exempt his family from service due in Israel.' Then David turned to his 26 neighbours and said, 'What is to be done for the man who kills this Philistine and wipes out our disgrace? And who is he, an uncircumcised Philistine, to defy the army of the living God?' The people told him how the matter 27 stood and what was to be done for the man who killed him. His elder brother 28 Eliab overheard David talking with the men and grew angry. 'What are you doing here?' he asked. 'And who have you left to look after those few sheep in the wilderness? I know you, you impudent young rascal; you have only come to see the fighting.' David answered, 29 'What have I done now? I only asked a question.' And he turned away from 30 him to someone else and repeated his question, but everybody gave him the same answer.

What David had said was overheard 31 and reported to Saul, who sent for him. David said to him, 'Do not lose heart, 32 sir. I will go and fight this Philistine.' Saul answered, 'You cannot go and 33 fight with this Philistine; you are only a lad, and he has been a fighting man all his life.' David said to Saul, 'Sir, I 34 am my father's shepherd; when a lion or bear comes and carries off a sheep from the flock, I go after it and attack 35 it and rescue the victim from its jaws. Then if it turns on me, I seize it by the beard and batter it to death. Lions I 36 have killed and bears, and this uncircumcised Philistine will fare no better than they; he has defied the army of the living God. The LORD who saved 37 me from the lion and the bear will save me from this Philistine.' 'Go then,' said Saul; 'and the LORD will be with you.' He put his own tunic on David, 38 placed a bronze helmet on his head and gave him a coat of mail to wear; he 39 then fastened his sword on David over his tunic. But David hesitated, because

k *Prob. rdg.; Heb. adds* Is this the man from Bethlehem in Judah?

action. This perhaps represents a different strategy by the Philistines, after their defeat in the region of Benjamin, ch. 14. **12–31:** This section seems to be a later insertion. Without it, the

he had not tried them, and said to Saul, 'I cannot go with these, because I have not tried them.' So he took them 40 off. Then he picked up his stick, chose five smooth stones from the brook and put them in a shepherd's bag which served as his pouch. He walked out to meet the Philistine with his sling in his hand.

41 The Philistine came on towards David, with his shield-bearer march-42 ing ahead; and he looked David up and down and had nothing but con-tempt for this handsome lad with his 43 ruddy cheeks and bright eyes.[1] He said to David, 'Am I a dog that you come out against me with sticks?' And he swore at him in the name of his god. 44 'Come on,' he said, 'and I will give your flesh to the birds and the beasts.' 45 David answered, 'You have come against me with sword and spear and dagger, but I have come against you in the name of the LORD of Hosts, the God of the army of Israel which you 46 have defied. The LORD will put you into my power this day; I will kill you and cut your head off and leave your carcass and the carcasses of the Philis-tines to the birds and the wild beasts; all the world shall know that there is a 47 God in Israel. All those who are gathered here shall see that the LORD saves neither by sword nor spear; the battle is the LORD's, and he will put you all into our power.'

48 When the Philistine began moving towards him again, David ran quickly 49 to engage him. He put his hand into his bag, took out a stone, slung it, and struck the Philistine on the forehead. The stone sank into his forehead, and he fell flat on his face on the ground. 50 So David proved the victor with his sling and stone; he struck Goliath down and gave him a mortal wound, though he had no sword. Then he ran to the 51 Philistine and stood over him, and grasping his sword, he drew it out of the scabbard, dispatched him and cut off his head. The Philistines, when they saw that their hero was dead, turned and ran. The men of Israel and Judah 52 at once raised the war-cry and hotly pursued them all the way to Gath and even to the gates of Ekron. The road that runs to Shaaraim, Gath, and Ekron was strewn with their dead. On 53 their return from the pursuit of the Philistines, the Israelites plundered their camp. David took Goliath's head 54 and carried it to Jerusalem, leaving his weapons in his tent.

Saul had said to Abner his com- 55 mander-in-chief, when he saw David going out against the Philistine, 'That boy there, Abner, whose son is he?' 'By your life, your majesty,' said Abner, 'I do not know.' The king said to 56 Abner, 'Go and find out whose son the lad is.' When David came back after 57 killing the Philistine, Abner took him and presented him to Saul with the Philistine's head still in his hand. Saul 58 asked him, 'Whose son are you, young man?', and David answered, 'I am the son of your servant Jesse of Bethlehem.'

That same day, when Saul had fin- 18 1-2 ished talking with David, he kept him and would not let him return any more to his father's house, for he saw that Jonathan had given his heart to David and had grown to love him as himself. So Jonathan and David made a solemn 3 compact because each loved the other as dearly as himself. And Jonathan 4 stripped off the cloak he was wearing and his tunic, and gave them to David, together with his sword, his bow, and his belt. David succeeded so well in 5 every venture on which Saul sent him

[1] *handsome . . . bright eyes: prob. rdg.; Heb. obscure.*

---

narrative would otherwise be largely compatible with 16.14–23. **54:** *Jerusalem* was then still an independent city-state; David, a Bethlehemite, had grown up in the shadow of its walls and may have had an intimate relation to it. **55–58:** As in vv. 12–31, David is hitherto unknown to Saul.

18.1–20.42: David's vicissitudes at Saul's court. The sequence of episodes here is rapid and complex. Each chapter begins with an episode involving Jonathan and David (18.1–4; 19.1–7; 20.1–42) followed in chs. 18 and 19 by notices of David's successes against the Philistines (18.5,14–16,30; 19.8), and Saul's jealous attacks upon David with his spear (18.10–13; 19.9–10). The three passages concerning Jonathan and David show a gradual disillusionment on Jona-than's part. Chs. 18 and 19 also relate David's marriage to Saul's daughter Michal (18.17–29) and her aid in his escape from Saul (19.11–17). **4:** The exchange of garments and weapons

that he was given a command in the army, and his promotion pleased the ordinary people, and even pleased Saul's officers.

6 At the home-coming of the army when David returned from the slaughter of the Philistines, the women came out from all the cities of Israel to look on, and the dancers came out to meet King Saul with tambourines, singing,
7 and dancing. The women as they made merry sang to one another:

> Saul made havoc among thousands
> but David among tens of thousands.

8 Saul was furious, and the words rankled. He said, 'They have given David tens of thousands and me only thousands; what more can they
9 do but make him king?' From that day forward Saul kept a jealous eye on David.

10 Next day an evil spirit from God seized upon Saul; he fell into a frenzy[m] in the house, and David played the harp to him as he had before.
11 Saul had his spear in his hand, and he hurled it at David, meaning to pin him to the wall; but twice David
12 swerved aside. After this Saul was afraid of David, because he saw that the LORD had forsaken him and was
13 with David. He therefore removed David from his household and appointed him to the command of a thousand men. David led his men into action,
14 and succeeded in everything that he undertook, because the LORD was with
15 him. When Saul saw how successful he was, he was more afraid of him
16 then ever; all Israel and Judah loved him because he took the field at their head.

17 Saul said to David, 'Here is my elder daughter Merab; I will give her to you in marriage, but in return you must serve me valiantly and fight the LORD's battles.' For Saul meant David to meet his end at the hands of the
18 Philistines and not himself. David answered Saul, 'Who am I and what

are my father's people, my kinsfolk, in Israel, that I should become the king's son-in-law?' However, when 19 the time came for Saul's daughter Merab to be married to David, she had already been given to Adriel of Meholah. But Michal, Saul's other 20 daughter, fell in love with David, and when Saul was told of this, he saw that it suited his plans. He said to himself, 21 'I will give her to him; let her be the bait that lures him to his death at the hands of the Philistines.' So Saul proposed a second time to make David his son-in-law, and ordered his courtiers 22 to say to David privately, 'The king is well disposed to you and you are dear to us all; now is the time for you to marry into the king's family.' When 23 Saul's people spoke in this way to David, he said to them, 'Do you think that marrying the king's daughter is a matter of so little consequence that a poor man of no consequence, like myself, can do it?' Saul's courtiers re- 24 ported what David had said, and he 25 replied, 'Tell David this: all the king wants as the bride-price is the fore-skins of a hundred Philistines, by way of vengeance on his enemies.' Saul was counting on David's death at the hands of the Philistines. The courtiers told 26 David what Saul had said, and marriage with the king's daughter on these terms pleased him well. Before the appointed time, David went out with 27 his men and slew two hundred Philistines; he brought their foreskins and counted them out to the king in order to be accepted as his son-in-law. So Saul married his daughter Michal to David. He saw clearly that the LORD 28 was with David, and knew that Michal his daughter had fallen in love with him; and so he grew more and more 29 afraid of David and was his enemy for the rest of his life.

The Philistine officers used to come 30 out to offer single combat; and whenever they did, David had more success

[m] *Or* fell into prophetic rapture.

---

effected a bond of souls. **7:** This old poetic refrain may have originally had no suggestion of invidious comparison between Saul and David, the second line being simply a poetic parallel to the first. In later times, this song was used to account for the jealousy on Saul's part. The saying was well known; see 21.11; 29.5. **25:** Since the Philistines were uncircumcised, *fore-*

against them than all the rest of Saul's men, and he won a great name for himself.

19 SAUL SPOKE TO JONATHAN HIS SON AND all his household about killing David. But Jonathan was devoted to David 2 and told him that his father Saul was looking for an opportunity to kill him. 'Be on your guard tomorrow morning,' he said; 'conceal yourself, and remain 3 in hiding. Then I will come out and join my father in the open country where you are and speak to him about you, and if I discover anything I will 4 tell you.' Jonathan spoke up for David to his father Saul and said to him, 'Sir, do not wrong your servant David; he has not wronged you; his conduct towards you has been beyond reproach. 5 Did he not take his life in his hands when he killed the Philistine, and the LORD won a great victory for Israel? You saw it, you shared in the rejoicing; why should you wrong an innocent man and put David to death without cause?' Saul listened to Jonathan and swore 6 solemnly by the LORD that David should not be put to death. So Jonathan 7 called David and told him all this; then he brought him to Saul, and he was in attendance on the king as before.
8 War broke out again, and David attacked the Philistines and dealt them such a blow that they ran before him.
9 An evil spirit from the LORD came upon Saul as he was sitting in the house with his spear in his hand; and 10 David was playing the harp. Saul tried to pin David to the wall with the spear, but he avoided the king's thrust so that Saul drove the spear into the wall. David escaped and got safely away. 11 That night Saul sent servants to keep watch on David's house, intending to kill him in the morning, but David's wife Michal warned him to get away that night, 'or tomorrow', she said, 12 'you will be a dead man.' She let David

down through a window and he slipped away and escaped. Michal took 13 their household gods and put them on the bed; at its head she laid a goat's-hair rug and covered it all with a cloak. When the men arrived to arrest David 14 she told them he was ill. Saul sent 15 them back to see David for themselves. 'Bring him to me, bed and all,' he said, 'and I will kill him.' When 16 they came, there were the household gods on the bed and the goat's-hair rug at its head. Then Saul said to Michal, 17 'Why have you played this trick on me and let my enemy get safe away?' And Michal answered, 'He said to me, "Help me to escape or I will kill you."'

Meanwhile David made good his 18 escape and came to Samuel at Ramah, and told him how Saul had treated him. Then he and Samuel went to Naioth and stayed there. Saul was 19 told that David was there, and he 20 sent a party of men to seize him. When they saw the company of prophets in rapture, with Samuel standing at their head, the spirit of God came upon them and they fell into prophetic rapture. When this was reported to Saul he 21 sent another party. These also fell into a rapture, and when he sent more men a third time, they did the same. Saul himself then set out for Ramah 22 and came to the great cistern in Secu. He asked where Samuel and David were and was told that they were at Naioth in Ramah. On his way there 23 the spirit of God came upon him too and he went on, in a rapture as he went, till he came to Naioth in Ramah. There 24 he too stripped off his clothes and like the rest fell into a rapture before Samuel and lay down naked all that day and all that night. That is why men say, 'Is Saul also among the prophets?'

Then David made his escape from 20 Naioth in Ramah and came to Jonathan. 'What have I done?' he asked.

---

skins made a grisly trophy of battle. **19.1–7:** Jonathan's intercession delays Saul's open hostility to David. **3:** The meeting in the *open country* is notably similar to the narrative of ch. 20. **9–10:** The king's jealousy breaks out again. **17:** Saul is defeated in his attempts on David by both his son and his daughter, an indirect effect of divine favor toward David. **18–24:** This legend of the great force of Samuel's charismatic power is peripheral to the main narrative but supplies another explanation for the popular proverb about Saul among the prophets; compare 10.11–12. **20.1–42:** This is the fullest elaboration of Saul's deviousness and of Jona-

'What is my offence? What does your father think I have done wrong, that he seeks my life?' Jonathan answered him, 'God forbid! There is no thought of putting you to death. I am sure my father will not do anything whatever without telling me. Why should my father hide such a thing from me? 3 I cannot believe it!' David said, 'I am ready to swear to it: your father has said to himself, "Jonathan must not know this or he will resent it", because he knows that you have a high regard for me. As the LORD lives, your life upon it, there is only a step between 4 me and death.' Jonathan said to David, 'What do you want me to do 5 for you?' David answered, 'It is new moon tomorrow, and I ought to dine with the king. Let me go and lie hidden in the fields until the third 6 evening. If your father happens to miss me, then say, "David asked me for leave to pay a rapid visit to his home in Bethlehem, for it is the annual sacri- 7 fice there for the whole family." If he says, "Well and good", that will be a good sign for me; but if he flies into a rage, you will know that he is set on 8 doing me wrong. My lord, keep faith with me; for you and I have entered into a solemn compact before the LORD. Kill me yourself if I am guilty. Why let me fall into your father's hands?' 9 'God forbid!' cried Jonathan. 'If I find my father set on doing you 10 wrong I will tell you.' David answered Jonathan, 'How will you let me know 11 if he answers harshly?' Jonathan said, 'Come with me into the fields.' So they 12 went together into the fields, and Jonathan said to David, 'I promise you, David, in the sight of the LORD the God of Israel, this time tomorrow I will sound my father for the third time and, if he is well disposed to you, I 13 will send and let you know. If my father means mischief, the LORD do the same to me and more, if I do not let you know and get you safely away. The LORD be with you as he has 14 been with my father! I know that as long as I live you will show me faithful

friendship, as the LORD requires; and if I should die, you will continue 15 loyal to my family for ever. When the LORD rids the earth of all David's enemies, may the LORD call him to 16 account if he and his house are no longer my friends.' Jonathan pledged 17 himself afresh to David because of his love for him, for he loved him as himself. Then he said to him, 'Tomorrow 18 is the new moon, and you will be missed when your place is empty. So 19 go down at nightfall for the third time to the place where you hid on the evening of the feast and stay by the mound there. Then I will shoot three 20 arrows towards it, as though I were aiming at a mark. Then I will send 21 my boy to find the arrows. If I say to him, "Look, the arrows are on this side of you, pick them up", then you can come out of hiding. You will be quite safe, I swear it; for there will be nothing amiss. But if I say to the lad, 22 "Look, the arrows are on the other side of you, further on", then the LORD has said that you must go; the LORD stand witness between us 23 for ever to the pledges we have exchanged.'

So David hid in the fields. The new 24 moon came, the dinner was prepared, and the king sat down to eat. Saul took 25 his customary seat by the wall, and Abner sat beside him; Jonathan too was present, but David's place was empty. That day Saul said nothing, for he 26 thought that David was absent by some chance, perhaps because he was ritually unclean. But on the second 27 day, the day after the new moon, David's place was still empty, and Saul said to his son Jonathan, 'Why has not the son of Jesse come to the feast, either yesterday or today?' Jonathan 28 answered Saul, 'David asked permis- sion to go to Bethlehem. He asked my 29 leave and said, "Our family is holding a sacrifice in the town and my brother himself has ordered me to be there. Now, if you have any regard for me, let me slip away to see my brothers." That is why he has not come to dine

---

than's loyalty to David. **18–23:** These plans assume that someone will be with Jonathan, so that he must use signals. That fits 19.2–3, but not what follows here in vv. 40–42, where Jona- than and David can talk openly.

30 with the king.' Saul was angry with Jonathan, 'You son of a crooked and unfaithful mother! You have made friends with the son of Jesse only to bring shame on yourself and dishonour on your mother; I see how it will be.
31 As long as Jesse's son remains alive on earth, neither you nor your crown will be safe. Send at once and fetch him;
32 he deserves to die.' Jonathan answered his father, 'Deserves to die! Why? What
33 has he done?' At that, Saul picked up his spear and threatened to kill him; and he knew that his father was bent
34 on David's death. Jonathan left the table in a rage and ate nothing on the second day of the festival; for he was indignant on David's behalf because his father had humiliated him.
35 Next morning, Jonathan went out into the fields to meet David at the appointed time, taking a young boy
36 with him. He said to the boy, 'Run and find the arrows; I am going to shoot.' The boy ran on, and he shot the arrows
37 over his head. When the boy reached the place where Jonathan's arrows had fallen, Jonathan called out after him, 'Look, the arrows are beyond
38 you. Hurry! No time to lose! Make haste!' The boy gathered up the arrows and brought them to his
39 master; but only Jonathan and David knew what this meant; the boy knew
40 nothing. Jonathan handed his weapons to the boy and told him to take them
41 back to the city. When the boy had gone, David got up from behind the mound and bowed humbly three times. Then they kissed one another and shed tears together, until David's grief was
42 even greater than Jonathan's. Jonathan said to David, 'Go in safety; we have pledged each other in the name of the LORD who is witness for ever between you and me and between your descendants and mine.'

David went off at once, while
21 Jonathan returned to the city. David

made his way to the priest Ahimelech at Nob, who hurried out to meet him and said, 'Why have you come alone and no one with you?' David an- 2 swered Ahimelech, 'I am under orders from the king: I was to let no one know about the mission on which he was sending me or what these orders were. When I took leave of my men I told them to meet me in such and such a place. Now, what have you got by 3 you? Let me have five loaves, or as many as you can find.' The priest 4 answered David, 'I have no ordinary bread available. There is only the sacred bread; but have the young men kept themselves from women?' David answered the priest, 'Women 5 have been denied us hitherto, when I have been on campaign, even an ordinary campaign, and the young men's bodies have remained holy; and how much more will they be holy today?' So, as there was no other bread 6 there, the priest gave him the sacred bread, the Bread of the Presence, which had just been taken from the presence of the LORD to be replaced by freshly baked bread on the day that the old was removed. One of Saul's servants 7 happened to be there that day, detained before the LORD; his name was Doeg the Edomite, and he was the strongest of all Saul's herdsmen. David said 8 to Ahimelech, 'Have you a spear or sword here at hand? I have no sword or other weapon with me, because the king's business was urgent.' The priest 9 answered, 'There is the sword of Goliath the Philistine whom you slew in the Vale of Elah; it is wrapped up in a cloak behind the ephod. If you wish to take that, take it; there is no other weapon here.' David said, 'There is no sword like it; give it to me.'

That day, David went on his way, 10 eluding Saul, and came to Achish king of Gath. The servants of Achish 11 said to him, 'Surely this is David, the

21.1–23.13: David becomes a fugitive. Several episodes here form a transition from David at Saul's court to David as leader of an outlaw band in the Judean wilderness. 1–9: David gets assistance from Ahimelech, a descendant of the priestly line of Shiloh (22.9; 14.3 n.). 2: Ahimelech does not knowingly assist a fugitive. 6: *The Bread of the Presence* was set before God in the sanctuary and periodically replaced. Only priests could eat it; compare Lev.24.5–9. 7: *Doeg the Edomite* was to prove an informer and executioner; 22.9–23. 10–15: David's fugitive period is opened and closed by stays with Achish of Gath; see 27.1–6. 11: On the song see

king of his country, the man of whom they sang as they danced:

Saul made havoc among thousands
but David among tens of thousands.'

12 These words were not lost on David, and he became very much afraid of
13 Achish king of Gath. So he altered his behaviour in public and acted like a lunatic in front of them all, scrabbling on the double doors of the city gate
14 and dribbling down his beard. Achish said to his servants, 'The man is mad!
15 Why bring him to me? Am I short of madmen that you bring this one to plague me? Must I have this fellow in my house?'

22 DAVID MADE HIS ESCAPE AND WENT from there to the cave of Adullam. When his brothers and all his family heard that he was there, they joined
2 him. Men in any kind of distress or in debt or with a grievance gathered round him, about four hundred in number, and he became their chief.
3 From there David went to Mizpeh in Moab and said to the king of Moab, 'Let my father and mother come and take shelter with you until
4 I know what God will do for me.' So he left them at the court of the king of Moab, and they stayed there as long as David was in his stronghold.
5 The prophet Gad said to David, 'You must not stay in your stronghold; go at once into Judah.' So David went
6 as far as the forest of Hareth. News that David and his men had been seen reached Saul while he was in Gibeah, sitting under the tamarisk-tree on the hill-top with his spear in his hand and all his retainers standing about
7 him. He said to them, 'Listen to me, you Benjamites: do you expect the son of Jesse to give you all fields and vineyards, or make you all officers over units
8 of a thousand and a hundred? Is that why you have all conspired against me? Not one of you told me when my son made a compact with the son of Jesse; none of you spared a thought

for me or told me that my son had set my own servant against me, who is lying in wait for me now.'

9 Then Doeg the Edomite, who was standing with the servants of Saul, spoke: 'I saw the son of Jesse coming to Nob, to Ahimelech son of Ahitub.
10 Ahimelech consulted the LORD on his behalf, then gave him food and handed over to him the sword of Goliath the Philistine.' The king sent
11 for Ahimelech the priest and his family, who were priests at Nob, and they all came into his presence. Saul said,
12 'Now listen, you son of Ahitub', and the man answered, 'Yes, my lord?' Then
13 Saul said to him, 'Why have you and the son of Jesse plotted against me? You gave him food and the sword too, and consulted God on his behalf; and now he has risen against me and is at this moment lying in wait for me.' 'And who among all your ser-
14 vants', answered Ahimelech, 'is like David, a man to be trusted, the king's son-in-law, appointed to your staff and holding an honourable place in your household? Have I on this
15 occasion done something profane in consulting God on his behalf? God forbid! I trust that my lord the king will not accuse me or my family; for I know nothing whatever about it.' But
16 the king said, 'Ahimelech, you must die, you and all your family.' He then
17 turned to the bodyguard attending him and said, 'Go and kill the priests of the LORD; for they are in league with David, and, though they knew that he was a fugitive, they did not tell me.' The king's men, however, were unwilling to raise a hand against the priests of
18 the LORD. The king therefore said to Doeg the Edomite, 'You, Doeg, go and fall upon the priests'; so Doeg went and fell upon the priests, killing that day with his own hand eighty-five men
19 who could carry the ephod. He put to the sword every living thing in Nob, the city of priests: men and women, children and babes in arms, oxen,
20 asses, and sheep. One son of Ahimelech named Abiathar made his escape and

---

18.7 n. **22.1–5:** David accepts his situation as fugitive, organizes a band of outlaws, and secures his family against Saul. **5:** *The prophet Gad* appears also in 2 Sam.24.11–14, rather suddenly in both cases. **6–23:** Saul avenges himself on Ahimelech, brother of his own priest Ahijah

21 joined David. He told David how Saul had killed the priests of the Lord. 22 Then David said to him, 'When Doeg the Edomite was there that day, I knew that he would inform Saul. I have gambled with the lives of all your 23 father's family. Stay here with me, have no fear; he who seeks your life seeks mine, and you will be safe with me.'

23 The Philistines were fighting against Keilah and plundering the threshing- 2 floors; and when David heard this, he consulted the Lord and asked whether he should go and attack the Philistines. The Lord answered, 'Go, attack them, 3 and relieve Keilah.' But David's men said to him, 'As we are now, we have enough to fear from Judah. How much worse if we challenge the Philistine 4 forces at Keilah!' David consulted the Lord once again and the Lord answered him, 'Go to Keilah; I will give 5 the Philistines into your hands.' So David and his men went to Keilah and fought the Philistines, they carried off their cattle, inflicted a heavy defeat on them and relieved the inhabitants. 6 Abiathar son of Ahimelech made good his escape and joined David at Keilah, bringing the ephod with him. Saul was 7 told that David had entered Keilah, and he said, 'God has put him into my hands; for he has walked into a trap by entering a walled town with gates 8 and bars.' He called out the levy to march on Keilah and besiege David and 9 his men. When David learnt how Saul planned his undoing, he told Abiathar 10 the priest to bring the ephod, and then he prayed, 'O Lord God of Israel, I thy servant have heard news that Saul intends to come to Keilah and destroy 11 the city because of me. Will the citizens of Keilah surrender me to him? Will Saul come as I have heard? O Lord God of Israel, I pray thee, tell thy servant.' The Lord answered, 12 'He will come.' Then David asked,

'Will the citizens of Keilah surrender me and my men to Saul?', and the Lord answered, 'They will.' Then 13 David left Keilah at once with his men, who numbered about six hundred, and moved about from place to place. When the news reached Saul that David had escaped from Keilah, he made no further move.

While David was living in the fast- 14 nesses of the wilderness of Ziph, in the hill-country, Saul searched for him day after day, but God did not put him into his power. David well knew 15 that Saul had come out to seek his life; and while he was at Horesh in the wilderness of Ziph, Saul's son Jonathan 16 came to him there and gave him fresh courage in God's name: 'Do not be 17 afraid,' he said; 'my father's hand shall not touch you. You will become king of Israel and I shall hold rank after you; and my father knows it.' The two of them made a solemn com- 18 pact before the Lord; then David remained in Horesh and Jonathan went home. While Saul was at Gibeah 19 the Ziphites brought him this news: 'David, we hear, is in hiding among us in the fastnesses of Horesh on the hill of Hachilah, south of Jeshimon. Come 20 down, your majesty, come whenever you will, and we are able to surrender him to you.' Saul said, 'The Lord has 21 indeed blessed you; you have saved me a world of trouble. Go now and make 22 further inquiry, and find out exactly where he is and who saw him there. They tell me that he by himself is crafty enough to outwit me. Find out 23 which of his hiding-places he is using; then come back to me at such and such a place, and I will go along with you. So long as he stays in this country, I will hunt him down, if I have to go through all the clans of Judah one by one.' They set out for Ziph without 24 delay, ahead of Saul; David and his men were in the wilderness of Maon

---

(14.3). **23.1–13**: David's band begins to be a force in the south. He carefully consults the Lord concerning all his movements. **1**: *Keilah* was an independent town southwest of Judah. **11–12**: The oracle answered one question at a time, yes or no.

23.14–24.22: **The chase in the Wilderness.** David's Wilderness period was a popular narrative topic. **14**: *Ziph* was a rough region a few miles south and east of Hebron. **16–18**: *Jonathan*, now fully aware of his father's intent, here predicts and consents to David's future establishment as king. Several other speeches in these chapters view David's kingship as the inevitable out-in the Arabah to the south of Jeshimon. 25 Saul set off with his men to look for him; but David got wind of it and went down to a refuge in the rocks, and there he stayed in the wilderness of Maon. Hearing of this, Saul went into the 26 wilderness after him; he was on one side of the hill, David and his men on the other. While David and his men were trying desperately to get away and Saul and his followers were closing 27 in for the capture, a runner brought a message to Saul: 'Come at once! the 28 Philistines are harrying the land.' So Saul called off the pursuit and turned back to face the Philistines. This is why that place is called the Dividing Rock. 29 David went up from there and lived in the fastnesses of En-gedi.

24 When Saul returned from the pursuit of the Philistines, he learnt that David 2 was in the wilderness of En-gedi. So he took three thousand men picked from the whole of Israel and went in search of David and his men to the east of the 3 Rocks of the Wild Goats. There beside the road were some sheepfolds, and near by was a cave, at the far end of which David and his men were sitting concealed. Saul came to the cave and 4-7^n went in to relieve himself. His men said to David, 'The day has come: the LORD has put your enemy into your hands, as he promised he would, and you may do what you please with him.' David said to his men, 'God forbid that I should harm my master, the LORD's anointed, or lift a finger against him; he is the LORD's anointed.' So David reproved his men severely and would not let them attack Saul. He himself got up stealthily and cut off a piece of Saul's cloak; but when he had cut it off, his conscience smote him. Saul rose, left the cave and went on his 8 way; whereupon David also came out of the cave and called after Saul, 'My lord the king!' When Saul looked round, David prostrated himself in obeisance and said to him, 'Why do you 9 listen when they say that David is out to do you harm? Today you can see 10 for yourself that the LORD put you into my power in the cave; I had a mind to kill you, but no, I spared your life and said, "I cannot lift a finger against my master, for he is the LORD's anointed." Look, my dear lord, look at this 11 piece of your cloak in my hand. I cut it off, but I did not kill you; this will show you that I have no thought of violence or treachery against you, and that I have done you no wrong; yet you are resolved to take my life. May the 12 LORD judge between us! but though he may take vengeance on you for my sake, I will never lift my hand against you; "One wrong begets another", as 13 the old saying goes, yet I will never lift my hand against you. Who has the 14 king of Israel come out against? What are you pursuing? A dead dog, a mere flea. The LORD will be judge and decide 15 between us; let him look into my cause, he will plead for me and will acquit me.'

When David had finished speaking, 16 Saul said, 'Is that you, David my son?', and he wept. Then he said, 'The right is 17 on your side, not mine; you have treated me so well, I have treated you so badly. Your goodness to me this day has passed 18 all bounds: the LORD put me at your mercy but you did not kill me. Not 19 often does a man find his enemy and let him go safely on his way; so may the LORD reward you well for what you have done for me today! I know now 20 for certain that you will become king, and that the kingdom of Israel will flourish under your rule. Swear to me 21 by the LORD then that you will not exterminate my descendants and blot out my name from my father's house.' David swore an oath to Saul; and Saul 22 went back to his home, while David and his men went up to their fastness.

n Verses 4–7 are re-arranged thus: 4a, 6, 7a, 4b, 5, 7b.

---

come of these events. **26–28:** The pressure of the *Philistines* continued, interrupting Saul in the nick of time. *The Dividing Rock* was later said to be named for this escape. **29:** *En-gedi* was in the most barren part of Judah, just west of the Dead Sea. **24.1:** The *Philistines* are treated here as no more than a brief interlude in Saul's real enterprise. **3:** The narrative which begins here verges on the burlesque. **4–7:** David's speech moves from irony into a serious statement of *the LORD's anointed.* The sanctity of that office was not to be violated under any circumstances, according to the view of the writers toward the kingship in Jerusalem. **8–22:** The tone changes from the humor of the opening in v. 3. **20:** See 23.16–18 n.

25 SAMUEL DIED, AND ALL ISRAEL CAME TO-
gether to mourn for him, and he was
buried in his house in Ramah. Afterwards David went down to the wilderness of Paran.

2 There was a man at Carmel in
Maon, who had great influence and
owned three thousand sheep and a
thousand goats; and he was shearing
3 his flocks in Carmel. His name was
Nabal and his wife's name Abigail; she
was a beautiful and intelligent woman,
but her husband, a Calebite, was surly
4 and mean. David heard in the wilderness that Nabal was shearing his flocks,
5 and sent ten of his men, saying to
them, 'Go up to Carmel, find Nabal and
6 give him my greetings. You are to say,
"All good wishes for the year ahead!
Prosperity to yourself, your house-
7 hold, and all that is yours! I hear that
you are shearing. Your shepherds have
been with us lately and we did not
molest them; nothing of theirs was
missing all the time they were in Car-
8 mel. Ask your own people and they
will tell you. Receive my men kindly,
for this is an auspicious day with us,
and give what you can to David your
9 son and your servant."' David's servants came and delivered this message
to Nabal in David's name. When they
10 paused, Nabal answered, 'Who is
David? Who is this son of Jesse? In
these days every slave who breaks
away from his master sets himself up
11 as a chief.*o* Am I to take my food and
my wine and the meat I have provided
for my shearers and give it to men
who come from I know not where?'
12 David's men turned and made their
way back to him and told him all this.
13 He said to his men, 'Buckle on your
swords, all of you.' So they buckled on
their swords and followed David, four
hundred of them, while two hundred
stayed behind with the baggage.

One of the young men said to 14
Abigail, Nabal's wife, 'David sent
messengers from the wilderness to ask
our master politely for a present, and
he flew out*p* at them. The men have 15
been very good to us and have not
molested us, nor did we miss anything
all the time we were going about with
them in the open country. They were 16
as good as a wall round us, night and
day, while we were minding the flocks.
Think carefully what you had better 17
do, for it is certain ruin for our master
and his whole family; he is such a
good-for-nothing that it is no good
talking to him.' So Abigail hastily 18
collected two hundred loaves and two
skins of wine, five sheep ready dressed,
five measures of parched grain, a
hundred bunches of raisins, and two
hundred cakes of dried figs, and loaded
them on asses, but told her husband 19
nothing about it. Then she said to her
servants, 'Go on ahead, I will follow
you.' As she made her way on her 20
ass, hidden by the hill, there were
David and his men coming down
towards her, and she met them. David 21
had said, 'It was a waste of time to
protect this fellow's property in the
wilderness so well that nothing of his
was missing. He has repaid me evil for
good.' David swore a great oath: 22
'God do the same to me and more if I
leave him a single mother's son alive
by morning!'

When Abigail saw David she dis- 23
mounted in haste and prostrated herself before him, bowing low to the 24
ground at his feet, and said, 'Let me
take the blame, my lord, but allow me,
your humble servant, to speak out
and let my lord give me a hearing. How 25
can you take any notice of this good-
for-nothing? He is just what his name

*o Or In these days there are many slaves who break
away from their master.*
p flew out: or screamed.

25.1–44: David and Abigail. This delightful narrative stands in the midst of the Wilderness
period to convey the flavor of David's life there. **1:** Samuel's king-making work has been done
since ch. 16, but he will appear yet once more (ch. 28). **2:** *Maon* was a few miles south of Ziph.
It was a region where grazing lands bordered on agricultural lands. **3:** *Nabal* is the noun "fool"
used as a name; see v. 25. **6–8:** David's speech is very courteous, but the request for a "protection"
payment is clear. **10:** David was apparently renowned as a rebel against Saul. **16:** David is
depicted as a kind of Robin Hood whose band constituted an informal peace keeping force.
On those terms, there would be some justice in his request of gifts from Nabal. **19:** Abigail
understands both her husband's character and the crisis of the moment. **24–35:** Abigail argues
(v. 26) that if David kills Nabal, the *bloodshed* can imperil the sanctity of his future kingship

Nabal means: "Churl" is his name,
and churlish his behaviour. I did not
26 myself, sir, see the men you sent. And
now, sir, the LORD has restrained you
from bloodshed and from giving vent
to your anger. As the LORD lives, your
life upon it, your enemies and all
who want to see you ruined will be
27 like Nabal. Here is the present which I,
your humble servant, have brought;
give it to the young men under your
28 command. Forgive me, my lord, if I am
presuming; for the LORD will establish
your family for ever, because you have
fought his wars. No calamity shall
29 overtake you as long as you live. If
any man sets out to pursue you and
take your life, the LORD your God will
wrap your life up and put it with his
own treasure, but the lives of your
enemies he will hurl away like stones
30 from a sling. When the LORD has
made good all his promises to you,
31 and has made you ruler of Israel, there
will be no reason why you should stumble or your courage falter because you
have shed innocent blood or given way
to your anger. Then when the LORD
makes all you do prosper, you will
32 remember me, your servant.' David
said to Abigail, 'Blessed is the LORD
the God of Israel who has sent you
33 today to meet me. A blessing on your
good sense, a blessing on you because
you have saved me today from the guilt
of bloodshed and from giving way to
34 my anger. For I swear by the life of the
LORD the God of Israel who has kept
me from doing you wrong: if you had
not come at once to meet me, not a
man of Nabal's household, not a single
mother's son, would have been left alive
35 by morning.' Then David took from her
what she had brought him and said, 'Go
home in peace, I have listened to you
and I grant your request.'
36   On her return she found Nabal holding a banquet in his house, a banquet
fit for a king. He grew merry and
became very drunk, so drunk that his
wife said nothing to him, trivial or

serious, till daybreak. In the morning, 37
when the wine had worn off, she told
him everything, and he had a seizure
and lay there like a stone. Ten days 38
later the LORD struck him again and
he died. When David heard that 39
Nabal was dead he said, 'Blessed be the
LORD, who has himself punished
Nabal for his insult, and has kept
me his servant from doing wrong. The
LORD has made Nabal's wrongdoing
recoil on his own head.' David then sent
to make proposals that Abigail should
become his wife. And his servants came 40
to Abigail at Carmel and said to her,
'David has sent us to fetch you to be
his wife.' She rose and prostrated 41
herself with her face to the ground,
and said, 'I am his slave to command,
I would wash the feet of my lord's
servants.' So Abigail made her prep- 42
arations with all speed and, with her
five maids in attendance, accompanied
by David's messengers, rode away on
an ass; and she became David's wife.
David had also married Ahinoam of 43
Jezreel; both these women became
his wives. Saul meanwhile had given 44
his daughter Michal, David's wife, to
Palti son of Laish from Gallim.

THE ZIPHITES CAME TO SAUL AT GIBEAH **26**
to report that David was in hiding
on the hill at Hachilah overlooking
Jeshimon. Saul went down at once to 2
the wilderness of Ziph, taking with
him three thousand picked men, to
search for David there. He encamped 3
beside the road on the hill of Hachilah
overlooking Jeshimon, while David
was still in the wilderness. As soon
as David knew that Saul had come to
the wilderness in pursuit of him, he 4
sent out scouts and found that Saul
had reached such and such a place.
Without delay, he went to the place 5
where Saul had pitched his camp and
observed where Saul and Abner son of
Ner, the commander-in-chief, were
lying. Saul lay within the lines with his
troops encamped in a circle round him.

(on such speeches see 23.16–18 n.) David agrees and is grateful to Abigail for restraining him
from the *guilt of bloodshed* (v. 33). **39:** In these stories God is understood to be working out
the destiny leading to David's kingship, including his royal family (see 2 Sam.3.3). **44:** *Michal*,
first supportive of David (19.11–17), later changed (2 Sam.3.14 16; 6.20–23)
26.1–25: David again spares Saul's life. This narrative was originally an alternative version

6 David turned to Ahimelech the Hittite and Abishai son of Zeruiah, Joah's brother, and said, 'Who will venture with me into the camp, to go to Saul?'
7 Abishai answered, 'I will.' David and Abishai entered the camp at night and found Saul lying asleep within the lines with his spear thrust into the ground by his head. Abner and the army were
8 lying all round him. Abishai said to David, 'God has put your enemy into your power today; let me strike him and pin him to the ground with one thrust of the spear; I shall not have to
9 strike twice.' David said to him, 'Do him no harm; who has ever lifted a finger against the LORD's anointed
10 and gone unpunished? As the LORD lives,' went on David, 'the LORD will strike him down; either his time will come and he will die, or he will go
11 down to battle and meet his end. God forbid that I should lift a finger against the LORD's anointed! But now let us take the spear which is by his
12 head, and the water-jar, and go.' So David took the spear and the water-jar from beside Saul's head and they went. The whole camp was asleep; no one saw him, no one knew anything, no one even woke up. A heavy sleep sent by the LORD had fallen on them.
13 Then David crossed over to the other side and stood on the top of a hill a long way off; there was no little
14 distance between them. David shouted across to the army and hailed Abner, 'Answer me, Abner!' He answered, 'Who are you to shout to the king?'
15 David said to Abner, 'Do you call yourself a man? Is there anyone like you in Israel? Why, then, did you not keep watch over your lord the king, when someone came to harm your
16 lord the king? This was not well done. As the LORD lives, you deserve to die, all of you, because you have not kept watch over your master the LORD's anointed. Look! Where are the king's spear and the water-jar that were by his head?'
17 Saul recognized David's voice and said, 'Is that you, David my son?'
'Yes, sir, it is', said David. 'Why must 18 your majesty pursue me? What have I done? What mischief am I plotting? Listen, my lord, to what I have to 19 say. If it is the LORD who has set you against me, may an offering be acceptable to him; but if it is men, a curse on them in the LORD's name; for they have ousted me today from my share in the LORD's inheritance and have banished me to serve other gods! Do 20 not let my blood be shed on foreign soil, far from the presence of the LORD, just because the king of Israel came out to look for a flea, as one might hunt a partridge over the hills.'
Saul answered, 'I have done wrong; 21 come back, David my son. You have held my life precious this day, and I will never harm you again. I have been a fool, I have been sadly in the wrong.'
David answered, 'Here is the king's 22 spear; let one of your men come across and fetch it. The LORD who rewards 23 uprightness and loyalty will reward the man into whose power he put you today, when I refused to lift a finger against the LORD's anointed. As I held your life precious today, so 24 may the LORD hold mine precious and deliver me from every distress.' Then 25 Saul said to David, 'A blessing is on you, David my son. You will do great things and be victorious.' So David went on his way and Saul returned home.

David thought, 'One of these days I 27 shall be killed by Saul. The best thing for me to do will be to escape into Philistine territory; then Saul will lose all further hope of finding me anywhere in Israel, search as he may, and I shall escape his clutches.' So David 2 and his six hundred men crossed the frontier forthwith to Achish son of Maoch king of Gath. David settled in 3 Gath with Achish, taking with him his men and their families and his two wives, Ahinoam of Jezreel and Abigail of Carmel, Nabal's widow. Saul was 4 told that David had escaped to Gath,

of 23.14–24.22. **9–11:** On David's speech, see 24.4–7 n. Saul's *spear* is recurrently prominent; see 18.10–11; 19.9–10; 22.6. **12:** The *heavy sleep* introduces a miraculous element not really required by the story.
27.1–28.2: David becomes a vassal of Achish of Gath. The narrow escapes in the Wilderness

5 and he gave up the search. David said to Achish, 'If I stand well in your opinion, grant me a place in one of your country towns where I may settle. Why should I remain in the royal city 6 with your majesty?' Achish granted him Ziklag on that day: that is why Ziklag still belongs to the kings of Judah.

7 David spent a year and four months 8 in Philistine country. He and his men would sally out and raid the Geshurites, the Gizrites, and the Amalekites, for it was they who inhabited the country from Telaim*q* all the way to 9 Shur and Egypt. When David raided the country he left no one alive, man or woman; he took flocks and herds, asses and camels, and clothes too, and 10 then came back again to Achish. When Achish asked, 'Where was your raid today?', David would answer, 'The Negeb of Judah' or 'The Negeb of the Jerahmeelites' or 'The Negeb of the 11 Kenites'. Neither man nor woman did David bring back alive to Gath, for fear that they should denounce him and his men for what they had done. This was his practice as long as he remained with the Philistines. 12 Achish trusted David, thinking that he had won such a bad name among his own people the Israelites that he would remain his subject all his life.

Saul and his sons killed

28 IN THOSE DAYS THE PHILISTINES MUSTERED their army for an attack on Israel. Achish said to David, 'You know that you and your men must take the 2 field with me.' David answered Achish, 'Good, you will learn what your servant can do.' And Achish said to David, 'I will make you my bodyguard for life.'

By this time Samuel was dead, and all 3 Israel had mourned for him and buried him in Ramah, his own city; and Saul had banished from the land all who trafficked with ghosts and spirits. The 4 Philistines mustered and encamped at Shunem, and Saul gathered all the Israelites and encamped on Gilboa; and when Saul saw the Philistine force, 5 fear struck him to the heart. He 6 inquired of the LORD, but the LORD did not answer him, whether by dreams or by Urim or by prophets. So he said to his servants, 'Find me 7 a woman who has a familiar spirit, and I will go and inquire through her.' His servants told him that there was such a woman at En-dor. Saul put 8 on different clothes and went in disguise with two of his men. He came to the woman by night and said, 'Tell me my fortunes by consulting the dead, and call up the man I name to you.' But the woman answered, 9 'Surely you know what Saul has done, how he has made away with those who call up ghosts and spirits; why do you press me to do what will lead to my death?' Saul swore her an oath: 10 'As the LORD lives, no harm shall come to you for this.' The woman 11 asked whom she should call up, and Saul answered, 'Samuel.' When the 12 woman saw Samuel appear, she shrieked and said to Saul, 'Why have you deceived me? You are Saul!' The 13 king said to her, 'Do not be afraid. What do you see?' The woman answered, 'I see a ghostly form coming up from the earth.' 'What is it like?' 14 he asked; she answered, 'Like an old man coming up, wrapped in a cloak.' Then Saul knew it was Samuel, and he bowed low with his face to the ground, and prostrated himself. Samuel said to 15 Saul, 'Why have you disturbed me

q from Telaim: prob. rdg.; Heb. from of old.

---

finally drive David (again) to the protection of the Philistines; see 21.10–15. **5–6**: David had a feudal relation to Achish; he owed certain military duties (28.1) in return for the benefits of the territory of *Ziklag*. **7–8**: David's raids were in regions south of Judah. **10**: *Jerahmeelites* and *Kenites* were clans eventually absorbed into the tribe of Judah; see 1 Chr.2.25, 55. *Negeb* means "dry country"; here it is applied to a small local region.
28.3–25: **Saul and the ghost of Samuel.** The collapse of Saul's personality and character reaches its climax. **3**: Consultation of *ghosts* and *spirits* of the dead was consistently opposed in Israelite religious practice; see Lev.19.31; 20.6,27; Deut.18.10–11; 2 Kgs.23.24. **4**: The movement of *the Philistines* anticipates ch. 29. **6**: To be auspicious, important decisions needed divine sanction; compare 14.18,36–37; 23.1–13. **13**: *Coming up from the earth* means up from

and brought me up?' Saul answered, 'I am in great trouble; the Philistines are pressing me and God has turned away; he no longer answers me through prophets or through dreams, and I
16 should do.' Samuel said, 'Why do you ask me, now that the LORD has turned from you and become your
17 adversary? He has done what he foretold through me. He has torn the kingdom from your hand and given it
18 to another man, to David. You have not obeyed the LORD, or executed the judgement of his fury against the Amalekites; that is why he has done
19 this to you today. For the same reason the LORD will let your people Israel fall into the hands of the Philistines and, what is more, tomorrow you and your sons shall be with me. Yes, indeed, the LORD will give the Israelite army into the hands of the Philistines.'
20 Saul was overcome and fell his full length to the ground, terrified by Samuel's words. He had no strength left, for he had eaten nothing all day and all night.
21 The woman went to Saul and saw that he was much disturbed, and she said to him, 'I listened to what you said and I risked my life to obey you.
22 Now listen to me: let me set before you a little food to give you strength for
23 your journey.' But he refused to eat anything. When his servants joined the woman in pressing him, he yielded, rose from the ground and sat on the
24 couch. The woman had a fatted calf at home, which she quickly slaughtered. She took some meal, kneaded it and
25 baked unleavened cakes, which she set before Saul and his servants. They ate the food and departed that same night.

29 The Philistines mustered all their troops at Aphek, while the Israelites
2 encamped at En-harod*r* in Jezreel. The Philistine princes were advancing with their troops in units of a hundred and

a thousand; David and his men were in the rear of the column with Achish.
3 The Philistine commanders asked, 'Why are those Hebrews there?' Achish answered, 'This is David, the servant of Saul king of Israel who has been with me now for a year or more. I have had no fault to find in him ever since he came over to me.' The Philis-
4 tine commanders were indignant and said to Achish, 'Send the man back to the town which you allotted to him. He shall not fight side by side with us, or he may turn traitor in the battle. What better way to buy his master's favour, than at the price of our lives?
5 This is that David of whom they sang, as they danced:

Saul made havoc among thousands
but David among tens of thousands.'

6 Achish summoned David and said to him, 'As the LORD lives, you are an upright man and your service with my troops has well satisfied me. I have had no fault to find with you ever since you joined me, but the other princes
7 are not willing to accept you. Now go home in peace, and you will then be doing nothing that they can regard as wrong.' David protested, 'What have I
8 done, or what fault have you found in me from the day I first entered your service till now, that I should not come and fight against the enemies of my lord the king?' Achish answered
9 David, 'I agree that you have been as true to me as an angel of God, but the Philistine commanders insist that you shall not fight alongside them. Now rise
10 early in the morning with those of your lord's subjects who have followed you, and go to the town which I allotted to you; harbour no evil thoughts, for I am well satisfied with you. Rise early and start as soon as it is light.' So
11 David and his men rose early to start

r Prob. rdg.; Heb. at the spring.

Sheol, the underground abode of the dead; see 2.6 n. **17–18:** This may be a later writer's harmonization with ch. 15. There (15.28) the *man* was anonymous; here he is named as *David.*
   29.1–11: David's exclusion by the Philistines from the war against Saul. 1: The Philistines aimed at occupying the valley of Jezreel that cuts across from the Mediterranean to the Jordan Valley. Saul seeks to stop them at the narrowest part of that valley. **3–6:** The Philistines mistrust David. On *Hebrews*, see 14.21 n. **5:** See 18.7 n.

that morning on their way back to the land of the Philistines, while the Philistines went on to Jezreel.

30 On the third day David and his men reached Ziklag. Now the Amalekites had made a raid into the Negeb, 2 attacked Ziklag and set fire to it; they had carried off all the women, high and low, without putting one of them to death. These they drove with them 3 and continued their march. When David and his men approached the town, they found it destroyed by fire, and their wives, their sons, and their daughters 4 carried off. David and the people with him wept aloud until they could weep 5 no more. David's two wives, Ahinoam of Jezreel and Abigail widow of Nabal of Carmel, were among the captives. 6 David was in a desperate position because the people, embittered by the loss of their sons and daughters, threatened to stone him. So David sought strength 7 in the LORD his God. He told Abiathar the priest, son of Ahimelech, to bring the ephod. When Abiathar had brought 8 the ephod, David inquired of the LORD, 'Shall I pursue these raiders? and shall I overtake them?' The answer came, 'Pursue them: you will over- 9 take them and rescue everyone.' So David and his six hundred men set out and reached the ravine of Besor. [s] 10 Two hundred of them who were too weary to cross the ravine stayed behind, and David with four hundred pressed on in pursuit.

11 In the open country they came across an Egyptian and took him to David. They gave him food to eat and water 12 to drink, also a lump of dried figs and two bunches of raisins. When he had eaten these he revived; for he had had nothing to eat or drink for three 13 days and nights. David asked him, 'Whose slave are you? and where have you come from?' 'I am an Egyptian boy,' he answered, 'the slave of an Amalekite, but my master left me behind because I fell ill three days 14 ago. We had raided the Negeb of the Kerethites, part of Judah, and the

Negeb of Caleb; we also set fire to Ziklag,' David asked, 'Can you guide 15 me to this band?' 'Swear to me by God', he answered, 'that you will not put me to death or hand me back to my master, and I will guide you to them.' So he led him down, and there they 16 were scattered everywhere, eating and drinking and celebrating the capture of the great mass of spoil taken from Philistine and Judaean territory.

David attacked from dawn till dusk 17 and continued till next day; only four hundred young men mounted on camels made good their escape. David 18 rescued all those whom the Amalekites had taken, including his two wives. No one was missing, high or low, sons 19 or daughters, and none of the spoil, nor anything they had taken for themselves: David recovered every- thing. They took all the flocks and 20 herds, drove the cattle before him[t] and said, 'This is David's spoil.' When 21 David returned to the two hundred men who had been too weak to follow him and whom he had left behind at the ravine of Besor, they came forward to meet him and his men. David greeted them all, inquiring how things were with them. But some of those who 22 had gone with David, worthless men and scoundrels, broke in and said, 'These men did not go with us; we will not allot them any of the spoil that we have retrieved, except that each of them may take his own wife and children and then go.' 'That you shall 23 never do,' said David, 'considering what the LORD has given us, and how he has kept us safe and given the raiding party into our hands. Who 24 could agree with what you propose? Those who stayed with the stores shall have the same share as those who went into battle. They shall share and share alike.' From that time onwards, this 25 has been the established custom in Israel down to this day.

s *Prob. rdg.; Heb. adds* those who were left over remained.
t They took . . . before him: *prob. rdg.; Heb.* David took all the flocks and herds; they drove before that cattle.

30.1–31: David's reprisal against the Amalekites. Saul's campaign (15.1–9) did not prevent the Amalekites from harassing the southern Judean clans. **6:** Compare David's situation here with that of Moses in Exod.17.4. **7–8:** David is again scrupulous in consulting the LORD; see 23.1–13. **14:** The *Kerethites* were Cretans, closely related to the Philistines; see Zeph.2.5 and

26 When David reached Ziklag, he sent some of the spoil to the elders of Judah and to his friends, with this message: 'This is a present for you out of the spoil taken from the LORD's

27 enemies.' He sent to those in Bethuel,
28 in Ramoth-negeb, in Jattir, in Ararah,[u]
29 in Siphmoth, in Eshtemoa, in Rachal, in the cities of the Jerahmeelites, in
30 the cities of the Kenites, in Hormah,
31 in Borashan, in Athak, in Hebron, and in all the places over which he and his men had ranged.

311[v] The Philistines fought a battle against Israel, and the men of Israel were routed, leaving their dead on Mount

2 Gilboa. The Philistines hotly pursued Saul and his sons and killed the three sons, Jonathan, Abinadab and Mal-

3 chishua. The battle went hard for Saul, for some archers came upon him and he was wounded in the belly

4 by the archers. So he said to his armour-bearer, 'Draw your sword and run me through, so that these uncircumcised brutes may not come and taunt me and make sport of me.' But the armour-bearer refused, he dared not; whereupon Saul took his own

5 sword and fell on it. When the armour-bearer saw that Saul was dead, he too fell on his sword and died with him.

6 Thus they all died together on that day, Saul, his three sons, and his armour-bearer, as well as his men. And all the 7 Israelites in the district of the Vale and of the Jordan, when they saw that the other Israelites had fled and that Saul and his sons had perished, fled likewise, abandoning their cities, and the Philistines went in and occupied them.

Next day, when the Philistines came 8 to strip the slain, they found Saul and his three sons lying dead on Mount Gilboa. They cut off his head and 9 stripped him of his weapons; then they sent messengers through the length and breadth of their land to take the good news to idols and people alike. They deposited his armour in 10 the temple of Ashtoreth and nailed his body on the wall of Beth-shan. When the inhabitants of Jabesh- 11 gilead heard what the Philistines had done to Saul, the bravest of them 12 journeyed together all night long and recovered the bodies of Saul and his sons from the wall of Beth-shan; they brought them back to Jabesh and anointed them there with spices. Then 13 they took their bones and buried them under the tamarisk-tree in Jabesh, and fasted for seven days.

u Prob. rdg.; Heb. Aroer.
v Verses 1–13: cp. 1 Chr. 10. 1–12.

Ezek.25.16. The *Negeb of Caleb* was in the vicinity of Hebron; see Josh.15.13–19. **26–31:** David is currying favor preparatory to becoming king. On the *Jerahmeelites* and *Kenites*; see 27.10 n.

31.1–13: The death of Saul. Saul had made some headway against the Philistines and here sought to prevent their occupation of the central valley; see 29.1 n. The result, however, was disastrous. **10:** *Ashtoreth*; see 7.4 n. *Beth-shan*: probably the Canaanite city in the eastern part of the valley, near Mount Gilboa (v. 8). **11–13:** The inhabitants of *Jabesh-gilead* were grateful to Saul for his rescue of them; see ch. 11.

THE SECOND BOOK OF
SAMUEL

Without a break, the story begun in 1 Samuel continues in 2 Samuel (see Introduction to 1 Samuel). The focus of the narrative is on David the king, first (chs. 1–8) on the establishment of his rule in Judah and in Israel, then (chs. 9–20) on events largely related to the issue of succession to the throne. Chapters 21–24 appear to be an intrusive appendix concerning David's reign (see 21.1–24.25 n.), but the throne succession narrative is concluded in 1 Kings chs. 1–2.

Beginning with 8.1–18, the relationship of the report in 2 Samuel to that in the books of Chronicles is such that the annotations which cross-reference to the latter work deserve special attention.

David's rule at Hebron

1 WHEN DAVID RETURNED FROM his victory over the Amalekites, he spent two days in Ziklag. 2 And on the third day after Saul's death a man came from the army with his clothes rent and dust on his head. When he came into David's presence 3 he fell to the ground in obeisance, and David asked him where he had come from. He answered, 'I have escaped 4 from the army of Israel.' And David said to him, 'What news? Tell me.' 'The army has been driven from the field,' he answered, 'and many have fallen in battle. Saul and Jonathan his 5 son are dead.' David said to the young man who brought the news, 'How do you know that Saul and Jonathan 6 are dead?' The man answered, 'It so happened that I was on Mount Gilboa and saw Saul leaning on his spear with the chariots and horsemen closing in 7 upon him. He turned round and, seeing me, called to me. I said, "What 8 is it, sir?" He asked who I was, and I 9 said, "An Amalekite." Then he said to me, "Come and stand over me and dispatch me. I still live, but the throes 10 of death have seized me." So I stood over him and gave him the death-blow; for I knew that, broken as he

was, he could not live. Then I took the crown from his head and the armlet from his arm, and I have brought them here to you, sir.' At that David 11 caught at his clothes and rent them, and so did all the men with him. They 12 beat their breasts and wept, because Saul and Jonathan his son and the people of the LORD, the house of Israel, had fallen in battle; and they fasted till evening. David said to the 13 young man who brought the news, 'Where do you come from?', and he answered, 'I am the son of an alien, an Amalekite.' 'How is it', said David, 14 'that you were not afraid to raise your hand to slay the LORD's anointed?' And he summoned one of his own 15 young men and ordered him to fall upon the man. So the young man struck him down and killed him; and David 16 said, 'Your blood be on your own head; for out of your own mouth you condemned yourself when you said, "I killed the LORD's anointed."'

David made this lament over Saul 17 and Jonathan his son; and he ordered 18 that this dirge over them should be taught to the people of Judah. It was written down and may be found in the Book of Jashar:[a]

---

[a] Or the Book of the Upright.

1.1–5.25: David acquires the kingship. This is the concluding section of the history of the rise of David (see 1 Sam.16.1–2 Sam.5.25 n.). Though strongly favorable toward David, it is a fine piece of balanced historical writing.
1.1–27: David learns of Saul's death. Throughout the account of his rise David is viewed as maintaining scrupulous loyalty toward Saul. That emphasis here reaches its strongest expression. 1: The narrative resumes from the end of 1 Sam. ch. 30. 2: Compare the messenger in 1 Sam.4.12. 6: On Saul's *spear*, see 1 Sam.26.9–11 n. 8: The *Amalekite* was a mercenary in the Israelite army. 14: On *the LORD's anointed*, see 1 Sam.14.4–7 n. 17–27: Since David was a harpist (1 Sam.16.14–23) this *dirge* may indeed go back to him. It is lyric poetry without any particular religious aspect. 18: *Jashar*: "Upright." On *the Book of Jashar* see Josh.10,13 n.

318

19 O prince of Israel, laid low in
       death!
    How are the men of war fallen!

20 Tell it not in Gath,
    proclaim it not in the streets of
       Ashkelon,
    lest the Philistine women rejoice,
    lest the daughters of the
       uncircumcised exult.

21 Hills of Gilboa, let no dew or rain
       fall on you,
    no showers on the uplands[b]!
    For there the shields of the warriors
       lie tarnished,
    and the shield of Saul, no longer
       bright with oil.

22 The bow of Jonathan never held back
    from the breast of the foeman, from
       the blood of the slain;
    the sword of Saul never returned
    empty to the scabbard.

23 Delightful and dearly loved were
       Saul and Jonathan;
    in life, in death, they were not
       parted.
    They were swifter than eagles,
       stronger than lions.

24 Weep for Saul, O daughters of
       Israel!
    who clothed you in scarlet and rich
       embroideries,
    who spangled your dress with jewels
       of gold.

25 How are the men of war fallen,
       fallen on the field!
    O Jonathan, laid low in death!

26 I grieve for you, Jonathan my
       brother;

dear and delightful you were to
   me;
your love for me was wonderful,
   surpassing the love of women.

Fallen, fallen are the men of war;   27
and their armour left on the field.

After this David inquired of the **2**
LORD, 'Shall I go up into one of the
cities of Judah?' The LORD answered,
'Go.' David asked, 'To which city?',
and the answer came, 'To Hebron.'
So David went to Hebron with **2**
his two wives, Ahinoam of Jezreel
and Abigail widow of Nabal of Carmel.
David also brought the men who had **3**
joined him, with their families, and
they settled in the city[c] of Hebron.
The men of Judah came, and there **4**
they anointed David king over the house
of Judah.

Word came to David that the men
of Jabesh-gilead had buried Saul, and **5**
he sent them this message: 'The LORD
bless you because you kept faith with
Saul your lord and buried him. For **6**
this may the LORD keep faith and
truth with you, and I for my part will
show you favour too, because you
have done this. Be strong, be valiant, **7**
now that Saul your lord is dead, and the
people of Judah have anointed me to
be king over them.'

Meanwhile Saul's commander-in- **8**
chief, Abner son of Ner, had taken
Saul's son Ishbosheth, brought him
across the Jordan to Mahanaim, and **9**
made him king over Gilead, the Asherites, Jezreel, Ephraim, and Benjamin,

b *showers on the uplands:* prob. rdg.; Heb. *fields of
   offerings.*
c Prob. rdg.; Heb. *cities.*

Its contents may have been *taught to the people*, probably by recitation at assemblies and
festivals. **20:** *Uncircumcised*: see 1 Sam.14.6 n. **21:** The place of Saul's death should be afflicted
with drought. The leather *shields* were kept in good condition with *oil*.
   2.1–7: David becomes king of Judah. 1–3: David again carefully consults the LORD about
his movements; see 1 Sam.23.1–13; 30.7–8. With Saul gone, *the men of Judah* take their own
steps against the Philistines. **4b–7:** David's message to *the men of Jabesh-gilead* had its political
motivations, for it was in the territory of the remnant kingdom of Saul's son.
   2.8–5.5: All Israel comes to David. There is a twofold concern throughout this narrative:
to show how events worked inevitably toward David's becoming king of all Israel, but also
that he himself remained blameless of bloodshed and other offenses in the process. **8:** The name
literally means "man (*ish*) of shame (*bosheth*)"; the *bosheth* was originally "baal," and then the
name meant "man of Baal." Late editors eliminated here the abhorred name of the Canaanite
deity; the change was not made in Chr. ("Eshbaal," 1 Chr.8.33; 9.39). *Mahanaim* was a prominent city in Gilead. It also served as a refuge for David when he had to flee to the east (17.24).
9: That *Ishbosheth* actually ruled over *all Israel* is an exaggeration, an instance of court etiquette.

10 and all Israel. Ishbosheth was forty years old when he became king over Israel, and he reigned two years. The tribe of Judah, however, followed
11 David. David's rule over Judah in Hebron lasted seven years and a half.
12 Abner son of Ner, with the troops of Saul's son Ishbosheth, marched out
13 from Mahanaim to Gibeon, and Joab son of Zeruiah marched out with David's troops from Hebron. They met at the pool of Gibeon and took up their positions one on one side of the pool and the other on the other side.
14 Abner said to Joab, 'Let the young men come forward and join in single combat before us.' Joab answered,
15 'Yes, let them.' So they came up, one by one, and took their places, twelve for Benjamin and for Ishbosheth and twelve
16 from David's men. Each man seized his opponent by the head and thrust his sword into his side; and thus they fell together. That is why that place, which lies in Gibeon, was called the Field of Blades.
17 There ensued a fierce battle that day, and Abner and the men of Israel were
18 defeated by David's troops. All three sons of Zeruiah were there, Joab, Abishai and Asahel. Asahel, who was
19 swift as a gazelle on the plains, ran straight after Abner, swerving neither
20 to right nor left in his pursuit. Abner turned and asked, 'Is it you, Asahel?'
21 Asahel answered, 'It is.' Abner said, 'Turn aside to right or left, tackle one of the young men and win his belt for yourself.' But Asahel would not
22 abandon the pursuit. Abner again urged him to give it up. 'Why should I kill you?' he said. 'How could I look
23 Joab your brother in the face?' When he still refused to turn aside, Abner struck him in the belly with a back-thrust of his spear*d* so that the spear came out behind him, and he fell dead in his tracks. All who came to the place where Asahel lay dead stopped
24 there. But Joab and Abishai kept up the pursuit of Abner, until, at sunset, they reached the hill of Ammah, opposite Giah on the road leading to the pastures of Gibeon.

25 The Benjamites rallied to Abner and, forming themselves into a single company, took up their stand on the top of the hill of Ammah.*e* Abner called
26 to Joab, 'Must the slaughter go on for ever? Can you not see that it will be all the more bitter in the end? Will you never recall the people from the pursuit of their kinsmen?' Joab answered,
27 'As God lives, if you had not spoken, the people would not have given up the pursuit till morning.' Then Joab
28 sounded the trumpet, and all the people abandoned the pursuit of the men of Israel and the fighting ceased.
29 Abner and his men moved along the Arabah all that night, crossed the Jordan and went on all the morning
30 till they reached Mahanaim. When Joab returned from the pursuit of Abner, he assembled his troops and found that, besides Asahel, nineteen
31 of David's men were missing. David's forces had routed the Benjamites and the followers of Abner, killing three hundred and sixty of them. They took
32 up Asahel and buried him in his father's tomb at Bethlehem. Joab and his men marched all night, and as day broke they reached Hebron.

3 THE WAR BETWEEN THE HOUSES OF SAUL and David was long drawn out, David growing steadily stronger while the house of Saul became weaker and weaker.

2*f* Sons were born to David at Hebron. His eldest was Amnon, whose mother
3 was Ahinoam of Jezreel; his second Chileab, whose mother was Abigail widow of Nabal of Carmel; the third Absalom, whose mother was Maacah daughter of Talmai king of Geshur;
4 the fourth Adonijah, whose mother

d a back-thrust of his spear: prob. rdg.; Heb. obscure.
e the hill of Ammah: prob. rdg., cp. verse 24; Heb. a single hill.
f Verses 2–5: cp. 1 Chr. 3. 1–4.

10–11: The chronology here is difficult. But if Ishbosheth reigned only two years, and then David became king of all Israel, David's wars with the Philistines (5.17–25) probably preceded his conquest of Jerusalem (5.6–10); thereby we can possibly understand the *seven years and a half* of his reign at Hebron. **16:** The exact nature of this combat is obscure. **22:** *Abner* wishes to avoid a blood feud with his respected opponent. **29:** *Arabah,* "dry place," is the southern Jordan Valley. **3.2–5:** This is an editorial addition to the main narrative. **7:** To take a king's

was Haggith; the fifth Shephatiah,
5 whose mother was Abital; and the
sixth Ithream, whose mother was
David's wife Eglah. These were all
born to David at Hebron.

6 As the war between the houses of
Saul and David went on, Abner made
his position gradually stronger in the
7 house of Saul. Now Saul had had a
concubine named Rizpah daughter of
Aiah. Ishbosheth asked Abner, 'Why
have you slept with my father's con-
8 cubine?' Abner was very angry at this
and exclaimed, 'Am I a baboon in the
pay of Judah? Up to now I have been
loyal to the house of your father Saul,
to his brothers and friends, and I have
not betrayed you into David's hands;
yet you choose this moment to charge
me with disloyalty over this woman.
9 But now, so help me God, I will do all
I can to bring about what the LORD
10 swore to do for David: I will set to
work to bring down the house of Saul
and to put David on the throne over
Israel and Judah from Dan to Beer-
11 sheba.' Ishbosheth could not say
another word; he was too much afraid
12 of Abner. Then Abner, seeking to
make friends where he could, instead of
going to David himself sent envoys with
this message: 'Let us come to terms, and
I will do all I can to bring the whole
13 of Israel over to you.' David sent
answer: 'Good, I will come to terms
with you, but on this one condition,
that you do not come into my presence
without bringing Saul's daughter Mi-
14 chal to me.' David also sent messengers
to Saul's son Ishbosheth with the
demand: 'Hand over to me my wife
Michal to whom I was betrothed at
the price of a hundred Philistine fore-
15 skins.' Thereupon Ishbosheth sent and
took her away from her husband,
16 Paltiel son of Laish. Paltiel followed
her as far as Bahurim, weeping all the
way, until Abner ordered him to go back
home, and he went.

Abner now approached the elders 17
of Israel and said, 'For some time
past you have wanted David for your
king; now is the time to act, for this 18
is the word of the LORD about David:
"By the hand of my servant David I
will deliver my people Israel from the
Philistines and from all their enemies." ' Abner spoke also to the Ben- 19
jamites and then went on to report to
David at Hebron all that the Israelites
and the Benjamites had agreed. When 20
Abner was admitted to David's presence, there were twenty men with him
and David gave a feast for them all.
Then Abner said to David, 'I shall now 21
go and bring the whole of Israel over
to your majesty, and they shall make a
covenant with you. Then you will be
king over a realm after your own heart.'
David dismissed Abner, granting him
safe conduct.

David's men and Joab returned 22
from a raid bringing a great deal of
plunder with them, and by this time
Abner, after his dismissal, was no
longer with David in Hebron. So when 23
Joab and his raiding party arrived,
they were greeted with the news that
Abner son of Ner had been with the
king and had departed under safe
conduct. Joab went in to the king 24
and said, 'What have you done?
Here you have had Abner with you.
How could you let him go? He has got
clean away! You know Abner son of 25
Ner: he came meaning to deceive you,
to learn all about your movements and
to find out what you are doing.' When 26
he left David's presence, Joab sent
messengers after Abner and they
brought him back from the Pool of
Sirah; but David knew nothing of all
this. On Abner's return to Hebron, 27
Joab drew him aside in the gateway,
as though to speak privately with him,
and there, in revenge for his brother
Asahel, he stabbed him in the belly,
and he died. When David heard the 28

concubine was an act of treason; compare 16.20–22; 1 Kgs.2.13–24. **14:** David's interest in
Michal was for a claim, as son-in-law, of continuity with Saul. **19:** In this entire narrative *the
Benjamites* are depicted as remarkably independent, probably because they were Saul's
tribe. **22–27:** Joab's killing of Abner threatened to undo David's plans to become king of all
Israel; hence David's great anger. **28–39:** The violent outbreak and conspicuous mourning
over *Abner* reflect David's need to persuade the Israelites of his own innocence. David may
curse *Joab* (v. 29), but Joab is far too valuable to execute, as had been done to the Amalekite

news he said, 'I and my realm are for ever innocent in the sight of the LORD 29 of the blood of Abner son of Ner. May it recoil upon the head of Joab and upon all his family! May the house of Joab never be free from running sore or foul disease, nor lack a son fit only to ply the distaff or doomed to die by 30 the sword or beg his bread!' So Joab and Abishai his brother slew Abner because he had killed their brother 31 Asahel in battle at Gibeon. Then David ordered Joab and all the people with him to rend their clothes, put on sackcloth and beat their breasts for Abner, and the king himself walked 32 behind the bier. They buried Abner in Hebron and the king wept aloud at the tomb, while all the people wept 33 with him. The king made this lament for Abner:

Must Abner die so base a death?
34   Your hands were not bound,
     your feet not thrust into fetters;
     you fell as one who falls at a
         ruffian's hands.

And the people wept for him again.
35   They came to persuade David to eat something; but it was still day and he swore, 'So help me God! I will not touch food of any kind before sunset.'
36 The people took note of this and approved; indeed, everything the king 37 did pleased them. Everyone throughout Israel knew on that day that the king had had no hand in the murder of 38 Abner son of Ner. The king said to his servants, 'Do you not know that a warrior, a great man, has fallen this 39 day in Israel? King though I am, I feel weak and powerless in face of these ruthless sons of Zeruiah; they are too much for me; the LORD will requite the wrongdoer as he deserves.'

4   When Saul's son Ishbosheth heard that Abner had been killed in Hebron, his courage failed him and all Israel 2 was dismayed. Now Ishbosheth had[g]

two officers, who were captains of raiding parties, and whose names were Baanah and Rechab; they were Benjamites, sons of Rimmon of Beeroth, Beeroth being reckoned part of Ben- 3 jamin; but the Beerothites had fled to Gittaim, where they have lived ever since.

(Saul's son Jonathan had a son lame 4 in both feet. He was five years old when word of the death of Saul and Jonathan came from Jezreel. His nurse had picked him up and fled, but in her hurry to get away he fell and was crippled. His name was Mephibosheth.)

Rechab and Baanah, the sons of 5 Rimmon of Beeroth, came to the house of Ishbosheth in the heat of the day and went in, while he was taking his midday rest. Now the door-keeper had 6 been sifting wheat, but she had grown drowsy and fallen asleep, so Rechab and his brother Baanah crept in, found 7 their way to the room where he was asleep on the bed, and struck him dead. They cut off his head and took it with them, and, making their way along the Arabah all night, came to Hebron. They brought Ishbosheth's 8 head to David at Hebron and said to the king, 'Here is the head of Ishbosheth son of Saul, your enemy, who sought your life. The LORD has avenged your majesty today on Saul and on his family.' David answered Rechab 9 and his brother Baanah, the sons of Rimmon of Beeroth, with an oath: 'As the LORD lives, who has rescued me from all my troubles! I seized the 10 man who brought me word that Saul was dead and thought it good news; I killed him in Ziklag, and that was how I rewarded him for his news. How much more when ruffians have 11 killed an innocent man on his bed in his own house? Am I not to take vengeance on you now for the blood you have shed, and rid the earth of

g had: *prob. rdg.; Heb. om.*

(1.15) and was to be done to the assassins of Ishbosheth (4.12). **29**: A *distaff* was an instrument used in spinning thread from wool, a womanly task. **4.2**: *Beeroth* was a village of the old city-state of Gibeon (Josh.9.17), with which Saul had some kind of feud (21.1), and which may have led to *Beeroth being reckoned part of Benjamin*. **4**: Another editorial addition; it prepares for ch. 9. *Mephibosheth* is a distortion of the original Meribbaal; see 2.8 n. **11**. David does not speak of Ishbosheth as the Lord's anointed, as he did of Saul (1 Sam.24.4–7 n.), but only as an

12 you?' David gave the word, and the young men killed them; they cut off their hands and feet and hung them up beside the pool in Hebron, but the head of Ishbosheth they took and buried in Abner's tomb at Hebron.

David king in Jerusalem

5 1[h] NOW ALL THE TRIBES OF ISRAEL CAME to David at Hebron and said to him, 'We are your own flesh and blood. 2 In the past, while Saul was still king over us, you led the forces of Israel to war and you brought them home again. And the LORD said to you, "You shall be shepherd of my people Israel; 3 you shall be their prince."' All the elders of Israel came to the king at Hebron; there David made a covenant with them before the LORD, and they 4 anointed David king over Israel. David came to the throne at the age of thirty 5 and reigned for forty years. In Hebron he had ruled over Judah for seven years and a half, and for thirty-three years he reigned in Jerusalem over Israel and Judah together.

6 The king and his men went to Jerusalem to attack the Jebusites, whose land it was. The Jebusites said to David, 'Never shall you come in here; not till you have disposed of the blind and the lame', meaning that 7 David should never come in. None the less David did capture the stronghold of Zion, and it is now known as the 8 City of David. David said on that day, 'Everyone who would kill a Jebusite, let him use his grappling-iron to reach the lame and the blind, David's bitter enemies.' That is why they say, 'No blind or lame man shall come into the LORD's house.'

David took up his residence in the 9 stronghold and called it the City of David. He built the city[i] round it, starting at the Millo and working inwards. So David steadily grew 10 stronger, for the LORD the God of Hosts was with him.

Hiram king of Tyre sent an embassy 11[j] to David; he sent cedar logs, and with them carpenters and stonemasons, who built David a house. David knew by 12 now that the LORD had confirmed him as king over Israel and had made his royal power stand higher for the sake of his people Israel.

After he had moved from Hebron 13 he took more concubines and wives from Jerusalem; and more sons and daughters were born to him. These 14[k] are the names of the children born to him in Jerusalem: Shammua, Shobab, Nathan, Solomon, Ibhar, Elishua, 15 Nepheg, Japhia, Elishama, Eliada and 16 Eliphelet.

When the Philistines learnt that 17 David had been anointed king over Israel, they came up in force to seek him out. David, hearing of this, took refuge in the stronghold. The Philistines 18 had come and overrun the Vale of Rephaim. So David inquired of the 19 LORD, 'If I attack the Philistines, wilt thou deliver them into my hands?'

h Verses 1–3, 6–10: cp. 1 Chr. 11. 1–9.
i the city: prob. rdg., cp. 1 Chr. 11. 8; Heb. om.
j Verses 11–25: cp. 1 Chr. 14. 1–16.
k Verses 14–16: cp. 1 Chr. 3. 5–8; 14. 4–7.

innocent man! **5.2:** On *prince*, see 1 Sam.9.15–16 n. **3:** In contrast to David's rule of Jerusalem, this is a kingship by *covenant*, not by conquest. The *covenant* was subject to renewal by each new king; see 1 Kgs.12.1. **4–5:** The *forty years* of David's reign may be a round number, but it is approximately correct. His conquest of Jerusalem occurred very near the year 1000 B.C.
5.6–10: Jerusalem becomes the City of David. *Jerusalem* was a very ancient settlement or city as much as a thousand years earlier than the age of David. Biblical traditions about it vary. In Judg.19.10 its name is Jebus, and it is there a Jebusite city; in Josh.10.1–10 its forces are defeated; it is captured in Judg.1.8 and then burned. The account here seems unaware of the capture of Jerusalem in Judg.1.8. David was seeking a base that had no previous alliance with either Israel to the north or Judah to the south. By capturing the city in the way he did it became his private property, the *City of David*. He did not destroy the city or kill its population (for contrast, see 1 Kgs.9.16). **7:** *Zion:* a hill crest in Jerusalem, it is a poetic term for the city, frequent in the Psalms and prophetic writings but rare in prose texts. The name Zion became attached to the area where Solomon's Temple was built.
5.11–25: David secures his kingdom. 11: That *Hiram king of Tyre* took these measures indicates that David, after defeating the Philistines, became a power to be reckoned with. **17–25:** These two notices of defeats of *the Philistines* are regrettably laconic, interested primarily in

And the LORD answered, 'Go, I will deliver the Philistines into your hands.'
20 So he went up and attacked them at Baal-perazim and defeated them there. 'The LORD has broken through my enemies' lines,' David said, 'as a river breaks its banks.' That is why the place
21 was named Baal-perazim.[l] The Philistines left their idols behind them there, and David and his men carried them off.
22 The Philistines made another attack and overran the Vale of Rephaim.
23 David inquired of the LORD, who said, 'Do not attack now but wheel round and take them in the rear opposite the
24 aspens. As soon as you hear a rustling sound in the tree-tops, then act at once; for the LORD will have gone out before you to defeat the Philistine
25 army.' David did as the LORD had commanded, and drove the Philistines in flight all the way from Geba to Gezer.

6 After that David again summoned the picked men of Israel, thirty thous-
2[m] and in all, and went with the whole army to Baalath-judah[n] to fetch the Ark of God which bears the name of the LORD of Hosts, who is enthroned
3 upon the cherubim. They mounted the Ark of God on a new cart and conveyed it from the house of Abinadab on the hill, with Uzzah and Ahio, sons of Abinadab, guiding the cart.
4 They took it with the Ark of God upon it from Abinadab's house on the hill,
5 with Ahio walking in front. David and all Israel danced for joy before the LORD without restraint to the sound of singing,[o] of harps and lutes, of tambourines and castanets and cymbals.
6 But when they came to a certain threshing-floor, the oxen stumbled, and Uzzah reached out to the Ark of
7 God and took hold of it. The LORD was angry with Uzzah and struck him down there for his rash act. So he

died there beside the Ark of God. David was vexed because the LORD's 8 anger had broken out upon Uzzah, and he called the place Perez-uzzah,[p] the name it still bears. David was afraid 9 of the LORD that day and said, 'How can I harbour the Ark of the LORD after this?' He felt he could not take 10 the Ark of the LORD with him to the City of David, but turned aside and carried it to the house of Obed-edom the Gittite. Thus the Ark of the LORD 11 remained at Obed-edom's house for three months, and the LORD blessed Obed-edom and all his family.

When they told David that the LORD 12[q] had blessed Obed-edom's family and all that was his because of the Ark of God, he went and brought up the Ark of God from the house of Obed-edom to the City of David with much rejoicing. When the bearers of the Ark 13 of the LORD had gone six steps he sacrificed an ox and a buffalo. David, 14 wearing a linen ephod, danced without restraint before the LORD. He and all 15 the Israelites brought up the Ark of the LORD with shouting and blowing of trumpets. But as the Ark of the 16 LORD was entering the City of David, Saul's daughter Michal looked down through a window and saw King David leaping and capering before the LORD, and she despised him in her heart. When they had brought in the 17 Ark of the LORD, they put it in its place inside the tent that David had pitched for it, and David offered whole-offerings and shared-offerings before the LORD. After David had completed 18 these sacrifices, he blessed the people in the name of the LORD of Hosts and 19

l That is Baal of Break-through.
m Verses 2–11: cp. 1 Chr. 13. 6–14.
n to Baalath-judah: prob. rdg., cp. 1 Chr. 13. 6; Heb. from the lords of Judah.
o without . . . singing: prob. rdg., cp. 1 Chr. 13. 8; Heb. to the beating of batons.
p That is Outbreak on Uzzah.
q Verses 12–19: cp. 1 Chr. 15. 25—16. 3.

David's guidance by the LORD. No writer pursued this topic in the way that was done with another of David's wars, that against the Ammonites and the Arameans (ch. 10 and 12.26–31).
    6.1–23: David brings the Ark to Jerusalem. The account of the Ark was suspended at 1 Sam. 7.1, giving way to the topic of kingship; see 1 Sam.4.1b–7.1 n. and 8.1–15.35 n. The Ark here moves from the outskirts of Judah to the great sacred city of the future, Jerusalem. **1:** *Thirty thousand* is another number that gives an impression rather than a report; see 1 Sam.13.5 n. **2:** *Ark . . . enthroned:* see 1 Sam.4.4 n. **3:** The *new cart* was a ritual requirement; see 1 Sam.6.7 n. **7:** The uncontrollable and dangerous aspect of the deity is prominent in the Ark story; see 1 Sam.6.19 20. **10:** *Obed-edom* was a *Gittite,* that is, a man of Gath, the Philistine city. **12–19:** The occasion was one of great festivity. In addition to the procession, dancing, and

gave food to all the people, a flat loaf of bread, a portion of meat, and a cake of raisins, to every man and woman in the whole gathering of the Israelites.

20 Then all the people went home. When David returned to greet his household, Michal, Saul's daughter, came out to meet him and said, 'What a glorious day for the king of Israel, when he exposed his person in the sight of his servants' slave-girls like any empty-

21 headed fool!' David answered Michal, 'But it was done in the presence of the LORD, who chose me instead of your father and his family and appointed me prince over Israel, the people of the LORD. Before the LORD I will dance

22 for joy, yes, and I will earn yet more disgrace and lower myself still more in your eyes. But those girls of whom

23 you speak, they will honour me for it.' Michal, Saul's daughter, had no child to her dying day.

7 1 *r* As soon as the king was established in his house and the LORD had given him security from his enemies on all

2 sides, he said to Nathan the prophet, 'Here I live in a house of cedar, while the Ark of God is housed in curtains.'

3 Nathan answered the king, 'Very well, do whatever you have in mind, for the

4 LORD is with you.' But that night the word of the LORD came to Nathan:

5 'Go and say to David my servant, "This is the word of the LORD: Are you the man to build me a house to

6 dwell in? Down to this day I have never dwelt in a house since I brought Israel up from Egypt; I made my journey in

7 a tent and a tabernacle. Wherever I journeyed with Israel, did I ever ask any of the judges[s] whom I appointed shepherds of my people Israel why

they had not built me a house of cedar?"

8 Then say this to my servant David: "This is the word of the LORD of Hosts: I took you from the pastures, and from following the sheep, to be

9 prince over my people Israel. I have been with you wherever you have gone, and have destroyed all the enemies in your path. I will make you a great name among the great ones of

10 the earth. I will assign a place for my people Israel; there I will plant them, and they shall dwell in their own land. They shall be disturbed no more, never again shall wicked men oppress

11 them as they did in the past, ever since the time when I appointed judges over Israel my people; and I will give you peace from all your enemies. The LORD has told you that he would build up

12 your royal house. When your life ends and you rest with your forefathers, I will set up one of your family, one of your own children, to succeed you and

13 I will establish his kingdom. It is he shall build a house in honour of my name, and I will establish his royal

14 throne for ever. I will be his father, and he shall be my son. When he does wrong, I will punish him as any father

15 might, and not spare the rod. My love will never be withdrawn from him as I withdrew it from Saul, whom I re-

16 moved from your path. Your family shall be established and your kingdom shall stand for all time in my sight, and your throne shall be established for ever." '

17 Nathan recounted to David all that had been said to him and all that had

18 been revealed. Then King David went

r Verses 1–29: cp. 1 Chr. 17. 1–27.
s Prob. rdg., cp. 1 Chr. 17. 6; Heb. tribes.

---

shouting, the many sacrifices supplied meat for banquets, and David concluded the event with gifts to all the people. **20:** David was apparently dressed only in the linen ephod (v. 14), a kind of priestly apron.

7.1–29: The establishment of the house of David. This is the climax to all that precedes in the books of Samuel. After the legitimacy of kingship was established through Samuel and Saul (1 Sam. chs. 8–14), what remained to establish was the legitimacy of the Davidic dynasty. **1–7:** David proposes to build a temple. An old tradition about the LORD not dwelling in a permanent house is drawn upon to oppose that plan. That the Ark dwelt in a temple at Shiloh (1 Sam. 3.3) is ignored. **2:** *Nathan the prophet* first appears here. Since he always appears in Jerusalem and was a close associate of the priest Zadok (1 Kgs. 1.32), he may have been a native of Jerusalem. **8–16:** There is a deliberate wordplay on *house:* David will not build the LORD a house (the Temple), but the LORD will build David a house (dynasty). **12–15:** These verses, concerned with the conduct of later kings, are probably a late expansion of the passage. **17–29:** The prayer is often regarded as reflecting a time later than that of David, for it deals with David's *house,* that is, the dynasty of his descendants.

into the presence of the LORD and took his place there and said, 'What am I, Lord GOD, and what is my family, that thou hast brought me thus far? 19 It was a small thing in thy sight to have planned for thy servant's house in days long past. But such, O Lord GOD, is the lot of a man embarked on a high 20 career.[t] And now what more can I say? for well thou knowest thy servant 21 David, O Lord GOD. Thou hast made good thy word; it was thy purpose to spread thy servant's fame, and so thou 22 hast raised me to this greatness. Great indeed art thou, O Lord GOD; we have never heard of one like thee; there is no 23 god but thee. And thy people Israel, to whom can they be compared? Is there any other nation on earth whom thou, O God, hast set out to redeem from slavery to be thy people? Any other for whom thou hast done great and terrible things to win fame for thyself? Any other whom thou hast redeemed for thyself from Egypt by driving out other nations and their 24 gods to make way for them? Thou hast established thy people Israel as thy own for ever, and thou, O LORD, hast 25 become their God. But now, LORD God, perform what thou hast promised for thy servant and his house, and for all time; make good what thou hast 26 said. May thy fame be great for evermore and let men say, "The LORD of Hosts is God over Israel." So shall the house of thy servant David be estab- 27 lished before thee. O LORD of Hosts, God of Israel, thou hast shown me thy purpose, in saying to thy servant, "I will build up your house"; and therefore I have made bold to offer this 28 prayer to thee. Thou, O Lord GOD, art God; thou hast made these noble promises to thy servant, and thy prom- 29 ises come true; be pleased now to bless thy servant's house that it may continue always before thee; thou, O Lord GOD,

hast promised, and thy blessing shall rest upon thy servant's house for evermore.'

After this David defeated the Philis- 8 1[u] tines and conquered them, and took from them Metheg-ha-ammah. He 2 defeated the Moabites, and he made them lie along the ground and measured them off with a length of cord; for every two lengths that were to be put to death one full length was spared. The Moabites became subject to him and paid him tribute. David also 3 defeated Hadadezer the Rehobite, king of Zobah, who was on his way to re-erect his monument of victory by[v] the river Euphrates. From him David 4 captured seventeen hundred horse and twenty thousand foot; he hamstrung all the chariot-horses, except a hundred which he retained. When the Aramae- 5 ans of Damascus came to the help of Hadadezer king of Zobah, David destroyed twenty-two thousand of them, and established garrisons among 6 these Aramaeans; they became subject to him and paid him tribute. Thus the LORD gave David victory wherever he went. David took the gold quivers 7 borne by Hadadezer's servants and brought them to Jerusalem; and he 8 also took a great quantity of bronze[w] from Hadadezer's cities, Betah and Berothai.

When Toi king of Hamath heard 9 that David had defeated the entire army of Hadadezer, he sent his son 10 Joram to King David to greet him and to congratulate him on defeating Hadadezer in battle (for Hadadezer had been at war with Toi); and he brought with him vessels of silver, gold, and copper, which King David dedi- 11 cated to the LORD. He dedicated also

t embarked on a high career: *prob. rdg., cp. 1 Chr. 17. 17; Heb. om.*
u *Verses 1–14: cp. 1 Chr. 18. 1–13.*
v re-erect ... victory by: *or* recover control of the crossings of ...
w *Or* copper.

8.1–18: **David's wars and administration.** This list of notices stands between the long narrative of David's rise to power (1 Sam. ch. 16–2 Sam. ch. 5) and the dramatic narrative of David's sons and the succession to the throne (chs. 9–20, concluded in 1 Kgs. chs. 1–2). (From this point on, cross-references to the books of Chronicles should be noted.) 1: *Metheg-ha-ammah* is probably not a proper name. 1 Chr.18.1 reads "Gath with its villages," a reading appropriate here, too. 2: No reason for the severity here toward the *Moabites* is given; it is surprising in view of 1 Sam.22.3–4. 3–10: These conquests were all to the north and east, subduing the *Aramaeans*, who were, however, to remain a thorn in Israel's side until the Assyrian conquest in the eighth century. 4: Unlike his son Solomon (1 Kgs.10.26–29), David did not exploit

the silver and gold taken from all the
12 nations he had subdued, from Edom
and Moab, from the Ammonites, the
Philistines, and Amalek, as well as
part of the spoil taken from Hadadezer
the Rehobite, king of Zobah.
13 David made a great name for himself by the slaughter of eighteen
thousand Edomites in the Valley of
14 Salt, and on returning he stationed
garrisons throughout Edom, and all
the Edomites were subject to him.
Thus the LORD gave victory to David
wherever he went.
15ˣ David ruled over the whole of Israel
and maintained law and justice among
16 all his people. Joab son of Zeruiah
was in command of the army; Jehoshaphat son of Ahilud was secretary of
17 state; Zadok and Abiathar son of
Ahimelech, son of Ahitub,ʸ were priests;
18 Seraiah was adjutant-general; Benaiah
son of Jehoiada commanded the Kerethite and Pelethite guards. David's sons
were priests.

9 David asked, 'Is any member of
Saul's family left, to whom I can show
true kindness for Jonathan's sake?'
2 There was a servant of Saul's family
named Ziba; and he was summoned
to David. The king asked, 'Are you
Ziba?', and he answered, 'Your ser-
3 vant, sir.' So the king said, 'Is no
member of Saul's family still alive
to whom I may show the kindness
that God requires?' 'Yes,' said Ziba,
'there is a son of Jonathan still alive;
he is a cripple, lame in both feet.'
4 'Where is he?' said the king, and
Ziba answered, 'He is staying with
Machir son of Ammiel in Lo-debar.'
5 So the king sent and fetched him
from Lo-debar, from the house of
6 Machir son of Ammiel, and when

Mephibosheth, son of Jonathan and
Saul's grandson, entered David's presence, he prostrated himself and did
obeisance. David said to him, 'Mephibosheth', and he answered, 'Your
servant, sir.' Then David said, 'Do not 7
be afraid; I mean to show you kindness
for your father Jonathan's sake, and I
will give you back the whole estate of
your grandfather Saul; you shall have
a place for yourself at my table.'
So Mephibosheth prostrated himself 8
again and said, 'Who am I that you
should spare a thought for a dead dog
like me?' Then David summoned 9
Saul's servant Ziba to his presence and
said to him, 'I assign to your master's
grandson all the property that belonged to Saul and his family. You 10
and your sons and your slaves must
cultivate the land and bring in the
harvest to provide for your master's
household, but Mephibosheth your
master's grandson shall have a place
at my table.' This man Ziba had
fifteen sons and twenty slaves. Then 11
Ziba answered the king, 'I will do all
that your majesty commands.' So
Mephibosheth took his place in the
royal household like one of the king's
sons. He had a young son, named 12
Mica; and the members of Ziba's
household were all Mephibosheth's
servants, while Mephibosheth lived in 13
Jerusalem and had his regular place at
the king's table, crippled as he was in
both feet.

Some time afterwards the king of 10ᶻ
the Ammonites died and was succeeded
by his son Hanun. David said, 'I must 2

x *Verses 15–18: cp. 20. 23–26; 1 Kgs. 4. 2–6; 1 Chr. 18.
14–17.*
y *and Abiathar . . . Ahitub: prob. rdg., cp. 1 Sam. 22.
11, 20; 2 Sam. 20. 25; Heb. son of Ahitub and
Ahimelech son of Abiathar.*
z *Verses 1–19: cp. 1 Chr. 19. 1–19.*

chariot warfare. **17:** *Zadok and Abiathar* represented two priestly traditions, Abiathar the old
line of Eli at Shiloh (1 Sam.23.6; 22.9; 14.3), Zadok the priestly line of Jerusalem. **18:** *The
Kerethite and Pelethite guards* were mercenaries, sometimes more loyal to the king than his
own countrymen; compare 15.17–22. Kerethites and Pelethites were, in origin, from Mediterranean islands.
9.1–20.22: David's children and the succession to the throne. This narrative of court intrigue
and rebellion, which has its conclusion in 1 Kgs. chs. 1–2, is commonly regarded as the finest
piece of purely historical writing in the OT.
9.1–13: David cares for Jonathan's son. The king's kindness probably was motivated by
political wisdom as well as friendship. By keeping Saul's heir under control, David was assured
that no rebellion could form around Mephibosheth. **1:** *For Jonathan's sake:* see 1 Sam.20.42.
3: *Cripple:* see 4.4. **4:** *Lo-debar* was east of the Jordan: see 17.27. **6:** For *Mephibosheth,* see 4.4 n.
10.1–11.1: The Ammonite war. Though this seems to be a digression, it provides the setting
and the occasion for David's relation to Bathsheba in ch. 11. **2:** *Nahash* was the Ammonite

keep up the same loyal friendship with Hanun son of Nahash as his father showed me', and he sent a mission to condole with him on the death of his father. But when David's envoys entered the country of the Ammon-3 ites, the Ammonite princes said to Hanun their lord, 'Do you suppose David means to do honour to your father when he sends you his con-dolences? These men of his are spies whom he has sent to find out how to 4 overthrow the city.' So Hanun took David's servants, and he shaved off half their beards, cut off half their garments up to the buttocks, and 5 dismissed them. When David heard how they had been treated, he sent to meet them, for they were deeply humiliated, and ordered them to wait in Jericho and not to return until their 6 beards had grown again. The Am-monites knew that they had fallen into bad odour with David, so they hired the Aramaeans of Beth-rehob and of Zobah to come to their help with twenty thousand infantry; they also hired the king of Maacah with a thousand men, and twelve thousand 7 men from Tob. When David heard of it, he sent out Joab and all the fighting 8 men. The Ammonites came and took up their position at the entrance to the city, while the Aramaeans of Zobah and of Rehob and the men of Tob and Maacah took up theirs in the open 9 country. When Joab saw that he was threatened both front and rear, he detailed some picked Israelite troops and drew them up facing the Aramae-10 ans. The rest of his forces he put under his brother Abishai, who took up a 11 position facing the Ammonites. 'If the Aramaeans prove too strong for me,' he said, 'you must come to my relief; and if the Ammonites prove too strong for you, I will come to yours.

Courage! Let us fight bravely for our 12 people and for the cities*a* of our God. And the LORD's will be done.' But 13 when Joab and his men came to close quarters with the Aramacans, they put them to flight; and when the 14 Ammonites saw them in flight, they too fled before Abishai and entered the city. Then Joab returned from the battle against the Ammonites and came to Jerusalem. The Aramaeans saw that 15 they had been worsted by Israel; but they rallied their forces, and Hadadezer 16 sent to summon other Aramaeans from the Great Bend of the Euphrates, and they advanced to Helam under Sho-bach, commander of Hadadezer's army. Their movement was reported to 17 David, who immediately mustered all the forces of Israel, crossed the Jordan and advanced to meet them at Helam. There the Aramaeans took up positions facing David and engaged him, but 18 were put to flight by Israel. David slew seven hundred Aramaeans in chariots and forty thousand horsemen, mortally wounding Shobach, who died on the field. When all the vassal kings of 19 Hadadezer saw that they had been worsted by Israel, they sued for peace and submitted to the Israelites. The Aramaeans never dared help the Am-monites again.

AT THE TURN OF THE YEAR, WHEN KINGS **11** take the field, David sent Joab out with his other officers and all the Israelite forces, and they ravaged Ammon and laid siege to Rabbah, while David remained in Jerusalem. One evening David got up from his 2 couch and, as he walked about on the roof of the palace, he saw from there a woman bathing, and she was very beautiful. He sent to inquire who she 3

a Or altars.

king defeated by Saul (1 Sam. ch. 11). Perhaps David's earlier friendship was based on their mutual enmity toward Saul. **6:** *Aramaeans:* see 8.3–10. They wished to prevent David from gaining control of the north-south trade routes east of the Jordan, a source of considerable wealth. **7:** *The fighting men:* the professional army. In v. 17 David drafts additional forces. **19:** The *vassal kings* were often little more than chiefs of tribes; see 1 Kgs.20.1. **11.1:** Having won the battles in the field, David now seeks to capture *Rabbah* itself, the capital city of the Ammonites.
11.2–27: David, Bathsheba, and Uriah. The story of intrigue and violence in David's family now begins in earnest. His ensuing setbacks are interpreted as the fruit of his sin here. **2–5:** The relation to *Bathsheba* is passed over briefly; it is the relation to *Uriah,* her husband, that

was, and the answer came, 'It must be Bathsheba daughter of Eliam and wife 4 of Uriah the Hittite.' So he sent messengers to fetch her, and when she came to him, he had intercourse with her, though she was still being purified after her period, and then she went 5 home. She conceived, and sent word to 6 David that she was pregnant. David ordered Joab to send Uriah the Hittite to him. So Joab sent him to David, 7 and when he arrived, David asked him for news of Joab and the troops and how 8 the campaign was going; and then said to him, 'Go down to your house and wash your feet after your journey.' As he left the palace, a present from the 9 king followed him. But Uriah did not return to his house; he lay down by the palace gate with the king's slaves. 10 David heard that Uriah had not gone home, and said to him, 'You have had a long journey, why did you not go 11 home?' Uriah answered David, 'Israel and Judah are under canvas,*b* and so is the Ark, and my lord Joab and your majesty's officers are camping in the open; how can I go home to eat and drink and to sleep with my wife? By 12 your life, I cannot do this!' David then said to Uriah, 'Stay here another day, and tomorrow I will let you go.' So Uriah stayed in Jerusalem that day. 13 The next day David invited him to eat and drink with him and made him drunk. But in the evening Uriah went out to lie down in his blanket*c* among the king's slaves and did not go home.

14 The following morning David wrote a letter to Joab and sent Uriah with it. 15 He wrote in the letter, 'Put Uriah opposite the enemy where the fighting is fiercest and then fall back, and leave 16 him to meet his death.' Joab had been watching the city, and he stationed Uriah at a point where he knew they 17 would put up a stout fight. The men of the city sallied out and engaged Joab, and some of David's guards fell; Uriah the Hittite was also killed. Joab sent David a dispatch with all the 18 news of the battle and gave the mes- 19 senger these instructions: 'When you have finished your report to the king, if he is angry and asks, "Why did you 20 go so near the city during the fight? You must have known there would be shooting from the wall. Remember 21 who killed Abimelech son of Jerub-besheth. It was a woman who threw down an upper millstone on to him from the wall of Thebez and killed him! Why did you go so near the wall?"— if he asks this, then tell him, "Your servant Uriah the Hittite also is dead."'

So the messenger set out and, when 22 he came to David, he made his report as Joab had instructed. David was angry with Joab and said to the mes-senger, 'Why did you go so near the city during the fight? You must have known you would be struck down from the wall. Remember who killed Abime-lech son of Jerubbesheth. Was it not a woman who threw down an upper mill-stone on to him from the wall of Thebez and killed him? Why did you go near the wall?' He answered, 'The 23 enemy massed against us and sallied out into the open; we pressed them back as far as the gateway. There the 24 archers shot down at us from the wall and some of your majesty's men fell; and your servant Uriah the Hittite is dead.' David said to the man, 'Give 25 Joab this message: "Do not let this distress you—there is no knowing where the sword will strike; press home your attack on the city, and you will take it and raze it to the ground"; and tell him to take heart.'

When Uriah's wife heard that her 26 husband was dead, she mourned for

b under canvas: or at Succoth.
c in his blanket: or on his pallet.

---

forms the real drama. **4:** On menstrual purification, see Lev.15.19–24. **6–13:** David tries to get Uriah to spend a night at home with his wife, to cover up his deed. There is both sardonic humor and pathos in Uriah's stubborn loyalty to duty. **9:** Uriah avoids his wife in order to remain qualified for battle, for which sexual abstinence was required; see 1 Sam.21.5. **14–25:** David's general, Joab, was ever ready to shed blood in David's behalf; see 3.26–30; 18.9–15. **21:** *Abimelech*: The account is in Judg. ch.9. *Jerubbesheth* is a distorted form of Jerubbaal; see 2.8 n. and Judg.9.1. Apparently Joab took unwise risks in order to carry out David's plot. **26:** The period of mourning was short enough that Bathsheba's pregnancy could be

27 him; and when the period of mourning was over, David sent for her and brought her into his house. She became his wife and bore him a son. But what David had done was wrong in the eyes of the LORD.

12 The LORD sent Nathan the prophet to David, and when he entered his presence, he said to him, 'There were once two men in the same city, one 2 rich and the other poor. The rich man 3 had large flocks and herds, but the poor man had nothing of his own except one little ewe lamb. He reared it himself, and it grew up in his home with his own sons. It ate from his dish, drank from his cup and nestled in his arms; it was like a daughter to him. 4 One day a traveller came to the rich man's house, and he, too mean to take something from his own flocks and herds to serve to his guest, took the poor man's lamb and served up 5 that.' David was very angry, and burst out, 'As the LORD lives, the man who 6 did this deserves to die! He shall pay for the lamb four times over, because he has done this and shown no pity.' 7 Then Nathan said to David, 'You are the man. This is the word of the LORD the God of Israel to you: "I anointed you king over Israel, I rescued 8 you from the power of Saul, I gave you your master's daughter*d* and his wives to be your own, I gave you the daughters of Israel and Judah; and, had this not been enough, I would have 9 added other favours as great. Why then have you flouted the word of the LORD by doing what is wrong in my eyes? You have struck down Uriah the Hittite with the sword; the man himself you murdered by the sword of the Ammonites, and you have stolen his 10 wife. Now, therefore, since you have despised me and taken the wife of Uriah the Hittite to be your own wife, your family shall never again have rest 11 from the sword." This is the word of

the LORD: "I will bring trouble upon you from within your own family; I will take your wives and give them to another man before your eyes, and he will lie with them in broad daylight. What you did was done in 12 secret; but I will do this in the light of day for all Israel to see." ' David said to 13 Nathan, 'I have sinned against the LORD.' Nathan answered him, 'The LORD has laid on another the consequences of your sin: you shall not die, but, because in this you have 14 shown your contempt for the LORD,*e* the boy that will be born to you shall die.'

When Nathan had gone home, the 15 LORD struck the boy whom Uriah's wife had borne to David, and he was very ill. David prayed to God for the 16 child; he fasted and went in and spent the night fasting, lying on the ground. The older men of his household tried 17 to get him to rise from the ground, but he refused and would eat no food with them. On the seventh day the boy 18 died, and David's servants were afraid to tell him. 'While the boy was alive,' they said, 'we spoke to him, and he did not listen to us; how can we now tell him that the boy is dead? He may do something desperate.' But David 19 saw his servants whispering among themselves and guessed that the boy was dead. He asked, 'Is the boy dead?, and they answered, 'He is dead.' Then David rose from the 20 ground, washed and anointed himself, and put on fresh clothes; he entered the house of the LORD and prostrated himself there. Then he went home, asked for food to be brought, and when it was ready, he ate it. His servants 21 asked him, 'What is this? While the boy lived you fasted and wept for him, but now that he is dead you rise up and eat.' He answered, 'While the boy 22

d Prob. rdg.; Heb. house.
e the LORD: *prob. rdg.; Heb.* the enemies of the LORD.

---

attributed to her new marriage. **27:** The narrator's observation is most laconic and thereby the more forceful.

12.1–14: Nathan's rebuke and prophecy. An effective courtier had to know how to lead a king into judging himself; compare 14.1–23. Nathan's parable achieves this exceedingly well. **7–12:** This prophecy is the narrator's statement of the theme of his work. Vv. 11–12 may be a later addition.

12.15–25: Death of the first son and birth of Solomon. 16: *Lying on the ground:* probably at an

was still alive I fasted and wept, thinking, "It may be that the LORD will be gracious to me, and the boy may live." But now that he is dead, 23 why should I fast? Can I bring him back again? I shall go to him; he will not come back to me.' David consoled 24 Bathsheba his wife; he went to her and had intercourse with her, and she gave birth to a son and called him Solomon. And because the LORD loved him, he sent word through Nathan the 25 prophet that for the LORD's sake he should be given the name Jedidiah.*f*

26*g*   Joab attacked the Ammonite city of Rabbah and took the King's Pool. He 27 sent messengers to David with this report: 'I have attacked Rabbah and have taken the pool. You had better 28 muster the rest of the army yourself, besiege the city and take it; otherwise I shall take the city and the name to be proclaimed over it will be mine.' David accordingly mustered his 29 whole forces, marched to Rabbah, attacked it and took it. He took the 30 crown from the head of Milcom, which weighed a talent of gold and was set with a precious stone, and this he placed on his own head. He also removed a great quantity of booty from the city; he took its inhabitants 31 and set them to work with saws and other iron tools, sharp and toothed, and made them work in the brick-kilns. David did this to all the cities of the Ammonites; then he and all his people returned to Jerusalem.

Absalom's rebellion and other conflicts

13 NOW DAVID'S SON ABSALOM HAD A BEAU-tiful sister named Tamar, and Amnon,

another of David's sons, fell in love with her. Amnon was so distressed that 2 he fell sick with love for his half-sister; for he thought it an impossible thing to approach her since she was a virgin. But he had a friend named Jonadab, 3 son of David's brother Shimeah, who was a very shrewd man. He said to 4 Amnon, 'Why are you so low-spirited morning after morning, my lord? Will you not tell me?' So Amnon told him that he was in love with Tamar, his brother Absalom's sister. Jonadab said 5 to him, 'Take to your bed and pretend to be ill. When your father comes to visit you, say to him, "Please let my sister Tamar come and give me my food. Let her prepare it in front of me, so that I may watch her and then take it from her own hands."' So Amnon 6 lay down and pretended to be ill. When the king came to visit him, he said, 'Sir, let my sister Tamar come and make a few cakes in front of me, and serve them to me with her own hands.' So David sent a message to 7 Tamar in the palace: 'Go to your brother Amnon's quarters and prepare a meal for him.' Tamar came to her 8 brother and found him lying down; she took some dough and kneaded it, made the cakes in front of him and baked them. Then she took the pan 9 and turned them out before him. But Amnon refused to eat and ordered everyone out of the room. When they had all left, he said to Tamar, 'Bring 10 the food over to the recess so that I may eat from your own hands.' Tamar took the cakes she had made and brought them to Amnon in the recess. But when she offered them to 11

f That is Beloved of the LORD.
g Verses 26–31: cp. 1 Chr. 20. 1–3.

---

altar. **23:** The child would go down to Sheol (1 Sam.2.6 n.) from which he would not return (Job 7.9–10). **24–25:** The second son lived and was *loved* by the LORD. Solomon's second name reflects the practice of assuming a throne name at the accession; see 2 Kgs.23.34; 24.17; Jer.22.11.
  12.26–31: The conclusion of the Ammonite war. 26: *The King's Pool* was probably the city's water supply. After its capture, the city would shortly have to capitulate. **28:** Joab was constantly more solicitous of David's interests than his own. **30:** *Milcom* was the god of the Ammonites. A *talent* was over sixty pounds; this makes it hard to imagine on David's *head*.
  13.1–22: The rape of Tamar. The drama now turns to David's oldest sons, those from among whom the next king would presumably come. *Amnon* was the eldest son, Absalom the third, but the second son Chileab seems to have dropped from the scene, probably by an early death; compare 3.2–3. V. 13 indicates that marriage to a half-sister was not yet generally prohibited, as it was later; see Lev.18.9,11; Deut.27.22. **6:** The Heb. word for *cakes* is related to the noun "heart." Some special healing powers may have been attributed to them. **9:** *Amnon* might claim that the conditions for the healing ritual were not right until *everyone* was *out of the room*.

him, he caught hold of her and said,
10 'Come to bed with me, sister.' But she
answered, 'No, brother, do not dishonour me, we do not do such things
in Israel; do not behave like a beast.
13 Where could I go and hide my disgrace?—and you would sink as low
as any beast in Israel. Why not speak
to the king for me? He will not refuse
14 you leave to marry me.' He would not
listen, but overpowered her, dishonoured her and raped her.
15 Then Amnon was filled with utter
hatred for her; his hatred was stronger
than the love he had felt, and he said
16 to her, 'Get up and go.' She answered,
'No. It is wicked to send me away.
This is harder to bear than all you have
done to me.' He would not listen to
17 her, but summoned the boy who
attended him and said, 'Get rid of this
woman, put her out and bolt the door
18 after her.' She had on a long, sleeved
robe, the usual dress of unmarried
princesses; and the boy turned her out
19 and bolted the door. Tamar threw ashes
over her head, rent the long, sleeved
robe that she was wearing, put her
hands on her head and went away, sob-
20 bing as she went. Her brother Absalom
asked her, 'Has your brother Amnon
been with you? Keep this to yourself,
he is your brother; do not take it to
heart.' So Tamar remained in her
brother Absalom's house, desolate.
21 When King David heard the whole
story he was very angry; but he would
not hurt Amnon because he was his
22 eldest son and he loved him. Absalom
did not speak a single word to Amnon,
friendly or unfriendly; he hated him
for having dishonoured his sister
Tamar.
23 Two years later Absalom invited all
the king's sons to his sheep-shearing
24 at Baal-hazor, near Ephron.[h] He
approached the king and said, 'Sir,
I am shearing; will your majesty and
25 your servants come?' The king answered, 'No, my son, we must not all

come and be a burden to you.' Absalom pressed him, but David was still
unwilling to go and dismissed him with
his blessing. But Absalom said, 'If 26
you cannot, may my brother Amnon
come with us?' 'Why should he go with
you?' the king asked; but Absalom 27
pressed him again, so he let Amnon
and all the other princes go with him.
Then Absalom prepared a feast fit 28
for a king. He gave his servants these
orders: 'Bide your time, and when
Amnon is merry with wine I shall say
to you, "Strike." Then kill Amnon.
You have nothing to fear, these are my
orders; be bold and resolute.' Absalom's 29
servants did as he had told them,
whereupon all the king's sons mounted
their mules in haste and set off for
home.
While they were on their way, a 30
rumour reached David that Absalom
had murdered all the royal princes
and that not one was left alive. The 31
king stood up and rent his clothes and
then threw himself on the ground; all
his servants were standing round him
with their clothes rent. Then Jonadab, 32
son of David's brother Shimeah, said,
'Your majesty must not think that they
have killed all the young princes; only
Amnon is dead; Absalom has looked
black ever since Amnon ravished his
sister Tamar. Your majesty must not 33
pay attention to a mere rumour that
all the princes are dead; only Amnon
is dead.'
Absalom made good his escape. 34
Meanwhile the sentry looked up and
saw a crowd of people coming down
the hill from the direction of Horonaim.[i] He came and reported to the
king, 'I see men coming down the hill
from Horonaim.' Then Jonadab said 35
to the king, 'Here come the royal
princes, just as I said they would.'
As he finished speaking, the princes 36
came in and broke into loud lamenta-

h *Prob. rdg.; Heb.* Ephraim.
i *Prob. rdg.; Heb.* from a road behind him.

13.23–39: **Absalom's revenge. 23:** *Absalom* waits *two years* to allay suspicion, though David
may still suspect something; see v. 26. The princes, who are clearly adult men here, would have
received possessions in the realm from their father. Thus, Absalom has a farm *at Baal-hazor*.
The *sheep-shearing* was a time of festivity and potential violence; see Gen.31.19–54; 38.12–26;
1 Sam.25.4–13,36–38. **32:** *Jonadab*, having had a hand in the original deed of *Amnon*, vv. 3–5,
understands the situation and is not mislead by rumors. **34:** *Horonaim* means "the two horons,"

tions; the king and all his servants also wept bitterly.

47 But Absalom went to take refuge with Talmai son of Ammihur king of Geshur; and for a long while the 38 king mourned for Amnon. Absalom, having escaped to Geshur, stayed there 39 for three years; and David's heart went out to him with longing, for he became reconciled to the death of Amnon.

14 Joab son of Zeruiah saw that the 2 king's heart was set on Absalom, so he sent to Tekoah and fetched a wise woman. He said to her, 'Pretend to be a mourner; put on mourning, go without anointing yourself, and behave like a bereaved woman who has been 3 long in mourning. Then go to the king and repeat what I tell you.' He then told her exactly what she was to say. 4 When the woman from Tekoah came into the king's presence, she threw herself, face downwards, on the ground and did obeisance, and cried, 5 'Help, your majesty!' The king asked, 'What is it?' She answered, 'O sir, I 6 am a widow; my husband is dead. I had two sons; they came to blows out in the country where there was no one to part them, and one of them struck 7 the other and killed him. Now, sir, the kinsmen have risen against me and they all cry, "Hand over the man who has killed his brother, so that we can put him to death for taking his brother's life, and so cut off the succession." If they do this, they will stamp out my last live ember and leave my husband no name and no descendant upon 8 earth.' 'Go home,' said the king to the woman, 'and I will settle your case.' 9 But the woman continued, 'The guilt be on me, your majesty, and on my father's house; let the king and his 10 throne be blameless.' The king said, 'If anyone says anything more to you,

bring him to me and he shall never 11 molest you again.' Then the woman went on, 'Let your majesty call upon the LORD your God, to prevent his kinsmen bound to vengeance from doing their worst and destroying my son.' The king swore, 'As the LORD lives, not a hair of your son's head shall fall to the ground.'

The woman then said, 'May I add 12 one word more, your majesty?' 'Say on', said the king. So she continued, 13 'How then could it enter your head to do this same wrong to God's people? Out of your own mouth, your majesty, you condemn yourself: you have refused to bring back the man you have banished. We shall all 14 die; we shall be like water that is spilt on the ground and lost; but God will spare the man who does not set himself to keep the outlaw in banishment. I came to say this to your majesty 15 because the people have threatened me. I thought, "If I can only speak to the king, perhaps he will attend to my case; for he will listen, and he will save 16 me from the man who is seeking to cut off me and my son together from Israel, God's own possession." I 17 thought too that the words of my lord the king would be a comfort to me; for your majesty is like the angel of God and can decide between right and wrong. The LORD your God be with you!' Then the king said to the 18 woman, 'Tell me no lies: I shall now ask you a question.' 'Speak on, your majesty', she said. So he asked, 'Is the 19 hand of Joab behind you in all this?' 'Your life upon it, sir!' she answered; 'when your majesty asks a question, there is no way round it, right or left. Yes, your servant Joab did prompt me; it was he who put the whole story into my mouth. He did it to give a new 20

Upper Beth-horon and Lower Beth-horon, a few miles northwest of Jerusalem. **37:** *Talmai* was Absalom's maternal grandfather; see 3.3. **39:** David's favor shifted to whichever son was in line for the throne.

14.1–24: Joab secures Absalom's return. The king is induced to give in to his true feelings toward Absalom and recall the prince to Jerusalem. **1:** *A wise woman* was skilled in speech, especially in decision making; see the important position of the wise woman in 20.14–22 and Solomon's wisdom in 1 Kgs.3.16–28. **8:** David is reluctant to use his royal authority to override tribal customs concerning bloodshed. The woman persists in vv. 9–11, and the king finally swears to protect the son. **12–17:** In a series of hints and flattery, the *woman* reveals to David that her case was a parable of Absalom and Amnon; see v. 20; 12.1–14 n.; 19.27.

turn to this affair. Your majesty is as wise as the angel of God and knows all that goes on in the land.'

21 The king said to Joab, 'You have my consent; go and fetch back the young 22 man Absalom.' Then Joab humbly prostrated himself, took leave of the king with a blessing and said, 'Now I know that I have found favour with your majesty, because you have granted 23 my humble petition.' Joab went at once to Geshur and brought Absalom to 24 Jerusalem, but the king said, 'Let him go to his own quarters; he shall not come into my presence.' So Absalom went to his own quarters and did not enter the king's presence.

25 No one in all Israel was so greatly admired for his beauty as Absalom; he was without flaw from the crown 26 of his head to the sole of his foot. His hair, when he cut his hair (as he had to do every year, for he found it heavy), weighed two hundred shekels by the 27 royal standard. Three sons were born to Absalom, and a daughter named Tamar, who was a very beautiful woman.

28 Absalom remained in Jerusalem for two whole years without entering the 29 king's presence. He summoned Joab to send a message by him to the king, but Joab refused to come; he sent for him a second time, but he still refused. 30 Then Absalom said to his servants, 'You know that Joab has a field next to mine with barley growing in it; go and set fire to it.' So Absalom's servants 31 set fire to the field. Joab promptly came to Absalom in his own quarters and said to him, 'Why have your 32 servants set fire to my field?' Absalom answered Joab, 'I had sent for you to come here, so that I could ask you to give the king this message from me: "Why did I leave Geshur? It would be better for me if I were still there. Let me

now come into your majesty's presence and, if I have done any wrong, put me to death."' When Joab went to 33 the king and told him, he summoned Absalom, who came and prostrated himself humbly before the king; and he greeted Absalom with a kiss.

AFTER THIS, ABSALOM PROVIDED HIM- 15 self with a chariot and horses and an escort of fifty men. He made it a 2 practice to rise early and stand beside the road which runs through the city gate. He would hail every man who had a case to bring before the king for judgement and would ask him what city he came from. When he answered, 'I come, sir, from such and such a tribe of Israel', Absalom would say to him, 'I 3 can see that you have a very good case, but you will get no hearing from the king.' And he would add, 'If only I 4 were appointed judge in the land, it would be my business to see that every-one who brought a suit or a claim got justice from me.' Whenever a man 5 approached to prostrate himself, Absalom would stretch out his hand, take hold of him and kiss him. By 6 behaving like this to every Israelite who sought the king's justice, Absalom stole the affections of the Israelites.

At the end of four years, Absalom 7 said to the king, 'May I have leave now to go to Hebron to fulfil a vow there that I made to the LORD? For 8 when I lived in Geshur, in Aram, I made this vow: "If the LORD brings me back to Jerusalem, I will become a wor-shipper of the LORD in Hebron."' 9 The king answered, 'Certainly you may go'; so he set off for Hebron at once. 10 Absalom sent runners through all the tribes of Israel with this message: 'As soon as you hear the sound of the trumpet, then say, "Absalom is king in Hebron."' Two hundred men 11

14.25–33: Absalom's restoration. Absalom finds a way to regain full standing in David's court. **26:** *Two hundred shekels* would be just over four pounds. **28–33:** *Absalom* is, if anything, even more strongheaded than Amnon was. The now aged *king* gives in.

15.1–12: Absalom's rebellion. Absalom would have become king on David's death. He either became too impatient or was embittered by the circumstances of the preceding years. **1:** Absalom's *chariot, horses,* and *escort* give him the airs of a king-to-be. **7–12:** These *four years* extend the Absalom story over eleven years; see 13.23,39; 14.28. By moving from *Hebron,* the former capital of Judah, Absalom made sure David would not have his old territory to retreat to. **10:** *The trumpet* was normally sounded at the coronation of a new king; see 1 Kgs. 1.39. **12:** *Giloh* was a village near Hebron.

accompanied Absalom from Jerusalem; they were invited and went in all innocence, knowing nothing of the
12 affair. Absalom also sent to summon Ahithophel the Gilonite, David's counsellor, from Giloh his city, where he was offering the customary sacrifices. The conspiracy gathered strength, and Absalom's supporters increased in number.

13 When news reached David that the men of Israel had transferred their
14 allegiance to Absalom, he said to those who were with him in Jerusalem, 'We must get away at once; or there will be no escape from Absalom for any of us. Make haste, or else he will soon be upon us and bring disaster on us, showing
15 no mercy to anyone in the city.' The king's servants said to him, 'As your majesty thinks best; we are ready.'

16 When the king departed, all his household followed him except ten concubines, whom he left in charge
17 of the palace. At the Far House the king and all the people who were with
18 him halted. His own servants then stood*j* beside him, while the Kerethite and Pelethite guards and Ittai*k* with the six hundred Gittites under him marched
19 past the king. The king said to Ittai the Gittite, 'Are you here too? Why are you coming with us? Go back and stay with the new king, for you are a foreigner and, what is more, an exile
20 from your own country. You came only yesterday, and today must you be compelled to share my wanderings? I do not know where I am going. Go back home and take your countrymen with you; and may the LORD ever be
21 your steadfast friend.' Ittai swore to the king, 'As the LORD lives, your life upon it, wherever you may be, in life or in death, I, your servant, will be
22 there.' David said to Ittai, 'It is well, march on!' So Ittai the Gittite marched on with his whole company and all the
23 dependants who were with him. The

whole country-side re-echoed with their weeping. And the king remained standing*l* while all the people crossed the gorge of the Kidron before him, by way of the olive-tree in the wilderness.*m*

24 Zadok also was there with all the Levites; they were carrying the Ark of the Covenant of God, which they set down beside Abiathar*n* until all the people had passed out of the city.
25 But the king said to Zadok, 'Take the Ark of God back to the city. If I find favour with the LORD, he will bring me back and will let me see the Ark and its
26 dwelling-place again. But if he says he does not want me, then here I am; let him do what he pleases with me.'
27 The king went on to say to Zadok the priest, 'Can you make good use of your eyes? You may safely go back to the city, you and Abiathar,*o* and take with you the two young men, Ahimaaz your son and Abiathar's son Jonathan.
28 Do not forget: I will linger at the Fords of the Wilderness until you can send word to me.' Then Zadok and Abiathar
29 took the Ark of God back to Jerusalem and stayed there.

30 David wept as he went up the slope of the Mount of Olives; he was bareheaded and went bare-foot. The people with him all had their heads uncovered and wept as they went.
31 David had been told that Ahithophel was among the conspirators with Absalom, and he prayed, 'Frustrate, O LORD, the counsel of Ahithophel.'
32 As David was approaching the top of the ridge where it was the custom to prostrate oneself to God, Hushai the Archite was there to meet him with his tunic rent and earth on his head.
33 David said to him, 'If you come with

j Prob. rdg.; Heb. passed.
k and Ittai: prob. rdg.; Heb. om.
l Prob. rdg.; Heb. passing.
m by way . . . wilderness: prob. rdg.; Heb. obscure.
n beside Abiathar: prob. rdg.; Heb. and Abiathar went up.
o you and Abiathar: prob. rdg., cp. verse 29; Heb. om.

15.13–16.14: David's flight from Jerusalem. The narrative dwells at some length on this action. The question of loyalty to David is developed through a series of scenes. **16:** On the *ten concubines*, see 16.21–23. **17:** *The Far House* was a boundary point of the city. **18:** The international makeup of the royal court is conspicuous here. *Kerethite:* Cretan; *Pelethite:* Philistine; *Ittai:* a Philistine banished from his own city, as was David in the period of Saul's reign. **24:** *All the Levites* is a later addition to conform to the theory that only Levites carried the Ark; see 1 Chr.15.12–15. **30:** David leads a mourning procession up *the Mount of Olives*. **32:** This sanctuary on the south side of the Mount of Olives was later regarded as idolatrous;

34 me you will only be a hindrance; but you can help me to frustrate Ahithophel's plans if you go back to the city and say to Absalom, "I will be your majesty's servant; up to now I have been your father's servant, and now I 35 will be yours." You will have with you, as you know, the priests Zadok and Abiathar; tell them everything that 36 you hear in the king's household. They have with them Zadok's son Ahimaaz and Abiathar's son Jonathan, and through them you may pass on to me 37 everything you hear.' So Hushai, David's friend, came to the city as Absalom was entering Jerusalem.

16 When David had moved on a little from the top of the ridge, he was met by Ziba the servant of Mephibosheth, who had with him a pair of asses saddled and loaded with two hundred loaves, a hundred clusters of raisins, a hundred bunches of summer fruit, 2 and a flagon of wine. The king said to him, 'What are you doing with these?' Ziba answered, 'The asses are for the king's family to ride on, the bread and the summer fruit are for the servants to eat, and the wine for anyone who becomes exhausted in the 3 wilderness.' The king asked, 'Where is your master's grandson?' 'He is staying in Jerusalem,' said Ziba, 'for he thought that the Israelites might now restore 4 to him his grandfather's throne.' The king said to Ziba, 'You shall have everything that belongs to Mephibosheth.' Ziba said, 'I am your humble servant, sir; may I continue to stand well with you.'

5 As King David approached Bahurim, a man of Saul's family, whose name was Shimei son of Gera, came 6 out, cursing as he came. He showered stones right and left on David and on all the king's servants and on every-7 one, soldiers and people alike. This is what Shimei said as he cursed him: 'Get out, get out, you scoundrel! you

man of blood! The LORD has taken 8 vengeance on you for the blood of the house of Saul whose throne you stole, and he has given the kingdom to your son Absalom. You murderer, see how your crimes have overtaken you!'

Then Abishai son of Zeruiah said to 9 the king, 'Why let this dead dog curse your majesty? I will go across and knock off his head.' But the king said, 'What 10 has this to do with you, you sons of Zeruiah? If he curses and if the LORD has told him to curse David, who can question it?' David said to Abishai and 11 to all his servants, 'If my son, my own son, is out to kill me, who can wonder at this Benjamite? Let him be, let him curse; for the LORD has told him to do it. But perhaps the LORD will 12 mark my sufferings and bestow a blessing on me in place of the curse laid on me this day.' David and his 13 men continued on their way, and Shimei moved along the ridge of the hill parallel to David's path, cursing as he went and hurling stones across the valley at him and kicking up the dust. When the king and all the people 14 with him reached the Jordan, they were worn out; and they refreshed themselves there.

By now Absalom and all his Israelites 15 had reached Jerusalem, and Ahithophel with him. When Hushai the 16 Archite, David's friend, met Absalom he said to him, 'Long live the king! Long live the king!' But Absalom 17 retorted, 'Is this your loyalty to your friend? Why did you not go with him?' Hushai answered Absalom, 'Because I 18 mean to attach myself to the man chosen by the LORD, by this people, and by all the men of Israel, and with him I will remain. After all, whom 19 ought I to serve? Should I not serve the son? I will serve you as I have served your father.' Then Absalom 20 said to Ahithophel, 'Give us your advice: how shall we act?' Ahithophel 21

---

compare 1 Kgs.11.7; 2 Kgs.23.13–14. **16.1:** *Ziba:* see ch. 9. **3–4:** This conflicts with *Mephibosheth's* own story in 19.24–30, where David allows him the benefit of the doubt. **8:** The *blood* Shimei refers to may be that of 21.1–14. **10–12:** See David's attitude in 15.25–26.

16.15–17.23: Absalom forms a strategy. The king judged between alternative courses of action proposed by wise counselors. *Hushai,* actually still loyal to David (15.32–34), and *Ahithophel* compete as counselors. **16–19:** Such deceit was assumed and not particularly condemned in court intrigues of this kind. **20–22:** On the importance of royal concubines, see

answered, 'Have intercourse with your father's concubines whom he left in charge of the palace. Then all Israel will come to hear that you have given great cause of offence to your father, and this will confirm the resolution of 22 your followers.' So they set up a tent for Absalom on the roof, and he lay with his father's concubines in the sight 23 of all Israel. In those days a man would seek counsel of Ahithophel as readily as he might make an inquiry of the word of God; that was how Ahithophel's counsel was esteemed by David and Absalom.

17 Ahithophel said to Absalom, 'Let me pick twelve thousand men, and I 2 will pursue David tonight. I shall overtake him when he is tired and dispirited; I will cut him off from his people and they will all scatter; and I 3 shall kill no one but the king. I will bring all the people over to you as a bride is brought to her husband. It is only one man's life that you are seeking; the rest of the people will be unharmed.' 4 Absalom and all the elders of Israel 5 approved of Ahithophel's advice; but Absalom said, 'Summon Hushai the Archite and let us hear what he too 6 has to say.' Hushai came, and Absalom told him all that Ahithophel had said and asked him, 'Shall we do what he says? If not, say what you think.' 7 Hushai said to Absalom, 'For once the counsel that Ahithophel has given 8 is not good. You know', he went on, 'that your father and the men with him are hardened warriors and savage as a bear in the wilds robbed of her cubs. Your father is an old campaigner and will not spend the night with the main 9 body; even now he will be lying hidden in a pit or in some such place. Then if any of your men are killed at the outset, anyone who hears the news will say, "Disaster has over-10 taken the followers of Absalom." The courage of the most resolute and lion-hearted will melt away, for all Israel knows that your father is a man of war and has determined men with 11 him. My advice is this. Wait until the

whole of Israel, from Dan to Beer-sheba, is gathered about you, countless as grains of sand on the sea-shore, and then you shall march with them in person. Then we shall come upon him 12 somewhere, wherever he may be, and descend on him like dew falling on the ground, and not a man of his family or of his followers will be left alive. If 13 he retreats into a city, all Israel will bring ropes to that city, and we will drag it into a ravine until not a stone can be found on the site.' Absalom 14 and all the men of Israel said, 'Hushai the Archite gives us better advice than Ahithophel.' It was the LORD's purpose to frustrate Ahithophel's good advice and so bring disaster upon Absalom.

Hushai told Zadok and Abiathar 15 the priests all the advice that Ahitho-phel had given to Absalom and the elders of Israel, and also his own. 'Now send quickly to David,' he said, 16 'and warn him not to spend the night at the Fords of the Wilderness but to cross the river at once, before a blow can be struck at the king and his followers.' Jonathan and Ahimaaz 17 were waiting at En-rogel, and a servant girl would go and tell them what happened and they would pass it on to King David; for they could not risk being seen entering the city. But this 18 time a lad saw them and told Absalom; so the two of them hurried to the house of a man in Bahurim. He had a pit in his courtyard, and they climbed down into it. The man's wife took a covering, 19 spread it over the mouth of the pit and strewed grain over it, and no one was any the wiser. Absalom's servants 20 came to the house and asked the woman, 'Where are Ahimaaz and Jonathan?' She answered, 'They went beyond the pool.' The men searched but could not find them; so they went back to Jerusalem. When they 21 had gone the two climbed out of the pit and went off to report to King David and said, 'Over the water at once, make haste!', and they told him Ahithophel's plan against him. So 22

3.7 n. **17.1–14:** Ahithophel's advice was best, but Hushai's prevailed, since it was *the LORD's purpose* (v. 14) to defeat Absalom. **15–22:** David's escape is made good by those still loyal to

David and all his company began at once to cross the Jordan; by daybreak there was not one who had not reached the other bank.

23 When Ahithophel saw that his advice had not been taken he saddled his ass, went straight home to his own city, gave his last instructions to his household, and hanged himself. So he died and was buried in his father's grave.

24 By the time that Absalom had crossed the Jordan with the Israelites, David 25 was already at Mahanaim. Absalom had appointed Amasa as commander-in-chief instead of Joab; he was the son of a man named Ithra, an Ishmaelite, by Abigal daughter of Nahash and sister to Joab's mother Zeruiah. 26 The Israelites and Absalom camped 27 in the district of Gilead. When David came to Mahanaim, he was met by Shobi son of Nahash from the Ammonite town Rabbah, Machir son of Ammiel from Lo-debar, and Barzillai 28 the Gileadite from Rogelim, bringing mattresses and blankets, bowls and jugs.[p] They brought also wheat and barley, meal and parched grain, beans 29 and lentils, honey and curds, sheep and fat cattle, and offered them to David and his people to eat, knowing that the people must be hungry and thirsty and weary in the wilderness.

18 David mustered the people who were with him, and appointed officers over units of a thousand and a hun- 2 dred. Then he divided the army in three, one division under the command of Joab, one under Joab's brother Abishai son of Zeruiah, and the third under Ittai the Gittite. The king announced to the army that he was coming out himself with them to 3 battle. But they said, 'No, you must not come out; if we turn and run, no one will take any notice, nor will they, even if half of us are killed; but you are worth ten thousand of us, and it would be better now for you to remain

in the city in support.' 'I will do what 4 you think best', answered the king; and he then stood beside the gate, and the army marched past in their units of a thousand and a hundred. The king gave orders to Joab, Abishai, 5 and Ittai: 'Deal gently with the young man Absalom for my sake.' The whole army heard the king giving all his officers this order to spare Absalom.

The army took the field against the 6 Israelites and the battle was fought in the forest of Ephron.[q] There the Israel- 7 ites were routed before the onslaught of David's men; so great was the rout that twenty thousand men fell that day. The fighting spread over the whole 8 country-side, and the forest took toll of more people that day than the sword.

Now some of David's men caught 9 sight of Absalom. He was riding a mule and, as it passed beneath a great oak,[r] his head was caught in its boughs; he found himself in mid air and the mule went on from under him. One 10 of the men who saw it went and told Joab, 'I saw Absalom hanging from an oak.' While the man was telling him, 11 Joab broke in, 'You saw him? Why did you not strike him to the ground then and there? I would have given you ten pieces of silver and a belt.' The man 12 answered, 'If you were to put in my hands a thousand pieces of silver, I would not lift a finger against the king's son; for we all heard the king giving orders to you and Abishai and Ittai that whoever finds himself near the young man Absalom must take great care of him. If I had dealt him a 13 treacherous blow, the king would soon have known, and you would have kept well out of it.' 'That is a lie!' said Joab. 14 'I will make a start and show you.'[s] So he picked up three stout sticks and drove them against Absalom's chest

[p] bringing . . . jugs: *prob. rdg.*; *Heb.* a couch, bowls and a potter's vessel.
[q] *Prob. rdg.*; *Heb.* Ephraim.   [r] *Or* terebinth.
[s] I will . . . show you: *or* I can waste no more time on you like this.

him at Jerusalem. **23:** *Ahithophel's* suicide is mentioned immediately after David has made good his escape, since that was the final frustration of his counsel.

17.24–19.8: The battle in Gilead and Absalom's death. 27: Many of David's supporters were non-Israelites. On *Nahash*, see 10.2 n.; on *Machir*, see 9.4; on *Barzillai*, see 19.31–39. **18.1–4:** The king's safety was decisive; compare 21.15–17. **5:** David's excessive attachment to successive favorite sons was one of his weaknesses; see 13.21,39. **6:** *Forest:* in ancient times there were forests on the Gilead highlands. **9:** Absalom's great head of hair (14.26) may have helped get him caught in the tree. **14:** *Against Absalom's chest,* more literally rendered, is "in Absalom's

15 while he was held fast in the tree and still alive. Then ten young men who were Joab's armour bearers closed in on Absalom, struck at him, and killed 16 him. Joab sounded the trumpet, and the army came back from the pursuit of Israel because he had called it off. 17 They took Absalom's body and flung it into a great pit in the forest, and raised over it a huge pile of stones. The Israelites all fled to their homes.

18 The pillar in the King's Vale had been set up by Absalom in his lifetime, for he said, 'I have no son to carry on my name.' He had named the pillar after himself; and to this day it is called Absalom's Monument.

19 Ahimaaz son of Zadok said, 'Let me run and take the news to the king that the LORD has avenged him and deliv-20 ered him from his enemies.' But Joab replied, 'This is no day for you to be the bearer of news. Another day you may have news to carry, but not today, 21 because the king's son is dead.' Joab told a Cushite to go and report to the king what he had seen. The Cushite bowed low before Joab and set off 22 running. Ahimaaz pleaded again with Joab, 'Come what may,' he said, 'let me run after the Cushite.' 'Why should you, my son?' asked Joab. 'You will 23 get no reward for your news.' 'Come what may,' he said, 'I will run.' 'Go, then', said Joab. So Ahimaaz ran by the road through the Plain of the Jordan and outstripped the Cushite.

24 David was sitting between the two gates when the watchman went up to the roof of the gatehouse by the wall and, looking out, saw a man running 25 alone. The watchman called to the king and told him. 'If he is alone,' said the king, 'then he has news.' The man 26 came nearer and nearer. Then the watchman saw another man running. He called down to the gate-keeper and said, 'Look, there is another man running alone.' The king said, 'He too

brings news.' The watchman said, 'I 27 see by the way he runs that the first runner is Ahimaaz son of Zadok.' The king said, 'He is a good fellow and shall earn the reward for good news.' Ahim- 28 aaz called out to the king, 'All is well!' He bowed low before him and said, 'Blessed be the LORD your God who has given into your hands the men who rebelled against your majesty.' The 29 king asked, 'Is all well with the young man Absalom?' Ahimaaz answered, 'Sir, your servant Joab sent me,*t* I saw a great commotion, but I did not know what had happened.' The king told him 30 to stand on one side; so he turned aside and stood there. Then the 31 Cushite came in and said, 'Good news, your majesty! The LORD has avenged you this day on all those who rebelled against you.' The king said to the 32 Cushite, 'Is all well with the young man Absalom?' The Cushite answered, 'May all the king's enemies and all rebels who would do you harm be as that young man is.' The king was deeply 33 moved and went up to the roof-chamber over the gate and wept, crying out as he went, 'O, my son! Absalom my son, my son Absalom! If only I had died instead of you! O Absalom, my son, my son.'

Joab was told that the king was **19** weeping and mourning for Absalom; and that day victory was turned to 2 mourning for the whole army, because they heard how the king grieved for his son; they stole into the city like men 3 ashamed to show their faces after a defeat in battle. The king hid his face 4 and cried aloud, 'My son Absalom; O 5 Absalom, my son, my son.' But Joab came into the king's quarters and said to him, 'You have put to shame this day all your servants, who have saved you and your sons and daughters, your wives and your concubines. You love 6

t Sir . . . sent me: prob. rdg.; Heb. At the sending of Joab the king's servant and your servant.

heart." Joab, knowing that David sometimes let his sentiment override his best judgment, dispatched Absalom without hesitation. **18:** This verse reflects popular tradition about a *pillar in the King's Vale,* the Kidron Valley just east of Jerusalem (contrast 14.27). **19:** *Ahimaaz:* see 15.27; 17.17–21. **21:** That *a Cushite,* from upper Egypt, was in David's army is further evidence of its international character. **29:** *Ahimaaz* was more discreet about Absalom's death than the Cushite (v. 32). **19.1–8:** Joab persuaded David to take a realistic attitude. David did not reward Joab very graciously; see v. 13.

those that hate you and hate those that love you; you have made us feel, officers and men alike, that we are nothing to you; for it is plain that if Absalom were still alive and all of us dead, you 7 would be content. Now go at once and give your servants some encouragement; if you refuse, I swear by the LORD that not a man will stay with you tonight, and that would be a worse disaster than any you have suffered 8 since your earliest days.' Then the king rose and took his seat in the gate; and when the army was told that the king was sitting in the gate, they all appeared before him.

Various events of David's reign

MEANWHILE THE ISRAELITES HAD ALL 9 scattered to their homes. Throughout all the tribes of Israel people were discussing it among themselves and saying, 'The king has saved us from our enemies and freed us from the power of the Philistines, and now he has fled the country because of Absalom. 10 But Absalom, whom we anointed king, has fallen in battle; so now why have we no plans for bringing the king back? 11 What all Israel was saying came to the king's ears.*u* So he sent word to Zadok and Abiathar the priests: 'Ask the elders of Judah why they should be the last to bring the king back to his 12 palace. Tell them, "You are my brothers, my flesh and my blood; why 13 are you last to bring me back?" And tell Amasa, "You are my own flesh and blood. You shall be my commander-in-chief, so help me God, for the rest of your life in place of Joab."' 14 David's message won all hearts in Judah, and they sent to the king, urging him to return with all his men.
15   So the king came back to the Jordan; and the men of Judah came to Gilgal

to meet him and escort him across the river. Shimei son of Gera the Ben- 16 jamite from Bahurim hastened down among the men of Judah to meet King David with a thousand men from 17 Benjamin; Ziba was there too, the servant of Saul's family, with his fifteen sons and twenty servants. They rushed into the Jordan under the king's eyes and crossed to and fro conveying his 18 household in order to win his favour. Shimei son of Gera, when he had crossed the river, fell down before the king and said to him, 'I beg your 19 majesty not to remember how disgracefully your servant behaved when your majesty left Jerusalem; do not hold it against me or take it to heart. For I humbly acknowledge that I did 20 wrong, and today I am the first of all the house of Joseph to come down to meet your majesty.' But Abishai son of 21 Zeruiah objected, 'Ought not Shimei to be put to death because he cursed the LORD's anointed prince?' David 22 answered, 'What right have you, you sons of Zeruiah, to oppose me today? Why should any man be put to death this day in Israel? I know now that I am king of Israel.' Then the king said to 23 Shimei, 'You shall not die', and confirmed it with an oath.

Saul's grandson Mephibosheth also 24 went down to meet the king. He had not dressed his feet, combed his beard or washed his clothes, from the day the king went out until he returned victorious. When he came from Jerusa- 25 lem to meet the king, David said to him, 'Why did you not go with me, Mephibosheth?' He answered, 'Sir, 26 my servant deceived me; I did intend to harness my ass and ride with the king (for I am lame), but his stories set your 27 majesty against me. Your majesty is like the angel of God; you must do

---

u What . . . ears: prob. rdg.; Heb. has these words after back to his palace and adds to his palace.

19.9–43: Bringing David back. Once it was clear that Absalom's rebellion had failed, the issue became the reconciliation of the warring factions. Israel and Judah—here treated as two distinct groups—and also individual petitioners had to make their peace with the king who was clearly going to regain his throne. **11–15:** David takes the side of Judah against Israel. **13:** David bribes *Amasa*, Absalom's commander-in-chief; see 17.25. **16–39:** David makes very lenient settlements with those whose loyalty during the rebellion was questionable: *Shimei son of Gera*, who had cursed David at his departure (16.5–13), vv. 16–23; *Mephibosheth*, son of Jonathan, whose loyalty had been challenged by his servant *Ziba* (16.1–4), vv. 24–36; for his old friend *Barzillai*, the only question was how to reward his loyalty (17.27), vv. 31–39.

28 what you think right. My father's whole family, one and all, deserved to die at your majesty's hands, but you gave me, your servant, my place at your table. What further favour can I expect of 29 the king?' The king answered, 'You have said enough. My decision is that you and Ziba are to share the estate.' 30 Mephibosheth said, 'Let him have it all, now that your majesty has come home victorious.'

31 　　Barzillai the Gileadite too had come down from Rogelim, and he went as far as the Jordan with the king to send 32 him on his way. Now Barzillai was very old, eighty years of age; it was he who had provided for the king while he was at Mahanaim, for he was a man of high 33 standing. The king said to Barzillai, 'Cross over with me and I will provide for your old age in my household in 34 Jerusalem.' Barzillai answered, 'Your servant is far too old to go up with your 35 majesty to Jerusalem. I am already eighty; and I cannot tell good from bad. I cannot taste what I eat or drink; I cannot hear the voices of men and women singing. Why should I be a burden any longer on your majesty? 36 Your servant will attend the king for a short way across the Jordan; and why should the king reward me so hand-37 somely? Let me go back and end my days in my own city near the grave of my father and mother. Here is my son Kimham; let him cross over with your majesty, and do for him what you 38 think best.' The king answered, 'Kimham shall cross with me and I will do for him whatever you think best; and I will do for you whatever you ask.' 39 　　All the people crossed the Jordan while the king waited. The king then kissed Barzillai and gave him his blessing. Barzillai went back to his own 40 home; the king crossed over to Gilgal, Kimham with him. All the people of Judah escorted the king over the river, and so did half the people of Israel. 41 　　The men of Israel came to the king in a body and said, 'Why should our brothers of Judah have got possession of the king's person by joining King David's own men and then escorting him and his household across the Jordan?' The men of Judah replied, 42 'Because his majesty is our near kinsman. Why should you resent it? Have we eaten at the king's expense? Have we received any gifts?' The men of Israel 43 answered, 'We have ten times your interest in the king and, what is more, we are senior to you; why do you disparage us? Were we not the first to speak of bringing the king back?' The men of Judah used language even fiercer than the men of Israel.

　　There happened to be a man there, **20** a scoundrel named Sheba son of Bichri, a man of Benjamin. He blew the trumpet and cried out:

What share have we in David?
　We have no lot in the son of Jesse.
Away to your homes, O Israel.

The men of Israel all left David, to 2 follow Sheba son of Bichri, but the men of Judah stood by their king and followed him from the Jordan to Jerusalem.

　　When David came home to Jeru-3 salem he took the ten concubines whom he had left in charge of the palace and put them under guard; he maintained them but did not have intercourse with them. They were kept in confinement to the day of their death, widowed in the prime of life.

　　The king said to Amasa, 'Call up the 4 men of Judah and appear before me again in three days' time.' So Amasa 5 went to call up the men of Judah, but it took longer than the time fixed by the king. David said to Abishai, 'Sheba 6 son of Bichri will give us more trouble than Absalom; take the royal bodyguard and follow him closely. If he has occupied some fortified cities, he may escape us.' Abishai was followed 7 by Joab[v] with the Kerethite and Pelethite guards and all the fighting men; they left Jerusalem in pursuit of Sheba son of Bichri. When they reached the 8

v Abishai . . . Joab: *prob. rdg.; Heb.* Some men of Joab followed him.

20.1–22: Another rebellion of Israel. A rebellion of the Israelite tribes, called for by the Benjaminite *Sheba*, is portrayed as a sequel to the disagreements over the return of David. **1:** This call to rebellion is used again in 1 Kgs.12.16. **8–13:** Joab again resorts to bloodshed,

great stone in Gibeon, Amasa came towards them. Joab was wearing his tunic and over it a belt supporting a sword in its scabbard. He came for-
9 ward, concealing his treachery, and said to Amasa, 'I hope you are well, my brother', and with his right hand he grasped Amasa's beard to kiss him.
10 Amasa was not on his guard against the sword in Joab's hand. Joab struck him with it in the belly and his entrails poured out to the ground; he did not strike a second blow, for Amasa was dead. Joab and his brother Abishai went on in pursuit of Sheba son of
11 Bichri. One of Joab's young men stood over Amasa and called out, 'Follow Joab, all who are for Joab and for
12 David!' Amasa's body lay soaked in blood in the middle of the road, and when the man saw how all the people stopped, he rolled him off the road into the field and threw a cloak over him; for everyone who came by saw
13 the body and stopped. When he had been dragged from the road, they all went on after Joab in pursuit of Sheba son of Bichri.
14 Sheba passed through all the tribes of Israel until he came to Abel-beth-maacah,ʷ and all the clan of Bichriˣ rallied to him and followed him into
15 the city. Joab's forces came up and besieged him in Abel-beth-maacah, raised a siege-ramp against it and began undermining the wall to bring it
16 down. Then a wise woman stood on the rampartʸ and called from the city, 'Listen, listen! Tell Joab to step forward
17 and let me speak with him.' So he came forward and the woman said, 'Are you Joab?' He answered, 'I am.' 'Listen to what I have to say, sir', she went on, to which he replied, 'I am listening.'

'In the old days', she said, 'there was a 18 saying, "Go to Abel for the answer", and that settled the matter. My city is 19 known to be one of the most peaceable and loyalᶻ in Israel; she is like a watch-ful mother in Israel, and you are seeking to kill her. Would you destroy the LORD's own possession?' Joab an- 20 swered, 'God forbid, far be it from me to ruin or destroy! That is not our 21 aim; but a man from the hill-country of Ephraim named Sheba son of Bichri has raised a revolt against King David; surrender this one man, and I will retire from the city.' The woman said to Joab, 'His head shall be thrown to you over the wall.' Then the woman 22 withdrew, and her wisdom won over the assembled people; they cut off Sheba's head and threw it to Joab. Then he sounded the trumpet and the whole army left the city and dispersed to their homes, while Joab went back to the king of Jerusalem.

Joab was in command of the army,ᵃ 23ᵇ and Benaiah son of Jehoiada com-manded the Kerethite and Pelethite guards. Adoram was in charge of the 24 forced levy, and Jehoshaphat son of Ahilud was secretary of state. Sheva 25 was adjutant-general, and Zadok and Abiathar were priests; Ira the Jairite 26 was David's priest.

IN DAVID'S REIGN THERE WAS A FAMINE 21 that lasted year after year for three years. So David consulted the LORD, and he answered, 'Blood-guilt rests on

w *Prob. rdg., cp. verse 15; Heb.* Abel and Beth-maacah.
x *Prob. rdg.; Heb.* Beri.
y stood . . . rampart: *transposed from verse 15.*
z My city . . . loyal: *prob. rdg.; Heb.* I am the requited ones of the loyal ones.
a *Prob. rdg., cp. 8. 16; Heb.* adds Israel.
b *Verses 23–26: cp. 8. 16–18; 1 Kgs. 4. 2–6; 1 Chr. 18. 15–17.*

this time to regain his position as head of the army. **14:** *Sheba* either lacked the time to gather sufficient forces for an engagement, or else Israelites, other than *the clan of Bichri*, failed to respond. *Abel-beth-maacah* was in the far north, near Dan. **19:** Cities were often spoken of as *mothers* and their dependent villages as "daughters." The term "metropolis" (mother city), still reflects this idiom. **22:** The people of the city had consented to give Sheba refuge. Faced with Joab's ultimatum, they recanted.

20.23–26: David's officers. This is a parallel to 8.16–18.

21.1–24.25: A miscellany of David's reign. This is a group of items pertaining to David's reign that collectors did not want to lose. They are arranged in an "envelope form"; (1) a cultic narrative (21.1–14), (2) heroic anecdotes (21.15–22), (3) a royal song (22.1–51), (3′) a royal song (23.1–7), (2′) more heroic anecdotes (23.8–39), and (1′) another cultic narrative. The whole miscellany forms an appendix to the throne succession narrative of chs. 9–20.

21.1–14: Expiation of Saul's blood-guilt. The ancient notion that *famine*, drought, or other disasters indicated some divine wrath to be assuaged long persisted. **1:** Nothing is otherwise

Saul and on his family because he put
2 the Gibeonites to death.' (The Gibeonites were not of Israelite descent, they
were a remnant of Amorite stock whom
the Israelites had sworn that they
would spare. Saul, however, had sought
to exterminate them in his zeal for
Israel and Judah.) King David sum-
3 moned the Gibeonites, therefore, and
said to them, 'What can be done for
you? How can I make expiation, so
that you may have cause to bless the
4 LORD's own people?' The Gibeonites
answered, 'Our feud with Saul and his
family cannot be settled in silver and
gold, and there is no one man in
Israel whose death would content us.'
'Then what do you want me to do for
5 you?' asked David. They answered,
'Let us make an end of the man who
caused our undoing and ruined us, so
that he shall never again have his place
6 within the borders of Israel. Hand over
to us seven of that man's sons, and we
will hurl them down to their death
before*c* the LORD in Gibeah of Saul,
the LORD's chosen king.' The king
7 agreed to hand them over, but he
spared Mephibosheth son of Jonathan,
son of Saul, because of the oath that
had been taken in the LORD's name
by David and Saul's son Jonathan.
8 The king then took the two sons whom
Rizpah daughter of Aiah had borne
to Saul, Armoni and Mephibosheth,
and the five sons whom Merab, Saul's
daughter, had borne to Adriel son of
9 Barzillai of Meholah. He handed them
over to the Gibeonites, and they flung
them down from the mountain before
the LORD; the seven of them fell
together. They were put to death in
the first days of harvest at the begin-
10 ning of the barley harvest. Rizpah
daughter of Aiah took sackcloth and
spread it out as a bed for herself on the
rock, from the beginning of harvest
until the rains came and fell from
heaven upon the bodies. She allowed
no bird to set upon them by day nor
any wild beast by night. When David 11
was told what Rizpah daughter of Aiah
the concubine of Saul had done, he 12
went and took the bones of Saul and his
son Jonathan from the citizens of
Jabesh-gilead, who had stolen them
from the public square at Beth-shan,
where the Philistines had hung them
on the day they defeated Saul at Gilboa.
He removed the bones of Saul and Jona- 13
than from there and gathered up the
bones of the men who had been hurled
to death. They buried the bones of 14
Saul and his son Jonathan in the
territory of Benjamin at Zela, in the
grave of his father Kish. Everything
was done as the king ordered, and
thereafter the LORD was willing to
accept prayers offered for the country.

Once again war broke out between 15
the Philistines and Israel. David and
his men went down to the battle, but as
he fought with the Philistines he fell
exhausted. Then Benob, one of the race 16
of the Rephaim, whose bronze spear
weighed three hundred shekels*d* and
who wore a belt of honour, took
David prisoner and was about to kill
him. But Abishai son of Zeruiah came 17
to David's help, struck the Philistine
down and killed him. Then David's
officers took an oath that he should
never again go out with them to war,
for fear that the lamp of Israel might
be extinguished.

Some time later war with the Philis- 18*e*
tines broke out again in Gob: it was
then that Sibbechai of Hushah killed
Saph, a descendant of the Rephaim.

c Or for.
d shekels: prob. rdg.; Heb. weight.
e Verses 18–22: cp. 1 Chr. 20. 4–7.

known of Saul's action against *the Gibeonites*, but see 4.2 n. **2:** See Josh. ch. 9. **4–6:** Since the
offense to be expiated was sacral, it was the priests of Gibeon who laid down these terms. The
sanctuary of Gibeon was highly venerated by Jerusalemites; see 1 Kgs.3.4. **8:** On *Rizpah*,
see 3.7. *Merab* appears in 1 Sam.18.17–19; her children are not otherwise mentioned. **9:** This
was a ritual execution carried out *before the LORD. The first days of harvest* were around April.
10: *Rizpah* had to keep her vigil for some months, until the autumn rains. The coming of the
rains showed that the expiation was complete. **11–14:** David's action suggests some ambi-
valence on his part about consenting to the Gibeonite demand.

21.15–22: Anecdotes from the Philistine wars. These events were earlier than those of the
throne succession narrative (chs. 9–20). **16:** *The Rephaim*, legendary inhabitants of southern
and eastern Canaan, were remarkable for their unusual stature. **17:** See 18.2–4. This seems to

19 In another war with the Philistines in Gob, Elhanan son of Jair[f] of Bethlehem killed Goliath of Gath, whose spear had a shaft like a weaver's
20 beam. In yet another war in Gath there appeared a giant with six fingers on each hand and six toes on each foot, twenty-four in all. He too was de-
21 scended from the Rephaim; and, when he defied Israel, Jonathan son of David's brother Shimeai killed him.
22 These four giants were the descendants of the Rephaim in Gath, and they all fell at the hands of David and his men.

22 THESE ARE THE WORDS OF THE SONG David sang to the LORD on the day when the LORD delivered him from the power of all his enemies and from the power of Saul:

2[g] The LORD is my stronghold, my fortress and my champion,
3 my God, my rock where I find safety;
   my shield, my mountain fastness,
     my strong tower,
   my refuge, my deliverer, who saves me from violence.
4 I will call on the LORD to whom all praise is due,
   and I shall be delivered from my enemies.
5 When the waves of death swept round me,
   and torrents of destruction overtook me,
6 the bonds of Sheol tightened about me,
   the snares of death were set to catch me;
7 then in anguish of heart I cried to the LORD,
   I called for help to my God;
   he heard me from his temple,
   and my cry rang in his ears.
8 The earth heaved and quaked,
   heaven's foundations shook;
   they heaved, because he was angry.
9 Smoke rose from his nostrils,

devouring fire came out of his mouth,
   glowing coals and searing heat.
10 He swept the skies aside as he descended,
   thick darkness lay under his feet.
11 He rode on a cherub, he flew through the air;
   he swooped[h] on the wings of the wind.
12 He curtained himself in darkness and made dense vapour his canopy.
13 Thick clouds came out of the radiance before him;
   glowing coals burned brightly.
14 The LORD thundered from the heavens
   and the voice of the Most High spoke out.
15 He loosed his arrows, he sped them far and wide,
   his lightning shafts, and sent them echoing.
16 The channels of the sea-bed were revealed,
   the foundations of earth laid bare
   at the LORD's rebuke,
   at the blast of the breath of his nostrils.
17 He reached down from the height and took me,
   he drew me out of mighty waters,
18 he rescued me from my enemies, strong as they were,
   from my foes when they grew too powerful for me.
19 They confronted me in the hour of my peril,
   but the LORD was my buttress.
20 He brought me out into an open place,
   he rescued me because he delighted in me.
21 The LORD rewarded me as my righteousness deserved;
   my hands were clean, and he requited me.

f Jair: *prob. rdg.*, cp. 1 *Chr.* 20. 5; Heb. Jaare-oregim.
g Verses 2–51: cp. Ps. 18. 2–50.
h Prob. rdg., cp. Ps. 18. 10; Heb. was seen.

have been an earlier occasion. **19:** The slaying of *Goliath* was romanticized in later times as a deed of David himself; see 1 Sam.17.1–58 n.
     22.1–51: The song of David. See 1.17–27 n. This song also appears as Ps.18; see the annotations there. The speaker is a king who was first delivered from cosmic powers by a theophany of the LORD (vv. 1–20), who then celebrates the character of the LORD and his own righteousness (vv. 21–31), and who finally achieves spectacular victory because the LORD is his support (vv. 32–51).

22 For I have followed the ways of the
　LORD
　and have not turned wickedly from
　my God;
23 all his laws are before my eyes,
　I have not failed to follow his
　decrees.
24 In his sight I was blameless
　and kept myself from wilful sin;
25 the LORD requited me as my
　righteousness deserved
　and my purity in his eyes.

26 With the loyal thou showest thyself
　loyal
　and with the blameless man blameless.
27 With the savage man thou showest
　thyself savage,
　and[i] tortuous with the perverse.
28 Thou deliverest humble folk,
　thou lookest with contempt upon
　the proud.
29 Thou, LORD, art my lamp,
　and the LORD will lighten my
　darkness.
30 With thy help I leap over a bank,
　by God's aid I spring over a wall.

31 The way of God is perfect,
　the LORD's word has stood the test;
　he is the shield of all who take
　refuge in him.
32 What god is there but the LORD?
　What rock but our God?—
33 the God who girds me[j] with
　strength
　and makes my way blameless,[k]
34 who makes me swift as a hind
　and sets me secure on the
　mountains;
35 who trains my hands for battle,
　and my arms aim an arrow tipped
　with bronze.

36 Thou hast given me the shield of
　thy salvation,
　in thy providence thou makest me
　great.
37 Thou givest me room for my steps,
　my feet have not faltered.
38 I pursue my enemies and destroy
　them,
　I do not return until I have made an
　end of them.
39 I make an end of them, I strike
　them down;

they rise no more, they fall beneath
　my feet,
40 Thou dost arm me with strength for
　the battle
　and dost subdue my foes before me.
41 Thou settest[l] my foot on my
　enemies' necks,
　and I bring to nothing those that
　hate me.
42 They cry out[m] and there is no one
　to help them,
　they cry to the LORD and he does
　not answer.
43 I will pound them fine as dust on
　the ground,
　like mud in the streets will I trample
　them.[n]
44 Thou dost deliver me from the
　clamour of the people,
　and makest me master of the
　nations.
　A people I never knew shall be my
　subjects.
45 Foreigners shall come cringing to me;
　as soon as they hear tell of me, they
　shall obey me.
46 Foreigners shall be brought captive
　to me,
　and come limping from their
　strongholds.
47 The LORD lives, blessed is my rock,
　high above all is God my rock and
　safe refuge.

48 O God, who grantest me vengeance,
　who dost subdue peoples under me,
49 who dost snatch me from my foes
　and set me over my enemies,
　thou dost deliver me from violent
　men.
50 Therefore, LORD, I will praise thee
　among the nations
　and sing psalms to thy name,
51 to one who gives his king great
　victories
　and in all his acts keeps faith with
　his anointed king,
　with David and his descendants for
　ever.

i With the savage ... savage, and: *or* With the pure
thou showest thyself pure, but ...
j who girds me: *prob. rdg., cp. Ps. 18. 32; Heb.* my
refuge *or* my strength.
k and makes ... blameless: *prob. rdg., cp. Ps. 18. 32;
Heb. unintelligible.*
l Prob. rdg., cp. Ps. 18. 40; Heb. unintelligible.
m cry out: *prob. rdg., cp. Ps. 18. 41; Heb.* look.
n Prob. rdg., cp. Ps. 18. 42; Heb. adds will I stamp them
down.

23 These are the last words of David:

> The very word of David son of Jesse,
> the very word of the man whom the
> 　High God raised up,
> the anointed prince of the God of
> 　Jacob,
> and the singer of Israel's psalms:
> **2** the spirit of the LORD has spoken
> 　　through me,
> and his word is on my lips.
> **3** The God of Israel spoke,
> the Rock of Israel spoke of me:
> 'He who rules men in justice,
> who rules in the fear of God,
> **4** is like the light of morning at
> 　　sunrise,
> a morning that is cloudless after
> 　rain
> and makes the grass sparkle from
> 　the earth.'
>
> **5** Surely, surely my house is true to
> 　　God;
> for he has made a pact with me for
> 　all time,
> its terms spelled out and faithfully
> 　kept,
> my whole salvation, all my*o* delight.
> **6** But the ungodly put forth no shoots,
> they are all like briars tossed aside;
> none dare put out his hand to pick
> 　them up,
> **7** none touch them but*p* with tool of
> 　　iron or of wood;
> they are fit only for burning in the
> 　fire.*q*

8*r* THESE ARE THE NAMES OF DAVID'S
heroes. First came Ishbosheth the
Hachmonite,*s* chief of the three; it was
he who brandished his spear*t* over
eight hundred dead, all slain at one
9 time. Next to him was Eleazar son of
Dodo the Ahohite,*u* one of the heroic
three. He was with David at Pas-
dammim where the Philistines*v* had
gathered for battle. When the Israel-
10 ites fell back, he stood his ground and
rained blows on the Philistines until,
from sheer weariness, his hand stuck
fast to his sword; and so the LORD
brought about a great victory that
day. Afterwards the people rallied
behind him, but it was only to strip
the dead. Next to him was Shammah **11**
son of Agee a Hararite. The Philistines
had gathered at Lehi, where there was
a field with a fine crop of lentils; and,
when the Philistines put the people to
flight, he stood his ground in the field, **12**
saved it*w* and defeated them. So the
LORD again brought about a great
victory.

Three of the thirty went down **13**
towards the beginning of harvest to
join David at the cave of Adullam,
while a band of Philistines was encamped in the Vale of Rephaim. At **14**
that time David was in the stronghold
and a Philistine garrison held Bethlehem. One day a longing came over **15**
David, and he exclaimed, 'If only I
could have a drink of water from the
well*x* by the gate of Bethlehem!' At this **16**
the heroic three made their way
through the Philistine lines and drew
water from the well by the gate of
Bethlehem and brought it to David.
But David refused to drink it; he
poured it out to the LORD and said, **17**
'God forbid that I should do such a
thing! Can I drink*y* the blood of these
men who risked their lives for it?' So
he would not drink it. Such were the
exploits of the heroic three.

Abishai the brother of Joab son of **18**
Zeruiah was chief of the thirty. He once
brandished his spear over three

o Prob. rdg.; Heb. om.
p but: prob. rdg.; Heb. he shall be filled.
q Prob. rdg.; Heb. adds in sitting.
r Verses 8–39: cp. 1 Chr. 11. 10–41.
s Prob. rdg.; Heb. Josheb-basshebeth a Tahchemonite.
t who ... spear: prob. rdg., cp. 1 Chr. 11. 11; Heb. unintelligible.
u the Ahohite: prob. rdg., cp. 1 Chr. 11. 12; Heb. son of Ahohi.
v He was ... Philistines: prob. rdg., cp. 1 Chr. 11. 13; Heb. With David when they taunted them among the Philistines.
w saved it: or cleared it of the Philistines.
x Or cistern.
y I drink: prob. rdg., cp. 1 Chr. 11. 19; Heb. om.

23.1–7: The last words of David. The text of this song is rather uncertain; it has a good claim
to be from David himself. **1:** *High God:* see 1 Sam.2.10 n. **3:** On *Rock*, see 1 Sam.2.2 n.
5: This may be the earliest reference to the *pact* ("perpetual covenant") between the LORD
and David; compare ch. 7.
23.8–39: David's warriors. The heroic deeds are probably touched up, but David commanded
the loyalty of a powerful following. The organization in *the three* and *the thirty* reflects a
ten-to-one ratio that often appears in military, labor force, and cultic groups; see 1 Kgs.5.16;

hundred dead, and he was famous
19 among the thirty. Some think he even
surpassed the rest of the thirty[z] in
reputation, and he became their
captain, but he did not rival the three.
20 Benaiah son of Jehoiada, from Kabzeel, was a hero of many exploits. It
was he who smote the two champions
of Moab, and who went down into a
pit and killed a lion on a snowy day.
21 It was he who also killed the Egyptian,
a man of striking appearance armed
with a spear: he went to meet him with
a club, snatched the spear out of the
Egyptian's hand and killed him with his
22 own weapon. Such were the exploits of
Benaiah son of Jehoiada, famous
23 among the heroic thirty.[z] He was more
famous than the rest of the thirty, but
he did not rival the three. David
appointed him to his household.
24 Asahel the brother of Joab was one
of the thirty, and Elhanan son of
25 Dodo from Bethlehem; Shammah from
26 Harod, and Elika from Harod; Helez
from Beth-pelet,[a] and Ira son of
27 Ikkesh from Tekoa; Abiezer from
Anathoth, and Mebunnai from Hu-
28 shah; Zalmon the Ahohite, and
29 Maharai from Netophah; Heled son of
Baanah from Netophah, and Ittai son
of Ribai from Gibeah of Benjamin;
30 Benaiah from Pirathon, and Hiddai
31 from the ravines of Gaash; Abi-albon
from Beth-arabah,[b] and Azmoth from
32 Bahurim;[c] Eliahba from Shaalbon,
and Hashem the Gizonite; Jonathan
33 son of[d] Shammah the Hararite, and
Ahiam son of Sharar the Hararite;[e]
34 Eliphelet son of Ahasbai son of the
Maacathite, and Eliam son of Ahitho-
35 phel the Gilonite; Hezrai from Carmel,
36 and Paarai the Arbite; Igal son of
Nathan from Zobah, and Bani the
37 Gadite; Zelek the Ammonite, and
Naharai from Beeroth, armour-bearer
38 to Joab son of Zeruiah; Ira the Ithrite,
39 Gareb the Ithrite, and Uriah the
Hittite: there were thirty-seven in all.

ONCE AGAIN THE ISRAELITES FELT THE **24** 1[f]
LORD's anger, when he incited David
against them and gave him orders that
Israel and Judah should be counted.
So he instructed Joab and the officers 2
of the army[g] with him to go round all
the tribes of Israel, from Dan to Beersheba, and make a record of the
people and report the number to him.
Joab answered, 'Even if the LORD 3
your God should increase the people a
hundredfold and your majesty should
live to see it, what pleasure would that
give your majesty?' But Joab and the 4
officers were overruled by the king
and they left his presence in order to
count the people. They crossed the 5
Jordan and began at Aroer and the
level land of the gorge, proceeding
towards Gad[h] and Jazer. They came 6
to Gilead and to the land of the
Hittites, to Kadesh, and then to Dan
and Iyyon[i] and so round towards
Sidon. They went as far as the walled 7
city of Tyre and all the towns of the
Hivites and Canaanites, and then
went on to the Negeb of Judah at
Beersheba. They covered the whole 8
country and arrived back at Jerusalem
after nine months and twenty days.
Joab reported to the king the total 9
number of people: the number of able-
bodied men, capable of bearing arms,
was eight hundred thousand in Israel
and five hundred thousand in Judah.
After he had counted the people 10
David's conscience smote him, and he
said to the LORD, 'I have done a very
wicked thing: I pray thee, LORD, remove thy servant's guilt, for I have

z *Prob. rdg.; Heb.* three.
a *Prob. rdg., cp. Josh.* 15. 27; *Heb.* from Pelet.
b *Prob. rdg., cp. Josh.* 18. 22; *Heb.* from Arabah.
c *Prob. rdg., cp. 1 Chr.* 11. 33; *Heb.* from Barhum.
d Hashem . . . son of: *prob. rdg., cp. 1 Chr.* 11. 34; *Heb.*
the sons of Jashen, Jonathan.
e *Prob. rdg., cp. 1 Chr.* 11. 35; *Heb.* Ararite.
f *Verses 1–25: cp. 1 Chr.* 21. 1–27.
g Joab . . . army: *prob. rdg., cp. 1 Chr.* 21. 2; *Heb.*
Joab the officer of the army.
h began at . . . Gad: *prob. rdg.; Heb.* encamped in Aroer
on the right of the level land of the gorge Gad.
i *Prob. rdg., cp. 1 Kgs.* 15. 20; *Heb.* Yaan.

9.23 and the ratio of sheep to bulls in 2 Chr.35.7,9. **24–39:** There are thirty-one names here,
plus *Abishai* and *Benaiah* in vv. 18–23. The list may include names of men who belonged to
the elite *thirty* at different times, some replacing others.
24.1–25: David's census and the Jerusalem altar. This "sacred story" sanctions the site of the
altar of the Solomonic Temple. **1:** *The LORD's anger* must be assuaged, as in 21.1–14. **4:** David
insists on the census; it was a step toward effective government of his realm, but intruded upon
the independence of tribal groups. **9:** The numbers are improbable, even for David's time. **10:**
The interest of the narrative is cultic; hence, consistency of conduct on David's part is sacrificed

11 been very foolish.' He rose next morning, and meanwhile the command of the LORD had come to the 12 prophet Gad, David's seer, to go and speak to David: 'This is the word of the LORD: I have three things in store for you; choose one and I will bring it 13 upon you.' So Gad came to David and repeated this to him and said, 'Is it to be three years of famine in your land, or three months of flight with the enemy at your heels, or three days of pestilence in your land? Consider carefully what answer I am to take back 14 to him who sent me.' Thereupon David said to Gad, 'I am in a desperate plight; let us fall into the hands of the LORD, for his mercy is great; and let me not 15 fall into the hands of men.' So the LORD sent a pestilence throughout Israel from morning till the hour of dinner, and from Dan to Beersheba seventy thousand of the people died. 16 Then the angel stretched out his arm towards Jerusalem to destroy it; but the LORD repented of the evil and said to the angel who was destroying the people, 'Enough! Stay your hand.' At that moment the angel of the LORD was standing by the threshing-floor of Araunah the Jebusite. 17 When David saw the angel who was striking down the people, he said to the LORD, 'It is I who have done wrong, the sin is mine; but these poor sheep, what have they done? Let thy hand fall upon me and upon my family.' 18 That same day Gad came to David and said to him, 'Go and set up an altar to the LORD on the threshing-floor 19 of Araunah the Jebusite.' David did what Gad told him to do, and went up as the LORD had commanded. 20 When Araunah looked down and saw the king and his servants coming over towards him, he went out, prostrated 21 himself low before the king and said, 'Why has your majesty come to visit his servant?' David answered, 'To buy the threshing-floor from you to build an altar to the LORD, so that the plague which has attacked the people may be stopped.' 22 Araunah answered David, 'I beg your majesty to take it and sacrifice what you think fit. I have here the oxen for a whole-offering, and their harness and the threshing-sledges for the fuel.' Araunah*j* gave it all to the 23 king for his own use and said to him, 'May the LORD your God accept you.' 24 But the king said to Araunah, 'No, I will buy it from you; I will not offer to the LORD my God whole-offerings that have cost me nothing.' So David bought the threshing-floor and the 25 oxen for fifty shekels of silver. He built an altar to the LORD there and offered whole-offerings and shared-offerings. Then the LORD yielded to his prayer for the land; and the plague in Israel stopped.

j Prob. rdg.; Heb. adds the king.

to that interest. **11:** *The prophet Gad:* see 1 Sam.22.5. **17:** David's piety is similar to that expressed in the throne succession narrative; compare 15.25–26; 16.10–12. **18:** That *the threshing-floor of Araunah* became the place of the altar of the Temple is only implicit here, but is made explicit in 1 Chr.21.28–22.1.

THE FIRST BOOK OF
KINGS

1 and 2 Kings are a single book in Hebrew, related to 1 and 2 Samuel and the whole "Deuteronomic history" (see Introduction to 1 Sam.). The establishment of David's dynasty and the building of Solomon's Temple bring to a completion the LORD's work of establishing Israel in Canaan (1 Kgs. chs. 1–10).

Israel's prosperity has a condition, however: that the LORD's commandments be carefully obeyed. Hence, the rest of Kings tells how disaster finally came upon the Israelite kingdoms through their failure to meet that condition. While individual kings were guilty of various offenses, two particular violations of the LORD's cultic requirements condemned the two kingdoms. In the Northern Kingdom of Israel, the violation was the "sin" of Jeroboam I, namely, his establishment of the cult of the golden calves at Bethel; this constituted a worship of the LORD, but an improper one (see 1 Kgs.12.25–33; 2 Kgs.17.21–23). In Judah, the violation was permitting the local sanctuaries, called the hill-shrines, to continue after the Temple was built (see, e.g. 1 Kgs.3.2–3; 22.41–43).

Only two kings of the late period, Hezekiah and Josiah, are fully approved, this because they removed the hill-shrines (2 Kgs.18.3–4; 23.8).

1 Kings opens with the conclusion (chs. 1–2) of the narrative of the succession to David's throne; earlier parts of that same source are in 2 Sam. chs. 9–20. At different points some other literary sources are referred to: "the annals of Solomon" (1 Kgs.11.41), "the annals of the kings of Israel" (14.19), and "the annals of the kings of Judah" (14.29). Data from these annals are given in regular formulas for each king (see, e.g. 14.21–22; 15.25–26). Also drawn upon, without explicit reference, were one or more sources on the history of the Temple (e.g. 6.2–36; 2 Kgs.12.4–16; 16.10–18) and collections of prophetic legends (e.g. 1 Kgs. chs. 13; 17–19; 2 Kgs. chs. 2–8; 18.17–20.19). Also, the Deuteronomic historians contributed speeches and reflections in their distinctive style (e.g. 1 Kgs.8.14–61; 2 Kgs.17.7–23).

A "first edition" of these materials may have been composed during Josiah's reign, before his death (609 B.C.). The point of that edition would have been to show that the previous history of the kings justified Josiah's religious reform (see 2 Kgs.22.3–23.24). Later (about 550 B.C.), after the kingdom of Judah had fallen, a "second edition" of Kings, extending the account, was incorporated into the larger Deuteronomic history.

The death of David and accession of Solomon

1 KING DAVID WAS NOW A VERY OLD man and, though they wrapped clothes round him, he could not 2 keep warm. So his household said to him, 'Let us find a young virgin for your majesty, to attend you and take care of you; and let her lie in your 3 bosom, sir, and make you warm.' So they searched all over Israel for a beautiful maiden and found Abishag, a Shunammite, and brought her to the 4 king. She was a very beautiful girl, and she took care of the king and waited on him, but he had no intercourse with her.

Now Adonijah, whose mother was 5 Haggith, was boasting that he was to be king; and he had already provided himself with chariots and horsemen[a] and fifty outrunners. Never in his life 6 had his father corrected him or asked why he behaved as he did. He was a very handsome man, too, and was next in age to Absalom. He talked with 7 Joab son of Zeruiah and with Abiathar the priest, and they gave him their strong support; but Zadok the priest, 8 Benaiah son of Jehoiada, Nathan the

[a] Or a chariot and horses.

1.1–2.46: Solomon's succession to the throne. This is the conclusion of the throne succession narrative in 2 Sam. chs. 9–20.

1.1–53: Two parties struggle for the kingship. 1: *Very old:* about seventy at this time. **5–6:** *Adonijah,* as *next in age to Absalom* (now dead), had good reason to suppose he would succeed David; compare 2 Sam.15.1. **7–10:** Adonijah was born during David's Hebron period and was therefore supported by David's leading men of that time, *Joab,* commander of the army (2 Sam.2.13 is his first appearance), and *Abiathar,* the priest who escaped Saul's wrath and dwelt with David during the fugitive years in the Wilderness (1 Sam.22.20; 23.6). Solomon's support,

prophet, Shimei, Rei, and David's bodyguard of heroes, did not take his
9 side. Adonijah then held a sacrifice of sheep, oxen, and buffaloes at the stone Zoheleth beside En-rogel, and he invited all his royal brothers and all those officers of the household who
10 were of the tribe of Judah. But he did not invite Nathan the prophet, Benaiah and the bodyguard, or Solomon his brother.

11 Then Nathan said to Bathsheba, the mother of Solomon, 'Have you not heard that Adonijah son of Haggith has become king, all unknown to our
12 lord David? Now come, let me advise you what to do for your own safety and for the safety of your son Solomon.
13 Go in and see King David and say to him, "Did not your majesty swear to me, your servant, that my son Solomon should succeed you as king; that it was he who should sit on your throne? Why then has Adonijah become king?"
14 Then while you are still speaking there with the king, I will follow you in and tell the whole story.'
15 So Bathsheba went to the king in his private chamber; he was now very old, and Abishag the Shunammite was
16 waiting on him. Bathsheba bowed before the king and prostrated herself. 'What do you want?' said the king.
17 She answered, 'My lord, you swore to me your servant, by the LORD your God, that my son Solomon should succeed you as king, and that he
18 should sit on your throne. But now, here is Adonijah become king, all
19 unknown to your majesty. He has sacrificed great numbers of oxen, buffaloes, and sheep, and has invited to the feast all the king's sons, and Abiathar the priest, and Joab the commander-in-chief, but he has not
20 invited your servant Solomon. And now, your majesty, all Israel is looking to you to announce who is to succeed
21 you on the throne. Otherwise, when

you, sir, rest with your forefathers, my son Solomon and I shall be treated as criminals.' She was still speaking to 22 the king when Nathan the prophet arrived. The king was told that 23 Nathan was there; he came into the presence and prostrated himself with his face to the ground. 'My lord,' he 24 said, 'your majesty must, I suppose, have declared that Adonijah should succeed you and that he should sit on your throne. He has today gone down 25 and sacrificed great numbers of oxen, buffaloes, and sheep, and has invited to the feast all the king's sons, Joab the commander-in-chief, and Abiathar the priest; and at this very moment they are eating and drinking in his presence and shouting, "Long live King Adonijah!" But he has not 26 invited me your servant, Zadok the priest, Benaiah son of Jehoiada, or your servant Solomon. Has this been 27 done by your majesty's authority, while we[b] your servants have not been told who should succeed you on the throne?' Thereupon King David said, 28 'Call Bathsheba', and she came into the king's presence and stood before him. Then the king swore an oath to 29 her: 'As the LORD lives, who has delivered me from all my troubles: I 30 swore by the LORD the God of Israel that Solomon your son should succeed me and that he should sit on my throne, and this day I give effect to my oath.' Bathsheba bowed low to the king and 31 prostrated herself; and she said, 'May my lord King David live for ever!'

Then King David said, 'Call Zadok 32 the priest, Nathan the prophet, and Benaiah son of Jehoiada.' They came into the king's presence and he gave 33 them these orders: 'Take the officers of the household with you; mount my son Solomon on the king's mule and escort him down to Gihon. There 34

b Has this ... while we: *or* If this has been done by your majesty's authority, then we ...

---

on the other hand, came from leaders who only appeared after David's settlement in Jerusalem: *Zadok*, the other leader of the priests (2 Sam.8.17 n.), *Nathan* the prophet (see 2 Sam.7.2 n.; 12.1–14 n.), and *Benaiah*, commander of David's Philistine palace guard (2 Sam.8.18; 20.23). *Solomon* was, of course, born in David's Jerusalem period to a Jerusalemite mother (2 Sam.12. 24–25). The two parties represented a tension that would persist through the centuries (see 2 Kgs.21.23–24) between the old city-state of Jerusalem and the new kingdom of Judah. **9:** *En-rogel*; a spring southeast of the city (2 Sam.17.17). **11–31:** *Nathan* sees the crisis and knows that through *Bathsheba* a counter-stroke can be affected. **33:** *Gihon* was a sacred spring to the

Zadok the priest and Nathan the prophet shall anoint him king over Israel. Sound the trumpet and shout,
35 "Long live King Solomon!" Then escort him home again, and he shall come and sit on my throne and reign in my place; for he is the man that I have appointed prince over Israel and
36 Judah.' Benaiah son of Jehoiada answered the king, 'It shall be done. And may the LORD, the God of my lord the
37 king, confirm it! As the LORD has been with your majesty, so may he be with Solomon; may he make his throne even greater than the throne of
38 my lord King David.' So Zadok the priest, Nathan the prophet, and Benaiah son of Jehoiada, together with the Kerethite and Pelethite guards, went down and mounted Solomon on King David's mule and escorted him to
39 Gihon. Zadok the priest took the horn of oil from the Tent of the LORD and anointed Solomon; they sounded the trumpet and all the people shouted,
40 'Long live King Solomon!' Then all the people escorted him home in procession, with great rejoicing and playing of pipes, so that the very earth split with the noise.
41   Adonijah and his guests had finished their banquet when the noise reached their ears. Joab, hearing the sound of the trumpet, exclaimed, 'What is all this uproar in the city? What has
42 happened?' While he was still speaking, Jonathan son of Abiathar the priest arrived. 'Come in', said Adonijah. 'You are an honourable man and
43 bring good news.' 'Far otherwise,' Jonathan replied; 'our lord King David
44 has made Solomon king and has sent with him Zadok the priest, Nathan the prophet, and Benaiah son of Jehoiada, together with the Kerethite and Peleth-

ite guards; they have mounted him on the king's mule, and Zadok the priest 45 and Nathan the prophet have anointed him king at Gihon, and they have now escorted him home rejoicing, and the city is in an uproar. That was the noise you heard. More than that, 46 Solomon has taken his seat on the royal throne. Yes, and the officers of 47 the household have been to greet our lord King David with these words: "May your God make the name of Solomon your son more famous than your own and his throne even greater than yours", and the king bowed upon his couch. What is more, he said 48 this: "Blessed be the LORD the God of Israel who has set a successor on my throne this day while I am still alive to see it."' Then Adonijah's guests all 49 rose in panic and scattered. Adonijah 50 himself, in fear of Solomon, sprang up and went to the altar and caught hold of its horns. Then a message was sent 51 to Solomon: 'Adonijah is afraid of King Solomon; he has taken hold of the horns of the altar and has said, "Let King Solomon first swear to me that he will not put his servant to the sword."' Solomon said, 'If he proves 52 himself a man of worth, not a hair of his head shall fall to the ground; but if he is found to be troublesome, he shall die.' Then King Solomon sent and had 53 him brought down from the altar; he came in and prostrated himself before the king, and Solomon ordered him home.

When the time of David's death 2 drew near, he gave this last charge to his son Solomon: 'I am going the way 2 of all the earth. Be strong and show yourself a man. Fulfil your duty to the 3 LORD your God; conform to his ways, observe his statutes and his command-

---

east of the city, in the Kidron Valley. **36–37:** *Benaiah*, as commander of the guard, occupied the key position here. **38:** *The Kerethite and Pelethite guards* were Cretan and Philistine mercenaries. The king's *mule* had special significance in the royal rituals of the city; compare Zech.9.9. **39:** The city *priest* anoints the new king with *oil* preserved in the sanctuary for ritual purposes. On anointing *oil*, see Exod.30.22–33. For *the Tent of the LORD*, see 2 Sam.6.17; 7.1–7. **40:** The *procession* went to the royal palace where Solomon was seated on the throne, the decisive conclusion to the coronation; see v. 46. **41–53:** When it was clear that Solomon's supporters had carried out their coup and that the king fully concurred (v. 48), Adonijah and his followers fled in *panic* (v. 50). **52–53:** Solomon wished to avoid an open confrontation between the two parties. He would subsequently find ways to secure his own party.
    2.1–46: David's death and the securing of Solomon's throne. 1–9: Old scores and debts, which for various reasons David had not settled, were bequeathed to Solomon. **3–4:** This reflects

ments, his judgements and his solemn precepts, as they are written in the law of Moses, so that you may prosper in whatever you do and whichever way 4 you turn, and that the LORD may fulfil this promise that he made about me: "If your descendants take care to walk faithfully in my sight with all their heart and with all their soul, you shall never lack a successor on the throne 5 of Israel." You know how Joab son of Zeruiah treated me and what he did to two commanders-in-chief in Israel, Abner son of Ner and Amasa son of Jether. He killed them both, breaking the peace by bloody acts of war; and with that blood he stained the belt about my waist and the sandals on my 6 feet. Do as your wisdom prompts you, and do not let his grey hairs go 7 down to the grave in peace. Show constant friendship to the family of Barzillai of Gilead; let them have their place at your table; they befriended me when I was a fugitive from 8 your brother Absalom. Do not forget Shimei son of Gera, the Benjamite from Bahurim, who cursed me bitterly the day I went to Mahanaim. True, he came down to meet me at the Jordan, and I swore by the LORD that I would 9 not put him to death. But you do not need to let him go unpunished now; you are a wise man and will know how to deal with him; bring down his grey hairs in blood to the grave.'

10 So David rested with his forefathers and was buried in the city of David, 11 having reigned over Israel for forty years, seven in Hebron and thirty-12 three in Jerusalem; and Solomon succeeded his father David as king and was firmly established on the throne.

The reign of Solomon

13 THEN ADONIJAH SON OF HAGGITH CAME to Bathsheba, the mother of Solomon.

'Do you come as a friend?' she asked. 'As a friend,' he answered; 'I have 14 something to say to you.' 'Tell me', she said. 'You know', he went on, 'that 15 the throne was mine and that all Israel was looking to me to be king; but I was passed over and the throne has gone to my brother; it was his by the LORD's will. And now I have one 16 request to make of you; do not refuse me.' 'What is it?' she said. He an-17 swered, 'Will you ask King Solomon (he will never refuse you) to give me Abishag the Shunammite in marriage?' 'Very well,' said Bathsheba, 'I will speak 18 for you to the king.' So Bathsheba went 19 in to King Solomon to speak for Adonijah. The king rose to meet her and kissed her, and seated himself on his throne. A throne was set for the king's mother and she sat at his right hand. Then she said, 'I have one small 20 request to make of you; do not refuse me.' 'What is it, mother?' he replied; 'I will not refuse you.' 'It is this, that 21 Abishag the Shunammite should be given to your brother Adonijah in marriage.' At that Solomon answered 22 his mother, 'Why do you ask for Abishag the Shunammite as wife for Adonijah? you might as well ask for the throne, for he is my elder brother and has both Abiathar the priest and Joab son of Zeruiah on his side.' Then 23 King Solomon swore by the LORD: 'So help me God, Adonijah shall pay for this with his life. As the LORD lives, 24 who has established me and set me on the throne of David my father and has founded a house for me as he promised, this very day Adonijah shall be put to death!' Thereupon King Sol-25 omon gave Benaiah son of Jehoiada his orders, and he struck him down and he died.

Abiathar the priest was told by the 26 king to go off to Anathoth to his own estate. 'You deserve to die,' he said,

the piety of the Deuteronomic historians. **5–6**: *Joab* had slain *Abner* (2 Sam.3.22–27) and *Amasa* (2 Sam.20.8–10), both of whom were commanders who had previously opposed David (2 Sam.2.8–10,12–13; 17.25; 19.13). It is striking, however, that David does not here blame *Joab* for killing Absalom (2 Sam.18.9–17). That Joab always labored in behalf of David is beyond question, even when bloodshed was required. A Solomonic viewpoint, however, has condemned him. **7**: On *Barzillai*, see 2 Sam.17.27 and 19.31–39. **8**: On *Shimei*, see 2 Sam.16.5–14 and 19.15–23. **17**: As v. 22 shows, Adonijah's request for David's concubine *Abishag* would have serious political implication; see 2 Sam.3.7 n. **19**: The queen mother occupied a very important position in Jerusalem and thus had a *throne* at her son's *right hand*. **24**: Adonijah's

'but in spite of this day's work I shall not put you to death, for you carried the Ark of the Lord GOD before my father David, and you shared in all
27 the hardships that he endured.' So Solomon dismissed Abiathar from his office as priest of the LORD, and so fulfilled the sentence that the LORD had pronounced against the house of Eli in Shiloh.
28 News of all this reached Joab, and he fled to the Tent of the LORD and caught hold of the horns of the altar; for he had sided with Adonijah, though not
29 with Absalom. When King Solomon learnt that Joab had fled to the Tent of the LORD and that he was by the altar, he sent Benaiah son of Jehoiada with orders to strike him down.
30 Benaiah came to the Tent of the LORD and ordered Joab in the king's name to come away; but he said, 'No; I will die here.' Benaiah reported Joab's
31 answer to the king, and the king said, 'Let him have his way; strike him down and bury him, and so rid me and my father's house of the guilt for the
32 blood that he wantonly shed. The LORD will hold him responsible for his own death, because he struck down two innocent men who were better men than he, Abner son of Ner, commander of the army of Israel, and Amasa son of Jether, commander of the army of Judah, and ran them through with the sword, without my
33 father David's knowledge. The guilt of their blood shall recoil on Joab and his descendants for all time; but David and his descendants, his house and his throne, will enjoy perpetual
34 prosperity from the LORD.' So Benaiah son of Jehoiada went up to the altar and struck Joab down and killed him, and he was buried in his house on the

edge of the wilderness. Thereafter the 35 king appointed Benaiah son of Jehoiada to command the army in his place, and installed Zadok the priest in place of Abiathar.

Next the king sent for Shimei and 36 said to him, 'Build yourself a house in Jerusalem and stay there; you are not to leave the city for any other place. If ever you leave it and cross the gorge 37 of the Kidron, you shall die; make no mistake about that. Your blood will be on your own head.' And Shimei 38 said to the king, 'I accept your sentence; I will do as your majesty commands.' So for a long time Shimei remained in Jerusalem; but three years 39 later two of his slaves ran away to Achish son of Maacah, king of Gath. When Shimei heard that his slaves 40 were in Gath, he immediately saddled his ass and went there to Achish in search of his slaves; he came to Gath and returned with them. When King 41 Solomon was told that Shimei had gone from Jerusalem to Gath and back, he sent for him and said, 'Did I not 42 require you to swear by the LORD? Did I not give you this solemn warning: "If ever you leave this city for any other place, you shall die; make no mistake about it"? And you said, "I accept your sentence; I obey." Why 43 then have you not kept the oath which you swore by the LORD, and the order which I gave you? Shimei, you 44 know in your own heart all the mischief you did to my father David; the LORD is now making that mischief recoil on your own head. But King 45 Solomon is blessed and the throne of David will be secure before the LORD for all time.' The king then gave 46 orders to Benaiah son of Jehoiada, and he went out and struck Shimei down;

assassination was the first in a series of executions intended to remove dangerous antagonists from the scene. **26–27:** *Abiathar* the *priest* was next to be removed. The prophet Jeremiah was descended from these priests at *Anathoth* (Jer.1.1). *The sentence that the* LORD *had pronounced* concerning Eli appears in 1 Sam.2.35–36. **28–35:** No new high-handed action by *Joab* is reported, but he too had to die; see vv. 5–6 n. **35:** *The edge of the wilderness* was near Bethlehem, where Joab's father and brother were buried (2 Sam.2.32). **36–46:** *Three years* passed before *Shimei*, the last opponent, slipped; with his death Solomon's *royal power was . . . established.*

3.1–11.43: The reign of Solomon. This complex section, which has little affinity with the two preceding chs., is based on three kinds of material: popular narratives of Solomon's character, annalistic materials concerning his administration and works, and statistics and speeches concerning the establishment of the Temple. The whole is arranged in an "envelope" (1,2,3,2,1) structure: (1) narratives of Solomon's divine favor, ch. 3; (2) details of his administration and wisdom, ch. 4; (3) the Temple, 5.1–9.9; (2') details of administration, wisdom,

and he died. Thus Solomon's royal power was securely established.

3 Solomon allied himself to Pharaoh king of Egypt by marrying his daughter. He brought her to the City of David, until he had finished building his own house and the house of the LORD and 2 the wall round Jerusalem. The people however continued to sacrifice at the hill-shrines, for till then no house had been built in honour of the name 3 of the LORD. Solomon himself loved the LORD, conforming to the precepts laid down by his father David; but he too slaughtered and burnt sacrifices at the hill-shrines.

4 Now King Solomon went to Gibeon to offer a sacrifice, for that was the chief hill-shrine, and he used to offer a thousand whole-offerings on its altar. 5*c* There that night the LORD God appeared to him in a dream and said, 6 'What shall I give you? Tell me.' And Solomon answered, 'Thou didst show great and constant love to thy servant David my father, because he walked before thee in loyalty, righteousness, and integrity of heart; and thou hast maintained this great and constant love towards him and hast now given him a son to succeed him on the 7 throne. Now, O LORD my God, thou hast made thy servant king in place of my father David, though I am a mere 8 child, unskilled in leadership. And I am here in the midst of thy people, the people of thy choice, too many to be 9 numbered or counted. Give thy servant, therefore, a heart with skill to listen,

so that he may govern thy people justly and distinguish good from evil. For who is equal to the task of governing this great people of thine?' The Lord 10 was well pleased that Solomon had asked for this, and he said to him, 11 'Because you have asked for this, and not for long life for yourself, or for wealth, or for the lives of your enemies, but have asked for discernment in administering justice, I grant 12 your request; I give you a heart so wise and so understanding that there has been none like you before your time nor will be after you. I give you 13 furthermore those things for which you did not ask, such wealth and honour*d* as no king of your time can match. And if you conform to my 14 ways and observe my ordinances and commandments, as your father David did, I will give you long life.' Then he 15 awoke, and knew it was a dream.

Solomon came to Jerusalem and stood before the Ark of the Covenant of the Lord; there he sacrificed whole-offerings and brought shared-offerings, and gave a feast to all his household.

Then there came into the king's 16 presence two women who were prostitutes and stood before him. The first 17 said, 'My lord, this woman and I share the same house, and I gave birth to a child when she was there with me. On the third day after my 18 baby was born she too gave birth to a child. We were quite alone; no one

c Verses 5–14: cp. 2 Chr. 1. 7–12.
d Or riches.

---

and wealth, 9.10–10.29; and (1') Solomon's divine disfavor, ch. 11. The resulting impression—that the building of the Temple was the great and central work of the reign and that it was only late in the reign that Solomon took foreign wives and supported foreign religious establishments—is the viewpoint of later interpreters primarily interested in the exclusive claims of the Jerusalem Temple.

3.1–28: Solomon chooses wisdom and uses it. After brief introductory comments, two popular narratives of Solomon's surpassing wisdom introduce his reign. **1:** The *Pharaoh* whose *daughter* was Solomon's wife must have belonged to the weak twenty-first dynasty, since Shishak (about 935–914 B.C.), the first king of the twenty-second dynasty, was hostile to Judah (14.25). *The City of David* was the old city. Solomon, through his building campaigns, was to double its size. **2–3:** From the late compilers' viewpoint, *hill-shrines* (including local city sanctuaries) were legitimate sanctuaries of the LORD before the Jerusalem Temple was built, but not afterward. Failure to eliminate these shrines is to be the basis for condemning most of the kings of Judah. **4–15:** *Gibeon:* once one of a group of allied Canaanite cities related to Jerusalem (Josh. 10.3–5). Cultic relations between such cities persisted into Israelite times; compare 2 Sam.21.1–14 n. Gibeon and Gibeah were two different places, at times confused with each other by ancient copyists of the Heb. text (e.g. 2 Sam.21.64). *A thousand whole-offerings* is either a great exaggeration or covers a considerable period of time. **6–9:** Solomon as imagined in seventh-century piety speaks here. **15:** This late comment is designed to reassert the religious importance of *Jerusalem* after the reference to Gibeon as "the chief hill-shrine" (v. 4). **16–28:** The wisdom

19 else was with us in the house; only the two of us were there. During the night this woman's child died because 20 she overlaid it, and she got up in the middle of the night, took my baby from my side while I, your servant, was asleep, and laid it in her bosom, 21 putting her dead child in mine. When I got up in the morning to feed my baby, I found him dead; but when I looked at him closely, I found that it was not the child that I had borne.' 22 The other woman broke in, 'No; the living child is mine; yours is the dead one', while the first retorted, 'No; the dead child is yours; mine is the living one.' So they went on arguing in the 23 king's presence. The king thought to himself, 'One of them says, "This is my child, the living one; yours is the dead one." The other says, "No; it is your child that is dead and mine that 24 is alive."' Then he said, 'Fetch me a 25 sword.' They brought in a sword and the king gave the order: 'Cut the living child in two and give half to one 26 and half to the other.' At this the woman who was the mother of the living child, moved with love for her child, said to the king, 'Oh! sir, let her have the baby; whatever you do, do not kill it.' The other said, 'Let neither 27 of us have it; cut it in two.' Thereupon the king gave judgement: 'Give the living baby to the first woman; 28 do not kill it. She is its mother.' When Israel heard the judgement which the king had given, they all stood in awe of him; for they saw that he had the wisdom of God within him to administer justice.

4 KING SOLOMON REIGNED OVER ISRAEL. 2[e] His officers were as followers:

In charge of the calendar:[f] Azariah son of Zadok the priest.
3 Adjutant-general:[g] Ahijah son[h] of Shisha.
Secretary of state: Jehoshaphat son of Ahilud.

Commander of the army: Benaiah 4 son of Jehoiada.
Priests: Zadok and Abiathar.
Superintendent of the regional go- 5 vernors: Azariah son of Nathan.
King's Friend: Zabud son of Nathan.
Comptroller of the household: Ahi- 6 shar.
Superintendent of the forced levy: Adoniram son of Abda.

Solomon had twelve regional gover- 7 nors over Israel and they supplied the food for the king and the royal household, each being responsible for one month's provision in the year. These were their names: 8

Ben-hur in the hill-country of Ephraim.
Ben-dekar in Makaz, Shaalbim, Beth- 9 shemesh, Elon, and Beth-hanan.
Ben-hesed in Aruboth; he had 10 charge also of Socoh and all the land of Hepher.
Ben-abinadab, who had married Sol- 11 omon's daughter Taphath, in all the district of Dor.
Baana son of Ahilud in Taanach and 12 Megiddo, all Beth-shean as far as Abel-meholah beside Zartanah, and from Beth-shean below Jezreel as far as Jokmeam.
Ben-geber in Ramoth-gilead, includ- 13 ing the tent-villages of Jair son of Manasseh in Gilead and the region of Argob in Bashan, sixty large walled cities with gate-bars of bronze.
Ahinadab son of Iddo in Mahanaim. 14
Ahimaaz in Naphtali; he also had 15 married a daughter of Solomon, Basmath.
Baanah son of Hushai in Asher and 16 Aloth.
Jehoshaphat son of Paruah in Issa- 17 char.
Shimei son of Elah in Benjamin. 18

e Verses 2–6: cp. 2 Sam. 8. 16–18; 20. 23–26; 1 Chr. 18. 15–17.
f In ... calendar: prob. rdg.; Heb. Elihoreph.
g Prob. rdg., cp. 1 Chr. 18. 16; Heb. Adjutants-general.
h Prob. rdg.; Heb. sons.

bestowed by the LORD results in judgments manifestly just; see Isa.11.2–5. **19:** *Overlaid:* accidentally smothered in covering the baby.
4.1–34: Solomon's administration and wisdom. 1–6: Compare 2 Sam.8.16–18 and 20.23–26.
7–19: The division of the northern part of the kingdom (*Israel*) replaced local tribal leadership with more dependable *regional governors* and resulted in more efficient support of the large

19 Geber son of Uri in Gilead, the land of Sihon king of the Amorites and of Og king of Bashan.

In addition, one governor over all the governors[i] in the land.

20 The people of Judah and Israel were countless as the sands of the sea; they ate and they drank, and enjoyed life.
21 Solomon ruled over all the kingdoms from the river Euphrates to Philistia and as far as the frontier of Egypt; they paid tribute and were subject to him all his life.
22 Solomon's provision for one day was thirty kor of flour and sixty kor
23 of meal, ten fat oxen and twenty oxen from the pastures and a hundred sheep, as well as stags, gazelles, roebucks, and
24 fattened fowl. For he was paramount over all the land west of the Euphrates from Tiphsah to Gaza, ruling all the kings west of the river; and he en-
25 joyed peace on all sides. All through his reign Judah and Israel continued at peace, every man under his own vine and fig-tree, from Dan to Beersheba.
26 Solomon had forty thousand chariot-horses in his stables and twelve thousand cavalry horses.
27 The regional governors, each for a month in turn, supplied provisions for King Solomon and for all who came to his table; they never fell short in
28 their deliveries. They provided also barley and straw, each according to his duty, for the horses and chariot-horses where it was required.
29 And God gave Solomon depth of wisdom and insight, and understanding as wide as the sand on the sea-shore,
30 so that Solomon's wisdom surpassed that of all the men of the east and of
31 all Egypt. For he was wiser than any man, wiser than Ethan the Ezrahite,

and Heman, Kalcol, and Darda, the sons of Mahol; his fame spread among all the surrounding nations.
32 He uttered three thousand proverbs, and his songs numbered a thousand
33 and five. He discoursed of trees, from the cedar of Lebanon down to the marjoram that grows out of the wall, of beasts and birds, of reptiles and fishes. Men of all races came to listen to
34 the wisdom of Solomon, and from all the kings of the earth who had heard of his wisdom he received gifts.

5 WHEN HIRAM KING OF TYRE HEARD that Solomon had been anointed king in his father's place, he sent envoys to him, because he had always been a friend of David. Solomon sent this
2[j] answer to Hiram: 'You know that my
3 father David could not build a house in honour of the name of the LORD his God, because he was surrounded by armed nations until the LORD made them subject to him. But now on every
4 side the LORD my God has given me peace; there is no one to oppose me,
5 I fear no attack. So I propose to build a house in honour of the name of the LORD my God, following the promise given by the LORD to my father David: "Your son whom I shall set on the throne in your place will build the house in honour of my
6 name." If therefore you will now give orders that cedars be felled and brought from Lebanon, my men will work with yours, and I will pay you for your men whatever sum you fix; for, as you know, we have none so skilled at felling timber as your Sidonians.'
7 When Hiram received Solomon's

i over ... governors: *prob. rdg.; Heb. om.*
j Verses 2–11: *cp. 2 Chr. 2. 3–16.*

palace establishment (vv. 27–28). **20–28:** The extent of his empire, the magnitude of his daily provisions, and the peace of his reign confer praise on Solomon and his wisdom. **22–23:** *Kor:* five bushels. These supplies may have been for royal service in several cities (see 9.15–19). **26:** Solomon maintained a large military force (compare 10.26) with which he preserved peace throughout his reign. Unlike David (compare 2 Sam.8.4), Solomon made extensive use of chariotry, as the Canaanite city-state kings had done before him (see Judg.4.12–16; Josh.11.1–9). **29–34:** Solomon's reputation for wisdom made him the hero of Wisdom literature (Prov.1.1) as David was of the Psalms. **30:** *The men of the east:* north Arabians; see Job 1.3.
5.1–9.9: The building and dedication of the Temple. This central part of the presentation of Solomon's reign is drawn from old court records (in "the annals of Solomon," 11.41) and Temple records, with inserted speeches expressing the viewpoint of the late monarchic period.
5.1–18: Preparing the materials. When *Hiram* ruled in Tyre (about 969–936 B.C.), Phoenicia

message, he was greatly pleased and said, 'Blessed be the LORD today who has given David a wise son to rule over
8 this great people.' And he sent this reply to Solomon: 'I have received your message. In this matter of timber, both cedar and pine, I will do all you
9 wish. My men shall bring down the logs from Lebanon to the sea and I will make them up into rafts to be floated to the place you appoint; I will have them broken up there and you can remove them. You, on your part, will meet my wishes if you provide the
10 food for my household.' So Hiram kept Solomon supplied with all the
11 cedar and pine that he wanted, and Solomon supplied Hiram with twenty thousand kor of wheat as food for his household and twenty kor of oil of pounded olives; Solomon gave this
12 yearly to Hiram. (The LORD had given Solomon wisdom as he had promised him; there was peace between Hiram and Solomon and they concluded an
13 alliance.) King Solomon raised a forced levy from the whole of Israel amounting
14 to thirty thousand men. He sent them to Lebanon in monthly relays of ten thousand, so that the men spent one month in Lebanon and two at home; Adoniram was superintendent of the
15 whole levy. Solomon had also seventy thousand hauliers and eighty thousand
16 quarrymen, apart from the three thousand three hundred foremen in charge of the work who superintended
17 the labourers. By the king's orders they quarried huge, massive blocks for laying the foundation of the

LORD's house in hewn stone. Solomon's 18 and Hiram's builders and the Gebalites shaped the blocks and prepared both timber and stone for the building of the house.

It was in the four hundred and 6 1[k] eightieth year after the Israelites had come out of Egypt, in the fourth year of Solomon's reign over Israel, in the second month of that year, the month of Ziv, that he began to build the house of the LORD.

The house which King Solomon 2 built for the LORD was sixty cubits long by twenty cubits broad, and its height was thirty cubits. The vestibule in 3 front of the sanctuary was twenty cubits long, spanning the whole breadth of the house, while it projected ten cubits in front of the house; and he 4 furnished the house with embrasures. Then he built a terrace against its 5 wall round both the sanctuary and the inner shrine. He made arcades all round: the lowest arcade was five 6 cubits in depth, the middle six, and the highest seven; for he made rebates all round the outside of the main wall so that the bearer beams might not be set into the walls. In the building of the 7 house, only blocks of undressed stone direct from the quarry were used; no hammer or axe or any iron tool whatever was heard in the house while it was being built.

The entrance to the lowest arcade 8 was in the right-hand corner of the house; there was access by a spiral stairway from that to the middle

k Verses 1–3: cp. 2 Chr. 3. 2–4.

---

began its great commercial success in the Mediterranean. Alliances between Tyre and land powers that controlled trade routes with the east and with Arabia were necessary for its commercial policies. **2–6:** This speech depends on 2 Sam. ch. 7. **13:** On *forced* labor see 9.20–23. **16:** *Three thousand three hundred foremen:* a foreman served over ten men, with a supervisor over ten foremen, and so on to higher officials. **18:** *Gebalites:* from the old Phoenician city Gebal; Greeks called it Byblos, the Gr. term for papyrus. Byblos, altered in spelling, yields "bible" and the prefix "biblio–."
   6.1–13: The external structure of the Temple. 1: *The fourth year of Solomon's reign was 957* B.C. or shortly after. *Four hundred and eightieth:* this number is artificial, equaling twelve generations of forty years each. *Ziv:* the old Canaanite name for *the second month* (April-May). **2:** *Cubit:* eighteen inches. **3:** *Vestibule:* an enclosed porch. **4:** *Embrasures:* openings in thick walls with sides slanting outward. **5:** *Terrace:* a platform built around the sides and rear of the Temple upon which the *arcades* were built. *The sanctuary:* the large main room of the Temple (vv. 32–35). *The inner shrine:* the holiest place of the Temple, a small chamber at the rear where the Ark would rest (see vv. 19–22; 8.6–8). The arcades were three stories high, the chambers of the lower stories narrower because their thicker walls provided support for the upper ones. The chambers in the arcades were for storage (see Neh.13.4–5). **7:** The use of an *iron tool* on the stones would have profaned them; see Exod.20.25. Iron was too new a

arcade, and from the middle arcade to the highest. So he built the house and finished it, having constructed the terrace five cubits high against the whole building, braced the house with struts of cedar and roofed it with beams and coffering of cedar.

11 Then the word of the LORD came 12 to Solomon, saying, 'As for this house which you are building, if you are obedient to my ordinances and conform to my precepts and loyally observe all my commands, then I will fulfil my promise to you, the promise I 13 gave to your father David, and I will dwell among the Israelites and never forsake my people Israel.'

14 So Solomon built the LORD's house 15 and finished it. He lined the inner walls of the house with cedar boards, covering the interior from floor to rafters with wood; the floor he laid 16 with boards of pine. In the innermost part of the house he partitioned off a space of twenty cubits with cedar boards from floor to rafters and made of it an inner shrine, to be the Most 17 Holy Place. The sanctuary in front of 18 this was forty cubits long. The cedar inside the house was carved with open flowers and gourds; all was cedar, no stone was left visible.

19 He prepared an inner shrine in the furthest recesses of the house to receive the Ark of the Covenant of the 20 LORD. This inner shrine was twenty cubits square and it stood twenty cubits high; he overlaid it with red gold and made an altar of cedar. 21 And Solomon overlaid the inside of the house with red gold and drew a Veil[l] with golden chains across in front 22 of the inner shrine.[m] The whole house he overlaid with gold until it was all covered; and the whole of the altar by the inner shrine he overlaid with gold.

23[n] In the inner shrine he made two cherubim of wild olive, each ten cubits 24 high. Each wing of the cherubim was five cubits long, and from wing-tip to wing-tip was ten cubits. Similarly the 25 second cherub measured ten cubits; the two cherubim were alike in size and shape, and each ten cubits high. He put 26,27 the cherubim within the shrine at the furthest recesses and their wings were outspread, so that a wing of the one cherub touched the wall on one side and a wing of the other touched the wall on the other side, and their other wings met in the middle; and he over-28 laid the cherubim with gold.

Round all the walls of the house 29 he carved figures of cherubim, palm-trees, and open flowers, both in the inner chamber and in the outer. The 30 floor of the house he overlaid with gold, both in the inner chamber and in the outer. At the entrance to the 31 inner shrine he made a double door of wild olive; the pilasters and the[o] doorposts were pentagonal. The doors 32 were of wild olive, and he carved cherubim, palms, and open flowers on them, overlaying them with gold and hammering the gold upon the cherubim and the palms. Similarly for 33 the doorway of the sanctuary he made a square frame of wild olive and a 34 double door of pine, each leaf having two swivel-pins. On them he carved 35 cherubim, palms, and open flowers, overlaying them evenly with gold over the carving.

He built the inner court with three 36 courses of dressed stone and one course of lengths of cedar.

In the fourth year of Solomon's 37 reign the foundation of the house of the LORD was laid, in the month of Ziv; and in the eleventh year, in the month 38 of Bul, which is the eighth month, the house was finished in all its details according to the specification. It had taken seven years to build.

l a Veil: *prob. rdg.; Heb. om.*
m Prob. rdg.; Heb. adds and overlaid it with gold.
n Verses 23–28: cp. 2 Chr. 3. 10–13.
o and the: *prob. rdg.; Heb. om.*

metal to have attained the sanctity of bronze in this Temple. **11–13:** This brief oracle anticipates 9.1–9.
6.14–38: The internal structure of the Temple. The inside of the Temple was seen only by priests, some prophets, and royalty. The description here is idealized. That *cedar* covered all the *stone* is doubtful, and that all important parts were *overlaid . . . with red gold* is a later glorification. **23:** *Cherubim:* compare Exod. 25.18–22. **38:** *Bul:* another old Canaanite month name, *the eighth month* (October–November); see also v. 1.

7 Solomon had been engaged on his building for thirteen years by the time
2 he had finished it. He built the House of the Forest of Lebanon, a hundred cubits long, fifty broad, and thirty high, constructed of four rows of cedar columns, over which were laid
3 lengths of cedar. It had a cedar roof, extending over the beams, which rested on the columns, fifteen in each row; and the number of the beams was
4 forty-five. There were three rows of window-frames, and the windows corresponded to each other at three
5 levels. All the doorways and the windows had square frames, and window corresponded to window at three levels.
6 He made also the colonnade, fifty cubits long and thirty broad,*p* with a cornice above.
7 He built the Hall of Judgement, the hall containing the throne where he was to give judgement; this was panelled in cedar from floor to rafters.
8 His own house where he was to reside, in a court set back from the colonnade, and the house he made for Pharaoh's daughter whom he had married, were constructed like the hall.
9 All these were made of heavy blocks of stone, hewn to measure and trimmed with the saw on the inner and outer sides, from foundation to coping and from the court of the house*q* as far as
10 the great court. At the base were heavy stones, massive blocks, some ten and
11 some eight cubits in size, and above were heavy stones dressed to measure,
12 and cedar. The great court had three courses of dressed stone all around and a course of lengths of cedar; so had the inner court of the house of the LORD, and so had the vestibule of the house.
13 King Solomon fetched from Tyre
14 Hiram, the son of a widow of the tribe of Naphtali. His father, a native of

Tyre, had been a worker in bronze, and he himself was a man of great skill and ingenuity, versed in every kind of craftsmanship in bronze. Hiram came to King Solomon and executed all his works.

He cast in a mould the two bronze 15*r* pillars. One stood eighteen cubits high and it took a cord twelve cubits long to go round it; it was hollow, and the metal was four fingers thick.*s* The second pillar was the same. He made 16 two capitals of solid copper to set on the tops of the pillars, each capital five cubits high. He made two bands of 17 ornamental network, in festoons of chain-work, for the capitals on the tops of the pillars, a band of network for each capital. Then he made pome- 18 granates in two rows all round on top of the ornamental network of the one pillar; he did the same with the other capital. (The capitals at the tops of the 19 pillars in the vestibule were shaped like lilies and were four cubits high.) Upon the capitals at the tops of the two 20 pillars, immediately above the cushion, which was beyond the network up- wards, were two hundred pome- granates in rows all round on the two capitals.*t* Then he erected the pillars 21 at the vestibule of the sanctuary. When he had erected the pillar on the right side, he named it Jachin;*u* and when he had erected the one on the left side, he named it Boaz.*v* On the 22 tops of the pillars was lily-work. Thus the work of the pillars was finished.

He then made the Sea of cast metal; 23*w* it was round in shape, the diameter from rim to rim being ten cubits; it stood five cubits high, and it took a line thirty cubits long to go round it.

p Prob. rdg.; Heb. adds and a colonnade and pillars in front of them.
q Prob. rdg., cp. verse 12; Heb. from outside.
r Verses 15–21: cp. 2 Chr. 3. 15–17.
s it was . . . thick: prob. rdg., cp. Jer. 52. 21; Heb. om.
t the two capitals: prob. rdg.; Heb. the second capital.
u Or Jachun, meaning It shall stand.
v Or Booz, meaning In strength.
w Verses 23–26: cp. 2 Chr. 4. 2–5.

7.1–12: The rest of the palace complex. The Temple was only one part of the entire palace. *The great court* of v. 9 enclosed the whole, within which "the inner court" of the Temple was only one area (6.36). **9:** The stones of the rest of the palace could be *trimmed with the saw,* unlike the Temple itself (6.7).
7.13–51: The bronze fixtures of the Temple court. These are again parts of the Temple com- plex visible to the lay worshiper. The bronze *trolleys* (v. 27), *basins* (v. 38), *pots, shovels,* and *tossing-bowls* (v. 40) were used in the preparation of various sacrificial materials and in the daily work of maintaining the altar.

24 All round the Sea on the outside under its rim, completely surrounding the thirty*x* cubits of its circumference, were two rows of gourds, cast in one piece 25 with the Sea itself. It was mounted on twelve oxen, three facing north, three west, three south, and three east, their hind quarters turned inwards; the 26 Sea rested on top of them. Its thickness was a hand-breadth; its rim was made like that of a cup, shaped like the calyx of a lily; it held two thousand bath of water.

27 He also made the ten trolleys of bronze; each trolley was four cubits 28 long, four wide, and three high. This was the construction of the trolleys. 29 They had panels set in frames; on these panels were portrayed lions, oxen, and cherubim, and similarly on the frames. Above and below the lions, oxen, and cherubim*y* were fillets of 30 hammered work of spiral design. Each trolley had four bronze wheels with axles of bronze; it also had four flanges and handles beneath the laver, and these handles were of cast metal with a 31 spiral design on their sides. The opening for the basin was set within a crown which projected one cubit; the opening was round with a level edge,*z* and it had decorations in relief. (The panels of the trolleys were square, not 32 round.) The four wheels were beneath the panels, and the wheel-forks were made in one piece with the trolleys; the height of each wheel was a cubit and a 33 half. The wheels were constructed like those of a chariot, their axles, hubs, spokes, and felloes being all of cast 34 metal. The four handles were at the four corners of each trolley, of one 35 piece with the trolley. At the top of the trolley there was a circular band half a cubit high; the struts and panels on*a* the trolley were of one piece with it. 36 On the plates, that is on the panels,*b* he carved cherubim, lions, and palm-trees, wherever there was a blank space, with spiral work all round it. 37 This is how the ten trolleys were made; all of them were cast alike, having the same size and the same shape.

38 He then made ten bronze basins, each holding forty bath and measuring four cubits; there was a basin for each of the ten trolleys. He put five 39 trolleys on the right side of the house and five on the left side, and he put the Sea in the south-east corner of it.

Hiram made also the pots, the shovels, 40*c* and the tossing-bowls. So he finished all the work which he had undertaken for King Solomon on the house of the LORD: the two pillars; the two 41 bowl-shaped capitals on the tops of the pillars; the two ornamental networks to cover the two bowl-shaped capitals on the tops of the pillars; the 42 four hundred pomegranates for the two networks, two rows of pomegranates for each network, to cover the bowl-shaped capitals on the two pillars; the ten trolleys and the ten basins 43 on the trolleys; the one Sea and the 44 twelve oxen which supported it; the 45 pots, the shovels, and the tossing-bowls—all these objects in the house of the LORD which Hiram made for King Solomon being of bronze, burnished work. In the Plain of the Jordan the 46 king cast them, in the foundry between Succoth and Zarethan.

Solomon put all these objects in 47 their places; so great was the quantity of bronze used in their making that the weight of it was beyond all reckoning. He made also all the furnishings 48 for the house of the LORD: the golden altar and the golden table upon which was set the Bread of the Presence; the 49 lamp-stands of red gold, five on the right side and five on the left side of the inner shrine; the flowers, lamps, and tongs, of gold; the cups, snuffers, 50 tossing-bowls, saucers, and firepans, of red gold; and the panels for the doors of the inner sanctuary, the Most Holy Place, and for the doors of the house,*d* of gold.

When all the work which King 51 Solomon did for the house of the LORD was completed, he brought in the sacred treasures of his father David, the silver, the gold, and the vessels, and deposited them in the storehouses of the house of the LORD.

8 1*e* THEN SOLOMON SUMMONED THE ELDERS of Israel, all the heads of the tribes who were chiefs of families in Israel, to assemble in Jerusalem, in order to bring up the Ark of the Covenant of the LORD from the City of David, which 2 is called Zion. All the men of Israel assembled in King Solomon's presence at the pilgrim-feast in the month 3 Ethanim, the seventh month. When the elders of Israel had all come, the 4 priests took the Ark of the LORD and carried it up with the Tent of the Presence and all the sacred furnishings of the Tent: it was the priests and the Levites together who carried them up. 5 King Solomon and the whole congregation of Israel, assembled with him before the Ark, sacrificed sheep and oxen in numbers past counting 6 or reckoning. Then the priests brought in the Ark of the Covenant of the LORD to its place, the inner shrine of the house, the Most Holy Place, beneath the wings of the cherubim. 7 The cherubim spread their wings over the place of the Ark; they formed a screen above the Ark and its poles. 8 The poles projected, and their ends could be seen from the Holy Place immediately in front of the inner shrine,

but from nowhere else outside; they are there to this day. There was 9 nothing inside the Ark but the two tablets of stone which Moses had deposited there at Horeb, the tablets of the covenant which the LORD made with the Israelites when they left Egypt.

Then the priests came out of the 10 Holy Place, since the cloud was filling the house of the LORD, and they could 11 not continue to minister because of it, for the glory of the LORD filled his house. And Solomon said: 12*f*

O LORD who hast set the sun in
  heaven,
but hast chosen to dwell in thick
  darkness,
here have I built thee a lofty house, 13
a habitation for thee to occupy for
  ever.

And as they stood waiting, the 14 king turned round and blessed all the assembly of Israel in these words: 15 'Blessed be the LORD the God of Israel who spoke directly to my father David and has himself fulfilled his promise.

e Verses 1–9: cp. 2 Chr. 5. 2–10.
f Verses 12–50: cp. 2 Chr. 6. 1–39.

8.1–66: The dedication of the Temple. This chapter (together with the LORD's response in 9.1–9) presents the second great development in the LORD's relation to Israel as the Deuteronomic historians viewed it. The first was the emergence of kingship, approved by the LORD in the form of the Davidic dynasty; see 2 Sam.7.8–16. There was also a tradition in the older period that the LORD did not dwell in a house of cedar (2 Sam.7.5–7). The Deuteronomic historians show as the second development how the LORD agreed to a change in his mode of dwelling; that change reaches its climax here with the dedication of the Temple of Solomon. This chapter consists of elements of an old report of Solomon's transfer of the Ark to the new Temple, of some Deuteronomic and priestly glosses added to that report, and of extensive speeches from a Deuteronomic viewpoint put into Solomon's mouth. **1–13:** *The Ark of the Covenant* represented the presence of the LORD. Its movement from one sanctuary to another was an awesome, even hazardous, operation (compare 2 Sam. ch. 6). **1:** The writer emphasizes that all the leaders of *Israel* participated in the ceremonies of the movement of the Ark. *The City of David* was the old city, greatly expanded on the north side by Solomon's building activities. **2:** A *pilgrim-feast* was a time when Israelites were required to appear before the LORD with offerings (Exod.23.14–17; 34.18,22–24; Deut.16.1–17). This pilgrim-feast is identified with Tabernacles, set in the later Israelite calendars at full moon of *the seventh month* (Sept.-Oct.), the old Canaanite name of which was *Ethanim*. This feast is explained as derived from a Canaanite new year festival at which the kingship of God over the powers of chaos and drought was symbolically celebrated; some associate Pss.93, 97 with the festival. Eleven months elapsed between the completion (6.38) and the dedication. **4:** This mention of *the Tent of the Presence* and *the Levites* is regarded as a late priestly gloss. **8:** The formula *to this day* was often employed in popular explanations and here may reflect a time earlier than the writer of the Deuteronomic history. **9:** A relatively late tradition combined the much older separate traditions of the *tablets of stone* (Exod.24.12; 34.1,27–29) and of the *Ark* (Num.10.35–36; 1 Sam.4.3–5); see Deut.10.1–5. *Horeb* is the usual Deuteronomic name for the mountain of God (Deut.1.6; 5.2, etc.), though it was also used in earlier traditions (Exod.3.1; 1 Kgs.19.8). **10–11:** *The cloud* of *the glory of the LORD* here is modeled after the tradition in Exod.40.34–35; compare Ezek. chs. 9–11 and 43.1–5. **12–13:** This is a piece from one of the very old Israelite collections of songs, perhaps the "Book of Jashar"; see Josh.10.13 n. and 2 Sam.1.18 n. **14–21:** In this blessing Solomon speaks in the

16 For he said, "From the day when I brought my people Israel out of Egypt, I chose no city out of all the tribes of Israel where I should build a house for my Name to be there, but I chose David to be over my people Israel."

17 My father David had in mind to build a house in honour of the name of the

18 LORD the God of Israel, but the LORD said to him, "You purposed to build a house in honour of my name; and

19 your purpose was good. Nevertheless, you shall not build it; but the son who is to be born to you, he shall build the

20 house in honour of my name." The LORD has now fulfilled his promise: I have succeeded my father David and taken his place on the throne of Israel, as the LORD promised; and I have built the house in honour of the name of the

21 LORD the God of Israel. I have assigned therein a place for the Ark containing the Covenant of the LORD, which he made with our forefathers when he brought them out of Egypt.'

22 Then Solomon, standing in front of the altar of the LORD in the presence of the whole assembly of Israel, spread out his hands towards heaven and said,

23 'O LORD God of Israel, there is no god like thee in heaven above or on earth beneath, keeping covenant with thy servants and showing them constant love while they continue faithful to thee

24 in heart and soul. Thou hast kept thy promise to thy servant David my father; by thy deeds this day thou hast fulfilled what thou didst say to him in words.

25 Now therefore, O LORD God of Israel, keep this promise of thine to thy servant David my father: "You shall never want for a man appointed by me to sit on the throne of Israel, if only your sons look to their ways and walk before me as

26 you have walked before me." And now, O God of Israel, let the words which thou didst speak to thy servant David my father be confirmed.

27 'But can God indeed dwell on earth? Heaven itself, the highest heaven, cannot contain thee; how much less this

28 house that I have built! Yet attend to the prayer and the supplication of thy servant, O LORD my God, listen to the cry and the prayer which thy servant

29 utters this day, that thine eyes may ever be upon this house night and day, this place of which thou didst say, "My Name shall be there"; so mayest thou hear thy servant when he prays

30 towards this place. Hear the supplication of thy servant and of thy people Israel when they pray towards this place. Hear thou in heaven thy dwelling and, when thou hearest, forgive.

31 'When a man wrongs his neighbour and he is adjured to take an oath, and the adjuration is made before thy

32 altar in this house, then do thou hear in heaven and act: be thou thy servants' judge, condemning the guilty man and bringing his deeds upon his own head, acquitting the innocent and rewarding him as his innocence may deserve.

33 'When thy people Israel are defeated by an enemy because they have sinned against thee, and they turn back to thee, confessing thy name and making their prayer and supplication to thee

34 in this house, do thou hear in heaven; forgive the sin of thy people Israel and restore them to the land which thou gavest to their forefathers.

35 'When the heavens are shut up and there is no rain because thy servant and thy people Israel have sinned against thee, and when they pray towards this place, confessing thy name and forsaking their sin when they feel

36 thy punishment, do thou hear in heaven and forgive their sin; so mayest thou teach them the good way which they should follow; and grant rain to thy land which thou hast given to thy people as their own possession.

37 'If there is famine in the land, or pestilence, or black blight or red, or locusts new-sloughed or fully grown; or if their enemies besiege them in any of their cities; or if plague or sickness

38 befall them, then hear the prayer or supplication of every man among thy people Israel, as each one, prompted by the remorse of his own heart, spreads

39 out his hands towards this house: hear

light of 2 Sam.7.1–16. **27–53:** A Deuteronomic theology of the Temple. A finely wrought meditation on the spatial relation of the LORD to the Temple (vv. 27 30) is followed by petitions that the LORD will hearken when the faithful will pray *towards* it in times of typical human

it in heaven thy dwelling and forgive, and act, And, as thou knowest a man's heart, reward him according to his deeds, for thou alone knowest the hearts 40 of all men; and so they will fear thee all their lives in the land thou gavest to our forefathers.

41 'The foreigner too, the man who does not belong to thy people Israel, but has come from a distant land 42 because of thy fame (for men shall hear of thy great fame and thy strong hand and arm outstretched), when he comes 43 and prays towards this house, hear in heaven thy dwelling and respond to the call which the foreigner makes to thee, so that like thy people Israel all peoples of the earth may know thy fame and fear thee, and learn that this house which I have built bears thy name.

44 'When thy people go to war with an enemy, wherever thou dost send them, when they pray to the LORD, turning towards this city which thou hast chosen and towards this house which I have 45 built in honour of thy name, do thou in heaven hear their prayer and supplication, and grant them justice. 46 'Should they sin against thee (and what man is free from sin?) and shouldst thou in thy anger give them over to an enemy, who carries them captive to his 47 own land, far or near; if in the land of their captivity they learn their lesson and make supplication again to thee in that land and say, "We have sinned and acted perversely and wickedly", 48 if they turn back to thee with heart and soul in the land of their captors, and pray to thee, turning towards their land which thou gavest to their fore-forefathers and towards this city which thou didst choose and this house which I have built in honour of thy 49 name; then in heaven thy dwelling do thou hear their prayer and supplication, 50 and grant them justice. Forgive thy

people their sins and transgressions against thee; put pity for them in their captors' hearts. For they are thy pos- 51 session, thy people whom thou didst bring out of Egypt, from the smelting-furnace, and so thine eyes are ever open 52 to the entreaty of thy servant and of thy people Israel, and thou dost hear whenever they call to thee. Thou thyself hast 53 singled them out from all the peoples of the earth to be thy possessions; so thou didst promise through thy servant Moses when thou didst bring our fore-fathers from Egypt, O Lord GOD.'

When Solomon had finished this 54 prayer and supplication to the LORD, he rose from before the altar of the LORD, where he had been kneeling with his hands spread out to heaven, stood 55 up and in a loud voice blessed the whole assembly of Israel: 'Blessed be 56 the LORD who has given his people Israel rest, as he promised: not one of the promises he made through his servant Moses has failed. The LORD our 57 God be with us as he was with our forefathers; may he never leave us nor forsake us. May he turn our hearts 58 towards him, that we may conform to all his ways, observing his commandments, statutes, and judgements, as he commanded our forefathers. And 59 may the words of my supplication to the LORD be with the LORD our God day and night, that, as the need arises day by day, he may grant justice to his servant and justice to his people Israel. So all the peoples of the earth 60 will know that the LORD is God, he and no other, and you will be perfect in 61 loyalty to the LORD our God as you are this day, conforming to his statutes and observing his commandments.'

When the king and all Israel came 62 to offer sacrifices before the LORD, Sol-omon offered as shared-offerings to the 63 LORD twenty-two thousand oxen and a hundred and twenty thousand sheep;

---

crises. **46–53:** This passage deals with Exile. It is commonly viewed as an addition from the time of the Exile to Babylonia after 587. Yet the possibility of exile (and the terms of return) were issues of importance from shortly after the fall of the Northern Kingdom (722 B.C.). Hence, though the present form of vv. 46–53 may come after 587, its leading ideas are probably much older, possibly as old as Hezekiah, about 715–687 B.C.; see 2 Kgs.18.3–8; 2 Chr.30.1–31.1. For other passages anticipating exile, see Lev.26.32–45; Deut.4.25–31; 30.1–10. **54–61:** A second benediction refers to the promises *through . . . Moses* rather than those to David; see vv. 14–21. **62–66:** The numbers in v. 63 are exaggerated. *The bronze altar* (v. 64) is curiously lacking from

thus it was that the king and the Israelites dedicated the house of the Lord.
64[g] On that day also the king consecrated the centre of the court which lay in front[h] of the house of the Lord; there he offered the whole-offering, the grain-offering, and the fat portions of the shared-offerings, because the bronze altar which stood before the Lord was too small to take them all, the whole-offering, the grain-offering, and the fat portions of the shared-offerings.
65 So Solomon and all Israel with him, a great assembly from Lebo-hamath to the Torrent of Egypt, celebrated the pilgrim-feast at that time before the
66 Lord our God for seven days. On the eighth day he dismissed the people; and they blessed the king, and went home happy and glad at heart for all the prosperity granted by the Lord to his servant David and to his people Israel.

9[i] WHEN SOLOMON HAD FINISHED THE house of the Lord and the royal palace and all the plans for building on
2 which he had set his heart, the Lord appeared to him a second time, as he
3 had appeared to him at Gibeon. The Lord said to him, 'I have heard the prayer and supplication which you have offered me; I have consecrated this house which you have built, to receive my Name for all time, and my eyes and my heart shall be fixed on it
4 for ever. And if you, on your part, live in my sight as your father David lived, in integrity and uprightness, doing all I command you and observing my statutes and my judgements,
5 then I will establish your royal throne over Israel for ever, as I promised your father David when I said, "You shall never want for a man upon the throne

of Israel." But if you or your sons 6 turn back from following me and do not observe my commandments and my statutes which I have set before you, and if you go and serve other gods and prostrate yourselves before them, then I will cut off Israel from the 7 land which I gave them; I will renounce this house which I have consecrated in honour of my name, and Israel shall become a byword and an object lesson among all peoples. And 8 this house will become a ruin; every passer-by will be appalled and gasp at the sight of it; and they will ask, "Why has the Lord so treated this land and this house?" The answer will 9 be, "Because they forsook the Lord their God, who brought their forefathers out of Egypt, and clung to other gods, prostrating themselves before them and serving them; that is why the Lord has brought this great evil on them."'

Solomon had taken twenty years to 10[j] build the two houses, the house of the Lord and the royal palace. Hiram king 11 of Tyre had supplied him with all the timber, both cedar and pine, and all the gold, that he desired, and King Solomon gave Hiram twenty cities in the land of Galilee. But when Hiram 12 went from Tyre to inspect the cities which Solomon had given him, they did not satisfy him, and he said, 13 'What kind of cities are these you have given me, my brother?' And so he called them the Land of Cabul,[k] the name they still bear. Hiram sent a 14 hundred and twenty talents of gold to the king.

g *Verses 64–66: cp. 2 Chr. 7. 7–10.*
h *Or to the east.*
i *Verses 1–9: cp. 2 Chr. 7. 11–22.*
j *Verses 10–28: cp. 2 Chr. 8. 1–18.*
k *That is* Sterile Land.

---

the description of the Temple court fixtures in 7.13–46. **65:** *Lebo-hamath* was north of the Lebanon mountain range in Syria.
9.1–9: The Lord sanctions the Temple. Of all the kings treated in this history, it is only to Solomon that the Lord speaks directly; otherwise he speaks through prophets. The Deuteronomic historians portray the Lord's approval of the Jerusalem Temple, and the conditions on which that approval is given. They saw the meaning of the history of the kingdoms epitomized in the recurrent failures to meet those conditions. **2:** *Gibeon:* see 3.4–15. **5:** For the promise to *David,* see 2 Sam.7.8–16.
9.10–10.29: Solomon's works, wisdom, and wealth. The materials of this section balance those of ch. 4; see 3.1–11.43 n. **10–14:** The reasons for Solomon's sale of *cities* (actually only villages) are unknown, though overexpenditure in building programs is a likely explanation. A playful folk etymology explains the town name *Cabul* (v. 13) as meaning "like nothing."

15 This is the record of the forced labour which King Solomon conscripted to build the house of the LORD, his own palace, the Millo, the wall of Jerusalem, and Hazor, Megiddo, and
16 Gezer. Gezer had been attacked and captured by Pharaoh king of Egypt, who had burnt it to the ground, put its Canaanite inhabitants to death, and given it as a marriage gift to his
17 daughter, Solomon's wife; and Solomon rebuilt it. He also built Lower
18 Beth-horon, Baalath, and Tamar in
19 the wilderness, as well as all his store-cities, and the towns where he quartered his chariots and horses; and he carried out all his cherished plans for building in Jerusalem, in the Lebanon, and
20 throughout his whole dominion. All the survivors of the Amorites, Hittites, Perizzites, Hivites, and Jebusites, who
21 did not belong to Israel—that is their descendants who survived in the land, wherever the Israelites had been unable to annihilate them—were employed by Solomon on perpetual forced
22 labour, as they still are. But Solomon put none of the Israelites to forced labour; they were his fighting men,[l] his captains and lieutenants, and the commanders of his chariots and of his
23 cavalry. The number of officers in charge of the foremen over Solomon's work was five hundred and fifty; these superintended the people engaged on the work.
24 Then Solomon brought Pharaoh's daughter up from the City of David to her own house which he had built for her; later on he built the Millo.
25 Three times a year Solomon used to offer whole-offerings and shared-offerings on the altar which he had built to the LORD, making smoke-offerings before the LORD. So he completed the house.
26 King Solomon built a fleet of ships at Ezion-geber, near Eloth[m] on the shore of the Red Sea,[n] in Edom.
27 Hiram sent men of his own to serve

with the fleet, experienced seamen, to work with Solomon's men; and they 28 went to Ophir and brought back four hundred and twenty talents of gold, which they delivered to King Solomon.

THE QUEEN OF SHEBA HEARD OF SOL- 10 1[o] omon's fame[p] and came to test him with hard questions. She arrived in Jeru- 2 salem with a very large retinue, camels laden with spices, gold in great quantity, and precious stones. When she came to Solomon, she told him everything she had in her mind, and Solomon 3 answered all her questions; not one of them was too abstruse for the king to answer. When the queen of Sheba 4 saw all the wisdom of Solomon, the house which he had built, the food on 5 his table, the courtiers sitting round him, and his attendants standing behind in their livery, his cupbearers, and the whole-offerings which he used to offer in the house of the LORD, there was no more spirit left in her. Then 6 she said to the king, 'The report which I heard in my own country about you and your wisdom was true, but I did not believe it until I 7 came and saw for myself. Indeed I was not told half of it; your wisdom and your prosperity go far beyond the report which I had of them. Happy 8 are your wives, happy these courtiers of yours who wait on you every day and hear your wisdom! Blessed be the 9 LORD your God who has delighted in you and has set you on the throne of Israel; because he loves Israel for ever, he has made you their king to maintain law and justice.' Then she 10 gave the king a hundred and twenty talents of gold, spices in great abundance, and precious stones. Never again came such a quantity of spices as the queen of Sheba gave to King Solomon.

l *Prob. rdg.; Heb. adds* and his servants.
m *Or* Elath.   n *Or* the Sea of Reeds.
o *Verses 1–25: cp.* 2 *Chr.* 9. 1–24.
p *Prob. rdg., cp.* 2 *Chr.* 9. 1; *Heb. adds* to the name of the LORD.

15–23: *The forced labour* for Solomon's projects was probably drawn largely from non-Israelite inhabitants of Canaan, but some Israelites were apparently also drawn upon; see 5.13; 11.28; 12.4. From a later viewpoint, the continued presence of non-Israelites in the promised land required special explanation; see Josh.9.22–27; Judg.2.20–3.6. **24:** See 3.1 n. **25:** *Three times a year:* see 8.2 n. **26–28:** Commerce rather than conquest was the key to Solomon's wealth. **10.1–13:** This narrative is a popular magnification of Solomon's wisdom. *Sheba* was a region

11 Besides all this, Hiram's fleet of ships, which had brought gold from Ophir, brought in also from Ophir cargoes of
12 almug wood and precious stones. The king used the wood to make stools for the house of the LORD and for the royal palace, as well as harps and lutes for the singers. No such almug wood has ever been imported or even seen since that time.
13 And King Solomon gave the queen of Sheba all she desired, whatever she asked, in addition to all that he gave her of his royal bounty. So she departed and returned with her retinue to her own land.
14 Now the weight of gold which Solomon received yearly was six
15 hundred and sixty-six talents, in addition to the tolls levied by the customs officers and profits on foreign trade, and the tribute of*q* the kings of Arabia and the regional governors.
16 King Solomon made two hundred shields of beaten gold, and six hundred shekels of gold went to the making of
17 each one; he also made three hundred bucklers of beaten gold, and three minas of gold went to the making of each buckler. The king put these into the House of the Forest of Lebanon.
18 The king also made a great throne of ivory and overlaid it with fine gold.
19 Six steps led up to the throne; at the back of the throne there was the head of a calf. There were arms on each side of the seat, with a lion standing beside
20 each of them, and twelve lions stood on the six steps, one at either end of each step. Nothing like it had ever
21 been made for any monarch. All Solomon's drinking vessels were of gold, and all the plate in the House of the Forest of Lebanon was of red gold; no silver was used, for it was reckoned

of no value in the days of Solomon.
22 The king had a fleet of merchantmen at sea with Hiram's fleet; once every three years this fleet of merchantmen came home, bringing gold and silver, ivory, apes and monkeys.
23 Thus King Solomon outdid all the kings of the earth in wealth and wis-
24 dom, and all the world courted him, to hear the wisdom which God had put
25 in his heart. Each brought his gift with him, vessels of silver and gold, garments, perfumes and spices, horses and mules, so much year by year.
26 And Solomon got together many*r* chariots and horses; he had fourteen hundred chariots and twelve thousand horses, and he stabled some in the chariot-towns and kept others at hand
27 in Jerusalem. The king made silver as common in Jerusalem as stones, and cedar as plentiful as sycomore-fig in
28 the Shephelah. Horses were imported from Egypt and Coa for Solomon; the royal merchants obtained them
29 from Coa by purchase. Chariots were imported from Egypt for six hundred silver shekels each, and horses for a hundred and fifty; in the same way the merchants obtained them for export from all the kings of the Hittites and the kings of Aram.

11 King Solomon was a lover of women, and besides Pharaoh's daughter he married many foreign women, Moab-
2 ite, Ammonite, Edomite, Sidonian, and Hittite, from the nations with whom the LORD had forbidden the Israelites to intermarry, 'because', he said, 'they will entice you to serve their gods.' But Solomon was devoted to them and
3 loved them dearly. He had seven hundred wives, who were princesses,

q and the tribute of: prob. rdg.; Heb. and all.
r Verses 26–29: cp. 2 Chr. 1. 14–17; 9. 25–28.

in Arabia, renowned for wisdom; see 4.30 n. **11:** *Almug wood:* sandalwood, used for ornamental carving and incense. **13:** The Ethiopian tradition of their king's descent from David is based on interpreting *all she desired* as including an heir. **14–29:** These verses indicate the sources and the uses of Solomon's great wealth. **28:** *Coa:* Cilicia, in southern Asia Minor.

11.1–43: Solomon's divine disfavor. This chapter is a special construction of the Deutero-nomic historians. They balanced a positive view of Solomon as wise ruler and devout Temple builder with a negative view of him as taking foreign wives, sponsoring foreign cults, and beginning the process of apostasy that was eventually to undo Israel (compare Deut.17.14–20; 7.1–4). The view here is that the apostasy resulting from his foreign wives arose only late in his reign. However, his son and successor Rehoboam was born of an Ammonite wife one year before Solomon came to the throne, for Rehoboam was forty-one (14.21) when he succeeded Solomon, who reigned forty years (11.42). Solomon married his Egyptian wife during the first twenty years of his reign (3.1; 6.1; 9.10). The Deuteronomic historians suggest that rebellions

and three hundred concubines, and they turned his heart from the truth. 4 When he grew old, his wives turned his heart to follow other gods, and he did not remain wholly loyal to the LORD his God as his father David had 5 been. He followed Ashtoreth, goddess of the Sidonians, and Milcom, the loath-6 some god of the Ammonites. Thus Solomon did what was wrong in the eyes of the LORD, and was not loyal 7 to the LORD like his father David. He built a hill-shrine for Kemosh, the loathsome god of Moab, on the height to the east of Jerusalem, and for Molech, the loathsome god of the 8 Ammonites. Thus he did for the gods to which all his foreign wives burnt 9 offerings and made sacrifices. The LORD was angry with Solomon because his heart had turned away from the LORD the God of Israel, who had 10 appeared to him twice and had strictly commanded him not to follow other gods; but he disobeyed the LORD's 11 command. The LORD therefore said to Solomon, 'Because you have done this and have not kept my covenant and my statutes as I commanded you, I will tear the kingdom from you and 12 give it to your servant. Nevertheless, for the sake of your father David I will not do this in your day; I will tear it 13 out of your son's hand. Even so not the whole kingdom; I will leave him one tribe for the sake of my servant David and for the sake of Jerusalem, my chosen city.'

14 Then the LORD raised up an adversary for Solomon, Hadad the Edomite, of 15 the royal house of Edom. At the time when David reduced Edom, his commander-in-chief Joab had destroyed every male in the country when he went 16 into it to bury the slain. He and the armies of Israel remained there for six months, until he had destroyed every 17 male in Edom. Then Hadad, who was still a boy, fled the country with

some of his father's Edomite servants, intending to enter Egypt. They set out 18 from Midian, made their way to Paran and, taking some men from there, came to Pharaoh king of Egypt, who assigned Hadad a house and maintenance and made him a grant of land. Hadad found great favour with 19 Pharaoh, who gave him in marriage a sister of Queen Tahpenes his wife. She bore him his son Genubath; 20 Tahpenes weaned the child in Pharaoh's house, and he lived there along with Pharaoh's children. When Hadad 21 heard in Egypt that David rested with his forefathers and that his commander-in-chief Joab was also dead, he said to Pharaoh, 'Let me go so that I may return to my own country.' 'What is 22 it that you find wanting in my country', said Pharaoh, 'that you want to go back to your own?' 'Nothing,' said Hadad, 'but do, pray, let me go.' He 25 remained an adversary for Israel all through Solomon's reign. This is the harm that Hadad caused: he maintained a stranglehold on Israel and became king of Edom.

Then God raised up another ad-23 versary against Solomon, Rezon son of Eliada, who had fled from his master Hadadezer king of Zobah. He gathered 24 men about him and became a captain of freebooters, who came to Damascus and occupied it; he became king there.

Jeroboam son of Nebat, one of 26[s] Solomon's courtiers, an Ephrathite from Zeredah, whose widowed mother was named Zeruah, rebelled against the king. And this is the story of his 27 rebellion. Solomon had built the Millo and closed the breach in the wall of the city of his father David. Now this 28 Jeroboam was a man of great energy; and Solomon, seeing how the young man worked, had put him in charge of all the labour-gangs in the tribal

s Verse 25 transposed to follow verse 22.

against Solomon reflected the LORD's abandoning him (vv. 14–40). **5–7:** *Milcom* and *Molech* are variants of *melek*, "king," used as a name for the Ammonite god. These shrines remained for more than three hundred years; see 2 Kgs.23.13. **13:** *David* and *Jerusalem* are the primary objects of interest in the Deuteronomic history. **14–25:** All that is known of *Hadad the Edomite* is related here. Though *Edom* was not a serious threat during Solomon's reign, a resistance group may have arisen there. **18:** The change of dynasties in Egypt (see 3.1 n.) almost certainly affected Solomon's political relations; see also v. 40. **23:** *Hadadezer*: see 2 Sam.10.15–19.

29 district of Joseph. On one occasion Jeroboam had left Jerusalem, and the prophet Ahijah from Shiloh met him on the road. The prophet was wrapped in a new cloak, and the two of them 30 were alone in the open country. Then Ahijah took hold of the new cloak he was wearing, tore it into twelve pieces 31 and said to Jeroboam, 'Take ten pieces, for this is the word of the LORD the God of Israel: "I am going to tear the kingdom from the hand of Solomon 32 and give you ten tribes. But one tribe will remain his, for the sake of my servant David and for the sake of Jerusalem, the city I have chosen out 33 of all the tribes of Israel. I have done this because Solomon has forsaken me; he has prostrated himself before Ashtoreth goddess of the Sidonians, Kemosh god of Moab, and Milcom god of the Ammonites, and has not conformed to my ways. He has not done what is right in my eyes or observed my statutes and judgements as David his 34 father did. Nevertheless I will not take the whole kingdom from him, but will maintain his rule as long as he lives, for the sake of my chosen servant David, who did observe my commandments 35 and statutes. But I will take the kingdom, that is the ten tribes, from his 36 son and give it to you. One tribe I will give to his son, that my servant David may always have a flame burning before me in Jerusalem, the city which 37 I chose to receive my Name. But I will appoint you to rule over all that you can desire, and to be king over Israel. 38 If you pay heed to all my commands, if you conform to my ways and do what is right in my eyes, observing my statutes and commandments as my servant David did, then I will be with you. I will establish your family for

ever as I did for David; I will give Israel to you, and punish David's 39 descendants as they have deserved, but not for ever."'

After this Solomon sought to kill 40 Jeroboam, but he fled to King Shishak in Egypt and remained there till Solomon's death.

The other acts and events of Sol- 41*t* omon's reign, and all his wisdom, are recorded in the annals of Solomon. The 42 reign of King Solomon in Jerusalem over the whole of Israel lasted forty years. Then he rested with his fore- 43 fathers and was buried in the city of David his father, and he was succeeded by his son Rehoboam.

The divided kingdom

REHOBOAM WENT TO SHECHEM, FOR ALL 12 1*u* Israel had gone there to make him king. When Jeroboam son of Nebat, who 2 was still in Egypt, heard of it, he re-mained there, having taken refuge there to escape King Solomon. They now re- 3 called him, and he and all the assembly of Israel came to Rehoboam and said, 'Your father laid a cruel yoke upon 4 us; but if you will now lighten the cruel slavery he imposed on us and the heavy yoke he laid on us, we will serve you.' 'Give me three days,' he 5 said, 'and come back again.' So the people went away. King Rehoboam 6 then consulted the elders who had been in attendance on his father Solomon while he lived: 'What answer do you advise me to give to this people?' And they said, 'If today you 7 are willing to serve this people, show yourself their servant now and speak

t Verses 41–43: cp. 2 Chr. 9. 29–31.
u Verses 1–19: cp. 2 Chr. 10. 1–19.

Rezon was probably only a rebellious vassal of Solomon. **29–39:** Here appears the first instance of a pattern repeated throughout Kgs.: The LORD sends a prophet to announce in advance a change in dynasty, thus giving a divine sanction to the change and to the new dynasty. Thus, the northern dynasties of Jeroboam, Baasha, and Jehu had divine sanction; the dynasty of Omri did not, nor did any of the kings who ruled after the fall of the Jehu dynasty. This theory of legitimacy is presented in 14.7–11,14; 15.25–29; 16.1–4,9–12; 19.15–18; 21.17–22; 2 Kgs.9.1–10; 10.30–31; 15.8–12. **30–32:** *Twelve* was the traditional number of the tribes; but by this time Judah had absorbed Simeon and the two were spoken of as only *one tribe.*
12.1–16.34: The first period of the two kingdoms. Here the compilers of Kgs. begin their parallel account of the two kingdoms. The sources drawn upon are the royal annals of Judah and Israel (14.19,29) and collections of prophetic legends.
12.1–24: The division of the two kingdoms. 1: David ruled over Israel by covenant (2 Sam.5.3); apparently that kingship had to be renewed at the beginning of each reign. **3:** More than one

kindly to them, and they will be your
8 servants ever after.' But he rejected
the advice which the elders gave him.
He next consulted those who had
grown up with him, the young men
9 in attendance, and asked them, 'What
answer do you advise me to give to
this people's request that I should
lighten the yoke which my father laid
10 on them?' The young men replied,
'Give this answer to the people who
say that your father made their yoke
heavy and ask you to lighten it; tell them:
"My little finger is thicker than my
11 father's loins. My father laid a heavy
yoke on you; I will make it heavier.
My father used the whip on you; but
12 I will use the lash."' Jeroboam and the
people all came back to Rehoboam
on the third day, as the king had
13 ordered. And the king gave them a
harsh answer. He rejected the advice
14 which the elders had given him and
spoke to the people as the young men
had advised: 'My father made your
yoke heavy, I will make it heavier.
My father used the whip on you; but I
15 will use the lash.' So the king would not
listen to the people; for the LORD had
given this turn to the affair, in order
that the word he had spoken by Ahijah
of Shiloh to Jeroboam son of Nebat
might be fulfilled.
16   When all Israel saw that the king
would not listen to them, they answered:

What share have we in David?
We have no lot in the son of Jesse.
Away to your homes, O Israel;
  now see to your own house, David.

17 So Israel went to their homes, and
Rehoboam ruled over those Israelites
who lived in the cities of Judah.
18   Then King Rehoboam sent out Adoram, the commander of the forced

levies, but the Israelites stoned him to
death; thereupon King Rehoboam
mounted his chariot in haste and
fled to Jerusalem. From that day 19
to this, the whole of Israel has been
in rebellion against the house of
David.
   When the men of Israel heard that 20
Jeroboam had returned, they sent and
called him to the assembly and made
him king over the whole of Israel. The
tribe of Judah alone followed the
house of David.
   When Rehoboam reached Jerusalem, 21*v*
he assembled all the house of Judah,
the tribe of Benjamin also, a hundred
and eighty thousand chosen warriors,
to fight against the house of Israel and
recover his kingdom. But the word 22
of God came to Shemaiah the man of
God: 'Say to Rehoboam son of 23
Solomon, king of Judah, and to the
house of Judah and to Benjamin and
the rest of the people, "This is the 24
word of the LORD: You shall not go
up to make war on your kinsmen the
Israelites. Return to your homes, for
this is my will."' So they listened to
the word of the LORD and returned
home, as the LORD had told them.
   Then Jeroboam rebuilt Shechem in 25
the hill-country of Ephraim and took
up residence there; from there he went
out and built Penuel. 'As things now 26
stand,' he said to himself, 'the kingdom will revert to the house of David.
If this people go up to sacrifice in the 27
house of the LORD in Jerusalem, it will
revive their allegiance to their lord
Rehoboam king of Judah, and they
will kill me and return to King Rehoboam.' After giving thought to the 28
matter he made two calves of gold and
said to the people, 'It is too much
trouble for you to go up to Jerusalem;

v Verses 21–24: cp. 2 Chr. 11. 1–4.

---

account of *Jeroboam* has been drawn upon; this verse conflicts with v. 20. **15:** *Ahijah*: see
11.29–39. **16:** See the similar summons in 2 Sam.20.1. **19:** *From that day to this:* a formula
not always used literally; see 8.8 n. **21–24:** A prophetic oracle forces *Rehoboam* to accept the
division of the kingdoms.
   12.25–33: Jeroboam's religious establishment. Jeroboam, to secure his kingdom, fortified
Shechem, making it his capital city west of the Jordan, and then securing a similar military
base east of the Jordan, at *Penuel* in Gilead. Dan and Bethel (vv. 29–30) were at the northern
and southern extremes of his kingdom. **28:** Images of *calves* or bulls were associated with
worship of the Canaanite deity Baal. Tradition also traced such an image to Aaron, however;
see Exod.32.1–6. Speaking of *gods* in the plural is intended to express an alien viewpoint;

here are your gods, Israel, that brought
29 you up from Egypt.' One he set up at
Bethel and the other he put at Dan,
30 and this thing became a sin in Israel;
the people went to Bethel to worship
the one, and all the way to Dan to wor-
31 ship the other. He set up shrines on the
hill-tops also and appointed priests
from every class of the people, who
32 did not belong to the Levites. He instituted a pilgrim-feast on the fifteenth
day of the eighth month like that in
Judah, and he offered sacrifices upon
the altar. This he did at Bethel, sacrificing to the calves that he had made and
compelling the priests of the hill-shrines,
which he had set up, to serve at Bethel.
33 So he went up to the altar that he had
made at Bethel on the fifteenth day of
the eighth month; there, in a month
of his own choosing, he instituted for
the Israelites a pilgrim-feast and himself went up to the altar to burn the
sacrifice.

13 As Jeroboam stood by the altar to
burn the sacrifice, a man of God from
Judah, moved by the word of the
2 LORD, appeared at Bethel. He inveighed
against the altar in the LORD's name,
crying out, 'O altar, altar! This is the
word of the LORD: "Listen! A child
shall be born to the house of David,
named Josiah. He will sacrifice upon
you the priests of the hill-shrines who
make offerings upon you, and he will
3 burn human bones upon you."' He
gave a sign the same day: 'This is
the sign which the LORD has ordained:
This altar will be rent in pieces and the
4 ashes upon it will be spilt.' When King
Jeroboam heard the sentence which
the man of God pronounced against
the altar at Bethel, he pointed to him
from the altar and said, 'Seize that
man!' Immediately the hand which he
had pointed at him became paralysed,
5 so that he could not draw it back. The
altar too was rent in pieces and the
ashes were spilt, in fulfilment of the
sign that the man of God had given

at the LORD's command. The king 6
appealed to the man of God to pacify
the LORD his God and pray for him
that his hand might be restored. The
man of God did as he asked; his hand
was restored and became as it had been
before. Then the king said to the man 7
of God, 'Come home and take refreshment at my table, and let me
give you a present.' But the man of 8
God answered, 'If you were to give me
half your house, I would not enter it
with you: I will eat and drink nothing
in this place, for the LORD's command 9
to me was to eat and drink nothing,
and not to go back by the way I came.'
So he went back another way; he did 10
not return by the road he had taken to
Bethel.

At that time there was an aged proph- 11
et living in Bethel. His sons came and
recounted to him all that the man of
God had done in Bethel that day;
they also told their father what he had
said to the king. Their father said to 12
them, 'Which road did he take?' They
pointed out the road taken by the
man of God who had come from Judah.
He said to his sons, 'Saddle an ass for 13
me.' They saddled the ass, and he
mounted it and went after the man of 14
God. He found him seated under a
terebinth and said to him, 'Are you the
man of God who came from Judah?'
And he said, 'Yes, I am.' 'Come 15
home and eat with me', said the
prophet. 'I cannot go back with you 16
or enter your house', said the other;
'I can neither eat nor drink with you 17
in this place, for it was told me by the
word of the LORD: "You shall eat
and drink nothing there, nor shall you
go back the way you came."' And the 18
old man said to him, 'I also am a
prophet, as you are; and an angel
commanded me by the word of the
LORD to bring you home with me to
eat and drink with me.' He was
lying; but the man of Judah went back 19
with him and ate and drank in his

---

compare 1 Sam.4.8. **31–33:** Besides the cultic objects and sanctuaries, Jeroboam established
his own priesthood, his own pilgrim-feast (one month later than in Jerusalem; see 8.2 n.),
and he himself offered the sacrifices.
 13.1–34: The man of God from Judah. A prophetic legend reflects divine condemnation of
Jeroboam's altar and anticipates Josiah's destruction of it over three hundred years later.
2: See 2 Kgs.23.15. **4–6:** On such prophetic miracles, compare 2 Kgs.2.19–25; 4.38–44.

20 house. While they were still seated at table the word of the LORD came to the prophet who had brought him
21 back, and he cried out to the man of God from Judah, 'This is the word of the LORD: "You have defied the word of the LORD your God and have not
22 obeyed his command; you have come back to eat and to drink in the place where he forbade it; therefore your body shall not be laid in the grave of your forefathers."'

23 After they had eaten and drunk, he saddled an ass for the prophet whom
24 he had brought back. As he went on his way a lion met him and killed him, and his body was left lying in the road, with the ass and the lion both
25 standing beside it. Some passers-by saw the body lying in the road and the lion standing beside it, and they brought the news to the city where the
26 old prophet lived. When the prophet who had caused him to break his journey heard it, he said, 'It is the man of God who defied the word of the LORD. The LORD has given him to the lion, and it has broken his neck and killed him in fulfilment of the word of the
27 LORD.' He told his sons to saddle an
28 ass and, when they had saddled it, he set out and found the body lying in the road with the ass and the lion standing beside it; the lion had neither devoured the body nor broken the back
29 of the ass. Then the prophet lifted the body of the man of God, laid it on the ass and brought it back to his own city to mourn over it and bury it. He laid
30 the body in his own grave and they mourned for him, saying, 'My brother,
31 my brother!' After burying him, he said to his sons, 'When I die, bury me in the grave where the man of God lies buried; lay my bones beside his; for the sen-
32 tence which he pronounced at the LORD's command against the altar in Bethel and all the hill-shrines of Samaria shall be carried out.'

33 After this Jeroboam still did not abandon his evil ways but went on appointing priests for the hill-shrines from all classes of the people; any man who offered himself he would conse-
34 crate to be priest of a hill-shrine. By doing this he brought guilt upon his own house and doomed it to utter destruction.

At that time Jeroboam's son Abijah **14** fell ill, and Jeroboam said to his wife, 2 'Come now, disguise yourself so that people may not be able to recognize you as my wife, and go to Shiloh. Ahijah the prophet is there, the man who said I was to be king over this people. Take 3 with you ten loaves, some raisins, and a flask of syrup, and go to him; he will tell you what will happen to the child.' Jeroboam's wife did so; she set 4 off at once for Shiloh and came to Ahijah's house. Now Ahijah could not see, for his eyes were fixed in the blindness of old age, and the LORD 5 had said to him, 'The wife of Jeroboam is on her way to consult you about her son, who is ill; you shall give her such and such an answer.' When she came in, concealing who she was, and Ahijah heard her footsteps at the door, 6 he said, 'Come in, wife of Jeroboam. Why conceal who you are? I have heavy news for you. Go and tell Jer- 7 oboam: "This is the word of the LORD the God of Israel: I raised you out of the people and appointed you prince over my peole Israel; I tore away 8 the kingdom from the house of David and gave it to you; but you have not been like my servant David, who kept my commands and followed me with his whole heart, doing only what was right in my eyes. You have outdone 9 all your predecessors in wickedness; you have provoked me to anger by making for yourself other gods and images of cast metal; and you have turned your back on me. For this I will bring disaster on the house of 10 Jeroboam and I will destroy them all, every mother's son, whether still under the protection of the family or not, and I will sweep away the house of Jeroboam in Israel, as a man sweeps up dung until none is left. Those of 11

14.1–20: Prophetic condemnation of Jeroboam. This legend enhances the prophets (vv. 4–6, 12,17); it is used here to convey a second stage of the Deuteronomic theory about northern kingship (vv. 7–11; compare 11.29–39 n.). **1:** *Jeroboam* sends to the prophet who had originally sanctioned his kingship (11.29–39). **11:** The stereotyped curse here means that no member of that house who die in the city shall be food for the dogs, and those who die in the country shall be food for the birds. It is the word of the LORD."

12 'You must go home now; the moment you set foot in the city, the

13 child will die. All Israel will mourn for him and bury him; he alone of all Jeroboam's family will have proper burial, because in him alone could the LORD the God of Israel find

14 anything good. Then the LORD will set up a king over Israel who shall put an end to the house of Jeroboam. This

15 first; and what next? The LORD will strike Israel, till it trembles like a reed in the water; he will uproot its people from this good land which he gave to their forefathers and scatter them beyond the Euphrates, because they have made their sacred poles and provoked

16 the LORD's anger. And he will abandon Israel for the sins that Jeroboam has committed and has led Israel to

17 commit.' Jeroboam's wife went home at once to Tirzah and, as she crossed the threshold of the house, the boy

18 died. They buried him, and all Israel mourned over him; and thus the word of the LORD was fulfilled which he had spoken through his servant Ahijah the prophet.

19 The other events of Jeroboam's reign, in war and peace, are recorded in the annals of the kings of Israel.

20 He reigned twenty-two years; then he rested with his forefathers and was succeeded by his son Nadab.

21 IN JUDAH REHOBOAM SON OF SOLOMON had become king. He was forty-one years old when he came to the throne, and he reigned for seventeen years in Jerusalem, the city which the LORD had chosen out of all the tribes of Israel to receive his Name. Rehoboam's mother was a woman of Ammon

22 called Naamah. Judah did what was wrong in the eyes of the LORD, rousing his jealous indignation by the sins they committed, beyond anything that

23 their forefathers had done. They erected hill-shrines, sacred pillars, and sacred poles, on every high hill and

24 under every spreading tree. Worse still, all over the country there were male prostitutes attached to the shrines, and the people adopted all the abominable practices of the nations whom the LORD had dispossessed in favour of Israel.

25 In the fifth year of Rehoboam's reign Shishak king of Egypt attacked

26 Jerusalem. He removed the treasures of the house of the LORD and of the royal palace, and seized everything, including all the shields of gold that

27 Solomon had made. King Rehoboam replaced them with bronze shields and entrusted them to the officers of the escort who guarded the entrance of

28 the royal palace. Whenever the king entered the house of the LORD, the escort carried them; afterwards they returned them to the guard-room.

29 The other acts and events of Rehoboam's reign are recorded in the annals

30 of the kings of Judah. There was continual fighting between him and

31 Jeroboam. He rested with his forefathers and was buried with them in the city of David. (His mother was a woman of Ammon, whose name was Naamah.) He was succeeded by his son Abijam.

15 In the eighteenth year of the reign of Jeroboam son of Nebat, Abijam

2 became king of Judah. He reigned in Jerusalem for three years; his mother was Maacah granddaughter of Abi-

3 shalom. All the sins that his father had committed before him he committed too, nor was he faithful to the LORD his God as his ancestor David had been.

w Verses 25–28: cp. 2 Chr. 12. 9–11.
x Verses 29–31: cp. 2 Chr. 12. 13–16.

the family would have an honorable burial; compare v. 13. **14b–16:** This Deuteronomic comment anticipates the exile of the leading citizens of the Northern Kingdom in 722 B.C. **17:** For an unknown reason Jeroboam had moved his capital to *Tirzah*, a few miles northeast of Shechem.

14.21–31: The reign of Rehoboam of Judah. The usual condemnation in Kgs. for cultic offenses is well illustrated here. **25–26:** On *Shishak*, first king of the twenty-second Egyptian dynasty, see 3.1 n. and 11.40. Shishak also conquered several cities in Israel at this time.

15.1–24: The reigns of Abijam and Asa in Judah. 1–8: *Abijam was a son of Maacah, granddaughter of Abishalom*, the latter probably David's son Absalom (see, on Maacah, 2 Sam.5.3).

4 But for David's sake the LORD his God gave him a flame to burn in Jerusalem, by establishing his dynasty and making 5 Jerusalem secure, because David had done what was right in the eyes of the LORD and had not disobeyed any of his commandments all his life, except in the matter of Uriah the Hittite.[y] 7 The other acts and events of Abijam's reign are recorded in the annals of the kings of Judah. There was fighting 8 between Abijam and Jeroboam. And Abijam rested with his forefathers and was buried in the city of David; and he was succeeded by his son Asa.

9 In the twentieth year of Jeroboam king of Israel, Asa became king of 10 Judah. He reigned in Jerusalem for forty-one years; his grandmother was Maacah granddaughter of Abishalom. 11 Asa did what was right in the eyes of the LORD, like his ancestor David. 12 He expelled from the land the male prostitutes attached to the shrines and did away with all the idols which his 13[z] predecessors had made. He even deprived his own grandmother Maacah of her rank as queen mother because she had an obscene object made for the worship of Asherah; Asa cut it down and burnt it in the gorge of the Kidron. 14 Although the hill-shrines were allowed to remain, Asa himself remained faithful 15 to the LORD all his life. He brought into the house of the LORD all his father's votive offerings and his own, gold and silver and sacred vessels.

16 Asa was at war with Baasha king of 17[a] Israel all through their reigns. Baasha king of Israel invaded Judah and fortified Ramah to cut off all access 18 to Asa king of Judah. So Asa took all the gold and silver that remained in the treasuries of the house of the LORD and of the royal palace, and sent his servants with them to Ben-hadad son of Tabrimmon, son of Hezion, king of Aram, whose capital was Damascus, with instructions to say, 19 'There is an alliance between us, as

there was between our fathers. I now send you this present of silver and gold; break off your alliance with Baasha king of Israel, so that he may abandon his campaign against me.' Ben-hadad listened willingly to King 20 Asa; he ordered the commanders of his armies to move against the cities of Israel, and they attacked Iyyon, Dan, Abel-beth-maacah, and that part of Kinnereth which marches with the land of Naphtali. When Baasha heard of it, 21 he stopped fortifying Ramah and fell back on Tirzah. Then King Asa issued 22 a proclamation requiring every man in Judah to join in removing the stones of Ramah and the timbers with which Baasha had fortified it; no one was exempted; and he used them to fortify Geba of Benjamin and Mizpah.

All the other events of Asa's reign, 23[b] his exploits and his achievements, and the cities he built, are recorded in the annals of the kings of Judah. But in his old age his feet were crippled by disease. He rested with his forefathers 24 and was buried with them in the city of his ancestor David; and he was succeeded by his son Jehoshaphat.

Nadab son of Jeroboam became 25 king of Israel in the second year of Asa king of Judah, and he reigned for two years. He did what was wrong in 26 the eyes of the LORD and followed in his father's footsteps, repeating the sin which he had led Israel to commit. Baasha son of Ahijah, of the house of 27 Issachar, conspired against him and attacked him at Gibbethon, a Philistine city, which Nadab was besieging with all his forces. And Baasha slew him 28 and usurped the throne in the third year of Asa king of Judah. As soon as 29 he became king, he struck down all the family of Jeroboam, destroying every living soul and leaving not one survivor. Thus the word of the LORD was

y *Prob. rdg.; Heb. adds* (6) There was war between Rehoboam and Jeroboam all his days (*cp. 14. 30*).
z *Verses 13–15: cp. 2 Chr. 15. 16–18.*
a *Verses 17–22: cp. 2 Chr. 16. 1–6.*
b *Verses 23, 24: cp. 2 Chr. 16. 11–14.*

This Maacah was a woman of great influence; see vv. 11–13; 2 Chr. 13.2 n. **14:** *Asa* is the first of several Judean kings who are approved of by the compilers, except that they did not remove the *hill-shrines*. **16–24:** Once the two Hebrew kingdoms were at odds rather than coordinated under one king, *Damascus* became an independent and threatening power in the northeast.

15.25–16.7: Nadab and Baasha of Israel. These two kings are treated in stereotyped terms; see 11.29–39 n.

fulfilled which he spoke through his servant Ahijah the Shilonite. This happened because of the sins of Jeroboam and the sins which he led Israel to commit, and because he had provoked the anger of the LORD the 31 God of Israel. The other events of Nadab's reign and all his acts are recorded in the annals of the kings of 32 Israel. Asa was at war with Baasha king of Israel all through their reigns.

33 In the third year of Asa king of Judah, Baasha son of Ahijah became king of all Israel in Tirzah and reigned 34 twenty-four years. He did what was wrong in the eyes of the LORD and followed in Jeroboam's footsteps, repeating the sin which he had led **16** Israel to commit. Then the word of the LORD came to Jehu son of Hanani 2 concerning Baasha: 'I raised you from the dust and made you a prince over my people Israel, but you have followed in the footsteps of Jeroboam and have led my people Israel into sin, and have provoked me to anger 3 with their sins. Therefore I will sweep away Baasha and his house and will deal with it as I dealt with the house 4 of Jeroboam son of Nebat. Those of Baasha's family who die in the city shall be food for the dogs, and those who die in the country shall be food 5 for the birds.' The other events of Baasha's reign, his achievements and his exploits, are recorded in the annals 6 of the kings of Israel. Baasha rested with his forefathers and was buried in Tirzah; and he was succeeded by his 7 son Elah. Moreover the word of the LORD concerning Baasha and his family came through the prophet Jehu son of Hanani, because of all the wrong that he had done in the eyes of the LORD, thereby provoking his anger: because he had not only sinned like the house of Jeroboam, but had also brought destruction upon it.

8 In the twenty-sixth year of Asa king of Judah, Elah son of Baasha became king of Israel and he reigned in Tirzah 9 two years. Zimri, who was in his service commanding half the chariotry,

plotted against him. The king was in Tirzah drinking himself drunk in the house of Arza, comptroller of the household there, when Zimri broke in 10 and attacked him, assassinated him and made himself king. This took place in the twenty-seventh year of Asa king of Judah. As soon as he had become 11 king and was enthroned, he struck down all the family of Baasha and left not a single mother's son alive, kinsman or friend. He destroyed the whole 12 family of Baasha, and thus fulfilled the word of the LORD concerning Baasha, spoken through the prophet Jehu. This was what came of all the sins which 13 Baasha and his son Elah had committed and the sins into which they had led Israel, provoking the anger of the LORD the God of Israel with their worthless idols. The other events and 14 acts of Elah's reign are recorded in the annals of the kings of Israel.

In the twenty-seventh year of Asa 15 king of Judah, Zimri reigned in Tirzah for seven days. At the time the army was investing the Philistine city of Gibbethon. When the Israelite troops 16 in the field heard of Zimri's conspiracy and the murder of the king, there and then in the camp they made their commander Omri king of Israel by common consent. Then Omri and 17 his whole force withdrew from Gibbethon and laid siege to Tirzah. Zimri, 18 as soon as he saw that the city had fallen, retreated to the keep of the royal palace, set the whole of it on fire over his head and so perished. This was 19 what came of the sin he had committed by doing what was wrong in the eyes of the LORD and following in the footsteps of Jeroboam, repeating the sin into which he had led Israel. The 20 other events of Zimri's reign, and his conspiracy, are recorded in the annals of the kings of Israel.

Thereafter the people of Israel were 21 split into two factions: one supported Tibni son of Ginath, determined to make him king; the other supported Omri. Omri's party proved the stronger; 22 Tibni lost his life and Omri became king.

16.8–34: **The establishment of the dynasty of Omri.** Though this was the greatest dynasty of the north, it is slighted by the Deuteronomic historians. **13:** See 11.29–39 n. **15–20:** The episode of *Zimri* was no more than a palace revolt. **21–22:** The following six years witnessed

23 It was in the thirty-first year of Asa king of Judah that Omri became king of Israel and he reigned twelve years, 24 six of them in Tirzah. He bought the hill of Samaria from Shemer for two talents of silver and built a city on it which he named Samaria after Shemer 25 the owner of the hill. Omri did what was wrong in the eyes of the LORD; he outdid all his predecessors in wicked- 26 ness. He followed in the footsteps of Jeroboam son of Nebat, repeating the sins which he had led Israel to commit, so that they provoked the anger of the LORD their God with their worthless 27 idols. The other events of Omri's reign, and his exploits, are recorded in the 28 annals of the kings of Israel. So Omri rested with his forefathers and was buried in Samaria; and he was suc- ceeded by his son Ahab.

Ahab and Elijah

29 AHAB SON OF OMRI BECAME KING OF Israel in the thirty-eighth year of Asa king of Judah, and he reigned over Israel 30 in Samaria for twenty-two years. He did more that was wrong in the eyes of the LORD than all his predecessors. As 21 if it were not enough for him to follow the sinful ways of Jeroboam son of Nebat, he contracted a marriage with Jezebel daughter of Ethbaal king of Sidon, and went and worshipped Baal; he prostrated himself before him and 32 erected an altar to him in the temple of Baal which he built in Samaria. He 33 also set up a sacred pole; indeed he did more to provoke the anger of the LORD the God of Israel than all the kings of Israel before him. In his days 34 Hiel of Bethel rebuilt Jericho; laying its foundations cost him his eldest son Abiram, and the setting up of its gates cost him Segub his youngest son. Thus was fulfilled what the LORD had spoken through Joshua son of Nun.

Elijah the Tishbite, of Tishbe in 17 Gilead, said to Ahab, 'I swear by the life of the LORD the God of Israel, whose servant I am, that there shall be neither dew nor rain these coming years unless I give the word.' Then the word of the 2 LORD came to him: 'Leave this place 3 and turn eastwards; and go into hiding in the ravine of Kerith east of

a genuine civil war, which the compilers of Kgs. pass over in a phrase. **23–34:** *Omri* and his son *Ahab* devised a new policy for the Northern Kingdom. Whereas the two Hebrew kingdoms had been at war with each other for fifty years after Solomon's death (14.30; 15.32), the dynasty of Omri made peace with the kingdom of Judah and even established a marriage tie between the two royal houses (2 Kgs.8.26). The two kingdoms then collaborated in wars to dominate the kingdoms east of the Jordan (see 1 Kgs. ch. 22 and 2 Kgs. ch. 3), probably to control the inland trade routes. The policy of Omri and Ahab also included peaceful relations with the maritime power of Tyre, strengthened by the marriage of *Jezebel* to Ahab (16.31). This alliance introduced into Israel strong influences from the religious practices of Tyre, especially the worship of Baal. From the later historians' viewpoint, Baal worship was the worst kind of apostasy, and they judge the leading kings of the dynasty of Omri accordingly (16.26,30–33). **23–24:** A new capital city *Samaria* was to symbolize the new policy. **32:** *The temple of Baal* was certainly a part of Omri's original plan for the city (the city was less than six years old at the time of Omri's death). **34:** A direct reference to Josh.6.26.

17.1–2 Kgs.10.36: The religious crisis of the ninth century. During the two generations of the prophets Elijah and Elisha a sharp conflict of greatest importance arose between partisans of the LORD (Yahweh), the God of old Israel, and of the Baal, the god of Canaan and Phoenicia. Elijah led the fight for the LORD; Jezebel, the Phoenician wife of Ahab, Omri's son, with her group of prophets, fought for the Baal. The conflict led finally to the overthrow of the Omri dynasty. The account in Kgs. draws on a cycle of Elijah stories (1 Kgs. chs. 17–19, 21; 2 Kgs. ch. 1), a cycle of Elisha stories (2 Kgs.2.1–8.15), more selections from royal annals (e.g. 1 Kgs.22.39–53; 2 Kgs.8.16–27), and historical narratives about Ahab's wars with Damascus (1 Kgs. chs. 20, 22) and Jehu's overthrow of the Omri dynasty (2 Kgs. chs. 9–10).

17.1–19.21: Elijah's work. A series of stories about Elijah relates the first stage of the over- throw of the dynasty of Omri. The parallels between Elijah and Moses, and between Elisha and Joshua, are deliberate. In chs. 17–19 three groups of materials have been combined: episodes concerning the drought that Elijah announced and ended (17.1–18.16,41–46); the contest with the prophets of Baal on Mount Carmel (18.17–40); and the pilgrimage to Horeb, the mountain of God (ch. 19).

17.1–18.16: Elijah brings a severe drought. The issue was which of the two gods controls the rain. **1:** The compilers used only parts of their older source; hence the abruptness of the appearance of Elijah here. **2–16:** The drought soon leads to famine. Where the holy man goes,

4 the Jordan. You shall drink from the stream, and I have commanded the
5 ravens to feed you there.' He did as the LORD had told him: he went and stayed in the ravine of Kerith east of
6 the Jordan, and the ravens brought him bread and meat morning and evening, and he drank from the stream.
7 After a while the stream dried up, for there had been no rain in the land.
8 Then the word of the LORD came to
9 him: 'Go now to Zarephath, a village of Sidon, and stay there; I have commanded a widow there to feed you.'
10 So he went off to Zarephath. When he reached the entrance to the village, he saw a widow gathering sticks, and he called to her and said, 'Please bring me a little water in a pitcher to drink.'
11 As she went to fetch it, he called after her, 'Bring me, please, a piece of
12 bread as well.' But she said, 'As the LORD your God lives, I have no food to sustain me except a handful of flour in a jar and a little oil in a flask. Here I am, gathering two or three sticks to go and cook something for my son
13 and myself before we die.' 'Never fear,' said Elijah; 'go and do as you say; but first make me a small cake from what you have and bring it out to me; and after that make something
14 for your son and yourself. For this is the word of the LORD the God of Israel: "The jar of flour shall not give out nor the flask of oil fail, until the
15 LORD sends rain on the land."' She went and did as Elijah had said, and there was food for him and for her and
16 her family for a long time. The jar of flour did not give out nor did the flask of oil fail, as the word of the LORD foretold through Elijah.
17   Afterwards the son of this woman, the mistress of the house, fell ill and grew worse and worse, until at last his
18 breathing ceased. Then she said to Elijah, 'What made you interfere, you man of God? You came here to bring
19 my sins to light and kill my son!' 'Give

me your son', he said. He took the boy from her arms and carried him up to the roof-chamber where his lodging was, and laid him on his own bed. Then 20 he called out to the LORD, 'O LORD my God, is this thy care for the widow with whom I lodge, that thou hast been so cruel to her son?' Then he breathed 21 deeply[c] upon the child three times and called on the LORD, 'O LORD my God, let the breath of life, I pray, return to the body of this child.' The LORD 22 listened to Elijah's cry, and the breath of life returned to the child's body, and he revived; Elijah lifted him up 23 and took him down from the roof into the house, gave him to his mother and said, 'Look, your son is alive.' Then she said to Elijah, 'Now I know 24 for certain that you are a man of God and that the word of the LORD on your lips is truth.'

Time went by, and in the third year **18** the word of the LORD came to Elijah: 'Go and show yourself to Ahab, and I will send rain upon the land.' So 2 he went to show himself to Ahab. At this time the famine in Samaria was at its height, and Ahab summoned 3 Obadiah, the comptroller of his household, a devout worshipper of the LORD. When Jezebel massacred the prophets 4 of the LORD, he had taken a hundred of them and hidden them in caves, fifty by fifty, giving them food and drink to keep them alive. Ahab said to 5 Obadiah, 'Let us go through the land, both of us, to every spring and gully; if we can find enough grass we may keep the horses and mules alive and lose none of our cattle.' They divided 6 the land between them for their survey, Ahab going one way by himself and Obadiah another.

As Obadiah was on his way, Elijah 7 met him. Obadiah recognized him and fell prostrate before him and said, 'Can it be you, my lord Elijah?' 'Yes,' 8 he said, 'it is I; go and tell your master

c *Or* stretched himself.

there is miraculous provision of food; compare 2 Kgs.4.1–7. **17–24:** The *woman* thinks the holy man's presence causes punishment for her *sins*. Compare 2 Kgs.4.18–37. **24:** The compilers were particularly interested in showing the power of *the word of the LORD* through the prophets. **18.3–4:** The intensity of the religious conflict is shown by the slaughtering of prophets on both sides (v. 40). **7–16:** *Elijah* had a reputation for elusiveness; *Obadiah* tactfully seeks assurance that he will remain.

9 that Elijah is here.' 'What wrong have I done?' said Obadiah. 'Why should you give me into Ahab's hands? He will
10 put me to death. As the LORD your God lives, there is no nation or kingdom to which my master has not sent in search of you. If they said, "He is not here", he made that kingdom or nation swear on oath that they could
11 not find you. Yet now you say, "Go and tell your master that Elijah is
12 here." What will happen? As soon as I leave you, the spirit of the LORD will carry you away, who knows where? I shall go and tell Ahab, and when he fails to find you, he will kill me. Yet I have been a worshipper of the LORD
13 from boyhood. Have you not been told, my lord, what I did when Jezebel put the LORD's prophets to death, how I hid a hundred of them in caves, fifty by fifty, and kept them alive with food
14 and drink? And now you say, "Go and tell your master that Elijah is here"!
15 He will kill me.' Elijah answered, 'As the LORD of Hosts lives, whose servant I am, I swear that I will show myself
16 to him this very day.' So Obadiah went to find Ahab and gave him the message, and Ahab went to meet Elijah.
17 As soon as Ahab saw Elijah, he said to him, 'Is it you, you troubler of
18 Israel?' 'It is not I who have troubled Israel,' he replied, 'but you and your father's family, by forsaking the commandments of the LORD and
19 following Baal. But now, send and summon all Israel to meet me on Mount Carmel, and the four hundred and fifty prophets of Baal with them and the four hundred prophets of the goddess Asherah, who are Jezebel's
20 pensioners.' So Ahab sent out to all the Israelites and assembled the

prophets on Mount Carmel. Elijah 21 stepped forward and said to the people, 'How long will you sit on the fence? If the LORD is God, follow him; but if Baal, then follow him.' Not a word did they answer. Then Elijah said 22 to the people, 'I am the only prophet of the LORD still left, but there are four hundred and fifty prophets of Baal. Bring two bulls; let them choose one for 23 themselves, cut it up and lay it on the wood without setting fire to it, and I will prepare the other and lay it on the wood without setting fire to it. You 24 shall invoke your god by name and I will invoke the LORD by name; and the god who answers by fire, he is God.' And all the people shouted their approval.

Then Elijah said to the prophets of 25 Baal, 'Choose one of the bulls and offer it first, for there are more of you; invoke your god by name, but do not set fire to the wood.' So they took the 26 bull provided for them and offered it, and they invoked Baal by name from morning until noon, crying, 'Baal, Baal, answer us'; but there was no sound, no answer. They danced wildly beside the altar they had set up. At 27 midday Elijah mocked them: 'Call louder, for he is a god; it may be he is deep in thought, or engaged, or on a journey; or he may have gone to sleep and must be woken up.' They 28 cried still louder and, as was their custom, gashed themselves with swords and spears until the blood ran. All 29 afternoon they raved and ranted till the hour of the regular sacrifice, but still there was no sound, no answer, no sign of attention.

Then Elijah said to all the people, 30 'Come here to me.' They all came,

18.17–46: The contest on Mount Carmel. 17–18: When *Ahab* introduced the worship of *Baal* into the Northern Kingdom he did not cease to worship the LORD; see 22.5–6. It was such religious tolerance or pluralism that *Elijah* was attacking. From Ahab's viewpoint, therefore, Elijah was a *troubler of Israel*. **19:** *Prophets* throughout these narratives usually means followers or disciples, living at court or in separate communities; see, e.g. 2 Kgs.6.1–3. **21:** Ahab's policy was to avoid this alternative. **22:** *Elijah* was not *the only prophet of the LORD still left*, but he may have been the only one willing to come forward as such. **23–24:** The contest is cast in terms of a tradition about the holy fire of the altar; see Lev.6.2–6; 9.24; 1 Chr.21.26; 2 Chr.7.1–3; 2 Macc.1.18–22. **26:** The dancing was a ritual action consisting of limping motions. **27:** This fierce satire may be even stronger if, as is likely, *engaged* is a euphemism for seeing to bodily needs. **28:** *Gashed themselves*: a ritual action done in an ecstatic state (compare Hos.7.14), usually associated with mourning for the dead (Jer.16.6), a practice forbidden to Israelites (Deut.14.1). **29:** *The hour of the regular sacrifice* was roughly 3:00 P.M. **30–35:** Much symbolism is involved here; the *twelve stones* and twelve *jars* of *water*, and the complex of *altar* (land)

and he repaired the altar of the LORD
31 which had been torn down. He took
twelve stones, one for each tribe of the
sons of Jacob, the man named Israel
32 by the word of the LORD. With these
stones he built an altar in the name of
the LORD; he dug a trench round it
big enough to hold two measures of
33 seed; he arranged the wood, cut up
34 the bull and laid it on the wood. Then
he said, 'Fill four jars with water and
pour it on the whole-offering and on
the wood.' They did so, and he said,
'Do it again.' They did it again, and he
said, 'Do it a third time.' They did it a
35 third time, and the water ran all
round the altar and even filled the
36 trench. At the hour of the regular sacrifice the prophet Elijah came forward
and said, 'LORD God of Abraham, of
Isaac, and of Israel, let it be known
today that thou art God in Israel and
that I am thy servant and have done all
37 these things at thy command. Answer
me, O LORD, answer me and let this
people know that thou, LORD, art
God and that it is thou that hast
38 caused them to be backsliders.'[d] Then
the fire of the LORD fell. It consumed
the whole-offering, the wood, the
stones, and the earth, and licked up
39 the water in the trench. When all the
people saw it, they fell prostrate and
cried, 'The LORD is God, the LORD is
40 God.' Then Elijah said to them, 'Seize
the prophets of Baal; let not one of
them escape.' They seized them, and
Elijah took them down to the Kishon
and slaughtered them there in the
valley.
41   Elijah said to Ahab, 'Go back now,
eat and drink, for I hear the sound of
42 coming rain.' He did so, while Elijah
himself climbed to the crest of Carmel.
There he crouched on the ground with
43 his face between his knees. He said to
his servant, 'Go and look out to the
west.' He went and looked; 'There is
nothing to see', he said. Seven times
Elijah ordered him back, and seven

times he went. The seventh time he 44
said, 'I see a cloud no bigger than a
man's hand, coming up from the
west.' 'Now go', said Elijah,' and tell
Ahab to harness his chariot and be off,
or the rain will stop him.' Meanwhile 45
the sky had grown black with clouds,
the wind rose, and heavy rain began to
fall. Ahab mounted his chariot and set
off for Jezreel; but the power of the 46
LORD had come upon Elijah: he tucked
up his robe and ran before Ahab all
the way to Jezreel.

Ahab told Jezebel all that Elijah **19**
had done and how he had put all the
prophets to death with the sword. Jez- 2
ebel then sent a messenger to Elijah to
say, 'The gods do the same to me and
more, unless by this time tomorrow I
have taken your life as you took
theirs.' He was afraid and fled for his 3
life. When he reached Beersheba in
Judah, he left his servant there and 4
himself went a day's journey into the
wilderness. He came upon a broom-
bush, and sat down under it and
prayed for death: 'It is enough,' he
said; 'now, LORD, take my life, for I
am no better than my fathers before
me.' He lay down under the bush and, 5
while he slept, an angel touched him
and said, 'Rise and eat.' He looked, 6
and there at his head was a cake
baked on hot stones, and a pitcher of
water. He ate and drank and lay down
again. The angel of the LORD came 7
again and touched him a second time,
saying, 'Rise and eat; the journey is
too much for you.' He rose and ate 8
and drank and, sustained by this food,
he went on for forty days and forty
nights to Horeb, the mount of God. He 9
entered a cave and there he spent the
night.

Suddenly the word of the LORD
came to him: 'Why are you here,
Elijah?' 'Because of my great zeal for 10
the LORD the God of Hosts', he said.
'The people of Israel have forsaken

d Or thou that dost bring them back to their allegiance.

---

and the *trench* (water) probably symbolize the cosmic order. **38:** *The fire of the* LORD: see vv.
23–24 n. **41–46:** The narrative of the drought, dropped at v. 16, is concluded here. **46:** The
distance to *Jezreel* was over fifteen miles.
   19.1–21: Elijah at Mount Horeb. 1–4: *Elijah's* triumph was only momentary; *Jezebel* still
has the balance of power. Elijah flees, therefore, and then falls into a mood of depression.
5–8: *At his head . . . cake . . . and water:* on food and water in the Wilderness, see Exod. chs. 16–17.

thy covenant, torn down thy altars and put thy prophets to death with the sword, I alone am left, and they seek 11 to take my life.' The answer came: 'Go and stand on the mount before the LORD.' For the LORD was passing by: a great and strong wind came rending mountains and shattering rocks before him, but the LORD was not in the wind; and after the wind there was an earthquake, but the LORD was not 12 in the earthquake; and after the earthquake fire, but the LORD was not in the fire; and after the fire a low 13 murmuring sound. When Elijah heard it, he muffled his face in his cloak and went out and stood at the entrance of the cave. Then there came a voice: 14 'Why are you here, Elijah?' 'Because of my great zeal for the LORD the God of Hosts', he said. 'The people of Israel have forsaken thy covenant, torn down thy altars and put thy prophets to death with the sword. I alone am left, and they seek to take my life.' 15 The LORD said to him, 'Go back by way of the wilderness of Damascus, enter the city and anoint Hazael to be 16 king of Aram; anoint Jehu son[e] of Nimshi to be king of Israel, and Elisha son of Shaphat of Abel-meholah to be 17 prophet in your place. Anyone who escapes the sword of Hazael Jehu will slay, and anyone who escapes the 18 sword of Jehu Elisha will slay. But I will leave seven thousand in Israel, all who have not bent the knee to Baal, all whose lips have not kissed him.' 19 Elijah departed and found Elisha son of Shaphat ploughing; there were twelve pair of oxen ahead of him, and he himself was with the last of them. As Elijah passed, he threw his cloak 20 over him, and Elisha, leaving his oxen, ran after Elijah and said, 'Let me kiss my father and mother goodbye, and then I will follow you.' 'Go back,' he replied; 'what have I done to prevent 21 you?' He followed him no further but went home, took his pair of oxen, slaughtered them and burnt the wooden gear to cook the flesh, which he gave to the people to eat. Then he followed Elijah and became his disciple.

BEN-HADAD KING OF ARAM, HAVING **20** mustered all his forces, and taking with him thirty-two kings with their horses and chariots, marched against Samaria to take it by siege or assault. He sent envoys into the city to Ahab 2 king of Israel to say, 'Hear what 3 Ben-hadad says: Your silver and gold are mine, your wives and your splendid sons are mine.'[f] The king of Israel 4 answered, 'As you say, my lord king, I am yours and all that I have.' The 5 envoys came again and said, 'Hear what Ben-hadad says: I demand that you hand over your silver and gold, your wives and your sons. This time 6 tomorrow I will send my servants to search your house and your subjects' houses and to take possession of everything you prize, and remove it.' The 7 king of Israel then summoned the elders of the land and said, 'You see this? The man is plainly picking a quarrel; for I did not demur when he sent to claim my wives and my sons, my silver and gold.' All the elders and 8 all the people answered, 'Do not listen to him; you must not consent.' So he 9 gave this reply to Ben-hadad's envoys: 'Say to my lord the king: I accepted your majesty's demands on the first occasion; but what you now ask I cannot do.' The envoys went away and reported to their master, and Ben- 10 hadad sent back word: 'The gods do the same to me and more, if there is enough dust in Samaria to provide a handful for each of my men.' The king 11 of Israel made reply, 'Remind him of the saying: "The lame must not think himself a match for the nimble."' This

e Or grandson (*cp. 2 Kgs. 9. 2*).
f Or are your wives and your sons any good to me?

11–14: Compare with the natural phenomena of Exod. ch. 19. **12:** The *low murmuring sound*: possibly the experience of prophetic inspiration. **15–18:** A program and divine sanction are here provided for overthrowing the dynasty of Omri; see vv. 19–21; 2 Kgs.8.7–15; 9.1–13.
   20.1–43: Episodes of the Syrian wars. Vv. 1–34 present Ahab in quite a different light from the Elijah materials (see 17.1–2 Kgs.10.36 n.). Ahab is here a popular king supported by the prophets of the LORD. **1:** Minor rulers of small cities or tribes could be called *kings*. **2–9:** *Ahab* responds to *Ben-hadad*'s demand with the formality proper to one king as vassal of another. Ben-hadad insists on more than formality, and Ahab is incited to serious resistance.

12 message reached Ben-hadad while he and the kings were drinking in their quarters.^y At once he ordered his men to attack the city, and they did so.

13 Meanwhile a prophet had come to Ahab king of Israel and said to him, 'This is the word of the LORD: "You see this great rabble? Today I will give it into your hands and you shall 14 know that I am the LORD."' 'Whom will you use for that?' asked Ahab. 'The young men who serve the district officers', was the answer. 'Who will draw up the line of battle?' asked the 15 king. 'You', said the prophet. Then Ahab called up these young men, two hundred and thirty-two all told, and behind them the people of Israel, seven 16 thousand in all. They went out at midday, while Ben-hadad and his allies, those thirty-two kings, were drinking themselves drunk in their 17 quarters.^g The young men sallied out first, and word was sent to Ben-hadad that a party had come out of Samaria. 18 'If they have come out for peace,' he said, 'take them alive; if for battle, take them alive.'

19 So out of the city the young men 20 went, and the army behind them; each struck down his man, and the Aramaeans fled. The Israelites pursued them, but Ben-hadad king of Aram escaped on horseback with some of the cavalry. 21 Then the king of Israel advanced and captured the horses and chariots, inflicting a heavy defeat on the Aramaeans.

22 Then the prophet came to the king of Israel and said to him, 'Build up your forces; you know what you must do. At the turn of the year the king of 23 Aram will renew the attack.' But the king of Aram's ministers gave him this advice: 'Their gods are gods of the hills; that is why they defeated us. Let us fight them in the plain; and then 24 we shall have the upper hand. What you must do is to relieve the kings of their command and appoint other officers 25 in their place. Raise another army like the one you have lost. Bring your

cavalry and chariots up to their former strength, and then let us fight them in the plain, and we shall have the upper hand.' He listened to their advice and acted on it.

26 At the turn of the year Ben-hadad 27 mustered the Aramaeans and advanced to Aphek to attack Israel. The Israelites too were mustered and formed into companies, and then went out to meet them and encamped opposite them. They seemed no better than a pair of new-born kids, while the Aramaeans covered the country-side. 28 The man of God came to the king of Israel and said, 'This is the word of the LORD: The Aramaeans may think that the LORD is a god of the hills and not a god of the valleys; but I will give all this great rabble into your hands and you shall know that I am the LORD.'

29 They lay in camp opposite one another for seven days; on the seventh day battle was joined and the Israelites destroyed a hundred thousand of the Aramaean infantry in one day. 30 The survivors fled to Aphek, into the citadel, and the city wall fell upon the twenty-seven thousand men who were left. Ben-hadad took refuge in the citadel, retreating into an inner room; 31 and his attendants said to him, 'Listen; we have heard that the kings of Israel are men to be trusted. Let us therefore put sackcloth round our waists and wind rough cord round our heads and go out to the king of Israel. It may be that he will spare your life.' So they 32 fastened on the sackcloth and the cord, and went to the king of Israel and said, 'Your servant Ben-hadad pleads for his life.' 'My royal cousin,' he said, 'is he still alive?' The men, 33 taking the word for a favourable omen, caught it up at once and said, 'Your cousin, yes, Ben-hadad.' 'Go and fetch him', he said. Then Ben-hadad came out and Ahab invited him into his chariot. And Ben-hadad said to him, 34 'I will restore the cities which my father

_{g in their quarters: or at Succoth.}

13–28: The prophets are portrayed as playing a large role in the struggle against Damascus. **24–25:** The administration of the military force had to be made more professional; compare 4.7–19 n. **26:** In the next year, the battle is around *Aphek*, east of the Sea of Galilee. **29–30:** The numbers are exaggerated. **32:** *My royal cousin:* not a family tie but their common royalty.

took from your father, and you may establish for yourself a trading quarter in Damascus, as my father did in Samaria.' 'On these terms', said Ahab, 'I will let you go.' So he granted him a treaty and let him go.

35 One of a company of prophets, at the command of the LORD, ordered a certain man to strike him, but the man
36 refused. 'Because you have not obeyed the LORD,' said the prophet, 'when you leave me, a lion will attack you.' When the man left, a lion did meet him and
37 attacked him. The prophet fell in with another man and ordered him to strike
38 him. He struck and wounded him. Then the prophet went off, with a bandage over his eyes, and thus disguised waited
39 by the wayside for the king. As the king was passing, he called out to him, 'Sir, I went into the thick of the battle, and a soldier came over to me with a prisoner and said, "Take charge of this fellow. If by any chance he gets away, your life shall be forfeit, or you shall
40 pay a talent of silver." As I was busy with one thing and another, sir, he disappeared.' The king of Israel said to him, 'You deserve to die.' And he said to the king of Israel,*h* 'You have passed
41 sentence on yourself.' Then he tore the bandage from his eyes, and the king of Israel saw that he was one of the
42 prophets. And he said to the king, 'This is the word of the LORD: "Because you let that man go when I had put him under a ban, your life shall be forfeit for his life, your people for his
43 people."' The king of Israel went home sullen and angry and entered Samaria.

21 NABOTH OF JEZREEL HAD A VINEYARD near the palace of Ahab king of
2 Samaria. One day Ahab made a proposal to Naboth: 'Your vineyard is close to my palace; let me have it for a garden; I will give you a better vineyard in exchange for it or, if you prefer,
3 its value in silver.' But Naboth answered,

'The LORD forbid that I should let you have land which has always been in my family.' So Ahab went home sullen and 4 angry because Naboth would not let him have his ancestral land. He lay down on his bed, covered his face and refused to eat. His wife Jezebel came 5 in to him and said, 'What makes you so sullen and why do you refuse to eat?' He told her, 'I proposed to 6 Naboth of Jezreel that he should let me have his vineyard at its value or, if he liked, in exchange for another; but he would not let me have the vineyard.' 'Are you or are you not king in 7 Israel?' said Jezebel. 'Come, eat and take heart; I will make you a gift of the vineyard of Naboth of Jezreel.' So 8 she wrote a letter in Ahab's name, sealed it with his seal and sent it to the elders and notables of Naboth's city, who sat in council with him. She wrote: 9 'Proclaim a fast and give Naboth the seat of honour among the people. And 10 see that two scoundrels are seated opposite him to charge him with cursing God and the king, then take him out and stone him to death.' So 11 the elders and notables of Naboth's city, who sat with him in council, carried out the instructions Jezebel had sent them in her letter: they proclaimed a 12 fast and gave Naboth the seat of honour, and these two scoundrels came 13 in, sat opposite him and charged him publicly with cursing God and the king. Then they took him outside the city and stoned him, and sent word to Jezebel 14 that Naboth had been stoned to death.

As soon as Jezebel heard that Naboth 15 had been stoned and was dead, she said to Ahab, 'Get up and take possession of the vineyard which Naboth refused to sell you, for he is no longer alive; Naboth of Jezreel is dead.' When 16 Ahab heard that Naboth was dead, he got up and went to the vineyard to

---

h You deserve . . . Israel: *prob. rdg.; Heb. om.*

35–43: Some prophets took a more hostile view of Ahab. **40:** The king must be induced to pass *sentence* on himself unwittingly; see 2 Sam.12.1–6. **41:** *One of the prophets:* members of the prophetic groups had identifying marks on their foreheads.
   21.1–29: The crime of Naboth's vineyard. This story of the abuse of royal authority is the occasion for Elijah's condemnation of Ahab's dynasty. **3:** *Always been in my family:* by religious law Naboth could not permanently alienate his land; see Lev.25.10.13. **13:** See Exod.22.28.

17 take possession. Then the word of the
18 LORD came to Elijah the Tishbite: 'Go down at once to Ahab king of Israel, who is in Samaria; you will find him in Naboth's vineyard, where he has
19 gone to take possession. Say to him, "This is the word of the LORD: Have you killed your man, and taken his land as well?" Say to him, "This is the word of the LORD: Where dogs licked the blood of Naboth, there dogs shall
20 lick your blood." ' Ahab said to Elijah, 'Have you found me, my enemy?' 'I have found you', he said, 'because you have sold yourself to do what is
21 wrong in the eyes of the LORD. I will bring[i] disaster upon you; I will sweep you away and destroy every mother's son of the house of Ahab in Israel, whether under protection of the family
22 or not. And I will deal with your house as I did with the house of Jeroboam son of Nebat and of Baasha son of Ahijah, because you have provoked
23 my anger and led Israel into sin.' And the LORD went on to say of Jezebel, 'Jezebel shall be eaten by dogs by the
24 rampart of Jezreel. Of the house of Ahab, those who die in the city shall be food for the dogs, and those who die in the country shall be food for the
25 birds.' (Never was a man who sold himself to do what is wrong in the LORD's eyes as Ahab did, and all at the
26 prompting of Jezebel his wife. He committed gross abominations in going after false gods, doing everything that the Amorites did, whom the LORD had
27 dispossessed in favour of Israel.) When Ahab heard this, he rent his clothes, put on sackcloth and fasted; he lay down in his sackcloth and went about
28 muttering to himself. Then the word of the LORD came to Elijah the Tish-
29 bite: 'Have you seen how Ahab has humbled himself before me? Because he has thus humbled himself, I will not bring disaster upon his house in his own lifetime, but in his son's.'

FOR THREE YEARS THERE WAS NO WAR **22** between the Aramaeans and the Israelites, but in the third year Jehoshaphat 2[j] king of Judah went down to visit the king of Israel. The latter said to his 3 courtiers, 'You know that Ramothgilead belongs to us, and yet we do nothing to recover it from the king of Aram.' He said to Jehoshaphat, 'Will 4 you join me in attacking Ramothgilead?' Jehoshaphat said to the king of Israel, 'What is mine is yours: myself, my people, and my horses.' Then Jehosh- 5 aphat said to the king of Israel, 'First let us seek counsel from the LORD.' The 6 king of Israel assembled the prophets, some four hundred of them, and asked them, 'Shall I attack Ramoth-gilead or shall I refrain?' 'Attack,' they answered; 'the Lord will deliver it into your hands.' Jehoshaphat asked, 'Is 7 there no other prophet of the LORD here through whom we may seek guidance?' 'There is one more', the king 8 of Israel answered, 'through whom we may seek guidance of the LORD, but I hate the man, because he prophesies no good for me; never anything but evil. His name is Micaiah son of Imlah.' Jehoshaphat exclaimed, 'My lord king, let no such word pass your lips!' So the king of Israel called one of 9 his eunuchs and told him to fetch Micaiah son of Imlah with all speed.

The king of Israel and Jehoshaphat 10 king of Judah were seated on their thrones, in shining armour, at the entrance to the gate of Samaria, and all the prophets were prophesying before them. One of them, Zedekiah son of 11 Kenaanah, made himself horns of iron and said, 'This is the word of the LORD: "With horns like these you shall gore the Aramaeans and make an end of them."' In the same vein all the 12 prophets prophesied, 'Attack Ramothgilead and win the day; the LORD will

i he said, ... bring: or he said. 'Because you ... LORD, I am bringing ...
j Verses 2–35: cp. 2 Chr. 18. 2–34.

Two witnesses were required; see Deut.17.6–7. **27–29:** The Deuteronomic historians offer Ahab's repentance as the reason the dynasty did not fall immediately.
    22.1–40: Ahab's last campaign and Micaiah the prophet. The view of Ahab here, as in ch. 20, is laudatory. **1:** Assyrian records establish that Ahab was in alliance with *the Aramaeans* against the Assyrians at the battle of Qarqar in 853 B.C.; later in 853 Israel and Damascus were again at war. **2:** On *Jehoshaphat*, see v. 41–53 n. **3:** *Ramoth-gilead* was the key to control of important trade routes in northern Transjordan. **6:** The issue here is between true and false prophets of Yahweh (unlike 18.17–40, where it is between Yahweh and Baal). **11:** *Horns:*

13 deliver it into your hands.' The messenger sent to fetch Micaiah told him that the prophets had with one voice given the king a favourable answer. 'And mind you agree with them', he
14 added. 'As the LORD lives,' said Micaiah, 'I will say only what the LORD tells me to say.'
15 When Micaiah came into the king's presence, the king said to him, 'Micaiah, shall we attack Ramoth-gilead or shall we refrain?' 'Attack and win the day,' he said; 'the LORD will deliver it
16 into your hands.' 'How often must I adjure you', said the king, 'to tell me nothing but the truth in the name of
17 the LORD?' Then Micaiah said, 'I saw all Israel scattered on the mountains, like sheep without a shepherd; and I heard the LORD say, "They have no master, let them go home in peace."'
18 The king of Israel said to Jehoshaphat, 'Did I not tell you that he never prophesies good for me, nothing but
19 evil?' Micaiah went on, 'Listen now to the word of the LORD. I saw the LORD seated on his throne, with all the host of heaven in attendance on his right
20 and on his left. The LORD said, "Who will entice Ahab to attack and fall on^k Ramoth-gilead?" One said one thing
21 and one said another; then a spirit came forward and stood before the LORD and said, "I will entice him."
22 "How?" said the LORD. "I will go out", he said, "and be a lying spirit in the mouth of all his prophets." "You shall entice him," said the LORD, "and you
23 shall succeed; go and do it." You see, then, how the LORD has put a lying spirit in the mouth of all these prophets of yours, because he has decreed dis-
24 aster for you.' Then Zedekiah son of Kenaanah came up to Micaiah and struck him in the face: 'And how did the spirit of the LORD pass from me to
25 speak to you?' he said. Micaiah answered, 'That you will find out on the day when you run into an inner room
26 to hide yourself.' Then the king of

Israel ordered Micaiah to be arrested and committed to the custody of Amon the governor of the city and Joash the king's son.^{l} 'Lock this fellow up', 27 he said, 'and give him prison diet of bread and water until I come home in safety.' Micaiah retorted, 'If you do 28 return in safety, the LORD has not spoken by me.'

So the king of Israel and Jehoshaphat 29 king of Judah marched on Ramoth-gilead, and the king of Israel said to 30 Jehoshaphat, 'I will disguise myself to go into battle, but you shall wear your royal robes.' So he went into battle in disguise. Now the king of Aram had 31 commanded the thirty-two captains of his chariots not to engage all and sundry but the king of Israel alone. When the captains saw Jehoshaphat, 32 they thought he was the king of Israel and turned to attack him. But Jehoshaphat cried out and, when the captains 33 saw that he was not the king of Israel, they broke off the attack on him. But 34 one man drew his bow at random and hit the king of Israel where the breastplate joins the plates of the armour. So he said to his driver, 'Wheel round and take me out of the line; I am wounded.' When the day's fighting 35 reached its height, the king was facing the Aramaeans propped up in his chariot, and the blood from his wound flowed down upon the floor of the chariot; and in the evening he died. At sunset the herald went through 36 the ranks, crying, 'Every man to his city, every man to his country.' Thus 37 died the king. He was brought to Samaria and they buried him there. The chariot was swilled out at the 38 pool of Samaria, and the dogs licked up the blood, and the prostitutes washed themselves in it, in fulfilment of the word the LORD had spoken.

Now the other acts and events of 39 Ahab's reign, the ivory house and all the cities he built, are recorded in the

k Or at.   l son: or deputy.

symbols of military power; see Deut.33.17; Zech.1.18–21. Compare Jeremiah's dramatic action in Jer. chs. 27–28. **17–23:** Micaiah's speech is an effort to dissuade the king, not simply to prophesy his death. **19:** Compare Isa. ch. 6. **20–23:** This is one of several instances of the theme of divine enticement to sin or disaster; compare 2 Sam.24.1; 1 Chr.21.1. **38:** If by *the word of the LORD* 21.21–24 is meant, the details are treated rather loosely. **39:** As with Omri (16.8–34 n.), much of Ahab's activity is quickly passed over, in keeping with the compilers' bent.

40 annals of the kings of Israel. So Ahab rested with his forefathers and was succeeded by his son Ahaziah.

41 *m* Jehoshaphat son of Asa had become king of Judah in the fourth year of 42 Ahab king of Israel. He was thirty-five years old when he came to the throne, and he reigned in Jerusalem for twenty-five years; his mother was Azubah 43 daughter of Shilhi. He followed in the footsteps of Asa his father and did not swerve from them; he did what was right in the eyes of the LORD. But the hill-shrines were allowed to remain; the people continued to slaughter and 44 burn sacrifices there. Jehoshaphat remained at peace with the king of 45 Israel. The other events of Jehoshaphat's reign, his exploits and his wars, are recorded in the annals of the kings 46 of Judah. But he did away with such of the male prostitutes attached to the shrines as were still left over from the days of Asa his father.

47 There was no king in Edom, only*n* 48 a viceroy of Jehoshaphat; he built merchantmen to sail to Ophir for gold, but they never made the journey because they were wrecked at Ezion-geber. Ahaziah son of Ahab proposed 49 to Jehoshaphat that his own men should go to sea with his; but Jehoshaphat would not consent.

Jehoshaphat rested with his fore- 50 fathers and was buried with them in the city of David his father, and was succeeded by his son Joram.

Ahaziah son of Ahab became king of 51 Israel in Samaria in the seventeenth year of Jehoshaphat king of Judah, and reigned over Israel for two years. He did what was wrong in the eyes of 52 the LORD, following in the footsteps of his father and mother and in those of Jeroboam son of Nebat, who had led Israel into sin. He served Baal and 53 worshipped him, and provoked the anger of the LORD the God of Israel, as his father had done.

m Verses 41–43: cp. 2 Chr. 20. 31–33.
n only: prob. rdg.; Heb. om.

22.41–53: Jehoshaphat of Judah and Ahaziah of Israel. Jehoshaphat was the first new king of Judah after the dynasty of Omri came to power in Israel. He cooperated with Omri's and Ahab's master policy to control Syria-Palestine (see 16.23–34 n.), and accordingly married his son and heir to Ahab's daughter Athaliah (2 Kgs.8.16–18, 25–28) and cooperated with the military campaigns of Ahab (vv. 1–40) and his successors (2 Kgs. ch. 3). **43–46:** In the light of Jehoshaphat's open collaboration with wicked Ahab, it is surprising that he is approved. **50–53:** On *Ahaziah,* see 2 Kgs. ch. 1.

THE SECOND BOOK OF
KINGS

2 Kings is not actually a second book but the continuation of 1 Kings. Here, the violations of the requirements of the LORD lead to the end which the Deuteronomic historian sees as inevitable: the fall of Israel (ch. 17) and of Judah (ch. 25). See the Introduction to 1 Kings.

Elisha and the end of the house of Ahab

1 AFTER AHAB'S DEATH MOAB REbelled against Israel.

2 Ahaziah fell through a latticed window in his roof-chamber in Samaria and injured himself; he sent messengers to inquire of Baal-zebub the god of Ekron whether he would recover 3 from his illness. The angel of the LORD ordered Elijah the Tishbite to go and meet the messengers of the king of Samaria and say to them, 'Is there no god in Israel, that you go to inquire of Baal-zebub the god of Ekron? 4 This is the word of the LORD to your master: "You shall not rise from the bed where you are lying; you will 5 die."' Then Elijah departed. The messengers went back to the king. When asked why they had returned, they 6 answered that a man had come to meet them and had ordered them to return and say to the king who had sent them, 'This is the word of the LORD: "Is there no god in Israel, that you send to inquire of Baal-zebub the god of Ekron? In consequence, you shall not rise from the bed where 7 you are lying; you will die."' The king asked them what kind of man it was who had met them and said this. 'A 8 hairy man', they answered, 'with a leather apron round his waist.' 'It is Elijah the Tishbite', said the king. 9 Then the king sent a captain to him with his company of fifty. He went up and found the prophet sitting on a hill-top and said to him, 'Man of God, the king orders you to come down.' Elijah answered the captain, 10 'If I am a man of God, may fire fall from heaven and consume you and your company!' Fire fell from heaven and consumed the officer and his fifty men. The king sent another captain 11 of fifty with his company, and he went up and said to the prophet, 'Man of God, this is the king's command: Come down at once.' Elijah answered, 12 'If I am a man of God, may fire fall from heaven and consume you and your company!' God's fire fell from heaven and consumed the man and his company. The king sent the captain 13 of a third company with his fifty men, and this third captain went up the hill to Elijah and knelt down before him and pleaded with him: 'Man of God, consider me and these fifty servants of yours, and set some value on our lives. Fire fell from heaven 14 and consumed the other two captains of fifty and their companies; but let my life have some value in your eyes.' The angel of the LORD said to Elijah, 15 'Go down with him. Do not be afraid.' So he rose and went down with him to the king, and he said, 'This is the 16 word of the LORD: "You have sent to inquire of Baal-zebub the god of Ekron, and therefore you shall not rise from the bed where you are lying; you will die."' The word of the LORD 17 which Elijah had spoken was fulfilled, and Ahaziah died; and because he had

1.1–10:36: **The climax of the religious crisis.** Further materials (chs. 1–2; 8–10) relevant to the religious crisis of the ninth century are arranged around a collection of miracle stories about Elisha (chs. 3–7). See 1 Kgs.17.1–2 Kgs.10.36 n.
1.1–18: **Elijah condemns Ahaziah.** Two prophetic legends (vv. 2–8,16–17 and vv. 9–15) are merged; compare vv. 9–15 with 1 Sam.19.18–24 and vv. 2–8, 16–17 with 2 Kgs.14.1–18. **1:** This verse, here apparently misplaced by a copyist, is repeated in 3.5. **2:** *Baal-zebub*, meaning "lord of flies," is a distorted, contemptuous alteration of Baal-zebul, "Baal the Prince." **9–14:** *Elijah* has heavenly fire at his disposal; Samuel, in a similar situation, employed only prophetic ecstasy, 1 Sam.19.18–24. **17:** The Deuteronomic emphasis on the fulfillment of the prophetic *word* continues; see also 1 Kgs.17.24. The chronological data of 1.17 and 3.1 are inconsistent.

no son, his brother Jehoram succeeded him in the second year of Joram son of Jehoshaphat king of Judah.

18 The other events of Ahaziah's reign are recorded in the annals of the kings of Israel.

2 The time came when the LORD would take Elijah up to heaven in a whirlwind. Elijah and Elisha left 2 Gilgal, and Elijah said to Elisha, 'Stay here; for the LORD has sent me to Bethel.' But Elisha said, 'As the LORD lives, your life upon it, I will not leave you.' So they went down country to 3 Bethel. There a company of prophets came out to Elisha and said to him, 'Do you know that the LORD is going to take your lord and master from you today?' 'I do know,' he replied; 'say 4 no more.' Then Elijah said to him, 'Stay here, Elisha; for the LORD has sent me to Jericho.' But he replied, 'As the LORD lives, your life upon it, I will not leave you.' So they went to 5 Jericho. There a company of prophets came up to Elisha and said to him, 'Do you know that the LORD is going to take your lord and master from you today?' 'I do know,' he said; 'say no 6 more.' Then Elijah said to him, 'Stay here; for the LORD has sent me to the Jordan.' The other replied, 'As the LORD lives, your life upon it, I will not leave you.' So the two of them went on. 7 Fifty of the prophets followed them, and stood watching from a distance as the two of them stopped by the Jordan. 8 Elijah took his cloak, rolled it up and struck the water with it. The water divided to right and left, and they both crossed over on dry ground. 9 While they were crossing, Elijah said to Elisha, 'Tell me what I can do for you before I am taken from you.' Elisha said, 'Let me inherit a double 10 share of your spirit.' 'You have asked a hard thing', said Elijah. 'If you see me taken from you, may your wish be granted; if you do not, it shall not be

granted.' They went on, talking as they 11 went, and suddenly there appeared chariots of fire and horses of fire, which separated them one from the other, and Elijah was carried up in the whirlwind to heaven. When Elisha saw it, 12 he cried, 'My father, my father, the chariots and the horsemen of Israel!', and he saw him no more. Then he took hold of his mantle and rent it in two, and he picked up the cloak which had 13 fallen from Elijah, and came back and stood on the bank of the Jordan. There 14 he too struck the water with Elijah's cloak and said, 'Where is the LORD the God of Elijah?' When he struck the water, it was again divided to right and left, and he crossed over. The 15 prophets from Jericho, who were watching, saw him and said, 'The spirit of Elijah has settled on Elisha.' So they came to meet him, and fell on their faces before him and said, 'Your ser- 16 vants have fifty stalwart men. Let them go and search for your master; perhaps the spirit of the LORD has lifted him up and cast him on some mountain or into some valley.' But he said, 'No, you must not send them.' They pressed him, 17 however, until he had not the heart to refuse. So they sent out the fifty men but, though they searched for three days, they did not find him. When they 18 came back to Elisha, who had re- mained at Jericho, he said to them, 'Did I not tell you not to go?'

The people of the city said to Elisha, 19 'You can see how pleasantly our city is situated, but the water is polluted and the country is troubled with mis- carriages.' He said, 'Fetch me a new 20 bowl and put some salt in it.' When they had fetched it, he went out to the 21 spring and, throwing the salt into it, he said, 'This is the word of the LORD: "I purify this water. It shall cause no more death or miscarriage."' The water 22 has remained pure till this day, in ful- filment of Elisha's word.

2.1–25: **Elisha succeeds Elijah.** Elijah is taken up by God in the same geographical locale in which Moses was buried (see Deut.34.5–6), and Elisha recrosses the Jordan in the same manner that Joshua led Israel across; compare vv. 13–15 with Josh.3.9–4.14. **2**: This *Gilgal* was in Ephraim, different from the one near Jericho. **3**: *A company of prophets*: see 1 Kgs. 18.19 n. **19–25**: These two miracle stories are brief versions of the types that appear in chs. 4–7. These legends stress the power and holiness of the prophet, occasionally even (v. 24) at the cost of humaneness.

23 He went up from there to Bethel and, as he was on his way, some small boys came out of the city and jeered at him, saying, 'Get along with you, bald head, 24 get along.' He turned round and looked at them and he cursed them in the name of the LORD; and two she-bears came out of a wood and mauled forty- 25 two of them. From there he went on to Mount Carmel, and thence back to Samaria.

3 In the eighteenth year of Jehoshaphat king of Judah, Jehoram son of Ahab became king of Israel in Samaria, and 2 he reigned for twelve years. He did what was wrong in the eyes of the LORD, though not as his father and his mother had done; he did remove the sacred pillar of the Baal which his 3 father had made. Yet he persisted in the sins into which Jeroboam son of Nebat had led Israel, and did not give them up.

4 Mesha king of Moab was a sheep-breeder, and he used to supply the king of Israel regularly with the wool of a hundred thousand lambs and a 5 hundred thousand rams. When Ahab died, the king of Moab rebelled against 6 the king of Israel. Then King Jehoram came from Samaria and mustered 7 all Israel. He also sent this message to Jehoshaphat king of Judah: 'The king of Moab has rebelled against me. Will you join me in attacking Moab?' 'I will,' he replied; 'what is mine is yours: myself, my people, and my 8 horses.' 'From which direction shall we attack?' Jehoram asked. 'Through the wilderness of Edom', replied the 9 other. So the king of Israel set out with the king of Judah and the king of Edom. When they had been seven days on the march, they had no water left 10 for the army or the pack-animals. Then the king of Israel said, 'Alas, the LORD has brought together three kings, only to put us at the mercy of the Moabites.' 11 But Jehoshaphat said. 'Is there not a

prophet of the LORD here through whom we may seek guidance of the LORD?' One of the officers of the king of Israel answered, 'Elisha son of Shaphat is here, the man who poured water on Elijah's hands.' 'The word of 12 the LORD is with him', said Jehoshaphat. So the king of Israel and Jehoshaphat and the king of Edom went down to Elisha. Elisha said to the king of 13 Israel, 'Why do you come to me? Go to the prophets of your father and your mother.' But the king of Israel said to him, 'No; the LORD has called us three kings out to put us at the mercy of the Moabites.' 'As the LORD of Hosts lives, 14 whom I serve,' said Elisha, 'I would not spare a look or a glance for you, if it were not for my regard for Jehoshaphat king of Judah. But now, fetch me a 15 minstrel.' They fetched a minstrel, and while he was playing, the power of the LORD came upon Elisha and he said, 16 'This is the word of the LORD: "Pools will form all over this ravine." The 17 LORD has decreed that you shall see neither wind nor rain, yet this ravine shall be filled with water for you and your army and your pack-animals to drink. But that is a mere trifle in the 18 sight of the LORD; what he will also do, is to put Moab at your mercy. You 19 will raze to the ground every fortified town and every noble city; you will cut down all their fine trees; you will stop up all the springs of water; and you will spoil every good piece of land by littering it with stones.' In the 20 morning at the hour of the regular sacrifice they saw water flowing in from the direction of Edom, and the land was flooded.

Meanwhile all Moab had heard 21 that the kings had come up to fight against them, and every man, young and old, who could carry arms, was called out and stationed on the frontier. When they got up next morning and the 22 sun had risen over the water, the

---

3.1–27: **Israel's campaign against Mesha of Moab.** In the alliance of Israel and Judah that was a part of Omri's policy (see 1 Kgs.16.23–34 n.), Judah dominated Edom (1 Kgs.22.47) while Israel dominated Moab (vv. 4–5), and the two cooperated in maintaining their dominance. **2:** *The sacred pillar* Jehoram removed was presumably in Samaria. **5:** A Moabite account of the successful revolt by *Mesha*, carved in stone, was discovered in 1868. **7:** See similar words in 1 Kgs.22.4. **8:** The strategy was to circle the south side of the Dead Sea. **15:** The *minstrel, . . . playing*, suggests the use of music to induce the ecstatic state in which the *power of the Lord* was experienced. **22:** The *red* seen by *the Moabites* arises from the red sandstone common in

387

Moabites saw the water in front of them red like blood and cried out, 'It is blood. The kings must have quarrelled and attacked one another. Now to the plunder, Moab!' When they came to the Israelite camp, the Israelites turned out and attacked them and drove the Moabites headlong in flight, and themselves entered the land of Moab, destroying as they went. They razed the cities to the ground; they littered every good piece of land with stones, each man casting one stone on to it; they stopped up every spring of water; they cut down all their fine trees; and they harried Moab until only in Kir-hareseth were any buildings left standing, and even this city the slingers surrounded and attacked.

26 When the king of Moab saw that the war had gone against him, he took seven hundred men with him, armed with swords, to cut a way through to the king of Aram, but they failed in 27 the attempt. Then he took his eldest son, who would have succeeded him, and offered him as a whole-offering upon the city wall. The Israelites were filled with such consternation at this sight,[a] that they struck camp and returned to their own land.

4 The wife of a member of a company of prophets appealed to Elisha. 'My husband, your servant, has died', she said. 'You know that he was a man who feared the LORD; but a creditor has come to take away my two boys 2 as his slaves.' Elisha said to her, 'How can I help you? Tell me what you have in the house.' 'Nothing at all', she 3 answered, 'except a flask of oil.' 'Go out then', he said, 'and borrow vessels from all your neighbours; get as many 4 empty ones as you can. Then, when you come home, shut yourself in with your sons, pour from the flask into all these vessels and, as they are filled,

set them aside.' She left him and shut 5 herself in with her sons. As they brought her the vessels she filled them. When 6 they were all full, she said to one of her sons, 'Bring me another.' 'There is not one left', he said. Then the flow of oil ceased. She came out and told the 7 man of God, and he said, 'Go and sell the oil and redeem your boys who are being taken as pledges,[b] and you and they can live on what is left.'

It happened once that Elisha went 8 over to Shunem. There was a great lady there who pressed him to accept her hospitality, and so, whenever he came that way, he stopped to take food there. One day she said to her husband, 9 'I know that this man who comes here regularly is a holy man of God. Why not build up the wall to make 10 him a little roof-chamber, and put in it a bed, a table, a seat, and a lamp, and let him stay there whenever he comes to us?' Once when he arrived 11 and went to this roof-chamber and lay down to rest, he said to Gehazi, his 12 servant, 'Call this Shunammite woman.' He called her and, when she appeared before the prophet, he said to his servant, 'Say to her, "You have taken all 13 this trouble for us. What can I do for you? Shall I speak for you to the king or to the commander-in-chief?"' But she replied, 'I am content where I am, among my own people.' He said, 'Then 14 what can be done for her?' Gehazi said, 'There is only this: she has no child and her husband is old.' 'Call 15 her back', Elisha said. When she was called, she appeared in the doorway, and he said, 'In due season, this time 16 next year, you shall have a son in your arms.' But she said, 'No, no, my lord, you are a man of God and would not lie to your servant.' Next year in due 17

a The Israelites ... sight: *or* There was such great anger against the Israelites ...
b redeem ... pledges: *or* pay off your debt.

Edom. **25:** Elisha's prophecy (v. 19) is nearly fulfilled here, but the Israelites do not gain final victory. **26:** *The king of Aram* (Damascus) was always interested in aiding rebels against Israel. **27:** The sacrifice of a prince was a last extreme step. On human sacrifice see Exod.22.29–30; Judg.11.30–39; 1 Kgs.16.34.
4.1–8.6: Various miracles of Elisha. This collection of stories (see also 2.19–25) magnifies the prophetic power of Elisha. Not until the Gospels does a comparable collection of miracle stories appear in biblical literature.
4.1–37: Elisha's prophetic powers. 1–7: This story is parallel to Elijah's first miracle during the drought (1 Kgs.17.8–16). **8–37:** Elisha is related to the *great lady* of *Shunem* in several episodes (the concluding one is in 8.1–6). **8–17:** The childless woman eventually bears a child;

season the woman conceived and bore a son, as Elisha had foretold.

18 When the child was old enough, he went out one day to the reapers where 19 his father was. All of a sudden he cried out to his father, 'O my head, my head!' His father told a servant to carry him 20 to his mother. He brought him to his mother; the boy sat on her lap till 21 midday, and then he died. She went up and laid him on the bed of the man of God, shut the door and went out. 22 She called her husband and said, 'Send me one of the servants and a she-ass, I must go to the man of God as fast as 23 I can, and come straight back.' 'Why go to him today?' he asked. 'It is neither new moon nor sabbath.'c 'Never 24 mind that', she answered. When the ass was saddled, she said to her servant, 'Lead on and do not slacken pace unless 25 I tell you.' So she set out and came to the man of God on Mount Carmel. The man of God spied her in the distance and said to Gehazi, his servant, 'That is the Shunammite 26 woman coming. Run and meet her, and ask, "Is all well with you? Is all well with your husband? Is all well with the boy?"' She answered, 'All is 27 well.' When she reached the man of God on the hill, she clutched his feet. Gehazi came forward to push her away, but the man of God said, 'Let her alone; she is in great distress, and the LORD has concealed it from me 28 and not told me.' 'My lord,' she said, 'did I ask for a son? Did I not beg you not to raise my hopes and then dash 29 them?' Then he turned to Gehazi: 'Hitch up your cloak; take my staff with you and run. If you meet anyone on the way, do not stop to greet him; if anyone greets you, do not answer him. Lay my staff on the boy's face.' 30 But the mother cried, 'As the LORD lives, your life upon it, I will not leave you.' So he got up and followed her.d 31 Gehazi went on ahead of them and laid the staff on the boy's face, but there was no sound and no sign of

life. So he went back to meet Elisha and told him that the boy had not 32 roused. When Elisha entered the house, there was the boy dead, on the bed where he had been laid. He went into 33 the room, shut the door on the two of them and prayed to the LORD. Then, 34 getting on to the bed, he lay upon the child, put his mouth to the child's mouth, his eyes to his eyes and his hands to his hands; and, as he pressede upon him, the child's body grew warm. Elisha got up and walked once up and 35 down the room; then, getting on to the bed again, he pressede upon him and breathed into himf seven times; and the boy opened his eyes. The prophet 36 summoned Gehazi and said, 'Call this Shunammite woman.' She answered his call and the prophet said, 'Take your child.' She came in and fell 37 prostrate before him. Then she took up her son and went out.

Elisha returned to Gilgal at a time 38 when there was a famine in the land. One day, when a group of prophets was sitting at his feet, he said to his servant, 'Set the big pot on the fire and prepare some broth for the company.' One of them went out into the fields to 39 gather herbs and found a wild vine, and filled the skirt of his garment with bitter-apples.g He came back and sliced them into the pot, not knowing what they were. They poured it out for the 40 men to eat, but, when they tasted it, they cried out, 'Man of God, there is death in the pot', and they could not eat it. The prophet said, 'Fetch 41 some meal.' He threw it into the pot and said, 'Now pour out for the men to eat.' This time there was no harm in the pot.

A man came from Baal-shalisha, 42 bringing the man of God some of the new season's bread, twenty barley loaves, and fresh ripe ears of corn.h Elisha said, 'Give this to the people to

c *Or* full moon.   d *Or* went with her.
e *Prob. rdg.; Heb.* crouched.
f *and breathed into him: or and the boy sneezed.*
g *Or* poisonous wild gourds.
h *fresh . . . corn: prob. rdg.; Heb. unintelligible.*

---

compare Gen.18.1–15; 1 Sam. ch. 1. **18–37:** The child miraculously born to the woman is later revived after an accidental death. The story parallels 1 Kgs.17.17–24.
  4.38–44: Two food miracles. Elisha here does with food what he did with water in 2.19–22. The multiplying of the loaves of *bread* resembles the later miracles of Jesus (Mt.14.13–21; 15.32–38).

43 eat.' But his disciple protested, 'I cannot set this before a hundred men.' Still he repeated, 'Give it to the people to eat; for this is the word of the LORD: "They will eat and there will 44 be some left over."' So he set it before them, and they ate and left some over, as the LORD had said.

5 NAAMAN, COMMANDER OF THE KING OF Aram's army, was a great man highly esteemed by his master, because by his means the LORD had given victory to 2 Aram; but he was a leper.*ⁱ* On one of their raids the Aramaeans brought back as a captive from the land of Israel a little girl, who became a servant 3 to Naaman's wife. She said to her mistress, 'If only my master could meet the prophet who lives in Samaria, he would get rid of the disease for him.' 4 Naaman went in and reported to his master word for word what the girl 5 from the land of Israel had said. 'Very well, you may go,' said the king of Aram, 'and I will send a letter to the king of Israel.' So Naaman went, taking with him ten talents of silver, six thousand shekels of gold, and ten 6 changes of clothing. He delivered the letter to the king of Israel, which read thus. 'This letter is to inform you that I am sending to you my servant Naaman, and I beg you to rid him of his 7 disease.' When the king of Israel read the letter, he rent his clothes and said, 'Am I a god*ʲ* to kill and to make alive, that this fellow sends to me to cure a man of his disease? Surely you must see that he is picking a quarrel with 8 me.' When Elisha, the man of God, heard how the king of Israel had rent his clothes, he sent to him saying, 'Why did you rend your clothes? Let the man come to me, and he will know 9 that there is a prophet in Israel.' So Naaman came with his horses and chariots and stood at the entrance to 10 Elisha's house. Elisha sent out a messenger to say to him, 'If you will go and wash seven times in the Jordan, your flesh will be restored and you will be clean.' Naaman was furious and 11 went away, saying, 'I thought he would at least have come out and stood, and invoked the LORD his God by name, waved his hand over the place and so rid me of the disease. Are not Abana 12 and Pharpar, rivers of Damascus, better than all the waters of Israel? Can I not wash in them and be clean?' So he turned and went off in a rage. But his 13 servants came up to him and said, 'If the prophet had bidden you do something difficult, would you not do it? How much more then, if he tells you to wash and be clean?' So 14 he went down and dipped himself in the Jordan seven times as the man of God had told him, and his flesh was restored as a little child's, and he was clean.

Then he and his retinue went back 15 to the man of God and stood before him; and he said, 'Now I know that there is no god anywhere on earth except in Israel. Will you accept a token of gratitude from your servant?' 'As the LORD lives, whom I serve,' 16 said the prophet, 'I will accept nothing.' He was pressed to accept, but he refused. 'Then if you will not,' said 17 Naaman, 'let me, sir, have two mules' load of earth. For I will no longer offer whole-offering or sacrifice to any god but the LORD. In this one matter 18 only may the LORD pardon me: when my master goes to the temple of Rimmon to worship, leaning on my arm, and I worship in the temple of Rimmon when he worships there, for this let the LORD pardon me.' And 19 Elisha bade him farewell.

Naaman had gone only a short distance on his way, when Gehazi, the 20 servant of Elisha the man of God, said to himself, 'What? Has my master let this Aramaean, Naaman, go scot-free,

i he was a leper: *or* his skin was diseased.
j Or Am I God.

5.1–27: Elisha cures Naaman's leprosy. The narrative speaks simply of *the king of Aram* and *the king of Israel* without names, a usual mark of legendary materials. 5: The money amounts to an enormous sum. 7: The narrative assumes that Damascus dominated *Israel*; this would be after the overthrow of the Omri dynasty; see 10.32–33; 13.3. 15–19: This viewpoint is on the verge of explicit monotheism; yet, *the LORD* must be worshiped on soil from his own land. *Rimmon*, a title of Hadad, the god of Damascus, was also known in Canaan (Zech 12.11).

and not accepted what he brought? As the LORD lives, I will run after him 21 and get something from him.' So Gehazi hurried after Naaman. When Naaman saw him running after him, he jumped down from his chariot to meet him and said, 'Is anything wrong?' 22 'Nothing,' said Gehazi, 'but my master sent me to say that two young men of the company of prophets from the hill-country of Ephraim have just arrived. Could you provide them with a talent of silver and two changes of 23 clothing?' Naaman said, 'By all means; take two talents.' He pressed[k] him to take them; so he tied up the two talents of silver in two bags, and the two changes of clothing, and gave them to his two servants, and they walked 24 ahead carrying them. When Gehazi came to the citadel[l] he took them from the two servants, deposited them in the house and dismissed the men; 25 and they departed. When he went in and stood before his master, Elisha said, 'Where have you been, Gehazi?' 26 'Nowhere', said Gehazi. But he said to him, 'Was I not with you in spirit when the man turned back from his chariot to meet you? Is it not true that you have the money? You may buy gardens with it,[m][n] and olive-trees and vineyards, sheep and oxen, slaves 27 and slave-girls; but the disease of Naaman will fasten on you and on your descendants for ever.' Gehazi left his presence, his skin diseased, white as snow.

6 A COMPANY OF PROPHETS SAID TO Elisha, 'You can see that this place where our community is living, under 2 you as its head, is too small for us. Let us go to the Jordan and each fetch a log, and make ourselves a place to 3 live in.' The prophet agreed. Then one of them said, 'Please, sir, come with 4 us.' 'I will', he said, and he went with them. When they reached the Jordan,

they began cutting down trees; but it 5 chanced that, as one man was felling a trunk, the head of his axe flew off into the water. 'Oh, master!' he exclaimed, 'it was a borrowed one.' 'Where did it fall?' asked the man of 6 God. When he was shown the place, he cut off a piece of wood and threw it in and made the iron float. Then he 7 said, 'There you are, lift it out.' So he stretched out his hand and took it.

Once, when the king of Aram was 8 making war on Israel, he held a conference with his staff at which he said, 'I mean to attack in such and such a direction.' But the man of God warned 9 the king of Israel: 'Take care to avoid this place, for the Aramaeans are going down that way.' So the king of Israel 10 sent to the place about which the man of God had given him this warning; and the king took special precautions every time he found himself near that place. The king of Aram was greatly perturbed at this and, summoning his staff, 11 he said to them, 'Tell me, one of you, who has betrayed us to the king of Israel?' 'None of us, my lord king,' 12 said one of his staff; 'but Elisha, the prophet in Israel, tells the king of Israel the very words you speak in your bedchamber.' 'Go and find out where 13 he is,' said the king, 'and I will send and seize him.' He was told that the prophet was at Dothan, and he sent 14 a strong force there with horses and chariots. They came by night and surrounded the city.

When the disciple of the man of God 15 rose early in the morning and went out, he saw a force with horses and chariots surrounding the city. 'Oh, master,' he said, 'which way are we to turn?' He answered, 'Do not be 16 afraid, for those who are on our side are more than those on theirs.' Then 17

k *Prob. rdg.; Heb.* broke out on.
l *Or* hill.
m *gardens with it: prob. rdg.; Heb.* garments.
n *Is it not ... with it: or* Was it time to get the money and to get garments?

22: A *talent* (over sixty pounds) *of silver* (see p. 1035) was an extravagant amount for *two* needy *young men*. 24–27: The prophet's divine powers enforced justice among his adherents. 6.1–7: The floating axe head. This episode, showing only the prophet's miraculous power, is like those in 2.19–25 and ch. 4. 6.8–23: Elisha foils Aramaean raids. 8–10: As 8.7 shows, prophets could come and go between Israel and Damascus. The story does not mean, however, that Elisha conducted an efficient spy network. His knowledge was due to his supernatural powers. 17: *Horses and chariots of fire*

Elisha offered this prayer: 'O LORD, open his eyes and let him see.' And the LORD opened the young man's eyes, and he saw the hills covered with horses and chariots of fire all round

18 Elisha. As they came down towards him, Elisha prayed to the LORD: 'Strike this host, I pray thee, with blindness'; and he struck them blind as Elisha

19 had asked. Then Elisha said to them, 'You are on the wrong road; this is not the city. Follow me and I will lead you to the man you are looking for.' And he

20 led them to Samaria. As soon as they had entered Samaria, Elisha prayed, 'O LORD, open the eyes of these men and let them see again.' And he opened their eyes and they saw that they were inside

21 Samaria. When the king of Israel saw them, he said to Elisha, 'My father, am

22 I to destroy them?' 'No, you must not do that', he answered. 'You may destroy*o* those whom you have taken prisoner with your own sword and bow, but as for these men, give them food and water, and let them eat and drink, and then go back to their

23 master.' So he prepared a great feast for them, and they ate and drank and then went back to their master. And Aramaean raids on Israel ceased.

24   But later, Ben-hadad king of Aram called up his entire army and marched

25 to the siege of Samaria. The city was near starvation, and they besieged it so closely that a donkey's head was sold for eighty shekels of silver, and a quarter of a kab of locust-beans for five

26 shekels. One day, as the king of Israel was walking along the city wall, a woman called to him, 'Help, my lord

27 king!' He said, 'If the LORD will not bring you help, where can I find any for you? From threshing-floor or from

28 winepress? What is your trouble?' She replied, 'This woman said to me, "Give up your child for us to eat today, and

29 we will eat mine tomorrow." So we cooked my son and ate him; but when

I said to her the next day, "Now give up your child for us to eat", she had hidden him.' When he heard the 30 woman's story, the king rent his clothes. He was walking along the wall at the time, and when the people looked, they saw that he had sackcloth underneath, next to his skin. Then he 31 said, 'The LORD do the same to me and more, if the head of Elisha son of Shaphat stays on his shoulders today.'

Elisha was sitting at home, the elders 32 with him. The king had dispatched one of his retinue but, before the messenger arrived, Elisha said to the elders, 'See how this son of a murderer has sent to behead me! Take care, when the messenger comes, to shut the door and hold it fast against him. Can you not hear his master following on his heels?' While he was still speaking, 33 the king*p* arrived and said, 'Look at our plight! This is the LORD's doing. Why should I wait any longer for him to help us?' But Elisha answered, 'Hear 7 this word of the LORD: By this time tomorrow a shekel will buy a measure of flour or two measures of barley in the gateway of Samaria.' Then the 2 lieutenant on whose arm the king leaned said to the man of God, 'Even if the LORD were to open windows in the sky, such a thing could not happen!' He answered, 'You will see it with your own eyes, but none of it will you eat.'

At the city gate were four lepers.*q* 3 They said to one another, 'Why should we stay here and wait for death? If we 4 say we will go into the city, there is famine there, and we shall die; if we say we will stay here, we shall die just the same. Well then, let us go to the camp of the Aramaeans and give ourselves up: if they spare us, we shall live; if they put us to death, we can but die.' And so in the twilight they 5 set out for the Aramaean camp;

o Prob. rdg.; Heb. Would you destroy.
p Prob. rdg.; Heb. messenger.
q Or men suffering from skin-disease.

---

are often motifs in the Elijah-Elisha stories; see 2.11; 1.9–14 n. **22–23:** The prisoners captured by supernatural means are evidence that divine power resists the *Aramaean raids*.
    6.24–7.20: Episodes in a siege of Samaria. 24: *Ben-hadad:* there were several kings of *Aram* who bore this name. The name of the Israelite king is not given. Prophetic legends tend to lack precise historical references. **25:** The prices were extremely high; see p. 1035. **30:** The king's *sackcloth* showed how much he was concerned with the distress of his people. **31:** Possibly Elisha was blamed because he was thought to embody anti-Aramaean policies that

but when they reached the outskirts,
6 they found no one there; for the Lord
had caused the Aramaean army to
hear a sound like that of chariots and
horses and of a great host, so that the
word went round: 'The king of Israel
has hired the kings of the Hittites and
7 the kings of Egypt to attack us.' They
had fled at once in the twilight, abandoning their tents, their horses and asses,
and leaving the camp as it stood, while
8 they fled for their lives. When the four
men came to the outskirts of the
camp, they went into a tent and ate and
drank and looted silver and gold and
clothing, and made off and hid them.
Then they came back, went into another
tent and rifled it, and made off and hid
9 the loot. Then they said to one another,
'What we are doing is not right. This is
a day of good news and we are keeping
it to ourselves. If we wait till morning,
we shall be held to blame. We must go
now and give the news to the king's
10 household.' So they came and called
to the watch at the city gate and described how they had gone to the
Aramaean camp and found not a single
man in it and had heard no sound:
nothing but horses and asses tethered,
11 and the tents left as they were. Then the
watch called out and gave the news to
12 the king's household in the palace. The
king rose in the night and said to his
staff, 'I will tell you what the Aramaeans have done. They know that
we are starving, and they have left their
camp to go and hide in the open
country, expecting us to come out, and
then they can take us alive and enter
13 the city.' One of his staff said, 'Send
out a party of men with some of
the horses that are left; if they live,
they will be as well off as all the other
Israelites who are still left; if they die,[r]
they will be no worse off than all those
who have already perished. Let them
14 go and see what has happened.' So they
picked two mounted men, and the
king dispatched them in the track of
the Aramaean army with the order to
go and find out what had happened.
15 They followed as far as the Jordan and
found the whole road littered with
clothing and equipment which the
Aramaeans had flung aside in their
haste. The messengers returned and
reported this to the king. Then the
16 people went out and plundered the
Aramaean camp, and a measure of
flour was sold for a shekel and two
measures of barley for a shekel, so
that the word of the LORD came true.
17 Now the king had appointed the
lieutenant on whose arm he leaned to
take charge of the gate, and the people
trampled him to death there, just as the
man of God had foretold when the king
18 visited him. For when the man of God
said to the king, 'By this time tomorrow
a shekel will buy two measures of barley
or one measure of flour in the gateway
19 of Samaria', the lieutenant had answered, 'Even if the LORD were to open
windows in the sky, such a thing could
not happen!' And the man of God had
20 said, 'You will see it with your own eyes,
but none of it will you eat.' And this is
just what happened to him: the people
trampled him to death at the gate.

8 Elisha said to the woman whose
son he had restored to life, 'Go away
at once with your household and find
lodging where you can, for the LORD
has decreed a seven years' famine and
it has already come upon the land.'
2 The woman acted at once on the word
of the man of God and went away with
her household; and she stayed in the
Philistine country for seven years.
3 When she came back at the end of the
seven years, she sought an audience
of the king to appeal for the return of
her house and land. Now the king was
4 questioning Gehazi, the servant of the
man of God, about all the great things
5 Elisha had done; and, as he was
describing to the king how he had
brought the dead to life, the selfsame
woman began appealing to the king
for her house and her land. 'My lord

[r] *if they live ... if they die: prob. rdg.; Heb. obscure.*

had reduced Samaria to dire straits. **7.17:** Elisha's prophecies always come true, even if somewhat grimly.
8.1–6: The Shunammite woman as witness. This episode resumes the story of Elisha and the Shunammite woman from 4.37. **4:** As yet *Gehazi* does not seem to have suffered the leprosy of 5.24–27.

king,' said Gehazi, 'this is the very
woman, and this is her son whom
6 Elisha brought to life.' The king asked
the woman about it, and she told him.
Then he entrusted the case to a eunuch
and ordered him to restore all her property to her, with all the revenues from
her land from the time she left the
country till that day.
7 Elisha came to Damascus, at a time
when Ben-hadad king of Aram was ill;
and when he was told that the man of
8 God had arrived, he bade Hazael take
a gift with him and go to the man of
God and inquire of the LORD through
him whether he would recover from
9 his illness. Hazael went, taking with
him as a gift all kinds of wares of
Damascus, forty camel-loads. When
he came into the prophet's presence,
he said, 'Your son Ben-hadad king of
Aram has sent me to you to ask whether
10 he will recover from his illness.' 'Go
and tell him that he will recover,' he
answered; 'but the LORD has revealed
11 to me that in fact he will die.' The man
of God stood there with set face like a
man stunned, until he could bear it no
12 longer; then he wept. 'Why do you
weep, my lord?' said Hazael. He answered, 'Because I know the harm you
will do to the Israelites: you will set
their fortresses on fire and put their
young men to the sword; you will dash
their children to the ground and you
will rip open their pregnant women.'
13 But Hazael said, 'But I am a dog, a
mere nobody; how can I do this great
thing?' Elisha answered, 'The LORD
has revealed to me that you will be
14 king of Aram.' Hazael left Elisha and
returned to his master, who asked
him what Elisha had said. 'He told me
that you would recover', he replied.
15 But the next day he took a blanket and,
after dipping it in water, laid it over the
king's face, and he died; and Hazael
succeeded him.

In the fifth year of Jehoram son of 16
Ahab king of Israel, Joram son of
Jehoshaphat king of Judah became
king. He was thirty-two years old 17[s]
when he came to the throne, and he
reigned in Jerusalem for eight years.
He followed the practices of the kings 18
of Israel as the house of Ahab had
done, for he had married Ahab's
daughter; and he did what was wrong
in the eyes of the LORD. But for his 19
servant David's sake the LORD was unwilling to destroy Judah, since he had
promised to give him and his sons a
flame, to burn for all time.
During his reign Edom revolted 20
against Judah and set up its own king.
Joram crossed over to Zair with all 21
his chariots. He and his chariot-
commanders set out by night, but they
were surrounded by the Edomites and
defeated,[t] whereupon the people fled
to their tents. So Edom has remained 22
independent of Judah to this day; Libnah also revolted at the same time.
The other acts and events of Joram's 23
reign are recorded in the annals of the
kings of Judah. So Joram rested with 24
his forefathers and was buried with
them in the city of David, and his son
Ahaziah succeeded him.
In the twelfth year of Jehoram son 25[u]
of Ahab king of Israel, Ahaziah son of
Joram king of Judah became king.
Ahaziah was twenty-two years old 26
when he came to the throne, and he
reigned in Jerusalem for one year; his
mother was Athaliah granddaughter of
Omri king of Israel. He followed the 27
practices of the house of Ahab and
did what was wrong in the eyes of the
LORD like the house of Ahab, for he
was connected with that house by
marriage. He allied himself with 28
Jehoram son of Ahab to fight against
Hazael king of Aram at Ramoth-

s *Verses 17–22: cp. 2 Chr. 21. 5–10.*
t *and defeated: prob. rdg.; Heb. and he defeated Edom.*
u *Verses 25–29: cp. 2 Chr. 22. 1–6.*

8.7–15: Elisha and revolution in Damascus. The Elisha stories now return to the larger account
of the overthrow of the dynasty of Omri. The second of the three commissions given to Elijah
at Mount Horeb (1 Kgs.19.15–16) is here carried out. **10:** The deception of Ben-hadad is
God's will. **12:** Elisha foresees the events of 10.32–33 and 13.3.
8.16–29: The last years of the Omri dynasty. *Joram* of *Judah* followed the policy of collaboration with the Northern Kingdom and the religious tolerance involved in that policy (v. 18). The
power of the two kingdoms was declining; Israel had lost control of Moab (3.27), and now
Judah loses control of *Edom* (vv. 20–22). **26:** *Athaliah*, daughter of Jezebel, was to prove much
more powerful than her son *Ahaziah*; see ch. 11.

gilead; but King Jehoram was wounded
29 by the Aramaeans, and returned to
Jezreel to recover from the wounds
which were inflicted on him at Ramoth
in battle with Hazael king of Aram;
and because of his illness Ahaziah son
of Joram king of Judah went down to
Jezreel to visit him.

9 ELISHA THE PROPHET SUMMONED ONE
of the company of prophets and said
to him, 'Hitch up your cloak, take this
flask of oil with you and go to Ramoth-
2 gilead. When you arrive, you will find
Jehu son of Jehoshaphat, son of Nimshi; go in and call him aside from his
fellow-officers, and lead him through
3 to an inner room. Then take the flask
and pour the oil on his head and say,
"This is the word of the LORD: I
anoint you king over Israel"; then open
4 the door and flee for your life.' So the
young prophet went to Ramoth-gilead.
5 When he arrived, he found the officers
sitting together and said, 'Sir, I have
a word for you.' 'For which of us?'
asked Jehu. 'For you, sir', he said.
6 He rose and went into the house, and
the prophet poured the oil on his head,
saying, 'This is the word of the LORD
the God of Israel: "I anoint you king
over Israel, the people of the LORD.
7 You shall strike down the house of
Ahab your master, and I will take vengeance on Jezebel for the blood of my
servants the prophets and for the blood
8 of all the LORD's servants. All the house
of Ahab shall perish and I will destroy
every mother's son of his house in
Israel, whether under the protection of
9 the family or not. And I will make the
house of Ahab like the house of Jeroboam son of Nebat and the house of
10 Baasha son of Ahijah. Jezebel shall be
devoured by dogs in the plot of
ground at Jezreel and no one will
bury her."' Then he opened the door
11 and fled. When Jehu rejoined the
king's officers, they said to him, 'Is all

well? What did this crazy fellow want
with you?' 'You know him and the way
his thoughts run', he said. 'Nonsense!' 12
they replied; 'tell us what happened.'
'I will tell you exactly what he said:
"This is the word of the LORD: I
anoint you king over Israel."' They 13
snatched up their cloaks and spread
them under him on the stones[v] of the
steps, and sounded the trumpet and
shouted, 'Jehu is king.'

Then Jehu son of Jehoshaphat, son 14
of Nimshi, laid his plans against Jehoram, while Jehoram and the Israelites
were defending Ramoth-gilead against
Hazael king of Aram. King Jehoram
had returned to Jezreel to recover from 15
the wounds inflicted on him by the
Aramaeans when he fought against
Hazael king of Aram. Jehu said to
them, 'If you are on my side, see that
no one escapes from the city to tell the
news in Jezreel.' He mounted his
chariot and drove to Jezreel, for Je- 16
horam was laid up there, and Ahaziah
king of Judah had gone down to visit
him.

The watchman standing on the 17
watch-tower in Jezreel saw Jehu and his
troop approaching and called out, 'I
see a troop of men.' Then Jehoram
said, 'Fetch a horseman and send to
find out if they come peaceably.' The 18
horseman went to meet him and said,
'The king asks, "Is it peace?"' Jehu
said, 'Peace? What is peace to you?
Fall in behind me.' Thereupon the
watchman reported, 'The messenger
has met them but he is not coming
back.' A second horseman was sent; 19
when he met them, he also said, 'The
king asks, "Is it peace?"' 'Peace?' said
Jehu. 'What is peace to you? Fall in
behind me.' Then the watchman re- 20
ported, 'He has met them but he is not
coming back. The driving is like the
driving of Jehu son[w] of Nimshi, for he

v Prob. rdg.; Heb. obscure.
w Or grandson (cp. verse 2).

9.1–10.36: Jehu overthrows the dynasty of Omri. The third and last commission to Elijah
at Horeb (1 Kgs.19.15–18) is carried out here. This fine piece of historical writing is without
legendary coloring.
    9.1–13: The anointing of Jehu. 1: *Elisha* must work in secret; therefore, he sends one of his
disciples to anoint Jehu. **6–7:** On the LORD's sanction of Jehu's dynasty, see 1 Kgs.11.29–39 n.
    9.14–37: Jehu kills the reigning kings. 15: *Jezreel* served as a second capital of the Northern
Kingdom, nearer the war front than Samaria. **17:** *Jezreel* was about forty miles from Ramoth-
gilead. It overlooked the valley going down to the Jordan River. **18–22:** *Jehoram* is concerned

21 drives furiously.' 'Harness my chariot', said Jehoram. They harnessed it, and Jehoram king of Israel and Ahaziah king of Judah went out each in his own chariot to meet Jehu, and met him 22 by the plot of Naboth of Jezreel. When Jehoram saw Jehu, he said, 'Is it peace, Jehu?' But he replied, 'Do you call it peace while your mother Jezebel keeps up her obscene idol-worship and mon- 23 strous sorceries?' Jehoram wheeled about and fled, crying out to Ahaziah, 24 'Treachery, Ahaziah!' Jehu seized his bow and shot Jehoram between the shoulders; the arrow pierced his heart 25 and he sank down in his chariot. Then Jehu said to Bidkar, his lieutenant, 'Pick him up and throw him into the plot of land belonging to Naboth of Jezreel; remember how, when you and I were riding side by side behind Ahab his father, the LORD pronounced this 26 sentence against him: "It is the very word of the LORD: as surely as I saw yesterday the blood of Naboth and the blood of his sons, I will requite you in this plot." So pick him up and throw him into it and thus fulfil the word of 27 the LORD.' When Ahaziah king of Judah saw this, he fled by the road to Beth-haggan. Jehu went after him and said, 'Make sure of him too.' They shot him down in his chariot on the road up the valley*x* near Ibleam, but he escaped to Megiddo and died there. 28 His servants conveyed his body to Jerusalem and buried him in his tomb with his forefathers in the city of David. 29 In the eleventh year of Jehoram son of Ahab, Ahaziah became king over Judah. 30 Jehu came to Jezreel. Now Jezebel had heard what had happened; she had painted her eyes and dressed her hair, and she stood looking down from 31 a window. As Jehu entered the gate, she said, 'Is it peace, you Zimri, you 32 murderer of your master?' He looked

up at the window and said, 'Who is on my side, who?' Two or three eunuchs looked out, and he said, 'Throw 33 her down.' They threw her down, and some of her blood splashed on to the wall and the horses, which tram- pled her underfoot. Then he went in 34 and ate and drank. 'See to this accursed woman,' he said, 'and bury her; for she is a king's daughter.' But when they 35 went to bury her they found nothing of her but the skull, the feet, and the palms of the hands; and they went back 36 and told him. Jehu said, 'It is the word of the LORD which his servant Elijah the Tishbite spoke, when he said, "In the plot of ground at Jezreel the dogs shall devour the flesh of Jezebel, and 37 Jezebel's corpse shall lie like dung upon the ground in the plot at Jezreel so that no one will be able to say: This is Jezebel." '

Now seventy sons of Ahab were left **10** in Samaria. Jehu therefore sent a letter to Samaria, to the elders, the rulers of the city, and to the tutors of Ahab's children, in which he wrote: 'Now, when 2 this letter reaches you, since you have in your care your master's family as well as his chariots and horses, fortified cities and weapons, choose the best and 3 the most suitable of your master's family, set him on his father's throne, and fight for your master's house.' They were panic-stricken and said, 'The 4 two kings could not stand against him; what hope is there that we can?' Therefore the comptroller of the 5 household and the governor of the city, with the elders and the tutors, sent this message to Jehu: 'We are your servants. Whatever you tell us we will do; but we will not make anyone king. Do as you think fit.' Then he 6 wrote them a second letter: 'If you are on my side and will obey my orders, then bring the heads of your master's

x the valley: prob. rdg.; Heb. to Gur.

---

here about news from the war front. **25–26:** The prophecy of 1 Kgs.21.19–29 is fulfilled. **27:** *Ahaziah*, though *king of Judah*, was both grandson of Jezebel and ally of Jehoram. **30–37:** *Jezebel* was now an elderly queen mother. **31:** On *Zimri*, see 1 Kgs.16.8–12. **36–37:** See 1 Kgs.21.23.

10.1–14: The execution of the royal families. The whole dynasty of Israel and its Judean allies had to be removed or else the religious issue would not be settled. **1:** The *seventy sons of Ahab*: leading members of the royal family, not literally sons of Ahab, see similar groups

sons to me at Jezreel by this time tomorrow.' Now the royal princes, seventy in all, were with the nobles of the city who were bringing them up.

7 When the letter reached them, they took the royal princes and killed all seventy; they put their heads in baskets and sent them to Jehu in Jezreel.

8 When the messenger came to him and reported that they had brought the heads of the royal princes, he ordered them to be put in two heaps and left at the entrance of the city gate till morning.

9 In the morning he went out, stood there and said to all the people, 'You are fair judges. If I conspired against my master and killed him, who put

10 all these to death? Be sure then that every word which the LORD has spoken against the house of Ahab shall be fulfilled, and that the LORD has now done what he spoke through his servant

11 Elijah.' So Jehu put to death all who were left of the house of Ahab in Jezreel, as well as all his nobles, his close friends, and his priests, until he had left not one survivor.

12 Then he set out for Samaria, and on the way there, when he had reached a

13 shepherds' shelter,*y* he came upon the kinsmen of Ahaziah king of Judah and said, 'Who are you?' 'We are kinsmen of Ahaziah,' they replied; 'and we have come down to greet the families of the king and of the queen mother.'

14 'Take them alive', he said. So they took them alive; then they slew them and flung them into the pit that was there, forty-two of them; they did not leave a single survivor.

15 When he had left that place, he found Jehonadab son of Rechab coming to meet him. He greeted him and said, 'Are you with me heart and soul, as I am with you?' 'I am', said Jehonadab. 'Then if you are,' said Jehu, 'give me your hand.' He gave him his hand and Jehu helped him up into his chariot.

16 'Come with me,' he said, 'and you will see my zeal for the LORD.' So he took

him with him in his chariot. When he 17 came to Samaria, he put to death all of Ahab's house who were left there and so blotted it out, in fulfilment of the word which the LORD had spoken to Elijah. Then Jehu called all the 18 people together and said to them, 'Ahab served the Baal a little; Jehu will serve him much. Now, summon 19 all the prophets of Baal, all his ministers and priests; not one must be missing. For I am holding a great sacrifice to Baal, and no one who is missing from it shall live.' In this way Jehu outwitted the ministers of Baal in order to destroy them. So Jehu said, 'Let a 20 sacred ceremony for Baal be held.' They did so, and Jehu himself sent 21 word throughout Israel, and all the ministers of Baal came; there was not a man left who did not come. They went into the temple of Baal and it was filled from end to end. Then he said to the 22 person who had charge of the wardrobe, 'Bring out robes for all the ministers of Baal'; and he brought them out. Then Jehu and Jehonadab 23 son of Rechab went into the temple of Baal and said to the ministers of Baal, 'Look carefully and make sure that there are no servants of the LORD here with you, but only the ministers of Baal.' Then they went in to offer 24 sacrifices and whole-offerings. Now Jehu had stationed eighty men outside and said to them, 'I am putting these men in your charge, and any man who lets one escape shall answer for it with his life.' When he had finished 25 offering the whole-offering, Jehu ordered the guards and the lieutenants to go and cut them all down, and let not one of them escape; so they slew them without quarter. The escort and the lieutenants then rushed into the keep of the temple of Baal and brought 26 out the sacred pole*z* from the temple

y a shepherds' shelter: *or* Beth-eker of the Shepherds.
z *Prob. rdg.; Heb.* sacred pillars.

---

in Judg. 8.30; 9.5; 12.13; Num.11.16–17,24–30. **9:** Jehu wished it to appear that not he alone was guilty of shedding royal blood.
    10.15–36: Jehu's religious purge. Overt, and official, Baalism was destroyed in Israel. **15:** *Jehonadab son of Rechab:* the leader of a religious order bound by vows of abstinence from certain features of settled life in Canaan; see Jer.35.1–11. **21:** *The temple of Baal* was built by Ahab (1 Kgs.16.32). **22:** The *robes* were ritual garments kept in the holy precincts.

27 of Baal and burnt it; and they pulled down the sacred pillar of the Baal and the temple itself and made a privy of
28 it—as it is today. Thus Jehu stamped
29 out the worship of Baal in Israel. He did not however abandon the sins of Jeroboam son of Nebat who led Israel into sin, but he maintained the worship of the golden calves of Bethel and Dan.
30   Then the LORD said to Jehu, 'You have done well what is right in my eyes and have done to the house of Ahab all that it was in my mind to do. Therefore your sons to the fourth generation shall sit on the throne of
31 Israel.' But Jehu was not careful to follow the law of the LORD the God of Israel with all his heart; he did not abandon the sins of Jeroboam who led Israel into sin.
32   In those days the LORD began to work havoc on Israel, and Hazael struck at them in every corner of their ter-
33 ritory eastwards from the Jordan: all the land of Gilead, Gad, Reuben, and Manasseh, from Aroer which is by the gorge of the Arnon, including Gilead and Bashan.
34   The other events of Jehu's reign, his achievements and his exploits, are recorded in the annals of the kings of
35 Israel. So Jehu rested with his fore-fathers and was buried in Samaria; and he was succeeded by his son
36 Jehoahaz. Jehu reigned over Israel in Samaria for twenty-eight years.

Kings of Israel and Judah

11 1ᵃ AS SOON AS ATHALIAH MOTHER OF Ahaziah saw that her son was dead, she set out to destroy all the royal line.

But Jehosheba daughter of King 2 Joram, sister of Ahaziah, took Ahaziah's son Joash and stole him away from among the princes who were being murdered; she putᵇ him and his nurse in a bedchamber where he was hidden from Athaliah and was not put to death. He remained concealed with 3 her in the house of the LORD for six years, while Athaliah ruled the country. In the seventh year Jehoiada sent for 4 the captains of units of a hundred, both of the Carites and of the guards, and he brought them into the house of the LORD; he made an agreement with them and put them on their oath in the house of the LORD, and showed them the king's son, and gave them the 5 following orders: 'One third of you who are on duty on the sabbath are to be on guard in the palace; the rest of 6 you are to be on special duty in the house of the LORD, one third at the Sur Gate and the other third at the gate withᶜ the outrunners. Your two com- 7 panies who are off duty on the sabbath shall be on duty for the king in the house of the LORD. So you shall be on 8 guard round the king, each man with his arms at the ready, and anyone who comes near the ranks is to be put to death; you must be with the king wherever he goes.'

The captains carried out the orders 9 of Jehoiada the priest to the letter. Each took his men, both those who came on duty on the sabbath and those who came off, and came to Jehoiada. The priest handed out to the captains 10 King David's spears and shields, which were in the house of the LORD. Then 11 the guards took up their stations, each

a Verses 1–20: cp. 2 Chr. 22.10—23. 21.
b she put: prob. rdg., cp. 2 Chr. 22. 11; Heb. om.
c Or behind.

27: *The sacred pillar of the Baal:* 3.2 reports it as removed by Jehoram; apparently it had been re-erected. 30: See 1 Kgs.11.29–39 n. 32–33: Jehu's revolution meant the complete breakdown of Omri's policy and the dissolution of alliances with Phoenicia and Judah (see 1 Kgs. 16.23–34 n.). Isolated thereby, Israel had no hope of holding Transjordan against Damascus.

11.1–17.41: **The second period of the two kingdoms.** From the viewpoint of the compilers, the period of Elijah and Elisha had settled the question that Yahweh, not the Baal, was the god of Israel. The question that remained was the persistence of the cult of the golden calves of Bethel and Dan; see 1 Kgs.12.25–33; 2 Kgs.10.31.

11.1–20: **Athaliah overthrown in Jerusalem.** The revolution in Israel against the house of Omri was not immediately effective in the kingdom of Judah. 1: After *Ahaziah* was killed in the north (9.27) his mother *Athaliah*, daughter of Jezebel, determined to hold power in Jerusalem. No other queen is known to have ruled without a king in the two Hebrew kingdoms. 2: *Jehosheba* was wife of the priest Jehoiada according to 2 Chr.22.11; thus, she had access to the Temple chambers. 4: *Carites:* foreign mercenaries; see 2 Sam.8.18 n. 6: The location of

man carrying his arms at the ready, from corner to corner of the house to north and south,[d] surrounding the
12 king. Then he brought out the king's son, put the crown on his head, handed him the warrant and anointed him king. The people clapped their hands and shouted, 'Long live the king.'
13 When Athaliah heard the noise made by the guards and the people, she came into the house of the LORD where the
14 people were and found the king standing, as was the custom, on the dais,[e] amidst outbursts of song and fanfares of trumpets in his honour, and all the populace rejoicing and blowing trumpets. Then Athaliah rent her clothes and cried, 'Treason! Treas-
15 on!' Jehoiada the priest gave orders to the captains in command of the troops: 'Bring her outside the precincts and put to the sword anyone in attendance on her'; for the priest said, 'She shall not be put to death
16 in the house of the LORD.' So they laid hands on her and took her out by the entry for horses to the royal palace, and there she was put to death.
17   Then Jehoiada made a covenant between the LORD and the king and people that they should be the LORD's people, and also between the king and
18 the people. And all the people went into the temple of Baal and pulled it down; they smashed to pieces its altars and images, and they slew Mattan the priest of Baal before the altars. Then Jehoiada set a watch over the house of
19 the LORD; he took the captains of units of a hundred, the Carites and the guards and all the people, and they escorted the king from the house of the LORD through the Gate of the Guards to the royal palace, and seated him on
20 the royal throne. The whole people rejoiced and the city was tranquil.

That is how Athaliah was put to the sword in the royal palace.

Joash was seven years old when he 21[f] became king. In the seventh year of 12 Jehu, Joash became king, and he reigned in Jerusalem for forty years; his mother was Zibiah of Beersheba. He did what was right in the eyes of 2 the LORD all his days, as Jehoiada the priest had taught him. The hill-shrines, 3 however, were allowed to remain; the people still continued to sacrifice and make smoke-offerings there.

Then Joash ordered the priests to take 4 all the silver brought as holy-gifts into the house of the LORD, the silver for which each man was assessed,[g] the silver for the persons assessed under his name, and any silver which any man brought voluntarily to the house of the LORD. He ordered the priests, 5 also, each to make a contribution from his own funds, and to repair the house wherever it was found necessary. But 6 in the twenty-third year of the reign of Joash the priests had still not carried out the repairs to the house. King 7 Joash summoned Jehoiada the priest and the other priests and said to them, 'Why are you not repairing the house? Henceforth you need not contribute from your own funds for the repair of the house.' So the priests agreed 8 neither to receive money from the people nor to undertake the repairs of the house. Then Jehoiada the priest 9 took a chest and bored a hole in the lid and put it beside the altar on the right side going into the house of the LORD, and the priests on duty at the entrance put in it all the money brought into the house of the LORD. And whenever they saw that the chest 10 was well filled, the king's secretary and

d Prob. rdg.; Heb. adds of the altar and the house.
e Or by the pillar.
f 11. 21—12. 15: cp. 2 Chr. 24. 1–14.
g the silver . . . assessed: prob. rdg.; Heb. obscure.

these gates is uncertain. 12: The warrant was probably a document giving the king's royal titles and divine sanction, a usage derived from Egypt. 14: The populace is literally "the people of the land," a phrase designating the landed citizens of the kingdom, especially outside Jerusalem. They were to play an increasingly important role in the late history of Judah; see vv. 18–20; 15.5 n.; 16.15; 21.24; 23.30,35; 25.3,19. 17: The covenant established the same religious policy for Judah as Jehu had established in the north.
12.1–21: Joash of Judah. 1: Forty years: about 835–796 B.C. 3: Just as the failure to remove Jeroboam's golden calves was the great fault of northern kings, so the failure to remove the hill-shrines was the fault of the kings of Judah, until Hezekiah (18.4) and Josiah (23.4–20). 4–16: This section comes from a source concerned with the history of the Temple; see 22.3–7.

the high priest came and melted down the silver found in the house of the
11 LORD and weighed it. When it had been checked, they gave the silver to the foremen over the work in the house of the LORD and they paid the carpenters and the builders working on
12 the temple and the masons and the stone-cutters; they used it also to buy timber and hewn stone for the repairs and for all other expenses connected
13 with them. They did not use the silver brought into the house of the LORD to make silver cups, snuffers, tossing-bowls, trumpets, or any gold or silver
14 vessels; but they paid it to the work-
15 men and used it for the repairs. No account was demanded from the foremen to whom the money was given for the payment of the workmen, for
16 they were acting on trust. Money from guilt-offerings and sin-offerings was not brought into the house of the LORD: it belonged to the priests.
17   Then Hazael king of Aram came up and attacked Gath and took it; and he
18 moved on against Jerusalem. But Joash king of Judah took all the holy-gifts that Jehoshaphat, Joram, and Ahaziah his forefathers, kings of Judah, had dedicated, and his own holy-gifts, and all the gold that was found in the treasuries of the house of the LORD and in the royal palace, and sent them to Hazael king of Aram; and he withdrew from Jerusalem.
19   The other acts and events of the reign of Joash are recorded in the
20[h] annals of the kings of Judah. His servants revolted against him and struck him down in the house of
21 Millo on the descent to Silla. It was his servants Jozachar son of Shimeath and Jehozabad son of Shomer who struck the fatal blow; and he was buried with his forefathers in the city of David. He was succeeded by his son Amaziah.

In the twenty-third year of Joash son 13 of Ahaziah king of Judah, Jehoahaz son of Jehu became king over Israel in Samaria and he reigned seventeen years. He did what was wrong in the 2 eyes of the LORD and continued the sinful practices of Jeroboam son of Nebat who led Israel into sin, and did not give them up. So the LORD was 3 roused to anger against Israel and he made them subject for some years to Hazael king of Aram and Ben-hadad son of Hazael. Then Jehoahaz sought 4 to placate the LORD, and the LORD heard his prayer, for he saw how the king of Aram oppressed Israel. The 5 LORD appointed a deliverer for Israel, who rescued them from the power of Aram, and the Israelites settled down again in their own homes. But they did 6 not give up the sinful practices of the house of Jeroboam who led Israel into sin, but continued in them; the goddess Asherah[i] remained in Samaria. Hazael 7 had left Jehoahaz no armed force except fifty horsemen, ten chariots, and ten thousand infantry; all the rest the king of Aram had destroyed and made like dust under foot.

The other events of the reign of 8 Jehoahaz, and all his achievements and his exploits, are recorded in the annals of the kings of Israel. So Jehoahaz 9 rested with his forefathers and was buried in Samaria; and he was succeeded by his son Jehoash.

In the thirty-ninth year of Joash king 10 of Judah, Jehoash son of Jehoahaz became king over Israel in Samaria and reigned sixteen years. He did what 11 was wrong in the eyes of the LORD; he did not give up any of the sinful practices of Jeroboam son of Nebat who led Israel into sin, but continued in them. The other events of the reign 12 of Jehoash, all his achievements, his

h *Verses 20, 21: cp. 2 Chr. 24. 25–27.*
i *the goddess Asherah: or the sacred pole.*

17–18: Judah also suffered from the breakdown of the alliance by Omri (1 Kgs. 16.23–34 n.). It was oppressed by Hazael, as was the kingdom of Israel (10.32–33 n.). 20–21: The issues behind Joash's assassination are unknown. The crown prince was already of age (14.2).
    13.1–25: Jehoahaz and Jehoash of Israel. These two reigns covered (roughly) 814–782 B.C. Israel was still suffering under the power of Damascus, but under Jehoash a recovery began, largely because Damascus was severely pressed by renewed Assyrian power. 4–5: The shift in power is attributed to Jehoahaz's contriteness. The *deliverer* is probably Adad-nirari III of Assyria (811–783 B.C.), who decisively defeated Damascus in 802 B.C. 6: *The goddess Asherah* was not purged, even from the public cult, to the same degree Baal had been. 12: On *Jehoash's*

exploits and his war with Amaziah king of Judah, are recorded in the annals of
13 the kings of Israel. So Jehoash rested with his forefathers and was buried in Samaria with the kings of Israel, and Jeroboam sat upon his throne.

14 Elisha fell ill and lay on his death-bed, and Jehoash king of Israel went down to him and wept over him and said, 'My father! My father, the chariots and the horsemen of Israel!'
15 'Take bow and arrows', said Elisha,
16 and he took bow and arrows. 'Put your hand to the bow', said the prophet. He did so, and Elisha laid his
17 hands on those of the king. Then he said, 'Open the window toward the east'; he opened it and Elisha told him to shoot, and he shot. Then the prophet said, 'An arrow for the LORD's victory, an arrow for victory over Aram! You will defeat Aram utterly at
18 Aphek'; and he added, 'Now take up your arrows.' When the king had taken them, Elisha said, 'Strike the ground with them.' He struck three times and
19 stopped. The man of God was furious with him and said, 'You should have struck five or six times; then you would have defeated Aram utterly; as it is, you will strike Aram three times and no more.'

20 Then Elisha died and was buried. Year by year Moabite raiders used
21 to invade the land. Once some men were burying a dead man when they caught sight of the raiders. They threw the body into the grave of Elisha and made off; when the body touched the prophet's bones, the man came to life and rose to his feet.

22 All through the reign of Jehoahaz, Hazael king of Aram oppressed Israel.
23 But the LORD was gracious and took pity on them; because of his covenant with Abraham, Isaac, and Jacob, he looked on them with favour and was unwilling to destroy them; nor has he even yet banished them from his sight.

When Hazael king of Aram died and 24 was succeeded by his son Ben-hadad, Jehoash son of Jehoahaz recaptured 25 the cities which Ben-hadad had taken in war from Jehoahaz his father; three times Jehoash defeated him and recovered the cities of Israel.

In the second year of Jehoash son of 14[j] Jehoahaz king of Israel, Amaziah son of Joash king of Judah succeeded his father. He was twenty-five years old 2 when he came to the throne, and he reigned in Jerusalem for twenty-nine years; his mother was Jehoaddin of Jerusalem. He did what was right in 3 the eyes of the LORD, yet not as his forefather David had done; he followed his father Joash in everything. The 4 hill-shrines were allowed to remain; the people continued to slaughter and burn sacrifices there. When the royal 5 power was firmly in his grasp, he put to death those of his servants who had murdered the king his father; but 6 he spared the murderers' children in obedience to the LORD's command written in the law of Moses: 'Fathers shall not be put to death for their children, nor children for their fathers; a man shall be put to death only for his own sin.' He defeated ten thousand 7 Edomites in the Valley of Salt and captured Sela; he gave it the name Joktheel, which it still bears.

Then Amaziah sent messengers to 8[k] Jehoash son of Jehoahaz, son of Jehu, king of Israel, to propose a meeting. But Jehoash king of Israel sent this 9 answer to Amaziah king of Judah: 'A thistle in Lebanon sent to a cedar in Lebanon to say, "Give your daughter in marriage to my son." But a wild beast in Lebanon, passing by, trampled on the thistle. You have defeated 10 Edom, it is true; and it has gone to your head. Stay at home and enjoy your triumph. Why should you in-

j Verses 1–6: cp. 2 Chr. 25. 1–4.
k Verses 8–14: cp. 2 Chr. 25. 17–24.

---

war with *Amaziah king of Judah*, see 14.8–14. **14–20:** Two brief prophetic legends about Elisha are allocated to Jehoash's reign. *Three* Israelite victories against *Aram* (Damascus) are attributed to magical rituals performed by Elisha; see vv. 24–25. **23:** *Even yet:* the late compilers hold out some hope that both Israel and Judah can return from exile; compare 1 Kgs.8.27–53 n. and Jer. chs.30–31.
14.1–22: Amaziah of Judah. This was one of the more aggressive kings. **6:** *The law of Moses:* see Deut.24.15. **7:** Amaziah moved to reestablish Judean power in the south; compare 8.20–22. **8:** *Meeting:* a face-to-face encounter; a trial of strength. **9–10:** *Jehoash* knew that the two

volve yourself in disaster and bring yourself to the ground, and Judah with you?'

11 But Amaziah would not listen; so Jehoash king of Israel marched out, and he and Amaziah king of Judah met one another at Beth-shemesh in 12 Judah. The men of Judah were routed 13 by Israel and fled to their homes. But Jehoash king of Israel captured Amaziah king of Judah, son of Joash, son of Ahaziah, at Beth-shemesh. He went to Jerusalem and broke down the city wall from the Gate of Ephraim to the Corner Gate, a distance of four 14 hundred cubits. He also took all the gold and silver and all the vessels found in the house of the LORD and in the treasuries of the royal palace, as well as hostages, and returned to Samaria. 15 The other events of the reign of Jehoash, and all his achievements, his exploits and his wars with Amaziah king of Judah, are recorded in the 16 annals of the kings of Israel. So Jehoash rested with his forefathers and was buried in Samaria with the kings of Israel; and he was succeeded by his son Jeroboam.

17[l] Amaziah son of Joash, king of Judah, outlived Jehoash son of Jehoahaz, king of Israel, by fifteen years. 18 The other events of Amaziah's reign are recorded in the annals of the kings 19 of Judah. A conspiracy was formed against him in Jerusalem and he fled to Lachish; but they sent after him to Lachish and put him to death there. 20 Then his body was conveyed on horseback to Jerusalem, and there he was buried with his forefathers in the 21 city of David. The people of Judah took Azariah, now sixteen years old, and made him king in succession to 22 his father Amaziah. It was he who built Elath and restored it to Judah after the king rested with his forefathers.

In the fifteenth year of Amaziah son 23 of Joash king of Judah, Jeroboam son of Jehoash king of Israel became king in Samaria and reigned for forty-one years. He did what was wrong in the 24 eyes of the LORD; he did not give up the sinful practices of Jeroboam son of Nebat who led Israel into sin. He re- 25 established the frontiers of Israel from Lebo-hamath to the Sea of the Arabah, in fulfilment of the word of the LORD the God of Israel spoken by his servant the prophet Jonah son of Amittai, of Gath-hepher. For the LORD had seen 26 how bitterly Israel had suffered; no one was safe, whether under the protection of his family or not, and Israel was left defenceless. But the LORD had 27 made no threat to blot out the name of Israel under heaven, and he saved them through Jeroboam son of Jehoash. The other events of Jeroboam's reign, 28 and all his achievements, his exploits, the wars he fought and how he recovered Damascus and Hamath in Jaudi for[m] Israel, are recorded in the annals of the kings of Israel. So Jerob- 29 oam rested with his forefathers the kings of Israel; and he was succeeded by his son Zechariah.

In the twenty-seventh year of Jerob- **15** oam king of Israel, Azariah[n] son of Amaziah king of Judah became king. He was sixteen years old when he came 2[o] to the throne, and he reigned in Jerusalem for fifty-two years; his mother was Jecoliah of Jerusalem. He did what 3 was right in the eyes of the LORD, as Amaziah his father had done. But the 4 hill-shrines were allowed to remain; the people still continued to slaughter and burn sacrifices there. The LORD 5[p] struck the king with leprosy,[q] which he had till the day of his death; he

l Verses 17–22: cp. 2 Chr. 25. 25—26. 2.
m in Jaudi for: prob. rdg.; Heb. to Judah in.
n Uzziah in verses 13, 30, 32, 34.
o Verses 2, 3: cp. 2 Chr. 26. 3, 4.
p Verses 5–7: cp. 2 Chr. 26. 21–23.
q Or a skin-disease.

kingdoms could be powerful only when allied. **15–16:** This repeats 13.12–13. **19–21:** The reasons for the *conspiracy* are not known.

   14.23–15.7: Jeroboam II of Israel and Azariah (Uzziah) of Judah. Under these two kings the Israelite kingdoms attained, for the third and last time, a dominance over Syria-Palestine. As in the case of Omri, some kings of great historical significance receive scant treatment by the compilers of Kgs. **28:** *Jaudi* may have been a minor kingdom in Syria. **15.2:** *Fifty-two years:* These include several years of coregency by Azariah with his father before the latter's assassination. Azariah's death (compare Isa.6.1) brought an era to an end. **5:** *Regent:* lit. "he judged the people of the land"; see 11.14 n.

was relieved of all duties and lived in his own house, while his son Jotham was comptroller of the household and 6 regent. The other acts and events of Azariah's reign are recorded in the 7 annals of the kings of Judah. So he rested with his forefathers and was buried with them in the city of David; and he was succeeded by his son Jotham.

8 In the thirty-eighth year of Azariah king of Judah, Zechariah son of Jeroboam became king over Israel in Samaria 9 and reigned six months. He did what was wrong in the eyes of the LORD, as his forefathers had done; he did not give up the sinful practices of Jeroboam son of Nebat who led Israel into sin. 10 Shallum son of Jabesh formed a conspiracy against him, attacked him in Ibleam, killed him and usurped the 11 throne. The other events of Zechariah's reign are recorded in the annals of 12 the kings of Israel. Thus the word of the LORD spoken to Jehu was fulfilled: 'Your sons to the fourth generation shall sit on the throne of Israel.'

13 Shallum son of Jabesh became king in the thirty-ninth year of Uzziah king of Judah, and he reigned one full month 14 in Samaria. Then Menahem son of Gadi came up from Tirzah to Samaria, attacked Shallum son of Jabesh there, killed him and usurped the throne. 15 The other events of Shallum's reign and the conspiracy that he formed are recorded in the annals of the kings of Israel.

16 Then Menahem, starting out from Tirzah, destroyed Tappuah and everything in it and ravaged its territory; he ravaged it because it had not opened its gates to him, and he ripped open all the pregnant women.

17 In the thirty-ninth year of Azariah king of Judah, Menahem son of Gadi became king over Israel and he reigned in Samaria for ten years. He did what 18 was wrong in the eyes of the LORD; he did not give up the sinful practices of Jeroboam son of Nebat who led Israel into sin. In his days Pul king of Assyria 19 invaded the country, and Menahem gave him a thousand talents of silver to obtain his help in strengthening his hold on the kingdom. Menahem laid 20 a levy on all the men of wealth in Israel, and each had to give the king of Assyria fifty silver shekels. Then the king of Assyria withdrew without occupying the country. The other acts and events 21 of Menahem's reign are recorded in the annals of the kings of Israel. So 22 Menahem rested with his forefathers; and he was succeeded by his son Pekahiah.

23 In the fiftieth year of Azariah king of Judah, Pekahiah son of Menahem became king over Israel in Samaria and reigned for two years. He did what 24 was wrong in the eyes of the LORD; he did not give up the sinful practices of Jeroboam son of Nebat who led Israel into sin. Pekah son of Remaliah, 25 his lieutenant, formed a conspiracy against him and, with the help of fifty Gileadites, attacked him in Samaria in the citadel of the royal palace,[r] killed him and usurped the throne. The 26 other acts and events of Pekahiah's reign are recorded in the annals of the kings of Israel.

In the fifty-second year of Azariah 27 king of Judah, Pekah son of Remaliah became king over Israel in Samaria and reigned for twenty years. He did 28 what was wrong in the eyes of the LORD; he did not give up the sinful practices of Jeroboam son of Nebat who led Israel into sin. In the days of Pekah 29 king of Israel, Tiglath-pileser king of Assyria came and seized Iyyon, Abel-beth-maacah, Janoah, Kedesh, Hazor,

r Prob. rdg.; Heb. adds Argob and Arieh.

15.8–38: The decline of Israel. After Jeroboam II's long reign, the dynasty of Jehu was overthrown. No stable regime was again established in the north. **12:** See 10.31 and 1 Kgs. 11.29–39 n. **19:** *Pul:* the Babylonian throne name of the Assyrian king Tiglath-pileser III (745–727 B.C.). *Menahem* represented a policy of vassalage to Assyria; his contemporary opponent Pekah pursued an anti-Assyrian policy; see v. 27 n. **25:** *Gileadites* disturbed the Israelite throne more than once; see 1 Kgs.17.1. **27:** Pekah's *twenty years* are counted from the death of Zechariah, the last king of the Jehu dynasty. He was a claimant to the throne throughout the reigns of Shallum, Menahem, and Pekahiah. His victory was the signal for an uprising in alliance with Damascus against Assyria; see v. 37; Isa.7.1–9. **29–30:** The rebellion against Tiglath-pileser was a great failure, and Israel lost all its northern territory. Such a disaster

Gilead, and Galilee, with all the land of Naphtali, and deported the people to
30 Assyria. Then Hoshea son of Elah formed a conspiracy against Pekah son of Remaliah, attacked him, killed him and usurped the throne in the twentieth year of Jotham son of
31 Uzziah. The other acts and events of Pekah's reign are recorded in the annals of the kings of Israel.
32 In the second year of Pekah son of Remaliah king of Israel, Jotham son of Uzziah king of Judah became king.
33s He was twenty-five years old when he came to the throne, and he reigned in Jerusalem for sixteen years; his mother
34 was Jerusha daughter of Zadok. He did what was right in the eyes of the LORD, as his father Uzziah had done;
35 but the hill-shrines were allowed to remain and the people continued to slaughter and burn sacrifices there. It was he who constructed the upper gate
36 of the house of the LORD. The other acts and events of Jotham's reign are recorded in the annals of the kings of
37 Judah. In those days the LORD began to make Rezin king of Aram and Pekah son of Remaliah attack Judah.
38 And Jotham rested with his forefathers and was buried with them in the city of David his forefather; and he was succeeded by his son Ahaz.

Downfall of the northern kingdom

16 IN THE SEVENTEENTH YEAR OF PEKAH son of Remaliah, Ahaz son of Jotham
2t king of Judah became king. Ahaz was twenty years old when he came to the throne, and he reigned in Jerusalem for sixteen years. He did not do what was right in the eyes of the LORD his
3 God like his forefather David, but followed in the footsteps of the kings of Israel; he even passed his son

through the fire, adopting the abominable practice of the nations whom the LORD had dispossessed in favour of the Israelites. He slaughtered and burnt 4 sacrifices at the hill-shrines and on the hill-tops and under every spreading tree.

Then Rezin king of Aram and Pekah 5 son of Remaliah king of Israel attacked Jerusalem and besieged Ahaz but could not bring him to battle. At that time 6 the king of Edomu recovered Elath and drove the Judaeans out of it; so the Edomites entered the city and have occupied it to this day. Ahaz sent 7 messengers to Tiglath-pileser king of Assyria to say, 'I am your servant and your son. Come and save me from the king of Aram and from the king of Israel who are attacking me.' Ahaz 8 took the silver and gold found in the house of the LORD and in the treasuries of the royal palace and sent them to the king of Assyria as a bribe. The king 9 of Assyria listened to him; he advanced on Damascus, captured it, deported its inhabitants to Kir and put Rezin to death.

When King Ahaz went to meet 10 Tiglath-pileser king of Assyria at Damascus, he saw there an altar of which he sent a sketch and a detailed plan to Uriah the priest. Accordingly, Uriah 11 built an altar, following all the instructions that the king had sent him from Damascus, and had it ready against the king's return. When the king re- 12 turned from Damascus, he saw the altar, approached it and mounted the steps; there he burnt his whole-offering 13 and his grain-offering and poured out his drink-offering, and he flung the blood of his shared-offerings against it. The bronze altar that was before 14

s *Verses 33–35: cp. 2 Chr. 27. 1–3.*
t *Verses 2–4: cp. 2 Chr. 28. 1–4.*
u *the king of Edom: prob. rdg.; Heb. Rezin king of Aram.*

---

invited yet another coup by a leader willing to come to terms with Assyria. **30:** *The twentieth year of Jotham:* v. 33 gives *Jotham* only sixteen years; he must have reigned for some years as coregent with his father.
    16.1–20: Ahaz of Judah. 3: In the late monarchic period some very primitive cult practices were revived; compare 3.27; Jer.7.30–31. **5–9:** Compare Isa.7.1–9. **6:** Because of pressure on Judah from the north, *Edom* was able again (see 8.20–22) to escape its domination. *Elath:* the harbor on the Gulf of Aqabah. **10–18:** This passage is taken from a source about the history of the Temple; see 12.4–16. *Ahaz* had to make these changes because he became a vassal of Assyria. **14:** *The bronze altar* was from Solomon's time; see 1 Kgs.8.64. **15:** On *the people of the land*, see 11.14 n.

the LORD he removed from the front of the house, from between this altar and the house of the LORD, and put it on the north side of this altar. Then 15 King Ahaz gave these instructions to Uriah the priest: 'Burn on the great altar the morning whole-offering and the evening grain-offering, and the king's whole-offering and his grain-offering, and the whole-offering of all the people of the land, their grain-offering and their drink-offerings, and fling against it all the blood of the sacrifices. But the bronze altar shall be 16 mine, to offer morning sacrifice.' Uriah the priest did all that the king told 17 him. Then King Ahaz broke up the trolleys and removed the panels, and he took down the basin and the Sea of bronze from the oxen which supported 18 it and put it on a stone base. In the house of the LORD he turned round the structure they had erected for use on the sabbath, and the outer gate for the king, to satisfy the king of Assyria. 19*v* The other acts and events of the reign of Ahaz are recorded in the annals of 20 the kings of Judah. So Ahaz rested with his forefathers and was buried with them in the city of David; and he was succeeded by his son Hezekiah.

17 In the twelfth year of Ahaz king of Judah, Hoshea son of Elah became king over Israel in Samaria and reigned 2 nine years. He did what was wrong in the eyes of the LORD, but not as the previous kings of Israel had done. 3 Shalmaneser king of Assyria made war upon him and Hoshea became 4 tributary to him. But when the king of Assyria discovered that Hoshea was being disloyal to him, sending messengers to the king of Egypt at So,*w* and withholding the tribute which he had been paying year by year, the king of Assyria arrested him and put 5 him in prison. Then he invaded the whole country and, reaching Samaria, 6 besieged it for three years. In the ninth year of Hoshea he captured Samaria and deported its people to Assyria and

settled them in Halah and on the Habor, the river of Gozan, and in the cities of Media.

All this happened to the Israelites 7 because they had sinned against the LORD their God who brought them up from Egypt, from the rule of Pharaoh king of Egypt; they paid homage to other gods and observed the laws and 8 customs of the nations whom the LORD had dispossessed before them and 9 uttered blasphemies against the LORD their God; they built hill-shrines for themselves in all their settlements, from watch-tower to fortified city, and set up sacred pillars and sacred poles on 10 every high hill and under every spreading tree, and burnt sacrifices at all the 11 hill-shrines there, as the nations did whom the LORD had displaced before them. By this wickedness of theirs they provoked the LORD's anger. They 12 worshipped idols, a thing which the LORD had forbidden them to do. Still 13 the LORD solemnly charged Israel and Judah by every prophet and seer, saying, 'Give up your evil ways; keep my commandments and statutes given in the law which I enjoined on your forefathers and delivered to you through my servants the prophets.' They would not listen, however, but 14 were as stubborn and rebellious as their forefathers had been, who refused to put their trust in the LORD their God: they rejected his statutes and 15 the covenant which he had made with their forefathers and the solemn warnings which he had given to them; they followed worthless idols and became worthless themselves; they imitated the nations round about them, a thing which the LORD had forbidden them to do. Forsaking every commandment 16 of the LORD their God, they made themselves images of cast metal, two calves, and also a sacred pole; they prostrated themselves to all the host of heaven and worshipped the Baal, and

v Verses 19, 20: cp. 2 Chr. 28. 26, 27.
w to the king of Egypt at So: prob. rdg.; Heb. to So king of Egypt.

17.1–41: The fall of Israel. The Deuteronomist attributes the fall of the Northern Kingdom to apostasy; he scorns the syncretistic religious practices of the population of the conquered area. **3:** *Shalmaneser* V (727–722 B.C.) began the siege of Samaria but the conquest was completed under Sargon II (722–705 B.C.). **6:** In his own inscriptions, Sargon claims to have deported 27,290 Israelites. **7–23:** Here the Deuteronomic compilers speak as commentators;

17 they made their sons and daughters pass through the fire. They practised augury and divination; they sold themselves to do what was wrong in the eyes of the LORD and so provoked his anger.

18   Thus it was that the LORD was incensed against Israel and banished them from his presence; only the tribe
19 of Judah was left. Even Judah did not keep the commandments of the LORD their God but followed the practices
20 adopted by Israel; so the LORD rejected the whole race of Israel and punished them and gave them over to plunderers and finally flung them out of his sight.
21 When he tore Israel from the house of David, they made Jeroboam son of Nebat king, who seduced Israel from their allegiance to the LORD and led
22 them into grave sin. The Israelites persisted in all the sins that Jeroboam had committed and did not give them
23 up, until finally the LORD banished the Israelites from his presence, as he had threatened through his servants the prophets, and they were carried into exile from their own land to Assyria; and there they are to this day.
24   Then the king of Assyria brought people from Babylon, Cuthah, Avva, Hamath, and Sepharvaim, and settled them in the cities of Samaria in place of the Israelites; so they occupied
25 Samaria and lived in its cities. In the early years of their settlement they did not pay homage to the LORD; and the LORD sent lions among them, and
26 the lions preyed upon them. The king was told that the deported peoples whom he had settled in the cities of Samaria did not know the established usage of the god of the country, and that he had sent lions among them which were preying upon them because
27 they did not know this. The king of Assyria, therefore, gave orders that one of the priests deported from Samaria should be sent back to live there and teach the people the usage
28 of the god of the country. So one of the

deported priests came and lived at Bethel, and taught them how they should pay their homage to the LORD. But each of the nations made its 29 own god, and they set them up within*ˣ* the hill-shrines which the Samaritans had made, each nation in its own settlements. Succoth-benoth was wor- 30 shipped by the men of Babylon, Nergal by the men of Cuth, Ashima by the men of Hamath, Nibhaz and Tartak 31 by the Avvites; and the Sepharvites burnt their children as offerings to Adrammelech and Anammelech, the gods of Sepharvaim. While still pay- 32 ing homage to the LORD, they appointed people from every class to act as priests of the hill-shrines and they resorted to them there. They paid 33 homage to the LORD while at the same time they served their own gods, according to the custom of the nations from which they had been carried into exile.

They keep up these old practices to 34 this day; they do not pay homage to the LORD, for they do not keep his*ʸ* statutes and his*ʸ* judgements, the law and commandment, which he enjoined upon the descendants of Jacob whom he named Israel. When the LORD 35 made a covenant with them, he gave them his commandment: 'You shall not pay homage to other gods or bow down to them or serve them or sacrifice to them, but you shall pay homage to 36 the LORD who brought you up from Egypt with great power and with outstretched arm; to him you shall bow down, to him you shall offer sacrifice. You shall faithfully keep the statutes, 37 the judgements, the law, and the commandments which he wrote for you, and you shall not pay homage to other gods. You shall not forget the 38 covenant which I made with you; you shall not pay homage to other gods. But to the LORD your God you shall 39 pay homage, and he will preserve you from all your enemies.' However, they 40

x Or in niches at.   *y Prob. rdg.; Heb.* their.

usually they put a speech into the mouth of a famous leader or prophet. **19–20:** At the time of the writing (see Introduction to 1 Kgs.) Judah has also fallen. **24–41:** The imported population possessed a mixture of religious identities and practices, that later marked the *Samaritans* (v. 29); the practices were improper from the standpoint of later Judean norms. **41:** *To this day:* the time of the Judean exile.

would not listen but continued their
41 former practices. While these nations
paid homage to the LORD they continued to serve their images, and their
children and their children's children
have maintained the practice of their
forefathers to this day.

18 [z] IN THE THIRD YEAR OF HOSHEA SON OF
Elah king of Israel, Hezekiah son of
2 Ahaz king of Judah became king. He
was twenty-five years old when he came
to the throne, and he reigned in
Jerusalem for twenty-nine years; his
mother was Abi daughter of Zechariah.
3 He did what was right in the eyes of the
LORD, as David his forefather had done.
4 It was he who suppressed the hill-
shrines, smashed the sacred pillars,
cut down every sacred pole and broke
up the bronze serpent that Moses had
made; for up to that time the Israelites
had been burning sacrifices to it; they
5 called it Nehushtan. He put his trust
in the LORD the God of Israel; there
was nobody like him among all the
kings of Judah who succeeded him or
among those who had gone before
6 him. He remained loyal to the LORD
and did not fail in his allegiance to him,
and he kept the commandments which
7 the LORD had given to Moses. So the
LORD was with him and he prospered
in all that he undertook; he rebelled
against the king of Assyria and was
8 no longer subject to him. He conquered the Philistine country as far as
Gaza and its boundaries, alike the
watch-tower and the fortified city.
9 In the fourth year of Hezekiah's
reign (that was the seventh year of
Hoshea son of Elah king of Israel)

Shalmaneser king of Assyria made an
attack on Samaria, invested it and 10
captured it after a siege of three years;
it was in the sixth year of Hezekiah
(the ninth year of Hoshea king of
Israel) that Samaria was captured.
The king of Assyria deported the 11
Israelites to Assyria and settled them
in Halah and on the Habor, the river
of Gozan, and in the cities of Media,
because they did not obey the LORD 12
their God but violated his covenant
and every commandment that Moses
the servant of the LORD had given them;
they would not listen and they would
not obey.

In the fourteenth year of the reign 13 [a]
of Hezekiah, Sennacherib king of
Assyria attacked and took all the fortified cities of Judah. Hezekiah king of 14
Judah sent a message to the king of
Assyria at Lachish: 'I have done wrong;
withdraw from my land, and I will pay
any penalty you impose upon me.' So
the king of Assyria laid on Hezekiah
king of Judah a penalty of three
hundred talents of silver and thirty
talents of gold; and Hezekiah gave them 15
all the silver found in the house of the
LORD and in the treasuries of the royal
palace. At that time Hezekiah broke up 16
the doors of the temple of the LORD
and the door-frames which he himself
had plated, and gave them to the king
of Assyria.

From Lachish the king of Assyria 17
sent the commander-in-chief, the chief
eunuch, and the chief officer[b] with a
strong force to King Hezekiah at Jeru-

z *Verses 1–3: cp. 2 Chr. 29. 1, 2.*
a *Verses 13–17: cp. Isa. 36. 1–22; 2 Chr. 32. 1–19.*
b *the commander-in-chief, the chief eunuch, and the chief officer: or Tartan, Rab-saris, and Rab-shakeh.*

18.1–20.21: The reign of Hezekiah. The dating of Hezekiah's reign is one of the most difficult chronological problems in Kgs. According to 18.1 it began in 729 B.C.; according to 18.14, in 716/715, for Sennacherib's siege is known to have occurred in 701 B.C. The account of the reign consists of annalistic data (18.1–8,13–16) and stories involving the prophet Isaiah at the siege of Jerusalem in 701 B.C. (18.17–20.21).
18.1–16: Hezekiah in the annals. When the Assyrian king Sargon II died in 705, Hezekiah timed his rebellion to coincide with that of Merodach-baladan in Babylonia (see 20.12). The religious purge included removing local sanctuaries (the hill-shrines) in Judah in favor of the sole sanctuary in Jerusalem and purging venerated but superstitious practices from the cult at Jerusalem itself (v. 4). **4:** The *hill-shrines* are suppressed for the first time; compare 1 Kgs.3.2 and, e.g. 1 Kgs.22.43. *The bronze serpent that Moses had made* was destroyed; the story of its supposed origin is preserved in Num.21.4–9. **9–12:** A brief summary of ch. 17. **13–16:** This realistic report is contradicted in Sennacherib's own inscription only by his claim to have received eight hundred instead of *three hundred talents of silver* (v. 14).
18.17–19.37: The siege and deliverance of Jerusalem. Within the totality of the Deuteronomic history (Deut.–2 Kgs.), this is the last time the LORD intervenes by prophecy and marvelous action on Israel's behalf. **17:** For more details about *the conduit of the Upper Pool* see Isa.7.3.

Downfall of the northern kingdom

salem, and they went up and came to Jerusalem and halted by the conduit of the Upper Pool on the causeway
18 which leads to the Fuller's Field. When they called for the king, Eliakim son of Hilkiah, the comptroller of the household, came out to them, with Shebna the adjutant-general and Joah son of
19 Asaph, the secretary of state. The chief officer said to them, 'Tell Hezekiah that this is the message of the Great King, the king of Assyria: "What ground have you for this confidence
20 of yours? Do you think fine words can take the place of skill and numbers? On whom then do you rely for support in your rebellion against me? On Egypt?
21 Egypt is a splintered cane that will run into a man's hand and pierce it if he leans on it. That is what Pharaoh king of Egypt proves to all who rely on him.
22 And if you tell me that you are relying on the LORD your God, is he not the god whose hill-shrines and altars Hezekiah has suppressed, telling Judah and Jerusalem that they must prostrate themselves before this altar in Jerusalem?"
23 'Now, make a bargain with my master the king of Assyria: I will give you two thousand horses if you can
24 find riders for them. Will you reject the authority of even the least of my master's servants and rely on Egypt
25 for chariots and horsemen? Do you think that I have come to attack this place and destroy it without the consent of the LORD? No; the LORD himself said to me, "Attack this land and destroy it."'
26 Eliakim son of Hilkiah, Shebna, and Joah said to the chief officer, 'Please speak to us in Aramaic, for we understand it; do not speak Hebrew to us within earshot of the people on the
27 city wall.' The chief officer answered, 'Is it to your master and to you that my master has sent me to say this? Is it not to the people sitting on the wall who, like you, will have to eat their own dung and drink their own
28 urine?' Then he stood and shouted in Hebrew, 'Hear the message of the

Great King, the king of Assyria. These 29 are the king's words: "Do not be taken in by Hezekiah. He cannot save you from me. Do not let him persuade 30 you to rely on the LORD, and tell you that the LORD will save you and that this city will never be surrendered to the king of Assyria." Do not listen to 31 Hezekiah; these are the words of the king of Assyria: "Make peace with me. Come out to me, and then you shall each eat the fruit of his own vine and his own fig-tree, and drink the water of his own cistern, until I come and take 32 you to a land like your own, a land of grain and new wine, of corn and vineyards, of olives, fine oil, and honey— life for you all, instead of death. Do not listen to Hezekiah; he will only mislead you by telling you that the LORD will save you. Did the god of any of 33 these nations save his land from the king of Assyria? Where are the gods of 34 Hamath and Arpad? Where are the gods of Sepharvaim, Hena, and Ivvah? Where are the gods of Samaria? Did they save Samaria from me? Among 35 all the gods of the nations is there one who saved his land from me? And how is the LORD to save Jerusalem?"'

The people were silent and answered 36 not a word, for the king had given orders that no one was to answer him. Eliakim son of Hilkiah, comptroller of 37 the household, Shebna the adjutant-general, and Joah son of Asaph, secretary of state, came to Hezekiah with their clothes rent and reported what the chief officer had said.

When King Hezekiah heard their **19**[c] report, he rent his clothes and wrapped himself in sackcloth, and went into the house of the LORD. He sent Eliakim 2 comptroller of the household, Shebna the adjutant-general, and the senior priests, all covered in sackcloth, to the prophet Isaiah son of Amoz, to 3 give him this message from the king: 'This day is a day of trouble for us, a day of reproof and contempt. We are like a woman who has no strength to

c Verses 1–37: cp. Isa. 37. 1–38; 2 Chr. 32. 20–22.

18: *Shebna:* see Isa.22.15–19. **26:** *Aramaic* was becoming the common language of commerce and diplomacy. **19.1:** The penitent attitude is to gain the LORD's favor. **6–7:** Isaiah's prophecy is only partially fulfilled in what follows; it does not include striking down the Assyrian army;

bear the child that is coming to the
4 birth. It may be that the LORD your
God heard all the words of the chief
officer whom his master the king of
Assyria sent to taunt the living God,
and will confute what he, the LORD
your God, heard. Offer a prayer for
5 those who still survive.' King Hezekiah's
6 servants came to Isaiah, and he told
them to say this to their master: 'This
is the word of the LORD: "Do not be
alarmed at what you heard when the
lackeys of the king of Assyria blas-
7 phemed me. I will put a spirit in him
and he shall hear a rumour and withdraw to his own country; and there I
will make him fall by the sword."'

8 So the chief officer withdrew. He
heard that the king of Assyria had left
Lachish, and he found him attacking
9 Libnah. But when the king learnt that
Tirhakah king of Cush was on the way
to make war on him, he sent messengers
10 again to Hezekiah king of Judah, to say
to him. 'How can you be deluded by
your god on whom you rely when he
promises that Jerusalem shall not fall
into the hands of the king of Assyria?
11 Surely you have heard what the kings
of Assyria have done to all countries,
exterminating their people; can you
12 then hope to escape? Did their gods
save the nations which my forefathers
destroyed, Gozan, Harran, Rezeph,
and the people of Beth-eden living in
13 Telassar? Where are the kings of
Hamath, of Arpad, and of Lahir, Sepharvaim, Hena, and Ivvah?'
14 Hezekiah took the letter from the
messengers and read it; then he went
up into the house of the LORD, spread
15 it out before the LORD and offered
this prayer: 'O LORD God of Israel,
enthroned on the cherubim, thou alone
art God of all the kingdoms of the
earth; thou hast made heaven and earth.
16 Turn thy ear to me, O LORD, and listen;
open thine eyes, O LORD, and see;
hear the message that Sennacherib has

sent to taunt the living God. It is true, 17
O LORD, that the kings of Assyria
have ravaged the nations and their
lands, that they have consigned their 18
gods to the fire and destroyed them;
for they were no gods but the work
of men's hands, mere wood and stone.
But now, O LORD our God, save us 19
from his power, so that all the kingdoms of the earth may know that
thou, O LORD, alone art God.'

Isaiah son of Amoz sent to Hezekiah 20
and said, 'This is the word of the
LORD the God of Israel: I have heard
your prayer to me concerning Sennacherib king of Assyria. This is the 21
word which the LORD has spoken
concerning him:

The virgin daughter of Zion disdains
    you,
  she laughs you to scorn;
the daughter of Jerusalem tosses her
    head
    as you retreat.
Whom have you taunted and 22
    blasphemed?
  Against whom have you
    clamoured,
casting haughty glances at the Holy
    One of Israel?
You have sent your messengers to 23
    taunt the Lord,
    and said:
I have mounted my chariot and
    done mighty deeds:
I have gone high up in the
    mountains,
    into the recesses of Lebanon.
I have cut down its tallest cedars,
    the best of its pines,
I have reached its farthest corners,
    forest and meadow.
I have dug wells 24
and drunk the waters of a foreign
    land,
and with the soles of my feet I have
    dried up
    all the streams of Egypt.

---

compare vv. 35–37. **8–13:** This second ultimatum to Hezekiah, plus the fact that *Tirhakah* did
not become king of Egypt before 690 B.C., has led some to think there were two different sieges
of Jerusalem by Sennacherib, the second taking place around 689–688 B.C. A duplication of
reports of the same siege is more likely. **14–19:** Hezekiah's *prayer* here is much less related to
the immediate situation than vv. 3–4. **15:** *Enthroned on the cherubim;* see 1 Sam.4.4 n. **20–28:**
Isaiah's taunt song against Sennacherib is similar to the prophecy in Isa. 10.5–19, probably
delivered on the occasion of Sennacherib's siege of Jerusalem in 701 B.C. **21:** *Zion:* the city is

25 Have you not heard long ago?
    I did it all.
In days gone by I planned it
and now I have brought it about,
making fortified cities tumble down
    into heaps of rubble.*d*
26 Their citizens, shorn of strength,
    disheartened and ashamed,
were but as plants in the field, as
    green herbs,
as grass on the roof-tops blasted
    before the east wind.*e*
27 I know your rising up*f* and your
    sitting down,
your going out and your coming
    in.
28 The frenzy of your rage against me*g*
    and your arrogance
have come to my ears.
I will put a ring in your nose
    and a hook in your lips,
and I will take you back by the
      road
    on which you have come.

29 This shall be the sign for you: this year you shall eat shed grain and in the second year what is self-sown; but in the third year sow and reap, plant
30 vineyards and eat their fruit. The survivors left in Judah shall strike fresh root under ground and yield
31 fruit above ground, for a remnant shall come out of Jerusalem and survivors from Mount Zion. The zeal of the LORD will perform this.

32 'Therefore, this is the word of the LORD concerning the king of Assyria:

He shall not enter this city
    nor shoot an arrow there,
he shall not advance against it with
      shield
    nor cast up a siege-ramp against it.
33 By the way on which he came he
      shall go back;
    this city he shall not enter.
This is the very word of the
      LORD.
34 I will shield this city to deliver it,

for my own sake and for the sake of
    my servant David.'

That night the angel of the LORD 35 went out and struck down a hundred and eighty-five thousand men in the Assyrian camp; when morning dawned, they all lay dead. So Sennacherib 36 king of Assyria broke camp, went back to Nineveh and stayed there. One day, while he was worshipping in 37 the temple of his god Nisroch, Adrammelech and Sharezer his sons murdered him and escaped to the land of Ararat. He was succeeded by his son Esarhaddon.

At this time Hezekiah fell dangerous- 20 *h* ly ill and the prophet Isaiah son of Amoz came to him and said, 'This is the word of the LORD: Give your last instructions to your household, for you are a dying man and will not recover.' Hezekiah turned his face to 2 the wall and offered this prayer to the LORD: 'O LORD, remember how I 3 have lived before thee, faithful and loyal in thy service, always doing what was good in thine eyes.' And he wept bitterly. But before Isaiah had left the 4 citadel, the word of the LORD came to him: 'Go back and say to Hezekiah, 5 the prince of my people: "This is the word of the LORD the God of your father David: I have heard your prayer and seen your tears; I will heal you and on the third day you shall go up to the house of the LORD. I will add 6 fifteen years to your life and deliver you and this city from the king of Assyria, and I will protect this city for my own sake and for my servant David's sake."' Then Isaiah told them 7 to apply a fig-plaster; so they made one and applied it to the boil, and he

d heaps of rubble: prob. rdg., cp. Isa. 37. 26: Heb. obscure.
e the east wind: prob. rdg., cp. Isa. 37. 27; Heb. it is mature.
f your rising up: prob. rdg., cp. Isa. 37. 28; Heb. om.
g Prob. rdg., cp. Isa. 37. 29; Heb. repeats the frenzy of your rage against me.
h Verses 1–11: cp. Isa. 38. 1–8, 21, 22.

personified as a goddess. **27–28:** The LORD speaks again, to Assyria. **32–34:** This oracle speaks to a situation prior to the last desperate siege. **35:** This miracle has neither been prepared for nor is it referred to elsewhere. **37:** Sennacherib died in 681 B.C., twenty years after the siege of Jerusalem.
20.1–21: Two legends of Isaiah. 6: That *fifteen years* are added to Hezekiah's life is probably related to the problem of the chronology in Hezekiah's reign; compare 18.1–20.21 n.

8 recovered. Then Hezekiah asked Isaiah what sign the LORD would give him that he would be cured and would go up into the house of the LORD on the
9 third day. And Isaiah said, 'This shall be your sign from the LORD that he will do what he has promised; shall the shadow go forward ten steps or
10 back ten steps?' Hezekiah answered, 'It is an easy thing for the shadow to move forward ten steps; rather let it
11 go back ten steps.' Isaiah the prophet called to the LORD, and he made the shadow go back ten steps where it had advanced down the stairway of Ahaz.
12*i* At this time Merodach-baladan son of Baladan king of Babylon sent envoys with a gift to Hezekiah; for he had
13 heard that he had been ill. Hezekiah welcomed them and showed them all his treasury, silver and gold, spices and fragrant oil, his armoury and everything to be found among his treasures; there was nothing in his house and in all his realm that Hezekiah did not
14 show them. Then the prophet Isaiah came to King Hezekiah and asked him, 'What did these men say and where have they come from?' 'They have come from a far-off country,' Hezekiah
15 answered, 'from Babylon.' Then Isaiah asked, 'What did they see in your house?' 'They saw everything,' Hezekiah replied; 'there was nothing among my treasures that I did not show them,'
16 Then Isaiah said to Hezekiah, 'Hear
17 the word of the LORD: The time is coming, says the LORD, when everything in your house, and all that your forefathers have amassed till the present day, will be carried away to Bab-
18 ylon; not a thing shall be left. And some of the sons who will be born to you, sons of your own begetting, shall be taken and shall be made eunuchs in the palace of the king of Babylon.'

19 Hezekiah answered, 'The word of the LORD which you have spoken is good'; thinking to himself that peace and security would last out his lifetime.
20 The other events of Hezekiah's reign, his exploits, and how he made the pool and the conduit and brought water into the city, are recorded in the annals of the kings of Judah.
21 So Hezekiah rested with his forefathers and was succeeded by his son Manasseh.

The last kings of Judah

21*j* MANASSEH WAS TWELVE YEARS OLD when he came to the throne, and he reigned in Jerusalem for fifty-five years;
2 his mother was Hephzi-bah. He did what was wrong in the eyes of the LORD, in following the abominable practices of the nations which the LORD had dispossessed in favour of
3 the Israelites. He rebuilt the hill-shrines which his father Hezekiah had destroyed, he erected altars to the Baal and made a sacred pole as Ahab king of Israel had done, and prostrated himself before all the host of
4 heaven and worshipped them. He built altars in the house of the LORD, that house of which the LORD had said, 'Jerusalem shall receive my Name.'
5 He built altars for all the host of heaven in the two courts of the house of the
6 LORD; he made his son pass through the fire, he practised soothsaying and divination, and dealt with ghosts and spirits. He did much wrong in the eyes of the LORD and provoked his anger;
7 and the image that he had made of the goddess Asherah he put in the house, the place of which the LORD had said to David and Solomon his son, 'This

i Verses 12–19: cp. Isa. 39. 1–8.
j Verses 1–9: cp. 2 Chr. 33. 1–9.

8–11: The *sign* given is the backward movement of the sun's shadow on some stairs; this was a normal time-keeping device. **12–19:** *Merodach-baladan* rebelled against Sennacherib at the same time as Hezekiah; see 18.1–16 n. An actual eighth-century embassy to coordinate the rebellion is here combined with a more legendary prophetic story about Isaiah, which reflects a much later time (after 605 B.C.) when Babylon became a threat to, rather than an ally of, Judean independence. **18:** No *sons* of Hezekiah's *begetting* became Babylonian prisoners; Babylon as well as Judah was subject to Assyria.
21.1–18: Manasseh and Judah. The Northern Kingdom had fallen because the sins of Jeroboam were never removed. Manasseh's *fifty-five years* began with a coregency with Hezekiah (697 B.C.), not long after Sennacherib's defeat of the rebellion. **7:** *Asherah:* see 13.6.

411

house and Jerusalem, which I chose out of all the tribes of Israel, shall re-
8 ceive my Name for all time. I will not again make Israel outcasts from the land which I gave to their forefathers, if only they will be careful to observe all my commands and all the law that
9 my servant Moses gave them.' But they did not obey, and Manasseh misled them into wickedness far worse than that of the nations which the LORD had exterminated in favour of the Israelites.
10 Then the LORD spoke through his
11 servants the prophets: 'Because Manasseh king of Judah has done these abominable things, outdoing the Amorites before him in wickedness, and because he has led Judah into sin with
12 his idols, this is the word of the LORD the God of Israel: I will bring disaster on Jerusalem and Judah, disaster which will ring in the ears of all
13 who hear of it. I will mark down every stone of Jerusalem with the plumbline of Samaria and the plummet of the house of Ahab; I will wipe away Jerusalem as when a man wipes his
14 plate and turns it upside down, and I will cast off what is left of my people, my own possession, and hand them over to their enemies. They shall be plundered and fall a prey to all their
15 enemies; for they have done what is wrong in my eyes and have provoked my anger from the day their forefathers left Egypt up to the present day.
16 And this Manasseh shed so much innocent blood that he filled Jerusalem full to the brim, not to mention the sin into which he led Judah by
17 doing what is wrong in my eyes.' The other events and acts of Manasseh's reign, and the sin that he committed, are recorded in the annals of the kings
18 of Judah. So Manasseh rested with his forefathers and was buried in the

garden-tomb of his family, in the garden of Uzza; he was succeeded by his son Amon.

Amon was twenty-two years old 19[k] when he came to the throne, and he reigned in Jerusalem for two years; his mother was Meshullemeth daughter of Haruz of Jotbah. He did what was 20 wrong in the eyes of the LORD as his father Manasseh had done. He 21 followed in his father's footsteps and served the idols that his father had served and prostrated himself before them. He forsook the LORD the God 22 of his fathers and did not conform to his ways. King Amon's courtiers con- 23 spired against him and murdered him in his house; but the people of the 24 land killed all the conspirators and made his son Josiah king in his place. The 25 other events of Amon's reign are recorded in the annals of the kings of Judah. He was buried in his grave in 26 the garden of Uzza; he was succeeded by his son Josiah.

Josiah was eight years old when he 22 1[l] came to the throne, and he reigned in Jerusalem for thirty-one years; his mother was Jedidah daughter of Adaiah of Bozkath. He did what was right in 2 the eyes of the LORD; he followed closely in the footsteps of his forefather David, swerving neither right nor left.

In the eighteenth year of his reign 3[m] Josiah sent Shaphan son of Azaliah, son of Meshullam, the adjutant-general, to the house of the LORD. 'Go 4 to the high priest Hilkiah,' he said, 'and tell him to melt down the silver that has been brought into the house of the LORD, which those on duty at the entrance have received from the people, and to hand it over to the foremen 5

k Verses 19–24: cp. 2 Chr. 33. 21–25.
l Verses 1, 2: cp. 2 Chr. 34. 1, 2.
m Verses 3–20: cp. 2 Chr. 34. 8–28.

10–16: The condemnation is anonymous, spoken simply *through his servants the prophets.* **11:** *Amorites:* see Gen.15.16 n.

    21.19–26: Amon of Judah. 19: Amon's *mother*, Manasseh's most important wife, was from Jotbah. **23:** This assassination probably had some relation to the policy toward Assyria. **24:** *The people of the land:* see 11.14 n.

    22.1–23.30: Josiah. With this king the Deuteronomic history reached its climax. *Josiah* carries out what all earlier kings are blamed for failing to do. He removes the hill-shrines in Judah and destroys the cult center in Bethel. Religiously, his program was deemed entirely correct, but—from the final viewpoint of Kgs.—he came one generation too late, for the divine decision about Judah had been made; see 21.10–15; 23.26–27. **3–7:** *Josiah* instructs

in the house of the LORD, to pay the workmen who are carrying out repairs
6 in it, the carpenters, builders, and masons, and to purchase timber and
7 hewn stones for its repair. They are not to be asked to account for the money that has been given them; they are act-
8 ing on trust.' The high priest Hilkiah told Shaphan the adjutant-general that he had discovered the book of the law in the house of the LORD, and he gave it
9 to him, and Shaphan read it. Then Shaphan came to report to the king and told him that his servants had melted down the silver in the house of the LORD and handed it over to the
10 foremen there. Then Shaphan the adjutant-general told the king that the high priest Hilkiah had given him a book, and he read it out in the king's
11 presence. When the king heard what was in the book of the law, he rent his
12 clothes, and ordered the priest Hilkiah, Ahikam son of Shaphan, Akbor son of Micaiah, Shaphan the adjutant-
13 general, and Asaiah the king's attendant, to go and seek guidance of the LORD for himself, for the people, and for all Judah, about what was written in this book that had been discovered. 'Great is the wrath of the LORD', he said, 'that has been kindled against us, because our forefathers did not obey the commands in this book and do all that is laid upon us.'
14 So Hilkiah the priest, Ahikam, Akbor, Shaphan, and Asaiah went to Huldah the prophetess, wife of Shallum son of Tikvah, son of Harhas, the keeper of the wardrobe, and consulted her at her home in the second
15 quarter of Jerusalem. 'This is the word of the LORD the God of Israel,' she answered: 'Say to the man who sent
16 you to me, "This is the word of the LORD: I am bringing disaster on this place and its inhabitants as foretold in the book which the king of
17 Judah has read, because they have forsaken me and burnt sacrifices to other gods, provoking my anger with all the idols they have made with their own hands; therefore, my wrath is kindled against this place and will not be quenched." This is what you shall say 18 to the king of Judah who sent you to seek guidance of the LORD: "This is the word of the LORD the God of Israel: You have listened to my words and 19 shown a willing heart, you humbled yourself before the LORD when you heard me say that this place and its inhabitants would become objects of loathing and scorn, you rent your clothes and wept before me. Because of all this, I for my part have heard you. This is the very word of the LORD. Therefore, I will gather you to 20 your forefathers, and you will be gathered to your grave in peace; you will not live to see all the disaster which I am bringing upon this place."' So they brought back word to the king.

Then the king sent and called all the 23 [n] elders of Judah and Jerusalem together, and went up to the house of the 2 LORD; he took with him the men of Judah and the inhabitants of Jerusalem, the priests and the prophets, the whole population, high and low. There he read out to them all the book of the covenant discovered in the house of the LORD; and then, standing 3 on the dais,[o] the king made a covenant before the LORD to obey him and keep his commandments, his testimonies, and his statutes, with all his heart and soul, and so fulfil the terms of the covenant written in this book. And all the people pledged themselves to the covenant.

Next, the king ordered the high priest 4 Hilkiah, the deputy high priest,[p] and those on duty at the entrance, to remove from the house of the LORD all the objects made for Baal and Asherah and all the host of heaven;

n *Verses 1–3: cp. 2 Chr. 34. 29–32.*
o *Or by the pillar.*
p *Prob. rdg.; Heb. priests.*

Shaphan to institute the Temple repairs; compare 12.4–16. **8–13:** The king's response to the *book* implies that it contained divine requirements not previously known. **14–20:** The punishment promised in the book is inescapable, but because of the faithfulness of Josiah it is to be postponed until after his death. **23.1–3:** *The book of the covenant* becomes authorized as the law of the land; the *book* is often taken to be the central portion of Deuteronomy, chs. 5–28. **4–14:** The cult objects and sites of temples were regarded as illicit both from the viewpoint

he burnt these outside Jerusalem, in the open country by the Kidron, and carried the ashes to Bethel. He suppressed the heathen priests whom the kings of Judah had appointed to burn sacrifices at the hill-shrines in the cities of Judah and in the neighbourhood of Jerusalem, as well as those who burnt sacrifices to Baal, to the sun and moon and planets and all the host of heaven. He took the symbol of Asherah*q* from the house of the Lord to the gorge of the Kidron outside Jerusalem, burnt it there and pounded it to dust, which was then scattered over the common burial-ground. He also pulled down the houses of the male prostitutes attached to the house of the Lord, where the women wove vestments in honour of Asherah.

He brought in all the priests from the cities of Judah and desecrated the hill-shrines where they had burnt sacrifices, from Geba to Beersheba, and dismantled the hill-shrines of the demons*r* in front of the gate of Joshua, the governor of the city, to the left of the city gate. These priests, however, never came up to the altar of the Lord in Jerusalem but used to eat unleavened bread with the priests of their clan. He desecrated Topheth in the Valley of Ben-hinnom, so that no one might make his son or daughter pass through the fire in honour of Molech.*s* He destroyed the horses that the kings of Judah had set up in honour of the sun at the entrance to the house of the Lord, beside the room of Nathan-melek the eunuch in the colonnade, and he burnt the chariots of the sun. He pulled down the altars made by the kings of Judah on the roof by the upper chamber of Ahaz and the altars made by Manasseh in the two courts of the house of the Lord; he pounded them to dust and threw it into the gorge of the Kidron. Also, on the east of Jerusalem, to the south of the Mount of Olives, the king desecrated the hill-shrines which Solomon the king of Israel had built for Ashtoreth the loathsome goddess of the Sidonians, and for Kemosh the loathsome god of Moab, and for Milcom the abominable god of the Ammonites; he broke down the sacred pillars and cut down the sacred poles and filled the places where they had stood with human bones.

At Bethel he dismantled the altar by*t* the hill-shrine made by Jeroboam son of Nebat who led Israel into sin, together with the hill-shrine itself; he broke its stones in pieces, crushed them to dust and burnt the sacred pole. When Josiah set eyes on the graves which were there on the hill, he sent and took the bones from them and burnt them on the altar to desecrate it, thus fulfilling the word of the Lord announced by the man of God when Jeroboam stood by the altar at the feast. But when he caught sight of the grave of the man of God who had foretold these things, he asked, 'What is that monument I see there?' The people of the city answered, 'The grave of the man of God who came from Judah and foretold all that you have done to the altar at Bethel.' 'Leave it alone,' he said; 'let no one disturb his bones.' So they spared his bones and also those of the prophet who came from Samaria. Further, Josiah suppressed all the hill-shrines in the cities of Samaria, which the kings of Israel had set up and thereby provoked the Lord's anger, and he did to them what he had done at Bethel. He slaughtered on the altars all the priests of the hill-shrines who were there, and he burnt human bones upon them. Then he went back to Jerusalem.

The king ordered all the people to keep the Passover to the Lord their God, as this book of the covenant pre-

q symbol of Asherah: or sacred pole.   r Or satyrs.
s in honour of Molech: or for an offering.
t Prob. rdg.; Heb. om.

---

of Josiah and of those who in postexilic times were faithful to the norms here set forth. **8–9:** While *hill-shrines* were eliminated, their *priests* were incorporated into a more complex Jerusalemite priesthood. **13:** Compare 1 Kgs.11.7. **15–20:** Later in his reign, after Assyria had collapsed, Josiah moved to take over the territory of the former Northern Kingdom. He defended that territory against Pharaoh Necho II, at the cost of his life (vv. 29–30; compare 2 Chr.35.20–25). **16–18:** See 1 Kgs.13.2,30–32. **21–23:** The *Passover* observance was the occasion

22 scribed; no such Passover had been kept either when the Judges were ruling Israel or during the times of the kings 23 of Israel and Judah. But in the eighteenth year of Josiah's reign this Passover was kept to the LORD in Jerusalem. 24 Further, Josiah got rid of all who called up ghosts and spirits, of all household gods and idols and all the loathsome objects seen in the land of Judah and in Jerusalem, so that he might fulfil the requirements of the law written in the book which the priest Hilkiah had discovered in the house of the LORD. 25 No king before him had turned to the LORD as he did, with all his heart and soul and strength, following the whole law of Moses; nor did any king like him appear again.

26 Yet the LORD did not abate his fierce anger; it still burned against Judah because of all the provocation which Manasseh had given him. 27 'Judah also I will banish from my presence', he declared, 'as I banished Israel; and I will cast off this city of Jerusalem which once I chose, and the house where I promised that my Name should be.'

28 The other events and acts of Josiah's reign are recorded in the annals of the 29 kings of Judah. It was in his reign that Pharaoh Necho king of Egypt set out for the river Euphrates to help the king of Assyria. King Josiah went to meet him; and when they met at Megiddo, 30*u* Pharaoh Necho slew him. His attendants conveyed his body in a chariot from Megiddo to Jerusalem and buried him in his own burial place. Then the people of the land took Josiah's son Jehoahaz and anointed him king in place of his father.

31 Jehoahaz was twenty-three years old when he came to the throne, and he reigned in Jerusalem for three months; his mother was Hamutal daughter of Jeremiah of Libnah. He did what was 32 wrong in the eyes of the LORD, as his forefathers had done. Pharaoh Necho 33 removed him from the throne*v* in Jerusalem, and imposed on the land a fine of a hundred talents of silver and one talent of gold. Pharaoh Necho made 34 Josiah's son Eliakim king in place of his father and changed his name to Jehoiakim. He took Jehoahaz and brought him to Egypt, where he died. Jehoiakim paid the silver and gold to 35 Pharaoh, taxing the country to meet Pharaoh's demands; he exacted it from the people, from every man according to his assessment, so that he could pay Pharaoh Necho.

Jehoiakim was twenty-five years old 36 when he came to the throne, and he reigned in Jerusalem for eleven years; his mother was Zebidah daughter of Pedaiah of Rumah. He did what was 37 wrong in the eyes of the LORD, as his forefathers had done. During his reign **24** Nebuchadnezzar king of Babylon took the field, and Jehoiakim became his vassal; but three years later he broke with him and revolted. The LORD 2 launched against him raiding-parties of Chaldaeans, Aramaeans, Moabites, and Ammonites, letting them range through Judah and ravage it, as the LORD had foretold through his servants the prophets. All this happened to 3 Judah in fulfilment of the LORD's purpose to banish them from his presence, because of all the sin that Manasseh had committed and because of the 4 innocent blood that he had shed; he had drenched Jerusalem with innocent

u Verses 30–34: cp. 2 Chr. 36. 1–4.
v removed ... throne: prob. rdg., cp. 2 Chr. 36. 3; Heb. bound him at Riblah in the land of Hamath when he was king ...

on which the people reconstituted themselves as the people of God; compare 2 Chr. ch. 30 and Ezra 6.19–22. **26–27:** See 21.10–15; 22.16–20. **29–30:** By the account in 2 Chr.35.20–25 Josiah was moving to impede Necho's aid for the Assyrians at Carchemish. The Babylonians took and held that city, thanks, perhaps, to Josiah's delaying tactics against the Egyptians. **30:** *The people of the land* were Josiah's primary support; see 11.14 n.

23.31–24.20: The last kings of Judah. 31–35: *Jehoahaz* was Josiah's second son, born to his second wife (vv. 31,36). After Josiah's death he, rather than Jehoiakim, the eldest son, was put on the throne by "the people of the land" (v. 30). Accordingly, Necho put the older son on the throne (609 B.C.) and imposed a heavy fine on the people of the land, who had been the mainstay of Josiah's movement; see 11.14 n. **24.1:** *Nebuchadnezzar* won the battle of Carchemish in 605 (see Jer.46.2), driving Egyptian forces out of Syria. *Jehoiakim* took the first opportunity, however, to rebel against the new Babylonian master. **2:** See Jer.25.9 **3–4:** See 21.10–15.

blood, and the LORD would not forgive
5 him. The other events and acts of
Jehoiakim's reign are recorded in the
6 annals of the kings of Judah. He rested
with his forefathers, and was succeeded
7 by his son Jehoiachin. The king of
Egypt did not leave his own land again,
because the king of Babylon had
stripped him of all his possessions, from
the Torrent of Egypt to the river
Euphrates.

Downfall of the southern kingdom

8w JEHOIACHIN WAS EIGHTEEN YEARS OLD
when he came to the throne, and he
reigned in Jerusalem for three months;
his mother was Nehushta daughter of
9 Elnathan of Jerusalem. He did what
was wrong in the eyes of the LORD, as
10 his father had done. At that time the
troops of Nebuchadnezzar king of
Babylon advanced on Jerusalem and
11 besieged the city. Nebuchadnezzar
arrived while his troops were besieging
12 it, and Jehoiachin king of Judah, his
mother, his courtiers, his officers, and
his eunuchs, all surrendered to the
king of Babylon. The king of Babylon,
now in the eighth year of his reign,
13 took him prisoner; and, as the LORD
had foretold, he carried off all the treasures of the house of the LORD and of
the royal palace and broke up all the
vessels of gold which Solomon king of
Israel had made for the temple of the
14 LORD. He carried the people of Jerusalem into exile, the officers and the
fighting men, ten thousand in number,
together with all the craftsmen and
smiths; only the weakest class of people
15 were left. He deported Jehoiachin to
Babylon; he also took into exile from
Jerusalem to Babylon the king's mother
and his wives, his eunuchs and the
16 foremost men of the land. He also
deported to Babylon all the men of substance, seven thousand in number,
and a thousand craftsmen and smiths,

all of them able-bodied men and
skilled armourers. He made Mattaniah, 17
uncle of Jehoiachin, king in his place
and changed his name to Zedekiah.

Zedekiah was twenty-one years old 18x
when he came to the throne, and he
reigned in Jerusalem for eleven years;
his mother was Hamutal daughter of
Jeremiah of Libnah. He did what was 19
wrong in the eyes of the LORD, as
Jehoiakim had done. Jerusalem and 20
Judah so angered the LORD that in the
end he banished them from his sight;
and Zedekiah rebelled against the
king of Babylon.

In the ninth year of his reign, in the 25[1]y
tenth month, on the tenth day of the
month, Nebuchadnezzar king of Babylon advanced with all his army against
Jerusalem, invested it and erected
watch-towers against it on every side;
the siege lasted till the eleventh year of 2
King Zedekiah. In the fourth month 3
of that year,z on the ninth day of the
month, when famine was severe in the
city and there was no food for the
common people, the city was thrown 4
open. When Zedekiah king of Judah
saw this,a he and all his armed escort
left the city and fled by night through
the gate called Between the Two Walls,
near the king's garden. They escaped
towards the Arabah, although the Chaldaeans were surrounding the city. But 5
the Chaldaean army pursued the king
and overtook him in the lowlands of
Jericho; and all his company was
dispersed. The king was seized and 6
brought before the king of Babylon at
Riblah, where he pleaded his case
before him. Zedekiah's sons were slain 7
before his eyes; then his eyes were put
out, and he was brought to Babylon
in fetters of bronze.

In the fifth month, on the seventh 8
day of the month, in the nineteenth year

w *Verses 8–17: cp. 2 Chr. 36. 9, 10.*
x *24. 18—25. 21: cp. Jer. 52. 1–27.*
y *Verses 1–12: cp. Jer. 39. 1–10; verses 1–17: cp. 2 Chr. 36. 17–20.*
z *In . . . year: prob. rdg., cp. Jer. 52. 6; Heb. om.*
a *When . . . this: prob. rdg., cp. Jer. 39. 4; Heb. om.*

10–17: Jehoiakim had rebelled against *Nebuchadnezzar*, but he died before the inevitable surrender. His young son *Jehoiachin* thus bore the brunt of the anti-Babylonian policy. 18–20:
Zedekiah appears repeatedly in the Book of Jer., e.g. Jer.21.1–7; 38.14–28; 39.1–10.

25.1–30: The destruction of Jerusalem. 2–4: *Jerusalem* fell on July 29, 587 B.C.; some scholars,
assuming an autumn new year, give the year as 586. The city was destroyed one month later
(v. 8). Some records were seemingly removed during that month and were thus available to the
Deuteronomic historians. *The common people* (v. 4) were "the people of the land"; see 11.14 n.

of Nebuchadnezzar king of Babylon, Nebuzaradan, captain of the king's
9 bodyguard, came to Jerusalem and set fire to the house of the LORD and the royal palace; all the houses in the city, including the mansion of Gedaliah,[b]
10 were burnt down. The Chaldaean forces with the captain of the guard pulled down the walls all round Jeru-
11 salem. Nebuzaradan captain of the guard deported the rest of the people left in the city, those who had deserted to the king of Babylon and any re-
12 maining artisans.[c] He left only the weakest class of people to be vine-dressers and labourers.

13 The Chaldaeans broke up the pillars of bronze in the house of the LORD, the trolleys, and the Sea of bronze, and
14 took the metal to Babylon. They took also the pots, shovels, snuffers, saucers, and all the vessels of bronze used in the
15 service of the temple. The captain of the guard took away the precious metal, whether gold or silver, of which the fire-pans and the tossing-bowls were made.
16 The bronze of the two pillars, the one Sea, and the trolleys, which Solomon had made for the house of the LORD,
17 was beyond weighing. The one pillar was eighteen cubits high and its capital was bronze; the capital was three cubits high, and a decoration of network and pomegranates ran all round it, wholly of bronze. The other pillar, with its network, was exactly like it.
18 The captain of the guard took Seraiah the chief priest and Zephaniah the deputy chief priest and the three
19 on duty at the entrance; he took also from the city a eunuch who was in charge of the fighting men, five of those with right of access to the king who were still in the city, the adjutant-general[d] whose duty was to muster the people for war, and sixty men of the
20 people who were still there. These Nebuzaradan captain of the guard brought to the king of Babylon at

Riblah. There, in the land of Hamath, 21
the king of Babylon had them flogged and put to death. So Judah went into exile from their own land.

Nebuchadnezzar king of Babylon 22
appointed Gedaliah son of Ahikam, son of Shaphan, governor over the few people whom he had left in Judah.
When the captains of the armed bands 23
and their men heard that the king of Babylon had appointed Gedaliah governor, they all came to him at Mizpah: Ishmael son of Nethaniah, Johanan son of Kareah, Seraiah son of Tanhumeth of Netophah, and Jaaz-aniah of Beth-maacah. Then Ged- 24
aliah gave them and their men this assurance: 'Have no fear of the Chal-daean officers. Settle down in the land and serve the king of Babylon; and then all will be well with you.' But in the 25
seventh month Ishmael son of Neth-aniah, son of Elishama, who was a member of the royal house, came with ten men and murdered Gedaliah and the Jews and Chaldaeans who were with him at Mizpah. Thereupon all the 26
people, high and low, and the captains of the armed bands, fled to Egypt for fear of the Chaldaeans.

In the thirty-seventh year of the 27[e]
exile of Jehoiachin king of Judah, on the twenty-seventh day of the twelfth month, Evil-merodach[f] king of Babylon in the year of his accession showed favour to Jehoiachin king of Judah.
He brought him out of prison, treated 28
him kindly and gave him a seat at table above the kings with him in Bab-ylon. So Jehoiachin discarded his prison 29
clothes and lived as a pensioner of the king for the rest of his life. For his 30
maintenance, a regular daily allowance was given him by the king as long as he lived.

b *Gedaliah*: prob. rdg.; *Heb.* a great man.
c *any remaining artisans*: prob. rdg., cp. Jer. 52. 15; *Heb.* the remaining crowd.
d Prob. rdg.; *Heb.* adds commander-in-chief.
e *Verses 27–30*: cp. Jer. 52. 31–34. f Or Ewil-marduk.

13–17: The *bronze* work of the Temple court is described in 1 Kgs.7.15–46 and 7.13–51 n. **19**: That there was an officer responsible for mustering the people ("the people of the land"; see 11.14 n.) *for war* indicates the dependence of the Judean monarchy on a draft in its later years. **22**: It should be noted that *Gedaliah* was the grandson of Josiah's adjutant-general (22.3), sharing a pro-Babylonian orientation with Josiah. **23–26**: Compare Jer. chs. 41–44. **27–30**: Compare Jer.52.31–34. This last hopeful word of the Deuteronomic history may be a later appendix. It reaffirms a motif of the whole work, that the LORD will not forever abandon the house of David.

THE FIRST BOOK OF THE
CHRONICLES

The books of 1 and 2 Chronicles are the first and larger part of a comprehensive work continued in the books of Ezra and Nehemiah. The entire work is concerned with the proper service of the LORD at the Temple in Jerusalem: how that service was established by David (1 Chr.), how it was finally lost through the folly of the kings of Judah (2 Chr.), and how it was restored by Ezra and Nehemiah. The writing was completed some time during the fourth century B.C.

The Chronicler made extensive use of the books of Samuel and Kings, often taking over long passages without major change; the annotations to those books can be consulted. He also made use of historical sources not otherwise known (see, e.g. 2 Chr.11.5–12; 26.11–13). He reproduced genealogical lists which probably reflect conditions earlier than his own time (see, e.g. 1 Chr. chs. 23–27).

David is the center of attention in 1 Chronicles. After a genealogical survey of history until David (chs. 1–9), David is treated in four blocks of material: his accession to the throne (chs. 10–12), his bringing the Ark into Jerusalem (chs. 13–16), his military achievements (chs. 18–20), and his elaborate preparation for the building of the Temple before his death (chs. 21–29). 2 Chronicles carries on the account of David's dynasty.

While some of the sources used have great historical value, the Chronicler's work itself should not be read as precise history. He presents, rather, a liturgical history of the City of David, with a prevalent mood and atmosphere of joyful veneration of a sacred past, centered in the Temple. Most of the numbers which he gives and the battles which he describes are more like figures in stained-glass windows than in real life. The heroes of his work are the faithful servants of the sanctuary, the Levites, and especially the singers. It is usually thought that the Chronicler was himself one of these singers.

Genealogies from Adam to Saul

1,2[a] ADAM, SETH, ENOSH, KENAN, MAHA-
3 lalel, Jared, Enoch, Methuselah,
4 Lamech, Noah.

The sons of Noah: Shem, Ham and Japheth.

5[b] The sons of Japheth: Gomer, Magog, Madai, Javan,[c] Tubal, Meshech and
6 Tiras. The sons of Gomer: Ashkenaz,
7 Diphath and Togarmah. The sons of Javan: Elishah, Tarshish, Kittim[d] and Rodanim.

8[e] The sons of Ham: Cush, Mizraim,[f]
9 Put and Canaan. The sons of Cush: Seba, Havilah, Sabta, Raama and Sabtecha. The sons of Raama: Sheba
10 and Dedan. Cush was the father of Nimrod, who began to show himself a
11[g] man of might on earth. From Mizraim sprang the Lydians, Anamites, Leha-

bites, Naphtuhites, Pathrusites, Caslu- 12 hites, and the Caphtorites, from whom the Philistines were descended.

Canaan was the father of Sidon, 13 who was his eldest son, and Heth,[h] the 14 Jebusites, the Amorites, the Girgash- ites, the Hivites, the Arkites, the Sin- 15 ites, the Arvadites, the Zemarites, and 16 the Hamathites.

The sons of Shem: Elam, Asshur, 17[i] Arphaxad, Lud[j] and Aram. The sons of Aram: Uz, Hul, Gether and Mash. Arphaxad was the father of Shelah, 18 and Shelah the father of Eber. Eber 19 had two sons: one was named Peleg,[k]

a Verses 2–4: cp. Gen. 5. 9–32.
b Verses 5–7: cp. Gen. 10. 2–4.
c Or Greece.
d Or Tarshish of the Kittians.
e Verses 8–10: cp. Gen. 10. 6–8.
f Or Egypt.
g Verses 11–16: cp. Gen. 10. 13–18.
h Or the Hittites.   i Verses 17–23: cp. Gen. 10. 22–29.
j Or the Lydians.   k That is Division.

1.1–9.44: Genealogical prologues. To his liturgical history of the City of David, the Chronicler gave a universal setting by assembling the genealogies of 1 Chr. chs. 1–9, recording the line from Adam to David, with whom the liturgical history really began. Within this overall plan, some of the sources utilized had their own purposes, as is noted. A striking feature is the almost total absence of narrative here; world history simply moves through the families of man until it reaches David.
1.1–54: From Adam to Israel. Here the materials are from Genesis; special materials from the Chronicler's own circle (see Introduction) either were not required or were not available.
1–4: The Chronicler provides only the briefest list of the names of the antediluvians, omitting data, such as their ages at the birth of their sons given in Gen.5.3–31. 5–23: This is a catalogue

because in his time the earth was divided, and his brother's name was 20 Joktan. Joktan was the father of Almo-21 dad, Sheleph, Hazarmoth, Jerah, Had-22 oram, Uzal, Diklah, Ebal,[l] Abimael, 23 Sheba, Ophir, Havilah and Jobab. All these were sons of Joktan.

24[m] The line of[n] Shem: Arphaxad, Shelah, 25,26 Eber, Peleg, Reu, Serug, Nahor, Terah, 27,28 Abram, also known as Abraham, whose sons were Isaac and Ishmael.

29[o] The sons of[p] Ishmael in the order of their birth: Nebaioth the eldest, then 30 Kedar, Adbeel, Mibsam, Mishma, 31 Dumah, Massa, Hadad, Teman, Jetur, Naphish and Kedemah. These were Ishmael's sons.

32[q] The sons of Keturah, Abraham's concubine: she bore him Zimran, Jokshan, Medan, Midian, Ishbak and Shuah. The sons of Jokshan: Sheba and 33 Dedan. The sons of Midian: Ephah, Epher, Enoch, Abida and Eldaah. All these were descendants of Keturah.

34 Abraham was the father of Isaac, and Isaac's sons were Esau and Israel. 35[r] The sons of Esau: Eliphaz, Reuel, 36 Jeush, Jalam and Korah. The sons of Eliphaz: Teman, Omar, Zephi, Gatam, 37 Kenaz, Timna and Amalek. The sons of Reuel: Nahath, Zerah, Shammah and Mizzah.

38[s] The sons of Seir: Lotan, Shobal, Zibeon, Anah, Dishon, Ezer and 39 Dishan. The sons of Lotan: Hori and Homam; and Lotan had a sister named 40 Timna. The sons of Shobal: Alvan,

Manahath, Ebal, Shephi and Onam. The sons of Zibeon: Aiah and Anah. The son[t] of Anah: Dishon. The sons of 41 Dishon: Amram, Eshban, Ithran and Cheran. The sons of Ezer: Bilhan, 42 Zavan and Akan. The sons of Dishan: Uz and Aran.

These are the kings who ruled over 43[u] Edom before there were kings in Israel: Bela son of Beor, whose city was named Dinhabah. When he died, he 44 was succeeded by Jobab son of Zerah of Bozrah. When Jobab died, he was 45 succeeded by Husham of Teman. When 46 Husham died, he was succeeded by Hadad son of Bedad, who defeated Midian in Moabite country. His city was named Avith. When Hadad died, 47 he was succeeded by Samlah of Mas-rekah. When Samlah died, he was 48 succeeded by Saul of Rehoboth on the River. When Saul died, he was suc- 49 ceeded by Baal-hanan son of Akbor. When Baal-hanan died, he was suc- 50 ceeded by Hadad. His city was named Pai; his wife's name was Mehetabel daughter of Matred a woman of Me-zahab.[v]

After Hadad died the chiefs in Edom 51

l Or Obal, cp. Gen. 10. 28.
m Verses 24–27: cp. Gen. 11. 10–26.
n The line of: prob. rdg.; Heb. om.
o Verses 29–31: cp. Gen. 25. 13–16.
p The sons of: prob. rdg., cp. Gen. 25. 13; Heb. om.
q Verses 32, 33: cp. Gen. 25. 1–4.
r Verses 35–37: cp. Gen. 36. 4, 5, 9–13.
s Verses 38–42: cp. Gen. 36. 20–28.
t Prob. rdg.; Heb. sons; the same correction is made in several other places in chs. 1–9.
u Verses 43–54: cp. Gen. 36. 31–43.
v Or daughter of Mezahab.

of nations rather than simply a genealogy; compare Gen. ch. 10. **24–27:** The genealogy from *Shem* through *Abraham* is given. Just as there were ten generations before the flood, so there were ten from the flood to Abraham. **29–54:** Here the Chronicler rearranges the genealogies found in Genesis. He consistently lists first the descendants who do not lead to David. **29–34:** The offspring of Abraham are given in three groups; each son was from a different wife, Hagar, Keturah, and Sarah. See v. 32 n. **31:** The Chronicler does not comment here (as does Gen.25.16) that the twelve names of 1.29–30 were tribal and territorial groups. The twelve tribes of *Ishmael* at some time formed a union like that of the twelve tribes of Israel. **32:** The Chronicler mentions specifically *Keturah*, but not Hagar or Sarah. **33:** Gen.25.3 includes two sons of *Dedan*, omitted here, probably inadvertently. **34:** The Chronicler regularly uses the name *Israel* rather than Jacob. **35–54:** The longer treatment given to the descendants of *Esau* is probably due to the extent of the materials available in Gen.36.31–43 rather than to any special importance of their own. **35–37:** The Chronicler greatly abbreviates Gen.36.1–14, mainly by eliminating some repetitions and the references to the Canaanite wives of *Esau*. **36:** The Chronicler, or his source, mistakes *Timna* for a son instead of a concubine; see Gen.36.12. **38–42:** The Chronicler skips the lists of chiefs of the tribes of Edom (Gen.36.15–19). Instead, surprisingly, he gives lists of the clans of pre-Edomite inhabitants, *the sons of Seir* (Seir was a mountainous region south of Judah), called Horites in the Genesis source. **43–50:** It is remarkable that Israelites should have preserved this careful list of *the kings* of *Edom*. The form of the Edomite monarchy apparently required that the kingship pass from one family to another, as no dynastic principle was observed. Since the city of each king is also listed, that too was apparently a point of importance. **51–54:** The Chronicler makes these *chiefs* successors to the kings; in his source

52 were: chief Timna, chief Aliah, chief
Jetheth, chief Oholibamah, chief Eluh,
53 chief Pinon, chief Kenaz, chief Teman,
54 chief Mibzar, chief Magdiel and chief
Iram. These were the chiefs of Edom.

2 These were the sons of Israel: Reuben, Simeon, Levi, Judah, Issachar,
2 Zebulun, Dan, Joseph, Benjamin, Naphtali, Gad and Asher.
3 The sons of Judah: Er, Onan and
Shelah; the mother of these three was
a Canaanite woman, Bathshua.*w* Er,
Judah's eldest son, displeased the LORD
4 and the LORD slew him. Then Tamar,
Judah's daughter-in-law, bore him
Perez and Zerah, making in all five
5 sons of Judah. The sons of Perez:
6 Hezron and Hamul. The sons of Zerah:
Zimri, Ethan, Heman, Calcol and
7 Darda, five in all. The son of Zimri:
Carmi.*x* The son of Carmi: Achar,
who troubled Israel by his violation of
8 the sacred ban. The son of Ethan:
9 Azariah. The sons of Hezron: Jerah-
10 meel, Ram and Caleb. Ram was the
father of Amminadab, Amminadab
father of Nahshon prince of Judah.
11 Nahshon was the father of Salma,
12 Salma father of Boaz, Boaz father of
13 Obed, Obed father of Jesse. The eldest
son of Jesse was Eliab, the second

Abinadab, the third Shimea, the 14
fourth Nethaneel, the fifth Raddai, the 15
sixth Ozem, the seventh David; their 16
sisters were Zeruiah and Abigail. The
sons of Zeruiah: Abishai, Joab and
Asahel, three in all. Abigail was the 17
mother of Amasa; his father was Jether
the Ishmaelite.

Caleb son of Hezron had Jerioth by 18
Azubah his wife;*y* these were her
sons: Jesher, Shobab and Ardon.
When Azubah died, Caleb married 19
Ephrath, who bore him Hur. Hur was 20
the father of Uri, and Uri father of
Bezalel. Later, Hezron, then sixty years 21
of age, had intercourse with the
daughter of Machir father of Gilead,
having married her, and she bore
Segub. Segub was the father of Jair, 22
who had twenty-three cities in Gilead.
Geshur and Aram took from them 23
Havvoth-jair, and Kenath and its dependent villages, a total of sixty towns.
All these were descendants of Machir
father of Gilead. After the death of 24
Hezron, Caleb had intercourse with
Ephrathah and she bore him Ashhur
the founder of Tekoa.

w Bathshua: *or* daughter of Shua.
x The son ... Carmi: *prob. rdg.* (*cp. Josh. 7. 1, 18*);
 Heb. *om.*
y his wife: *prob. rdg.; Heb.* a woman and.

(Gen. 36.51–54) they simply form an alternative list of earlier chiefs; the significance of this alternative list is no longer clear.
2.1–55: The offspring of Judah. The details of the lists provided here present complexities. **1–2:** There is considerable variety in the sequence in which the twelve *sons of Israel* are listed in Scripture; see, e.g. Gen. 29.32–30.24 (Benjamin in 35.16–18); 35.23–25; and 46.8–25. The list here is close to Gen. 35.23–25 and Exod. 1.2–4, though *Dan* could well be linked with *Naphtali*, as sons of the same mother. **3–17:** An initial genealogy carries the main line from *the sons of Judah* to the generation of *David* and his contemporary relatives; no part of the genealogies was more important to the Chronicler. **3–5:** For the names and events referred to here, see Gen. ch. 38. **5:** The *Perez-Hezron* line is most important; see vv. 9–15. **6:** Here some traditional names of wise men and singers are incorporated into the minor Judean line of *Zerah*; see *Ethan* and *Heman* as inspired musicians in 15.17–18 and 25.1 (Jeduthun = Ethan). Compare 1 Kgs. 4.31 (which has no mention of *Zimri*). **7:** *Zimri* is included here as a son of Zerah (see v. 6 n.), in order to link the Judahite genealogy of the "troubler" *Achar* with the minor Judean clan of Zerah; compare Josh. 7.1,18. Achar and Achon, and Zimri and Zabdi (of Josh. 7.1, etc.) are pronunciation or copyist variants of the same names. **9–12:** The three *sons of Hezron* are particularly important because the rest of this genealogy of Judah traces their descendants separately: *Ram* (vv. 10–17), *Caleb* (vv. 18–24), and *Jerahmeel* (vv. 25–41). **11–12:** *Nahshon* is listed as the chief of the Judahites during Israel's Wilderness sojourn (Num. 1.7), but the same position is occupied by Caleb in another tradition (Num. 13.6). On *Boaz, Obed,* and *Jesse,* the immediate ancestors of David, see Ruth 4.13–17. **13:** On the sons of *Jesse,* see 1 Sam. 16.1–13. **16:** The main account of *the sons of Zeruiah* and their role in the rise of David is in 2 Sam. chs. 2–3; see especially 2 Sam. 2.18–24. **18–24:** *Caleb* was a name claimed as an ancestor by many clans in Judah with Hebron as their major city; see Josh. 14.6–15; 15.13–19. Several different lists of Calebite clans and villages arranged as family trees were seemingly available to the Chronicler: he used them even though they were not fully consistent; see vv. 42–55 and 4.11–15. **18:** The different wives of an ancestor stand for different groupings of clans or villages within the one tribe or tribal division. **20:** On *Bezalel,* artisan of the Tabernacle, see Exod. 31.2. **21–23:** The area of northeastern Transjordan (*Gilead*) was partially colonized by Israelites from west of the Jordan, though the colonists are not otherwise identified as Judeans; see

25 The sons of Jerahmeel eldest son of Hezron by[z] Ahijah were Ram the 26 eldest, Bunah, Oren and Ozem. Jerahmeel had another wife, whose name was Atarah; she was the mother of 27 Onam. The sons of Ram eldest son of Jerahmeel: Maaz, Jamin and Eker. 28 The sons of Onam: Shammai and Jada. The sons of Shammai: Nadab 29 and Abishur. The name of Abishur's wife was Abihail; she bore him Ahban 30 and Molid. The sons of Nadab: Seled and Ephraim; Seled died without 31 children. Ephraim's son was Ishi, Ishi's son Sheshan, Sheshan's son Ahlai. 32 The sons of Jada brother of Shammai: Jether and Jonathan; Jether died 33 without children. The sons of Jonathan: Peleth and Zaza. These were the descendants of Jerahmeel.

34 Sheshan had daughters but no sons. He had an Egyptian servant named 35 Jarha; he gave his daughter in marriage to this Jarha, and she bore him 36 Attai. Attai was the father of Nathan, 37 Nathan father of Zabad, Zabad father 38 of Ephlal, Ephlal father of Obed, Obed father of Jehu, Jehu father of Azariah, 39 Azariah father of Helez, Helez father 40 of Elasah, Elasah father of Sisamai, 41 Sisamai father of Shallum, Shallum father of Jekamiah, and Jekamiah father of Elishama.

42 The sons of Caleb brother of Jerahmeel: Mesha the eldest, founder of Ziph, and[a] Mareshah founder of Heb-43 ron. The sons of Hebron: Korah, Tap-44 puah, Rekem and Shema. Shema was the father of Raham father of Jorkoam, and Rekem was the father of 45 Shammai. The son of Shammai was Maon, and Maon was the founder 46 of Beth-zur. Ephah, Caleb's concubine, was the mother of Haran, Moza and Gazez; Haran was the father of Gazez. The sons of Jahdai: Regem, 47 Jotham, Geshan, Pelet, Ephah and Shaaph. Maacah, Caleb's concubine, 48 was the mother of Sheber and Tirhanah; she bore also Shaaph founder 49 of Madmannah, and Sheva founder of Machbenah and Gibea. Caleb also had a daughter named Achsah.

The descendants of Caleb: the sons 50 of Hur, the eldest son of Ephrathah: Shobal the founder of Kiriath-jearim, Salma the founder of Bethlehem, and 51 Hareph the founder of Beth-gader. Shobal the founder of Kiriath-jearim 52 was the father of Reaiah[b] and the ancestor of half the Manahethites.[c]

The clans of Kiriath-jearim: Ithrites, 53 Puhites, Shumathites, and Mishraites, from whom were descended the Zareathites and the Eshtaulites.

The descendants of Salma: Bethle-54 hem, the Netophathites, Ataroth, Bethjoab, half the Manahethites, and the Zorites.

The clans of Sophrites[d] living at 55 Jabez: Tirathites, Shimeathites, and Suchathites. These were Kenites who were connected by marriage with the ancestor of the Rechabites.

These were the sons of David, born 3¹[e] at Hebron: the eldest Amnon, whose mother was Ahinoam of Jezreel; the second Daniel, whose mother was Abigail of Carmel; the third Absalom, 2 whose mother was Maacah daughter of Talmai king of Geshur; the fourth Adonijah, whose mother was Haggith; the fifth Shephatiah, whose mother 3

z by: *prob. rdg.; Heb. om.*
a *Prob. rdg.; Heb.* adds the sons of.
b *Prob. rdg., cp.* 4. 2; *Heb.* the seer.
c *Prob. rdg., cp. verse* 54; *Heb.* Menuhoth.
d *Or* secretaries.
e *Verses* 1–4: *cp.* 2 *Sam.* 3. 2–5.

Josh.13.29–31. **25–41:** *The sons of Jerahmeel* were another group of clans that were eventually absorbed into Judah by taking a place in the genealogy of *Hezron* alongside Ram and Caleb (see v. 9). **34–41:** A mixture of Canaanite and *Egyptian* (slave) people in southern Palestine is historically probable. **42–54:** The additional *Caleb* genealogies show special interest in place names (used as if they were personal names) and in the founding of towns. *Hebron*, for example, appears as the city in v. 42 and as an ancestor in v. 43, while *Bethlehem* appears as a son of *Salma* in v. 54. **55:** By mentioning *Sophrites* ("scribes"), the Chronicler may be drawing on a list of professional accountants, in effect, lawyers. Compare the function of Baruch, the scribe, in Jer.32.9–12. *The Rechabites* presumably refers to the sons of Rechab who appear in 2 Kgs. 10.15–16 and Jer.35.1–11. This verse suggests a link between the old *Kenite* clan to which Moses' father-in-law belonged (Judg.4.11) and the Rechabites of later times.
　　3.1–24: The line of David. This is a continuation of the line of Ram from 2.17. **1–9:** *The sons of David* are listed as in 2 Sam.3.2–5 and 5.14–16. A comparison of minor differences in the three lists of David's sons born at Jerusalem (2 Sam.5.14–16; 1 Chr.3.5–8; 14.4–7) is

was Abital; the sixth Ithream, whose
4 mother was David's wife Eglah. These
six were born at Hebron, where David
reigned seven years and six months.
In Jerusalem he reigned thirty-three
5*f* years, and there the following sons
were born to him: Shimea, Shobab,
Nathan and Solomon; these four were
sons of Bathsheba daughter of Am-
6 miel. There were nine others: Ibhar,
7 Elishama, Eliphelet, Nogah, Nepheg,
8 Japhia, Elishama, Eliada and Eliphelet.
9 These were all the sons of David, with
their sister Tamar, in addition to his
sons by concubines.

10   Solomon's son was Rehoboam, his
son Abia, his son Asa, his son Jehosha-
11 phat, his son Joram, his son Ahaziah,
12 his son Joash, his son Amaziah, his
son Azariah, his son Jotham, his son
13 Ahaz, his son Hezekiah, his son Manas-
14 seh, his son Amon, and his son Josiah.
15 The sons of Josiah: the eldest was
Johanan, the second Jehoiakim, the
third Zedekiah, the fourth Shallum.
16 The sons of Jehoiakim: Jeconiah and
17 Zedekiah. The sons of Jeconiah, a pris-
18 oner:*g* Shealtiel, Malchiram, Pedaiah,
Shenazzar, Jekamiah, Hoshama and
19 Nedabiah. The sons of Pedaiah: Zerubbabel and Shimei. The sons of Zerubbabel: Meshullam and Hananiah; they
20 had a sister, Shelomith. There were five
others; Hashubah, Ohel, Berechiah,
21 Hasadiah and Jushab-hesed. The sons
of Hananiah: Pelatiah and Isaiah; his
son was Rephaiah, his son Arnan, his
22 son Obadiah, his son Shecaniah. The
sons of Shecaniah: Shemaiah,*h* Hattush,
Igeal, Bariah, Neariah and Shaphat, six
23 in all. The sons of Neariah: Elioenai,
Hezekiah and Azrikam, three in all.

24 The sons of Elioenai: Hodaiah, Eliashib, Pelaiah, Akkub, Johanan, Dalaiah
and Anani, seven in all.

4   The sons of Judah: Perez, Hezron,
2 Carmi, Hur and Shobal. Realah son of
Shobal was the father of Jahath,
Jahath father of Ahumai and Lahad.
These were the clans of the Zorathites.
3-4   The sons of Etam: Jezreel, Ishma,
Idbash, Penuel the founder of Gedor,
and Ezer the founder of Hushah; they
had a sister named Hazelelponi. These
were the sons of Hur: Ephrathah the
eldest, the founder of Bethlehem.

5   Ashhur the founder of Tekoa had
6 two wives, Helah and Naarah. Naarah
bore him Ahuzam, Hepher, Temeni and
Haahashtari.*i* These were the sons of
7 Naarah. The sons of Helah: Zereth,
8 Jezoar, Ethnan and Coz. Coz was the
father of Anub and Zobebah and the
clans of Aharhel son of Harum.

9   Jabez ranked higher than his brothers;
his mother called him Jabez because,
as she said, she had borne him in
10 pain. Jabez called upon the God of
Israel and said, 'I pray thee, bless me
and grant me wide territories. May
thy hand be with me, and do me no
harm, I pray thee, and let me be free
from pain'; and God granted his
petition.

11   Kelub brother of Shuah was the
father of Mehir the father of Eshton.
12 Eshton was the father of Beth-rapha,
Paseah, and Tehinnah father of Ir-
nahash. These were the men of Rechah.
13   The sons of Kenaz: Othniel and

f Verses 5–8: cp. 14. 4–7; 2 Sam. 5. 14–16.
g Jeconiah, a prisoner: or Jeconiah: Assir, . . .
h Prob. rdg.; Heb. adds and the sons of Shemaiah.
i Temeni and Haahashtari: or the Temanite and the
Ahashtarite.

---

instructive for the difficulties facing ancient writers in transmitting such lists. **10–14:** The
kings of Judah from *Solomon* to *Josiah* are listed without reference to brothers or other members
of the royal family. Athaliah (2 Kgs. ch. 11), the one queen to rule over Judah, and an evil
woman, is omitted. **14–16:** The order and number of the *sons of Josiah* are confused. No *Johanan*
is otherwise known; *Jehoiakim* was the eldest son, though *Shallum* (with the throne name
Jehoahaz) reigned three months before *Jehoiakim* came to the throne; see 2 Kgs.23.28–37.
Also, *Zedekiah* was *Jehoiakim's* younger brother, not his son; see 2 Kgs.24.17–18. **17–24:** For
the descendants of David after *Jeconiah* (Jehoiachin), the Chronicler is the only extant source,
though *Shealtiel* is mentioned in Ezra 3.2, and *Zerubbabel* is known to have been governor
when the Temple was rebuilt in Jerusalem; see Hag.1.1,12; 2.2 (see also Sheshbazzar in Ezra
1.8). The number of generations listed here after *Jeconiah* may be significant for the date of
the final form of the book; eleven are listed. If twenty years is calculated between the birth
of first sons, the list will come down to about 375 B.C., a probable date on other grounds for
the Chronicler's work.
   4.1–23: Further lists of the clans of Judah. The tribes were very fluid entities, constantly
absorbing and losing smaller clan or family units. Consequently, enumerations of the families

Seraiah. The sons of Othniel: Hathath and Meonothai.

14 Meonothai was the father of Ophrah. Seraiah was the father of Joab founder of Ge-harashim,[j] for they were craftsmen.

15 The sons of Caleb son of Jephunneh: Iru, Elah and Naam. The son of Elah: Kenaz.

16 The sons of Jehaleleel: Ziph and Ziphah, Tiria and Asareel.

17-18 The sons of Ezra: Jether, Mered, Epher and Jalon. These were the sons of Bithiah daughter of Pharaoh, whom Mered had married; she conceived and gave birth to[k] Miriam, Shammai and Ishbah founder of Eshtemoa. His Jewish wife was the mother of Jered founder of Gedor, Heber founder of Soco, and Jekuthiel founder of Zanoah.

19 The sons of his[l] wife Hodiah sister of Naham were Daliah father of Keilah the Garmite, and Eshtemoa the Maacathite.

20 The sons of Shimon: Amnon, Rinnah, Ben-hanan and Tilon.

The sons of Ishi: Zoheth and Ben-zoheth.

21 The sons of Shelah son of Judah: Er founder of Lecah, Laadah founder of Mareshah, the clans of the guild of 22 linen-workers at Ashbea, Jokim, the men of Kozeba, Joash, and Saraph who fell out with Moab and came back to Bethlehem.[m] (The records are 23 ancient.) They were the potters, and those who lived at Netaim and Gederah were there on the king's service.

24 The sons of Simeon: Nemuel, Jamin, 25 Jarib, Zerah, Saul, his son Shallum, his son Mibsam and his son Mishma. 26 The sons of Mishma: his son Hamuel, his son Zaccur and his son Shimei. 27 Shimei had sixteen sons and six daughters, but others of his family had fewer children, and the clan as a whole did not increase as much as the tribe of 28 Judah. They lived at Beersheba, Mola-

dah, Hazar-shual, Bilhah, Ezem, Tolad, 29 Bethuel, Hormah, Ziklag, Beth-mar- 30,31 caboth, Hazar-susim, Beth-birei, and Shaaraim. These were their cities until David came to the throne. Their settle- 32 ments[n] were Etam, Ain, Rimmon, Tochen, and Ashan, five cities in all. They had also hamlets round these 33 cities as far as Baal. These were the places where they lived.

The names on their register were: Meshobab, Jamlech, Joshah son of 34 Amaziah, Joel, Jehu son of Josibiah, 35 son of Seraiah, son of Asiel, Elioenai, 36 Jaakobah, Jeshohaiah, Asaiah, Adiel, Jesimiel, Benaiah, Ziza son of Shiphi, 37 son of Allon, son of Jedaiah, son of Shimri, son of Shemaiah, whose names 38 are recorded as princes in their clans, and their families had greatly increased. They then went from the approaches 39 to Gedor east of the valley in search of pasture for their flocks. They found 40 rich and good pasture in a wide stretch of open country where everything was quiet and peaceful; before then it had been occupied by Hamites. During 41 the reign of Hezekiah king of Judah these whose names are written above came and destroyed the tribes of Ham[o] and the Meunites whom they found there. They annihilated them so that no trace of them has remained to this day; and they occupied the land in their place, for there was pasture for their flocks. Of their number five 42 hundred Simeonites invaded the hill-country of Seir, led by Pelatiah, Neariah, Rephaiah, and Uzziel, the sons of Ishi. They destroyed all who were left 43 of the surviving Amalekites; and they live there still.

The sons of Reuben, the eldest of 5

j *Or* the Valley of Craftsmen.
k and gave birth to: *prob. rdg.; Heb. om.*
l his: *prob. rdg.; Heb. om.*
m and came ... Bethlehem: *prob. rdg.; Heb. unintelligible.*
n *Prob. rdg.; Heb.* hamlets.
o the tribes of Ham: *prob. rdg., cp. verse 40; Heb.* their tribes.

of the same tribe would vary at different times. In the time of the Chronicler, only the tribe of *Judah* was still organized in anything like the old fashion. For that tribe many materials were available, but they were not reducible to a coherent picture.

4.24–43: The sons of Simeon. *Simeon* had ceased to be a separate tribe long before the Chronicler's time. **41–43:** The military actions and migrations suggested here are not otherwise known.

5.1–26: The tribes east of the Jordan. After three chapters on the descendants of Judah, attention is given much more briefly to the other sons of Israel. **1–10:** Vv. 2–3 explain the order in which the first genealogies are given. The firstborn son (*Reuben*) would normally be

Israel's sons. (He was, in fact, the first son born, but because he had committed incest with a wife of his father's the rank of the eldest was transferred to the sons of Joseph, Israel's son, who, however, could not 2 be registered as the eldest son. Judah held the leading place among his brothers because he fathered a ruler, and the rank of the eldest was his, not[p] Jo- 3 seph's.) The sons of Reuben, the eldest of Israel's sons: Enoch, Pallu, Hezron 4 and Carmi. The sons of Joel: his son Shemaiah, his son Gog, his son Shimei, 5 his son Micah, his son Reaia, his son 6 Baal, his son Beerah, whom Tiglath-pileser king of Assyria carried away into exile; he was a prince of the 7 Reubenites. His kinsmen, family by family, as registered in their tribal lists: 8 Jeiel the chief, Zechariah, Bela son of Azaz, son of Shema, son of Joel. They lived in Aroer, and their lands stretched 9 as far as Nebo and Baal-meon. Eastwards they occupied territory as far as the edge of the desert which stretches from the river Euphrates, for they had large numbers of cattle in Gilead. 10 During Saul's reign they made war on the Hagarites, whom they conquered, occupying their encampments over all the country east of Gilead.

11   Adjoining them were the Gadites, occupying the district of Bashan as far 12 as Salcah: Joel the chief; second in rank, Shapham; then Jaanai and Sha- 13 phat in Bashan. Their fellow-tribesmen belonged to the families of Michael, Meshullam, Sheba, Jorai, Jachan, Zia 14 and Heber, seven in all. These were the sons of Abihail son of Huri, son of Jaroah, son of Gilead, son of Michael, son of Jeshishai, son of Jahdo, son of 15 Buz. Ahi son of Abdiel, son of Guni, 16 was head of their family; they lived in Gilead, in Bashan and its villages, in all the common land of Sharon as far

as it stretched. These registers were 17 all compiled in the reigns of Jotham king of Judah and Jeroboam king of Israel.

The sons of Reuben, Gad, and half 18 the tribe of Manasseh: of their fighting men armed with shield and sword, their archers and their battle-trained soldiers, forty-four thousand seven hundred and sixty were ready for active service. They made war on the Hagar- 19 ites, Jetur, Nephish, and Nodab. They 20 were given help against them, for they cried to their God for help in the battle, and because they trusted him he listened to their prayer, and the Hagarites and all their allies surrendered to them.[q] They drove off their 21 cattle, fifty thousand camels, two hundred and fifty thousand sheep, and two thousand asses, and they took a hundred thousand captives. Many had 22 been killed, for the war was of God's making, and they occupied the land instead of them until the exile.

Half the tribe of Manasseh lived 23 in the land from Bashan to Baal-hermon, Senir, and Mount Hermon, and were numerous also in Lebanon. The heads of their families were: Epher, 24 Ishi, Eliel, Azriel, Jeremiah, Hodaviah, and Jahdiel, all men of ability and repute, heads of their families. But they 25 sinned against the God of their fathers, and turned wantonly to worship the gods of the peoples whom God had destroyed before them. So the God of 26 Israel stirred up Pul king of Assyria, that is Tiglath-pileser king of Assyria, and he carried into exile Reuben, Gad, and half the tribe of Manasseh. He took them to Halah, Habor, Hara, and the river Gozan, where they are to this day.

p his, not: *prob. rdg.; Heb. om.*
q They were . . . surrendered to them: *or* They attacked them boldly, and the Hagarites and all their allies surrendered to them, for they cried . . . to their prayer.

---

given first; but *Judah* had *fathered a ruler*, David, and therefore his genealogy was given first. **4–7:** There are two lists, one giving the succession of sons (vv. 4–6) and one the three contemporary *families* (v. 7). **10:** *Hagarites:* see vv. 18–22. **11–17:** *Gadites:* there are again two lists, one of *families* and one of generations. **17:** These genealogies are brought down to the time of the exile of the Northern Kingdom, the late eighth century; see vv. 6,22,26. The lists are, in fact, not long enough to cover such a period of time. **18–22:** The tribes east of the Jordan had conflicts with north Arabian tribes, *Hagarites,* related to Hagar, Abraham's servant wife; see Gen. ch. 16 and 21.9–21. **23–24:** Eastern *Manasseh:* only *families* are given here; the main genealogy is in 7.14–18. **26:** On the conquest (in 733 B.C.), see 2 Kgs.15.29. *Pul* and *Tiglath-pileser* are different names for the same king.

6 THE SONS OF LEVI: GERSHON,[r] KOHATH
2 and Merari. The sons of Kohath:
Amram, Izhar, Hebron and Uzziel.
3 The children of Amram: Aaron, Moses
and Miriam. The sons of Aaron: Na-
4[s] dab, Abihu, Eleazar and Ithamar. Eleazar was the father of Phinehas, Phinehas
5 father of Abishua, Abishua father of
6 Bukki, Bukki father of Uzzi, Uzzi
father of Zerahiah, Zerahiah father of
7 Meraioth, Meraioth father of Amariah,
8 Amariah father of Ahitub, Ahitub
father of Zadok, Zadok father of Ahi-
9 maaz, Ahimaaz father of Azariah, Azar-
10 iah father of Johanan, and Johanan
father of Azariah, the priest who
officiated in the LORD's house which
11 Solomon built at Jerusalem. Azariah
was the father of Amariah, Amariah
12 father of Ahitub, Ahitub father of
Zadok, Zadok father of Shallum,
13 Shallum father of Hilkiah, Hilkiah
14 father of Azariah, Azariah father of
Seraiah, and Seraiah father of Jehoza-
15 dak. Jehozadak went into exile when
the LORD sent Judah and Jerusalem
into exile under Nebuchadnezzar.

16[t]   The sons of Levi: Gershom, Kohath
17 and Merari. The sons of Gershom:
18 Libni and Shimei. The sons of Kohath:
Amram, Izhar, Hebron and Uzziel.
19 The sons of Merari: Mahli and Mushi.
The clans of Levi, family by family:
20[u] Gershom: his son Libni, his son Jahath,
21 his son Zimmah, his son Joah, his son
Iddo, his son Zerah, his son Jeaterai.
22[v] The sons of Kohath: his son Amminadab, his son Korah, his son Assir,
23 his son Elkanah, his son Ebiasaph,
24 his son Assir, his son Tahath, his son
Uriel, his son Uzziah, his son Saul.
25 The sons of Elkanah: Amasai and
26 Ahimoth, his son Elkanah, his son
27 Zophai, his son Nahath, his son Eliab,
his son Jeroham, his son Elkanah.

The sons of Samuel: Joel the eldest 28
and Abiah the second. The sons of 29
Merari: his son Mahli, his son Libni,
his son Shimei, his son Uzza, his son 30
Shimea, his son Haggiah, his son
Asaiah.

These are the men whom David 31
appointed to take charge of the music
in the house of the LORD when the
Ark should be deposited there. They 32
performed their musical duties before
the Tent of the Presence until Solomon
built the house of the LORD in Jerusalem, and took their regular turns of
duty there. The following, with their 33
descendants, took this duty. Of the
line of Kohath: Heman the musician,
son of Joel, son of Samuel, son of 34
Elkanah, son of Jeroham, son of Eliel,
son of Toah, son of Zuph, son of Elka- 35
nah, son of Mahath, son of Amasai,
son of Elkanah, son of Joel, son of 36
Azariah, son of Zephaniah, son of 37
Tahath, son of Assir, son of Ebiasaph,
son of Korah, son of Izhar, son of 38
Kohath, son of Levi, son of Israel.
Heman's colleague Asaph stood at his 39
right hand. He was the son of Berachiah, son of Shimea, son of Michael, 40
son of Baaseiah, son of Malchiah,
son of Ethni, son of Zerah, son of Ada- 41[w]
iah, son of Ethan, son of Zimmah, 42
son of Shimei, son of Jahath, son of 43
Gershom, son of Levi. On their left 44
stood their colleague of the line of
Merari: Ethan son of Kishi, son of
Abdi, son of Malluch, son of Hashab- 45
iah, son of Amaziah, son of Hilkiah,
son of Amzi, son of Bani, son of 46
Shamer, son of Mahli, son of Mushi, 47
son of Merari, son of Levi. Their 48

r *Gershom in verses 16 and 17.*
s *Verses 4–8: cp. verses 50–53.*
t *Verses 16–19: cp. Exod. 6. 16–19.*
u *Verses 20, 21: cp. verses 41–43.*
v *Verses 22–28: cp. verses 33–38.*
w *Verses 41–43: cp. verses 20, 21.*

6.1–81: The genealogies and settlements of the Levites. The genealogies of the clans of *the Levites* were of as great interest to the Chronicler as the ancestry of David. Among *the sons of Levi, the sons of Aaron* occupied a special place as priests; the rest of the three main clans had other liturgical functions. These lists are genealogies, giving the succession of generations. In chs. 23–26, lists of the same clans are given according to contemporary family groups. **3–15:** The Aaronites are listed to the time of the Judean Exile in 587 B.C. **8:** *Zadok* was not originally an Aaronite, but came to be regarded as such in the late monarchic period; see 2 Sam.8.17 n.; Ezek.44.9–16. **16–30:** Though the organization of the Levites into these three clans was postexilic (with, however, older beginnings), these lists go down only to the time of David. See 23.8–23 n. for other lists of Levites. **23–27:** The fourth *Elkanah* is intended as *Samuel's* father, though it is clear from 1 Sam.1.1 that he was not a Levite. **31–48:** The genealogies of the Chronicler's favorite Levites, the musicians, are full and careful; compare

kinsmen the Levites were dedicated to all the service of the Tabernacle, the house of God.

49 But it was Aaron and his descendants who burnt the sacrifices on the altar of whole-offering and the altar of incense, in fulfilment of all the duties connected with the most sacred gifts, and to make expiation for Israel, exactly as Moses the servant of God had 50[x] commanded. The sons of Aaron: his son Eleazar, his son Phinehas, his son 51 Abishua, his son Bukki, his son Uzzi, 52 his son Zerahiah, his son Meraioth, 53 his son Amariah, his son Ahitub, his son Zadok, his son Ahimaaz.

54 These are their settlements in encampments in the districts assigned to the descendants of Aaron, to the clan of Kohath, for it was to them that the 55 lot had fallen: they gave them Hebron in Judah, with the common land round 56 it, but they assigned to Caleb son of Jephunneh the open country belonging 57[y] to the town and its hamlets. They gave to the sons of Aaron: Hebron the city[z] of refuge, Libnah, Jattir, Eshte- 58,59 moa, Hilen, Debir, Ashan, and Beth-shemesh, each with its common land. 60 And from the tribe of Benjamin: Geba, Alemeth, and Anathoth, each with its common land, making thirteen cities in all by their clans.

61 They gave to the remaining clans of the sons of Kohath ten cities by lot 62 from the half tribe of Manasseh. To the sons of Gershom according to their clans they gave thirteen cities from the tribes of Issachar, Asher, Naphtali, and 63 Manasseh in Bashan. To the sons of Merari according to their clans they gave by lot twelve cities from the tribes of Reuben, Gad, and Zebulun. 64 Israel gave these cities, each with its 65 common land, to the Levites. (The cities mentioned above, from the tribes of Judah, Simeon, and Benjamin, were assigned by lot.)

66 Some of the clans of Kohath had 67 cities allotted[a] to them. They gave them the city[b] of refuge, Shechem in the hill-country of Ephraim, Gezer, 68,69 Jokmeam, Beth-horon, Aijalon, and Gath-rimmon, each with its common land. From the half tribe of Manasseh, 70 Aner and Bileam, each with its common land, were given to the rest of the clans of Kohath.

To the sons of Gershom they gave 71 from the half tribe of Manasseh: Golan in Bashan, and Ashtaroth, each with its common land. From the tribe of 72 Issachar: Kedesh, Daberath, Ramoth, 73 and Anem, each with its common land. From the tribe of Asher: Mashal, 74 Abdon, Hukok, and Rehob, each with 75 its common land. From the tribe of 76 Naphtali: Kedesh in Galilee, Hammon, and Kiriathaim, each with its common land.

To the rest of the sons of Merari they 77 gave from the tribe of Zebulun: Rimmon and Tabor, each with its common land. On the east of Jordan, opposite 78 Jericho, from the tribe of Reuben: Bezer-in-the-wilderness, Jahzah, Kede- 79 moth, and Mephaath, each with its common land. From the tribe of Gad: 80 Ramoth in Gilead, Mahanaim, Hesh- 81 bon, and Jazer, each with its common land.

The sons of Issachar: Tola, Pua, 7 1[c] Jashub and Shimron, four. The sons of 2 Tola: Uzzi, Rephaiah, Jeriel, Jahmai, Jibsam, and Samuel, all able men and heads of families by paternal descent from Tola according to their tribal lists; their number in David's time was twenty-two thousand six hundred. The son of Uzzi: Izrahiah. The sons of 3 Izrahiah: Michael, Obadiah, Joel and Isshiah, making a total of five, all of them chiefs. In addition there were 4 bands of fighting men recorded by families according to the tribal lists to

x *Verses 50–53: cp. verses 4–8.*
y *Verses 57–81: cp. Josh. 21. 13–39.*
z *Prob. rdg., cp. Josh. 21. 13; Heb. cities.*
a *allotted: prob. rdg., cp. Josh. 21. 20; Heb. of their frontier.*
b *Prob. rdg., cp. Josh. 21. 21; Heb. cities.*
c *Verses 1, 6, 13, 30 and 8. 1–5: cp. Gen. 46. 13, 17, 21–24.*

15.16–22; 16.4–42; ch. 25. **49–53:** A second genealogy of *Aaron* shows that the special sacrificial duties passed down to *Zadok*. **54–81:** The Chronicler draws materials concerning the Levite settlements from Josh. ch. 21. In theory there were forty-eight Levite cities (see the numbers in vv. 60–65), but forty-eight names are not given.

7.1 40: The northern tribes. For the remaining tribes, except Benjamin, the Chronicler gives a few generations for each tribe; he emphasizes their military strength at the time David became

the number of thirty-six thousand, for they had many wives and children. 5 Their fellow-tribesmen in all the clans of Issachar were able men, eighty-seven thousand; every one of them was registered.

6 The sons of Benjamin: Bela, Becher 7 and Jediael, three. The sons of Bela: Ezbon, Uzzi, Uzziel, Jerimoth and Iri, five. They were heads of their families and able men; the number registered was twenty-two thousand and thirty-8 four. The sons of Becher: Zemira, Joash, Eliezer, Elioenai, Omri, Jeremoth, Abiah, Anathoth and Alemeth; 9 all these were sons of Becher according to their tribal lists, heads of their families and able men; and the number registered was twenty-thousand two 10 hundred. The son of Jediael: Bilhan. The sons of Bilhan: Jeush, Benjamin, Ehud, Kenaanah, Zethan, Tarshish and 11 Ahishahar. All these were descendants of Jediael, heads of*[d]* families and able men. The number was seventeen thousand two hundred men, fit for active service in war.

12 The sons of Dan:*[e]* Hushim and the sons of Aher.*[f]*

13 The sons of Naphtali: Jahziel, Guni, Jezer, Shallum. These were sons of Bilhah.

14*[g]* The sons of Manasseh,*[h]* born of his concubine, an Aramaean: Machir 15 father of Gilead. Machir married a woman whose name was*[i]* Maacah. The second son was named Zelophehad, and Zelophehad had daughters. 16 Maacah wife of Machir had a son whom she named Peresh. His brother's name was Sheresh, and his sons were 17 Ulam and Rakem. The son of Ulam: Bedan. These were the sons of Gilead 18 son of Machir, son of Manasseh. His sister Hammoleketh was the mother of 19 Ishhod, Abiezer and Mahalah. The sons of Shemida: Ahian, Shechem, Likhi and Aniam.

20 The sons of Ephraim: Shuthelah, his son Bered, his son Tahath, his son

21 Eladah, his son Tahath, his son Zabad, his son Shuthelah. Ephraim's other sons Ezer and Elead were killed by the native Gittites when they came down to lift their cattle. Their father Ephraim 22 long mourned for them, and his kinsmen came to comfort him. Then he had 23 intercourse with his wife; she conceived and had a son whom he named Beriah (because disaster*[j]* had come on his family). He had a daughter named 24 Sherah; she built Lower and Upper Beth-horon and Uzzen-sherah. He also 25 had a son named Rephah; his son was Resheph, his son Telah, his son Tahan, his son Laadan, his son Ammihud, his 26 son Elishama, his son Nun, his son 27 Joshua.

Their lands and settlements were: 28 Bethel and its dependent villages, to the east Naaran, to the west Gezer, Shechem, and Gaza, with their villages. In the possession of Manasseh 29 were Beth-shean, Taanach, Megiddo, and Dor, with their villages. In all of these lived the descendants of Joseph the son of Israel.

The sons of Asher: Imnah, Ishvah, 30 Ishvi and Beriah, together with their sister Serah. The sons of Beriah: Heber 31 and Malchiel father of Birzavith. Heber 32 was the father of Japhlet, Shomer, Hotham, and their sister Shua. The 33 sons of Japhlet: Pasach, Bimhal and Ashvath. These were the sons of Japhlet. The sons of Shomer: Ahi, 34 Rohgah, Jehubbah and Aram. The 35 sons of his brother Hotham:*[k]* Zophah, Imna, Shelesh and Amal. The sons of 36 Zophah: Suah, Harnepher, Shual, Beri, Imrah, Bezer, Hod, Shamma, 37 Shilshah, Ithran and Beera. The sons of 38 Jether: Jephunneh, Pispah and Ara. The sons of Ulla: Arah, Haniel and 39

d Prob. rdg.; Heb. to the heads of.
e The sons of Dan: *prob. rdg., cp. Gen.* 46. 23; *Heb.* And Shuppim and Huppim, the sons of Ir.
f Or another.
g Verses 14–19: cp. Num. 26. 29–33.
h Prob. rdg.; Heb. adds Asriel.
i whose name was: *prob. rdg.; Heb.* to Huppim and Shuppim, and his sister's name was . . .
j Heb. beraah.
k Prob. rdg., cp. verse 32; Heb. Helem.

king; compare ch. 12. As is mostly the case, the numbers are exaggerated. **6:** Instead of *Benjamin*, this is the list for Zebulun, otherwise the only tribe missing. Benjamin is given in ch. 8. **12–13:** Apparently little tradition survived about *Dan* and *Naphtali*. **14:** *Manasseh* is regarded as the grandfather of *Gilead* because of an early colonization of Gilead east of the Jordan by settlers from Manasseh west of it. *Machir* had an *Aramaean* mother because *Gilead* often shared territory with the Aramaeans.

40 Rezia. All these were descendants of Asher, heads of families, picked men of ability, leading princes. They were enrolled among the fighting troops; the total number was twenty-six thousand men.

8 The sons of Benjamin were: the eldest Bela, the second Ashbel, the 2 third Aharah, the fourth Nohah and 3 the fifth Rapha. The sons of Bela: 4 Addar, Gera father of Ehud.[l] Abishua, 5 Naaman, Ahoah, Gera, Shephuphan 6 and Huram. These were the sons of Ehud, heads of families living in Geba, who were removed to Mana- 7 hath: Naaman, Ahiah, and Gera—he it was who removed them. He was the 8 father of Uzza and Ahihud. Shaharaim had sons born to him in Moabite country, after putting away his wives Maha- 9 sham and Baara. By his wife Hodesh he had Jobab, Zibia, Mesha, Malcham, 10 Jeuz, Shachia and Mirmah. These were 11 his sons, heads of families. By Mahasham he had had Abitub and Elpaal. 12 The sons of Elpaal: Eber, Misham, Shamed who built Ono and Lod with 13 its villages, also Beriah and Shema who were heads of families living in Aijalon, having expelled the inhabitants of 14,15 Gath. Ahio, Shashak, Jeremoth, Zeb- 16 adiah, Arad, Ader, Michael, Ispah, 17 and Joha were sons of Beriah; Zeb- 18 adiah, Meshullam, Hezeki, Heber, Ishmerai, Jezliah, and Jobab were sons of 19,20 Elpaal; Jakim, Zichri, Zabdi, Elienai, 21 Zilthai, Eliel, Adaiah, Beraiah, and 22 Shimrath were sons of Shimei; Ishpan, 23 Heber, Eliel, Abdon, Zichri, Hanan, 24,25 Hananiah, Elam, Antothiah, Iphedeiah, and Penuel were sons of Shashak; 26,27 Shamsherai, Shehariah, Athaliah, Jaresiah, Eliah, and Zichri were sons of 28 Jeroham. These were enrolled in the tribal lists as heads of families, chiefs living in Jerusalem.

29[m] Jehiel founder of Gibeon lived at Gibeon; his wife's name was Maacah. 30 His eldest son was Abdon, followed 31 by Zur, Kish, Baal, Nabad, Gedor, 32 Ahio, Zacher and Mikloth. Mikloth was the father of Shimeah; they lived alongside their kinsmen in Jerusalem.

33 Ner was the father of Kish, Kish father of Saul, Saul father of Jonathan, Malchishua, Abinadab and 34 Eshbaal. Jonathan's son was Meribbaal, and he was the father of Micah. 35 The sons of Micah: Pithon, Melech, 36 Tarea and Ahaz. Ahaz was the father of Jehoaddah, Jehoaddah father of Alemeth, Azmoth and Zimri. Zimri 37 was the father of Moza, and Moza father of Binea; his son was Raphah, his son Elasah, and his son Azel. Azel 38 had six sons, whose names were Azrikam, Bocheru, Ishmael, Sheariah, Obadiah and Hanan. All these were sons of Azel. The sons of his brother 39 Eshek: the eldest Ulam, the second Jeush, the third Eliphelet. The sons of 40 Ulam were able men, archers, and had many sons and grandsons, a hundred and fifty. All these were descendants of Benjamin.

The restored community

So ALL ISRAEL WERE REGISTERED AND 9 recorded in the book of the kings of Israel; but Judah for their sins were carried away to exile in Babylon. The 2[n] first to occupy their ancestral land in their cities were lay Israelites, priests, Levites, and temple-servitors. Jerusa- 3 lem was occupied partly by Judahites, partly by Benjamites, and partly by men of Ephraim and Manasseh. Judah- 4 ites:[o] Uthai son of Ammihud, son of Omri, son of Imri, son of Bani, a

l father of Ehud: prob. rdg., cp. Judg. 3. 15; Heb. Abihud.
m Verses 29–38: cp. 9. 35–44.
n Verses 2–22: cp. Neh. 11. 3–22.
o Prob. rdg.; Heb. om.

8.1–40: **Benjamin.** The Chronicler's materials show greater interest in *Benjamin* than in any other of the tribes except Judah and Levi. In the postexilic period much of the former territory of Benjamin was attached to Judah; thus Benjaminites were prominent in the postexilic community around Jerusalem; see 9.7–9 and Neh.7.27–38; 11.7–9. **33–40:** The mention of *Saul* (v. 33) prepares for ch. 10; the Chronicler, however, carries the genealogy through the monarchic period.

9.1–44: **The restored community.** This chapter forms an appendix to chs. 1–8. It lists the families, especially of the Temple personnel, resettled after the Exile. Lists were compiled from sources such as Neh. ch. 11. **1:** *The book of the kings of Israel:* this probably refers to chs. 1–8, understanding that the official tribal lists were once the particular concern of kings.

descendant of Perez son of Judah.
5 Shelanites: Asaiah the eldest and his
6 sons. The sons of Zerah: Jeuel and six
hundred and ninety of their kinsmen.
7 Benjamites: Sallu son of Meshullam,
son of Hodaviah, son of Hassenuah,
8 Ibneiah son of Jeroham, Elah son of
Uzzi, son of Micri, Meshullam son
of Shephatiah, son of Reuel, son of
9 Ibniah, and their recorded kinsmen
numbering nine hundred and fifty-six,
all heads of families.
10   Priests: Jedaiah, Jehoiarib, Jachin,
11 Azariah son of Hilkiah, son of Meshullam, son of Zadok, son of Meraioth,
son of Ahitub, the officer in charge of
12 the house of God, Adaiah son of Jeroham, son of Pashhur, son of Malchiah,
Maasai son of Adiel, son of Jahzerah,
son of Meshullam, son of Meshille-
13 mith, son of Immer, and their colleagues, heads of families numbering
one thousand seven hundred and
sixty, men of substance and fit for the
work connected with the service of the
house of God.
14   Levites: Shemaiah son of Hasshub,
son of Azrikam, son of Hashabiah, a
15 descendant of Merari, Bakbakkar,
Heresh, Galal, Mattaniah son of Mica,
16 son of Zichri, son of Asaph, Obadiah
son of Shemaiah, son of Galal, son of
Jeduthun, and Berechiah son of Asa,
son of Elkanah, who lived in the hamlets of the Netophathites.
17   The door-keepers were Shallum,
Akkub, Talmon, and Ahiman; their
18 brother Shallum was the chief. Until
then they had all been door-keepers in
the quarters of the Levites at the king's
19 gate, on the east. Shallum son of Kore,
son of Ebiasaph, son of Korah, and
his kinsmen of the Korahite family
were responsible for service as guards
of the thresholds of the Tabernacle;
their ancestors had performed the
duty of guarding the entrances to the
20 camp of the LORD. Phinehas son of
Eleazar had been their overseer in the
21 past—the LORD be with him! Zechariah
son of Meshelemiah was the door-
keeper of the Tent of the Presence.
22 Those picked to be door-keepers

numbered two hundred and twelve
in all, registered in their hamlets.
David and Samuel the seer had installed them because they were trustworthy. They and their sons had 23
charge, by watches, of the gates of the
house, the tent-dwelling of the LORD.
The door-keepers were to be on four 24
sides, east, west, north, and south.
Their kinsmen from their hamlets had 25
to come on duty with them for seven
days at a time in turn. The four principal 26
door-keepers were chosen for their
trustworthiness; they were Levites and
had charge of the rooms and the stores
in the house of God. They always slept 27
in the precincts of the house of God
(for the watch was their duty) and they
had charge of the key for opening the
gates every morning. Some of them had 28
charge of the vessels used in the service
of the temple, keeping count of them
as they were brought in and taken out.
Some of them were detailed to take 29
charge of the furniture and all the
sacred vessels, the flour, the wine, the
oil, the incense, and the spices.
   Some of the priests compounded the 30
ointment for the spices. Mattithiah 31
the Levite, the eldest son of Shallum
the Korahite, was in charge of the
preparation of the wafers because he
was trustworthy. Some of their Kohathite kinsmen were in charge of setting 32
out the rows of the Bread of the
Presence every sabbath.
   These, the musicians, heads of 33
Levite families, were lodged in rooms
set apart for them, because they were
liable for duty by day and by night.
   These are the heads of Levite families, 34
chiefs according to their tribal lists,
living in Jerusalem.
   Jehiel founder of Gibeon lived at 35*p*
Gibeon; his wife's name was Maacah,
and his sons were Abdon the eldest, 36
Zur, Kish, Baal, Ner, Nadab, Gedor, 37
Ahio, Zechariah and Mikloth. Mikloth 38
was the father of Shimeam; they lived
alongside their kinsmen in Jerusalem.*q*
Ner was the father of Kish, Kish father 39

p Verses 35–44: cp. 8. 29–38.
q Prob. rdg.; Heb. adds with their kinsmen.

17–32: This attention to *the door-keepers* is out of proportion to that given to the other groups.
The Chronicler esteemed very highly their functions as well as their trustworthiness; compare
ch. 26. **35–44:** A repetition of 8.29–38; it prepares for ch. 10.

of Saul, Saul father of Jonathan, Malchishua, Abinadab and Eshbaal.
40 The son of Jonathan was Meribbaal, and Meribbaal was the father of
41 Micah. The sons of Micah: Pithon,
42 Melech, Tahrea and Ahaz. Ahaz was the father of Jarah, Jarah father of Alemeth, Azmoth, and Zimri; Zimri
43 father of Moza, and Moza father of Binea; his son was Rephaiah, his son
44 Elasah, his son Azel. Azel had six sons, whose names were Azrikam, Bocheru, Ishmael, Sheariah, Obadiah and Hanan. These were the sons of Azel.

The death of Saul

10 1r THE PHILISTINES FOUGHT A BATTLE against Israel, and the men of Israel were routed, leaving their dead on
2 Mount Gilboa. The Philistines hotly pursued Saul and his sons and killed the three sons, Jonathan, Abinadab
3 and Malchishua. The battle went hard for Saul, for some archers came upon him and he was wounded by them.
4 So he said to his armour-bearer, 'Draw your sword and run me through, so that these uncircumcised brutes may not come and make sport of me.' But the armour-bearer refused, he dared not; whereupon Saul took his own sword
5 and fell on it. When the armour-bearer saw that Saul was dead, he too
6 fell on his sword and died. Thus Saul died and his three sons; his whole house
7 perished at one and the same time. And all the Israelites in the Vale, when they saw that their army had fled and that Saul and his sons had perished, fled likewise, abandoning their cities, and

the Philistines went in and occupied them.
Next day, when the Philistines came 8 to strip the slain, they found Saul and his sons lying dead on Mount Gilboa. They stripped him, cut off his head 9 and took away his armour; then they sent messengers through the length and breadth of their land to take the good news to idols and people alike. They deposited his armour in the 10 temple of their god,*s* and nailed up his skull in the temple of Dagon. When 11 the people of Jabesh-gilead heard all that the Philistines had done to Saul, the bravest of them set out together to 12 recover the bodies of Saul and his sons; they brought them back to Jabesh and buried their bones under the oak-tree there, and fasted for seven days. Thus Saul paid with his life for his 13 unfaithfulness: he had disobeyed the word of the LORD and had resorted to ghosts for guidance. He had not sought 14 guidance of the LORD, who therefore destroyed him and transferred the kingdom to David son of Jesse.

David king over Israel

THEN ALL ISRAEL ASSEMBLED AT HEBRON 11 1t to wait upon David. 'We are your own flesh and blood', they said. 'In the past, 2 while Saul was still king, you led the forces of Israel to war, and you brought them home again. And the LORD your God said to you, "You shall be shepherd of my people Israel,

r *Verses 1–12: cp. 1 Sam. 31. 1–13.*
s *Or gods.*
t *Verses 1–9: cp. 2 Sam. 5. 1–3, 6–10.*

10.1–12.40: David established as king. The first block of David materials (see Introduction) shows how Israel unanimously acknowledged David's kingship. Materials drawn from 1 and 2 Sam. were reorganized to give the following sequence: death of Saul; David made king of Israel at Hebron; the capture of Jerusalem, which becomes David's capital; and an enumeration of the chiefs and heroes who made David king (chs. 10–11). Additional lists of warriors and of military contingents from the twelve tribes (ch. 12) are given from sources other than 1 and 2 Sam.

10.1–14: Saul is removed. The account of Saul's death is taken from 1 Sam. ch. 31. The circumstances leading to the death scene, so richly developed there, are ignored by the Chronicler here. He treats Saul as only an obstacle to David's kingship. **6:** Saul's *whole house* did not perish at the battle of Gilboa (2 Sam.2.8–10; ch. 9). However, the Chronicler does not narrate the subsequent demise of that house (see 2 Sam.21.1–14). **13–14:** This is the Chronicler's succinct summary. He knew of the accounts in 1 Sam. chs. 15 and 28 but omitted them.

11.1–9: David, as king, takes Jerusalem. The Chronicler retains his excerpts from 2 Sam. in the order in which they appear in that book (5.1–3,6–10; 23.8–39), even though his own additions (ch. 12) pertain to slightly earlier events. He organized his material more by topic

3 you shall be their prince."' All the elders of Israel came to the king at Hebron; there David made a covenant with them before the LORD, and they anointed David king over Israel, as the LORD had said through the lips of Samuel.

4 Then David and all Israel went to Jerusalem (that is Jebus, where the Jebusites, the inhabitants of the land, 5 lived). The people of Jebus said to David, 'Never shall you come in here'; none the less David did capture the stronghold of Zion, and it is now known 6 as the City of David. David said, 'The first man to kill a Jebusite shall become a commander or an officer', and the first man to go up was Joab son of Zeruiah; so he was given the command.

7 David took up his residence in the stronghold: that is why they called it 8 the City of David. He built the city round it, starting at the Millo and including its neighbourhood, while Joab reconstructed the rest of the city. 9 So David steadily grew stronger, for the LORD of Hosts was with him.

10*u* Of David's heroes these were the chief, men who lent their full strength to his government and, with all Israel, joined in making him king; such was 11 the LORD's decree for Israel. First came Jashobeam the Hachmonite, chief of the three; he it was who brandished his spear over three hundred, all 12 slain at one time. Next to him was Eleazar son of Dodo the Ahohite, one 13 of the heroic three. He was with David at Pas-dammim where the Philistines had gathered for battle in a field carrying a good crop of barley; and when the people had fled from the Philistines 14 he stood his ground in the field, saved it*v* and defeated them. So the LORD brought about a great victory.

15 Three of the thirty chiefs went down to the rock to join David at the cave of Adullam, while the Philistines were encamped in the Vale of Rephaim. At that time David was in the strong- 16 hold, and a Philistine garrison held Bethlehem. One day a longing came 17 over David, and he exclaimed, 'If only I could have a drink of water from the well*w* by the gate of Bethlehem!' At this the three made their way through 18 the Philistine lines and drew water from the well by the gate of Bethlehem, and brought it to David. But David refused to drink it; he poured it out to the LORD and said, 'God forbid that I 19 should do such a thing! Can I drink the blood of these men? They have brought it at the risk of their lives.' So he would not drink it. Such were the exploits of the heroic three.

Abishai the brother of Joab was 20 chief of the thirty. He once brandished his spear over three hundred dead, and he was famous among the thirty. He held higher rank than the 21 rest of the thirty and became their captain, but he did not rival the three. Benaiah son of Jehoiada, from Kab- 22 zeel, was a hero of many exploits. It was he who smote the two champions of Moab, and who went down into a pit and killed a lion on a snowy day. It 23 was he who also killed the Egyptian, a giant seven and a half feet high armed with a spear as big as the beam of a loom; he went to meet him with a club, snatched the spear out of the Egyptian's hand and killed him with his own weapon. Such were the exploits 24 of Benaiah son of Jehoiada, famous among the heroic thirty.*x* He was more 25 famous than the rest of the thirty, but did not rival the three. David appointed him to his household.

u Verses 10–41: cp. 2 Sam. 23. 8–39.
v saved it: or cleared it of the Philistines.
w Or cistern.
x Prob. rdg.; Heb. three.

than by chronology. **3:** The reference to *Samuel*'s prophecy is an addition to the excerpt from 2 Sam. **5–6:** The text simplifies some textual problems in 2 Sam.5.6–8. **8:** *Joab:* an addition to the Samuel source.
    11.10–47: David's warrior heroes. The Chronicler uses the list of David's heroes from 2 Sam. ch. 23 without significant change but with a new purpose, expressed in v. 10. **10–14:** The Chronicler omits the third of *the three*, Shammah (2 Sam.23.11). **15–19:** The confusion as to whether these were *three of the thirty chiefs* (v. 15) or *the heroic three* (v. 19) derives from the source in 2 Sam.23.13–17. *The heroic three* is most likely meant. **20–21:** The *thirty* and *three* reflect a ten-to-one ratio among commanders, similar to that employed in the administration of the labor forces; compare 1 Kgs.5.16 n. **25:** David's *household* is enumerated in 18.14–17.

26 These were his valiant heroes: Asahel the brother of Joab, and Elhanan 27 son of Dodo from Bethlehem; Shammoth from Harod," and Helez from a 28 place unknown; Ira son of Ikkesh from Tekoa, and Abiezer from Anathoth; 29 Sibbecai from Hushah, and Ilai the 30 Ahohite; Maharai from Netophah, and Heled son of Baanah from Neto- 31 phah; Ithai son of Ribai from Gibeah of Benjamin, and Benaiah from Pira- 32 thon; Hurai from the ravines of Gaash, 33 and Abiel from Beth-arabah; Azmoth from Bahurim, and Eliahba from Shaal- 34 bon; Hashem the Gizonite, and Jonathan son of Shage the Hararite; 35 Ahiam son of Sacar the Hararite, and 36 Eliphal son of Ur; Hepher from Mecherah, and Ahijah from a place 37 unknown; Hezro from Carmel, and 38 Naari son of Ezbai; Joel the brother of Nathan, and Mibhar the son of Hag- 39 geri; Zelek the Ammonite, and Naharai from Beeroth, armour-bearer to 40 Joab son of Zeruiah; Ira the Ithrite, 41 and Gareb the Ithrite; Uriah the Hit- 42 tite, and Zabad son of Ahlai. Adina son of Shiza the Reubenite, a chief of the Reubenites, was over these thirty. 43 Also Hanan son of Maacah, and Josh- 44 aphat the Mithnite; Uzzia from Ashtaroth, Shama and Jeiel the sons of 45 Hotham from Aroer; Jediael son of Shimri, and Joha his brother, the 46 Tizite; Eliel the Mahavite, and Jeribai and Joshaviah sons of Elnaam, and 47 Ithmah the Moabite; Eliel, Obed, and Jasiel, from Zobah.*z*

12 These are the men who joined David at Ziklag while he was banned from the presence of Saul son of Kish. They ranked among the warriors 2 valiant in battle. They carried bows and could sling stones or shoot arrows with the left hand or the right; they were Benjamites, kinsmen of Saul. The 3 foremost were Ahiezer and Joash, the sons of Shemaah the Gibeathite; Jeziel and Pelet, men of Beth-azmoth; Berachah and Jehu of Anathoth; Ishmaiah 4 the Gibeonite, a hero among the thirty and a chief among them; Jeremiah, Jahaziel, Johanan, and Josabad of Gederah; Eluzai, Jerimoth, Bealiah, 5 Shemariah, and Shephatiah the Haruphite; Elkanah, Isshiah, Azareel, 6 Joezer, Jashobeam, the Korahites; and Joelah and Zebadiah sons of 7 Jeroham, of Gedor.

Some Gadites also joined David at 8 the stronghold in the wilderness, valiant men trained for war, who could handle the heavy shield and spear, grim as lions and swift as gazelles on the hills. Ezer was their chief, Obadiah the 9 second, Eliab the third; Mishmannah 10 the fourth and Jeremiah the fifth; Attai 11 the sixth and Eliel the seventh; Jo- 12 hanan the eighth and Elzabad the ninth; Jeremiah the tenth and Mach- 13 banai the eleventh. These were chiefs 14 of the Gadites in the army, the least of them a match for a hundred, the greatest a match for a thousand. These 15 were the men who in the first month crossed the Jordan, which was in full flood in all its reaches, and wrought havoc in the valleys, east and west.

Some men of Benjamin and Judah 16 came to David at the stronghold. David 17 went out to them and said, 'If you come as friends to help me, join me and welcome; but if you come to betray me to my enemies, innocent though I am of any crime of violence, may the God of our fathers see and judge.' At 18

y Prob. rdg., cp. 2 Sam. 23. 25; Heb. Haror.
z from Zobah: prob. rdg.; Heb. obscure.

26-41: *Valiant heroes:* thirty-one names are from 2 Sam.23.24–39, where it is said (v. 39) that there were thirty-seven heroes in all. **42–47:** Sixteen names are added by the Chronicler from another source. If a group of thirty leading warriors was maintained constantly over a period of many years, far more than just thirty men would have been required. The longer list may reflect that fact.

12.1–40: The contingents that came to David. The Chronicler's purpose is to show a progressive transfer of allegiance to David on the part of Israel's military forces. There are five stages in the process; the Chronicler supplies a list of warriors for each, except the third. **1–7:** The first contingent. While David was at *Ziklag* (as a vassal of Achish, king of Gath; see 1 Sam. ch. 27), some of Saul's own best warriors joined him. **8–15:** The second contingent. *The stronghold* where David was a fugitive (1 Sam.22.4) was near Moab. The territory of the *Gadites* was north of Moab in Transjordan. **15:** The Gadites had to cross *the Jordan* to reach Judah. On the flood in *the first month*, see Josh.3.15; 4.19. **16–18:** The third contingent: *men of Benjamin and Judah.* No list is given here, but the unqualified devotion of the new supporters

that a spirit took possession of Amasai, the chief of the thirty, and he said:

We are on your side, David!
We are with you, son of Jesse!
Greetings, greetings to you
and greetings to your ally!
For your God is your ally.

So David welcomed them and attached them to the columns of his raiding parties.

19 Some men of Manasseh had deserted to David when he went with the Philistines to war against Saul, though he did not, in fact, fight on the side of the Philistines. Their princes brusquely dismissed him, saying to themselves that he would desert them for his master Saul, and that would cost them 20 their heads. The men of Manasseh who deserted to him when he went to Ziklag were these: Adnah, Jozabad, Jediael, Michael, Jozabad, Elihu, and Zilthai, each commanding his thousand in 21 Manasseh. It was they who stood valiantly by David against the raiders, for they were all good fighters, and they were given commands in his forces. 22 From day to day men came in to help David, until he had gathered an immense army.

23 These are the numbers of the armed bands which joined David at Hebron to transfer Saul's sovereignty to him, 24 as the LORD had said: men of Judah, bearing heavy shield and spear, six thousand eight hundred, drafted for 25 active service; of Simeon, fighting men drafted for active service, seven 26 thousand one hundred; of Levi, four 27 thousand six hundred, together with Jehoiada prince of the house of Aaron and three thousand seven hundred men, 28 and Zadok a valiant fighter, with twenty-29 two officers of his own clan; of Benjamin, Saul's kinsmen, three thousand, though most of them had hitherto remained loyal to the house of Saul; 30 of Ephraim, twenty thousand eight hundred, fighting men, famous in their 31 own clans; of the half tribe of Manasseh, eighteen thousand, who had been nominated to come and make David 32 king; of Issachar, whose tribesmen were skilled in reading the signs of the times to discover what course Israel should follow, two hundred chiefs, with all their kinsmen under their 33 command; of Zebulun, fifty thousand troops well-drilled for battle, armed with every kind of weapon, bold and 34 single-minded; of Naphtali, a thousand officers with thirty-seven thousand men bearing heavy shield and spear; 35 of the Danites, twenty-eight thousand 36 six hundred well-drilled for battle; of Asher, forty thousand troops well-37 drilled for battle; of the Reubenites and the Gadites and the half tribe of Manasseh east of Jordan, a hundred and twenty thousand, armed with every kind of weapon.

38 All these warriors, bold men in battle, came to Hebron, loyally determined to make David king over the whole of Israel; the rest of Israel, too, had but one thought, to make him king. 39 They spent three days there with David, eating and drinking, for their kinsmen 40 made provision for them. Their neighbours also round about, as far away as Issachar, Zebulun, and Naphtali, brought food on asses and camels, on mules and oxen, supplies of meal, fig-cakes, raisin-cakes, wine and oil, oxen and sheep, in plenty; for there was rejoicing in Israel.

DAVID CONSULTED THE OFFICERS OVER **13** units of a thousand and a hundred on every matter brought forward. Then he 2 said to the whole assembly of Israel, 'If you approve, and if the LORD our

---

is emphasized. **19–22:** The fourth contingent. When the crisis between Saul and the Philistines reached its height (1 Sam. ch. 29), more of Saul's followers, in this case *men of Manasseh*, went over to David at *Ziklag* and aided against *the raiders*; see 1 Sam. ch. 30. **23–37:** The fifth contingent. After Saul's death, all Israel came over to *David at Hebron* (see 2 Sam.5.1–5). Thus, the Chronicler gives a list of forces from all twelve tribes (plus contingents of Levites and priests, vv. 26–28). Old data from muster lists of Israelite militia (possibly in the time of Josiah) probably lie behind the list. The terms *thousand* and *hundred* were originally conventional terms for military units, not actual numbers.

13.1–16.43: The Ark is established in Jerusalem. The second block of Davidic material (see Introduction) turns to David's establishing the proper service of the LORD in Jerusalem. In

God opens a way, let us[a] send to our kinsmen who have stayed behind, in all the districts of Israel, and also to the priests and Levites in the cities where they have common lands, bidd-3 ing them join us. Let us fetch the Ark of our God, for while Saul lived we 4 never resorted to it.' The whole assembly resolved to do this; the entire nation approved it.

5 So David assembled all Israel from the Shihor in Egypt to Lebo-hamath, in order to fetch the Ark of God from 6[b] Kiriath-jearim. Then David and all Israel went up to Baalah, to Kiriath-jearim, which belonged to Judah, to fetch the Ark of God, the LORD enthroned upon the cherubim, the Ark 7 which bore his name.[c] And they conveyed the Ark of God on a new cart from the house of Abinadab, with 8 Uzza and Ahio guiding the cart. David and all Israel danced for joy before God without restraint to the sound of singing, of harps and lutes, of tambourines, and cymbals and trumpets. 9 But when they came to the threshing-floor of Kidon, the oxen stumbled, and Uzza put out his hand to hold the 10 Ark. The LORD was angry with Uzza and struck him down because he had put out his hand to the Ark. So he died 11 there before God. David was vexed because the LORD's anger had broken out upon Uzza, and he called the place Perez-uzza,[d] the name it still 12 bears. David was afraid of God that day and said, 'How can I harbour the Ark 13 of God after this?' So he did not take the Ark with him into the City of David, but turned aside and carried it to the 14 house of Obed-edom the Gittite. Thus the Ark of God remained beside the house of Obed-edom, in its tent,[e] for three months, and the LORD blessed the family of Obed-edom and all that he had.

141[f] Hiram king of Tyre sent an embassy to David; he sent cedar logs, and masons and carpenters with them to build him a house. David knew by now 2 that the LORD had confirmed him as king over Israel and had made his royal power stand higher for the sake of his people Israel.

David married more wives in Jeru-3 salem, and more sons and daughters were born to him. These are the names 4[g] of the children born to him in Jerusalem: Shammua, Shobab, Nathan, Solomon, Ibhar, Elishua, Elpelet, 5 Nogah, Nepheg, Japhia, Elishama, 6,7 Beeliada and Eliphelet.

When the Philistines learnt that 8 David had been anointed king over the whole of Israel, they came up in force to seek him out. David, hearing of this, went out to face them. Now 9 the Philistines had come and raided the Vale of Rephaim. So David in-10 quired of God, 'If I attack the Philistines, wilt thou deliver them into my hands?' And the LORD answered, 'Go; I will deliver them into your hands.' So he went up and attacked them at 11 Baal-perazim and defeated them there. 'God has used me to break through my enemies' lines,' David said, 'as a river breaks its banks'; that is why the place was named Baal-perazim.[h] The 12 Philistines left their gods behind them there, and by David's orders these were burnt.

The Philistines made another raid 13 on the Vale. Again David inquired of 14 God, and God said to him, 'No, you must go up towards their rear; wheel round without making contact and[i] come upon them opposite the aspens.

a and if... let us: *or* and if it is from the LORD our God, let us seize the opportunity and ...
b Verses 6–14: cp. 2 Sam. 6. 2–11.
c which bore his name: *prob. rdg.; Heb. obscure.*
d *That is* Outbreak on Uzza.
e *Or* in his tent.
f Verses 1–16: cp. 2 Sam. 5. 11–25.
g Verses 4–7: cp. 3. 5–8.
h *That is* Baal of Break-through.
i No ... contact and: *or* Do not go up to the attack; withdraw from them and then ...

---

2 Sam. ch. 6 the two movements of the Ark are related successively. The Chronicler retains the first movement without change (13.5–14) but inserts other materials from 2 Sam. ch. 14 before the second movement (chs. 15–16). He elaborates the second movement with special materials of his own.
    13.1–14: The first movement of the Ark. The Chronicler adds his own introduction, vv. 1–4, which emphasizes the unison of Israel's action; the main account, however, simply follows 2 Sam.6.2–11.
    14.1–17: David secures his position. This chapter is mostly drawn from 2 Sam., but the Chronicler inserts it between the two Ark movements. 4–7: Compare 3.1–9 n.

15 Then, as soon as you hear a rustling sound in the tree-tops, you shall give battle, for God will have gone out before you to defeat the Philistine army.' 16 David did as God commanded, and they drove the Philistine army in flight 17 all the way from Gibeon to Gezer. So David's fame spread through every land, and the LORD inspired all nations with dread of him.

15 DAVID BUILT HIMSELF QUARTERS IN THE City of David, and prepared a place for the Ark of God and pitched a tent 2 for it. Then he decreed that only Levites should carry the Ark of God, since they had been chosen by the LORD to carry it and to serve him^j for ever. 3 Next David assembled all Israel at Jerusalem, to bring up the Ark of the LORD to the place he had prepared for 4 it. He gathered together the sons of 5 Aaron and the Levites: of the sons of Kohath, Uriel the chief with a hundred 6 and twenty of his kinsmen; of the sons of Merari, Asaiah the chief with two hundred and twenty of his kins- 7 men; of the sons of Gershom, Joel the chief with a hundred and thirty of his 8 kinsmen; of the sons of Elizaphan, Shemaiah the chief with two hundred 9 of his kinsmen; of the sons of Hebron, Eliel the chief with eighty of his kins- 10 men; of the the sons of Uzziel, Amminadab the chief with a hundred and 11 twelve of his kinsmen. And David summoned Zadok and Abiathar the priests, together with the Levites, Uriel, Asaiah, Joel, Shemaiah, Eliel, and 12 Amminadab, and said to them, 'You who are heads of families of the Levites, hallow yourselves, you and your kinsmen, and bring up the Ark of the LORD the God of Israel to the 13 place which I have prepared for it. It was because you were not present the

first time, that the LORD our God broke out upon us. For we had not sought his guidance as we should have done.' So the priests and the Levites 14 hallowed themselves to bring up the Ark of the LORD the God of Israel, and 15 the Levites carried the Ark of God, bearing it on their shoulders with poles as Moses had prescribed at the command of the LORD.

David also ordered the chiefs of the 16 Levites to install as musicians those of their kinsmen who were players skilled in making joyful music on their instruments, lutes and harps and cymbals. So the Levites installed Heman 17 son of Joel and, from his kinsmen, Asaph son of Berechiah; and from their kinsmen the Merarites, Ethan son of Kushaiah, together with their kins- 18 men of the second degree, Zechariah, Jaaziel, Shemiramoth, Jehiel, Unni, Eliab, Benaiah, Maaseiah, Mattithiah, Eliphelehu, and Mikneiah, and the door-keepers Obed-edom and Jeiel. They installed the musicians Heman, 19 Asaph, and Ethan to sound the cymbals of bronze; Zechariah, Jaaziel, 20 Shemiramoth, Jehiel, Unni, Eliab, Maaseiah, and Benaiah to play on lutes;^k Mattithiah, Eliphelehu, Mik- 21 neiah, Obed-edom, Jeiel, and Azaziah to play on harps.^l Kenaniah, officer 22 of the Levites, was precentor in charge of the music because of his proficiency. Berechiah and Elkanah were door- 23 keepers for the Ark, while the priests Shebaniah, Jehoshaphat, Nethaneel, 24 Amasai, Zechariah, Benaiah, and Eliezer sounded the trumpets before the Ark of God; and Obed-edom and Jehiah also were door-keepers for the Ark.

j Or it.
k Prob. rdg.; Heb. adds al alamoth, possibly a musical term.
l Prob. rdg.; Heb. adds al hashsheminith lenasseah, possibly musical terms.

15.1–16.43: The Ark and its Levitical service. The account of the bringing up of the Ark in 2 Sam.6.12–19 is greatly expanded by the Chronicler's interest in the Levites, and especially the Levitical musicians. **1–15:** In the Chronicler's view, the outbreak of the LORD against Uzza in 13.7–11 was because the Levites were not carrying the Ark; see v. 13. Therefore, on the second attempt to bring up the Ark, the Levites had to carry it. **4–10:** Normally there are only three families of Levites, not six; compare 6.16–30; 23.6–23. *Hebron* and *Uzziel* appear as sons of *Kohath*, 6.18; 23.12; and, more rarely, *Elizaphan* is listed as a son of Uzziel, Lev.10.4 (here spelled "Elzaphan"); Num.3.30; 2 Chr.29.13. **16–24:** The provision for carefully defined groups of musicians is a late development, mostly from the postexilic organization of the Temple, though based on older monarchic practice. Vv. 17–18 give the basic list, vv. 19–24 supplementary lists and comments. The lists are not completely consistent with each other.

25[m] Then David and the elders of Israel and the captains of units of a thousand went to bring up the Ark of the Covenant of the LORD with much rejoicing from the house of Obed-
26 edom. Because God had helped the Levites who carried the Ark of the Covenant of the LORD, they sacrificed seven bulls and seven rams.
27 Now David and all the Levites who carried the Ark, and the musicians, and Kenaniah the precentor,[n] were arrayed in robes of fine linen; and
28 David had on a linen ephod. All Israel escorted the Ark of the Covenant of the LORD with shouts of acclamation, blowing on horns and trumpets, clashing cymbals and playing on
29 lutes and harps. But as the Ark of the Covenant of the LORD was entering the city of David, Saul's daughter Michal looked down through a window and saw King David dancing and making merry, and she despised him in her heart.

16 1[o] When they had brought in the Ark of God, they put it inside the tent that David had pitched for it, and they offered whole-offerings and shared-
2 offerings before God. After David had completed these sacrifices, he blessed the people in the name of the LORD
3 and gave food, a loaf of bread, a portion of meat, and a cake of raisins, to each
4 Israelite, man or woman. He appointed certain Levites to serve before the Ark of the LORD, to repeat the Name, to confess and to praise the LORD the
5 God of Israel. Their leader was Asaph; second to him was Zechariah; then came Jaaziel,[p] Shemiramoth, Jehiel, Mattithiah, Eliab, Benaiah, Obed-edom, and Jeiel, with lutes and harps, Asaph, who sounded the cymbals;
6 and Benaiah and Jahaziel the priests, who blew the trumpets before the

Ark of the Covenant of God continuously throughout that day. It was 7 then that David first ordained the offering of thanks to the LORD by Asaph and his kinsmen:

Give the LORD thanks and invoke 8[q]
    him by name,
make his deeds known in the world
    around.
Pay him honour with song and 9
    psalm
and think upon all his wonders.
Exult in his hallowed name; 10
    let those who seek the LORD be
    joyful in heart.
Turn to the LORD, your strength,[r] 11
seek his presence always.
Remember the wonders that he 12
    has wrought,
his portents and the judgements
    he has given,
O offspring of Israel his servants, O 13
    chosen sons of Jacob.

He is the LORD our God; 14
    his judgements fill the earth.
He called to mind his covenant 15
    from long ago,[s]
the promise he extended to a
    thousand generations—
    the covenant made with Abraham, 16
    his oath given to Isaac,
the decree by which he bound 17
    himself for Jacob,
his everlasting covenant with
    Israel:
'I will give you the land of 18
    Canaan', he said,
    'to be your possession, your
    patrimony.'

m Verses 25–29: cp. 2 Sam. 6. 12–16.
n the precentor: prob. rdg.; Heb. obscure.
o Verses 1–3: cp. 2 Sam. 6. 17–19.
p Prob. rdg., cp. 15. 18, 20; Heb. Jeiel.
q Verses 8–22: cp. Ps. 105. 1–15.
r your strength: or the symbol of his strength; lit. and his strength.
s from long ago: or for ever.

15.25–16.3: After the liturgical arrangements, the Ark is brought in. 2 Sam. 6.12–19 is revised.
26: The Chronicler makes *the Levites* the reason for the sacrifices. **27:** In the Chronicler's version, all the officiants wear ritual garments and David's modesty is preserved; contrast 2 Sam.6.14,20. **29:** *Michal*'s motives are eliminated here; compare 2 Sam.6.20. **16.4–36:** There were three guilds of Levitical musicians; those of Heman, *Asaph*, and Ethan or Jeduthun (6.33–47; 15.17–18; 25.1–8). Only that of *Asaph*, however, was assigned to the service of the Ark because, from the Chronicler's viewpoint, the other two guilds were still serving at the Tabernacle in Gibeon; see vv. 39–42. **5–6:** Including the two *priests, who blew trumpets,* twelve musicians are listed. On the *trumpets,* see Num.10.1–10. **7:** The Chronicler is familiar with a regular order of *offering of thanks* at the Temple, an order attributed to David. **8–36:** The Chronicler or one of his sources composed a hymn of praise by drawing on parts of hymns now

19   A small company it was,
         few in number, strangers in that
              land,
20   roaming from nation to nation,
         from one kingdom to another;
21   but he let no man ill-treat them,
         for their sake he admonished
              kings:
22   'Touch not my anointed servants,
         do my prophets no harm.'

23[t] Sing to the LORD, all men on earth,
         proclaim his triumph day by day.
24   Declare his glory among the
              nations,
         his marvellous deeds among all
              peoples.
25   Great is the LORD and worthy of all
              praise;
         he is more to be feared than all
              gods.
26   For the gods of the nations are
              idols every one;
         but the LORD made the heavens.
27   Majesty and splendour attend
              him,
         might and joy are in his dwelling.

28   Ascribe to the LORD, you families
              of nations,
         ascribe to the LORD glory and
              might;
29   ascribe to the LORD the glory due
              to his name,
         bring a gift and come before him.
         Bow down to the LORD in the
              splendour of holiness,[u]
30   and dance in his honour, all
              men on earth.
         He has fixed the earth firm,
              immovable.
31   Let the heavens rejoice and the
              earth exult,
         let men declare among the nations,
              'The LORD is king.'
32   Let the sea roar and all the creatures
              in it,
         let the fields exult and all that is
              in them;
33   then let the trees of the forest
              shout for joy

         before the LORD when he comes to
              judge the earth.

         It is good to give thanks to the   34[v]
              LORD,
         for his love endures for ever.
         Cry, 'Deliver us, O God our   35[w]
              saviour,
         gather us in and save us from the
              nations
         that we may give thanks to thy
              holy name
         and make thy praise our pride.'

         Blessed be the LORD the God of   36
              Israel
         from everlasting to everlasting.

And all the people said 'Amen' and
'Praise the LORD.'
David left Asaph and his kinsmen   37
there before the Ark of the Covenant
of the LORD, to perform regular service
before the Ark as each day's duty required; as door-keepers he left Obed- 38
edom son of Jeduthun, and Hosah.
(Obed-edom and his kinsmen were
sixty-eight in number.) He left Zadok 39
the priest and his kinsmen the priests
before the Tabernacle of the LORD
at the hill-shrine in Gibeon, to make 40
offerings there to the LORD upon the
altar of whole-offering regularly morning and evening, exactly as it is written
in the law enjoined by the LORD upon
Israel. With them he left Heman and   41
Jeduthun and the other men chosen
and nominated to give thanks to the
LORD, 'for his love endures for ever.'
They had trumpets and cymbals for   42
the players, and the instruments used
for sacred song. The sons of Jeduthun
kept the gate.
So all the people went home, and   43
David returned to greet his household.

AS SOON AS DAVID WAS ESTABLISHED IN   17 1[x]
his house, he said to Nathan the

t Verses 23–33: cp. Ps. 96. 1–13.
u Or in holy vestments.
v Verse 34: cp. Ps. 107. 1.
w Verses 35, 36: cp. Ps. 106. 47, 48.
x Verses 1–27: cp. 2 Sam. 7. 1–29.

contained in the canonical book of Psalms. Only a concluding note of lamentation (v. 35)
suggests a different mood. **37–42:** From the Chronicler's viewpoint, the service of the Mosaic
Tabernacle was still in *Gibeon* while the new Davidic service of *the Ark* was in Jerusalem.
The two services were to be merged in Solomon's time; see 2 Chr.1.2–6; 5.4.
   17.1–27: The LORD establishes David's house. The remaining two blocks of material con-

prophet, 'Here I live in a house of cedar, while the Ark of the Covenant of the LORD is housed in curtains.'

2 Nathan answered David, 'Do whatever you have in mind, for God is with

3 you.' But that night the word of God

4 came to Nathan: 'Go and say to David my servant, "This is the word of the LORD: It is not you who shall build

5 me a house to dwell in. Down to this day I have never dwelt in a house since I brought Israel up from Egypt; I lived in a tent and a tabernacle.*y*

6 Wherever I journeyed with Israel, did I ever ask any of the judges whom I appointed shepherds of my people why they had not built me a house of

7 cedar?" Then say this to my servant David: "This is the word of the LORD of Hosts: I took you from the pastures, and from following the sheep, to be

8 prince over my people Israel. I have been with you wherever you have gone, and have destroyed all the enemies in your path. I will make you as famous

9 as the great ones of the earth. I will assign a place for my people Israel; there I will plant them, and they shall dwell in their own land. They shall be disturbed no more, never again shall wicked men wear them down as they

10 did from the time when I first appointed judges over Israel my people, and I will subdue all your enemies. But I will make you great and the LORD shall

11 build up your royal house. When your life ends and you go to join your forefathers, I will set up one of your family, one of your own sons, to succeed you, and I will establish his

12 kingdom. It is he shall build me a house, and I will establish his throne for

13 all time. I will be his father, and he shall be my son. I will never withdraw my love from him as I withdrew it from

14 your predecessor. But I will give him a sure place in my house and kingdom for all time, and his throne shall be established for ever."'

15 Nathan recounted to David all that had been said to him and all that had

16 been revealed. Then King David went into the presence of the LORD and took his place there and said, 'What am I, LORD God, and what is my family, that thou hast brought me thus far?

17 It was a small thing in thy sight, O God, to have planned for thy servant's house in days long past, and now thou lookest upon me as a man already embarked on a high career, O LORD

18 God. What more can David say to thee of the honour thou hast done thy servant, well though thou knowest

19 him? For the sake of thy servant, LORD, and according to thy purpose, thou hast brought me to all this

20 greatness. O LORD, we have never heard of one like thee; there is no god

21 but thee. And thy people Israel, to whom can they be compared? Is there any other nation on earth whom God has gone out to redeem from slavery, to make them his people? Thou hast won a name for thyself by great and terrible deeds, driving out nations before thy people whom thou didst redeem from Egypt. Thou hast made

22 thy people Israel thy own for ever, and thou, O LORD, hast become their

23 God. But now, LORD, let what thou hast promised for thy servant and his house stand fast for all time; make good what

24 thou hast said. Let it stand fast, that thy fame may be great for ever, and let men say, "The LORD of Hosts, the God of Israel, is Israel's God." So shall the house of thy servant David be estab-

25 lished before thee. Thou, my God, hast shown me thy purpose to build up thy servant's house; therefore I have

26 been able to pray before thee. Thou, O LORD, art God, and thou hast made these noble promises to thy servant;

27 thou hast been pleased to bless thy servant's house, that it may continue always before thee; thou it is who hast blessed it, and it shall be blessed for ever.'

y I lived ... tabernacle: *prob. rdg.; Heb.* I have been from tent to tent and from a tabernacle.

cerning David (chs. 18–20, 21–29) are introduced by ch. 17. 2 Sam. ch. 7 is drawn on to show that David was a man of war (the motif presented in chs. 18–20) and that, consequently, not he but his son would build the LORD's house. Nevertheless, David makes all the preparations for the Temple (chs. 21–29). This latter view is stated explicitly in the Chronicler's speech in 22.7–10. Contrast ch. 17 with 2 Sam. ch. 24.

18 1² After this David defeated the Philistines and conquered them, and took 2 from them Gath with its villages; he defeated the Moabites, and they became subject to him and paid him 3 tribute. He also defeated Hadadezer king of Zobah-hamath, who was on his way to set up a monument of 4 victory by the river Euphrates. From him David captured a thousand chariots, seven thousand horsemen and twenty thousand foot; he hamstrung all the chariot-horses, except a 5 hundred which he retained. When the Aramaeans of Damascus came to the help of Hadadezer king of Zobah, David destroyed twenty-two thousand 6 of them, and established garrisons among these Aramaeans; they became subject to him and paid him tribute. Thus the LORD gave David victory 7 wherever he went. David took the gold quivers borne by Hadadezer's servants and brought them to Jerusa- 8 lem. He also took a great quantity of bronze*ᵃ* from Hadadezer's cities, Tibhath and Kun; from this Solomon made the Sea of bronze,*ᵃ* the pillars, and the bronze*ᵃ* vessels.

9 When Tou king of Hamath heard that David had defeated the entire army of Hadadezer king of Zobah, 10 he sent his son Hadoram to King David to greet him and to congratulate him on defeating Hadadezer in battle (for Hadadezer had been at war with Tou); and he brought with him vessels of gold, 11 silver, and copper, which King David dedicated to the LORD. He dedicated also the silver and the gold which he had carried away from all the other nations, from Edom and Moab, from the Ammonites and the Philistines, and from Amalek.

12 Edom was defeated by Abishai son of Zeruiah, who destroyed eighteen thousand of them in the Valley of Salt 13 and stationed garrisons in the country. All the Edomites now became subject to David. Thus the LORD gave victory to David wherever he went.

14ᵇ David ruled over the whole of Israel and maintained law and justice among all his people. Joab son of Zeruiah was 15 in command of the army; Jehoshaphat son of Ahilud was secretary of state; Zadok and Abiathar son of Ahime- 16 lech, son of Ahitub,*ᶜ* were priests; Shavsha was adjutant-general; Ben- 17 aiah son of Jehoiada commanded the Kerethite and Pelethite guards. The eldest sons of David were in attendance on the king.

19 1ᵈ Some time afterwards Nahash king of the Ammonites died and was suc- 2 ceeded by his son. David said, 'I must keep up the same loyal friendship with Hanun son of Nahash as his father showed me', and he sent a mission to condole with him on the death of his father. But when David's envoys entered the country of the Ammonites 3 to condole with Hanun, the Ammonite princes said to Hanun, 'Do you suppose David means to do honour to your father when he sends you his condolences? These men of his are spies whom he has sent to find out how to overthrow the country.' So 4 Hanun took David's servants, and he shaved them, cut off half their garments up to the hips, and dismissed them. 5 When David heard how they had been treated, he sent to meet them, for they were deeply humiliated, and ordered them to wait in Jericho and not to return until their beards had grown again. The Ammonites knew that they 6 had brought themselves into bad odour with David, so Hanun and the Ammonites sent a thousand talents of silver to hire chariots and horsemen from Aram-naharaim,*ᵉ* Maacah, and Aram-

z Verses 1–13: cp. 2 Sam. 8. 1–14.
a Or copper.
b Verses 14–17: cp. 2 Sam. 8. 15–18; 20. 23–26; 1 Kgs. 4. 2–4.
c and Abiathar ... Ahitub: prob. rdg., cp. 2 Sam. 8. 17; Heb. son of Ahitub and Abimelech son of Abiathar.
d Verses 1–19: cp. 2 Sam. 10. 1–19.
e That is Aram of Two Rivers.

18.1–19.19: David's imperial victories. The Chronicler includes the accounts of David's victories from 2 Sam. chs. 8, 10, 12, and 21. However, he omits the stories of David's court life related in 2 Sam. chs. 11–20. **4:** The numbers differ from those of 2 Sam. 8.4. **8:** The Chronicler infers that this *bronze* must have been put to a good use, i.e. the making of such objects as Solomon's *Sea of bronze*. **17:** The Chronicler has views of priesthood that prohibit David's sons from being priests, as they are in 2 Sam. 8.18; therefore, here they are only *in attendance on the king.*

7 zobah.*f* They hired thirty-two thousand chariots and the king of Maacah and his people, who came and encamped before Medeba, while the Ammonites came from their cities and 8 mustered for battle. When David heard of it, he sent out Joab and all the 9 fighting men. The Ammonites came and took up their position at the entrance to the city, while the allied kings took 10 up theirs in the open country. When Joab saw that he was threatened both front and rear, he detailed some picked Israelite troops and drew them up 11 facing the Aramaeans. The rest of his forces he put under his brother Abishai, who took up a position facing the 12 Ammonites. 'If the Aramaeans prove too strong for me,' he said, 'you must come to my relief; and if the Ammonites prove too strong for you, I 13 will relieve you. Courage! Let us fight bravely for our people and for the cities*g* of our God. And the LORD's 14 will be done.' But when Joab and his men came to close quarters with the Aramaeans, they put them to flight; 15 and when the Ammonites saw them in flight, they too fled before his brother Abishai and entered the city. Then 16 Joab came to Jerusalem. The Aramaeans saw that they had been worsted by Israel, and they sent messengers to summon other Aramaeans from the Great Bend of the Euphrates under Shophach, commander of Hadadezer's 17 army. Their movement was reported to David, who immediately mustered all the forces of Israel, crossed the Jordan and advanced against them and took up battle positions. The Aramaeans likewise took up positions facing 18 David and engaged him, but were put to flight by Israel. David slew seven thousand Aramaeans in chariots and forty thousand infantry, killing Sho- 19 phach the commander of the army.

When Hadadezer's men saw that they had been worsted by Israel, they sued for peace and submitted to David. The Aramaeans were never again willing to give support to the Ammonites.

AT THE TURN OF THE YEAR, WHEN **20**1*h* kings take the field, Joab led the army out and ravaged the Ammonite country. He came to Rabbah and laid siege to it, while David remained in Jerusalem; he reduced the city and razed it to the ground. David took the 2 crown from the head of Milcom and found that it weighed a talent of gold and was set with a precious stone, and this he placed on his own head. He also removed a great quantity of booty from the city; he took its inhabitants 3 and set them to work with saws and other iron tools, sharp and toothed. David did this to all the cities of the Ammonites; then he and all his people returned to Jerusalem.

Some time later war with the 4*i* Philistines broke out in Gezer; it was then that Sibbechai of Hushah killed Sippai, a descendant of the Rephaim, and the Philistines were reduced to submission. In another war with the 5 Philistines, Elhanan son of Jair killed Lahmi brother of Goliath of Gath, whose spear had a shaft like a weaver's beam. In yet another war in Gath, 6 there appeared a giant with six fingers on each hand and six toes on each foot, twenty-four in all; he too was descended from the Rephaim, and, 7 when he defied Israel, Jonathan son of David's brother Shimea killed him. These giants were the descendants of 8 the Rephaim in Gath, and they all fell at the hands of David and his men.

f Maacah, and Aram-zobah: *prob. rdg.; Heb.* Aram-maacah, and Zobah.
g Or altars.
h Verses 1–3: cp. 2 Sam. 12. 26–31.
i Verses 4–7: cp. 2 Sam. 21. 18–22.

20.1–8: War with the Ammonites and Philistines. While the dramatic military action of ch. 19 is unchanged from its source (2 Sam. ch. 10), care is taken to avoid any hint of the Bathsheba-Uriah story (2 Sam. chs. 11–12), and even of Joab's efforts to insure that David was the conqueror of Rabbah in person; compare 2 Sam.12.26–29. **4–8:** Materials about the exploits of David's heroes not previously used by the Chronicler find their appropriate place here. **4:** *The Rephaim:* legendary inhabitants of southern and eastern Palestine noted for their unusual stature. **5:** The Chronicler does not narrate the David and Goliath story; however, he eliminates the inconsistency between that story and 2 Sam.21.19 by making *Elhanan* the slayer of the *brother of Goliath* rather than of Goliath himself. **6:** *Gath;* see 1 Sam.5.8. **7:** *Shimea:* Shammah of 1 Sam.16.9

21 1 NOW SATAN, SETTING HIMSELF AGAINST Israel, incited David to count the 2 people. So he instructed Joab and his public officers to go out and number Israel, from Beersheba to Dan, and to 3 report the number to him. Joab answered, 'Even if the LORD should increase his people a hundredfold, would not your majesty still be king and all the people your slaves? Why should your majesty want to do this? 4 It will only bring guilt on Israel.' But Joab was overruled by the king; he set out and went up and down the whole country. He then came to Jerusalem 5 and reported to David the numbers recorded: those capable of bearing arms were one million one hundred thousand in Israel, and four hundred 6 and seventy thousand in Judah. Levi and Benjamin were not counted by Joab, so deep was his repugnance against the king's order.

7 God was displeased with all this and 8 proceeded to punish Israel. David said to God, 'I have done a very wicked thing: I pray thee remove thy servant's guilt, for I have been very foolish.' 9 And the LORD said to Gad, David's 10 seer, 'Go and tell David, "This is the word of the LORD: I have three things to offer you; choose one of them and I 11 will bring it upon you."' So Gad came to David and said to him, 'This is the word of the LORD: "Make your choice: 12 three years of famine, three months of harrying by your foes and close pursuit by the sword of your enemy, or three days of the LORD's own sword, bringing pestilence throughout the country, and the LORD's angel working destruction in all the territory of Israel." Consider now what answer I am to take 13 back to him who sent me.' Thereupon David said to Gad, 'I am in a desperate plight; let me fall into the hands of the LORD, for his mercy is very great; and let me not fall into the hands of 14 man.' So the LORD sent a pestilence

throughout Israel, and seventy thousand men of Israel died. And God sent 15 an angel to Jerusalem to destroy it; but, as he was destroying it, the LORD saw and repented of the evil, and said to the destroying angel at the moment when he was standing beside the threshing-floor of Ornan the Jebusite, 'Enough! Stay your hand.'

When David looked up and saw the 16 angel of the LORD standing between earth and heaven, with his sword drawn in his hand and stretched out over Jerusalem, he and the elders, clothed in sackcloth, fell prostrate to the ground; and David said to God, 'It 17 was I who gave the order to count the people. It was I who sinned, I, the shepherd,[k] who did wrong. But these poor sheep, what have they done? O LORD my God, let thy hand fall upon me and upon my family, but check this plague on the people.'[l]

The angel of the LORD, speaking 18 through the lips of Gad, commanded David to go to the threshing-floor of Ornan the Jebusite and to set up there an altar to the LORD. David went up 19 as Gad had bidden him in the LORD's name. Ornan's four sons who were with 20 him hid themselves, but he was busy threshing his wheat when he turned and saw the angel. As David approached, 21 Ornan looked up and, seeing the king, came out from the threshing-floor and prostrated himself before him. David said to Ornan, 'Let me 22 have the site of the threshing-floor that I may build on it an altar to the LORD; sell it me at the full price, that the plague which has attacked my people may be stopped.' Ornan answered 23 David, 'Take it and let your majesty do as he thinks fit; see, here are the oxen for whole-offerings, the threshing-sledges for the fuel, and the wheat for

j Verses 1–27: cp. 2 Sam. 24. 1–25.
k I, the shepherd: *prob. rdg.; Heb.* doing wrong.
l check . . . people: *prob. rdg.; Heb.* among thy people, not for a plague.

21.1–22.1: The consecration of the Temple site. This is taken from the story of the altar site of the Solomonic Temple (2 Sam. ch. 24). The story serves here as the introduction to David's preparations for the Temple that Solomon would build (chs. 22–29), after the empire will have been secured; see 17.1–27 n. **1:** *Satan* means "the Adversary." See the role he plays in Job 1.6–12; compare 1 Kgs.22.19–23; Zech.3.1–2; and, in a poetic context, Ps.82. **5:** Compare the numbers in 2 Sam.24.9. **6:** *Levi* was not a tribal territory; to count Levites (local priests) was not the same as to count the men of a tribe. Why *Benjamin* should be omitted is not clear. **22–25:** Compare David's refusal to take the site as a gift, for religious reasons, with Abram's

the grain-offering; I give you every-thing.' But King David said to Ornan, 'No, I will pay the full price; I will not present to the Lord what is yours, or offer a whole-offering which 25 has cost me nothing.' So David gave Ornan six hundred shekels of gold for 26 the site, and built an altar to the Lord there; on this he offered whole-offerings and shared-offerings, and called upon the Lord, who answered him with fire falling from heaven on the 27 altar of whole-offering. Then, at the Lord's command, the angel sheathed his sword.

28 It was when David saw that the Lord had answered him at the threshing-floor of Ornan the Jebusite that he 29 offered sacrifice there. The tabernacle of the Lord and the altar of whole-offering which Moses had made in the wilderness were then at the hill-shrine 30 in Gibeon; but David had been un-able to go there and seek God's guid-ance, so shocked and shaken was he 22 at the sight of the angel's sword. Then David said, 'This is to be the house of the Lord God, and this is to be an altar of whole-offering for Israel.'

The temple and its organization

2 DAVID NOW GAVE ORDERS TO ASSEMBLE the aliens resident in Israel, and he set them as masons to dress hewn stones 3 and to build the house of God. He laid in a great store of iron to make nails and clamps for the doors, more 4 bronze than could be weighed and cedar-wood without limit; the men of Sidon and Tyre brought David an 5 ample supply of cedar. David said, 'My son Solomon is a boy of tender

years, and the house that is to be built to the Lord must be exceedingly magnificent, renowned and celebrated in every land; therefore I must make preparations for it myself.' So David made abundant preparation before his death.

He sent for Solomon his son and 6 charged him to build a house for the Lord the God of Israel. 'Solomon, 7 my son,' he said, 'I had intended to build a house in honour of the name of the Lord my God; but the Lord 8 forbade me and said, "You have shed much blood in my sight and waged great wars; for this reason you shall not build a house in honour of my name. But you shall have a son who 9*m* shall be a man of peace; I will give him peace from all his enemies on every side; his name shall be Solomon, 'Man of Peace', and I will grant peace and quiet to Israel in his days. He shall 10 build a house in honour of my name; he shall be my son and I will be a father to him, and I will establish the throne of his sovereignty over Israel for ever." Now, Solomon my son, the 11 Lord be with you! May you prosper and build the house of the Lord your God, as he promised you should. But 12 may the Lord grant you wisdom and discretion, so that when he gives you authority in Israel you may keep the law of the Lord your God. You will pros- 13 per only if you are careful to observe the decrees and ordinances which the Lord enjoined upon Moses for Israel; be strong and resolute, neither faint-hearted nor dismayed.

'In spite of all my troubles, I have 14 here ready for the house of the Lord

m Verse 9: cp. 1 Kgs. 5. 4.

response to the king of Sodom in Gen.14.21–24. **26:** On the tradition of the *fire from heaven*, see 1 Kgs. 18.38 n. **21.28–22.1:** This is the Chronicler's own comment on the episode he has taken from 2 Sam.
22.2–29.30: The preparations for the Temple. These materials are derived from different sources preserved in the Chronicler's circle. Ch. 22 is mostly repeated in chs. 28–29; the two sections are probably two renderings of the same topic. Chs. 23–27, lists of Levites and other groups, are not closely connected to the speeches in the surrounding chapters. Such lists probably existed separately in the Chronicler's circle.
22.2–19: A survey of the preparations. David assembles the workers and materials, addresses Solomon (see 28.20–21), and gives a charge to the officers of Israel (see 28.1–10). **2:** On the *aliens* as a source of labor, see 1 Kgs.9.15–23 n. **8:** The Chronicler did not alter the Samuel account when he gave it in ch. 17; there the Lord declined a house of cedar because he had always dwelt in a tent (17.4–6). Here, the Chronicler gives his own reason: that David shed much blood in the conquest of his empire. **9:** In contrast to David, *Solomon* was a "*Man of Peace*"; the Heb. Solomon (*Shelōmōh*) is related to the noun *peace* (*shalōm*). **14:** The *troubles*

442

a hundred thousand talents of gold and a million talents of silver, with great quantities of bronze and iron, more than can be weighed; timber and stone, too, I have got ready; and you may 15 add to them. Besides, you have a large force of workmen, masons, sculptors, and carpenters, and countless men 16 skilled in work of every kind, in gold and silver, bronze and iron. So now to work, and the LORD be with you!'

17 David ordered all the officers of Israel 18 to help Solomon his son: 'Is not the LORD your God with you? Will he not give you peace on every side? For he has given the inhabitants of the land into my power, and they will be subject 19 to the LORD and his people. Devote yourselves, therefore, heart and soul, to seeking guidance of the LORD your God, and set about building his sanctuary, so that the Ark of the Covenant of the LORD and God's holy vessels may be brought into a house built in honour of his name.'

23 David was now an old man, weighed down with years, and he appointed 2 Solomon his son king over Israel. He gathered together all the officers of Is-3 rael, the priests, and the Levites. The Levites were enrolled from the age of thirty upwards, their males being 4 thirty-eight thousand in all. Of these, twenty-four thousand were to be responsible for the maintenance and service of the house of the LORD, six thousand to act as officers and magis-5 trates, four thousand to be door-keepers, and four thousand to praise the LORD on the musical instruments which David had made for the service 6 of praise. David organized them in divisions, called after Gershon, Kohath, and Merari, the sons of Levi.

The sons of Gershon: Laadan and 7 Shimei. The sons of Laadan: Jehiel 8 the chief, Zethan and Joel, three.[n] These were the heads of the families 9 grouped under Laadan. The sons of 10 Shimei: Jahath, Ziza, Jeush and Beriah, four. Jahath was the chief and Ziza 11 the second, but Jeush and Beriah, having few children, were reckoned for duty as a single family.

The sons of Kohath: Amram, Izhar, 12 Hebron and Uzziel, four. The sons of 13 Amram: Aaron and Moses. Aaron was set apart, he and his sons in perpetuity, to dedicate the most holy gifts,[o] to burn sacrifices before the LORD, to serve him, and to give the blessing in his name for ever, but the 14 sons of Moses, the man of God, were to keep the name of Levite. The sons of 15 Moses: Gershom and Eliezer. The sons 16 of Gershom: Shubael the chief. The 17 sons of Eliezer: Rehabiah the chief. Eliezer had no other sons, but Rehabiah had very many. The sons of 18 Izhar: Shelomoth the chief. The sons of 19 Hebron: Jeriah the chief, Amariah the second, Jahaziel the third and Jekameam the fourth. The sons of 20 Uzziel: Micah the chief and Isshiah the second.

The sons of Merari: Mahli and 21 Mushi. The sons of Mahli: Eleazar and Kish. When Eleazar died, he left 22 daughters but no sons, and their cousins, the sons of Kish, married them. The sons of Mushi: Mahli, Eder 23 and Jeremoth, three.

n *Prob. rdg.; Heb. adds* The sons of Shimei: Shelomith, Haziel and Haran, three.
o to dedicate . . . gifts: *or* to be hallowed as most holy.

---

may be the acute family problems and rebellions related in 2 Sam. chs. 12–20 but omitted by the Chronicler.

23.1–26.32: The divisions of the religious personnel. Other than the genealogies of chs. 1–10, this is the most "technical" section of 1 and 2 Chr., and important to the Chronicler's circle in that the family lists of Levites and priests established the legitimacy of and the priorities for the many personnel involved in the service and benefits of the postexilic Temple.

23.1–32: The Levites. 3–6: These statements apply to all the Levitical groups to be listed. Here, the Levites did not begin active service until *the age of thirty*. Later, when more men were needed in active service, the age was lowered to twenty-five (Num.8.24), and even to twenty (23.24,27). **8–23:** For other genealogies of the Levites, see Exod.6.16–25; Num.3.17–39; 1 Chr.6.19–29; 24.20–30. The three main clans, *Gershon, Kohath,* and *Merari,* are firm in all lists. The third generation is also very consistent, though *Gershon's* first son otherwise appears as Libni instead of *Laadan*. Except for the genealogies of Aaron (see ch. 24), only Chr. gives names beyond the third generation, and those names differ in each list. This list gives the families active at one time within the several Levitical clans. The list in 1 Chr.6.19–29, on the other hand, traces the lineage of each clan through several generations. When one of the sons is

24 Such were the Levites, grouped by families in the father's line whose heads were entered in the detailed list, they performed duties in the service of the house of the LORD, from 25 the age of twenty upwards. For David said, 'The LORD the God of Israel has given his people peace and has made 26 his abode in Jerusalem for ever. The Levites will no longer have to carry the Tabernacle or any of the vessels for its 27 service.' By these last words of David the Levites were enrolled from the age 28 of twenty upwards. Their duty was to help the sons of Aaron in the service of the house of the LORD: they were responsible for the care of the courts and the rooms, for the cleansing of all holy things, and the general service of 29 the house of God; for the rows of the Bread of the Presence, the flour for the grain-offerings, unleavened wafers, cakes baked on the griddle, and pastry, and for the weights and 30 measures. They were to be on duty continually before the LORD every morning and evening, giving thanks 31 and praise to him, and at every offering of whole-offerings to the LORD, on sabbaths, new moons and at the appointed seasons, according to their 32 prescribed number. The Levites were to have charge of the Tent of the Presence and of the sanctuary, but the sons of Aaron their kinsmen were charged with the service of worship in the house of the LORD.

24 The divisions of the sons of Aaron: his sons were Nadab and Abihu, Eleazar 2 and Ithamar. Nadab and Abihu died before their father, leaving no sons; therefore Eleazar and Ithamar held 3 the office of priest. David, acting with Zadok of the sons of Eleazar and with Ahimelech of the sons of Ithamar,

organized them in divisions for the discharge of the duties of their office. The male heads of families proved to 4 be more numerous in the line of Eleazar than in that of Ithamar, so that sixteen heads of families were grouped under the line of Eleazar and eight under that of Ithamar. He organized 5 them by drawing lots among them, for there were sacred officers^p and officers of God in the line of Eleazar and in that of Ithamar. Shemaiah the 6 clerk, a Levite, son of Nethaneel, wrote down the names in the presence of the king, the officers, Zadok the priest, and Ahimelech son of Abiathar, and of the heads of the priestly and levitical families, one priestly family being taken from the line of Eleazar and one from that of Ithamar. The first lot fell to 7 Jehoiarib, the second to Jedaiah, the 8 third to Harim, the fourth to Seorim, the fifth to Malchiah, the sixth to 9 Mijamin, the seventh to Hakkoz, the 10 eighth to Abiah, the ninth to Jeshua, 11 the tenth to Shecaniah, the eleventh to 12 Eliashib, the twelfth to Jakim, the 13 thirteenth to Huppah, the fourteenth to Jeshebeab, the fifteenth to Bilgah, 14 the sixteenth to Immer, the seven- 15 teenth to Hezir, the eighteenth to Aphses, the nineteenth to Pethahiah, 16 the twentieth to Jehezekel, the twenty- 17 first to Jachin, the twenty-second to Gamul, the twenty-third to Delaiah, 18 and the twenty-fourth to Maaziah. This was their order of duty for the 19 discharge of their service when they entered the house of the LORD, accord- ing to the rule prescribed for them by their ancestor Aaron, who had re- ceived his instructions from the LORD the God of Israel.

p sacred officers: or officers of the sanctuary.

referred to as *chief*, it means he was the leader for that group in carrying out its Temple duties. If only the last generation of each family is counted, twenty-one families are listed. However, two families were merged because neither was large enough to carry out its duties separately (v. 11), and one family had no male descendants (v. 22). **25–26:** On the earlier duties of the Levites, see Num. chs. 3–4. **27:** On the age, see vv. 3–6 n. The *last words* here are meant to acknowledge that though *David* once said thirty years, his last word was *twenty*.

24.1–31: The divisions of the priests. The genealogy of Aaron, tracing the line of the chief priests, is given in 6.1–15. Here, the names of the priestly families who alternated in service at the Temple are given. The twenty-four families probably each served from Sabbath to Sabbath according to an established order; see 9.25 and Lk.1.5–10. The income from the altar service went partly to all *the sons of Aaron* and partly to the priests who were presiding at any given time; compare Lev.2.3,10; 7.14,32–35. **6:** Solemn measures were taken to assure a proper

20 Of the remaining Levites: of the sons of Amram: Shubael. Of the sons of
21 Shubael: Jehdeiah. Of Rehabiah: Is-
22 shiah, the chief of Rehabiah's sons. Of the line of Izhar: Shelomoth. Of the sons
23 of Shelomoth: Jahath. The sons of Hebron: Jeriah the chief, Amariah the second, Jahaziel the third and Jekam-
24 eam the fourth. The sons of Uzziel: Micah. Of the sons of Micah: Shamir;
25 Micah's brother: Isshiah. Of the sons
26 of Isshiah: Zechariah. The sons of Merari: Mahli and Mushi and also*q*
27 Jaaziah his son. The sons of Merari: of Jaaziah: Beno, Shoham, Zaccur and
28 Ibri. Of Mahli: Eleazar, who had no
29 sons; of Kish: the sons of Kish: Jerah-
30 meel; and the sons of Mushi: Mahli, Eder and Jerimoth. These were the
31 Levites by families. These also, side by side with their kinsmen the sons of Aaron, cast lots in the presence of King David, Zadok, Ahimelech, and the heads of the priestly and levitical families, the senior and junior houses casting lots side by side.

25 David and his chief officers assigned special duties to the sons of Asaph, of Heman, and of Jeduthun, leaders in inspired prophecy to the accompaniment of harps, lutes, and cymbals; the number of the men who performed this work in the temple was as follows.
2 Of the sons of Asaph: Zaccur, Joseph, Nethaniah and Asarelah; these were under Asaph, a leader in inspired
3 prophecy under the king. Of the sons of Jeduthun: Gedaliah, Izri,*r* Isaiah, Shimei, Hashabiah, Mattithiah, these six under their father Jeduthun, a leader in inspired prophecy to the accompaniment of the harp, giving
4 thanks and praise to the LORD. Of the sons of Heman: Bukkiah, Mattaniah, Uzziel, Shubael, Jerimoth, Hananiah,

Hanani, Eliathah, Giddalti, Romamti-ezer, Joshbekashah, Mallothi, Hothir, and Mahazioth; all these were sons 5 of Heman the king's seer, given to him through the promises of God for his greater glory. God had given Heman fourteen sons and three daughters, and they all served under their father 6 for the singing in the house of the LORD; they took part in the service of the house of God, with cymbals, lutes, and harps, while Asaph, Jeduthun, and Heman were under the king. Reckoned with their kinsmen, trained 7 singers of the LORD, they brought the total number of skilled musicians up to two hundred and eighty-eight. They 8 cast lots for their duties, young and old, master-singer and apprentice side by side.

The first lot fell*s* to Joseph: he and 9 his brothers and his sons, twelve.*t* The second to Gedaliah: he and his brothers and his sons, twelve. The third 10 to Zaccur: his sons and his brothers, twelve. The fourth to Izri: his sons and 11 his brothers, twelve. The fifth to Neth- 12 aniah: his sons and his brothers, twelve. The sixth to Bukkiah: his sons 13 and his brothers, twelve. The seventh 14 to Asarelah: his sons and his brothers, twelve. The eighth to Isaiah: his sons 15 and his brothers, twelve. The ninth to 16 Mattaniah: his sons and his brothers, twelve. The tenth to Shimei: his sons 17 and his brothers, twelve. The eleventh 18 to Azareel: his sons and his brothers, twelve. The twelfth to Hashabiah: 19 his sons and his brothers, twelve. The 20 thirteenth to Shubael: his sons and his brothers, twelve. The fourteenth to 21 Mattithiah: his sons and his brothers,

q and also: prob. rdg.; Heb. the sons of.
r Prob. rdg.; cp. verse 11; Heb. Zeri.
s Prob. rdg.; Heb. adds to Asaph.
t he ... twelve: prob. rdg.; Heb. om.

---

priestly service and to give each family its due. **20–31:** An appendix containing an alternative list to 23.16–23.
    25.1–31: The singers and musicians. 1: The name of the third guild varies: it is Ethan in 6.31–48 and 15.16–24, but Jeduthun in 16.41; 25.3,6; 2 Chr.5.12; 29.14; and Neh.11.17. The two names became identified; it is unknown whether originally they reflected two separate clans. *Asaph* appears in the Heb. headings of Pss.50,73–83; Ethan, Ps.89; and *Jeduthun*, Pss.39,62,77. These headings are not given in the New English Bible; see p. xxi. *Prophecy:* see 5 n. **5:** *Seer:* there is reflected the kinship between music and prophecy; compare 2 Chr.20.14 and 2 Kgs.3.14–16. **7:** *Two hundred and eighty-eight:* twelve singers for each of the twenty-four divisions, matching the divisions of the priests in ch. 24. A different number, four thousand, is given in 23.5. **9–31:** The twenty-four names are given in the order of their duty as determined by lot (see the same for the priests in 24.5–6).

22 twelve. The fifteenth to Jeremoth: his
23 sons and his brothers, twelve. The
sixteenth to Hananiah: his sons and his
24 brothers, twelve. The seventeenth to
Joshbekashah: his sons and his brothers,
25 twelve. The eighteenth to Hanani:
26 his sons and his brothers, twelve. The
nineteenth to Mallothi: his sons and his
27 brothers, twelve. The twentieth to Eliathah: his sons and his brothers, twelve.
28 The twenty-first to Hothir: his sons
29 and his brothers, twelve. The twenty-
second to Giddalti: his sons and his
30 brothers, twelve. The twenty-third to
Mahazioth: his sons and his brothers,
31 twelve. The twenty-fourth to Romamti-
ezer: his sons and his brothers, twelve.

26   The divisions of the door-keepers:
Korahites: Meshelemiah son of Kore,
2 son of Ebiasaph.*u* Sons of Meshelemiah: Zechariah the eldest, Jediael the
second, Zebediah the third, Jathniel
3 the fourth, Elam the fifth, Jehohanan
4 the sixth, Elioenai the seventh. Sons of
Obed-edom: Shemaiah the eldest,
Jehozabad the second, Joah the third,
Sacar the fourth, Nethaneel the fifth,
5 Ammiel the sixth, Issachar the seventh,
Peulthai the eighth (for God had
6 blessed him). Shemaiah, his son, was
the father of sons who had authority
in their family, for they were men of
7 great ability. Sons of Shemaiah:
Othni, Rephael, Obed, Elzabad and his
brothers Elihu and Semachiah, men of
8 ability. All these belonged to the family
of Obed-edom; they, their sons and
brothers, were men of ability, fit for
service in the temple; total: sixty-two.
9 Sons and brothers of Meshelemiah,
10 all men of ability, eighteen. Sons of
Hosah, a Merarite: Shimri the chief
(he was not the eldest, but his father
11 had made him chief), Hilkiah the
second, Tebaliah the third, Zechariah
the fourth. Total of Hosah's sons and
brothers: thirteen.
12   The male heads of families constituted the divisions of the door-

keepers; their duty was to serve in the
house of the LORD side by side with
their kinsmen. Young and old, family 13
by family, they cast lots for the gates.
The lot for the east gate fell to She- 14
lemiah; then lots were cast for his son
Zechariah, a prudent counsellor, and
he was allotted the north gate. To 15
Obed-edom was allotted the south
gate, and the gatehouse to his sons.
Hosah*v* was allotted the west gate, to- 16
gether with the Shallecheth gate on
the ascending causeway. Guard corresponded to guard. Six Levites were on 17
duty daily on the east side, four on the
north and four on the south, and two
at each gatehouse; at the western colon- 18
nade there were four at the causeway
and two at the colonnade itself. These 19
were the divisions of the door-keepers,
Korahites and Merarites.

Fellow-Levites were in charge of the 20
stores of the house of God and of the
stores of sacred gifts. Of the children 21
of Laadan, descendants of the Gershonite line through Laadan, heads of
families in the group of Laadan the Gershonite, Jehiel and*w* his brothers Zetham 22
and Joel were in charge of the stores of
the house of the LORD. Of the families 23
of Amram, Izhar, Hebron and Uzziel,
Shubael son of Gershom, son of Moses, 24
was overseer of the stores. The line of 25
Eliezer his brother: his son Rehabiah,
his son Isaiah, his son Joram, his son
Zichri, and his son Shelomoth. This 26
Shelomoth and his kinsmen were in
charge of all the stores of the sacred
gifts dedicated by David the king, the
heads of families, the officers over
units of a thousand and a hundred, and
other officers of the army. They had 27
dedicated some of the spoils taken in
the wars for the upkeep of the house
of the LORD. Everything which Samuel 28

*u son of Ebiasaph: prob. rdg.; Heb. from the sons of
Asaph.*
v Hosah: prob. rdg.; Heb. Shuppim and Hosah.
*w Jehiel and: prob. rdg.; Heb. Jehieli. The sons of
Jehieli . . .*

26.1–32: The door-keepers and other Levites. Compare 9.17–24; 15.23–24; 16.37–42. **1–11:**
The leaders of the clans of *door-keepers—Meshelemiah* (v. 1), *Obed-edom* (v. 4), and *Hosah*
(v. 10)—are only minor figures in Levite lists. The overlap of names with those of musical clans
perhaps suggests a close relationship between gatekeepers and musicians. **12–19:** The structure
of the Temple as reflected in these guard posts envisions the postexilic age of the Chronicler,
not Solomon's Temple; compare 9.17–32. **20–32:** The Levites engaged in administrative tasks.
21–22: Three officials were *in charge of stores* in the Temple. **23 24:** The *overseer(s) of the stores*
were from different families, perhaps to insure fairness in handling them. **26:** A still different

the seer, Saul son of Kish, Abner son of Ner, and Joab son of Zeruiah had dedicated, in short every sacred gift, was under the charge of Shelomoth
29 and his kinsmen. Of the family of Izhar, Kenaniah and his sons acted as clerks and magistrates in the secular
30 affairs of Israel. Of the family of Hebron, Hashabiah and his kinsmen, men of ability to the number of seventeen hundred, had the oversight of Israel west of the Jordan, both in the work of the LORD and in the
31 service of the king. Also of the family of Hebron, Jeriah was the chief. (In the fortieth year of David's reign search was made in the family histories of the Hebronites, and men of great ability were found among them at Jazer in
32 Gilead.) His kinsmen, all men of ability, two thousand seven hundred of them, heads of families, were charged by King David with the oversight of the Reubenites, the Gadites, and the half tribe of Manasseh, in religious and civil affairs alike.

27 THE NUMBER OF THE ISRAELITES—THAT is to say, of the heads of families, the officers over units of a thousand and a hundred, and the clerks who had their share in the king's service in the various divisions which took monthly turns of duty throughout the year—was twenty-four thousand in each division.
2   First, Jashobeam son of Zabdiel commanded the division for the first month with twenty-four thousand in
3 his division; a member of the house of Perez, he was chief officer of the temple
4 staff for the first month. Eleazar son of*x* Dodai the Ahohite commanded the division for the second month with twenty-four thousand in his division.
5 Third, Benaiah son of Jehoiada the chief priest, commander of the army, was the officer for the third month with twenty-four thousand in his division
6 (he was the Benaiah who was one of the

thirty warriors and was a chief among the thirty); but his son Ammizabad commanded his division. Fourth, Asa- 7 hel, the brother of Joab, was the officer commanding for the fourth month with twenty-four thousand in his division; and his successor was Zebediah his son. Fifth, Shamhuth the 8 Zerahite*y* was the officer commanding for the fifth month with twenty-four thousand in his division. Sixth, Ira son 9 of Ikkesh, a man of Tekoa, was the officer commanding for the sixth month with twenty-four thousand in his division. Seventh, Helez an Ephraimite, 10 from a place unknown, was the officer commanding for the seventh month with twenty-four thousand in his division. Eighth, Sibbecai the Husha- 11 thite, of the family of Zerah, was the officer commanding for the eighth month with twenty-four thousand in his division. Ninth, Abiezer, from 12 Anathoth in Benjamin, was the officer commanding for the ninth month with twenty-four thousand in his division. Tenth, Maharai the Netophathite, of 13 the family of Zerah, was the officer commanding for the tenth month with twenty-four thousand in his division. Eleventh, Benaiah the Pirathonite, 14 from Ephraim, was the officer commanding for the eleventh month with twenty-four thousand in his division. Twelfth, Heldai the Netophathite, of 15 the family of Othniel, was the officer commanding for the twelfth month with twenty-four thousand in his division.

The following were the principal 16 officers in charge of the tribes of Israel: of Reuben, Eliezer son of Zichri; of Simeon, Shephatiah son of Maacah; of Levi, Hashabiah son of Kemuel; of 17 Aaron, Zadok; of Judah, Elihu a kins- 18 man of David; of Issachar, Omri son

x Eleazar son of: *prob. rdg., cp. 11. 12; Heb. om.*
y the Zerahite: *prob. rdg.; Heb. the Izrah.*

family was *in charge of . . . the sacred gifts.* **29–32:** Three other groups of Levites conducted secular judicial and administrative tasks outside of Jerusalem: *clerks and magistrates* (v. 29); administrators *west of the Jordan* (v. 30); and administrators east of the Jordan (vv. 31–32). Compare 2 Chr.19.18–11 and Deut.17.8–13.
    27.1–34: Officials of the realm. 1–15: In his own time, David was in no position to rule through such a schematic arrangement; also, the postexilic period offered no opportunity for such exaggerated numbers as twenty-four thousand people in each of the twelve divisions. **16–22:** The tribe of Asher is omitted, yet *Aaron* is included (v. 17) as if a tribe; contrast 12.26–27,

19 of Michael; of Zebulun, Ishmaiah son of Obadiah; of Naphtali, Jerimoth

20 son of Azriel; of Ephraim, Hoshea son of Azaziah; of the half tribe of Manas-

21 seh, Joel son of Pedaiah; of the half of Manasseh in Gilead, Iddo son of Zechariah; of Benjamin, Jaasiel son of

22 Abner; of Dan, Azareel son of Jeroham. These were the officers in charge of the tribes of Israel.

23 David took no census of those under twenty years of age, for the LORD had promised to make the Israelites as many

24 as the stars in the heavens. Joab son of Zeruiah did begin to take a census but he did not finish it; this brought harm upon Israel, and the census was not entered in the chronicle of King David's reign.

25 Azmoth son of Adiel was in charge of the king's stores; Jonathan son of Uzziah was in charge of the stores in the country, in the cities, in the

26 villages and in the fortresses. Ezri son of Kelub had oversight of the workers

27 on the land; Shimei of Ramah was in charge of the vine-dressers, while Zabdi of Shephem had charge of the produce of the vineyards for the wine-cellars.

28 Baal-hanan the Gederite supervised the wild olives and the sycomore-figs in the Shephelah; Joash was in charge of

29 the oil-stores. Shitrai of Sharon was in charge of the herds grazing in Sharon, Shaphat son of Adlai of the herds in

30 the vales. Obil the Ishmaelite was in charge of the camels, Jehdeiah the Mero-

31 nothite of the asses. Jaziz the Hagerite was in charge of the flocks. All these were the officers in charge of King

32 David's possessions. David's favourite nephew Jonathan, a counsellor, a discreet and learned man, and Jehiel the Hachmonite, were tutors to the

33 king's sons. Ahithophel was a king's counsellor; Hushai the Archite was

34 the King's Friend. Ahithophel was succeeded by Jehoiada son of Benaiah, and Abiathar. Joab was commander of the army.

DAVID ASSEMBLED AT JERUSALEM ALL **28** the officers of Israel, the officers over the tribes, over the divisions engaged in the king's service, over the units of a thousand and a hundred, and those in charge of all the property and the cattle of the king and of his sons, as well as the eunuchs, the heroes and all the men of ability. Then King David 2 rose to his feet and said, 'Hear me, kinsmen and people. I had in mind to build a house as a resting-place for the Ark of the Covenant of the LORD which might serve as a footstool for the feet of our God, and I made preparations to build it. But God said to me, 3 "You shall not build a house in honour of my name, for you have been a fighting man and you have shed blood." Never- 4 theless, the LORD the God of Israel chose me out of all my father's family to be king of Israel in perpetuity; for it was Judah that he chose as ruling tribe, and, out of the house of Judah, my father's family; and among my father's sons it was I whom he was pleased to make king over all Israel. And out of all my sons— for the LORD 5 gave me many sons—he chose Solomon to sit upon the throne of the LORD's sovereignty over Israel; and he said 6 to me, "It is Solomon your son who shall build my house and my courts, for I have chosen him to be a son to me and I will be a father to him. I will 7 establish his sovereignty in perpetuity, if only he steadfastly obeys my commandments and my laws as they are now obeyed." Now therefore, in the 8 presence of all Israel, the assembly of the LORD, and within the hearing of our God, I bid you all study carefully the commandments of the LORD your God, that you may possess this good land and hand it down as an inheritance for all time to your children after you. And you, Solomon my son, acknowl- 9 edge your father's God and serve him with whole heart and willing mind, for the LORD searches all hearts and dis-

where Aaron is listed but not counted as a tribe. **23–24:** On the census, see 21.1–6. **32–34:** This *Jonathan* is elsewhere unmentioned, as is the case with *Jehiel*. On *Ahithophel* see 2 Sam.15.31; 16.23; 17.23. On *Hushai*, 2 Sam.15.32–37; 16.16–19; 17.5–16. On *Abiathar*, 1 Sam.22.20–23; on *Joab*, 2 Sam. 2.12–17.
  28.1–29.30: David's farewell addresses and his death. This whole block of material is an elaboration of David as founder of the dynasty and the preparer for the Temple, but not its

cerns every invention of men's thoughts. If you search for him, he will let you find him, but if you forsake him, he will 10 cast you off for ever. Remember, then, that the LORD has chosen you to build a house for a sanctuary: be steadfast and do it.'

11   David gave Solomon his son the plan of the porch of the temple[z] and its buildings, strong-rooms, roof-chambers and inner courts, and the shrine 12 of expiation;[a] also the plans of all he had in mind for the courts of the house of the LORD and for all the rooms around it, for the stores of God's house and 13 for the stores of the sacred gifts, for the divisions of the priests and the Levites, for all the work connected with the service of the house of the LORD and for all the vessels used in its 14 service. He prescribed the weight of gold for all the gold vessels[b] used in the various services, and the weight of silver[c] for all the silver vessels used in 15 the various services; and the weight of gold for the gold lamp-stands and their lamps; and the weight of silver for the silver lamp-stands, the weight required for each lamp-stand and its lamps according to the use of each; 16 and the weight of gold for each of the tables for the rows of the Bread of the Presence, and of silver for the silver 17 tables. He prescribed also the weight of pure gold for the forks, tossing-bowls and cups, the weight of gold for each of the golden dishes and of silver[c] for 18 each of the silver dishes; the weight also of refined gold for the altar of incense, and of gold for the model of the chariot, that is the cherubim with their wings outspread to screen the Ark of 19 the Covenant of the LORD. 'All this was drafted by the LORD's own hand,' said David; 'my part was to consider the detailed working out of the plan.' 20   Then David said to Solomon his son, 'Be steadfast and resolute and do it; be neither faint-hearted nor dismayed, for the LORD God, my God, will be

with you; he will neither fail you nor forsake you, until you have finished all the work needed for the service of the house of the LORD. Here are the 21 divisions of the priests and the Levites, ready for all the service of the house of God. In all the work you will have the help of every willing craftsman for any task; and the officers and all the people will be entirely at your command.'

King David then said to the whole 29 assembly, 'My son Solomon is the one chosen by God, Solomon alone, a boy of tender years; and this is a great work, for it is a palace not for man but for the LORD God. Now to the 2 best of my strength I have made ready for the house of my God gold for the gold work, silver for the silver, bronze for the bronze, iron for the iron, and wood for the woodwork, together with cornelian and other gems for setting, stones for mosaic work, precious stones of every sort, and marble in plenty. Further, because I delight in the house 3 of my God, I give my own private store of gold and silver for the house of my God—over and above all the store which I have collected for the sanctuary—namely three thousand talents 4 of gold, gold from Ophir, and seven thousand talents of fine silver for overlaying the walls of the buildings, for 5 providing gold for the gold work, silver for the silver, and for any work to be done by skilled craftsmen. Now who is willing to give with open hand to the LORD today?'

Then the heads of families, the 6 officers administering the tribes of Israel, the officers over units of a thousand and a hundred, and the officers in charge of the king's service, responded willingly and gave for the 7 work of the house of God five thousand talents of gold, ten thousand darics,

z of the temple: *prob. rdg.; Heb. om.*
a the shrine . . . expiation: *or* the place for the Ark with its cover.
b for . . . vessels: *prob. rdg.; Heb.* for gold.
c of silver: *prob. rdg.; Heb. om.*

---

builder. **11–19:** Just as Moses received a divine plan for the first sanctuary (Exod.25.9), so David is the recipient of a divine pattern for the Temple (v. 19). **18:** *The Ark* is called a *chariot* because originally it was a mobile throne; see 1 Sam.4.4. **21:** These farewell speeches take account of the lists in chs. 23–27, as the speeches in ch. 22 do not. **29.1–5:** Compare David's provisions in 22.3–4,14–15. **6–9:** On the extravagant generosity by the people, compare Exod. 35.4–29. **7:** *Darics* were Persian coins, indicating a date of origin of the passage not earlier

ten thousand talents of silver, eighteen thousand talents of bronze, and a
8 hundred thousand talents of iron. Further, those who possessed precious stones gave them to the treasury of the house of the LORD, into the charge of
9 Jehiel the Gershonite. The people rejoiced at this willing response, because in the loyalty of their hearts they had given willingly to the LORD;
10 King David also was full of joy, and he blessed the LORD in the presence of all the assembly and said, 'Blessed art thou, LORD God of our father Israel,
11 from of old and for ever. Thine, O LORD, is the greatness, the power, the glory, the splendour, and the majesty; for everything in heaven and on earth is thine;*d* thine, O LORD, is the sovereignty, and thou art exalted
12 over all as head. Wealth and honour come from thee; thou rulest over all; might and power are of thy disposing; thine it is to give power and strength
13 to all. And now, we give thee thanks, our God, and praise thy glorious name.
14 'But what am I, and what is my people, that we should be able to give willingly like this? For everything comes from thee, and it is only of thy
15 gifts that we give to thee. We are aliens before thee and settlers, as were all our fathers; our days on earth are like a shadow, we have no abiding
16 place. O LORD our God, from thee comes all this wealth that we have laid up to build a house in honour of thy holy name, and everything is
17 thine. I know, O my God, that thou dost test the heart and that plain honesty pleases thee; with an honest heart I have given all these gifts willingly, and have rejoiced now to see thy people
18 here present give willingly to thee. O LORD God of Abraham, Isaac and Israel our fathers, maintain this purpose for ever in thy people's thoughts and
19 direct their hearts toward thyself. Grant

that Solomon my son may loyally keep thy commandments, thy solemn charge, and thy statutes, that he may fulfil them all and build the palace for which I have prepared.'
20 Then, turning to the whole assembly, David said, 'Now bless the LORD your God.' So all the assembly blessed the LORD the God of their fathers, bowing low and prostrating themselves before
21 the LORD and the king. The next day they sacrificed to the LORD and offered whole-offerings to him, a thousand oxen, a thousand rams, a thousand lambs, with the prescribed drink-offerings, and abundant sacrifices for
22 all Israel. So they ate and drank before the LORD that day with great rejoicing. They then appointed Solomon, David's son, king a second time and anointed him as the LORD's prince, and Zadok
23 as priest. So Solomon sat on the LORD's throne as king in place of his father David, and he prospered and
24 all Israel obeyed him. All the officers and the warriors, as well as all the sons of King David, swore fealty to
25 King Solomon. The LORD made Solomon stand very high in the eyes of all Israel, and bestowed upon him sovereignty such as no king in Israel had had before him.
26 David son of Jesse had ruled over the
27 whole of Israel, and the length of his reign over Israel was forty years; he ruled for seven years in Hebron, and for thirty-three in Jerusalem. He died
28 in ripe old age, full of years, wealth, and honour; and Solomon his son ruled
29 in his place. The events of King David's reign from first to last are recorded in the books of Samuel the seer, of Nathan the prophet, and of Gad the seer, with a full account of his reign,
30 his prowess, and of the times through which he and Israel and all the kingdoms of the world had passed.

d is thine: prob. rdg.; Heb. om.

than 400 B.C. **8:** *Jehiel:* see 26.21. **10–19:** The speech of an ideal king, from the postexilic perspective. Such a speech by David is found in the Deuteronomic history in 2 Sam.7.18–29. **18:** *God of Abraham, Isaac and Israel:* a phrasing favored by the Chronicler; see 2 Chr.30.6 (also Elijah's prayer in 1 Kgs.18.36). **22–25:** The enthronement of Solomon; see 23.1. **22:** The high priest Zadok was *anointed* because in postexilic practice, the high priest had the civil functions which in preexilic times belonged to the king. **29:** *The books of Samuel* and *Nathan* may be 1 Sam. and most of 2 Sam. respectively; the book of *Gad* could be 2 Sam. chs. 21–24, used by the Chronicler in 1 Chr. chs. 11, 17, and 20.

THE SECOND BOOK OF THE
CHRONICLES

2 Chronicles is part of an idealized history of the elect people, especially of the kingdom of Judah (see Introduction to 1 Chronicles). The segment of that history encompassed in 2 Chronicles extends from Solomon to the Babylonian Exile.

The most distinctive feature of 2 Chronicles is the speeches attributed to faithful kings and prophets (see, e.g. 13.5–12 and ch. 20). Such speeches were often placed in the mouths of worthy figures of the monarchic age by the later period in which they were composed.

The Chronicler frequently interprets the past of which he tells in the light of the piety that flourished at Jerusalem after the Exile.

The reign of Solomon and dedication of the temple

1 KING SOLOMON, DAVID'S SON, strengthened his hold on the kingdom, for the LORD his God was with him and made him very great.

2 Solomon spoke to all Israel, to the officers over units of a thousand and of a hundred, the judges and all the leading men of Israel, the heads of families; 3 and he, together with all the assembled people, went to the hill-shrine at Gibeon; for the Tent of God's Presence, which Moses the LORD's servant had made in the wilderness, was 4 there. (But David had brought up the Ark of God from Kiriath-jearim to the place which he had prepared for it, for he had pitched a tent for it in 5 Jerusalem.) The altar of bronze also, which Bezalel son of Uri, son of Hur, had made, was there in front of the Tabernacle of the LORD; and Solomon 6 and the assembly resorted to it.[a] There Solomon went up to the altar of bronze before the LORD in the Tent of the Presence and offered on it a 7[b] thousand whole-offerings. That night God appeared to Solomon and said, 'What shall I give you? Tell me.' 8 Solomon answered, 'Thou didst show

great and constant love to David my father and thou hast made me king in his place. Now, O LORD God, let thy 9 word to David my father be confirmed, for thou hast made me king over a people as numerous as the dust on the earth. Give me now wisdom 10 and knowledge, that I may lead this people; for who is fit to govern this great people of thine?' God answered 11 Solomon, 'Because this is what you desire, because you have not asked for wealth or possessions or honour[c] or the lives of your enemies or even long life for yourself, but have asked for wisdom and knowledge to govern my people over whom I have made you king, wisdom and knowledge are given 12 to you; I shall also give you wealth and possessions and honour[c] such as no king has had before you and none shall have after you.' Then Solomon returned 13 from the hill-shrine at Gibeon, from before the Tent of the Presence, to Jerusalem and ruled over Israel.

Solomon got together many chariots 14[d] and horses; he had fourteen hundred chariots and twelve thousand horses, and he stabled some in the chariot-towns and kept others at hand in Jerusalem. The king made silver and 15

a resorted to it: or worshipped him.
b Verses 7–12: cp. 1 Kgs. 3. 5–14.   c Or riches.
d Verses 14–17: cp. 9. 25–28; 1 Kgs. 10. 26–29.

1.1–9.31: Solomon and the Temple. The Chronicler draws most of his material concerning *Solomon* from 1 Kgs. chs. 3–10. He omits the struggle for David's throne in 1 Kgs. chs. 1–2. Thereby, he comes quickly to the building and dedication of the Temple.

1.1–17: Solomon's wisdom and wealth. *Solomon's* dream at *Gibeon* (vv. 7–13) is abbreviated from the 1 Kgs.3.4–10 source; an excerpt is also given (14–17) to document Solomon's *wealth* which God said would be given as well as *wisdom* (1 Kgs.10.26–29). **3–4:** Because a *hill-shrine*, was normally pagan, and it could appear unseemly for Solomon to have gone to a pagan shrine, v. 3 mentions the Mosaic *Tent of God's Presence;* yet v. 4 then comments that the Ark was not in this tent, but on hand at Jerusalem! The Tent of God's Presence and the Ark come together in 5.4–5. **14–17:** This passage on Solomon's wealth also occurs in 9.25–28.

gold as common in Jerusalem as stones, and cedar as plentiful as syco16 more-fig in the Shephelah. Horses were imported from Egypt and Coa for Solomon; the royal merchants obtained them from Coa by purchase.
17 Chariots were imported from Egypt for six hundred silver shekels each, and horses for a hundred and fifty; in the same way the merchants obtained them for export from all the kings of the Hittites and the kings of Aram.

2 Solomon resolved to build a house in honour of the name of the LORD,
2 and a royal palace for himself. He engaged seventy thousand hauliers and eighty thousand quarrymen, and three thousand six hundred men to
3e superintend them. Then Solomon sent this message to Huram king of Tyre: 'You were so good as to send my father David cedar-wood to build his royal
4 residence. Now I am about to build a house in honour of the name of the LORD my God and to consecrate it to him, so that I may burn fragrant incense in it before him, and present the rows of the Bread of the Presence regularly, and whole-offerings morning and evening, on the sabbaths and the new moons and the appointed festivals of the LORD our God; for this is a duty
5 laid upon Israel for ever. The house I am about to build will be a great house, because our God is greater than all
6 gods. But who is able to build him a house when heaven itself, the highest heaven, cannot contain him? And who am I that I should build him a house, except that I may burn sacrifices
7 before him? Send me then a skilled craftsman, a man able to work in gold and silver, copper*f* and iron, and in purple, crimson, and violet yarn, who is also an expert engraver and will work with my skilled workmen in Judah and in Jerusalem who were provided
8 by David my father. Send me also cedar, pine, and algum timber from Lebanon, for I know that your men are expert at felling the trees of

Lebanon; my men will work with yours to get an ample supply of timber 9 ready for me, for the house which I shall build will be great and wonder10 ful. I will supply provisions for your servants, the woodmen who fell the trees: twenty thousand kor of wheat and twenty thousand kor of barley, with twenty thousand bath of wine and twenty thousand bath of oil.'

Huram king of Tyre sent this answer 11 by letter to Solomon: 'It is because of the love which the LORD has for his people that he has made you king over them.' The letter went on to say, 12 'Blessed is the LORD the God of Israel, maker of heaven and earth, who has given to King David a wise son, endowed with intelligence and understanding, to build a house for the LORD and a royal palace for himself. I now send you a skilful and ex- 13 perienced craftsman, master Huram. He is the son of a Danite woman, his 14 father a Tyrian; he is an experienced worker in gold and silver, copper*f* and iron, stone and wood, as well as in purple, violet, and crimson yarn, and in fine linen; he is also a trained engraver who will be able to work with your own skilled craftsmen and those of my lord David your father, to any design submitted to him. Now then, 15 let my lord send his servants the wheat and the barley, the oil and the wine, which he promised; we will fell all the 16 timber in Lebanon that you need and float it as rafts to the roadstead at Joppa, and you will convey it from there up to Jerusalem.'

Solomon took a census of all the 17 aliens resident in Israel, similar to the census which David his father had taken; these were found to be a hundred and fifty-three thousand six hundred. He made seventy thousand 18 of them hauliers and eighty thousand quarrymen, and three thousand six hundred superintendents to make the people work.

e Verses 3–16: cp. 1 Kgs. 5. 2–11.   f Or bronze.

2.1–18: **Preparation for building the Temple. 4–6:** The Chronicler adds to his source his own view of the religious service; compare 1 Kgs.5.1–6. **3:** *Huram* here and Hiram of Kgs. are the same man. **11–12:** The Chronicler heightens Huram's praise of *the LORD* and of *Solomon* (1 Kgs.5.7). **17–18:** The source, 1 Kgs.5.13–18, makes no mention of these *aliens;* rather, it is Israelites there who do the work.

3 Then Solomon began to build the house of the LORD in Jerusalem on Mount Moriah, where the LORD had appeared to his father David, on the site which David had prepared on the threshing-floor of Ornan the Jebusite. 2[g] He began to build in the second month 3 of the fourth year of his reign. These are the foundations which Solomon laid for building the house of God: the length, according to the old standard of measurement, was sixty 4 cubits and the breadth twenty. The vestibule in front of the house[h] was twenty cubits long, spanning the whole breadth of the house, and its height was twenty; on the inside he overlaid 5 it with pure gold. He panelled the large chamber with pine, covered it with fine gold and carved on it palm-6 trees and chain-work. He adorned the house with precious stones for decoration, and the gold he used was from 7 Parvaim. He covered the whole house with gold, its rafters and frames, its walls and doors; and he carved cherubim on the walls.

8 He made the Most Holy Place twenty cubits long, corresponding to the breadth of the house, and twenty cubits broad. He covered it all with 9 six hundred talents of fine gold, and the weight of the nails was fifty shekels of gold. He also covered the upper chambers with gold. 10[i] In the Most Holy Place he carved two images of cherubim and over-11 laid them with gold. The total span of the wings of the cherubim was twenty cubits. A wing of the one cherub extended five cubits to reach the wall of the house, while its other wing reached out five cubits to meet a wing 12 of the other cherub. Similarly, a wing of the second cherub extended five cubits to reach the other wall of the house, while its other wing met a wing of the first cherub. The wings of 13 these cherubim extended twenty cubits; they stood with their feet on the ground, facing the outer chamber. He made the Veil of violet, purple, and 14 crimson yarn, and fine linen, and embroidered cherubim on it.

In front of the house he erected two 15[j] pillars eighteen cubits high, with an architrave five cubits high on top of each. He made chainwork like a neck-16 lace[k] and set it round the tops of the pillars, and he carved a hundred pomegranates and set them in the chain-work. He erected the two 17 pillars in front of the temple, one on the right and one on the left; the one on the right he named Jachin[l] and the one on the left Boaz.[m]

He then made an altar of bronze, **4** twenty cubits long, twenty cubits broad, and ten cubits high. He also made the 2[n] Sea of cast metal; it was round in shape, the diameter from rim to rim being ten cubits; it stood five cubits high, and it took a line thirty cubits long to go round it. Under the Sea, on every side, 3 completely surrounding the thirty[o] cubits of its circumference, were what looked like gourds,[p] two rows of them, cast in one piece with the Sea itself. It was mounted on twelve oxen, three 4 facing north, three west, three south, and three east, their hind quarters turned inwards; the Sea rested on top of them. Its thickness was a hand-5

g *Verses 2–4: cp. 1 Kgs. 6. 1–3.*
h *house: prob. rdg.; Heb. length.*
i *Verses 10–13: cp. 1 Kgs. 6. 23–28.*
j *Verses 15–17: cp. 1 Kgs. 7. 15–21.*
k *necklace: prob. rdg.; Heb. obscure.*
l *Or Jachun, meaning It shall stand.*
m *Or Booz, meaning In strength.*
n *Verses 2–5: cp. 1 Kgs. 7. 23–26.*
o *Prob. rdg.; Heb. ten.*
p *Prob. rdg., cp. 1 Kgs. 7. 24; Heb. oxen.*

3.1–5.1: The construction of the Temple. The Chronicler greatly reduces from 1 Kgs.6.1–7.22 the description of the basic structure of the Temple; he omits altogether the building of Solomon's palace (1 Kgs.7.1–12). **1:** *Moriah:* Rabbinic tradition uses the mention here of Moriah to identify it with Mount Zion; compare too Gen.22.2. Possibly this rabbinic identification is as old as the age of the Chronicler. **4:** *Its height was twenty* (see Tfn. *h*): note that the figure is taken from the Sept., but the MT reads "a hundred and twenty"; this latter is either an error or else an exaggeration characteristic of the Chronicler. The source, 1 Kgs.6.2, reads "thirty." **5:** *Pine* is given here instead of the cedar of 1 Kgs.6.18. That all the wood was *covered with fine gold* (six hundred talents' worth, see v. 8) is an embroidered exaggeration. **14:** *The Veil* is possibly the Chronicler's own contribution, reflecting the postexilic temple of his time; the source (1 Kgs.6.2,31) speaks of doors, though the Wilderness Tabernacle (Exod.16.31) had a Veil (Exod.36.35). See Mt.27.51; Mk.15.38; Lk.23.45. **17:** See Tfn. *j*. **4.1:** The *altar of bronze* is not directly mentioned in 1 Kgs. ch. 7, but see 1 Kgs.8.64 and n. there.

breadth; its rim was made like that of a cup, shaped like the calyx of a lily; when full it held three thousand 6 baths. He also made ten basins for washing, setting five on the left side and five on the right; in these they rinsed everything used for the whole-offering. The Sea was made for the priests to wash in.

7 He made ten golden lamp-stands in the prescribed manner and set them in the temple, five on the right side and 8 five on the left. He also made ten tables and placed them in the temple, five on the right and five on the left; and he made a hundred golden tossing-bowls.

9 He made the court of the priests and the great precinct and the doors for it, and overlaid the doors of both 10 with copper; he put the Sea at the right side, at the south-east corner of the temple.

11*q* Huram made the pots, the shovels, and the tossing-bowls. So he finished the work which he had undertaken for King 12 Solomon on the house of God. The two pillars; the two bowl-shaped capitals*r* on the tops of the pillars; the two ornamental networks to cover the two bowl-shaped capitals on the tops of the 13 pillars; the four hundred pomegranates for the two networks, two rows of pomegranates for each network, to cover the two bowl-shaped 14 capitals on the two*s* pillars; the ten*t* trolleys and the ten*t* basins on the 15 trolleys; the one Sea and the twelve 16 oxen which supported it; the pots, the shovels, and the tossing-bowls*u*—all these*v* objects master Huram made of bronze, burnished work for King Solomon for the house of the LORD. 17 In the Plain of the Jordan the king cast them, in the foundry between 18 Succoth and Zeredah. Solomon made great quantities of all these objects; the weight of the copper*w* used was beyond reckoning.

19 Solomon made also all the furnishings for the house of God: the golden altar, the tables upon which was set the 20 Bread of the Presence, the lamp-stands

of red gold whose lamps burned before the inner shrine in the prescribed man ner, the flowers and lamps and tongs of 21 solid gold, the snuffers, tossing-bowls, saucers, and firepans of red gold, and, at the entrance to the house, the inner doors leading to the Most Holy Place and those leading to the sanctuary, of gold.

When all the work which Solomon 5 did for the house of the LORD was completed, he brought in the sacred treasures of his father David, the silver, the gold, and the vessels, and deposited them in the storehouses of the house of God.

THEN SOLOMON SUMMONED THE ELDERS 2*x* of Israel, and all the heads of the tribes who were chiefs of families in Israel, to assemble in Jerusalem, in order to bring up the Ark of the Covenant of the LORD from the City of David, which is called Zion. All the men of 3 Israel assembled in the king's presence at the pilgrim-feast in the seventh month. When the elders of Israel had 4 all come, the Levites took the Ark and carried it up with the Tent of the 5 Presence and all the sacred furnishings of the Tent: it was the priests and the Levites together who carried them up. King Solomon and the whole con- 6 gregation of Israel, assembled with him before the Ark, sacrificed sheep and oxen in numbers past counting or reckoning. Then the priests brought 7 in the Ark of the Covenant of the LORD to its place, the inner shrine of the house, the Most Holy Place, beneath the wings of the cherubim. The 8 cherubim spread their wings over the place of the Ark, and formed a cover-ing above the Ark and its poles. The 9 poles projected, and their ends could

q 4. 11—5. 1: cp. 1 Kgs. 7. 40–51.
r bowl-shaped capitals: prob. rdg., cp. 1 Kgs. 7. 41; Heb. the bowls and the capitals.
s two: prob. rdg., cp. 1 Kgs. 7. 42; Heb. surface of the.
t the ten: prob. rdg., cp. 1 Kgs. 7. 43; Heb. he made the . . .
u tossing-bowls: prob. rdg., cp. 1 Kgs. 7. 45; Heb. forks.
v Prob. rdg., cp. 1 Kgs. 7. 45; Heb. their.
w Or bronze.
x Verses 2–10: cp. 1 Kgs. 8. 1–9.

6: *Basins:* See 1 Kgs.7.38–39. That *the Sea* was used *to wash in* is the Chronicler's contribution.
5.2–7.22: The dedication and divine acceptance of the Temple. The source is 1 Kgs.8.1–9.9.
2–14: *The Ark* is brought into the Temple. See 11 13 n. **3 4:** The Chronicler omits Ethanim (1 Kgs.8.2), the Canaanite name of *the seventh month* September-October; he replaces priests

be seen from the Holy Place immediately in front of the inner shrine, but
from nowhere else outside; they are
10 there to this day. There was nothing
inside the Ark but the two tablets which
Moses had put there at Horeb, the
tablets of the covenant*y* which the
LORD made with the Israelites when
they left Egypt.

11 Now when the priests came out of the
Holy Place (for all the priests who were
present had hallowed themselves with-
12 out keeping to their divisions), all the
levitical singers, Asaph, Heman, and
Jeduthun, their sons and their kinsmen, clothed in fine linen, stood with
cymbals, lutes, and harps, to the east
of the altar, together with a hundred
and twenty priests who blew trumpets.
13 Now the trumpeters and the singers
joined in unison to sound forth praise
and thanksgiving to the LORD, and the
song was raised with trumpets, cymbals,
and musical instruments, in praise of the
LORD, because 'that*z* is good, for his
love endures for ever'; and the house
was filled with the cloud of the glory
14 of the LORD. The priests could not
continue to minister because of the
cloud, for the glory of the LORD filled
61ᵃ the house of God. Then Solomon
said:

O LORD who hast chosen to dwell
   in thick darkness,
2 here have I built thee a lofty house,
   a habitation for thee to occupy for
      ever.

3   And as they stood waiting, the king
turned round and blessed all the
4 assembly of Israel in these words:
'Blessed be the LORD the God of Israel
who spoke directly to my father
David and has himself fulfilled his
5 promise. For he said, "From the day
when I brought my people out of Egypt,
I chose no city out of all the tribes of
Israel where I should build a house for
my Name to be there, nor did I choose
any man to be prince over my people

Israel. But I chose Jerusalem for my 6
Name to be there, and I chose David
to be over my people Israel." My father 7
David had in mind to build a house in
honour of the name of the LORD the
God of Israel, but the LORD said to 8
him, "You purposed to build a house
in honour of my name; and your purpose was good. Nevertheless, you shall 9
not build it; but the son who is to be
born to you, he shall build the house in
honour of my name." The LORD has 10
now fulfilled his promise: I have succeeded my father David and taken his
place on the throne of Israel, as the
LORD promised; and I have built the
house in honour of the name of the
LORD the God of Israel. I have installed 11
there the Ark containing the covenant
of the LORD which he made with Israel.'

Then Solomon, standing in front of 12
the altar of the LORD, in the presence
of the whole assembly of Israel, spread
out his hands. He had made a bronze*b* 13
platform, five cubits long, five cubits
broad, and three cubits high, and had
placed it in the centre of the precinct.
He mounted it and knelt down in the
presence of the assembly, and, spreading
out his hands towards heaven, he 14
said, 'O LORD God of Israel, there is no
god like thee in heaven or on earth,
keeping covenant with thy servants and
showing them constant love while they
continue faithful to thee in heart and
soul. Thou hast kept thy promise to 15
thy servant David my father; by thy
deeds this day thou hast fulfilled what
thou didst say to him in words. Now, 16
therefore, O LORD God of Israel, keep
this promise of thine to thy servant
David my father: "You shall never
want for a man appointed by me to sit
on the throne of Israel, if only your
sons look to their ways and conform to
my law, as you have done in my
sight." And now, O LORD God of Israel, 17

y the tablets of the covenant: prob. rdg., cp. 1 Kgs. 8. 9; Heb. om.
z Or he.
a Verses 1–39: cp. 1 Kgs. 8. 12–50.
b Or copper.

(1 Kgs.8.3) with *Levites* as the bearers of *the Ark;* see 1 Chr.15.1–15. **11–13:** The Chronicler
adds the role of Levites and the musicians here as he did at David's bringing up of the Ark
in 1 Chr.15.16–22; 16.4–6. **14:** *The cloud of the glory:* see 1 Kgs.8.10–11 n. **6.1–42:** The
Chronicler makes few alterations in the benediction and prayer of *Solomon* as given in
1 Kgs.8.12–50. **13:** The *bronze platform*, added by the Chronicler, is not mentioned in 1 Kgs.

let the word which thou didst speak to thy servant David be confirmed.

18 'But can God indeed dwell with man on the earth? Heaven itself, the highest heaven, cannot contain thee; how much

19 less this house that I have built! Yet attend to the prayer and the supplication of thy servant, O Lord my God; listen to the cry and the prayer which

20 thy servant utters before thee, that thine eyes may ever be upon this house day and night, this place of which thou didst say, "It shall receive my Name"; so mayest thou hear thy servant when he prays towards this

21 place. Hear thou the supplications of thy servant and of thy people Israel when they pray towards this place. Hear from heaven thy dwelling and, when thou hearest, forgive.

22 'When a man wrongs his neighbour and he is adjured to take an oath, and the adjuration is made before thy

23 altar in this house, then do thou hear from heaven and act: be thou thy servants' judge, requiting the guilty man and bringing his deeds upon his own head, acquitting the innocent and rewarding him as his innocence may deserve.

24 'When thy people Israel are defeated by an enemy because they have sinned against thee, and they turn back to thee, confessing thy name and making their prayer and supplication before thee

25 in this house, do thou hear from heaven; forgive the sin of thy people Israel and restore them to the land which thou gavest to them and to their forefathers.

26 'When the heavens are shut up and there is no rain, because thy servant and thy people Israel have sinned against thee, and when they pray towards this place, confessing thy name and forsaking their sin when they feel thy

27 punishment, do thou hear in heaven and forgive their sin; so mayest thou teach them the good way which they should follow, and grant rain to thy land which thou hast given to thy people as their own possession.

28 'If there is famine in the land, or pestilence, or black blight or red, or locusts new sloughed or fully grown, or if their enemies besiege them in any[c]

of their cities, or if plague or sickness

29 befall them, then hear the prayer of supplication of every man among thy people Israel, as each one, prompted by his own suffering and misery, spreads

30 out his hands towards this house; hear it from heaven thy dwelling and forgive. And, as thou knowest a man's heart, reward him according to his deeds, for thou alone knowest the hearts of all

31 men; and so they will fear and obey thee all their lives in the land thou gavest to our forefathers.

32 'The foreigner too, the man who does not belong to thy people Israel, but has come from a distant land because of thy great fame and thy strong hand and arm outstretched, when he comes

33 and prays towards this house, hear from heaven thy dwelling and respond to the call which the foreigner makes to thee, so that like thy people Israel all peoples of the earth may know thy fame and fear thee, and learn that this house which I have built bears thy name.

34 'When thy people go to war with their enemies, wherever thou dost send them, and they pray to thee, turning towards this city which thou hast chosen and towards this house which I have

35 built in honour of thy name, do thou from heaven hear their prayer and supplication, and grant them justice.

36 'Should they sin against thee (and what man is free from sin?) and shouldst thou in thy anger give them over to an enemy, who carries them

37 captive to a land far or near; if in the land of their captivity they learn their lesson and turn back and make supplication to thee in that land and say, "We have sinned and acted perversely

38 and wickedly", if they turn back to thee with heart and soul in the land of their captivity to which they have been taken, and pray, turning towards their land which thou gavest to their forefathers and towards this city which thou didst choose and this house which I

39 have built in honour of thy name; then from heaven thy dwelling do thou hear their prayer and supplications and grant them justice. Forgive thy people their

c In any: *prob. rdg.; Heb.* in the land.

40 sins against thee. Now, O my God, let thine eyes be open and thy ears attentive to the prayer made in this place.

41 Arise now, O LORD God, and come to thy place of rest, thou and the Ark of thy might. Let thy priests, O LORD God, be clothed with salvation and thy

42 saints rejoice in prosperity. O LORD God, reject not thy anointed prince; remember thy servant David's loyal service.'*d*

7 When Solomon had finished this prayer, fire came down from heaven and consumed the whole-offering and the sacrifices, while the glory of the

2 LORD filled the house. The priests were unable to enter the house of the LORD because the glory of the LORD

3 had filled it. All the Israelites were watching as the fire came down with the glory of the LORD on the house, and where they stood on the paved court they bowed low to the ground and worshipped and gave thanks to the LORD, because 'that*e* is good, for his love endures for ever.'

4 Then the king and all the people

5 offered sacrifice before the LORD. King Solomon offered a sacrifice of twenty-two thousand oxen and a hundred and twenty thousand sheep; in this way the king and all the people dedicated

6 the house of God. The priests stood at their appointed posts; so too the Levites with their musical instruments for the LORD's service, which King David had made for giving thanks to the LORD—'for his love endures for ever'—whenever he rendered praise with their help; opposite them, the priests sounded their trumpets; and all the Israelites were standing there.

7*f* Then Solomon consecrated the centre of the court which lay in front*g* of the house of the LORD; there he

offered the whole-offerings and the fat portions of the shared-offerings, because the bronze altar which he had made could not take the whole-offering, the grain-offering, and the fat

8 portions. So Solomon and all Israel with him, a very great assembly from Lebo-hamath to the Torrent of Egypt, celebrated the pilgrim-feast at that time for seven days. On the eighth day

9 they held a closing ceremony; for they had celebrated the dedication of the altar for seven days; the pilgrim-feast lasted seven days. On the twenty-third

10 day of the seventh month he sent the people to their homes, happy and glad at heart for all the prosperity granted by the LORD to David and Solomon and to his people Israel.

11 When Solomon had finished the house of the LORD and the royal palace and had successfully carried out all that he had planned for the house of the

12 LORD and the palace, the LORD appeared to him by night and said, 'I have heard your prayer and I have chosen this place to be my place of sacrifice. When I shut up the heavens

13 and there is no rain, or command the locusts to consume the land, or send a pestilence against my people, if my

14 people whom I have named my own submit and pray to me and seek me and turn back from their evil ways, I will hear from heaven and forgive their sins and heal their land. Now my eyes

15 will be open and my ears attentive to the prayers which are made in this place. I have chosen and consecrated

16 this house, that my Name may be there for all time and my eyes and my

d thy servant . . . service: *or* thy constant love for David thy servant.
e *Or* he.
f *Verses 7–22: cp. 1 Kgs. 8. 64—9. 9.*
g *Or* to the east.

40–42: These verses follow not the Kgs. source, but Ps.132.8–10. **41–42:** These verses are added. V. 42 reverts to David; see 1 Chr.28.1–29.30 n. Solomon is the *anointed prince.* **7.1–3:** 1 Kgs.8.54–66 has a second benediction instead of an immediate divine response to Solomon's *prayer.* The Chronicler gives a second divine sign, drawing on the tradition of *fire from heaven* to consecrate an altar; compare Lev.9.24; 1 Kgs.18.38; 1 Chr.21.26. The *glory* sanctioned the house; the *fire* sanctioned the altar. **7–8:** Compare 1 Kgs.8.64–65. **9–10:** The Chronicler is concerned to make clear the different sacred times involved; see 1 Kgs.8.66. On his understanding, there were two seven-day periods, one to dedicate the altar (compare Ezek.43.18–27) and one to observe the regular autumn festival of Tabernacles, which lasted from the fifteenth through the twenty-first day of the seventh month. *The eighth day* of the Tabernacles festival was to be specially consecrated (Lev.23.36). Only on *the twenty-third day* of the month, therefore, were the people dismissed. **11–22:** From 1 Kgs.9.1–9; but vv. 13–15 are here added to furnish hope.

17 heart be fixed on it for ever. And if you, on your part, live in my sight as your father David lived, doing all I command you, and observing my 18 statutes and my judgements, then I will establish your royal throne, as I promised by a covenant granted to your father David when I said, "You shall never want for a man to rule over 19 Israel." But if you turn away and forsake my statutes and my commandments which I have set before you, and if you go and serve other gods and prostrate yourselves before them, 20 then I will uproot you from my land which I gave you, I will reject this house which I have consecrated in honour of my name, and make it a byword and an object-lesson among all peoples. 21 And this house will become a ruin; every passer-by will be appalled at the sight of it, and they will ask, "Why has the LORD so treated this land and 22 this house?" The answer will be, "Because they forsook the LORD the God of their fathers, who brought them out of Egypt, and clung to other gods, prostrating themselves before them and serving them; that is why the LORD has brought this great evil on them."'

8 1*h* Solomon had taken twenty years to build the house of the LORD and his 2 own palace, and he rebuilt the cities which Huram had given him and 3 settled Israelites in them. He went to 4 Hamath-zobah and seized it, and rebuilt Tadmor in the wilderness and all the store-cities which he had built in 5 Hamath. He also built Upper Beth-horon and Lower Beth-horon as fortified cities with walls and barred 6 gates, and Baalath, as well as all his store-cities, and all the towns where he quartered his chariots and horses; and he carried out all his cherished plans for building in Jerusalem, in the Lebanon, and throughout his whole 7 dominion. All the survivors of the Hittites, Amorites, Perizzites, Hivites, and Jebusites, who did not belong to Israel—that is their descendants who 8 survived in the land, wherever the Israelites had been unable to exterminate them—were employed by Solomon on forced labour, as they still are. He put 9 none of the Israelites to forced labour for his public works; they were his fighting men, his captains and lieutenants, and the commanders of his chariots and of his cavalry. These were 10 King Solomon's officers, two hundred and fifty of them, in charge of the foremen who superintended the people.

Solomon brought Pharaoh's daughter 11 up from the City of David to the house he had built for her, for he said, 'No wife of mine shall live in the house of David king of Israel, because this place which the Ark of the LORD has entered is*i* holy.'

Then Solomon offered whole-offer- 12 ings to the LORD on the altar which he had built to the east of the vestibule, according to what was required for 13 each day, making offerings according to the law of Moses for the sabbaths, the new moons, and the three annual appointed feasts—the pilgrim-feasts of Unleavened Bread, of Weeks, and of Tabernacles.*j* Following the practice 14 of his father David, he drew up the roster of service for the priests and that for the Levites for leading the praise and for waiting upon the priests, as each day required, and that for the door-keepers at each gate; for such was the instruction which David the man of God had given. The instructions 15 which David had given concerning the priests and the Levites and concerning the treasuries were not forgotten.

By this time all Solomon's work was 16 achieved, from the foundation of the house of the LORD to its completion; the house of the LORD was perfect. Then Solomon went to Ezion-geber 17

h Verses 1–18: cp. 1 Kgs. 9. 10–28.
i this place which . . . is: prob. rdg.; Heb. those which . . . are.
j Or Booths.

8.1–9.31: Solomon's works, wisdom, and wealth. The Chronicler makes only slight changes in his source. 1–28: Compare 1 Kgs.9.10–28. 2–4: In 1 Kgs.9.10–11 it was Solomon who gave *cities* to *Huram*, not the reverse. The source did not mention the campaign to the north (vv. 3–4). 11: Compare 1 Kgs.9.24. Solomon's comment is added by the Chronicler. 13: The Chronicler adds the occasions on which the sacrifices are to be offered according to Mosaic legislation; see Lev. ch. 23 and Num. chs. 28–29. 14–15: The priestly and Levitical organizations

and to Eloth on the coast of Edom,
18 and Huram sent ships under the command of his own officers and manned by crews of experienced seamen; and these, in company with Solomon's servants, went to Ophir and brought back four hundred and fifty talents of gold, which they delivered to King Solomon.

9 1[k] THE QUEEN OF SHEBA HEARD OF SOLO-mon's fame and came to test him with hard questions. She arrived in Jerusalem with a very large retinue, camels laden with spices, gold in abundance, and precious stones. When she came to Solomon, she told him everything
2 she had in her mind, and Solomon answered all her questions; not one of them was too abstruse for him to
3 answer. When the queen of Sheba saw the wisdom of Solomon, the house
4 which he had built, the food on his table, the courtiers sitting round him, his attendants and his cupbearers in their livery standing behind, and the stairs by which he went up to the house of the LORD, there was no more spirit
5 left in her. Then she said to the king, 'The report which I heard in my own country about you and your wisdom
6 was true, but I did not believe what they told me until I came and saw for myself. Indeed, I was not told half of the greatness of your wisdom; you surpass
7 the report which I had of you. Happy are your wives, happy these courtiers of yours who wait on you every day and
8 hear your wisdom! Blessed be the LORD your God who has delighted in you and has set you on his throne as his king; because in his love your God has elected Israel to make it endure for ever, he has made you king over it to maintain law and justice.'
9 Then she gave the king a hundred and twenty talents of gold, spices in great abundance, and precious stones. There had never been any spices to equal those which the queen of Sheba gave to King Solomon.
10 Besides all this, the servants of Huram and of Solomon, who had brought gold from Ophir, brought also

cargoes of algum wood and precious stones. The king used the wood to 11 make stands for the house of the LORD and for the royal palace, as well as harps and lutes for the singers. The like of them had never before been seen in the land of Judah.

King Solomon gave the queen of 12 Sheba all she desired, whatever she asked, besides his gifts in return for[l] what she had brought him. Then she departed and returned with her retinue to her own land.

Now the weight of gold which 13 Solomon received yearly was six hundred and sixty-six talents, in addition 14 to the tolls levied on merchants and on traders who imported goods; all the kings of Arabia and the regional governors also[m] brought gold and silver to the king.

King Solomon made two hundred 15 shields of beaten gold, and six hundred shekels of gold went to the making of each one; he also made three hundred 16 bucklers of beaten gold, and three hundred shekels of gold went to the making of each buckler. The king put these into the House of the Forest of Lebanon.

The king also made a great throne of 17 ivory and overlaid it with pure gold. Six steps and a footstool for the throne 18 were all encased in gold. There were arms on each side of the seat, with a lion standing beside each of them, and 19 twelve lions stood on the six steps, one at either end of each step. Nothing like it had ever been made for any monarch. All Solomon's drinking vessels 20 were of gold, and all the plate in the House of the Forest of Lebanon was of red gold; silver was reckoned of no value in the days of Solomon. The 21 king had a fleet of ships plying to Tarshish with Huram's men; once every three years this fleet of merchantmen came home, bringing gold and silver, ivory, apes, and monkeys.

Thus King Solomon outdid all the 22

k Verses 1–24: cp. 1 Kgs. 10. 1–25.
l his gifts . . . for: prob. rdg.; Heb. om.
m all . . . also: or and on all the kings of Arabia and the regional governors who . . .

ascribed to *David* in 1 Chr. chs. 23–26 are referred to. **9.1–28**: These reports are taken over

kings of the earth in wealth and
22 wisdom, and all the kings of the earth
courted him, to hear the wisdom which
24 God had put in his heart. Each brought
his gift with him, vessels of silver and
gold, garments, perfumes and spices,
horses and mules, so much year by
year.
25[n] Solomon had standing for four
thousand horses and chariots, and
twelve thousand cavalry horses, and he
stabled some in the chariot-towns and
26 kept others at hand in Jerusalem. He
ruled over all the kings from the
Euphrates to the land of the Philistines
27 and the border of Egypt. He made
silver as common in Jerusalem as
stones, and cedar as plentiful as
28 sycomore-fig in the Shephelah. Horses
were imported from Egypt and from
all countries for Solomon.
29[o] The rest of the acts of Solomon's
reign, from first to last, are recorded in
the history of Nathan the prophet, in
the prophecy of Ahijah of Shiloh, and
in the visions of Iddo the seer concern-
30 ing Jeroboam son of Nebat. Solomon
ruled in Jerusalem over the whole of
31 Israel for forty years. Then he rested
with his forefathers and was buried in
the city of David his father, and he was
succeeded by his son Rehoboam.

The kings of Judah from
Rehoboam to Ahaz

10 1[p] REHOBOAM WENT TO SHECHEM, FOR ALL
Israel had gone there to make him
2 king. When Jeroboam son of Nebat
heard of it in Egypt, where he had taken
refuge to escape Solomon, he returned
3 from Egypt. They now recalled him,
and he and all Israel came to Rehob-
4 oam and said, 'Your father laid a
cruel yoke upon us; but if you will now
lighten the cruel slavery he imposed
on us and the heavy yoke he laid on us,

we will serve you.' 'Give me three days,' 5
he said, 'and come back again.' So the
people went away. King Rehoboam 6
then consulted the elders who had been
in attendance on his father Solomon
while he lived: 'What answer do you
advise me to give to this people?' And 7
they said, 'If you show yourself well-
disposed to this people and gratify them
by speaking kindly to them, they will
be your servants ever after.' But he 8
rejected the advice which the elders
gave him. He next consulted those who
had grown up with him, the young
men in attendance, and asked them, 9
'What answer do you advise me to give
to this people's request that I should
lighten the yoke which my father laid
on them?' The young men replied, 10
'Give this answer to the people who say
that your father made their yoke heavy
and ask you to lighten it; tell them:
"My little finger is thicker than my
father's loins. My father laid a heavy 11
yoke on you; I will make it heavier.
My father used the whip on you; but I
will use the lash."' Jeroboam and the 12
people all came back to Rehoboam on
the third day, as the king had ordered.
And the king gave them a harsh answer. 13
He rejected the advice which the
elders had given him and spoke to the 14
people as the young men had advised:
'My father made your yoke heavy; I
will make it heavier. My father used
the whip on you; but I will use the
lash.' So the king would not listen to 15
the people; for the LORD had given this
turn to the affair, in order that the word
he had spoken by Ahijah of Shiloh to
Jeroboam son of Nebat might be
fulfilled.
When all Israel saw[q] that the king 16
would not listen to them, they answered:

n Verses 25–28: cp. 1. 14–17; 1 Kgs. 10. 26–29.
o Verses 29–31: cp. 1 Kgs. 11. 41–43.
p Verses 1–19: cp. 1 Kgs. 12. 1–19.
q saw: prob. rdg., cp. 1 Kgs. 12. 16; Heb. om.

almost unchanged from 1 Kgs.10.1–25. **29–31:** The Chronicler omits the entire negative side
of Solomon's reign as given in 1 Kgs.11.1–40. He lists some prophetic sources, though none
of these is mentioned in 1 Kgs.11.41; see 1 Chr.29.29 n. *Ahijah of Shiloh* is included even
though the Chronicler omits the account of his prophecy; compare 1 Kgs.11.29–39. *Iddo the
seer* is also mentioned in 12.15 and 13.22, but is otherwise unknown.
    10.1–28.27: The kings of Judah from Rehoboam to Ahaz. 10.1–11.4: The beginning of the
reign of *Rehoboam*. The account here is taken over without change from 1 Kgs.12.12–19,21–24.
In omitting 1 Kgs.12.20 the Chronicler also omits the crowning of Jeroboam, an event
distasteful to him.

What share have we in David?
We have no lot in the son of Jesse
Away to your homes, O Israel;
now see to your own house, David.

17 So all Israel went to their homes, and Rehoboam ruled over those Israelites who lived in the cities of Judah. 18 Then King Rehoboam sent out Hadoram, the commander of the forced levies, but the Israelites stoned him to death; whereupon King Rehoboam mounted his chariot in haste and fled 19 to Jerusalem. From that day to this, Israel has been in rebellion against the house of David.

11 1*r* When Rehoboam reached Jerusalem, he assembled the tribes of Judah and Benjamin, a hundred and eighty thousand chosen warriors, to fight against 2 Israel and recover his kingdom. But the word of the LORD came to Shemaiah 3 the man of God: 'Say to Rehoboam son of Solomon, king of Judah, and to all the Israelites in Judah and Ben- 4 jamin, "This is the word of the LORD: You shall not go up to make war on your kinsmen. Return to your homes, for this is my will."' So they listened to the word of the LORD and abandoned their campaign against Jeroboam.

5 Rehoboam resided in Jerusalem and built up the defences of certain cities in 6 Judah. The cities in Judah and Benjamin which he fortified were Beth- 7 lehem, Etam, Tekoa, Beth-zur, Soco, 8 Adullam, Gath, Mareshah, Ziph, 9,10 Adoraim, Lachish, Azekah, Zorah, 11 Aijalon, and Hebron. He strengthened the fortifications of these fortified cities, and put governors in them, as well as 12 supplies of food, oil, and wine. Also he stored shields and spears in every one of the cities, and strengthened their fortifications. Thus he retained possession of Judah and Benjamin.

Now the priests and the Levites 13 throughout the whole of Israel resorted to Rehoboam from all their territories; for the Levites had left all their com- 14 mon land and their own patrimony and had gone to Judah and Jerusalem, because Jeroboam and his successors rejected their services as priests of the LORD, and he appointed his own priests 15 for the hill-shrines, for the demons,*s* and for the calves which he had made. Those, from all the tribes of Israel, 16 who were resolved to seek the LORD the God of Israel followed the Levites to Jerusalem to sacrifice to the LORD the God of their fathers. So they 17 strengthened the kingdom of Judah and for three years made Rehoboam son of Solomon secure, because he followed the example of David and Solomon during that time.

Rehoboam married Mahalath, whose 18 father was Jerimoth son of David and whose mother was Abihail daughter of Eliab son of Jesse. His sons by her 19 were: Jeush, Shemaiah and Zaham. Next he married Maacah granddaughter 20 of Absalom, who bore him Abijah, Attai, Ziza and Shelomith. Of all his 21 wives and concubines, Rehoboam loved Maacah most; he had in all eighteen wives and sixty concubines and became the father of twenty-eight sons and sixty daughters. He appointed 22 Abijah son of Maacah chief among his brothers, making him crown prince and planning to make him his successor on the throne. He showed discretion 23 in detailing his sons to take charge of all the fortified cities throughout the whole territory of Judah and Benjamin; he also made generous provision for them and procured them*t* wives.

When the kingdom of Rehoboam 12

r Verses 1–4: cp. 1 Kgs. 12. 21–24. *s Or satyrs.*
t procured them: prob. rdg.; Heb. asked for a multitude of . . .

11.5–12.16: The rest of the reign of Rehoboam. The Chronicler proceeds (vv. 5–12) to use a source otherwise unknown but quite credible historically (with the exception, at times, of the numbers given). **13–16:** The Chronicler portrays the faithfulness of *the Levites;* they abandon the apostate Northern Kingdom. Historically, circles of *Levites* remained in the Northern Kingdom until its fall in 722/21; after that they became important in reform movements in the surviving Southern Kingdom. **14:** See 1 Kgs.12.31. **17:** *Rehoboam* was first faithful to the LORD in the manner of *David and Solomon;* afterward he was unfaithful and brought trouble upon himself. Thus is established a pattern also exemplified by other kings; see Asa, 16.7–10; Joash, 24.1–24; Amaziah, 25.14–24; and Uzziah, 26.16–21. **18–23:** The source is unknown. The Chronicler gives here the abundance of Rehoboam's wives, but he has previously omitted Solomon's abundance, 1 Kgs.11.3. **12.1–12:** 1 Kgs. treated the invasion of *Shishak* as simply

was on a firm footing and he became strong, he forsook the law of the LORD, he and all Israel with him. In the 2 fifth year of Rehoboam's reign, because of this disloyalty to the LORD, Shishak king of Egypt attacked Jerusalem 3 with twelve hundred chariots and sixty thousand horsemen, and brought with him from Egypt an innumerable following of Libyans, Sukkites, and 4 Cushites.*u* He captured the fortified cities of Judah and reached Jerusalem. 5 Then Shemaiah the prophet came to Rehoboam and the leading men of Judah, who had assembled in Jerusalem before the advance of Shishak, and said to them, 'This is the word of the LORD: You have abandoned me; therefore I now abandon 6 you to Shishak.' The princes of Israel and the king submitted and said, 'The 7 LORD is just.' When the LORD saw that they had submitted, there came from him this word to Shemaiah: 'Because they have submitted I will not destroy them, I will let them barely escape; my wrath shall not be poured out on 8 Jerusalem by means of Shishak, but they shall become his servants; then they will know the difference between serving me and serving the rulers of 9*v* other countries.' Shishak king of Egypt in his attack on Jerusalem removed the treasures of the house of the LORD and of the royal palace. He seized everything, including the shields 10 of gold that Solomon had made. King Rehoboam replaced them with bronze shields and entrusted them to the officers of the escort who guarded the entrance 11 of the royal palace. Whenever the king entered the house of the LORD, the escort entered, carrying the shields;

afterwards they returned them to the guard-room. Because Rehoboam sub- 12 mitted, the LORD's wrath was averted from him, and he was not utterly destroyed; Judah enjoyed prosperity.

Thus King Rehoboam increased his 13*w* power in Jerusalem. He was forty-one years old when he came to the throne, and he reigned for seventeen years in Jerusalem, the city which the LORD had chosen out of all the tribes of Israel as the place to receive his Name. Rehoboam's mother was a woman of Ammon called Naamah. He did what was wrong, he did not 14 make a practice of seeking guidance of the LORD. The events of Rehoboam's 15 reign, from first to last, are recorded in the histories of Shemaiah the prophet and Iddo the seer.*x* There was continual fighting between Rehoboam and Jeroboam. He rested with his fore- 16 fathers and was buried in the city of David; and he was succeeded by his son Abijah.

IN THE EIGHTEENTH YEAR OF KING JER- **13** oboam's reign Abijah became king of Judah. He reigned in Jerusalem for 2 three years; his mother was Maacah daughter of Uriel of Gibeah. There was fighting between Abijah and Jeroboam. Abijah drew up his army 3 of four hundred thousand picked troops in order of battle, while Jeroboam formed up against him with eight hundred thousand picked troops. Abijah 4 took up position on the slopes of Mount Zemaraim in the hill-country of Ephraim and called out, 'Hear me, Jeroboam and all Israel: Ought you not 5

u Or Nubians. *v Verses 9–11: cp. 1 Kgs. 14. 25–28.*
w Verses 13–16: cp. 1 Kgs. 14. 29–31.
x Prob. rdg.; Heb. adds to be enrolled by genealogy.

---

an event of Rehoboam's reign; the Chronicler sees it as a punishment for some fault and explains that it is a result of *Rehoboam's* forsaking the LORD. **4–8:** The repentance of the Judeans and the consequent limitation of the punishment are characteristic motifs of the Chronicler's history. **15:** The Chronicler tends to cite sources written by prophets rather than court annals; contrast 1 Kgs.14.29.

13.1–14.1: The reign of Abijah. A longer account is given here than the brief mention in 1 Kgs.15.1–8 (there Abijah's name is spelled Abijam). **2:** Here Abijah's mother is a daughter of *Uriel of Gibeah* whereas in 1 Kgs.15.2 she is the daughter (probably granddaughter) of Abishalom, who was probably David's rebellious son Absalom (2 Sam. chs. 13–18). The Chronicler may have wanted to avoid having Absalom an ancestor of later kings. The mother's name is given both as Micaiah and *Maacah*. In 15.16, she is called mother of Asa, with mother to be understood as grandmother. **3:** The Chronicler shows interest in the numbers of Judean armies and the armies of their enemies, usually to glorify the Judean kings or their God. The numbers are unreliable. **5–12:** The speech presents the two motifs of greatest concern to the Chronicler: the validity of the dynasty of *David* as the one proper kingship in *Israel*, and the

to know that the LORD the God of Israel gave the kingship over Israel to David and his descendants in perpetuity 6 by a covenant of salt? Yet Jeroboam son of Nebat, the servant of Solomon son of David, rose in rebellion 7 against his lord, and certain worthless scoundrels gathered round him, who stubbornly opposed Solomon's son Rehoboam when he was young and inexperienced, and he was no match 8 for them. Now you propose to match yourselves against the kingdom of the LORD as ruled by David's sons, you and your mob of supporters and the golden calves which Jeroboam has made to be 9 your gods. Have you not dismissed from office the Aaronites, priests of the LORD, and the Levites, and followed the practice of other lands in appointing priests? Now, if any man comes for consecration with an offering of a young bull and seven rams, you accept him as 10 a priest to a god that is no god. But as for us, the LORD is our God and we have not forsaken him; we have Aaronites as priests ministering to the LORD with the Levites, duly dis- 11 charging their office. Morning and evening, these burn whole-offerings and fragrant incense to the LORD and offer the Bread of the Presence arranged in rows on a table ritually clean; they also kindle the lamps on the golden lamp-stand every evening. Thus we do indeed keep the charge of the LORD our God, whereas you have forsaken 12 him. God is with us at our head, and his priests stand there with trumpets to signal the battle-cry against you. Men of Israel, do not fight the LORD

the God of your fathers; you will have no success.'

Jeroboam sent a detachment of his 13 troops to go round and lay an ambush in the rear, so that his main body faced Judah while the ambush lay behind them. The men of Judah turned to find 14 that they were engaged front and rear. Then they cried to the LORD for help. The priests sounded their trumpets, and the men of Judah raised a shout, 15 and when they did so, God put Jeroboam and all Israel to rout before Abijah and Judah. The Israelites fled before 16 the men of Judah, and God delivered them into their power. So Abijah and 17 his men defeated them with very heavy losses, and five hundred thousand picked Israelites fell in the battle. After 18 this, the Israelites were reduced to submission, and Judah prevailed because they relied on the LORD the God of their fathers. Abijah followed 19 up his victory over Jeroboam and captured from him the cities of Bethel, Jeshanah, and Ephron, with their villages. Jeroboam did not regain his power 20 during the days of Abijah; finally the LORD struck him down and he died.

But Abijah established his position; 21 he married fourteen wives and became the father of twenty-two sons and sixteen daughters. The other events of 22 Abijah's reign, both what he said and what he did, are recorded in the story of the prophet Iddo. Abijah rested with **14** his forefathers and was buried in the city of David; and he was succeeded on the throne by his son Asa. In his days the land was at peace for ten years.

Asa did what was good and right in 2

---

validity of the *Aaronite* priesthood and the service of *the Levites* at Jerusalem. Compare 1 Chr. 29.10–19. The Northern Kingdom, given more serious treatment in the Book of Kings, is dealt with negatively and only partially by the Chronicler. **5:** *A covenant of salt* was an eternal agreement (Num.18.19) sealed by both parties eating of the same food. **8:** The origin of the *golden calves* (1 Kgs.12.26–30) was deliberately omitted; the mention here is therefore strange. **11:** The ritual service assumed here is that of the Mosaic Tabernacle; compare 2.4–6 and Exod.25.23–40; 29.38–42; 30.1–10. **13–20:** This battle account expresses the Chronicler's view of battles; see also 20.22–27. The LORD throws the enemy army into panic or confusion, and the (smaller) army of the righteous is victorious because of divine intervention. The numbers involved are typical of the Chronicler's exaggerations. **20:** Actually, Jeroboam survived Abijah (1 Kgs.15.8–9). **21:** The statistics of *Abijah's* family are quite credible for a Judean king. **22:** *Iddo*: see 9.29–31 n. **14.1:** The *ten years* of *peace* refer to the first ten years of Asa's reign.
  14.2–16.14: The reign of Asa. Two main occurrences were reported concerning Asa in 1 Kgs.: his religious reform (1 Kgs.15.9–15) and his successful war against Baasha of Israel (1 Kgs. 15.16–22). These lead the Chronicler to a lengthy account (chs. 14–16), absent from Kgs., of Asa's faithfulness to the LORD, including a divinely given military victory (14.2–15.19; see 13.13–20 n.), and a shorter period of warfare (16.1–14) in which his reliance on foreign alliances instead of the LORD brings him suffering from disease (16.12). **2–7:** The Chronicler sees the

3 the eyes of the LORD his God. He suppressed the foreign altars and the hill-shrines, smashed the sacred pillars and hacked down the sacred poles, 4 and ordered Judah to seek guidance of the LORD the God of their fathers and to keep the law and the com- 5 mandments. He also suppressed the hill-shrines and the incense-altars in all the cities, and the kingdom was at 6 peace under him. He built fortified cities in Judah, for the land was at peace. He had no war to fight during those years, because the LORD had given 7 him security. He said to the men of Judah, 'Let us build these cities and fortify them, with walls round them, and towers and barred gates. The land still lies open before us. Because we have sought guidance of the LORD our God, he has sought us and given us security on every side.' So they built and prospered.

8   Asa had an army equipped with shields and spears; three hundred thousand men came from Judah, and two hundred and eighty thousand from Benjamin, shield-bearers and archers; 9 all were valiant warriors. Zerah the Cushite came out against them with an army a million strong and three hundred chariots. When he reached 10 Mareshah, Asa came out to meet him and they took up position in the 11 valley of Zephathah at Mareshah. Asa called upon the LORD his God and said, 'There is none like thee, O LORD, to help men, whether strong or weak; help us, O LORD our God, for on thee we rely and in thy name we have come out against this horde. O LORD, thou art our God, how can man vie with 12 thee?' So the LORD gave Asa and Judah victory over the Cushites and 13 they fled, and Asa and his men pursued them as far as Gerar. The Cushites broke before the LORD and his army, and many of them fell mortally wounded; and Judah carried off great loads

of spoil. They destroyed all the cities 14 around Gerar, for the LORD had struck the people with panic; and they plundered the cities, finding rich spoil in them all. They also killed the herds- 15 men and seized many sheep and camels, and then they returned to Jerusalem.

The spirit of God came upon Azariah **15** son of Oded, and he went out to meet 2 Asa and said to him, 'Hear me, Asa and all Judah and Benjamin. The LORD is with you when you are with him; if you look for him, he will let himself be found; if you forsake him, he will forsake you. For a long time 3 Israel was without the true God, without a priest to interpret the law and without law.y But when, in their dis- 4 tress, they turned to the LORD the God of Israel and sought him, he let himself be found by them. At those times there 5 was no safety for people as they went about their business; the inhabitants of every land had their fill of trouble; there was ruin on every side, nation 6 at odds with nation, city with city, for God harassed them with every kind of distress. But now you must be strong 7 and not let your courage fail; for your work will be rewarded.' When Asa 8 heard these words,z he resolutely suppressed the loathsome idols in all Judah and Benjamin and in the cities which he had captured in the hill-country of Ephraim; and he repaired the altar of the LORD which stood before the vestibule of the LORD's house.a Then 9 he assembled all Judah and Benjamin and all who had come from Ephraim, Manasseh, and Simeon to reside among them; for great numbers had come over to him from Israel, when they saw that the LORD his God was with him. So they assembled at 10 Jerusalem in the third month of the fifteenth year of Asa's reign, and that 11

y without law; *or* without the law.
z *Prob. rdg.; Heb. adds* and the prophecy, Oded the prophet.
a house: *prob. rdg.; Heb. om.*

reform of religious practice as the cause of the period of *peace.* **5:** Contrast 15.17, and its source (1 Kgs.15.14). **9:** *Zerah the Cushite:* his identity is uncertain. Cush is sometimes Ethiopia, but also an Arabian tribe, as is probable here. This account is another example of the stylized combat in which the LORD intervenes for the victory of the righteous people; see 13.13–20 n.
     15.1–19: Asa's religious reform. 1–7: One of the typical speeches developed within the Chronicler's circle; see Introduction to 2 Chr. **1:** *Azariah son of Oded* is otherwise unknown. A prophet Oded is mentioned in 28.9. Notice v. 8 and Tin. *z.* **10:** *The third month (Sivan)* was

day they sacrificed to the LORD seven hundred oxen and seven thousand sheep from the spoil which they had brought. 12 And they entered into a covenant to seek guidance of the LORD the God of their fathers with all their heart and 13 soul; all who would not seek the LORD the God of Israel were to be put to death, young and old, men and women alike. 14 Then they bound themselves by an oath to the LORD, with loud shouts of acclamation while trumpets and horns 15 sounded; and all Judah rejoiced at the oath, because they had bound themselves with all their heart and had sought him earnestly, and he had let himself be found by them. So the LORD 16[b] gave them security on every side. King Asa also deprived Maacah his grandmother of her rank as queen mother because she had an obscene object made for the worship of Asherah; Asa cut it down, ground it to powder and burnt it in the gorge of the Kidron. 17 Although the hill-shrines were allowed to remain in Israel, Asa himself re-18 mained faithful all his life. He brought into the house of God all his father's votive offerings and his own, gold and silver and sacred vessels. And there was no more war until the thirty-fifth year of Asa's reign.

161[c]   In the thirty-sixth year of the reign of Asa, Baasha king of Israel invaded Judah and fortified Ramah to cut off all 2 access to Asa king of Judah. So Asa brought out silver and gold from the treasuries of the house of the LORD and the royal palace, and sent this request to Ben-hadad king of Aram, whose capital 3 was Damascus: 'There is an alliance between us, as there was between our fathers. I now send you herewith silver and gold; break off your alliance with Baasha king of Israel, so that he may abandon his campaign against me.' 4 Ben-hadad listened willingly to King Asa and ordered the commanders of

his armies to move against the cities of Israel, and they attacked Iyyon, Dan, Abel-mayim, and all the store-cities of Naphtali. When Baasha heard of it, he 5 ceased fortifying Ramah and stopped all work on it. Then King Asa took 6 with him all the men of Judah and they carried away the stones of Ramah and the timbers with which Baasha had fortified it; and he used them to fortify Geba and Mizpah.

At that time the seer Hanani came to 7 Asa king of Judah and said to him, 'Because you relied on the king of Aram and not on the LORD your God, the army of the king of Israel has escaped. The 8 Cushites and the Libyans, were they not a great army with a vast number of chariots and horsemen? Yet, because you relied on the LORD, he delivered them into your power. The eyes of the 9 LORD range through the whole earth, to bring aid and comfort to those whose hearts are loyal to him. You have acted foolishly in this affair; you will have wars from now on.' Asa was 10 angry with the seer and put him in the stocks; for these words of his had made the king very indignant. At the same time he treated some of the people with great brutality.

The events of Asa's reign, from first 11[d] to last, are recorded in the annals of the kings of Judah and Israel. In the 12 thirty-ninth year of his reign Asa became gravely affected with gangrene in his feet; he did not seek guidance of the LORD but resorted to physicians. He rested with his forefathers, in the 13 forty-first year of his reign, and was 14 buried in the tomb which he had bought[e] for himself in the city of David, being laid on a bier[f] which had been heaped with all kinds of spices skilfully

b Verses 16–18: cp. 1 Kgs. 15. 13–15.
c Verses 1–6: cp. 1 Kgs. 15. 17–22.
d Verses 11–14: cp. 1 Kgs. 15. 23, 24.
e Or dug.
f Or in a niche.

June-July, the time of the grain harvest. The reference may be to the early summer pilgrim-feast, called Harvest, or Weeks (Exod.23.16; 34.22). The sacrificial *sheep* often have a ten-to-one ratio to the *oxen*.
  16.1–14: War and apostasy. 1–6: There is little change from 1 Kgs.15.17–22. **7–10:** The Chronicler adds a homily to his source material. It prepares for v. 12. *Hanani* figures only here; his son, the prophet Jehu, figures in 19.2; 20.34 and 1 Kgs.16.1,7; but Jehu's time was a half century earlier. *The eyes . . . that range through the whole earth* recall Zech.4.4–5. **11–14:** The Chronicler adds here to 1 Kgs.15.23–24 the comments about *physicians, the tomb, the bier,* and the *great fire.* **14:** An unusually full funeral description.

compounded; and they kindled a great fire in his honour.

17 ASA WAS SUCCEEDED BY HIS SON JE-hoshaphat, who determined to resist 2 Israel by force. He posted troops in all the fortified cities of Judah and stationed officers*g* throughout Judah and in the cities of Ephraim which 3 his father Asa had captured. The LORD was with Jehoshaphat, for he followed the example his father had set in his early years and did not resort to the 4 Baalim; he sought guidance of the God of his father and obeyed his commandments and did not follow the 5 practices of Israel. So the LORD established the kingdom under his rule, and all Judah brought him gifts, and his wealth and fame*h* became very 6 great. He took pride in the service of the LORD; he also suppressed the hill-shrines and the sacred poles in Judah.

7 In the third year of his reign he sent his officers, Ben-hayil, Obadiah, Zechariah, Nethaneel, and Micaiah, to 8 teach in the cities of Judah, together with the Levites, Shemaiah, Nethaniah, Zebadiah, Asahel, Shemiramoth, Jehonathan, Adonijah, Tobiah, and Tobadonijah,*i* accompanied by the priests 9 Elishama and Jehoram. They taught in Judah, having with them the book of the law of the LORD; they went round the cities of Judah, teaching the people.

10 So the dread of the LORD fell upon all the rulers of the lands surrounding Judah, and they did not make war 11 on Jehoshaphat. Certain Philistines brought a gift, a great quantity of silver, to Jehoshaphat; the Arabs too brought him seven thousand seven hundred rams and seven thousand 12 seven hundred he-goats. Jehoshaphat

became ever more powerful and built fortresses and store-cities in Judah; and he had much work on hand in 13 the cities of Judah. He had regular, seasoned troops in Jerusalem, en- 14 rolled according to their clans in this way: of Judah, the officers over units of a thousand: Adnah the commander, together with three hundred thousand seasoned troops; and next to him the 15 commander Johanan, with two hundred and eighty thousand; and next to 16 him Amasiah son of Zichri, who had volunteered for the service of the LORD, with two hundred thousand seasoned troops; and of Benjamin: an 17 experienced soldier Eliada, with two hundred thousand men armed with bows and shields; next to him Jehoza- 18 bad, with a hundred and eighty thousand fully-armed men. These were 19 the men who served the king, apart from those whom the king had posted in the fortified cities throughout Judah.

When Jehoshaphat had become very **18** wealthy and famous,*j* he allied himself with Ahab by marriage. Some years 2*k* afterwards he went down to visit Ahab in Samaria, and Ahab slaughtered many sheep and oxen for him and his retinue, and incited him to attack Ramoth-gilead. What Ahab king of Israel said 3 to Jehoshaphat king of Judah was this: 'Will you join me in attacking Ramoth-gilead?' And he answered, 'What is mine is yours, myself and my people; I will join with you in the war.' Then Jehoshaphat said to the king 4 of Israel, 'First let us seek counsel from the LORD.' The king of Israel assembled 5 the prophets, some four hundred of them, and asked them, 'Shall I attack Ramoth-gilead or shall I refrain?'

g Or garrisons.   *h* Or riches.
i Prob. rdg.; Heb. adds the Levites.
j Or rich.   *k* Verses 2–34: cp. 1 Kgs. 22. 2–35.

17.1–20.37: The reign of Jehoshaphat. The only incident of *Jehoshaphat's* reign related at any length in Kgs. is the battle in which Ahab was killed, presented here in ch. 18. Jehoshaphat was one of the great kings of Judah, however, and the Chronicler greatly expands the account of him.
17.1–19.11: Organizing the righteous kingdom. The account of Jehoshaphat's alliance with Ahab (ch. 18) is placed between descriptions of Jehoshaphat's good administration of the kingdom. **1b–6:** This is not in Kgs. **6:** Yet according to 20.33 *the hill-shrines* were not removed. Compare 1 Kgs.15.24. **7–9:** The king's instruction of the people here is an added element. **10–19:** Again this is an added element. The *troops* attributed to *Jehoshaphat* add up to 1,160,000 men. The numbers reflect the exaggerations usual in the Chronicler's writing. **18.1–34:** The affairs of the Northern Kingdom are usually neglected by the Chronicler, but the dramatic narrative of *Ahab's* death is here included for the sake of *Jehoshaphat's* part in it. Apart from vv. 1–2, the material is mostly from 1 Kgs.22.1–35. **1:** See 2 Kgs.8.18,25–27. **2:** The verse expands

6 'Attack,' they answered; 'God will deliver it into your hands.' Jehoshaphat asked, 'Is there no other prophet of the LORD here through whom we may 7 seek guidance?' 'There is one more', the king of Israel answered, 'through whom we may seek guidance of the LORD, but I hate the man, because he never prophesies any good for me; never anything but evil. His name is Micaiah son of Imla.' Jehoshaphat exclaimed, 'My lord king, let no such 8 word pass your lips!' So the king of Israel called one of his eunuchs and told him to fetch Micaiah son of Imla with all speed.

9 The king of Israel and Jehoshaphat king of Judah were seated on their thrones, clothed in their royal robes and in shining armour, at the entrance to the gate of Samaria, and all the prophets were prophesying before 10 them. One of them, Zedekiah son of Kenaanah, made himself horns of iron and said, 'This is the word of the LORD: "With horns like these you shall gore the Aramaeans and make an end 11 of them."' In the same vein all the prophets prophesied, 'Attack Ramoth-gilead and win the day; the LORD will 12 deliver it into your hands.' The messenger sent to fetch Micaiah told him that the prophets had with one voice given the king a favourable answer. 'And mind you agree with them', he 13 added. 'As the LORD lives,' said Micaiah, 'I will say only what my God tells me to say.'

14 When Micaiah came into the king's presence, the king said to him, 'Micaiah, shall I attack Ramoth-gilead or shall I refrain?' 'Attack and win the day,' he said, 'and it will fall into 15 your hands.' 'How often must I adjure you', said the king, 'to tell me nothing but the truth in the name of the LORD?' 16 Then Micaiah said, 'I saw all Israel scattered on the mountains, like sheep without a shepherd; and I heard the LORD say, "They have no master; let 17 them go home in peace." ' The king of Israel said to Jehoshaphat, 'Did I not tell you that he never prophesies good for me, nothing but evil?' Micaiah 18

went on, 'Listen now to the word of the LORD; I saw the LORD seated on his throne, with all the host of heaven in attendance on his right and on his left. The LORD said, "Who will entice 19 Ahab to attack and fall on*l* Ramoth-gilead?" One said one thing and one 20 said another; then a spirit came forward and stood before the LORD and said, "I will entice him." "How?" said 21 the LORD. "I will go out", he said, "and be a lying spirit in the mouth of all his prophets." "You shall entice him," said the LORD, "and you shall succeed; go and do it." You see, then, 22 how the LORD has put a lying spirit in the mouth of all these prophets of yours, because he has decreed disaster for you.' Then Zedekiah son of Kenaanah 23 came up to Micaiah and struck him in the face: 'And how did the spirit of the LORD pass from me to speak to you?' he said. Micaiah answered, 'That you 24 will find out on the day when you run into an inner room to hide yourself.' Then the king of Israel ordered Micaiah 25 to be arrested and committed to the custody of Amon the governor of the city and Joash the king's son.*m* 'Lock 26 this fellow up', he said, 'and give him prison diet of bread and water until I come home in safety.' Micaiah re- 27 torted, 'If you do return in safety, the LORD has not spoken by me.'*n*

So the king of Israel and Jehoshaphat 28 king of Judah marched on Ramoth-gilead, and the king of Israel said to 29 Jehoshaphat, 'I will disguise myself to go into battle, but you shall wear your royal robes.' So he went into battle in disguise. Now the king of Aram had 30 commanded the captains of his chariots not to engage all and sundry but the king of Israel alone. When the cap- 31 tains saw Jehoshaphat, they thought he was the king of Israel and wheeled to attack him. But Jehoshaphat cried out, and the LORD came to his help; and God drew them away from him. When the captains saw that he was not 32 the king of Israel, they broke off the attack on him. But one man drew his 33

l Or at.   m son: or deputy.
n Prob. rdg.; Heb. adds and he said, 'Listen, peoples, all together.'

1 Kgs.22.2. **31:** The LORD's overt intervention is the Chronicler's addition; see 1 Kgs.22.33.

bow at random and hit the king of Israel where the breastplate joins the plates of the armour. So he said to his driver, 'Wheel round and take me out
34 of the line; I am wounded.' When the day's fighting reached its height, the king of Israel was facing the Aramaeans, propped up in his chariot; he remained so till evening, and at sunset he died.

19 As Jehoshaphat king of Judah returned in safety to his home in Jeru-
2 salem, Jehu son of Hanani, the seer, went out to meet him and said, 'Do you take delight in helping the wicked and befriending the enemies of the LORD? The LORD will make you suffer
3 for this. Yet there is some good in you, for you have swept away the sacred poles from the land and have made a practice of seeking guidance of God.'
4 Jehoshaphat had his residence in Jerusalem, but he went out again among his people from Beersheba to the hill-country of Ephraim and brought them back to the LORD the God of their
5 fathers. He appointed judges through-out the land, one in each of the
6 fortified cities of Judah, and said to them, 'Be careful what you do; you are there as judges, to please not man but the LORD, who is with you when
7 you pass sentence. Let the dread of the LORD be upon you, then; take care what you do, for the LORD our God will not tolerate injustice, partiality, or bribery.'
8 In Jerusalem Jehoshaphat appointed some of the Levites and priests and some heads of families by paternal descent in Israel to administer the law of the LORD and to arbitrate in law-suits among the inhabitants*o* of the
9 city, and he gave them these instructions: 'You must always act in the fear of the LORD, faithfully and with single-
10 ness of mind. In every suit which comes before you from your kinsmen, in

whatever city they live, whether cases of bloodshed or offences against the law or the commandments, against statutes or regulations, you shall warn them to commit no offence against the LORD; otherwise you and your kinsmen will suffer for it. If you act thus, you will be free of all offence. Your authority 11 in all matters which concern the LORD is Amariah the chief priest, and in those which concern the king it is Zebediah son of Ishmael, the prince of the house of Judah; the Levites are your officers. Be strong and resolute, and may the LORD be on the side of the good!'

It happened some time afterwards 20 that the Moabites, the Ammonites, and some of the Meunites made war on Jehoshaphat. News was brought to him 2 that a great horde of them was attacking him from beyond the Dead Sea, from Edom, and was already at Hazazon-tamar, which is En-gedi. Jehoshaphat 3 in his alarm resolved to seek guidance of the LORD and proclaimed a fast for all Judah. Judah gathered together to 4 ask counsel of the LORD; from every city of the land they came to consult him. Jehoshaphat stood up in the 5 assembly of Judah and Jerusalem in the house of the LORD, in front of the New Court, and said, 'O LORD God of 6 our fathers, art not thou God in heaven? Thou rulest over all the kingdoms of the nations; in thy hand are strength and power, and there is none who can withstand thee. Didst not thou, O God 7 our God, dispossess the inhabitants of this land in favour of thy people Israel, and give it for ever to the descendants of Abraham thy friend? So they lived in it 8 and have built a sanctuary in it in honour of thy name and said, "Should 9 evil come upon us, war or flood,*p* pestilence or famine, we will stand

o in . . . inhabitants: prob. rdg.: Heb. obscure.
p Prob. rdg.; Heb. judgement.

19.1–3: *Jehoshaphat* is reprimanded in this expansion by a prophet, Jehu, for collaborating with the Northern Kingdom, as was his father Asa; see 16.7–10 n. **5–7:** This is an expansion by the Chronicler. On instruction to the *judges*, compare Deut.1.16–17. **8–11:** The Chronicler adds that supreme courts were appointed *in Jerusalem* with highest authority for both religious and civil cases. **8:** *Israel* here is the entire people, not just the Northern Kingdom.
   20.1–37: Jehoshaphat's great victory. This full narrative is typical of the Chronicler's expansions. They are, as usual, the religious speech (vv. 5-12,20) made by the king or else a prophet (vv. 15–17), and are ascribed to successive stages of the action. **1:** *Meunites* were an Arab tribe. The Heb. reads "Ammonites," but is corrected, as in other modern translations,

before this house and before thee, for in this house is thy Name, and we will cry to thee in our distress and thou
10 wilt hear and save." Thou didst not allow Israel, when they came out of Egypt, to enter the land of the Ammonites, the Moabites, and the people of the hill-country of Seir, so they turned aside and left them alone and
11 did not destroy them. Now see how these people repay us: they are coming to drive us out of thy possession
12 which thou didst give to us. Judge them, O God our God, for we have no strength to face this great horde which is invading our land; we know not what we ought to do; we lift our eyes to thee.'
13 So all Judah stood there before the LORD, with their dependants, their
14 wives and their children. Then, in the midst of the assembly, the spirit of the LORD came upon Jahaziel son of Zechariah, son of Benaiah, son of Jeiel, son of Mattaniah, a Levite of the
15 line of Asaph, and he said, 'Attend, all Judah, all inhabitants of Jerusalem, and King Jehoshaphat; this is the word of the LORD to you: "Have no fear; do not be dismayed by this great horde, for the battle is in God's hands,
16 not yours. Go down to meet them tomorrow; they will come up by the Ascent of Ziz. You will find them at the end of the valley, east of the
17 wilderness of Jeruel. It is not you who will fight this battle; stand firm and wait, and you will see the deliverance worked by the LORD: he is on your side, O Judah and Jerusalem. Do not fear or be dismayed; go out tomorrow to face them; for the LORD is on your
18 side." ' Jehoshaphat bowed his face to the ground, and all Judah and the inhabitants of Jerusalem fell down before the LORD to make obeisance to
19 him. Then the Levites of the lines of Kohath and Korah stood up and praised the LORD the God of Israel with a mighty shout.
20 So they rose early in the morning and went out to the wilderness of Tekoa; and, as they were starting, Jehoshaphat

took his stand and said, 'Hear me, O Judah and inhabitants of Jerusalem: hold firmly to your faith in the LORD your God and you will be upheld; have faith in his prophets and you will prosper.' After consulting with the 21 people, he appointed men to sing to the LORD and praise the splendour of his holiness*q* as they went before the armed troops, and they sang:

Give thanks to the LORD,
for his love endures for ever.

As soon as their loud shouts of praise 22 were heard, the LORD deluded the Ammonites and Moabites and the men of the hill-country of Seir, who were invading Judah, and they were defeated. It turned out that the Am- 23 monites and Moabites had taken up a position against the men of the hill-country of Seir, and set themselves to annihilate and destroy them; and when they had exterminated the men of Seir, they savagely attacked one another. So when Judah came to the 24 watch-tower in the wilderness and looked towards the enemy horde, there they were all lying dead upon the ground; none had escaped. When Je- 25 hoshaphat and his men came to collect the booty, they found a large number of cattle, goods, clothing, and precious things, which they plundered until they could carry away no more. They spent three days collecting the booty, there was so much of it. On the fourth day 26 they assembled in the Valley of Bera-kah,*r* the name that it bears to this day because they blessed the LORD there. Then all the men of Judah and 27 Jerusalem, with Jehoshaphat at their head, returned home to the city in triumph; for the LORD had given them cause to triumph over their enemies. They entered Jerusalem with lutes, 28 harps, and trumpets playing, and went into the house of the LORD. So the 29 dread of God fell upon the rulers of every country, when they heard that

q Or singers in sacred vestments to praise the LORD.
r That is Valley of Blessing.

from 26.7. **10:** Compare Deut.2.1–19. *Seir* is the area from which the Meunites came; here it does not mean Edom, as elsewhere it does. **17:** See 13.13–20 n. **22, 28:** Note the music before and after the battle. **23:** Some internal dissension seems to have arisen. The Meunites are slain

the LORD had fought against the 30 enemies of Israel; and the realm of Jehoshaphat was at peace, God giving him security on all sides.

31⁸ Thus Jehoshaphat reigned over Judah. He was thirty-five years old when he came to the throne, and he reigned in Jerusalem for twenty-five years; his mother was Azubah daughter 32 of Shilhi. He followed in the footsteps of Asa his father and did not swerve from them; he did what was 33 right in the eyes of the LORD. But the hill-shrines were allowed to remain, and the people did not set their hearts 34 upon the God of their fathers. The other events of Jehoshaphat's reign, from first to last, are recorded in the history of Jehu son of Hanani, which is included in the annals of the kings of Israel.

35 Later Jehoshaphat king of Judah allied himself with Ahaziah king of 36 Israel; he did wrong in joining with him to build ships for trade with Tarshish; these were built in Ezion-37 geber. But Eliezer son of Dodavahu of Mareshah denounced Jehoshaphat with this prophecy: 'Because you have joined with Ahaziah, the LORD will bring your work to nothing.' So the ships were wrecked and could not make the voyage to Tarshish.

21 JEHOSHAPHAT RESTED WITH HIS FORE-fathers and was buried with them in the city of David. He was succeeded by his 2 son Joram, whose brothers were Azariah, Jehiel, Zechariah, Azariah, Michael, and Shephatiah, sons of Jehoshaphat. All of them were sons of 3 Jehoshaphat king of Judah, and their father gave them many gifts, silver and

gold and other costly things, as well as fortified cities in Judah; but the king-ship he gave to Joram because he was the eldest.

When Joram was firmly established 4 on his father's throne, he put to the sword all his brothers and also some of the princes of Israel. He was thirty-5ᵗ two years old when he came to the throne, and he reigned in Jerusalem for eight years. He followed the practices 6 of the kings of Israel as the house of Ahab had done, for he had married Ahab's daugher; and he did what was wrong in the eyes of the LORD. But 7 for the sake of the covenant which he had made with David, the LORD was unwilling to destroy the house of David, since he had promised to give him and his sons a flame, to burn for all time.

During his reign Edom revolted 8 against Judah and set up its own king. Joram, with his commanders and all 9 his chariots, advanced into Edom. He and his chariot-commanders set out by night, but they were surrounded by the Edomites and defeated.ᵘ So Edom 10 has remained independent of Judah to this day. Libnah revolted against him at the same time, because he had for-saken the LORD the God of his fathers, and because he had built hill-shrines 11 in the hill-country of Judah and had seduced the inhabitants of Jerusalem into idolatrous practices and corrupted Judah.

A letter reached Joram from Elijah 12 the prophet, which ran thus: 'This is the word of the LORD the God of David your father: "You have not

s Verses 31–33: cp. 1 Kgs. 22. 41–43.
t Verses 5–10: cp. 2 Kgs. 8. 17–22.
u and defeated: prob. rdg.; Heb. and he defeated them.

---

by their erstwhile allies. **31–35:** The passage is rewritten from 1 Kgs.22.41–49, *Israel* here strangely replacing Judah there. **35–37:** Here the motif is added that Jehoshaphat's alliance with *Ahaziah* was evil, and caused the *ships* to be *wrecked*. *Eliezer* is mentioned only here. *Ezion-geber* (v. 36) is identified with Elath on the Gulf of Aqabah, which gave access to the Red Sea. *Tarshish* is often identified with Spain (possibly correctly; see Jonah 1.3), but Spain is hardly possible here, since it is on the Mediterranean.
21.1–24.27: A period of failures. The Chronicler now deals with a succession of four reigns disastrous to Judah. At points he greatly amplifies his source to increase the wickedness of the kings (2 Kgs.8.16–11.20), but also omits an abundance of material. **1–20:** *Joram's* reign. **2–4:** Joram's killing of his *brothers* is not otherwise attested; it is hard to know whether the material is historical, or whether the Chronicler has increased Joram's misdeeds, and thereby his consequent punishment. **10–11:** The reasons given for *Libnah's* revolt are the Chronicler's own contribution. **12–20:** The letter from *Elijah* and the ensuing defeats were added by the Chronicler. Apparently the figure of Elijah, magnified in later legend, was already a com-manding one.

followed in the footsteps of Jehoshaphat your father and of Asa king of
13 Judah, but have followed the kings of Israel and have seduced Judah and the inhabitants of Jerusalem, as the house of Ahab did; and you have put to death your own brothers, sons of your father's house, men better than your-
14 self. Because of all this, the LORD is about to strike a heavy blow at your people, your children, your wives, and
15 all your possessions, and you yourself will suffer from a chronic disease of the bowels, until they prolapse and be-
16 come severely ulcerated.'' Then the LORD aroused against Joram the anger of the Philistines and of the Arabs who
17 live near the Cushites, and they invaded Judah and made their way right through it, carrying off all the property which they found in the king's palace, as well as his sons and wives; not a son was left to him except the youngest,
18 Jehoahaz. It was after all this that the LORD struck down the king with an
19 incurable disease of the bowels. It continued for some time, and towards the end of the second year the disease caused his bowels to prolapse, and the painful ulceration brought on his death. But his people kindled no fire in his honour as they had done for his
20 fathers. He was thirty-two years old when he became king, and he reigned in Jerusalem for eight years. His passing went unsung, and he was buried in the city of David, but not in the burial-place of the kings.

22 1*v*   Then the inhabitants of Jerusalem made Ahaziah, his youngest son, king in his place, for the raiders who had joined the Arabs in the campaign had killed all the elder sons. So Ahaziah son of Joram became king of Judah.
2 He was forty-two years old when he came to the throne, and he reigned in Jerusalem for one year; his mother was Athaliah granddaughter of Omri.
3 He too followed the practices of the house of Ahab, for his mother was his
4 counsellor in wickedness. He did what was wrong in the eyes of the LORD like the house of Ahab, for they had

been his counsellors after his father's death, to his undoing. He followed 5 their counsel also in the alliance he made with Jehoram son of Ahab king of Israel, to fight against Hazael king of Aram at Ramoth-gilead. But Jehoram was wounded by the Aramaeans, and returned to Jezreel to recover from 6 the wounds which were inflicted on him at Ramoth in battle with Hazael king of Aram.

Because of Jehoram's illness Ahaziah son of Joram king of Judah went down to Jezreel to visit him. It was God's will 7 that the visit of Ahaziah to Jehoram should be the occasion of his downfall. During the visit he went out with Jehoram to meet Jehu son of Nimshi, whom the LORD had anointed to bring the house of Ahab to an end. So it came about that Jehu, who was 8 then at variance with the house of Ahab, found the officers of Judah and the kinsmen of Ahaziah who were his attendants, and killed them. Then he 9 searched out Ahaziah himself, and his men captured him in Samaria, where he had gone into hiding. They brought him to Jehu and put him to death; they gave him burial, for they said, 'He was a son of Jehoshaphat who sought the guidance of the LORD with his whole heart.' Then the house of Ahaziah had no one strong enough to rule.

As soon as Athaliah mother of Aha- 10*w* ziah saw that her son was dead, she set out to extirpate the royal line of the house of Judah. But Jehosheba daughter 11 of King Joram took Ahaziah's son Joash and stole him away from among the princes who were being murdered; she put him and his nurse in a bed-chamber. Thus Jehosheba, daughter of King Joram and wife of Jehoiada the priest, because she was Ahaziah's sister, hid Joash from Athaliah so that she did not put him to death. He remained 12 concealed with them in the house of God for six years, while Athaliah ruled the country.

v Verses 1–6: cp. 2 Kgs. 8. 25–29.
w 22. 10—23. 21: cp. 2 Kgs. 11. 1–20.

22.1–12: **Ahaziah. 2:** He was twenty-two (2 Kgs.8.26), not *forty-two*, at his accession. **7:** The comment about *God's will* is the Chronicler s addition. The account of *Jehu's* revolution (2 Kgs.9.1–10.31) is here greatly compressed, with much of the material in Kgs. omitted.

23 In the seventh year Jehoiada felt himself strong enough to make an agreement with Azariah son of Jeroham, Ishmael son of Jehohanan, Azariah son of Obed, Maaseiah son of Adaiah, and Elishaphat son of Zichri, all captains of units of a hundred. 2 They went all through Judah and gathered to Jerusalem the Levites from the cities of Judah and the heads of clans in Israel, and they came to 3 Jerusalem. All the assembly made a compact with the king in the house of God, and Jehoiada said to them, 'Here is the king's son! He shall be king, as the LORD promised that the sons of 4 David should be. This is what you must do: a third of you, priests and Levites, as you come on duty on the sabbath, are to be on guard at the 5 threshold gates, another third are to be in the royal palace, and another third are to be at the Foundation Gate, while all the people will be in the courts of 6 the house of the LORD. Let no one enter the house of the LORD except the priests and the attendant Levites; they may enter, for they are holy, but all the people shall continue to keep the 7 LORD's charge. The Levites shall mount guard round the king, each with his weapons at the ready; anyone who tries to enter the house is to be put to death. They shall stay with the king wherever he goes.'

8 The Levites and all Judah carried out the orders of Jehoiada the priest to the letter. Each captain took his men, both those who came on duty on the sabbath and those who came off, for Jehoiada the priest had not released the 9 outgoing divisions. And Jehoiada the priest handed out to the captains King David's spears, shields, and bucklers, which were in the house of God; 10 and he posted all the people, each man carrying his weapon at the ready, from corner to corner of the house to north 11 and south,^x surrounding the king. Then they brought out the king's son, put the crown on his head, handed him the warrant and proclaimed him king, and Jehoiada and his sons anointed him;

and a shout went up: 'Long live the king.' When Athaliah heard the noise 12 of the people as they ran about cheering for the king, she came into the house of the LORD where the people were and found the king standing on 13 the dais^y at the entrance, amidst outbursts of song and fanfares of trumpets in his honour; all the populace were rejoicing and blowing trumpets, and singers with musical instruments were leading the celebrations. Athaliah rent her clothes and cried, 'Treason! Treason!' Jehoiada the priest gave orders 14 to^z the captains in command of the troops: 'Bring her outside the precincts and let anyone in attendance on her be put to the sword'; for the priest said, 'Do not kill her in the house of the LORD.' So they laid hands on 15 her and took her to the royal palace and killed her there at the passage to the Horse Gate.

Then Jehoiada made a covenant 16 between the LORD^a and the whole people and the king, that they should be the LORD's people. And all the people 17 went into the temple of Baal and pulled it down; they smashed its altars and images, and they slew Mattan the priest of Baal before the altars. Then 18 Jehoiada committed the supervision of the house of the LORD to the charge of the priests and the Levites whom David had allocated to the house of the LORD, to offer whole-offerings to the LORD as prescribed in the law of Moses, with the singing and rejoicing as handed down from David. He 19 stationed the door-keepers at the gates of the house of the LORD, to prevent anyone entering who was in any way unclean. Then he took the captains of 20 units of a hundred, the nobles, and the governors of the people, and all the people of the land, and they escorted the king from the house of the LORD through the Upper Gate to the royal palace, and seated him on the royal throne. The whole people rejoiced and 21

x *Prob. rdg.; Heb. adds* of the altar and the house.
y *Prob. rdg., cp.* 2 Kgs. 11. 14; *Heb.* by his pillar.
z *gave orders to: prob. rdg., cp.* 2 Kgs. 11. 15; *Heb.* brought out.
a *the* LORD: *prob. rdg., cp.* 2 Kgs. 11. 17; *Heb.* him.

23.1–21: Athaliah. 1–3: The Chronicler added proper names as well as all references to *the Levites*. 18 19: Some revision of, and addition to, the source, 2 Kgs.11.1–16, brings the account into line with the Chronicler's view of *Levites*, singers, *door-keepers*, and *the law of Moses*.

the city was tranquil. That is how Athaliah was put to the sword.

24 Joash was seven years old when he became king, and he reigned in Jerusalem for forty years; his mother was 2 Zibiah of Beersheba. He did what was right in the eyes of the LORD as long as 3 Jehoiada the priest was alive. Jehoiada chose him two wives, and he had a family of sons and daughters.

4 Some time after this, Joash decided 5 to repair the house of the LORD. So he assembled the priests and the Levites and said to them, 'Go through the cities of Judah and collect the annual tax from all the Israelites for the restoration of the house of your God, and do it quickly.' But the Levites did not 6 act quickly. The king then called for Jehoiada the chief priest and said to him, 'Why have you not required the Levites to bring in from Judah and Jerusalem the tax imposed by Moses the servant of the LORD and by the assembly of Israel for the Tent of the 7 Tokens?' For the wicked Athaliah and her adherents had broken into the house of God and had devoted all its holy things to the service of the 8 Baalim. So the king ordered them to make a chest and to put it outside the 9 gate of the house of the LORD; and proclamation was made throughout Judah and Jerusalem that the people should bring to the LORD the tax imposed on Israel in the wilderness by 10 Moses the servant of God. And all the leaders and all the people gladly brought their taxes and cast them 11 into the chest until it was full. Whenever the chest was brought to the king's officers by the Levites and they saw that it was well filled, the king's secretary and the chief priest's officer would come to empty it, after which it was carried back to its place. This they did daily, and they collected a 12 great sum of money. The king and Jehoiada gave it to those responsible for carrying out the work in the house of the LORD, and they hired masons and carpenters to do the repairs, as well as craftsmen in iron

and copper[c] to restore the house. So the 13 workmen proceeded with their task and the new work progressed under their hands; they restored the house of God according to its original design and strengthened it. When they had 14 finished, they brought what was left of the money to the king and to Jehoiada, and it was made into vessels for the house of the LORD, both for service and for sacrificing, saucers and other vessels of gold and silver. While Jehoiada lived, whole-offerings were offered in the house of the LORD continually.

Jehoiada, now old and weighed down 15 with years, died at the age of a hundred and thirty and was buried with the 16 kings in the city of David, because he had done good in Israel and served God and his house.

After the death of Jehoiada the 17 leading men of Judah came and made obeisance to the king. He listened to them, and they forsook the house of the 18 LORD the God of their fathers and worshipped sacred poles and idols. And Judah and Jerusalem suffered for this wickedness. But the LORD sent 19 prophets to bring them back to himself, prophets who denounced them and were not heeded. Then the spirit of 20 God took possession of Zechariah son of Jehoiada the priest, and he stood looking down on the people and said to them, 'This is the word of God: "Why do you disobey the commands of the LORD and court disaster? Because you have forsaken the LORD, he has forsaken you."' But they made 21 common cause against him, and on orders from the king they stoned him to death in the court of the house of the LORD. King Joash did not remem- 22 ber the loyalty of Zechariah's father Jehoiada but killed his son, who said as he was dying, 'May the LORD see this and exact the penalty.'

At the turn of the year an Aramaean 23 army advanced against Joash; they invaded Judah and Jerusalem and massacred all the officers, so that the

b Verses 1–14: cp. 2 Kgs. 11. 21—12. 15.   c Or bronze.

24.1–27: **Joash.** The source is 2 Kgs. ch. 12. **15–22:** This is entirely from the Chronicler. As elsewhere, a good king turns bad toward the end of his reign and receives punishment; compare 11.17 n. **23–24:** This revision of 2 Kgs.12.17–18 (which see) adds the motif of punishment.

army ceased to exist, and sent all their
21 spoil to the king of Damascus. Although the Aramaeans had invaded
with a small force, the LORD delivered
a very great army into their hands,
because the people had forsaken the
LORD the God of their fathers; and
Joash suffered just punishment.
25ᵈ When the Aramaeans had withdrawn, leaving the king severely
wounded, his servants conspired
against him to avenge the death of the
son of Jehoiada the priest; and they
killed him on his bed. Thus he died
and was buried in the city of David,
but not in the burial-place of the
26 kings. The conspirators were Zabad
son of Shimeath an Ammonite woman
and Jehozabad son of Shimrith a
27 Moabite woman. His children, the
many oracles about him, and his
reconstruction of the house of God are
all on record in the story given in the
annals of the kings. He was succeeded
by his son Amaziah.

25 1ᵉ AMAZIAH WAS TWENTY-FIVE YEARS OLD
when he came to the throne, and he
reigned in Jerusalem for twenty-nine
years; his mother was Jehoaddan of
2 Jerusalem. He did what was right in
the eyes of the LORD, but not whole-
3 heartedly. When the royal power was
firmly in his grasp, he put to death those
of his servants who had murdered the
4 king his father; but he spared their
children, in obedience to the LORD's
command written in the law of Moses:
'Fathers shall not die for their children,
nor children for their fathers; a man
shall die only for his own sin.'
5 Then Amaziah assembled the men of
Judah and drew them up by families, all
Judah and Benjamin as well, under
officers over units of a thousand and a
hundred. He mustered those of twenty

years old and upwards and found their
number to be three hundred thousand,
all picked troops ready for service, able
to handle spear and shield. He also 6
hired a hundred thousand seasoned
troops from Israel for a hundred talents
of silver. But a man of God came to 7
him and said, 'My lord king, do not
let the Israelite army march with you;
the LORD is not with Israel—all these
Ephraimites! For, if you make these 8
peopleᶠ your allies in the war, God will
overthrow you in battle; he has power
to help or to overthrow.' Then Amaziah 9
said to the man of God, 'What am I
to do about the hundred talents which
I have spent on the Israelite army?' The
man of God answered, 'It is in the
LORD's power to give you much more
than that.' So Amaziah detached the 10
troops which had come to him from
Ephraim and sent them home; that
infuriated them against Judah and they
went home in a rage.
Then Amaziah took heart and led 11
his men to the Valley of Salt and there
killed ten thousand men of Seir. The 12
men of Judah captured another ten
thousand men alive, brought them to
the top of a cliffᵍ and hurled them
over so that they were all dashed to
pieces. Meanwhile the troops which 13
Amaziah had sent home without
allowing them to take part in the battle
raided the cities of Judah from Samaria
to Beth-horon, massacred three thous-
and people in them and carried off
quantities of booty.
After Amaziah had returned from the 14
defeat of the Edomites, he brought the
gods of the people of Seir and, setting
them up as his own gods, worshipped
them and burnt sacrifices to them. The 15

d Verses 25–27: *cp. 2 Kgs. 12. 20, 21.*
e Verses 1–4: *cp. 2 Kgs. 14. 1–6.*
f these people: *prob. rdg.; Heb. obscure.*
g a cliff: *or Sela.*

26: That the two assassins were sons of an *Ammonite woman* and a *Moabite woman* is the Chronicler's own comment. For him, evil influence is likely to come from foreigners.

25.1–28.27: Four kings assessed concerning their faithfulness. The Chronicler continues his recasting of the source, 2 Kgs.14.1–16.21, sometimes drastically adding incidents to show that only faithfulness to the LORD leads to welfare and peace. The first two kings, Amaziah and Uzziah, are faithful at first and then unfaithful; the third, Jotham, is faithful, the fourth, Ahaz, completely unfaithful.

25.1–28: Amaziah. The source is 2 Kgs.14.1–20. The brief report of *Amaziah*'s Edomite campaign in the source is here expanded by the Chronicler in four respects: the king's military force is listed (vv. 5–6); a prophet dissuades him from employing northern mercenaries (vv. 7–10); the military destruction is increased (vv. 11–13); and *Amaziah*'s veneration of the

LORD was angry with Amaziah for this and sent a prophet who said to him, 'Why have you resorted to gods who could not save their own people from

16 you?' But while he was speaking, the king said to him, 'Have we appointed you counsellor to the king? Stop! Why risk your life?' The prophet did stop, but first he said, 'I know that God has determined to destroy you because you have done this and have not listened to my counsel.'

17ʰ Then Amaziah king of Judah, after consultation, sent messengers to Jehoash son of Jehoahaz, son of Jehu, king of Israel, to propose a meeting.

18 But Jehoash king of Israel sent this answer to Amaziah king of Judah: 'A thistle in Lebanon sent to a cedar in Lebanon to say, "Give your daughter in marriage to my son." But a wild beast in Lebanon, passing by, trampled

19 on the thistle. You have defeated Edom, you say, but it has gone to your head. Enjoy your glory at home and stay there. Why should you involve yourself in disaster and bring yourself to the ground, and Judah with you?'

20 But Amaziah would not listen; and this was God's doing in order to give Judah into the power of Jehoash, because they had resorted to the gods

21 of Edom. So Jehoash king of Israel marched out, and he and Amaziah king of Judah met one another at Beth-

22 shemesh in Judah. The men of Judah were routed by Israel and fled to their

23 homes. But Jehoash king of Israel captured Amaziah king of Judah, son of Joash, son of Jehoahaz, at Beth-shemesh, and brought him to Jerusalem. There he broke down the city wall from the Gate of Ephraim to the Corner Gate,

24 a distance of four hundred cubits; he also tookⁱ all the gold and silver and all the vessels found in the house of God, in the care of Obed-edom, and the treasures of the royal palace, as well as hostages, and returned to Samaria.

25ʲ Amaziah son of Joash, king of Judah,

outlived Jehoash son of Jehoahaz, king of Israel, by fifteen years. The other

26 events of Amaziah's reign, from first to last, are recorded in the annals of the kings of Judah and Israel. From

27 the time when he turned away from the LORD, there was conspiracy against him in Jerusalem and he fled to Lachish; but they sent after him to Lachish and put him to death there.

28 Then his body was conveyed on horseback to Jerusalem, and there he was buried with his forefathers in the city of David.

26 All the people of Judah took Uzziah, now sixteen years old, and made him king in succession to his father Amaziah.

2 It was he who built Eloth and restored it to Judah after the king rested with his forefathers.

3ᵏ Uzziah was sixteen years old when he came to the throne, and he reigned in Jerusalem for fifty-two years; his

4 mother was Jecoliah of Jerusalem. He did what was right in the eyes of the LORD, as Amaziah his father had done.

5 He set himself to seek the guidance of God in the days of Zechariah, who instructed him in the fear of God; as long as he sought guidance of the LORD, God caused him to prosper.

6 He took the field against the Philistines and broke down the walls of Gath, Jabneh, and Ashdod; and he built cities in the territory of Ashdod and among the Philistines. God aided him

7 against them, against the Arabs who lived in Gur-baal, and against the

8 Meunites. The Ammonites brought gifts to Uzziah and his fame spread to the borders of Egypt, for he had become very powerful. Besides, he built

9 towers in Jerusalem at the Corner Gate, at the Valley Gate, and at the escarpment, and fortified them. He

10 built other towers in the wilderness and dug many cisterns, for he had large

h Verses 17–24: cp. 2 Kgs. 14. 8–14.
i he also took: prob. rdg., cp. 2 Kgs. 14. 14; Heb. om.
j 25. 25—26. 2: cp. 2 Kgs. 14. 17–22.
k Verses 3, 4: cp. 2 Kgs. 15. 2, 3.

---

captured Edomite idols becomes the occasion of divine disfavor (vv. 14–16). **20:** The Chronicler adds the comment that *Amaziah*'s rashness was God's punishment for the apostasy referred to in vv. 14–16.

26.1–23: Uzziah. In 2 Kgs.15.1–34 he is usually called Azariah; one name may be personal, the other a throne name. **1:** *Eloth*: Elath. **6–15:** The Chronicler expands here, following sources other than 2 Kgs. Those sources gave an accurate view, however, of *Uzziah*'s historical im-

herds of cattle both in the Shephelah and in the plain. He also had farmers and vine-dressers in the hill-country and in the fertile lands, for he loved the soil.

11 Uzziah had an army of soldiers trained and ready for service, grouped according to the census made by Jeiel the adjutant-general and Maaseiah the clerk under the direction of Hananiah,
12 one of the king's commanders. The total number of heads of families which supplied seasoned warriors was two
13 thousand six hundred. Under their command was an army of three hundred and seven thousand five hundred, a powerful fighting force to aid
14 the king against his enemies. Uzziah prepared for the whole army shields, spears, helmets, coats of mail, bows,
15 and*l* sling-stones. In Jerusalem he had machines designed by engineers for use upon towers and bastions, made to discharge arrows and large stones. His fame spread far and wide, for he was so wonderfully gifted that he became very powerful.
16 But when he grew powerful his pride led to his own undoing:*m* he offended against the LORD his God by entering the temple of the LORD to burn incense
17 on the altar of incense. Azariah the priest and eighty others of the LORD's priests, courageous men, went in after
18 King Uzziah, confronted him and said, 'It is not for you, Uzziah, to burn incense to the LORD, but for the Aaronite priests who have been consecrated for that office. Leave the sanctuary; for you have offended, and that will certainly bring you no honour from
19 the LORD God.' The king, who had a censer in his hand ready to burn incense, was indignant; and because of his indignation at the priests, leprosy broke out on his forehead in the presence of the priests, there in the house of the LORD, beside the altar of
20 incense. When Azariah the chief priest and the other priests looked towards

him, they saw that he had leprosy on his forehead and they hurried him out of the temple, and indeed he himself hastened to leave, because the LORD had struck him with the disease. And
21*n* King Uzziah remained a leper till the day of his death; he lived in his own house as a leper, relieved of all duties and excluded from the house of the LORD, while his son Jotham was comptroller of the household and regent. The other events of Uzziah's reign,
22 from first to last, are recorded by the prophet Isaiah son of Amoz. So he
23 rested with his forefathers and was buried in a burial-ground, but not that of the kings; for they said, 'He is a leper'; and he was succeeded by his son Jotham.

Jotham was twenty-five years old **27**1*o* when he came to the throne, and he reigned in Jerusalem for sixteen years; his mother was Jerushah daughter of Zadok. He did what was right in the
2 eyes of the LORD, as his father Uzziah had done, but unlike him he did not enter the temple of the LORD; the people, however, continued their corrupt practices. He constructed the
3 upper gate of the house of the LORD and built extensively on the wall at Ophel. He built cities in the hill-
4 country of Judah, and forts and towers on the wooded hills. He made war on
5 the king of the Ammonites and defeated him; and that year the Ammonites gave him a hundred talents of silver, ten thousand kor of wheat and ten thousand of barley. They paid him the same tribute in the second and third years. Jotham became very pow-
6 erful because he maintained a steady course of obedience to the LORD his God. The other events of Jotham's
7 reign, all that he did in war and in peace, are recorded in the annals of

l Prob. rdg.; Heb. adds for.
m his pride ... undoing: or he became so proud that he acted corruptly.
n Verses 21–23: cp. 2 Kgs. 15. 5–7.
o Verses 1–3: cp. 2 Kgs. 15. 33–35.

---

portance. **12–13:** This is one of the few instances in which the numbers given by the Chronicler are not artificial and schematic, for the Chronicler had older, written sources at his disposal. **16–23:** The source simply reported *Uzziah's leprosy;* the Chronicler here explains it as a result of a cultic offense on Uzziah's part. **22:** *Isaiah:* 2 Kgs.15.6 speaks rather of the "annals of the kings of Judah." *From first to last* exaggerates the attention to Uzziah found in Isaiah.
    27.1–28.27: Jotham and Ahaz. *Jotham* receives only favorable treatment (27.1–9); *Ahaz* (28.1–27) only unfavorable. **2:** The king is portrayed as faithful; the infidelity is on the part

8 the kings of Israel and Judah. He was
twenty-five years old when he came
to the throne, and he reigned in
9 Jerusalem for sixteen years. He rested
with his forefathers and was buried
in the city of David; and he was
succeeded by his son Ahaz.

28 1[p] AHAZ WAS TWENTY YEARS OLD WHEN
he came to the throne, and he reigned
in Jerusalem for sixteen years. He did
not do what was right in the eyes of the
2 LORD like his forefather David, but
followed in the footsteps of the kings of
Israel, and cast metal images for the
3 Baalim. He also burnt sacrifices in the
Valley of Ben-hinnom; he even burnt
his sons in the fire according to the
abominable practice of the nations
whom the LORD had dispossessed in
4 favour of the Israelites. He slaughtered
and burnt sacrifices at the hill-shrines
and on the hill-tops and under every
spreading tree.

5 The LORD his God let him suffer at
the hands of the king of Aram, and the
Aramaeans defeated him, took many
captives and brought them to Damascus; he was also made to suffer at the
hands of the king of Israel, who inflicted
6 a severe defeat on him. This was Pekah
son of Remaliah, who killed in one
day a hundred and twenty thousand
men of Judah, seasoned troops, because
they had forsaken the LORD the God of
7 their fathers. And Zichri, an Ephraimite hero, killed Maaseiah the king's
son[q] and Azrikam the comptroller of
the household and Elkanah the king's
8 chief minister. The Israelites took captive from their kinsmen two hundred
thousand women and children; they
also took a large amount of booty and
brought it to Samaria.

9 A prophet of the LORD was there,
Oded by name; he went out to meet
the army as it returned to Samaria and
said to them, 'It is because the LORD
the God of your fathers is angry with
Judah that he has given them into your
power; and you have massacred them
in a rage that has towered up to heaven.
10 Now you propose to force the people
of Judah and Jerusalem, male and
female, into slavery. Are not you also
guilty men before the LORD your God?
Now, listen to me. Send back those 11
you have taken captive from your
kinsmen, for the anger of the LORD
is roused against you.' Next, some 12
Ephraimite chiefs, Azariah son of
Jehohanan, Berechiah son of Meshillemoth, Hezekiah[r] son of Shallum, and
Amasa son of Hadlai, met those who
were returning from the war and said 13
to them, 'You must not bring these
captives into our country; what you
are proposing would make us guilty
before the LORD and add to our sins
and transgressions. We are guilty enough
already, and there is fierce anger
against Israel.' So the armed men left 14
the captives and the spoil with the
officers and the assembled people.
The captives were put in charge of 15
men nominated for this duty, who
found clothes from the spoil for all
who were naked. They clothed them
and shod them, gave them food and
drink, and anointed them; those who
were tottering from exhaustion they
conveyed on the backs of asses, and
so brought them to their kinsmen in
Jericho, in the Vale of Palm Trees. Then
they themselves returned to Samaria.

At that time King Ahaz sent to the 16
king of Assyria for help. The Edomites 17
had invaded again and defeated Judah
and taken away prisoners; and the 18
Philistines had raided the cities of the
Shephelah and of the Negeb of Judah
and had captured Beth-shemesh, Aijalon, and Gederoth, as well as Soco,
Timnah, and Gimzo with their villages,
and occupied them. The LORD had re- 19
duced Judah to submission because of
Ahaz king of Judah; for his actions in
Judah had been unbridled and he had
been grossly unfaithful to the LORD. 20
Then Tiglath-pileser king of Assyria
marched against him and, so far from
assisting him, pressed him hard. Ahaz 21
stripped the house of the LORD, the
king's palace and the houses of his

p *Verses 1–4: cp. 2 Kgs. 16. 2–4.*
q son: *or* deputy.
r *Or* Jehizkiah.

of the people. This latter is added by the Chronicler. **28.6–15:** This episode is the Chronicler's own contribution. **16–21:** The Chronicler has eliminated the positive assistance the Assyrian king rendered *Ahaz;* compare 2 Kgs.16.5–9. He gives instead the viewpoint found in Isa.7.1–17.

officers, and gave the plunder to the king of Assyria; but all to no purpose.
22 This King Ahaz, when hard pressed, became more and more unfaithful to
23 the LORD; he sacrificed to the gods of Damascus who had defeated him and said, 'The gods of the kings of Aram helped them; I will sacrifice to them so that they may help me.' But in fact they caused his downfall and that of all
24 Israel. Then Ahaz gathered together the vessels of the house of God and broke them up, and shut the doors of the house of the LORD; he made himself
25 altars at every corner in Jerusalem, and at every single city of Judah he made hill-shrines to burn sacrifices to other gods and provoked the anger of the LORD the God of his fathers.
26⁸ The other acts and all the events of his reign, from first to last, are recorded in the annals of the kings of Judah and
27 Israel. So Ahaz rested with his forefathers and was buried in the city of Jerusalem, but was not given burial with the kings of Judah. He was succeeded by his son Hezekiah.

The kings of Judah from Hezekiah to the exile

29 1ᵗ HEZEKIAH WAS TWENTY-FIVE YEARS OLD when he came to the throne, and he reigned in Jerusalem for twenty-nine years; his mother was Abijah daughter
2 of Zechariah. He did what was right in the eyes of the LORD, as David his forefather had done.
3 In the first year of his reign, in the first month, he opened the gates of the house of the LORD and repaired them.
4 He brought in the priests and the Levites and gathered them together in
5 the square on the east side, and said to them, 'Levites, listen to me. Hallow yourselves now, hallow the house of the LORD the God of your fathers, and remove the pollution from the sanc-
6 tuary. For our forefathers were unfaithful and did what was wrong in the eyes of the LORD our God: they forsook him, they would have nothing to do with his dwelling-place, they turned their backs on it. They shut the doors
7 of the porch and extinguished the lamps, they ceased to burn incense and offer whole-offerings in the sanctuary
8 to the God of Israel. Therefore the anger of the LORD fell upon Judah and Jerusalem and he made them repugnant, an object of horror and derision,
9 as you see for yourselves. Hence it is that our fathers have fallen by the sword, our sons and daughters and our wives are in captivity. Now I intend
10 that we should pledge ourselves to the LORD the God of Israel, in order that his anger may be averted from us. So,
11 my sons, let no time be lost; for the LORD has chosen you to serve him and to minister to him, to be his ministers and to burn sacrifices.'
12 Then the Levites set to work— Mahath son of Amasai and Joel son of Azariah of the family of Kohath; of the family of Merari, Kish son of Abdi and Azariah son of Jehalelel; of the family of Gershon, Joah son of
13 Zimmah and Eden son of Joah; of the family of Elizaphan, Shimri and Jeiel; of the family of Asaph, Zechariah and Mattaniah; of the family of Heman,
14 Jehiel and Shimei; and of the family of
15 Jeduthun, Shemaiah and Uzziel. They assembled their kinsmen and hallowed themselves, and then went in, as the king had instructed them at the LORD's command, to purify the house of the
16 LORD. The priests went inside to purify the house of the LORD; they removed all the pollution which they found in

s *Verses 26, 27; cp. 2 Kgs. 16. 19, 20.*
t *Verses 1, 2: cp. 2 Kgs. 18. 1–3.*

29.1–32.33: The reign of Hezekiah. *Hezekiah* is portrayed in Kgs. as one of the most faithful kings; the Chronicler greatly elaborates the account of his reign, with chs. 29–31 entirely his addition. Ch. 32, on the other hand, is an abbreviated version of 2 Kgs.18.13–20.21. In the Chronicler's account, Hezekiah gave more attention to the Temple and its service than any king since Solomon; see 30.26.

29.1–36: Restoration of the Temple service. After the apostasy of Ahaz (28.24), *Hezekiah*'s first act was to restore the proper Temple service. The Chronicler's special interest in *the Levites* and *singers* reappears (vv. 12–14,25–26,34). After sixteen days of renovating the Temple (vv. 3–19), the renewal of service consisted of sacrifices by the king and leaders (vv. 20–30) and then by all the assembled people (vv. 31–36).

the temple into the court of the house of the LORD, and the Levites took it from them and carried it outside to
17 the gorge of the Kidron. They began the rites on the first day of the first month, and on the eighth day they reached the porch; then for eight days they consecrated the house of the LORD, and on the sixteenth day of the
18 first month they finished. Then they went into the palace and said to King Hezekiah, 'We have purified the whole of the house of the LORD, the altar of whole-offering with all its vessels, and the table for the Bread of the Presence arranged in rows with all its vessels;
19 and we have put in order and consecrated all the vessels which King Ahaz cast aside during his reign, when he was unfaithful. They are now in place before the altar of the LORD.'
20 Then King Hezekiah rose early, assembled the officers of the city and went up to the house of the LORD.
21 They brought seven bulls, seven rams, and seven lambs for the whole offering,*u* and seven he-goats as a sin-offering for the kingdom, for the sanctuary, and for Judah; these he commanded the priests of Aaron's line
22 to offer on the altar of the LORD. So the bulls were slaughtered, and the priests took their blood and flung it against the altar; the rams were slaughtered, and their blood was flung against the altar; the lambs were slaughtered, and their blood was flung against the altar.
23 Then the he-goats for the sin-offering were brought before the king and the assembly, who laid their hands on
24 them; and the priests slaughtered them and used their blood as a sin-offering on the altar to make expiation for all Israel. For the king had commanded that the whole-offering and the sin-offering should be made for all Israel.
25 He posted the Levites in the house of the LORD with cymbals, lutes, and harps, according to the rule prescribed by David, by Gad the king's seer and Nathan the prophet; for this rule had come from the LORD through his
26 prophets. The Levites stood ready with

the instruments of David, and the priests with the trumpets. Hezekiah 27 gave the order that the whole-offering should be offered on the altar. At the moment when the whole-offering began, the song to the LORD began too, with the trumpets, led by the instruments of David king of Israel. The 28 whole assembly prostrated themselves, the singers sang and the trumpeters sounded; all this continued until the whole-offering was complete. When 29 the offering was complete, the king and all his company bowed down and prostrated themselves. And King 30 Hezekiah and his officers commanded the Levites to praise the LORD in the words of David and of Asaph the seer. So they praised him most joyfully and bowed down and prostrated themselves.

Then Hezekiah said, 'You have now 31 given to the LORD with open hands; approach with your sacrifices and thank-offerings for the house of the LORD.' So the assembly brought sacrifices and thank-offerings, and every man of willing spirit brought whole-offerings. The number of whole- 32 offerings which the assembly brought was seventy bulls, a hundred rams, and two hundred lambs; all these made a whole-offering to the LORD. And the 33 consecrated offerings were six hundred bulls and three thousand sheep. But 34 the priests were too few and could not flay all the whole-offerings; so their colleagues the Levites helped them until the work was completed and all the priests had hallowed themselves— for the Levites had been more scrupulous than the priests in hallowing themselves. There were indeed whole- 35 offerings in abundance, besides the fat of the shared-offerings and the drink-offerings for the whole-offerings. In this way the service of the house of the LORD was restored; and Hezekiah and 36 all the people rejoiced over what God had done for the people and because it had come about so suddenly.

Then Hezekiah sent word to all Israel 30 and Judah, and also wrote letters to

u for the whole-offering: prob. rdg.; Heb. om.

30.1–27: Hezekiah's great Passover in Jerusalem. The Chronicler did not relate the fall of the Northern Kingdom (compare 2 Kgs.18.9–12); this chapter reflects *Hezekiah's* effort to unite the divided kingdoms into a single one centered in the Davidic monarchy and the Jerusalem

Ephraim and Manasseh, inviting them to come to the house of the LORD in Jerusalem to keep the Passover of the 2 LORD the God of Israel. The king and his officers and all the assembly in Jerusalem had agreed to keep the 3 Passover in the second month, but they had not been able to keep it at that time, because not enough priests had hallowed themselves and the people 4 had not assembled in Jerusalem. The proposal was acceptable to the king and 5 the whole assembly. So they resolved to make a proclamation throughout all Israel, from Beersheba to Dan, that the people should come to Jerusalem to keep the Passover of the LORD the God of Israel. Never before had so many kept it according to the prescribed 6 form. Couriers went throughout all Israel and Judah with letters from the king and his officers, proclaiming the royal command: 'Turn back, men of Israel, to the LORD the God of Abraham, Isaac, and Israel, so that he may turn back to those of you who escaped capture by the kings of Assyria. 7 Do not be like your forefathers and your kinsmen, who were unfaithful to the LORD the God of their fathers, so that he made them an object of horror, 8 as you yourselves saw. Do not be stubborn as your forefathers were; submit yourselves to the LORD and enter his sanctuary which he has sanctified for ever, and worship the LORD your God, so that his anger may be averted from 9 you. For when you turn back to the LORD, your kinsmen and your children will win compassion from their captors and return to this land. The LORD your God is gracious and compassionate, and he will not turn away from you if you turn back to him.'

10   So the couriers passed from city to city through the land of Ephraim and Manasseh and as far as Zebulun, but they were treated with scorn and 11 ridicule. However, a few men of Asher, Manasseh, and Zebulun submitted and 12 came to Jerusalem. Further, the hand of God moved the people in Judah with one accord to carry out what the king and his officers had ordered at the LORD's command.

Many people, a very great assembly, 13 came together in Jerusalem to keep the pilgrim-feast of Unleavened Bread in the second month. They began by re- 14 moving the altars in Jerusalem; they removed the altars for burning sacrifices and threw them into the gorge of the Kidron. They killed the passover lamb 15 on the fourteenth day of the second month; and the priests and the Levites were bitterly ashamed. They hallowed themselves and brought whole-offerings to the house of the LORD. They took 16 their accustomed places, according to the direction laid down for them in the law of Moses the man of God; the priests flung against the altar the blood which they received from the Levites. But many in the assembly had not hal- 17 lowed themselves; therefore the Levites had to kill the passover lamb for every one who was unclean, in order to hallow him to the LORD. For a majority 18 of the people, many from Ephraim, Manasseh, Issachar, and Zebulun, had not kept themselves ritually clean, and therefore kept the Passover irregularly. But Hezekiah prayed for them, saying, 'May the good LORD grant pardon to 19 every one who makes a practice of seeking guidance of God, the LORD the God of his fathers, even if he has not observed the rules for the purifica- tion of the sanctuary.' The LORD heard 20 Hezekiah and healed the people. And 21 the Israelites who were present in Jerusalem kept the feast of Unleavened Bread for seven days with great re- joicing, and the Levites and the priests praised the LORD every day with un- restrained fervour.*v* Hezekiah spoke 22 encouragingly to all the Levites who had shown true understanding in the service of the LORD. So they spent the seven days of the festival sacrificing

v with unrestrained fervour: prob. rdg.; Heb. with powerful instruments.

Temple; see his appeal in vv. 6–9. None of this material is in 2 Kgs. **2:** A *Passover in the second month:* compare Num.9.1–14. The festival of *Unleavened Bread* (v. 13) was not normally held in the second month. **14:** In the first month (ch. 29) the Temple was purified; now the city is cleansed. **15–20:** Only the daytime Passover rituals are reported; the nocturnal meal (see Exod.12.1–14) is not relevant to the Chronicler's purpose.

shared-offerings and making confession to^w the LORD the God of their fathers,

23 Then the whole assembly agreed to keep the feast for another seven days; so they kept it for another seven days 24 with general rejoicing. For Hezekiah king of Judah set aside for the assembly a thousand bulls and seven thousand sheep, and his officers set aside for the assembly a thousand bulls and ten thousand sheep; and priests hallowed 25 themselves in great numbers. So the whole assembly of Judah, including the priests and the Levites, rejoiced, together with all the assembly which came out of Israel, and the resident aliens from Israel and those who lived in 26 Judah. There was great rejoicing in Jerusalem, the like of which had not been known there since the days of Solomon son of David king of Israel. 27 Then the priests and the Levites stood to bless the people: the LORD listened to their cry, and their prayer came to God's holy dwelling-place in heaven.

31 When this was over, all the Israelites present went out to the cities of Judah and smashed the sacred pillars, hacked down the sacred poles and broke up the hill-shrines and the altars throughout Judah and Benjamin, Ephraim and Manasseh, until they had made an end of them. That done, the Israelites returned, each to his own patrimony in his own city.

2 Then Hezekiah installed the priests and the Levites in office, division by division, allotting to each priest or Levite his own particular duty, for whole-offerings or shared-offerings, to give thanks or to sing praise, or to serve in the gates of the several quarters in the LORD's house.

3 The king provided from his own resources, as the share due from him, the whole-offerings for both morning and evening, and for sabbaths, new moons, and appointed seasons, as pre- 4 scribed in the law of the LORD. He ordered the people living in Jerusalem

to provide the share due from the priests and the Levites, so that they might devote themselves entirely to the law of the LORD. As soon as the king's 5 order was issued to the Israelites, they gave generously from the firstfruits of their corn and new wine, oil and honey, all the produce of their land; they brought a full tithe of everything. The 6 Israelites and the Judaeans living in the cities of Judah also brought a tithe of cattle and sheep, and a tithe of all produce as offerings dedicated to the LORD their God, and they stacked the produce in heaps. They began to 7 deposit the heaps in the third month and completed them in the seventh. When Hezekiah and his officers came 8 and saw the heaps, they blessed the LORD and his people Israel. Hezekiah 9 asked the priests and the Levites about these heaps, and Azariah the chief 10 priest, who was of the line of Zadok, answered, 'From the time when the people began to bring their contribution into the house of the LORD, they have had enough to eat, enough and to spare; indeed, the LORD has so greatly blessed them that they have this great store left over.'

Then Hezekiah ordered store-rooms 11 to be prepared in the house of the LORD, and this was done; and the people 12 honestly brought in their contributions, the tithe, and their dedicated gifts. The overseer in charge of them was Conaniah the Levite, with Shimei his brother as his deputy; Jehiel, Azaziah, 13 Nahath, Asahel, Jerimoth, Jozabad, Eliel, Ismachiah, Mahath, and Benaiah were appointed by King Hezekiah and Azariah, the chief overseer of the house of God, to assist Conaniah and Shimei his brother. And Kore son of Imnah 14 the Levite, keeper of the East Gate, was in charge of the freewill offerings to God, to apportion the contributions made to the LORD and the most sacred offerings. Eden, Miniamin, Jeshua, 15

w making confession to: or confessing.

31.1–21: The support of the Temple service. Hezekiah's first act had prepared the Temple (ch. 29) and his second, the city as the center for all Israel (ch. 30); here his third act prepares the land for the support of the proper service of the LORD. The land is first cleansed of offensive religious objects (v. 1), then its abundant produce is amassed for support of the Temple (vv. 2–10), and finally the king reorganizes the Temple personnel for a just distribution of that produce (vv. 11–19).

Shemaiah, Amariah, and Shecaniah in the priestly cities assisted him in the fair distribution of portions to their kinsmen, young and old*x* alike, by 16 divisions. Irrespective of their registration, shares were distributed to all males three years of age and upwards who entered the house of the LORD to take their daily part in the service, according to their divisions, as their 17 office demanded. The priests were registered by families, the Levites from twenty years of age and upwards by 18 their offices in their divisions. They were registered with all their dependants, their wives, their sons, and their daughters, the whole company of them, because in virtue of their permanent standing they had to keep themselves 19 duly hallowed. As for the priests of Aaron's line in the common lands attached to their cities, in every city men were nominated to distribute portions to every male among the priests and to every one who was registered with the Levites.

20 Such was the action taken by Hezekiah throughout Judah; he did what was good and right and loyal in 21 the sight of the LORD his God. Whatever he undertook in the service of the house of God and in obedience to the law and the commandment to seek guidance of his God, he did with all his heart, and he prospered.

32¹*y* After these events and this example of loyal conduct, Sennacherib king of Assyria invaded Judah and encamped against the fortified cities, believing that he could attach them to himself. 2 When Hezekiah saw that he had come and was determined to attack Jerusa- 3 lem, he consulted his civil and military officers about blocking up the springs outside the city; and they encouraged 4 him. They gathered together a large number of people and blocked up all the springs and the stream which flowed through the land. 'Why,' they said, 'should Assyrian kings come here and 5 find plenty of water?' Then the king acted boldly; he made good every breach in the city wall and erected

towers on it; he built another wall outside it and strengthened the Millo of the city of David; he also collected a great quantity of weapons and shields. He appointed military commanders 6 over the people and assembled them in the square by the city gate and spoke encouragingly to them in these words: 'Be strong; be brave. Do not let the 7 king of Assyria or the rabble he has brought with him strike terror or panic into your hearts. We have more on our side than he has. He has human 8 strength; but we have the LORD our God to help us and to fight our battles.' So spoke Hezekiah king of Judah, and the people were buoyed up by his words.

After this, Sennacherib king of 9 Assyria, while he and his high command were at Lachish, sent envoys to Jerusalem to deliver this message to Hezekiah king of Judah and to all the Judaeans in Jerusalem: 'Sennacherib 10 king of Assyria says, "What gives you confidence to stay in Jerusalem under siege? Hezekiah is misleading you into 11 risking death by famine or thirst where you are, when he tells you that the LORD your God will save you from the grip of the Assyrian king. Was it not 12 Hezekiah himself who suppressed the LORD's hill-shrines and altars and told the people of Judah and Jerusalem that they must prostrate themselves before one altar only and burn sacrifices there? You know very well what I and 13 my forefathers have done to all the peoples of the lands. Were the gods of these nations able to save their lands from me? Not one of the gods of these 14 nations, which my forefathers exterminated, was able to save his people from me. Much less will your god save you! How, then, can Hezekiah deceive 15 you or mislead you like this? How can you believe him, for no god of any nation or kingdom has been able to save his people from me or my forefathers? Much less will your gods save you!"'

x Or high and low.
y Verses 1–19: cp. 2 Kgs. 18. 13–37; Isa. 36. 1–22.

32.1–33: Sennacherib's assault and Hezekiah's response. The Chronicler shortens the account in 2 Kgs.18.13–20.19 but also adds comments of his own, e.g. vv. 3–8, 22–23, and 27–31.

16 The envoys of Sennacherib spoke still more against the LORD God and 17 against his servant Hezekiah. And the king himself wrote a letter to defy the LORD the God of Israel, in these terms: 'Just as the gods of other nations could not save their people from me, so the god of Hezekiah will not save his 18 people from me.' Then they shouted in Hebrew at the top of their voices at the people of Jerusalem on the wall, to strike them with fear and terror, hoping 19 thus to capture the city. They described the god[z] of Jerusalem as being like the gods of the other peoples of the earth—things made by the hands of men.

20[a] In this plight King Hezekiah and the prophet Isaiah son of Amoz cried 21 to heaven in prayer. So the LORD sent an angel who cut down all the fighting men, as well as the leaders and the commanders, in the camp of the king of Assyria, so that he went home disgraced to his own land. When he entered the temple of his god, certain of his own sons struck him down with their swords. 22 Thus the LORD saved Hezekiah and the inhabitants of Jerusalem from Sennacherib king of Assyria and all their enemies; and he gave them respite 23 on every side. Many people brought to Jerusalem offerings for the LORD and costly gifts for Hezekiah king of Judah. From then on he was held in high honour by all the nations.

24 About this time Hezekiah fell dangerously ill and prayed to the LORD; the LORD said, 'I will heal you',[b] and 25 granted him a sign. But, being a proud man, he was not grateful for the good done to him, and Judah and Jerusalem 26 suffered for it. Then, proud as he was, Hezekiah submitted, and the people of Jerusalem with him, and the LORD's anger did not fall on them again in Hezekiah's time.

27 Hezekiah enjoyed great wealth and fame.[c] He built for himself treasuries for silver and gold, precious stones and spices, shields and other costly things; 28 and barns for the harvests of corn, new wine, and oil; and stalls for every kind of cattle, as well as sheepfolds. He 29 amassed[d] a great many flocks and herds; God had indeed given him vast riches. It was this same Hezekiah who 30 blocked the upper outflow of the waters of Gihon and directed them downwards and westwards to the city of David. In fact, Hezekiah was successful in everything he attempted, even in the 31 affair of the envoys sent by the king[e] of Babylon—the envoys who came to inquire about the portent which had been seen in the land at the time when God left him to himself, to test him and to discover all that was in his heart.

The other events of Hezekiah's reign, 32 and his works of piety, are recorded in the vision of the prophet Isaiah son of Amoz and in the annals of the kings of Judah and Israel. So Hezekiah rested 33 with his forefathers and was buried in the uppermost of the graves of David's sons; all Judah and the people of Jerusalem paid him honour when he died, and he was succeeded by his son Manasseh.

MANASSEH WAS TWELVE YEARS OLD 33 1[f] when he came to the throne, and he reigned in Jerusalem for fifty-five years. He did what was wrong in the eyes of 2 the LORD, in following the abominable practices of the nations which the LORD had dispossessed in favour of the Israelites. He rebuilt the hill-shrines 3 which his father Hezekiah had dismantled, he erected altars to the Baalim and made sacred poles, he prostrated himself before all the host of heaven and worshipped them. He built 4 altars in the house of the LORD, that house of which the LORD had said, 'In Jerusalem shall my Name be for

z *Or gods.*
a *Verses 20–22: cp. 2 Kgs. 19. 1–37; Isa. 37. 1–38.*
b *I will heal you: prob. rdg., cp. 2 Kgs. 20. 5; Heb. om.*
c *Or riches.*   d *Prob. rdg.; Heb. adds cities.*
e *Prob. rdg., cp. 2 Kgs. 20. 12; Heb. officers.*
f *Verses 1–9: cp. 2 Kgs. 21. 1–9.*

24–26: The verses abridge 2 Kgs.20.1–9, to suggest that worthy Hezekiah was less than perfect; compare Isa.38.1–39.8.
33.1–25: Manasseh and Amon. In 2 Kgs. *Manasseh* is the worst king of the Davidic dynasty. It was during his reign that the LORD finally gave up on Jerusalem and Judah (2 Kgs.21.10–16). Here, however, Manasseh repents and is restored. This theme possibly arises from the very long reign of *fifty-five years*, which the Chronicler may have thought was due to some good on the

5 ever.' He built altars for all the host of heaven in the two courts of the house 6 of the LORD; he made his sons pass through the fire in the Valley of Ben-hinnom, he practised soothsaying, divination, and sorcery, and dealt with ghosts and spirits. He did much wrong in the eyes of the LORD and provoked 7 his anger; and the image that he had carved in relief he put in the house of God, the place of which God had said to David and Solomon his son, 'This house and Jerusalem, which I chose out of all the tribes of Israel, shall 8 receive my Name for all time. I will not again displace Israel from the land which I assigned to their forefathers, if only they will be careful to observe all that I commanded them through Moses, all the law, the statutes, and the 9 rules.' But Manasseh misled Judah and the inhabitants of Jerusalem into wickedness far worse than that of the nations which the LORD had exterminated in favour of the Israelites.

10 The LORD spoke to Manasseh and to 11 his people, but they paid no heed. So the LORD brought against them the commanders of the army of the king of Assyria; they captured Manasseh with spiked weapons, and bound him with fetters, and brought him to Babylon. 12 In his distress he prayed to the LORD his God and sought to placate him, and made his humble submission before 13 the God of his fathers. He prayed, and God accepted his petition and heard his supplication. He brought him back to Jerusalem and restored him to the throne; and thus Manasseh learnt that the LORD was God.

14 After this he built an outer wall for the city of David, west of Gihon in the gorge, and extended it to the entrance by the Fish Gate, enclosing Ophel; and he raised it to a great height. He also put military commanders in all 15 the fortified cities of Judah. He removed the foreign gods and the carved image from the house of the LORD and all the altars which he had built on the temple mount and in Jerusalem, and threw them out of the city. Moreover, 16 he repaired the altar of the LORD and sacrificed at it shared-offerings and thank-offerings, and commanded Judah to serve the LORD the God of Israel. But the people still continued to sacri- 17 fice at the hill-shrines, though only to the LORD their God.

The rest of the acts of Manasseh, his 18 prayer to his God, and the discourses of the seers who spoke to him in the name of the LORD the God of Israel, are recorded in the chronicles of the kings of Israel. His prayer and the 19 answer he received to it, and all his sin and unfaithfulness, and the places where he built hill-shrines and set up sacred poles and carved idols, before he submitted, are recorded in the chronicles of the seers. So Manasseh rested 20 with his forefathers and was buried in the garden-tomb of[g] his family; he was succeeded by his son Amon.

Amon was twenty-two years old 21[h] when he came to the throne, and he reigned in Jerusalem for two years. He 22 did what was wrong in the eyes of the LORD as his father Manasseh had done. He sacrificed to all the images that his father Manasseh had made, and worshipped them. He was not submissive 23 before the LORD like his father Manasseh; his guilt was much greater. His courtiers conspired against him 24 and murdered him in his house; but the 25 people of the land killed all the conspirators and made his son Josiah king in his place.

JOSIAH WAS EIGHT YEARS OLD WHEN HE 34 1[i] came to the throne, and he reigned in Jerusalem for thirty-one years. He did 2 what was right in the eyes of the LORD; he followed in the footsteps of his forefather David, swerving neither right nor left. In the eighth year of his reign, 3

g the garden-tomb of: *prob. rdg., cp. 2 Kgs. 21. 18; Heb. om.*
h Verses 21–25: *cp. 2 Kgs. 21. 19–24.*
i Verses 1, 2. *cp. 2 Kgs. 22, 1, 2.*

king's part. 18: The Gr. translation adds the penitential prayer of Manasseh, found in the Apocrypha.
34.1–35.27: Josiah, the faithful king (2 Kgs. chs. 22–23). In 2 Kgs. *Josiah's* great religious reform was a concentrated event after the discovery of the *book of the law;* here his purge of pagan practices preceded that discovery (14–18) and, indeed, lasted six years (3 7). The

when he was still a boy, he began to seek guidance of the God of his forefather David; and in the twelfth year he began to purge Judah and Jerusalem of the hill-shrines and the sacred poles, and the carved idols and the images of 4 metal. He saw to it that the altars for the Baalim were destroyed and he hacked down the incense-altars which stood above them; he broke in pieces the sacred poles and the carved and metal images, grinding them to powder and scattering it on the graves of those who had sacrificed to them. He also burnt 5 the bones of the priests on their altars and purged Judah and Jerusalem. In 6 the cities of Manasseh, Ephraim, and Simeon, and as far as Naphtali, he burnt down their houses wherever he 7 found them; he destroyed the altars and the sacred poles, ground the idols to powder, and hacked down the incense-altars throughout the land of Israel. Then he returned to Jerusalem.

8ʲ   In the eighteenth year of his reign, after he had purified the land and the house, he sent Shaphan son of Azaliah and Maaseiah the governor of the city and Joah son of Joahaz the secretary of state to repair the house of the LORD 9 his God. They came to Hilkiah the high priest and gave him the silver that had been brought to the house of God, the silver which the Levites, on duty at the threshold, had gathered from Manasseh, Ephraim, and all the rest of Israel, as well as from Judah and Benjamin and the inhabitants of 10 Jerusalem. It was then handed over to the foremen in charge of the work in the house of the LORD, and these men, working in the house, used it for repairing and strengthening the fabric; 11 they gave it also to the carpenters and builders to buy hewn stone, and timber for rafters and beams, for the buildings which the kings of Judah had allowed 12-13 to fall into ruin. The men did their work honestly under the direction of Jahath and Obadiah, Levites of the line of Merari, and Zechariah and Meshullam, members of the family of Kohath. These also had control of the

porters and directed the workmen of every trade. The Levites were all skilled musicians, and some of them were secretaries, clerks, or door-keepers. When they fetched the silver which had 14 been brought to the house of the LORD, the priest Hilkiah discovered the book of the law of the LORD which had been given through Moses. Then Hilkiah told 15 Shaphan the adjutant-general, 'I have discovered the book of the law in the house of the LORD.' Hilkiah gave the book to Shaphan, and he brought it 16 to the king and reported to him: 'Your servants are doing all that was entrusted to them. They have melted 17 down the silver in the house of the LORD and have handed it over to the foremen and the workmen.' Shaphan 18 the adjutant-general also told the king that the priest Hilkiah had given him a book; and he read it out in the king's presence. When the king heard what 19 was in the book of the law, he rent his clothes, and ordered Hilkiah, Ahikam 20 son of Shaphan, Abdon son of Micah, Shaphan the adjutant-general, and Asaiah the king's attendant, to go and 21 seek guidance of the LORD, for himself and for all who still remained in Israel and Judah, about the contents of the book that had been discovered. 'Great is the wrath of the LORD,' he said, 'and it has been poured out upon us because our forefathers did not observe the command of the LORD and do all that is written in this book.'

So Hilkiah and those whom the king 22 had instructed went to Huldah the prophetess, wife of Shallum son of Tikvah,ᵏ son of Hasrah, the keeper of the wardrobe, and consulted her at her home in the second quarter of Jerusalem. 'This is the word of the LORD 23 the God of Israel,' she answered: 'Say to the man who sent you to me, "This 24 is the word of the LORD: I am bringing disaster on this place and its inhabitants, fulfilling all the imprecations recorded in the book which was read in the presence of the king of Judah,

j Verses 8–32: cp. 2 Kgs. 22. 3—23. 3.
k Prob. rdg., cp. 2 Kgs. 22. 14; Heb. Tokhath.

Chronicler's view is probably correct. **8–13:** Greater attention is paid here to the Levites and Temple workers than in the source, 2 Kgs. 22. 3–7. **9:** *The silver:* see 24.4. **29–33:** This is based

25 because they have forsaken me and burnt sacrifices to other gods, provoking my anger with all the idols they have made with their own hands; therefore my wrath is poured out upon this place and will not be quenched."

26 This is what you shall say to the king of Judah who sent you to seek guidance of the LORD: "This is the word of the LORD the God of Israel: You have

27 listened to my words and shown a willing heart, you humbled yourself before God when you heard what I said about this place and its inhabitants; you humbled yourself and rent your clothes and wept before me. Because of all this,*l* I for my part have heard you. This is the very word of the LORD.

28 Therefore, I will gather you to your forefathers, and you will be gathered to your grave in peace; you will not live to see all the disaster which I am bringing upon this place and upon its inhabitants."' So they brought back word to the king.

29 Then the king sent and called all the elders of Judah and Jerusalem together, and went up to the house of the LORD;

30 he took with him all the men of Judah and the inhabitants of Jerusalem, the priests and the Levites, the whole population, high and low. There he read them the whole book of the covenant discovered in the house of the

31 LORD; and then, standing on the dais, the king made a covenant before the LORD to obey him and keep his commandments, his testimonies, and his statutes, with all his heart and soul, and so fulfil the terms of the covenant

32 written in this book. Then he swore an oath with all who were present in Jerusalem to keep the covenant.*m* Thereafter the inhabitants of Jerusalem did obey the covenant of God, the God

33 of their fathers. Josiah removed all abominable things from all the territories of the Israelites, so that everyone living in Israel might serve the LORD his God. As long as he lived they did not fail in their allegiance to the LORD the God of their fathers.

Josiah kept a Passover to the LORD **35** in Jerusalem, and the passover lamb was killed on the fourteenth day of the first month. He appointed the priests 2 to their offices and encouraged them to perform the service of the house of the LORD. He said to the Levites, the 3 teachers of Israel, who were dedicated to the LORD, 'Put the holy Ark in the house which Solomon son of David king of Israel built; it is not to be carried about on your shoulders. Now is the time to serve the LORD your God and his people Israel: prepare 4 yourselves by families according to your divisions, following the written instructions of David king of Israel and those of Solomon his son; and 5 stand in the Holy Place as representatives of the family groups of the lay people, your brothers, one division of Levites to each family group. Kill the 6 passover lamb and hallow yourselves and prepare for your brothers to fulfil the word of the LORD given through Moses.'

Josiah contributed on behalf of all 7 the lay people present thirty thousand small cattle, that is young rams and goats, for the Passover, in addition to three thousand bulls; all these were from the king's own resources. And 8 his officers contributed willingly for the people, the priests, and the Levites. Hilkiah, Zechariah, and Jehiel, the chief officers of the house of God, gave on behalf of the priests two thousand six hundred small cattle for the Passover, in addition to three hundred bulls. And Conaniah, Shemaiah and 9 Nethaneel his brothers, and Hashabiah, Jeiel, and Jozabad, the chiefs of the Levites, gave on behalf of the Levites for the Passover five thousand small cattle in addition to five hundred bulls.

l Because of all this: *prob. rdg.; Heb. om.*
m to keep the covenant: *prob. rdg., cp. 2 Kgs. 23. 3; Heb.* and Benjamin.

on 2 Kgs.23.1–20. **35.1–19:** The Chronicler expands the brief report of a *Passover* observance in 2 Kgs.23.21–23. As usual, he emphasizes the part of *the Levites* and the *singers*. **3:** The statement here seems to imply that the *Ark* had been regularly moved for religious ceremonies prior to Josiah's time; contrast 1 Chr.13.15–16. The exact function of the *Ark* in the older Temple service is obscure; see Jer.3.16. **4:** *Written instructions of David:* see 1 Chr. chs. 23–26. **7–9:** Similar gifts are described in 1 Chr.29.6–9. **10–15:** Characteristically, the Chronicler

10 When the service had been arranged, the priests stood in their places and the Levites in their divisions, according to 11 the king's command. They killed the passover victim, and the priests flung the blood against the altar as the 12 Levites flayed the animals. Then they removed the fat flesh,[n] which they allocated to the people by groups of families for them to offer to the LORD, as prescribed in the book of Moses; 13 and so with the bulls. They cooked the passover victim over the fire according to custom, and boiled the holy offerings in pots, cauldrons, and pans, and served them quickly to all the people. 14 After that they made the necessary preparations for themselves and the priests, because the priests of Aaron's line were engaged till nightfall in offering whole-offerings and the fat portions; so the Levites made the necessary preparations for themselves and for the priests of Aaron's line. 15 The singers, the sons of Asaph, were in their places according to the rules laid down by David and by Asaph, Heman, and Jeduthun, the king's seers. The door-keepers stood, each at his gate; there was no need for them to leave their posts, because their kinsmen the Levites had made the preparations for them.

16 In this manner all the service of the LORD was arranged that day, to keep the Passover and to offer whole-offerings on the altar of the LORD, according to the command of King 17 Josiah. The people of Israel who were present kept the Passover at that time and the pilgrim-feast of Unleavened 18 Bread for seven days. No Passover like it had been kept in Israel since the days of the prophet Samuel; none of the kings of Israel had ever kept such a Passover as Josiah kept, with the priests and Levites and all Judah and Israel who were present and the inhab- itants of Jerusalem. In the eighteenth 19 year of Josiah's reign this Passover was kept.

After Josiah had thus organized all 20 the service of the house, Necho king of Egypt marched up to attack Car- chemish on the Euphrates; and Josiah went out to confront him. But Necho 21 sent envoys to him, saying, 'What do you want with me, king of Judah? I have no quarrel with you today, only with those with whom I am at war. God has purposed to speed me on my way, and God is on my side; do not stand in his way, or he will destroy you.' Josiah would not be deflected from his 22 purpose but insisted on fighting; he refused to listen to Necho's words spoken at God's command, and he sallied out to join battle in the vale of Megiddo. The archers shot at him; 23 he was severely wounded and told his bodyguard to carry him off. They lifted 24 him out of his chariot and carried him in his viceroy's chariot to Jerusalem. There he died and was buried among the tombs of his ancestors, and all Judah and Jerusalem mourned for him. Jeremiah also made a lament for 25 Josiah; and to this day the minstrels, both men and women, commemorate Josiah in their lamentations. Such laments have become traditional in Israel, and they are found in the written collections.

The other events of Josiah's reign, 26 and his works of piety, all performed in accordance with what is laid down in the law of the LORD, and his acts, 27 from first to last, are recorded in the annals of the kings of Israel and Judah.

THE PEOPLE OF THE LAND TOOK JOSIAH'S **36**[o] son Jehoahaz and made him king in

n fat flesh: or whole-offering.
o Verses 1–4: cp. 2 Kgs. 23. 30–34.

---

reports the importance, absent from his source, of the Levites and other Temple workers. **16–19:** Based on 2 Kgs.23.22–23. **18:** *Since the days of the prophet Samuel:* the meaning is, since the beginning of the monarchy; compare 2 Kgs.23.22. This unique *Passover* expressed the unity of all *Israel*, otherwise lacking throughout the monarchic period. **21–22:** Historically, *Josiah*'s policy of resistance to *Necho* arose from his collaboration with the Babylonians; see 2 Kgs.23.29–30 n. Here that collaboration is viewed as a violation of God's will, expressed by the foreign king himself. This addition, by the Chronicler, explains how the otherwise righteous Josiah fell in battle. **25:** *Jeremiah* goes unmentioned in Kgs. Compare Jer.22.10–11,15.

    36.1–23: The end of the Judean monarchy. The Chronicler condenses the account in 2 Kgs. 23.30–24.15, yet also adds to it, for example, v. 14. **1–4:** The account of Jehoahaz is much

2 place of his father in Jerusalem. He was twenty-three years old when he came to the throne, and he reigned in
3 Jerusalem for three months. Then Necho king of Egypt deposed him and fined the country a hundred talents of
4 silver and one talent of gold, and made his brother Eliakim king over Judah and Jerusalem in his place, changing his name to Jehoiakim; he also carried away his brother Jehoahaz to Egypt.
5 Jehoiakim was twenty-five years old when he came to the throne, and he reigned in Jerusalem for eleven years. He did what was wrong in the eyes of
6 the LORD his God. So Nebuchadnezzar king of Babylon marched against him and put him in fetters and took him
7 to Babylon. He also removed to Babylon some of the vessels of the house of the LORD and put them into
8 his own palace there. The other events of Jehoiakim's reign, including the abominations he committed, and everything of which he was held guilty, are recorded in the annals of the kings of Israel and Judah. He was succeeded by his son Jehoiachin.
9p   Jehoiachin was eight years old when he came to the throne, and he reigned in Jerusalem for three months and ten days. He did what was wrong in the
10 eyes of the LORD. At the turn of the year King Nebuchadnezzar sent and brought him to Babylon, together with the choicest vessels of the house of the LORD, and made his father's brother Zedekiah king over Judah and Jerusalem.
11   Zedekiah was twenty-one years old when he came to the throne, and he reigned in Jerusalem for eleven years.
12 He did what was wrong in the eyes of the LORD his God; he did not defer to the guidance of the prophet Jeremiah,
13 the spokesman of the LORD. He also

rebelled against King Nebuchadnezzar, who had laid on him a solemn oath of allegiance. He was obstinate and stubborn and refused to return to the
14 LORD the God of Israel. All the chiefs of Judah and the priests and the people became more and more unfaithful, following all the abominable practices of the other nations; and they defiled the house of the LORD which he had hallowed in Jerusalem. The LORD God
15 of their fathers had warned them betimes through his messengers, for he took pity on his people and on his
16 dwelling-place; but they never ceased to deride his messengers, scorn his words and scoff at his prophets, until the anger of the LORD burst out against his people and could not be appeased.
17q So he brought against them the king of the Chaldaeans, who put their young men to the sword in the sanctuary and spared neither young man nor maiden, neither the old nor the weak; God gave them all into his power. And he brought
18 all the vessels of the house of God, great and small, and the treasures of the house of the LORD and of the king and his officers—all these he brought to Babylon. And they burnt down the
19 house of God, razed the city wall of Jerusalem and burnt down all its stately mansions and all their precious possessions until everything was destroyed.
20 Those who escaped the sword he took captive to Babylon, and they became slaves to him and his sons until the sovereignty passed to the Persians,
21 while the land of Israel ran the full term of its sabbaths. All the time that it lay desolate it kept the sabbath rest, to complete seventy years in fulfilment of the word of the LORD by the prophet Jeremiah.

p *Verses 9, 10: cp. 2 Kgs. 24. 8–17.*
q *Verses 17–20: cp. 2 Kgs. 25. 1–17.*

---

condensed; see 2 Kgs.23.30–34. *Jehoiakim*: see 2 Kgs.23.36–24.6. **6**: *Jehoiakim* actually died before the Babylonian king could capture and exile him; compare 2 Kgs.24.1–6. **7**: This has been added by the Chronicler, see v. 10. **9–10**: *Jehoiachin*: again condensation (of 2 Kgs. 24.8–17) is present. **9**: *Eight*: The correct number is eighteen, as in 2 Kgs.24.8. **11–13**: *Zedekiah*: This is much changed from 2 Kgs.24.18–20, with the names of his mother and grandfather omitted. **12**: See 35.25 n. On the reference here to *Jeremiah*, see Jer.32.1–5; 37.1–10; 38.28. **14**: In the source, the blame for the end of the monarchy was placed on the wicked kings, not, as here, on *chiefs*, *priests*, and the *people*. Note that the Levites go unmentioned here. **15–16**: The ignoring of the prophets appears repeatedly, e.g. 12.5–8; 15.1–8; 19.1–3; and elsewhere. **17–21**: The account of the fall of Jerusalem and the beginning of the Exile is greatly abridged from 2 Kgs.25.1–21. **21**: On *the sabbath rest*, see Lev.26.33–45 and Jer.25.11–12.

22ʳ   Now in the first year of Cyrus king of Persia, so that the word of the LORD spoken through Jeremiah might be fulfilled, the LORD stirred up the heart of Cyrus king of Persia; and he issued a proclamation throughout his kingdom, both by word of mouth and in writing, to this effect:

Persia: The LORD the God of heaven has given me all the kingdoms of the earth, and he himself has charged me to build him a house at Jerusalem in Judah. To every man of his people now among you I say, the LORD his God beˢ with him, and let him go up.

23   This is the word of Cyrus king of

r *Verses 22, 23: cp. Ezra 1. 1–3.*
s *be: prob. rdg., cp. Ezra 1. 3; Heb. om.*

22–23: These verses appear also in Ezra 1.1–3, an indication that the single book, Ezra-Neh., was the continuation of Chr. Apparently the verses were first written, but later repeated and incorporated here to abstain from an ending so negative as v. 21. In the MT, 2 Chr. is the last book; it was characteristic of later rabbinic thought that even passages of doom must end in hope.

THE BOOK OF
EZRA

The books of Chronicles, Ezra, and Nehemiah were originally a single unit which came to be separated (see Introduction to 1 Chronicles). The Book of Ezra deals with several episodes of the return to Zion by Judeans after the Babylonian Exile (587–539 B.C.); these episodes took place in both the sixth and the fifth centuries, and focus on Sheshbazzar, Zerubbabel, Ezra (who made two trips), and Nehemiah (who made two trips).

The book poses a number of historical and literary problems, the chief of which is that of sources and the sequence of materials. Two main sources used by the author, usually called the Chronicler, are the "Memoirs of Ezra" and the "Memoirs of Nehemiah" (narratives using first person forms). But some of the Nehemiah material appears in the Book of Ezra and some of the Ezra material is in the Book of Nehemiah, suggesting that materials were dislocated in the course of their transmission.

As a consequence, uncertainty attends the effort to determine whether Ezra and Nehemiah were contemporaries. If they were not, then problems arise as to whose career came first. In the order of the books in the Hebrew Bible, the Book of Ezra precedes the Book of Nehemiah, and the general impression suggests that priority belonged to Ezra. But serious doubts have been raised; for example, if Ezra came first, why does Nehemiah seem to ignore him? (See also 10.6 n.) Hence, a frequent view adopted here concludes that Nehemiah preceded Ezra. Accordingly, the king of 7.1 is likely Artaxerxes II (404–359 B.C.); the king at the time of Nehemiah was Artaxerxes I (464–424 B.C.).

On the date of composition, probably the fourth pre-Christian century is to be adopted; see Introduction to 1 Chronicles.

Chapters 1–6 are not about Ezra but deal with a return from Babylonia led by Sheshbazzar (about 538 B.C.), and with further events of the time of Zerubbabel (about 516 B.C.); some scholars term these early chapters "The Book of Zerubbabel."

The material on Ezra himself is in Ezra chs. 7–10 and Neh. chs. 8–9.

Despite the problems, the prevailing interest in the book is clear. The returned exiles represent to the author the remnant of Israel who must exhibit fullest fidelity to, and conformity with, the Law of Moses. Hence, the community needed to reconstruct Jerusalem and the Temple, and to maintain its sanctity in the midst of foreign peoples.

The return of the exiles to Jerusalem

1 NOW IN THE FIRST YEAR OF CYRUS king of Persia, so that the word of the LORD spoken through Jeremiah might be fulfilled, the LORD stirred up the heart of Cyrus king of Persia; and he issued a proclamation throughout his kingdom, both by word of mouth and in writing, to this effect:

2 This is the word of Cyrus king of Persia: The LORD the God of heaven has given me all the kingdoms of the earth, and he himself has charged me to build him a house at Jerusalem in Judah. To every man of his people 3 now among you I say, God be with him, and let him go up to Jerusalem in Judah, and rebuild the house of the LORD the God of Israel, the God whose city is Jerusalem. And every 4 remaining Jew, wherever he may be living, may claim aid from his neighbours in that place, silver and gold, goods*a* and cattle, in addition to the voluntary offerings for the house of God in Jerusalem.

a Or pack-animals.

1.1–11: The return of the exiles to Jerusalem under Sheshbazzar. 1–3: These verses duplicate 2 Chr.36.22–23; see annotation there. 1: *The first year of Cyrus* was 538 B.C. Cyrus II's rule over Persia actually began in 557 B.C.; 538 is the date from the perspective of the Babylonians. *The word of the Lord spoken through Jeremiah:* what to the Persians was undoubtedly an act of political expediency was to the Jews the fulfillment of God's promise as taught by Jeremiah (see Jer.25.11–14; 29.10; compare Isa.44.28; 45.1). Notices *in writing* were posted in public places. 2–4: Compare the decree of Cyrus in vv. 2–4, which is in Heb., with the Aram. parallel in 6.3–5. The somewhat different versions both conform with what is known of the diplomatic policies of the early Persian Achaemenid kings (sixth-fourth centuries B.C.). 4: *Remaining:*

5 Thereupon the heads of families of Judah and Benjamin, and the priests and the Levites, answered the summons, all whom God had moved to go up to rebuild the house of the LORD in 6 Jerusalem. Their neighbours all assisted them with gifts of every kind, silver[b] and gold, goods[a] and cattle and valuable gifts in abundance,[c] in addi- 7 tion to any voluntary service. Moreover, Cyrus king of Persia produced the vessels of the house of the LORD which Nebuchadnezzar had removed from Jerusalem and placed in the temple 8 of his god; and he handed them over into the charge of Mithredath the treasurer, who made an inventory of them for Sheshbazzar the ruler of 9 Judah. This was the list: thirty gold basins, a thousand silver basins, twenty- 10 nine vessels of various kinds, thirty golden bowls, four hundred and ten silver bowls of various types, and a 11 thousand other vessels. The vessels of gold and silver amounted in all to five thousand four hundred, and Sheshbazzar took them all up to Jerusalem, when the exiles were brought back from Babylon.

2,1[d]   Of the captives whom Nebuchadnezzar king of Babylon had taken into exile in Babylon, these were the people of the province who returned to Jerusalem and Judah, each to his own 2 city, led by Zerubbabel, Jeshua,[e] Nehemiah, Seraiah, Reelaiah, Mordecai, Bilshan, Mispar, Bigvai, Rehum and Baanah.

The roll of the men of the people of 3 Israel: the family of Parosh, two thousand one hundred and seventy- 4 two; the family of Shephatiah, three 5 hundred and seventy-two; the family of Arah, seven hundred and seventy- 6 five; the family of Pahath-moab, namely the families of Jeshua and[f] Joab, two thousand eight hundred and 7 twelve; the family of Elam, one thousand two hundred and fifty-four;

the family of Zattu, nine hundred and 8 forty-five, the family of Zaccai, seven 9 hundred and sixty; the family of Bani, 10 six hundred and forty-two; the family 11 of Bebai, six hundred and twenty-three; the family of Azgad, one thousand two 12 hundred and twenty-two; the family of 13 Adonikam, six hundred and sixty-six; the family of Bigvai, two thousand and 14 fifty-six; the family of Adin, four 15 hundred and fifty-four; the family of 16 Ater, namely that of Hezekiah, ninety-eight; the family of Bezai, three 17 hundred and twenty-three; the family 18 of Jorah, one hundred and twelve; the 19 family of Hashum, two hundred and twenty-three; the family of Gibbar, 20 ninety-five. The men[g] of Bethlehem, 21 one hundred and twenty-three; the 22 men of Netophah, fifty-six; the men 23 of Anathoth, one hundred and twenty-eight; the men of Beth-azmoth,[h] forty- 24 two; the men of Kiriath-jearim,[i] 25 Kephirah, and Beeroth, seven hundred and forty-three; the men[j] of Ramah 26 and Geba, six hundred and twenty-one; the men of Michmas, one hundred 27 and twenty-two; the men of Bethel and 28 Ai, two hundred and twenty-three; the 29 men[k] of Nebo, fifty-two; the men of 30 Magbish, one hundred and fifty-six; the men of the other Elam, one 31 thousand two hundred and fifty-four; the men of Harim, three hundred and 32 twenty; the men of Lod, Hadid, and 33 Ono, seven hundred and twenty-five; the men of Jericho, three hundred and 34 forty-five; the men of Senaah, three 35 thousand six hundred and thirty.

Priests: the family of Jedaiah, of the 36

a Or pack-animals.
b with gifts . . . silver: *prob. rdg., cp. 1 Esdras 2. 9; Heb.* with vessels of silver.
c in abundance: *prob. rdg., cp. 1 Esdras. 2. 9; Heb.* apart.
d Verses 1–70: cp. Neh. 7. 6–73.
e Or Joshua (*cp. Hag. 1. 1*).
f and: *prob. rdg., cp. Neh. 7. 11; Heb. om.*
g Prob. rdg., cp. Neh. 7. 26; Heb. family.
h Prob. rdg., cp. Neh. 7. 28; Heb. the family of Azmoth.
i Prob. rdg., cp. Neh. 7. 29; Heb. the family of Kiriath-arim.
j Prob. rdg., cp. Neh. 7. 30; Heb. family.
k Prob. rdg.; Heb. family (*also in verses 30–35*).

surviving (2 Chr.36.20). **8:** *Mithredath:* Cyrus' treasurer. *Sheshbazzar* may be identical with a son of Jeconiah whose name in 1 Chr.3.18 is given as Shenazzar and elsewhere as Shenabasar or Sheshbazzar. *Ruler:* leader. **11:** *In all:* see 1 Esd.2.13–15.

2.1–70: The census of returnees, paralleled in Neh.7.6–73. **2:** Possibly a composite list of men who at different times led groups of exiles home. **3–67:** Enumeration of the heads of families of Israel (Judah and Benjamin, see 1.5), various Temple officials (vv. 36–63) and servants, and animals (vv. 64–67). Some returnees are listed according to the name of the father, others accord-

line of Jeshua, nine hundred and
37 seventy three; the family of Immer,
38 one thousand and fifty-two: the family
of Pashhur, one thousand two hundred
39 and forty-seven; the family of Harim,
one thousand and seventeen.
40 Levites: the families of Jeshua and
Kadmiel, of the line of Hodaviah,
41 seventy-four. Singers: the family of
Asaph, one hundred and twenty-eight.
42 The guild of door-keepers: the family
of Shallum, the family of Ater, the
family of Talmon, the family of Akkub,
the family of Hatita, and the family of
Shobai, one hundred and thirty-nine
in all.
43 Temple-servitors: the family of Ziha,
the family of Hasupha, the family of
44 Tabbaoth, the family of Keros, the
family of Siaha, the family of Padon,
45 the family of Lebanah, the family of
46 Hagabah, the family of Akkub, the
family of Hagab, the family of Shamlai,[l]
47 the family of Hanan, the family of
Giddel, the family of Gahar, the family
48 of Reaiah, the family of Rezin, the
family of Nekoda, the family of
49 Gazzam, the family of Uzza, the family
50 of Paseah, the family of Besai, the
family of Asnah, the family of the
Meunim,[m] the family of the Nephu-
51 sim,[n] the family of Bakbuk, the family
52 of Hakupha, the family of Harhur, the
family of Bazluth, the family of
53 Mehida, the family of Harsha, the
family of Barkos, the family of Sisera,
54 the family of Temah, the family of
Neziah, and the family of Hatipha.
55 Descendants of Solomon's servants:
the family of Sotai, the family of
Hassophereth, the family of Peruda,
56 the family of Jaalah, the family of
57 Darkon, the family of Giddel, the
family of Shephatiah, the family of
Hattil, the family of Pochereth-
hazzebaim, and the family of Ami.
58 The temple-servitors and the descendants of Solomon's servants amounted

to three hundred and ninety-two in all.
59 The following were those who
returned from Tel-melah, Tel-harsha,
Kerub, Addan, and Immer, but could
not establish their father's family nor
whether by descent they belonged to
60 Israel: the family of Delaiah, the
family of Tobiah, and the family of
Nekoda, six hundred and fifty-two.
61 Also of the priests: the family of
Hobaiah, the family of Hakkoz, and
the family of Barzillai who had
married a daughter of Barzillai the
Gileadite and went by his[o] name.
62 These searched for their names among
those enrolled in the genealogies, but
they could not be found; they were
disqualified for the priesthood as
63 unclean, and the governor forbade
them to partake of the most sacred
food until there should be a priest able
to consult the Urim and the Thummim.
64 The whole assembled people numbered forty-two thousand three hun-
65 dred and sixty, apart from their slaves,
male and female, of whom there were
seven thousand three hundred and
thirty-seven; and they had two hundred
singers, men and women. Their horses
66 numbered seven hundred and thirty-
six, their mules two hundred and forty-
67 five, their camels four hundred and
thirty-five, and their asses six thousand
seven hundred and twenty.
68 When they came to the house of the
LORD in Jerusalem, some of the heads
of families volunteered to rebuild the
house of God on its original site.
69 According to their resources they gave
for the fabric fund a total of sixty-one
thousand drachmas of gold, five thous-
and minas of silver, and one hundred
priestly robes.
70 The priests, the Levites, and some
of the people lived in Jerusalem and its

l Or Shalmai *(cp. Neh. 7. 48).*
m Or Meinim.
n Or Nephisim.
o Prob. rdg., cp. 1 Esdras 5. 38; Heb. their.

ing to place of origin. **41–42:** *Singers* and *door-keepers:* functionaries among the Levites. **43:**
Servitors: Heb. *nethinim.* **63:** *Governor:* Sheshbazzar (1.8). The statement *until there should be
a priest able to consult the Urim and the Thummim* (see 1 Sam.14.41) refers ostensibly to the
future when the use of the sacred lot would be reinstated, but the author apparently knew that
that ancient practice was never reintroduced, as is clear from later rabbinic sources. **64:** The
figure for *the whole assembled people* apparently included those from tribes not specified above.
65: The *two hundred* were not the Temple singers of v. 41, but entertainers (see 2 Sam.19.35
or 2 Chr.35.25), here morale boosters for the long journey. **69:** *Fabric fund:* a reserve fund for
building maintenance and repair. For contrast see Neh.7.70–71.

suburbs;*p* the singers, the door-keepers, and temple-servitors,*q* and all other Israelites, lived in their own towns.

Worship restored and the temple rebuilt

3 WHEN THE SEVENTH MONTH CAME, THE Israelites now being settled in their towns, the people assembled as one 2 man in Jerusalem. Then Jeshua son of Jozadak and his fellow-priests, and Zerubbabel son of Shealtiel and his kinsmen, set to work and built the altar of the God of Israel, in order to offer upon it whole-offerings as prescribed in the law of Moses the man of God. 3 They put the altar in place first, because they lived in fear of the foreign population; and they offered upon it whole-offerings to the LORD, both morning 4 and evening offerings. They kept the pilgrim-feast of Tabernacles*r* as ordained, and offered whole-offerings every day in the number prescribed for 5 each day, and, in addition to these, the regular whole-offerings and the offerings for sabbaths,*s* for new moons and for all the sacred seasons appointed by the LORD, and all voluntary 6 offerings brought to the LORD. The offering of whole-offerings began from the first day of the seventh month, although the foundation of the temple 7 of the LORD had not yet been laid. They gave money for the masons and carpenters, and food and drink and oil for the Sidonians and the Tyrians to fetch cedar-wood from the Lebanon to the roadstead at Joppa, by licence from Cyrus king of Persia. 8 In the second year after their return to the house of God in Jerusalem, and in the second month, Zerubbabel son of Shealtiel and Jeshua son of Jozadak started work, aided by all their fellow-

Israelites, the priests and the Levites and all who had returned from captivity to Jerusalem. They appointed Levites from the age of twenty years and upwards to supervise the work of the house of the LORD. Jeshua with his 9 sons and his kinsmen, Kadmiel, Binnui, and Hodaviah,*t* together assumed control of those responsible for the work on the house of God.*u* When the builders had laid the 10 foundation of the temple of the LORD, the priests in their robes took their places with their trumpets, and the Levites, the sons of Asaph, with their cymbals, to praise the LORD in the manner prescribed by David king of Israel; and they chanted praises and 11 thanksgiving to the LORD, singing, 'It is good to give thanks to the LORD,*v* for his love towards Israel endures for ever.' All the people raised a great shout of praise to the LORD because the foundation of the house of the LORD had been laid. But many of the 12 priests and Levites and heads of families, who were old enough to have seen the former house, wept and wailed aloud when they saw the foundation of this house laid, while many others shouted for joy at the top of their voice. The people could not 13 distinguish the sound of the shout of joy from that of the weeping and wailing, so great was the shout which the people were raising, and the sound could be heard a long way off.

When the enemies of Judah and Ben- 4 jamin heard that the returned exiles

p in Jerusalem and its suburbs: *prob. rdg., cp. 1 Esdras. 5. 46; Heb. om.*
q Prob. rdg.; Heb. adds in their towns.
r Or Booths.
s for sabbaths: prob. rdg., cp. 1 Esdras 5. 52; Heb. om.
t Binnui, and Hodaviah: prob. rdg.; Heb. and his sons the family of Judah.
u Prob. rdg.; Heb. adds the family of Henadad, their family and their kinsmen the Levites.
v to give thanks to the LORD: prob. rdg., cp. Ps. 106. 1; Heb. om.

3.1–13: Worship restored and the Temple rebuilt. 1: *The seventh month:* Tishri (September-October); the date is regarded by some as 538 B.C., the first year of Cyrus (see 1.1 n.), but by others as 520, the second year of Darius. **3:** After *they put the altar in place*, the sacrifices for the sacred days could be offered (vv. 3–6). **7:** *Sidonians* and *Tyrians:* Phoenicians. Compare the account of Solomon's building of the Temple in 2 Chr.2.1–16. **8:** *The second month:* Iyyar (April-May). **11:** *Prescribed by David:* see 2 Chr.29.25–30.
 4.1–6.22: Opposition to the efforts to rebuild. 4.1–5 record opposition to rebuilding the *temple,* but vv. 6–23 to rebuilding the *walls* of Jerusalem. 4.1–5 reflect the reigns of Cyrus, Cambyses (not mentioned in the book), and Darius I (though only the beginning), that is, the period 538–520 B.C. 4.6–23, however, reflect the reign of Artaxerxes, namely, 464–424, and intrude into and interrupt the account in 4.1–6.22. **1:** *Enemies:* the Samaritans. **2:** See 2 Kgs.17.24–28 on

were building a temple to the LORD the God of Israel, they approached Zerubbabel and Jeshua[w] and the heads of families and said to them, 'Let us join you in building, for like you we seek your God, and we have been sacrificing to him ever since the days of Esarhaddon king of Assyria, who 3 brought us here.' But Zerubbabel and Jeshua and the rest of the heads of families in Israel said to them. 'The house which we are building for our God is no concern of yours. We alone will build it for the LORD the God of Israel, as his majesty Cyrus king of Persia commanded us.'

4 Then the people of the land caused the Jews to lose heart and made them 5 afraid to continue building; and in order to defeat their purpose they bribed officials at court to act against them. This continued throughout the reign of Cyrus and into the reign of Darius king of Persia.

6 At the beginning of the reign of Ahasuerus, the people of the land brought a charge in writing against the inhabitants of Judah and Jerusalem.

7 And in the days of Artaxerxes king of Persia, with the agreement of Mithredath, Tabeel and all his colleagues wrote to him; the letter was written in Aramaic and read aloud in Aramaic.

8[x] Rehum the high commissioner and Shimshai the secretary wrote a letter to King Artaxerxes concerning Jerusalem in the following terms:

9 From Rehum the high commissioner, Shimshai the secretary, and all their colleagues, the judges, the commissioners, the overseers, and chief officers, the men of Erech and Babylon, and the Elamites in Susa, 10 and the other peoples whom the great and renowned Asnappar[y] deported and settled in the city of Samaria and in the rest of the province of Beyond-Euphrates.

Here follows the text of their letter: 11

To King Artaxerxes from his servants, the men of the province of Beyond-Euphrates:

Be it known to Your Majesty that 12 the Jews who left you and came to these parts have reached Jerusalem and are rebuilding that wicked and rebellious city; they have surveyed[z] the foundations and are completing the walls. Be it known to Your 13 Majesty that, if their city is rebuilt and the walls are completed, they will pay neither general levy, nor poll-tax, nor land-tax, and in the end[a] they will harm the monarchy. Now, because we eat the king's salt 14 and it is not right that we should witness the king's dishonour, therefore we have sent to inform Your Majesty, in order that search may be 15 made in the annals of your predecessors. You will discover by searching through the annals that this has been a rebellious city, harmful to the monarchy and its provinces, and that sedition has long been rife within its walls, That is why the city was laid waste. We submit to Your 16 Majesty that, if it is rebuilt and its walls are completed, the result will be that you will have no more footing in the province of Beyond-Euphrates.

The king sent this answer: 17

w *and Jeshua: prob. rdg., cp. 1 Esdras 5. 68; Heb. om.*
x *From 4. 8 to 6. 18 the text is in Aramaic.*
y *Or Osnappar.*
z *have surveyed: prob. rdg.; Aram. are surveying.*
a *in the end: or certainly.*

---

the non-Jewish origin of the Samaritans. **6:** *Ahasuerus:* Xerxes I (485–465). The verse, not part of vv.7–23, seems out of place, but where it may belong is uncertain. **7–23:** The section appears to be misplaced, but it is no longer possible to determine its proper location. **7:** *Mithredath:* not to be confused with the man mentioned in 1.8. *With the agreement of:* Heb. *bishlam,* regarded by some as a proper name of a man to be associated with Mithredath and Tabeel. *Written . . . and read aloud in Aramaic:* probably the meaning is that the letter was both in the Aramaic language and also written in the Aramaic script (rather than in another alphabet). **9:** The terms *judges, commissioners, overseers, and chief officers* translate words of uncertain meaning; they may be names of local peoples (such as *Erech* and *Babylon*) rather than official titles. **10:** *Asnappar:* probably Ashurbanipal (668–627 B.C.). **11–22:** The complaint (vv. 11–16) and the royal reply (vv. 17–22). **23:** The cessation of building.

To Rehum the high commissioner, Shimshai the secretary, and all your colleagues resident in Samaria and in the rest of the province of Beyond-Euphrates, greeting. The letter which 18 you sent to me has now been read clearly in my presence. I have given 19 orders and search has been made, and it has been found that the city in question has a long history of revolt against the monarchy, and that rebellion and sedition have been rife in it. Powerful kings have ruled 20 in Jerusalem, exercising authority over the whole province of Beyond-Euphrates, and general levy, poll-tax, and land-tax have been paid to them. Therefore, issue orders that 21 these men must desist. This city is not to be rebuilt until a decree to that effect is issued by me. See that you do 22 not neglect your duty in this matter, lest more damage and harm be done to the monarchy.

When the text of the letter from 23 King Artaxerxes was read before Rehum the high commissioner, Shimshai the secretary, and their colleagues, they hurried to Jerusalem and forcibly compelled the Jews to stop work. From 24 then onwards the work on the house of God in Jerusalem stopped; and it remained at a standstill till the second year of the reign of Darius king of Persia.

5 But the prophets Haggai[b] and Zechariah grandson of Iddo upbraided the Jews in Judah and Jerusalem, prophesying in the name of the God of Israel. Then Zerubbabel son of Shealtiel and 2 Jeshua son of Jozadak at once began to rebuild the house of God in Jerusalem, and the prophets of God were with them and supported them. Tattenai, 3 governor of the province of Beyond-Euphrates, Shethar-bozenai, and their colleagues promptly came to them and said, 'Who issued a decree permitting you to rebuild this house and complete

its furnishings?' They also asked them 4 for the names of the men engaged in the building. But the elders of the Jews 5 were under God's watchful eye, and they were not prevented from continuing the work, until such time as a report should reach Darius and a royal letter should be received in answer.

Here follows the text of the letter sent 6 by Tattenai, governor of the province of Beyond-Euphrates, Shethar-bozenai, and his colleagues, the inspectors in the province of Beyond-Euphrates, to King Darius. This is the written report that 7 they sent:

To King Darius, all greetings. Be 8 it known to Your Majesty that we went to the province of Judah and found the house of the great God being rebuilt by the Jewish elders,[c] with massive stones and timbers laid in the walls. The work was being done thoroughly and was making good progress under their direction. We asked these elders who had issued 9 a decree for the rebuilding of this house and the completion of the furnishings. We also asked them for 10 their names, so that we might make a list of the leaders for your information. This was their reply: 'We are 11 the servants of the God of heaven and earth, and we are rebuilding the house originally built many years ago; a great king of Israel built it and completed it. But because our fore-12 fathers provoked the anger of the God of heaven, he put them into the the power of Nebuchadnezzar the Chaldaean, king of Babylon, who pulled down this house and carried the people captive to Babylon. However, Cyrus king of Babylon in 13 the first year of his reign issued a decree that this house of God should be rebuilt. Moreover, there were gold 14 and silver vessels of the house of God,

b Prob. rdg., cp. 1 Esdras 6. 1; Aram. adds the prophet.
c by . . . elders: prob. rdg., cp. 1 Esdras 6. 8; Aram. om.

4.24–5.17: The resumption of rebuilding. 24: See 4.1–6.22 n. **5.1:** *Haggai and Zechariah:* prophets whose books are preserved in Scripture. **8–17:** The report to the king seeks to ascertain whether proper channels have been consulted and proper authorization obtained. We are in the realm of bureaucracy, not hostility. **11:** *Great king:* Solomon. **12–14:** The conduct of the Chaldeans, who had destroyed the Temple, and the Persian Achaemenids, who allowed its rebuilding, is skillfully contrasted.

which Nebuchadnezzar had taken from the temple in Jerusalem and put in the temple in Babylon; and these King Cyrus took out of the temple in Babylon. He gave them to a man named Sheshbazzar whom he had appointed governor, and said 15 to him, "Take these vessels; go and restore them to the temple in Jerusalem, and let the house of God there 16 be rebuilt on its original site." Then this Sheshbazzar came and laid the foundation of the house of God in Jerusalem; and from that time until now the rebuilding has continued, 17 but it is not yet finished.' Now, therefore, if it please Your Majesty, let search be made in the royal archives in Babylon, to discover whether a decree was issued by King Cyrus for the rebuilding of this house of God in Jerusalem. Then let the king send us his wishes in the matter.

6 Then King Darius issued an order, and search was made in the archives where the treasures were deposited in 2 Babylon. But it was in Ecbatana, in the royal residence in the province of Media, that a scroll was found, on which was written the following memorandum:

3   In the first year of King Cyrus, the king issued this decree concerning the house of God in Jerusalem: Let the house be rebuilt as a place where sacrifices are offered and fire-offerings brought. Its height shall be sixty cubits and its breadth sixty 4 cubits, with three courses of massive stones and one^d course of timber, the cost to be defrayed from the royal 5 treasury. Also the gold and silver vessels of the house of God, which Nebuchadnezzar took out of the temple in Jerusalem and brought to Babylon, shall be restored; they shall all be taken back to the temple in Jerusalem, and restored each to its place in the house of God.

6 Then King Darius issued this order:^e

Now, Tattenai, governor of the province of Beyond-Euphrates, Shethar-bozenai, and your colleagues, the inspectors in the province of Beyond-Euphrates, you are to keep away from the place, and to leave 7 the governor of the Jews and their elders free to rebuild this house of God; let them rebuild it on its original site. I also issue an order pre- 8 scribing what you are to do for these elders of the Jews, so that the said house of God may be rebuilt. Their expenses are to be defrayed in full from the royal funds accruing from the taxes of the province of Beyond-Euphrates, so that the work may not be brought to a standstill. And let 9 them have daily without fail whatever they want, young bulls, rams, or lambs as whole-offerings for the God of heaven, or wheat, salt, wine, or oil, as the priests in Jerusalem demand, so that they may 10 offer soothing sacrifices to the God of heaven, and pray for the life of the king and his sons. Furthermore, 11 I decree that, if any man tampers with this edict, a beam shall be pulled out of his house and he shall be fastened erect to it and flogged; and, in addition, his house shall be forfeit.^f And may the God who made 12 that place a dwelling for his Name overthrow any king or people that shall presume to tamper with this edict or to destroy this house of God in Jerusalem. I Darius have issued a decree; it is to be carried out to the letter.

Then Tattenai, governor of the prov- 13 ince of Beyond-Euphrates, Shethar-bozenai, and their colleagues carried out to the letter the instructions which King Darius had sent them, and the 14 elders of the Jews went on with the rebuilding. As a result of the prophecies

d *Prob. rdg., cp. 1 Esdras 6. 25; Aram. a new.*
e *Then . . . order: prob. rdg., cp. 1 Esdras 6. 27; Aram. om.*
f *Or made into a dunghill (mng. of Aram. word uncertain).*

6.1–22: Completion of the Temple and celebration of Passover. 2: *Ecbatana*, modern Hamadan, was the summer residence of the Persian kings. **4:** *Stones . . . timber:* such construction was usual. **7:** *Governor:* possibly Zerubbabel (see Hag.2.21). **14:** Artaxerxes (see Tfn. *g*) is mentioned in error, for he ruled after Darius I, and hence subsequent to the completion of

of Haggai the prophet and Zechariah grandson of Iddo they had good success and finished the rebuilding as commanded by the God of Israel and according to the decrees of Cyrus and

15 Darius;*g* and the house was completed on the twenty-third*h* day of the month Adar, in the sixth year of King Darius.

16 Then the people of Israel, the priests and the Levites and all the other exiles who had returned, celebrated the dedication of the house of God with

17 great rejoicing. For its dedication they offered one hundred bulls, two hundred rams, and four hundred lambs, and as a sin-offering for all Israel twelve he-goats, corresponding to the number of

18 the tribes of Israel. And they re-established the priests in their groups and the Levites in their divisions for the service of God in Jerusalem, as prescribed in the book of Moses.

19 On the fourteenth day of the first month the exiles who had returned kept

20 the Passover. The priests and the Levites, one and all, had purified them selves; all of them were ritually clean, and they killed the passover lamb for all the exiles who had returned, for their fellow-priests and for themselves.

21 It was eaten by the Israelites who had come back from exile and by all who had separated themselves from the peoples of the land and their un-cleanness and sought the LORD the God

22 of Israel. And they kept the pilgrim-feast of Unleavened Bread for seven days with rejoicing; for the LORD had given them cause for joy by changing the disposition of the king of Assyria towards them, so that he encouraged them in the work of the house of God, the God of Israel.

Ezra's mission to Jerusalem

7 NOW AFTER THESE EVENTS, IN THE REIGN of Artaxerxes king of Persia, there came up from Babylon one Ezra son of

2 Seraiah, son of Azariah, son of Hilkiah, son of Shallum, son of Zadok, son*i*

3 of Ahitub, son of Amariah, son of

4 Azariah, son of Meraioth, son of Zerahiah, son of Uzzi, son of Bukki,

5 son of Abishua, son of Phinehas, son of Eleazar, son of Aaron the chief

6 priest. He was a scribe*j* learned in the law of Moses which the LORD the God of Israel had given them; and the king granted him all that he asked, for the hand of the LORD his God was upon

7 him. In the seventh year of King Artaxerxes, other Israelites, priests, Levites, singers, door-keepers, and temple-servitors went up with him to

8 Jerusalem; and they reached Jerusalem in the fifth month, in the seventh year

9 of the king. On the first day of the first month Ezra fixed the day for departure from Babylon, and on the first day of the fifth month he arrived at Jerusalem, for the gracious hand of his God was

10 upon him. For Ezra had devoted him-self to the study and observance of the law of the LORD and to teaching statute and ordinance in Israel.

11 This is a copy of the royal letter which King Artaxerxes had given to Ezra the priest and scribe, a scribe versed in questions concerning the commandments and the statutes of the LORD laid upon Israel:

12 Artaxerxes, king of kings, to Ezra*k*

g Prob. rdg.; Aram. adds and Artaxerxes king of Persia.
h Prob. rdg., cp. 1 Esdras 7. 5; Aram. third.
i Or grandson.   j Or doctor of the law.
k The text of verses 12–26 is in Aramaic.

---

the Temple. **15:** The date (see Tnf. *h*) corresponds to late March, 516 B.C. **16–18:** Compare 1 Kgs. ch. 8. **18:** No provision exists in the Pentateuch for the *priests in their groups* and *Levites in their divisions*. **19:** *First month:* Nisan, corresponding to March-April. Passover (the fourteenth of Nisan) falls three weeks after the twenty-third of Adar mentioned in v. 15. **22:** The end of "The Book of Zerubbabel"; see Introduction. *King of Assyria* is anachronistic, for Assyria had fallen in 612 B.C., about a hundred years earlier; but the phrase may simply mean a distant emperor ruling over what had been Assyria.

7.1–10.16: Ezra's mission to Jerusalem. "The Memoir of Ezra" seems extracted from the personal diaries of Ezra himself; see Introduction. The entire biblical book received its name from these chapters. It is likely that this section belongs chronologically after Neh. chs. 1–7; the "Memoir" continues (still in the first person) in Neh. chs. 8–10. **1:** *Artaxerxes:* see Introduction. **6:** *Scribe:* see Tfn. *j*. It means teacher, rather than copyist. **9:** *The first month* was Nisan (March-April); *the fifth month* was Ab (July-August).

7.11–26: Artaxerxes' letter. Scholars disagree as to the precise nature and extent of Ezra's authority here granted, whether it was restricted to religious matters pertaining only to the

the priest and scribe learned in the law of the God of heaven;

13 This is my decision. I hereby issue a decree that any of the people of Israel or of its priests or Levites in my kingdom who volunteer to go to

14 Jerusalem may go with you. You are sent by the king and his seven counsellors to find out how things stand in Judah and Jerusalem with regard to the law of your God with which

15 you are entrusted. You are also to convey the silver and gold which the king and his counsellors have freely offered to the God of Israel whose

16 dwelling is in Jerusalem, together with any silver and gold that you may find throughout the province of Babylon, and the voluntary offerings of the people and of the priests which they freely offer for the house of their

17 God in Jerusalem. In pursuance of this decree you shall use the money solely for the purchase of bulls, rams, and lambs, and the proper grain-offerings and drink-offerings, to be offered on the altar in the house of

18 your God in Jerusalem. Further, should any silver and gold be left over, you and your colleagues may use it at your discretion according

19 to the will of your God. The vessels which have been given you for the service of the house of your God you shall hand over to the God of

20 Jerusalem; and if anything else should be required for the house of your God, which it may fall to you to provide, you may provide it out of the king's treasury.

21 And I, King Artaxerxes, issue an order to all treasurers in the province of Beyond-Euphrates that whatever is demanded of you by Ezra the priest, a scribe learned in the law of the God of heaven, is to be supplied

22 exactly, up to a hundred talents of silver, a hundred kor of wheat, a hundred bath of wine, a hundred bath of oil, and salt without reck-

23 oning. Whatever is demanded by the God of heaven, let it be diligently carried out for the house of the God of heaven; otherwise wrath may fall upon the realm of the king and his

24 sons. We also make known to you that you have no authority to impose general levy, poll-tax, or land-tax on any of the priests, Levites, musicians, door-keepers, temple-servitors, or other servants of this house of God.

25 And you, Ezra, in accordance with the wisdom of your God with which you are entrusted, are to appoint arbitrators and judges to judge all your people in the province of Beyond-Euphrates, all who acknowledge the laws of your God,[l] and you and they are to instruct those who do not acknowledge them.

26 Whoever will not obey the law of your God and the law of the king, let judgement be rigorously executed upon him, be it death, banishment, confiscation of property, or imprisonment.

27 Then Ezra said,[m] 'Blessed be the LORD the God of our fathers who has prompted the king thus to add glory to the house of the LORD in Jerusalem,

28 and has made the king and his counsellors and all his high officers well disposed towards me!'
So, knowing that the hand of the LORD my God was upon me, I took courage and assembled leading men out of Israel to go up with me.

8 These are the heads of families, as registered, family by family, of those who went up with me from Babylon in

2 the reign of King Artaxerxes: of the family of Phinehas, Gershom; of the family of Ithamar, Daniel; of the

3 family of David, Hattush son of[n] Shecaniah; of the family of Parosh, Zechariah, and with him a hundred

4 and fifty males in the register; of the family of Pahath-moab, Elihoenai son

l to judge ... your God: *or* all of them versed in the laws of your God, to judge all the people in the province of Beyond-Euphrates.
m Then Ezra said: *prob. rdg., cp.* 1 Esdras 8. 25; *Heb. om.*
n son of: *prob. rdg.; Heb.* of the family of.

---

returnees, or whether it included broad political powers over the entire province. **24:** The tax exemption of Temple functionaries. **25:** *Laws of your God* hearkens back to vv. 6 and 14.
7.27–28: Ezra's thanksgiving prayer.
8.1–14: A list of returnees is given here, just as one is also given in ch. 2 for earlier returnees.

of Zerahiah, and with him two hundred
5 males; of the family of Zattu,[o] Shecaniah son of Jahaziel, and with him
6 three hundred males; of the family of
Adin, Ebed son of Jonathan, and with
7 him fifty males; of the family of Elam,
Isaiah son of Athaliah, and with him
8 seventy males; of the family of Shephatiah, Zebadiah son of Michael, and
9 with him eighty males; of the family of
Joab, Obadiah son of Jehiel, and
with him two hundred and eighteen
10 males; of the family of Bani,[p] Shelomith son of Josiphiah, and with him a
11 hundred and sixty males; of the family
of Bebai, Zechariah son of Bebai, and
12 with him twenty-eight males; of the
family of Azgad, Johanan son of
Hakkatan, and with him a hundred
13 and ten males. The last were the family
of Adonikam, and these were their
names: Eliphelet, Jeiel, and Shemaiah,
14 and with them sixty males; and the
family of Bigvai, Uthai and Zabbud,
and with them seventy males.

15 I assembled them by the river which
flows toward Ahava; and we encamped
there three days. When I reviewed the
people and the priests, I found no
16 Levite there. So I sent Eliezer, Ariel,
Shemaiah, Elnathan, Jarib, Elnathan,
Nathan, Zechariah, and Meshullam,
prominent men, and Joiarib and
17 Elnathan, men of discretion, with
instructions to go to Iddo, the chief
man of the settlement at Casiphia; and
I gave them a message for him and his
kinsmen, the temple-servitors there,
asking for servitors for the house of
18 our God to be sent to us. And, because
the gracious hand of our God was
upon us, they let us have Sherebiah, a
man of discretion, of the family of
Mahli son of Levi, son of Israel,
together with his sons and kinsmen,
19 eighteen men; also Hashabiah, together
with Isaiah of the family of Merari, his
kinsmen and their sons, twenty men;
besides two hundred and twenty 20
temple servitors (this was an order
instituted by David and his officers to
assist the Levites). These were all indicated by name.

Then I proclaimed a fast there by the 21
river Ahava, so that we might mortify
ourselves before our God and ask from
him a safe journey for ourselves, our
dependants, and all our possessions.
For I was ashamed to ask the king for 22
an escort of soldiers and horsemen to
help us against enemies on the way,
because we had said to the king, 'The
hand of our God is upon all who seek
him, working their good; but his fierce
anger is on all who forsake him.' So 23
we fasted and asked our God for a safe
journey, and he answered our prayer.

Then I separated twelve of the chiefs 24
of the priests, together with[q] Sherebiah
and Hashabiah and ten of their kinsmen, and handed over to them the silver 25
and gold and the vessels which had
been set aside by the king, his counsellors and his officers and all the
Israelites who were present, as their
contribution to the house of our God.
I handed over to them six hundred and 26
fifty talents of silver, a hundred silver
vessels weighing two talents, a hundred
talents of gold, twenty golden bowls 27
worth a thousand drachmas, and two
vessels of a fine red copper,[r] precious
as gold. And I said to the men, 'You 28
are dedicated to the LORD, and the
vessels too are sacred, the silver and
gold are a voluntary offering to the
LORD the God of your fathers. Watch 29
over them and guard them, until you
hand them over in the presence of the
chiefs of the priests and the Levites and
the heads of families of Israel in Jerusalem, in the rooms of the house of
the LORD.'

[o] of Zattu: *prob. rdg., cp. 1 Esdras 8. 32; Heb. om.*
[p] of Bani: *prob. rdg., cp. 1 Esdras 8. 36; Heb. om.*
[q] together with: *prob. rdg., cp. 1 Esdras 8. 54; Heb. om.*
[r] red copper: *or* orichalc.

8.15–20: Recruitment of Levites. The locations of the canal/*river* and *Ahava* cannot be ascertained. **15:** *No Levite:* in the list of earlier returnees the Levites (2.40) appear to have been few. **16:** There may be an erroneous duplication of the same names; *Elnathan* surprisingly occurs three times. **17:** *Casiphia:* its location is unknown.

8.21–36: The preparation for leaving (vv. 21–30); the journey (31–32); the arrival in Jerusalem (33–36). **21–23:** The *fast* and prayer were usual devotional preparations for a new venture. **22:** *Ashamed to ask:* Ezra, a priest, believed that God would protect his people, without need of soldiers; Nehemiah, designated the governor (Neh.12.26), went to Jerusalem with an escort of army officers with cavalry (Neh.2.9). **26–27:** The amounts here are regarded as exaggerated.

30 So the priests and Levites received the consignment of silver and gold and vessels, to be taken to the house of our 31 God in Jerusalem; and on the twelfth day of the first month we left the river Ahava bound for Jerusalem. The hand of our God was upon us, and he saved us from enemy attack and from 32 ambush on the way. When we arrived at Jerusalem, we rested for three days. 33 And on the fourth day the silver and gold and the vessels were deposited in the house of our God in the charge of Meremoth son of Uriah the priest, who had with him Eleazar son of Phinehas, and they had with them the Levites Jozabad son of Jeshua and 34 Noadiah son of Binnui. Everything was checked as it was handed over, and at the same time a written record was made of the whole consignment. 35 Then those who had come home from captivity, the exiles who had returned, offered as whole-offerings to the God of Israel twelve bulls for all Israel, ninety-six rams and seventy-two[s] lambs, with twelve he-goats as a sin-offering; all these were offered as a whole-offering 36 to the LORD. They also delivered the king's commission to the royal satraps and governors in the province of Beyond-Euphrates; and these gave support to the people and the house of God.

9 When all this had been done, some of the leaders approached me and said, 'The people of Israel, including priests and Levites, have not kept themselves apart from the foreign population and from the abominable practices of the Canaanites, the Hittites, the Perizzites, the Jebusites, the Ammonites, the Moabites, the Egyptians, and the 2 Amorites. They have taken women of these nations as wives for themselves and their sons, so that the holy race has become mixed with the foreign population; and the leaders and magistrates have been the chief offenders.'

When I heard this news, I rent my robe 3 and mantle, and tore my hair and my beard, and I sat dumbfounded, and all 4 who went in fear of the words of the God of Israel rallied to me because of the offence of these exiles. I sat there dumbfounded till the evening sacrifice.

Then, at the evening sacrifice, I rose 5 from my humiliation and, in my rent robe and mantle, I knelt down and spread out my hands to the LORD my God and said, 'O my God, I am 6 humiliated, I am ashamed to lift my face to thee, my God; for we are sunk in our iniquities, and our guilt is so great that it reaches high heaven. From the 7 days of our fathers down to this present day our guilt has been great. For our iniquities we, our kings, and our priests have been subject to death, captivity, pillage, and shameful humiliation at the hands of foreign kings, and such is our present plight. But now, for a brief 8 moment, the LORD our God has been gracious to us, leaving us some survivors and giving us a foothold in his holy place. He has brought light to our eyes again and given us some chance to renew our lives in our slavery. For slaves we are; nevertheless, our 9 God has not forsaken us in our slavery, but has made the kings of Persia so well disposed towards us as to give us the means of renewal, so that we may repair the house of our God and rebuild its ruins, and to give us a wall of defence in[t] Judah and Jerusalem. Now, O our God, what are we to say 10 after this? For we have neglected the commands which thou gavest through 11 thy servants the prophets, when thou saidst, "The land which you are entering and will possess is a polluted land, polluted by the foreign population with their abominable practices, which have made it unclean from end to end. Therefore, do not give your daughters 12

s *Prob. rdg., cp. 1 Esdras 8. 65; Heb.* seventy-seven.
t *Or* thereby giving us a wall of defence for . . .

31–32: See 7.9; the journey took four months. **36:** *The king's commission* presumably spelled out to the local rulers the precise extent of Ezra's authority.
   9.1–15: Mixed marriages. 2: *Holy race:* see v. 11–12.
   9.10–15: Ezra's prayer for forgiveness. 11–12: *When thou saidst:* an exact quotation from Scripture is expected, but does not appear, as is the case too in Neh.1.8–9; only an echo of general ideas (e.g. Lev.18.24–30 or Deut.7.1–3) is given. **11:** The Heb. word for *polluted* is used in Lev. ch. 15 (and elsewhere) for sexual impurity, a result of the *abominable practices* indulged in by the natives.

in marriage to their sons, and do not marry your sons to their daughters, and never seek their welfare or prosperity. Thus you will be strong and enjoy the good things of the land, and pass it on to your children as an everlasting
13 possession." Now, after all that we have suffered for our evil deeds and for our great guilt—although thou, our God, hast punished us less than our iniquities deserved and hast allowed us to survive
14 as now we do—shall we again disobey thy commands and join in marriage with peoples who indulge in such abominable practices? Would not thy anger against us be unrelenting, until
15 no remnant, no survivor was left? O LORD God of Israel, thou art righteous; now as before, we are only a remnant that has survived. Look upon us, guilty as we are in thy sight; for because of our guilt none of us can stand in thy presence.'

10 While Ezra was praying and making confession, prostrate in tears before the house of God, a very great crowd of Israelites assembled round him, men, women, and children, and they all wept
2 bitterly. Then Shecaniah son of Jehiel, one of the family of Elam, spoke up and said to Ezra, 'We have committed an offence against our God in marrying foreign wives, daughters of the foreign population. But in spite of this, there is
3 still hope for Israel. Now, therefore, let us pledge ourselves to our God to dismiss all these women and their brood, according to your advice, my lord, and the advice of those who go in fear of the command of our God; and let us act as the law prescribes.
4 Up now, the task is yours, and we will support you. Take courage and act.'
5 Ezra stood up and made the chiefs of the priests, the Levites, and all the Israelites swear to do as had been said;
6 and they took the oath. Then Ezra left his place in front of the house of God and went to the room of Jehohanan

grandson of Eliashib and lodged[u] there; he neither ate bread nor drank water, for he was mourning for the offence committed by the exiles who had returned. Next, there was issued 7 throughout Judah and Jerusalem a proclamation that all the exiles should assemble in Jerusalem, and that if 8 anyone did not arrive within three days, it should be within the discretion of the chief officers and the elders to confiscate all his property and to exclude him from the community of the exiles. So 9 all the men of Judah and Benjamin assembled in Jerusalem within the three days; and on the twentieth day of the ninth month the people all sat in the forecourt of the house of God, trembling with apprehension and shivering in the heavy rain. Ezra the priest 10 stood up and said, 'You have committed an offence in marrying foreign wives and have added to Israel's guilt. Make your confession now to the 11 LORD the God of your fathers and do his will, and separate yourselves from the foreign population and from your foreign wives.' Then all the 12 assembled people shouted in reply, 'Yes; we must do what you say. But 13 there is a great crowd of us here, and it is the rainy season; we cannot go on standing out here in the open. Besides, this business will not be finished in one day or even two, because we have committed so grave an offence in this matter. Let our leading men act for the 14 whole assembly, and let all in our cities who have married foreign women present themselves at appointed times, each man with the elders and judges of his own city, until God's anger against us on this account is averted.' Only 15 Jonathan son of Asahel and Jahzeiah son of Tikvah, supported by Meshullam and Shabbethai the Levite, opposed this.

So the exiles acted as agreed, and 16

[u] *Prob. rdg., cp. 1 Esdras 9. 2; Heb. went.*

10.1–44: The divorce of Gentile wives. The drastic step was deemed necessary to preserve the Hebrew faith unadulterated (compare also 1 Kgs. 11.1–14). **3:** *The law prescribes:* see Deut.7.3. **6:** The Heb. *ben* can mean grandson as well as son. Despite some uncertainties, it would seem from Neh.13.28 that *Jehohanan* was the grandson of *Eliashib* and son of Jehoiada. In Neh.3.1, Eliashib is identified as contemporaneous with Nehemiah. Here the grandson is contemporaneous with Ezra. **9:** *The ninth month* was Kislev (November-December), a rainy period. **15:** These opponents (*Jonathan, Jahzeiah, Meshullam, Shabbethai*) are not otherwise identified.

Ezra the priest selected[v] certain men, heads of households representing their families, all of them designated by name. They began their formal inquiry into the matter on the first day of the **17** tenth month, and by the first day of the first month they had finished their inquiry into all the marriages with foreign women.

18 Among the members of priestly families who had married foreign women were found Maaseiah, Eliezer, Jarib, and Gedaliah of the family of Jeshua son of Jozadak and his brothers.

19 They pledged themselves to dismiss their wives, and they brought a ram from the flock as a guilt-offering for **20** their sins. Of the family of Immer: **21** Hanani and Zebadiah. Of the family of Harim: Maaseiah, Elijah, Shemaiah, **22** Jehiel and Uzziah. Of the family of Pashhur: Elioenai, Maaseiah, Ishmael, Nethaneel, Jozabad and Elasah.

23 Of the Levites: Jozabad, Shimei, Kelaiah (that is Kelita), Pethahiah, **24** Judah and Eliezer. Of the singers: Eliashib. Of the door-keepers: Shallum, Telem and Uri.

25 And of Israel: of the family of Parosh: Ramiah, Izziah, Malchiah, Mijamin, Eleazar, Malchiah and **26** Benaiah. Of the family of Elam: Mattaniah, Zechariah, Jehiel, Abdi, **27** Jeremoth and Elijah. Of the family of Zattu: Elioenai, Eliashib, Mattaniah, Jeremoth, Zabad and Aziza. Of the **28** family of Bebai: Jehohanan, Hananiah, Zabbai and Athlai. Of the family of **29** Bani: Meshullam, Malluch, Adaiah, Jashub, Sheal and Jeremoth. Of the **30** family of Pahath-moab: Adna, Kelal, Benaiah, Maaseiah, Mattaniah, Bezalel, Binnui and Manasseh. Of the **31** family of Harim: Eliezer, Isshijah, Malchiah, Shemaiah, Simeon, Benja- **32** min, Malluch and Shemariah. Of the **33** family of Hashum: Mattenai, Mattattah, Zabad, Eliphelet, Jeremai, Manasseh and Shimei. Of the family of Bani: **34** Maadai, Amram and Uel, Benaiah, **35** Bedeiah and Keluhi, Vaniah, Mere- **36** moth, Eliashib, Mattaniah, Mattenai **37** and Jaasau. Of the family of[w] Binnui: **38** Shimei, Shelemiah, Nathan and **39** Adaiah, Maknadebai, Shashai and **40** Sharai, Azareel, Shelemiah and Shem- **41** ariah, Shallum, Amariah and Joseph. **42** Of the family of Nebo: Jeiel, Matti- **43** thiah, Zabad, Zebina, Jaddai, Joel and Benaiah. All these had married foreign **44** women, and they dismissed them, together with their children.[x]

---

v and Ezra the priest selected: *prob. rdg., cp. 1 Esdras 9.16; Heb. obscure.*
w Of the family of: *prob. rdg., cp. 1 Esdras 9.34; Heb. and Bani and.*
x and they . . . children: *prob. rdg., cp. 1 Esdras 9.36; Heb.* and some of them were women; and they had borne sons.

16: *Tenth month:* Tebeth (December–January). **17:** *The first month* was Nisan (March-April). **18–43:** The list numbers over one hundred offenders, a fraction of the total populace. Perhaps only the names of the prominent persons are given, but others too were implicated. **19:** *A guilt-offering* is not specifically prescribed in Scripture for marriage to a non-Israelite spouse; it could have been an ad hoc decision by the leaders of v. 16. **44:** *Children:* see Tfn. *x*.

THE BOOK OF
NEHEMIAH

The books of Ezra and Nehemiah are part of the same writing; the Introduction to Ezra treats literary and chronological problems of Nehemiah too.

The events described in the Book of Nehemiah (except chs. 8–9) took place during the reign of the Persian king, Artaxerxes I (464–424 B.C.). Nehemiah, who lived in Susa, the Persian capital, made two visits to Jerusalem. The first was in 445/444 B.C. (1.1; 2.1), and lasted for twelve years (until 433/432); see 5.14. The second visit was some time after this, but before the death of Artaxerxes I (13.6–7).

The material here, like that in Ezra, consists of several distinct genres. Nehemiah's memoirs provide personal reflections on the events of the day, a number of prayers, and accounts of his determination to ameliorate the position of the downtrodden Judeans. In addition, there are census lists, a psalm of confession and repentance, and a record of rededication to the service of God.

Nehemiah's commission

1 THE NARRATIVE OF NEHEMIAH SON of Hacaliah.

In the month Kislev in the twentieth year, when I was in Susa the 2 capital city, it happened that one of my brothers, Hanani, arrived with some others from Judah; and I asked them about Jerusalem and about the Jews, the families still remaining of those 3 who survived the captivity. They told me that those still remaining in the province who had survived the captivity were facing great trouble and reproach; the wall of Jerusalem was broken down and the gates had been 4 destroyed by fire. When I heard this news, I sat down and wept; I mourned for some days, fasting and praying to 5 the God of heaven. This was my prayer: 'O LORD God of heaven, O great and terrible God who faithfully keepest covenant with those who love thee and observe thy commandments,

let thy ear be attentive and thine eyes 6 open, to hear my humble prayer which I make to thee day and night on behalf of thy servants the sons of Israel. I confess the sins which we Israelites have all committed against thee, and of which I and my father's house are also guilty. We have wronged thee and 7 have not observed the commandments, statutes, and rules which thou didst enjoin upon thy servant Moses. Re- 8 member what thou didst impress upon him in these words: "If you are unfaithful, I will disperse you among the nations; but if you return to me and 9 observe my commandments and fulfil them, I will gather your children who have been scattered to the ends of the earth and will bring them home to the place which I have chosen as a dwelling for my Name." They are thy servants 10 and thy people, whom thou hast redeemed with thy great might and thy strong hand. O Lord, let thy ear be 11 attentive to my humble prayer, and to

---

1.1–2.10: Nehemiah's commission: *Susa* was the winter residence of the Persian kings after 521 B.C. Nehemiah, the royal cupbearer (2.1 here, but 1.11 in the MT), was an influential court figure. 1: *Kislev:* (November-December) *the twentieth year* alludes to the reign of Artaxerxes I (mentioned in 2.1) and would be 445/444 B.C. Nisan (March-April), is described as still "in the twentieth year" in 2.1, where we would expect the twenty-first, for the Babylonian year ran from spring to spring. But possibly the years here are reckoned from Tishri (September-October) and are regnal years, differing from ordinary calendar years. 2: While *brothers* can mean friends or colleagues, 7.2 suggests that Hanani was a real brother. *The families still remaining* had continued in Jerusalem when substantial parts of the population went into exile after 587 B.C. 3: *Broken down . . . destroyed:* this seems to allude to an obscure disaster after the time of Cyrus (538–529 B.C.); Nehemiah has had no prior knowledge of it. 5–11: The structure of Nehemiah's prayer is praise, supplication, confession, supplication. 8–9: An exact quotation from the Pentateuch is expected but does not appear; perhaps Deut.30.1–5 is being echoed. 11: *Let thy ear be attentive* is not a needless repetition of the same phrase in v. 6, but, rather, climaxes Nehemiah's prayer. *This man's heart* refers to Artaxerxes I. See 2.1.

the prayer of thy servants who delight to revere thy name. Grant me good success this day, and put it into this man's heart to show me kindness.'

2 Now I was the king's cupbearer, and one day, in the month Nisan, in the twentieth year of King Artaxerxes, when his wine was ready, I took it up and handed it to the king, and as I stood before him I was feeling very 2 unhappy. He said to me, 'Why do you look so unhappy? You are not ill; it can be nothing but unhappiness.' I was 3 much afraid and answered, 'The king will live for ever. But how can I help looking unhappy when the city where my forefathers are buried lies waste 4 and its gates are burnt?' 'What are you asking of me?' said the king. I prayed 5 to the God of heaven, and then I answered, 'If it please your majesty, and if I enjoy your favour, I beg you to send me to Judah, to the city where my forefathers are buried, so that I may 6 rebuild it.' The king, with the queen consort sitting beside him, asked me, 'How long will the journey last, and when will you return?' Then the king approved the request and let me go, and I told him how long I should be. 7 Then I said to the king, 'If it please your majesty, let letters be given me for the governors in the province of Beyond-Euphrates with orders to grant me all the help I need for my journey 8 to Judah. Let me have also a letter for Asaph, the keeper of your royal forests, instructing him to supply me with timber to make beams for the gates of the citadel, which adjoins the palace, and for the city wall, and for the palace which I shall occupy.' The king granted my requests, for the gracious hand of 9 my God was upon me. I came in due course to the governors in the province of Beyond-Euphrates and presented to them the king's letters; the king had given me an escort of army officers with cavalry. But when Sanballat the 10 Horonite and the slave Tobiah, an Ammonite, heard this, they were much vexed that someone should have come to promote the interests of the Israelites.

The walls of Jerusalem rebuilt

WHEN I ARRIVED IN JERUSALEM, I WAITED 11 three days. Then I set out by night, 12 taking a few men with me; but I told no one what my God was prompting me to do for Jerusalem. I had no beast with me except the one on which I myself rode. I went out by night through 13 the Valley Gate towards the Dragon Spring and the Dung Gate, and I inspected the places where the walls of Jerusalem had been broken down and her gates burnt. Then I passed on to the 14 Fountain Gate and the King's Pool; but there was no room for me to ride through. I went up the valley in the 15 night and inspected the city wall; then I re-entered the city by the Valley Gate. So I arrived back without the magi- 16 strates knowing where I had been or what I was doing. I had not yet told the Jews, the priests, the nobles, the magistrates, or any of those who would be responsible for the work.

Then I said to them, 'You see our 17 wretched plight. Jerusalem lies in ruins, its gates destroyed by fire. Come, let us rebuild the wall of Jerusalem and be rid of the reproach.' I told them how 18 the gracious hand of my God had been upon me and also what the king had said to me. They replied, 'Let us start the rebuilding.' So they set about the work vigorously and to good purpose.

But when Sanballat the Horonite, To- 19 biah the Ammonite slave, and Geshem the Arab heard of it, they jeered at

---

2.1–10: Beginning of Nehemiah's mission in Jerusalem. 1: On the date, see 1.1 n. Note the similarity in the *cupbearer* of 2.1 to Gen.40.1, and "Why do you look so unhappy?" (2.2) to Gen.40.7. **8:** *Citadel* is mentioned again in 7.2. **10:** *Sanballat, Tobiah:* see 2.19 n.
    2.11–3.32: The walls of Jerusalem rebuilt. 12: *By night:* a secret inspection. **13:** Nehemiah begins at the *Valley Gate*, apparently at the southwest corner of the walled city, and proceeds eastward, then northward. **19:** The three opponents were very influential men. *Sanballat the Horonite* (mentioned in the Elephantine papyri of the late fifth century B.C.) was governor of Samaria; he was related by marriage to the High Priest, Eliashib (13.28). *Tobiah* was a *slave*, not to Sanballat, but to the Persian king; *the Ammonite slave* here probably means agent (perhaps even governor), with jurisdiction in Ammon.

us, asking contemptuously, 'What is this you are doing? Is this a rebellion
20 against the king?' But I answered them, 'The God of heaven will give us success. We, his servants, are making a start with the rebuilding. You have no stake, or claim, or traditional right in Jerusalem.'

3 Eliashib the high priest and his fellow-priests started work and rebuilt the Sheep Gate. They laid its beams[a] and set its doors in place; they carried the work as far as the Tower of the Hundred, as far as the Tower of
2 Hananel, and consecrated it. Next to Eliashib the men of Jericho worked; and next to them Zaccur son of Imri.
3 The Fish Gate was built by the sons of Hassenaah; they laid its tie-beams and set its doors in place with their
4 bolts and bars. Next to them Meremoth son of Uriah, son of Hakkoz, repaired his section; next to them Meshullam son of Berechiah, son of Meshezabel; next to them Zadok son of Baana did
5 the repairs; and next again the men of Tekoa did the repairs, but their nobles would not demean themselves to serve their governor.
6 The Jeshanah Gate[b] was repaired by Joiada son of Paseah and Meshullam son of Besodeiah; they laid its tie-beams and set its doors in place with
7 their bolts and bars. Next to them Melatiah the Gibeonite and Jadon the Meronothite, the men of Gibeon and Mizpah, did the repairs as far as the seat of the governor of the province
8 of Beyond-Euphrates. Next to them Uzziel son of Harhaiah, a goldsmith, did the repairs, and next Hananiah, a perfumer; they reconstructed Jerusalem
9 as far as the Broad Wall. Next to them Rephaiah son of Hur, ruler of half the district of Jerusalem, did the repairs.
10 Next to them Jedaiah son of Harumaph did the repairs opposite his own house; and next Hattush son of Hashabniah.
11 Malchiah son of Harim and Hasshub son of Pahath-moab repaired a second section including the Tower of the

Ovens.[c] Next to them Shallum son of 12 Hallohesh, ruler of half the district of Jerusalem, did the repairs with the help of his daughters.

The Valley Gate was repaired by 13 Hanun and the inhabitants of Zanoah; they rebuilt it and set its doors in place with their bolts and bars, and they repaired a thousand cubits of the wall as far as the Dung Gate. The Dung 14 Gate itself was repaired by Malchiah son of Rechab, ruler of the district of Beth-hakkerem; he rebuilt[d] it and set its doors in place with their bolts and bars. The Fountain Gate was repaired 15 by Shallun son of Col-hozeh, ruler of the district of Mizpah; he rebuilt[d] it and roofed it and set its doors in place with their bolts and bars; and he built the wall of the Pool of Shelah next to the king's garden and onwards as far as the steps leading down from the City of David.

After him Nehemiah son of Azbuk, 16 ruler of half the district of Beth-zur, did the repairs as far as a point opposite the burial-place of David, as far as the artificial pool and the House of the Heroes.[e] After him the Levites did 17 the repairs: Rehum son of Bani and next to him Hashabiah, ruler of half the district of Keilah, did the repairs for his district. After him their kinsmen 18 did the repairs: Binnui son of Henadad, ruler of half the district of Keilah; next 19 to him Ezer son of Jeshua, ruler of Mizpah, repaired a second section opposite the point at which the ascent meets the escarpment; after him Baruch 20 son of Zabbai repaired a second section, from the escarpment to the door of the house of Eliashib the high priest. After him Meremoth son of Uriah, son 21 of Hakkoz, repaired a second section, from the door of the house of Eliashib to the end of the house of Eliashib.

After him the priests of the neigh- 22

a laid its beams: *prob. rdg., Heb.* consecrated it.
b The Jeshanah Gate: *or* The gate of the Old City.
c *Or* Furnaces.   d *Prob. rdg.; Heb.* he will rebuild.
e *Or* and the barracks.

3.1–32: The reconstruction of the wall. The description indicates that the construction began at the northern part of the city and moved in a counterclockwise direction. **1:** *Eliashib* was the grandson of the high priest Jeshua (12.10; see Zech.3.1) and grandfather of Jehohanan, a later high priest (Ezra 10.6). **3–32:** The groupings of the builders are according to priestly or levitical identity, place of origin, or membership in a craft guild.

bourhood of Jerusalem did the repairs.
23 Next Benjamin and Hasshub did the repairs opposite their own house; and next Azariah son of Maaseiah, son of Ananiah, did the repairs beside his
24 house. After him Binnui son of Henadad repaired a second section, from the house of Azariah as far as the escarp-
25 ment and the corner. Palal son of Uzai worked opposite the escarpment and the upper tower which projects from the king's house and belongs to the court of the guard. After him Pedaiah
26 son of Parosh*f* worked as far as a point on the east opposite the Water Gate
27 and the projecting tower. Next the men of Tekoa repaired a second section, from a point opposite the great projecting tower as far as the wall of Ophel.
28 Above the Horse Gate the priests did the repairs opposite their own
29 houses. After them Zadok son of Immer did the repairs opposite his own house; after him Shemaiah son of Shecaniah, the keeper of the East Gate,
30 did the repairs. After him Hananiah son of Shelemiah and Hanun, sixth son of Zalaph, repaired a second section. After him Meshullam son of Berechiah did the repairs opposite his room.
31 After him Malchiah, a goldsmith, did the repairs as far as the house of the temple-servitors and the merchants, opposite the Mustering Gate, as far as
32 the roof-chamber at the corner. Between the roof-chamber at the corner and the Sheep Gate the goldsmiths and merchants did the repairs.

4 WHEN SANBALLAT HEARD THAT WE were rebuilding the wall, he was very indignant; in his anger he jeered at the
2 Jews and said in front of his companions and of the garrison in Samaria, 'What do these feeble Jews think they are doing? Do they mean to reconstruct the place? Do they hope to offer sacrifice and finish the work in a day? Can they make stones again out of heaps
3 of rubble, and burnt at that?' Tobiah the Ammonite, who was beside him, said, 'Whatever it is they are building,

if a fox climbs up their stone walls, it will break them down.'

Hear us, our God, for they treat us 4 with contempt. Turn back their reproach upon their own heads and let them become objects of contempt in a land of captivity. Do not condone 5 their guilt or let their sin be struck off the record, for they have openly provoked the builders.

We built up the wall until it was 6 continuous all round up to half its height; and the people worked with a will. But when Sanballat and Tobiah, 7 the Arabs and Ammonites and Ashdodites, heard that the new work on the walls of Jerusalem had made progress and that the filling of the breaches had begun, they were very angry; and they all banded together 8 to come and attack Jerusalem and to create confusion. So we prayed to our 9 God, and posted a guard day and night against them.

But the men of Judah said, 'The 10 labourers' strength has failed, and there is too much rubble; we shall never be able to rebuild the wall by ourselves.' And our adversaries said, 11 'Before they know it or see anything, we shall be upon them and kill them, and so put an end to the work.' When 12 the Jews who lived among them came in to the city, they warned us many times that they would gather from every place where they lived to attack us, and that they would station themselves on the lowest levels below the 13 wall, on patches of open ground. Accordingly I posted my people by families, armed with swords, spears, and bows. Then I surveyed the position 14 and at once addressed the nobles, the magistrates, and all the people. 'Do not be afraid of them', I said. 'Remember the Lord, great and terrible, and fight for your brothers, your sons and daughters, your wives and your homes.' Our enemies heard that every- 15 thing was known to us, and that God

f Prob. rdg.; Heb. adds and the temple-servitors lodged on Ophel (*cp. 11. 21*).

4.1–23: The attempts to impede. 4–5: The narrative is interrupted by a curse pronounced against the enemies. **10–15:** Even some Jews join against the builders. **16–23:** The protection

had frustrated their plans; and we all returned to our work on the wall.

16   From that day forward half the men under me were engaged in the actual building, while the other half stood by holding their spears, shields, and bows, and wearing coats of mail; and officers supervised all the people of Judah 17 who were engaged on the wall. The porters carrying the loads had one hand on the load and a weapon in the 18 other. The builders had their swords attached to their belts as they built; 19 the trumpeter was beside me. I addressed the nobles, the magistrates, and all the people: 'The work is great and covers much ground', I said. 'We are isolated on the wall, each man at some distance from his neighbour. 20 Wherever the trumpet sounds, rally to us there, and our God will fight for 21 us.' So we continued with the work, half the men holding the spears, from 22 daybreak until the stars came out. At the same time I had said to the people, 'Let every man and his servant pass the night in Jerusalem, to act as a guard for us by night and a working 23 party by day.' So neither I nor my kinsmen nor the men under me nor my bodyguard ever took off our clothes, each keeping his right hand on*g* his weapon.

5 THERE CAME A TIME WHEN THE COMMON people, both men and women, raised a great outcry against their fellow-Jews. 2 Some complained that they were giving their sons and daughters as pledges*h* for food to keep themselves alive; 3 others that they were mortgaging their fields, vineyards, and houses to buy 4 corn in the famine; others again that they were borrowing money on their fields and vineyards to pay the king's 5 tax. 'But', they said, 'our bodily needs are the same as other people's, our children are as good as theirs; yet here we are, forcing our sons and daughters

to become slaves. Some of our daughters are already enslaved, and there is nothing we can do, because our fields and vineyards now belong to others.' I 6 was very angry when I heard their outcry and the story they told. I mastered my 7 feelings and reasoned with the nobles and the magistrates. I said to them, 'You are holding your fellow-Jews as pledges for debt.' I rebuked them severely and said, 'As far as we have 8 been able, we have bought back our fellow-Jews who had been sold to other nations; but you are now selling your own fellow-countrymen, and they will have to be bought back by us!' They were silent and had not a word to say. I went on, 'What you are doing is 9 wrong. You ought to live so much in the fear of God that you are above reproach in the eyes of the nations who are our enemies. Speaking for 10 myself, I and my kinsmen and the men under me are advancing them money and corn. Let us give up this taking of persons as pledges for debt. Give 11 back today to your debtors their fields and vineyards, their olive-groves and houses, as well as the income*i* in money, and in corn, new wine, and oil.' 'We 12 will give them back', they promised, 'and exact nothing more. We will do what you say.' So, summoning the priests, I put the offenders on oath to do as they had promised. Then I 13 shook out the fold of my robe and said, 'So may God shake out from his house and from his property every man who does not fulfil this promise. May he be shaken out like this and emptied!' And all the assembled people said 'Amen' and praised the LORD. And they did as they had promised.

Moreover, from the time when I 14 was appointed governor in the land of

g keeping his right hand on: *prob. rdg.; Heb. obscure.*
h that they . . . as pledges: *prob. rdg.; Heb. that they, their sons and daughters were many.*
i *Prob. rdg.; Heb. hundredth.*

---

of the workers. **18:** *The trumpeter was beside me:* presumably others were also stationed around the wall to give the alarm from any quarter.
5.1–13: The plight of the poor. The chapter seems out of place and not directly connected with the building of the wall, which it interrupts. **1–5:** The exploitation of the poor by the rich. **6–13:** Nehemiah's response. **7–10:** The charging of interest is prohibited in Deut.23.20. **13:** *Shook out:* a symbolic gesture meant to reinforce the oath of the offenders.
5.14–19: Nehemiah defends his governorship. The section emphasizes his concern not to harass the poor through personal demands. The occasion for the apologia is not known.

Judah, from the twentieth to the thirty-second year of King Artaxerxes, a period of twelve years, neither I nor my kinsmen drew the governor's allow-
15 ance of food. Former governors had laid a heavy burden on the people, exacting from them a daily toll*ʲ* of bread and wine to the value of forty shekels of silver. Further, the men under them had tyrannized over the people; but, for fear of God, I did not
16 behave like this. I also put all my energy into the work on this wall, and I acquired no land; and all my men were gathered there for the work.
17 Also I had as guests at my table a hundred and fifty Jews, including the magistrates, as well as men who came
18 to us from the surrounding nations. The provision which had to be made each day was an ox and six prime sheep; fowls also were prepared for me, and every ten days skins of wine in abundance. Yet, in spite of all this, I did not draw the governor's allowance, because the people were so heavily
19 burdened. Remember for my good, O God, all that I have done for this people.

6 When the news came to Sanballat, Tobiah, Geshem the Arab, and the rest of our enemies, that I had rebuilt the wall and that not a single breach remained in it, although I had not yet
2 set up the doors in the gates, Sanballat and Geshem sent me an invitation to come and confer with them at Hakkephirim in the plain of Ono; this was a ruse on their part to do me harm.
3 So I sent messengers to them with this reply: 'I have important work on my hands at the moment; I cannot come down. Why should the work be brought to a standstill while I leave it and come
4 down to you?' They sent me a similar invitation four times, and each time I
5 gave them the same answer. On a fifth occasion Sanballat made a similar approach, but this time his messenger

came with an open letter. It ran as 6
follows: 'It is reported among the nations—and Gashmu*ᵏ* confirms it— that you and the Jews are plotting rebellion, and it is for this reason that you are rebuilding the wall, and—so the report goes—that you yourself want to be king. You are also said to have 7
put up prophets to proclaim in Jerusalem that Judah has a king, meaning yourself. The king will certainly hear of this. So come at once and let us talk the matter over.' Here 8
is the reply I sent: 'No such thing as you allege has taken place; you have made up the whole story.' They were all 9
trying to intimidate us, in the hope that we should then relax our efforts and that the work would never be finished. So I applied myself to it with greater energy.

One day I went to the house of 10
Shemaiah son of Delaiah, son of Mehetabel, for he was confined to his house. He said, 'Let us meet in the house of God, within the sanctuary, and let us shut the doors, for they are coming to kill you—they are coming to kill you by night.' But I said, 'Should 11
a man like me run away? And can a man like me go into the sanctuary and survive*ˡ*? I will not go in.' Then it dawned 12
on me: God had not sent him. His prophecy aimed at harming me, and Tobiah and Sanballat had bribed him to utter it. He had been bribed to frighten 13
me into compliance and into committing sin; then they could give me a bad name and discredit me. Remember 14
Tobiah and Sanballat, O God, for what they have done, and also the prophetess Noadiah and all the other prophets who have tried to intimidate me.

On the twenty-fifth day of the month 15
Elul the wall was finished; it had taken fifty-two days. When our enemies 16
heard of it, and all the surrounding

j a daily toll: prob. rdg.; Heb. obscure.
k Geshem in 2. 19 and 6. 1, 2.
l and survive: or to save his life.

6.1–19: The plots of the enemy. 2: *Hakkephirim* is an unknown village; *the plain of Ono* is located near the seacoast, some distance from Jerusalem. **5–9:** Accusation of rebellion. **5:** The *open letter*, if recorded on a clay tablet, had no clay envelope; if on papyrus or parchment, it was not folded or sealed. In either case, the senders obviously intended no secrecy. Compare Jer.32.14. **10–14:** *Shemaiah* plots against Nehemiah. **11:** *A man like me:* a political leader must neither show cowardice nor commit sacrilege (see Num.3.10; 18.7). **15–19:** Completion of the wall. **15:** *Elul:* August-September, 444 B.C. **16:** The verse reflects understandable exaggeration.

nations saw it,[m] they thought it a very wonderful achievement,[n] and they recognized that this work had been accomplished by the help of our God.

17 All this time the nobles in Judah were sending many letters to Tobiah, 18 and receiving replies from him. For many in Judah were in league with him, because he was a son-in-law of Shecaniah son of Arah, and his son Jehohanan had married a daughter of 19 Meshullam son of Berechiah. They were always praising[o] him in my presence and repeating to him what I said. Tobiah also wrote to me to intimidate me.

7 Now when the wall had been rebuilt, and I had set the doors in place and the gate-keepers[p] had been 2 appointed, I gave the charge of Jerusalem to my brother Hanani, and to Hananiah, the governor of the citadel, for he was trustworthy and 3 God-fearing above other men. And I said to them, 'The entrances to Jerusalem are not to be left open during the heat of the day; the gates must be kept shut and barred while the gate-keepers are standing at ease. Appoint guards from among the inhabitants of Jerusalem, some on sentry-duty and others posted in front of their own homes.'

4 The city was large and spacious; there were few people in it and no 5 houses had yet been rebuilt. Then God prompted me to assemble the nobles, the magistrates, and the people, to be enrolled family by family. And I found the book of the genealogies of those who had been the first to come back. 6[q] This is what I found written in it: Of the captives whom Nebuchadnezzar king of Babylon had taken into exile, these are the people of the province who have returned to Jerusalem and 7 Judah, each to his own town, led by Zerubbabel, Jeshua,[r] Nehemiah, Azariah, Raamiah, Nahamani, Mordecai, Bilshan, Mispereth, Bigvai, Nehum and Baanah.

The roll of the men of the people of Israel: the family of Parosh, two 8 thousand one hundred and seventy-two; the family of Shephatiah, three 9 hundred and seventy-two; the family 10 of Arah, six hundred and fifty-two; the family of Pahath-moab, namely 11 the families of Jeshua and Joab, two thousand eight hundred and eighteen; the family of Elam, one thousand two 12 hundred and fifty-four; the family of 13 Zattu, eight hundred and forty-five; the family of Zaccai, seven hundred and 14 sixty; the family of Binnui, six hundred 15 and forty-eight; the family of Bebai, 16 six hundred and twenty-eight; the 17 family of Azgad, two thousand three hundred and twenty-two; the family 18 of Adonikam, six hundred and sixty-seven; the family of Bigvai, two 19 thousand and sixty-seven; the family 20 of Adin, six hundred and fifty-five; the 21 family of Ater, namely that of Hezekiah, ninety-eight; the family of Hash- 22 um, three hundred and twenty-eight; the family of Bezai, three hundred and 23 twenty-four; the family of Harif, one 24 hundred and twelve; the family of 25 Gibeon, ninety-five. The men of Beth- 26 lehem and Netophah, one hundred and eighty-eight; the men of Anathoth, one 27 hundred and twenty-eight; the men of 28 Beth-azmoth, forty-two; the men of 29 Kiriath-jearim, Kephirah, and Beeroth, seven hundred and forty-three; the 30 men of Ramah and Geba, six hundred and twenty-one; the men of Michmas, 31 one hundred and twenty-two; the men of 32 Bethel and Ai, one hundred and twenty-three; the men of[s] Nebo, fifty- 33 two; the men[t] of the other Elam, one 34 thousand two hundred and fifty-four; the men of Harim, three hundred and 35 twenty; the men of Jericho, three 36 hundred and forty-five; the men of 37 Lod, Hadid and Ono, seven hundred

m Or were afraid.
n they thought . . . achievement: *prob. rdg.; Heb.* they fell very much in their own eyes.
o Or repeating rumours about . . .
p Prob. rdg.; Heb. adds the singers and the Levites.
q Verses 6–73: *cp.* Ezra 2. 1–70.
r Or Joshua (*cp.* Hag. 1. 1).
s Prob. rdg., cp. Ezra 2. 29; *Heb.* adds the other.
t Prob. rdg.; Heb. family (*also in verses* 35–38).

17–19: For further data on *Tobiah* and his Jewish connections—his chamber in the temple—see 13.4–9.
  7.1–73a: **Guards and patrols. 2:** *Hanani:* see 1.2 n. *Citadel:* mentioned in 2.8. **4–5:** The taking of a census. **6–73a:** This list of returning Judeans duplicates, with slight variations, that of Ezra 2.1–70.

30 and twenty-one; the men of Senaah, three thousand nine hundred and thirty.

39 Priests: the family of Jedaiah, of the line of Jeshua, nine hundred and 40 seventy-three; the family of Immer, 41 one thousand and fifty-two; the family of Pashhur, one thousand two hundred 42 and forty-seven; the family of Harim, one thousand and seventeen.

43 Levites: the families of Jeshua and*u* Kadmiel, of the line of Hodvah, 44 seventy-four. Singers: the family of Asaph, one hundred and forty-eight. 45 Door-keepers: the family of Shallum, the family of Ater, the family of Talmon, the family of Akkub, the family of Hatita, and the family of Shobai, one hundred and thirty-eight in all.

46 Temple-servitors: the family of Ziha, the family of Hasupha, the family of 47 Tabbaoth, the family of Keros, the 48 family of Sia, the family of Padon, the family of Lebanah, the family of 49 Hagabah, the family of Shalmai, the family of Hanan, the family of Giddel, 50 the family of Gahar, the family of Reaiah, the family of Rezin, the family 51 of Nekoda, the family of Gazzam, the family of Uzza, the family of Paseah, 52 the family of Besai, the family of the Meunim, the family of the Nephish-53 esim,*v* the family of Bakbuk, the family of Hakupha, the family of Harhur, 54 the family of Bazlith,*w* the family of Mehida, the family of Harsha, the 55 family of Barkos, the family of Sisera, 56 the family of Temah, the family of Neziah, and the family of Hatipha.

57 Descendants of Solomons' servants: the family of Sotai, the family of 58 Sophereth, the family of Perida, the family of Jaalah, the family of Darkon, 59 the family of Giddel, the family of Shephatiah, the family of Hattil, the family of Pochereth-hazzebaim, and the family of Amon.

60 The temple-servitors and the descendants of Solomon's servants amounted to three hundred and ninety-two in all.

61 The following were those who returned from Tel-melah, Tel-harsha,

Kerub, Addon, and Immer, but could not establish their father's family nor whether by descent they belonged to 62 Israel. the family of Delaiah, the family of Tobiah, the family of Nekoda, 63 six hundred and forty-two. Also of the priests: the family of Hobaiah, the family of Hakkoz, and the family of Barzillai who had married a daughter of Barzillai the Gileadite and went by 64 his*x* name. These searched for their names among those enrolled in the genealogies, but they could not be found; they were disqualified for the 65 priesthood as unclean, and the governor forbade them to partake of the most sacred food until there should be a priest able to consult the Urim and the Thummim.

66 The whole assembled people numbered forty-two thousand three hundred and sixty, apart from their slaves, 67 male and female, of whom there were seven thousand three hundred and thirty-seven; and they had two hundred and forty-five singers, men and women. 68 Their horses numbered seven hundred and thirty-six, their mules two hundred 69 and forty-five, their camels four hundred and thirty-five, and their asses six thousand seven hundred and twenty.

70 Some of the heads of families gave contributions for the work. The governor gave to the treasury a thousand drachmas of gold, fifty tossing-bowls, and five hundred and thirty priestly robes. Some of the heads of families 71 gave for the fabric fund twenty thousand drachmas of gold and two thousand two hundred minas of silver. What 72 the rest of the people gave was twenty thousand drachmas of gold, two thousand minas of silver, and sixty-seven priestly robes.

73 The priests, the Levites, and some of the people lived in Jerusalem and its suburbs;*y* the door-keepers, the singers, the temple-servitors, and all other Israelites, lived in their own towns.

u and: prob. rdg.; cp. Ezra 2. 40; Heb. to.
v Or Nephushesim.
w Or Bazluth (cp. Ezra 2. 52).
x Prob. rdg., cp. 1 Esdras 5. 38; Heb. their.
y in Jerusalem and its suburbs: prob. rdg., cp. 1 Esdras 5. 46; Heb. om.

7.73b–8.12: The law read by Ezra and the covenant renewed. The section 7.73b 9.37 is misplaced (see Introduction to Ezra); it is about Ezra. Perhaps it should follow directly after

The law read by Ezra and the covenant renewed

8 WHEN THE SEVENTH MONTH CAME, AND the Israelites were now settled in their towns, the people assembled as one man in the square in front of the Water Gate, and Ezra the scribe[z] was asked to bring the book of the law of Moses, which the LORD had enjoined upon 2 Israel. On the first day of the seventh month, Ezra the priest brought the law before the assembly, every man and woman, and all who were capable of 3 understanding what they heard.[a] He read from it, facing the square in front of the Water Gate, from early morning till noon, in the presence of the men and the women, and those who could understand;[b] all the people listened attentively to the book of the law. 4 Ezra the scribe stood on a wooden platform made for the purpose,[c] and beside him stood Mattithiah, Shema, Anaiah, Uriah, Hilkiah, and Maaseiah on his right hand; and on his left Pedaiah, Mishael, Malchiah, Hashum, Hashbaddanah, Zechariah and Me-5 shullam. Ezra opened the book in the sight of all the people, for he was standing above them; and when he 6 opened it, they all stood. Ezra blessed the LORD, the great God, and all the people raised their hands and answered, 'Amen, Amen'; and they bowed their heads and prostrated themselves hum-7 bly before the LORD. Jeshua, Bani, Sherebiah, Jamin, Akkub, Shabbethai, Hodiah, Maaseiah, Kelita, Azariah, Jozabad, Hanan, Pelaiah, the Levites,[d] expounded the law to the people while 8 they remained in their places. They read from the book of the law of God clearly, made its sense plain and gave instruction in what was read. 9 Then Nehemiah the governor and Ezra the priest and scribe, and the Levites who instructed the people, said to them all, 'This day is holy to the LORD your God; do not mourn or weep.' For all the people had been weeping while they listened to the words of the law. Then he said to them, 'You 10 may go now; refresh yourselves with rich food and sweet drinks, and send a share to all who cannot provide for themselves; for this day is holy to our Lord. Let there be no sadness, for joy in the LORD is your strength.' The 11 Levites silenced the people, saying, 'Be quiet, for this day is holy; let there be no sadness.' So all the people went 12 away to eat and to drink, to send shares to others and to celebrate the day with great rejoicing, because they had understood what had been explained to them.

On the second day the heads of 13 families of the whole people, with the priests and the Levites, assembled before Ezra the scribe to study the law. And they found written in the law that 14 the LORD had given commandment through Moses that the Israelites should live in arbours[e] during the feast of the seventh month, and that 15 they should make proclamation throughout all their cities and in Jerusalem: 'Go out into the hills and fetch branches of olive and wild olive, myrtle and palm, and other leafy boughs to make arbours, as prescribed.' So the people went out and fetched 16 them and made arbours for themselves, each on his own roof, and in their courts and in the courts of the house of God, and in the square at the Water Gate and the square at the Ephraim Gate. And the whole community of 17 those who had returned from the captivity made arbours and lived in

[z] Or doctor of the law.
[a] were capable . . . heard: or would teach them to understand.
[b] could understand: or were to instruct.
[c] Or for the address. [d] Prob. rdg.; Heb. and the Levites.
[e] Or tabernacles or booths.

Ezra chs. 9–10. **8.1:** *The book of the law of Moses:* not the entire Pentateuch as we now know it, but selections from it. **2:** *The first day of the seventh month:* Tishri (September-October); compare Lev.23.24 and Num.29.1. The first day of Tishri is observed by Jews as the new year day, a term rare in the OT. **7–8:** The law was in Heb.; the language of the Judeans after the sixth century B.C. was Aram. Hence the Levites, after reading in Heb., *expounded* in the Aram., giving *instruction in what was read.*

8.13–18: Renewal of the celebration of the Festival of Booths. **14: Arbour:** see Tfn. *e;* compare Lev.23.33–43. **15:** Five species of plants are prescribed here; Lev.23.40 prescribes four species; only two species are common; the differences seem due to varying practices concerning this pilgrim feast. Both family and community booths seem described.

them, a thing that the Israelites had not done from the days of Joshua son of Nun to that day; and there was very 18 great rejoicing. And day by day, from the first day to the last, the book of the law of God was read. They kept the feast for seven days, and on the eighth day there was a closing ceremony, according to the rule.

9 ON THE TWENTY-FOURTH DAY OF THIS month the Israelites assembled for a fast, clothed in sackcloth and with 2 earth on their heads. Those who were of Israelite descent separated themselves from all the foreigners; they took their places and confessed their sins and the iniquities of their forefathers. 3 Then they stood up in their places, and the book of the law of the LORD their God was read for one fourth of the day, and for another fourth they confessed and did obeisance to the LORD their 4 God. Upon the steps assigned to the Levites stood Jeshua, Bani, Kadmiel, Shebaniah, Bunni, Sherebiah, Bani, and Kenani, and they cried aloud to 5 the LORD their God. Then the Levites, Jeshua, Kadmiel, Bani, Hashabniah, Sherebiah, Hodiah, Shebaniah, and Pethahiah, said, 'Stand up and bless the LORD your God, saying: From everlasting to everlasting thy glorious name is blessed*f* and exalted above all 6 blessing and praise. Thou alone art the LORD; thou hast made heaven, the highest heaven with all its host, the earth and all that is on it, the seas and all that is in them. Thou preservest all of them, and the host of heaven wor- 7 ships thee. Thou art the LORD, the God who chose Abram and brought him out of Ur of the Chaldees and named 8 him Abraham. Thou didst find him faithful to thee and didst make a covenant with him to give to him and to his descendants the land of the Canaanites, the Hittites, the Amorites, the Perizzites, the Jebusites, and the

Girgashites; and thou didst fulfil thy promise, for thou art just.

'And thou didst see the misery of 9 our forefathers in Egypt and didst hear their cry for help at the Red Sea,*g* and 10 didst work signs and portents against Pharaoh, all his courtiers and all the people of his land, knowing how arrogantly they treated our forefathers, and thou didst win for thyself a name that lives on to this day. Thou didst 11 tear the sea apart before them so that they went through the middle of it on dry ground; but thou didst cast their pursuers into the depths, like a stone cast into turbulent waters. Thou didst 12 guide them by a pillar of cloud in the day-time and by a pillar of fire at night to give them light on the road by which they travelled. Thou didst descend upon 13 Mount Sinai and speak with them from heaven, and give them right judgements and true laws, and statutes and commandments which were good, and thou 14 didst make known to them thy holy sabbath and give them commandments, statutes, and laws through thy servant Moses. Thou gavest them bread from 15 heaven to stay their hunger and thou broughtest water out from a rock for them to quench their thirst, and thou didst bid them enter and take possession of the land which thou hadst solemnly sworn to give them. But they, our fore- 16 fathers, were arrogant and stubborn, and disobeyed thy commandments. They refused to obey and did not 17 remember the miracles which thou didst accomplish among them; they remained stubborn, and they appointed a man to lead them back to slavery in Egypt. But thou art a forgiving god, gracious and compassionate, long-suffering and ever constant, and thou didst not forsake them. Even when 18 they made the image of a bull-calf in metal and said, "This is your god who

f thy glorious name is blessed: *prob. rdg.; Heb.* and let them bless thy glorious name.
g Or the Sea of Reeds.

9.1–5: A day of fasting. This cannot be the Day of Atonement, which fell on the tenth day of the seventh month (Lev.23.26–32; Num.29.7–9). Indeed, the Day of Atonement is not mentioned; some speculate that its introduction came at a later time.

9.6–37: The confession and prayer, a skillfully designed tapestry of historical reminiscence, an acknowledgment of backsliding, and an appeal to God's compassion, was probably once an independent psalm. **6:** The Gk. has the words, "And Ezra said," before the opening line of the prayer, *Thou . . . the LORD.*

brought you up from Egypt", and were
19 guilty of great blasphemies, thou in
thy great compassion didst not forsake
them in the wilderness. The pillar of
cloud did not fail to guide them on
their journey by day nor the pillar
of fire by night to give them light on
20 the road by which they travelled. Thou
gavest thy good spirit to instruct them;
thy manna thou didst not withhold
from them, and thou gavest them water
21 to quench their thirst. Forty years long
thou didst sustain them in the wilderness, and they lacked nothing; their
clothes did not wear out and their feet
were not swollen.
22 'Thou gavest them kingdoms and
peoples, allotting these to them as
spoils of war. Thus they took possession
of the land of Sihon king of Heshbon
and the land of Og king of Bashan.
23 Thou didst multiply their descendants
so that they became countless as the
stars in the sky, bringing them into the
land which thou didst promise to give
to their forefathers as their possession.
24 When their descendants entered the
land and took possession of it, thou
didst subdue before them the Canaanites who inhabited it and gavest these,
kings and peoples alike, into their
hands to do with them whatever they
25 wished. They captured fortified cities
and a fertile land and took possession
of houses full of all good things, rock-
hewn cisterns, vineyards, olive-trees,
and fruit-trees in abundance; so they
ate and were satisfied and grew fat and
found delight in thy great goodness.
26 But they were defiant and rebelled
against thee; they turned their backs
on thy law and killed thy prophets,
who solemnly warned them to return
to thee, and they were guilty of great
27 blasphemies. Because of this thou
didst hand them over to their enemies
who oppressed them. But when in the
time of their oppression, they cried to
thee for help, thou heardest them from
heaven and in thy great compassion
didst send them saviours to save them
28 from their enemies. But when they had
had a respite, they once more did what

was wrong in thine eyes; and thou didst
abandon them to their enemies who
held them in subjection. But again they
cried to thee for help, and many times
over thou heardest them from heaven
and in thy compassion didst save them.
Thou didst solemnly warn them to 29
return to thy law, but they grew
arrogant and did not heed thy commandments; they sinned against thy
ordinances, which bring life to him
who keeps them. Stubbornly they
turned away in mulish obstinacy and
would not obey. Many years thou wast 30
patient with them and didst warn them
by thy spirit through thy prophets;
but they would not listen. Therefore
thou didst hand them over to foreign
peoples. Yet in thy great compassion 31
thou didst not make an end of them
nor forsake them; for thou art a gracious and compassionate god.
'Now therefore, our God, thou great 32
and mighty and terrible God, who
faithfully keepest covenant, do not
make light of the hardships that have
befallen us—our kings, our princes,
our priests, our prophets, our forefathers, and all thy people—from the
days of the kings of Assyria to this day.
In all that has befallen us thou hast been 33
just, thou hast kept faith, but we have
done wrong. Our kings, our princes, 34
our priests, and our forefathers did not
keep thy law nor heed thy commandments and the warnings which thou
gavest them. Even under their own 35
kings, while they were enjoying the
great prosperity which thou gavest
them and the broad and fertile land
which thou didst bestow upon them,
they did not serve thee; they did not
abandon their evil ways. Today we are 36
slaves, slaves here in the land which
thou gavest to our forefathers so that
they might eat its fruits and enjoy its
good things. All its produce now goes 37
to the kings whom thou hast set over
us because of our sins. They have power
over our bodies, and they do as they
please with our beasts, while we are in
dire distress.
'Because of all this we make a 38

9.38–10.39: Renewal of the covenant, and its obligations. The structure resembles that of
similar stipulations of loyalty found in clay tablets: writing and sealing, list of witnesses, oath,
and enumeration of particulars. The stress against intermarriage in this "covenant renewal"

binding declaration in writing, and our princes, our Levites, and our priests witness the sealing.

10 'Those who witness the sealing are Nehemiah the governor, son of Ha-
2 caliah, Zedekiah, Seraiah, Azariah, Jer-
3 emiah, Pashhur, Amariah, Malchiah,
4,5 Hattush, Shebaniah, Malluch, Harim,
6 Meremoth, Obadiah, Daniel, Ginne-
7 thon, Baruch, Meshullam, Abiah, Mi-
8 jamin, Maaziah, Bilgai, Shemaiah;
9 these are the priests. The Levites:
Jeshua[h] son of Azaniah, Binnui of the
10 family of Henadad, Kadmiel; and their
brethren, Shebaniah, Hodiah,[i] Kelita,
11 Pelaiah, Hanan, Mica, Rehob, Hasha-
12 biah, Zaccur, Sherebiah, Shebaniah,
13,14 Hodiah, Bani, Beninu. The chiefs of
the people: Parosh, Pahath-moab,
15 Elam, Zattu, Bani, Bunni, Azgad, Bebai,
16,17 Adonijah, Bigvai, Adin, Ater, Heze-
18 kiah, Azzur, Hodiah, Hashum, Bezai,
19,20 Hariph, Anathoth, Nebai,[j] Magpiash,
21 Meshullam, Hezir, Meshezabel, Zadok,
22,23 Jaddua, Pelatiah, Hanan, Anaiah, Ho-
24 shea, Hananiah, Hasshub, Hallohesh,
25 Pilha, Shobek, Rehum, Hashabnah,
26,27 Maaseiah, Ahiah, Hanan, Anan, Malluch, Harim, Baanah.
28 'The rest of the people, the priests, the Levites, the door-keepers, the singers, the temple-servitors, with their wives, their sons, and their daughters, all who are capable of understanding, all who for the sake of the law of God have kept themselves apart from the
29 foreign population, join with the leading brethren,[k] when the oath is put to them, in swearing to obey God's law given by Moses the servant of God, and to observe and fulfil all the command-ments of the LORD our Lord, his rules and his statutes.
30 'We will not give our daughters in marriage to the foreign population or
31 take their daughters for our sons. If on the sabbath these people bring in merchandise, especially corn, for sale,

we will not buy from them on the sabbath or on any holy day. We will forgo the crops of the seventh year and release every person still held as a pledge for debt.

'We hereby undertake the duty of 32 giving yearly the third of a shekel for the service of the house of our God, for the Bread of the Presence, the regular grain-offering and whole- 33 offering, the sabbaths, the new moons, the appointed seasons, the holy-gifts, and the sin-offerings to make expiation on behalf of Israel, and for all else that has to be done in the house of our God. We, the priests, the Levites, and the 34 people, have cast lots for the wood-offering, so that it may brought into the house of our God by each family in turn, at appointed times, year by year, to burn upon the altar of the LORD our God, as prescribed in the law. We 35 undertake to bring the firstfruits of our land and the firstfruits of every fruit-tree, year by year, to the house of the LORD; also to bring to the house of 36 our God, to the priests who minister in the house of our God, the first-born of our sons and of our cattle, as pre-scribed in the law, and the first-born of our herds and of our flocks; and to 37 bring to the priests the first kneading of our dough, and the first of the fruit of every tree, of the new wine and of the oil, to the store-rooms in the house of our God; and to bring to the Levites the tithes from our land, for it is the Levites who collect the tithes in all our farming villages. The Aaronite priest 38 shall be with the Levites when they collect the tithes; and the Levites shall bring up one tenth of the tithes to the house of our God, to the appropriate rooms in the storehouse. For the 39 Israelites and the Levites shall bring

h Prob. rdg.; Heb. and Jeshua.
i Or, with Ezra 2. 40, Hodaviah.
j Or Nobai.
k the leading brethren: prob. rdg.; Heb. their brethren, their leading men.

(it is mentioned first) should be seen against the background of the harassment of the sur-rounding nations and the pressing security needs of the small Jerusalem community. Later ages introduced proselytizing. **10.30–31:** For the prohibition of intermarriage, see Deut.7.3; of work on the Sabbath day, see Exod.20.8–11; of planting during the release year, see Exod.23.10–11; for the release of pledges, Deut.15.2. **32:** The offering of *the third of a shekel* for the Temple seems voluntary; the legislation of Exod.30.13 stipulated a compulsory half shekel, to which the voluntary was added. **34:** On *wood* for *the altar*, see Lev.6.13, which does not mention the casting of lots found here. **35–37:** *Firstfruits:* see Exod.23.19. *First-born:* see Exod.13.13. *Tithes*, see Lev.27.30–33 and Num.18.25–32.

the contribution of corn, new wine, and oil to the rooms where the vessels of the sanctuary are kept, and where the ministering priests, the door-keepers, and the singers are lodged. We will not neglect the house of our God.'

11 THE LEADERS OF THE PEOPLE SETTLED IN Jerusalem; and the rest of the people cast lots to bring one in every ten to live in Jerusalem, the holy city, while the remaining nine lived in other 2 towns. And the people were grateful to all those who volunteered to live in Jerusalem.

3   These are the chiefs of the province who lived in Jerusalem; but, in the towns of Judah, other Israelites, priests, Levites, temple-servitors, and descendants of Solomon's servants lived on their own property, in their own towns. 4 Some members of the tribes of Judah and Benjamin lived in Jerusalem. Of Judah: Athaiah son of Uzziah, son of Zechariah, son of Amariah, son of Shephatiah, son of Mahalalel of the 5 family of Perez, all of whose family, to the number of four hundred and sixty-eight men of substance, lived in Jeru- 6 salem; and Maaseiah son of Baruch, son of Col-hozeh, son of Hazaiah, son of Adaiah, son of Joiarib, son of Zechariah of the Shelanite family.

7   These were the Benjamites: Sallu son of Meshullam, son of Joed, son of Pedaiah, son of Kolaiah, son of Maaseiah, son of Ithiel, son of Isaiah, 8 and his kinsmen Gabbai and Sallai, nine hundred and twenty-eight in all. 9 Joel son of Zichri was their overseer, and Judah son of Hassenuah was second over the city.[l]

10   Of the priests: Jedaiah son of 11 Joiarib, son of[m] Seraiah, son of Hilkiah, son of Meshullam, son of Zadok, son of Meraioth, son of Ahitub, supervisor 12 of the house of God, and his[n] brethren responsible for the work in the temple, eight hundred and twenty-two in all; and Adaiah son of Jeroham, son of Pelaliah, son of Amzi, son of Zechariah,

son of Pashhur, son of Malchiah, and 13 his brethren, heads of fathers' houses, two hundred and forty-two in all; and Amasai[o] son of Azarel, son of Ahzai, son of Meshillemoth, son of Immer, and his brethren, men of substance, a 14 hundred and twenty-eight in all; their overseer was Zabdiel son of Hagge-dolim.

And of the Levites: Shemaiah son of 15 Hasshub, son of Azrikam, son of Hashabiah, son of Bunni; and Shabbe- 16 thai and Jozabad of the chiefs of the Levites, who had charge of the external business of the house of God; and 17 Mattaniah son of Micah, son of Zabdi, son of Asaph, who as precentor led the prayer of thanksgiving, and Bakbukiah who held the second place among his brethren; and Abda son of Shammua, son of Galal, son of Jeduthun. The 18 number of Levites in the holy city was two hundred and eighty-four in all.

The gate-keepers who kept guard at 19 the gates were Akkub, Talmon, and their brethren, a hundred and seventy-two. The rest of the Israelites[p] were in 20 all the towns of Judah, each man on his own inherited property. But the 21 temple-servitors lodged on Ophel, and Ziha and Gishpa were in charge of them.

The overseer of the Levites in 22 Jerusalem was Uzzi son of Bani, son of Hashabiah, son of Mattaniah, son of Mica, of the family of Asaph the singers, for the supervision of the business of the house of God. For they 23 were under the king's orders, and there was obligatory duty for the singers every day. Pethahiah son of Meshe- 24 zabel, of the family of Zerah son of Judah, was the king's adviser on all matters affecting the people.

As for the hamlets with their sur- 25 rounding fields: some of the men of Judah lived in Kiriath-arba and its

l second over the city: or over the second quarter of the city.
m son of: prob. rdg.; Heb. obscure.
n Prob. rdg.; Heb. their.
o Prob. rdg.; Heb. Amashsai.
p Prob. rdg.; Heb. adds the levitical priests.

11.1–24: Repopulation of Jerusalem. A parallel list, 1 Chr. ch. 9, provides a similar order: chiefs, priests, Levites, and people with other functions. Some scholars connect this chapter with Neh.7.5a as continuing the "Memoirs of Nehemiah."
   11.25–36: Population of the surrounding Judean area. The borders of Judea extend to *Beersheba* in the south, and *Lachish* and *Ziklag*, towns closer to the coast in the southwest.

villages, in Dibon and its villages, and
26 in Jekabzeel and its hamlets, in Jeshua,
27 Moladah, and Bethpelet, in Hazar-
shual, and in Beersheba and its villages,
28 in Ziklag and in Meconah and its
29 villages, in Enrimmon, Zorah, and
30 Jarmuth, in Zanoah, Adullam, and
their hamlets, in Lachish and its fields
and Azekah and its villages. Thus they
occupied the country from Beersheba
to the Valley of Hinnom.
31   The men of Benjamin lived in[q] Geba,
Michmash, Aiah, and Bethel with its
32 villages, in Anathoth, Nob, and Ana-
33 niah, in Hazor, Ramah, and Gittaim,
34,35 in Hadid, Zeboim, and Neballat, in
36 Lod, Ono, and[r] Ge-harashim.[s] And
certain divisions of the Levites in Judah
were attached to Benjamin.

12   These are the priests and the Levites
who came back with Zerubbabel son
of Shealtiel, and Jeshua:[t] Seraiah,
2 Jeremiah, Ezra, Amariah, Malluch,
3 Hattush, Shecaniah, Rehum, Mere-
4,5 moth, Iddo, Ginnethon, Abiah, Mi-
6 jamin, Maadiah, Bilgah, Shemaiah,
7 Joiarib, Jedaiah, Sallu, Amok, Hilkiah,
Jedaiah. These were the chiefs of the
priests and of their brethren in the days
of Jeshua.
8   And the Levites: Jeshua, Binnui,
Kadmiel, Sherebiah, Judah, and Mattaniah, who with his brethren was in
charge of the songs of thanksgiving.
9 And Bakbukiah and Unni their brethren stood opposite them in the service.
10 And Jeshua was the father of Joiakim,
Joiakim the father of Eliashib, Eliashib
11 of Joiada, Joiada the father of Jonathan, and Jonathan the father of
12 Jaddua. And in the days of Joiakim the
priests who were heads of families were:
of Seraiah, Meraiah; of Jeremiah, Han-
13 aniah; of Ezra, Meshullam; of Ama-
14 riah, Jehohanan; of Malluch,[u] Jon-
15 athan; of Shebaniah, Joseph; of Harim,
16 Adna; of Meraioth, Helkai; of Iddo,
Zechariah; of Ginnethon, Meshullam;
17 of Abiah, Zichri; of Miniamin[v]; of

Moadiah, Piltai; of Bilgah, Shammua; 18
of Shemaiah, Jehonathan; of Joiarib, 19
Mattenai; of Jedaiah, Uzzi; of Sallu,[w] 20
Kallai; of Amok, Eber; of Hilkiah, 21
Hashabiah; of Jedaiah, Nethaneel.
    [x]The heads of the priestly families[y] 22
in the days of Eliashib, Joiada,
Johanan, and Jaddua were recorded
down to the reign of Darius the Persian.
The heads of the levitical families were 23
recorded in the annals only down to
the days of Johanan the grandson of
Eliashib. And the chiefs of the Levites: 24
Hashabiah, Sherebiah, Jeshua, Binnui,[z]
Kadmiel, with their brethren in the
other turn of duty, to praise and to
give thanks, according to the commandment of David the man of God,
turn by turn. Mattaniah, Bakbukiah, 25
Obadiah, Meshullam, Talmon, and
Akkub were gate-keepers standing
guard at the gatehouses. This was the 26
arrangement in the days of Joiakim
son of Jeshua, son of Jozadak, and in
the days of Nehemiah the governor and
of Ezra the priest and scribe.
    At the dedication of the wall of 27
Jerusalem they sought out the Levites
in all their settlements, and brought
them to Jerusalem to celebrate the
dedication with[a] rejoicing, with thanksgiving and song, to the accompaniment
of cymbals, lutes, and harps. And the 28
Levites,[b] the singers, were assembled
from the district round Jerusalem and
from the hamlets of the Netophathites;
also from Beth-gilgal and from the 29
region of Geba and Beth-azmoth;[c] for
the singers had built themselves hamlets
in the neighbourhood of Jerusalem.

q *Prob. rdg.; Heb.* from.   r *and: prob. rdg.; Heb. om.*
s *Or* and the Valley of Woods *or* and the Valley of
Craftsmen.
t *Or* Joshua.
u *Prob. rdg.; Heb.* Malluchi, *or* Melichu.
v *A name is missing here.*
w *Prob. rdg., cp. verse; 7; Heb.* Sallai.
x *Prob. rdg.; Heb. prefixes* The Levites.
y heads . . . families: *prob. rdg.; Heb.* heads of the
families and the priests.
z Jeshua, Binnui: *prob. rdg.; Heb.* and Jeshua son of.
a *Prob. rdg.; Heb.* and.
b the Levites: *prob. rdg.; Heb.* the sons of.
c Beth-azmoth: *prob. rdg., cp. 7. 28; Heb.* Azmoth.

11.31–36: The towns of Benjamin. These are located north and west of Jerusalem; the farthest
of these (Ono) was about thirty miles away.
    12.1–26: List of priests and Levites. A later hand has appended this additional list. **10–11:**
The genealogy of high priests. *Jonathan* is often regarded as an error for Jehohanan; see
Ezra 10.6 n. **22:** The historian Josephus tells that *Jaddua* was high priest in 332, in the time of
the conquest by Alexander the Great. *Darius* may be Darius III who ruled 335–331 B.C.
    12.27–43: Dedication of the walls. 33: The mentions of *Ezra* here and in v. 36 are regarded as
interpolations; see Introduction to Ezra on dislocations of materials.

30 The priests and the Levites purified themselves; and they purified the
31 people, the gates, and the wall. Then I brought the leading men of Judah up on to the city wall, and appointed two great choirs to give thanks. One went in procession*d* to the right, going along
32 the wall to the Dung Gate; and after it went Hoshaiah with half the leading
33 men of Judah, and Azariah, Ezra,
34 Meshullam, Judah, Benjamin, She-
35 maiah, and Jeremiah; and certain of the priests with trumpets: Zechariah son of Jonathan, son of Shemaiah, son of Mattanaiah, son of Micaiah, son of
36 Zaccur, son of Asaph, and his kinsmen, Shemaiah, Azarel, Milalai, Gilalai, Maai, Nethaneel, Judah, and Hanani, with the musical instruments of David the man of God; and Ezra the scribe
37 led them. They went past the Fountain Gate and thence straight forward by the steps up to the City of David, by the ascent to the city wall, past the house of David, and on to the Water Gate on
39 the east. The other thanksgiving choir went to the left,*e* and I followed it with half the leading men of*f* the people, continuing along the wall, past the Tower of the Ovens*g* to the Broad Wall,
39 and past the Ephraim Gate, and over the Jeshanah Gate,*h* and over the Fish Gate, taking in the Tower of Hananel and the Tower of the Hundred, as far as the Sheep Gate; and they halted at
40 the Gate of the Guardhouse. So the two thanksgiving choirs took their place in the house of God, and I and
41 half the magistrates with me; and the priests Eliakim, Maaseiah, Miniamin, Micaiah, Elioenai, Zechariah, and
42 Hananiah, with trumpets; and Maaseiah, Shemaiah, Eleazar, Uzzi, Jehohanan, Malchiah, Elam, and Ezer. The singers, led by Izrahiah, raised their
43 voices. A great sacrifice was celebrated that day, and they all rejoiced because God had given them great cause for rejoicing; the women and children rejoiced with them. And the rejoicing

in Jerusalem was heard a long way off.

On that day men were appointed to 44 take charge of the store-rooms for the contributions, the firstfruits, and the tithes, to gather in the portions required by the law for the priests and Levites according to the extent of the farmlands round the towns; for all Judah was full of rejoicing at the ministry of the priests and Levites. And they performed the service of their 45 God and the service of purification, as did the singers and the door-keepers, according to the rules laid down by David and his son Solomon. For it was 46 in the days of David that Asaph took the lead as chief of the singers and director*i* of praise and thanksgiving to God. And in the days of Zerubbabel 47 and of Nehemiah all Israel gave the portions for the singers and the door-keepers as each day required; and they set apart the portion for the Levites, and the Levites set apart the portion for the Aaronites.

Nehemiah's reforms

On that day at the public reading 13 from the book of Moses, it was found to be laid down that no Ammonite or Moabite should ever enter the assembly of God, because they did not meet the 2 Israelites with food and water but hired Balaam to curse them, though our God turned the curse into a blessing. When the people heard the law, they 3 separated from Israel all who were of mixed blood.

But before this, Eliashib the priest, 4 who was appointed over the store-rooms of the house of our God, and who was connected by marriage with Tobiah, had provided for his use a 5 large room where formerly they had

d One . . . procession: *prob. rdg.; Heb.* Processions.
e to the left: *prob. rdg.; Heb.* to the front.
f the leading men of: *prob. rdg.; Heb. om.*
g Or Furnaces.
h the Jeshanah Gate: *or* the gate of the Old City.
i Prob. rdg.; Heb. song.

12.44–47: The admirable functioning of the cult. 45: See also 2 Chr.8.14, dependent on 1 Chr. chs. 23–26. **47:** The mention of Zerubbabel instead of Ezra has influenced scholars to conclude that Ezra was not contemporaneous with Nehemiah. See Introduction to Ezra.
    13.1–31: Nehemiah's reforms. 1–3: These verses connect the chapter with 8.18. **1:** See Deut.23.3–5. **2:** *Balaam:* see Num. chs. 22–24. **4–9:** The expulsion of *Tobiah* the Ammonite (2.10) is important to the author, so that the community could maintain an unadulterated

kept the grain-offering, the incense, the temple vessels, the tithes of corn, new wine, and oil prescribed for the Levites, singers, and door-keepers, and the 6 contributions for the priests. All this time I was not in Jerusalem because, in the thirty-second year of Artaxerxes king of Babylon, I had gone to the king. Some time later, I asked permission 7 from him and returned to Jerusalem. There I discovered the wicked thing that Eliashib had done for Tobiah's sake in providing him with a room 8 in the courts of the house of God. I was greatly displeased and threw all Tobiah's belongings out of the room. 9 Then I gave orders that the room should be purified, and that the vessels of the house of God, with the grain-offering and incense, should be put back into it.

10 I also learnt that the Levites had not been given their portions; both they and the singers, who were responsible for their respective duties, had made 11 off to their farms. So I remonstrated with the magistrates and said, 'Why is the house of God deserted?' And I recalled the men and restored them to 12 their places. Then all Judah brought the tithes of corn, new wine, and oil into 13 the storehouses; and I put in charge of them Shelemiah the priest, Zadok the accountant, and Pedaiah a Levite, with Hanan son of Zaccur, son of Mattaniah, as their assistant, for they were considered trustworthy men; their duty was the distribution of their shares 14 to their brethren. Remember this, O God, to my credit, and do not wipe out of thy memory the devotion which I have shown in the house of my God and in his service.

15 In those days I saw men in Judah treading winepresses on the sabbath, collecting quantities of produce and piling it on asses—wine, grapes, figs, and every kind of load, which they brought into Jerusalem on the sabbath; and I protested to them about selling 16 food on that day. Tyrians living in Jerusalem also brought in fish and all kinds of merchandise and sold them on the sabbath to the people of Judah, even in Jerusalem. Then I complained 17 to the nobles of Judah and said to them, 'How dare you profane the sabbath in this wicked way? Is not this just what 18 your fathers did, so that our God has brought all this evil on us and on this city? Now you are bringing more wrath upon Israel by profaning the sabbath.' When the entrances to Jerusalem had 19 been cleared in preparation for the sabbath, I gave orders that the gates should be shut and not opened until after the sabbath. And I appointed some of the men under me to have charge of the gates so that no load might enter on the sabbath. Then on 20 one or two occasions the merchants and all kinds of traders camped just outside Jerusalem, but I cautioned 21 them. 'Why are you camping in front of the city wall?' I asked. 'If you do it again, I will take action against you.' After that they did not come on the sabbath again. And I commanded the 22 Levites who were to purify themselves and take up duty as guards at the gates, to ensure that the sabbath was kept holy. Remember this also to my credit, O God, and spare me in thy great love.

In those days also I saw that some 23 Jews had married women from Ashdod, Ammon, and Moab. Half their children 24 spoke the language of Ashdod or of the other peoples and could not speak the language of the Jews. I argued 25 with them and reviled them, I beat them and tore out their hair; and I made them swear in the name of God: 'We will not marry our daughters to their sons, or take any of their daughters in marriage for our sons or for ourselves.' 'Was it not for such 26 women', I said, 'that King Solomon of Israel sinned? Among all the nations there was no king like him; he was loved by his God, and God made him king over all Israel; nevertheless even he was led by foreign women into sin.

worship of God. **6:** *Some time later:* Nehemiah was in Susa from 433 to 424. The king is Artaxerxes I, 464–424/3. **10–14:** The *tithes:* contrast 12.47, where tithes seem given freely. **15–22:** *The sabbath:* disregard for the Sabbath law was considered to be the cause for exile and enslavement to foreign kings. Compare Jer.17.19–27, possibly hearkened back to in v. 18. **23–29:** On mixed marriages, see 10.30 and Ezra 9.1–5; 10.2. **26:** *Solomon.* see 1 Kgs.11.1 8.

27 Are we then to follow your example and commit this grave offence, breaking faith with our God by marrying foreign women?'

28 Now one of the sons of Joiada son of Eliashib the high priest had married a daughter of Sanballat the Horonite; therefore I drove him out of my presence. 29 Remember, O God, to their shame that they have defiled the priesthood and the covenant of the priests[j] and the Levites.

Thus I purified them from every-30 thing foreign, and I made the Levites and the priests resume the duties of their office; I also made provision for 31 the wood-offering, at appointed times, and for the firstfruits. Remember me for my good, O God.

[j] Or priesthood.

28: *Sanballat* was a personal foe; see 2.10; 4.1–2,7–8; 6.1–14. **30–31**: Closing verses and prayer.

ESTHER

This book tells how Esther, a young Jewish girl, delivers the Jews in Persia when they are threatened with extermination by Haman, the chief minister of the Persian king. Esther, who has become queen, acts on the advice of her cousin, Mordecai, the principal object of Haman's anger. A complete reversal of positions results; Haman is hanged, Mordecai assumes his office, and the Jews massacre their enemies. To commemorate this victory, the annual feast of Purim is instituted.

Esther is often considered to have been written in the Persian period (538–333 B.C.), though some view it as much later, perhaps even in the Maccabean period. Although Persian customs are familiar to the author and details about the city of Susa and the palace are confirmed by archaeology, it is impossible to find historical confirmation of the events recounted. However, an official at Susa under King Xerxes I is named Marduka, which is close to Mordecai. In the Hebrew Bible, Esther is the last of the five Megilloth, or Scrolls, for reading at the great festivals; it is read on Purim.

Although God's name is not mentioned, there is an obvious implicit trust in his guidance, as 4.13–17 makes clear. Because religious themes are not explicitly stressed, some ancient rabbis opposed the book's reception into Scripture. In the Greek some additions are found which modify the secular tone of the Hebrew; see "The Rest of the Chapters of the Book of Esther" in the Apocrypha.

Esther chosen as queen by the Persian king

1 THE EVENTS HERE RELATED HAP-pened in the days of Ahasuerus, the Ahasuerus who ruled from India to Ethiopia, a hundred and 2 twenty-seven provinces. At this time he sat on his royal throne in Susa the 3 capital city. In the third year of his reign he gave a banquet for all his officers and his courtiers; and when his army of Persian and Medes, with his nobles and provincial governors, were 4 in attendance, he displayed the wealth of his kingdom and the pomp and splendour of his majesty for many days, 5 a hundred and eighty in all. When these days were over, the king gave a banquet for all the people present in Susa the capital city, both high and low; it was held in the garden court of the royal pavilion and lasted seven days. 6 There were white curtains and violet hangings fastened to silver rings with bands of fine linen and purple;[a] there were alabaster pillars and couches of gold and silver set on a mosaic pave-ment of malachite and alabaster, of mother-of-pearl and turquoise. Wine 7 was served in golden cups of various patterns: the king's wine flowed freely as befitted a king, and the law of the 8 drinking was that there should be no compulsion, for the king had laid it down that all the stewards of his palace should respect each man's wishes. In 9 addition, Queen Vashti gave a banquet for the women in the royal apartments of King Ahasuerus.

On the seventh day, when he was 10 merry with wine, the king ordered Mehuman, Biztha, Harbona, Bigtha, Abagtha, Zethar, and Carcas, the seven eunuchs who were in attendance on the king's person, to bring Queen 11 Vashti before him wearing her royal crown, in order to display her beauty to the people and the officers; for she was indeed a beautiful woman. But 12 Queen Vashti refused to come in an-swer to the royal command conveyed by the eunuchs. This greatly incensed the king, and he grew hot with anger.

Then the king conferred with his wise 13

a bands . . . purple: or white and purple cords.

1.1–9: **Ahasuerus' banquet.** 1: *Ahasuerus* (see Ezra 4.6; Dan.9.1) seems to be Xerxes I (485–464 B.C.), whose empire extended from *India* to *Ethiopia*, and included some twenty satrapies, subdivided into *provinces*. 2: *Susa*, in Elam, was the king's winter residence; Persepolis was the capital of Persia. 3: Greek authors mention the great banquets given by Persian kings. 5: Archaeologists have uncovered such *a court* at Susa. 9: Xerxes' queen was Amestris; *Vashti* was perhaps a royal concubine. No mention of Vashti or Esther is to be found outside this book. 1.10–2.4: **Vashti deposed.** 13: The *wise men* are possibly his seven counsellors (Ezra 7.14).

men versed in misdemeanours;[b] for it was his royal custom to consult all who were versed in law and religion,

14 those closest to him being Carshena, Shethar, Admatha, Tarshish, Meres, Marsena, and Memucan, the seven princes of Persia and Media who had access to the king and held first place

15 in the kingdom. He asked them, 'What does the law require to be done with Queen Vashti for disobeying the command of King Ahasuerus brought to

16 her by the eunuchs?' Then Memucan made answer before the king and the princes: 'Queen Vashti has done wrong, and not to the king alone, but also to all the officers and to all the peoples in all the provinces of King Ahasuerus.

17 Every woman will come to know what the queen has done, and this will make them treat their husbands with contempt; they will say, "King Ahasuerus ordered Queen Vashti to be brought before him and she did not come."

18 The great ladies of Persia and Media, who have heard of the queen's conduct, will tell all the king's officers about this day, and there will be endless disrespect

19 and insolence! If it please your majesty, let a royal decree go out from you and let it be inscribed in the laws of the Persians and Medes, never to be revoked, that Vashti shall not again appear before King Ahasuerus; and let the king give her place as queen to another woman who is more worthy of

20 it than she. Thus when this royal edict is heard through the length and breadth of the kingdom, all women will give honour to their husbands, high and

21 low alike.' Memucan's advice pleased the king and the princes, and the king

22 did as he had proposed. Letters were sent to all the royal provinces, to every province in its own script and to every people in their own language, in order that each man might be master in his own house and control all his own womenfolk.[c]

Later, when the anger of King 2 Ahasuerus had died down, he remembered Vashti and what she had done and what had been decreed against her. So the king's attendants 2 said, 'Let beautiful young virgins be sought out for your majesty; and let 3 your majesty appoint commissioners in all the provinces of your kingdom to bring all these beautiful young virgins into the women's quarters in Susa the capital city. Let them be committed to the care of Hegai, the king's eunuch in charge of the women, and let cosmetics be provided for them; and let the one who is most acceptable 4 to the king become queen in place of Vashti.' This idea pleased the king and he acted on it.

Now there was in Susa the capital 5 city a Jew named Mordecai son of Jair, son of Shimei, son of Kish, a Benjamite; he had been carried into exile 6 from Jerusalem among those whom Nebuchadnezzar king of Babylon had carried away with Jeconiah king of Judah. He had a foster-child Hadassah, 7 that is Esther, his uncle's daughter, who had neither father nor mother. She was a beautiful and charming girl, and after the death of her father and mother Mordecai had adopted her as his own daughter. When the king's 8 order and his edict were published, and many girls were brought to Susa the capital city to be committed to the care of Hegai, Esther too was taken to the king's palace to be entrusted to Hegai, who had charge of the women. She attracted his notice and received 9 his special favour: he readily provided her with her cosmetics and her allow-

[b] Or *times.*
[c] *and control . . . womenfolk: prob. rdg.; Heb.* and speak in his own language.

19: Reference to laws *never to be revoked* is also made in 8.8 and in Dan.6.8,12,15. There may be some irony in the allusion that in both Esther and Dan, the irrevocable decrees against the Jews are ineffective. **22:** The verse seems to be a humorous exaggeration.

2.5–23: The selection of Esther. Mordecai and Esther have names derived from the Babylonian deities Marduk and Ishtar, who also were cousins. That Mordecai, like Saul, was a Benjaminite is stressed to foreshadow the enmity of Haman, an Amalekite of the Agag family, Saul's enemy, 1 Sam.15.1–9. **5:** On these remote ancestors see 2 Sam.16.5–8, *Shimei;* and 1 Sam.9.1–2, *Kish,* the father of Saul. **6:** *Jeconiah* is also known as Jehoiachin (2 Kgs.24.6). Modern critics regard the author as unconcerned with precise chronology, for Mordecai's age here would appear to be at least one hundred and fifteen years. **7:** *Hadassah* is a Heb. word meaning

ance of food, and also with seven picked maids from the king's palace, and he gave her and her maids privileges in the women's quarters.

10 Esther had not disclosed her race or her family, because Mordecai had 11 forbidden her to do so. Every day Mordecai passed along by the forecourt of the women's quarters to learn how Esther was faring and what was happening to her.

12 The full period of preparation prescribed for the women was twelve months, six months with oil and myrrh and six months with perfumes and cosmetics. When the period was complete, each girl's turn came to go to 13 King Ahasuerus, and she was allowed to take with her whatever she asked, when she went from the women's 14 quarters to the king's palace. She went into the palace in the evening and returned in the morning to another part of the women's quarters, to be under the care of Shaashgaz, the king's eunuch in charge of the concubines. She did not again go to the king unless he expressed a wish for her; then she was summoned by name.

15 When the turn came for Esther, daughter of Abihail the uncle of Mordecai her adoptive father, to go to the king, she asked for nothing to take with her except what was advised by Hegai, the king's eunuch in charge of the women; and Esther charmed all 16 who saw her. When she was taken to King Ahasuerus in the royal palace, in the seventh year of his reign, in the tenth month, that is the month Tebeth, 17 the king loved her more than any of his other women and treated her with greater favour and kindness than the rest of the virgins. He put a royal crown on her head and made her queen in 18 place of Vashti. Then the king gave a great banquet for all his officers and courtiers, a banquet in honour of Esther. He also proclaimed a holiday[d]

throughout the provinces and distributed gifts worthy of a king.

Mordecai was in attendance at court; 19 on his instructions Esther had not 20 disclosed her family or her race, she had done what Mordecai told her, as she did when she was his ward. One 21 day when Mordecai was in attendance at court, Bigthan and Teresh, two of the king's eunuchs, keepers of the threshold, who were disaffected, were plotting to lay hands on King Ahasuerus. This 22 became known to Mordecai, who told Queen Esther; and she told the king, mentioning Mordecai by name. The 23 affair was investigated and the report confirmed; the two men were hanged on the gallows. All this was recorded in the royal chronicle in the presence of the king.

Haman's plot against the Jews

AFTER THIS, KING AHASUERUS PROMOTED 3 Haman son of Hammedatha the Agagite, advancing him and giving him precedence above all his fellow-officers. So the king's attendants at 2 court all bowed down to Haman and did obeisance, for so the king had commanded; but Mordecai did not bow down to him or do obeisance. Then the 3 attendants at court said to Mordecai, 'Why do you flout his majesty's command?' Day by day they challenged 4 him, but he refused to listen to them; so they informed Haman, in order to discover if Mordecai's refusal would be tolerated, for he had told them that he was a Jew. When Haman saw that 5 Mordecai was not bowing down to him or doing obeisance, he was infuriated. On learning who Mordecai's 6 people were, he scorned to lay hands on him alone, and looked for a way to destroy all the Jews throughout the whole kingdom of Ahasuerus, Mordecai and all his race.

d Or an amnesty.

"myrtle." **10:** The requirement of the plot in ch. 6 is the likely reason why *Esther had not disclosed her race or her family*. **11:** We are not told precisely how Mordecai received information. See also vv. 19–23. **16:** *Tebeth* (December–January) is a Babylonian month name. **18:** A *holiday:* see Tfn. *d.* **21:** The *keepers of the threshold* guarded the king's private apartment. Xerxes died by assassination in just such a plot. **23:** The delay in a reward for Mordecai foreshadows 6.1–13. *Royal chronicle:* see 10.2.
   3.1–5.14: Haman's plot against the Jews. 3.1: The identification of Haman as an Agagite

7 In the twelfth year of King Ahasuerus, in the first month, Nisan, they cast lots, Pur as it is called, in the presence of Haman, taking day by day and month by month, and the lot fell on the thirteenth day of the twelfth 8 month,*e* the month Adar. Then Haman said to King Ahasuerus, 'There is a certain people, dispersed among the many peoples in all the provinces of your kingdom, who keep themselves apart. Their laws are different from those of every other people; they do not keep your majesty's laws. It does not befit your majesty to tolerate them. 9 If it please your majesty, let an order be made in writing for their destruction; and I will pay ten thousand talents of silver to your majesty's officials, to be 10 deposited in the royal treasury.' So the king took the signet-ring from his hand and gave it to Haman son of Hammedatha the Agagite, the enemy of the 11 Jews; and he said to him, 'The money and the people are yours; deal with them as you wish.'

12 On the thirteenth day of the first month the king's secretaries were summoned and, in accordance with Haman's instructions, a writ was issued to the king's satraps and the governor of every province, and to the officers over each separate people: for each province in its own script and for each people in their own language. It was drawn up in the name of King Ahasuerus and sealed with the king's signet. 13 Thus letters were sent by courier to all the king's provinces with orders to destroy, slay, and exterminate all Jews, young and old, women and children, in one day, the thirteenth day of the twelfth month, the month Adar, and 14 to plunder their possessions. A copy of the writ was to be issued as a decree in every province and to be published to all the peoples, so that they might be 15 ready for that day. The couriers were dispatched post-haste at the king's

command, and the decree was issued in Susa the capital city. The king and Haman sat down to drink; but the city of Susa was thrown into confusion.

When Mordecai learnt all that had 4 been done, he rent his clothes, put on sackcloth and ashes, and went through the city crying loudly and bitterly. He 2 came within sight of the palace gate, because no one clothed with sackcloth was allowed to pass through the gate. In every province reached by the royal 3 command and decree there was great mourning among the Jews, with fasting and weeping and beating of the breast. Most of them made their beds of sackcloth and ashes. When Queen Esther's 4 maids and eunuchs came and told her, she was distraught, and sent garments for Mordecai, so that they might take off the sackcloth and clothe him with them; but he would not accept them. Then Esther summoned Hathach, one 5 of the king's eunuchs who had been appointed to wait upon her, and ordered him to find out from Mordecai what the trouble was and what it meant. Hathach went to Mordecai in the city 6 square in front of the palace gate, and 7 Mordecai told him all that had happened to him and how much money Haman had offered to pay into the royal treasury for the destruction of the Jews. He also gave him a copy of the 8 writ for their destruction issued in Susa, so that he might show it to Esther and tell her about it, bidding her go to the king to plead for his favour and entreat him for her people. Hathach 9 went and told Esther what Mordecai had said, and she sent him back with 10 this message: 'All the king's courtiers 11 and the people of the provinces are aware that if any person, man or woman, enters the king's presence in the inner court unbidden, there is one law only: that person shall be put to

e and the lot . . . twelfth month: prob. rdg., cp. verse 13; Heb. the twelfth.

(see 2.5–23 n.) subtly emphasizes the hostility between Mordecai and Haman. **7:** *Pur* is a Babylonian word meaning *lot*. The lot was to determine the best day for the pogrom. *Adar* is in March–April. **9:** Experts think that the amount of *silver* here would represent almost two-thirds of the annual income of the Persian Empire. **10:** The *signet-ring* sealed official documents; it gave Haman unlimited power. **11:** The king apparently accepts the bribe. **12:** The *writ was issued* on the thirteenth of Nisan, the day before Passover. **15:** The *couriers* belonged to the famous Persian post service; see 8.10 n.
4.1–17: Mordecai appeals to Esther. 11: Prohibition to enter without a summons was possibly

death, unless the king stretches out to him the golden sceptre; then and then only shall he live. It is now thirty days since I myself was called to go to the
12 king.' But when they told Mordecai
13 what Esther had said, he bade them go back to her and say, 'Do not imagine that you alone of all the Jews will escape because you are in the royal
14 palace. If you remain silent at such a time as this, relief and deliverance for the Jews will appear from another quarter, but you and your father's family will perish. Who knows whether it is not for such a time as this that you
15 have come to royal estate?' Esther gave them this answer to take back to
16 Mordecai: 'Go and assemble all the Jews to be found in Susa and fast for me; take neither food nor drink for three days, night or day, and I and my maids will fast as you do. After that I will go to the king, although it is against
17 the law; and if I perish, I perish.' So Mordecai went away and did exactly as Esther had bidden him.

5   On the third day Esther put on her royal robes and stood in the inner court of the king's palace, facing the palace itself; the king was seated on his royal throne in the palace, facing the
2 entrance. When the king caught sight of Queen Esther standing in the court, she won his favour and he stretched out to her the golden sceptre which he was holding. Thereupon Esther approached and touched the head of the sceptre.
3 Then the king said to her, 'What is it, Queen Esther? Whatever you ask of me, up to half my kingdom, shall be
4 given to you.' 'If it please your majesty,' said Esther, 'will you come today, sire, and Haman with you, to a banquet which I have made ready for you?'
5 The king gave orders that Haman

should be fetched quickly, so that Esther's wish might be fulfilled; and the king and Haman went to the banquet which she had prepared. Over 6 the wine the king said to Esther, 'Whatever you ask of me shall be given to you. Whatever you request of me, up to half my kingdom, it shall be done.' Esther said in answer, 'What I 7 ask and request of you is this. If I have 8 won your majesty's favour, and if it please you, sire, to give me what I ask and to grant my request, will your majesty and Haman come tomorrow to the banquet which I shall prepare for you both? Tomorrow I will do as your majesty has said.'

So Haman went away that day in 9 good spirits and well pleased with himself. But when he saw Mordecai in attendance at court and how he did not rise nor defer to him, he was filled with rage; but he kept control of himself 10 and went home. Then he sent for his friends and his wife Zeresh and held 11 forth to them about the splendour of his wealth and his many sons, and how the king had promoted him and advanced him above the other officers and courtiers. 'That is not all,' said Haman; 12 'Queen Esther invited no one but myself to accompany the king to the banquet which she had prepared; and she has invited me again tomorrow with the king. Yet all this means 13 nothing to me so long as I see that Jew Mordecai in attendance at court.' Then 14 his wife Zeresh and all his friends said to him, 'Let a gallows seventy-five feet high be set up, and recommend to the king in the morning to have Mordecai hanged upon it. Then go with the king to the banquet in good spirits.' Haman thought this an excellent plan, and he set up the gallows.

for security reasons. **14:** *Another quarter* seems to be a veiled allusion to God. The question *"Who knows whether . . . ?"* implies that Esther's position is providential. See The Rest of the Chapters of the Book of Esther in the Apocrypha. **16:** To *fast* has long been regarded as a pious act which wins divine favor.
5.1–8: Esther before the king. 2: The gesture of stretching *out to her the golden sceptre* is explained in 4.11. **3:** *Up to half my kingdom* is gross exaggeration. **4–8:** The early banquets with Haman the only guest, and Esther passing up two opportunities to intercede for her people, are literary devices necessary for working out the plot of the story. **8:** For additional details, see 6.14; 7.3; 8.5.
5.9–14: Haman's gallows. 14: The height of the *gallows* seems exaggerated, unless it was on a high building or hill for all to see. *Haman . . . set up the gallows,* all the while gleefully thinking it was intended for *Mordecai.*

Haman's downfall and
Mordecai's triumph

6 THAT NIGHT SLEEP ELUDED THE KING, so he ordered the chronicle of daily events to be brought; and it was read 2 to him. Therein was recorded that Mordecai had given information about Bigthana and Teresh, the two royal eunuchs among the keepers of the threshold who had plotted to lay hands 3 on King Ahasuerus. Whereupon the king said, 'What honour or dignity has been conferred on Mordecai for this?' The king's courtiers who were in attendance told him that nothing had 4 been done for Mordecai. The king asked, 'Who is that in the court?' Now Haman had just entered the outer court of the palace to recommend to the king that Mordecai should be hanged on the gallows which he had 5 prepared for him. The king's servants answered, 'It is Haman standing there'; 6 and the king bade him enter. He came in, and the king said to him, 'What should be done for the man whom the king wishes to honour?' Haman said to himself, 'Whom would the king wish 7 to honour more than me?' And he said to the king, 'For the man whom the 8 king wishes to honour, let there be brought royal robes which the king himself wears, and a horse which the king rides, with a royal crown upon its 9 head. And let the robes and the horse be delivered to one of the king's most honourable officers, and let him attire the man whom the king wishes to honour and lead him mounted on the horse through the city square, calling out as he goes: "See what is done for the man whom the king wishes to 10 honour."' Then the king said to Haman, 'Fetch the robes and the horse at once, as you have said, and do all this for Mordecai the Jew who is in attendance at court. Leave nothing 11 undone of all that you have said.' So

Haman took the robes and the horse, attired Mordecai, and led him mounted through the city square, calling out as he went: 'See what is done for the man whom the king wishes to honour.' Then Mordecai returned to court 12 and Haman hurried off home mourn- 13 ing, with head uncovered. He told his wife Zeresh and all his friends everything that had happened to him. And this was the reply of his friends and his wife Zeresh: 'If Mordecai, in face of whom your fortunes begin to fall, belongs to the Jewish race, you will not get the better of him; he will see your utter downfall.'

While they were still talking with 14 Haman, the king's eunuchs arrived and hurried him away to the banquet which Esther had prepared.

So the king and Haman went to dine **7** with Queen Esther. Again on that 2 second day, over the wine, the king said, 'Whatever you ask of me will be given to you, Queen Esther. Whatever you request of me, up to half my kingdom, it shall be done.' Queen 3 Esther answered, 'If I have found favour with your majesty, and if it please your majesty, my request and petition is that my own life and the lives of my people may be spared. For 4 we have been sold, I and my people, to be destroyed, slain, and exterminated. If it had been a matter of selling us, men and women alike, into slavery, I should have kept silence; for then our plight would not be such as to injure the king's interests.' Then King Ahasuerus 5 said to Queen Esther, 'Who is he, and where is he, who has presumed to do such a thing as this?' 'An adversary and 6 an enemy,' said Esther, 'this wicked Haman.' At that Haman was dumbfounded in the presence of the king and the queen. The king rose from the 7 banquet in a rage and went to the garden of the pavilion, while Haman remained where he was, to plead for

---

6.1–14: Haman's downfall and Mordecai's triumph. 1: The insomnia of kings, a common theme in eastern literature, is here treated comically. **5:** That *Haman* was *standing there* (during the night!) is a necessity of the plot. **8:** The bestowal of *royal robes* was common in ancient times; see Gen.41.42. Horses wearing royal crowns are pictured on Persian monuments. **13:** The *reply* to Haman here is another reference to Providence; see 4.14 n. **14:** It was Oriental custom for the guests to be escorted.
  7.1–10: Haman's end. 4: *Sold:* a reference to the bribe (3.9–10); Esther could tolerate *slavery*

his life with Queen Esther; for he saw that in the king's mind his fate was
8 determined. When the king returned from the garden to the banqueting hall, Haman had flung himself across the couch on which Esther was reclining. The king exclaimed, 'Will he even assault the queen here in my presence?' No sooner had the words left the king's mouth than Haman hid his face in
9 despair.*f* Then Harbona, one of the eunuchs in attendance on the king, said, 'At Haman's house stands the gallows, seventy-five feet high, which he himself has prepared for Mordecai, who once served the king well.' 'Hang
10 Haman on it', said the king. So they hanged him on the gallows that he himself had prepared for Mordecai. After that the king's rage abated.

8 On that day King Ahasuerus gave Queen Esther the house of Haman, enemy of the Jews; and Mordecai came into the king's presence, for Esther had told him how he was related
2 to her. Then the king took off his signet-ring, which he had taken back from Haman, and gave it to Mordecai. And Esther put Mordecai in charge of Haman's house.
3 Once again Esther spoke before the king, falling at his feet in tears and pleading with him to avert the calamity planned by Haman the Agagite and to
4 frustrate his plot against the Jews. The king stretched out the golden sceptre to Esther, and she rose and stood before
5 the king, and said, 'May it please your majesty: if I have found favour with you, and if the proposal seems right to your majesty and I have won your approval, let a writ be issued to recall the letters which Haman son of Hammedatha the Agagite wrote in pursuance of his plan to destroy the Jews in all the
6 royal provinces. For how can I bear to see the calamity which is coming upon

my race? Or how can I bear to see the destruction of my family?' Then King 7 Ahasuerus said to Queen Esther and to Mordecai the Jew, 'I have given Haman's house to Esther, and he has been hanged on the gallows, because he threatened the lives of the Jews. Now you shall issue a writ concerning 8 the Jews in my name, in whatever terms you think fit, and seal it with the royal signet; for an order written in the name of the king and sealed with the royal signet cannot be revoked.'

And so, on the twenty-third day of 9 the third month, the month Sivan, the king's secretaries were summoned; and a writ was issued to the Jews, exactly as Mordecai directed, and to the satraps, the governors, and the officers in the provinces from India to Ethiopia, a hundred and twenty-seven provinces, for each province in its own script and for each people in their own language, and also for the Jews in their own script and language. The writ was 10 drawn up in the name of King Ahasuerus and sealed with the royal signet, and letters were sent by mounted couriers riding on horses from the royal stables. By these letters the king 11 granted permission to the Jews in every city to unite and defend themselves, and to destroy, slay, and exterminate the whole strength of any people or province which might attack them, women and children too, and to plunder their possessions, throughout 12 all the provinces of King Ahasuerus, in one day, the thirteenth day of the twelfth month, the month Adar. A 13 copy of the writ was to be issued as a decree in every province and published to all peoples, and the Jews were to be ready for that day, the day of vengeance on their enemies. So the couriers, 14

f Haman . . . despair: prob. rdg.; Heb. they covered Haman's face.

occasioned by the bribe, but *to be destroyed, slain, and exterminated* was intolerable. **9:** *Mordecai, who once served the king well:* Haman has tried to kill a benefactor of the king, and hence all the more merits hanging.

    8.1–17: The calamity averted. 2: The transfer of the *signet-ring* gives Mordecai the same powers as Haman had; see 3.10 n. **5:** Esther emphasizes that the edict against the Jews was from Haman, not the king. **8–17:** Note the general similarity of this passage to 3.9–4.3. The wording in 9–14 is very similar to 3.12–15; the main difference is that it is aimed at the enemies of the Jews. A Persian king would hardly have allowed such a slaughter of his people; this section is not history but theology, legend, emphasizing retributive justice. **9:** *Sivan* is May–June. **10:** Greek writers mention the *horses* of the Persian postal system. **12:** The date is given precisely

mounted on their royal horses, were dispatched post haste at the king's urgent command; and the decree was issued also in Susa the capital city.

15 Mordecai left the king's presence in royal robes of violet and white, wearing a great golden crown and a cloak of fine linen and purple, and all the city 16 of Susa shouted for joy. For the Jews there was light and joy, gladness and 17 honour. In every province and every city reached by the royal command and decree, there was joy and gladness for the Jews, feasting and holiday. And many of the peoples of the land professed themselves Jews, because fear of the Jews had seized them.

9 ON THE THIRTEENTH DAY OF THE twelfth month Adar, the time came for the king's command and his edict to be carried out. The very day on which the enemies of the Jews had hoped to gain the upper hand over them was to become the day when the Jews should gain the upper hand over 2 those who hated them. On that day the Jews united in their cities in all the provinces of King Ahasuerus to fall upon those who had planned their ruin. No one could resist them, because fear 3 of them had seized all peoples. All the officers of the provinces, the satraps and the governors, and all the royal officials, aided the Jews, because fear 4 of Mordecai had seized them. Mordecai had become a great personage in the royal palace; his fame had spread throughout all the provinces as the power of the man grew steadily greater. 5 So the Jews put their enemies to the sword, with great slaughter and destruction; they worked their will on 6 those who hated them. In Susa, the capital city, the Jews killed five hundred 7 men and destroyed them; and they killed also Parshandatha, Dalphon and Aspatha, Poratha, Adalia and Ari-datha, Parmashta, Arisai, Aridai and 8,9 Vaizatha, the ten sons of Haman son 10 of Hammedatha, the enemy of the Jews; but they did not touch the plunder.

11 That day when the number of those killed in Susa the capital city came to the notice of the king, he said to Queen 12 Esther, 'In Susa, the capital city, the Jews have killed and destroyed five hundred men and the ten sons of Haman. What have they done in the rest of the king's provinces? Whatever you ask further will be given to you; whatever more you seek shall be done.' Esther answered him, 'If it please your 13 majesty, let tomorrow be granted to the Jews in Susa to do according to the edict for today; and let the bodies of Haman's ten sons be hung up on the gallows.' The king gave orders for this 14 to be done; the edict was issued in Susa and Haman's ten sons were hung up on the gallows. The Jews in Susa 15 united again on the fourteenth day of the month Adar and killed three hundred men in Susa; but they did not touch the plunder.

16 The rest of the Jews in the king's provinces had united to defend themselves; they took vengeance on*g* their enemies by killing seventy-five thousand of those who hated them; but they did not touch the plunder. This was on the 17 thirteenth day of the month Adar, and they rested on the fourteenth day and made that a day of feasting and joy. The Jews in Susa had united on 18 the thirteenth and fourteenth days of the month, and rested on the fifteenth day and made that a day of feasting and joy. This is why isolated Jews who 19 live in remote villages keep the four-teenth day of the month Adar in joy and feasting, as a holiday on which they send presents of food to one another.

g Prob. rdg.; Heb. got respite from.

since it helps date the Purim festival. **15:** The *crown* is the turban of the vizier. **17:** Some interpret the verse to mean conversion to Judaism; some think not conversion, but only association with the Jews took place; see 9.27. Still others regard the verse as just a literary enhancement of the story.

9.1–32: The inauguration of the feast of Purim. 7: In MT manuscripts the names of Haman's sons are written in a column one under the other, a peculiar arrangement (similar to Josh. 12.9–23); the reason is unknown, but may reflect triumphalism. **10:** The emphasis here and in vv. 15–16 that *they did not touch the plunder,* despite the permission of 8.11, seems to be a deliberate echo of, and dissent from, 1 Sam.15.9–35, the Agag story, in which Israel took plunder, to their harm. **15–19:** These verses explain different customs in the observance of

20 Then Mordecai set these things on record and sent letters to all the Jews in all the provinces of King Ahasuerus, 21 far and near, binding them to keep the fourteenth and fifteenth days of the 22 month Adar, year by year, as the days on which the Jews obtained relief from their enemies and as the month which was changed for them from sorrow into joy, from a time of mourning to a holiday. They were to keep them as days of feasting and joy, days for sending presents of food to one another and gifts to the poor.

23 So the Jews undertook to continue the practice that they had begun in accordance with Mordecai's letter. 24 This they did because Haman son of Hammedatha the Agagite, the enemy of all the Jews, had plotted to destroy the Jews and had cast lots, Pur as it is called, with intent to crush and destroy 25 them. But when the matter came before the king, he issued written orders that the wicked plot which Haman had devised against the Jews should recoil on his own head, and that he and his sons should be hanged on the gallows. 26 Therefore, these days were named Purim after the word Pur. Accordingly, because of all that was written in this letter, because of all they had seen and 27 experienced in this affair, the Jews resolved and undertook, on behalf of themselves, their descendants, and all who should join them, that they would without fail keep these two days as a yearly festival in the prescribed manner 28 and at the appointed time; that these

days should be remembered and kept, generation after generation, in every family, province, and city, that the days of Purim should always be observed among the Jews, and that the memory of them should never cease among their descendants.

29 Queen Esther daughter of Abihail gave full authority in writing to[h] Mordecai the Jew, to confirm this second letter about Purim. 30 Letters wishing peace and security were sent to all the Jews in the hundred and twenty-seven provinces of King Ahasuerus, making the observance of these 31 days of Purim at their appointed time binding on them, as Mordecai the Jew[i] had prescribed. In the same way they had prescribed regulations for fasts and lamentations for themselves and their descendants. 32 The command of Esther confirmed these regulations for Purim, and the record is preserved in writing.

10 King Ahasuerus imposed forced labour on the land and the coasts and 2 islands. All the king's acts of authority and power, and the dignities which he conferred on Mordecai, are written in the annals of the kings of Media and 3 Persia. For Mordecai the Jew was second only to King Ahasuerus; he was a great man among the Jews and was popular with the mass of his countrymen, for he sought the good of his people and promoted the welfare of all their descendants.[j]

[h] *Prob. rdg.; Heb.* and.
[i] *Prob. rdg.; Heb. adds* and Queen Esther.
[j] *Or* and was in friendly relations with all his race.

Purim, city Jews having a two-day celebration but village Jews only one day. **20–32:** This summary of how Purim became part of the Jewish religious calendar seems to be an addition to the book. It is comprised of Mordecai's letter (vv. 20–22), the deliberate resolve of the Jews (vv. 23–28), and the confirmatory letter of Esther and Mordecai (vv. 29–32). **31:** *Fasts:* the date is not specified here, but the thirteenth of Adar, set by Haman for the pogrom (3.13), naturally suggests itself; this date is known in the Jewish calendar as "the fast of Esther."

10.1–3: Conclusion. These verses, also an addition (see 9.20–32 n.), exalt the power of Xerxes and his high elevation of Mordecai.

THE BOOK OF
JOB

In the Book of Job, a gifted poet and theologian examines the problem of a just God allowing the innocent to suffer. While the literary form may be modeled after the Babylonian "discussion literature"—rather than after Greek tragedy, as is sometimes suggested—the story itself possibly derives from an ancient Edomite folktale. External similarities to the Mesopotamian literary works, "The Babylonian Theodicy," "I Will Praise the Lord of Wisdom," and "Man and His God," are worthy of notice, but Job surpasses them in theological depth, human insight, and literary skill.

The structure of the book is as follows: (1) Introduction: a mythological presentation of a meeting in the heavenly court between God and the angels, among whom is Satan (chs. 1–2); (2) Poetic dialogue: the central poem containing three cycles of speeches (chs. 3–31). Into this core have been inserted later additions, namely a hymn on the inaccessibility of Wisdom (ch. 28) and speeches by an extraneous character, Elihu, a spokesman for a later orthodoxy that found the arguments of Job blasphemous (chs. 32–37); (3) Divine resolution (chs. 38–42), including an epilogue (ch. 42).

The poet boldly challenges the Deuteronomist theology that the good man is rewarded with material prosperity and the wicked man punished with temporal suffering. While the merit of this position is acknowledged, the poet creates a dialogue in which Job maintains that man's integrity in the face of disaster must not be sacrificed to social convention, nor even to its established concepts of the deity as upheld by his friends. In the end, Job discovers that his own God as well as that of his friends is too small. Nevertheless, because of his integrity, Job is exonerated and stands before God as intercessor for his friends. And perhaps the key to the book is the view that the suffering righteous man stands in the presence of God.

The date of the writing is most uncertain. The core dialogue (chs. 3.1–31.40; 38.1–42.6) was possibly recorded from older material in the sixth or fifth century B.C. The Elihu material (32.1–37.24) is often viewed as a later addition, and the present prologue (chs. 1–2) regarded as recorded even later.

Prologue

1 THERE LIVED IN THE LAND OF UZ A man of blameless and upright life named Job, who feared God and 2 set his face against wrongdoing. He had seven sons and three daughters; 3 and he owned seven thousand sheep and three thousand camels, five hundred yoke of oxen and five hundred asses, with a large number of slaves. Thus Job was the greatest man in all the East.

4 Now his sons used to foregather and give, each in turn, a feast in his own house; and they used to send and invite their three sisters to eat and drink with them. Then, when a round of feasts 5 was finished, Job sent for his children and sanctified them, rising early in the morning and sacrificing a whole-offering for each of them; for he thought that they might somehow have sinned against God and committed blasphemy in their hearts. This he always did.

The day came when the members of 6 the court of heaven took their places

---

1.1–2.13: The prologue. Job, a devout and prosperous man, is tested for his integrity by calamity and disaster. **1:** *Uz* probably means Edom, although northern Transjordan is possible (see Gen.36.28 and Jer.25.20 for the former and Gen.10.23; 22.21, and 1 Chr.1.17 for the latter). *Blameless:* lit. whole; the import is not sinless perfection. The etymology of the name Job can be "inveterate foe" or else the "penitent one," thus indicating the role of Job and the content of the book. **2:** A family consisting of *seven sons and three daughters* (see Ruth 4.15) was deemed ideal. **3:** The wealth described is that of a seminomadic sheikh (note the absence of such items as precious stones or metal). **4:** The *feast* is possibly to be understood as an annual festival celebration. **5:** *Sanctified:* ceremonial removal of ritual uncleanness in preparation for worship; see Exod.19.15; Lev.11.39–47; Num.11.18. **6:** For the ancients, human events were decided in divine councils; see 1 Kgs.22.19–22; Isa.6.8. *Satan*, lit. "adversary," or "accuser," is apparently a legal term (Ps.109.6), and not yet the proper name for an evil being it was to become later. This title and function possibly derive from the Persian secret police and his duties would compare to those of a district attorney in the United States. He is

in the presence of the LORD, and
7 Satan*a* was there among them. The
LORD asked him where he had been.
'Ranging over the earth', he said, 'from
8 end to end.' Then the LORD asked
Satan, 'Have you considered my servant
Job? You will find no one like him on
earth, a man of blameless and upright
life, who fears God and sets his face
9 against wrongdoing.' Satan answered
the LORD, 'Has not Job good reason
10 to be God-fearing? Have you not
hedged him round on every side with
your protection, him and his family
and all his possessions? Whatever he
does you have blessed, and his herds
11 have increased beyond measure. But
stretch out your hand and touch all
that he has, and then he will curse you
12 to your face.' Then the LORD said to
Satan, 'So be it. All that he has is in
your hands; only Job himself you must
not touch.' And Satan left the LORD's
presence.
13   When the day came that Job's sons
and daughters were eating and drinking
14 in the eldest brother's house, a messenger came running to Job and said,
'The oxen were ploughing and the
15 asses were grazing near them, when the
Sabaeans swooped down and carried
them off, after putting the herdsmen
to the sword; and I am the only one to
16 escape and tell the tale.' While he was
still speaking, another messenger
arrived and said, 'God's fire flashed
from heaven. It struck the sheep and
the shepherds and burnt them up; and
I am the only one to escape and tell
17 tale.' While he was still speaking,
another arrived and said, 'The Chaldaeans, three bands of them, have made
a raid on the camels and carried them
off, after putting the drivers to the
sword; and I am the only one to escape
18 and tell the tale.' While this man was
speaking, yet another arrived and said,
'Your sons and daughters were eating

and drinking in the eldest brother's
house, when suddenly a whirlwind 19
swept across from the desert and struck
the four corners of the house, and it
fell on the young people and killed
them; and I am the only one to escape
and tell the tale.' At this Job stood up 20
and rent his cloak; then he shaved his
head and fell prostrate on the ground,
saying: 21

Naked I came from the womb,
naked I shall return whence I came.
The LORD gives and the LORD takes
        away;
blessed be the name of the LORD.

Throughout all this Job did not sin; 22
he did not charge God with unreason.
   Once again the day came when the **2**
members of the court of heaven took
their places in the presence of the LORD,
and Satan was there among them. The 2
LORD asked him where he had been.
'Ranging over the earth', he said, 'from
end to end.' Then the LORD asked 3
Satan, 'Have you considered my servant
Job? You will find no one like him on
earth, a man of blameless and upright
life, who fears God and sets his face
against wrongdoing. You incited me to
ruin him without a cause, but his
integrity is still unshaken.' Satan 4
answered the LORD, 'Skin for skin!
There is nothing the man will grudge
to save himself. But stretch out your 5
hand and touch his bone and his flesh,
and see if he will not curse you to your
face.'
   Then the LORD said to Satan, 'So be 6
it. He is in your hands; but spare his
life.' And Satan left the LORD's 7
presence, and he smote Job with running sores from head to foot, so that 8
he took a piece of a broken pot to
scratch himself as he sat among the
ashes. Then his wife said to him, 'Are 9
a Or the adversary.

---

the enemy of man, not of God. **10:** *Hedged him round:* the barrier of thorns would keep adversity away from Job's territory (see Hos.2.6 for the figure). **15:** *Sabaeans:* nomads from
Arabia. **16:** The author makes skillful use of a refrain, "*I am the only one . . .*" here and in the
following verses. *God's fire:* lightning. **17:** *Chaldaeans:* the biblical word for Babylonians. The
import here is wandering marauders, not invaders. **19:** *Whirlwind:* a wind much more violent
than the sirocco (*hamsin*). **21:** *The womb* is likened to mother earth. **2.4:** *Skin for skin:* a
proverbial expression meaning "value for value." **7:** It is impossible to determine the illness;
some sort of skin boil is suggested. **9:** Death was not an immediate result of cursing God; the

you still unshaken in your integrity?
Curse God and die!' But he answered,
10 'You talk as any wicked fool of a
woman might talk. If we accept good
from God, shall we not accept evil?'
Throughout all this, Job did not utter
one sinful word.

11   When Job's three friends, Eliphaz of
Teman, Bildad of Shuah, and Zophar
of Naamah, heard of all these calamities
which had overtaken him, they left their
homes and arranged to come and con-
12 dole with him and comfort him. But
when they first saw him from a distance,
they did not recognize him; and they
wept aloud, rent their cloaks and tossed
13 dust into the air over their heads. For
seven days and seven nights they sat
beside him on the ground, and none of
them said a word to him; for they saw
that his suffering was very great.

Job's complaint to God

3 1 2 After this Job broke silence and cursed
the day of his birth:

3   Perish the day when I was born
and the night which said, 'A man is
conceived'!
4   May that day turn to darkness; may
God above not look for it,
nor light of dawn shine on it.
5   May blackness sully it, and murk and
gloom,
cloud smother that day, swift darkness
eclipse its sun.
6   Blind darkness swallow up that night;
count it not among the days of the
year,
reckon it not in the cycle of the
months.
7   That night, may it be barren for ever,
no cry of joy be heard in it.

Cursed be it by those whose magic   8
binds even the monster of the
deep,
who are ready to tame Leviathan
himself with spells.
May no star shine out in its twilight;   9
may it wait for a dawn that never
comes,
nor ever see the eyelids of the
morning,
because it did not shut the doors of   10
the womb that bore me
and keep trouble away from my sight.
Why was I not still-born,   11
why did I not die when I came out
of the womb?
Why was I ever laid on my mother's   12
knees
or put to suck at her breasts?
Why was I not hidden like an   16
untimely birth,
like an infant that has not lived to
see the light?
For then I should be lying in the   13
quiet grave,
asleep in death, at rest,
with kings and their ministers   14
who built themselves palaces,
with princes rich in gold   15
who filled their houses with silver.
There the wicked man chafes no   17[b]
more,
there the tired labourer rests;
the captive too finds peace there   18
and hears no taskmaster's voice;
high and low are there,   19
even the slave, free from his master.

Why should the sufferer be born to   20
see the light?
Why is life given to men who find it
so bitter?
They wait for death but it does not   21
come,

b Verse 16 transposed to follow verse 12.

---

hope here is that death may soon follow. **11:** *Teman:* see Jer.49.7 n. *Shuah:* perhaps Edom or
Arabia (see Gen.25.2; 1 Chr.1.32). *Naamah:* an unknown place (but see Josh.15.41).
    3.1–26: Job's complaint to God. Two subtle links unite the poetry with the folk narrative,
namely the curse (which is against Job's day of birth rather than God) and an ironic reference
to God's hedging in of Job on all sides (1.10), now no longer a sign of favor (v. 23). **1:** Compare
Jer.20.14–18. **8:** Astrologers and magicians were reputed to have dominance, by means of
incantations, over the dragon of chaos, *Leviathan;* the mythological monster, mentioned
frequently in Canaanite literature, plays a prominent role in Israelite poetry as the embodiment
of disorder (Job 7.12; 9.13 n.; Pss.74.13–14; 104.26; Isa.27.1, etc.). In the Babylonian
creation story, the god Marduk slays the monster. **12:** The repeated *why* (vv. 12,16,20,23)
shows Job confused over the meaning of his suffering but not questioning the justice of God.
His friends raise that issue (4.7–9). **13:** The positive attitude toward Sheol (see 7.9 n.) as pro-

they seek it more eagerly than^c hidden treasure.

They are glad when they reach the tomb,
and when they come to the grave they exult.

23 Why should a man be born to wander blindly,
hedged in by God on every side?

24 My sighing is all my food,
and groans pour from me in a torrent.

25 Every terror that haunted me has caught up with me,
and all that I feared has come upon me.

26 There is no peace of mind nor quiet for me;
I chafe in torment and have no rest.

First cycle of speeches

4 Then Eliphaz the Temanite began:

2 If one ventures to speak with you, will you lose patience?
For who could hold his tongue any longer?

3 Think how once you encouraged those who faltered,
how you braced feeble arms,

4 how a word from you upheld the stumblers
and put strength into weak knees.

5 But now that adversity comes upon you, you lose patience;
it touches you, and you are unmanned.

6 Is your religion no comfort to you?
Does your blameless life give you no hope?

7 For consider, what innocent man has ever perished?

Where have you seen the upright destroyed?

This I know, that those who plough   8
mischief and now trouble
reap as they have sown;
they perish at the blast of God   9
and are shrivelled by the breath of his nostrils.

The roar of the lion, the whimpering   10
of his cubs, fall silent;
the teeth of the young lions are broken;
the lion perishes for lack of prey   11
and the whelps of the lioness are abandoned.

A word stole into my ears,   12
and they caught the whisper of it;
in the anxious visions of the night,   13
when a man sinks into deepest sleep,
terror seized me and shuddering;   14
the trembling of my body frightened me.

A wind brushed my face   15
and made the hairs bristle on my flesh;
and a figure stood there whose shape   16
I could not discern,
an apparition loomed before me,
and I heard the sound of a low voice:
'Can mortal man be more righteous   17
than God,
or the creature purer than his Maker?
If God mistrusts his own servants   18
and finds his messengers at fault,
how much more those that dwell in   19
houses whose walls are clay,
whose foundations are dust,
which can be crushed like a bird's nest

c *Or* seek it among . . .

---

viding anticipated rest is in contrast to the Semite's usual fear of the underworld and underlines Job's present misery. **23:** *Hedged in:* see 3.1–26 n.
4.1–14.22: First cycle of speeches.
4.1–5.27: Eliphaz's first speech. Gently Eliphaz broaches the central ideas that will recur throughout the friends' speeches: man cannot be more righteous than God, and even celestial beings have no claim to purity in God's sight. **2:** Note the courtesy here. "The Babylonian Theodicy," a somewhat similar work, is replete with politeness, even while the argument is vehement. Eliphaz is not above harsh innuendo (vv. 5–7) and even open attack (vv. 8–9). **7:** The view expressed that the righteous do not suffer is an implied slur, a vicious one, and Job is later (12.4) portrayed responding to it. (See the similar formulations in Ps.37.25, Prov. 12.22, Ecclus.2.10, etc.) **12–21:** The appeal to subjective *visions of the night* is a subtle admission that the Wisdom tradition which drew its conclusions from empirical evidence had no cogent answer to suffering. The *visions* are in the tradition of professional prophecy which was at this time in disrepute. See Ezek.13.6–16. **18:** *Messengers*. angels. **19:** *Houses:* the human body. In later literature, e.g. Wis.9.15, there is development of the idea in this verse, there influenced by

20 or torn down between dawn and dark,
how much more shall such men
      perish outright and unheeded,
21 *d*die, without ever finding wisdom?'

5 Call if you will; is there any to
      answer you?
To which of the holy ones will you
      turn?
2 The fool is destroyed by his own
      angry passions,
and the end of childish resentment is
      death.
3 I have seen it for myself: a fool
      uprooted,
his home in sudden ruin about him,*e*
4 his children past help,
browbeaten in court with none to
      save them.
5 *f*Their rich possessions are snatched
      from them;
what they have harvested others
      hungrily devour;
the stronger man seizes it from the
      panniers,
panting, thirsting for their wealth.
6 Mischief does not grow out of the
      soil
nor trouble spring from the earth;
7 man is born to trouble,
as surely as birds fly*g* upwards.

8 For my part, I would make my
      petition to God
and lay my cause before him,
9 who does great and unsearchable
      things,
marvels without number.
10 He gives rain to the earth
and sends water on the fields;
11 he raises the lowly to the heights,
the mourners are uplifted by victory;
12 he frustrates the plots of the crafty,
and they win no success,
13 he traps the cunning in their
      craftiness,
and the schemers' plans are thrown
      into confusion.

In the daylight they run into   14
      darkness,
and grope at midday as though it
      were night
He saves the destitute from their   15
      greed,
and the needy from the grip of the
      strong;
so the poor hope again,   16
and the unjust are sickened.

Happy the man whom God rebukes! 17
therefore do not reject the discipline
      of the Almighty.
For, though he wounds, he will bind 18
      up;
the hands that smite will heal.
You may meet disaster six times, and 19
      he will save you;
seven times, and no harm shall touch
      you.
In time of famine he will save you   20
      from death,
in battle from the sword.
You will be shielded from the lash   21
      of slander,*h*
and when violence comes you need
      not fear.
You will laugh at violence and   22
      starvation
and have no need to fear wild beasts;
for you have a covenant with the   23
      stones to spare your fields,
and the weeds have been constrained
      to leave you at peace.
You will know that all is well with   24
      your household,
you will look round your home and
      find nothing amiss;
you will know, too, that your   25
      descendants will be many
and your offspring like grass, thick
      upon the earth.
You will come in sturdy old age to   26
      the grave

d Prob. rdg.; transposing Their rich possessions are
snatched from them *to follow 5. 4.*
e ruin about him: *prob. rdg.; Heb. obscure.*
f Line transposed from 4. 21. g Or as sparks shoot.
h from . . . slander: *or* when slander is rife.

strands of Greek thought in which anything material was devalued. **5.1:** *Holy ones:* members of
the heavenly court; see 1.6 n. **2:** This verse quotes or paraphrases a proverb like 29.11. **4:** The
word translated *court* means "gates"; justice was administered at the gates of the city. **17:**
Divine *discipline* of man, *musar* in Heb., is emphasized by Elihu in 33.14–30; 36.7–15. **18:** The
theme of discipline as a means of education and correction is frequent in Wisdom literature;
see Ecclus.4.17; 32.14. The *Almighty* himself will heal Job if he does *not reject* his suffering
as a correction for his evil-doing. **19:** *Six . . . seven:* a frequent numerical device meaning
"totality." It originates from the pattern of poetic parallelism. **23:** Job's acceptance of correction
will insure a *covenant*, i.e. harmony, with the *stones* and *weeds* since they too obey God. Stones

as sheaves come in due season to
    the threshing-floor.

27 We have inquired into all this, and
    so it is;
    this we have heard, and you may
        know it for the truth.

6 Then Job answered:

2 O that the grounds for my resentment
        might be weighed,
    and my misfortunes set with them on
        the scales!
3 For they would outweigh the sands
        of the sea:
    what wonder if my words are wild?[i]
4 The arrows of the Almighty find their
        mark in me,
    and their poison soaks into my spirit;
    God's onslaughts wear me away.
5 Does the wild ass bray when he has
        grass
    or the ox low when he has fodder?
6 Can a man eat tasteless food
        unseasoned with salt,
    or find any flavour in the juice of
        mallows?
7 Food that should nourish me sticks
        in my throat,
    and my bowels rumble with an
        echoing sound.

8 O that I might have my request,
    that God would grant what I hope
        for:
9 that he would be pleased to crush me,
    to snatch me away with his hand and
        cut me off!
10 For that would bring me relief,
    and in the face of unsparing anguish
    I would leap for joy.[j]
11 Have I the strength to wait?
    What end have I to expect, that I
        should be patient?

12 Is my strength the strength of stone,
    or is my flesh bronze?
13 Oh how shall I find help within
        myself?
    The power to aid myself is put out
        of my reach.

14 Devotion is due from his friends
    to one who despairs and loses faith
        in the Almighty;
15 but my brothers have been
        treacherous as a mountain
        stream,
    like the channels of streams that
        run dry,
16 which turn dark with ice
    or are hidden with piled-up snow;
17 or they vanish the moment they are
        in spate,
    dwindle in the heat and are gone.
18 Then the caravans, winding hither
        and thither,
    go up into the wilderness and
        perish;[k]
19 the caravans of Tema look for their
        waters,
    travelling merchants of Sheba hope
        for them;
20 but they are disappointed, for all
        their confidence,
    they reach them only to be balked.
21 So treacherous have you now been
        to me:[l]
    you felt dismay and were afraid.
22 Did I ever say, 'Give me this or that;
    open your purses to save my life;
23 rescue me from my enemy;
    ransom me out of the hands of
        ruthless men'?
24 Tell me plainly, and I will listen in
        silence;

[i] *what ... wild?: or therefore words fail me.*
[j] *Prob. rdg.; Heb. adds* I have not denied the words
   of the Holy One.
[k] *Or and are lost.*
[l] *So ... to me: prob. rdg.; Heb. obscure.*

are the bane of the Palestinian fields whose soil is very shallow. **27**: Eliphaz here reinforces his earlier mention of God's way and discipline (12–17) by an appeal to what he has learned from experience.
6.1–7.21: Job's answer. His distress has come from God, unjustly. He will not abstain from expressing his bitterness. **3–12:** Job's *wild words* are as involuntary and physical as the lowing of an ox when hungry, for his flesh is not *bronze*. **4:** While fire *arrows* were used in the Ancient Near East, there is no OT evidence of poison arrows outside this verse. The metaphor of God as an archer occurs frequently (Deut.32.23; Ezek.5.16; Ps.7.13). **15–20:** Streams in Palestine rush into the plain filled with water from *mountain* rain and *snow* but quickly lose themselves as they *run dry* in the *heat* and sand of the desert. One who follows their banks in security suddenly finds himself without water. **22–23:** Job does not ask his friend to take any risks to

show me where I have erred.

25 How harsh are the words of the
upright man!
What do the arguments of wise
men[m] prove?

26 Do you mean to argue about words
or to sift the utterance of a man
past hope?

27 Would you assail an orphan[n]?
Would you hurl yourselves on a
friend?

28 So now, I beg you, turn and look at
me:
am I likely to lie to your faces?

29 Think again, let me have no more
injustice;
think again, for my integrity is in
question.

30 Do I ever give voice to injustice?
Does my sense not warn me when
my words are wild?

7 Has not man hard service on earth,
and are not his days like those of a
hired labourer,

2 like those of a slave longing for the
shade
or a servant kept waiting for his
wages?

3 So months of futility are my portion,
troubled nights are my lot.

4 When I lie down, I think,
'When will it be day that I may rise?'
When the evening grows long and I
lie down,
I do nothing but toss till morning
twilight.

5 My body is infested with worms,
and scabs cover my skin.[o]

6 My days are swifter than a shuttle[p]
and come to an end as the thread
runs out.[q]

7 Remember, my life is but a breath of
wind;
I shall never again see good days.

Thou wilt behold me no more with a 8
seeing eye;
under thy very eyes I shall disappear.

As clouds break up and disperse, 9
so he that goes down to Sheol never
comes back;

he never returns home again, 10
and his place will know him no more.[r]

But I will not hold my peace; 11
I will speak out in the distress of my
mind
and complain in the bitterness of my
soul.

Am I the monster of the deep, am I 12
the sea-serpent,
that thou settest a watch over me?

When I think that my bed will 13
comfort me,
that sleep will relieve my
complaining,

thou dost terrify me with dreams 14
and affright me with visions.

I would rather be choked outright; 15
I would prefer death to all my
sufferings.

I am in despair, I would not go on 16
living;
leave me alone, for my life is but a
vapour.

What is man that thou makest much 17
of him
and turnest thy thoughts towards
him,

only to punish him morning by 18
morning
or to test him every hour of the day?

Wilt thou not look away from me for 19
an instant?

Wilt thou not let me be while I
swallow my spittle?

If I have sinned, how do I injure 20
thee,

m wise men: *prob. rdg.; Heb. unintelligible.*
n *Or* a blameless man.
o *Prob. rdg.; Heb. adds* it is cracked and discharging.
p *Or* a fleeting odour. q as . . . out: *or without hope.*
r *Or* and he will not be noticed any more in his place.

---

save his *life*, he asks only for compassion. **26–27:** Job accuses his friends of being heartless with a man in despair and of a power play against an *orphan*, a helpless *friend*. **7.1–6:** Job universalizes his experience. **1:** *Service:* the image seems to derive from military duty. **6:** As a shuttle runs out of thread, so Job's life is being emptied of hope. **9:** *Sheol:* the netherworld. **12:** Job, here addressing God, in effect is saying: "Am I a threat to divine order like the chaos *monster* (see 3.8 n) who requires constant surveillance?" **17–18:** The traditional sublime celebration of God's concern for man (see Ps.8) here becomes a parody, for Job wishes God to abstain from taking thought of him; beneficent providence has been replaced by divine harassment. **19–21:** Job finds even God's gaze oppressive. He declares that it is unworthy of God to punish a fragile being like man, even though he be guilty, since he does not *injure* God. **20:** *Watcher of the hearts of men* is meant as a rebuke, not as adoration.

thou watcher of the hearts of men?
Why hast thou made me thy butt,
and why have I become thy target?

21 Why dost thou not pardon my
　　offence
and take away my guilt?
But now I shall lie down in the
　　grave;
seek me, and I shall not be.

8 Then Bildad the Shuhite began:

2 How long will you say such things,
the long-winded ramblings of an old
　　man?

3 Does God pervert judgement?
Does the Almighty pervert justice?

4 Your sons sinned against him,
so he left them to be victims of their
　　own iniquity.

5 If only you will seek God betimes
and plead for the favour of the
　　Almighty,

6 if you are innocent and upright,
then indeed will he watch over you
and see your just intent fulfilled.

7 Then, though your beginnings were
　　humble,
your end will be great.

8 Inquire now of older generations
and consider the experience of their
　　fathers;

9 for we ourselves are of yesterday and
are transient;
our days on earth are a shadow.

10 Will not they speak to you and teach
　　you
and pour out the wisdom of their
　　hearts?

11 Can rushes grow where there is no
　　marsh?
Can reeds flourish without water?

12 While they are still in flower and
　　not ready to cut,*s*
they wither earlier than*t* any green
　　plant.

13 Such is the fate of all who forget
　　God;
the godless man's life-thread breaks
　　off;

14 his confidence is gossamer,
and the ground of his trust a
　　spider's web.

15 He leans against his house but it
　　does not stand;
he clutches at it but it does not hold
　　firm.

16 His is the lush growth of a plant in
　　the sun,
pushing out shoots over the garden;

17 but its roots become entangled in a
　　stony patch
and run against a bed of rock.

18 Then someone uproots it from its
　　place,
which*u* disowns it and says, 'I have
　　never known you.'

19 That is how its life withers away,
and other plants spring up from
　　the earth.

20 Be sure, God will not spurn the
　　blameless man,
nor will he grasp the hand of the
　　wrongdoer.

21 He will yet fill your mouth with
　　laughter,
and shouts of joy will be on your
　　lips;

22 your enemies shall be wrapped in
　　confusion,
and the tents of the wicked shall
　　vanish away.

s and . . . cut: *or* they are surely cut.
t Or wither like . . .
u Or and.

8.1–22: Bildad's first speech, an appeal not to his own experience, but to that of the race of man. 4: Compare the accusation against Job's children with their innocence in 1.4–5. 5–7: Picking up Job's mention of God's watchfulness (7.19), Bildad assures Job that innocence coupled with repentance will lead to restoration. 8–10: Lessons, distilled from experience, that have stood the test of time and the scrutiny of the ancients are more worthy to be considered *wisdom* than the subjective experience that is still in flux like *a shadow*. 8–9: See 8.1–22 n. Lessons derived from experience are preserved by the wise. 11–13: The law of retribution is as certain as the order of nature. 14–19: Neither the root nor the fruit, i.e. house, of a wicked man's life has sufficient substance to give security. 17: The metaphor of plants growing in stony ground is also used in Mk.4.3–9. 20: To *grasp the hand* is a symbol of divine election to a favored position and of support in it; see Isa.42.6; 51.18. 21–22: God *will fill your mouth with laughter . . . and the tents of the wicked shall vanish away*. Thus, after his earlier harsh criticism of Job, Bildad softens his tone and assures him that God will be just after all if he, Job, will change his attitude.

9 Then Job answered:

2 Indeed this I know for the truth,
   that no man can win his case against
      God.
3 If a man chooses to argue with him,
   God will not answer one question
      in a thousand.*v*
4 He is wise, he is powerful;
   what man has stubbornly resisted him
      and survived?
5 It is God who moves mountains,
      giving them no rest,
   turning them over in his wrath;
6 who makes the earth start from its
      place
   so that its pillars are convulsed;
7 who commands the sun's orb not to
      rise
   and shuts up the stars under his seal;
8 who by himself spread out the
      heavens
   and trod on the sea-monster's back;*w*
9 who made Aldebaran and Orion,
   the Pleiades and the circle of the
      southern stars;
10 who does great and unsearchable
      things,
   marvels without number.

11 He passes by me, and I do not see
      him;
   he moves on his way undiscerned by
      me;
12 if he hurries on, who can bring him
      back?
   Who will ask him what he does?
13 God does not turn back his wrath;
   the partisans of Rahab lie prostrate
      at his feet.
14 How much less can I answer him

or find words to dispute with him?
Though I am right, I get no answer,   15
   though I plead with my accuser for
      mercy.
If I summoned him to court and he   16
      responded,
I do not believe that he would listen
      to my plea—
for he bears hard upon me for a   17
      trifle
and rains blows on me without
      cause;
he leaves me no respite to recover   18
      my breath
but fills me with bitter thoughts.
If the appeal is to force, see how   19
      strong he is;
if to justice, who can compel him to
      give me a hearing?
Though I am right, he condemns me   20
      out of my own mouth;
though I am blameless, he twists my
      words.
Blameless, I say; of myself   21
I reck nothing, I hold my life cheap
But it is all one; therefore I say,   22
   'He destroys blameless and wicked
      alike.'
When a sudden flood brings death,   23
   he mocks the plight of the innocent.
The land is given over to the power   24
      of the wicked,
and the eyes of its judges are
      blindfold.*x*

My days have been swifter than a   25
      runner,

v If a man . . . thousand: or If God is pleased to argue with him, man cannot answer one question in a thousand.
w Or on the crests of the waves.
x Prob. rdg.; Heb. adds if not he, then who?

9.1–10.22: Job's response. The praise of God's majesty (5–10) gives way (9.11–10.22) to an accusation of divine malice of intent; Job feels the necessity (9.33–35) of calling in an arbitrator between himself and God. **3:** The phrase "one in a thousand" is a hyperbole; see also Eccles. 7.28. **5–10:** The so-called "doxologies" in Amos 4.13; 5.8–9; 9.5–6 are strikingly similar to this hymn. **5:** *Move mountains:* earthquake. These are often described as accompanying a theophany, e.g. Judg.5.4. **6:** *Pillars:* the seven columns supporting the cosmic house (see Prov.9.1). **7:** The *sun's orb* does *not rise* and the *stars* are *under a seal* at God's command in an overcast sky. **8:** Note Tfn. *w,* "crests of the waves." **9:** The precise identity of these constellations is uncertain. **10:** See 5.9. Job's praise of God's grandeur here seems to surpass that of Eliphaz in a similar hymn in 5.9–16. **11–12:** God cannot be accosted or called into question in any way. **13:** *Rahab:* in folklore the mythological ocean-chaos monster, elsewhere called Leviathan or Tannin, slain by the deity (compare 26.12; Isa.51.9; Ps.89.10). In Isa.30.7 and Ps.87.4 Rahab and Egypt are identified. **14–20:** An imaginary courtroom, with God pictured as judge and prosecuting attorney. **15:** *Right:* innocent. That is, even when the verdict of innocence is pronounced, Job must beg for mercy. **19:** Here the crucial point is made that God is a law unto himself (Jer.12.1). **20–24:** These bitter verses indict God's governing of the universe as callous indifference, if not malevolence. Job here abandons the basic premise of all ancient wisdom, namely, an order sustained by the Creator. **20:** Job, despite his innocence,

they have slipped away and seen no
   prosperity;
26 they have raced by like reed-built
   skiffs,
   swift as vultures swooping on carrion.
27 If I think, 'I will forget my griefs,
   I will show a cheerful face and smile',
28 I tremble in every nerve;*y*
   I know that thou wilt not hold me
     innocent.
29 If I am to be accounted guilty,
   why do I labour in vain?
30 Though I wash myself with soap
   or cleanse my hands with lye,
31 thou wilt thrust me into the mud
   and my clothes will make me
     loathsome.

32 He is not a man as I am, that I can
     answer him
   or that we can confront one another
     in court.
33 If only there were one to arbitrate
     between us
   and impose his authority on us both,
34 so that God might take his rod from
     my back,
   and terror of him might not come on
     me suddenly.
35 I would then speak without fear of
     him;
   for I know I am not what I am
     thought to be.

10 I am sickened of life;
   I will give free rein to my griefs,
   I will speak out in bitterness of soul.
2 I will say to God, 'Do not condemn
     me,
   but tell me the ground of thy
     complaint against me.
3 Dost thou find any advantage in
     oppression,
   in spurning the fruit of all thy labour
   and smiling on the policy of wicked
     men?
4 Hast thou eyes of flesh

or dost thou see as mortal man sees?
Are thy days as those of a mortal 5
or thy years as the life of a man,
that thou lookest for guilt in me 6
and dost seek in me for sin,
though thou knowest that I am 7
     guiltless
and have none to save me from thee?

'Thy hands gave me shape and made 8
     me;
and dost thou at once turn and
     destroy me?
Remember that thou didst knead me 9
     like clay;
and wouldst thou turn me back into
     dust?
Didst thou not pour me out like milk 10
and curdle me like cheese,
clothe me with skin and flesh 11
and knit me together with bones and
     sinews?
Thou hast given me life and 12
     continuing favour,
and thy providence has watched over
     my spirit.
Yet this was the secret purpose of 13
     thy heart,
and I know that this was thy intent:
that, if I sinned, thou wouldst be 14
     watching me
and wouldst not acquit me of my
     guilt.
If I indeed am wicked, the worse for 15
     me!
If I am righteous, even so I may lift
     up my head;*z*
if I am proud as a lion, thou dost 16
     hunt me down
and dost confront me again with
     marvellous power;
thou dost renew thy onslaught upon 17
     me,
and with mounting anger against me
bringest fresh forces to the attack.

y Or I am afraid of all that I must suffer.
z Prob. rdg.; Heb. adds filled with shame and steeped
in my affliction.

---

has no defense against God's power. **30–31:** The image of sin as filth is frequent, e.g. Zech.3.3–5.
32–35: Job pleads that he be allowed to present his case as a man without being compared to
God and without having to deal with his awesome might and holiness which he acknowledges.
An arbitrator could bring this about and Job will call for him again; see 16.21. **34:** The divine
rod is here no comfort; contrast Ps.23.4. **10.2:** *Complaint:* that is, a lawsuit. This figure of
speech is common, especially in prophetic literature. **4–7:** For God to hunt for sin in Job is to
act like another man who sees only the externals without understanding the depths of human
life. God should try to understand man's limitations and predicaments. **13–22:** God, in granting
man life, constantly scrutinizes him for his guilt or innocence. So relentlessly does he punish
man that it seems better for man not to have been born—unless he has some respite.

18 Why didst thou bring me out of the womb?
    O that I had ended there and no eye had seen me,
19 that I had been carried from the womb to the grave
    and were as though I had not been born.
20 Is not my life short and fleeting?
    Let me be, that I may be happy for a moment,
21 before I depart to a land of gloom, a land of deep darkness, never to return,
22 a land of gathering shadows, of deepening darkness,
    lit by no ray of light,*a* dark*b* upon dark.'

11 Then Zophar the Naamathite began:

2   Should this spate of words not be answered?
    Must a man of ready tongue be always right?
3   Is your endless talk to reduce men to silence?
    Are you to talk nonsense and no one rebuke you?
4   You claim that your opinions are sound;
    you say to God, 'I am spotless in thy sight.'
5   But if only he would speak
    and open his lips to talk with you,
6   and expound to you the secrets of wisdom,
    for wonderful are its effects!
    [Know then that God exacts from you less than your sin deserves.]
7   Can you fathom the mystery of God,
    can you fathom the perfection of the Almighty?
8   It is higher than heaven; you can do nothing.
    It is deeper than Sheol; you can know nothing.

9   Its measure is longer than the earth and broader than the sea.
10 If he passes by, he may keep secret his passing;
    if he proclaims it, who can turn him back?
11 He surely knows which men are false, and when he sees iniquity, does he not take note of it?*c*
12 Can a fool grow wise?
    can a wild ass's foal be born a man?
13 If only you had directed your heart rightly
    and spread out your hands to pray to him!
14 If you have wrongdoing in hand, thrust it away;
    let no iniquity make its home with you.
15 Then you could hold up your head without fault,
    a man of iron, knowing no fear.
16 Then you will forget your trouble;
    you will remember it only as flood-waters that have passed;
17 life will be lasting, bright as noonday,
    and darkness will be turned to morning.
18 You will be confident, because there is hope;
    sure of protection, you will lie down in confidence;*d*
19 great men will seek your favour.
20 Blindness will fall on the wicked;
    the ways of escape are closed to them,
    and their hope is despair.

Then Job answered: **12**

2   No doubt you are perfect men*e*
    and absolute wisdom is yours!
3   But I have sense as well as you;
    in nothing do I fall short of you;

a lit . . . light: or a place of disorder.
b Prob. rdg.; Heb. obscure.
c does . . . of it? or he does not stand aloof.
d Prob. rdg.; Heb. adds and you will lie down unafraid.
e Prob. rdg.; Heb. No doubt you are people.

11.1–20: Zophar's first speech. He rebukes Job for presuming to understand God's unfathomable character, and exhorts Job to repent. **11:** In Exod.32.32 and Mal.3.16–18 the mention of divine record keeping is quite explicit. Late Judaism embellished this idea. **12:** Apparently a popular proverb. Some scholars suggest a change of MT, altering *born a man* to "come to learn." **13–20:** The rewards for repentance are great; hence, Job should repent for his sins.

12.1–14.22: Job's response. He is no less wise than his friends, for even dumb animals understand shallow matters. To lie on behalf of God is wrong, and will be punished no less. Let God directly confront Job and let Job speak. Man is frail and has only one life to live; why, then, is God so severe? **2:** *Perfect men and absolute wisdom:* the words are sarcastic. See also 13.2.

what gifts indeed have you that others
have not?

4 Yet I am a laughing-stock to my
friend—
a laughing-stock, though I am
innocent and blameless,
one that called upon God, and he
answered.*f*

5 Prosperity and ease look down on
misfortune,
on the blow that fells the man who
is already reeling,

6 while the marauders' tents are left
undisturbed
and those who provoke God live safe
and sound.*g*

7 Go and ask the cattle,
ask the birds of the air to inform
you,

8 or tell the creatures that crawl to
teach you,
and the fishes of the sea to give you
instruction.

9 Who cannot learn from all these
that the LORD's own hand has done
this?

11*h* (Does not the ear test what is
spoken
as the palate savours food?

12 There is wisdom, remember, in age,
and long life brings understanding.)

10 In God's hand are the souls of all
that live,
the spirits of all human kind.

13 Wisdom and might are his,
with him are firmness and
understanding.

14 If he pulls down, there is no
rebuilding;
if he imprisons, there is no release.

15 If he holds up the waters, there is
drought;
if he lets them go, they turn the land
upside down.

16 Strength and success belong to him,
deceived and deceiver are his to use.

He makes counsellors behave like   17
idiots
and drives judges mad;
he looses the bonds imposed by   18
kings
and removes the girdle of office from
their waists;
he makes priests behave like idiots   19
and overthrows men long in office;
those who are trusted he strikes   20
dumb,
he takes away the judgement of old
men;
he heaps scorn on princes   21
and abates the arrogance of nobles.
He leads peoples astray and destroys   23*i*
them,
he lays them low, and there they lie.
He takes away their wisdom from   24
the rulers of the nations
and leaves them wandering in a
pathless wilderness;
they grope in the darkness without   25
light
and are left to wander like a
drunkard.
He uncovers mysteries deep in   22
obscurity
and into thick darkness he brings
light.

All this I have seen with my own eyes, **13**
with my own ears I have heard it, and
understood it.
What you know, I also know;   2
in nothing do I fall short of you.
But for my part I would speak with   3
the Almighty
and am ready to argue with God,
while you like fools are smearing   4
truth with your falsehoods,
stitching a patchwork of lies, one and
all.
Ah, if you would only be silent   5
and let silence be your wisdom!

f Or and he afflicted me.
*g Prob. rdg.; Heb. adds He brings it in full measure
to whom he will (cp. 21. 17).*
h Verse 10 transposed to follow verse 12.
i Verse 22 transposed to follow verse 25.

4–6: As in society everywhere it is much easier to make a scapegoat of a helpless person for some
trivial fault than to confront a powerful person for a serious wrong. **7–9:** Job observes that such
profound knowledge as his visitors have shown is known to the lowest creatures. **9:** LORD:
Nowhere else in Job (except at 28.28) does the poetry use the divine name Yahweh, whereas the
prose prologue and epilogue employ it regularly. *Hand has done this:* compare Isa.41.20.
12: Some interpreters regard this not as a statement but as an ironic question: "Is there wisdom
in old age, and does long life bring understanding?" **10,13–25:** The fate which God decrees for
man or nations is not subject to alteration, and his causality is all-pervasive. **13.5:** In Egyptian

6 Now listen to my arguments
and attend while I put my case.

7 Is it on God's behalf that you speak
so wickedly,
or in his defence that you allege what
is false?

8 Must you take God's part,
or put his case for him?

9 Will all be well when he examines
you?
Will you quibble with him as you
quibble with a man?

10 He will most surely expose you
if you take his part by falsely accusing
me.

11 Will not God's majesty strike you
with dread,
and terror of him overwhelm you?

12 Your pompous talk is dust and ashes,
your defences will crumble like clay.

13 Be silent, leave me to speak my mind,
and let what may come upon me!

14 I will put my neck in the noose
and take my life in my hands.

15 If he would slay me, I should not
hesitate;
I should still argue my cause to his
face.

16 This at least assures my success,
that no godless man may appear
before him.

17 Listen then, listen to my words,
and give a hearing to my exposition.

18 Be sure of this: once I have stated my
case
I know that I shall be acquitted.

19 Who is there that can argue so
forcibly with me
that he could reduce me straightway
to silence and death?

20 Grant me these two conditions only,
and then I will not hide myself out
of thy sight:

21 take thy heavy hand clean away
from me
and let not the fear of thee strike me
with dread.

22 Then summon me, and I will answer;

or I will speak first, and do thou
answer me.

23 How many iniquities and sins are
laid to my charge?
let me know my offences and my sin.

24 Why dost thou hide thy face
and treat me as thy enemy?

25 Wilt thou chase a driven leaf,
wilt thou pursue dry chaff,

26 prescribing punishment for me
and making me heir to the iniquities
of my youth,

27 putting my feet in the stocks*j*
and setting a slave-mark on the
arches of my feet?*k*

14 Man born of woman is short-lived
and full of disquiet.

2 He blossoms like a flower and then
he withers;
he slips away like a shadow and does
not stay;
*l*he is like a wine-skin that perishes
or a garment that moths have eaten.

3 Dost thou fix thine eyes on such a
creature,
and wilt thou bring him into court
to confront thee?*m*

5 The days of his life are determined,
and the number of his months is
known to thee;
thou hast laid down a limit, which
he cannot pass.

6 Look away from him therefore and
leave him alone
counting the hours day by day like
a hired labourer.

7 If a tree is cut down,
there is hope that it will sprout again
and fresh shoots will not fail.

8 Though its roots grow old in the
earth,
and its stump is dying in the ground,

j Prob. rdg.; Heb. adds keeping a close watch on all
I do.
k Prob. rdg.; Heb. adds verse 28, he is like . . . have
eaten, *now transposed to follow 14. 2.*
l he is like . . . have eaten: *13. 28 transposed here.*
m So one Heb. MS.; others add (4) Who can produce
pure out of unclean? No one.

Wisdom literature "the silent one" is an epithet for the sage, as over against "the passionate one."
7–12: Job's friends are accused of defending God with lies. **10:** Job here argues on the basis of a
just God, an idea he has previously rejected. **15:** An older (and traditional) translation incorrectly
renders the verse as expressive of unflagging trust in God: "Though he slay me, I shall wait for
him." **15–16:** Some interpreters view this passage as the key to the book, namely, confidence
that no sinner can stand before God; since God later appears to him, Job is vindicated. **27:** For
purposes of tracking a runaway slave, *marks* were cut on the bottoms of his feet. **14.1–22:** Man's

9 if it scents water it may break into
   bud
   and make new growth like a young
   plant.

10 But a man dies, and he disappears;[n]
   man comes to his end, and where is
   he?

11 As the waters of a lake dwindle,
   or as a river shrinks and runs dry,

12 so mortal man lies down, never to
   rise
   until the very sky splits open.
   If a man dies, can he live again?[o]
   He shall never be roused from his
   sleep.

13 If only thou wouldst hide me in
   Sheol
   and conceal me till thy anger turns
   aside,
   if thou wouldst fix a limit for my time
   there, and then remember me!

14 [p]Then I would not lose hope,
   however long my service,
   waiting for my relief to come.

15 Thou wouldst summon me, and I
   would answer thee;
   thou wouldst long to see the
   creature thou hast made.

16 But now thou dost count every step
   I take,
   watching all my course.

17 Every offence of mine is stored in
   thy bag;
   thou dost keep my iniquity under
   seal.

18 Yet as a falling mountain-side is
   swept away,
   and a rock is dislodged from its
   place,

19 as water wears away stones,
   and a rain-storm scours the soil from
   the land,

so thou hast wiped out the hope of
frail man;
thou dost overpower him finally, and 20
he is gone;
his face is changed, and he is
banished from thy sight.
His flesh upon him becomes black,   22[q]
and his life-blood dries up within
him.[r]
His sons rise to honour, and he sees 21
nothing of it;
they sink into obscurity, and he
knows it not.

Second cycle of speeches

Then Eliphaz the Temanite answered: **15**

Would a man of sense give vent to   2
such foolish notions
and answer with a bellyful of wind?
Would he bandy useless words   3
and arguments so unprofitable?
Why! you even banish the fear of   4
God from your mind,
usurping the sole right to speak in
his presence;
your iniquity dictates what you say,   5
and deceit is the language of your
choice.
You are condemned out of your own   6
mouth, not by me;
your own lips give evidence against
you.

Were you born first of mankind?   7
were you brought forth before the
hills?

n *Or and is powerless.*
o *Line transposed from beginning of verse 14.*
p *See note on verse 12.* q *Verses 21 and 22 transposed.*
r *His flesh . . . within him: or His own kin, maybe,*
regret him, and his slaves mourn his loss.

---

life is limited and his death is his end. **12:** *Until the sky splits open* is here a symbol of the hope-lessness of a person ever returning from Sheol. It is not an apocalyptic symbol for the end of the world and the resurrection from the dead. **13:** Job sees his plight as a temporary *anger* on God's part which would abate if he could but escape God's sight. Since in Israelite belief God was absent from Sheol, Job asks to be hidden there for a fixed time, rather than in death from which he can *never be roused*. **15:** Job recognizes that God could love him since he could long to see him, *his creature;* therefore the underlying principle of the relationship to God is not justice but love. **17:** *Bag:* tiny stones may have been used for counting sheep; the bag, then, connotes tabulation and recording (see 11.11 n.). **20:** A person's *face is changed* either in anger, fear, or consternation; compare Dan.5.6,9,10. **22:** *Flesh* turned *black* is a sign of catastrophe and great mourning; see 30.30; Lam.5.10.
   15.1–21.34: Second cycle of speeches.
   15.1–35: Eliphaz's second speech. Offended by Job's contentions, Eliphaz asserts that the apparent prosperity of the wicked is only temporary, and then disaster strikes them. Job is accused of despising the three basic institutions of Israel's religious life: wisdom (vv. 2–3), piety (vv. 4–5), and prophecy (v. 11). **4:** There is no Heb. term for "religion." *Fear of God*

8 Do you listen in God's secret council
   or usurp all wisdom for yourself
       alone?
9 What do you know that we do not
       know?
   What insight have you that we do not
       share?
10 We have age and white hairs in our
       company,
   men older than your father.
11 Does not the consolation of God
       suffice you,
   a word whispered quietly in your ear?
12 What makes you so bold at heart,
   and why do your eyes flash,
13 that you vent your anger on God
   and pour out such a torrent of
       words?
14 What is frail man that he should be
       innocent,
   or any child of woman that he should
       be justified?
15 If God puts no trust in his holy ones,
   and the heavens are not innocent in
       his sight,
16 how much less so is man, who is
       loathsome and rotten
   and laps up evil like water!

17 I will tell you, if only you will listen,
   and I will describe what I have seen
18 [what has been handed down by
       wise men
   and was not concealed from them by
       their fathers;
19 to them alone the land was given,
   and no foreigner settled among
       them]:
20 the wicked are racked with anxiety
       all their days,
   the ruthless man for all the years in
       store for him.
21 The noise of the hunter's scare rings
       in his ears,
   and in time of peace the raider falls
       on him;

22 he cannot hope to escape from dark
       death;
   he is marked down for the sword;
23 he is flung out as food for vultures;
   such a man knows that his
       destruction is certain.
24 Suddenly a black day comes upon
       him,
   distress and anxiety overwhelm him
   [like a king ready for battle];
25 for he has lifted his hand against God
   and is pitting himself against the
       Almighty,
26 charging him head down,
   with the full weight of his bossed
       shield.

27 Heavy though his jowl is and gross,
   and though his sides bulge with fat,
28 the city where he lives will lie in
       ruins,
   his house will be deserted;
   it will soon become a heap of rubble.
29 He will no longer be rich, his wealth
       will not last,
   and he will strike no root in the
       earth;*
30 scorching heat will shrivel his shoots,
   and his blossom will be shaken off
       by the wind.
31 He deceives himself, trusting in his
       high rank,
   for all his dealings will come to
       nothing.
32 His palm-trees will wither
       unseasonably,
   and his branches will not spread;
33 he will be like a vine that sheds its
       unripe grapes,
   like an olive-tree that drops its
       blossom.
34 For the godless, one and all, are
       barren,
   and their homes, enriched by
       bribery, are destroyed by fire;

s Prob. rdg.; Heb. adds he will not escape from darkness.

---

is a near equivalent. **8:** *Council:* see 1.6 n. **10:** Job is apparently younger than his visitors; he has not reached the age of a grandfather. **11:** Suffering is seen as an occasion for a mystical experience of a message from God, bringing its own *consolation.* **14:** This verse is not directly related to the later doctrine of original sin but maintains that man is already subject to sin at birth. **16:** Perhaps this is a proverb describing man's evil propensity. **18:** In the Egyptian book "Instructions" also much is made of the necessity of handing down the teachings of the wise from one generation to another. **20–24:** Pangs of conscience and fear of *dark death* were considered to be the hidden punishments of the wicked who seemed to prosper. **29–34:** The traditional teaching held that the wicked who seemed to prosper would *strike no root in the earth* either by being *barren* or through losing their children by sudden death, like *blossoms shaken off by the wind;* see Ps.109.12–13.

35   they conceive mischief and give birth
          to trouble,
      and the child of their womb is deceit.

16 Then Job answered:

2   I have heard such things often before,
      you who make trouble, all of you,
          with every breath,
      saying, 'Will this windbag never have
3   done?
      What makes him so stubborn in
          argument?'
4   If you and I were to change places,
      I could talk like you;
      how I could harangue you
      and wag my head at you!
5   But no, I would speak words of
          encouragement,
      and then my condolences would flow
          in streams.
6   If I speak, my pain is not eased;
      if I am silent, it does not leave me.
7   Meanwhile, my friend wearies me
          with false sympathy;
8   they tear me to pieces, he and his[t]
          fellows.
      He has come forward to give
          evidence against me;
      the liar testifies against me to my
          face,
9   in his wrath he wears me down, his
          hatred is plain to see;
      he grinds his teeth at me.

      My enemies look daggers at me,
10   they bare their teeth to rend me,
      they slash my cheeks with knives;
      they are all in league against me.
11   God has left me at the mercy of
          malefactors
      and cast me into the clutches of
          wicked men.
12   I was at ease, but he set upon me
          and mauled me,
      seized me by the neck and worried me.
      He set me up as his target;
13   his arrows rained upon me from
          every side;

pitiless, he cut deep into my vitals,
he spilt my gall on the ground.
He made breach after breach in my   14
    defences;
he fell upon me like a fighting man.

I stitched sackcloth together to   15
    cover my body
and I buried my forelock in the dust;
my cheeks were flushed with weeping 16
and dark shadows were round my
    eyes,
yet my hands were free from violence 17
and my prayer was sincere.

O earth, cover not my blood   18
and let my cry for justice find no
    rest!
For look! my witness is in heaven;   19
there is one on high ready to answer
    for me.
My appeal will come before God,   20
while my eyes turn again and again
    to him.
If only there were one to arbitrate   21
    between man and God,
as between a man and his neighbour!
For there are but few years to come   22
before I take the road from which I
    shall not return.

My mind is distraught, my days are   **17**
    numbered,
and the grave is waiting for me.
Wherever I turn, men taunt me,   2
and my day is darkened by their
    sneers.
Be thou my surety with thyself,   3
for who else can pledge himself for
    me?
Thou wilt not let those men triumph,   4
whose minds thou hast sunk in
    ignorance;
if such a man denounces his friends   5
    to their ruin,
his sons' eyes shall grow dim.

I am held up as a byword in every   6
    land,

t Prob. rdg.; Heb. my.

16.1–17.16: Job's answer laments the lack of sympathy and understanding in his friends and
repeats that his disaster has come from God. **4:** To *wag the head* was a sign of gloating over the
misfortune of another; see Mt.27.39–40. **9:** *Grinds his teeth:* a sign of scornful hatred and
hostility; see Lam.2.16; Pss.35.16; 37.12. **15:** *Sackcloth . . . and dust:* signs of grief and mourning; see Ezek.27.30–31. **18:** According to Gen.4.10–11 spilled *blood* of an innocent victim cries
out to the Lord of Justice (see also Jonah 1.14). **17.3:** This is a key sentence in which Job shows

a portent for all to see;

7 my eyes are dim with grief,
my limbs wasted to a shadow.

8 Honest men are bewildered at this,
and the innocent are indignant at my
plight.

9 In spite of all, the righteous man
maintains his course,
and he whose hands are clean grows
strong again.

10 But come on, one and all, try again!
I shall not find a wise man among
you.

11 My days die away like an echo;
my heart-strings*u* are snapped.

12 Day is turned into night,
and morning*v* light is darkened
before me.

13 If I measure Sheol for my house,
if I spread my couch in the darkness,

14 if I call the grave my father
and the worm my mother or my
sister,

15 where, then, will my hope be,
and who will take account of my
piety?

16 I cannot take them down to Sheol
with me,
nor can they descend with me into
the earth.

18 Then Bildad the Shuhite answered:

2 How soon will you bridle*w* your
tongue?
Do but think, and then we will talk.

3 What do you mean by treating us as
cattle?
Are we nothing but brute beasts to
you?*x*

4 Is the earth to be deserted to prove
you right,

or the rocks to be moved from their
place?

5 No, it is the wicked whose light is
extinguished,
from whose fire no flame will rekindle;

6 the light fades in his tent,
and his lamp dies down and fails him.

7 In his iniquity his steps totter,
and his disobedience trips him up;

8 he rushes headlong into a net
and steps through the hurdle that
covers a pit;

9 his heel is caught in a snare,
the noose grips him tight;

10 a cord lies hidden in the ground for
him
and a trap in the path.

11 The terrors of death suddenly beset
him
and make him piss over his feet.

12 For all his vigour he is paralysed
with fear;
strong as he is, disaster awaits him.

13 Disease eats away his skin,
Death's eldest child devours his
limbs.

14 He is torn from the safety of his
home,
and Death's terrors escort him to
their king.*y*

15 Magic herbs lie strewn about his tent,
and his home is sprinkled with
sulphur to protect it.

16 His roots beneath dry up,
and above, his branches wither.

17 His memory vanishes from the face
of the earth
and he leaves no name in the world.

18 He is driven from light into darkness
and banished from the land of the
living.

u Prob. rdg.; Heb. the desires of my heart.
v morning: prob. rdg.; Heb. near.
w bridle: prob. rdg.; Heb. unintelligible.
x Prob. rdg.; Heb. adds rending himself in his anger.
y Or and you conduct him to the king of terrors.

---

his faith by asking God to be Job's pledge with the deity, as he had stated in 16.19–20. **9:** Some
interpreters view this verse as a later pious addition, others as a sarcastic quotation of his
friends' view. **15–16:** A bitter comment that both hope and piety disappear at a man's death.
   18.1–21: Bildad's second speech. The sinner, dying horribly, leaves neither positive memory
nor progeny. **2:** The *you* is plural in the MT, as if the author is addressing the wicked in general.
4: The allegation is that Job seeks an alteration in the order of nature just to vindicate him.
5–6: *Light* here is a figure for the life-force in man (see also Prov.13.9; 20.20; 24.20). **13–14:** Far
from being a place of rest and even solace, Sheol can be a constant terror; see 26.5–6. *Death's
eldest child:* this seems to reflect mythology and to allude to Mot, the Canaanite god of death.
Perhaps, though, *eldest child* is a fatal illness, or the fear of dying. **15:** Such practices, to cure
diseases, or restore ritual purity, are familiar from Canaanite and Mesopotamian texts. The
verse seems to hearken back to v. 13.

19 He leaves no issue or offspring
        among his people,
    no survivor in his earthly home;
20 in the west men hear of his doom
        and are appalled;
    in the east they shudder with horror.
21 Such is the fate of the dwellings of
        evildoers,
    and of the homes of those who care
        nothing for God.

19 Then Job answered:

2 How long will you exhaust me
    and pulverize me with words?
3 Time and time again you have
        insulted me
    and shamelessly done me wrong.
4 If in fact I had erred,
    the error would still be mine.
5 But if indeed you lord it over me
    and try to justify the reproaches
        levelled at me,
6 I tell you, God himself has put me
        in the wrong,
    he has drawn the net round me.
7 If I cry 'Murder!' no one answers;
    if I appeal for help, I get no justice.
8 He has walled in my path so that I
        cannot break away,
    and he has hedged in the road before
        me.
9 He has stripped me of all honour
    and has taken the crown from my
        head.
10 On every side he beats me down and
        I am gone;
    he has pulled up my tent-rope^z like
        a tree.
11 His anger is hot against me
    and he counts me his enemy.
12 His raiders gather in force^a
    and encamp about my tent.

13 My brothers hold aloof from me,
    my friends are utterly estranged from
        me;

my kinsmen and intimates fall away,   14-15
    my retainers have forgotten me;
my slave-girls treat me as a stranger,
    I have become an alien in their eyes.
I summon my slave, but he does not   16
        answer,
    though I entreat him as a favour.
My breath is noisome to my wife,   17
    and I stink in the nostrils of my own
        family.
Mere children despise me   18
    and, when I rise, turn their backs on
        me;
my intimate companions loathe me,   19
    and those whom I love have turned
        against me.
My bones stick out through my   20
        skin,^b
    and I gnaw my under-lip with my
        teeth.

Pity me, pity me, you that are my   21
        friends;
    for the hand of God has touched me.
Why do you pursue me as God   22
        pursues me?
    Have you not had your teeth in me
        long enough?
O that my words might be inscribed,   23
O that they might be engraved in an
        inscription,
cut with an iron tool and filled with   24
        lead
to be a witness^c in hard rock!
But in my heart I know that my   25
        vindicator lives
and that he will rise last to speak in
        court;
and I shall discern my witness   26
        standing at my side^d
    and see my defending counsel, even
        God himself,
whom I shall see with my own eyes,   27
    I myself and no other.

z *Or* he has uprooted my hope.
a *Prob. rdg.; Heb. adds* they raise an earthwork against
me.
b *Prob. rdg.; Heb. adds* and my flesh.
c to . . . witness: *or* for ever.
d my witness . . . side: *prob. rdg.; Heb. unintelligible.*

19.1–29: Job's reply. He describes eloquently the wrongs done him by God (1–23), yet a
vindicator will emerge to defend him: God himself. **3:** *Time and time:* "ten times" in Heb.
17: The allusion to family, if taken literally, stands in tension with the earlier passage (1.18–19)
reporting the death of his children. **23–24:** Job wants his words to be *engraved* on a *rock*
so that his case may be judged by others who are more honest than his friends. For
inscription filled with lead, compare Behistun stone. **25:** In ancient *court* trials the witness for
the defense stood at the accused person's right *side* and the accuser stood at his left; compare
Ps.109.31. The rendering here, *in court*, is an interpretation of the MT "on the dust." **26–27:**
These verses are so poorly preserved that it is impossible to discern the exact meaning. It is

28 My heart failed me when you said,
'What a train of disaster he has
brought on himself!
The root of the trouble lies in him.'
29 Beware of the sword that points at
you,
the sword that sweeps away all
iniquity;
then you will know that there is a
judge.*e*

20 Then Zophar the Naamathite answered:

2 My distress of mind forces me to
reply,
and this is why*f* I hasten to speak:
3 I have heard arguments that are a
reproach to me,
a spirit beyond my understanding
gives me the answers.
4 Surely you know that this has been so
since time began,
since man was first set on the earth:
5 the triumph of the wicked is short-
lived,
the glee of the godless lasts but a
moment?
6 Though he stands high as heaven,
and his head touches the clouds,
7 he will be swept utterly away like his
own dung,
and all that saw him will say, 'Where
is he?'
8 He will fly away like a dream and be
lost,
driven off like a vision of the night;
9 the eye which glimpsed him shall do
so no more
and shall never again see him in his
place.
11*g* The youth and strength which filled
his bones
shall lie with him in the dust.
10 His sons will pay court to the poor,
and their*h* hands will give back his
wealth.

12 Though evil tastes sweet in his
mouth,
and he savours it, rolling it round
his tongue,
13 though he lingers over it and will not
let it go,
and holds it back on his palate,
14 yet his food turns in his stomach,
changing to asps' venom within him.
15 He gulps down wealth, then vomits
it up,
or God makes him discharge it.
16 He sucks the poison of asps,
and the tongue of the viper kills him.
17 Not for him to swill down rivers of
cream*i*
or torrents of honey and curds;
18 he must give back his gains without
swallowing them,
and spew up his profit undigested;
19 for he has hounded and harassed the
poor,
he has seized houses which he did not
build.
20 Because his appetite gave him no rest,
and he cannot escape his own desires,
21 nothing is left for him to eat,
and so his well-being does not last;
22 with every need satisfied his troubles
begin,
and the full force of hardship strikes
him.
23 God vents his anger upon him
and rains on him cruel blows.
24 He is wounded by weapons of iron
and pierced by a bronze-tipped
arrow;
25 out at his back the point comes,
the gleaming tip from his gall-bladder.
26 Darkness unrelieved awaits him,
a fire that needs no fanning will
consume him.
[Woe betide any survivor in his tent!]
27 The heavens will lay bare his guilt,

e Or judgement.
f this is why: *prob. rdg.; Heb. obscure.*
g Verses 10 and 11 transposed.
h Prob. rdg.; Heb. his.
i rivers of cream: *prob. rdg.; Heb. obscure.*

clear, however, that Job expresses his certainty that somehow and somewhere he will be shown
to have been innocent. **28–29:** His friends will in time be punished for their false accusations.
See 42.7.
20.1–29: Zophar's second speech. The bad fate of the wicked is certain, with short-lived
triumph giving way to extreme punishment. **2–3:** *Beyond my understanding:* not human
experience or that of the race (5.27 and 8.8–10), but a supernatural *spirit* is said to guide his
words. **16:** *Poison:* a figure of speech. **26:** For a similar threat on *darkness*, see 18.18. On a
punishing fire, see Pss.21.9 and 140.10. **27:** Compare Deut.31.28.

and earth will rise up to condemn
    him.
28 A flood will sweep away his house,
    rushing waters on the day of wrath.
29 Such is God's reward for the wicked
    man
    and the lot appointed for the rebel*j*
      by God.

21 Then Job answered:

2 Listen to me, do but listen,
    and let that be the comfort you offer
      me.
3 Bear with me while I have my say;
    when I have finished, you may mock.
4 May not I too voice*k* my thoughts?
    Have not I as good cause to be
      impatient?
5 Look at my plight, and be aghast;
    clap your hand to your mouth.
6 When I stop to think, I am filled
      with horror,
    and my whole body is convulsed.

7 Why do the wicked enjoy long life,
    hale in old age, and great and
      powerful?
8 They live to see their children settled,
    their kinsfolk and descendants
      flourishing;
9 their families are secure and safe;
    the rod of God's justice does not
      reach them.
10 Their bull mounts and fails not of
      its purpose;
    their cow calves and does not
      miscarry.
11 Their children like lambs run out to
      play,
    and their little ones skip and dance;
12 they rejoice with tambourine and
      harp
    and make merry to the sound of the
      flute.
13 Their lives close in prosperity,
    and they go down to Sheol in peace.
14 To God they say, 'Leave us alone;
    we do not want to know your ways.

What is the Almighty that we should 15
    worship him,
or what should we gain by seeking
    his favour?'

Is not the prosperity of the wicked 16
    in their own hands?
Are not their purposes very
    different from God's*l*?
How often is the lamp of the wicked 17
    snuffed out,
and how often does their ruin come
    upon them?
How often does God in his anger deal
    out suffering,
bringing it in full measure to whom
    he will?*m*
How often is that man like a wisp of 18
    straw before the wind,
like chaff which the storm-wind
    whirls away?
You say, 'The trouble he has earned, 19
    God will keep for his sons';
no, let him be paid for it in full and
    be punished.
Let his own eyes see damnation come 20
    upon him,
and the wrath of the Almighty be the
    cup he drinks.
What joy shall he have in his 21
    children after him,
if his very months and days are
    numbered?
Can any man teach God, 22
God who judges even those in heaven
    above?

One man, I tell you, dies crowned 23
    with success,
lapped in security and comfort,
his loins full of vigour 24
and the marrow juicy in his bones;
another dies in bitterness of soul 25
and never tastes prosperity;
side by side they are laid in earth, 26
and worms are the shroud of both.

j the rebel: prob. rdg.; Heb. his word.
k May . . . voice: prob. rdg.; Heb. obscure.
l God's: prob. rdg.; Heb. mine.
m Line transposed from 12. 6.

21.1–34: Job's answer. Against his friends' arguments, Job asserts that the wicked do prosper,
and only rarely undergo misfortune. **14–15:** The wicked presume to scorn God. **16:** Job appears
to quote his friends' words (e.g. 18.5–21) only to refute them. **19–20:** Against Zophar's argument
(20.10, echoing Exod.34.7) that the punishment of the wicked is visited on *his sons*, Job demands
a justice in which the wicked *drinks* the *cup* of his own punishment; see Jer.31.29; Ezek.18.2–4.
22: Perhaps this verse is a gloss, or else irony. It could, however, be an expression of despair

27 I know well what you are thinking
and the arguments you are
marshalling against me;

28 I know you will ask, 'Where is the
great man's home now,
what has become of the home of the
wicked?'

29 Have you never questioned
travellers?
Can you not learn from the signs
they offer,

30 that the wicked is spared when
disaster comes
and conveyed to safety before the
day of wrath?

31 No one denounces his conduct to
his face,
no one requites him for what he
has done.

32–33 When he is carried to the grave,
all the world escorts him, before and
behind;
the dust of earth is sweet to him,
and thousands keep watch at his
tomb.

34 How futile, then, is the comfort you
offer me!
How false your answers ring!

Third cycle of speeches

22 Then Eliphaz the Temanite answered:

2 Can man be any benefit to God?
Can even a wise man benefit him?

3 Is it an asset to the Almighty if you
are righteous?
Does he gain if your conduct is
perfect?

4 Do not think that he reproves you
because you are pious,
that on this count he brings you to
trial.

5 No: it is because you are a very
wicked man,
and your depravity passes all
bounds.

6 Without due cause you take a brother
in pledge,
you strip men of their clothes and
leave them naked.

7 When a man is weary, you give him
no water to drink
and you refuse bread to the hungry.

8 Is the earth, then, the preserve of
the strong
and a domain for the favoured
few?

9 Widows you have sent away empty-
handed,
orphans you have struck defenceless.

10 No wonder that there are pitfalls in
your path,
that scares are set to fill you with
sudden fear.

11 The light is turned into darkness, and
you cannot see;
the flood-waters cover you.

12 Surely God is at the zenith of the
heavens
and looks down on all the stars, high
as they are.

13 But you say, 'What does God
know?
Can he see through thick darkness to
judge?

14 His eyes cannot pierce the curtain of
the clouds
as he walks to and fro on the vault of
heaven.'

15 Consider the course of the wicked
man,
the path the miscreant treads:

16 see how they are carried off before
their time,
their very foundation flowing away
like a river;

---

over the necessity to instruct God in elementary human justice. **27–34:** *Arguments:* their syllogism is that God is pleased with goodness; he favors the good man; therefore, the good man fares well. The broadest human experience refutes such arguments, so that their comfort of him (v. 34) is futile. **28:** See 2.21; 8.22. **30:** Contrast 20.28; Prov.16.4; Rom.2.5.
    22.1–27.23: Third cycle of speeches.
    22.1–30: Eliphaz's third speech. He insists that Job has definitely trespassed, perhaps in mistreating widows and orphans (vv. 5–7) and has thought that a thick cloud shielded him from God's eyes (12–14). Hence Job must repent (21–30). **2–3:** God has no need of any man, even the *wise* or the *righteous* (see 35.7), and hence can have no ulterior motive for punishing Job. **6:** *Clothes:* a poor man's outer garment taken in pledge had to be returned by nightfall, since it was his protection from the cold (Exod.22.26; Deut.24.10–13). **9:** *Widows* and *orphans* are frequently linked together in the OT; their cause is also championed in the Hammurabi code, Canaanite texts, Egyptian wisdom literature (Amen-em-ope). **14:** The *vault of heaven* was

17 these men said to God, 'Leave us
        alone;
   what can the Almighty do to us?'
18 Yet it was he that filled their houses
        with good things,
   although their purposes and his were
        very different.
19 The righteous see their fate and
        exult,
   the innocent make game of them;
20 for their riches are swept away,
   and the profusion of their wealth is
        destroyed by fire.

21 Come to terms with God and you
        will prosper;
   that is the way to mend your
        fortune.
22 Take instruction from his mouth
   and store his words in your heart.
23 If you come back to the Almighty in
        true sincerity,
   if you banish wrongdoing from your
        home,
24 if you treat your precious metal as
        dust*n*
   and the gold of Ophir as stones from
        the river-bed,
25 then the Almighty himself will be
        your precious metal;
   he will be your silver in double
        measure.
26 Then, with sure trust in*o* the
        Almighty,
   you will raise your face to God;
27 you will pray to him, and he will hear
        you,
   and you will have cause to fulfil your
        vows.
28 In all your designs you will
        succeed,
   and light will shine on your path;
29 but God brings down the pride of
        the haughty*p*
   and keeps safe the man of modest
        looks.
30 He will deliver the innocent,*q*
   and you will be delivered, because
        your hands are clean.

Then Job answered: **23**

My thoughts today are resentful,   2
for God's hand is heavy on me in my
        trouble.
If only I knew how to find him,   3
how to enter his court,
I would state my case before him   4
and set out my arguments in full;
then I should learn what answer he   5
        would give
and find out what he had to say.
Would he exert his great power to   6
        browbeat me?
No; God himself would never bring
        a charge against me.
There the upright are vindicated   7
        before him,
and I shall win from my judge an
        absolute discharge.
If I go forward,*r* he is not there;   8
if backward,*s* I cannot find him;
when I turn*t* left,*u* I do not descry   9
        him;
I face right,*v* but I see him not.
But he knows me in action or at rest;   10
when he tests me, I prove to be gold.
My feet have kept to the path he has   11
        set me,
I have followed his way and not
        turned from it.
I do not ignore the commands that   12
        come from his lips,
I have stored in my heart what he
        says.
He decides,*w* and who can turn him   13
        from his purpose?
He does what his own heart desires.
What he determines, that he carries   14
        out;
his mind is full of plans like these.
Therefore I am fearful of meeting   15
        him;

n *Prob. rdg.; Heb.* if you put your precious metal on
dust.
o with . . . in: *or* delighting in.
p but . . . haughty: *prob. rdg.; Heb. obscure.*
q *Prob. rdg.; Heb.* the not innocent.
r *Or* east.   s *Or* west.
t *Prob. rdg.; Heb.* he turns.
u *Or* north.   v *Or* south.
w He decides: *prob. rdg.; Heb.* He in one.

regarded as if it were solid; see Ezek.1.22 n.; Gen.1.6. **21:** *Come to terms:* be reconciled.
24: *Ophir:* the proverbial source of *gold*, identified differently as India, south Arabia, or South
Africa.
    23.1–24.25: Job's answer. If only it were possible to encounter God in a court of law, Job
would emerge vindicated by God himself, for he is innocent; in a true court of law, the wicked
are convicted. **2:** *God's hand* was thought *heavy* when a person was struck with disease or other
tragedy; see 1 Sam.5.6–7; Ps.32.3–4. **3–6:** The view that God is hidden or is hiding is a frequent

when I think about him,[x] I am afraid;

16 it is God who makes me faint-hearted
and the Almighty who fills me with
fear,

17 yet I am not reduced to silence by
the darkness
nor[y] by the mystery which hides him.

24 [z]The day of reckoning is no secret to
the Almighty,
though those who know him have no
hint of its date.

2 Wicked men move boundary-stones
and carry away flocks and their
shepherds.

6[a] In the field they reap what is not
theirs,
and filch the late grapes from the
rich[b] man's vineyard.

3 They drive off the orphan's ass
and lead away the widow's ox with
a rope.

9 They snatch the fatherless infant from
the breast
and take the poor man's child in
pledge.

4 They jostle the poor out of the way;
the destitute huddle together, hiding
from them.

5 The poor rise early like the wild ass,
when it scours the wilderness for
food;
but though they work till nightfall,[c]
their children go hungry.[d]

7 Naked and bare they pass the night;
in the cold they have nothing to cover
them.

8 They are drenched by rain-storms
from the hills
and hug the rock, their only shelter.

10 Naked and bare they go about their
work,
and hungry they carry the sheaves;

11 they press the oil in the shade where
two walls meet,
they tread the winepress but
themselves go thirsty.

12 Far from the city, they groan like
dying men,
and like wounded men they cry out;

but God pays no heed to their prayer.

Some there are who rebel against the 13
light of day,
who know nothing of its ways
and do not linger in the paths of
light.

The murderer rises before daylight 14
to kill some miserable wretch.[e]

The seducer watches eagerly for 15
twilight,
thinking, 'No eye will catch sight of
me.'

The thief prowls[f] by night,[g]
his face covered with a mask,
and in the darkness breaks into 16
houses
which he has marked down in the
day.

One and all,[h] they are strangers to
the daylight,
but dark night is morning to them; 17
and in the welter of night they are at
home.

Such men are scum on the surface of 18
the water,
their fields have a bad name
throughout the land,
and no labourer will go near their
vineyards.

As drought and heat make away with 19
snow,
so the waters of Sheol[i] make away
with the sinner.

The womb forgets him, the worm 20
sucks him dry;
he will not be remembered ever
after.[j]

He may have wronged the barren 21
childless woman
and been no help to the widow;

x when . . . him: or I stand aloof.
y yet I am not . . . nor: or indeed I am . . . and . . .
z Prob. rdg.; Heb. prefixes Why.
a Verses 3–9 re-arranged to restore the natural order.
b Or wicked.
c Prob. rdg.; Heb. Arabah.
d go hungry: prob. rdg.; Heb. to it food.
e See note on verse 15.
f The thief prowls: prob. rdg.; Heb. Let him be like a
thief.
g Line transposed from end of verse 14.
h One and all: transposed from after but in next verse.
i snow . . . Sheol: prob. rdg.; Heb. snow-water, Sheol.
j Prob. rdg.; Heb. here adds iniquity is snapped like
a stick (see note on verse 24).

theme in the OT; see, e.g. Isa.6.11–64.2 and Ps.22.1–2. **17:** *Mystery:* lit. thick darkness.
24.1–17: The misdeeds of the wicked. **24.1:** Only God knows when the *day of reckoning,* that is,
the death, of each individual is to come. **13:** *Light of day* is a sign of uprightness having a
real connection with it; see Ps.97.11; Prov.4.18–19. **18–25:** Some interpreters believe these
verses belong with 27.11–23; see 27.11–23 n. The third cycle of speeches is apparently preserved
in great disorder. **21:** *Barren, childless:* see the similar repetition intoned in Isa.54.1, this to

22 yet God in his strength carries off
    even the mighty;
they may rise, but they have no firm
    hope of life.

23 He lulls them into security and
    confidence;
but his eyes are fixed on their ways.

24 For a moment they rise to the
    heights, but are soon gone;
iniquity is snapped like a stick.*k*
They are laid low and wilt like a
    mallow-flower;
they droop like an ear of corn on the
    stalk.

25 If this is not so, who will prove me
    wrong
and make nonsense of my argument?

25 Then Bildad the Shuhite answered:

2 Authority and awe rest with him
who has established peace in his realm
    on high.

3 His squadrons are without number;
at whom will they not spring from
    ambush?

4 How then can a man be justified in
    God's sight,
or one born of woman be innocent?

5 If the circling moon is found wanting,
and the stars are not innocent in his
    eyes,

6 much more so man who is but a
    maggot,
mortal man who is only a worm.

26 Then Job answered:

2 What help you have given to the man
    without resource,
what deliverance you have brought
    to the powerless!

3 What counsel you offer to a man at
    his wit's end,

what sound advice to the foolish!
Who has prompted you to say such   4
    things,
and whose spirit is expressed in your
    speech?

In the underworld the shades writhe   5
    in fear,
the waters and all that live in them
    are struck with terror.*l*
Sheol is laid bare,   6
and Abaddon uncovered before
    him.
God spreads the canopy of the sky   7
    over chaos
and suspends earth in the void.
He keeps the waters penned in dense   8
    cloud-masses,
and the clouds do not burst open
    under their weight.
He covers the face of the full
    moon,*m*   9
unrolling his clouds across it.
He has fixed the horizon on the   10
    surface of the waters
at the farthest limit of light and
    darkness.
The pillars of heaven quake   11
and are aghast at his rebuke.
With his strong arm he cleft the sea-   12
    monster,
and struck down the Rahab by his
    skill.
At his breath the skies are
    clear,   13
and his hand breaks the twisting*n*
    sea-serpent.
These are but the fringe of his
    power;   14
and how faint the whisper that we
    hear of him!
[Who could fathom the thunder of
    his might?]

k Line transposed from end of verse 20.
l are struck with terror: prob. rdg.; Heb. om.
m Or He overlays the surface of his throne.
n Or primeval.

intensify the poetic effect of the passage. **23:** God is often pictured as seducing men into mistaken confidence in themselves (compare Jer.20.7; Isa.6.9–10), especially through false prophets (Ezek.14.9).
    25.1–6: Bildad's third speech. So brief is this speech, and so little new is in it, that some interpreters believe that a part of it has been lost, or that 26.5–14 continues it. **3:** *Squadrons:* of angels.
    26.1–27.10: Job's reply. Anger moves Job to wish upon his friends the fate of the wicked; again he reminds them that a sinner would never challenge God to a trial. **2–4:** The irony here is remarkably bitter. **5–14:** Perhaps Bildad's speech. See 25.1–6 n. **6:** *Abaddon:* another name for Sheol, meaning place of "destruction" (see Prov.15.11). **7:** *Canopy:* lit. *zaphon*, i.e. the north, the mythological dwelling of heavenly beings, especially those hostile to Israel; compare

27 Then Job resumed his discourse:

2 I swear by God, who has denied me
      justice,
  and by the Almighty, who has filled
      me with bitterness:
3 so long as there is any life left in me
  and God's breath is in my nostrils,
4 no untrue word shall pass my lips
  and my tongue shall utter no
      falsehood.
5 God forbid that I should allow you
      to be right;
  till death, I will not abandon my
      claim to innocence.
6 I will maintain the rightness of my
      cause, I will never give up;
  so long as I live, I will not change.

7 May my enemy meet the fate of the
      wicked,
  and my antagonist the doom of the
      wrongdoer!
8 What hope has a godless man, when
      he is cut off,[o]
  when God takes away his life?
9 Will God listen to his cry
  when trouble overtakes him?
10 Will he trust himself to the Almighty
   and call upon God at all times?

11 I will teach you what is in God's
      power,
   I will not conceal the purpose of the
      Almighty.
12 If all of you have seen these things,
   why then do you talk such empty
      nonsense?

13 This is the lot prescribed by God for
      the wicked,
   and the ruthless man's reward from
      the Almighty.
14 He may have many sons, but they
      will fall by the sword,

and his offspring will go hungry;
the survivors will be brought to the   15
      grave by pestilence,
and no widows will weep for them.
He may heap up silver like dirt   16
and get himself piles of clothes;
he may get them, but the righteous   17
      will wear them,
and his silver will be shared among
      the innocent.
The house he builds is flimsy as a   18
      bird's nest
or a shelter put up by a watchman.
He may lie down rich one day, but   19
      never again;
he opens his eyes and all is gone.
Disaster overtakes him like a flood,   20
and a storm snatches him away in
      the night;
the east wind lifts him up and he is   21
      gone;
it whirls him far from home;
it flings itself on him without mercy,   22
and he is battered and buffeted by
      its force;
it snaps its fingers at him   23
and whistles over him wherever he
      may be.

God's unfathomable wisdom

There are mines for silver   **28**
and places where men refine gold;
where iron is won from the earth   2
and copper smelted from the ore;
the end of the seam lies in darkness,   3
and it is followed to its farthest limit.[p]
Strangers cut the galleries;[q]   4
they are forgotten as they drive
      forward far from men.[r]

o *Or* What is a godless man's thread of life when it
is cut . . .
p *Prob. rdg.; Heb. adds* stones of darkness and deep
darkness.
q Strangers . . . galleries: *prob. rdg.; Heb. obscure.*
r *Prob. rdg.; Heb. adds* languishing without foothold.

Isa.14.13; Ezek.39.2. **27.1:** *Resumed:* only here is a speech interrupted. Perhaps this verse is a consequence of the disorder in the third cycle of speeches and is a copyist's note identifying what ensues as a continuation of 26.1–14. **2:** Despite his accusations, Job swears by the accused deity.
   27.11–23: The lot of the wicked. Some interpreters believe that this is part, or all of Zophar's third speech; if not, then strangely there is no third speech by Zophar. Note that ch. 28 is almost universally regarded as an interpolation into the book, indicative of disorder in the text. The description of the fate of the wicked comes very close to Job's own situation. **20:** *Flood* (Heb. *kamayim*): a slight change in the Heb. would substitute *yōman*, "by day," yielding a better parallel for *in the night*.
   28.1–28: God's unfathomable wisdom. This poem is probably a later addition; it marvels at man's ingenuity in extracting precious ore hidden in the heart of the earth but his inability

5 While corn is springing from the
      earth above,
   what lies beneath is raked over like a
      fire,
6 and out of its rocks comes lapis lazuli,
      dusted with flecks of gold.
7 No bird of prey knows the way there,
   and the falcon's keen eye cannot
      descry it;
8 proud beasts do not set foot on it,
   and no serpent comes that way.
9 Man sets his hand to the granite rock
   and lays bare the roots of the
      mountains;
10 he cuts galleries in the rocks,
   and gems of every kind meet his eye;
11 he dams up the sources of the
      streams
   and brings the hidden riches of the
      earth to light.
12 But where can wisdom be found?
   And where is the source of
      understanding?
13 No man knows the way to it;
   it is not found in the land of living
      men.
14 The depths of ocean say, 'It is not
      in us',
   and the sea says, 'It is not with me.'
15 Red gold cannot buy it,
   nor can its price be weighed out in
      silver;
16 it cannot be set in the scales against
      gold of Ophir,
   against precious cornelian or lapis
      lazuli;
17 gold and crystal are not to be
      matched with it,
   no work in fine gold can be bartered
      for it;
18 black coral and alabaster are not
      worth mention,
   and a parcel of wisdom fetches more
      than red coral;
19 topaz*s* from Ethiopia is not to be
      matched with it,
   it cannot be set in the scales against
      pure gold.
20 Where then does wisdom come from,

and where is the source of
   understanding?
No creature on earth can see it,   21
and it is hidden from the birds of the
   air.
Destruction and death say,   22
'We know of it only by report.'
But God understands the way to it,   23
he alone knows its source;
for he can see to the ends of the   24
   earth
and he surveys everything under
   heaven.
When he made a counterpoise for   25
   the wind
and measured out the waters in
   proportion,
when he laid down a limit for the rain 26
and a path for the thunderstorm,
even then he saw wisdom and took   27
   stock of it,
he considered it and fathomed its
   very depths.
And he said to man: 28
   The fear of the Lord is wisdom,
   and to turn from evil is
      understanding.

Job's final survey of his case

Then Job resumed his discourse: **29**

If I could only go back to the old   2
   days,
to the time when God was watching
   over me,
when his lamp shone above my head,   3
and by its light I walked through the
   darkness!
If I could be as in the days of my   4
   prime,
when God protected my home,
while the Almighty was still there at   5
   my side,
and my servants stood round me,
while my path flowed with milk,   6
and the rocks streamed oil!
s Or chrysolite.

---

to find even a trace of wisdom. **12**: This refrain recurs in v. 20 in slightly different form. **28**: The
verse is a sort of motto; compare Prov.1.7. It probably postdates the poem itself. *LORD*: Heb.,
adonai, not Yahweh; only here is this form used in Job.
   29.1–31.40: Job's final survey of his case. Remembering his gratifying life before God's blow
fell (ch. 29), Job describes the contrast of his decline and the attendant scorn (30.1–19). Piteously
he pleads with God (30.20–31; 31.2–4) and sets forth his past ethical conduct (31.5,1,6 37).
4: *Prime*: lit. "autumn days." The meaning is clearly the prime period of fruitful harvest, not

7 If I went through the gate out of
the town
to take my seat in the public square,

8 young men saw me and kept out of
sight;
old men rose to their feet,

9 men in authority broke off their talk
and put their hands to their lips;

10 the voices of the nobles died away,
and every man held his tongue.

21[t] They listened to me expectantly
and waited in silence for my opinion.

22 When I had spoken, no one spoke
again;
my words fell gently on them;

23 they waited for them as for rain
and drank them in like showers in
spring.

24 When I smiled on them, they took
heart;
when my face lit up, they lost their
gloomy looks.

25 I presided over them, planning their
course,
like a king encamped with his
troops.[u]

11 Whoever heard of me spoke in my
favour,
and those who saw me bore witness
to my merit,

12 how I saved the poor man when he
called for help
and the orphan who had no protector.

13 The man threatened with ruin blessed
me,
and I made the widow's heart sing for
joy.

14 I put on righteousness as a garment
and it clothed me;
justice, like a cloak or a turban,
wrapped me round.

15 I was eyes to the blind
and feet to the lame;

16 I was a father to the needy,
and I took up the stranger's cause.

17 I broke the fangs of the miscreant
and rescued the prey from his teeth.

18 I thought, 'I shall die with my
powers unimpaired
and my days uncounted as the
grains of sand,[v]

with my roots spreading out to the   10
water
and the dew lying on my branches,
with the bow always new in my grasp 20
and the arrow ever ready to my
hand.'[w]

But now I am laughed to scorn   **30**
by men of a younger generation,
men whose fathers I would have
disdained
to put with the dogs who kept my
flock.

What use were their strong arms to   2
me,
since their sturdy vigour had wasted
away?

They gnawed roots[x] in the desert,   3
gaunt with want and hunger,[y]
they plucked saltwort and   4
wormwood
and root of broom[z] for their food.

Driven out from the society of men,[a] 5
pursued like thieves with hue and cry,
they lived in gullies and ravines,   6
holes in the earth and rocky clefts;
they howled like beasts among the   7
bushes,
huddled together beneath the scrub,
vile base-born wretches,   8
hounded from the haunts of men.

Now I have become the target of   9
their taunts,
my name is a byword among them.

They loathe me, they shrink from me, 10
they dare to spit in my face.

They run wild and savage[b] me;   11
at sight of me they throw off all
restraint.

On my right flank they attack in a   12
mob;[c]
they raise their siege-ramps against
me,

---

t Verses 21–25 transposed to this point.
u Prob. rdg.; Heb. adds as when one comforts mourners.
v Or as those of the phoenix.
w Verses 21–25 transposed to follow verse 10.
x roots: prob. rdg.; Heb. om.
y Prob. rdg.; Heb. adds yesterday waste and derelict
land.
z root of broom: probably fungus on broom root.
a the society of men: prob. rdg.; Heb. obscure.
b They run . . . savage: prob. rdg.; Heb. He runs . . .
savages.
c Prob. rdg.; Heb. adds they let loose my feet.

---

man's fading years. **7–10,21–25,11–20:** The erstwhile prestige of Job described here surpasses
that of the prologue, 1.1–3. The translators' rearrangement should be noted. **11–17:** The good
deeds Job claims here contradict the accusations made by Eliphaz in 22.5–9. **18:** The fabled
phoenix (see Tfn. *v*) arose to new life from the ashes of its funeral pyre. **20:** The *bow* and *arrow*

13 they tear down my crumbling
    defences to my undoing,
and scramble up against me
    unhindered;

14 they burst in through the gaping
    breach;
at the moment of the crash they
    come rolling in.

15 Terror upon terror overwhelms me,
it sweeps away my resolution like
    the wind,
and my hope of victory vanishes like
    a cloud.

16 So now my soul is in turmoil within
    me,
and misery has me daily in its grip.

17 By night pain pierces my very bones,
and there is ceaseless throbbing in
    my veins;

18 my garments are all bespattered with
    my phlegm,
which chokes me like the collar of
    a shirt.

19 God himself*d* has flung me down in
    the mud,
no better than dust or ashes.

20 I call for thy help, but thou dost not
    answer;
I stand up to plead, but thou sittest
    aloof;

21 thou hast turned cruelly against me
and with thy strong hand pursuest
    me in hatred;

22 thou dost snatch me up and set me
    astride the wind,
and the tempest*e* tosses me up and
    down.

23 I know that thou wilt hand me over
    to death,
to the place appointed for all mortal
    men.

24 Yet no beggar held out his hand
but was relieved*f* by me in his
    distress.

25 Did I not weep for the man whose
    life was hard?
Did not my heart grieve for the poor?

26 Evil has come though I expected
    good;
I looked for light but there came
    darkness.

27 My bowels are in ferment and know
    no peace;
days of misery stretch out before me.

28 I go about dejected and friendless;
I rise in the assembly, only to appeal
    for help.

29 The wolf is now my brother,
the owls of the desert have become
    my companions.

30 My blackened skin peels off,
and my body is scorched by the heat.

31 My harp has been tuned for a dirge,
my flute to the voice of those who
    weep.

31 2*g* What is the lot prescribed by God
    above,
the reward from the Almighty on
    high?

3 Is not ruin prescribed for the
    miscreant
and calamity for the wrongdoer?

4 Yet does not God himself see my
    ways
and count my every step?

5 I swear I have had no dealings with
    falsehood
and have not embarked on a course
    of deceit.

1 I have come to terms with my eyes,
never to take notice of a girl.

6 Let God weigh me in the scales of
    justice,
and he will know that I am innocent!

7 If my steps have wandered from the
    way,
if my heart has followed my eyes,
or any dirt stuck to my hands,

8 may another eat what I sow,
and may my crops be pulled up by
    the roots!

d God himself: prob. rdg.; Heb. om.
e the tempest: prob. rdg.; Heb. unintelligible.
f was relieved: prob. rdg.; Heb. unintelligible.
g Verse 1 transposed to follow verse 5.

---

may here and in Ecclus.26.12 have overtones of sexual potency. **30.22:** Irony is intended, Job
being punished by being put *astride* the wind, a role elsewhere deemed the great prerogative
of the LORD (see Ps.18.9–10) and also of the Canaanite Baal. **24–28:** Job's claim is that no
needy person was ever refused help by him, yet now no one, not even God, listens to his
appeal for help; thereby God is less compassionate than Job. Compare 32.2–3. **31.1–37:** Job's
record of ethical conduct. **1:** See also Ecclus.9.5. It might be useful to compare Mt 5.27–28 to
note that the NT is not the sole repository of interior ethics, as is sometimes claimed. **7:** *Dirt:*

9 If my heart has been enticed by a
  woman
  or I have lain in wait at my
  neighbour's door,
10 may my wife be another man's slave,
  and may other men enjoy her.
11 [But that is a wicked act, an offence
  before the law;
12 it would be a consuming and
  destructive fire,
  raging*h* among my crops.]
13 If I have ever rejected the plea of my
  slave
  or of my slave-girl, when they brought
  their complaint to me,
14 what shall I do if God appears?
  What shall I answer if he intervenes?
15 Did not he who made me in the
  womb make them?
  Did not the same God create us in
  the belly?
16 If I have withheld their needs from
  the poor
  or let the widow's eye grow dim with
  tears,
17 if I have eaten my crust alone,
  and the orphan has not shared it
  with me—
18 the orphan who from boyhood
  honoured me like a father,
  whom I guided from the day of his*i*
  birth—
19 if I have seen anyone perish for lack
  of clothing,
  or a poor man with nothing to cover
  him,
20 if his body had no cause to bless me,
  because he was not kept warm with a
  fleece from my flock,
21 if I have raised*j* my hand against the
  innocent,*k*
  knowing that men would side with me
  in court,
22 then may my shoulder-blade be torn
  from my shoulder,
  my arm be wrenched out of its socket!
23 But the terror of God was heavy
  upon me,*l*
  and for fear of his majesty I could do
  none of these things.
24 If I have put my faith in gold
  and my trust in the gold of Nubia,
25 if I have rejoiced in my great wealth

and in the increase of riches;
if I ever looked on the sun in   26
  splendour
or the moon moving in her glory,
and was led astray in my secret heart   27
and raised my hand in homage;
this would have been an offence   28
  before the law,
for I should have been unfaithful to
  God on high.
If my land has cried out in reproach   38*m*
  at me,
and its furrows have joined in weeping,
if I have eaten its produce without   39
  payment
and have disappointed my creditors,
may thistles spring up instead of   40
  wheat,
and weeds instead of barley!

Have I rejoiced at the ruin of the man 29
  that hated me
or been filled with malice when
  trouble overtook him,
even though I did not allow my   30
  tongue to sin
by demanding his life with a curse?
Have the men of my household never   31
  said,
'Let none of us speak ill of him!
No stranger has spent the night in   32
  the street'?
For I have kept open house for the
  traveller.
Have I ever concealed my misdeeds   33
  as men do,
keeping my guilt to myself,
because I feared the gossip of the   34
  town
or dreaded the scorn of my fellow-
  citizens?
Let me but call a witness in my   35
  defence!
Let the Almighty state his case
  against me!
If my accuser had written out his
  indictment,
I would not keep silence and remain
  indoors.*n*

*h Prob. rdg.; Heb. uprooting.   i Prob. rdg.; Heb. my.
j Or waved.   k Or orphan.
l Prob. rdg.; Heb. A fear towards me is a disaster from
God.
m Verses 38–40 transposed (but see note p, page 558).
n Line transposed from verse 34.*

perhaps an allusion to land-grabbing practices (see Amos 2.7). **11–12:** The verses are probably
a gloss to reject the content of vv. 9–10. **18:** See Tfn. *i.* **24:** *Nubia:* Ethiopia. **38:** *Land has cried
out:* see Gen.4.10.

36 No! I would flaunt it on my shoulder
and wear it like a crown on my head;
37 I would plead the whole record of
my life
and present that in court as my
defence.*o*

Job's speeches are finished.*p*

Speeches of Elihu

32 So these three men gave up answering
Job; for he continued to think himself
2 righteous. Then Elihu son of Barakel
the Buzite, of the family of Ram, grew
angry; angry because Job had made
himself out more righteous than God,*q*
3 and angry with the three friends because
they had found no answer to Job and
4 had let God appear wrong.*r* Now
Elihu had hung back while they were
talking with Job because they were
5 older than he; but, when he saw that the
three had no answer, he could no longer
6 contain his anger. So Elihu son of
Barakel the Buzite began to speak:

I am young in years,
and you are old;
that is why I held back and shrank
from displaying my knowledge in
front of you.
7 I said to myself, 'Let age speak,
and length of years expound wisdom.'
8 But the spirit of God himself is in man,
and the breath of the Almighty gives
him understanding;
9 it is not only the old who are wise
or the aged who understand what is
right.
10 Therefore I say: Listen to me;

I too will display my knowledge.
Look, I have been waiting upon your 11
words,
listening for the conclusions of your
thoughts,
while you sought for phrases;
I have been giving thought to your 12
conclusions,
but not one of you refutes Job or
answers his arguments.
Take care then not to claim that you 13
have found wisdom;
God will rebut him, not man.
I will not string*s* words together like 14
you*t*
or answer him as you have done.

If these men are confounded and no 15
longer answer,
if words fail them,
am I to wait because they do not 16
speak,
because they stand there and no
longer answer?
I, too, have a furrow to plough; 17
I will express my opinion;
for I am bursting with words, 18
a bellyful of wind gripes me.
My stomach is distended as if with 19
wine,
bulging like a blacksmith's bellows;
I must speak to find relief, 20
I must open my mouth and answer;
I will show no favour to anyone, 21
I will flatter no one, God or man;*u*
for I cannot use flattering titles, 22

*o Verses 38–40 transposed to follow verse 28 (but see
note p).*
p The last line of verse 40 retained here.
q Or had justified himself with God.
*r Prob. original rdg., altered in Heb. to and had not
proved Job wrong.*
s Prob. rdg.; Heb. He has not strung.
t Prob. rdg.; Heb. towards me.
u Prob. rdg.; Heb. I will not flatter man.

32.1–37.24: The speeches of Elihu. These chapters interrupt the context, introduce a new
character unmentioned elsewhere, and repeat many of the friends' arguments, while addressing
themselves more directly to Job's objections. Probably a later addition to the poetic text, they
emphasize the disciplinary nature of suffering and life as divine gift.
    32.1–6a: Prose introduction. 1: The three had earlier been called "friends," but here *men*,
suggesting a different author. **2:** *Elihu* means "he is my God." *Barakel* means "God has blessed,"
a frequent name in Akkadian texts, possibly indicating some connection with Babylonian
literature. *Buzite:* perhaps a clan living on the Persian gulf (Gen.22.21). *Ram:* see Ruth 4.19;
1 Chr.2.9,25,27. It is usual in OT narrative patterns to record the father's name and that of the
clan. **3:** *God:* see Tfn. *q.* The substitution of *Job* for God in the MT is one of the eighteen
recorded alterations by ancient Jewish scribes.
    32.6b–37.24: The poems of Elihu. 6b–22: Elihu feels that he must speak in order to make
up for the ineffectiveness of the friends. The tone here appears to be comic. **10:** The imperative
listen is in the singular as if addressed to Job alone as in 33.1, but the friends are addressed
in the plural in *your words* and in *not one of you* in v. 12 and other instances. **22:** "The Babylonian
Theodicy" makes generous use of *flattering titles*, though it has sharp verbal retorts.

or my Maker would soon do away
with me.

33 Come now, Job, listen to my words
and attend carefully to everything I
say.
2 Look, I am ready to answer;
the words are on the tip of my
tongue.
3 My heart assures me that I speak with
knowledge,
and that my lips speak with sincerity.
4 For the spirit of God made me,
and the breath of the Almighty gave
me life.
5 Answer me if you can,
marshal your arguments and confront
me.
6 In God's sight^v I am just what you
are;
I too am only a handful of clay.
7 Fear of me need not abash you,
nor any pressure from me overawe
you.
8 You have said your say and I heard
you;
I have listened to the sound of your
words:
9 'I am innocent', you said, 'and free
from offence,
blameless and without guilt.
10 Yet God finds occasions to put me
in the wrong
and counts me his enemy;
11 he puts my feet in the stocks
and keeps a close watch on all I do.'
12 Well, this is my answer: You are
wrong.
God is greater than man;
13 why then plead your case with him?
for no one can answer his arguments.
14 Indeed, once God has spoken
he does not speak a second time to
confirm it.
15 In dreams, in visions of the night,
when deepest sleep falls upon men,
16 while they sleep on their beds, God
makes them listen,

and his correction strikes them with
terror.
To turn a man from reckless conduct, 17
to check the pride^w of mortal man,
at the edge of the pit he holds him 18
back alive
and stops him from crossing the
river of death.
Or again, man learns his lesson on a 19
bed of pain,
tormented by a ceaseless ague in his
bones;
he turns from his food with loathing 20
and has no relish for the choicest
meats;
his flesh hangs loose upon him, 21
his bones are loosened and out of
joint,
his soul draws near to the pit, 22
his life to the ministers of death.
Yet if an angel, one of thousands, 23
stands by him,
a mediator between him and God,
to expound what he has done right
and to secure mortal man his due;^{x}
if he speaks in the man's favour and 24
says, 'Reprieve him,
let him not go down to the pit, I
have the price of his release';
then that man will grow sturdier^y 25
than he was in youth,
he will return to the days of his
prime.
If he entreats God to show him 26
favour,
to let him see his face and shout for
joy;^{z}
if he declares before all men, 'I have 27
sinned,
turned right into wrong and thought
nothing of it';
then he saves himself from going 28
down to the pit,
he lives and sees the light.
All these things God may do to a 29
man,

v In God's sight: or In strength.
w the pride: prob. rdg.; Heb. obscure.
x Line transposed from verse 26.
y will grow sturdier: prob. rdg.; Heb. unintelligible.
z See note on verse 23.

33.1–35.16: A reply to Job. The passage cites Job's assertions (vv. 9–11) in a context of refuting
him. **1:** The three friends never addressed Job by name as Elihu does here and in v. 31. **7:**
Pointedly, Elihu asserts that, unlike God, he cannot *overawe* Job. **12:** Elihu's argument is: "If
you admit that *God is greater than man* (which Job has admitted, 9.1–12; 12.13–25), then how can
you bring a law *case* against him." **15:** This verse cites the words of Eliphaz in 4.13; Elihu often
quotes portions of earlier speeches. **22–28:** Angels as *ministers of death* appear early in Israelite
literature; see 2 Sam.24.16. Angels as mediators who *expound* God's will and intercede also

again and yet again,

30 bringing him back from the pit
to enjoy the full light of life.

31 Listen, Job, and attend to me;
be silent, and I myself will speak.

32 If you have any arguments, answer
me;
speak, and I would gladly find you
proved right;

33 but if you have none, listen to me:
keep silence, and I will teach you
wisdom.

34 Then Elihu went on to say;

2 Mark my words, you wise men;
you men of long experience, listen to
me;

3 for the ear tests what is spoken
as the palate savours food.

4 Let us then examine for ourselves
what is right;
let us together establish the true
good.

5 Job has said, 'I am innocent,
but God has deprived me of justice,

6 he has falsified my case;
my state is desperate, yet I have done
no wrong.'

7 Was there ever a man like Job
with his thirst for irreverent talk,

8 choosing bad company to share his
journeys,
a fellow-traveller with wicked men?

9 For he says that it brings a man no
profit
to find favour with God.

10 But listen to me, you men of good
sense.
Far be it from God to do evil
or the Almighty to play false!

11 For he pays a man according to his
work
and sees that he gets what his
conduct deserves.

12 The truth is, God does no wrong,
the Almighty does not pervert justice.

13 Who committed the earth to his
keeping?
Who but he established the whole
world?

14 If he were to turn his thoughts
inwards
and recall his life-giving spirit,

15 all that lives would perish on the
instant,
and man return again to dust.

16 Now Job, if you have the wit,
consider this;
listen to the words I speak.

17 Can it be that a hater of justice holds
the reins?
Do you disparage a sovereign whose
rule is so fair,

18 who will say to a prince, 'You
scoundrel',
and call his magnates blackguards to
their faces;

19 who does not show special favour
to those in office
and thinks no more of rich than of
poor?

20 All alike are God's creatures,
who may die in a moment, in the
middle of the night;
at his touch the rich are no more,
and the mighty vanish though no
hand is laid on them.

21 His eyes are on the ways of men,
and he sees every step they take;

22 there is nowhere so dark, so deep
in shadow,
that wrongdoers may hide from him.

25 Therefore he repudiates all that they
do;
he turns on them in the night, and
they are crushed.

23 There are no appointed days for men
to appear before God for judgement.

24 He holds no inquiry, but breaks the
powerful
and sets up others in their place.

26ᵃ For their crimes he strikes them
downᵇ
and makes them disgorge their
bloated wealth,ᶜ

27 because they have ceased to obey him
and pay no heed to his ways.

28 Then the cry of the poor reaches his
ears,

a Verse 25 transposed to follow verse 22.
b he strikes them down: prob. rdg.; Heb. om.
c Or and chastises them where people see.

appear; see Josh.5.13–14; Dan.8.15–17. **34.1–37**: Job is wrong in imputing injustice to God.
3: Repeats 12.11 almost verbatim. **5–6**: These verses echo 27.2 and 33.9. **21**: See 24.23 and 31.4.
23–25: Since God observes everything under the sun, he does not need to go through a legal
process such as Job demands, i.e. *inquiry* or *appointed days . . . for judgement* in court, but his

and he hears the cry of the distressed.

29-30 [Even if he is silent, who can
condemn him?
If he looks away, who can find fault?
What though he makes a godless man
king
over a stubborn nation and all its
people?]

31 But suppose you were to say to God,
'I have overstepped the mark; I will
do no more*d* mischief.
32 Vile wretch that I am, be thou my
guide;
whatever wrong I have done, I will do
wrong no more.'
33 Will he, at these words, condone your
rejection of him?
It is for you to decide, not me:
but what can you answer?
34 Men of good sense will say,
any intelligent hearer will tell me,
35 'Job talks with no knowledge,
and there is no sense in what he says.
36 If only Job could be put to the test
once and for all
for answers that are meant to make
mischief!
37 He is a sinner and a rebel as well*e*
with his endless ranting against God.'

35 Then Elihu went on to say:

2 Do you think that this is a sound plea
or maintain that you are in the right
against God?—
3 if you say, 'What would be the
advantage to me?
how much should I gain from
sinning?'
4 I will bring arguments myself against
you,
you and your three friends.
5 Look up at the sky and then consider,
observe the rain-clouds towering
above you.
6 How does it touch him if you have
sinned?
However many your misdeeds, what

does it mean to him?
7 If you do right, what good do you
bring him,
or what does he gain from you?
8 Your wickedness touches only men,
such as you are;
the right that you do affects none but
mortal man.

9 Men will cry out beneath the burdens
of oppression
and call for help against the power of
the great;
10 but none of them asks, 'Where is
God my Maker
who gives protection by night,
11 who grants us more knowledge than
the beasts of the earth
and makes us wiser than the birds of
the air?'
12 So, when they cry out, he does not
answer,
because they are self-willed and proud.
13 All to no purpose! God does not
listen,
the Almighty does not see.

14 The worse for you when you say, 'He
does not see me'!
Humble yourself*f* in his presence and
wait for his word.
15 But now, because God does not grow
angry and punish
and because he lets folly pass
unheeded,
16 Job gives vent to windy nonsense
and makes a parade of empty words.

36 Then Elihu went on to say:

2 Be patient a little longer, and let me
enlighten you;
there is still something more to be
said on God's side.
3 I will search far and wide to support
my conclusions,
as I defend the justice of my Maker.

d more: prob. rdg.; Heb. obscure.
e Prob. rdg.; Heb. adds between us it is enough.
f Humble yourself: prob. rdg.; Heb. Judge.

sentence is sudden, out of *the night.* **31–37:** Elihu states that Job's violent language is a *ranting
rejection* of God that will merit further punishment even if he were now to repent of it. Job will
repent (42.6) but the punishment does not follow, which may be a key to the whole story.
35.4: Elihu attacks the three friends not because they agree with Job, but because their arguments against him are so feeble. **9–16:** This passage replies to Job's contention that God does
not reply to Job's challenge to come to a trial (13.20–24; 30.20–21). In due time God responds
to man.
   36.1–19,21: God does not allow the wicked to prosper forever. Those who learn from suffering

4 There are no flaws in my reasoning;
   before you stands one whose
     conclusions are sound.

5 God,[g] I say, repudiates the high
   and[h] mighty
6 and does not let the wicked prosper,
   but allows the just claims of the poor
     and suffering;
7 he does not deprive the sufferer of
     his due.[i]
   Look at kings on their thrones:
   when God gives them sovereign
     power, they grow arrogant.
8 Next you may see them loaded with
     fetters,
   held fast in captives' chains:
9 he denounces their conduct to them,
   showing how insolence and tyranny
     was their offence;
10 his warnings sound in their ears
   and summon them to turn back from
     their evil courses.
11 If they listen to him, they spend[j]
     their days in prosperity
   and their years in comfort.
12 But, if they do not listen, they die,
     their lesson unlearnt,
   and cross the river of death.
13 Proud men rage against him
   and do not cry to him for help when
     caught in his toils;
14 so they die in their prime,
   like male prostitutes,[k] worn out.[l]

15 Those who suffer he rescues through
     suffering
   and teaches them by the discipline of
     affliction.

16 Beware, if you are tempted to
     exchange hardship for comfort,[m]
   for unlimited plenty spread before
     you, and a generous table;
17 if you eat your fill of a rich man's
     fare
   when you are occupied with the
     business of the law,
18 do not be led astray by lavish gifts of
     wine
   and do not let bribery warp your
     judgement.

19 Will that wealth of yours, however
     great, avail you,
   or all the resources of your high
     position?
21[n] Take care not to turn to mischief;
   for that is why you are tried by
     affliction.

20 Have no fear if in the breathless
     terrors of the night
   you see nations vanish where they
     stand.
22 God towers in majesty above us;
   who wields such sovereign power as
     he?
23 Who has prescribed his course for
     him?
   Who has said to him, 'Thou hast
     done wrong'?
24 Remember then to sing the praises
     of his work,
   as men have always sung them.
25 All men stand back from[o] him;
   the race of mortals look on from afar.
26 Consider; God is so great that we
     cannot know him;
   the number of his years is beyond
     reckoning.
27 He draws up drops of water from the
     sea[p]
   and distils rain from the mist he has
     made;
28 the rain-clouds pour down in
     torrents,[q]
   they descend in showers on mankind;
31 thus he sustains the nations
   and gives them food in plenty.
29 Can any man read the secret of the
     sailing clouds,
   spread like a carpet under[r] his
     pavilion?
30 See how he unrolls the mist across
     the waters,
   and its streamers[s] cover the sea.

---

g Prob. rdg.; Heb. adds a mighty one and not.
h and: prob. rdg.; Heb. om.
i deprive . . . due: or withdraw his gaze from the
  righteous.
j Prob. rdg.; Heb. adds they end.   k Cp. Deut. 23. 17.
l worn out: prob. rdg.; Heb. unintelligible.
m for comfort: prob. rdg.; Heb. om.
n Verses 20 and 21 transposed.   o Or gaze at.
p from the sea: prob. rdg.; Heb. om.
q in torrents: prob. rdg.; Heb. which.
r spread . . . under: prob. rdg.; Heb. crashing noises.
s its streamers: prob. rdg.; Heb. the roots of.

---

attain contentment. **14**: *Male prostitutes* had a role in the fertility rites of pagan temples. In
times of religious decline they were attached to the Israelite temple and shrines; see Tfn. *k*
and *l*; also 2 Kgs.23.7. The orgiastic excesses of male prostitutes led to an early death.
   36.20,22–37.24: God's power over nature is such that mere man cannot truly understand him;

32[t] He charges the thunderbolts with flame
and launches them straight[u] at the mark;

33 in his anger he calls up the tempest,
and the thunder is the herald of its coming.[v]

37 This too makes my heart beat wildly
and start from its place.

2 Listen, listen to the thunder of God's voice
and the rumbling of his utterance.

3 Under the vault of heaven he lets it roll,
and his lightning reaches the ends of the earth;

4 there follows a sound of roaring
as he thunders with the voice of majesty.[w]

5 God's voice is marvellous in its working;[x]
he does great deeds that pass our knowledge.

6 For he says to the snow, 'Fall to earth',
and to the rainstorms, 'Be fierce.'
And when his voice is heard,
the floods of rain pour down unchecked.[y]

7 He shuts every man fast indoors,[z]
and all men whom he has made must stand idle;

8 the beasts withdraw into their lairs
and take refuge in their dens.

9 The hurricane bursts from its prison,
and the rain-winds bring bitter cold;

10 at the breath of God the ice-sheet is formed,
and the wide waters are frozen hard as iron.

11 He gives the dense clouds their load of moisture,
and the clouds spread his mist abroad,

12 as they travel round in their courses,
steered by his guiding hand
to do his bidding
all over the habitable world.[a]

14 Listen, Job, to this argument;
stand still, and consider God's wonderful works.

Do you know how God assigns them 15 their tasks,
how he sends light flashing from his clouds?

Do you know why the clouds hang 16 poised overhead,
a wonderful work of his consummate skill,
sweating there in your stifling 17 clothes,
when the earth lies sultry under the south wind?

Can you beat out the vault of the 18 skies, as he does,
hard as a mirror of cast metal?

Teach us then what to say to him; 19
for all is dark, and we cannot marshal our thoughts.

Can any man dictate to God when 20 he is[b] to speak?
or command him to make proclamation?

At one moment the light is not seen, 21
it is overcast with clouds and rain;
then the wind passes by and clears them away,
and a golden glow comes from the 22 north.[c]

But the Almighty we cannot find; 23
his power is beyond our ken,
and his righteousness not slow to do justice.

Therefore mortal men pay him 24 reverence,
and all who are wise look to him.

God's answer and Job's submission

Then the LORD answered Job out of **38** the tempest:

t *Verse 31 transposed to follow verse 28.*
u *and . . . straight: prob. rdg.; Heb. and gives orders concerning it.*
v *in his anger . . . coming: prob. rdg.; Heb. obscure.*
w *See note on verse 6.*
x *Prob rdg.; Heb. thundering.*
y *And when . . . unchecked: prob. rdg.; some words in these lines transposed from verse 4.*
z *indoors: prob. rdg.; Heb. obscure.*
a *Prob. rdg.; Heb. adds (13) whether he makes him attain the rod, or his earth, or constant love.*
b *Prob. rdg.; Heb. I am.*
c *Prob. rdg.; Heb. adds this refers to God, terrible in majesty.*

man can only marvel at God's greatness. (Note transposition of vv. 20 and 21.) **37.22**: *North*: Heb., *zaphon*, the mountain habitation of the gods (see 26.7 n.).
    38.1–40.2: God's answer and Job's submission.
    38.1–40.2: God's answer from the whirlwind. God's argument seems to be that in the beauty, majesty, power, and wonder of the world, Job's situation cannot be the one thing out of joint. Surely Job cannot deny that his condition must fit into the mysteries of the universe which Job

2 Who is this whose ignorant words
    cloud my design in darkness?
3 Brace yourself and stand up like a
    man;
    I will ask questions, and you shall
    answer.
4 Where were you when I laid the
    earth's foundations?
    Tell me, if you know and understand.
5 Who settled its dimensions? Surely
    you should know.
    Who stretched his measuring-line over
    it?
6 On what do its supporting pillars
    rest?
    Who set its corner-stone in place,
7 when the morning stars sang
    together
    and all the sons of God shouted
    aloud?
8 Who watched over the birth of the
    sea,[d]
    when it burst in flood from the
    womb?—
9 when I wrapped it in a blanket of
    cloud
    and cradled it in fog,
10 when I established its bounds,
    fixing its doors and bars in place,
11 and said, 'Thus far shall you come
    and no farther,
    and here your surging waves shall
    halt.'[e]
12 In all your life have you ever called
    up the dawn
    or shown the morning its place?
13 Have you taught it to grasp the
    fringes of the earth
    and shake the Dog-star from its
    place;
14 to bring up the horizon in relief as
    clay under a seal,
    until all things stand out like the
    folds of a cloak,
15 when the light of the Dog-star is
    dimmed

and the stars of the Navigator's Line
    go out one by one?
16 Have you descended to the springs of
    the sea
    or walked in the unfathomable deep?
17 Have the gates of death been revealed
    to you?
    Have you ever seen the door-keepers
    of the place of darkness?
18 Have you comprehended the vast
    expanse of the world?
    Come, tell me all this, if you know.
19 Which is the way to the home of
    light
    and where does darkness dwell?
20 And can you then take each to its
    appointed bound
    and escort it on its homeward path?
21 Doubtless you know all this; for you
    were born already,
    so long is the span of your life!
22 Have you visited the storehouse of
    the snow
    or seen the arsenal where hail is
    stored,
23 which I have kept ready for the day
    of calamity,
    for war and for the hour of battle?
24 By what paths is the heat spread
    abroad
    or the east wind carried far and wide
    over the earth?
25 Who has cut channels for the
    downpour
    and cleared a passage for the thunder-
    storm,
26 for rain to fall on land where no man
    lives
    and on the deserted wilderness,
27 clothing lands waste and derelict with
    green

[d] Who . . . sea: *prob. rdg.*; *Heb.* And he held back
the sea with two doors.
[e] *Prob. rdg.*; *Heb.* here one shall set on your surging
waves.

---

cannot penetrate and yet cannot blame God for making them incomprehensible. The form of the
passage is derived from nature wisdom, encyclopedic data under the care of the sages (in Egypt
especially). The passage ignores the accusations made against God, and focuses on Job's
inevitable, human ignorance. **1:** Whereas *the tempest* had brought Job's calamity in the beginning (1.19, *whirlwind*), it is now the occasion for his vindication. The passage ensues directly
on 31.37, abstaining from comment on the Elihu speeches (see 32.1–37.24 n.). **3:** *Brace:* the
word means to prepare for warfare, and may derive from belt wrestling. **7:** Light is a symbol of
rejoicing; compare Ps.97.11–12. Because of their brilliance in the surrounding darkness, the
heavenly bodies are often personified as rejoicing and praising God; see Pss.18.1–6; 148.3–4.
21: Further irony: Job may be comparing himself to Wisdom, which existed in the beginning
with God (see Prov.8.22 n.). **22–23:** *Hail:* compare Josh.10.11 and Ecclus.46.6. **30:** *Expanse of*

and making grass grow on thirsty
    ground*f*?

28 Has the rain a father?
    Who sired the drops of dew?

29 Whose womb gave birth to the ice,
    and who was the mother of the frost
        from heaven,

30 which lays a stony cover over the
        waters
    and freezes the expanse of ocean?

31 Can you bind the cluster of the
        Pleiades
    or loose Orion's belt?

32 Can you bring out the signs of the
        zodiac in their season
    or guide Aldebaran and its train?

33 Did you proclaim the rules that
        govern the heavens,
    or determine the laws of nature on
        earth?

34 Can you command the dense clouds
    to cover you with their weight of
        waters?

35 If you bid lightning speed on its
        way,
    will it say to you, 'I am ready'?

36 Who put wisdom in depths of
        darkness
    and veiled understanding in secrecy*g*?

37 Who is wise enough to marshal the
        rain-clouds
    and empty the cisterns of heaven,

38 when the dusty soil sets hard as
        iron,
    and the clods of earth cling together?

39 Do you hunt her prey for the lioness
    and satisfy the hunger of young lions,

40 as they crouch in the lair
    or lie in wait in the covert?

41 Who provides the raven with its
        quarry
    when its fledglings croak*h* for lack of
        food?

39 Do you know when the mountain-
        goats are born
    or attend the wild doe when she is
        in labour?

2 Do you count the months that they
        carry their young
    or know the time of their delivery,

3 when they crouch down to open their
        wombs

and bring their offspring to the
    birth,

4 when the fawns grow and thrive in
    the open forest,
    and go forth and do not return?

5 Who has let the wild ass of Syria
    range at will
    and given the wild ass of Arabia its
        freedom?—

6 whose home I have made in the
        wilderness
    and its lair in the saltings;

7 it disdains the noise of the city
    and is deaf to the driver's shouting;

8 it roams the hills as its pasture
    and searches for anything green.

9 Does the wild ox consent to serve
    you,
    does it spend the night in your stall?

10 Can you harness its strength*i* with
    ropes,
    or will it harrow the furrows*i* after
        you?

11 Can you depend on it, strong as it is,
    or leave your labour to it?

12 Do you trust it to come back
    and bring home your grain to the
        threshing-floor?

13 The wings of the ostrich are stunted;*j*
    *k*her pinions and plumage are so
        scanty*l*

14 that she abandons her eggs to the
        ground,
    letting them be kept warm by the sand.

15 She forgets that a foot may crush
    them,
    or a wild beast trample on them;

16 she treats her chicks heartlessly as if
    they were not hers,
    not caring if her labour is wasted

17 (for God has denied her wisdom
    and left her without sense),

18 while like a cock she struts over the
    uplands,
    scorning both horse and rider.

f thirsty ground: prob. rdg.; Heb. source.
g secrecy: *prob. rdg.; Heb.* word unknown.
h Prob. rdg.; Heb. adds they cry to God.
i Prob. rdg.; Heb. transposes strength *and* furrows.
j are stunted: *prob. rdg.; Heb. unintelligible.*
k Prob. rdg.; Heb. prefixes if.
l Prob. rdg.; Heb. godly *or* stork.

---

ocean: lit. the surface of the deep, i.e. any deep body of water such as the Sea of Galilee. **32:**
This verse seems to allude to the Great Bear and Little Bear. **36:** The text is disturbed here.
Perhaps the meaning is that even *darkness* of which the Israelite was afraid had a purpose.
39.13–18: Perhaps this means that God could be no less compassionate to Job than to the

19 Did you give the horse his strength?
Did you clothe his neck with a mane?

20 Do you make him quiver like a
locust's wings,
when his shrill neighing strikes terror?

21 He shows his mettle as he paws and
prances;
he charges the armoured line with
all his might.

22 He scorns alarms and knows no
dismay;
he does not flinch before the sword.

23 The quiver rattles at his side,
the spear and sabre flash.

24 Trembling with eagerness, he devours
the ground
and cannot be held in when he hears
the horn;

25 at the blast of the horn he cries 'Aha!'
and from afar he scents the battle.*m*

26 Does your skill teach the hawk to
use its pinions
and spread its wings towards the
south?

27 Do you instruct the vulture to fly
high
and build its nest aloft?

28 It dwells among the rocks and there
it lodges;
its station is a crevice in the rock;

29 from there it searches for food,
keenly scanning the distance,

30 that its brood may be gorged with
blood;
and where the slain are, there the
vulture is.

411*n* Can you pull out the whale*o* with a
gaff
or can you slip a noose round its
tongue?

2 Can you pass a cord through its nose
or put a hook through its jaw?

3 Will it plead with you for mercy
or beg its life with soft words?

4 Will it enter into an agreement with
you
to become your slave for life?

5 Will you toy with it as with a bird

or keep it on a string like a song-
bird for your maidens?

Do trading-partners haggle over it   6
or merchants share it out?

Then the LORD said to Job: **40**

Is it for a man who disputes with the 2
Almighty to be stubborn?
Should he that argues with God
answer back?

And Job answered the LORD: 3

What reply can I give thee, I who   4
carry no weight?
I put my finger to my lips.
I have spoken once and now will   5
not answer again:
twice have I spoken, and I will do so
no more.

Then the LORD answered Job out of 6
the tempest:

Brace yourself and stand up like a   7
man;
I will ask questions, and you shall
answer.
Dare you deny that I am just   8
or put me in the wrong that you may
be right?
Have you an arm like God's arm,   9
can you thunder with a voice like
his?
Deck yourself out, if you can, in   10
pride and dignity,
array yourself in pomp and splendour;
unleash the fury of your wrath,   11
look upon the proud man and
humble him;
look upon every proud man and   12
bring him low,

*m Prob. rdg.; Heb. adds the thunder of the captains
and the shouting.*
n 41. 1–6 (in Heb. 40. 25–30) transposed to this point.
o Or Leviathan.

---

ostrich. **19–25:** The *horse* was considered extremely valuable in warfare, as Canaanite texts
indicate. **40.2:** Two interpretations of the text are possible, namely, (a) that for Job to *answer
back* would be further impudence; or (b) an invitation to Job to answer God if he can.
     40.3–5: Job's reply is that he is moved to silence.
     40.6–41.34: God's second speech. In addition to man's ignorance, man is unable to humble the
proud man or to master the crocodile and whale as God has done. The subdued animal is to be
understood both literally and as recalling the primeval sea monster of mythology (3.8 and
26.12–13; compare Ps.74.14). **6:** See 38.1. **7:** See 38.1 n. and 38.3 n. **15:** In Tfn. *p.* Behemoth in

throw down the wicked where they
　　stand;

13　hide them in the dust together,
　　and shroud them in an unknown
　　　grave.

14　Then I in my turn will acknowledge
　　that your own right hand can save you.

15　Consider the chief of the beasts, the
　　　crocodile,[p]
　　who devours cattle as if they were
　　　grass:[q]

16　what strength is in his loins!
　　what power in the muscles of his
　　　belly!

17　His tail is rigid as[r] a cedar,
　　the sinews of his flanks are closely
　　　knit,

18　his bones are tubes of bronze,
　　and his limbs like bars of iron.

19　He is the chief of God's works,
　　made to be a tyrant over his peers;[s]

20　for he takes[t] the cattle of the hills
　　　for his prey
　　and in his jaws he crunches all wild
　　　beasts.

21　There under the thorny lotus he lies,
　　hidden in the reeds and the marsh;

22　the lotus conceals him in its shadow,
　　the poplars of the stream surround
　　　him.

23　If the river is in spate, he is not
　　　scared,
　　he sprawls at his ease though the
　　　stream is in flood.

24　Can a man blind[u] his eyes and take him
　　or pierce his nose with the teeth of
　　　a trap?

417[v]　Can you fill his skin with harpoons
　　or his head with fish-hooks?

8　If ever you lift your hand against
　　　him,
　　think of the struggle that awaits you,
　　　and let be.

9　No, such a man is in desperate case,
　　hurled headlong at the very sight of
　　　him.

10　How fierce he is when he is roused!
　　Who is there to stand up to him?

11　Who has ever attacked him[w] unscathed?
　　Not a man[x] under the wide heaven.

I will not pass over in silence his　　12
　　limbs,
his prowess and the grace of his
　　proportions.
Who has ever undone his outer　　13
　　garment
or penetrated his doublet of hide?
Who has ever opened the portals of　　14
　　his face?
for there is terror in his arching teeth.
His back[y] is row upon row of shields,　　15
enclosed in a wall[z] of flints;
one presses so close on the other　　16
that air cannot pass between them,
each so firmly clamped to its　　17
　　neighbour
that they hold and cannot spring apart.
His sneezing sends out sprays of　　18
　　light,
and his eyes gleam like the shimmer
　　of dawn.
Firebrands shoot from his mouth,　　19
and sparks come streaming out;
his nostrils pour forth smoke　　20
like a cauldron on a fire blown to
　　full heat.
His breath sets burning coals ablaze,　　21
and flames flash from his mouth.
Strength is lodged in his neck,　　22
and untiring energy dances ahead of
　　him.
Close knit is his underbelly,　　23
no pressure will make it yield.
His heart is firm as a rock,　　24
firm as the nether millstone.
When he raises himself, strong men[a]　　25
　　take fright,
bewildered at the lashings of his tail.
Sword or spear, dagger or javelin,　　26
if they touch him, they have no effect.
Iron he counts as straw,　　27
and bronze as rotting wood.
No arrow can pierce him,　　28
and for him sling-stones are turned
　　into chaff;

p chief . . . crocodile: prob. rdg.; Heb. beasts (behemoth) which I have made with you.
q cattle . . . grass: prob. rdg.; Heb. grass like cattle.
r Or He bends his tail like . . .
s Prob. rdg.; Heb. his sword.
t Prob. rdg.; Heb. they take.
u Can a man blind: prob. rdg.; Heb. obscure.
v Verses 1–6 transposed to follow 39. 30.
w Prob. rdg.; Heb. me. x Prob. rdg.; Heb. He is mine.
y Prob. rdg.; Heb. pride. z Prob. rdg.; Heb. seal.
a strong men: or leaders or gods.

Heb. is an intensive plural for majesty, but denotes a singular, as in older translations. **17:** The reference to *his tail* suggests a crocodile, rather than the hippopotamus found in some older commentaries.

29 to him a club is a mere reed,
and he laughs at the swish of the
sabre.
30 Armoured beneath with jagged sherds,
he sprawls on the mud like a
threshing-sledge.
31 He makes the deep water boil like
a cauldron,
he whips up the lake like ointment in
a mixing-bowl.
32 He leaves a shining trail behind him,
and the great river is like white hair
in his wake.
33 He has no equal on earth;
for he is made quite without fear.
34 He looks down on all creatures,
even the highest;
he is king over all proud beasts.

42 Then Job answered the LORD:

2 I know that thou canst do all things
and that no purpose is beyond thee.
3 But I have spoken of great things
which I have not understood,
things too wonderful for me to
know.*b*
5 I knew of thee then only by report
but now I see thee with my own eyes.
6 Therefore I melt away;*c*
I repent in dust and ashes.

Epilogue

7 When the LORD had finished speaking
to Job, he said to Eliphaz the Temanite,
'I am angry with you and your two
friends, because you have not spoken
as you ought about me, as my servant
8 Job has done. So now take seven bulls

and seven rams, go to my servant Job
and offer a whole-offering for yourselves, and he will intercede for you;
I will surely show him favour by not
being harsh with you because you have
not spoken as you ought about me, as
he has done.' Then Eliphaz the Temanite 9
and Bildad the Shuhite and Zophar the
Naamathite went and carried out the
LORD's command, and the LORD
showed favour to Job when he had
interceded for his friends. So the LORD 10
restored Job's fortunes and doubled all
his possessions.

Then all Job's brothers and sisters 11
and his former acquaintance came and
feasted with him in his home, and they
consoled and comforted him for all the
misfortunes which the LORD had
brought on him; and each of them
gave him a sheep*d* and a gold ring.
Furthermore, the LORD blessed the end 12
of Job's life more than the beginning;
and he had fourteen thousand head of
small cattle and six thousand camels, a
thousand yoke of oxen and as many
she-asses. He had seven*e* sons and three 13
daughters; and he named his eldest 14
daughter Jemimah, the second Keziah
and the third Keren-happuch. There 15
were no women in all the world so
beautiful as Job's daughters; and their
father gave them an inheritance with
their brothers.

Thereafter Job lived another hundred 16
and forty years, he saw his sons and his
grandsons to four generations, and 17
died at a very great age.

b Prob. rdg.; Heb. adds (4) O listen, and let me speak;
    I will ask questions, and you shall answer.
c Or despise myself.
d Or piece of money.
e Or fourteen.

42.1–6: Job's repentance. Job's silence (40.3–5) now gives way to the immediacy of God's presence and brings him to repentance. **3–4:** See Tfn. *b*. Job quotes from God's initial speech (38.2–3) to admit the validity of the divine charge. **5–6:** Job's knowledge of God was a conceptual one acquired from tradition *by report;* now he has a vivid personal encounter. As a consequence he recognizes not only his limitations in understanding but comes to acknowledge that God's actions in ordering the universe go beyond a system of justice as men know it. Job experienced God as bounty (38.41–39.12), beauty (38.12–15), freedom (38.5–6), and grace (41.9–31).

42.7–17: Epilogue. Job is restored to his former glory. The epilogue, like the prologue (chs. 1–2), is in prose. **9:** The suffering righteous man stands before God as intercessor. **11:** The *gold ring* was for the ear or the nose. **13:** More than three daughters would have been a liability. See Ecclus.26.10–12; 42.9–11. Several manuscripts read fourteen sons (Tfn. *e*), in line with the doubling of his property. **14:** *Jemimah:* dove (S. of S.2.14). *Keziah:* cinnamon (Prov.7.17). *Keren-happuch:* horn of eye cosmetics. **15:** The specific mention of daughters receiving an inheritance is unique in the OT, but see Num.26.33; 27.1–8; 36.1–12. **16–17:** Job's life span becomes double the usual expectation (Ps.90.10). *Four generations:* compare Ps.128.6. The language here is reminiscent of descriptions of the patriarchs in Gen.25.8; 35.29; 50.23.

PSALMS

In the psalms there are many voices, from various times and places, from Joshua to Ezra, and from Jerusalem to Babylon. Gathered by unknown men, often called "the sages of Israel," the psalms were used in ancient worship as they have continued to live in both synagogue and church.

When Israel came to Canaan she encountered and absorbed a living poetic tradition; hence many psalms reveal much that Israel had in common with her predecessors and neighbors. At times, however, some of Israel's poets skillfully shaped the language with intuitive insight greater even than the very language itself; these are the occasions which are always exciting for the student who is interested in the singular thrust of Israel's creative literary achievement. But the historian must also recognize that the less striking aspects, the common elements themselves, could be of great significance too in the late biblical age.

Some of the poetic voices seem muffled by our own world view, yet others break through such barriers, for in many passages the Hebrew poets sang of a reality which is only on the horizon of our comprehension.

The Book of Psalms is divided into five books. In the Hebrew Masoretic Text, there is a superscription or heading for many psalms. In the present translation, as is noted in the Introduction to the Old Testament (p. xxi), "The headings of the Psalms . . . have been omitted; they are almost certainly not original." In the annotations it has at times been useful to refer to these omitted superscriptions. Two recurrent words, "Selah" and "Amen," have also been omitted (e.g. from 3.2,4). These words appear to be instructions inserted when the psalms were used liturgically. Perhaps Selah, whose meaning is unclear, was a signal for an instrumental interlude. Amen (e.g. 41.13), likewise uncertain in its original use, seems to instruct the participants in the liturgy to assent to the passage read to them.

The classification of each psalm is to be regarded as summary, and meant to be useful rather than complete. Thus, the "Laments" are not here classified into subcategories such as "individual" and "group" Laments. The procedure in the notes is to designate the following types: Lament, Thanksgiving, Hymn, Enthronement Hymn, Royal Psalm, Wisdom Psalm, Prophetic Judgment, Vow, Liturgy, and Benediction. Some psalms are really only fragments of known types and others are impossible to classify at all.

A Lament, the most abundant type, was sung in time of great trouble. It usually contains a statement of the poet's distress, a word of trust, an appeal to God, a declaration about the poet's obedience, and his vow to sing a Thanksgiving (see Pss. 22 and 26; also compare 56.8,12; 107.22). A Thanksgiving Psalm thanks God for what he had done in specific historical circumstances to save an individual or the nation. A Hymn praises God for what he is accustomed to do in nature or history for the welfare of mankind. An Enthronement Hymn was used to celebrate the kingship of God. Royal Psalms dealt with the human king; many were used at the time of his coronation and one is a Wedding Song. The Wisdom Psalms reflect the teaching of the sages of Israel. Other types are rather rare, and are explained in the notes.

Tradition ascribes the book of Psalms to David (2 Sam.23.1); about half are so ascribed in the superscriptions. Modern scholarship rejects a view held three generations ago which supposed that no psalms were as early as David; indeed, some were written even before his time. The Psalter is a collection, indeed, probably a collection of collections, of poems from all periods of Israel's history. It has, with justice, been called "The Prayer Book of the Second Temple," for in that later period (after 520 B.C.) the psalms were used in the liturgy.

BOOK 1

1

1 Happy is the man
  who does not take the wicked for
    his guide

nor walk the road that sinners tread
nor take his seat among the scornful;
the law of the LORD is his delight, 2
the law his meditation night and day.
He is like a tree 3
planted beside a watercourse,
which yields its fruit in season
and its leaf never withers:

Ps. 1: The LORD watches over the way of the righteous. This Wisdom Psalm (see Introduction) contrasts the two ways open to man—good and evil—and their consequences—happiness and misery. Thus, it is a summary of the moral teaching of the Psalter; hence, its place at the beginning of the Psalms. **1–3:** *Happy is the man:* a common Wisdom phrase; see Ps.41.1 and the

569

in all that he does he prospers.

4 Wicked men are not like this;
   they are like chaff driven by the
      wind.
5 So when judgement comes the
      wicked shall not stand firm,
   nor shall sinners stand in the
      assembly of the righteous.
6 The LORD watches over the way of
      the righteous,
   but the way of the wicked is doomed.

2

1 Why are the nations in turmoil?
   Why do the peoples hatch their
      futile plots?
2   The kings of the earth stand
         ready,
   and the rulers conspire together
   against the LORD and his anointed
      king.
3 'Let us break their fetters,' they cry,
   'let us throw off their chains!'
4 The Lord who sits enthroned in
      heaven
   laughs them to scorn;
5 then he rebukes them in anger,
   he threatens them in his wrath.
6 Of me he says, 'I have enthroned
      my king
   on Zion my holy mountain.'
7 I will repeat the LORD's decree:
   'You are my son,' he said;
   'this day I become your father.
8 Ask of me what you will:

I will give you nations as your
   inheritance,
the ends of the earth as your
   possession.
You shall break them with a rod of 9
   iron,
you shall shatter them like a clay
   pot.'
Be mindful then, you kings;   10
   learn your lesson, rulers of the
      earth:
worship the LORD with reverence;   11–12
tremble, and kiss the king,*
lest the LORD be angry and you are
   struck down in mid course;
for his anger flares up in a moment.
Happy are all who find refuge in
   him.

3

LORD, how my enemies have   1
   multiplied!
Many rise up against me,
many there are who say of me,   2
   'God will not bring him victory.'
But thou, LORD, art a shield to   3
   cover me:
thou art my glory, and thou dost
   raise my head high.
I cry aloud to the LORD,   4
   and he answers me from his
      holy mountain.
I lie down and sleep,   5

a tremble . . . king: *prob. rdg.; lit.* tremble and kiss
the mighty one; *Heb. obscure.*

---

beatitudes of Jesus (Mt.5.1–12). See also Jer.17.7–8. *A tree . . . beside a watercourse* is a symbol
of the fullness of life in arid Palestine where trees are generally dwarfed for lack of moisture;
compare Ezek.47.1–12; Ecclus.24.14–31. **6:** The confident assertion that the LORD *watches over
the way of the righteous* is found in many psalms, especially Wisdom Psalms. Even though in
the Laments the psalmist recognizes the paradox of the just man suffering, he trusts that
deliverance always comes; see Ps.22.
   Ps. 2: I have enthroned my king on Zion. A Royal Psalm used at the time of coronation. For
comparable psalms see Pss.72, 101, 110, and 132. **1–2:** The accession of a new emperor was
the time usually picked by subject *kings* to revolt. Because the emperor-king was considered
chosen by God, for subjects to *conspire* against him was to conspire against the LORD. The word
king is not found here in the Heb. The Heb. word for *anointed* is *messiah.* This word, in later
Jewish tradition, came to stand for the ideal king who would accomplish God's purposes and
Israel's destiny. Perhaps because of this connotation this psalm is placed here at the head of the
Psalter. The passage is cited in Acts 4.25–29. **7:** *You are my son:* a formula apparently used at the
time of the coronation (see 2 Sam.7.14; Ps.89.26–27). For Christian interpretation, see Lk.3.22
and, more explicitly, Acts 13.33.
   Ps. 3: I cry aloud to the LORD. A Lament, this psalm has characteristics usually found in all
psalms of this category: (a) a cry to God (v. 1); (b) narration of his trouble (vv.1–2); (c) expression of trust in God (vv. 3–6); (d) a plea for God's help (vv. 7–8). The superscription (see
Introduction) ascribes this psalm to David when he fled from his rebellious son Absalom
(2 Sam.15.13–15). Pss.3–41 are all ascribed to, or are about, David. **4:** *Holy mountain:* Mount
Zion, the place of the Temple, symbolic of God's heavenly abode.

and I wake again, for the LORD
   upholds me.
6 I will not fear the nations in their
   myriads
who set on me from all sides.

7 Rise up, LORD; save me, O my God.
   Thou dost strike all my foes across
      the face
   and breakest the teeth of the
      wicked.
8   Thine is the victory, O LORD,
and may[b] thy blessing rest upon
   thy people.

4

1 Answer me when I call, O God,
   maintainer of my right,
I was hard pressed, and thou didst
   set me at large;
be gracious to me now and hear
   my prayer.
2 Mortal men, how long will you pay
    me not honour but dishonour,
or set your heart on trifles and run
   after lies?
3 Know that the LORD has shown me[c]
   his marvellous love;
the LORD hears when I call to him.
4   However angry your hearts, do not
    do wrong;
though you lie abed resentful,[d] do
   not break silence:
5 pay your due of sacrifice, and trust in
   the LORD.

6 There are many who say, 'If only we
    might be prosperous again!
But the light of thy presence has fled
   from us, O LORD.'
7 Yet in my heart thou hast put more
   happiness
than they enjoyed when there was
   corn and wine in plenty.

Now I will lie down in peace, and   9
   sleep;
for thou alone, O LORD, makest me
   live unafraid.

5

Listen to my words, O LORD,   1
   consider my inmost thoughts;
heed my cry for help, my king and   2
   my God.
In the morning, when I say my   3
   prayers,
   thou wilt hear me.
I set out my morning sacrifice[e]
   and watch for thee, O LORD.
For thou art not a God who   4
   welcomes wickedness;
   evil can be no guest of thine.[f]
There is no place for arrogance   5
   before thee;
thou hatest evildoers,
thou makest an end of all liars.   6

The LORD detests traitors and men
   of blood.
But I, through thy great love, may   7
   come into thy house,
and bow low toward thy holy
   temple in awe of thee.
Lead me, LORD, in thy   8
   righteousness,
   because my enemies are on the
   watch;
give me a straight path to follow.
There is no trusting what they say,   9
   they are nothing but wind.
Their throats are an open[g]
   sepulchre;
smooth talk runs off their tongues.

b Thine . . . and may: or O LORD of salvation, may . . .
c Prob. rdg.; Heb. him.
d lie abed resentful: prob. rdg.; Heb. say on your beds.
e Or plea.
f who welcomes . . . thine: or who protects a wicked
man; an evil man cannot be thy guest.
g Or inscribed.

Ps. 4: Answer me when I call, O God. Partly a Lament, and partly exultation on delivery from
distress. **4-5:** The virtue of obedience. Note the mention of sacrifices; the obedience advised
is ritual as well as ethical. **6:** *Presence:* lit. "face," an idiom, originally royal, often applied to
God. A king could show pleasure by allowing his subjects to "seek his face," or by making his
face shine on someone; as used of God see Pss.31.16; 67.1 and Num.6.25.
    Ps. 5: Listen to my words, O LORD. A Lament. **1-2:** In asking God to *consider* his *inmost
thoughts* the poet acknowledges his guilt (which is amplified in vv. 4-6) and asks God's *help* for
uprightness in the future (see v. 8 for elaboration). **3:** A *sacrifice* was prescribed for various
sins (see Lev.3.1-17; 4.27-6.7), here possibly after a vigil in the Temple. To *watch for . . . LORD*
meant to look for signs of God's forgiveness and approval in the events of life. **7:** The psalmist
acknowledges that he does not meet the conditions to enter the *house* of the LORD, the Temple;

10 Bring ruin on them, O God;
let them fall by their own devices.
Cast them out, after all their
rebellions,
for they have defied thee.
11 But let all who take refuge in thee
rejoice,
let them for ever break into shouts
of joy;
shelter those who love thy name,
that they may exult in thee.
12 For thou, O LORD, wilt bless the
righteous;
thou wilt hedge him round with
favour as with a shield.

6

1 O LORD, do not condemn me in
thy anger,
do not punish me in thy fury.
2 Be merciful to me, O LORD, for I
am weak;
heal me, my very bones are shaken;
3 my soul quivers in dismay.
And thou, O LORD—how long?
4 Come back, O LORD; set my soul free,
deliver me for thy love's sake.
5 None talk of thee among the dead;
who praises thee in Sheol?

6 I am wearied with groaning;
all night long my pillow is wet
with tears,
I soak my bed with weeping.
7 Grief dims my eyes;
they are worn out with all my
woes.
8 Away from me, all you evildoers,
for the LORD has heard the sound
of my weeping.

The LORD has heard my entreaty; 9
the LORD will accept my prayer.
All my enemies shall be confounded 10
and dismayed;
they shall turn away in sudden
confusion.

7

O LORD my God, in thee I find 1
refuge;
save me, rescue me from my
pursuers,
before they tear at my throat like 2
a lion
and carry me off beyond hope of
rescue.
O LORD my God, if I have done 3
any of these things—
if I have stained my hands with
guilt,
if I have repaid a friend evil for 4
good
or set free an enemy who
attacked me without cause,
may my adversary come after me 5
and overtake me,
trample my life to the ground
and lay my honour in the dust!

Arise, O LORD, in thy anger, 6
rouse thyself in wrath against
my foes.
Awake, my God who hast ordered
that justice be done;
let the peoples assemble around 7
thee,
and take thou thy seat on high
above them.
O LORD, thou who dost pass 8
sentence on the nations,

---

see Ps.15 for conditions. God's love experienced as an *awe* of *the holy* and therefore a forgiveness, makes such entry possible; compare Isa.6.5–7. **11–12:** Transition from cries of sorrow to *shouts of joy* is a sign of God's *love* and *favour*.

Ps. 6: Be merciful to me, O LORD. A Lament (see Introduction), seemingly to be uttered in the time of a severe illness (vv. 2–7). **1–3:** *Bones are shaken . . . soul quivers:* probably chills and shivering resulting from a fever. Illness was considered a sign of God's *anger* and a punishment for sin; compare Jn.9.2–3. **4:** *Soul* is the Heb. *nephesh*, meaning the totality of life which is enslaved by illness. **5:** The motive for God's healing is that death would mean the end of praising God, for there is no worship of God in *Sheol*, the place of the dead. **9–10:** The psalm ends with a usual note of confidence. The *enemies* may be sickness, rather than men.

Ps. 7: Rescue me from my pursuers. A Lament (see Introduction). The background seems that of a prisoner awaiting trial, or of an innocent man pleading with God for justice. **5:** The crime of which the psalmist is accused seems to demand payment with *life. Lay honour in the dust:* to die in dishonor; compare Isa.53.9–12. **6–9:** This section has the flavor of the Book of Job. **6:** Compare 44.23 n. In the face of manifest injustice, God is seen as one who needs to *awake* from sleep. **7–8:** God here is asked to vindicate the psalmist's innocence before the peoples.

O LORD, judge me as my
righteousness deserves,
for I am clearly innocent.

9 Let wicked men do no more harm,
establish the reign of righteousness,[h]
thou who examinest both heart and
mind,
thou righteous God.

10 God, the High God, is my shield
who saves men of honest heart.

11 God is a just judge,
every day he requites the raging
enemy.

12 He sharpens his sword,
strings his bow and makes it ready.

13 He has prepared his deadly shafts
and tipped his arrows with fire.

14 But the enemy is in labour with
iniquity;
he conceives mischief, and his brood
is lies.

15 He has made a pit and dug it deep,
and he himself shall fall into the
hole that he has made.

16 His mischief shall recoil upon
himself,
and his violence fall on his own
head.

17 I will praise the LORD for his
righteousness
and sing a psalm to the name of
the LORD Most High.

8

1 O LORD our sovereign,
how glorious is thy name in all the
earth!
Thy majesty is praised high as the
heavens.

2 Out of the mouths of babes, of

infants at the breast,
thou hast rebuked[i] the mighty,
silencing enmity and vengeance to
teach thy foes a lesson.

3 When I look up at thy heavens, the
work of thy fingers,
the moon and the stars set in their
place by thee,

4 what is man that thou shouldst
remember him,
mortal man that thou shouldst
care for him?

5 Yet thou hast made him little less
than a god,
crowning him with glory and
honour.

6 Thou makest him master over all
thy creatures;
thou hast put everything under his
feet:

7 all sheep and oxen, all the wild
beasts,

8 the birds in the air and the fish
in the sea,
and all that moves along the
paths of ocean.

9 O LORD our sovereign,
how glorious is thy name in all the
earth!

9–10

1 I will praise thee, O LORD, with all
my heart,
I will tell the story of thy
marvellous acts.

2 I will rejoice and exult in thee,
I will praise thy name in psalms, O
thou Most High,

3 when my enemies turn back,
when they fall headlong and
perish at thy appearing;

h the reign of righteousness: or the cause of the righteous.
i Prob. rdg.; Heb. founded.

15: The theme of a wicked man falling into the *pit* he has *dug* is frequent in Wisdom literature. **17:** Many Laments end with a vow to praise or thank the LORD for what he will surely do.

Ps. 8: How glorious is thy name in all the earth. This Hymn, drawing its inspiration from the beauties of the night, glorifies God's majesty and power (v. 3). **1:** God's *name* is *glorious* when his power is manifest and acknowledged. **4–5:** The poet is here affirmative about man; elsewhere (144.3–4) the mood is one of discouragement about man and his estate; compare Job 7.17–19. **6–8:** The verses echo the idea in Gen.1.26–29. **9:** The repetition of v. 1 is the literary device known as "Inclusion," designed to extend the idea of God's glory to all that is between the two statements.

Pss. 9–10: Have pity on me, O LORD. A Lament (see Introduction). Most scholars take these two psalms as a single poem, as in the Sept. It is an alphabetic acrostic, though not perfectly so preserved; see Ps.111 n. The nations (9.5,15–19; 10.16) are possibly best interpreted as personal enemies. The vow (9.1–2) and expression of confidence (vv. 3–12), normally in the midst of

4 for thou hast upheld my right and
     my cause,
   seated on thy throne, thou
     righteous judge.
5 Thou hast rebuked the nations and
     overwhelmed the ungodly,
   thou hast blotted out their name for
     all time.
6 The strongholds of the enemy are
     thrown down for evermore;
   thou hast laid their cities in ruins,
     all memory of them is lost.
7 The LORD thunders,^*j* he sits enthroned
     for ever:
   he has set up his throne, his
     judgement-seat.
8 He it is who will judge the world
     with justice
   and try the cause of the peoples
     fairly.
9 So may the LORD be a tower of
     strength for the oppressed,
   a tower of strength in time of need,
10 that those who acknowledge thy
     name may trust in thee;
   for thou, LORD, dost not forsake
     those who seek thee.
11 Sing psalms to the LORD who
     dwells in Zion,
   proclaim his deeds among the
     nations.
12 For the Avenger of blood has
     remembered men's desire,
   and has not forgotten the cry of
     the poor.

13 Have pity on me, O LORD; look
     upon my affliction,
   thou who hast lifted me up^*k* and
     caught me back from the gates
     of death,
14 that I may repeat all thy praise
   and exult at this deliverance in the
     gates of Zion's city.

15 The nations have plunged into a
     pit of their own making;
   their own feet are entangled in the
     net which they hid.

16 Now the LORD makes himself
     known. Justice is done:
   the wicked man is trapped in his
     own devices.
17 They rush blindly down to Sheol,
     the wicked,
   all the nations who are heedless
     of God.
18 But the poor shall not always be
     unheeded
   nor the hope of the destitute be
     always vain.
19 Arise, LORD, give man no chance to
     boast his strength;
   summon the nations before thee for
     judgement.
20 Strike them with fear, O LORD,
   let the nations know that they are
     but men.

10 Why stand so far off, LORD,
   hiding thyself in time of need?
2 The wicked man in his pride hunts
     down the poor:
   may his crafty schemes be his own
     undoing!
3 The wicked man is obsessed with
     his own desires,
   and in his greed gives wickedness
     his blessing;
4 arrogant as he is, he scorns the
     LORD
   and leaves no place for God in all
     his schemes.
5 His ways are always devious;
   thy judgements are beyond his
     grasp,^*l*
   and he scoffs at all restraint.
6 He says to himself, 'I shall never be
     shaken;
   no misfortune can check my
     course.'^*m*
7 His mouth is full of lies and violence;
   mischief and trouble lurk under his
     tongue.
8 He lies in ambush in the villages

---

j thunders: *prob. rdg.; Heb. unintelligible.*
k thou . . . me up: *prob. rdg.; Heb.* from those who
   hate me.
l beyond his grasp: *prob. rdg.; Heb.* on high before him.
m my course: *prob. rdg.; Heb.* which.

Laments, are here at the beginning. **4:** The LORD's kingship is stressed in 9.7 and 10.16; in
9.11 "dwells" means enthroned. **7–9:** God is enthroned to vindicate the rights of the oppressed.
12: The duty of avenging a murdered or wronged person fell upon the nearest relative. God is
the *Avenger of the blood . . . of the poor;* compare Gen.4.10; Num.35.23–29. **13:** *Gates of
death:* Sheol, the place of the dead, under the image of a fortified city; compare Mt.16.18.
15–16: See 7.15. **10.2–6:** The meaning of life is totally beyond the *grasp* of the *wicked.*
4: *Place for God:* not atheists, but those who deny all moral force or scrutiny. See v. 13; 14.1 n.

and murders innocent men by stealth,
He is watching[n] intently for some
poor wretch;

9 he seizes him and drags him away
in his net;
he crouches stealthily, like a lion in
its lair
crouching to seize its victim;

10 the good man[o] is struck down and
sinks to the ground,
and poor wretches fall into his toils.

11 He says to himself, 'God has
forgotten;
he has hidden his face and has seen
nothing.'

12 Arise, LORD, set[p] thy hand to the
task;
do not forget the poor, O God.

13 Why, O God, has the wicked man
rejected thee
and said to himself that thou dost
not care?

14 Thou seest that mischief and trouble
are his companions,
thou takest the matter into thy own
hands.
The poor victim commits himself to
thee;
fatherless, he finds in thee his helper.

15 Break the power of wickedness and
wrong;
hunt out all wickedness until thou
canst find no more.

16 The LORD is king for ever and ever;
the nations have vanished from his
land.

17 Thou hast heard the lament of the
humble, O LORD,
and art attentive to their heart's
desire,

18 bringing justice to the orphan and
the downtrodden
that fear may never drive men from
their homes again.

11

In the LORD I have found my   1
refuge; why do you say to me,
'Flee to the mountains like a bird;
see how the wicked string their bows   2
and fit the arrow to the string,
to shoot down honest men out of
the darkness'?
When foundations are undermined,   3
what can the good man do?
The LORD is in his holy temple,   4
the LORD's throne is in heaven.
His eye is upon mankind, he takes
their measure at a glance.
The LORD weighs just and unjust   5
and hates with all his soul the lover
of violence.
He shall rain down red-hot coals   6
upon the wicked;
brimstone and scorching winds shall
be the cup they drink.
For the LORD is just and loves just   7
dealing;
his face is turned towards the
upright man.

12

Help, LORD, for loyalty is no more;   1
good faith between man and man
is over.
One man lies to another: 2
they talk with smooth lip and
double heart.
May the LORD make an end of   3
such smooth lips
and the tongue that talks so
boastfully!
They said, 'Our tongue can win   4
the day.
Words are our ally; who can master
us?'

n Prob. rdg.; Heb. storing up.
o the good man: prob. rdg.; Heb. om.
p Or who settest.

11: Here the *face* of God is *hidden* in order not to see; see 4.6 n. and 11.7 for another meaning.
  Ps. 11: The LORD is just. Some scholars classify this poem as a Song of Trust; it is kindred
to the statement of confidence contained in most Laments (see Introduction). **1:** The mountains
are often considered a place of refuge in calamity; see Gen.19.17; Mk.13.14. **4:** *In his holy
temple . . . throne in heaven:* not a contradiction to the psalmist. That God is in Zion (9.11),
the site of the Jerusalem Temple, does not exclude his domain in heaven from whence he can
look upon mankind. **6:** *Scorching winds* brought death from the desert, considered a punishment
from God; see Hos.13.15. *Cup* is a figure for destiny, generally unpleasant; compare Jer.25.15.
  Ps. 12: Help, LORD, for man is unreliable. A Lament (see Introduction). This psalm may
have been spoken in drama form in the Temple liturgy. **1–3:** Possibly spoken by a chorus.
2: *Double heart:* two-faced. **4:** *They said:* possibly a cue, to bring on another group of voices.

5 'For the ruin of the poor, for the
    groans of the needy,
now I will arise,' says the LORD,
'I will place him in the safety for
    which he longs.'

6 The words of the LORD are pure
    words:
silver refined in a crucible,
gold*q* seven times purified.
7 Do thou, LORD, protect us
and guard us from a profligate and
    evil generation.*r*
8 The wicked flaunt themselves on
    every side,
while profligacy stands high
    among mankind.

13

1 How long, O LORD, wilt thou quite
    forget me?
How long wilt thou hide thy face
    from me?
2 How long must I suffer anguish in
    my soul,
grief in my heart, day and night?
How long shall my enemy lord it
    over me?
3 Look now and answer me, O LORD
    my God.
Give light to my eyes lest I sleep the
    sleep of death,
4 lest my adversary say, 'I have
    overthrown him',
and my enemies rejoice at my
    downfall.
5 But for my part I trust in thy true
    love.

My heart shall rejoice, for thou
    hast set me free.
I will sing to the LORD, who has   6
    granted all my desire.

14

The impious fool says in his heart,   1*s*
    'There is no God.'
How vile men are, how depraved
    and loathsome;
not one does anything good!
The LORD looks down from heaven   2
    on all mankind
to see if any act wisely,
    if any seek out God.
But all are disloyal, all are rotten to   3
    the core;
not one does anything good,
    no, not even one.

Shall they not rue it,   4
all evildoers who devour my people
    as men devour bread,
and never call upon the LORD?
There they were in dire alarm;   5
for God was in the brotherhood of
    the godly.
The resistance of their victim was   6
    too much for them,
because the LORD was his refuge.
If only Israel's deliverance might come   7
    out of Zion!
When the LORD restores his
    people's fortunes,
let Jacob rejoice, let Israel be glad.

q gold: prob. rdg.; Heb. to the earth.
r a profligate and evil generation: prob. rdg.; Heb.
the generation which is for ever.
s Verses 1–7: cp. Ps. 53. 1–6.

5: *I will arise:* this expression, and others like it, is found repeatedly to depict the action of the
LORD, as in Num.10.35; see Ps.44.23 n. *Says the LORD:* could be spoken by a priest. **6–8:**
Another chorus, indicated by the word *us.* **6:** *Pure words:* in contrast to man's *smooth lip* (v. 2).
    Ps. 13: How long, O LORD? A very typical Lament (see Introduction) with distress (vv. 1–2),
request (vv. 3–4), trust (v. 5), and vow (v. 6). Note the force of the repetition of *How long.*
1: *Hide thy face:* compare 10.11 n.
    Ps. 14: If only deliverance might come from God. This Lament (see Introduction) is almost
identical with Ps.53. The poet says in despair (v. 13) that all men are vile; yet he speaks in
v. 5 of *the brotherhood of the godly.* **1:** *Impious fool:* a single word in Heb. In biblical language
the fool is the sinner. *Says in his heart:* decides in his conscience to act as if there is *no God;*
he is not an atheist. See 10.4 n. **2–6:** God's help enables the godly man to resist the wicked.
2: *To seek God* is to *act wisely:* a theme of Wisdom literature; see Wis.1.1. **4:** *Devour my people:*
to exploit them; see Ezek.34.9–10. *Call upon the LORD:* worship God. **7:** *Zion:* Mount Zion,
the location of the Temple; hence it means deliverance from God. *Jacob ... Israel:* the two
names of the ancestor of the Jews are each applied to the nation; see Gen.32.27–28.
    Ps. 15: Who may dwell on thy holy mountain? This psalm, difficult to classify (see Introduction),
is best considered a Wisdom poem on purity as a requirement for participating in the Temple
worship. **1:** *Who ... who:* possibly this was connected with the liturgy of entrance into the
Temple, the questions being asked by pilgrims and the answer given by a priest. *Lodge ...*

15

1 O LORD, who may lodge in thy
      tabernacle?
   Who may dwell on thy holy
      mountain?
2 The man of blameless life, who does
      what is right
   and speaks the truth from his
      heart;
3 who has no malice on his tongue,
   who never wrongs a friend
   and tells no tales against his
      neighbour;
4 the man who shows his scorn for
      the worthless
   and honours all who fear the LORD;
   who swears to his own hurt and does
      not retract;
5 who does not put his money out to
      usury
   and takes no bribe against an
      innocent man.
   He who does these things shall never
      be brought low.

16

1 Keep me, O God, for in thee have
      I found refuge.
2   I have said to the LORD,
   'Thou, Lord, art my felicity.'
3 The gods whom earth holds sacred
      are all worthless,
   and cursed are all who make them
      their delight;[t]
4 those who run after them[u] find
      trouble without end.
   I will not offer them libations of
      blood
   nor take their names upon my lips.
5 Thou, LORD, my allotted portion,
      thou my cup,
   thou dost enlarge my boundaries:

the lines fall for me in pleasant   6
      places,
indeed I am well content with my
      inheritance.
I will bless the LORD who has given 7
      me counsel:
in the night-time wisdom comes to
      me in my inward parts.
I have set the LORD continually   8
      before me:
with him[v] at my right hand I
      cannot be shaken.
Therefore my heart exults   9
      and my spirit rejoices,
my body too rests unafraid;
for thou wilt not abandon me to   10
      Sheol
nor suffer thy faithful servant to see
      the pit.
Thou wilt show me the path of   11
      life;
in thy presence is the fullness of
      joy,
in thy right hand pleasures for
      evermore.

17

Hear, LORD, my plea for justice,   1
      give my cry a hearing,
   listen to my prayer,
   for it is innocent of all deceit.
Let judgement in my cause issue   2
      from thy lips,
   let thine eyes be fixed on justice.
Thou hast tested my heart and   3
      watched me all night long;
   thou hast assayed me and found in
      me no mind to evil.
I will not speak of the deeds of men; 4
   I have taken good note of all thy
      sayings.

t are all worthless . . . delight: prob. rdg.; Heb. obscure.
u after them: prob. rdg.; Heb. obscure.
v with him: prob. rdg.; Heb. om.

---

dwell: the words are to be taken as hyperbole, not literally. **2–5:** The descriptive statements number ten; hence, they are often regarded as related in some way to the Ten Commandments.
   Ps. 16: Keep me, O God. This psalm is difficult to classify (see Introduction). **3–4:** A curse on idolators. **4:** *Blood* of animals was poured upon the altar as part of sacrificial ritual. To *take* the name of a god on the *lips* meant to call on him in worship; see Gen.13.4. **5:** *My cup:* destiny, here in an infrequent pleasant sense. *Enlarge my boundaries:* a figure of speech for abundant blessings. **6–11:** The blessedness of the faithful. **6:** *Lines:* a surveyor's measure. **7:** *Inward parts:* lit. the loins, considered the center of emotions and feelings. **8:** In a trial the defendants of an accused person stood at his *right hand;* here it is God. *Cannot be shaken:* the Heb. is the same as 15.5, there rendered "be brought low." **10:** *Sheol* and *pit* are synonymous; they refer to the place of the dead.
   Ps. 17: Listen to my prayer. A Lament (see Introduction). **1–5:** In courtroom language the

5 I have not strayed from the course
   of duty;
   I have followed thy path and
   never stumbled.
6 I call upon thee, O God, for thou
   wilt answer me.
   Bend down thy ear to me, listen to
   my words.
7   Show me how marvellous thy
   true love can be,
   who with thy hand dost save
   all who seek sanctuary from
   their enemies.
8 Keep me like the apple of thine eye;
   hide me in the shadow of thy
   wings
9   from the wicked who obstruct me,
   from deadly foes who throng round
   me.
10 They have stifled all compassion;
   their mouths are full of pride;
11 they press me hard,*w* now they hem
   me in,
   on the watch to bring me to the
   ground.
12 The enemy is like a lion eager for
   prey,
   like a young lion crouching in
   ambush.
13 Arise, LORD, meet him face to face
   and bring him down.
   Save my life from the wicked;
14   make an end of them*x* with thy
   sword.
   With thy hand, O LORD, make an
   end of them;*x*
   thrust them out of this world in
   the prime of their life,
   gorged as they are with thy good
   things,
   blest with many sons
   and leaving their children wealth in
   plenty.
15 But my plea is just: I shall see thy
   face,

and be blest with a vision of thee
   when I awake.

18

I love thee, O LORD my strength.   1
The LORD is my stronghold, my   2*y*
   fortress and my champion,
my God, my rock where I find safety,
my shield, my mountain refuge, my
   strong tower.
I will call on the LORD to whom all   3
   praise is due,
and I shall be delivered from my
   enemies.
When the bonds of death held me   4
   fast,
destructive torrents overtook me,
the bonds of Sheol tightened round   5
   me,
the snares of death were set to
   catch me;
then in anguish of heart I cried to   6
   the LORD,
I called for help to my God;
he heard me from his temple,
and my cry reached his ears.
The earth heaved and quaked,   7
the foundations of the mountains
   shook;
they heaved, because he was angry.
Smoke rose from his nostrils,   8
devouring fire came out of his
   mouth,
glowing coals and searing heat.
He swept the skies aside as he   9
   descended,
thick darkness lay under his feet.
He rode on a cherub, he flew   10
   through the air;
he swooped on the wings of the
   wind.

w they press me hard: prob. rdg.; Heb. our footsteps.
x make an end of them: prob. rdg.; Heb. unintelligible.
y Verses 2–50: cp. 2 Sam. 22. 2–51.

psalmist proclaims his innocence in calling on the LORD for justice and help. **8:** *Apple:* lit. the pupil, the most essential part of the eye. *Shadow of thy wings:* the image is of an eagle hovering over its young, with a reference to God's protection of Israel in the Exodus; compare Deut.32.10–11. **15:** Darkness is viewed as a time of trial, when evil is on the loose and God is absent; the dawn brings a new *vision* of God and his presence.
   Ps. 18: The LORD keeps faith with his king. A Thanksgiving. This psalm is also found in 2 Sam. ch. 22. There, and in the superscription (see Introduction), it is said that David sang this psalm when the LORD delivered him from all his enemies and from Saul. **1–3:** The poem begins by praising the LORD. **4–6:** Next, as in such psalms, the poet refers to troubles which were his. **4:** *Bonds of death* is a synonymous parallelism for *bonds of Sheol,* i.e. some mortal danger. **7–19:** God appears in response. The description of the appearance of the Deity reflects words and terms of Canaanite mythological language. **9–14:** The LORD is viewed as the storm god; see also Ps.29. **10:** *He rode on a cherub:* compare 68.4 n. and 104.3, where God rides on the

11 He made darkness around him his
hiding place
and dense^z vapour his canopy.^a

12 Thick clouds came out of the
radiance before him,
hailstones and glowing coals.

13 The LORD thundered from the
heavens
and the voice of the Most High
spoke out.^b

14 He loosed his arrows, he sped them
far and wide,
he shot forth lightning shafts and
sent them echoing.

15 The channels of the sea-bed were
revealed,
the foundations of earth laid bare
at the LORD's rebuke,
at the blast of the breath of his^c
nostrils.

16 He reached down from the height
and took me,
he drew me out of mighty waters,

17 he rescued me from my enemies,
strong as they were,
from my foes when they grew too
powerful for me.

18 They confronted me in the hour of
my peril,
but the LORD was my buttress.

19 He brought me out into an open
place,
he rescued me because he delighted
in me.

20 The LORD rewarded me as my
righteousness deserved;
my hands were clean, and he requited
me.

21 For I have followed the ways of the
LORD
and have not turned wickedly from
my God;

22 all his laws are before my eyes,
I have not failed to follow his decrees.

23 In his sight I was blameless
and kept myself from wilful sin;

24 the LORD requited me as my
righteousness deserved
and the purity of my life in his eyes.

25 With the loyal thou showest thyself
loyal

and with the blameless man
blameless.

26 With the savage man thou showest
thyself savage,
and^d tortuous with the perverse.

27 Thou deliverest humble folk,
and bringest proud looks down to
earth.

28 Thou, LORD, dost make my lamp
burn bright,
and my God will lighten my darkness.

29 With thy help I leap over a bank,
by God's aid I spring over a wall.

30 The way of God is perfect,
the LORD's word has stood the test;
he is the shield of all who take refuge
in him.

31 What god is there but the LORD?
What rock but our God?—

32 the God who girds me with strength
and makes my way blameless,

33 who makes me swift as a hind
and sets me secure on the
mountains;

34 who trains my hands for battle,
and my arms aim an arrow tipped
with bronze.

35 Thou hast given me the shield of thy
salvation,
thy hand sustains me, thy providence
makes me great.

36 Thou givest me room for my steps,
my feet have not faltered.

37 I pursue my enemies and overtake
them,
I do not return until I have made an
end of them.

38 I strike them down and they will
never rise again;
they fall beneath my feet.

39 Thou dost arm me with strength for
the battle
and dost subdue my foes before me.

40 Thou settest my foot on my enemies'
necks,

z Prob. rdg., cp. 2 Sam. 22. 12; Heb. dark.
a Prob. rdg.; Heb. adds thick clouds.
b Prob. rdg.; Heb. adds hailstones and glowing coals.
c Prob. rdg.; Heb. thy.
*d With the savage . . . savage, and: or With the pure
thou showest thyself pure, but . . .*

---

clouds. **13–19:** In mythology thunder and lightning are the symbols of the storm god's power
over the forces of chaos which he subdues when he becomes the Creator-King. Israelite poets
borrowed such motifs (see Introduction). The LORD defeats the powers of chaos, delivering
the man in distress. **20–29:** The deliverance was merited because God is just. **30–45:** God is

and I bring to nothing those that
    hate me.

41 They cry out and there is no one to
    help them,
they cry to the LORD and he does
    not answer.

42 I will pound them fine as dust before
    the wind,
like mud in the streets will I trample
    them.*e*

43 Thou dost deliver me from the
    clamour of the people,
and makest me master of the nations.
A people I never knew shall be my
    subjects;

44 as soon as they hear tell of me, they
    shall obey me,
and foreigners shall come cringing
    to me.

45 Foreigners shall be brought captive
    to me,
and emerge from their strongholds.

46 The LORD lives, blessed is my rock,
high above all is God who saves me.

47 O God, who grantest me vengeance,
who layest nations prostrate at my
    feet,

48 who dost rescue me from my foes
    and set me over my enemies,
thou dost deliver me from violent
    men.

49 Therefore, LORD, I will praise thee
    among the nations
and sing psalms to thy name,

50 to one who gives his king great
    victories
and in all his acts keeps faith with
    his anointed king,
with David and his descendants for
    ever.

19

1 The heavens tell out the glory of God,
the vault of heaven reveals his
    handiwork.

2 One day speaks to another,
night with night shares its knowledge,

3 and this without speech or
    language
or sound of any voice.

4 Their music goes out through all
    the earth,
their words reach to the end of
    the world.
In them a tent is fixed for the sun,

5 who comes out like a bridegroom
    from his wedding canopy,
rejoicing like a strong man to run
    his race.

6 His rising is at one end of the
    heavens,
his circuit touches their farthest
    ends;
and nothing is hidden from his
    heat.

7 The law of the LORD is perfect and
    revives the soul.
The LORD's instruction never fails,
and makes the simple wise.

8 The precepts of the LORD are right
    and rejoice the heart.
The commandment of the LORD
    shines clear
and gives light to the eyes.

9 The fear of the LORD is pure and
    abides for ever.
The LORD's decrees are true and
    righteous every one,

10 more to be desired than gold, pure
    gold in plenty,
sweeter than syrup or honey from
    the comb.

11 It is these that give thy servant
    warning,
and he who keeps them wins a
    great reward.

12 Who is aware of his unwitting
    sins?
Cleanse me of any secret fault.

13 Hold back thy servant also from

---

e Prob. rdg., cp. 2 Sam. 22. 43; Heb. will I empty
them out.

invincible in battle. **46–50:** This is an additional praise and vow. **50:** *His anointed king*
is *David.*
    Ps. 19: The glory of God. A Hymn. All creation reveals God's handiwork. Indeed, nature,
law, history, and the personal problems of the individual must be combined in terms of God's
kingdom. **4:** In Wisdom literature the *sun* is a symbol of justice and of wisdom itself; see
Wis.5.6; 7.29. **7–11:** The *law* is wisdom itself; and these *give* (v. 11) a more important *light*
(v. 8) than the sun. **12–14:** Man, even when inspired and guided, may still sin. Hence, the
worshiper asks forgiveness of God.

sins of self-will,
lest they get the better of me.
Then I shall be blameless
and innocent of any great
transgression.

14 May all that I say and think be
acceptable to thee,
O LORD, my rock and my redeemer!

20

1 May the LORD answer you in the
hour of trouble!
The name of Jacob's God be your
tower of strength,
2 give you help from the sanctuary
and send you support from Zion!
3 May he remember all your
offerings
and look with favour on your
rich sacrifices,
4 give you your heart's desire
and grant success to all your
plans!
5 Let us sing aloud in praise of
your victory,
let us do homage to the name of
our God!
The LORD grant all you ask!

6 Now I know
that the LORD has given victory to
his anointed king:
he will answer him from his holy
heaven
with the victorious might of his
right hand.
7 Some boast of chariots and some of
horses,
but our boast is the name of the
LORD our God.
8 They totter and fall,
but we rise up and are full of
courage.
9 O LORD, save the king,
and answer us in the hour of our
calling.

21

1 The king rejoices in thy might, O
LORD:
well may he exult in thy victory,
2 for thou hast given him his heart's
desire
and hast not refused him what
he asked.
3 Thou dost welcome him with
blessings and prosperity
and set a crown of fine gold upon
his head.
4 He asked of thee life, and thou didst
give it him,
length of days for ever and ever.
5 Thy salvation has brought him
great glory;
thou dost invest him with majesty
and honour,
6 for thou bestowest blessings on
him for evermore
and dost make him glad with joy
in thy presence.
7 The king puts his trust in the LORD;
the loving care of the Most High
holds him unshaken.

8 Your hand shall reach all your
enemies:
your right hand shall reach those
who hate you;
9 at your coming you shall plunge
them into a fiery furnace;
the LORD in his anger will strike
them down,
and fire shall consume them.
10 It will exterminate their offspring
from the earth
and rid mankind of their
posterity.
11 For they have aimed wicked blows
at you,
they have plotted mischief but
could not prevail;
12 but you will catch them round the
shoulders
and will aim with your bow-strings
at their faces.

Ps. 20: O LORD, save the king. A psalm, possibly Royal, of public supplication used in the
Temple liturgy before a battle. 1–5: A prayer for God's support of the king. 2: *The sanctuary*
and *Zion* are synonymous. 5: Choral response to the petitions. 6: Possibly an oracle pronounced
by a priest or cult prophet. 7–9: Choral response.
Ps. 21: The LORD gives life. A Royal Psalm of thanksgiving, as if in gratitude for the victory
prayed for in Ps.20. It is very similar in structure and content to Ps.18, though much briefer.
1–7: Motives for thanksgiving. 8–12: Perhaps an oracle by a priest or a cultic prophet.

13 Be exalted, O LORD, in thy might;
　we will sing a psalm of praise to
　　thy power.

22

1 My God, my God, why hast thou
　　forsaken me
　and art so far from saving me,
　　from heeding my groans?
2 O my God, I cry in the day-time
　　but thou dost not answer,
　in the night I cry but get no respite.
3 And yet thou art enthroned in
　　holiness,
　　thou art he whose praises Israel
　　　sings.
4 In thee our fathers put their trust;
　　they trusted, and thou didst
　　　rescue them.
5 Unto thee they cried and were
　　delivered;
　in thee they trusted and were not
　　put to shame.
6 But I am a worm, not a man,
　　abused by all men, scorned by
　　　the people.
7 All who see me jeer at me,
　make mouths at me and wag their
　　heads:
8 'He threw himself on the LORD for
　　rescue;
　let the LORD deliver him, for he
　　holds him dear!'
9 But thou art he who drew me from
　　the womb,
　who laid me at my mother's
　　breast.
10 Upon thee was I cast at birth;
　from my mother's womb thou hast
　　been my God.
11 Be not far from me,
　for trouble is near, and I have no
　　helper.
12 A herd of bulls surrounds me,

　great bulls of Bashan beset me.
13 Ravening and roaring lions
　open their mouths wide against me.
14 My strength drains away like
　　water
　and all my bones are loose.
　My heart has turned to wax and
　　melts within me.
15 My mouth[f] is dry as a potsherd,
　and my tongue sticks to my jaw;
　I am laid[g] low in the dust of
　　death.
16 The huntsmen are all about me;
　a band of ruffians rings me round,
　and they have hacked off[h] my hands
　　and my feet.
17 I tell my tale of misery,
　while they look on and gloat.
18 They share out my garments among
　　them
　and cast lots for my clothes.
19 But do not remain so far away, O
　　LORD;
　O my help, hasten to my aid.
20 Deliver my very self from the sword,
　my precious life from the axe.
21 Save me from the lion's mouth,
　my poor body[i] from the horns of
　　the wild ox.

22 I will declare thy fame to my
　　brethren;
　I will praise thee in the midst of
　　the assembly.
23 Praise him, you who fear the
　　LORD;
　all you sons of Jacob, do him
　　honour;
　stand in awe of him, all sons of
　　Israel.
24 For he has not scorned the
　　downtrodden,

f Prob. rdg.; Heb. My strength.
g I am laid: prob.rdg .; Heb. thou wilt lay me.
h and they have hacked off: prob. rdg.; Heb. like a lion.
i my poor body: prob. rdg.; Heb. thou hast answered me.

13: Antiphonal acclamation by the bystanders. For such recurring expressions, see Ps.57.5,11. **Ps. 22: My God, my God, why hast thou forsaken me?** The classic example of a Lament. **1:** Introduction: invocation of the divine name; see Mk.15.34. **2–19:** Motives for deliverance, apparently from serious illness: (a) God's deliverance of ancestors (vv. 2–5); (b) the poet's present abject and helpless state. **3:** God was considered *enthroned* above the Ark of the Covenant in the Temple; see Isa.6.1–3. **7:** *Wag their heads:* sign of derision. **8:** The poet's enemies deride his call for God's help since illness was considered a punishment from God for sin. **12:** *Bashan:* grazing area south of Damascus noted for its large cattle. **14–15:** Symptoms of an illness accompanied by a severe fever are evident. **18:** Assured of his death, the poet's enemies divide his possessions. **22–27:** A hymn of praise anticipating the healing and the fulfillment of a *vow* (v. 25). **29:** See 6.5 n.

nor shrunk in loathing from his
plight,
nor hidden his face from him,
but gave heed to him when he cried
out.

25 Thou dost inspire my praise in the
full assembly;
and I will pay my vows before all
who fear thee.

26 Let the humble eat and be satisfied.
Let those who seek the LORD
praise him
and be in good heart for ever.

27 Let all the ends of the earth remember
and turn again to the LORD;
let all the families of the nations
bow down before him.

28 For kingly power belongs to the
LORD,
and dominion over the nations
is his.

29 How can those buried in the earth
do him homage,
how can those who go down to the
grave bow before him?
But I shall live for his sake,

30 my posterity*j* shall serve him.
This shall be told of the Lord to
future generations;

31 and they shall justify him,
declaring to a people yet unborn
that this was his doing.

23

1 The LORD is my shepherd; I shall
want nothing.

2 He makes me lie down in green
pastures,
and leads me beside the waters of
peace;

he renews life within me,   3
and for his name's sake guides me
in the right path.

Even though I walk through a   4
valley dark as death
I fear no evil, for thou art with me,
thy staff and thy crook are my
comfort.

Thou spreadest a table for me in the   5
sight of my enemies;
thou hast richly bathed my head
with oil,
and my cup runs over.

Goodness and love unfailing, these   6
will follow me
all the days of my life,
and I shall dwell in the house of
the LORD
my whole life long.

24

The earth is the LORD's and all   1
that is in it,
the world and those who dwell
therein.

For it was he who founded it upon   2
the seas
and planted it firm upon the
waters beneath.

Who may go up the mountain of   3
the LORD?
And who may stand in his holy
place?
He who has clean hands and a   4
pure heart,
who has not set his mind on
falsehood,

j But I . . . posterity: *prob. rdg.; Heb. obscure.*

Ps. 23: The LORD is my shepherd and host. A Hymn, or possibly psalm of pilgrimage to the Temple. **1:** God is often considered a *shepherd*; see Ezek. ch. 34. *Want:* lack. **2:** *Green pastures* are scarce in Palestine. *Waters of peace:* pools of calm water fed by a spring and not the dangerous, turbulent streams formed by a downpour of rain. **3:** *Name's sake:* the "name" gives the nature of a person or a god. **4:** *Dark* reflects deep ravines of Judean hills. A Palestinian shepherd sometimes has a *staff*, a cudgel, to ward off wild animals, as well as a *crook* for guiding sheep. **5:** *The table* was probably where a sacrifice was eaten in the Temple in the *sight of . . . enemies. Cup runs over:* abundant blessing and joy. The head of an honored guest was anointed with oil in the Near East; see Lk.7.46. **6:** The joy and *goodness* experienced in the Temple will carry over into daily *life*. The poet will continue to *dwell* in the Temple in desire and in worship.
   Ps. 24: The LORD is Creator-King. A Liturgy used in the Temple worship. **1–2:** As the pilgrims go through the countryside they observe that the LORD is the possessor and creator of the earth. Myth in the Ancient Near East viewed God as defeating the sea, or chaos, in order to build the earth on the sea. *Waters beneath:* underground reservoir of water from which springs arise; compare Gen.7.11. **3:** As pilgrims approach the Temple they ask who is worthy to *stand in the holy place*. **4:** Conditions for entry are moral rather than ritual cleanliness.

and has not committed perjury.
5 He shall receive a blessing from
　　the LORD,
　and justice from God his saviour.
6 Such is the fortune of those who
　　seek him,
　who seek the face of the God of
　　Jacob.

7 Lift up your heads, you gates,
　　lift yourselves up, you everlasting
　　doors,
　that the king of glory may come in.
8 Who is the king of glory?
　The LORD strong and mighty,
　the LORD mighty in battle.
9 Lift up your heads, you gates,
　　lift them up, you everlasting
　　doors,
　that the king of glory may come
　　in.
10 Who then is the king of glory?
　The king of glory is the LORD of
　　Hosts.

25

1 Unto thee, O LORD my God, I lift
　　up my heart.
2 In thee I trust: do not put me to
　　shame,
　let not my enemies exult over me.
3 No man who hopes in thee is put
　　to shame;
　but shame comes to all who break
　　faith without cause.
4 Make thy paths known to me,
　　O LORD;
　teach me thy ways.
5 Lead me in thy truth and teach me;
　　thou art God my saviour.
　For thee I have waited all the day
　　long,
　for the coming of thy goodness,
　　LORD.*k*

6 Remember, LORD, thy tender care
　and thy love unfailing,
　shown from ages past.
7 Do not remember the sins and
　　offences of my youth,
　but remember me in thy unfailing
　　love.
8 The LORD is good and upright;
　therefore he teaches sinners the way
　　they should go.
9 He guides the humble man in doing
　　right,
　he teaches the humble his ways.
10 All the ways of the LORD are loving
　　and sure
　to men who keep his covenant
　　and his charge.
11 For the honour of thy name,
　　O LORD,
　forgive my wickedness, great as it is.
12 If there is any man who fears the
　　LORD,
　he shall be shown the path that he
　　should choose;
13 he shall enjoy lasting prosperity,
　and his children after him shall
　　inherit the land.
14 The LORD confides his purposes
　　to those who fear him,
　and his covenant is theirs to know.
15 My eyes are ever on the LORD,
　who alone can free my feet from
　　the net.

16 Turn to me and show me thy favour,
　for I am lonely and oppressed.
17 Relieve the sorrows of my heart
　　and bring me out of my distress.
18 Look at my misery and my trouble
　　and forgive me every sin.
19 Look at my enemies, see how many
　　they are
　and how violent their hatred for
　　me.

k for the coming . . . LORD: *transposed from end of*
verse 7.

5: *Seek the face of . . . God:* visit the Temple. **7–10:** This seems to reflect a processional liturgy with the Ark of the Covenant, in which antiphonal singing takes place. **7:** The procession with the Ark stops in front of the closed doors of the Temple; hence the dramatic request, *Lift*. **8a:** This question comes from within. **8b–9:** The answer comes from those bearing the Ark. **10:** Question and answer repeated.
　Ps. 25: Defend me and deliver me. A Lament (see Introduction); an alphabetical acrostic, each verse beginning with a successive letter of the Heb. alphabet (see Ps.111 n.). **1–3:** The poet's distress. **4–14:** He prays for God's guidance and help as in the past (4–9) for those faithful to his covenant (10–14). **13–14:** To *inherit the land* was a sign of God's blessing, especially after the return from the Babylonian Exile of 587, and was a reward for keeping the *covenant.* **15–22:** He pleads for deliverance from his sorrows.

20 Defend me and deliver me,
        do not put me to shame when I
            take refuge in thee.
21 Let integrity and uprightness
            protect me,
        for I have waited for thee, O
            LORD.
22 O God, redeem Israel from all his
            sorrows.

26

1 Give me justice, O LORD,
        for I have lived my life without
            reproach,
        and put unfaltering trust in the
            LORD.
2 Test me, O LORD, and try me;
        put my heart and mind to the
            proof.
3 For thy constant love is before my
            eyes,
        and I live in thy truth.
4 I have not sat among worthless
            men,
        nor do I mix with hypocrites;
5 I hate the company of evildoers
        and will not sit among the
            ungodly.
6 I wash my hands in innocence
        to join in procession round thy
            altar, O LORD,
7 singing of thy marvellous acts,
        recounting them all with thankful
            voice.
8 O LORD, I love the beauty of thy
            house,
        the place where thy glory dwells.
9 Do not sweep me away with sinners,
        nor cast me out with men who
            thirst for blood,
10 whose fingers are active in
            mischief,
        and their hands are full of bribes.
11 But I live my life without reproach;
        redeem me, O LORD, and show me
            thy favour.

12 When once my feet are planted on
            firm ground,
        I will bless the LORD in the full
            assembly.

27

1 The LORD is my light and my
            salvation;
        whom should I fear?
The LORD is the refuge of my life;
        of whom then should I go in
            dread?
2 When evildoers close in on me to
            devour me,
        it is my enemies, my assailants,
        who stumble and fall.
3 If an army should encamp against
            me,
        my heart would feel no fear;
        if armed men should fall upon me,
        even then I should be undismayed.
4 One thing I ask of the LORD,
        one thing I seek:
        that I may be constant in the
            house of the LORD
        all the days of my life,
        to gaze upon the beauty of the
            LORD
        and to seek him[1] in his temple.
5 For he will keep me safe beneath
            his roof
        in the day of misfortune;
        he will hide me under the cover of
            his tent;
        he will raise me beyond reach of
            distress.
6 Now I can raise my head high
        above the enemy all about me;
        so will I acclaim him with sacrifice
            before his tent
        and sing a psalm of praise to the
            LORD.

7 Hear, O LORD, when I call aloud;
        show me favour and answer me.

1 Or and to pay my morning worship.

Ps. 26: Redeem me, O LORD. A Lament (see Introduction). 1–3: A cry for justice. 4–7: A
protestation of innocence. 5: To *sit among the ungodly*: to be identified with their values.
6–7: To *wash* the *hands* was a dramatic protestation of innocence, possibly a condition for
joining a Temple procession; compare Deut.21.6. 9: *Thy glory*: the sense of God's majesty.
12: The usual vow.
    Ps. 27: Hear, O LORD, when I call aloud. The classification of this psalm is difficult; perhaps
it is a Lament or Hymn (see Introduction). 1–6: Such a statement of trust could be a part of
either a Lament or a Thanksgiving. 5: *Tent*: poetic word for Temple alluding to the Tabernacle
used for worship in the desert; see Lam.2.6; also v. 6. 7–14: A plea to God. The tone is more

8 'Come,' my heart has said,
'seek his face.'[m]
I will seek thy face, O LORD;
9 do not hide it from me,
nor in thy anger turn away thy
servant,
whose help thou hast been;
do not cast me off or forsake me,
O God my saviour.
10 Though my father and my mother
forsake me,
the LORD will take me into his
care.
11–12 Teach me thy way, O LORD;
do not give me up to the greed of
my enemies;
lead me by a level path
to escape my watchful foes;
liars stand up to give evidence
against me,
breathing malice.
13 Well I know that I shall see the
goodness of the LORD
in the land of the living.

14 Wait for the LORD; be strong, take
courage,
and wait for the LORD.

28

1 To thee, O LORD, I call;
O my Rock, be not deaf to my cry,
lest, if thou answer me with
silence,
I become like those who go down
to the abyss.
2 Hear my cry for mercy
when I call to thee for help,
when I lift my hands to thy holy
shrine.
3 Do not drag me away with the
ungodly, with evildoers,
who speak civilly to neighbours,
with malice in their hearts.

Reward them for their works, their 4
evil deeds;
reward them for what their hands
have done;
give them their deserts.
Because they pay no heed to the 5
works of the LORD
or to what his hands have done,
may he tear them down and
never build them up!

Blessed be the LORD, 6
for he has heard my cry for mercy.
The LORD is my strength, my shield, 7
in him my heart trusts;
so I am sustained, and my heart
leaps for joy,
and I praise him with my whole
body.[n]
The LORD is strength to his people, 8
a safe refuge for his anointed king.

O save thy people and bless thy own, 9
shepherd them, carry them for ever.

29

Ascribe to the LORD, you gods, 1
ascribe to the LORD glory and might.
Ascribe to the LORD the glory due 2
to his name;
bow down to the LORD in the
splendour of holiness.[o]
The God of glory thunders: 3
the voice of the LORD echoes
over the waters,
the LORD is over the mighty
waters.
The voice of the LORD is power. 4
The voice of the LORD is majesty.
The voice of the LORD breaks the 5
cedars,

m seek his face: *prob. rdg.; Heb.* seek ye my face.
n with my whole body: *prob. rdg.; Heb.* from my song.
o the splendour of holiness: *or* holy vestments.

typical of the Lament than of the Hymn. **8:** To *seek* the LORD's *face* originally meant to consult him by means of an oracle; see 2 Sam.21.1. Later it meant to seek him by faithful service and hence to seek his favor. See 4.6 n.
    Ps. 28: Hear my cry for mercy. A Lament (see Introduction), including Thanksgiving to be sung when the LORD has heard the cry of the psalmist. **1–3:** The appeal to God. **4–5:** Let God punish the wicked. **6–9:** The Thanksgiving.
    Ps. 29: The God of glory thunders. This hymn describes an awesome storm as it rises over the Mediterranean, crosses the Lebanon mountains in Phoenicia, the Anti-Lebanon in Syria, and spends itself in the desert. This poem is often viewed by modern students as an ancient Canaanite poem written originally to the storm god, Baal, and adapted by Israel with the necessary change in the divine name and other alterations. **3:** *Mighty waters:* Mediterranean Sea. **4:** *Voice of*

the LORD splinters the cedars of
   Lebanon.

6 He makes Lebanon skip like a calf,
   Sirion like a young wild ox.

7 The voice of the LORD makes flames
   of fire burst forth,

8 the voice of the LORD makes the
   wilderness writhe in travail;
the LORD makes the wilderness of
   Kadesh writhe.

9 The voice of the LORD makes the
   hinds calve
and brings kids early to birth;
and in his temple all cry, 'Glory!'

10 The LORD is king above*p* the flood,
the LORD has taken his royal seat as
   king for ever.

11 The LORD will give strength to his
   people;
the LORD will bless his people with
   peace.

my mountain refuge;
thou didst hide thy face, and I was
   struck with dismay.
I called unto thee, O LORD,   8
   and I pleaded with thee, Lord,
   for mercy:
'What profit in my death if I go down 9
   into the pit?
Can the dust confess thee or
   proclaim thy truth?
Hear, O LORD, and be gracious   10
   to me;
LORD, be my helper.'
Thou hast turned my laments into   11
   dancing;
thou hast stripped off my sackcloth
   and clothed me with joy,
that my spirit may sing psalms to   12
   thee and never cease.
I will confess thee for ever, O LORD
   my God.

30

1 I will exalt thee, O LORD;
   thou hast lifted me up
and hast not let my enemies make
   merry over me.

2 O LORD my God, I cried to thee and
   thou didst heal me.

3 O LORD, thou hast brought me up
   from Sheol
and saved my life as I was
   sinking into the abyss.*q*

4 Sing a psalm to the LORD, all you
   his loyal servants,
   and give thanks to his holy name.

5 In his anger is disquiet, in his favour
   there is life.
Tears may linger at nightfall,
   but joy comes in the morning.

6 Carefree as I was, I had said,
   'I can never be shaken.'

7 But, LORD, it was thy will to shake

31

With thee, O LORD, I have sought   1
   shelter,
   let me never be put to shame.
Deliver me in thy righteousness;
bow down and hear me,   2
   come quickly to my rescue;
be thou my rock of refuge,
   a stronghold to keep me safe.
Thou art to me both rock and   3
   stronghold;
lead me and guide me for the
   honour of thy name.
Set me free from the net men have   4
   hidden for me;
   thou art my refuge,
into thy keeping I commit my spirit. 5
Thou hast redeemed me, O LORD
   thou God of truth.

p Or since.
*q and saved . . . abyss: or and rescued me alive from
among those who go down to the abyss.*

---

the LORD: thunder. **6:** *Sirion:* Mount Hermon in Syria. *Skip like a calf:* reverberation of the
thunder. **8:** *Kadesh:* the desert east of the Syrian city of Kadesh. **9:** *The hinds calve* prematurely
from fright. **10:** *Above the flood:* the reservoir of waters above the vault of heaven from which,
according to Semitic thought, the rains came; see Gen.1.6–7; 7.12.
    Ps. 30: Thou hast turned my laments into dancing. A Thanksgiving, or a "declarative" Hymn
of praise. Perhaps it reflects recovery from serious illness. **3:** The entrance to *Sheol* was viewed
as an opening to a well into which the poet was already falling when pulled out by God. **11:**
The transition from sickness to health is expressed in a change from *sackcloth,* the clothing of
penance and grief, to festive garments of *joy.*
    Ps. 31: Be gracious to me, O LORD. A Lament, or, indeed, two separate Laments, the one
vv. 1–8, and the other vv. 9–24. Each Lament (see Introduction) contains Thanksgivings to
ensue after God has delivered the distressed man (vv. 5–8 and 21–24). **2:** Solid *rock* is the only
secure foothold on the shallow and pebbly or sandy soil of Palestine; compare Mt.7.24.

6 Thou hatest all who worship useless
    idols,
but I put my trust in the LORD.
7 I will rejoice and be glad in thy
    unfailing love;
for thou hast seen my affliction
    and hast cared for me in my
    distress.
8 Thou hast not abandoned me to
    the power of the enemy
but hast set me free to range at will.
9 Be gracious to me, O LORD, for I
    am in distress,
and my eyes are dimmed with grief.*r*
10 My life is worn away with sorrow
    and my years with sighing;
strong as I am, I stumble under my
    load of misery;
    there is disease in all my bones.
11 I have such enemies that all men
    scorn me;*s*
    my neighbours find me a burden,
    my friends shudder at me;
when they see me in the street they
    turn quickly away.
12 I am forgotten, like a dead man out
    of mind;
I have come to be like something
    lost.
13 For I hear many men whispering
    threats from every side,
in league against me as they are
    and plotting to take my life.
14 But, LORD, I put my trust in thee;
I say, 'Thou art my God.'
15 My fortunes are in thy hand;
rescue me from my enemies and
    those who persecute me.
16 Make thy face shine upon thy
    servant;
save me in thy unfailing love.
17 O LORD, do not put me to shame
    when I call upon thee;
let the wicked be ashamed, let them
    sink into Sheol.
18 Strike dumb the lying lips
which speak with contempt against

the righteous
in pride and arrogance.
19 How great is thy goodness,
stored up for those who fear thee,
made manifest before the eyes of men
for all who turn to thee for
    shelter.
20 Thou wilt hide them under the
    cover of thy presence
from men in league together;
thou keepest them beneath thy
    roof,
safe from contentious men.

21 Blessed be the LORD,
who worked a miracle of unfailing
    love for me
when I was in sore straits.*t*
22 In sudden alarm I said,
    'I am shut out from thy sight.'
But thou didst hear my cry for
    mercy
when I called to thee for help.
23 Love the LORD, all you his loyal
    servants.
The LORD protects the faithful
but pays the arrogant in full.
24 Be strong and take courage,
all you whose hope is in the
    LORD.

32

1 Happy the man whose
    disobedience is forgiven,
whose sin is put away!
2 Happy is a man when the LORD lays
    no guilt to his account,
and in his spirit there is no deceit.

3 While I refused to speak, my body
    wasted away
with moaning all day long.

r Prob. rdg.; Heb. adds my soul and my body.
s I have . . . scorn me: *or* I am scorned by all my
enemies.
t when . . . straits: *prob. rdg.; Heb.* like a city besieged.

7: *Unfailing love:* a single word, *hesed*, in Heb. *Hesed* is a key word in the OT. At times translated as "steadfast love" or "loving kindness," it has the connotation of a love arising out of a covenant or a bond, and manifested in concrete action; see also vv. 16 and 21. **9–13:** Compare with this passage Job 30.1–15. The distress is the loneliness of a man fallen from heights to a low estate, and fearful of plots against his life. The latter possibly is to be taken figuratively, but compare Jer.20.10. **16:** *Make thy face shine:* see 4.6 n. **20:** Compare 27.5.
Ps. 32: **Happy is a man who is forgiven.** A Thanksgiving Psalm, probably used as a Wisdom Psalm (see Introduction). An ancient idea that sickness was a consequence of sin is clearly implied (vv. 3–5). The poem proceeds (vv. 6–11) to commend to others the poet's experience of forgiveness and recovery from illness. **3:** *Refused to speak:* a refusal to acknowledge or confess

4   For day and night
thy hand was heavy upon me,
the sap in me dried up as in summer
    drought.

5   Then I declared my sin, I did not
    conceal my guilt.
I said, 'With sorrow I will confess
    my disobedience to the LORD';
then thou didst remit the penalty of
    my sin.

6   So every faithful heart shall pray to
    thee
in the hour of anxiety,[u] when great
    floods threaten.
Thou art a refuge for me from
    distress
so that it cannot touch me;[v]

7   thou dost guard me[w] and enfold
    me in salvation
beyond all reach of harm,[x]

8   I will teach you, and guide you in
    the way you should go.
I will keep you under my eye.

9   Do not behave like horse or mule,
    unreasoning creatures;
whose course must be checked with
    bit and bridle.

10   Many are the torments of the
    ungodly;
but unfailing love enfolds him who
    trusts in the LORD.

11   Rejoice in the LORD and be glad,
    you righteous men,
and sing aloud, all men of upright
    heart.

33

1   Shout for joy before the LORD, you
    who are righteous;
praise comes well from the upright.

Give thanks to the LORD on the   2
    harp;
sing him psalms to the ten-stringed
    lute.

Sing to him a new song;   3
strike up with all your art and
    shout in triumph.

    The word of the LORD holds true,   4
    and all his work endures.

The LORD loves righteousness and   5
    justice,
his love unfailing fills the earth.

The LORD's word made the heavens,   6
all the host of heaven was made at
    his command.

He gathered the sea like water in a   7
    goatskin;
he laid up the deep in his store-
    chambers.

Let the whole world fear the LORD   8
and all men on earth stand in awe
    of him.

For he spoke, and it was;   9
he commanded, and it stood firm.

The LORD brings the plans of   10
    nations to nothing;
he frustrates the counsel of the
    peoples.

But the LORD's own plans shall   11
    stand for ever,
and his counsel endure for all
    generations.

Happy is the nation whose God is   12
    the LORD,
the people he has chosen for his
    own possession.

The LORD looks out from heaven,   13
he sees the whole race of men;
he surveys from his dwelling-place   14
    all the inhabitants of earth.

u of anxiety: *prob. rdg.; Heb. unintelligible.*
v *Prob. rdg.; Heb.* him.
w *Prob. rdg.; Heb. adds an unintelligible word.*
x beyond . . . harm: *transposed from end of verse 9.*

---

sin, a condition for healing in traditional Israelite theology; see Prov.28.13. **4:** The *hand* of God is *heavy*, especially with calamity, when he touches someone's life. **8–11:** Possibly an oracle spoken by a priest in the Temple. **10:** *Love:* see 31.7 n.
    Ps. 33: Shout for joy. A Hymn (see Introduction), in praise and description of God. The praise (vv. 1–3) turns into praise of God as creator and ruler (4–11). **3:** *Shout in triumph:* one word in Heb.; the battle cry of an attacking army (Josh.6.5); later it meant a liturgical acclamation of God as king of Israel and of the nations (as here; compare Num.23.21), and as savior (compare Isa.44.23). **4–5:** The four terms, *holds true* (i.e. is faithful), *righteousness, justice,* and *love unfailing,* are used most consistently in the OT to describe God and his activities; compare Hos.2.19. **6:** *His command:* lit. "the wind of his mouth"; compare the "mighty wind" of Gen.1.2. **7:** *Water* was often carried in a whole *goatskin* of which the orifices were tied, the skins being lighter and more convenient than earthenware. Out of chaos (the combat in which God defeats the sea), there comes order. **8:** *Fear:* that is, religion, for which creation is the basis. **10–19:** God's universal rule. **10:** *Counsel of the peoples:* human wisdom and diplomacy. **12:** Israel in the context of many nations. In virtue of the mighty deeds at the Exodus by which

15 It is he who fashions the hearts of
    all men alike,
    who discerns all that they do.

16 A king is not saved by a great army,
    nor a warrior delivered by great
    strength.

17 A man cannot trust his horse to
    save him,
    nor can it deliver him for all its
    strength.

18 The LORD's eyes are turned towards
    those who fear him,
    towards those who hope for his
    unfailing love

19 to deliver them from death,
    to keep them alive in famine.

20 We have waited eagerly for the
    LORD;
    he is our help and our shield.

21 For in him our hearts are glad,
    because we have trusted in his
    holy name.

22 Let thy unfailing love, O LORD, rest
    upon us,
    as we have put our hope in thee.

34

1 I will bless the LORD continually;
   his praise shall be always on my
   lips.

2 In the LORD I will glory;
   the humble shall hear and be glad.

3 O glorify the LORD with me,
   and let us exalt his name together.

4 I sought the LORD's help and he
   answered me;
   he set me free from all my terrors.

5 Look towards him and shine with
   joy;
   no longer hang your heads in
   shame.

6 Here was a poor wretch who cried
   to the LORD;

he heard him and saved him from
    all his troubles.

7 The angel of the LORD is on
   guard
   round those who fear him, and
   rescues them.

8 Taste, then, and see that the LORD
   is good.
   Happy the man who finds refuge in
   him!

9 Fear the LORD, all you his holy
   people;
   for those who fear him lack nothing.

10 Unbelievers suffer want and go
    hungry,
    but those who seek the LORD lack
    no good thing.

11 Come, my children, listen to me:
    I will teach you the fear of the
    LORD.

12 Which of you delights in life
    and desires a long life to enjoy all
    good things?

13 Then keep your tongue from evil
    and your lips from uttering lies;

14 turn from evil and do good,
    seek peace and pursue it.

15 The eyes of the LORD are upon
    the righteous,
    and his ears are open to their
    cries.

16 The LORD sets his face against
    evildoers
    to blot out their memory from the
    earth.

17 When men cry for help, the LORD
    hears them
    and sets them free from all their
    troubles.

18 The LORD is close to those whose
    courage is broken
    and he saves those whose spirit is
    crushed.

19 The good man's misfortunes may
    be many,

God redeemed her from Egypt, Israel is his *possession*. 20–22: God alone is the hope of Israel.
Ps. 34: The LORD ransoms the lives of his servants. A Thanksgiving, and an alphabetic
acrostic (see Ps.25 n.). Both this psalm and Ps.25, also an acrostic, provide, after the alphabet
is complete, an extra verse which begins with the Heb. word for "ransom" or "redeem." Such
acrostic psalms were useful in instruction, and were connected to the experiences of Israel's
kings. Thus, the superscription (see Introduction) connects it with the time when David feigned
madness (1 Sam.21.11–16). **1–3:** The praise of God. **4–8:** God's deliverance. **7:** An *angel* to
guard it was promised to Israel at the Exodus; see Exod.23.20,23. The theme was developed
extensively during the persecution of the Maccabean period; compare Tob.5.6–27; 2 Macc.11.6–
8. **8:** To *taste* is to surrender to God's care and to distinguish true *good* from the apparent;
compare Job 34.3–6; Ps.37.4–6. **9–22:** The way of God with the righteous. **10:** *Unbelievers*:
older versions abstain from a minor correction of the Heb., adopted here, and hence read
instead, "young lions." *Lack no good thing*: compare 23.1.

the LORD delivers him out of them all.

20 He guards every bone of his body,
and not one of them is broken.

21 Their own misdeeds are death to the wicked,
and those who hate the righteous are brought to ruin.

22 The LORD ransoms the lives of his servants,
and none who seek refuge in him are brought to ruin.

35

1 Strive, O LORD, with those who strive against me;
fight against those who fight me.

2 Grasp shield and buckler,
and rise up to help me.

3 Uncover the spear and bar the way against my pursuers.
Let me hear thee declare,
'I am your salvation.'

4 Shame and disgrace be on those who seek my life;
and may those who plan to hurt me retreat in dismay!

5 May they be like chaff before the wind,
driven by the angel of the LORD!

6 Let their way be dark and slippery
as the angel of the LORD pursues them!

7 For unprovoked they have hidden a net^y for me,
unprovoked they have dug a pit to trap me.

8 May destruction unforeseen come on him;
may the net which he hid catch him;
may he crash headlong into it!

9 Then I shall rejoice in the LORD
and delight in his salvation.

10 My very bones cry out,
'LORD, who is like thee?—
thou saviour of the poor from those

too strong for them,
the poor and wretched from those who prey on them.'

11 Malicious witnesses step forward;
they question me on matters of which I know nothing.

12 They return me evil for good,
lying in wait^z to take my life.

13 And yet when they were sick, I put on sackcloth,
I mortified myself with fasting.
When my prayer came back unanswered,

14 I walked with head bowed in grief as if for a brother;
as one in sorrow for his mother I lay prostrate in mourning.

15 But when I stumbled, they crowded round rejoicing,
they crowded about me;
nameless ruffians^a jeered at me and nothing would stop them.

16 When I slipped, brutes who would mock even a hunchback
ground their teeth at me.

17 O Lord, how long wilt thou look on at those who hate me for no reason^b?

Rescue me out of their cruel grasp,
save my precious life from the unbelievers.

18 Then I will praise thee before a great assembly,
I will extol thee where many people meet.

19 Let no treacherous enemy gloat over me
nor leer at me in triumph.^{c}

20 No friendly greeting do they give to peaceable folk.
They invent lie upon lie,

21 they open their mouths at me:
'Hurrah!' they shout in their joy,
feasting their eyes on me.

22 Thou hast seen all this, O LORD,
do not keep silence;

y Prob. rdg., transposing a pit from this line to follow have dug.
z lying in wait: prob. rdg.; Heb. bereavement.
a nameless ruffians: or ruffians who give me no rest.
b Line transposed from verse 19. c See note on verse 17.

Ps. 35: O LORD, be not far from me. A Lament (see Introduction). Some would see three Laments in this psalm (vv. 1–10,11–18,19–28), yet the structure of the Lament was never so firm as to bar the variations found here. Rather, the whole psalm seems to be a single Lament, but with a three-fold vow. The first part (vv. 1–8) contains a cry for deliverance and vengeance, plus the first vow (9–10); the second (vv. 11–17), a cry of innocence and a plea for help, plus the second vow (v. 18); and the third (vv. 19–27), a complaint and a cry for justice, plus the third vow (v. 28). **5:** *Angel of the LORD:* see Ps.34.7 n. **13:** *Sackcloth:* sign of grief; *fasting:* expression of supplication; compare Joel 1.13–14. **16:** *Ground their teeth:* sign of hatred and malicious

O Lord, be not far from me.
23   Awake, bestir thyself, to do me
         justice,
     to plead my cause, my Lord and
         my God.
24   Judge me, O LORD my God, as thou
         art true;
     do not let them gloat over me.
25   Do not let them say to themselves,
         'Hurrah!
     We have swallowed him up at
         one gulp.'
26   Let them all be disgraced and
         dismayed
     who rejoice at my fall;
     let them be covered with shame and
         dishonour
     who glory over me.
27   But let all who would see me
         righted shout for joy,
     let them cry continually,
     'All glory to the LORD
     who would see his servant thrive!'
28   So shall I talk of thy justice
     and of thy praise all the day long.

36

1   Deep in his heart, sin whispers to
         the wicked man
     who cherishes no fear of God.
2   For he flatters himself in his own
         opinion
     and, when he is found out, he does
         not mend his ways.[d]
3   All that he says is mischievous and
         false;
     he has turned his back on wisdom;
4   in his bed he plots how best to do
         mischief.
     So set is he on his wrong courses
         that he rejects nothing evil.
5   But thy unfailing love, O LORD,
         reaches to heaven,

thy faithfulness to the skies.
Thy righteousness is like the lofty   6
     mountains,
thy judgements are like the great
     abyss;
O LORD, who savest man and beast,
how precious is thy unfailing   7
     love!
Gods and men seek refuge in the
     shadow of thy wings.
They are filled with the rich   8
     plenty of thy house,
and thou givest them water from
     the flowing stream of thy
     delights;
for with thee is the fountain of   9
     life,
and in thy light we are bathed
     with light.
Maintain thy love unfailing over   10
     those who know thee,
and thy justice toward men of
     honest heart.
Let not the foot of pride come   11
     near me,
no wicked hand disturb me.
There they lie, the evildoers,   12
they are hurled down and cannot
     rise.

37

Do not strive to outdo the   1
     evildoers
or emulate those who do wrong.
For like grass they soon wither,   2
     and fade like the green of spring.
Trust in the LORD and do good;   3
settle in the land and find safe
     pasture.
Depend upon the LORD,   4
and he will grant you your heart's
     desire.

---

d he does . . . ways: *prob. rdg.; Heb. unintelligible.*

---

aggressiveness; compare Lam.2.16; Acts 7.54. **23–24:** *Justice . . . Judge . . . true:* qualities of
God by which he saves the oppressed.
   Ps. 36: Maintain thy love unfailing. Perhaps a Lament, though a common element, the vow,
is missing (see Introduction); it might be classified as a Wisdom Psalm, depicting the two ways,
the lonely way of evil and the union with God, the way of the good. **1:** *Fear of God* is the
beginning of Wisdom, according to the sages, and the sinner is a fool; see Prov.13.6. **5–6:** God's
faithfulness, righteousness, judgements are qualities by which he saves both *man* and *beast.*
8–9: A *fountain* of *water* in arid Palestine is a symbol of God's life-giving qualities; compare
Jer.2.13; Ezek.47.1–12.
   Ps. 37: The righteous shall possess the land. A Wisdom Psalm, in acrostic form (see Ps.111 n.).
V. 40 has the idea, but not the identical words, found in 25.22 and 34.22, that the LORD will save.
Just as some Laments can be related to the challenging speeches of Job, so a psalm such as this

5   Commit your life to the LORD;
       trust in him and he will act.
6   He will make your righteousness
          shine clear as the day
      and the justice of your cause like
          the sun at noon.
7   Wait quietly for the LORD, be
          patient till he comes;
      do not strive to outdo the
          successful
      nor envy him who gains his ends.
8   Be angry no more, have done with
          wrath;
          strive not to outdo in evildoing.
9   For evildoers will be destroyed,
      but they who hope in the LORD
          shall possess the land.
10 A little while, and the wicked will
          be no more;
      look well, and you will find their
          place is empty.
11   But the humble shall possess the
          land
      and enjoy untold prosperity.
12 The wicked mutter against the
          righteous man
      and grind their teeth at the sight of
          him;
13   the Lord shall laugh at them,
      for he sees that their time is coming.
14 The wicked have drawn their swords
          and strung their bows
      to bring low the poor and needy
      and to slaughter honest men.
15 Their swords shall pierce their own
          hearts
      and their bows be broken.
16 Better is the little which the
          righteous has
      than the great wealth of the
          wicked.
17 For the strong arm of the wicked
          shall be broken,
      but the LORD upholds the righteous.
18 The LORD knows each day of the
          good man's life,
      and his inheritance shall last for
          ever.
19   When times are bad, he shall not
          be distressed,
      and in days of famine he shall
          have enough.

But the wicked shall perish,   20
and their children shall beg their
   bread.[e]
The enemies of the LORD, like fuel
   in a furnace,[f]
are consumed in smoke.
The wicked man borrows and does   21
   not pay back,
but the righteous is a generous giver.
All whom the LORD has blessed shall 22
   possess the land,
   and all who are cursed by him
      shall be destroyed.
It is the LORD who directs a man's   23
   steps,
   he holds him firm and watches
      over his path.
Though he may fall, he will not   24
   go headlong,
for the LORD grasps him by the
   hand.
I have been young and am now   25
   grown old,
and never have I seen a righteous
   man forsaken [g]
Day in, day out, he lends   26
   generously,
   and his children become a
      blessing.
Turn from evil and do good,   27
   and live at peace for ever;
   for the LORD is a lover of justice 28
      and will not forsake his loyal
         servants.
The lawless are banished for ever
   and the children of the wicked
      destroyed.
The righteous shall possess the land 29
and shall live there at peace for ever.
The righteous man utters words of   30
   wisdom
and justice is always on his lips.
   The law of his God is in his   31
      heart,
   his steps do not falter.
The wicked watch for the righteous   32
   man
   and seek to take his life;

e *Line transposed from verse 25.*
f *like . . . furnace: prob. rdg.; Heb. like the worth of
rams.*
g *See note on verse 20.*

---

can be related to the "orthodox" view of Job's "friends," that the righteous will be rewarded
but the wicked perish (compare vv. 20 and 25). Because the psalm is an acrostic, it presents a
variety of views, rather than a single, well-developed view. **11:** Compare Mt.5.5. **12:** *Grind
teeth:* see 35.16 n. **18:** *Knows each day:* is in control of it. **22:** For the significance of a curse see

33 but the LORD will not leave him in
    their power
  nor let him be condemned before
    his judges.
34 Wait for the LORD and hold to his
    way;
  he will keep you[h] safe from
    wicked men[i]
  and will raise you to be master of
    the land.
  When the wicked are destroyed, you
    shall be there to see.
35 I have watched a wicked man at
    his work,
  rank as a spreading tree in its
    native soil.
36 I passed by one day, and he was
    gone;
  I searched for him, but he could
    not be found.
37 Now look at the good man, watch
    him who is honest,
  for the man of peace leaves
    descendants;
38 but transgressors are wiped out one
    and all,
  and the descendants of the wicked
    are destroyed.
39 Deliverance for the righteous comes
    from the LORD,
  their refuge in time of trouble.
40 The LORD will help them and
    deliver them;[j]
  he will save them because they
    seek shelter with him.

38

1 O LORD, do not rebuke me in thy
    anger,
  nor punish me in thy wrath.
2 For thou hast aimed thy arrows[k]
    at me,
  and thy hand weighs heavy
    upon me.
3 Thy indignation has left no part
    of my body unscarred;

there is no health in my whole
  frame because of my sin.
For my iniquities have poured over   4
  my head;
they are a load heavier than I can
  bear.
My wounds fester and stink because   5
  of my folly.
I am bowed down and utterly   6
  prostrate.
All day long I go about as if in
  mourning,
for my loins burn with fever,   7
  and there is no wholesome flesh
  in me.
All battered and benumbed,   8
  I groan aloud in my heart's
  longing.
O Lord, all my lament lies open   9
  before thee
and my sighing is no secret to thee.
My heart beats fast, my strength has 10
  ebbed away,
  and the light has gone out of my
  eyes.
My friends and my companions   11
  shun me in my sickness,
and my kinsfolk keep far away.
Those who wish me dead defame   12
  me,
those who mean to injure me spread
  cruel gossip
and mutter slanders all day long.
But I am deaf, I do not listen;   13
I am like a dumb man who cannot
  open his mouth.
I behave like a man who cannot   14
  hear
  and whose tongue offers no
  defence.
On thee, O LORD, I fix my hope;   15
thou wilt answer, O Lord my God.
I said, 'Let them never rejoice over 16
  me
who exult when my foot slips.'

h Prob. rdg.; Heb. them.
i he will . . . wicked men: *transposed from verse 40.*
j See note on verse 34.
k thou . . . arrows: *prob. rdg.; Heb.* thy arrows have
come down.

Num.22.6. **36–38:** In a number of biblical books, the view occurs that the scandal of seeing a
wicked man prospering would be removed by the sudden death of the wicked or the extermination of his *descendants.*
  Ps. 38: Lord, do not thou forsake me. A Lament (see Introduction). The psalmist asserts that
his sickness (v. 3) is the result of sin and folly. **2:** God's *hand* is *heavy* upon a person when he
visits him with affliction and trial; compare 32.4 and see n. **3:** The poet attributes loss of *health*
to his *sin* and to God's consequent *indignation.* **10:** *Heart beats fast,* etc.: symptoms of the
illness. **12:** *Spread . . . slanders:* possibly conjectures as to the sin that is causing the illness.

17 I am indeed prone to stumble,
       and suffering is never far away.
18   I make no secret of my iniquity
       and am anxious at the thought
          of my sin.
19 But many are my enemies, all
          without cause,[l]
    and many those who hate me
          wrongfully.
20 Those who repay good with evil
    oppose me because my purpose is
          good.
21   But, LORD, do not thou forsake
          me;
    keep not far from me, my God.
22 Hasten to my help, O Lord my
          salvation.

39

1 I said: I will keep close watch
          over myself
       that all I say may be free from sin.
    I will keep a muzzle on my mouth,
       so long as wicked men confront
          me.
2 In dumb silence I held my peace.
    So my agony was quickened,
3   and my heart burned within me.
    My mind wandered as the fever
          grew,
    and I began to speak:
4 LORD, let me know my end
       and the number of my days;
    tell me how short my life must be.
5 I know thou hast made my days a
          mere span long,
    and my whole life is nothing in
          thy sight.
    Man, though he stands upright, is
       but a puff of wind,
6 he moves like a phantom;
    the riches[m] he piles up are no
          more than vapour,

he does not know who will enjoy
       them.
And now, Lord, what do I wait for? 7
My hope is in thee.
    Deliver me from all who do me   8
       wrong,
    make me no longer the butt of
       fools.
I am dumb, I will not open my   9
       mouth,
    because it is thy doing.
Plague me no more;   10
I am exhausted by thy blows.
When thou dost rebuke a man to   11
       punish his sin,
all his charm festers and drains
       away;
    indeed man is only a puff of wind.
Hear my prayer, O LORD;   12
    listen to my cry,
hold not thy peace at my tears;
for I find shelter with thee,
I am thy guest, as all my fathers
       were.
Frown on me no more and let me   13
       smile again,
before I go away and cease to be.

40

I waited, waited for the LORD,   1
he bent down to me and heard my
       cry.
He brought me up out of the muddy   2
       pit,
out of the mire and the clay;
he set my feet on a rock
       and gave me a firm footing;
and on my lips he put a new song,   3
    a song of praise to our God.
Many when they see will be filled
    with awe

l all . . . cause: prob. rdg.; Heb. living.
m the riches: prob. rdg.; Heb. they murmur.

18: In traditional theology restoration to health required the confession of *sin*. Compare 32.3–5.
    Ps. 39: Plague me no more. A Lament (see Introduction), but a rather strange one, for it begins by asserting that the poet had earlier stifled his complaint (vv. 1–3). Indeed, this silence increased his agony. Aware that life is short (*span* is a measurement, about three inches, v. 5) and riches unyielding (v. 6), he prays for healing from his sickness, even if he may receive only a brief respite (vv. 7–13). **12–13:** It was the duty of a host, here God, to defend his *guest* against any avenger and even to hold back his own vengeance, if it were deserved, until the guest went *away*.
    Ps. 40: My desire is to do thy will, O LORD. A Thanksgiving, though ending with a Lament (vv. 12–17); see Introduction. Vv. 13–17 are almost identical with Ps.70. Like other psalms at the end of Book 1 (see Introduction), this psalm echoes Wisdom poems, as in v. 4, *happy is the man*. **2:** The psalmist viewed himself as already sinking into the *pit*, i.e. Sheol, when God drew

and will learn to trust in the
LORD:
4   happy is the man
who makes the LORD his trust,
and does not look to brutal and
treacherous men.
5 Great things thou hast done,
O LORD my God;
thy wonderful purposes are all for
our good;
none can compare with thee;
I would proclaim them and speak
of them,
but they are more than I can tell.
6 If thou hadst desired sacrifice and
offering
thou wouldst have given me ears
to hear.
If thou hadst asked for whole-
offering and sin-offering
7   I would have said, 'Here I am.'*n*
8 My desire is to do thy will, O God,
and thy law is in my heart.
9 In the great assembly I have
proclaimed what is right,
I do not hold back my words,
as thou knowest, O LORD.
10 I have not kept thy goodness
hidden in my heart;
I have proclaimed thy faithfulness
and saving power,
and not concealed thy unfailing
love and truth
from the great assembly.
11   Thou, O LORD, dost not withhold
thy tender care from me;
thy unfailing love and truth for ever
guard me.

12   For misfortunes beyond counting
press on me from all sides;
my iniquities have overtaken me,
and my sight fails;
they are more than the hairs of my
head,
and my courage forsakes me.
13*o* Show me favour, O LORD, and
save me;
hasten to help me, O LORD.
14   Let those who seek to take my
life

be put to shame and dismayed one
and all;
let all who love to hurt me shrink
back disgraced;
let those who cry 'Hurrah!' at my   15
downfall
be horrified at their reward of
shame.
But let all those who seek thee   16
be jubilant and rejoice in thee;
and let those who long for thy saving
help ever cry,
'All glory to the LORD!'

But I am poor and needy;   17
O Lord, think of me.*p*
Thou art my help and my salvation;
O my God, make no delay.

41

Happy the man who has a concern   1
for the helpless!
The LORD will save him in time of
trouble.
The LORD protects him and gives   2
him life,
making him secure in the land;
the LORD never leaves him*q* to the
greed of his enemies.
He nurses him on his sick-bed;   3
he turns his bed when he is ill.

But I said, 'LORD, be gracious to me; 4
heal me, for I have sinned against
thee.'
'His case is desperate,' my enemies   5
say;
'when will he die, and his line become
extinct?'
All who visit me speak from an   6
empty heart,
alert to gather bad news;
then they go out to spread it abroad.

---

n Prob. rdg.; Heb. adds in a scroll of a book it is prescribed for me.
o Verses 13–17: cp. Ps. 70. 1–5.
p O Lord . . . me: prob. rdg.; Heb. may the Lord think
of me.
q never leaves him: prob. rdg.; Heb. do thou not give
him up . . .

---

him out and set him on a *rock*. **6–8**: The righteous man esteems God's *will* above ritual sacrifice.
This passage is quoted in Heb.10.5–7. On Tfn. *n*, see 56.8 and Exod.32.33.
    Ps. 41: Thou keepest me for ever in thy sight. A mixture of Thanksgiving and Lament; see
Introduction. Possibly the psalm has been reworked as a conclusion to Book 1 (see Introduction).
It begins in the same way as Ps.1: *Happy is the man*. **4–9**: The Lament, possibly of some king,

7 All who hate me whisper together
    about me
  and love to make the worst of
    everything:
8 'An evil spell is cast upon him;
  he is laid on his bed, and will rise no
    more.'
9 Even the friend whom I trusted, who
    ate at my table,ʳ
  exults over my misfortune.
10 O Lᴏʀᴅ, be gracious and restore me,
  that I may pay them out to the full.ˢ
11 Then I shall know that thou
    delightest in me
  and that my enemy will not triumph
    over me.
12 But I am upheld by thee because of
    my innocence;
  thou keepest me for ever in thy
    sight.

13 Blessed be the Lᴏʀᴅ, the God of
    Israel,
  from everlasting to everlasting.

Amen, Amen.

BOOK 2

42–43

1 As a hind longs for the running
    streams,
  so do I long for thee, O God.
2 With my whole being I thirst for
    God, the living God.
  When shall I come to God and
    appear in his presence?
3 Day and night, tears are my food;

'Where is your God?' they ask me
    all day long.
As I pour out my soul in distress,   4
    I call to mind
how I marched in the ranks of the
    great to the house of God,
among exultant shouts of praise, the
    clamour of the pilgrims.
How deep I am sunk in misery,   5
    groaning in my distress:
yet I will wait for God;
I will praise him continually,
    my deliverer, my God.
I am sunk in misery, therefore will I   6
    remember thee,
though from the Hermons and the
    springs of Jordan,
    and from the hill of Mizar,
deep calls to deep in the roar of thy   7
    cataracts,
and all thy waves, all thy breakers,
    pass over me.
The Lᴏʀᴅ makes his unfailing love   8
    shine forthᵗ
    alike by day and night;
his praise on my lips is a prayer
    to the God of my life.
I will say to God my rock, 'Why   9
    hast thou forgotten me?'
Why must I go like a mourner
    because my foes oppress me?
My enemies taunt me, jeeringᵘ at   10
    my misfortunes;
'Where is your God?' they ask me all
    day long.
How deep I am sunk in misery,   11
    groaning in my distress:
yet I will wait for God;

r who . . . table: or slanders me.
s to the full: transposed from end of verse 9.
t makes . . . forth: or entrusts me to his unfailing love.
u jeering: prob. rdg.; Heb. obscure.

often interpreted as David; the *friend* (v. 9) has been traditionally seen as Ahithophel (2 Sam.15.30–31). **5**: The extinction of *his line* was the greatest tragedy and punishment from God that could befall a person. **9**: *Ate at my table:* the height in betrayal; see Jn.13.18. **13**: This verse, not truly a part of the psalm, marks the end of Book 1. Compare 72.18–20; 89.52; 106.48, which end, respectively, Books 2, 3, and 4.
  Pss. 42–43: Send forth thy light. These two psalms make up a single Lament which has three parts. (Note the repeated refrain, vv. 5,11; 43.5. Compare the three-part structure of Ps.35.) The psalmist lives in the far north, near the sources of the Jordan (42.6); sick, he cannot join the pilgrims on their way to Jerusalem but hopes to do so in the future (43.3–4). The poems in Book 2 (see Introduction) emphasize the importance of Jerusalem and the Temple, and hence this psalm is an appropriate beginning. **2**: God's presence was considered especially realized above the Ark of the Covenant in the Temple; see 1 Chr.13.6. **3**: *Where is your God?:* the rhetorical question is intended as a reproach to a man in distress, as with the implication that God has deserted him if sin caused his illness. See the repetition in v. 10. See Job 35.10. **6**: *Hermons:* A mountain in northern Palestine, usually written Hermon, but here in the plural because of its three peaks. *Mizar:* a hill probably near Hermon, its exact location is unknown.

I will praise him continually,
my deliverer, my God.

43 Plead my cause and give me
    judgement against an impious
    race;
save me from malignant men and
    liars, O God.
2 Thou, O God, art my refuge; why
    hast thou rejected me?
Why must I go like a mourner
    because my foes oppress me?
3 Send forth thy light and thy truth
    to be my guide
and lead me to thy holy hill, to thy
    tabernacle,
4 then shall I come to the altar of
    God, the God of my joy,
and praise thee on the harp, O God,
    thou God of my delight.
5 How deep I am sunk in misery,
    groaning in my distress:
yet I will wait for God;
I will praise him continually,
my deliverer, my God.

44

1 O God, we have heard for ourselves,
    our fathers have told us
all the deeds which thou didst in
    their days,
2 all the work of thy hand in days of
    old.
Thou didst plant them in the land
    and drive the nations out,
thou didst make them strike root,
    breaking up the peoples;
3 it was not our fathers' swords won
    them the land,
nor their arm that gave them the
    victory,
but thy right hand and thy arm
and the light of thy presence; such
    was thy favour to them.
4 Thou art my king and my God;
at thy bidding Jacob is victorious.

By thy help we will throw back our   5
    enemies,
in thy name we will trample down
    our adversaries.
I will not trust in my bow,   6
nor will my sword win me the
    victory;
for thou dost deliver us from our   7
    foes
and put all our enemies to shame.
In God have we gloried all day long,   8
and we will praise thy name for ever.
But now thou hast rejected and   9
    humbled us
and dost no longer lead our armies
    into battle.
Thou hast hurled us back before   10
    the enemy,
and our foes plunder us as they will.
Thou hast given us up to be   11
    butchered like sheep
 and hast scattered us among the
    nations.
Thou hast sold thy people for next   12
    to nothing
and had no profit from the sale.
Thou hast exposed us to the taunts   13
    of our neighbours,
to the mockery and contempt of all
    around.
Thou hast made us a byword among   14
    the nations,
 and the peoples shake their heads
    at us;
so my disgrace confronts me all   15
    day long,
and I am covered with shame
 at the shouts of those who taunt   16
    and abuse me
as the enemy takes his revenge.
All this has befallen us, but we do   17
    not forget thee
and have not betrayed thy covenant;
we have not gone back on our   18
    purpose,
nor have our feet strayed from thy
    path.

43.3: *Holy hill:* this is the site of the Temple, where the psalmist prays to be sent.
Ps. 44: Arise and come to our help. A collective Lament, after a bitter military defeat suffered
by the nation. **2:** Compare Exod.15.17. **3:** That God fought and won the victory for Israel at
the time of the Exodus is a frequent theme; compare Josh.24.6–11. **9:** Perhaps this is a reference
to the time when the Ark of the Covenant was taken by *armies into battle;* compare 1 Sam.4.1–11.
The Ark was lost during the destruction of Jerusalem in 587 B.C. **10–16:** The conditions described
here fit the period after the destruction of Jerusalem when Israel was scattered *among the
nations;* see Ezek.36.1–8. **12:** God received *no profit* from handing over Israel into captivity
because the nations gave credit for it to their gods, not to him. See Isa.52.3. **17–22:** The conditions described here fit the Maccabean period (about 165 B.C.) when Israel was persecuted

19 Yet thou hast crushed us as the sea-
    serpent was crushed
and covered us with the darkness of
    death.
20 If we had forgotten the name of our
    God
and spread our hands in prayer to
    any other,
21 would not God find this out,
for he knows the secrets of the heart?
22 Because of thee we are done to
    death all day long,
and are treated as sheep for
    slaughter.
23 Bestir thyself, Lord; why dost thou
    sleep?
Awake, do not reject us for ever.
24 Why dost thou hide thy face,
heedless of our misery and our
    sufferings?
25 For we sink down to the dust
and lie prone on the earth.
26 Arise and come to our help;
    for thy love's sake set us free.

45

1 My heart is stirred by a noble theme,
in a king's honour I utter the song I
    have made,
and my tongue runs like the pen of
    an expert scribe.

2 You surpass all mankind in beauty,
your lips are moulded in grace,
so you are blessed by God for ever.
3 With your sword ready at your side,
    warrior king,
4 your limbs resplendent*v* in their
    royal armour,
ride on to execute true sentence and
    just judgement.

Your right hand shall show you a
    scene of terror!
your sharp arrows flying, nations   5
    beneath your feet,
the courage of the king's foes
    melting away!*w*

Your throne is like God's throne,   6
    eternal,
your royal sceptre a sceptre of
    righteousness.
You have loved right and hated   7
    wrong;
so God, your God, has anointed you
    above your fellows with oil, the
    token of joy.
Your robes are all fragrant with   8
    myrrh and powder of aloes,
and the music of strings greets you
    from a palace panelled with ivory.
A princess takes her place among   9
    the noblest of your women,
a royal lady at your side in gold
    of Ophir.

Listen, my daughter, hear my words 10
    and consider them:
forget your own people and your
    father's house;
and, when the king desires your   11
    beauty,
remember that he is your lord.
Do him obeisance, daughter of Tyre, 12
and the richest in the land will
    court you with gifts.

In the palace honour awaits her;*x* 13
she is a king's daughter,
arrayed in cloth-of-gold richly   14
    embroidered.

v your limbs resplendent: *prob. rdg.*; *Heb.* and in
  your pomp prosper.
w the courage . . . away: *prob. rdg.*; *Heb.* obscure.
x honour awaits her: *prob. rdg.*; *Heb.* all honoured.

---

because of her loyalty to the Covenant; see 1 Macc.1.25–64. **19:** With the Babylonian Exile
Israel ceased to exist as a nation and was lost in the *darkness of death;* compare Lam.3.6;
Ezek.37.1–14. **23:** The poet believed so strongly in the justice of Israel's cause and in God's
power to deliver it that no other reason suited the human emotions except that the *Lord* was
in *sleep* even though only alien gods were considered to slumber; see 7.6; 35.23; Isa.51.9.
Contrast Ps.121.4. **24:** *Hide thy face:* see 10.11 n.
    Ps. 45: Blessed by God forever. A Royal Psalm, a wedding song for a king and his bride. It
is a unique psalm. It consists of an introduction (v. 1), words about the king (vv. 2–9), words
about the queen (vv.10–15), and the conclusion (vv. 16–17). **2–9:** This section may have been
used before the wedding at a feast for the king and his friends (see Gen.29.22). **6:** It was the
king's duty to establish the righteousness of God; see 1 Sam.10.1. **8:** The *palaces* of the kings
of the Northern Kingdom are described as *ivory* either because they abounded in ivory utensils
or because the stone of which they were made resembled ivory. **10–15:** This passage may have
traditionally been read to the bride and her friends before she was brought to the king (see
Gen.29.23).

Virgins shall follow her into the
    presence of the king;
    her companions shall be brought
      to her,
15 escorted with the noise of revels
    and rejoicing
    as they enter the king's palace.
16 You shall have sons, O king, in
    place of your forefathers
    and will make them rulers over all
    the land.[y]
17 I will declare your fame to all
    generations;
    therefore the nations will praise you
    for ever and ever.

46

1 God is our shelter and our refuge,
    a timely help in trouble;
2 so we are not afraid when the earth
    heaves
    and the mountains are hurled into
    the sea,
3 when its waters seethe in tumult
    and the mountains quake before
    his majesty.
4 There is a river whose streams
    gladden the city of God,[z]
    which the Most High has made his
    holy dwelling;
5 God is in that city; she will not be
    overthrown,
    and he will help her at the break
    of day.
6 Nations are in tumult, kingdoms
    hurled down;
    when he thunders, the earth surges
    like the sea.

7 The LORD of Hosts is with us,
    the God of Jacob our high
    stronghold.

8 Come and see what the LORD has
    done,
    the devastation he has brought
    upon earth,
9 from end to end of the earth he
    stamps out war:
    he breaks the bow, he snaps the spear
    and burns the shield in the fire.

10 Let be then: learn that I am God,
    high over the nations, high above
    earth.
11 The LORD of Hosts is with us,
    the God of Jacob our high
    stronghold.

47

1 Clap your hands, all you nations;
    acclaim our God with shouts of joy.
2 How fearful is the LORD Most High,
    great sovereign over all the earth!
3 He lays the nations prostrate
    beneath us,
    he lays peoples under our feet;
4 he chose our patrimony for us,
    the pride of Jacob whom he loved.

5 God has gone up with shouts of
    acclamation,
    the LORD has gone up with a
    fanfare of trumpets.
6 Praise God,[a] praise him with
    psalms;

y over all the land: or in all the earth.
z the city of God: or a wondrous city.
a Praise God: or Praise, you gods.

Ps. 46: The LORD of Hosts is with us. A Hymn, probably glorifying God's power as it will be manifested in the final judgment over the world. The vision of the future is based on the mythology of creation borrowed from non-Israelite sources. The centrality of Jerusalem in the poem (vv. 4–5) has prompted a phrase, "songs of Zion," from 137.3, to allude to this and other psalms emphasizing Jerusalem. **1–3:** God will abide in the upheavals to take place at the end of time. **1:** This verse inspired Luther's hymn, "A Mighty Fortress." **4–5:** *That city:* Jerusalem. Here it is apparently under siege, but God will deliver it as the climax to history. **4:** *A river:* that is, the place of the divine throne. In the mythology of Ancient Near East, God, after defeating chaos, sits upon the sea or water (see 29.10). Also, a river or some kind of water is often mentioned in connection with his throne or temple (see Ezek.47.1–12; Zech.14.8–9; or Rev.22.1–2). **8–11:** A vision of universal peace, after the punishing upheavals.

Ps. 47: God is King of all the earth. An Enthronement Hymn, celebrating the kingship of God. Enthronement Hymns are believed to have been sung on a festival, probably Booths. Other such hymns are Pss.93,96–99. A view, often disputed, supposes that behind such hymns lies the folklore of a dying and resurrected god, with the Enthronement in reality the reascension of the throne by the resurrected deity. **5–9:** The passage has a liturgical ring. **5–7:** The Ark of the Covenant was carried in liturgical procession with *shouts*, *psalms*, clapping of *hands* (v. 1) and

praise our king, praise him with
    psalms.

7 God is king of all the earth;
    sing psalms with all your art.

8 God reigns over the nations,
    God is seated on his holy throne.

9   The princes of the nations
      assemble
    with the families of Abraham's
      line;[b]
for the mighty ones of earth belong
    to God,
and he is raised above them all.

48

1 The LORD is great and worthy of
    our praise
    in the city of our God, upon his
    holy hill.

2 Fair and lofty, the joy of the whole
    earth
    is Zion's hill, like the farthest
    reaches of the north,[c]
    the hill of the great King's city.

3 In her palaces God is known for a
    tower of strength.

4 See how the kings all gather round
    her,
    marching on in company.

5 They are struck with amazement
    when they see her,
    they are filled with alarm and
    panic;

6 they are seized with trembling,
    they toss in pain like a woman
    in labour,

7 like the ships of Tarshish
    when an east wind wrecks them.

8 All we had heard we saw with our
    own eyes
    in the city of the LORD of Hosts,
    in the city of our God,
    the city which God plants firm for
    evermore.

O God, we re-enact the story of thy 9
    true love
    within thy temple;
the praise thy name deserves, O God, 10
    is heard at earth's farthest
    bounds.
Thy hand is charged with justice,
    and the hill of Zion rejoices, 11
Judah's daughter-cities exult
    in thy judgements.

Make the round of Zion in 12
    procession,
    count the number of her towers,
take good note of her ramparts, 13
    pass her palaces in review,
that you may tell generations yet
    to come:
    Such is God, 14
our God for ever and ever;
    he shall be our guide eternally.

49

Hear this, all you nations, 1
listen, all who inhabit this world,
all mankind, every living man, 2
rich and poor alike;
for the words that I speak are wise, 3
    my thoughtful heart is full of
    understanding.

I will set my ear to catch the moral 4
    of the story
and tell on the harp how I read the
    riddle;
why should I be afraid in evil times, 5
beset by the wickedness of
    treacherous foes,
who trust in their riches 6
and boast of their great wealth?
Alas! no man can ever ransom 7
    himself

b the families of Abraham's line: *prob. rdg.; Heb.*
the God of Abraham.
c *Or of Zaphon.*

---

fanfare of trumpets; see 2 Sam.6.12–19. **9:** God is the true King, and hence the King of kings.
    Ps. 48: The joy of the whole earth is Zion's hill. A Hymn, a "Song of Zion" (see Ps.46 n.).
The psalm exultantly expresses confidence in the formidable power of Jerusalem as a fortress
city. **2:** *North:* lit. Zaphon (Tfn. *c*), to be identified with Mount Casius, north of the ancient
city of Ugarit, site of a temple of Baal, where the Canaanite pantheon dwelled. To Zion are
ascribed the majestic qualities which mythology ascribed to Zaphon. **7:** *The ships of Tarshish*
were used for the transport of metals from the western Mediterranean to Phoenicia (1 Kgs.10.22).
Tarshish is often supposed to have been in southern Spain. *East wind:* a violent wind arising
in the desert.
    Ps. 49: No man can ever ransom himself. A Wisdom Psalm. Quite beyond the usual Wisdom
theme of the merits of the righteous, this meditation asserts that not only is life short but also

nor pay God the price of that
      release;

8 his ransom would cost too much,
      for ever beyond his power to pay,

9 the ransom that would let him live
      on always
   and never see the pit of death.

10 But remember this:[d] wise men
       must die;
    stupid men, brutish men, all perish.[e]

11 The grave is their eternal home,
       their dwelling for all time to come;
    they may give their own names to
       estates,
    but they must leave their riches to
       others.[f]

12 For men are like oxen whose life
       cannot last,
    they are like cattle whose time is
       short.

13 Such is the fate of foolish men
    and of all who seek to please them;

14 like sheep they run headlong into
       Sheol, the land of Death;
    he is their shepherd and urges
       them on;
    their flesh must rot away[g]
    and their bodies be wasted by Sheol,
       stripped of all honour.

15 But God will ransom my life,
       he will take me from the power
       of Sheol.

16 Do not envy a man when he grows
       rich,
    when the wealth of his family
       increases;

17 for he will take nothing when he
       dies,
    and his wealth will not go with him.

18 Though in his lifetime he counts
       himself happy
    and men praise him in his[h]
       prosperity,

19 he[i] will go to join the company of
       his forefathers
    who will never again see the light.

For men are like oxen whose life   20
   cannot last,
they are like cattle whose time is
   short.

50

God, the LORD God, has spoken   1
and summoned the world from the
      rising to the setting sun.
God shines out from Zion, perfect   2
      in beauty.
Our God is coming and will not   3
      keep silence:
consuming fire runs before him
and wreathes him closely round.[j]
He summons heaven on high and   4
      earth
to the judgement of his people:
'Gather to me my loyal servants,   5
all who by sacrifice have made a
      covenant with me.'
The heavens proclaim his justice,   6
for God himself is the judge.

Listen, my people, and I will speak;   7
I will bear witness against you, O
      Israel:
I am God, your God,
shall I not[k] find fault with your   8
      sacrifices,
though[l] your offerings are before
      me always?
I need take no young bull from   9
      your house,
      no he-goat from your folds;
for all the beasts of the forest are   10
      mine

d But remember this: *prob. rdg.; Heb.* But he will
  remember this.
e *Line transposed from here to follow verse 11.*
f *Line transposed from verse 10.*
g and urges . . . rot away: *prob. rdg.; Heb. obscure.*
h him . . . his: *prob. rdg.; Heb.* you . . . your.
i he: *prob. rdg.; Heb.* you.
j and wreathes him closely round: *or* and rages round
  him.
k *Or* I will not.
l *Or* for.

no one can buy salvation. A man need not fear the rich, for they too die. A refrain occurs
twice (vv. 12,20). **11**: The giving of *names to estates* was a common practice. **15**: *Take me from
the power of Sheol:* most scholars hold that this passage speaks only about deliverance from
present trouble. *Sheol* is the place of the dead; hence, to some interpreters it seems quite possible
that the psalmist here speaks of an afterlife with God. But compare v. 19.
   Ps. 50: God has summoned the world. A prophetic judgment. The prophets often used the
figure of the courtroom. Here, God, the judge, will summon the world to the courtroom and
there present his case against his people, indicting them on two counts: (a) formalism in worship
(vv. 8–15); and (b) transgression of the moral law (vv. 16–22). **1**: *God, the LORD God:* lit. God
of gods is the LORD (compare Josh.22.22 and Ps.136.1–3). **8**: *Shall I not:* there is some uncertainty whether the passage is a question, or a statement (see Tfn. *k*). Regardless of this

and the cattle in thousands on
my hills
11 I know every bird on those hills,
the teeming life of the fields is my
care.
12 If I were hungry, I would not tell
you,
for the world and all that is in it
are mine.
13 Shall I eat the flesh of your bulls
or drink the blood of he-goats?
14 Offer to God the sacrifice of
thanksgiving
and pay your vows to the Most
High.
15 If you call upon me in time of
trouble,
I will come to your rescue, and
you shall honour me.

16 God's word to the wicked man is
this:
What right have you to recite
my laws
and make so free with the words
of my covenant,
17 you who hate correction
and turn your back when I am
speaking?
18 If you meet a thief, you choose him
as your friend;
you make common cause with
adulterers;
19 you charge your mouth with
wickedness
and harness your tongue to slander.
20 You are for ever talking against
your brother,
stabbing your own mother's son in
the back.
21 All this you have done, and shall I
keep silence?
You thought that I was another
like yourself,
but point by point I will rebuke you

to your face.
Think well on this, you who forget   21
God,
or I will tear you in pieces and no
one shall save you.
He who offers a sacrifice of   23
thanksgiving
does me due honour,
and to him who follows my way[m]
I will show the salvation of God.

51

Be gracious to me, O God, in thy   1
true love;
in the fullness of thy mercy blot
out my misdeeds.

Wash away all my guilt   2
and cleanse me from my sin.
For well I know my misdeeds,   3
and my sins confront me all the
day long.
Against thee, thee only, I have   4
sinned
and done what displeases thee,
so that thou mayest be proved
right in thy charge
and just in passing sentence.

In iniquity I was brought to birth   5
and my mother conceived me in
sin;
yet, though thou hast hidden the   6
truth in darkness,
through this mystery thou dost
teach me wisdom.
Take hyssop[n] and sprinkle me, that   7
I may be clean;
wash me, that I may become whiter
than snow;

m him who follows my way: *prob. rdg.; Heb.* him who
puts a way.
n *Or* marjoram.

problem, *sacrifices* in general are not deemed important. **12:** Animal sacrifices satisfied no
need of God, such as hunger, as was thought in pagan sacrifices. **14,23:** *Sacrifice of thanksgiving:*
it is possible that Thanksgiving Psalms were used in accompaniment of thanksgiving sacrifices
at the Temple. **16:** While the indictment for ritualism applied to the whole nation, what follows
is addressed only to the *wicked*. **21:** God, in effect, keeps silence if he leaves evil unpunished.
   Ps. 51: Be gracious to me, O God. A Lament, in confession of sin. The superscription (see
Introduction) gives the occasion for the psalm as the time when Nathan came to David after
his affair with Bathsheba (2 Sam.12.1–10). Illness ("broken bones," v. 8) was a token of sin,
confessed to in a general way in vv. 1–9, followed by a plea for forgiveness and restoration
(10–12) in terms of genuine contrition (13–17); an addition (vv. 18–19) validates worthy sacrifices
seemingly deemed worthless in v. 16. **5:** Man is already a sinner at conception and surrounded
by iniquity at birth, a condition which the poet puts forth as a motive of forgiveness. **7:** *Hyssop:*
leaves of an aromatic plant, used in ceremonies for purging guilt; see Exod.12.22; Lev.14.49–53.

8   let me hear the sounds of joy and
         gladness,
     let the bones dance which thou hast
         broken.
9   Turn away thy face from my sins
         and blot out all my guilt.

10   Create a pure heart in me, O God,
         and give me a new and steadfast
             spirit;
11   do not drive me from thy
             presence
         or take thy holy spirit from me;
12   revive in me the joy of thy
             deliverance
         and grant me a willing spirit to
             uphold me.

13   I will teach transgressors the ways
         that lead to thee,
     and sinners shall return to thee
         again.
14   O LORD God, my deliverer, save me
         from bloodshed,°
     and I will sing the praises of thy
         justice.
15   Open my lips, O Lord,
         that my mouth may proclaim thy
             praise.
16   Thou hast no delight in sacrifice;
     if I brought thee an offering, thou
         wouldst not accept it.
17   My sacrifice, O God, is a broken
             spirit;
     a wounded heart, O God, thou
         wilt not despise.
18   Let it be thy pleasure to do good
         to Zion,
         to build anew the walls of
             Jerusalem.
19   Then only shalt thou delight in the
         appointed sacrifices;°
     then shall young bulls be offered
         on thy altar.

52

Why make your wickedness your   1–2
    boast, you man of might,
forging wild lies all day against God's
    loyal servant?
Your slanderous tongue is sharp as
    a razor.
You love evil and not good,   3
    falsehood, not speaking the truth;
cruel gossip you love and slanderous 4
    talk.
So may God�q pull you down to the   5
    ground,
sweep you away, leave you ruined
    and homeless,
    uprooted from the land of the
        living.
The righteous will look on,   6
    awestruck,
    and laugh at his plight:
'This is the man', they say,   7
'who does not make God his
    refuge,
but trusts in his great wealth
    and takes refuge in wild lies.'
But I am like a spreading olive-tree 8
    in God's house;
for I trust in God's true love for
    ever and ever.
I will praise thee for ever for what 9
    thou hast done,
and glorify thy name among thy
    loyal servants;
    for that is good.

53

The impious fool says in his heart,   1ʳ
    'There is no God.'

o Or from punishment by death.
p Prob. rdg.; Heb. adds a whole-offering and one
   wholly consumed.
q Or So God will.
r Verses 1–6: cp. Ps. 14. 1–7.

Here the request is that God figuratively purge the sinner. **8**: *The bones . . . broken* seems to refer to a physical illness which will give way to *dance*, the transition from guilt to forgiveness. **10**: Creation of a *pure heart* and a *new . . . spirit* meant a total transformation of man which could be accomplished only by God; compare Ezek.36.25–27. **16**: *Thou hast no delight in sacrifice*: the statement is sweeping, and is modified in the last verses. **17**: *Broken spirit*: afflicted and humbled. **18–19**: This modification of v. 16 is probably an addition. **18**: *Build anew the walls*: see Neh. chs. 1–3, which rebuilding is possibly alluded to here.

    Ps. 52: I am like a spreading olive-tree. A psalm difficult to classify (see Introduction) and a Lament only in that a righteous man is denouncing a wicked one, and it ends in the typical vow (v. 9). The tone is righteous, even vindictive (vv. 5–6). *Man of might* (vv. 1 and 7) is unclear, but is surely someone highly placed and wealthy, accused of slander and falsehood (vv. 3–4).

    Ps. 53: If only Israel's deliverance might come out of Zion. A Lament, with the usual vow (v, 6), See Ps.14, with which this psalm is almost identical. They differ in that the use here is of *Elohim* (God), and in Ps.14 it is *Yahweh* (LORD).

How vile men are, how depraved
and loathsome;
not one does anything good!

2 God looks down from heaven
on all mankind
to see if any act wisely,
if any seek out God.

3 But all are unfaithful, all are rotten
to the core;
not one does anything good,
no, not even one.

4 Shall they not rue it,
these evildoers who devour my
people
as men devour bread,
and never call upon God?

5 There they were in dire alarm
when God scattered them.
The crimes of the godless were
frustrated;[s]
for God had rejected them.

6 If only Israel's deliverance might
come out of Zion!
When God restores his people's
fortunes,
let Jacob rejoice, let Israel be glad.

54

1 Save me, O God, by the power of
thy name,
and vindicate me through thy
might.

2 O God, hear my prayer,
listen to my supplication.

3 Insolent men rise to attack me,
ruthless men seek my life;
they give no thought to God.

4 But God is my helper,
the Lord the mainstay of my life.

5 May their own malice recoil on my
watchful foes;
silence them by thy truth, O LORD.

6 I will offer thee a willing sacrifice
and praise thy name, for that is
good;

God has rescued me from every 7
trouble,
and I look on my enemies' downfall
with delight.

55

Listen, O God, to my pleading, 1
do not hide thyself when I pray.
Hear me and answer, 2
for my cares give me no peace.
I am panic-stricken at the shouts of 3
my enemies,
at the shrill clamour of the wicked;
for they heap trouble on me
and they revile me in their anger.
My heart is torn with anguish 4
and the terrors of death come upon
me.
Fear and trembling overwhelm me 5
and I shudder from head to foot.
[t]Oh that I had the wings of a dove 6
to fly away and be at rest!
I should escape far away 7
and find a refuge in the
wilderness;
soon I should find myself a 8
sanctuary
from wind and storm,
from the blasts of calumny, O Lord, 9
from my enemies' contentious
tongues.
I have seen violence and strife in the
city;
day and night they encircle it, 10
all along its walls;
it is filled with trouble and mischief,
alive with rumour and scandal, 11
and its public square is never free
from violence and spite.
It was no enemy that taunted me, 12
or I should have avoided him;
no adversary that treated me with
scorn,
or I should have kept out of his
way.

s The crimes . . . frustrated: prob. rdg.; Heb. obscure.
t Prob. rdg.; Heb. prefixes And I said.

Ps. 54: O God, hear my prayer. A Lament (see Introduction), possibly the prayer of a king as
in Ps.20. 1–2: A plea for help. 3–4: The distress caused by evildoers. 5: Against the foe. 6–7:
The vow usual in a Lament. 6: A willing sacrifice: see Num.15.3. 7: The conclusion is straightforward in its vindictiveness.
Ps. 55: Hear me and answer. A Lament (see Introduction), with a vindictive tone. 1–2: A
plea for God's response. 3–15: The poet's distress. 3–9a: The impulse to flee. 7: A refuge in the
wilderness: see Jer.9.2. 9b–11: The vice in the city. 12–15a: On such betrayal, compare 41.9 n.

13 It was you, a man of my own sort,
      my comrade, my own dear friend,
14-15 with whom I kept pleasant company
      in the house of God.

May death strike them,
and may they[u] perish in confusion,
may they go down alive into Sheol;
   for their homes are haunts of
      evil!

16 But I will call upon God;
      the LORD will save me.
17 Evening and morning and at noon
      I nurse my woes, and groan.
18 He has heard my cry, he rescued me
      and gave me back my peace,
   when they beset me like archers,[v]
      massing against me,
19 like Ishmael and the desert tribes
      and those who dwell in the East,
   who have no respect for an oath
      nor any fear of God.
20 Such men do violence to those at
         peace with them
   and break their promised word;
21 their speech is smoother than
         butter
   but their thoughts are of war;
   their words are slippery as oil
      but sharp as drawn swords.
22 Commit your fortunes to the LORD,
      and he will sustain you;
   he will never let the righteous be
         shaken.
23 Cast them, O God, into the pit of
         destruction;
   bloodthirsty and treacherous,
   they shall not live out half their
         days;
   but I will put my trust in thee.

56

1 Be gracious to me, O God, for the
      enemy persecute me,
   my assailants harass me all day long.

All the day long my watchful foes   2
      persecute me;
countless are those who assail me.
Appear on high[w] in my day of fear; 3
I put my trust in thee.
With God to help me I will shout   4
      defiance,
in God I trust and shall not be
      afraid;
what can mortal men do to me?
All day long abuse of me is their   5
      only theme,
   all their thoughts are hostile.
In malice they are on the look-out, 6
      and watch for me,
   they dog my footsteps;
but, while they lie in wait for me,
   it is they who will not[x] escape.   7
O God, in thy anger bring ruin on
   the nations.

Enter my lament in thy book,[y]   8
store every tear in thy flask.[z]
Then my enemies will turn back   9
   on the day when I call upon
      thee;[a]
for this I know, that God is on my
      side,
with God to help me I will shout   10
      defiance.[b]
In God I trust and shall not be   11
      afraid;
what can man do to me?
I have bound myself with vows to   12
      thee, O God,
and will redeem them with due
      thank-offerings;
for thou hast rescued me from   13
      death[c]
to walk in thy presence, in the
      light of life.

u Prob. rdg.; Heb. we.
v when . . . archers: prob. rdg.; Heb. obscure.
w Appear on high: prob. rdg.; Heb. Height.
x it is . . . not: prob. rdg.; Heb. for iniquity.
y Enter . . . book: prob. rdg.; Heb. obscure.
z Prob. rdg.; Heb. adds is it not in thy book?
a Enter . . . thee: or Thou hast entered my lament
   in thy book, my tears are put in thy flask. Then my
   enemies turned back, when I called upon thee.
b Prob. rdg.; Heb. adds With the LORD to help me I
   will shout defiance.
c Prob. rdg.; Heb. adds is it not my feet from stumbling (cp. Ps. 116. 8).

15b: A curse. Sheol: the netherworld. 16-21: God's deliverance. 19: Ishmael: compare Gen.
16:11-12. The translation rests on the frequently corrected Heb. text. 22-23: The word of trust.
   Ps. 56: Be gracious to me, O God. A Lament (see Introduction), similar to the others (Pss.51-
61), but somewhat less plaintive. The distress is in vv. 1-2 and 5-6, the expression of trust in
vv. 3-4, and the vow in v. 12. The latter part of v. 7 is a plea for vengeance. 8: On a heavenly
record book, see Exod.32.33. 12: Thank-offerings: see Ps.50.14,23 n. 13: God's presence is the
light that gives meaning and value to life, just as darkness is death because devoid of worthwhile
activity; compare Isa.5.9-10.

57

1 Be gracious to me, O God, be
        gracious;
    for I have made thee my refuge.
    I will take refuge in the shadow of
        thy wings
        until the storms are past.
2 I will call upon God Most High,
    on God who fulfils his purpose for
        me.
3 He will send his truth and his love
        that never fails,
    he will send from heaven and save
        me.
    God himself will frustrate my
        persecutors;
4 for I lie down among lions, man-
        eaters,
    whose teeth are spears and arrows
    and whose tongues are sharp
        swords.
5 Show thyself, O God, high above
        the heavens;
    let thy glory shine over all the
        earth.
6 Men have prepared a net to catch
        me as I walk,
    but I bow my head to escape
        from it;
    they have dug a pit in my path
        but have fallen into it themselves.

7*d* My heart is steadfast, O God,
        my heart is steadfast.
    I will sing and raise a psalm;
8   awake, my spirit,
    awake, lute and harp,
    I will awake at dawn of day.*e*
9 I will confess thee, O Lord, among
        the peoples,
    among the nations I will raise a
        psalm to thee,

10 for thy unfailing love is wide as the
        heavens
    and thy truth reaches to the skies.
11 Show thyself, O God, high above
        the heavens;
    let thy glory shine over all the
        earth.

58

1 Answer, you rulers:*f* are your
        judgements just?
    Do you decide impartially between
        man and man?
2 Never! Your hearts devise all kinds
        of wickedness
    and survey the violence that you
        have done on earth.

3 Wicked men, from birth they have
        taken to devious ways;
    liars, no sooner born than they go
        astray,
4 venomous with the venom of
        serpents,
    of the deaf asp which stops its ears
5 and will not listen to the sound of
        the charmer,
        however skilful his spells may be.

6 O God, break the teeth in their
        mouths.
    Break, O LORD, the jaws of the
        unbelievers.*g*
7 May they melt, may they vanish
        like water,
    may they wither like trodden grass,*h*
8 like an abortive birth which melts
        away

d Verses 7–11: cp. Ps. 108. 1–5.
e at dawn of day: or the dawn.
f Or you gods.
g the jaws of the unbelievers: or the lions' fangs.
h like trodden grass: prob. rdg.; Heb. obscure.

Ps. 57: Be gracious to me, O God. A Lament (see Introduction), the poet's plea to God and his trust in him. **1–6:** The poet's distress. **1:** The figure of an eagle protecting its young under its *wings* to represent God giving refuge to the innocent goes back to the trials of the Exodus from Egypt; see Exod.19.4; Deut.32.10–11. **3–4:** The poet's tribulation is that he was attacked by slanderous *tongues* and he asks God's *truth* to ward off the evil. Teeth biting flesh is the symbol of slander; compare Job 19.22. **5:** A refrain. **6:** One could escape a trap made of a net by keeping the *head* low to the ground, i.e. by being humble. **7–11:** A combined vow and utterance of thanks, virtually identical with Ps.108.1–5. **7:** *Raise a psalm:* see Ps.50.14, 23 n. **8:** The poet's confidence in God is so great that he anticipates his restoration by a thanksgiving on *lute* and *harp* at the earliest opportunity, i.e. *dawn.* **11:** A refrain.
    Ps. 58: O God, break the teeth in their mouths. A Lament (see Introduction), violent in its outburst of wrath. The curse uttered in v. 6 is often viewed as responsive to a curse that enemies have put on the poet, alluded to in the word "charmer" in v. 5. It is uncertain, however, just who the enemies are in vv. 1–5, which allude to them. The curse (vv. 6–9) is followed by an assurance of vengeance (vv. 10–11). **1:** *Rulers:* gods (Tfn. *f*); in either case the translation rests

or a still-born child which never
   sees[i] the sun!

9 All unawares, may they be rooted
   up like[j] a thorn-bush,
like weeds which a man angrily[k]
   clears away!

10 The righteous shall rejoice that he
   has seen vengeance done
and shall wash his feet in the
   blood of the wicked,

11   and men shall say,
'There is after all a reward for the
   righteous;
after all, there is a God that judges
   on earth.'

59

1 Rescue me from my enemies, O my
   God,
be my tower of strength against all
   who assail me,

2   rescue me from these evildoers,
deliver me from men of blood.

3 Savage men lie in wait for me,
they lie in ambush ready to attack
   me;
for no fault or guilt of mine, O
   LORD,

4-5 innocent as I am, they run to take
   post against me.
But thou, LORD God of Hosts,
   Israel's God,
do thou bestir thyself at my call,
   and look:
awake, and punish all the nations.
Have no mercy on villains and
   traitors,

6 who run wild at nightfall like
   dogs,
snarling and prowling round the
   city,

15[l] wandering to and fro in search of
   food,
and howling if they are not satisfied.

From their mouths comes a stream   7
   of nonsense;
'But who will hear?' they murmur.
But thou, O LORD, dost laugh at   8
   them,
and deride all the nations.
O my strength,[m] to thee I turn in   9
   the night-watches;
for thou, O God, art my strong
   tower.
My God, in his true love, shall be   10
   my champion;
with God's help, I shall gloat over
   my watchful foes.
Wilt thou not kill them, lest my   11
   people forget?
Scatter them by thy might and
   bring them to ruin.
Deliver them,[n] O Lord, to be   12
   destroyed
by their own sinful words;
let what they have spoken entrap
   them in their pride.
Let them be cut off for their cursing
   and falsehood;
bring them to an end in thy   13
   wrath,
and they will be no more;
then they will know that God is
   ruler in Jacob,
even to earth's farthest limits.[o] [p]
But I will sing of thy strength,   16
and celebrate thy love when
   morning comes;
for thou hast been my strong tower
and a sure retreat in days of trouble.
O thou my strength, I will raise a   17
   psalm to thee;
for thou, O God, art my strong
   tower.

i sees: *prob. rdg.; Heb.* they see.
j may they be rooted up like: *prob. rdg.; Heb.* your pots
k angrily: *prob. rdg.; Heb.* like anger.
l *Verse transposed*
m *Or* refuge.
n Deliver them: *prob. rdg.; Heb.* Our shield.
o *Prob. rdg.; Heb. adds* (14) who run wild at nightfall like dogs, snarling and prowling round the city (*cp.* verse 6.)
p *Verse 15 transposed to follow verse 6.*

on a usual correction of the Heb. **10:** *Wash his feet in the blood of the wicked:* the Canaanite goddess Anat is described after a battle with her enemies, in a text from Ugarit, as follows: "She washes her hands of the blood of warriors, her fingers of the gore of troops."
   Ps. 59: Rescue me from my enemies, O my God. A Lament, which seems to veer from the personal (vv. 1–4a) to the national (4b–7), unless "nations" is a figure of speech for personal enemies. The usual trust is in vv. 8–10, the plea for vengeance in 11–13, and the vow in 16–17. Note that v. 15 has been moved and v. 14 put into Tfn. *o.* **4–5:** *Bestir thyself . . . awake:* compare Ps.44.23 n. **8:** *Laugh:* compare Ps.2.4. **9:** The parts of the city walls that were the weakest, e.g. gates, were furnished with *strong towers* from which defenders could repel the attackers; see v. 17. **12:** *Cut off:* brought to a sudden death.

60

1 O God, thou hast cast us off and
    broken us;
  thou hast been angry and rebuked
    us cruelly.
2 Thou hast made the land quake and
    torn it open;
  it gives way and crumbles into
    pieces.
3 Thou hast made thy people drunk
    with a bitter draught,
  thou hast given us wine that makes
    us stagger.
4 But thou hast given a warning to
    those who fear thee,
  to make their escape before the
    sentence falls.

5^q Deliver those that are dear to thee;
  save them with thy right hand, and
    answer.
6 God has spoken from his sanctuary:^r
  'I will go up now and measure out
    Shechem;
  I will divide the valley of Succoth
    into plots;
7 Gilead and Manasseh are mine;
  Ephraim is my helmet, Judah my
    sceptre;
8 Moab is my wash-bowl, I fling my
    shoes at Edom;
  Philistia is the target of my anger.'

9 Who can bring me to the fortified
    city,
  who can guide me to Edom,
10 since thou, O God, hast abandoned
    us
  and goest not forth with our
    armies?

Grant us help against the enemy,   11
  for deliverance by man is a vain
    hope.
With God's help we shall do   12
  valiantly,
and God himself will tread our
  enemies under foot.

61

Hear my cry, O God, listen to my   1
  prayer.
From the end of the earth I call to   2
  thee with fainting heart;
lift me up and set me upon a rock.
For thou hast been my shelter,   3
  a tower for refuge from the
    enemy.
In thy tent will I make my home   4
  for ever
and find my shelter under the
  cover of thy wings.
For thou, O God, hast heard my   5
  vows
and granted the wish^s of all who
  revere thy name.

To the king's life add length of days,   6
  year upon year for many
    generations;
may he dwell in God's presence for   7
  ever,
may true and constant love preserve
  him.

So will I ever sing psalms in   8
  honour of thy name
as I fulfil my vows day after day.

q Verses 5–12: cp. Ps. 108. 6–13.
r from his sanctuary: or in his holiness.
s Prob. rdg.; Heb. the inheritance.

Ps. 60: Deliver those that are dear to thee. A Lament, after a national humiliation. **1a:** The
Lament begins, as usual, with an invocation of the divine name. **1b–3:** The national tribulation,
a military humiliation, is depicted in the apocalyptic imagery of a cosmic catastrophe; compare
Isa.24.19–20. **4:** *A warning:* compare Amos 5.6. **5:** The supplication for deliverance asks for an
answer in the form of an oracle. **6–8:** In the oracle, *spoken* probably by a priest, assurance is
given that even though the lands of *Shechem, Succoth, Gilead* and *Manasseh* are in the hands
of foreigners, they belong to God and he will *measure* them *out* again as an inheritance to his
people; compare Jer.32.42–44. The cause of *Ephraim* and *Judah* is God's cause for they are
his instruments of judgment and warfare, *helmet* and *sceptre. Moab, Edom* and *Philistia,*
which now oppress the land, are objects of scorn and *anger.* The conditions fit the period after
the destruction of Jerusalem in 587 B.C.; compare Ezek.25.8–17. **9:** *Me:* probably the king is
meant. **10:** Perhaps an allusion to the fact that the Ark of the Covenant was lost after 587 B.C.
and no longer taken to battle as in early days; see 1 Sam.4.3–11.

Ps. 61: Hear my cry, O God. A Lament (see Introduction) by someone far from Judea, who
yearns for the Temple in Jerusalem, possibly a Levite or a priest who had been attached to the
Temple. **2:** *End of the earth:* outside the Holy Land. **4:** *Tent:* an ancient word for tabernacle or
temple; see 27.6. *Cover of thy wings:* see Ps.57.1 n. **6–7:** The prayer for the king appears to be an
interpolation; it recalls Nathan's prophecy in 2 Sam.7.16.

62

1 Truly my heart waits silently for
    God;
    my deliverance comes from him.
2 In truth he is my rock of deliverance,
    my tower of strength, so that I
    stand unshaken.
3 How long will you assail a man
    with your threats,
    all battering on a leaning wall?
4 In truth men plan to topple him
    from his height,
    and stamp on the fallen stones.*t*
    With their lips they bless him, the
    hypocrites,
    but revile him in their hearts.
5 Truly my heart waits silently for
    God;
    my hope of deliverance comes
    from him.
6 In truth he is my rock of deliverance,
    my tower of strength, so that I am
    unshaken.
7 My deliverance and my honour
    depend upon God,
    God who is my rock of refuge and
    my shelter.
8 Trust always in God, my people,
    pour out your hearts before him;
    God is our shelter.

9 In very truth men are a puff of
    wind,
    all men are faithless,
    put them in the balance and they
    can only rise,
    all of them lighter than wind.
10 Put no trust in extortion,
    do not be proud of stolen goods;
    though wealth breeds wealth, set
    not your heart on it.
11 One thing God has spoken,
    two things I have learnt:

'Power belongs to God'
and 'True love, O Lord, is thine';   12
thou dost requite a man for his
    deeds.

63

O God, thou art my God, I seek thee   1
    early
with a heart that thirsts for thee
and a body wasted with longing for
    thee,
like a dry and thirsty land that has
    no water.
So longing, I come before thee in   2
    the sanctuary
to look upon thy power and glory.
Thy true love is better than life;   3
    therefore I will sing thy praises.
And so I bless thee all my life   4
and in thy name lift my hands in
    prayer.
I am satisfied as with a rich and   5
    sumptuous feast
and wake the echoes with thy praise.
When I call thee to mind upon my   6
    bed
and think on thee in the watches of
    the night,
remembering how thou hast been   7
    my help
and that I am safe in the shadow
    of thy wings,
then I humbly follow thee with all   8
    my heart,
and thy right hand is my support.

Those who seek my life, bent on evil,   9
    shall sink into the depths of the
    earth;
they shall be given over to the   10
    sword;
they shall be carrion for jackals.

t the fallen stones: transposed from end of verse 3.

Ps. 62: **Power belongs to God.** A poem of trust, kindred to a Wisdom Psalm, though echoing the Lament. Its theme is that not men and wealth, but only God can help. The distress of the poet (vv. 3–4) comes in between two assertions of trust in God (1–2 and 5–7), followed by the counsel to others also to trust in God (8–12). **10:** Wisdom literature often warns against setting the heart on riches. **11:** *One thing . . . two things:* compare Prov.6.16; 30.15–31. This numerical progression is common in Wisdom literature.
    Ps. 63: **I seek thee, O God.** A Wisdom Psalm emphasizing the poet's *longing* for God. **1:** A thirst for God and for Wisdom is a frequent theme in Wisdom literature. See Ecclus.24.23–34; Isa.55.1. **5:** Wisdom, as a quality of God, is presented as a *sumptuous feast;* see Prov.9.1–5. **6:** *Watches of the night* were divided into three shifts. **7:** *Shadow of thy wings:* see Ps.57.1 n. **9–10:** The sinner *bent on evil* is a fool, for his life ends in the *earth.* **11:** Especially in need of Wisdom is the *king;* see Wis.1.1.

11   The king shall rejoice in God,
and whoever swears by God's name
shall exult;
the voice of falsehood shall be
silenced.

65

We owe thee praise, O God, in Zion; 1–2
thou hearest prayer, vows shall be
paid to thee.
All men shall lay their guilt before 3
thee:
our sins are too heavy for us;
only thou canst blot them out.
Happy is the man of thy choice, 4
whom thou dost bring
to dwell in thy courts;
let us enjoy the blessing of thy
house,
thy holy temple.
By deeds of terror answer us with 5
victory,
O God of our deliverance,
in whom men trust from the ends
of the earth
and far-off seas;
thou art girded with strength, 6
and by thy might dost fix the
mountains in their place,
dost calm the rage of the seas and 7
their raging waves.*a*
The dwellers at the ends of the 8
earth
hold thy signs in awe;
thou makest morning and evening
sing aloud in triumph.

Thou dost visit the earth and give 9
it abundance,
as often as thou dost enrich it
with the waters of heaven, brimming
in their channels,
providing rain*b* for men.

64

1   Hear me, O God, hear my lament;
keep me safe from the threats of the
enemy.
2   Hide me from the factions of the
wicked,
from the turbulent mob of
evildoers,
3   who sharpen their tongues like
swords
and wing their cruel words like
arrows,*u*
4   to shoot down the innocent from
cover,
shooting suddenly, themselves
unseen.
5   They boldly*v* hide their snares,
sure that none will see them;
6   they hatch their secret plans*w* with
skill and cunning,
with evil*x* purpose and deep design.
7   But God with his arrow shoots
them down,
and sudden is their overthrow.

8   They may repeat their wicked tales,*y*
but their mischievous tongues*z* are
their undoing.
All who see their fate take fright
at it,
9   every man is afraid;
'This is God's work', they declare;
they learn their lesson from what
he has done.
10 The righteous rejoice and seek refuge
in the LORD
and all the upright exult.

u and wing . . . arrows: *prob. rdg.; Heb.* they tread
their arrow a cruel word.
v See first note on verse 8.
w their secret plans: *prob. rdg.; Heb.* unintelligible.
x evil: *prob. rdg.; Heb.* man.
y They . . . tales: *transposed from after* boldly *in verse 5.*
z their mischievous tongues: *prob. rdg.; Heb.* against
them their tongues.
a Prob. rdg.; Heb. adds and tumult of people.
b Or corn.

Ps. 64: Hear me, O God, hear my plea. A Lament on the evil of the wicked. A plea (vv. 1–2) is
followed by a description of the wicked (5–6), whom God overthrows (7–9), to the gratification
of the righteous (10). **3:** *Cruel words:* either slander, or else curses believed to have magical
force. **6:** The poet is the object of backbiting and calumny.
   Ps. 65: We owe thee praise, O God. A Thanksgiving Hymn because it praises God for what
he always does for man (vv. 6–10). It was recited in the context of a pilgrimage to the Temple
(v. 4) which probably took place at the Feast of Weeks; see Deut.16.9–12. Hence, it can also be
classified as a pilgrimage psalm. **4:** *Dwell:* visit. **6–8:** One of frequent allusions to God the
warrior who at creation defeated chaos; compare 24.1–2 n. **7:** *The rage of the seas:* compare
Ps.74.12–14. **8:** *Morning and evening sing aloud:* the psalmist joins the chorus of all creation in
praise of the creator. **9:** *Waters of heaven:* water falling from the reservoir above the vault of
heaven; see Gen.1.6–7. The much needed *rain* is a blessing to the crops. See Pss.68.9,10; 104.14.

For this is thy provision for it,
10 watering its furrows, levelling its
ridges,
softening it with showers and
blessing its growth.
11 Thou dost crown the year with thy
good gifts
and the palm-trees drip with sweet
juice;
12 the pastures in the wild are rich
with blessing
and the hills wreathed in happiness,
13 the meadows are clothed with
sheep
and the valleys mantled in corn,
so that they shout, they break
into song.

66

1 Acclaim our God, all men on earth;
2 let psalms declare the glory of
his name,
make glorious his praise.
3 Say unto God, 'How fearful are thy
works!
Thy foes cower before the greatness
of thy strength.
4 All men on earth fall prostrate in
thy presence,
and sing to thee, sing psalms in
honour of thy name.'
5 Come and see all that God has
done,
tremendous in his dealings with
mankind.
6 He turned the waters into dry land
so that his people passed through
the sea on foot;
there did we rejoice in him.^c

7 He rules for ever by his power,
his eye rests on the nations;
let no rebel rise in defiance.

Bless our God, all nations;   8
let his praise be heard far and
near.
He set us in the land of the living;   9
he keeps our feet from stumbling.
For thou, O God, hast put us to   10
the proof
and refined us like silver.
Thou hast caught us in a net,   11
thou hast bound our bodies fast;
thou hast let men ride over our   12
heads.
We went through fire and water,
but thou hast brought us out
into liberty.

I will bring sacrifices into thy   13
temple
and fulfil my vows to thee,
vows which I made with my own   14
lips
and swore with my own mouth
when in distress.
I will offer thee fat beasts as   15
sacrifices
and burn rams as a savoury
offering;
I will make ready oxen and
he-goats.

Come, listen, all who fear God,   16
and I will tell you all that he has
done for me;
I lifted up my voice in prayer,   17
his high praise was on my lips.
If I had cherished evil thoughts,   18
the Lord would not have heard
me;
but in truth God has heard   19
and given heed to my prayer.
Blessed is God   20
who has not withdrawn his love and
care from me.

c there . . . him: *or* where we see this, we will rejoice
in him.

11–13: As the pilgrims go through the fields teeming with life just before the harvest, they are
overwhelmed with joy and a feeling of thanksgiving.
   Ps. 66: Let psalms declare the glory of his name. Verses 1–12 are a corporate Thanksgiving
Hymn (see vv. 1–4), vv. 13–20 a personal, private one. The two portions are fused together, both
beginning with the invitation "come" (5,16). **1:** The invitation to *all men* to *acclaim God* is the
typical beginning of a Hymn. **6:** This verse recalls the Exodus from Egypt and the entry into
the land of Canaan. **10–12:** Perhaps these verses echo either the Babylonian Exile, or the bitter
experiences of the Maccabean revolt. **13–15:** The large numbers of sacrifices referred to such
as would be offered by a prince or a ruler; see Ezek.46.4–7. **16–20:** The verses seem to hearken
back to vv. 1–2. **16:** *Fear:* the word reflects not fright but dutiful worship. To fear God or to
love God are synonymous in the Heb. Bible. **18:** The prayers of even the devout will not be
answered if *evil thoughts* are *cherished*.

67

1 God be gracious to us and bless us,
  God make his face shine upon us,
2 that his ways may be known on
    earth
  and his saving power among all
    the nations.
3 Let the peoples praise thee, O God;
  let all peoples praise thee.
4 Let all nations rejoice and shout in
    triumph;
  for thou dost judge the peoples
    with justice
  and guidest the nations of the earth.
5 Let the peoples praise thee, O God;
  let all peoples praise thee.
6 The earth has given its increase
  and God, our God, will bless us.
7   God grant us his blessing,
  that all the ends of the earth may
    fear him.

68

1 God arises and his enemies are
    scattered;
  those who hate him flee before him,
2 driven away like smoke in the
    wind;
  like wax melting at the fire,
  the wicked perish at the presence
    of God.
3 But the righteous are joyful, they
    exult before God,
  they are jubilant and shout for
    joy.

4 Sing the praises of God, raise a
    psalm to his name,
  extol him who rides over the desert
    plains.*d*

Be joyful*e* and exult before him,
  father of the fatherless, the widow's   5
    champion—
  God in his holy dwelling-place.
God gives the friendless a home   6
  and brings out the prisoner safe
    and sound;
  but rebels must live in the scorching
    desert.

O God, when thou didst go forth   7
    before thy people,
  marching across the wilderness,
earth trembled, the very heavens   8
    quaked
before God the lord of Sinai, before
  God the God of Israel.

Of thy bounty, O God, thou dost   9
    refresh with rain
  thy own land in its weariness,
  the land which thou thyself didst
    provide,
  where thy own people made their   10
    home,
  which thou, O God, in thy goodness
    providest for the poor.

The Lord proclaims good news:*f*   11–13
  'Kings with their armies have fled
    headlong.'
O mighty host, will you linger among
    the sheepfolds
  while the women in your tents divide
    the spoil—
  an image of a dove, its wings
    sheathed in silver
  and its pinions in yellow gold—
  while the Almighty scatters kings   14
    far and wide
  like snowflakes falling on Zalmon?

d over the desert plains: *or* on the plains.
e Be joyful: *prob. rdg.; Heb.* In the LORD is his name.
f proclaims good news: *or* gives the word, women
bearing good news.

Ps. 67: Let all the people praise thee. A Hymn of Praise, kindred to a blessing (compare
Num.6.24–27 which is here echoed). **1**: *Make his face shine*: compare Ps.4.6 n. **6–7**: The occasion
seems to be a rich harvest; compare Ps.65.11–13.
  Ps. 68: Sing the praises of God. The psalm is a Hymn in which God is praised for his deeds
in the liberation of Israel from Egypt, her establishment in the Land, and victories over
attackers in later history. Since different historical events are alluded to in poetic form, the
impression is given of disconnected fragments which some scholars see collected here. **1–3**:
Narrative of what God is accustomed to do in behalf of the *righteous*. **4–10**: Allusion to the
Exodus and the conquest of the Land. **4**: A slight correction of the Heb., proposed by some
scholars, would yield "clouds" rather than *desert plains*. "Rider of the clouds" is a phrase used
also of the Canaanite god Baal; see v. 33. On the other hand, desert plains would be an allusion
to God's traveling with Israel to Sinai, and then to Canaan (Judg.5.4). **5**: Israel saw herself as a
fatherless girl abandoned in the desert and found by God; see Ezek.16.1–6. **7–8**: *Heavens
quaked:* Exod.19.16–25. **11–14**: The allusion is to the victory over the Canaanite *kings* after

15 The hill of Bashan is a hill of
        God indeed,
    a hill of many peaks is Bashan's
        hill.

16 But, O hill of many peaks, why gaze
        in envy
    at the hill where the LORD delights
        to dwell,
    where the LORD himself will live
        for ever?

17 Twice ten thousand were God's
        chariots, thousands upon
        thousands,
    when the Lord came in holiness
        from Sinai.*g*

18 Thou didst go up to thy lofty home
        with captives in thy train,
    having received tribute from men;
    in the presence of the LORD God no
        rebel could live.

19   Blessed is the Lord:
    he carries us day by day,
        God our salvation.

20 Our God is a God who saves us,
    in the LORD God's hand lies escape
        from death.*h*

21 God himself will smite*i* the head of
        his enemies,
    those proud sinners with their
        flowing locks.

22 The Lord says, 'I will return from
        the Dragon,*j*
    I will return from the depths of
        the sea,

23 that you may dabble your feet in
        blood,
    while the tongues of your dogs are
        eager*k* for it.'

24 Thy procession, O God, comes
        into view,

the procession of my God and
    King into the sanctuary:
at its head the singers, next come   25
    minstrels,
girls among them playing on
    tambourines.

In the great concourse they bless   26
    God,
all Israel assembled*l* bless the LORD.
There is the little tribe of Benjamin   27
    leading them,
there the company of Judah's
    princes,
the princes of Zebulun and of
    Naphtali.

O God, in virtue of thy power*m*—   28
that godlike power which has acted
    for us—
command kings to bring gifts to thee   29
    for the honour of thy temple in
    Jerusalem.
Rebuke those wild beasts of the   30
    reeds, that herd of bulls,
    the bull-calf warriors of the
    nations;*n*
scatter these nations which revel in
    war;
make them bring tribute from   31
    Egypt,
precious stones and silver from
    Pathros;*o*
let Nubia stretch out*p* her hands to
    God.

g came . . . from Sinai: *prob. rdg.; Heb. obscure.*
h in the LORD God's hand . . . death: *or* death is ex-
    pelled by the LORD God.
i will smite: *or* smites.
j the Dragon: *or* Bashan.
k are eager: *prob. rdg.; Heb.* from enemies.
l assembled: *prob. rdg.; Heb. obscure.*
m O God . . . power: *prob. rdg.; Heb.* Your God your
    power.
n See first note on verse 31.
o precious . . . Pathros: *prob. rdg., transposed from*
    verse 30 and slightly altered.
p stretch out: *prob. rdg.; Heb. obscure.*

much hesitation on the part of some tribes to leave their *sheepfolds;* see Judg.5.16–20. **15–18:**
The allusion seems to be to the victory over the Ammonites either by Jephthah (Judg.11.4–33),
or by Saul (1 Sam.11.1–11), or by David (2 Sam.10.1–12.31). **15:** The Syrians from the territory
of *Bashan* joined the Ammonites in the fight against David; see 2 Sam.10.6. Mount Hermon
with its three *peaks* personifies the Syrian rulers. Because of its height and majesty it was considered the *hill of God,* vying with Mount Zion for glory. **21:** The desert warriors left their hair
flowing loose when they went to battle; see Judg.5.1 and Tfn. *j* there. **22:** See Tfn. *j.* God comes
back victorious from the *Dragon* (Bashan) and from the depths of the Red Sea where he conquered Egypt. **23:** Compare 58.10 and see n. **24–35:** A liturgical celebration in which the victories
of God are reenacted in a Temple procession, possibly with the Ark of the Covenant at its head.
27: Men of *Benjamin* are first in the procession, either because of their role in the victory over
the Canaanites (Judg.5.14) or because Saul of Benjamin was victorious over the Ammonites
(1 Sam.11.1–11). David of *Judah* defeated the Ammonites; see vv.15–18 n. *Zebulun* and *Naphtali*
were the leading tribes in the victory over the Canaanites; see Judg.4.6–7. **30:** *Beasts of the*
reeds: Egyptians. *Herd of bulls:* warriors (Syrians) from Bashan, a place known for its cattle.
31: *Pathos* and *Nubia* adjoined Egypt. **32–35:** A Hymn of praise; compare Ps.29. **33:** See v. 4 n.

32 All you kingdoms of the world, sing
    praises to God,
    sing psalms to the Lord,
33 to him who rides on the heavens,
    the ancient heavens.
Hark! he speaks in the mighty
    thunder.
34 Ascribe all might to God, Israel's
    High God,
Israel's pride and might throned in
    the skies.
35 Terrible is God as he comes from
    his sanctuary;
he is Israel's own God,
who gives to his people might and
    abundant power.

Blessed be God.

69

1 Save me, O God;
    for the waters have risen up to my
    neck.
2 I sink in muddy depths and have no
    foothold;
I am swept into deep water, and the
    flood carries me away.
3 I am wearied with crying out, my
    throat is sore,
my eyes grow dim as I wait for God
    to help me.
4 Those who hate me without reason
    are more than the hairs of my head;
they outnumber my hairs, those who
    accuse me falsely.
How can I give back what I have
    not stolen?
5 O God, thou knowest how foolish
    I am,
and my guilty deeds are not hidden
    from thee.
6 Let none of those who look to thee
    be shamed on my account,
    O Lord GOD of Hosts;
let none who seek thee be humbled
    through my fault,
    O God of Israel.
7 For in thy service I have suffered
    reproach;

I dare not show my face for shame.
8 I have become a stranger to my
    brothers,
    an alien to my own mother's
    sons;
9 bitter enemies of thy temple tear me
    in pieces;q
those who reproach thee reproach
    me.
10 I have broken my spirit with fasting,
only to lay myself open to many
    reproaches.
11 I have made sackcloth my clothing
and have become a byword among
    them.
12 Those who sit by the town gate
    talk about me;
drunkards sing songs about me in
    their cups.
13 But I lift up this prayer to thee,
    O LORD:
accept mer now in thy great love,
answer me with thy sure deliverance,
    O God.
14 Rescue me from the mire, do not
    let me sink;
let me be rescued from the muddy
    depths,s
15 so that no flood may carry me
    away,
    no abyss swallow me up,
    no deep close over me.
16 Answer me, O LORD, in the goodness
    of thy unfailing love,
turn towards me in thy great
    affection.
17 I am thy servant, do not hide thy
    face from me.
Make haste to answer me, for I am
    in distress.
18 Come near to me and redeem me;
    ransom me, for I have many
    enemies.

19 Thou knowest what reproaches I
    bear,
all my anguish is seen by thee.
20 Reproach has broken my heart,

q bitter . . . pieces: or zeal for thy temple has eaten me
up (cp. John 2. 17).
r Prob. rdg.; Heb. acceptance.
s from . . . depths: prob. rdg.; Heb. from my haters
and from the depths.

Ps. 69: Save me, O God. A Lament, probably written by an exile (in Babylon) in the sixth
century B.C., as suggested by v. 35. The figure of a man sunken into the mire is most vivid.
1–6: The poet's distress. The mire (vv. 1–3) is figurative; it is repeated in vv. 14–15. 7–21: His
experience of humiliation. 9: The allusion is uncertain, but see Ezra 4.4–5,23–24; 5.2–3. The use
may be noted in Jn.2.17. 13–18: An intervening prayer. 17: Hide thy face: compare 10.11 and 27.9.

my shame and my dishonour[t] are
   past hope;
I looked for consolation and
   received none,
   for comfort and did not find any.

21 They put poison in my food
   and gave me vinegar when I was
    thirsty.

22 May their own table be a snare to
    them
   and their sacred feasts lure them to
    their ruin;

23 may their eyes be darkened so that
    they do not see,
   let a continual ague shake their
    loins.

24 Pour out thine indignation upon
    them
   and let thy burning anger
    overtake them.

25 May their settlements be desolate,
   and no one living in their tents;

26 for they pursue him whom thou
    hast struck down
and multiply the torments of those
   whom thou hast wounded.

27 Give them the punishment their
    sin deserves;[u]
   exclude them from thy righteous
    mercy;

28 let them be blotted out from the
    book of life
   and not be enrolled among the
    righteous.

29 But by thy saving power, O God,
    lift me high
   above my pain and my distress,

30 then I will praise God's name in
    song
   and glorify him with thanksgiving;

31 that will please the LORD more than
    the offering of a bull,
   a young bull with horn and cloven
    hoof.

32 See and rejoice, you humble folk,
   take heart, you seekers after God;

33 for the LORD listens to the poor
   and does not despise those bound

to his service.
Let sky and earth praise him,   34
the seas and all that move in them,
for God will deliver Zion   35–36
   and rebuild the cities of Judah.
His servants' children shall inherit
   them;
they shall dwell there in their own
   possession
   and all who love his name shall
   live in them.

70

Show me favour,[v] O God, and save   1[w]
   me;
hasten to help me, O LORD.
Let all who seek my life be brought   2
   to shame and dismay,
let all who love to hurt me shrink
   back disgraced;
let those who cry 'Hurrah!' at my   3
   downfall
turn back at the shame they incur,
   but let all who seek thee   4
   be jubilant and rejoice in thee,
and let those who long for thy
   saving help ever cry,
   'All glory to God!'

But I am poor and needy;   5
   O God, hasten to my aid.
Thou art my help, my salvation;
   O LORD, make no delay.

71

In thee, O LORD, I have taken   1
   refuge;
never let me be put to shame.
As thou art righteous rescue me   2
   and save my life;
hear me and set me free,
be a rock of refuge for me,   3

t my shame and my dishonour: *transposed from after*
reproaches in verse 19.
u Give them . . . deserves: *or* Add punishment to
punishment.
v Show me favour: *prob. rdg., cp. Ps. 40. 13; Heb. om.*
w Verses 1–5: *cp. Ps. 40. 13–17.*

21: Compare Mt.27.34,48; Mk.15.36; Lk.23.36; Jn.19.29. **22–28:** A curse. **25:** See Acts 1.20.
28: *The book of life:* compare 56.8 n.; 109.15. **29–31:** A prayer and vow. Normally the vow is
favorable to animal sacrifice. **32–36:** The psalmist's trust in God. **35:** An allusion to the situation
after the Babylonian conquest (597 B.C.) and the Exile (587–520).
   Ps. 70: O God, hasten to my aid. A Lament (see Introduction) almost identical to Ps.40.13–17.
   Ps. 71: Forsake me not, O God. A Lament (see Introduction), apparently of an old man in

where I may ever find safety at thy
call;
for thou art my towering crag and
stronghold.
4 O God, keep my life safe from the
wicked,
from the clutches of unjust and
cruel men.

5 Thou art my hope, O Lord,
my trust, O LORD, since boyhood.
6 From birth I have leaned upon thee,
my protector since I left[x] my
mother's womb.[y]
7 To many I seem a solemn warning;
but I have thee for my strong refuge.
8 My mouth shall be full of thy
praises,
I shall tell of thy splendour all
day long.
9 Do not cast me off when old age
comes,
nor forsake me when my strength
fails,
10 when my enemies' rancour bursts
upon me[z]
and those who watch me whisper
together,
11 saying, 'God has forsaken him;
after him! seize him; no one will
rescue him.'
12 O God, do not stand aloof from
me;
O my God, hasten to my help.
13 Let all my traducers be shamed and
dishonoured,
let all who seek my hurt be covered
with scorn.
14 But I will wait in continual hope,
I will praise thee again and yet
again;
15 all day long thy righteousness,
thy saving acts, shall be upon
my lips.
Thou shalt ever be the theme of my
praise,[a]
although I have not the skill of a
poet.

I will begin with a tale of great   16
deeds, O Lord GOD,
and sing of thy righteousness, thine
alone.
O God, thou hast taught me from   17
boyhood,
all my life I have proclaimed thy
marvellous works;
and now that I am old and my hairs 18
are grey,
forsake me not, O God,
when I extol thy mighty arm to
future generations,
thy power and righteousness, O God, 19
to highest heaven;
for thou hast done great things.
Who is like thee, O God?
Thou hast made me pass through   20
bitter and deep distress,
yet dost revive me once again
and lift me again from earth's
watery depths.
Restore me to honour, turn and   21
comfort me,
then I will praise thee on the lute 22
for thy faithfulness, O God;
I will sing psalms to thee with the
harp,
thou Holy One of Israel;
songs of joy shall be on my lips;   23
I will sing thee psalms, because thou
hast redeemed me.
All day long my tongue shall tell of 24
thy righteousness;
shame and disgrace await those
who seek my hurt.

72

O God, endow the king with thy   1
own justice,
and give thy righteousness to a
king's son,

x my . . . left: or who didst bring me out from.
y See note on verse 15.
z enemies' . . . me: prob. rdg.; Heb. enemies say of me.
a Line transposed from verse 6.

serious trouble who reminds God of his past faithfulness. 7–11: The general belief of the OT,
that troubles were due to a rejection by God because of some sin, made the psalmist's troubled
life (v. 20) seem a solemn warning to would-be sinners. 14–24: The vow here to praise as a motive
for God's favorable action is longer than usual. 20: The earth's watery depths are the underground place of the dead into which the man seems already sunk. 22: Though not a poet
(v. 15), the psalmist offers this musical praise as the content of his vow.
   Ps. 72: May the king live long. A Royal Psalm. The superscription (see Introduction) describes
this as a psalm of Solomon. Vv. 18–20 are an editorial addition to close Book 2 (see Ps.41.13 n.
for other closings). Royal or Wisdom psalms are common at the beginnings and at the ends

2 that he may judge thy people
rightly
and deal out justice to the poor
and suffering.

3 May hills and mountains afford thy
people
peace and prosperity in
righteousness.

4 He shall give judgement for the
suffering
and help those of the people that
are needy;
he shall crush the oppressor.

5 He shall live as long as the sun
endures,
long as the moon, age after age.

6 He shall be like rain falling on early
crops,
like showers watering[b] the earth.

7 In his days righteousness shall
flourish,
prosperity abound until the moon
is no more.

8 May he hold sway from sea to sea,
from the River to the ends of the
earth.

9 Ethiopians shall crouch low before
him;
his enemies shall lick the dust.

10 The kings of Tarshish and the islands
shall bring gifts,
the kings of Sheba and Seba shall
present their tribute,

11 and all kings shall pay him homage,
all nations shall serve him.

12 For he shall rescue the needy from
their rich oppressors,
the distressed who have no
protector.

13 May he have pity on the needy and
the poor,
deliver the poor from death;

14 may he redeem them from
oppression and violence

and may their blood be precious
in his eyes.

May the king live long   15
and receive gifts of gold[c] from
Sheba;
prayer be made for him continually,
blessings be his all the day long.

May there be abundance of corn in   16
the land,
growing in plenty to the tops of
the hills;
may the crops flourish like
Lebanon,
and the sheaves[d] be numberless
as blades of grass.

Long may the king's name endure,   17
may it live for ever like the sun;
so shall all peoples pray to be
blessed as he was,
all nations tell of his happiness.

Blessed be the LORD God, the God   18
of Israel,
who alone does marvellous things;
blessed be his glorious name for ever, 19
and may his glory fill all the earth.
                    Amen, Amen.

Here end the prayers of David son   20
of Jesse.

BOOK 3

73

How good God is to the upright![e]   1
How good to those who are pure
in heart!

b *like showers watering: prob. rdg.; Heb. unintelligible.*
c *Or frankincense.*
d *the sheaves: prob. rdg.; Heb. from a city.*
e *How . . . upright: prob. rdg.; Heb. How good it is to Israel!*

of the five books (see Pss.1,2,41,73,89,90,91). This psalm could have been used at a coronation or at its annual celebration. **1–2:** To *judge* meant to vindicate the rights of the poor and to relieve suffering. Thus, the king was also a judge, and therefore needed to be just. **6–7:** *Early crops* were those that matured before the drought of summer came and hence needed much rain. In Near Eastern ideas of the king, even the fertility of the land depended on him. **8–11:** The desired territory for the Israelite king. **8:** *River:* the Euphrates (1 Kgs.4.21). **9:** *Ethiopians,* elsewhere called also Cushites, were considered fierce warriors; see Jer.46.9. *To lick dust* was a symbol of utter defeat. **10:** *Tarshish:* probably in Spain. *Sheba and Seba:* in South Arabia. **12–14:** The king, like God (v. 1), was to *redeem* people from *oppression.* The absolute kings of the Near East tended to shed the blood of the weak with little remorse; see Ezek.24.1–13. **15–17:** A prayer on behalf of the king. **17:** Many kings in the Ancient Near East were called "the Sun" and still more were compared to the sun. **18–19:** A prayer, not part of the original psalm, but added by an editor to close (v. 20) the second collection of psalms.
   Ps. 73: How good God is to the upright. A Wisdom Psalm, used as the introduction to Book 3

2   My feet had almost slipped,
      my foothold had all but given way,
3   because the boasts of sinners roused
         my envy
      when I saw how they prosper.
4   No pain, no suffering is theirs;
      they are sleek and sound in limb;
5   they are not plunged in trouble as
         other men are,
      nor do they suffer the torments of
         mortal men.
6   Therefore pride is their collar of
         jewels
      and violence the robe that wraps
         them round.
7   Their eyes gleam through folds of
         fat;
      while vain fancies pass through their
         minds.
8   Their talk is all sneers and malice;
      scornfully they spread their
         calumnies.
9   Their slanders reach up to heaven,
      while their tongues ply to and fro
         on earth.
10   And so my people follow their lead*f*
      and find nothing to blame in them,*g*
11   even though they say, 'What does
         God know?
      The Most High neither knows nor
         cares.'
12   So wicked men talk, yet still they
         prosper,
      and rogues*h* amass great wealth.
13   So it was all in vain that I kept my
         heart pure
      and washed my hands in innocence.
14   For all day long I suffer torment
      and am punished every morning.
15   Yet had I let myself talk on in this
         fashion,
      I should have betrayed the family of
         God.
16   So I set myself to think this out

but I found it too hard for me,
   until I went into God's sacred   17
      courts;
   there I saw clearly what their end
      would be.

How often thou dost set them on   18
   slippery ground
   and drive them headlong into
      ruin!
Then in a moment how dreadful   19
   their end,
   cut off root and branch by death
      with all its terrors,
   like a dream when a man rouses   20
      himself, O Lord,
   like images in sleep which are
      dismissed on waking!

When my heart was embittered   21
   I felt the pangs of envy,
I would not understand, so brutish   22
      was I,
I was a mere beast in thy sight, O
      God.
Yet I am always with thee,   23
   thou holdest my right hand;
thou dost guide me by thy counsel   24
   and afterwards wilt receive me
      with glory.
Whom have I in heaven but thee?   25
And having thee,*i* I desire nothing
      else on earth.
Though heart and body fail,   26
   yet God is my possession for ever.
They who are far from thee are lost;   27
   thou dost destroy all who wantonly
      forsake thee.
But my chief good is to be near   28
      thee, O God;
I have chosen thee, Lord GOD, to
      be my refuge.*j*

*f their lead: prob. rdg.; Heb. hither.
g and find . . . in them: prob. rdg.; Heb. obscure.
h yet . . . rogues: prob. rdg.; Heb. those at ease for ever.
i Or And compared with thee.
j Prob. rdg.; Heb. adds to tell all thy works.*

(see Introduction). The psalm falls into two major divisions. The first (vv. 2–15) asks why the wicked prosper and the righteous suffer; the second (vv. 16–28) asserts that after a visit to the Temple, the psalmist learned that the prosperity of the wicked is only temporary and that the righteous enjoy the constant guidance of God. **6–7**: *Fat* connotes an insensitive heart which indulges in *violence*. **11**: The assertion of the wicked, that God is indifferent to man and his behavior, is a practical "atheism"; the theoretical denial of God's existence does not occur in the Bible. **13–15**: The claim that a *pure heart*, i.e. upright life, is *in vain* and useless, is to attack the foundation of Israel's existence and so a betrayal of her hopes; see Deut.6.1–3. **17**: *God's courts*: the Temple. **22–23**: A *brutish* man is moved only by physical force in pain and is insensitive to God's touch in leading him by the *hand;* compare Ps.32.8–10. **24–27**: The final reward of the just man is to be in dialogue with God and to receive his counsel; compare Job 38.1–42.6; Pss.27.4; 32.8; 63.1–11.

74

1 Why hast thou cast us off, O God?
　　Is it for ever?
Why art thou so stern, so angry
　　with the sheep of thy flock?
2 Remember the assembly of thy
　　people,
taken long since for thy own,[k]
and Mount Zion, which was thy
　　home.
3 Now at last[l] restore what was
　　ruined beyond repair,
the wreck that the foe has made of
　　thy sanctuary.

4 The shouts of thy enemies filled the
　　holy place,[m]
they planted their standards there
　　as tokens of victory.
5 They brought it crashing down,[n]
　　like woodmen plying their axes
　　in the forest;
6 they ripped the carvings clean out,
they smashed them with hatchet
　　and pick.
7 They set fire to thy sanctuary,
tore down and polluted the shrine
　　sacred to thy name.
8 They said to themselves, 'We will
　　sweep them away',
and all over the land they burnt
　　God's holy places.[o]

9 We cannot see what lies before us,[p]
　　we have no prophet now;
we have no one who knows how
　　long this is to last.
10 How long, O God, will the enemy
　　taunt thee?
Will the adversary pour scorn on
　　thy name for ever?
11 Why dost thou hold back thy hand,
why keep thy right hand within thy
　　bosom?

12 But thou, O God, thou king from
　　of old,
　　thou mighty conqueror all the
　　world over,
13 by thy power thou didst cleave the
　　sea-monster in two
and break the sea-serpent's heads
　　above the waters;
14 thou didst crush Leviathan's many
　　heads
and throw him to the sharks[q] for
　　food.
15 Thou didst open channels for spring
　　and torrent;
thou didst dry up rivers never
　　known to fail.
16 The day is thine, and the night is
　　thine also,
thou didst ordain the light of moon
　　and sun;
17 thou hast fixed all the regions of
　　the earth;
summer and winter, thou didst create
　　them both.

18 Remember, O LORD, the taunts of
　　the enemy,
the scorn a savage nation pours on
　　thy name.
19 Cast not to the beasts the soul that
　　confesses thee;
forget not for ever the sufferings of
　　thy servants.
20 Look upon thy creatures:[r] they are
　　filled with hatred,
and earth is the haunt of violence.
21 Let not the oppressed be shamed
　　and turned away;

k *Prob. rdg.; Heb. adds* thou didst redeem the tribe of thy possession.
l Now at last: *prob. rdg.; Heb.* Thy steps.
m the holy place: *or* thy meeting place.
n They . . . down: *prob. rdg.; Heb. unintelligible.*
o holy places: *or* meeting places.
p what . . . us: *prob. rdg.; Heb.* our signs.
q to the sharks: *prob. rdg.; Heb.* to a people, desert-dwellers.
r thy creatures: *prob. rdg.; Heb.* the covenant, because.

Ps. 74: Forget not forever the sufferings of the servants. A Lament over the destruction of the Temple by a foreign invader whom some scholars identify as the Babylonians under Nebuchadnezzar in 587 B.C. and others as the Greeks under Antiochus Epiphanes in 167 B.C. (1 Macc.4.38). **9:** The lack of a *prophet* seems to indicate Maccabean times as the period of composition, since prophets did continue their activity after the Babylonian destruction; see 1 Macc.9.27. **11:** *Hold back thy hand:* refrain from acting in behalf of Israel. **12–17:** God's power in restoring dispersed Israel is often compared to the creation of the universe and described in the mythological imagery of the Ancient Near East; compare Isa.51.9–16. God is here a great warrior who defeats primitive chaos identified as the *sea-monster, sea-serpent, Leviathan,* so that he may bring about a benevolent order of *day* and *night,* etc. **18–23:** A prayer for deliverance, the motive being to end the *taunts of the enemy* against God. The vow usual in a Lament is absent, perhaps because it involved a sacrifice which was impossible because the Temple was in ruins.

let the poor and the downtrodden
 praise thy name.
22 Rise up, O God, maintain thy own
 cause;
remember how brutal men taunt
 thee all day long.
23 Ignore no longer the cries of thy
 assailants,
the mounting clamour of those who
 defy thee.

75

1 We give thee thanks, O God, we give
 thee thanks;
thy name is brought very near to us
in the story of thy wonderful deeds.

2 I seize the appointed time
and then I judge mankind with justice.
3 When the earth rocks, with all who
 live on it,
I make its pillars firm.
4 To the boastful I say, 'Boast no
 more',
and to the wicked, 'Do not toss
 your proud horns:
5 toss not your horns against high
 heaven
nor speak arrogantly against your
 Creator.'
6 No power from the east nor from
 the west,
no power from the wilderness, can
 raise a man up.
7 For God is judge;
he puts one man down and raises
 up another.
8 The LORD holds a cup in his hand,
and the wine foams in it, hot with
 spice;
he offers it to every man for drink,
and all the wicked on earth must
 drain it to the dregs.
9 But I will glorify him for ever;

I will sing praises to the God of
 Jacob.

I will break off the horns of the   10
 wicked,
but the horns of the righteous shall
 be lifted high.

76

In Judah God is known,   1
his name is great in Israel;
his tent is pitched in Salem,   2
in Zion his battle-quarters are set up.ˢ
He has broken the flashing arrows, 3
shield and sword and weapons of
 war.

Thou art terrible, O Lord, and   4
 mighty:
men that lust for plunder stand   5
 aghast,
the boldest swoon away,
and the strongest cannot lift a hand.
At thy rebuke, O God of Jacob,   6
rider and horse fall senseless.
Terrible art thou, O Lord;   7
who can stand in thy presence when
 thou art angry?
Thou didst give sentence out of   8
 heaven;
the earth was afraid and kept
 silence.
O God, at thy risingᵗ in judgement 9
to deliver all humble men on the
 earth,
for all her fury Edom shall confess 10
 thee,
and the remnant left in Hamath
 shall dance in worship.

Make vows to the LORD your God, 11
 and pay them duly;

s are set up: *prob. rdg.; Heb.* thither (*at beginning of
 verse 3*).
t O God . . . rising: *prob. rdg.; Heb.* When God rises.

Ps. 75: We give thee thanks, O God. This is classified by some as a Thanksgiving but by others
as a Wisdom Psalm of exhortation. **1:** Gratitude due God. **2–5,10:** God is the speaker. **4:**
Horns: a symbol of power. **6–9:** God alone is the true judge, and his judgment is sure to come.
8: On the *cup* of judgment, compare Isa.51.22–23; Jer.25.15; Lk.22.42.
 Ps. 76: Terrible art thou, O Lord. A Hymn, after a military victory (v. 3). The introduction
(vv. 1–3) is followed by allusions to an unknown battle (vv. 6–10), and ended by an exhortation
to thank God (vv. 11–12). This is one of the songs of Zion (see Ps.46 n.). **2:** *Salem:* mentioned
in Gen.14.18; tradition, as here, identifies it with Jerusalem. **4:** *Terrible:* the translation is
based on a correction of the Heb.; "terrible" means able to elicit terror. **10:** *Edom* to the southeast and *Hamath* to the north. This translation is based on minor corrections of the MT.
11: *Vows:* in Laments, the poet usually vows to express his gratitude through offering a sacrifice.

let the peoples all around him
  bring their tribute;[u]
12 for he breaks the spirit of princes,
  he is the terror of the kings on
  earth.

77

1   I cried aloud to God,
  I cried to God, and he heard me.
2 In the day of my distress I sought
  the Lord,
  and by night I lifted[v] my outspread
  hands in prayer.
  I lay sweating and nothing would
  cool me;
  I refused all comfort.
3 When I called God to mind, I
  groaned;
  as I lay thinking, darkness came over
  my spirit.
4 My eyelids were tightly closed;
  I was dazed and I could not speak.
5 My thoughts went back to times
  long past,
  I remembered forgotten years;
6 all night long I was in deep distress,
  as I lay thinking, my spirit was sunk
  in despair.

7 Will the Lord reject us for evermore
  and never again show favour?
8 Has his unfailing love now failed us
  utterly,
  must his promise time and again be
  unfulfilled?
9 Has God forgotten to be gracious,
  has he in anger withheld his mercies?
10 'Has his right hand', I said, 'lost its
  grasp?
  Does it hang powerless,[w] the arm
  of the Most High?'

11 But then, O LORD, I call to mind
  thy deeds;[x]

I recall thy wonderful acts in times
  gone by.
I meditate upon thy works   12
  and muse on all that thou hast
  done.
O God, thy way is holy;   13
what god is so great as our God?
Thou art the God who workest   14
  miracles;
thou hast shown the nations thy
  power.
With thy strong arm thou didst   15
  redeem thy people,
  the sons of Jacob and Joseph.

The waters saw thee, O God,   16
  they saw thee and writhed in
  anguish;
  the ocean was troubled to its
  depths.
The clouds poured water, the skies   17
  thundered,
  thy arrows flashed hither and
  thither.
The sound of thy thunder was in the   18
  whirlwind,[y]
  thy lightnings lit up the world,
  earth shook and quaked.
Thy path was through the sea, thy   19
  way through mighty waters,
  and no man marked thy
  footsteps.
Thou didst guide thy people like a   20
  flock of sheep,
  under the hand of Moses and
  Aaron.

78

Mark my teaching, O my people,   1
  listen to the words I am to speak.

u Prob. rdg.; Heb. adds for the terror *(cp. verse* 12).
v I lifted: *prob. rdg.; Heb. om.*
w lost . . . powerless: *prob. rdg.; Heb. unintelligible.*
x Prob. rdg.; Heb. then I call to mind the deeds of
  the LORD, for.
y Or in the chariot-wheels.

Ps. 77: I cried aloud to God but then I recalled his wonderful acts. A Lament that has a hymn
of praise (vv. 11–20), in place of the usual vow, as a motive in eliciting God's saving action.
2–4: *Sweating* and a *dazed* condition indicate either the fever of a physical illness or great
anxiety of spirit; compare Lk.22.44. **9–10:** Two questions about God arise in the face of human
suffering: (a) Is God *gracious*, i.e. good and concerned enough about man to want to help him?
(b) Is he able or is he *powerless* to help? **11–15:** A Hymn, extolling God's *way* as *holy* in redeeming
his *people* in the past, affirms his goodness. **16–19:** An ancient Hymn describing creation in
mythological images—the sea serpent writhes *in anguish*—affirms God's power to help. See
74.13–14. **20:** Since God's goodness and power were manifested to the *people* in the Exodus,
they need to be displayed again now.
  Ps. 78: From Moses to David. A historical psalm (see also Pss.105,106,135,136). Israel's

2 I will tell you a story with a
      meaning,
   I will expound the riddle of things
      past,
3 things that we have heard and
      know,
   and our fathers have repeated to us.
4 From their sons we will not hide
   the praises of the LORD and his
      might
   nor the wonderful acts he has
      performed;
   then they shall repeat them to the
      next generation.
5 He laid on Jacob a solemn charge
   and established a law in Israel,
   which he commanded our fathers
      to teach their sons,
6 that it might be known to a future
      generation,
      to children yet unborn,
   and these would repeat it to their
      sons in turn.
7 He charged them to put their trust
      in God,
   to hold his great acts ever in mind
      and to keep all his commandments;
8 not to do as their fathers did,
   a disobedient and rebellious race,
   a generation with no firm purpose,
   with hearts not fixed steadfastly
      on God.

9 The men of Ephraim, bowmen all
      and marksmen,
   turned and ran in the hour of
      battle.
10 They had not kept God's covenant
   and had refused to live by his law;
11 they forgot all that he had done
   and the wonderful acts which he
      had shown them.

12 He did wonders in their fathers'
      sight

in the land of Egypt, the country
   of Zoan:
he divided the sea and took them   13
   through it,
making the water stand up like
   banks on either side.
He led them with a cloud by day   14
and all night long with a glowing
   fire.
He cleft the rock in the wilderness 15
and gave them water to drink,
   abundant as the sea;
he brought streams out of the cliff 16
and made water run down like
   rivers.
But they sinned against him yet   17
   again:
in the desert they defied the Most
   High,
they tried God's patience wilfully, 18
demanding food to satisfy their
   hunger.
They vented their grievance against 19
   God and said,
'Can God spread a table in the
   wilderness?'
When he struck a rock, water   20
   gushed out
until the gullies overflowed;
they said, 'Can he give bread as well,
can he provide meat for his people?'
When he heard this, the LORD was   21
   filled with fury:
fire raged against Jacob,
anger blazed up against Israel,
because they put no trust in God   22
and had no faith in his power to
   save.
Then he gave orders to the skies   23
   above
   and threw open heaven's doors,
he rained down manna for them to   24
   eat
and gave them the grain of heaven.
So men ate the bread of angels;   25

story was undoubtedly told again and again by her poets and for various reasons. An emphasis
here is the condemnation of Ephraim (9–11,67), the leading tribe of the Northern Kingdom.
The historical allusions are quite clear, especially in the light of information in the Pentateuch.
Perhaps the psalm was used on a festival day; perhaps, too, vv.1–9,67 are an addition. **1–4:**
This introduction is kindred to Wisdom writings (see 49.1–4); the *teaching* is offered so that the
present generation will perpetuate its legacy. **2:** This verse is paraphrased in Mt.13.35. **5–8:**
The Sinai episode, Exod. chs. 19–24. **6:** Compare Deut.6.7. **9–11:** The allusion to *in the hour
of battle* is obscure. The major denunciation, though, is in 10–11. **12–53:** A review of the Exodus
and the Wilderness experience emphasizes God's wondrous deeds related in Exod. and Num.
The usual trespasses of Israel (17–20 and 32–40) balanced God's great deeds with men's de-
ficiencies. **12:** *Zoan:* called Rameses in Exod.1.11. **15–16:** See Exod.17.6 and Num.20.10–13.
17–25: See Exod.15.23–16.8. **17:** See Deut.9.22; Heb.3.16. **18:** See Num.20.11. **24:** See Jn.6.31.

he sent them food to their heart's
desire.

26 He let loose the east wind from
heaven
and drove the south wind by his
power;

27 he rained meat like a dust-storm
upon them,
flying birds like the sand of the
sea-shore,

28 which he made settle all over the
camp
round the tents where they lived.

29 So the people ate and were well
filled,
for he had given them what they
craved.

30 Yet they did not abandon their
complaints^z
even while the food was in their
mouths.

31 Then the anger of God blazed up
against them;
he spread death among their
stoutest men
and brought the young men of
Israel to the ground.

32 In spite of all, they persisted in their
sin
and had no faith in his wonderful
acts.

33 So in one moment he snuffed out
their lives
and ended their years in calamity.

34 When he struck them, they began to
seek him,
they would turn and look eagerly for
God;

35 they remembered that God was their
Creator,
that God Most High was their
deliverer.

36 But still they beguiled him with
words
and deceived him with fine speeches;

37 they were not loyal to him in their
hearts
nor were they faithful to his
covenant.

38 Yet he wiped out their guilt
and did not smother his own^a
natural affection;
often he restrained his wrath

and did not rouse his anger to its
height.

39 He remembered that they were only
mortal men,
who pass by like a wind and never
return.

40 How often they rebelled against him
in the wilderness
and grieved him in the desert!

41 Again and again they tried God's
patience
and provoked the Holy One of
Israel.

42 They did not remember his prowess
on the day when he saved them
from the enemy,

43 how he set his signs in Egypt,
his portents in the land of Zoan.

44 He turned their streams into blood,
and they could not drink the running
water.

45 He sent swarms of flies which
devoured them,
and frogs which brought devastation;

46 he gave their harvest over to locusts
and their produce to the grubs;

47 he killed their vines with hailstones
and their figs with torrents of rain;

48 he abandoned their cattle to the
plague
and their beasts to the arrows of
pestilence.

49 He loosed upon them the violence
of his anger,
wrath and enmity and rage,
launching those messengers of evil

50-51 to open a way for his fury.
He struck down all the first-born in
Egypt,
the flower of their manhood in the
tents of Ham,
not shielding their lives from death
but abandoning their bodies to the
plague.

52 But he led out his own people like
sheep
and guided them like a flock in the
wilderness.

53 He led them in safety and they were
not afraid,
and the sea closed over their enemies.

z Or craving.
a his own: prob. rdg.; Heb. om.

27.39: Num.11.31–34. 42–53: The sequence of the plagues differs from that of Exod. chs. 7–12.

54 He brought them to his holy
    mountain,
the hill which his right hand had won;
55 he drove out nations before them,
he allotted their lands to Israel as a
    possession
and settled his tribes in their
    dwellings.
56 Yet they tried God's patience and
    rebelled against him;
they did not keep the commands of
    the Most High;
57 they were renegades, traitors like
    their fathers,
they changed, they went slack like a
    bow.
58 They provoked him to anger with
    their hill-shrines
and roused his jealousy with their
    carved images.
59 When God heard this, he put them
    out of mind
and utterly rejected Israel.
60 He forsook his home at Shiloh,
the tabernacle in which he dwelt
    among men;
61 he surrendered the symbol of his
    strength into captivity
and his pride into enemy hands;
62 he gave his people over to the sword
and put his own possession out of
    mind.
63 Fire devoured his young men,
and his maidens could raise no
    lament for them;
64 his priests fell by the sword,
and his widows could not weep.

65 Then the Lord awoke as a sleeper
    awakes,
like a warrior heated with wine;
66 he struck his foes in the back parts
and brought perpetual shame upon
    them.
67 He despised the clan of Joseph

and did not choose the tribe of
    Ephraim,
he chose the tribe of Judah   68
and Mount Zion which he loved;
he built his sanctuary high as the   69
    heavens,
founded like the earth to last for ever.
He chose David to be his servant   70
and took him from the sheepfolds;
he brought him from minding the   71
    ewes
to be the shepherd of his people
    Jacob;[b]
and he shepherded them in   72
    singleness of heart
and guided them with skilful hand.

79

O God, the heathen have set foot in   1
    thy domain,
defiled thy holy temple
and laid Jerusalem in ruins.
They have thrown out the dead   2
    bodies of thy servants
to feed the birds of the air;
they have made thy loyal servants
    carrion for wild beasts.
Their blood is spilled all round   3
    Jerusalem like water,
and there they lie unburied.
We suffer the contempt of our   4
    neighbours,
the gibes and mockery of all
    around us.

How long, O Lord, wilt thou be   5
    roused to such fury?
Must thy jealousy rage like a fire?
Pour out thy wrath over nations   6
    which do not know thee
and over kingdoms which do not
    invoke thee by name;

b *Prob. rdg.; Heb. adds* and Israel his possession.

54–64: These vv. deal with the conquest of the land of Canaan and the age of the Judges. God gave Israel the land, but infidelity did not cease. **54:** *Holy mountain:* Zion. **55:** Josh. chs. 13–17. **60:** *Shiloh:* See Josh.18.1; Judg.18.31; 1 Sam. chs. 1–4. On its abandonment, see Jer.7.12–14; 26.6. **61:** *The symbol of his strength:* the Ark of the Covenant, captured by the Philistines; see 1 Sam.4.1–7.1. **65–72:** Perhaps this section refers to the destruction of the Northern Kingdom in 721 B.C., 2 Kgs.17.3–6; perhaps, as some suggest, it reflects the Samaritan schism of the age of Ezra and Nehemiah. **65:** *The Lord awoke:* compare 44.23 n. and 59.5. **66:** *Back parts:* see 1 Sam.5.6–12. **68:** *Judah:* the tribe to which David belonged. **69:** 1 Kgs. chs. 6–8. **70–71:** 1 Sam.16.1–16.

    Ps. 79: How long, O Lord. A national Lament after invaders have defiled the Temple and devastated Jerusalem. For the occasion see Ps.74 n. **3:** An *unburied* corpse was a great indignity to the dead person (Tob.1.17–19) and made the whole place unclean; see Num.19.11–16. **5:** Israel aroused God to *jealousy* by her acceptance of other gods and religious practices;

7 see how they have devoured Jacob
and laid waste his homesteads.

8 Do not remember against us the
guilt of past generations
but let thy compassion come swiftly
to meet us,
we have been brought so low.

9 Help us, O God our saviour, for the
honour of thy name;
for thy name's sake deliver us and
wipe out our sins.

10 Why should the nations ask, 'Where
is their God?'
Let thy vengeance for the bloody
slaughter of thy servants
fall on those nations before our
very eyes.

11 Let the groaning of the captives
reach thy presence
and in thy great might set free
death's prisoners.

12 As for the contempt our neighbours
pour on thee, O Lord,
turn it back sevenfold on their own
heads.

13 Then we thy people, the flock
which thou dost shepherd,
will give thee thanks for ever
and repeat thy praise to every
generation.

80

1 Hear us, O shepherd of Israel,
who leadest Joseph like a flock of
sheep.
Show thyself, thou that art throned
on the cherubim,
2 to Ephraim and to Benjamin.
Rouse thy victorious might from
slumber,*c*
come to our rescue.

3 Restore us, O God,
and make thy face shine upon us that
we may be saved.

4 O LORD God of Hosts,
how long wilt thou resist thy people's
prayer?
5 Thou hast made sorrow their
daily bread
and tears of threefold grief their
drink.
6 Thou hast humbled us before our
neighbours,
and our enemies mock us to their
hearts' content.

7 O God of Hosts, restore us;
make thy face shine upon us that we
may be saved.

8 Thou didst bring a vine out of Egypt,
thou didst drive out nations and
plant it;
9 thou didst clear the ground before
it,
so that it made good roots and filled
the land.
10 The mountains were covered with
its shade,
and its branches were like those
of mighty cedars.
11 It put out boughs all the way to the
Sea
and its shoots as far as the River.
12 Why hast thou broken down the
wall round it
so that every passer-by can pluck
its fruit?
13 The wild boar from the thickets
gnaws it,
and swarming insects from the
fields feed on it.
14 O God of Hosts, once more look
down from heaven,
take thought for this vine and
tend it,

c from slumber: prob. rdg.; Heb. and Manasseh.

see Deut.4.23–24; 5.9. **7:** *Jacob,* the father of the twelve patriarchs, is the ancestor of the
Israelites and here a symbol for the nation. **8:** Solidarity in guilt between parents and children
was a belief of the OT and carried over into the NT; see Deut.5.9; Jn.9.2.
    Ps. 80: Hear us, O shepherd of Israel. A group Lament, probably composed in the Northern
Kingdom as suggested by the tribes named (vv. 2–3). The time may have been shortly after the
fall of the Northern Kingdom in 721 B.C. The parts are indicated by the refrain found three
times (vv. 3,7,19); see Ps.4.6 n. for this phrase. **1:** For God to *show* himself to someone is to
bring life and joy to that person. *Cherubim:* see 1 Sam.4.4. **2:** *Ephraim* and Manasseh were the
sons of Joseph who gave their names to the two principal tribes of the Northern Kingdom.
The tribe of *Benjamin,* Joseph's younger brother, was often associated with them. **8–16:** Israel
is the *vine,* a frequent figure; see Hos 10.1 and compare Isa.5.1–7. **11:** *The Sea:* the Mediterranean. *The River:* the Euphrates. **12:** *The wall round it* serves as God's protection.

15 this stock that thy right hand has
planted.*d*

16 Let them that set fire to it or cut it
down
perish before thy angry face.

17 Let thy hand rest upon the man at
thy right side,
the man whom thou hast made
strong for thy service.

18 We have not turned back from thee,
so grant us new life, and we will
invoke thee by name.

19 LORD God of Hosts, restore us;
make thy face shine upon us that
we may be saved.

81

1 Sing out in praise of God our
refuge,*e*
acclaim the God of Jacob.

2 Take pipe and tabor,
take tuneful harp and lute.

3 Blow the horn for the new month,
for the full moon on the day of
our pilgrim-feast.

4 This is a law for Israel,
an ordinance of the God of Jacob,

5 laid as a solemn charge on Joseph
when he came out of Egypt.*f*

6 When I lifted the load from his
shoulders,
his hands let go the builder's basket.

7 When you cried to me in distress, I
rescued you;
unseen, I answered you in
thunder.
I tested you at the waters of
Meribah,
where I opened your mouths and
filled them.*g*

I fed Israel*h* with the finest wheat-   16*i*
flour
and satisfied him with honey from
the rocks.

Listen, my people, while I give you   8
a solemn charge—
do but listen to me, O Israel:
you shall have no strange god   9
nor bow down to any foreign god;
I am the LORD your God   10
who brought you up from Egypt.*j*

But my people did not listen to my   11
words
and Israel would have none of me;
so I sent them off, stubborn as   12
they were,
to follow their own devices.

If my people would but listen to   13
me,
if Israel would only conform to
my ways,
I would soon bring their enemies   14
to their knees
and lay a heavy hand upon their
persecutors.
Let those who hate them*k* come   15
cringing to them,
and meet with everlasting troubles.*l*

82

God takes his stand in the court   1
of heaven
to deliver judgement among the
gods themselves.

d Prob. rdg.; Heb. adds and on the son whom thou
hast made strong for thy service (*cp. verse 17*).
e Or strength.
f Prob. rdg.; Heb. adds I hear an unfamiliar language.
g Line transposed from end of verse 10.
h I fed Israel: *prob. rdg.; Heb.* He fed him.
i Verse transposed.   j See note on verse 7.
k those . . . them: *prob. rdg.; Heb.* those who hate
the LORD.
l Verse 16 transposed to follow verse 7.

17: This may be a prayer for the king, or else the man a figure for Israel. **18:** The vow usual in a
Lament is here a promise to invoke God's name. It is overshadowed by the refrain in v. 19.
Ps. 81: Acclaim the God of Jacob. A Didactic Psalm used for a festival (possibly Passover or
Booths), consisting of ritual prescriptions (vv. 1–5) and prophetic exhortation (vv. 6–15).
3: It is not clear which *pilgrim-feast* is meant of the three ordained in the Pentateuch: Passover,
Booths, or Weeks (Deut.16.16). The first two fit the *full moon* prescription. **6–12:** The divine
words were possibly spoken as an exhortation by a cultic prophet in a liturgical recitation. This
latter may begin with the words of v. 5 found in Tfn. *f* which would mean that God begins by
saying that he met Israel as strangers (they were speaking the Egyptian language). **7:** *When you
cried to me:* see Exod.3.7. *Thunder:* i.e. at Sinai. *Meribah:* see Exod.17.7 and Ps.95.8. **9–10:**
No strange god: the first of the Ten Commandments; Exod.20.2–3. **13–15:** God's benefits to
Israel are conditional on Israel's obedience and fidelity; compare 95.7–11.
Ps. 82: Arise, O God and judge the earth. A Lament, or a Wisdom Psalm, possibly in a liturgical setting, in which a prophetic judgment against the unjust rulers of the world is given.
1: *Court of heaven* as an assembly of *gods* (Heb. *elohim*), superhuman beings lesser than God,

2   How long will you judge unjustly
      and show favour to the wicked?
3   You ought to give judgement for
      the weak and the orphan,
      and see right done to the destitute
      and downtrodden,
4   you ought to rescue the weak and
      the poor,
      and save them from the clutches
      of wicked men.
5   But you know nothing, you
      understand nothing,
      you walk in the dark
      while earth's foundations are
      giving way.
6   This is my sentence: Gods you
      may be,
      sons all of you of a high god,*m*
7   yet you shall die as men die;*n*
      princes fall, every one of them, and
      so shall you.

8   Arise, O God, and judge the earth;
      for thou dost pass all nations
      through thy sieve.

83

1   Rest not, O God;
      O God, be neither silent nor still,
2   for thy enemies are making a
      tumult,
      and those that hate thee carry their
      heads high.
3   They devise cunning schemes
      against thy people
      and conspire against those thou
      hast made thy treasure:
4   'Come, away with them,' they cry,
      'let them be a nation no longer,

let Israel's name be remembered no
      more,'
With one mind they have agreed   5
      together
to make a league against thee:
      the families of Edom, the   6
      Ishmaelites,
      Moabites and Hagarenes,
Gebal, Ammon and Amalek,   7
      Philistia and the citizens of Tyre,
Asshur too their ally,   8
all of them lending aid to the
      descendants of Lot.
Deal with them as with Sisera,   9
      as with Jabin by the torrent of
      Kishon,
who fell vanquished as Midian*o* fell   10
      at En-harod,*p*
      and were spread on the battlefield
      like dung.
Make their princes like Oreb and   11
      Zeeb,
      make all their nobles like Zebah
      and Zalmunna;
for they said, 'We will seize for   12
      ourselves
      all the pastures of God's people.'
Scatter them, O God, like   13
      thistledown,
      like chaff before the wind.
Like fire raging through the forest   14
      or flames which blaze across the
      hills,
hunt them down with thy tempest,   15
      and dismay them with thy storm-
      wind.
Heap shame upon their heads, O   16
      LORD,

m Or of the Most High.
n Or as Adam died.
o as Midian: transposed from previous verse.
p En-harod: prob. rdg., cp. Judg. 7. 1; Heb. Endor.

---

is found also in 89.5–7; Job 1.6 and elsewhere. Some scholars interpret "gods" (here and in v. 6) literally as a mythological motif taken over from Canaanite literature. Others see it as a reference to human judges, as in Jn.10.34. **2–7:** One explanation of evil in the world was that heavenly beings abused the power over the world given them by God; compare Col.2.6–15. The divine words, possibly spoken by a prophet in a temple ceremony, contain a condemnation of these beings by God; this takes the place of the lamentation and the vow usual in a Lament.
     Ps. 83: Rest not, O God. A Lament calling for vengeance on the nations which intended to destroy Israel. The exact historic situation is unclear; a loose connection with Ps.79 is possible. A call for help (v. 1) arises from the aggressive plans of the nations (vv. 2–8); a plea follows for their destruction (vv. 9–18) as other foes were once destroyed (vv. 9–11). **6–7:** The enemies are neighboring nations, often mentioned in Scripture, except for the unclear *Hagarenes*. Since the Ishmaelites were descended from Hagar (Gen.16.15), the name may be a synonym for Ishmaelites, a desert people. *Gebal* probably means the Phoenician city Byblos. An interesting variant from Masada reads "the gods of Edom" instead of *the families of Edom*. **8:** *Asshur* is clearly Assyria, but the allusion is not clear. Lot's *descendants* were Ammon and Moab (Gen.19 30–38). **9:** *Sisera and Jabin:* see Judg. chs. 4–5. **10:** *Midian:* compare Judg. chs. 6–8. **11:** *Oreb . . . Zeeb:* Judg.7.25. *Zebah and Zalmunna:* Judg.8.21. **12–19:** A characteristic curse.

until they confess the greatness
of thy name.

17 Let them be abashed, and live in
perpetual dismay;
let them feel their shame and
perish.

18 So let them learn that thou alone
art LORD,
God Most High over all the earth.

84

1 How dear is thy dwelling-place,
thou LORD of Hosts!
2 I pine, I faint with longing
for the courts of the LORD's
temple;
my whole being cries out with joy
to the living God.
3 Even the sparrow finds a home,
and the swallow has her nest,
where she rears her brood beside
thy altars,
O LORD of Hosts, my King and
my God.
4 Happy are those who dwell in thy
house;
they never cease from praising
thee.
5 Happy the men whose refuge is in
thee,
whose hearts are set on the
pilgrim ways*q*!
6 As they pass through the thirsty
valley
they find water from a spring;
and the LORD provides even men
who lose their way
with pools to quench their thirst.*r*
7 So they pass on from outer wall to
inner,
and the God of gods shows himself
in Zion.
8 O LORD God of Hosts, hear my
prayer;
listen, O God of Jacob.
9 O God, look upon our lord the king

and accept thy anointed prince
with favour.

Better one day in thy courts   10
than a thousand days at home;
better to linger by the threshold of
God's house
than to live in the dwellings of
the wicked.
The LORD God is a battlement and   11
a shield;
grace and honour are his to give.
The LORD will hold back no good
thing
from those whose life is blameless.

O LORD of Hosts,   12
happy the man who trusts in thee!

85

LORD, thou hast been gracious to   1
thy land
and turned the tide of Jacob's
fortunes.
Thou hast forgiven the guilt of   2
thy people
and put away all their sins.
Thou hast taken back all thy   3
anger
and turned from thy bitter wrath.

Turn back to us, O God our   4
saviour,
and cancel thy displeasure.
Wilt thou be angry with us for ever? 5
Must thy wrath last for all
generations?
Wilt thou not give us new life   6
that thy people may rejoice in thee?
O LORD, show us thy true love   7
and grant us thy deliverance.

Let me hear the words of the LORD: 8
are they not*s* words of peace,

q are set . . . ways: *or* high praises fill.
r they find . . . thirst: *prob. rdg.; Heb. obscure.*
s of the LORD: are they not: *prob. rdg.; Heb.* of God
the LORD.

Ps. 84: **Happy are those who dwell in thy house.** A Hymn, probably sung by a pilgrim at the
Temple on a festival. A prayer for the king (vv. 8–9) may be an addition. The praise of the
Temple (vv. 1–4) is followed by an allusion to the pilgrim's journey (vv. 5–7), and an exaltation
of the Temple (vv. 10–12) closes the psalm. 6: *Thirsty:* older translations interpreted the Heb.
to mean "valley of weeping."
Ps. 85: **Wilt thou not give us new life?** A national Lament (see Introduction), possibly composed during the difficult times following the return from the Exile, as seems indicated by v. 12;

peace to his people and his loyal
servants
and to all who turn and trust in
him?

9 Deliverance is near to those who
worship him,
so that glory may dwell in our
land.

10 Love and fidelity have come
together;
justice and peace join hands.

11 Fidelity springs up from earth
and justice looks down from
heaven.

12 The LORD will add prosperity,
and our land shall yield its harvest.

13 Justice shall go in front of him
and the path before his feet shall
be peace.[t]

86

1 Turn to me, LORD, and answer;
I am downtrodden and poor.

2 Guard me, for I am constant and
true;
save thy servant who puts his trust
in thee.

3 O Lord my God,[u] show me thy
favour;
I call to thee all day long.

4 Fill thy servant's heart with joy,
O Lord,
for I lift up my heart to thee.

5 Thou, O Lord, art kind and forgiving,
full of true love for all who cry
to thee.

6 Listen, O LORD, to my prayer
and hear my pleading.

7 In the day of my distress I call
on thee;
for thou wilt answer me.

8 Among the gods not one is like
thee, O Lord,
no deeds are like thine.

9 All the nations thou hast made,
O Lord, will come,

will bow down before thee and
honour thy name;

10 for thou art great, thy works are
wonderful,
thou alone art God.

11 Guide me, O LORD,
that I may be true to thee and
follow thy path;
let me be one in heart
with those who revere thy name.

12 I will praise thee, O Lord my God,
with all my heart
and honour thy name for ever.

13 For thy true love stands high above
me;
thou hast rescued my soul from the
depths of Sheol.

14 O God, proud men attack me;
a mob of ruffians seek my life
and give no thought to thee.

15 Thou, Lord, art God, compassionate
and gracious,
forbearing, ever constant and true.

16 Turn towards me and show me thy
favour;
grant thy slave protection
and rescue thy slave-girl's son.

17 Give me proof of thy kindness;
let those who hate thee see to their
shame
that thou, O LORD, hast been my
help and comfort.

87[v]

1-2 The LORD loves the gates of Zion
more than all the dwellings of
Jacob;
her[w] foundations are laid upon
holy hills,

4-5 and he has made her his home.[x]

[t] and the path . . . peace: prob. rdg.; Heb. so that he
may put his feet to the way.
[u] my God: transposed from previous verse.
[v] The text of this psalm is disordered, and several verses
have been re-arranged.
[w] Prob. rdg.; Heb. his.
[x] his home: prob. rdg.; Heb. most high.

see Neh.5.1–5. 9: Glory may refer to the presence of God in the Temple. His presence left
Jerusalem at the Exile and returned with the captives; see Ezek.11.23–24; 43.1–2. 10–11: God's
love and Israel's fidelity are seen as a dialogue between heaven and earth.
     Ps. 86: Listen, O Lord, to my prayer. A Lament. 1: Downtrodden: perhaps to be taken
literally, but more likely the usual language of self-abasement. 13: Rescued my soul from Sheol:
saved my life from death. 16: Thy slave-girl's son is the psalmist.
     Ps. 87: O city of God. A Hymn. It has long been recognized as transmitted defectively; see
Tfn. v. Zion, the city of God, is the mother of the faithful of all the world. 4: Egypt: Heb

I will count Egypt and Babylon
   among my friends;
Philistine, Tyrian and Nubian shall
   be[y] there;
and Zion shall be called a mother
in whom men of every race are born.
6 The LORD shall write against each
   in the roll of nations:
'This one was born in her.'
7 Singers and dancers alike all chant[z]
   your praises,
3 proclaiming glorious things of you,
   O city of God.

88

1 O LORD, my God, by day I call
   for help,[a]
by night I cry aloud in thy presence.
2 Let my prayer come before thee,
hear my loud lament;
3 for I have had my fill of woes,
   and they have brought me to the
   threshold of Sheol.
4 I am numbered with those who go
   down to the abyss
and have become like a man
   beyond help,
5 like a man who lies dead[b]
   or the slain who sleep in the
   grave,
whom thou rememberest no more
because they are cut off from thy
   care.
6 Thou hast plunged me into the
   lowest abyss,
in dark places, in the depths.
7 Thy wrath rises against me,
thou hast turned on me the full
   force of thy anger.[c]
8 Thou hast taken all my friends far
   from me,
and made me loathsome to them.
I am in prison and cannot escape;
9 my eyes are failing and dim with
   anguish.
I have called upon thee, O LORD,
   every day

and spread out my hands in prayer
   to thee.
10 Dost thou work wonders for the
   dead?
Shall their company rise up and
   praise thee?
11 Will they speak of thy faithful love
   in the grave,
of thy sure help in the place of
   Destruction?
12 Will thy wonders be known in the
   dark,
thy victories in the land of
   oblivion?

13 But, LORD, I cry to thee,
my prayer comes before thee in the
   morning.
14 Why hast thou cast me off, O LORD,
why dost thou hide thy face from
   me?
15 I have suffered from boyhood and
   come near to death;
I have borne thy terrors, I cower
   beneath thy blows.
16 Thy burning fury has swept over me,
   thy onslaughts have put me to
   silence;
17 all the day long they surge round
   me like a flood,
they engulf me in a moment.
18 Thou hast taken lover and friend
   far from me,
   and parted me from my
   companions.

89

1 I will sing the story of thy love, O
   LORD, for ever;
I will proclaim thy faithfulness to all
   generations.

y Prob. rdg.; Heb. adds this one was born (cp. verse 6).
z all chant: prob. rdg.; Heb. all my springs.
a I call for help: prob. rdg.; Heb. my deliverance.
b who lies dead: prob. rdg.; Heb. obscure.
c anger: or waves.

Rahab, the sea dragon, a frequent figure for Egypt. 6: *Against each*: respecting each. *Born in her*: her citizens.
   Ps. 88: Hear my loud lament. An extremely bitter Lament of a man desperately ill, perhaps from a life-long sickness (v. 15). 3–5: He considers himself all but dead, *Sheol* and *abyss* being the place of the dead. 10–12: A classic description of Sheol. The motive for securing God's healing is that no one can *praise* God in the *grave*. 13: The usual vow is the promise of *prayer*.
   Ps. 89: How long must thy wrath blaze like fire? A Lament with a complicated structure, including a hymn and a royal prayer for a lasting line (v. 36). 1–8: A hymn of praise to the Creator-King.

2 Thy true love is firm as the ancient
    earth,[d]
thy faithfulness fixed as the heavens.

5[e] The heavens praise thy wonders,
    O LORD,
and the council of the holy ones
    exalts thy faithfulness.

6 In the skies who is there like the
    LORD,
who like the LORD in the court of
    heaven,

7 like God who is dreaded among the
    assembled holy ones,
great and terrible above all who
    stand about him?

8 O LORD God of Hosts, who is like
    thee?
Thy strength[f] and faithfulness, O
    LORD, surround thee.

9 Thou rulest the surging sea,
calming the turmoil[g] of its waves.

10 Thou didst crush the monster Rahab
    with a mortal blow
and scatter thy enemies with thy
    strong arm.

11 Thine are the heavens, the earth is
    thine also;
the world with all that is in it is of
    thy foundation.

12 Thou didst create Zaphon and
    Amanus;[h]
Tabor and Hermon echo thy name.

13 Strength of arm and valour are
    thine;
thy hand is mighty, thy right hand
    lifted high;

14 thy throne is built upon righteous-
    ness and justice,
true love and faithfulness herald thy
    coming.

15 Happy the people who have learnt
    to acclaim thee,
who walk, O LORD, in the light of
    thy presence!

16 In thy name they shall rejoice all
    day long;
thy righteousness shall lift them up.

17 Thou art thyself the strength in
which they glory;
through thy favour we hold our
    heads high.

18 The LORD, he is our shield;
the Holy One of Israel, he is our
    king.

19 Then didst thou announce in a
    vision
and declare to thy faithful servants:

3 I have made a covenant with him
    I have chosen,
I have sworn to my servant
    David;

4 'I will establish your posterity for
    ever,
I will make your throne endure for
    all generations.'
I have endowed a warrior with
    princely gifts,
so that the youth I have chosen
    towers over his people.

20 I have discovered David my servant;
I have anointed him with my holy
    oil.

21 My hand shall be ready to help him
and my arm to give him strength.

22 No enemy shall strike at him
and no rebel bring him low;

23 I will shatter his foes before him
and vanquish those who hate him.

24 My faithfulness and true love shall
    be with him
and through my name he shall hold
    his head high.

25 I will extend his rule over the Sea
and his dominion as far as the
    River.

26 He will say to me, 'Thou art my
    father,
my God, my rock and my safe
    refuge.'

27 And I will name him my first-born,
highest among the kings of the
    earth.

d Thy . . . earth: prob. rdg.; Heb. Thou hast said for
ever true love shall be made firm.
e Verses 3 and 4 transposed to follow servants in verse 19.
f Thy strength: prob. rdg.; Heb. obscure.
g turmoil: prob. rdg.; Heb. obscure.
h Amanus: prob. rdg.; Heb. right hand or south.

5–7: See 82.1 n. *Terrible:* inspires terror. **9–10:** On the mythical language of creation see 74.12–17 n.; Isa.51.9–10. **12:** The four mountains, *Zaphon* (48.2 n.), *Amanus* in southern Turkey, *Tabor* in northern Israel, and *Hermon* in Syria, near Damascus, were considered sacred in ancient myths as residences of the gods. **14:** *Righteousness, justice, true love,* and *faithfulness* are the most characteristic attributes of God in his covenant dealings with Israel. **18:** *Shield:* protector. **19–37:** God's words which proclaimed an eternal dynasty for David and his descendants, even should the latter fall into *disobedience* (v. 32). **26–27:** *First-born:* the position of highest favor.

28 I will maintain my love for him for
      ever
    and be faithful in my covenant with
      him.
29 I will establish his posterity for ever
      and his throne as long as the
      heavens endure.
30 If his sons forsake my law
      and do not conform to my
      judgements,
31 if they renounce my statutes
      and do not observe my
      commands,
32 I will punish their disobedience
      with the rod
      and their iniquity with lashes.
33 Yet I will not deprive him of my
      true love
      nor let my faithfulness prove
      false;
34 I will not renounce my covenant
      nor change my promised purpose.
35 I have sworn by my holiness once
      and for all,
    I will not break my word to
      David:
36 his posterity shall continue for ever,
      his throne before me like the sun;
37 it shall be sure for ever as the
      moon's return,
    faithful so long as the skies remain.*i*

38 Yet thou hast rejected thy anointed
      king,
      thou hast spurned him and raged
      against him,*j*
39 thou hast denounced the covenant
      with thy servant,
      defiled his crown and flung it to the
      ground.
40 Thou hast breached his walls
      and laid his fortresses in ruin;
41 all who pass by plunder him,
      and he suffers the taunts of his
      neighbours.
42 Thou hast increased the power of
      his enemies
      and brought joy to all his foes;
43 thou hast let his sharp sword be
      driven back
      and left him without help in the
      battle.

44 Thou hast put an end to his
      glorious rule*k*
      and hurled his throne to the ground;
45 thou hast cut short the days of his
      youth and vigour
      and covered him with shame.

46 How long, O LORD, wilt thou hide
      thyself from sight?
    How long must thy wrath blaze
      like fire?
47 Remember that I shall not live for
      ever;*l*
    hast thou created man in vain?
48 What man shall live and not see death
      or save himself from the power of
      Sheol?
49 Where are those former acts of thy
      love, O Lord,
      those faithful promises given to
      David?
50 Remember, O Lord, the taunts
      hurled at thy servant,
    how I have borne in my heart the
      calumnies of the nations;*m*
51 so have thy enemies taunted us,
      O LORD,
    taunted the successors of thy
      anointed king.

Blessed is the LORD for ever.   52

              Amen, Amen.

              BOOK 4

                  90

Lord, thou hast been our refuge   1
      from generation to generation.
Before the mountains were brought   2
      forth,
    or earth and world were born in
      travail,

i so long . . . remain: *prob. rdg.; Heb.* a witness in the
skies.
j raged against him: *or* put him out of mind.
k his glorious rule: *prob. rdg.; Heb.* from his purity.
l live for ever: *prob. rdg.; Heb.* obscure.
m the calumnies . . . nations: *prob. rdg.; Heb.* all of
many peoples.

38–45: A military defeat seems to have ended the king's *glorious rule* and nullified *the covenant*.
46: God's *wrath blazes* when he hides himself from man's *sight*, i.e. experience. **47–51:** The
fragility of *man* and God's faithfulness to his *promises* are motives for deliverance.
   Ps. 90: Teach us to order our days. A Lament of the community in which the description of

from age to age everlasting thou art
　　God.

3　Thou turnest man back into dust;
　　'Turn back,' thou sayest, 'you sons
　　　of men';

4　for in thy sight a thousand years
　　are as yesterday;

5　a night-watch passes, and thou hast
　　　cut them off;
　　they are like a dream at daybreak,

6　they fade like grass which springs
　　　up[n] with the morning
　　but when evening comes is parched
　　　and withered.

7　So we are brought to an end by thy
　　　anger
　　and silenced by thy wrath.

8　Thou dost lay bare our iniquities
　　　before thee
　　and our lusts in the full light of
　　　thy presence.

9　All our days go by under the
　　　shadow of thy wrath;
　　our years die away like a murmur.

10　Seventy years is the span of our
　　　life,
　　eighty if our strength holds;[o]
　　the hurrying years are labour and
　　　sorrow,
　　so quickly they pass and are
　　　forgotten.

11　Who feels the power of thy anger,
　　who feels thy wrath like those that
　　　fear thee?

12　Teach us to order our days rightly,
　　that we may enter the gate of
　　　wisdom.

13　How long, O LORD?
　　Relent, and take pity on thy
　　　servants.

14　Satisfy us with thy love when
　　　morning breaks,
　　that we may sing for joy and be
　　　glad all our days.

15　Repay us days of gladness for our
　　　days of suffering,
　　for the years thou hast humbled us.

16　Show thy servants thy deeds
　　and their children thy majesty.

May all delightful things be ours, O　17
　　Lord our God;
establish firmly all we do.

91

You that live in the shelter of　　　1
　　the Most High
and lodge under the shadow of
　　the Almighty,
who say, 'The LORD is my safe　　　2
　　retreat,
my God the fastness in which I
　　trust';
he himself will snatch you away　　3
　　from fowler's snare or raging
　　tempest.
He will cover you with his pinions,　4
　　and you shall find safety beneath
　　his wings;
you shall not fear the hunters' trap　5
　　by night
or the arrow that flies by day,
the pestilence that stalks in darkness　6
　　or the plague raging at noonday.
A thousand may fall at your side,　　7
　　ten thousand close at hand,
　　but you it shall not touch;
　　his truth[p] will be your shield and
　　　your rampart.[q]
With your own eyes you shall see　　8
　　all this;
　　you shall watch the punishment
　　of the wicked.
For you, the LORD is a[r] safe retreat;　9
　　you have made the Most High
　　your refuge.
No disaster shall befall you,　　　10
　　no calamity shall come upon your
　　home.
For he has charged his angels　　　11
　　to guard you wherever you go,
　　to lift you on their hands　　　12
for fear you should strike your foot
　　against a stone.

n Prob. rdg.; Heb. adds and passes away.
o Or eighty at the most.　　p Or his arm.
q his truth . . . rampart: transposed from end of verse 4.
r Prob. rdg.; Heb. my.

the grievance is a wisdomlike reflection on the transient condition of human life (vv. 3–12). This
psalm, standing at the beginning of Book 4, resembles in form and content Pss. 42–43, which
begin Book 2. 13–17: The petition for deliverance has as its motive the prolonged suffering of the
past.
　　Ps. 91: I will satisfy him with long life. A psalm of trust in the Wisdom tradition. **1:** *Most
High, Almighty, LORD, God* represent different Heb. names for God. To know the name of a
person indicates a deep knowledge of, and special power over, the person; see v. 14. **6:** *Pestilence*
and *plague:* considered demonic powers in Israelite belief. **11–12:** Used in Mt.4 6; Lk.4.10–11.

13 You shall step on asp and cobra,
    you shall tread safely on snake and
      serpent.

14 Because his love is set on me, I will
    deliver him;
    I will lift him beyond danger, for he
      knows me by my name.
15 When he calls upon me, I will
      answer;
    I will be with him in time of
      trouble;
      I will rescue him and bring him
      to honour.
16 I will satisfy him with long life
    to enjoy the fullness of my salvation.

92

1 O LORD, it is good to give thee
      thanks,
    to sing psalms to thy name, O
      Most High,
2 to declare thy love in the morning
    and thy constancy every night,
3 to the music of a ten-stringed lute,
    to the sounding chords of the
      harp.
4 Thy acts, O LORD, fill me with
      exultation;
    I shout in triumph at thy mighty
      deeds.
5 How great are thy deeds, O LORD!
    How fathomless thy thoughts!

6 He who does not know this is a
      brute,
    a fool is he who does not under-
    stand this:

7 that though the wicked grow like
      grass
    and every evildoer prospers,
      they will be destroyed for ever.
8 While thou, LORD, dost reign on
      high eternally,
9 thy foes will surely perish,
    all evildoers will be scattered.

10 I lift my head high, like a wild ox
      tossing its horn;
    I am anointed richly with oil.
11 I gloat over all who speak ill of me,
    I listen for the downfall of my cruel
      foes.
12 The righteous flourish like a palm-
      tree,
    they grow tall as a cedar on
      Lebanon;
13 planted as they are in the house
      of the LORD,
    they flourish in the courts of our
      God,
14 vigorous in old age like trees full of
      sap,
    luxuriant, wide-spreading,
15 eager to declare that the LORD is
      just,
    the LORD my rock,[s] in whom there
      is no unrighteousness.

93

1 The LORD is king; he is clothed in
      majesty;
    the LORD clothes himself with might
      and fastens on his belt of wrath.

[s] *Or* creator.

14–16: The words are God's, perhaps in an oracle spoken by a priest in the Temple; they reflect the Wisdom teaching that God tests the virtuous by their suffering, but in the end *will deliver* them.

    Ps. 92: It is good to give thanks. A Thanksgiving Psalm which has a hymn of praise for intro-duction (vv. 1–5) and a Wisdom-tradition description of the "two ways of human life," good rewarded and evil punished. **8–9:** God, Creator-King, reigns forever because he has defeated the cosmic powers. This is one of several echoes in Psalms of a common ancient myth. The MT equivalent to v. 9 has three portions instead of the usual two: (1) For lo, thy enemies, O LORD, (2) for lo thy enemies will surely perish, (3) all evildoers will be scattered. Many scholars view the MT version as a parallel to a "tricolon" found in a Ugaritic text (68.8–9) describing Baal's defeat of the Sea: "Lo, your enemies, O Baal, Lo your enemies you will smite, Lo, you will vanquish your foes." **10:** *Ox tossing its horn:* symbol of strength; *anointed with oil:* symbol of well-being and prosperity. **13:** Other passages (e.g. 52.8; Exod.15.17) speak of righteous people as *planted* in God's house.
    Ps. 93: The LORD is King. An Enthronement Hymn, as are also Pss. 95–99 and 47; see 47 n. The theme of enthronement (vv. 1–2) moves (3–4) to a recollection of the cosmic warfare (symbolized by the control of the sea); see 74.12–17; 104.7–9; Job 38.8–11. **1:** The *belt* is that of the warrior, as if to say that God is valiant in warfare; compare Exod.15.3; Isa 42.13. "King," "warrior," and "creator" are many times synonymous, and all are implied in this

Thou hast fixed the earth
  immovable and firm,
2   thy throne firm from of old;
from all eternity thou art God.
3 O Lord, the ocean lifts up, the
  ocean lifts up its clamour;
the ocean lifts up^t its pounding
  waves.
4   The Lord on high is mightier
    far
than the noise of great waters,
mightier than the breakers of
  the sea.

5 Thy law stands firm, and holiness is
  the beauty of thy temple,
while time shall last, O Lord.

94

1   O Lord, thou God of vengeance,
  thou God of vengeance, show
    thyself.
2   Rise up, judge of the earth;
punish the arrogant as they deserve.
3 How long shall the wicked, O Lord,
how long shall the wicked exult?
4 Evildoers are full of bluster,
boasting and swaggering;
5 they beat down thy people,
  O Lord,
and oppress thy chosen nation;
6 they murder the widow and the
    stranger
and do the fatherless to death;
7 they say, 'The Lord does not see,
  the God of Jacob pays no heed.'
8   Pay heed yourselves, most brutish
  of the people;
  you fools, when will you be wise?
9 Does he that planted the ear not
    hear,
he that moulded the eye not see?
10   Shall not he that instructs the
  nations correct them?
The teacher of mankind, has he
  no^u knowledge?

The Lord knows the thoughts of 11
  man,
that they are but a puff of wind.

Happy the man whom thou dost 12
  instruct, O Lord,
and teach out of thy law,
giving him respite from adversity 13
until a pit is dug for the wicked.
The Lord will not abandon his 14
  people
nor forsake his chosen nation;
for righteousness still informs 15
  his judgement,^{v}
and all upright men follow it.

Who is on my side against these 16
  sinful men?
Who will stand up for me against
  these evildoers?
If the Lord had not been my helper, 17
I should soon have slept in the silent
  grave.
When I felt that my foot was 18
  slipping,
thy love, O Lord, held me up.
Anxious thoughts may fill my 19
  heart,
but thy presence is my joy and
  my consolation.
Shall sanctimonious calumny 20
  call thee partner,
or he that contrives a mischief
  under cover of law?
For they put the righteous on 21
  trial^w for his life
and condemn to death innocent
  men.
But the Lord has been my strong 22
  tower,
and God my rock of refuge;
our God requites the wicked for 23
  their injustice,

t the ocean lifts up: *or* let the ocean lift up.
u no: *prob. rdg.; Heb. om.*
v for . . . judgement: *prob. rdg.; Heb.* for judgement
  will return as far as righteousness.
w they put . . . trial: *prob. rdg.; Heb.* they cut the
  righteous.

Hymn. **2–4:** God controls the sea, and hence secures order in all creation. **5:** *Holiness* is the divine quality of being removed from and beyond the profane and human.
  Ps. 94: Thy love, O Lord, held me up. It is difficult to say whether this psalm is a Thanksgiving in which former trials are described, or a Lament in which deliverance and thanksgiving are anticipated. There is an invocation of God to help (vv. 1–3); the description of the trials (if a Lament) is in the Wisdom motif of the "two ways"—the evil and their punishment (vv. 4–11) and the virtuous being tested and their reward (vv. 12–15). **20–21:** Under pious pretense of carrying out God's *law,* the powerful oppress the innocent weak; see 1 Kgs.21.1–14; Job 13.4–7.

the LORD puts them to silence for
their misdeeds.

95	**96**

¹ Come! Let us raise a joyful song to
the LORD,
a shout of triumph to the Rock of
our salvation.

² Let us come into his presence with
thanksgiving,
and sing him psalms of triumph.

³ For the LORD is a great God,
a great king over all gods;

⁴ the farthest places of the earth are
in his hands,
and the folds of the hills are
his;

⁵ the sea is his, he made it;
the dry land fashioned by his hands
is his.

⁶ Come! Let us throw ourselves at
his feet in homage,
let us kneel before the LORD who
made us;

⁷ for he is our God,
we are his people, we the flock he
shepherds.
You shall know^x his power today
if you will listen to his voice.

⁸ Do not grow stubborn, as you
were at Meribah,^y
as at the time of Massah^z in the
wilderness,

⁹ when your forefathers challenged
me,
tested me and saw for themselves
all that I did.

¹⁰ For forty years I was indignant
with that generation, and I said:
They are a people whose hearts are
astray,
and they will not discern my ways.

As I swore in my anger: 11
They shall never enter my rest.

Sing a new song to the LORD;   1^a
sing to the LORD, all men on earth.

Sing to the LORD and bless his name, 2
proclaim his triumph day by day.

Declare his glory among the nations, 3
his marvellous deeds among all
peoples.

Great is the LORD and worthy of all   4
praise;
he is more to be feared than all
gods.

For the gods of the nations are   5
idols every one;
but the LORD made the heavens.

Majesty and splendour attend him,   6
might and beauty are in his
sanctuary.

Ascribe to the LORD, you families   7
of nations,
ascribe to the LORD glory and might;
ascribe to the LORD the glory due   8
to his name,
bring a gift and come into his
courts.

Bow down to the LORD in the   9
splendour of holiness,^b
and dance in his honour, all men
on earth.

Declare among the nations, 'The   10
LORD is king.
He has fixed the earth firm,
immovable;
he will judge the peoples justly.'

Let the heavens rejoice and the earth 11
exult,

x *You shall know: prob. rdg.; Heb. om.*
y *That is Dispute.*
z *That is Challenge.*
a *Verses 1–13: cp. 1 Chr. 16. 23–33.*
b *the splendour of holiness: or holy vestments.*

Ps. 95: The LORD is a great God. An Enthronement Hymn (see Ps. 47 n.) with the motif of
God as king, expressed in a liturgical ceremony. **1:** God is the *Rock of our salvation.* This is
either in reference to the rock which gave water in the desert (Exod.17.1–7) or the rock on which
the Temple stood (2 Sam.24.18). **3–7:** God is *king* in virtue of being the Creator. **3:** *Gods:* see
82.1 n. **7:** *Know his power:* experience his helping presence. Israel listened to God's *voice*
speaking in nature and in the covenant. Vv. 7b–11 are quoted in Heb.3.7–11; 4.3–11. **8–9:** For
the event at *Meribah* see Exod.17.1–7; Num.20.1–13. **10:** *Forty years* is usually symbolic of
one *generation;* see Num.14.33. **11:** *My rest:* land of Canaan; see Deut.3.20; 12.10.
Ps. 96: The LORD is King. An Enthronement Hymn; see Ps. 47 n. It is found also in 1
Chr.16.23–33 though the order of lines is different. There it appears as occasion of the
the movement of the Ark of the Covenant to Jerusalem. **4–6:** *Than all gods:* see 82.1 n.; 89.5–7.
God as Creator is a usual motif in Enthronement psalms, as is his *sanctuary.* **10–13:** A description of God as the divine *king*, Creator and *judge.*

let the sea roar and all the creatures
in it,
12 let the fields exult and all that is in
them;
then let all the trees of the forest
shout for joy
13 before the LORD when he comes to
judge the earth.
He will judge the earth with
righteousness
and the peoples in good faith.

The LORD loves[d] those who hate   10
evil;
he keeps his loyal servants safe
and rescues them from the
wicked.
A harvest of light is sown for the   11
righteous,
and joy for all good men.
You that are righteous, rejoice in   12
the LORD
and praise his holy name.

97

1 The LORD is king, let the earth be
glad,
let coasts and islands all rejoice.
2 Cloud and mist enfold him,
righteousness and justice
are the foundation of his throne.
3 Fire goes before him
and burns up his enemies all
around.
4 The world is lit up beneath his
lightning-flash;
the earth sees it and writhes in
pain.
5 The mountains melt like wax as the
LORD approaches,
the Lord of all the earth.
6 The heavens proclaim his
righteousness,
and all peoples see his glory.
7 Let all who worship images, who
vaunt their idols,
be put to shame;
bow down, all gods,[c] before him.

8 Zion heard and rejoiced, the cities of
Judah were glad
at thy judgements, O LORD.
9 For thou, LORD, art most high over
all the earth,
far exalted above all gods.

98

Sing a new song to the LORD,   1
for he has done marvellous deeds;
his right hand and holy arm have
won him victory.
The LORD has made his victory   2
known;
he has displayed his righteousness
to all the nations.
He has remembered his constancy,   3
his love for the house of Israel.
All the ends of the earth have seen
the victory of our God.

Acclaim the LORD, all men on   4
earth,
break into songs of joy, sing psalms.
Sing psalms in the LORD's honour   5
with the harp,
with the harp and with the music
of the psaltery.
With trumpet and echoing horn   6
acclaim the presence of the LORD
our king.
Let the sea roar and all its creatures, 7
the world and those who dwell
in it.
Let the rivers clap their hands,   8
let the hills sing aloud together

c bow ... gods: or all gods bow down ...
d The LORD loves: prob. rdg.; Heb. Lovers of the
LORD.

Ps. 97: The LORD is King. An Enthronement Hymn with motifs of God's future final victory
and rule over all peoples (vv. 1–7); see Ps.47 n. **2–6:** The images employed here occur in other
psalms; see 18.7–15; 50.1–3. **9:** *Above all gods:* see 82.1 n.; 89.6–7.
   Ps. 98: The LORD our King. An Enthronement Hymn (Ps.47 n.) with motifs of God's final
judgment and establishment of "peoples in justice" (v. 9). The themes in this and other Enthronement psalms are frequent in Isa. chs. 40–55, e.g. 41.1–5. **1:** *God's right hand ... won him
victory,* both initially and most decisively, over chaos at the time of creation. **2–3:** God's
creative power is continued by his characteristic qualities in dealing with Israel: *righteousness,
constancy, love,* justice (v. 9). **5–6:** A flourish of *trumpets* accompanies God's enthronement
here as it did at the making of the covenant on Sinai (Exod.19.16), in the manner of the coronation of the kings of Israel; see 2 Sam.15.10; 1 Kgs.1.34. **7–9:** Compare, e.g. 96.7–13 and
Isa.14.23; 52.10.

9 before the LORD; for he comes
to judge the earth
He will judge the world with
righteousness
and the peoples in justice.

99

1 The LORD is king, the peoples are
perturbed;
he is throned on the cherubim, earth
quivers.
2 The LORD is great in Zion;
he is exalted above all the peoples.
3 They extol his[e] name as great and
terrible;
4 he is holy, he is mighty,
a king who loves justice.

Thou hast established justice and
equity;
thou hast dealt righteously in Jacob.
5 Exalt the LORD our God,
bow down before his footstool;
he is holy.

6 Moses and Aaron among his
priests,
and Samuel among those who
call on his name,
called to the LORD, and he answered.
7 He spoke to them in a pillar of
cloud;
they followed his teaching and kept
the law he gave them.
8 Thou, O LORD our God, thou didst
answer them;
thou wast a God who forgave all
their misdeeds
and held them innocent.
9 Exalt the LORD our God,
bow down towards his holy hill;
for the LORD our God is holy.

100

1 Acclaim the LORD, all men on
earth,
2 worship the LORD in gladness,
enter his presence with songs of
exultation.
3 Know that the LORD is God;
he has made us and we are his own,
his people, the flock which he
shepherds.
4 Enter his gates with thanksgiving
and his courts with praise.
Give thanks to him and bless his
name;
5 for the LORD is good and his love is
everlasting,
his constancy endures to all
generations.

101

1 I sing of loyalty and justice;
I will raise a psalm to thee, O
LORD.[f]
2 I will follow a wise and blameless
course,
whatever may befall me.[g]
I will go about my house in purity
of heart.
3 I will set before myself no sordid
aim;
I will hate disloyalty, I will have
none of it.
4 I will reject all crooked thoughts;
I will have no dealings with evil.
5 I will silence those who spread tales
behind men's backs,

e *Prob. rdg.; Heb.* thy.
f I sing . . . O LORD: *or* I will follow a course of justice
and loyalty; I will hold thee in awe, O LORD.
g whatever may befall me; *prob. rdg.; Heb.* when
comest thou to me?

Ps. 99: The LORD is King. An Enthronement Hymn; see 47 n. There is more emphasis than
usual on God's distance from Israel because "he is holy," yet at the same time his closeness to
Israel in historical events is presented. Note the refrain "he is holy" in vv. 4,5, and 9. **1**: *Cherubim:*
see Exod.25.18–22. **4**: God is *holy* because he is beyond the reach of the mundane. **6–8**: *Moses*
(Exod.32.30–35), *Aaron* (Num.16.46–50), and *Samuel* (1 Sam.7.8–9) interceded with God and
were favorably answered. It is unusual for Moses to be included among the *priests.*
Ps. 100: The LORD is God. An Enthronement Hymn (see 47 n.), or a part of an incomplete one.
Some regard it as a deliberate close of the collection of Enthronement hymns: Pss. 93, 95–99.
It carries on the themes of these other, longer psalms.
Ps. 101: A wise and blameless course. A Royal Psalm. It may represent the king's vow at the
time of the coronation; compare Ps.45. In much biblical thought, the king is viewed as God's
representative on earth. Hence, a proper king needed to display the qualities attributed to God
himself. Here the king offers such assurance. **2**: *Purity of heart:* sincerity and single-heartedness.

I will not sit at table with proud,
pompous men,

6 I will choose the most loyal for my
companions;
my servants shall be men whose lives
are blameless.

7 No scandal-monger shall live in my
household;
no liar shall set himself up where I
can see him.

8 Morning after morning I will put
all wicked men to silence
and will rid the LORD's city of all
evildoers.

102

1 LORD, hear my prayer
and let my cry for help reach thee.

2 Hide not thy face from me
when I am in distress.
Listen to my prayer
and, when I call, answer me soon;

3 for my days vanish like smoke,
my body is burnt up as in an oven.

4 I am stricken, withered like grass;
I cannot find the strength to eat.

5 Wasted away,[h] I groan aloud
and my skin hangs on my bones.

6 I am like a desert-owl in the
wilderness,
an owl that lives among ruins.

7 Thin and meagre, I wail in solitude,
like a bird that flutters on the
roof-top.

8 My enemies insult me all the day
long;
mad with rage, they conspire
against me.

9 I have eaten ashes for bread
and mingled tears with my drink.

10 In thy wrath and fury
thou hast taken me up and flung
me aside.

11 My days decline as the shadows
lengthen,
and like grass I wither away.

12 But thou, LORD, art enthroned for
ever
and thy fame shall be known to all
generations.

13 Thou wilt arise and have mercy on
Zion;
for the time is come[i] to pity her.

14 Her very stones are dear to thy
servants,
and even her dust moves them
with pity.

15 Then shall the nations revere thy
name, O LORD;
and all the kings of the earth thy
glory,

16 when the LORD builds up Zion again
and shows himself in his glory.

17 He turns to hear the prayer of the
destitute
and does not scorn them when
they pray.

18 This shall be written down for future
generations,
and a people yet unborn shall praise
the LORD.

19 The LORD looks down from his
sanctuary on high,
from heaven he surveys the earth

20 to listen to the groaning of the
prisoners
and set free men under sentence of
death;

21 so shall the LORD's name be on
men's lips in Zion
and his praise shall be told in
Jerusalem,

22 when peoples are assembled
together,
peoples and kingdoms, to serve the
LORD.

23 My strength is broken in mid
course;

24 the time allotted me is short.
Snatch me not away before half
my days are done,

h Wasted away: *transposed from previous verse.*
i Prob. rdg.; *Heb. adds* season.

8: *The LORD's city:* probably Jerusalem, but it can refer more restrictedly to the Temple and palace quarter.
  Ps. 102: Let my cry for help reach thee. A Lament (see Introduction). The first section (vv. 1–11) contains an individual's cry for help from his sickness and loneliness; next (vv. 12–22) there is an appeal to God to have mercy on and rebuild Zion. Finally (vv. 23–28) there is another individual cry for help, as from an ill man; it contrasts the brevity of human life with the eternity of God in the manner of Wisdom literature (see Ecclus. ch. 17). 2: *Hide not thy face:* see 4.6 n. and 10.11. 14: *Stones . . . dust:* possibly an allusion to the Temple lying in ruins. 19: *Sanctuary*

for thy years last through all
generations.

25 Long ago thou didst lay the
foundations of the earth,
and the heavens were thy
handiwork.

26 They shall pass away, but thou
endurest;
like clothes they shall all grow old;
thou shalt cast them off like a
cloak,
and they shall vanish;

27 but thou art the same and thy years
shall have no end;

28 thy servants' children shall
continue,
and their posterity shall be
established in thy presence.

103

1 Bless the LORD, my soul;
my innermost heart, bless his
holy name.

2 Bless the LORD, my soul,
and forget none of his benefits.

3 He pardons all my guilt
and heals all my suffering.

4 He rescues me from the pit of death
and surrounds me with constant love,
with tender affection;

5 he contents me with all good in the
prime of life,
and my youth is ever new like an
eagle's.

6 The LORD is righteous in his acts;
he brings justice to all who have
been wronged.

7 He taught Moses to know his way
and showed the Israelites what
he could do.

8 The LORD is compassionate and
gracious,

long-suffering and for ever
constant;

9 he will not always be the accuser
or nurse his anger for all time.

10 He has not treated us as our sins
deserve
or requited us for our misdeeds.

11 For as the heaven stands high above
the earth,
so his strong love stands high over
all who fear him.

12 Far as east is from west,
so far has he put our offences away
from us.

13 As a father has compassion on
his children,
so has the LORD compassion on all
who fear him.

14 For he knows how we were made,
he knows full well that we are dust.

15 Man's days are like the grass;
he blossoms like the flowers of the
field:

16 a wind passes over them, and they
cease to be,
and their place knows them no
more.

17 But the LORD's love never fails those
who fear him;
his righteousness never fails their
sons and their grandsons

18 who listen to his voice[j] and keep
his covenant,
who remember his command-
ments and obey them.

19 The LORD has established his throne
in heaven,
his kingly power over the whole
world.

20 Bless the LORD, all his angels,
creatures of might who do his
bidding.

[j] who listen to his voice: *transposed from end of verse 20.*

---

on high: God's abode in heaven. **25–27:** These verses are used in Heb.1.10–12. **27:** *The same:*
lit. "Thou art he." See Isa.43.10,13,25 for this expression. **28:** Assurance, if not to a man, to
his children.

Ps. 103: Bless the LORD, all created things. A Hymn in which the poet's thanksgiving for his
own healing (vv. 3–5) overflows into a universal praise of God for all his goodness to Israel
(vv. 6–10) and to all men (vv. 11–18). **1:** *Bless the LORD:* praise and thank him. *Soul . . . heart:*
totality of a person's life, nonrational as well as intellectual. **3:** *Guilt* and *suffering* were linked
together in a causal relationship. **5:** An *eagle's* strength was thought to be renewed with molting.
6–8: These verses contain the heart of OT piety, for they show the characteristic qualities of
God's dealing with Israel as revealed to Moses: *righteous, compassionate, gracious, long-
suffering, ever constant,* bringing *justice* to the *wronged;* see Exod.34.6. **16:** The hot *wind* from
the desert wilts all vegetation in its path. **19:** *Throne in heaven:* compare 102.19.

21 Bless the LORD, all his hosts,
   his ministers who serve his will.
22 Bless the LORD, all created things,
   in every place where he has
     dominion.

Bless the LORD, my soul.

104

1 Bless the LORD, my soul:
   O LORD my God, thou art great
     indeed,
   clothed in majesty and splendour,
2 and wrapped in a robe of light.
   Thou hast spread out the heavens
     like a tent
3 and on their waters laid the beams
     of thy pavilion;
   who takest the clouds for thy
     chariot,
   riding on the wings of the wind;
4 who makest the winds thy
     messengers
   and flames of fire thy servants;
5 thou didst fix the earth on its
     foundation
   so that it never can be shaken;
6 the deep overspread it like a
     cloak,
   and the waters lay above the
     mountains.
7 At thy rebuke they ran,
   at the sound of thy thunder they
     rushed away,
8 flowing over the hills,
   pouring down into the valleys
   to the place appointed for them.
9 Thou didst fix a boundary which
     they might not pass;
   they shall not return to cover the
     earth.

10 Thou dost make springs break out
     in the gullies,

so that their water runs between
  the hills.
11 The wild beasts all drink from them,
the wild asses quench their thirst;
12 the birds of the air nest on their
  banks
and sing among the leaves.

13 From thy high pavilion thou dost
  water the hills;
the earth is enriched by thy
  provision.
14 Thou makest grass grow for the
  cattle
and green things for those who
  toil for man,
bringing bread out of the earth
15 and wine to gladden men's hearts,
oil to make their faces shine
and bread to sustain their strength.
16 The trees of the LORD are green
  and leafy,
the cedars of Lebanon which he
  planted;
17 the birds build their nests in them,
the stork makes her home in their
  tops.*k*
18 High hills are the haunt of the
  mountain-goat,
and boulders a refuge for the rock-
  badger.

19 Thou hast made the moon to
  measure the year
and taught the sun where to set.
20 When thou makest darkness and it
  is night,
all the beasts of the forest come forth;
21 the young lions roar for prey,
seeking their food from God.
22 When thou makest the sun rise, they
  slink away
and go to rest in their lairs;
23 but man comes out to his work
and to his labours until evening.

k in their tops: *prob. rdg.; Heb.* the pine-trees.

Ps. 104: Thou hast made all by thy wisdom. A creation Hymn often compared to the
Egyptian "Hymn to Aton" and to the Mesopotamian "Enuma Elish" since it uses similar
mythological language. Ps.104 begins and closes in the same way as Ps.103. Perhaps Pss.104–105
were used together in the Temple liturgy, providing a sequence of movement from God's
majesty in the universe (Ps.104) to his historic deeds on behalf of Israel (105.5–45); see
vv. 31–35 n.
3: The *beams* of God's *pavilion*, i.e. his dwelling, were thought to rest above the reservoir of
water contained in the vault of heaven (29.10), just as the earth is established on the waters
below it; see Gen.1.6–8. **6–9:** God controls the sea, having fixed a *boundary* for it, making
Leviathan, the wild sea monster who symbolizes the unruly sea of the original chaos, into a
"plaything" (v. 26); compare 74.12–17 n. **10–26:** The order God brought out of chaos is

24 Countless are the things thou hast
      made, O Lord.
   Thou hast made all by thy wisdom;
   and the earth is full of thy creatures,
25 beasts great and small

   Here is the great immeasurable sea,
   in which move creatures beyond
      number.
26 Here ships sail to and fro,
   here is Leviathan whom thou hast
      made thy plaything.[l]
27 All of them look expectantly to
      thee
   to give them their food at the
      proper time;
28 what thou givest them they gather
      up;
   when thou openest thy hand, they
      eat their fill.
29 Then thou hidest thy face, and they
      are restless and troubled;
   when thou takest away their breath,
      they fail
   [and they return to the dust from
      which they came];
30 but when thou breathest into them,
      they recover;
   thou givest new life to the earth.

31 May the glory of the Lord stand
      for ever
   and may he rejoice in his works!
32 When he looks at the earth, it
      quakes;
   when he touches the hills, they
      pour forth smoke.

33 I will sing to the Lord as long as I
      live,
   all my life I will sing psalms to my
      God.
34 May my meditation please the
      Lord,
   as I show my joy in him!

35 Away with all sinners from the
      earth
   and may the wicked be no more!

   Bless the Lord, my soul.

   O praise the Lord.

105

1[m] Give the Lord thanks and invoke
      him by name,
   make his deeds known in the world
      around.
2 Pay him honour with song and psalm
   and think upon all his wonders.
3 Exult in his hallowed name;
   let those who seek the Lord be
      joyful in heart.
4 Turn to the Lord, your strength,
   seek his presence always.
5 Remember the wonders that he has
      wrought,
   his portents and the judgements
      he has given,
6 O offspring of Abraham his servant,
      O chosen sons of Jacob.

7 He is the Lord our God;
   his judgements fill the earth.
8 He called to mind his covenant
      from long ago,[n]
   the promise he extended to a
      thousand generations—
9 the covenant made with Abraham,
   his oath given to Isaac,
10 the decree by which he bound
      himself for Jacob,
   his everlasting covenant with Israel:
11 'I will give you the land of Canaan',
      he said,
   'to be your possession, your
      patrimony.'

l thy plaything: or that it may sport in it.
m Verses 1–15: cp. 1 Chr. 16. 8–22.
n from long ago: or for ever.

---

marvelous and benign. **27–30:** God continued his creative presence to prevent a return to chaos. **29:** God's *breath*, spirit, is the source of all *life* (v. 30); see Gen.1.2 and Tfn. *b* there; 2.7. **31–35:** A prayer that all may continue beneficently for the righteous. It ends with *Bless the Lord, my soul*, thus beginning and closing in the same way. The final phrase, *O praise the Lord* (in Heb. Hallelujah) may belong to Ps.105 as its beginning.

Ps. 105: Remember the wonders that God has wrought. A Hymn celebrating God's action in Israel's history. It could have been used at any of the major festivals; vv. 1–15 are used in 1 Chr.16.8–22 for the transfer of the Ark of the Covenant to Jerusalem. While nothing is mentioned specifically of the events at Sinai, the themes of covenant (v. 8) and of laws and statutes (v. 45) presuppose Sinai and form the framework of the historical recital. **5:** *Judgements:* God's decisive actions in behalf of Israel, the *sons of Jacob.* **8–15:** The *roaming* of *Abraham, Isaac* and

12 A small company it was,
few in number, strangers in that
land,
13 roaming from nation to nation,
from one kingdom to another;
14 but he let no one ill-treat them,
for their sake he admonished kings:
15 'Touch not my anointed servants,
do my prophets no harm.'

16 He called down famine on the land
and cut short their daily bread.
17 But he had sent on a man before
them,
Joseph, who was sold into slavery;
18 he was kept a prisoner with fetters
on his feet
and an iron collar clamped on his
neck.
19 He was tested by the LORD's
command
until what he foretold came true.
20 Then the king sent and set him free,
the ruler of nations released him;
21 he made him master of his
household
and ruler over all his possessions,
22 to correct his officers at will
and teach his counsellors wisdom.
23 Then Israel too went down into
Egypt
and Jacob came to live in the land
of Ham.
24 There God made his people very
fruitful,
he made them stronger than
their enemies,
25 whose hearts he turned to hatred of
his people
and double-dealing with his
servants.
26 He sent his servant Moses
and Aaron whom he had chosen.
27 They were his mouthpiece to
announce his signs,
his portents in the land of Ham.
28 He sent darkness, and all was dark,
but still they resisted his commands.
29 He turned their waters into blood
and killed all their fish.
30 Their country swarmed with frogs,

even their princes' inner chambers.
31 At his command came swarms of
flies
and maggots the whole land
through.
32 He changed their rain into hail
and flashed fire over their country.
33 He blasted their vines and their
fig-trees
and splintered the trees
throughout the land.
34 At his command came locusts,
hoppers past all number,
35 they consumed every green thing in
the land,
consumed all the produce of the
soil.
36 Then he struck down all the
first-born in Egypt,
the firstfruits of their manhood;
37 he led Israel out, laden with silver
and gold,
and among all their tribes no
man fell.
38 The Egyptians were glad when they
went,
for fear of Israel had taken hold
of them.
39 He spread a cloud as a screen,
and fire to light up the night.
40 They asked, and he sent them
quails,
he gave them bread from heaven
in plenty.
41 He opened a rock and water gushed
out,
a river flowing in a parched land;
42 for he had remembered his solemn
promise
given to his servant Abraham.
43 So he led out his people rejoicing,
his chosen ones in triumph.
44 He gave them the lands of heathen
nations
and they took possession where
others had toiled,
45 so that they might keep his
statutes
and obey his laws.

O praise the LORD.

Jacob from nation to nation is narrated in Gen.12.1–37.1. **15**: The patriarchs are called *anointed servants* inasmuch as they were filled with the spirit of the LORD, like the *prophets;* compare Isa.61.1. **16–23**: The story of *Joseph;* see Gen. chs. 37, 39–50. **24–43**: The Exodus and God's guidance in the Wilderness; see Exod.1.1–17.6. **27**: *Ham:* Egypt, as in 78.5; see Gen.10.6. **44–45**: The gift of *lands* and the *laws:* an allusion to Joshua.

106

1 O praise the LORD.

It is good to give thanks to the
    LORD;
for his love endures for ever.

2 Who will tell of the LORD's mighty
    acts
and make his praises heard?

3 Happy are they who act justly
    and do right at all times!

4 Remember me, LORD, when thou
    showest favour to thy people,
look upon me when thou savest
    them,

5 that I may see the prosperity of
    thy chosen,
rejoice in thy nation's joy and exult
    with thy own people.

6 We have sinned like our forefathers,
    we have erred and done wrong.

7 Our fathers in Egypt took no
    account of thy marvels,
they did not remember thy many
    acts of faithful love,
but in spite of all*o* they rebelled by
    the Red Sea.*p*

8 Yet the LORD delivered them for
    his name's sake
and so made known his mighty
    power.

9 He rebuked the Red Sea and it
    dried up,
he led his people through the deeps
    as through the wilderness.

10 So he delivered them from those
    who hated them,
and claimed them back from the
    enemy's hand.

11 The waters closed over their
    adversaries,
not one of them survived.

12 Then they believed his promises and
    sang praises to him.

13 But they quickly forgot all he had
    done

and would not wait to hear his
    counsel;

14 their greed was insatiable in the
    wilderness,
they tried God's patience in the
    desert.

15 He gave them what they asked
but sent a wasting sickness among
    them.*q*

16 They were envious of Moses in the
    camp,
and of Aaron, who was consecrated
    to the LORD.

17 The earth opened and swallowed
    Dathan,
it closed over the company of
    Abiram;

18 fire raged through their company,
    the wicked perished in flames.

19 At Horeb they made a calf
    and bowed down to an image;

20 they exchanged their Glory*r*
for the image of a bull that feeds
    on grass.

21 They forgot God their deliverer,
who had done great deeds in Egypt,

22 marvels in the land of Ham,
    terrible things at the Red Sea.

23 So his purpose was to destroy
    them,
but Moses, the man he had chosen,
threw himself into the breach
to turn back his wrath lest it
    destroy them.

24 They made light of the pleasant
    land,
disbelieving his promise;

25 they muttered treason in their
    tents
and would not obey the LORD.

26 So with uplifted hand he swore
to strike them down in the
    wilderness,

o in spite of all: prob. rdg.; Heb. obscure.
p Or the Sea of Reeds.
q among them: or in their throats.
r their Glory: or the glory of God (cp. Jer. 2. 11;
*   Romans 1. 23).*

Ps. 106: Deliver us, O LORD our God. A Lament (see Introduction) of the community, in a
liturgical setting, in which the recitation of the adversity is a national confession of sins which
brought on various punishments, ending in the crowning adversity of being scattered among the
nations in the Exile. The psalm closes Book 4. **1–5:** The invitation to *praise the LORD* seems to
be in the course of a worship. **6:** To have *sinned* against God is the greatest calamity to have
befallen Israel; this is the theme of the psalm. **7–12:** Story of the Exodus; see 105.24–43 n.
13–15: Manna and the quail: Num.11.4–15,31–34. **16–18:** *Dathan* and *Abiram:* Num. ch. 16.
19–23: *Horeb:* Sinai; for the golden *calf* incident, see Exod. ch. 32. **24–27:** Refusal to enter

27 to scatter their descendants among
     the nations
     and disperse them throughout
     the world.

28 They joined in worshipping the
     Baal of Peor
     and ate meat sacrificed to lifeless
     gods.
29 Their deeds provoked the LORD
     to anger,
     and plague broke out amongst them;
30 but Phinehas stood up and
     interceded,
     so the plague was stopped.
31 This was counted to him as
     righteousness
     throughout all generations for ever.

32 They roused the LORD to anger at
     the waters of Meribah,
     and Moses suffered because of them;
33 for they had embittered his spirit
     and he had spoken rashly.

34 They did not destroy the peoples
     round about,
     as the LORD had commanded them
     to do,
35 but they mingled with the nations,
     learning their ways;
36 they worshipped their idols
     and were ensnared by them.
37 Their sons and their daughters
     they sacrificed to foreign demons;
38 they shed innocent blood,
     the blood of sons and daughters
     offered to the gods of Canaan,
     and the land was polluted with
     blood.
39 Thus they defiled themselves by
     their conduct
     and they followed their lusts and
     broke faith with God.
40 Then the LORD grew angry with his
     people

and loathed them, his own chosen
     nation;
so he gave them into the hands   41
     of the nations,
and they were ruled by their foes,
     their enemies oppressed them   42
and made them subject to their
     power.
Many times he came to their rescue,   43
but they were disobedient and
     rebellious still.*s*
And yet, when he heard them wail   44
     and cry aloud,
he looked with pity on their
     distress;
he called to mind his covenant   45
     with them
and, in his boundless love,
     relented;
he roused compassion for them   46
     in the hearts of all their captors.

Deliver us, O LORD our God,   47
     and gather us in from among
     the nations
that we may give thanks to thy
     holy name
and make thy praise our pride.

Blessed be the LORD the God of   48
     Israel
     from everlasting to everlasting;
and let all the people say 'Amen.'

O praise the LORD.

BOOK 5

107

It is good to give thanks to the LORD, 1
     for his love endures for ever.

s *Prob. rdg.; Heb. adds* and were brought low by
their guilt.

---

the promised land shows disloyalty; Num. ch. 14. **28–31:** In Num. ch. 25, Phinehas slays the
offending Israelite; the episode is embellished here. **32–33:** The incident of the *waters of Meribah*
has also been embellished; see Num.20.2–13. **34–46:** Summary of the events in the Book of
Judges. **34:** *The LORD had commanded:* compare Exod.23.23–33; Deut.7.1–5. **38:** The precise
incident of polluting *the land with blood* is not clear in Judg.; however, compare 1 Kgs.16.34.
The prohibition seems to counter a common practice; see Num.35.33–34; Lev.18.25–29. **47:** This
verse seems to indicate that the psalm was written during the Babylonian Exile, i.e. after
587 B.C.; compare Ps.74 n. **48:** *Let all the people say* seems to be a liturgical prescription. This
verse appears to be an addition to the psalm, either to adapt it to public worship or to close
the collection of psalms in Book 4.
  Ps. 107: Let them thank the LORD. A Thanksgiving of the community sung either by captives

2 So let them say who were redeemed
　　by the LORD,
　　redeemed by him from the power
　　of the enemy

3 　　and gathered out of every land,
　　from east and west, from north and
　　south.

4 Some lost their way in desert wastes;
　　they found no road to a city to
　　live in;

5 hungry and thirsty,
　　their spirit sank within them.

6 So they cried to the LORD in their
　　trouble,
　　and he rescued them from their
　　distress;

7 he led them by a straight and easy way
　　until they came to a city to live in.

8 Let them thank the LORD for his
　　enduring love
　　and for the marvellous things he
　　has done for men:

9 he has satisfied the thirsty
　　and filled the hungry with good
　　things.

10 Some sit in darkness, dark as death,
　　prisoners bound fast in iron,

11 because they had rebelled against
　　God's commands
　　and flouted the purpose of the
　　Most High.

12 Their spirit was subdued by hard
　　labour;
　　they stumbled and fell with none
　　to help them.

13 So they cried to the LORD in their
　　trouble,
　　and he saved them from their
　　distress;

14 he brought them out of darkness,
　　dark as death,
　　and broke their chains.

15 Let them thank the LORD for his
　　enduring love
　　and for the marvellous things he
　　has done for men:

16 he has shattered doors of bronze,
　　bars of iron he has snapped in
　　two.

17 Some were fools, they took to
　　rebellious ways,
　　and for their transgression they
　　suffered punishment.

18 They sickened at the sight of food
　　and drew near to the very gates
　　of death.

19 So they cried to the LORD in their
　　trouble,
　　and he saved them from their
　　distress;

20 he sent his word to heal them
　　and bring them alive out of the
　　pit of death.*t*

21 Let them thank the LORD for his
　　enduring love
　　and for the marvellous things he
　　has done for men.

22 Let them offer sacrifices of
　　thanksgiving
　　and recite his deeds with shouts
　　of joy.

23 Others there are who go to sea in
　　ships
　　and make their living on the wide
　　waters.

24 These men have seen the acts of the
　　LORD
　　and his marvellous doings in the
　　deep.

25 At his command the storm-wind rose
　　and lifted the waves high.

26 Carried up to heaven, plunged down
　　to the depths,
　　tossed to and fro in peril,

27 they reeled and staggered like
　　drunken men,
　　and their seamanship was all in
　　vain.

28 So they cried to the LORD in their
　　trouble,

t alive . . . death: prob. rdg.; Heb. from their corruption.

returning from the Babylonian Exile or by pilgrims to Jerusalem who had been delivered from
various dangers. Wisdom motifs are prominent (vv. 33–43) as in other psalms which stand at
the beginning of collections: Pss.1 (Book 1), 73 (Book 3) and 90 (Book 4). **1**: A frequent
exclamation of praise in the liturgy of the Temple; see 118.1; 1 Chr.16.34; 1 Macc.4.24. **2–3**: A
universal gathering out of all nations of those whom God calls and delivers; compare Isa.43.5–6;
49.12. The four sections that follow perhaps symbolize the four quarters of the earth. **4–32**:
Thanksgiving of those delivered from perils of the desert (vv. 4–7), from prison (vv. 10–16),
from sickness (vv. 17–22), from the dangers of the sea (vv. 23–32). **8–9**: A refrain that is repeated
and adapted to each situation; see vv. 15–16; 21–22; 31–32. **22**: *Sacrifices:* probably to fulfill

and he brought them out of their
   distress.

29 The storm sank to a murmur
   and the waves of the sea were
     stilled.

30 They were glad then that all was
     calm,
   as he guided them to the harbour
     they desired.

31 Let them thank the LORD for his
     enduring love
   and for the marvellous things he has
     done for men.

32 Let them exalt him in the assembly
     of the people
   and praise him in the council of
     the elders.

33 He turns rivers into desert
   and springs of water into thirsty
     ground;

34 he turns fruitful land into salt
     waste,
   because the men who dwell there
     are so wicked.

35 Desert he changes into standing
     pools,
   and parched land into springs of
     water.

36 There he gives the hungry a home,
   and they build themselves a city
     to live in;

37 they sow fields and plant vineyards
   and reap a fruitful harvest.

38 He blesses them and their numbers
     increase,
   and he does not let their herds
     lose strength.

39 Tyrants*u* lose their strength and are
     brought low
   in the grip of misfortune and
     sorrow;

40 he brings princes into contempt
   and leaves them wandering in a
     trackless waste.

41 But the poor man he lifts clear of
     his troubles
   and makes families increase like
     flocks of sheep.

42 The upright see it and are glad,
   while evildoers are filled with
     disgust.

43 Let the wise man lay these things to
     heart,
   and ponder the record of the
     LORD's enduring love.

108

1 My heart is steadfast, O God,*v*
     my heart is steadfast.
   I will sing and raise a psalm;
     awake,*w* my spirit,

2 awake, lute and harp,
   I will awake at dawn of day.*x*

3 I will confess thee, O LORD, among
     the peoples,
   among the nations I will raise a
     psalm to thee;

4 for thy unfailing love is wider than
     the heavens
   and thy truth reaches to the skies.

5 Show thyself, O God, high above
     the heavens;
   let thy glory shine over all the
     earth.

6 Deliver those that are dear to thee;*y*
   save with thy right hand and
     answer.

7 God has spoken from his sanctuary:*z*
   'I will go up now and measure out
     Shechem;
   I will divide the valley of Succoth
     into plots;

8 Gilead and Manasseh are mine;
   Ephraim is my helmet, Judah my
     sceptre;

9 Moab is my wash-bowl, I fling my
     shoes at Edom;
   Philistia is the target of my anger.'

10 Who can bring me to the impregnable
     city,
   who can guide me to Edom,

11 since thou, O God, hast abandoned
     us
   and goest not forth with our
     armies?

u Prob. rdg.; Heb. om.
v Verses 1–5: cp. Ps. 57. 7–11.
w awake: prob. rdg.; Heb. also.
x at dawn of day: or the dawn.
y Verses 6–13: cp. Ps. 60. 5–12.
z from his sanctuary: or in his holiness.

vows made during distress. **33–43:** The Wisdom themes of the two ways, "good and evil," and
the reversal of situations in rewarding the *upright* and humiliating the *evildoers* are elaborated.
   Ps. 108: I will raise a psalm to thee. A vow; vv. 1–5 are almost identical with 57.7–11 and
vv. 6–13 with 60.5–12. See the annotations to those passages.

12 Grant us help against the enemy,
      for deliverance by man is a vain
         hope.
13 With God's help we shall do
         valiantly,
      and God himself will tread our
         enemies under foot.

109

1 O God of my praise, be silent no
         longer,
2   for wicked men heap calumnies
         upon me.
   They have lied to my face
3   and ringed me round with words
         of hate.
   They have attacked me without a
         cause[a]
4   and accused me though I have
         done nothing unseemly.[b]
5 They have repaid me evil for good
      and hatred in return for my love.
6 They say, 'Put up some rascal to
         denounce him,
      an accuser to stand at his right
         side.'
7 But when judgement is given, that
         rascal will be exposed
      and his follies accounted a sin.
8 May his days be few;
      may his hoarded wealth[c] fall to
         another!
9 May his children be fatherless,
      his wife a widow!
10 May his children be vagabonds and
         beggars,
      driven from their homes!
11 May the money-lender distrain on
         all his goods
      and strangers seize his earnings!
12 May none remain loyal to him,
      and none have mercy on his
         fatherless children!

May his line be doomed to   13
      extinction,
   may their name be wiped out
      within a generation!
May the sins of his forefathers be 14
      remembered
   and his mother's wickedness never
      be wiped out!
May they remain on record before   15
      the LORD,
   but may he extinguish their name
      from the earth!
For that man never set himself   16
      to be loyal to his friend
   but persecuted the downtrodden
      and the poor
   and hounded the broken-hearted
      to their death.
Curses he loved: may the curse fall 17
      on him!
He took no pleasure in blessing:
   may no blessing be his!
He clothed himself in cursing like a 18
      garment:
   may it seep into his body like water
      and into his bones like oil!
May it wrap him round like the   19
      clothes he puts on,
   like the belt which he wears every
      day!
May the LORD so requite my   20
      accusers
   and those who speak evil against
      me!

But thou, O LORD God,   21
deal with me as befits thy honour;
   in the goodness of thy unfailing
      love deliver me,
for I am downtrodden and poor,   22
   and my heart within me is
      distracted.

a Prob. rdg.; Heb. adds in return for my love.
b though . . . unseemly: prob. rdg.; Heb. obscure.
c hoarded wealth: or charge, cp. Acts 1. 20.

Ps. 109: Help me, O LORD my God. A Lament (see Introduction) of an individual who is falsely accused of causing the death of someone (v. 16). It is divided into three distinct sections; the first (vv.1–5) and the third (vv.20–31) are supplications for deliverance, the second (vv. 6–19) is a series of curses against an individual by his enemies. **1:** No one is left to *praise* the psalmist, i.e. to take his part, but *God*, and he is *silent*. **6–19:** These verses seem to be spoken by the poet's enemies, for there is a profound emotional change—from meekness of vv. 1–5 into hatred, as well as a pronominal change from "they" of vv. 1–5, to *his*. The curses all say one thing: "may he be put to death." **6:** Ordinarily the accuser stood at the left of the accused and his defender at the right: see v. 31; 110.5; 120.5. **8:** See Tfn. *c.* **13:** For his *name* to be wiped out in one *generation* was the Israelite's greatest tragedy; compare Isa.53.12 for the opposite. **16–17:** It seems that the psalmist was accused of accomplishing someone's *death* by a *curse.* **20:** Other translations of this verse are possible; in this one the psalmist invokes the law of the talion,

23   I fade like a passing shadow,
     I am shaken off like a locust.

24   My knees are weak with fasting
     and my flesh wastes away, so
       meagre is my fare.

25   I have become the victim of their
       taunts;
     when they see me they toss their
       heads.

26   Help me, O LORD my God;
     save me, by thy unfailing love,

27   that men may know this is thy doing
     and thou alone, O LORD, hast
       done it.

28   They may curse, but thou dost
       bless;
     may my opponents be put to
       shame,
     but may thy servant rejoice!

29   May my accusers be clothed with
       dishonour,
     wrapped in their shame as in a
       cloak!

30   I will lift up my voice to extol the
       LORD,
     and before a great company I
       will praise him.

31   For he stands at the poor man's
       right side
     to save him from his adversaries.*d*

110

1   The LORD said to my lord,
     'You shall sit*e* at my right hand
     when*f* I make your enemies the
       footstool under your feet.'

2   When the LORD from Zion hands
       you the sceptre, the symbol of
       your power,
     march forth through the ranks of*g*
       your enemies.

3   At birth*h* you were endowed with
       princely gifts

and*i* resplendent*j* in holiness.
You have shone with the dew of youth
     since your mother bore you.
The LORD has sworn and will not   4
     change his purpose:
'You are a priest for ever,
in the succession of Melchizedek.'
The Lord at your right hand   5
has broken kings in the day of his
     anger.
So the king in his majesty,*k*   6
     sovereign of a mighty land,
     will punish nations;*l*
he will drink from the torrent   7
     beside the path
and therefore will hold his head
     high.

111

O praise the LORD.   1

With all my heart will I praise the
     LORD
in the company of good men, in the
     whole congregation.
Great are the doings of the LORD;   2
all men study them for their delight.
His acts are full of majesty and   3
     splendour;
righteousness is his for ever.
He has won a name by his   4
     marvellous deeds;
the LORD is gracious and
     compassionate.
He gives food to those who fear him, 5
he keeps his covenant always in
     mind.

d Prob. rdg.; Heb. his judges.   *e* You shall sit: *or* Sit.
f Or until *or* while.   *g Or* reign in the midst of.
h At birth: *or* On the day of your power.
i you were . . . and: *or* your people offered themselves
willingly; *mng. of Heb. uncertain.*
j Or apparelled.
k So . . . majesty: *poss. rdg.; Heb.* full of corpses, he
crushed.
l So . . . nations: *or* He shall punish the nations—
heaps of corpses, broken heads—over a wide expanse.

---

i.e. "an eye for an eye" against his accusers. **23:** Locusts were either *shaken off* to the ground and killed or swept away by the wind; see Exod.10.19. **25:** To *toss* the head was a sign of derision and hostility.
     Ps. 110: Sit at my right hand. A Royal Psalm, probably used at the coronation ceremonies for kings (compare Ps.2). **1:** *The LORD:* Yahweh. *My lord:* the king who is taking office. *Footstool:* a figure for complete domination. **4:** *The succession of Melchizedek:* the king will also serve as priest, like a predecessor Melchizedek, the Canaanite priest-king of Jerusalem (Gen.14.18–20). The verse is used in a very different way in Heb.5.6 and 7.1,17. **5:** *Right hand:* chief support, as in v. 1.
     Ps. 111: The beginning of Wisdom. A Hymn with Wisdom themes. It is an acrostic; hence each of the twenty-two half verses begins with a successive letter of the Heb. alphabet. The opening phrase, *O praise the LORD* (Heb. Hallelujah), is not part of the alphabetic structure; Pss.112

6 He showed his people what his
strength could do,
bestowing on them the lands of
other nations.
7 His works are truth and justice;
his precepts all stand on firm
foundations,
8 strongly based to endure for ever,
their fabric goodness and truth.
9 He sent and redeemed his people;
he decreed that his covenant should
always endure.
Holy is his name, inspiring awe.
10 The fear of the LORD is the
beginning[m] of wisdom,
and they who live by it grow in
understanding.
Praise will be his for ever.

his goodness shall be remembered
for all time.
Bad news shall have no terrors for   7
him,
because his heart is steadfast,
trusting in the LORD.
His confidence is strongly based, he   8
will have no fear;
and in the end he will gloat over
his enemies.
He gives freely to the poor;   9
righteousness shall be his for ever;
in honour he carries his head high.
The wicked man shall see it with   10
rising anger
and grind his teeth in despair;
the hopes of wicked men shall come
to nothing.

112

1 O praise the LORD.

Happy is the man who fears the LORD
and finds great joy in his
commandments.
2 His descendants shall be the mightiest
in the land,
a blessed generation of good men.
3 His house shall be full of wealth and
riches;
righteousness shall be his for ever.
4 He is gracious, compassionate, good,
a beacon in darkness for honest
men.
5 It is right for a man to be gracious
in his lending,
to order his affairs with judgement.
6 Nothing shall ever shake him;

113

O praise the LORD.   1

Praise the LORD, you that are his
servants,
praise the name of the LORD.
Blessed be the name of the LORD   2
now and evermore.
From the rising of the sun to its   3
setting
may the LORD's name be praised.
High is the LORD above all nations,   4
his glory above the heavens.
There is none like the LORD our God   5–6
in heaven or on earth,
who sets his throne so high
but deigns to look down so low;

m Or chief part.

and 113 also begin with this ritual proclamation. 9: *Inspiring awe:* compare 76.4 n. 10: Compare
Prov.1.7 and Job 28.28.
   Ps. 112: Happy is the man who fears the LORD. A Wisdom Psalm in acrostic form; see Ps.111 n.
It continues the previous psalm, being linked to it by the phrase "fear of the LORD" (v. 1;
111.10), which it elaborates and applies to practical life. Attributes assigned to God in Ps.111
are here ascribed to the virtuous man who acts as God does (v. 4). 1: *Praise the LORD:* see
Ps.111 n. 3–5: *Righteousness*, graciousness, compassion, goodness, *judgement* are all attributes
that are applied ordinarily to God in his dealings with all men and in particular with Israel;
see 111.3–4; 103.6–8,13,17. 3: *Righteousness* here is the state of being in proper order with God
and of possessing the happiness that flows from it. 5: To act *with judgement* is to work truth and
justice (111.7) by delivering the oppressed, giving freely to the poor (v.9) to bring about righteousness. 8: *Strongly based:* compare 111.7–8. 10: *Grind teeth:* an expression of extreme and
malicious anger and/or frustration; see Lam.3.16; Mt.8.12; Acts 7.54.
   Ps. 113: Praise the LORD. A Hymn, the first of a collection (Pss.113–118) known as the
"Hallel" (praise). This collection (often called the "Egyptian Hallel") was used on the great
festivals: Booths, Passover, and Weeks. At the Passover seder service, Pss.113–114 are sung
before the meal and Pss.115–118 after it. See Mt.26.30; Mk.14.26. 2–4: The response of an
assembly to the call to praise the LORD (v. 1). 5–6: A key concept in Israel's relation to God was
that he was exalted *so high* as to be beyond reach, yet came *so low* as to live in their midst; see

7 who lifts the weak out of the dust
 and raises the poor from the
 dunghill,

8 giving them a place among princes,
 among the princes of his people;

9 who makes the woman in a childless
 house
 a happy mother of children.[n]

114

1 O praise the LORD.[o]

 When Israel came out of Egypt,
 Jacob from a people of outlandish
 speech,

2 Judah became his sanctuary,
 Israel his dominion.

3 The sea looked and ran away;
 Jordan turned back.

4 The mountains skipped like rams,
 the hills like young sheep.

5 What was it, sea? Why did you run?
 Jordan, why did you turn back?

6 Why, mountains, did you skip like
 rams,
 and you, hills, like young sheep?

7 Dance, O earth, at the presence of
 the Lord,
 at the presence of the God of
 Jacob,

8 who turned the rock into a pool of
 water,
 the granite cliff into a fountain.

115

1 Not to us, O LORD, not to us,
 but to thy name ascribe the glory,

for thy true love and for thy
 constancy.

2 Why do the nations ask,
 'Where then is their God?'

3 Our God is in high heaven;
 he does whatever pleases him.

4 Their idols are silver and gold,
 made by the hands of men.

5 They have mouths that cannot
 speak,
 and eyes that cannot see;

6 they have ears that cannot hear,
 nostrils, and cannot smell;

7 with their hands they cannot feel,
 with their feet they cannot walk,
 and no sound comes from their
 throats.

8 Their makers grow to be like them,
 and so do all who trust in them.

9 But Israel trusts in the LORD;
 he is their helper and their shield.

10 The house of Aaron trusts in the
 LORD;
 he is their helper and their shield.

11 Those who fear the LORD trust in
 the LORD;
 he is their helper and their shield.

12 The LORD remembers us, and he
 will bless us;
 he will bless the house of Israel,
 he will bless the house of Aaron.

13 The LORD will bless all who fear
 him,
 high and low alike.

14 May the LORD give you increase,
 both you and your sons.

[n] O praise the LORD *transposed to the beginning of
Ps. 114.*
[o] *See note on Ps. 113. 9.*

Ezek.48.35. **7:** *Dunghill:* sign of abject rejection and ritual uncleanness. **9:** Barrenness was
considered a curse and disgrace; see Gen.16.4–5; 1 Sam.1.6.
 Ps. 114: Judah became his sanctuary. A Thanksgiving, although some classify it as a Hymn.
This psalm, which continues the Hallel, is a psalm of praise proclaiming how God saved Israel
at the Exodus. **2:** *Judah:* name of the southern portion; *Israel:* name of the northern portion.
3–6: Wondrous events accompanied the Exodus at the Red *sea* (Exod. ch. 14), at the *Jordan*
River (Josh. ch. 3) and at Sinai (Exod.19.16–20). **7–8:** The entire world is to enter into the joy
of vv. 3–6. **8:** See Exod.17.6 and Num.20.11.
 Ps. 115: To thy name ascribe the glory. A Liturgy, part of the Hallel (Ps.113 n.), contrasts the
invisible God with the idols of the heathen. **1:** God's glory is his *true love;* compare 1 Jn.4.7–9.
2–8: Israel's God is invisible to the *nations* but his actions of constant love are evident; the idols
are visible but their actions are not. **9–11:** These verses perhaps were sung antiphonally, i.e. one
chorus said the first part of the verse and another the second. Three classes of people take part:
Israel are all the lay people; *house of Aaron* are the priestly class; *those who fear the LORD* are
either the converts from the pagan nations or the first two classes combined. **12–13:** An oracle
perhaps pronounced by a Temple prophet. **14–15:** A blessing pronounced by a priest. **14:** See
Deut.1.11 on *increase.* An abundance of children was seen as a sign of God's beneficent favor.

15 You are blessed by the LORD,
      the LORD who made heaven and
      earth.
16 The heavens, they are the LORD's;
      the earth he has given to all
      mankind.
17 It is not the dead who praise the
      LORD,
      not those who go down into
      silence;
18 but we, the living, bless the LORD,
      now and for evermore.

   O praise the LORD.

116

1 I love the LORD, for he has heard me
      and listens to my prayer;
2 for he has given me a hearing
      whenever I have cried to him.
3 The cords of death bound me,
      Sheol held me in its grip.
   Anguish and torment held me fast;
4   so I invoked the LORD by name,
   'Deliver me, O LORD, I beseech thee;
      for I am thy slave.'p
5 Gracious is the LORD and righteous,
      our God is full of compassion.
6 The LORD preserves the simple-
      hearted;
   I was brought low and he saved me.
7 Be at rest once more, my heart,
      for the LORD has showered gifts
      upon you.
8 He has rescued me from death
      and my feet from stumbling.
9 I will walk in the presence of the
      LORD
      in the land of the living.

I was sure that I should be swept   10
      away,
      and my distress was bitter.
In panic I cried,   11
      'How faithless all men are!'
How can I repay the LORD   12
      for all his gifts to me?
I will take in my hands the cup of   13
      salvation
      and invoke the LORD by name.
I will pay my vows to the LORD   14
      in the presence of all his people.
A precious thing in the LORD's   15
      sight
   is the death of those who die
      faithful to him.
qI am thy slave, thy slave-girl's son; 16
      thou hast undone the bonds that
      bound me.
To thee will I bring a thank-offering 17
      and invoke the LORD by name.
I will pay my vows to the LORD   18
      in the presence of all his people,
   in the courts of the LORD's house, 19
      in the midst of you, Jerusalem.

   O praise the LORD.

117

Praise the LORD, all nations,   1
      extol him, all you peoples;
for his love protecting us is strong, 2
      the LORD's constancy is
      everlasting.

   O praise the LORD.

p for . . . slave: transposed from the beginning of verse 16;
  Heb. adds O LORD.
q Prob. rdg.; Heb. prefixes For I am thy slave, O
  LORD; see note on verse 4.

17: In Sheol, the underworld of the *dead*, there is only *silence*; see Job 3.13,18. **18:** See Ps.113.2.
  Ps. 116: I love the LORD, for he has heard me. A Thanksgiving Psalm, part of the Hallel; see
Ps.113 n. It supposes a recovery from serious illness (vv. 2–4) and the ensuing fulfillment of a
vow to offer a sacrifice of thanks in the Temple (vv. 17–20). **3:** *Sheol*, the place of the dead, is
pictured as a trapper that has snared the poet in the *cords* of his noose. **4:** Calling a person, here
the LORD, by name not only expresses a submission to him (v. 13) but also draws power from
him. **5:** The key attributes of God in dealing with men: graciousness, righteousness, *full of
compassion;* see 103.6–8 n. **10–11:** The poet describes as *faithless* either himself because he lost
confidence in God (v. 9) or his friends who left him helpless in his illness. **13:** *Cup of salvation:*
possibly a figurative expression or possibly an allusion to a sacrificial libation in fulfillment of a
vow such as mentioned in Num.15.1–10. **14:** The *vows* are fulfilled in the Temple *in the presence
of people.* **15:** In the Hebrew concept of Sheol, *death* severed all contact between God and the
faithful whom he loves (117.2) and so their death is precious, i.e. costly to him. Another possible
interpretation is that they are like gold purified in the fire and hence costly; see Wis.3.1–8.
17: *Thank-offering:* see Lev.7.12–15. **19:** *LORD's house:* the Temple.
  Ps. 117: Praise the LORD. A Hymn, probably part of the Temple liturgy. The shortest of the
psalms, it is part of the Hallel (see Ps.113 n.). **2:** *O praise the LORD* may belong with Ps.118 as
its opening words.

118

1 It is good to give thanks to the
    LORD,
    for his love endures for ever.
2 Declare it, house of Israel:
    his love endures for ever.
3 Declare it, house of Aaron:
    his love endures for ever.
4 Declare it, you that fear the LORD:
    his love endures for ever.
5 When in my distress I called to the
    LORD,
    his answer was to set me free.
6 The LORD is on my side, I have no
    fear;
    what can man do to me?
7 The LORD is on my side, he is my
    helper,
    and I shall gloat over my enemies.
8 It is better to find refuge in the LORD
    than to trust in men.
9 It is better to find refuge in the LORD
    than to trust in princes.
10 All nations surround me,
    but in the LORD's name I will
    drive them away.
11 They surround me on this side and
    on that,
    but in the LORD's name I will
    drive them away.
12 They surround me like bees at the
    honey;
    they attack me, as fire attacks
    brushwood,
    but in the LORD's name I will
    drive them away.
13 They thrust hard against me so
    that I nearly fall;

but the LORD has helped me.
The LORD is my refuge and defence, 14
    and he has become my deliverer.
Hark! Shouts of deliverance 15
    in the camp of the victors[r]!
With his right hand the LORD does
    mighty deeds,
    the right hand of the LORD raises 16
    up.
I shall not die but live 17
    to proclaim the works of the
    LORD.
The LORD did indeed chasten me, 18
    but he did not surrender me to
    Death.

Open to me the gates of victory;[s] 19
    I will enter by them and praise
    the LORD.
This is the gate of the LORD; 20
    the victors[t] shall make their entry
    through it.
I will praise thee, for thou hast 21
    answered me
    and hast become my deliverer.
The stone which the builders rejected 22
    has become the chief corner-stone.
This is the LORD's doing; 23
    it is marvellous in our eyes.
This is the day on which the LORD 24
    has acted:[u]
    let us exult and rejoice in it.
We pray thee, O LORD, deliver us; 25
    we pray thee, O LORD, send us
    prosperity.
Blessed in the name of the LORD 26
    are all who come;

r Or righteous.   s Or righteousness.
t Or righteous.   u Or which the LORD has made.

Ps. 118: This is the LORD's doing. A Thanksgiving, originally possibly a king's thanksgiving hymn for victory in battle (vv. 10–14), sung in the Temple. However, as the last of the "Egyptian Hallel" (see Ps.113 n.), it was appropriate for use at the Passover. The psalm seems to be a dramatic ceremonial (see Neh.12.27–43) with the following structure: a procession forms outside the Temple and is invited to praise the LORD (vv. 1–4); the king or another individual in the name of the group describes dramatically how God came to the rescue when the nation confidently implored his help (vv. 5–18); a dialogue between the leader of the procession outside the Temple gates and the priests within (vv. 19–25); the blessing given by the priest to the procession gathered round the altar (vv. 26–27); resumption of the invitation (v. 1) to praise the LORD (vv. 28–29). 2–4: House of Israel . . . Aaron . . . you that fear the LORD: see 115.10–12 n. 10–12: In the LORD's name: by the power of the LORD. 20–21: The condition for entering the Temple is a righteous life which is attested by the fact that God has answered in time of need. 22: In the context of the Exodus feasts—Passover, Weeks, and Booths—Israel was the stone rejected by the empire builders, Egypt. The verse is quoted frequently in the NT; see Mt.21.42; Acts 4.11. 24: Israelite festivals came to be viewed as a contemporary reenactment of a day on which God acted in past events: Passover as the Exodus; Weeks, the Sinai episode; Booths, the Wilderness. Christian liturgy interprets "the day" to mean the Resurrection of Christ. 25: Deliver us: Heb. "Hosanna"; see Mt.21.9 and parallels. 27: Light: possibly a reminiscence of a primitive celebration held at dawn. The four elevations at the corners of the altar were called horns; see Exod.27.2; Lev.4.7.

we bless you from the house of
   the LORD.
27 The LORD is God; he has given
   light to us,
   the ordered line of pilgrims by the
   horns of the altar.
28 Thou art my God and I will praise
   thee;
   my God, I will exalt thee.
29 It is good to give thanks to the LORD,
   for his love endures for ever.

119

1 Happy are they whose life is
   blameless,
   who conform to the law of the
   LORD.
2 Happy are they who obey his
   instruction,
   who set their heart on finding
   him;
3 who have done no wrong
   and have lived according to his
   will.
4 Thou, Lord, hast laid down thy
   precepts
   for men to keep them faithfully.
5 If only I might hold a steady course,
   keeping thy statutes!
6 I shall never be put to shame
   if I fix my eyes on thy commandments.
7 I will praise thee in sincerity of heart
   as I learn thy just decrees.
8 Thy statutes will I keep faithfully;
   O do not leave me forsaken.

9 How shall a young man steer an
   honest course?
   By holding to thy word.
10 With all my heart I strive to find
   thee;

let me not stray from thy
   commandments.
I treasure thy promise in my heart, 11
   for fear that I might sin against thee.
Blessed art thou, O LORD; 12
   teach me thy statutes.
I say them over, one by one, 13
   the decrees that thou hast
   proclaimed.
I have found more joy along the 14
   path of thy instruction
   than in any kind of wealth.
I will meditate on thy precepts 15
   and keep thy paths ever before
   my eyes.
In thy statutes I find continual 16
   delight;
   I will not forget thy word.

Grant this to me, thy servant: let 17
   me live
   and, living, keep thy word.
Take the veil from my eyes, that I 18
   may see
   the marvels that spring from thy
   law.
I am but a stranger here on earth,*v* 19
   do not hide thy commandments
   from me.
My heart pines with longing 20
   day and night for thy decrees.
The proud have felt thy rebuke; 21
   cursed are those who turn from
   thy commandments.
Set me free from scorn and insult, 22
   for I have obeyed thy instruction.
The powers that be sit scheming 23
   together against me;
   but I, thy servant, will study thy
   statutes.
Thy instruction is my continual 24
   delight;
   I turn to it for counsel.

v Or in the land.

Ps. 119: Thy law, O LORD, is my continual delight. A Wisdom meditation, didactic in nature, with many motifs of a Lament. Its unparalleled length arises from its being an acrostic (see Ps.111 n.) with eight verses for each of the twenty-two letters of the Heb. alphabet. The word "law" and its synonyms—instruction, will, precept, statutes, commandments, decrees, word, promise, paths—occur in every verse. Frequent also is the plea that God teach his Law that man may be faithful to him. Law and its synonyms are understood in the wide sense of divine teaching as found in the Pentateuch and in the prophets. There is very little logical development of thought but ideas are strung together loosely. The main thrust appears to be "How I love thy precepts, O LORD." The elements of a Lament are: description of troubles and enemies, pleas for deliverance, vows both explicit and implicit (vv. 106,175). The psalm is considered to be a late composition. **18:** Only an extraneous obstruction of vision, a *veil*, prevents a person from seeing the benefits of the *law.* **19:** The poet needs to be taught the native law of God's *earth* since every man comes into the world as a *stranger.* **21:** The *proud* are the most averse to God's commandments. **23:** *Powers that be:* lit. princes. The joy of keeping God's *statutes* is the

25　I lie prone in the dust;
　　　grant me life according to thy
　　　word.
26　I tell thee all I have done and thou
　　　dost answer me;
　　　teach me thy statutes.
27　Show me the way set out in thy
　　　precepts,
　　　and I will meditate on thy wonders.
28　I cannot rest for misery;
　　　renew my strength in accordance
　　　with thy word.
29　Keep falsehood far from me
　　　and grant me the grace of living
　　　by thy law.
30　I have chosen the path of truth
　　　and have set thy decrees before me.
31　I hold fast to thy instruction;
　　　O Lord, let me not be put to
　　　shame.
32　I will run the course set out in thy
　　　commandments,
　　　for they gladden my heart.

33　Teach me, O Lord, the way set out
　　　in thy statutes,
　　　and in keeping them I shall find
　　　my reward.
34　Give me the insight to obey thy law
　　　and to keep it with all my heart;
35　make me walk in the path of thy
　　　commandments,
　　　for that is my desire.
36　Dispose my heart toward thy
　　　instruction
　　　and not toward ill-gotten gains;
37　turn away my eyes from all that is
　　　vile,
　　　grant me life by thy word.
38　Fulfil thy promise for thy servant,
　　　the promise made to those who
　　　fear thee.
39　Turn away the censure which I
　　　dread,
　　　for thy decrees are good.
40　How I long for thy precepts!
　　　In thy righteousness grant me life.

41　Thy love never fails; let it light on
　　　me, O Lord,
　　　and thy deliverance, for that was
　　　thy promise;
42　then I shall have my answer to the
　　　man who taunts me,

because I trust in thy word.
Rob me not of my power to speak　43
　　the truth,
　　for I put my hope in thy decrees.
I will heed thy law continually,　44
　　for ever and ever;
I walk in freedom wherever I will,　45
　　because I have studied thy
　　precepts.
I will speak of thy instruction　46
　　before kings
　　and will not be ashamed;
in thy commandments I find　47
　　continuing delight;
　　I love them with all my heart.
I will welcome thy commandments[w]　48
　　and will meditate on thy statutes.

Remember the word spoken to me,　49
　　thy servant,
　　on which thou hast taught me to
　　fix my hope.
In time of trouble my consolation　50
　　is this,
　　that thy promise has given me life.
Proud men treat me with insolent　51
　　scorn,
　　but I do not swerve from thy law.
I have cherished thy decrees all my　52
　　life long,
　　and in them I find consolation,
　　O Lord.
Gusts of anger seize me as I think　53
　　of evil men
　　who forsake thy law.
Thy statutes are the theme of my　54
　　song[x]
　　wherever I make my home.
In the night I remember thy name,　55
　　O Lord,
　　and dwell upon thy law.
This is true of me,　56
　　that I have kept thy precepts.

Thou, Lord, art all I have;　57
　　I have promised to keep thy word.
With all my heart I have tried to　58
　　please thee;
　　fulfil thy promise and be gracious
　　to me.
I have thought much about the　59
　　course of my life

w *Prob. rdg.; Heb. adds* which I love.
x the theme of my song: *or* wonderful to me.

immediate reward of the docile. **48:** *Will welcome:* lit. "stretch out my hand to." **55:** For the

and always turned back to thy
   instruction;

60 I have never delayed but always
   made haste
   to keep thy commandments.

61 Bands of evil men close round me,
   but I do not forget thy law.

62 At midnight I rise to give thee
   thanks
   for the justice of thy decrees.

63 I keep company with all who fear
   thee,
   with all who follow thy precepts.

64 The earth is full of thy never-failing
   love;
   O LORD, teach me thy statutes.

65 Thou hast shown thy servant much
   kindness,
   fulfilling thy word, O LORD.

66 Give me insight, give me knowledge,
   for I put my trust in thy
   commandments.

67 I went astray before I was punished;
   but now I pay heed to thy
   promise.

68 Thou art good and thou doest
   good;
   teach me thy statutes.

69 Proud men blacken my name with
   lies,
   yet I follow thy precepts with all
   my heart;

70 their hearts are thick and gross;
   but I continually delight in thy
   law.

71 How good it is for me to have been
   punished,
   to school me in thy statutes!

72 The law thou hast ordained means
   more to me
   than a fortune in gold and silver.

73 Thy hands moulded me and made
   me what I am;
   show me how I may learn thy
   commandments.

74 Let all who fear thee be glad when
   they see me,
   because I hope for the fulfilment
   of thy word.

75 I know, O LORD, that thy decrees
   are just
   and even in punishing thou
   keepest faith with me.

76 Let thy never-failing love console me,
   as thou hast promised me, thy
   servant.

77 Extend thy compassion to me, that
   I may live;
   for thy law is my continual
   delight.

78 Put the proud to shame, for with
   their lies they wrong me;
   but I will meditate on thy
   precepts.

79 Let all who fear thee turn to me,
   all who cherish thy instruction.

80 Let me give my whole heart to thy
   statutes,
   so that I am not put to shame.

81 I long with all my heart for thy
   deliverance,
   hoping for the fulfilment of thy
   word;

82 my sight grows dim with looking
   for thy promise
   and still I cry, 'When wilt thou
   comfort me?'

83 Though I shrivel like a wine-skin in
   the smoke,
   I do not forget thy statutes.

84 How long has thy servant to wait
   for thee to fulfil thy decree
   against my persecutors?

85 Proud men who flout thy law
   spread tales about me.

86 Help me, for they hound me with
   their lies,
   but thy commandments all stand
   for ever.

87 They had almost swept me from
   the earth,
   but I did not forsake thy precepts;

88 grant me life, as thy love is
   unchanging,
   that I may follow all thy
   instruction.

89 Eternal is thy word, O LORD,
   planted firm in heaven.

Semite, darkness of *night* connotes the absence of God. **70:** *Thick* and *gross hearts* are dull, insensitive and cruel. **75:** If God's *decrees are just* their observance is beneficial to men and God keeps *faith with* men in punishing transgressions. **83:** Leather flasks containing wine were hung from the ceiling, out of reach of children and rodents, where, exposed to heat and *smoke*, they eventually became brittle and useless. Though the psalmist is shrivelled by age like an old

90 Thy promise^y endures for all time,
   stable as the earth which thou
      hast fixed.
91 This day, as ever, thy decrees stand
      fast;
   for all things serve thee.
92 If thy law had not been my
      continual delight,
   I should have perished in all my
      troubles;
93 never will I forget thy precepts,
   for through them thou hast
      given me life.
94 I am thine; O save me,
   for I have pondered thy precepts.
95 Evil men lie in wait to destroy me;
   but I will give thought to thy
      instruction.
96 I see that all things come to an end,
   but thy commandment has no
      limit.

97 O how I love thy law!
   It is my study all day long.
98 Thy commandments are mine for
      ever;
   through them I am wiser than my
      enemies.
99 I have more insight than all my
      teachers,
   for thy instruction is my study;
100 I have more wisdom than the old,
   because I have kept thy precepts.
101 I set no foot on any evil path
   in my obedience to thy word;
102 I do not swerve from thy decrees,
   for thou thyself hast been my
      teacher.
103 How sweet is thy promise in my
      mouth,
   sweeter on my tongue than honey!
104 From thy precepts I learn wisdom;
   therefore I hate the paths of
      falsehood.

105 Thy word is a lamp to guide my feet
   and a light on my path;
106 I have bound myself by oath and
      solemn vow
   to keep thy just decrees.
107 I am cruelly afflicted;

O LORD, revive me and make
   good thy word.
Accept, O LORD, the willing tribute 108
   of my lips
and teach me thy decrees.
Every day I take my life in my 109
   hands,
   yet I never forget thy law.
Evil men have set traps for me, 110
   but I do not stray from thy
      precepts.
Thy instruction is my everlasting 111
   inheritance;
   it is the joy of my heart.
I am resolved to fulfil thy statutes; 112
   they are a reward that never fails.

I hate men who are not single- 113
   minded,
   but I love thy law.
Thou art my shield and hiding-place; 114
I hope for the fulfilment of thy
   word.
Go, you evildoers, and leave me to 115
   myself,
   that I may keep the command-
      ments of my God.
Support me as thou hast promised, 116
   that I may live;
   do not disappoint my hope.
Sustain me, that I may see 117
   deliverance;
   so shall I always be occupied with
      thy statutes.
Thou dost reject those who stray 118
   from thy statutes,
   for their talk is all malice and lies.
In thy sight all the wicked on earth 119
   are scum;
   therefore I love thy instruction.
The dread of thee makes my flesh 120
   creep,
   and I stand in awe of thy decrees.

I have done what is just and right; 121
   thou wilt not abandon me to my
      oppressors.
Stand surety for the welfare of thy 122
   servant;

y *Prob. rdg.; Heb.* Thy constancy.

wineskin, he can still meditate on the law in good vigor. **99:** In the study of the Law, God is the
inner teacher so that the psalmist has more *insight* than his academic *teachers*. **100:** Even though
wisdom and old age were equated, the young who *kept* the Law acquired *more wisdom* than
the old who did not. **109:** The threat to *life* itself does not distract him from attention to the Law.
113: *Not single-minded:* those whose allegiance is divided, who have ambivalent feelings about

let not the proud oppress me.[z]

123 My sight grows dim with looking
for thy deliverance
and waiting for thy righteous
promise.

124 In all thy dealings with me, LORD,
show thy true love
and teach me thy statutes.

125 I am thy servant; give me insight
to understand thy instruction.

126 It is time to act, O LORD;
for men have broken thy law.

127 Truly I love thy commandments
more than the finest gold.

128 It is by thy precepts that I find the
right way;
I hate the paths of falsehood.

129 Thy instruction is wonderful;
therefore I gladly keep it.

130 Thy word is revealed, and all is
light;
it gives understanding even to
the untaught.

131 I pant, I thirst,
longing for thy commandments.

132 Turn to me and be gracious,
as thou hast decreed for those
who love thy name.

133 Make my step firm according to
thy promise,
and let no wrong have the
mastery over me.

134 Set me free from man's oppression,
that I may observe thy precepts.

135 Let thy face shine upon thy servant
and teach me thy statutes.

136 My eyes stream with tears
because men do not heed thy
law.

137 How just thou art, O LORD!
How straight and true are thy
decrees!

138 How just is the instruction thou
givest!
It is fixed firm and sure.

139 I am speechless with resentment,
for my enemies have forgotten
thy words.

140 Thy promise has been tested
through and through,
and thy servant loves it.

141 I may be despised and of little
account,
but I do not forget thy precepts.

142 Thy justice is an everlasting justice,
and thy law is truth.

143 Though I am oppressed by trouble
and anxiety,
thy commandments are my
continual delight.

144 Thy instruction is ever just;
give me understanding that I
may live.

145 I call with my whole heart; answer
me, LORD.
I will keep thy statutes.

146 I call to thee; O save me
that I may heed thy instruction.

147 I rise before dawn and cry for
help;
I hope for the fulfilment of thy
word.

148 Before the midnight watch also my
eyes are open
for meditation on thy promise.

149 Hear me, as thy love is unchanging,
and give me life, O LORD, by thy
decree.

150 My pursuers in their malice are
close behind me,
but they are far from thy law.

151 Yet thou art near, O LORD,
and all thy commandments are
true.

152 I have long known from thy
instruction
that thou hast given it eternal
foundations.

153 See in what trouble I am and set
me free,
for I do not forget thy law.

154 Be thou my advocate and win
release for me;
true to thy promise, give me life.

155 Such deliverance is beyond the
reach of wicked men,
because they do not ponder thy
statutes.

156 Great is thy compassion, O LORD;
grant me life by thy decree.

[z] oppress me: *or* charge me falsely.

the Law. **135:** *Let thy face shine:* regard favorably. **140:** *Tested:* proved valid. **150:** Though
evildoers may apprehend the psalmist, they cannot overpower the Law which is his support.

157 Many are my persecutors and
enemies,
but I have not swerved from thy
instruction.
158 I was cut to the quick when I saw
traitors
who had no regard for thy
promise.
159 See how I love thy precepts, O
LORD!
Grant me life, as thy love is
unchanging.
160 Thy word is founded in truth,
and thy just decrees are
everlasting.

161 The powers that be persecute me
without cause,
yet my heart thrills at thy word.
162 I am jubilant over thy promise,
like a man carrying off much
booty.
163 Falsehood I detest and loathe,
but I love thy law.
164 Seven times a day I praise thee
for the justice of thy decrees.
165 Peace is the reward of those who
love thy law;
no pitfalls beset their path.
166 I hope for thy deliverance, O LORD,
and I fulfil thy commandments;
167 gladly I heed thy instruction
and love it greatly.
168 I heed thy precepts and thy
instruction,
for all my life lies open before
thee.

169 Let my cry of joy reach thee, O
LORD;
give me understanding of thy
word.
170 Let my supplication reach thee;

be true to thy promise and save
me.
Let thy praise pour from my lips, 171
because thou teachest me thy
statutes;
let the music of thy promises be 172
on my tongue,
for thy commandments are
justice itself.
Let thy hand be prompt to help me, 173
for I have chosen thy precepts;
I long for thy deliverance, O 174
LORD,
and thy law is my continual
delight.
Let me live and I will praise thee; 175
let thy decrees be my support.
I have strayed like a lost sheep; 176
come, search for thy servant,
for I have not forgotten thy
commandments.

120

I called to the LORD in my distress, 1
and he answered me.
'O LORD,' I cried, 'save me from 2
lying lips
and from the tongue of slander.'
What has he in store for you, 3
slanderous tongue?
What more has he for you?
Nothing but a warrior's sharp 4
arrows
or red-hot charcoal.
Hard is my lot, exiled in Meshech, 5
dwelling by the tents of Kedar.
All the time that I dwelt 6
among men who hated peace,
I sought peace; but whenever I 7
spoke of it,
they were for war.

164: *Seven times:* either a symbolic number meaning "always" (compare Mt.18.21), or an allusion to a pious regimen of prayer.
   Ps. 120: He answered me. Either a Thanksgiving (v. 1) which contains a past lamentation (vv. 2–7) or a Lament with God's assurance of deliverance. The superscriptions in the MT (see Introduction) designate Pss.120–134 as "Songs of Ascents." The phrase could mean the ascent of pilgrims to the city of Jerusalem, one of the highest points in Palestine, and hence a song for one of the great annual pilgrim feasts designated in Exod.23.14–17; Deut.16.16. It could also mean the ascent of a procession within Jerusalem up the steps leading to the Temple; hence the interpretation of the superscription as "Psalms of the Steps." The theme of exile (v. 5) among a hostile people (vv. 6–7) with the resultant longing for Jerusalem, the city of peace, possibly made this a Pilgrim Song. **3:** *What more:* a formula commonly used for a curse in Heb.; compare 1 Sam.25.22. **4:** *Sharp arrows:* death in battle. **5:** *Meshech:* an ancient people to the north of Palestine (Gen.10.2) from whom the final enemy of Israel would come; see Ezek.38.2. *Kedar:* a land in the Syrian desert, perhaps a symbol of hardship or barbarism; see S. of S.1.5–6. **7:** See 55–21.

121

1 If I lift up my eyes to the hills,
     where shall I find help?
2 Help comes only from the LORD,
     maker of heaven and earth.
3 How could he let your foot stumble?
     How could he, your guardian,
       sleep?
4 The guardian of Israel
     never slumbers, never sleeps.
5 The LORD is your guardian,
     your defence at your right hand;
6 the sun will not strike you by day
     nor the moon by night.
7 The LORD will guard you against
       all evil;
     he will guard you, body and soul.
8 The LORD will guard your going
       and your coming,
     now and for evermore.

122

1 I rejoiced when they said to me,
     'Let us go to the house of the
       LORD.'
2 Now we stand within your gates,
     O Jerusalem:
3 Jerusalem that is built to be a city
     where people come together in
       unity;
4 to which the tribes resort, the tribes
       of the LORD,
     to give thanks to the LORD
       himself,
     the bounden duty of Israel.
5 For in her are set the thrones of
       justice,

the thrones of the house of David.
Pray for the peace of Jerusalem: 6
'May those who love you prosper;
peace be within your ramparts   7
  and prosperity in your palaces.'
For the sake of these my brothers   8
  and my friends,
I will say, 'Peace be within you.'
For the sake of the house of the   9
  LORD our God
I will pray for your good.

123

I lift my eyes to thee   1
  whose throne is in heaven.
As the eyes of a slave follow his   2
    master's hand
  or the eyes of a slave-girl her
    mistress,
so our eyes are turned to the
  LORD our God
  waiting for kindness from him.
Deal kindly with us, O LORD, deal   3
    kindly,
  for we have suffered insult enough;
too long have we had to suffer   4
  the insults of the wealthy,
  the scorn of proud men.

124

If the LORD had not been on our   1
    side,
  Israel may now say,
if the LORD had not been on our   2
    side
  when they assailed us,

Ps. 121: The guardian of Israel. A Hymn, another Song of Ascents (see Ps.120 n.), pointing to Mount Zion as the source of protection in the dangers of the pilgrimage to Jerusalem (vv. 2–6) as well as in life (vv. 7–8). **1:** Sanctuaries were built on *hills*, both to the pagan Baals (2 Kgs.23.5) and to the God of Israel for whom the Temple on Mount Zion was built. **4:** *Never sleeps:* the affirmation is in sharp contrast with the anxiety in 44.23. **5:** The defendant of an accused man stood at his *right hand* at a trial. **8:** *Going and coming:* the performance of one's daily work; see Deut.28.6.
Ps. 122: Pray for the peace of Jerusalem. A Hymn, sung by admiring pilgrims at their departure as they still stood within the walls of Jerusalem. **3:** Jerusalem was the center of political *unity* since it belonged to no tribe when David made it his capital (2 Sam.5.6–10); it was the center of religious unity, in whose Temple alone could sacrifices be legitimately offered; see Deut.12.5–7; 2 Kgs. ch. 23. **5:** *Thrones of justice:* where the king held court (1 Kgs.7.7). **6–9:** Pilgrims *pray* for Jerusalem as they leave. **6:** *Peace:* in Heb. "shalom," has wide-ranging positive meaning, namely, well-being, happiness, and prosperity.
Ps. 123: Deal kindly with us, O LORD. A Lament of the community which returned humbled and lowly from the Exile and was exposed to the contempt of its pagan neighbors; see Neh.2.19. **1:** See Ps.121.1. **3–4:** A plea for help.
Ps. 124: Our help is in the name of the LORD. A Thanksgiving. See Ps.120 n. on Songs of

3 they would have swallowed us alive
    when their anger was roused
    against us.
4 The waters would have carried us
    away
    and the torrent swept over us;
5 over us would have swept
    the seething waters.
6 Blessed be the LORD, who did not
    leave us
    to be the prey between their teeth.
7 We have escaped like a bird
    from the fowler's trap;
    the trap broke, and so we escaped.
8 Our help is in the name of the LORD,
    maker of heaven and earth.

125

1 Those who trust in the LORD are
    like Mount Zion,
    which cannot be shaken but stands
    fast for ever.
2 As the hills enfold Jerusalem,
    so the LORD enfolds his people, now
    and evermore.
3 The sceptre of wickedness shall
    surely find no home
    in the land allotted to the
    righteous,
    so that the righteous shall not set
    their hands to injustice.
4 Do good, O LORD, to those who
    are good
    and to those who are upright in
    heart.
5 But those who turn aside into
    crooked ways,
    may the LORD destroy them, as he
    destroys all evildoers!

    Peace be upon Israel!

126

When the LORD turned the tide of   1
    Zion's fortune,
    we were like men who had found
    new health.*a*
Our mouths were full of laughter   2
    and our tongues sang aloud for joy.
Then word went round among the
    nations,
    'The LORD has done great things
    for them.'
Great things indeed the LORD then   3
    did for us,
    and we rejoiced.

Turn once again our fortune, LORD,   4
    as streams return in the dry south.
Those who sow in tears   5
    shall reap with songs of joy.
A man may go out weeping,   6
    carrying his bag of seed;
    but he will come back with songs
    of joy,
    carrying home his sheaves.

127

Unless the LORD builds the house,   1
    its builders will have toiled in vain.
Unless the LORD keeps watch over
    a city,
    in vain the watchman stands on
    guard.
In vain you rise up early   2
    and go late to rest,
    toiling for the bread you eat;
    he supplies the need of those he
    loves.*b*
Sons are a gift from the LORD   3

a like. . health: or like dreamers.
b Prob. rdg.; Heb. adds an unintelligible word.

Ascents. The theme is the deliverance of the nation from its foes. **4–5**: The metaphor of *waters* is also found in 69.1–2,15. **8**: Compare 121.2.
   Ps. 125: Peace be upon Israel. A Lament; a Song of Ascents (see 120 n.). **1–3**: The security of those who trust in God is as solid as Mount Zion, the rock on which the Temple stood. **3**: *Sceptre of wickedness:* a foreign conqueror. The allusion is, however, quite vague. **4–5**: A plea for help.
   Ps. 126. Turn once again our fortune, O LORD. A Lament with a prayer for deliverance, possibly from the hardships the community experienced in the first years after the return from Exile; see Neh.5.1–5. **1–2**: To the returned Exiles their new life of freedom at first seemed like a dream (see Tfn. *a*) as they *sang*, in contrast to their stay in Babylon; compare 137.2–4. **4**: In the *south* of Palestine water courses, dry during most of the year, all at once fill up with streams of water from sudden rains in winter.
   Ps. 127: Without the LORD all is in vain. A Wisdom Psalm. Since this Song of Ascents (see Ps.120 n.) is a Wisdom Psalm, it is ascribed to Solomon in the superscription of the MT (see Introduction). **1–2**: God is the true source of security and blessing. **3–5**: The blessing of having

and children a reward from him.

4 Like arrows in the hand of a
fighting man
are the sons of a man's youth.

5 Happy is the man
who has his quiver full of them;
such men shall not be put to shame
when they confront their enemies
in court.

128

1 Happy are all who fear the LORD,
who live according to his will.

2 You shall eat the fruit of your own
labours,
you shall be happy and you shall
prosper.

3 Your wife shall be like a fruitful
vine
in the heart of your house;
your sons shall be like olive-shoots
round about your table.

4 This is the blessing in store for the
man
who fears the LORD.

5 May the LORD bless you from Zion;
may you share the prosperity of
Jerusalem
all the days of your life,

6 and live to see your children's
children!

Peace be upon Israel!

129

1 Often since I was young have men
attacked me—
let Israel now say—

2 often since I was young have men
attacked me,
but never have they prevailed.

3 They scored my back with scourges,
like ploughmen driving long
furrows.

4 Yet the LORD in his justice
has cut me loose from the bonds
of the wicked.

5 Let all enemies of Zion
be thrown back in shame;

6 let them be like grass growing on
the roof,
which withers before it can shoot,

7 which will never fill a mower's hand
nor yield an armful for the
harvester,

8 so that passers-by will never say to
them,
'The blessing of the LORD be
upon you!
We bless you in the name of the
LORD.'

130

1 Out of the depths have I called to
thee, O LORD;

2 Lord, hear my cry.
Let thy ears be attentive
to my plea for mercy.

3 If thou, LORD, shouldest keep
account of sins,
who, O LORD, could hold up his
head?

4 But in thee is forgiveness,
and therefore thou art revered.

5 I wait for the LORD with all my
soul,
I hope for the fulfilment of his
word.

many sons. 5: In an Israelite *court*, which was held in an open forum, the larger a man's family, the greater influence he had.

Ps. 128: May the LORD bless you from Zion. A Wisdom Psalm; see Ps.120 n. **1–4:** It is a frequent theme of Wisdom teaching that the faithful are blessed with a devoted family. **5–6:** A prayer for Jerusalem and for peace.

Ps. 129: Let all enemies of Zion be thrown back in shame. A Lament of the community in which an individual speaks for the whole nation, apparently in a cultic setting. See Ps.120 n. **1:** Israel was *young* in the Exodus from Egypt and in the wandering in the desert. **3:** *Ploughmen driving long furrows:* apparently a popular metaphor (also found in a Ugaritic text 62.4–5). **5–8:** A curse, prompted by the danger from foes. **6:** In Palestine a house has a flat *roof* made of clay from which *grass* sprouts after a rain but quickly *withers* in the sunshine that follows. See Ps.37.2. **8:** See Ps.118.26; Ruth 2.4.

Ps. 130: LORD, hear my cry. A Lament; see Ps.120 n. This psalm is one of the seven "Penitential Psalms" (others are: Pss. 6, 32, 38, 51, 102, 143), so called because they are used in the Christian liturgy on occasions of mourning as an expression of repentance. **1:** *Depths:* affliction of the spirit because of sinfulness rather than physical misery. **4:** God is revered because he is

6 My soul waits*c* for the Lord
    more eagerly than watchmen for
    the morning.
    Like men who watch for the
    morning,
7 O Israel, look for the LORD.
    For in the LORD is love unfailing,
    and great is his power to set men
    free.
8 He alone will set Israel free
    from all their sins.

131

1 O LORD, my heart is not proud,
    nor are my eyes haughty;
    I do not busy myself with great
    matters
    or things too marvellous for me.
2 No; I submit myself, I account
    myself lowly,
    as a weaned child clinging to its
    mother.*d*
3 O Israel, look for the LORD
    now and evermore.

132

1 O LORD, remember David
    in the time of his adversity,
2 how he swore to the LORD
    and made a vow to the Mighty
    One of Jacob:
3 'I will not enter my house
    nor will I mount my bed,
4 I will not close my eyes in sleep
    or my eyelids in slumber,
5 until I find a sanctuary for the LORD,

    a dwelling for the Mighty One of
    Jacob.'
    We heard of it in Ephrathah;   6
    we came upon it in the region of
    Jaar.
    Let us enter his dwelling,   7
    let us fall in worship at his
    footstool.
    Arise, O LORD, and come to thy   8
    resting-place,
    thou and the ark of thy power.
    Let thy priests be clothed in   9
    righteousness
    and let thy loyal servants shout
    for joy.
    For thy servant David's sake   10
    reject not thy anointed king.
    The LORD swore to David   11
    an oath which he will not break:
    'A prince of your own line
    will I set upon your throne.
    If your sons keep my covenant   12
    and heed the teaching that I give
    them,
    their sons in turn for all time
    shall sit upon your throne.'
    For the LORD has chosen Zion   13
    and desired it for his home:
    'This is my resting-place for ever;   14
    here will I make my home, for
    such is my desire.
    I will richly bless her destitute*e*   15
    and satisfy her needy with bread.
    With salvation will I clothe her   16
    priests;
    her loyal servants shall shout for
    joy.

---

c waits: *transposed from after the* LORD *in verse 5.*
d Prob. rdg.; Heb. *adds* as a weaned child clinging
to me.
e her destitute: *prob. rdg.;* Heb. her provisions.

---

forgiving and not because he is vindictive. **6–7:** Men keeping a military or shepherd's *watch*
during the darkest hours before dawn *eagerly* await the security of the *morning.* **8:** *Set Israel
free:* compare Isa.44.22.
    Ps. 131: I submit myself. A fragment of a Song of Ascents; see Ps.120 n. **1b:** The allusion in
these words of humility is unclear. **2:** For the suggestion that God is like a *mother* see Isa.66.7–13.
    Ps. 132: The LORD swore to David. A Royal Psalm. It was probably used in a liturgical
setting, possibly at a coronation ceremony or at a processional ceremony, to commemorate
the finding of the Ark (vv. 6–8; see 1 Sam.6.13) and its transfer to Jerusalem (2 Sam. ch. 6.)
This latter use put it into the category of the Ascents; see Ps.120 n. **2:** *Mighty One:* a name
for God. **5:** *Dwelling:* a shrine to house the Ark of the Covenant above which God was
considered to be present in a special way; see Exod.25.22. **6:** *Ephrathah:* Bethlehem, David's
birth-place. *Jaar:* Kiriath-jearim, a city in Judah to which the Philistines returned the Ark
after capturing it in battle; see 1 Sam.6.13–7.2. **7:** *His footstool:* the Ark; see v. 5. **8:** *Arise,
O LORD:* a ceremonial exclamation when moving the Ark; see 68.1 and compare Num.10.35. **9:**
This is possibly a rubric for the *priests* to put on sacred vestments, i.e. be *clothed in righteousness,*
and for the assembly to *shout for joy,* i.e. start singing as the procession begins. **11–18:** Possibly
an oracle by a Temple prophet proclaiming God's promises to David and to Zion. **17:** God
lights *a lamp* for David by establishing his successor (see 1 Kgs.11.36).

17 There will I renew the line of
David's house
and light a lamp for my anointed
king;
18 his enemies will I clothe with shame,
but on his head shall be a shining
crown.'

133

1 How good it is and how pleasant
for brothers to live*f* together!
2 It is fragrant as oil poured upon
the head
and falling over the beard,
Aaron's beard, when the oil runs down
over the collar of his vestments.
3 It is like the dew of Hermon falling
upon the hills of Zion.
There the LORD bestows his blessing,
life for evermore.

134

1 Come, bless the LORD,
all you servants of the LORD,
who stand night after night
in the house of the LORD.
2 Lift up your hands in the sanctuary
and bless the LORD.
3 The LORD, maker of heaven and
earth,
bless you from Zion!

135

1 O praise the LORD.

Praise the name of the LORD;

praise him, you servants of the
LORD,
who stand in the house of the LORD, 2
in the temple courts of our God.
Praise the LORD, for that is good; 3
honour his name with psalms,
for that is pleasant.
The LORD has chosen Jacob to be 4
his own
and Israel as his special treasure.
I know that the LORD is great, 5
that our LORD is above all gods.
Whatever the LORD pleases, 6
that he does, in heaven and on
earth,
in the sea, in the depths of ocean.
He brings up the mist from the 7
ends of the earth,
he opens rifts*g* for the rain,
and brings the wind out of his
storehouses.
He struck down all the first-born in 8
Egypt,
both man and beast.
In Egypt he sent signs and portents 9
against Pharaoh and all his
subjects.
He struck down mighty nations 10
and slew great kings,
Sihon king of the Amorites, Og the 11
king of Bashan,
and all the princes of Canaan,
and gave their land to Israel, 12
to Israel his people as their
patrimony.
O LORD, thy name endures for ever; 13
thy renown, O LORD, shall last for
all generations.
The LORD will give his people 14
justice

f Or to worship.   *g Prob. rdg.; Heb.* lightnings.

Ps. 133: How pleasant for brothers to live together. A Wisdom Psalm; see Introduction. The united community of Israel is seen to be as beneficent as the oil that conferred the blessings of the priesthood and the dew that brought refreshment in the heat. **2:** *Oil upon the head* was part of the ceremony of priestly consecration which brought a person into a brotherly relationship of Temple ministers; see Exod.29.7. **3:** *Hermon* is the highest mountain in Syria, whose peak is almost always covered with snow and lost in mist. It was believed by the ancients to be the source of the refreshing *dew* that settled on the parched countryside to the south of Palestine.
Ps. 134: The LORD bless you from Zion. A Benediction which closes the Songs of Ascents (Ps.120 n.) with a blessing. It consists of a liturgical dialogue between pilgrims who leave and the priests who remain on duty in the Temple at night. **1–2:** Encouragement given to the priests, the *servants of the LORD*, by the pilgrims. **3:** Blessing imparted by the priests in the name of the LORD, from whom all blessings in *heaven* and on *earth* come. *Maker of heaven and earth:* also used in 121.2 and 124.8.
Ps. 135: O praise the LORD. A Hymn which begins and ends with a ritual call to worship. It is composed almost entirely of allusions to, or borrowings from, other psalms and passages of the Bible. **7:** In the absence of meteorological science, the formation of *mist* was a mystery. Also, rain was thought to fall from *rifts* opened by God in the vault containing the waters above the heaven; see Gen.1.6–8. **8–12:** God's deeds in history. **10:** For the defeat of *kings* see Num.

and have compassion on his servants.

15 The gods of the nations are idols of silver and gold,
   made by the hands of men.

16 They have mouths that cannot speak and eyes that cannot see;

17 they have ears that do not hear, and there is no breath in their nostrils.[h]

18 Their makers grow like them, and so do all who trust in them.

19 O house of Israel, bless the LORD;
   O house of Aaron, bless the LORD.

20 O house of Levi, bless the LORD;
   you who fear the LORD, bless the LORD.

21 Blessed from Zion be the LORD who dwells in Jerusalem.

O praise the LORD.

136

1 It is good to give thanks to the LORD,
   for his love endures for ever.

2 Give thanks to the God of gods;
   his love endures for ever.

3 Give thanks to the Lord of lords;
   his love endures for ever.

4 Alone he works great marvels;
   his love endures for ever.

5 In wisdom he made the heavens;
   his love endures for ever.

6 He laid the earth upon the waters;
   his love endures for ever.

7 He made the great lights,
   his love endures for ever,

8 the sun to rule by day,
   his love endures for ever,

9 the moon and the stars to rule by night;
   his love endures for ever.

10 He struck down the first-born of the Egyptians,

his love endures for ever,
and brought Israel from among them; 11
his love endures for ever.

With strong hand and outstretched arm, 12
his love endures for ever,

he divided the Red Sea in two, 13
his love endures for ever,

and made Israel pass through it, 14
his love endures for ever;

but Pharaoh and his host he swept 15
into the sea;
his love endures for ever.

He led his people through the 16
wilderness;
his love endures for ever.

He struck down great kings; 17
his love endures for ever.

He slew mighty kings, 18
his love endures for ever,

Sihon king of the Amorites, 19
his love endures for ever,

and Og the king of Bashan; 20
his love endures for ever.

He gave their land to Israel, 21
his love endures for ever,

to Israel his servant as their 22
patrimony;
his love endures for ever.

He remembered us when we were 23
cast down,
his love endures for ever,

and rescued us from our enemies; 24
his love endures for ever.

He gives food to all his creatures; 25
his love endures for ever.

Give thanks to the God of heaven, 26
for his love endures for ever.

137

By the rivers of Babylon we sat 1
down and wept

h *Prob. rdg.; Heb.* mouths.

21.21–35. **15–18:** Similar to 115.3–8. **19–21:** For the house of *Israel, Aaron*, etc., see 115.9–11 n.

Ps. 136: His love endures forever. A Hymn. In the Jewish liturgy it is called "the Great Hallel" since it was recited at the Passover meal after the "Lesser Hallel," i.e. Pss.113–118. In structure it is a litany; that is, the refrain, "his love endures forever," in the second half of every verse, was sung by the congregation in response to the first half of the verse sung by a soloist. The basic structure is an introduction (vv. 1–3), God's majesty in creation (vv. 4–9), his greatness in the Exodus (vv. 10–15), in the Wilderness (vv. 16–20), in the Conquest (vv. 21–22), his deliverance in the time of the Judges (vv. 23–25), and a conclusion (v. 26). **17–20:** Num.21.21–35; compare Ps.135.11. **23–25:** Compare 135.13–18.

Ps. 137: We sat down and wept. A Lament sung in the Exile after the destruction of Jerusalem by the Babylonians in 587 B.C. **1:** *Rivers of Babylon:* the Tigris and Euphrates and the irrigation

when we remembered Zion.

9 There on the willow-trees[i]
we hung up our harps,

3 for there those who carried us off
demanded music and singing,
and our captors called on us to be
merry:
'Sing us one of the songs of Zion.'

4 How could we sing the LORD's song
in a foreign land?

5 If I forget you, O Jerusalem,
let my right hand wither away;

6 let my tongue cling to the roof of
my mouth
if I do not remember you,
if I do not set Jerusalem
above my highest joy.

7 Remember, O LORD, against the
people of Edom
the day of Jerusalem's fall,
when they said, 'Down with it,
down with it,
down to its very foundations!'

8 O Babylon, Babylon the destroyer,
happy the man who repays you
for all that you did to us!

9 Happy is he who shall seize your
children
and dash them against the rock.

138

1 I will praise thee, O LORD, with all
my heart;
boldly, O God, will I sing psalms
to thee.[j]

2 I will bow down towards thy holy
temple,
for thy love and faithfulness I will
praise thy name;
for thou hast made thy promise wide
as the heavens.

When I called to thee thou didst   3
answer me
and make me bold and valiant-
hearted.

Let all the kings of the earth praise[k] 4
thee, O LORD,
when they hear the words thou
hast spoken;

and let them sing of[l] the LORD's   5
ways,
for great is the glory of the LORD.

For the LORD, high as he is, cares   6
for the lowly,
and from afar he humbles the
proud.

Though I walk among foes thou dost   7
preserve my life,
exerting thy power against the rage
of my enemies,
and with thy right hand thou
savest me.

The LORD will accomplish his   8
purpose for me.
Thy true love, O LORD, endures
for ever;
leave not thy work unfinished.

139

LORD, thou hast examined me and   1
knowest me.

Thou knowest all, whether I sit   2
down or rise up;
thou hast discerned my thoughts
from afar.

Thou hast traced my journey and   3
my resting places,
and art familiar with all my paths.

For there is not a word on my   4
tongue

i Or poplars.
j boldly . . . thee: or I will sing psalms to thee before
the gods.
k Or confess.   l Or walk in.

ditches which branched off from them. 3: A group of psalms which extol Jerusalem, the "city
of God" are called the *songs*, or canticles, *of Zion;* they are Pss. 46, 48, 76, 84, 87, and 122.
7: *The people of Edom* (a country to the southeast of Judah), allied themselves with the Babylonians in plundering Jerusalem after the *day* of its capture in June–July, 587 B.C.; see Ezek.35.5;
Obad. 10–14. 9: In ancient warfare *children* were often cruelly killed.

Ps. 138: I will praise thee, O LORD. A Thanksgiving Psalm, probably a royal one sung in the
Temple. 1: The word "gods" in Tfn. *j* can also mean godlike beings and may be translated as
"angels"; some versions interpret it "kings" or "judges." 2: *Promise wide as the heavens:* God
offers everything to man, including himself. 6: Not only does God stay *afar* from the *proud*,
those who aspire to be his equals, but he also humbles them, in bringing them lower than they
were.

Ps. 139: Slay the wicked. A Lament (see Introduction). Man's life is mysterious; and since
God has shown himself all-wise and all-powerful in creating man, he knows intimately the
inner soul of the poet and his need for guidance. 2: *Sit down or rise up:* all of man's actions.

but thou, LORD, knowest them all.^m

5 Thou hast kept close guard before
me and behind
and hast spread thy hand over me.

6 Such knowledge is beyond my
understanding,
so high that I cannot reach it.

7 Where can I escape from thy spirit?
Where can I flee from thy
presence?

8 If I climb up to heaven, thou art
there;
if I make my bed in Sheol, again I
find thee.

9 If I take my flight to the frontiers
of the morning
or dwell at the limit of the western
sea,

10 even there thy hand will meet me
and thy right hand will hold me
fast.

11 If I say, 'Surely darkness will steal
over me,
night will close around me',

12 darkness is no darkness for thee
and night is luminous as day;
to thee both dark and light are one.

13 Thou it was who didst fashion my
inward parts;
thou didst knit me together in my
mother's womb.

14 I will praise thee, for thou dost fill
me with awe;
wonderful thou art, and wonderful
thy works.
Thou knowest me through and
through:

15 my body is no mystery to thee,
how I was secretly kneaded into
shape
and patterned in the depths of the
earth.

16 Thou didst see my limbs unformed
in the womb,
and in thy book they are all
recorded;

day by day they were fashioned,
not one of them was late in
growing.ⁿ

17 How deep I find thy thoughts, O
God,
how inexhaustible their themes!

18 Can I count them? They outnumber
the grains of sand;
to finish the count, my years must
equal thine.

19 O God, if only thou wouldst slay
the wicked!
If those men of blood would but
leave me in peace—

20 those who provoke thee with
deliberate evil
and rise in vicious rebellion
against thee!

21 How I hate them, O LORD, that
hate thee!
I am cut to the quick when they
oppose thee;

22 I hate them with undying hatred;
I hold them all my enemies.

23 Examine me, O God, and know my
thoughts;
test me, and understand my
misgivings.

24 Watch lest I follow any path that
grieves thee;
guide me in the ancient^o ways.

140

1 Rescue me, O LORD, from evil men:
keep me safe from violent men,

2 whose heads are full of wicked
schemes,
who stir up contention day after day.

3 Their tongues are sharp as serpents'
fangs;

m For . . . them all: *or* If there is any offence on my
tongue, thou, LORD, knowest it all.
n was late in growing: *prob. rdg.; Heb. om.*
o *Or* everlasting.

8: Although God's knowledge encompassed *Sheol* (Job 26.6), he was ordinarily considered
absent from it (Job 3.13–19), the view here being unique. **9:** The great mysteries for the ancient
man affecting his life daily were the *frontiers of the morning,* "the home of light" and the limit
of the western sea, the Mediterranean, the "dwelling of darkness"; see Job 38.12–20. **15:** *Depths
of the earth:* the womb, the emphasis being on the mystery of the process that is at work.
16: *Thy book:* see 56.8 n. **22:** For the Hebrew, God's cause is the cause of his faithful, and vice
versa; compare Mt.12.30. **24:** *Ancient ways:* the fidelity of the patriarchs to God even when
his guidance was a mystery to them.
    Ps. 140: Rescue me, O LORD. A Lament (see Introduction), a lengthy appeal for deliverance
from enemies. **1–2:** A prayer for help. **3–7:** The entrapment by the wicked. **3:** *Tongues:* possibly

on their lips is spiders' poison.

1 Guard me, O LORD, from wicked men;
keep me safe from violent men,
who plan to thrust me out of the
way.

5 Arrogant men set hidden traps for
me,
rogues spread their nets
and lay snares for me along the
path.

6 I said, 'O LORD, thou art my God;
O LORD, hear my plea for mercy.

7 O LORD God, stronghold of my
safety,
thou hast shielded my head in the
day of battle.

8–9 Frustrate, O LORD, their designs
against me;
never let the wicked gain their
purpose.
If any of those at my table rise
against me,
let their own conspiracies be
their undoing.

10 Let burning coals be tipped upon
them;
let them be plunged into the
miry depths,
never to rise again.

11 Slander shall find no home in the
land;
evil and violence shall be hounded
to destruction.'

12 I know that the LORD will give their
due to the needy
and justice to the downtrodden.

13 Righteous men will surely give
thanks to thy name;
the upright will worship in thy
presence.

141

1 O LORD, I call to thee, come
quickly to my aid;
listen to my cry when I call to
thee.

2 Let my prayer be like incense duly
set before thee
and my raised hands like the
evening sacrifice.

3 Set a guard, O LORD, over my
mouth;
keep watch at the door of my lips.

4 Turn not my heart to sinful thoughts
nor to any pursuit of evil courses.
The evildoers appal me;*p*
not for me the delights of their
table.

5 I would rather be buffeted by the
righteous
and reproved by good men.
My head shall not be anointed with
the oil of wicked men,
for that would make me a party to
their crimes.

6 They shall founder on the rock of
justice
and shall learn how acceptable
my words are.

7 Their bones shall be scattered at the
mouth of Sheol,
like splinters of wood or stone on
the ground.

8 But my eyes are fixed on thee, O
LORD God;
thou art my refuge; leave me not
unprotected.

9 Keep me from the trap which they
have set for me,
from the snares of evildoers.

10 Let the wicked fall into their own
nets,
whilst I pass in safety, all alone.

142

1 I cry aloud to the LORD;
to the LORD I plead aloud for
mercy.

p appal me: prob. rdg.; Heb. with men.

an allusion to a curse; compare 109.28. **6:** His plea is based on his confession: *thou art my God.*
8–11: A curse on the enemies. **8–9:** *My table:* compare 41.9. **12–13:** The psalmist's trust.
Ps. 141: **Listen to my cry.** A Lament (see Introduction), with the usual vow absent. **2:** The
fragrant smoke of *incense* rising from the altar was a symbol of *prayer* acceptable to God; see
Rev.5.8. *Raised hands* are a gesture of supplication which the poet prays may be acceptable as
an *evening sacrifice* which God had commanded; see Exod.29.38–42. **3:** *Guard over mouth:*
against sinful words. **4:** Anointing oneself with oil was a sign of prosperity and festivity; see
23.5; Ezek.16.9. **6:** God is often called the *rock* on which the wicked founder; see 18.2; compare
Lk.20.18. **7:** *Bones at the mouth of Sheol:* symbol of shameful death.
Ps. 142: **I cry to thee. O LORD.** A Lament (see Introduction). See Ps.30.8 and 77.1.

2 I pour out my complaint before him
   and tell over my troubles in his
      presence.

3 When my spirit is faint within me,
   thou art there to watch over my
      steps.
   In the path that I should take
   they have hidden a snare.

4 I look to my right hand,
   I find no friend by my side;
   no way of escape is in sight,
   no one comes to rescue me.

5 I cry to thee, O LORD,
   and say, 'Thou art my refuge;
   thou art all I have
   in the land of the living.

6 Give me a hearing when I cry,
   for I am brought very low;
   save me from my pursuers,
   for they are too strong for me.

7 Set me free from my prison,
   so that I may praise thy name.'
   The righteous shall crown me with
      garlands,*q*
   when thou givest me my due
      reward.

143

1 LORD, hear my prayer;
   be true to thyself, and listen to my
      pleading;
   then in thy righteousness answer
      me.

2 Bring not thy servant to trial before
      thee;
   against thee no man on earth can
      be right.

3 An enemy has hunted me down,
   has ground my living body under
      foot
   and plunged me into darkness like
      a man long dead,

so that my spirit fails me   4
   and my heart is dazed with
      despair.
I dwell upon the years long past,   5
   upon the memory of all that thou
      hast done;
   the wonders of thy creation fill
      my mind.
To thee I lift my outspread hands,   6
   athirst for thee in a thirsty land.
LORD, make haste to answer,   7
   for my spirit faints.
Do not hide thy face from me
   or I shall be like those who go down
      to the abyss.
In the morning let me know thy   8
      true love;
   I have put my trust in thee.
Show me the way that I must take;
   to thee I offer all my heart.
Deliver me, LORD, from my enemies,   9
   for with thee have I sought refuge.
Teach me to do thy will, for thou   10
      art my God;
   in thy gracious kindness, show me
      the level road.
Keep me safe, O LORD, for the   11
      honour of thy name
and, as thou art just, release me
   from my distress.
In thy love for me, reduce my   12
      enemies to silence
and bring destruction on all who
      oppress me;
   for I am thy servant.

144

Blessed is the LORD, my rock,   1
   who trains my hands for war,
   my fingers for battle;
my help that never fails, my fortress,   2

q crown me with garlands: or crowd round me.

4: *Right hand:* see 109.6 n. 5: *Land of the living:* this earth. 7–8: The vow usual in a Lament.
7: *Prison:* probably meant figuratively for the feeling of being hemmed in by enemies. *Praise thy
name:* the vow as a motive for deliverance. *Reward:* liberation and restoration to an honorable
status surrounded by the *righteous.*
   Ps. 143: LORD, make haste to answer. A Lament (see Introduction). This is the last of the
so-called "Penitential Psalms" (see Ps.130 n.). The poet confesses that because of his sins he
does not deserve to be heard in strict justice (vv. 1–2) but only in God's love (vv. 8,10,12).
1: God will be *true* to himself when he listens to the pleas of the psalmist since his attributes are:
righteousness, true love (v. 8), and gracious kindness (v. 10); see 86.15 n. **7:** *Hide thy face:* see
10.11 n. *Abyss:* Sheol, the place of the dead. **8–12:** An appeal to God's love for deliverance and
for the destruction of the enemies. **8:** In the darkness and loneliness of night God seemed
absent, but *morning* was the true indication of God's *love.*
   Ps. 144: Rescue me from the cruel sword. A Lament (see Introduction), probably by a king
(vv. 10–11). The first part, vv. 1–11, is almost completely borrowed from, or inspired by, other

my strong tower and my refuge,
my shield in which I trust,
he who puts nations under my
  feet.

3 O LORD, what is man that thou
  carest for him?
What is mankind? Why give a
  thought to them?
4 Man is no more than a puff of wind,
  his days a passing shadow.
5 If thou, LORD, but tilt the heavens,
  down they come;
touch the mountains, and they
  smoke.
6 Shoot forth thy lightning flashes,
  far and wide,
and send thy arrows whistling.
7 Stretch out thy hands from on high
  to rescue me
and snatch me from great waters.[r]

9 I will sing a new song to thee, O
  God,
psalms to the music of a ten-stringed
  lute.
10 O God who gavest victory to kings
  and deliverance to thy servant
  David,
rescue me from the cruel sword;
11 snatch me from the power of
  foreign foes,
whose every word is false
and all their oaths are perjury.

12 Happy[s] are we whose sons in their
  early prime
stand like tall towers,
our daughters like sculptured
  pillars
at the corners of a palace.
13 Our barns are full and furnish
  plentiful provision;
our sheep bear lambs in thousands
  upon thousands;
14 the oxen in our fields are fat and
  sleek;
there is no miscarriage or untimely
  birth,

no cries of distress in our public
  places.
15 Happy are the people in such a
  case as ours;
happy the people who have the
  LORD for their God.

145

1 I will extol thee, O God my king,
  and bless thy name for ever and
  ever.
2 Every day will I bless thee
  and praise thy name for ever and
  ever.
3 Great is the LORD and worthy of
  all praise;
his greatness is unfathomable.
4 One generation shall commend thy
  works to another
and set forth thy mighty deeds.
5 My theme shall be thy marvellous
  works,
the glorious splendour of thy
  majesty.
6 Men shall declare thy mighty acts
  with awe
and tell of thy great deeds.
7 They shall recite the story of thy
  abounding goodness
and sing of thy righteousness
  with joy.

8 The LORD is gracious and
  compassionate,
forbearing, and constant in his
  love.
9 The LORD is good to all men,
  and his tender care rests upon all
  his creatures.

10 All thy creatures praise thee, LORD,
  and thy servants bless thee.
11 They talk of the glory of thy kingdom
  and tell of thy might,

r Prob. rdg.; Heb. adds from the power of foreign foes, (8) whose every word is false and all their oaths are perjury (cp. verse. 11).
s Prob. rdg.; Heb. Who.

psalms: vv. 1–2 = 18.2–3; v. 3 = 8.4–5; v. 4 = 39.5; v. 5 = 18.10; v. 9 = 18.49–50. **9:** The vow usual in a Lament. **12–14:** The blessing of peace and prosperity promised to Israel for obeying the Law; see Deut.28.1–12. **12:** *Like sculptured pillars:* statuesque.
  Ps. 145: I will extol thee, O God my king. A Hymn, many of whose phrases are similar to other psalms and other parts of the Bible. It extols the goodness and greatness of God. The preceding six psalms (139–144) are Laments, but the ensuing and last six (145–150) are Hymns. This acrostic psalm (see Ps.111 n.) lacks a verse for the Heb. letter *nun* in the MT, possibly as a result of a copyist's omission; its place would be between vv. 13 and 14. **8–9:** The unique attri-

12 they proclaim to their fellows how
        mighty are thy deeds,
    how glorious the majesty of thy
        kingdom.
13 Thy kingdom is an everlasting
        kingdom,
    and thy dominion stands for all
        generations.

14 In all his promises the LORD keeps
        faith,
    he is unchanging in all his works;
    the LORD holds up those who
        stumble
    and straightens backs which are
        bent.
15 The eyes of all are lifted to thee in
        hope,
    and thou givest them their food
        when it is due;
16 with open and bountiful hand
    thou givest what they desire*t* to
        every living creature.
17 The LORD is righteous in all his ways,
        unchanging in all that he does;
18 very near is the LORD to those
        who call to him,
    who call to him in singleness of
        heart.
19 He fulfils their desire if only they
        fear him;
    he hears their cry and saves them.
20 The LORD watches over all who
        love him
    but sends the wicked to their
        doom.
21 My tongue shall speak out the
        praises of the LORD,
    and all creatures shall bless his
        holy name
    for ever and ever.

146

1   O praise the LORD.

Praise the LORD, my soul.
As long as I live I will praise the   1
    LORD;
I will sing psalms to my God all
    my life long.
Put no faith in princes,   3
    in any man, who has no power
    to save.
He breathes his last breath,   4
    he returns to the dust;
and in that same hour all his
    thinking ends.

Happy the man whose helper is the   5
    God of Jacob,
    whose hopes are in the LORD his
        God,
maker of heaven and earth,   6
    the sea, and all that is in them;
who serves wrongdoers as he has
    sworn
    and deals out justice to the   7
        oppressed.
The LORD feeds the hungry
    and sets the prisoner free.
The LORD restores sight to the   8
    blind
    and straightens backs which are
        bent;
the LORD loves the righteous
    and watches over the stranger;   9
the LORD gives heart to the orphan
    and widow
but turns the course of the wicked
    to their ruin.
The LORD shall reign for ever,   10
    thy God, O Zion, for all
    generations.

    O praise the LORD.

147

    O praise the LORD.   1

t they desire: *or* thou wilt.

---

butes of God in his dealing with Israel and all men; see 86.15 n. **14–20:** God's responsive
attention to the needs of the faithful. **21:** The praise of God, an echo of vv. 1–4.
    Ps. 146: Praise the LORD, my soul. A Hymn. The last five of the psalms (146–150) begin and
end with *O praise the LORD*, Heb. "Hallelujah". **1–2:** The praise of God. **3–4:** Compare 144.3–4.
4: *Returns to the dust:* see Gen.3.19. *His thinking:* his planning and projects. **5–10:** The great
deeds, past and present, of God the Creator. **6–9:** In extolling God's deeds on behalf of the
poor in the present there is a subtle allusion to his deeds on behalf of Israel, *the oppressed*, *the
hungry*, *the prisoner*, the *bent* of back in the Exodus.
    Ps. 147: How good it is to sing psalms to our God. A Hymn, possibly two separate psalms
joined together; the Sept. and Vg. treat this psalm as two (vv. 1–11 and 12–20) with a Hallelujah
(see Ps.146 n.) in vv. 1 and 20. **1:** The praise of God. **2–11:** His power in history and over nature;

How good it is to sing psalms to
  our God!
How pleasant to praise him!

2 The LORD is rebuilding Jerusalem;
  he gathers in the scattered sons of
    Israel.
3 It is he who heals the broken in
    spirit
  and binds up their wounds,
4 he who numbers the stars one by
    one
  and names them one and all.
5 Mighty is our Lord and great his
    power,
  and his wisdom beyond all
    telling.
6 The LORD gives new heart to the
    humble
  and brings evildoers down to the
    dust.
7 Sing to the LORD a song of
    thanksgiving,
  sing psalms to the harp in honour
    of our God.
8 He veils the sky in clouds
  and prepares rain for the earth;
  he clothes the hills with grass
    and green plants for the use of
      man.
9 He gives the cattle their food
  and the young ravens all that they
    gather.
10 The LORD sets no store by the
    strength of a horse
  and takes no pleasure in a
    runner's legs;
11 his pleasure is in those who fear
    him,
  who wait for his true love.

12 Sing to the LORD, Jerusalem;
  O Zion, praise your God,
13 for he has put new bars in your
    gates;
  he has blessed your children
    within them.
14 He has brought peace to your realm
  and given you fine wheat in
    plenty.

15 He sends his command to the ends
    of the earth,
  and his word runs swiftly.
16 He showers down snow, white as
    wool,
  and sprinkles hoar-frost thick as
    ashes;
17 crystals of ice he scatters like
    bread-crumbs;
  he sends the cold, and the water
    stands frozen,
18 he utters his word, and the ice is
    melted;
  he blows with his wind and the
    waters flow.
19 To Jacob he makes his word known,
  his statutes and decrees to Israel;
20 he has not done this for any other
    nation,
  nor taught them his decrees.

O praise the LORD.

148

O praise the LORD.   1

Praise the LORD out of heaven;
  praise him in the heights.
Praise him, all his angels;   2
  praise him, all his host.
Praise him, sun and moon;   3
  praise him, all you shining stars;
praise him, heaven of heavens,   4
  and you waters above the heavens.
Let them all praise the name of the   5
    LORD,
for he spoke the word and they
    were created;
he established them for ever and ever   6
  by an ordinance which shall never
    pass away.

Praise the LORD from the earth,   7
  you water-spouts and ocean
    depths;
fire and hail, snow and ice,   8
  gales of wind obeying his voice;

his goodness to the faithful. **2:** A clue to the postexilic date of the poem. **12–20:** God's special
care of Jerusalem and Israel. **15:** God's word here is presented as a messenger, an active power
in the world.
  Ps. 148: Let all praise the name of the LORD. A Hymn; see Ps.146 n. **1–12:** All that God has
created should praise him. **2:** *Host:* the armies of angels; compare Mt.26.53. **3:** *Heaven of
heavens:* the highest heaven, i.e. God's dwelling, where he is enthroned above the vault and
the heavenly reservoir of waters: see Gen.1.6–8. **5:** *He spoke the word:* compare Gen. ch. 1

9   all mountains and hills;
      all fruit-trees and all cedars;
10 wild beasts and cattle,
      creeping things and winged birds;
11 kings and all earthly rulers,
      princes and judges over the whole
        earth;
12 young men and maidens,
      old men and young together.
13 Let all praise the name of the LORD,
      for his name is high above all
        others,
      and his majesty above earth and
        heaven;
14 he has exalted his people in the
        pride of power
      and crowned with praise his loyal
        servants,
      all Israel, the people nearest him.

    O praise the LORD.

149

1   O praise the LORD.

    Sing to the LORD a new song,
      sing his praise in the assembly of
        the faithful;
2   let Israel rejoice in his maker
      and the sons of Zion exult in their
        king.
3   Let them praise his name in the
        dance,
      and sing him psalms with tambourine
        and harp.
4   For the LORD accepts the service of
        his people;
      he crowns his humble folk with
        victory.
5   Let his faithful servants exult in
        triumph;

    let them shout for joy as they kneel
      before him.
    Let the high praises of God be on   6
      their lips
      and a two-edged sword in their
        hand,
    to wreak vengeance on the nations   7
      and to chastise the heathen;
    to load their kings with chains   8
      and put their nobles in irons;
    to execute the judgement decreed   9
      against them—
    this is the glory of all his faithful
      servants.

    O praise the LORD.

150

    O praise the LORD.   1

    O praise God in his holy place,
      praise him in the vault of heaven,
        the vault of his power;
    praise him for his mighty works,   2
      praise him for his immeasurable
        greatness.
    Praise him with fanfares on the   3
        trumpet,
      praise him upon lute and harp;
    praise him with tambourines and   4
        dancing,
      praise him with flute and strings;
    praise him with the clash of cymbals,   5
      praise him with triumphant
        cymbals;
    let everything that has breath   6
      praise the LORD!

    O praise the LORD.

---

and Ps.33.6. **13–14:** Israel has a very special place but should not be alone in praising the name of the LORD.
   Ps. 149: Sing to the LORD a new song. A Hymn; see Ps.146 n. It reflects a liturgical setting. **3:** *Dance* seems to be prescribed as part of the religious ceremony; see 2 Sam.6.14; Exod.15.20. **4–9:** A military victory appears to be reflected.
   Ps. 150: O praise God in his holy place. A Hymn. This is the last of Hallelujah psalms (see Ps.146 n.) and it also is a final doxology to Book 5 and to all the psalms. A festival seems to be the background (vv. 3–5). **1:** *Holy place:* the Temple. **3–5:** The various musical instruments used in the Temple liturgy are indicated. **6:** *Praise* from all living beings, the note on which the Psalter closes.

PROVERBS

The Book of Proverbs is a distillate of centuries of Israelite instruction in the home, court, and school. Called by some a foreign body in the Bible, Proverbs ignores major religious themes (covenant, patriarchs, Exodus, Sinai) and makes creative use of non-Israelite wisdom traditions, particularly Egyptian. In substance, it represents the results of a search for a divinely sustained order in the lessons derived from human experience. Prudence plus knowledge are thought to have been conferred by God, and these are regarded as an authoritative repository, entrusted to the care of fathers, teachers, and royal counselors. All insight being deemed a gift of God, Proverbs was thought of as revealed wisdom and hence was incorporated into Scripture.

Four long collections and five short appendixes are represented. Several headings indicate royal patronage (1.1; 10.1; 25.1); these and others (22.17; 24.23; 30.1; 31.1) testify to many centuries in which material accumulated. Chs. 1–9, by far the most religious collection, are the latest; these chapters have stylistic affinities with Deuteronomy and prophecy. The oldest collections, surely preexilic, are 10.1–22.16 and 25.1–29.27; these are basically "secular." The teachings generally reflect an agricultural economy and are "this worldly" and optimistic despite a rigid principle of retribution. There is a characteristic tendency toward sharp contrast, such as rich/poor, wise/fool, good/evil.

Advice to the reader

1 The proverbs of Solomon son of
David, king of Israel,
2 by which men will come to wisdom
and instruction
and will understand words that bring
understanding,
3 and by which they will gain a well-
instructed intelligence,
righteousness, justice, and probity.
4 The simple will be endowed with
shrewdness
and the young with knowledge and
prudence.
5 If the wise man listens, he will
increase his learning,
and the man of understanding will
acquire skill
6 to understand proverbs and parables,
the sayings of wise men and their
riddles.

The fear of the LORD is the 7
beginning[a] of knowledge,
but fools scorn wisdom and discipline.

Attend, my son, to your father's 8
instruction
and do not reject the teaching of
your mother;
for they are a garland of grace on 9
your head
and a chain of honour round your
neck.

My son, bad men may tempt you[b] and 10,11
say,

a Or chief part.
b Prob. rdg.; Heb. adds do not come, or, with some
MSS., do not consent.

1.1–7.27: Advice to the reader. This section differs both stylistically and thematically from the subsequent ones. Only here are there discussions of single topics in long paragraphs and also reflections of Deut. and the Prophets. The personification of Wisdom and Folly is a major theme of the chapters; the picture of Lady Wisdom is a derivative of the portrait of Dame Folly. It is not fully clear how one is to view the allusions to the "foreign woman," whether: (1) she may be a participant in a fertility cult, that is, a sacred prostitute; or (2) simply a loose woman, foreign because her bad behavior sets her apart. In either case, the chapters burn with the intense conviction that since all knowledge derives from God it instructs man in the path of life. The superscription (1.1) recalls a tradition, 1 Kgs.4.29–34, that Solomon composed or compiled proverbs and songs.

1.2–6: Introduction to the several collections. The editor gives reasons for studying the proverbial traditions. **6:** The Heb. word for proverb (*mashal*) implies a "likeness" or an author-itative word, while that for riddle (*hidah*) suggests an enigmatic saying.

1.7–9: Recommendation of wisdom. 7: This motto of the book occurs again at 9.10, and in expanded form in Job 28.28 and Ecclus.1.14. It is in creative tension with the anthropocentricity ("centering on man") of most wisdom texts. *Fools:* a moral rather than an intellectual judgment. **8:** A metaphor for student, *my son* derives from the family setting in which the father instructed his children in the way of the wise. The term is used frequently in Egyptian wisdom literature for "pupil." **9:** *Garland:* a motif common in Egyptian wisdom literature.

1.10–19: Warning against the sinner's style of life. The attractiveness of evil is negated by its

675

'Come with us; let us lie in wait for
someone's blood,
let us waylay[c] an innocent man who
has done us no harm.
12 Like Sheol we will swallow them
alive;
though blameless, they shall be like
men who go down to the abyss.
13 We shall take rich treasure of every
sort
and fill our homes with booty;
14 throw in your lot with us,
and we will have a common purse.'
15 My son, do not go along with them,
keep clear of their ways;
16 they hasten hot-foot into crime,
impatient to shed blood.

17 In vain is a net spread wide
if any bird that flies can see it.

18 These men lie in wait for their own
blood
and waylay[c] no one but themselves.
19 This is the fate[d] of men eager for
ill-gotten gain:
it robs those who get it of their lives.

20 Wisdom cries aloud in the open air,
she raises her voice in public places;
21 she calls at the top of the busy street
and proclaims at the open gates of
the city:
22 'Simple fools, how long will you be
content with your simplicity?[e]
23 If only you would respond to my
reproof,
I would give you my counsel
and teach you my precepts.
24 But because you refused to listen
when I called,
because no one attended when I
stretched out my hand,
25 because you spurned all my advice

and would have nothing to do with
my reproof,
26 I in my turn will laugh at your
doom
and deride you when terror comes
upon you,
27 when terror comes upon you like a
hurricane
and your doom descends like a
whirlwind.[f]
Insolent men delight in their
insolence;
stupid men hate knowledge.[g]
28 When they call upon me, I will not
answer them;
when they search for me, they shall
not find me.
29 Because they hate knowledge
and have not chosen to fear the
LORD,
30 because they have not accepted my
counsel
and have spurned all my reproof,
31 they shall eat the fruits of their
behaviour
and have a surfeit of their own
devices;
32 for the simpleton turns a deaf ear
and comes to grief,
and the stupid are ruined by their
own complacency.
33 But whoever listens to me shall live
without a care,
undisturbed by fear of misfortune.'

2 My son, if you take my words to
heart
and lay up my commands in your
mind,

c *Prob. rdg.; Heb.* store up.
d *This . . . fate: prob. rdg.; Heb.* Such are the courses.
e *The rest of verse 22 transposed to follow verse 27.*
f *Prob. rdg.; Heb. adds* when anguish and distress
come upon you.
g *Insolent . . . knowledge: transposed from end of*
verse 22.

---

ultimate result; compare Wis.2.1–20. **12:** *Sheol:* the shadowy realm of the dead. **17:** A popular
proverb enforces the warning against gullibly paying heed to the enticing criminal.
    1.20–33: Wisdom in the role of prophetess. In striking prophetic style personified Wisdom
pleads for a hearing and rebukes those who pay her no heed. **20–21:** Unafraid of competition,
Wisdom speaks publicly at the *gates,* the center of economic and judicial activity. **23:** *Give you
my counsel:* lit. "I will pour out my spirit upon you . . . ," recalling prophetic language, e.g.
Isa.44.3. **24:** The *hand* of God may be *stretched out* either to strengthen or save a people or else
to punish them; the former is intended here, and resembles numerous prophetic texts (see the
refrain in Isa.5.25; 9.17,21; 10.4). The outstretched hand is a frequent Deuteronomic expression
for God's saving deeds in defeating the enemies of his people. **32:** *Turns a deaf ear:* turns away,
i.e. waywardness. **33:** See 3.24–26.
    2.1 22: The fruits of wisdom. By diligent attention to the precepts of the sages one becomes
heir to (1) insight into religious knowledge; (2) divine protection, both from evil ways and from

2 giving your attention to wisdom
and your mind to understanding,
3 if you summon discernment to your
aid
and invoke understanding,
4 if you seek her out like silver
and dig for her like buried treasure,
5 then you will understand the fear of
the LORD
and attain to the knowledge of God;
6 for the LORD bestows wisdom
and teaches knowledge and
understanding.
7 Out of his store he endows the
upright with ability
as a shield for those who live
blameless lives;
8 for he guards the course of justice
and keeps watch over the way of his
loyal servants.

9 Then you will understand what is
right and just
and keep*h* only to the good man's
path;
10 for wisdom will sink into your mind,
and knowledge will be your heart's
delight.
11 Prudence will keep watch over you,
understanding will guard you,
12 it will save you from evil ways
and from men whose talk is
subversive,
13 who forsake the honest course
to walk in ways of darkness,
14 who rejoice in doing evil
and exult in evil and subversive acts,
15 whose own ways are crooked,
whose tracks are devious.
16 It will save you from the adulteress,
from the loose woman with her
seductive words,
17 who forsakes the teaching of her
childhood
and has forgotten the covenant of
her God;
18 for her path*i* runs downhill towards
death,

and her course is set for the land of
the dead.
No one who resorts to her*j* finds his 19
way back
or regains the path to life.

See then that you follow the   20
footsteps of good men
and keep to the course of the
righteous;
for the upright shall dwell on earth, 21
and blameless men remain there;
but the wicked shall be uprooted   22
from it
and traitors weeded out.

My son, do not forget my teaching,   3
but guard my commands in your
heart;
for long life and years in plenty   2
will they bring you, and prosperity
as well.
Let your good faith and loyalty   3
never fail,
but bind them about your neck.
Thus will you win favour and   4
success
in the sight of God and man.

Put all your trust in the LORD   5
and do not rely on your own
understanding.
Think of him in all your ways,   6
and he will smooth your path.
Do not think how wise you are,   7
but fear the LORD and turn from
evil.
Let that be the medicine to keep you   8
in health,
the liniment for your limbs.
Honour the LORD with your wealth   9
as the first charge on all your
earnings;
then your granaries will be filled   10
with corn*k*

h keep: prob. rdg.; Heb. uprightness.
i Prob. rdg.; Heb. house.
j resorts to her: or takes to them.
k with corn: or to overflowing.

the adulteress; and (3) the promise of the land, i.e. possessions. **3:** *Invoke understanding:*
this passage comes near to personifying wisdom; see 1.1–7.27 n. **9:** The insight is moral, what
is *right* and *just*. **16:** *Loose:* lit. alien; a moral rather than an ethnic term. **17:** As frequently
elsewhere, *covenant* is the term for the relation between God and man.
   3.1–12: Divine trustworthiness. The LORD's discipline, like that of one's natural parents,
has man's best interests at heart. **3:** The New English Bible, with the Sept., omits a third clause
found in the MT: "Write them upon the tablet of your heart." **9:** *First charge:* lit. first fruit
(see Exod.22.29). This is the sole cultic injunction in Prov.

and your vats bursting with new
wine.

11 My son, do not spurn the LORD's
correction
or take offence at his reproof;

12 for those whom he loves the LORD
reproves,
and he punishes a favourite son.

13 Happy he who has found wisdom,
and the man who has acquired
understanding;

14 for wisdom is more profitable than
silver,
and the gain she brings is better than
gold.

15 She is more precious than red coral,
and all your jewels are no match for
her.

16 Long life is in her right hand,
in her left hand are riches and
honour.

17 Her ways are pleasant ways
and all her paths lead to prosperity.

18 She is a staff of life to all who grasp
her,
and those who hold her fast are
safe.

19 In wisdom the LORD founded the
earth
and by understanding he set the
heavens in their place;

20 by his knowledge the depths burst
forth
and the clouds dropped dew.

21 My son, keep watch over your ability
and prudence,
do not let them slip from sight;

22 they shall be a charm hung about
your neck
and an ornament on your breast.

23 Then you will go your way without
a care,

and your feet will not stumble.

24 When you sit, you need have no
fear;
when you lie down, your sleep will
be pleasant.

25 Do not be afraid when fools are
frightened
or when ruin comes upon the
wicked;

26 for the LORD will be at your side,
and he will keep your feet clear of
the trap.

27 Refuse no man any favour that you
owe him
when it lies in your power to pay it.

28 Do not say to your friend, 'Come
back again;
you shall have it tomorrow'—when
you have it already.

29 Plot no evil against your friend,
your unsuspecting neighbour.

30 Do not pick a quarrel with a man
for no reason,
if he has not done you a bad turn.

31 Do not emulate a lawless man,
do not choose to follow his
footsteps;

32 for one who is not straight is
detestable to the LORD,
but upright men are in God's
confidence.

33 The LORD's curse rests on the house
of the evildoer,
while he blesses the home of the
righteous.

34 Though God himself meets the
arrogant with arrogance,
yet he bestows his favour on the
meek.*l*

35 Wise men are adorned with*m*
honour,
but the coat*n* on a fool's back is
contempt.

l Or wretched.
m are adorned with: prob. rdg.; Heb. shall inherit.
n the coat: prob. rdg.; Heb. obscure.

3.13–18: Praise of Wisdom. In the style almost of a hymn the author extols Wisdom as a precious treasure. **13:** *Happy:* the word that usually introduces beatitudes, as in "wisdom psalms" (Pss.1,32, etc.). **16:** The image is likely that of the Egyptian goddess Maat, who holds in her *right hand* the symbol of life and in her *left hand* the scepter, symbolizing wealth and dignity. **18:** *Staff:* lit. tree.

3.19–20: Wisdom's role at creation. Wisdom was at God's side when he created the universe. This motif is elaborated in 8.22–31. **20:** *Depths:* underground springs (see Gen.7.11; 2 Sam.1.21). In Israelite thought the sources of water were three: rain, dew, and underground streams.

3.21–35: Admonition and warning. A series of exhortations to commendable behavior is followed by specific prohibitions, particularly in regard to the treatment of neighbors. **32:** *Detestable:* the word in the cultic sense is usually rendered "abomination," and is frequent in Deut. Originally it had the limited sense of ritual uncleanness.

4 Listen, my sons, to a father's
    instruction,
   consider attentively how to gain
    understanding;

2 for it is sound learning I give you;
   so do not forsake my teaching.

3 I too have been a father's son,
   tender in years, my mother's only
    child.

4 He taught me and said to me:
   Hold fast to my words with all your
    heart,
   keep my commands and you will
    have life.

5 Do not forget or turn a deaf ear to
    what I say.

7 The first thing[o] is to acquire
    wisdom;
   gain understanding though it cost
    you all you have.

6 Do not forsake her, and she will
    keep you safe;
   love her, and she will guard you;

8 cherish her, and she will lift you
    high;
   if only you embrace her, she will
    bring you to honour.

9 She will set a garland of grace on
    your head
   and bestow on you a crown of glory.

10 Listen, my son, take my words to
    heart,
   and the years of your life shall be
    multiplied.

11 I will guide you in the paths of
    wisdom
   and lead you in honest ways.

12 As you walk you will not slip,
   and, if you run, nothing will bring
    you down.

13 Cling to instruction and never let it
    go;
   observe it well, for it is your life.

14 Do not take to the course of the
    wicked
   or follow the way of evil men;

15 do not set foot on it, but avoid it;
   turn aside and go on your way.

16 For they cannot sleep unless they
    have done some wrong;
   unless they have been someone's
    downfall they lose their sleep

17 The bread they eat is the fruit of
    crime
   and they drink wine got by violence.

18 The course of the righteous is like
    morning light,
   growing brighter till it is broad day;

19 but the ways of the wicked are like
    darkness at night,
   and they do not know what has
    been their downfall.

20 My son, attend to my speech,
   pay heed to my words;

21 do not let them slip out of your
    mind,
   keep them close in your heart;

22 for they are life to him who finds
    them,
   and health to his whole body.

23 Guard your heart more than any
    treasure,
   for it is the source of all life.

24 Keep your mouth from crooked
    speech
   and your lips from deceitful talk.

25 Let your eyes look straight before
    you,
   fix your gaze upon what lies ahead.

26 Look out for the path that your feet
    must take,
   and your ways will be secure.

27 Swerve neither to right nor left,
   and keep clear of every evil thing.

5 My son, attend to my wisdom
   and listen to my good counsel,

2 so that you may observe proper
    prudence
   and your speech be informed with
    knowledge.

3 For though the lips of an adulteress
    drip honey
   and her tongue is smoother than oil,

4 yet in the end she is more bitter than
    wormwood,

o Prob. rdg.; Heb. adds wisdom.

4.1–27: Threefold recommendation of Wisdom. She is the supreme acquisition, indeed a lover
or bride (vv. 1–9); a path of light enabling one to walk in the right way (10–19); and the pathway
itself (20–27). **3:** *I, too . . . :* This formula, one of self-abnegation, is also found in Wis.7.1.
    5.1–23: Warning against the loose woman. Belying her beautiful appearance, the adulteress
leads a youth to his destruction. He must be able to recognize her deceitfulness (vv. 1–6) in order
to steer clear of embarrassment and loss (7–14), particularly since he should be faithful to his

and sharp as a two-edged sword,
5 Her feet go downwards on the path
to death,
her course is set for Sheol.
6 She does not watch for the road
that leads to life;
her course turns this way and that,
and what does she care?*p*

7 Now, my son, listen to me
and do not ignore what I say:
8 keep well away from her
and do not go near the door of her
house;
9 or you will lose your dignity in the
eyes of others
and your honour before strangers;
10 strangers will batten on your
wealth,
and your hard-won gains pass to
another man's family.
11 The end will be that you will starve,
you will shrink to mere skin and
bones.
12 Then you will say, 'Why did I hate
correction
and set my heart against reproof?
13 I did not listen to the voice of my
teachers
or pay attention to my masters.
14 I soon earned*q* a bad name
and was despised in the public
assembly.'

15 Drink water from your own cistern
and running water from your own
spring;
16 do not let your*r* well overflow into
the road,
your runnels of water pour into the
street;
17 let them be yours alone,
not shared with strangers.
18 Let your fountain, the wife of your
youth,
be blessed, rejoice in her,
19 a lovely doe, a graceful hind, let her
be your companion;

you will at all times be bathed in her
love,
and her love will continually wrap
you round.
Wherever you turn, she will guide
you;
when you lie in bed, she will watch
over you,
and when you wake she will talk
with you.*s*
20 Why, my son, are you wrapped up
in the love of an adulteress?
Why do you embrace a loose
woman?
21 For a man's ways are always in the
LORD's sight
who watches for every path that he
must take.
22 The wicked man is caught in his
own iniquities
and held fast in the toils of his own
sin;
23 he will perish for want of discipline,
wrapped in the shroud of his
boundless folly.

6 My son, if you pledge yourself to
another man
and stand surety for a stranger,
2 if you are caught by your promise,
trapped by some promise you have
made,
3 do what I now tell you
and save yourself, my son:
when you fall into another man's
power,
bestir yourself, go and pester the
man,
4 give yourself no rest,
allow yourself no sleep.
5 Save yourself like a gazelle from the
toils,
like a bird from the grasp of the
fowler.

p what . . . care?: or she is restless.
q Or I almost earned.
r do not let your: prob. rdg.; Heb. shall your.
*s Wherever . . . with you: transposed from ch. 6 (verse
22).*

solicitous wife (15–23). **6:** The metaphor is that of restless turning *this way and that*, characteristic of the opportunist, who, irresponsible, does not *care*. **15:** *Cistern:* a metaphor for wife
(see v. 18); a cistern was important for storing precious water. **21:** That God's *sight* takes in
all the ways of a man is a theme in the Egyptian work by Amen-em-ope and in Mesopotamian
hymns to the sun-god Shamash. That God sees everything is essential to the belief in a judgment
after life, a theme prominent in Egypt.
    6.1–19: Various admonitions. Do everything possible to be free of standing surety for another's
debt (vv. 1–5), do not be a sluggard (vv. 6–11; compare 24.30–34); avoid scoundrels who by
gestures belie their words (vv. 12–15); shun detestable habits (vv. 16–19; these are described by

6 Go to the ant, you sluggard,
watch her ways and get wisdom.

7 She has no overseer,
no governor or ruler;

8 but in summer she prepares her store of food
and lays in her supplies at harvest.

9 How long, you sluggard, will you lie abed?
When will you rouse yourself from sleep?

10 A little sleep, a little slumber,
a little folding of the hands in rest,

11 and poverty will come upon you like a robber,
want like a ruffian.

12 A scoundrel, a mischievous man, is he
who prowls about with crooked talk—

13 a wink of the eye,
a touch with the foot,
a sign with the fingers.

14 Subversion is the evil that he is plotting,
he stirs up quarrels all the time.

15 Down comes disaster suddenly upon him;
suddenly he is broken beyond all remedy.

16 Six things the LORD hates,
seven things are detestable to him:

17 a proud eye, a false tongue,
hands that shed innocent blood,

18 a heart that forges thoughts of mischief,
and feet that run swiftly to do evil,

19 a false witness telling a pack of lies,
and one who stirs up quarrels between brothers.

20 My son, observe your father's commands
and do not reject the teaching of your mother;

21 wear them always next your heart
and bind them close about your neck;

23[t] for a command is a lamp, and teaching a light,
reproof and correction point the way of life,

24 to keep you from the wife of another man,
from the seductive tongue of the loose woman.

25 Do not desire her beauty in your heart
or let her glance provoke you;

26 for a prostitute can be had for the price of a loaf,
but a married woman is out for bigger game.

27 Can a man kindle fire in his bosom without burning his clothes?

28 If a man walks on hot coals, will his feet not be scorched?

29 So is he who sleeps with his neighbour's wife;
no one can touch such a woman and go free.

30 Is not a thief contemptible when he steals
to satisfy his appetite, even if he is hungry?

31 And, if he is caught, must he not pay seven times over
and surrender all that his house contains?

32 So one who commits adultery is a senseless fool:
he dishonours the woman and ruins himself;

33 he will get nothing but blows and contumely
and will never live down the disgrace;

t Verse 22 transposed to follow wrap you round *in 5. 19.*

---

metaphors of the body in vv. 16–18). **16:** *Six . . . seven:* a common literary device (see 30.15–31), perhaps growing out of the parallel structure of a Heb. verse (see 10.1–22.16 n.). The device usually means "the totality of," rather than the specific number mentioned. **19:** The climax of the section is in *false witness* and *one who stirs up quarrels*. . . .
6.20–35: Warning against adultery. What a young man learns in the family setting can shield him from adultery. He who succumbs to the allurements of the married woman cannot expect forgiveness from the woman's husband. **23:** The commandment is a *lamp*, that is, more than simply a mechanical law. The psalms similarly throb with joyous exultation over the gift of the divine commandments. See too Deut.6.4–7. **27:** This appears to be an old proverb about *fire* and its ill effects, applied to the destructive effects of passions left unrestrained. **31:** *Seven times over:* contrast Exod.22.1–4.

34 for a husband's anger is a jealous
    anger
    and in the day of vengeance he will
    show no mercy;
35 compensation will not buy his
    forgiveness;*u*
    no bribe, however large, will
    purchase his connivance.

7 My son, keep my words,
    store up my commands in your
    mind.
2   Keep my commands if you would
    live,
    and treasure my teaching as the
    apple of your eye.
3   Wear them like a ring on your
    finger;
    write them on the tablet of your
    memory.
4   Call Wisdom your sister,
    greet Understanding as a familiar
    friend;
5   then they will save you from the
    adulteress,
    from the loose woman with her
    seductive words.

6   I glanced*v* out of the window of my
    house,
    I looked down through the lattice,
7   and I saw among simple youths,
    there amongst the boys I noticed
    a lad, a foolish lad,
8   passing along the street, at the
    corner,
    stepping out in the direction of her
    house
9   at twilight, as the day faded,
    at dusk as the night grew dark;
10 suddenly a woman came to meet
    him,
    dressed like a prostitute, full of
    wiles,
11 flighty and inconstant,
    a woman never content to stay at
    home,
12 lying in wait at every corner,
    now in the street, now in the public
    squares.

She caught hold of him and kissed   13
    him;
    brazenly she accosted him and said,
    'I have had a sacrifice, an offering, to   14
    make
    and I have paid my vows today;
    that is why I have come out to meet   15
    you,
    to watch for you and find you.
    I have spread coverings on my bed   16
    of coloured linen from Egypt.
    I have sprinkled my bed with   17
    myrrh,
    my clothes*w* with aloes and cassia.
    Come! Let us drown ourselves in   18
    pleasure,
    let us spend a whole night of love;
    for the man of the house is away,   19
    he has gone on a long journey,
    he has taken a bag of silver with   20
    him;
    until the moon is full he will not be
    home.'
    Persuasively she led him on,   21
    she pressed him with seductive
    words.
    Like a simple fool he followed her,   22
    like an ox on its way to the
    slaughter-house,
    like an antelope bounding into the
    noose,
    like a bird hurrying into the trap;   23
    he did not know that he was
    risking his life
    until the arrow pierced his vitals.

But now, my son, listen to me,   24
    attend to what I say.
    Do not let your heart entice you   25
    into her ways,
    do not stray down her paths;
    many has she pierced and laid low,   26
    and her victims are without
    number.
    Her house is the entrance to Sheol,   27
    which leads down to the halls of
    death.

u compensation . . . forgiveness: *prob. rdg.; Heb. obscure.*
v I glanced: *prob. rdg.; Heb. om.*
w my clothes: *prob. rdg.; Heb. om.*

7.1–27: Wisdom as a defense against the loose woman. The words of the sages will protect one from the seductress. Her way of working is described by an observer, safely from a distance. **4:** *Sister:* probably bride, as in S. 4.9–10,12, and in Egyptian love literature. **14:** Having had an animal *sacrifice,* the seductress is now ready to enjoy the subsequent feast; see Lev.3.1–5 and 7.15. Irony is intended in the contrast of ritual observance and personal dissoluteness. See also 15.8 and Isa.1.12–17.

Wisdom and folly contrasted

8 Hear how Wisdom lifts her voice
and Understanding cries out.

2 She stands at the cross-roads,
by the wayside, at the top of the
hill;

3 beside the gate, at the entrance to
the city,
at the entry by the open gate she
calls aloud:

4 'Men, it is to you I call,
I appeal to every man:

5 understand, you simple fools, what
it is to be shrewd;
you stupid people, understand what
sense means.

6 Listen! For I will speak clearly,
you will have plain speech from me;

7 for I speak nothing but truth
and my lips detest wicked talk.

8 All that I say is right,
not a word is twisted or crooked.

9 All is straightforward to him who
can understand,
all is plain to the man who has
knowledge.

10 Accept instruction and not silver,
knowledge rather than pure gold;

11 for wisdom is better than red coral,
no jewels can match her.

12 I am Wisdom, I bestow shrewdness
and show the way to knowledge and
prudence.

13 *x*Pride, presumption, evil courses,
subversive talk, all these I hate.

14 I have force, I also have ability;
understanding and power are mine.

15 Through me kings are sovereign
and governors make just laws.

16 Through me princes act like princes,
from me all rulers on earth derive
their nobility.

17 Those who love me I love,
those who search for me find me.

18 In my hands are riches and honour,
boundless wealth and the rewards of
virtue.

19 My harvest is better than gold, fine
gold,
and my revenue better than pure
silver.

20 I follow the course of virtue,
my path is the path of justice;

21 I endow with riches those who love
me
and I will fill their treasuries.

22 'The LORD created me the beginning
of his works,
before all else that he made, long
ago.

23 Alone, I was fashioned in times
long past,
at the beginning, long before earth
itself.

24 When there was yet no ocean I was
born,
no springs brimming with water.

25 Before the mountains were settled
in their place,
long before the hills I was born,

26 when as yet he had made neither
land nor lake
nor the first clod*y* of earth.

27 When he set the heavens in their
place I was there,
when he girdled the ocean with the
horizon,

28 when he fixed the canopy of clouds
overhead
and set the springs of ocean firm in
their place,

29 when he prescribed its limits for the
sea*z*
and knit together earth's
foundations.

30 Then I was at his side each day,
his darling and delight,

x Prob. rdg.; Heb. prefixes The fear of the LORD is to
hate evil.
y the first clod: or the sum of the clods.
z Prob. rdg.; Heb. adds and the water shall not disobey his command.

8.1–9.18: Wisdom and Folly contrasted. Wisdom seeks out men where they usually congregate,
and hence is readily available to, and clearly understandable by, all who wish to respond (8.1–
13). She enables monarchs to rule as befits true kings (vv. 14–16). Those who seek her find her,
and gain wealth and rewards beyond wealth (vv. 17–21). Created as the first of God's works, she
is God's delight as man is hers (vv. 22–36). Like a gracious hostess, she invites men to her home
and table (9.1–6). The insolent reject her, the wise accept her (vv. 7–12). By contrast, Lady
Stupidity (vv. 13–18) invites fools to destruction. **13:** The verse has suffered in ancient copying.
It was probably once a numerical saying, possibly reading: "Three things I hate, indeed four I
loathe; pride, presumption, evil courses, and subversive talk." **22:** The emphasis on Wisdom's
role *before all else* came into being is common in Egyptian and Babylonian texts; see also Col.
1.15–16 and Jn.1.1–3. *Created:* acquired, possessed. **30:** *Darling:* the Heb. is uncertain; perhaps

playing in his presence continually,
31 playing on the earth, when he had
       finished it,
while my delight was in mankind.

32-33 'Now, my sons, listen to me,
listen to instruction and grow wise,
       do not reject it.
Happy is the man who keeps to my
       ways,
34 happy the man who listens to me,
watching daily at my threshold
with his eyes on the doorway;
35 for he who finds me finds life
and wins favour with the LORD,
36 while he who finds me not, hurts
       himself,
and all who hate me are in love with
       death.'

9 Wisdom has built her house,
she has hewn her seven pillars;
2 she has killed a beast and spiced her
       wine,
and she has spread her table.
3 She has sent out her maidens to
       proclaim
from the highest part of the town,
4 'Come in, you simpletons.'
She says also to the fool,
5 'Come, dine with me
and taste the wine that I have
       spiced.
6 Cease to be silly, and you will live,
you will grow in understanding.'

7 Correct an insolent man, and be
       sneered at for your pains;
correct a bad man, and you will put
       yourself in the wrong.
8 Do not correct the insolent or they
       will hate you;

correct a wise man, and he will be
       your friend.
Lecture a wise man, and he will   9
       grow wiser;
teach a righteous man, and his
       learning will increase.

The first step to wisdom is the fear of   10
       the LORD,
and knowledge of the Holy One is
       understanding;
for through me your days will be   11
       multiplied
and years will be added to your life.
If you are wise, it will be to your   12
       own advantage;
if you are haughty, you alone are to
       blame.
The Lady Stupidity is a flighty   13
       creature;
the simpleton, she cares for nothing.
She sits at the door of her house,   14
on a seat in the highest part of the
       town,
to invite the passers-by indoors   15
as they hurry on their way:
'Come in, you simpletons', she says.   16
She says also to the fool,
'Stolen water is sweet   17
and bread got by stealth tastes
       good.'
Little does he know that death lurks   18
       there,
that her guests are in the depths of
       Sheol.

A collection of wise sayings

The proverbs of Solomon: **10**

A wise son brings joy to his father;

---

the meaning is master workman or confidant. If darling, the figure is of a child playing in the presence of a loving father. The personification of Wisdom is of profound theological significance, for it corrects a faulty notion that God was thought of in Wisdom literature as somewhat remote from his creation. A development in the idea of personification can be traced from Job ch. 28, which asks about Wisdom's hiding place, through 8.22-31 (and 3.19-20), to Ecclus.24.1-24 and Wis.7.22-8.21. In Ecclus.24.1 Wisdom is identified with Torah; in Wis. she is viewed, in a Greek manner, as an emanation of God. **9.1:** From the mention of *seven pillars* it has been conjectured that the house is really the world and the pillars are those which support the sky. Yet the figure seems modeled after vv. 14-15. **10:** Contrast Wisdom as something to be learned with the inner knowledge of God as in Jer.31.33-34. **17:** Lady Stupidity quotes an old proverb, to which may be compared the Arabic saying that "everything forbidden is sweet."

10.1-22.16: A collection of wise sayings. The section consists of observations from experience in the form of miscellaneous one-line maxims. Each verse is in parallelism, i.e. it consists of two balanced parts, as is usual in Heb. verse. The observations have a secular tone, and their date is preexilic. These proverbs may have been used for instruction in the home and in school.

a foolish son is his mother's bane.

2 Ill-gotten wealth brings no profit;
uprightness is a safeguard against
death.

3 The LORD does not let the righteous
go hungry,[a]
but he disappoints the cravings[b] of
the wicked.

4 Idle hands make a man poor;
busy hands grow rich.

5 A thoughtful son puts by in
summer;
a son who sleeps at harvest is a
disgrace.

6 Blessings are showered on the
righteous;
the wicked are choked by their own
violence.

7 The righteous are remembered in
blessings;
the name of the wicked turns rotten.

8 A wise man takes a command to
heart;
a foolish talker comes to grief.

9 A blameless life makes for security;
crooked ways bring a man down.

10 To wink at a fault causes trouble;
a frank rebuke leads to peace.

11 The words of good men are a
fountain of life;
the wicked are choked by their own
violence.

12 Hate is always picking a quarrel,
but love turns a blind eye to every
fault.

13 The man of understanding has
wisdom on his lips;
a rod is in store for the back of the
fool.

14 Wise men lay up knowledge;
when a fool speaks, ruin is near.

15 A rich man's wealth is his strong
city,
but poverty is the undoing of the
helpless.

16 The good man's labour is his
livelihood;
the wicked man's earnings bring him
to a bad end.

17 Correction is the high road to life;
neglect reproof and you miss the way.

18 There is no spite in a just man's
talk;
it is the stupid who are fluent with
calumny.

19 When men talk too much, sin is
never far away;
common sense holds its tongue.

20 A good man's tongue is pure silver;
the heart of the wicked is trash.

21 The lips of a good man teach many,
but fools perish for want of sense.

22 The blessing of the LORD brings
riches
and he sends no sorrow with them.

23 Lewdness is sport for the stupid;
wisdom a delight to men of
understanding.

24 The fears of the wicked will
overtake them;
the desire of the righteous will be
granted.

25 When the whirlwind has passed by,
the wicked are gone;
the foundations of the righteous are
eternal.

26 Like vinegar on the teeth or smoke
in the eyes,
so is the lazy servant to his master.

27 The fear of the LORD brings length
of days;
the years of the wicked are few.

28 The hope of the righteous blossoms;
the expectation of the wicked withers
away.

29 The way of the LORD gives refuge to
the honest man,
but dismays those who do evil.

30 The righteous man will never be
shaken;
the wicked shall not remain on
earth.

31 Wisdom flows from the mouth of
the righteous;
the subversive tongue will be rooted
out.

32 The righteous man can suit his
words to the occasion;
the wicked know only subversive
talk.

a Or be afraid.
b Or the clamour.

The mention of Solomon does not imply his authorship, but rather his royal sponsorship, or else possibly a literary type. **2:** Premature death was thought to be an indication of divine disfavor. **3:** See also Ps.37.25. **6:** The doctrine of reward and punishment is here almost mechanical, in that calamity is understood as punishment for sin. **25:** *Whirlwind:* God uses natural phenomena to punish those with whom he is angry (see especially Ecclus.39.28–31

11 False scales are the LORD's
    abomination;
correct weights are dear to his heart.
2 When presumption comes in, in
    comes contempt,
but wisdom goes with sagacity.
3 Honesty is a guide to the upright,
but rogues are balked by their own
    perversity.
4 Wealth is worth nothing in the day
    of wrath,
but uprightness is a safeguard
    against death.
5 By uprightness the blameless keep
    their course,
but the wicked are brought down by
    their wickedness.
6 Uprightness saves the righteous,
but rogues are trapped in their own
    greed.
7 When a man dies, his thread of life
    ends,
and with it ends the hope of
    affluence.
8 A righteous man is rescued from
    disaster,
and the wicked man plunges into it.
9 By his words a godless man tries to
    ruin others,
but they are saved when the
    righteous plead for them.
10 A city rejoices in the prosperity of
    the righteous;
there is jubilation when the wicked
    perish.
11 By the blessing of the upright a city
    is built up;
the words of the wicked tear it
    down.
12 A man without sense despises
    others,
but a man of understanding holds
    his peace.
13 A gossip gives away secrets,
but a trusty man keeps his own
    counsel.
14 For want of skilful strategy an army
    is lost;
victory is the fruit of long planning.
15 Give a pledge for a stranger and
    know no peace;
refuse to stand surety and be safe.
16 Grace in a woman wins honour,

but she who hates virtue makes a
    home for dishonour.
Be timid in business and come to
    beggary;
be bold and make a fortune.
Loyalty brings its own reward; 17
a cruel man makes trouble for his
    kin.
A wicked man earns a fallacious[c] 18
    profit;
he who sows goodness reaps a sure
    reward.[d]
A man set on righteousness finds 19
    life,
but the pursuit of evil leads to death.
The LORD detests the crooked heart, 20
but honesty is dear to him.
Depend upon it: an evil man shall 21
    not escape punishment;
the righteous and all their offspring
    shall go free.
Like a gold ring in a pig's snout 22
is a beautiful woman without good
    sense.
The righteous desire only what is 23
    good;
the hope of the wicked comes to
    nothing.
A man may spend freely and yet 24
    grow richer;
another is sparing beyond measure,
    yet ends in poverty.
A generous man grows fat and 25
    prosperous,
and he who refreshes others will
    himself be refreshed.
He who withholds his grain is cursed 26
    by the people,
but he who sells his corn is blessed.
He who eagerly seeks what is good 27
    finds much favour,
but if a man pursues evil it turns
    upon him.
Whoever relies on his wealth is 28
    riding for a fall,
but the righteous flourish like the
    green leaf.
He who brings trouble on his family 29
    inherits the wind,
and a fool becomes slave to a wise
    man.

c Or fraudulent.
d a sure reward: *or* the reward of honesty.

and Wis.16–19). **11.9:** *Saved:* in the courts, when the righteous *plead* as advocates of the weak.
21: The strong statement seems to counter doubt about retribution (compare 24.16), as if one
cannot always or truly depend on it; such questioning of the justice of God is a recurrent theme

30 The fruit of righteousness is a tree
　　of life,
　but violence means the taking away
　　of life.
31 If the righteous in the land get their
　　deserts,
　how much more the wicked man
　　and the sinner!

12 He who loves correction loves
　　knowledge;
　he who hates reproof is a mere
　　brute.
2 A good man earns favour from the
　　LORD;
　the schemer is condemned.
3 No man can establish himself by
　　wickedness,
　but good men have roots that
　　cannot be dislodged.
4 A capable wife is her husband's
　　crown;
　one who disgraces him is like rot in
　　his bones.
5 The purposes of the righteous are
　　lawful;
　the designs of the wicked are full of
　　deceit.
6 The wicked are destroyed*e* by their
　　own words;
　the words of the good man are his
　　salvation.
7 Once the wicked are down, that is
　　the end of them,
　but the good man's line continues.
8 A man is commended for his
　　intelligence,
　but a warped mind is despised.
9 It is better to be modest*f* and earn
　　one's living
　than to be conceited*g* and go hungry.
10 A righteous man cares for his beast,
　but a wicked man is cruel at heart.
11 He who tills his land has enough to
　　eat,
　but to follow idle pursuits is
　　foolishness.
12 The stronghold of the wicked
　　crumbles like clay,*h*
　but the righteous take lasting root.
13 The wicked man is trapped by his
　　own falsehoods,

but the righteous comes safe through
　　trouble.
One man wins success by his words; 14
another gets his due reward by the
　　work of his hands.
A fool thinks that he is always right; 15
wise is the man who listens to advice.
A fool shows his ill humour at once; 16
a clever man slighted conceals his
　　feelings.
An honest speaker comes out with 17
　　the truth,
but the false witness is full of deceit.
Gossip can be sharp as a sword, 18
but the tongue of the wise heals.
Truth spoken stands firm for ever, 19
but lies live only for a moment.
Those who plot evil delude 20
　　themselves,
but there is joy for those who seek
　　the common good.
No mischief will befall the righteous, 21
but wicked men get their fill of
　　adversity.
The LORD detests a liar 22
but delights in the honest man.
A clever man conceals his knowledge, 23
but a stupid man broadcasts his
　　folly.
Diligence brings a man to power, 24
but laziness to forced labour.
An anxious heart dispirits a man, 25
and a kind word fills him with joy.
A righteous man recoils from evil,*i* 26
but the wicked take a path that
　　leads them astray.
The lazy hunter puts up no game, 27
but the industrious man reaps a rich
　　harvest.*j*
The way of honesty leads to life, 28
but there is a well-worn path to
　　death.

A wise man sees the reason for his **13**
　　father's correction;
an arrogant man will not listen to
　　rebuke.

e Prob. rdg.; Heb. are an ambush for blood.
f Or scorned.
g Or honoured.
h Prob. rdg.; Heb. A wicked man covets a stronghold
　of crumbling earth.
i recoils from evil: *prob. rdg.; Heb.* let him spy out
　his friend.
j but . . . harvest: *prob. rdg.; Heb.* obscure.

in Eccles. and the major theme of Job. **30:** *Tree of life* (see Gen.3.22–24): a symbol for eternal
life found also in Egypt and Babylonia. Here eternal life arises from righteous living. The motif
of the beneficial effect of correction is frequent in Prov. and underwent further development

2 A good man enjoys the fruit of
  righteousness,
  but violence is meat and drink for
   the treacherous.

3 He who minds his words preserves
  his life;
  he who talks too much comes to
   grief.

4 A lazy man is torn by appetite
  unsatisfied,
  but the diligent grow fat and
   prosperous.

5 The righteous hate falsehood;
  the doings of the wicked are foul
   and deceitful.

6 To do right is the protection of an
  honest man,
  but wickedness brings sinners to
   grief.*k*

7 One man pretends to be rich,
  although he has nothing;
  another has great wealth but goes in
   rags.*l*

8 A rich man must buy himself off,
  but a poor man is immune from
   threats.

9 The light of the righteous burns
  brightly;
  the embers of the wicked will be put
   out.

10 A brainless fool causes strife by his
  presumption;
  wisdom is found among friends in
   council.

11 Wealth quickly come by dwindles
  away,
  but if it comes little by little, it
   multiplies.

12 Hope deferred makes the heart sick;
  a wish come true is a staff of life.

13 To despise a word of advice is to ask
  for trouble;
  mind what you are told, and you
   will be rewarded.

14 A wise man's teaching is a fountain
  of life
  for one who would escape the snares
   of death.

15 Good intelligence wins favour,
  but treachery leads to disaster.

16 A clever man is wise and conceals
  everything,
  but the stupid parade their folly.

17 An evil messenger causes trouble,*m*
  but a trusty envoy makes all go well
   again.

18 To refuse correction brings poverty
  and contempt;
  one who takes a reproof to heart
   comes to honour.

19 Lust indulged sickens a man;*n*
  stupid people loathe to mend their
   ways.

20 Walk with the wise and be wise;
  mix with the stupid and be misled.

21 Ill fortune follows the sinner close
  behind,
  but good rewards the righteous.

22 A good man leaves an inheritance
  to his descendants,
  but the sinner's hoard passes to the
   righteous.

23 Untilled land might yield food
  enough for the poor,
  but even that may be lost through
   injustice.

24 A father who spares the rod hates
  his son,
  but one who loves him keeps him in
   order.

25 A righteous man eats his fill,
  but the wicked go hungry.

14 The wisest women build up their
  homes;
  the foolish pull them down with
   their own hands.

2 A straightforward man fears the
  LORD;
  the double-dealer scorns him.

3 The speech of a fool is a rod for his
  back;*o*
  a wise man's words are his
   safeguard.

4 Where there are no oxen the barn is
  empty,
  but the strength of a great ox
   ensures rich crops.

5 A truthful witness is no liar;
  a false witness tells a pack of lies.

k brings . . . grief: *or* plays havoc with a man.
l One man . . . rags: *Or* One man may grow rich though
he has nothing; another may grow poor though he
has great wealth.
m causes trouble: *or* is unsuccessful.
n Lust . . . a man: *or* Desire fulfilled is pleasant to the
appetite.
o his back: *prob. rdg.; Heb.* pride.

in later literature. **13.23:** The land here is either that left uncultivated every seventh year
(Lev.25.1–7) or the marginal areas left for the poor (Lev.19.9–10). **14.4:** *Empty:* of fodder.

6 A conceited man seeks wisdom, yet
finds none;
to one of understanding, knowledge
comes easily.

7 Avoid a stupid man,
you will hear not a word of sense
from him.

8 A clever man has the wit to find the
right way;
the folly of stupid men misleads
them.

9 A fool is too arrogant to make
amends;
upright men know what
reconciliation means.

10 The heart knows its own bitterness,
and a stranger has no part in its joy.

11 The house of the wicked will be
torn down,
but the home of the upright
flourishes.

12 A road may seem straightforward to
a man,
yet may end as the way to death.

13 Even in laughter the heart may
grieve,
and mirth may end in sorrow.

14 The renegade reaps the fruit of his
conduct,
a good man the fruit of his own
achievements.

15 A simple man believes every word
he hears;
a clever man understands the need
for proof.

16 A wise man is cautious and turns
his back on evil;
the stupid is heedless and falls
headlong.

17 Impatience runs into folly;
distinction comes by careful
thought.*p*

18 The simple wear the trappings of
folly;
the clever are crowned with
knowledge.

19 Evil men cringe before the good,
wicked men at the righteous man's
door.

20 A poor man is odious even to his
friend;
the rich have friends in plenty.

21 He who despises a hungry man does
wrong,
but he who is generous to the poor
is happy.

22 Do not those who intend evil go
astray,
while those with good intentions are
loyal and faithful?

23 The pains of toil bring gain,
but mere talk brings nothing but
poverty.

24 Insight is the crown of the wise;
folly the chief ornament of the
stupid.

25 A truthful witness saves life;
the false accuser utters nothing but
lies.

26 A strong man who trusts in the fear
of the LORD
will be a refuge for his sons.

27 The fear of the LORD is the fountain
of life
for the man who would escape the
snares of death.

28 Many subjects make a famous king;
with none to rule, a prince is ruined.

29 To be patient shows great
understanding;
quick temper is the height of folly.

30 A tranquil mind puts flesh on a
man,
but passion rots his bones.

31 He who oppresses*q* the poor insults
his Maker;
he who is generous to the needy
honours him.

32 An evil man is brought down by his
wickedness;
the upright man is secure in his own
honesty.

33 Wisdom is at home in a discerning
mind,
but is ill at ease in the heart of a
fool.

34 Righteousness raises a people to
honour;
to do wrong is a disgrace to any
nation.

35 A king shows favour to an
intelligent servant,

p distinction . . . thought: *prob. rdg.; Heb.* a man of
careful thought is hated.
q Or slanders.

31: The attitude to the poor is ambivalent in Wisdom literature, for it is usually assumed that
one's external circumstances indicate his interior life, and hence a rich man was enjoying God's
reward and a poor man his punishment. On the other hand, the wise championed the cause of
the widow, the orphan, and the poor. **33**: The harsh judgment on the *fool* is moral, associating

but his displeasure strikes down those who fail him.

15 A soft answer turns away anger,
but a sharp word makes tempers hot.

2 A wise man's tongue spreads knowledge;
stupid men talk nonsense.

3 The eyes of the LORD are everywhere,
surveying evil and good men alike.

4 A soothing word is a staff of life,
but a mischievous tongue breaks the spirit.

5 A fool spurns his father's correction,
but to take a reproof to heart shows good sense.

6 In the righteous man's house there is ample wealth;
the gains of the wicked bring trouble.

7 The lips of a wise man promote knowledge;
the hearts of the stupid are dishonest.

8 The wicked man's sacrifice is abominable to the LORD;
the good man's prayer is his delight.

9 The conduct of the wicked is abominable to the LORD,
but he loves the seeker after righteousness.

10 A man who leaves the main road resents correction,
and he who hates reproof will die.

11 Sheol and Abaddon lie open before the LORD,
how much more the hearts of men!

12 The conceited man does not take kindly to reproof
and he will not consult the wise.

13 A merry heart makes a cheerful face;
heartache crushes the spirit.

14 A discerning mind seeks knowledge,
but the stupid man feeds on folly.

15 In the life of the downtrodden every day is wretched,
but to have a glad heart is a perpetual feast.

16 Better a pittance with the fear of the LORD
than great treasure and trouble in its train.

17 Better a dish of vegetables if love go with it
than a fat ox eaten in hatred.

18 Bad temper provokes a quarrel,
but patience heals discords.

19 The path of the sluggard is a tangle of weeds,
but the road of the diligent is a highway.

20 A wise son brings joy to his father;
a young fool despises his mother.

21 Folly may amuse the empty-headed;
a man of understanding makes straight for his goal.

22 Schemes lightly made come to nothing,
but with long planning they succeed.

23 A man may be pleased with his own retort;
how much better is a word in season!

24 For men of intelligence the path of life leads upwards
and keeps them clear of Sheol below.

25 The LORD pulls down the proud man's home
but fixes the widow's boundary-stones.

26 A bad man's thoughts are the LORD's abomination,
but the words of the pure are a delight.*r*

27 A grasping man brings trouble on his family,
but he who spurns a bribe will enjoy long life.

28 The righteous think before they answer;
a bad man's ready tongue is full of mischief.

29 The LORD stands aloof from the wicked,
he listens to the righteous man's prayer.

30 A bright look brings joy to the heart,
and good news warms a man's marrow.

31 Whoever listens to wholesome reproof
shall enjoy the society of the wise.

r the words . . . delight: or gracious words are pure.

---

folly with sin (13.10; 14.9; 15.5,7). **15.3:** *Eyes . . . everywhere:* God's scrutiny of men (see also 15.11; 20.27; 24.11–12) assures the working out of divine retribution (10.6). **8:** See also 21.3. **11.** *Abaddon:* lit. destruction or perdition. That is, God who sees into the realm of the dead surely sees into the hearts of living men. **25:** *Fixes:* that is, the LORD preserves her property

32 He who refuses correction is his own
worst enemy,
but he who listens to reproof learns
sense.

33 The fear of the LORD is a training in
wisdom,
and the way to honour is humility.

16 A man may order his thoughts,
but the LORD inspires the words he
utters.

2 A man's whole conduct may be pure
in his own eyes,
but the LORD fixes a standard for
the spirit of man.

3 Commit to the LORD all that you
do,
and your plans will be fulfilled.

4 The LORD has made each thing for
its own end;
he made even the wicked for a day
of disaster.

5 Proud men, one and all, are
abominable to the LORD;
depend upon it; they will not escape
punishment.

6 Guilt is wiped out by faith and
loyalty,
and the fear of the LORD makes men
turn from evil.

7 When the LORD is pleased with a
man and his ways,
he makes even his enemies live at
peace with him.

8 Better a pittance honestly earned
than great gains ill gotten.

9 Man plans his journey by his own
wit,
but it is the LORD who guides his
steps.

10 The king's mouth is an oracle,
he cannot err when he passes
sentence.

11 Scales[s] and balances[t] are the LORD's
concern;

all the weights in the bag are his
business.

12 Wickedness is abhorrent to kings,
for a throne rests firm on
righteousness.

13 Honest speech is the desire of kings,
they love a man who speaks the
truth.

14 A king's anger is a messenger of
death,
and a wise man will appease it,

15 In the light of the king's
countenance is life,
his favour is like a rain-cloud in the
spring.

16 How much better than gold it is to
gain wisdom,
and to gain discernment is better
than pure silver.

17 To turn from evil is the highway of
the upright;
watch your step and save your life.

18 Pride comes before disaster,
and arrogance before a fall.

19 Better sit humbly with those in need
than divide the spoil with the proud.

20 The shrewd man of business will
succeed well,
but the happy man is he who trusts
in the LORD.

21 The sensible man seeks advice from
the wise,
he drinks it in and increases his
knowledge.[u]

22 Intelligence is a fountain of life to
its possessors,
but a fool is punished by his own
folly.

23 The wise man's mind guides his
speech,
and what his lips impart increases
learning.[v]

s *Or* Pointer.   t *Prob. rdg.; Heb.* balances of justice.
u he drinks . . . knowledge: *or* and he whose speech
is persuasive increases learning.
v and what . . . learning: *or* and increases the learning
of his utterance.

intact. **16.1:** Man proposes but God disposes; compare the Egyptian Amen-em-ope 20.5–6,
"If the tongue of man [be] the rudder of the boat, the All-Lord is its pilot." **2:** A similar saying
occurs in 21.2; see also v. 25. Compare the statement in a Babylonian work that what is good
with man is evil with the gods, and what is evil to him is proper to a god. **4:** The second half
of the verse expresses the view that God is the source of evil as well as good. This view is
characteristic of Hebrew "monism," namely, that the ultimate source of evil as well as good
is God (see Isa.45.6–7). **9:** Wisdom recognizes its limits (see 30.4). The limitation on the nature
of human knowledge can induce some despair in the sage, for he can no longer perceive any
purpose in life. This despair is increased greatly in Eccles. **10:** The king functions as the ultimate
source of appeal for redress (20.8; see 1 Kgs.3.16–28). **12:** The idea of righteousness as a royal
pedestal is an Egyptian motif as well. **15:** *Rain-cloud:* the seasonal rain was eagerly awaited to
assure the grain crop; hence the comparison with the favorable countenance of the king.

24 Kind words are like dripping honey,
   sweetness on the tongue and health
   for the body.

25 A road may seem straightforward to
   a man,
   yet may end as the way to death.

26 The labourer's appetite is always
   plaguing him,
   his hunger spurs him on.

27 A scoundrel repeats evil gossip;
   it is like a scorching fire on his lips.

28 Disaffection stirs up quarrels,
   and tale-bearing breaks up
   friendship.

29 A man of violence draws others on
   and leads them into lawless ways.

30 The man who narrows his eyes is
   disaffected at heart,
   and a close-lipped man is bent on
   mischief.

31 Grey hair is a crown of glory,
   and it is won by a virtuous life.

32 Better be slow to anger than a
   fighter,
   better govern one's temper than
   capture a city.

33 The lots may be cast into the lap,
   but the issue depends wholly on the
   LORD.

17 Better a dry crust and concord with it
   than a house full of feasting and
   strife.

2 A wise slave may give orders to a
   disappointing son
   and share the inheritance with the
   brothers.

3 The melting-pot is for silver and the
   crucible for gold,
   but it is the LORD who assays the
   hearts of men.

4 A rogue gives a ready ear to
   mischievous talk,
   and a liar listens to slander.

5 A man who sneers at the poor
   insults his Maker,
   and he who gloats over another's
   ruin will answer for it.

6 Grandchildren are the crown of old
   age,
   and sons are proud of their fathers.

7 Fine talk is out of place in a boor,

how much more is falsehood in the
   noble!

He who offers a bribe finds it work   8
   like a charm,
he prospers in all he undertakes.

He who conceals another's offence   9
   seeks his goodwill,
but he who harps on something
   breaks up friendship.

A reproof is felt by a man of   10
   discernment
more than a hundred blows by a
   stupid man.

An evil man is set only on   11
   disobedience,
but a messenger without mercy will
   be sent against him.

Better face a she-bear robbed of her   12
   cubs
than a stupid man in his folly.

If a man repays evil for good,   13
evil will never quit his house.

Stealing water starts a quarrel;   14
drop a dispute before you bare your
   teeth.

To acquit the wicked and condemn   15
   the righteous,
both are abominable in the LORD's
   sight.

What use is money in the hands of   16
   a stupid man?
Can he buy wisdom if he has no
   sense?

A friend is a loving companion at   17
   all times,
and a brother is born to share
   troubles.

A man is without sense who gives a   18
   guarantee
and surrenders himself to another as
   surety.

He who loves strife loves sin.   19
He who builds a lofty entrance
   invites thieves.

A crooked heart will come to no   20
   good,
and a mischievous tongue will end
   in disaster.

A stupid man is the bane of his   21
   parent,
and his father has no joy in a
   boorish son.

30: *Narrows:* restricts himself to his evil purpose, and, being *close-lipped*, acts secretly to achieve his aim. **33:** The decision of God was learned by casting *lots* (called Urim and Thummim, Exod.28.15 n.) which were in the care of priests. **17.8:** *Bribe:* the meaning here is a proper gift,

22 A merry heart makes a cheerful
   countenance,
   but low spirits sap a man's strength.
23 A wicked man accepts a bribe under
   his cloak
   to pervert the course of justice.
24 Wisdom is never out of sight of a
   discerning man,
   but a stupid man's eyes are roving
   everywhere.
25 A stupid son exasperates his father
   and is a bitter sorrow to the mother
   who bore him.
26 Again, to punish the righteous is not
   good
   and it is wrong to inflict blows on
   men of noble mind.
27 Experience uses few words;
   discernment keeps a cool head.
28 Even a fool, if he holds his peace, is
   thought wise;
   keep your mouth shut and show your
   good sense.

18 The man who holds aloof seeks
   every pretext
   to bare his teeth in scorn at
   competent people.
2 The foolish have no interest in
   seeking to understand,
   but prefer to display their wit.
3 When wickedness comes in, in
   comes contempt;
   with loss of honour comes reproach.
4 The words of a man's mouth are a
   gushing torrent,
   but deep is the water in the well of
   wisdom.ʷ
5 It is not good to show favour to the
   wicked
   or to deprive the righteous of justice.
6 When the stupid man talks,
   contention follows;
   his words provoke blows.
7 The stupid man's tongue is his
   undoing;
   his lips put his life in jeopardy.
8 A gossip's whispers are savoury
   morsels,
   gulped down into the inner man.
9 Again, the lazy worker is own
   brother

to the man who enjoys destruction.
The name of the Lord is a tower of   10
   strength,
where the righteous may run for
   refuge.
A rich man's wealth is his strong   11
   city,
a towering wall, so he supposes.
Before disaster comes, a man is   12
   proud,
but the way to honour is humility.
To answer a question before you   13
   have heard it out
is both stupid and insulting.
A man's spirit may sustain him in   14
   sickness,
but if the spirit is wounded, who
   can mend it?
Knowledge comes to the discerning   15
   mind;
the wise ear listens to get knowledge.
A gift opens the door to the giver   16
and gains access to the great.
In a lawsuit the first speaker seems   17
   right,
until another steps forward and
   cross-questions him.
Cast lots, and settle a quarrel,   18
and so keep litigants apart.
A reluctant brother is more   19
   unyielding than a fortress,
and quarrels are stubborn as the
   bars of a castle.
A man may live by the fruit of his   20
   tongue,
his lips may earn him a livelihood.
The tongue has power of life and   21
   death;
make friends with it and enjoy its
   fruits.
Find a wife, and you find a good   22
   thing;
so you will earn the favour of the
   Lord.
The poor man speaks in a tone of   23
   entreaty,
and the rich man gives a harsh
   answer.
Some companions are good only for   24
   idle talk,
but a friend may stick closer than a
   brother.

w The words . . . wisdom: *prob. rdg.; inverting phrases.*

not a dishonest one; the verse commends generosity. **18.10–11:** The trust in God, here expressed
in *name*, is more dependable than a trust in wealth. See 2 Sam.22.3; Ps.18.2. **24:** See 17.17.

19 Better be poor and above reproach
than rich and crooked in speech.

2 Again, desire without knowledge is
not good;
the man in a hurry misses the way.

3 A man's own folly wrecks his life,
and then he bears a grudge against
the LORD.

4 Wealth makes many friends,
but a man without means loses the
friend he has.

5 A false witness will not escape
punishment,
and one who utters nothing but lies
will not go free.

6 Many curry favour with the great;
a lavish giver has the world for his
friend.

7 A poor man's brothers all dislike him,
how much more is he shunned by
his friends!
Practice in evil makes the perfect
scoundrel;
the man who talks too much meets
his deserts.

8 To learn sense is true self-love;
cherish discernment and make sure
of success.

9 A false witness will not escape
punishment,
and one who utters nothing but lies
will perish.

10 A fool at the helm is out of place,
how much worse a slave in
command of men of rank!

11 To be patient shows intelligence;
to overlook faults is a man's glory.

12 A king's rage is like a lion's roar,
his favour like dew on the grass.

13 A stupid son is a calamity to his
father;
a nagging wife is like water dripping
endlessly.

14 Home and wealth may come down
from ancestors,
but an intelligent wife is a gift from
the LORD.

15 Laziness is the undoing of the
worthless;
idlers must starve.

16 To keep the commandments keeps a
man safe,
but scorning the way of the LORD
brings death.

17 He who is generous to the poor
lends to the LORD;

he will repay him in full measure.

18 Chasten your son while there is hope
for him,
but be careful not to flog him to
death.

19 A man's ill temper brings its own
punishment;
try to save him, and you make
matters worse.

20 Listen to advice and accept
instruction,
and you will die a wise man.

21 A man's heart may be full of
schemes,
but the LORD's purpose will prevail.

22 Greed is a disgrace to a man;
better be a poor man than a liar.

23 The fear of the LORD is life;
he who is full of it will rest
untouched by evil.

24 The sluggard plunges his hand in the
dish
but will not so much as lift it to his
mouth.

25 Strike an arrogant man, and he
resents it like a fool;
reprove an understanding man, and
he understands what you mean.

26 He who talks his father down vexes
his mother;
he is a son to bring shame and
disgrace on them.

27 A son who ceases to accept
correction
is sure to turn his back on the
teachings of knowledge.

28 A rascally witness perverts justice,
and the talk of the wicked fosters
mischief.

29 There is a rod in pickle for the
arrogant,
and blows ready for the stupid man's
back.

20 Wine is an insolent fellow, and
strong drink makes an uproar;
no one addicted to their company
grows wise.

2 A king's threat is like a lion's roar;
one who ignores it is his own worst
enemy.

3 To draw back from a dispute is
honourable;
it is the fool who bares his teeth.

4 The sluggard who does not plough
in autumn

goes begging at harvest and gets nothing.

5 Counsel in another's heart is like deep water,
but a discerning man will draw it up.

6 Many a man protests his loyalty,
but where will you find one to keep faith?

7 If a man leads a good and upright life,
happy are the sons who come after him!

8 A king seated on the judgement-throne
has an eye to sift all that is evil.

9 Who can say, 'I have a clear conscience;
I am purged from my sin'?

10 A double standard in weights and measures
is an abomination to the LORD.

11 Again, a young man is known by his actions,
whether his conduct is innocent or guilty.*x*

12 The ear that hears, the eye that sees,
the LORD made them both.

13 Love sleep, and you will end in poverty;
keep your eyes open, and you will eat your fill.

14 'A bad bargain!' says the buyer to the seller,
but off he goes to brag about it.

15 There is gold in plenty and coral too,
but a wise word is a rare jewel.

16 Take a man's garment when he pledges his word for a stranger
and hold that as a pledge for the unknown person.

17 Bread got by fraud tastes good,
but afterwards it fills the mouth with grit.

18 Care is the secret of good planning;
wars are won by skilful strategy.

19 A gossip will betray secrets;*y*
have nothing to do with a tattler.

20 If a man reviles father and mother,
his lamp will go out when darkness comes.

21 If you begin by piling up property in haste,
it will bring you no blessing in the end.

22 Do not think to repay evil for evil,
wait for the LORD to deliver you.

23 A double standard in weights is an abomination to the LORD,
and false scales are not good in his sight.

24 It is the LORD who directs a man's steps;
how can mortal man understand the road he travels?

25 It is dangerous to dedicate a gift rashly
or to make a vow and have second thoughts.

26 A wise king sifts out the wicked
and turns back for them the wheel of fortune.

27 The LORD shines into a man's very soul,
searching out his inmost being.

28 A king's guards are loyalty and good faith,
his throne is upheld by righteousness.

29 The glory of young men is their strength,
the dignity of old men their grey hairs.

30 A good beating purges the mind,
and blows chasten the inmost being.

21 The king's heart is under the LORD's hand;
like runnels of water, he turns it wherever he will.

2 A man may think that he is always right,
but the LORD fixes a standard for the heart.

3 Do what is right and just;
that is more pleasing to the LORD than sacrifice.

4 Haughty looks and a proud heart—
these sins mark a wicked man.

5 Forethought and diligence are sure of profit;
the man in a hurry is as sure of poverty.

x Prob. rdg.; Heb. upright.
y Or He who betrays secrets is a gossip.

20.16: *A man's garment:* demand a significant pledge if it is made by a man on behalf of a stranger. Ordinarily a garment taken in pledge had to be returned at sundown (Exod.22.26). **25:** Gifts *dedicated* to sanctuaries were accompanied by solemn oaths, not to be taken lightly; see Ps.15.4. **27:** *Shines:* God plants moral discernment within every man. **21.3:** See Hos.6.6.

6 He who makes a fortune by telling
lies
runs needlessly into the toils of
death.

7 The wicked are caught up in their
own violence,
because they refuse to do what is
just.

8 The criminal's conduct is tortuous;
straight dealing is a sign of integrity.

9 Better to live in a corner of the
house-top
than have a nagging wife and a
brawling household.

10 The wicked man is set on evil;
he has no pity to spare for his
friend.

11 The simple man is made wise when
he sees the insolent punished,
and learns his lesson when the wise
man prospers.

12 The just God*z* makes the wicked
man's home childless;*a*
he overturns the wicked and ruins
them.

13 If a man shuts his ears to the cry of
the helpless,
he will cry for help himself and not
be heard.

14 A gift in secret placates an angry
man;
a bribe slipped under the cloak
pacifies great wrath.

15 When justice is done, all good men
rejoice,
but it brings ruin to evildoers.

16 A man who takes leave of common
sense
comes to rest in the company of the
dead.

17 Love pleasure and you will beg your
bread;
a man who loves wine and oil will
never grow rich.

18 The wicked man serves as a ransom
for the righteous,
so does a traitor for the upright.

19 Better to live alone in the desert
than with a nagging and ill-
tempered wife.

20 The wise man has his home full of
fine and costly treasures;
the stupid man is a mere spendthrift.

21 Persevere in right conduct and
loyalty
and you shall find life and honour.

22 A wise man climbs into a city full of
armed men
and undermines its strength and its
confidence.

23 Keep a guard over your lips and
tongue
and keep yourself out of trouble.

24 The conceited man is haughty, his
name is insolence;
conceit and impatience are in all he
does.

25 The sluggard's cravings will be the
death of him,
because his hands refuse to work;

26 all day long his cravings go
unsatisfied,
while the righteous man gives
without stint.

27 The wicked man's sacrifice is an
abomination to the LORD;
how much more when he offers it
with vileness at heart!

28 A lying witness will perish,
but he whose words ring true will
leave children behind him.

29 A wicked man puts a bold face on it,
whereas the upright man secures his
line of retreat.

30 Face to face with the LORD,
wisdom, understanding, counsel go
for nothing.

31 A horse may be made ready for the
day of battle,
but victory comes from the LORD.

22 A good name is more to be desired
than great riches;
esteem is better than silver or gold.

2 Rich and poor have this in common:
the LORD made them both.

3 A shrewd man sees trouble coming
and lies low;
the simple walk into it and pay the
penalty.

4 The fruit of humility is the fear of
God
with riches and honour and life.

z Or The just man.
a makes . . . childless: *prob. rdg.; Heb.* considers the
wicked man's home.

9: *Corner:* may mean a room apart. 18: *Ransom:* the price society pays; righteous men are
clearly discerned by comparison with the unrighteous.

5　The crooked man's path is set with
　　snares and pitfalls;
　　the cautious man will steer clear of
　　　them.
6　Start a boy on the right road,
　　and even in old age he will not
　　　leave it.
7　The rich lord it over the poor;
　　the borrower becomes the lender's
　　　slave.
　　The man who sows injustice reaps
　　　trouble,
　　and the end of his work will be the
　　　rod.*b*
9　The kindly man will be blessed,
　　for he shares his food with the poor.
10　Drive out the insolent man, and
　　　strife goes with him;
　　if he sits on the bench, he makes a
　　　mockery of justice.
11　The Lord loves a sincere man;
　　but you will make a king your
　　　friend with your fine phrases.
12　The Lord keeps watch over every
　　　claim at law,
　　and overturns the scoundrel's case.
13　The sluggard protests, 'There's a
　　　lion outside;
　　I shall get myself killed in the
　　　street.'
14　The words of an adulteress are like
　　　a deep pit;
　　those whom the Lord has cursed
　　　will fall into it.
15　Folly is deep-rooted in the heart of
　　　a boy;
　　a good beating will drive it right out
　　　of him.
16　Oppression of the poor may bring
　　　gain to a man,
　　but giving to the rich leads only to
　　　penury.

Thirty wise sayings

17　The sayings of the wise:

　　Pay heed and listen to my words,

open your mind to the knowledge I
　　impart;
to keep them in your heart will be a　18
　　pleasure,
and then you will always have them
　　ready on your lips.
I would have you trust in the Lord　19
and so I tell you these things this
　　day for your own good.
Here I have written out for you　　20
　　thirty sayings,
full of knowledge and wise advice,
to impart to you a knowledge of the　21
　　truth,
that you may take back a true
　　report*c* to him who sent you.

Never rob a helpless man because　22
　　he is helpless,
nor ill-treat a poor wretch in court;
for the Lord will take up their cause　23
and rob him who robs them of their
　　livelihood.
Never make friends with an angry　24
　　man
nor keep company with a bad-
　　tempered one;
be careful not to learn his ways,　　25
or you will find yourself caught in a
　　trap.
Never be one to give guarantees,　　26
or to pledge yourself as surety for
　　another;
for if you cannot pay, beware:　　　27
your bed will be taken from under
　　you.
Do not move the ancient boundary-　28
　　stone
which your forefathers set up.
You see a man skilful at his craft:　29
he will serve kings, he will not serve
　　common men.

When you sit down to eat with a　　**23**
　　ruling prince,
be sure to keep your mind on what
　　is before you,

b the rod: or the threshing.
c Prob. rdg.; Heb. adds words of truth.

22.17–24.22(34): Thirty wise sayings. This section is dependent on the Egyptian work by
Amen-em-ope, from which ten sayings have been derived and adapted to the Israelite setting.
17–21: A prologue. The MT's reading (v. 20), formerly rendered "excellent things," has been
corrected to "thirty sayings"—a very minor change in the Heb.—on the basis of the Amen-em-
ope, where, as here, there are found both prologue and conclusion (for the latter see 24.21–22).
17: *To my words:* MT reads "to the words of the wise," possibly a superscription belonging
elsewhere and misplaced here. **28:** The prohibition against removing a landmark is in Amen-
em-ope, ch. 6; compare Prov.23.10; Deut.19.14 and 27.17. **23.1:** *What:* i.e. who: in whose

2   and if you are a greedy man,
     cut your throat first.

3   Do not be greedy for his dainties,
     for they are not what they seem.

4   Do not slave to get wealth;*d*
     be a sensible man, and give up.

5   Before you can look round, it will
          be gone;
     it will surely grow wings
     like an eagle, like a bird in the
          sky.

6   Do not go to dinner with a miser,*e*
     do not be greedy for his dainties;

7   for they will stick in your*f* throat
          like a hair.
     He will bid you eat and drink,
     but his heart is not with you;

8   you will bring up the mouthful you
          have eaten,
     and your winning words will have
          been wasted.

9   Hold your tongue in the hearing of
          a stupid man;
     for he will despise your words of
          wisdom.

10   Do not move the ancient boundary-
          stone
     or encroach on the land of orphans:

11   they have a powerful guardian
     who will take up their cause against
          you.

12   Apply your mind to instruction
     and open your ears to knowledge
          when it speaks.

13   Do not withhold discipline from a
          boy;
     take the stick to him, and save him
          from death.

14   If you take the stick to him yourself,
     you will preserve him from the jaws
          of death.

15   My son, if you are wise at heart,
     my heart in its turn will be glad;

16   I shall rejoice with all my soul
     when you speak plain truth.

17   Do not try to emulate sinners;

envy only those who fear the LORD
          day by day;

18   do this, and you may look forward
     to the future,
     and your thread of life will not be
          cut short.

19   Listen, my son, listen, and become
          wise;
     set your mind on the right course.

20   Do not keep company with
          drunkards
     or those who are greedy for the
          flesh-pots;

21   for drink and greed will end in
          poverty,
     and drunken stupor goes in rags.

22   Listen to your father, who gave you
          life,
     and do not despise your mother
          when she is old.

23   Buy truth, never sell it;
     buy wisdom, instruction, and
          understanding.

24   A good man's father will rejoice
     and he who has a wise son will
          delight in him.

25   Give your father and your mother
          cause for delight,
     let her who bore you rejoice.

26   My son, mark my words,
     and accept my guidance with a will.

27   A prostitute is a deep pit,
     a loose woman a narrow well;

28   she lies in wait like a robber
     and betrays her husband with man
          after man.

29   Whose is the misery? whose the
          remorse?
     Whose are the quarrels and the
          anxiety?
     Who gets the bruises without
          knowing why?
     Whose eyes are bloodshot?

d to get wealth: or for an invitation to a feast.
e Or a man with an evil eye.
f Prob. rdg.; Heb. his.

presence you are. **2:** *Cut your throat:* curb your appetite. **5:** *Eagle:* Amen-em-ope here reads geese, but since Palestine has no such fowl, the Heb. text substitutes eagle. **10:** *Ancient:* Amen-em-ope reads widow (in Heb. *'almana*); *'olam,* "ancient," is a scribe's error; "widow's bound-ary" is a more suitable parallel for *the land of orphans.* **11:** The next-of-kin was responsible for the welfare of the defenseless victim of the powerful (see Lev.25.25; Ruth 4.1–6); here the *guardian* is God. **20:** Meat was eaten by most people only on special occasions; hence the danger of greed when it was served. **27:** *Deep pit:* dug as a trap for wild animals. **28:** See 7.12.

30 Those who linger late over their
        wine,
    those who are always trying some
        new spiced liquor.
31 Do not gulp down the wine, the
        strong red wine,
    when the droplets form on the side
        of the cup;*g*
32 in the end it will bite like a snake
    and sting like a cobra.
33 Then your eyes see strange sights,
    your wits and your speech are
        confused;
34 you become like a man tossing out
        at sea,
    like one who clings to*h* the top of
        the rigging;
35 you say, 'If it lays me flat, what do
        I care?
    If it brings me to the ground, what
        of it?
    As soon as I wake up,
    I shall turn to it again.'

24 Do not emulate wicked men
    or long to make friends with them;
2   for violence is all they think of,
    and all they say means mischief.

3   Wisdom builds the house,
    good judgement makes it secure,
4   knowledge furnishes the rooms
    with all the precious and pleasant
        things that wealth can buy.

5   Wisdom prevails over strength,
    knowledge over brute force;
6   for wars are won by skilful
        strategy,
    and victory is the fruit of long
        planning.

7   Wisdom is too high for a fool;
    he dare not open his mouth in court.

8   A man who is bent on mischief
    gets a name for intrigue;
9   the intrigues of foolish men misfire,
    and the insolent man is odious to
        his fellows.

10 If your strength fails on a lucky*i*
        day,

how helpless will you be on a day
    of disaster!

When you see a man being dragged   11
    to be killed, go to his rescue,
and save those being hurried away
    to their death.
If you say, 'But I do not know this   12
    man',
God, who fixes a standard for the
    heart, will take note.
God who watches you—be sure he
    will know;
he will requite every man for what
    he does.

Eat honey, my son, for it is good,   13
and the honeycomb so sweet upon
    the tongue.
Make wisdom too your own;   14
if you find it, you may look forward
    to the future,
and your thread of life will not be
    cut short.

Do not lie in wait like a felon at the   15
    good man's house,
or raid his farm.
Though the good man may fall seven   16
    times, he is soon up again,
but the rascal is brought down by
    misfortune.
Do not rejoice when your enemy   17
    falls,
do not gloat when he is brought
    down;
or the LORD will see and be   18
    displeased with you,
and he will cease to be angry with
    him.

Do not vie with evildoers   19
or emulate the wicked;
for wicked men have no future to   20
    look forward to;
their embers will be put out.

My son, fear the LORD and grow   21
    rich,
but have nothing to do with men of
    rank,

g Prob. rdg.; Heb. adds it runs smoothly to and fro.
h clings to: prob. rdg.; Heb. lies on.
i lucky: prob. rdg.; Heb. om.

24.11–22: Passive virtue is inadequate. See Ps.82.4; Isa.58.6,7; 1 Jn.3.16. **16:** V.22; Ps.34.19.
17: See Job 31.29; Obad.12.

22   they will bring about disaster
      without warning;
      who knows what ruin such men
          may cause*j*?

More proverbs of Solomon transcribed **25**
by the men of Hezekiah king of Judah:

23   More sayings of wise men:

      Partiality in dispensing justice is not
          good.

The glory of God is to keep things   2
    hidden
but the glory of kings is to fathom
    them.

24   A judge who pronounces a guilty
          man innocent
      is cursed by all nations, all peoples
          execrate him;

The heavens for height, the earth*k*   3
    for depth:
unfathomable is the heart of a king.

25   but for those who convict the guilty
          all will go well,
      they will be blessed with prosperity.

Rid silver of its impurities,   4
then it may go to*l* the silversmith;
rid the king's presence of wicked men, 5
and his throne will rest firmly on
    righteousness.

26   A straightforward answer
      is as good as a kiss of friendship.

Do not put yourself forward in the   6
    king's presence

27   First put all in order out of doors
      and make everything ready on the
          land;
      then establish your house and home.

or take your place among the great;
for it is better that he should say to   7
    you, 'Come up here',
than move you down to make room
    for a nobleman.

28   Do not be a witness against your
          neighbour without good reason
      nor misrepresent him in your
          evidence.

Be in no hurry to tell everyone what   8
    you have seen,
or it will end in bitter reproaches
    from your friend.

29   Do not say,
      'I will do to him what he has done
          to me;
      I will requite him for what he has
          done.'

Argue your own case with your   9
    neighbour,
but do not reveal another man's
    secrets,
or he will reproach you when he   10
    hears of it

30   I passed by the field of an idle man,
      by the vineyard of a man with no
          sense.

and your indiscretion will then be
    beyond recall.

31   I looked, and it was all dried up,
      it was overgrown with thistles
      and covered with weeds,
      and the stones of its walls had been
          torn down.

Like apples of gold set in silver   11
    filigree
is a word spoken in season.

Like a golden earring or a necklace   12
    of Nubian gold
is a wise man whose reproof finds
    attentive ears.

32   I saw and I took good note,
      I considered and learnt the lesson:

33   a little sleep, a little slumber,
          a little folding of the hands in rest,

34   and poverty will come upon you
          like a robber,
      want like a ruffian.

Like the coolness of snow in harvest   13
is a trusty messenger to those who
    send him.*m*

j they . . . cause: *or* they will come to sudden disaster;
    who knows what the ruin of such men will be.
k *Or* the underworld.
l then it may go to: *or* and it will come out bright for.
m *Prob. rdg.; Heb. adds* refreshing his master.

24.23–34: Miscellaneous proverbs, plus a narrative about a sluggard. **30–31:** Compare
Isa.5.1–7. **34:** Identical with 6.11.
25.1–31.9: Other collections of wise sayings. Chs. 25–29 are a second collection of "Proverbs
of Solomon." The reign of Hezekiah was 715–687 B.C. The official phrase *men of Hezekiah*
suggests that this king took an active interest in the welfare of the Wisdom tradition, as had
Solomon before him. **7:** Compare Lk.14.7–11. **12:** *Nubian:* Ethiopic. **14:** In a subtropical
climate the first *clouds* promising *rain* after the many dry months are greeted eagerly and become

14　Like clouds and wind that bring no
　　　rain
　　is the man who boasts of gifts he
　　　never gives.

15　A prince may be persuaded by
　　　patience,
　　and a soft tongue may break down
　　　solid bone.[n]

16　If you find honey, eat only what you
　　　need,
　　too much of it will make you sick;

17　be sparing in visits to your
　　　neighbour's house,
　　if he sees too much of you, he will
　　　dislike you.

18　Like a club or a sword or a sharp
　　　arrow
　　is a false witness who denounces his
　　　friend.

19　Like a tooth decayed or a foot
　　　limping
　　is a traitor relied on in the day of
　　　trouble.

20　Like one who dresses[o] a wound with
　　　vinegar,
　　so is the sweetest of singers to the
　　　heavy-hearted.

21　If your enemy is hungry, give him
　　　bread to eat;
　　if he is thirsty, give him water to
　　　drink;

22　so you will heap glowing coals on
　　　his head,
　　and the LORD will reward you.

23　As the north wind holds back the
　　　rain,
　　so an angry glance holds back
　　　slander.

24　Better to live in a corner of the
　　　house-top
　　than have a nagging wife and a
　　　brawling household.

25　Like cold water to the throat when
　　　it is dry
　　is good news from a distant land.

26　Like a muddied spring or a tainted
　　　well
　　is a righteous man who gives way to
　　　a wicked one.

27　A surfeit of honey is bad for a man,
　　and the quest for honour is
　　　burdensome.

28　Like a city that has burst out of its
　　　confining walls[p]
　　is a man who cannot control his
　　　temper.

26　Like snow in summer or rain at
　　　harvest,
　　honour is unseasonable in a stupid
　　　man.

2　Like a fluttering sparrow or a
　　　darting swallow,
　　groundless abuse gets nowhere.

3　The whip for a horse, the bridle for
　　　an ass,
　　the rod for the back of a fool!

4　Do not answer a stupid man in the
　　　language of his folly,
　　or you will grow like him;

5　answer a stupid man as his folly
　　　deserves,
　　or he will think himself a wise man.

6　He who sends a fool on an errand
　　cuts his own leg off and displays the
　　　stump.

7　A proverb in the mouth of stupid
　　　men
　　dangles helpless as a lame man's
　　　legs.

8　Like one who gets the stone caught
　　　in his sling
　　is he who bestows honour on a fool.

9　Like a thorn that pierces a
　　　drunkard's hand
　　is a proverb in a stupid man's
　　　mouth.

10　Like an archer who shoots at any
　　　passer-by[q]
　　is one who hires a stupid man or a
　　　drunkard.

11　Like a dog returning to its vomit
　　is a stupid man who repeats his
　　　folly.

12　Do you see that man who thinks
　　　himself so wise?
　　There is more hope for a fool than
　　　for him.

13　The sluggard protests, 'There is a
　　　lion[r] in the highway,
　　a lion at large in the streets.'

[n] solid bone: *or* authority.
[o] *Prob. rdg.; Heb. adds* a garment on a cold day.
[p] *Or* that is breached and left unwalled.
[q] passer-by: *transposed from end of verse.*
[r] *Or* snake.

---

particularly disappointing when no rain falls. **15:** Compare Ecclus.28.17. **22:** *Glowing coals* may have had a cultic origin in Egypt. The figure is used in Rom.12.20. **26.1:** Rainfall in Palestine is limited to certain seasons, so that the weather is highly predictable. **4–5:** The two

14 A door turns on its hinges,
   a sluggard on his bed.

15 A sluggard plunges his hand in the
   dish
   but is too lazy to lift it to his mouth.

16 A sluggard is wiser in his own eyes
   than seven men who answer
   sensibly.

17 Like a man who seizes a passing cur
   by the ears
   is he who meddles in another's
   quarrel.

19*s* A man who deceives another
   and then says, 'It was only a joke',

18 is like a madman shooting at
   random
   his deadly darts and arrows.

20 For lack of fuel a fire dies down
   and for want of a tale-bearer a
   quarrel subsides.

21 Like bellows for the coal and fuel
   for the fire
   is a quarrelsome man for kindling
   strife.

22 A gossip's whispers are savoury
   morsels
   gulped down into the inner man.

23 Glib speech that covers a spiteful
   heart
   is like glaze spread on earthenware.

24 With his lips an enemy may speak
   you fair
   but inwardly he harbours deceit;

25 when his words are gracious, do not
   trust him,
   for seven abominations fill his heart;

26 he may cloak his enmity in
   dissimulation,
   but his wickedness is shown up
   before the assembly.

27 If he digs a pit, he will fall into it;
   if he rolls a stone, it will roll back
   upon him.

28 A lying tongue makes innocence
   seem guilty,
   and smooth words conceal their
   sting.

27 Do not flatter yourself about
   tomorrow,
   for you never know what a day will
   bring forth.

2 Let flattery come from a stranger,
   not from yourself,
from the lips of an outsider and not
   from your own

3 Stone is a burden and sand a dead
   weight,
   but to be vexed by a fool is more
   burdensome than either.

4 Wrath is cruel and anger is a
   deluge;
   but who can stand up to jealousy?

5 Open reproof is better
   than love concealed.

6 The blows a friend gives are well
   meant,
   but the kisses of an enemy are
   perfidious.

7 A man full-fed refuses honey,
   but even bitter food tastes sweet to
   a hungry man.

8 Like a bird that strays far from its
   nest
   is a man far from his home.

9 Oil and perfume bring joy to the
   heart,
   but cares torment a man's very soul.

10 Do not neglect your own friend or
   your father's;*t*
   a neighbour at hand is better than a
   brother far away.

11 Be wise, my son, then you will bring
   joy to my heart,
   and I shall be able to forestall my
   critics.

12 A shrewd man sees trouble coming
   and lies low;
   the simple walk into it and pay the
   penalty.

13 Take a man's garment when he
   pledges his word for a stranger
   and hold that as a pledge for the
   unknown person.

14 If one man greets another too
   heartily,
   he may give great offence.

15 Endless dripping on a rainy day—
   that is what a nagging wife is like.

16 As well try to control the wind as to
   control her!
   As well try to pick up oil in one's
   fingers!

17 As iron sharpens iron,
   so one man sharpens the wits of
   another.

s Verses 18 and 19 transposed.
t Prob. rdg.; Heb. adds or how should you enter your
brother's house in the day of your ruin?

---

proverbs supplement each other: they are not in contradiction. **27.13:** See 20.16. **15:** See 19.13.

18 He who guards the fig-tree will eat
    its fruit,
    and he who watches his master's
    interests will come to honour.

19 As face answers face reflected in the
    water,
    so one man's heart answers
    another's.

20 Sheol and Abaddon are insatiable;
    a man's eyes too are never satisfied.

21 The melting-pot is for silver and the
    crucible for gold,
    but praise is the test of character.

22 Pound a fool with pestle and
    mortar,*u*
    his folly will never be knocked out
    of him.

23 Be careful to know your own sheep
    and take good care of your flocks;

24 for possessions do not last for ever,
    nor will a crown endure to endless
    generations.

25 The grass disappears, new shoots are
    seen
    and the green growth on the hills is
    gathered in;

26 the lambs clothe you,
    the he-goats are worth the price of a
    field,

27 while the goats' milk is enough for
    your food
    and nourishment for your maidens.

28 The wicked man runs away with no
    one in pursuit,
    but the righteous is like a young
    lion in repose.

2 It is the fault of a violent man that
    quarrels start,
    but they are settled by a man of
    discernment.

3 A tyrant oppressing the poor
    is like driving rain which ruins the
    crop.

4 The lawless praise wicked men;
    the law-abiding contend with them.

5 Bad men do not know what justice
    is,
    but those who seek the LORD know
    everything good.

6 Better be poor and above reproach
    than rich and crooked.

7 A discerning son observes the law,

but one who keeps riotous company
    wounds his father.

8 He who grows rich by lending at
    discount or at interest
    is saving for another who will be
    generous to the poor.

9 If a man turns a deaf ear to the law,
    even his prayers are an
    abomination.

10 He who tempts the upright into
    evil courses
    will himself fall into the pit he has
    dug.
    The honest shall inherit a fortune,
    but the wicked shall inherit nothing.

11 The rich man may think himself
    wise,
    but a poor man of discernment sees
    through him.

12 When the just are in power, there
    are great celebrations,*v*
    but when the wicked come to the
    top, others are downtrodden.

13 Conceal your faults, and you will
    not prosper;
    confess and give them up, and you
    will find mercy.

14 Happy the man who is scrupulous
    in conduct,
    but he who hardens his heart falls
    into misfortune.

15 Like a starving lion or a thirsty bear
    is a wicked man ruling a helpless
    people.

16 The man who is stupid and grasping
    will perish,
    but he who hates ill-gotten gain will
    live long.

17 A man charged with bloodshed
    will jump into a well to escape
    arrest.

18 Whoever leads an honest life will be
    safe,
    but a rogue will fail, one way or
    another.

19 One who cultivates his land has
    plenty to eat;
    idle pursuits lead to poverty.

20 A man of steady character will
    enjoy many blessings,
    but one in a hurry to grow rich will
    not go unpunished.

u Prob. rdg.; Heb. adds with groats.
v Or there is great pageantry.

28.6: See 14.31 n. **13:** *Mercy:* from men. Divine mercy plays little role in Wisdom literature.

21 To show favour is not good;
    but men will do wrong for a mere
        crust of bread.

22 The miser*w* is in a hurry to grow
        rich,
    never dreaming that want will
        overtake him.

23 Take a man to task and in the end
        win more thanks
    than the man with a flattering
        tongue.

24 To rob your father or mother and
        say you do no wrong
    is no better than wanton destruction.

25 A self-important*x* man provokes
        quarrels,
    but he who trusts in the LORD grows
        fat and prosperous.

26 It is plain stupidity to trust in one's
        own wits,
    but he who walks the path of wisdom
        will come safely through.

27 He who gives to the poor will never
        want,
    but he who turns a blind eye gets
        nothing but curses.

28 When the wicked come to the top,
        others are pulled down;*y*
    but, when they perish, the righteous
        come into power.

29 A man who is still stubborn after
        much reproof
    will suddenly be broken past
        mending.

2   When the righteous are in power
        the people rejoice,
    but they groan when the wicked
        hold office.

3   A lover of wisdom brings joy to his
        father,
    but one who keeps company with
        harlots squanders his wealth.

4   By just government a king gives his
        country stability,
    but by forced contributions he
        reduces it to ruin.

5   A man who flatters his neighbour
    is spreading a net for his feet.

6   An evil man is ensnared by his sin,*z*
    but a righteous man lives and
        flourishes.

7   The righteous man is concerned for
        the cause of the helpless,
    but the wicked understand no such
        concern.

8   Arrogance can inflame a city,
    but wisdom averts the people's
        anger.

9   If a wise man goes to law with a
        fool,
    he will meet abuse or derision, but
        get no remedy.

10 Men who have tasted blood hate an
        honest man,
    but the upright set much store by
        his life.

11 A stupid man gives free rein to his
        anger;
    a wise man waits and lets it grow
        cool.

12 If a prince listens to falsehood,
    all his servants will be wicked.

13 Poor man and oppressor have this
        in common:
    what happiness each has comes from
        the LORD.

14 A king who steadfastly deals out
        justice to the weak
    will be secure for ever on his throne.

15 Rod and reprimand impart wisdom,
    but a boy who runs wild brings
        shame on his mother.

16 When the wicked are in power, sin
        is in power,
    but the righteous will gloat over
        their downfall.

17 Correct your son, and he will be a
        comfort to you
    and bring you delights of every kind.

18 Where there is no one in authority,*a*
        the people break loose,
    but a guardian of the law keeps
        them on the straight path.

19 Mere words will not keep a slave
        in order;
    he may understand, but he will not
        respond.

20 When you see someone over-eager
        to speak,*b*
    there will be more hope for a fool
        than for him.

21 Pamper a slave from boyhood,
    and in the end he will prove
        ungrateful.

22 A man prone to anger provokes a
        quarrel
    and a hot-head is always doing
        wrong.

w Or The man with the evil eye.   *x Or* grasping.
y are pulled down: *or* hide themselves.
z An evil . . . sin: *or* When an evil man steps out a
    trap awaits him.
a Or no vision.   *b Or* someone hasty in business.

23 Pride will bring a man low;
a man lowly in spirit wins honour.
24 He who goes shares with a thief is
his own enemy:
he hears himself put on oath and
dare not give evidence.
25 A man's fears will prove a snare to
him,
but he who trusts in the LORD has
a high tower of refuge.
26 Many seek audience of a prince,
but in every case the LORD decides.
27 The righteous cannot abide an
unjust man,
nor the wicked a man whose
conduct is upright.

30 Sayings of Agur son of Jakeh from
Massa:*c*

This is the great man's very word:
I am weary, O God,
I am weary and worn out;
2 I am a dumb brute, scarcely a man,
without a man's powers of
understanding;
3 I have not learnt wisdom
nor have I received knowledge from
the Holy One.
4 Who has ever gone up to heaven
and come down again?
Who has cupped the wind in the
hollow of his hands?
Who has bound up the waters in the
fold of his garment?
Who has fixed the boundaries of the
earth?
What is his name or his son's name,
if you know it?

5 God's every promise has stood the
test:
he is a shield to all who seek refuge
with him.
6 Add nothing to his words,
or he will expose you for a liar.
7 Two things I ask of thee;
do not withhold them from me
before I die.

8 Put fraud and lying far from me;
give me neither poverty nor wealth,
provide me only with the food I
need.
9 If I have too much, I shall deny thee
and say, 'Who is the LORD?'
If I am reduced to poverty, I shall
steal
and blacken the name of my God.

10 Never disparage a slave to his
master,
or he will speak ill of you, and you
will pay for it.

11 There is a sort of people who
defame their fathers
and do not speak well of their own
mothers;
12 a sort who are pure in their own
eyes
and yet are not cleansed of their
filth;
13 a sort—how haughty are their looks,
how disdainful their glances!
14 A sort whose teeth are swords,
their jaws are set with knives,
they eat the wretched out of the
country
and the needy out of house and
home.*d*

15 The leech has two daughters;
'Give', says one, and 'Give', says the
other.

Three things there are which will never
be satisfied,
four which never say, 'Enough!'
16 The grave and a barren womb,*e*
a land thirsty for water
and fire that never says, 'Enough!'

17 The eye that mocks a father or
scorns a mother's old age*f*
will be plucked out by magpies
or eaten by the vulture's young.

c from Massa: prob. rdg.; (cp. 31. 1); Heb. the oracle.
d house and home: prob. rdg.; Heb. man.
e Or a woman's desire.
f old age: prob. rdg.; Heb. unintelligible.

30.1–9: The skeptical words of Agur (vv. 1–4), a non-Israelite (Tfn. *c*), followed by pious advice
(5–6) and a prayer (7–9), form an appendix. **1:** *Massa:* probably a place in Arabia (Gen.25.14).
The word also means "oracle." *Weary . . . worn out:* Some interpreters read here the proper
names Ithiel and Ucal; the translation has altered the extremely difficult text. **3–4:** The style
is ironical, scorning those who know too much about God, but the mood is agonized sadness.
30.10–33: Another appendix. Some of these numerical sayings may originally have been

18 Three things there are which are too
    wonderful for me,
    four which I do not understand:
19 the way of a vulture in the sky,
    the way of a serpent on the rock,
    the way of a ship out at sea,
    and the way of a man with a girl.

20 The way of an unfaithful wife is this:
    she eats, then she wipes her mouth
    and says, 'I have done no harm.'

21 At three things the earth shakes,
    four things it cannot bear:
22 a slave turned king,
    a churl gorging himself,
23 a woman unloved when she is
    married,
    and a slave-girl displacing her
    mistress.

24 Four things there are which are
    smallest on earth
    yet wise beyond the wisest:
25 ants, a people with no strength,
    yet they prepare their store of food
    in the summer;
26 rock-badgers, a feeble folk,
    yet they make their home among the
    rocks;
27 locusts, which have no king,
    yet they all sally forth in detachments;
28 the lizard, which can be grasped in
    the hand,
    yet is found in the palaces of kings.

29 Three things there are which are
    stately in their stride,
    four which are stately as they move:
30 the lion, a hero among beasts,
    which will not turn tail for anyone;
31 the strutting cock and the he-goat;
    and a king going forth to lead his
    army.*g*

32 If you are churlish and arrogant
    and fond of filthy talk, hold your
    tongue;

33 for wringing out the milk produces
    curd
    and wringing the nose produces blood,
    so provocation leads to strife.

Sayings of Lemuel king of Massa, **31**
which his mother taught him:

What, O my son, what shall I say to 2
    you,
    you, the child of my womb and
    answer to my prayers?
Do not give the vigour of your 3
    manhood to women
    nor consort with those who make
    eyes at*h* kings.
It is not for kings, O Lemuel, not 4
    for kings to drink wine
    nor for princes to crave strong
    drink;
if they drink, they will forget rights 5
    and customs
    and twist the law against their
    wretched victims.
Give strong drink to the desperate 6
    and wine to the embittered;
such men will drink and forget their 7
    poverty
    and remember their trouble no
    longer.
Open your mouth and speak up for 8
    the dumb,
    against the suit of any that oppose
    them;
open your mouth and pronounce 9
    just sentence
    and give judgement for the wretched
    and the poor.

A capable wife

Who can find a capable wife? 10
Her worth is far beyond coral.

---

g going forth to lead his army: prob. rdg.: Heb. un-
intelligible.
h who make eyes at: prob. rdg.; Heb. unintelligible.

---

riddles (e.g. vv. 15b–16). **18–19**: The point seems to be the absence of all trace of the movement
made. **20**: *Eats*: commits adultery. The words are to be taken as symbolic of sex relations.
    31.1–9: The advice of the queen mother, here an appendix, is paralleled in Egyptian royal
instructions. **1**: *Lemuel*: he is unknown. **4–9**: Those whose situation is desperate resort to
strong drink; the king must not imbibe, for he is to vindicate the cause of the *poor* and so is
not to impair his *judgement* by strong drink. **8–9**: A characteristic Hebrew concern for the lowly.
    31.10–31: A capable wife. An acrostic poem on the ideal wife, possibly meant as instruction
to girls (for other alphabetic poems see Lam. chs. 1–4; Pss.9–10; 119, etc.). **10**: *Who . . . wife*: a
rhetorical question, equivalent to the statement, "A man who finds a capable wife . . ."

11   Her husband's whole trust is in her, when he takes his seat with the
      and children are not lacking.   elders of the land.

12   She repays him with good, not evil, She weaves linen and sells it,   24
      all her life long.   and supplies merchants with their

13   She chooses wool and flax   sashes.
      and toils at her work.   She is clothed in dignity and power   25

14   Like a ship laden with merchandise, and can afford to laugh at
      she brings home food from far off.   tomorrow.

15   She rises while it is still night   When she opens her mouth, it is to   26
      and sets meat before her household.*i*   speak wisely,

16   After careful thought she buys a   and loyalty is the theme of her
         field   teaching.
      and plants a vineyard out of her   She keeps her eye on the doings of   27
         earnings.   her household

17   She sets about her duties with   and does not eat the bread of
         vigour   idleness.
      and braces herself for the work.   Her sons with one accord call her   28

18   She sees that her business goes well,   happy;
      and never puts out her lamp at   her husband too, and he sings her
         night.   praises:

19   She holds the distaff in her hand, 'Many a woman shows how capable   29
      and her fingers grasp the spindle.   she is;*j*

20   She is open-handed to the wretched but you excel them all.'
      and generous to the poor.   Charm is a delusion and beauty   30

21   She has no fear for her household   fleeting;
         when it snows,   It is the God-fearing woman who is
      for they are wrapped in two cloaks.   honoured.

22   She makes her own coverings,   Extol her for the fruit of all her toil, 31
      and clothing of fine linen and   and let her labours bring her honour
         purple.   in the city gate.

23   Her husband is well known in the   *i Prob. rdg.; Heb. adds* and a prescribed portion for
         city gate   her maidens.
                                          j Or Many daughters show how capable they are.

707

ECCLESIASTES

This book stands alone in the Hebrew Bible, both in theology and style. It asserts that God and his ways are inscrutable, and that this recognition is the only valid intellectual stance for man, who cannot comprehend why the same fate befalls the good and the bad, man and beast. Since death ignores all distinctions, life in the long run is empty, profitless.

As in Egyptian royal instructions, the style depends on frequent references to personal experience and reflection. Despair over existence is expressed in repeated refrains and phrases, brief stories and maxims. In service of his basic pessimistic outlook, the author's favorite expressions are "emptiness," "under the sun," "labor and toil," "chasing the wind," "man's portion."

The book predates the entrance of vivid views of afterlife into Jewish thought. However, the Hebrew employed here is a late type (fourth or third century B.C.). The ascription of the book to Solomon is, therefore, unlikely; yet Solomon's name may have opened the way for its inclusion in the canon, while at the same time reinforcing the theme of life's emptiness.

The noun applied to the author, Hebrew *Qoheleth*, here rendered "Speaker," is taken by some to be a proper name. But the noun seems related to a root which means "to assemble," and the Greek name Ecclesiastes derives from the idea of someone addressing an assembly (see 1.1 n.). The place of composition was probably Palestine.

The book moves a step beyond Job in attacking man's overconfidence about his wisdom; yet it encourages man to enjoy life while he has the strength to do so. Glosses which relieve the gloom (and, indeed, the impiety) of the book seem to have been added in later times at 3.17; 7.18; 8.12–13; 11.9b; 12.9–11.

The emptiness of all endeavour

1 THE WORDS OF THE SPEAKER, THE son of David, king in Jerusalem.
2 Emptiness, emptiness, says the
3 Speaker, emptiness, all is empty. What does man gain from all his labour and
4 his toil here under the sun? Generations come and generations go, while the earth endures for ever.
5 The sun rises and the sun goes down; back it returns to its place*a* and rises
6 there again. The wind blows south, the wind blows north, round and round it
7 goes and returns full circle. All streams run into the sea, yet the sea never overflows; back to the place from which the streams ran they return to run again.
8 All things are wearisome;*b* no man can speak of them all. Is not the eye surfeited with seeing, and the ear sated
9 with hearing? What has happened will happen again, and what has been done will be done again, and there is nothing new under the sun. Is there anything of **10** which one can say, 'Look, this is new'? No, it has already existed, long ago before our time. The men of old are not **11** remembered, and those who follow will not be remembered by those who follow them.

I, the Speaker, ruled as king over **12** Israel in Jerusalem; and in wisdom I **13** applied my mind to study and explore all that is done under heaven. It is a sorry business that God has given men to busy themselves with. I have seen all **14** the deeds that are done here under the sun; they are all emptiness and chasing the wind. What is crooked cannot **15** become straight; what is not there cannot be counted. I said to myself, 'I have **16** amassed great wisdom, more than all my predecessors on the throne in Jerusalem; I have become familiar with wisdom and knowledge.' So I **17**

a back . . . place: prob. rdg.; Heb. to its place panting.
b Prob. rdg.; Heb. weary.

1.1–6.12: **The emptiness of all endeavor.** Inasmuch as meaningless repetition characterizes life, there is no profit to toil.

1.1–11: **Title and prologue. 1:** The unusual Heb. form for "*the speaker*" indicates that an office, not a name, is meant. **2:** The Heb. phrase *emptiness, emptiness* is a superlative, just as Song of Songs means "the best song." **3:** *Under the sun:* on earth. **4:** *Earth endures* while the "lord of the earth," man, passes on; see Gen.1.28. **8:** *Things:* or words.

1.12–2.26: **Neither wisdom nor pleasure is profitable.** Since one fate comes to all, there is no gain in work, knowledge, or sensuality. **13:** The occupation of the wise man is dismissed as *sorry business,* even if a gift of God. **14:** *Chasing:* with nothing to show for one's effort (Hos. 12.1). **16:** *Predecessors:* the fiction of Solomonic authorship is here abandoned; Solomon had

708

applied my mind to understand wisdom and knowledge, madness and folly, and I came to see that this too is chasing the wind. For in much wisdom is much vexation, and the more a man knows, the more he has to suffer.

2 I said to myself, 'Come, I will plunge into pleasures and enjoy myself'; but this too was emptiness. Of laughter I said, 'It is madness!' And of pleasure, 'What is the good of that?' So I sought to stimulate myself with wine, in the hope of finding out what was good for men to do under heaven throughout the brief span of their lives. But my mind was guided by wisdom, not blinded by*c* folly. I undertook great works; I built myself houses and planted vineyards; I made myself gardens and parks and planted all kinds of fruit-trees in them; I made myself pools of water to irrigate a grove of growing trees; I bought slaves, male and female, and I had my home-born slaves as well; I had possessions, more cattle and flocks than any of my predecessors in Jerusalem; I amassed silver and gold also, the treasure of kings and provinces; I acquired singers, men and women, and all that man delights in.*d* I was great, greater than all my predecessors in Jerusalem; and my wisdom stood me in good stead. Whatever my eyes coveted, I refused them nothing, nor did I deny myself any pleasure. Yes indeed, I got pleasure from all my labour, and for all my labour this was my reward. Then I turned and reviewed all my handiwork, all my labour and toil, and I saw that everything was emptiness and chasing the wind, of no profit under the sun.

I set myself to look at wisdom and at madness and folly.*e* Then I perceived that wisdom is more profitable than folly, as light is more profitable than darkness: the wise man has eyes in his head, but the fool walks in the dark. Yet I saw also that one and the same fate overtakes them both. So I said to myself, 'I too shall suffer the fate of the fool. To what purpose have I been wise? What*f* is the profit of it? Even this', I said to myself, 'is emptiness. The wise man is remembered no longer than the fool, for, as the passing days multiply,*g* all will be forgotten. Alas, wise man and fool die the same death!' So I came to hate life, since everything that was done here under the sun was a trouble to me; for all is emptiness and chasing the wind. So I came to hate all my labour and toil here under the sun, since I should have to leave its fruits to my successor. What sort of a man will he be who succeeds me, who inherits what others have acquired?*h* Who knows whether he will be a wise man or a fool? Yet he will be master of all the fruits of my labour and skill here under the sun. This too is emptiness.

Then I turned and gave myself up to despair, reflecting upon all my labour and toil here under the sun. For anyone who toils with wisdom, knowledge, and skill must leave it all to a man who has spent no labour on it. This too is emptiness and utterly wrong. What reward has a man for all his labour, his scheming, and his toil here under the sun? All his life long his business is pain and vexation to him; even at night his mind knows no rest. This too is emptiness. There is nothing better for a man to do than to eat and drink and enjoy himself in return for his labours. And yet I saw that this comes from the hand of God. For without him who can enjoy his food, or who can be anxious? God gives wisdom and knowledge and joy to the man who pleases him, while to the sinner is given the trouble of gathering and amassing wealth only to hand it over to someone else who pleases God. This too is emptiness and chasing the wind.

c not blinded by: *prob. rdg.; Heb.* to grasp.
d Prob. rdg.; Heb. adds two unintelligible words.
e The rest of verse 12 transposed to follow verse 18.
f Prob. rdg.; Heb. Then.
g for . . . multiply: *prob. rdg.; Heb.* because already.
h What sort . . . acquired: *see note on verse 12.*

only one predecessor in Jerusalem (contrast 2.7,9). **2.10:** The author intends his readers to assume that the king possessed the means and power of fulfilling his will, yet at the same time he renders a negative judgment on "Solomon and all his glory." **23:** *Rest* is forbidden even the good man. **24:** Similar advice is given in the Babylonian text, Gilgamesh Epic; see also Isa.22.13. **26:** Except for the refrain this may be a pious gloss, or a quotation to be refuted.

3 FOR EVERYTHING ITS SEASON, AND FOR
every activity under heaven its time:

2 a time to be born and a time to die;
   a time to plant and a time to uproot;
3 a time to kill and a time to heal;
   a time to pull down and a time to
      build up;
4 a time to weep and a time to laugh;
   a time for mourning and a time for
      dancing;
5 a time to scatter stones and a time to
      gather them;
   a time to embrace and a time to
      refrain from embracing;
6 a time to seek and a time to lose;
   a time to keep and a time to throw
      away;
7 a time to tear and a time to mend;
   a time for silence and a time for
      speech;
8 a time to love and a time to hate;
   a time for war and a time for peace.

9 What profit does one who works get
10 from all his labour? I have seen the
   business that God has given men to
11 keep them busy. He has made everything to suit its time; moreover he has
   given men a sense of time past and
   future, but no comprehension of God's
12 work from beginning to end. I know
   that there is nothing good for man[i]
   except to be happy and live the best life
13 he can while he is alive. Moreover, that
   a man should eat and drink and enjoy
   himself, in return for all his labours, is
14 a gift of God. I know that whatever
   God does lasts for ever; to add to it or
   subtract from it is impossible. And he
   has done it all in such a way that men
15 must feel awe in his presence. Whatever
   is has been already,[j] and whatever is to
   come has been already, and God
   summons each event back in its turn.
16 Moreover I saw here under the sun
   that, where justice ought to be, there
   was wickedness, and where righteous-

ness ought to be, there was wickedness.
I said to myself, 'God will judge the just 17
man and the wicked equally; every
activity and[k] every purpose has its
proper time.' I said to myself, 'In deal- 18
ing with men it is God's purpose[l] to
test them and to see what they truly
are.[m] For man is a creature of chance 19
and the beasts are creatures of chance,
and one mischance awaits them all:
death comes to both alike. They all
draw the same breath. Men have no
advantage over beasts; for everything
is emptiness. All go to the same place: 20
all came from the dust, and to the dust
all return. Who knows whether the 21
spirit[n] of man goes upward or whether
the spirit[n] of the beast goes downward
to the earth?' So I saw that there is 22
nothing better than that a man should
enjoy his work, since that is his lot. For
who can bring him through to see what
will happen next?

Again, I considered all the acts of **4**
oppression here under the sun; I saw
the tears of the oppressed, and I saw
that there was no one to comfort them.
Strength was on the side of their
oppressors, and there was no one to
avenge them. I counted the dead happy 2
because they were dead, happier than
the living who are still in life. More for- 3
tunate than either I reckoned the man
yet unborn, who had not witnessed the
wicked deeds done here under the sun.
I considered all toil and all achievement 4
and saw that it comes from rivalry between man and man. This too is
emptiness and chasing the wind. The 5
fool folds his arms and wastes away.
Better one hand full and peace of mind, 6
than both fists full and toil that is
chasing the wind.

i for man: prob. rdg., cp. 2. 24; Heb. in them.
j Or Whatever has been already is.
k Prob. rdg.; Heb. and upon.
l it is God's purpose: prob. rdg.; Heb. obscure.
m Prob. rdg.; Heb. adds they to them.
n Or breath.

3.1–15: On timeliness. Every deed, thought, or feeling has an appropriate moment, but man
cannot discover it. **11:** *Time past and future:* man can know the facts of history and in a sense
the events of the immediate future, yet can fail to grasp God's role in history.
3.16–4.3: Tears of the oppressed. Injustice abounds, and none comes to the defense of the
weak, so that death is to be preferred to life. **16:** *Wickedness:* perhaps bribery at the court.
19: Although man rules the beast, *death* strikes both man and beast indiscriminately. **21:** The
sage is agnostic, recognizing that life after death is problematic. **4.1:** Compare Isa.25.8 for the
prophetic word of comfort to the tearful.
4.4–16: Advantages of community. Concerted effort is better than solitary endeavor. **5–6:** Two

7 Here again, I saw emptiness under
8 the sun: a lonely man without a friend, without son or brother, toiling endlessly yet never satisfied with his wealth—'For whom', he asks, 'am I toiling and denying myself the good things of life?' This too is emptiness, a
9 sorry business. Two are better than one; they receive a good reward for
10 their toil, because, if one falls, the other[o] can help his companion up again; but alas for the man who falls alone with no partner to help him up.
11 And, if two lie side by side, they keep each other warm; but how can one
12 keep warm by himself? If a man is alone, an assailant may overpower him, but two can resist; and a cord of three strands is not quickly snapped.
13 Better a young man poor and wise than a king old and foolish who will
14 listen to advice no longer. A man who leaves prison may well come to be king, though born a pauper in his future
15 kingdom. But I have studied all life here under the sun, and I saw his place
16 taken by yet another young man, and no limit set to the number of the subjects whose master he became. And he in turn will be no hero to those who come after him. This too is emptiness and chasing the wind.
5 Go carefully when you visit the house of God. Better draw near in obedience than offer the sacrifice of
2 fools, who sin without a thought. Do not rush into speech, let there be no hasty utterance in God's presence. God is in heaven, you are on earth; so let
3 your words be few. The sensible man has much business on his hands; the fool talks and it is so much chatter.
4 When you make a vow to God, do not be slow to pay it, for he has no use for
5 fools; pay whatever you vow. Better not vow at all than vow and fail to pay.
6 Do not let your tongue lead you into sin, and then say before the angel of God that it was a mistake; or God will

be angry at your words, and all your achievements will be brought to nothing.[p] You must fear God.   7
If you witness in some province the   8
oppression of the poor and the denial of right and justice, do not be surprised at what goes on, for every official has a higher one set over him, and the highest[q] keeps watch over them all. The best thing for a country is a king   9
whose[r] own lands are well tilled.
The man who loves money can never   10
have enough, and the man who is in love with great wealth enjoys no return from it. This too is emptiness. When   11
riches multiply, so do those who live off them; and what advantage has the owner, except to look at them? Sweet 12
is the sleep of the labourer whether he eats little or much; but the rich man owns too much and cannot sleep. There 13
is a singular evil here under the sun which I have seen: a man hoards wealth to his own hurt, and then that   14
wealth is lost through an unlucky venture, and the owner's son left with nothing. As he came from the womb of 15
mother earth, so must he return, naked as he came; all his toil produces nothing which he can take away with him. This 16
too is a singular evil: exactly as he came, so shall he go, and what profit does he get when his labour is all for the wind? What is more, all his days   17
are overshadowed; gnawing anxiety and great vexation are his lot, sickness[s] and resentment. What I have seen is   18
this: that it is good and proper for a man to eat and drink and enjoy himself in return for his labours here under the sun, throughout the brief span of life which God has allotted him. Moreover, 19
it is a gift of God that every man to

o if one falls, the other: *prob. rdg.*; *Heb. obscure.*
p *Prob. rdg.*; *Heb. adds* for in a multitude of dreams and empty things and many words.
q for every . . . the highest: *or though every . . . over him, the Highest . . .*
r whose: *prob. rdg.*; *Heb. for.*
s sickness: *prob. rdg.*; *Heb. and his sickness.*

proverbs are employed in a didactic setting. **9–10:** In companionship there is *reward*, some profit to one's action. **16:** Since memory is short, the *hero* is soon forgotten.
   5.1–7: Passive ethics. Act so as not to call God's attention to you. **6:** *Angel:* that is, the angel responsible for collecting what was vowed. **7:** The wise man's motto was *fear* of God according to Prov.1.7 and 9.10.
   5.8–6.12: Oppression and anxiety. Society is so ordered that injustice will be observed by high officials; in money there is no profit, only sleeplessness. **15:** This verse may be a citation

Wisdom and folly compared

whom he has granted wealth and riches and the power to enjoy them should accept his lot and rejoice in his labour.
20 He will not dwell overmuch upon the passing years; for God fills his*t* time with joy of heart.

6 Here is an evil under the sun which I have seen, and it weighs heavy upon
2 men. Consider the man to whom God grants wealth, riches, and substance,*u* and who lacks nothing that he has set his heart on: if God has not given him the power to enjoy these things, but a stranger enjoys them instead, that is
3 emptiness and a grave disorder. A man may have a hundred children and live a long life; but however many his days may be, if he does not get satisfaction from the good things of life and in the end receives no burial, then I maintain that the still-born child is in better case
4 than he. Its coming is an empty thing, it departs into darkness, and in darkness
5 its name is hidden; it has never seen the sun or known anything,*v* yet its state is
6 better than his. What if a man should live a thousand years twice over, and never prosper? Do not both go to one place?
7 The end of all man's toil is but to fill his belly, yet his appetite is never satis-
8 fied. What advantage then in facing life has the wise man over the fool, or the
9 poor man for all his experience? It is better to be satisfied with what is before your eyes than give rein to desire; this too is emptiness and chasing the wind.
10 Whatever has already existed has been given a name, its nature is known; a man cannot contend with what is
11 stronger than he. The more words one uses the greater is the emptiness of it all; and where is the advantage to a man?
12 For who can know what is good for a man in this life, this brief span of empty existence through which he passes like a shadow? Who can tell a man what is to happen next here under the sun?

A GOOD NAME SMELLS SWEETER THAN 7 the finest ointment, and the day of death is better than the day of birth. Better to visit the house of mourning 2 than the house of feasting; for to be mourned is the lot of every man, and the living should take this to heart. Grief is better than laughter: a sad face 3 may go with a cheerful heart. Wise 4 men's thoughts are at home in the house of mourning, but a fool's thoughts in the house of mirth. It is better to listen 5 to a wise man's rebuke than to the praise of fools. For the laughter of a 6 fool is like the crackling of thorns under a pot. This too is emptiness. Slander 7 drives a wise man crazy and breaks a strong man's*w* spirit. Better the end of 8 anything than its beginning; better patience than pride. Do not be quick 9 to show resentment; for resentment is nursed by fools. Do not ask why the 10 old days were better than these; for that is a foolish question. Wisdom is better 11 than possessions and an advantage to all who see the sun. Better have wisdom 12 behind you than money; wisdom profits men by giving life to those who know her.

Consider God's handiwork; who can 13 straighten what he has made crooked? When things go well, be glad; but when 14 things go ill, consider this: God has set the one alongside the other in such a way that no one can find out what is to happen next.*x* In my empty existence I 15 have seen it all, from a righteous man perishing in his righteousness to a wicked man growing old in his wicked-ness. Do not be over-righteous and do 16 not be over-wise. Why make yourself a laughing-stock? Do not be over-wicked 17 and do not be a fool. Why should you die before your time? It is good to hold 18

t his: prob. rdg.; Heb. om.   u Or honour.   v Or it.
w strong man's: prob. rdg.; Heb. obscure.
x find out . . . next: or hold him responsible.

---

of Job 1.21. **19:** *Lot:* fate; lot and fate are close in idea. **6.3:** *Long life* and many *children* were signs of God's favor and hence sources of happiness. A lack of proper *burial* was considered a curse. **4:** On the advantage of the *still-born*, see Job 3.11.

7.1–12: Seven proverbs on relative value. The task of the wise man was to evaluate various alternatives, in essence, to make distinctions as to better options. **12b:** This part of the verse may be a gloss, inasmuch as the author elsewhere (7.23–24) denies that Wisdom can be known or that she profits man.

7.13–29: On premature death. Man should not so behave as to bring about an early death, despite the fact that no woman is trustworthy (and few men!). **14:** The practice of divining

on to the one thing and not lose hold of the other; for a man who fears God will
19 succeed both ways. Wisdom makes the wise man stronger than the ten rulers of
20 a city. The world contains no man so righteous that he can do right always
21 and never do wrong.*y* Moreover, do not pay attention to everything men say, or you may hear your servant
22 disparage you; for you know very well how many times you yourself have
23 disparaged others. All this I have put to the test of wisdom. I said, 'I am resolved to be wise', but wisdom was beyond my
24 grasp—whatever has happened lies beyond our grasp, deep down, deeper than man can fathom.

25   I went on to reflect, I set my mind*z* to inquire and search for wisdom and for the reason in things, only to discover that it is folly to be wicked and madness
26 to act like a fool. The wiles of a woman I find mightier*a* than death; her heart is a trap to catch you and her arms are fetters. The man who is pleasing to God may escape her, but she will catch a
27 sinner. 'See,' says the Speaker, 'this is what I have found, reasoning things
28 out one by one, after searching long without success: I have found one man in a thousand worth the name, but I have not found one woman among
29 them all. This alone I have found, that God, when he made man, made him straightforward, but man invents endless subtleties of his own.'

8 Who is wise enough for all this? Who knows the meaning of anything? Wisdom lights up a man's face, but grim
2 looks make a man hated.*b* Do as the king commands you, and if you have to swear by God, do not be precipitate.
3 Leave the king's presence and do not persist in a thing which displeases him;
4 he does what he chooses. For the king's word carries authority. Who can
5 question what he does? Whoever obeys a command will come to no harm. A wise man knows in his heart the right

time and method for action. There is a 6 time and a method for every enterprise, although man is greatly troubled by 7 ignorance of the future; who can tell him what it will bring? It is not in man's 8 power to restrain the wind,*c* and no one has power over the day of death. In war no one can lay aside his arms, no wealth will save its possessor. All this 9 I have seen, having applied my mind to everything done under the sun. There was a time when one man had power over another and could make him suffer. It was then that I saw wicked 10 men approaching and even entering*d* the holy place; and they went about the city priding themselves on having done right. This too is emptiness. It is be- 11 cause sentence upon a wicked act is not promptly carried out that men do evil so boldly. A sinner may do wrong*e* and 12 live to old age, yet I know that it will be well with those who fear God: their fear of him ensures this, but it will not 13 be well with a wicked man nor will he live long; the man who does not fear God is a mere shadow. There is an 14 empty thing found on earth: when the just man gets what is due to the unjust, and the unjust what is due to the just. I maintain that this too is emptiness. So I commend enjoyment, since there is 15 nothing good for a man to do here under the sun but to eat and drink and enjoy himself; this is all that will remain with him to reward his toil throughout the span of life which God grants him here under the sun. I 16 applied my mind to acquire wisdom and to observe the business which goes on upon earth, when man never closes an eye in sleep day or night; and always 17 I perceived that God has so ordered it that man should not be able to discover

y can do . . . wrong: *or* prospers without ever making a mistake.
z *Prob. rdg.; Heb.* adds to know and.
a *Or* more bitter.
b make . . . hated: *prob. rdg.; Heb. obscure.*
c *Or* to retain the breath of life.
d approaching . . . entering: *prob. rdg.; Heb. obscure.*
e *Prob. rdg.; Heb.* adds an unintelligible word.

---

the future is attacked. **26:** See Prov.7.10–27. **28:** Ecclus.25.13–24 advances this misogynistic attitude considerably (see also Zech.5.7–8). **29:** This verse affirms the goodness of man at creation.

   8.1–9.6: The king and his subjects. Respect for royal authority is prudent, even though injustice prevails. **12–13:** These verses seem to be a gloss affirming divine justice. **17:** God has sealed off from the wise man the object of his inquiry; hence the sage may be deceived because of the partial knowledge permitted him.

what is happening here under the sun. However hard a man may try, he will not find out; the wise man may think that he knows, but he will be unable to find the truth of it.

9 I applied my mind to all this, and I understood that the righteous and the wise and all their doings are under God's control; but is it love or hatred? No man knows. Everything that con-
2 fronts him, everything is empty, since one and the same fate befalls every one, just and unjust alike, good and bad, clean and unclean, the man who offers sacrifice and the man who does not. Good man and sinner fare alike, the man who can take an oath and the man
3 who dares not. This is what is wrong in all that is done here under the sun: that one and the same fate befalls every man. The hearts of men are full of evil; madness fills their hearts all through their lives, and after that they go down
4 to join the dead. But for a man who is counted among the living there is still hope: remember, a live dog is better
5 than a dead lion. True, the living know that they will die; but the dead know nothing. There are no more rewards for them; they are utterly forgotten.
6 For them love, hate, ambition,*f* all are now over. Never again will they have any part in what is done here under the sun.
7 Go to it then, eat your food and enjoy it, and drink your wine with a cheerful heart; for already God has accepted
8 what you have done. Always be dressed in white and never fail to anoint your
9 head. Enjoy life with a <u>woman you love</u> <u>all the days of your allotted span here</u> <u>under the sun, empty as they are;*g* for</u> <u>that is your lot while you live and</u>
10 <u>labour here under the sun.</u> Whatever task lies to your hand, do it with all your might; because in Sheol, for which you are bound, there is neither doing nor thinking, neither understanding
11 nor wisdom. One more thing I have observed here under the sun: speed does not win the race nor strength the battle. Bread does not belong to the wise, nor wealth to the intelligent, nor success to the skilful; time and chance
12 govern all. Moreover, no man knows when his hour will come; like fish caught in a net, like a bird taken in a snare, so men are trapped when bad times come suddenly.

13 This too is an example of wisdom as I have observed it here under the sun,
14 and notable I find it. There was a small town with few inhabitants, and a great king came to attack it; he besieged it and constructed great siege-works
15 against it. There was in it a poor wise man, and he alone might have saved the town by his wisdom, but no one remembered that poor wise man.
16 'Surely', I said to myself, 'wisdom is better than strength.' But the poor man's wisdom was despised, and his
17 words went unheeded. A wise man who speaks his mind calmly is more to be heeded than a commander shouting
18 orders among fools. Wisdom is better than weapons of war, and one mistake can undo many things done well.

10 Dead flies make the perfumer's sweet ointment turn rancid and ferment; so can a little folly make wisdom lose its
2 worth. The mind of the wise man faces right, but the mind of the fool faces left.
3 Even when he walks along the road, the fool shows no sense and calls everyone else*h* a fool. If your ruler breaks out in
4 anger against you, do not resign your post; submission makes amends for
5 great mistakes. There is an evil that I have observed here under the sun, an error for which a ruler is responsible:
6 the fool given high office, but*i* the great
7 and the rich in humble posts. I have seen slaves on horseback and men of high rank going on foot like slaves.

f Or passion.
g Prob. rdg.; Heb. adds all your days, empty as they are.
h calls everyone else: or tells everyone he is.
i but: prob. rdg.; Heb. om.

9.7–12: The wise man's counsel. Enjoy your wife, since time and chance befall everyone. **8:** The festive garment and the *anointed head* are signs of the good life. **10:** *Sheol:* the land of the dead, of shadowy existence, but not, in Hebrew thought, of punishment.

    9.13–18: The waste of wisdom. The point of this passage is that a ready means of deliverance, the *wisdom* of a *poor man,* was not called on. **18:** The sense of *and* here is equivalent to "but."

    10.1–20: Maxims derived from experience. The whole of life is brought under Wisdom's control. **2:** *Right and left* are to be understood here in a moral sense. For a somewhat different use of *right* and *left,* see Mt.25.33–46.

8 The man who digs a pit may fall into it, and he who pulls down a wall may be 9 bitten by a snake. The man who quarries stones may strain himself, and the woodcutter runs a risk of injury. 10 When the axe is blunt and has not first[j] been sharpened, then one must use more force; the wise man has a better 11 chance of success. If a snake bites before it is charmed, the snake-charmer loses his fee.

12 A wise man's words win him favour, 13 but a fool's tongue is his undoing. He begins by talking nonsense and ends in 14 mischief run mad. The fool talks on and on; but no man knows what is coming, and who can tell him what will come 15 after that? The fool wearies himself to death[k] with all his labour, for he does not know the way to town.

16 Woe betide the land when a slave has become its king, and its princes feast in 17 the morning. Happy the land when its king is nobly born, and its princes feast at the right time of day, with self- 18 control, and not as drunkards. If the owner is negligent the rafters collapse, and if he is idle the house crumbles 19 away. The table has its pleasures, and wine makes a cheerful life; and money 20 is behind it all. Do not speak ill of the king in your ease, or of a rich man in your bedroom; for a bird may carry your voice, and a winged messenger may repeat what you say.

11 Send your grain across the seas, and 2 in time you will get a return. Divide your merchandise among seven ventures, eight maybe, since you do not know what disasters may occur on 3 earth.[l] If the clouds are heavy with rain, they will discharge it on the earth; whether a tree falls south or north, it 4 must lie as it falls. He who watches the wind will never sow, and he who keeps an eye on the clouds will never reap. 5 You do not know how a pregnant woman comes to have a body and a living spirit in her womb; nor do you know how God, the maker of all things, works. In the morning sow your seed 6 betimes, and do not stop work until evening, for you do not know whether this or that sowing will be successful, or whether both alike will do well.

Advice to a young man

THE LIGHT OF DAY IS SWEET, AND 7 pleasant to the eye is the sight of the sun; if a man lives for many years, he 8 should rejoice in all of them. But let him remember that the days of darkness will be many. Everything that is to come will be emptiness. Delight in your 9 boyhood, young man, make the most of the days of your youth; let your heart and your eyes show you the way; but remember that for all these things God will call you to account. Banish dis- 10 content from your mind, and shake off the troubles of the body; boyhood and the prime of life are mere emptiness.

Remember your Creator in the days 12 of your youth, before the time of trouble comes and the years draw near when you will say, 'I see no purpose in them.'[m] Remember him before the sun 2 and the light of day give place to darkness, before the moon and the stars grow dim, and the clouds return with the rain—when the guardians of the 3 house tremble, and the strong men stoop, when the women grinding the meal cease work because they are few, and those who look through the windows look no longer, when the street- 4 doors are shut, when the noise of the mill is low, when the chirping of the sparrow grows faint[n] and the songbirds fall silent;[o] when men are afraid 5

j first: *prob. rdg.; Heb.* face.
k fool . . . death: *prob. rdg.; Heb.* obscure.
l *Or* on land.
m *Or* I have no pleasure in them.
n grows faint: *prob. rdg.; Heb.* obscure.
o *Prob. rdg.; Heb.* sink low.

11.1–10: Admonitions. One cannot foresee the result of a course of action, but he must be willing to take the risk of failure. Youth is to be especially prized. **8:** *Darkness:* Sheol; see 9.10 n.
12.1–8: An allegory on old age. By means of a rich store of metaphors, not all of them fully clear, the author characterizes the twilight years. **1:** The unusual Heb. word translated *Creator* can have a double meaning, one, "cistern," referring to one's wife (as in Prov.5.15,18–19), the other "grave," thus hinting at the positive and negative themes of the book. **2:** *Clouds* may refer to poor eyesight. **3:** The *guardians* . . . are the arms; the *strong men* are the knees; the *women grinding* are the teeth; and the *windows* are the eyes. **4:** The *doors* are the ears, the *chirping* . . . is sleeplessness, the *songbirds* are the voice. **5:** *Almond* . . . : gray hair; *locust*, creaking of bones.

of a steep place and the street is full of terrors, when the blossom whitens on the almond-tree and the locust's paunch is swollen and caper-buds have no more zest. For man goes to his everlasting home, and the mourners go about the 6 streets. Remember him before the silver cord is snapped*p* and the golden bowl is broken, before the pitcher is shattered at the spring and the wheel broken at 7 the well, before the dust returns to the earth as it began and the spirit*q* returns 8 to God who gave it. Emptiness, emptiness, says the Speaker, all is empty.

9 So the Speaker, in his wisdom, continued to teach the people what he knew. He turned over many maxims in 10 his mind and sought how best to set them out. He chose his words to give pleasure, but what he wrote was the honest truth. The sayings of the wise 11 are sharp as goads, like nails driven home; they lead the assembled people, for they come from one shepherd. One 12 further warning, my son: the use of books is endless, and much study is wearisome.

This is the end of the matter: you 13 have heard it all. Fear God and obey his commands; there is no more to man than this. For God brings every- 14 thing we do to judgement, and every secret, whether good or bad.

p is snapped: *prob. rdg.; Heb. unintelligible.*
q Or breath.

6: *Cord* and *bowl:* life, and when broken, death. **7:** *To God who gave it:* 3.20–21. See also Gen.3.19.
12.9–14: Postscript. One addition (vv. 9–12) praises the author for his integrity, and even suggests that the wisdom set forth is sufficient; hence *the use of books is endless.* Earlier translations read, "of making many books there is no end." **13–14:** A second addition reflects a usual piety, and is in tension with the rest of the book.

THE SONG OF SONGS

Unique in the Bible, this collection of songs sensitively touches several major chords in the love life of a young man and a maiden. It is an anthology which plays on a wide range of themes: love's awakening, the description of the beloved, the enticement, the surrender of the embrace, the pain of separation, the joy of coming together again, the wedding ceremony. The book was early regarded as fully allegorical, a view not surprising because of the presence of some obvious symbolism, as is noted.

In its own way, the book extols the virtues of deep rather than transient love. There is no discernible overall flow of action or plot, although the positioning of the various songs creates a definite dramatic effect.

The traditional ascription of authorship to King Solomon (1.1) may have come about because of the several appearances of his name in the text. Scholars have dated the songs as early as the tenth century B.C. and as late as the Greek period, the fourth century B.C., with a postexilic date at least for the final redaction the usual view. There are no historical allusions; the geographical ones are mainly from the Northern Kingdom (see 1.14 n.); the images are decidedly rural. The book is often referred to as Canticles.

Bride[a]

1 I will sing the song of all songs to
  Solomon

2 that he may[b] smother me with kisses.

Your love is more fragrant than wine,
3 fragrant is[c] the scent of your perfume,
and your name like perfume poured
  out;[d]
for this the maidens love you.

4 Take me with you, and we will run
  together;
bring me into your chamber, O king.

Companions
Let us rejoice and be glad for you;
Let us praise your love more than
  wine,
  and your caresses more than any
  song.

Bride
5 I am dark but lovely, daughters of
  Jerusalem,
  like the tents of Kedar
  or the tent-curtains of Shalmah.
6 Do not look down on me; a little
  dark I may be
  because I am scorched by the sun.

My mother's sons were displeased
  with me,
they sent me to watch over the
  vineyards;
so I did not watch over my own
  vineyard.
Tell me, my true love,   7
  where you mind your flocks,
where you rest them at midday,
that I may not be left picking lice
  as I sit among your companions'
  herds.

Bridegroom
If you yourself do not know,   8
  O fairest of women,
go, follow the tracks of the sheep
and mind your kids by the shepherds'
  huts.

I would compare you, my dearest,   9
  to Pharaoh's chariot-horses.
Your cheeks are lovely between   10
  plaited tresses,
  your neck with its jewelled chains.

a The Hebrew text implies, by its pronouns, different speakers, but does not indicate them; they are given, however, in two MSS. of Sept.
b I will . . . that he may: or The song of all songs which was Solomon's; may he . . .
c Or more fragrant than.
d poured out: prob. rdg.; Heb. word uncertain.

1.1–11: Opening songs of man and woman, telling of their love. *Bride* (Tfn. a): the maiden appears more like a young lover than a bride, but the songs would be appropriate for a wedding, recalling early love and courtship. **1:** *Song of all songs:* Heb. idiom for the best of songs. **4:** The girl is often portrayed as taking the initiative. *King:* bridegroom; see 3.11 n. **5:** *Dark but lovely:* she is more sunburned than city girls, but no less pretty. *Daughters of Jerusalem:* used in 2.7 and passim. This is an answer to the chorus-companions of v. 4 where the chorus is female, perhaps consisting of wedding guests (see 5.1 n.); in 8.8–9 the chorus is male. *Kedar:* in northern Arabia. *Shalmah:* a frequent correction of the text, which reads Solomon; possibly it was near Kedar. **7:** *That . . . lice:* the Heb. text here is obscure.

Companions

11   We will make you braided plaits of
        gold
           set with beads of silver.

Bride

12   While the king reclines on his
        couch,
        my spikenard gives forth its scent.

13   My beloved is for me a bunch of
        myrrh
        as he lies on my breast,

14   my beloved is for me a cluster of
        henna-blossom
        from the vineyards of En-gedi.

Bridegroom

15   How beautiful you are, my dearest,
        O how beautiful,
        your eyes are like doves!

Bride

16   How beautiful you are, O my love,
        and how pleasant!

Bridegroom

    Our couch is shaded with branches;
17   the beams of our house are of
        cedar,
        our ceilings are all of fir.

Bride

2   I am an asphodel in Sharon,
        a lily growing in the valley.

Bridegroom

2   No, a lily among thorns
    is my dearest among girls.

Bride

3   Like an apricot-tree among the
        trees of the wood,
    so is my beloved among boys.
    To sit in its shadow was my
        delight,
    and its fruit was sweet to my taste.

4   He took me into the wine-garden
    and gave me loving glances.

5 He refreshed me with raisins, he
        revived me with apricots;
    for I was faint with love.

His left arm was under my head, his   6
    right arm was round me,

Bridegroom

    I charge you, daughters of Jerusalem,   7
    by the spirits and the goddesses[e] of
        the field:
    Do not rouse her, do not disturb my
        love
    until she is ready.[f]

Bride

    Hark! My beloved! Here he comes,   8
    bounding over the mountains, leaping
        over the hills.
    My beloved is like a gazelle   9
        or a young wild goat:
    there he stands outside our wall,
    peeping in at the windows, glancing
        through the lattice.

    My beloved answered, he said to me: 10
    Rise up, my darling;
    my fairest, come away.
    For now the winter is past,   11
    the rains are over and gone;
    the flowers appear in the country- 12
        side;
    the time is coming when the birds
        will sing,
    and the turtle-dove's cooing will be
        heard in our land;
    when the green figs will ripen on the 13
        fig-trees
    and the vines[g] give forth their
        fragrance.
    Rise up, my darling;
    my fairest, come away.

Bridegroom

    My dove, that hides in holes in the 14
        cliffs
        or in crannies on the high
        ledges,
    let me see your face, let me hear
        your voice;
    for your voice is pleasant, your face
        is lovely.

e by . . . goddesses: *or* by the gazelles and the hinds.
f until . . . ready: *or* while she is resting.
g *Prob. rdg.; Heb. adds* blossom.

1.12–2.7: The lovers together. 14: *En-gedi:* on the western edge of the Dead Sea, the only
southern Israelite reference, except for Jerusalem, in the book. **2.1:** *Asphodel:* a flower; perhaps
a daffodil. *Sharon:* the coastal plain in north central Israel. **7:** A refrain (see 3.5; 8.4), perhaps
marking the end of a section. *Goddesses:* see Tfn. *e*.
    2.8–17: The season for love. 11: It is spring, which is the time for love the world over.

Companions

16 Catch for us the jackals, the little
jackals,[h]
that spoil our vineyards, when the
vines are in flower.

Bride

16 My beloved is mine and I am his;
he delights in the lilies.

17 While the day is cool and the shadows
are dispersing,
turn, my beloved, and show yourself
a gazelle or a young wild goat
on the hills where cinnamon
grows.[i]

3 Night after night on my bed
I have sought my true love;
I have sought him but not found
him,
I have called him but he has not
answered.

2 I said, 'I will rise and go the rounds of
the city,
through the streets and the squares,
seeking my true love.'
I sought him but I did not find him,
I called him but he did not answer.

3 The watchmen, going the rounds of
the city, met me,
and I asked, 'Have you seen my true
love?'

4 Scarcely had I left them behind me
when I met my true love.
I seized him and would not let him go
until I had brought him to my
mother's house,
to the room of her who conceived
me.

Bridegroom

5 I charge you, daughters of
Jerusalem,
by the spirits and the goddesses[j] of
the field:

Do not rouse her, do not disturb my
love
until she is ready.[k]

Companions

What is this coming up from the   6
wilderness
like a column of smoke
from burning myrrh or
frankincense,
from all the powdered spices that
merchants bring?
Look; it is Solomon carried in   7
his litter;
sixty of Israel's chosen warriors
are his escort,
all of them skilled swordsmen,   8
all trained to handle arms,
each with his sword ready at his side
to ward off the demon of the night.

The palanquin which King Solomon   9
had made for himself
was of wood from Lebanon.
Its poles he had made of silver,   10
its head-rest of gold;
its seat was of purple stuff,
and its lining was of leather.

Come out, daughters of Jerusalem;   11
you daughters of Zion, come out and
welcome King Solomon,
wearing the crown with which his
mother has crowned him,
on his wedding day, on his day of joy.

Bridegroom

How beautiful you are, my dearest, 4
how beautiful!
Your eyes behind your veil are like
doves,

h Or fruit-bats.
i on . . . grows: *or on the rugged hills or on the hills of*
Bether.
j by . . . goddesses: *or by the gazelles and the hinds.*
k until . . . ready: *or while she is resting.*

15: The import of the verse is unclear; it is directed against someone or something interfering
with the lovers. The image of the *vineyards* is used for the maiden's physical charms; see 7.12,
and, in 6.2, gardens.
3.1–5: Separation and reunion. Here the maiden finds her beloved; in a similar passage,
5.2–8, she does not. **4:** *I seized him:* see 1.4 n. *Mother's. . . .room:* to bind symbolically her
love making to that of her parents; see 8.2,5. **5:** See 2.7 n.
3.6–11: Solomon's wedding procession. The legendary style of Solomon was perhaps the
model for every groom to aspire to, the way he would want a poet to picture his wedding.
For another description of a royal wedding, see Ps.45. **6:** *What is this:* the rhetorical question
is used often as a stylistic device; see 5.9; 6.10. **11:** Perhaps the *crown* the groom wears as "king"
on his wedding day in the Near East today still accounts for the allusions to the king and
Solomon in the book; the maiden is nowhere referred to as queen.
4.1–12: The lover's description of the maiden. See also 6.4–10; 7.1–9 for similar endearments.

your hair like a flock of goats
    streaming down Mount Gilead.
2 Your teeth are like a flock of ewes
    just shorn
which have come up fresh from
    the dipping;
each ewe has twins and none has cast
    a lamb.
3 Your lips are like a scarlet thread,
    and your words are delightful;[l]
your parted lips behind your veil
    are like a pomegranate cut open.
4 Your neck is like David's tower,
    which is built with winding
    courses;
a thousand bucklers hang upon it,
    and all are warriors' shields.
5 Your two breasts are like two fawns,
    twin fawns of a gazelle.[m]
6 While the day is cool and the
    shadows are dispersing,
I will go to the mountains of myrrh
    and to the hills of frankincense.
7 You are beautiful, my dearest,
    beautiful without a flaw.

8 Come from Lebanon, my bride;
    come with me from Lebanon.
Hurry down from the top of
    Amana,
    from Senir's top and Hermon's,
    from the lions' lairs, and the hills
    the leopards haunt.

9 You have stolen my heart,[n] my
    sister,
you have stolen it,[o] my bride,
with one of your eyes, with one
    jewel of your necklace.
10 How beautiful are your breasts, my
    sister, my bride!
Your love is more fragrant than
    wine,
and your perfumes sweeter than any
    spices.
11 Your lips drop sweetness like the
    honeycomb, my bride,
syrup and milk are under your
    tongue,

and your dress has the scent of
    Lebanon.
Your two cheeks[p] are an orchard 13[q]
    of pomegranates,
an orchard full of rare fruits:[r]
spikenard and saffron, sweet-cane 14
    and cinnamon
with every incense-bearing tree,
    myrrh and aloes
with all the choicest spices.
My sister, my bride, is a garden 12
    close-locked,
a garden close-locked, a fountain
    sealed.

Bride
The fountain in my garden[s] is a 15
    spring of running water
    pouring down from Lebanon.
Awake, north wind, and come, south 16
    wind;
blow upon my garden that its
    perfumes may pour forth,
that my beloved may come to his
    garden
    and enjoy its rare fruits.

Bridegroom
I have come to my garden, my sister **5**
    and bride,
and have plucked my myrrh with
    my spices;
I have eaten my honey and my syrup,
I have drunk my wine and my milk.
Eat, friends, and drink,
    until you are drunk with love.

Bride
I sleep but my heart is awake. 2
Listen! My beloved is knocking:

'Open to me, my sister, my dearest,
    my dove, my perfect one;

l Or and your mouth is lovely.
m Prob. rdg.; Heb. adds which delight in the lilies.
n stolen my heart: *or* put heart into me.
o stolen it: *or* put heart into me.
p Your two cheeks: *prob. rdg.; Heb.* Your shoots.
q Verse 12 transposed to follow verse 14.
r Prob. rdg.; Heb. adds henna with spikenard.
s my garden: *prob. rdg.; Heb.* gardens.

6: *Mountains . . . hills:* breasts. **8:** Many commentators hold that this is an old poem from Lebanon, and hence the mention of Lebanese mountaintops. **9:** *My sister:* a term of endearment as in ancient Egypt, and used in 4.9–5.2; compare Prov.7.4. *Bride:* See 1.1–11 n. **12:** *Garden close-locked:* her charms are closed to all but her beloved.
    4.15–5.1: Sensitive metaphors. The maiden invites her young man to make love and he responds. **5.1:** *Friends:* the wedding guests; compare 8.13 n.
    5.2–8: The maiden's dream song. A short dramatic dream sequence. It is kindred to 3.1–5, both passages dealing with the pain of separation and the search for the lover, here fruitless.

for my head is drenched with dew,
my locks with the moisture of the
night.'

3 'I have stripped off my dress; must I
put it on again?
I have washed my feet; must I soil
them again?'

4 When my beloved slipped his hand
through the latch-hole,
my bowels stirred within me.

5 When I arose to open for my
beloved,
my hands dripped with myrrh;
the liquid myrrh from my fingers
ran over the knobs of the bolt.

6 With my own hands I opened to my
love,
but my love had turned away and
gone by;
my heart sank when he turned his
back.
I sought him but I did not find him,
I called him but he did not answer.

7 The watchmen, going the rounds of
the city, met me;
they struck me and wounded me;
the watchman on the walls took away
my cloak.

8 I charge you, daughters of Jerusalem,
if you find my beloved, will you not
tell him[t]
that I am faint with love?

Companions
9 What is your beloved more than any
other,
O fairest of women?
What is your beloved more than any
other,
that you give us this charge?

Bride
10 My beloved is fair and ruddy,
a paragon among ten thousand.
11 His head is gold, finest gold;
his locks are like palm-fronds.[u]
12 His eyes are like doves beside brooks
of water,
splashed by the milky water
as they sit where it is drawn.

His cheeks are like beds of spices or   13
chests full of perfumes;
his lips are lilies, and drop liquid
myrrh;
his hands are golden rods set in   14
topaz;
his belly a plaque of ivory overlaid
with lapis lazuli.
His legs are pillars of marble in   15
sockets of finest gold;
his aspect is like Lebanon, noble as
cedars.
His whispers are[v] sweetness itself,   16
wholly desirable.
Such is my beloved, such is my
darling,
daughters of Jerusalem.

Companions
Where has your beloved gone,   6
O fairest of women?
Which way did your beloved go,
that we may help you to seek him?

Bride
My beloved has gone down to his   2
garden,
to the beds where balsam grows,
to delight in the garden[w] and to pick
the lilies.
I am my beloved's, and my beloved   3
is mine,
he who delights in the lilies.

Bridegroom
You are beautiful, my dearest, as   4
Tirzah,
lovely as Jerusalem.[x]
Turn your eyes away from me;   5
they dazzle me.
Your hair is like a flock of goats
streaming down Mount Gilead;
your teeth are like a flock of ewes   6
come up fresh from the dipping,
each ewe has twins and none has cast
a lamb.
Your parted lips behind your veil   7
are like a pomegranate cut open.

[t] *will you . . . him: or* what will you tell him?
[u] *Prob. rdg.; Heb. adds* black as the raven.
[v] *Or* His nature is.
[w] *Prob. rdg.; Heb.* gardens.
[x] *Prob. rdg.; Heb. adds* majestic as the starry heavens
(*see verse* 10).

7: Perhaps they mistook her for a woman of the streets; contrast 3.3. **8:** See 2.7; 3.5; 2.5.
5.9–7.9: Descriptions of the beloved. 10–16: The maiden describes the man, as he has described
her in 4.1–7. **6.1:** The same theme as in 3.3 and 5.6. **4–10:** A description of the maiden; see
4.1–12 n. **4:** *Tirzah:* the early residence of the northern kings (1 Kgs.15.33). The maiden is

8   There may be sixty princesses,
eighty concubines, and young women
       past counting,
9   but there is one alone, my dove, my
       perfect one,
  her mother's only child,
  devoted to the mother who bore her;
  young girls see her and call her happy,
  princesses and concubines praise her.
10 Who is this that looks out like the
       dawn,
  beautiful as the moon, bright as the
       sun,
  majestic as the starry heavens?

11 I went down to a garden of nut-trees
    to look at the rushes by the stream,
  to see if the vine had budded
  or the pomegranates were in
       flower.
12 I did not know myself;
  she made me feel more than a
       prince
  reigning over the myriads*y* of his
       people.

Companions
  Come back, come back, Shulammite
13   maiden,
  come back, that we may gaze upon you.

Bridegroom
  How you love to gaze on the
       Shulammite maiden,
  as she moves between the lines of
       dancers!

7 How beautiful are your sandalled feet,
    O prince's daughter!
  The curves of your thighs are like
       jewels,
  the work of a skilled craftsman.
2   Your navel is a rounded goblet
  that never shall want for spiced
       wine.
  Your belly is a heap of wheat
  fenced in by lilies.

Your two breasts are like two fawns, 3
  twin fawns of a gazelle.
Your neck is like a tower of ivory.   4
Your eyes are the pools in Heshbon,
  beside the gate of the crowded
      city.*z*
Your nose is like towering Lebanon
  that looks towards Damascus.
You carry your head like Carmel;   5
  the flowing hair on your head is
      lustrous black,
  your tresses are braided with
      ribbons.
How beautiful, how entrancing   6
  you are,
my loved one, daughter of delights!
You are stately as a palm-tree,   7
  and your breasts are the clusters
      of dates.
I said, 'I will climb up into the palm 8
  to grasp its fronds.'
May I find your breasts like clusters
  of grapes on the vine,
  the scent of your breath like
      apricots,
and your whispers like spiced wine   9
  flowing smoothly to welcome my
      caresses,
gliding down through lips and teeth.

Bride
I am my beloved's, his longing is all   10
  for me.
Come, my beloved, let us go out into 11
  the fields
  to lie among the henna-bushes;
let us go early to the vineyards   12
and see if the vine has budded or its
      blossom opened,
  if the pomegranates are in flower.
There will I give you my love,
  when the mandrakes give their   13
      perfume,
  and all rare fruits are ready at our
      door,

y Prob. rdg.; Heb. chariots.
z Or the gate of Beth-rabbim.

---

compared to two capital cities. **8–9:** She excels all the women of a king's harem. Perhaps
1 Kgs.11.3, Solomon's harem, is here echoed. **10:** The praise spoken by the harem women.
11–12: Perhaps a fragment of a longer poem. V. 12 is obscure. **6.13–7.9:** Another praise of the
beauty of the maiden. **13:** *Shulammite:* the name occurs only here in the book. It seems related
to the Heb. for Solomon. The meaning, often guessed at, is uncertain. The *dancers* are the
wedding dancers. **7.4:** *Heshbon:* a city in Moab east of the Jordan. **5:** *Carmel:* a famous
mountain on the coast, in the north.
    7.10–8.4: Love's fulfillment. 10–13: The flowers are probably all symbols of awakening
passion. **12:** See 2.15 n. **13:** *Mandrakes:* an aphrodisiac; they were also an assurance of fertility
(see Gen.30.14–17). **8.2:** *Room of* [my] *mother:* see 3.4 n. **4:** See 2.7 n.

fruits new and old
which I have in store for you, my
  love.

8 If only you were my own true
    brother
  that sucked my mother's breasts!
  Then, if I found you outside, I would
    kiss you,
  and no man would despise me.
2 I would lead you to the room of the
    mother who bore me,
  bring you to her house for you to
    embrace me;[a]
  I would give you mulled wine to
    drink
  and the fresh juice of pomegranates,
3 your[b] left arm under my head and
    your[b] right arm round me.

Bridegroom
4 I charge you, daughters of Jerusalem:
  Do not rouse her, do not disturb my
    love
  until she is ready.[c]

Companions
5 Who is this coming up from the
    wilderness
  leaning on her beloved?

Bridegroom
  Under the apricot-trees I roused
    you,
  there where your mother was in
    labour with you,
  there where she who bore you was
    in labour.
6 Wear me as a seal upon your heart,
    as a seal upon your arm;
  for love is strong as death,
  passion cruel as the grave;
  it blazes up like blazing fire,
  fiercer than any flame.
7 Many waters cannot quench love,
    no flood can sweep it away;
  if a man were to offer for love

the whole wealth of his house,
  it would be utterly scorned.

Companions
  We have a little sister   **8**
  who has no breasts;
  what shall we do for our sister
  when she is asked in marriage?
  If she is a wall,   **9**
  we will build on it a silver parapet,
    but[d] if she is a door,
  we will close it up with planks of cedar.

Bride
  I am a wall and my breasts are like   **10**
    towers;
  so in his eyes I am as one who brings
    contentment.
  Solomon has a vineyard at Baal-   **11**
    hamon;
  he has let out his vineyard to
    guardians,
  and each is to bring for its fruit
    a thousand pieces of silver.
  But my vineyard is mine to give;   **12**
  the thousand pieces are yours,
    O Solomon,
  and the guardians of the fruit shall
    have two hundred.

Bridegroom
  My bride, you who sit in my   **13**
    garden,
  what is it that my friends[e] are
    listening to?
  Let me also hear your voice.

Bride
  Come into the open, my beloved,   **14**
  and show yourself like a gazelle or a
    young wild goat
  on the spice-bearing mountains.

a for you to embrace me: *or* to teach me how to love
  you.
b *Prob. rdg.; Heb.* his.
c until . . . ready: *or* while she is resting.
d *Or* and.
e my garden . . . friends: *prob. rdg.; Heb.* the gardens,
  friends.

8.5a: A suggestion of a procession, perhaps the bridal march, using the same words as 3.6.
8.5b–7: Authentic love. These verses could well be considered the theme of the whole book.
  8.8–12: The little sister. To her brothers who seek to protect her, the maiden responds with a
statement of her chastity. **11:** *Solomon:* see 3.11 n. *Baal-hamon:* an unknown place. **12:**
Vineyard: see 2.15 n. *Mine to give:* lit. my own before me. The verse perhaps means that the
king sells the fruit of his vineyard for whatever he pleases, even great amounts, but her richer
love is her own to give to whomever she pleases; see 8.7b. *Two hundred:* possibly the dowry.
  8.13–14: The lovers together. Perhaps a joyous wedding game is reflected. **13:** *My bride:*
the words are not in the Heb. text, but have been added for clarity. *Friends:* see 5.1 n. The
Heb. word here is a synonym of that in 5.1. **14:** See 2.9; 4.6 n.

THE BOOK OF THE PROPHET
ISAIAH

There are three major collections of literature in the book of Isaiah reflecting different periods of Israel's history. Most of the material in chapters 1–39 is related to Isaiah of Jerusalem, the advisor of kings, a poet of genius, and an eloquent religious spokesman whose career coincided with a series of four kings of Judah: Uzziah, 783–742 B.C. (1.1; 6.1), Jotham, 742–735 B.C. (1.1); Ahaz, 735–715 B.C. (1.1; 7.1–12), and Hezekiah, 715–687 B.C. (1.1; 38.1–6).

The advance of the Assyrian Empire toward Egypt disturbed the balance of power in the Near East, causing political intrigue and rebellions that swallowed up the Northern Kingdom of Israel (721 B.C.) and threatened to engulf Judah (see ch. 7). Isaiah spoke out against political involvements which compromised the covenant with the LORD, and against the oppression of the poor by the rich and the mighty. In language that is both powerful and of poetic beauty, he pleaded for a renewed faith in God.

Collections of Isaiah's prophecies seem to have existed separately. When these were gathered into one book, the words of the collector-editors and of later writers (perhaps disciples; see 8.16) seem to have been added. Many units in these chapters, therefore, are easily recognized as not those of Isaiah, but written in a different style and reflecting a later historical situation.

Chapters 40–55 are from an unknown prophet, now called Second Isaiah, active in Babylon toward the end of the Exile (587–539 B.C.), whose words were joined to those of Isaiah. This conclusion is based on the difference in historical situation, namely exiles receiving the promises of a return to their homeland, and not the inhabitants of Palestine threatened with imminent invasion. The glowing promises of this section have led to its often being called the "Book of the Consolation of Israel." One discerns in moving from the first (chs. 1–39) into this section, a change in religious ideas, especially now a clear affirmation, in theological language, of monotheism and a religious universalism. Moreover, a different vocabulary is used, and the style has become more rhetorical and complex.

The final chapters of the book (56–66) reflect for the most part the life and thought of the post-exilic community struggling against discouragement to reestablish its life in the promised land. The varying styles, religious ideas, and historical situations reflect diverse authors writing over a longer period of time. This section is often called "Trito-Isaiah" or "Third Isaiah."

Judah arraigned

1 THE VISION RECEIVED BY ISAIAH SON of Amoz concerning Judah and Jerusalem during the reigns of Uzziah, Jotham, Ahaz, and Hezekiah, kings of Judah.

2 Hark you heavens, and earth give ear,
    for the LORD has spoken:
I have sons whom I reared and brought up,
    but they have rebelled against me.
3 The ox knows its owner
    and the ass its master's stall;
but Israel, my own people,
    has no knowledge, no discernment.

4 O sinful nation, people loaded with iniquity,
    race of evildoers, wanton destructive children
who have deserted the LORD,
    spurned the Holy One of Israel
    and turned your backs on him.
5 Where can you still be struck
    if you will be disloyal still?
Your head is covered with sores,
    your body diseased;

1.1–5.30: Judah arraigned. Isaiah's charge is that Israel has rejected her sovereign LORD and loving father.
   1.1: Superscription. The prophetic message frequently is designated as a *vision* (see 6.1–13; Ezek.1.1–3; Amos 1.1) to indicate that it was a revelation from God. On the *kings of Judah,* see Introduction. *Uzziah:* compare 6.1.
   1.2–31: A collection of speeches. Diverse speeches from different periods in Isaiah's life. They are a compendium of the prophet's thought. **2–3:** The prophetic message often takes the form of a lawsuit in which God is both plaintiff and judge with the *heavens and earth* as witnesses. The indictment is lack of *knowledge,* i.e. insensitivity to God's benefits. **4–9:** A woe (v. 4) indictment is elaborated into a warning to the people of Judah and Jerusalem. First comes the people's sinfulness, then the results of their rebellion, and finally, they are reminded that the LORD has stopped short of total destruction. **4:** *O:* lit. "woe" (see 5.8-23 n.). **5:** See 9.13.

6 from head to foot there is not a
    sound spot in you—
nothing but bruises and weals and
    raw wounds
which have not felt compress or
    bandage
    or soothing oil.

7 Your country is desolate, your cities
    lie in ashes.
Strangers devour your land before
    your eyes;
it is desolate as Sodom*a* in its
    overthrow.

8   Only Zion is left,
like a watchman's shelter in a
    vineyard,
a shed in a field of cucumbers,
    a city well guarded.

9 If the LORD of Hosts had not left us
    a remnant,
we should soon have been like
    Sodom,
    no better than Gomorrah.

10 Hear the word of the LORD, you
    rulers of Sodom,
attend, you people of Gomorrah, to
    the instruction of our God:

11 Your countless sacrifices, what are
    they to me?
    says the LORD.
I am sated with whole-offerings of
    rams
and the fat of buffaloes;
I have no desire for the blood of
    bulls,
    of sheep and of he-goats.

12–13 Whenever you come to enter my
    presence—
who asked you for this?
No more shall you trample my
    courts.

The offer of your gifts is useless,
the reek of sacrifice is abhorrent to 13
    me.
New moons and sabbaths and
    assemblies,
sacred seasons and ceremonies, I
    cannot endure.

I cannot tolerate your new moons 14
    and your festivals;
they have a become a burden to me,
and I can put up with them no
    longer.
When you lift your hands outspread 15
    in prayer,
I will hide my eyes from you.
Though you offer countless prayers,
    I will not listen.
There is blood on your hands;
    wash yourselves and be clean. 16
Put away the evil of your deeds,
    away out of my sight.
Cease to do evil and learn to do right, 17
pursue justice and champion the
    oppressed;
give the orphan his rights, plead the
    widow's cause.

Come now, let us argue it out, 18
    says the LORD.
Though your sins are scarlet,
    they may become white as snow;
though they are dyed crimson,
    they may yet be like wool.
Obey with a will, 19
and you shall eat the best that
    earth yields;
but, if you refuse and rebel, 20
    locust-beans shall be your only
    food.*b*
The LORD himself has spoken.

a Sodom: *prob. rdg.; Heb.* strangers.
b locust-beans . . . food: *or, with Scroll,* you shall
be eaten by the sword.

7–8: This description of the destruction refers either to the invasion of Tiglath-pileser III in
734–732 B.C. (see 7.1–9 n.) or Sennacherib in 701 B.C. (see 36.1). **8:** In Palestine stones gathered
in a vineyard are made into a small tower from which the *watchman* protects the fruit by
warding off thieves and destructive animals. This *shelter* is useless when the vines are destroyed;
just so is *Zion*, Jerusalem, in a land which will be devastated. The description here of Jerusalem's
isolation is similar to Sennacherib's report of his siege of the city. **9:** Judah is compared to
Sodom and *Gomorrah* both in their depravity (Gen.18.20–33) and in their total destruction
(Gen.19.24–29), except that God leaves Judah a *remnant*. **10–17:** Instructions on the relationship
between ritual and social justice (see Amos 5.21–27). **10:** *Instruction:* that is, "Torah," or
"Law." **11–15:** The LORD rejects the rituals of the cult. **11:** The *fat* and the *blood* of animals
were not to be eaten but used only for sacrifices, the former because it was considered a choice
morsel, the latter because it was the vehicle of life; see Lev. 3.12–16. **12:** *My presence:* the
Temple. **13:** New *moons* occurred on the first day of each month; these days, like the *sabbaths*,
were days of rest; see Num.28.11–15. **15:** *Hide my eyes:* refuse to look at. *Outspread hands* do
not draw God's benevolent gaze because there is *blood* on them. **16–17:** Instructions concerning
the LORD's expectations. **18–20:** If Israel repents she will be saved; if she continues to *rebel*, she

21 How the faithful city has played the
whore,
once the home of justice where
righteousness dwelt—
but now murderers!

22 Your silver has turned into base
metal
and your liquor is diluted with
water.

23 Your very rulers are rebels,
confederate with thieves;
every man of them loves a bribe
and itches for a gift;
they do not give the orphan his
rights,
and the widow's cause never comes
before them.

24 This therefore is the word of the
Lord, the LORD of Hosts, the Mighty
One of Israel:

Enough! I will secure a respite from
my foes
and take vengeance on my
enemies.

25 Once again I will act against you
to refine away your base metal as
with potash
and purge all your impurities;

26 I will again make your judges what
once they were
and your counsellors like those
of old.
Then at length you shall be called
the home of righteousness, the
faithful city.

27 Justice shall redeem Zion

and righteousness her repentant
people.

Rebels and sinners shall be broken   28
together
and those who forsake the LORD
shall cease to be.

For the sacred oaks in which you   29
delighted shall fail you,
the garden-shrines of your fancy
shall disappoint you.

You shall be like a terebinth whose   30
leaves have withered,
like a garden without water;

the strongest tree*c* shall become like 31
tow,
and what is made of it*d* shall go
up in sparks,
and the two shall burst into flames
together
with no one to quench them.

This is the word which Isaiah son of **2**
Amoz received in a vision concerning
Judah and Jerusalem.

In days to come   2*e*
the mountain of the LORD's house
shall be set over all other
mountains,
lifted high above the hills.
All the nations shall come
streaming to it,
and many peoples shall come and   3
say,
'Come, let us climb up on to the
mountain of the LORD,

c Or the strong man.
d Or what he makes.
e Verses 2–4: cp. Mic. 4. 1–3.

---

will be punished. **21–28**: The corruption of Jerusalem (vv. 21–23) and judgment which will
purge and purify the city (vv. 24–28). **21–23**: These verses are written in a meter used for
lamentations and dirges, thus expressing grief over the decay of Judah's religious life as in the
metaphor, *silver* to *base metal*. **21**: *The faithful city*: Jerusalem; see also v. 26. **25–27**: These
verses contain the heart of the message of First Isaiah (see Introduction): after a period of
purification Judah will be restored. The last word is hope not doom. *Justice*, the quality by
which a king rescues the oppressed, and *righteousness*, the state of right order and harmony in
relationships, will be given by God. **27**: *Zion* was originally the mount where the Temple was
built; it became another name for Jerusalem. **29–31**: *The sacred oaks* (lit. "oaks"), the *garden-
shrines* (lit. "gardens"), and the *terebinth* are the sacred places and symbols of fertility religion.
This is one of the few passages in Isa. chs. 1–39 where judgment is announced on Israel because
of pagan practices.
    2.1: A second superscription. This verse probably served as the original title to a collection
of Isaiah's speeches, perhaps Isa. chs. 2–5. Both the individual utterances of the prophets and
the collections of their speeches are characterized as *the word*. *Vision*: see 1.1 n.
    2.2–5: An announcement of eternal peace. The new age will begin when Mount Zion is elevated
above *all other mountains*, i.e. recognized as the most holy place. The same vision of peace is
found in Mic.4.1–4; it is strikingly reversed in Joel 3.9–12. **2**: The *mountain* is Zion; the LORD's
house is the Temple in Jerusalem. On the importance and holiness of Zion, see Pss.48.1–2;
78.69; 87.1–7. **3**: As they approach Zion the *peoples* will be singing a pilgrim song (see Ps.122).
Zion is the source of both *instruction* (or "Torah," or "Law"), ordinarily understood as the

to the house of the God of Jacob,
that he may teach us his ways
and we may walk in his paths.'
For instruction issues from Zion,
and out of Jerusalem comes the
word of the LORD;
4 he will be judge between nations,
arbiter among many peoples.
They shall beat their swords into
mattocks
and their spears into pruning-
knives;*f*
nation shall not lift sword against
nation
nor ever again be trained for war.

5   O people of Jacob, come,
let us walk in the light of the LORD.
6 Thou hast abandoned thy people the
house of Jacob;
for they are crowded with traders*g*
and barbarians like the Philistines,
and with the children of foreigners
everywhere.
7 Their land is filled with silver and
gold,
and there is no end to their
treasure;
their land is filled with horses,
and there is no end to their
chariots;
8 their land is filled with idols,
and they bow down to the work of
their own hands,
to what their fingers have made.
9 Mankind shall be brought low,
all men shall be humbled;
and how can they raise themselves?*h*
10 Get you into the rocks and hide
yourselves in the ground
from the dread of the LORD and the
splendour of his majesty.

Man's proud eyes shall be humbled, 11
the loftiness of men brought low,
and the LORD alone shall be exalted
on that day.

For the LORD of Hosts has a day 12
of doom waiting
for all that is proud and lofty,
for all that is high and lifted up,
for all the cedars of Lebanon, lofty 13
and high,
and for all the oaks of Bashan,
for all lofty mountains and for all 14
high hills,
for every high tower and for every 15
sheer wall,
for all ships of Tarshish and all the 16
dhows of Arabia.
Then man's pride shall be 17
brought low,
and the loftiness of man shall be
humbled,
and the LORD alone shall be exalted
on that day,
while the idols shall pass away 18
utterly.
Get you into caves in the rocks 19
and crevices in the ground
from the dread of the LORD and the
splendour of his majesty,
when he rises to inspire the earth
with fear.
On that day a man shall fling away 20
his idols of silver and his idols of
gold
which he has made for himself to
worship;
he shall fling them to the dung-
beetles and the bats,
and creep into clefts in the rocks 21

f They shall beat . . . pruning-knives: cp. Joel 3. 9–12.
g Or hawkers.
h Prob. rdg.; Heb. and do not forgive them.

responsibility of the priest, and the *word of the LORD*, the message of the prophet. **4:** Peace can
result because there will be but one *judge* and *arbiter*, namely, Israel's God. See 11.3–4. **5:** The
language of v. 3 is used in an admonition. On *light* as a symbol of the presence of the LORD,
see 60.1–3.
    2.6–22: The coming Day of the LORD. On the day when the LORD comes to judge pride and
idolatry, men will flee from his wrath. The organization of the unit is difficult to discern, but
there are refrains throughout (compare vv. 9, 11 with v. 17, and v. 10 with vv. 19, 21). V. 22 is
omitted from the Sept. **6–11:** An announcement of judgment because of foreign corruption,
specifically, idolatry. **6–9:** The words are addressed to God. *Barbarians:* the Gk. reads "soothsayers"; divination was illegal (see Lev.20.27; Deut.18.10–11), yet was practiced (see 1 Sam.
28.3–20). **11:** As v. 12 indicates, *that day* is the Day of the LORD, when, in popular expectation
(Amos 5.18–20), the LORD would punish the enemies of Israel; the prophets of the eighth
century declare, rather, that *on that day* the LORD would, instead, judge his own people. (See
also 13.6; 4.1; Amos 2.16; compare Jer.17.16–18; Ezek.30.3). **12–19:** The Day of the LORD is a
day of doom for all that is proud in man and nature. **13:** *Bashan* is a region in northeastern
Trans-Jordan, known for its *oaks.* **16:** On *ships of Tarshish* see Isa.23.1.14; 60.9; Ezek.27.25;

and crannies in the cliffs
from the dread of the LORD and the
splendour of his majesty,
when he rises to inspire the earth
with fear.
22 Have no more to do with man, for
what is he worth?
He is no more than the breath in
his nostrils.

3 Be warned: the Lord, the LORD of
Hosts,
is stripping Jerusalem and Judah
of every prop and stay,*i*
2 warrior and soldier,
judge and prophet, diviner and elder,
3 captains of companies and men of
rank,
counsellor, magician, and cunning
enchanter.
4 Then I will appoint mere boys to
be their captains,
who shall govern as the fancy takes
them;
5 the people shall deal harshly
each man with his fellow and with
his neighbour;
children shall break out against
their elders,
and nobodies against men of
substance.
6 If a man takes hold of his brother
in his father's house,
saying, 'You have a cloak, you shall
be our chief;
our stricken family shall be under
you',
7 he will cry out that day and say,
'I will not be your master;
there is neither bread nor cloak in
my house,
and you shall not make me head
of the clan.'

Jerusalem is stricken and Judah   8
fallen
because they have spoken and
acted against the LORD,
rebelling against the glance of his
glorious eye.
The look on their faces testifies   9
against them;
like Sodom they proclaim their sins
and do not conceal them.*j*
Woe upon them! they have earned
their own disaster.
Happy*k* the righteous man! all   10
goes well with him,
for such men enjoy the fruit of
their actions.
Woe betide the wicked! with him all   11
goes ill,
for he reaps the reward that he has
earned.
Money-lenders strip my people bare,   12
and usurers lord it over them.
O my people! your guides lead you
astray
and confuse the path that you
should take.
The LORD comes forward to argue   13
his case
and stands to judge his people.
The LORD opens the indictment   14
against the elders of his people and
their officers:
You have ravaged the vineyard,
and the spoils of the poor are in
your houses.
Is it nothing to you that you crush   15
my people
and grind the faces of the poor?
This is the very word of the Lord,
the LORD of Hosts.

i Prob. rdg.; Heb. adds all stay of bread and all stay of
water.
j like . . . them: *or* and their sins, like those of Sodom, denounce them; they do not deny them.
k Prob. rdg.; Heb. Say.

Ps.48.7. *Dhows:* sailing vessels. **22:** *He is . . . the breath in his nostrils;* see Gen. 2.7; Ps.104.29.
3.1–12: A threat of anarchy. The LORD will take away from Jerusalem and Judah all their
leaders, and chaos will result. **1:** *Be warned:* lit. "for behold." *Prop* and *stay* refer to the leaders
of the people. The phrase, "all stay of bread and all stay of water" (Tfn. *i*), interprets the prop
and stay as referring to what supports life. **2:** The prophet lists all who might give any direction,
government officials, military leaders and charismatics. **4:** Compare Eccles.10.16. *Captains:*
that is, princes. **5:** Oppression and disorder result from the removal of leaders. **6–7:** When
leaders, qualified either because of training or talents, disappear, the only requirement for
election as *chief* will be the possession of a decent outer *cloak.* The struggle for individual
survival will be so intense that no one will take the responsibility of providing for the welfare of
a *clan.* **8–12:** The *guides* who confuse the path are the elders (v. 14) who despoil the food.
3.13–15: The LORD's indictment of the leaders. On the "lawsuit" form of prophecy see
1.2–3 n. **13:** Technical legal language is used to describe the LORD's appearance. *People:* The
New English Bible reads a singular with the Sept. **14:** *Officers:* princes. On the *vineyard* as a
figure of speech representing Israel, see 5.1–7.

16   Then the LORD said:
Because the women of Zion hold
    themselves high
and walk with necks outstretched
    and wanton glances,
moving with mincing gait
    and jingling feet,
17   the Lord will give the women of
        Zion bald heads,
    the LORD will strip the hair from
        their foreheads.

18   In that day the Lord will take away
    all finery: anklets, discs, crescents,
19,20 pendants, bangles, coronets, head-
    bands, armlets, necklaces, lockets,
21,22 charms, signets, nose-rings, fine dresses,
23   mantles, cloaks, flounced skirts, scarves
    of gauze, kerchiefs of linen, turbans,
    and flowing veils.

24   So instead of perfume you shall
        have the stench of decay,
    and a rope in place of a girdle,
    baldness instead of hair elegantly
        coiled,
    a loin-cloth of sacking instead of a
        mantle,
    and branding instead of beauty.
25   Your men shall fall by the sword,
        and your warriors in battle;
26   then Zion's gates shall mourn and
        lament,
    and she shall sit on the ground
        stripped bare.

4   Then on that day
seven women shall take hold of one
    man and say,

'We will eat our own bread and
    wear our own clothes
if only we may be called by your
    name;
    take away our disgrace.'

On that day the plant that the LORD 2
    has grown
shall become glorious in its beauty,
and the fruit of the land shall be
    the pride and splendour
    of the survivors of Israel.

Then those who are left in Zion, who 3
remain in Jerusalem, every one enrolled in the book of life, shall be called
holy. If the Lord washes away the 4
filth of the women of Zion and cleanses
Jerusalem from the blood that is in it
by a spirit of judgement, a consuming
spirit, then over every building on 5
Mount Zion and on all her places of
assembly the LORD will create a cloud
of smoke by day and a bright flame of
fire by night; for glory shall be spread
over all as a covering and a canopy, a 6
shade from the heat by day, a refuge
and a shelter from rain and tempest.

I will sing for my beloved   5
    my love-song about his vineyard:
My beloved had a vineyard
    high up on a fertile hill-side.
He trenched it and cleared it of 2
        stones
    and planted it with red vines;
he built a watch-tower in the middle
    and then hewed out a winepress
    in it.

3.16–24: Announcement of judgment against the ladies of Jerusalem. First, reasons for punishment are given in terms of evil pride of the *women of Zion*; next, sentence is passed which fits
the crime (vv. 17–24). **17,24:** The humiliations which the women will suffer are common to
military defeat and exile. **18–23:** The list of *finery* is a prose elaboration of vv. 17,24.
    3.25–4.1: Judgment against Jerusalem and her women. 25: The repeated pronoun *your* is
feminine singular, referring to Jerusalem; compare v. 26. **4.1:** With men killed in war (v. 25),
women will be without husbands and children, a reproach in the society of that day. To *take
away* the *disgrace,* women will break all tradition and beg men to marry them. On *disgrace,*
see 54.4; Gen.30.23; 2 Sam.13.13.
    4.2–6: A promise of Jerusalem's renewal. The hope for the future lies in *survivors* who have
been purged through punishment. **2:** The *plant* and the *fruit* are the *survivors* or the remnant.
See 1.9 n. **3:** *Enrolled in the book of life:* compare Exod.32.32; Mal.3.16; Dan.12.1. **5–6:** The
cloud and the *fire* were symbols of God's presence and guidance in the Wilderness during the
flight from Egypt; see Exod.13.21–22. The *glory* is a technical name for God's protective
presence in a perceptible yet hidden manner; compare Exod.40.34–38; Ezek.10.4.
    5.1–7: The parable of the vineyard. Israel is indicted for her failure to respond to the LORD's
nurture. The prophet first sings a love song (vv. 1–2) and then assumes the role of the vineyard's
owner presenting a lawsuit (vv. 3–6). **1:** The *vineyard* is a common metaphor in love poetry
(see S. of S.1.6; 7.12; 8.12). **2:** The soil in Palestine is shallow and full of *stones*; these the good
farmer gathers and makes a *tower* from which he keeps *watch* over the vineyard. The vinepress

He looked for it to yield grapes,
but it yielded wild grapes.

3 Now, you who live in Jerusalem,
and you men of Judah,
judge between me and my vineyard.

4 What more could have been done
for my vineyard
that I did not do in it?
Why, when I looked for it to yield
grapes,
did it yield wild grapes?

5 Now listen while I tell you
what I will do to my vineyard:
I will take away its fences and let it
be burnt,
I will break down its walls and let it
be trampled underfoot,

6 and so I will leave it derelict;
it shall be neither pruned nor hoed,
but shall grow thorns and briars.
Then I will command the clouds
to send no more rain upon it.

7 The vineyard of the LORD of Hosts
is Israel,
and the men of Judah are the plant
he cherished.
He looked for justice and found it
denied,
for righteousness but heard cries of
distress.

8 Shame on you! you who add house
to house
and join field to field,
until not an acre remains,
and you are left to dwell alone in
the land.

9 The LORD of Hosts has sworn*l* in
my hearing:
Many houses shall go to ruin,
fine large houses shall be uninhabited.

10 Five acres of vineyard shall yield
only a gallon,
and ten bushels of seed return only a
peck.

11 Shame on you! you who rise early
in the morning
to go in pursuit of liquor
and draw out the evening inflamed
with wine,

12 at whose feasts there are harp and
lute,
tabor and pipe and wine,
who have no eyes for the work of
the LORD,
and never see the things that he
has done.

13 Therefore my people are dwindling
away
all unawares;
the nobles are starving to death,
and the common folk die of thirst.

14 Therefore Sheol gapes with straining
throat
and has opened her measureless
jaws:
down go nobility and common
people,
their noisy bustling mob.*m*

15 Mankind is brought low, men are
humbled,
humbled are haughty looks.

16 But the LORD of Hosts sits high in
judgement,
and by righteousness the holy God
shows himself holy.

17 Young rams shall feed where fat
bullocks once pastured,
and kids shall graze broad acres
where cattle grew fat.*n*

18 Shame on you! you who drag
wickedness along like a
tethered sheep
and sin like a heifer on a rope,

19 who say, 'Let the LORD make haste,
let him speed up his work for us to
see it,

l has sworn: *prob. rdg.; Heb. om.*
m nobility . . . mob: *or* nobility, common people and noisy mob, and are restless there.
n Young . . . grew fat: *prob. rdg.; Heb. unintelligible.*

---

is a hollow excavation made in the bedrock in which the grapes are pressed. *Wild:* i.e. sour. **3–6:** The vineyard's owner calls for the court to convene (v. 3), argues the reasonableness of his complaint (vv. 4–5), and gives his judgment. **5:** From the gathered stones *fences* are built as boundaries and *walls* to retain the terraces. **7:** The Heb. contains two plays on words, *mishpat . . . mispah* ("justice" . . . "denied") and *tzedakah . . . tze'akah* ("righteousness" . . . "cries of distress"). *Justice* and *righteousness* are often used in parallel (see 1.21; Amos 5.24) to characterize the standards of behavior which the LORD expects (see also 1.17,26–27; 9.7; 16.5).
   5.8–23: A series of woe indictments. Each accusation begins with the cry *shame on you* (lit. "woe," vv. 8,11,18,20,21,22). Isa.10.1–4 may also belong to this series. Each unit describes a group in terms of its immoral actions. **8–10:** Against the rich who take the land of the poor. **11–17:** Against those whose pursuit of pleasure obscures their perception of the LORD's activity and the needs of his *people.* **14:** *Sheol:* netherworld. **18–19:** Against those who dare the LORD

let the purpose of the Holy One of
Israel
be soon fulfilled, so that we may
know it.'

20 Shame on you! you who call evil
good and good evil,
who turn darkness into light and
light into darkness,
who make bitter sweet and sweet
bitter.

21 Shame on you! you who are wise
in your own eyes
and prudent in your own esteem.

22 Shame on you! you mighty topers,
valiant mixers of drink,

23 who for a bribe acquit the guilty
and deny justice to those in the
right.

26*o* So he will hoist a signal to a nation
far away,
he will whistle to call them from the
end of the earth;
and see, they come, speedy and
swift;

27 none is weary, not one of them
stumbles,
not one slumbers or sleeps.
None has his belt loose about his
waist
or a broken thong to his sandals.

28 Their arrows are sharpened and
their bows all strung,
their horses' hooves flash like
shooting stars,

their chariot-wheels are like the
whirlwind.

29 Their growling is the growling of a
lioness,
they growl like young lions,
which roar as they seize the prey
and carry it beyond reach of
rescue.

30 They shall roar over it on that day
like the roaring of the sea.
If a man looks over the earth, behold,
darkness closing in,
and the light darkened on the
hill-tops*p*!

The call of Isaiah

6 IN THE YEAR OF KING UZZIAH'S DEATH
I saw the Lord seated on a throne, high
and exalted, and the skirt of his robe
filled the temple. About him were 2
attendant seraphim, and each had six
wings; one pair covered his face and
one pair his feet, and one pair was
spread in flight. They were calling 3
ceaselessly to one another,

Holy, holy, holy is the LORD of
Hosts:
the whole earth is full of his
glory.

o Verses 24 and 25 transposed to follow 10. 4.
p hill-tops: *or* clouds.

---

to act in demonstration of his power. **20:** Against those who distort moral law. **21:** Against
those who are proud of their wisdom. **22–23:** Against drunkards who pervert justice.
 5.26–30: An announcement of judgment. The prophet alludes to one of several Assyrian
invasions which took place during his career, namely, by Tiglath-pileser III in 734–732 B.C.;
Shalmeneser in 722 B.C.; Sargon, 711 B.C.; Sennacherib in 701 B.C. The invaders are regarded
as called in by God to punish his people. **26:** The invaders obey God as a dog obeys the *whistle*
of his master. **27–28:** No comfort should be taken in the wishful thinking that the invaders
will become weary or ill-equipped or softened by the long march; compare Jos.9.1–15. **30:** *That
day:* see 2.11 n. The invaders will leave the land in the same chaos over which, before creation,
darkness and the *sea* spread; compare Gen.1.1–2.
 6.1–13: Isaiah's report of his call. This inaugural vision in which Isaiah receives his call to
prophesy should probably be at the beginning of the book as are the calls of other prophets;
compare Jer.1.4–9; Ezek. chs. 1–3. It may be at this place either because the following chapters,
often known as the "Book of Immanuel," existed as a separate collection which an editor who
compiled the whole book put at the wrong place; or because the editor thought the previous
chapters (1–5), which magnificently describe the majesty of God, were a better introduction to
the whole book. The vision report authenticates that the prophet is commissioned as the LORD's
spokesman; also, it justifies the prophet's uncompromising message of doom. **1:** *King Uzziah's
death* was in 742 B.C. God's *throne* was considered to be above the Ark in the *temple*; see
Exod. 25.16–22; Ezek.10.1–5. The *skirt of his robe* was possibly the cloud of smoke that came
from sacrifices and from the incense; compare 2 Chr.7.1–3. **2:** The *seraphim* (lit. "fiery ones")
perhaps are to be associated with the cherubim who appear as the LORD's attendants in Ezek.
ch. 1 and elsewhere are associated with the Ark (Exod.25.18–20). The seraph *covered his face*
for fear of seeing God. *Feet* is a euphemism for sexual organs. The triple *holy* is an intensive
superlative. Isaiah frequently speaks of the LORD as "the holy one of Israel" (1.4; 5.19,24;

4 And, as each one called, the threshold shook to its foundations, while the 5 house was filled with smoke. Then I cried,

> Woe is me! I am lost,
> for I am a man of unclean lips
> and I dwell among a people of
>   unclean lips;
> yet with these eyes I have seen the
>   King, the LORD of Hosts.

6 Then one of the seraphim flew to me carrying in his hand a glowing coal which he had taken from the altar with 7 a pair of tongs. He touched my mouth with it and said,

> See, this has touched your lips;
>   your iniquity is removed,
>   and your sin is wiped away.

8 Then I heard the Lord saying, Whom shall I send? Who will go for me? And I answered, Here am I; send me. 9 He said, Go and tell this people:

> You may listen and listen, but you
>   will not understand.*q*
> You may look and look again,
>   but you will never know.*r*
> 10 This people's wits are dulled,
> their ears are deafened and their
>   eyes blinded,
>   so that they cannot see with their
>   eyes
>   nor listen with their ears
>   nor understand with their wits,
> so that they may turn and be
>   healed.

Then I asked, How long, O Lord? And 11 he answered,

> Until cities fall in ruins and are
>   deserted,
> houses are left without people,
> and the land goes to ruin and lies
>   waste,
> until the LORD has sent all   12
>   mankind far away,
> and the whole country is one vast
>   desolation.
> Even if a tenth part of its people   13
>   remain there,
> they too will be exterminated
> [like an oak or a terebinth,
> a sacred pole thrown out from its
>   place in a hill-shrine*s*].

Prophecies during the Syro-Ephraimite war

WHILE AHAZ SON OF JOTHAM AND **7** grandson of Uzziah was king of Judah, Rezin king of Aram with Pekah son of Remaliah, king of Israel, marched on Jerusalem, but could not force a battle. When the house of David heard that 2 the Aramaeans had come to terms with the Ephraimites, king and people were shaken like forest trees in the wind. Then the LORD said to Isaiah, Go out 3 with your son Shear-jashub*t* to meet Ahaz at the end of the conduit of the Upper Pool by the causeway leading to

q Or but how will you understand?
r Or but how will you know?
s a sacred pole . . . hill-shrine: prob. rdg.; Heb. obscure.
t That is A remnant shall return.

10.20). **4**: The *smoke* in the *house* (that is, the Temple) should be associated with the "cloud" (Exod.19.9) on Mount Sinai where the "glory of the LORD" was present; compare Ezek.10.1–4. **5**: Human lips are deemed *unclean* to speak on behalf of God. Furthermore, according to OT tradition, no one could see God and live (Exod.33.20). **6–7**: See Jer.1.9–10; Ezek.3.1–3. **8**: *Me:* lit. "us." The questions are not addressed to the prophet; he overhears the LORD speaking to the heavenly council (see Ps.82). **9–10**: The Heb. (see Tfn. *q* and *r*) reads literally as a commission to the prophet deliberately to prevent the people from hearing, seeing, understanding, and thus repenting. **11–13**: Isaiah's response is a prayer of intercession, but the LORD offers no hope until the land will have been destroyed.
7.1–9: Assurance given to Ahaz. Assyria invaded the lands to the west in 735 B.C. The kings of Israel, the Northern Kingdom, and of Aram, i.e. Syria, had tried to organize a coalition of small nations to stop the invasion. When Ahaz, king of Judah, refused to join the coalition, the two kings laid siege to Jerusalem (about 734–732 B.C.). Ahaz decided to ask Assyria for help; thereupon Isaiah emerged to counsel Ahaz neither to fear the besiegers nor to seek the human help of Assyria, but rather to look to the LORD for aid. For the historical context, see 2 Kgs.16.1–20. **1**: *Ahaz* reigned 735–715 B.C. *Aram:* Syria, with its capital at Damascus. **2**: *The house of David*, i.e. Judah, the Southern Kingdom, was *shaken* with fear because it was no military match for either of the attackers. **3**: *Shear-jashub:* see Tfn. *t*. Isaiah's son is a living reminder of God's promise to David (2 Sam.7.15–16) that a *remnant will return*; see 10.21–22.

4 the Fuller's Field, and say to him, Be on your guard, keep calm; do not be frightened or unmanned by these two smouldering stumps of firewood, because Rezin and his Aramaeans with Remaliah's son are burning with rage. 5 The Aramaeans with Ephraim and Remaliah's son have laid their plans 6 against you, saying, Let us invade Judah and break her spirit;*u* let us make her join with us, and set the son of 7 Tabeal on the throne. Therefore the Lord GOD has said:

This shall not happen now, and
    never shall,
8 for all that the chief city of Aram
    is Damascus,
  and Rezin is the chief of
    Damascus;
  within sixty-five years
  Ephraim shall cease to be a nation,
9   for all that Samaria is the chief
    city of Ephraim,
  and Remaliah's son the chief of
    Samaria.
Have firm faith, or you will not
    stand firm.

10   Once again the LORD spoke to Ahaz 11 and said, Ask the LORD your God for a sign, from lowest Sheol or from 12 highest heaven. But Ahaz said, No, I will not put the LORD to the test by asking for a sign. Then the answer 13 came: Listen, house of David. Are you not content to wear out men's patience? Must you also wear out the patience of my God? Therefore the Lord himself 14 shall give you a sign: A young woman is with child, and she will bear a son, and will*v* call him Immanuel.*w* By the 15 time that he has learnt to reject evil and choose good, he will be eating curds and honey;*x* before that child 16 has learnt to reject evil and choose good, desolation will come upon the land before whose two kings you cower now. The LORD will bring on 17 you, your people, and your house, a time the like of which has not been seen since Ephraim broke away from Judah.*y*

On that day the LORD will whistle 18 for the fly from the distant streams of Egypt and for the bee from Assyria. They shall all come and settle in the 19 precipitous ravines and in the clefts of the rock; camel-thorn and stinkwood shall be black with them. On that day 20 the Lord shall shave the head and body with a razor hired on the banks of the Euphrates,*z* and it shall remove the beard as well. On that day a man shall 21 save alive a young cow and two ewes;

u Or and parley with her.   v Or you will.
w That is God is with us.
x he will . . . honey: or curds and honey will be eaten.
y Prob. rdg.; Heb. adds the king of Assyria.
z Prob. rdg.; Heb. adds with the king of Assyria.

4: *Smouldering stumps:* a scornful allusion to the destructive power of the two kings as being already extinguished. 6: *The son of Tabeal*—his own name is not given—probably was a rebel in Judah who agreed with the anti-Assyrian policies of the coalition. 8–9: No *nation,* whatever its *chief city* and whoever its human *chief,* can prevail against Jerusalem, the city of God, whose chief is the LORD. 9: *Firm faith* (Heb. *ta'aminu*) and *stand firm* (*te'amenu*) are different forms of the same verb; this play on words underscores that the only security for Judah is faith in God, not reliance upon human help.

7.10–17: **The sign of Immanuel.** The historical context is the same as in 7.1–9. Here the prophet assures Ahaz that within a short time Aram and Israel will be destroyed. 10: *The LORD spoke:* that is, through the prophet. 11–12: A *sign* was an event so extraordinary that in it one could recognize the hand of God. *Put the LORD to the test:* i.e. expect God to perform an extraordinary feat on demand. Here Ahaz, by refusing the sign Isaiah offers him, prompts the prophet to conclude that Ahaz prefers to rely on Assyria rather than on God for deliverance from Israel and Aram. 14: *A young woman:* lit. "the young woman." The Heb. here, *'almah* (feminine of *'elem,* young man), refers to a girl of marriageable age, or one recently married (see Gen.24.43; Exod.2.8; Prov.30.19; S. of S.6.8). The NT references (Mt.1.23; see also Lk.1.27) to this verse are based on the early Gk. rendering of the passage. Many identifications have been proposed of the *young woman* and her *son:* the wife of Ahaz and her son the future king Hezekiah; the wife of Isaiah; collective Israel personified and sometimes called "virgin"; compare Jer.14.17; Amos 5.2. 15–16: *Curds and honey* are simple foods and perhaps contain an allusion to difficult times. Nevertheless, before the child ceases to be a toddler, the threat by the two kings will be ended.

7.18–25: **The Day of the LORD.** Each announcement is introduced by *on that day* (vv. 18,20, 21,23); the phrase is commonly used by the prophets to indicate God's decisive future action in establishing his justice. 20: To *shave the head* was a sign of disgrace and/or mourning; see Neh.13.25; Jer.48.37. *Body:* lit. "feet," a euphemism for pubic hair.

22 and he shall get so much milk that he eats curds, for all who are left in the
23 land shall eat curds and honey. On that day every place where there used to be a thousand vines worth a thousand pieces of silver shall be given over to
24 thorns and briars. A man shall go there only to hunt with bow and arrows, for thorns and briars cover the whole land;
25 and no one who fears thorns and briars shall set foot on any of those hills once worked with the hoe. Oxen shall be turned loose on them, and sheep shall trample them.

8 The LORD said to me, Take a large tablet and write on it in common
2 writing,*a* Maher-shalal-hash-baz;*b* and fetch Uriah the priest and Zechariah son of Jeberechiah for me as trust-
3 worthy witnesses. Then I lay with the prophetess, and she conceived and bore a son; and the LORD said to me, Call
4 him Maher-shalal-hash-baz. Before the boy can say Father or Mother, the wealth of Damascus and the spoils of Samaria shall be carried off and presented to the king of Assyria.
5 Once again the LORD said to me:

6 Because this nation has rejected
the waters of Shiloah, which run so
softly and gently,*c*
7 therefore the Lord will bring up
against it
the strong, flooding waters of the
Euphrates,
the king of Assyria and all his glory;
it shall run up all its channels
and overflow all its banks;
8 it shall sweep through Judah in a
flood,

pouring over it and rising shoulder-
high.
The whole expanse of the land shall
be filled,
so wide he spreads his wings; for
God is with us.*d*
Take note, you nations, and be   9
dismayed.
Listen, all you distant parts of the
earth:
you may arm yourselves but will
be dismayed;
you may arm yourselves but will
be dismayed.
Make your plans, but they will be   10
foiled,
propose what you please, but it
shall not stand;
for God is with us.*d*

These were the words of the LORD   11
to me, for his hand was strong upon
me; and he warned me not to follow*e*
the ways of this people: You shall not say   12
'too hard' of everything that this people
calls hard; you shall neither dread nor
fear that which they fear. It is the LORD   13
of Hosts whom you must count 'hard';*f*
he it is whom you must fear and dread.
He shall become your 'hardship',*f* a   14
boulder and a rock which the two
houses of Israel shall run against and
over which they shall stumble, a trap
and a snare to those who live in
Jerusalem; and many shall stumble   15
over them, many shall fall and be

a in common writing: or with an ordinary stylus.
b That is Speed-spoil-hasten-plunder.
c Prob. rdg.; Heb. adds Rezin and the son of Remaliah.
d God is with us: Heb. Immanuel.
e Or and he turned me from following . . .
*f 'hard' and 'hardship': prob. rdg.; Heb. unintelligible
in this context.*

8.1–4: The sign of Maher-shalal-hash-baz (speedy-spoiling-prompt-plundering). The prophet reports two symbolic "sign acts" (see 7.11–12 n.), the writing of the name of a child before his conception, and the name of the child himself. The message of the name is that the threat to Judah (see 7.1–9 n.) will be ended by Assyria; the message of the inscription is that the promise can be trusted as a word of the LORD since it is known in advance. For other "sign acts" see also Hos.1.2; Ezek.4.1,9; 5.1; 37.16; Jer.13.4; etc. **1**: *Common writing:* intelligible to ordinary people. **2**: *Uriah:* see 2 Kgs.16.10–16. **3**: The *prophetess* would have been Isaiah's wife, but elswhere the term refers to a woman performing some official function; see 2 Kgs.22.14; Exod.15.20; Judg.4.4; Neh.6.14.
   8.5–10: Judgments against the enemies of the LORD. 6: *This nation:* Judah. *Waters of Shiloah:* the stream fed by the spring Gihon which flowed alongside the hill Ophel and brought clean drinking water into a pool (7.3) in Jerusalem. *Flowing softly* and *gently* is meant to signify God's life-giving providence. **7–8**: *Assyria*, whose aid Ahaz unwisely solicited (2 Kgs.16.5–9), will overrun the *land* like the *Euphrates* which, unlike Shiloah, overflows all its *channels*, including those made by man for irrigation. **9–10**: Contrary to appearances, the *plans* of God are being carried out and those of Assyria *foiled.*
   8.11–22: The role of the prophet among people who will not hear. 11–15: The prophet reports a private message concerning his role; he is to *fear* (v. 13) only the LORD, who causes the unfaith-

broken, many shall be snared and caught.

16   Fasten up the message,
         seal the oracle with my teaching;[g]
17   and I will wait for the LORD
      who hides his face from the house
         of Jacob;
      I will watch for him.
18   See, I and the sons whom the LORD
         has given me
      are to be signs and portents in
         Israel,
      sent by the LORD of Hosts who
         dwells on Mount Zion.
19   But men will say to you,
      'Seek guidance of ghosts and
         familiar spirits
      who squeak and gibber;
      a nation may surely seek guidance
         of its gods,
      of the dead on behalf of the living,
20   for an oracle or a message?'
      They will surely say some such
         thing as this;
      but what they say is futile.
21   So despondency and fear will come
         over them,
      and then, when they are afraid and
         fearful,
      they will turn against their king
         and their gods.
22   Then, whether they turn their gaze
         upwards or look down,
      everywhere is distress and darkness
         inescapable,
      constraint and gloom that cannot
         be avoided;
9   for there is no escape for an
         oppressed people.

   For, while the first invader has dealt
lightly with the land of Zebulun and
the land of Naphtali, the second has
dealt heavily with Galilee of the
Nations on the road beyond Jordan
to the sea.

      The people who walked in darkness   2
         have seen a great light:
      light has dawned upon them,
         dwellers in a land as dark as death.
      Thou hast increased their joy and[h]   3
         given them great gladness;
      they rejoice in thy presence as men
         rejoice at harvest,
      or as they are glad when they share
         out the spoil;
      for thou hast shattered the yoke   4
         that burdened them,
         the collar that lay heavy on their
            shoulders,
      the driver's goad, as on the day of
         Midian's defeat.
      All the boots of trampling soldiers   5
         and the garments fouled with blood
      shall become a burning mass, fuel
         for fire.
      For a boy has been born for us, a   6
         son given to us
      to bear the symbol of dominion on
         his shoulder;
      and he shall be called
         in purpose wonderful, in battle
            God-like,
      Father for all time,[i] Prince of
         peace.
      Great shall the dominion be,   7
         and boundless the peace
      bestowed on David's throne and on
         his kingdom,
      to establish it and sustain it
         with justice and righteousness
      from now and for evermore.
      The zeal of the LORD of Hosts shall
         do this.

g *Or* among my disciples.
h *their joy and: prob. rdg.; Heb.* the nation, not.
i *Or of* a wide realm.

ful to *stumble* (v. 14; compare 6.9–10 n.). **16–20:** These words are addressed to the prophet's disciples (see Tfn. *g*). **17:** Since the LORD *hides his face* there is no prophetic word to give. **18:** *The sons* are the ones mentioned in 7.3; 8.1–4; and possibly also 7.14. *Sign:* see 7.11–12 n. **19–20:** *Squeak and gibber:* probably a mocking imitation of sounds made by necromancers to convey the alleged voice of the dead. When people reject the words of a living prophet, they turn to *ghosts.* For the prohibition of consulting the dead, see Deut.8.10–15.
9.1–7: The great light, a new king. After an introductory note (v. 1), this poem captures the celebration and hope following the birth of a new prince to continue the line of David. Three reasons for celebration are given: (1) the *yoke* of the oppressor has been broken (v. 4), (2) the gear of battle has been destroyed (v. 5), and (3) a new crown prince has been born (vv. 6–7). **1:** *Zebulun, Naphtali,* and *Galilee* probably refer to territories taken by the Assyrians after 734 B.C. **4:** On *Midian's defeat,* see Judg. 7.15–25. **6:** The verse begins with a birth announcement (Job 3.3; Jer.20.15); it closes with a series of four crown names. **7:** *Peace* means more than the absence of war; it means the presence of *justice and righteousness.*

Prophecies addressed to Israel

8 The Lord has sent forth his word
against Jacob
and it shall fall on Israel;
9 all the people shall be humbled,
Ephraim and the dwellers in Samaria,
though in their pride and arrogance
they say,
10 The bricks are fallen, but we will
build in hewn stone;
the sycomores are hacked down,
but we will use cedars instead.
11 The LORD has raised their foes[j] high
against them
and spurred on their enemies,
12 Aramaeans from the east and
Philistines from the west,
and they have swallowed Israel in
one mouthful.
For all this his anger has not
turned back,
and his hand is stretched out still.
13 Yet the people did not come back
to him who struck them,
or seek guidance of the LORD of
Hosts;
14 therefore on one day the LORD cut
off from Israel
head and tail, palm and reed.[k]
16 This people's guides have led them
astray;
those who should have been
guided are in confusion.
17 Therefore the Lord showed no
mercy to their young men,
no tenderness to their orphans and
widows;
all were godless and evildoers,
every one speaking profanity.
For all this his anger has not
turned back,
and his hand is stretched out still.

18 Wicked men have been set ablaze
like a fire

fed with briars and thorns,
kindled in the forest thickets;
they are wrapped in a murky
pall of smoke.
The land is scorched by the fury of 19
the LORD of Hosts,
and the people have become fuel
for the fire.[l]
On the right, one man eats his fill 20
but yet is hungry;
on the left, another devours but is
not satisfied;
each feeds on his own children's
flesh,
and neither spares his own
brother.[m]
[n]For all this his anger has not 21
turned back,
and his hand is stretched out still.

Shame on you! you who make **10**
unjust laws
and publish burdensome decrees,
depriving the poor of justice, 2
robbing the weakest of my people
of their rights,
despoiling the widow and plundering
the orphan.
What will you do when called to 3
account,
when ruin from afar confronts you?
To whom will you flee for help
and where will you leave your
children,
so that they do not cower before 4
the gaoler
or fall by the executioner's hand?
For all this his anger has not
turned back,
and his hand is stretched out still.

j *their foes: prob. rdg.; Heb.* the foes of Rezin.
k *Prob. rdg.; Heb. adds* (15) The aged and honoured
are the head, and the prophet who gives false instruction is the tail.
l *See note on verse 20.*
m *and neither . . . brother: transposed from end of
verse 19.*
n *Prob. rdg.; Heb. prefixes* Manasseh devours Ephraim,
and Ephraim Manasseh; together they are against
Judah.

9.8–10.4; 5.24–25: The LORD's outstretched hand. A series of five stanzas (9.8–12,13–17,18–21;
10.1–4; 5.24–25), each concluding with the same refrain, announces the LORD's unrelenting
judgment upon his people. For a similar series see Amos 4.6–12. Repeated disasters have not
brought repentance; therefore the punishment continues. **8:** The *word* of the *Lord* spoken
through a prophet is considered to be God's active power which sets in motion the fulfillment
of the prophecy. **9:** *Ephraim* was the Northern Kingdom named after the leading tribe; *Samaria*
was the capital city. **10–13:** The destruction of houses made of *bricks* and *sycomores* has not
humbled the people who boast that they will build with *hewn stone,* in this way rejecting God's
warning and his *guidance.* **14:** *Head and tail:* rulers and subjects, rich and poor. The MT
(see Tfn. *k*) is a gloss interpreting the meaning of head and tail. **18–21:** The disaster is so severe
that cannibalism results. See Jer.19.9. **10.1–4:** This woe indictment (see 5.8–23) explains the

736

[24⁰] So, as tongues of fire lick up the
     stubble
  and the heat of the flame dies down,
  their root shall moulder away,
  and their shoots vanish like dust;
  for they have spurned the instruction
    of the LORD of Hosts
  and have rejected the word of the
    Holy One of Israel.

[25⁰] So the anger of the LORD is roused
    against his people,
  he has stretched out his hand against
    them and struck them down;
  the mountains trembled,
  and their corpses lay like offal in
    the streets.
  For all this his anger has not
    turned back,
  and his hand is stretched out still.

5 The Assyrian! He is the rod that I
    wield in my anger,
  and the staff of my wrath is in his
    hand.ᵖ

6 I send him against a godless nation,
  I bid him march against a people
    who rouse my wrath,
  to spoil and plunder at will
  and trample them down like mud
    in the streets.

7 But this man's purpose is lawless,
  lawless are the plans in his mind;
  for his thought is only to destroy
  and to wipe out nation after nation.

8 'Are not my officers all kings?' he says;
9 'see how Calno has suffered the
    fate of Carchemish.
  Is not Hamath like Arpad, and
    Samaria like Damascus?

10 Before now I have found kingdoms
    full of idols,
  with more images than Jerusalem
    and Samaria,

11 and now, what I have done to
    Samaria and her worthless gods,

I will do also to Jerusalem and her
  idols.'

When the Lord has finished all that   12
he means to do on Mount Zion and in
Jerusalem, he will punish the king of
Assyria for this fruit of his pride and
for his arrogance and vainglory, be-   13
cause he said:

By my own might I have acted
  and in my own wisdom I have laid
    my schemes;
  I have removed the frontiers of
    nations
  and plundered their treasures,
  like a bull I have trampled on their
    inhabitants.
  My hand has found its way to the   14
    wealth of nations,
  and, as a man takes the eggs from
    a deserted nest,
  so have I taken every land;
  not a wing fluttered,
  not a beak gaped, no chirp was
    heard.

Shall the axe set itself up against   15
    the hewer,
  or the saw claim mastery over the
    sawyer,
  as if a stick were to brandish him
    who wields it,
  or a staff of wood to wield one
    who is not wood?

Therefore the Lord, the LORD of   16
    Hosts, will send disease
  on his sturdy frame, from head to
    toe,�q
  and within his fleshʳ a fever like fire
    shall burn.

o *These are verses 24 and 25 of ch. 5, transposed to*
this point.
p *and . . . hand: prob. rdg.; Heb. obscure.*
q *from . . . toe: transposed from verse 18.*
r *within his flesh: or in his strong body.*

---

punishment as arising from failure to give the *poor* (v. 2) their legal rights. **5.24–25** (see Tfn. *o*):
Punishment will be total. *Stubble* is destroyed completely by a fire, *root and shoots*, unlike a
tree which can sprout again.
   10.5–19: Assyria, rod of God's anger. Assyria is the LORD's means of punishing his people,
but she too will be judged for her arrogance. **5:** *The Assyrian:* lit. "woe Assyria." **6–7:** God's
purpose to punish Israel, carried out by Assyria, is just, but Assyria's own purpose *to plunder
at will* is *lawless*. **9:** *Calno, Carchemish, Hamath*, and *Arpad* are cities in northern Syria taken
by Tiglath-pileser III in 734 B.C. **13–14:** The *king of Assyria* (v. 12) is quoted as boasting that
everything he did was his own plan. **13:** *Frontiers:* as the Assyrians advanced they included
conquered nations as provinces of their empire. They were notorious for their cruelty to conquered *inhabitants.* **15:** The question is rhetorical; Assyria is just a tool in the hand of the LORD.
16–19: After the LORD, *the light of Israel*, has used the Assyrians (v. 12) for his purposes, he
will destroy them, leaving only a tiny *remnant.*

17 The light of Israel shall become a
    fire
    and his Holy One a flame,
which in one day shall burn up and
    consume
    his thorns and his briars;
18 the glory of forest and meadow shall
    be destroyed
    as when a man falls in a fit;
19 and the remnant of trees in the
    forest shall be so few
    that a child may count them one
    by one.

20 On that day the remnant of Israel,
the survivors of Jacob, shall cease to
lean on him that proved their destroyer,
but shall loyally lean on the LORD, the
Holy One of Israel.

21 A remnant shall turn again, a
    remnant of Jacob,
    to God their champion.
22 Your people, Israel, may be many
    as the sands of the sea,
    but only a remnant shall turn
    again,
    the instrument of final destruction,
    justice in full flood;[s]
23 for the Lord, the LORD of Hosts,
    will bring final destruction
    upon all the earth.

24 Therefore these are the words of the
Lord, the LORD of Hosts: My people
who live in Zion, you must not be
afraid of the Assyrians, though they
beat you with their rod and lift their
staff against you as the Egyptians did;
25 for soon, very soon, my anger will come
to an end, and my wrath will all be
26 spent.[t] Then the LORD of Hosts will
brandish his whip over them as he did
when he struck Midian at the Rock of

Oreb, and will lift his staff against the
River as he did against Egypt.

27 On that day
    the burden they laid on your
        shoulder shall be removed
    and their yoke shall be broken
        from your neck.
28 An invader from Rimmon[u] has
        come to Aiath,
        has passed by Migron,
    and left his baggage-train at
        Michmash;
29 he has passed by Maabarah
    and camped for the night at Geba.
    Ramah is anxious, Gibeah of Saul
        is in panic.
30 Raise a shrill cry, Bath-gallim;
    hear it, Laish, and answer her,
        Anathoth:
31 'Madmenah is in flight; take refuge,
        people of Gebim.'
32 Today he is due to pitch his camp
        in Nob;
    he gives the signal to advance
        against the mount of the daughter
        of Zion,
        the hill of Jerusalem.

33 Look, the Lord, the LORD of Hosts,
    cleaves the trees with a flash of
        lightning,
    the tallest are hewn down, the lofty
        laid low,
34 the heart of the forest is felled with
        the axe,
    and Lebanon with its noble trees
        has fallen.

11 Then a shoot shall grow from the
        stock of Jesse,

s the instrument . . . flood: or wasting with sickness,
   yet overflowing with righteousness.
t will . . . spent: prob. rdg.; Heb. obscure.
u and their yoke . . . Rimmon: prob. rdg.; Heb. and
   their yoke from upon your neck, and a yoke shall
   be broken because of oil. He . . .

10.20–23: A remnant shall return. On the Day of the LORD (*that day*, see 2.11 n.) those who are left in Israel will trust the LORD and not Assyria. **21–22:** *A remnant shall turn again*, or, "a remnant shall return." The sentence is the name of Isaiah's son, Shear-jashub (7.3). The idea of a remnant, a group which would survive the judgment, is very important in Isaiah's thought (see 4.2–3; 11.11,16; 28.5–6; 37.4,31–32).

10.24–27: Deliverance from Assyria. The people of Jerusalem (*Zion*, v. 24) are not to fear the *Assyrians*, for the LORD will treat them as he did the *Egyptians* (v. 24). **26:** *Midian:* see Judg. chs. 6–7; *Oreb:* Judg.7.25. *River:* the Euphrates, symbolic here of Assyria.

10.28–34: The advance of the Assyrians. The route of the invader (vv. 28–32) is described as he approaches from the north toward Jerusalem. **30–34:** The destruction is the work of the LORD.

11.1–9: The appearance of the Davidic king. The prophet first announces the coming of a new king (v. 1), describes him as the perfect king (vv. 2–5), and characterizes the results of his reign as perfect and complete peace throughout all of nature (vv. 6–9). See 9.1–7. **1:** *Jesse* was

and a branch shall spring from his
roots

2 The spirit of the LORD shall rest
upon him,
a spirit of wisdom and
understanding,
a spirit of counsel[v] and power,
a spirit of knowledge and the fear
of the LORD.[w]

3 He shall not judge by what he sees
nor decide by what he hears;

4 he shall judge the poor with
justice
and defend the humble in the land
with equity;
his mouth shall be a rod to strike
down the ruthless,[x]
and with a word he shall slay the
wicked.

5 Round his waist he shall wear the
belt of justice,
and good faith shall be the girdle
round his body.

6 Then the wolf shall live with the
sheep,
and the leopard lie down with the
kid;
the calf and the young lion shall
grow up together,
and a little child shall lead them;

7 the cow and the bear shall be
friends,
and their young shall lie down
together.
The lion shall eat straw like cattle;

8 the infant shall play over the hole of
the cobra,
and the young child dance over the
viper's nest.

9 They shall not hurt or destroy in all
my holy mountain;
for as the waters fill the sea,

so shall the land be filled with the
knowledge of the LORD.

10 On that day a scion from the root
of Jesse
shall be set up as a signal to the
peoples;
the nations shall rally to it,
and its resting-place shall be
glorious.

11 On that day the Lord will make his
power more glorious by recovering the
remnant of his people, those who are
still left, from Assyria and Egypt, from
Pathros, from Cush and Elam, from
Shinar, Hamath and the islands of the
sea.

12 Then he will raise a signal to the
nations
and gather together those driven
out of Israel;
he will assemble Judah's scattered
people
from the four corners of the
earth.

13 Ephraim's jealousy shall vanish,
and Judah's enmity shall be
done away.
Ephraim shall not be jealous of
Judah,
nor Judah the enemy of Ephraim.

14 They shall swoop down on the
Philistine flank in the west
and together they shall plunder the
tribes of the east;
Edom and Moab shall be within
their grasp,
and Ammon shall obey them.

v Or force.
w Prob. rdg.; Heb. adds and his delight shall be in the
fear of the LORD. *x Prob. rdg.; Heb.* land.

---

the father of David (1 Sam.16.1–20); the new king continues the dynasty of David in fulfillment
of the promise reported in 1 Sam. ch. 7. **2:** The same Heb. word (*ruah*) is translated by "spirit"
and "breath." The *spirit*, or breath, of the LORD is found throughout the Bible as an active
and creative presence of God. It swept over the abyss at creation (Gen.1.2); it inspired his
servants (42.1; 61.1), judges (Judg.3.10; 6.34), kings (1 Sam.11.6), and prophets (2 Kgs.2.9,
Mic.3.8), enabling them to accomplish deeds beyond their human capacities. The future king
would possess the powers of the greatest men of Israel. **3–5:** The king was responsible for *justice*,
especially the protection of the *poor* and the *humble.* See Ps.72. **6–9:** The rise of this messianic
ruler has cosmic implications; all creatures, even natural enemies, will be at peace with one
another.
    11.10–16: The return of the exiles. The passage assumes the dispersion of the people of Israel
among the nations and looks toward the day of their return. **10:** *A scion from the root of Jesse:*
lit. "the root of Jesse"; see 11.1 n. **11:** Most of the known countries of the civilized world (that
is, the Near East) are listed. *Pathros* (see Jer.44.1,15) was a section of upper Egypt; *Cush,*
Ethiopia; *Shinar,* a name for Babylonia; *the islands of the Sea* included the islands of the
Mediterranean as well as the Aegean coast. **13–14:** The kingdom, reunited, will conquer its

15 The LORD will divide the tongue of
　　the Egyptian sea
and wave his hand over the River
　　to bring a scorching wind;
he shall split it into seven channels
　　and let men go across dry-shod.
16 So there shall be a causeway for the
　　remnant of his people,
for the remnant rescued from
　　Assyria,
as there was for Israel when they
　　came up out of Egypt.

12 You shall say on that day:
　　I will praise thee, O LORD,
　　though thou hast been angry
　　　　with me;
　　thy anger has turned back,
　　　　and thou hast comforted me.
2 God is indeed my deliverer.
　　I am confident and unafraid;
for the LORD is my refuge and
　　defence
　　and has shown himself my
　　　　deliverer.
3 And so you shall draw water with
　　joy
　　from the springs of deliverance.

4 You shall all say on that day:
　　Give thanks to the LORD and invoke
　　　　him by name,
　　make his deeds known in the world
　　　　around;
　　declare that his name is supreme.
5 Sing psalms to the LORD, for he has
　　triumphed,
　　and this must be made known in
　　　　all the world.

Cry out, shout aloud, you that 6
　　dwell in Zion,
for the Holy One of Israel is among
　　you in majesty.

*Prophecies relating
to foreign nations*

BABYLON: AN ORACLE WHICH ISAIAH 13
son of Amoz received in a vision.

Raise the standard on a windy 2
　　height,
roar out your summons,
beckon with arm upraised to the
　　advance,
　　draw your swords, you nobles.
I have given my warriors their 3
　　orders
and summoned my fighting men to
　　launch my anger;
　　they are eager for my triumph.
Hark, a tumult in the mountains, 4
　　the sound of a vast multitude;
hark, the roar of kingdoms, of
　　nations gathering!
The LORD of Hosts is mustering a
　　host for war,
men from a far country, from 5
　　beyond the horizon.
It is the LORD with weapons of
　　his wrath
coming to lay the whole land
　　waste.
Howl, for the Day of the LORD is 6
　　at hand;
it comes, a mighty blow from
　　Almighty God.

---

traditional enemies. **15–16:** The return of the *remnant* will be a new exodus, with natural phenomena more glorious than the first; see Exod.14.21–22; Josh.3.13–17. **15:** *The River:* the Euphrates. *The tongue of the Egyptian Sea:* the modern Gulf of Suez.

　　12.1–6: Two Thanksgiving hymns. Two brief hymns similar in form to psalms of Enthronement of the LORD (Pss.47; 97) mark the end of the first major section of the book of Isa. Each is introduced by ceremonial instructions to the congregation (vv. 1a and 4a) which link the songs to the previous section (11.11–16). **2b:** The language is common in hymns of Thanksgiving; see Exod.15.2; Ps.18.14. **3:** The verse can be read with 4a as liturgical instruction to Temple priests. **4–6:** Typical invitations to give thanks and to sing; see Pss.105.1; 148.13.

　　13.1–23.18: Prophecies against foreign nations. Most major sections are introduced with the word *oracle*, or "burden." See 13.1; 15.1; 17.1; 19.1; 21.1,11,13; 22.1; 23.1; 30.6.

　　13.1–22: Judgment on Babylon. Since Babylon did not develop into a ruling power until 612 B.C. when it destroyed Nineveh, the capital of Assyria, this oracle is probably later than Isaiah. The Medes, mentioned in v. 17, were united to the Persians under Cyrus in 550 B.C. Together they conquered Babylon in 539 B.C. Therefore, the prophecy belongs somewhere between the Exile in 587 B.C. and the conquest of Babylon by Cyrus. The oracle is in the poetic form of a dirge, i.e. a funeral lament, over Babylon. **3:** *My warriors:* the Medes (v. 17) and Persians who carry out God's purpose of overthrowing Babylon to bring back the captives from Exile. **5:** *Far country:* Persia. *Whole land:* Babylonian empire. **6:** *Day of the LORD:* see 2.11 n. Since Israel has been punished by God with the Exile, here the *Day* is a judgment on its

7   Thereat shall every hand hang limp,
    every man's courage shall melt
        away,
8   his stomach hollow with fear;
    anguish shall grip them, like a
        woman in labour.
    One man shall look aghast at another
    and their faces shall burn with
        shame.
9   The Day of the LORD is coming
        indeed,
    that cruel day of wrath and fury,
    to make the land a desolation
    and exterminate its wicked people.
10 The stars of heaven in their
        constellations shall give no light,
    the sun shall be darkened at its
        rising,
    and the moon refuse to shine.
11 I will bring disaster upon the world
    and their due punishment upon the
        wicked,
    I will check the pride of the
        haughty
        and bring low the arrogance of
        ruthless men.
12 I will make men scarcer than fine
        gold,
    rarer than gold of Ophir.
13 Then the heavens shall shudder,[y]
    and the earth shall be shaken from
        its place
    at the fury of the LORD of Hosts, on
        the day of his anger.
14   Then, like a gazelle before the
        hunter
    or a flock with no man to round
        it up,
    each man will go back to his own
        people,
    every one will flee to his own land.
15   All who are found will be
        stabbed,
    all who are taken will fall by the
        sword;

16 their infants will be dashed to the
        ground before their eyes,
    their houses rifled and their wives
        ravished.
17 I will stir up against them the
        Medes,
    who care nothing for silver and are
        not tempted by gold,[z]
18 who have no pity on little children
    and spare no mother's son;
19   and Babylon, fairest of kingdoms,
        proud beauty of the Chaldaeans,
    shall be like Sodom and Gomorrah
        when God overthrew them.
20   Never again shall she be
        inhabited,
    no man shall dwell in her through
        all the ages;
    there no Arab shall pitch his tent,
    no shepherds fold their flocks.
21 There marmots shall have their
        lairs,
    and porcupines shall overrun her
        houses;
    there desert owls shall dwell,
    and there he-goats shall gambol;
22 jackals shall occupy her mansions,[a]
    and wolves her gorgeous palaces.
    Her time draws very near,
    and her days have not long to run.

The LORD will show compassion for **14**
Jacob and will once again make Israel
his choice. He will settle them on their
own soil, and strangers will come to
join them and attach themselves to
Jacob. Many nations shall escort Israel 2
to her place, and she shall employ them
as slaves and slave-girls on the land of
the LORD; she shall take her captors
captive and rule over her task-masters.

y Prob. rdg.; Heb. Then I will make the heavens
shudder.
z Prob. rdg.; Heb. adds bows shall dash young men to
the ground.
a Prob. rdg.; Heb. her widows.

---

enemies who afflicted it beyond measure. Before the Exile the Day was a judgment exclusively
on Israel; compare Amos 5.18. **10–15:** God's decisive judgments are accompanied by a dis-
ruption of order in *heaven* as well as the civil order established by man, since he is master of all.
16: Children were treated cruelly in ancient warfare; see Ps.137.8–9. **17:** *Medes:* 13.1–22 n.
above. **19:** *Chaldaeans:* the inhabitants of the southern part of Mesopotamia at the head of
the Persian Gulf, who extended their rule over all of Babylonia and Assyria under Nabopolassar,
the father of Nebuchadnezzar. *Sodom and Gomorrah:* see Gen.19.23–25. **20:** The land on which
an *Arab* pitched *his tent* was a desert, unsuitable for habitation.
   14.1–23: The return of the exiles and a satire on the fall of their oppressor. 1–2: Since this
unit refers to the return from Exile and the conversion of pagan *nations,* it has affinities with
the second part of Isaiah, namely, chs. 40–55, and perhaps its date of composition is the same
(see Introduction). *Strangers:* converts to Judaism, a characteristic of postexilic prophecy.

3   When the LORD gives you relief
from your pain and your fears and from
4   the cruel slavery laid upon you, you
will take up this song of derision over
the king of Babylon:

See how the oppressor has met his
     end and his frenzy ceased!
5   The LORD has broken the rod of the
     wicked,
     the sceptre of the ruler
6   who struck down peoples in his rage
     with unerring blows,
     who crushed nations in anger
     and persecuted them unceasingly.
7   The whole world has rest and is at
     peace;
     it breaks into cries of joy.
8   The pines themselves and the cedars
     of Lebanon exult over you:
Since you have been laid low, they
     say,
no man comes up to fell us.

9   Sheol below was all astir
     to meet you at your coming;
     she roused the ancient dead to meet
     you,
     all who had been leaders on
     earth;
     she made all who had been kings
     of the nations
     rise from their thrones.
10   One and all they greet you with
     these words:
So you too are weak as we are,
     and have become one of us!
11   Your pride and all the music of
     your lutes
     have been brought down to
     Sheol;*b*
     maggots are the pallet beneath you,
     and worms your coverlet.

12   How you have fallen from heaven,
     bright morning star,

felled to the earth, sprawling
     helpless across the nations!
You thought in your own mind,   13
     I will scale the heavens;
I will set my throne high above the
     stars of God,
I will sit on the mountain where
     the gods meet
     in the far recesses of the north.
I will rise high above the cloud-   14
     banks
     and make myself like the Most
     High.
Yet you shall be brought down to   15
     Sheol,
     to the depths of the abyss.
Those who see you will stare at you,   16
     they will look at you and
     ponder:
Is this, they will say, the man who
     shook the earth,
     who made kingdoms quake,
who turned the world into a desert   17
     and laid its cities in ruins,
who never let his prisoners go free
     to their homes,
     the kings of every land?   18
Now they lie all of them in honour,
     each in his last home.
But you have been flung out   19
     unburied,
     mere loathsome carrion,
     companion to the slain pierced by
     the sword
who have gone down to the stony
     abyss.
And you, a corpse trampled
     underfoot,
shall not share burial with them,   20
for you have ruined your land and
     slaughtered your people.
Such a brood of evildoers shall
     never be seen again.

b Or Your pride has been brought down to Sheol to the
crowding throng of your dead.

3–23: This dirge is referred to the king of Babylon in its prose introduction (vv. 3–4a) and
conclusion (vv. 22–23), but it could have been applied to any of Israel's oppressors. **8:** *The
cedars of Lebanon* were in great demand for building of palaces (1 Kgs.5.6) and were lavishly
cut down as spoils of war. **9:** *Sheol:* the underworld where the "shades" of the dead dwelled.
See Ezek.32.17–32; Ps.88. **12–15:** The tyrant placed himself *above the stars* (v. 13) and now
lies beneath the earth. **12:** *Bright morning star:* Heb. "Helal son of Shahar," possibly meaning
"Day Star, son of Dawn," and reflecting the names of deities. **13:** *Mountain where the gods meet:*
lit. "Mountain of assembly"; in Canaanite mythology a place (usually Mount Zaphon, Pss.48.3;
89.12) where the gods met in council. **19–20:** To be left *unburied* as *carrion* was considered to
be a loathsome curse which pursued and troubled a person even beyond death. Those *pierced
by the sword* died an untimely death with their lives unfulfilled and so in some way were cursed

21　Make the shambles ready for his
　　　　sons
　　　butchered for their fathers' sin;
　　they shall not rise up and possess
　　　　the world
　　nor cover the face of the earth with
　　　　cities.

22　I will rise against them, says the
　　LORD of Hosts; I will destroy the name
　　of Babylon and what remains of her,
　　her offspring and posterity, says the
23　LORD; I will make her a haunt of the
　　bustard, a waste of fen, and sweep her
　　with the besom of destruction. This is
　　the very word of the LORD of Hosts.

24　The LORD of Hosts has sworn:
　　In very truth, as I planned, so shall
　　　　it be;
　　　as I designed, so shall it fall out:
25　I will break the Assyrian in my
　　　　own land
　　　and trample him underfoot upon
　　　　my mountains;
　　his yoke shall be lifted from you,
　　his burden taken from your shoulders.
26　This is the plan prepared for the
　　　　whole earth,
　　this the hand stretched out over all
　　　the nations.
27　For the LORD of Hosts has prepared
　　　his plan:
　　　who shall frustrate it?
　　His is the hand stretched out, and
　　　who shall turn it back?

28　In the year that King Ahaz died this
　　oracle came from God:

29　Let none of you rejoice, you
　　　　Philistines,

because the rod that chastised
　you is broken;
for a viper shall be born of a snake
　as a plant from the root,
and its fruit shall be a flying
　serpent.
But the poor shall graze their　　30
　flocks in my meadows,
and the destitute shall lie down in
　peace;
but the offspring of your roots I
　will kill by starvation,
and put the remnant of you to
　death.
Howl in the gate, cry for help in the　31
　city,
let all Philistia be in turmoil;
for a great enemy is coming from
　the north,
not a man straying from his
　ranks.
What answer is there for the　　32
　envoys of the nation?
This, that the LORD has fixed Zion
　in her place,
and the afflicted among his people
　shall take refuge there.

Moab: an oracle.　　**15**

On the night when Ar is sacked,
　　Moab meets her doom;
on the night when Kir is sacked,
　　Moab meets her doom.
The people of Dibon go up*c* to the　　2
　hill-shrines to weep;
Moab howls over Nebo and over
　Medeba.

c The people . . . go up: prob. rdg.; Heb. He has gone
up to the house and Dibon.

---

by God. **21:** That *sons* be cut off from life at an early age was considered to be a particularly
heavy punishment for the *sin* of a father.
　14.24–27: Judgment against Assyria. 24: *The LORD . . . planned* to act against Assyria; in
doing so he will deliver his people. **27:** God's *hand is stretched* out in punishment of Assyria.
　14.28–32: Judgment against the Philistines. 28: *Ahaz died* about 715 B.C. **29:** Although the
Philistines ceased to be a power in the time of David, they continued to exist as a thorn in
Israel's side, rejoicing in his misfortunes and taking advantage of them; see Ezek.25.15–17.
The *rod that chastised* the Philistines probably was Sargon II, who died in 705 B.C. The *snake*
is probably the Assyrian nation that will give birth to another tyrant ruler, or *viper*. **32:** *Zion*
was deemed to be impregnable and inviolable.
　15.1–16.14: Lament over Moab. Moab was the country immediately to the east of the Dead
Sea. According to Gen.19.36–38, the Moabites are descended from Lot and so related to the
Israelites. The relations between the two peoples vacillated between close friendship and bitter
hostility; see Ruth 1.1–2; 1 Sam.22.3–4; 2 Sam.8.2. This song at points carries a tone of authentic
lament, but at others (16.6,12) shows no regret over Moab's destruction. See Jer. ch. 48. **2–3:**
weep, howls, hair torn, beard shaved, sackcloth: these were conventional signs of mourning.

The hair is torn from every head,
and every beard shaved off.
3 In the streets men go clothed with
sackcloth,
they cry out on the roofs;
in the public squares every man
howls,
weeping as he goes through them.
4 Heshbon and Elealeh cry for help,
their voices are heard as far as
Jahaz.
Thus Moab's stoutest warriors
become cowards,
and her courage ebbs away.
5 My heart cries out for Moab,
whose nobles have fled*d* as far as
Zoar.*e*
On the ascent to Luhith men go up
weeping;
on the road to Horonaim there are
cries of 'Disaster!'
6 The waters of Nimrim are desolate
indeed;
the grass is parched, the herbage
dead,
not a green thing is left;
7 and so the people carry off across
the gorge of the Arabim
their hard-earned wealth and all
their savings.
8 The cry for help echoes round the
frontiers of Moab,
their howling reaches Eglaim and
Beer-elim.
9 The waters of Dimon already run
with blood;
yet I have more troubles in store for
Dimon,
for I have a vision*f* of the
survivors of Moab,
of the remnant of Admah.
16 The rulers of the country send a
present of lambs
from Sela in the wilderness
to the hill of the daughter of Zion;
2 the daughters of Moab at the fords
of the Arnon
shall be like fluttering birds, like
scattered nestlings.
3 'Take up our cause with all your
might;
let your shadow shield us at high
noon, dark as night.

Shelter the homeless, do not betray
the fugitive;
let the homeless people of Moab   4
find refuge with you;
hide them from the despoiler.'

When extortion has done its work
and the looting is over,
when the heel of the oppressor has
vanished from the land,
a throne shall be set up in mutual   5
trust in David's tent,
and on it there shall sit a true judge,
one who seeks justice and is swift
to do right.

We have heard tell of Moab's pride, 6
how great it is,
we have heard of his pride, his
overweening pride;
his talk is full of lies.
For this all Moab shall howl;   7
Moab shall howl indeed;
he*g* shall mourn for the prosperous
farmers of Kir-hareseth,
utterly ruined;
the orchards of Heshbon,   8
the vines of Sibmah languish,
though their red grapes once laid
low the lords of the nations,
though they reached as far as Jazer
and trailed out to the wilderness,
though their branches spread abroad
and crossed the sea.
Therefore I will weep for Sibmah's   9
vines as I weep for Jazer.
I will drench you with my tears,
Heshbon and Elealeh;
for over your summer-fruits and
your harvest
the shouts of the harvesters are
ended.
Joy and gladness shall be banished 10
from the meadows,
no more shall men shout and sing
in the vineyards,
no more shall they tread wine in
the winepresses;
I have silenced the shouting of
the harvesters.

d have fled: prob. rdg.; Heb. om.
e Prob. rdg.; Heb. adds Eglath Shelishiya.
f I have a vision: prob. rdg.; Heb. a lion.
g Prob. rdg.; Heb. you.

9: The Heb. words for *Dimon* and *blood* are very similar; hence the play on words. **16.4:**
David's tent: the dynasty of David. **8:** *Wilderness:* the Arabian desert to the east of Moab.
Sea: the Dead Sea.

11　Therefore my heart throbs
　　　like a harp for Moab,
　　and my very soul for Kir-hareseth.[h]
12　When Moab comes to worship
　　　and wearies himself at the hill-
　　　　shrines,
　　when he enters his sanctuary to pray,
　　　he will gain nothing.

13　These are the words which the LORD
14　spoke long ago about Moab; and now
he says, In three years, as a hired
labourer counts them off, the glory of
Moab shall become contemptible for
all his vast numbers; a handful shall
be left and those of no account.

17　　　　　　Damascus: an oracle.

Damascus shall be a city no longer,
　　she shall be but a heap of ruins.
2　For ever desolate, flocks shall have
　　　her for their own,
　　and lie there undisturbed.
3　No longer shall Ephraim boast a
　　　fortified city,
　　or Damascus a kingdom;
the remnant of Aram and the glory
　　of Israel, their fate is one.
This is the very word of the LORD
　　of Hosts.

4　On that day Jacob's weight shall
　　　dwindle
　　and the fat on his limbs waste
　　　away,
5　as when the harvester gathers up the
　　　standing corn
　　and reaps the ears in armfuls,
　　or as when a man gleans the ears in
6　　　the Vale of Rephaim,
　　　or as when one beats an olive-tree
　　and only gleanings are left on it,
two or three berries on the top of a
　　　branch,

four or five on the boughs of the
　　fruiting tree.
This is the very word of the LORD
　　the God of Israel.

On that day men shall look to their　7
Maker and turn their eyes to the Holy
One of Israel; they shall not look to the　8
altars made by their own hands nor to
anything that their fingers have made,
sacred poles or incense-altars.

On that day their strong cities shall　9
be deserted like the cities of the Hivites
and the Amorites, which they abandoned when Israel came in; all shall be
desolate.

For you forgot the God who　　　10
　　delivered you,
and did not remember the rock,
　　your stronghold.
Plant them, if you will, your gardens
　　in honour of Adonis,
　　strike your cuttings for a foreign
　　　god;
protect your gardens on the day you　11
　　plant them,
　　and next day make the seed sprout.
But the crop will be scorched when
　　wasting disease comes
　　in the day of incurable pain.

Listen! it is the thunder of many　　12
　　peoples,
they thunder with the thunder of
　　the sea.
Listen! it is the roar of nations
roaring with the roar of mighty
　　waters.
When he rebukes them, away they　13
　　fly,
driven like chaff on the hills before
　　the wind,
　　like thistledown before the storm.
At evening all is confusion,　　　14

h *Prob. rdg.; Heb.* Kir-hares.

17.1–6: Judgment on the Syro-Ephraimitic coalition. In the context of the threat to Judah from Syria (*Aram*, v. 3) and Israel (*Ephraim*, v. 3), the prophet announces judgment on these enemies. The date is 734–732 B.C.; see 7.1–9 n. **1**: *Damascus:* capital of Syria. **3**: *The glory of Israel* perhaps refers to her capital, Samaria. **5**: The *Vale of Rephaim* was northwest of Jerusalem; see Josh.15.8; 18.16.
　17.7–11: Concerning idolatry. 7–8: One day men will choose *their Maker* over what they have made. **8**: *Sacred poles:* lit. "Asherim," cultic objects representing a Canaanite goddess. **9–11**: Idolatry results in desolation. **10**: *Adonis* (lit. "pleasant plants") was a god of vegetation.
　17.12–14: The thunder of the enemy. While the passage may refer to the unsuccessful Assyrian attack on Jerusalem (2 Kgs.19.35–36) in 701 B.C., the language and concepts are common enough to lack a direct reference.

and before morning they are gone.
Such is the fate of our plunderers,
the lot of those who despoil us.

in summer the birds shall make
their home there,
in winter every beast of the earth.

18 There is a land of sailing ships,
a land beyond the rivers of Cush

2 which sends its envoys by the
Nile,
journeying on the waters in vessels
of reed.
Go, swift messengers,
go to a people tall and smooth-
skinned,
to a people dreaded near and far,
a nation strong and proud,
whose land is scoured by rivers.

3 All you who dwell in the world,
inhabitants of earth,
shall see when the signal is hoisted
on the mountains
and shall hear when the trumpet
sounds.

4 These were the words of the LORD to
me:

From my dwelling-place I will look
quietly down
when the heat shimmers in the
summer sun,
when the dew is heavy at harvest
time.

5 Before the vintage, when the
budding is over
and the flower ripens into a berry,
the shoots shall be cut down with
knives,
the branches struck off and cleared
away.

6 All shall be left to birds of prey on
the hills
and to beasts of the earth;

At that time tribute shall be brought 7
to the LORD of Hosts from a people
tall and smooth-skinned, dreaded near
and far, a nation strong and proud,
whose land is scoured by rivers. They
shall bring it to Mount Zion, the place
where men invoke the name of the
LORD of Hosts.

Egypt: an oracle.   **19**

See how the LORD comes riding
swiftly upon a cloud,
he shall descend upon Egypt;
the idols of Egypt quail before him,
Egypt's courage melts within her.
I will set Egyptian against Egyptian, 2
and they shall fight one against
another,
neighbour against neighbour,
city against city and kingdom
against kingdom.
Egypt's spirit shall sink within her, 3
and I will throw her counsels
into confusion.
They may resort to idols and
oracle-mongers,
to ghosts and spirits,
but I will hand Egypt over to a   4
hard master,
and a cruel king shall rule over
them.
This is the very word of the Lord,
the LORD of Hosts.

The waters of the Nile shall drain 5
away,

18.1–20.6: Relations with Egypt.
18.1–7: The proposal of the envoys. This section ensues on an attempt by an Egyptian embassy
to establish a coalition against Assyria, about 714 B.C. Isaiah speaks against the attempt, holding that God, not human treaties, controls history. **1:** *Beyond . . . Cush:* the Pharaohs of the
Twenty-fifth Dynasty who, coming from the area south of Egypt, are regarded as Ethiopians;
Cush is the ordinary Heb. name for Ethiopia. **2:** *Vessels of reed:* the Egyptians used boats
made of papyrus, lined with pitch. **4–6:** As the seasons turn, the LORD will act in his time.
19.1–15: Judgment against Egypt. The LORD will bring internal chaos in Egypt, dry up the
Nile, and cause all who depended on it to suffer (vv. 1–10). The crucial decisions in history are
made in the *counsels* of the LORD to which the prophets are privy and the wise *counsellors*
of kings are not (vv. 11–15). **1:** In Canaanite mythology too the god Baal often is called "cloud
rider"; see Pss.104.3; 68.4 n. **2:** *Egyptian against Egyptian* may allude to the turbulent period at
the beginning of the Twenty-fifth Dynasty begun by the Ethiopian king Piankhi, or else to an
invasion of Egypt by the Assyrians (under Sargon II in 711 B.C. or Esarhaddon in 671 B.C.)
which some Egyptians may have welcomed as liberation from the Ethiopian rule. **4:** The *hard
master* may be one of the rulers mentioned in v. 2. **5–6:** Egypt depended upon the regular floods

the river shall be parched and run
   dry,

6   its channels shall stink,
the streams of Egypt shall be parched
   and dry up,
reeds and rushes shall wither away;

7   the lotus too beside the Nile[i]
and all that is sown along the Nile
   shall dry up,
   shall be blown away and vanish.

8   The fishermen shall groan and
   lament,
all who cast their hooks into the
   Nile
and those who spread nets on the
   water shall lose heart.

9   The flax-dressers shall hang their
   heads,
the women carding and the weavers
   shall grow pale,

10   Egypt's spinners shall be downcast,
and all her artisans sick at heart.

11   Fools that you are, you princes of
   Zoan!
Wisest of Pharaoh's counsellors you
   may be,
but stupid counsellors you are.
How can you say to Pharaoh,
'I am the heir of wise men and
   spring from ancient kings'?

12   Where are your wise men,
   Pharaoh,
to teach you and make known to
   you
what the LORD of Hosts has planned
   for Egypt?

13   Zoan's princes are fools, the princes
   of Noph are dupes;
the chieftains of her clans have led
   Egypt astray.

14   The LORD has infused into them
   a spirit that warps their
   judgement;
they make Egypt miss her way in
   all she does,

as a drunkard will miss his footing as
   he vomits.

15 There shall be nothing in Egypt that
   any man can do,
head or tail, palm or rush.

16 When that day comes the Egyptians
shall become weak as women; they
shall fear and tremble when they see the
LORD of Hosts raise his hand against
them, as raise it he will. The land of 17
Judah shall strike terror into Egypt;
its very name shall cause dismay,
because of the plans that the LORD of
Hosts has laid against them.

18 When that day comes there shall be
five cities in Egypt speaking the
language of Canaan and swearing allegiance to the LORD of Hosts, and one
of them shall be called the City of the
Sun.[j]

19 When that day comes there shall be
an altar to the LORD in the heart of
Egypt, and a sacred pillar set up for the
LORD upon her frontier. It shall stand 20
as a token and a reminder to the LORD
of Hosts in Egypt, so that when they
appeal to him against their oppressors,
he may send a deliverer to champion
their cause, and he shall rescue them.
The LORD will make himself known to 21
the Egyptians; on that day they shall
acknowledge the LORD and do him
service with sacrifice and grain-
offering, make vows to him and pay
them. The LORD will strike down 22
Egypt, healing as he strikes; then they
will turn back to him and he will hear
their prayers and heal them.

23 When that day comes there shall be
a highway between Egypt and Assyria;
Assyrians shall come to Egypt and
Egyptians to Assyria: then Egyptians
shall worship with[k] Assyrians.

i Prob. rdg.; Heb. adds on the mouth of the Nile.
j the City of the Sun: or Heliopolis.
k Or shall be slaves to.

---

of the Nile. The anticipated disaster is more serious than a mere drought. **11:** *Zoan:* the Greek
Tanis, a city on the Nile delta; see Num.13.22; Ezek.30.14. The wise men of Egypt were renowned; see 1 Kgs.4.30. **13:** *Noph:* Memphis, one of the ancient capitals of Egypt. **15:** Everyone
in Egypt, from the highly placed (the *head,* the *palm*) to the lowest (the *tail, rush* in the water)
will be helpless.

    19.16–25: Hope for the salvation of Egypt. Five paragraphs, each beginning with the same
phrase (*When that day comes*), have been appended to the poem against Egypt. **16:** *That day:*
Day of the LORD; see 2.11 n. **18:** *City of the Sun:* the translation and identification are problematic. *Heliopolis* (Tfn. *j*) was a later name for the city of On, center of sun worship and
renowned as an educational center. **22:** The LORD will treat Egypt as he does Israel, i.e. he will
strike her with a *healing* punishment, unlike that of the dire punishment visited on Egypt at the

24 When that day comes Israel shall rank with Egypt and Assyria, those three, and shall be a blessing in the 25 centre of the world. So the LORD of Hosts will bless them: A blessing be upon Egypt my people, upon Assyria the work of my hands, and upon Israel my possession.

20 SARGON KING OF ASSYRIA SENT HIS commander-in-chief*l* to Ashdod, and 2 he took it by storm. At that time the LORD said to Isaiah son of Amoz, Come, strip the sackcloth from your waist and take your sandals off. He did so, and went about naked and barefoot. 3 The LORD said, My servant Isaiah has gone naked and barefoot for three years as a sign and a warning to Egypt 4 and Cush; just so shall the king of Assyria lead the captives of Egypt and the exiles of Cush naked and barefoot, their buttocks shamefully exposed, 5 young and old alike. All men shall be dismayed, their hopes in Cush and their 6 pride in Egypt humbled. On that day those who dwell along this coast will say, So much for all our hopes on which we relied for help and deliverance from the king of Assyria; what escape have we now?

21   A wilderness: an oracle.

Rough weather, advancing like a
    storm in the south,
coming from the wilderness, from a
    land of terror!
2   Grim is the vision shown to me:
the traitor betrayed, the spoiler
    himself despoiled.
Up, Elam; up, Medes, to the siege,
    no time for weariness!

At this my limbs writhe in anguish,   3
I am gripped by pangs like a woman
    in labour.
I am distraught past hearing, dazed
    past seeing,
my mind reels, sudden convulsions   4
    seize me.

The cool twilight I longed for has
    become a terror:
the banquet is set out, the rugs are   5
    spread;
    they are eating and drinking—
rise, princes, burnish your shields.
For these were the words of the   6
    Lord to me:
Go, post a watchman to report
    what he sees.
He sees chariots, two-horsed   7
    chariots,
riders on asses, riders on camels.
He is alert, alert, always on the
    alert.
Then the look-out cried: 8
All day long I stand on the Lord's
    watch-tower
and night after night I keep my
    station.
See, there come men in a chariot, a   9
    two-horsed chariot.
    And a voice calls back:
Fallen, fallen is Babylon,
and all the images of her gods lie
    shattered on the ground.
    O my people,   10
once trodden out and winnowed on
    the threshing-floor,
what I have heard from the LORD
    of Hosts,
from the God of Israel, I have told
    you.

l Or sent Tartan.

Exodus. 24–25: *Israel, Egypt, and Assyria,* traditional enemies, will be reconciled on *that day* and the promise of Gen.12.3 to Abraham of *blessing* will be fulfilled.

20.1–6: A sign of Egypt's humiliation. When Egypt attempted to unite the small states of Palestine against Assyria (714–711 B.C.; see 14.28–32; 18.1–7), Isaiah walked naked and barefoot, proclaiming himself as a sign of Egypt's failure. **1:** *Sargon:* Sargon II (722–705 B.C.). *Ashdod* was one of the Philistine cities taken by the Assyrians in 711 B.C. **3–6:** The prophet would have proclaimed these words as the interpretation of his behavior. **3:** *Sign:* see 7.11–12 n. **4:** See 2 Sam.10.1–5. **6:** The Palestinian coastal states which trusted Egypt have no escape.

21.1–10: A vision of the fall of Babylon. The poem was written by an anonymous prophet, active at the time of Babylon's fall in 539 B.C., who awaits a messenger with the news of the oppressor's demise. **2:** *Elam* and the *Medes,* powers east of Babylon, together with Persia, overcame Babylon. **5:** According to a tradition found in Daniel ch. 5 and in the Gk. historian Herodotus, an orgy of *eating* and *drinking* was in progress so that Babylon was attacked and fell without a battle. **10:** The news is for the *people* of Israel who have experienced the punishment of exile.

11   Dumah: an oracle.

One calls to me from Seir:
Watchman, what is left of the
        night?
Watchman, what is left?
12   The watchman answered:
Morning comes, and also night.*m*
Ask if you must; then come back
        again.

13   With the Arabs: an oracle.

You caravans of Dedan, that camp in
        the scrub with the Arabs,
14 bring water to meet the thirsty.
You dwellers in Tema, meet the
        fugitives with food,
15 for they flee from the sword, the
        sharp edge of the sword,
from the bent bow, and from the
        press of battle.

16   For these are the words of the Lord
to me: Within a year, as a hired
labourer counts off the years, all the
glory of Kedar shall come to an end;
17 few shall be the bows left to the
warriors of Kedar.
        The LORD the God of Israel has
spoken.

22   The Valley of Vision:*n* an oracle.

Tell me, what is amiss
that you have all climbed on to the
        roofs,
2 O city full of tumult, town in ferment
        and filled with uproar,
whose slain were not slain with the
        sword
        and did not die in battle?

Your commanders are all in flight,   3
        huddled together out of bowshot;
all your stoutest warriors are
        huddled together,
        they have taken to their heels.
Then I said, Turn your eyes away   4
        from me;
leave me to weep in misery.
Do not thrust consolation on me
        for the ruin of my own people.

For the Lord, the LORD of Hosts,   5
has ordained a day of tumult, a day of
trampling and turmoil in the Valley of
Vision,*n* rousing cries for help that
echo among the mountains.

Elam took up his quiver,   6
        horses were harnessed to the
        chariots of Aram,*o*
Kir took the cover from his shield.
Your fairest valleys were overrun by   7
        chariots and horsemen,
        the gates were hard beset,
        the heart of Judah's defence was   8
        laid open.

On that day you looked to the
weapons stored in the House of the
Forest; you filled all the many pools in   9
the City of David, collecting water from
the Lower Pool.*p* Then you surveyed   10
the houses in Jerusalem, tearing some
down to make the wall inaccessible,
and between the two walls you made a   11
cistern for the Waters of the Old Pool;
        but you did not look to the
        Maker of it all
or consider him who fashioned it
        long ago.

m and also night: *or* and the night is full spent.
n *Or* of Calamity.   *o* *Prob. rdg.; Heb.* man.
p you filled . . . Lower Pool: *or* you took note of the
cracks, many as they were, in the wall of the City
of David, and you collected water from the Lower
Pool.

21.11–17: Speeches concerning Arabia. With the exception of *Seir* (Edom), the places mentioned are in Arabia.

22.1–14: The LORD's Day of judgment upon his people. The events here probably occurred in 701 B.C. when Sennacherib of Assyria invaded Judah and besieged Jerusalem, but left without destroying the city (2 Kgs.19.35–36). **1:** *Valley of Vision:* the allusion is uncertain; some interpret it as a euphemism for the Valley of Slaughter, spoken of in Jer.7.30–32. **2:** The *tumult* may have been the cries of alarm as the siege began, or the celebration when the siege was lifted. **5–13:** The prophet sees the approach of the enemy as the coming *day* of the LORD's judgment. **6:** *Elam, Aram* (the text is uncertain) and *Kir* (an unknown locality in Mesopotamia) may represent troops in the Assyrian army. **8–13:** The people of Jerusalem trusted in their siege preparations instead of the LORD; they ate and drank (v. 13) instead of praying and lamenting. **8:** The *House of the Forest* was an armory built by Solomon (1 Kgs.7.2; 10.17). **9–11:** According to 2 Kgs.20.20 (which see) Hezekiah built a reservoir and water conduit; such water systems were common in Palestinian cities, built in such a way as to provide water

12 On that day the Lord, the LORD of
    Hosts,
    called for weeping and beating the
    breast,
    for shaving the head and putting
    on sackcloth;
13 but instead there was joy and
    merry-making,
    slaughtering of cattle and killing of
    sheep,
    eating of meat and drinking of wine,
    as you thought,
    Let us eat and drink; for tomorrow
    we die.

14   The LORD of Hosts has revealed
    himself to me; in my hearing he swore:

    Your wickedness shall never be purged
    until you die.
    This is the word of the Lord, the
    LORD of Hosts.

15 These were the words of the Lord, the
    LORD of Hosts.

    Go to this steward,
    to Shebna, comptroller of the
    household, and say:
16 What right, what business, have you
    here,
    that you have dug yourself a grave
    here,
    cutting out your grave on a height
    and carving yourself a resting-place
    in the rock?
17 The LORD will shake you out,
    shake you as a garment*q* is shaken
    out
    to rid it of lice;
18 then he will bundle you tightly and
    throw you
    like a ball into a great wide land.
    There you shall die,
    and there shall lie your chariot of
    honour,

an object of contempt to your
    master's household.
I will remove you from office and   19
    drive you from your post.

    On that day I will send for my   20
servant Eliakim son of Hilkiah; I will   21
invest him with your robe, gird him
with your sash; and hand over your
authority to him. He shall be a father
to the inhabitants of Jerusalem and
the people of Judah. I will lay the key   22
of the house of David on his shoulder;
what he opens no man shall shut, and
what he shuts no man shall open. He   23
shall be a seat of honour for his father's
family; I will fasten him firmly in place
like a peg. On him shall hang all the   24
weight of the family, down to the
lowest dregs—all the little vessels, both
bowls and pots. On that day, says the   25
LORD of Hosts, the peg which was
firmly fastened in its place shall be
removed; it shall be hacked out and
shall fall, and the load of things hanging
on it shall be destroyed. The LORD has
spoken.

                Tyre: an oracle.   **23**

The ships of Tarshish howl, for the
    harbour is sacked;
the port of entry from Kittim is
    swept away.
The people of the sea-coast, the   2–3
    merchants of Sidon, wail,
people whose agents cross the great
    waters,
    whose harvest*r* is the grain of the
    Shihor
    and their revenue the trade of
    nations.

q Prob. rdg.; Heb. man.
r whose harvest: *prob. rdg.; Heb.* the harvest of the
Nile.

---

in case of siege. **12–13:** The city celebrates the completion of fortifications with sacrifices, the
slaughtering of cattle, instead of seeing the impending siege as a call to repentance.
  22.15–25: Against an arrogant official. *Shebna*, the highest government official under the king
(Jer.20.1–6), has behaved arrogantly; he will not be buried in the magnificent grave he has
prepared for himself, but will be exiled after losing his office (vv. 15–19). He will be replaced by
Eliakim (vv. 20–25; see 36.3,11,22; 37.2). **15:** The *comptroller of the household* (lit. "the one
over the household") was the prime minister (see Gen.41.40). **21–24:** The symbols of authority
and the duties of the prime minister are described. **25:** The verse is enigmatic; it suggests that
Eliakim himself eventually will be removed from office.
  23.1–18: Judgment against Tyre and Sidon. These were Phoenician seaports. **1–7:** The location
of *Tarshish* is uncertain; it was a distant Mediterranean port, perhaps on the southern coast

4 Sidon, the sea-fortress,[s] cries in her
  disappointment,[t]
  I no longer feel the anguish of labour
  or bear children;
  I have no young sons to rear, no
  daughters to bring up.
5 When the news is confirmed in Egypt
  her people sway in anguish at the
  fate of Tyre.
6   Make your way to Tarshish, they
  say,
  howl, you who dwell by the sea-
  coast.
7 Is this your busy city, ancient in
  story,
  on whose voyages you were carried
  to settle far away?

8 Whose plan was this against Tyre,
  the city of battlements,
  whose merchants were princes
  and her traders the most
  honoured men on earth?
9 The LORD of Hosts planned it to
  prick every noble's pride
  and bring all the most honoured
  men on earth into contempt.
10 Take to the tillage of your fields,
  you people of Tarshish;
  for your market[u] is lost.
11 The LORD has stretched out his hand
  over the sea
  and shaken kingdoms,
  he has given his command to
  destroy the marts of Canaan;
12 and he has said, You shall busy
  yourselves no more,
  you, the sorely oppressed virgin
  city of Sidon.
  Though you arise and cross over to
  Kittim,
  even there you shall find no rest.

13   Look at this land, the destined home
  of ships[v]! The Chaldaeans[w] erected
  their[x] siege-towers, dismantled its palaces and laid it in ruins.

Howl, you ships of Tarshish; 11
for your haven is sacked.

From that day Tyre shall be for- 15
gotten for seventy years, the span of
one king's life. At the end of the
seventy years her plight shall be that of
the harlot in the song:

Take your harp, go round the city, 16
poor forgotten harlot;
touch the strings sweetly, sing all
your songs,
make them remember you again.

At the end of seventy years, the LORD 17
will turn again to Tyre; she shall go
back to her old trade and hire herself
out to every kingdom on earth. The 18
profits of her trading will be dedicated
to the LORD; they shall not be hoarded
or stored up, but shall be given to those
who worship the LORD, to purchase
food in plenty and fine attire.

The LORD's judgement on the earth

Beware, the LORD will empty the **24**
earth,
split it open and turn it upside down,
and scatter its inhabitants.
Then it will be the same for priest 2
and people,
the same for master and slave,
mistress and slave-girl,
seller and buyer,
borrower and lender, debtor and
creditor.
The earth is emptied clean away 3
and stripped clean bare.

s the sea-fortress: *prob. rdg.; Heb.* the sea, sea-fortress, saying.
t in her disappointment: *prob. rdg.; Heb.* be dis-appointed.
u *Prob. rdg.; Heb.* girdle.
v *Or* marmots.
w *Prob. rdg.; Heb. adds* this was the people; it was not Assyria.
x *Prob. rdg.; Heb.* his.

of Spain and so a symbol for the end of the earth. *Kittim:* probably Cyprus. **13:** This verse, the text of which is corrupt, relates the destruction to the Babylonian period (see Ezek. chs. 27–28). **15:** *Seventy years* is symbolic of a long time.
  24.1–27.13: The new age. The diverse materials collected in this section are strongly eschato-logical in character, looking toward the final triumph of the LORD. There are announcements of the final judgment, prayers of petition, and hymns. The literary style with the tendency toward apocalyptic (vv. 21–23) and the theological perspective of final judgment (v. 21) indicate that this collection originated long after Isaiah of Jerusalem (see Introduction).
  24.1–23: The LORD's judgment on the earth. The first (vv. 1–6) and final (vv. 18b–23) sections of this chapter constitute a single announcement of the LORD's intervention against all of

For this is the word that the LORD
  has spoken.

4 The earth dries up and withers,
  the whole world withers and grows
    sick;
  the earth's high places sicken,
5 and earth itself is desecrated by the
    feet of those who live in it,
  because they have broken the laws,
  and violated the eternal covenant.
6 For this a curse has devoured the
    earth
  and its inhabitants stand aghast.
  For this those who inhabit the
    earth dwindle
  and only a few men are left.

7 The new vine dries up, the vines
    sicken,
  and all the revellers turn to sorrow.
8 Silent the merry beat of tambourines,
  hushed the shouts of revelry,
  the merry harp is silent.
9 No one shall drink wine to the
    sound of song;
  the liquor will be bitter to the man
  who drinks it.
10   The city of chaos is a broken city,
  every house barred, that no one
    may enter.
11 Men call for wine in the streets;
  all revelry is darkened,
  and mirth is banished from the
    land.

12 Desolation alone is left in the city
  and the gate is broken into pieces.
13 So shall it be in all the world, in
    every nation,
  as when an olive-tree is beaten and
    stripped,
  as when the vintage is ended.

14 Men raise their voices and cry aloud,
  they shout in the west,*y* so great is
    the LORD's majesty.

15 Therefore let the LORD be glorified
  in the regions of the east,
  and the name of the LORD the
    God of Israel
  in the coasts and islands of the
    west.

16 From the ends of the earth we have
    heard them sing,
  How lovely is righteousness!
  But I thought, Villainy, villainy!
  Woe to the traitors and their
    treachery!
  Traitors double-dyed they are indeed!
17 The hunter's scare, the pit, and the
    trap
  threaten all who dwell in the land;
18 if a man runs from the rattle of the
    scare
  he will fall into the pit;
  if he climbs out of the pit
  he will be caught in the trap.
  When the windows of heaven above
    are opened
  and earth's foundations shake,
19 the earth is utterly shattered,
  it is convulsed and reels wildly.
20 The earth reels to and fro like a
    drunken man
  and sways like a watchman's
    shelter;
  the sins of men weigh heavy upon it,
  and it falls to rise no more.

21 On that day the LORD will punish
  the host of heaven in heaven, and
    on earth the kings of the earth,
22 herded together, close packed like
    prisoners in a dungeon;
  shut up in gaol, after a long time they
    shall be punished.
23 The moon shall grow pale and the
    sun hide its face in shame;
  for the LORD of Hosts has become
    king

y in the west: or more loudly than the sea.

---

creation. The remainder of the chapter (vv. 7–18a) consists of additions to that poem. **5:** *The eternal covenant* may allude to the one with Noah (Gen.9.1–17), but in view of the reference to the *laws* and *statutes*, may well reflect the covenant on Sinai (Exod. chs. 19–24). **7–13:** As nature suffers, *the city* (vv. 10,12), probably Jerusalem, will become desolate; the same tragedy will occur throughout the earth (v. 13). **14–18a:** Some are heard to praise the LORD and *righteousness* (v. 16), or "the righteous one," but this is deceptive. **17–18a:** There is no escape from God's judgment; compare Amos 5.18–20. **18b–23:** The judgment has cosmic dimensions; afterward the LORD will become king in Jerusalem. **18b:** *Windows of heaven:* see Gen.7.11. **21:** *Host of heaven:* the stars, here conceived of as deities. See Jer.19.13; Zeph.1.5; Ps.82.1,6–7. **23:** On the enthronement of the LORD, see Pss.47,93,96.

on Mount Zion and in Jerusalem,
and shows his glory before their
    elders.

The deliverance and
ingathering of Judah

25 O LORD, thou art my God;
I will exalt thee and praise thy name;
for thou hast accomplished a
    wonderful purpose,
certain and sure, from of old.
2 For thou hast turned cities into
    heaps of ruin,
and fortified towns into rubble;
every mansion in the cities is swept
    away,
    never to be rebuilt.
3 For this a cruel nation holds thee
    in honour,
the cities of ruthless nations fear thee.
4 Truly thou hast been a refuge to
    the poor,
a refuge to the needy in his trouble,
shelter from the tempest and shade
    from the heat.
For the blast of the ruthless is like
    an icy storm
5 or a scorching drought;
thou subduest the roar of the
    foe,^{z}
and the song of the ruthless dies
    away.

6 On this mountain the LORD of Hosts
    will prepare
a banquet of rich fare for all the
    peoples,
a banquet of wines well matured
    and richest fare,
well-matured wines strained clear.

On this mountain the LORD will 7
    swallow up
that veil that shrouds all the peoples,
the pall thrown over all the nations;
he will swallow up death for ever. 8
Then the Lord GOD will wipe away
    the tears
    from every face
and remove the reproach of his people
    from the whole earth.
The LORD has spoken.

On that day men will say, 9
See, this is our God
for whom we have waited to deliver us;
this is the LORD for whom we have
    waited;
let us rejoice and exult in his
    deliverance.
For the hand of the LORD will rest 10
    on this mountain,
but Moab shall be trampled under
    his feet
as straw is trampled into a midden.
In it Moab shall spread out his 11
    hands
as a swimmer spreads his hands to
    swim,
but he shall sink his pride with every
    stroke of his hands.
The LORD has thrown down the 12
    high defences of your walls,
has levelled them to the earth
and brought them down to the dust.

On that day this song shall be sung in **26**
Judah:

We have a strong city
whose walls and ramparts are our
    deliverance.

z Prob. rdg.; Heb. adds heat in the shadow of a cloud.

25.1–5: A hymn of thanksgiving. Compare Ps.145. **2–4:** God, and not man's *fortified towns*
and *cities,* is the ultimate source of security and he is especially a *refuge to the poor.* **5:** The
dominance of the *ruthless* is as fleeting as a *song.*
    25.6–12: Promise of the LORD's banquet. The unit is an announcement of salvation, with
strong eschatological tones. The inclusion of *Moab* (vv. 10b–12) seems out of place and may be
an addition, a symbol for all of Israel's enemies. **6:** *This mountain:* Zion. Shared-offering sacrifices were those in which a part of the animal was burned on the altar to God, a part given to
the priests, and a part eaten at the shrine by the offerer and his family as a sign of a loving
communion with the deity; see Num.7.16–36; 1 Sam.9.12. Here this cultic feast is extended to
symbolize the great, universal *banquet* given by God in which man and God will live in communion and harmony; compare Lk.14.12–25; Isa.55.1–3. **8:** This is one of the rare OT passages
expressing the hope for the end of *death.*
    26.1–6: A hymn of trust. See Ps.24, especially vv. 7–10. The themes of 25.1–5 are resumed:
Judah has confidence in the LORD because he has destroyed the enemy and cares for the *oppressed
and the poor* (v. 6). **1–2:** An entrance or processional liturgy begins the psalm: see Ps.118.19–20.
1: The *strong city* is Jerusalem.

2 Open the gates to let a righteous
     nation in,
     a nation that keeps faith.
3 Thou dost keep in peace men of
     constant mind,
     in peace because they trust in thee.
4 Trust in the LORD for ever;
     for the LORD himself is an
     everlasting rock.
5 He has brought low all who dwell
     high in a towering city;
     he levels it to the ground and lays
     it in the dust,
6 that the oppressed and the poor may
     tread it underfoot.
7 The path of the righteous is level,
     and thou markest out the right way
     for the upright.
8 We too look to the path prescribed
     in thy laws, O LORD;
     thy name and thy memory are
     our heart's desire.
9 With all my heart I long for thee
     in the night,
     I seek thee eagerly when dawn
     breaks;
     for, when thy laws prevail in the land,
     the inhabitants of the world learn
     justice.
10 The wicked are destroyed, they have
     never learnt justice;
     corrupt in a land of honest ways,
     they do not regard the majesty of
     the LORD.

11 O LORD, thy hand is lifted high,
     but the bitter enemies of thy
     people do not see it;[a]
     let the fire of thy enmity destroy them.
12 O LORD, thou wilt bestow prosperity
     on us;
     for in truth all our works are thy doing.
13 O LORD our God,
     other lords than thou have been
     our masters,
     but thee alone do we invoke by name.
14 The dead will not live again,
     those long in their graves will not
     rise;

to this end thou hast punished them
     and destroyed them,
     and made all memory of them
     perish.
15 Thou hast enlarged the nation, O
     LORD,
     enlarged it and won thyself honour,
     thou hast extended all the frontiers
     of the land.
16 In our distress, O LORD, we[b] sought
     thee out,
     chastened by the mere whisper of
     thy rebuke.
17 As a woman with child, when her
     time is near,
     is in labour and cries out in her pains,
     so were we in thy presence, O LORD.
18 We have been with child, we
     have been in labour,
     but have brought forth wind.
     We have won no success for the land,
     and no one will be born to inhabit
     the world.
19 But thy dead live, their bodies will
     rise again.
     They that sleep in the earth will
     awake and shout for joy;
     for thy dew is a dew of sparkling
     light,
     and the earth will bring those long
     dead to birth again.

20 Go, my people, enter your rooms
     and shut your doors behind you;
     withdraw for a brief while, until
     wrath has gone by.
21 For see, the LORD is coming from
     his place
     to punish the inhabitants of the
     earth for their sins;
     then the earth shall uncover her
     blood-stains
     and hide her slain no more.

27 On that day the LORD will punish
     with his cruel sword, his mighty and
     powerful sword,

a *Prob. rdg.; Heb. adds* let them see and be ashamed.
b *Prob. rdg.; Heb.* they.

26.7–19: Prayers of petition and meditations. 8: For the ancients, the *name* somehow contained the reality of a person or thing. **11:** The *enemies* of God's *people* do not recognize in their calamity the *hand* of the LORD instructing them to salvation and so they are destroyed by it. **14:** *The dead* here seem to be individuals who have died in hostility to God. **19:** The words concerning resurrection may refer to individuals; see Dan.12.2; however, they may be only figurative, referring to the restoration of the nation whose suffering has been described in the previous verses; see Ezek. ch. 37.
     26.20–27.1: The LORD's judgment on the dragon. 27.1: *Leviathan* and other sea monsters,

Leviathan that twisting[c] sea-serpent,
that writhing serpent Leviathan,
and slay the monster of the deep.

2 On that day sing to the pleasant
vineyard,
3 I the LORD am its keeper,
moment by moment I water it for
fear its green leaves fail.
Night and day I tend it,
4 but I get no wine;
I would as soon have briars and thorns,
then I would wage war upon it and
burn it all up,
5 unless it grasps me as its refuge and
makes peace with me—
unless it makes peace with me.

6 In time to come Jacob's offspring
shall take root
and Israel shall bud and blossom,
and they shall fill the whole earth
with fruit.

7 Has God struck him down as he
struck others down?
Has the slayer been slain as he slew
others?
8–10[d] This then purges Jacob's iniquity,
this[e] has removed his sin;
that he grinds all altar stones to
powder like chalk;
no sacred poles and incense-altars
are left standing.

The fortified city is left solitary,
and his quarrel with her ends in
brushing her away,[f]
removing her by a cruel blast when

the east wind blows;
it is a homestead stripped bare,
deserted like a wilderness;
there the calf grazes and there lies
down,
and crops every twig.
Its boughs snap off when they grow dry, 11
and women come and light their
fires with them.
For they are a people without sense;
therefore their maker will show
them no mercy,
he who formed them will show
them no favour.

On that day the LORD will beat out 12
the grain,
from the streams of the Euphrates
to the Torrent of Egypt;
but you Israelites will be gleaned
one by one.

On that day 13
a blast shall be blown on a great
trumpet,
and those who are lost in Assyria
and those dispersed in Egypt will
come in
and worship the LORD on the holy
mountain, in Jerusalem.

Assyria and Judah

Oh, the proud garlands of the 　　**28**
drunkards of Ephraim

c *Or* primeval.
d *Verses 8–10 re-arranged thus: 9, 10a, 8, 10b.*
e *Prob. rdg.; Heb. adds* all fruit.
f *Prob. rdg.; Heb. adds* by dismissing her.

well-known in Canaanite and Mesopotamian mythology, occasionally appear in the OT,
especially in Pss., as symbols of the chaos and evil overcome by God; see 51.9–10; Amos 9.3;
Ps.74.13; Job 26.12–13. The struggle against the monster or monsters is usually associated
either with creation or with the end of the world.

27.2–13: Words of salvation and judgment. The section is not a unified whole, but a collection
of various speeches announcing the LORD's intentions. **2–6:** The poem is a reinterpretation of
the metaphors of the *vineyard* in 5.1–7; announcement of judgment has become promise of
salvation. **7–11:** The New English Bible rearrangement of the verses is an attempt to make
sense of a very confusing passage. The first part sees the judgment upon Israel as a purging
punishment; the second part is an announcement of total judgment upon an unidentified *fortified
city* which symbolizes the forces of evil. **12–13:** The *day* of the LORD will be a day of harvest
when the exiles will be brought home. **12:** *Torrent of Egypt:* a stream, dry except during the
rainy season, flowing from the Sinai peninsula into the Mediterranean fifty miles south of Gaza.
It was considered to be the southern boundary of Judah. **13:** The *great trumpet*, the horn which
called people to worship, will summon the exiles home to *Jerusalem*.

28.1–33.24: Assyria and Judah. The historical context of many of these speeches is the Assyrian
crisis of 705–701 B.C. when Hezekiah allied himself with Egypt against Assyria. The prophet
criticized those who favored the alliance and warned of disaster. Many of the speeches in this
unit begin in Hebrew with a cry "Woe," which the New English Bible translates in various
ways; see 28.1; 29.1; 29.15; 30.1; 31.1; 33.1.

and the flowering sprays, so lovely
    in their beauty,
on the heads of revellers dripping
    with perfumes,
    overcome with wine!

2 See, the Lord has one at his bidding,
        mighty and strong,
    whom he sets to work with violence
        against the land,
    like a sweeping storm of hail, like a
        destroying tempest,
    like a torrent of water in overwhelming
        flood.

3   The proud garlands of Ephraim's
            drunkards
        shall be trampled underfoot,

4 and the flowering sprays, so lovely
        in their beauty
    on the heads dripping with perfumes,
    shall be like early figs ripe before
        summer;
    he who sees them plucks them,
    and their bloom is gone while they
        lie in his hand.

5 On that day the LORD of Hosts shall
        be a lovely garland,
    a beautiful diadem for the remnant
        of his people,

6 a spirit of justice for one who
        presides in a court of justice,
    and of valour for^g those who repel
        the enemy at the gate.

7   These too are addicted to wine,
            clamouring in their cups:
    priest and prophet are addicted to
        strong drink
    and bemused with wine;
    clamouring in their cups, confirmed
        topers,^{h}
        hiccuping in drunken stupor;

8 every table is covered with vomit,
        filth that leaves no clean spot.

9 Who is it that the prophet hopes to
        teach,

to whom will what they hear make
    sense?
Are they babes newly weaned, just
    taken from the breast?
It is all harsh cries and raucous   10
    shouts,
'A little more here, a little there!'
So it will be with barbarous speech   11
    and strange tongue
that this people will hear God
    speaking,
    this people to whom he once said,   12
'This is true rest; let the exhausted
    have rest.
This is repose', and they refused to
    listen.
Now to them the word of the LORD   13
    will be
harsh cries and raucous shouts,
'A little more here, a little there!'—
and so, as they walk, they will
    stumble backwards,
they will be injured, trapped and
    caught.

Listen then to the word of the LORD,   14
    you arrogant men
who rule this people in Jerusalem.
You say, 'We have made a treaty   15
    with Death
and signed a pact with Sheol:
so that, when the raging flood sweeps
    by, it shall not touch us;
for we have taken refuge in lies
    and sheltered behind falsehood.'
These are the words of the   16
    Lord GOD:
Look, I am laying a stone in Zion, a
    block of granite,
a precious corner-stone for a firm
    foundation;

g for: *prob. rdg.; Heb. om.*
h *These too . . . topers: or* These too lose their way
through wine and are set wandering by strong drink:
priest and prophet lose their way through strong
drink and are fuddled with wine; are set wandering
by strong drink, lose their way through tippling.

28.1–6: Judgment against the Northern Kingdom. The speech probably dates before the fall
of Samaria (2 Kgs.17.6) in 722–721 B.C. which signaled the end of the Northern Kingdom,
Ephraim. **2:** The *one* must be an Assyrian king. **5–6:** This promise of salvation for the *remnant*
is a later addition.
28.7–22: Judgment because of false prophets, priests, and leaders. The prophet ridicules
drunken priests and prophets, holding them responsible for his people's trouble. **9–10:** The
drunkards mimic the language of *the prophet*, namely Isaiah, as if his language were the unintelligible babbling of infants, which the Heb. words imitate. **11–13:** The leaders refusing to
listen to *God* through Isaiah, will be forced to listen to him through the *harsh*, unintelligible
shouts of the Assyrians, their conquerors. **14:** The *word* is now addressed to those who *rule*,
that is, the king and his advisers. **15:** The *treaty* (or "covenant") which Isaiah ridicules may
have been an agreement with Egypt for mutual aid against Assyria. **16:** *Faith:* see 7.9 n.

he who has faith shall not waver.

17 I will use justice as a plumb-line
and righteousness as a plummet;
hail shall sweep away your refuge
of lies,
and flood-waters carry away your
shelter.

18 Then your treaty with Death shall
be annulled
and your pact with Sheol shall not
stand;
the raging waters will sweep by,
and you will be like land swept by
the flood.

19 As often as it sweeps by, it will
take you;
morning after morning it will
sweep by,
day and night.
The very thought of such tidings
will bring nothing but dismay;

20 for 'The bed is too short for a man
to stretch,
and the blanket too narrow to
cover him.'

21 But the LORD shall arise as he rose
on Mount Perazim
and storm with rage as he did in the
Vale of Gibeon
to do what he must do—how
strange a deed!
to perform his work—how outlandish
a work!

22 But now have done with your
arrogance,
lest your bonds grow tighter;
for I have heard destruction
decreed
by the Lord GOD of Hosts for the
whole land.

23 Listen and hear what I say,
attend and hear my words.

24 Will the ploughman continually
plough for the sowing,

breaking his ground and harrowing
it?

25 Does he not, once he has levelled it,
broadcast the dill and scatter the
cummin?
Does he not plant the wheat in rows
with barley[i] and spelt along the
edge?

26 Does not his God instruct him and
train him aright?

27 Dill is not threshed with a sledge,
and the cartwheel is not rolled over
cummin;
dill is beaten with a rod,
and cummin with a flail.

28 Corn is crushed, but not to the
uttermost,
not with a final crushing;
his cartwheels rumble over it and
break it up,
but they do not grind it fine.

29 This message, too, comes from the
LORD of Hosts,
whose purposes are wonderful
and his power great.

29 Alas for Ariel! Ariel,
the city where David encamped.
Add year to year,
let the pilgrim-feasts run their
round,

2 and I will bring Ariel to sore
straits,
when there shall be moaning and
lamentation.
I will make her my Ariel indeed,
my fiery altar.

3 I will throw my army round you
like a wall;
I will set a ring of outposts all
round you
and erect siege-works against you.

4 You shall be brought low, you will
speak out of the ground

i Prob. rdg.; Heb. adds an unintelligible word.

17: *Plumb-line:* see Amos 7.7–9. **20:** The proverb cited illustrates the point: the treaty is not sufficient to save Israel. **21:** *Mount Perazim* was the site of one of David's victories over the Philistines (2 Sam.5.17–21). *Gibeon* was in Benjamin (Josh.18.25); the allusion is uncertain, though Josh. 10.1–10 may be meant.

28.23–29: The parable of the farmer. No direct interpretation or application, such as in 5.1–7 and 2 Sam.12.1–6, is given here; the point (v. 29) is that the farmer's wisdom symbolizes the divine *purposes*. **27:** In the Near East even today large grains like wheat, barley, etc. (British: *corn*) are threshed under a sledge pulled over the ears by oxen or donkeys. *Dill* and *cummin* are too small and soft and could be lost or crushed in such a process. **28:** As *corn is crushed, but not to the uttermost,* neither is Israel's weakness by God.

29.1–8: Jerusalem under siege. 1–4: The occasion is probably Sennacherib's invasion of Judah in 701 B.C. (2 Kgs.18.13–35). **1:** *Ariel,* which probably means "lion of God," is a special

and your words will issue from the
earth;
your voice will come like a ghost's
from the ground,
and your words will squeak out of
the earth.
5 Yet the horde of your enemies shall
crumble into dust,
the horde of ruthless foes shall fly
like chaff.
Then suddenly, all in an instant,
6 punishment shall come from the
LORD of Hosts
with thunder and earthquake and a
great noise,
with storm and tempest and a flame
of devouring fire;
7 and the horde of all the nations
warring against Ariel,
all their baggage-trains and siege-
works,
and all her oppressors themselves,
shall fade as a dream, a vision of
the night.
8 Like a starving man who dreams
and thinks that he is eating,
but wakes up to find himself empty,
or a thirsty man who dreams
and thinks that he is drinking,
but wakes up to find himself thirsty
and dry,
so shall the horde of all the nations
be
that war against Mount Zion.

9 Loiter and be dazed, enjoy yourselves
and be blinded,
be drunk but not with wine, reel but
not with strong drink;
10 for the LORD has poured upon you
a spirit of deep stupor;
he has closed your eyes, the prophets,
and muffled your heads, the seers.

11 All prophetic vision has become for
you like a sealed book. Give such a
book to one who can read and say,
'Come, read this'; he will answer, 'I

cannot', because it is sealed. Give it to 12
one who cannot read and say, 'Come,
read this'; he will answer, 'I cannot
read.'

Then the Lord said: 13

Because this people approach me
with their mouths
and honour me with their lips
while their hearts are far from me,
and their religion is but a precept of
men, learnt by rote,
therefore I will yet again shock this 14
people,
adding shock to shock:
the wisdom of their wise men shall
vanish
and the discernment of the
discerning shall be lost.

Shame upon those who seek to   15
hide their purpose
too deep for the LORD to see,
and who, when their deeds are
done in the dark,
say, 'Who sees us? Who knows of
us?'
How you turn things upside   16
down,
as if the potter ranked no higher
than the clay!
Shall the thing made say of its
maker, 'He did not make me'?
Shall the pot say of the potter, 'He
has no skill'?
The time is but short   17
before Lebanon goes back to
grassland
and the grassland is no better than
scrub.

On that day deaf men shall hear   18
when a book is read,
and the eyes of the blind shall see
out of impenetrable darkness.
The lowly shall once again rejoice in 19
the LORD,
and the poorest of men exult in the

---

name for Jerusalem, used only by Isaiah. **5–8:** Promises of salvation from the enemy alternate
with the promise of punishment, but the final word is that Jerusalem will be delivered. According
to his own reports, Sennacherib besieged Jerusalem but left without destroying it. See 37.21–36.
29.9–24: Human ignorance and the LORD's plans. 9–10: The failure to see and hear comes
from the LORD; see 6.9–10 n. **11–12:** This seems to be a later prose addition to explain vv. 9–10.
13–14: The punishment for religious rites without depth is a loss of *wisdom.* **13:** See Mt.15.8–9;
Mk.7.6 7. *Religion:* lit. "their fear of me." **15–17:** Not trusting God's help but seeking instead
help from military alliances (as the kings of Judah did) is like the *pot* accusing the *potter* of
having *no skill;* see 30.1–2. **17:** *Lebanon* was proverbially very fertile. **18–21:** The time will

Holy One of Israel.
20 The ruthless shall be no more, the
    arrogant shall cease to be;
    those who are quick to see mischief,
21   those who charge others with a sin
    or lay traps for him who brings the
      wrongdoer into court
    or by falsehood deny justice to the
      righteous—
    all these shall be exterminated.

22   Therefore these are the words of the
    LORD the God of the house of Jacob,
    the God who ransomed Abraham:

    This is no time for Jacob to be
      shamed,
    no time for his face to grow pale;
23   for his descendants will hallow my
      name
    when they see what I have done in
      their nation.
    They will hallow the Holy One of
      Jacob
    and hold the God of Israel in awe;
24   those whose minds are confused will
      gain understanding,
    and the obstinate will receive
      instruction.

30   Oh, rebel sons! says the LORD,
    you make plans, but not of my
      devising,
    you weave schemes, but not
      inspired by me,
    piling sin upon sin;
2   you hurry down to Egypt without
      consulting me,
    to seek protection under Pharaoh's
      shelter
    and take refuge under Egypt's
      wing.
3   Pharaoh's protection will bring you
      disappointment
    and refuge under Egypt's wing
      humiliation;

for, though his officers are at   4
  Zoan
and his envoys reach as far as
  Hanes,
all are left in sorry plight by that   5
  unprofitable nation,
no help they find, no profit, only
  disappointment and disgrace.

The Beasts of the South: an oracle.   6

Through a land of hardship and
  distress
the tribes of lioness and roaring
  lion,
sand-viper and venomous flying
  serpent,
carry their wealth on the backs of
  asses
and their treasures on camels'
  humps
to an unprofitable people.
Vain and worthless is the help of   7
  Egypt;
therefore have I given her this
  name,
  Rahab Quelled.
Now come and write it on a tablet,   8
engrave it as an inscription before
  their eyes,
that it may be there in future days,
  a testimony for all time.
For they are a race of rebels, disloyal 9
  sons,
sons who will not listen to the
  LORD's instruction;
they say to the seers, 'You shall   10
  not see',
and to the visionaries, 'You shall
  have no true visions;
give us smooth words and seductive
  visions.
Turn aside, leave the straight path,   11
  and rid us for ever of the Holy One
    of Israel.'

---

come when, hearing and sight restored, the *lowly* (v. 19) will have cause for celebration, and the *ruthless* and *arrogant* (v. 20) will be destroyed.
    30.1–18: The fruits of rebellion. These pronouncements are related to the period of Judah's alliance with Egypt against Assyria, 705–701 B.C. **4:** *Zoan* and *Hanes* were in the Nile delta. **6–7:** It is vain to seek the help of Egypt (*Beasts of the South*). **7:** *Rahab Quelled* is a sarcastic title based on one of the names of the chaos dragon slain by the deity. See 27.1 n. Rahab is often a synonym for Egypt. **8–18:** Several speeches concerning the danger of rebellion against the LORD support the prophet's warnings against the Egyptian alliance. **8–11:** Isaiah is commanded to write down his words so that when they come true it will be known that he was a prophet. **8:** See 8.1–4,16–18. **9:** *Disloyal sons* deny the goodness of their father, the LORD, by seeking help from Egypt or Assyria. **10:** Seductive visions are false prophecies that confirm

12 These are the words of the Holy One of
Israel:

> Because you have rejected this
> warning
> and trust in devious and dishonest
> practices,
> resting on them for support,
13 therefore you shall find this iniquity
> will be
> like a crack running down
> a high wall, which bulges
> and suddenly, all in an instant,
> comes crashing down,
14 as an earthen jar is broken with a
> crash,
> mercilessly shattered,
> so that not a shard is found among
> the fragments
> to take fire from the glowing
> embers,
> or to scoop up water from a pool.

15 These are the words of the Lord GOD
the Holy One of Israel:

> Come back, keep peace, and you
> will be safe;
> in stillness and in staying quiet, there
> lies your strength.
16 But you would have none of it; you
> said, No,
> we will take horse and flee;
> therefore you shall be put to flight:
> We will ride apace;
> therefore swift shall be the pace of
> your pursuers.
17 When a thousand flee at the
> challenge of one,
> you shall all flee at the challenge
> of five, until you are left
> like a pole on a mountain-top, a
> signal post on a hill.
18 Yet the LORD is waiting to show you
> his favour,
> yet he yearns to have pity on you;
> for the LORD is a God of justice.
> Happy are all who wait for
> him!

19 O people of Zion who dwell in
Jerusalem, you shall weep no more.
The LORD will show you favour and
answer you when he hears your cry for
help. The Lord may give you bread of 20
adversity and water of affliction, but
he who teaches you shall no longer be
hidden out of sight, but with your own
eyes you shall see him always. If you 21
stray from the road to right or left you
shall hear with your own ears a voice
behind you saying, This is the way;
follow it. You will reject, as things 22
unclean, your silvered images and
your idols sheathed in gold; you will
loathe them like a foul discharge and
call them ordure.*j* The Lord will give 23
you rain for the seed you sow, and as
the produce of your soil he will give
you heavy crops of corn in plenty.
When that day comes the cattle shall
graze in broad pastures; the oxen and 24
asses that work your land shall be fed
with well-seasoned fodder, winnowed
with shovel and fork. On each high 25
mountain and each lofty hill shall be
streams of running water, on the day
of massacre when the highest in the
land fall. The moon shall shine with a 26
brightness like the sun's, and the sun
with seven times his wonted brightness,
seven days' light in one, on the day
when the LORD binds up the broken
limbs of his people and heals their
wounds.

> See, the name of the LORD comes   27
> from afar,
> his anger blazing and his doom
> heavy.
> His lips are charged with wrath
> and his tongue is a devouring fire.
> His breath is like a torrent in spate, 28
> rising neck-high,
> a yoke to force the nations to their
> ruin,
> a bit in the mouth to guide the
> peoples astray.

j call them ordure: *or* say to them, Be off.

---

human wisdom, inclination, whim, or fancy; see 1 Kgs.22.8–28. **13:** Lack of faith is like a
crack in a *high wall* which gives way under pressure. **15:** See 7.9. **16:** See Amos 2.14–16. **17:**
Signal post: Jerusalem under siege.
   30.19–26: Healing beyond punishment. Those who suffer *adversity* (v. 20) are encouraged to
remain faithful by the assurance that a punishment will purge them and by the promise of
restored prosperity. The section reflects the circumstances of the Exile; vv. 19–26 may be a late
expansion of v. 18.
   30.27–33: Judgment against Assyria. The approach of the LORD to punish Assyria is an-

29 But for you there shall be songs,
 as on a night of sacred pilgrimage,
your hearts glad, as the hearts of
 men who walk to the sound of
  the pipe
on their way to the LORD's hill, to
 the rock of Israel.
30 Then the LORD shall make his voice
 heard in majesty
and show his arm sweeping down in
 fierce anger
with devouring flames of fire,
with cloudburst and tempests of
 rain and hailstones;
31 for at the voice of the LORD
 Assyria's heart fails her,
 as she feels the stroke of his rod.
32 Tambourines and harps and shaking
 sistrums
 shall keep time
with every stroke of his rod,
of the chastisement which the LORD
 inflicts on her.
33 Long ago was Topheth made ready,*k*
 made deep and broad,
its fire-pit a blazing mass of logs,
and the breath of the LORD like a
 stream of brimstone
 blazing in it.

31 Shame upon those who go down to
 Egypt for help
and rely on horses,
putting their trust in chariots many
 in number
and in horsemen in their thousands,
but do not look to the Holy One
 of Israel
or seek guidance of the LORD!
2 Yet the LORD too in his wisdom can
 bring about trouble
and he does not take back his
 words;
he will rise up against the league of
 evildoers,

against all who help those who do
 wrong
The Egyptians are men, not God,*l*   3
their horses are flesh, not spirit;
and, when the LORD stretches out
 his hand,
the helper will stumble and he who
 is helped will fall,
and they will all vanish together.

This is what the LORD has said to me: 4

As a lion or a young lion growls over
 its prey
when the muster of shepherds is
 called out against it,
 and is not scared at their noise
 or cowed by their clamour,
so shall the LORD of Hosts come
 down to do battle
for Mount Zion and her high
 summit.
Thus the LORD of Hosts, like a bird   5
 hovering over its young,
will be a shield over Jerusalem;
 he will shield her and deliver her,
 standing over her and delivering
 her.
O Israel, come back to him whom   6
 you have so deeply offended,
for on that day when you spurn,   7
 one and all,
the idols of silver and the idols of
 gold
which your own sinful hands have
 made,
Assyria shall fall by the sword, but   8
 by no sword of man;
a sword that no man wields shall
 devour him.
He shall flee before the sword,
and his young warriors shall be
 put to forced labour,

k Prob. rdg.; Heb. adds is that prepared also for the
king?
l Or gods.

---

nounced. **33:** The oracle is probably about 701 B.C. *Topheth* was a place just outside of Jerusalem
where human sacrifices had been offered to the pagan deity Molech; see Lev.18.21; 2 Kgs.23.10.
Assyria apparently will be slaughtered and burned there.
 31.1–3: Against reliance on Egypt. The prophet again indicts those leaders who made a treaty
with Egypt. **2–3:** The LORD *in his wisdom* controls history; it is ridiculous to trust in these
mere men. **2:** *League:* an allusion to the treaty parties, i.e. Egyptians, *who help,* and Israel,
who do wrong; see 30.1–18 n.
 31.4–9: A promise to protect Jerusalem. The LORD will *come down* on Zion and fight against
Assyria. The speech should be associated with Sennacherib's invasion of 701 B.C. See 29.1–8;
37.21–38. **5:** The LORD will continue his protective role, *hovering* over *Jerusalem* like an eagle
over *its young,* picking her up to *deliver* her from danger; compare Deut.32.11. **6–7:** The verses
probably are a late addition.

9   his officers shall be helpless from
            terror
    and his captains too dismayed to
            flee.
    This is the very word of the LORD
    whose fire blazes in Zion,
    and whose furnace is set up in
            Jerusalem.

32 Behold, a king shall reign in
            righteousness
    and his rulers rule with justice,
2   and a man shall be a refuge from
            the wind
        and a shelter from the tempest,
        or like runnels of water in dry
            ground,
    like the shadow of a great rock in a
            thirsty land.
3   The eyes that can see will not be
            clouded,
    and the ears that can hear will
            listen;
4   the anxious heart will understand
            and know,
    and the man who stammers will at
            once speak plain.
5   The scoundrel will no longer be
            thought noble,
        nor the villain called a prince;
6   for the scoundrel will speak like a
            scoundrel
    and will hatch evil in his heart;
        he is an impostor in all his
            actions,
    and in his words a liar even to the
            LORD;
        he starves the hungry of their food
        and refuses drink to the thirsty.
7   The villain's ways are villainous
    and he devises infamous plans
    to ruin the poor with his lies
    and deny justice to the needy.
8   But the man of noble mind forms
            noble designs
    and stands firm in his nobility.

9   You women that live at ease,
            stand up

and hear what I have to say.
You young women without a care,
        mark my words.
You have no cares now, but when   10
        the year is out, you will
        tremble,
for the vintage will be over and no
        produce gathered in.
        You who are now at ease, be   11
            anxious;
        tremble, you who have no cares.
        Strip yourselves bare;
        put a cloth round your waists
        and beat your breasts   12
    for the pleasant fields and fruitful
        vines.
On the soil of my people shall spring   13
        up thorns and briars,
    in every happy home and in the
        busy town,
for the palace is forsaken and the   14
        crowded streets deserted;
citadel*m* and watch-tower are turned
        into open heath,
the joy of wild asses ever after and
        pasture for the flocks,
until a spirit from on high is   15
        lavished upon us.
Then the wilderness will become
        grassland
    and grassland will be cheap as
        scrub;
    then justice shall make its home in 16
        the wilderness,
    and righteousness dwell in the
        grassland;
    when righteousness shall yield   17
        peace
    and its fruit be quietness and
        confidence for ever.
    Then my people shall live in a   18
        tranquil country,
dwelling in peace, in houses full of
        ease;
    it will be cool on the slopes of the 19
        forest then,
    and cities shall lie peaceful in the
        plain.

m Or hill; Heb. Ophel.

32.1–8: A promise of justice and righteousness. When Israel's government is based on *justice*, fools will be seen for what they are. See Prov.16.12–15. 1: See 9.7; 11.3–5. 5: In Wisdom thought the *scoundrel* is a fool and the *noble* man, especially a ruler, is wise.

32.9–14: A warning to complacent women. The women, now carefree (probably at the *vintage* festival, v. 10) will, in a *year*, mourn the destruction of their fields and cities. See 3.16–24; Amos 4.1–3. 14: *Citadel:* the fortified hills in the old city of David.

32.15–20: A promise of peace with justice. The outpouring of the *spirit* reverses the desolation wrought by human complacency outlined in the previous section.

20 Happy shall you be, sowing every
    man by the water-side,
    and letting ox and ass run free.

33 Ah! you destroyer, yourself
    undestroyed,
    betrayer still unbetrayed,
    when you cease to destroy you will
      be destroyed,
    after all your betrayals, you will
      be betrayed yourself.

2 O LORD, show us thy favour; we
      hope in thee.
    Uphold us every morning,
    save us when troubles come.
3 At the roar of the thunder the
      peoples flee,
    at thy rumbling nations are
      scattered;
4 their spoil is swept up as if young
      locusts had swept it,
    like a swarm of locusts men swarm
      upon it.

5 The LORD is supreme, for he dwells
      on high;
    if you fill Zion with justice and with
      righteousness,
6 then he will be the mainstay of the
      age:*n*
    wisdom and knowledge are the
      assurance of salvation;
    the fear of the LORD is her*o* treasure.

7 Hark, how the valiant cry aloud
      for help
    and those sent to sue for peace
      weep bitterly!
8 The highways are deserted, no
      travellers tread the roads.
    Covenants are broken, treaties are
      flouted;
    man is of no account.
9 The land is parched and wilting,
    Lebanon is eaten away and
      crumbling;
    Sharon has become a desert,
    Bashan and Carmel are stripped
      bare.

10 Now, says the LORD, I will rise up.
    Now I will exalt myself, now lift
      myself up.
11 What you conceive and bring to
      birth is chaff and stubble;
    a wind like fire shall devour you.
12 Whole nations shall be heaps of
      white ash,
    or like thorns cut down and set on
      fire.
13 You who dwell far away, hear what
      I have done;
    acknowledge my might, you who
      are near.
14 In Zion sinners quake with terror,
    the godless are seized with trembling
      and ask,
    Can any of us live with a devouring
      fire?
    Can any live in endless burning?
15 The man who lives an upright life
      and speaks the truth,
    who scorns to enrich himself by
      extortion,
    who snaps his fingers at a bribe,
    who stops his ears to hear nothing
      of bloodshed,
    who closes his eyes to the sight of
      evil—
16 that is the man who shall dwell on
      the heights,
    his refuge a fastness in the cliffs,
    his bread secure and his water never
      failing.

17 Your eyes shall see a king in his
      splendour
    and will look upon a land of far
      distances.
18 You will call to mind what once
      you feared:
    'Where then is he that counted,
      where is he that weighed,
    where is he that counted the
      treasures?'
19 You will no longer see that
      barbarous people,

---

n the age: *prob. rdg.*; *Heb.* your times.
o Prob. rdg.; *Heb.* his.

33.1–24: An exilic liturgy. It is impossible to identify the precise historical context of this psalm. The apparently disjointed units in this collection of prayers probably reflect the use of the chapter in worship after the time of Isaiah. **1:** The *destroyer*, Babylon in 21.1–10, is not identified here. **5–6:** A hymn of praise. **7–9:** In the absence of the fear of the LORD the order made by *man is of no account* and nature itself is *wilting*. **10–14:** Announcement of the LORD's intervention. **17–20:** This poem is considered postexilic. *King:* God or a restored Davidic king.

that people whose speech was so
     hard to catch,
whose stuttering speech you could
     not understand.

20 Look upon Zion, city of our solemn
        feasts,
    let your eyes rest on Jerusalem,
    a land of comfort, a tent that shall
        never be shifted,
    whose pegs shall never be pulled
        up,
    not one of its ropes cast loose.
21 There we have the LORD's majesty;[p]
    it will be a place[q] of rivers and
        broad streams;
    but[r] no galleys shall be rowed
        there,
    no stately ship sail by.
22 For the LORD our judge, the LORD
        our law-giver,
    the LORD our king—he himself will
        save us.
23 [Men may say, Your rigging is
        slack;
    it will not hold the mast firm in its
        socket,
    nor can the sails be spread.]
    Then the blind man shall have a full
        share of the spoil
    and the lame shall take part in the
        pillage;
24 no man who dwells there shall say,
        'I am sick';
    and the sins of the people who live
        there shall be pardoned.

Edom and Israel

34 Approach, you nations, to listen,
        and attend, you peoples;
    let the earth listen and everything
        in it,
    the world and all that it yields;
2   for the LORD's anger is turned
        against all the nations

and his wrath against all the host
     of them:
he gives them over to slaughter and
     destruction.
Their slain shall be flung out,   3
the stench shall rise from their
     corpses,
and the mountains shall stream
     with their blood.
All the host of heaven shall   4
     crumble into nothing,
the heavens shall be rolled up like
     a scroll,
and the starry host fade away,
as the leaf withers from the vine
     and the ripening fruit from the
     fig-tree;
for the sword of the LORD[s] appears   5
     in heaven.
See how it descends in judgement
     on Edom,
on the people whom he dooms[t] to
     destruction.
The LORD has a sword steeped in   6
     blood,
     it is gorged with fat,
the fat of rams' kidneys, and the
     blood of lambs and goats;
for he has a sacrifice in Bozrah,
a great slaughter in Edom.
Wild oxen shall come down and   7
     buffaloes[u] with them,
     bull and bison together,
and the land shall drink deep of
     blood
and the soil be sated with fat.
For the LORD has a day of   8
     vengeance,
the champion of Zion has a year
     when he will requite.
Edom's torrents shall be turned into   9
     pitch
and its soil into brimstone,

p *Or* threshing-floor.
q *it . . . place: or* instead.
r *Or* and.
s the sword of the LORD: *prob. rdg.; Heb.* my sword.
t *Prob. rdg.; Heb.* I doom.
u and buffaloes: *prob. rdg.; Heb. om.*

Stuttering speech: a reversal of the doom pronounced in 28.12–13. **21–24:** In the messianic
age not man's economy dependent on *stately ships* but one dependent on the LORD's majesty
will prevail: *no man* will be *sick* in body or oppressed by want or sins; compare Ezek.34.11–31;
47.1–12; Mt.11.5.
  34.1–35.10: Edom and Israel. Two poems, both of them exilic or postexilic, are juxtaposed
to contrast the expected devastation of *Edom* (34.1–17) with the glorious future in store for the
exiles (35.1–10).
  34.1–17: The doom of Edom. Compare Ps.137.7–9. **5–8:** He is coming to destroy *Edom*, as
men slaughter animals for sacrifice. **5:** *Sword:* see Ezek. ch. 21. **6:** *Bozrah* was a major city in
northern Edom. **9–15:** As the result of divine intervention, *Edom* will return to a state of chaos.

and the land shall become blazing
  pitch,
10 which night and day shall never be
  quenched,
and its smoke shall go up for ever.
From generation to generation it
  shall lie waste,
and no man shall pass through it
  ever again.
11 Horned owl and bustard shall make
  their home in it,
screech-owl and raven shall haunt it.
He has stretched across it a
  measuring-line of chaos,
12 and its frontiers shall be a jumble
  of stones.
No king shall be acclaimed there,
and all its princes shall come to
  nought.
13 Thorns shall sprout in its palaces;
nettles and briars shall cover its
  walled towns.
It shall be rough land fit for wolves,
  a haunt of desert-owls.
14 Marmots shall consort with jackals,
and he-goat shall encounter he-goat.
There too the nightjar shall rest
and find herself a place for repose.
15 There the sand-partridge shall
  make her nest,
lay her eggs and hatch them
and gather her brood under her
  wings;
there shall the kites gather,
  one after another.
16 Consult the book of the LORD and
  read it;
not one of these shall be lacking,
  not one miss its fellow,
for with his own mouth he has
  ordered it
and with his own breath he has
  brought them together.
17 He it is who has allotted each its
  place,
and his hand has measured out
  their portions;
they shall occupy it for ever
and dwell there from generation
  to generation.

Let the wilderness and the thirsty   35
  land be glad,
let the desert rejoice and burst into
  flower.
Let it flower with fields of asphodel,   2
let it rejoice and shout for joy.
The glory of Lebanon is given to it,
  the splendour too of Carmel and
  Sharon;
these shall see the glory of the LORD,
  the splendour of our God.
Strengthen the feeble arms,   3
steady the tottering knees;
say to the anxious, Be strong and   4
  fear not.
See, your God comes with
  vengeance,
with dread retribution he comes to
  save you.
Then shall blind men's eyes be   5
  opened,
  and the ears of the deaf unstopped.
Then shall the lame man leap like   6
  a deer,
  and the tongue of the dumb
  shout aloud;
for water springs up in the
  wilderness,
and torrents flow in dry land.
The mirage becomes a pool,   7
  the thirsty land bubbling springs;
  instead of reeds and rushes, grass
  shall grow
  in the rough land where wolves
  now lurk.
And there shall be a causeway there   8
  which shall be called the Way of
  Holiness,
  and the unclean shall not pass
  along it;
it shall become a pilgrim's way,*v*
  no fool shall trespass on it.
No lion shall come there,   9
  no savage beast climb on to it;
  not one shall be found there.
By it those he has ransomed shall
  return
  and the LORD's redeemed come   10
  home;
  v a pilgrim's way: *prob. rdg.; Heb. unintelligible.*

11: *Chaos:* see Jer.4.23–28. **16–17:** The announcement is trustworthy, for it is written in the *book of the* LORD (probably prophetic books).
  35.1–10: God comes in judgment to save the exiles. This poem of the return from Exile resembles Second Isaiah; see 40.1–11; 42.17–18. **4:** *The anxious:* those discouraged by the long captivity. **7:** Like a *mirage* turned into a real *pool* of water was the announcement of the return from Exile; compare Ps.126.1. **8:** *Causeway:* highway.

they shall enter Zion with shouts of
      triumph,
crowned with everlasting gladness.
Gladness and joy shall be their
      escort,
and suffering and weariness shall
      flee away.

Jerusalem delivered from Sennacherib

361[w] IN THE FOURTEENTH YEAR OF THE REIGN
of Hezekiah, Sennacherib king of
Assyria attacked and took all the
2 fortified cities of Judah. From Lachish
he sent the chief officer[x] with a strong
force to King Hezekiah at Jerusalem;
and he halted by the conduit of the
Upper Pool on the causeway which
3 leads to the Fuller's Field. There
Eliakim son of Hilkiah, the comptroller of the household, came out to
him, with Shebna the adjutant-general
and Joah son of Asaph, the secretary
4 of state. The chief officer said to them,
'Tell Hezekiah that this is the message
of the Great King, the king of Assyria:
"What ground have you for this con-
5 fidence of yours? Do you think fine
words can take the place of skill and
numbers? On whom then do you rely
for support in your rebellion against
6 me? On Egypt? Egypt is a splintered
cane that will run into a man's hand
and pierce it if he leans on it. That is
what Pharaoh king of Egypt proves to
7 all who rely on him. And if you tell me
that you are relying on the LORD your
God, is he not the god whose hill-
shrines and altars Hezekiah has suppressed, telling Judah and Jerusalem
that they must prostrate themselves
before this altar alone?"

8   'Now, make a bargain with my
master the king of Assyria: I will give
you two thousand horses if you can find
9 riders for them. Will you reject the
authority of even the least of my
master's servants and rely on Egypt

for chariots and horsemen? Do you 10
think that I have come to attack this
land and destroy it without the consent
of the LORD? No, the LORD himself
said to me, "Attack this land and
destroy it."'

Eliakim, Shebna, and Joah said to 11
the chief officer, 'Please speak to us in
Aramaic, for we understand it; do not
speak Hebrew to us within earshot of
the people on the city wall.' The chief 12
officer answered, 'Is it to your master
and to you that my master has sent me
to say this? Is it not to the people
sitting on the wall who, like you, will
have to eat their own dung and drink
their own urine?' Then he stood and 13
shouted in Hebrew, 'Hear the message
of the Great King, the king of Assyria.
These are the king's words: "Do not be 14
taken in by Hezekiah. He cannot save
you. Do not let him persuade you to rely 15
on the LORD, and tell you that the LORD
will save you and that this city will never
be surrendered to the king of Assyria."
Do not listen to Hezekiah; these are the 16
words of the king of Assyria: "Make
peace with me. Come out to me, and then
you shall each eat the fruit of his own
vine and his own fig-tree, and drink the
water of his own cistern, until I come 17
and take you to a land like your own,
a land of grain and new wine, of corn
and vineyards. Beware lest Hezekiah 18
mislead you by telling you that the
LORD will save you. Did the god of any
of these nations save his land from the
king of Assyria? Where are the gods of 19
Hamath and Arpad? Where are the
gods of Sepharvaim? Where are the
gods of Samaria? Did they save
Samaria from me? Among all the gods 20
of these nations is there one who saved
his land from me? And how is the
LORD to save Jerusalem?"'

The people were silent and answered 21
not a word, for the king had given

*w Verses 1–22: cp. 2 Kgs. 18. 13–37; 2 Chr. 32. 1–19.
x Or sent Rab-shakeh.*

36.1–39.8: An appendix. With some variants, this material, with the exception of 38.9–20,
is found in 2 Kgs.18.13–20.19. The main theme is the relationship between Isaiah and King
Hezekiah through several crises.
   36.1–22: First account of Sennacherib's attack. See 2 Kgs.18.13–27. This account omits the
report in 2 Kgs.18.14–16 of Hezekiah's submission and tribute to the Assyrians. **1:** The *fourteenth
year* of Hezekiah was 701 B.C. **2:** See 7.3. **3:** See 22.15–25. **6:** A reference to the alliance with
Egypt; see 31.1–3. **11:** *Aramaic:* the international language of the Assyrian empire. **13:** *In
Hebrew:* lit. "in Jewish" or "in the Judean language."

orders that no one was to answer him

22 Eliakim son of Hilkiah, comptroller of the household, Shebna the adjutant-general, and Joah son of Asaph, secretary of state, came to Hezekiah with their clothes rent and reported what the chief officer had said.

37₁ʸ When King Hezekiah heard their report, he rent his clothes and wrapped himself in sackcloth, and went into the 2 house of the LORD. He sent Eliakim comptroller of the household, Shebna the adjutant-general, and the senior priests, all covered in sackcloth, to the 3 prophet Isaiah son of Amoz, to give him this message from the king: 'This day is a day of trouble for us, a day of reproof and contempt. We are like a woman who has no strength to bear the child that is coming to the birth. 4 It may be that the LORD your God heard the words of the chief officer whom his master the king of Assyria sent to taunt the living God, and will confute what he, the LORD your God, heard. Offer a prayer for those who 5 still survive.' King Hezekiah's servants 6 came to Isaiah, and he told them to say this to their master: 'This is the word of the LORD: "Do not be alarmed at what you heard when the lackeys of 7 the king of Assyria blasphemed me. I will put a spirit in him, and he shall hear a rumour and withdraw to his own country; and there I will make him fall by the sword."'

8 So the chief officer withdrew. He heard that the king of Assyria had left Lachish, and he found him attacking 9 Libnah. But when the king learnt that Tirhakah king of Cush was on the way to make war on him, he sent messengers 10 againᶻ to Hezekiah king of Judah, to say to him, 'How can you be deluded by your god on whom you rely when he promises that Jerusalem shall not fall into the hands of the king of

Assyria? Surely you have heard what 11 the kings of Assyria have done to all countries, exterminating their people; can you then hope to escape? Did their 12 gods save the nations which my forefathers destroyed, Gozan, Harran, Rezeph, and the people of Beth-eden living in Telassar? Where are the kings 13 of Hamath, of Arpad, and of Lahir, Sepharvaim, Hena, and Ivvah?'

Hezekiah took the letter from the 14 messengers and read it; then he went up into the house of the LORD, spread it out before the LORD and offered this 15 prayer: 'O LORD of Hosts, God of 16 Israel, enthroned on the cherubim, thou alone art God of all the kingdoms of the earth; thou hast made heaven and earth. Turn thy ear to me, O LORD, 17 and listen; open thine eyes, O LORD, and see; hear the message that Sennacherib has sent to taunt the living God. It is true, O LORD, that the kings of 18 Assyria have laid waste every country, that they have consigned their gods to 19 the fire and destroyed them; for they were no gods but the work of men's hands, mere wood and stone. But now, 20 O LORD our God, save us from his power, so that all the kingdoms of the earth may know that thou, O LORD, alone art God.'

Isaiah son of Amoz sent to Hezekiah 21 and said, 'This is the word of the LORD the God of Israel: I have heard your prayer to me concerning Sennacherib king of Assyria. This is the word which 22 the LORD has spoken concerning him:

The virgin daughter of Zion disdains
    you,
  she laughs you to scorn;
the daughter of Jerusalem tosses her
    head
  as you retreat.

y Verses 1–38: cp. 2 Kgs. 19. 1–37; 2 Chr. 32. 20–22.
z again: prob. rdg., cp. 2 Kgs. 19. 9; Heb. and he heard.

37.1–7: **Hezekiah turns to Isaiah.** See 2 Kgs.19.1–7. The king and his officials, afraid and in mourning, consult Isaiah who announces the end of the siege and the death of Sennacherib. **1:** *Rent his clothes:* sign of consternation and despair. *Sackcloth:* symbol of mourning and repentance.
37.8–20: **A second account of Sennacherib's attack.** See 2 Kgs.19.9–19. This narrative is another tradition of the events reported in 36.1–37.7. **9:** *Tirhakah* was a member of the royal house of Ethiopia, *Cush,* which gained control over Egypt to become the Twenty-fifth Dynasty. **12:** *Nations:* places in Mesopotamia. **14–20:** Instead of summoning Isaiah, Hezekiah goes to the Temple to pray for help.
37.21–38: **Isaiah's intervention.** See 2 Kgs.19.20–34. **22:** *Virgin daughter of Zion:* prophetic

22 Whom have you taunted and
   blasphemed?
   Against whom have you
   clamoured,
   casting haughty glances at the Holy
   One of Israel?

24 You have sent your servants to
   taunt the Lord,
   and said:
   With my countless chariots I have
   gone up
   high in the mountains, into the
   recesses of Lebanon.
   I have cut down its tallest cedars,
   the best of its pines,
   I have reached its highest limit of
   forest and meadow.*a*

25 I have dug wells
   and drunk the waters of a foreign
   land,
   and with the soles of my feet I have
   dried up
   all the streams of Egypt.

26 Have you not heard long ago?
   I did it all.
   In days gone by I planned it
   and now I have brought it about,
   making fortified cities tumble down
   into heaps of rubble.

27 Their citizens, shorn of strength,
   disheartened and ashamed,
   were but as plants in the field, as
   green herbs,
   as grass on the roof-tops blasted
   before the east wind.

28 I know your rising up and your
   sitting down,
   your going out and your coming in.

29 The frenzy of your rage against me
   and your arrogance
   have come to my ears.
   I will put a ring in your nose
   and a hook in your lips,
   and I will take you back by the road
   on which you have come.

This shall be the sign for you: this 30
year you shall eat shed grain and in the
second year what is self-sown; but in
the third year sow and reap, plant
vineyards and eat their fruit. The sur- 31
vivors left in Judah shall strike fresh
root under ground and yield fruit
above ground, for a remnant shall come 32
out of Jerusalem and survivors from
Mount Zion. The zeal of the LORD of
Hosts will perform this.

'Therefore, this is the word of the 33
LORD concerning the king of Assyria:

   He shall not enter this city
      nor shoot an arrow there,
   he shall not advance against it with
      shield
      nor cast up a siege-ramp against it.
   By the way on which he came he   34
      shall go back;
   this city he shall not enter.
      This is the very word of the
      LORD.
   I will shield this city to deliver it, 35
      for my own sake and for the sake
      of my servant David.'

The angel of the LORD went out and 36
struck down a hundred and eighty-five
thousand men in the Assyrian camp;
when morning dawned, they all lay
dead. So Sennacherib king of Assyria 37
broke camp, went back to Nineveh and
stayed there. One day, while he was 38
worshipping in the temple of his god
Nisroch, Adrammelech and Sharezer
his sons murdered him and escaped to
the land of Ararat. He was succeeded
by his son Esarhaddon.

At this time Hezekiah fell dan- 38 1*b*
gerously ill and the prophet Isaiah son
of Amoz came to him and said, 'This
is the word of the LORD: Give your

a and meadow: prob. rdg.; Heb. its meadow.
b Verses 1–8, 21, 22: cp. 2 Kgs. 20. 1–11.

term for Jerusalem. *Tosses her head:* gesture of contempt. **24:** *Tallest cedars of Lebanon:* the
most poweful and exalted kings; compare Ezek.31.3–14. **25:** To dry up *streams . . . with the
soles of* the *feet* is a figure of speech for easy victory over Egypt whose power is in the Nile River.
26: Achievements claimed by Assyria were *planned* and *brought about* by God. **27:** Grass sprang
up on the mud *roof-tops* of Palestinian houses but dried up quickly in the *east wind* from the
desert. **29:** Under God's power Sennacherib is as helpless as a prisoner led into captivity with
a *hook in* his *lips.* **30:** Either the sign is that after two years conditions of life will be normal;
or it may be a proverb that the change from adversity to prosperity is gradual. **32:** *Remnant:*
see 10.21–22 n. **36:** An *angel of the LORD* appears in the Bible either as the LORD himself
(Exod.3.2–6) or as a messenger or agent of God's will in some event.
   38.1–22: Hezekiah's illness. See 2 Kgs.20.1–11. **3:** Hezekiah uses the language of the Lament;

last instructions to your household, for you are a dying man and will not 2 recover.' Hezekiah turned his face to the wall and offered this prayer to the 3 LORD: 'O LORD, remember how I have lived before thee, faithful and loyal in thy service, always doing what was good in thine eyes.' And he wept 4 bitterly. Then the word of the LORD 5 came to Isaiah: 'Go and say to Hezekiah: "This is the word of the LORD the God of your father David: I have heard your prayer and seen your tears; I will add fifteen years to 6 your life. I will deliver you and this city from the king of Assyria and will 21[c] protect this city."' Then Isaiah told them to apply a fig-plaster; so they made one and applied it to the boil, and 22 he recovered. Then Hezekiah said, 'By what sign shall I know that I shall go 7 up into the house of the LORD?' And Isaiah said,[d] 'This shall be your sign from the LORD that he will do what he 8 has promised. Watch the shadow cast by the sun on the stairway of Ahaz: I will bring backwards ten steps the shadow which has gone down on the stairway.' And the sun went back ten steps on the stairway down which it had gone.

9 A poem of Hezekiah king of Judah after his recovery from his illness, as it was written down:

10 I thought: In the prime of life I
    must pass away;
for the rest of my years I am
    consigned to the gates of Sheol.
11 I said: I shall no longer see the
    LORD
    in the land of the living;
never again, like those who live in
    the world,
    shall I look on a man.
12 My dwelling is taken from me,
    pulled up like a shepherd's tent;
thou hast cut short my life like a
    weaver
who severs the web from the
    thrum.

From morning to night thou
    tormentest me,
then I am racked with pain till   13
    the morning.
All my bones are broken, as a lion
    would break them;
from morning to night thou
    tormentest me.
I twitter as if I were a swallow,   14
    I moan like a dove.
My eyes falter as I look up to the
    heights;
O Lord, pay heed, stand surety for
    me.
How can I complain, what can I say   15
    to the LORD
    when he himself has done this?
I wander to and fro all my life long
    in the bitterness of my soul.
Yet, O Lord, my soul shall live with   16
    thee;
do thou give my spirit rest.[e]
Restore me and give me life.
Bitterness had indeed been my lot   17
    in place of prosperity;
but thou by thy love hast brought
    me back
    from the pit of destruction;
for thou hast cast all my sins
    behind thee.
Sheol cannot confess thee,   18
Death cannot praise thee,
nor can they who go down to the
    abyss
    hope for thy truth.
The living, the living alone can   19
    confess thee
    as I do this day,
as a father makes thy truth known,
    O God, to his sons.
The LORD is at hand to save me;   20
    so let us sound the music of our
    praises
all our life long in the house of the
    LORD.[f]

At this time Merodach-baladan son 39[g]
of Baladan king of Babylon sent

c Verses 21, 22 transposed.
d And Isaiah said: prob. rdg., cp. 2 Kgs. 20. 9; Heb. om.
e Yet . . . rest: prob. rdg.; Heb. unintelligible.
f Verses 21, 22 transposed to follow verse 6.
g Verses 1–8: cp. 2 Kgs. 20. 12–19.

see Introduction to Pss. **9–20:** The song ascribed here to Hezekiah is a typical individual thanksgiving psalm, used in the Temple service of thanksgiving for deliverance from suffering. See Pss.32; 116. **11:** *See the* LORD*:* visit the Temple. **18–19:** According to Hebrew thought, it was impossible to *confess,* i.e. *praise,* God or relate to him, after death.
39.1–8: Hezekiah and ambassadors from Babylon. See 2 Kgs.20.12–19. The Babylonian king

envoys with a gift to Hezekiah; for he had heard that he had been ill and was
2 well again. Hezekiah welcomed them and showed them all his treasury, silver and gold, spices and fragrant oil, his entire armoury and everything to be found among his treasures; there was nothing in his house and in all his realm that Hezekiah did not show
3 them. Then the prophet Isaiah came to King Hezekiah and asked him, 'What did these men say and where have they come from?' 'They have come from a far-off country,' Hezekiah
4 answered, 'from Babylon.' Then Isaiah asked, 'What did they see in your house?' 'They saw everything,' Hezekiah replied; 'there was nothing among my treasures that I did not show them.'
5 Then Isaiah said to Hezekiah, 'Hear
6 the word of the LORD of Hosts: The time is coming, says the LORD, when everything in your house, and all that your forefathers have amassed till the present day, will be carried away to
7 Babylon; not a thing shall be left. And some of the sons who will be born to you, sons of your own begetting, shall be taken and shall be made eunuchs in the palace of the king of Babylon.'
8 Hezekiah answered, 'The word of the LORD which you have spoken is good'; thinking to himself that peace and security would last out his lifetime.

News of the returning exiles

40   Comfort, comfort my people;[h]
     —it is the voice of your God;
2   speak tenderly to Jerusalem[i]
    and tell her this,
  that she has fulfilled, her term of
    bondage,
  that her penalty is paid;

she has received at the LORD's hand
  double[j] measure for all her sins.

There is a voice that cries: 3
Prepare a road for the LORD
  through the wilderness,
clear a highway across the desert for
  our God.
Every valley shall be lifted up,   4
every mountain and hill brought
  down;
rugged places shall be made smooth
  and mountain-ranges become a
  plain.
Thus shall the glory of the LORD   5
  be revealed,
and all mankind together shall see it;
  for the LORD himself has spoken.

A voice says, 'Cry',   6
and another asks, 'What shall I cry?'
'That all mankind is grass,
they last no longer than a flower of
  the field.
The grass withers, the flower fades,   7
when the breath of[k] the LORD blows
  upon them;[l]
the grass withers, the flowers fade,   8
  but the word of our God endures
  for evermore.'

You who bring Zion good news,[m] up   9
  with you to the mountain-top;
lift up your voice and shout,
you who bring good news to
  Jerusalem,[n]
lift it up fearlessly;
cry to the cities of Judah, 'Your
  God is here.'

h Comfort . . . people: *or* Comfort, O my people, comfort.
i speak . . . Jerusalem: *or* bid Jerusalem be of good heart.
j double: *or* full.
k the breath of: *or* a wind from.
l *Prob. rdg.; Heb. adds* surely the people are grass.
m You . . . news: *or* O Zion, bringer of good news.
n you . . . Jerusalem: *or* O Jerusalem, bringer of good news.

sent *envoys* to Hezekiah, ostensibly to inquire about his health, but probably to encourage rebellion against Assyria. The date is probably 705–703 B.C. Isaiah criticizes the welcome given the Babylonians and announces judgment against Hezekiah.
  40.1–55.13: Words of hope. On Second Isaiah, see Introduction.
  40.1–11: The prophet's commission. 1: This second part of Isaiah is known as "The Consolation of Israel" because the prophet brings *comfort* to the captives in the Exile. **2:** *Fulfilled . . . bondage:* the Exile is over. **3:** The *voice that cries,* here and in v. 6, is that of the LORD giving the prophet his mission (6.8; Jer.1.7–10; Ezek.2.1–3) to prepare the return from the captivity across the desert as in the Exodus. **4:** God will eliminate all difficulties from the path of the returning captives. **5:** *The glory of the LORD,* i.e. the presence and power of God, will become manifest to all nations in the restoration of Israel. **6–8:** Like First Isaiah (6.1–13), this prophet overhears the discussion in the heavenly council. **6:** *Another:* the prophet.

10   Here is the Lord God coming in
     might,
   coming to rule with his right arm.
     His recompense comes with him,
     he carries his reward before him.

11   He will tend his flock like a
     shepherd
   and gather them together with
     his arm;
   he will carry the lambs in his bosom
   and lead the ewes to water.

Israel delivered and redeemed

12   Who has gauged the waters in the
     palm of his hand,
   or with its span set limits to the
     heavens?
   Who has held all the soil of earth
     in a bushel,
   or weighed the mountains on a
     balance
   and the hills on a pair of scales?

13   Who has set limits to the spirit of
     the Lord?
   What counsellor stood at his side
     to instruct him?

14   With whom did he confer to gain
     discernment?
   Who taught him how to do justice
   or gave him lessons in wisdom?

15   Why, to him nations are but drops
     from a bucket,
   no more than moisture on the
     scales;
   coasts and islands weigh as light as
     specks of dust.

16   All Lebanon does not yield wood
     enough for fuel
   or beasts enough for a sacrifice.

17   All nations dwindle to nothing
     before him,
   he reckons them mere nothings, less
     than nought.

18   What likeness will you find for God
   or what form to resemble his?

19   Is it an image which a craftsman
     sets up,

and a goldsmith covers with plate
and fits with studs of silver as a
     costly gift?

20   Or is it mulberry-wood that will
     not rot which a man chooses,
seeking out a skilful craftsman for it,
to mount an image that will not fall?

   Each workman helps the others,   [6°]
   each man encourages his fellow.
   The craftsman urges on the   [7°]
     goldsmith,
   the gilder urges the man who beats
     the anvil,
   he declares the soldering to be
     sound;
   he fastens the image with nails
   so that it will not fall down.

21   Do you not know, have you not
     heard,
were you not told long ago,
have you not perceived ever since
     the world began,

22   that God sits throned on the vaulted
     roof of earth,
     whose inhabitants are like
     grasshoppers*p*?
He stretches out the skies like a
     curtain,
   he spreads them out like a tent to
     live in;

23   he reduces the great to nothing
   and makes all earth's princes less
     than nothing.

24   Scarcely are they planted, scarcely
     sown,
scarcely have they taken root in the
     earth,
   before he blows upon them and
     they wither away,
   and a whirlwind carries them off
     like chaff.

25   To whom then will you liken me,
     whom set up as my equal?
   asks the Holy One.

26   Lift up your eyes to the heavens;
   consider who created it all,

*o These are verses 6 and 7 of ch. 41, transposed to this
point.*
p Or locusts.

40.12–31: The majestic Creator. 12–14: Rhetorical questions stress the majesty (v. 12) and
the wisdom (vv. 13–14) of God. **15–17:** All nations are nothing before him. **15:** *Coasts and
islands:* lit. "islands." **16:** *Lebanon* had the biggest forest of the largest trees known to ancient
man. **18–20:** Probably an interpolation, with 41.6–7. No *image* resembles God. **21–24:** God
controls the destinies of men. **22:** The *vaulted roof* is the horizon or the dome over the earth.
25–26: *Holy One* of Israel, the characteristic title given to God by Second Isaiah, has its foun-

led out their host one by one
and called them all by their names,
through his great might, his
might and power,
not one is missing.

27 Why do you complain, O Jacob,
and you, Israel, why do you say,
'My plight is hidden from the LORD
and my cause has passed out of
God's notice'?

28 Do you not know, have you not
heard?
The LORD, the everlasting God,
creator of the wide world,
grows neither weary nor faint;
no man can fathom his
understanding.

29 He gives vigour to the weary,
new strength to the exhausted.

30 Young men may grow weary and
faint,
even in their prime they may
stumble and fall;

31 but those who look to the LORD
will win new strength,
they will grow wings like eagles;
they will run and not be weary,
they will march on and never grow
faint.

41 Keep silence before me, all you
coasts and islands;
let the peoples come to meet me.*q*
Let them come near, then let them
speak;
we will meet at that place of
judgement, I and they.

2 Tell me, who raised up that one
from the east,
one greeted by victory wherever he
goes?
Who is it that puts nations into his
power
and makes kings go down before
him,*r*

he scatters them with his sword like
dust
and with his bow like chaff before
the wind,
he puts them to flight and passes 3
on unscathed,
swifter than any traveller on foot?
Whose work is this, I ask, who has 4
brought it to pass?
Who has summoned the generations
from the beginning?
It is I, the LORD, I am the first,
and to the last of them I am He.
Coasts and islands saw it and were 5
afraid,
the world trembled from end to
end.*s*

But you, Israel my servant, 8*t*
you, Jacob whom I have chosen,
race of Abraham my friend,
I have taken you up, 9
have fetched you from the ends of
the earth,
and summoned you from its
farthest corners,
I have called you my servant,
have chosen you and not cast you
off;
fear nothing, for I am with you; 10
be not afraid, for I am your God.
I strengthen you, I help you,
I support you with my victorious
right hand.

Now shall all who defy you 11
be disappointed and put to shame;
all who set themselves against you
shall be as nothing; they shall
vanish.

q come to meet me: *prob. rdg., transposing, with slight
change, from end of verse 5; Heb.* win new strength
(repeated from 40. 31).
r before him: *prob. rdg.; Heb. om.*
s See note on verse 1.
t Verses 6 and 7 transposed to follow 40. 20.

---

dation in the inaugural vision of Isaiah of Jerusalem; see 6.3. It signifies that God is and acts
beyond all earthly and/or profane causality and motivation. Hence, the terms "creator" and
created are used more frequently by Second Isaiah than by any other OT writer; see 41.20,
42.5, etc. **28**: See Pss. 90.2; 147.5. **31**: See Pss. 103.5.
    41.1–29: The LORD in court. The framework of the chapter is a courtroom scene (*place of
judgement,* v. 1) in which the LORD himself argues the case that he controls historical events.
1: *Coasts and islands:* all the earth to the farthest reaches of the Mediterranean Sea, the then
known world. **2:** The *one from the east* of whom these first four verses speak is Cyrus, whom the
ancient world welcomed as a benevolent liberator from the harsh Babylonians. **4:** God will be
there when the *last generations* of men will cease to be. **8:** In Second Isaiah, Israel is represented
as a *servant chosen* anew by God, never to be *cast off* again to the mercy of the nations. The title
servant was applied to the patriarchs, *Abraham* and *Jacob* (Gen.26.24; 28.25), and to prophets

12 You will look for your assailants
       but not find them;
   all who take up arms against you
   shall be as nothing, nothing at all.
13 For I, the LORD your God,
   take you by the right hand;
   I say to you, Do not fear;
   It is I who help you,
14 fear not, Jacob you worm and
       Israel poor louse.
   It is I who help you, says the LORD,
       your ransomer, the Holy One of
       Israel.
15 See, I will make of you a sharp
       threshing-sledge,
       new and studded with teeth;
   you shall thresh the mountains and
       crush them
   and reduce the hills to chaff;
16 you shall winnow them, the wind
       shall carry them away
   and a great gale shall scatter them.
   Then shall you rejoice in the LORD
   and glory in the Holy One of
       Israel.

17 The wretched and the poor look for
       water and find none,
   their tongues are parched with
       thirst;
   but I the LORD will give them an
       answer,
   I, the God of Israel, will not
       forsake them.
18 I will open rivers among the sand-
       dunes
       and wells in the valleys;
   I will turn the wilderness into pools
   and dry land into springs of water;
19 I will plant cedars in the wastes,
       and acacia and myrtle and wild
       olive;
   the pine shall grow on the barren
       heath
   side by side with fir and box,
20 that men may see and know,
   may once for all give heed and
       understand

that the LORD himself has done this,
   that the Holy One of Israel has
   performed it.

21 Come, open your plea, says the LORD,
   present your case, says Jacob's King;
22 let them come forward, these idols,
   let them foretell the future.
   Let them declare the meaning of
       past events
       that we may give our minds to it;
   let them predict things that are to be
       that we may know their outcome.
23 Declare what will happen hereafter;
   then we shall know you are gods.
   Do what you can, good or ill,
   anything that may grip us with
       fear and awe.
24 You cannot! You are sprung from
       nothing,
   your works are rotten;
   whoever chooses you is vile as you
   are.
25 I roused one from the north, and
       he obeyed,
   I called one from the east,
       summoned him in[u] my name,
   he marches over viceroys as if they
       were mud,
   like a potter treading his clay.
26 Tell us, who declared this from the
       beginning, that we might know
       it,
   or told us beforehand so that we
       could say, 'He was right'?
   Not one declared, not one foretold,
   not one heard a sound from you.
27 Here is one who will speak first as
       advocate for Zion,
   here I appoint defending counsel
       for Jerusalem;
28 but from the other side no advocate
       steps forward
   and, when I look, there is no one
       there.
29 I ask a question and no one answers;
   see what empty things they are!

u summoned him in: or who will call on.

and kings, especially David. **14**: The *ransomer* (Heb. *goel*) was the closest relative, whose duty it was to be the "avenger of blood" (Num.35.19–29) in a murder, or to buy back a kinsman from slavery (Lev.25.48), or to pay his debt. The LORD is Israel's nearest kin who first ransomed them from Egypt by his mighty deeds of the Exodus and now will repeat the wonders. **18**: The return from captivity will be more wonderful than the Exodus because the LORD will not only furnish water in the desert (Num.20.8–12) but will transform it into *pools*. **21**: *Plea . . . case:* language of a juridical process. **25**: *One from the north . . . east:* Cyrus from Persia. **27**: The LORD is the *one* who speaks as the *advocate* (lawyer) for Israel, **28–29**: On the expression of monotheism, see Introduction. **29**: A final sarcastic denial of the existence of other gods.

Nothing that they do has any
worth,
their images are wind, mere
nothings.

42 Here is my servant, whom I uphold,
my chosen one in whom I delight,
I have bestowed my spirit upon
him,
and he will make justice shine on
the nations.

2 He will not call out or lift his voice
high,
or*v* make himself heard in the open
street.

3 He will not break a bruised reed,
or snuff out a smouldering wick;
he will make justice shine on every
race,*w*

4 never faltering, never breaking
down,*x*
he will plant justice on earth,
while coasts and islands wait for
his teaching.

5 Thus speaks the LORD who is God,
he who created the skies and
stretched them out,
who fashioned the earth and all
that grows in it,
who gave breath to its people,
the breath of life to all who walk
upon it:

6 I, the LORD, have called you with
righteous purpose
and taken you by the hand;
I have formed you, and
appointed you
to be a light*y* to all peoples,
a beacon for the nations,

7 to open eyes that are blind,
to bring captives out of prison,
out of the dungeons where they
lie in darkness.

I am the LORD; the LORD*z* is my   8
name;
I will not give my glory to another
god,
nor my praise to any idol.

See how the first prophecies have   9
come to pass,
and now I declare new things;
before they break from the bud I
announce them to you.

Sing a new song to the LORD,   10
sing his praise throughout the
earth,
you that sail the sea, and all
sea-creatures,
and you that inhabit the coasts and
islands.

Let the wilderness and its towns   11
rejoice,
and the villages of the tribe of
Kedar.
Let those who live in Sela shout for
joy
and cry out from the hill-tops.

You coasts and islands, all uplift   12
his praises;
let all ascribe glory to the LORD.

The LORD will go forth as a   13
warrior,
he will rouse the frenzy of battle
like a hero;
he will shout, he will raise the
battle-cry
and triumph over his foes.

Long have I lain still,   14
I kept silence and held myself in
check;
now I will cry like a woman in
labour,

v He will not . . . or: *or* In very truth he will call out
and lift his voice high, and . . .
w on every race: *or* in truth.
x never faltering . . . down: *or* he will neither rebuke
nor wound.
y Or a covenant. *z* the LORD: *or* He.

42.1–43.7: Israel, the servant of God. These poems (except possibly the hymn in 42.10–13)
speak of the relationship between God and his servant, and of the role of that servant.
42.1–4: First servant song. This and three other passages in Second Isaiah are generally
acknowledged to have a unique orientation; the other three are 49.1–6; 50.4–11; 52.13–53.12.
Here God himself speaks to introduce his *servant*. Some scholars argue that the servant is a
particular individual but without agreement concerning his identity; both the language and
context of this song, however, urge that he is Israel. **1:** *Spirit:* see 11.2 n. **2–4:** The servant will
be gentle of *voice* and sympathetic to those in desperate spiritual straits, the *bruised reed* and
smouldering wick. **4:** *Teaching,* or "Law" (Heb. *Torah*), parallels *justice.* The servant will bring
it to all peoples, the *coasts and islands.*
42.5–43.7: The Creator and his servant Israel. 6: *With righteous purpose:* according to the
divine plan. *Formed* is the same word used in Gen.2.7 for the making of man, i.e. a potter
molding clay. **10–11:** *Kedar* and *Sela,* remote inhabited places in the desert of Arabia, the
former to the north and the latter to the south, will praise the LORD along with the remote

whimpering, panting and gasping.
15 I will lay waste mountains and hills
    and shrivel all their green herbs;
    I will turn rivers into desert
        wastes*a*
    and dry up all the pools.
16 Then will I lead blind men on their
        way*b*
    and guide them by paths they do
        not know;
    I will turn darkness into light before
        them
        and straighten their twisting
            roads.
    All this I will do and leave nothing
        undone.
17   Those who trust in an image,
    those who take idols for their gods
    turn tail in bitter shame.

18   Hear now, you that are deaf;
    you blind men, look and see:
19 yet who is blind but my servant,
    who so deaf as the messenger whom
        I send?
    Who so blind as the one who holds
        my commission,
        so deaf as the servant of the
            LORD?
20 You have seen much but
        remembered little,
    your ears are wide open but nothing
        is heard.
21 It pleased the LORD, for the
        furtherance of his justice,
    to make his law a law of surpassing
        majesty;
22 yet here is a people plundered and
        taken as prey,
    all of them ensnared, trapped in
        holes,
        lost to sight in dungeons,
    carried off as spoil without hope of
        rescue,
    as plunder with no one to say,
        'Give it back.'
23 Hear this, all of you who will,
    listen henceforward and give me a
        hearing:
24 who gave away Jacob for plunder,
    who gave Israel away for spoil?

Was it not the LORD? They sinned
        against him,
they would not follow his ways
    and refused obedience to his law;
so in his anger he poured out upon   25
        Jacob
his wrath and the fury of battle.
It wrapped him in flames, yet still
    he did not learn the lesson,
scorched him, yet he did not lay it
    to heart.

But now this is the word of the   **43**
        LORD,
the word of your creator, O Jacob,
    of him who fashioned you, Israel:
Have no fear; for I have paid your
        ransom;
I have called you by name and you
    are my own.
When you pass through deep waters,   2
    I am with you,
    when you pass through rivers,
    they will not sweep you away;
walk through fire and you will not
    be scorched,
through flames and they will not
    burn you.
For I am the LORD your God,   3
    the Holy One of Israel, your
        deliverer;
for your ransom I give Egypt,
Nubia and Seba are your price.
You are more precious to me than   4
        the Assyrians,
you are honoured and I have loved
        you,
I would give the Edomites in
        exchange for you,
and the Leummim for your life.

Have no fear; for I am with you;   5
I will bring your children from the
        east
    and gather you all from the west.
I will say to the north, 'Give them   6
        up',
    and to the south, 'Do not hold
        them back.

a desert wastes: prob. rdg.; Heb. coasts and islands.
b Prob. rdg.; Heb. adds which they do not know.

---

places to the west, the *coasts and islands*. **18–19:** God heals the deaf and blind Israelites, his *servant*, thereby reversing the action performed by Isaiah at his command in 6.10. **22:** *People . . . taken as prey:* Israel in the Exile. No human power, but only God will say to Babylon: *"Give back* the captives." **43.3:** God gave *Egypt* and *Nubia* (in Africa) and *Seba* (in Arabia) into the hands of the Persians so that Israel might be allowed to return from the Exile. **6–7:** Israel

Bring my sons and daughters from
    afar,
  bring them from the ends of the
    earth;
7 bring every one who is called by
    my name,
  all whom I have created, whom
    I have formed,
all whom I have made for my glory.'
8   Bring out this people,
  a people who have eyes but are
    blind,
who have ears but are deaf.
9 All the nations are gathered
    together
  and the peoples assembled.
Who amongst them can expound
    this thing
  and interpret for us all that has
    gone before?
Let them produce witnesses to
    prove their case,
  or let them listen and say, 'That is
    the truth.'
10 My witnesses, says the LORD, are
    you, my servants,
you whom I have chosen
  to know me and put your faith in
    me
and understand that I am He.
Before me there was no god fashioned
  nor ever shall be after me.
11 I am the LORD, I myself,
  and none but I can deliver.
12 I myself have made it known in
    full, and declared it,
  I and no alien god amongst you,
and you are my witnesses, says the
    LORD.
13 I am God; from this very day I am
    He.
  What my hand holds, none can
    snatch away;
  what I do, none can undo.

14 Thus says the LORD your ransomer,
  the Holy One of Israel:

For your sakes I have sent to
  Babylon;
I will lay the Chaldaeans prostrate
  as they flee,
and their cry of triumph will turn
  to groaning.
I am the LORD, your Holy One,   15
  your creator, Israel, and your
  King.

Thus says the LORD,   16
who opened a way in the sea
and a path through mighty waters,
who drew on chariot and horse to   17
  their destruction,
a whole army, men of valour;
there they lay, never to rise again;
they were crushed, snuffed out like
  a wick:
Cease to dwell on days gone by   18
and to brood over past history.
Here and now I will do a new   19
  thing;
this moment it will break from
  the bud.
Can you not perceive it?
I will make a way even through the
  wilderness
and paths in the barren desert;
the wild beasts shall do me   20
  honour,
the wolf and the ostrich;
for I will provide water in the
  wilderness
and rivers in the barren desert,
where my chosen people may
  drink.
I have formed this people for   21
  myself
and they shall proclaim my
  praises.
Yet you did not call upon me, O   22
  Jacob;
much less did you weary yourself in
  my service, O Israel.
You did not bring me sheep as   23
  whole-offerings

---

brought back from Exile is a people newly *created* by God—begotten by him, they are his *sons*
and *daughters* and can be called by his *name*.
    43.8–44.8: Israel can witness that the LORD is God. As in 41.1–29, the framework of these
poems is the legal process; the court will decide who is God and whether the LORD is a just
God. **8–10:** In this court scene God calls *blind* and *deaf* Israel as *witnesses* to prove that he
alone is God. **14:** *Ransomer:* see 41.14 n. The LORD has *sent* his power *to Babylon* to act on
behalf of Israel. *Holy One:* see 40.25–26 n. **15:** The *King* in the Ancient Near East was an
absolute ruler having the power of life and death. Only the LORD has such power in Israel
because he was her *creator.* **19–21:** The return from Exile is a creative act by which a *new thing,*
i.e. the redeemed people of Israel, is *formed.* **23:** The Law did require *sacrifices,* but neither the

or honour me with sacrifices;
I asked you for no burdensome
    offerings
and wearied you with no demands
    for incense.
24 You did not buy me sweet-cane with
    your money
or glut me with the fat of your
    sacrifices;
rather you burdened me with your
    sins
and wearied me with your
    iniquities.
25 I alone, I am He,
who for his own sake wipes out
    your transgressions,
who will remember your sins no
    more.
26 Cite me by name, let us argue it
    out;
set forth your pleading and justify
    yourselves.
27 Your first father transgressed,
your spokesmen rebelled against
    me,
28 and your princes profaned my
    sanctuary;
so I sent Jacob to his doom
    and left Israel to execration.

44 Hear me now, Jacob my servant,
    hear me, my chosen Israel.
2 Thus says the LORD your maker,
your helper, who fashioned you
    from birth:
have no fear, Jacob my servant,
Jeshurun whom I have chosen,
3 for I will pour down rain on a
    thirsty land,
    showers on the dry ground.
I will pour out my spirit on your
    offspring
and my blessing on your children.
4 They shall spring up like a green
    tamarisk,
like poplars by a flowing stream.

This man shall say, 'I am the LORD's 5
    man',
that one shall call himself a son of
    Jacob,
another shall write the LORD's name
    on his hand
and shall add the name of Israel to
    his own.

Thus says the LORD, Israel's King, 6
    the LORD of Hosts, his ransomer:
I am the first and I am the last,
    and there is no god but me.
Who is like me? Let him stand up, 7
let him declare himself and speak
    and show me his evidence.
let him announce beforehand[c]
    things to come,
let him[d] declare what is yet to
    happen.
Take heart, do not be afraid. 8
Did I not foretell this long ago?
I declared it, and you are my
    witnesses.
Is there any god beside me,
    or any creator, even one I do not
    know?
Those who make idols are less than 9
    nothing;
    all their cherished images profit
    nobody;
their worshippers are blind,
    sheer ignorance makes fools of
    them.
If a man makes a god or casts an 10
    image,
    his labour is wasted.
Why! its votaries show their folly; 11
    the craftsmen too are but men.
Let them all gather together and
    confront me,
    all will be afraid and look the fools
    they are.

c let him announce beforehand: *prob. rdg.; Heb.*
since my appointing an ancient people and . . .
d Prob. rdg.; Heb. them.

Law nor the prophets looked upon these as the basic bonds in Israel's relation to her God
(see 1.11; Exod.20.23–23.19; Jer.7.21–23). **24:** *Sweet-cane:* an aromatic plant used in making
incense and sacred anointing oil; see Exod.30.23–25. **26:** The LORD wants Israel (compare
Job 13.15–27; 16.21) to *cite* him to a lawsuit, if it feels unjustly oppressed. **27:** *First father:*
Jacob (Gen.27.1–29; Hos.12.2–4). *Your spokesmen:* rulers, priests, and prophets. **44.2:** *Jeshurun:*
a name for Israel; it appears also in Deut.32.15; 33.5,26. **3:** *Spirit:* see 11.1 n. **5:** The *name* of
his owner was tattooed *on* the *hand* of a Babylonian slave (see Rev.13.16). **6:** *Ransomer:* see
41.14 n.
  44.9–20: Idols and idolaters are ridiculous. This biting satire on idolatry appears to be an
addition to the preceding verses as a commentary on them. In the MT, the entire unit is understood as prose. **9–11:** All *who make idols* are *fools.* **10:** See 41.29; 45.20. **11:** See 1.29; 42.17.

12 The blacksmith sharpens a graving
tool and hammers out his work*e* hot
from the coals and shapes it with his
strong arm; when he grows hungry his
strength fails, if he has no water to
13 drink he tires. The woodworker draws
his line taut and marks out a figure
with a scriber; he planes the wood and
measures it with callipers, and he carves
it to the shape of a man, comely as the
human form, to be set up presently in a
house.*f*
14 A man plants a cedar and the rain
makes it grow, so that later on he will
have cedars to cut down; or he chooses
an ilex or an oak to raise a stout tree
15 for himself in the forest. It becomes
fuel for his fire: some of it he takes and
warms himself, some he kindles and
bakes bread on it, and some he makes
into a god and prostrates himself,
shaping it into an idol and bowing
16 down before it. The one half of it he
burns in the fire and on this he roasts
meat, so that he may eat his roast and
be satisfied; he also warms himself at
it and he says, 'Good! I can feel the
17 heat, I am growing warm.' Then what
is left of the wood he makes into a god
by carving it into shape; he bows down
to it and prostrates himself and prays
to it, saying, 'Save me; for thou art my
18 god.' Such people neither know nor
understand, their eyes made too blind
to see, their minds too narrow to
19 discern. Such a man will not use his
reason, he has neither the wit nor the
sense to say, 'Half of it I have burnt,
yes, and used its embers to bake bread;
I have roasted meat on them too and
eaten it; but the rest of it I turn into
this abominable thing and so I am
20 worshipping a log of wood.' He feeds
on ashes indeed! His own deluded
mind has misled him, he cannot rec-
ollect himself so far as to say, 'Why!
this thing in my hand is a sham.'

21 Remember all this, Jacob,
remember, Israel, for you are my
servant,

I have fashioned you, and you are
to serve me;
you shall not forget me, Israel.
I have swept away your sins like a   22
dissolving mist,
and your transgressions are
dispersed like clouds;
turn back to me; for I have
ransomed you.
Shout in triumph, you heavens, for   23
it is the LORD's doing;
cry out for joy, you lowest depths
of the earth;
break into songs of triumph, you
mountains,
you forest and all your trees;
for the LORD has ransomed Jacob
and made Israel his masterpiece.

Thus says the LORD, your ransomer, 24
who fashioned you from birth:
I am the LORD who made all things,
by myself I stretched out the skies,
alone I hammered out the floor of
the earth.
I frustrate false prophets and their   25
signs
and make fools of diviners;
I reverse what wise men say
and make nonsense of their
wisdom.
I make my servants' prophecies   26
come true
and give effect to my messengers'
designs.
I say of Jerusalem,
'She shall be inhabited once
more',
and of the cities of Judah, 'They
shall be rebuilt;
all their ruins I will restore.'
I say to the deep waters, 'Be dried   27
up;
I will make your streams run dry.'
I say to Cyrus, 'You shall be my   28
shepherd
to carry out all my purpose,
so that Jerusalem may be rebuilt
and the foundations of the temple
may be laid.'

e his work: prob. rdg.; Heb. he works.   *f Or a shrine.*

12–20: The procedures for making idols are reviewed to show that they are nothing but
human creations.
44.21–45.17: The election of Cyrus. The LORD announces that his means of ransoming Israel
is through a foreign king. 24: *Ransomer:* see 41.14 n. 25: *Signs:* see 7.11–12 n. 28: *Cyrus,* king
of Persia (559–529 B.C.) and victor over Babylon (539 B.C.), issued the edict that *Jerusalem* and

45 Thus says the LORD to Cyrus his
anointed,
Cyrus whom he has taken by the
hand
to subdue nations before him
and undo the might of kings;
before whom gates shall be opened
and no doors be shut:

2 I will go before you
and level the swelling hills;
I will break down gates of bronze
and hack through iron bars.

3 I will give you treasures from dark
vaults,
hoarded in secret places,
that you may know that I am the
LORD,
Israel's God who calls you by
name.

4 For the sake of Jacob my servant
and Israel my chosen
I have called you by name
and given you your title, though
you have not known me.

5 I am the LORD, there is no other;
there is no god beside me.
I will strengthen you though you
have not known me,

6 so that men from the rising and the
setting sun
may know that there is none but I:
I am the LORD, there is no other;

7 I make the light, I create
darkness,
author alike of prosperity and
trouble.
I, the LORD, do all these things.

8 Rain righteousness, you heavens,
let the skies above pour down;
let the earth open to receive it,
that it may bear the fruit of
salvation
with righteousness in blossom at its
side.
All this I, the LORD, have created.

9 Will the pot contend*g* with the
potter,
or the earthenware,*h* with the hand
that shapes it?
Will the clay ask the potter what he
is making?
or his*i* handiwork say to him, 'You
have no skill'?
Will the babe say*j* to his father,   10
'What are you begetting?',
or to his mother, 'What are you
bringing to birth?'

Thus says the LORD, Israel's Holy   11
One, his maker:
Would you dare question me
concerning my children,
or instruct me in my handiwork?
I alone, I made the earth   12
and created man upon it;
I, with my own hands, stretched out
the heavens
and caused all their host to shine.
I alone have roused this man in   13
righteousness,
and I will smooth his path before
him;
he shall rebuild my city
and let my exiles go free—
not for a price nor for a bribe,
says the LORD of Hosts.

Thus says the LORD: 14
Toilers of Egypt and Nubian
merchants
and Sabaeans bearing tribute*k*
shall come into your power and be
your slaves,
shall come and march behind you in
chains;
they shall bow down before you in
supplication, saying,
'Surely God is among you and there
is no other,
no other god.
How then canst thou be a god that   15
hidest thyself,
O God of Israel, the deliverer?'

g Will . . . contend: *prob. rdg.; Heb.* Ho! he has con-
tended.
h *Or* shard.
i *Prob. rdg.; Heb.* your.
j Will . . . say: *prob. rdg.; Heb.* Ho! you that say.
k bearing tribute: *or* men of stature.

---

the *temple* be rebuilt; see Ezra 1.1–4. *Shepherd:* king; see Ezek. ch. 34. **45.1:** *Anointed* is the
English equivalent of the Heb. *mashiah* (from which the word "Messiah" comes) and of the
Gk. *christos* from which "Christ" is derived. Hebrew priests (Lev.8.12–13) and kings (1 Sam.
6.12–13) were anointed with oil, signifying a special gift of the spirit to carry out a commission
given them by God. Cyrus is the only non-Israelite called "anointed" because he carried out
God's purpose of liberating his people. God himself leads Cyrus *by the hand* so that he may
accomplish his task without fail. **4:** *Your title:* "anointed." **13:** *This man:* Cyrus.

16 Those who defy him are confounded
      and brought to shame,
   those who make idols perish in
      confusion.
17   But Israel has been delivered by
         the LORD,
      delivered for all time to come;
   they shall not be confounded or put
      to shame for all eternity.

18 Thus says the LORD, the creator of
      the heavens,
      he who is God,
   who made the earth and fashioned it
      and himself fixed it fast,
   who created it no empty void,
      but made it for a place to dwell in:
   I am the LORD, there is no other.
19 I do not speak in secret, in realms
      of darkness,
   I do not say to the sons of Jacob,
      'Look for me in the empty void.'
   I the LORD speak what is right,
      declare what is just.
20   Gather together, come, draw near,
         all you survivors of the nations,
      you fools, who carry your wooden
         idols in procession
      and pray to a god that cannot save
         you.
21   Come forward and urge your case,
         consult together:
      who foretold this in days of old,
         who stated it long ago?
      Was it not I the LORD?
      There is no god but me;
      there is no god other than I,
         victorious and able to save.
22   Look to me and be saved,
         you peoples from all corners of
            the earth,
      for I am God, there is no other.
23   By my life I have sworn,
      I have given a promise of victory,
         a promise that will not be broken,
      that to me every knee shall bend
         and by me every tongue shall
            swear.

In the LORD alone, men shall say,   24
   are victory and might
and all who defy him
   shall stand ashamed in his presence,
but all the sons of Israel shall stand   25
   victorious
and find their glory in the LORD.

Bel has crouched down, Nebo has   **46**
   stooped low:
their images, once carried in your
   processions,
have been loaded on to beasts and
   cattle,
a burden for the weary creatures;
   they stoop and they crouch;   2
not for them to bring the burden to
   safety;
the gods themselves go into captivity.
Listen to me, house of Jacob   3
and all the remnant of the house
   of Israel,
a load on me from your birth,
   carried by me from the womb:
till you grow old I am He,   4
and when white hairs come, I will
   carry you still;
I have made you and I will bear the
   burden,
I will carry you and bring you to
   safety.
To whom will you liken me? Who   5
   is my equal?
With whom can you compare me?
   Where is my like?
Those who squander their bags of   6
   gold
and weigh out their silver with a
   balance
hire a goldsmith to fashion them
   into a god;
then they worship it and fall
   prostrate before it;
they hoist it shoulder-high and carry   7
   it home;
   they set it down on its base;
there it must stand, it cannot stir
   from its place.

45.18–25: Lawsuit against idolators. 18: The *empty void* (better, "chaos") preceded, and is the
alternative to, creation. **20–21a:** Idolators are summoned as if to a court; see 41.21. **21b–25:**
Note the clear statement of monotheism.
   46.1–13: The LORD and the gods of Babylon. 1–7: The downfall of the Babylonian gods.
1: *Bel* ("lord") is one of the titles of Marduk, the main Babylonian deity; *Nebo* (Babylonian
Nabu), the god of wisdom, was considered Marduk's son. The liturgies of Babylonian cultic
festivities, among them the New Year's celebration, included *processions* of *their images*. See
also v. 7. **2–4:** Babylon's gods had to be carried to *safety* when Cyrus captured the city. In
contrast the LORD has *carried* Israel from the time of her *birth* at the Exodus. **6–7:** See 44.9–20.

Let a man cry to it as he will, it
  never answers him;
  it cannot deliver him from his
    troubles.

8 Remember this, you rebels,
  consider it well, and abandon hope,
9 remember all that happened long
    ago;
  for I am God, there is no other,
  I am God, and there is no one like
    me;
10 I reveal the end from the beginning,
  from ancient times I reveal what is
    to be;
  I say, 'My purpose shall take effect,
  I will accomplish all that I please.'
11 I summon a bird of prey[l] from the
    east,
  one from a distant land to fulfil my
    purpose.
  Mark this; I have spoken, and I
    will bring it about,
  I have a plan to carry out, and
    carry it out I will.
12 Listen to me, all you stubborn
    hearts,
  for whom victory is far off:
13 I bring my victory near, it is not
    far off,
  and my deliverance shall not be
    delayed;
  I will grant deliverance in Zion
  and give my glory to Israel.[m]

47 Down with you, sit in the dust,
  virgin daughter of Babylon.
  Down from your throne, sit on the
    ground,
    daughter of the Chaldaeans;
  never again shall men call you
    soft-skinned and delicate.
2 Take up the millstone, grind meal,
    uncover your tresses;
  strip off your skirt, bare your thighs,
    wade through rivers,
3 so that your nakedness may be
    plain to see

and your shame exposed.
I will take vengeance, I will treat
  with none of you,
says the Holy One of Israel, our 4
  ransomer,
whose name is the LORD of Hosts.

Sit silent, 5
be off into the shadows, daughter
  of the Chaldaeans;
for never again shall men call you
  queen of many kingdoms.
When I was angry with my 6
  people,
I dishonoured my own possession
and gave them into your power.
You showed them no mercy,
you made your yoke weigh heavy on
  the aged.
You said then, 'I shall reign a queen 7
  for ever',
while[n] you gave no thought to this
and did not consider how it would
  end.
Now therefore listen to this, 8
you lover of luxury, carefree on
  your throne.
You say to yourself,
'I am, and who but I?
No widow's weeds for me, no deaths
  of children.'
Yet suddenly, in a single day, 9
these two things shall come upon
  you;
they shall both come upon you in
  full measure:[o]
children's deaths and widowhood,
for all your monstrous sorceries,
  your countless spells.
Secure in your wicked ways you 10
  thought, 'No one is looking.'
Your wisdom betrayed you,
  omniscient as you were,
and you said to yourself,
'I am, and who but I?'

l a bird of prey: or a massed host.
m and give my glory to Israel: or for Israel my glory.
n for ever', while: or of a wide realm, for all time'
but.
o in full measure: or at random.

11: The one *from the east* is Cyrus; see 41.2; in 44.28 he is "my shepherd"; in 45.1, "his anointed."
47.1–15: A funeral song for Babylon. The city of Babylon, personified as a dethroned queen
reduced to slavery, is commanded to mourn, for nothing can stop the punishment the LORD
plans for her. The poem is a taunt song in *qinah* ("dirge") form. 1: *Daughter of Babylon:* better,
"daughter Babylon." 2: To *grind meal* was the work of slaves whose task required them to
strip off outer clothes, especially in working around irrigation *rivers,* i.e. canals. 4: *Holy One:*
see 40.25–26 n. *Ransomer:* see 41.14 n. 8: Babylon describes herself in the same terms as did the
LORD; see 43.13. 9–12: Magic, divination, and rituals for warding off evil were important elements in Babylonian religion. 10: Her famous *wisdom* was not able to reveal to Babylon her

11 Therefore evil shall come upon you,
    and you will not know how to
        master it;
    disaster shall befall you,
        and you will not be able to charm
            it away;
        ruin all unforeseen
    shall come suddenly upon you.
12 Persist in your spells and your
        monstrous sorceries,*p*
    maybe you can get help from them,
        maybe you will yet inspire awe.
13 But no! in spite of your many wiles
        you are powerless.
    Let your astrologers, your star-
        gazers
    who foretell your future month by
        month,
    persist, and save you!
14 But look, they are gone like chaff;
        fire burns them up;
    they cannot snatch themselves from
        the flames;
        this is no glowing coal to warm
            them,
    no fire for them to sit by.
15 So much for your magicians
        with whom you have trafficked all
            your life:
    they have stumbled off, each his
        own way,
        and there is no one to save you.

48 Hear this, you house of Jacob,
        you who are called by the name
            of Israel,
    you who spring from the seed of
        Judah;
    who swear by the name of the
        LORD
        and boast in the God of Israel,
    but not in honesty or sincerity,
2 although you call yourselves citizens
        of a holy city
    and lean for support on the God
        of Israel;
    his name is the LORD of Hosts.
3 Long ago I announced what would
        first happen,
    I revealed it with my own mouth;

suddenly I acted and it came about.
I knew that you were stubborn,   4
    your neck stiff as iron, your brow
        like bronze,
therefore I told you of these things   5
    long ago,
and declared them before they
    came about,
so that you could not say, 'This
    was my idol's doing;
my image, the god that I fashioned,
    he ordained them.'
You have heard what I said;   6
    consider it well,
and you must admit the truth of it.
Now I show you new things,
    hidden things which you did not
        know before.
They were not created long ago,   7
    but in this very hour;
you had never heard of them
    before today.
You cannot say, 'I know them
    already.'
You neither heard nor knew,   8
    long ago your ears were closed;
for I knew that you were
    untrustworthy, treacherous,
a notorious rebel from your birth.
For the sake of my own name I   9
    was patient,*q*
rather than destroy you I held
    myself in check.
See how I tested you, not as silver   10
    is tested,
    but in the furnace of affliction;
    there I purified you.
For my honour, for my own   11
    honour I did it;
let them disparage my past
    triumphs*r* if they will:
I will not give my glory to any
    other god.

Hear me, Jacob,   12
    and Israel whom I called:
I am He; I am the first,

p Prob. rdg.; Heb. adds with which you have trafficked
all your life (*cp. verse 15*).
q See note on verse 11.
r my past triumphs: *transposed from verse 9.*

---

basic weakness and consequent fall. **13:** Astrology was a sophisticated art in Mesopotamia.
48.1–22: Hear what the LORD will do. Just as he controlled the past, so the God of Israel
controls the future. **3:** *With my own mouth:* that is, through the prophets. **4–5:** The purpose of
prophecy was to show that the LORD alone controls history. **6:** *New things:* the message of
deliverance in Second Isaiah. **10:** See 1.25. *The furnace of affliction* was the Babylonian Exile.
12–16: The LORD promises to call Cyrus (*he whom I love,* v. 14) to destroy Babylon. **12:** See 41.4.

I am the last also.

13 With my own hands I founded the
earth,
with my right hand I formed the
expanse of sky;
when I summoned them,
they sprang at once into being.

14 Assemble, all of you, and listen to
me;
which of you has declared what is
coming,
that he whom I love shall wreak
my[s] will on Babylon
and the Chaldaeans shall be
scattered?

15 I, I myself, have spoken, I have called
him,
I have made him appear, and
wherever he goes he shall
prosper.

16 Draw near to me and hear this:
from the beginning I have never
spoken in secret;
from the moment of its first
happening I was there.[t]

17 Thus says the LORD your ransomer,
the Holy One of Israel:
I am the LORD your God:
I teach you for your own
advantage
and lead you in the way you must
go.

18 If only you had listened to my
commands,
your prosperity would have rolled
on like a river in flood
and your just success like the
waves of the sea;

19 in number your children would
have been like the sand
and your descendants countless as
its grains;
their name would never be erased or
blotted from my sight.

20 Come out of Babylon, hasten away
from the Chaldaeans;
proclaim it with loud songs of
triumph,
crying the news to the ends of the
earth;

tell them, 'The LORD has ransomed
his servant Jacob.'
21 Though he led them through desert
places they suffered no thirst,
for them he made water run from
the rock,
for them he cleft the rock and
streams gushed forth.

22 There is no peace for the wicked,
says the LORD.

Israel a light to the nations

49 Listen to me, you coasts and
islands,
pay heed, you peoples far away:
from birth the LORD called me,
he named me from my mother's
womb.
2 He made my tongue his sharp sword
and concealed me under cover of
his hand;
he made me a polished arrow
and hid me out of sight in his
quiver.
3 He said to me, 'You are my servant,
Israel through whom I shall win
glory';
so I rose to honour in the LORD's
sight
and my God became my strength.[u]
4 Once I said, 'I have laboured in vain;
I have spent my strength for nothing,
to no purpose';
yet in truth my cause is with the
LORD
and my reward is in God's hands.
5 And now the LORD who formed me
in the womb to be his servant,
to bring Jacob back to him
that Israel should be gathered to
him,[v]
now the LORD calls me again:[w]
6 it is too slight a task for you, as
my servant,

s Or his.
t Prob. rdg.; Heb. adds and now the Lord GOD has
sent me, and his spirit.
u so I rose . . . strength: transposed from end of verse 5.
v be gathered to him: or not be swept away.
w See note on verse 3.

20: *Servant Jacob:* see 41.8 n. **18:** *Your prosperity:* welfare, well-being. **22:** Probably a gloss.
49.1–6: Second servant song. See 42.1–4 n. The servant himself speaks concerning his call and
mission. In vv. 1–4, though the servant speaks as an individual, he is identified as Israel;
however, in vv. 5–6 his mission is to *restore* Israel. Hence, he is identified by some as the ideal
Israel or the faithful Israel, the remnant. **1,5:** *Mother's womb:* see Jer.1.5. *Named me:* see 43.1.

to restore the tribes of Jacob,
to bring back the descendants of
    Israel:
I will make you a light to the
    nations,
to be my salvation*x* to earth's
    farthest bounds.

7   Thus says the Holy One, the LORD
    who ransoms Israel,
to one who thinks little of himself,
  whom every nation abhors,
  the slave of tyrants:
When they see you kings shall rise,
princes shall rise and bow down,
because of the LORD who is faithful,
because of the Holy One of Israel
  who has chosen you.

8   Thus says the LORD:
  In the hour of my favour I
    answered you,
  and I helped you on the day of
    deliverance,*y*
  putting the land to rights
and sharing out afresh its desolate
    fields;
9   I said to the prisoners, 'Go free',
and to those in darkness, 'Come
    out and be seen.'
They shall find pasture in the
    desert sands*z*
and grazing on all the dunes.
10   They shall neither hunger nor
    thirst,
no scorching heat or sun shall
    distress them;
  for one who loves them shall
    lead them
  and take them to water at
    bubbling springs.
11   I will make every hill a path
  and build embankments for my
    highways.
12   See, they come; some from far
    away,
these from the north and these from
    the west
  and those from the land of Syene.
13   Shout for joy, you heavens, rejoice,
    O earth,

you mountains, break into songs of
    triumph,
for the LORD has comforted his
    people
  and has had pity on his own in
    their distress.

But Zion says,   14
'The LORD has forsaken me; my
    God has forgotten me.'
Can a woman forget the infant at   15
    her breast,
or a loving mother the child of her
    womb?
Even these forget, yet I will not
    forget you.
Your walls are always before my   16
    eyes,
I have engraved them on the palms
    of my hands.
Those who are to rebuild you make 17
    better speed
  than those who pulled you down,
while those who laid you waste depart.
Raise your eyes and look around   18
    you:
see how they assemble, how they are
    flocking back to you.
By my life I, the LORD, swear it,
you shall wear them proudly as
    your jewels,
  and adorn yourself with them
    like a bride;
I did indeed make you waste and 19
    desolate,
  I razed you to the ground,
but your boundaries*a* shall now be
    too narrow
  for your inhabitants—
  and those who laid you in ruins
    are far away.
The children born in your   20
    bereavement shall yet say in
    your hearing,
'This place is too narrow; make
    room for me to live in.'
Then you will say to yourself,   21

x to be my salvation: or that my salvation may reach.
y Prob. rdg.; Heb. adds I have formed you, and ap-
pointed you to be a light to all peoples (cp. 42. 6).
z desert sands: prob. rdg.; Heb. ways.
a I did . . . boundaries: or your wasted and desolate
land, your ruined countryside.

49.7–26: The glorious return. 9a: *Prisoners . . . darkness:* the exiles in Babylon. **9b–10:** The
desert between Babylon and Israel will provide water and food as Israel returns, as did the
desert at the Exodus. **12:** *Syene:* a town at the southern end of Egypt; see Ezek.29.10. **14–26:**
The LORD has not forgotten Jerusalem; Israel will return and *rebuild it.* **18:** *By my life:* an
oath formula; see Amos 4.2. **19–21:** The city cannot contain the enlarged population. **20:** *In*

'All these children, how did I come
   by them,
bereaved and barren as I was?
Who reared them
when I was left alone, left by myself;
   where did I get them all?'

22   The LORD God says,
Now is the time: I will beckon to
   the nations
and hoist a signal to the peoples,
and they shall bring your sons in
   their arms
and carry your daughters on their
   shoulders;
23   kings shall be your foster-fathers
and their princesses shall be your
   nurses.
They shall bow to the earth before you
and lick the dust from your feet;
and you shall know that I am the LORD
and that none who look to me will
   be disappointed.

24   Can his prey be taken from the
   strong man,
or the captive be rescued from the
   ruthless?
25   And the LORD answers,
The captive shall be taken even
   from the strong,
and the prey of the ruthless shall
   be rescued;
I will contend with all who contend
   against you
and save your children from them.
26   I will force your oppressors to feed
   on their own flesh
and make them drunk with their own
   blood as if with fresh wine,
and all mankind shall know
that it is I, the LORD, who save you,
I your ransomer, the Mighty One
   of Jacob.

50   The LORD says,
Is there anywhere a deed of divorce

by which I have put your mother
   away?
Was there some creditor of mine
to whom I sold you?
No; it was through your own
   wickedness that you were sold
and for your own misconduct that
   your mother was put away.
Why, then, did I find no one when 2
   I came?
Why, when I called, did no one
   answer?
Did you think my arm too short to
   redeem,
did you think I had no power to
   save?
Not so. By my rebuke I dried up the sea
and turned rivers into desert;
their fish perished for lack of water
and died on the thirsty ground;
I clothed the skies in mourning 3
and covered them with sackcloth.

The Lord GOD has given me 4
   the tongue of a teacher
and skill to console the weary
   with a word in the morning;
he sharpened my hearing
that I might listen like one who is
   taught.
The Lord GOD opened my ears 5
and I did not disobey or turn back
   in defiance.
I offered my back to the lash, 6
   and let my beard be plucked
   from my chin,
I did not hide my face from spitting
   and insult;
but the Lord GOD stands by to help 7
   me;
therefore no insult can wound me.
I have set my face like flint,
   for I know that I shall not be put
   to shame,
because one who will clear my name 8
   is at my side.

---

bereavement: in Exile, separated from the Temple, the special presence of God. **22:** The *signal*, formerly a sign of danger (5.26; 13.2; 18.3; compare Jer.6.1), is now a call for the return. **23:** See 49.7. **26:** *Ransomer*: see 41.14 n.

50.1–3: Separation, not divorce. The Exile did not mark the end of the LORD's relationship with Israel, as some say; he can do what he wills. **1:** *Put your mother away*: see Hos.2.2–13; Jer.3.1–10. *Deed of divorce*: see Deut.24.1–4. The covenant is not broken since no *creditor* takes precedence over God. **2:** See Exod. chs. 14–15.

50.4–9: Third servant song. See 42.1–4 n. The servant speaks concerning his mission (v. 4) and his response to suffering (vv. 5–9). **4:** The prophet perhaps identifies himself with the servant, but it is still possible to regard the servant as Israel, or at least faithful Israel. *Teacher:* or "disciple." **8:** The language comes from the court process.

Who dare argue against me? Let us
  confront one another.
Who will dispute my cause? Let him
  come forward.
9 The Lord GOD will help me;
  who then can prove me guilty?
They will all wear out like a garment,
  the moths will eat them up.

10 Which of you fears the LORD and
  obeys his servant's commands?
The man who walks in dark places
  with no light,
yet trusts in the name of the LORD
  and leans on his God.

11 But you who kindle a fire and set
  fire-brands alight,
go, walk into your own fire
and among the fire-brands you
  have set ablaze.
This is your fate at my hands:
  you shall lie down in torment.

51 Listen to me, all who follow the
  right and seek the LORD:
look to the rock from which you
  were hewn,
to the quarry from which you
  were dug;
2 look to your father Abraham
  and to Sarah who gave you birth:
when I called him he was but one,
I blessed him and made him many.
3 The LORD has indeed comforted Zion,
  comforted all her ruined homes,
turning her wilderness into an Eden,
  her thirsty plains into a garden of
  the LORD.
Joy and gladness shall be found in
  her,
  thanksgiving and melody.
4 Pay heed to me, my people,
and hear me, O my nation;
for my law shall shine forth
and I will flash the light of my
  judgement over the nations.
5 My victory is near, my deliverance
  has gone*b* forth

and my arm shall rule the nations;
for the coasts and islands shall wait
  and they shall look to me for
  protection.
Lift your eyes to the heavens,   6
look at the earth beneath:
the heavens grow murky as smoke;
the earth wears into tatters like a
  garment,
and those who live on it die like
  maggots;
but my deliverance is everlasting
  and my saving power shall never
  wane.

Listen to me, my people who know   7
  what is right,
you who lay my law to heart:
  do not fear the taunts of men,
  let no reproaches dismay you;
for the grub will devour them like   8
  a garment
and the moth as if they were wool,
but my saving power shall last for
  ever
  and my deliverance to all
  generations.

Awake, awake, put on your strength, 9
  O arm of the LORD,
awake as you did long ago, in days
  gone by.
Was it not you
who hacked the Rahab in pieces and
  ran the dragon through?
  Was it not you   10
who dried up the sea, the waters of
  the great abyss,
and made the ocean depths a path
  for the ransomed?
So the LORD's people shall come   11
  back, set free,
and enter Zion with shouts of
  triumph,
  crowned with everlasting joy;
joy and gladness shall overtake
  them as they come,

b Or shone.

50.10–11: Follow the servant. Israel is admonished to be obedient like the servant, trusting
in the LORD and not in herself.
  51.1–16: Comfort to Zion. Several poems of different types present a common theme, Zion's
salvation. *1–2: Abraham* and *Sarah, the rock from which* Israel was *hewn,* were *made many* in
accord with God's promise (Gen.12.1–3); the same promise and power are still active. **3:** The
restoration of *Zion* will be like the creation of *Eden* out of the primeval desert; see Gen.2.5–9;
Ezek.36.35. **5:** Israel's restoration will inaugurate a new era for all *nations* who will look to the
LORD for *protection.* **9:** *Rahab, the dragon:* see 30.7 n. **10:** The crossing of the sea at the Exodus
was also a new creation, like the slaying of the dragon of the great abyss at the original creation

and sorrow and sighing shall flee
away.
12 I, I myself, am he that comforts
you.
Why then fear man, man who must
die,
man frail as grass?
13 Why have you forgotten the LORD
your maker,
who stretched out the skies and
founded the earth?
Why are you continually afraid,
all the day long,
why dread the fury of oppressors
ready to destroy you?
Where is that fury?
14 He that cowers under it shall soon
stand upright and not die,
he shall soon reap the early crop
and not lack bread.

15 I am the LORD your God, the LORD
of Hosts is my name. I cleft the sea and
16 its waves roared, that I might fix the
heavens in place and form the earth
and say to Zion, 'You are my people.'
I have put my words in your mouth
and kept you safe under the shelter of
my hand.

17 Awake, awake; rise up, Jerusalem.
You have drunk from the LORD's
hand
the cup of his wrath,
drained to its dregs the bowl of
drunkenness;
18 of all the sons you have borne there
is not one to guide you,
of all you have reared, not one to
take you by the hand.
19 These two disasters have overtaken
you;
who can console you?—
havoc and ruin, famine and the
sword;
who can comfort you?
20 Your sons are in stupor, they lie at

the head of every street,
like antelopes caught in the net,
glutted with the wrath of the
LORD,
the rebuke of your God.
Therefore listen to this, in your 21
affliction,
drunk that you are, but not with
wine:
thus says the LORD, your Lord and 22
your God,
who will plead his people's
cause:
Look, I take from your hand
the cup of drunkenness;
you shall never again drink from the
bowl of my wrath,
I will give it instead to your 23
tormentors and oppressors,
those who said to you, 'Lie down
and we will walk over you';
and you made your backs like the
ground beneath them,
like a roadway for passers-by.

Awake, awake, put on your strength, **52**
O Zion,
put on your loveliest garments, holy
city of Jerusalem;
for never shall the uncircumcised and
the unclean enter you again.
Rise up, captive Jerusalem, shake 2
off the dust;
loose your neck from the collar
that binds it,
O captive daughter of Zion.

The LORD says, You were sold but 3
no price was paid, and without payment you shall be ransomed. The Lord 4
GOD says, At the beginning my people
went down into Egypt to live there,
and at the end it was the Assyrians who
oppressed them; but now what do I 5
find here? says the LORD. My people
carried off and no price paid, their
rulers derided, and my name reviled all

14: The *early crop* was the result of the "blessing" of an early rain. **16:** *You are my people:*
see Hos.1.8; 2.23.
  51.17–52.2: Awake, Jerusalem. The holy city earlier had been drunk with the LORD's wrath.
Compare Jer.13.13; 25.15–18; Ezek.23.32–34; Lam.4.21. **17:** Pleasure and pain are pictured in
the Bible as a *cup* that is offered to a person by God, emphasizing God's control of man's
destiny; compare Pss.11.6; 16.5–6; Mk.10.38–39. **18:** *Take you by the hand:* give guidance and
support. **52.1–2:** The opening call to *awake* is reiterated, now looking to the future instead of
the past. **1:** *Uncircumcised:* foreigners. *Unclean:* Jews who do not observe the ritual laws of
cleanliness.
  52.3–6: Israel sold and ransomed without money. A prose insertion. **4–5:** *Egypt* paid the price

6 day long, says the LORD. But on that
day my people shall know my name;
they shall know that it is I who speak;
here I am.

7 How lovely on the mountains are
      the feet of the herald
  who comes to proclaim prosperity
      and bring good news,
      the news of deliverance,
  calling to Zion, 'Your God is king.'
8 Hark, your watchmen raise their
      voices
      and shout together in triumph;
  for with their own eyes they shall
      see
      the LORD returning in pity to Zion.
9 Break forth together in shouts of
      triumph,
      you ruins of Jerusalem;
  for the LORD has taken pity on his
      people
      and has ransomed Jerusalem.
10 The LORD has bared his holy arm
      in the sight of all nations,
  and the whole world from end to end
      shall see the deliverance of our God.
11 Away from Babylon; come out,
      come out,
      touch nothing unclean.
  Come out from Babylon, keep
      yourselves pure,
      you who carry the vessels of the
      LORD.
12 But you shall not come out in
      urgent haste
      nor leave like fugitives;
  for the LORD will march at your
      head,
      your rearguard will be Israel's
      God.

Behold, my servant shall prosper,   13
  he shall be lifted up, exalted to the
      heights.

Time was when many*e* were aghast   14
      at you, my people;*d*
  so now many nations*e* recoil at   15
      sight of him,
  and kings curl their lips in disgust.
  For they see what they had never
      been told
  and things unheard before fill their
      thoughts.

Who could have believed what we   **53**
      have heard,
  and to whom has the power of the
      LORD been revealed?

He grew up before the LORD like a   2
      young plant
  whose roots are in parched ground;
  he had no beauty, no majesty to
      draw our eyes,
      no grace to make us delight in him;
  his form, disfigured, lost all the
      likeness of a man,
  his beauty changed beyond
      human semblance.*f*
He was despised, he shrank from   3
      the sight of men,
  tormented and humbled by
      suffering;
  we despised him, we held him of
      no account,
  a thing from which men turn
      away their eyes.
Yet on himself he bore our   4
      sufferings,

c Or the great.   *d See note on 53. 2.*
e Or great nations.
f his form . . . semblance: *transposed from end of 52. 14.*

---

of Israel's slavery by the plagues and death of its firstborn, but Babylon *paid no price* when it
carried them *off* into Exile. **6:** *That day:* see 7.18–25 n. *Know my name:* see 43.1.
    52.7–12: A pilgrim victory hymn. This is a continuation of the song, interrupted after v. 2,
which celebrates the joyful return of the LORD and his people to the holy city. **7:** *God is king:*
see 43.15 n. **8–9:** *Watchmen* are the people left in the *ruins of Jerusalem* at the time of its destruction by the Babylonians in 587 B.C. (2 Kgs.25.8–12). They look for the return of *the LORD*
who was considered to have gone to Babylon with the captives; compare Ezek.11.22–25;
43.1–7. **12:** The Israelites on their return from Babylon did not ask for an escort of soldiers but
trusted that the LORD would be their guard: see Ezra 8.21–23.
    52.13–53.12: Fourth servant song. The suffering servant. See 42.1–4 n. Israel, the servant of
God, has suffered as a humiliated individual. However, the servant endured without complaint
because it was vicarious suffering (suffering for others). **13–15:** *Nations* and *kings* will be
surprised to see the servant *exalted.* **53.1:** The crowds, pagan nations, among whom the servant
(Israel) lived, speak here (through v. 9), saying that the significance of Israel's humiliation and
exaltation is hard to believe. **2:** In traditional Hebrew thought, the good man prospers like a
tree by water but the wicked is like a *plant* growing in *parched ground;* see Ps.1.3–6. **3:** *Turn
away their eyes:* lit. hide their faces, an expression used in relation to lepers, whose sickness,
considered a sign of sin, made them *despised.* **4–5:** The vicarious suffering expressed here is in

our torments he endured,
while we counted him smitten by
　　God,
struck down by disease and
　　misery;
5　but he was pierced for our
　　transgressions,
　　tortured for our iniquities;
the chastisement he bore is health
　　for us
and by his scourging we are healed.
6　We had all strayed like sheep,
each of us had gone his own way;
but the LORD laid upon him
　　the guilt of us all.
7　He was afflicted, he submitted to
　　be struck down
　　and did not open his mouth;
he was led like a sheep to the
　　slaughter,
like a ewe that is dumb before the
　　shearers.*g*
8　Without protection, without justice,*h*
　　he was taken away;
and who gave a thought to his fate,
how he was cut off from the
　　world of living men,
stricken to the death for my people's
　　transgression?
9　He was assigned a grave with the
　　wicked,
a burial-place among the refuse of
　　mankind,
though he had done no violence
　　and spoken no word of treachery.
10　Yet the LORD took thought for his
　　tortured servant
and healed him who had made
　　himself*i* a sacrifice for sin;
so shall he enjoy long life and see
　　his children's children,
and in his hand the LORD's cause
　　shall prosper.
11　After all his pains he shall be
　　bathed in light,

after his disgrace he shall be fully
　　vindicated;
so shall he, my servant, vindicate
　　many,
himself bearing the penalty of their
　　guilt.
Therefore I will allot him a portion　12
　　with the great,
and he shall share the spoil with
　　the mighty,
because he exposed himself to face
　　death*j*
　　and was reckoned among
　　transgressors,
because he bore the sin of many
　　and interceded for their
　　transgressions.

Sing aloud, O barren woman who　　**54**
　　never bore a child,
break into cries of joy, you who
　　have never been in labour;
for the deserted wife has more sons
　　than she who lives in wedlock,
　　says the LORD
Enlarge the limits of your home,　　2
　　spread wide the curtains of your
　　tent;
let out its ropes to the full
　　and drive the pegs home;
for you shall break out of your　　3
　　confines right and left,
your descendants shall dispossess
　　wide regions,*k*
and re-people cities now desolate.
Fear not; you shall not be put to　　4
　　shame,
you shall suffer no insult, have no
　　cause to blush.

*g Prob. rdg.; Heb. adds and he would not open his
mouth.*
*h Without protection, without justice: or After arrest
and sentence.*
*i healed . . . himself: prob. rdg.; Heb. he made sick,
if you make.*
j Or because he poured out his life to the death.
k wide regions: or the nations.

---

contrast both to the traditional solidarity in guilt of Exod.20.5 and to individual responsibility
proposed by the prophets at the time of the Exile; see Jer.31.30; Ezek. ch. 18. **5:** *Health for us:*
lit. "our peace," which means "general welfare." **6–7:** The servant is *led like a sheep* in contrast
to the peoples going their *own* way. **8:** Although some legal process seems to be involved, the
servant does not receive *justice;* see Jer.39.5–6. **9:** The death probably refers to the destruction
and Exile of Israel. Compare Ezek. ch. 37. **10–12:** The theme of 52.13 is resumed. Israel, which
has suffered for all mankind, will now be granted her rightful place. **10:** *Long life* and *children's
children* are the signs of a final vindication before God; see Job 42.16–17. **11:** *Bathed in light:*
enjoying God's favor; see Ps.80.3.
　　54.1–17: Reassurance to Israel. A series of metaphors is used to repeat the promise that the
nation will be rebuilt and Israel's relationship to the LORD restored. **1:** The *deserted wife*
represents Israel in Exile; the one *in wedlock* represents preexilic Israel. **4:** *Shame of your*

It is time to forget the shame of
    your younger days
and remember no more the
    reproach of your widowhood,
5 for your husband is your maker,
    whose name is the LORD of Hosts;
your ransomer is the Holy One of
    Israel
who is called God of all the earth.
6 The LORD has acknowledged you a
    wife again,
once deserted and heart-broken,
your God has called you a bride
    still young
though once rejected.
7 On the impulse of a moment I
    forsook you,
but with tender affection I will bring
    you home again.
8   In sudden anger
I hid my face from you for a
    moment;
but now have I pitied you with a
    love which never fails,
says the LORD who ransoms you.
9 These days recall for me the days
    of Noah:
as I swore that the waters of
    Noah's flood
should never again pour over the
    earth,
so now I swear to you
never again to be angry with you
    or reproach you.
10 Though the mountains move and
    the hills shake,
my love shall be immovable and
    never fail,
and my covenant of peace shall
    not be shaken.
So says the LORD who takes pity
    on you.

11 O storm-battered city, distressed
    and disconsolate,
now I will set your stones in the
    finest mortar
and your foundations in lapis
    lazuli;

I will make your battlements of red 12
    jasper,[l]
and your gates of garnet;[m]
all your boundary-stones shall
    be jewels.
Your masons shall all be 13
    instructed by the LORD,
and your sons shall enjoy great
    prosperity;
and in triumph[n] shall you be 14
    restored.
You shall be free from oppression
    and have no fears,
free from terror, and it shall not
    come near you;
should any attack you, it will not be 15
    my doing,
the aggressor, whoever he be, shall
    perish for his attempt.
It was I who created the smith 16
    to fan the coals in the furnace
    and forge weapons each for its
    purpose,
and I who created the destroyer to
    lay waste;
but now no weapon made to harm 17
    you shall prevail,
and you shall rebut every charge
    brought against you.
Such is the fortune of the servants
    of the LORD;
their vindication comes from me.
This is the very word of the
    LORD.

Come, all who are thirsty, come, **55**
    fetch water;
come, you who have no food, buy
    corn and eat;
come and buy, not for money, not
    for a price.[o]
Why spend money and get what is 2
    not bread,
why give the price of your labour
    and go unsatisfied?
Only listen to me and you will have
    good food to eat,

l Or carbuncle.   *m Or* firestone.
n Or in righteousness.
o Prob. rdg.; Heb. adds wine and milk.

younger days: see Ezek. ch. 16. **7:** *Tender affection:* lit. the affection of a mother for the child of her womb. **8:** *Love which never fails* is the covenant love based on the bond of parent and child between the LORD and Israel; see 43.6–7 n. *Ransoms:* see 41.14 n. **9:** See Gen.9.8–17; compare Gen.8.21–22. **10:** *Covenant of peace:* see Ezek.34.25.
    55.1–13: Admonitions and reassurance. The Book of the Consolation of Israel (chs. 40–55) concludes with this poem celebrating God's liberality (vv. 1–2), faithfulness (vv. 3–5), transcendence (vv. 6–9), and power (vv. 10–13). **1–2:** See 25.6–12 n. All are invited to the LORD's table. The language is both metaphorical and literal; those who *listen* (vv. 2–3) to the LORD

and you will enjoy the fat of the land.
3 Come to me and listen to my words,
hear me, and you shall have life:
I will make a covenant with you,
this time for ever,
to love you faithfully as I loved David.
4 I made him a witness to all races,
a prince and instructor of peoples;
5 and you in turn shall summon
nations you do not know,
and nations that do not know you
shall come running to you,
because the LORD your God,
the Holy One of Israel, has glorified
you.

6 Inquire of the LORD while he is
present,
call upon him when he is close at
hand.
7 Let the wicked abandon their ways
and evil men their thoughts:
let them return to the LORD, who will
have pity on them,
return to our God, for he will freely
forgive.
8 For my thoughts are not your
thoughts,
and your ways are not my ways.
This is the very word of the LORD.
9 For as the heavens are higher than
the earth,
so are my ways higher than your ways
and my thoughts than your
thoughts;
10 and as the rain and the snow come
down from heaven
and do not return until they have
watered the earth,
making it blossom and bear fruit,
and give seed for sowing and bread
to eat,
11 so shall the word which comes from
my mouth prevail;
it shall not return to me fruitless
without accomplishing my purpose
or succeeding in the task I gave it.
12 You shall indeed go out with joy
and be led forth in peace.

Before you mountains and hills shall
break into cries of joy,
and all the trees of the wild shall
clap their hands,
pine-trees shall shoot up in place of 13
camel-thorn,
myrtles instead of briars;
all this shall win the LORD a great
name,
imperishable, a sign for all time.

Warnings to keep the moral law

These are the words of the LORD: **56**
Maintain justice, do the right;
for my deliverance is close at hand,
and my righteousness will show
itself victorious.
Happy is the man who follows these 2
precepts,
happy the mortal who holds them
fast,
who keeps the sabbath undefiled,
who refrains from all wrong-doing!
The foreigner who has given his 3
allegiance to the LORD must
not say,
'The LORD will keep me separate
from his people for ever';
and the eunuch must not say,
'I am nothing but a barren tree.'
For these are the words of the 4
LORD:
The eunuchs who keep my sabbaths,
who choose to do my will and hold
fast to my covenant,
shall receive from me something 5
better than sons and daughters,
a memorial and a name in my own
house and within my walls;
I will give them an everlasting name,
a name imperishable for all time.
So too with the foreigners who give 6
their allegiance to me, the LORD,
to minister to me and love my name
and to become my servants,
all who keep the sabbath undefiled
and hold fast to my covenant:

---

will be fed. **3–5**: The *words* of the LORD give *life*. **3**: The irrevocable *covenant* with David (2
Sam. ch. 7) is extended to the people as a whole. **6**: *Inquire*: to request an oracle. See Amos
5.5–6,14. *Call upon him*: to pray. **12–13**: Nature will celebrate as Israel comes out of Babylon.
56.1–66.24: A collection of postexilic poems. See Introduction. **56.1–8: The house of prayer for
all nations.** Converts to Judaism are welcomed and encouraged to obey the ritual laws. **3**:
Barren tree: no offspring to give to the community of God's people. **4–5**: The law of Deut.23.1–6
is superseded. **5**: Inscription and service among God's people will earn a *name* more lasting

7   them will I bring to my holy hill
      and give them joy in my house of
      prayer.
   Their offerings and sacrifices shall be
      acceptable on my altar;
   for my house shall be called
   a house of prayer for all nations.
8   This is the very word of the Lord
      GOD,
   who brings home the outcasts of
      Israel:
   I will yet bring home all that remain
      to be brought in.

9   Come, beasts of the plain, beasts of
      the forest,
    come, eat your fill,
10 for Israel's watchmen are blind, all
      of them unaware.
   They are all dumb dogs who cannot
      bark,
   stretched on the ground, dreaming,
      lovers of sleep,
11 greedy dogs that can never have
      enough.
   They are shepherds who understand
      nothing,
   absent each of them on his own
      pursuits,
   each intent on his own gain wherever
      he can find it.
12 'Come,' says each of them, 'let me
      fetch wine,
   strong drink, and we will drain
      it down;
   let us make tomorrow like today,
   or greater far!'

57   The righteous perish,
   and no one takes it to heart;
   men of good faith are swept away,
      but no one cares,
   the righteous are swept away before
      the onset of evil,
2   but they enter into peace;
   they have run a straight course
   and rest in their last beds.

3 Come, stand forth, you sons of a
    soothsayer.
 You spawn of an adulterer and a
    a harlot,
4 who is the target of your jests?
 Against whom do you open your
    mouths
 and wag your tongues,
 children of sin that you are, spawn
    of a lie,
5 burning with lust under the
    terebinths,
 under every spreading tree,
 and sacrificing children in the gorges,
    under the rocky clefts?
6 And you, woman,
 your place is with the creatures of
    the gorge;
    that is where you belong.
 To them you have dared to pour a
    libation
 and present an offering of grain.*p*
7 On a high mountain-top
    you have made your bed;
 there too you have gone up to offer
    sacrifice.
 In spite of all this am I to relent?*q*
8 Beside door and door-post you have
    put up your sign.
 Deserting me, you have stripped
    and lain down
    on the wide bed which you have
      made,
 and you drove bargains with men
    for the pleasure of sleeping
      together,
 and you have committed countless
    acts of fornication
    in the heat of your lust.
9 You drenched your tresses in oil
    blended with many perfumes;
 you sent out your procurers far and
    wide
    even down to the gates of Sheol.

p See note on verse 7.
q Line transposed from end of verse 6.

---

than begetting *sons and daughters*. **7:** *Holy hill:* Mount Zion, on which the Temple was built. The future community of God will exclude no one because of arbitrary physical or ethnic conditions but will include all nations. **8:** *Who brings home the outcasts of Israel:* see 11.12; 27.12; Ps.147.2.
   56.9–57.13: Against corruption. 56.9–57.2: Israel's leaders fail in their duty. **9:** *Beasts:* the hostile nations; see Ezek.34.5–6; 39.17. **11:** *Shepherds:* rulers; see Ezek. ch. 34. **57.3:** Idolatry was considered adultery against God. The Israelites practicing idolatry are not children of the LORD but *spawn of an adulterer*. **5:** *Terebinths:* trees used in pagan fertility cults. *Sacrificing children:* see 30.33. **7–11:** This alludes either literally to sexual immorality connected with the fertility cult sacrifice or figuratively to the courting of foreign alliances and friendships with pagan nations, as in Ezek. ch. 16. **7:** See Ezek.16.16; 23.41. **8:** *Sign:* idol placed at the en-

10 Worn out by your unending
       excesses,
   even so you never said, 'I am past
       hope.'
   You earned a livelihood
   and so you had no anxiety.

11 Whom do you fear so much, that
       you should be false,
   that you never remembered me or
       gave me a thought?
   Did I not hold my peace and seem
       not to see
   while you showed no fear of me?

12 Now I will denounce your conduct
   that you think so righteous.

13 These idols of yours shall not help
       when you cry;
   no idol shall save you.
   The wind shall carry them off, one
       and all,
   a puff of air shall blow them away;
   but he who makes me his refuge
       shall possess the earth
   and inherit my holy hill.

14   Then a voice shall be heard:
   Build up a highway, build it and
       clear the track,
   sweep away all that blocks my
       people's path.

15 Thus speaks the high and exalted
       one,
   whose name is holy, who lives forever:
   I dwell in a high and holy place
       with him who is broken and
           humble in spirit,
       to revive the spirit of the humble,
       to revive the courage of the
           broken.

16 I will not be always accusing,
   I will not continually nurse my
       wrath.
   For a breath of life passed out from
       me,
   and by my own act I created living
       creatures.

17 For a time I was angry at the guilt
       of Israel;
   I smote him in my anger and
       withdrew my favour.
   But he ran wild and went his wilful
       way.

18 Then I considered his ways,
   I cured him and gave him relief,
   and I brought him comfort in full
       measure,

19 brought peace to those who
       mourned for him,
   by the words that issue from my lips,
   peace for all men, both near and far,
   and so I cured him, says the LORD.

20 But the wicked are like a troubled
       sea,
   a sea that cannot rest,
   whose troubled waters cast up mud
       and filth.

21 There is no peace for the wicked,
       says the LORD.

58 Shout aloud without restraint;
   lift up your voice like a trumpet.
   Call my people to account for their
       transgression
   and the house of Jacob for their
       sins,

2 although they ask counsel of me
       day by day
   and say they delight in knowing
       my ways,
   although, like nations which have
       acted rightly
   and not forsaken the just laws of
       their gods,
   they ask me for righteous laws
   and say they delight in
       approaching God.

3 Why do we fast, if thou dost not
       see it?
   Why mortify ourselves, if thou
       payest no heed?

---

trance of a house as an invitation to wanton pleasure seekers. **13**: *Holy hill:* Zion, Jerusalem; see 56.7 n.; 65.10.

57.14–21: Consolation to the humble. God addresses the *broken and humble in spirit* (v. 15) to assure them that they will be healed. **15**: *Name is holy:* see 40.25–26 n. **18**: Those *who mourned* for Israel are either the repentant Israelites or peoples sympathetic to Israel's tragedy, like the Persians. **19**: *Men . . . near:* proselytes.

58.1–12: The true fasts, a prophetic Torah. This is a postexilic oracle (v. 12). Its insistence on justice along with outward religious acts is in the tradition of the great prophets (Jer.7.21–28). **1**: A *voice like a trumpet* is that of the prophet to warn people of danger; see Ezek.33.3–4. **3**: A *fast* was prescribed by the Law only on the Day of Atonement (Lev.23.26–32). Later other fasts were added to commemorate public calamities (e.g. destruction of the Temple in the fifth month; Zech.8.18–19) or to beg God's mercy when disaster threatened (Joel 2.1–15). There

Since you serve your own interest
only on your fast day
and make all your men work the
harder,

4 since your fasting leads only to
wrangling and strife
and dealing vicious blows with the
fist,
on such a day you are keeping no fast
that will carry your cry to heaven.

5 Is it a fast like this that I require,
a day of mortification such as this,
that a man should bow his head
like a bulrush
and make his bed on sackcloth and
ashes?
Is this what you call a fast,
a day acceptable to the LORD?

6 Is not this what I require of you
as a fast:
to loose the fetters of injustice,
to untie the knots of the yoke,
to snap every yoke
and set free those who have been
crushed?

7 Is it not sharing your food with the
hungry,
taking the homeless poor into your
house,
clothing the naked when you meet
them
and never evading a duty to your
kinsfolk?

8 Then shall your light break forth like
the dawn
and soon you will grow healthy like
a wound newly healed;
your own righteousness shall be
your vanguard
and the glory of the LORD your
rearguard.

9 Then, if you call, the LORD will
answer;
if you cry to him, he will say,
'Here I am.'
If you cease to pervert justice,
to point the accusing finger and lay
false charges,

10 if you feed the hungry from your
own plenty

and satisfy the needs of the
wretched,
then your light will rise like dawn
out of darkness
and your dusk be like noonday,
the LORD will be your guide   11
continually
and will satisfy your needs in the
shimmering heat;
he will give you strength of limb;
you will be like a well-watered
garden,
like a spring whose waters never fail.
The ancient ruins will be restored   12
by your own kindred
and you will build once more on
ancestral foundations;
you shall be called Rebuilder of
broken walls,
Restorer of houses in ruins.

If you cease to tread the sabbath   13
underfoot,
and keep my holy day free from
your own affairs,
if you call the sabbath a day of joy
and the LORD's holy day a day to
be honoured,
if you honour it by not plying
your trade,
not seeking your own interest
or attending to your own affairs,
then you shall find your joy in the   14
LORD,
and I will set you riding on the
heights of the earth,
and your father Jacob's patrimony
shall be yours to enjoy;
the LORD himself has spoken it.

The LORD'S arm is not so short that **59**
he cannot save
nor his ear too dull to hear;
it is your iniquities that raise a   2
barrier
between you and your God,
because of your sins he has hidden
his face
so that he does not hear you.
Your hands are stained with blood   3

---

were also fasts out of private devotion; see Mt.6.16; Lk.18.12. **5:** *Bow his head:* sign of sadness;
sackcloth and ashes: sign of mortification and mourning.
  58.13–14: The rewards of observing the Sabbath. See Exod.20.8–11; Deut.5.12–15.
  59.1–21: A liturgy of repentance. The parts which comprise this unit may have once existed
separately, but together they are the words of a liturgical act of confession and forgiveness.
1–9: *It is your iniquities:* the prophet begins the service by indicting Israel for her sins.

and your fingers with crime;
your lips speak lies
and your tongues utter injustice.
4 No man sues with just cause,
no man goes honestly to law;
all trust in empty words, all tell lies,
conceive mischief and give birth to
trouble.
5 They hatch snakes' eggs, they weave
cobwebs;
eat their eggs and you will die,
for rotten eggs hatch only
rottenness.
6 As for their webs, they will never
make cloth,
no one can use them for clothing;
their works breed trouble
and their hands are busy with
deeds of violence.
7 They rush headlong into crime
in furious haste to shed innocent
blood;
their schemes are schemes of mischief
and leave a trail of ruin and
devastation.
8 They do not know the way to
peace,
no justice guides their steps;
all the paths they follow are
crooked;
no one who walks in them enjoys
true peace.

9 Therefore justice is far away from us,
right does not reach us;
we look for light but all is darkness,
for the light of dawn, but we walk
in deep gloom.
10 We grope like blind men along a
wall,
feeling our way like men without
eyes;
we stumble at noonday as if it were
twilight,
like dead men in the ghostly
underworld.
11 We growl like bears,
like doves we moan incessantly,
waiting for justice, and there is
none;
for deliverance, but it is still far
away.

12 Our acts of rebellion against thee
are past counting
and our sins bear witness against us;
we remember our many rebellions,
we know well our guilt:
13 we have rebelled and broken faith
with the Lord,
we have relapsed and forsaken our
God;
we have conceived lies in our hearts
and repeated them
in slanderous and treacherous words.
14 Justice is rebuffed and flouted
while righteousness stands aloof;
truth stumbles in the market-place
and honesty is kept out of court,
15 so truth is lost to sight,
and whoever shuns evil is thought
a madman.

The Lord saw, and in his eyes it
was an evil thing,
that there was no justice;
16 he saw that there was no man to help
and was outraged that no one
intervened;
so his own arm brought him victory
and his own integrity upheld him.
17 He put on integrity as a coat of
mail
and the helmet of salvation on his
head;
he put on garments of vengeance
and wrapped himself in a cloak of
jealous anger.
18 High God of retribution that he is,
he pays in full measure,
wreaking his anger on his foes,
retribution on his enemies.
19 So from the west men shall fear his
name,
fear his glory from the rising of
the sun;
for it shall come like a shining river,
the spirit of the Lord hovering
over it,
20 come as the ransomer of Zion
and of all in Jacob who repent of
their rebellion.
This is the very word of the Lord.

21 This, says the Lord, is my covenant,

5–6: This is probably a proverb. *Snakes' eggs:* malicious evil deeds; *weave cobwebs:* useless, unproductive schemes and plans. **10:** The *dead* in the *underworld* were thought to be weak and in a state of torpor. **19:** *Spirit of the Lord:* see 11.2 n. **20:** *Ransomer:* see 41.14 n. **21:** This verse, which is a later addition, affirms a *covenant* which shall not end.

which I make with them: My spirit
which rests on you and my words which
I have put into your mouth shall never
fail you from generation to generation
of your descendants from now onward
for ever. The LORD has said it.

Promise of the new Jerusalem

60   Arise, Jerusalem,
rise clothed in light; your light has
     come
and the glory of the LORD shines
     over you.
2 For, though darkness covers the
     earth
and dark night the nations,
the LORD shall shine upon you
and over you shall his glory appear;
3 and the nations shall march towards
     your light
and their kings to your sunrise.

4 Lift up your eyes and look all around:
they flock together, all of them,
     and come to you;
your sons also shall come from
     afar,
your daughters walking beside them
     leading the way.
5 Then shall you see, and shine with
     joy,
then your heart shall thrill with
     pride;
the riches of the sea shall be lavished
     upon you
and you shall possess the wealth of
     nations.

6   Camels in droves shall cover the
     land,
dromedaries of Midian and Ephah,
all coming from Sheba
laden with golden spice*r* and
     frankincense,
heralds of the LORD's praise.
7 All Kedar's flocks shall be gathered
     for you,

rams of Nebaioth shall serve your
     need,
acceptable offerings on my altar,
and glory shall be added to glory
in my temple.

Who are these that sail along like   8
     clouds,
that fly like doves to their
     dovecotes?
They are vessels assembling from   9
     the coasts and islands,
ships from Tarshish leading the
     convoy;
they bring your sons from afar,
their gold and their silver with
     them,
to the honour of the LORD your
     God,
the Holy One of Israel;
for he has made you glorious.

Foreigners shall rebuild your walls   10
and their kings shall be your
     servants;
for though in my wrath I struck
     you down,
now I have shown you pity and
     favour.
Your gates shall be open   11
     continually,
they shall never be shut day or
     night,
that through them may be brought
     the wealth of nations
and their kings under escort.

For the nation or kingdom which   12
refuses to serve you shall perish, and
wide regions shall be laid utterly waste.

The wealth of Lebanon shall come   13
     to you,
pine, fir,*s* and boxwood,*t* all together,
to bring glory to my holy sanctuary,
to honour the place where my
     feet rest.

r golden spice: or gold.
s Or elm.
t Or cypress.

60.1–22: The new Jerusalem. The LORD addresses the holy city, promising restoration and a
glory greater than in the past. The style and thought here resemble the Book of the Consolation
of Israel, i.e. chs. 40–55. **1–3:** *Jerusalem* will *shine* with the *glory of the LORD.* **6–7:** The riches
of Arabia come by *camels* across the desert. **8–9:** The riches of the west, *coasts and islands,* will
come by ship. *Like clouds . . . doves:* white sails of *ships from Tarshish.* **10:** The great reversal:
walls destroyed by *foreigners* will be rebuilt by them; their *kings,* once tyrants, will now be
servants. **13:** *Wealth of Lebanon:* the cedar trees used by Solomon to build the first Temple;

14 The sons of your oppressors shall
    come forward to do homage,
all who reviled you shall bow low at
    your feet;
they shall call you the City of the
    LORD,
    the Zion of the Holy One of Israel.

15   No longer will you be deserted,
    a wife hated and unvisited;*u*
    I will make you an eternal pride
    and a never-ending joy.
16   You shall suck the milk of nations
    and be suckled at the breasts of
    kings.
So you shall know that I the LORD
    am your deliverer,
your ransomer the Mighty One of
    Jacob.

17 For bronze*v* I will bring you gold
and for iron I will bring silver,
bronze*v* for timber and iron for stone;
and I will make your government
    be peace
    and righteousness rule over you
18 The sound of violence shall be heard
    no longer in your land,
or ruin and devastation within your
    borders;
but you shall call your walls
    Deliverance
and your gates Praise.

19 The sun shall no longer be your
    light by day,
nor the moon shine on you when
    evening falls;
the LORD shall be your everlasting
    light,
    your God shall be your glory.
20 Never again shall your sun set
    nor your moon withdraw her
    light;
but the LORD shall be your
    everlasting light
and the days of your mourning
    shall be ended.

Your people shall all be righteous 21
and shall for ever possess the land,
    a shoot of my own planting,
a work of my own hands to bring
    me glory.
The few shall become ten thousand, 22
    the little nation great.
I am the LORD;
soon, in the fullness of time, I will
    bring this to pass.

The spirit of the Lord GOD is upon **61**
    me
because the LORD has anointed me;
he has sent me to bring good news
    to the humble,
    to bind up the broken-hearted,
to proclaim liberty to captives
    and release to those in prison;
to proclaim a year of the LORD's 2
    favour
    and a day of the vengeance of
    our God;
to comfort all who mourn,*w*
to give them garlands instead of 3
    ashes,
    oil of gladness instead of
    mourners' tears,
    a garment of splendour for the
    heavy heart.
They shall be called Trees of
    Righteousness,
    planted by the LORD for his glory.
Ancient ruins shall be rebuilt 4
    and sites long desolate restored;
    they shall repair the ruined cities
and restore what has long lain
    desolate.
Foreigners shall serve as shepherds 5
    of your flocks,
and aliens shall till your land and
    tend your vines;
but you shall be called priests of 6
    the LORD
    and be named ministers of our
    God;

u Or divorced and unmated.
v Or copper.
w Prob. rdg.; Heb. adds to appoint to Zion's mourners.

---

1 Kgs.5.6–10. **16:** *Ransomer:* see 41.14 n. **18:** Ancient as well as modern *walls* and *gates* of
Jerusalem had names. Here they are symbolic, *Deliverance* being God's action protecting the
city, and *Praise* being the people's action in entering God's protection. The life of the city will
be completely changed. **19–20:** The LORD will be a *light* of the city; compare vv. 1–3. **21–22:**
The *people* shall be reestablished in the *land*. **21:** Jerusalem is a new plant, a new creation, at
the LORD's *hands;* see 43.6–7 n. **22:** *Fullness of time:* lit. "its time."
    61.1–11: Good news to the exiles. A prophetic voice proclaims consolation and salvation.
1: *Spirit of the LORD:* see 11.2 n. **3:** *Righteousness:* see 5.7 n. **4–9:** The prophet announces the
restoration and return. **4:** See Amos 9.14. **5–6:** Since *foreigners* will do the secular work, the

you shall enjoy the wealth of
other nations
and be furnished[x] with their
riches.

7 And so, because shame in double
measure
and jeers and insults[y] have been
my people's lot,
they shall receive in their own land
a double measure of wealth,
and everlasting joy shall be theirs.
8 For I, the LORD, love justice
and hate robbery and wrong-doing;
I will grant them a sure reward
and make an everlasting covenant
with them;
9 their posterity will be renowned
among the nations
and their offspring among the
peoples;
all who see them will acknowledge
in them
a race whom the LORD has blessed.

10 Let me rejoice in the LORD with all
my heart,
let me exult in my God;
for he has robed me in salvation
as a garment
and clothed me in integrity as a
cloak,
like a bridegroom with his priestly
garland,
or a bride decked in her jewels.
11 For, as the earth puts forth her
blossom
or bushes in the garden burst into
flower,
so shall the Lord GOD make
righteousness and praise
blossom before all the nations.

62 For Zion's sake I will not keep
silence,
for Jerusalem's sake I will speak
out,
until her right shines forth like the
sunrise,
her deliverance like a blazing torch,

until the nations see the triumph of 2
your right
and all kings see your glory.
Then you shall be called by a new
name
which the LORD shall pronounce
with his own lips;
you will be a glorious crown in the 3
LORD's hand,
a kingly diadem in the hand of
your God.
No more shall men call you Forsaken, 4
no more shall your land be called
Desolate,
but you shall be named Hephzi-bah[z]
and your land Beulah;[a]
for the LORD delights in you
and to him your land is wedded.
For, as a young man weds a 5
maiden,
so you shall wed him who
rebuilds you,
and your God shall rejoice over you
as a bridegroom rejoices over the
bride.
I have posted watchmen on your 6
walls, Jerusalem,
who shall not keep silence day or
night:
'You who invoke the LORD's name,
take no rest, give him no rest 7
until he makes Jerusalem
a theme of endless praise on earth.'

The LORD has sworn with raised 8
right hand and mighty arm:
Never again will I give your grain
to feed your foes
or let foreigners drink the new wine
for which you have toiled;
but those who bring in the corn 9
shall eat and praise the LORD,
and those who gather the grapes
shall drink in my holy courts.

Go out of the gates, go out, 10
prepare a road for my people;

x be furnished: *prob. rdg.; Heb.* unintelligible.
y and insults: *prob. rdg.; Heb.* they shout in triumph.
z *That is* My delight is in her. a *That is* Wedded.

Israelites will be their *priests*, i.e. intermediaries between them and the LORD, offering sacrifices
for them and giving them the Torah, or teaching; see Exod.19.5–6. **10–11:** The prophet (or
perhaps Israel) responds to the promises with a hymn.
62.1–12: New names for Jerusalem. See 60.1–22; 51.1–52.12. **1:** *New name:* signifies a new
status; see 43.1; Ezek.48.35. **4:** Israel's *land* is an integral part of the promise and covenant
with God; Gen.15.18–20; Deut.6.10–24. **6–7:** Compare 21.12–13. The *watchmen* (prophets)
must keep praying, giving God *no rest* until he fulfills his promises. **10–12:** 60.1–62.9 are
summarized here.

build a highway, build it up,
  clear away the boulders;
raise a signal to the peoples.

11 This is the LORD's proclamation
  to earth's farthest bounds:
Tell the daughter of Zion,
Behold, your deliverance has come.
  His recompense comes with him;
  he carries his reward before him;
12 and they shall be called a Holy People,
  the Ransomed of the LORD,
a People long-sought, a City not
  forsaken.

63 'Who is this coming from Edom,
  coming from Bozrah, his garments
    stained red?
Under his clothes his muscles stand
    out,
  and he strides, stooping in his
    might.'
It is I, who announce that right has
    won the day,
  I, who am strong to save.
2 'Why is your clothing all red,
like the garments of one who treads
    grapes in the vat?'
3 I have trodden the winepress alone;
  no man, no nation was with me.
I trod them down in my rage,
  I trampled them in my fury;
and their life-blood spurted over my
    garments
  and stained all my clothing.
4 For I resolved on a day of
    vengeance;
  the year for ransoming my own
    had come.
5 I looked for a helper but found
    no one,
I was amazed that there was no
    one to support me;
yet my own arm brought me
    victory,
  alone my anger supported me.
6 I stamped on nations in my fury,
  I pierced them in my rage

and let their life-blood run out upon
  the ground.

7 I will recount the LORD's acts of
    unfailing love
  and the LORD's praises as High
    God,
all that the LORD has done for us
  and his great goodness to the house
    of Israel,
all that he has done for them in
    his tenderness
  and by his many acts of love.
8 He said, 'Surely they are my people,
  my sons who will not play me
    false';
9 and he became their deliverer in all
    their troubles.
It was no envoy, no angel, but he
    himself that delivered them;
he himself ransomed them by his
    love and pity,
  lifted them up and carried them
  through all the years gone by.
10 Yet they rebelled and grieved his
    holy spirit;
  only then was he changed into their
    enemy
  and himself fought against them.
11 Then men remembered days long
    past
  and him who drew out[b] his people:
Where is he who brought them up
    from the Nile
  with the shepherd[c] of his flock?
Where is he who put within him
    his holy spirit,
12 who made his glorious power march
    at the right hand of Moses,
dividing the waters before them,
to win for himself an everlasting name,
13 causing them to go through the
    depths
  sure-footed as horses in the
    wilderness,

b *That is* Moses *whose name resembles the Heb. verb meaning* draw out, *cp.* Exod. 2. 10 *and the note there.*
c *Or* shepherds.

63.1–6: The approach of the divine warrior. The prophet as watchman (62.6) asks a question (v. 1a) and the LORD, as a figure covered with the blood of his enemies, responds (1b–6). He alone has destroyed the nations in order to save his people; see ch. 34. **1:** *Bozrah:* see 34.6 n. **2–3:** As one treading *grapes* to squeeze out the juice for wine stains his *garments*, so the LORD *trampled* on the *nations* and *stained* his *clothing* with their *blood.*
  63.7–64.12: Praise and petition. This prayer begins with an emphasis upon praising God for his saving acts (63.7–14) and turns to pleas that he act again to restore Jerusalem and the Temple (63.15–64.12). **7:** Hymns often begin with an expression of the intention to praise. See Ps.89.1. **9–14:** The account of God's acts corresponds to Israel's history. **11:** *Spirit:* see 11.2 n.; Ps.106.4. **12:** See Exod. chs. 14–15, especially 14.21 and 15.6. **13:** See also Ps. 106.9.

14 like cattle moving down into a
        valley without stumbling,
        guided by the spirit of the LORD?
    So didst thou lead thy people
        to win thyself a glorious name.

15 Look down from heaven and behold
        from the heights where thou dwellest
        holy and glorious.
    Where is thy zeal, thy valour,
        thy burning and tender love?
16 Stand not aloof;*d* for thou art our
        father,
    though Abraham does not know us
        nor Israel acknowledge us.
    Thou, LORD, art our father;
    thy name is our Ransomer*e* from
        of old.
17 Why, LORD, dost thou let us wander
        from thy ways
    and harden our hearts until we
        cease to fear thee?
    turn again for the sake of thy
        servants,
        the tribes of thy patrimony.
18 Why have wicked men trodden
        down thy sanctuary,*f*
    why have our enemies trampled on
        thy shrine?
19 We have long been reckoned as
        beyond thy sway,
    as if we had not been named thy
        own.

64 Why didst thou not rend the
        heavens and come down,
    and make the mountains shudder
        before thee
2   as when fire blazes up in brushwood
        or fire makes water boil?
    then would thy name be known to
        thy enemies
    and nations tremble at thy coming.
3   When thou didst terrible things that
        we did not look for,
    the mountains shuddered before thee.
4   Never has ear heard*g* or eye seen
    any other god taking the part of
        those who wait for him.

Thou dost welcome him who rejoices 5
    to do what is right,
    who remembers thee in thy ways.
Though thou wast angry, yet we
    sinned,
in spite of it we have done evil
    from of old,
we all became like a man who is 6
    unclean
and all our righteous deeds like a
    filthy rag;
we have all withered*h* like leaves
and our iniquities sweep us away
    like the wind.
There is no one who invokes 7
    thee by name
or rouses himself to cling to thee;
for thou hast hidden thy face from us
    and abandoned us to our
        iniquities.
But now, LORD, thou art our father; 8
we are the clay, thou the potter,
    and all of us are thy handiwork.
Do not be angry beyond measure, 9
    O LORD,
and do not remember iniquity for
    ever;
look on us all, look on thy people.
Thy holy cities are a wilderness, 10
Zion a wilderness, Jerusalem desolate;
    our sanctuary, holy and glorious, 11
    where our fathers praised thee,
    has been burnt to the ground
and all that we cherish is a ruin.
After this, O LORD, wilt thou hold 12
    back,
wilt thou keep silence and punish
    us beyond measure?

I was there to be sought by a people **65**
    who did not ask,
to be found by men who did not
    seek me.
I said, 'Here am I, here am I',

d Stand not aloof: prob. rdg.; Heb. obscure in context.
e Or our Kinsman.
*f Why . . . sanctuary: prob. rdg.; Heb. For a little
while they possessed thy holy people.*
*g Never . . . heard: prob. rdg.; Heb. They have never
heard or listened.*
h have all withered: or are all carried away.

15–19: The petitioner asks for reasons for God's absence. **16:** *Ransomer:* see 41.14 n. **17:**
Harden our hearts: since God controls all things, he must have caused Israel to go astray.
Compare Exod.14.4. **19:** *Named:* see 43.6–7 n. **64.12:** When the LORD answers man with *silence*
he leaves him to his own resources, i.e. doom, which is punishment *beyond measure;* see Ps.28.1.
  65.1–25: The answer to the prayer. In the inherited organization of the book, this chapter
appears as God's response to the previous petition; sinners will be judged but the faithful
redeemed. **1–2:** Far from keeping silence, God makes his presence known by shouting *"Here am*

to a nation that did not invoke me
    by name.
2 I spread out my hands all day
    appealing to an unruly people
who went their evil way,
    following their own devices,
3 a people who provoked me
    continually to my face,
offering sacrifice in gardens, burning
    incense on brick altars,
4 crouching among graves, keeping
    vigil all night long,
eating swine's flesh, their cauldrons
    full of a tainted brew.
5 'Stay where you are,' they cry,
'do not dare touch me; for I am too
    sacred for you.'
Such people are a smouldering fire,
    smoking in my nostrils all day long.
6 All is on record before me: I will not
    keep silence;
7 I will repay[i] your iniquities,
yours and your fathers', all at once,
    says the LORD,
because they burnt incense[j] on the
    mountains
and defied me on the hills;
I will first measure out their reward
and then pay them in full.

8 These are the words of the LORD:
As there is new wine in a cluster of
    grapes
and men say, 'Do not destroy it;
    there is a blessing in it',
so will I do for my servants' sake:
I will not destroy the whole nation.
9 I will give Jacob children to come
    after him
and Judah heirs who shall possess
    my mountains;
    my chosen shall inherit them
and my servants shall live there.
10 Flocks shall range over Sharon,
    and the Vale of Achor be a
    pasture for cattle;
    they shall belong to my people
    who seek me.
11 But you that forsake the LORD and
    forget my holy mountain,
who spread a table for the god of
    Fate,

and fill bowls of spiced wine in
    honour of Fortune,
12 I will deliver you to your fate, to
    execution,
and you shall all bend the neck to
    the sword,
because I called and you did not
    answer,
I spoke and you did not listen;
and you did what was wrong in my
    eyes
and you chose what was against my
    will.
13 Therefore these are the words of the
    Lord GOD:
My servants shall eat but you shall
    starve;
my servants shall drink but you
    shall go thirsty;
my servants shall rejoice but you
    shall be put to shame;
14 my servants shall shout in triumph
    in the gladness of their hearts,
but you shall cry from sorrow
    and wail from anguish of spirit;
15 your name shall be used as an oath
    by my chosen,
and the Lord GOD shall give you
    over to death;
but his servants he shall call by
    another name.
16 He who invokes a blessing on
    himself in the land
shall do so by the God whose
    name is Amen,
and he who utters an oath in the
    land
shall do so by the God of Amen;
the former troubles are forgotten
    and they are hidden from my
    sight.
17 For behold, I create
new heavens and a new earth.
    Former things shall no more be
    remembered
    nor shall they be called to mind.
18 Rejoice and be filled with delight,
you boundless realms which I
    create;
for I create Jerusalem to be a delight

i *Prob. rdg., transposing* and then pay *to follow* reward.
j *Or* sacrifices.

I'' *and stretching out his hands to a* people *that is silent.* 3: *Sacrifice . . . incense:* that is, participation in fertility cults. 4: *Crouching among graves* probably refers to consulting the spirits of
the dead. *Keeping vigil:* awaiting a dream revelation; see Jer.23.25–32. *Eating swine's flesh* was
a violation of dietary law; see Deut.14.8. 11: *Fate, Fortune:* Aramaean gods. 15: *Oath:* i.e.

and her people a joy;

19 I will take delight in Jerusalem and
    rejoice in my people;
    weeping and cries for help
shall never again be heard in her.

20 There no child shall ever again die an
    infant,
no old man fail to live out his life;
every boy shall live his hundred
    years before he dies,
whoever falls short of a hundred
    shall be despised.*k*

21 Men shall build houses and live to
    inhabit them,
plant vineyards and eat their fruit;

22 they shall not build for others to
    inhabit
nor plant for others to eat.
My people shall live the long life of
    a tree,
and my chosen shall enjoy the fruit
    of their labour.

23 They shall not toil in vain or raise
    children for misfortune.
For they are the offspring of the
    blessed of the LORD
and their issue after them;

24 before they call to me, I will answer,
and while they are still speaking I
    will listen.

25 The wolf and the lamb shall feed
    together
and the lion shall eat straw like
    cattle.*l*
They shall not hurt or destroy in all
    my holy mountain,
    says the LORD.

66 These are the words of the LORD:
Heaven is my throne and earth my
    footstool.
Where will you build a house for me,
where shall my resting-place be?

2 All these are of my own making
and all these are mine.
    This is the very word of the LORD.

The man I look to is a man down-
    trodden and distressed,
one who reveres my words.

3 But to sacrifice an ox or to*m* kill a
    man,

slaughter a sheep or break a dog's
    neck,
offer grain or offer pigs' blood,
burn incense as a token and worship
    an idol—
all these are the chosen practices of
    men
who*n* revel in their own loathsome
    rites.

4 I too will practise those wanton rites
    of theirs
and bring down on them the very
    things they dread;
for I called and no one answered,
I spoke and no one listened.
They did what was wrong in my eyes
and chose practices not to my liking.

5 Hear the word of the LORD, you who
    revere his word:
Your fellow-countrymen who
    hate you,
who spurn you because you bear
    my name, have said,
'Let the LORD show his glory,
then we shall see you rejoice';
but they shall be put to shame.

6 That roar from the city, that uproar
    in the temple,
is the sound of the LORD dealing
    retribution to his foes.

7 Shall a woman bear a child without
    pains?
give birth to a son before the onset
    of labour?

8 Who has heard of anything like
    this?
Who has seen any such thing?
Shall a country be born after one
    day's labour,
shall a nation be brought to birth
    all in a moment?
But Zion, at the onset of her pangs,
    bore her sons.

9 Shall I bring to the point of birth
    and not deliver?

---

k Or cursed.
l Prob. rdg.; Heb. adds and the food of the snake shall
be dust.
m to sacrifice an ox or to: *or* those who sacrifice an ox
and . . .
n are the chosen practices of men who: *or* have chosen
their own devices and . . .

---

curse. **21**: See Amos 9.14. See also Ezek.28.26; 45.4; Hos.11.11. **25**: Isa.11.9 is quoted at the end.
    66.1–24: A collection of speeches. 1–2a: The LORD, who speaks, cannot be confined to one
place. **2b–4:** Those who sacrifice to idols will themselves be sacrificed. **5–9:** God's intervention
has already begun and will soon be evident. **5–6:** He is dealing with his *foes*. **7 9:** Israel is

the LORD says;
shall I who deliver close the womb?
your God has spoken.

10 Rejoice with Jerusalem and exult in
 her,
 all you who love her;
 share her joy with all your heart,
 all you who mourn over her.
11 Then you may suck and be fed from
 the breasts that give comfort,
 delighting in her plentiful milk.
12 For thus says the LORD:
 I will send peace flowing over her
 like a river,
 and the wealth of nations like a
 stream in flood;
 it shall suckle you,
 and you shall be carried in their
 arms
 and dandled on their knees.
13 As a mother comforts her son,
 so will I myself comfort you,
 and you shall find comfort in
 Jerusalem.
14 This you shall see and be glad at
 heart,
 your limbs shall be as fresh as
 grass in spring;
 the LORD shall make his power
 known among his servants
 and his indignation felt among
 his foes.
15 For see, the LORD is coming in fire,
 with his chariots like a whirlwind,
 to strike home with his furious
 anger
 and with the flaming fire of his
 reproof.
16 The LORD will judge by fire,
 with fire he will test all living
 men,
 and many will be slain by the
 LORD;
17 those who hallow and purify
 themselves in garden-rites,

one after another in a magic ring,
those who eat the flesh of pigs and
 rats*o* and all vile vermin,
shall meet their end, one and all,
says the LORD,
for I know their deeds and their   18
 thoughts.

Then I myself will come to gather
 all nations and races,
 and they shall come and see my
 glory;
and I will perform a sign among   19
 them.
I will spare some of them and send
 them to the nations,
 to Tarshish, Put, and Lud,*p*
 to Meshek, Rosh,*q* Tubal, and
 Javan,*r*
distant coasts and islands which have
 never yet heard of me
 and have not seen my glory;
these shall announce that glory
 among the nations.
From every nation they shall bring   20
 your countrymen
 on horses, in chariots and wagons,
 on mules and dromedaries,
 as an offering to the LORD,
 on my holy mountain Jerusalem,
 says the LORD,
as the Israelites bring offerings
 in pure vessels to the LORD's house;
and some of them I will take for   21
 priests, for Levites,
 says the LORD.
For, as the new heavens and the new 22
 earth
which I am making shall endure in
 my sight,
 says the LORD,
so shall your race and your name
 endure;

o Or jerboas.
p Or Lydia.
q Meshek, Rosh: prob. rdg.; Heb. those who draw the bow.
r Or Greece.

being reborn. Unlike the *labour* of childbirth, God will deliver the new Israel without prolonged *birth pangs* of further calamity and Israel will continue to be fruitful in bearing children. **10–16:** God is coming to bring *peace* (v. 12) to his people and punishment to his enemies. **18–24:** God will *gather all nations and races* to Jerusalem. **18:** Not only Israel but all nations will see the *glory* of the LORD; see v. 5. **19:** *Sign:* see 7.11–12 n. The glory of the LORD will be made known to the nations farthest west, *coasts and islands* of the Mediterranean world, by non-Israelites, since the Jews were not a seafaring people. *Tarshish:* possibly Spain, at the extreme edge of the then known world; *Put* and *Lud:* northern Africa; *Javan:* Ionia; *Meshek, Rosh, Tubal:* at the extremities of Asia Minor to the north of Palestine. **20–21:** All peoples will be the *countrymen* of the Jews in the new Israel, some of them even becoming *priests*. **22:** The *race* and *name* of Israel will *endure* forever as a *new* creation in a new world; see also 65.17.

23   and month by month at the new
       moon,
    week by week on the sabbath,
    all mankind shall come to bow
      down before me,
    says the LORD;
24   and they shall come out and see

the dead bodies of those who have
    rebelled against me;
their worm shall not die nor their
    fire be quenched,
and they shall be abhorred by all
    mankind.

24: The punishment of the wicked shall not end. Outside the city there will be a place of refuse, *dead bodies* and smoldering *fire*, as it was in the Valley of Hinnom outside of the old Jerusalem.

THE BOOK OF THE PROPHET

JEREMIAH

Jeremiah prophesied in Jerusalem mostly before the Babylonians destroyed the Temple there in 587 B.C. but also for a short while after that event, and even, briefly, in Egypt among the fugitives from Judah. He foresaw this fall of the Southern Kingdom which occurred something over a century after the fall of the Northern Kingdom, Israel. He was no uninvolved spectator; loving his people, compelled by his God and undeterred either by ridicule or by persecution, he sought to salvage what he could from the national calamity. His major accomplishment as a prophet was his contribution to his people's maturation: Judah could survive, he knew, even without the Jerusalem sanctuary.

Chapters 1 to 20 contain two related types of matter: the tender prophet pleads with Israel for an appropriately loyal response, one that would enable a pardoning God to withhold a merited punishment; and he also reveals his dismay and sorrow at her stubbornly heedless behavior and rebels against his need to pursue his seemingly futile mission to her. In chapters 21 to 45 a biographer, probably the prophet's disciple Baruch, records the dramatic course of Jeremiah's frustrating ministry. Both here and in the remaining section (chs. 46–52), messages of hope and consolation occasionally relieve the dreary forebodings.

Persons other than the prophet and his biographer may be responsible for certain passages, especially within the "prophecies against the nations" (chs. 46–51), but also elsewhere in the book. Some of the passages are written after the manner of Deuteronomy or in the style of the later chapters of Isaiah.

1 THE WORDS OF JEREMIAH SON OF Hilkiah, one of the priests at 2 Anathoth in Benjamin. The word of the LORD came to him in the thirteenth year of the reign of Josiah son 3 of Amon, king of Judah; also during the reign of Jehoiakim son of Josiah, king of Judah, until the eleventh year of Zedekiah son of Josiah, king of Judah, was completed. In the fifth month the people of Jerusalem were carried away into exile.

Jeremiah's call and two visions

4 THE WORD OF THE LORD CAME TO ME: 5 'Before I formed you in the womb I knew you for my own; before you were 6 born I consecrated you, I appointed you a prophet to the nations.' 'Ah! Lord GOD,' I answered, 'I do not know how to speak; I am only a child.' But 7 the LORD said, 'Do not call yourself a child; for you shall go to whatever people I send you and say whatever I tell you to say. Fear none of them, for 8 I am with you and will keep you safe.' This was the very word of the LORD. Then the LORD stretched out his hand 9 and touched my mouth, and said to me, 'I put my words into your mouth. This 10 day I give you authority over nations and over kingdoms, to pull down and to uproot, to destroy and to demolish, to build and to plant.'

The word of the LORD came to me: 11 'What is it that you see, Jeremiah?' 'An almond in early bloom',[a] I answered. 'You are right,' said the LORD to me, 12 'for I am early on the watch[b] to carry

a *Heb.* shaked.
b *Heb.* shoked.

1.1–3: A title page. 1: *Anathoth:* about three miles north of Jerusalem. *One of the priests:* a member of a priestly family (see 1 Kgs.2.26–27) though seemingly not of the Jerusalem priesthood. **2:** *Thirteenth year of Josiah:* 627 B.C. **3:** *Eleventh year of Zedekiah:* 587 B.C. *In the fifth month:* see 2 Kgs.25.8,11. But chs. 40–44 imply that Jeremiah's activity actually extended into later years.
1.4–19: The beginning of Jeremiah's career: 5: *I consecrated you:* set you apart. *To the nations:* chs. 46–51 are against the nations. **6:** *I am only a child* suggests inadequacy, not early youth. **7:** *Say whatever I tell you to say:* the thought is dramatized in v. 9. **8:** *Fear none of them:* God fortifies his prophet in advance against his people's opposition, a thought which is developed in vv. 17–19. **10:** *To pull down . . . uproot . . . build . . . plant:* God's message has two aspects, the threat of disaster and consolation after calamity. **11–12:** What God threatens through his prophet he brings to sure fulfillment. The early blooming *almond (shaked)* reminds Jeremiah

13 out my purpose.' The word of the LORD came to me a second time: 'What is it that you see?' 'A cauldron', I said, 'on a fire, fanned by the wind; it is tilted
14 away from the north.' The LORD said:

From the north disaster shall flare up
    against all who live in this land;
15 for now I summon all peoples and
      kingdoms of the north,
    says the LORD.
Their kings shall come and each shall
    set up his throne
before the gates of Jerusalem,
against her walls on every side,
and against all the cities of Judah.
16 I will state my case against my
    people
    for all the wrong they have done
      in forsaking me,
in burning sacrifices to other gods,
    worshipping the work of their
      own hands.
17 Brace yourself, Jeremiah;
    stand up and speak to them.
Tell them everything I bid you,
do not let your spirit break at sight
    of them,
    or I will break you before their
      eyes.
18 This day I make you a fortified city,
    a pillar of iron, a wall of bronze,
    to stand fast against the whole
      land,
against the kings and princes of
    Judah,
    its priests and its people.
19 They will make war on you but
      shall not overcome you,
for I am with you and will keep you
    safe.
This is the very word of the LORD.

Exhortations to Israel and Judah

2 THE WORD OF THE LORD CAME TO ME:
2 Go, make a proclamation that all Jerusalem shall hear: These are the words of the LORD:

I remember the unfailing devotion of
    your youth,
    the love of your bridal days,
when you followed me in the
    wilderness,
through a land unsown.
Israel then was holy to the LORD, 3
    the firstfruits of his harvest;
no one who devoured her went
    unpunished,
evil always overtook them.
    This is the very word of the LORD.

Listen to the word of the LORD, 4
people of Jacob, families of Israel, one
and all. These are the words of the 5
LORD:

What fault did your forefathers find
    in me,
that they wandered far from me,
pursuing empty phantoms and
    themselves becoming empty;
that they did not ask, 'Where is the   6
    LORD,
who brought us up from Egypt,
and led us through the wilderness,
through a country of deserts and
    shifting sands,
a country barren and ill-omened,
    where no man ever trod,
no man made his home?'
I brought you into a fruitful land 7
to enjoy its fruit and the goodness
    of it;
but when you entered upon it you
    defiled it
and made the home I gave you
    loathsome.
The priests no longer asked, 'Where 8
    is the LORD?'
Those who handled the law had no
    thought of me,
the shepherds of the people rebelled
    against me;

---

that God is "watchful" (*shoked*) *to carry out his purpose.* **13–16:** Disaster looms from the north. **13:** In steam from a boiling *cauldron* the prophet sees an omen of national calamity. **15:** *Peoples and kingdoms of the north:* the enemy, Babylon, is not directly identified until 20.4. While some, indeed, speculate that the distant Scythians are intended, more probably Jeremiah had in mind the Babylonians, the currently dominant Mesopotamian power. Similarly, in Amos 6.14, an unnamed nation can be identified as Assyria.

    2.1–37: Israel's apostasy a fateful error. 2–3: *In the wilderness . . . a land unsown:* before the entry into Canaan, Israel served God with undivided loyalty, and he protected her. **5–8:** In agricultural Canaan, the *fruitful land*, Israel forgot God's solicitude, confused him with the god

the prophets prophesied in the
    name of Baal
and followed gods powerless to help.

9 Therefore I will bring a charge
    against you once more,
    says the LORD,
against you and against your
    descendants.

10 Cross to the coasts and islands of
    Kittim and see,
send to Kedar and consider well,
see whether there has been anything
    like this:

11 has a nation ever changed its gods,
    although they were no gods?
But my people have exchanged their
    Glory
for a god altogether powerless.

12 Stand aghast at this, you heavens,
    tremble in utter despair,
    says the LORD.

13 Two sins have my people committed:
    they have forsaken me,
a spring of living water,
and they have hewn out for
    themselves cisterns,
cracked cisterns that can hold no
    water.

14 Is Israel a slave? Was he born in
    slavery?
If not, why has he been despoiled?

15 Why do lions roar and growl at
    him?
Why has his land been laid waste,
why are his cities razed to the ground
    and abandoned?

16 Men of Noph and Tahpanhes
    will break your heads.

17 Is it not your desertion of the LORD
    your God
that brings all this upon you?

18 And now, why should you make off
    to Egypt
to drink the waters of the Shihor?

Or why make off to Assyria
    to drink the waters of the River?

19 It is your own wickedness that will
    punish you,
your own apostasy that will
    condemn you.
See for yourselves how bitter a thing
    it is and how evil,
to forsake the LORD your God and
    revere me no longer.
This is the very word of the Lord
    GOD of Hosts.

20 Ages ago you broke your yoke and
    snapped your traces,
crying, 'I will not be your slave';
and you sprawled in promiscuous
    vice
on all the hill-tops, under every
    spreading tree.

21 I planted you as a choice red vine,
    true stock all of you,
yet now you are turned into a vine
    debased and worthless!

22 The stain of your sin is still there and
    I see it,
though you wash with soda and do
    not stint the soap.
    This is the very word of the Lord
    GOD.

23 How can you say, 'I am not polluted,
    not I!
I have not followed the Baalim'?
Look how you conducted yourself in
    the valley;
remember what you have done.
You have been like a she-camel,
twisting and turning as she runs,

24 rushing alone into*c* the wilderness,
snuffing the wind in her lust;
who can restrain her in her heat?
No one need tire himself out in
    pursuit of her;

c rushing alone into: *prob. rdg.*; *Heb.* a wild-ass
taught in.

Baal, and forfeited his care. **8:** *Priests . . . shepherds* (rulers), and *prophets* all went astray.
9–13: It was wholly unnatural behavior in that not even worshipers of idols, *no gods*, exchange
those phantoms for others. **10:** *Kittim:* Cyprus. *Kedar:* in Arabia, east of Edom. **11:** *Their
glory:* God. **13:** Water sources were either a *spring* flowing from underground, or *cisterns*, dug
out and plastered to collect and hold rainwater. **14–15:** The consequences of Israel's apostasy
already in evidence. *Despoiled . . . razed . . . abandoned:* the allusions are either to the ruin
wrought by Assyria about 721 B.C. in the Northern Kingdom, or else to the effects of some
more recent invasion, possibly Necho's in 609 B.C.; see 22.10 n. **16:** *Noph and Tahpanhes:*
Memphis and Daphne in Lower Egypt. **18:** *Shihor:* a branch of the Nile. *The River:* the
Euphrates. Playing international politics is also disloyalty to God. **20:** *Promiscuous vice:* an
example of, and a metaphor for, religious apostasy. **21:** Compare the vineyard parable in
Isa.5.1–7. **23:** *Baalim:* the gods of the Canaanites. *The valley:* its name was Ben-hinnom; see

she is easily found at mating time.
25 Why not save your feet from stony
        ground
    and your throats from thirst?
    But you said, 'No, I am desperate,
    I love foreign gods and I must go
        after them.'
26 As a thief is ashamed when he is
        found out,
    so the people of Israel feel ashamed,
    they, their kings, their princes,
        their priests and their prophets;
27 they say 'You are our father' to a
        block of wood
    and cry 'Mother' to a stone.
    But on me they have turned their
        backs
    and averted their faces from me.
    And now on the day of disaster they
        say,
    'Rise up and save us.'
28 Where are they, those gods you made
        for yourselves?
    Let them come and save you in the
        day of disaster.
    For you, Judah, have as many gods
        as you have towns.*d*
29   The LORD answers,
    Why argue your case with me?
    You are rebels, every one of you.
30 In vain I struck down your sons,
        the lesson was not learnt;
    still your own sword devoured your
        prophets
    like a ravening lion.
31 *e*Have I shown myself inhospitable
        to Israel
    like some wilderness or waterless
        land?
    Why do my people say, 'We have
        broken away;
    we will never come back to thee'?

32 Will a girl forget her finery
        or a bride her ribbons?
    Yet my people have forgotten
        me
    over and over again.
33 How well you pick your way in

search of lovers!
Why! even the worst of women can
    learn from you.
Yes, and there is blood on the   *ı*
    corners of your robe—
the life-blood of the innocent poor.
You did not get it by
    housebreaking
but by your sacrifices under every
    oak.
You say, 'I am innocent;   35
surely his anger has passed away.'
But I will challenge your claim
    to have done no sin.
Why do you so lightly change your   36
    course?
Egypt will fail you as Assyria did;
you shall go out from here,   37
    each of you with his hands above
        his head,
for the LORD repudiates those in
    whom you trusted,
and from them you shall gain nothing.

If a man puts away his wife   **3**
    and she leaves him,
and if she then becomes another's,
    may he go back to her again?
Is not that woman defiled,
    a forbidden thing?
You have played the harlot with
    many lovers;
can you come back to me?
says the LORD.
Look up to the high bare places   2
    and see:
where have you not been
    ravished?
You sat by the wayside to catch
    lovers,
    like an Arab lurking in the desert,
and defiled the land
    with your fornication and your
        wickedness.
Therefore the showers were   3
    withheld

d towns: or blood-spattered altars.
e Prob. rdg.; Heb. prefixes You, O generation, see the
word of the LORD.

7.31. **27:** *Block of wood ... a stone:* idols. **30:** *In vain I struck down your sons:* brought defeat
to your armies. *The lesson* that I was displeased *was not learned;* see 3.3 n. *Your prophets,* e.g.
Uriah (26.20–23). **34:** *The life-blood of the innocent poor:* see 5.28. Social injustice too is
infidelity. **36:** *Egypt ... Assyria:* see vv. 16 and 18. **37:** *His hands above his head:* disgraced;
see 2 Sam.13.19. *Those in whom you trusted:* possibly Egypt; see 37.7.
　　3.1–10: A persistently inconstant people. Jeremiah condemns Judah, the wife faithless to God.
1: A twice divorced woman may not remarry her first husband; see Deut.24.1–4. **3:** *Showers*

and the spring rain failed.
But yours was a harlot's brow,
    and you were resolved to show no
      shame.
4 Not so long since, you called me
      'Father,
    dear friend of my youth',
5 thinking, 'Will he be angry for ever?
    Will he rage eternally?'
  This is how you spoke; you have
      done evil
    and gone unchallenged.

6 In the reign of King Josiah, the LORD
said to me, Do you see what apostate
Israel did? She went up to every hill-top
and under every spreading tree, and
7 there she played the whore. Even after
she had done all this, I said to her,
Come back to me, but she would not.
That faithless woman, her sister Judah,
8 saw it all; she saw too that I had put
apostate Israel away and given her a
note of divorce because she had committed adultery. Yet that faithless
woman, her sister Judah, was not
afraid; she too has gone and played the
9 whore. She defiled the land with her
thoughtless harlotry and her adulterous
10 worship of stone and wood. In spite of
all this that faithless woman, her sister
Judah, has not come back to me in good
faith, but only in pretence. This is the
very word of the LORD.
11 The LORD said to me, Apostate Israel
is less to blame than that faithless
12 woman Judah. Go and proclaim this
message to the north:

  Come back to me, apostate Israel,
    says the LORD,
  I will no longer frown on you.
  For my love is unfailing, says the
      LORD,
    I will not be angry for ever.
13 Only you must acknowledge your
      wrongdoing,
    confess your rebellion against the

LORD your God.
  Confess your promiscuous traffic
    with foreign gods
  under every spreading tree,
  confess that you have not obeyed
      me.
    This is the very word of the LORD.

Come back to me, apostate children, 14
says the LORD, for I am patient with
you, and I will take you, one from a
city and two from a clan, and bring you
to Zion. There will I give you shepherds 15
after my own heart, and they shall lead
you with knowledge and understanding. In those days, when you have in- 16
creased and become fruitful in the land,
says the LORD, men shall speak no more
of the Ark of the Covenant of the LORD;
they shall not think of it nor remember
it nor resort to it; it will be needed no
more. At that time Jerusalem shall be 17
called the Throne of the LORD. All
nations shall gather in Jerusalem to
honour the LORD's name; never again
shall they follow the promptings of
their evil and stubborn hearts. In those 18
days Judah shall join Israel, and together they shall come from a northern
land into the land I gave their fathers
as their patrimony.

I said, How gladly would I treat you 19
    as a son,
  giving you a pleasant land,
    a patrimony fairer than that of
      any nation!
  I said, You shall call me Father
    and never cease to follow me.
  But like a woman who is unfaithful 20
    to her lover,
  so you, Israel, were unfaithful to me.
    This is the very word of the LORD.
  Hark, a sound of weeping on the 21
    bare places,
  Israel's people pleading for mercy!
  For they have taken to crooked ways
    and ignored the LORD their God.

---

were withheld but this proved ineffective as discipline (see Amos 4.7–8). **6:** *The reign of King
Josiah:* 640–609 B.C., in Jeremiah's earlier period. **7–9:** *Judah saw that I had* delivered *Israel*
over to the armies of Assyria (2 Kgs.18.9–12) but did not learn from that early example. **10:**
Has . . . come back . . . but only in pretence: this may refer to the reformation under Josiah in
621 B.C. (2 Kgs.22.8–23.25); if so, the reformation is judged as halfhearted.
  3.11–4.2: An invitation to return, coupled with gleaming messianic promise. 11: *Apostate Israel is
less to blame:* the Northern Kingdom had no such earlier example to learn from (vv. 7–9 n.).
12: *To the north:* in the Assyrian captivity, Israel still survives as the ten tribes. (Later these

22 Come back to me, wayward*f* sons;
    I will heal your apostasy.

    O Lord, we come! We come to
      thee;
    for thou art our God.
23 There is no help in worship on the
      hill-tops,
    no help from clamour on the
      heights;
    truly in the Lord our God
    is Israel's only salvation.
24 From our early days
    Baal, god of shame, has devoured
    the fruits of our fathers' labours,
    their flocks and herds, their sons and
      daughters.
25 Let us lie down in shame, wrapped
      round by our dishonour,
    for we have sinned against the Lord
      our God,
    both we and our fathers,
    from our early days till now,
    and we have not obeyed the Lord
      our God.

4 If you will but come back, O Israel,
    if you will but come back to me,
      says the Lord,
    if you will banish your loathsome
      idols from my sight,
    and stray no more,
2 if you swear by the life of the
      Lord,
    in truth, in justice and uprightness,
    then shall the nations pray to be
      blessed like you*g*
    and in you*g* shall they boast.

3 These are the words of the Lord to
the men of Judah and Jerusalem:

    Break up your fallow ground,
      do not sow among thorns,
4 circumcise yourselves to the service
      of the Lord,

circumcise your hearts,
    men of Judah and dwellers in
      Jerusalem,
lest the fire of my fury blaze up and
      burn unquenched,
    because of your evil doings.
Tell this in Judah,   5
    proclaim it in Jerusalem,
blow the trumpet throughout the
      land,
    sound the muster,
give the command, Stand to!—and
      let us fall back
    on the fortified cities.
Raise the signal—To Zion!   6
    make for safety, lose no time,
for I bring disaster out of the north,
    and dire destruction.
A lion has come out from his lair,   7
    the destroyer of nations;
he has struck his tents, he has
      broken camp,
    to harry your land
and lay your cities waste and
      unpeopled.
Well may you put on sackcloth,   8
    beat the breast and wail,
for the anger of the Lord
    is not averted from us.
On that day, says the Lord,   9
    the hearts of the king and his
      officers shall fail them,
    priests shall be struck with horror
      and prophets dumbfounded.

And I said, O Lord God, thou surely   10
didst deceive this people and Jerusalem
in saying, 'You shall have peace', while
the sword is at our throats.
At that time this people and Jeru-   11
salem shall be told:

A scorching wind from the high
    bare places in the wilderness
    sweeps down upon my people,

f Or apostate.   g Prob. rdg.; Heb. him.

were deemed "lost.") **22–25:** Jeremiah imagines the response he desires. **22:** *Come back:*
reconciliation was still possible.
    4.3–4: The peril of stubborn disobedience. Ancient psychology located the emotions in the
lower viscera, and the mind in the heart; "uncircumcised heart" means a stubbornly closed
mind. Jeremiah pleads for open minds. The thought of v. 4 is repeated with a different symbol
in v. 14.
    4.5–31: More about the devastating foe from the north. See 1.13–16. Mostly the prophet
speaks for God, but in v. 13 (end), in vv. 19–21, and in v. 31 (end), he puts the words of
anguished lamentation into the mouths of his people, while in v. 10 and vv. 23–26 he breaks
in with his own exclamations of dismay. **6:** God names himself as the moving force behind
the invading armies. **9:** *Prophets:* these claim, like Jeremiah, to speak for God, but, unlike

no breeze for winnowing or for
  cleansing;
12 a wind too strong for these
  will come at my bidding,
  and now I will state my case
  against them.

13 Like clouds the enemy advances
  with a whirlwind of chariots;
  his horses are swifter than eagles—
  alas, we are overwhelmed!
14 O Jerusalem, wash the wrongdoing
  from your heart
  and you may yet be saved;
  how long will you cherish
  your evil schemes?
15 Hark, a runner from Dan,
  tidings of evil from Mount
  Ephraim!
16 Tell all this to the nations,
  proclaim the doom of Jerusalem:
  hordes of invaders come from a
  distant land,
  howling against the cities of Judah.
17 Their pickets are closing in all
  round her,
  because she has rebelled against me.
  This is the very word of the LORD.
18 Your own ways, your own deeds
  have brought all this upon you;
  this is your punishment,
  and all this comes of your
  rebellion.ʰ
19 Oh, the writhing of my bowels
  and the throbbing of my heart!
  I cannot keep silence.
  I hear the sound of the trumpet,
  the sound of the battle-cry.
20 Crash upon crash,
  the land goes down in ruin,
  my tents are thrown down,
  their coverings torn to shreds.
21 How long must I see the standard
  raised
  and hear the trumpet call?
22 My people are fools, they know
  nothing of me;
  silly children, with no understanding,
  they are clever only in wrongdoing,

and of doing right they know
  nothing.

23 I saw the earth, and it was without
  form and void;
  the heavens, and their light was
  gone.
24 I saw the mountains, and they
  reeled;
  all the hills rocked to and fro.
25 I saw, and there was no man,
  and the very birds had taken
  flight.
26 I saw, and the farm-land was
  wilderness,
  and the towns all razed to the
  ground,
  before the LORD in his anger.
27 These are the words of the LORD:
  The whole land shall be desolate,
  though I will not make an end
  of it.
28 Therefore the earth will mourn
  and the heavens above turn black.
  For I have made known my purpose;
  I will not relent or change my mind.

29 At the sound of the horsemen and
  archers
  the whole country is in flight;
  they creep into caves, they hide in
  thickets,
  they scramble up the crags.
  Every town is forsaken,
  no one dwells there.

30 And you, what are you doing?
  When you dress yourself in scarlet,
  deck yourself out with golden
  ornaments,
  and make your eyes big with
  antimony,
  you are beautifying yourself to
  no purpose.
  Your lovers spurn you
  and are out for your life.
31 I hear a sound as of a woman in
  labour,

h your rebellion: prob. rdg.; Heb. obscure.

Jeremiah, say: "You shall have peace" (v. 10). **14:** *Heart:* see vv. 3–4 n. **15:** *Dan . . . Mount
Ephraim:* places north of Jerusalem, the first to fall to the invader. **22:** *My people:* after the
imagined lamentation Jeremiah speaks again as if for God; in vv. 23–26, the prophet puts his
vision of the event in "apocalyptic" terms, depicting a catastrophe whereby all becomes void
as things were before creation. **27–28:** Here again appear *the words of the LORD,* followed in
v. 29 with another reference to the invader. **27:** Some regard the last clause as one of several
comforting additions, like 5.10,18; 48.47a. **30:** *To no purpose:* flirtation with prospective
military allies (*your lovers*) will not avail.

the sharp cry of one bearing her
   first child.
It is Zion, gasping for breath,
   clenching her fists.
Ah me! I am weary,
   weary of slaughter.

5   Go up and down the streets of
     Jerusalem
   and see for yourselves;
search her wide squares:
   can you find any man who acts
     justly,
   who seeks the truth,
that I may forgive that city?
2   Men may swear by the life of the
     LORD,
but they only perjure themselves.
3   O LORD, are thine eyes not set upon
     the truth?
Thou didst strike them down,
   but they took no heed;
didst pierce them to the heart,
   but they refused to learn.
They set their faces harder than flint
   and refused to come back.
4   I said, 'After all, these are the poor,
     these are stupid folk,
who do not know the way of the
     LORD,
   the ordinances of their God.
5   I will go to the great
   and speak with them;
for they will know the way of the
     LORD,
   the ordinances of their God.'
But they too have broken the yoke
   and snapped their traces.
6   Therefore a lion out of the scrub
     shall strike them down,
   a wolf from the plains shall ravage
     them;
a leopard shall prowl about their
     cities
and maul any who venture out.
For their rebellious deeds are many,
   their apostasies past counting.
7   How can I forgive you for all this?

Your sons have forsaken me and
   sworn by gods
   that are no gods.
I gave them all they needed, yet they
   preferred adultery,
   and haunted the brothels;
each neighs after another man's wife,   8
   like a well-fed and lusty stallion.
Shall I not punish them for this?   9
   the LORD asks.
Shall I not take vengeance
   on such a people?
Go along her rows of vines and   10
     slash them,
   yet do not make an end of them.
Hack away her green branches,
   for they are not the LORD's.
Faithless are Israel and Judah,   11
   both faithless to me.
   This is the very word of the LORD.
They have denied the LORD,   12
   saying, 'He does not exist.
No evil shall come upon us;
   we shall never see sword or famine.
The prophets will prove mere wind,   13
   the word not in them.'

And so, because you talk in this way,   14
these are the words of the LORD the
God of Hosts to me:

I will make my words a fire in your
     mouth;
and it shall burn up this people like
     brushwood.

I bring against you, Israel, a nation   15
   from afar,
an ancient people established long ago,
   says the LORD.
A people whose language you do
     not know,
   whose speech you will not
     understand;
they are all mighty warriors,   16
   their jaws are a grave, wide open,
to devour your harvest and your   17
   bread,

5.1–31: Deserved calamities. The people are at fault. **1:** The merit of even a few who act justly would enable God to *forgive* Jerusalem; compare Gen.18.28,32. **3:** *Refused to learn:* disciplinary punishment had gone unheeded (see 2.30 n.). **10:** *Go:* here and in v. 14 God seems to be making Jeremiah himself his own executioner. The *vines* are figurative; see 2.21 n. *Yet do make an end of them:* possibly a comforting addition; see 4.27 n. **11:** *Israel and Judah:* both kingdoms are mentioned, though Israel has already long been in captivity. **12–13:** A challenge and a retort. *He does not exist* is to be understood as denying the authenticity of the prophet's threatening *words.* "Atheism" in the Bible is largely a denial of divine activity, not of God's existence. **14:** *To me:* to the prophet. *Fire in your mouth:* see v. 10 n. **15:** *From afar:* see 1.15 n.

to devour your sons and your
daughters,
to devour your flocks and your
herds,
to devour your vines and your
fig-trees.
They shall batter down the cities in
which you trust,[i]
walled though they are.

18 But in those days, the LORD declares,
I will still not make an end of you.
19 When you ask, 'Why has the LORD our
God done all this to us?' I shall answer,
'As you have forsaken me and served
alien gods in your own land, so shall
you serve foreigners[j] in a land that is
not yours.'

20 Tell this to the people of Jacob,
proclaim it in Judah:
21 Listen, you foolish and senseless
people,
who have eyes and see nothing,
ears and hear nothing.
22 Have you no fear of me? says the
LORD;
will you not shiver before me,
before me, who made the shivering
sand to bound the sea,
a barrier it never can pass?
Its waves heave and toss but they
are powerless;
roar as they may, they cannot pass.
23 But this people has a rebellious and
defiant heart,
rebels they have been and now
they are clean gone.
24 They did not say to themselves,
'Let us fear the LORD our God,
who gives us the rains of autumn
and spring showers in their turn,
who brings us unfailingly
fixed seasons of harvest.'
25 But your wrongdoing has upset
nature's order,
and your sins have kept from you
her kindly gifts.

26 For among my people there are
wicked men,
who lay snares like a fowler's net[k]
and set deadly traps to catch men.
27 Their houses are full of fraud,
as a cage is full of birds.
They grow rich and grand,
bloated and rancorous;
28 their thoughts are all of evil,
and they refuse to do justice,
the claims of the orphan they do not
put right
nor do they grant justice to the poor.
29 Shall I not punish them for this?
says the LORD;
shall I not take vengeance
on such a people?

30 An appalling thing, an outrage,
has appeared in this land:
31 prophets prophesy lies and priests go
hand in hand with them,
and my people love to have it so.
How will you fare at the end of
it all?

6 Save yourselves, men of Benjamin,
come out of Jerusalem,
blow the trumpet in Tekoa,
fire the beacon on Beth-hakkerem,
for calamity looms from the north
and great disaster.
2 Zion, delightful and lovely:
her end is near—
3 she to whom the shepherds come
and bring their flocks with them.
There they pitch their tents all round
her,
each grazing his own strip of
pasture.
4 Declare war solemnly against her;
come, let us attack her at noon.
Too late! the day declines
and the shadows lengthen.
5 Come then, let us attack her by night
and destroy her palaces.

i *Prob. rdg.; Heb. adds* with the sword.
j *Or* foreign gods.
k who . . . net: *prob. rdg.; Heb. unintelligible.*

18: *A comforting addition; see* 4.27 n. **21–23:** *See* nothing . . . hear nothing . . . rebellious and
defiant heart. They are a people ignorant of the LORD of creation and willfully obtuse; see vv.
30–31 and 4.3–4 n. **22:** Shiver . . . shivering sand. *The translation imitates a play on words in
the Hebrew original; shiver is* taḥīlu, *and sand* ḥōl, *the pun associating* ḥīl *and* ḥōl. **27:** Full
of fraud: *full of possessions obtained by fraud.* **29:** *A refrain, see v.* 9. **30–31:** *These verses
resume the thought of vv.* 21–23. *A similar theme is found in* 6.13–15.

6.1–30: Calamity is near. 1: *Jerusalem is no refuge for the tribe of Benjamin, and when Zion
(Jerusalem) falls,* Tekoa *and* Beth-hakkerem *to the south will be exposed to attack.* **3:** Shepherds
. . . their flocks: *used ironically for the hostile kings with their armies.* **4–5:** *These words*

6 These are the words of the LORD of
      Hosts:
   Cut down the trees of Jerusalem
      and raise siege-ramps against her,
   the city whose name is Licence,
   oppression is rampant in her.
7 As a well keeps its water fresh,
   so she keeps her evil fresh.
   Violence and outrage echo in her
      streets;
   sickness and wounds stare me in the
      face.
8   Learn your lesson, Jerusalem,
   lest my love for you be torn from
      my heart,
   and I leave you desolate,
   a land where no one can live.
9 These are the words of the LORD of
      Hosts:
   Glean the remnant of Israel
      like a vine,
   pass your hand like a vintager one
      last time
   over the branches.
10   To whom can I address myself,
   to whom give solemn warning?
   Who will hear me?
   Their ears are uncircumcised;
      they cannot listen;
   they treat the LORD's word as a
      reproach;
   they show no concern with it.
11   But I am full of the anger of the
      LORD,
   I cannot hold it in.
   I must pour it out on the children
      in the street
   and on the young men in their
      gangs.
   Man and wife alike shall be caught
      in it,
   the greybeard and the very old.
12   Their houses shall be turned over
      to others,
   their fields and their women alike.
   For I will raise my hand, says the
      LORD,

against the people of the country.
   For all, high and low,   13
   are out for ill-gotten gain;
   prophets and priests are frauds,
   every one of them,
   they dress my people's wound, but   14
      skin-deep only,
   with their saying, 'All is well.'
   All well? Nothing is well!
   Are they ashamed when they   15
      practise their abominations?
   Ashamed? Not they!
   They can never be put out of
      countenance.
   Therefore they shall fall with a great
      crash,*l*
   and be brought to the ground on the
      day of my reckoning.
   The LORD has said it.

These are the words of the LORD: 16
Stop at the cross-roads; look for the
ancient paths; ask, 'Where is the way
that leads to what is good?' Then take
that way, and you will find rest for
yourselves. But they said, 'We will not.'
Then I will appoint watchmen to direct   17
you; listen for their trumpet-call. But
they said, 'We will not.' Therefore hear,   18
you nations, and take note, all you who
witness it, of the plight of this people.
Listen, O earth, I bring ruin on them,   19
the harvest of all their scheming; for
they have given no thought to my
words and have spurned my instruction.
What good is it to me if frankincense is   20
brought from Sheba and fragrant spices
from distant lands? I will not accept
your whole-offerings, your sacrifices do
not please me. Therefore these are the   21
words of the LORD:

I will set obstacles before this people
   which shall bring them to the
      ground;

*l with a great crash: or where they fall or among the
fallen.*

---

are placed in the mouths of these "shepherds." **6–8:** *Oppression . . . evil . . . violence and
outrage* will bring on the city's fate, unless she heeds the *lesson;* see 2.30 n. **10–12:** The prophet
has no choice but to speak, while his people, unconcerned, cover their ears. **10:** *Their ears are
uncircumcised;* see 4.4. **11:** The prophet's *anger* is a part of God's anger, and beyond the
prophet's control; it spills over, causing havoc. **13–15:** *Prophets and priests are frauds:* the
thought of 5.31 is more fully developed here; see 5.30–31 n. **16–21:** The fate of an unheeding
people, for God asks obedience more than incense and offerings. Israel spurns his *instruction*
(v. 19) and will perish. **16:** *Ancient paths:* Jeremiah does not claim to be proposing a new doctrine.
Find rest: he shares the common human yearning for security. **17:** *Watchmen:* prophets.
20: *Sheba* was in Arabia. **22–26:** Another dramatic projection of the northern foe (see 1.13–16;

fathers and sons, friends and
neighbours
shall all perish together.

22 These are the words of the LORD:

See, a people is coming from a
northern land,
a great nation rouses itself from
earth's farthest corners.
23 They come with bow and sabre,
cruel men and pitiless,
bestriding their horses, they sound
like the thunder of the sea,
they are like men arrayed for battle
against you, Zion.
24 We have heard tell of them
and our hands hang limp,
agony grips us, the anguish of a
woman in labour.
25 Do not go out into the country;
do not walk by the high road;
for the foe, sword in hand,
is a terror let loose.
26 Daughter of my people, wrap
yourself in sackcloth,
sprinkle ashes over yourself, wail
bitterly,
as one who mourns an only son;
in an instant shall the marauder be
upon us.

27 I have appointed you an assayer of
my people;
you will know how to test them and
will assay their conduct;
28 arch-rebels all of them,
mischief-makers, corrupt to a man.
29 The bellows puff and blow, the
furnace glows;
in vain does the refiner smelt the
ore,
lead, copper and iron*m* are not
separated out.
30 Call them spurious silver;
for the LORD has spurned them.

False religion and its punishment

THIS WORD CAME FROM THE LORD TO 7
Jeremiah. Stand at the gate of the 2
LORD's house and there make your
proclamation: Listen to the words of
the LORD, all you men of Judah who
come in through these gates to worship
him. These are the words of the LORD 3
of Hosts the God of Israel: Mend your
ways and your doings, that I may let
you live in this place. You keep saying, 4
'This place*n* is the temple of the LORD,
the temple of the LORD, the temple of
the LORD!' This catchword of yours is
a lie; put no trust in it. Mend your ways 5
and your doings, deal fairly with one
another, do not oppress the alien, the 6
orphan, and the widow, shed no innocent blood in this place, do not run
after other gods to your own ruin.
Then will I let you live in this place, in 7
the land which I gave long ago to your
forefathers for all time. You gain noth- 8
ing by putting your trust in this lie.
You steal, you murder, you commit 9
adultery and perjury, you burn sacrifices to Baal, you run after other gods
whom you have not known; then you 10
come and stand before me in this house,
which bears my name, and say, 'We
are safe'; safe, you think, to indulge in
all these abominations. Do you think 11
that this house, this house which bears
my name, is a robbers' cave? I myself
have seen all this, says the LORD. Go 12
to my shrine at Shiloh, which once I
made a dwelling for my Name, and
see what I did to it because of the
wickedness of my people Israel. And 13
now you have done all these things,
says the LORD; though I took pains to
speak to you, you did not listen, and
though I called, you gave no answer.

m copper and iron: *transposed from after* mischief-
makers *in verse 28.*
n This place: *prob. rdg.; Heb.* Those.

4.5–31); vv. 24 and 25 are exclamations of the dismayed Judeans. 27–30: God speaks to
Jeremiah. The prophet, like an *assayer,* tests his people, and finds them to be utterly lacking in
value.
   7.1–10.25: False religion and its punishment.
   7.1–8.3: The Temple sermon (vv. 1–15), with supplements. To the Judeans assembled for worship at the Jerusalem Temple Jeremiah brings the alarming message that their confidence is misplaced, for God rejects their worship and will reduce his Temple and their land to ruins. The
thought is expanded in vv. 21–26, 29–34, and 8.1–3. **1:** *The LORD's house:* the Jerusalem
Temple. **3:** *Mend your ways . . . that I may:* he appeals for repentence. **9–10:** You break half
of the Ten Commandments, and yet say, "We are safe," because you are in the sanctuary. **12:**
Shiloh: an earlier sanctuary. It was probably destroyed by the Philistines after the battle of

14 Therefore what I did to Shiloh I will do to this house which bears my name, the house in which you put your trust, the place I gave to you and your fore-
15 fathers; I will fling you away out of my sight, as I flung away all your kinsfolk, the whole brood of Ephraim.

16 Offer up no prayer, Jeremiah, for this people, raise no plea or prayer on their behalf, and do not intercede with me;
17 for I will not listen to you. Do you not see what is going on in the cities of Judah and in the streets of Jerusalem?
18 Children are gathering wood, fathers lighting fires, women kneading dough to make crescent-cakes in honour of the queen of heaven; and drink-offerings are poured out to other gods than me—
19 all to provoke and hurt me. But is it I, says the LORD, whom they hurt? No; it is themselves, covering their own
20 selves with shame. Therefore, says the Lord GOD, my anger and my fury shall fall on this place, on man and beast, on trees and crops, and it shall burn unquenched.

21 These are the words of the LORD of Hosts the God of Israel: Add whole-offerings to sacrifices and eat the flesh
22 if you will. But when I brought your forefathers out of Egypt, I gave them no commands about whole-offering and sacrifice; I said not a word about them.
23 What I did command them was this: If you obey me, I will be your God and you shall be my people. You must conform to all my commands, if you would
24 prosper. But they did not listen; they paid no heed, and persisted in disobedience with evil and stubborn hearts; they looked backwards and not
25 forwards, from the day when your forefathers left Egypt until now. I took pains to send to them all my servants
26 the prophets; they did not listen to me,

they paid no heed, but were obstinate and proved even more wicked than their forefathers. When you tell them this, 27 they will not listen to you; if you call them, they will not answer. Then you 28 shall say to them, This is the nation that did not obey the LORD its God nor accept correction; truth has perished, it is heard no more on their lips.

O Jerusalem, cut off your hair,   29
  the symbol of your dedication,
    and throw it away;
raise up a lament on the high bare
  places.

For the LORD has spurned the generation which has roused his wrath, and has abandoned them. For the men of 30 Judah have done what is wrong in my eyes, says the LORD. They have defiled with their loathsome idols the house that bears my name, they have built a 31 shrine of Topheth in the Valley of Ben-hinnom, at which to burn their sons and daughters; that was no command of mine, nor did it ever enter my thought. Therefore a time is coming, 32 says the LORD, when it shall no longer be called Topheth or the Valley of Ben-hinnom, but the Valley of Slaughter; for the dead shall be buried in Topheth because there is no room elsewhere. So 33 the bodies of this people shall become food for the birds of the air and the wild beasts, and there will be no one to scare them away. From the cities of 34 Judah and the streets of Jerusalem I will banish all sounds of joy and gladness, the voice of the bridegroom and the bride; for the land shall become desert.

At that time, says the LORD, men **8** shall bring out from their graves the bones of the kings of Judah, of the

Eben-ezer (1 Sam. ch. 4). **15:** *Ephraim:* the Northern Kingdom, Israel (compare 2 Kgs.18.9–12), of which Ephraim was the leading tribe. **16:** *Offer up no prayer* (see 14.12) suggests that Jeremiah would have done so if it were not prohibited, and that God would have found it hard to refuse him (see 15.1–2 n.). **17–18; 30–31:** These verses enlarge on the offensive acts listed briefly in v. 9, of running "after other gods." **18:** *Queen of heaven* was an astral deity variously identified as Ishtar, Venus, or some other love goddess of the Ancient Near East. See also 44.17–19 and 32.29. **22:** *No commands about . . . sacrifice:* Jeremiah seems to reflect a tradition at direct variance with much of the Pentateuch. **23:** *I will be your God . . . you . . . my people;* the covenant arrangement is contingent, not on the temple cult, but on obedience to such ethical demands as those in vv. 5 and 6. **29:** *Your hair . . . symbol of . . . dedication:* see Num.6.1–8. **30–31:** *The house:* the Temple. *Topheth in the Valley of Ben-hinnom* was outside the south wall of Jerusalem. **7.33–8.3:** For those long dead to lie unburied constituted a grave indignity to the person and a defilement of the land (see 22.19).

officers, priests, and prophets, and of
2 all who lived in Jerusalem. They shall
expose them to the sun, the moon, and
all the host of heaven, whom they loved
and served and adored, to whom they
resorted and bowed in worship. Those
bones shall not be gathered up nor
buried but shall become dung on the
3 ground. All the survivors of this wicked
race, wherever I have banished them,
would rather die than live. This is the
very word of the LORD of Hosts.

4   You shall say to them, These are the
words of the LORD:

If men fall, can they not also rise?
If a man breaks away, can he not
    return?
5 Then why are this people so wayward,
    incurable in their waywardness?
Why have they clung to their
    treachery
and refused to return to their
    obedience?
6 I have listened to them
    and heard not one word of truth,
not one sinner crying remorsefully,
'Oh, what have I done?'
Each one breaks away[o] in headlong
    career
as a war-horse plunges in battle.

7 The stork in the sky
    knows the time to migrate,
the dove and the swift and the
    wryneck
    know the season of return;
but my people do not know the
    ordinances of the LORD.
8 How can you say, 'We are wise,
    we have the law of the LORD',
when scribes with their lying pens
    have falsified it?
9 The wise are put to shame, they are
    dismayed and have lost their wits.
They have spurned the word of the
    LORD,
    and what sort of wisdom is theirs?
10 Therefore will I give their wives to
    other men

and their lands to new owners.
For all, high and low,
    are out for ill-gotten gain;
prophets and priests are frauds,
    every one of them;
they dress my people's wound, but   11
    skin-deep only,
with their saying, 'All is well.'
All well? Nothing is well!
Are they ashamed when they   12
    practise their abominations?
Ashamed? Not they!
They can never be put out of
    countenance.
Therefore they shall fall with a great
    crash,[p]
and be brought to the ground on the
    day of my reckoning.
The LORD has said it.
I would gather their harvest, says   13
    the LORD,
but there are no grapes on the vine,
no figs on the fig-tree;
even their leaves are withered.
Why do we sit idle? Up, all of you   14
    together,
let us go into our walled cities and
    there meet our doom.
For the LORD our God has struck
    us down,
he has given us a draught of bitter
    poison;
for we have sinned against the
    LORD.
Can we hope to prosper when   15
    nothing goes well?
Can we hope for respite when the
    terror falls suddenly?
The snorting of his horses is heard   16
    from Dan;
at the neighing of his stallions the
    whole land trembles.
The enemy come; they devour the
    land and all its store,
    city and citizens alike.
Beware, I am sending snakes against   17
    you,

o breaks away: or is wayward.
p with a great crash: or where they fall or among the
    fallen.

8.4–13: Unnatural conduct and its consequence. 8–9: They allow themselves to be misled by
scribes with . . . lying pens: a possible disparaging reference to Josiah's reform; see 3.10 n.
10–12: These verses repeat 6.12–15 almost verbatim.
    8.14–17: Consternation at the destroyer's approach. The people, or some among them, are
speaking in vv. 14–16; God speaks in v. 17. **16:** *Dan* was in the north, at the headwaters of
the Jordan. **17:** *Vipers:* figurative for irretrievable disaster.

vipers, such as no man can charm,
  and they shall bite you.
    This is the very word of the LORD.

18 How can I bear my sorrow?*q*
  I am sick at heart.
19 Hark, the cry of my people
  from a distant land:
  'Is the LORD not in Zion?
    Is her King no longer there?'
  Why do they provoke me with their
    images
  and foreign gods?
20 Harvest is past, summer is over,
  and we are not saved.
  I am wounded at the sight of my
    people's wound,
21 I go like a mourner, overcome with
    horror.
22 Is there no balm in Gilead,
  no physician there?
  Why has no new skin grown over
    their wound?

9 Would that my head were all water,
  my eyes a fountain of tears,
  that I might weep day and night
  for my people's dead!

2 Oh that I could find in the wilderness
  a shelter by the wayside,
  that I might leave my people and
    depart!
  Adulterers are they all, a mob of
    traitors.
3 The tongue is their weapon, a bow
    ready bent.
  Lying, not truth, is master in the
    land.
  They run from one sin to another,
  and for me they care nothing.
    This is the very word of the LORD.

4 Be on your guard, each man against
    his friend;
  put no trust even in a brother.

Brother supplants brother,*r*
and friend slanders friend.
They make game of their friends   5
  but never speak the truth;
they have trained their tongues to lie,
deep in their sin, they cannot
  retrace their steps.
Wrong follows wrong, deceit follows   6
  deceit;
  they refuse to acknowledge me.
    This is the very word of the LORD.
Therefore these are the words of the   7
    LORD of Hosts:
I am their refiner and will assay them.
How can I disregard my people?
Their tongue is a cruel arrow,   8
their mouths speak lies.
One speaks amicably to another,
  while inwardly he plans a trap for
    him.
Shall I not punish them for this?   9
  says the LORD;
shall I not take vengeance
  on such a people?

Over the mountains will I raise   10
  weeping and wailing,
and over the desert pastures will I
  chant a dirge.
They are scorched and untrodden,
  they hear no lowing of cattle;
birds of the air and beasts have fled
  and are gone.

I will make Jerusalem a heap of   11
  ruins, a haunt of wolves,
and the cities of Judah an unpeopled
  waste.

What man is wise enough to under- 12
stand this, to understand what the LORD
has said and to proclaim it? Why has
the land become a dead land, scorched
like the desert and untrodden? The 13

q How . . . sorrow?: prob. rdg.; Heb. unintelligible.
r Brother supplants brother: or Every brother is a
supplanter like Jacob (cp. Gen. 27. 35 and note).

8.18–9.1: An elegy. Jeremiah envisions his people in captivity and laments. God interrupts
the captives' dismayed exclamation with a challenge: *Why do they provoke me?* 22: *Is there
no balm in Gilead?* This was probably a proverbial expression. Gilead was perhaps a distribution
point for the healing balm.
    9.2–22: The fate in store for a chaotic society caring nothing for God. Cheating, treachery,
slander, and deceit are deeply engrained (vv. 2–6 and 8); *therefore* God will *assay* and *punish*
them (vv. 7,9,11). **2:** Repelled by his people's corruption, Jeremiah would *find a refuge in the
wilderness.* **9:** See 5.29 n. **10:** Jeremiah bemoans the envisioned fate of his people as in 8.21
and 9.1. **13:** *My law:* perhaps an allusion to Deut., which formed the basis of Josiah's reform;
see 3.10 n. If so, unlike 3.10 and 8.8, this passage (vv. 12–16) urges compliance with that law.
It is often suggested that this and similar passages are a later editor's attempt to make of

LORD said, It is because they forsook my law which I set before them; they neither obeyed me nor conformed to it.
14 They followed the promptings of their own stubborn hearts, they followed the Baalim as their forefathers had taught
15 them. Therefore these are the words of the LORD of Hosts the God of Israel: I will feed this people with wormwood and give them bitter poison to drink.
16 I will scatter them among nations whom neither they nor their forefathers have known; I will harry them with the sword until I have made an end of them.
17 These are the words of the LORD of Hosts:

Summon the wailing women to come,
    send for the women skilled in
        keening
18 to come quickly and raise a lament
        for us,
    that our eyes may run with tears
        and our eyelids be wet with
            weeping.
19 Hark, hark, lamentation is heard in
        Zion:
    How fearful is our ruin! How great
        our shame!
    We have left our lands, our houses
        have been pulled down.
20 Listen, you women, to the words of
        the LORD,
    that your ears may catch what he
        says.
    Teach your daughters the lament,
    let them teach one another this
        dirge:
21 Death has climbed in through our
        windows,
    it has entered our palaces,
    it sweeps off the children in the
        open air
    and drives the young men from
        the streets.

This is the word of the LORD: 22

The corpses of men shall fall and lie
    like dung in the fields,
    like swathes behind the reaper, but
        no one shall gather them.

These are the words of the LORD: 23

Let not the wise man boast of his
        wisdom
    nor the valiant of his valour;
    let not the rich man boast of his
        riches;
    but if any man would boast, let him 24
        boast of this,
    that he understands and knows me.
For I am the LORD, I show unfailing
        love,
    I do justice and right upon the
        earth;
    for on these I have set my heart.
    This is the very word of the LORD.

The time is coming, says the LORD, 25
    when I will punish all the circumcised,
Egypt and Judah, Edom and Ammon, 26
Moab, and all who haunt the fringes of
    the desert;[s] for all alike, the nations
    and Israel, are uncircumcised in heart.
    Listen, Israel, to this word that the 10
LORD has spoken against you:

Do not fall into the ways of the 2
        nations,
    do not be awed by signs in the
        heavens;
    it is the nations who go in awe of
        these.
For the carved images of the nations 3
    are a sham,
    they are nothing but timber cut
        from the forest,

[s] who . . . desert: *or* the dwellers in the desert who clip the hair on their temples.

Jeremiah a supporter of the reform. **14**: *Baalim:* gods (5.19). **15**: *Wormwood:* a bitter drug **17–21**: A continuation of the lament begun in v. 10. **17**: *Women skilled in keening:* professionally trained for ritual weeping and wailing. **19**: *How fearful . . . pulled down:* words attributed to the stricken inhabitants of Zion.

9.23–26: Closed minds. 23–24: To "know" God is to do as he does (22.16). **25–26**: The thought of 4.3–4, there applied to Judah alone, is here generalized to include all the willfully obtuse. *Egypt . . . Edom, Ammon, Moab:* except for the Philistines, all of Israel's neighbors practiced circumcision, but, like *Judah,* were also *uncircumcised in heart.*

10.1–16: The folly of idolatry and of other "ways of the nations." This passage is closely related in thought to the satiric attack on the Babylonian gods and their deluded "witnesses" in Isa. chs. 40–48 (see especially Isa.44.9–20). **1–2**: *Do not be awed by signs in the heavens.* "Omens" were connected with the prohibited worship of astral deities. **3–5**: See Isa.40.18–20;

worked with his chisel by a
craftsman;

4 he adorns it with silver and gold,
fastening them on with hammer and
nails
so that they do not fall apart.

5 They can no more speak than a scarecrow in a plot of cucumbers;
they must be carried, for they
cannot walk.
Do not be afraid of them: they can
do no harm,
and they have no power to do good.

6 Where can one be found like thee,
O Lord?
Great thou art and great the might
of thy name.

7 Who shall not fear thee, king of the
nations?
for fear is thy fitting tribute.
Where among the wisest of the
nations and all their royalty
can one be found like thee?

8 They are fools and blockheads one
and all,
learning their nonsense from a log
of wood.

9 The beaten silver is brought from
Tarshish
and the gold from Ophir;
all are the work of craftsmen and
goldsmiths.
They are draped in violet and
purple,
all the work of skilled men.

10 But the Lord is God in truth,
a living god, an eternal king.
The earth quakes under his wrath,
nations cannot endure his fury.

11 [You shall say this to them: The gods
who did not make heaven and earth
shall perish from the earth and from
under these heavens.]

12*t* God made the earth by his power,
fixed the world in place by his
wisdom,

unfurled the skies by his
understanding.

13 At the thunder of his voice the waters
in heaven are amazed;*u*
he brings up the mist from the ends
of the earth,
he opens rifts*v* for the rain
and brings the wind out of his
storehouses.

14 All men are brutish and ignorant;
every goldsmith is discredited by his
idol;
for the figures he casts are a sham,
there is no breath in them.

15 They are worth nothing, mere
mockeries,
which perish when their day of
reckoning comes.

16 God, Jacob's creator, is not like
these;
for he is the maker of all.
Israel is the people he claims as
his own;
the Lord of Hosts is his name.

17 Put your goods together and carry
them out of the country,
living as you are under siege.

18 For these are the words of the
Lord:
This time I will uproot
the whole population of the land,
and I will press them hard and
squeeze them dry.

19 O the pain of my wounds!
Cruel are the blows I suffer.
But this is my plight, I said, and I
must endure it.

20 My home is ruined, my tent-ropes all
severed,
my sons have left me and are gone,
there is no one to pitch my tent
again,
no one to put up its curtains.

t Verses 12–16: cp. 51. 15–19.
*u At the thunder . . . amazed: prob. rdg.; Heb. At
the sound of his giving tumult of waters in heaven.*
v rifts: prob. rdg.; Heb. lightnings.

46.1–7. **9:** *Tarshish . . . Ophir:* regions not clearly identifiable, proverbially a source of precious metals. Tarshish is identified by some as in Spain; Ophir as in India, Arabia, or Africa. **11:** The verse is bracketed because it appears to be a later addition. Jer. is in Heb. except for this one verse in Aram. **16:** The climactic point of the passage is made in this verse.

10.17–25: The threat of total captivity, the distress of the victims, and a plea for equity. 17–18: It is uncertain which of two sieges is meant, the first (597) or the second (587). *This time* suggests the latter. **19–20:** The heartfelt words *this is my plight, I said, and I must endure it,* seem to be spoken by Jeremiah himself. The subsequent words of v. 20 are the imagined anguished cry of his collective people, personified as an individual. Jeremiah had no *sons:* see 16.2. The

21 The shepherds of the people are
　　mere brutes;
　they never consult the LORD,
　　and so they do not prosper,
and all their flocks at pasture are
　　scattered.

22 Hark, a rumour comes flying,
　　then a mounting uproar from the
　　　land of the north,
　an army to make Judah's cities
　　desolate, a haunt of wolves.

23 I know, O LORD,
　　that man's ways are not of his own
　　　choosing;
　nor is it for a man to determine his
　　course in life.

24 Correct us, O LORD, but with
　　justice, not in anger,
　　lest thou bring us almost to
　　　nothing.

25 Pour out thy fury on nations
　　that have not acknowledged thee,
　on tribes that have not invoked thee
　　by name;
　for they have devoured Jacob and
　　made an end of him
　and have left his home a waste.

Warnings and punishment

11 THE WORD WHICH CAME TO JEREMIAH
2 from the LORD: Listen to the terms of
this covenant and repeat them to the
men of Judah and the inhabitants of
3 Jerusalem. Tell them, These are the
words of the LORD the God of Israel:
A curse on the man who does not ob-
4 serve the terms of this covenant by
which I bound your forefathers when
I brought them out of Egypt, from the
smelting-furnace. I said, If you obey
me and do all that I tell you, you shall
become my people and I will become
5 your God. And I will thus make good
the oath I swore to your forefathers,

that I would give them a land flowing
with milk and honey, the land you now
possess. I answered, 'Amen, LORD.'
Then the LORD said: Proclaim all these 6
terms in the cities of Judah and in the
streets of Jerusalem. Say, Listen to the
terms of this covenant and carry them
out. I have protested to your forefathers 7
since I brought them out of Egypt, till
this day; I took pains to warn them:
Obey me, I said. But they did not obey; 8
they paid no attention to me, but each
followed the promptings of his own
stubborn and wicked heart. So I
brought on them all the penalties laid
down in this covenant by which I had
bound them, whose terms they did not
observe.

The LORD said to me, The men of 9
Judah and the inhabitants of Jerusalem
have entered into a conspiracy: they 10
have gone back to the sins of their
earliest forefathers and refused to listen
to me. They have followed other gods
and worshipped them; Israel and Judah
have broken the covenant which I
made with their fathers. Therefore these 11
are the words of the LORD: I now bring
on them disaster from which they cannot escape; though they cry to me for
help I will not listen. The inhabitants of 12
the cities of Judah and of Jerusalem
may go and cry for help to the gods to
whom they have burnt sacrifices; they
will not save them in the hour of disaster. For you, Judah, have as many gods 13
as you have towns; you have set up as
many altars to burn sacrifices to Baal
as there are streets in Jerusalem. So 14
offer up no prayer for this people; raise
no cry or prayer on their behalf, for I
will not listen when they call to me in
the hour of disaster.

What right has my beloved in my　　15
　　house
　with her shameless ways?

---

people speak again in v. 24. **21:** *Shepherds:* kings. **23–25:** *Jacob:* the collective people. See
Ps.79.6–7 which may be the source of this verse.
　　11.1–15.9: Warnings and punishment.
　　11.1–17: The penalty of a breach of faith. Some scholars deny this section to Jeremiah because
of its conventional style and substance. **3:** The terms of a covenant include the penalty (*curse*)
which the party incurs who fails to meet his obligations. **5:** *Amen:* Heb. for "so be it." **8:** *All
the penalties:* the "curse" in v. 3. **9:** *The men of Judah:* your own generation. **11–14:** *I will
not listen . . . offer up no prayer:* see 7.16 n. **15–16:** A metaphor of irrevocable doom. The
offerings brought to the Temple will not avail, for Judah, the choice *olive-tree*, is to be utterly
consumed.

Can the flesh of fat offerings on the
  altar
ward off the disaster that threatens
  you?

16 Once the LORD called you an olive-
  tree,
  leafy and fair;
but now with a great roaring noise
  you will feel sharp anguish;*w*
fire sets its leaves alight
  and consumes*x* its branches.

17 The LORD of Hosts who planted you
has threatened you with disaster, because of the harm Israel and Judah
brought on themselves when they provoked me to anger by burning sacrifices
to Baal.

18 It was the LORD who showed me, and
so I knew; he opened my eyes to what
19 they were doing. I had been like a sheep
led obedient to the slaughter; I did not
know that they were hatching plots
against me and saying, 'Let us cut down
the tree while the sap is in it; let us destroy him out of the living, so that his
very name shall be forgotten.'

20 O LORD of Hosts who art a
  righteous judge,
  testing the heart and mind,
I have committed my cause to thee;
  let me see thy vengeance upon them.

21 Therefore these are the words of the
LORD about the men of Anathoth who
seek to take my life, and say, 'Prophesy
no more in the name of the LORD or
22 we will kill you'—these are his words:
I will punish them: their young men
shall die by the sword, their sons and
23 daughters shall die by famine. Not one
of them shall survive; for in the year of
their reckoning I will bring ruin on the
men of Anathoth.

O LORD, I will dispute with thee, for **12**
  thou art just;
yes, I will plead my case before thee.
Why do the wicked prosper
and traitors live at ease?
Thou hast planted them and their   2
  roots strike deep,
they grow up and bear fruit.
Thou art ever on their lips,
  yet far from their hearts.
But thou knowest me, O LORD, thou   3
  seest me;
thou dost test my devotion to thyself.
Drag them away like sheep to the
  shambles;
set them apart for the day of
  slaughter.

How long must the country lie   4
  parched
and its green grass wither?
No birds and beasts are left, because
  its people are so wicked,
because they say, 'God will not see
  what we are doing.'

If you have raced with men and the 5
  runners have worn you down,
how then can you hope to vie
  with horses?
If you fall headlong in easy country,
how will you fare in Jordan's dense
  thickets?
All men, your brothers and kinsmen, 6
  are traitors to you,
they are in full cry after you;
trust them not, for all the fine words
  they give you.

I have forsaken the house of Israel, 7
  I have cast off my own people.
I have given my beloved into the
  power of her foes.

w you will feel sharp anguish: *transposed from end of
  verse 15.*
x consumes: *prob. rdg.; Heb.* they consume.

11.18–12.6: A prayer of Jeremiah and what he learns. Jeremiah hears of plots against his
life, seeks God's help, and is reassured. **18–19:** A narrative preamble. **20:** The prayer itself.
21–23: The answer. **20:** *Heart:* lit. "kidneys," see 4.3–4 n. **21:** It is the people of his own village,
Anathoth (1.1), who have threatened to kill him for his prophesying.
  12.1–6: Prayer and response. This passage, related in form and substance to 11.18–23, is in
some disorder. Vv. 1–3 and the end of v. 4 are Jeremiah's prayer; v. 5 is what he takes to be
the answer to his prayer. In v. 4 *How long . . . wicked* concerns "the drought"; see 14.1–6.
V. 6 would follow best on 11.18. **1–2:** Jeremiah is not here asking the broader question about
the suffering of the righteous raised in Job; here the *wicked,* the *traitors* are specifically the
men who hatch plots against him; see v. 6 and 11.19. **4:** *God will not see:* see 5.12–13 n. **5:** *If
you:* you, Jeremiah. You have proved too soft for your task (see 20.14–18; 15.19–21 n.); but
weightier challenges lie ahead.
  12.7–13: God explains the lamentable disaster. The conduct of his *own people* left him no

8 My own people have turned on me
       like a lion from the scrub,
   roaring against me, therefore I hate
       them.
9   Is this land of mine a hyena's
           lair,
       with birds of prey hovering all
           around it?
   Come, you wild beasts; come, all of
       you, flock to the feast.

10 Many shepherds have ravaged my
       vineyard
       and trampled down my field,
   they have made my pleasant field a
       desolate wilderness,
11 made it a waste land, waste and
       waterless, to my sorrow.
   The whole land is waste, and no one
       cares.

12 Plunderers have swarmed across the
   high bare places in the wilderness, a
   sword of the LORD devouring the land
   from end to end; no creature can find
   peace.

13 Men sow wheat and reap thistles;
       they sift but get no grain.
   They are disappointed of their*y*
       harvest
   because of the anger of the
       LORD.

14 These are the words of the LORD
   about all those evil neighbours who are
   laying hands on the land which I gave
   to my people Israel as their patrimony:
16*z* I will uproot them from that*a* soil. Yet,
   if they will learn the ways of my people,
   swearing by my name, 'By the life of
   the LORD', as they taught my people to
   swear by the Baal, they shall form
17 families among my people. But if they
   will not listen, I will uproot that people,

uproot and destroy them. Also I will
uproot Judah from among them; but 15
after I have uprooted them, I will have
pity on them again and will bring each
man back to his patrimony and his
land. This is the very word of the
LORD.
    These were the words of the LORD to 13
me: Go and buy yourself a linen girdle
and put it round your waist, but do not
let it come near water. So I bought it 2
as the LORD had told me and put it
round my waist. The LORD spoke to 3
me a second time: Take the girdle 4
which you bought and put round your
waist; go at once to Perath and hide it
in a crevice among the rocks. So I went 5
and hid the girdle at*b* Perath, as the
LORD had told me. After a long time the 6
LORD said to me: Go at once to Perath
and fetch back the girdle which I told
you to hide there. So I went to Perath 7
and looked for the place where I had
hidden it, but when I picked it up, I
saw that it was spoilt, and no good for
anything. Again the LORD spoke to me 8
and these were his words: Thus will I 9
spoil the gross pride of Judah, the gross
pride of Jerusalem. This wicked nation 10
has refused to listen to my words; they
have followed other gods, serving them
and bowing down to them. So it shall
be*c* like this girdle, no good for anything. For, just as a girdle is bound 11
close to a man's waist, so I bound all
Israel and all Judah to myself, says the
LORD, so that they should become my
people to win a name for me, and
praise and glory; but they did not
listen.

y Prob. rdg.; Heb. your.
*z The rest of verse 14 and verse 15 transposed to follow
    destroy them in verse 17.*
a Prob. rdg.; Heb. their.
b Or by.
c Prob. rdg.; Heb. And let it be.

choice but to bring on the enemy and lay waste the land. 9–10: *Many shepherds:* foreign kings
and their armies. *Pleasant field:* the land of Judah. God speaks in vv. 7–11; in 12–13 the prophet
interprets the events.
   12.14–17: An inclusive covenant. Were even Israel's *evil neighbours* to learn faithfully to worship God alone, they would form *families* (lit. "be built up") within God's people. Otherwise
general havoc must ensue, but the latter would be followed in the end by a reconciled world.
The passage is related to the "Prophecies against the nations" in chs. 46–51, and may be an
addition here.
   13.1–14: The waistcloth and the wine-jars, two symbols. 1–11: As Jeremiah bound the *girdle*
about his waist, thus intimately God took Israel to himself in covenant. Israel spurned his love
and would rot away like that garment. 4–7: *Perath:* usually the river Euphrates, but here
perhaps a nearer place with a like-sounding name. 11: *To win a name for me:* for the broad
purpose of making God known among the nations; compare Isa.5.55; Ezek.36.23–24.

12 You shall say this to them: These are the words of the LORD the God of Israel: Wine-jars should be filled with wine. They will answer, 'We know quite well that wine-jars should be 13 filled with wine.' Then you shall say to them, These are the words of the LORD: I will fill all the inhabitants of this land with wine until they are drunk—kings of David's line who sit on his throne, priests, prophets, and all who live in 14 Jerusalem. I will dash them to pieces one against another, fathers and sons alike, says the LORD, I will show them no compassion or pity or tenderness; nor refrain from destroying them.*d*

15 Hear and attend. Be not too proud
       to listen,
   for it is the LORD who speaks.
16 Ascribe glory to the LORD your
       God
   before the darkness falls,
   before your feet stumble
       on the twilit hill-sides,
   before he turns the light you look
       for
   to deep gloom and thick
       darkness.
17 If in those depths of gloom you will
       not listen,
   then for very anguish I can only
       weep and shed tears,*e*
   my eyes must stream with tears;
       for the LORD's flock is carried
       away into captivity.
18 Say to the king and the queen
       mother:*f*
   Down, take a humble seat,
   for your proud crowns are fallen from
       your heads.
19 Your cities in the Negeb are
       besieged,
   and no one can relieve them;
   all Judah has been swept into exile,
       swept clean away.
20 Lift up your eyes and see
       those who are coming from the
       north.

Where is the flock that was entrusted
    to you,
    the flock you were so proud of?
What will you say when you suffer   21
    because your leaders*g* cannot be
    found,
though it was you who trained them
    to be your head?
Will not pangs seize you,
    like the pangs of a woman in
    labour,
when you wonder,   22
'Why has this come upon me?'
For your many sins your skirts are
    torn off you,
    your limbs uncovered.

Can the Nubian change his skin,   23
    or the leopard its spots?
And you? Can you do good,
    you who are schooled in evil?
Therefore I will scatter you*h* like   24
    chaff
    driven by the desert wind.
This is your lot, the portion of the 25
    rebel,
    measured out by me, says the
    LORD,
because you have forsaken me
    and trusted in false gods.
So I myself have stripped off your   26
    skirts
    and laid bare your shame.
Your adulteries, your lustful   27
    neighing,
your wanton lewdness, are an
    offence to me.*i*
On the hills and in the open
    country
    I have seen your foul deeds.
Alas, Jerusalem, unclean that you
    are!
How long, how long will you
    delay?*j*

d nor refrain . . . them: *or* so corrupt are they.
e If . . . shed tears: *or* If you will not listen to this, for
very anguish I must weep in secret.
f Or queen.
g leaders: *transposed from next line.*
h Prob. rdg.; *Heb.* them.
i an offence to me (*Heb.* you): *transposed from verse 26.*
j How . . . delay?: *prob. rdg.; Heb. unintelligible.*

12–14: A new meaning for an old saying: As *wine-jars* are *filled with wine*, so too would the people of Jerusalem, who thereafter would be shattered.
   13.15–27: A frantic plea to trust in God. 15–17: *Hear* before it is too late, or else I must weep *for very anguish.* The mood is elegiac as in 9.1 and elsewhere. **18–22:** One blow has already fallen, and another comes. **18:** *The king:* probably Jehoiachin. **19:** *Negeb:* southern Judah. **20:** *Entrusted to you:* to Jerusalem. **23:** The power of habit. *Nubian:* a black-skinned people from the upper Nile region.

14 This came to Jeremiah as the word of the LORD concerning the drought:

2 Judah droops, her cities languish,
  her men sink to the ground;
  Jerusalem's cry goes up.
3 Their flock-masters send their boys
      for water;
  they come to the pools but find no
      water there.
  Back they go, with empty vessels;
4 the produce[k] of the land has failed,
  because there is no rain.
  The farmer's hopes are wrecked,
  they uncover their heads for grief.
5 The hind calves in the open country
      and forsakes her young
  because there is no grass;
6 for lack of herbage, wild asses stand
      on the high bare places
  and snuff the wind for moisture,
  as wolves do, and their eyes begin
      to fail.
7 Though our sins testify against us,
  yet act,[l] O LORD, for thy own
      name's sake.
  Our disloyalties indeed are many;
      we have sinned against thee.
8 O hope of Israel, their saviour in
      time of trouble,
  must thou be a stranger in the land,
  a traveller pitching his tent for a
      night?
9 Must thou be like a man suddenly
      overcome,
  like a man powerless to save himself?
  Thou art in our midst, O LORD,
  and thou hast named us thine; do
      not forsake us.

10 The LORD speaks thus of this people:
They love to stray from my ways, they
wander where they will. Therefore he
has no more pleasure in them; he remembers their guilt now, and punishes
11 their sins. Then the LORD said to me,
Do not pray for the well-being of this
12 people. When they fast, I will not listen
to their cry; when they sacrifice whole-
offering and grain-offering, I will not

accept them. I will make an end of them
with sword, with famine and pestilence.
But I said, O Lord GOD, the prophets 13
tell them that they shall see no sword
and suffer no famine; for thou wilt give
them lasting prosperity in this place.
The LORD answered me, The prophets 14
are prophesying lies in my name. I have
not sent them; I have given them no
charge; I have not spoken to them.
The prophets offer them false visions,
worthless augury, and their own deluding fancies. Therefore these are the 15
words of the LORD about the prophets
who, though not sent by me, prophesy
in my name and say that neither sword
nor famine shall touch this land: By
sword and by famine shall those
prophets meet their end. The people to 16
whom they prophesy shall be flung out
into the streets of Jerusalem, victims
of famine and sword; they, their wives,
their sons, and their daughters, with no
one to bury them: I will pour down
upon them the evil they deserve.

So this is what you shall say to   17
    them:
Let my eyes stream with tears,
ceaselessly, day and night.
For the virgin daughter of my people
has been broken in pieces,
struck by a cruel blow.
If I go out into the country,   18
I see men slain by the sword;
if I enter the city, I see the ravages
    of famine;
prophet and priest alike
go begging round the land and are
    never at rest.
Hast thou spurned Judah utterly?   19
Dost thou loathe Zion?
Why hast thou wounded us, and
    there is no remedy;
why let us hope for better days, and
    we find nothing good,
for a time of healing, and all is
    disaster?

[k] the produce: *prob. rdg.*; *Heb. obscure.*
[l] *Or* turn away.

14.1–15.9: Concerning the drought and other calamities. 7–9: Public confession and supplication. *For thy own name's sake:* that is, God should act for his own reasons because of who
he is, to enhance his glory among men. **12:** *Their cry:* the accompaniment of the ritual fasting,
for relief from drought. **13:** *The prophets tell them;* see 4.9 n. **17–18:** *So this is what you shall
say to them* is probably not in place, as a result of a copyist's blunder; the rest of vv. 17 and
18 is Jeremiah's private lament. **19–22:** Again a public prayer, as in vv. 7–9. **21:** *The place where*

20 We acknowledge our wickedness,
the guilt of our forefathers;
O LORD, we have sinned against
thee.
21 Do not despise the place where thy
name dwells
nor bring contempt on the throne
of thy glory.
Remember thy covenant with us and
do not make it void.
22 Can any of the false gods of the
nations give rain?
Or do the heavens send showers of
themselves?
Art thou not God, O LORD,
that we may hope in thee?
It is thou only who doest*m* all these
things.

15 The LORD said to me, Even if Moses
and Samuel stood before me, I would
not be moved to pity this people.
Banish them from my presence; let
2 them be gone. When they ask where
they are to go, you shall say to them,
These are the words of the LORD:

Those who are for death shall go
to their death,
and those for the sword to the
sword;
those who are for famine to famine,
and those for captivity to captivity.

3 Four kinds of doom do I ordain for
them, says the LORD: the sword to kill,
dogs to tear, birds of prey from the
skies and beasts from their lairs to
4 devour and destroy. I will make them
repugnant to all the kingdoms of the
earth, because of the crimes of Manasseh son of Hezekiah, king of Judah, in
Jerusalem.

5 Who will take pity on you,
Jerusalem,
who will offer you consolation?

Who will turn aside to wish you
well?
You cast me off, says the LORD, 6
you turned your backs on me.
So I stretched out my hand and
ruined you;
I was weary of relenting.
I winnowed them and scattered 7
them
through the cities of the land;
I brought bereavement on them, I
destroyed my people,
for they would not abandon their
ways.
I made widows among them more 8
in number
than the sands of the sea;
I brought upon them a horde of
raiders*n*
to plunder at high noon.
I made the terror of invasion fall
upon them
all in a moment.
The mother of seven sons grew 9
faint,
she sank into a swoon;
her light was quenched while it was
yet day;
she was left humbled and shamed.
All the remnant I gave to perish by
the sword
at the hand of their enemies.
This is the very word of the LORD.

Confessions and addresses

Alas, alas, my mother, that you ever 10
gave me birth!
a man doomed to strife, with the
whole world against me.
I have borrowed from no one, I
have lent to no one,
yet all men abuse me.

m Or madest.
n I brought . . . raiders: prob. rdg.; Heb. obscure.

thy name dwells: the usual Deuteronomic designation of the Temple in Jerusalem. **22:** The reference to *rain* ties the prayer in with the context of drought (v. 1). **15.1–2:** Because of their reputed success in providing water and calling down a storm, Moses and Samuel (Exod.17.1–7 and 1 Sam.7.7–13) are cited as examples of men who had influence with God. Now not even they, much less Jeremiah, could relieve the drought. **4:** The reference to King *Manasseh*, whose evil excesses his grandson Josiah sought to counter, may be a Deuteronomic addition (see 2 Kgs.21.1–18). **5–9:** Probably written after 597 (possibly even after 587) since the calamity has already occurred; compare 9.12. **9:** *Mother of seven:* the populous city Jerusalem is here personified.

15.10–21: The prophet's lament and God's response. 10: Jeremiah gives vent to self-pity; see

11 The LORD answered,

But I will greatly strengthen you,
in time of distress and in time of
disaster
I will bring the enemy to your feet.
12 Can iron break steel from the north?*o*
15 LORD, thou knowest;
remember me, LORD, and come to
visit me,
take vengeance for me on my
persecutors
Be patient with me and take me not
away,
see what reproaches I endure for thy
sake.
16 I have to suffer those who despise
thy words,
but thy word is joy and happiness to
me,
for thou hast named me thine,
O LORD, God of Hosts.
17 I have never kept company with any
gang of roisterers,
or made merry with them;
because I felt thy hand upon me I
have sat alone;
for thou hast filled me with
indignation.
18 Why then is my pain unending,
my wound desperate and incurable?
Thou art to me like a brook that is
not to be trusted,
whose waters fail.

19 This was the LORD'S answer:

If you will turn back to me, I will
take you back
and you shall stand before me.
If you choose noble utterance and
reject the base,
you shall be my spokesman.
This people will turn again to you,
but you will not turn to them.

To withstand them I will make you   20
impregnable,
a wall of bronze.
They will attack you but they will not
prevail,
for I am with you to deliver you
and save you, says the LORD;
I will deliver you from the wicked,   21
I will rescue you from the ruthless.

The word of the LORD came to me: **16**
You shall not marry a wife; you shall 2
have neither son nor daughter in this
place. For these are the words of the 3
LORD concerning sons and daughters
born in this place, the mothers who
bear them and the fathers who beget
them in this land: When men die, struck 4
down by deadly ulcers, there shall be
no wailing for them and no burial; they
shall be like dung lying upon the
ground. When men perish by sword or
famine, their corpses shall become food
for birds and for beasts.

For these are the words of the LORD: 5
Enter no house where there is a
mourning-feast; do not go in to wail
or to bring comfort, for I have withdrawn my peace from this people, says
the LORD, my love and affection. High 6
and low shall die in this land, but there
shall be no burial, no wailing for them;
no one shall gash himself, or shave his
head. No one shall give the mourner a 7
portion of bread to console him for the
dead, nor give him the cup of consolation, even for his father or mother.
Nor shall you enter a house where there 8
is feasting, to sit eating and drinking
there. For these are the words of the 9

o *Prob. rdg.; Heb. adds* and bronze. *Heb. also adds*
(13) I will give away your wealth as spoil, and your
treasure for no payment, because of your sin throughout your country. (14) I will make your enemies
pass through a land you do not know; for my anger
is a blazing fire and it shall burn for ever (*cp. 17. 3, 4*).

also 20.14–18. **11:** The precise meaning of this is obscure. The verse may belong with the prayer
continued in v. 15. **12–14:** These verses seem to be a confused intrusion from 17.1–4. **15–18:**
Jeremiah pleads before God like a man on trial before a judge. **18:** *Why . . . ?* Jeremiah charges
that God is not being fair, nor even trustworthy, like Judean brooks which disappear in the
dry season; see, too, Job 6.15–21. **19–21:** *The LORD's answer:* God has not failed him; he has
failed God. Jeremiah has been running away (see 12.5 n.) and must *turn back.* **19:** *Spokesman:*
prophet. **20:** *Wall of bronze:* as in 1.18–19.
16.1–9: Jeremiah the solitary prophet. With no family of his own (vv. 1–4), alienated from
his parental home (11.21; 12.6), renouncing human companionship (vv. 5 and 8), Jeremiah is
the figure of a lonely man. **5:** Like God, his prophet is to withdraw his *peace, love, and affection.*
6: *Gash himself, or shave his head:* rites of mourning. See 41.5; 47.5. **7:** Compare Ezek.24.17;
Hos.9.4. **8:** See 15.17.

LORD of Hosts, the God of Israel: In your own days, in the sight of you all, and in this very place, I will silence all sounds of joy and gladness, and the voice of bridegroom and bride.

10 When you tell this people all these things they will ask you, 'Why has the LORD decreed that this great disaster is to come upon us? What wrong have we done? What sin have we committed 11 against the LORD our God?' You shall answer, Because your forefathers forsook me, says the LORD, and followed other gods, serving them and bowing down to them. They forsook me and 12 did not keep my law. And you yourselves have done worse than your forefathers; for each of you follows the promptings of his wicked and stubborn 13 heart instead of obeying me. So I will fling you headlong out of this land into a country unknown to you and to your forefathers; there you can serve other gods day and night, for I will show you 14 no favour. Therefore, says the LORD, the time is coming when men shall no longer swear, 'By the life of the LORD who brought the Israelites up from 15 Egypt', but, 'By the life of the LORD who brought the Israelites back from a northern land and from all the lands to which he had dispersed them'; and I will bring them back to the soil which I gave to their forefathers.

16 I will send for many fishermen, says the LORD, and they shall fish for them. After that I will send for many hunters, and they shall hunt them out from every mountain and hill and from the crevices 17 in the rocks. For my eyes are on all their ways; they are not hidden from my sight, nor is their wrongdoing concealed 18 from me. I will first make them pay in full[p] for the wrong they have done and the sin they have committed by defiling with the dead lumber of their idols the land which belongs to me, and by filling it with their abominations.

O LORD, my strength and my stronghold, 19
my refuge in time of trouble,
to thee shall the nations come
from the ends of the earth and say,
Our forefathers inherited only a sham,
an idol vain and useless.
Can man make gods for himself? 20
They would be no gods.
Therefore I am teaching them, 21
once for all will I teach them
my power and my might,
and they shall learn that my name
is the LORD.

The sin of Judah is recorded with an 17 iron tool, engraved on the tablet of their heart with a point of adamant and carved on the horns of their altars to 2 bear witness against them.[q] Their altars and their sacred poles stand by every spreading tree, on the heights and the 3 hills in the mountain country. I will give away your wealth as spoil, and all your treasure for no payment,[r] because of your[s] sin throughout your country. You will lose possession[t] of the pat- 4 rimony which I gave you. I will make you serve your enemies as slaves in a land you do not know; for my anger is a blazing fire[u] and it shall burn for ever.

These are the words of the LORD: 5

A curse on the man who trusts in man
and leans for support on human kind,
while his heart is far from the LORD!
He shall be like a juniper in the 6
desert;

p in full: *or* double.
q to bear . . . them: *prob. rdg.; Heb.* as their sons remember.
r for no payment: *prob. rdg., cp.* 15. 13; *Heb.* your hill-shrines.
s your: *prob. rdg., cp.* 15. 13; *Heb. om.*
t You . . . possession: *prob. rdg.; Heb.* obscure.
u for . . . fire: *prob. rdg., cp.* 15. 14; *Heb.* for you have kindled a fire in my anger.

16.10–21: Mingled threat and promise. 10–13: The sense and language of threat are Deuteronomic; see 15.4 n. **13:** *Serve other gods:* contrast with this verse Jeremiah's message to the exiles in Babylonia in 29.12. **14–15:** Restoration promised; as in Isa.52.10–12, the return from Babylonian captivity is equated with the ancient Exodus from Egypt. **16–18:** See 10.3–5,8–9,14–16. **19–21:** *The nations:* compare the broader purpose of calamity in 12.14–17 n. and 13.11 n.
17.1–18: Observations and prayers. 1–4: Judah, habituated in evil, is doomed. **1:** *Their heart:* compare 4.3–4 n. and 31.33. *Horns:* the elevated corners of an altar. **5–8:** A clear affirmation

when good comes he shall not see it.
He shall dwell among the rocks in
the wilderness,
in a salt land where no man can live.

7 Blessed is the man who trusts in the
LORD,
and rests his confidence upon him.

8 He shall be like a tree planted by the
waterside,
that stretches its roots along the
stream,
When the heat comes it has nothing
to fear;
its spreading foliage stays green.
In a year of drought it feels no care,
and does not cease to bear fruit.

9 The heart is the most deceitful of all
things,
desperately sick;*v* who can fathom it?

10 I, the LORD, search the mind
and test the heart,
requiting man for his conduct,
and as his deeds deserve.

11 Like a partridge which gathers
into its nest
eggs which it has not laid,
so is the man who amasses wealth
unjustly.
Before his days are half done he
must leave it,
and prove but a fool at the last.

12 O throne of glory, exalted from the
beginning,
the place of our sanctuary,

13 O LORD on whom Israel's hope is
fixed,
all who reject thee shall be put to
shame;
all in this land who forsake thee
shall be humbled,*w*
for they have rejected the fountain of
living water.*x*

14 Heal me, O LORD, and I shall be
healed,
save me and I shall be saved;
for thou art my praise.

They say to me, 'Where is the word   15
of the LORD?
Let it come if it can!'

It is not the thought of disaster that   16
makes me press after thee;
never did I desire this day of
despair.
Thou knowest all that has passed
my lips;
it was approved by thee.

Do not become a terror to me;   17
thou art my only refuge on the day
of disaster.

May my persecutors be foiled,   18
not I;
may they be terrified, not I.
Bring on them the day of disaster;
destroy them, destroy them utterly.

These were the words of the LORD to   19
me: Go and stand in the Benjamin*y*
Gate, through which the kings of Judah
go in and out, and in all the gates of
Jerusalem. Say, Hear the words of the   20
LORD, you princes of Judah, all you
men of Judah, and all you inhabitants
of Jerusalem who come in through
these gates. These are the words of the   21
LORD: Observe this with care, that you
do not carry any load on the sabbath or
bring it through the gates of Jerusalem.
You shall not bring any load out of   22
your houses or do any work on the
sabbath, but you shall keep the sabbath
day holy as I commanded your forefathers. Yet they did not obey or pay   23
attention, but obstinately refused to
hear or learn their lesson. Now if you   24
will obey me, says the LORD, and refrain from bringing any load through
the gates of this city on the sabbath,
and keep that day holy by doing no
work on it, then kings shall come   25
through the gates of this city, kings*z*

v the most . . . sick: or too deceitful for any man.
w humbled: prob. rdg.; Heb. written.
x Prob. rdg.; Heb. adds the LORD.
y Benjamin: prob. rdg.; Heb. sons of the people.
z Prob. rdg.; Heb. adds and officers.

---

of individual retribution; compare Ps.1. **9–10:** Only God can clearly know the motives behind
a man's conduct; man's organs of thought and feeling are open to him. **10:** *As his deeds deserve*
connects 9–10 with 5–8. **12:** *The place:* the Temple in Jerusalem;
contrast 7.4 with its scorn of the Temple. **13:** *Living water:* see, too, 2.13. **14–18:** A private
prayer. **15:** "*. . . Let it come if it can!*": see 5.12–13 n. **16:** *Never did I desire this day of despair:*
see 8.18–9.1 n.
17.19–27: The importance of Sabbath rest. The passage seems not to come from Jeremiah,
but comes from a time like that of Nehemiah when the Sabbath received particular emphasis;
see Neh.13.15–22. **25:** *David's throne:* apparently it is conceived of as vacant at the time.

who shall sit on David's throne. They shall come riding in chariots or on horseback, escorted by their captains, by the men of Judah and the inhabitants of Jerusalem; and this city shall be in-

26 habited for ever. People shall come from the cities of Judah, the country round Jerusalem, the land of Benjamin, the Shephelah, the hill-country and the Negeb, bringing whole-offerings, sacrifices, grain-offerings, and frankincense, bringing also thank-offerings to the

27 house of the LORD. But if you do not obey me by keeping the sabbath day holy and by not carrying any load as you come through the gates of Jerusalem on the sabbath, then I will set fire to those gates; it shall consume the palaces of Jerusalem and shall not be put out.

18 These are the words which came to

2 Jeremiah from the LORD: Go down at once to the potter's house, and there I

3 will tell you what I have to say. So I went down to the potter's house and

4 found him working at the wheel. Now and then a vessel he was making out of the clay would be spoilt in his hands, and then he would start again and mould it into another vessel to his

5 liking. Then the word of the LORD

6 came to me: Can I not deal with you, Israel, says the LORD, as the potter deals with his clay? You are clay in my hands like the clay in his, O house of

7 Israel. At any moment I may threaten to uproot a nation or a kingdom, to

8 pull it down and destroy it. But if the nation which I have threatened turns back from its wicked ways, then I shall think better of the evil I had in mind

9 to bring on it. Or at any moment I may decide to build or to plant a nation or

10 a kingdom. But if it does evil in my sight and does not obey me, I shall think better of the good I had in mind

11 for it. Go now and tell the men of Judah and the inhabitants of Jerusalem that these are the words of the LORD: I am the potter; I am preparing evil for you and perfecting my designs against

you. Turn back, every one of you, from his evil course; mend your ways and your doings. But they answer, 'Things 12 are past hope. We will do as we like, and each of us will follow the promptings of his own wicked and stubborn heart.' Therefore these are the words 13 of the LORD:

Inquire among the nations: who ever
    heard the like of this?
The virgin Israel has done a thing
    most horrible.
Will the snow cease to fall on the   14
    rocky slopes of Lebanon?
Will the cool rain streaming in
    torrents ever fail?
No, but my people have forgotten   15
    me;
  they burn sacrifices to a mere idol,
so they stumble in their paths, the
    ancient ways,
and they take to byways and
    unmade roads;
their own land they lay waste,   16
and men will jeer at it for ever in
    contempt.
All who go by will be horror-struck
    and shake their heads.
  Like a wind from the east   17
I will scatter them before their
    enemies.
  In the hour of their downfall
I will turn my back towards them
    and not my face.

'Come, let us decide what to do with 18 Jeremiah', men say. 'There will still be priests to guide us, still wise men to advise, still prophets to proclaim the word. Come, let us invent some charges against him; let us pay no attention to his message.'

But do thou, O LORD, pay attention, 19
    and hear what my opponents are
    saying against me.
Is good to be repaid with evil?[a]   20

a *Prob. rdg.; Heb. adds* they have dug a pit for me (*cp. verse* 22).

18.1–17: **A lesson from the potter's shop.** A last minute pardon is possible; before 587, an appropriate response could yet avert the doom, and hence the plea (v. 11): *turn back . . . from this evil course.* 12: *Things are past hope:* because of the unnatural conduct of this unfaithful people it is now too late; see vv. 16–17.
18.18–23: **A private prayer.**

Remember how I stood before thee,
pleading on their behalf
to avert thy wrath from them.

21 Therefore give their sons over to
famine,
leave them at the mercy of the
sword.
Let their women be childless and
widowed,
let death carry off their men,
let their young men be cut down in
battle.

22 Bring raiders upon them without
warning,
and let screams of terror ring out
from their houses.
For they have dug a pit to catch me
and have hidden snares for my feet.

23 Well thou knowest, O LORD,
all their murderous plots against me.
Do not blot out their wrongdoing
or annul their sin;
when they are brought stumbling
into thy presence,
deal with them on the day of thy
anger.

19 These are the words of the LORD:
Go and buy an earthenware jar. Then
take with you some of the elders of the
2 people and of the priests, and go out
to the Valley of Ben-hinnom, on which
the Gate of the Potsherds opens, and
3 there proclaim what I tell you. Say,
Hear the word of the LORD, you princes
of Judah and inhabitants of Jerusalem.
These are the words of the LORD of
Hosts the God of Israel: I will bring on
this place a disaster which shall ring in
4 the ears of all who hear of it. For they
have forsaken me, and treated this place
as if it were not mine, burning sacrifices
to other gods whom neither they nor
their fathers nor the kings of Judah
have known, and filling this place with
5 the blood of the innocent. They have
built shrines to Baal, where they burn
their sons as whole-offerings to Baal.
It was no command of mine; I never

spoke of it; it never entered my
thought. Therefore, says the LORD, the 6
time is coming when this place shall no
longer be called Topheth or the Valley
of Ben-hinnom, but the Valley of
Slaughter. In this place I will shatter 7
the plans of Judah and Jerusalem as a
jar is shattered; I will make the people
fall by the sword before their enemies,
at the hands of those who would kill
them, and I will give their corpses to
the birds and beasts to devour. I will 8
make this city a scene of horror and
contempt, so that every passer-by will
be horror-struck and jeer in contempt
at the sight of its wounds. I will compel 9
men to eat the flesh of their sons and
their daughters; they shall devour one
another's flesh in the dire straits to
which their enemies and those who
would kill them will reduce them in the
siege. Then you must shatter the jar 10
before the eyes of the men who have
come with you and say to them, These 11
are the words of the LORD of Hosts:
Thus will I shatter this people and this
city as one shatters an earthen vessel so
that it cannot be mended, and the dead
shall be buried in Topheth because
there is no room elsewhere to bury
them. This is what I will do to this 12
place, says the LORD, and to those who
live there: I will make this city like
Topheth. Because of their defilement, 13
the houses of Jerusalem and those of
the kings of Judah shall be like Topheth, every one of the houses on
whose roofs men have burnt sacrifices
to the host of heaven and poured drink-
offerings to other gods.

Jeremiah came in from Topheth, 14
where the LORD had sent him to
prophesy, and stood in the court of the
LORD's house. He said to all the people,
These are the words of the LORD of 15
Hosts the God of Israel: I am bringing
on this city and on all its blood-
spattered altars every disaster with
which I have threatened it, for its

19.1–20.6: A dramatic pronouncement and its consequences. 1: *An earthenware jar:* it is
dramatically reserved for the climax in v. 10. *Elders . . . and . . . priests:* they are both audience
and witnesses. 2: *Valley of Ben-hinnom* is chosen for its association with human sacrifice; see
7.30–31 n. *Gate of the Potsherds:* the mention of pottery fragments anticipates the shattering of
jars in vv. 10–11. 4–5: *The innocent: their sons* (compare 15.4 and 2 Kgs.21.1–7). 10–11: The
shattering of the *jar* could have been interpreted as more than a dramatic gesture, and may
have reflected a view that regarded it as a marginal, hostile act. See v. 1 n.; Ps.2.9. 14: See 26.2.

people have remained obstinate and refused to listen to me.

20 When Pashhur son of Immer the priest, the chief officer in the house of the LORD, heard Jeremiah prophesying 2 these things, he had him flogged*b* and put him into the stocks at the Upper Gate of Benjamin, in the house of the 3 LORD. The next morning he released him, and Jeremiah said to him, The LORD has called you not Pashhur but 4 Magor-missabib.*c* For these are the words of the LORD: I will make you a terror to yourself and to all your friends; they shall fall by the sword of the enemy before your very eyes. I will hand over all Judah to the king of Babylon, and he will deport them to Babylon and put them to the sword. 5 I will give all this city's store of wealth and riches and all the treasures of the kings of Judah to their enemies; they shall seize them as spoil and carry them 6 off to Babylon. You, Pashhur, and all your household shall go into captivity and come to Babylon. There shall you die and there shall you be buried, you and all your friends to whom you have been a false prophet.

7 O LORD, thou hast duped me, and
    I have been thy dupe;
  thou hast outwitted me and hast
    prevailed.
  I have been made a laughing-stock
    all the day long,
  everyone mocks me.
8 Whenever I speak I must needs cry
    out
  and proclaim violence and
    destruction.
  I am reproached and mocked all the
    time
  for uttering the word of the LORD.
9 Whenever I said, 'I will call him to
    mind no more,
  nor speak in his name again',
  then his word was imprisoned in my
    body,

like a fire blazing in my heart,
and I was weary with holding it
    under,
and could endure no more.
10 For I heard many whispering,*d*
  'Denounce him! we will denounce
    him.'
All my friends were on the watch for
    a false step,
saying, 'Perhaps he may be tricked,
    then we can catch him
  and take our revenge.'
11 But the LORD is on my side, strong
    and ruthless,
therefore my persecutors shall
    stumble and fall powerless.
Bitter shall be their abasement when
    they fail,
  and their shame shall long be
    remembered.
12 O LORD of Hosts, thou dost test the
    righteous
and search the depths of the heart;
to thee have I committed my cause,
let me see thee take vengeance on
    them.
13 Sing to the LORD, praise the LORD;
for he rescues the poor from those
    who would do them wrong.

14 A curse on the day when I was
    born!
  Be it for ever unblessed,
    the day when my mother bore me!
15 A curse on the man who brought
    word to my father,
  'A child is born to you, a son',
    and gladdened his heart!
16 That man shall fare like the cities
  which the LORD overthrew without
    mercy.
He shall hear cries of alarm in the
    morning
  and uproar at noon,
17 because death did not claim me
    before birth,

b had him flogged: or struck him.
c That is Terror let loose.
d Prob. rdg.; Heb. adds Terror let loose.

20.3–6: When Jeremiah is *released* he puts an individual curse on his torturer, but without revoking his threat to all Judah.

20.7–13: A personal plaintive prayer. 7–9: God has misused his prophet. He would cease speaking in God's name were the compulsion not beyond his power to resist. **10:** *Friends:* ironic. **11–12:** He needs the LORD on his *side* and is torn between the wish to flee and the need to find refuge with his God.

20.14–18: Inner fury. 14: See Job 3.3. He avoids a curse on his parents. **16:** *Cities:* Sodom and Gomorrah. See Gen.19.24–25.

and my mother did not become my
    grave,
        her womb great with me for ever.
18   Why did I come forth from the
        womb
    to know only sorrow and toil,
    to end my days in shame?

Kings and prophets denounced

21 THE WORD WHICH CAME FROM THE LORD
to Jeremiah when King Zedekiah sent
to him Pashhur son of Malchiah and
Zephaniah the priest, son of Maasciah,
2 with this request: 'Nebuchadrezzar king
of Babylon is making war on us; inquire
of the LORD on our behalf. Perhaps the
LORD will perform a miracle as he has
done in past times, so that Nebu-
3 chadrezzar may raise the siege.' But
Jeremiah answered them, Tell Zede-
4 kiah, these are the words of the LORD
the God of Israel: I will turn back upon
you your own weapons with which you
are fighting the king of Babylon and
the Chaldaeans besieging you outside
the wall; and I will bring them into the
5 heart of this city. I myself will fight
against you in burning rage and great
fury, with an outstretched hand and a
6 strong arm. I will strike down those
who live in this city, men and cattle
alike; they shall die of a great pes-
7 tilence. After that, says the LORD, I will
take Zedekiah king of Judah, his courtiers and the people, all in this city who
survive pestilence, sword, and famine,
and hand them over to Nebuchadrezzar
the king of Babylon, to their enemies
and those who would kill them. He
shall put them to the sword and shall
show no pity, no mercy or compassion.
8   You shall say further to this people,
These are the words of the LORD: I
offer you now a choice between the way
9 of life and the way of death. Whoever
remains in this city shall die by sword,
by famine, or by pestilence, but who-

ever goes out to surrender to the
Chaldaeans, who are now besieging
you, shall survive; he shall take home
his life, and nothing more. I have set 10
my face against this city, meaning to
do them harm, not good, says the
LORD. It shall be handed over to the
king of Babylon, and he shall burn it
to the ground.

To the royal house of Judah.   11
    Listen to the word of the LORD:
    O house of David, these are the   12
        words of the LORD:
    Administer justice betimes,
    rescue the victim from his
        oppressor,
lest the fire of my fury blaze up and
        burn unquenched
because of your evil doings.

    The LORD says,   13
I am against you who lie in the
        valley,
    you, the rock in the plain,
you who say, 'Who can come down
        upon us?
    Who can penetrate our lairs?'
I will punish you as you deserve,   14
        says the LORD,
I will kindle fire on the heathland
        around you,
and it shall consume everything
        round about.

These were the words of the LORD: **22**
Go down to the house of the king of
Judah and say this: Listen to the words 2
of the LORD, O king of Judah, you who
sit on David's throne, you and your
courtiers and your people who come
in at these gates. These are the words 3
of the LORD: Deal justly and fairly,
rescue the victim from his oppressor,
do not ill-treat or do violence to the
alien, the orphan or the widow, do not
shed innocent blood in this place. If 4
you obey, and only if you obey, kings
who sit on David's throne shall yet

21.1–23.8: The kings are denounced. 1–7: Jeremiah answers Zedekiah. **1:** *Pashhur:* not
the same person as in 20.1. **2:** *Nebuchadrezzar* is closer to the Akkadian original, *Nabû-kudurri-
uṣur*, than the more familiar spelling, Nebuchadnezzar (see 2 Kgs.24.1). *Making war:* the final
siege of Jerusalem was in 588–587. The king hopes for a *miracle* like the deliverance from Egypt.
5: *Outstretched hand...strong arm:* these words are here bitterly ironical; they commonly
signify deliverance for Israel, as in Deut.4.34. **7:** See 2 Kgs.25.6–7,18–21. **12:** *House of David:*
all the Judean kings were of Davidic lineage. **13–14:** These verses are apparently not in their
original context. **13:** *Valley:* Jerusalem. **22.1–7:** These verses develop the thought of 21.11–12.

come riding through these gates in
chariots and on horses, with their
5 retinue of courtiers and people. But if
you do not listen to my words, then by
myself I swear, says the LORD, this
house shall become a desolate ruin.
6 For these are the words of the LORD
about the royal house of Judah:

Though you are dear to me as Gilead
or as the heights of Lebanon,
I swear that I will make you a
wilderness,
a land of unpeopled cities.
7 I will dedicate an armed host to
fight against you,
a ravening horde;
they shall cut your choicest cedars
down
and fling them on the fire.

8 Men of many nations shall pass by
this city and say to one another, 'Why
has the LORD done this to such a great
9 city?' The answer will be, 'Because they
forsook their covenant with the LORD
their God; they worshipped other gods
and served them.'

10 Weep not for the dead nor brood
over his loss.
Weep rather for him who has gone
away,
for he shall never return,
never again see the land of his birth.

11 For these are the words of the LORD
concerning Shallum son of Josiah, king
of Judah, who succeeded his father on
the throne and has gone away: He shall
12 never return; he shall die in the place of
his exile and never see this land again.

13 Shame on the man who builds his
house by unjust means
and completes its roof-chambers by
fraud,
making his countrymen work
without payment,

giving them no wage for their
labour!
Shame on the man who says, 'I will   14
build a spacious house
with airy roof-chambers,
set windows in it, panel it with cedar
and paint it with vermilion'!
If your cedar is more splendid,   15
does that prove you a king?
Think of your father: he ate and
drank,
dealt justly and fairly; all went well
with him.
He dispensed justice to the lowly   16
and poor;*e*
did not this show he knew me? says
the LORD.
But you have no eyes, no thought   17
for anything but gain,
set only on the innocent blood you
can shed,
on cruel acts of tyranny.

Therefore these are the words of the   18
LORD concerning Jehoiakim son of
Josiah, king of Judah:

For him no mourner shall say, 'Alas,
brother, dear brother!'
no one say, 'Alas, lord and master!'
He shall be buried like a dead ass,   19
dragged along and flung out
beyond the gates of Jerusalem.

Get up into Lebanon and cry aloud,   20
make your voice heard in Bashan,
cry aloud from Abarim, for all who
befriend you are broken.
I spoke to you in your days of   21
prosperous ease,
but you said, 'I will not listen.'
This is how you behaved since your
youth;
never have you obeyed me.
The wind shall carry away all your   22
friends,*f*

*e Prob. rdg.; Heb. adds all went well (repeated from
verse 15).*
f Or shepherds.

6: *Gilead* and *Lebanon* are symbols for flourishing habitations; so, too, *cedars*, v. 7. **10–12:**
Concerning Jehoahaz the son of Josiah. **10:** *For the dead:* this is King Josiah, whom Pharaoh
Necho killed at Megiddo (2 Kgs.23.28–30). *For him who has gone away:* this is Jehoahaz who
succeeded his father, Josiah, only to be deposed by Necho and brought to Egypt where he
died (2 Kgs.23.30–34). **11:** *Shallum* is the name here and in 1 Chr.3.15. **13–19:** Concerning
Jehoiakim, son of Josiah, whom Necho made king after deposing Jehoahaz (see v. 18 and 2
Kgs.23.34–36). **17 19:** Words addressed to Jehoiakim. **20–30:** The kings of Judah in exile.
20: *Lebanon, Bashan,* and *Abarim* (the latter in Moab): these areas were to the north and the

your lovers shall depart into exile.
Then you will be put to shame and
abashed
for all your evil deeds.*g*

23 You dwellers in Lebanon, who make
your nests among the cedars,
how you will groan when the pains
come upon you,
like the pangs of a woman in
labour!

24 By my life, says the LORD, Coniah
son of Jehoiakim, king of Judah, shall
be the signet-ring on my right hand no
longer. Yes, Coniah, I will pull you off.
25 I will hand you over to those who seek
your life, to those you fear, to Nebuchadrezzar king of Babylon and to the
26 Chaldaeans. I will fling you headlong,
you and the mother who gave you
birth, into another land, a land where
you were not born; and there shall you
27 both die. They shall never come back
to their own land, the land for which
they long.
28 This man, Coniah, then, is he a mere
puppet, contemptible and broken, only
a thing unwanted? Why else are he and
his children flung out headlong and
hurled into a country they do not
know?
29 O land, land, land, hear the words of
30 the LORD: These are the words of the
LORD: Write this man down as stripped
of all honour, one who in his own life
shall not prosper, nor shall he leave
descendants to sit in prosperity on
David's throne or rule again in Judah.

23 Shame on the shepherds who let the
sheep of my flock scatter and be lost!
2 says the LORD. Therefore these are the
words of the LORD the God of Israel
about the shepherds who tend my
people: You have scattered and dispersed my flock. You have not watched
over them; but I am watching you to
punish you for your evil doings, says
3 the LORD. I will myself gather the
remnant of my sheep from all the lands
to which I have dispersed them. I will
bring them back to their homes, and
they shall be fruitful and increase. I will 4
appoint shepherds to tend them; they
shall never again know fear or dismay
or punishment. This is the very word of
the LORD.

The days are now coming, says the 5
LORD,
when I will make a righteous Branch
spring from David's line,
a king who shall rule wisely,
maintaining law and justice in the land.
In his days Judah shall be kept safe, 6
and Israel shall live undisturbed.
This is the name to be given to him:
The LORD is our Righteousness.

Therefore the days are coming, says 7
the LORD, when men shall no longer
swear, 'By the life of the LORD who
brought Israel up from Egypt', but, 8
'By the life of the LORD who brought
the descendants of the Israelites back
from a northern land and from all the
lands to which he had dispersed them,
to live again on their own soil.'

On the prophets. 9

Deep within me my heart is broken,
there is no strength in my bones;
because of the LORD, because of his
dread words
I have become like a drunken man,
like a man overcome with wine.
For the land is full of adulterers, 10
and because of them the earth lies
parched,
the wild pastures have dried up.
The course that they run is evil,
and their powers are misused.
For prophet and priest alike are 11
godless;
I have come upon the evil they are
doing even in my own house.
This is the very word of the LORD.

g Or calamities.

east, the direction of exile or of flight. **21:** God speaks in this verse. **24–30:** Concerning Jehoiachin (called *Coniah* here, but Jeconiah in 24.2 and 1 Chr.3.16). **24:** *Signet-ring:* a symbol of
authority (see Gen.41.42; Hag.2.23). **25–27:** See 2 Kgs.24.8–17. **27:** *They* (by anticipation):
this is possibly an allusion to the *descendants* of Jehoiachin, who are denied rulership in v. 30.
23.1–4: The *shepherds* (kings) whom God *will appoint;* see Ezek.34.1–10. **5:** *Branch* is used
also in Isa.11.1 and Zech.3.9 to designate the hoped for ideal ruler from the tree of Jesse,
father of David. **7–8:** A promise repeated from 16.14–15.
23.9–40: Concerning prophets and prophecy. 10–12: Here God is speaking. See 5.7,8; 6.13.

12 Therefore the path shall turn slippery
      beneath their feet;
    they shall be dispersed in the dark
      and shall fall there.
    For I will bring disaster on them when
      their day of reckoning comes.
    This is the very word of the LORD.
13 I found the prophets of Samaria
      men of no sense:
    they prophesied in Baal's name and
      led my people Israel astray.
14 In the prophets of Jerusalem I see a
      thing most horrible:
    adulterers and hypocrites that they
      are,
      they encourage evildoers,
    so that no man turns back from his
      sin;
    to me all her inhabitants are like
      Sodom and Gomorrah.

15 These then are the words of the LORD
    of Hosts concerning the prophets:

    I will give them wormwood to eat
      and a bitter poison to drink;
    for a godless spirit has spread over
      all the land
    from the prophets of Jerusalem.

16 These are the words of the LORD of
    Hosts:

    Do not listen to what the prophets
      say,
      who buoy you up with false hopes;
    the vision they report springs from
      their own imagination,
      it is not from the mouth of the
      LORD.
17 They say to those who spurn the
      word of the LORD,
      'Prosperity shall be yours';
    and to all who follow the promptings
      of their own stubborn heart
      they say,
    'No disaster shall befall you.'
18 But which of them has stood in the
      council of the LORD,

seen him and heard his word?
  Which of them has listened to his
    word and obeyed?
See what a scorching wind has gone   19
  out from the LORD,
  a furious whirlwind;
  it whirls round the heads of the
    wicked.
The LORD's anger is not to be   20
  turned aside,
until he has accomplished and
  fulfilled his deep designs.
In days to come you will fully
  understand.
I did not send these prophets, yet   21
  they went in haste;
I did not speak to them, yet they
  prophesied.
If they have stood in my council,   22
  let them proclaim my words to my
    people
and turn them from their evil course
  and their evil doings.
Am I a god only near at hand, not   23
  far away?
Can a man hide in any secret place   24
  and I not see him?
Do I not fill heaven and earth?
  This is the very word of the LORD.

I have heard what the prophets say,   25
the prophets who speak lies in my
name and cry, 'I have had a dream, a
dream!' How long will it be till they 26
change their tune, these prophets who
prophesy lies and give voice to their
own inventions? By these dreams which 27
they tell one another these men think
they will make my people forget my
name, as their fathers forgot my name
for the name of[h] Baal. If a prophet has 28
a dream, let him tell his dream; if he
has my word, let him speak my word in
truth. What has chaff to do with grain?
says the LORD. Do I not my words   29
scorch[i] like fire? says the LORD. Are
they not like a hammer that splinters

h for the name of: *or* by their worship of.
i scorch: *prob. rdg.; Heb.* thus.

13–15: *Prophets of Samaria* is an allusion to times past, for, by Jeremiah's day, the *people Israel*
had long been exiled, this after the Assyrian conquest in 722. **19:** The *furious whirlwind* of the
LORD's anger (v. 20) is not to be turned aside by optimistic slogans. **22:** A prophet who has
truly been admitted to intimacy with God (*stood in my council*) brings word to his people
designed to *turn them from their evil course.* **25–32:** Misdeeds of the self-appointed prophets.
25: They pass off mere *dreams* for true prophetic words. **26:** They *prophesy lies* and *give voice
to their own* fantasies, leading the people to apostasy. **29:** *Chaff . . . grain:* they are ignorant

30 rock? I am against the prophets, says
the LORD, who steal my words from
31 one another for their own use. I am
against the prophets, says the LORD,
who concoct words of their own and
32 then say, 'This is his very word.' I am
against the prophets, says the LORD,
who dream lies and retail them, misleading my people with wild and reckless falsehoods. It was not I who sent
them or commissioned them, and they
will do this people no good. This is the
very word of the LORD.
33　　When you are asked by this people or
by a prophet or priest what the burden
of the LORD's message is, you shall
answer, You are his burden, and I
shall throw you down, says the LORD.
34 If prophet or priest or layman uses the
term 'the LORD's burden', I will punish
35 that man and his family. The form of
words you shall use in speaking
amongst yourselves is: 'What answer
has the LORD given?' or, 'What has the
36 LORD said?' You shall never again
mention 'the burden of the LORD';
that is reserved for the man to whom
he entrusts his message. If you do, you
will make nonsense of the words of the
living God, the LORD of Hosts our God.
37 This is the form you shall use in speaking to a prophet: 'What answer has the
LORD given?' or, 'What has the LORD
38 said?' But to any of you who do say,
'the burden of the LORD', the LORD
speaks thus: Because you say, 'the
burden of the LORD', though I sent to
39 tell you not to say it, therefore I myself
will carry you like a burden and throw
you down, casting out of my sight both
you and the city which I gave to you
40 and to your forefathers. I will inflict on
you endless reproach, endless shame
which shall never be forgotten.

Two visions

THIS IS WHAT THE LORD SHOWED ME: I **24**
saw two baskets of figs set out in front
of the sanctuary of the LORD. This was
after Nebuchadrezzar king of Babylon
had deported from Jerusalem Jeconiah
son of Jehoiakim, king of Judah, with
the officers of Judah, the craftsmen and
the smiths,*j* and taken them to Babylon.
In one basket the figs were very good, 2
like the figs that are first ripe; in the
other the figs were very bad, so bad
that they were not fit to eat. The LORD 3
said to me, 'What are you looking at,
Jeremiah?' 'Figs,' I answered, 'the
good very good, and the bad so bad
that they are not fit to eat.' Then this 4
word came to me from the LORD:
These are the words of the LORD the 5
God of Israel: I count the exiles of
Judah whom I sent away from this
place to the land of the Chaldaeans as
good as these good figs. I will look 6
upon them meaning to do them good,
and I will restore them to their land; I
will build them up and not pull them
down, plant them and not uproot them.
I will give them the wit to know me, for 7
I am the LORD; they shall become my
people and I will become their God, for
they will come back to me with all their
heart. But Zedekiah king of Judah, his 8
officers and the survivors of Jerusalem,
whether they remain in this land or live
in Egypt—all these I will treat as bad
figs, says the LORD, so bad that they are
not fit to eat. I will make them repug- 9
nant to all the kingdoms of the earth, a
reproach, a by-word, an object-lesson
and a thing of ridicule wherever I drive
them. I will send against them sword, 10
famine, and pestilence until they have

j the smiths: *or* the harem.

---

of the true intensity and power of God's words (see v. 9 and 20.9). **30:** *Steal my words:* they
quote but distort the words of true prophets. **33–38:** In v. 33, there is a play on words, for
masa' in Heb. is both something heavy to carry and also a prophetic message. In vv. 36, 38,
the phrase *burden of the LORD* is regarded as offensive, an affront to the word of God, for it
is not an unwelcome "burden." Hence, one should ask about God's *answer;* not his *burden.*
　24.1–10: Two baskets of figs suggests two groups within the people. One, the Judean exiles,
will eventually be restored; the second, *survivors* still in *Jerusalem* (v. 8), will yet experience
exile. For the literary form used here compare 1.11–12,13–16. **1:** *In front of the sanctuary:* like
firstfruit offerings; see Deut.26.1–4. *Jeconiah* (see 22.24–30 n.) was deported in 597 B.C. (2
Kgs.24.8–17). **6:** *Build them up . . . plant them:* after the threat comes the promise; see 1.10.
8: This verse anticipates the events in ch. 43, with the wider dispersion of the conquered
Judahites. See also 44.26–30. *Treat as bad figs:* See 29.17. **9:** *Repugnant:* see 15.4; 29.18;
34.17. **10:** See 21.9; 27.8; Isa.51.19.

vanished from the land which I gave to them and to their forefathers.

25 This came to Jeremiah as the word concerning all the people of Judah in the fourth year of Jehoiakim son of Josiah, king of Judah (that is the first year of Nebuchadrezzar king of Baby- 2 lon). This is what the prophet Jeremiah said to all Judah and all the inhabitants 3 of Jerusalem: For twenty-three years, from the thirteenth year of Josiah son of Amon, king of Judah, to the present day, I have been receiving the words of the LORD and taking pains to speak to you, but you have not 4 listened. The LORD has taken pains to send you his servants the prophets, but you have not listened or shown any 5 inclination to listen. If each of you will turn from his wicked ways and evil courses, he has said, then you shall for ever live on the soil which the LORD gave to you and to your forefathers. 6 You must not follow other gods, serving and worshipping them, nor must you provoke me to anger with the idols your hands have made; then 7 I will not do you harm. But you did not listen to me, says the LORD; you provoked me to anger with the idols your hands had made and so brought harm upon yourselves.

8 Therefore these are the words of the LORD of Hosts: Because you have not 9 listened to my words, I will summon all the tribes of the north, says the LORD: I will send for my servant Nebuchadrezzar king of Babylon. I will bring them against this land and all its inhabitants and all these nations round it; I will exterminate them and make them a thing of horror and derision, a scandal 10 for ever. I will silence all sounds of joy and gladness among them, the voices of bridegroom and bride, and the sound of the handmill; I will quench the light of every lamp. For seventy 11 years this whole country shall be a scandal and a horror; these nations shall be in subjection to the king of Babylon. When those seventy years are 12 completed, I will punish the king of Babylon and his people, says the LORD, for all their misdeeds and make the land of the Chaldaeans a waste for ever. I will bring upon that country all I have 13 said, all that is written in this book, all that Jeremiah has prophesied against these peoples. They will be the victims[k] 14 of mighty nations and great kings, and thus I will repay them for their actions and their deeds.

These were the words of the LORD 15 the God of Israel to me: Take from my hand this cup of fiery wine and make all the nations to whom I send you drink it. When they have drunk it they 16 will vomit and go mad; such is the sword which I am sending among them. Then I took the cup from the LORD's 17 hand, gave it to all the nations to whom he sent me and made them drink it: to 18 Jerusalem, the cities of Judah, its kings and officers, making them a scandal, a thing of horror and derision and an object of ridicule, as they still are: to 19 Pharaoh king of Egypt, his courtiers, his officers, all his people, and all his 20 rabble of followers, all the kings of the land of Uz, all the kings of the Philistines: to Ashkelon, Gaza, Ekron, and the remnant of Ashdod: also to Edom, 21 Moab, and the Ammonites, all the 22 kings of Tyre, all the kings of Sidon, and the kings of the coasts and islands: to Dedan, Tema, Buz, and all who 23 roam the fringes of the desert,[l] all the 24

k They . . . victims: *prob. rdg.; Heb.* They were the victims.
l who roam . . . desert: *or* who clip the hair on their temples.

25.1–14: Ineffective warnings. Jeremiah, summarizing a twenty-three year effort, calls it a failure; he now foresees only disaster. **1:** *Fourth year:* 605 B.C., the year when Jeremiah dictated his prophecies to Baruch (36.1). The reference in v. 13 to "this book" suggests that possibly 25.1–14 is the conclusion of, or else the preface to, the second copy of the "book" mentioned in 36.27–32. **3:** *From the thirteenth year of Josiah:* see 1.2. **9:** *Babylon:* see 1.15 n. **11:** *Seventy:* actually Babylon fell in 539 B.C., fewer than *seventy years* from the destruction of Jerusalem in 587. Perhaps the seventy are reckoned (after the fact) to the rededication of the Temple about 516 B.C. (see Ezra 6.15).

25.15–38: Worldwide devastation. All Judah's foes will sink in ruin along with her—a small measure of comfort. **15:** *Cup:* a frequent figure for experience; see Isa.51.22–23; Mk.14.36. *Fiery wine:* a captured city was often burned. Hence, fiery wine means a great disaster. **18:** *As they still are:* the words suggest a time of continuing decline. **20:** *Uz:* a place near Damascus. *Ashkelon, Gaza, Ekron, Ashdod:* Philistine cities. **23:** *Dedan, Tema, and Buz* were in central

kings of Arabia living in the wilderness,
26 all the kings of Zimri, all the kings of
Elam, and all the kings of the Medes,
26 all the kings of the north, neighbours
or far apart, and all the kingdoms on
the face of the earth. Last of all the
27 king of Sheshak[m] shall drink. You shall
say to them, These are the words of the
LORD of Hosts the God of Israel:
Drink this, get drunk and be sick; fall,
to rise no more, before the sword which
28 I am sending among you. If they refuse
to take the cup from you and to drink,
say to them, These are the words of the
LORD of Hosts: You must and shall
29 drink. I will first punish the city which
bears my name; do you think that you
can be exempt? No, you cannot be
exempt, for I am invoking the sword
against all that inhabit the earth. This
is the very word of the LORD of Hosts.
30   Prophesy to them and tell them all I
have said:

> The LORD roars from Zion on high
> and thunders from his holy
>   dwelling-place.
> Yes, he roars across the heavens,
>   his home;
> an echo comes back like the shout of
>   men treading grapes.
31 The great noise reaches to the ends
>   of the earth
>   and all its inhabitants.
> For the LORD brings a charge
>   against the nations,
> he goes to law with all mankind
> and has handed the wicked over to
>   the sword.
> This is the very word of the LORD.

32 These are the words of the LORD of
>   Hosts:
> Ruin spreads from nation to nation,
> a mighty tempest is blowing up from
>   the ends of the earth.

33 In that day those whom the LORD
has slain shall lie like dung on the

ground from one end of the earth to
the other, no one shall wail for them,
they shall not be taken up and buried.

> Howl, shepherds, cry aloud,   34
> sprinkle yourselves with ashes, you
>   masters of the flock.
> It is your turn to go to the slaughter,
>   and you shall fall like fine rams.
> The shepherds shall have nowhere   35
>   to flee,
>   the flockmasters no way of escape.
> Hark, the shepherds cry out, the   36
>   flockmasters howl,
>   for the LORD is ravaging their
>   pasture,
> and their peaceful homesteads lie in   37
>   ruins beneath his anger.
> They flee like a young lion   38
>   abandoning his lair,
> for their land has become a waste,
> wasted by the cruel sword and by his
>   anger.

Jerusalem laid under a curse

AT THE BEGINNING OF THE REIGN OF **26**
Jehoiakim son of Josiah, king of Judah, this word came to Jeremiah from
the LORD: These are the words of the 2
LORD: Stand in the court of the
LORD's house and speak to the inhabitants of all the cities of Judah who
come to worship there. You shall tell
them everything that I command you
to say to them, keeping nothing back.
Perhaps they may listen, and every man 3
may turn back from his evil courses.
Then I will relent, and give up my
purpose to bring disaster on them for
their evil deeds. You shall say to them, 4
These are the words of the LORD: If
you do not obey me, if you do not
follow the law I have set before you,
and listen to the words of my servants 5
the prophets, the prophets whom I have
taken pains to send to you, but you
_____
m *A name for Babylon.*

Arabia. **25:** *Zamri is unknown.* **29:** *City which bears my name:* Jerusalem. *All that inhabit the
earth* is an apocalyptic phrase; see following note. **30–38:** This whole passage has the flavor of
"apocalypse," the prediction of a violent intervention of God into human history for judgment.
34: *Shepherds:* rulers.

    26.1–24: Jeremiah's arrest and release. Accused of a capital offense, Jeremiah is brought to
trial, defends himself, finds support in a precedent, and is acquitted, though another prophet
is executed for the same offense. **1:** *The beginning of the reign of Jehoiakim:* 609 B.C. **2–6:** An

6 have never listened to them, then I will make this house like Shiloh and this city an object of ridicule to all nations on earth.

7 The priests, the prophets, and all the people heard Jeremiah say this in the 8 LORD's house and, when he came to the end of what the LORD had commanded him to say to them, priests, prophets, and people seized him and threatened 9 him with death. 'Why', they demanded, 'have you prophesied in the LORD's name that this house shall become like Shiloh and this city waste and uninhabited?' The people all gathered against Jeremiah in the LORD's house. 10 The officers of Judah heard what was happening, and they went up from the royal palace to the LORD's house and took their places there at the entrance 11 of the new gate. Then the priests and the prophets said to the officers and all the people, 'Condemn this fellow to death. He has prophesied against this city: you have heard it with your own 12 ears.' Then Jeremiah said to the officers and the people, 'The LORD sent me to prophesy against this house and this 13 city all that you have heard. If you now mend your ways and your doings and obey the LORD your God, then he may relent and revoke the disaster with 14 which he has threatened you. But I am in your hands; do with me whatever 15 you think right and proper. Only you may be certain that, if you put me to death, you and this city and all who live in it will be guilty of murdering an innocent man; for in very truth the LORD has sent me to you to say all this in your hearing.'

16 Then the officers and all the people said to the priests and the prophets, 'This man ought not to be condemned to death, for he has spoken to us in the 17 name of the LORD our God.' Some of the elders of the land also stood up and said to the assembled people, 'In the 18 time of Hezekiah king of Judah, Micah of Moresheth was prophesying and said to all the people of Judah: "These are the words of the LORD of Hosts:

Zion shall become a ploughed field,
     Jerusalem a heap of ruins,
     and the temple-hill rough heath."

Did King Hezekiah and all Judah put 19 him to death? Did not the king show reverence for the LORD and seek to placate him? Then the LORD relented and revoked the disaster with which he had threatened them. Are we to bring great disaster on ourselves?'

There was another man who proph- 20 esied in the name of the LORD, Uriah son of Shemaiah, from Kiriath-jearim. He also prophesied against this city and this land, just as Jeremiah had done. King Jehoiakim with all his 21 officers and his bodyguard heard what he said and sought to put him to death. When Uriah heard of it, he was afraid and fled to Egypt. King Jehoiakim sent 22 Elnathan son of Akbor with others to 23 fetch Uriah from Egypt, and they brought him to the king. He had him put to death by the sword, and his body flung into the burial-place of the common people. But Ahikam son of 24 Shaphan used his influence on Jeremiah's behalf to save him from death at the hands of the people.

A rising against Nebuchadrezzar checked

AT THE BEGINNING OF THE REIGN OF **27** Zedekiah son of Josiah, king of Judah, this word came from the LORD to Jeremiah: These are the words of the 2 LORD to me: Take the cords and bars of a yoke and put them on your neck. Then send to the kings of Edom, Moab, 3

---

abstract of the Temple sermon, more fully quoted in 7.1–15. **9:** Though Jeremiah said much more, what the people heard was: *This house shall become like Shiloh* (7.12 n.). The prophet had just laid the city under a curse; they must destroy him. **11:** *The officers and all the people* sit as a court in the Temple gate. **12–15:** Jeremiah repeats the threat. **15:** *In very truth the LORD has sent me* (see 1.4–10). His affirmation is here made explicit. **18–19:** *Hezekiah:* 715–687 B.C., about a century before this time. *Micah of Moresheth:* see Mic.1.1. *Zion shall become . . . rough heath:* see Mic.3.12. Hezekiah's *reverence for the LORD* is related not in the book of Mic. but in Isa.37.14–21. **20:** *Uriah* is known only from this passage.

27.1–22: Jeremiah declares Nebuchadrezzar's success. 1: *Zedekiah* became king in 597 B.C. **3:** *Send:* send word. *The envoys* have come to draw Judah into an anti-Babylonian alliance.

Ammon, Tyre, and Sidon by the envoys who have come from them to Zedekiah
4 king of Judah in Jerusalem, and give them the following message for their masters: These are the words of the LORD of Hosts the God of Israel:
5 Say to your masters: I made the earth with my great strength and with outstretched arm, I made man and beast on the face of the earth, and I give it to
6 whom I see fit. I now give all these lands to my servant Nebuchadrezzar king of Babylon, and I give him also all the beasts of the field to serve him.
7 All nations shall serve him, and his son and his grandson, until the destined hour of his own land comes, and then mighty nations and great kings shall
8 use him as they please. If any nation or kingdom will not serve Nebuchadrezzar king of Babylon or submit to his yoke, I will punish them with sword, famine, and pestilence, says the LORD, until I
9 leave them entirely in his power. Therefore do not listen to your prophets, your diviners, your wise women, your soothsayers, and your sorcerers when they tell you not to serve the king of
10 Babylon. They are prophesying falsely to you; and so you will be carried far from your own land, and I shall banish
11 you and you will perish. But if any nation submits to the yoke of the king of Babylon and serves him, I will leave them on their own soil, says the LORD; they shall cultivate it and live there.
12 I have said all this to Zedekiah king of Judah: If you will submit to the yoke of the king of Babylon and serve him and his people, then you shall save
13 your lives. Why should you and your people die by sword, famine, and pestilence, the fate with which the LORD has threatened any nation which does
14 not serve the king of Babylon? Do not listen to the prophets who tell you not to become subject to the king of Babylon; they are prophesying falsely
15 to you. I have not sent them, says the LORD; they are prophesying falsely in

my name, and so I shall banish you and you will perish, you and these prophets who prophesy to you.
16 I said to the priests and all the people, These are the words of the LORD: Do not listen to your prophets who tell you that the vessels of the LORD's house will very soon be brought back from Babylon; they are only prophesying falsely to you. Do not
17 listen to them; serve the king of Babylon, and save your lives. Why
18 should this city become a ruin? If they are prophets, and if they have the word of the LORD, let them intercede with the LORD of Hosts to grant that the vessels still left in the LORD's house, in the royal palace, and in Jerusalem, may
19 not be carried off to Babylon. For these are the words of the LORD of Hosts concerning the pillars, the sea, the trolleys, and all the other vessels still left in
20 this city, which Nebuchadrezzar king of Babylon did not take when he deported Jeconiah son of Jehoiakim, king of Judah, from Jerusalem to Babylon, together with all the nobles of Judah
21 and Jerusalem. These indeed are the words of the LORD of Hosts the God of Israel concerning the vessels still left in the LORD's house, in the royal palace,
22 and in Jerusalem: They shall be taken to Babylon and stay there until I recall them, says the LORD; then I will bring them back and restore them to this place.

28 That same year,[n] in the fifth month of the first[o] year of the reign of Zedekiah king of Judah, Hananiah son of Azzur, the prophet from Gibeon, said to me in the house of the LORD, in the presence of the priests and all the
2 people, 'These are the words of the LORD of Hosts the God of Israel: I have broken the yoke of the king of
3 Babylon. Within two years I will bring back to this place all the vessels of the LORD's house which Nebuchadrezzar

[n] *Prob. rdg.; Heb. adds* at the beginning of the reign.
[o] *Prob. rdg.; Heb.* fourth.

7: *The destined hour of his own land:* when Cyrus of Persia will break the power of Babylon (539 B.C.). **9:** *Prophets:* of these pagan nations. **12–15:** Jeremiah's word to Zedekiah, king of Judah. **16–22:** Jeremiah's word to the priests and people. **16:** *The vessels* were taken as loot in 597 (see vv. 19–20). *Very soon:* within two years, according to 28.3. **17:** See 21.8–10.

28.1–17: Two types of prophets in conflict. Hananiah disputes Jeremiah's claims and hears God's adverse judgment. **1:** The same year, 597, as the events in ch. 27. **3:** Temple treasures.

king of Babylon took from here and
4 carried off to Babylon. I will also bring
back to this place, says the LORD,
Jeconiah son of Jehoiakim, king of
Judah, and all the exiles of Judah who
went to Babylon; for I will break the
5 yoke of the king of Babylon.' The
prophet Jeremiah said to Hananiah the
prophet in the presence of the priests
and all the people standing in the
6 LORD's house: 'May it be so! May the
LORD indeed do this: may he fulfil all
that you have prophesied, by bringing
back the vessels of the LORD's house
and all the exiles from Babylon to this
7 place! Only hear what I have to say to
8 you and to all the people: the prophets
who preceded you and me from earliest
times have foretold war, famine, and
pestilence for many lands and for great
9 kingdoms. If a prophet foretells prosperity, when his words come true it will
be known that the LORD has sent him.'

10   Then the prophet Hananiah took the
yoke from the neck of the prophet
11 Jeremiah and broke it, saying before all
the people, 'These are the words of the
LORD: Thus will I break the yoke of
Nebuchadrezzar king of Babylon; I
will break it off the necks of all nations
within two years';*p* and the prophet
12 Jeremiah went his way. After Hananiah
had broken the yoke which had been on
Jeremiah's neck, the word of the LORD
13 came to Jeremiah: Go and say to
Hananiah, These are the words of the
LORD: You have broken bars of wood;
in their place you shall get bars of iron.
14 For these are the words of the LORD of
Hosts the God of Israel: I have put a
yoke of iron on the necks of all these
nations, making them serve Nebuchadrezzar king of Babylon. They shall
serve him, and I have given him even
15 the beasts of the field. Then Jeremiah
said to Hananiah, 'Listen, Hananiah.
The LORD has not sent you, and you
have led this nation to trust in false
16 prophecies. Therefore these are the

words of the LORD: Beware, I will
remove you from the face of the earth;
you shall die within the year, because
you have preached rebellion against the
LORD.' The prophet Hananiah died that 17
same year, in the seventh month.

Jeremiah sent a letter from Jerusalem 29
to the remaining elders among the
exiles, to the priests and prophets, and
to all the people whom Nebuchadrezzar
had deported from Jerusalem to Babylon, after King Jeconiah had left 2
Jerusalem with the queen mother and
the eunuchs, the officers of Judah and
Jerusalem, the craftsmen and the
smiths.*q* The prophet entrusted the 3
letter to Elasah son of Shaphan and
Gemariah son of Hilkiah, whom Zedekiah king of Judah had sent to Babylon
to King Nebuchadrezzar. This is what
he wrote: These are the words of the 4
LORD of Hosts the God of Israel: To all
the exiles whom I have carried off from
Jerusalem to Babylon: Build houses 5
and live in them; plant gardens and eat
their produce. Marry wives and beget 6
sons and daughters; take wives for
your sons and give your daughters to
husbands, so that they may bear sons
and daughters and you may increase
there and not dwindle away. Seek the 7
welfare of any city to which I have
carried you off, and pray to the LORD
for it; on its welfare your welfare will
depend. For these are the words of the 8
LORD of Hosts the God of Israel: Do
not be deceived by the prophets or the
diviners among you, and do not listen
to the wise women whom you set to
dream dreams. They prophesy falsely 9
to you in my name; I did not send them.
This is the very word of the LORD.

These are the words of the LORD: 10
When a full seventy years has passed
over Babylon, I will take up your cause
and fulfil the promise of good things I
made you, by bringing you back to this

*p within two years: or while there are still two full
years to run.*
q the smiths: or the harem.

6: *"May it be so...!":* the Heb. word is *amen.* *"...May the* LORD *indeed do this!"* Although
Jeremiah believes that it will not come about, he wishes that it would. **8–9:** Only when the
words of a prophet, one foretelling prosperity, *come true,* will the prophecy be recognized as
authentic; see Deut.18.21–22. **16:** *You shall die ... because you have preached rebellion against
the* LORD*:* see Deut.13.5.
    29.1–32: Messages to the exiles. 1–23: The first letter. **2:** The time is after the first deportation
in 597. **3:** The opportunity is the sending of envoys to Nebuchadrezzar. **10:** Babylon's *seventy
years* are possibly reckoned (approximately) from the battle of Carchemish in 605 to the fall

11 place. I alone know my purpose for you, says the LORD, prosperity and not misfortune, and a long line of children
12 after you. If you invoke me and pray
13 to me, I will listen to you: when you seek me, you shall find me; if you
14 search with all your heart, I will let you find me, says the LORD. I will restore your fortunes and gather you again from all the nations and all the places to which I have banished you, says the LORD, and bring you back to the place from which I have carried you into exile.
15 You say that the LORD has raised up
16 prophets for you in Babylon. These are the words of the LORD concerning the king who sits on the throne of David and all the people who live in this city, your fellow-countrymen who have not
17 gone into exile with you. These are the words of the LORD of Hosts: I bring upon them sword, famine, and pestilence, and make them like rotten figs,
18 too bad to be eaten. I pursue them with sword, famine, and pestilence, and make them repugnant to all the kingdoms of the earth, an object of execration and horror, of derision and reproach, among all the nations to which
19 I have banished them. Just as they did not listen to my words, says the LORD, when I took pains to send them my servants the prophets, so you did not
20 listen, says the LORD. But now, you exiles whom I have sent from Jerusalem to Babylon, listen to the words of the
21 LORD. These are the words of the LORD of Hosts the God of Israel concerning Ahab son of Kolaiah and Zedekiah son of Maaseiah, who prophesy falsely to you in my name. I will hand them over to Nebuchadrezzar king of Babylon, and he will put them to death before
22 your eyes. Their names shall be used by all the exiles of Judah in Babylon when they curse a man; they shall say, May the LORD treat you like Zedekiah and Ahab, whom the king of Babylon

roasted in the fire! For their conduct 23 in Israel was an outrage: they committed adultery with other men's wives, and without my authority prophesied in my name, and what they prophesied was false. I know; I can testify. This is the very word of the LORD.

To Shemaiah the Nehelamite.[r] These 24,25 are the words of the LORD of Hosts the God of Israel: You have sent a letter in your own name to Zephaniah son of Maaseiah the priest, in which you say: 'The LORD has appointed you to be 26 priest in place of Jehoiada the priest, and it is your duty, as officer in charge of the LORD's house, to put every madman who sets up as a prophet into the stocks and the pillory. Why, then, have 27 you not reprimanded Jeremiah of Anathoth, who poses as a prophet before you? On the strength of this he 28 has sent to us in Babylon and said, "Your exile will be long; build houses and live in them, plant gardens and eat their produce." ' Zephaniah the priest 29 read this letter to Jeremiah the prophet, and the word of the LORD came to 30 Jeremiah: Send and tell all the exiles 31 that these are the words of the LORD concerning Shemaiah the Nehelamite: Because Shemaiah has prophesied to you, though I did not send him, and has led you to trust in false prophecies, these are now the words of the LORD: 32 I will punish Shemaiah and his children. He shall have no one to take his place in this nation and enjoy the prosperity which I will bestow on my people, says the LORD, because he has preached rebellion against me.

Hopes for the restoration of Jerusalem

THE WORD WHICH CAME TO JEREMIAH 30 from the LORD. These are the words of 2 the LORD the God of Israel: Write in a book all that I have said to you, for this 3

r *Prob. rdg.; Heb. adds* you shall say, saying.

of Babylon in 539. **12:** *If you . . . pray to me I will listen to you:* even in Babylonia. **16–18:** *This city:* Jerusalem; still populous between the first and second deportations, it was yet to experience defeat and ruin; see 24.8–10. **21–23:** *Ahab . . . and Zedekiah:* two prophets in Babylonia not mentioned elsewhere. **22:** *May the Lord treat you like . . . :* this is a formula used in a curse, the counterpart of the formula for blessing in Gen.48.20. **24–32:** The second letter. **28:** He (correctly) understood Jeremiah to be saying: *"Your exile will be long,"* that is, longer than Hananiah's predicted two years (28.3).
30.1–31.40: Hopes for the restoration of Jerusalem. It is sometimes argued that these chapters

is the very word of the LORD: The time is coming when I will restore the fortunes of my people Israel and Judah, says the LORD, and bring them back to the land which I gave to their forefathers; and it shall be their possession.

4 This is what the LORD has said to
5 Israel and Judah. These are the words of the LORD:

You shall hear a cry of terror, of fear
    without relief.
6 Ask and see: can a man bear a child?
    Why then do I see every man
    gripping his sides like a woman in
        labour,
    every face changed, all turned pale?
7 Awful is that day:
        when has there been its like?
    A time of anguish for Jacob,
        yet he shall come through it safely.

8 In that day, says the LORD of Hosts,
    I will break their yoke off their necks
    and snap their cords; foreigners shall
9 no longer use them as they please; they
    shall serve the LORD their God and
    David their king, whom I will raise up
    for them.

10 And you, Jacob my servant, have no
        fear;
    despair not, O Israel, says the LORD.
    For I will bring you back safe from
        afar
    and your offspring from the land
        where they are captives;
    and Jacob shall be at rest once more,
        prosperous and unafraid.
11 For I am with you and will save
        you, says the LORD.
    I will make an end of all the
        nations
    amongst whom I have scattered
        you,
    but I will not make an end of you;
        though I punish you as you
        deserve,
    I will not sweep you clean away.

For these are the words of the LORD to 12
    Zion:
    Your injury is past healing,
        cruel was the blow you suffered.
There can be no[s] remedy for your 13
        sore,
    the new skin cannot grow.
All your lovers have forgotten 14
        you;
    they look for you no longer.
    I have struck you down
        as an enemy strikes, and punished
        you cruelly;
    for your wickedness is great and your
        sins are many.
Why complain of your injury, 15
        that your sore cannot be healed?[t]
    I have done this to you,
        because your wickedness is great and
        your sins are many.

Yet all who devoured you shall 16
        themselves be devoured,
    all your oppressors shall go into
        captivity.
Those who plunder you shall be
        plundered,
    and those who despoil you I will
        give up to be spoiled.
I will cause the new skin to grow 17
    and heal your wounds, says the
        LORD,
    although men call you the Outcast,
        Zion, nobody's friend.

These are the words of the LORD: 18

Watch; I will restore the fortunes of
        Jacob's clans
    and show my love for all his
        dwellings.
Every city shall be rebuilt on its
        mound of ruins,
    every mansion shall have its familiar
        household.
From them praise shall be heard 19

s *Prob. rdg.; Heb. adds* one judging your case.
t *Why . . . healed?: or* Cry not for help in your injury.
  Your sore cannot be healed.

---

originally held out hope for the exiles of the Northern Kingdom alone. As we have them now, they clearly speak to the exiles of the Southern Kingdom, too. References to the restoration of Judah are necessarily later than the fall of Jerusalem. **4–7:** The concluding line, *Yet he shall come through it safely*, contains the consolation that an extreme crisis has been overcome. **8–11:** The bright future. **9:** *David their king:* the restoration of the monarchy to a descendant of David. **12–17:** Again, Zion's disaster overcome. **18–24:** The ruins will be restored and the kingdom reconstituted. **18:** *Jacob's clans:* the ten northern tribes, not yet considered "lost"

and sounds of merrymaking.
I will increase them, they shall not
    diminish,
I will raise them to honour, they shall
    no longer be despised.
20 Their sons shall be what they once
    were,
and their community shall be
    established in my sight.
I will punish all their oppressors;
21 a ruler shall appear, one of
    themselves,
a governor shall arise from their
    own number.
I will myself bring him*u* near and so
he*v* shall approach me;
for no one ventures of himself to
    approach me,
    says the Lord.
22 So you shall be my people,
and I will be your God.
23 See what a scorching wind has gone
    out from the Lord,
a sweeping whirlwind.
It whirls round the heads of the
    wicked;
24 the Lord's anger is not to be turned
    aside,
till he has finished and achieved his
    heart's desire.
In days to come you will understand.

31 At that time, says the Lord, I will
become God of all the families of Israel,
2 and they shall become my people. These
are the words of the Lord:

A people that survived the sword
    found favour in the wilderness;
Israel journeyed to find rest;
3 long ago*w* the Lord appeared to
    them:
I have dearly loved you from of old,
and still I maintain my unfailing care
    for you.
4 I will build you up again, O virgin
    Israel,
and you shall be rebuilt.
Again you shall adorn yourself with
    jingles,

and go forth with the merry
    throng of dancers.
Again you shall plant vineyards on   5
    the hills of Samaria,
vineyards which those who planted
    them defiled;
for a day will come when the watch-   6
    men on Ephraim's hills cry out,
Come, let us go up to Zion, to the
    Lord our God.

For these are the words of the Lord: 7

Break into shouts of joy for Jacob's
    sake,
lead the nations, crying loud and
    clear,
sing out your praises and say,
The Lord has saved his people,
    and preserved a remnant of Israel.
See how I bring them from the land   8
    of the north;
I will gather them from the ends of
    the earth,
their blind and lame among them,
    women with child and women in
    labour,
a great company.
They come home, weeping as they   9
    come,
    but I will comfort them and be
    their escort.
I will lead them to flowing streams;
they shall not stumble, their path will
    be so smooth.
For I have become a father to Israel,
and Ephraim is my eldest son.

Listen to the word of the Lord, you 10
    nations,
announce it, make it known to coasts
    and islands far away:
He who scattered Israel shall
    gather them again
and watch over them as a shepherd
    watches his flock.
For the Lord has ransomed Jacob   11
and redeemed him from a foe too
    strong for him.

u Or them. v Or they. w long ago: or from afar.

(3.12 n.). **21:** *A ruler . . . from their own number;* the end of foreign domination. **22:** *My people
. . . your God:* this ancient formula reaffirms the covenant. **23–24:** *The wicked* are those who
hold God's people in captivity; see v. 16. The verses repeat 23.19–20. **31.1–22:** God's constant
love for the Northern Kingdom. **4:** Dancing in *vineyards* was an ancient ritual; see Judg.21.19–21.
5: *Samaria:* the capital of the Northern Kingdom. **6:** *Ephraim:* see 7.15 n. *Zion:* The mention
here suggests a future reunion of the two Hebrew kingdoms. **8:** *The land of the north:* the

12 They shall come with shouts of joy
    to Zion's height,
  shining with happiness at the
    bounty of the LORD,
  the corn, the new wine, and the oil,
    the young of flock and herd.
  They shall become like a watered
    garden
  and they shall never want again.
13 Then shall the girl show her joy in
    the dance,
  young men and old shall rejoice;
  I will turn their mourning into
    gladness,
  I will relent and give them joy to
    outdo their sorrow.
14 I will satisfy the priests with the fat
    of the land
  and fill my people with my bounty.
    This is the very word of the
    LORD.

15 These are the words of the LORD:

  Hark, lamentation is heard in
    Ramah, and bitter weeping,
  Rachel weeping for her sons.
  She refuses to be comforted: they
    are no more.

16 These are the words of the LORD:

  Cease your loud weeping,
    shed no more tears;
  for there shall be a reward for your
    toil,
    they shall return from the land of
    the enemy.
17 You shall leave descendants after
    you;*x*
  your sons shall return to their own
    land.
18 I listened; Ephraim was rocking in
    his grief:
  'Thou hast trained me to the yoke
    like an unbroken calf,
  and now I am trained;
    restore me, let me return,
  for thou, LORD, art my God.

Though I broke loose I have   19
    repented:
  now that I am tamed I beat my
    breast,
  in shame and remorse
  I reproach myself for the sins of my
    youth.'
Is Ephraim still my dear son,   20
  a child in whom I delight?
  As often as I turn my back on
    him
  I still remember him;
and so my heart yearns for him,
  I am filled with tenderness
    towards him.
  This is the very word of the
    LORD.
Build cairns to mark your way,   21
set up sign-posts;
make sure of the road,
  the path which you will tread.
  Come back, virgin Israel,
come back to your cities.
How long will you twist and turn,   22
  my wayward child?
For the LORD has created a new
    thing in the earth:
  a woman turned into a man.

These are the words of the LORD of   23
Hosts the God of Israel: Once more
shall these words be heard in the land
of Judah and in her cities, when I
restore their fortunes:

  The LORD bless you,
  the LORD, your true goal,*y* your
    holy mountain.
Ploughmen and shepherds who   24
    wander with their flocks
shall live together there.*z*
For I have given deep draughts to   25
    the thirsty,
  and satisfied those who were faint
    with hunger.

x You shall . . . you: or There shall be hope for your
   posterity.
y the LORD . . . goal: or O home of righteousness.
z Prob. rdg.; Heb. adds Judah and all his cities.

---

distant regions of Assyria; see 2 Kgs.17.6. **15:** *Ramah:* a place in Benjamin. *Rachel* was the
mother of Benjamin and Joseph, and the grandmother of Ephraim and Manasseh, tribes of
the Northern Kingdom. **18–20:** Ephraim's penitent words. **18:** See Hos.11.8. **22:** *A woman
turned into a man:* The meaning is obscure. Perhaps it is a witty reference to the mixed figure
that the *virgin Israel* (v. 21) is God's *dear son* (v. 20), or that the kingdom, conceived as female,
acts a male's role. **23 25:** The restoration of Judah. **23:** *The LORD, your true goal:* the alternative
translation (see Tfn.*y*), "O home of righteousness," is a probable designation for Jerusalem,

26 Thereupon I woke and looked about me, and my dream[a] had been pleasant.
27 The time is coming, says the LORD, when I will sow Israel and Judah with the seed of man and the seed of cattle.
28 As I watched over them with intent to pull down and to uproot, to demolish and destroy and harm, so now will I watch over them to build and to plant. This is the very word of the LORD.
29 In those days it shall no longer be said,

'The fathers have eaten sour grapes
　and the children's teeth are set on
　　edge';

30 for a man shall die for his own wrongdoing; the man who eats sour grapes shall have his own teeth set on edge.
31 The time is coming, says the LORD, when I will make a new covenant with
32 Israel and Judah. It will not be like the covenant I made with their forefathers when I took them by the hand and led them out of Egypt. Although they broke my covenant, I was patient with
33 them, says the LORD. But this is the covenant which I will make with Israel after those days, says the LORD; I will set my law within them and write it on their hearts; I will become their God
34 and they shall become my people. No longer need they teach one another to know the LORD; all of them, high and low alike, shall know me, says the LORD, for I will forgive their wrongdoing and remember their sin no more.
35 These are the words of the LORD, who gave the sun for a light by day and the moon and stars for a light by night, who cleft the sea and its waves roared; the LORD of Hosts is his name:

36 If this fixed order could vanish out
　　of my sight,
　　　says the LORD,
　then the race of Israel too could

cease for evermore
　to be a nation in my sight.

These are the words of the LORD: If 37 any man could measure the heaven above or fathom the depths of the earth beneath, then I could spurn the whole race of Israel because of all they have done. This is the very word of the LORD.
The time is coming, says the LORD, 38 when the city shall be rebuilt in the LORD's honour from the Tower of Hananel to the Corner Gate. The 39 measuring line shall then be laid straight out over the hill of Gareb and round Goath.[b] All the valley and every field 40 as far as the gorge of the Kidron to the corner by the Horse Gate eastwards shall be holy to the LORD. It shall never again be pulled down or demolished.

The word which came to Jeremiah **32** from the LORD in the tenth year of Zedekiah king of Judah (the eighteenth year of Nebuchadrezzar). At that time 2 the forces of the Babylonian king were besieging Jerusalem, and the prophet Jeremiah was imprisoned in the court of the guard-house attached to the royal palace. Zedekiah king of Judah 3 had imprisoned him after demanding what he meant by this prophecy: 'These are the words of the LORD: I will deliver this city into the hands of the king of Babylon, and he shall take it. Zedekiah 4 king of Judah will not escape from the Chaldaeans but will be surrendered to the king of Babylon; he will speak with him face to face and see him with his own eyes. Zedekiah will be taken to 5 Babylon and will remain there until I turn my thoughts to him, says the LORD. However much you fight against the Chaldaeans you will have no success.'
Jeremiah said, The word of the LORD 6 came to me: Hanamel son of your 7 uncle Shallum is coming to see you and

a Or sleep. *b Or* Goah.

your holy mountain; see 33.16 for another use of righteousness. **26:** The prophet, or a reader, reflects on the preceding lines. **27–40:** The fulfillment of gleaming promises. **28:** See 1.10. **31–34:** *A new covenant:* unlike a usual covenant, it will not depend on external knowledge, nor be recorded on stone tablets, but will be internal, written on men's *hearts.* **35–37:** That God could reject Israel is not conceivable. **38–40:** The places mentioned were in or near Jerusalem.
32.1–44: Jeremiah's confidence in a restored Judah. 1: *Tenth year:* 588, the year before Jerusalem fell; see 2 Kgs.25.1–4. **2:** *Imprisoned* (see 38.2–6,13). Yet Jeremiah had considerable freedom of movement. **7:** *Anathoth:* see 1.1. *Right of redemption:* land remained within the

will say, 'Buy my field at Anathoth; you have the right of redemption, as
8 next of kin, to buy it.' As the LORD had foretold, my cousin Hanamel came to the court of the guard-house and said, 'Buy my field at Anathoth in Benjamin. You have the right of redemption and possession as next of kin; buy it.' I knew that this was the LORD's message;
9 so I bought the field at Anathoth from my cousin Hanamel and weighed out
10 the price, seventeen shekels of silver. I signed and sealed the deed and had it witnessed; then I weighed out the
11 money on the scales. I took my copies of the deed of purchase, both the sealed
12 and the unsealed, and gave them to Baruch son of Neriah, son of Mahseiah, in the presence of Hanamel my cousin, of the witnesses whose names were on the deed of purchase, and of the Judaeans sitting in the court of the
13 guard-house. In the presence of them all I gave my instructions to Baruch:
14 These are the words of the LORD of Hosts the God of Israel: Take these copies of the deed of purchase, the sealed and the unsealed, and deposit them in an earthenware jar so that they
15 may be preserved for a long time. For these are the words of the LORD of Hosts the God of Israel: The time will come when houses, fields, and vineyards will again be bought and sold in
16 this land. After I had given the deed of purchase to Baruch son of Neriah, I
17 prayed to the LORD: O Lord GOD, thou hast made the heavens and the earth by thy great strength and with thy outstretched arm; nothing is impossible
18 for thee. Thou keepest faith with thousands and thou dost requite the sins of fathers on to the heads of their sons. O great and mighty God whose
19 name is the LORD of Hosts, great are thy purposes and mighty thy actions.

Thine eyes watch all the ways of men, and thou rewardest each according to his ways and as his deeds deserve. Thou 20 didst work signs and portents in Egypt and hast continued them to this day, both in Israel and amongst all men, and hast won for thyself a name that lives on to this day. Thou didst bring 21 thy people Israel out of Egypt with signs and portents, with a strong hand and an outstretched arm, and with terrible power. Thou didst give them 22 this land which thou didst promise with an oath to their forefathers, a land flowing with milk and honey. They 23 came and took possession of it, but they did not obey thee or follow thy law, they disobeyed all thy commands; and so thou hast brought this disaster upon them. Look at the siege-ramps, 24 the men who are advancing to take the city, and the city given over to its assailants from Chaldaea, the victim of sword, famine, and pestilence. The word thou hast spoken is fulfilled and thou dost see it. And yet thou hast 25 bidden me buy the field, O Lord GOD, and have the deed witnessed, even though the city is given to the Chaldaeans.

These are the words of the LORD to 26 Jeremiah: I am the LORD, the God of 27 all flesh; is anything impossible for me? Therefore these are the words of 28 the LORD: I will deliver this city into the hands of the Chaldaeans and of Nebuchadrezzar king of Babylon, and he shall take it. The Chaldaeans who 29 are fighting against this city will enter it, set it on fire and burn it down, with the houses on whose roofs sacrifices have been burnt to Baal and drink-offerings poured out to other gods, by which I was provoked to anger.

From their earliest days Israel and 30 Judah have been doing what is wrong

---

family; if any man had to sell his property the *next of kin* had the duty, as well as the right, to purchase it; see Lev.25.25. **8:** When it happened *as the LORD had foretold* (v. 7) Jeremiah *knew that this was the LORD's message.* **11:** *The sealed and the unsealed:* clay tablets in Mesopotamia and papyrus rolls in Egypt were completed, with one copy open and one sealed for security. *Baruch:* see 36.4. **14:** *In an earthenware jar:* the Qumran (Dead Sea) Scrolls were similarly preserved. **15:** The meaning is that since not all of the people would be taken captive nor the kingdom be destroyed forever, one would make use of the land he bought. **16–44:** The rest of the chapter enlarges on the theme already clearly stated and is thought to be a later supplement; the language is conventional. **16–25:** A prayer for enlightenment: God's actions are beyond challenge; *and yet* (v. 25) he has led his prophet to perform a wholly irrational act, so that one must wonder. **26–44:** God responds: After Judah has fared as she has indeed

in my eyes, provoking me to anger by
31 their actions, says the LORD. For this
city has so roused my anger and my
fury, from the time it was built down
to this day, that I would rid myself of
32 it. Israel and Judah, their kings, officers,
priests, prophets, and everyone living
in Jerusalem and Judah have provoked
33 me to anger by their wrongdoing. They
have turned their backs on me and
averted their faces; though I took pains
to teach them, they would not hear or
34 learn their lesson. They set up their
loathsome idols in the house which
35 bears my name and so defiled it. They
built shrines to Baal in the Valley of
Ben-hinnom, to surrender their sons
and daughters to Molech. It was no
command of mine, nor did it ever enter
my thought to do this abominable thing
and lead Judah into sin.

36　Now, therefore, these are the words
of the LORD the God of Israel to this
city of which you say, 'It is being given
over to the king of Babylon, with sword,
37 famine, and pestilence': I will gather
them from all the lands to which I
banished them in my anger, rage, and
fury, and I will bring them back to this
place and let them dwell there undis-
38 turbed. They shall become my people
39 and I will become their God. I will give
them one heart and one way of life so
that they shall fear me at all times, for
their own good and the good of their
40 children after them. I will enter into an
eternal covenant with them, to follow
them unfailingly with my bounty; I will
fill their hearts with fear of me, and so
41 they will not turn away from me. I will
rejoice over them, rejoice to do them
good, and faithfully with all my heart
and soul I will plant them in this land.
42 For these are the words of the LORD:
As I brought on this people such great
disaster, so will I bring them all the
prosperity which I now promise them.
43 Fields shall again be bought and sold

in this land of which you now say, 'It
is desolate, without man or beast; it is
given over to the Chaldaeans.' Fields 44
shall be bought and sold, deeds signed,
sealed, and witnessed, in Benjamin, in
the neighbourhood of Jerusalem, in the
cities of Judah, of the hill-country, of
the Shephelah, and of the Negeb; for I
will restore their fortunes. This is the
very word of the LORD.

The word of the LORD came to 33
Jeremiah a second time while he was
still imprisoned in the court of the
guard-house: These are the words of 2
the LORD who made the earth, who
formed it and established it; the LORD
is his name: If you call to me I will 3
answer you, and tell you great and
mysterious things which you do not
understand. These are the words of the 4
LORD the God of Israel concerning the
houses in this city and the royal palace,
which are to be razed to the ground,
concerning siege-ramp and sword, and 5
attackers[c] who fill the houses with the
corpses of those whom he struck down
in his furious rage: I hid my face from
this city because of their wicked ways,
but now I will bring her healing: I will 6
heal and cure Judah and Israel, and will
let my people see an age of peace and
security. I will restore their fortunes 7
and build them again as once they were.
I will cleanse them of all the wickedness 8
and sin that they have committed; I
will forgive all the evil deeds they have
done in rebellion against me. This city 9
will win me a name[d] and praise and
glory before all the nations on earth,
when they hear of all the blessings I
bestow on her; and they shall be moved
and filled with awe because of the
blessings and the peace which I have
brought upon her.

These are the words of the LORD: 10
You say of this place, 'It is in ruins,

c Prob. rdg.; Heb. adds the Chaldaeans.
d Prob. rdg.; Heb. adds of joy.

deserved, survivors will again become God's people, and he their God. **35:** See 19.4–5. There
"Baal," the Canaanite god, stands in place of the Moabite god *Molech* here. **39–40:** God will
give them a *heart;* he will *fill their hearts with fear* of him, by such divine initiative excluding
all contingency from the arrangement. *An eternal covenant* is, in fact, a divine commitment;
see 31.31–34 n.
33.1–26: More comforting thoughts. These supplement chs. 30–32. With vv. 1–9 compare
32.36–44. **4:** *Which are to be razed:* the destruction was still in prospect. **8:** *I will cleanse them:*
as in 31.34 God takes the initiative. **9:** *This city will win me a name:* see 13.11 n. **10:** The
destruction is no longer a prospect, but now a reality; accordingly, the passage comes after 587.

and neither man nor beast lives in the cities of Judah or in the streets of Jerusalem. It is all a waste, inhabited by neither man nor beast.¹ Yet in this

11 place shall be heard once again the sounds of joy and gladness, the voice of the bridegroom and the bride; here too shall be heard voices shouting, 'Praise the LORD of Hosts, for he is good, for his love endures for ever', as they offer praise and thanksgiving in the house of the LORD. For I will restore the fortunes of the land as once they were. This is the word of the LORD.

12 These are the words of the LORD of Hosts: In this place and in all its cities, now ruined and inhabited by neither man nor beast, there shall once more be a refuge where shepherds may fold

13 their flocks. In the cities of the hill-country, of the Shephelah, of the Negeb, in Benjamin, in the neighbourhood of Jerusalem and the cities of Judah, flocks will once more pass under the shepherd's hand as he counts them. This is the word of the LORD.

14 Wait, says the LORD, the days are coming when I will bestow on Israel and Judah all the blessings I have

15 promised them. In those days, at that time, I will make a righteous Branch of David spring up; he shall maintain law

16 and justice in the land. In those days Judah shall be kept safe and Jerusalem shall live undisturbed; and this shall be her name: The LORD is our Righteousness.

17 For these are the words of the LORD: David will never lack a successor on

18 the throne of Israel, nor will the levitical priests lack a man who shall come before me continually to present whole offerings, to burn grain-offerings and to make other offerings.

19 This word came from the LORD to

20 Jeremiah: These are the words of the LORD: If the law that I made for the day and the night could be annulled so

that they fell out of their proper order,
21 then my covenant with my servant David could be annulled so that none of his line should sit upon his throne; so also could my covenant with the levitical priests who minister to me.

22 Like the innumerable host of heaven or the countless sands of the sea, I will increase the descendants of my servant David and the Levites who minister to me.

23 The word of the LORD came to

24 Jeremiah: Have you not observed how this people have said, 'It is the two families whom he chose that the LORD has spurned'? So others will despise my people and no longer regard them

25 as a nation. These are the words of the LORD: If I had not made my law for day and night nor established a fixed

26 order in heaven and earth, then I would spurn the descendants of Jacob and of my servant David, and would not take any of David's line to be rulers over the descendants of Abraham, Isaac and Jacob. But now I will restore their fortunes and have compassion upon them.

Events under Jehoiakim and Zedekiah

34 THE WORD WHICH CAME TO JEREMIAH from the LORD when Nebuchadrezzar king of Babylon and his army, with all his vassal kingdoms and nations, were fighting against Jerusalem and all her

2 towns: These are the words of the LORD the God of Israel: Go and say to Zedekiah king of Judah, These are the words of the LORD: I will give this city into the hands of the king of Babylon

3 and he will burn it down. You shall not escape, you will be captured and handed over to him. You will see him face to face, and he will speak to you in person; and you shall go to Babylon.

4 But listen to the LORD's word to you,

11: *"Praise the LORD of Hosts..."*: this phrase is a variant of Ps.136.1. *Offer...thanksgiving*: the sacrifice of a thank offering (Lev.22.29) as acknowledgment of blessings received. **14–16:** See 23.5–6 and 31.23 n. **17–22:** The abiding stability of the Davidic and Levitical lines. **17:** That *David will never lack a successor* (see 2 Sam.7.11–16) was an article of faith frequently invoked in postexilic times. **18:** *Nor will the levitical priests lack a man*: see 1 Sam.2.35. **23–26:** God will never *spurn . . . the descendants of Abraham, Isaac, and Jacob* or leave them without a legitimate ruler.
   34.1–7: A warning to Zedekiah about his captivity. 1: The time is just before the final siege. **3:** See the realities in 39.6–7. **5:** *You shall not die by the sword:* Jeremiah offers only this comfort

Zedekiah king of Judah. This is his word: You shall not die by the sword; you will die a peaceful death, and they will kindle fires in your honour like the fires kindled in former times for the kings your ancestors who preceded you. 'Alas, my lord!' they will say as they beat their breasts in mourning for you. This I have spoken. This is the very word of the LORD. The prophet Jeremiah repeated all this to Zedekiah king of Judah in Jerusalem when the army of the king of Babylon was attacking Jerusalem and the remaining cities of Judah, namely Lachish and Azekah. These were the only fortified cities left in Judah.

8 The word that came to Jeremiah from the LORD after Zedekiah had made a covenant with all the people in Jerusalem to proclaim an act of freedom for the slaves. All who had Hebrew slaves, male or female, were to set them free; they were not to keep their fellow Judaeans in servitude. All the officers and people, having made this covenant to set free their slaves, both male and female, and not to keep them in servitude any longer, fulfilled its terms and let them go. Afterwards, however, they changed their minds and forced back again into slavery the men and women whom they had freed. Then this word came from the LORD to Jeremiah: These are the words of the LORD the God of Israel: I made a covenant with your forefathers on the day that I brought them out of Egypt, out of the land of slavery. These were its terms: 'Within seven years each of you shall set free any Hebrew who has sold himself to you as a slave and has served you for six years; you shall set him free.' Your forefathers did not listen to me or obey me. You, on the contrary, recently proclaimed an act of freedom for the slaves and made a covenant in my presence, in the house that bears my name, and so have done what is right in my eyes. But you too have profaned my 16 name. You have all taken back the slaves you had set free and you have forced them, both male and female, to be your slaves again. Therefore these 17 are the words of the LORD: After you had proclaimed an act of freedom, a deliverance for your kinsmen and your neighbours, you did not obey me; so I will proclaim a deliverance for you, says the LORD, a deliverance over to sword, to pestilence, and to famine, and I will make you repugnant to all the kingdoms of the earth. You have 18 disregarded my covenant and have not fulfilled the terms to which you yourselves had agreed; so I will make you like the calf of the covenant when they cut it into two and passed between the pieces. Those who passed between the 19 pieces of the calf were the officers of Judah and Jerusalem, the eunuchs and priests and all the people of the land. I 20 will give them up to their enemies who seek their lives, and their bodies shall be food for birds of prey and wild beasts. I will deliver Zedekiah king of 21 Judah and his officers to their enemies who seek their lives and to the army of the king of Babylon, which is now raising the siege. I will give the command, 22 says the LORD, and will bring them back to this city. They shall attack it and take it and burn it down, and I will make the cities of Judah desolate and unpeopled.

The word which came to Jeremiah 35 from the LORD in the days of Jehoiakim son of Josiah, king of Judah: Go and 2 speak to the Rechabites, bring them to one of the rooms in the house of the LORD and offer them wine to drink. So I fetched Jaazaniah son of Jeremiah, 3 son of Habaziniah, with his brothers

---

to the king; compare his minimal promise (21.9) to those who would surrender to the Chaldeans. Ceremonial *fires in your honour*: contrast with 22.18–19. **7:** *Lachish and Azekah*: southwest of Jerusalem.

34.8–22: The evils of slavery. 14: *Within seven years*: see Deut.15.12. **16:** The betrayal of the classes was a profanation of God's *name*. **17:** *Deliverance for you*: this is bitter irony. **18:** The dismembered covenant animal suggests the fate of one who breaches the covenant; see Gen.15.10. **21:** The *raising* of *the siege* at the advance of an Egyptian army coming to Jerusalem's relief had produced the illusion of victory; thereupon the slaveholders, regretting their generous impulse, denounced the covenant (v. 8). **22:** The thought is more fully developed in 37.7–10. There, Pharaoh's diversionary campaign has failed and Jerusalem's end is in sight.

35.1–19: A lesson in loyalty. The members of the Rechabite order remain faithful to the rules

and all his sons and all the family of
4 the Rechabites. I brought them into the
house of the LORD to the room of the
sons of Hanan son of Igdaliah, the man
of God; this adjoins the officers' room
above that of Maaseiah son of Shallum,
5 the keeper of the threshold. I set bowls
full of wine and drinking-cups before
the Rechabites and invited them to
6 drink wine; but they said, 'We will not
drink wine, for our forefather Jonadab
son of Rechab laid this command on
us: "You shall never drink wine, neither
7 you nor your children. You shall not
build houses or sow seed or plant vineyards; you shall have none of these
things. Instead, you shall remain tent-
dwellers all your lives, so that you may
live long in the land where you are
8 sojourners." We have honoured all the
commands of our forefather Jonadab
son of Rechab and have drunk no wine
all our lives, neither we nor our wives,
9 nor our sons, nor our daughters. We
have not built houses to live in, nor
have we possessed vineyards or sown
10 fields. We have lived in tents, obeying
and observing all the commands of our
11 forefather Jonadab. But when Nebuchadrezzar king of Babylon invaded
the land we said, "Come, let us go to
Jerusalem before the advancing Chaldaean and Aramaean armies." And we
have stayed in Jerusalem.'
12 Then the word of the LORD came to
13 Jeremiah: These are the words of the
LORD of Hosts the God of Israel: Go
and say to the men of Judah and the
inhabitants of Jerusalem, You must
accept correction and obey my words,
14 says the LORD. The command of
Jonadab son of Rechab to his descendants not to drink wine has been
honoured; they have not drunk wine
to this day, for they have obeyed their
ancestor's command. But I have taken
especial pains to warn you and yet you

have not obeyed me. I sent my servants 15
the prophets especially to say to you,
'Turn back every one of you from his
evil course, mend your ways and cease
to follow other gods and worship them;
then you shall remain on the land that
I have given to you and to your forefathers.' Yet you did not obey or listen
to me. The sons of Jonadab son of 16
Rechab have honoured their ancestor's
command laid on them, but this people
have not listened to me. Therefore, 17
these are the words of the LORD the
God of Hosts, the God of Israel: Because they did not listen when I spoke
to them, nor answer when I called them,
I will bring upon Judah and upon all
the inhabitants of Jerusalem the disaster
with which I threatened them. To the 18
Rechabites Jeremiah said, These are the
words of the LORD of Hosts the God
of Israel: Because you have kept the
command of Jonadab your ancestor
and obeyed all his instructions and
carried out all that he told you to do,
therefore these are the words of the 19
LORD of Hosts the God of Israel:
Jonadab son of Rechab shall not want
a descendant to stand before me for all
time.

IN THE FOURTH YEAR OF JEHOIAKIM SON **36**
of Josiah, king of Judah, this word
came to Jeremiah from the LORD: Take 2
a scroll and write on it every word that
I have spoken to you about Jerusalem
and Judah and all the nations, from the
day that I first spoke to you in the reign
of Josiah down to the present day. Per- 3
haps the house of Judah will be warned
of the calamity that I am planning to
bring on them, and every man will
abandon his evil course; then I will
forgive their wrongdoing and their sin.
So Jeremiah called Baruch son of 4
Neriah, and he wrote on the scroll at
Jeremiah's dictation all the words

---

laid down by their founder but Israel shows no such loyalty to God; compare Isa.1.3. **6–7:**
The group traced their beginnings to *Jonadab son of Rechab*. The Rechabites are otherwise
known only from 2 Kgs.10.15–28 and 1 Chr.2.55. The abstentions mentioned are features of a
nomadic society, *tent-dwellers;* see 2.2. Nazirites, too, abstained from products of the vine; see
Num.6.1–4 and Judg.13.2–5. **16:** This verse contains the point of the chapter. **18–19:** On
individual survival in the midst of general disaster, see also 39.16–18 and 45.5.

　36.1–32: Jeremiah, amid difficulties, records his words. 1: *Fourth year:* 605 B.C. **2:** *The day
that I first spoke to you:* see 1.2. **3:** The word *perhaps* suggests Jeremiah's motivation in that
he goes on hoping that his repeated appeal may yet effect a change; see v. 7. **4–6:** Baruch's
instruction. Jeremiah was probably hiding, fearing a fate like that of Uriah; see 26.21–23. The

which the LORD had spoken to him.
5 He gave Baruch this instruction: 'I am prevented from going to the LORD's
6 house. You must go there in my place on a fast-day and read the words of the LORD in the hearing of the people from the scroll you have written at my dictation. You shall read them in the hearing of all the men of Judah who come in
7 from their cities. Then perhaps they will present a petition to the LORD and every man will abandon his evil course; for the LORD has spoken against this people in great anger and wrath.'
8 Baruch son of Neriah did all that the prophet Jeremiah had told him to do, and read the words of the LORD in the LORD's house out of the book.
9 In the ninth month of the fifth year of the reign of Jehoiakim son of Josiah, king of Judah, all the people in Jerusalem and all who came there from the cities of Judah proclaimed a fast before
10 the LORD. Then Baruch read Jeremiah's words in the house of the LORD out of the book in the hearing of all the people; he read them from the room of Gemariah son of the adjutant-general Shaphan in the upper court at the entrance to the new gate of the LORD's
11 house. Micaiah son of Gemariah, son of Shaphan, heard all the words of the
12 LORD out of the book and went down to the palace, to the adjutant-general's room where all the officers were gathered—Elishama the adjutant-general, Delaiah son of Shemaiah, Elnathan son of Akbor, Gemariah son of Shaphan, Zedekiah son of Hananiah
13 and all the other officers. There Micaiah repeated all the words he had heard when Baruch read out of the book in
14 the people's hearing. Then the officers sent Jehudi son of Nethaniah, son of Shelemiah, son of Cushi, to Baruch with this message: 'Come here and bring the scroll from which you read in the people's hearing.' So Baruch son of
15 Neriah brought the scroll to them, and they said, 'Sit down and*e* read it to us.'

16 When they heard what he read, they turned to each other trembling and said, 'We must report this to the king.'
17 They asked Baruch to tell them how he
18 had come to write all this. He said to them, 'Jeremiah dictated every word of it to me, and I wrote it down in ink in the book.' The officers said to Baruch,
19 'You and Jeremiah must go into hiding so that no one may know where you
20 are.' When they had deposited the scroll in the room of Elishama the adjutant-general, they went to the court and reported everything to the king.
21 The king sent Jehudi to fetch the scroll. When he had fetched it from the room of Elishama the adjutant-general, he read it to the king and to all the
22 officers in attendance. It was the ninth month of the year, and the king was sitting in his winter apartments with a fire burning in a brazier in front of
23 him. When Jehudi had read three or four columns of the scroll, the king cut them off with a penknife and threw them into the fire in the brazier. He went on doing so until the whole scroll
24 had been thrown on the fire. Neither the king nor any of his courtiers who heard these words showed any fear or
25 rent their clothes; and though Elnathan, Delaiah, and Gemariah begged the king not to burn the scroll, he
26 would not listen to them. The king then ordered Jerahmeel, a royal prince,*f* Seraiah son of Azriel, and Shelemiah son of Abdeel to fetch the scribe Baruch and the prophet Jeremiah; but the LORD had hidden them.
27 After the king had burnt the scroll with all that Baruch had written on it at Jeremiah's dictation, the word of the LORD came to Jeremiah: Now take
28 another scroll and write on it all the words that were on the first scroll which
29 Jehoiakim king of Judah burnt. You shall say to Jehoiakim king of Judah, These are the words of the LORD: You

e Sit down and: *or* This time.
f a royal prince: *or* the king's deputy.

---

unspecified *fast-day* provides Baruch with a gathering of hearers. **8:** *The book:* the scroll of v. 1. **9:** *Fifth year:* probably a mistake for the "fourth"; see 25.1 n. **12:** *Other officers:* see 26.10. **16:** *Trembling:* see 26.9 n. The words were in themselves a threat to the people and the city. **19:** *Go into hiding:* the officers were not overtly hostile (see v. 25), but only frightened. **22:** *Ninth month:* Kislev, in midwinter. **23:** *Cut them . . . threw them into the fire:* he hoped to remove the curse by destroying the words. **24:** Once they had burned up the words they no

burnt this scroll and said, Why have you written here that the king of Babylon shall come and destroy this land and exterminate both men and 30 beasts? Therefore these are the words of the LORD about Jehoiakim king of Judah: He shall have no one to succeed him on the throne of David, and his dead body shall be exposed to scorching 31 heat by day and frost by night. I will punish him and also his offspring and his courtiers for their wickedness, and I will bring down on them and on the inhabitants of Jerusalem and on the men of Judah all the calamities with which I threatened them, and to which 32 they turned a deaf ear. Then Jeremiah took another scroll and gave it to the scribe Baruch son of Neriah, who wrote on it at Jeremiah's dictation all the words of the book which Jehoiakim king of Judah had burnt; and much else was added to the same effect.

37 King Zedekiah son of Josiah was set on the throne of Judah by Nebuchadrezzar king of Babylon, in succession to Coniah son of Jehoiakim. 2 Neither he nor his courtiers nor the people of the land listened to the words which the LORD spoke through the prophet Jeremiah.

3 King Zedekiah sent Jehucal son of Shelemiah and the priest Zephaniah son of Maaseiah to the prophet Jeremiah to say to him, 'Pray for us to the LORD our 4 God.' At the time Jeremiah was free to come and go among the people; he had 5 not yet been thrown into prison. Meanwhile, Pharaoh's army had marched out of Egypt, and when the Chaldaeans who were besieging Jerusalem heard of 6 it they raised the siege. Then this word came from the LORD to the prophet 7 Jeremiah: These are the words of the LORD the God of Israel: Say to the king of Judah who sent you to consult me, Pharaoh's army which marched out to help you is on its way back to Egypt, its own land, and the Chaldaeans will 8 return to the attack. They will capture this city and burn it to the ground. 9 These are the words of the LORD: Do not deceive yourselves, do not imagine that the Chaldaeans will go away and leave you alone. They will not go: for 10 even if you defeated the whole Chaldaean force with which you are now fighting, and only the wounded were left lying in their tents, they would rise and burn down the city.

When the Chaldaean army had raised 11 the siege of Jerusalem because of the advance of Pharaoh's army, Jeremiah 12 was on the point of leaving Jerusalem to go into Benjamite territory and take possession of his patrimony in the presence of the people there. Irijah son 13 of Shelemiah, son of Hananiah, the officer of the guard, was in the Benjamin Gate when Jeremiah reached it, and he arrested the prophet, accusing him of going over to the Chaldaeans. 'It is a lie,' said Jeremiah; 'I am not 14 going over to the Chaldaeans.' Irijah would not listen to him but arrested him and brought him before the officers. The officers were indignant with 15 Jeremiah; they flogged him and imprisoned him in the house of Jonathan the scribe, which they had converted into a prison; for Jeremiah had been 16 put into a vaulted pit beneath the house, and here he remained for a long time.

King Zedekiah had Jeremiah brought 17 to him and consulted him privately in the palace, asking him if there was a word from the LORD. 'Indeed there is,' said Jeremiah; 'you shall fall into the hands of the king of Babylon.' Then 18 Jeremiah said to King Zedekiah, 'What wrong have I done to you or your courtiers or this people? Why have you thrown me into prison? Where are 19 your prophets who prophesied that the

---

longer *showed any fear*. **32**: *Another scroll:* see 25.1 n. *Much else:* the written record continues beyond the fourth year (v. 1.).
  37.1–10: Jeremiah disappoints the king. 1: See 2 Kgs.24.15–17. **3:** *Pray for us:* Zedekiah attributes to Jeremiah special intercessory qualities; see 7.16 n. and 15.1–2 n. **4:** *Not yet ... thrown into prison;* see v. 15. **5–8:** See 34.21–22.
  37.11–16: Jeremiah is accused of desertion and imprisoned. 11: See v. 5. **12:** *His patrimony:* a part of the family inheritance from which, in 32.6–15, he buys a field. **13:** *The Benjamin gate:* in the direction of Anathoth. **15:** *They flogged him:* see 20.2. **16:** *A vaulted pit:* apparently, according to v. 20, a dungeonlike, unwholesome place.
  37.17–21: Jeremiah speaks bluntly. 19: *Prophets:* like Hananiah (ch. 28).

king of Babylon would not attack you 20 or your country? I pray you now, my lord king, give me a hearing and let my petition be presented: do not send me back to the house of Jonathan the 21 scribe, or I shall die there.' Then King Zedekiah gave the order and Jeremiah was committed to the court of the guard-house and was granted a daily ration of one loaf from the Street of the Bakers, until the bread in the city was all gone. So Jeremiah remained in the court of the guard-house.

38 Shephatiah son of Mattan, Gedaliah son of Pashhur, Jucal son of Shelemiah, and Pashhur son of Malchiah heard what Jeremiah was saying to all the 2 people: These are the words of the LORD: Whoever remains in this city shall die by sword, by famine, or by pestilence, but whoever goes out to surrender to the Chaldaeans shall survive; he shall survive, he shall take 3 home his life and nothing more. These are the words of the LORD: This city will fall into the hands of the king of Babylon's army, and they will capture 4 it. Then the officers said to the king, 'The man must be put to death. By talking in this way he is discouraging the soldiers and the rest of the people left in the city. He is pursuing not the 5 people's welfare but their ruin.' King Zedekiah said, 'He is in your hands; 6 the king is powerless against you.' So they took Jeremiah and threw him into the pit,*g* in the court of the guard-house, letting him down with ropes. There was no water in the pit, only mud, and 7-8 Jeremiah sank in the mud. Now Ebed-melech the Cushite, a eunuch, who was in the palace, heard that they had thrown Jeremiah into the pit and went to tell the king, who was seated in the 9 Benjamin Gate. 'Your majesty,' he said, 'these men have shown great wickedness in their treatment of the prophet Jeremiah. They have thrown him into the pit, and when there is no more

bread in the city he will die of hunger where he lies.' Thereupon the king told 10 Ebed-melech the Cushite to take three men with him and hoist Jeremiah out of the pit before he died. So Ebed- 11 melech went to the palace with the men and took some tattered, cast-off clothes from the wardrobe*h* and let them down with ropes to Jeremiah in the pit. Ebed- 12 melech the Cushite said to Jeremiah, 'Put these old clothes under your arm-pits to ease the ropes.' Jeremiah did this, and they pulled him up out of the 13 pit with the ropes; and he remained in the court of the guard-house.

King Zedekiah had the prophet 14 Jeremiah brought to him by the third entrance to the LORD's house and said to him, 'I want to ask you something; hide nothing from me.' Jeremiah an- 15 swered, 'If I speak out, you will certainly put me to death; if I offer you any advice, you will not take it.' But 16 King Zedekiah swore to Jeremiah privately, 'By the life of the LORD who gave us our lives, I will not put you to death, nor will I hand you over to these men who are seeking to take your life.' Jeremiah said to Zedekiah, 'These are 17 the words of the LORD the God of Hosts, the God of Israel: If you go out and surrender to the officers of the king of Babylon, you shall live and this city shall not be burnt down; you and your family shall live. But if you do not sur- 18 render to the officers of the king of Babylon, the city shall fall into the hands of the Chaldaeans, and they shall burn it down, and you will not escape them.' King Zedekiah said to 19 Jeremiah, 'I am afraid of the Judaeans who have gone over to the enemy. I fear the Chaldaeans will give me up to them and I shall be roughly handled.' Jeremiah answered, 'They will not give 20 you up. If you obey the LORD in every-

g Prob. rdg.; Heb. adds Malchiah son (*or* deputy) of the king.
h the wardrobe: prob. rdg.; Heb. underneath the treasury.

38.1–13: Jeremiah is charged with sedition. 1: *Pashhur son of Malchiah:* he is mentioned in 21.1. **2–3:** Jeremiah's allegedly seditious speech may have been more extensive than the two verses quoted here. The same address probably appears in excerpts in 21.8–10, 32.3–5, and 34.2–5. **4:** *He is discouraging the soldiers:* perhaps; but Jeremiah's goal is national survival. **5:** *Powerless:* the king vacillates, first assenting to the attempt on Jeremiah's life and then (v. 10) to his deliverance from mortal danger. **7:** *Cushite:* from Cush in Upper Egypt. **9:** *He will die of hunger:* beyond hunger, there was the likelihood of dying of suffocation in the mud. **38.14–28: Zedekiah again consults the prophet. 15:** The substance is paraphrased in Lk.22.67–68.

thing I tell you, all will be well with you
21 and you shall live. But if you refuse to
go out and surrender, this is what the
22 LORD has shown me: all the women left
in the king of Judah's palace will be led
out to the officers of the king of Babylon
and they will say:

Your own friends have misled you
    and have been too strong for you;
they have let your feet sink in the mud
    and have turned away and left you.

23 All your women and children will be led
out to the Chaldaeans, and you will not
escape; you will be seized by the king of
Babylon and this city will be burnt
24 down.' Zedekiah said to Jeremiah, 'Let
no one know about this, and you shall
25 not be put to death. If the officers hear
that I have been speaking with you and
they come to you and say, "Tell us
what you said to the king and what he
said to you; hide nothing from us, and
26 we will not put you to death", then
answer, "I was presenting a petition to
the king not to send me back to the
27 house of Jonathan to die there." ' The
officers all came to Jeremiah and questioned him, and he said to them just
what the king had told him to say; so
their talk came to an end and they were
28 none the wiser. Jeremiah remained in
the court of the guard-house till the day
Jerusalem fell.

39 1*i* IN THE TENTH MONTH OF THE NINTH YEAR
of the reign of Zedekiah king of Judah,
Nebuchadrezzar advanced with all his
army against Jerusalem, and they laid
2 siege to it. In the fourth month of the
eleventh year of Zedekiah, on the ninth
day of the month, the city was thrown
3 open. All the officers of the king of
Babylon came in and took their seats
in the middle gate: Nergalsarezer of
Simmagir, Nebusarsekim*j* the chief
eunuch,*k* Nergalsarezer the commander
of the frontier troops,*l* and all the other
4 officers of the king of Babylon. When

Zedekiah king of Judah saw them, he
and all his armed escort left the city and
fled by night by way of the king's garden
through the gate called Between the
Two Walls. They escaped towards the
Arabah, but the Chaldaean army pur- 5
sued them and overtook Zedekiah in
the lowlands of Jericho. The king was
seized and brought before Nebuchadrezzar king of Babylon at Riblah in the
land of Hamath, and he pleaded his
case before him. The king of Babylon 6
slew Zedekiah's sons before his eyes at
Riblah; he also put to death the nobles
of Judah. Then Zedekiah's eyes were 7
put out, and he was bound in fetters
of bronze to be brought to Babylon.
The Chaldaeans burnt the royal palace 8
and the house of the LORD and the
houses*m* of the people, and pulled down
the walls of Jerusalem. Nebuzaradan 9
captain of the bodyguard deported to
Babylon the rest of the people left in
the city, those who had deserted to him
and any remaining artisans.*n* At the 10
same time the captain of the guard left
behind the weakest class of the people,
those who owned nothing at all, and
made them vine-dressers and labourers.

Nebuchadrezzar king of Babylon sent 11
orders about Jeremiah to Nebuzaradan
captain of the guard. 'Take him,' he 12
said; 'take special care of him, and do
him no harm of any kind, but do for
him whatever he says.' So Nebuzaradan 13
captain of the guard sent Nebushazban
the chief eunuch, Nergalsarezer the
commander of the frontier troops, and
all the chief officers of the king of
Babylon, and they fetched Jeremiah 14
from the court of the guard-house and
handed him over to Gedaliah son of
Ahikam, son of Shaphan, to take him
out to the Residence. So he stayed with
his own people.

i Verses 1–10: cp. 52. 4–16 and 2 Kgs. 25. 1–12.
j Probably a different form of Nebushazban (verse 13).
k the chief eunuch: or Rab-saris.
l the commander . . . troops: or Rab-mag.
m of the LORD and the houses: prob. rdg.; Heb. om.
*n artisans: prob rdg., cp. 52. 15; Heb. people who were
left.*

22–23: The ladies of the court will taunt the king, but their fate will be no better. See 39.6;
41.10. **28:** See 39.14.
    39.1–14: Jeremiah is spared when Jerusalem falls. Vv. 1–2 and 4–10 appear also in 52.4–16
and 2 Kgs.25.1–12, the latter where they stood originally. Only 11–14 here concern Jeremiah.
14: *Gedaliah son of Ahikam:* the puppet governor appointed by Nebuchadrezzar; see 40.7. *The
Residence:* for the governor at Mizpah (40.6). The royal palace had been destroyed (v. 8).

15 The word of the LORD had come to Jeremiah while he was under arrest in
16 the court of the guard-house: Go and say to Ebed-melech the Cushite, These are the words of the LORD of Hosts the God of Israel: I will make good the words I have spoken against this city, foretelling ruin and not prosperity, and when that day comes you will be there
17 to see it. But I will preserve you on that day, says the LORD, and you shall not
18 be handed over to the men you fear. I will keep you safe and you shall not fall a victim to the sword; because you trusted in me you shall escape, you shall take home your life and nothing more. This is the very word of the LORD.

Jeremiah after the capture of Jerusalem

40 THE WORD WHICH CAME FROM THE LORD concerning Jeremiah: Nebuzaradan captain of the guard had taken him in chains to Ramah along with the other exiles from Jerusalem and Judah who were being deported to Babylon; and
2 there he set him free, and took it upon himself to say to Jeremiah, 'The LORD your God threatened this place with
3 disaster, and has duly carried out his threat that this should happen to all of you because you have sinned against the
4 LORD and not obeyed him. But as for you, Jeremiah, today I remove the fetters from your wrists. Come with me to Babylon if you wish, and I will take special care of you; but if you prefer not to come, well and good. The whole country lies before you; go wherever
5 you think best.' Jeremiah had not yet answered when Nebuzaradan went on,*o* 'Go back to Gedaliah son of Ahikam, son of Shaphan, whom the king of Babylon has appointed governor of the cities of Judah, and stay with him openly; or else go wherever you choose.' Then the captain of the guard

granted him an allowance of food, and gave him a present, and so took leave
6 of him. Jeremiah then came to Gedaliah son of Ahikam at Mizpah and stayed with him among the people left in the land.

7 When all the captains of the armed bands in the country-side and their men heard that the king of Babylon had appointed Gedaliah son of Ahikam governor of the land, and had put him in charge of the weakest class of the population, men, women, and children who had not been deported to Babylon,
8 they came to him at Mizpah; Ishmael son of Nethaniah came, and Johanan and Jonathan sons of Kareah, Seraiah son of Tanhumeth, the sons of Ephai*p* from Netophah, and Jezaniah of Beth-
9 maacah, with their men. Gedaliah son of Ahikam, son of Shaphan, gave them all this assurance: 'Have no fear of the Chaldaean officers. Settle down in the land and serve the king of Babylon; and then all will be well with you. I am
10 to stay in Mizpah and attend upon the Chaldaeans whenever they come, and you are to gather in the summer-fruits, wine, and oil, store them in jars, and settle in the towns you have taken over.'
11 The Judaeans also, in Moab, Ammon, Edom and other countries, heard that the king of Babylon had left a remnant in Judah and that he had set over them Gedaliah son of Ahikam,
12 son of Shaphan. The Judaeans, therefore, from all the places where they were scattered, came back to Judah and presented themselves before Gedaliah at Mizpath; and they gathered in a considerable store of fruit and wine.
13 Johanan son of Kareah and all the captains of the armed bands from the country-side came to Gedaliah at Mizpah and said to him, 'Do you know
14 that Baalis king of the Ammonites has sent Ishmael son of Nethaniah to assas-

o Jeremiah . . . went on: prob. rdg.; Heb. unintelligible in context.
p Or Ophai.

39.15–18: Jeremiah praises Ebed-melech. See 38.8–13. **15:** *Had come:* before the fall of Jerusalem.
　　40.1–6: Jeremiah after the capture of Jerusalem. 1: *Ramah:* in Benjamin, a few miles north of Jerusalem. **2–3:** Nebuzaradan's language here is much like that of Jeremiah in 44.2–6. **5:** *Ahikam, son of Shaphan:* he is mentioned in 26.24 and 2 Kgs.22.12. **6:** *Mizpah:* see 39.14 n.
　　40.7–41.18: The assassination of Gedaliah. The date was probably 582 B.C. Some scholars call the event the "third revolt." The story is told more succinctly in 2 Kgs.25.22–26. **9:** Compare this with Jeremiah's counsel in 27–12. **10:** *Attend upon the Chaldaeans:* Gedaliah would represent

sinate you?' But Gedaliah son of

15 Ahikam did not believe them. Then Johanan son of Kareah said in private to Gedaliah, 'Let me go, unknown to anyone else, and kill Ishmael son of Nethaniah. Why allow him to assassinate you, and so let all the Judaeans who have rallied round you be scattered and the remnant of Judah lost?'

16 Gedaliah son of Ahikam answered him, 'Do no such thing. Your story about Ishmael is a lie.'

41 In the seventh month Ishmael son of Nethaniah, son of Elishama, who was a member of the royal house, came with ten men to Gedaliah son of Ahikam at Mizpah. While they were at table with

2 him there, Ishmael son of Nethaniah and the ten men with him rose to their feet and assassinated Gedaliah son of Ahikam, son of Shaphan, whom the king of Babylon had appointed gover-

3 nor of the land. They also murdered the Judaeans with him in Mizpah and the Chaldaeans who happened to be there.

4 The second day after the murder of Gedaliah, while it was not yet common

5 knowledge, there came eighty men from Shechem, Shiloh, and Samaria. They had shaved off their beards, their clothes were rent and their bodies gashed, and they were carrying grain-offerings and frankincense to take to

6 the house of the LORD. Ishmael son of Nethaniah came out weeping from Mizpah to meet them and, when he met them, he said, 'Come to Gedaliah son

7 of Ahikam.' But as soon as they reached the centre of the town, Ishmael son of Nethaniah and his men murdered them

8 and threw their bodies into a pit, all except ten of them who said to Ishmael, 'Do not kill us, for we have a secret hoard in the country, wheat and barley, oil and honey.' So he held his hand and

9 did not kill them with the others. The pit into which he threw the bodies of

those whose death he had caused by using Gedaliah's name was the pit which King Asa had made when threatened by Baasha king of Israel,

10 and the dead bodies filled it. He rounded up the rest of the people in Mizpah, that is the king's daughters and all who remained in Mizpah when Nebuzaradan captain of the guard appointed Gedaliah son of Ahikam governor; and with these he set out to

11 cross over into Ammon. When Johanan son of Kareah and all the captains of the armed bands heard of the crimes committed by Ishmael son of

12 Nethaniah, they took all the men they had and went to attack him. They found him by the great pool in Gibeon.

13 The people with Ishmael were glad when they saw Johanan son of Kareah and the captains of the armed bands

14 with him; and all whom Ishmael had taken prisoner at Mizpah turned and

15 joined Johanan son of Kareah. But Ishmael son of Nethaniah escaped from Johanan with eight men, and they made their way to the Ammonites.

16 Johanan son of Kareah and all the captains of the armed bands took from Mizpah the survivors whom he had rescued from Ishmael son of Nethaniah after the murder of Gedaliah son of Ahikam—men, armed and unarmed, women, children, and eunuchs, whom he had brought back from Gibeon.

17 They started out and broke their journey at Kimham's holding near Bethlehem, on their way into Egypt to

18 escape the Chaldaeans. They were afraid because Ishmael son of Nethaniah had assassinated Gedaliah son of Ahikam, whom the king of Babylon had appointed governor of the country.

42 All the captains of the armed bands, including Johanan son of Kareah and Azariah son of Hoshaiah, together with the people, high and low, came to the

them to the Chaldeans. **41.4:** *Shechem, Shiloh . . . Samaria:* These were once prominent northern cities, now again settled after war and destruction. **4–5:** Since Gedaliah's murder was *not yet common knowledge,* the mourning rites were perhaps in observance of a fast day of the seventh month. Seemingly, parts of *the house of the LORD* were still standing, or else they had been restored. **9:** *King Asa:* around 900 B.C.; see 1 Kgs.15.16–22. **11–18:** The defeat of Ishmael. **12:** The *pool* in Gibeon is mentioned also in 2 Sam.2.13. **17:** *Kimham's* father was named Barzillai; see 2 Sam.19.37–40 and 1 Kgs.2.7. *Bethlehem* was on the way to Egypt. *Escape:* the motive for the group's flight to Egypt was the fear of Babylonian reprisals for Ishmael's rebellious acts.

42.1–43.7: The fugitives consult Jeremiah, whether to proceed to Egypt for safety, or whether

2 prophet Jeremiah and said to him, 'May our petition be acceptable to you. Pray to the LORD your God on our behalf and on behalf of this remnant; for, as you see for yourself, only a few 3 of us remain out of many. Pray that the LORD your God may tell us which way we ought to go and what we ought to 4 do.' Then the prophet Jeremiah said to them, 'I have heard your request and will pray to the LORD your God as you desire, and whatever answer the LORD gives I will tell you; I will keep nothing 5 back.' They said to Jeremiah, 'May the LORD be a true and faithful witness against us if we do not keep our oath! We swear that we will do whatever the LORD your God sends you to tell us. 6 Whether we like it or not, we will obey the LORD our God to whom we send you, in order that it may be well with us; we will obey the LORD our God.'

7 Within ten days the word of the LORD 8 came to Jeremiah; so he summoned Johanan son of Kareah, all the captains of the armed bands with him, and all 9 the people, both high and low. He said to them, These are the words of the LORD the God of Israel, to whom you 10 sent me to present your petition: If you will stay in this land, then I will build you up and not pull you down, I will plant you and not uproot you; I grieve for the disaster which I have brought 11 upon you. Do not be afraid of the king of Babylon whom you now fear. Do not be afraid of him, says the LORD; for I am with you, to save you and deliver 12 you from his power. I will show you compassion, and he too will have compassion on you; he will let you stay on 13 your own soil. But it may be that you will disobey the LORD your God and 14 say, 'We will not stay in this land. No, we will go to Egypt, where we shall see no sign of war, never hear the sound of the trumpet, and not starve for want of 15 bread; and there we will live.' Then hear the word of the LORD, you remnant of Judah. These are the words of the LORD of Hosts the God of Israel: If you are bent on going to Egypt, if

you do settle there, then the sword you 16 fear will overtake you in Egypt, and the famine you dread will still be with you, even in Egypt, and there you will die. All the men who are bent on going 17 to Egypt and settling there will die by sword, by famine, or by pestilence; not one shall escape or survive the calamity which I will bring upon them. These are 18 the words of the LORD of Hosts the God of Israel: As my anger and my wrath were poured out upon the inhabitants of Jerusalem, so will my wrath be poured out upon you when you go to Egypt; you will become an object of execration and horror, of ridicule and reproach; you will never see this place again. To you, then, remnant of Judah, 19 the LORD says, Do not go to Egypt. Make no mistake, I can bear witness against you this day. You deceived 20 yourselves when you sent me to the LORD your God and said, 'Pray for us to the LORD our God; tell us all that the LORD our God says and we will do it.' I have told you everything today; 21 but you have not obeyed the LORD your God in what he sent me to tell you. So now be sure of this: you will die by 22 sword, by famine, and by pestilence in the place where you desire to go and make your home.

When Jeremiah had finished reciting **43** to the people all that the LORD their God had sent him to say, Azariah son 2 of Hoshaiah and Johanan son of Kareah and their party had the effrontery to say to*q* Jeremiah, 'You are lying; the LORD our God has not sent you to forbid us to go and make our home in Egypt. Baruch son of Neriah 3 has incited you against us in order to put us in the power of the Chaldaeans, so that they may kill us or deport us to Babylon.' Johanan son of Kareah and 4 the captains of the armed bands and all the people refused to obey the LORD and stay in Judah. So Johanan son of 5 Kareah and the captains collected the remnant of Judah, all who had returned from the countries among which

q to say to: or to say: It is being said to.

---

it would be safe to remain in Judea, but reject his answer. **2:** *Your:* Jeremiah's God, as though there was a special tie between him and Jeremiah. **4:** *To the LORD your God:* Jeremiah makes no distinction between their God and his. **10:** *Stay in this land:* see 32.6–15. **14:** *The trumpet:* the ram's horn warning of peril; see Ezek.33.3. **19–20:** See vv. 5–6. **43.3:** The fugitives, strangely,

they had been scattered to make their home in Judah men, women and children, including the king's daughters, all the people whom Nebuzaradan captain of the guard had left with Gedaliah son of Ahikam, son of Shaphan, as well as the prophet Jeremiah and Baruch 7 son of Neriah; these all went to Egypt and came to Tahpanhes, disobeying the LORD.

8 The word of the LORD came to 9 Jeremiah at Tahpanhes: Take some large stones and set them in cement in the pavement at the entrance to Pharaoh's palace in Tahpanhes. Let 10 the Judaeans see you do it and say to them, These are the words of the LORD of Hosts the God of Israel: I will send for my servant Nebuchadrezzar king of Babylon, and he will place his throne on these stones that I have set there, and 11 spread his canopy over them. He will then proceed to strike Egypt down, killing those doomed to death, taking captive those who are for captivity, and putting to the sword those who are for 12 the sword. He will set fire to the temples of the Egyptian gods, burning the buildings and carrying the gods into captivity. He will scour the land of Egypt as a shepherd scours his clothes to rid them of lice. He will leave Egypt 13 with his purpose achieved. He will smash the sacred pillars of Beth-shemesh in Egypt and burn down the temples of the Egyptian gods.

44 The word that came to Jeremiah for all the Judaeans who were living in Egypt, in Migdol, Tahpanhes, Noph, 2 and the district of Pathros: These are the words of the LORD of Hosts the God of Israel: You have seen the calamity that I brought upon Jerusalem and all the cities of Judah: today they are laid 3 waste and left uninhabited, all because of the wickedness of those who provoked me to anger by going after other gods, gods unknown to them, by burning sacrifices to them. It was you and

your fathers who did this. I took pains 4 to send all my servants the prophets to you with this warning: 'Do not do this abominable thing which I hate.' But your fathers would not listen; they 5 paid no heed. They did not give up their wickedness or cease to burn sacrifices to other gods; so my anger and 6 wrath raged like a fire through the cities of Judah and the streets of Jerusalem, and they became the desolate ruin that they are today.

Now these are the words of the LORD 7 the God of Hosts, the God of Israel: Why bring so great a disaster upon yourselves? Why bring destruction upon Judaeans, men and women, children and babes, and leave yourselves without a survivor? This is what comes 8 of your provoking me by all your idolatry in burning sacrifices to other gods in Egypt where you have made your home. You will destroy yourselves and become an object of ridicule and reproach to all the nations of the earth. Have you forgotten all the 9 wickedness committed by your forefathers, by the kings of Judah and their wives, by yourselves and your wives in the land of Judah and in the streets of Jerusalem? To this day you have shown 10 no remorse, no reverence; you have not conformed to the law and the statutes which I set before you and your forefathers. These, therefore, are the words 11 of the LORD of Hosts the God of Israel: I have made up my mind to bring calamity upon you and exterminate the people of Judah. I will deal with the 12 remnant of Judah who were bent on going to make their home in Egypt; in Egypt they shall all meet their end. Some shall fall by the sword, others will meet their end by famine. High and low alike will die by sword or by famine and will be an object of execration and horror, of ridicule and reproach. I will 13 punish those who live in Egypt as I punished those in Jerusalem, by sword,

hold Baruch responsible for Jeremiah's unwelcome answer. **6:** *Jeremiah and Baruch:* they were taken to Egypt, apparently against their will. **7:** *Tahpanhes:* Daphne, just west of the Sinai-Egypt border (2.16).

43.8–44.30: Jeremiah in Egypt. 8–13: He forecasts Nebuchadrezzar's invasion of Egypt. **9:** *Stones:* to dramatize the message. **12:** *Will scour the land:* will leave no survivors. **13:** *Beth-shemesh:* lit. "house of the sun (God)." It was also called On (Gen.41.45), and later, Heliopolis. It was near Tahpanhes. Nebuchadrezzar's forces did invade Egypt about 567 B.C. **44.1–30:** The faithlessness of the Judeans in Egypt. **1:** *Migdol:* near *Tahpanhes;* both were east of *Noph*

14 famine, and pestilence. Those who had remained in Judah came to make their home in Egypt, confident that they would return and live once more in Judah. But they shall not return;*r* not one of them shall survive, not one escape.

15 Then all the men who knew that their wives were burning sacrifices to other gods and the crowds of women stand-

16 ing by*s* answered Jeremiah, 'We will not listen to what you tell us in the

17 name of the LORD. We intend to fulfil all the promises by which we have bound ourselves: we will burn sacrifices to the queen of heaven and pour drink-offerings to her as we used to do, we and our fathers, our kings and our princes, in the cities of Judah and in the streets of Jerusalem. We then had food in plenty and were content; no calamity

18 touched us. But from the time we left off burning sacrifices to the queen of heaven and pouring drink-offerings to her, we have been in great want, and in the end we have fallen victims to sword

19 and famine.' And the women said, 'When we burnt sacrifices to the queen of heaven and poured drink-offerings to her, our husbands knew full well that we were making crescent-cakes marked with her image and pouring

20 drink-offerings to her.' When Jeremiah received this answer from these men and women and all the people, he said,

21 'The LORD did not forget those sacrifices which you and your fathers, your kings and princes and the people of the land burnt in the cities of Judah and in the streets of Jerusalem, and they

22 mounted up in his mind until he could no longer tolerate them, so wicked were your deeds and so abominable the things you did. Your land became a desolate waste, an object of horror and ridicule, with no inhabitants, as it still

23 is. This calamity has come upon you because you burnt these sacrifices and

sinned against the LORD and did not obey the LORD or conform to his laws, statutes, and teachings.'

21 Jeremiah further said to all the people and to the women, Listen to the word of the LORD, all you from Judah

25 who live in Egypt. These are the words of the LORD of Hosts the God of Israel: You women have made your actions match your words. 'We will carry out our vows', you said, 'to burn sacrifices to the queen of heaven and to pour drink-offerings to her.' Well then, fulfil your vows by all means, and make your words good. But listen to the

26 word of the LORD, all you from Judah who live in Egypt. I have sworn by my great name, says the LORD, that my name shall never again be on the lips of the men of Judah; they shall no longer swear in Egypt, 'By the life of the Lord GOD.' I am on the watch to bring

27 you evil and not good, and all the men of Judah who are in Egypt shall meet their end by sword and by famine until not one is left.*t* It is then that all the

28 survivors of Judah who have made their home in Egypt shall know whose word prevails, theirs or mine.

29 This is the sign I give you, says the LORD, that I intend to punish you in this place, so that you may learn that my words against you will prevail to bring evil upon you: These are the

30 words of the LORD: I will hand over Pharaoh Hophra king of Egypt to his enemies and to those who seek his life, just as I handed over Zedekiah king of Judah to his enemy Nebuchadrezzar king of Babylon who was seeking to take his life.

THE WORD WHICH THE PROPHET **45** Jeremiah spoke to Baruch son of Neriah when he wrote these words in a

r Prob. rdg.; Heb. adds except fugitives.
s Prob. rdg.; Heb. adds and all the people who lived in Egypt, in Pathros.
t Prob. rdg.; Heb. adds Few will escape the sword in Egypt to return to Judah.

(Memphis), while *Pathros* was in the south of Egypt. **17:** *Queen of heaven:* see 7.18 n. **18:** *The time:* this is probably not an allusion to Josiah's reform (621 B.C.), but to some more recent period, such as the fall of Jerusalem in 587, or possibly even the earlier deportation in 597. **26–27:** *Meet their end:* contrast the doom on the exiles to Egypt with the hope extended to the exiles in Babylonia (24.6). **28:** *Prevails:* the *word* that is *theirs* is in vv. 16–17a. **29–30:** Jeremiah proposes a sign, that when Pharaoh *Hophra* will be taken by his enemies, God's punishment of these Judeans will be imminent. Hophra was deposed in 569, lost his life in 566. This prediction concludes the story of the Judeans in Egypt and the biography of Jeremiah.
  45.1–5: The experience of Baruch. A warning against aggrandizement. See also ch. 36.

book at Jeremiah's dictation in the fourth year of Jehoiakim son of Josiah, 2 king of Judah: These are the words of the LORD the God of Israel concerning 3 you, Baruch: You said, 'Woe is me, for the LORD has added grief to all my trials. I have worn myself out with my 4 labours and have had no respite.' This is what you shall say to Baruch, These are the words of the LORD: What I have built, I demolish; what I have planted, I uproot. So it will be with the 5 whole earth. You seek great things for yourself. Leave off seeking them; for I will bring disaster upon all mankind, says the LORD, and I will let you live wherever you go, but you shall save your life and nothing more.

Prophecies against the nations

46 THIS CAME TO THE PROPHET JEREMIAH as the word of the LORD concerning the nations.

2 Of Egypt: concerning the army of Pharaoh Necho king of Egypt at Carchemish on the river Euphrates, which Nebuchadrezzar king of Babylon defeated in the fourth year of Jehoiakim son of Josiah, king of Judah.

3　　Hold shield and buckler ready
　　　and advance to battle;
4　harness the horses, let the riders
　　　mount;
　　form up, your helmets on, your lances
　　　burnished;
　　on with your coats of mail!
5　　But now, what sight is this?
　　They are broken and routed,
　　　their warriors beaten down;
　　they have turned to flight and do not
　　　look behind them.

Terror let loose!
This is the very word of the LORD.

Can the swift escape, can the warrior　*u*
　save himself?
In the north, by the river Euphrates,
　they stumble and fall.

Who is this rising like the Nile,　　7
　like its streams turbulent in
　　flood?
Egypt is rising like the Nile,　　　8
　like its streams turbulent in flood.

He*u* says:

I will rise and cover the earth,
I will destroy both city and people.

Charge, horsemen! On, you flashing　9
　chariots, on!
　Forward, the warriors,
Cushites and men of Put carrying
　shields,
Lydians grasping their bent bows!
This is the day of the Lord, the GOD　10
　of Hosts,
a day of vengeance, vengeance on
　his enemies;
the sword shall devour and be sated,
　drunk with their blood.
For the GOD of Hosts, the Lord,
　holds sacrifice
　in a northern land, by the river
　Euphrates.
Go up into Gilead and fetch balm,　11
　O virgin people of Egypt.
You have tried many remedies, all
　in vain;
no skin shall grow over your
　wounds.
The nations have heard your cry,　12
　and the earth echoes with your
　screams;
u Or It.

4: God also knows failure and grief. 5: Baruch needs to be satisfied simply to survive.
　46.1–51.64: Heathen nations will be destroyed. Compare 25.15–38. The book of Jer. ends on a note of comfort. Unlike the comfort in chs. 30–34 which stressed God's forgiving love and looked to the rehabilitation of his exiled people, these chapters offer comfort through the elimination of actively or potentially hostile nations. The prevailing tone is spiteful, yet sympathy is not lacking. 1: The verse ascribes the ensuing chapters to Jeremiah; compare 1.5,10. Some scholars, however, question his authorship of the whole, others of the individual parts. 2–26: Two taunt songs (vv. 2–12 and 13–26) against Egypt. The proud might of Egypt (vv. 3–4 and 7–9) suffers inglorious defeat (5–6 and 11–12) at Carchemish. 2: *Carchemish:* a place on the upper Euphrates. There, in 605 B.C., *Nebuchadrezzar* of Babylonia defeated and wiped out *the army of Pharaoh Necho* (II), an ally of the waning Assyrian power. 3: Egypt is addressed. 9: *Put:* in North Africa. *The day of the Lord:* in an old tradition the day was to be, as here, a time of God's triumph over enemies, the foes of his people Israel. 11: *Balm:* a healing medicine;

warrior stumbles against warrior
and both fall together.

13 The word which the LORD spoke to
the prophet Jeremiah when Nebuchadrezzar king of Babylon was coming
to harry the land of Egypt:

14 Announce it in Egypt, proclaim it in
Migdol,
proclaim it in Noph and Tahpanhes.
Say, Stand to! Be ready!
for a sword devours all around you.
15 Why does Apis flee, why does your
bull-god not[v] stand fast?
The LORD has thrust him out.
16 The rabble of Egypt stumbles and
falls,
man against man;
each says, 'Quick, back to our people,
to the land of our birth, far from the
cruel sword!'
17 Give Pharaoh of Egypt the title King
Bombast,
the man who missed his moment.
18 By my life, says the King
whose name is the LORD of Hosts,
one shall come mighty as Tabor
among the hills,
as Carmel by the sea.
19 Make ready your baggage for exile,
you native people of Egypt;
for Noph shall become a waste,
ruined and unpeopled.

20 Egypt was a lovely heifer,
but a gadfly from the north descended
on her.
21 The mercenaries in her land were like
stall-fed calves;
but they too turned and fled,
not one of them stood his ground.
The hour of their downfall has come
upon them,
their day of reckoning.
22 Hark, she is hissing like a snake,
for the enemy has come in all his
force.

They fall upon her with axes
like woodcutters at their work.
They cut down her forest, says the   23
LORD,
and it flaunts itself no more;
for they are many as locusts and past
counting.
The Egyptians are put to shame,   24
enslaved to a northern race.
The LORD of Hosts the God of Israel 25
has spoken:
I will punish Amon god of No,[w]
Egypt with her gods and her princes,
Pharaoh and all who trust in him.
I will deliver them to those bent on   26
their destruction,
to Nebuchadrezzar king of Babylon
and his troops;
yet in after time the land shall be
peopled as of old.
This is the very word of the LORD.

But you Jacob my servant, have no   27
fear,
despair not, O Israel;
for I will bring you back safe from
afar
and your offspring from the land
where they are captives;
and Jacob shall be at rest once more,
prosperous and unafraid.
O Jacob my servant, have no fear,   28
says the LORD; for I am with you.
I will make an end of all the nations
amongst whom I have banished
you;
but I will not make an end of you;
though I punish you as you
deserve,
I will not sweep you clean away.

This came to the prophet Jeremiah as **47**
the word of the LORD concerning the
Philistines before Pharaoh's harrying
of Gaza: The LORD has spoken: 2

v Why does Apis . . . not: *or* Why is your bull-god
routed, why does he not . . .
w *Prob. rdg.; Heb. adds* and Pharaoh.

see 8.22. **13:** The precise occasion of the passage is uncertain. It may be that of 567 B.C.; see
43.13 n. **15:** *Apis:* a bull god, one of the chief deities of Egypt. With the scorn here, compare
Isa.46.1–2. **16:** The people speaking are foreign mercenaries. **18:** *Mighty:* these Palestinian
mountains, *Carmel* and *Tabor,* dominate their vicinities. **25:** *Amon:* a god worshiped at *No*
(Thebes) in southern Egypt. **26:** The latter part of the verse is probably an addition, softening
the judgment; see 48.47 and 49.6. **27–28:** Reassurance to Israel; see 30.1–11.
   47.1–7: Concerning the Philistines. Pharaoh is mentioned only in v. 1. *From the north* (v. 2)
suggests Babylon, not Egypt, as the agent of God (v. 4) being sent to destroy Philistia. The
chapter could refer to any of the frequent occasions when Philistia was ground between the

See how waters are rising from the
    north
and swelling to a torrent in spate,
flooding the land and all that is in it,
cities and all who live in them.
    Men shall shriek in alarm
and all who live in the land shall
    howl.
3 Hark, the pounding of his chargers'
    hooves,
the rattle of his chariots and their
    rumbling wheels!
Fathers spare no thought for their
    children;
    their hands hang powerless,
4 because the day is upon them when
    Philistia will be despoiled,
and Tyre and Sidon destroyed to the
    last defender;
for the LORD will despoil the
    Philistines,
    that remnant of the isle of
    Caphtor.
5 Gaza is shorn bare, Ashkelon ruined.
    Poor remnant of their strength,
how long will you gash yourselves
    and cry:
6 Ah, sword in the hand of the LORD,
    how long will it be before you rest?
Sheathe yourself, rest and be quiet.
7 How can it rest? for the LORD has
    given it work to do
against Ashkelon and the plain
    by the sea;
there he has assigned the sword
    its task.

48 Of Moab. The LORD of Hosts the God
of Israel has spoken:

    Alas for Nebo! it is laid waste;
    Kiriathaim is put to shame and
        captured,
    Misgab reduced to shame and
        dismay;
2   Moab is renowned no longer.
    In Heshbon they plot evil against her:

Come, destroy her, and leave her no
    longer a nation.
And you who live in Madmen shall
    be struck down,
your people pursued by the sword.
    Hark to the cries of anguish from   3
    Horonaim:
great havoc and disaster!
    Moab is broken.   4
Their cries are heard as far as Zoar.
    On the ascent of Luhith   5
    men go up weeping bitterly;
on the descent of Horonaim
    cries of 'Disaster!' are heard.
Flee, flee for your lives   6
like a sand-grouse in the wilderness.
Because you have trusted in your   7
    defences and your arsenals,
    you too will be captured,
and Kemosh will go into exile,
    his priests and his captains with him;
and a spoiler shall descend on every   8
    city.
No city shall escape,
valley and tableland will be laid waste
    and plundered;
    the LORD has spoken.

Let a warning flash to Moab,^x^   9
for she shall be laid in ruins^y^
and her cities shall become waste
    places
    with no inhabitant.
A curse on him who is slack in doing 10
    the LORD's work!
A curse on him who withholds his
    sword from bloodshed!

All his life long, Moab has lain   11
    undisturbed
like wine settled on its lees,
not emptied from vessel to vessel;
    he has not gone into exile.
Therefore the taste of him is
    unaltered,

x Let . . . Moab: *or* Doom Moab to become saltings.
y laid in ruins: *prob. rdg.; Heb. obscure.*

---

two major powers, e.g. during Necho's campaign in 609 (see 2 Kgs.23.29). **4:** *Tyre and Sidon*,
Phoenician cities, seemingly allied with the Philistines (27.3). *Caphtor:* Crete, or possibly Asia
Minor; see Amos 9.7. *Gaza . . . Ashkelon:* Philistine cities. **6:** Philistia speaks here.
   48.1–47: *Of Moab.* A collection of compositions concerning Moab, some threatening
calamities, others lamenting that people's distress. Neither the occasions nor the human agents
of destruction are specified. During the latter half of the seventh century and early in the sixth,
Moab suffered from incursions of Arab tribes from the east. When Jerusalem fell in 587, Moab
afforded refuge to fugitives from Judah (see 40.11–12). **1–6:** The chapter begins with what
sounds like a dirge, sympathy for Moab in her plight; compare Isa.15.1–8. **7:** The tone becomes
more hostile. *Kemosh:* the Moabite god; see vv. 13 and 46. *Will go into exile:* see also Isa.46.2.

and the flavour stays unchanged.

12 Therefore the days are coming, says
the LORD,
when I will send men to tilt the jars;
they shall tilt them
and empty his vessels and smash his
jars;
13 and Moab shall be betrayed by
Kemosh,
as Israel was betrayed by Bethel,
a god in whom he trusted.

14 How can you say, 'We are warriors
and men valiant in battle'?
15 The spoiler of Moab and her cities
has come up,
and the flower of her army goes
down to the slaughter.

This is the very word of the King whose
name is the LORD of Hosts.

16 The downfall of Moab is near at
hand,
disaster rushes swiftly upon him.
17 Grieve for him, all you his
neighbours
and all you who acknowledge him,
and say, 'Alas! The commander's
staff is broken,
broken is the baton of honour.'
18 Come down from your place of
honour,
sit on the thirsty ground, you natives
of Dibon;
for the spoiler of Moab has come
upon you
and destroyed your citadels.
19 You that live in Aroer, stand on the
roadside and watch,
ask the fugitives, the man running,
the woman escaping,
ask them, 'What has happened?'

20 Moab is reduced to shame and
dismay:
howl and shriek,
proclaim by the Arnon that Moab is
despoiled,
21 and that judgement has come to the

tableland, to Holon and Jahazah, Mephaath and Dibon, Nebo and Beth- 22
diblathaim and Kiriathaim, Beth-gamul, 23
Beth-meon, Kirioth and Bozrah, and to 24
all the cities of Moab far and near.

Moab's horn is hacked off 25
and his strong arm is broken,
says the LORD.

Make Moab drunk—he has defied 26
the LORD—
until he overflows with his vomit
and even he becomes a butt for
derision.
But was Israel ever your butt? 27
Was he ever in company with
thieves,
that whenever you spoke of him you
should shake your head?
Leave your cities, you inhabitants of 28
Moab,
and find a home among the crags;
become like a dove which nests
in the rock-face at the mouth of a
cavern.

We have heard of Moab's pride, and 29
proud indeed he is,
proud, presumptuous, overbearing,
insolent.
I know his arrogance, says the LORD; 30
his boasting is false, false are his
deeds.
Therefore I will howl over Moab 31
and cry in anguish at the fate of
every soul in Moab;
I will moan over the men of
Kir-heres.
I will weep for you more than I 32
wept for Jazer,
O vine of Sibmah
whose branches spread out to the
sea
and stretch as far as Jazer.
The despoiler has fallen on your fruit
and on your vintage,
gladness and joy are taken away 33
from the meadows of Moab,
and I have stopped the flow of wine
from the vats;

12: *Smash his jars:* see 13.12–14. 13: *Bethel:* see Gen.31.13. Here the word is a name for a
deity rather than the place of a sanctuary. The betrayal alluded to is obscure. 17–24: Further
sympathy for Moab. *Alas!:* the same Heb. word (*echah*) begins Lamentations. 25–39: Again
the hostile words are interspersed with sympathetic murmurs (see vv. 31–32,34). 27: *Shake your
head:* this motion is a sign of scorn. 29–33,36: These verses largely echo those of Isa.16.6–11.

nor shall shout follow shout from the harvesters—not one shout,

11 Heshbon and Elealeh utter cries of anguish which are heard in Jahaz; the sound carries from Zoar to Horonaim and Eglath-shelishiyah; for the waters of Nimrim have become a desolate **35** waste. In Moab I will stop their sacrificing at hill-shrines and burning of offerings to their gods, says the LORD. **36** Therefore my heart wails for Moab like a reed-pipe, wails like a pipe for the men of Kir-heres. Their hard-**37** earned wealth has vanished. Every man's head is shorn in mourning, every beard shaved, every hand gashed, and **38** every waist girded with sackcloth. On Moab's roofs and in her broad streets nothing is heard but lamentation; for I have broken Moab like a useless thing.[a]
39 Moab in her dismay has shamefully turned to flight. Moab has become a butt of derision and a cause of dismay to all her neighbours.
40 For the LORD has spoken:

A vulture shall swoop down
and spread out his wings over Moab.
41 The towns are captured, the
    strongholds taken;
on that day the spirit of Moab's
    warriors shall fail
like the spirit of a woman in
    childbirth.
42 Then Moab shall be destroyed, no
    more to be a nation;
for he defied the LORD.
43 The hunter's scare, the pit, and the
    trap
threaten all who dwell in Moab,
    says the LORD.
44 If a man runs from the scare
    he will fall into the pit;
if he climbs out of the pit
    he will be caught in the trap.
All this will I bring on Moab in the
    year of their reckoning.
    This is the very word of the LORD.

In the shadow of Heshbon the   **45**
    fugitives stand helpless;
for fire has blazed out from
    Heshbon,
flames have shot out from the
    palace of Sihon;
they devour the homeland of Moab
    and the country of the sons of
    tumult.
Alas for you, Moab! the people of   **46**
    Kemosh have vanished,
for your sons are taken into
    captivity
and your daughters led away
    captive.
Yet in days to come I will restore   **47**
    Moab's fortunes.
    This is the very word of the LORD.

Here ends the sentence on Moab.

Of the people of Ammon. Thus says **49**
the LORD:

Has Israel no sons? Has he no heir?
Why has Milcom inherited the land
    of Gad,
and why do his people live in the
    cities of Gad?
Look, therefore, a time is coming,   **2**
    says the LORD,
when I will make Rabbath Ammon
    hear the battle-cry,
when it will become a desolate
    mound of ruins
and its villages will be burnt to
    ashes,
and Israel shall disinherit those who
    disinherited him,
    says the LORD.

Howl, Heshbon, for Ai is despoiled. **3**
    Cry aloud, you villages round
    Rabbath Ammon,
put on sackcloth and beat your
    breast,
and score your bodies with gashes.

z and: prob. rdg., cp. Isa. 15. 4; Heb. as far as.
a Prob. rdg.; Heb. adds says the LORD.

34: Sites in Moab. **36:** *Kir-heres* (Kir-hareseth) ancient capital of Moab. **40–46:** Moab is to undergo irretrievable disaster. With vv. 43–44 compare Isa.24.17–18. **45–46:** On Moab's sad plight, see also Num.21.28–29. **45:** *Heshbon:* a border city. It is here in Moab, but in 49.3 it is in Ammon. *Sihon:* a Moabite king (Num.21.21–31). *Sons of tumult:* see Num.24.17b.
   49.1–39: The seizure by the people of Ammon of Israelite territory will not go unpunished. The exact occasion is not known. **1:** *Gad:* on Ammon's northern border, east of the Jordan. *Milcom:* the Ammonite god. **2:** *Rabbath Ammon:* the capital city, modern Amman. **3:** *Heshbon:* see

For Milcom will go into exile,
and with him his priests and officers.

4 Why do you boast of your resources,
you whose resources are melting
away,
you wayward people who trust in
your arsenals,
and say, 'Who will dare attack me?'

5 Beware, I am bringing fear upon you
from every side,[b]
and every one of you shall be driven
headlong
with no man to round up the
stragglers.

6 Yet after this I will restore the
fortunes of Ammon.
This is the very word of the LORD.

7 Of Edom. The LORD of Hosts has
said:

Is wisdom no longer to be found in
Teman?
Have her sages no skill in counsel?
Has their wisdom decayed?

8 The people of Dedan have turned
and fled
and taken refuge in remote places;
for I will bring Esau's calamity
upon him
when his day of reckoning comes.

9[c] When the vintagers come to you
they will surely leave gleanings;
and if thieves raid your early crop
in the night,
they will take only as much as
they want.

10 But I have ransacked Esau's treasure,
I have uncovered his hiding-places,
and he has nowhere to conceal
himself;
his children, his kinsfolk and his
neighbours are despoiled;
there is no one to help him.

11 What! am I to save alive your
fatherless children?
Are your widows to trust in me?

For the LORD has spoken: Those 12
who were not doomed to drink the cup
shall drink it none the less. Are you
alone to go unpunished? You shall not
go unpunished; you shall drink it. For 13
by my life, says the LORD, Bozrah shall
become a horror and reproach, a byword and a thing of ridicule; and all
her towns shall be a byword for ever.

When a herald was sent among the 14[d]
nations, crying,
'Gather together and march against
her,
rouse yourselves for battle',
I heard this message from the LORD:

Look, I make you the least of all 15
nations,
an object of all men's contempt.
Your overbearing arrogance and 16
your insolent heart
have led you astray,
you who haunt the crannies among
the rocks
and keep your hold on the heights
of the hills.
Though you build your nest high as
a vulture,
thence I will bring you down.
This is the very word of the LORD.
Edom shall become a scene of 17
horror,
all who pass that way shall be
horror-struck
and shall jeer in derision at the blows
she has borne,
overthrown like Sodom and Gomor- 18
rah and their neighbours,[e]
says the LORD.
No man shall live there,
no mortal make a home in her.
Look, like a lion coming up 19
from Jordan's dense thickets to the
perennial pastures,

b *Prob. rdg.; Heb. adds* says the Lord GOD of Hosts.
c *Verses 9 and 10: cp.* Obad. 5, 6.
d *Verses 14–16: cp.* Obad. 1–4.   e *Or* inhabitants.

48.45 n. **6**: See, similarly, 48.47. **7–22**: *Of Edom:* except for her "arrogance" (v. 16) Edom's
offense is not here specified. After the fall of Jerusalem and during the early Persian Period
(sixth century), the Nabateans, nomadic peoples from Arabia, invaded and pushed the Edomites
westward into southern Judah. **7**: "Men of the east," including *Edom,* were widely reputed for
their *wisdom;* see 1 Kgs.4.29–30. *Teman:* an Edomite city, at times used synonymously with
Edom. **8**: *Esau:* the ancestor of Edom; see Gen.25.29–30;36.1. **9**: *Vintagers:* harvesters of
grapes. **10**: *Ransacked:* see Obad.5–6. **12**: *Those who were not doomed:* i.e. not specifically
"sentenced"; probably they are included in the category of: "all that inhabit the earth" in
25.29. **13**: *Bozrah:* a fortress city in the northern part of Edom. **14–16**: See Obad.1–4. **18**:
Sodom and Gomorrah and their neighbours: see Deut.29.23. **19**: *From Jordan's dense thickets:*

in a moment I will chase every one
away
and round up the choicest of*f* her
rams.

For who is like me? Who is my
equal?
What shepherd can stand his ground
before me?

20   Therefore listen to the LORD's whole
purpose against Edom and all his plans
against the people of Teman:

The young ones of the flock shall
be carried off,
and their pasture shall be horrified
at their fate.
21   At the sound of their fall the land
quakes;
it cries out, and the cry is heard at
the Red Sea.*g*

22   A vulture shall soar and swoop
down
and spread out his wings over
Bozrah,
and on that day the spirit of Edom's
warriors shall fail
like the spirit of a woman in
labour.

23   Of Damascus.

Hamath and Arpad are in
confusion,
for they have heard news of
disaster;
they are tossed up and down in
anxiety
like the unresting sea.
24   Damascus has lost heart and turns to
flight;
trembling has seized her,
the pangs of childbirth have gripped
her.
25   How forlorn is the town of joyful
song,
the city of gladness!
26   Therefore her young men shall fall in
her streets

and all her warriors lie still in death
that day
This is the very word of the LORD
of Hosts.
Then will I kindle a fire against the   27
wall of Damascus
and it shall consume the palaces of
Ben-hadad.

Of Kedar and the royal princes*h* of   28
Hazer which Nebuchadrezzar king of
Babylon subdued. The LORD has said:

Come, attack Kedar,
despoil the Arabs of the east.
Carry off their tents and their flocks,   29
their tent-hangings and all their
vessels,
drive off their camels too,
and a cry shall go up: 'Terror let
loose!'
Flee, flee; make haste,   30
take refuge in remote places, O
people of Hazer,
for the king of Babylon has laid his
plans
and formed a design against you,
says the LORD.
Come, let us attack a nation living at   31
peace,
in fancied security,
with neither gates nor bars,
sufficient to themselves.
Their camels shall be carried off as   32
booty,
their vast herds of cattle as
plunder;
I will scatter them before the wind to
roam the fringes of the desert,*i*
and bring ruin upon them from
every side.
Hazer shall become a haunt of   33
wolves,
for ever desolate;
no man shall live there,
no mortal make a home in her.
This is the very word of the LORD.

f the choicest of: prob. rdg.; Heb. who is chosen?
g Or the Sea of Reeds.
h royal princes: or kingdom.
*i them . . . desert: or to the wind those who clip the
hair on their temples.*

God, like a lion, attacks Edom's *rams*, her leaders. **23–27:** *Damascus:* the capital of Syria.
23: Except in v. 27, which is quoted from Amos 1.4, no reason for, or source of, the *disaster*
is given. *Hamath* and *Arpad* are neighboring cities. *Ben-hadad:* a royal Syrian name. **28–33:**
Kedar: an area in the east of Palestine. **28:** *Hazer:* a place unknown, but apparently in, or
near, Kedar. **29:** *'Terror let loose!':* see 6.25; 46.5. **30:** See 25.9. **31:** See Ezek.38.11; Deut.33.28.
32: See Ezek.12.14,15. **33:** *Wolves:* the exact identification is uncertain here and in 10.22.

34 This came to the prophet Jeremiah
on the word of the LORD concerning
Elam, at the beginning of the reign of
35 Zedekiah king of Judah: Thus says the
LORD of Hosts:

Listen, I will break the bow of
Elam,
the chief weapon of their might;
36 I will bring four winds against Elam
from the four quarters of heaven;
I will scatter them before these four
winds,
and there shall be no nation
to which the exiles from Elam shall
not come.
37 I will break Elam before their foes,
before those who are bent on
their destruction;
I will vent my anger upon them in
disaster;
I will harry them with the sword
until I make an end of them.
38 Then I will set my throne in Elam,
and there I will destroy the king and
his officers.
This is the very word of the LORD.
39 Yet in days to come I will restore the
fortunes of Elam.
This is the very word of the LORD.

50 The word which the LORD spoke
concerning Babylon, concerning the
land of the Chaldaeans, through the
prophet Jeremiah:

2 Declare and proclaim among the
nations,
keep nothing back, spread the news:
Babylon is taken,
Bel is put to shame, Marduk is in
despair;
the idols of Babylon are put to
shame,
her false gods are in despair.

3 For a nation out of the north has
fallen upon her,
they will make her land a desolate
waste
where neither man nor beast shall
live.

4 In those days, at that time, says the
LORD, the people of Israel and the
people of Judah shall come together
and go in tears to seek the LORD their
5 God; they shall ask after Zion, turning
their faces towards her, and they shall
come and join themselves to the LORD
in an everlasting covenant which shall
not be forgotten.
6 My people were lost sheep, whose
shepherds let them stray and run wild
on the mountains; they went from
mountain to hill and forgot their fold.
7 Whoever found them devoured them,
and their enemies said, 'We incur no
guilt, because they have sinned against
the LORD, the LORD who is the true
goal and the hope of all their fathers.'

8 Flee from Babylon, from the land
of the Chaldaeans;
go forth, and be like he-goats leading
the flock.
9 For I will stir up a host of mighty
nations
and bring them against Babylon,
marshalled against her from a
northern land;
and from the north she shall be
captured.
Their arrows shall be like a practised
warrior
who never comes back empty-
handed;
10 the Chaldaeans shall be plundered,
and all who plunder them shall take
their fill.
This is the very word of the LORD.

34–39: *Elam:* a country east of Babylonia, bordering on Media and Persia, and a protec-
torate of Media, but having no known contact with Judah. **34:** *Zedekiah:* he began to reign
around 597 B.C. **38:** *Throne:* see also 1.15. **39:** A comforting addition.
  50.1–51.64: Concerning Babylon. Around 550 B.C. her capital fell before Cyrus the Persian.
In part, chs. 50–51 anticipate those events, without, however, naming Persia, and in part they
look back to them, but it is not always clear whether the intention is future or past. **2:** Babylon
is taken. But in vv. 3 and 9 the land is yet to be conquered. *Bel,* "great god," is a title of
Marduk (Merodach), god of the city of Babylon. **3:** *A nation out of the north:* Media lay north
of Babylon, Persia to the southeast: by 539, Cyrus of Persia had incorporated the northern
peoples into his expanding empire. **4–7:** The reunion of *Israel and . . . Judah:* these verses
interrupt the material concerning Babylon. **8:** *Flee from Babylon:* this is addressed to captive
Judeans. **9–10:** God assembles the nations of the north; see 51.27–28 n. The time is future.

11 You ravaged my patrimony; but
    though you rejoice and exult,
  though you run free like a heifer
    after threshing,
  though you neigh like a stallion,
12 your mother shall be cruelly
    disgraced,
  she who bore you shall be put to
    shame.
    Look at her, the mere rump of the
    nations,
  a wilderness, parched and desert,
13 unpeopled through the wrath of the
    LORD,
  nothing but a desolate waste;
  all who pass by Babylon shall be
    horror-struck
  and jeer in derision at the sight of
    her wounds.

14 Marshal your forces against Babylon,
    on every side,
  you whose bows are ready strung;
  shoot at her, spare no arrows.
15 Shout in triumph over her, she has
    thrown up her hands,
  her bastions are down, her walls
    demolished;
  this is the vengeance of the LORD.
    Take vengeance on her;
  as she has done, so do to her.
16 Destroy every sower in Babylon,
  every reaper with his sickle at
    harvest-time.
  Before the cruel sword every man
    will go back to his people,
  every man flee to his own land.

17 Israel is a scattered flock
    harried and chased by lions:
  as the king of Assyria was the first
    to feed on him,
  so the king of Babylon was the last
    to gnaw his bones.

18 Therefore the LORD of Hosts the God
  of Israel says this:

    I will punish the king of Babylon
    and his country

  as I have punished the king of
    Assyria.
19 I will bring Israel back to his
    pasture,
  and he shall graze on Carmel and
    Bashan;
  in the hills of Ephraim and Gilead he
    shall eat his fill.

20 In those days, says the LORD, when
that time comes, search shall be made
for the iniquity of Israel but there shall
be none, and for the sin of Judah but it
shall not be found; for those whom I
leave as a remnant I will forgive.

21   Attack the land of Merathaim;
  attack it and the inhabitants of
    Pekod;
  put all to the sword and destroy
    them,
  and do whatever I bid you.
    This is the very word of the LORD.

22 Hark, the sound of war in the land
    and great destruction!
23 See how the hammer of all the
    earth
  is hacked and broken in pieces,
  how Babylon has become
    a horror among the nations.
24 O Babylon, you have laid a snare to
    be your own undoing;
  you have been trapped, all unawares;
  there you are, you are caught,
    because you have challenged the
    LORD.
25 The LORD has opened his arsenal
    and brought out the weapons of
    his wrath;
  for this is work for the Lord the GOD
    of Hosts
  in the land of the Chaldaeans.
26 Her harvest-time has come:
  throw open her granaries,[j] pile her
    in heaps;
  destroy her, let no survivor be left.
27 Put all her warriors to the sword;
  let them be led to the slaughter.

    j Or cattle-pens.

11: *My patrimony:* the land of Judah. **12:** *Your mother:* Babylon, the capital city. **16:** *Every man:* from a foreign land. **17–20:** Concern for Israel and Judah; see vv. 4–7. God has already dealt with Assyria which had conquered Israel; now he will punish Babylonia. He will bring Israel back to its land, forgiven. **19:** *Carmel and Bashan . . . Ephraim and Gilead:* areas west and east of the Jordan, formerly occupied by the Northern Kingdom. **21:** The attention reverts to Babylonia. **23:** The conquests of Babylon, *the hammer of all the earth,* have been ended.

Woe upon them! for their time has
come,
their day of reckoning.
28 I hear the fugitives escaping from the
land of Babylon
to proclaim in Zion the vengeance of
the LORD our God.

29 Let your arrows be heard whistling
against Babylon,
all you whose bows are ready
strung.
Pitch your tents all around her
so that no one escapes.
Pay her back for all her misdeeds;
as she has done, so do to her,
for she has insulted the LORD the
Holy One of Israel.
30 Therefore her young men shall fall
in her streets,
and all her warriors shall lie still in
death that day.
This is the very word of the LORD.

31 I am against you, insolent city;
for your time has come, your day of
reckoning.
This is the very word of the Lord
GOD of Hosts.
32 Insolence shall stumble and fall
and no one shall lift her up,
and I will kindle fire in the heath
around her
and it shall consume everything
round about.

33 The LORD of Hosts has said this:

The peoples of Israel and Judah
together are oppressed;
their captors hold them firmly and
refuse to release them.
34 But they have a powerful
advocate,
whose name is the LORD of
Hosts;
he himself will plead their cause,
bringing distress on Babylon and
turmoil on its people.

35 A sword hangs over the Chaldaeans,

over the people of Babylon, her
officers and her wise men,
says the LORD.
A sword over the false prophets,   36
and they are made fools,
a sword over her warriors, and they
despair,
a sword over her horses and her   37
chariots
and over all the rabble within her,
and they shall become like
women;
a sword over her treasures, and they
shall be plundered,
a sword over her waters, and they   38
shall dry up;
for it is a land of idols
that glories in its dreaded gods.*k*

Therefore marmots and jackals shall   39
skulk in it, desert-owls shall haunt it,
nevermore shall it be inhabited by men
and no one shall dwell in it through all
the ages. As when God overthrew   40
Sodom and Gomorrah and their neighbours,*l* says the LORD, no man shall
live there, no mortal make a home in
her.

See, a people is coming from the   41
north, a great nation,
mighty*m* kings rouse themselves from
earth's farthest corners;
armed with bow and sabre, they are   42
cruel and pitiless;
bestriding horses, they sound like the
thunder of the sea;
they are like men arrayed for battle
against you, Babylon.
The king of Babylon has heard news   43
of them
and his hands hang limp;
agony grips him, anguish as of a
woman in labour.
Look, like a lion coming up   44
from Jordan's dense thickets to the
perennial pastures,
in a moment I will chase every one
away

k dreaded gods: or dire portents.
l Or inhabitants.
m Or many.

28: At the end the Heb. adds "vengeance for his temple," as in 51.11. **40,44–46:** These verses
quote 49.18–21, substituting Babylon here for Edom there. **41–43:** These verses quote 6.22–24
almost exactly, here substituting Babylon for Zion. **44:** See vv. 40,44–46 n. God brings the Medes
(51.11) to destroy Babylon and avenge the destruction of his Temple; see Isa.13.17–19. After
Media's defeat about 550 B.C., by Cyrus of Persia, the latter was a real threat to Babylon.

and round up the choicest of[n] the
rams.
For who is like me? Who is my
equal?
What shepherd can stand his ground
before me?

45 Therefore listen to the LORD's whole
purpose against Babylon and all his
plans against the land of the Chaldaeans:

The young ones of the flock shall be
carried off
and their pasture shall be horrified at
their fate.
46 At the sound of the capture of
Babylon
the land quakes and her cry is heard
among the nations.

51 For thus says the LORD:

I will raise a destroying wind
against Babylon and those who live
in Kambul,[o]
2 and I will send winnowers to
Babylon,
who shall winnow her and empty
her land;
for they shall assail her on all sides
on the day of disaster.
3 How shall the archer then string his
bow
or put on his coat of mail?

Spare none of her young men, destroy
all her host,
4 and let them fall dead in the land of
the Chaldaeans,
pierced through in her streets.
5 Israel and Judah are not left widowed
by their God, by the LORD of Hosts;
but the land of the Chaldaeans is
full of guilt,
condemned by the Holy One of
Israel.

6 Flee out of Babylon, every man for
himself,
or you will be struck down for
her sin;

for this is the LORD's day of
vengeance,
and he is paying her full
recompense.
7 Babylon has been a gold cup in the
LORD's hand
to make all the earth drunk;
the nations have drunk of her wine,
and that has made them mad.
8 Babylon falls suddenly and is broken.
Howl over her,
fetch balm for her wound;
perhaps she will be healed.
9 We would have healed Babylon, but
she would not be[p] healed.
Leave her and let us be off, each to
his own country;
for her doom reaches to heaven
and mounts up to the skies.
10 The LORD has made our innocence
plain to see;
come, let us proclaim in Zion
what the LORD our God has done.

11 Sharpen the arrows, fill the quivers.
The LORD has roused the spirit of the
king of the Medes;
for the LORD's purpose against
Babylon is to destroy it,
and his vengeance is the avenging of
his temple.
12 Raise the standard against Babylon's
walls,
mount a strong guard, post a watch,
set an ambush;
for the LORD has both planned and
carried out
what he threatened to do to the
people of Babylon.
13 O opulent city, standing beside great
waters,
your end has come, your destiny is
certain.
14 The LORD of Hosts has sworn by
himself, saying,
Once I filled you with men, countless
as locusts,
yet a song of triumph shall be
chanted over you.

n the choicest of: *prob. rdg.; Heb.* who is chosen?
o Kambul: *prob. rdg.; Heb.* the heart of my opponents.
p would not be: *or* was not.

51.1: *Kambul:* Chaldea. 5: *Not left widowed by their God:* the same metaphor is in Isa.54.4–6.
6: *Flee out of Babylon:* this is addressed to the foreigners and the mercenaries; see 46.16 n.
7: *Cup:* see 25.15–16. 10: *Our innocence:* the words are spoken by the Judean exiles; see 50.28.
11: *The avenging of his temple:* see 50.28 n. 13: *Great waters* refers to the Euphrates river.

15[q] God made the earth by his power,
    fixed the world in place by his
      wisdom,
    unfurled the skies by his
      understanding.
16 At the thunder of his voice the waters
    in heaven are amazed;[r]
    he brings up the mist from the ends
      of the earth,
    he opens rifts[s] for the rain
    and brings the wind out of his
      storehouses.
17 All men are brutish and ignorant,
    every goldsmith is discredited by his
      idol;
    for the figures he casts are a sham,
    there is no breath in them.
18 They are worth nothing, mere
      mockeries,
    which perish when their day of
      reckoning comes.
19 God, Jacob's creator, is not like
      these;
    for he is the maker of all.
    Israel is the people he claims as
      his own;
    the LORD of Hosts is his name.

20 You are my battle-axe, my weapon
      of war;
    with you I will break nations in pieces,
    and with you I will destroy kingdoms.
21 With you I will break horse and
      rider,
    with you I will break chariot and
      rider,
22 with you I will break man and
      woman,
    with you I will break young and old,
    with you I will break young man and
      maiden,
23 with you I will break shepherd and
      flock,
    with you I will break ploughman and
      team,
    with you I will break viceroys and
      governors.
24 So will I repay Babylon and the
      people of Chaldaea
    for all the wrong which they did in

Zion in your sight,
    This is the very word of the LORD.

I am against you, O destroying   25
    mountain,[t]
you who destroy the whole earth,
and I will stretch out my hand
    against you
and send you tumbling from
    your terraces
and make you a burnt-out mountain.
No stone of yours shall be used as a   26
    corner-stone,
    no stone for a foundation;
but you shall be desolate, for ever
    waste.
    This is the very word of the LORD.

Raise a standard in the land,[u]   27
blow the trumpet among the nations,
hallow the nations for war against
    her,
summon the kingdoms of Ararat,
    Minni, and Ashkenaz,
appoint a commander-in-chief
    against her,
bring up the horses like a dark
    swarm of locusts;[v]
hallow the nations for war against   28
    her,
the king of the Medes, his viceroys
    and governors,
and all the lands of his realm.
The earth quakes and writhes;   29
for the LORD's designs against
    Babylon are fulfilled,
to make the land of Babylon desolate
    and unpeopled.
Babylon's warriors have given up   30
    the fight,
    they skulk in the forts;
their courage has failed, they have
    become like women.
Her buildings are set on fire, the bars
    of her gates broken.
Runner speeds to meet runner,   31

q Verses 15–19: cp. 10. 12–16.
r At the thunder . . . amazed: prob. rdg.; Heb. At
the sound of his giving tumult of waters in heaven.
s rifts: prob. rdg.; Heb. lightnings.
t Or O Mount of the Destroyer.
u Or earth.   v Or hoppers.

15–19: Note Tfn. *q.* **20–24**: Continues vv. 1–14. The Medes (or Persians) are God's *weapon* against
Babylon. **25–33**: God summons a company of nations to avenge his people and destroy
Babylon. **25**: *Mountain*: Babylon, so called because of a landmark, a terraced tower (ziggurat)
of the Marduk temple there. **27–28**: *Ararat, Minni, and Ashkenaz:* they were far to the north.
Defeated by the Medes, they were later added to the empire of Cyrus. The Heb. term for
commander-in-chief is a loan word from the Babylonian. **31**: Relay *runners* report to the king,

messenger to meet messenger,
bringing news to the king of Babylon
that every quarter of his city is taken,
32 the river-crossings are seized,
the guard-towers set on fire
and the garrison stricken with panic.

33 For the LORD of Hosts the God of Israel
has spoken:

Babylon is like a threshing-floor when
it is trodden;
soon, very soon, harvest-time will
come.

34 'Nebuchadrezzar king of Babylon
has devoured me
and sucked me dry,
he has set me aside like an empty
jar.
Like a dragon he has gulped me
down;
he has filled his maw with my
delicate flesh
and spewed me up.
35 On Babylon be the violence done to
me,
the vengeance taken upon me!',
Zion's people shall say.
'My blood be upon the
Chaldaeans!',
Jerusalem shall say.

36 Therefore the LORD says:

I will plead your cause, I will avenge
you;
I will dry up her sea*w* and make her
waters fail;
37 and Babylon shall become a heap of
ruins, a haunt of wolves,
a scene of horror and derision, with
no inhabitant.

38 Together they roar like young lions,
they growl like the whelps of a
lioness.
39 I will cause their drinking bouts to
end in fever
and make them so drunk that they
will writhe and toss,

then sink into unending sleep,
never to wake.
This is the very word of the LORD.
I will bring them like lambs to the
slaughter,
rams and he-goats together.
Sheshak*x* is captured, 41
the pride of the whole earth taken;
Babylon has become a horror
amongst the nations!
The sea has surged over Babylon, 42
she is covered by its roaring
waves.
Her cities have become waste places, 43
a land dried up and desert,
a land in whose cities no man lives
and through which no mortal travels.
I will punish Bel in Babylon 44
and make him bring up what he has
swallowed;
nations shall never again come
streaming to him.
The wall of Babylon has fallen;
come out of her, O my people, 45
and let every man save himself
from the anger of the LORD.
Then beware of losing heart, 46
fear no rumours spread abroad in the
land,
as rumour follows rumour,
each year a new one:
violence on earth and ruler against
ruler.
Therefore a time is coming 47
when I will punish Babylon's
idols,
and all her land shall be put to
shame,
and all her slain shall lie fallen in
her midst.
Heaven and earth and all that is in 48
them
shall sing in triumph over
Babylon;
for marauders from the north shall
overrun her.
This is the very word of the LORD.
Babylon must fall for the sake of*y* 49
Israel's slain,

w *Possibly the Euphrates.*
x *A name for Babylon.*
y *for the sake of: prob. rdg.; Heb. om.*

Nabonidus, who was probably away at his oasis at Tema in Arabia when Babylon fell. **33:**
Trodden: grain was separated from straw by the treading of animals (Deut.25.4). **34–35:**
Jerusalem's plea. **36–58:** God responds. Babylon is doomed (if not already taken, vv. 41,44).
41: *Sheshak:* Babylonia. **44:** *Bel:* also called Marduk, the god of Babylon; see Isa.46.1–2.
45: *Come out . . . my people:* from your captivity; compare Isa.48.20. **48:** *From the north:*

as the slain of all the world fell for
the sake of Babylon.

50 You who have escaped from her
    sword, off with you, do not
    linger.
Remember the LORD from afar
and call Jerusalem to mind.

51 We are put to shame by the
    reproaches we have heard,
and our faces are covered with
    confusion:
strangers have entered the sacred
    courts of the LORD's house.

52 A time is coming therefore, says the
    LORD,
when I will punish her idols,
and all through the land there shall
    be the groaning of the wounded.

53 Though Babylon should reach to the
    skies
and make her high towers
    inaccessible,
I will send marauders to overrun her.
    This is the very word of the LORD.

54 Hark, cries of agony from Babylon!
Sounds of destruction from the
    land of the Chaldaeans!

55 For the LORD is despoiling Babylon
and will silence the hum of the city,
before the advancing wave that
    booms and roars
    like mighty waters.

56 For marauders march on Babylon
    herself,
her warriors are captured and their
    bows are broken;
for the LORD, a God of retribution,
    will repay in full.

57 I will make her princes and her wise
    men drunk,
her viceroys and governors and
    warriors,
and they shall sink into unending
    sleep, never to wake.
This is the very word of the King,
whose name is the LORD of Hosts.

The LORD of Hosts says: 58

The walls of broad Babylon shall be
    razed to the ground,
her lofty gates shall be set on fire.
Worthless now is the thing for which
    the nations toiled;
the peoples wore themselves out for
    a mere nothing.

The instructions given by the prophet 59
Jeremiah to the quartermaster Seraiah
son of Neriah and grandson of Mahseiah, when he went to Babylon with
Zedekiah king of Judah in the fourth
year of his reign.
Jeremiah, having written down in a^z 60
book^a a full description of the disaster
which would come upon Babylon, said 61
to Seraiah, 'When you come to Babylon,
look at this, read it all and then say, 62
"Thou, O LORD, hast declared thy
purpose to destroy this place and leave
it with no one living in it, man or
beast; it shall be desolate, for ever
waste." When you have finished reading 63
the book, tie a stone to it and throw it
into the Euphrates, and then say, "So 64
shall Babylon sink, never to rise again
after the disaster which I shall bring
upon her." '

Thus far are the collected sayings of
Jeremiah.

Historical note about the fall of Jerusalem

ZEDEKIAH WAS TWENTY-ONE YEARS OLD **52**₁^b
when he came to the throne, and he
reigned in Jerusalem for eleven years;
his mother was Hamutal daughter of

z *Or one.*
a *Prob. rdg.; Heb. adds* all these things which are written concerning Babylon.
b *Verses 1–27: cp. 39. 1–10 and 2 Kgs. 24. 18–25. 21.*

---

vv. 27–28 n. **51:** *We:* the speaker and his fellow exiles. **53:** *High towers:* see v. 25 n. and Gen.11.4 n.
56: Israel's *God of retribution* will repay Babylon for her cruelty to his people; compare
Isa.47.6. **59–64:** A curse on Babylon. **59:** *Seraiah:* he appears to have been a brother to
Jeremiah's disciple Baruch; see 32.12. *With king Zedekiah:* such a journey is unknown. The
king may have gone in person to pay a vassal's homage to Nebuchadrezzar; see 29.3. **63:** *Throw
it into the Euphrates:* set the process in motion. Compare the rinsing of the written curse in
Num.5.23. **64b:** *Thus far...Jeremiah:* this half verse, apparently, once followed v. 58.
    **52.1–34: An appendix recapitulating Zedekiah's reign, Jerusalem's fall, deportations, Je-
hoichin's release.** Only vv. 28–30 are new; the remainder of this chapter is taken almost verbatim from, one may see, 2 Kgs.24.18–25.21,27–30. Vv. 4–16 occur also in Jer.39.1–2,4–10.

2 Jeremiah of Libnah. He did what was wrong in the eyes of the Lord, as 3 Jehoiakim had done. Jerusalem and Judah so angered the Lord that in the end he banished them from his sight; and Zedekiah rebelled against the king of Babylon.

4 In the ninth year of his reign, in the tenth month, on the tenth day of the month, Nebuchadrezzar king of Babylon advanced with all his army against Jerusalem, invested it and erected watch-towers against it on every side; 5 the siege lasted till the eleventh year of 6 King Zedekiah. In the fourth month of that year, on the ninth day of the month, when famine was severe in the city and there was no food for the 7 common people, the city was thrown open. When Zedekiah king of Judah saw this, he and*c* all his armed escort left the city and fled by night through the gate called Between the Two Walls, near the king's garden. They escaped towards the Arabah, although the Chaldaeans were surrounding the city. 8 But the Chaldaean army pursued the king and overtook him in the lowlands of Jericho; and all his company was 9 dispersed. The king was seized and brought before the king of Babylon at Riblah in the land of Hamath, where he 10 pleaded his case before him. The king of Babylon slew Zedekiah's sons before his eyes; he also put to death all the 11 princes of Judah in Riblah. Then the king of Babylon put Zedekiah's eyes out, bound him with fetters of bronze, brought him to Babylon and committed him to prison till the day of his death.

12 In the fifth month, on the tenth day of the month, in the nineteenth year of Nebuchadrezzar king of Babylon, Nebuzaradan, captain of the king's 13 bodyguard,*d* came to Jerusalem and set fire to the house of the Lord and the royal palace; all the houses in the city, including the mansion of Geda-14 liah,*e* were burnt down. The Chaldaean forces with the captain of the guard pulled down the walls all round Jeru-15 salem. *f*Nebuzaradan captain of the guard deported the rest of the people left in the city, those who had deserted to the king of Babylon and any re-maining artisans. The captain of the 16 guard left only the weakest class of people to be vine-dressers and labourers.

The Chaldaeans broke up the pillars 17 of bronze in the house of the Lord, the trolleys, and the sea of bronze, and took the metal to Babylon. They took 18 also the pots, shovels, snuffers, tossing-bowls, saucers, and all the vessels of bronze used in the service of the temple. The captain of the guard took 19 away the precious metal, whether gold or silver, of which the cups, firepans, tossing-bowls, pots, lamp-stands, saucers, and flagons were made. The 20 bronze of the two pillars, of the one sea and of the twelve oxen supporting it, which King Solomon had made for the house of the Lord, was beyond weighing. The one pillar was eighteen cubits 21 high and twelve cubits in circumference; it was hollow and the metal was four fingers thick. It had a capital 22 of bronze, five cubits high, and a decoration of network and pomegranates ran all round it, wholly of bronze. The other pillar, with its pomegranates, was exactly like it. Ninety-six pomegranates were exposed 23 to view and there were a hundred in all on the network all round.

The captain of the guard took Seraiah 24 the chief priest and Zephaniah the deputy chief priest and the three on duty at the entrance; he took also from 25 the city a eunuch who was in charge of the fighting men, seven of those with right of access to the king who were still in the city, the adjutant-general*g* whose duty was to muster the people for war, and sixty men of the people who were still there. These Nebuzaradan 26 captain of the guard brought to the king of Babylon at Riblah. There, in the 27 land of Hamath, the king of Babylon had them flogged and put to death. So Judah went into exile from their own land.

28 These were the people deported by Nebuchadrezzar. In the seventeenth[h] year: three thousand and twenty-three
29 Judaeans. In his eighteenth year, eight hundred and thirty-two people from
30 Jerusalem; in his twenty-third year, seven hundred and forty-five Judaeans were deported by Nebuzaradan the captain of the bodyguard: all together four thousand six hundred people.

31[i] In the thirty-seventh year of the exile of Jehoiachin king of Judah, on the twenty-fifth day of the twelfth month, Evil-merodach king of Babylon in the year of his accession showed favour to Jehoiachin king of Judah. He brought him out of prison, treated him kindly 32 and gave him a seat at table above the kings with him in Babylon. So 33 Jehoiachin discarded his prison clothes and lived as a pensioner of the king for the rest of his life. For his maintenance 34 a regular daily allowance was given him by the king of Babylon as long as he lived, to the day of his death.

h Prob. rdg.; Heb. seventh.
i Verses 31–34: cp. 2 Kgs. 25. 27–30.

28–30: The dates are 588, 587, and 582 B.C. The Heb. text reads seventh, 598 B.C., but this is usually corrected to *seventeenth*, 588. The events of 582 B.C. are unknown and unrecorded; perhaps there was some aftermath to the (undated) assassination of Gedaliah (40.7–41.8). No great numbers were deported, 4600 in all. **31–34:** The same as 2 Kgs.25.27–30.

LAMENTATIONS

This collection of five carefully structured poems is unified by a common theme: lamentation over the fall of Jerusalem and its Temple to the Babylonians in 587 B.C. Each poem except the last is an alphabetic acrostic.

With dirge-type rhythm, the mood is set by a number of unnamed voices. One voice comments on the condition of the city (1.1–11b), while another is that of the city herself, whose personification heightens the pathos (1.11c–22). A third voice is that of a man who, though crushed, maintains an attitude of hope (ch. 3). At times the voice speaks in the plural, as in ch. 5. All these separate voices blend as one.

A very old tradition that Jeremiah was the author is based upon some similarities between his writings and Lamentations, but there are also profound differences; the poems have closer affinities to the national "laments," such as Pss. 44, 74, 80. The exact date after 587 and the place of composition are difficult to determine because the style and themes were used for many hundreds of years, even in Mesopotamian compositions antedating Hebrew literature.

Lamentations probably came to be used in the Temple in liturgical mourning, a practice which continues in Jewish synagogue worship today.

Sorrows of captive Zion

1 How solitary lies the city, once so
    full of people!
Once great among nations, now
    become a widow;
once queen among provinces, now
    put to forced labour!
2 Bitterly she weeps in the night,
    tears run down her cheeks;
she has no one to bring her comfort
    among all that love her;
all her friends turned traitor
    and became her enemies.
3 Judah went into the misery of exile
    and endless servitude.
Settled among the nations,
    she found no resting-place;
all her persecutors fell upon her
    in her sore straits.
4 The paths to Zion mourn,
    for none attend her sacred feasts;
all her gates are desolate.
    Her priests groan and sigh,
    her virgins are cruelly treated.
How bitter is her fate!
5 Her adversaries have become her
    masters,
    her enemies take their ease,
for the LORD has cruelly punished
    her
because of misdeeds without number;

her young children have gone,
    driven away captive by the enemy.
All majesty has vanished 6
    from the daughter of Zion.
Her princes have become like deer
    that can find no pasture
and run on, their strength all spent,
    pursued by the hunter.
Jerusalem has remembered 7
    her days of misery and wandering,[a]
when her people fell into the power
    of the adversary
and there was no one to help her.
The adversary saw and mocked
    at her fallen state.
Jerusalem had sinned greatly, 8
    and so she was treated like a filthy
    rag;
all those who had honoured her
    held her cheap,
for they had seen her nakedness.
What could she do but sigh
    and turn away?
Uncleanness clung to her skirts, 9
    and she gave no thought to her fate.
Her fall was beyond belief
and there was no one to comfort
    her.
Look, LORD, upon her misery,
    see how the enemy has triumphed.

[a] *Prob. rdg.; Heb. adds* all her treasures which have been from days of old.

1.1–22: The desolation of Zion (Jerusalem). This general lament introduces many of the themes of the book. **1:** *How:* lit. "alas, how . . . " From *great*ness to *widow*hood, from a *queen* to a slave are typical of the poet's stylistic contrasts. **3:** Even though *Judah* as a whole sometimes appears, the main focus is on Jerusalem and the Temple. **5:** *Misdeeds without number:* this theme of sin is to be contrasted with that of innocence, as in 3.52; or the sin of a specific group, as in 4.13; or the sins of the fathers, as in 5.7. **6:** *Daughter of Zion:* a term of endearment for Zion, personifying the Temple mount area. **7:** The backward look seems to come after the

10 The adversary stretched out his hand
       to seize all her treasures;
    then it was that she saw Gentiles
       entering her sanctuary,
    Gentiles forbidden by thee to enter
       the assembly, for it was thine.
11 All her people groaned,
       they begged for bread;
    they sold their treasures for food
       to give them strength again.

    Look, O Lord, and see
       how cheap I am accounted.
12 Is it of no concern to you who
       pass by?
    If only you would look and see:
    is there any agony like mine,
       like these my torments
    with which the Lord has cruelly
       punished me
    in the day of his anger?
13 He sent down fire from heaven,
       it ran through my bones;
    he spread out a net to catch my
       feet,
       and turned me back,
    he made me an example of
       desolation,
       racked with sickness all day long.
14 My transgressions were bound[b]
       upon me,
    his own hand knotted them round
       me;
    his yoke was lifted on to my neck,
       my strength failed beneath its
       weight;
    the Lord abandoned me to its hold,[c]
       and I could not stand.
15 The Lord treated with scorn
    all the mighty men within my walls;
    he marshalled rank on rank
       against me
       to crush my young warriors.
    The Lord trod down, like grapes
       in the press,
       the virgin daughter of Judah.
16 For these things I weep over my
       plight,[d]
       my eyes run with tears;

    for any to comfort me and renew
       my strength
       are far to seek;
    my sons are an example of
       desolation,
       for the enemy is victorious.

17 Zion lifted her hands in prayer,
       but there was no one to comfort
       her;
    the Lord gave Jacob's enemies the
       order
       to beset him on every side.
    Jerusalem became a filthy rag in
       their midst.

18 The Lord was in the right;
       it was I who rebelled against his
       commands.
    Listen, O listen, all you nations,
       and look on my agony:
    my virgins and my young men are
       gone into captivity.
19 I called to my lovers, they broke
       faith with me;
    my priests and my elders in the city
       went hungry and could find
       nothing,
    although they sought food for
       themselves
       to renew their strength.
20 See, Lord, how sorely I am
       distressed.
    My bowels writhe in anguish
    and my stomach turns within me,
       because I wantonly rebelled.
    The sword makes orphans in the
       streets,
       as plague does within doors.
21 Hear me when I groan
       with no one to comfort me.
    All my enemies, when they heard
       of my calamity,
    rejoiced at what thou hadst done;
    but hasten the day thou hast
       promised
       when they shall become like me.

b bound: *prob rdg.; Heb. word unknown.*
c its hold: *prob. rdg.; Heb. obscure.*
d my plight: *prob. rdg.; Heb. my eye.*

passing of many years. **10:** This verse is a stereotyped description of the enemy; see Ps. 74.4–8. **1.11c–22: The voice is now the city herself speaking. 12:** *You who pass by:* perhaps the other nations; see v. 18. **15:** *Rank on rank against me:* the role of the Lord as an enemy warrior, as in Isa.10.5–11. **17:** Here the observer in 1.1–11b again comments. **18:** The city's confession of sin; see Deut.28.15–68. *Into captivity:* see 2 Kgs.25.11. **21:** *Hasten the day:* though somewhat incongruous with v. 15, this is a call for God's wrath on the enemy, as in 3.64–66; see also Pss.60.12; 83.9–18.

22 Let all their evil deeds come before
thee;
torment them in their turn,
as thou hast tormented me
for all my transgressions;
for my sighs are many and my heart
is faint.

Zion's hope of relief after punishment

2 What darkness the Lord in his anger
has brought upon the daughter
of Zion!
He hurled down from heaven to
earth
the glory of Israel,
and did not remember in the day
of his anger
that Zion was his footstool.
2 The Lord overwhelmed without pity
all the dwellings of Jacob.
In his wrath he tore down
the strongholds of the daughter of
Judah;
he levelled with the ground and
desecrated
the kingdom and its rulers.
3 In his anger he hacked down
the horn of Israel's pride,
he withdrew his helping hand
when the enemy came on;
and he blazed in Jacob like flaming
fire
that rages far and wide.
4 In enmity he strung his bow;
he took his stand like an adversary
and with his strong arm he slew
all those who had been his delight;
he poured his fury out like fire
on the tent of the daughter of
Zion.
5 The Lord played an enemy's part
and overwhelmed Israel.
He overwhelmed all their towered
mansions
and brought down their
strongholds in ruins;

sorrow upon sorrow he brought
to the daughter of Judah.
He stripped his tabernacle as a vine 6
is stripped
and made the place of assembly
a ruin.
In Zion the LORD blotted out all
memory
of festal assembly*e* and of
sabbath;
king and priest alike he scorned
in the grimness of his anger.
The Lord spurned his own altar 7
and laid a curse upon his
sanctuary.
He delivered the walls of her
mansions
into the power of the enemy;
in the LORD's very house they
raised shouts of victory
as on a day of festival.
The LORD was minded to bring 8
down in ruins
the walls of the daughter of Zion;
he took their measure with his
line
and did not scruple to demolish
her;
he made rampart and wall lament,
and both together lay dejected.
Her gates are sunk into the earth, 9
he has shattered and broken their
bars;
her king and her rulers are among
the Gentiles,
and there is no law;
her prophets too have received
no vision from the LORD.
The elders of the daughter of 10
Zion
sit on the ground and sigh;
they have cast dust on their heads
and clothed themselves in
sackcloth;
the virgins of Jerusalem
bow their heads to the ground.

e festal assembly: or appointed seasons.

2.1–4.22: A compassionate God judges suffering Zion. Dire as the sufferings are, the Lord
will have compassion.
2.1–10: The fullness of calamity. 1: *What:* lit. "alas, how"; so too 1.1 and 4.1. The verse
reminds God of past favors, especially his partiality for the Temple, which here, and in
1 Chr.28.2, is likened to a *footstool*, a figure of affectionate comfort. **3:** *Horn:* perhaps of the
altar, as in Amos 3.14; see also Ps.75.10. **4–5:** See 1.15 n. **6:** *Blotted out all memory:* see 1.7 n.
7: *Shouts of victory:* as in Ps.74.4. **9bc:** Revelation and prophecy have ceased; compare
Mic.3.5–6.

11 My eyes are blinded with tears,
　　my bowels writhe in anguish.
In my bitterness my bile is spilt on
　　the earth
　　because of my people's wound,
when children and infants faint
　　in the streets of the town
12 and cry to their mothers,
'Where can we get corn and wine?'—
when they faint like wounded things
　　in the streets of the city,
gasping out their lives
　　in their mothers' bosom.

13 How can I cheer you? Whose
　　plight is like yours,
　　daughter of Jerusalem?
To what can I compare you for
　　your comfort,
　　virgin daughter of Zion?
For your wound gapes wide as the
　　ocean;
　　who can heal you?
14 The visions that your prophets saw
　　for you
　　were false and painted shams;
they did not bring home to you
　　your guilt
　　and so reverse your fortunes.
The visions that they saw for you
　　were delusions,
　　false and fraudulent.*f*
15 All those who pass by
　　snap their fingers at you;
they hiss and wag their heads at you,
　　daughter of Jerusalem:
'Is this the city once called Perfect
　　in beauty,
　　Joy of the whole earth?'
16 All your enemies
　　make mouths and jeer at you;
they hiss and grind their teeth,
　　saying, 'Here we are,
this is the day we have waited for;
　　we have lived to see it.'

17 The LORD has done what he planned
　　to do,
　　he has fulfilled his threat,

all that he ordained from days of
　　old.
He has demolished without pity
and let the enemy rejoice over you,
filling your adversaries with pride.
Cry with a full heart*g* to the Lord,　18
　　O wall of the daughter of Zion;
let your tears run down like a
　　torrent
　　by day and by night.
Give yourself not a moment's rest,
　　let your tears never cease.
Arise and cry aloud in the night;　19
　　at the beginning of every watch
pour out your heart like water
　　in the Lord's very presence.
Lift up your hands to him
　　for the lives of your children.*h*

Look, LORD, and see:　20
　　who is it that thou hast thus
　　tormented?
Must women eat the fruit of their
　　wombs,
　　the children they have brought
　　safely to birth?
Shall priest and prophet be slain
　　in the sanctuary of the Lord?
There in the streets young men　21
　　and old
　　lie on the ground.
My virgins and my young men
　　have fallen
by sword and by famine;
thou hast slain them in the day of
　　thy anger,
　　slaughtered them without pity.
Thou didst summon my enemies　22
　　against me from every side,
　　like men assembling for a
　　festival;
not a man escaped, not one
　　survived
　　in the day of the LORD's anger.
All whom I brought safely to birth
　　and reared
were destroyed by my enemies.

f fraudulent: *or* causing banishment.
g Cry . . . heart: *prob. rdg.; Heb.* Their heart cried.
h Prob. rdg.; Heb. adds who faint with hunger at
every street-corner.

2.11–16: An observer witnesses the distress. 12: The hunger: see 4.4–10. **13:** *Virgin:* the
figure appears also in Amos 5.2. **14:** *Your prophets:* here the false prophets, who prophesied
peace; see Jer.14.13–16. The true prophets spoke of destruction; see Jer.28.8. **15:** *All those who
pass by:* recalling the words of 1.12.
　　2.17–19: Let the city weep. 17: *All that he ordained:* compare Jer.23.20.
　　2.20–22: The city's plea to God. 21: The day of the LORD (v. 22), anticipated by many
prophets, is viewed here as having occurred; see Joel 1.14–15 n.

3 I am the man who has known
    affliction,
  I have felt the rod of his wrath.

2 It was I whom he led away and
    left to walk
  in darkness, where no light is.

3 Against me alone he has turned his
    hand,
  and so it is all day long.

4 He has wasted away my flesh and
    my skin
  and broken all my bones;

5 he has built up walls around me,
    behind and before,

6 and has cast me into a place of
    darkness
  like a man long dead.

7 He has walled me in so that I
    cannot escape,
  and weighed me down with fetters;

8 even when I cry out and call for help,
  he rejects my prayer.

9 He has barred my road with blocks
    of stone
  and tangled up my way.

10 He lies in wait for me like a bear
  or a lion lurking in a covert.

11 He has made my way refractory
    and lamed me
  and left me desolate.

12 He has strung his bow
  and made me the target for his
    arrows;

13 he has pierced my kidneys with
    shafts
  drawn from his quiver.

14 I have become a laughing-stock to
    all nations,
  the target of their mocking songs
    all day.

15 He has given me my fill of bitter
    herbs
  and made me drunk with
    wormwood.

16 He has broken my teeth on gravel;
  fed on ashes, I am racked with
    pain;

peace has gone out of my life,   17
  and I have forgotten what
  prosperity means.

Then I cry out that my strength   18
  has gone
  and so has my hope in the LORD.

The memory of my distress and   19
    my wanderings
  is[i] wormwood and gall.
Remember, O remember,   20
  and stoop down to me.[j][k]
All this I take to heart   21
  and therefore I will wait patiently:
the LORD's true love is surely not   22
    spent,[l]
  nor has his compassion failed;
they are new every morning,   23
  so great is his constancy.
The LORD, I say, is all that I have;   24
  therefore I will wait for him
    patiently.
The LORD is good to those who   25
    look for him,
  to all who seek him;
it is good to wait in patience and sigh 26
  for deliverance by the LORD.
It is good, too, for a man   27
  to carry the yoke in his youth.
Let him sit alone and sigh   28
  if it is heavy upon him;
let him lay his face in the dust,   29
  and there may yet be hope.
Let him turn his cheek to the smiter   30
  and endure full measure of abuse;
for the Lord will not cast off   31
  his servants[m] for ever.
He may punish cruelly, yet he will   32
  have compassion
  in the fullness of his love;
he does not willingly afflict   33
  or punish any mortal man.

i The memory . . . is: *or* Remember my distress and my
wanderings, the . . .
j stoop down to me: *prob. original rdg., altered in Heb.*
to I sink down.
k Remember . . . me: *or* I remember, I remember
them and sink down.
l spent: *prob. rdg.; Heb. unintelligible.*
m his servants: *prob. rdg.; Heb. om.*

3.1–66: An individual in distress bemoans his plight. See the similar themes in such psalms
of lamentation as Pss.22; 69. The individual has traditionally been identified as Jeremiah; see
Introduction.
  3.1–18: What his life has become. 1: *His wrath:* the Lord's, as in 2.4–5. **2–16:** Many metaphors
describe the techniques of the punishing God, literally inconsistent with one another, but
thematically in accord. **14:** *Laughing-stock:* see Jer.20.7.
  3.19–33: A sensitive outpouring of trust in the Lord. The positive attitude here is unique in
the book. **21:** *Wait patiently:* the idea, a key one, recurs often in this section, but not elsewhere
in the book; compare Pss.69.3; 42.5. **29:** *Hope:* equivalent to waiting. **30:** Compare Isa.50.6;
Mt.5.39.

34 To trample underfoot
any prisoner in the land,
35 to deprive a man of his rights
in defiance of the Most High,
36 to pervert justice in the courts—
such things the Lord has never
approved.

37 Who can command and it is done,
if the Lord has forbidden it?
38 Do not both bad and good proceed
from the mouth of the Most High?
39 Why should any man living
complain,
any mortal who has sinned?
40 Let us examine our ways and put
them to the test
and turn back to the LORD;
41 let us lift up our hearts, not our
hands,
to God in heaven.
42 We ourselves have sinned and
rebelled,
and thou hast not forgiven.
43 In anger thou hast turned[n] and
pursued us
and slain without pity;
44 thou hast hidden thyself behind
the clouds
beyond reach of our prayers;
45 thou hast treated us as offscouring
and refuse
among the nations.
46 All our enemies make mouths
and jeer at us.
47 Before us lie hunter's scare and pit,
devastation and ruin.
48 My eyes run with streams of water
because of my people's wound.
49 My eyes stream with unceasing tears
and refuse all comfort,
50 while the LORD in heaven looks
down
and watches my affliction,[o]
51 while the LORD torments[p] me
with the fate of all the daughters
of my city.

52 Those who for no reason were
my enemies

drove me cruelly like a bird;
53 they thrust me alive into the silent
pit,
and they closed it over me with
a stone;
54 the waters rose high above my head,
and I said, 'My end has come.'
55 But I called on thy name, O LORD,
from the depths of the pit;
56 thou heardest my voice; do not turn
a deaf ear
when I cry, 'Come to my relief.'
57 Thou wast near when I called to
thee;
thou didst say, 'Have no fear.'
58 Lord, thou didst plead my cause
and ransom my life;
59 thou sawest, LORD, the injustice
done to me
and gavest judgement in my
favour;
60 thou sawest their vengeance,
all their plots against me.
61 Thou didst hear their bitter taunts,
O LORD,
their many plots against me,
62 the whispering, the murmurs of my
enemies
all the day long.
63 See how, whether they sit or stand,
they taunt me bitterly.
64 Pay them back for their deeds,
O LORD,
pay them back what they deserve.
65 Show them how hard thy heart
can be,
how little concern thou hast for
them.
66 Pursue them in anger and
exterminate them
from beneath thy heavens, O
LORD.

4 How dulled is the gold,
how tarnished the fine gold!
The stones of the sanctuary[q] lie strewn
at every street-corner.

n Prob. rdg.; Heb. hidden.
o my affliction: prob. rdg.; Heb. my eye.
p the LORD torments: prob. rdg.; Heb. tormenting.
q The stones of the sanctuary: or Bright gems.

3.34–47: **The city or nation speaks as a prophet. 41:** A de-emphasis on worship and a stress on morality, as in Isa.1.15–17.
3.48–51: **The afflicted individual again. 51:** The only direct mention of the city in this chapter.
3.52–66: **The innocent one is hurt. 52:** *No reason:* this motif is common in the psalms of lamentation, as in Ps.69.4. **64:** See 1.21 n.
4.1–16: **A return to the distressing conditions in Jerusalem,** but here on a more personal level.

2 See Zion's precious sons,
    once worth their weight in finest
        gold,
    now counted as pitchers of
        earthenware
    made by any potter's hand.
3 Even whales[r] uncover the teat
    and suckle their young;
    but the daughters of my people are
        cruel
    as ostriches in the desert.
4 The sucking infant's tongue
    cleaves to its palate from thirst;
    young children beg for bread
    but no one offers them a crumb.
5 Those who once fed delicately
    are desolate in the streets,
    and those nurtured in purple
    now grovel on dunghills.
6 The punishment[s] of my people is
        worse
    than the penalty[t] of Sodom,
    which was overthrown in a moment
    and no one wrung his hands.
7 Her crowned princes[u] were once
        purer than snow,
    whiter than milk;
    they were ruddier than branching
        coral,[v]
    and their limbs were lapis lazuli.
8 But their faces turned blacker than
        soot,
    and no one knew them in the
        streets;
    the skin was drawn tight over their
        bones,
    dry as touchwood.
9 Those who died by the sword were
        more fortunate
    than those who died of hunger;
    these wasted away, deprived
    of the produce of the field.
10 Tender-hearted women with their
        own hands
    boiled their own children;
    their children became their food
    in the day of my people's
        wounding.
11 The LORD glutted his rage

and poured forth his anger;
    he kindled a fire in Zion,
    and it consumed her foundations.
12 This no one believed, neither the
        kings of the earth
    nor anyone that dwelt in the world:
    that enemy or invader would enter
    the gates of Jerusalem.
13 It was for the sins of her prophets
    and for the iniquities of her priests,
    who shed within her walls
    the blood of the righteous.
14 They wandered blindly in the streets,
    so stained with blood
    that men would not touch
    even their garments.
15 'Away, away; unclean!' men cried
    to them.
    'Away, do not come near.'
    They hastened away, they wandered
        among the nations,[w]
    unable to find any resting-place.
16 The LORD himself scattered them,
    he thought of them no more;
    he showed no favours to priests,
    no pity for elders.

17 Still we strain our eyes,
    looking in vain for help.
    We have watched and watched
    for a nation powerless to save us.
18 When we go out, we take to
    by-ways
    to avoid the public streets;
    our days are all but finished,[x]
    our end has come.
19 Our pursuers have shown
    themselves swifter
    than vultures in the sky;
    they are hot on our trail over the
        hills,
    they lurk to catch us in the
        wilderness.
20 The LORD's anointed, the breath
    of life to us,

r Prob. rdg.; Heb. jackals.   *s Or* iniquity.
t Or sin.   *u* crowned princes: *or* Nazirites.
v than . . . coral: *prob. rdg.; Heb.* branch than coral.
w Prob. rdg.; Heb. adds they said.
x our . . . finished: *prob. rdg.; Heb.* our end has drawn
near, our days are complete.

3–10: A vivid portrayal of the results of hunger. **3:** *Cruel:* see v. 10. *As ostriches:* see Job
39.13–18. **6:** *Sodom:* the oft-used example of a wicked city; see Gen.19.1–26. **10:** *Their own
children:* see 2.20. **13:** See 1.5 n. Here the blame is laid at the feet of the leaders: prophets
(false, see 2.14 n.), priests, and elders (v. 16).
    4.17–20: A poet again cries out. The passage, deeply personal and sorrowful, is in the plural.
17: *A nation powerless·* perhaps Egypt; see Jer.37.5–7. **19–20:** Perhaps this is related to the
incident told of the king, that is, the LORD's anointed, in 2 Kgs.25.4–7.

was caught in their machinations;
although we had thought to live
among the nations, safe under his
protection.

21 Rejoice and be glad, daughter of
Edom,
you who live in the land of Uz.
Yet the cup shall pass to you in
your turn,
and when you are drunk you will
expose yourself to shame.
22 The punishment for your sin, daughter
of Zion, is now complete,
and never again shall you be carried
into exile.
But you, daughter of Edom, your
sin shall be punished,
and your guilt revealed.

A prayer for remembrance and restoration

Remember, O LORD, what has
5 befallen us;
look, and see how we are scorned.
2 Our patrimony is turned over to
strangers
and our homes to foreigners.
3 We are like orphans, without a
father;
our mothers are like widows.
4 We must buy our own water to
drink,
our own wood can only be had at a
price.
5 The yoke is on our necks, we are
overdriven;
we are weary and are given no rest.
6 We came to terms, now with the
Egyptians,
now with the Assyrians, to provide
us with food.
7 Our fathers sinned and are no more,

and we bear the burden of their guilt.
Slaves have become our rulers, א
and there is no one to rescue us
from them.
We must bring in our food from 9
the wilderness,
risking our lives in the scorching
heat.*y*
Our skins are blackened as in a 10
furnace
by the ravages of starvation.
Women were raped in Zion, 11
virgins raped in the cities of Judah.
Princes were hung up by their hands, 12
and elders received no honour.
Young men toil to grind corn, 13
and boys stumble under loads of
wood.
Elders have left off their sessions 14
in the gate,
and young men no longer pluck
the strings.
Joy has fled from our hearts, 15
and our dances are turned to
mourning.
The garlands have fallen from 16
our heads;
woe betide us, sinners that we are.
For this we are sick at heart, 17
for all this our eyes grow dim:
because Mount Zion is desolate 18
and over it the jackals run wild.

O LORD, thou art enthroned for ever, 19
thy throne endures from one
generation to another.
Why wilt thou quite forget us 20
and forsake us these many days?
O LORD, turn us back to thyself, 21
and we will come back;
renew our days as in times long past.
For if thou hast utterly rejected us, 22
then great indeed has been thy
anger against us.

y in the scorching heat: *or* by the sword.

4.21–22: Criticism of Edom for her action at the time of the fall; see Obad.10–14; Ps.137.7.
22: *Punishment . . . complete:* this theme is also found in Isa.40.2.
5.1–18: A prayer for remembrance and restoration. Many verses are paraphrases of passages
in chs. 1; 2; 4. **6:** *Assyrians:* this is anachronistic; the Babylonians, conquerors of the Assyrians,
had control at the time of the fall of the city. The mention shows a powerful remembrance of
the Assyrian conquest of the Northern Kingdom (721 B.C.) and the siege of Jerusalem; see
2 Kgs. chs. 17–19. **7:** *Our fathers sinned:* another explanation of the fall. On the sins of the
fathers being visited upon the children, see Jer.31.29; see also 1.5 n. **14–18:** For a similar passage,
see Isa.24.7–13.
5.19–22: A final prayer for rescue. 21: *Turn us back:* unless the LORD himself causes the city
to return to him, she will have no success in doing so. **22:** The conclusion is indefinite, fittingly
cautious after the mournful words of the rest of the book.

THE BOOK OF THE PROPHET
EZEKIEL

Ezekiel, priest and prophet, began his ministry in the last years of the Kingdom of Judah and ended it during the Babylonian captivity following upon the destruction of Jerusalem in 587 B.C. His ministry bridges the greatest catastrophe and transformation the religion of Israel ever experienced: the transition from a religion identified with a land and a temple, with its sacrifices, to a religion identified with a community of people, thus leading ultimately to the full development of the synagogue where the study of the Law is paramount, the essential Judaism of today.

Beginning with the inaugural vision, dated 593 B.C. (1.2), and ending with the last securely dated oracle, 571 B.C. (29.17), Ezekiel contains the most complete chronology of any prophetic book. The dates do not follow in order, however, and only the oracle immediately following a given date can be attached to it with certainty. The dating of the oracles according to contemporary chronology in the annotations is an approximation, correlating the lunar calendar followed by the ancients with the modern solar calendar.

Ezekiel, the most unusual among a unique class of men, the prophets of Israel, dramatized his prophecies by bizarre actions that some interpreters see as simply literary devices to emphasize his message, but which others see as reflecting pathological states. Further, though he seems to be with the captives in Babylon (1.1–3; 3.11, etc.) he sometimes addresses his message to the Palestinian Jews (11.1–3), so that interpreters are divided between postulating a double ministry (first to the people in Palestine before the captivity and then to the captives in Babylonia after the destruction of Jerusalem) and holding a single ministry, but attributing the gift of clairvoyance to Ezekiel by which he was in contact with people and events in Palestine.

The key to Ezekiel's message is a very exalted idea of God; a God beyond man's comprehension (1.4–28); a God whose hand guides the destinies of nations (chs. 25–32); a God whose "holy name" is upon man to forgive transgression and to give his own "spirit" to him (36.22–26). Earlier prophets saw in man's life a cause and effect chain with this sequence: sin—punishment—repentance (condition)—redemption (at a price). Ezekiel sees the sequence as: sin—punishment—redemption (gratuitous)—repentance (free). Thus, with redemption once assured, man is free to choose repentance without the coercion of punishment; Ezekiel's message, therefore, stresses also freedom of choice and human responsibility (ch. 18).

The MT account of Ezekiel is longer and more repetitious than that of the Sept., which is more concise and more strongly supported by the other versions, suggesting that the MT has undergone disturbance and dislocation in many passages. Moreover, chs. 40–48 are regarded by many scholars as an addition from a later hand and a later time (see 40.1–48.35 n.).

Ezekiel's call to be a prophet

1 ON THE FIFTH DAY OF THE FOURTH month in the thirtieth year, while I was among the exiles by the river Kebar,[a] the heavens were opened and I saw a vision of God. On the fifth 2 day of the month in the fifth year of the exile of King Jehoiachin, the word of 3

a Or the Kebar canal.

1.1–3.21: Ezekiel empowered. He receives his commission to prophesy doom to the Israelites. **1.1–3: Superscription. 1–2:** There is difficulty understanding the *thirtieth year*, especially in view of the *fifth year* (v. 2), since both dates seem to refer to the same event, i.e. the call of the prophet. The point of reference for both dates seems to be the capture of *Jehoiachin* by Nebuchadnezzar, king of Babylon, in 597 B.C. (2 Kgs.24.10–17). The first date then becomes 568 B.C. and the second 593 B.C. Scholars think that the thirtieth year refers either to a second call of the prophet, the one in Babylonia (see Introduction); or possibly, though less likely, to the date of the compilation of Ezekiel's many messages into a single book. Some conjecture that the call of another prophet whose work was in some way associated with that of Ezekiel was added. The *river Kebar*, an irrigation canal mentioned in Babylonian records, flowed from the Euphrates through the old city of Nippur, where excavations revealed ancient business contracts with Jewish names. See Ps.137.1–6. There were two groups of *exiles*. The first, referred to here, was taken to Babylonia with King Jehoiachin. The second was deported by Nebuchadnezzar after his destruction of Jerusalem (12.11–12; 2 Kgs.25.3–12); this date is set by some at 586, by others at 587 B.C. Jehoiachin was considered the rightful king, if a restoration were to take place; hence his captivity is the point of departure for all the dates in the book. **3:** *Ezekiel* means "God strengthens." *Hand of the LORD* is the symbol for Ezekiel's consciousness that he is divinely moved to action. Compare 8.1–9,11. *Chaldaea*: southern part of Babylonia.

the LORD came to Ezekiel son of Buzi the priest, in Chaldaea, by the river Kebar, and there the hand of the LORD came upon him.

4 I saw a storm wind coming from the north, a vast cloud with flashes of fire and brilliant light about it; and within was a radiance like brass, glowing in 5 the heart of the flames. In the fire was the semblance of four living creatures 6 in human form. Each had four faces 7 and each four wings; their legs were straight, and their hooves were like the hooves of a calf, glittering like a disc of 8 bronze. Under the wings on each of the four sides were human hands; all four 9 creatures had faces and wings, and their wings touched one another. They did not turn as they moved; each creature 10 went straight forward. Their faces were like this: all four had the face of a man and the face of a lion on the right, on the left the face of an ox and the face of 11 an eagle. Their wings were spread; each living creature had one pair touching its neighbours',[b] while one pair covered 12 its body. They moved straight forward in whatever direction the spirit[c] would go; they never swerved in their course. 13 The appearance of the creatures was as if fire from burning coals or torches were darting to and fro among them; the fire was radiant, and out of the fire came lightning.[d]

15 As I looked at the living creatures, I saw wheels on the ground, one beside 16 each of the four.[e] The wheels sparkled like topaz, and they were all alike: in form and working they were like a 17 wheel inside a wheel, and when they moved in any of the four directions they 18 never swerved in their course. All four had hubs and each hub had a projection which had the power of sight,[f] and the rims of the wheels were full of eyes all

round. When the living creatures 19 moved, the wheels moved beside them; when the creatures rose from the ground, the wheels rose; they moved in 20 whatever direction the spirit[c] would go; and the wheels rose together with them, for the spirit of the living creatures was in the wheels. When the one 21 moved, the other moved; when the one halted, the other halted; when the creatures rose from the ground, the wheels rose together with them, for the spirit of the creatures was in the wheels.

Above the heads of the living creatures 22 was, as it were, a vault glittering like a sheet of ice, awe-inspiring, stretched over their heads above them. Under the 23 vault their wings were spread straight out, touching one another, while one pair covered the body of each. I heard, 24 too, the noise of their wings; when they moved it was like the noise of a great torrent or of a cloud-burst,[g] like the noise of a crowd or of an armed camp; when they halted their wings dropped. A sound was heard above the vault over 25 their heads, as they halted with drooping wings. Above the vault over their 26 heads there appeared, as it were, a sapphire[h] in the shape of a throne, and high above all, upon the throne, a form in human likeness. I saw what might 27 have been brass glowing like fire in a furnace from the waist upwards; and from the waist downwards I saw what looked like fire with encircling radiance. Like a rainbow in the clouds on a rainy 28 day was the sight of that encircling

b *its neighbours': prob. rdg.; Heb. unintelligible.*
c *Or wind.*
d *Prob. rdg., cp. Sept.; Heb. adds* (14) and the living creatures went out (*prob. rdg.; Heb. obscure*) and in like rays of light.
e *one . . . four: prob. rdg.; Heb. obscure.*
f *the power of sight: prob. rdg.; Heb. fear.*
g *Or of the Almighty.*
h *Or lapis lazuli.*

1.4–28a: The throne-chariot vision. God's incomprehensible majesty, power, and mobility are conveyed in a visual metaphor that overwhelms the imagination and, moreover, is a fitting summary of God's activity in the book. **4:** *North:* mythological symbol for the dwelling of the gods; see Isa.14.13. *Wind, cloud, fire* are all signs of God's presence as in Exod.19.16; Ps.18.10–14. **12:** *The Spirit* is God's purposeful power directing the activity of the universe and of man; see 1.20. **15–21:** *Wheels* are symbols of cosmic mobility, and the *eyes all around* signify an all-seeing intelligence guiding the movement of the most insensitive elements in the universe which respond to the same active spirit that moves the prophet, e.g. 3.14. **22:** The ancients considered the sky a *vault* (Gen.1.6), i.e. a solid roof over the world supporting a great *torrent* of *flood* waters above which God was enthroned Lord over the universe and all in it. Compare Ps.29.10. **28:** *Like . . . the glory of the LORD* indicates that the description is a subjective vision rather than an objective presence of God such as that experienced at Sinai by all the people. See Exod.19.17–20.

radiance; it was like the appearance of the glory of the Lord.

When I saw this I threw myself on my face, and heard a voice speaking to 2 me: Man, he said, stand up, and let me 2 talk with you. As he spoke, a spirit came into me and stood me on my feet, 3 and I listened to him speaking. He said to me, Man, I am sending you to the Israelites, a nation of rebels who have rebelled against me. Past generations of them have been in revolt against me to 4 this very day, and this generation to which I am sending you is stubborn and obstinate. When you say to them, 'These are the words of the Lord GOD', 5 they will know that they have a prophet among them, whether they listen or whether they refuse to listen, because 6 they are rebels. But you, man, must not be afraid of them or of what they say, though they are rebels against you and renegades, and you find yourself sitting on scorpions. There is nothing to fear in what they say, and nothing in their looks to terrify you, rebels 7 though they are. You must speak my words to them, whether they listen or whether they refuse to listen, rebels that 8 they are. But you, man, must listen to what I say and not be rebellious like them. Open your mouth and eat what I give you.

9 Then I saw a hand stretched out to 10 me, holding a scroll. He unrolled it before me, and it was written all over on both sides with dirges and laments 3 and words of woe. Then he said to me, 'Man, eat what is in front of you, eat this scroll; then go and speak to the 2 Israelites.' So I opened my mouth and 3 he gave me the scroll to eat. Then he said, 'Man, swallow this scroll I give

you, and fill yourself full.' So I ate it, and it tasted as sweet as honey.

Man, he said to me, go and tell the 4 Israelites what I have to say to them. You are sent not to people whose 5 speech is thick and difficult, but to Israelites. No; I am not sending you to 6 great nations whose speech is so thick and so difficult that you cannot make out what they say; if however I had sent you to them they would have listened to you. But the Israelites will 7 refuse to listen to you, for they refuse to listen to me, so brazen are they all and stubborn. But I will make you a 8 match for them. I will make you as brazen as they are and as stubborn as they are. I will make your brow like 9 adamant, harder than flint. Never fear them, never be terrified by them, rebels though they are. And he said to me, 10 Listen carefully, man, to all that I have to say to you, and take it to heart. Go 11 to your fellow-countrymen in exile and speak to them. Whether they listen or refuse to listen, say, 'These are the words of the Lord GOD.'

Then a spirit[i] lifted me up, and I 12 heard behind me a fierce rushing sound as the glory of the LORD rose[j] from his place. I heard the sound of the living 13 creatures' wings brushing against one another, the sound of the wheels beside them, and a fierce rushing sound. A 14 spirit[i] lifted me and carried me along, and I went full of exaltation, the hand of the LORD strong upon me. So I came 15 to the exiles at Tel-abib who were settled by the river Kebar. For seven days I stayed with them, dumbfounded.

i Or wind.
j rose: *prob. rdg.; Heb. obscure.*

1.28b–3.21: Prophetic experience of the call and five commissions. There are four calls: 1.28b–3.9; 3.10–11; 3.16–21; 3.22–27, which contain five commissions. **2.1:** *Man*, lit. "son of man," used over ninety times, contrasts human frailty with God's might and glory. Compare Job 14.1–5. **2:** *Spirit . . . stood me*, i.e. bridged the distance between God and the prophet, and gave such power to his words and actions that the people *will know*, i.e. be unable to ignore, the reality of the divine message even though they *refuse to listen*. **2.8–3.3:** The *scroll* contains only *dirges* and *words of woe* because a prophet preaching peace is suspect; see 13.10–16. Eating the scroll signifies assimilating God's message; the sweetness is the sense of fulfillment it brings; compare Pss.19.9–10; 119.100–103. **4–9:** Ezekiel's boldness is attributed to God because it was acquired in carrying out his commission. **10–21:** Some interpreters conjecture that this repetition is a second call of Ezekiel; others, that it is the call of another man whose prophecy is added to that of Ezekiel's (see 1.1–2 n.); still others reason that it is editorial duplication. See Introduction. **14:** *Full of exaltation:* lit. "bitter in the fury of my spirit," the ecstasy of a religious experience. **15:** *Tel-abib:* a Jewish settlement in Babylonia. In 1.1, Ezekiel is already among the exiles when the vision takes place; here he is arriving after the vision.

16 At the end of seven days, the word of
17 the LORD came to me: Man, I have made you a watchman for the Israelites; you will take messages from me and
18 carry my warnings to them. It may be that I pronounce sentence of death on a wicked man:[k] if you do not warn him to give up his wicked ways and so save his life, the guilt is his; because of his wickedness he shall die, but I will hold
19 you answerable for his death. But if you have warned him and he still continues in his wicked and evil ways, he shall die because of his wickedness, but you will
20 have saved yourself. Or it may be that a righteous man turns away and does wrong, and I let that be the cause of his downfall; he will die because you have not warned him. He will die for his sin; the righteous deeds he has done will not be taken into account, and I will
21 hold you answerable for his death. But if you have warned the righteous man not to sin and he has not sinned, then he will have saved his life because he has been warned, and you will have saved yourself.

The impending ruin of Jerusalem

22 THE HAND OF THE LORD CAME UPON ME there, and he said to me, Rise up; go out into the plain, and there I will speak
23 to you. So I rose and went out into the plain; the glory of the LORD was there, like the glory which I had seen by the river Kebar, and I threw myself down
24 on my face. Then a spirit came into me and stood me on my feet, and spoke to me: Go, he said, and shut yourself up
25 in your house. You shall be tied and bound with ropes, man, so that you cannot go out among the people. I will
26 fasten your tongue to the roof of your mouth and you will be unable to speak; you will not be the one to rebuke them, rebels though they are. But when I have
27 something to say to you, I will give you back the power of speech. Then you will say to them, 'These are the words of the Lord GOD.' If anyone will listen, he may listen, and, if he refuses to listen, he may refuse; for they are rebels.

4 Man, take a tile and set it before you. Draw a city on it, the city of Jerusalem:
2 lay siege to it, erect watch-towers against it, raise a siege-ramp, put mantelets in position, and bring batter-ing-rams against it all round. Then
3 take an iron griddle, and put it as a wall of iron between you and the city. Keep your face turned towards the city; it will be the besieged and you the besieger. This will be a sign to the Israelites.
4 Now lie on your left side, and I will lay Israel's iniquity on you; you shall bear their iniquity for as many days as you lie on that side. Allowing one day
5 for every year of their iniquity, I ordain that you bear it for one hundred and ninety days; thus you shall bear Israel's iniquity. When you have completed all
6 this, lie down a second time on your right side, and bear Judah's iniquity for forty days; I count one day for
7 every year. Then turn your face to-wards the siege of Jerusalem and bare
8 your arm, and prophesy against it. See how I tie you with ropes so that you cannot turn over from one side to the other until you complete the days of your distress.

[k] *Prob. rdg.; Heb. adds* if you do not warn him.

For possible explanation see vv. 10–12. **16:** How *the word of the LORD came* to Ezekiel is not clear; it need only imply his conviction that he spoke God's message to the people. **17–21:** The prophet as *watchman* has a long tradition in Israel; compare Isa.21.6–12. Here it applies Ezekiel's principle of personal responsibility (see 18.1–32) to the prophetic office.
   3.22–27: Ezekiel confined. To be *bound with ropes* (v. 25) may mean actual physical restraints; more probably it means discouragement, deterring the prophet from speaking and acting except when moved by special inspiration from God. Compare Ps.22.15.
   4.1–5.17: Actions symbolic of the judgment of Jerusalem. The prophecies given here as actions seem impossible to perform and so are probably dramatic allegories. Ezekiel, having received a command "to speak . . . in allegory and parable" (17.2), acquired a reputation of dealing "only in parables"; see 20.49. **1:** *Tile:* clay tablet. **3:** *Israelites*, lit. "house of Israel," embraces both the Northern Kingdom of Israel, as in v. 4, taken into captivity in 721 B.C. by the Assyrians, and the Southern Kingdom of Judah, as in v. 6; Ezekiel envisions the ultimate restoration and reunion of the two. **4:** *Bear their iniquity:* be a symbol of their punishment. **5–6:** The number symbolism is uncertain, possibly referring to the duration of the exiles of the two kingdoms.

9 Then take wheat and barley, beans and lentils, millet and spelt. Mix them all in one bowl and make your bread out of them. You are to eat it during the one hundred and ninety days you 10 spend lying on your side. And you must weigh out your food; you may eat twenty shekels' weight a day, taking it 11 from time to time. Measure out your drinking water too; you may drink a sixth of a hin a day, taking it from time 12 to time. You are to eat your bread baked like barley cakes, using human dung as fuel, and you must bake it 13 where people can see you. Then the LORD said, 'This is the kind of bread, unclean bread, that the Israelites will eat in the foreign lands into which I 14 shall drive them.' But I said, 'O Lord GOD, I have never been made unclean, never in my life have I eaten what has died naturally or been killed by wild beasts; no tainted meat has ever passed 15 my lips.' So he allowed me to use cow-dung instead of human dung to bake my bread.

16 Then he said to me, Man, I am cutting short their daily bread in Jerusalem; people will weigh out anxiously the bread they eat, and measure with dismay the water they 17 drink. So their food and their water will run short until they are dismayed at the sight of one another; they will waste away because of their iniquity.

5 Man, take a sharp sword, take it like a barber's razor and run it over your head and your chin. Then take scales 2 and divide the hair into three. When the siege comes to an end, burn one third of the hair in a fire in the centre of the city; cut up one third with the sword all round the city; scatter one third to the wind, and I will follow it 3 with drawn sword. Take a few of these hairs and tie them up in a fold of your 4 robe. Then take others of them, throw them into the fire and burn them, and

out of them fire will come upon all Israel.

5 These are the words of the Lord GOD: This city of Jerusalem I have set among the nations, with other countries around her, and she has rebelled 6 against my laws and my statutes more wickedly than those nations and countries; for her people have rejected my laws and refused to conform to my statutes.

7 Therefore the Lord GOD says: Since you have been more ungrateful than the nations around you and have not conformed to my statutes and have not kept my laws or even the laws of the 8 nations around you, therefore, says the Lord GOD, I, in my turn, will be against you; I will execute judgements in your 9 midst for the nations to see, such judgements as I have never executed before nor ever will again, so abominable 10 have your offences been. Therefore, O Jerusalem, fathers will eat their children and children their fathers in your midst; I will execute judgements on you, and any who are left in you I will scatter to 11 the four winds. As I live, says the Lord GOD, because you have defiled my holy place with all your vile and abominable rites, I in my turn will consume you without pity; I in my turn will not 12 spare you. One third of your people shall die by pestilence and perish by famine in your midst; one third shall fall by the sword in the country round about; and one third I will scatter to the four winds and follow with drawn 13 sword. Then my anger will be spent, I will abate my fury against them and be calm; when my fury is spent they will know that it is I, the LORD, who spoke in jealous passion. I have made 14 you a scandal[l] and a reproach to the nations around you, and all who pass 15 by will see it. You will be an object of reproach and abuse, a terrible lesson to the nations around you, when I pass

l Or desolation.

9: Mixing different grains *all in one bowl* signifies the last of the food supply, the threat of famine. 12: Contact with *human dung* made a person unclean (Deut.23.13); here it indicates the ritual uncleanness of Babylon where pure cultic life was impossible. 5.1–17: Shearing the prophet's hair and beard—symbols of dignity (2 Sam.10.4–5) and of life (Num.6.1–9)—is a sign of the degradation and massacre following the horrible siege. God treats Israel with the *jealous passion* of a rejected lover; this theme is central in the book. For examples, read 6.13; 7.3, 8; 8.18; 14.21; 20.8; 28.23.

sentence on you and do judgement in anger and fury. I, the Lord, have
16 spoken. When I shoot the deadly arrows of famine against you,*m* arrows of destruction, I will shoot to destroy you. I will bring famine upon you and
17 cut short your daily bread; I will unleash famine and beasts of prey upon you, and they will leave you childless. Pestilence and slaughter will sweep through you, and I will bring the sword upon you. I, the Lord, have spoken.

6 These were the words of the Lord to
2 me: Man, look towards the mountains of Israel, and prophesy to them:
3 Mountains of Israel, hear the word of the Lord God. This is his word to mountains and hills, watercourses and valleys: I am bringing a sword against you, and I will destroy your hill-shrines.
4 Your altars will be made desolate, your incense-altars shattered, and I will fling
5 down your slain before your idols. I will strew the corpses of the Israelites before their idols, and I will scatter
6 your bones about your altars. In all your settlements the blood-spattered altars*n* shall be laid waste and the hill-shrines made desolate. Your altars will be waste and desolate and your idols shattered and useless, your incense-altars hewn down, and all your works
7 wiped out; with the slain falling about you, you shall know that I am the
8 Lord. But when they fall,*o* I will leave you, among the nations, some who survive the sword. When you are
9 scattered in foreign lands, these survivors, in captivity among the nations, will remember how I was grieved because their hearts had turned wantonly from me and their eyes had gone roving wantonly after idols. Then they will loathe themselves for all the evil they have done with their abomina-
10 tions. So they will know that I am the

Lord, that I was uttering no vain threat when I said that I would bring this evil upon them.

These are the words of the Lord 11 God: Beat your hands together, stamp with your foot, bemoan your vile abominations, people of Israel. Men will fall by sword, famine, and pestilence. Far away they will die by pestilence; at 12 home they will fall by the sword; any who survive or are spared will die by famine, and so at last my anger will be spent. You will know that I am the 13 Lord when their slain fall among the idols round their altars, on every high hill, on all mountain-tops, under every spreading tree, under every leafy terebinth, wherever they have brought offerings of soothing odour for their idols one and all. So I will stretch out 14 my hand over them and make the land a desolate waste in all their settlements, more desolate than the desert of Riblah.*p* They shall know that I am the Lord.

The word of the Lord came to me: 7 Man, the Lord God says this to the 2 land of Israel: An end is coming, the end is coming upon the four corners of the land.*q* The end is now upon you; 3 I will unleash my anger against you; I will call you to account for your doings and bring your abominations upon your own heads. I will neither 4 pity nor spare you: I will make you suffer for your doings and the abominations that continue in your midst. So you shall know that I am the Lord.

These are the words of the Lord 5 God: Behold, it comes, disasters one upon another; the end, the end, it 6 comes, it comes.*r* Doom is coming 7 upon you, dweller in the land; the time is coming, the day is near, with

m Prob. rdg.; Heb. them.
n blood-spattered altars: or cities.
o when they fall: prob. rdg.; Heb. obscure.
p Prob. rdg.; Heb. Diblah.   q Or earth.
r Prob. rdg.; Heb. adds it wakes up, behold it comes.

6.1–7.27: Oracles of judgment. Here punishment is announced in words rather than in symbolic actions. **3:** *Hill-shrines:* lit. "high places," associated with mountaintops where worship was carried on. They were proscribed after Hezekiah centralized the cult in the Jerusalem Temple (2 Kgs.18.4), because the rituals tended toward the cult of the fertility gods of the Canaanites. **5:** The touch of *corpses* which made a person unclean for worship will pollute the very altars. **8:** *Some who survive:* the "remnant" (Isa.4.3) will be the seed of the restoration. **11:** *Sword, famine, pestilence* are the traditional scourges by which God punishes his people; see Jer.14.12; 27.8. **13:** *Leafy terebinth:* certain trees were especially associated with female deities in fertility rites, the terebinth among them. See Deut.16.21.
7.1–27: Judgment against the land. The day is near when all practitioners of evil in Israel will be destroyed and all human security will disintegrate: social life, vv. 10–11; economic life,

confusion and the crash of thunder.*

8 Now, in an instant, I will vent my rage upon you and let my anger spend itself. I will call you to account for your doings and bring your abominations 9 upon your own heads. I will neither pity nor spare; I will make you suffer for your doings and the abominations that continue in your midst. So you shall know that it is I, the LORD, who strike the blow.

10 Behold, the day! the doom is here, it has burst upon them. Injustice buds, 11 insolence blossoms, violence shoots up into injustice and wickedness. And it is all their fault, the fault of their turmoil and tumult and all their restless ways. 12 The time has come, the day has arrived; the buyer has no reason to be glad, and the seller none for regret, for 13 I am angry at all their turmoil. The seller will never go back on his bargain while either of them lives; for the bargain will never be reversed because of the turmoil, and no man will exert himself, even in his iniquity, as long as 14 he lives. The trumpet has sounded and all is ready, but no one goes out to war.

15 Outside is the sword, inside are pestilence and famine; in the country men will die by the sword, in the city famine 16 and pestilence will carry them off. If any escape and take to the mountains, like moaning doves, there will I slay 17 them, each for his iniquity, while their hands hang limp and their knees run 18 with urine. They will go in sackcloth, shuddering from head to foot, with faces downcast and heads close shaved. 19 They shall fling their silver into the streets and cast aside their gold like filth; their silver and their gold will be powerless to save them on the day of the LORD's fury. Their hunger will not be satisfied nor their bellies filled; for their iniquity will be the cause of their 20 downfall. They have fed their pride on their beautiful jewels, which they made into vile and abominable images.

Therefore I will treat their jewels like 21 filth, I will hand them over as plunder to foreigners and as booty to the most evil people on earth, and these will 22 defile them. I will turn my face from them and let my treasured land be profaned; brigands will come in and defile it.

Clench your fists, for the land is full 23 of bloodshed† and the city full of violence. I will let in the scum of 24 nations to take possession of their houses; I will quell the pride of the strong, and their sanctuaries shall be profaned. Shuddering will come over 25 them, and they will look in vain for peace. Tempest shall follow upon 26 tempest and rumour upon rumour. Men will go seeking a vision from a prophet; there will be no more guidance from a priest, no counsel from elders. The king will mourn, the prince 27 will be clothed with horror, the hands of the common people will shake with fright. I will deal with them as they deserve, and call them to account for their doings; and so they shall know that I am the LORD.

Jerusalem's guilt and punishment

ON THE FIFTH DAY OF THE SIXTH MONTH **8** in the sixth year, I was sitting at home and the elders of Judah were with me. Suddenly the hand of the Lord GOD came upon me, and I saw what looked 2 like a man. He seemed to be all fire from the waist down and to shine and glitter like brass from the waist up. He 3 stretched out what seemed a hand and seized me by the forelock. A spirit*u* lifted me up between heaven and earth, carried me to Jerusalem in a vision of God and put me down at the entrance to the inner gate facing north, where stands the image of Lust to rouse

s and the crash of thunder: *prob. rdg.; Heb. unintelligible.*
t bloodshed: *prob. rdg.; Heb.* the judgement of bloodshed.   *u Or* wind.

12–19; religious life, 20–26; political life, 27. **12–14:** Neither the *buyer* getting a good bargain can rejoice nor the *seller* suffering a loss will grieve; total disaster will permanently nullify all loss or gain. **26–27:** In the catastrophe to follow, of all the community functions, only the work of the *prophet* will remain, it being a divine communication rather than a human effort.
    8.1–11.25: God punishes Jerusalem for her abominations. 1–18: Pagan rites such as these are also mentioned elsewhere, e.g. 2 Kgs.21.7; Hos.10.1–2. **1:** *Sixth year:* September 17, 592 B.C. **3:** The *image of Lust* was probably that of the fertility goddess, Asherah, mentioned in

4 lustful passion. The glory of the God of Israel was there, like the vision I had
5 seen in the plain. The LORD said to me, 'Man, look northwards.' I did so, and there to the north of the altar gate, at the entrance, was that image of Lust.
6 'Man,' he said, 'do you see what they are doing? The monstrous abominations which the Israelites practise here are driving me far from my sanctuary, and you will see even more such abominations.'
7 Then he brought me to the entrance of the court, and I looked and found a
8 hole in the wall. 'Man,' he said to me, 'dig through the wall.' I did so, and it
9 became an opening. 'Go in,' he said, 'and see the vile abominations they
10 practise here.' So I went in and saw figures of reptiles, beasts, and vermin, and all the idols of the Israelites,
11 carved round the walls. Seventy elders of Israel were standing in front of them, with Jaazaniah son of Shaphan in the middle, and each held a censer from which rose the fragrant smoke of
12 incense. 'Man,' he said to me, 'do you see what the elders of Israel are doing in darkness, each at the shrine of his own carved image? They think that the LORD does not see them, or that he
13 has forsaken the country. You will see', he said, 'yet more monstrous abominations which they practise.'
14 Then he brought me to that gateway of the LORD's house which faces north; and there I saw women sitting and
15 wailing for Tammuz. 'Man, do you see that?' he asked me. 'But you will see abominations more monstrous than
16 these.' So he took me to the inner court of the LORD's house, and there, by the entrance to the sanctuary of the LORD, between porch and altar, were some twenty-five men with their backs to the sanctuary and their faces to the east, prostrating themselves to the rising
17 sun. He said to me, 'Man, do you see that? Is it because they think these

abominations a trifle, that the Jews have filled the country with violence?
18 They provoke me further to anger, even while they seek to appease me; I will turn upon them in my rage; I will neither pity nor spare. Loudly as they may cry to me, I will not listen.'
9 A loud voice rang in my ears: 'Here they come, those appointed to punish the city, each carrying his weapon of
2 destruction.' Then I saw six men approaching from the road that leads to the upper northern gate, each carrying a battle-axe, one man among them dressed in linen, with pen and ink at his waist; and they halted by the altar
3 of bronze. Then the glory of the God of Israel rose from above the cherubim. He came to the terrace of the temple and called to the man dressed in linen with pen and ink at his waist. 'Go
4 through the city, through Jerusalem,' said the LORD, 'and put a mark on the foreheads of those who groan and lament over the abominations practised
5 there.' Then I heard him say to the others, 'Follow him through the city and kill without pity; spare no one.
6 Kill and destroy them all, old men and young, girls, little children and women, but touch no one who bears the mark. Begin at my sanctuary.' So they began with the elders in front of the temple.
7 'Defile the temple,' he said, 'and fill the courts with dead bodies; then go out into the city and kill.'
8 While they did their work, I was left alone; and I threw myself upon my face, crying out, 'O Lord GOD, must thou destroy all the Israelites who are left, pouring out thy anger on Jerusa-
9 lem?' He answered, 'The iniquity of Israel and Judah is great indeed; the land is full of murder, the city is filled with injustice. They think the LORD has forsaken this country; they think he sees nothing. But I will neither pity nor
10 spare them; I will make them answer for all they have done.' Then the man
11

2 Kgs.21.7. 7–11: The imagery recalls the Egyptian Book of the Dead, with its descriptions of the cult of the god Osiris. 14–15: *Tammuz*, the Babylonian god of fertility, whose annual descent into the underworld brought death to vegetation, was mourned especially by *women*. 17: *Violence* is seen as the result of idolatry.
  9.1–11: Purge of idolaters in Jerusalem. 2: *Linen:* a ritually clean cloth worn by those in immediate service of God, priests in the Temple (Lev.16.3–4) and angels in heaven (Dan.10.5; Rev.15.6). **7:** *Dead bodies* made the Temple unfit for any worship, legitimate or idolatrous.

dressed in linen with pen and ink at his waist came and made his report: 'I have done what thou hast commanded.'

10 Then I saw, above the vault over the heads of the cherubim, as it were a throne of sapphire*v* visible above them.
2 The LORD said to the man dressed in linen, 'Come in between the circling wheels under the cherubim, and take a handful of the burning embers lying among the cherubim; then toss them over the city.' So he went in before my eyes.
3 The cherubim stood on the right side of the temple as a man enters, and a
4 cloud filled the inner court. The glory of the LORD rose high from above the cherubim and moved on to the terrace; and the temple was filled with the cloud, while the radiance of the glory of
5 the LORD filled the court. The sound of the wings of the cherubim could be heard as far as the outer court, as loud as if God Almighty were speaking.
6 Then he told the man dressed in linen to take fire from between the circling wheels and among the cherubim; the
7 man came and stood by a wheel, and a cherub from among the cherubim put its hand into the fire that lay among them, and, taking some fire, gave it to the man dressed in linen; and he received it and went out.
8 Under the wings of the cherubim there appeared what seemed a human
9 hand. And I saw four wheels beside the cherubim, one wheel beside each cherub. They had the sparkle of topaz,
10 and all four were alike, like a wheel
11 inside a wheel. When the cherubim moved in any of the four directions, they never swerved in their course; they went straight on in the direction in which their heads were turned, never
12 swerving in their course. Their whole

bodies, their backs and hands and wings, as well as the wheels, were full of eyes all round the four of them.*w*
13 The whirring of the wheels sounded in
14 my ears. Each had four faces: the first was that of a cherub, the second that of a man, the third that of a lion, and the fourth that of an eagle.
15 Then the cherubim raised themselves up, those same living creatures I had
16 seen by the river Kebar. When the cherubim moved, the wheels moved beside them; when the cherubim lifted their wings and rose from the ground, the wheels did not turn away from
17 them. When the one halted, the other halted; when the one rose, the other rose; for the spirit of the creatures was in the wheels. Then the glory of the
18 LORD left the temple terrace and halted
19 above the cherubim. The cherubim lifted their wings and raised themselves from the ground; I watched them go with the wheels beside them. They halted at the eastern gateway of the LORD's house, and the glory of the God of Israel was over them.
20 These were the living creatures I had seen beneath the God of Israel at the river Kebar; I knew that they were
21 cherubim. Each had four faces and four wings and the semblance of human
22 hands under their wings. Their faces were like those I had seen in vision by the river Kebar;*x* they moved, each one of them, straight forward.

11 A spirit*y* lifted me up and brought me to the eastern gate of the LORD's house, the gate that faces east. By the doorway were twenty-five men, and I saw among them two of high office, Jaazaniah son of Azzur and Pelatiah son of Benaiah. The LORD said to me,
2

v Or lapis lazuli. w Prob. rdg.; Heb. adds their wheels.
x Prob. rdg.; Heb. adds and them.   y Or wind.

10.1–22: God leaves the Temple. In the Bible, abandonment by the Lord is the most terrible punishment known; see Deut.31.16–17; Ps.27.8–10. **3–4:** Unlike the subjective vision of 1.28, *the glory of the LORD* here is Israel's shared experience of the objective majesty of God. The symbolism of *cloud* conveys his hiddenness (Exod.16.10) and the brilliance of sapphire manifests his majesty (Exod.24.9–10). Compare Isa.6.1–5. **7:** Jerusalem, desecrated and put under the ban (Josh.6.17 n.), must be completely destroyed by *fire* (5.2) coming from God's throne itself; a new city, holy to the LORD, may then rise in its place; see 40.2. **19:** The LORD leaves by the *eastern gateway* because he is going eastward to the captives already in Babylon. The vision continues in 11.22–24.
11.1–25: False security of the inhabitants of Jerusalem. Jehoiachin and the most important people of Jerusalem were taken captive to Babylon in 597; those who remained congratulated themselves that they had God's favor and were therefore safe. Compare Jer.24.1–10. **2–3:** The princes, as secure and contented as *meat* in a bubbling *stewpot*, express a confidence that

Man, it is these who are planning mischief and plotting trouble in this city, 3 saying to themselves, 'There will be no building of houses yet awhile; the city is a stewpot and we are the meat in it.' 4 Therefore, said he, prophesy against 5 them, prophesy, O man. Then the spirit of the LORD came suddenly upon me, and he told me to say, These are the words of the LORD: This is what you are saying to yourselves, you men of Israel; well do I know the thoughts 6 that rise in your mind. You have killed and killed in this city and heaped the 7 streets with the slain. These, therefore, are the words of the Lord GOD: The bodies of the slain that you have put there, it is they that are the meat. The city is indeed the stewpot, but I will 8 take you out of it. It is a sword that you fear, and a sword I will bring upon 9 you, says the Lord GOD. I will take you out of it; I will give you over to a foreign power; I will bring you to 10 justice. You too shall fall by the sword when I judge you on the frontier of Israel; thus you shall know that I am 11 the LORD. So the city will not be your stewpot, nor you the meat in it. On the 12 frontier of Israel I will judge you; thus you shall know that I am the LORD. You have not conformed to my statutes nor kept my laws, but you have followed the laws of the nations around you. 13 While I was prophesying, Pelatiah son of Benaiah fell dead; and I threw myself upon my face, crying aloud, 'O Lord GOD, must thou make an end of all the Israelites who are left?' 14 The word of the LORD came to me:

Man, they are your brothers, your 15 brothers and your kinsmen, this whole people of Israel, to whom the men who now live in Jerusalem have said, 'Keep your distance from the LORD; the land has been made over to us as our property.' Say therefore, These are the 16 words of the Lord GOD: When I sent them far away among the nations and scattered them in many lands, for a while I became their sanctuary in the countries to which they had gone. Say 17 therefore, These are the words of the Lord GOD: I will gather them from among the nations and assemble them from the countries over which I have scattered them, and I will give them the soil of Israel. When they come into it, 18 they will do away with all their vile and abominable practices. I will give them a 19 different heart and put a new spirit into them; I will take the heart of stone out of their bodies and give them a heart of flesh. Then they will conform to my 20 statutes and keep my laws. They will become my people, and I will become their God. But as for those whose heart 21 is set upon[z] their vile and abominable practices, I will make them answer for all they have done. This is the very word of the Lord GOD.

Then the cherubim lifted their 22 wings, with the wheels beside them and the glory of the God of Israel above them. The glory of the LORD rose up 23 and left the city, and halted on the mountain to the east of it. And a spirit[a] 24 lifted me up and brought me to the exiles in Chaldaea. All this came in a vision sent by the spirit of God, and

z Prob. rdg.; Heb. adds the heart of. *a Or* wind.

---

houses will be built in the city after *awhile*, thus giving the lie to Ezekiel's warning in 7.12–13. The key to this allegory is found in 24.3–7, 9–13. **7–9:** Those unjustly slain in Jerusalem by the princes are the *meat* in the *stewpot*, i.e. their bodies will remain in Palestine, but the nobility will be taken beyond the *frontier of Israel* for examination: judgment. **13:** Pelatiah's death in the presence of the prophesying Ezekiel is considered proof by some interpreters of the prophet's double ministry, first before the destruction of Jerusalem in 587 B.C. and subsequently in Babylon. Those who admit only a Babylonian ministry explain the whole verse either as a vision the prophet had in Babylonia or as one he added when the oracles were gathered together in 563 B.C. See 1.1–2 n. **14–15:** The northern tribes having been in captivity since 721 B.C. (2 Kgs.17.6) and a large portion of Judah since 597 B.C., the men who *now live in Jerusalem* consider the *whole people of Israel* as at a *distance from the LORD*, i.e. away from his presence in the Temple. Hence, in their false security, they claim all the land as their exclusive property. **16–17:** Though distant from the Temple, the captives have the LORD himself (vv. 22–24) as *their sanctuary* until he, as their next-of-kin, delivers them from captivity and gives them anew the *soil* of Palestine. **19–20:** Following a new Exodus (vv. 16–17), *God* will renew his covenant with Israel; by giving them a *new spirit* and a *heart of flesh*, he will make them his *people*. **23:** To fulfill the promises made in vv. 16–17,19–20, the *glory of the LORD* leaves Jerusalem to be with the exiles in the *east*.

then the vision that I had seen left me.
13 I told the exiles all that the LORD had revealed to me.

Jerusalem's downfall certain

12 THE WORD OF THE LORD CAME TO ME:
2 Man, you live among a rebellious people. Though they have eyes they will not see, though they have ears they will not hear, because they are a
3 rebellious people. Therefore, man, pack up what you need for a journey into exile, by day before their eyes; then set off on your journey. When you leave home and go off into exile before their eyes, it may be they will see that they
4 are rebels. Bring out your belongings, packed as for exile; do it by day, before their eyes, and then at evening, still before their eyes, leave home, as if you
5 were going into exile. Next, before their eyes, break a hole through the wall, and carry your belongings out
6 through it. When dusk falls, take your pack on your shoulder, before their eyes, and carry it out, with your face covered so that you cannot see the ground. I am making you a warning sign for the Israelites.
7 I did exactly as I had been told. By day I brought out my belongings, packed as for exile, and at evening I broke through the wall with my hands. When dusk fell, I shouldered my pack and carried it out before their eyes.
8 Next morning, the word of the LORD
9 came to me: Man, he said, have not the Israelites, that rebellious people, asked
10 you what you are doing? Tell them that these are the words of the Lord GOD: This oracle concerns the prince in Jerusalem, and all the Israelites there-

in.[b] Tell them that you are a sign to 11 warn them; what you have done will be done to them; they will go into exile and captivity. Their prince will shoulder 12 his pack in the dusk and go through a hole made to let him out, with his face covered so that he cannot be seen nor himself see the ground. But I will cast 13 my net over him, and he will be caught in the meshes. I will bring him to Babylon, the land of the Chaldaeans, though he will not see it; and there he will die. I will scatter his bodyguard 14 and drive all his squadrons to the four winds; I will follow them with drawn sword. Then they shall know that I am 15 the LORD, when I disperse them among the nations and scatter them through many lands. But I will leave 16 a few of them who will escape sword, famine, and pestilence, to tell the whole story of their abominations to the peoples among whom they go; and they shall know that I am the LORD.

And the word of the LORD came to 17 me: Man, he said, as you eat you must 18 tremble, and as you drink you must shudder with dread. Say to the com- 19 mon people. These are the words of the Lord GOD about those who live in Jerusalem and about the land of Israel: They will eat with dread and be filled with horror as they drink; the land shall be filled with horror because it is sated with the violence of all who live there. Inhabited cities shall be deserted, 20 and the land shall become a waste. Thus you shall know that I am the LORD.

The word of the LORD came to me: 21 Man, he said, what is this proverb 22 current in the land of Israel: 'Time runs on, visions die away'? Say to them, 23

[b] therein: *prob. rdg.; Heb.* among them.

12.1–24.27: Jerusalem's fate predicted. This section contains further prophecies against all whose conduct makes Jerusalem's doom inevitable: the city's rulers and people, priests and prophets.

12.1–20: More symbols of exile. According to some interpreters, the prophet acts out his prediction of exile before the inhabitants of Jerusalem in Palestine; according to others, he is in Babylon before the captives. **6:** The *face* was *covered* as a sign of grief, or to avoid recognition and thus escape ridicule. **12:** Ezekiel's dramatization (vv. 3–7) was already applied to Israel's departure into exile (vv. 10–11). Its reapplication here to the attempted escape of King Zedekiah (2 Kgs.25.4–5) is probably a later addition, but possibly by the prophet himself. **13:** *There he will die:* the words seem to indicate that the writer is in Palestine, not Babylonia.

12.21–13.23: True and false prophecy. Without objective criteria to distinguish true from false prophecy, the common people are left confused. See 1 Kgs.22.1–28; Jer.28.1–15; Mic.3.5. Two oracles (the first, vv. 21–25, and the second, 26–28) reflect both ridicule suffered by the prophet and his own keen sensitivity and hurt. **22:** *Visions die away:* they are not fulfilled.

These are the words of the Lord GOD: I have put an end to this proverb, it shall never be heard in Israel again. Say rather to them, The time, with all the vision means, is near. There will be

24 no more false visions, no specious

25 divination among the Israelites, for I, the LORD, will say what I will, and it shall be done. It shall be put off no longer: in your lifetime, you rebellious people, I will speak, I will act. This is the very word of the Lord GOD.

26   The word of the LORD came to me:

27 Man, he said, the Israelites say that the vision you now see is not to be fulfilled for many years: you are prophesying

28 of a time far off. Say to them, These are the words of the Lord GOD: No word of mine shall be delayed; even as I speak it shall be done. This is the very word of the Lord GOD.

13 1,2   The LORD said to me, Man, prophesy of the prophets of Israel; prophesy, and say to those who prophesy out of their own hearts, Hear what the LORD says:

3 These are the words of the Lord GOD: Oh, the wicked folly of the prophets! Their inspiration comes from them-

4 selves; they have seen no vision. Your prophets, Israel, have been like jackals

5 among ruins. They have not gone up into the breach to repair the broken wall round the Israelites, that they may stand firm in battle on the day of the

6 LORD. Oh, false vision and lying divination! Oh, those prophets who say, 'It is the very word of the LORD', when it is not the LORD who has sent them; yet they expect their words to control the

7 event. Is it not a false vision that you prophets have seen? Is not your divination a lie? You call it the very word of the LORD, but it is not I who have spoken.

8   These, then, are the words of the

Lord GOD: Because your words are false and your visions a lie, I am against you, says the Lord GOD. I will raise my 9 hand against the prophets whose visions are false, whose divinations are a lie. They shall have no place in the counsels of my people; they shall not be entered in the roll of Israel nor set foot upon its soil. Thus you shall know that I am the Lord GOD. Rightly, for 10 they have misled my people by saying that all is well when all is not well. It is as if they were building a wall and used whitewash for the daubing. Tell these 11 daubers that it will fall; rain will pour down in torrents, and I will send hailstones hard as rock streaming down and I will unleash a stormy wind. When the building falls, men will ask, 12 'Where is the plaster you should have used?' So these are the words of the 13 Lord GOD: In my rage I will unleash a stormy wind; rain will come in torrents in my anger, hailstones hard as rock in my fury, until all is destroyed. I will 14 demolish the building which you have daubed with whitewash and level it to the ground, so that its foundations are laid bare. It shall fall, and you shall be destroyed within it; thus you shall know that I am the LORD. I will spend my 15 rage on the building and on those who daubed it with wash; and people[c] will say, 'The building is gone and the men who daubed it are gone, those prophets 16 of Israel who prophesied to Jerusalem, who saw visions of prosperity when there was no prosperity.' This is the very word of the Lord GOD.

Now turn, man, to the women of 17 your people who prophesy out of their own hearts, and prophesy to them. Say to them, These are the words of the 18 Lord GOD: I loathe you, you women

[c] *Prob. rdg.; Heb.* I.

25: Ezekiel feels that he speaks what the *LORD* wishes to *say*, i.e. that he is the mouth of God. **13.1–5:** Those who *prophesy out of their own hearts*, i.e. make schemes in their minds, are moved by their greed, and, far from exposing the community's weaknesses, conceal and exploit them; thus they live like *jackals* off the calamity of others. For the ancients the heart was the seat of the intellect. **6:** In *divination*, man, on his own initiative and for his own gain, seeks to discover the will of God; by contrast, the true prophet is moved by God, against his will and to his own danger; see 3.4–10; Jer.1.4–10. Divination, arising out of self-interest, tends easily toward *lying.* **10–11:** Plaster, not *whitewash*, gives mud-brick walls a hard, water-resistant coat that does not merely hide the faults of the wall. So, too, a true prophet strengthens the community against a day of reckoning by not hiding its evil. **17–23:** Certain *women* seem to have practiced, for payment by *handfuls of barley and scraps of bread* (v. 19), idolatrous magic, divination, and sorcery of an unknown nature. See 1 Sam.28.7–19; Mic.3.5–11.

who hunt men's lives by sewing magic bands upon the wrists and putting veils over the heads of persons of every age; are you to hunt the lives of my people and keep your own lives safe? 19 You have violated my sanctity before my people with handfuls of barley and scraps of bread. You bring death to those who should not die, and life to those who should not live, by lying to this people of mine who listen to lies. 20 So these are the words of the Lord GOD: I am against your magic bands with which you hunt men's lives for the excitement of it. I will tear them from your arms and set those lives at liberty, lives that you hunt for the excitement 21 of it. I will tear up your long veils and save my people from you; you shall no longer have power to hunt them. Thus you shall know that I am the 22 LORD. You discouraged the righteous man with lies, when I meant him no hurt; you so strengthened the wicked that he would not abandon his evil 23 ways and be saved; and therefore you shall never see your false visions again nor practise your divination any more. I will rescue my people from your power; and thus you shall know that I am the LORD.

14 Some of the elders of Israel came to 2 visit me, and while they sat with me the 3 LORD said to me, Man, these people have set their hearts on their idols and keep their eyes fixed on the sinful things that cause their downfall. Am I to let 4 such men consult me? Speak to them and tell them that these are the words of the Lord GOD: If any Israelite, with his heart set on his idols and his eyes fixed on the sinful things that cause his downfall, comes to a prophet, I, the LORD, in my own person, shall be constrained to answer him, despite his 5 many idols. My answer will grip the hearts of the Israelites, estranged from me as they are, one and all, through 6 their idols. So tell the Israelites that

these are the words of the Lord GOD: Turn away, turn away from your idols; turn your backs on all your abominations. If any man, Israelite or alien, 7 renounces me, sets his heart upon idols and fixes his eyes upon the vile thing that is his downfall—if such a man comes to consult me through a prophet, I, the LORD, in my own person, shall be constrained to answer him. I will set 8 my face against that man; I will make him an example and a byword; I will rid my people of him. Thus you shall know that I am the LORD. If a prophet 9 is seduced into making a prophecy, it is I the LORD who have seduced him; I will stretch out my hand and rid my people Israel of him. Both shall be 10 punished; the prophet and the man who consults him alike are guilty. And 11 never again will the Israelites stray from their allegiance, never again defy my will and bring pollution upon themselves; they will become my people, and I will become their God. This is the very word of the Lord GOD.

These were the words of the LORD 12 to me: Man, when a country sins by 13 breaking faith with me, I will stretch out my hand and cut short its daily bread. I will send famine upon it and destroy both men and cattle. Even if 14 those three men were living there, Noah, Danel[d] and Job, they would save none but themselves by their righteousness. This is the very word of the Lord GOD. If I should turn wild 15 beasts loose in a country to destroy its inhabitants, until it became a waste through which no man would pass for fear of the beasts, then, if those three 16 men were living there, as I live, says the Lord GOD, they would not save even their own sons and daughters; they would save themselves alone, and the country would become a waste. Or 17 if I should bring the sword upon that country and command it to go through

d *Or, as otherwise read,* Daniel.

14.1–23: Duplicity and personal responsibility. 7: If anyone, while still practicing idolatry, comes to consult a prophet he will receive an answer not from the prophet, but from the LORD —in punishment! **9:** A prophet who gives an answer to a known idolater is regarded as his accomplice. God, who as LORD of all allowed it, is considered to have *seduced* him in order to destroy him and *rid* the community of his influence. **14:** Three men famous in the ancient world for their virtue and intercessory power. *Noah* (Gen.6.9), *Job* (Job 42.7–10), and *Daniel*, a Canaanite hero, or possibly Daniel the biblical hero (Dan.3.22–27). These men were not able to save their wicked contemporaries from God's anger in time of calamity. They

the land and should destroy men and
18 cattle, then, if those three men were
living there, as I live, says the Lord
GOD, they could save neither son nor
daughter; they would save themselves
19 alone. Or if I should send pestilence on
that land and pour out my fury upon
it in blood, to destroy men and cattle,
20 then, if Noah, Danel and Job were
living there, as I live, says the Lord
GOD, they would save neither son nor
daughter; they would save themselves
alone by their righteousness.
21 These were the words of the Lord
GOD: How much less hope is there for
Jerusalem when I inflict on her these
four punishments of mine, sword and
famine, wild beasts and pestilence, to
22 destroy both men and cattle! Some will
be left in her, some survivors to be
brought out, both sons and daughters.
Look at them as they come out to you,
and see how they have behaved and
what they have done. This will be some
comfort to you for all the harm I have
done to Jerusalem and all I have in-
23 flicted upon her. It will bring you comfort when you see how they have
behaved and what they have done; for
you will know that it was not without
reason that I dealt thus with her. This is
the very word of the Lord GOD.

15 These were the words of the LORD
to me:

2 Man, how is the vine better than any
other tree,
than a branch from a tree in the forest?
3 Is wood got from it
fit to make anything useful?
Can men make it into a peg
and hang things on it?
4 If it is put on the fire for fuel,
if its two ends are burnt by the fire
and the middle is charred,

is it fit for anything useful?
Nothing useful could be made of it
even when whole;
how much less, when it is burnt by
the fire and charred,
can it be made into anything useful!

6 So these are the words of the Lord
GOD:

I treat the vine, as against forest-trees,
only as fuel for the fire,
even so I treat the people of Jerusalem;
I set my face against them.   7
Though they escape from the fire,
fire shall burn them up.
Thus you shall know that I am the
LORD
when I set my face against them,
making the land a waste   8
because they have broken faith.
This is the very word of the Lord
GOD.

The word of the LORD came to me: 16
Man, he said, make Jerusalem see her 2
abominable conduct. Tell her that these 3
are the words of the Lord GOD to her:
Canaan is the land of your ancestry
and there you were born; an Amorite
was your father and a Hittite your
mother. This is how you were treated 4
at birth: when you were born, your
navel-string was not tied, you were not
bathed in water ready for the rubbing,
you were not salted as you should have
been nor wrapped in swaddling clothes.
No one cared for you enough to do 5
any of these things or, indeed, to have
any pity for you; you were thrown out
on the bare ground in your own filth
on the day of your birth. Then I came 6
by and saw you kicking helplessly in
your own blood; I spoke to you, there
in your blood, and bade you live. I 7

---

would not be able to do so in the present situation. **21–23:** The *survivors* of the coming
catastrophe will be evidence that God does not punish *without reason*. That he does not will
be a source of hope to the exiles.
    15.1–8: Parable of the wood of the vine. Israel is the vine cultivated by God, in contrast to
the big trees, the nations. Unlike the big trees, a vine is valued only for its fruit and not for
its wood, especially if it has been charred by flames, as Israel has been by sin and her punishment, the Exile. See Judg.9.12–13; Jn.15.1–11.
    16.1–63: The marriage allegory of Jerusalem. The city's history is compared, in erotic
imagery, to the biography of a woman in distinct stages of her life. **1–7:** Unlike other cities,
Jerusalem had no epic legend of being founded by some god's commission. Rather, like an
illegitimate foundling, she was left as the result of the Amorite and Hittite movements in
Palestine, known now as occurring in the second millennium B.C. The LORD *bade* Jerusalem

tended you like an evergreen plant, like something growing in the fields; you throve and grew. You came to full womanhood; your breasts became firm and your hair grew, but still you were naked and exposed.

8 Again I came by and saw that you were ripe for love. I spread the skirt of my robe over you and covered your naked body. Then I plighted my troth and entered into a covenant with you, says the Lord GOD, and you became 9 mine. Then I bathed you in water and washed off the blood and anointed you 10 with oil. I gave you robes of brocade and sandals of stout hide; I fastened a linen girdle round you and dressed you 11 in lawn. For jewellery I put bracelets on your arms and a chain round your 12 neck; I gave you a nose-ring, I put pendants in your ears and a beautiful 13 coronet on your head. You had ornaments of gold and silver, your dresses were of linen, lawn, and brocade. You had flour and honey and olive oil for food, and you grew very 14 beautiful, you grew into a queen. The fame of your beauty went all over the world, for the splendour with which I decked you made it perfect. This is the very word of the Lord GOD.

15 But you trusted to your beauty and prostituted your fame; you committed fornication, offering yourself freely to any passer-by for your beauty to 16 become his. You took some of your clothes and decked a platform for yourself in gay colours and there you committed fornication; you had intercourse with him for your beauty to 17 become his.[e] You took the splendid ornaments of gold and silver which I had given you, and made for yourself male images with which you com- 18 mitted fornication. You covered them with your robes of brocade and offered

up my oil and my incense before them. You took the food I had given you, the 19 flour, the oil, and the honey, with which I had fed you, and set it before them as an offering of soothing odour. This is the very word of the Lord GOD.

You took the sons and daughters 20 whom you had borne to me, and sacrificed them to these images for their food. Was this of less account than your fornication? No! you slaugh- 21 tered my children and handed them over, you surrendered them to your images. With all your abominable 22 fornication you forgot those early days when you lay naked and exposed, kicking helplessly in your own blood.

After all the evil you had done (Oh! 23 the pity of it, says the Lord GOD), you 24 built yourself a couch and constructed a high-stool in every open place. You 25 built up your high-stools at the top of every street and disgraced your beauty, offering your body to any passer-by in countless acts of fornication. You 26 committed fornication with your gross neighbours, the Egyptians, and you provoked me to anger by your countless acts of fornication.

I stretched out my hand against you 27 and cut down your portion. Then I gave you up to women who hated you, Philistine women, who were so disgusted by your lewd ways. Not content 28 with this, you committed fornication with the Assyrians, led them into fornication and still were not content. You committed countless acts of 29 fornication in Chaldaea, the land of commerce, and even with this you were not content.

How you anger me! says the Lord 30 GOD. You have done all this like the imperious whore you are. You have 31 built your couch at the top of every

[e] you had intercourse . . . his: *prob. rdg.; Heb. obscure.*

live, by not destroying her during Joshua's conquest; see Josh.15.63. **8–14:** The espoused maiden: Jerusalem, being *ripe for love* when taken by David (2 Sam.5.6–8), became the "spouse" of the Lord when the Ark of the *Covenant* was moved into it (2 Sam.6.12–19); she was given *ornaments* when the Temple and the palaces were built by Solomon (1 Kgs.6.1–9.1). **15–19:** The flirtatious bride: her head turned by commerce with other nations, Jerusalem committed the double fornication of being unfaithful to God and of adopting the ritualistic prostitution of fertility cults (2 Kgs.21.1–18; Hos.4.13–14). **20–22:** An unfeeling mother: even human sacrifices of her children were offered; see 2 Kgs.16.3; 17.17; Jer.7.31. **23–34:** The adulterous wife: Jerusalem squandered the wealth of the Lord, her husband, in order to attract partners for her illicit love affairs of commerce and idolatry, thus being worse than a prostitute who offers herself to gain wealth (2 Kgs.16.7–18; 21.1–22). *High-stools* are the "high places,"

street and constructed your stool in every open place, but, unlike the common prostitute, you have scorned a fee. An adulterous wife who owes 32 obedience to her husband takes a fee 33 from*ᶠ* strangers. The prostitute also takes her fee; but you give presents to all your lovers, you bribe them to come from all quarters to commit fornication 34 with you. You are the very opposite of other women in your fornication: no one runs after you, you do not receive a fee, you give it. You are the very opposite.

35 Listen to the words of the LORD, 36 whore that you are. These are the words of the Lord GOD: You have been prodigal in your excesses, you have exposed your naked body in fornication with your lovers. In return for your abominable idols and for the slaughter of the children you have given 37 them, I will gather all those lovers to whom you made advances,*ᵍ* all whom you loved and all whom you hated. I will gather them in from all quarters against you; I will strip you naked before them, and they shall see your 38 whole body naked. I will put you on trial for adultery and murder, and I will charge you with*ʰ* blood shed in 39 jealousy and fury. Then I will hand you over to them. They will demolish your couch and pull down your high-stool; they will strip your clothes off, take away your splendid ornaments, and 40 leave you naked and exposed. They will bring up the mob against you and stone you, they will hack you to pieces 41 with their swords. They will burn down your houses and execute judgement on you, and many women shall see it. I will put an end to your fornication, and you shall never again give a fee to 42 your lovers. Then I will abate my fury, and my jealousy will turn away from you. I will be calm and will no longer 43 be provoked to anger. For you had forgotten the days of your youth and exasperated me with all your doings: so I in my turn brought retribution

upon you for your deeds. This is the very word of the Lord GOD.

Did you not commit these obscenities, as well as all your other abominations? Dealers in proverbs will say of 44 you, 'Like mother, like daughter.' You 45 are a true daughter of a mother who loathed her husband and children. You are a true sister of your sisters who loathed their husbands and children. You are all daughters of a Hittite mother and an Amorite father. Your 46 elder sister was Samaria, who lived with her daughters to the north of you; your younger sister, who lived with her daughters to the south of you, was Sodom. Did you not behave as they 47 did and commit the same abominations? You came very near to doing even worse than they. As I live, says the 48 Lord GOD, your sister Sodom and her daughters never behaved as you and your daughters have done. This was 49 the iniquity of your sister Sodom: she and her daughters had pride of wealth and food in plenty, comfort and ease, and yet she never helped the poor and wretched. They grew haughty and 50 did deeds abominable in my sight, and I made away with them, as you have seen. Samaria was never half the sinner 51 you have been; you have committed more abominations than she, abominations which have made your sister seem innocent. You must bear the humilia- 52 tion which you thought your sisters deserved. Your sins are so much more abominable than theirs that they appear innocent in comparison with you; and now you must bear your shame and humiliation and make your sisters seem innocent.

But I will restore the fortunes of 53 Sodom and her daughters and of Samaria and her daughters, and I will restore yours at the same time. Even 54 though you bring them comfort, you will bear your shame, you will be disgraced for all you have done; but when 55

f a fee from: *prob. rdg.; Heb. om.*
g to whom . . . advances: *or* whom you charmed.
h charge you with: *prob. mng.; Heb.* give you.

sanctuaries of illicit worship; see 6.3 n.; 2 Kgs.21.3. **35–43:** The castoff and condemned woman: Jerusalem, having lost the concerned jealousy of her husband, gained instead the cruel contempt of her paramours, Egypt and Babylon, nations which despoiled her. **45–52:** Jerusalem's sins exceed those of her sister cities Samaria and Sodom, and therefore, so will her *shame and humiliation.* **53–63:** Reconciliation, conversion, and new espousals await Jerusalem when once

your sister Sodom and her daughters become what they were of old, and when your sister Samaria and her daughters become what they were of old, then you and your daughters will
56 be restored. Did you not hear and talk much of your sister Sodom in the days
57 of your pride, before your wickedness was exposed, in the days when the daughters of Aram with those about her were disgraced, and the daughters of the Philistines round about, who so
58 despised you? Now you too must bear the consequences of your lewd and abominable conduct. This is the very word of the LORD.
59 These are the words of the Lord GOD: I will treat you as you have deserved, because you violated a covenant and made light of a solemn
60 oath. But I will remember the covenant I made with you when you were young, and I will establish with you a
61 covenant which shall last for ever. And you will remember your past ways and feel ashamed when you receive your sisters, the elder and the younger. For I will give them to you as daughters, and they shall not be outside your
62 covenant.*i* Thus I will establish my covenant with you, and you shall know
63 that I am the LORD. You will remember, and will be so ashamed and humiliated that you will never open your mouth again once I have accepted expiation for all you have done. This is the very word of the Lord GOD.

17 These were the words of the LORD
2 to me: Man, speak to the Israelites in
3 allegory and parable. Tell them that these are the words of the Lord GOD:

    A great eagle
    with broad wings and long pinions,

    in full plumage, richly patterned,
      came to Lebanon.
    He took the very top of a cedar
      tree,
    he plucked its highest twig;
    he carried it off to a land of
      commerce,
    and planted it in a city of
      merchants.
5 Then he took a native seed
    and put it in nursery-ground;
    he set it like a willow,
    a shoot beside abundant water.
6 It sprouted and became a vine,
    sprawling low along the ground
    and bending its trailing boughs
      towards him*j*
    with its roots growing beneath him.
    So it became a vine, it branched out
    and put forth shoots.
7 But there was another great eagle
    with broad wings and thick plumage;
    and this vine gave its roots
      a twist towards him;*j*
    it pushed out its trailing boughs
      towards him,
    seeking drink from the bed where it
      was planted,
8 though it had been set
    in good ground beside abundant
      water
    that it might bear shoots and be
      fruitful
    and become a noble vine.

9 Tell them that these are the words of the Lord GOD:

    Can such a vine flourish?
    Will not its roots be broken off
      and its fruit be stripped,

i and they . . . covenant: or though not on the ground of your covenant.   j Or inwards.

---

she will recognize and return to her original condition. *Daughters of Aram:* perhaps the Assyrian cities of Asshur and Nineveh destroyed in 614 and 612 respectively. *Solemn oath:* oath of loyalty to Nebuchadnezzar broken by Zedekiah; see 17.12–18.

17.1–24: Allegory of the cedar and the eagles portrays the drama of Zedekiah, the weak king of Judah, caught between the aggressiveness of the king of Babylon and the king of Egypt. **3–5:** Since allegory is an extended metaphor, a narrative with a continuous system of equivalents, the following identifications can possibly be made: *great eagle,* Nebuchadnezzar; *Lebanon,* city of Jerusalem; *top of a cedar tree,* dynasty of David; *highest twig,* King Jehoiachin; *land of commerce,* Babylonia; *city of merchants,* Babylon; *native seed,* Zedekiah, Jehoiachin's uncle, placed upon the throne by Nebuchadnezzar in 597 B.C. (2 Kgs.24.17). **6:** *Roots growing beneath him* is explained in v. 13, namely, when the king of Babylon put Zedekiah "on his oath." The kingdom was *sprawling low,* because most of its exalted citizens had been taken into captivity and Zedekiah's power was very limited even over his princes (Jer.38.5). **7:** *Another great eagle:* the Pharaoh Psammetichus II of Egypt (594–588 B.C.). Zedekiah's request for

and all its fresh sprouting leaves
wither,
until it is uprooted and carried away
with little effort and few hands?

10 If it is transplanted, can it flourish?
Will it not be utterly shrivelled,
as though by the touch of the east
wind,
on the bed where it ought to
sprout?

11 These were the words of the LORD
12 to me: Say to that rebellious people,
Do you not know what this means?
The king of Babylon came to Jerusalem,
took its king and its officers and
had them brought to him at Babylon.
13 He took a prince of the royal line and
made a treaty with him, putting him on
his oath. He took away the chief men
14 of the country, so that it should
become a humble kingdom unable to
raise itself but ready to observe the
15 treaty and keep it in force. But the
prince rebelled against him and sent
messengers to Egypt, asking for horses
and men in plenty. Can such a man
prosper? Can he escape destruction if
he acts in this way? Can he violate a
16 covenant and escape? As I live, says
the Lord GOD, I swear that he shall die
in the land of the king who put him
on the throne; he made light of his
oath and violated the covenant he
made with him. He shall die in Babylon.
17 Pharaoh will send no large army, no
great host, to protect him in battle; no
siege-ramp will be raised, no watch-
tower put up, nor will the lives of many
18 men be lost. He has violated a covenant
and has made light of his oath. He had
submitted, and yet he did all these
things; he shall not escape.
19 These then are the words of the Lord
GOD: As I live, he has made light of the
oath he took by me and has violated
the covenant I made with him. I will

bring retribution upon him; I will cast 20
my net over him, and he shall be caught
in its meshes. I will carry him to
Babylon and bring him to judgement
there, because he has broken faith with
me. In all his squadrons every com- 21
mander shall fall by the sword; those
who are left will be scattered to the four
winds. Thus you shall know that it is I,
the LORD, who have spoken.

These are the words of the Lord 22
GOD:

I, too, will take a slip
from the lofty crown of the cedar
and set it in the soil;
I will pluck a tender shoot from the
topmost branch
and plant it.
I will plant it high on a lofty 23
mountain,
the highest mountain in Israel.
It will put out branches, bear its fruit,
and become a noble cedar.
Winged birds of every kind will
roost under it,
they will roost in the shelter of its
sweeping boughs.
All the trees of the country-side 24
will know
that it is I, the LORD,
who bring low the tall tree
and raise the low tree high,
who dry up the green tree
and make the dry tree put forth
buds.
I, the LORD, have spoken and will
do it.

THESE WERE THE WORDS OF THE LORD 18
to me: What do you all mean by 2
repeating this proverb in the land of
Israel:

'The fathers have eaten sour grapes,
and the children's teeth are set on
edge'?

military aid from Egypt (v. 15) is the *twist towards him*. **19**: Ezekiel considers Zedekiah's breach
of his loyalty oath to Nebuchadnezzar a rejection of God's *covenant*. **22–24**: God's action in
history—to *pluck* and to *plant*—is decisive, not the maneuverings of kings.
18.1–32: The Lord's way is freedom. Maintaining right relations with God frees a man from:
(a) the past of his parents, vv. 1–20; (b) the past of his own life, vv. 21–32. Although individual
responsibility is asserted by biblical authors before Ezekiel, as in Deut.24.16; 2 Kgs.14.6;
Jer.31.29–30, Ezekiel's challenging affirmation here stands in clear contrast to the strong
formulations of the inherited doctrine found in Exod.34.7; Lev.26.39–40; Deut.5.9. **2**: *This
proverb*, restating, though somewhat cynically, the teaching of Exod.20.5 and 34.7, seems to
imply that the nation's recent calamities were an unjust application of the teaching by God.

3 As I live, says the Lord God, this proverb shall never again be used in 4 Israel. Every living soul belongs to me; father and son alike are mine. The soul that sins shall die.

5 Consider the man who is righteous 6 and does what is just and right. He never feasts at mountain-shrines, never lifts his eyes to the idols of Israel, never dishonours another man's wife, never approaches a woman during her 7 periods. He oppresses no man, returns the debtor's pledge, he never robs. He gives bread to the hungry and 8 clothes to those who have none. He never lends either at discount or at interest. He shuns injustice and deals 9 fairly between man and man. He conforms to my statutes and loyally observes my laws. Such a man is righteous: he shall live, says the Lord God.

10 He may have a son who is a man of violence and a cut-throat who turns 11 his back on these rules.*k* He obeys none of them, he feasts at mountain-shrines, 12 he dishonours another man's wife, he oppresses the unfortunate and the poor, he is a robber, he does not return the debtor's pledge, he lifts his eyes to 13 idols and joins in abominable rites; he lends both at discount and at interest. Such a man shall not live. Because he has committed all these abominations he shall die, and his blood will be on his own head.

14 This man in turn may have a son who sees all his father's sins; he sees, 15 but he commits none of them. He never feasts at mountain-shrines, never lifts his eyes to the idols of Israel, never 16 dishonours another man's wife. He oppresses no man, takes no pledge, does not rob. He gives bread to the hungry and clothes to those who have 17 none. He shuns injustice, he never lends either at discount or at interest. He keeps my laws and conforms to my statutes. Such a man shall not die for his father's wrongdoing; he shall live.

18 His father may have been guilty of oppression and robbery and may have lived an evil life among his kinsfolk, and so has died because of his iniquity.

19 You may ask, 'Why is the son not punished for his father's iniquity?' Because he has always done what is just and right and has been careful to obey all my laws, therefore he shall live. 20 It is the soul that sins, and no other, that shall die; a son shall not share a father's guilt, nor a father his son's. The righteous man shall reap the fruit of his own righteousness, and the wicked man the fruit of his own wickedness.

21 It may be that a wicked man gives up his sinful ways and keeps all my laws, doing what is just and right. That man shall live; he shall not die. None 22 of the offences he has committed shall be remembered against him; he shall live because of his righteous deeds. 23 Have I any desire, says the Lord GOD, for the death of a wicked man? Would I not rather that he should mend his ways and live?

24 It may be that a righteous man turns back from his righteous ways and commits every kind of abomination that the wicked practise; shall he do this and live? No, none of his former righteousness will be remembered in his favour; he has broken his faith, he 25 has sinned, and he shall die. You say that the Lord acts without principle? Listen, you Israelites, it is you who act without principle, not I. If a righteous 26 man turns from his righteousness, takes to evil ways and dies,*l* it is because of these evil ways that he dies. Again, 27 if a wicked man turns from his wicked ways and does what is just and right, he will save his life. If he sees his 28 offences as they are and turns his back on them all, then he shall live; he shall not die.

29 'The Lord acts without principle', say the Israelites. No, Israelites, it is you who act without principle, not I. Therefore, Israelites, says the Lord 30 GOD, I will judge every man of you on his deeds. Turn, turn from your offences, or your iniquity will be your downfall. Throw off the load of your 31 past misdeeds; get yourselves a new

k who turns . . . rules: prob. rdg.; Heb. unintelligible.
l Prob. rdg.; Heb. adds because of them.

31–32: After repeated assurances that a man of "righteous deeds" will "surely live" (vv.

heart and a new spirit. Why should you
32 die, you men of Israel? I have no desire
for any man's death. This is the very
word of the Lord GOD.

19 Raise a lament over the princes of
2 Israel and say:

> Your mother was a lioness
>   among the lions!
> She made her lair among the young
>   lions
>   and many were the cubs she bore.
3 One of her cubs she raised,
>   and he grew into a young lion.
> He learnt to tear his prey,
>   he devoured men.
4 Then the nations shouted at[m] him
>   and he was caught in their pit,
> and they dragged him with hooks to
>   the land of Egypt.
5 His case, she saw, was desperate, her
>   hope was lost;
> so she took another of her cubs
>   and made him a young lion.
6 He prowled among the lions
>   and acted like a young lion.
> He learnt to tear his prey,
>   he devoured men;
7 he broke down their palaces, laid
>   their cities in ruins.
> The land and all that was in it
>   was aghast at the noise of his
>   roaring.
8 From the provinces all round
>   the nations raised the hue and cry;
> they cast their net over him
>   and he was caught in their pit.
9 With hooks they drew him into a
>   cage
> and brought him to the king of
>   Babylon,
> who flung him into prison,
> that his voice might never again be
>   heard
>   on the mountains of Israel.

10 Your mother was a vine in a
>   vineyard[n]
> planted by the waterside.

> It grew fruitful and luxuriant,
>   for there was water in plenty.
> It had stout branches,   11
>   fit to make sceptres for those who
>   bear rule.
> It grew tall, finding its way through
>   the foliage,
> and conspicuous for its height and
>   many trailing boughs.
> But it was torn up in anger and   12
>   thrown to the ground;
> the east wind blighted it,
>   its fruit was blown off,
>   its strong branches were blighted,
>   and fire burnt it.
> Now it is replanted in the   13
>   wilderness,
> in a dry and thirsty land;
> and fire bursts forth from its own   14
>   branches
>   and burns up its shoots.[o]
> It has no strong branch any more
>   to make a sceptre for those who
>   bear rule.

This is the lament and as a lament it
passed into use.

ON THE TENTH DAY OF THE FIFTH **20**
month in the seventh year, some of the
elders of Israel came to consult the
LORD and were sitting with me. Then 2
this word came to me from the LORD:
Man, say to the elders of Israel, This 3
is the word of the Lord GOD: Do you
come to consult me? As I live, I will
not be consulted by you. This is the
very word of the Lord GOD.
Will you judge them? Will you judge 4
them, O man? Then tell them of the
abominations of their forefathers and 5
say to them, These are the words of the
Lord GOD: When I chose Israel, with
uplifted hand I bound myself by oath
to the race of Jacob and revealed myself
to them in Egypt; I lifted up my hand
and declared: I am the LORD your God.

m shouted at: *or* heard a report about.
n in a vineyard: *prob. rdg.; Heb. obscure in context.*
o *Prob. rdg.; Heb. adds* its fruit.

9,17,22), Ezekiel exhorts his reader to *get a new heart and a new spirit* and so turn and live;
the prophet's message seems to have implications beyond the physical life of this world.
19.1–14: Laments on the royal house. The calamities of the Davidic dynasty are depicted
allegorically in mournful poetic meter. **2:** *Lioness:* Judah (Gen.49.9). **3:** *One of her cubs:* King
Jehoahaz, taken captive by Pharaoh Necho in 609; see 2 Kgs.23.30–34. **10:** *Vine:* Judah.
11: *Stout branches:* either Zedekiah or Jehoiachin.
20.1–44: Theology of Israel's history. The history of Israel, in the prophet's view, is the
history of God's self-revelation, so that Israel might have life. **1:** August 14, 591 B.C. Compare

6 On that day I swore with hand uplifted that I would bring them out of Egypt Into the land I had sought out for them, a land flowing with milk and honey, 7 fairest of all lands. I told them, every one, to cast away the loathsome things on which they feasted their eyes and not to defile themselves with the idols of Egypt. I am the LORD your God, I said.

8 But they rebelled against me, they refused to listen to me, and not one of them cast away the loathsome things on which he feasted his eyes or forsook the idols of Egypt. I had thought to pour out my wrath and exhaust my 9 anger on them in Egypt. I acted for the honour of my name, that it might not be profaned in the sight of the nations among whom Israel was living: I revealed myself to them by bringing 10 Israel out of Egypt. I brought them out of Egypt and led them into the wilder-11 ness. There I gave my statutes to them and taught them my laws, so that by keeping them men might have life. 12 Further, I gave them my sabbaths as a sign between us, so that they should know that I, the LORD, was hallowing 13 them for myself. But the Israelites rebelled against me in the wilderness; they did not conform to my statutes, they rejected my laws, though by keeping them men might have life, and they utterly desecrated my sabbaths. So again I thought to pour out my wrath on them in the wilderness to destroy 14 them. I acted for the honour of my name, that it might not be profaned in the sight of the nations who had seen me bring them out. 15 Further, I swore to them in the wilderness with uplifted hand that I would not bring them into the land I had given them, that land flowing with milk and honey, fairest of all lands. 16 For they had rejected my laws, they would not conform to my statutes and they desecrated my sabbaths, because they loved to follow idols of their own. 17 Yet I pitied them too much to destroy

them and did not make an end of them in the wilderness. I commanded their 18 sons in the wilderness not to conform to their fathers' statutes, nor observe their laws, nor defile themselves with their idols. I said, I am the LORD your 19 God, you must conform to my statutes; you must observe my laws and act according to them. You must keep 20 my sabbaths holy, and they will become a sign between us; so you will know that I am the LORD your God.

But the sons too rebelled against me. 21 They did not conform to my statutes or observe my laws, though any who had done so would have had life through them, and they desecrated my sabbaths. Again I thought to pour out my wrath and exhaust my anger on them in the wilderness. I acted for the 22 honour of my name, that it might not be profaned in the sight of the nations who had seen me bring them out. Yes, 23 and in the wilderness I swore to them with uplifted hand that I would disperse them among the nations and scatter them abroad, because they had dis-24 obeyed my laws, rejected my statutes, desecrated my sabbaths, and turned longing eyes toward the idols of their forefathers. I did more; I imposed on 25 them statutes that were not good statutes, and laws by which they could not win life. I let them defile themselves 26 with gifts to idols; I made them surrender their eldest sons to them so that I might fill them with horror. Thus they would know that I am the LORD.

Speak then, O man, to the Israelites 27 and say to them, These are the words of the Lord GOD: Once again your forefathers insulted me and broke faith with me: when I brought them into 28 the land which I had sworn with uplifted hand to give them, they marked down every hill-top and every leafy tree, and there they offered their sacrifices, they made the gifts which roused my anger, they set out their offerings of soothing odour and poured out their drink-offerings. I asked them, 29

1.1; 8.1; 24.1. **9:** *Honour* of his *name:* not vain concern for reputation, but acute awareness that Israel's welfare flows from, and is identified with, the name, i.e. the reality, of God. **20:** The observance of the *sabbaths* became at this time, and especially in captivity, a visible *sign* of fidelity to the covenant. **25–26:** The *surrender* of the *eldest sons* as *gifts to idols* is seen as one of the *laws* from God, inasmuch as he directs even the evil deeds of men to their own good. Sacrifices

What is this hill-shrine to which you are going up? And 'hill-shrine' has been its name ever since.

30 So tell the Israelites, These are the words of the Lord GOD: Are you defiling yourselves as your forefathers did? Are you wantonly giving your-selves to their loathsome gods? When 31 you bring your gifts, when you pass your sons through the fire, you are still defiling yourselves in the service of your crowd of idols. How can I let you consult me, men of Israel? As I live, says the Lord GOD, I will not be con-32 sulted by you. When you say to your-selves, 'Let us become like the nations and tribes of other lands and worship wood and stone', you are thinking of 33 something that can never be. As I live, says the Lord GOD, I will reign over you with a strong hand, with arm 34 outstretched and wrath outpoured. I will bring you out from the peoples and gather you from the lands over which you have been scattered by my strong hand, my outstretched arm and out-35 poured wrath. I will bring you into the wilderness of the peoples; there will I confront you, and there will I state my 36 case against you. Even as I did in the wilderness of Egypt against your fore-fathers, so will I state my case against you. This is the very word of the Lord GOD.

37 I will pass you under the rod and bring you within the bond*p* of the 38 covenant. I will rid you of those who revolt and rebel against me. I will take them out of the land where they are now living, but they shall not set foot on the soil of Israel. Thus shall you know that I am the LORD.

39 Now, men of Israel, these are the words of the Lord GOD: Go, sweep away your idols, every man of you. So in days to come you will never be dis-obedient to me or desecrate my holy name with your gifts and your idol-40 atries. But on my holy hill, the lofty

hill of Israel, says the Lord GOD, there shall the Israelites serve me in the land, every one of them. There will I receive them with favour; there will I demand your contribution and the best of your offerings, with all your consecrated gifts. I will receive your offerings of 41 soothing odour, when I have brought you out from the peoples and gathered you from the lands where you have been scattered. I, and only I, will have your worship, for all the nations to see.

You will know that I am the LORD, 42 when I bring you home to the soil of Israel, to the land which I swore with uplifted hand to give your forefathers. There you will remember your past ways 43 and all the wanton deeds with which you have defiled yourselves, and will loathe yourselves for all the evils you have done. You will know that I am 44 the LORD, when I have dealt with you, O men of Israel, not as your wicked ways and your vicious deeds deserve but for the honour of my name. This is the very word of the Lord GOD.

These were the words of the LORD 45 to me: Man, turn and face towards 46 Teman*q* and pour out your words to the south; prophesy to the rough country of the Negeb. Say to it, Listen 47 to the words of the LORD. These are the words of the Lord GOD: I will set fire to you, and the fire will consume all the wood, green and dry alike. Its fiery flame shall not be put out, but from the Negeb northwards every face will be scorched by it. All men will see 48 that it is I, the LORD, who have set it ablaze; it shall not be put out. 'Ah no! 49 O Lord GOD,' I cried; 'they say of me, "He deals only in parables."'

These were the words of the LORD 21 to me: Man, turn and face towards 2 Jerusalem, and pour out your words against her sanctuary;*r* prophesy against the land of Israel. Say to the 3

p Or muster.   *q Or* face southward.
r her sanctuary: *prob. rdg.; Heb.* sanctuaries.

of human infants are condemned in v. 31 and in 16.20; also in Lev.18.21; Jer.7.31. **34–39:** The return from exile through the *wilderness of the peoples,* i.e. the desert of Syria, will be like the Sinai experience relived.
 20.45–21.32: Parable of the forest fire is the oracle of doom in vv. 45–48. When the people object that Ezekiel is *dealing only in parables* (v. 49), he gives an explanation (21.1–7). **46:** According to some interpreters, Ezekiel, if in Babylon, could not *face south* and look toward Judah. See Introduction. *Negeb:* the southern part of Judah. **21.3:** The consuming fire (20.47) is the *sword* which destroys Israel, both of which are attributed to God as the Lord of history.

land of Israel, These are the words of the LORD: I am against you; I will draw my sword from the scabbard and cut off from you both righteous and 4 wicked. It is because I would cut off your righteous and your wicked equally that my sword will be drawn from the scabbard against all men, from the 5 Negeb northwards. All men shall know that I the LORD have drawn my sword; 6 it shall never again be sheathed. Groan in their presence, man, groan bitterly 7 until your lungs are bursting. When they ask you why you are groaning, say to them, 'I groan at the thing I have heard; when it comes, all hearts melt, all courage fails, all hands fall limp, all men's knees run with urine. It is coming. It is here.' This is the very word of the Lord GOD.

8   These were the words of the LORD to 9 me: Prophesy, man, and say, This is the word of the Lord:

A sword, a sword is sharpened and
   burnished,
10   sharpened to kill and kill again,
   burnished to flash[s] like lightning.
Ah! the club is brandished, my son,
   to defy all wooden idols!
11   The sword is given to be burnished
   ready for the hand to grasp.
The sword—it is sharpened,
   it is burnished,
ready to be put into the slayer's hand.

12   Cry, man, and howl; for all this falls on my people, it falls on Israel's princes who are delivered over to the sword and are slain with my people. Therefore 13 beat your breast in remorse, for it is the test—and what if it is not in truth the club of defiance? This is the very word of the Lord GOD.

14   But you, man, prophesy and clap
   your hands together;
swing the sword twice, thrice:
   it is the sword of slaughter,
the great sword of slaughter whirling
   about them.

That their hearts may be troubled 15
   and many stumble and fall,
I have set the threat of the sword at
   all their gates,
the threat of the sword[t] made to
   flash like lightning
   and drawn to kill.
Be sharpened, turn right; be un- 16
   sheathed, turn left,
wherever your point is aimed.

I, too, will clap my hands together and 17 abate my anger. I, the LORD, have spoken.

   These were the words of the LORD 18 to me: Man, trace out two roads by 19 which the sword of the king of Babylon may come, starting both of them from the same land. Then carve a signpost, carve it at the point where the highway forks. Mark out a road for the sword 20 to come to the Ammonite city of Rabbah, to Judah, and to Jerusalem at the heart of it. For the king of Babylon 21 halts to take the omens at the parting of the ways, where the road divides. He casts lots with arrows, consults teraphim[u] and inspects the livers of beasts. The augur's arrow marked 22 'Jerusalem' falls at his right hand: here, then,[v] he must raise a shout and sound the battle-cry, set battering-rams against the gates, pile siege-ramps and build watch-towers. It may well seem 23 to the people that the auguries are false, whereas they will put me in mind of their wrongdoing, and they will fall into the enemies' hand. These therefore 24 are the words of the Lord GOD: Because you have kept me mindful of your wrongdoing by your open rebellion, and your sins have been revealed in all your acts, because you have kept yourselves in my mind, you will fall into the enemies' hand by force.

   You, too, you impious and wicked 25 prince of Israel, your fate has come upon you in the hour of final punishment. These are the words of the Lord 26

s to flash: *prob. rdg.; Heb. unintelligible.*
t the threat of the sword: *prob. rdg.; Heb. obscure in context.*   *u Or* household gods.
v Prob. rdg.; Heb. adds he must set battering-rams.

8–17: This song of *the sword* is a poetic description of the coming catastrophe. **20:** *Rabbah* is modern Amman, the capital of Jordan. **21:** Three forms of divination are used; the result of only one is given: arrows inscribed with alternatives, shaken in a quiver, and then drawn. **23–24:** The *auguries* do not bind the Lord but only *put* him *in mind* of Israel's *rebellion* against him. **25:** *Wicked prince:* Zedekiah. See 7.2, 3, 7; 12.10; 17.19; 35.5; 2 Chr.36.11–13; Jer.52.2.

GOD: Put off your diadem, lay aside your crown. All is changed; raise the 27 low and bring down the high. Ruin! Ruin! I will bring about such ruin as never was before, until the rightful sovereign comes. Then I will give him all.

28 Man, prophesy and say, These are the words of the Lord GOD to the Ammonites and to their shameful god:

A sword, a sword drawn for slaughter,
burnished for destruction,*w*
to flash like lightning!
29 Your visions are false, your
auguries a lie,
which bid you bring it*x* down
upon the necks of impious and
wicked men,
whose fate has come upon them
in the hour of final punishment.
30 Sheathe it again.
I will judge you in the place where
you were born,
the land of your origin.
31 I will pour out my rage upon you;
I will breathe out my blazing wrath
over you.
I will hand you over to brutal men,
skilled in destruction.
32 You shall become fuel for fire,
your blood shall be shed within
the land
and you shall leave no memory
behind.

For I, the LORD, have spoken.

22 These were the words of the LORD
2 to me: Man, will you judge her, will you judge the murderous city and bring home to her all her abominable
3 deeds? Say to her, These are the words of the Lord GOD: Alas for the city that sheds blood within her walls and brings her fate upon herself, the city that makes herself idols and is defiled
4 thereby! The guilt is yours for the

blood you have shed, the pollution is on you for the idols you have made. You have shortened your days by this and brought the end of your years nearer. This is why I exposed you to the contempt of the nations, the mockery of every country. Lands far 5 and near will taunt you with your infamy and gross disorder. In you the 6 princes of Israel, one and all, have used their power to shed blood; men have 7 treated their fathers and mothers with contempt, they have oppressed the alien and ill-treated the orphan and the widow. You have disdained what is 8 sacred to me and desecrated my sabbaths. In you, Jerusalem, informers 9 have worked to procure bloodshed; in you are men who have feasted at mountain-shrines and have committed lewdness. In you men have exposed 10 their fathers' nakedness; they have violated women during their periods; they have committed an outrage with 11 their neighbours' wives and have lewdly defiled their daughters-in-law; they have ravished their sisters, their own fathers' daughters. In you men 12 have accepted bribes to shed blood, and they have exacted discount and interest on their loans. You have oppressed your fellows for gain, and you have forgotten me. This is the very word of the Lord GOD.

See, I strike with my clenched fist in 13 anger at your ill-gotten gains and at the bloodshed within your walls. Will 14 your strength or courage stand when I deal with you? I, the LORD, have spoken and I will act. I will disperse you 15 among the nations and scatter you abroad; thus will I rid you altogether of your defilement. I will sift you*y* in 16 the sight of the nations, and you will know that I am the LORD.

w *for destruction: prob. rdg.; Heb. obscure.*
x *Prob. rdg.; Heb. you.*
y *I will sift you: or You will be profaned.*

28–32: The song of the *sword* depicts for Ammon the same fate as for Judah in vv. 8–17.
22.1–31: The docket of crimes committed by the city and by various classes of citizens. Three indictments are given, in legal form, each followed by an appropriate sentence: vv. 1–12, against the population of Jerusalem in general, vv. 13–16 being the sentence; 17–18, against other Israelites who took refuge in the city, with the sentence in 19–22; 23–30, against specific classes for their various abuses of civic, religious and social authority or responsibility, with v. 31 as the sentence. **3:** *Sheds blood:* bloody violence, or sins which demand the death penalty as in vv. 10–11. **10–11:** These acts, according to Lev.18.6–30, are prohibited. **12:** Two forms of exacting *interest* were apparently in use: *discount* (Heb. "bite"), taking a cut at the time of loan; and *interest* (Heb. "increase"), demanding at time of payment more than was lent.

17 These were the words of the LORD
18 to me: Man, to me all Israelites are an
alloy, their silver alloyed with copper,
19 tin, iron, and lead.ᶻ Therefore, these
are the words of the Lord GOD:
because you have all become alloyed,
I will gather you together into Jeru-
20 salem, as a mass of silver, copper, iron,
lead, and tin is gathered into a crucible
for the fire to be blown to full heat to
melt them. So will I gather you in my
anger and wrath, set you there and
21 melt you; I will collect you and blow up
the fire of my anger until you are melted
22 within it. You will be melted as silver
is melted in a crucible, and you will
know that I, the LORD, have poured
out my anger upon you.

23 These were the words of the LORD
24 to me: Man, say to Jerusalem, You are
like a land on which no rain has fallen;
no shower has come down upon youᵃ
25 in the days of indignation. The princes
within her are like lions growling as
they tear their prey. They have
devoured men, and seized their treasure and all their wealth; they have
widowed many women within her
26 walls. Her priests have done violence
to my lawᵇ and profaned what is
sacred to me. They make no distinction
between sacred and common, and lead
men to see no difference between clean
and unclean. They have disregarded
my sabbaths, and I am dishonoured
27 among them. Her officers within her
are like wolves tearing their prey,
shedding blood and destroying men's
28 lives to acquire ill-gotten gain. Her
prophets use whitewash instead of
plaster;ᶜ their vision is false and their
divination a lie. They say, 'This is the
word of the Lord GOD', when the LORD
29 has not spoken. The common people
are bullies and robbers; they ill-treat

the unfortunate and the poor, they are
unjust and cruel to the alien. I looked 30
for a man among them who could build
up a barricade, who could stand before
me in the breach to defend the land
from ruin; but I found no such man.
I poured out my indignation upon them 31
and utterly destroyed them in the fire
of my wrath. Thus I brought on them
the punishment they had deserved.
This is the very word of the Lord GOD.

The word of the LORD came to me: 23
Man, he said, there were once two 2
women, daughters of the same mother.
They played the whore in Egypt, 3
played the whore while they were
still girls; for there they let their
breasts be fondled and their virgin
bosoms pressed. The elder was named 4
Oholah, her sister Oholibah. They
became mine and bore me sons and
daughters. 'Oholah' is Samaria, 'Oholibah' Jerusalem. While she owed me 5
obedience Oholah played the whore
and was infatuated with her Assyrian
lovers, staff officers in blue,ᵈ viceroys 6
and governors, handsome young cavaliers all of them, riding on horseback.
She played the whore with all of them, 7
the flower of the Assyrian youth; and
she let herself be defiled with all their
idols, wherever her lust led her. She 8
never gave up the whorish ways she had
learnt in Egypt, where men had lain
with her when young, had pressed her
virgin bosom and overwhelmed her
with their fornication. So I abandoned 9
her to her lovers, the Assyrians, with
whom she was infatuated. They rav- 10
ished her, they took her sons and
daughters, and they killed her with the
sword. She became a byword among

ᶻ *their silver . . . lead: prob. rdg.; Heb.* copper, tin,
iron, and lead inside a crucible; they are an alloy,
silver.   ᵃ *Prob. rdg.; Heb.* it.
ᵇ *Or* instruction.   ᶜ *Cp. 13. 8–16.*   ᵈ *Or* violet.

20: *Into Jerusalem:* possibly an allusion to refugees fleeing before the advancing Babylonian
army.
   23.1–49: Allegorical tale of two cities. Similar in literary form to ch. 16, but there the emphasis
is on cultic infidelity, here on political instability. **1–3:** The *two women* are the two capital
cities: Samaria standing for the Northern Kingdom Israel, and Jerusalem for the Southern
Kingdom Judah. *Played the whore in Egypt* as *girls:* the patriarchs, ancestors of the two kingdoms,
descended into Egypt in search of food. Their progeny, making use of Egypt's power and
wealth (see Gen. chs. 40–50), presumably fell into idolatry and were subsequently enslaved
(Exod.1.1–14). Such events set the pattern, allegorically, of the two women's adult life. **4:**
Oholah: lit. "she who has a tent" (or: "her [own] tent"), that is, the Northern Kingdom;
Oholibah: lit. "my tent [is] in her," is the Southern. "Tent" probably means the place of
worship, Oholah having her own schismatic worship (see 1 Kgs.12.25–33), and Oholibah being
the sanctuary in Jerusalem where the Ark was kept (2 Sam.6.17). **5–10:** Because political

women, and judgement was passed upon her.

11 Oholibah, her sister, had watched her, and she gave herself up to lust and played the whore worse than her sister. 12 She, too, was infatuated with Assyrians, viceroys, governors and staff officers, all handsome young cavaliers, in full 13 dress, riding on horseback. I found that she too had let herself be defiled; both 14 had gone the same way; but she carried her fornication to greater lengths: she saw male figures carved on the wall, sculptured forms of Chaldaeans, picked 15 out in vermilion. Belts were round their waists, and on their heads turbans with dangling ends. All seemed to be high officers and looked like Babylonians, 16 natives of Chaldaea. As she looked she was infatuated with them, so she sent 17 messengers to Chaldaea for them. And the Babylonians came to her to share her bed, and defiled her with fornication; she was defiled by them until she 18 was filled with revulsion. She made no secret that she was a whore but let herself be ravished until I was filled with revulsion against her as I was against 19 her sister. She played the whore again and again, remembering how in her youth she had played the whore in 20 Egypt. She was infatuated with their male prostitutes, whose members were like those of asses and whose seed came 21 in floods like that of horses. So, Oholibah, you relived the lewdness of your girlhood in Egypt when you let your bosom be pressed and your breasts fondled.*e*

22 Therefore these are the words of the Lord GOD: I will rouse them against you, Oholibah, those lovers of yours who have filled you with revulsion, and bring them upon you from every side, 23 the Babylonians and all those Chaldaeans, men of Pekod, Shoa, and Koa, and all the Assyrians with them. Handsome young men they are, viceroys and governors, commanders and staff officers,*f* riding on horseback. 24 They will come against you with war-

horses, with chariots and wagons, with a host drawn from the nations, armed with shield, buckler, and helmet; they will beset you on every side. I will give them authority to judge, and they will use that authority to judge you. I will 25 turn my jealous wrath loose on you, and they will make you feel their fury. They will cut off your nose and your ears, and in the end you*g* will fall by the sword.*h* They will strip you of your 26 clothes and take away all your finery. So I will put a stop to your lewdness 27 and the way in which you learnt to play the whore in Egypt. You will never cast longing eyes on such things again, never remember Egypt any more.

These are the words of the Lord 28 GOD: I am handing you over to those whom you hate, those who have filled you with revulsion; and they will make 29 you feel their hatred. They will take all you have earned and leave you naked and exposed; that body with which you have played the whore will be ravished. It is your lewdness and your fornication that have brought this upon you, 30 it is because you have followed alien peoples and played the whore and have allowed yourself to be defiled with their idols. You have followed in your sister's 31 footsteps, and I will put her cup into your hand.

These are the words of the Lord 32 GOD:

You shall drink from your sister's
    cup,
  a cup deep and wide,
charged with mockery and scorn,
  more than ever cup can hold.
It*i* will be full of drunkenness and   33
    grief,
  a cup of ruin and desolation,
the cup of your sister Samaria;
  and you shall drink it to the dregs.   34

e fondled: prob. rdg.; Heb. unintelligible.
f staff officers: prob. rdg., cp. verses 5 and 12; Heb. obscure.
g in the end you: or your successors.
h Prob. rdg.; Heb. adds They will take your sons and daughters, and in the end you will be burnt.
i Prob. rdg.; Heb. You.

alliances implied a lack of trust in God's power, the prophets considered reliance on them as playing the *whore*. God *abandoned* Samaria in 721 B.C., when she was destroyed by the Assyrians and her people taken into captivity; see 2 Kgs.17.5–6. **12:** Oholibah (Judah) was *infatuated* with *Assyrians*, when Ahaz, king of Judah (735–715 B.C.), courted their favor (2 Kgs.16.7–9). **32:** Samaria's fate (destruction of 721 B.C.) will be Jerusalem's *cup* in the destruction and

Then you will chew[j] it in pieces
and tear out your breasts.
This is my verdict, says the Lord GOD.

35 Therefore, these are the words of the
Lord GOD: Because you have forgotten me and flung me behind your
back, you must bear the guilt of your
lewdness and your fornication.

36 The LORD said to me, Man, will you
judge Oholah and Oholibah? Then
37 tax them with their vile offences. They
have committed adultery, and there is
blood on their hands. They have committed adultery with their idols and
offered my children to them for food,
38 the children they had borne me. This
too they have done to me: they have
polluted my sanctuary and desecrated
39 my sabbaths. They came into my
sanctuary and desecrated it by slaughtering their sons as an offering to their
idols; this they did in my own house.
40 They would send for men from a far-off
country; and the men came at the
messenger's bidding. You bathed your
body for these men, you painted your
eyes, decked yourself in your finery,
41 you sat yourself upon a bed of state
and had a table put ready before it and
laid my own incense and my own oil
42 on it. Loud were the voices of the light-
hearted crowd; and besides ordinary
folk Sabaeans were there, brought from
the wilderness; they put bracelets on
the women's hands and beautiful gar-
43 lands on their heads. I thought: Ah
that woman, grown old in adultery!
Now they will commit fornication with
44 her—with her of all women! They
resorted to her as a prostitute; they
resorted to Oholah and Oholibah,
45 those lewd women. Upright men will
condemn them for their adultery and
bloodshed; for adulterous they are, and
blood is on their hands.

46 These are the words of the Lord
GOD: Summon the invading host;

abandon them to terror and rapine.
Let the host stone them and hack them 47
to pieces with their swords, kill their
sons and daughters and burn down
their houses. Thus I will put an end 48
to lewdness in the land, and other
women shall be taught not to be as
lewd as they. You shall pay the penalty 49
for your lewd conduct and be punished
for your idolatries, and you will know
that I am the Lord GOD.

These were the words of the LORD, **24**
spoken to me on the tenth day
of the tenth month in the ninth year:
Man, write down a name for this day, 2
this very day: This is the day the king
of Babylon invested Jerusalem. Sing a 3
song of derision to this people of
rebels; say to them, These are the
words of the Lord GOD:

Set a cauldron on the fire,
  set it on and pour water into it.
Into it collect the pieces, 4
  all the choice pieces,
cram it with leg and shoulder and
  the best of the bones;
  take the best of the flock. 5
Pack the logs[k] round it underneath;
  seethe the stew
and boil the bones in it.

O city running with blood, 6
O pot green with corrosion,
  corrosion that will never be clean!

Therefore these are the words of the
Lord GOD:

Empty it, piece after piece,
  though no lot is cast for any of them.
The city had blood in her midst 7
and she poured it out on the
  gleaming rock,
not on the ground: she did not pour
  it there
for the dust to cover it.

[j] *Or* dash.   [k] *Prob. rdg., cp. verse* 10; *Heb.* bones.

---

captivity of 587 B.C. **40–44:** Unknown contemporary political events seem to be indicated.
42: *Sabaeans:* inhabitants of Sheba, a land of traders in the southwest corner of the Arabian
peninsula, probably modern Yemen.
    24.1–27: Jerusalem is besieged: Verses 1–14 are an elaboration and interpretation of 11.3–13.
1: The date is probably January 18, 588 B.C.; compare 2 Kgs.25.1. **3–5:** Into the *cauldron*
(Jerusalem) are collected the *choice pieces* (the nobility); the Babylonians apply the *fire* (siege),
thus fulfilling in a tragic sense the optimistic allegory of 11.3. **6:** Their expected security
destroyed, the nobles will be taken out *piece after piece* indiscriminately because the cauldron
is full of *corrosion.* **7:** *Blood,* the source of life, and thus somehow divine, is to be covered by

8 But I too have spilt blood on the
    gleaming white rock
   so that it cannot be covered,
to make anger flare up and to call
   down vengeance.

9 Therefore these are the words of the
Lord GOD:

O city running with blood,
  I too will make a great fire-pit.
10 Fill it with logs, light the fire;
   make an end of the meat,
pour out all the broth*l* and the
   bones with it.*m*
11 Then set the pot empty on the
   coals
so that its copper may be heated
   red-hot,
  and then the impurities in it may
   be melted
  and its corrosion burnt off.
12 Try as you may,*n*
the corrosion is so deep that it will
   not come off;
  only fire will rid it of corrosion
   for you.
13 Even so, when I cleansed you in
   your filthy lewdness,
you did not become clean from it,
  and therefore you shall never
   again be clean
until I have satisfied my anger
   against you.

14 I, the LORD, have spoken; the time
is coming, I will act. I will not refrain
nor pity nor relent; I will judge you for
your conduct and for all that you have
done. This is the very word of the Lord
GOD.

15 These were the words of the LORD
16 to me: Man, I am taking from you at
one blow the dearest thing you have,
but you must not wail or weep or give
17 way to tears. Keep in good heart; be
quiet, and make no mourning for the
dead; cover your head as usual and
put sandals on your feet. You shall not

cover your upper lip in mourning nor
eat the bread of despair.

18 I spoke to the people in the morning,
and that very evening my wife died.
19 Next morning I did as I was told. The
people asked me to say what meaning
20 my behaviour had for them. I answered, These were the words of the
21 LORD to me: Tell the Israelites, This is
the word of the Lord GOD: I will
desecrate my sanctuary, which has been
the pride of your strength, the delight
of your eyes and your heart's desire;
and the sons and daughters whom you
have left behind shall fall by the
22 sword. But, I said, you shall do as I
have done: you shall not cover your
upper lip in mourning nor eat the
23 bread of despair. You shall cover your
head and put sandals on your feet; you
shall not wail nor weep. Because of
your wickedness you will pine away
24 and will lament to*o* one another. The
LORD says, Ezekiel will be a sign to
warn you, and when it happens you will
do as he has done, and you will know
that I am the Lord GOD.

25 And now, man, a word for you: I am
taking from them that fortress whose
beauty so gladdened them, the delight
of their eyes, their heart's desire; I am
taking their sons and their daughters.
26 Soon fugitives will come and tell you
27 their news by word of mouth. At once
you will recover the power of speech
and speak with the fugitives; you will
no longer be dumb. So will you be a
portent to them, and they shall know
that I am the LORD.

Prophecies against foreign nations

25 THESE WERE THE WORDS OF THE LORD
2 to me: Man, look towards the Ammonites and prophesy against them.

l pour . . . broth: prob. rdg.; Heb. mix ointment.
m with it: prob. rdg.; Heb. will be scorched.
n Try as you may: prob. rdg.; Heb. obscure.
o Or for.

---

dust and forbidden to human contact. See Gen.9.4–6; Lev.17.13–14. Blood *poured* on *gleaming
rock* shows flagrant disregard for life and its divine origin. **15–24:** Ezekiel, at the double tragedy
of his wife's death and the impending destruction of the Temple, is so numbed by grief that
he cannot perform the ordinary rituals of mourning (v. 17) so important in the Near East.
26: *Soon:* lit. "on the very day." That fugitives could arrive so quickly again raises the question
of where Ezekiel was preaching, in Babylon or in Palestine. See Introduction.
   25.1–32.32: Judgment passed against enemy nations. The sin of the nations is twofold: the
arrogance of powerful nations like Egypt, Tyre, and Babylon that exalt themselves at the

3 Say to the Ammonites, Listen to the word of the Lord GOD. These are his words: Because you cried 'Aha!' when you saw my holy place desecrated, the soil of Israel laid waste and the people 4 of Judah sent into exile, I will hand you over as a possession to the tribes of the east. They shall pitch their camps and put up their dwellings among you; they shall eat your crops; 5 they shall drink your milk. I will make Rabbah a camel-pasture and Ammon a sheep-walk. Thus you shall know that 6 I am the LORD. These are the words of the Lord GOD: Because you clapped your hands and stamped your feet, and exulted over the land of Israel with 7 single-minded scorn, I will stretch out my hand over you and make you the prey of the nations and cut you off from all other peoples; in every land I will exterminate you and bring you to utter ruin. Thus you shall know that I am the LORD.

8 These are the words of the Lord GOD: Because Moab said, 'Judah is 9 like all the rest', I will expose the flank of Moab and lay open its cities,*p* from one end to the other—the fairest of its cities: Beth-jeshimoth, Baal-meon and 10 Kiriathaim. I will hand over Moab and Ammon together to the tribes of the east to be their possession, so that the Ammonites shall not be remembered 11 among the nations, and so that I may execute judgement upon Moab. Thus they shall know that I am the LORD.

12 These are the words of the Lord GOD: Because Edom took deliberate revenge on Judah and by so doing incurred lasting guilt, I will stretch my 13 hand out over Edom, says the Lord GOD, and destroy both man and beast in it, laying waste the land from Teman as far as Dedan; they shall fall by the sword. I will wreak my vengeance upon 14 Edom through my people Israel. They will deal with Edom as my anger and fury demand, and it shall feel my vengeance. This is the very word of the Lord GOD.

These are the words of the Lord 15 GOD: Because the Philistines have taken deliberate revenge and have avenged themselves with single-minded scorn, giving vent to their age-long enmity in destruction, I will stretch out 16 my hand over the Philistines, says the Lord GOD, I will wipe out the Kerethites and destroy all the rest of the dwellers by the sea. I will take fearful 17 vengeance upon them and punish them in my fury. When I take my vengeance, they shall know that I am the LORD.

These were the words of the LORD to **26** me on the first day of the first month in the eleventh year: Man, Tyre has 2 said of Jerusalem,

Aha! she that was the gateway of
    the nations
   is broken,
her gates swing open to me;
I grow rich, she lies in ruins.

p and lay . . . cities: prob. rdg.; Heb. from the cities, from its cities.

---

expense of God; and the meanness of Israel's weak neighbors, Edom and Moab, that exalt themselves by preying on God's people. The first act in the restoration of Israel is the judgment passed upon the nations. See 36.7.

25.1–17: Oracles against Israel's neighbors. Apparently written after the destruction of Jerusalem, these oracles are cast in the form of a lawsuit against the nations, i.e. an indictment and a sentence: "because . . . therefore." **1–7:** *Ammonites:* people inhabiting the east side of the Jordan just north of the Dead Sea. Partners with Judah in the conspiracy against Nebuchadnezzar, they despoiled their prostrate ally; see Jer.49.1–2. **4:** *Tribes of the east* are nomadic Arabs. **8–11:** *Moab:* directly south of Ammon and east of the Dead Sea. Most of its cities were situated on the *flank of Moab*, the steep but rounded eastern shore of that sea. **12–14:** Inhabiting the region south of the Dead Sea before the destruction of Jerusalem, *Edom* profited from Judah's tragedy by occupying the southern half of her territory. For traditional hostility between Judah and Edom see Gen.27.41; 36.6–8. *Teman . . . Dedan:* Edomite cities to the southeast of the Dead Sea. **15–17:** The *Philistines* and their kinsmen the *Kerethites* (both living on the Mediterranean coast, though by then greatly diminished) also plundered prostrate Judah.

26.1–21: Tyre will be swept from the sea. Tyre, an ancient Phoenician port (in modern Lebanon) was the heart of a commercial and cultural empire. Its traditional friendship with Israel (1 Kgs. ch. 5) wins it a fate less harsh. **1:** *Eleventh year:* approximately April 22, 587 B.C. **2:** Caravans to

3 Therefore these are the words of the Lord GOD:

I am against you, Tyre,
and will bring up many nations
　　against you
as the sea brings up its waves;
4 they will destroy the walls of Tyre
　　and pull down her towers.
I will scrape the soil off her
and make her a gleaming rock,
5 she shall be an islet where men
　　spread their nets;
I have spoken, says the Lord GOD.
She shall become the prey of
　　nations,
6 and her daughters*q* shall be slain by
　　the sword in the open country.

Thus they shall know that I am the LORD.

7 These are the words of the Lord GOD: I am bringing against Tyre from the north Nebuchadrezzar king of Babylon, king of kings. He will come with horses and chariots, with cavalry and a great army.

8 Your daughters in the open
　　country
　he will put to the sword.
He will set up watch-towers against
　　you,
　pile up siege-ramps against you
and raise against you a screen of
　　shields.
9 He will launch his battering-rams on
　　your walls
and break down your towers with
　　his axes.
10 He will cover you with dust from the
　　thousands of his cavalry;
at the thunder of his horses
　and of his chariot-wheels
your walls will quake when he
　　enters your gates
as men enter a city that is breached.
11 He will trample all your streets
　　with the hooves of his horses
and put your people to the sword,
and your strong pillars will fall to
　　the ground.

12 Your wealth will become spoil,
your merchandise will be
　　plundered,
your walls levelled,
your pleasant houses pulled down,
your stones, your timber and your
　　rubble
will be dumped into the sea.
13 So I will silence the clamour of
　　your songs,
and the sound of your harps shall be
　　heard no more.
14 I will make you a gleaming rock,
a place for fishermen to spread
　　their nets,
and you shall never be rebuilt.
I, the LORD, have spoken.
This is the very word of the Lord
GOD.

15 These are the words of the Lord GOD to Tyre: How the coasts and islands will shake at the sound of your downfall, while the wounded groan, and the slaughter goes on in your midst! 16 Then all the sea-kings will come down from their thrones, and lay aside their cloaks, and strip off their brocaded robes. They will wear coarse loin-cloths; they will sit on the ground, shuddering at every moment, horror-struck at your fate. 17 Then they will raise this dirge over you:

How you are undone, swept from
　　the sea,
　O famous city!
You whose strength lay in the sea,
　you and your inhabitants,
who spread their terror throughout
　　the mainland.*r*
18 Now the coast-lands tremble on the
　　day of your downfall,
and the isles of the sea are appalled
　　at your passing.

19 For these are the words of the Lord GOD: When I make you a desolate city, like a city where no man can live, when I bring up the primeval ocean

q *Or* daughter-towns.
r the mainland: *prob. rdg.; Heb.* her inhabitants.

Tyre from Mesopotamia, Arabia, and Egypt had to pay duty to use Israelite territory as a *gateway*. **3:** *Tyre*, built on an island a half mile from shore, will be overrun by *nations*, just as it is washed by the *sea waves* in a storm. **4:** *Rock:* a play on words since "rock" and "Tyre" are identical in Heb. **8:** A *screen of shields:* probably an offensive military technique. **14:** Tyre

against you and the great waters cover
20 you, I will thrust you down with those
that descend to the abyss, to the dead
of all the ages. I will make you dwell in
the underworld as in places long
desolate, with those that go down to
the abyss. So you will never again be
inhabited or take your place in the land
21 of the living. I will bring you to a
fearful end, and you shall be no more;
men may look for you but will never
find you again. This is the very word of
the Lord GOD.

27 These were the words of the LORD to
2,3 me: Man, raise a dirge over Tyre and
say, Tyre, throned above your harbours, you who carry the trade of the
nations to many coasts and islands,
these are the words of the Lord GOD:

    O Tyre, you said,
        'I am perfect in beauty.'
4   Your frontiers are on the high seas,
        your builders made your beauty
            perfect;
5   they fashioned all your timbers
            of pine from Senir;
        they took a cedar from Lebanon
        to raise up a mast over you.
6   They made your oars of oaks from
            Bashan;
        they made your deck strong[s] with
            box-wood
        from the coasts of Kittim.
7   Your canvas was linen,
        patterned linen from Egypt
        to make your sails;
        your awnings were violet and purple
        from the coasts of Elishah.
8   Men of Sidon and Arvad became your
            oarsmen;
        you had skilled men within you, O
            Tyre,
        who served as your helmsmen.
9   You had skilled veterans from Gebal
        caulking your seams.
    You had all sea-going ships and their
            sailors
        to market your wares;

men of Pharas,[t] Lud,[u] and Put,   10
    served
    as warriors in your army;
    they hung shield and helmet around
        you,
    and it was they who gave you your
        glory.
Men of Arvad and Cilicia manned   11
    all your walls,
    men of Gammad were posted on
        your towers
    and hung their shields around your
        battlements;
    it was they who made your beauty
        perfect.

Tarshish was a source of your   12
commerce, from its abundant resources
offering silver and iron, tin and lead,
as your staple wares. Javan,[v] Tubal,   13
and Meshech dealt with you, offering
slaves and vessels of bronze as your
imports. Men from Togarmah offered   14
horses, mares, and mules as your staple
wares. Rhodians dealt with you, great   15
islands were a source of your commerce, paying what was due to you in
ivory and ebony. Edom was a source of   16
your commerce, so many were your
undertakings, and offered purple garnets, brocade and fine linen, black coral
and red jasper,[w] for your staple wares.
Judah and Israel dealt with you, offer-   17
ing wheat from Minnith, and meal,
syrup, oil, and balsam, as your imports.
Damascus was a source of your   18
commerce, so many were your undertakings, from its abundant resources
offering wine of Helbon and wool of
Suhar, and casks of wine from Izalla,[x]   19
for your staple wares; wrought iron,
cassia, and sweet cane were among
your imports. Dedan dealt with you in   20
coarse woollens for saddle-cloths.
Arabia and all the chiefs of Kedar were   21
the source of your commerce in lambs,
rams, and he-goats; this was your trade

s strong: *prob. rdg.; Heb.* ivory.   t *Or* Persia.
u *Or* Lydia.   v *Or* Ionia.   w *Or* and carbuncles.
x casks . . . Izalla: *prob. rdg.; Heb.* obscure.

---

was not *rebuilt* after its destruction by Alexander in 332 B.C. **20**: *Abyss:* Sheol, the place of
the dead; see 31.15–18.
    27.1–28.19: Dirge over Tyre. The lament is in traditional dirge meter called the *qinah.* Tyre
is like a stately ship, carrying an expert crew, rich passengers and rare cargo, that founders.
5: *Senir:* Mount Hermon near Damascus. **6**: *Bashan:* plateau east of the Sea of Galilee
mentioned for its oaks in Isa.2.13. *Kittim:* Cyprus. **10–25a**: This section, in which the metaphor
shifts from a ship to a fortified city and the language from poetry to prose, is possibly an

22 with them. Dealers from Sheba and
Raamah dealt with you, offering the
choicest spices, every kind of precious
stone and gold, as your staple wares.
23 Harran, Kanneh, and Eden, dealers
from Asshur and all Media, dealt with
24 you; they were your dealers in gorgeous
stuffs, violet cloths and brocades, in
stores of coloured fabric rolled up and
tied with cords; your dealings with
them were in these.

25 Ships of Tarshish were the caravans
   for your imports;
   you were deeply laden with full
      cargoes
   on the high seas.
26 Your oarsmen brought you into
      many waters,
   but on the high seas an east wind
      wrecked you.
27 Your wealth, your staple wares,
      your imports,
      your sailors and your helmsmen,
   your caulkers, your merchants, and
      your warriors,
   all your ship's company,
      all who were with you,
   were flung into the sea on the day
      of your disaster;
28 at the cries of your helmsmen the
      troubled waters tossed.

29 When all the rowers disembark from
      their ships,
   when the sailors, the helmsmen all
      together, go ashore,
30 they exclaim over your fate,
      they cry out bitterly;
   they throw dust on their heads
      and sprinkle themselves with
         ashes.
31 They tear out their hair at your
      plight
      and put on sackcloth;
   they weep bitterly over you,
      bitterly wailing.
32 In their lamentation they raise a
      dirge over you,
      and this is their dirge:
   Who was like Tyre,
   with her buildings piled*y* off shore?

When your wares were unloaded off 33
   the sea
you met the needs of many nations;
   with your vast resources and
      your imports
   you enriched the kings of the
      earth.
Now you are broken by the sea   34
   in deep water;
your wares and all your company are
   gone overboard.
All who dwell on the coasts and   35
   islands
   are aghast at your fate;
horror is written on the faces of
   their kings
   and their hair stands on end.
Among the nations the merchants   36
   jeer in derision at you;
you have come to a fearful end and
   shall be no more for ever.

These were the words of the LORD to **28**
me: Man, say to the prince of Tyre, 2
This is the word of the Lord GOD:

In your arrogance you say,
   'I am a god;
I sit throned like a god on the high
   seas.'
Though you are a man and no god,
   you try to think the thoughts of a
      god.
What? are you wiser than Danel*z*? 3
Is no secret too dark for you?
Clever and shrewd as you are,   4
   you have amassed wealth for
      yourself,
   you have amassed gold and silver in
      your treasuries;
by great cleverness in your trading 5
   you have heaped up riches,
   and with your riches your arrogance
      has grown.

Therefore these are the words of the 6
Lord GOD:

Because you try to think the thoughts
   of a god

y with her buildings piled: prob. rdg.; Heb. obscure.
z Or, as otherwise read, Daniel; cp. 14. 14, 20.

---

interpolation. **26:** The *east wind*, death-dealing on sea (Ps.48.7) and land (Jer.18.17) alike,
probably symbolizes Nebuchadnezzar, as in 17.10. **28.1–3:** Blinded by *arrogance*, the city
scorned its national hero *Danel*, who, a model of true wisdom (14.14 n.), had placed his sagacity
at the service of the gods, of widows and orphans. **4–10:** Thinking its power and *wisdom*

7 I will bring strangers against you,
     the most ruthless of nations,
   who will draw their swords against
       your fine wisdom
     and lay your pride in the dust,
8 sending you down to the pit*a* to die
     a death of disgrace on the high seas.
9 Will you dare to say that you are
       a god
     when you face your assailants,
   though you are a man and no god
     in the hands of those who lay
       you low?
10 You will die strengthless
     at the hands of strangers.

For I have spoken. This is the very
word of the Lord GOD.
11 These were the words of the LORD to
12 me: Man, raise this dirge over the king
of Tyre, and say to him, This is the
word of the Lord GOD:

   You set the seal on perfection;
   full of wisdom you were and
     altogether beautiful.
13 You were in an Eden, a garden of
     God,
   adorned with gems of every kind:
   sardin and chrysolite and jade,
   topaz, cornelian and green jasper,
   lapis lazuli,*b* purple garnet and
     green felspar.
   Your jingling beads were of gold,
   and the spangles you wore were
     made for you
     on the day of your birth.
14 I set you with a towering cherub*c*
     as guardian;
   you were on God's holy hill
   and you walked proudly among
     stones that flashed with fire.
15 You were blameless in all your ways
     from the day of your birth
   until your iniquity came to light.
16 Your commerce grew so great,
   lawlessness filled your heart and you
     went wrong,

so I brought you down in disgrace
   from the mountain of God,
   and the guardian cherub banished
     you*d*
   from among the stones that
     flashed like fire.
Your beauty made you arrogant,   17
you misused your wisdom to increase
     your dignity.
   I flung you to the ground,
I left you there, a sight for kings
     to see.
So great was your sin in your wicked   18
     trading
   that you desecrated your
     sanctuaries.
So I kindled a fire within you,
   and it devoured you.
I left you as ashes on the ground
   for all to see.
All among the nations who knew   19
     you were aghast:
you came to a fearful end and shall
     be no more for ever.

These were the words of the LORD to   20
me: Man, look towards Sidon and   21
prophesy against her. These are the   22
words of the Lord GOD:

   Sidon, I am against you
   and I will show my glory in your
     midst.

Men will know that I am the LORD
   when I execute judgement upon her
   and thereby prove my holiness.
I will let loose pestilence upon her   23
   and bloodshed in her streets;
   the slain will fall in her streets,
   beset on all sides by the sword;
   then men will know that I am the
     LORD.

No longer shall the Israelites suffer   24

a Or to destruction.   b Or sapphire.
c I set . . . cherub: prob. rdg.; Heb. You were a tower-
ing cherub whom I set.
d and the . . . you: or and I parted you, O guardian
cherub, . . .

---

unlimited, as it *amassed wealth* for its own glorification, Tyre will find a fool's fate. **11–19:**
Though Tyre had, like a *cherub* in the Temple (*God's holy hill*), enjoyed familiarity with God,
he scorned such honor in favor of his own *dignity*, achieved by *wicked trading*. Some interpreters
see in the passage allusions to unknown creation myths; others, an allegory on Tyre's ancient
and long-standing alliance with Israel (1 Kgs.5.1–18), ended when the high priest Jehoiada
cast Queen Athaliah—daughter of the Tyrian princess Jezebel—out of the temple. See 2
Kgs.11.13–16. Cut off from God's people, Tyre's doom was sealed.
    28.20–24: Sidon denounced. Sidon, a Phoenician city north of Tyre, merits punishment as
an accomplice in the fatal rebellion against Babylon; see Jer.27.3.

from the scorn of their neighbours, the pricking of briars and scratching of thorns, and they shall know that I am the Lord God.

25 These are the words of the Lord God: When I gather the Israelites from the peoples among whom they are scattered, I shall thereby prove my holiness in the sight of all nations. They shall live on their native soil, which I
26 gave to my servant Jacob. They shall live there in peace of mind, build houses and plant vineyards; they shall live there in peace of mind when I execute judgement on all their scornful neighbours. Thus they shall know that I am the Lord their God.

29 These are the words of the Lord to me on the twelfth day of the tenth
2 month in the tenth year: Man, look towards Pharaoh king of Egypt and prophesy against him and all his
3 country. Say, These are the words of the Lord God:

I am against you,
 Pharaoh king of Egypt,
  you great monster,
 lurking in the streams of the Nile.
 You have said, 'My Nile is my own;
  it was I who made it.'
4 I will put hooks in your jaws
 and make them cling[e] to your scales.
 I will hoist you out of its streams
  with all its fish clinging to your scales.
5 I will fling you into the
   wilderness,
 you and all the fish in your streams;
 you will fall on the bare ground
  with none to pick you up and bury
   you;
 I will make you food
  for beasts and for birds.

So all who live in Egypt will know 6
 that I am the Lord,
 for the support that you gave to
  the Israelites
 was no better than a reed,
which splintered in the hand when 7
  they grasped you,
 and tore their armpits;
 when they leaned upon you, you
  snapped
 and their limbs gave way.

This therefore is the word of the 8
Lord God: I am bringing a sword upon you to destroy both man and beast. The land of Egypt shall become a 9 desolate waste, and they shall know that I am the Lord, because you said, 'The Nile is mine; it was I who made it.' I am against you therefore, you and 10 your Nile, and I will make Egypt desolate, wasted by drought, from Migdol to Syene and up to the very frontier of Cush. No foot of man 11 shall pass through it, no foot of beast; it shall lie uninhabited for forty years. I will make the land of Egypt the most 12 desolate of desolate lands; her cities shall lie derelict among the ruined cities. For forty years shall they lie derelict, and I will scatter the Egyptians among the nations and disperse them among the lands.

These are the words of the Lord 13 God: At the end of forty years I will gather the Egyptians from the peoples among whom they are scattered. I will 14 turn the fortunes of Egypt and bring them back to Pathros, the land of their origin, where they shall become a petty kingdom. She shall be the most 15 paltry of kingdoms and never again

[e] make them cling: *prob. rdg.; Heb.* make the fish of your streams cling.

28.25–26: Israel, restored, will experience God's holiness, and will witness it to the nations.
29.1–32.32: Egypt shall become a desolate waste. From Israel's beginning as a nation, Egypt either oppressed it like a slave master or abused it by fickle alliances; see 29.6–7. The reed conveys the latter idea for it was abundant in the Nile and hence a symbol of Egypt. It promised support, but would break and pierce the hand.
29.1–9: Oracle against Pharaoh, the monster and reed of the Nile. 1: January 7, 587 B.C.
3: *Streams of the Nile:* the Nile's several mouths in the delta. *Great monster:* the crocodile.
4: *Clinging fish:* the dependent nations. **6–7:** The *support no better than a reed* given to the Israelites reflects Pharaoh Hophra's failure to drive the Babylonians from Palestine, a little less than a year before this oracle. See Jer.37.1–10. The Babylonians' siege was briefly lifted; see Jer.34.21–22.
29.10–16: Israelites will never trust Egypt again. When finally converted, Israel will have a "new heart" and a "new spirit" from the Lord; it will then depend entirely on him. **10:** *Migdol:* at the northern boundary of Egypt. *Syene:* modern Aswan on the southern frontiers, near *Cush*, i.e. Ethiopia. **12:** *Forty years:* a round number.

exalt herself over the nations, for I will make the Egyptians too few to rule over
16 them. The Israelites will never trust Egypt again; this will be a reminder to them of their sin in turning to Egypt for help. They shall know that I am the Lord GOD.

17 These were the words of the LORD to me on the first day of the first month
18 in the twenty-seventh year: Man, long did Nebuchadrezzar king of Babylon keep his army in the field against Tyre, until every head was rubbed bare and every shoulder chafed. But neither he nor his army gained anything from Tyre for their long service against her.
19 This, therefore, is the word of the Lord GOD: I am giving the land of Egypt to Nebuchadrezzar king of Babylon. He shall carry off its wealth, he shall spoil and plunder it, and so his army will be
20 paid. I have given him the land of Egypt as the wages for his service because they have disregarded me. This is the very word of the Lord GOD.
21 At that time I will make Israel put out fresh shoots, and give you back the power to speak among them, and they will know that I am the LORD.

30 These were the words of the LORD to
2 me: Man, prophesy and say, These are the words of the Lord GOD:

Woe, woe for the day!
3   for a day is near,
a day of the LORD is near,
a day of cloud, a day of reckoning for the nations.
4   Then a sword will come upon Egypt, and there will be anguish in Cush, when the slain fall in Egypt, when its wealth is taken and its foundations are torn up.
5   Cush and Put and Lud,*f* all the Arabs and Libyans and the peoples of allied lands, shall fall with them by the sword.

These are the words of the LORD: 6

All who support Egypt shall fall, and her boasted might be brought low;
from Migdol to Syene men shall fall by the sword.
This is the very word of the Lord GOD.

They shall be the most desolate of 7 desolate lands, and their cities shall lie derelict among the ruined cities. When 8 I set Egypt on fire and all her helpers are broken, they will know that I am the LORD. When that time comes 9 messengers shall go out in haste from my presence to alarm Cush, still without a care, and anguish shall come upon her in Egypt's hour. Even now it is on the way.
These are the words of the Lord 10 GOD:

I will make an end of Egypt's hordes
by the hands of Nebuchadrezzar king of Babylon.
He and his people with him, the   11 most ruthless of nations,
will be brought to ravage the land.
They will draw their swords against Egypt
and fill the land with the slain.
I will make the streams of the Nile 12 dry land
and sell Egypt to evil men;
I will lay waste the land and everything in it by foreign hands.
I, the LORD, have spoken.

These are the words of the Lord 13 GOD:

I will make an end of the lordlings*g*

f Or Lydia.   g Or idols.

29.17–21: Egypt as wages for Nebuchadrezzar. 17: The latest date for any oracle is April 26, 571 B.C., this date is also the latest secure one in the book. Since other oracles with earlier dates will follow, this one is placed here because its topic is the same as that of the preceding. **20:** In humbling Tyre, Nebuchadrezzar carries out God's purposes in history, and so deserves *wages*. **21:** *Fresh shoots* are symbols of restoration, either in messianic (Isa.11.1) or political perspective (17.22).
    30.1–19: Day of the LORD for Egypt is near. 3: In the early prophetic writings, the *day* or the *day of the LORD* is the time of God's future decisive judgment when he will bring doom either for Israel (Amos 5.18–20) or for the nations (Isa.2.12). Later it represented the vindication of Israel against the nations (Joel 3.1–3).

and wipe out the princelings[h] of
Noph;
and never again shall a prince arise
in Egypt.
Then I will put fear in that land,
14 I will lay Pathros waste and set fire
to Zoan
and execute judgement on No.
15 I will pour out my rage upon Sin,
the bastion of Egypt,
and destroy the horde of Noph.
16 I will set Egypt on fire,
and Syene shall writhe in anguish;
the walls of No shall be breached
and flood-waters shall burst into
it.
17 The young men of On and Pi-beseth[i]
shall fall by the sword
and the cities themselves go into
captivity.
18 Daylight shall fail in Tahpanhes
when I break the yoke of Egypt
there;
then her boasted might shall be
subdued;
a cloud shall cover her,
and her daughters[j] shall go into
captivity.
19 Thus I will execute judgement on
Egypt,
and they shall know that I am the
LORD.

20 This was the word of the LORD to me
on the seventh day of the first month
21 in the eleventh year: Man, I have
broken the arm of Pharaoh king of
Egypt. See, it has not been bound up
with dressings and bandage to give it
22 strength to wield a sword. These,
therefore, are the words of the Lord
GOD: I am against Pharaoh king of
Egypt; I will break both his arms, the
sound and the broken, and make the
23 sword drop from his hand. I will
scatter the Egyptians among the nations
and disperse them over many lands.
24 Then I will strengthen the arms of the
king of Babylon and put my sword in
his hand; but I will break Pharaoh's

arms, and he shall lie wounded and
groaning before him. I will give 25
strength to the arms of the king of
Babylon, but the arms of Pharaoh will
fall. Men will know that I am the
LORD, when I put my sword in the
hand of the king of Babylon, and he
stretches it out over the land of Egypt.
I will scatter the Egyptians among the 26
nations and disperse them over many
lands, and they shall know that I am
the LORD.

On the first day of the third month 31
in the eleventh year this word came to
me from the LORD: Man, say to 2
Pharaoh king of Egypt and all his
horde:

What are you like in your greatness?

Look at Assyria: it was a cedar in   3
Lebanon,
whose fair branches overshadowed
the forest,
towering high with its crown finding
a way through the foliage.
Springs nourished it, underground   4
waters gave it height,
their streams washed the soil all
round it
and sent forth their rills to every tree
in the country.
So it grew taller than every other tree. 5
Its boughs were many, its branches
spread far;
for water was abundant in the
channels.
In its boughs all the birds of the air   6
had their nests,
under its branches all wild creatures
bore their young,
and in its shadow all great nations
made their home.
A splendid great tree it was, with   7
its long spreading boughs,
for its roots were beside abundant
waters.
No cedar in God's garden   8
overshadowed it,

h *Or* false gods.   i *Or* Bubastis.   j *Or* daughter-towns.

30.20–26: The sword drops from Pharaoh's arm. 20: April 29, 587 B.C. **21:** Pharaoh's *sword
arm* was broken the year before when he was compelled to abandon his effort to lift the siege
of Jerusalem. See 29.6–7 n. **22:** *Both his arms* will be broken when Egypt will sink to complete
military insignificance. This happened following its conquest by Cambyses in 525 B.C.
31.1–18: Egypt, proud cedar of Lebanon, will be hewed down like Assyria. 8: Many commentators see in *God's garden* a reference to a mythological earthly paradise; others, a symbol

no fir could compare with its boughs,
and no plane-tree had such branches;
not a tree in God's garden
could rival its beauty.

9   I, the Lord, gave it beauty
with its mass of spreading boughs,
the envy of all the trees in Eden,
the garden of God.

10   Therefore these are the words of the
Lord GOD: Because it grew so high
and pushed its crown up through the
foliage, and its pride mounted as it
11 grew, therefore I handed it over to a
prince of the nations to deal with it;
I made an example of it as its wicked-
12 ness deserved. Strangers from the most
ruthless of nations hewed it down and
flung it away. Its sweeping boughs fell
on the mountains and in all the valleys,
and its branches lay broken beside all
the streams in the land. All nations of
the earth came out from under its shade
13 and left it. All the birds of the air
settled on its fallen trunk; the wild crea-
14 tures all stood by its branches. Never
again, therefore, shall the well-watered
trees grow so high or push their
crowns up through the foliage. Nor
shall the strongest of them, well
watered though they be, stand erect in
their full height; for all have been given
over to death, to the world below, to
share the common doom and go down
to the abyss.
15   These are the words of the Lord
GOD: When he went down to Sheol,
I closed the deep over him as a gate, I
dammed its rivers, the great waters
were held back. I put Lebanon in
mourning for him, and all the trees of
16 the country-side wilted. I made nations
shake with the crash of his fall, when I
brought him down to Sheol with those
who go down to the abyss. From this
all the trees of Eden, all the choicest

and best of Lebanon, all the well-
watered trees, drew comfort in the
world below. They too, like him, had 17
gone down to Sheol, to those slain with
the sword; and those who had lived in
his shadow were scattered among the
nations. Which among the trees of 18
Eden was like you in glory and greatness? Yet you will be brought down
with the trees of Eden to the world
below; you will lie with those who have
been slain by the sword, in the company
of the strengthless dead. This stands
for Pharaoh and all his horde. This is
the very word of the Lord GOD.

On the first day of the twelfth month **32**
in the twelfth year the word of the
LORD came to me: Man, raise a dirge 2
over Pharaoh king of Egypt and say
to him:

Young lion of the nations, you are
undone.
You were like a monster in the waters
of the Nile
scattering the water with its snout,[k][l]
churning the water with its feet
and fouling the streams.

These are the words of the Lord 3
GOD: When many nations are gathered
together I will spread my net over you,
and you will be dragged up in its
meshes. I will fling you on land, dashing 4
you down on the bare ground. I will let
all the birds of the air settle upon you
and all the wild beasts gorge themselves
on your flesh. Your flesh I will lay on 5
the mountains, and fill the valleys with
the worms that feed on it. I will drench 6
the land with your discharge, drench it
with your blood to the very mountain-
tops, and the watercourses shall be full
of you. When I put out your light I will 7

k snout: *prob. rdg.; Heb.* streams.
l scattering . . . snout: *or* heaving itself up in the streams.

of God's care (Isa.51.3) for the nations in endowing them with material resources. **12:** Assyria's
far-reaching administration broke down like *sweeping branches* when the trunk is cut; so too
will Egypt's. **15:** When Egypt *went down to Sheol* all the dependent nations shook and *wilted*.
18: *Slain by the sword:* those who suffered an untimely death.
    32.1–32: A dirge over Egypt. This final prophecy against Egypt contains two oracles: vv. 1–16,
a continuation of the monster allegory of ch. 29, and vv. 17–32, a dirge on the descent into
Sheol of Pharaoh and his hordes to join the company of the dishonored dead. **1:** March 3,
585 B.C. **2:** *Fouling the streams:* doing violence to other nations by its violence. **3–4:** The monster
Egypt will be *dragged* out of the Nile onto the *bare ground*, to be seen and despoiled by the
nations, called here *beasts* that *gorge* themselves on carrion. **5:** To leave the *flesh* of the dead
unburied was a great curse for the ancients. **7:** These phenomena suggest the judgment of the

veil the sky and blacken its stars; I will veil the sun with a cloud, and the moon 8 shall not give its light. I will darken all the shining lights of the sky above you and bring darkness over your land. This is the very word of the Lord GOD.

9 I will disquiet many peoples when I bring your broken army among the nations into lands you have never 10 known. I will appal many peoples with your fate; when I brandish my sword in the faces of their kings, their hair shall stand on end. In the day of your downfall each shall tremble for his own 11 fate from moment to moment. For these are the words of the Lord GOD: The sword of the king of Babylon shall 12 come upon you. I will make the whole horde of you fall by the sword of warriors who are of all men the most ruthless. They shall make havoc of the pride of Egypt, and all its horde shall 13 be wiped out. I will destroy all their cattle beside many waters. No foot of man, no hoof of beast, shall ever churn 14 them up again. Then will I let their waters settle and their streams run smooth as oil. This is the very word of 15 the Lord GOD. When I have laid Egypt waste, and the whole land is devastated, when I strike down all who dwell there, they shall know that I am the LORD.

16 This is a dirge, and the women of the nations shall sing it as a dirge. They shall sing it as a dirge, as a dirge over Egypt and all its horde. This is the very word of the Lord GOD.

17 On the fifteenth day of the first month in the twelfth year, the word of the LORD came to me:

18 Man, raise a lament, you and the
daughters of the nations,
over the hordes of Egypt and
her nobles,
whom I will bring down[m] to the
world below
with those that go down to the
abyss.

19 Are you better favoured than
others?

Go down and be laid to rest with the strengthless dead.

20 A sword stands ready. Those who marched with her, and all her horde, shall fall into the midst of those slain by the sword. 21 Warrior chieftains in Sheol speak to Pharaoh and those who aided him:

The strengthless dead, slain by the sword, have come down and are laid to rest. 22 There is Assyria with all her company, her buried around her, all of them slain and fallen by the sword. 23 Her graves are set in the recesses of the abyss, with her company buried around her, all of them slain, fallen by the sword, men who once filled the land of the living with terror. 24 There is Elam, with all her hordes buried around her, all of them slain, fallen by the sword; they have gone down strengthless to the world below, men who struck terror into the land of the living but now share the disgrace of those that go down to the abyss. 25 In the midst of the slain a resting-place has been made for her, with all her hordes buried around her; all of them strengthless, slain by the sword. For they who once struck terror into the land of the living now share the disgrace of those that go down to the abyss; they are assigned a place in the midst of the slain. 26 There are Meshech and Tubal with all their hordes, with their buried around them, all of them strengthless and slain by the sword, men who once struck terror into the land of the living. 27 Do they not rest with warriors fallen strengthless,[n] who have gone down to Sheol with their weapons, their swords under their heads and their shields over their bones,[o] though the terror of their prowess once lay on the land of the living? 28 You also, Pharaoh, shall lie broken in the company of the strengthless dead, resting with those slain by the sword. 29 There is Edom, her kings and all her princes, who, for all their

m her nobles . . . down: *prob. rdg.; Heb. obscure.*
n Prob. rdg.; Heb. from strengthless ones.
o and . . . bones: *prob. rdg.; Heb. unintelligible.*

day of the Lord; see Joel 2.1–2. **17:** April 27, 586 B.C. **21:** *Strengthless:* lit. "uncircumcised," and therefore excluded from the community of Israel and its God, even after death. The Israelites are not included in this multitude even though two degrees of existence are mentioned: honorable and dishonorable.

prowess, have been lodged with those slain by the sword; they shall rest with the strengthless dead and with those
30 that go down to the abyss. There are all the princes of the North and all the Sidonians, who have gone down in shame with the slain, for all the terror they inspired by their prowess. They rest strengthless with those slain by the sword, and they share the disgrace of those that go down to the abyss.
31 Pharaoh will see them and will take comfort for his lost hordes—Pharaoh who, with all his army, is slain by the
32 sword, says the Lord GOD; though he spread[p] terror throughout the land of the living, yet he with all his horde is laid to rest with those that are slain by the sword, in the company of the strengthless dead. This is the very word of the Lord GOD.

The remnant of Israel in the land

33 THESE WERE THE WORDS OF THE LORD
2 to me: Man, say to your fellow-countrymen, When I set armies in motion against a land, its people choose one of themselves to be a watchman.
3 When he sees the enemy approaching and blows his trumpet to warn the
4 people, then if anyone does not heed the warning and is overtaken by the enemy, he is responsible for his own
5 fate. He is responsible because, when he heard the alarm, he paid no heed to it; if he had heeded it, he would have
6 escaped. But if the watchman does not blow his trumpet or warn the people when he sees the enemy approaching, then any man who is killed is caught with all his sins upon him; but I will hold the watchman answerable for his death.
7 Man, I have appointed you a watchman for the Israelites. You will take messages from me and carry my warn-

ings to them. It may be that I pro- 8
nounce sentence of death on a man because he is wicked; if you do not warn him to give up his ways, the guilt is his and because of his wickedness he shall die, but I will hold you answerable for his death. But if you have warned 9
him to give up his ways, and he has not given them up, he will die because of his wickedness, but you will have saved yourself.
Man, say to the Israelites, You 10
complain, 'We are burdened by our sins and offences; we are pining away because of them; we despair of life.' So tell them: As I live, says the Lord 11
GOD, I have no desire for the death of the wicked. I would rather that a wicked man should mend his ways and live. Give up your evil ways, give them up; O Israelites, why should you die?
Man, say to your fellow-countrymen, 12
When a righteous man goes wrong, his righteousness shall not save him. When a wicked man mends his ways, his former wickedness shall not bring him down. When a righteous man sins, all his righteousness cannot save his life. It may be that, when I tell the righteous 13
man that he will save his life, he presumes on his righteousness and does wrong; then none of his righteous acts will be remembered: he will die for the wrong he has done. It may be that when 14
I pronounce sentence of death on the wicked, he mends his ways and does what is just and right: if he then 15
restores the pledges he has taken, repays what he has stolen, and, doing no more wrong, follows the rules that ensure life, he shall live and not die. None of 16
the sins he has committed shall be remembered against him; he shall live, because he does what is just and right.
Your fellow-countrymen are saying, 17
'The Lord acts without principle', but

p Prob. rdg.; Heb. I have spread.

33.1–37.28: Israel to be restored; the kingdom established. The prophet assures Israel that the Lord will accomplish her redemption.
    33.1–20: A prophet's responsibility. Ideas from preceding chapters are paralleled here: With 33.1–6, compare 3.4–11; with 33.7–9, compare 3.16–21; with 33.10–20, compare 18.1–32; with 33.23–29, compare 12.17–20. **1–6:** This particular definition of prophetic role is unique to Ezekiel. Nebuchadnezzar's advancing *armies* (v. 2) probably suggested the oracle; life or death depended possibly on the warning of a watchman. On the watchman's importance in the hills of Palestine, see 2 Kgs.9.17–28. **7–9:** Ezekiel is here presumably in Palestine, not in Babylonia. See Introduction. **10–20:** Compare with 18.2.–30.

19 it is their ways that are unprincipled. When a righteous man gives up his righteousness and does wrong, he shall

19 die because of it; and when a wicked man gives up his wickedness and does what is just and right, he shall live.

20 How, Israel, can you say that the Lord acts without principle, when I judge every man of you on his deeds?

21 On the fifth day of the tenth month in the twelfth year of our captivity, fugitives came to me from Jerusalem and told me that the city had fallen.

22 The evening before they arrived, the hand of the LORD had come upon me, and by the time they reached me in the morning the LORD had given me back my speech. My speech was restored and I was no longer dumb.

23 These were the words of the LORD to
24 me: Man, the inhabitants of these wastes on the soil of Israel say, 'When Abraham took possession of the land he was but one; now we are many, and the land has been granted to us in

25 possession.' Tell them, therefore, that these are the words of the Lord GOD: You eat meat with the blood in it, you lift up your eyes to idols, you shed*q* blood; and yet you expect to possess

26 the land! You trust to the sword, you commit abominations, you defile one another's wives; and you expect to

27 possess the land! Tell them that these are the words of the Lord GOD: As I live, among the ruins they shall fall by the sword; in the open country I will give them for food to beasts: in dens and caves they shall die by pestilence.

28 I will make the land a desolate waste; her boasted might shall be brought to nothing, and the mountains of Israel

29 shall be an untrodden desert. When I make the land a desolate waste because of all the abominations they have

committed, they will know that I am the LORD.

30 Man, your fellow-countrymen gather in groups and talk of you under walls and in doorways and say to one another, 'Let us go and see what mes-

31 sage there is from the LORD.' So my people will come crowding in, as people do, and sit down in front of you. They will hear what you have to say, but they will not do it. 'Fine words*r*!' they will say, but their hearts are set on selfish gain. You are no more to them

32 than a singer of fine songs*s* with a lovely voice, or a clever harpist; they will listen to what you say but will certainly

33 not do it. But when it comes, as come it will, they will know that there has been a prophet in their midst.

34 These were the words of the LORD to
2 me: Prophesy, man, against the shepherds of Israel; prophesy and say to them, You shepherds, these are the words of the Lord GOD: How I hate the shepherds of Israel who care only for themselves! Should not the shep-

3 herd care for the sheep? You consume the milk, wear the wool, and slaughter the fat beasts, but you do not feed the

4 sheep. You have not encouraged the weary, tended the sick, bandaged the hurt, recovered the straggler, or searched for the lost; and even the

5 strong you have driven with ruthless severity. They are scattered, they have no shepherd, they have become the

6 prey of wild beasts. My sheep go straying over the mountains and on every high hill, my flock is dispersed over the whole country, with no one to ask after them or search for them.

7 Therefore, you shepherds, hear the
8 words of the LORD. As surely as I live,

q Or pour out.
r Fine words: or Love songs.
s fine songs: or love songs.

33.21–22: Jerusalem's fall. The date varies; where the MT reads *twelfth* year or January 8, 585 B.C., the Syr. and Sept. read "eleventh" or January 19, 586 B.C. See 24.26 n. **22:** See 3.26–27 where Ezekiel seems not to be completely mute but only forbidden by the Lord to speak in certain circumstances. Compare 24.18–21,26–27.

33.28: The desolation. Since the prediction of *a desolate waste* must be for the future, these words were spoken prior to the destruction of 587 B.C. The dates of v. 21 do not apply to this oracle.

33.30–33: The people listen, but do not heed. Such dubious pietism, blending *selfish gain* into a search for God's *message*, seems in vogue after the first capture of Jerusalem in 597 B.C.

34.1–31: The Lord as shepherd of his flock, Israel, is an image which Ezekiel inherited (Isa.40.10–11; Jer.23.1–6) and passed on to those who followed him (Zech.13.7), including Jesus (Mt.18.12–14; Jn.10.1–18). **6:** Worship at illicit *hill* shrines was encouraged or tolerated by most kings. See 2 Kgs.12.3; 21.3; Jer.50.6. **8:** *Wild beasts:* the hostile neighboring peoples.

says the Lord GOD, because my sheep are ravaged by wild beasts and have become their prey for lack of a shepherd, because my shepherds have not asked after the sheep but have cared only for themselves and not for the 9 sheep—therefore, you shepherds, hear 10 the words of the LORD. These are the words of the Lord GOD: I am against the shepherds and will demand my sheep from them. I will dismiss those shepherds: they shall care only for themselves no longer; I will rescue my sheep from their jaws, and they shall feed on them no more.

11　For these are the words of the Lord GOD: Now I myself will ask after my 12 sheep and go in search of them. As a shepherd goes in search of his sheep when his flock is dispersed all around him, so I will go in search of my sheep and rescue them, no matter where they were scattered in dark and cloudy days. 13 I will bring them out from every nation, gather them in from other lands, and lead them home to their own soil. I will graze them on the mountains of Israel, by her streams and in all her 14 green fields. I will feed them on good grazing-ground, and their pasture shall be the high mountains of Israel. There they will rest, there in good pasture, and find rich grazing on the mountains 15 of Israel. I myself will tend my flock, I myself pen them in their fold, says the 16 Lord GOD. I will search for the lost, recover the straggler, bandage the hurt, strengthen the sick, leave the healthy and strong to play, and give them their proper food.

17　As for you, my flock, these are the words of the Lord GOD: I will judge between one sheep and another. You 18 rams and he-goats! Are you not satisfied with grazing on good herbage, that you must trample down the rest with your feet? Or with drinking clear water, that you must churn up the rest with your feet? My flock has to eat 19 what you have trampled and drink what you have churned up. These, 20 therefore, are the words of the Lord GOD to them: Now I myself will judge between the fat sheep and the lean. You hustle the weary with flank and 21 shoulder, you butt them with your horns until you have driven them away and scattered them abroad. Therefore 22 I will save my flock, and they shall be ravaged no more; I will judge between one sheep and another. Then I will set 23 over them one shepherd to take care of them, my servant David; he shall care for them and become their shepherd. I, the LORD, will become their God, and 24 my servant David shall be a prince among them. I, the LORD, have spoken. I will make a covenant with them to 25 ensure prosperity; I will rid the land of wild beasts, and men shall live in peace of mind on the open pastures and sleep in the woods. I will settle them in the 26 neighbourhood of my hill and send them rain in due season, blessed rain. Trees in the country-side shall bear 27 their fruit, the land shall yield its produce, and men shall live in peace of mind on their own soil. They shall know that I am the LORD when I break the bars of their yokes and rescue them from those who have enslaved them. They shall never be ravaged by the 28 nations again nor shall wild beasts devour them; they shall live in peace of mind, with no one to alarm them. I will 29 give prosperity to their plantations; they shall never again be victims of famine in the land nor any longer bear the taunts of the nations. They shall 30 know that I, the LORD their God, am with them, and that they are my people Israel, says the Lord GOD. You are my 31

10: A play upon ideas; lit.: "I will stop them from feeding the flock so that they may no longer feed themselves [upon it]." **11–14:** God will *tend* his *flock:* a continuation of his saving action performed in the Exodus from Egypt. Compare Isa.63.7–19. **17:** The Lord's judging *between one sheep and another* is a concrete application of the principle—not found explicit in other prophets —of individual responsibility (see 33.8–9). **18:** *Churn up:* abuse of power by exploiting the weak; see 32.2 for the same indictment of Egypt. **19:** The *fat sheep* are the self-satisfied, hardhearted and insensitive people; see Deut.32.15; Jer.5.28. **23:** The *one shepherd* points to a renewed dynasty of David, uniting the two kingdoms separated after Solomon (see Hos.1.11). **24:** Ezekiel envisions a restored Israel politically similar to the period after the Exodus. The ruler will be a *prince*, not an absolute king with power to dictate (2 Kgs.16.10–18) in matters of worship and conduct as the kings had done. Compare 45.13–17 n.

flock, my people, the flock I feed, and I am your God. This is the very word of the Lord GOD.

35 These were the words of the LORD to 2 me. Man, look towards the hill-country of Seir and prophesy against it. Say, 3 These are the words of the Lord GOD;

O hill-country of Seir, I am against
   you:
I will stretch out my hand over you
   and make you a desolate waste.
4 I will lay your cities in ruins
   and you shall be made desolate;
   thus you shall know that I am the
      LORD.
5 For you have maintained an
      immemorial feud
  and handed over the Israelites to the
      sword
   in the hour of their doom,
   at the time of their final
      punishment.

6 Therefore, as I live, says the Lord
      GOD,
I make blood your destiny, and blood
      shall pursue you;
  you are most surely guilty of
      blood,
  and blood shall pursue you.
7 I will make the hill-country of Seir a
      desolate waste
  and put an end to all in it who pass
      to and fro;
8 I will fill your hills and your valleys
      with its slain,
  and those slain by the sword shall
      fall into your streams.
9 I will make you desolate for ever,
  and your cities shall not be
      inhabited;
  thus you shall know that I am the
      LORD.

10 You say, The two nations and the two countries shall be mine and I will take possession of them, though the LORD is[t] there. Therefore, as I live, 11 says the Lord GOD, your anger and jealousy shall be requited, for I will do to you what you have done in your hatred against them. I shall be known among you when I judge you; you 12 shall know that I am the LORD. I have heard all your blasphemies; you have said, 'The mountains of Israel are desolate and have been given to us to devour.' You have set yourselves up 13 against me and spoken recklessly against me. I myself have heard you. These are the words of the Lord GOD: 14 I will make you so desolate that the whole world will gloat over you. I will 15 do to you as you did to Israel my own possession when you gloated over its desolation. O hill-country of Seir, you will be desolate, and it will be the end of all Edom. Thus men will know that I am the LORD.

And do you, man, prophesy to the 36 mountains of Israel and say, Mountains of Israel, hear the words of the LORD. These are the words of the Lord GOD: 2 The enemy has said, 'Aha! now the everlasting highlands are ours.' There- 3 fore prophesy and say, These are the words of the Lord GOD: You moun- tains of Israel, all round you men gloated over you and trampled you down when you were seized and occupied by the rest of the nations; your name was bandied about in the common talk of men. Therefore, listen 4 to the words of the Lord GOD when he speaks to the mountains and hills, to the streams and valleys, to the desolate palaces and deserted cities, all plun- dered and despised by the rest of the nations round you. These are the words 5 of the Lord GOD: In the fire of my jealousy I have spoken plainly against the rest of the nations, and against Edom above all. For Edom, swollen with triumphant scorn, seized on my

[t] Or has been.

35.1–15: The indictment of Edom. 1–5: A lawsuit is prepared for the recovery of the mountains of Israel (ch. 36). The defendant is *the hill-country of Seir*, which is Edom. The accusation is the oppression of Judah by occupying its lands extensively in *its hour of doom*, the destruction of 587 B.C. Compare Obad.1–21. 6: The verdict is: *guilty of blood;* and the sentence: *blood shall pursue you*, with the Lord himself as avenger. 10: *Shall be mine:* second indictment. 11: The verdict: *guilty of anger and jealousy;* the sentence: exact retaliation; see Exod.21.23–25.

36.1–38: Mountains of Israel will be like a garden of Eden. 1–11: The mountains of Israel are personified as successful plaintiffs. The verdict is the *fire of* the Lord's *jealousy against the rest of the nations* (v. 5); the mountains in compensation are *to yield fruit* and have the Lord

land to hold it up to public contempt.
⁶ Therefore prophesy over the soil of
Israel and say to the mountains and
hills, the streams and valleys, These
are the words of the Lord GOD: I have
spoken my mind in jealousy and anger
because you have had to endure the
⁷ taunts of all nations. Therefore, says
the Lord GOD, I have sworn with
uplifted hand that the nations round
about shall be punished for[u] their
⁸ taunts. But you, mountains of Israel,
you shall put forth your branches and
yield your fruit for my people Israel,
⁹ for their home-coming is near. See
now, I am for you, I will turn to you,
¹⁰ and you shall be tilled and sown. I will
plant many men upon you—the whole
house of Israel. The cities shall again
be inhabited and the palaces rebuilt.
¹¹ I will plant many men and beasts upon
you; they shall increase and be fruitful.
I will make you populous as in days of
old and more prosperous than you
were at first. Thus you will know that
¹² I am the LORD. I will make men—my
people Israel—tread your paths again.
They shall settle in you, and you shall
be their possession; but you shall never
again rob them of their children.
¹³   These are the words of the Lord
GOD: People say that you are a land
that devours men and robs your tribes
¹⁴ of their children. But you shall never
devour men any more nor rob your
tribes of their children, says the Lord
¹⁵ GOD. I will never let you hear the
taunts of the nations again nor shall
you have to endure the reproaches of
the peoples. This is the very word of
the Lord GOD.
¹⁶   These were the words of the LORD to
¹⁷ me: Man, when the Israelites lived on
their own soil they defiled it with their
ways and deeds; their ways were foul
¹⁸ and disgusting in my sight. I poured
out my fury upon them because of the
blood they had poured out upon the
land, and the idols with which they

had defiled it. I scattered them among ¹⁹
the nations, and they were dispersed
among different countries; I passed on
them the sentence which their ways and
deeds deserved. When they came among ²⁰
those nations, they caused my holy
name to be profaned wherever they
came: men said of them, 'These are the
people of the LORD, and it is from his
land that they have come.' And I spared ²¹
them for the sake of my holy name
which the Israelites had profaned among
the nations to whom they had gone.
    Therefore tell the Israelites that these ²²
are the words of the Lord GOD: It is not
for your sake, you Israelites, that I am
acting, but for the sake of my holy
name, which you have profaned among
the peoples where you have gone. I will ²³
hallow my great name, which has been
profaned among those nations. When
they see that I reveal my holiness
through you, the nations will know
that I am the LORD, says the Lord
GOD. I will take you out of the nations ²⁴
and gather you from every land and
bring you to your own soil. I will ²⁵
sprinkle clean water over you, and you
shall be cleansed from all that defiles
you; I will cleanse you from the taint
of all your idols. I will give you a new ²⁶
heart and put a new spirit within you;
I will take the heart of stone from your
body and give you a heart of flesh. I ²⁷
will put my spirit into you and make
you conform to my statutes, keep my
laws and live by them. You shall live in ²⁸
the land which I gave to your ancestors;
you shall become my people, and I will
become your God. I will save you ²⁹
from all that defiles you; I will call to
the corn and make it plentiful; I will
bring no more famine upon you. I will ³⁰
make the trees bear abundant fruit and
the ground yield heavy crops, so that
you will never again have to bear the
reproach of famine among the nations.
You will recall your wicked ways and ³¹

[u] *be punished for*: *or* bear.

---

plant many men on them (v. 10), thus reversing the oracles of Israel's doom pronounced in
chs. 6 and 7. **26–27**: The heart being for the ancients the seat of the conscious processes of
knowing and willing, a *heart of stone* is imperceptive and one which chooses not to be aware
of what the Lord has done, what his demands are, and does not know how to respond; by
contrast *a heart of flesh* is a sensitive human heart fully aware of its relationship with God,
and so capable of receiving a new measure of his life-giving activity, a *new spirit*. **29–31**: In
other prophets, the process of redemption involved the people's sin, their punishment, and,
upon doing penance, their restoration. Ezekiel promises that God will redeem Israel out of his

evil deeds, and you will loathe yourselves because of your wickedness and
32 your abominations. It is not for your
sake that I am acting; be sure of that,
says the Lord GOD. Feel, then, the
shame and disgrace of your ways, men
of Israel.

33 These are the words of the Lord
GOD: When I cleanse you of all your
wickedness, I will re-people the cities,
34 and the palaces shall be rebuilt. The
land now desolate shall be tilled,
instead of lying waste for every passer-
35 by to see. Men will say that this same
land which was waste has become like
a garden of Eden, and people will make
their homes in the cities once ruined,
wasted, and shattered, but now well
36 fortified. The nations still left around
you will know that it is I, the LORD,
who have rebuilt the shattered cities
and planted anew the waste land; I, the
LORD, have spoken and will do it.

37 These are the words of the Lord
GOD: Yet again will I let the Israelites
ask me to act in their behalf. I will
make their men numerous as sheep,
38 like the sheep offered as holy-gifts, like
the sheep in Jerusalem at times of
festival. So shall their ruined cities be
filled with human flocks, and they shall
know that I am the LORD.

37 The hand of the LORD came upon
me, and he carried me out by his spirit
and put me down in a plain full of
2 bones. He made me go to and fro
across them until I had been round
them all;[v] they covered the plain,
countless numbers of them, and they
3 were very dry. He said to me, 'Man, can
these bones live again?' I answered,
'Only thou knowest that, Lord GOD.'
4 He said to me, 'Prophesy over these
bones and say to them, O dry bones,
5 hear the word of the LORD. This is the

word of the Lord GOD to these bones:
I will put breath[w] into you, and you
shall live. I will fasten sinews on you, 6
bring flesh upon you, overlay you with
skin, and put breath in you, and you
shall live; and you shall know that I
am the LORD.' I began to prophesy as 7
he had bidden me, and as I prophesied
there was a rustling sound and the
bones fitted themselves together. As I 8
looked, sinews appeared upon them,
flesh covered them, and they were
overlaid with skin, but there was no
breath in them. Then he said to me, 9
'Prophesy to the wind, prophesy, man,
and say to it, These are the words of
the Lord GOD: Come, O wind, come
from every quarter and breathe into
these slain, that they may come to life.'
I began to prophesy as he had bidden 10
me: breath came into them; they came
to life and rose to their feet, a mighty
host. He said to me, 'Man, these bones 11
are the whole people of Israel. They
say, "Our bones are dry, our thread of
life is snapped, our web is severed from
the loom."[x] Prophesy, therefore, and 12
say to them, These are the words of the
Lord GOD: O my people, I will open
your graves and bring you up from
them, and restore you to the land of
Israel. You shall know that I am the 13
LORD when I open your graves and
bring you up from them, O my people.
Then I will put my spirit[y] into you and 14
you shall live, and I will settle you on
your own soil, and you shall know that
I the LORD have spoken and will act.
This is the very word of the LORD.'

These were the words of the LORD 15
to me: Man, take one leaf of a wooden 16
tablet and write on it, 'Judah and his

v He made . . . all: *or* He made me pass all round them.
w *Or* wind *or* spirit.
x our web . . . loom: *prob. rdg.; Heb.* we are completely
cut off.
y *Or* breath.

sheer goodness, "for the sake of my holy name" (vv. 21–22), leading the people thereafter
to repent.
37.1–14: The dry bones of Israel's hopes will live again. Central to the passage is a remarkable
play on the Heb. word *ruah*, with its basic meaning, "breath," being applied in three contexts:
(a) wind, the life-giving breath in nature; (b) the life-supporting breath of the nostrils in
animals and man; (c) spirit, the life-creating power of God. Ezekiel does not refer directly to
personal resurrection. His emphasis on individual responsibility and a person's continued life
with God, which parallels national survival, at least raises the question. **2:** *Very dry:* lifeless a
long time. **8–9:** The perfect and more enduring new creation of man also occurs in two stages;
compare Gen.2.7. **11:** Israel's *bones are dry*, being *completely cut off* (Tfn. *x*) from the core of
life, the covenant.
37.15–28: One nation (Israel), one king (David), and one God (the Lord). 16: *Joseph* is a
synonym for the Northern Kingdom, Israel, sometimes called Ephraim after its leading tribe.

associates of Israel.' Then take another leaf and write on it, 'Joseph, the leaf of Ephraim and all his associates of 17 Israel.' Now bring the two together to form one tablet; then they will be a 18 folding tablet in your hand. When your fellow-countrymen ask you to tell them 19 what you mean by this, say to them, These are the words of the Lord GOD: I am taking the leaf of Joseph, which belongs to Ephraim and his associate tribes of Israel, and joining*z* to it the leaf of Judah. Thus I shall make them one tablet, and they shall be one in my hand. 20 The leaves on which you write shall be visible in your hand for all to see. 21 Then say to them, These are the words of the Lord GOD: I am gathering up the Israelites from their places of exile among the nations; I will assemble them from every quarter and restore 22 them to their own soil. I will make them one single nation in the land, on the mountains of Israel, and they shall have one king; they shall no longer be two nations or divided into two king- 23 doms. They shall never again be defiled with their idols, their loathsome ways and all their disloyal acts; I will rescue them from all their sinful backsliding and purify them. Thus they shall become my people, and I will become 24 their God. My servant David shall become king over them, and they shall have one shepherd. They shall conform to my laws, they shall observe and carry 25 out my statutes. They shall live in the land which I gave my servant Jacob, the land where your fathers lived. They and their descendants shall live there for ever, and my servant David shall 26 for ever be their prince. I will make a covenant with them to bring them prosperity; this covenant shall be theirs for ever.*a* I will greatly increase their numbers, and I will put my sanctuary 27 for ever in their midst. They shall live

under the shelter of my dwelling; I will become their God and they shall become my people. The nations shall 28 know that I the LORD am keeping Israel sacred to myself, because my sanctuary is in the midst of them for ever.

God's triumph over the world

THESE WERE THE WORDS OF THE LORD **38** to me: Man, look towards Gog, the 2 prince of Rosh, Meshech, and Tubal, in the land of Magog, and prophesy against him. Say, These are the words 3 of the Lord GOD: I am against you, Gog, prince of Rosh, Meshech, and Tubal. I will turn you about, I will put 4 hooks in your jaws. I will lead you out, you and your whole army, horses and horsemen, all fully equipped, a great host with shield and buckler, every man wielding a sword, and with them 5 the men of Pharas, Cush, and Put, all with shield and helmet; Gomer and all 6 its squadrons, Beth-togarmah with its squadrons from the far recesses of the north—a great concourse of peoples with you. Be prepared; make ready, 7 you and all the host which has gathered to join you, and hold yourselves in reserve for me.*b* After many days you 8 will be summoned; in years to come you will enter a land restored from ruin, whose people are gathered from many nations upon the mountains of Israel that have been desolate so long. The Israelites, brought out from the nations, will all be living undisturbed; and you 9 will come up, driving in like a hurri- cane; you will cover the land like a cloud, you and all your squadrons, a great concourse of peoples.

This is the word of the Lord GOD: 10

z Prob. rdg.; Heb. adds them.
a Prob. rdg.; Heb. adds and I will put them.
b and hold . . . me: or and you shall be their rallying-point.

21–28: God will unite the *two kingdoms* to himself by a new *covenant*. The description of the new land and new Temple (chs. 40–48) should logically follow here.

38.1–39.29: Gog will be destroyed. God's triumph over the world includes primarily the triumph of Israel over all hostile evil forces. Resembling other biblical apocalypses (Isa. chs. 24–27; Dan. chs. 9–14; Zech. chs. 9–14), these verses are an early form of the genre.

38.1–39.7: Universal terror against Gog, who sets in motion against Israel all the forces of evil and hostility. **2:** *Gog* resembles all Israel's persecutors, a symbol of all wickedness menacing it, but neither he nor the land of *Magog* nor its place names can be identified with certainty. **4–13:** The *army of Gog* is composed of elements from the four corners of the author's world: Gomer, north; Ethiopia, south; Tarshish, west; Dedan, east; it is called out from the *far*

At that time a thought will enter your
11 head and you will plan evil. You will
say, 'I will attack a land of open
villages, I will fall upon a people living
quiet and undisturbed, undefended by
12 walls, with neither gates nor bars.' You
will expect to come plundering, spoil-
ing, and stripping bare the ruins where
men now live again, a people gathered
out of the nations, a people acquiring
cattle and goods, and making their
home at the very centre of the world.
13 Sheba and Dedan, the traders of
Tarshish and her leading merchants,
will say to you, 'Is it for plunder that
you have come? Have you gathered
your host to get spoil, to carry off
silver and gold, to seize cattle and
goods, to collect rich spoil?'
14 Therefore, prophesy, man, and say
to Gog, These are the words of the
Lord GOD: In that day when my
people Israel is living undisturbed, will
15 you not awake and come with many
nations from your home in the far
recesses of the north, all riding on
horses, a great host, a mighty army?
16 You will come up against my people
Israel; and in those future days you
will be like a cloud covering the earth.
I will bring you against my land, that
the nations may know me, when they
see me prove my holiness at your
expense, O Gog.
17 This is the word of the Lord GOD:
When I spoke in days of old through
my servants the prophets, who prophesied in those days unceasingly, it was
you whom I threatened to bring
18 against Israel. On that day, when at
length Gog comes against the land of
Israel, says the Lord GOD, my wrath
19 will boil over. In my jealousy and in
the heat of my anger I swear that on
that day there shall be a great earthquake throughout the land of Israel.
20 The fish in the sea and the birds in the
air, the wild animals and all reptiles
that move on the ground, all mankind
on the face of the earth, all shall be
shaken before me. Mountains shall be
torn up, the terraced hills collapse, and

every wall crash to the ground. I will 21
summon universal terror against Gog,
says the Lord GOD, and his men shall
turn their swords against one another.
I will bring him to judgement with 22
pestilence and bloodshed; I will pour
down teeming rain, hailstones hard as
rock, and fire and brimstone, upon him,
upon his squadrons, upon the whole
concourse of peoples with him. Thus 23
will I prove myself great and holy and
make myself known to many nations;
they shall know that I am the LORD.

And you, man, prophesy against **39**
Gog and say, These are the words of
the Lord GOD: I am against you, Gog,
prince of Rosh, Meshech, and Tubal.
I will turn you about and drive you, I 2
will fetch you up from the far recesses
of the north and bring you to the
mountains of Israel. I will strike the 3
bow from your left hand and dash the
arrows from your right hand. There 4
on the mountains of Israel you shall
fall, you, all your squadrons, and your
allies; I will give you as food to the
birds of prey and the wild beasts. You 5
shall fall on the bare ground, for it is I
who have spoken. This is the very word
of the Lord GOD. I will send fire on 6
Magog and on those who live undisturbed in the coasts and islands, and
they shall know that I am the LORD.
My holy name I will make known in 7
the midst of my people Israel and will
no longer let it be profaned; the
nations shall know that in Israel I, the
LORD, am holy.

Behold, it comes; it shall be, says the 8
Lord GOD, the day of which I have
spoken. The dwellers in the cities of 9
Israel shall come out and gather
weapons to light their fires, buckler and
shield, bow and arrows, throwing-stick
and lance, and they shall kindle fires
with them for seven years. They shall 10
take no wood from the fields nor cut it
from the forests but shall light their
fires with the weapons. Thus they will
plunder their plunderers and spoil their
spoilers. This is the very word of the
Lord GOD.

---

recesses of the north, the mythological dwelling of good and evil. **12:** *Centre of the world:*
Jerusalem; see 5.5. **39.7:** To *know* God or his *name* is to experience God's reality and to
acknowledge it by obedience.
　39.8–20: Evil turned to good in the complete slaughter of Gog. 8: The verse hearkens back to 38.17.

11 In that day I will give to Gog, instead of ᶜ a burial ground in Israel, the valley of Abarim east of the Sea.ᵈ There they shall bury Gog and all his horde, and all Abarim will be blocked; and they shall call it the Valley of Gog's 12 Horde. For seven months the Israelites shall bury them and purify the land; 13 all the people shall take their share in the burying. The day that I win myself honour shall be a memorable day for them. This is the very word of the Lord 14 GOD. Men shall be picked for the regular duty of going through the country and searching forᵉ any left above ground, to purify the land; they shall begin their search at the end of the 15 seven months. They shall go through the country, and whenever one of them sees a human bone he shall put a marker beside it until it has been buried 16 in the Valley of Gog's Horde. So no more shall be heard of that great horde,ᶠ and the land will be purified.

17 Man, these are the words of the Lord GOD: Cry to every bird that flies and to all the wild beasts: Come, assemble, gather from every side to my sacrifice, the great sacrifice I am making for you on the mountains of Israel; eat flesh 18 and drink blood, eat the flesh of warriors and drink the blood of princes of the earth; all these are your rams and sheep, he-goats and bulls, and 19 buffaloes of Bashan. You shall cram yourselves with fat and drink yourselves drunk on blood at the sacrifice 20 which I am preparing for you. At my table you shall eat your fill of horses and riders, of warriors and all manner of fighting men. This is the very word of the Lord GOD.

21 I will show my glory among the nations; all shall see the judgement that I execute and the heavy hand that I lay upon them. From that day forwards 22 the Israelites shall know that I am the LORD their God. The nations shall 23 know that the Israelites went into exile for their iniquity, because they were faithless to me. So I hid my face from them and handed them over to their enemies, and they fell, every one of them, by the sword. I dealt with them 24 as they deserved, defiled and rebellious as they were, and hid my face from them.

These, therefore, are the words of the 25 Lord GOD: Now I will restore the fortunes of Jacob and show my affection for all Israel, and I will be jealous for my holy name. They shall forget 26 their shame and all their unfaithfulness to me, when they are at home again on their own soil, undisturbed, with no one to alarm them. When I bring them 27 home out of the nations and gather them from the lands of their enemies, I will make them an example of my holiness, for many nations to see. They 28 will know that I am the LORD their God, because I who sent them into exile among the nations will bring them together again on the soil of their own land and leave none of them behind. No longer will I hide my face 29 from them, I who have poured out my spirit upon Israel. This is the very word of the Lord GOD.

The restored theocracy

AT THE BEGINNING OF THE YEAR, ON **40** the tenth day of the month, in the

c Prob. rdg.; Heb. adds there.
d That is the Dead Sea.
e searching for: prob. rdg.; Heb. burying those who are passing through.
f So . . . horde: prob. rdg.; Heb. obscure.

11: *Abarim:* play on words with *oberim*, Heb. "travelers," who will be *blocked* and so reminded of God's action. The *Sea* is the Dead Sea. **15:** Unburied bodies make the land unclean. **17–20:** An evil army other than Gog's, which has been buried, is slaughtered and then offered as sacrifices for wild beasts, thus reversing the usual practice of animal sacrifices offered for men. The significance of this is not clear. **39.21–29: End of the oracles.** The only relation between this passage and Gog is the theme of Israel's exaltation after exile and the vindication of God's holiness in accomplishing it. **40.1–48.35: Revelation of "Utopia."** It is described in a vision extending over eight chapters. Containing precise building plans, rubrics for ritual, and legal enactments—none of which was ever realized, and perhaps not meant to be—the passage aims to portray graphically the religious, social and political structures of a society termed "The-Lord-is-there" (*Jehovah-shammah,* 48.35). It is a religious Utopia, the ideal postexilic Jewish community in its relations with the Lord. Most interpreters agree that some of this material is not Ezekiel's but comes from the postexilic community that developed following his inspiration.

twenty-fifth year of our exile, that is fourteen years after the destruction of the city, on that very day, the hand of the LORD came upon me and he brought 2 me there. In a vision God brought me to the land of Israel and set me on a very high mountain, where I saw what seemed the buildings of a city facing 3 me. He led me towards it, and I saw a man like a figure of bronze holding a cord of linen thread and a measuring- 4 rod, and standing at the gate. 'Man,' he said to me, 'look closely and listen carefully; mark well all that I show you, for this is why you have been brought here. Tell the Israelites all that you see.'

5 Round the outside of the temple ran a wall. The length of the rod which the man was holding was six cubits, reckoning by the long cubit which was one cubit and a hand's breadth. He measured the thickness and the height 6 of the wall; each was one rod. He came to a gate which faced eastwards, went up its steps and measured the threshold of the gateway, its depth was one rod. 7 Each cell was one rod long and one rod wide; the space between the cells five cubits, and the threshold of the gateway at the end of the vestibule on the side 8 facing the temple one rod. He measured the vestibule of the gate and found it 9 eight cubits, with pilasters two cubits thick; the vestibule of the gateway lay 10 at the end near the temple. Now the cells of the gateway, looking back eastwards, were three in number on each side; all three of the same size, and their pilasters on each side of the same 11 size also. He measured the entrance into the gateway; it was ten cubits wide, and the gateway itself throughout its 12 length thirteen cubits wide. In front of the cells on each side lay a kerb, one cubit wide; each cell was six cubits by 13 six. He measured the width of the gateway through the cell doors which faced

one another, from the back of one cell to the back of the opposite cell, he made it twenty-five cubits, and the 14 vestibule twenty cubits, across; the gateway on every side projected into[g] the court. From the front of the 15 entrance-gate to the outer face of the vestibule of the inner gate the distance was fifty cubits. Both cells and pilasters 16 had loopholes all round inside the gateway, and the vestibule had windows all round within and palms carved on each pilaster.

He brought me to the outer court, 17 and I saw rooms and a pavement all round the court: in all, thirty rooms on the pavement. The pavement ran up 18 to the side of the gateways, as wide as they were long; this was the lower pavement. He measured the width of 19 the court from the front of the lower gateway to the outside of the inner gateway; it was a hundred cubits. He led me round to the north and I saw a 20 gateway facing northwards, belonging to the outer court, and he measured its length and its breadth. Its cells, three 21 on each side, together with its pilasters and its vestibule, were the same size as those of the first gateway, fifty cubits long by twenty-five wide. So too its 22 windows, and those of[h] its vestibule, and its palms were the same size as those of the gateway which faced east; it was approached by seven steps with its vestibule facing them. A gate like 23 that on the east side led to the inner court opposite the northern gateway; he measured from gateway to gateway, and it was a hundred cubits. Then he 24 led me round to the south, and I found a gateway facing southwards. He measured its cells, its pilasters, and its vestibule, and found it the same size

g *Prob. rdg.; Heb. adds* pilaster.
h *those of: prob. rdg.; Heb. om.*

40.1–47: The new Temple: its enclosure. 1: *Beginning of the year:* Heb., r'oš haššana. In modern Judaism this phrase would indicate the Feast of the New Year which is celebrated on the first day of the month of Tishri (September-October). In Ezekiel all dates are derived from the ancient religious calendar in which the year began in the spring. Hence the *tenth day of the month* is probably April 28, 573 B.C. **5:** *The length of the rod* was about 10 feet 4 inches long. The long cubit, an ancient standard, was seven hands' breadth or 20.60 inches, and the newer cubit was six hands' breadth or 17.5 inches. In choosing the ancient measure, Ezekiel indicates a return to ancient standards (and/or possibly principles) in the new community. **6:** *Gate:* of the new Temple. Built on a high mountain (17.23), the new Temple rose above successive elevations of seven, eight and ten steps; see vv. 22,26,31,34,49. The Temple stood on the last

25 as the others, fifty cubits long by twenty-five wide. Both gateway and vestibule had windows all round like the others. It was approached by seven steps with a vestibule facing them and

27 palms carved on each pilaster. The inner court had a gateway facing southwards, and he measured from gateway to gateway; it was a hundred cubits.

28 He brought me into the inner court through the southern gateway, measured it and found it the same size as

29 the others. So were its cells, pilasters, and vestibule, fifty cubits long by twenty-five wide. It and its vestibule

31 had windows all round.*i* Its vestibule faced the outer court; it had palms carved on its pilasters, and eight steps led up to it.

32 Then he brought me into the inner court, towards the east, and measured the gateway and found it the same size

33 as the others. So too were its cells, pilasters, and vestibule; it and its vestibule had windows all round, and it was fifty cubits long by twenty-five

34 wide. Its vestibule faced the outer court and had a palm carved on each

35 pilaster; eight steps led up to it. Then he brought me to the north gateway and measured it and found it the same

36 size as the others. So were its cells, pilasters, and vestibule, and it had windows all round; it was fifty cubits

37 long by twenty-five wide. Its vestibule faced the outer court and had palms carved on the pilaster at each side; eight steps led up to it.

38 There was a room opening out from the vestibule of the gateway;*j* here the

39 whole-offerings were washed. In the vestibule of the gateway were two tables on each side, at which to slaughter the whole-offering, the sin-offering,

40 and the guilt-offering. At the corner on the outside, as one goes up to the opening of the northern gateway, stood two tables, and two more at the other corner of the vestibule of the gateway.

Another four stood on each side at the 41 corner of the gateway, eight tables in all at which slaughtering was done. Four tables used for the whole-offering 42 were of hewn stone, each a cubit and a half long by a cubit and a half wide and a cubit high; and on them they put the instruments used for the whole-offering and other sacrifices. The flesh 43 of the offerings was on the tables, and ledges a hand's breadth in width were fixed all round facing inwards.

Then he brought me right into the 44 inner court, and I saw two rooms in the inner court, one at the corner of the northern gateway, facing south, and one at the corner of the southern gateway, facing north. This room facing 45 south, he told me, is for the priests who have charge of the temple. The room 46 facing north is for the priests who have charge of the altar; these are the sons of Zadok, who alone of the Levites may come near to serve the LORD. He 47 measured the court; it was square, a hundred cubits each way, and the altar lay in front of the temple.

Then he brought me into the 48 vestibule of the temple, and measured a pilaster of the vestibule; it was five cubits on each side, the width of the gateway fourteen cubits and that of the corners of the gateway three cubits in each direction. The vestibule was 49 twenty cubits long by twelve wide; ten steps led up to it, and by the pilasters rose pillars, one on each side.

Then he brought me into the sanc- **41** tuary and measured the pilasters; they were six cubits wide on each side. The 2 opening was ten cubits wide and its corners five cubits wide in each direction. He measured its length; it was forty cubits, and its width twenty. He 3 went inside and measured the pilasters at the opening: they were two cubits;

i So some MSS.; others add (30) It had vestibules all round, and it was twenty-five cubits long by five wide.
j the vestibule of the gateway: prob. rdg.; Heb. pilasters, the gates.

elevation crowning the land as the Lord's throne; see 43.7. **25:** The *gateway* and *windows all round* enabled guards to keep out any one who might profane the Temple. **39:** The emphasis on *sin-offering* and *guilt-offering*, expiatory sacrifices, stems from a keener sense of culpability and responsibility following the Exile. **45–46:** The *Levites* are divided into two ranks, those having *charge of the temple*, performing work formerly done by foreign slaves, and a superior rank in *charge of altar* sacrifices; see 43.19; 44.10–15.
40.48 42.20: The new Temple, like other ancient temples, had three well defined areas: the vestibule (vv. 48–49); the sanctuary (41.1–2); the Holy of Holies (41.4). **49:** Two *pillars* stood in

the opening itself was six cubits, and the corners of the opening were seven 4 cubits in each direction. Then he measured the room at the far end of the sanctuary; its length and its breadth were each twenty cubits. He said to me, 'This is the Holy of Holies.'

5 He measured the wall of the temple; it was six cubits high, and each arcade all round the house was four cubits 6 wide. The arcades were arranged in three tiers, each tier in thirty sections. In the wall all round the temple there were intakes for the arcades, so that they could be supported without being fastened into the wall of the temple. 7 The higher up the arcades were, the broader they were all round by the addition of the intakes, one above the other all round the temple; the temple itself had a ramp running upwards on a base, and in this way one went up from the lowest to the highest tier by way of the middle tier.

8 Then I saw a raised pavement all round the temple, and the foundations of the arcades were flush with it and measured a full rod, six cubits high. 9 The outer wall of the arcades was five cubits thick. There was an unoccupied area beside the terrace[k] which was 11[l] adjacent to the temple, and the arcades opened on to this area, one opening facing northwards and one southwards; the unoccupied area was five 10 cubits wide on all sides. There was a free space[m] twenty cubits wide all 12 round the temple. On the western side, at the far end of the free space, stood a building seventy cubits wide; its wall was five cubits thick all round, and its length ninety cubits.

13 He measured the temple; it was a hundred cubits long; and the free space, the building, and its walls, a hundred 14 cubits in all. The eastern front of the temple and the free space was a 15 hundred cubits wide. He measured the length of the building at the far end of the free space to the west of the

temple, and its corridors on each side: a hundred cubits.

The sanctuary, the inner shrine and the outer vestibule were panelled; the 16 embrasures all round the three of them were framed with wood all round. From the ground up to the windows 17 and above the door, both in the inner and outer chambers, round all the walls, inside and out, were carved 18 figures,[n] cherubim and palm-trees, a palm between every pair of cherubim. Each cherub had two faces: one the 19 face of a man, looking towards one palm-tree, and the other the face of a lion, looking towards another palm-tree. Such was the carving round the whole of the temple. The cherubim and 20 the palm-trees were carved from the ground up to the top of the doorway and on the wall of the sanctuary. The 21 door-posts of the sanctuary were square.[o]

In front of[p] the Holy Place was what seemed an altar of wood, three cubits 22 high and two cubits long; it was fitted with cornerposts, and its base and sides also were of wood. He told me that this was the table which stood before the LORD. The sanctuary had a 23 double door, and the Holy Place also had a double door: the double doors 24 had swinging leaves, a pair for each door. Cherubim and palm-trees like 25 those on the walls were carved on them.[q] Outside there was a wooden cornice over the vestibule; on both 26 sides of the vestibule were loopholes, with palm-trees carved at the corners.[r]

Then he took me to the outer court 42 round by the north and brought me to the rooms facing the free space and

k beside the terrace: *prob. rdg.; Heb.* between the arcades.
l *Verses 10 and 11 transposed.*
m There . . . space: *prob. rdg.; Heb.* Between the rooms.
n carved figures: *prob. rdg.; Heb.* measures and carving.
o The door-posts . . . square: *prob. rdg.; Heb.* unintelligible.
p In front of: *prob. rdg.; Heb.* The face of.
q *Prob. rdg.; Heb.* adds on the doors of the sanctuary.
r *Prob. rdg.; Heb.* adds and the arcades of the temple and the cornices.

front of Solomon's Temple; see 1 Kgs.7.21,41. **41.12:** *On the western side. . .a building:* possibly a place for keeping animals destined for sacrifice. **22:** The *altar of wood* seems to be either the altar of incense or the *table* of the Presence bearing the twelve cakes of pure wheat flour, a witness to the covenant between the Lord and the twelve tribes; see Lev.24.5–9; 1 Kgs.6.20–22. **42.1–14:** Accessory structures provide rooms for priests to eat their share of the sacrifices, for storing vestments and other supplies. The shape and disposition of the buildings are unclear.

2 facing the buildings to the north. The length along the northern side was a hundred cubits, and the breadth fifty. 3 Facing the free space measuring twenty cubits, which adjoined the inner court, and facing the pavement of the outer court, were corridors at three levels 4 corresponding to each other. In front of the rooms a passage, ten cubits wide and a hundred cubits long, ran towards the inner court; their entrances faced 5 northwards. The upper rooms were shorter than the lower and middle rooms, because the corridors took 6 building space from them. For they were all at three levels and had no pillars as the courts had, so that the lower and middle levels were recessed 7 from the ground upwards. An outside wall, fifty cubits long, ran parallel to the rooms and in front of them, on the 8 side of the outer court. The rooms adjacent to the outer court were fifty cubits long, and those facing the 9 sanctuary a hundred cubits. Below these rooms was an entry from the east as one entered them from the outer court 10 where the wall of the court began.[s] On the south side, passing by the free space and the building, were other 11 rooms with a passage in front of them. These rooms corresponded, in length and breadth and in general character, 12 to those facing north, whose exits and entrances were the same as those of the rooms on the south. As one[t] went eastwards, where the passages began, there was an entrance in the face of the 13 inner[u] wall. Then he said to me, 'The northern and southern rooms facing the free space are the consecrated rooms where the priests who approach the LORD may eat the most sacred offerings. There they shall put these offerings as well as the grain-offering, the sin-offering, and the guilt-offering; for the place is holy. 14 When the priests have entered the Holy Place they shall not go into the outer court again without leaving here the

garments they have worn while performing their duties, for these are holy. They shall put on other garments when they approach the place assigned to the people.'

15 When he had finished measuring the inner temple, he brought me out towards the gateway which faces eastwards and measured the whole area. 16 He measured the east side with the measuring-rod, and it was five hundred 17 cubits. He turned and measured the north side with his rod, and it was five 18 hundred cubits. He turned to the south side and measured it with his rod; it 19 was five hundred cubits. He turned to the west and measured it with his rod; 20 it was five hundred cubits. So he measured all four sides; in each direction the surrounding wall measured five hundred cubits. This marked off the sacred area from the profane.

43 He led me to the gate, the gate facing 2 eastwards, and I beheld the glory of the God of Israel coming from the east. His voice was like the sound of a mighty torrent, and the earth shone with his 3 glory. The form that I saw was the same as that which I had seen when he came to destroy the city, and as that which I had seen by the river Kebar,[v] 4 and I fell on my face. The glory of the LORD came up to the temple towards the gate which faced eastwards. A 5 spirit[w] lifted me up and brought me into the inner court, and the glory of the LORD filled the temple. Then I heard 6 one speaking to me from the temple, and the man was standing at my side. 7 He said, Man, do you see the place of my throne, the place where I set my feet, where I will dwell among the Israelites for ever? Neither they nor their kings shall ever defile my holy name again with their wanton disloyalty, and with the corpses[x] of their

s began: prob. rdg.; Heb. breadth.
t Prob. rdg.; Heb. they.
u Prob. rdg.; Heb. word unknown.
v Or the Kebar canal.
w Or wind.   x Or effigies.

15–20: The Temple area is holy, 500 cubits square, surrounded by a wall separating it from the profane, secular life.
43.1–12: **The glory of the LORD returns to consecrate the new city.** This occurrence is the high point of the vision. 1: *Glory;* see 10.3–4 n. 2: *The east:* the direction in which he had departed in 11.23. 3: There is here no appearance of a man, no living creatures as in 1.4–28. 7: Now the Lord will *set* his *feet* permanently in Jerusalem because it is his, planned and built by him; earlier, since it was Canaanite in origin, he had entered it as a sojourner. See 16.3.

8 kings when they die. They set their threshold by mine and their door-post beside mine, with a wall between me and them, and they defiled my holy name with the abominations they committed, and I destroyed them in
9 my anger. But now they shall abandon their wanton disloyalty and remove the corpses[x] of their kings far from me, and I will dwell among them for ever.
10 So tell the Israelites, man, about this temple, its appearance and proportions,
11 that they may be ashamed of their iniquities. If they are ashamed of all they have done, you shall describe to them the temple and its fittings, its exits and entrances, all the details and particulars of its elevation and plan; explain them and draw them before their eyes, so that they may keep them in mind and
12 carry them out. This is the plan of the temple to be built on the top of the mountain; all its precincts on every side shall be most holy.
13 These were the dimensions of the altar in cubits (the cubit that is a cubit and a hand's breadth). This was the height of the altar: the base was a cubit high[y] and projected a cubit; on its edge
14 was a rim one span deep. From the base to the cubit-wide ridge of the lower pedestal-block was two cubits, and from this shorter pedestal-block to the cubit-wide ridge of the taller
15 pedestal-block was four cubits. The altar-hearth was four cubits high and was surmounted by four horns a cubit
16 high. The hearth was twelve cubits long and twelve cubits wide, being a perfect
17 square. The upper pedestal-block was fourteen cubits long and fourteen cubits wide along its four sides, and the rim round it was half a cubit deep. The base of the altar projected a cubit, and there were steps facing eastwards.

He said to me, Man, these are the 18 words of the Lord GOD: These are the regulations for the altar when it has been made, for sacrificing whole-offerings on it and flinging the blood against it. The levitical priests of the 19 family of Zadok, and they alone, may come near to me to serve me, says the Lord GOD. You shall assign them a young bull for a sin-offering; you shall 20 take some of the blood and put it on the four horns of the altar, on the four corners of the upper pedestal and all round the rim, and so purify it and make expiation for it. Then take the 21 bull assigned as the sin-offering, and they shall destroy it by fire in the proper place within the precincts but outside the Holy Place. On the second day you 22 shall present a he-goat without blemish as a sin-offering, and with it they shall purify the altar as they did with the bull. When you have completely puri- 23 fied the altar, you shall present a young bull without blemish and a ram without blemish from the flock. You shall 24 present them before the LORD; the priests shall throw salt on them and sacrifice them as a whole-offering to the LORD. For seven days you shall provide 25 as a daily sin-offering a goat, a young bull, and a ram from the flock; all of them shall be provided free from blemish. For seven days they shall make 26 expiation for the altar, and pronounce it ritually clean, and consecrate it. At 27 the end of that time, on the eighth day and onwards, the priests shall sacrifice on the altar your whole-offerings and your shared-offerings, and I will accept you. This is the very word of the Lord GOD.

x *Or* effigies.
y the base . . . high: *prob. rdg.; Heb.* the base of the cubit.

8: Unlike Solomon's Temple, the new Temple will not be a dependency of the king, surrounded by his buildings; see 1 Kgs.7.1–12; 2 Kgs.16.7–20.
　　43.13–27: **Shape of the altar and its consecration.** Since in cultic acts the altar represents God (Exod.24.6–8), it will be a sign of his permanent presence. 13–17: Built in tiers on three platforms—16, 14, and 12 cubits square—the altar resembles the Babylonian ziggurat, or sacred tower (Gen.11.4 n.); it is 12 cubits or about 20½ ft. high. 15: The significance of the *horns*, projections from the four corners of the altar, is not known. 18–26: Zadokite *priests* were the descendants of Zadok, the priest who remained loyal to David (1 Kgs.1.5–40). They will *consecrate* the *altar*—lit. "fill its hands" (with offerings), terminology used in consecrating priests—setting it aside for sacred use. Compare Exod.29.1–46. 27: *Accept you:* be pleased with you. *Whole offerings:* the sacrifice was completely burned. *Shared offerings:* the offerer received a portion of it back and ate it as a sign of his communion with God.

44 He again brought me round to the outer gate of the sanctuary facing
2 eastwards, and it was shut. The LORD said to me, This gate shall be kept shut; it must not be opened. No man may enter by it, for the LORD the God of Israel has entered by it. It shall be kept
3 shut. The prince, however, when he is here as prince, may sit there to eat food in the presence of the LORD; he shall come in and go out by the vestibule of the gate.

4 He brought me round to the northern gate facing the temple, and I saw the glory of the LORD filling the LORD's
5 house, and I fell on my face. The LORD said to me, Mark well, man, look closely, and listen carefully to all that I say to you, to all the rules and regulations for the house of the LORD. Mark well the entrance to the house of the LORD and all the exits from the
6 sanctuary. Say to that rebel people of Israel, These are the words of the Lord GOD: Enough of all these abominations
7 of yours, you Israelites! You have added to them by bringing foreigners, uncircumcised in mind and body, to stand in my sanctuary and defile my house when you present my food to me, both fat and blood, and they have
8 made my covenant void. Instead of keeping charge of my holy things yourselves, you have chosen to put these men in charge of my sanctuary.

9 These are the words of the Lord GOD: No foreigner, uncircumcised in mind and body, shall enter my sanctuary, not even a foreigner living
10 among the Israelites. But the Levites, though they deserted me when the Israelites went astray after their idols and had to bear the punishment of
11 their iniquity, shall yet do service in my sanctuary. They shall take charge of the gates of the temple and do service there. They shall slaughter the whole-offering and the sacrifice for the people and shall be in attendance to serve

12 them. Because they served them in the presence of their idols and brought Israel to the ground by their iniquity, says the Lord GOD, I have sworn with uplifted hand that they shall bear the punishment of their iniquity. They shall
13 not have access to me, to serve me as priests; they shall not come near to my holy things or to the Holy of Holies; they shall bear the shame of the abominable deeds they have done. I
14 will put them in charge of the temple with all the service which must be performed there.

15 But the levitical priests of the family of Zadok remained in charge of my sanctuary when the Israelites went astray from me; these shall approach me to serve me. They shall be in attendance on me, presenting the fat
16 and the blood, says the Lord GOD. It is they who shall enter my sanctuary and approach my table to serve me and
17 observe my charge. When they come to the gates of the inner court they shall dress in linen; they shall wear no wool when they serve me at the gates
18 of the inner court and within. They shall wear linen turbans, and linen drawers on their loins; they shall not fasten their clothes with a belt so that
19 they sweat. When they go out to the people in the outer court, they shall take off the clothes they have worn while serving, leave them in the sacred rooms and put on other clothes; otherwise they will transmit the sacred influence to the people through their clothing.

20 They shall neither shave their heads nor let their hair grow long; they shall
21 only clip their hair. No priest shall drink wine when he is to enter the inner
22 court. He may not marry a widow or a divorced woman; he may marry a virgin of Israelite birth. He may, however, marry the widow of a priest.

23 They shall teach my people to distinguish the sacred from the profane,

44.1–31: The personnel of the new Temple receive guidelines for a worship free from profanation. **3:** *The prince* could be in the Temple *as prince*, not for the priestly function of the former kings; see 2 Chr.26.16–19. For sacred meals following a sacrifice see Deut.12.4–7. **7:** The Bible notes several instances of foreigners being taken into Temple service; most to the point are Josh.9.23–27; Ezra 2.43,55; 8.20; Neh.7.57,60; 11.3,21. Circumcision *of the body* is a sign of circumcision *of mind:* a willingness to love and serve the Lord by keeping his Law (see Deut.10.12–20); foreigners, uncircumcised in both, would profane the new covenant. **10–16:** Ezekiel seems to be a transition between Deut. (18.1–8) where all Levites are priests, and the

and show them the difference between
24 clean and unclean. When disputes
break out, they shall take their place in
court, and settle the case according to
my rules. At all my appointed seasons
they shall observe my laws and statutes.
They shall keep my sabbaths holy.
25 They shall not defile themselves by
contact with any dead person, except[z]
father or mother, son or daughter,
26 brother or unmarried sister. After
purification, they shall count seven
27 days and then be clean. When they
enter the inner court to serve in the
Holy Place, they shall present their sin-
offering, says the Lord GOD.
28 They shall own no patrimony in
Israel; I am their patrimony. You shall
grant them no holding in Israel; I am
29 their holding. The grain-offering, the
sin-offering, and the guilt-offering shall
be eaten by them, and everything in
Israel devoted to God shall be theirs,
30 The first of all the firstfruits and all
your contributions of every kind shall
belong wholly to the priests. You shall
give the first lump of your dough to
the priests, that a blessing may rest
31 upon your home. The priests shall eat
no carrion, bird or beast, whether it
has died naturally or been killed by a
wild animal.

45 When you divide the land by lot
among the tribes for their possession,
you shall set apart from it a sacred
reserve for the LORD, twenty-five
thousand cubits in length and twenty
thousand in width; the whole en-
2 closure shall be sacred. Of this a square
plot, five hundred cubits each way,
shall be devoted to the sanctuary, with
3 fifty cubits of open land round it. From
this area you shall measure out a space
twenty-five thousand by ten thousand
cubits, in which the sanctuary, the
4 holiest place of all, shall stand. This

space is for the priests who serve in
the sanctuary and who come nearest
in serving the LORD. It shall include
space for their houses and a sacred plot
for the sanctuary. An area of twenty- 5
five thousand by ten thousand cubits
shall belong to the Levites, the temple
servants; on this shall stand the towns
in which they live. You shall give to 6
each town an area of five thousand by
twenty-five thousand cubits alongside
the sacred reserve; this shall belong to
all Israel. On either side of the sacred 7
reserve and of the city's holding the
prince shall have a holding facing the
sacred reserve and the city's holding,
running westwards on the west and
eastwards on the east. It shall run
alongside one of the tribal portions, and
stretch to the western limit of the land
and to the eastern. It shall be his 8
holding in Israel; the princes of Israel
shall never oppress my people again
but shall give the land to Israel, tribe
by tribe.

THESE ARE THE WORDS OF THE LORD 9
GOD: Enough, princes of Israel! Put
an end to lawlessness and robbery;
maintain law and justice; relieve my
people and stop your evictions, says
the Lord GOD. Your scales shall be 10
honest, your bushel and your gallon
shall be honest. There shall be one 11
standard for each, taking each as the
tenth of a homer, and the homer shall
have its fixed standard. Your shekel 12
weight shall contain twenty gerahs;
your mina shall contain weights of
ten[a] and twenty-five and fifteen shekels.
These are the contributions you shall 13
set aside: out of every homer of wheat
or of barley, one sixth of an ephah.

z any . . . except: *or* anyone else's dead, but only their
own . . .
a *Prob. rdg.; Heb.* twenty.

---

later Priestly source (Num.3.5–10; 18.2) where they are assistants to the priests. **29:** *Devoted
to God,* lit. "under the ban," Heb. *herem,* is anything strictly reserved for sacred cultic use.
31: *Carrion* is meat with blood in it; hence forbidden.

45.1–8: The new distribution of the land. Beginning here and ending in ch. 48, there is a
graphic portrayal of the ideals of theocracy, a political system in which God is held to be the
supreme ruler. **4:** Priests held such a position relative to the Tent of the Presence in the desert;
see Num.3.38. **7–8:** The prince's property is so great because he must provide offerings for the
cult; see v. 17. The prince's role in the new nation is ambiguous, no mention being made of
a king; see 44.3 n.; 45.13–17 n.

45.9–12: Weights and measures are standardized for use in the new Temple.

45.13–46.24: Sacrifices, feasts, and ritual. The cult outlined in great detail. **13–17:** Out of

14 For oil the rule is[b] one tenth of a bath from every kor (at ten bath to the kor); 15 one sheep in every flock of two hundred is to be reserved by every Israelite clan. For a grain-offering, a whole-offering, and a shared-offering, to make expiation for them, says the 16 Lord GOD, all the people of the land shall bring[c] this contribution to the 17 prince in Israel; and the prince shall be responsible for the whole-offering, the grain-offering, and the drink-offering, at pilgrim-feasts, new moons, sabbaths, and every sacred season observed by Israel. He himself is to provide the sin-offering and the grain-offering, the whole-offering and the shared-offering, needed to make expiation for Israel.

18 These are the words of the Lord GOD: On the first day of the first month you shall take a young bull without blemish, and purify the sanc- 19 tuary. The priest shall take some of the blood from the sin-offering and put it on the door-posts of the temple, on the four corners of the altar pedestal and on the gate-posts of the inner court. 20 You shall do the same on the seventh day of the month;[d] in this way you shall make expiation for the temple.

21 On the fourteenth day of the first month you shall hold the Passover, the pilgrim-feast of seven days; bread 22 must be eaten unleavened. On that day the prince shall provide a bull as a sin-offering for himself and for all the 23 people. During the seven days of the feast he shall offer daily as a whole-offering to the LORD seven bulls and seven rams without blemish, and a 24 he-goat as a daily sin-offering. With every bull and ram he shall provide a grain-offering of one ephah, together 25 with a hin of oil for each ephah. He shall do the same thing also on the fifteenth day of the seventh month at the pilgrim-feast; this also shall last seven days, and he shall provide the same sin-offering and whole-offering

and the same quantity of grain and oil.

These are the words of the Lord 46 GOD: The eastern gate of the inner court shall remain closed for the six working days; it may be opened only on the sabbath and at new moon. When the prince comes through the 2 porch of the gate from the outside, he shall halt at the door-post, and the priests shall sacrifice his whole-offering and shared-offerings. On the terrace he shall bow down at the gate and then go out, but the gate shall not be shut till the evening. On sabbaths and at new 3 moons the people also shall bow down before the LORD at the entrance to that gate.

The whole-offering which the prince 4 sacrifices to the LORD shall be as follows: on the sabbath, six sheep without blemish and a ram without blemish; the grain-offering shall be an 5 ephah with the ram and as much as he likes with the sheep, together with a hin of oil for every ephah. At the new 6 moon it shall be a young bull without blemish, six sheep and a ram, all with-out blemish. He shall provide as the 7 grain-offering to go with the bull one ephah and with the ram one ephah, with the sheep as much as he can afford, adding a hin of oil for every ephah.

When the prince comes in, he shall 8 enter through the porch of the gate and come out by the same way. But 9 on festal days when the people come before the LORD, a man who enters by the northern gate to bow down shall leave by the southern gate, and a man who enters by the southern gate shall leave by the northern gate. He shall not turn back and go out through the gate by which he came in but shall go straight on. The prince shall then be 10 among them, going in when they go in

b *Prob. rdg.; Heb. adds* the bath, the oil.
c all . . . bring: *prob. rdg.; Heb. unintelligible.*
d *Prob. rdg.; Heb. adds* This comes from a man who is wrong and foolish. *Cp. Lev. 23. 24; Num. 29. 1.*

taxes he receives, the prince provides for certain sacrifices; in contrast to the meddling of past kings, this is the only privilege and duty allowed him; see 2 Kgs.16.10–18. **18–20:** The rite here for purifying *the sanctuary* does not accord with Lev.16.1–34. Comparable discrepancies in relation to the prescriptions of the Pentateuch concerning sacrifices created problems about the eligibility of the entire book for the canon, the official list of Judaism's biblical books, as is known from rabbinic literature. **21:** *Passover:* see Exod.23.15; Lev.23.4–8; Deut.16.1–8. **25:** Feast of Tabernacles; see Exod.23.16; Lev.23.33–36; Deut.16.13–15. **46.1–2:** The prince may enter the *inner court* to watch the *priests* offer the *sacrifice* which he has provided.

and coming out when they come out.

11 At pilgrim feasts and on festal days the grain-offering shall be an ephah with a bull, an ephah with a ram and as much as he likes with a sheep, together with a hin of oil for every ephah.

12 When the prince provides a whole-offering or shared-offerings as a voluntary sacrifice to the LORD, the eastern gate shall be opened for him,[e] and he shall make his whole-offering and his shared-offerings as he does on the sabbath; when he goes out the gate shall be closed[f] behind him.

13 You shall provide a yearling sheep without blemish daily as a whole-offering to the LORD; you shall provide

14 it morning by morning. With it every morning you shall provide as a grain-offering one sixth of an ephah with a third of a hin of oil to moisten the flour; the LORD's grain-offering is an observ-

15 ance prescribed for all time. Morning by morning, as a regular whole-offering, they shall offer a sheep with the grain-offering and the oil.

16 These are the words of the Lord GOD: When the prince makes a gift out of his property to any of his sons, it shall belong to his sons, since it is part

17 of the family property. But when he makes such a gift to one of his slaves, it shall be his only till the year of manumission, when it shall revert to the prince; it is the property of his sons and shall belong to them.

18 The prince shall not oppress the people by taking part of their holdings; he shall give his sons an inheritance from his own holding of land, so that my people may not be scattered and separated from their holdings.

19 Then he brought me through the entrance by the side of the gate to the rooms which face north (the sacred rooms reserved for the priests), and,

pointing to a place on their western side, he said to me, 'This is the place 20 where the priests shall boil the guilt-offering and the sin-offering and bake the grain-offering; they shall not take it into the outer court for fear they transmit the sacred influence to the people.' Then he brought me into the 21 outer court and took me across to the four corners of the court, at each of which there was a further court. These 22 four courts were vaulted and were the same size, forty cubits long by thirty cubits wide. Round each of the four 23 was a row of stones, with fire-places constructed close up against the rows. He said to me, 'These are the kitchens 24 where the attendants shall boil the people's sacrifices.'

He brought me back to the gate of 47 the temple, and I saw a spring of water issuing from under the terrace of the temple towards the east; for the temple faced east. The water was running down along the right side, to the south of the altar. He took me out through 2 the northern gate and brought me round by an outside path to the eastern gate of the court, and water was trickling from the right side. When 3 the man went out eastwards he had a line in his hand. He measured a 4 thousand cubits and made me walk through the water; it came up to my ankles. He measured another thousand and made me walk through the water; it came up to my knees. He measured another thousand and made me walk through the water; it was up to my waist. Another thousand, and it was a 5 torrent I could not cross, for the water had risen and was now deep enough to swim in; it had become a torrent that could not be crossed. 'Mark this, man', 6 he said, and led me back to the bank of

e the eastern . . . him: or he shall open the gate facing east.
f the gate . . . closed: or he shall close the gate.

13–15: This daily morning sacrifice was unfailingly offered in the Temple until the last days of Jerusalem in 70 A.D., when, according to Josephus (*B.J.* VI,2,1), it was discontinued. In the *year of manumission*—probably every fiftieth or Jubilee year—all lands reverted to original patrimony; see Lev.25.8–55. **18:** Compare 34.5–6. **20:** *Sacred influence* is the Lord's exclusive holiness sometimes attached spatially to places and things connected with the cult, as here, and sometimes attached to the persons totally dedicated to the cult, the priests (Lev.21.6–8).
    47.1–48.35: Life in the new land and the new city. Both land and city are to be so arranged that the vitality emanating from God in his Temple may keep the tribes in unity.
    47.1–12: Life-giving water flowing from the Temple is a symbolism found in Ps.36.8–9; Joel 3.18; Zech.14.8; Rev.22.1–2. **3–6:** In powerful contrast to this visionary stream which increases

7 the torrent. When we came back to the bank I saw a great number of trees on

8 each side. He said to me, 'This water flows out to the region lying east, and down to the Arabah; at last it will reach that sea whose waters are foul, and they

9 will be sweetened. When any one of the living creatures that swarm upon the earth comes where the torrent flows, it shall draw life from it. The fish shall be innumerable; for these waters come here so that the others may be sweetened, and where the torrent flows

10 everything shall live. From En-gedi as far as En-eglaim fishermen shall stand on its shores, for nets shall be spread there. Every kind of fish shall be there in shoals, like the fish of the Great Sea;

11 but its swamps and pools shall not have their waters sweetened but shall be left

12 as salt-pans. Beside the torrent on either bank all trees good for food shall spring up. Their leaves shall not wither, their fruit shall not cease; they shall bear early every month. For their water comes from the sanctuary; their fruit is for food and their foliage for enjoyment.'

13 These are the words of the Lord GOD: These are the boundary lines within which the twelve tribes of Israel shall enter into possession of the land,

14 Joseph receiving two portions. The land which I swore with hand uplifted to give to your fathers you shall divide with each other; it shall be assigned to

15 you by lot as your patrimony. This is the frontier: on its northern side, from the Great Sea through Hethlon, Lebo-

16 hamath, Zedad, Berutha, and Sibraim, which are between the frontiers of Damascus and Hamath, to Hazar-enan,

17 near the frontier of Hauran. So the frontier shall run from the sea to Hazar-enan on the frontier of Damascus and northwards, this is its northern

18 side. The eastern side runs alongside the territories of Hauran, Damascus, and Gilead, and alongside the territory of Israel; Jordan sets the boundary to the eastern sea, to Tamar. This is the

19 eastern side. The southern side runs from Tamar to the waters of Meribah-by-Kadesh; the region assigned to you reaches the Great Sea. This is the

20 southern side towards the Negeb. The western side is the Great Sea, which forms a boundary as far as a point opposite Lebo-hamath. This is the

21 western side. You shall distribute this

22 land among the tribes of Israel and assign it by lot as a patrimony for yourselves and for any aliens living in your midst who leave sons among you. They shall be treated as native-born in Israel and with you shall receive a patrimony by lot among the tribes of

23 Israel. You shall give the alien his patrimony with the tribe in which he is living. This is the very word of the Lord GOD.

48 These are the names of the tribes: In the extreme north, in the direction of Hethlon, to Lebo-hamath and Hazar-enan, with Damascus on the northern frontier in the direction of Hamath, and so from the eastern side to the western, shall be Dan: one portion.

2 Bordering on Dan, from the eastern side to the western, shall be Asher: one portion.

3 Bordering on Asher, from the eastern side to the western, shall be Naphtali: one portion.

4 Bordering on Naphtali, from the eastern side to the western, shall be Manasseh: one portion.

5 Bordering on Manasseh, from the

as it flows from the Temple into the desert is the spring Gihon, which still emerges from the hillside under the Temple area and quickly dries out in the valley of the brook Kidron, which is ordinarily a wadi or a dry wash. **8-9:** *Arabah* is the geological rifting forming the Dead Sea and the valley south of it, a barren desert. Even the Dead Sea, in whose *foul waters* (26 percent salt, besides a high mineral content) no life can survive, will *be sweetened* and will give life. The image symbol is the whole earth's receiving life and nourishment from the Lord's presence in his Temple. **10:** *En-gedi, En-eglaim:* oases on the western shore of the Dead Sea at the mouth of the wadi Kidron, just south of Qumran. *Great Sea* is the Mediterranean.
    47.13–48.35. Israel's boundaries and the tribal portions. Except along the River Jordan, these boundaries approximate the greatest extent of the kingdom under David, the ideal king. Since, in the past, the tribes east of the Jordan tended to isolate themselves, no territories are assigned there. See Josh.22.10–29; Judg.5.15–17. **21–23:** Other codes provide that *aliens* be treated like Israelites, but only here are they given a *patrimony* among the tribes of Israel. **48.1–8:** Since they minister in the sanctuary, the portion of priests and Levites is adjacent to it. *Judah*, the

eastern side to the western, shall be Ephraim: one portion.

6 Bordering on Ephraim, from the eastern side to the western, shall be Reuben: one portion.

7 Bordering on Reuben, from the eastern side to the western, shall be Judah: one portion.

8 Bordering on Judah, from the eastern side to the western, shall be the reserve which you shall set apart. Its breadth shall be twenty-five thousand cubits and its length the same as that of the other portions, from the eastern side to the western, and the sanctuary shall be in the middle of it.

9 The reserve which you shall set apart for the LORD shall measure twenty-five thousand cubits by twenty[g]

10 thousand. The reserve shall be apportioned thus: the priests shall have an area measuring twenty-five thousand cubits on the north side, ten thousand on the west, ten thousand on the east, and twenty-five thousand on the south side; the sanctuary of the LORD shall

11 be in the middle of it. It shall be for the consecrated priests, the sons of Zadok, who kept my charge and did not follow the Israelites when they

12 went astray, as the Levites did. The area set apart for the priests from the reserved territory shall be most sacred, reaching the frontier of the Levites.

13 The Levites shall have a portion running parallel to the border of the priests. It shall be twenty-five thousand cubits long by ten thousand wide; altogether, the length shall be twenty-five thousand cubits and the breadth

14 ten thousand. They shall neither sell nor exchange any part of it, nor shall the best of the land be alienated; for it is holy to the LORD.

15 The strip which is left, five thousand cubits in width by twenty-five thousand, is the city's secular land for dwellings and common land, and the city shall

16 be in the middle of it. These shall be its dimensions: on the northern side four thousand five hundred cubits, on the

southern side four thousand five hundred cubits, on the eastern side four thousand five hundred cubits, on the western side four thousand five hun-

17 dred cubits. The common land belonging to the city shall be two hundred and fifty cubits to the north, two hundred and fifty to the south, two hundred and fifty to the east, and two hundred and

18 fifty to the west. What is left parallel to the reserve, ten thousand cubits to the east and ten thousand to the west,[h] shall provide food for those who work

19 in the city. Those who work in the city shall cultivate it; they may be drawn from any of the tribes of Israel.

20 You shall set apart the whole reserve, twenty-five thousand cubits square, as sacred, as far as the holding

21 of the city. What is left over on each side of the sacred reserve and the holding of the city shall be assigned to the prince. Eastwards, what lies over against the reserved twenty-five thousand cubits, as far as the eastern side, and westwards, what lies over against the twenty-five thousand cubits to the western side, parallel to the tribal portions, shall be assigned to the prince; the sacred reserve and the sanctuary itself shall be in the centre.

22 The[i] holding of the Levites and the[i] holding of the city shall be in the middle of that which is assigned to the prince; it shall be between the frontiers of Judah and Benjamin.

23 The rest of the tribes: from the eastern side to the western shall be Benjamin: one portion.

24 Bordering on Benjamin, from the eastern side to the western, shall be Simeon: one portion.

25 Bordering on Simeon, from the eastern side to the western, shall be Issachar: one portion.

26 Bordering on Issachar, from the eastern side to the western, shall be Zebulun: one portion.

g Prob. rdg.; Heb. ten.
h Prob. rdg.; Heb. adds and it shall be parallel to the sacred reserve.
i Prob. rdg.; Heb. Some of the.

leading southern tribe, is closest to the sanctuary. It is placed among the northern tribes with whom it had formerly lived in hostile rivalry, to show the harmony in the new nation. **15:** Land used for daily existence, i.e. unconnected with the cult, is *secular*, and so separated from the sanctuary by the priests' land. **16–19:** Jerusalem, much larger in extent than at any time in history—5000 cubits or 1.6 miles square—will be a "federal" district, with the names of all

27   Bordering on Zebulun, from the eastern side to the western, shall be Gad: one portion.

28   Bordering on Gad, on the side of the Negeb, the border on the south stretches from Tamar to the waters of Meribah-by-Kadesh, to the Brook as far as the Great Sea.

29   This is the land which you shall allot as a patrimony to the tribes of Israel, and these shall be their lots. This is the very word of the Lord GOD.

30-31   These are to be the ways out of the city, and they are to be named after the tribes of Israel. The northern side, four thousand five hundred cubits long,

shall have three gates, those of Reuben, Judah, and Levi; the eastern side, four 32 thousand five hundred cubits long, three gates, those of Joseph, Benjamin, and Dan; the southern side, four thou- 33 sand five hundred cubits long, three gates, those of Simeon, Issachar, and Zebulun; the western side, four thou- 34 sand five hundred cubits long, three gates, those of Gad, Asher, and Naphtali. The perimeter of the city 35 shall be eighteen thousand cubits, and the city's name for ever after shall be Jehovah-shammah.*j*

j That is the LORD *is there.*

---

the twelve tribes on its gates (vv. 30–34). **35:** Unnamed till now, the city will be called in Heb. *Jehovah-shammah,* a contrast in assonance to its old Canaanite name *Yerushalaim.* For other names given Jerusalem by prophets as a sign of future transformation, see Isa.1.26; 60.14; 62.2–4; Jer.3.17; Zech.8.3. The new city with its name expresses the concept of God's absolute transcendence and his intimate closeness.

THE BOOK OF
DANIEL

The reports about Daniel in this book may contain elements about an older figure, or figures, with the same name: a king in an Ugaritic legend of the fourteenth century B.C.; the example, along with Noah and Job, of a righteous man in Ezek.14.14; and a wise man who knows secrets in Ezek.28.3; these three Daniels may reflect an ancient tradition about a single figure.

The book divides neatly into two parts. In chs. 1–6, Daniel is a young Jew at a foreign court, who, by his ability to interpret royal dreams, and through divine revelation, becomes a vizier to kings. In chs. 8–12, Daniel himself has the visions, and must turn to angels for interpretation. Chapter 7, belonging with chs. 1–6 in its idea of a succession of kingdoms, but also containing the first of the visions characteristic of the second section, unites the two parts. In language, too, ch. 7 provides a bridge between the two parts: Aramaic, rather than Hebrew, is found in 2.4–7.28; see 2.4 n. In chs. 1–6 Daniel has many of the characteristics of Joseph at the Pharaoh's court in Gen. ch. 41; in chs. 7–12 the author builds on elements from the Book of the Prophet Ezekiel to fashion the most fully developed example of apocalyptic literature in the Old Testament; see 8.17 n., 12.1 n., and the heavenly figures of ch. 7.

The stories and visions are set in the Babylonian and Persian periods (sixth–fourth centuries B.C.), but they reflect a later time, primarily that of the successors to Alexander the Great. Antiochus IV Epiphanes (175–163 B.C.) and his wars with the Egyptians (see 7.8 n.) are especially in view. In chs. 7–12, Antiochus, though anonymous as befits apocalyptic literature, emerges in more and more detail as the oppressor of the Jews. In the face of his intense persecution, the book gives great encouragement to Jews by promising God's ultimate vindication of the righteous.

Additional stories in the Daniel tradition are found in the Sept. expansion of the book, and appear in the Apocrypha in The Song of the Three; Daniel and Susanna; and Daniel, Bel, and the Snake.

Jews at the court of Nebuchadnezzar

1 IN THE THIRD YEAR OF THE REIGN OF Jehoiakim king of Judah, Nebuchadnezzar king of Babylon came 2 to Jerusalem and laid siege to it. The Lord delivered Jehoiakim king of Judah into his power, together with all that was left of the vessels of the house of God; and he carried them off to the land of Shinar, to the temple of his god, where he deposited the vessels 3 in the treasury. Then the king ordered Ashpenaz, his chief eunuch, to take certain of the Israelite exiles, of the 4 blood royal and of the nobility, who were to be young men of good looks and bodily without fault, at home in all branches of knowledge, well-informed, intelligent, and fit for service in the royal court; and he was to instruct them in the literature and language of the Chaldaeans. The king 5 assigned them a daily allowance of food and wine from the royal table. Their training was to last for three years, and at the end of that time they would[a] enter the royal service.

Among them there were certain 6 young men from Judah called Daniel, Hananiah, Mishael and Azariah; but 7 the master of the eunuchs gave them new names: Daniel he called Belteshazzar, Hananiah Shadrach, Mishael Meshach and Azariah Abed-nego. Now 8 Daniel determined not to contaminate himself by touching the food and wine assigned to him by the king, and he begged the master of the eunuchs not to make him do so. God made the 9 master show kindness and goodwill to

a at the end ... would: or all of them were to.

1.1–21: Daniel as a young man at a foreign court. See Introduction. The chronology is uncertain, and dates given are not necessarily precise. **1:** *Third year of Jehoiakim:* 607 or 606 B.C. *Nebuchadnezzar* became king in 605; but see 2 Kgs.24.1–6. The first deportation took place in 598; see 2 Kgs.24.10–17. **2:** *Shinar* was in southern Mesopotamia. **3:** *Ashpenaz* is otherwise unknown. **6:** *Hananiah, Mishael and Azariah* were common names; Azariah appears in Neh.10.2, and Hananiah in Neh.10.22. **7:** This was also the case with Joseph in Gen.41.45. **8:** *Determined not to contaminate himself:* compare 1 Macc.1.62; see Ezek.4.13; Hos.9.3.

10 Daniel, and he said to him, 'I am afraid of my lord the king: he has assigned you your food and drink, and if he sees you looking dejected, unlike the other young men of your own age,

11 it will cost me my head.' Then Daniel said to the guard whom the master of the eunuchs had put in charge of Hananiah, Mishael, Azariah and him-

12 self, 'Submit us to this test for ten days. Give us only vegetables to eat and

13 water to drink; then compare our looks with those of the young men who have lived on the food assigned by the king, and be guided in your treatment of us

14 by what you see.'*b* The guard listened to what they said and tested them for

15 ten days. At the end of ten days they looked healthier and were better nourished than all the young men who had lived on the food assigned them by

16 the king. So the guard took away the assignment of food and the wine they were to drink, and gave them only the vegetables.

17 To all four of these young men God had given knowledge and understanding of books and learning of every kind, while Daniel had a gift for interpreting visions and dreams of

18 every kind. The time came which the king had fixed for introducing the young men to court, and the master of the eunuchs brought them into the

19 presence of Nebuchadnezzar. The king talked with them and found none of them to compare with Daniel, Hananiah, Mishael and Azariah; so they

20 entered the royal service. Whenever the king consulted them on any matter calling for insight and judgement, he found them ten times better than all the magicians and exorcists in his

21 whole kingdom. Now Daniel was there till the first year of King Cyrus.

2 In the second year of his reign

Nebuchadnezzar had dreams, and his mind was so troubled that he could not sleep. Then the king gave orders to 2 summon the magicians, exorcists, sorcerers, and Chaldaeans to tell him what he had dreamt. They came in and stood in the royal presence, and the king said 3 to them, 'I have had a dream and my mind has been troubled to know what my dream was.' The Chaldaeans, 4 speaking in Aramaic, said, *c*'Long live the king! Tell us what you dreamt and we will tell you the interpretation.' The 5 king answered. 'This is my declared intention. If you do not tell me both dream and interpretation, you shall be torn in pieces and your houses shall be forfeit.*d* But if you can tell me the 6 dream and the interpretation, you will be richly rewarded and loaded with honours. Tell me, therefore, the dream and its interpretation.' They answered 7 a second time, 'Let the king tell his servants the dream, and we will tell him the interpretation.' The king answered, 'It is clear to me that you are 8 trying to gain time, because you see that my intention has been declared. If you do not make known to me the 9 dream, there is one law that applies to you, and one only. What is more, you have agreed among yourselves to tell me a pack of lies to my face in the hope that with time things may alter. Tell me the dream, therefore, and I shall know that you can give me the interpretation.' The Chaldaeans answered 10 in the presence of the king, 'Nobody on earth can tell your majesty what you wish to know; no great king or prince has ever made such a demand of magician, exorcist, or Chaldaean. What your majesty requires of us is too 11

b be guided . . . see: *or treat us as you see fit.*
c The Aramaic text begins here and continues to the end of ch. 7.
d Or made into a dunghill *(mng. of Aram. word uncertain).*

12: The total abstinence from meat was a safeguard against eating forbidden meats such as pork. **17:** *Visions and dreams:* the practice of dream interpretation in Mesopotamia, and the special significance attributed to them, goes back to the third millennium. **20:** This verse anticipates the plots in chs. 2; 4; 5. *Magicians and exorcists:* the Heb. terms are borrowed from the ancient Akkadian, meaning, respectively, "interpreters of dreams" and "incantation officials." **21:** *First years of King Cyrus:* 539 B.C., sixty-eight years after the date (607 or 606) in v. 1.

    2.1–49: The revelation of the future history of five world kingdoms. 1: *Second year:* 604 B.C. **2:** *Chaldaeans:* wise men, rather than simply people from Chaldea. Chaldeans were found in great numbers in the Grecian lands, usually as astrologers and magicians. **4:** *In Aramaic:* either the author is deliberately following the format of the Book of Ezra, in which the center chapters are in Aram., or else the stories in this section were handed down in Aram. **11:** *No one but*

hard; there is no one but the gods, who dwell remote from mortal men, who

12 can give you the answer.' At this the king lost his temper and in a great rage ordered the death of all the wise men

13 of Babylon. A decree was issued that the wise men were to be executed, and accordingly men were sent to fetch Daniel and his companions for execution.

14 When Arioch, the captain of the king's bodyguard, was setting out to execute the wise men of Babylon,

15 Daniel approached him cautiously and with discretion and said, 'Sir, you represent the king; why has his majesty issued such a peremptory decree?'

16 Arioch explained everything; so Daniel went in to the king's presence and begged for a certain time by which he would give the king the interpretation.

17 Then Daniel went home and told the whole story to his companions, Hana-

18 niah, Mishael and Azariah. They should ask the God of heaven in his mercy, he said, to disclose this secret, so that they and he with the rest of the wise men of Babylon should not be put

19 to death. Then in a vision by night the secret was revealed to Daniel, and he

20 blessed the God of heaven in these words:

Blessed be God's name from age
    to age,
for all wisdom and power are his.

21 He changes seasons and times;
he deposes kings and sets them up;
he gives wisdom to the wise
and all their store of knowledge to
    the men who know;

22 he reveals deep mysteries;
he knows what lies in darkness,
and light has its dwelling with him.

23 To thee, God of my fathers, I give
    thanks and praise,
for thou hast given me wisdom and
    power;
thou hast now revealed to me what
    we asked,
and told us what the king is
    concerned to know.

24 Daniel therefore went to Arioch who had been charged by the king to put to death the wise men of Babylon and said to him, 'Do not put the wise men of Babylon to death. Take me into the king's presence, and I will now tell him the interpretation of the dream.' Arioch 25 in great trepidation brought Daniel before the king and said to him, 'I have found among the Jewish exiles a man who will make known to your majesty the interpretation of your dream.' Thereupon the king said to Daniel (who 26 was also called Belteshazzar), 'Can you tell me what I saw in my dream and interpret it?' Daniel answered in the 27 king's presence, 'The secret about which your majesty inquires no wise man, exorcist, magician, or diviner can disclose to you. But there is in heaven 28 a god who reveals secrets, and he has told King Nebuchadnezzar what is to be at the end of this age. This is the dream and these the visions that came into your head: the thoughts that came 29 to you, O king, as you lay on your bed, were thoughts of things to come, and the revealer of secrets has made known to you what is to be. This secret has 30 been revealed to me not because I am wise beyond all living men, but because your majesty is to know the interpretation and understand the thoughts which have entered your mind.

'As you watched, O king, you saw a 31 great image. This image, huge and dazzling, towered before you, fearful to behold. The head of the image was 32 of fine gold, its breast and arms of silver, its belly and thighs of bronze,[e] its 33 legs of iron, its feet part iron and part clay. While you looked, a stone was 34 hewn from a mountain, not by human hands; it struck the image on its feet of iron and clay and shattered them. Then the iron, the clay, the bronze, the 35 silver, and the gold, were all shattered to fragments and were swept away like chaff before the wind from a threshing-floor in summer, until no trace of them remained. But the stone which struck

e Or copper.

---

the gods: this anticipates v. 47, in which the king recognizes Daniel's words as divinely given.
28: *A god who reveals secrets:* see v. 22. **32:** The theme of a descending scale of metals representing ages of world history is also found in Greece, in Hesiod's "Works and Days";

36 the image grew into a great mountain filling the whole earth. That was the dream. We shall now tell your majesty 37 the interpretation. You, O king, king of kings, to whom the God of heaven has given the kingdom with all its 38 power, authority, and honour; in whose hands he has placed men and beasts and birds of the air, wherever they dwell, granting you sovereignty over them all—you are that head of gold. 39 After you there shall arise another kingdom, inferior to yours, and yet a third kingdom, of bronze, which shall have sovereignty over the whole world. 40 And there shall be a fourth kingdom, strong as iron; as iron shatters and destroys all things, it shall break and 41 shatter the whole earth.*f* As, in your vision, the feet and toes were part potter's clay and part iron, it shall be a divided kingdom. Its core shall be partly of iron just as you saw iron 42 mixed with the common clay; as the toes were part iron and part clay, the kingdom shall be partly strong and 43 partly brittle. As, in your vision, the iron was mixed with common clay, so shall men mix with each other by intermarriage, but such alliances shall not be stable: iron does not mix with 44 clay. In the period of those kings the God of heaven will establish a kingdom which shall never be destroyed; that kingdom shall never pass to another people; it shall shatter and make an end of all these kingdoms, while it shall 45 itself endure for ever. This is the meaning of your vision of the stone being hewn from a mountain, not by human hands, and then shattering the iron, the bronze, the clay, the silver, and the gold. The mighty God has made known to your majesty what is to be hereafter. The dream is sure and the interpretation to be trusted.' 46 Then King Nebuchadnezzar pros-

trated himself and worshipped Daniel, and gave orders that sacrifices and soothing offerings should be made to him. 'Truly,' he said, 'your god is 47 indeed God of gods and Lord over kings, a revealer of secrets, since you have been able to reveal this secret.' Then the king promoted Daniel, 48 bestowed on him many rich gifts, and made him regent over the whole province of Babylon and chief prefect over all the wise men of Babylon. Moreover at Daniel's request the king 49 put Shadrach, Meshach and Abed-nego in charge of the administration of the province of Babylon. Daniel himself, however, remained at court.

KING NEBUCHADNEZZAR MADE AN IMAGE **3** of gold, ninety feet high and nine feet broad. He had it set up in the plain of Dura in the province of Babylon. Then 2 he sent out a summons to assemble the satraps, prefects, viceroys, counsellors, treasurers, judges, chief constables, and all governors of provinces to attend the dedication of the image which he had set up. So they assembled—the satraps, 3 prefects, viceroys, counsellors, treasurers, judges, chief constables, and all governors of provinces—for the dedication of the image which King Nebuchadnezzar had set up; and they stood before the image which Nebuchadnezzar had set up. Then the herald 4 loudly proclaimed, 'O peoples and nations of every language, you are commanded, when you hear the sound 5 of horn, pipe, zither, triangle, dulcimer, music, and singing of every kind, to prostrate yourselves and worship the golden image which King Nebuchadnezzar has set up. Whoever does not 6 prostrate himself and worship shall forthwith be thrown into a blazing

f the whole earth: *prob. rdg.; Aram.* and like iron which shatters all these.

---

in ancient Hindu mythology; and elsewhere. **37–40:** The four kingdoms are usually taken to be the Babylonian, the Median, the Persian, and the Macedonian Greek; compare 8.20–21. There is no confirming evidence for the opinion (9.1), found in Jer.51.11,28 as well, that the Medes existed as a world power quite separate from the Persians. **44:** The fifth kingdom will bring an end to world history as then known. **47:** V. 22, alluded to here and in v. 28, is thereby a key theme of the story. **48:** Daniel's appointment is similar to that of Joseph in Gen.41.41.
    3.1–30: God delivers the three young men from the fiery furnace. The three are presented here as Daniel-like figures (see ch. 6), but do not appear again after this chapter. **1:** *An image:* the account does not give the exact nature of the statue but indicates that it is a major Babylonian god. *Dura:* a place name common in ancient Babylonia; the exact location cannot be

7 furnace.' Accordingly, no sooner did all the peoples hear the sound of horn, pipe, zither, triangle, dulcimer, music, and singing of every kind, than all the peoples and nations of every language prostrated themselves and worshipped the golden image which King Nebuchadnezzar had set up.

8 It was then that certain Chaldaeans came forward and brought a charge 9 against the Jews. They said to King Nebuchadnezzar, 'Long live the king! 10 Your majesty has issued an order that every man who hears the sound of horn, pipe, zither, triangle, dulcimer, music, and singing of every kind shall fall down and worship the image of 11 gold. Whoever does not do so shall be 12 thrown into a blazing furnace. There are certain Jews, Shadrach, Meshach and Abed-nego, whom you have put in charge of the administration of the province of Babylon. These men, your majesty, have taken no notice of your command; they do not serve your god, nor do they worship the golden image 13 which you have set up.' Then in rage and fury Nebuchadnezzar ordered Shadrach, Meshach and Abed-nego to be fetched, and they were brought into 14 the king's presence. Nebuchadnezzar said to them, 'Is it true, Shadrach, Meshach and Abed-nego, that you do not serve my god or worship the 15 golden image which I have set up? If you are ready at once to prostrate yourselves when you hear the sound of horn, pipe, zither, triangle, dulcimer, music, and singing of every kind, and to worship the image that I have set up, well and good. But if you do not worship it, you shall forthwith be thrown into the blazing furnace; and what god is there that can save you 16 from my power?' Shadrach, Meshach and Abed-nego said to King Nebuchadnezzar, 'We have no need to 17 answer you on this matter. If there is a god who is able to save us from the blazing furnace, it is our God whom

we serve, and he will save us from your power, O king; but if not, be it known 18 to your majesty that we will neither serve your god nor worship the golden image that you have set up.'

Then Nebuchadnezzar flew into a 19 rage with Shadrach, Meshach and Abed-nego, and his face was distorted with anger. He gave orders that the furnace should be heated up to seven times its usual heat, and commanded 20 some of the strongest men in his army to bind Shadrach, Meshach and Abed-nego and throw them into the blazing furnace. Then those men in their 21 trousers, their shirts, and their hats and all their other clothes, were bound and thrown into the blazing furnace. Because the king's order was urgent 22 and the furnace exceedingly hot, the men who were carrying Shadrach, Meshach and Abed-nego were killed by the flames that leapt out; and those three 23 men, Shadrach, Meshach and Abed-nego, fell bound into the blazing furnace.

Then King Nebuchadnezzar was 24 amazed and sprang to his feet in great trepidation. He said to his courtiers, 'Was it not three men whom we threw bound into the fire?' They answered the king, 'Assuredly, your majesty.' He answered, 'Yet I see four men 25 walking about in the fire free and unharmed; and the fourth looks like a god.' Nebuchadnezzar approached the 26 door of the blazing furnace and said to the men, 'Shadrach, Meshach and Abed-nego, servants of the Most High God, come out, come here.' Then Shadrach, Meshach and Abed-nego came out from the fire. And the 27 satraps, prefects, viceroys, and the king's courtiers gathered round and saw how the fire had had no power to harm the bodies of these men; the hair of their heads had not been singed, their trousers were untouched, and no smell of fire lingered about them.

Then Nebuchadnezzar spoke out, 28

determined. **17–18:** *But if not:* that is, even if God does not save us. The intention is not to imply that God cannot save, but that they can be saved only by the God they worship. **23:** At this point the Sept. introduces Shadrach, Meshach, and Abed-nego. Roman Catholic Bibles retain it here, but Protestant Bibles include it as a separate book of the Apocrypha, in this version called "The Song of the Three." **25:** *Like a god:* in v. 28, this fourth "person" is called an angel. **28–29:** The king's acknowledgment here is similar to the endings in 2.47; 4.37; 6.26–7.

'Blessed is the God of Shadrach, Meshach and Abed-nego. He has sent his angel to save his servants who put their trust in him, who disobeyed the royal command and were willing to yield themselves to the fire rather than to serve or worship any god other than 29 their own God. I therefore issue a decree that any man, to whatever people or nation he belongs, whatever his language, if he speaks blasphemy against the God of Shadrach, Meshach and Abed-nego, shall be torn to pieces and his house shall be forfeit;*g* for there is no other god who can save 30 men in this way.' Then the king advanced the fortunes of Shadrach, Meshach and Abed-nego in the province of Babylon.

4 KING NEBUCHADNEZZAR TO ALL PEOPLES and nations of every language living in the whole world: May all prosperity 2 be yours! It is my pleasure to recount the signs and marvels which the Most High God has worked for me:

3 How great are his signs,
 and his marvels overwhelming!
 His kingdom is an everlasting kingdom,
 his sovereignty stands to all
  generations.

4 I, Nebuchadnezzar, was living peacefully at home in the luxury of my 5 palace. As I lay on my bed, I saw a dream which terrified me; and fantasies and visions which came into my head 6 dismayed me. So I issued an order summoning into my presence all the wise men of Babylon to make known to me the interpretation of the dream. 7 Then the magicians, exorcists, Chaldaeans, and diviners came in, and in their presence I related my dream. But 8 they could not interpret it. And yet another came into my presence, Daniel, who is called Belteshazzar after the name of my god, a man possessed by

the spirit of the holy gods. To him, too, I related the dream: 'Belteshazzar, 9 chief of the magicians, whom I myself know to be possessed by the spirit of the holy gods, and whom no secret baffles, listen to the vision I saw in a dream, and tell me its interpretation.

'Here is the vision which came into 10 my head as I was lying upon my bed:

 As I was looking,
I saw a tree of great height at the
  centre of the earth;
 the tree grew and became strong, 11
reaching with its top to the sky
 and visible to earth's farthest
  bounds.
 Its foliage was lovely, 12
 and its fruit abundant;
and it yielded food for all.
Beneath it the wild beasts found
  shelter,
 the birds lodged in its branches,
and from it all living creatures fed.

'Here is another vision which came 13 into my head as I was lying upon my bed:

As I was watching, there was a
  Watcher,
a Holy One coming down from
  heaven.
He cried aloud and said, 14
"Hew down the tree, lop off the
  branches,
strip away the foliage, scatter the
  fruit.
Let the wild beasts flee from its
  shelter
 and the birds from its branches,
but leave the stump with its roots in 15
  the ground.
So, tethered with an iron ring,
let him eat his fill of the lush grass;
let him be drenched with the dew
  of heaven

g *Or* made into a dunghill (*mng. of Aram. word uncertain*).

4.1–37: **Nebuchadnezzar loses and regains the throne.** This chapter has the form of a letter; it turns from the first to the third person in vv. 19–33. **3:** The king's earlier reverence for Daniel's God (2.47 and 3.28–29) here emerges into full praise. **8:** *Belteshazzar:* the author either mistakenly or according to folk etymology considers *Belteshazzar* to contain the *name* of the Babylonian *god* Bel. Actually it is a shortened form of a simple name, "Balatshuuzur," meaning "guards his life." **13:** *Watcher, Holy One* are synonyms for "angel." The first is not found in the Bible outside this chapter, but appears often in the Book of Enoch (in the "Pseudepigrapha") as a term for archangel. The second is used in Dan.8.13 for angel. **15:** The

and share the lot of the beasts in
   their pasture;
16 let his mind cease to be a man's
      mind,
    and let him be given the mind of a
      beast.
    Let seven times pass over him.
17 The issue has been determined by
      the Watchers
    and the sentence pronounced by
      the Holy Ones.

Thereby the living will know that
the Most High is sovereign in the
kingdom of men: he gives the kingdom
to whom he will and he may set over
it the humblest of mankind."
18 'This is the dream which I, King
Nebuchadnezzar, have dreamed; now,
Belteshazzar, tell me its interpretation;
for, though all the wise men of my
kingdom are unable to tell me what it
means, you can tell me, since the spirit
of the holy gods is in you.'
19 Daniel, who was called Belteshazzar,
was dumbfounded for a moment,
dismayed by his thoughts; but the king
said, 'Do not let the dream and its
interpretation dismay you.' Belteshazzar answered, 'My lord, if only the
dream were for those who hate you
and its interpretation for your enemies!
20 The tree which you saw grow and
become strong, reaching with its top to
the sky and visible to earth's farthest
21 bounds, its foliage lovely and its fruit
abundant, a tree which yielded food
for all, beneath which the wild beasts
dwelt and in whose branches the birds
22 lodged, that tree, O king, is you. You
have grown and become strong. Your
power has grown and reaches the sky;
your sovereignty stretches to the ends
23 of the earth. Also, O king, you saw a
Watcher, a Holy One, coming down
from heaven and saying, "Hew down
the tree and destroy it, but leave its
stump with its roots in the ground. So,
tethered with an iron ring, let him eat
his fill of the lush grass; let him be
drenched with the dew of heaven and

share the lot of the beasts until seven
times pass over him." This is the 24
interpretation, O king—it is a decree
of the Most High which touches my
lord the king. You will be banished 25
from the society of men; you will have
to live with the wild beasts; you will
feed on grass like oxen and you will be
drenched with the dew of heaven.
Seven times will pass over you until
you have learnt that the Most High is
sovereign over the kingdom of men
and gives it to whom he will. The 26
command was given to leave the stump
of the tree with its roots. By this you
may know that from the time you
acknowledge the sovereignty of heaven
your rule will endure. Be advised by me, 27
O king: redeem your sins by charity
and your iniquities by generosity to the
wretched. So may you long enjoy
peace of mind.'
All this befell King Nebuchadnezzar. 28
At the end of twelve months the king 29
was walking on the roof of the royal
palace at Babylon, and he exclaimed, 30
'Is not this Babylon the great which I
have built as a royal residence by my
own mighty power and for the honour
of my majesty?' The words were still 31
on his lips, when a voice came down
from heaven: 'To you, King Nebuchadnezzar, the word is spoken: the
kingdom has passed from you. You are 32
banished from the society of men and
you shall live with the wild beasts; you
shall feed on grass like oxen, and seven
times will pass over you until you have
learnt that the Most High is sovereign
over the kingdom of men and gives it
to whom he will.' At that very moment 33
this judgement came upon Nebuchadnezzar. He was banished from the
society of men and ate grass like oxen;
his body was drenched by the dew of
heaven, until his hair grew long like
goats' hair and his nails like eagles'
talons.[h]

---

h goats' hair . . . eagles' talons: *prob. rdg.; Aram.*
eagles' and his nails like birds'.

---

metaphor changes from a tree to a beast to a human. **16:** *Times:* years, as in 7.25. **25:** *The
Most High is sovereign:* see v. 30 n. **26:** *Heaven* as a "euphemism" for God, common in the
Apocrypha, is not found elsewhere in the OT. **30:** The sin of pride is here given as the reason
for his fall, as in Ezek.31.10; see v. 27. **33:** A temporary lapse in the reign of Nebuchadnezzar
is unknown, but does fit the last Babylonian king, Nabonidus, who (inexplicably) spent part of

34 At the end of the appointed time, I, Nebuchadnezzar, raised my eyes to heaven and I returned to my right mind. I blessed the Most High, praising and glorifying the Ever-living One:

His sovereignty is never-ending
and his rule endures through all
        generations;
35 all dwellers upon earth count for
        nothing
and he deals as he wishes with the
        host of heaven;[i]
no one may lay hand upon him
and ask him what he does.

36 At that very time I returned to my right mind and my majesty and royal splendour were restored to me for the glory of my kingdom. My courtiers and my nobles sought audience of me. I was established in my kingdom and 37 my power was greatly increased. Now I, Nebuchadnezzar, praise and exalt and glorify the King of heaven; for all his acts are right and his ways are just and those whose conduct is arrogant he can bring low.

Belshazzar's feast

5 BELSHAZZAR THE KING GAVE A BANQUET for a thousand of his nobles and was drinking wine in the presence of the 2 thousand. Warmed by the wine, he gave orders to fetch the vessels of gold and silver which his father Nebuchadnezzar had taken from the sanctuary at Jerusalem, that he and his nobles, his concubines and his courtesans, might 3 drink from them. So the vessels of gold and silver from the sanctuary in the house of God at Jerusalem were brought in, and the king and his nobles, his concubines and his courtesans, 4 drank from them. They drank wine and praised the gods of gold and silver, of bronze and iron, and of wood and 5 stone. Suddenly there appeared the fingers of a human hand writing on the plaster of the palace wall opposite the lamp, and the king could see the back of the hand as it wrote. At this the 6 king's mind was filled with dismay and he turned pale, he became limp in every limb and his knees knocked together. He called loudly for the exorcists, 7 Chaldaeans, and diviners to be brought in; then, addressing the wise men of Babylon, he said, 'Whoever can read this writing and tell me its interpretation shall be robed in purple and honoured with a chain of gold round his neck and shall rank as third in the kingdom.' Then all the king's wise men 8 came in, but they could not read the writing or interpret it to the king. King 9 Belshazzar sat there pale and utterly dismayed, while his nobles were perplexed.

The king and his nobles were talking 10 when the queen entered the banqueting-hall: 'Long live the king!' she said. 'Why this dismay, and why do you look so pale? There is a man in your 11 kingdom who has in him the spirit of the holy gods, a man who was known in your father's time to have a clear understanding and godlike wisdom. King Nebuchadnezzar, your father, appointed him chief of the magicians, exorcists, Chaldaeans, and diviners. This same Daniel, whom the king 12 named Belteshazzar, is known to have a notable spirit, with knowledge and understanding, and the gift of interpreting dreams, explaining riddles and unbinding spells;[j] let him be summoned now and he will give the interpretation.' Daniel was then brought into the 13 king's presence and the king said to him, 'So you are Daniel, one of the Jewish exiles whom the king my father brought from Judah. I have heard that 14 you possess the spirit of the holy gods and that you are a man of clear understanding and peculiar wisdom. The wise men, the exorcists, have just 15 been brought into my presence to read this writing and tell me its interpreta-

i *Prob. rdg.; Aram. adds* and the dwellers upon earth.
j *Or* and solving problems.

---

his reign at the north Arabian oasis of Taima. **34b–35:** These verses are an expansion of v. 3.
  5.1–31: Corruption punished. 1: *Belshazzar* was the son of Nabonidus, but is never referred to as king in Babylonian texts; he ruled as vice-regent while his father was away from the country; see 4.33 n. **7:** *Shall rank as third:* that is, after the king and crown prince; compare 2.48.

tion, and they have been unable to
16 interpret it. But I have heard it said of
you that you are able to give interpretations and to unbind spells.[k] So now,
if you are able to read the words and
tell me what they mean, you shall be
robed in purple and honoured with a
chain of gold round your neck and
shall rank as third in the kingdom.'
17 Then Daniel answered in the king's
presence, 'Your gifts you may keep for
yourself; or else give your rewards to
another. Nevertheless I will read the
writing to your majesty and tell you its
18 interpretation. My lord king, the Most
High God gave your father Nebuchadnezzar a kingdom and power and glory
19 and majesty; and, because of this power
which he gave him, all peoples and
nations of every language trembled
before him and were afraid. He put to
death whom he would and spared
whom he would, he promoted them at
20 will and at will degraded them. But,
when he became haughty, stubborn and
presumptuous, he was deposed from his
royal throne and his glory was taken
21 from him. He was banished from the
society of men, his mind became like
that of a beast, he had to live with the
wild asses and to eat grass like oxen,
and his body was drenched with the
dew of heaven, until he came to know
that the Most High God is sovereign
over the kingdom of men and sets up
22 over it whom he will. But you, his son
Belshazzar, did not humble your heart,
23 although you knew all this. You have
set yourself up against the Lord of
heaven. The vessels of his temple have
been brought to your table; and you,
your nobles, your concubines, and your
courtesans have drunk from them. You
have praised the gods of silver and
gold, of bronze and iron, of wood and
stone, which neither see nor hear nor
know, and you have not given glory to
God, in whose charge is your very
breath and in whose hands are all your

ways. This is why that hand was sent 24
from his very presence and why it wrote
this inscription. And these are the 25
words of the writing which was
inscribed: *Mene mene tekel u-pharsin.*
Here is the interpretation: *mene*:[l] God 26
has numbered the days of your
kingdom and brought it to an end;
tekel:[m] you have been weighed in the 27
balance and found wanting; *u-pharsin*:[n] 28
and your kingdom has been divided
and given to the Medes and Persians.'
Then Belshazzar gave the order and 29
Daniel was robed in purple and
honoured with a chain of gold round
his neck, and proclamation was made
that he should rank as third in the
kingdom.

That very night Belshazzar king of 30
the Chaldaeans was slain, and Darius 31
the Mede took the kingdom, being then
sixty-two years old.

Daniel in the lions' pit

IT PLEASED DARIUS TO APPOINT SATRAPS 6
over the kingdom, a hundred and
twenty in number in charge of the
whole kingdom, and over them three 2
chief ministers, to whom the satraps
should send reports so that the king's
interests might not suffer; of these three,
Daniel was one. In the event Daniel 3
outshone the other ministers and the
satraps because of his ability, and the
king had it in mind to appoint him
over the whole kingdom. Then the 4
chief ministers and the satraps began
to look round for some pretext to
attack Daniel's administration of the
kingdom, but they failed to find any
malpractice on his part; for he was
faithful to his trust. Since they could 5
discover no neglect of duty or
malpractice, they said, 'There will be

k *Or and to solve problems.*
l *That is numbered.*
m *That is shekel or weight.*
n *Prob. rdg.; Aram.* pheres. *There is a play on three
possible meanings* halves *or* divisions *or* Persians.

18–21: A summary of ch. 4. 25: *Mene mene tekel u-pharsin: tekel,* Heb. *shekel,* was a sixtieth
of a *mene,* Heb. *mina. U* means "and"; *pharsin* means two *pheres,* with one *pheres* being a
half-shekel. The weights, or coins, are here in descending value; this is in accord with the
comparable descending values of the metals in 2.32. The weights are symbolic of the five kings
after Nebuchadnezzar, including Belshazzar. 31: See 2.37–40 n. No Darius is known as king
of the Medes. The Persian king Darius ruled 521–486 B.C.
  6.1–28: Daniel impresses Darius. The plot is a variant of that of ch. 3. 1: *Darius:* see 5.31 n.
2: *A hundred and twenty:* Persian sources refer to numbers of satrapies (province states) only

no charge to bring against this Daniel unless we find one in his religion.'

6 These chief ministers and satraps watched for an opportunity to approach the king, and said to him,
7 'Long live King Darius! All we, the ministers of the kingdom, prefects, satraps, courtiers, and viceroys, have taken counsel and agree that the king should issue a decree and bring an ordinance into force, that whoever within the next thirty days shall present a petition to any god or man other than the king shall be thrown
8 into the lions' pit. Now, O king, issue the ordinance and have it put in writing, so that it may be unalterable, for the law of the Medes and Persians
9 stands for ever.' Accordingly King Darius issued the ordinance in written form.
10 When Daniel learnt that this decree had been issued, he went into his house. He had had windows made in his roof-chamber looking towards Jerusalem; and there he knelt down three times a day and offered prayers and praises to his God as his custom had always been.
11 His enemies watched for an opportunity to catch Daniel and found him at his prayers making supplication to
12 his God. Then they came into the king's presence and reminded him of the ordinance. 'Your majesty,' they said, 'have you not issued an ordinance that any person who, within the next thirty days, shall present a petition to any god or man other than your majesty shall be thrown into the lions' pit?' The king answered, 'Yes, it is fixed. The law of the Medes and
13 Persians stands for ever.' So in the king's presence they said, 'Daniel, one of the Jewish exiles, has ignored the ordinance issued by your majesty, and is making petition to his god three
14 times a day.' When the king heard this, he was greatly distressed. He tried to think of a way to save Daniel, and
15 continued his efforts till sunset; then those same men watched for an oppor-

tunity to approach the king, and said to him, 'Your majesty must know that by the law of the Medes and Persians no ordinance or decree issued by the
16 king may be altered.' So the king gave orders and Daniel was brought and thrown into the lions' pit; but he said to Daniel, 'Your own God, whom you serve continually, will save you.' A
17 stone was brought and put over the mouth of the pit, and the king sealed it with his signet and with the signets of his nobles, so that no one might intervene to rescue Daniel.
18 The king went back to his palace and spent the night fasting; no woman was brought to him and sleep eluded
19 him. At dawn, as soon as it was light, he rose and went in fear and trembling
20 to the pit. When the king reached it, he called anxiously to Daniel, 'Daniel, servant of the living God, has your God whom you serve continually been able to save you from the lions?' Then
21 Daniel answered, 'Long live the king!
22 My God sent his angel to shut the lions' mouths so that they have done me no injury, because in his judgement I was found innocent;[o] and moreover,
23 O king, I had done you no injury.' The king was overjoyed and gave orders that Daniel should be lifted out of the pit. So Daniel was lifted out and no trace of injury was found on him, because he had put his faith in his God.
24 By order of the king Daniel's accusers were brought and thrown into the lions' pit with their wives and children, and before they reached the floor of the pit the lions were upon them and crunched them up, bones and all.
25 Then King Darius wrote to all peoples and nations of every language throughout the whole world: 'May your prosperity increase! I have issued
26 a decree that in all my royal domains men shall fear and reverence the God of Daniel;

o *in his judgement . . . innocent: or* before him success was granted me.

up to twenty-nine; this text uses a typical biblical round number; compare Esther 8.9. **7:** A drastic form of punishment was to be thrown into *the lions' pit*. **8:** *The law of the Medes and the Persians:* this phrase has passed into our everyday language to mean something unchangeable. **10:** *Looking towards Jerusalem:* the sacred direction for Jewish prayer, as in 1 Kgs.8.44. **14:** Darius here knows Daniel immediately, which is in contrast to situations in earlier chapters.

for he is the living God, the
everlasting,
whose kingly power shall not be
weakened;
whose sovereignty shall have no
end—
27 a saviour, a deliverer, a worker of
signs and wonders
in heaven and on earth,
who has delivered Daniel from the
power of the lions.'

28 So this Daniel prospered during the
reigns of Darius and Cyrus the Persian.

Daniel's visions

7 IN THE FIRST YEAR OF BELSHAZZAR KING
of Babylon, as Daniel lay on his bed,
dreams and visions came into his head.
Then he wrote down the dream, and
here his account begins:
2 In my visions of the night I, Daniel,
was gazing intently and I saw a great
sea churned up by the four winds of
3 heaven, and four huge beasts coming
up out of the sea, each one different
4 from the others. The first was like a
lion but had an eagle's wings. I
watched until its wings were plucked
off and it was lifted from the ground
and made to stand on two feet like a
man; it was also given the mind of a
5 man. Then I saw another, a second
beast, like a bear. It was half crouching
and had three ribs in its mouth,
between its teeth. The command was
given: 'Up, gorge yourself with flesh.'
6 After this as I gazed I saw another, a
beast like a leopard with four bird's
wings on its back; this creature had
four heads, and it was invested with
7 sovereign power. Next in my visions
of the night I saw a fourth beast,

dreadful and grisly, exceedingly strong,
with great iron teeth and bronze
claws.*p* It crunched and devoured, and
trampled underfoot all that was left.
It differed from all the beasts which
preceded it in having ten horns. While 8
I was considering the horns I saw
another horn, a little one, springing up
among them, and three of the first
horns were uprooted to make room for
it. And in that horn were eyes like the
eyes of a man, and a mouth that spoke
proud words. I kept looking, and then 9

thrones were set in place and one
ancient in years took his seat,
his robe was white as snow and the
hair of his head like cleanest
wool.
Flames of fire were his throne and
its wheels blazing fire;
a flowing river of fire streamed out 10
before him.*q*
Thousands upon thousands served
him
and myriads upon myriads attended
his presence.
The court sat, and the books were
opened.

Then because of the proud words 11
that the horn was speaking, I went on
watching until the beast was killed and
its carcass destroyed: it was given to
the flames. The rest of the beasts, 12
though deprived of their sovereignty,
were allowed to remain alive for a time
and a season. I was still watching in 13
visions of the night and I saw one like
a man coming with the clouds of
heaven; he approached the Ancient in
Years and was presented to him.

p Or it.
q and bronze claws: prob. rdg. cp.verse 19; Aram. om.,

26b–27: This general hymn, similar to 4.34b–35, ends with a motif taken from the story; this
is also the case in 2.23b. 28: See 5.31 n.
7.1–12.13: **Final manifestations.** These form the second half of the book. Two separate themes
—the four beasts and the heavenly visions—become united. 2: *A great sea:* the ocean was viewed
as the chaos dragon, slain by the deity; see e.g. Job 7.12; Isa.27.1; and Ps.89.9–10 n. 4–7:
Compare the four creatures in Ezek.1.5–10. According to v. 17, the beasts probably represent
kingdoms; see 2.37–40. 8: *A little horn:* the ten horns would represent a round number of
successors of Alexander the Great in the Near East; see v. 24. The little horn would be the
contemporaneous persecutor of the Jews, Antiochus IV Epiphanes (see Introduction). See also
1 Macc.1.41–50. 9–10: A vision of heaven. 9: *Ancient in years:* God. On the scene depicted
here, see 1 Kgs.22.19 and Ezek.1.26–28. 10: *The court . . . the books:* the picture of a courtroom
scene is found in other writings, such as Enoch 47.3. 11–12: A continuation of v. 8. 13–14: A
continuation of vv. 9–10. 13: *One like a man:* lit. one like a son of man. The term "son of

14 Sovereignty and glory and kingly power were given to him, so that all people and nations of every language should serve him; his sovereignty was to be an everlasting sovereignty which should not pass away, and his kingly power such as should never be impaired.

15 My spirit within me was troubled, and, dismayed by the visions which

16 came into my head, I, Daniel, approached one of those who stood there and inquired from him what all this meant; and he told me the interpreta-

17 tion. 'These great beasts, four in number,' he said, 'are four kingdoms

18 which shall rise from the ground. But the saints[r] of the Most High shall receive the kingly power and shall retain it for ever, for ever and ever.'

19 Then I desired to know what the fourth beast meant, the beast that was different from all the others, very dreadful with its iron teeth and bronze claws, crunching and devouring and

20 trampling underfoot all that was left. I desired also to know about the ten horns on its head and the other horn which sprang up and at whose coming three of them fell—the horn that had eyes and a mouth speaking proud words and appeared larger than the

21 others. As I still watched, that horn was waging war with the saints and

22 overcoming them until the Ancient in Years came. Then judgement was given in favour of the saints of the Most High, and the time came when the saints gained possession of the

23 kingly power. He gave me this answer: 'The fourth beast signifies a fourth kingdom which shall appear upon earth. It shall differ from the other kingdoms and shall devour the whole

24 earth, tread it down and crush it. The ten horns signify the appearance of

ten kings in this kingdom, after whom another king shall arise, differing from his predecessors; and he shall bring low three kings. He shall hurl defiance 25 at the Most High and shall wear down the saints of the Most High. He shall plan to alter the customary times and law; and the saints shall be delivered into his power for a time and times and half a time. Then the court shall 26 sit, and he shall be deprived of his sovereignty, so that in the end it may be destroyed and abolished. The kingly 27 power, sovereignty, and greatness of all the kingdoms under heaven shall be given to the people of the saints of the Most High. Their kingly power is an everlasting power and all sovereignties shall serve them and obey them.'

Here the account ends. As for me, 28 Daniel, my thoughts dismayed me greatly and I turned pale; and I kept these things in my mind.

[s]In the third year of the reign of **8**1-2 King Belshazzar, while I was in Susa, the capital city of the province of Elam, a vision appeared to me, Daniel, similar to my former vision. In this vision I was watching beside the stream of the Ulai. I raised my 3 eyes and there I saw a ram with two horns standing between me and the stream. The two horns were long, the one longer than the other, growing up behind. I watched the ram butting 4 west and north and south. No beasts could stand before it, no one could rescue from its power. It did what it liked, making a display of its strength. While I pondered this, suddenly a 5 he-goat came from the west skimming over the whole earth without touching the ground; it had a prominent horn between its eyes. It approached the 6

r *Or* holy ones.
s *Here the Hebrew text resumes (see note at 2. 4).*

---

man" does not carry here all the levels of meaning it later acquired, such as "messiah." **14:** The prerogatives are to be effective forever for the one like a man (v. 13), as anticipated in 2.44. **15:** A continuation of v. 12. **18:** *The saints:* the people persecuted by Antiochus Epiphanes; see v. 27. In v. 14 such power was given to "the one like a man." **21:** *The Ancient in Years:* God would save the saints, as he had delivered the young men in chs. 3 and 6. **25:** *A time and times and half a time:* three and a half years. *Time* means year; *times*, two years; see 4.16.

8.1–27: The ram, the goat and the little horn. This chapter (it reverts to Heb.) alludes to the same events as ch. 7, though on a lower level of literary quality. **1:** *Susa:* a royal city in southern Persia, the area being named Elam after the ancient Elamites. *My former vision:* that of ch. 7. **2:** *Ulai:* a river at or near Susa. **3:** *Ram* and the "goat" of v. 5 were probably signs of the zodiac. **5:** Alexander the Great's conquest of the East was remarkably swift, 334–323 B.C.

two-horned ram which I had seen standing between me and the stream and rushed at it with impetuous force.
7 I saw it advance on the ram, working itself into a fury against it, then strike the ram and break its two horns; the ram had no strength to resist. The he-goat flung it to the ground and trampled on it, and there was no one to save the ram.

8 Then the he-goat made a great display of its strength. Powerful as it was, its great horn snapped and in its place there sprang out towards the four quarters of heaven four prominent
9 horns. Out of one of them there issued one small horn, which made a prodigious show of strength south and east and towards the fairest of all
10 lands. It aspired to be as great as the host of heaven, and it cast down to the earth some of the host and some of the
11 stars and trod them underfoot. It aspired to be as great as the Prince of the host, suppressed his regular offering and even threw down his sanctuary.
12 The heavenly hosts were delivered up, and it raised itself[t] impiously against the regular offering and threw true religion to the ground; in all that it did
13 it succeeded. I heard a holy one speaking and another holy one answering him, whoever he was. The one said, 'For how long will the period of this vision last? How long will the regular offering be suppressed, how long will impiety cause desolation,[u] and both the Holy Place and the fairest of all lands[v] be given over to be
14 trodden down?' The answer came, 'For two thousand three hundred evenings and mornings; then the Holy Place shall emerge victorious.'
15 All the while that I, Daniel, was seeing the vision, I was trying to understand it. Suddenly I saw standing before me one with the semblance of a
16 man; at the same time I heard a human voice calling to him across the

bend of the Ulai, 'Gabriel, explain the vision to this man.' He came up to 17 where I was standing; I was seized with terror at his approach and threw myself on my face. But he said to me, 'Understand, O man: the vision points to the time of the end.' When he spoke 18 to me, I fell to the ground in a trance; but he grasped me and made me stand up where I was. And he said, 'I shall 19 make known to you what is to happen at the end of the wrath; for there is an end to the appointed time. The two- 20 horned ram which you saw signifies the kings of Media and Persia, the 21 he-goat is the kingdom[w] of the Greeks and the great horn on his forehead is the first king. As for the horn which 22 was snapped off and replaced by four horns: four kingdoms shall rise out of that nation, but not with power comparable to his.

In the last days of those kingdoms, 23
　　when their sin is at its height,
a king shall appear, harsh and grim,
　　a master of stratagem.
His power shall be great, he shall 24
　　work havoc untold;
he shall succeed in whatever he
　　does.
He shall work havoc among great
　　nations and upon a holy people.
His mind shall be ever active, 25
and he shall succeed in his crafty
　　designs;
he shall conjure up great plans
and, when they least expect it, work
　　havoc on many.
He shall challenge even the Prince
　　of princes
and be broken, but not by human
　　hands.
This revelation which has been 26
　　given

---

t and it raised itself: *prob. rdg.; Heb. om.*
u will impiety cause desolation: *prob. rdg.; Heb. obscure.*
v fairest of all lands: *prob. rdg., cp. verse 9; Heb. host.*
w *Prob. rdg.; Heb.* king.

8: *Four...horns:* the successors to Alexander in Greece, Asia Minor, Syria and points east, and Egypt. **9:** Antiochus IV Epiphanes; see 7.8 n. **10–11:** See Isa.14.12–16. **13:** *Regular offering suppressed:* as described in 1 Macc.1.45. **14:** *Evenings and mornings:* this amounts to 1,150 days, a little less than the three and a half years of 7.25. **15:** *Semblance of a man:* not to be confused with the figure of 7.13. **16:** *Gabriel:* the name of an archangel; he appears often in the Book of Enoch. **17:** *The end* of time, when God would finally judge the world. A concern with what would happen at the end of time was a major theme of apocalyptic literature. **23–25:** See 7.8 n. **23:** *Last days:* see v. 17. **25:** *Not by human hands:* a theme in 7.26.

of the evenings and the mornings
is true;
but you must keep the vision secret,
for it points to days far ahead.'

27 As for me, Daniel, my strength failed me and I lay sick for a while. Then I rose and attended to the king's business. But I was perplexed by the revelation and no one could explain it.

9 IN THE FIRST YEAR OF THE REIGN OF Darius son of Ahasuerus (a Mede by birth, who was appointed king over 2 the kingdom of the Chaldaeans) I, Daniel, was reading the scriptures and reflecting on the seventy years which, according to the word of the LORD to the prophet Jeremiah, were to pass 3 while Jerusalem lay in ruins. Then I turned to the Lord God in earnest prayer and supplication with fasting 4 and sackcloth and ashes. I prayed to the LORD my God, making confession thus:

'Lord, thou great and terrible God who faithfully keepest the covenant with those who love thee and observe 5 thy commandments, we have sinned, we have done what was wrong and wicked; we have rebelled, we have turned our backs on thy command- 6 ments and thy decrees. We have not listened to thy servants the prophets, who spoke in thy name to our kings and princes, to our forefathers and to 7 all the people of the land. O Lord, the right is on thy side; the shame, now as ever, belongs to us, the men of Judah and the citizens of Jerusalem, and to all the Israelites near and far in every land to which thou hast banished them 8 for their treachery towards thee. O LORD, the shame falls on us as on our kings, our princes and our forefathers; 9 we have all sinned against thee. Com- passion and forgiveness belong to the Lord our God, though we have rebelled 10 against him. We have not obeyed the LORD our God, we have not con- formed to the laws which he laid down for us through his servants the proph-

ets. All Israel has broken thy law and 11 not obeyed thee, so that the curses set out in the law of Moses thy servant in the adjuration and the oath have rained down upon us; for we have sinned against him. He has fulfilled all 12 that he said about us and about our rulers, by bringing upon us and upon Jerusalem a calamity greater than has ever happened in all the world. It was 13 all foreshadowed in the law of Moses, this calamity which has come upon us; yet we have done nothing to propitiate the LORD our God; we have neither repented of our wrongful deeds nor remembered that thou art true to thy word. The LORD has been biding his 14 time and has now brought this calamity upon us. In all that he has done the LORD our God has been right; yet we have not obeyed him.

'And now, O Lord our God who 15 didst bring thy people out of Egypt by a strong hand, winning for thyself a name that lives on to this day, we have sinned, we have done wrong. O Lord, 16 by all thy saving deeds we beg that thy wrath and anger may depart from Jerusalem, thy city, thy holy hill; through our own sins and our fathers' guilty deeds Jerusalem and thy people have become a byword among all our neighbours. And now, our God, listen 17 to thy servant's prayer and supplica- tion; for thy own sake, O Lord, make thy face shine upon thy desolate sanctuary. Lend thy ear, O God, and 18 hear, open thine eyes and look upon our desolation and upon the city that bears thy name; it is not by virtue of our own saving acts but by thy great mercy that we present our supplica- tions before thee. O Lord, hear; O 19 Lord, forgive; O Lord, listen and act; for thy own sake do not delay, O God, for thy city and thy people bear thy name.'

Thus I was speaking and praying, 20 confessing my own sin and my people Israel's sin, and presenting my sup- plication before the LORD my God on behalf of his holy hill. While I was 21

9.1–27: Daniel's prayer, and another vision of things to come. 1: Continuing the chronology of ch. 6. **2:** *The scriptures:* this rare example of an interpretation of a scriptural text by another scriptural book apparently alludes to Jer.25.11–12; 29.10. **4–19:** This is a prayer of community confession of sins and a plea for forgiveness, formed from a series of biblical phrases; compare

praying, the man Gabriel, whom I had already seen in the vision, came close to[x] me at the hour of the evening 22 sacrifice, flying swiftly.[y] He spoke clearly to me and said, 'Daniel, I have now come to enlighten your under-23 standing. As you were beginning your supplications a word went forth; this I have come to pass on to you, for you are a man greatly beloved. Consider well the word, consider the vision: 24 Seventy weeks are marked out for your people and your holy city; then rebellion shall be stopped,[z] sin brought to an end,[a] iniquity expiated, everlasting right ushered in, vision and prophecy sealed, and the Most Holy 25 Place anointed. Know then and understand: from the time that the word went forth that Jerusalem should be restored and rebuilt, seven weeks shall pass till the appearance of one anointed, a prince; then for sixty-two weeks it shall remain restored, rebuilt with 26 streets and conduits. At the critical time, after the sixty-two weeks, one who is anointed shall be removed with no one to take his part; and the horde of an invading prince shall work havoc on city and sanctuary. The end of it shall be a deluge, inevitable war 27 with all its horrors. He shall make a firm league with the mighty[b] for one week; and, the week half spent, he shall put a stop to sacrifice and offering. And in the train of these abominations shall come an author of desolation; then, in the end, what has been decreed concerning the desolation will be poured out.'

10 IN THE THIRD YEAR OF CYRUS KING OF Persia a word was revealed to Daniel who had been given the name Belteshazzar. Though this word was true,

it cost him[c] much toil to understand it; nevertheless understanding came to him in the course of the vision.

In those days I, Daniel, mourned for 2 three whole weeks. I refrained from all 3 choice food; no meat or wine passed my lips, and I did not anoint myself until the three weeks had gone by. On 4 the twenty-fourth day of the first month, I found myself on the bank of the great river, that is the Tigris; I 5 looked up and saw a man clothed in linen with a belt of gold from Ophir round his waist. His body gleamed like 6 topaz, his face shone like lightning, his eyes flamed like torches, his arms and feet sparkled like a disc of bronze; and when he spoke his voice sounded like the voice of a multitude. I, Daniel, 7 alone saw the vision, while those who were near me did not see it, but great fear fell upon them and they stole away, and I was left alone gazing at 8 this great vision. But my strength left me; I became a sorry figure of a man, and retained no strength. I heard the 9 sound of his words and, when I did so, I fell prone on the ground in a trance. Suddenly a hand grasped me and 10 pulled me up on to my hands and knees. He said to me, 'Daniel, man 11 greatly beloved, attend to the words I am speaking to you and stand up where you are, for I am now sent to you.' When he addressed me, I stood up trembling and he said, 'Do not be 12 afraid, Daniel, for from the very first day that you applied your mind to understand and to mortify yourself before your God, your prayers have been heard, and I have come in answer to them. But the angel prince 13

x Or touched.
y flying swiftly: prob. rdg.; Heb. thoroughly wearied.
z Or restrained.
a Or sealed.　　　b Or many
c him: prob. rdg.; Heb. om.

Bar.1.15–3.8. **21:** See 8.16 n. **24:** *Seventy weeks:* meaning seven times seventy, equaling 490 years, the elapsed time since the destruction of Jerusalem (587 B.C.) mentioned in v. 2. The end will be like that in 7.26–27. **25:** *One anointed, a prince:* the first period of 49 years will be a time of waiting. The second period of 434 years will start with the appearance of one anointed as leader. **27:** The third period of 7 years will bring a religious persecution by a leader like the one described in 8.11–13. *The week half spent:* compare the three and a half years of 7.25. *The end:* see 8.17 n.
　10.1–12.13: A detailed vision of the reigns of Alexander and his successors and of the end. **1:** *Third year of Cyrus:* 536 B.C. **4:** Compare Ezek.1.1. **5–6:** The passage uses some of the same terms as Ezek.1.15–28. The *man* is probably the angel Gabriel. **7:** Compare Acts 9.7 for a vision seen by one person but not by his companions. **13:** *Michael,* the guardian angel of Israel, came to the aid of Gabriel (vv. 5–6 n.) when the latter was battling the *angel prince of the*

of the kingdom of Persia resisted me for twenty-one days, and then, seeing that I had held out there, Michael, one of the chief princes, came to help me against the prince of the kingdom of 14 Persia. And I have come to explain to you what will happen to your people in days to come; for this too is a vision for those days.'

15 While he spoke to me I hung my head 16 and was struck dumb. Suddenly one like a man touched my lips. Then I opened my mouth to speak and addressed him as he stood before me: 'Sir, this has pierced me to the heart, 17 and I retain no strength. How can my lord's servant presume to talk with such as my lord, since my strength has failed me and no breath is left in me?' 18 Then the figure touched me again and 19 restored my strength. He said, 'Do not be afraid, man greatly beloved; all will be well with you. Be strong, be strong.' When he had spoken to me, I recovered strength and said, 'Speak, sir, for you have given me strength.' 20 He said, 'Do you know why I have come to you? I am first going back to fight with the prince of Persia, and, as soon as I have left, the prince of 21- Greece will appear: I have no ally on 11₁ my side to help and support me, except Michael your prince.*d* However I will tell you what is written in the 2 Book of Truth. Here and now I will tell you what is true:

'Three more kings will appear in Persia, and the fourth will far surpass all the others in wealth; and when he has extended his power through his wealth, he will rouse the whole world 3 against the kingdom of Greece. Then there will appear a warrior king. He will rule a vast kingdom and will do 4 what he chooses. But as soon as he is established, his kingdom will be shattered and split up north, south, east and west. It will not pass to his descendants, nor will any of his success-ors have an empire like his; his kingdom will be torn up by the roots and given to others as well as to them. Then the king of the south will become 5 strong; but another of the captains will surpass him in strength and win a greater kingdom. In due course the two 6 will enter into a friendly alliance; to redress the balance the daughter of the king of the south will be given in marriage to the king of the north, but she will not maintain her influence and their line will not last. She and her escort, her child, and also her lord and master, will all be the victims of foul play. Then another shoot from the 7 same stock as hers will appear in his father's place, will penetrate the de-fences of the king of the north and enter his fortress, and will win a decisive victory over his people. He 8 will take back as booty to Egypt even the images of their gods cast in metal and their precious vessels of silver and gold. Then for some years he will refrain from attacking the king of the north. After that the king of the north 9 will overrun the southern kingdom but will retreat to his own land.

'His sons will press on to assemble a 10 great armed horde. One of them will sweep on and on like an irresistible flood. And after that he will press on as far as his enemy's stronghold. The 11 king of the south, his anger roused, will march out to do battle with the king of the north who, in turn, will raise a great horde, but it will be delivered into the hands of his enemy. When this horde has been captured, 12 the victor will be elated and he will slaughter tens of thousands, yet he will not maintain his advantage. Then the 13 king of the north will once more raise a horde even greater than the last and, when the years come round, will advance with a great army and a large

d Prob. rdg.; Heb. adds and as for me, in the first year of Darius the Mede.

---

kingdom of Persia. **20:** The battle of the angels reflects the battles of the people; *Greece* here is probably the kingdom of Antiochus IV Epiphanes, though it may be the empire of Alexander. **10.21–11.2:** *The Book of Truth revealed.* This was apparently an explanation of history and its fulfillment, and not the same as the book of 12.1. **11.2:** Since there were more than four kings in Persian history, it is not known which ones the author meant.
 11.3–45: Alexander and his successors. 3 4: See Introduction and 8.8. **5–45:** The south is the Egyptian Ptolemaic kingdom and the north is the Syrian Seleucid kingdom. The struggles between

14 baggage-train. During these times many will resist the king of the south, but some hotheads among your own people will rashly attempt to give substance to a vision and will come to
15 disaster. Then the king of the north will come and throw up siege-ramps and capture a fortified town, and the forces of the south will not stand up to him; even the flower of their army will
16 not be able to hold their ground. And so his adversary will do as he pleases and meet with no opposition. He will establish himself in the fairest of all lands and it will come wholly into his
17 power. He will resolve to subjugate all the dominions of the king of the south; and he will come to fair terms with him,*e* and he will give him a young woman in marriage, for the destruction of the kingdom; but she will not persist nor serve his purpose.
18 Then he will turn to the coasts and islands and take many prisoners, but a foreign commander*f* will put an end to his challenge by wearing him down;*g* thus he will throw back his challenge
19 on to him. He will fall back upon his own strongholds; there he will come to disaster and be overthrown and be seen no more.
20 'He will be succeeded by one who will send out an officer with a royal escort to extort tribute; after a short time this king too will meet his end, yet neither openly nor in battle.
21 'A contemptible creature will succeed but will not be given recognition as king; yet he will seize the kingdom by dissimulation and intrigue in time of
22 peace. He will sweep away all forces of opposition as he advances, and even the Prince of the Covenant will be
23 broken. He will enter into fraudulent alliances and, although the people behind him are but few, he will rise to
24 power and establish himself in time of peace. He will overrun the richest districts of the province and succeed in doing what his fathers and forefathers

failed to do, distributing spoil, booty, and property to his followers. He will lay his plans against fortresses, but only for a time.
25 'He will rouse himself in all his strength and courage and lead a great army against the king of the south, but the king of the south will press the campaign against him with a very great and numerous army; yet the king of the south will not persist, for
26 traitors will lay their plots. Those who eat at his board will be his undoing; his army will be swept away, and many
27 will fall on the field of battle. The two kings will be bent on mischief and, sitting at the same table, they will lie to each other with advantage to neither. Yet there will still be an end to the
28 appointed time. Then one will return home with a long baggage-train, and with anger in his heart against the Holy Covenant; he will work his will and return to his own land.
29 'At the appointed time he will once more overrun the south, but he will
30 not succeed as he did before. Ships from the west will sail against him, and he will receive a rebuff. He will turn and vent his fury against the Holy Covenant; on his way back he will take due note of those who have forsaken
31 it. Armed forces dispatched by him will desecrate the sanctuary and the citadel and do away with the regular offering. And there they will set up "the abominable thing that causes
32 desolation". He will win over by plausible promises those who are ready to condemn the covenant, but the people who are faithful to their God
33 will hold firm and fight back. Wise leaders of the nation will give guidance to the common people; yet for a while they will fall victims to fire and sword,
34 to captivity and pillage. But these victims will not want for help, though small, even if many who join them are

e and he . . . with him: prob. rdg.; Heb. obscure.
f Or consul or legate.
g by wearing him down: prob. rdg.; Heb. obscure.

---

the two countries is fairly accurately described. **21–45:** Antiochus IV Epiphanes, as in chs. 7–9, is the great oppressor. **22–23:** *Prince of the Covenant:* the Judean high priest Onias III deposed by Antiochus and supplanted by his brother Jason as part of the *fraudulent alliances.* **25–35:** The two campaigns of Antiochus against Egypt. **30:** *Ships from the west:* the Romans. They compelled Antiochus to withdraw from Egypt. On his return to Syria (168 B.C.), he desecrated the Temple in Jerusalem (v. 31; see 9.27). **32:** *Fight back:* the Maccabean revolt;

35 insincere. Some of these leaders will themselves fall victims for a time so that they may be tested, refined and made shining white. Yet there will still be an end[h] to the appointed time.
36 The king will do what he chooses; he will exalt and magnify himself above every god and against the God of gods he will utter monstrous blasphemies. All will go well for him until the time of wrath ends, for what is determined
37 must be done. He will ignore his ancestral gods, and the god beloved of women; to no god will he pay heed but will exalt himself above them all.
38 Instead he will honour the god of the citadel, a god unknown to his ancestors, with gold and silver, gems and
39 costly gifts. He will garrison his strongest fortresses with aliens, the people of a foreign god. Those whom he favours he will load with honour, putting them in office over the common people and distributing land at a price.
40 'At the time of the end, he and the king of the south will make feints at one another, and the king of the north will come storming against him with chariots and cavalry and many ships. He will overrun land after land, sweep-
41 ing over them like a flood, amongst them the fairest of all lands, and tens of thousands shall fall victims. Yet all these lands [including Edom and Moab and the remnant of the Ammonites]
42 will survive his attack. He will reach out to land after land, and Egypt will
43 not escape. He will gain control of her hidden stores of gold and silver and of all her treasures; Libyans and Cushites
44 will follow in his train. Then rumours from east and north will alarm him, and he will depart in a great rage to
45 destroy and to exterminate many. He will pitch his royal pavilion between the sea and the holy hill, the fairest of all hills; and he will meet his end with no one to help him.

At that moment Michael shall appear,   **12**
Michael the great captain,
who stands guard over your
    fellow-countrymen;
and there will be a time of
    distress
such as has never been
since they became a nation till
    that moment.
But at that moment your people will
    be delivered,[i]
every one who is written in the
    book:
many of those who sleep in the dust   2
    of the earth will wake,
    some to everlasting life
and some to the reproach of eternal
    abhorrence.
The wise leaders shall shine like the   3
    bright vault of heaven,
and those who have guided the
    people in the true path
shall be like the stars for ever and
    ever.

But you, Daniel, keep the words 4 secret and seal the book till the time of the end. Many will be at their wits' end, and punishment will be heavy.'
And I, Daniel, looked and saw two 5 others standing, one on this bank of the river and the other on the opposite bank. And I said to the man clothed 6 in linen who was above the waters of the river, 'How long will it be before these portents cease?' The man clothed 7 in linen above the waters of heaven lifted to heaven his right hand and his left, and I heard him swear by him who lives for ever: 'It shall be for a time, times, and a half. When the power of the holy people ceases to be dispersed, all these things shall come to an end.' I 8 heard but I did not understand, and so I said, 'Sir, what will the issue of these

[h] Yet . . . end: *prob. rdg.*; *Heb. has different word order.*
[i] *Or* will escape.

see 1 Macc. ch. 2. **35**: *End:* see 8.17 n. **36–45**: Wars to occur as a result of the arrogance of Antiochus. **43**: *Cushites:* the peoples living south of Egypt in Nubia (roughly today's Sudan) and Ethiopia.
    12.1–13: Concluding vision. 1: Apocalyptic literature seems to flow directly from historical events (here the wars brought on by Antiochus) to events of the end times. As in 9.26–27, the period before the very end would be the most distressful. *The book:* containing a list of the names of the saints, as in Ps.69.28; compare 10.21–11.2 n. **2:** This is a clear statement of resurrection, and unique in the OT. **4:** The book here seems to be that of 11.1, rather than 12.1. **6:** *Linen:* see Ezek.9.2. **7:** *Time, times, and a half:* three and a half years, as it is in 7.25.

9 things be?' He replied, 'Go your way, Daniel, for the winds are kept secret and sealed till the time of the end. 10 Many shall purify themselves and be refined, making themselves shining white, but the wicked shall continue in wickedness and none of them shall understand; only the wise leaders shall 11 understand. From the time when the regular offering is abolished and "the abomination of desolation" is set up, there shall be an interval of one thousand two hundred and ninety days. Happy the man who waits and lives to 12 see the completion of one thousand three hundred and thirty-five days! But go your way to the end and rest, 13 and you shall arise to your destiny at the end of the age.'

11–12: These figures, perhaps representing separate traditions, seem to be related to those of 7.25 and 8.14. **11:** See 9.27 n.

THE TWELVE PROPHETS

HOSEA

In the Hebrew Bible, the Minor Prophets (so named because their books are shorter than Isaiah, Jeremiah, and Ezekiel) are called the Book of the Twelve and are treated as a literary unit. The ancients arranged the twelve writings in what they considered chronological order; Hosea is in the first position. While modern scholars see reasons to date some of these writings at times other than the ancient sequence suggests, they regard Hosea as indeed the earliest writing.

The first verse places Hosea in the latter part of the eighth century B.C., when the Assyrians were about to overrun the Northern Kingdom of Israel. That menace gives the book, addressed to the north, its tension. The prophet knows both the people's corruption and Yahweh's love, and the book veers from judgment to love, from threats of destruction to promises of restoration.

A book such as Hosea can pose a problem for the reader in that it does not present a systematic argument. It consists of many poems and prose passages compiled into an anthology; hence there can be an impression of bewildering inconsistency. While it is uncertain that Hosea's message comes from his marriage, related in chs. 1–3, the experience narrated is searing and even bitter, though filled with his love. The portrait of the deity as partaking in man's feelings and agonies makes Hosea one of the most moving of Old Testament books.

---

1 THE WORD OF THE LORD WHICH came to Hosea son of Beeri during the reigns of Uzziah, Jotham, Ahaz, and Hezekiah, kings of Judah, and during the reign of Jeroboam son of Jehoash king of Israel.

Hosea's unfaithful wife

2 THIS IS THE BEGINNING OF THE LORD'S message by Hosea. He said, Go, take a wanton for your wife and get children of her wantonness; for like a wanton 3 this land is unfaithful to the LORD. So he went and took Gomer, a worthless woman;*a* and she conceived and bore 4 him a son. And the LORD said to him,

Call him Jezreel,*b* for in a little while I will punish the line of Jehu for the blood shed in Jezreel
and put an end to the kingdom of Israel.
5   On that day

I will break Israel's bow in the Vale of Jezreel.

She conceived again and bore a 6 daughter, and the LORD said to him,

Call her Lo-ruhamah;*c*
for I will never again show love to Israel,
never again forgive them.*d*

After weaning Lo-ruhamah, she con- 8 ceived and bore a son; and the LORD 9 said,

Call him Lo-ammi;*e*
for you are not my people,
and I will not be your God.
The Israelites shall become countless 10 as the sands of the sea

a a worthless woman: *or* daughter of Diblaim.
b *That is* God shall sow.
c *That is* Not loved.
d *Prob. rdg.; Heb. adds* (7) Then I will love Judah and will save them. I will save them not by bow or sword or weapon of war, by horses or by horsemen, but by the LORD their God.
e *That is* Not my people.

1.1: Introduction. *Hosea* means "rescue." The names of the kings place Hosea in the 740s B.C.
1.2–3.5: Hosea's unfaithful wife. The figure of the unhappy marriage sets forth God's dissatisfaction with Israel.
1.2–9: The three children. 2: *Wanton:* a harlot. **4:** *Jehu* became king in a bloody revolt at *Jezreel* in about 842 B.C. (see 2 Kgs.9.1–10.31). Jezreel was the name both of a town and of the valley between Galilee and Samaria. **5:** *Break Israel's bow:* destroy her power. **7:** See Tfn. *d.* This apparently was added so as to apply to the Southern Kingdom Hosea's message addressed to the Northern. **9:** *You are not my people:* the LORD renounces the covenant (compare Exod.6.7).
1.10–2.1: Restoration. 10: The substance of v. 9 is here reversed. See Gen.22.17 and 32.12.

which can neither be measured nor
    numbered;
it shall no longer be said, 'They are
    not my people',
they shall be called Sons of the
    Living God.

11 Then the people of Judah and of
    Israel shall be reunited
and shall choose for themselves a
    single head,
and they shall become masters
    of the earth;
for great shall be the day of
    Jezreel.

2 Then you will say to your brothers,
    'You are my people',
and to your sisters, 'You are
    loved.'

2 Plead my cause with your mother;
is she not my wife and I her
    husband?*f*
Plead with her to forswear those
    wanton looks,
to banish the lovers from her bosom.

3 Or I will strip her and expose her
    naked as the day she was born;
I will make her bare as the wilderness,
    parched as the desert,
and leave her to die of thirst.

4 I will show no love for her
    children;
they are the offspring of
    wantonness,

5 and their mother is a wanton.
She who conceived them is
    shameless;
she says, 'I will go after my lovers;
they give me my food and drink,
my wool and flax, my oil and my
    perfumes.'

6 Therefore I will block her road with
    thorn-bushes
and obstruct her path with a wall,
so that she can no longer follow her
    old ways.

7 When she pursues her lovers she will
    not overtake them,

when she looks for them she will
    not find them;
then she will say,
'I will go back to my husband again;
    I was better off with him than I am
    now.'

8 For she does not know that it is I
    who gave her
corn, new wine, and oil,
I who lavished upon her silver and
    gold
which they spent on the Baal.

9 Therefore I will take back
my corn at the harvest and my new
    wine at the vintage,
and I will take away the wool and
    the flax
which I gave her to cover her
    naked body;

10 so I will show her up for the lewd
    thing she is,
and no lover will want to steal her
    from me.

12*g* I will ravage the vines and the
    fig-trees,
which she says are the fee
with which her lovers have hired her,
and turn them into jungle where
    wild beasts shall feed.

11 I will put a stop to her
    merrymaking,
her pilgrimages and new moons, her
    sabbaths*h* and festivals.

13 I will punish her for the holy days
when she burnt sacrifices to the
    Baalim,
when she decked herself with
    earrings and necklaces,
ran after her lovers and forgot me.
This is the very word of the LORD.

14 But now listen,
I will woo her, I will go with her
    into the wilderness

*f is she . . . husband?: or for she is no longer my wife
nor I her husband.*
g Verses 11 and 12 transposed.
h Or her full moons.

11: *Reunited:* the division into two kingdoms came after Solomon (see 1 Kgs.12.1–20).
Jezreel is here the son, standing for God's restoration of Israel.
2.2–17: *Israel, the harlot wife.* **2:** *Plead my cause:* the phrase comes from the law court. *Is
she not my wife . . . ?:* compare Tfn. *f*, which implies a divorce proceeding. *Lovers* can often
mean foreign nations (compare Jer.4.30; Ezek. ch. 16); here it may also mean alien gods.
8: *Corn:* grain in general and not the American corn. *Baal:* the Canaanite fertility god,
whose worship was viewed as disloyalty to Yahweh. **11:** The list of rituals covers the various
kinds of public worship. *Pilgrimages* are the feasts commanded in Exod.23.14–17. **13:** *Baalim:*
the plural of Baal. **14–17:** *Wilderness:* the place of the first encounter between God and Israel,

and comfort her:

15 there I will restore her vineyards,
turning the Vale of Trouble into
the Gate of Hope,[i]
and there she will answer as in her
youth,
when she came up out of
Egypt.
On that day she shall call me 'My
husband'

16 and shall no more call me 'My
Baal';[j]

17 and I will wipe from her lips the
very names of the Baalim;
never again shall their names be
heard.
This is the very word of the
LORD.[k]

18 Then I will make a covenant on
behalf of Israel with the wild beasts,
the birds of the air, and the things that
creep on the earth, and I will break
bow and sword and weapon of war
and sweep them off the earth, so that
all living creatures may lie down

19 without fear. I will betroth you to
myself for ever, betroth you in lawful
wedlock with unfailing devotion and

20 love; I will betroth you to myself to
have and to hold, and you shall know

21 the LORD. At that time I will give
answer, says the LORD, I will answer
for the heavens and they will answer for

22 the earth, and the earth will answer
for the corn, the new wine, and the oil,

23 and they will answer for Jezreel. Israel
shall be my new sowing in the land,
and I will show love to Lo-ruhamah
and say to Lo-ammi, 'You are my
people', and he will say, 'Thou art my
God.'

The LORD said to me,   **3**

Go again and love a woman
loved by another man, an adulteress,
and love her as I, the LORD, love
the Israelites
although they resort to other gods
and love the raisin-cakes offered to
their idols.

So I got her back[l] for fifteen pieces of 2
silver, a homer of barley and a measure
of wine; and I said to her,   3

Many a long day you shall live in
my house
and not play the wanton,
and have no intercourse with a man,
nor I with you.

For the Israelites shall live many a   4
long day
without king or prince,
without sacrifice or sacred pillar,
without image or household gods;
but after that they will again seek   5
the LORD their God and David
their king,
and turn anxiously to the LORD for
his bounty in days to come.

God's case against Israel

Hear the word of the LORD, O   **4**
Israel;
for the LORD has a charge to bring
against the people of the land:

i turning . . . Hope: *or* Emek-achor to Pethah-tikvah.
j Also means My husband.
k This . . . LORD: *transposed from after* On that day *in
verse 16.*
l got her back: *or* bought her.

and viewed by the prophet as a time of perfect faith and ideal relations. Compare Jer.2.2–3.
15: *Vale of Trouble:* the Valley of Achor (see Josh.7.24–26). **16:** The word *Baal* means husband
as well as being the name of the god; hence its use is forbidden here.
   2.18–23: Restoring Israel's harmony with the earth. Yahweh will resume his relationship with
Israel, as shown in the image of the new betrothal and by the new love for the children (compare
1.10–2.1). **23:** *My new sowing:* a play on the word Jezreel, which means "God sows"; see 1.4
Tfn. *b.* Israel, not Jezreel, is God's sowing.
   3.1–5: Redemption of the wife is achieved by *love* (v. 1) and a high cost (v. 2). *Fifteen pieces
of silver* is about seven ounces, and a *homer* is nearly 11½ bushels; see p. 1035. Love entails
discipline: the *wanton* (v. 3) and Israel (v. 4) must be kept from further sin before receiving
Yahweh's full *bounty.* **4:** Israel's distress arises from corruption caused by kings and from
observing Canaanite religious rituals. *Sacred pillar:* doubtless a phallus, a symbol of Baal, a
god of fertility.
   4.1–9.17: God's case against Israel. The oracles in this section follow the literary form
of a court trial in which God presses charges (4.1), passes a judicial sentence (5.1), and imposes a
juridical penalty (5.9).

There is no good faith or mutual
trust,
no knowledge of God in the land,
2   oaths are imposed and broken, they
kill and rob;
there is nothing but adultery and
licence,[m]
one deed of blood after another.
3   Therefore the land shall be dried up,
and all who live in it shall pine away,
and with them the wild beasts and
the birds of the air;
even the fish shall be swept from
the sea.
4   But it is not for any man to
bring a charge,
it is not for him to prove a case;
the quarrel with you, false priest,
is mine.

5   Priest?[n] By day and by night you
blunder on,
you and the prophet with you.
6   My people are ruined for lack of
knowledge;
your own countrymen are
brought to ruin.[o]
You have rejected knowledge,
and I will reject you from serving
me as priest.
You have forgotten the teaching
of God,
and I, your God, will forget your
sons.

7   The more priests there are, the more
they sin against me;
their dignity I will turn into
dishonour.
8   They feed on the sin of my people
and batten on their iniquity.
9   But people and priest shall be
treated alike.
I will punish them for their conduct
and repay them for their deeds:

they shall eat but never be   10
satisfied,
behave wantonly but their lust will
never be overtaxed,
for they have forsaken the LORD
to give themselves to sacred   11
prostitution.
New wine and old steal my people's   12
wits:[p]
they ask advice from a block of
wood
and take their orders from a
fetish;
for a spirit of wantonness has led
them astray
and in their lusts they are unfaithful
to their God.
Your men sacrifice on mountain-   13
tops
and burn offerings on the hills,
under oak and poplar
and the terebinth's pleasant shade.
Therefore your daughters play the
wanton
and your sons' brides commit
adultery.
I will not punish your daughters   14
for playing the wanton
nor your sons' brides for their
adultery,
because your men resort to wanton
women
and sacrifice with temple-
prostitutes.
A people without understanding
comes to grief;
they are a mother turned wanton.   15
Bring no guilt-offering,[q] Israel;
do not come to Gilgal, Judah,

[m] and licence: *prob. rdg.; Heb.* they exceed.
[n] the quarrel . . . Priest?: *prob. rdg.; Heb.* and your
people are like those who quarrel with a priest.
[o] My people . . . ruin: *or* Your mother (Israel) is
destroyed, my people destroyed for lack of knowledge.
[p] steal . . . wits: *or* embolden my people.
[q] Bring no guilt-offering: *prob. rdg.; Heb.* Let him
not be guilty.

4.1–4: General charge. The nation has broken the covenant. **1:** *Mutual trust:* love between
persons growing out of fidelity to a covenant. *Knowledge of God:* the experience of God in
obedience and surrender, resulting in a close personal relationship (see Jer.9.23–24 n.). **2:** The
crimes are breaches of specific laws. **3:** The rupture of the covenant meant the loss of natural
vitality. Contrast 2.18–23, the vitality experienced in fidelity to the covenant.
4.5–5.7: Undermining religion. 5: The *prophet*, like the *priest*, is here a religious functionary,
and unlike the charismatic Hosea. See Jer.23.9–12. **6:** *Knowledge:* see 4.1 n. **11:** *Sacred
prostitution*, a fertility rite directed to Baal, was apparently practiced by Israel to gain control
over the reproductive powers of nature. **12:** *New wine and old:* an allusion to a pagan vintage
festival. **13:** Fertility worship (with sacred prostitutes) took place on *mountain-tops* and under
trees. **15:** *Gilgal:* an important shrine town near Jericho. *Beth-aven:* lit. "house of iniquity,"
a sarcastic name for Bethel, "house of God," Israel's religious center; Gen.28.16–19;

do not go up to Beth-aven to swear
by the life of the LORD,

16 since Israel has run wild, wild as a
heifer;
and will the LORD now feed this
people
like lambs in a broad meadow?

17 Ephraim, keeping company with
idols,

18 has held a drunken orgy,*r*
they have practised sacred
prostitution,
they have preferred dishonour to
glory.

19 The wind shall sweep them away,
wrapped in its wings,
and they will find their sacrifices
a delusion.

5 Hear this, you priests,
and listen, all Israel; let the royal
house mark my words.
Sentence is passed on you;
for you have been a snare at Mizpah,
and a net spread out on Tabor.

2 The rebels! they have shown base
ingratitude,
but I will punish them all.

3 I have cared for Ephraim
and I have not neglected Israel;
but now Ephraim has played the
wanton
and Israel has defiled himself.

4 Their misdeeds have barred their
way back to their God;
for a wanton spirit is in them,
and they care nothing for the
LORD.

5 Israel's arrogance cries out against
him;
*s*Ephraim's guilt is his undoing,
and Judah no less is undone.

6 They go with sacrifices of sheep
and cattle
to seek the LORD, but do not find
him.

He has withdrawn himself from
them;
for they have been unfaithful to 7
him,
and their sons are bastards.
Now an invader shall devour their
fields.

Blow the trumpet in Gibeah, 8
the horn in Ramah,
raise the battle-cry in Beth-aven:
'Benjamin, we are with you!'
On the tribes of Israel I have 9
proclaimed this unalterable
doom:
on the day of punishment Ephraim
shall be laid waste.
The rulers of Judah act like men who 10
move their neighbour's
boundary;
on them will I pour out my wrath
like a flood.
Ephraim is an oppressor trampling 11
on justice,
doggedly pursuing what is worthless.
But I am a festering sore to 12
Ephraim,
a canker to the house of Judah.
So when Ephraim found that he 13
was sick,
Judah that he was covered with
sores,
Ephraim went to Assyria,
he went in haste to the Great King;
but he has no power to cure you
or to heal your sores.
Yes indeed, I will be fierce as a 14
panther to Ephraim,
fierce as a lion to Judah—
I will maul the prey and go,
carry it off beyond hope of rescue—
I, the LORD.
I will go away and return to my 15
place

r a drunken orgy: prob. rdg.; Heb. unintelligible.
s Prob. rdg.; Heb. prefixes Israel.

---

1 Kgs.12.25–30. **17:** *Ephraim,* the main northern tribe, often means the whole Northern Kingdom.
5.1: What events *Mizpah* and *Tabor* allude to is not certain. **3–4:** *Cared:* lit. "known";
expressive of God's active concern for Israel's well-being. See 4.1 n. **7:** *Bastards:* because they
were born to parents who repudiated covenant with God, but also possibly because of actually
being born from fertility cult unions.
   5.8–6.6: Divine disappointment. The three parts of the poem are: punishment by political
upheavals (5.8–15), Israel's apparent remorse (6.1–3), and Yahweh's response (6.6). **8:** *Gibeah,
Ramah,* and *Beth-aven* (see 4.15 n.) were cities in *Benjamin,* possibly annexed by the Northern
Kingdom, and first targets of an invasion by the Southern Kingdom. **10:** The *rulers* of *Judah*
in calling the Assyrians against their brethren in Israel were, in effect, taking land away from
them; see 2 Kgs.16.7–9. **13:** *Great King* was a title assumed by Assyrian kings.

until in their horror they seek me,
and look earnestly for me in their
distress.

6 Come, let us return to the LORD;
for he has torn us and will heal us,
he has struck us and he will bind
up our wounds;
2   after two days he will revive us,
on the third day he will restore us,
that in his presence we may live.
3 Let us humble ourselves, let us
strive to know the LORD,
whose justice dawns like morning
light,[t]
and its dawning is as sure as the
sunrise.
It will come to us like a shower,
like spring rains that water the earth.

4   O Ephraim, how shall I deal with
you?
How shall I deal with you, Judah?
Your loyalty to me is like the
morning mist,
like dew that vanishes early.
5 Therefore have I lashed you through
the prophets
and torn you[u] to shreds with my
words;
6   loyalty is my desire, not sacrifice,
not whole-offerings but the
knowledge of God.

7   At Admah[v] they have broken my
covenant,
there they have played me false.
8 Gilead is a haunt of evildoers,
marked by a trail of blood;
9 like robbers lying in wait for a man,
priests are banded together
to do murder on the road to
Shechem;
their deeds are outrageous.
10 At Israel's sanctuary I have seen a
horrible thing:

there Ephraim played the wanton
and Israel defiled himself.
And for you, too, Judah, comes a   11
harvest of reckoning.

When I would reverse the fortunes
of my people,
when I would heal Israel,   7
then the guilt of Ephraim stands
revealed,
and all the wickedness of
Samaria;
they have not kept faith.
They are thieves, they break into
houses;[w]
they are robbers, they strip people
in the street,
little thinking that I have their   2
wickedness ever in mind.
Now their misdeeds beset them
and stare me in the face.
They win over the king with their   3
wickedness
and princes with their treachery,
lecherous all of them, hot as an oven 4
over the fire
which the baker does not stir
after kneading the dough until it is
proved.
On their king's festal day the   5
officers
begin to be inflamed with wine,
and he joins in the orgies of arrogant
men;
for their hearts are heated by it[x]   6
like an oven.
While they are relaxed all night
long
their passion slumbers,
but in the morning it flares up
like a blazing fire;
they all grow feverish, hot as an   7
oven,

t Line transposed from end of verse 5.
u Prob. rdg.; Heb. them.
v At Admah: prob. rdg.; Heb. Like Adam.
w houses: prob. rdg.; Heb. om.
x are heated by it: prob. rdg.; Heb. draw near.

6.1–6: Israel's apparent remorse. 1: *Torn:* the same Heb. word as maul (5.14). **2:** *Two days, third day:* that is, soon; possibly, instead, the days of a pagan ritual observance. **6:** *Loyalty, knowledge of God:* see 4.1 n. The qualities that maintain the covenant are beyond mere ritual, and hence Israel's repentance is unacceptable.
6.7–8.14: Israel's treachery. Influential persons, especially the king, have transgressed.
6.7–11: Murder and recklessness. 7: *Admah:* a city near the Dead Sea (see 11.8 n.). **8:** *Gilead:* east of the Jordan. **9:** *Shechem* was the ancient central shrine, site of the kingdom's most solemn festivities. **11:** The prophecy is now applied here to the Southern Kingdom.
7.1–16: The evils of the kings. 1: *Samaria:* the capital. **4–6:** The people of Israel hide the evil intrigue in their *hearts* like a *baker* who banks the *fire* in the *oven* after it has reached full intensity until the *dough* is *proved,* i.e. fully leavened and ready for baking. **7:** The kingdom

and devour their rulers.
King after king falls from power,
but not one of them calls upon me.

8 Ephraim and his aliens make a sorry
mixture;
Ephraim has become a cake half-baked.

9 Foreigners fed on his strength,
but he was unaware;
even his grey hairs turned white,
but he was unaware.

10 So Israel's arrogance cries out
against them;
but they do not return to the LORD
their God
nor seek him, in spite of it all.

11 Ephraim is a silly senseless pigeon,
now calling upon Egypt, now
turning to Assyria for help.

12 Wherever they turn, I will cast my
net over them
and will bring them down like
birds on the wing;
I will take them captive as soon
as I hear them flocking.

13 Woe betide them, for they have
strayed from me!
May disaster befall them for rebelling
against me!
I long to deliver them,
but they tell lies about me.

14 There is no sincerity in their cry
to me;
for all their howling on their pallets
and gashing of themselves over
corn and new wine,
they are turning away from me.

15 Though I support them, though I
give them strength of arm,
they plot evil against me.

16 Like a bow gone slack,
they relapse into the worship of
their high god;[y]
their talk is all lies,[z]
and so their princes shall fall by
the sword.

8 Put the trumpet to your lips!
A[a] vulture hovers over the
sanctuary of the LORD:

they have broken my covenant
and rebelled against my
instruction.
They cry to me for help; 2
'We know thee, God of Israel.'[b]
But Israel is utterly loathsome; 3
and therefore he shall run before
the enemy.
They make kings, but not by my 4
will;
they set up officers, but without
my knowledge;
they have made themselves idols of
their silver and gold.[c]

Your calf-gods stink, O Samaria; 5
my anger flares up against them.
Long will it be before they prove
innocent.
For what sort of a god is this 6
bull?
It is no god,
a craftsman made it;
the calf of Samaria will be broken
in fragments.

Israel sows the wind and reaps the 7
whirlwind;
there are no heads on the standing
corn, it yields no grain;
and, if it yielded any, strangers
would swallow it up.
Israel is now swallowed up, 8
lost among the nations,
a worthless nothing.
For, like a wild ass that has left the 9
herd,
they have run to Assyria.
Ephraim has bargained for lovers;
and, because they have bargained 10
among the nations,
I will now round them up,
and then they will soon abandon
this setting up of kings and princes.

y they relapse . . . god: *prob. rdg.; Heb. obscure.*
z Prob. rdg.; Heb. adds that is their stammering speech
in Egypt.
a Prob. rdg.; Heb. Like a.
b We . . . Israel: *prob. rdg.; Heb.* O my God, we know
thee, Israel.
c Prob. rdg.; Heb. adds so that he may be cut off.

---

devoured its *rulers*; three of the six who ruled in the previous twenty years were murdered. See
2 Kgs.15.8–26. **11:** Hoshea, the last king of Israel, became a vassal of *Assyria* but proved
disloyal in seeking help from *Egypt;* see 2 Kgs.17.1–6. **14:** *Howling* and *gashing* sarcastically
describe Canaanite rites (see 1 Kgs.18.25–29). *Corn:* see 2.8 n.
8.1–14: False religion. Specific missteps are given. **4:** Though one strand of the OT tradition
sees kingship as Yahweh's gift, another strand of it considers kingship as rebellion against
Yahweh. Hosea equates kingship with idolatry. **5:** *Calf* alludes sarcastically to the statue of a

11 For Ephraim in his sin has multiplied
    altars,
  altars have become his sin.
12 Though I give him countless rules
    in writing,
  they are treated as invalid.
13 Though they sacrifice flesh as offerings
    to me and eat them,
  I,[d] the LORD, will not accept them.
  Their guilt will be remembered
    and their sins punished.
  They shall go back to Egypt,
  or in Assyria they shall eat unclean
    food.

14 Israel has forgotten his Maker
    and built palaces,
  Judah has multiplied walled cities;
  but I will set fire to his cities,
    and it shall devour his castles.

  Do not rejoice, Israel, do not exult
9   like other peoples;
  for like a wanton you have forsaken
    your God,
  you have loved an idol[e]
  on every threshing-floor heaped
    with corn.
2 Threshing-floor and winepress
    shall know them no more,
  new wine shall disown[f] them.
3 They shall not dwell in the LORD's
    land;
  Ephraim shall go back to Egypt,
  or in Assyria they shall eat unclean
    food.
4 They shall pour out no wine to
    the LORD,
  they shall not bring their sacrifices
    to him;
  that would be mourners' fare for
    them,
  and all who ate it would be polluted.
  For their food shall only stay
    their hunger;

it shall not be offered in the
  house of the LORD.
What will you do for the festal day, 5
  the day of the LORD's pilgrim-
  feast?
For look, they have fled from a   6
  scene of devastation:
Egypt shall receive them,
Memphis shall be their grave;
the sands of Syrtes shall wreck
  them,
weeds shall inherit their land,
thorns shall grow in their
  dwellings.
The days of punishment are   7
  come,
the days of vengeance are come
  when Israel shall be humbled.
Then the prophet shall be made
  a fool
and the inspired seer a madman
  by your great guilt.
With great enmity Ephraim lies in   8
  wait for God's people
while the prophet is a fowler's trap
  by all their paths,
a snare in the very temple of God.
They lead them deep into sin as   9
  at the time of Gibeah.
Their guilt will be remembered and
  their sins punished.

I came upon Israel like grapes in   10
  the wilderness,
I looked on their forefathers
with joy like the first ripe figs;
but they resorted to Baal-peor
and consecrated themselves to a
  thing of shame,
and Ephraim became as loathsome   11
  as the thing he loved.
Their honour shall fly away like a
  bird:

d Prob. rdg.; Heb. he.
e an idol: or a harlot's fee.
f Or fail.

---

bull (see 1 Kgs.12.28–30). **13:** In captivity it will be impossible to observe laws of ritual
cleanliness because of contact with pagans, hence *unclean food.*
  9.1–13.16: Prosperity contrasted with exile. The poems use metaphors of agricultural plenty.
  9.1–9: Untoward results of false worship. 1: *Rejoice* and *exult* are cultic acts. *Threshing-floor:*
the place of pagan fertility worship at harvest time. **3:** *Egypt:* see 8.13 n. **5:** *Pilgrim-feast:* see
2.11 n. **6:** *Memphis, Syrtes:* Egyptian cities. **7–8:** A *prophet* attached to a *temple* was a *snare*
to the people in being concerned only with worship and in not warning people about their
guilt which would bring calamity, thereby making the prophet into a *fool.* See Ezek.13.1–16.
9: The allusion to *Gibeah* may mean Saul, whose throne was also there (1 Sam.10.26). See also
Judg. ch. 19.
  9.10–17: Israel's degeneration. 10: To find *grapes in the wilderness* was wondrous. *Baal-Peor:*
see Judg.2.11–13; Num.25.1–5; Ps.106.28; Jer.11.13. **11:** Childlessness was a dishonor.

no childbirth, no fruitful womb, no
   conceiving;
12 even if they rear their children,
    I will make them childless,
    without posterity.
Woe to them indeed when I turn
   away from them!

13 As lion-cubs emerge only to be
    hunted,*g*
so must Ephraim bring out his
   children for slaughter.
14 Give them, O LORD—what wilt
   thou give them?
Give them a womb that miscarries
   and dry breasts.

15 All their wickedness was seen at
    Gilgal; there did I hate them.
For their evil deeds I will drive
   them from my house,
I will love them no more: all their
   princes are in revolt.
16   Ephraim is struck down:
their root is withered, and they yield
   no fruit;
if ever they give birth,
I will slay the dearest offspring of
   their womb.

17   My God shall reject them,
   because they have not listened
    to him,
and they shall become wanderers
   among the nations.

God's judgement on Israel

10 Israel is like a rank vine
    ripening its fruit:
his fruit grows more and more, and
   more and more his altars;
the fairer his land becomes, the fairer
   he makes his sacred pillars.
2 They are crazy now, they are mad.
God himself will hack down their
   altars
and wreck their sacred pillars.

Well may they say, 'We have no   3
   king,
for we do not fear the LORD;
and what can the king do for us?'
There is nothing but talk,   4
imposing of oaths and making of
   treaties, all to no purpose;
and litigation spreads like a
   poisonous weed
along the furrows of the fields.
The inhabitants of Samaria tremble 5
   for the calf-god of Beth-aven;
the people mourn over it*h* and its
   priestlings howl,
distressed for their image, their
   glory,
which is carried away into exile.
It shall be carried to Assyria   6
as tribute to the Great King;
disgrace shall overtake Ephraim
and Israel shall feel the shame of
   their disobedience.
Samaria and her king are swept   7
   away
like flotsam on the water;
the hill-shrines of Aven are   8
   wiped out,
the shrines where Israel sinned;
thorns and thistles grow over her
   altars.
So they will say to the mountains,
   'Cover us',
and to the hills, 'Fall on us.'

Since the day of Gibeah Israel has 9
   sinned;
there they took their stand in
   rebellion.
Shall not war overtake them in
   Gibeah?
I have come against the rebels to 10
   chastise them,
and the peoples shall mass against
   them
in hordes for their two deeds of
   shame.

g As lion-cubs . . . hunted: prob. rdg.; Heb. unintelligible.
h the people mourn over it: or the high god and his people mourn.

15: *Gilgal:* see 4.15 n; 12.11. *Princes in revolt:* see 5.2, where they "have shown base ingratitude."

10.1–13.16: Israel's punishment and restoration. The LORD's efforts to redeem Israel have been frustrated.

10.1–8: The fruits of idolatry. Cultic misdeeds produce political disasters. **1:** *Sacred pillars:* see 3.4 n. **5:** *Calf-god:* see 8.5 n. *Priestlings:* idolatrous priests. **6:** *Great King:* see 5.13 n. **8:** *Aven:* see 4.15 n.

10.9–15: Punishment for rebellion. 9: *Gibeah:* see 9.9 n. **10:** Compare 4.9 and Ezek.5.13.

11 Ephraim is like a heifer broken in,
   which loves to thresh corn,
across whose fair neck I have laid a
   yoke;[i]
I have harnessed Ephraim to the
   pole that he[j] may plough,
that Jacob may harrow his land.
12 Sow for yourselves in justice,
   and you will reap what loyalty
      deserves.
Break up your fallow;
for it is time to seek the LORD,
seeking him till he comes and gives
   you just measure of rain.
13 You have ploughed wickedness
   into your soil,
and the crop is mischief;
you have eaten the fruit of
   treachery.

Because you have trusted in your
   chariots,
in the number of your warriors,
14 the tumult of war shall arise against
   your people,
and all your fortresses shall be
   razed
as Shalman razed Beth-arbel in the
   day of battle,
dashing the mother to the ground
   with her babes.
15 So it shall be done to you, Bethel,
   because of your evil scheming;
as sure as day dawns, the king of
   Israel shall be swept away.

11 When Israel was a boy, I loved
   him;
I called my son out of Egypt;
2 but the more I called, the further
   they went from me;
they must needs sacrifice to the
   Baalim
and burn offerings before carved
   images.
3 It was I who taught Ephraim to
   walk,
I who had taken them in my
   arms;
4 but they did not know that I harnessed
   them in leading-strings[k]
and led them with bonds of love[l]—

that I had lifted them like a little
   child[m] to my cheek,
that I had bent down to feed them.
Back they shall go to Egypt,   5
the Assyrian shall be their king;
for they have refused to return
   to me.
The sword shall be swung over   6
   their blood-spattered altars
and put an end to the prattling
   priests
and devour my people in return   7
   for all their schemings,
bent on rebellion as they are.
Though they call on their high god,
   even then he will not reinstate
      them.
How can I give you up, Ephraim,   8
   how surrender you, Israel?
How can I make you like Admah
   or treat you as Zeboyim?
My heart is changed within me,
my remorse kindles already.
I will not let loose my fury,   9
I will not turn round and destroy
   Ephraim;
for I am God and not a man,
   the Holy One in your midst;
I will not come with threats[n] like a   10
   roaring lion.
No; when I roar, I who am God,
my sons shall come with speed out
   of the west.
They will come speedily, flying like   11
   birds out of Egypt,
   like pigeons from Assyria,
and I will settle them in their
   own homes.
This is the very word of the LORD.
Ephraim besets me with treachery,   12
   the house of Israel besets me
      with deceit;
and Judah is still restive under God,
   still loyal to the idols he counts
      holy.
Ephraim is a shepherd whose flock
   is but[o] wind,   12

i a yoke: *prob. rdg.; Heb.* om.
j he: *prob. rdg.; Heb.* Judah.
k leading-strings: *or* cords of leather.
l bonds of love: *or* reins of hide.
m I had . . . child: *prob. rdg.; Heb.* like those who lift
   up a yoke.
n *Prob. rdg.; Heb. adds* they shall go after the LORD.
o is a . . . but: *or* feeds on.

12: *Fallow:* land uncultivated for a time, and by implication, hardened and unproductive.
14: The allusion to *Shalman's* destruction of *Beth-arbel* is obscure.
11.1–12.1: Fatherhood and ingratitude. 5: *Back . . . Egypt:* see 8.13 n. **8:** *Admah and Zeboyim:*
destroyed with Sodom and Gomorrah (Deut.29.23).

a hunter chasing the east wind all
day;*p*
he makes a treaty with Assyria
and carries tribute of oil to Egypt.

2 The LORD has a charge to bring
against Judah
and is resolved to punish Jacob for
his conduct;
he will requite him for his misdeeds.
3 Even in the womb Jacob over-
reached his brother,
and in manhood he strove with God.
4 The divine angel stood firm and
held his own;*q*
Jacob wept and begged favour for
himself.
Then God met him at Bethel
and there spoke with him.
5 The LORD the God of Hosts, the
LORD is his name.

6 Turn back all of you by God's help;
practise loyalty and justice
and wait always upon your God.
7 False scales are in merchants' hands,
and they love to cheat;
8 so Ephraim says,
'Surely I have become a rich man, I
have made my fortune';
but all his gains will not pay
for the guilt*r* of his sins.
9 Yet I have been the LORD your God
since your days in Egypt;
I will make you live in tents yet
again, as in the old days.

10 I spoke to the prophets,
it was I who gave vision after vision;
I spoke through the prophets in
parables.
11 Was there idolatry in Gilead?
Yes: they were worthless
and sacrificed to bull-gods in Gilgal;
their altars were common as heaps of
stones beside a ploughed field.

12 Jacob fled to the land of Aram;
Israel did service to win a wife,

to win a wife he tended sheep.

By a prophet the LORD brought up 13
Israel out of Egypt
and by a prophet he was tended.

Ephraim has given bitter 14
provocation;
therefore his Lord will make him
answerable
for his own death
and bring down upon his own
head the blame
for all that he has done.

When the Ephraimites mumbled 13
their prayers,
God himself denounced Israel;
they were guilty of Baal-worship
and died.
Yet now they sin more and more; 2
they have made themselves an image
of cast metal,
they have fashioned their silver
into idols,
nothing but the work of craftsmen;
men say of them,
'Those who kiss calf-images offer
human sacrifice.'

Therefore they shall be like the 3
morning mist
or like dew that vanishes early,
like chaff blown from the
threshing-floor
or smoke from a chimney.
But I have been the LORD your God 4
since your days in Egypt,
when you knew no other saviour
than me,
no god but me.
I cared for you in the wilderness, 5
in a land of burning heat, as if you 6
were in pasture.
So they were filled,
and, being filled, grew proud;

p *Prob. rdg.; Heb. adds* piling up treachery and havoc.
q The divine . . . own: *or* He stood firm against an
angel, but flagged.
r for the guilt: *prob. rdg.; Heb.* for me, guilt.

12.2–14: Jacob and Moses. 2–6: Just as *Jacob*, the tribal father in whom Israel glories, sinned
and *begged* God's *favour*, so his descendants should *turn back* and *wait* on *God*. See especially
Gen.25.21–26; 32.22–32; 35.2–7; or 28.10–22. **7–9:** Israel's ill-gotten *gains* on its land do not
have the power to prevent God from reducing her to the poverty and loyalty of *tents* of the
Exodus. **11:** In Palestine the soil is so shallow and stony that fields cleared for plowing are
hedged with *heaps of stones. Idolatry* was practiced in the whole land. *Gilead* was east of the
Jordan and *Gilgal*, west of it. **13:** *Prophet:* Moses.
13.1–16: Yahweh's patience ends. 1: *Baal:* see 2.8 n. **9–11:** See 8.4 n. **12:** God's lawsuit

and so they forgot me.

7 So now I will be like a panther to
     them,
  I will prowl like a leopard by the
     wayside;
8 I will meet them like a she-bear
     robbed of her cubs
  and tear their ribs apart,
  like a lioness I will devour them
     on the spot,
  I will rip them up like a wild
     beast.
9 I have destroyed you, O Israel; who
     is there to help you?
10 Where now is your king that he
     may save you,
  or the rulers in all your cities
  for whom you asked me,
  begging for king and princes?
11 I gave you a king in my anger,
  and in my fury took him away.

12 Ephraim's guilt is tied up in a
     scroll,
  his sins are kept on record.
13 When the pangs of his birth came
     over his mother,
  he showed himself a senseless child;
  for at the proper time he could
     not present himself
  at the mouth of the womb.
14 Shall I redeem him from Sheol?
  Shall I ransom him from death?
  Oh, for your plagues, O death! Oh,
     for your sting, Sheol!
  I will put compassion out of my
     sight.
15 Though he flourishes among the
     reeds,*s*
  an east wind shall come, a blast
     from the LORD,
  rising over the desert;
  Ephraim's spring will fail and his
     fountain run dry.
  It will carry away as spoil
  his whole store of costly
     treasures.
16 Samaria will become desolate because
  she has rebelled against her
  God;

her babes will fall by the sword and
     be dashed to the ground,
  her women with child shall be
     ripped up.

*Repentance, forgiveness,
and restoration*

Return, O Israel, to the LORD your   **14**
     God;
  for you have stumbled in your
     evil courses.
Come with your words ready,   2
  come back to the LORD;
say to him, 'Thou dost not endure
     iniquity.*t*
  Accept our plea,
  and we will pay our vows with
     cattle from our pens.
Assyria shall not save us, nor will we 3
     seek horses to ride;
  what we have made with our
     own hands
  we will never again call gods;
  for in thee the fatherless find a
     father's love.'

I will heal their apostasy; of my own   4
     bounty will I love them;
  for my anger is turned away from
     them.
I will be as dew to Israel   5
  that he may flower like the lily,
  strike root like the poplar*u*
  and put out fresh shoots,   6
  that he may be as fair as the
     olive
  and fragrant as Lebanon.
Israel shall again dwell in my*v*   7
     shadow
  and grow corn in abundance;
  they shall flourish like a vine
  and be famous as the wine of
     Lebanon.

s among the reeds: *prob. rdg.; Heb.* between (*or* a son
of) brothers.
t Thou . . . iniquity: *or* Thou wilt surely take away
iniquity.
u Prob. rdg.; Heb. like Lebanon.
v Prob. rdg.; Heb. its.

---

against Israel ends in a judicial conviction of *guilt*, sealed officially in a *scroll*, and entered on
record, as was the judiciary custom. See Isa.8.16. **13:** The verse seems to be a proverb for
congenital awkwardness and ineptitude ending in disaster. **14:** *Sheol:* place of the dead. *Oh,
for your plagues:* quoted in 1 Cor.15.55, though with the meaning altered from a rhetorical
question, implying a negative, into a strong affirmation. **15:** The *east wind* is dry and hot.
14.1–9: Repentence, forgiveness, and restoration. In a serenely confident poem, Hosea uses

8 What has Ephraim any more to do
   with idols?
I have spoken and I affirm it:
I am the pine-tree that shelters you;
to me you owe your fruit.

Let the wise consider these things
and let him who considers take note;
for the LORD's ways are straight and
the righteous walk in them, while
sinners stumble.

---

fertility images as signs of God's favor and Israel's restoration and new life. **9:** A pious postscript
from a later hand.

JOEL

Few books can match Joel for drama. From the opening description of locust plagues, through pictures of ruin and restoration, visions and cosmic omens, and the war of Yahweh against "multitudes in the Valley of Decision," the poetry crackles with energy and stretches the mind with the visionary power of a remarkably gifted prophet.

We know nothing about this astonishing person, not even the date of his book. Some scholars place it as early as 600 B.C., others as late as 350. The references in 3,4–8 to foreign nations are too vague to allow precise dating, nor can the locust plague described in ch. 1 be identified by date. The picture of religious observances in chs. 1–2 leads most scholars to place Joel in the time of the Second Temple, perhaps 450–400 B.C.

Joel concentrates on God's ultimate victory, pursuing the eschatological implications of the locust plague and other contemporary events, and using a visionary, highly symbolic style. In Joel the prophetic manner carries on from the past, as in Ezekiel and Zechariah (chs. 1–6), toward such later apocalyptic books as Daniel and Revelation.

1 The word of the LORD which came to Joel son of Pethuel.

The day of the LORD

2 Listen, you elders;
hear me, all you who live in the
land:
has the like of this happened in all
your days
or in your fathers' days?
3 Tell it to your sons and they may
tell theirs;
let them pass it on from generation
to generation.
4 What the locust has left the swarm
eats,
what the swarm has left the hopper
eats,
and what the hopper has left the
grub eats.
5 Wake up, you drunkards, and
lament your fate;
mourn for the fresh wine, all you
wine-drinkers,
because it is lost to you.
6 For a horde has overrun my land,
mighty and past counting;
their teeth are a lion's teeth;
they have the fangs of a lioness.
7 They have ruined my vines

and left my fig-trees broken and
leafless,
they have plucked them bare
and stripped them of their bark;
they have left the branches white.

8 Wail like a virgin wife in sackcloth,
wailing over the bridegroom of
her youth:
9 the drink-offering and grain-offering
are lost
to the house of the LORD.
Mourn, you priests, ministers of
the LORD,
10 the fields are ruined, the parched
earth mourns;
for the corn is ruined, the new wine
is desperate,
the oil has failed.
11 Despair, you husbandmen; you
vinedressers, lament,
because the wheat and the barley,
the harvest of the field, is lost.
12 The vintage is desperate, and the
fig-tree has failed;
pomegranate, palm, and apple,
all the trees of the country-side are
parched,
and none make merry over harvest.

13 Priests, put on sackcloth and beat
your breasts;

1.1: Title. The tone of the book may indicate that *Joel* was a Temple prophet.
1.2–2.17: The Day of the LORD (see 1.14–15 n.). A terrible locust plague seems the end of the world, and the people need to muster all their religious resources to meet it.
1.4–2.17: The locusts ruin the entire country-side, and all elements of the population are summoned to lament and repent. **4:** It is disputed whether the Heb. terms for *locust, swarm, hopper,* and *grub* mean various kinds of locusts or successive stages of growth of one kind. **6–7:** The description of the locusts' ravages is poetically powerful. **9:** The gravity of the situation is indicated by the cessation of the regular sacrifices of the *drink-offering* and *grain-offering*. **10:** *Corn:* grain; see Hos.2.8 n. **12:** The fall *harvest* was possibly the occasion for a *merry*

lament, you ministers of the altar;
come, lie in sackcloth all night long,
  you ministers of my God;
  for grain-offering and drink-
    offering
are withheld from the house of
  your God.

14 Proclaim a solemn fast, appoint a
    day of abstinence.
  You elders, summon all that live in
    the land
    to come together in the house of
      your God,
    and cry to the LORD.

15   Alas! the day is near,
  the day of the LORD: it comes,
  a mighty destruction from the
    Almighty.

16 Look! it stares us in the face;
  the house of our God has lost its
    food,
    lost all its joy and gladness.

17 The soil is parched,
  the dykes are dry,
  the granaries are deserted,
  the barns ruinous;
    for the rains have failed.

18 The cattle are exhausted,
  the herds of oxen distressed
  because they have no pasture;
  the flocks of sheep waste away.

19 To thee I cry, O LORD;
  for fire has devoured the open
    pastures
  and the flames have burnt up all the
    trees of the country-side.

20 The very cattle in the field look up
    to thee;
  for the water-channels are dried up,
  and fire has devoured the open
    pastures.

2 Blow the trumpet in Zion,
  sound the alarm upon my holy hill;
  let all that live in the land tremble,
    for the day of the LORD has come,

2 surely a day of darkness and
    gloom is upon us,
  a day of cloud and dense fog;

like a blackness spread over the
  mountains
a mighty, countless host appears;
  their like has never been known,
  nor ever shall be in ages to come;
  their vanguard a devouring fire,   3
  their rearguard leaping flame;
before them the land is a garden
    of Eden,
behind them a wasted wilderness;
nothing survives their march.
On they come, like squadrons of   4
    horse,
like war-horses they charge;
bounding over the peaks they advance 5
  with the rattle of chariots,
like flames of fire burning up the
    stubble,
like a countless host in battle array.
Before them nations tremble,   6
  every face turns pale.
  Like warriors they charge,   7
  they mount the walls like men at
    arms,
each marching in line,
  no confusion in the ranks,
  none jostling his neighbour,   8
  none breaking line.
They plunge through streams without
    halting their advance;
they burst into the city, leap on to   9
    the wall,
  climb into the houses,
  entering like thieves through the
    windows.
Before them the earth shakes,   10
  the heavens shudder,
sun and moon are darkened,
and the stars forbear to shine.
The LORD thunders before his host;   11
  his is a mighty army,
  countless are those who do his
    bidding.
Great is the day of the LORD and
    terrible,
  who can endure it?
And yet, the LORD says, even now   12
turn back to me with your whole
    heart,

religious festival. **14–15:** The Pentateuch prescribes only one *fast* a year, the recurring Day of Atonement; see Lev.23.27. The *day of the* LORD was the future day of final judgment on the nations, and the purification and restoration of Israel as described in chs. 3 and 4. Some see the plague of locusts as part of that future judgment, which is conceived of as already beginning to arrive. **2.1:** The *trumpet* (Heb., *shophar*) was blown on the most solemn occasions, especially at the new year. **10:** The plague of locusts in its density darkens the *sun* and *moon* which are the traditional conditions accompanying the day of the LORD in apocalyptic literature. See 2.30–31; Isa.13.10. **12–14:** Yahweh himself suggests the proper response, a genuine repentance

fast, and weep, and beat your
   breasts.

13 Rend your hearts and not your
   garments;
turn back to the LORD your God;
   for he is gracious and compassionate,
   long-suffering and ever constant,
always ready to repent of the
   threatened evil.

14 It may be he will turn back and
   repent
and leave a blessing behind him,
   blessing enough for grain-offering
   and drink-offering
for the LORD your God.

15 Blow the trumpet in Zion,
proclaim a solemn fast, appoint a
   day of abstinence;

16 gather the people together, proclaim
   a solemn assembly;
   summon the elders,
gather the children, yes, babes at the
   breast,
bid the bridegroom leave his chamber
   and the bride her bower.

17 Let the priests, the ministers of the
   LORD,
stand weeping between the porch
   and the altar
and say, 'Spare thy people, O LORD,
   thy own people,
expose them not to reproach,
lest other nations make them a
   byword
and everywhere men ask,
   "Where is their God?"'

Israel forgiven and restored

18 Then the LORD's love burned with
   zeal for his land,
and he was moved with
   compassion for his people.

19 He answered their appeal and said,

I will send you corn, and new wine,
   and oil,
   and you shall have your fill;
I will expose you no longer
   to the reproach of other nations.

20 I will remove the northern peril far
   away from you
and banish them into a land
   parched and waste,
their vanguard into the eastern sea
   and their rear into the western,
and the stench shall rise from their
   rotting corpses
because of their proud deeds!

21 Earth, be not afraid, rejoice and be
   glad;
for the LORD himself has done a
   proud deed.

22 Be not afraid, you cattle in the
   field;
for the pastures shall be green,
the trees shall bear fruit,
the fig and the vine yield their
   harvest.

23 O people of Zion,
rejoice and be glad in the LORD
   your God,
who gives you good food in due
   measure*a*
and sends down rain*b* as of old.

24 The threshing-floors shall be heaped
   with grain,
the vats shall overflow with new
   wine and oil.

25 So I will make good the years
   that the swarm has eaten,
hopper and grub and locust,
my great army which I sent against
   you;

26 and you shall eat, you shall eat
   your fill
and praise the name of the LORD
   your God

a *Or* gives you a sign pointing to prosperity.
b *Prob. rdg.; Heb. adds* spring rain and autumn rain.

(of the *heart*) and not merely an outward one (*garments*). *For he is gracious:* a frequent liturgical formula (compare Pss.86.15; 103.8; 145.8). *Repent:* God frequently so reverses his intentions; see Gen.6.6. *Blessing:* usually a tangible evidence of divine favor. **15–17:** The solemn ritual is proclaimed again. The *altar* stood in front of the temple. *Byword:* mockery (more generally, a sententious saying, like a proverb). If Israel is not spared, the Gentiles will infer that Israel's God is ineffectual.

    2.18–3.21: Israel repents and is delivered. The poems in this section are arranged thematically rather than chronologically.

    2.18–32: The day of the LORD has a positive side, for it is inaugurated by his *love*. **20:** Danger in Palestine usually came from the north (compare Jer.1.13–14; 4.6); the north is the mythological dwelling of evil (Isa.14.13); the *northern peril* is a mythological monster, whose carcass

who has done wonders for you,[c]
27 and you shall know that I am present
in Israel,
that I and no other am the LORD
your God;
and my people shall not again be
brought to shame.
28   Thereafter the day shall come
when I will pour out my spirit on
all mankind;
your sons and your daughters shall
prophesy,
your old men shall dream dreams
and your young men see visions;
29 I will pour out my spirit in those
days
even upon slaves and slave-girls.
30 I will show portents in the sky and
on earth,
blood and fire and columns of
smoke;
31 the sun shall be turned into
darkness
and the moon into blood
before the great and terrible day of
the LORD comes.
32 Then everyone who invokes the
LORD by name
shall be saved:
for when the LORD gives the word
there shall yet be survivors on
Mount Zion
and in Jerusalem a remnant[d]
whom the LORD will call.[e]

3   When that time comes, on that day
when I reverse the fortunes of Judah
and Jerusalem,
2 I will gather all the nations
together
and lead them down to the Valley
of the LORD's Judgement
and there bring them to judgement
on behalf of Israel, my own
possession;
for they have scattered my people

throughout their own countries,
have taken each their portion of
my land
and shared out my people by lot,   3
bartered a boy for a whore,
and sold a girl for wine and drunk
it down.

What are you to me, Tyre and Sidon 4
and all the districts of Philistia? Can
you pay me back for anything I have
done? Is there anything that you can
do to me? Swiftly and speedily I will
make your deeds recoil upon your own
heads; for you have taken my silver 5
and my gold and carried off my costly
treasures into your temples; you have 6
sold the people of Judah and Jerusalem
to the Greeks, and removed them far
beyond their own frontiers. But I will 7
rouse them to leave the places to which
you have sold them. I will make your
deeds recoil upon your own heads: I 8
will sell your sons and your daughters
to the people of Judah, and they shall
sell them to the Sabaeans, a nation far
away. The LORD has spoken.

Proclaim this amongst the nations: 9–12[f]
Declare a holy war, call your troops
to arms!
Beat your mattocks into swords
and your pruning-hooks into
spears.[g]
Rally to each other's help, all you
nations round about.
Let the weakling say, 'I am strong',
and let the coward show himself
brave.[h]

c *Prob. rdg.; Heb. adds* and my people shall not again
be brought to shame (*cp. verse* 27).
d a remnant: *prob. rdg.; Heb.* among the remnant.
e *Or* when the LORD calls.
f *The order of lines in verses 9–12 has been re-arranged
in several places.*
g Beat . . . spears: *cp. Isa. 2. 4; Mic. 4. 3.*
h and let . . . brave: *prob. rdg.; Heb.* O LORD bring
down thy warriors.

stretches from east to west; see Ezek.38.6. **28:** The LORD's *spirit*, the animating force behind
the prophets, is to come on all Israel; compare Ezek.36.26–27.
    3.1–8: Punishment on Judah's oppressors. 1–2: An element in the day of the LORD is the
reversal of the condition of the *nations*, the oppressor, and *Israel*, the oppressed; the nations
will be *gathered* for judgment, just as they *scattered* Israel in carrying out God's judgment on
them. **2:** *The Valley of the LORD's Judgement* is probably not any actual place but a hypothetical site for the final judgment. **4–8:** Merchants from *Tyre* and *Sidon* and the region of
Philistia came with the Seleucid armies to buy the Jews as slaves in order to *sell* them. See
1 Macc.3.41; 2 Macc.1.27; 8.11. But the *talion* (Exod.21.23–24) will operate. *Sabaeans*: a
people in Arabia.
    3.9–21: The return of Paradise. 9–12: A battle is expected to precede Yahweh's culminating
victory. *Beat your mattocks into swords*, etc., exactly reverses the familiar saying in Isa.2.4 and

Let all the nations hear the call to
  arms
and come to the Valley of the
  LORD's Judgement;
let all the warriors come and draw
  near
and muster there;
for there I will take my seat
and judge all the nations round
  about.

13 Ply the sickle, for the harvest is ripe;
  come, tread the grapes,
for the press is full and the vats
  overflow;
  great is the wickedness of the
  nations.
14 The roar of multitudes, multitudes,
  in the Valley of Decision!
The day of the LORD is at hand
  in the Valley of Decision;
15 sun and moon are darkened
  and the stars forbear to shine.
16 The LORD roars from Zion
  and thunders from Jerusalem;
heaven and earth shudder,
but the LORD is a refuge for his
  people
and the defence of Israel.

Thus you shall know that I am the   17
  LORD your God,
dwelling in Zion my holy mountain;
Jerusalem shall be holy,
and no one without the right shall
  pass through her again.
When that day comes,   18
the mountains shall run with fresh
  wine
and the hills flow with milk.
All the streams of Judah shall be full
  of water,
and a fountain shall spring from
  the LORD's house
and water the gorge of Shittim,
but Egypt shall become a desert   19
and Edom a deserted waste,
  because of the violence done to
  Judah
and the innocent blood shed in her
  land;
and I will spill their blood,   20-21
the blood I have not yet spilt.
Then there shall be people living in
  Judah for ever,
in Jerusalem generation after
  generation;
and the LORD will dwell in Zion.

Mic.4.3. **13:** The image of the vintage for the final day is echoed in Isa.63.1–3. **14:** *Decision:* against the nations and for Jerusalem. **17:** The LORD's *dwelling* in *Jerusalem* gives the city its holy character. **18:** The picture of overflowing nature is the antithesis of the ruin caused by the locusts (1.4–20; 2.3). *Shittim:* a valley some nineteen miles southwest of Jerusalem. Compare a similar vision elaborated in Ezek.47.1–12. **19:** *Egypt* and *Edom* will become sterile in contrast to Israel's fertility. Edom and Egypt receive special condemnation, Edom because it despoiled Judah after the latter was laid low by the Babylonians (587 B.C.) and Egypt because it deceived Judah with promised help against the same Babylonians. See Jer.49.7–22; Ezek.25.12–14; Obad.1–11.

AMOS

Amos speaks against the Northern Kingdom of Israel with a severity not exceeded in the stern denunciations delivered by other prophets.

The narrative of his confrontation with Amaziah the priest of Bethel (7.10–17) in the time of Jeroboam II places him in the vicinity of 750 B.C. At that time Israel was in the midst of a prosperity which would end with its devastating conquest by the Assyrians about 722. But along with the high prosperity there had arisen a social and moral corruption which appeared especially abominable to Amos, a native of the poorer Southern Kingdom of Judah and a shepherd and pruner of sycamore figs (7.14). Though in his view other nations were wicked (1.3–2.5), Israel was so deeply guilty of "countless sins" (5.12) that her doom, determined by the deity, was sealed and irrevocable.

Verses or passages here and there soften the unrelieved sternness of the words of Amos (for example, 5.14) by suggesting that a change of heart might still occur in time to save Israel from the divine judgment to come. Other passages (for example, 5.15) hold out at most a forlorn hope for Israel. More optimistically, the latter half of 9.8 and 9.13–15 assert that God's will to sustain Israel surpasses Israel's ability to go wrong. Such hopeful passages are often interpreted as additions to the book from a later hand. The "doxologies" in 4.13; 5.8–9; and 9.5–6 are sometimes also considered to be additions.

Although by his own statement (7.14) he was not the usual prophet, a striking series of visions (7.1–9; 8.1–3; 9.1–4) appear to reflect the personal experiences which culminated in his prophetic ministry, and determined the content of his message.

---

1 THE WORDS OF AMOS, ONE OF THE sheep-farmers of Tekoa, which he received in visions concerning Israel during the reigns of Uzziah king of Judah and Jeroboam son of Jehoash king of Israel, two years before the 2 earthquake. He said,

The LORD roars from Zion
and thunders from Jerusalem;
the shepherds' pastures are scorched
and the top of Carmel[a] is dried up.

The sins of Israel and her neighbours

3 These are the words of the LORD:

For crime after crime of Damascus
I will grant them no reprieve,
because they threshed Gilead under
threshing-sledges spiked with
iron.
4 Therefore will I send fire upon the
house of Hazael,

fire that shall eat up Ben-hadad's
palaces;
I will crush the great men of   5
Damascus
and wipe out those who live in the
Vale of Aven
and the sceptred ruler of
Beth-eden;
the people of Aram shall be exiled
to Kir.
It is the word of the LORD.

These are the words of the LORD: 6

For crime after crime of Gaza
I will grant them no reprieve,
because they deported a whole
band of exiles
and delivered them up to Edom.
Therefore will I send fire upon   7
the walls of Gaza,
fire that shall consume its palaces.
I will wipe out those who live in   8
Ashdod

---

a top of Carmel: *or* choicest farmland.

1.1: Title. *Sheep-farmers:* see 7.14 n. *Tekoa:* a small town southeast of Jerusalem. *Uzziah* reigned over Judah about 783–742 B.C. and *Jeroboam* (II) over Israel about 781–746 B.C. *Earthquake:* see Zech.14.5.
1.2–2.16: Judgment upon Israel and surrounding nations. After an opening threat (v. 2; compare Joel 3.16), the oracles traverse the nations surrounding Israel. On a map, the reader will see how the LORD's judgment circles closer and closer until it strikes Israel (2.6). The episodes alluded to in these oracles are now unknown. **3–5:** *Damascus:* a long-time enemy of Israel. *Gilead:* Israelite territory east of the Jordan. *Hazael* and *Ben-hadad* are royal names. *Aram:* Syria. *Kir:* see 9.7 n. **6–8:** *Gaza,* with *Ashdod, Ashkelon,* and *Ekron,* were Philistine cities. *Edom:* see

and the sceptred ruler of Ashkelon;
I will turn my hand against Ekron,
and the remnant of the Philistines
shall perish.
It is the word of the Lord God.

9 These are the words of the Lord:

For crime after crime of Tyre
I will grant them no reprieve,
because, forgetting the ties of
kinship,
they delivered a whole band of
exiles to Edom.
10 Therefore will I send fire upon the
walls of Tyre,
fire that shall consume its palaces.

11 These are the words of the Lord:

For crime after crime of Edom
I will grant them no reprieve,
because, sword in hand, they hunted
their kinsmen down,
stifling their natural affections.
Their anger raged unceasing,
their fury stormed unchecked.
12 Therefore will I send upon Teman,
fire that shall consume the palaces
of Bozrah.

13 These are the words of the Lord:

For crime after crime of the
Ammonites
I will grant them no reprieve,
because in their greed for land
they invaded the ploughlands of
Gilead.
14 Therefore will I set fire to the walls
of Rabbah,
fire that shall consume its palaces
amid war-cries on the day of
battle,
with a whirlwind on the day of
tempest;
15 then their king shall be carried into
exile,
he and his officers with him.
It is the word of the Lord.

These are the words of the Lord: 2

For crime after crime of Moab
I will grant them no reprieve,
because they burnt the bones of the
king of Edom to ash.[b]
Therefore will I send fire upon Moab, 2
fire that shall consume the palaces
in their towns;
Moab shall perish in uproar,
with war-cries and the sound of
trumpets,
and I will cut off the ruler from 3
among them
and kill all their officers with him.
It is the word of the Lord.

These are the words of the Lord: 4

For crime after crime of Judah
I will grant them no reprieve,
because they have spurned the law
of the Lord
and have not observed his decrees,
and have been led astray by the
false gods
that their fathers followed.
Therefore will I send fire upon 5
Judah,
fire that shall consume the palaces
of Jerusalem.

These are the words of the Lord: 6

For crime after crime of Israel
I will grant them no reprieve,
because they sell the innocent for
silver
and the destitute for a pair of
shoes.
They grind the heads of the poor 7
into the earth
and thrust the humble out of their
way.
Father and son resort to the same
girl,
to the profanation of my holy name.
Men lie down beside every altar 8
on garments seized in pledge,

b to ash: or for lime.

vv. 11–12. 9–10: *Tyre:* a Phoenician seaport. 11–12: Because *Edom* occupied Judah's territory
after the latter was conquered by the Babylonians in 587 B.C., the two became bitter enemies. Edom
lay south of Judah and southeast of the Dead Sea; its main cities were *Teman* and *Bozrah*.
13–15: Living adjacent to *Gilead*, east of the Jordan, the *Ammonites* had sporadic hostilities
with the Hebrews. *Rabbah:* the Ammonite capital. 2.1–3: *Moab* was south of Ammon.
8: *Garments seized in pledge* (as collateral) were to be returned to the owner at night

and in the house of their God[c] they
drink liquor
got by way of fines.

9 Yet it was I who destroyed the
Amorites before them,
though they were tall as cedars,
though they were sturdy as oaks,
I who destroyed their fruit above
and their roots below.

10 It was I who brought you up from
the land of Egypt,
I who led you in the wilderness forty
years,
to take possession of the land of
the Amorites;

11 I raised up prophets from your sons,
Nazirites from your young men.
Was it not so indeed, you men of
Israel?
says the LORD.

12 But you made the Nazirites drink
wine,
and said to the prophets, 'You shall
not prophesy.'

13 Listen, I groan under the burden
of you,
as a wagon creaks under a full load.

14 Flight shall not save the swift,
the strong man shall not rally his
strength.
The warrior shall not save himself,

15 the archer shall not stand his
ground;
the swift of foot shall not be saved,
nor the horseman escape;

16 on that day the bravest of warriors
shall be stripped of his arms and
run away.
This is the very word of the LORD.

Israel's sins and threatened
punishment

3 LISTEN, ISRAELITES, TO THESE WORDS
that the LORD addresses to you, to the
whole nation which he brought up
from Egypt:

For you alone have I cared 2
among all the nations of the world;
therefore will I punish you
for all your iniquities.

Do two men travel together 3
unless they have agreed?

Does a lion roar in the forest 4
if he has no prey?
Does a young lion growl in his den
if he has caught nothing?

Does a bird fall into a trap on the 5
ground
if the striker is not set for it?
Does a trap spring from the ground
and take nothing?

If a trumpet sounds the alarm, 6
are not the people scared?
If disaster falls on a city,
has not the LORD been at work?[d]

For the Lord GOD does nothing 7
without giving to his servants the
prophets knowledge of his plans.

The lion has roared; who is not 8
terrified?
The Lord GOD has spoken; who will
not prophesy?

Stand upon the palaces in Ashdod 9
and upon the palaces of Egypt,
and proclaim aloud:
'Assemble on the hills of Samaria,
look at the tumult seething among
her people
and at the oppression in her midst;
what do they care for honesty 10
who hoard in their palaces the gains
of crime and violence?'
This is the very word of the LORD.

Therefore these are the words of the 11
Lord GOD:

An enemy shall surround[e] the land;
your stronghold shall be thrown
down
and your palaces sacked.

c Or gods.
d If disaster ... work?: or If there is evil in a city, will
not the LORD act?
e shall surround: prob. rdg.; Heb. and round.

(Deut.24.12–13). **9:** The *Amorites* (Gen.15.16) were Canaanites. **11–12:** *Nazirites* vowed to
abstain from wine (see Num.6.2–4).
   3.1–6.14: Israel is pronounced guilty. The three parts of the section begin with the word
"Listen" (3.1; 4.1; 5.1).
   3.1–15: Promised destruction. 2: *Cared:* see Hos.5.3–4 n. **3–8:** A series of causes and effects
in the form of questions. V. 7 is in prose, and is regarded by some as a later addition since
the passage is mostly in meter. **9–11:** The imperatives in v. 9 are plural, perhaps addressed
to the prophets who are directed to *Ashdod* and *Egypt* as witnesses in a lawsuit against *Samaria*,

12 These are the words of the LORD:

As a shepherd rescues out of the
jaws of a lion
two shin bones or the tip of an ear,
so shall the Israelites who live in
Samaria be rescued
like a corner of a couch or a chip
from the leg of a bed.*f*
13 Listen and testify against the family
of Jacob.
This is the very word of the Lord
GOD, the God of Hosts.

14 On the day when I deal with Israel
for all their crimes,
I will most surely deal with the
altars of Bethel:
the horns of the altar shall be
hacked off
and shall fall to the ground.
15 I will break down both winter-house
and summer-house;
houses of ivory shall perish,
and great houses be demolished.
This is the very word of the LORD.

4 Listen to this,
you cows of Bashan who live on the
hill of Samaria,
you who oppress the poor and crush
the destitute,
who say to your lords, 'Bring us
drink':
2 the Lord GOD has sworn by his
holiness
that your time is coming
when men shall carry you away on
their shields*g*
and your children in fish-baskets.
3 You shall each be carried straight
out
through the breaches in the walls
and pitched on a dunghill.*h*
This is the very word of the LORD.

4 Come to Bethel—and rebel!
Come to Gilgal—and rebel the
more!

Bring your sacrifices for the morning,
your tithes within three days.
Burn your thank-offering without 5
leaven;
announce, proclaim your freewill
offerings;
for you love to do what is proper,
you men of Israel!
This is the very word of the Lord
GOD.

It was I who kept teeth idle 6
in all your cities,
who brought famine on all your
settlements;
yet you did not come back to me.
This is the very word of the LORD.

It was I who withheld the showers 7
from you
while there were still three months
to harvest.
I would send rain on one city
and no rain on another;
rain would fall on one field,
and another would be parched for
lack of it.
From this city and that, men would 8
stagger to another
for water to drink, but would not
find enough;
yet you did not come back to me.
This is the very word of the LORD.

I blasted you with black blight and 9
red;
I laid waste*i* your gardens and
vineyards;
the locust devoured your fig-trees
and your olives;
yet you did not come back to me.
This is the very word of the LORD.

I sent plague upon you like the 10
plagues of Egypt;
I killed with the sword

f or a chip . . . bed: *prob. rdg.; Heb. obscure.*
g Or baskets.
h a dunghill: *prob. rdg.; Heb.* the Harmon.
i I laid waste: *prob. rdg.; Heb.* to increase.

Israel's capital. The latter was ringed by *hills.* **12:** This bitterly ironic statement means that the
Israelites who will be rescued from the impending catastrophe will be merely a scrap, hardly
worth the effort. **14:** *Altars* had projecting corners, called *horns,* possessing special power.
15: The *houses* symbolize the corruption of wealth. *Ivory:* luxurious decorations.
 4.1–13: "Prepare to meet your God." 1–3: The *cows of Bashan* are the rich Samaritan women.
Bashan was famous for fine cattle (compare Ezek.39.18; Ps.22.12). **6a:** *Idle:* lit. "clean," never
soiled by food. **6b:** Hag.2.17. **7:** Deut.11.17. **10:** *Plagues:* compare Exod.7.14–11.10; 12.29–32.

your young men and your troops
of horses,
I made your camps stink in your
nostrils;
yet you did not come back to me.
This is the very word of the LORD.

11 I brought destruction amongst you
as God destroyed Sodom and
Gomorrah;
you were like a brand snatched from
the fire;
yet you did not come back to me.
This is the very word of the LORD.

12 Therefore, Israel, this is what I will
do to you;
and, because this is what I will do to
you,
Israel, prepare to meet your God.
13 It is he who forges the thunder and
creates the wind,
who showers abundant rain on the
earth,[j]
who darkens the dawn with thick
clouds
and marches over the heights of the
earth—
his name is the LORD the God of
Hosts.

5 Listen to these words; I raise a dirge
over you, O Israel:

2 She has fallen to rise no more,
the virgin Israel,
prostrate on her own soil, with no
one to lift her up.

3 These are the words of the Lord GOD:

The city that marched out to war a
thousand strong
shall have but a hundred left,
that which marched out a hundred
strong
shall have but ten men of Israel left.

4 These are the words of the LORD to the
people of Israel:

Resort to me, if you would live, not 5
to Bethel;
go not to Gilgal, nor pass on to
Beersheba;
for Gilgal shall be swept away
and Bethel brought to nothing.
If you would live, resort to the 6
LORD,
or he will break out against Joseph
like fire,
fire which will devour Israel with
no one to quench it;
he who made the Pleiades and 8[k]
Orion,
who turned darkness into morning
and darkened day into night,
who summoned the waters of the
sea
and poured them over the earth,
who makes Taurus rise after Capella 9
and Taurus set hard on the rising
of the Vintager[l]—
he who does this, his name is the
LORD.[m]
You that turn justice upside down[n] 7
and bring righteousness to the
ground,
you that hate a man who brings the 10
wrongdoer to court
and loathe him who speaks the
whole truth:
for all this, because you levy taxes 11
on the poor
and extort a tribute of grain from
them,
though you have built houses of
hewn stone,
you shall not live in them,
though you have planted pleasant
vineyards,
you shall not drink wine from
them.
For I know how many your crimes 12
are
and how countless your sins,

*j who showers . . . earth: prob. rdg.; Heb. who tells
his thoughts to mankind.*
k Verse 7 transposed to follow verse 9.
*l who makes . . . Vintager: prob. rdg.; Heb. who smiles
destruction on the strong, and destruction comes on
the fortified city.*
m his . . . LORD: transposed from end of verse 8.
n upside down: prob. rdg.; Heb. poison.

11: Compare Gen.19.24–28. **12:** An oath, in which the threat (*this is what I will do*) is unspecified.
13: The verse is hymnic in style.
    5.1–6.14: Death and exile. A miscellaneous group of poems unified by their pessimistic
outlook. **1–2:** The poetry of v. 2 has in Heb. the rhythm of the *dirge*.
    5.4–15: The possibility of life. The hope that the LORD holds out is hedged with qualifications.
Bethel and *Gilgal* were shrine towns in Benjamin; *Beersheba* a shrine town in Judah. As in

you who persecute the guiltless, hold
    men to ransom
and thrust the destitute out of court.
13 At that time, therefore, a prudent
    man will stay quiet,
    for it will be an evil time.

14 Seek good and not evil,
    that you may live,
that the LORD the God of Hosts may
    be firmly on your side,
    as you say he is.
15 Hate evil and love good;
    enthrone justice in the courts;
    it may be that the LORD the God
    of Hosts
will be gracious to the survivors of
    Joseph.

16 Therefore these are the words of the
LORD the God of Hosts:

    There shall be wailing in every
        street,
    and in all open places cries of woe.
    The farmer shall be called to
        mourning,
    and those skilled in the dirge to*o*
        wailing;
17 there shall be lamentation in every
        vineyard;
    for I will pass through the midst of
        you,
        says the LORD.

18 Fools who long for the day of the
        LORD,
    what will the day of the LORD
        mean to you?
    It will be darkness, not light.
19 It will be as when a man runs from
        a lion,
        and a bear meets him,
    or turns into a house and leans his
        hand on the wall,
        and a snake bites him.

The day of the LORD is indeed   20
    darkness, not light,
    a day of gloom with no dawn.

I hate, I spurn your pilgrim-feasts;   21
    I will not delight in your sacred
        ceremonies.
When you present your sacrifices   22
    and offerings
    I will not accept them,
    nor look on the buffaloes of your
        shared-offerings.
Spare me the sound of your songs;   23
    I cannot endure the music of your
        lutes.
Let justice roll on like a river   24
    and righteousness like an ever-
        flowing stream.
Did you bring me sacrifices and   25
    gifts,
you people of Israel, those forty
    years in the wilderness?
    No! but now you shall take up   26
        the shrine of your idol king
    and the pedestals of your images,*p*
    which you have made for yourselves,
    and I will drive you into exile   27
        beyond Damascus.

So says the LORD; the God of Hosts is
his name.

    Shame on you who live at ease in   **6**
        Zion,
    and you, untroubled on the hill of
        Samaria,
    men of mark in the first of nations,
    you to whom the people of Israel
        resort!
Go, look at Calneh,   2
travel on to Hamath the great,
    then go down to Gath of the
        Philistines—
are you better than these kingdoms?

o Prob. rdg.; Heb. places to before those skilled.
p Prob. rdg.; Heb. adds the star of your gods.

---

vv. 21–27, Amos rejects Israel's ritual worship. **14–15:** The word *seek* (*resort*, vv. 5–6) reflects
the ritual practice; the prophet insists that such seeking be fully genuine and not merely formal.
Amos goes beyond mere adherence to tradition, demanding instead a new attitude: *Hate evil
and love good.*
    5.16–27: Rejection of the cult. 18: *The day of the LORD:* see Joel 1.14–15 n. **21–27:** The
prophet rejects the entire system of ritual, denying (vv. 25–26) that it was truly part of Israel's
legacy from the formative Wilderness period. *Justice* and *righteousness* should replace the
unacceptable ritualism.
    6.1–7: "Are you better?" *Calneh*, perhaps the same as Calno (Isa.10.9) and Kanneh
(Ezek.27.23), was a town in northern Syria. *Hamath*, an important Syrian center, was captured
by the Assyrians in the 720s. *Gath*, one of the five Philistine cities, was destroyed many times.

Or is your*q* territory greater than
theirs*r*?

3 You who thrust the evil day aside
and make haste to establish
violence.*s*

4 You who loll on beds inlaid with
ivory
and sprawl over your couches,
feasting on lambs from the flock
and fatted calves,

5 you who pluck the strings of the
lute
and invent musical instruments like
David,

6 you who drink wine by the
bowlful
and lard yourselves with the
richest of oils,
but are not grieved at the ruin of
Joseph—

7 now, therefore,
you shall head the column of exiles;
that will be the end of sprawling
and revelry.

8 The Lord GOD has sworn by himself:

I loathe the arrogance of Jacob,
I loathe his palaces;
city and all in it I will abandon to
their fate.

9 If ten men are left in one house,
they shall die,

10 and a man's uncle and the embalmer
shall take him up
to carry his body out of the house
for burial,
and they shall call to someone in a
corner of the house,
'Any more there?', and he shall
answer, 'No.'
Then he will add, 'Hush!'—
for the name of the LORD must not
be mentioned.

11 For the LORD will command,
and at the shock the great house
will be rubble
and the cottage matchwood.

Can horses gallop over rocks? 12
Can the sea be ploughed with oxen?
Yet you have turned into venom
the process of law
and justice itself into poison,
you who are jubilant over a 13
nothing*t* and boast,
'Have we not won power*t* by our
own strength?'
O Israel, I am raising a nation 14
against you,
and they shall harry your land
from Lebo-hamath to the gorge of
the Arabah.
This is the very word of the LORD
the God of Hosts.

Visions foretelling doom upon Israel

THIS WAS WHAT THE LORD GOD SHOWED 7
me: a swarm of locusts hatched out
when the late corn, which comes after
the king's early crop, was beginning to
sprout. As they were devouring the 2
last of the herbage in the land, I said,
'O Lord GOD, forgive; what will Jacob
be after this? He is so small.' Then the 3
LORD relented and said, 'This shall not
happen.'
This was what the Lord GOD showed 4
me: the Lord GOD was summoning a
flame of fire*u* to devour the great abyss,
and to devour all creation. I said, 'O 5
Lord GOD, I pray thee, cease; what
will Jacob be after this? He is so
small.' The LORD relented and said, 6
'This also shall not happen.'
This was what the LORD showed me: 7
there was a man standing by a wall*v*
with a plumb-line in his hand. The 8
LORD said to me, 'What do you see,
Amos?' 'A plumb-line', I answered,
and the Lord said, 'I am setting a

q Prob. rdg.; Heb. their.
r Prob. rdg.; Heb. yours.
s You . . . violence: or You who invoke the day of
wrongdoing and bring near the sabbath of violence.
t a nothing and power: Heb. Lo-debar and Karnaim,
making a word-play on the two place-names.
u a flame of fire: prob. rdg.; Heb. to contend with fire.
v Prob. rdg.; Heb. adds of a plumb-line.

6.8–14: Punishment of Israel. The reduction of Israel to *rubble* (v. 11) is to be accompanied
by the demoralization of the people. **13:** *Nothing* and *power* represent city names; see Tfn. *t*.
14: *Lebo-hamath* was in the north, the *Arabah* in the south. The enemy overruns the land from
one end to the other.
7.1–9.8: Visions foretelling doom upon Israel. A series of symbolic but accurate visions is interspersed with a narrative and other oracles. **1–3:** A *locust* plague destroys the people's grain.
The king's early crop has already been harvested. **4–6:** *Abyss:* the waters beneath the earth;
see Ps.77.16–20. **7–9:** A *plumb-line* was used to make sure a wall was vertical and hence stable.

plumb-line to the heart of my people Israel; never again will I pass them by. The hill-shrines of Isaac shall be 9 desolated and the sanctuaries of Israel laid waste; I will rise, sword in hand, against the house of Jeroboam.'

10 Amaziah, the priest of Bethel, reported to Jeroboam king of Israel: 'Amos is conspiring against you in Israel; the country cannot tolerate what 11 he is saying. He says, "Jeroboam shall die by the sword, and Israel shall be deported far from their native land." '

12 To Amos himself Amaziah said, 'Be off, you seer! Off with you to Judah! You can earn your living and do your 13 prophesying there. But never prophesy again at Bethel, for this is the king's 14 sanctuary, a royal palace.' 'I am*w* no prophet,' Amos replied to Amaziah, 'nor am I a prophet's son; I am*w* a herdsman and a dresser of sycomore-15 figs. But the LORD took me as I followed the flock and said to me, "Go 16 and prophesy to my people Israel." So now listen to the word of the LORD. You tell me I am not to prophesy against Israel or go drivelling on 17 against the people of Isaac. Now these are the words of the LORD: Your wife shall become a city strumpet*x* and your sons and daughters shall fall by the sword. Your land shall be divided up with a measuring-line, you yourself shall die in a heathen country, and Israel shall be deported far from their native land and go into exile.'

8 This was what the Lord GOD showed me: there was a basket of summer 2 fruit, and he said, 'What are you looking at, Amos?' I answered, 'A basket of ripe summer*y* fruit.' Then the LORD said to me, 'The time is ripe*y* for my people Israel. Never again will 3 I pass them by. In that day, says the Lord GOD, the singing women in the palace shall howl, "So many dead men, flung out everywhere! Silence!" '

4 Listen to this, you who grind the destitute and plunder*z* the humble, 5 you who say, 'When will the new moon be over so that we may sell corn? When will the sabbath be past so that we may open our wheat again, giving short measure in the bushel and taking overweight in the silver, tilting the 6 scales fraudulently, and selling the dust of the wheat; that we may buy the poor for silver and the destitute 7 for a pair of shoes?' The LORD has sworn by the pride of Jacob: I will never forget any of their doings.

Shall not the earth shake for this? 8
Shall not all who live on it grieve?
All earth shall surge and seethe like the Nile
and subside like the river of Egypt.

On that day, says the Lord GOD, 9
I will make the sun go down at noon
and darken the earth in broad daylight.
I will turn your pilgrim-feasts into 10 mourning
and all your songs into lamentation.
I will make you all put sackcloth round your waists
and have all your heads shaved.
I will make it like mourning for an only son
and the end of it a bitter day.

The time is coming, says the Lord 11 GOD,
when I will send famine on the land,
not hunger for bread or thirst for water,

w Or was.
x become . . . strumpet: *or* be carried off as a prostitute in a raid.
y ripe summer *and* ripe: *a play on the Heb.* qais (summer) *and* qes (end).
z and plunder: *prob. rdg.; Heb.* to destroy.

7.10–17: Amos' confrontation with Amaziah. *Bethel* was the main royal shrine in Israel. The narrative is about Amos, not by him; its origin is obscure. The charge against Amos was sedition. **14:** Amos' reply, *I am no prophet . . . nor am I a prophet's son*, asserts that he was not the usual "professional" prophet (see 1 Sam.10.5), but rather someone specially called to prophesy. He terms himself *a herdsman and a dresser of sycomore-figs* (which had to be pricked to be edible); see 1.1, "sheep-farmer."
8.1–7: Summer fruit. This vision turns on a Heb. word-play (see Tfn. *y*). **4–7:** The mechanical observance of ritual, accompanied by derelictions from morality.
8.8–14: Cosmic catastrophe. 8: The allusion is to the annual flood of the *Nile*. **10:** *Pilgrim-feasts:* the festivals commanded in Exod.23.14–17. *Sackcloth* and *shaved heads* were signs of *mourning.* **11:** *Hunger for hearing the word:* lack of a prophet who speaks for the LORD.

but for hearing the word of the
  LORD.
12 Men shall stagger from north to
  south,*a*
  they shall range from east to west,
  seeking the word of the LORD,
  but they shall not find it.
13 On that day fair maidens and young
  men
  shall faint from thirst;
14 all who take their oath by Ashimah,
  goddess of Samaria,
  all who swear, 'By the life of your
  god, O Dan',
  and, 'By the sacred way to
  Beersheba',
  shall fall to rise no more.

9 I saw the LORD standing by the altar,
and he said:

  Strike the capitals so that the whole
  porch is shaken;
  I will smash them all into pieces*b*
  and I will kill them to the last man*c*
  with the sword.
  No fugitive shall escape,
  no survivor find safety;
2   if they dig down to Sheol,
  thence shall my hand take them;
  if they climb up to heaven,
  thence will I bring them down.
3   If they hide on the top of Carmel,
  there will I search out and take
  them;
  if they conceal themselves from me
  in the depths of the sea,
  there will I bid the sea-serpent bite
  them.
4 If they are herded into captivity by
  their enemies,
  there will I bid the sword slay them,
  and I will fix my eye on them
  for evil and not for good.

5   The Lord the GOD of Hosts,
  at whose touch the earth heaves,
  and all who dwell on it wither,*d*

it surges like the Nile,
  and subsides like the river of
  Egypt,
who builds his stair up to the   6
  heavens
and arches his ceiling over the
  earth,
who summons the waters of the
  sea
and pours them over the land—
  his name is the LORD.

Are not you Israelites like Cushites   7
  to me?
  says the LORD.
Did I not bring Israel up from
  Egypt,
the Philistines from Caphtor, the
  Aramaeans from Kir?
Behold, I, the Lord GOD,   8
have my eyes on this sinful kingdom,
and I will wipe it off the face of the
  earth.

A remnant spared and restored

Yet I will not wipe out the family of
  Jacob root and branch,
  says the LORD.
No; I will give my orders,   9
I will shake Israel to and fro through
  all the nations
as a sieve is shaken to and fro
and not one pebble falls to the
  ground.
They shall die by the sword, all the   10
  sinners of my people,
who say, 'Thou wilt not let disaster
  come near us
  or overtake us.'
On that day I will restore   11
  David's fallen house;
I will repair its gaping walls and
  restore its ruins;

a south: *prob. rdg.; Heb.* west.
b I will . . . pieces: *prob. rdg.; Heb.* I will hack them
on the heads of them all.
c them to the last man: *or* their children.
d *Or* mourn.

14: *Ashimah:* a fertility goddess. Since *Dan* was in the north and *Beersheba* in the south, when used together they were a frequent figure for all the land.
  9.1–8a: Destruction of the "chosen people." 2: *Sheol:* the place of the dead; compare Ps.139.8. **3:** *Carmel:* the famous mountain above modern Haifa. **7:** Since the LORD has dealt with other nations as he has with Israel, Israel is not "chosen." *Cushites:* Ethiopians. *Caphtor:* Crete. *Aramaeans:* compare 1.3–5. *Kir* was possibly in Mesopotamia; it appears both as the place of origin of the Aramaeans as here, and as the place to which they were exiled (1.5; 2 Kgs.16.9).
  9.8b–15: The future restoration of Israel. Many scholars believe that this glowing passage was added to give a positive ending. **11:** *Fallen* suggests the period of the Babylonian conquest

I will rebuild it as it was long ago,
12 that they may possess what is left of
    Edom
and all the nations who were once
    named mine.

This is the very word of the LORD, who
    will do this.

13 A time is coming, says the LORD,
    when the ploughman shall follow
        hard on the vintager,*e*
and he who treads the grapes after
    him who sows the seed.
The mountains shall run with fresh
    wine,

and every hill shall wave with corn.
I will restore the fortunes of my   11
    people Israel;
they shall rebuild deserted cities and
    live in them,
they shall plant vineyards and drink
    their wine,
make gardens and eat the fruit.
Once more I will plant them on   15
    their own soil,
and they shall never again be
    uprooted
from the soil I have given them.
It is the word of the LORD your
    God.

e Or reaper.

(587 B.C.) after which David's dynasty came to an end. **12:** On the enmity of Judah and *Edom*, see 1.11–12 n. **13:** Fertility would be so great that the labors of the agricultural seasons would press on each other.

OBADIAH

Nothing is known about this Obadiah. The similarities between vv. 1–9 and Jer. 49. 7–22 suggest a common time of origin for both passages, and possibly a common prophetic circle.

The book consists of short poems of diverse origin, unified by the prediction that Israel's and Edom's national situations will be reversed. In the tradition (Gen.25.30), Edom (Esau) was the twin brother of Israel (Jacob); according to Obadiah, Edom has not been his brother's keeper (v. 10), and now the LORD will punish Edom.

This latter theme suggests that the book originated shortly after the Babylonian sack of Jerusalem in 587 B.C., in which the Edomites apparently participated.

Edom's pride and downfall

1ᵃ The vision of Obadiah: what the
Lord GOD has said concerning Edom.

When a herald was sent out among
    the nations, crying,
'Rouse yourselves;
let us rouse ourselves to battle
    against Edom',
I heard this message from the LORD:

2 Look, I make you the least of all
    nations,
    an object of contempt.
3 Your proud, insolent heart has led
    you astray;
you who haunt the crannies
    among the rocks,
    making your home on the
    heights,
you say to yourself, 'Who can bring
    me to the ground?'
4 Though you soar as high as a
    vulture
and your nest is set among the stars,
    thence I will bring you down.
    This is the very word of the LORD.

5ᵇ If thieves or robbers come to you
    by night,
    though your loss be heavy,
they will steal only what they want;
if vintagers come to you,
    will they not leave gleanings?
6 But see how Esau's treasure is
    ransacked,

his secret wealth hunted out!
All your former allies march you to 7
    the frontier,
your confederates mislead you and
    bring you low,
your own kith and kin lay a snare
    for your feet,
a snare that works blindly,
    without wisdom.
And on that very day 8
I will destroy all the sages of Edom
and leave no wisdom on the
    mount of Esau.
This is the very word of the LORD.
Then shall your warriors, O 9
    Teman, be so enfeebled,
that every man shall be cut down
    on the mount of Esau.
For the murderous violence done 10
    to your brother Jacob
you shall be covered with shame and
    cut off for ever.
On the day when you stood aloof, 11
on the day when strangers carried
    off his wealth,
when foreigners trooped in by his
    gates
and parcelled out Jerusalem by lot,
you yourselves were of one mind
    with them.
Do not gloat over your brother on 12
    the day of his misfortune,
nor rejoice over Judah on his day
    of ruin;
do not boast on the day of distress,

a Verses 1–4: cp. Jer. 49. 14–16.
b Verses 5 and 6: cp. Jer. 49. 9, 10.

1: Title. Obadiah means "the LORD's servant."
1–4: Edom's pride and downfall. The poem describes the downfall by opposites: *contempt* and *proud, heights* and *the ground*. Edom's capital, Teman (v. 9), was in rocky hills.
5–7: Military conquest. 5: *Gleanings:* Harvesters were to leave fruit for the poor (Deut.24.19–21). 6: *Esau* was Edom's progenitor (Gen.36.1) as *Jacob* (Obad.10) was Israel's.
8–14: Edom's treachery. 8: Edom had a reputation for *wisdom;* the sages of 1 Kgs.4.31 are regarded by some as Edomites. 9: *Teman:* the main Edomite city. 12–14: On Edom's crimes at the time of the Babylonian sack of Jerusalem, see Ezek.35.1–36.7.

13   nor enter my people's gates on the
        day of his downfall,
     Do not gloat over his fall on the day
        of his downfall
     nor seize his treasure on the day of
        his downfall.
14   Do not wait at the cross-roads to
        cut off his fugitives
     nor betray the survivors on the day
        of distress.

15   For soon the day of the LORD will
        come on all the nations:
     you shall be treated as you have
        treated others,
     and your deeds will recoil on your
        own head.
16   The draught that you have drunk
        on my holy mountain
     all the nations shall drink
        continually;
     they shall drink and gulp down
     and shall be as though they had
        never been;
17   but on Mount Zion there shall be
        those that escape,
     and it shall be holy,
     and Jacob shall dispossess those
        that dispossessed them.

Then shall the house of Jacob be   18
   fire,
the house of Joseph flame,
and the house of Esua shall be
   chaff;
they shall blaze through it and
   consume it,
and the house of Esau shall have
   no survivor.
The LORD has spoken.
Then they shall possess the Negeb,   19
   the mount of Esau,
   and the Shephelah of the
      Philistines;
they shall possess the country-side
   of Ephraim and Samaria,
and Benjamin shall possess Gilead.
Exiles of Israel[c] shall possess[d] Canaan 20
   as far as Zarephath,
exiles of Jerusalem[e] shall possess the
   cities of the Negeb.
Those who find safety on Mount   21
   Zion shall go up
to hold sway over the mount of
   Esau,
and dominion shall belong to the
   LORD.

c *Prob. rdg.; Heb. adds* this army.
d shall possess: *prob. rdg.; Heb.* which.
e *Prob. rdg.; Heb. adds* who are in Sepharad.

15–21: The punishment. 15: *The day of the* LORD: the time of the LORD's judgment on men
and nations. **16:** *Draught:* a symbol of divine wrath (see Jer.25.15–28; Ps.75.8). **19–21:** The
areas mentioned are both in and around Israel. The *Negeb* was the southern wilderness,
Shephelah the Judean hills just east of the coastal plain. *Gilead* was east of the Jordan.
Zarephath was on the Phoenician coast. Sepharad (Tfn. *e*), in Asia Minor, is a later Heb. name
for Spain.

JONAH

Unlike the other prophetic books, Jonah takes the form of a story. The reader should begin by enjoying it as he would a short story, without concern about its historical accuracy; if, moreover, he views the story as in a satiric vein, he may enjoy it all the more.

A prophet Jonah is mentioned in 2 Kgs.14.25, yet with only the sketchiest information. We cannot be sure whether this story is or is not about that Jonah.

We cannot be certain of the date of composition of this book. The author's exaggerations (the size of Nineveh, 3.3; its response to Jonah's threat, 3.5–9) suggest that he wrote after Nineveh, destroyed in 612, was only a memory. This would mean a date at least later than 600 B.C. Since the book (like Ruth) opposes the exclusiveness found in Ezra and Nehemiah, it may have originated about 450–400 B.C.

The story has its own pungency. Traditionally, Jonah is viewed as a hero. Perhaps, however, as some modern scholars hold, the author had something other than a hero in mind, for his Jonah says the right things (1.9; 2.2–9; 4.2) but does not follow them. Jonah cannot conceive that God could care for anyone, man or beast, except an Israelite; he becomes quite upset when God forgives Nineveh. The book's message of God's universal concern is borne along by the irony of a petulant prophet who is disappointed by the success of his preaching.

Jonah's mission to Nineveh

1 THE WORD OF THE LORD CAME TO
2 Jonah son of Amittai: 'Go to the great city of Nineveh, go now and
3 denounce it, for its wickedness stares me in the face.' But Jonah set out for Tarshish to escape from the LORD. He went down to Joppa, where he found a ship bound for Tarshish. He paid his fare and went on board, meaning to travel by it to Tarshish out of reach of
4 the LORD. But the LORD let loose a hurricane, and the sea ran so high in the storm that the ship threatened to
5 break up. The sailors were afraid, and each cried out to his god for help. Then they threw things overboard to lighten the ship. Jonah had gone down into a corner of the ship and was lying sound
6 asleep when the captain came upon him. 'What, sound asleep?' he said. 'Get up, and call on your god; perhaps he will spare us a thought and we shall not perish.'
7 At last the sailors said to each other, 'Come and let us cast lots to find out who is to blame for this bad luck.' So they cast lots, and the lot fell on Jonah.
8 'Now then,' they said to him, 'what is your business? Where do you come from? What is your country? Of what nation are you?' 'I am a Hebrew,' he 9 answered, 'and I worship the LORD the God of heaven, who made both sea and land.' At this the sailors were even 10 more afraid. 'What can you have done wrong?' they asked. They already knew that he was trying to escape from the LORD, for he had told them so. 'What 11 shall we do with you', they asked, 'to make the sea go down?' For the storm grew worse and worse. 'Take me and 12 throw me overboard,' he said, 'and the sea will go down. I know it is my fault that this great storm has struck you.' The crew rowed hard to put back to 13 land but in vain, for the sea ran higher and higher. At last they called on the 14 LORD and said, 'O LORD, do not let us perish at the price of this man's life; do not charge us with the death of an innocent man. All this, O LORD, is thy set purpose.' Then they took Jonah 15 and threw him overboard, and the sea stopped raging. So the crew were filled 16 with the fear of the LORD and offered sacrifice and made vows to him. But 17 the LORD ordained that a great fish should swallow Jonah, and for three

---

1.1–16: Jonah's flight by ship. 2: Nineveh: the capital of Assyria, far to the east. 3: Tarshish: though often identified with Spain, it was probably a legendary place far to the west of Palestine. Jonah thus travels in the opposite direction from Nineveh. 9: Worship: in Heb., "fear." Jonah seems not to see the disparity between his adherence to the LORD who made both sea and land, and his attempt to escape by sea (vv. 3,10). 16: The sailors' fear is religiously more productive than Jonah's (see v. 9 n.).

1.17–2.10: In the belly of the fish. Not a whale but simply a great fish, it, unlike the prophet,

days and three nights he remained in
its belly.

2 Jonah prayed to the LORD his God
from the belly of the fish:

2 I called to the LORD in my distress,
and he answered me;
out of the belly of Sheol I cried
for help,
and thou hast heard my cry.

3 Thou didst cast me into the depths,
far out at sea,
and the flood closed round me;
all thy waves, all thy billows, passed
over me.

4 I thought I was banished from thy
sight
and should never see thy holy temple
again.

5 The water about me rose up to my
neck;
the ocean was closing over me.
Weeds twined about my head

6 in the troughs of the mountains;
I was sinking into a world
whose bars would hold me fast
for ever.
But thou didst bring me up alive
from the pit, O LORD my God.

7 As my senses failed me I remembered
the LORD,
and my prayer reached thee in thy
holy temple.

8 Men who worship false gods may
abandon their loyalty,

9 but I will offer thee sacrifice with
words of praise;
I will pay my vows; victory is the
LORD's.

10 Then the LORD spoke to the fish and
it spewed Jonah out on to the dry land.

The word of the LORD came to Jonah **3**
a second time: 'Go to the great city of 2
Nineveh, go now and denounce it in
the words I give you.' Jonah obeyed at 3–4
once and went to Nineveh. He began
by going a day's journey into the city,
a vast city, three days' journey across,
and then proclaimed: 'In forty days
Nineveh shall be overthrown!' The 5
people of Nineveh believed God's
word. They ordered a public fast and
put on sackcloth, high and low alike.
When the news reached the king of 6
Nineveh he rose from his throne,
stripped off his robes of state, put on
sackcloth and sat in ashes. Then he 7
had a proclamation made in Nineveh:
'This is a decree of the king and his
nobles. No man or beast, herd or flock,
is to taste food, to graze or to drink
water. They are to clothe themselves in 8
sackcloth and call on God with all
their might. Let every man abandon his
wicked ways and his habitual violence.
It may be that God will repent and turn 9
away from his anger: and so we shall
not perish.' God saw what they did, 10
and how they abandoned their wicked
ways, and he repented and did not
bring upon them the disaster he had
threatened.

Jonah was greatly displeased and **4**
angry, and he prayed to the LORD: 2
'This, O LORD, is what I feared when
I was in my own country, and to
forestall it I tried to escape to Tarshish;
I knew that thou art "a god gracious
and compassionate, long-suffering and
ever constant, and always willing to
repent of the disaster".*a* And now, 3
LORD, take my life: I should be better

a a god . . . disaster: cp. Exod. 34. 6.

---

does whatever God commands. **2.1–9:** Jonah's prayer, in form very like some of the psalms,
is felt by many scholars to have been added. The images of drowning, however, are appropriate
to the story, and the author himself may have used a psalm he already knew. *Sheol* (v. 2) and
the pit (v. 6) signify the place of the dead. In terms of the satire, v. 8 is deeply ironic, as is
perhaps *victory* (v. 9).
  3.1–10: The conversion of Nineveh. 1–2: This *second time*, Jonah is not told why he is to
denounce Nineveh, as he was before (1.2). **4–5:** Nineveh was a large city by ancient standards,
but not so *vast* as the storyteller measures. *Three days' journey* would be about fifty miles, a
gross exaggeration of the size of Nineveh but consistent with the author's satire. When Jonah
has gone only one-third of the way into the city, his work is finished! **10:** The sincerity of
Nineveh's response (like that of the sailors', ch. 1) prompts God on his own account to *repent*,
the word meaning to regret and to change a previous decision.
  4.1–11: Jonah's conversation with God. 1: Jonah is *angry* over his success! **2:** Jonah quotes a
conventional description of God's character, found in several other places (Exod.34.6;
Num.14.18; Pss.103.8; 145.8; Joel 2.13), but he clearly wishes God were not so. **3:** Compare
this death wish with those of Moses (Num.11.15), of Elijah (1 Kgs.19.4), and of Job (Job ch. 3).

4 dead than alive.' 'Are you so angry?'
5 said the LORD, Jonah went out and sat down on the east of the city. There he made himself a shelter and sat in its shade, waiting to see what would
6 happen in the city. Then the LORD God ordained that a climbing gourd[b] should grow up over his head to throw its shade over him and relieve his distress, and Jonah was grateful for the gourd.
7 But at dawn the next day God ordained that a worm should attack the gourd,
8 and it withered; and at sunrise God ordained that a scorching wind should blow up from the east. The sun beat down on Jonah's head till he grew

faint. Then he prayed for death and said, 'I should be better dead than alive.' At this God said to Jonah, 'Are you so angry over the gourd?' 'Yes,' he answered, 'mortally angry.' The 10 LORD said, 'You are sorry for the gourd, though you did not have the trouble of growing it, a plant which came up in a night and withered in a night. And should not I be sorry for 11 the great city of Nineveh, with its hundred and twenty thousand who cannot tell their right hand from their left, and cattle without number?'

b a climbing gourd: *or* a castor-oil plant.

6: As he had before ordained the fish (1.17), God now *ordained* a plant to shelter Jonah. *Gourd:* exactly what kind of plant is meant is unknown. The Heb. for *grateful* is lit. "very happy." 10: The basic idea of being *sorry* is that the tears flow in compassionate grief. 11: Since the *cattle* had previously repented (3.7–8), God is *sorry* for them too.

MICAH

If the prophets have a single message, it may be summed up thus: God can be counted on to care. When his people have succumbed to corruption or to overweening pride, his care shows itself in punishment; when they are in despair or have been overrun by an arrogant enemy, his care shows itself in encouraging and restoring them. So especially with Micah.

The unity of the book lies in presenting a God who is concerned with men and their life. That unity transcends a diversity of times and authors found in the book. Chapters 1–3 seem to come from the eighth century B.C., with portions from before 721, when the Assyrians demolished Israel and her capital, Samaria (see 1.5–6). Chapters 4–7 (except, perhaps, 5.5–6) seem to stem from the Babylonian Exile in the sixth century, or possibly even later.

The specific historical settings were helpful to the book's ancient readers, but not essential to them, for they were seeking its message of judgment and hope. These two elements appear alternately in the book. Judgment predominates in chs. 1–3, hope in chs. 4–5, judgment again in 6.1–7.6, and hope again in 7.7–20.

---

1 THIS IS THE WORD OF THE LORD which came to Micah of Moresheth during the reigns of Jotham, Ahaz, and Hezekiah, kings of Judah; which he received in visions concerning Samaria and Jerusalem.

The rulers of Israel and Judah denounced

2 Listen, you peoples, all together;
    attend, O earth and all who are in it,
  that the Lord GOD, the Lord from
    his holy temple,
    may bear witness against you.
3 For look, the LORD is leaving his
    dwelling-place;
  down he comes and walks on the
    heights of the earth.
4 Beneath him mountains dissolve
    like wax before the fire,
  valleys are torn open,
  as when torrents pour down the
    hill-side—
5 and all for the crime of Jacob and
    the sin of Israel.
  What is the crime of Jacob? Is it not
    Samaria?

What is the hill-shrine of Judah? Is
    it not Jerusalem?
  So I will make Samaria   6
  a heap of ruins in open country,
    a place for planting vines;
  I will pour her stones down into
    the valley
  and lay her foundations bare.
  All her carved figures shall be   7
    shattered,
  her images burnt one and all;
  I will make a waste heap of all her
    idols.
    She amassed them out of fees for
      harlotry,
    and a harlot's fee shall they
      become once more.
  Therefore I must howl and wail,   8
    go naked and distraught;
  I must howl like a wolf, mourn like
    a desert-owl.
    Her wound cannot be healed;   9
    for the stroke has bitten deep
      into Judah,
    it has fallen on the gate of my
      people,
    upon Jerusalem itself.
  Will you not weep your fill, weep   10
    your eyes out in Gath?

1.1: Title. *Micah* means "Who is like?" and is probably a contraction of Micaiah, "Who is like the LORD?" *Moresheth:* a town in Judah, about twenty-three miles southwest of Jerusalem. The names of the kings date the man Micah between about 740 and 700 B.C. *Samaria:* the capital of Israel, conquered by Assyria in 721 B.C.

1.2–3.12: The rulers of Israel and Judah denounced. Several of the poems accuse leaders, others deal with the people.

1.2–9: The crimes of Israel and Judah. The LORD himself *walks on the earth* to destroy *Samaria* and *Jerusalem.* 5: That *Samaria* is *the crime of Jacob* appears in v. 7. *Hill-shrine:* an open-air fertility shrine; the prophet implies that Jerusalem is a center of idolatrous worship. 6: When a city was razed by an enemy, the site was leveled by pushing ruined *stones* into the valley surrounding it. 8: The prophet probably acted out this verse; see Jer.27.2; 28.10–11.

1.10–16: An invasion of Judah. The names of the towns seem to depict an invader's advance from the southwest toward Jerusalem. 10: *Gath:* a Philistine town. *Beth-aphrah:* northwest of

In Beth-aphrah sprinkle yourselves
        with dust;
11 take the road, you that dwell in
        Shaphir;
have not the people of Zaanan gone
        out in shame from their city?
    Beth-ezel is a place of
        lamentation,
    she can lend you support no longer.
12 The people of Maroth are greatly
        alarmed,
    for disaster has come down from
        the LORD
        to the very gate of Jerusalem.
13 Harness the steeds to the chariot, O
        people of Lachish,
    for you first led the daughter of Zion
        into sin;
    to you must the crimes of Israel be
        traced.
14 Let Moresheth-gath be given her
        dismissal.
    Beth-achzib has*a* disappointed*b* the
        kings of Israel.
15 And you too, O people of Mareshah,
        I will send others to take your
        place;
    and the glory of Israel shall hide in
        the cave of Adullam.
16 Shave the hair from your head in
        mourning
    for the children of your delight;
    make yourself bald as a vulture,
    for they have left you and gone
        into exile.

2 Shame on those who lie in bed
        planning evil and wicked deeds
    and rise at daybreak to do them,
        knowing that they have the power!
2   They covet land and take it by
        force;
    if they want a house they seize it;

they rob a man of his home
    and steal every man's inheritance.

Therefore these are the words of the 3
    LORD:

Listen, for this whole brood I am
    planning disaster,
whose yoke you cannot shake from
    your necks
and walk upright; it shall be your
    hour of disaster.

    On that day   4
    they shall take up a poem about
        you
    and raise a lament thrice told,
    saying, 'We are utterly despoiled:
    the land of the LORD's*c* people
        changes hands.
    How shall a man have power*d*
    to restore our fields, now parcelled
        out*e*?'

Therefore there shall be no one to   5
    assign to you
any portion by lot in the LORD's
    assembly.

How they rant! They may say, 'Do   6
    not rant';
but this ranting is all their own,
these insults are their*f* own
    invention.

Can one ask, O house of Jacob,   7
    'Is the LORD's patience truly at an
    end?
    Are these his deeds?

a Beth-achzib has: *prob. rdg.; Heb.* The houses of
  Achzib have.
b *Heb.* achzab.
c the LORD's: *prob. rdg.; Heb.* my.
d have power: *prob. rdg.; Heb.* remove from me.
e now parcelled out: *prob. rdg.; Heb.* he will parcel out.
f *Prob. rdg.; Heb.* his.

Hebron; *dust* is a pun on its name, "house of dust." **11:** *Shaphir:* probably near Beth-aphrah.
Zaanan: perhaps near Lachish (v. 13); *gone out* is a pun on the name. *Beth-ezel:* to the south
of Beth-aphrah. **12:** *Maroth:* perhaps northeast of Beth-aphrah. **13:** *Lachish:* an important
fortress about thirty miles from Jerusalem; *to the chariot* may be a pun on the name. The
historical allusion is obscure. **14:** *Moresheth-gath:* the same as Moresheth, v. 1. *Beth-achzib:*
east of Moresheth; *disappointed* puns on the name. **15:** *Mareshah:* northeast of Lachish; *take
your place,* puns on the name. *Adullam:* east of Achzib; its *cave* was once David's headquarters
(2 Sam.23.13). **16:** To *shave the hair* was a sign of deep mourning.
    2.1–5: Punishment for evil schemes. Those who *plan* wickedness (v. 1) will find that the LORD
is *planning* for them (v. 3). *Disaster:* the same Heb. word as *wicked,* v. 1. **5:** A Hebrew acquired
valid possession of a *portion* of land by *lot:* see Num.26.55; Josh.14.2.
    2.6–11: False prophecy. 6: *Rant:* a sarcastic word for prophecy (in Amos 7.16 the Heb.
word which is here rendered "rant," is there translated "go drivelling on"). **7:** The false prophets
cannot understand how any *words* said in the name of the LORD would not be acceptable.
Vv. 8–10 show why.

Does not good come of the LORD's
words?
He is the upright man's best
friend.'

8 But you are no*g* people for me,
rising up as my enemy to my*h* face,
to strip the cloak from him that was
safe*i*
and take away the confidence of
returning warriors,
9 to drive the women of my people
from their pleasant homes
and rob the children of my glory
for ever.
10 Up and be gone; this is no resting-
place for you,
you that to defile yourselves would
commit any mischief,
mischief however cruel.

11 If anyone had gone about in a spirit
of falsehood and lies, saying, 'I will
rant to you of wine and strong drink',
his ranting would be what this people
like.

12 I will assemble you, the whole house
of Jacob;
I will gather together those that are
left in Israel.
I will herd them like sheep in a fold,
like a grazing flock which stampedes
at the sight of a man.
13 So their leader breaks out before
them,
and they all break through the gate
and escape,
and their king goes before them,
and the LORD leads the way.

3 And I said:

Listen, you leaders of Jacob, rulers
of Israel,
should you not know what is right?
2 You hate good and love evil,
you flay men alive and tear the very
flesh from their bones;
3 you devour the flesh of my people,
strip off their skin,
splinter their bones;

you shred them like flesh into a pot,
like meat into a cauldron,

Then they will call to the LORD, and   4
he will give them no answer;
when that time comes he will hide
his face from them,
so wicked are their deeds.

These are the words of the LORD 5
concerning the prophets who lead my
people astray, who promise prosperity
in return for a morsel of food, who
proclaim a holy war against them if
they put nothing into their mouths:

Therefore night shall bring you no   6
vision,
darkness no divination;
the sun shall go down on the prophets,
the day itself shall be black above
them.
Seers and diviners alike shall blush   7
for shame;
they shall all put their hands over
their mouths,
because there is no answer from God.

But I am full of strength,*j* of justice   8
and power,
to denounce his crime to Jacob
and his sin to Israel.
Listen to this, leaders of Jacob,   9
rulers of Israel,
you who make justice hateful
and wrest it from its straight course,
building Zion in bloodshed   10
and Jerusalem in iniquity.
Her rulers sell justice,   11
her priests give direction in return
for a bribe,
her prophets take money for their
divination,
and yet men rely on the LORD.
'Is not the LORD among us?' they
say;
'then no disaster can befall us.'
Therefore, on your account   12

g But . . . no: *prob. rdg.; Heb.* But yesterday.
h my: *prob. rdg.; Heb. om.*
i the cloak . . . safe: *prob. rdg.; Heb.* mantle, cloak.
j Prob. rdg.; Heb. adds the spirit of the LORD.

2.12–3.4: Against the leaders. The metaphor of a flock begins (2.12) as if a promise of
protection, but becomes (3.1) a denunciation of the rulers. **4:** *Them:* the rulers.
3.5–12: Against the prophets. Because the professional prophets suit their oracles to their
employers, they will get *no answer from God* (v. 7). **12:** The verse is quoted in Jeremiah's trial
(Jer.26.18) as proof that prophets may say offensive things without being punished.

Zion shall become a ploughed field,
Jerusalem a heap of ruins,
and the temple hill rough heath.

A remnant restored in
an age of peace

4 1^k   In days to come
the mountain of the LORD's house
shall be set over all other mountains,
lifted high above the hills.
Peoples shall come streaming to it,
2   and many nations shall come and say,
'Come, let us climb up on to the
mountain of the LORD,
to the house of the God of Jacob,
that he may teach us his ways
and we may walk in his paths.'
For instruction issues from Zion,
and out of Jerusalem comes the
word of the LORD;
3   he will be judge between many
peoples
and arbiter among mighty nations
afar.
They shall beat their swords into
mattocks
and their spears into pruning-
knives;
nation shall not lift sword against
nation
nor ever again be trained for war,
4   and each man shall dwell under his
own vine,
under his own fig-tree,
undisturbed.
For the LORD of Hosts himself has
spoken.

5   All peoples may walk, each in the
name of his god,
but we will walk in the name of the
LORD our God
for ever and ever.

On that day, says the LORD,   6
I will gather those who are lost;
I will assemble the exiles and I will
strengthen the weaklings.
I will preserve the lost as a remnant   7
and turn the derelict into a mighty
nation.
The LORD shall be their king on
Mount Zion
now and for ever.
And you, rocky bastion, hill of   8
Zion's daughter,
the promises to you shall be
fulfilled;
and your former sovereignty shall
come again,
the dominion of the daughter of
Jerusalem.

Why are you now filled with alarm? 9
Have you no king?
Have you no counsellor left,
that you are seized with writhing
like a woman in labour?
Lie writhing on the ground like a   10
woman in childbirth,
O daughter of Zion;
for now you must leave the city
and camp in the open country;
and so you will come to Babylon.
There you shall be saved,
there the LORD will deliver you from
your enemies.
But now many nations are massed   11
against you;
they say, 'Let her suffer outrage,
let us gloat over Zion.'
But they do not know the LORD's   12
thoughts
nor understand his purpose;
for he has gathered them like sheaves
to the threshing-floor.
Start your threshing, daughter of   13
Zion;

k *Verses 1–3: cp. Isa. 2. 2–4.*

4.1–5.15: A contrite people is restored in the LORD's favor. Because these poems seem, in part, to presuppose the Babylonian Exile (beginning in 587 B.C.) they do not come from Micah's time, though 5.5–6 may. **1–3:** Identical with Isa.2.2–4, the tone of the poem suggests a time after the sixth century B.C. **1:** *Mountain:* the hill on which the Jerusalem Temple stands will be elevated to the highest position in the world. **4:** A figure of peace and security; see 5.3 and compare Ezek.34.11–16. **9–11:** Suffering must be undergone in order that Judah *shall be saved.* **12–13:** Judah will now triumph over these enemies. *Horns* and *hooves:* The metaphor is of an animal tramping on grain to *thresh* it.

for I will make your horns of iron,
your hooves will I make of bronze,
and you shall crush many peoples.
You shall devote their ill-gotten
　　gain to the LORD,
their wealth to the Lord of all the
　　earth.

5 Get you behind your walls, you
　　people of a walled city;
the siege is pressed home against you:
Israel's ruler shall be struck on the
　　cheek with a rod.

2 But you, Bethlehem in Ephrathah,
small as you are to be among
　　Judah's clans,
out of you shall come forth a
　　governor for Israel,
one whose roots are far back in the
　　past, in days gone by.

3 Therefore only so long as a woman
　　is in labour
shall he give up Israel;
and then those that survive of
　　his race
shall rejoin their brethren.

4 He shall appear and be their
　　shepherd
in the strength of the LORD,
in the majesty of the name of the
　　LORD his God.
And they shall continue, for now his
　　greatness shall reach
to the ends of the earth;

5 and he shall be a man of peace.

When the Assyrian comes into our
　　land,
when he tramples our castles,
we will raise against him seven men
　　or eight
to be shepherds and princes.

6 They shall shepherd Assyria with
　　the sword
and the land of Nimrod with bare
　　blades;

they shall deliver us from the Assyrians
when they come into our land,
when they trample our frontiers.

All that are left of Jacob, surrounded
　　by many peoples,
shall be like dew from the LORD,
like copious showers on the grass,
which do not wait for man's
　　command
or linger for any man's bidding.
All that are left of Jacob among the **8**
　　nations,
surrounded by many peoples,
shall be like a lion among the beasts
　　of the forest,
like a young lion loose in a flock
　　of sheep;
as he prowls he will trample and
　　tear them,
with no rescuer in sight.
Your hand shall be raised high over **9**
　　your foes,
and all who hate you shall be destroyed.

On that day, says the LORD,　　　　**10**
I will destroy all your horses
　　among you
and make away with your chariots.
I will destroy the cities of your land **11**
and raze your fortresses.
I will destroy all your sorcerers,　　**12**
and there shall be no more
　　soothsayers among you.
I will destroy your images and all the **13**
　　sacred pillars in your land;
you shall no longer bow in reverence
　　before things your own hands
　　made.
I will pull down the sacred poles in　**14**
　　your land,
and demolish your blood-
　　spattered altars.
In anger and fury will I take　　　　**15**
　　vengeance
on all nations who disobey me.

5.1–6: A coming ruler. 1: *Struck:* some humiliation may have been part of the installation of a Hebrew king, as it was in Babylon. **2:** *Bethlehem in Ephrathah* was David's city; his family was called Ephrathite (see 1 Sam.17.12). The poem predicts the restoration (v. 4) of David's dynasty. The verse is paraphrased in Mt.2.6. **3:** *Those that survive:* the exiled Judeans. **5–6:** See Introduction. Judah will beat back an Assyrian threat. *Shepherds:* as in v. 4, probably a term for kings. *Nimrod:* equivalent to Assyria; see Gen.10.8–12.
　　5.7–15: Future security and fidelity. 10–15: Although the context appears to suggest that these verses are addressed to Assyria, the prophets often denounced Israel for such illicit practices as those in vv. 12–14 (see, e.g. Isa.2.6–8). If Israel, rather than Assyria, is addressed, these verses are a separate poem. **13:** *Sacred pillars:* phallic symbols. **14:** *Sacred poles:* objects representing the Canaanite goddess Asherah. Their precise nature is not known.

6 Hear now what the LORD is saying:

Up, state your case to the
mountains;
let the hills hear your plea.
2 Hear the LORD's case, you
mountains,
you everlasting pillars that bear
up the earth;
for the LORD has a case against his
people,
and will argue it with Israel.
3 O my people, what have I done to
you?
Tell me how I have wearied you;
answer me this.
4 I brought you up from Egypt,
I ransomed you from the land of
slavery,
I sent Moses and Aaron and Miriam
to lead you.
5 Remember, my people,
what Balak king of Moab schemed
against you,
and how Balaam son of Beor
answered him;
consider the journey*l* from Shittim
to Gilgal,
in order that you may know the
triumph of the LORD.

6 What shall I bring when I approach
the LORD?
How shall I stoop before God on
high?
Am I to approach him with whole-
offerings or yearling calves?
7 Will the LORD accept thousands of
rams
or ten thousand rivers of oil?
Shall I offer my eldest son for my
own wrongdoing,

my children for my own sin?

God*m* has told you what is good;   8
and what is it that the LORD asks
of you?
Only to act justly, to love loyalty,
to walk wisely before your God.

Hark, the LORD, the fear of whose   9
name brings success,
the LORD calls to the city.
Listen, O tribe of Judah and   10
citizens in assembly,*n*
can I overlook*o* the infamous false
measure,*p*
the accursed short bushel?
Can I connive at false scales or a   11
bag of light weights?
Your rich men are steeped in   12
violence,
your townsmen are all liars,
and their tongues frame deceit.
But now I will inflict a signal   13
punishment on you
to lay you waste for your sins:
you shall eat but not be satisfied,   14
your food shall lie heavy on your
stomach;
you shall come to labour but not
bring forth,
and even if you bear a child
I will give it to the sword;
you shall sow but not reap,   15
you shall press the olives but not use
the oil,
you shall tread the grapes but not
drink the wine.
You have kept the precepts of   16
Omri;
what the house of Ahab did, you
have done;

l consider the journey: *prob. rdg.; Heb. om.*
m God: *prob. rdg.; Heb. obscure.*
n citizens in assembly: *prob. rdg.; Heb. unintelligible.*
o can I overlook: *prob. rdg.; Heb. obscure.*
p Prob. rdg.; Heb. adds infamous treasures.

6.1–16: God accuses a wayward people. The poem takes its form from a lawsuit.
6.1–2: Preamble. The *mountains* and *hills* are called as witnesses to the trial. The Hebrews believed that the earth rested upon *pillars* (compare Prov.8.29).
6.3–16: The LORD's past deeds. 4: *Aaron and Miriam:* brother and sister of *Moses* (see Exod.4.14; 15.20). **5:** *Balaam,* the Mesopotamian diviner, was called by *Balak* to curse Israel but he blessed her instead; see Num. chs. 22–24. *Shittim:* east of the Jordan, where Israel was encamped after the Balaam episode (Num.25.1). *Gilgal:* Israel's first stopping place after crossing the Jordan under Joshua (Josh.4.19–5.9). The *journey* was the latter part of the Wilderness wandering before the conquest of Canaan. *Triumph:* the word also means "righteousness." **6:** *Stoop:* bow humbly. **7:** The overstatement suggests mild sarcasm or banter. *Eldest son:* Israelites at one time offered human sacrifices to Molech (see 2 Kgs.23.10; Jer.32.35). **8:** The answer to the question implies the validity of ritual as a fulfillment of God's demands. *Justly:* to obey the legal side of the covenant. The injunction is to *love,* rather than merely to practice *loyalty.* **13–16:** The punishment precludes any prosperity. **16:** *Omri:* king of Israel

you have followed all their ways.
So I will lay you utterly waste;
the nations shall jeer at your
citizens,
and their insults you shall bear.

Disappointment turned to hope

7 Alas! I am now like the last
gatherings of summer fruit,
the last gleanings of the vintage,
when there are no grapes left to
eat,
none of those early figs that I love.
2 Loyal men have vanished from the
earth,
there is not one upright man.
All lie in wait to do murder,
each man drives his own kinsman
like a hunter into the net.
3 They are bent eagerly on
wrongdoing,
the officer who presents the
requests,*q*
the judge who gives judgement*r* for
reward,
and the nobleman who harps on his
desires.
4 Thus their goodness is twisted*s* like
rank weeds
and their honesty like briars.*t*
As soon as thine eye sees, thy
punishment falls;
at that moment bewilderment seizes
them.
5 Trust no neighbour, put no confidence
in your closest friend;
seal your lips even from the wife of
your bosom.
6 For son maligns father,
daughter rebels against mother,
daughter-in-law against mother-
in-law,
and a man's enemies are his own
household.
7 But I will look for the LORD,
I will wait for God my saviour; my
God will hear me.

O my enemies, do not exult over 8
me;
I have fallen, but shall rise again;
though I dwell in darkness, the LORD
is my light.
I will bear the anger of the LORD, 9
for I have sinned against him,
until he takes up my cause and gives
judgement for me,
until he brings me out into light, and
I see his justice.
Then may my enemies see and be 10
abashed,
those who said to me, 'Where is he,
the LORD your God?'
Then shall they be trampled like mud
in the streets;
I shall gloat over them;
that will be a day for rebuilding 11
your walls,
a day when your frontiers will be
extended,
a day when men will come seeking 12
you
from Assyria to Egypt
and from Egypt to the Euphrates,
from every sea and every mountain;
and the earth with its inhabitants 13
shall be waste.
This shall be the fruit of their
deeds.

Shepherd thy people with thy crook, 14
the flock that is thy very own,
that dwells by itself on the heath and
in the meadows;
let them graze in Bashan and Gilead,
as in days gone by.
Show us*u* miracles as in the days 15
when thou camest out of Egypt;
let the nations see and be taken 16
aback for all their might,
let them keep their mouths shut,
make their ears deaf,
let them lick the dust like snakes, 17

q the requests: prob. rdg.; Heb. om.
r who gives judgement: prob. rdg.; Heb. om.
s twisted: prob. rdg.; Heb. obscure.
t their honesty like briars: prob. rdg.; Heb. obscure.
u Prob. rdg.; Heb. I will show him.

(1 Kgs.16.16–28), about 876–869 B.C., father of *Ahab* (1 Kgs.16.29–22.40). Exactly what is meant by *the precepts of Omri* is not certain. Ahab fostered Baal worship in Israel; see 1 Kgs.16.32–33.
7.1–20: Penance and expectation of fulfillment. 1–6: Social chaos is vividly portrayed, from corrupt officials (v. 3) to the failure of trust even within the family (vv. 5–6). **7–20:** Hope for the future comes from looking to the LORD, who will restore Israel. **14–20:** The restoration of Israel. **14:** The figure of the LORD as a *shepherd* (compare Ps.23) protecting his flock was a familiar one. *Bashan* and *Gilead* were fertile grazing areas. **15:** *Out of Egypt:* the Exodus. **17:** *Lick the dust* is a

like creatures that crawl upon the
    ground.
Let them come trembling and fearful
    from their strongholds,
let them fear thee, O LORD our God.

18 Who is a god like thee? Thou takest
        away guilt,
    thou passest over the sin of the
        remnant of thy own people,
    thou dost not let thy anger rage for
        ever

but delightest in love that will not
    change.
Once more thou wilt show us   19
    tender affection
and wash out our guilt,
    casting all our sins into the depths
        of the sea.
Thou wilt show good faith to   20
    Jacob,
    unchanging love to Abraham,
as thou didst swear to our fathers in
    days gone by.

---

figure for complete defeat; see Gen.3.14. **18:** *Love* is the same Heb. word as "loyalty," 6.8 n.
20: *Jacob* and *Abraham* are symbols for the descendants.

NAHUM

Nahum stands at the end of an epoch. For 150 years, Assyria has oppressed the Near Eastern world, but now (612 B.C.) Nineveh, its capital, has fallen to the Babylonians (chs. 2–3). The victory over the Assyrians belongs to the LORD, who moves both men and mountains (1.6). (Nahum does not seem to know that a terrible blow will fall on Judah from the Babylonians in 597 B.C.).

As a prophet, Nahum emphasizes two matters: Nineveh has received what it deserves at the LORD's hands, and, as a result, Judah can return to normal life. As a poet, Nahum is exceedingly gifted. Though neither especially profound nor original, he is capable of superb pictorial effects, as in 2.1–10, and of vivid metaphor, as in 2.11–13. The remains of an originally effective, though now disordered, acrostic poem (one in which each couplet begins with successive letters of the Hebrew alphabet) is to be found in 1.2–14.

---

1 An oracle about Nineveh: the book of the vision of Nahum the Elkoshite.

The vengeance of the LORD on his enemies

2[a] The LORD is a jealous god, a god of vengeance;
the LORD takes vengeance and is quick to anger.[b]

3 [c]In whirlwind and storm he goes on his way,
and the clouds are the dust beneath his feet.

4 He rebukes the sea and dries it up
and makes all the streams fail.
Bashan and Carmel languish,
and on Lebanon the young shoots wither.

5 The mountains quake before him,
the hills heave and swell,
and the earth, the world and all that lives in it,
are in tumult at his presence.

6 Who can stand before his wrath?
Who can resist his fury?
His anger pours out[d] like a stream of fire,
and the rocks melt[e] before him.

7 The LORD is a sure refuge
for those who look to him in time of distress;

he cares for all who seek his protection

and brings them safely[f] through the sweeping flood; 8
he makes a final end of all who oppose him
and pursues his enemies into darkness.

No adversaries dare oppose him twice; 9–11
all are burnt up[g] like tangled briars.

Why do you make plots against the LORD?
He himself will make an end of you all.

From you has come forth a wicked counsellor,
plotting evil against the LORD.
The LORD takes vengeance on his adversaries,
against his enemies he directs his wrath;
with skin scorched black, they are consumed
like stubble that is parched and dry.

---

a Verses 2–14 are an incomplete alphabetic acrostic poem; some parts have been re-arranged accordingly.
b The rest of verse 2, The LORD takes . . . wrath, transposed to verse 11.
c Prob. rdg.; Heb. inserts two lines The LORD is long-suffering and of great might, but the LORD does not sweep clean away.
d pours out: or fuses or melts.
e Prob. rdg.; Heb. are torn down.
f brings them safely: prob. rdg.; Heb. om.
g all are burnt up: prob. rdg.; Heb. for until.

1.1: Title. Nineveh: see Introduction. Nahum means "comforted." The location of Elkosh is unknown.

1.2–11: Turbulence, oppression, and revenge are rampant. An acrostic; see Introduction. The imagery is cosmic in character (e.g., whirlwind, storm, sea, earth, flood, darkness); the victory over the unnamed but universal enemy is also in a cosmic setting. 4: Bashan: east of the Jordan. Carmel: a mountain range on the northern coast. Lebanon: mountains northwest of Canaan. All three places were notably fertile. 6: Fire and rocks melting: frequent images of the LORD's appearance (see, e.g. Mic.1.4). 9–11: Wicked counsellor: obscure; probably no specific individual is meant, unless it is Sennacherib, as some interpreters would have it. Skin scorched: a sign of defeat and adversity; see Lam.5.10.

These are the words of the LORD:

13 Now I will break his yoke from
    your necks
    and snap the cords that bind you.
14 Image and idol will I hew down in
    the house of your God.
    This is what the LORD has ordained
      for you:
    never again shall your offspring be
      scattered;
    and I will grant you burial, fickle
      though you have been.
12   Has the punishment been so great?
    Yes, but it has passed away and is
      gone.
    I have afflicted you, but I will not
      afflict you again.

15 See on the mountains the feet of
    the herald
    who brings good news.
    Make your pilgrimages, O Judah,
    and pay your vows.
    For wicked men shall never again
      overrun you;
    they are totally destroyed.
2 2[h] The LORD will restore the pride of
    Jacob and Israel alike,
    although plundering hordes have
      stripped them bare
    and pillaged their vines.

Nineveh's enemies triumphant

1 The battering-ram is mounted
    against your bastions,
    the siege is closing in.
    Watch the road and brace yourselves;
    put forth all your strength.
3 The shields of their warriors are
    gleaming red,
    their soldiers are all in scarlet;
    their chariots, when the line is
      formed,
    are like flickering[i] fire;

squadrons of horse advance on the 4
    city in mad frenzy;[j]
they jostle one another in the
    outskirts, like waving torches;
    the leaders display their prowess[k] 5
    as they dash to and fro like
      lightning,
    rushing[l] in headlong career;
they hasten to the wall, and mantelets
    are set in position.
The sluices of the rivers are opened, 6
    the palace topples down;
    the train of captives goes into exile, 7
    their slave-girls are carried off,
    moaning like doves and beating
      their breasts;
    and Nineveh has become like a 8
      pool of water,
    like the waters round her, which
      are ebbing away.
    'Stop! Stop!' they cry; but none
      turns back.

Spoil is taken, spoil of silver and 9
    gold;
    there is no end to the store,
    treasure beyond the costliest that
      man can desire.
    Plundered, pillaged, stripped bare! 10
Courage melting and knees giving
    way,
    writhing limbs, and faces drained of
      colour!
    Where now is the lions' den, 11
    the cave[m] where the lion cubs
      lurked,
    where the lion and[n] lioness and
      young cubs
      went unafraid,
    the lion which killed to satisfy its 12
      whelps
    and for its mate broke the neck of
      the kill,

h Verses 1 and 2 transposed.
i flickering: prob. rdg.; Heb. obscure.
j Prob. rdg.; Heb. adds chariots.
k display their prowess: or shout their own names.
l Prob. rdg.; Heb. stumbling.
m Prob. rdg.; Heb. pasture.
n and: prob. rdg.; Heb. om.

1.13–15; 2.2: No more shall Israel and Judah be overrun. 13: Judah was Assyria's vassal from about 734 until into Josiah's reign (640–609 B.C.). **14:** To be denied *burial* was the final and most ignominious punishment of the LORD's enemies; compare Ezek.39.4. **15:** *See on the mountains:* compare Isa.52.7. *Pilgrimages:* the three yearly festivals of Exod.23.14–17; 34.23. **2.2:** Here, as elsewhere, the restoration of *Israel*, exiled after being overrun in 721 B.C., is predicted.
    2.1–3.19: The destruction of Nineveh. The poem is powerfully pictorial. We need not suppose that Nahum was present; an active imagination is enough. **6:** *Sluices:* the sluice-gates of the Tigris River, the opening of which caused Nineveh to be flooded. **11–13:** The *lion* is often a

mauling its prey to fill its lair,
  filling its den with the mauled
    prey?

13 I am against you, says the LORD of
      Hosts,
  I will smoke out your pride,[o]
  and a sword shall devour your cubs.
  I will leave you no more prey on
      the earth,
  and the sound of your feeding[p]
    shall no more be heard.

3 Ah! blood-stained city, steeped in
      deceit,
  full of pillage, never empty of prey!
2   Hark to the crack of the whip,
  the rattle of wheels and stamping of
      horses,
3 bounding chariots, chargers rearing,
    swords gleaming, flash of spears!
  The dead are past counting, their
      bodies lie in heaps,
  corpses innumerable, men stumbling
      over corpses—
4 all for a wanton's monstrous
      wantonness,
    fair-seeming, a mistress of sorcery,
  who beguiled nations and tribes
    by her wantonness and her
      sorceries.
5 I am against you, says the LORD of
      Hosts,
  I will uncover your breasts to your
      disgrace
  and expose your naked body to
      every nation,
    to every kingdom your shame.
6 I will cast loathsome filth over you,
  I will count you obscene and treat
      you like excrement.

7 Then all who see you will shrink
      from you and say,
  'Nineveh is laid waste; who will
      console her?'
  Where shall I look for anyone to
      comfort you?
8 Will you fare better than
      No-amon?—
    she that lay by the streams of the
      Nile,
    surrounded by water,

whose rampart was the Nile, waters
    her wall;
Cush and Egypt were her strength,   9
    and it was boundless,
Put and the Libyans brought her
    help.
She too became an exile and went   10
    into captivity,
  her infants too were dashed to the
      ground at every street-corner,
  her nobles were shared out by lot,
  all her great men were thrown into
      chains.
You too shall hire yourself out,   11
    flaunting your sex;
  you too shall seek refuge from the
      enemy.
Your fortifications are like figs when   12
    they ripen:
  if they are shaken, they fall into the
      mouth of the eater.
The troops[q] in your midst are a   13
    pack of women,
  the gates of your country stand open
      to the enemy,
  and fire consumes their bars.
Draw yourselves water for the siege,   14
    strengthen your fortifications;
  down into the clay, trample the
      mortar,
    repair the brickwork.
Even then the fire will consume you,   15
    and the sword will cut you down.[r]
Make yourselves many as the
    locusts,
  make yourselves many as the
      hoppers,
  a swarm which spreads out and   16
      then flies away.
You have spies as numerous as the
    stars in the sky;
  your secret agents are like locusts,   17
    your commanders like the hoppers
  which lie dormant in the walls on a
      cold day;
  but when the sun rises, they scurry
      off,
  and no one knows where they have
      gone.

o *your pride: prob. rdg.; Heb.* her chariot.
p *your feeding: prob. rdg.; Heb.* your messenger.
q *Or* people.
r *Prob. rdg.; Heb. adds* and consume you like the
locust (*or* hopper).

---

metaphor of a ruthless nation; the use here is ironic. Assyrian kings hunting lions are portrayed
on some relief sculptures. **3.8:** *No-amon:* Thebes in Egypt, captured by the Assyrians in 662
B.C. **9:** *Cush:* Ethiopia. *Put:* west of Egypt, as was Libya. **10:** *Captivity:* compare Isa.20.4;

18 Your shepherds slumber, O king of
        Assyria,
    your flock-masters lie down to
        rest;
    your troops[s] are scattered over the
        hills,
    and no one rounds them up.

19 Your wounds cannot be assuaged,
    your injury is mortal;
    all who have heard of your fate clap
        their hands in joy
    Are there any whom your ceaseless
        cruelty has not borne down?

    s Or people.

Shared out by lot: see Joel 3.3; Obad.11. **18–19:** Written in dirgelike rhythm, this poem is not
dirgelike in its gloating joy.

HABAKKUK

The end of Assyria as a world power (the Babylonians destroyed her capital, Nineveh, in 612 B.C.) seemed to many in Judah the beginning of a new age. But before long the conquering Babylonians (called Chaldeans in the Old Testament) made clear that they too were embarked on world domination. In 597 B.C. they conquered the Judeans. The allusion to the Chaldeans in 1.6 places 1.2–2.3 of this book within the period 612–597 B.C. We know nothing about Habakkuk other than his date.

The book's three sections are in different literary forms. 1.2–2.3 is a dialogue, in which the prophet seriously questions God's justice, that is, how he can allow the wicked Chaldeans to triumph. 2.4–20 is a series of denunciations of human injustice, which begin with "Woe." Chapter 3 has the form of a psalm. The differing styles, plus the book's brevity, obstruct certainty that one hand produced the entire book. However, the themes of God's justice and man's need of faithful confidence provide a basic unity.

The dialogue section, though focused on theodicy, contains vivid descriptions of invading forces (1.5–11) and a splendid metaphor of a fisherman (1.14–16). The denunciations (2.4–20) excel in shrewd characterizations. The psalm (ch. 3) abounds in colorful cosmic symbols and images.

1 An oracle which the prophet Habakkuk received in a vision.

Divine justice

2 How long, O LORD, have I cried to thee, unanswered?
I cry, 'Violence!', but thou dost not save.

3 Why dost thou let me see such misery,
why countenance*a* wrongdoing?

Devastation and violence confront me;
strife breaks out, discord raises its head,

4 and so law grows effete;
justice does not come forth victorious;
for the wicked outwit the righteous,
and so justice comes out perverted.

5 Look, you treacherous people, look:
here is what will astonish you and stun you,
for there is work afoot in your days
which you will not believe when it is told you.

6 It is this: I am raising up the Chaldaeans,
that savage and impetuous nation,
who cross the wide tracts of the earth
to take possession of homes not theirs.

7 Terror and awe go with them;
their justice and judgement are of their own making.

8 Their horses are swifter than hunting-leopards,
keener than wolves of the plain;*b*
their cavalry wait ready, they spring forward,
they come flying from afar
like vultures swooping to devour the prey.

9 Their whole army advances, violence in their hearts;
a sea of faces rolls on;
they bring in captives countless as the sand.

10 Kings they hold in derision,
rulers they despise;
they despise every fortress,
they raise siege-works and capture it.

11 Then they pass on like the wind and are gone;

a Or dost thou let me see.   *b Or* evening.

1.1: **Title.** The meaning of the name is unknown; but some associate it with a word meaning "to embrace." The name appears also in the apocryphal book of Dan. & Bel (vv. 33–39).

1.2–4: **Internal discord.** The prophet complains that God has allowed lawlessness to prevail in Judah. 4: *Effete*: sterile, without vigor.

1.5–11: **God's solution.** The *Chaldaeans*: the last dynasty of Babylon and often synonymous with it. They would punish Judah for its wickedness; yet they too were wicked. This "solution" by God is able to *astonish*, and to arouse the agonized questions in the next section.

and dismayed are all those whose
strength was their god.

12 Art thou not from of old, O
       LORD?—
    my God, the holy, the immortal.[c]
    O LORD, it is thou who hast appointed
       them to execute judgement;
    O mighty God, thou who hast
       destined them to chastise,
13 thou whose eyes are too pure to
       look upon evil,
    and who canst not countenance
       wrongdoing,
    why dost thou countenance the
       treachery of the wicked?
    Why keep silent when they devour
       men more righteous than they?
14 Why dost thou make men like the
       fish of the sea,
    like gliding creatures that obey no
       ruler?
15 They haul them up with hooks, one
       and all,
    they catch them in nets
       and drag them in their trawls;
    then they make merry and rejoice,
16 sacrificing to their nets
    and burning offerings[d] to their
       trawls;
    for by these they live sumptuously
       and enjoy rich fare.
17 Are they then to unsheathe the
       sword every day,
    to slaughter the nations without
       pity?

2   I will stand at my post,
    I will take up my position on the
       watch-tower,
    I will watch to learn what he will
       say through me,
    and what I shall reply when I am
       challenged.[e]

Then the LORD made answer: 2
Write down the vision, inscribe it on
   tablets,
ready for a herald to carry it with
   speed;[f]
for there is still a vision for the   3
   appointed time.
At the destined hour it will come in
   breathless haste,
   it will not fail.
If it delays, wait for it;
for when it comes will be no time
   to linger.

The reckless will be unsure of himself, 4
while the righteous man will live by
   being faithful;[g]
as for the traitor in his over-   5
   confidence,
still less will he ride out the storm,
   for all his bragging.
Though he opens his mouth as wide
   as Sheol
and is insatiable as Death,
gathering in all the nations,
making all peoples his own harvest,
surely they will all turn upon him   6
with insults and abuse, and say,
'Woe betide you who heap up wealth
   that is not yours[h]
and enrich yourself with goods
   taken in pledge!'
Will not your creditors suddenly   7
   start up,
   will not all awake who would
      shake you till you are empty,
   and will you not fall a victim to
      them?

c the immortal: *prob. original rdg., altered in Heb. to*
   we shall not die.
d *Or* incense.
e when I am challenged: *or concerning my complaint.*
f ready . . . speed: *or so that a man may read it easily.*
g *Or by his faithfulness (cp. Romans 1. 17; Galatians
   3. 11).*
h *Prob. rdg.; Heb. adds* till when.

1.12–2.1: Is God just? The first question (v. 12) carries a subtle uncertainty. Is God in charge?
Has he indeed *appointed* the Chaldeans for *judgement, to chastise?* How can he *countenance
wrongdoing?* How can he allow evil men to *devour men* more righteous? The images of fishing
(vv. 14–16) imply man's insignificance before God and God's seeming unconcern at the inhuman
tragedies in man's life. **2.1:** The prophet sees himself as the outpost of human consciousness
to pick up God's faintest message to man and regards himself as a responsible spokesman for
man before God.
    2.2–20: God's answer. 2: Habakkuk is to record the *vision,* so that others besides him can
know it. *Speed:* older translations read: "that he who runs may read." **4:** The vision contrasts
what will happen to the *reckless* (the Chaldeans) and to the *righteous man.* The verse is quoted
in Rom.1.17 and Gal.3.11, as well as in rabbinic literature; here, *being faithful* implies fidelity or
loyalty to the deity rather than a belief-centered faith. **5:** A delineation of the *traitor,* about whom
a series of woes begins in v. 6b, is given. *Sheol:* the place of the dead.
    2.6–8: First Woe. The exploiting creditor finds himself mercilessly exploited and despoiled.

8 Because you yourself have plundered
mighty[i] nations,
all the rest of the world will plunder
you,
because of bloodshed and
violence done in the land,
to the city and all its inhabitants.

9 Woe betide you who seek unjust
gain for your house,
to build your nest on a height,
to save yourself from the grasp of
wicked men!

10 Your schemes to overthrow mighty[i]
nations
will bring dishonour to your
house
and put your own life in jeopardy.

11 The very stones will cry out from
the wall,
and from the timbers a beam will
answer them.

12 Woe betide you who have built a
town with bloodshed
and founded a city on fraud,

13 so that nations toil for a pittance,
and peoples weary themselves for a
mere nothing!
Is not all this the doing of the LORD
of Hosts?

14 For the earth shall be full of the
knowledge of the glory of the
LORD
as the waters fill the sea.

15 Woe betide you who make your[j]
companions drink the
outpouring of your wrath,
making them drunk, that you may
watch their naked orgies!

16 Drink deep draughts of shame, not
of glory;
you too shall drink until you stagger.

The cup in the LORD's right hand
is passed to you,
and your shame will exceed[k] your
glory.

17 The violence done to Lebanon
shall sweep over you,
the havoc done to its beasts shall
break your own spirit,
because of bloodshed and violence
done in the land,
to the city and all its inhabitants.

18 What use is an idol when its maker
has shaped it?—
it is only an image, a source of
lies;
or when the maker trusts what he
has made?—
he is only making dumb idols.

19 Woe betide him who says to the
wood, 'Wake up',
to the dead stone, 'Bestir yourself'![l]
Why, it is firmly encased in gold and
silver
and has no breath in it.

20 But the LORD is in his holy temple;
let all the earth be hushed in his
presence.

A prayer for mercy

3 A prayer of the prophet Habakkuk.

2 O LORD, I have heard tell of thy
deeds;
I have seen, O LORD, thy work.[m]
In the midst of the years thou
didst make thyself known,

i Or many.
j Prob. rdg.; Heb. his.
k will exceed: prob. rdg.; Heb. unintelligible.
l Prob. rdg.; Heb. adds he will teach.
*m Prob. rdg.; Heb. adds in the midst of the years
quicken it.*

8a: See Isa.33.1; Zech.2.8. **8b:** The phrase, *to the city and all its inhabitants*, recurs in v. 17.
   2.9–11: Second Woe. The very attempts of the wicked to establish their honor and security
become for them shame and destruction.
   2.12–14: Third Woe. Against those who turn the conquered into slave labor. V. 14 is a
liturgical formula (see also v. 20).
   2.15–17: Fourth Woe. Against the conqueror's extreme cruelty. The cup of *wrath* is usually a
symbol of the LORD's anger (Isa.51.17–23; Jer.25.15–29); here the conqueror is usurping the
LORD's prerogative. *Lebanon:* mountains northwest of Israel.
   2.18–20: Fifth Woe. Against the folly of idolatry. **20:** A liturgical formula; see v. 14. *Be
hushed:* in awe; see also Zeph.1.7 and Zech.2.13.
   3.1–19: Habakkuk's supplication. The text is poorly preserved (and hence the unusually large
number of corrections the translators have made). The poem seems to be an old cultic prayer,
celebrating the LORD's march from the region of Sinai to save his people; see also Judg.5.4;

and in thy wrath thou didst
remember mercy.

3 God comes from Teman,
the Holy One from Mount Paran;
his radiance overspreads the skies,
and his splendour fills the earth.

4 He rises like the dawn,
with twin rays starting forth at
his side;
the skies are[n] the hiding-place of
his majesty,
and the everlasting[o] ways are for[p]
his swift flight.[q]

5 Pestilence stalks before him,
and plague comes forth behind.

6 He stands still and shakes the earth,
he looks and makes the nations
tremble;
the eternal mountains are riven,
the everlasting[r] hills subside,

7 the tents of Cushan are snatched
away,[s]
the tent-curtains of Midian flutter.

8 Art thou angry with the streams?
Is thy wrath against the sea, O
LORD?
When thou dost mount thy
horses,
thy riding is to victory.

9 Thou dost draw thy bow from its
case[t]
and charge thy quiver with shafts.
Thou cleavest the earth with rivers;

10–11 the mountains see thee and writhe
with fear.
The torrent of water rushes by,
and the deep sea thunders aloud.
The sun forgets to turn in his
course,[u]
and the moon stands still at her
zenith,
at the gleam of thy speeding arrows
and the glance of thy flashing
spear.

12 With threats thou dost bestride the
earth
and trample down the nations in
anger.

13 Thou goest forth to save thy
people,
thou comest to save thy anointed;
thou dost shatter the wicked man's
house from the roof down,[v]
uncovering its foundations to the
bare rock.[w]

14 Thou piercest their[x] chiefs with
thy[y] shafts,
and their leaders are torn from them
by the whirlwind,
as they open[z] their jaws
to devour their wretched victims in
secret.

15 When thou dost tread the sea with
thy horses
the mighty waters boil.

16 I hear, and my belly quakes;
my lips quiver at the sound;
trembling comes over my bones,
and my feet totter in their tracks;
I sigh for the day of distress
to dawn over my assailants.

17 Although the fig-tree does not
burgeon,
the vines bear no fruit,
the olive-crop fails,
the orchards yield no food,
the fold is bereft of its flock
and there are no cattle in the
stalls,

18 yet I will exult in the LORD
and rejoice in the God of my
deliverance.

19 The LORD God is my strength,
who makes my feet nimble as a
hind's
and sets me to range the heights.

n the skies are: *prob. rdg.; Heb.* there is.
o *Or* ancient.
p and . . . are for: *transposed from end of verse 6.*
q his swift flight: *transposed, with slight change, from
verse 7.*
r *Or* ancient.
s are snatched away: *prob. rdg.; Heb.* under wickedness.
t Thou . . . case: *prob. rdg.; Heb.* Thy bow was quite
bared.
u The sun . . . course: *prob. rdg.; Heb.* The sun raised
the height of his hands.
v the wicked . . . down: *prob. rdg.; Heb.* a head from
the house of the wicked.
w bare rock: *prob. rdg.; Heb.* neck.
x their: *prob. rdg.; Heb. om.*   y *Prob. rdg.; Heb.* his.
z from them . . . open: *prob. rdg.; Heb.* obscure.

Deut.33.2; and Ps.68.7–8. **3:** *Teman:* equivalent to Edom. *Paran:* see Num.10.11–12. **4:** *The
everlasting ways* are possibly the orbits of the planets. **7:** *Cushan . . . Midian:* countries
bordering on Edom. They lay along the route of the LORD's march (see 3.1–19 n.). **8:** See
Ps.89.10–11 and Isa.51.9. **9:** See Gen.49.24. **10:** *Deep sea:* see Exod.15.5–8. **13:** *Thy anointed:*
it is uncertain whether this alludes to the king or the people. **15:** See Ps.77.17–19; Isa.43.16–17.
18 19: These verses may not be part of the original poem. They express confidence in God
even in the face of adversity, perhaps referring to 2.4.

ZEPHANIAH

Two important events occurred during the reign of Josiah, when Zephaniah lived (1.1): Josiah's religious reform in 621 B.C. (see 2 Kgs.22.1–23.30); and Assyria's complete disappearance as a power (see Introduction to Nahum). Zephaniah seems to know of neither of these events (unless 2.13–15 reflects the second); he can, therefore, be dated shortly before 621 B.C.

Corruption is the order of the day, and the LORD must "sweep the earth clean" of it (1.2). The "day of the LORD" will bring an end to all this wickedness, both in Judah (1.4–18) and in other nations (2.1–15). Guilt falls on the ruling elements, who have deliberately pursued illicit religious practices (1.4–6; 3.4–5) and oppressed the common people (3.1–3). In destroying those responsible for Israel's misery, the LORD will entrust the land to the poor and humble, who better deserve it (3.11–20).

1 THIS IS THE WORD OF THE LORD which came to Zephaniah son of Cushi, son of Gedaliah, son of Amariah, son of Hezekiah, in the time of Josiah son of Amon king of Judah.

Doom on Judah and her neighbours

2 I will sweep the earth clean of all
    that is on it,
  says the LORD.
3 I will sweep away both man and
    beast,
  I will sweep the birds from the air
    and the fish from the sea,
  and I will bring the wicked to
    their knees*a*
  and wipe out mankind from the
    earth.
  This is the very word of the LORD.

4 I will stretch my hand over Judah
  and all who live in Jerusalem;
  I will wipe out from this place the
    last remnant of Baal
  and the very name of the heathen
    priests,
5 those who bow down upon the
    house-tops
  to worship the host of heaven
  and who swear by Milcom,

6 those who have turned their backs
    on the LORD,
  who have not sought the LORD or
    consulted him.

7 Silence before the Lord GOD!
  for the day of the LORD is near.
  The LORD has prepared a sacrifice
    and has hallowed his guests.
8 On the day of the LORD's sacrifice
  I will punish the royal house and
    its chief officers
  and all who ape outlandish fashions.
9 On that day
  I will punish all who dance on the
    temple terrace,
  who fill their master's*b* house with
    crimes of violence and fraud.

10 On that day, says the LORD,
  an outcry shall be heard from the
    Fish Gate,
  wailing from the second quarter
    of the city,
  a loud crash from the hills;
11 and*c* those who live in the Lower
    Town shall wail.
  For it is all over with the merchants,
  and all the dealers in silver are
    wiped out.

a I will bring . . . knees: *prob. rdg.; Heb.* the ruins with the wicked.
b *Or* their Lord's.   c and: *prob. rdg.; Heb. om.*

1.1: Title. *Zephaniah* means "the LORD protects." It is not sure that *Hezekiah* means the king of Judah of that name. *Josiah* reigned from about 640–609 B.C.
1.2–6: The great doom that is to come. A terrifyingly vivid portrayal of the end of Judah and of all mankind. 2–3: Contrast with the creation in Gen. ch. 1. 4–6: *Judah* and *Jerusalem* will be destroyed because of their idolatrous worship. *Baal:* the Canaanite fertility god. *Host of heaven:* stars personified as gods. *Milcom:* an Ammonite god, probably the same as Molech (or Moloch) to whom human sacrifice was made (see Lev.20.2–5; Jer.32.35).
1.7–18: The day of the LORD is the future day when the LORD will execute judgment over the earth; see Joel 1.14–15. Amos 5.18–20 implies that it was once thought to be a joyous day, but most of the prophets picture it as a time of terror. 7: *Sacrifice:* the LORD hallowed *his guests,* the Israelites, purifying them with punishment instead of ritual purifications; compare 1 Chr.15.14; Job 1.5; Isa.66.17. 10–11: Various parts of Jerusalem are named; the *Fish Gate* (Neh.3.3) was the northern gate in the *second quarter,* but the location of the *Lower Town* is

12   At that time
      I will search Jerusalem with a
          lantern
      and punish all who sit in stupor over
          the dregs of their wine,
      who say to themselves,
      'The LORD will do nothing, good or
          bad.'
13   Their wealth shall be plundered,
          their houses laid waste;
      they shall build houses but not live
          in them,
      they shall plant vineyards but not
          drink the wine from them.
14   The great day of the LORD is near,
          it comes with speed;
      no runner so fast as that day,
          no raiding band so swift.*d*
15   That day is a day of wrath,
          a day of anguish and affliction,
      a day of destruction and
          devastation,
      a day of murk and gloom,
          a day of cloud and dense fog,
16   a day of trumpet and battle-cry
      over fortified cities and lofty
          battlements.
17   I will bring dire distress upon
          men;
      they shall walk like blind men for
          their sin against the LORD.
      Their blood shall be spilt like dust
          and their bowels like dung;
18   neither their silver nor their gold
          shall avail to save them.
      On the day of the LORD's wrath, by
          the fire of his jealousy
      the whole land shall be consumed;
      for he will make an end, a swift end,
          of all who live in the land.

2   Gather together, you unruly nation,
          gather together,
2   before you are sent far away and
          vanish*e* like chaff,
    before the burning anger of the LORD
          comes upon you,
    before the day of the LORD's anger
          comes upon you.

Seek the LORD,   3
all in the land who live humbly by
    his laws,
seek righteousness, seek a humble
    heart;
it may be that you will find shelter
in the day of the LORD's anger.
For Gaza shall be deserted,   4
    Ashkelon left desolate,
the people of Ashdod shall be driven
    out*f* at noonday
    and Ekron uprooted.

Listen, you who live by the coast,   5
    you Kerethite settlers.
The word of the LORD is spoken
    against you;
I will subdue you,*g* land of the
    Philistines,
I will lay you waste and leave you
    without inhabitants,
and you, Kereth, shall be all   6
    shepherds' huts*h* and
    sheepfolds;
and the coastland shall belong to the 7
    survivors of Judah.
They shall pasture their flocks by
    the sea*i*
and lie down at evening in the
    houses of Ashkelon,
for the LORD their God will turn
    to them
    and restore their fortunes.

I have heard the insults of Moab,   8
    the taunts of Ammon,
how they have insulted my people
    and encroached on their frontiers.
Therefore, by my life,   9
says the LORD of Hosts, the God of
    Israel,
Moab shall be like Sodom,
    Ammon like Gomorrah,

d no runner . . . swift: *prob. rdg.; Heb.* hark, the day
of the LORD is bitter, there the warrior cries aloud.
e you are . . . vanish: *prob. rdg.; Heb.* obscure.
f the people . . . out: *or* Ashdod shall be made an
example.
g I . . . you: *prob. rdg.; Heb.* Canaan.
h you . . . huts: *Heb. has these words in a different
order.*
i by the sea: *prob. rdg.; Heb.* upon them.

uncertain. **15–18:** These verses are the basis of the medieval Latin hymn *Dies irae, dies illa*
("a day of wrath will that day be"), formerly (i.e. before Vatican Council II) part of the
Catholic Requiem Mass.
    2.1–3.10: Oracles against nations and Jerusalem. 1–3: Zephaniah's predictions against the
powerful (1.8,11,13; 3.3–4,6) are balanced by comfort for the poor.
    2.4–7: Against the Philistines. 4: Four Philistine cities are named. **5:** *Kereth* probably means
Crete, from which the Philistines came, settling on the *coastlands*.
    2.8–12: Against Moab, Ammon, and the Cushites. See Amos 1.13–15 n., 2.1–3 n. **9:** *Like*

a pile of weeds, a rotting heap of
  saltwort,
  waste land for evermore.
The survivors of my people shall
  plunder them,
  the remnant of my nation shall
  possess their land.

10 This will be retribution for their
pride, because they have insulted the
people of the LORD of Hosts and
11 encroached upon their rights. The
LORD will appear against them with
all his terrors; for he will reduce to
beggary all the gods of the earth, and
all the coasts and islands of the nations
will worship him, every man in his own
home.

12 You Cushites also shall be killed
  by the sword of the LORD.*j*
13 So let him stretch out his hand over
  the north
  and destroy Assyria,
  make Nineveh desolate,
  arid as the wilderness.
14 Flocks shall couch there,
  and all the beasts of the wild.
Horned owl and ruffed bustard shall
  roost on her capitals;
  the tawny owl shall hoot in the
  window,
  and the bustard stand in the
  porch.*k*
15 This is the city that exulted in fancied
  security,
  saying to herself, 'I am, and I alone.'
And what is she now? A waste, a
  haunt for wild beasts,
  at which every passer-by shall hiss
  and shake his fist.

3 Shame on the tyrant city, filthy and
  foul!
2 No warning voice did she heed, she
  took no rebuke to heart,
  she did not trust in the LORD or
  come near to her God.

Her officers were lions roaring in her 3
  midst,
  her rulers wolves of the plain*l*
  that did not wait*m* till morning,
  her prophets were reckless, no true 4
  prophets.
Her priests profaned the sanctuary
  and did violence to the law.
But the LORD in her midst is just; 5
  he does no wrong;
morning by morning he gives
  judgement,
  without fail at daybreak.*n*

I have wiped out the proud; 6
  their battlements are laid in ruin.
I have made their streets a desert
  where no one passes.
Their cities are laid waste, deserted,
  unpeopled.
In the hope that she would remember 7
  all my instructions,
I said, 'Do but fear me
  and take my rebuke to heart';
but they were up betimes and went
  about their evil deeds.

Wait for me, therefore, says the 8
  LORD,
wait for the day when I stand up
  to accuse you;
for mine it is to gather nations
  and assemble kingdoms,
to pour out on them my indignation,
  all the heat of my anger;
the whole earth shall be consumed
  by the fire of my jealousy.
I will give all peoples once again 9
  pure lips,
that they may invoke the LORD by
  name
and serve him with one consent.
From beyond the rivers of Cush 10
my suppliants of the Dispersion shall
  bring me tribute.

j the sword of the LORD: prob. rdg.; Heb. my sword.
k Prob. rdg.; Heb. adds an unintelligible phrase.
l Or evening.   m Or carry off.
*n Prob. rdg.; Heb. adds but the wrongdoer knows no
shame.*

Sodom . . . Gomorrah: i.e. destroyed; see Gen.19.24–28; Deut.29.23; Isa.1.9–10; Lam.4.6;
Amos 4.11. **10:** See v. 8; Isa.16.6; Jer.48.29. **11:** See Isa.45.23; Joel 2.11. **12:** *Cushites:* Ethiopians.
  2.13–15: Against Assyria. See Introduction. The oracle begins in looking forward to Nineveh's
destruction, but ends as though this has already happened.
  3.1–7: Against Jerusalem. In spite of warnings, the powerful (*officers, priests, prophets*) have
gone deeper into wickedness, both civil and religious.
  3.8–10: The call to wait. The judgment on all the nations will end with their redemption
(*pure lips*) and worshiping the LORD. *Dispersion:* probably foreign nations, not scattered
Judeans.

11 On that day, Jerusalem,
  you shall not be put to shame for
    all your deeds
  by which you have rebelled
    against me;
  for then I will rid you
    of your proud and arrogant
    citizens,
  and never again shall you flaunt
    your pride
    on my holy hill.
12 But I will leave in you a people
    afflicted and poor.
13 The survivors in Israel shall find
    refuge in the name of the LORD;
  they shall no longer do wrong or
    speak lies,
  no words of deceit shall pass their
    lips;
  for they shall feed and lie down
    with no one to terrify them.

14 Zion, cry out for joy;
  raise the shout of triumph, Israel;
  be glad, rejoice with all your
    heart,
  daughter of Jerusalem.
15 The LORD has rid you of your
    adversaries,
  he has swept away your foes;
  the LORD is among you as king, O
    Israel;
  never again shall you fear disaster.

16 On that day this shall be the message
  to Jerusalem:
  Fear not, O Zion; let not your hands
    fall slack.
17 The LORD your God is in your
    midst,
  like a warrior, to keep you safe;
  he will rejoice over you and be glad;
  he will show you his love once
    more;
  he will exult over you with a shout
    of joy
  as in days long ago.*o*
18 I will take your cries of woe*p* away
    from you;
  and you shall no longer endure
    reproach for her.
19 When that time comes, see,
  I will deal with all your oppressors.
  I will rescue the lost and gather the
    dispersed;
  I will win my people praise and
    renown
  in all the world where once they
    were despised.
20 When the time comes for me to
    gather you,*q*
  I will bring you home.
  I will win you renown and praise
    among all the peoples of the earth,
  when I bring back your prosperity;
  and you shall see it.
  It is the LORD who speaks.

o as . . . ago: *prob. rdg.; Heb. obscure.*
p cries of woe: *prob. rdg.; Heb. obscure.*
q When . . . you: *prob. rdg.; Heb.* and in the time, my
gathering you.

3.11–20: The humble shall inherit. 11–13: The fault of Jerusalem has lain in the *proud and arrogant*. With their removal, the city will be left for the *poor*. **14–15:** *Raise the shout . . . rejoice:* a reflection of ceremonies celebrating the *kingship* of the LORD. **16–20:** The LORD's care will produce security for Judah. The future will be as bright as the present is black.

HAGGAI

When the Exile in Babylon was lifted about 539 B.C., civil and religious life in Judah was at a low ebb. The Temple (destroyed in 587) was in ruins, and the economy scarcely better. While the Persian rule proved more lenient than that of Babylonia, a simple return to the situation before the Exile was not possible.

By 520, the standard of living had improved, but there had been no progress in religious reestablishment. Along with Zechariah (see Introduction to Zechariah) Haggai addressed himself to this latter problem with such zeal that the rebuilding of the Temple began within a month after his first oracle. Haggai saw a correlation between prosperity and piety, in that he tended to ascribe adverse conditions to the failure to build the Temple and to predict favorable ones as a result of its construction. Moreover, he considered the restoration of David's dynasty necessary to Judah's full life, and hence the promise of kingship to Zerubbabel (2.20–23). The rebuilding of the Temple was completed about 516, four years after Haggai revealed that it would be so.

Zerubbabel restorer of the temple

1 IN THE SECOND YEAR OF KING DARIUS, on the first day of the sixth month, the word of the LORD came through the prophet Haggai to Zerubbabel son of Shealtiel, governor of Judah, and to Joshua son of Jehozadak, the high 2 priest: These are the words of the LORD of Hosts: This nation says to itself that it is not yet time for the house of the 3 LORD to be rebuilt. Then this word 4 came through Haggai the prophet: Is it a time for you to live in your own well-roofed houses, while this house 5 lies in ruins? Now these are the words of the LORD of Hosts: Consider your 6 way of life. You have sown much but reaped little; you eat but never as much as you wish, you drink but never more than you need, you are clothed but never warm, and the labourer puts his wages into a purse with a hole in it. 7 These are the words of the LORD of 8 Hosts: Consider your way of life. Go up into the hills, fetch timber, and build a house acceptable to me, where I can show my glory,^a says the LORD. 9 You look for much and get little. At the moment when you would bring home the harvest, I blast it. Why? says the LORD of Hosts. Because my house lies in ruins, while each of you has a house that he can run to. It is your fault 10 that the heavens withhold their dew and the earth its produce. So I have 11 proclaimed a drought against land and mountain, against corn, new wine, and oil, and all that the ground yields, against man and cattle and all the products of man's labour.

Zerubbabel son of Shealtiel, Joshua 12 son of Jehozadak, the high priest, and the rest of the people listened to what the LORD their God had said and what the prophet Haggai said when the LORD their God sent him, and they were filled with fear because of the LORD. So Haggai the LORD's messen- 13 ger, as the LORD had commissioned him, said to the people: I am with you, says the LORD. Then the LORD stirred 14 up the spirit of Zerubbabel son of Shealtiel, governor of Judah, of Joshua son of Jehozadak, the high priest, and of the rest of the people; they came and began work on the house of the LORD of Hosts their God on the twenty- 15 fourth day of the sixth month.

2 In the second year of King Darius, on the twenty-first day of the seventh month, these words came from the LORD through the prophet Haggai:

a show my glory: or be honoured.

1.1–15: The first oracle, on the prompt rebuilding of the Temple, was designed to shame the people into beginning the work despite obstacles. The date was late August, 520 B.C. *Darius* began his reign as Persian emperor in 522. The Persians allowed *Zerubbabel* and *Joshua* to share in the local rule, dividing the civil and priestly offices between them (see Ezra 5.1–2; Zech. chs. 3–4). **2:** According to Ezra chs. 3–4, though the returned exiles began to rebuild the Temple on first coming to Jerusalem, they were compelled to stop. **9:** The nation's poor economic condition is attributed to the fact that the people have houses, but the LORD has not. **15:** The date is mid-September.
2.1–9: The second oracle urges the builders on in the face of discouragement. The date is

2 Say to Zerubbabel son of Shealtiel, governor of Judah, to Joshua son of Jehozadak, the high priest, and to the 3 rest of the people: Is there anyone still among you who saw this house in its former glory? How does it appear to you now? Does it not seem to you as if 4 it were not there? But now, Zerubbabel, take heart, says the LORD; take heart, Joshua son of Jehozadak, high priest. Take heart, all you people, says the LORD. Begin the work, for I am with 5 you, says the LORD of Hosts, and my spirit is present among you. Have no 6 fear. For these are the words of the LORD of Hosts: One thing more: I will shake heaven and earth, sea and land, 7 I will shake all nations; the treasure of all nations shall come hither, and I will fill this house with glory;*b* so says 8 the LORD of Hosts. Mine is the silver and mine the gold, says the LORD of 9 Hosts, and the glory*b* of this latter house shall surpass the glory*b* of the former, says the LORD of Hosts. In this place will I grant prosperity and peace. This is the very word of the LORD of Hosts.

10 In the second year of Darius, on the twenty-fourth day of the ninth month, this word came from the LORD to the 11 prophet Haggai: These are the words of the LORD of Hosts: Ask the priests 12 to give their ruling: If a man is carrying consecrated flesh in a fold of his robe, and he lets the fold touch bread or broth or wine or oil or any other kind of food, will that also become consecrated? And the priests answered, 13 'No.' Haggai went on, But if a person defiled by contact with a corpse touches any one of these things, will

that also become defiled? 'It will', answered the priests. Haggai replied, 14 So it is with this people and nation and all that they do, says the LORD; whatever offering they make here is defiled in my sight. And now look back 15 over recent times down to this day: before one stone was laid on another in the LORD's temple, what was your 16 plight? If a man came to a heap of corn expecting twenty measures, he found but ten; if he came to a wine-vat to draw fifty measures, he found but twenty. I blasted you and all your 17 harvest with black blight and red and with hail, and yet you had no mind to return to me, says the LORD. Consider, 18 from this day onwards, from this twenty-fourth day of the ninth month, the day when the foundations of the temple of the LORD are laid, consider: will the seed still be diminished*c* in the 19 barn? Will the vine and the fig, the pomegranate and the olive, still bear no fruit? Not so, from this day I will bless you.

On that day, the twenty-fourth day 20 of the month, the word of the LORD came to Haggai a second time: Tell 21 Zerubbabel, governor of Judah, I will shake heaven and earth; I will over- 22 throw the thrones of kings, break the power of heathen realms, overturn chariots and their riders; horses and riders shall fall by the sword of their comrades. On that day, says the LORD 23 of Hosts, I will take you, Zerubbabel son of Shealtiel, my servant, and will wear you as a signet-ring; for you it is that I have chosen. This is the very word of the LORD of Hosts.

b Or wealth.   *c* diminished: *prob. rdg.; Heb. om.*

---

early October, 520. **2:** *Former glory:* since Solomon's Temple was destroyed by the Babylonians in 587 B.C., some of the returnees might remember it. **6:** *Shake:* the verb often denotes an earthquake. Here it is used figuratively.

2.10–19: The third oracle comes on the day the foundations are laid (v. 18), in early December, 520. Its first part (vv. 10–14) has to do with ritual cleanliness. That which is *consecrated* (v. 12) does not affect what it touches, but that which is *defiled*, as a *corpse* is (v. 13), causes whatever it touches to become defiled. The second part (vv. 15–19) promises a change in economic fortune because of the work on the Temple.

2.20–23: The fourth oracle, dated also in December, 520, is addressed to *Zerubbabel*, grandson of the exiled king Jehoiachin (the Jeconiah of 1 Chr.3.17–19). By *shaking heaven and earth* God will crumple all human authority and effort, setting in their place his own choice, Judah. **23:** *Signet-ring:* a visible sign and seal which becomes the instrument of conveying authority and power. In Jer.22.24, a king is called a signet-ring. The symbol shows that Haggai considered Zerubbabel to be *chosen* by the LORD as the future king.

ZECHARIAH

Zechariah is really two books, not one. In the first, chs. 1–8, the setting is Jerusalem, beginning life anew after the Exile in Babylon and in the process of reestablishing herself as a living and worshiping city. The second book, chs. 9–14, takes place much later; the book is in prose and poetry, some perhaps stemming from a time after the Maccabean War, which ended about 160 B.C.

Zechariah, in chs. 1–8, is as anxious as his contemporary, Haggai (see Introduction to Haggai), to revive the social and religious order of Jerusalem. He states his message partly in oracles (especially in chs. 7–8), but mostly in visions of the LORD's purification of Jerusalem (chs. 1–6). These highly symbolic visions foreshadow the style that apocalyptic books, such as Daniel and Revelation, would later develop.

Chapters 9–14, often called Deutero-Zechariah, are so diverse as to defy any unified description. Ch.11.4–16 recalls the symbolic acts of earlier prophets (compare Jer.13.1–11; Ezek.4.1–5.4). The battle scene in 14.1–5 has an apocalyptic cast. Other oracles of threat and promise are quite similar to those of earlier prophets. But much of chs. 9–14 is extremely enigmatic.

Zechariah's commission

1 IN THE EIGHTH MONTH OF THE SECOND year of Darius, the word of the LORD came to the prophet Zechariah son of Berechiah, son of Iddo: 2 The LORD was very angry with your 3 forefathers. Say to the people, These are the words of the LORD of Hosts: Come back to me, and I will come back to you, says the LORD of Hosts. 4 Do not be like your forefathers. They heard the prophets of old proclaim, 'These are the words of the LORD of Hosts: Turn back from your evil ways and your evil deeds.' But they did not listen or pay heed to me, says the 5 LORD. And where are your forefathers now? And the prophets, do they live 6 for ever? But the warnings and the decrees with which I charged my servants the prophets—did not these overtake your forefathers? Did they not then repent and say, 'The LORD of Hosts has treated us as he purposed; as our lives and as our deeds deserved, so has he treated us'?

Eight visions with their interpretations

7 ON THE TWENTY-FOURTH DAY OF THE eleventh month, the month Shebat, in the second year of Darius, the word of the LORD came to the prophet Zechariah son of Berechiah, son of Iddo.

Last night I had a vision. I saw a 8 man on a bay horse standing among the myrtles in a hollow; and behind him were other horses, black, dappled, and white. 'What are these, sir?' I 9 asked, and the angel who talked with me answered, 'I will show you what they are.' Then the man standing 10 among the myrtles said, 'They are those whom the LORD has sent to range through the world.' They reported to 11 the angel of the LORD as he stood among the myrtles: 'We have ranged through the world; the whole world is still and at peace.' Thereupon the 12 angel of the LORD said, 'How long, O LORD of Hosts, wilt thou withhold thy compassion from Jerusalem and the cities of Judah, upon whom thou hast vented thy wrath these seventy years?' Then the LORD spoke kind and 13 comforting words to the angel who talked with me, and the angel said to 14 me, Proclaim, These are the words of the LORD of Hosts: I am very jealous for Jerusalem and Zion. I am full of 15 anger against the nations that enjoy their ease, because, while my anger was but mild, they heaped evil on evil.

1.1–6: Zechariah's commission. *Darius:* see Hag.1.1–15 n. The date is October–November, 520 B.C. *Zechariah* means "the LORD remembers."
1.7–6.15: Eight visions with their interpretations. 7: The date is early February, 519 B.C.
1.8–17: Vision of the horsemen. The vision (vv. 8–12) is of horsemen on *horses* of four different colors, who *range through the world* as a patrol. To the *angel's* urging that it is time that the *wrath* be lifted from Jerusalem, the answer is a *comforting* oracle (vv. 14–17). **14:** *Jealous:* exclusively concerned, or zealous. **15:** The LORD's *anger* against Jerusalem was *mild;* the

16 Therefore these are the words of the LORD: I have come back to Jerusalem with compassion, and my house shall be rebuilt in her, says the LORD of Hosts, and the measuring-line shall be 17 stretched over Jerusalem. Proclaim once more, These are the words of the LORD of Hosts: My cities shall again overflow with good things; once again the LORD will comfort Zion, once again he will make Jerusalem the city of his choice.

18 I lifted my eyes and there I saw four 19 horns. I asked the angel who talked with me what they were, and he answered, 'These are the horns which 20 scattered Judah[a] and Jerusalem.' Then 21 the LORD showed me four smiths. I asked what they were coming to do, and he said, 'Those horns scattered Judah and Jerusalem so completely that no man could lift his head. But these smiths have come to reunite them and to throw down the horns of the nations which had raised them against the land of Judah and scattered its people'.

2 I lifted my eyes and there I saw a 2 man carrying a measuring-line. I asked him where he was going, and he said, 'To measure Jerusalem and see what should be its breadth and length.' 3 Then, as the angel who talked with me was going away, another angel came 4 out to meet him and said to him, Run to the young man there and tell him that Jerusalem shall be a city without walls, so numerous shall be the men 5 and cattle within it. I will be a wall of fire round her, says the LORD, and a glory in the midst of her.

6 Away, away; flee from the land of the north, says the LORD, for I will make you spread your wings like the four winds of heaven, says the LORD. Away, escape, you people of Zion who 7 live in Babylon.

For these are the words of the LORD 8 of Hosts, spoken when he sent me on a glorious mission[b] to the nations who have plundered you, for whoever touches you touches the apple of his eye: I raise[c] my hand against them; 9 they shall be plunder for their own slaves. So you shall know that the LORD of Hosts has sent me. Shout 10 aloud and rejoice, daughter of Zion; I am coming, I will make my dwelling among you, says the LORD. Many 11 nations shall come over to the LORD on that day and become his people, and he will make his dwelling with you. Then you shall know that the LORD of Hosts has sent me to you. The LORD 12 will once again claim Judah as his own possession in the holy land, and make Jerusalem the city of his choice.

Silence, all mankind, in the presence 13 of the LORD! For he has bestirred himself out of his holy dwelling-place.

The angel who talked with me came **4** 1[d] back and roused me as a man is roused from sleep. He asked me what 2 I saw, and I answered, 'A lamp-stand all of gold with a bowl on it; it holds seven lamps, and there are seven pipes for the lamps on top of it, with two 3 olive-trees standing by it, one on the right of the bowl and another on the left.' I asked him, 'What are these two 11[e] olive-trees, the one on the right and

a *Prob. rdg.; Heb. adds* Israel.
b *on a glorious mission: prob. rdg.; Heb. after glory.*
c *Or* wave.
d *3. 1–10 transposed to follow 4. 14.*
e *4. 4–10 transposed to follow 3. 10.*

---

nations, his agents, went too far. **16:** *My house:* the Temple. *Measuring-line:* used in building, and hence a symbol of reconstruction.

1.18–21: Vision of the horns and smiths. *Horns* signify innate strength, especially as it is manifested in external activity, either good or evil; see Ps.75.10. *Four* is obscure, but seems to mean Babylonia. The symbolism of the *smiths*, though their action is clear, is uncertain; they may suggest counterdestruction.

2.1–5: Vision of the man with the measuring-line. The *measuring-line* implies limits on the size of the city; the *angel*, however, says that Jerusalem will have no limits. It will be protected not by walls but by a *wall of fire*, the indwelling *glory* of the LORD.

2.6–13: Oracle of promise to Jerusalem. 6–7: *Land of the north, Babylon:* see Joel 2.20 n. **10:** *Zion* was the hill on which the Temple stood; *daughter* is a figure of speech for Jerusalem.

4.1–3,11–14: Vision of the lamp-stand and olive-trees. The *lamp-stand* has *seven* branches, a bowl-shaped *lamp* on each, a *bowl* as an oil reservoir over the whole, and *pipes* conducting oil from the bowl to each lamp. *Seven* symbolizes completeness. The *olive-trees* probably stand for Joshua, the high priest, and Zerubbabel, the future king (see 4.6–10; 6.9–15 n.). By implication, the lamp-stand signifies the LORD's presence.

the other on the left of the lamp-stand?'

12 I asked also another question, 'What are the two sprays of olive beside the golden pipes which discharge the
13 golden oil from their bowls?' He said, 'Do you not know what these mean?'
14 'No, sir', I answered. 'These two', he said, 'are the two consecrated with oil who attend the Lord of all the earth.'

3 Then he showed me Joshua the high priest standing before the angel of the Lord, with the Adversary*f* standing at
2 his right hand to accuse him. The Lord said to the Adversary, 'The Lord rebuke you, Satan, the Lord rebuke you who are venting your spite on Jerusalem.*g* Is not this man a brand
3 snatched from the fire?' Now Joshua was wearing filthy clothes as he stood
4 before the angel; and the angel turned and said to those in attendance on him, 'Take off his filthy clothes.' Then he turned to him and said, 'See how I have taken away your guilt from you; I will clothe you in fine
5 vestments'; and he added, 'Let a clean turban be put on his head.' So they put a clean turban on his head and clothed him in clean garments, while the angel of the Lord stood by.
6 Then the angel of the Lord gave
7 Joshua this solemn charge: These are the words of the Lord of Hosts: If you will conform to my ways and carry out your duties, you shall administer my house and be in control of my courts, and I grant you the right to come and go amongst these in attendance here.
8 Listen, Joshua the high priest, you and your colleagues seated here before you, all you who are an omen of things to come: I will now bring my servant, the
9–10 Branch. In one day I will wipe away the guilt of the land. On that day, says the Lord of Hosts, you shall all of you

invite one another to come and sit each under his vine and his fig-tree.

Here is the stone that I set before Joshua, a stone in which are seven eyes. I will reveal its meaning to you, says the Lord of Hosts. Then I asked **4** 4*h* the angel of the Lord who talked with me, 'Sir, what are these?' And he 5 answered, 'Do you not know what these mean?' 'No, sir', I answered. 'These seven', he said, 'are the eyes of the Lord ranging over the whole earth.'*i*

Then he turned and said to me, This 6 is the word of the Lord concerning Zerubbabel: Neither by force of arms nor by brute strength, but by my spirit! says the Lord of Hosts. How 7 does a mountain, the greatest mountain, compare with Zerubbabel? It is no higher than a plain. He shall bring out the stone called Possession*j* while men acclaim its beauty. This word 8 came to me from the Lord: Zerubbabel 9 with his own hands laid the foundation of this house and with his own hands he shall finish it. So shall you know that the Lord of Hosts has sent me to you. Who has despised the day of small 10 things? He shall rejoice when he sees Zerubbabel holding the stone called Separation.*j*

I looked up again and saw a flying **5** scroll. He asked me what I saw, and 2 I answered, 'A flying scroll, twenty 3 cubits long and ten cubits wide.' This, he told me, is the curse which goes out over the whole land; for by the writing on one side every thief shall be swept clean away, and by the writing on the other every perjurer shall be swept clean away. I have sent it out, the 4

f Heb. the Satan.
g the Lord . . . Jerusalem: *or* the Lord who has chosen Jerusalem rebuke you.
h See note on 4. 11 *above.*
i These seven . . . earth: *transposed from verse 10.*
j Cp. Lev. 20. 24–26.

3.1–10; 4.4–5: Vision of Joshua's purification. In the trial, *the Adversary* (v. 1; see Tfn. *f*) is the title of an angelic figure who, as in Job chs. 1–2, accuses wrongdoers before the heavenly court. Joshua is purified of *guilt*, symbolized by his *filthy clothes*. **9–10:** *The Branch:* a title for the coming king, derived from Jer.23.5; 33.15. See also 6.9–15 n. The accession of the king and the purification of the priesthood prepare Jerusalem for restoration. To *invite* one's neighbor to *sit under his vine and his fig-tree* (v. 10) is a sign of unusual prosperity (compare Mic.4.4). *Seven eyes:* perhaps facets.
4.6–10: Oracle about Zerubbabel. *Zerubbabel* will build the Temple by the aid of the *spirit* of the Lord. The two stones, *Possession* and *Separation*, are taken to symbolize Judah's repossessing its land and being distinct from other peoples.
5.1–4: Vision of the flying scroll. The *scroll* contains *curses* designed to remove all crime from the land. **2:** *Cubit:* about seventeen inches.

LORD of Hosts has said, and it shall enter the house of the thief and the house of the man who has perjured himself in my name; it shall stay inside that house and demolish it, timbers and stones and all.

5 The angel who talked with me came out and said to me, 'Raise your eyes and look at this thing that comes forth.' 6 I asked what it was, and he said, 'It is a great barrel coming forth,' and he added, 'so great is their guilt in all the 7 land.' Then a round slab of lead was lifted, and a woman was sitting there 8 inside the barrel. He said, 'This is Wickedness', and he thrust her down into the barrel and rammed the leaden 9 weight upon its mouth. I looked up again and saw two women coming forth with the wind in their wings (for they had wings like a stork's), and they carried the barrel between earth and 10 sky. I asked the angel who talked with me where they were taking the barrel, 11 and he answered, 'To build a house for it*k* in the land of Shinar; when the house is ready, it*l* shall be set on the place prepared for it*k* there.'

6 I looked up again and saw four chariots coming out between two mountains, and the mountains were 2 made of copper.*m* The first chariot had 3 bay horses, the second black, the third 4 white, and the fourth dappled. I asked the angel who talked with me, 'Sir, 5 what are these?' He answered, 'These are the four winds of heaven which have been attending the Lord of the whole earth, and they are now going 6 forth. The chariot with the black horses is going to the land of the north, that with the white to the far west,*n* that with the dappled to the 7 south, and that with the roan to the land of the east.'*o* They were eager to

go and range over the whole earth; so he said, 'Go and range over the earth', and the chariots did so. Then he 8 called me to look and said, 'Those going to the land of the north have given my spirit rest in the land of the north.'

The word of the LORD came to me: 9 Take silver and gold from the exiles, 10 from Heldai, Tobiah, Jedaiah, and*p* Josiah son of Zephaniah, who have come back from Babylon. Take it and 11 make a crown; put the crown on the head of Joshua son of Jehozadak, the high priest,*q* and say to him, These are 12 the words of the LORD of Hosts: Here is a man named the Branch; he will shoot up from the ground where he is and will build the temple of the LORD. It is he who will build the temple of the 13 LORD, he who will assume royal dignity, will be seated on his throne and govern, with a priest at his right side, and concord shall prevail between them. The crown shall be in the 14 charge of Heldai, Tobiah, Jedaiah, and Josiah son of Zephaniah, as a memorial in the temple of the LORD.

Men from far away shall come and 15 work on the building of the temple of the LORD; so shall you know that the LORD of Hosts has sent me to you. If only you will obey the LORD your God!

Joy and gladness in the coming age

THE WORD OF THE LORD CAME TO 7 Zechariah in the fourth year of the reign of King Darius, on the fourth

k Or her. *l Or* she. *m Or* bronze.
n to the far west: *prob. rdg.; Heb.* behind them.
o to the land of the east: *prob. rdg.; Heb. om.*
p and: *prob. rdg.; Heb.* and go on that day yourself and go to the house of . . .
q Joshua . . . priest: *possibly an error for* Zerubbabel son of Shealtiel, *cp. 3. 5; 4. 9.*

5.5–11: Vision of the barrel. Wickedness is symbolically removed from Judah. **6:** *Barrel:* container for an ephah, a dry measure equal to about 1⅓ bushels. **11:** *House:* a temple. *Shinar:* Babylon. Wickedness is returned to the Exile where the Jews suffered.

6.1–15: Vision of the chariots. As in the first vision (1.8–17), four differently colored *horses* go in the four directions. The symbolism of the colors is unknown. The crucial point of the patrol is the *north*, the direction of danger. Everything is ready for reestablishing the dynasty of David. **9–15:** Almost certainly, *Joshua* (v. 11) is an error, or deliberate substitution, for Zerubbabel. See 3.8–9; the *Branch* (royal power) is not Joshua; and in 4.6–10, Zerubbabel is to build the Temple (compare v. 12). We do not know why the name Joshua was substituted. Some conjecture from 4.6 that Zerubbabel in some way offended.

7.1–8.23: Joy and gladness in the coming age. The oracles, taken together, give a wide-ranging answer to the question in 7.3, whether a fast in the *fifth month* (July–August) is still required. The date is mid-November, 518 B.C.

2 day of Kislev, the ninth month. Bethel-sharezer sent Regem-melech with his men to seek the favour of the LORD.
3 They were to say to the priests in the house of the LORD of Hosts and to the prophets, 'Am I to lament and abstain in the fifth month as I have done for
4 so many years?' Then the word of the
5 LORD of Hosts came to me: Say to all the people of the land and to the priests, When you fasted and lamented in the fifth and seventh months these seventy years, was it indeed in my
6 honour that you fasted? And when you ate and drank, was it not to
7 please yourselves? Was it not this that the LORD proclaimed through the prophets of old, while Jerusalem was populous and peaceful, as were the cities round her, and the Negeb and the Shephelah?
8 The word of the LORD came to
9 Zechariah: These are the words of the LORD of Hosts: Administer true justice, show loyalty and compassion to one
10 another, do not oppress the orphan and the widow, the alien and the poor, do not contrive any evil one against
11 another. But they refused to listen, they turned their backs on me in defiance, they stopped their ears and
12 would not hear. Their hearts were adamant; they refused to accept instruction and all that the LORD of Hosts had taught them by his spirit through the prophets of old; and they suffered under the anger of the LORD
13 of Hosts. As they did not listen when I*r* called, so I did not listen when they
14 called, says the LORD of Hosts, and I drove them out among all the nations to whom they were strangers, leaving their land a waste behind them, so that no one came and went. Thus they made their pleasant land a waste.

8 The word of the LORD of Hosts came
2 to me: These are the words of the LORD of Hosts: I have been very jealous for
3 Zion, fiercely jealous for her. Now, says the LORD, I have come back to

Zion and I will dwell in Jerusalem. Jerusalem shall be called the City of Truth, and the mountain of the LORD of Hosts shall be called the Holy
4 Mountain. These are the words of the LORD of Hosts: Once again shall old men and old women sit in the streets of Jerusalem, each leaning on a stick
5 because of their great age; and the streets of the city shall be full of boys
6 and girls, playing in the streets. These are the words of the LORD of Hosts: Even if it may seem impossible*s* to the survivors of this nation on that day, will it also seem impossible to me?*t* This is the very word of the LORD of
7 Hosts. These are the words of the LORD of Hosts: See, I will rescue my people from the countries of the east
8 and the west, and bring them back to live in Jerusalem. They shall be my people, and I will be their God, in truth and justice.

9 These are the words of the LORD of Hosts: Take courage, you who in these days hear, from the prophets who were present when the foundations were laid for the house of the LORD of Hosts, their promise that the temple is
10 to be rebuilt. Till that time there was no hiring either of man or of beast, no one could safely go about his business because of his enemies, and I set all men one against another. But now I
11 am not the same towards the survivors of this people as I was in former days, says the LORD of Hosts. For they shall
12 sow in safety; the vine shall yield its fruit and the soil its produce, the heavens shall give their dew; with all these things I will endow the survivors of this people. You, house of Judah
13 and house of Israel, have been the very symbol of a curse to all the nations; and now I will save you, and you shall become the symbol of a blessing. Courage! Do not be afraid.

r Prob. rdg.; Heb. he.
s Or wonderful.
t will . . . me?: *or* it will seem wonderful also to me.

7.4–14: **The first oracle** recapitulates the past. 5: *Seventy years:* the length of the Exile (compare Jer.25.11).
8.1–8: **The second oracle** describes a restored, *holy,* and happy Jerusalem. 2: *Jealous:* see 1.14 n. 8: *Justice:* lit. "righteousness."
8.9–13: **The third oracle** promises that the reconstruction of the Temple will bring *blessing* to Judah, prosperous crops and security of life.

14 For these are the words of the LORD of Hosts: Whereas I resolved to ruin you because your ancestors roused me to anger, says the LORD of Hosts, and I
15 did not relent, so in these days I have once more*u* resolved to do good to Jerusalem and to the house of Judah;
16 do not be afraid. This is what you shall do: speak the truth to each other, administer true and sound
17 justice in the city gate. Do not contrive any evil one against another, and do not love perjury, for all this I hate. This is the very word of the LORD.
18 The word of the LORD of Hosts
19 came to me: These are the words of the LORD of Hosts: The fasts of the fourth month and of the fifth, the seventh, and the tenth, shall become festivals of joy and gladness for the house of Judah. Love truth and peace.
20 These are the words of the LORD of Hosts: Nations and dwellers in great
21 cities shall yet come; people of one city shall come to those of another and say, 'Let us go and entreat the favour of the LORD, and resort to the LORD
22 of Hosts; and I will come too.' So great nations and mighty peoples shall resort to the LORD of Hosts in Jerusalem and entreat his favour.
23 These are the words of the LORD of Hosts: In those days, when ten men from nations of every language pluck up courage, they shall pluck the robe of a Jew and say, 'We will go with you because we have heard that God is with you.'

Judah's triumph over her enemies

9 An oracle: the word of the LORD.

He has come to the land of Hadrach

and*v* established himself in Damascus;
for the capital city*w* of Aram is the LORD's,
as are all the tribes of Israel.
*x*Sidon has closed her frontier   2
against Hamath,
for she is very wary.
Tyre has built herself a rampart;   3
she has heaped up silver like dust
and gold like mud in the streets.
But wait, the Lord will dispossess   4
her
and strike down the power of her ships,
and the city itself will be destroyed by fire.
Let Ashkelon see it and be afraid;   5
Gaza shall writhe in terror,
and Ekron's hope shall be extinguished;
kings shall vanish from Gaza,
and Ashkelon shall be unpeopled;
half-breeds shall settle in Ashdod,   6
and I will uproot the pride of the Philistine.
I will dash the blood of sacrifices   7
from his mouth
and his loathsome offerings from his teeth;
and his survivors shall belong*y* to our God
and become like a clan in Judah,
and Ekron like a Jebusite.
And I will post a garrison for my   8
house
so that no one may pass in or out,
and no oppressor shall ever overrun them.
[This I have lived to see with my own eyes.]

u once more: or changed my mind and.
v He has come . . . and: *prob. rdg.; Heb.* In the land of Hadrach he has . . .
w capital city: *or* chief part.
x Prob. rdg.; Heb. prefixes Tyre and.
y his survivors shall belong: *or* he shall become kin.

8.14–17: The fourth oracle sets out the quality of the social order. **16:** At the *city gate*, legal cases were heard and decided.
   8.18–19: The fifth oracle alters *fasts* from times at which to "lament and abstain" (7.3) to *festivals of joy and gladness.*
   8.20–23: The sixth oracle describes the growing adherence to the LORD of foreign nations. **23:** *Jew:* lit. a member of the tribe of Judah.
   9.1–14.21: Deutero-Zechariah. See Introduction on this portion of the book.
   9.1–8: The LORD's attack upon nations. 1: *Hadrach* and *Damascus* were in *Aram*, Syria. **2–4:** *Sidon* and *Tyre:* Phoenician ports on the Mediterranean. *Hamath:* a city inland from Sidon. **5–7:** *Ashkelon, Gaza, Ekron,* and *Ashdod* were *Philistine* cities, traditional enemies of Israel, which now become part of God's people. *Jebusite:* pre-Israelite inhabitants of Jerusalem who were assimilated into the Israelites after the capture of the city under David.

9 Rejoice, rejoice, daughter of Zion,
shout aloud, daughter of Jerusalem;
for see, your king is coming to you,
his cause won, his victory gained,
humble and mounted on an ass,
on a foal, the young of a she-ass.

10 He shall banish chariots from
Ephraim
and war-horses from Jerusalem;
the warrior's bow shall be banished.
He shall speak peaceably to every
nation,
and his rule shall extend from sea
to sea,
from the River to the ends of the
earth.

11 And as for you, by your covenant
with me sealed in blood
I release your prisoners from the
dungeon.*z*

12 (Come back to the stronghold, you
prisoners who wait in hope.)
Now is the day announced
when I will grant you twofold*a*
reparation.

13 For my bow is strung, O Judah;
I have laid the arrow to it, O
Ephraim;
I have roused your sons, O Zion,*b*
and made you into the sword of a
warrior.

14 The LORD shall appear above them,
and his arrow shall flash like
lightning;
the Lord GOD shall blow a blast on
the horn
and march with the storm-winds of
the south.

15 The LORD of Hosts will be their
shield;
they shall prevail, they shall trample
on the sling-stones;
they shall be roaring drunk as if
with wine,

brimful as a bowl, drenched like the
corners of the altar.

16 So on that day the LORD their God
will save them, his own people, like
sheep,
setting them all about his land,
like*c* jewels set to sparkle in a
crown.

17 What wealth, what beauty, is
theirs:
corn to strengthen young men,
and new wine for maidens!

10 Ask of the LORD rain in the autumn;
ask him for rain in the spring,
the LORD who makes the storm-
clouds,
and he will give you showers of rain
and to every man grass in his field;

2 for the household gods make
mischievous promises;
diviners see false signs,
they tell lying dreams*d*
and talk raving nonsense.
Men wander about like sheep
in distress for lack of a shepherd.

3 My anger is turned against the
shepherds,
and I will visit with punishment
the leaders of the flock;
but the LORD of Hosts will visit his
flock,
the house of Judah,
and make them his royal war-horses.

4 They shall be corner-stone and
tent-peg,
they shall be the bow ready for
battle,
and from them shall come every
commander.

z Prob. rdg.; Heb. adds no water in it.
a Or equal.
*b Prob. rdg.; Heb. adds against your sons, O Javan
(or Greece).*
c like: prob. rdg.; Heb. for.
*d they . . . dreams: or dreaming women make empty
promises.*

9.9–16: Judah goes to war. 9–10: *Daughter:* see 2.10 n. But here, it may be only a woman
of Jerusalem. Some scholars think the *king* is Alexander the Great, sweeping through Palestine
in 332 B.C. Others interpret the passage to mean a coming Jewish king (compare Mt.21.4–5).
Ephraim: the leading Israelite tribe of the Northern Kingdom, exiled in 722 B.C. *The River:*
Euphrates. **15:** *Roaring drunk:* figure for the ecstatic exuberance of victors in battle; see 10.7;
Ps.78.65–66. The Israelites, covered with blood of the slain enemy, are compared to *corners
of the altar* on which the blood of sacrifices was poured out daily, a symbol of overwhelming
victory.
9.17–10.12: The restoration of Israel. 10.1: Parched summers make early *rain in the autumn*
necessary to fill cisterns. Rains late *in spring* strengthened crops against the heat. **2:** *Household
gods:* idols, personal deities, who watched over families. Not they nor *diviners*, but the LORD
gives real prosperity (v. 1). *Shepherd:* a leader. **3:** The *anger* may be against specific leaders of Judah.

5 Together they shall be like warriors
  who tramp the muddy ways in
    battle,
and they will fight because the LORD
    is with them;
they will put horsemen shamefully
  to rout.
6 And I will give strength to the
  house of Judah
and grant victory to*e* the house of
  Joseph;
I will restore them, for I have
  pitied them,
and they shall be as though I had
  never cast them off;
for I am the LORD their God and I
  will answer them.
7 So Ephraim shall be like warriors,
glad like men cheerful with wine,
and their sons shall see and be glad;
so let their hearts exult in the LORD.
8 I will whistle to call them in, for I
  have redeemed them;
and they shall be as many as once
  they were.
9 If I disperse them*f* among the
  nations,
  in far-off lands they will remember
    me
and will rear their sons and then
  return.
10 Then will I fetch them home from
  Egypt
and gather them in from Assyria;
I will lead them into Gilead and
  Lebanon
until there is no more room for
  them.
11 Dire distress*g* shall come upon the
  Euphrates
and shall beat down its turbulent
  waters;
all the depths of the Nile shall run
  dry.

The pride of Assyria shall be
  brought down,
and the sceptre of Egypt shall pass
  away;
12 but Israel's strength shall be in
  the LORD,
and they shall march proudly in
  his name.
This is the very word of the LORD.

11 Throw open your gates, O Lebanon,
that fire may feed on your cedars.
2 Howl, every pine-tree; for the cedars
  have fallen,
mighty trees are ravaged.
Howl, every oak of Bashan;
for the impenetrable forest is laid
  low.
3 Hark to the howling of the
  shepherds,
for their rich pastures are ravaged.
Hark to the roar of the young lions,
for Jordan's dense thickets are
  ravaged.

4 These were the words of the LORD
my God: Fatten the flock for slaughter.
5 Those who buy will slaughter it and
incur no guilt; those who sell will say,
'Blessed be the LORD, I am rich!' Its
6 shepherds will have no pity for it. For
I will never again pity the inhabitants
of the earth, says the LORD. I will put
every man in the power of his neighbour and his king, and as each country
is crushed I will not rescue him from
their hands.
7 So I fattened the flock for slaughter
for the dealers. I took two staves: one
I called Favour and the other Union,
and so I fattened the flock. In one
8 month I got rid of the three shepherds,

e grant victory to: *or* expand.
f Or scatter them like seed.
g Dire distress: *or* An enemy.

Compare Ezek. ch. 34. **6:** *House of Joseph:* often a term for northern Israel (see Amos 5.6,15).
The predicted restoration includes the Northern Kingdom dispersed in 721 B.C., bringing the
nation to its former unity. **10:** The place of deportation in 721 was *Assyria.* After the Babylonian
Exile, a colony of Jews lived in *Egypt*, at Elephantine. *Gilead* and *Lebanon* are at the north
and northeastern edges of Israel's former territory, where the roads from Babylon and *Assyria*
entered. **11:** *Turbulent Euphrates* symbolizes warlike Assyria; *the depths of the Nile*, the wealth
and fertility of Egypt.
   11.1–3: A short poem threatening destruction. 1: *Cedars*, useful lumber, were the hallmark
of the prosperity of Lebanon. **2:** *Bashan:* fertile area east of the Sea of Galilee. **3:** Compare
Jer.49.19.
   11.4–14: An allegorical narrative in which a prophet tending sheep quits his job, breaking
his shepherd's staves, the action being symbolic of God, shepherd of men, breaking his
covenant, *Favour* (v. 10), with all men (Gen.9.1–17), and his special covenant, *Union* (v. 14),
with Israel (Exod.24.8). **8:** The *three shepherds* here are specific leaders who cannot be identified.

for I had lost patience with them and
9 they had come to abhor me. Then I
said to the flock, 'I will not fatten you
any more. Any that are to die, let them
die; any that stray, let them stray; and
10 the rest can devour one another.' I
took my staff called Favour and
snapped it in two, annulling the
covenant which the LORD[h] had made
11 with all nations. So it was annulled
that day, and the dealers who were
watching me knew that all this was the
12 word of the LORD. I said to them, 'If
it suits you, give me my wages;
otherwise keep them.' Then they
weighed out my wages, thirty pieces of
13 silver. The LORD said to me, 'Throw
it into the treasury.' I took the thirty
pieces of silver—that noble sum at
which I was valued and rejected by
them!—and threw them into the house
14 of the LORD, into the treasury. Then I
snapped in two my second staff called
Union, annulling the brotherhood
between Judah and Israel.
15 Then the LORD said to me, Equip
yourself again as a shepherd, a worth-
16 less one; for I am about to install a
shepherd in the land who will neither
miss any that are lost nor search for
those that have gone astray nor heal
the injured nor nurse the sickly, but
will eat the flesh of the fat beasts and
throw away their broken bones.

17 Alas for the worthless shepherd who
abandons the sheep!
A sword shall fall on his arm and
on his right eye;
his arm shall be shrivelled
and his right eye blinded.
13 7[i]   This is the very word of the
LORD of Hosts:
O sword, awake against my shepherd
and against him who works with me.
Strike the shepherd, and the sheep
will be scattered,
and I will turn my hand against the
shepherd boys.

This also is the very word of the 8
LORD:
It shall happen throughout the
land
that two thirds of the people shall be
struck down and die,
while one third of them shall be
left there.
Then I will pass this third through 9
the fire
and I will refine them as silver is
refined,
and assay them as gold is assayed.
Then they will invoke me by my
name,
and I myself will answer them;
I will say, 'They are my people',
and they shall say, 'The LORD is our
God.'

Jerusalem a centre of worship for all men

AN ORACLE. THIS IS THE WORD OF THE **12**
LORD concerning Israel, the very word
of the LORD who stretched out the
heavens and founded the earth, and
who formed the spirit of man within
him: I am making the steep approaches 2
to Jerusalem slippery for all the nations
pressing round her; and Judah will be
caught up in the siege of Jerusalem.
On that day, when all the nations of 3
the earth will be gathered against her,
I will make Jerusalem a rock too heavy
for any people to remove, and all who
try to lift it shall injure themselves. On 4
that day, says the LORD, I will strike
every horse with panic and its rider
with madness; I will keep watch over
Judah, but I will strike all the horses
of the other nations with blindness.
Then the clans of Judah shall say to 5
themselves, 'The inhabitants of Jerusalem find their strength[j] in the LORD
of Hosts their God.'

h the LORD: *prob. rdg.; Heb.* I.
i 13. 7–9 *transposed to this point.*
j The . . . strength: *prob. rdg.; Heb.* O inhabitants of
Jerusalem, I am strong.

12: In Exod.21.32, *thirty pieces of silver* is the value of a slave. Thirty pieces of silver appears in
Mt.26.14–16 and parallels.
    11.15–17; 13.7–9: A symbolic action and oracle against a coming king. *One-third* of Israel,
purified by fire, will remain as the *people* of the LORD.
    12.1–14.21: Jerusalem repents and is delivered by the LORD. The oracles convey the themes of
the LORD's triumph, not a chronology or systematic account. Some are extremely obscure.
3: *Rock:* compare Dan.2.33–35. **7:** Even the Davidic king's *glory* will not exceed that of the

6 On that day I will make the clans of Judah like a brazier in woodland, like a torch blazing among sheaves of corn. They shall devour all the nations round them, right and left, while the people of Jerusalem remain safe in 7 their city. The LORD will first set free all the families[k] of Judah, so that the glory of David's line and of the inhabitants of Jerusalem may not surpass that of Judah.

8 On that day the LORD will shield the inhabitants of Jerusalem; on that day the very weakest of them shall be like David, and the line of David like God, like the angel of the LORD going before them.

9 On that day I will set about destroy-10 ing all the nations that come against Jerusalem, but I will pour a spirit of pity and compassion into the line of David and the inhabitants of Jerusalem. Then

> They shall look on me, on him whom
> they have pierced,

and shall wail over him as over an only child, and shall grieve for him bitterly as for a first-born son.

11 On that day the mourning in Jerusalem shall be as great as the mourning over Hadad-rimmon in the 12 vale of Megiddo. The land shall wail, each family by itself: the family of David by itself and its women by themselves; the family of Nathan by 13 itself and its women by themselves; the family of Levi by itself and its women by themselves; the family of Shimei by 14 itself and its women by themselves; all the remaining families by themselves and their women by themselves.

13 On that day a fountain shall be opened for the line of David and for the inhabitants of Jerusalem, to remove all sin and impurity.

2 On that day, says the LORD of Hosts, I will erase the names of the idols from the land, and they shall be remembered no longer; I will also remove the prophets and the spirit of uncleanness from the land. Thereafter, if a man 3 continues to prophesy, his parents, his own father and mother, will say to him, 'You shall live no longer, for you have spoken falsely in the name of the LORD.' His own father and mother will pierce him through because he has prophesied. On that day every prophet 4 shall be ashamed of his vision when he prophesies, nor shall he wear a robe of coarse hair in order to deceive. He will 5 say, 'I am no prophet, I am a tiller of the soil who has been schooled in lust from boyhood.' 'What', someone will 6 ask, 'are these scars on your chest?' And he will answer, 'I got them in the house of my lovers.'[l]

A day is coming for the LORD to act, **14** and the plunder taken from you shall be shared out while you stand by. I 2 will gather all the peoples to fight against Jerusalem; the city shall be taken, the houses plundered and the women raped. Half the city shall go into exile, but the rest of the nation in the city shall not be wiped out. The 3 LORD will come out and fight against those peoples, as in the days of his prowess on the field of battle. On that 4 day his feet will stand on the Mount of Olives, which is opposite Jerusalem to the east, and the mountain shall be cleft in two by an immense valley running east and west; half the mountain shall move northwards and half southwards. The valley between 5 the hills[m] shall be blocked, for the new valley between them will reach as far as Asal. Blocked it shall be as it was blocked by the earthquake in the time of Uzziah king of Judah, and the LORD my God will appear with all the holy ones.

On that day there shall be neither 6

[k] *Or* tents.
[l] *Verses 7–9 transposed to follow 11.17.*
[m] *Prob. rdg.; Heb.* my hills.

---

people. **10:** *Him whom they have pierced:* probably a contemporary allusion, now unrecoverable. Compare Jn.19.37. **11:** *Hadad-rimmon:* a Canaanite fertility god, mourned in the seasonal death of vegetation. The *vale* was the most fertile plain near the city of *Megiddo* in northern Israel. **13.2–6:** The oracle marks the end of the professional *prophets.* **6:** *Scars* from ecstatic activities (compare Hos.7.14) are ascribed to a brothel brawl.

   14.1–21: The LORD's battle against Jerusalem's enemies. 5: *Valley:* named the Kidron, between Jerusalem and the Mount of Olives. *Earthquake:* compare Amos 1.1. *Holy ones:*

7 heat nor cold nor frost. It shall be all one day, whose coming is known only to the LORD, without distinction of day or night, and at evening-time there shall be light.

8 On that day living water shall issue from Jerusalem, half flowing to the eastern sea and half to the western, in summer and winter alike. Then the

9 LORD shall become king over all the earth; on that day the LORD shall be one LORD and his name the one name.

10 The whole land shall be levelled, flat as the Arabah from Geba to Rimmon southwards; but Jerusalem shall stand high in her place, and shall be full of people from the Benjamin Gate [to the point where the former gate stood,] to the Corner Gate, and from the Tower of Hananel to the king's wine-vats.

11 Men shall live in Jerusalem, and never again shall a solemn ban be laid upon

12 her; men shall live there in peace. The LORD will strike down all the nations who warred against Jerusalem, and the plague shall be this: their flesh shall rot while they stand on their feet, their eyes shall rot in their sockets, and their tongues shall rot in their mouths.

13 On that day a great panic, sent by the LORD, shall fall on them. At the very moment when a man would encourage his comrade his hand shall

14 be raised to strike him down. Judah too shall join in the fray in Jerusalem, and the wealth of the surrounding nations will be swept away—gold and silver and apparel in great abundance.

15 And slaughter shall be the fate of horse and mule, camel and ass, the fate of every beast in those armies.

16 All who survive of the nations which attacked Jerusalem shall come up year by year to worship the King, the LORD of Hosts, and to keep the pilgrim-feast of Tabernacles. If any of the families

17 of the earth do not go up to Jerusalem to worship the King, the LORD of Hosts, no rain shall fall upon them. If

18 any family of Egypt does not go up and enter the city, then the same disaster shall overtake it as that which the LORD will inflict on any nation which does not go up to keep the feast. This

19 shall be the punishment of Egypt and of any nation which does not go up to keep the feast of Tabernacles.

20 On that day, not a bell on a war-horse but shall be inscribed 'Holy to the LORD', and the pots in the house of the LORD shall be like the bowls

21 before the altar. Every pot in Jerusalem and Judah shall be holy to the LORD of Hosts, and all who sacrifice shall come and shall take some of them and boil the flesh in them. So when that time comes, no trader shall again be seen in the house of the LORD of Hosts.

---

probably angels. **8:** Compare Ezek.47.1–12; Joel 3.18. **10:** The elevation of *Jerusalem* is similar to Isa.2.2; Mic.4.1. **16–19:** As in 8.20–23, foreigners worship the LORD at Jerusalem. *Tabernacles:* the autumn vintage feast. **20–21:** In the new age, everything, however common, is sanctified. *Holy to the LORD:* also inscribed on the rosette on the high priest's forehead (Exod.28.36). **21:** *Trader:* lit. "Canaanite."

MALACHI

After the return of the Judeans from the Exile in Babylon and the rebuilding of the Temple was completed (see Introduction to Haggai), Judah, subject to the Persians, was without political defense, a royal dynasty, and other marks of a nation. Yet to live as the LORD's people, she had to formulate laws to govern both civil and religious conduct, as permitted by the Persians. The book of Malachi reflects aspects of the problems and hardships that arose about 500–450 B.C.

Malachi (see 1.1 n.) delivers his message in a rather systematic regular form. First he gives a declaration from the LORD, then he proposes a question from his audience; he answers the question in the name of the LORD. The statement criticizes the behavior of people or priests, while the answer to a question contains both judgment and promise. In his view, Judah must live by the Law to maintain the people's purity and devotion to the LORD. The final day of the LORD will separate good from bad. Indeed, the issue of determining what are good and bad acts and who are good and bad persons, dominates the latest stage of Old Testament religion. At the same time that this stage fostered a confining legalism, it also fostered a religious devotion of great power and purity.

1 An oracle. The word of the LORD to Israel through Malachi.[a]

Religious decline and hope of recovery

2 I LOVE YOU, SAYS THE LORD. YOU ASK, 'How hast thou shown love to us?' Is not Esau Jacob's brother? the LORD 3 answers. I love Jacob, but I hate Esau; I have turned his mountains into a waste and his ancestral home into a 4 lodging in the wilderness. When Edom says, 'We are beaten down; let us rebuild our ruined homes', these are the words of the LORD of Hosts: If they rebuild, I will pull down. They shall be called a realm of wickedness, a people whom the LORD has cursed for 5 ever. You yourselves will see it with your own eyes; you yourselves will say, 'The LORD's greatness reaches beyond the realm of Israel.'

6 A son honours his father, and a slave goes in fear of his master. If I am a father, where is the honour due to me? If I am a master, where is the fear due to me? So says the LORD of Hosts to you, you priests who despise my name.

You ask, 'How have we despised thy name?' Because you have offered 7 defiled food on my altar. You ask, 'How have we defiled thee?' Because you have thought that the table of the LORD may be despised, that if you 8 offer a blind victim, there is nothing wrong, and if you offer a victim lame or diseased, there is nothing wrong. If you brought such a gift to the governor, would he receive you or show you favour? says the LORD of Hosts. But 9 now, if you placate God, he may show you mercy; if you do this, will he withhold his favour from you? So the LORD of Hosts has spoken. Better far 10 that one of you should close the great door altogether, so that the light might not fall thus all in vain upon my altar! I have no pleasure in you, says the LORD of Hosts; I will accept no offering from you. From furthest east 11 to furthest west my name is great among the nations. Everywhere fragrant sacrifice and pure gifts are offered in my name; for my name is great among the nations, says the LORD of Hosts. But you profane it by 12

a Malachi: or my messenger.

1.1: Title. *Malachi* means "my messenger" or "my angel," and is probably not a proper name (compare 3.1).
1.2–3.12: Religious decline and hope for recovery.
1.2–5: The LORD's hatred of Esau. The Edomites were descended from Esau, the Israelites from Jacob. They were brother nations, but their relations were dominated by hostility. See Gen.25.19–23, Ezek. ch. 35, and Obad.
1.6–2.9: Against priests. Care for the details of sacrifice and ritual is a way to *honour* the LORD.
11: In contrast to the impurity of worship in Judah, the LORD is worshiped in purity by all the Gentile nations. See, too, v. 14. **12:** *Profane:* to treat an object set aside for worship as if

thinking that the table of the LORD may be defiled, and that you can offer
13 on it food you yourselves despise. You sniff at it, says the LORD of Hosts, and say, 'How irksome!' If you bring as - your offering victims that are mutilated, lame, or diseased, shall I accept them
14 from you? says the LORD. A curse on the cheat who pays his vows by sacrificing a damaged victim to the Lord, though he has a sound ram in his flock! I am the great king, says the LORD of Hosts, and my name is held in awe among the nations.

2 And now, you priests, this decree is
2 for you: if you will not listen to me and pay heed to the honouring of my name, says the LORD of Hosts, then I will lay a curse upon you. I will turn your blessings into a curse; yes, into a
3 curse, because you pay no heed. I will cut off your arm,*b* fling offal in your faces, the offal of your pilgrim-feasts, and I will banish you from my presence.
4 Then you will know that I have issued this decree against you. my covenant with Levi falls to the ground, says the
5 LORD of Hosts. My covenant was with him: I bestowed life and prosperity on him; I laid on him the duty of reverence, he revered me and lived in
6 awe of my name. The instruction he gave was true, and no word of injustice fell from his lips; he walked in harmony with me and in uprightness,
7 and he turned many back from sin. For men hang upon the words of the priest and seek knowledge and instruction from him, because he is the messenger
8 of the LORD of Hosts. But you have turned away from that course; you have made many stumble with your instruction; you have set at nought the covenant with the Levites, says the

LORD of Hosts. So I, in my turn, have 9 made you despicable and mean in the eyes of the people, in so far as you disregard my ways and show partiality in your instruction.

Have we not all one father? Did not 10 one God create us? Why do we violate the covenant of our forefathers by being faithless to one another? Judah 11 is faithless, and abominable things are done in Israel and in Jerusalem; Judah has violated the holiness of the LORD by loving and marrying daughters of a foreign god. May the LORD banish 12 any who do this from the dwellings of Jacob, nomads or settlers, even though they bring offerings to the LORD of Hosts.

Here is another thing that you do: 13 you weep and moan, and you drown the altar of the LORD with tears, but he still refuses to look at the offering or receive an acceptable gift from you. You ask why. It is because the LORD 14 has borne witness against you on behalf of the wife of your youth. You have been unfaithful to her, though she is your partner and your wife by solemn covenant. Did not the one God 15 make her, both flesh and spirit? And what does the one God require but godly children? Keep watch on your spirit, and do not be unfaithful to the wife of your youth. If a man divorces 16 or puts away his spouse, he overwhelms her with cruelty, says the LORD of Hosts the God of Israel. Keep watch on your spirit, and do not be unfaithful.

You have wearied the LORD with 17 your talk. You ask, 'How have we wearied him?' By saying that all evildoers are good in the eyes of the

b Or posterity.

---

it were a matter of secular business, subject to scheming and bargaining. **2.2:** The business of *priests* is to convey God's *blessings* to people; dishonorable priests will have their blessings turned into *curses* that will fall upon themselves. **3:** Contact with *offal* made one unfit for worship; here the blemished sacrifices do the same (1.13). **4:** *Levi* was the priestly tribe, and the *covenant* acknowledged Levi's priestly functions.

2.10–16: Responsibility of Judah. Two aspects of covenants are discussed, the first (vv. 10–12) is Judah's *covenant* obligating fidelity to the LORD, and the second (vv. 13–16), divorce. **11:** *Daughters of a foreign god:* though this may mean foreign women, it more probably refers to the worship of alien deities. **13–16:** Divorce violates the covenant, for it entails inhuman cruelty. **14:** *Wife of your youth:* this probably means that men were faithlessly divorcing older women to take up with young ones; it may possibly be a protest against forced divorces of foreign wives, narrated in Ezra ch. 10 and Neh.13.23–29, but this is unlikely.

2.17–3.5: The refinement of the priests. The prophet threatens that the priests, who ostensibly *seek* God's nearness, will be shocked and pained when he actually comes near.

LORD, that he is pleased with them, or by asking 'Where is the God of 3 justice?' Look, I am sending my messenger[c] who will clear a path before me. Suddenly the Lord whom you seek will come to his temple; the messenger of the covenant in whom you delight is here, here already, says 2 the LORD of Hosts. Who can endure the day of his coming? Who can stand firm when he appears? He is like a 3 refiner's fire, like fuller's soap; he will take his seat, refining and purifying;[d] he will purify the Levites and cleanse them like gold and silver, and so they shall be fit to bring offerings to the 4 LORD. Thus the offerings of Judah and Jerusalem shall be pleasing to the LORD as they were in days of old, in 5 years long past. I will appear before you in court, prompt to testify against sorcerers, adulterers, and perjurers, against those who wrong[e] the hired labourer, the widow, and the orphan, who thrust the alien aside and have no fear of me, says the LORD of Hosts. 6 I am the LORD, unchanging; and you, too, have not ceased to be sons of 7 Jacob. From the days of your forefathers you have been wayward and have not kept my laws. If you will return to me, I will return to you, says the LORD of Hosts. You ask, 'How can 8 we return?' May man defraud God, that you defraud me? You ask, 'How have we defrauded thee?' Why, in tithes 9 and contributions. There is a curse, a curse on you all, the whole nation of 10 you, because you defraud me. Bring the tithes into the treasury, all of them; let there be food in my house. Put me to the proof, says the LORD of Hosts, and see if I do not open windows in the sky and pour a blessing on you as 11 long as there is need. I will forbid pests to destroy the produce of your soil or make your vines barren, says the LORD

of Hosts. All nations shall count you 12 happy, for yours shall be a favoured land, says the LORD of Hosts.

Murmurers warned, the righteous triumphant

YOU HAVE USED HARD WORDS ABOUT 13 me, says the LORD, and then you ask, 'How have we spoken against thee?' You have said, 'It is useless to serve 14 God; what do we gain from the LORD of Hosts by observing his rules and behaving with deference? We ourselves 15 count the arrogant happy; it is evildoers who are successful; they have put God to the proof and come to no harm.'

Then those who feared the LORD 16 talked together, and the LORD paid heed and listened. A record was written before him of those who feared him and kept his name in mind. They 17 shall be mine, says the LORD of Hosts, my own possession against the day that I appoint, and I will spare them as a man spares the son who serves him. 18 You will again tell good men from bad, the servant of God from the man who does not serve him.

The day comes, glowing like a 4 furnace; all the arrogant and the evildoers shall be chaff, and that day when it comes shall set them ablaze, says the LORD of Hosts, it shall leave them neither root nor branch. But for 2 you who fear my name, the sun of righteousness shall rise with healing in his wings, and you shall break loose like calves released from the stall. On 3 the day that I act, you shall trample down the wicked, for they will be ashes under the soles of your feet, says the LORD of Hosts.

c my messenger: *Heb.* Malachi.
d Prob. rdg.; Heb. adds silver.
e Prob. rdg.; Heb. adds the wages of.

3.6–12: Fraud. *Sons of Jacob:* the people as a whole, not only the priests. *Tithe* is Heb. for a tenth. In Deut.14.28, the tithe of produce every third year is given to the Levites to support them.

3.13–18: How and when the good will triumph over the bad. To the complaint that *evildoers are successful* (compare Job ch. 21), the answer is that the good are in the LORD's *possession* and in his *day* and way, the *good* will be separated from the bad. **16:** *A record was written:* compare Exod. 32.32-34; Dan.12.1.

4.1–6: The day of the LORD. The *day* is the time of distinction between good and evil men, and its fire consumes rather than purifies; see Joel 1.14–15 n. The image of the *healing* winged

4 Remember the law of Moses my servant, the rules and precepts which I bade him deliver to all Israel at Horeb.

5 Look, I will send you the prophet Elijah before the great and terrible day of the LORD comes. He will reconcile 6 fathers to sons and sons to fathers, lest I come and put the land under a ban to destroy it.

---

sun (v. 2) may come, ultimately, from Egyptian symbolism. **4:** Obedience to the *law* is the criterion for surviving the day. *Horeb:* Mount Sinai. **5–6:** The expectation of the return of Elijah (2 Kgs.2.11) before the end may have already been a popular tradition, as it became later, based on this passage (Mt.11.13–14; Mk.9.11–13; and in the late Jewish expectations). He is probably not the same person as the messenger of 3.1. *Ban:* consignment to total destruction of anything or anyone connected with idolatry, including whole cities, as repugnant to God.

APPENDIX

MEASURES OF LENGTH

	span	cubit	rod[a]
span	1	. .	. .
cubit	2	1	. .
rod[a]	12	6	1

The 'short cubit' was traditionally the measure from the elbow to the knuckles of the closed fist; and what seems to be intended as a 'long cubit' measured a 'cubit and a hand-breadth', i.e. 7 instead of 6 hand-breadths (Ezek.40.5). What is meant by cubits 'according to the old standard of measurement' (2 Chr.3.3) is presumably this pre-exilic cubit of 7 hand-breadths. Modern estimates of the Hebrew cubit range from 12 to 25.2 inches, without allowing for varying local standards.

MEASURES OF CAPACITY

liquid measures	equivalences	dry measures
'log'	1 'log'	. .
. .	4 'log'	'kab'
. .	$7\frac{1}{5}$ 'log'	'omer'
'hin'	12 'log'	. .
'bath'	72 'log'	'ephah'
'kor'	720 'log'	'homer' or 'kor'

According to ancient authorities the Hebrew 'log' was of the same capacity as the Roman *sextarius*; this according to the best available evidence was equivalent to 0.99 pint of the English standard.

WEIGHTS AND COINS

	heavy (Phoenician) standard			light (Babylonian) standard		
	shekel	mina	talent	shekel	mina	talent
shekel	1	. .	. .	1	. .	. .
mina	50	1	. .	60	1	. .
talent	3,000	60	1	3,600	60	1

The 'gerah' was 1/20 of the sacred or heavy shekel and probably 1/24 of the light shekel.

[a] Hebrew literally 'reed', the length of Ezekiel's measuring-rod.

The 'sacred shekel' according to tradition was identical with the heavy shekel; while the 'shekel of the standard recognized by merchants' (Gen.23.16) was perhaps a weight stamped with its value as distinct from one not so stamped and requiring to be weighed on the spot.

The weight and value of the shekel varied so greatly according to the district and with the passing centuries that its evaluation in modern terms is impossible. Recent discoveries suggest that it may have weighed approximately 11.5 grammes.

Coins are not mentioned before the Exile. Only the 'daric' (1 Chr.29.7) and the 'drachma' (Ezra 2.69; Neh.7.70–72), if this is a distinct coin, are found in the Old Testament; the former is said to have been a month's pay for a soldier in the Persian army; while the latter will have been the Greek silver drachma, estimated at approximately 4.4 grammes. The 'shekel' of this period (Neh.5.15) as a coin was probably the Graeco-Persian *siglos* weighing 5.6 grammes.

THE NEW
ENGLISH BIBLE

THE APOCRYPHA
OXFORD STUDY EDITION

CONTENTS

INTRODUCTION
TO THE APOCRYPHA

The term 'Apocrypha', a Greek word meaning 'hidden (things)', was early used in different senses. It was applied to writings which were regarded as so important and precious that they must be hidden from the general public and reserved for the initiates, the inner circle of believers. It came to be applied to writings which were hidden not because they were too good but because they were not good enough, because, that is, they were secondary or questionable or heretical. A third usage may be traced to Jerome. He was familiar with the Scriptures in their Hebrew as well as their Greek form, and for him apocryphal books were those outside the Hebrew canon, hence the alternative term deutero-canonical.

The usage here adopted is based on that of Jerome. The Apocrypha in this translation consists of fifteen books or parts of books. They are:

1. The First Book of Esdras
2. The Second Book of Esdras
3. Tobit
4. Judith
5. The Rest of the Chapters of the Book of Esther
6. The Wisdom of Solomon
7. Ecclesiasticus or the Wisdom of Jesus Son of Sirach
8. Baruch
9. A Letter of Jeremiah
10. The Song of the Three
11. Daniel and Susanna
12. Daniel, Bel, and the Snake
13. The Prayer of Manasseh
14. The First Book of the Maccabees
15. The Second Book of the Maccabees

These works are outside the Palestinian canon; that is, they form no part of the Hebrew Scriptures, although the original language of some of them was Hebrew. With the exception, however, of the Second Book of Esdras, they are all in the Greek version of the Old Testament made for the Greek-speaking Jews in Egypt. As such they were accepted as biblical by the early Church and were quoted as Scripture by many early Christian writers, for their Bible was the Greek Bible.

In Greek and Latin manuscripts of the Old Testament these books are dispersed throughout the Old Testament, generally in the places most in accord with their contents. The practice of collecting them into a separate unit, a practice which dates back no farther than A.D. 1520, explains why certain of the items are but fragments; they are passages not found in the Hebrew Bible, and so have been removed from the books in which they occur in the Greek version. To help the reader over this disunity and lack of context the present translators have resorted to various devices. We have added the name Daniel to the titles of the stories of Susanna and of Bel and the Snake as a reminder that these tales are to be read with the Book of Daniel. A note we have inserted after the title, The Song of the Three, indicates that this item is to be found in the third chapter of the Greek form of Daniel. And the six additions to the Book of Esther are so disjointed and unintelligible as they stand in most editions of the Apocrypha that we have provided them with a context by rendering the whole of the Greek version of Esther.

The text used in this translation of the Apocrypha is that edited by H. B. Swete in *The Old Testament in Greek according to the Septuagint*. In places Swete includes two texts, and we have chosen to translate the Codex Sinaiticus text of Tobit and Theodotion's version of the additions to the Book of Daniel, namely, The Song of the Three, Daniel and Susanna, and Daniel, Bel, and the Snake. For Ecclesiasticus we have used, in addition to Codex Vaticanus as printed in Swete's edition, the text edited by J. H. A. Hart in *Ecclesiasticus: the Greek Text of Codex 248*, and constant reference has been made to the various forms of the Hebrew text. For the Second Book of Esdras, which apart from a few verses is not extant in a Greek form, we have based our translation on the Latin text of R. L. Bensly's *The Fourth Book of Ezra*. Throughout we have consulted the variant readings given in critical editions of the Greek, the texts of the versions, and the suggestions of editors and commentators.

Alternative readings cited from Greek manuscripts (referred to as *witnesses*) and the evidence of early translations (*Vss.*, that is Versions) are given, as footnotes, only when they are significant either for text or for meaning. In a few places where the text seems to have suffered in the course of transmission and in its present form is obscure or unintelligible we have made a slight change in the text and marked our rendering of it *probable reading*, and we have indicated any evidence other than the evidence afforded by the context. Where an alternative interpretation seemed to deserve serious consideration it has been recorded as a footnote with *Or* as indicator.

In order to preserve the verse numbering of the Authorized (King James) Version of 1611 we have, when necessary, added at the foot of the page those passages which are found in the manuscripts on which the Authorized Version ultimately rests but which are absent from the earlier manuscripts now available.

We have not sought to achieve consistency in the treatment of proper names any more than did our predecessors. We have continued to use familiar English forms, especially when the reference is to well-known Old Testament characters or places. Sometimes as an aid to the correct pronunciation we have had recourse to such expedients as the affixing of an acute accent to the word Sidé or the introduction of a diphthong, as in our Soud fur Sud. In general it may be said that Greek spellings have been Latinized, but the Greek forms of place-names have not been brought into line with the Hebrew.

We have not aimed at consistency in our treatment of weights and measures. We have rendered terms into the nearest English equivalents only when these seemed suitable and natural in the context.

In the text of the First and Second Books of the Maccabees the dates given are reckoned according to the Greek or Seleucid era. As a help to the reader we have added at the foot of the page the nearest dates according to the Christian era.

This translation of the Apocrypha shares with other parts of The New English Bible the aim of providing a rendering which will be both faithful to the text translated and genuinely English in idiom. The translators have endeavoured to convey the meaning of the original in language which will be the closest natural equivalent. They have tried to avoid free paraphrase on the one hand and, on the other, formal fidelity resulting in a translation which would read like a translation. It is their hope that by their labours these documents, valuable in themselves and indispensable for the study of the background of the New Testament, have been made more intelligible and more readily accessible.

W. D. McH.

The Place of the Apocrypha

The place of the Apocrypha in the biblical canon has long been the center of controversy.

Written between 200 (or somewhat earlier)–50 B.C., certain of the books contain doctrines not uniformly accepted at that time by Jews, namely, a clear teaching on the resurrection of the body (2 Macc.7.9–12) and angelology (Tob.12.15), both of which were opposed by the powerful party, the Sadducees (Acts 23.6–8). Questions concerning the Apocrypha raised among Jews were also raised in the same or divergent form in Christian circles, especially by those church writers who were in contact with the Hebrew tradition. Some Christian writers, Augustine among them, put these books on a par with the rest of the Old Testament and quoted them equally. Jerome, who in 390 A.D. was commissioned to make a new translation of the whole Bible into Latin, studied Hebrew with a rabbi. His avowed purpose was to translate the Old Testament according to the "Hebrew original" (*secundum Hebraicam veritatem*), with the result that he was opposed to translating the Apocrypha because they were not in the Hebrew. In the end, he yielded to the pressure of the bishops and included these writings in the translation which came to be known as the Vulgate and which remained the official translation of the Latin church for many centuries. Paradoxically, Jerome himself often quoted the Apocrypha without distinguishing them from the books of the Hebrew canon.

Following the decrees by the synods of Hippo (393 A.D.) and Carthage (397 A.D.), the Apocrypha were uniformly included in the canon of the Latin church. Nevertheless, questions concerning them continued to be raised right up to the Council of Trent in the sixteenth century.

It had been natural for the leaders of the Reformation in the sixteenth century, with their emphasis on the supremacy and the purity of the Bible, to reject the Apocrypha, especially because an appeal was made for these books by Catholics against some of the basic positions of the Reformation. In 1546 A.D. the Council of Trent published a list of books to be received "with equal devotion and reverence," which included the Apocrypha, with the exception of 1 and 2 Esdras and the Prayer of Manasseh. In time, the Apocrypha came to be designated by Roman Catholics as "deuterocanonical," in distinction to the "protocanonical" books of the Hebrew canon. This special designation is not intended to suggest an inferior status, but simply a reception into the canon later than the proto-canonical books. For the Eastern Orthodox Church, the Synod of Jerusalem (1672 A.D.) affirmed the validity of the longer canon; however, a universally binding conciliar decision has not been made, and hence a diversity of opinion still exists.

Today, the question of the canonical status of the Apocrypha is no longer so vehemently argued either in Protestant or Catholic circles. Scholarly biblical criticism has shown the presence of the same literary forms in both proto- and deuterocanonical writings. One of the results of biblical scholarship in the second half of the twentieth century has been to reduce the controversy, while not completely eliminating it, as witnessed by the inclusion of these books in the present Bible, though in a location and sequence different from those in Bibles published exclusively under Catholic auspices. Theologians now find themselves comfortable with a much more flexible concept of scriptural inerrancy, and consequently of inspiration, than was possible after the great religious controversies of the sixteenth century and before the era of modern biblical scholarship in the nineteenth and twentieth centuries. The usefulness of a book is less likely to be judged on the basis of its inclusion in, or exclusion from, the canon, but rather by the light it sheds for understanding the rest of the Bible. The Apocrypha have something in common with what came before them and with what followed them; they therefore act as a link between the Old and the New Testaments and so help us to understand both.

The conventional verse divisions in the Apocrypha date only from editions printed in the sixteenth century and have no basis in the manuscripts. Any system of division into numbered verses is foreign to the spirit of this translation, which is intended to convey the meaning in continuous natural English.

For purposes of reference, verse numbers are placed in the margin opposite the line in which the first word belonging to the verse in question appears. Sometimes, however, successive verses are combined in a continuous translation so that the precise point where a new verse begins cannot be fixed; in these cases the verse numbers, joined by a hyphen, are placed at the point where the passage begins.

THE FIRST BOOK OF
ESDRAS

1 Esdras presents the material found in 2 Chr. chs. 35–36, the Book of Ezra (with one minor omission), and Nehemiah 7.38–8.12, dealing with Ezra. This material is at places presented in a sequence different from that found in the Masoretic Text. One section, 3.1–5.6, a story of a debate at the Persian court, is exceptional in completely lacking a parallel in Old Testament texts.

1 Esdras is a Greek translation of a Hebrew-Aramaic original (no longer extant) that closely resembled the Masoretic Text. It differed, however, at several points (e.g. compare 1.11 n. and 2.13–15 n.), with some differences being enigmatic (e.g. 5.69 and 8.41). The exact relationship of the Hebrew-Aramaic original to the corresponding material in the Hebrew canon, and to a (hypothetical) common forerunner to these cannot be determined. 1 Esdras is not related to the Septuagint translation of Ezra and Nehemiah. It is a curiosity that Josephus, for his history of the period, followed 1 Esdras.

A possible point of confusion lies in the name: 1 Esdras has also been called 2 Esdras (with 1 Esdras then being reserved for the Septuagint translation of Ezra-Nehemiah, originally a single book) and 3 Esdras (as in the Vulgate, where Ezra is 1 Esdras and Nehemiah is 2 Esdras). Others have called it the "Greek Ezra" (*Esdras* being a Greek rendering of the Hebrew *Ezra*).

Many scholars believe that 1 Esdras was written between 200 B.C. and 90 A.D., with 150 B.C. a likely date.

The reader is invited to consult the annotations prepared for the parallel material in the Old Testament books, as indicated in the first paragraph above.

Exile and return

1 JOSIAH KEPT THE PASSOVER AT JERU-salem in honour of his Lord and sacrificed the Passover victims on the fourteenth day of the first month. 2 The priests, duly robed in their vestments, he stationed in the temple of the Lord according to the order of daily 3 service. He commanded the Levites, who served the temple in Israel, to purify themselves for the Lord, in order to place the holy Ark of the Lord in the house which was built by 4 King Solomon, son of David. Josiah said to them, 'You are no longer to carry it on your shoulders. Make yourselves ready now, family by family and clan by clan, to do service to the Lord your God and to minister to his 5 people Israel in the manner prescribed by King David and provided for so magnificently by his son Solomon. Take your places in the temple as Levites in the prescribed order of your families in the presence of your brother

Israelites; sacrifice the Passover vic- 6 tims, and prepare the sacrifices for your brothers. Observe the Passover according to the ordinance of the Lord which was given to Moses.'

To those who were present Josiah 7 made a gift of thirty thousand lambs and kids and three thousand calves. These he gave from the royal estates in fulfilment of his promise to the people and to the priests and Levites. The 8 temple-wardens, Chelkias, Zacharias, and Esyelus, gave the priests two thousand six hundred sheep and three hundred calves for the Passover. Jechonias, Samaeas, his brother Na- 9 thanael, Sabias, Ozielus, and Joram, army officers of high rank, gave the Levites five thousand sheep and seven hundred calves for the Passover.

This was the procedure. The priests 10 and the Levites, bearing the unleavened bread, stood in all their splendour before the people, in the order of their clans and families, to make offerings to 11 the Lord as is laid down in the book of

---

1.1–33: Josiah's Passover and his last days; parallel to 2 Chr.35.1–27. Why 1 Esd. begins with this account is not known. Some speculate that the author wished to highlight the role of Josiah, and possibly to show a connection between his worthy acts and the return from the Exile in the days of Cyrus. The conclusion at 9.55 seems abrupt, as if more material was once included; possibly the beginning was also lost. 4: *It:* the Ark. *Family and clan:* see 1 Chr. chs. 24–26. 8: *Esyelus:* 2 Chr.35.8 reads "Jehiel." 11: *In the morning:* 2 Chr.35.12 has "so with

Moses. This took place in the morning.
12 They roasted the Passover victims over
the fire in the prescribed way and
boiled the sacrifices in the vessels and
cauldrons, and a pleasant smell went
13 up; then they carried portions round to
the whole assembly. After this they
made preparations both for themselves
and for their brothers the priests, the
14 sons of Aaron. The priests went on
offering the fat until nightfall, while
the Levites made the preparations both
for themselves and for their brothers
15-16 the priests, the sons of Aaron. The
sons of Asaph, the temple singers, with
Asaph, Zacharias, and Eddinous of the
royal court, and the door-keepers at
each gateway remained at their station
according to the ordinances of David,
which prescribe that no one may lawfully default in his daily duty; their
brothers the Levites made the prep-
17 arations for them. All that pertained
to the Lord's sacrifice was completed
that day: the keeping of the Passover
18 and the offering of the sacrifices on the
altar of the Lord according to the
19 command of King Josiah. The Israelites
who were present on this occasion kept
the Passover and the Feast of Un-
20 leavened Bread for seven days. Such a
Passover had not been kept in Israel
since the time of the prophet Samuel;
21 none of the kings of Israel had kept
such a Passover as was kept by Josiah,
the priests and the Levites, the men of
Judah, and those Israelites who hap-
22 pened to be resident in Jerusalem. It
was in the eighteenth year of Josiah's
reign that this Passover was celebrated.
23 All that Josiah did he did rightly and
in whole-hearted devotion to his Lord.
24 The events of his reign are to be found
in ancient records which tell a story of
sin and rebellion against the Lord
graver than that of any other nation or
kingdom, and of offences against him
which brought down his judgement
upon Israel.
25 After all these doings of Josiah's it

happened that Pharaoh king of Egypt
was advancing to attack Carchemish
on the Euphrates, and Josiah took the
field against him. The king of Egypt 26
sent him this message: 'What is your
business with me, king of Judah? It is 27
not against you that the Lord God has
sent me to fight; my campaign is on the
Euphrates. The Lord is with me, the
Lord, I say, is with me, driving me on.
Withdraw, and do not oppose the
Lord.' Josiah did not turn his chariot 28
but went forward to the attack. He
disregarded what the Lord had said
through the prophet Jeremiah and 29
joined battle with Pharaoh in the plain
of Megiddo. Pharaoh's captains swept
down upon King Josiah. The king said 30
to his servants, 'Take me out of the
battle, for I am badly hurt.' At once
his servants took him out of the line
and lifted him into his second chariot. 31
He was brought back to Jerusalem, and
there he died and was buried in his
ancestral tomb.

All Judah mourned Josiah, and the 32
prophet Jeremiah lamented him. The
lamentation for Josiah has been observed by the chief men and their wives
from that day to this; it was proclaimed
that it should be a custom for ever for
the whole people of Israel. These things 33
are recorded in the book of the histories
of the kings of Judah; every deed that
Josiah did which won him fame and
showed his understanding of the law of
the Lord, both what he did earlier and
what is told of him here, is related in
the book of the kings of Israel and
Judah.

His compatriots took Joachaz the 34
son of Josiah and made him king in
succession to his father. He was twenty-
three years old, and he reigned over 35
Judah and Jerusalem for three months.
Then the king of Egypt deposed him,
fined the nation a hundred talents of 36
silver and one talent of gold, and 37
appointed his brother Joakim king of
Judah and Jerusalem. Joakim im- 38

---

the bulls"; the Heb. words for "morning" and "bulls," having identical consonants, were
easily confused. **22:** *The eighteenth year of Josiah's reign:* 621 B.C. **23–24:** Not paralleled in
2 Chr. **25:** *Pharaoh:* Necho (reigned 609–594 B.C.); 2 Chr.35.20. In 609 the Egyptians moved
north *to attack Carchemish*, to aid the Assyrians, who were making a last-ditch stand against
the Medes and Babylonians.
   1.34–58: The fall of Judah and Jerusalem; parallel to 2 Chr.36.1–21. **38:** A confused version

prisoned the leading men and had his brother Zarius arrested and brought back from Egypt.

39 Joakim was twenty-five years old when he became king of Judah and Jerusalem; he did what was wrong in
40 the eyes of the Lord. Nebuchadnezzar king of Babylon marched against him; he put him in chains of bronze and
41 took him to Babylon. Nebuchadnezzar also took some of the sacred vessels of the Lord, carried them off, and put
42 them in his temple in Babylon. The stories about Joakim, his sacrilegious and godless conduct, are recorded in the chronicles of the kings.

43 Joakim was succeeded on the throne by his eighteen-year-old son Joakim.
44 He reigned in Jerusalem for three months and ten days, and did what was wrong in the eyes of the Lord.

45 A year later Nebuchadnezzar had him deported to Babylon together with
46 the sacred vessels of the Lord. He made Zedekiah king of Judah and Jerusalem. Zedekiah was twenty-one years old and
47 reigned eleven years. He did what was wrong in the eyes of the Lord and disregarded what the Lord had said
48 through the prophet Jeremiah. King Nebuchadnezzar had made him take an oath of allegiance by the Lord, but he broke it and revolted. He was stubborn and defiant, and transgressed the commandments of the Lord, the God of Israel.

49 The leaders of the people and the chief priests committed many wicked and lawless acts, outdoing even the heathen in sacrilege, and they defiled the holy temple of the Lord in Jeru-
50 salem. The God of their fathers sent his messenger to reclaim them, because he wished to spare them and his
51 dwelling-place. But they derided his messengers, and on the very day when the Lord spoke they were scoffing at his
52 prophets. At last he was roused to fury against his people for their impieties,

and ordained that the kings of the Chaldaeans should attack them. These 53 put their young men to the sword all round the holy temple, sparing neither old nor young, neither boy nor girl; the Lord handed them all over to their enemies. All the sacred vessels of the 54 Lord, large and small, the furnishings of the Ark of the Lord, and the royal treasures were carried off to Babylon. The house of the Lord was set on fire, 55 the walls of Jerusalem destroyed, its towers burnt, and all its splendours 56 ruined. Nebuchadnezzar carried off to Babylon the survivors from the slaughter, and they remained slaves to him 57 and his sons until the Persians took his empire. This fulfilled the word of the Lord spoken by Jeremiah: 'Until the 58 land has run the full term of its sabbaths, it shall keep sabbath all the time of its desolation till the end of the seventy years.'

DURING THE FIRST YEAR OF CYRUS KING 2 1-2 of Persia, the Lord, in order to fulfil his word spoken through Jeremiah, moved Cyrus king of Persia to make a proclamation throughout his empire, which he also put in writing: 'This is the 3 decree of Cyrus king of Persia: The Lord of Israel, the most high Lord, has made me king of the world and has 4 directed me to build him a house at Jerusalem in Judaea. Whoever among 5 you belongs to his people, may his Lord be with him; let him go up to Jerusalem in Judaea and build the house of the Lord of Israel, the Lord who dwells in Jerusalem. Wherever each man 6 lives let his neighbours help him with gold and silver and other gifts, with 7 horses and pack-animals, together with other things set aside as votive offerings for the Lord's temple in Jerusalem.'

Then the chiefs of the clans of the 8 tribe of Judah and of Benjamin, the priests, the Levites, came forward, and

of 2 Chr.36.4; see 2 Chr.36.1–4, 9–11. The name *Zarius*, otherwise unknown, is likely an error for Zedekiah, the brother of Joakim and successor to his nephew Jehoiachin (vv. 45–48; 2 Kgs.24.17–25.7). The "bringing back" of Zarius-Zedekiah reflects further confusion. **43:** *Joakim . . . Joakim:* for the second *Joakim*, read "Jehoiachin"; *eighteen* is correct, not eight (2 Chr.36.9).
2.1–15: The ascendancy and decree of Cyrus; parallel to Ezra 1.1–11. **1:** *First year:* 539 B.C.
3: *The Lord of Israel:* Ezra 1.2 has "The LORD the God of heaven," a title perhaps more agree-

all whose spirit the Lord had moved to go up to build the Lord's temple in
9 Jerusalem. Their neighbours helped with everything, with silver and gold, horses and pack-animals; and many were also moved to help with votive
10 offerings in great quantity. King Cyrus brought out the sacred vessels of the Lord which Nebuchadnezzar had taken away from Jerusalem and set up in his
11 idolatrous temple. Cyrus king of Persia brought them out and delivered them
12 to Mithradates his treasurer, by whom they were delivered to Sanabassar, the
13 governor of Judaea. This is the inventory: a thousand gold cups, a thousand silver cups, twenty-nine silver censers, thirty gold bowls, two thousand four hundred and ten silver bowls, and a
14 thousand other articles. In all, five thousand four hundred and sixty-nine
15 gold and silver vessels were returned, and taken from Babylon to Jerusalem by Sanabassar together with the exiles.
16   In the time of Artaxerxes king of Persia, Belemus, Mithradates, Tabellius, Rathymus, Beeltethmus, Semellius the secretary, and their colleagues in office in Samaria and other places, wrote him a letter denouncing the inhabitants of Judaea and Jerusalem in the following terms:

17   To our Sovereign Lord Artaxerxes your servants Rathymus the recorder, Semellius the secretary, the other members of their council, and the magistrates in Coele-syria and Phoenicia:
18   This is to inform Your Majesty that the Jews who left you to come here have arrived in Jerusalem and

are rebuilding that wicked and rebellious city. They are repairing its streets and walls and laying the
19 foundation of the temple. If this city is rebuilt and the walls completed, they will cease paying tribute and will rebel against the royal
20 house. Since work on the temple is in hand, we have thought it well not
21 to neglect this important matter but to bring it to Your Majesty's notice, in order that, if it is Your Majesty's pleasure, search may be made in the records left by your predecessors.
22 You will find in the archives evidence about these matters and will learn that this is a city that has resisted authority and given trouble to kings and to other states, and has been a
23 centre of armed rebellion by the Jews from the earliest times. That is why it was laid in ruins. Now we submit
24 to Your Majesty that, if this city be rebuilt and its walls rise again, you will no longer have access to Coele-syria and Phoenicia.

Then the king wrote to Rathymus
25 the recorder, Beeltethmus, Semellius the secretary, and their colleagues in office in Samaria, Syria, and Phoenicia this reply:

I have read your letter. I ordered
26 search to be made and it was discovered that this city has always been opposed to its overlords, and its
27 inhabitants have raised rebellions and made wars. There were kings in Jerusalem, powerful and ruthless men, who in their time controlled Coele-syria and Phoenicia and ex-

---

able to the Persian rulers; see 2 Chr.36.23 and Ezra 5.11–12. **10:** *Idolatrous temple* is pointedly monotheistic; compare Ezra 1.7, which has "in the temple of his god." **12,15:** *Sanabassar* is Sheshbazzar in Ezra 1.8. **13–15:** The inventory here is probably more accurate than the parallel in Ezra 1.9–11. The total here, 5,469, is correct, not the figure 5,400 in Ezra, though a miscellaneous category "other vessels," is mentioned there.

   2.16–30: Opposition to rebuilding the Temple and the walls; parallel to Ezra 4.7,11–24. The account is somewhat confusing. V. 1 mentions Cyrus (died 529 B.C.) and v. 30, Darius I (521–486 B.C.); Cambyses (529–521 B.C.) is omitted. Artaxerxes (v. 16) reigned in 464–424 B.C. The section seems misplaced, perhaps belonging originally between the end of Ezra and the beginning of Nehemiah. **16:** *Beeltethmus:* the translator here mistook a title ("high commissioner," Ezra 4.9) for a personal name. **17:** The men ruled over the area which included Palestine; the area, from Persian perspective, is called "Beyond-Euphrates" (Ezra 4.10). **18:** *The temple* is not mentioned in Ezra 4.14; 4.24, however, speaks of the cessation of building it. Many scholars believe that the mention of the Temple here, in v. 30, and in Ezra 4.24 are late insertions, occasioned by the mention of sacred vessels (v. 10). The opposition at this time was to rebuilding the walls. **25:** *Beeltethmus:* see v. 16 n.

28 acted tribute from them. I therefore command that the men you mention be prevented from rebuilding the city, and that measures be taken to en-
29 force this order and to check the spread of an evil likely to be a nuisance to the royal house.

30 When the letter from King Artaxerxes had been read, Rathymus, Semellius the secretary, and their colleagues set out at once for Jerusalem with cavalry and a large body of other troops and stopped the builders. The building of the temple was broken off until the second year of the reign of Darius king of Persia.

A debate at the Persian court

3 KING DARIUS HELD A GREAT FEAST FOR all those under him, his household, the
2 chief men of Media and Persia, and the satraps and commanders and governors of his empire in the hundred and twenty-seven satrapies from India to
3 Ethiopia. When they had eaten and drunk their fill, they went away, and King Darius withdrew to his bedchamber; he went to sleep but woke up
4 again. Then the three young men of the king's personal bodyguard said to each
5 other: 'Let each one of us name the thing which he judges the strongest; and to the one whose opinion seems wisest King Darius will give rich gifts
6 and prizes: he shall be clothed in purple, drink from gold vessels, and sleep on a golden bed; and he shall have a chariot with gold-studded bridles, and a fine linen turban, and a
7 chain about his neck. His wisdom shall give him the right to sit next to Darius and to be given the title Kinsman of

Darius.' Then each wrote down his 8 own statement, sealed it, and put it under the king's pillow. 'When the king 9 wakes again,' they said, 'the writing will be given him. The king and the three chief men of Persia shall judge whose statement is wisest, and the award will be made on the merits of the written statement.'

One wrote 'Wine is strongest', the 10,11 second wrote 'The king is strongest', and the third wrote 'Women are 12 strongest, but truth conquers all'. When the king got up he was pre- 13 sented with what they had written. He read it, and summoned all the chief 14 men of Persia and Media, satraps, commanders, governors, and chief officers. Then he took his seat in the 15 council chamber, and what they had written was read out before them. He 16 said, 'Call the young men and let them expound their statements.' They were called and came in. They were asked, 17 'Tell us about what you have written.'

The first, who spoke about the strength of wine, began. 'Sirs,' he said, 18 'how true it is that wine is strongest! It sends astray the wits of all who drink it; king and orphan, slave and 19 free, rich and poor, it has the same effect on them all. It turns all thoughts 20 to revelry and mirth; it brings forgetfulness of grief and debt. It makes all 21 feel rich, cares nothing for king or satrap, and makes men always talk in millions. When they are in their cups, 22 they forget to be friendly to friends and relations, and are quick to draw their swords; when they have recovered from 23 their wine, they cannot remember what they have done. Sirs, is not wine the 24 strongest, seeing that it forces men to behave in this way?' With this he ended.

3.1–5.6: A debate at the Persian court. This interpolated story is unique to Esdras. It aggrandizes Zerubbabel. The author adapted a popular account of a debate, which originally contained only three statements (about wine, the king, and women). To that account he added the statement, "but truth conquers all" (v. 12), both in order to include a theme more akin to Jewish sensibilities, and also to introduce the return from the Babylonian Exile. The third speaker, Zerubbabel, proposes two separate statements, thus effacing the expected symmetry of three men and three statements.

3.1–17a: The setting of the debate. 1: *Darius* I, reigned 521–486 B.C. **2:** *The hundred and twenty-seven satrapies:* compare Esther 1.1; the number is greatly exaggerated; twenty would be accurate. **3:** *Went to sleep:* Josephus *Ant.* XI. 3.2 relates that the king suggested the debate after a sleepless night.

    3.17b–24: Wine is strongest. 18: *It sends astray the wits:* compare Ecclus.19.2.

4 Then the second, the one who spoke of the strength of the king, began his **2** speech: 'Sirs, is not man the strongest, man who masters the earth and the sea **3** and all that is in them? But the strongest of men is the king; he is their lord and master, and they obey all his **4** commands. If he bids them make war upon one another they do it; if he dispatches them against his enemies, they march and level mountains and **5** walls and towers. They kill and are killed; they do not disobey the king's order. If they are victorious they bring everything to the king, their spoils and **6** everything else. Or take those who do not serve as soldiers or go to war, but work the land: they sow and reap, and bring their produce to the king. They compel each other to bring him their **7** tribute. Though he is no more than one man, if he orders them to kill, they kill; if he orders them to release, they re- **8** lease; he orders them to attack and they attack, to lay waste and they lay waste, **9** to build and they build, to cut down and they cut down, to plant and they **10** plant. So all his people and his troops obey him. Besides this, while he himself sits at table, eats and drinks, and goes **11** to sleep, they stand in attendance round about him and none can leave and see to his own affairs; they never **12** disobey him in anything. Sirs, of course the king must be strongest when he commands such obedience!' So he stopped speaking.

13 The third, who spoke about women and truth—and this was Zerubbabel— **14** said: 'Sirs, it is true the king is great, men are many, and wine is strong, but who rules over them? Who is the **15** sovereign power? Women, surely! The king and all his people who rule land **16** and sea were born of women, and from them they came. Women brought up the men who planted the vineyards which yield the wine. They make **17** clothes for men and they bring honour to men; men cannot do without women. **18** If they have amassed gold and silver and all kinds of beautiful things, and then see a woman with a lovely face and figure, they leave all these things to **19** gape and stare at her with open mouth, and all choose her in preference to gold or silver or beautiful things. A man **20** will desert his father who brought him up, desert even his country, and become one with his wife. He forgets father, **21** mother, and country, and stays with his wife to the end of his days. Here is the **22** proof that women are your masters: do you not toil and sweat and then bring all you earn and give it to your wives? A man will take his sword and sally **23** forth to plunder and rob, to sail on sea and river; he faces lions, he travels in **24** the dark; and when he has robbed and plundered he brings the spoil home to his beloved.

'A man loves his wife more than his **25** father or mother. For women's sakes **26** many men have been driven out of their minds, many have been sold into slavery, many have died or come to **27** grief or ruined their lives. Do you **28** believe me now? Certainly the king wields great authority; no country dare lift a finger against him. Yet I watched **29** him with Apame, his favourite con- cubine, daughter of the famous Barta- cus. She was sitting on the king's right; she took the diadem off his head and **30** put it on her own, and slapped his face with her left hand; and the king only **31** gazed at her open-mouthed. When she laughed at him he laughed; when she was cross with him he coaxed her to make it up. Sirs, if women do as well **32** as this, how can their strength be denied?' The king and the chief men **33** looked at one another.

He then went on to speak about

4.1–12: **The king is strongest.** The passage is often misinterpreted as depicting the supposed arbitrary power of oriental kings; rather, it is a general discourse on the power of those who govern, whoever or wherever they may be. Sources indicate that oriental kings' powers were most usually circumscribed more effectively—though there were exceptions—than those of western kings.

4.13–33: **Women are strongest. 29:** The identity of this *Apame* is uncertain. An Apame, daughter of Spitamenes, was given as wife to Seleucus Nicator, the Syrian ruler; and an Apame, daughter of Artabazus, was given to Ptolemy I Soter, the Egyptian king. *Bartacus* appears in various forms in manuscripts; the words *the famous* may be a corruption of an ancestral name, rather than the implication that Bartacus was well-known.

34 truth: 'Sirs, we have seen that women are strong. The earth is vast, the sky is lofty, the sun swift in his course, for he moves through the circle of the sky and 35 speeds home in a single day. How great is he who does all this! But truth too 36 is great and stronger than all else. The whole earth calls on truth; the sky praises her. All created things shake and tremble; with her there is no injustice. There is injustice in wine, in kings, in women, in all men, and in all their works, and so 37 forth. There is no truth in them; they 38 shall perish in their injustice. But truth abides and is strong for ever; she lives 39 and rules for ever and ever. With her there is no favouritism or partiality; she chooses to do justice rather than what is unjust and evil. All approve her 40 works; in her judgements there is no injustice. Hers are strength and royalty, the authority and majesty of all ages. Praise be to the God of truth!'

41 So he ended his speech, and all the people shouted and said, 'Great is 42 truth: truth is strongest!' Then the king said to him, 'Ask what you will, even beyond what is in the writing, and I will grant it you. For you have been proved the wisest; and you shall sit by me and be called my Kinsman.'

43 Then he said to the king: 'Remember the vow you made on the day when you came to the throne. You promised 44 to rebuild Jerusalem and to send back all the vessels taken from it which Cyrus set aside. When he vowed to destroy Babylon he also vowed to re-45 store these vessels; and you too made a vow to rebuild the temple which the Edomites burnt when Judaea was 46 ravaged by the Chaldaeans. This is the favour that I now beg of you, my lord king, this is the magnanimity I request: that you should perform the vow which you made to the King of heaven.'

47 King Darius stood up and kissed him, and wrote letters for him to all the treasurers, governors, commanders, and satraps instructing them to give safe conduct to him and to all those who were going up with him to rebuild 48 Jerusalem. To all the governors in Coele-syria and Phoenicia and in Lebanon he wrote letters ordering them to transport cedar-wood from Lebanon to Jerusalem and join with Zerubbabel in building the city. He gave all Jews 49 going up from the kingdom to Judaea letters assuring their liberties: that no officer, satrap, governor, or treasurer should interfere with them, that all land 50 which they should acquire should be immune from taxation, and that the Edomites should surrender the villages they had seized from the Jews. Each 51 year twenty talents were to be contributed to the building of the temple until it was finished, and a further ten 52 talents annually for[a] burnt-offerings to be sacrificed daily upon the altar in accordance with their law. All those 53-54 who were going from Babylonia to build the city were to enjoy freedom, and their descendants after them. He gave written orders that all the priests going there should also receive maintenance and the vestments in which they would officiate; that the Levites 55 too should receive maintenance, until the day when the building of the temple and Jerusalem was completed; 56 and that all who guarded the city should be given land and pay. He sent 57 back all the vessels from Babylon which Cyrus had set aside. All that Cyrus had commanded, he reaffirmed, ordering everything to be restored to Jerusalem.

When the young man, Zerubbabel, 58 went out, he turned his face toward

a Some witnesses add seventeen.

4.34–42: Truth is strongest. 41: The Latin translation became an oft-quoted line: "Great is truth, and it prevails." **42:** *Sit by me and be called my Kinsman:* see 3.7.

4.43–60: Permission granted to rebuild Jerusalem. 43–46: *Darius' vow.* This section contains historical improbabilities. It is unlikely that Darius would have made a vow (v. 43) such as here, particularly on his coronation day! Next, the vessels had already been sent back to Jerusalem in the days of Cyrus (2.1–15). Again, the idea that Cyrus *vowed to destroy Babylon* (v. 44) is contradicted by the fact that the city yielded to him without a struggle. Furthermore, not the *Edomites* (v. 45) but the Babylonians destroyed Jerusalem. Hence, this section is a literary construction to introduce the theme of the return to Zion. **58–60:** Like Daniel, Zerubbabel *turned his face toward Jerusalem* (compare Dan.6.10). The prayer is kindred to that in Dan.2.20–23.

Jerusalem, looked up to heaven, and
59 praised the King of heaven. 'From
thee comes victory,' he said, 'from thee
comes wisdom; thine is the glory and
60 I am thy servant. All praise to thee who
hast given me wisdom; to thee I give
thanks, O Lord of our fathers.'
61 He took the letters and set off for
Babylon, where he told his fellow-Jews.
62 They praised the God of their fathers
because he had given them full freedom
63 to go and rebuild Jerusalem and the
temple called by his name, and they
feasted for a week with music and
rejoicing.

The temple rebuilt

5 AFTER THIS THE HEADS OF FAMILIES,
tribe by tribe, were chosen to go to
Jerusalem, with their wives, their sons
and daughters, their male and female
2 slaves, and their pack-animals. Darius
sent a thousand horsemen to accompany them until they had brought them
safely back to Jerusalem, with a band
3 of drums and flutes, and all their
brothers dancing. So he sent them off
with their escort.
4 These are the names of the men who
went to Jerusalem, according to their
5 families, tribes, and allotted duties. The
priests, the sons of Phineas son of
Aaron, with Jeshua son of Josedek son
of Saraeas, and Joakim his son; and[b]
Zerubbabel son of Salathiel of the
house of David of the line of Phares of
6 the tribe of Judah, who spoke wise
words before Darius king of Persia.
They went in the second year of his
reign, in Nisan the first month.
7 Now these are the men of Judah who
came up from amongst the captive
exiles, those whom Nebuchadnezzar
king of Babylon had transported to
8 Babylon. They returned to Jerusalem
and the rest of Judaea, each to his own
city: they came with Zerubbabel and
Jeshua, Nehemiah, Zaraeas, Resaeas,
Enenius, Mardochaeus, Beelsarus,

Aspharasus, Reelias, Romelius, and
Baana, their leaders. The numbers of 9
those from the nation who returned
with their leaders were: the line of
Phoros two thousand one hundred and
seventy-two; the line of Saphat four
hundred and seventy-two; the line of 10
Ares seven hundred and fifty-six; the 11
line of Phaath-moab, deriving from
the line of Jeshua and Joab, two
thousand eight hundred and twelve;
the line of Elam one thousand two 12
hundred and fifty-four; the line of
Zathui nine hundred and forty-five;
the line of Chorbe seven hundred and
five; the line of Banei six hundred and 13
forty-eight; the line of Bebae six
hundred and twenty-three; the line of
Astaa one thousand three hundred and
twenty-two. The line of Adonikam six 14
hundred and sixty-seven; the line of
Bagoi two thousand and sixty-six; the
line of Adinus four hundred and fifty-
four; the line of Ater son of Hezekias 15
ninety-two; the line of Keilan and
Azetas sixty-seven; the line of Azurus
four hundred and thirty-two; the line 16
of Annias one hundred and one; the
line of Arom and the line of Bassa three
hundred and twenty-three; the line of
Arsiphurith one hundred and twelve;
the line of Baeterus three thousand and 17
five. The line of Bethlomon one hundred and twenty-three; the men of 18
Netophae fifty-five; the men of Anathoth one hundred and fifty-eight; the
men of Bethasmoth forty-two; the men 19
of Cariathiarius twenty-five; the men of
Caphira and Beroth seven hundred and
forty-three; the Chadasians and Ammi- 20
daeans four hundred and twenty-two;
the men of Kirama and Gabbes six
hundred and twenty-one; the men of 21
Macalon one hundred and twenty-two;
the men of Betolio fifty-two; the line of
Phinis one hundred and fifty-six; the 22
line of Calamolalus and Onus seven
hundred and twenty-five; the line of

b his son; and: *probable reading (compare Nehemiah
12. 10).*

4.61–5.6: The departure from Babylon. The Judeans leave Babylon; the Persian capital, where
Zerubbabel served in the court, was presumably at Susa. Perhaps Zerubbabel went from Susa
to Babylon to find leaders and stimulate the return. 5.5: The genealogy of Zerubbabel clashes
with that in 1 Chr.3.17–24.
5.7–46: Tally of returnees; parallel to Ezra 2.1–70 and Neh.7.6–73, but with many differences.

Jerechus three hundred and forty-five;
22 the line of Sanaas three thousand three
hundred and thirty.

24 The priests: the line of Jeddu son of
Jeshua, deriving from the line of
Anasib, nine hundred and seventy-two.
The line of Emmeruth one thousand
25 and fifty-two. The line of Phassurus
one thousand two hundred and forty-
seven. The line of Charme one thousand and seventeen.

26 The Levites: the line of Jesue,
Cadmielus, Bannus, and Sudius seventy-
27 four. The temple singers: the line of
Asaph one hundred and twenty-eight.

28 The door-keepers: the line of Salum,
of Atar, of Tolman, of Dacubi, of
Ateta, of Sabi, in all one hundred and
thirty-nine.

29 The temple-servitors: the line of
Esau, of Asipha, of Taboth, of Keras,
of Susa, of Phaleas, of Labana, of
30 Aggaba, of Acud, of Uta, of Ketab, of
Gaba, of Subai, of Anan, of Cathua,
31 of Geddur, of Jairus, of Desan, of
Noeba, of Chaseba, of Gazera, of
Ozius, of Phinoe, of Asara, of Basthae,
of Asana, of Maani, of Naphisi, of
Acum, of Achipha, of Asur, of Phara-
32 kim, of Baaloth, of Meedda, of Coutha,
of Charea, of Barchue, of Serar, of
33 Thomi, of Nasith, of Atepha. The
descendants of Solomon's servants:
the line of Asapphioth, of Pharida, of
Jeeli, of Lozon, of Isdael, of Saphythi,
34 of Hagia, of Phacareth, of Sabie, of
Sarothie, of Masias, of Gas, of Addus,
of Subas, of Apherra, of Barodis, of
35 Saphat, of Adlon. All the temple-
servitors and the descendants of Solomon's servants numbered three hundred and seventy-two.

36 The following came from Thermeleth
and Thelsas with their leaders Chara-
37 athalar and Alar, and could not prove
by their families and genealogies that
they were Israelites: the line of Dalan,
the line of Ban, and the line of Necodan
six hundred and fifty-two.

38 From among the priests the claimants
to the priesthood whose record could
not be traced: the line of Obdia, of
Accos, of Joddus, who married Augia
one of the daughters of Zorzelleas, and
took his name; when search was made
39 for their family record in the register
it could not be traced, and so they were
40 excluded from priestly service. Nehemiah the governor[c] told them that they
should not participate in the sacred
offerings until a high priest arose
wearing the breast-piece of Revelation
and Truth.

41 They were in all: Israelites from
twelve years old, not counting slaves
male and female, forty-two thousand
three hundred and sixty; their slaves
42 seven thousand three hundred and
thirty-seven; musicians and singers two
hundred and forty-five; camels four
43 hundred and thirty-five, horses seven
thousand and thirty-six, mules two
hundred and forty-five, donkeys five
thousand five hundred and twenty-five.

44 Some of the heads of families, when
they arrived at the temple of God in
Jerusalem, made a vow to erect the
house again on its site as best they
could, and to give to the sacred trea-
45 sury for the fabric fund one thousand
minas of gold and five thousand minas
of silver and one hundred vestments.

46 The priests, the Levites, and some of
the people settled in Jerusalem and the
neighbourhood, with the temple musicians and the door-keepers; and all
Israel settled in their villages.

47 WHEN THE SEVENTH MONTH CAME AND
the Israelites were in their homes they
gathered as one man in the broad
square of the first gateway toward the
48 east. Jeshua son of Josedek and his
brother priests and Zerubbabel son of
Salathiel and his colleagues came forward and made ready the altar of the

c the governor: *probable meaning; Gk. and Attharias.*

24–25: The priestly divisions here number four, but twenty-four in 1 Chr.24.7–19. **40:** *Nehemiah the governor:* the name here (and in Neh.8.9) is a late insertion, for it is missing from Ezra 2.1–70 and Neh.7.6–73; see 9.49 n. *Revelation and Truth:* probably a rendering of Heb. "Urim" and "Thummim" (Exod.28.30).
   5.47–73: **The setting up of the altar and the attempted construction of the Temple;** parallel to Ezra 3.1–4.5. In Ezra we read only of the foundation of the Temple, whereas here there is apparently a more extensive effort, indeed, the construction of the entire edifice. **47:** *The seventh*

49 God of Israel, to offer on it whole burnt offerings according to the directions in the book of Moses the man 50 of God. They were joined*d* by men from the other peoples of the land and they set up the altar on its site (for the peoples in the land as a whole were hostile to them and were too strong for them); and they offered sacrifices to the Lord at the proper time, and whole burnt-offerings morning and evening. 51 They observed the Feast of Tabernacles as enjoined in the law, and the proper 52 sacrifices day by day; and thereafter the continual offerings, and sacrifices on sabbaths, at new moons, and on all 53 solemn feasts. All who had made a vow to God offered sacrifices to God from the new moon of the seventh month, although the temple of God was 54-55 not yet built. Money was paid to the stonemasons and carpenters; the Sidonians and Tyrians were supplied with food and drink, and with carts to bring cedar-trees from Lebanon, floating them down as rafts to the anchorage at Joppa, as decreed by Cyrus king of Persia.

56 In the second month of the second year, Zerubbabel son of Salathiel came to the temple of God in Jerusalem and started the work. There were with him Jeshua son of Josedek, their kinsmen, the levitical priests, and all who had 57 come to Jerusalem from the exile; and they laid the foundation of the temple of God. This was at the new moon, in the second month of the second year after they had returned to Judaea and 58 Jerusalem. The Levites from the age of twenty and upwards were set over the works of the Lord. Jeshua, his sons, his brothers, his brother Cadoel, the sons of Jeshua Emadabun, and the sons of Joda son of Iliadun with their sons and brothers, all the Levites, supervisors of the work, were active as one man on the works in the house of God.

While the builders built the temple of the Lord, the priests in their vestments 59 with musical instruments and trumpets, and the Levites (the sons of Asaph with their cymbals, stood singing to the 60 Lord and praising him as David king of Israel had appointed. They sang psalms 61 praising the Lord, 'for his goodness and glory is for ever toward all Israel'. 62 All the people blew their trumpets and gave a loud shout, singing to the Lord as the building rose.

The priests, the Levites, and heads 63 of families, the older men who had seen the former house, came to the building of this one with cries of lamentation; and so, while many were 64 sounding the trumpets loudly for joy— so loudly as to be heard far away—the 65 people could not hear the trumpets for the noise of lamentation.

The enemies of Judah and Benjamin 66 heard the noise of the trumpets and came to see what it meant. They found 67 the returned exiles building the temple for the Lord God of Israel; they came 68 to Zerubbabel and Jeshua and the leaders of the families, and said: 'We will build with you; for like you we 69 obey your Lord and have sacrificed to him from the time of Asbasareth king of Assyria who transported us here.' But Zerubbabel and Jeshua and the 70 leaders of the families of Israel replied: 'You can have no share in building the house for the Lord our God; we alone 71 will build for the Lord of Israel, as Cyrus king of Persia decreed.' But the 72 peoples of the land harassed*e* the men of Judaea, blockaded them, and interrupted the building. Their plots, agita- 73 tions, and riots held up the completion of the building all the lifetime of King Cyrus. They were prevented from building for two years until Darius became king.

d Or attacked; *the clauses are perhaps in a confused order.*
e *Probable reading; Gk. obscure.*

---

month: Tishri (September–October). **51:** *The Feast of Tabernacles as enjoined in the law:* Lev.23.33–43. *The proper sacrifices day by day:* Num.29.12–38. **52:** *The continual offerings . . . sabbaths . . . new moons . . . solemn feasts* follow the sequence of Num.28.1–29.11. **56:** *The second month:* Iyyar (April–May). **69:** Compare 2 Kgs.17.24–41. The name *Asbasareth* is hopelessly corrupt; the attempt at emendation (e.g. to Esarhaddon) is arbitrary. **73:** *For two years until Darius became king:* as at 2.16, the eight-year reign of Cambyses is ignored. Some scholars believe that two separate returns, one under Cyrus led by Sheshbazzar, and a second under Zerubbabel, have become merged.

6 In the second year of the reign of Darius, the prophets Haggai and Zechariah son of Addo prophesied to the Jews in Judaea and Jerusalem in the name of the Lord the God of Israel. ² Then Zerubbabel son of Salathiel and Jeshua son of Josedek began to rebuild the house of the Lord in Jerusalem. The prophets of the Lord were at their ³ side to help them. At that time Sisinnes, the governor-general of Syria and Phoenicia, with Sathrabuzanes and their colleagues, came to them and said: ⁴ 'Who has authorized you to put up this building, complete with roof and everything else? Who are the builders ⁵ carrying out this work?' But, thanks to the Lord who protected the returned ⁶ exiles, the elders of the Jews were not prevented from building during the time that Darius was being informed and directions issued.

⁷ Here is a copy of the letter written to Darius, and sent by Sisinnes, the governor-general of Syria and Phoenicia, with Sathrabuzanes and their colleagues the authorities in Syria and Phoenicia:

To King Darius our humble duty. ⁸ Be it known to our lord the king: we visited the district of Judaea and entered the city of Jerusalem, and there we found the elders of the Jews ⁹ returned from exile building a great new house for the Lord with costly hewn stone and with beams set in ¹⁰ the walls. This work was being done with all speed and the undertaking was making good progress; it was being executed in great splendour ¹¹ and with the utmost care. We then inquired of these elders by whose authority they were building this house and laying such foundations. ¹² We questioned them so that we could inform you in writing who their leaders were, and asked for a list of ¹³ their names. They answered as follows: 'We are servants of the Lord who made heaven and earth. This house was built and completed ¹⁴ many years ago by a great and powerful king of Israel. When our ¹⁵ fathers sinned against the heavenly Lord of Israel and provoked him, he delivered them over to Nebuchadnezzar, king of Babylon, king of the Chaldaeans; and they pulled ¹⁶ down the house, set it on fire, and took the people into exile in Babylon. In the first year of the reign of King ¹⁷ Cyrus over Babylonia, the king decreed that this house should be rebuilt. The sacred vessels of gold ¹⁸ and silver which Nebuchadnezzar had taken from the house in Jerusalem, and set up in his own temple, he brought back out of the temple in Babylon and delivered to Zerubbabel and Sanabassar the governor, with orders to take all these vessels ¹⁹ and to put them in the temple at Jerusalem, and to rebuild this temple of the Lord on the same site as before. Then Sanabassar came and laid ²⁰ the foundations of the house of the Lord in Jerusalem. From then till now the building has continued and is still unfinished.' Therefore, if it ²¹ is Your Majesty's pleasure, let search be made in the royal archives in Babylon, and if it is found that the ²² building of the house of the Lord in Jerusalem took place with the approval of king Cyrus, and if our lord the king so decide, let directions be issued to us on this subject.

Then King Darius ordered the ²³ archives in Babylon to be searched, and a scroll was found in the castle at Ecbatana in the province of Media which contained the following record:

In the first year of his reign King ²⁴ Cyrus ordered that the house of the Lord in Jerusalem, where they sacrifice with fire continually, should be rebuilt. Its height should be sixty ²⁵

6.1–7.15: **Building continued, correspondence with Darius, completion of the work,** parallel to Ezra 5.1–6.22. **1:** See Hag.1.1–4; 2.1–4; Zech.4.9; 6.15. Zech.1.1 reads "Zechariah son of Berechiah, son of Iddo." **2:** *Jeshua* is the same as Joshua. **7:** *Sisinnes* and *Sathrabuzanes* are Grecianized from Tattenai and Shethar-bozenai (Ezra 5.3). The "letter" (vv. 8–22) is one of bureaucratic inquiry rather than hostility. **14:** *King:* Solomon. **18:** *Zerubbabel*, not mentioned in Ezra 5.14, is probably an addition. **19–20:** *Sanabassar:* see 2.12,15 n. **23:** On *Ecbatana*, see

cubits and its breadth sixty cubits, with three courses of hewn stone to one of new local timber; the expenses to be met from the royal treasury.

26 The sacred gold and silver vessels of the house of the Lord which Nebuchadnezzar removed from the house in Jerusalem, and took to Babylon, should be restored to the house in Jerusalem and replaced where they formerly were.

27 Darius therefore instructed Sisinnes, the governor-general of Syria and Phoenicia, with Sathrabuzanes, their colleagues, and the governors in office in Syria and Phoenicia, to be careful not to interfere with the place, but to allow the servant of the Lord, Zerubbabel, governor of Judaea, and the elders of the Jews to build the house of 28 the Lord on its old site. 'I have also given instructions', he continued, 'that it should be completely rebuilt, and that they should not fail to co-operate with the returned exiles in Judaea until the house of the Lord is finished. 29 From the tribute of Coele-syria and Phoenicia let a contribution be duly given to these men for sacrifices to the Lord, payable to Zerubbabel the gover-30 nor, for bulls, rams, and lambs; and similarly wheat, salt, wine, and oil are to be provided regularly each year without question, as the priests in 31 Jerusalem may require day by day. Let all this be expended in order that sacrifices and libations may be offered to the Most High God for the king and his children, and that intercession may 32 be made on their behalf.' He also gave these orders: 'If anyone disobeys or neglects any of these orders written above or here set down, let a beam be taken from his own house and let him be hanged on it and his estate forfeited 33 to the king. May the Lord himself, therefore, to whom this temple is dedicated, destroy any king or people who shall lift a finger to delay or damage the Lord's house in Jerusalem.

I, Darius the king, decree that these 34 orders be obeyed to the letter.'

Then, in accordance with the orders 7 of King Darius, Sisinnes, governor general of Coele-syria and Phoenicia, with Sathrabuzanes and their colleagues, carefully supervised the sacred 2 works, co-operating with the elders of the Jews and the temple officers. With 3 the encouragement of the prophets Haggai and Zechariah, good progress was made with the sacred works, and 4 they were finished by the ordinance of the Lord God of Israel and with the approval of Cyrus, Darius, and Artaxerxes, kings of Persia. It was on the 5 twenty-third of Adar in the sixth year of King Darius that the house was completed. The Israelites, the priests, 6 the Levites, and the rest of the former exiles who had joined them carried out the directions in the book of Moses. For the dedication of the temple of 7 the Lord they offered a hundred bulls, two hundred rams, four hundred lambs, and twelve goats for the sin of 8 all Israel corresponding to the twelve patriarchs of Israel. The priests and the 9 Levites in their vestments stood family by family to preside over the services of the Lord God of Israel according to the book of Moses. The door-keepers took their stand at every gateway.

The Israelites who had returned 10 from exile kept the Passover on the fourteenth day of the first month. The priests and the Levites were purified together; not all the returned exiles 11 were purified with the priests, but *f* the Levites were. They slaughtered the 12 Passover victims for all the returned exiles and for their brother priests and for themselves. All those Israelites 13 participated who had returned from exile and had segregated themselves from the abominations of the peoples of the land to seek the Lord. They kept 14 the Feast of Unleavened Bread for seven days, rejoicing before the Lord;

f not all . . . but: *probable meaning; Gk. obscure; some witnesses omit* not.

Ezra 6.2 n. **32:** Contrast Ezra 6.11. **7.2:** *Carefully supervised . . . co-operating;* Ezra 6.13 depicts less enthusiasm, stating that the officials "carried out to the letter" their instructions. **4:** *Artaxerxes* (see 2.16 n.) is anachronistic. **5:** *The sixth year of Darius* was 516 B.C. **8:** *Twelve patriarchs:* Ezra 6.17 reads "tribes." **13:** Only those *who had returned from exile* celebrated, in contrast with Ezra 6.21, where "all who had separated themselves" are included. See also Neh.9.2; 10.28.

15 for he had changed the policy of the Assyrian king towards them and strengthened them for the service of the Lord the God of Israel.

Ezra in Jerusalem

8 AFTER THESE EVENTS, IN THE REIGN of Artaxerxes king of Persia, came Ezra, son of Saraeas, son of Ezerias, 2 son of Chelkias, son of Salemus, son of Zadok, son of Ahitub, son of Amarias, son of Ezias, son of Mareroth, son of Zaraeas, son of Savia, son of Bocca, son of Abishua, son of Phineas, son of Eleazar, son of Aaron 3 the chief priest. This Ezra came from Babylon as a talented scholar in the law of Moses which had been given by the 4 God of Israel. The king held him in high regard and looked with favour 5 upon all the requests he made. He was accompanied to Jerusalem by some Israelites, priests, Levites, temple singers, door-keepers, and temple- 6 servitors, in the fifth month of the seventh year of Artaxerxes' reign.[g] They left Babylon at the new moon in the first month and reached Jerusalem at the new moon in the fifth month; for the Lord gave them a safe journey. 7 Ezra's knowledge of the law of the Lord and the commandments was exact in every detail, so that he could teach all Israel the ordinances and judgements.
8 The following is a copy of the mandate from King Artaxerxes to Ezra the priest, doctor of the law of the Lord:

9 King Artaxerxes to Ezra the priest, doctor of the law of the Lord, greeting.
10 I have graciously decided, and now command, that those of the Jewish nation and of the priests and Levites, in our kingdom, who so choose, shall 11 go with you to Jerusalem. I and my council of seven Friends have de-cided that all who so desire may accompany you. Let them look to the 12 affairs of Judaea and Jerusalem in pursuance of the law of the Lord, and bring to Jerusalem for the Lord 13 of Israel the gifts which I and my Friends have vowed, all the gold and silver in Babylonia that may be found to belong to the Lord in Jerusalem, together with what has 14 been given by the nation for the temple of the Lord their God in Jerusalem. Let the gold and silver be expended upon[h] bulls, rams, lambs, and so forth, so that sacrifices may 15 be offered upon the altar of the Lord their God in Jerusalem. Make use of 16 the gold and silver in whatever ways you and your colleagues desire, according to the will of your God, and deliver the sacred vessels of the 17 Lord which have been given you for the use of the temple of your God in Jerusalem.
Any other expenses that you may 18 incur for the needs of the temple of your God you shall defray from the royal treasury. I, Artaxerxes the 19 king, direct the treasurers of Syria and Phoenicia to give without fail to Ezra the priest, doctor of the law of the Most High God, whatever he may request up to a hundred talents 20 of silver, and similarly up to a hundred sacks of wheat and a hundred casks of wine, and salt without limit. Let him diligently fulfil in 21 honour of the Most High God all the requirements of God's law, so that divine displeasure may not befall the kingdom of the king and of his descendants. You are also 22 informed that no tax or other impost is to be laid on the priests, the Levites, the temple singers, the door-keepers, the temple-servitors, and the lay officers of this temple; no one is permitted to impose any burden on them. You, Ezra, under God's 23

g *Probable reading; one witness adds* this was the king's second year.
h *Or* collected for.

15: *Assyrian king* is not meant to be taken literally; it merely denotes an emperor from beyond the Euphrates.
8.1–9.55: The story of Ezra (Ezra 7.1–10.44; Neh.7.73–8.12). Nehemiah is ignored. **1–67:** Ezra's return to Jerusalem, parallel to Ezra 7.1–8.36. **1:** *Artaxerxes* I reigned from 464–424 B.C. However, this is probably Artaxerxes II (404–359 B.C.); see Introduction to Ezra. **6:** *The fifth*

guidance, are to appoint judges and magistrates to judge all who know the law of your God in all Syria and Phoenicia, you yourself shall see to the instruction of those who do not 24 know it. All who transgress the law of your God and of the king shall be duly punished with death, degradation, fine, or exile.

25 Then Ezra said: All praise to the Lord alone, who put this into the king's mind, to glorify his house in Jerusalem. 26 He singled me out for honour before the king, his counsellors, and all his 27 Friends and dignitaries. I took courage from the help of the Lord my God and gathered men of Israel to go up with me.

28 These are the leaders according to clans and divisions who went with me from Babylon to Jerusalem in the reign 29 of King Artaxerxes: from the line of Phineas, Gershom; from the line of Ithamar, Gamael; from the line of 30 David, Attus son of Sechenias; from the line of Phoros, Zacharias and a hundred and fifty men with him 31 according to the register; from the line of Phaath-moab, Eliaonias son of Zaraeas and with him two hundred 32 men; from the line of Zathoe, Sechenias son of Jezelus and with him three hundred men; from the line of Adin, Obeth son of Jonathan and with him 33 two hundred and fifty men; from the line of Elam, Jessias son of Gotholias 34 and with him seventy men; from the line of Sophotias, Zaraeas son of Michael and with him seventy men; 35 from the line of Joab, Abadias son of Jezelus and with him two hundred and 36 twelve men; from the line of Bani, Assalimoth son of Josaphias and with 37 him a hundred and sixty men; from the line of Babi, Zacharias son of Bebae and with him twenty-eight men; 38 from the line of Astath, Joannes son of Hacatan and with him a hundred and

ten men; last came those from the line 39 of Adonikam, by name Eliphalatus, Jeuel, and Samaeas, and with them seventy men; from the line of Bogo, 40 Uthi son of Istalcurus and with him seventy men.

I assembled them at the river called 41 Theras, where we encamped for three days, and I inspected them. As I found 42 no one there who was of priestly or levitical descent, I sent to Eleazar, 43 Iduelus, Maasmas, Elnathan, Samaeas, 44 Joribus, Nathan, Ennatas, Zacharias, and Mosollamus, who were prominent and discerning men. I told them to go 45 to Doldaeus the chief man at the treasury. I instructed them to speak 46 with Doldaeus, his colleagues, and the treasurers there, and ask them to send us priests to officiate in the house of our Lord. Under the providence of 47 God they brought us discerning men from the line of Mooli son of Levi son of Israel, Asebebias and his sons and brothers, eighteen men in all, also 48 Asebias and Annunus and Hosaeas his brother. Those of the line of Chanunaeus and their sons amounted to twenty men; and those of the 49 temple-servitors whom David and the leading men appointed for the service of the Levites amounted to two hundred and twenty. A register of all these names was compiled.

There I made a vow that the young 50 men should fast before our Lord to beg him to give us a safe journey for ourselves, our children who accompanied us, and our pack-animals. I was 51 ashamed to ask the king for an escort of infantry and cavalry against our enemies; for we had told the king that 52 the strength of our Lord would ensure success for those who looked to him. So once more we laid all these things 53 before our Lord in prayer and found him gracious.

I set apart twelve men from among 54 the heads of the priestly families, and

---

month was Ab (July–August), *the first month* was Nisan (March–April). **41,61**: *Theras:* Ezra 8.21,31 reads "Ahava"; neither name can be identified, nor the location ascertained. **42**: *Of . . . levitical descent:* Ezra 8.15, in contrast, speaks of the absence of Levites among the people and the priests. Perhaps the Ezra version makes better sense; we can assume that the priests were anxious to return to resume their cultic duties in Jerusalem, whereas the subordinate Levites were less eager to leave their comforts in Babylonia. **51**: *I was ashamed:* contrast Neh.2.7–9 for a different response in a similar situation.

with them Sarabias and Asamias and 55 ten of their brother priests, I weighed out for them the silver, the gold, and the sacred vessels of the house of our Lord; these had been presented by the king himself, his counsellors, the chief 56 men, and all Israel. When I had weighed it all I handed over to them six hundred and fifty talents of silver, and vessels of silver weighing a hundred talents, a hundred talents of 57 gold, and twenty pieces of gold plate, and twelve vessels of brass so fine that 58 it gleamed like gold. I said to them: 'You are consecrated to the Lord, and so are the vessels; the silver and the gold are vowed to the Lord, the Lord 59 of our fathers. Be vigilant and keep guard until you hand them over at Jerusalem, in the priests' rooms in the house of our Lord, to the heads of the priestly and levitical families and to 60 the leaders of the clans of Israel.' The priests and the Levites who received the silver, the gold, and the vessels in Jerusalem brought them to the temple of the Lord.

61 We left the river Theras on the twelfth day of the first month, and under the powerful protection which our Lord gave us we reached Jerusalem. He guarded us against every enemy on our journey, and so we arrived at 62 Jerusalem. Three days passed, and on the fourth the silver and gold were weighed and handed over in the house of our Lord to the priest 63 Marmathi son of Uri, with whom was Eleazar son of Phineas. With them also were the Levites Josabdus son of Jeshua and Moeth son of Sabannus. Everything was numbered and weighed 64 and every weight recorded there and 65 then. The returned exiles offered sacrifices to the Lord the God of Israel, twelve bulls for all Israel, with ninety-66 six rams and seventy-two lambs, and also twelve goats for a peace-offering, the whole as a sacrifice to the Lord. 67 They delivered the king's orders to the royal treasurers and the governors of Coele-syria and Phoenicia, and so added lustre to the nation and the temple of the Lord.

WHEN THESE MATTERS HAD BEEN SETTLED 68 the leaders came to me and said, 'The 69 nation of Israel, the rulers, the priests, and the Levites, have not kept themselves apart from the alien population of the land with all their pollutions, that is to say the Canaanites, Hittites, Perizzites, Jebusites, Moabites, Egyptians, and Edomites. For they and their 70 sons have intermarried with the daughters of these peoples, and the holy race has been mingled with the alien population of the land; and the leaders and principal men have shared in this violation of the law from the very beginning.'

As soon as I heard of this I tore my 71 clothes and sacred vestment, plucked out the hair of my head and my beard, and sat down perplexed and miserable. Those who at that time were moved by 72 the word of the Lord of Israel gathered round me, while I grieved over this disregard of the law, and sat in my misery until the evening sacrifice. Then 73 I rose from my fast with my clothes and sacred vestment torn, and knelt down and, stretching out my hands to the Lord, said: 74

'O Lord, I am covered with shame and confusion in thy presence. Our 75-76 sins tower above our heads; from the time of our fathers our offences have reached the sky, and today we are as deep in sin as ever. Because of our 77 sins and the sins of our fathers, we and our brothers, our kings and our priests, were given over to the kings of the earth to be killed, taken prisoner, plundered, and humiliated down to this very day. And now, Lord, how 78 great is the mercy thou hast shown us! We still have a root and a name in the place of thy sanctuary, and thou hast 79 rekindled our light in the house of our Lord, and given us food in the time of our servitude. Even when we were 80 slaves we were not deserted by our Lord; for he secured for us the favour of the kings of Persia, who have provided our food and added lustre to 81 the temple of our Lord and restored the ruins of Zion, giving us a firm foothold in Judaea and Jerusalem. And 82

8.68–9.36: The problem of mixed marriages; parallel to Ezra 9.1–10.44. **69:** *Pollutions:*

now, Lord, what are we to say, we who have received all this? For we have broken thy commandments given us through thy servants the prophets. 83 Thou didst say: "The land which you are to occupy is a land defiled with the pollution of its heathen peoples; they 84 have filled it with their impurities. Do not marry your daughters to their sons nor take their daughters for your sons; 85 never try to make peace with them if you want to be strong and enjoy the good things of the land and take possession of it for your children for ever." 86 All our misfortunes have come upon us through our evil deeds and our great sins. Although thou, Lord, hast 87 lightened the burden of our sins and given us so firm a root, yet we have fallen away again and broken thy law by sharing in the impurities of the 88 heathen peoples of this land. But thou wast not so angry with us, Lord, as to 89 destroy us, root, seed, and name; thou keepest faith, O Lord of Israel; the 90 root is left, we are here today. Behold us, now before thee in our sins; because of all we have done we can no longer hold up our heads before thee.' 91 While Ezra prayed and made confession, weeping prostrate on the ground before the temple, a very large crowd gathered, men, women, and youths of Jerusalem, and there was widespread lamentation among the people. Jechon- 92 ias son of Jeel, one of the Israelites, called out to Ezra: 'We have sinned against the Lord in taking alien wives from the heathen population of this land; and yet there is still hope for 93 Israel. Let us take an oath to the Lord to expel all our wives of alien race 94 with their children, in accordance with your judgement and the judgement of all who are obedient to the law of the 95 Lord. Come now, set about it, it is in your hands; take strong action and 96 we are with you.' Ezra got up and laid an oath upon the principal priests and Levites of all Israel that they would act in this way, and they swore to it.

Ezra left the court of the temple and 9 entered the room of the priest Joanan son of Eliasibus. There he stayed, 2 eating no food and drinking no water, while he mourned over the serious violations of the law by the community. A proclamation was made 3 throughout Judaea and in Jerusalem to all the returned exiles that they should assemble at Jerusalem; those 4 who failed to arrive within two or three days, according to the decision of the elders in office, were to have their cattle confiscated for temple use and would themselves be excluded from the community of the returned exiles.

Three days later all Judah and 5 Benjamin had assembled in Jerusalem; the date was the twentieth of the ninth month. They all sat together in the 6 open space before the temple, shivering because winter had set in. Ezra stood 7 up and said to them: 'You have broken the law and married alien wives, bringing a fresh burden of guilt on Israel. Now make confession to the 8 Lord God of our fathers; do his will 9 and separate yourselves from the heathen population of this land and from your alien wives.'

The whole company answered with a 10 shout: 'We will do as you have said!' 'But', they said, 'our numbers are 11 great, and we cannot stay here in the open in this wintry weather. Nor is this the work of a day or two only; the offence is widespread among us. Let 12 the leaders of the community stay here, and let all members of our settlements who have alien wives attend at an appointed time along with the elders 13 and judges of each place, until we turn away the Lord's anger at what has been done.'

Jonathan son of Azael and Hezekias 14 son of Thocanus took charge on these terms, and Mosollamus, Levi, and Sabbataeus were their assessors. The 15 returned exiles duly carried all this out.

Ezra the priest selected men by name, 16 all chiefs of their clans, and on the new

---

customs viewed as idolatrous practices; see v. 83 n. **83:** *Thou didst say:* the quotation is not found in Scripture, but Lev.18.19–30, dealing with similar practices, contains like language. **9.1:** *Joanan* was actually the grandson of *Eliasibus*. **5:** *The twentieth of the ninth month:* Kislev (November–December). **6:** *Winter had set in:* Ezra 10.9 mentions "heavy rain." **16:** *The tenth month* was Tebeth (December–January).

17 moon of the tenth month they sat to investigate the matter. This affair of the men who had alien wives was settled by the new moon of the first month.

18 Among the priests some of those who had come together were found to 19 have alien wives; these were Mathelas, Eleazar, Joribus, and Joadanus of the line of Jeshua son of Josedek and his 20 brothers, who undertook to send away their wives and to offer rams in 21 expiation of their error. Of the line of Emmer: Ananias, Zabdaeus, Manes, 22 Samaeus, Jereel, and Azarias; of the line of Phaesus: Elionas, Massias, Ishmael, Nathanael, Okidelus, and 23 Saloas. Of the Levites: Jozabadus, Semis, Colius (this is Calitas), Pha-24 thaeus, Judah, and Jonas. Of the temple singers: Eliasibus, Bacchurus. 25 Of the door-keepers: Sallumus and Tolbanes.

26 Of the people of Israel there were, of the line of Phoros: Jermas, Jeddias, Melchias, Maelus, Elcazar, Asibias, 27 and Dannaeas. Of the line of Ela: Matthanias, Zacharias, Jezriclus, Oab-28 dius, Jeremoth, and Aedias. Of the line of Zamoth: Eliadas, Eliasimus, Othonias, Jarimoth, Sabathus, and 29 Zardaeas. Of the line of Bebae: Joannes, Ananias, Ozabadus, and Ema-30 this. Of the line of Mani: Olamus, Mamuchus, Jedaeus, Jasubus, Asaelus, 31 and Jeremoth. Of the line of Addi: Naathus, Moossias, Laccunus, Naidus, Matthanias, Sesthel, Balnuus, and 32 Manasseas. Of the line of Annas: Elionas, Asaeas, Melchias, Sabbaeas, 33 and Simon Chosomaeus. Of the line of Asom: Altannaeus, Mattathias, Bannaeus, Eliphalat, Manasses, and Semi. 34 Of the line of Baani: Jeremias, Momdis, Ismaerus, Juel, Mandae, Paedias, Anos, Carabasion, Enasibus, Mamnitanaemus, Eliasis, Bannus, Eliali, Somis, Selemias, and Nathanias. Of the line of Ezora: Sessis, Ezril, Azael, 35 Samatus, Zambris, and Josephus. Of the line of Nooma: Mazitias, Zaba-

36 daeas, Edaes, Juel, and Banaeas. All these had married alien wives, they sent them away with their children.

37 THE PRIESTS, THE LEVITES, AND SUCH Israelites as were in Jerusalem and its vicinity, settled down there on the new moon of the seventh month; the other Israelites remained in their settlements. 38 The entire body assembled as one in the open space before the east gateway 39 of the temple and asked Ezra the high priest and doctor of the law to bring the law of Moses given by the Lord God of Israel. On the new moon of 40 the seventh month he brought the law to all the multitude of men and women alike, and to the priests, for them to hear. He read it in the open 41 space before the temple gateway from daybreak until noon, in the presence of both men and women, and the whole body listened intently. Ezra the 42 priest and doctor of the law stood upon the wooden platform which had been prepared. There stood with him, 43 on his right, Mattathias, Sammus, Ananias, Azarias, Urias, Hezekias, and Baalsamus, and on his left, Phaldaeus, 44 Misael, Melchias, Lothasubus, Nabarias, and Zacharias. Ezra took up 45 the book of the law; everyone could see him, for he was seated in a conspicuous place in front of them all, and when he opened it they all stood 46 up. Ezra praised the Lord God the Most High God of hosts, the Almighty. All the multitude cried 'Amen, Amen', 47 and lifting up their hands fell to the ground and worshipped the Lord. Jeshua, Annus, Sarabias, Jadinus, Jacu-48 bus, Sabbataeas, Autaeas, Maeannas, Calitas, Azarias, Jozabdus, Ananias, and Phiathas, the Levites, taught the law of the Lord; they read the law of the Lord to the whole company, at the same time instilling into their minds what was read.

Then the governor[i] said to Ezra the 49

i Gk. Attharates.

9.37–55: The reading of the law; parallel to Neh.7.73–8.12. **37,40:** *The new moon of the seventh month:* the first day of Tishri (September–October) was a "day of sacred assembly" (Lev.23.24 and Num.29.1), later called Rosh Hashanah, the New Year festival. **39:** *High priest:* only here is Ezra so designated. **48:** *They read:* contrast v. 41, which states that Ezra *read* it. Apparently, the Levites relayed Ezra's words to those not within earshot, at the same time adding words of explanation and exhortation. **49:** The Heb. of Neh.8.9 reads "Nehemiah the tirshata" (i.e.

17

high priest and doctor of the law and to each of the Levites who taught the
50 multitude: 'This day is holy to the Lord.' All were weeping as they heard
51 the law. 'Go then, refresh yourselves with rich food and sweet wine, and send shares to those who have none;
52 for the day is holy to the Lord. Let there be no sadness; for the Lord will
53 give you glory.' The Levites issued the command to all the people: 'This day is holy, do not be sad.' So they all 54 departed to eat and drink and make merry, and to send shares to those who had none, and to hold a great celebration; because the teaching given them 55 had been instilled into their minds. They gathered together.*j*

j Probably the text originally carried on from this point; compare Nehemiah 8. 13.

governor). Since the name Nehemiah is missing here, the name is probably a late insertion in Neh.8.9 and in 1 Esd.5.40. **51,54:** The merriment and such phrases as *send shares to those who had none* are reminiscent of Esther 9.19 and 22, in connection with the Feast of Purim. **55:** The ending is so abrupt that it is believed that the continuation, probably paralleling Neh.8.13–18 (or further), has been lost.

THE SECOND BOOK OF
ESDRAS

This book is known in the Vulgate as 4 Esdras. *Esdras* is the Greek form of the name *Ezra*, to whom the book is attributed. The Second Book of Esdras is distinctive in the Apocrypha as an apocalyptic book. "Apocalypse" means "unveiling"; and apocalyptic literature usually involves the disclosure of previously unknown truths about reality and the future in visions and highly symbolic language. In this literary genre, the author, under the pseudonym of a famous person of the past, describes events that are taking place in his own day. In this way he tries to console innocent sufferers by showing that what is happening is under God's Providence and that injustices will be reversed at the end of time, which he proceeds to describe as also revealed.

2 Esdras contains a core of seven visions (chs. 3–14). To these were added a prefix (chs. 1–2) and a suffix (chs. 15–16) which differ markedly in content. The core section was probably written by a Palestinian Jew in Hebrew or Aramaic about 100 A.D.; the additions were written in Greek by Christian writers in the second and third centuries respectively.

A small fragment of the Greek has come down to us, but 2 Esdras survives only in ancient translations whose great number and variety reflect the popularity of the book in early centuries.

Echoing Old Testament Job and Habakkuk, the author of 2 Esdras dealt with the problem of human suffering. Though the writer is particularly concerned about the fall of Jerusalem and the triumphs of the persecuting Roman Empire, he also agonizes about the misery of human existence in general, finding some respite only in his conviction of restitution and reward in the world to come.

Roman Catholic tradition excludes 1 and 2 Esdras and the Prayer of Manasseh from its canon but accepts the rest of the Apocrypha.

Israel's rejection and glory to come

1 THE SECOND BOOK OF THE PROPHET Ezra, son of Seraiah, son of Azariah, son of Hilkiah, son of Shallum, son of Zadok, son of Ahitub, 2 son of Ahijah, son of Phinehas, son of Eli, son of Amariah, son of Aziah, son of Marimoth, son of Arna, son of Uzzi, son of Borith, son of Abishua, 3 son of Phinehas, son of Eleazar, son of Aaron, of the tribe of Levi.

I, EZRA, WAS A CAPTIVE IN MEDIA IN the reign of Artaxerxes, king of Persia, 4 when the word of the Lord came to 5 me: 'Go to my people and proclaim their crimes; tell their children how they have sinned against me, and let 6 them tell their children's children. They have sinned even more than their fathers; they have forgotten me and sacrificed to alien gods. Was it not I 7 who rescued them from Egypt, the country where they were slaves? And yet they have provoked me to anger and ignored my warnings.

'Now, Ezra, pluck out your hair and 8 let calamities loose upon these people who have disobeyed my law. They are beyond correction. How much longer 9 shall I endure them, I who have lavished on them such benefits? Many 10 are the kings I have overthrown for their sake; I struck down Pharaoh with his court and all his army. I 11 destroyed every nation that stood in their way, and in the east I routed the peoples of two provinces, Tyre and Sidon, and killed all the enemies of Israel.

1.1–2.48: Israel's rejection and glory to come. Israel's past infidelity and its dire consequences are enumerated. God's fidelity is shown in a promised restoration.

1.1–3a: Ezra's lineage. The list varies slightly from Ezra 7.1–5 and 1 Esd.8.1–2. **1:** *Ezra*, a priest and scribe in the OT (Ezra 7.11), is here termed a *prophet*.

1.3b–11: Ezra called to prophesy doom. 3: *Artaxerxes* II ruled from 404 to 359 B.C. **5:** *Proclaim their crimes:* make the people aware of their wickedness and condemn it; see Jer.1.16. **8:** *Pluck . . . hair:* sign of consternation and grief; see Ezra 9.3. **10:** *Pharaoh:* see Exod.14.28. **11:** *Tyre* and *Sidon* were Phoenician cities, not provinces, to the west of Media and not *east;* Tyre was not destroyed until the time of Alexander (332 B.C.), which was after the reign of Artaxerxes.

12 'Say to them, "These are the words
13 of the Lord. Was it not I who brought
you through the sea, and made safe
roads for you where no road had been?
I gave you Moses as your leader, and
14 Aaron as your priest; I gave you light
from a pillar of fire, and performed
great miracles among you. And yet
you have forgotten me, says the Lord.
15 ' "These are the words of the Lord
Almighty: I gave you the quails as a
sign; I gave you a camp for your
protection. But all you did there was
16 to grumble and complain—instead of
celebrating the victory I had given you
when I destroyed your enemies. From
that day to this you have never
17 stopped complaining. Have you forgotten what benefits I conferred on
you? When you were hungry and
thirsty in your journey through the
18 desert, you cried out to me, 'Why have
you brought us into this desert to kill
us? Better to have remained in Egypt
as slaves than to die here in the
19 desert!' I was grieved by your complaints, and gave you manna for food;
20 you ate the bread of angels. When you
were thirsty, I split open the rock, and
out flowed water in plenty. Against
the summer heat I gave you the
21 shelter of leafy trees. I gave you fertile
lands to divide among your tribes,
expelling the Canaanites, Perizzites,
and Philistines who opposed you.
What more could I do for you? says
the Lord.
22 ' "These are the words of the Lord
Almighty: When you were in the
desert, suffering thirst by the stream of
23 bitter water and cursing me, I did not
bring down fire upon you for your
blasphemy; I cast a tree into the
24 stream and made the water sweet. What
am I to do with you, Jacob? Judah,
you have refused to obey me. I will
turn to other nations; I will give them
my name, and they will keep my

statutes. Because you have deserted 25
me, I will desert you; when you cry for
mercy, I will show you none; when 26
you pray to me, I will not listen. You
have stained your hands with blood;
you run hot-foot to commit murder.
It is not I whom you have deserted, but 27
yourselves, says the Lord.
' "These are the words of the Lord 28
Almighty: Have I not pleaded with
you as a father with his sons, as a
mother with her daughters or a nurse
with her children? Have I not said, 'Be 29
my people, and I will be your God; be
my sons, and I will be your father'? I 30
gathered you as a hen gathers her
chickens under her wings. But now
what am I to do with you? I will toss
you away. When you offer me sacrifice, 31
I will turn from you; I have rejected
your feasts, your new moons, and your
circumcisions. I sent you my servants 32
the prophets, but you took them and
killed them, and mutilated their dead
bodies. For their murder I will call you
to account, says the Lord.
' "These are the words of the Lord 33
Almighty: Your house is abandoned. I
will toss you away like straw before the
wind. Your children shall have no 34
posterity, because like you they have
ignored my commandments and done
what I have condemned. I will hand 35
over your home to a people soon to
come; a people who will trust me,
though they have not known me; who
will do my bidding, though I gave
them no signs; who never saw the 36
prophets, and yet will keep in mind
what the prophets taught of old. I vow 37
that this people yet to come shall have
my favour. Their little ones shall jump
for joy. They have not seen me with
their eyes, but they shall perceive by
the spirit and believe all that I have
said."
'Now, father Ezra, look with triumph 38
at the nation coming from the east.

1.12–21: God's past mercies recounted; these are events of the Exodus. 13: See Exod.14.29;
3.10; 28.1. 14: See Exod.13.21. 15: See Exod.16.13. 18: See Num.14.2–3. 19: See Ps.78.25.
20: See Num.20.11.
1.22–32: Israel to be rejected. 22–23: See Exod.15.22–25. 24: *I will turn to other nations:*
compare Mt.21.43. Reflections of NT here show that the author of this preface was a Christian.
30–32: Compare Mt.23.34–37.
1.33–40: A new people replaces Israel. 35–37: *A people:* Gentile Christians; compare
1 Cor.2.6–15. 38: *Father:* in rabbinic Judaism, Ezra is equated in eminence with both the
patriarchs and prophets.

39 The leaders I shall give them are Abraham, Isaac, and Jacob, Hosea and Amos, Micah and Joel, Obadiah 40 and Jonah, Nahum, Habakkuk, and Zephaniah, Haggai and Zechariah, and Malachi, who is also called the Lord's Messenger.

2 'These are the words of the Lord: I freed this people from slavery, and gave them commandments through my servants the prophets; but they shut their ears to the prophets, and let my 2 precepts become a dead letter. The mother who bore them says to them: "Go, my sons; I am widowed and 3 deserted. Joyfully I brought you up; I have lost you with grief and sorrow, because you have sinned against the Lord God and done what I know to 4 be wrong. What can I do for you now, widowed and deserted as I am? Go, my sons, ask the Lord for mercy." 5 Now I call upon you, father Ezra, to add your testimony to hers, that her children have refused to keep my 6 covenant; and let your words bring confusion on them. May their mother be despoiled, and may they themselves 7 have no posterity. Condemn them to be scattered among the nations, and their name to vanish from the earth, because they have spurned my covenant.

8 'Woe to you, Assyria, for harbouring sinners! Remember, you wicked nation, what I did to Sodom and Gomorrah: 9 their land lies buried under lumps of pitch and heaps of ashes. That is how I will deal with those who have disobeyed me, says the Lord Almighty.

10 'These are the words of the Lord to Ezra: Tell my people that I will give to them the kingdom of Jerusalem which 11 once I offered to Israel. I will withdraw the splendour of my presence from Israel, and the home that was to be theirs for ever I will give to my own people. The tree of life shall spread its 12 fragrance over them; they shall not toil or grow weary. Ask, and you shall 13 receive; so pray that your short time of waiting may be made shorter still. The kingdom is ready for you now; be on the watch! Call heaven, call earth, to 14 witness: I have cancelled the evil and brought the good into being; for I am the Living One, says the Lord.

'Mother, cherish your sons. Rear 15 them joyfully as a dove rears her nestlings; teach them to walk without stumbling. You are my chosen one, says the Lord. I will raise up the dead 16 from their resting-places, and bring them out of their tombs, for I have acknowledged that they bear my name. Have no fear, mother of many sons; I 17 have chosen you, says the Lord.

'I will send my servants Isaiah 18 and Jeremiah to help you. As they prophesied, I have set you apart to be my people. I have made ready for you twelve trees laden with different kinds of fruit, twelve fountains flowing with 19 milk and honey, and seven great mountains covered with roses and lilies. There will I fill your sons with joy. Champion the widow, defend the 20 cause of the fatherless, give to the poor, protect the orphan, clothe the naked. Care for the weak and the helpless, and 21 do not mock at the cripple; watch over the disabled, and bring the blind to the vision of my brightness. Keep safe 22 within your walls both old and young.

'When you find the dead unburied, 23 mark them with the sign and commit them to the tomb; and then, when I cause the dead to rise, I will give you the chief place. Be calm, my people; for 24 your time of rest shall come. Care for 25 your children like a good nurse, and train them to walk without falling. Of 26

2.1–9: God to destroy sinful Israel. 6: Jerusalem, Israel's *"mother* city" (see Ezek. ch. 16), was *despoiled* in 70 A.D. The writer views this as just retribution. **8:** *Assyria* probably stands for Rome. *Sodom:* see Gen.19.24–25.

2.10–14: Israel's place given to others. 10: *My people:* the new people of 1.24,35,38. **12:** *Tree of life:* see Rev.2.7 n.; 22.2,14. **13:** *Ask:* compare Mt.7.7; *time of waiting:* Mt.24.22; *kingdom:* Mt.25.34.

2.15–32: The new people exhorted. The church, addressed as *mother* (contrast 2.6), is admonished to good works (vv. 20–25) and patient endurance (vv. 26–32). **18:** *Send . . . Isaiah and Jeremiah:* compare 1.39–40. *As they prophesied:* see Isa.65.1. *Twelve trees:* possibly an allusion to the twelve apostles. *Seven mountains:* seven deacons of the early church; compare Acts 6.1–6. **23:** To bury the *dead* was an act of piety; *the sign* was possibly a Christian symbol

Israel's rejection and glory to come

my servants whom I have given you not one shall be lost, I will demand them back from among your number. 27 Do not be anxious when the time of trouble and hardship comes; others shall lament and be sad, but you shall 28 have happiness and plenty. All nations shall envy you, but shall be powerless against you, says the Lord.

29 'My power shall protect you, and 30 save your sons from hell. Be joyful, mother, you and your sons, for I will 31 come to your rescue. Remember your children who sleep in the grave; I will bring them up from the depths of the earth, and show mercy to them; for I am merciful, says the Lord Almighty. 32 Cherish your children until I come, and proclaim my mercy to them; for my favour flows abundantly from springs that will never run dry.'

33 I, EZRA, RECEIVED ON MOUNT HOREB A commission from the Lord to go to Israel; but when I came, they scorned me and rejected the Lord's command- 34 ment. Therefore I say to you Gentiles, you who hear and understand: 'Look forward to the coming of your shepherd, and he will give you everlasting rest; for he who is to come at the end 35 of the world is close at hand. Be ready to receive the rewards of the kingdom; for light perpetual will shine upon you 36 for ever and ever. Flee from the shadow of this world, and receive the joy and splendour that await you. I 37 bear witness openly to my Saviour. It is he whom the Lord has appointed; receive him and be joyful, giving thanks to the One who has summoned you to 38 the heavenly realms. Rise, stand up, and see the whole company of those

who bear the Lord's mark and sit at his table. They have moved out of the 39 shadow of this world and have received shining robes from the Lord. Receive, 40 O Zion, your full number, and close the roll of those arrayed in white who have faithfully kept the law of the Lord. The number of your sons whom 41 you so long desired is now complete. Pray that the Lord's kingdom may come, so that your people, whom he summoned when the world began, may be set apart as his own.'

I, Ezra, saw on Mount Zion a crowd 42 too large to count, all singing hymns of praise to the Lord. In the middle 43 stood a very tall young man, taller than all the rest, who was setting a crown on the head of each one of them; he stood out above them all. I was enthralled at the sight, and asked 44 the angel, 'Sir, who are these?' He 45 replied, 'They are those who have laid aside their mortal dress and put on the immortal, those who acknowledged the name of God. Now they are being given crowns and palms.' And I asked 46 again, 'Who is the young man setting crowns on their heads and giving them palms?', and the angel replied, 'He is 47 the Son of God, whom they acknowledged in this mortal life.' I began to praise those who had stood so valiantly for the Lord's name. Then the angel 48 said to me: 'Go and tell my people all the great and wonderful acts of the Lord God that you have seen.'

The mystery of human destiny

IN THE THIRTIETH YEAR AFTER THE FALL 3 of Jerusalem, I, Salathiel (who am also

---

which identified the dead person as belonging to God's "people" (v. 38) and so protected by him; see Rev.14.1. **29:** *Hell:* lit. Gehenna, place of torment; compare Mk.9.42–48.

2.33–48: Ezra turns to Gentiles, envisioning a faithful multitude. This is the most overtly Christian section of the book. **33:** Ezra receives his *commission* as the leader of the "new people of God" at *Mount Horeb* where Moses was called; see Exod.3.1–12. **34:** The early Christians believed that *the end of the world* and the second coming of Jesus were *close at hand;* see 1 Thess.4.15–18; 2 Thess.2.1–2. **36:** The *shadow of this world* is the aspect of the world that passes away or changes; compare 1 Cor.7.29–31; 1 Jn.2.15–17. **38:** To *sit at table* may be a symbol for accepting Christianity (Lk.14.15–24; Rev.19.9) or for the Eucharist (see 1 Cor.10.21; 11.17–32). **40–41:** The *full number* of the righteous is regarded as determined by God. See 4.36–37 and compare Rev.6.11. **42:** *On Mount Zion:* compare Heb.12.22–23. *A crowd . . . singing:* compare Rev.7.9–12.

3.1–5.19: Vision I. 1–36: A difficult question is raised in these verses. Why does God allow Israel to suffer at the hands of a more wicked people? The writer prefaces the question by a survey of history stressing the origin of sin and the election of Israel. **1:** Mention of *the thirtieth*

Ezra), was in Babylon. As I lay on my bed I was troubled, my mind was 2 filled with perplexity, as I considered the desolation of Zion and the prosperity of those who lived in Babylon. 3 My spirit was deeply disturbed; and I uttered my fears to the Most High. 4 'My Lord, my Master,' I said, 'was it not you, and you alone, who in the beginning spoke the word that formed the world? You commanded the dust, 5 and Adam appeared. His body was lifeless; but yours were the hands that had moulded it, and into it you breathed the breath of life. So you 6 made him a living person. You led him into paradise, which you yourself had planted before the earth came into 7 being. You gave him your one commandment to obey; he disobeyed it, and thereupon you made him subject to death, him and his descendants.

'From him were born nations and tribes, peoples and families, too nu-8 merous to count. Each nation went its own way, sinning against you and scorning you; and you did not stop 9 them. But then again, in due time, you brought the flood upon the inhabitants 10 of the earth and destroyed them. The same doom came upon all: death upon Adam, and the flood upon that 11 generation. One man you spared—Noah, with his household, and all his righteous descendants.

12 'The population of the earth increased; families and peoples multiplied, nation upon nation. But then once again they began to sin, more 13 wickedly than those before them. When they sinned, you chose for yourself one of them, whose name was Abraham; 14 him you loved, and to him alone,

secretly, at dead of night, you showed how the world would end. You made 15 an everlasting covenant with him and promised never to abandon his descendants. You gave him Isaac, and to 16 Isaac you gave Jacob and Esau; of these you chose Jacob for yourself and rejected Esau; and Jacob grew to be a great nation.

'You rescued his descendants from 17 Egypt and brought them to Mount Sinai. There you bent the sky, shook[a] 18 the earth, moved the round world, made the depths shudder, and turned creation upside down. Your glory 19 passed through the four gates of fire and earthquake, wind and frost; and you gave the commandments of the law to the Israelites, the race of Jacob. But you did not take away their 20 wicked heart and enable your law to bear fruit in them. For the first man, 21 Adam, was burdened with a wicked heart; he sinned and was overcome, and not only he but all his descendants. So the weakness became inveterate. 22 Although your law was in your people's hearts, a rooted wickedness was there too; so that the good came to nothing, and what was bad persisted.

'Years went by, and when the time 23 came you raised up a servant for yourself, whose name was David. You 24 told him to build the city that bears your name and there offer to you in sacrifice what was already your own. This was done for many years; until 25 the inhabitants of the city went astray, behaving just like Adam and all his 26 line; for they had the same wicked heart. And so you gave your own city 27 over to your enemies.

a So some Vss.; Lat. fixed.

---

year after the destruction of Jerusalem by Nebuchadnezzar, i.e. 557/556 B.C. (see Jer.52.4–11), may suggest that the book was written thirty years after the fall of Jerusalem to the Romans in 70 A.D. *Salathiel* is the Gk. form of Shealtiel, oldest son of King Jehoiachin and father of Zerubbabel (1 Chr.3.17; Ezra 3.2). *Ezra* flourished a century after Shealtiel; the erroneous identification of the two may be an interpolation. **4–7:** Gen. chs. 1–3. According to rabbinic tradition, *paradise* was created before the *earth*. **7:** That Adam's sin made *him and his descendants subject to death* became heightened into the doctrine of "original sin." The view here is the earliest recording in Jewish literature; see vv. 20–22 for a fuller statement. **15:** The author stresses that God made *an everlasting covenant* with a representative of the fallen race, Abraham; see Gen.15.18;17.2–8. **19:** Speaking of God's appearance at Sinai (see Exod.19.16–18; Ps.68.7–8), the writer identifies *fire and earthquake, wind and frost* as *four gates* of heavenly regions, perhaps the gates of the four lowest of the "seven heavens" known in Jewish tradition. **20:** The *wicked heart* is the rabbinical "evil *yeṣer*" or "evil inclination," considered, like its counterpart, the "good *yeṣer*," to be implanted in man. That God had given Israel a law, but had not removed the evil nature inherited from Adam, the obstacle to its

28 'I said to myself: "Perhaps those in Babylon lead better lives, and that is 29 why they have conquered Zion." But when I arrived here, I saw more wickedness than I could reckon, and these thirty years I have seen many evil-doers with my own eyes. My 30 heart sank, because I saw how you tolerate sinners and spare the godless; how you have destroyed your own people, but protected your enemies. 31 You have given no hint whatever to anyone how to understand your ways.*b* Is Babylon more virtuous than Zion? 32 Has any nation except Israel ever known you? What tribes have put their trust in your covenants as the tribes of 33 Jacob have? But they have seen no reward, no fruit for their pains. I have travelled up and down among the nations, and have seen how they prosper, heedless though they are of 34 your commandments. So weigh our sins in the balance against the sins of the rest of the world; and it will be clear 35 which way the scale tips. Has there ever been a time when the inhabitants of the earth did not sin against you? Has any nation ever kept your com- 36 mandments like Israel? You may find one man here, one there; but nowhere a whole nation.'

4 The angel who was sent to me, whose 2 name was Uriel, replied: 'You are at a loss to explain this world; do you then expect to understand the ways of the 3 Most High?' 'Yes, my lord', I replied. 'I have been sent to propound to you three of the ways of this world,' he continued, 'to give you three illustra- 4 tions. If you can explain to me any one of them, then I will answer your question about the way of the Most High, and teach you why the heart is wicked.'

5 I said, 'Speak, my lord.' 'Come then,' he said, 'weigh me a pound of fire, measure me a bushel*c* of wind, or call back a day that has passed.'

'How can you ask me to do that?' I 6 replied; 'no man on earth can do it.' He said: 'Suppose I had asked you, 7 "How many dwellings are there in the heart of the sea? or how many streams to feed the deep? or how many water-courses above the vault of heaven? Where are the paths out of the grave, and the roads into*d* paradise?", you 8 might then have replied, "I have never been down into the deep, I have not yet gone down into the grave, I have never gone up into heaven." But, as it 9 is, I have only asked you about fire, about wind, and about yesterday, things you are bound to have met; and yet you have failed to tell me the answers.

'If then', he went on, 'you cannot 10 understand things you have grown up with, how can your small capacity 11 comprehend the ways of the Most High? A man corrupted by the corrupt world can never know the way of the incorruptible.'*e*

When I heard that, I fell*f* prostrate 12 and exclaimed: 'Better never to have come into existence than be born into a world of wickedness and suffering which we cannot explain!' He replied, 13 'I went out into a wood, and the trees of the forest were making a plan. They 14 said, "Come, let us make war on the sea, force it to retreat, and win ground for more woods." The waves of the sea 15 made a similar plan: they said, "Come, let us attack the trees of the forest, conquer them, and annex their terri-tory." The plan made by the trees came 16 to nothing, for fire came and burnt them down. The plan made by the 17

b how . . . ways: so some Vss.; Lat. obscure.
c So some Vss.; Lat. the blast.
d the grave . . . into: so some Vss.; Lat. omits.
e A man . . . incorruptible: reading based on other Vss.; Lat. obscure.
f When . . . fell: so some Vss.; Lat. defective.

obedience, adds a new dimension to the writer's troubling question. **28:** *Babylon* stands for Rome as in Rev.14.8. **30:** Having laid the foundation, the writer now poses his question in words reminiscent of Hab.1.12–17.

4.1–5.19: The response: Man cannot comprehend God's ways. The human spirit is limited. The future age will show the answer. **1:** *Uriel* ("God is my light") is one of seven archangels who are God's "watchers" in Enoch 20.1. **4:** *If you can explain:* Echoing Job chs.38–41, the passage goes on to stress man's total inability to understand God's ways (v. 11). **7:** *The vault of heaven* (Gen.1.6–7) was considered to support a reservoir of water fed by *watercourses;* compare Ps.29.10.

4.12–21: Parable of sea and forest depicts the folly of the quest. 21: Compare Isa.55.8–9.

waves failed just as badly, for the sand stood its ground and blocked their

18 way. If you had to judge between the two, which would you pronounce right, and which wrong?'

19 I answered, 'Both were wrong; their plans were impossible, for the land is assigned to the trees, and to the sea is allotted a place for its waves.'

20 'Yes,' he replied, 'you have judged rightly. Why then have you failed to do

21 so with your own question? Just as the land belongs to the trees and the sea to the waves, so men on earth can understand earthly things and nothing else; only those who live*g* above the skies can understand the things above the skies.'

22 'But tell me, my lord,' I said, 'why then have I been given the faculty of

23 understanding? My question is not about the distant heavens, but about the things which happen every day before our eyes. Why has Israel been made a byword among the Gentiles; why has the people you loved been put at the mercy of godless nations? Why has the law of our fathers been brought to nothing, and the written covenants

24 made a dead letter? We pass like a flight of locusts, our life is but a vapour, and we are not worth the

25 Lord's pity, though we bear his name; what then will he do for us? These are my questions.'

26 He answered: 'If you survive, you will see; if you live long enough, you will marvel.*h* For this present age is

27 quickly passing away; it is full of sorrow and frailties, too full to enjoy what is promised in due time for the

28 godly. The evil about which you ask me has been sown, but its reaping has

29 not yet come. Until the crop of evil has been reaped as well as sown, until the ground where it was sown has vanished, there will be no room for the field

30 which has been sown with the good. A grain of the evil seed was sown in the heart of Adam from the first; how

much godlessness has it produced already! How much more will it

31 produce before the harvest! Reckon this up: if one grain of evil seed has produced so great a crop of godless-

32 ness, how vast a harvest will there be when good seeds beyond number have been sown!'

33 I asked, 'But when? How long have we to wait? Why are our lives so short

34 and so miserable?' He replied, 'Do not be in a greater hurry than the Most High himself. You are in a hurry for yourself alone; the Most High for

35 many. Are not these the very questions which were asked by the righteous in the storehouse of souls: "How long must we stay here? When will the harvest begin, the time when we get our reward?" And the archangel Jere-

36 miel gave them this answer: "As soon as the number of those like yourselves is complete. For the Lord has weighed the world in a balance, he has measured

37 and numbered the ages; he will move nothing, alter nothing, until the appointed number is achieved." '

38 'But, my lord, my master,' I replied, 'we are all of us sinners through and

39 through. Can it be that because of us, because of the sins of mankind, the harvest and the reward of the just are

40 delayed?' 'Go,' he said, 'ask a pregnant woman whether she can keep the child in her womb any longer after the nine

41 months are complete.' 'No, my lord,' I said, 'she cannot.' He went on: 'The storehouses of souls in the world

42 below are like the womb. As a woman in travail is impatient to see the end of her labour, so they are impatient to give back all the souls committed to

43 them since time began. Then all your questions will be answered.'

44 I said, 'If it is possible for you to tell

45 and for me to understand, will you be gracious enough to disclose one thing more: which is the longer—the future

g Or he who lives.
h So one Vs.; Lat. live, you will often marvel.

4.22–25: The seer objects, continues to question.
4.26–32: The future age to show the answer. 30: *Evil seed:* the evil *yeṣer.* See 3.20 n.
4.33–50: The seer asks when the new age will dawn. 35: Talmudic sources speak of a *storehouse of souls* of the righteous dead beneath the throne of God. 36: *The archangel Jeremiel:* probably the archangel *Remiel* of Enoch 20.1–8. 37: *The appointed number:* see 2.40–41 n. 44: *Which is the longer:* the seer seeks to determine the end-time more closely.

still to come, or the past that has gone
46 by? What is past I know, but not what
47 is still to be.' 'Come and stand on my
right,' he said; 'you shall see a vision,
and I will explain what it means.'

48 So I stood and watched, and there
passed before my eyes a blazing fire;
when the flames had disappeared from
sight, there was still some smoke left.
49 After that a dark rain-cloud passed
before me; there was a heavy storm,
and when it had gone over, there were
50 still some raindrops left. 'Reflect on
this', said the angel. 'The shower of
rain filled a far greater space than the
drops of water, and the fire more than
the smoke. In the same way, the past
far exceeds the future in length; what
remains is but raindrops and smoke.'

51 'Pray tell me,' I said, 'do you think
that I shall live to see those days? Or
52 in whose lifetime will they come?' 'If
you ask me what signs will herald
them,' he said, 'I can tell you in part.
But the length of your own life I am
not commissioned to tell you; of that I
know nothing.

5 'But now to speak of the signs: there
will come a time when the inhabitants
of the earth will be seized with panic.[i]
The way of truth will be hidden from
sight, and the land will be barren of
2 faith. There will be a great increase in
wickedness, worse than anything you
3 now see or have ever heard of. The
country you now see governing the
world will become a trackless desert,
4 laid waste for all to see. After the
third period (if the Most High grants
you a long enough life) you will see
confusion everywhere. The sun will
suddenly begin to shine in the middle
of the night, and the moon in the
5 day-time. Trees will drip blood, stones
will speak, nations will be in confusion,
and the courses of the stars will be
6 changed. A king unwelcome to the
inhabitants of earth will succeed to the
throne; even the birds will all fly away.

The Dead Sea will cast up fish, and at 7
night a voice will sound, unknown to
the many but heard by all.[j] Chasms[k] 8
will open in many places and spurt out
flames incessantly. Wild beasts will
range far afield, women will give birth
to monsters, fresh springs will run with 9
salt water, and everywhere friends will
become enemies. Then understanding
will be hidden, and reason withdraw to
her secret chamber. Many will seek her, 10
but not find her; the earth will overflow
with vice and wickedness. One country 11
will ask another, "Has justice passed
your way, or any just man?", and it
will answer, "No." In those days men 12
will hope, but hope in vain; they will
strive, but never succeed.

'These are the signs I am allowed to 13
tell you. But turn again to prayer,
continue to weep and fast for seven
days; and then you shall hear further
signs, even greater than these.'

I awoke with a start, shuddering; my 14
spirit faltered, and I was near to
fainting. But the angel who had come 15
and talked to me gave me support and
strength, and set me on my feet.

The next night Phaltiel, the leader 16
of the people, came to me. 'Where
have you been?' he asked, 'and why
that sad look? Have you forgotten that 17
Israel in exile has been entrusted
to your care? Rouse yourself, take 18
nourishment. Do not abandon us like a
shepherd abandoning his flock to
savage wolves.' I replied: 'Leave me; 19
for seven days do not come near me,
then you may come again.' When he
heard this, he left me.

FOR SEVEN DAYS I FASTED, WITH TEARS 20
and lamentations, as the angel Uriel
had told me to do. By the end of the 21
seven days my mind was again deeply
disturbed, but I recovered the power 22

i So some Vss.; Lat. corrupt.
j Some Vss.; read and at night one whom the many
   do not know will utter his voice, and all will hear it.
k So one Vs.; Lat. Chaos.

4.51–5.12: Signs of end-time revealed. Compare Mt.24.4–35; Mk.13.3–31; Lk.21.7–33.
5.3: The *country . . . governing* is Rome. **6:** *Birds* were thought capable of foreseeing disaster.
7: *Fish* cannot live in the *Dead Sea*.
   5.13–19: Vision ended, but further revelations promised. 13: Fasting accompanied by *prayer*
and weeping seems to be set forth as a condition for receiving divine revelation. See 5.20;
6.35; 9.24; 12.51. **14:** *I awoke:* from the dream vision. **17–18:** The seer was regarded as the last
prophet left in Babylon (12.42) to whom *Israel* was *entrusted*.
   5.20–6.34: Vision II. 5.20–55: The seer's complaint and God's response. 20: *Fasted:* see 5.13 n.

of thought and spoke once more to the Most High.

23 'My Lord, my Master,' I said, 'out of all the forests of the earth, and all their trees, you have chosen one vine;
24 from all the lands in the whole world you have chosen one plot; and out of all the flowers in the whole world you
25 have chosen one lily. From all the depths of the sea you have filled one stream for yourself, and of all the cities ever built you have set Zion apart
26 as your own. From all the birds that were created you have named one dove, and from all the animals that were fashioned you have taken one
27 sheep. Out of all the countless nations, you have adopted one for your own, and to this chosen people you have given the law which all men have
28 approved. Why then, Lord, have you put this one people at the mercy of so many? Why have you humiliated[l] this one stock more than all others, and scattered your own people among the
29 hordes of heathen? Those who reject your promises have trampled on the
30 people who trust your covenants. If you so hate your people, they should be punished by your own hand.'
31 When I had finished speaking, the angel who had visited me that previous
32 night was sent to me again. 'Listen to me,' he said, 'and I will give you instruction. Attend carefully, and I
33 will tell you more.' 'Speak on, my lord', I replied.

He said to me, 'You are in great sorrow of heart for Israel's sake. Do you love Israel more than Israel's
34 Maker does?' 'No, my lord,' I said, 'but sorrow has forced me to speak; my heart is tortured every hour as I try to understand the ways of the Most High and to fathom some part of his judgements.'
35 He said to me, 'You cannot.' 'Why not, my lord?' I asked. 'Why then was I born? Why could not my mother's

womb have been my grave? Then I should never have seen Jacob's trials and the weariness of the race of Israel.'

He said to me, 'Count me those who 36 are not yet born, collect the scattered drops of rain, and make the withered flowers bloom again; unlock me the 37 storehouses and let loose the winds shut up there; or make visible the shape of a voice. Then I will answer your question about Israel's trials.'

'My lord, my master,' I said, 'how 38 can there be anyone with such knowledge except the One whose home is not among men? I am only a fool; how 39 then can I answer your questions?'

He said to me, 'Just as you cannot 40 do any of the things I have put to you, so you will not be able to find out my judgements or the ultimate purpose of the love I have promised to my people.'

I said, 'But surely, lord, your 41 promise[m] is to those who are alive at the end. What is to be the fate of those who lived before us, or of ourselves, or of those who come after us?'

He said to me, 'I will compare the 42 judgement to a circle: the latest will not be too late, nor the earliest too early.'

To this I replied, 'Could you not 43 have made all men, past, present, and future, at one and the same time? Then you could have held your assize with less delay.' But he answered, 'The 44 creation may not go faster than the Creator, nor could the world support at the same time all those created to live on it.'

'But, my lord,' I said, 'you have told 45 me that you will at one and the same time restore to life every creature you have made; how can that be? If it is going to be possible for all of them to be alive at the same time and for the world to support them all, then it

l So some Vss.; Lat. prepared.
m So one Vs.; Lat. obscure.

23–30: Drawing from OT imagery, the author stresses Israel's election as God's *chosen people*, v. 27. **35:** The seer is told that God's ways are beyond human comprehension. *Womb . . . grave:* compare Job 3.11; 10.18–19. **36–40:** Compare Job 38.24,28,34. If one cannot comprehend earthly things, how can he understand divine judgments? **40:** Instead of the angel (v. 31) God himself speaks to the troubled seer during the rest of Vision II. Such variation is found elsewhere (as in Gen. ch. 22) and is of limited significance, or none at all.
   5.41–55: The seer asks about the end-time. 42: Just as no one is first or last or in the middle of

46 could support all of them together now.' 'Put your question in terms of a woman's womb', he replied. 'Say to a woman, "If you give birth to ten children, why do you do so at intervals? Why not give birth to ten at one and 47 the same time?"' 'No, my lord, she cannot do that,' I said; 'the births must 48 take place at intervals.' 'True,' he answered; 'and I have made the earth's womb to bring forth at intervals those 49 conceived in it. An infant cannot give birth, nor can a woman who is too old; and I have made the same rule for the world I have created.'

50 I continued my questions. 'Since you have opened the way,' I said, 'may I now ask: is our mother that you speak of still young, or is she already 51 growing old?' He replied, 'Ask any 52 mother why the children she has lately borne are not like those born earlier, 53 but smaller. And she will tell you, "Those who were born in the vigour of my youth are very different from those born in my old age, when my 54 womb is beginning to fail." Think of it then like this: if you are smaller than 55 those born before you, and those who follow you are smaller still, the reason is that creation is growing old and losing the strength of youth.'

56 I said to him, 'If I have won your favour, my lord, show me through 6 whom you will visit your creation.' He said to me, 'Think of the beginning of this earth: the gates of the world had not yet been set up; no winds gathered 2 and blew, no thunder pealed, no lightning flashed; the foundations of 3 paradise were not yet laid, nor were its fair flowers there to see; the powers that move the stars were not established, nor the countless hosts of angels 4 assembled, nor the vast tracts of air set up on high; the divisions of the firmaments had not received their names. Zion had not yet been chosen 5 as God's own footstool; the present

age had not been planned; the schemes of its sinners had not yet been outlawed, nor had God's seal yet been set on those who have stored up a treasure 6 of fidelity. Then did I think my thought; and the whole world was created through me and through me alone. In the same way, through me and through me alone the end shall come.'

7 'Tell me', I went on, 'about the interval that divides the ages. When will the first age end and the next age 8 begin?' He said, 'The interval will be no bigger than that between Abraham and Abraham; for Jacob and Esau were his descendants, and Jacob's hand was grasping Esau's heel at the 9 moment of their birth. Esau represents the end of the first age, and Jacob 10 the beginning of the next age. The beginning of a man is his hand, and the end of a man is his heel.[n] Between the heel and the hand, Ezra, do not look for any interval.'

11 'My lord, my master,' I said, 'if I 12 have won your favour, make known to me the last of your signs, of which you showed me a part that former night.'

13 'Rise to your feet,' he replied, 'and you will hear a loud resounding voice. 14-15 When it speaks, do not be frightened if the place where you stand trembles and shakes; it speaks of the end, and the earth's foundations will understand that it is speaking of them. They will 16 tremble and shake; for they know that at the end they must be transformed.' 17 On hearing this I rose to my feet and listened; and a voice began to speak. Its sound was like the sound of rushing waters. The voice said: 18

'The time draws near when I shall come to judge those who live on the earth, the time when I shall inquire 19 into the wickedness of wrong-doers,

n The beginning of a man . . . heel: *reading based on other Vss.; Lat. defective.*

those standing on a circle's circumference, so God's judgment embraces living and dead in a simultaneous action. **50–55:** *That creation is growing old,* hence, soon to end, is shown by the smaller stature of recent generations.
5.56–6.34: Questions concerning the end-time. 6.6: See Gen. chs. 1 and 2; contrast Jn.1.3. **7–10:** As *Jacob's hand* grasped *Esau's heel* without interval (see Gen.25.26), so the new age will follow this one immediately. **12:** Compare 5.1–12. **17:** The roar of the *rushing waters* voices God's great power and majesty. See Ezek.1.24; Rev.1.15; 14.2; compare Ps.29.3–4.

the time when Zion's humiliation will
20 be over, the time when a seal will be
set on the age about to pass away.
Then I will perform these signs: the
books shall be opened in the sight of
heaven, and all shall see them at the
21 same moment. Children only one year
old shall be able to talk, and pregnant
women shall give birth to premature
babes of three and four months, who
22 shall live and leap about. Fields that
were sown shall suddenly prove unsown, and barns that were full shall
23 suddenly be found empty. There shall be
a loud trumpet-blast and it shall
24 strike terror into all who hear it. At
that time friends shall make war on
friends as though they were enemies,
and the earth and all its inhabitants
shall be terrified. Running streams shall
stand still; for three hours they shall
cease to flow.
25 'Whoever is left after all that I have
foretold, he shall be preserved, and
shall see the deliverance that I bring
26 and the end of this world of mine. They
shall all see the men who were taken up
into heaven without ever knowing
death. Then shall men on earth feel a
change of heart and come to a better
27 mind. Wickedness shall be blotted out
28 and deceit destroyed, but fidelity shall
flourish, corruption be overcome, and
truth, so long unfruitful, be brought to
light.'
29 While the voice was speaking to me,
the ground under me began to quake.*o*
30 Then the angel said to me, 'These,
then, are the revelations I have
31 brought you this night.*p* If once again
you pray and fast for seven days, then
I will return to tell you even greater
32 things.*q* For be sure your voice has
been heard by the Most High. The
Mighty God has seen your integrity
and the chastity you have observed all
33 your life. That is why he has sent me

to you with all these revelations, and
with this message: "Be confident, and
have no fear. Do not rush too quickly 34
into unprofitable thoughts now in the
present age; then you will not act
hastily when the last age comes." '

THEREUPON I WEPT AND FASTED AGAIN 35
for seven days in the same way as
before, thus completing the three
weeks enjoined on me. On the eighth 36
night I was again disturbed at heart,
and spoke to the Most High. With 37
spirit aflame and in great agony of
mind I said: 38
'O Lord, at the beginning of creation
you spoke the word. On the first day
you said, "Let heaven and earth be
made!", and your word carried out its
work. At that time the hovering spirit 39
was there, and darkness circled round;
there was silence, no sound as yet of
human voice.*r* Then you commanded a 40
ray of light to be brought out of your
store-chambers, to make your works
visible from that time onwards. On the 41
second day you created the angel*s* of
the firmament, and commanded him
to make a dividing barrier between the
waters, one part withdrawing upwards
and the other remaining below. On the 42
third day you ordered the waters to
collect in a seventh part of the earth;
the other six parts you made into dry
land, and from it kept some to be
sown and tilled for your service. Your 43
word went forth, and at once the work
was done. A vast profusion of fruits 44
appeared instantly, of every kind and
taste that can be desired, with flowers
of the most subtle colours and
mysterious scents. These were made on
the third day. On the fourth day by 45

o the ground . . . quake: reading based on other Vss.;
Lat. obscure.
p So one Vs.; Lat. this coming night.
q So other Vss.; Lat. adds in the day-time.
r So some Vss.; Lat. adds from you.
s Literally spirit.

20: *Books:* heavenly records of human deeds; see Dan.7.10; Rev.20.12. **23:** *Trumpet-blast:*
see 1 Cor.15.52; 1 Th.4.16 n. **26:** Enoch (Gen.5.24) and Elijah (2 Kgs.2.11) did not experience
death. Mal.4.5–6 pictures a second Elijah who leads men to repent, i.e. to *feel a change of*
heart. **29:** The quaking of the *ground* makes known God's presence in power; see Isa.6.4;
Jer.10.10. **31:** *Fast:* see 5.13 n.
6.35–9.25: Vision III. More questions about the end-time.
6.35–59: Was the world created for Israel? 35: *The three weeks:* apparently a week of fasting
preceded each of the first three visions. 38–54: Compare Gen. ch. 1. 41: A Jewish belief that
God governed the elements of the universe as well as people and nations through angels was
widespread at this time; hence, Gen.1.6 is here presumed to be addressed to an *angel of the*

your command you created the splendour of the sun, the light of the moon, and the stars in their appointed 46 places; and you ordered them to be at the service of man, whose creation was 47 about to take place. On the fifth day you commanded the seventh part, where the water was collected, to bring forth living things, birds and fishes. 48 And so, at your command, dumb lifeless water brought forth living creatures, and gave the nations cause 49 to tell of your wonders. Then you set apart two creatures: one you called Behemoth and the other Leviathan. 50 You put them in separate places, for the seventh part where the water was collected was not big enough to hold 51 them both. A part of the land which was made dry on the third day you gave to Behemoth as his territory, a 52 country of a thousand hills. To Leviathan you gave the seventh part, the water. You have kept them to be food for whom you will and when you 53 will. On the sixth day you ordered the earth to produce for you cattle, wild 54 beasts, and creeping things. To crown your work you created Adam, and gave him sovereignty over everything you had made. It is from Adam that we, your chosen people, are all descended. 55 'I have recited the whole story of the creation, O Lord, because you have said that you made this first world for 56 our sake, and that all the rest of the nations descended from Adam are nothing, that they are no better than spittle, and, for all their numbers, no 57 more than a drop from a bucket. And yet, O Lord, those nations which count for nothing are today ruling over us 58 and devouring us; and we, your people, have been put into their power—your people, whom you have called your first-born, your only son, your cham-59 pion, and your best beloved. Was the

world really made for us? Why, then, may we not take possession of our world? How much longer shall it be so?'

When I had finished speaking, the 7 same angel was sent to me as on the previous nights. He said to me, 'Rise 2 to your feet, Ezra, and listen to the message I have come to give you.' 'Speak, my lord', I said.   3

He said to me: 'Imagine a sea set in a vast open space, spreading far*t* and wide, but the entrance to it narrow 4 like the gorge of a river. If anyone is 5 determined to reach this sea, whether to set eyes on it or to gain command of it, he cannot arrive at its open waters except through the narrow gorge. Or again, imagine a city built in 6 a plain, a city full of everything you can desire, but the entrance to it 7 narrow and steep, with fire to the right and deep water to the left. There 8 is only the one path, between the fire and the water; and that is only wide enough for one man at a time. If some 9 man has been given this city as a legacy, how can he take possession of his inheritance except by passing through these dangerous approaches?' 'That is the only way, my lord', I 10 agreed.

He said to me: 'Such is the lot of Israel. It was for Israel that I made the 11 world, and when Adam transgressed my decrees the creation came under judgement. The entrances to this world 12 were made narrow, painful, and arduous, few and evil, full of perils and grinding hardship. But the entrances to 13 the greater world are broad and safe, and lead to immortality. All men must 14 therefore enter this narrow and futile existence; otherwise they can never attain the blessings in store. Why then, 15 Ezra, are you so deeply disturbed at the

t spreading far: reading based on other Vss.; Lat. deep.

---

firmament. Compare Jude 6; Rev.14.18; 16.5. **49**: *Behemoth . . . Leviathan:* compare Job 3.8; 40.15–41.34; Ps.74.12–14. **55**: *You made this first world for our sake:* see 7.11. Not found in the canonical OT, this idea was deduced by the rabbis from such texts as Deut.14.2. **58**: Israel is called the *first-born* and *only son* because the Lord brought it into existence at the Exodus, which he did for no other nation; see Hos.11.1; Jer.31.9. **59**: Apocalyptic and apocryphal literature which describes the end-time is in part an answer to this question: *How much longer before we take possession of our world?* See Ecclus.36.1–17.

7.1–25: Because of sin the path to the next world is arduous. 1: *The same angel:* Uriel (4.1 n.). **11**: *When Adam transgressed:* judgment brought by Adam's sin explains why Israel does not enjoy the world made for her. See 6.55–59; compare 3.7 n.; 4.30.

thought that you are mortal and must

18 die? Why have you not turned your mind to the future instead of the present?'

17 'My lord, my master,' I replied, 'in your law you have laid it down that the just shall come to enjoy these blessings but the ungodly shall be lost.

18 The just, therefore, can endure this narrow life and look for the spacious life hereafter; but those who have lived a wicked life will have gone through the narrows without ever reaching the open spaces.'

19 He said to me: 'You are not a better judge than God, nor wiser than the

20 Most High. Better that many now living should be lost, than that the law God has set before them should be

21 despised! God has given clear instructions for all men when they come into this world, telling them how to attain

22 life and how to escape punishment. But the ungodly have refused to obey him; they have set up their own empty ideas,

23 and planned deceit and wickedness; they have even denied the existence of the Most High and have not acknowl-

24 edged his ways. They have rejected his law and refused his promises, have neither put faith in his decrees nor done

25 what he commands. Therefore, Ezra, emptiness for the empty, fullness for the full!

26 'Listen! The time shall come when the signs I have foretold will be seen; the city which is now invisible*u* shall appear and the country now concealed

27 be made visible. Everyone who has been delivered from the evils I have foretold shall see for himself my

28 marvellous acts. My son the Messiah*v*

shall appear with his companions and bring four hundred years of happiness

29 to all who survive. At the end of that time, my son the Messiah shall die, and so shall all mankind who draw breath.

30 Then the world shall return to its original silence for seven days as at the beginning of creation, and no one

31 shall be left alive. After seven days the age which is not yet awake shall be roused and the age which is corruptible

32 shall die. The earth shall give up those who sleep in it, and the dust those who rest there in silence; and the store-houses shall give back the souls entrusted to them. Then the Most

33 High shall be seen on the judgement-seat, and there shall be an end of all pity and patience. Judgement alone

34 shall remain; truth shall stand firm and faithfulness be strong; requital*w*

35 shall at once begin and open payment be made; good deeds shall awake and wicked deeds shall not be allowed to sleep.*x* Then the place of torment shall [36] appear, and over against it the place of rest; the furnace of hell shall be displayed, and on the opposite side the paradise of delight.

'Then the Most High shall say to the [37] nations that have been raised from the dead: "Look and understand who it is you have denied and refused to serve, and whose commandment you have despised. Look on this side, then on [38] that: here are rest and delight, there

---

u So some Vss.; Lat. the city, the bride, which is now seen . . .
v So some Vss.; Lat. My son Jesus.
w Probable meaning; literally work.
x The passage from verse [36] to verse [105], missing from the text of the Authorized Version, but found in ancient witnesses, has been restored.

7.17–25: The angel answers concerning punishment of wicked. 17: The seer thinks not only of Israel but of all men. The rabbis held that the Gentiles rejected God's *law* before it was offered to Israel. **18–25:** Even though the wicked have to go through the *narrows* like the just, they will be *lost* because they *despised* the *law* and so *refused* God's *promises*.

7.26–[44]: The angel speaks of the messianic kingdom and the end of the world. 26: *The signs:* see 5.1–12; 6.20–24. *The city . . . the country:* the heavenly Jerusalem and paradise. See 8.52. **28:** In place of *four hundred years* some ancient versions have "thirty" or "one thousand," or omit the figure entirely. The idea of a temporary messianic reign is known from rabbinic sources. **31–32:** The age to come will awake when those who *sleep* in death will rise to new life. After the temporary messianic reign comes the resurrection (v. 32), and the judgment, hell and heaven (vv. 33–[44]). **32:** *The storehouses:* see 4.35 n. **34:** When the opportunity for obedience has passed, the final *judgement* is to be conducted with rigorous justice. **35:** Both *good* and *wicked deeds* will be brought to light and given the attention they deserve. **[36–105]:** These verses are missing from the standard Vg., and thus from the King James Version, but are found in two Latin MSS. and in several secondary versions. The passage may have been omitted from the Vg. for doctrinal reasons because it excludes prayer on behalf of the dead; see 7.[105] n.

7.[37–44]: Judgment Day described. Here judgment is not the end, but a prelude to subsequent blessings. See Mt.25.46, which summarizes the discourse in Mt. ch. 24 on Judgment Day.

fire and torments." That is what he will say to them on the day of judgement.

[39] 'That day will be a day without sun, [40] moon, or stars; without cloud, thunder, or lightning; wind, water, or air; [41] darkness, evening, or morning; without summer, spring, or winter; without heat, frost, or cold; without hail, rain, [42] or dew; without noonday, night, or dawn; without brightness, glow, or light. There shall be only the radiant glory of the Most High, by which all men will see everything that lies before [43] them. It shall last as it were for a week [44] of years. Such is the order that I have appointed for the Judgement. I have given this revelation to you alone.'

[45] I replied: 'My lord, I repeat what I said before: "How blest are the living who obey the decrees you have laid [46] down!" But as for those for whom I have been praying, is there any man alive who has never sinned, any man who has never transgressed your [47] covenant? I see now that there are few to whom the world to come will bring happiness, and many to whom it will [48] bring torment. For the wicked heart has grown up in us, which has estranged us from God's ways,ʸ brought us into corruption and the way of death, opened out to us the paths of ruin, and carried us far away from life. It has done this, not merely to a few, but to almost all who have been created.'

[49] The angel replied: 'Listen to me and I will give you further instruction and [50] correction. It is for this reason that the Most High has created not one world [51] but two. There are, you say, not many who are just, but only a few, whereas the wicked are very numerous; well [52] then, hear the answer. Suppose you had a very few precious stones; would you add to their number by putting common lead and clay among them²?' [53] 'No,' I said, 'no one would do that.' [54] 'Look at it also in this way,' he continued; 'speak to the earth and humbly ask her; she will give you the

answer. Say to her: "You produce [55] gold, silver, and copper, iron, lead, and clay. There is more silver than [56] gold, more copper than silver, more iron than copper, more lead than iron, more clay than lead." Then judge for [57] yourself which things are valuable and desirable—those that are common, or those that are rare.' 'My lord, my [58] master,' I said, 'the common things are cheaper, and the rarer are more valuable.' He replied, 'Consider then [59] what follows from that: the owner of something hard to get has more cause to be pleased than the owner of what is common. In the same way, at my [60] promised judgement,ᵃ I shall have joy in the few who are saved, because it is they who have made my glory prevail, and through them that my name has been made known. But I shall not [61] grieve for the many who are lost; for they are no more than a vapour, they are like flame or smoke; they catch fire, blaze up, and then die out.'

Then I said: 'Mother Earth, what [62] have you brought forth! Is the mind of man, like the rest of creation, a product of the dust? Far better then [63] if the very dust had never been created, and so had never produced man's mind! But, as it is, we grow up with [64] the power of thought and are tortured by it; we are doomed to die and we know it. What sorrow for mankind; [65] what happiness for the wild beasts! What sorrow for every mother's son; what gladness for the cattle and flocks! How much better their lot than ours! [66] They have no judgement to expect, no knowledge of torment or salvation after death. What good to us is the [67] promise of a future life if it is going to be one of torment? For every man [68] alive is burdened and defiled with wickedness, a sinner through and through. Would it not have been [69]

y Literally from these things.
z by putting . . . them: probable reading, based on other Vss.; Lat. obscure.
a Reading based on other Vss.; Lat. creation.

[42]: The radiant glory of God gives light at the judgment. Compare Isa.60.19–20; Rev.21.23.
7.[45–74]: That few are to be saved is justified by angel but lamented by seer. [48]: Wicked heart: see 3.20 n. [61]: The fire in which the wicked die out is not one of annihilation (see v. [67]), but one in which their worth goes up in smoke. [64–68]: The seer insists on the unity of the human race in doom, including himself in the wickedness and sorrow of every mother's

better for us if there had been no judgement awaiting us after death?'

[70] The angel replied: 'When the Most High was creating the world and Adam and his descendants, he first of all planned the judgement and what goes

[71] with it. Your own words, when you said that man grows up with the power of thought, will give you the answer.

[72] It was with conscious knowledge that the people of this world sinned, and that is why torment awaits them; they received the commandments but did not keep them, they accepted the law

[73] but violated it. What defence will they be able to make at the judgement, what

[74] answer at the last day? How patient the Most High has been with the men of this world, and for how long!—not for their own sake, but for the sake of the destined age to be.'

[75] Then I said: 'If I have won your favour, my lord, make this plain to me: at death, when every one of us gives back his soul, shall we be kept at rest until the time when you begin to create your new world, or does our

[76] torment begin at once?' 'I will tell you that also', he replied. 'But do not include yourself among those who have despised my law; do not count yourself with those who are to be

[77] tormented. For you have a treasure of good works stored up with the Most High, though you will not be shown it

[78] until the last days. But now to speak of death: when the Most High has given final sentence for a man to die, the spirit leaves the body to return to the One who gave it, and first of all to

[79] adore the glory of the Most High. But as for those who have rejected the ways of the Most High and despised his law,

[80] and who hate all that fear God, their spirits enter no settled abode, but roam thenceforward in torment, grief, and sorrow. And this for seven reasons.

[81] First, they have despised the law of

[82] the Most High. Secondly, they have lost their last chance of making a good

repentance and so gaining life. Thirdly, [83] they can see the reward in store for those who have trusted the covenants of the Most High. Fourthly, they [84] begin to think of the torment that awaits them at the end. Fifthly, they [85] see that angels are guarding the abode of the other souls in deep silence. Sixthly, they see that they are soon[b] to [86] enter into torment. The seventh cause [87] for grief, the strongest cause of all, is this: at the sight of the Most High in his glory, they break down in shame, waste away in remorse, and shrivel with fear remembering how they sinned against him in their lifetime, and how they are soon to be brought before him for judgement on the last day.

'As for those who have kept to the [88] way laid down by the Most High, this is what is appointed for them when their time comes to leave their mortal bodies. During their stay on earth they [89] served the Most High in spite of constant hardship and danger, and kept to the last letter the law given them by the lawgiver. Their reward is [90] this: first they shall exult to see the [91] glory of God who will receive them as his own, and then they shall enter into rest in seven appointed stages of joy. Their first joy is their victory in the [92] long fight against their inborn impulses to evil, which have failed to lead them astray from life into death. Their [93] second joy is to see the souls of the wicked wandering ceaselessly, and the punishment in store for them. Their [94] third joy is the good report given of them by their Maker, that throughout their life they kept the law with which they were entrusted. Their fourth joy [95] is to understand the rest which they are now to share in the storehouses, guarded by angels in deep silence, and the glory waiting for them in the next age. Their fifth joy is the contrast [96] between the corruptible world they have escaped and the future life that

b So some Vss.; Lat. obscure.

---

son; see also vv. [75–77]. [70]: According to rabbinic theology, paradise and hell which go with *judgement* were among seven things created before the world.

7.[75–101]: **State of the dead before judgment.** [77]: *Treasure of good works:* compare 8.33–36. [79–87]: Wicked spirits *roam ... in sorrow,* tormented by deep mental anguish. [85]: *The other souls:* the righteous.

7.[88–99]: **The destiny of the just.** [92]: *Inborn impulses* refers to the evil *yeser:* see 3.20 n.

is to be their possession, between the crumpled laborious[n] life from which they have been set free and the spacious life which will soon be their [97] to enjoy for ever and ever. Their sixth joy will be the revelation that they are to shine like stars, never to fade or die, [98] with faces radiant as the sun. Their seventh joy, the greatest joy of all, will be the confident and exultant assurance which will be theirs, free from all fear and shame, as they press forward to see face to face the One whom they served in their lifetime, and from whom they are now to receive their reward in glory.

[99] 'The joys I have been declaring are the appointed destiny for the souls of the just; the torments I described before are the sufferings appointed for the rebellious.'

[100] Then I asked: 'When souls are separated from their bodies, will they be given the opportunity to see what [101] you have described to me?' 'They will be allowed seven days,' he replied; 'for seven days they will be permitted to see the things I have told you, and after that they will join the other souls in their abodes.'

[102] Then I asked: 'If I have won your favour, my lord, tell me more. On the day of judgement will the just be able to win pardon for the wicked, or pray [103] for them to the Most High? Can fathers do so for their sons, or sons for their parents? Can brothers pray for brothers, relatives and friends[d] for their nearest and dearest?'

[104] 'You have won my favour,' he replied, 'and I will tell you. The day of judgement is decisive,[e] and sets its seal on the truth for all to see. In the present age a father cannot send his son in his place, nor a son his father, a master his slave, nor a man his best friend, to be ill[f] for him, or sleep, or [105] eat, or be cured for him. In the same way no one shall ever ask pardon for

another; when that day comes, every individual will be held responsible for his own wickedness or goodness.'

To this I replied: 'But how is it, 36[106] then, that we read of intercessions in scripture? First, there is Abraham, who prayed for the people of Sodom; then Moses, who prayed for our ancestors when they sinned in the desert. Next, 37[107] there is Joshua, who prayed for the Israelites in the time of Achan, then 38[108] Samuel in the time of Saul,[g] David during the plague,[h] and Solomon at the dedication of the temple. Elijah prayed 39[109] for rain for the people, and for a dead man that he might be brought back to life. Hezekiah prayed for the nation in 40[110] the time of Sennacherib; and there are many more besides. If, then, in the 41[111] time when corruption grew and wickedness increased, the just asked pardon for the wicked, why cannot it be the same on the day of judgement?'

The angel gave me this answer: 'The 42[112] present world is not the end, and the glory of God does not stay in it continually.[i] That is why the strong have prayed for the weak. But the day 43[113] of judgement will be the end of the present world and the beginning of the eternal world to come, a world in which corruption will be over, all excess 44[114] abolished, and unbelief uprooted, in which justice will be full-grown, and truth will have risen like the sun. On 45[115] the day of judgement, therefore, there can be no mercy for the man who has lost his case, no reversal for the man who has won it.'

I replied, 'But this is my point, my 46[116] first point and my last: how much better it would have been if the earth had never produced Adam at all, or,

c *So some Vss.; Lat.* obscure.
d friends: *so some Vss.; Lat.* the faithful.
e *So one Vs.; Lat.* stern.
f *So some Vss.; Lat.* to understand.
g in the time of Saul: *so some Vss.; Lat.* omits.
h during the plague: *so some Vss.; Lat.* for the destruction.
i does . . . continually: *so some Vss.; Lat.* regularly stays in it.

[97]: *Shine like stars, never to fade:* compare Dan.12.3; Mt.13.43. [101]: *Abodes:* see 4.35 n.
7.[102–115]: **No intercession can be made for the wicked at Judgment Day.** Compare Ezek. 18.4,20. [105]: See v. 35 n. That the practice, later popular, of prayer for the dead is here excluded probably accounts for the omission of this section from some MSS. Its restoration has necessitated the double numbering of subsequent verses. [106]: *Abraham:* see Gen.18.23–32. *Moses:* see Exod.32.11–14. [107]: *Joshua:* see Josh.7.6–9. [108]: *Samuel:* see 1 Sam.7.9; 12.19–25. *David:* see 2 Sam.24.17. *Solomon:* see 1 Kgs.8.22–30. [109]: *Elijah:* see 1 Kgs.18.41–45; 17.20–21. [110]: *Hezekiah:* see 2 Kgs.19.15–19. [112–115]: Compare v. 35 n.

47[117] since it has done so, if he had been restrained from sinning! For what good does it do us all to live in misery now and have nothing but punishment to 48[118] expect after death? O Adam, what have you done? Your sin was not your fall alone; it was ours also, the fall of all 49[119] your descendants. What good is the promise of immortality to us, when we 50[120] have committed mortal sins; or the hope of eternity, in the wretched and 51[121] futile state to which we have come; or the prospect of dwelling in health and safety, when we have lived such evil 52[122] lives? The glory of the Most High will guard those who have led a life of purity; but what help is that to us whose conduct has been so wicked? 53[123] What good is the revelation of paradise and its imperishable fruit, the source of perfect satisfaction and healing? 54[124] For we shall never enter it, since we 55[125] have made depravity our home. Those who have practised self-discipline shall shine with faces brighter than the stars; but what good is that to us whose faces are darker than the night? 56[126] For during a lifetime of wickedness we have never given a thought to the sufferings awaiting us after death.'

57[127] The angel replied, 'This is the thought for every man to keep in mind 58[128] during his earthly contest: if he loses, he must accept the sufferings you have mentioned, but if he wins, the rewards 59[129] I have been describing will be his. For that was the way which Moses in his time urged the people to take, when he 60[130] said, "Choose life and live!" But they did not believe him, nor the prophets after him, nor me when I spoke to 61[131] them. Over their damnation there will be no sorrow; there will only be joy for the salvation of those who have believed.'[j]

62[132] 'My lord,' I replied, 'I know that the Most High is called "compassionate", because he has compassion on those yet unborn; and called "merciful", 63[133] because he shows mercy to those who repent and live by his law; and 64[134] "patient", because he shows patience to those who have sinned, his own creatures as they are; and "benefactor", 65[135] because he prefers giving to taking; and 66[136] "rich in forgiveness", because again and again he forgives sinners, past, present, and to come. For without his 67[137] continued forgiveness there could be no hope of life for the world and its inhabitants. And he is called 68[138] "generous", because without his generosity in releasing sinners from their sins, not one ten-thousandth part of mankind could hope to be given life; and he is also called "judge", for 69[139] unless he grants pardon to those who have been created by his word, and blots out their countless offences, I 70[140] suppose that of the entire human race only very few would be spared.'

The angel said to me in reply: 'The **8** Most High has made this world for many, but the next world for only a few. Let me give you an illustration, 2 Ezra. Ask the earth, and it will tell you that it can produce plenty of clay for making earthenware, but very little gold-dust. The same holds good for the present world: many have been 3 created, but only a few will be saved.'

I SAID: 'MY SOUL, DRINK DEEP OF 4 understanding and eat your fill of wisdom! Without your consent[k] you 5 came here, and unwillingly you go away; only a brief span of life is given you. O Lord above, if I may be 6 allowed to approach you in prayer, plant a seed in our hearts and minds,

j *So some Vss.; Lat.* for those who are convinced of salvation.
k *Without your consent: so one Vs.; Lat.* To obey.

7.[116–131]: **Lament on man's sinful lot.** [118]: *O Adam:* see 3.7 n. [123]: The *imperishable fruit* comes from the restored tree of life. See Gen.3.22–24; Ezek.47.12; Rev.22.2. [125]: *Shall shine:* see Dan.12.3. [126]: *A lifetime of wickedness:* see [64–68]n. [129]: *Choose life:* see Deut. 30.19–20.

7.[132]–8.3: **The seer appeals to God's mercy.** [132–140]: The divine attributes are apparently derived from Exod.34.6–7 but here all involve the forgiveness of sin. [139]: God is called *judge* in the biblical sense of one who saves the oppressed, here from sin; compare Judg.2.16–18. 8.1–3: The seer is told strict justice will obtain and *few will be saved.* Compare 7.49–61 and Mt.22.14.

8.4–62: **The seer prays for mercy upon the wicked but is denied.** 4–19a: Why should men, so carefully created and sustained by God, be doomed to perish? 6: *Plant a seed:* give a sure

and make it grow until it bears fruit,
so that fallen man may obtain life.
7 For you alone are God, and we are all
shaped by you in one mould, as your
8 word declares. The body moulded in
the womb receives from you both life
and limbs; that which you create is
kept safe amid fire and water; for nine
months the body moulded by you
bears what you have created in it.
9 Both the womb which holds safely and
that which is safely held will be safe
only because you keep them so. And
after the womb has delivered up what
10 has been created in it, then from the
human body itself, that is from the
breasts, milk, the fruit of the breasts,
11 is supplied by your command. For a
certain time what has been made is
nourished in that way; and afterwards
12 it is still cared for by your mercy. You
bring it up to know your justice, train
it in your law, and correct it by your
13 wisdom. It is your creature and you
made it; you can put it to death or give
14 it life, as you please. But if you should
lightly destroy one who was fashioned
by your command with so much
labour, what was the purpose of
creating him?
15 'And now let me say this: about
mankind at large, you know best; but
it is for your own people that I grieve,
16 for your inheritance that I mourn; my
sorrow is for Israel and my distress for
17 the race of Jacob. For them and for
myself, therefore, I will address my
prayer to you, since I perceive how low
we have fallen, we dwellers on earth;
18 and I know well how quickly your
19 judgement will follow. Hear my words
then, and consider the prayer which I
make to you.'

Here begins the prayer which Ezra
made, before he was taken up to
heaven.

20 'O Lord, who dost inhabit eternity,
to whom the sky and the highest
21 heavens belong; whose throne is
beyond imagining, and whose glory is
past conceiving; who art attended by
the host of angels trembling as they 22
turn themselves into wind and fire at
thy bidding; whose word is true and
constant, whose commands are mighty
and terrible; whose glance dries up the 23
deeps, whose anger melts the mountains,
and whose truth stands for ever:[l] hear 24
thy servant's prayer, O Lord, listen to
my petition, for thou hast fashioned
me, and consider my words. While I 25
live I will speak; while understanding
lasts, I will answer.

'Do not look upon thy people's 26
offences, look on those who have
served thee faithfully; pay no heed to 27
the godless and their pursuits, but to
those who have observed thy covenant
and suffered for it. Do not think of 28
those who all their life have been
untrue to thee, but remember those
who have acknowledged and feared
thee from the heart. Do not destroy 29
those who have lived like animals, but
take account of those who have borne
shining witness to thy law. Do not be 30
angry with those judged to be worse
than beasts; but show love to those
who have put unfailing trust in thy
glory. For we and our fathers have 31
lived in mortal sin,[m] yet it is on our
account that thou art called merciful;
for if it is thy desire to have mercy on 32
us sinners, who have no just deeds to
our credit, then indeed thou shalt be
called merciful. For the reward which 33
will be given to the just, who have
many good works stored up with thee,
will be no more than their own deeds
have earned.

'What is man, that thou shouldst be 34
angry with him? or the race of mortals,
that thou shouldst treat them so
harshly? The truth is, no man was ever 35
born who did not sin; no man alive is
innocent of offence. It is through thy 36
mercy towards those with no store of
good deeds to their name that thy
justice and kindness, O Lord, will be
made known.'

l So some Vss.; Lat. bears witness.
m in mortal sin: *so some Vss.; Lat. obscure.*

---

inclination to righteousness which alone can offset the evil inclination in man's heart; see
3.7 and 3.20 nn. **16:** *My sorrow is for Israel:* see the opening complaint, 3.4–36. **19b:** Because of
its liturgical beauty, the following prayer appears separately in the special hymn section of
many Latin MSS. under the title *Confessio Esdrae.* Hence, the superscription in the text: *here
begins the prayer.* **34:** Man is so insignificant that it is unworthy of God to be *angry with him*

37 The angel said to me in reply: 'Much of what you have said is just, and it
38 will be as you say. Be sure that I shall not give any thought to sinners, to their creation, death, judgement, or
39 damnation; but I shall take delight in the just, in their creation, their departure from this world, their salvation,
40 and their final reward. So I have said,
41 and so it is. The farmer sows many seeds in the ground and plants many plants, but not all the seeds sown come up safely in season, nor do all the plants strike root. So too in the world of men: not all who are sown will be preserved.'

42 To that I replied: 'If I have won
43 your favour, let me speak. The farmer's seed may never come up because it is given no rain at the right time, or it may rot because of too much
44 rain. But man, who was formed by your hands and made in your image, and for whose sake you made everything—will you compare him with
45 seed sown by a farmer? Surely not, O Lord above! Spare your own people and pity them, for you will be pitying your own creation.'

46 He answered: 'The present is for those now alive, the future for those
47 yet to come. You cannot love my creation with a love greater than mine—far from it! But never again rank yourself among the unjust, as
48 you have so often done. Yet the Most
49 High approves of the modesty you have rightly shown; you have not sought great glory by including your-
50 self among the godly. In the last days, then, the inhabitants of the world will be punished for their arrogant lives by
51 bitter sufferings. But you, Ezra, should direct your thoughts to yourself and
52 the glory awaiting those like you. For all of you, paradise lies open, the tree of life is planted, the age to come is made ready, and rich abundance is in store; the city is already built, rest from toil is assured, goodness and
53 wisdom are brought to perfection. The root of evil has been sealed off from you; for you there is no more illness, death[n] is abolished, hell has fled, and
54 decay is quite forgotten. All sorrows are at an end, and the treasure of immortality has been finally revealed.
55 Ask no more questions, therefore,
56 about the many who are lost. For they were given freedom and used it to despise the Most High, to treat his law with contempt and abandon his ways.
57 Yes, and they trampled on his just
58 servants; they said to themselves, "There is no God", though well aware
59 that they must die. Yours, then, will be the joys I have predicted; theirs the thirst and torments which are prepared. It is not that the Most High has wanted any man to be lost, but that
60 those he created have themselves brought dishonour on their Creator's name, and shown ingratitude to the One who had put life within their reach. My day of judgement is now
61 close at hand, but I have not made
62 this known to all; only to you and a few like you.'

63 'My lord,' I replied, 'you have now revealed to me the many signs which you are going to perform in the last days; but you have not told me when that will be.'

9 The angel answered: 'Keep a careful count yourself; when you see that some of the signs predicted have
2 already happened, then you will understand that the time has come when the Most High will judge the world he has
3 created. When the world becomes the scene of earthquakes, insurrections, plots among the nations, unstable government, and panic among rulers,

n death: *so some Vss.; Lat. omits.*

---

or to treat fragile *mortals harshly*. **37:** *It will be as you say:* the seer's prayer, *pay no heed* (v. 27), is accepted, but is turned to an opposite meaning: God will forget the doomed sinners and rejoice in the righteous. **41:** The *farmer* rejoices in his crop and disregards *the seeds* that fail. **46:** The seer's objection (vv. 43–44) seems dismissed as inapplicable to the future age. **47:** The angel asserts that God's *love* for his *creation* includes the doing of justice in vindication of those who have been trampled (v. 57). **52:** Now in existence, *paradise lies open* for contemplation. *Tree of life:* see 7.[123] n. **53:** *The root of evil:* see 3.20 n. **62:** *A few like you:* prophets like the seer, called apocalyptists because they have claimed to draw back the veil hiding the end-time.
8.63–9.13: Description of the end. 63: *The many signs:* see 5.1–13; 6.18–24. The present passage is a resumé. **9.1:** Keeping *a careful count* of the signs will enable the seer to judge the

4 then you will recognize these as the events which the Most High has foretold since first the world began.
5 Just as everything that is done on earth has its beginning and end clearly
6 marked,[o] so it is with the times which the Most High has determined: their beginning is marked by portents and miracles, their end by manifestations of power.
7 'Whoever comes safely through and escapes destruction, thanks to his good
8 deeds or the faith he has shown, will survive all the dangers I have foretold and witness the salvation that I shall bring to my land, the country I have marked out from all eternity as my
9 own. Then those who have misused my law will be taken by surprise; their contempt for it will bring them
10 continual torment. All who in their lifetime failed to acknowledge me in spite of all the good things I had given
11 them, all who disdained my law while freedom still was theirs, who scornfully dismissed the thought of penitence
12 while the way was still open—all these will have to learn the truth through
13 torments after death. Do not be curious any more, Ezra, to know how the godless will be tormented, but only how and when the just will be saved; the world is theirs and it exists for their sake.'
14,15 I answered, 'I repeat what I have said again and again: the lost out-
16 number the saved as a wave exceeds a drop of water.'
17 The angel replied: 'The seed to be sown depends on the soil, the colour on the flower, the product on the work-man, and the harvest on the farmer.
18 There was once a time before the world had been created for men to dwell in; at that time I was planning it for the sake of those who now exist.
19 No one then disputed my plan, for no one existed. I supplied this world with

unfailing food and a mysterious law;
20 but those whom I created turned to a life of corruption. I looked at my world, and there it lay spoilt, at my
21 earth in danger from men's wicked thoughts; and at the sight I could scarcely bring myself to spare them. One grape I saved out of a cluster, one
22 tree out of a forest.[p] So then let it be: destruction for the many who were born in vain, and salvation for my grape and my tree, which have cost me such labour to bring to perfection.
23 'You, Ezra, must wait one more
24 week. Do not fast this time, but go to a flowery field where no house stands, and eat only what grows there—no
25 meat or wine—and pray unceasingly to the Most High. Then I will come and talk to you again.'

Visions of the last days

26 SO I WENT OUT, AS THE ANGEL TOLD ME, to a field called Ardat. There I sat among the flowers; my food was what grew in the field, and I ate to my
27 heart's content. The week ended, and I was lying on the grass, troubled again in mind with all the same perplexities. I broke my silence and
28 addressed the Most High. 'O Lord,' I
29 said, 'you showed yourself to our fathers in the desert at the time of the exodus from Egypt, when they were travelling through the barren and untrodden waste. You said, "Hear me,
30 Israel; listen to my words, race of Jacob. This is my law, which I sow
31 among you to bear fruit and bring you glory for ever." But our fathers who
32 received your law did not keep it; they did not observe your commandments. Not that the fruit of the law perished; that was impossible, for it was yours.

o has . . . marked: *so one Vs.; Lat. defective.*
p So some Vss.; Lat. tribe.

nearness of the end. **4:** The writer expects to see and to *recognize* the end in his lifetime. **12:** *Learn the truth:* the real meaning of their ruinous but willful rebellion.
 9.14–25: Summary. 14: *I repeat:* see 7.[140]. **21:** Because of corruption (vv. 19–20), to spare even *one grape* in a vineyard is a marvelous act of grace. **23:** *Do not fast:* see 6.35 n.
 9.26–10.59: Vision IV. Zion's present mourning and future glory. The transformation is sudden, complete, and terrifying.
 9.26–37: The seer ponders the law's permanence and Israel's instability. 26: *Ardat:* an unidentifiable place, perhaps of mystic significance. **29:** See Exod.19.9; 24.10; 24.15; Jer.2.2.

33 Those who received it perished, because they failed to keep safe the good seed
34 that had been sown in them. Now the usual way of things is that when seed is put into the earth, or a ship on the sea, or food or drink into a jar, then
35 if the seed, or the ship, or the contents of the jar should be destroyed, what held or contained them does not perish with them. But with us sinners it is
36 different. Destruction will come upon us, the recipients of the law, and upon our hearts, the vessel that held the law.
37 The law itself is not destroyed, but survives in all its glory.'
38 While these thoughts were in my mind, I looked round, and on my right I saw a woman in great distress, mourning and loudly lamenting; her dress was torn, and she had ashes on
39 her head. Abandoning my meditations,
40 I turned to her, and said: 'Why are you weeping? What is troubling you?'
41 'Sir,' she replied, 'please leave me to my tears and my grief; great is my bitterness of heart, great my distress.'
42 'Tell me,' I asked, 'what has happened
43 to you?' 'Sir,' she replied, 'I was barren and childless through thirty
44 years of marriage. Every hour of every day during those thirty years, day and night alike, I prayed to the Most High.
45 Then after thirty years, my God answered my prayer and had mercy on my distress; he took note of my sorrow and granted me a son. What happiness he brought to my husband and myself and to all our neighbours! What praise
46 we gave to the Mighty God! I took
47 great pains over his upbringing. When he came of age, I chose a wife for him, and fixed the date of the wedding.
10 'But when my son entered his wedding-chamber, he fell down dead.
2 So we all put out our lamps, and all my neighbours came to comfort me; I controlled my grief till the evening of
3 the following day. When they had all ceased urging me to take comfort and

control my grief, I rose and stole away in the night, and came here, as you can see, to this field. I have made up my 4 mind never to go back to the town, but to stay here eating nothing and drinking nothing, and to continue my mourning and fasting unbroken till I die.'
At that I interrupted the train of my 5 thoughts, and I spoke sternly to the woman: 'You are the most foolish 6 woman in the world,' I said; 'are you blind to the grief and sufferings of our nation? It is for the sorrow and 7 humiliation of Zion, the mother of us all, that you should mourn so deeply; you should share in our common 8 mourning and sorrow. But you are deep in sorrow for your one son. Ask the 9 earth and she will tell you; she must mourn for the thousands and thousands who come to birth upon her. From 10 her we all originally sprang, and there are more to come. Almost all her children go to perdition, and their 11 vast numbers are wiped out. Who then has the better right to be in mourning—the earth, who has lost such vast numbers, or you, whose sorrow is for 12 one alone? You may say to me, "But my grief is very different from the earth's grief; I have lost the fruit of my own womb, which I brought to 13 birth with pain and travail, but it is only in the course of nature that the vast numbers now alive on earth should depart in the same way as they have come." My answer to that is: at 14 the cost of pain you have been a mother, but in the same way the earth has always been the mother of mankind, bearing fruit to earth's creator.
'Keep your sorrow to yourself, 15 therefore, and bear your misfortunes bravely. If you will accept God's 16 decree as just, then in due time you will receive your son back again, and win an honoured name among women. So go back to the town and to your 17 husband.'

33: The whole generation that sinned at Sinai *perished* and did not enter the promised land; see Num.32.13.
9.38–10.28: The woman in mourning. 38: *Ashes on her head*, like the *torn dress*, were a sign of grief. **10.2:** Weddings took place at night, hence, the *lamps;* see Mt.25.1–13. **7:** *Zion, the mother:* compare Bar.4.8–20; Gal.4.26. **16:** To *accept God's decree as just* is to submit humbly to his will. The mother would receive her son back again after the resurrection in the new age; compare 2 Macc.7.9,23,29. *An honoured name:* childbearing was regarded as a blessing, barrenness as a

18 'No, I will not,' she replied; 'I will not go back to the town, I will stay here to die.'

19 But I continued to argue with her.
20 'Do not do what you say,' I urged; 'be persuaded because of Zion's misfortunes, and take comfort to yourself
21 from the sorrow of Jerusalem. You see how our sanctuary has been laid waste, our altar demolished, and our
22 temple destroyed. Our harps are unstrung, our hymns silenced, our shouts of joy cut short; the light of the sacred lamp is out, and the ark of our covenant has been taken as spoil; the holy vessels are defiled, and the name which God has conferred on us is disgraced; our leading men*q* have been treated shamefully, our priests burnt alive, and the Levites taken off into captivity; our virgins have been raped and our wives ravished, our godfearing men carried off, and our children abandoned; our youths have been enslaved, and our strong warriors
23 reduced to weakness. Worst of all, Zion, once sealed with God's own seal, has forfeited its glory and is in
24 the hands of our enemies. Then throw off your own heavy grief, and lay all your sorrows aside; may the Mighty God restore you to his favour, may the Most High give you rest and peace after your troubles!'
25 Suddenly, while I was still speaking to the woman, I saw her face begin to shine; her countenance flashed like lightning, and I shrank from her in terror. While I wondered what this
26 meant, she suddenly uttered a loud and terrible cry, which shook the
27 earth. I looked up and saw no longer a woman but a complete city, built*r* on massive foundations. I cried aloud in
28 terror, 'Where is the angel Uriel, who visited me before? It is his doing that I have fallen into this bewilderment, that all my hopes are shattered,*s* and all my prayers in vain.'
29 I was still speaking when the angel

appeared who had visited me before. When he saw me lying in a dead faint, 30 unconscious on the ground, he grasped me by my right hand, put strength into me, and raised me to my feet. 'What 31 is the matter?' he asked. 'Why are you overcome? What was it that disturbed your mind and made you faint?' 'It 32 was because you deserted me', I replied. 'I did what you told me: I came out to the field; and what I have seen here and can still see is beyond my power to relate.'

'Stand up like a man,' he said, 'and 33 I will explain it to you.'

'Speak, my lord,' I replied; 'only do 34 not abandon me and leave me to die unsatisfied. For I have seen and I hear 35 things beyond my understanding—unless this is all an illusion and a 36 dream. I beg you to tell me, my lord, 37 the meaning of my vision.'

'Listen to me,' replied the angel, 38 'while I explain to you the meaning of the things that terrify you; for the Most High has revealed many secrets to you. He has seen your blameless 39 life, your unceasing grief for your people, and your deep mourning over Zion. Here then is the meaning of the 40 vision. A little while ago you saw a 41 woman in mourning, and tried to give her comfort; now you no longer see 42 that woman, but a whole city. She 43 told you she had lost her son, and this is the explanation. The woman you 44 saw is Zion, which you now see as a city with all its buildings. She told you 45 she was childless for thirty years; that was because there were three thousand years in which sacrifices were not yet offered in Zion. But then, after the 46 three thousand years, Solomon built the city and offered the sacrifices; that was the time when the barren woman bore her son. She took great pains, she 47 said, over his upbringing; that was the

q So some Vss.; Lat. our children.
r Probable meaning, based on other Vss.; Lat. but a city was being built . . .
s Or that my destiny turns out to be corruption.

curse. **20–22:** These verses are a poignant enumeration of the misfortunes that attended the destruction of Jerusalem in 587 B.C.; see 2 Kgs.25.8–12. *Hymns silenced:* compare Ps.137.1–4. The *ark* of the *covenant* was lost in the destruction. The holy vessels were defiled by being put to pagan worship (Ezra 1.7) or to profane use (see Dan.5.2–3). **28:** *Uriel:* see 4.1 n.
   10.29–59: The vision interpreted. 30: *In a dead faint:* compare Rev.1.17. **33:** *Stand up:* see 5.15; 6.13,17. **44:** *City:* the heavenly Jerusalem. **46–48:** *Her son:* the earthly Jerusalem. His

48 Then she told you of the great loss she suffered, how her son died on the day he entered his wedding-chamber; that was the destruction which overtook 49 Jerusalem. Such then was the vision that you saw—the woman mourning for her son—and you tried to comfort her in her sufferings; this was the 50 revelation you had to receive. Seeing your sincere grief and heartfelt sympathy for the woman, the Most High is now showing you her radiant glory 51 and her beauty. That was why I told you to stay in a field where no house 52 stood, for I knew that the Most High 53 intended to send you this revelation. I told you to come to this field, where no foundation had been laid for any 54 building; for in the place where the city of the Most High was to be revealed, no building made by man could stand.

55 'Have no fear then, Ezra, and set your trembling heart at rest; go into the city, and see the magnificence of the buildings, so far as your eyes have 56 power to see it all. Then, after that, you shall hear as much as your ears 57 have power to hear. You are more blessed than most other men, and few have such a name with the Most High 58 as you have. Stay here till tomorrow 59 night, when the Most High will show you in dreams and visions what he intends to do to the inhabitants of earth in the last days.' I did as I was told and slept there that night and the next.

11 ON THE SECOND NIGHT I HAD A VISION in a dream; I saw, rising from the sea, an eagle with twelve wings and three 2 heads. I saw it spread its wings over the whole earth; and all the winds blew 3 on it, and the clouds*t* gathered. Out of its wings I saw rival wings sprout, which proved to be only small and 4 stunted. Its heads lay still; even the

middle head, which was bigger than the others, lay still between them. As I 5 watched, the eagle rose on its wings to set itself up as ruler over the earth and its inhabitants. I saw it bring into 6 subjection everything under heaven; it met with no opposition at all from any creature on earth. I saw the eagle stand 7 erect on its talons, and it spoke aloud to its wings: 'Do not all wake at once,' 8 it said; 'sleep in your places, and each wake up in turn; the heads are to be 9 kept till the last.' I saw that the 10 sound was not coming from its heads, but from the middle of its body. I 11 counted its rival wings, and saw that there were eight of them.

As I watched, one of the wings on 12 its right side rose and became ruler over the whole earth. After a time, its 13 reign came to an end, and it disappeared from sight completely. Then the next one arose and established its rule, which it held for a long time. When its reign was coming to an end 14 and it was about to disappear like the first one, a voice could be heard 15 saying to it: 'You have ruled the world 16 for so long; now listen to my message before your time comes to disappear. None of your successors will achieve a 17 reign as long as yours, nor even half as long.' Then the third wing arose, ruled 18 the world for a time like its predecessors, and like them disappeared. In the 19 same way all the wings came to power in succession, and in turn disappeared from sight.

As time went on, I saw the wings on 20 the left*u* side also raise themselves up to seize power. Some of them did so, and passed immediately from sight, while others arose but never came to 21 power. At this point I noticed that two 22 of the little wings were, like the twelve, no longer to be seen. Nothing was now 23

t the clouds: so some Vss.; Lat. omits.
u So one Vs.; Lat. right.

---

death symbolized Jerusalem's fall. **50:** Heavenly Zion continues, and its *radiant glory* will be seen; see Ezek.40.2; 48.35; Heb.11.10; Rev. 21.10.
   11.1–12.51: Vision V. Rome to be destroyed. This strange vision with its bizarre and mysterious details is more apocalyptic in tone than the previous ones.
   11.1–12.3a: The mighty eagle and the strong lion. 1: *Rising from the sea:* see Dan.7.3; Rev.13.1. As viewed from the east, Roman forces came from the Mediterranean. *An eagle:* the military emblem of Imperial Rome. **2:** *Spread its wings:* establish its dominion. **3:** *Rival wings* probably symbolize rebellious army officers. Being *small and stunted,* unequal to the task, the rebellion hopelessly failed. **12:** The *wings* and heads (vv. 4, 29) seem to represent successive Roman *rulers.*

left of the eagle's body except the three motionless heads and six little wings.
24 As I watched, two of the six little wings separated from the rest and took up a place under the head on the right. The other four remained where they were;
25 and I saw them planning to rise up and
26 seize power. One rose, but disappeared
27 immediately; so too did the second, vanishing even more quickly than the
28 first. I saw the last two planning to
29 seize the kingship for themselves. But while they were still plotting, suddenly one of the heads woke from sleep, the one in the middle, the biggest of the
30 three. I saw how it joined with the
31 other two heads, and along with them turned and devoured the two little wings which were planning to seize
32 power. This head got the whole earth into its grasp, establishing an oppressive rule over all its inhabitants and a world-wide kingdom mightier than any
33 of the wings had ruled. But after that I saw the middle head vanish just as
34 suddenly as the wings had done. There were two heads left, and they also seized power over the earth and its
35 inhabitants, but as I watched, the head on the right devoured the head on the left.
36 Then I heard a voice which said to me: 'Look carefully at what you see
37 before you.' I looked, and saw what seemed to be a lion roused from the forest; it roared as it came, and I heard it address the eagle in a human
38 voice. 'Listen to what I tell you', it
39 said. 'The Most High says to you: Are you not the only survivor of the four beasts to which I gave the rule over my world, intending through them to
40-41 bring my ages to their end? You are the fourth beast, and you have conquered all who went before, ruling over the whole world and holding it in the
42 grip of fear and harsh oppression. You have lived*v* long in the world, governing it with deceit and with no regard for

truth. You have oppressed the gentle and injured the peaceful, hating the truthful and loving liars; you have destroyed the homes of the prosperous, and razed to the ground the walls of those who had done you no harm.
43 Your insolence is known to the Most High, and your pride to the Mighty
44 One. The Most High has surveyed the periods he has fixed: they are now at an end, and his ages have reached
45 their completion. So you, eagle, must now disappear and be seen no more, you and your terrible great wings, your evil small wings, your cruel heads, your grim talons, and your whole
46 worthless body. Then all the earth will feel relief at its deliverance from your violence, and look forward hopefully to the judgement and mercy of its Creator.'
12 While the lion was still addressing
2 the eagle, I looked and saw the one remaining head disappear. Then the two*w* wings which had gone over to him arose and set themselves up as rulers. Their reign was short and
3 troubled, and when I looked at them they were already vanishing. Then the eagle's entire body burst into flames, and the earth was struck with terror.
4 So great was my alarm and fear that I awoke, and said to myself: 'See the result of your attempt to discover the
5 ways of the Most High! My mind is weary; I am utterly exhausted. The terrors of this night have completely
6 drained my strength. So I will now pray to the Most High for strength to hold out to the end.' Then I said: 'My
7 Master and Lord, if I have won your favour and stand higher in your approval than most men, if it is true that my prayers have reached your presence, then give me strength; reveal
8 to me, my Lord, the exact interpreta-

v You are the fourth . . . lived: *so some Vss.; Lat.* The fourth beast came and conquered . . . It has lived . . .
w So other Vss.; Lat. corrupt.

35: *The head . . . devoured:* successful insurrection. **37:** *A lion:* the Messiah; see 12.31–32. **39:** *The four beasts* are those of Dan.7.3 which the present passage recalls (12.11). **43:** *Your insolence:* compare Dan.5.20. **44:** The apocalyptic writers see the *periods* of human life before the *completion* of the end as *fixed* like the scenes of a pageant, brought on and removed from the stage of history by God, with no historical preparation, conditioning, or interconnection between them.
12.3b–39: The eagle vision interpreted. 11: *The fourth kingdom* of Dan.7.7,23 is here, as in

9 tion of this terrifying vision, and so bring full consolation to my soul. For you have already judged me worthy to be shown the end of the present age.'

10 He said to me: 'Here is the inter-
11 pretation of your vision. The eagle you saw rising from the sea represents the fourth kingdom in the vision seen by
12 your brother Daniel. But he was not given the interpretation which I am now giving you or have already given
13 you. The days are coming when the earth will be under an empire more
14 terrible than any before. It will be ruled by twelve kings, one after
15 another. The second to come to the throne will have the longest reign of
16 all the twelve. That is the meaning of the twelve wings you saw.

17 'As for the voice which you heard speaking from the middle of the eagle's body, and not from its heads, this is
18 what it means: After this second king's reign, great conflicts will arise, which will bring the empire into danger of falling; and yet it will not fall then, but will be restored to its original strength.

19 'As for the eight lesser wings which you saw growing from the eagle's
20 wings, this is what they mean: The empire will come under eight kings whose reigns will be trivial and short-
21 lived; two of them will come and go just before the middle of the period, four will be kept back until shortly before its end, and two will be left until the end itself.

22 'As for the three heads which you saw sleeping, this is what they mean:
23 In the last years of the empire, the Most High will bring to the throne three kings, who will restore much of its strength, and rule^x over the earth
24 and its inhabitants more oppressively

than anyone before. They are called 25 the eagle's heads, because they will complete and bring to a head its long series of wicked deeds. As for the 26 greatest head, which you saw disappear, it signifies one of the kings, who will die in his bed, but in great agony. The 27 two that survived will be destroyed by the sword; one of them will fall by 28 the sword of the other, who will himself fall by the sword in the last days.

'As for the two little wings that went 29 over to the head on the right side, this 30 is what they mean: They are the ones whom the Most High has reserved until the last days, and their reign, as you saw, was short and troubled.

'As for the lion which you saw 31 coming from the forest, roused from sleep and roaring, which you heard addressing the eagle, taxing it with its wicked deeds and words, this is the 32 Messiah whom the Most High has kept back until the end. He will address^y those rulers, taxing them openly with their sins, their crimes, and their defiance. He will bring them alive 33 to judgement; he will convict them and then destroy them. But he will be 34 merciful to those of my people that remain, all who have been kept safe in my land; he will set them free and give them gladness, until the final day of judgement comes, about which I told you at the beginning.

'That, then, is the vision which you 35 saw, and its meaning. It is the secret of 36 the Most High, which no one except yourself has proved worthy to be told. What you have seen you must therefore 37 write in a book and deposit it in a hiding-place. You must also disclose 38

x who . . . rule: so some Vss.; Lat. and he will restore . . . and they will rule . . .
y He will address: probable reading; Lat. defective.

---

rabbinic writings, understood to be the Roman Empire. **13:** The apocalyptic writers describe contemporary or past events as *days* that *are coming* to show that they had been foretold by the prophets and so were in God's plan. The objective was to provide consolation in the present trials and confidence in God's Providence for the future, as well as credibility in the descriptions of the end. Here the seer's visions are set in the exilic period (1.3; 3.1) even though he is describing events that followed it and continued up to his own day. **14:** *Twelve kings* are twelve emperors, beginning with Julius Caesar. **15:** *The second:* Augustus. **17:** See 11.10. **18:** The *great conflicts* seems to allude to the anarchy after Nero's death in 68 A.D. **19:** *Eight lesser wings:* see 11.3 n. **21:** *The period:* the duration of the empire. **22:** The three heads (see 11.1,4,29–35) may symbolize the Flavian emperors, Vespasian and his sons, Titus and Domitian. **31:** *The lion:* see 11.37–12.3. **32:** The verse implies the heavenly preexistence of *the Messiah;* compare Dan.7.13–14. **34:** *My people that remain* are those who survive the messianic woes. See 7.26–28. **37–38:** The book is to be put into a *hiding place* because of its esoteric contents which only the

these secrets to those of your people whom you know to be wise enough to understand them and to keep them
39 safe. But stay here yourself for seven more days, to receive whatever revelation the Most High thinks fit to send you.' Then the angel left me.
40 When all the people heard that seven days had passed without my returning to the town, they assembled
41 and came to me. 'What wrong or injury have we done you,' they asked me, 'that you have deserted us and
42 settled here? Out of all the prophets you are the only one left to us. You are like the last cluster in a vineyard, like a lamp in the darkness, or a safe
43 harbour for a ship in a storm. Have
44 we not suffered enough? If you desert us, we had far better have been destroyed in the fire that burnt up
45 Zion. We are no better than those who perished there.' Then they raised a loud lamentation.
46 I replied: 'Take courage, Israel; house of Jacob, lay aside your grief.
47 The Most High bears you in mind, and the Mighty One has not for ever*z*
48 forgotten you. I have not left you, nor abandoned you; I came here to pray for Zion in her distress, and to beg for mercy for your sanctuary that has
49 fallen so low. Go to your homes now, every one of you; and in a few days' time I will come back to you.'
50 So the people returned to the town
51 as I told them, while I remained in the field. I stayed there for seven days in obedience to the angel, eating nothing but what grew in the field, and living on that for the whole of the time.

13 THE SEVEN DAYS PASSED; AND THE NEXT
2 night I had a dream. In my dream, a wind came up out of the sea and set
3 the waves in turmoil. And this wind

brought a human figure rising from the depths,*a* and as I watched, this man came flying*b* with the clouds of heaven. Wherever he turned his eyes, everything that they fell on was seized with terror;
4 and wherever the sound of his voice reached, all who heard it melted like wax at the touch of fire.
5 Next I saw an innumerable host of men gathering from the four winds of heaven to wage war on the man who
6 had risen from the sea. I saw that the man hewed out a vast mountain for
7 himself, and flew up on to it. I tried to see from what quarter or place the mountain had been taken, but I could
8 not. Then I saw that all who had gathered to wage war against the man were filled with fear, and yet they
9 dared to fight against him. When he saw the hordes advancing to attack, he did not so much as lift a finger against
10 them. He had no spear in his hand, no weapon at all; only, as I watched, he poured what seemed like a stream of fire out of his mouth, a breath of flame from his lips, and a storm of
11 sparks from his tongue. All of them combined into one mass—the stream of fire, the breath of flame, and the great storm. It fell on the host advancing to join battle, and burnt up every man of them; suddenly all that enormous multitude had disappeared, leaving nothing but dust and ashes and a reek of smoke. I was dumbfounded at the sight.
12 After that, I saw the man coming down from the mountain and calling to himself a different company, a peaceful one. He was joined by great
13 numbers of men, some with joy on their faces, others with sorrow. Some came from captivity; some brought

z *So one Vs.; Lat.* in strife.
a *And . . . depths: so other Vss.; Lat.* defective.
b *So other Vss.; Lat.* grew strong.

wise, i.e. the initiated, can *understand* and be *safe* in reading. Hence, the name Apocrypha, lit. "hidden," given to this class of books.
   12.40–51: The seer comforts his people. 40: *Seven days:* see 9.23. **42:** The apocalyptic writer puts himself into the category of the *prophets;* see 5.17–18 n. *A lamp:* see 2 Pet.1.19. **50:** Compare v. 39 and 9.24–26.
   13.1–58: Vision VI. The Messiah's activity.
   13.1–20: The man risen from the sea. 3: *A human figure:* the Messiah, called God's son in v. 32. Compare Dan.7.13. **4:** *All . . . melted like wax* suggests a divine manifestation. See Ps.97.5; Mic.1.4. **6:** *Hewed out:* see Dan.2.34,45. **10:** *A breath of flame:* without weapon or allies the Messiah destroys his enemies supernaturally, i.e. by the words of judgment that come from his *mouth:* see Isa.11.4; 2 Th.2.8. **13:** *As an offering:* see Isa.66.20; compare Isa.19.22.

others to him as an offering. I woke up in terror, and prayed to the Most 14 High. I said, 'You have revealed these marvels to me, your servant, all the way through; you have judged me worthy to have my prayers answered. 15 Now show me the meaning of this 16 dream also. How terrible, to my thinking, it will be for all who survive to those days! But how much worse 17 for those who do not survive! Those who do not survive will have the 18 sorrow of knowing what is in store in 19 the last days and yet missing it. Those who do survive are to be pitied for the terrible dangers and trials which, as these visions show, they will have to 20 face. But perhaps after all it is better to endure the dangers and reach the goal than to vanish out of the world like a cloud and never see the events of the last days.'

21 'Yes,' he replied, 'I will explain the meaning of this vision, and tell you 22 all that you ask. As for your question about those who survive, this is the 23 answer: the very person from whom the danger will then come will protect in danger those who have works and fidelity laid up to their credit with the 24 Most High. You may be assured that those who survive are more highly blessed than those who die.

25 'This is what the vision means: The man you saw rising from the depths of 26 the sea is he whom the Most High has held in readiness through many ages; he will himself deliver the world he has made, and determine the lot of those 27 who survive. As for the breath, fire, and storm which you saw pouring 28 from the mouth of the man, so that without a spear or any weapon in his hand he destroyed the hordes advancing to wage war against him, this is the 29 meaning: The day is near when the Most High will begin to bring deliver-30 ance to those on earth. Then men will

all be filled with great alarm; they will 31 plot to make war on one another, city on city, region on region, nation on nation, kingdom on kingdom. When 32 this happens, and all the signs that I have shown you come to pass, then my son will be revealed, whom you saw as a man rising from the sea. On 33 hearing his voice, all the nations will leave their own territories and their separate wars, and unite in a countless 34 host, as you saw in your vision, with a common intent to go and wage war against him. He will take his stand on 35 the summit of Mount Zion, and Zion 36 will come into sight before all men, complete and fully built. This corresponds to the mountain which you saw hewn out, not by the hand of man. Then my son will convict of their 37 godless deeds the nations that confront him. This will correspond to the storm you saw. He will taunt them 38 with their evil plottings and the tortures they are soon to endure. This corresponds to the flame. And he will destroy them without effort by means of[c] the law—and that is like the fire.

'Then you saw him collecting a 39 different company, a peaceful one. They are the ten tribes which were 40 taken off into exile in the time of King Hoshea, whom Shalmaneser king of Assyria took prisoner. He deported them beyond the River, and they were taken away into a strange country. But 41 then they resolved to leave the country populated by the Gentiles and go to a distant land never yet inhabited by man, and there at last to be obedient 42 to their laws, which in their own country they had failed to keep. As 43 they passed through the narrow passages of the Euphrates, the Most 44 High performed miracles for them, stopping up the channels of the river until they had crossed over. Their 45

c *by means of: so one Vs.; Lat.* and.

18: *What is in store:* see 7.26–[44]; 9.1–12. **19:** Compare Mt.24.21–22. **20:** The just who *endure the dangers* of the *last days* seem to have an advantage over those who died before; compare 1 Th.4.15–18. See also v. 24. **13.21–58: The vision interpreted. 23:** *The very person* is the Messiah, whose coming is presaged by the messianic woes. **26:** See 12.32 n. **27:** See vv. 9–11. **32:** *My son will be revealed:* see 7.28; compare Mt.24.30. **36:** *Mount Zion* is thus the mountain hewed out (v. 6). *Zion:* the heavenly Jerusalem; see 7.26 and Rev.21.2–4. **40:** *The ten tribes:* the Northern Kingdom, 2 Kgs.17.3,6. Perhaps an ideal group, including proselytes, is meant. *The River:* the Euphrates. **44:** *The Most High performed miracles* as in the original entrance into Canaan (Josh.3.14–17). **45:** *Arzareth:*

journey through that region, which is called Arzareth, was long, and took a
46 year and a half. They have lived there ever since, until this final age. Now
47 they are on their way back, and once more the Most High will stop the channels of the river to let them cross. 'That is the meaning of the peaceful
48 assembly that you saw. With them too are the survivors of your own people, all who are found inside my sacred
49 boundary. So then, when the time comes for him to destroy the nations assembled against him, he will protect
50 his people who are left, and show them many prodigies.'
51 'My lord, my master,' I asked, 'explain to me why the man that I saw rose up out of the depths of the sea.'
52 He replied: 'It is beyond the power of any man to explore the deep sea and discover what is in it; in the same way no one on earth can see my son and his company until the appointed day.
53 Such then is the meaning of your vision. The revelation has been given
54 to you, and to you alone, because you have given up your own affairs, and devoted yourself entirely to mine, and
55 to the study of my law. You have taken wisdom as your guide in everything, and called understanding your
56 mother. That is why I have given this revelation to you; there is a reward in store for you with the Most High. In three days' time I will speak with you again, and tell you some momentous and wonderful things.'
57 So I went away to the field, giving worship and praise to the Most High for the wonders he performed from
58 time to time and for his providential control of the passing ages and what happens in them. There I remained for three days.

ON THE THIRD DAY I WAS SITTING 14 under an oak-tree, when a voice came to me from a bush, saying, 'Ezra, Ezra!' 'Here I am, Lord', I answered, 2 and rose to my feet. The voice went on: 3 'I revealed myself in the bush, and spoke to Moses, when my people Israel was in slavery in Egypt, and 4 sent him to lead my people out of Egypt. I brought him up on to Mount Sinai, and kept him with me for many days. I told him of many wonders, 5 showing him the secrets of the ages and the end of time, and instructed him what to make known and what to 6 conceal. So too I now give this order 7 to you: commit to memory the signs I 8 have shown you, the visions you have seen, and the explanations you have been given. You yourself are about to 9 be taken away from the world of men, and thereafter you will remain with my son and with those like you, until the end of time. The world has lost its 10 youth, and time is growing old. For the 11 whole of time is in twelve divisions; nine[d] divisions and half the tenth have already passed, and only two and a 12 half still remain. Set your house in 13 order, therefore; give warnings to your nation, and comfort to those in need of it; and take your leave of mortal life. Put away your earthly 14 cares, and lay down your human burdens; strip off your weak nature, set aside the anxieties that vex you, 15 and be ready to depart quickly from this life. However great the evils you 16 have witnessed, there are worse to come. As this ageing world grows 17 weaker and weaker, so will evils

d Probable reading; Lat. ten.

---

shortened transliteration of Heb. for "another land," taken from Deut.29.28. **47:** See Isa.11.15–16. **49:** *His people who are left:* righteous Israel enlarged by the return of the ten tribes. **50:** *Many prodigies* were to occur at the outset of the messianic age. See 5.1–13; 6.11–28. **52:** *His company:* probably angels, as in Mt.24.31; 25.31; 2 Th.1.7. **57:** *The field:* Ardat (9.26).
    14.1–48: Vision VII. The writing of the sacred books.
    14.1–18: God admonishes Ezra to prepare to leave this life. 1: *A bush:* see Exod.3.4. Ezra is set forth as a second Moses. **4:** *Many days:* forty days (Exod.34.28). **6:** *What to conceal:* see v. 46 n. **8:** *Signs . . . visions . . . explanations:* i.e. the contents of the preceding chapters. **9:** *To be taken away:* to be taken alive out of this world like Enoch and Elijah; see 6.26 n. **10:** Compare 5.50–55. **11–12:** *Nine divisions and half the tenth* had passed at the time the seer allegedly was writing, i.e. the reign of Artaxerxes II (404–359 B.C.; see 1.3 n.). What the measure of the divisions was is unknown but the two and a half divisions would have been greatly reduced at

18 increase for its inhabitants. Truth will move farther away, and falsehood come nearer. The eagle that you saw in your vision is already on the wing.'

19 'May I speak[e] in your presence,
20 Lord?' I replied. 'I am to depart, by your command, after giving warning to those of my people who are now alive. But who will give warning to those born hereafter? The world is shrouded in darkness, and its inhabi-
21 tants are without light. For your law was destroyed in the fire, and so no one can know about the deeds you have
22 done or intend to do. If I have won your favour, fill me with your holy spirit, so that I may write down the whole story of the world from the very beginning, everything that is contained in your law; then men will have the chance to find the right path, and, if they choose, gain life in the last days.'

23 'Go,' he replied, 'call the people together, and tell them not to look for
24 you for forty days. Have a large number of writing-tablets ready, and take with you Seraiah and Dibri, Shelemiah, Ethan, and Asiel, five men
25 all trained to write quickly. Then return here, and I will light a lamp of understanding in your mind, which will not go out until you have finished
26 all that you are to write. When your work is complete, some of it you must make public; the rest you must give to wise men to keep secret. Tomorrow at this time you shall begin to write.'

27 I went as I was ordered and sum-
28 moned all the people, and said: 'Israel,
29 listen to what I say. Our ancestors lived originally in Egypt as foreigners.
30 They were rescued from that land, and were given the law which offers life. But they disobeyed it, and you have
31 followed their example. Then you were given a land of your own, the land of Zion; but you, like your ancestors, sinned and abandoned the way laid down for you by the Most High. Because he is a just judge he took away 32 from you in due time what he had given. And so you are now here in 33 exile, and your fellow-countrymen are still farther away. If then you will 34 direct your understanding and instruct your minds, you shall be kept safe in life and meet with mercy after you die. For after death will come the judge- 35 ment; we shall be restored to life, and then the names of the just will be known and the deeds of the godless exposed. From this moment no one 36 must come to talk to me, nor look for me for the next forty days.'

I took with me the five men as I had 37 been told, and we went away to the field, and there we stayed. On the next 38 day I heard a voice calling me, which said: 'Ezra, open your mouth and drink what I give you.' So I opened my 39 mouth, and was handed a cup full of what seemed like water, except that its colour was the colour of fire. I took it 40 and drank, and as soon as I had done so my mind began to pour forth a flood of understanding, and wisdom grew greater and greater within me, for I retained my memory unimpaired. I 41 opened my mouth to speak, and I continued to speak unceasingly. The 42 Most High gave understanding to the five men, who took turns at writing down what was said, using characters[f] which they had not known before. They remained at work through the forty days, writing all day, and taking food only at night. But as for me, I 43 spoke all through the day; even at

e May I speak: *so other Vss.; Lat. omits.*
f *Probable reading, based on other Vss.; Lat. corrupt.*

---

the time when his book appeared, approximately 100 A.D. See Introduction. **18:** *Eagle:* see ch.11, especially 11.1 n.
14.19–26: The inspiration to restore Scriptures is granted. 20: *Without light:* without God's law (Ps.19.8). **21:** *The fire:* Jerusalem's destruction; see 2 Kgs.25.8–9. **23:** *Forty days:* see v. 1 n. and v. 4 n. **26:** *Some . . . make public:* publish the restored Heb. Scriptures (v. 45). *The rest . . . keep secret:* see v. 46. As Moses, according to tradition, handed down an oral law to the sages, so Ezra is to preserve a number of secret (apocryphal) books for the future. See 12.37–38 n.
14.27–36: Ezra's last admonition to the people. 33: *Your fellow-countrymen:* perhaps the ten tribes. See 13.40 n.,41. **36:** See v. 23.
14.37–48: Ezra rewrites the holy books. 39: A *cup* of inspiration is given to Ezra enabling him to restore perfectly the Scriptures; compare Ezek.3.1–3; Rev.10.9–11. **42:** Until the Exile, the Heb. language was written in the Phoenician script. Between the sixth and fourth centuries B.C., the Aram. script was adopted and from it developed the square *characters* still used in

44 night I was not silent. In the forty days,
45 ninety-four*g* books were written. At the end of the forty days the Most High spoke to me, 'Make public the books you wrote first,' he said, 'to be
46 read by good and bad alike. But the last seventy books are to be kept back, and given to none but the wise among
47 your people. They contain a stream of understanding, a fountain of wisdom,
48 a flood of knowledge.' And I did so.

Prophecies of doom

15 PROCLAIM TO MY PEOPLE THE WORDS of prophecy which I give you to
2 speak, says the Lord; and have them written down, because they are trust-
3 worthy and true. Have no fear of plots against you, and do not be troubled by the unbelief of those who
4 oppose you. For everyone who does not believe will die because of his unbelief.*h*
5 Beware, says the Lord, I am letting loose terrible evils on the world, sword and famine, death and destruc-
6 tion, because wickedness has spread over the whole earth and there is no room for further deeds of violence.
7,8 Therefore the Lord says, I will not keep silence about their godless sins; I will not tolerate their wicked deeds. See how the blood of innocent victims cries to me for vengeance, and the souls of the just never cease to plead
9 with me! I will most surely avenge them, says the Lord, and will hear the plea of all the innocent blood that has
10 been shed. My people are being led to the slaughter like sheep. I will no longer allow them to remain in Egypt,
11 but will use all my power to rescue them; I will strike the Egyptians with plagues, as I did before, and destroy
12 their whole land. How Egypt will mourn, shaken to its very foundations, when it is scourged and chastised by
13 the Lord! How the tillers of the soil will mourn, when the seed fails to grow, and when their trees are devastated by blight and hail and terrible
14 storm!*i* Alas for the world and its
15 inhabitants! The sword that will destroy them is not far away. Nation will draw sword against nation and go to war.
16 Stable government will be at an end; one faction will prevail over another, caring nothing in their day of power
17 for king or leading man of rank. A
18 man may want to visit a city, but will not be able to do so; for ambition and rivalry will have reduced cities to chaos, destroyed houses, and filled men
19 with panic. A man will violently assault his neighbour's house and plunder his goods; no pity will restrain him, when he is in the grip of famine and grinding misery.
20 See how I summon before me all the kings of the earth, says God, from sunrise and south wind, from east and south,*j* to turn back and repay what
21 they have been given. I will do to them as they are doing to my chosen people even to this day; I will pay them back in their own coin.
22 These are the words of the Lord God: I will show sinners no pity; the sword will not spare those murderers

g So other Vss.; Lat. corrupt.
h Or in his unbelief.
i Probable meaning; Lat. obscure.
j south: probable reading; Lat. Lebanon.

---

writing Heb. To give the new script a sacred quality it is presented as revealed by God. **44–45:** The *ninety-four books* comprise the twenty-four books of the present Heb. canon, those written *first to be read by good and bad*. These twenty-four equal the thirty-nine of the Christian canon where the double books of Sam., Kgs., and Chr., as well as Ezra-Neh., are counted separately and the minor prophets are counted as twelve instead of as one book as in the Hebrew. **46:** *The last seventy books* include apocryphal and apocalyptic works such as the present one, to which the writer here ascribes great value as well as the authority of Moses (see v. 6) and Ezra. They are for the *wise,* i.e. the initiated.

15.1–16.78: Prophecies of doom. This section is considered a Christian appendix.
15.1–27: The coming vengeance. 3: *Have no fear:* compare Jer.1.17; Ezek.2.6. Other expressions in vv. 1–4 also imitate the "calls" of OT prophets. **8–9:** The Lord is considered the avenger of *blood* in the case of the *innocent;* compare Gen.4.10–11; Rev.6.9–10; 19.2. **10:** See Ps.44.22. The chief wickedness to be avenged is the persecution of God's people. **11:** *I will strike the Egyptians* may allude to the famine which almost decimated the population of Alexandria in Gallienus' reign (260–268 A.D.). *As I did before* alludes to the ten plagues (Exod.7.14–11.10; 12.28–36). **15:** *Nation ... against nation:* compare Mt.24.7; Mk 13.8.

who stain the ground with innocent
23 blood. The Lord's anger has overflowed in fire to scorch the earth to its
foundations and consume sinners like
24 burning straw! Alas for sinners who
25 flout my commands! says the Lord; I
will show them no mercy. Away from
me, you rebels! Do not bring your
26 pollution near my holiness. The Lord
well knows all who sin against him,
and has consigned them to death and
27 destruction. Already disaster has fallen
upon the world, and you will never
escape it; God will refuse to rescue
you, because you have sinned against
him.
28 How terrible the sight of what is
29 coming from the east! Hordes of
dragons from Arabia will sally forth
with countless chariots, and from the
first day of their advance their hissing
will spread across the land, to fill all
who hear them with fear and consterna-
30 tion. The Carmanians, mad with rage,
will rush like wild boars out of the
forest, advancing in full force to join
battle with them, and will devastate
whole tracts of Assyria with their
31 tusks. But then the dragons will
summon up their native fury, and will
prove the stronger. They will rally and
join forces, and fall on them with
32 overwhelming might until they are
routed, until their power is silenced,
and every one of them turns to flight.
33 Then their way will be blocked by a
lurking enemy from Assyria, who will
destroy one of them. Fear and panic
will spread in their army, and wavering
among their kings.
34 See the clouds stretching from east
and north to south! Their appearance
is hideous, full of fury and tempest.
35 They will clash together, they will pour
over the land a vast storm;[k] blood,
shed by the sword, will reach as high
36 as a horse's belly, a man's thigh, or a
37 camel's hock. Terror and trembling
will cover the earth; all who see the

raging fury will shudder and be
stricken with panic. Then vast storm- 38
clouds will approach from north and
south, and others from the west. But 39
the winds from the east will be stronger
still, and will hold in check the raging
cloud and its leader; and the storm[k]
which was bent on destruction will be
fiercely driven back to the south and
west by the winds from the east. Huge 40
mighty clouds, full of fury, will
mount up and ravage the whole land
and its inhabitants; a terrible storm[k]
will sweep over the great and the
powerful, with fire and hail and flying 41
swords; and a deluge of water will
flood all the fields and rivers. They 42
will flatten to the ground cities and
walls, mountains and hills, trees in the
woods and crops in the fields. They 43
will advance all the way to Babylon,
and blot it out. When they reach it, 44
they will surround it, and let loose a
storm[k] in all its fury. The dust and
smoke will reach the sky, and all her
neighbours will mourn for Babylon.
Any of her survivors will be enslaved 45
by her destroyers.
And you, Asia, who have shared the 46
beauty and the splendour of Babylon,
alas for you, poor wretch! Like her 47
you have dressed up your daughters
as whores, to attract and catch your
lovers who have always lusted for you.
You have copied all the schemes and 48
practices of that vile harlot. Therefore
God says, I will bring upon you 49
terrible evils: widowhood and poverty,
famine, sword, and plague, bringing
ruin to your homes, bringing violence
and death. Your strength and splen- 50
dour will wither like a flower, when
that scorching heat bears down upon
you. Then you will be a poor weak 51
woman, bruised, beaten, and wounded,
unable to receive your wealthy lovers
any more. Should I be so fierce with 52
you, says the Lord, if you had not 53

k storm: *probable meaning; Lat. obscure.*

15.28–63: Syria, Rome threatened. After a general announcement of doom, the text speaks
of warfare against *Assyria*, i.e. the Roman province of Syria (v. 30). Again events of the third
century A.D. seem reflected (see v. 11 n.), especially the attack of the Persian King Shapur I
(241–273 A.D.) against Syria. **29:** *Dragons from Arabia* are apparently the armies of the Arabs
of Palmyra. **30:** *The Carmanians* are the Sassanid Persians, Carmania (Kerman) being a Persian
province. **43:** *Babylon:* Rome, as in Rev.18.10. **46:** *Asia:* perhaps the Roman province of
Asia, namely, the western end of Asia Minor, now Turkey. **48:** *That vile harlot:* see Rev.14.8;
17.4–5. **49:** See Rev.18.7–8.

killed my chosen ones continually, gloating over the blows you struck them, and hurling your drunken taunts at their corpses? 54 Paint your face; make yourself 55 beautiful! The harlot's pay shall be yours; you will get what you have 56 earned. What you do to my chosen people, God will do to you, says the Lord; he will consign you to a terrible 57 fate. Your children will die of hunger; you will fall by the sword, your cities will be blotted out, and all your people 58 will fall on the field of battle. Those who are up on the mountains will be dying of hunger, and their hunger and thirst will force them to gnaw their own flesh and drink their own blood. 59 You will be foremost in misery, and 60 still there will be more to come. As the victors go past on their way home from the sack of Babylon, they will smash your peaceful city, destroy a great part of your territory, and bring much of your splendour to an end. 61 They will destroy you—you will be 62 stubble, and they the fire. They will completely devour you and your cities, your land and your mountains, and will burn all your forests and your 63 fruit-trees. They will make your children prisoners and plunder your property; and not a trace will be left of your splendid beauty.

16 Alas for you, Babylon and Asia! 2 Alas for you, Egypt and Syria! Put on sackcloth and hair-shirt, and raise a howl of lamentation for your sons; 3 your doom is close at hand. The sword is let loose against you, and who 4 will turn it aside? Fire is let loose upon you, and who will put it out? 5 Calamities have been let loose against you, and who is there to stop them? 6 Can any man stop a hungry lion in a forest, or put out a fire among the stubble once it has begun to blaze? 7 Can any man stop an arrow shot by a 8 strong archer? When the Lord God sends calamities, who can stop them?

When his anger overflows in fire, who 9 can put it out? When the lightning 10 flashes, who will not tremble? When it thunders, who will not shake with dread? When it is the Lord who utters 11 his threats, is there any man who will not be crushed to the ground at his approach? The earth is shaken to its 12 very foundations, and the sea is churned up from its depths; the waves and all the fish with them are in turmoil before the presence of the Lord and the majesty of his strength. For strong is his arm which bends the 13 bow, and sharp the arrows which he shoots; once they are on their way, they will not stop before they reach the ends of the earth. Calamities are 14 let loose, and will not turn back before they strike the earth. The fire is alight 15 and will not be put out until it has burnt up earth's foundations. An 16 arrow shot by a powerful archer does not turn back; no more will the calamities be recalled which are let loose against the earth.

Alas, alas for me! Who will rescue 17 me on that day? When troubles come, 18 many will groan; when famine strikes, many will die; when wars break out, empires will tremble; when the calamities come, all will be filled with terror. What will men do then, in the face of calamity? Famine and plague, suffering 19 and hardship, are scourges sent to teach men better ways. But even so they 20 will not abandon their crimes, nor keep in mind their scourging. A time 21 will come when food grows cheap, so cheap that they will imagine they have been sent peace and prosperity. But at that very moment the earth will become a hotbed of disasters—sword, famine, and anarchy. Most of its inhabitants 22 will die in the famine; and those who survive the famine will be destroyed by the sword. The dead will be tossed out 23 like dung, and there will be no one to offer any comfort. For the earth will be left empty, and its cities a ruin. None 24

16.1–34: Various powers denounced. Chs. 15 and 16 emulate the oracles against foreign nations by OT prophets such as Isaiah and Jeremiah. **1:** *Babylon:* Rome, as in 15.43. *Asia:* see 15.46 n. *Egypt:* see 15.11–19. **2:** *Sackcloth* was a sign of mourning and wearing a *hairshirt* next to the body a way of doing penance. **5:** A profusion of biblical phrases and stock apocalyptic ideas comprises the vague calamities here enumerated. **15:** See 2 Pet.3.10 and Tfn. *g* there. **19:** *Scourges sent to teach men:* compare Heb.12.5–11.

will be left to till the ground and sow
25 it. The trees will bear their fruits, but
26 who will pick them? The grapes will
ripen, but who will tread them? There
27 will be vast desolation everywhere. A
man will long to see a human face or
28 hear a human voice. For out of a
whole city, only ten will survive; in the
country-side, only two will be left,
hiding in the forest or in holes in the
29 rocks. Just as in an olive-grove three
or four olives might be left on each
30 tree, or as a few grapes in a vineyard
might be overlooked by the sharp-eyed
31 pickers, so also in those days three or
four will be overlooked by those who
32 search the houses to kill. The earth
will be left a desert, and the fields will
be overrun with briers; thorns will
grow over all the roads and paths,
because there will be no sheep to tread
33 them. Girls will live in mourning with
none to marry them, women will
mourn because they have no husbands,
their daughters will mourn because
34 they have no one to support them. The
young men who should have married
them will be killed in the war, and the
husbands wiped out by the famine.

35 BUT LISTEN TO ME, YOU WHO ARE THE
Lord's servants, and take my words to
36 heart. This is the word of the Lord.
Receive it, and do not disbelieve what
37 he says. Calamities are here, close at
38 hand, and will not delay. When a
pregnant woman is in the ninth month,
and the moment of her child's birth is
drawing near, there will be two or
three hours in which her womb will
suffer pangs of agony, and then the
child will come from the womb without
39 a moment's delay; in the same way
calamities will come on the earth
without delay, and the world will groan
under the pangs that grip it.
40   Listen to my words, my people;
get ready for battle, and when the
calamities surround you, be as though
41 you were strangers on earth. The

seller must expect to have to run for
his life, the buyer to lose what he buys;
the merchant must expect to make no 42
profit, the builder never to live in the
house he builds. The sower must not 43
expect to reap, nor the pruner to gather
his grapes. Those who marry must 44
expect no children; the unmarried must
think of themselves as widowed. For 45
all labour is labour in vain. Their 46
fruits will be gathered by foreigners,
who will plunder their goods, pull
down their houses, and take their
children captive. If they have children,
they will have been bred only for
captivity and famine; any who make 47
money do so only to have it plundered.
The more care they lavish on their
cities, houses, and property, and on
their own persons, the fiercer will be 48
my indignation against their sins, says
the Lord. Like the indignation of a 49
virtuous woman towards a prostitute,
so will be the indignation of justice 50
towards wickedness with all her finery;
she will accuse her to her face, when
the champion arrives to expose all sin
upon earth. Do not imitate wickedness, 51
therefore, and her actions. For in a very 52
short time she will be swept from the
earth, and the reign of justice over us
will begin.
The sinner must not deny that he has 53
sinned; he will only bring burning
coals on to his own head if he says, 'I
have committed no sin against the
majesty of God.' For the Lord knows all 54
that men do; he knows their plans, their
schemes, and their inmost thoughts.
He said, 'Let the earth be made', and 55
it was made; and 'Let the heavens be
made', and they were made. It was by 56
the Lord's word that the stars were
fixed in their places; the number of
the stars is known to him. He looks 57
into the depths with their treasures; he
has measured the sea and everything it
contains. By his word he confined the 58
sea within the bounds of the waters,
and above the water he suspended the

16.35–52: God's people warned of the coming disasters. 38: *A pregnant woman:* compare 4.40.
Pangs of agony: calamities, as "birthpangs of the Messiah," presage the end of the present
order; compare Jn.16.21. **40–45:** In the *calamities* of the end, all stable economic and family
life will cease so that *labour* to make it secure will be *in vain;* compare 1 Cor.7.29–31. **51–52:**
Do not *imitate wickedness:* compare 2 Pet.3.11–13.
 16.53–67: Sin cannot be hidden from God. 55–60: See Gen.1.6–10.

59 land. He spread out the sky like a vault, and made it secure upon the
60 waters. He provided springs in the desert, and pools on the mountain-tops as the source of rivers flowing
61 down to water the earth. He created man, and placed a heart in the middle of his body; he gave him spirit, life,
62 and understanding, the very breath of Almighty God who created the whole world and searches out secret things in
63 secret places. He knows well your plans and all your inward thoughts. Alas for
64 sinners who try to hide their sins! The Lord will scrutinize all their deeds; he
65 will call you all to account. You will be covered with confusion, when your sins are brought into the open, and your wicked deeds stand up to accuse
66 you on that day. What can you do? How can you hide your sins from God
67 and his angels? God is your judge: fear him! Abandon your sins, and have done with your wicked deeds for ever! Then God will set you free from all distress.
68 Fierce flames are being kindled to burn you. A great horde will descend on you; they will seize some of you and make you eat pagan sacrifices.

Those who give in to them will be 69 derided, taunted, and trampled on. In 70 place after place[l] and in all the neigh-bourhood there will be a violent attack on those who fear the Lord. Their 71 enemies will be like madmen, plunder-ing and destroying without mercy all who still fear the Lord. They will 72 destroy and plunder their property, and throw them out of their homes. Then it will be seen that my chosen 73 people have stood the test like gold in the assayer's fire.

Listen, you whom I have chosen, 74 says the Lord; the days of harsh suffering are close at hand, but I will rescue you from them. Away with your 75 fears and doubts! For God is your leader. You who follow my command- 76 ments and instructions, says the Lord God, must not let your sins weigh you down, nor your wicked deeds get the better of you. Alas for those who are 77 entangled in their sins, and overrun with their wicked deeds! They are like a field overrun by bushes, with brambles across the path and no way through, completely shut off and 78 doomed to destruction by fire.

l In place after place: *possible meaning; Lat. obscure.*

16.68–78: God's persecuted people will be delivered. 68: *Fierce flames:* possibly the passage alludes to persecution of the Christians by the emperor Decius about 250 A.D.

TOBIT

This is the story of a pious Jew in exile who, after many misfortunes and trying events, finally sees the victory of God's Providence in a happy family reunion and a peaceful end.

Apart from the fascination of the tale itself, the book reflects aspects of Jewish piety in the period of history just prior to the birth of Christianity. The account is presented as history and as having taken place in Nineveh in the eighth pre-Christian century. The many discrepancies with known facts of history suggest that the author uses Nineveh as a literary device, intending the blind Tobit to represent collective Israel who, in exile, is sorely tempted to lose faith in divine providence. The Israelites are admonished to remain faithful to the Torah so that they too may "see" at the end how God works out his designs in the ambiguities of history. The story belongs, therefore, to the category of Wisdom literature.

The author of Tobit is unknown. The story seems to be very old; differing versions have survived. This version was probably written about the second century B.C. in Hebrew or Aramaic.

The troubles of Tobit

1 THIS IS THE STORY OF TOBIT, SON OF Tobiel, son of Hananiel, son of Aduel, son of Gabael, son of Raphael, son of Raguel, of the family 2 of Asiel, of the tribe of Naphtali. He was taken captive in the time of Shalmaneser[a] king of Assyria, from Thisbe which is south of Kedesh Naphtali in Upper Galilee above Hazor, behind the road to the west, north of Peor.

3 I, TOBIT, MADE TRUTH AND RIGHTEOUSness my lifelong guide; I did many acts of charity for my kinsmen, those of my nation who had gone into captivity 4 with me at Nineveh in Assyria. When I was quite young in my own country, Israel, the whole tribe of Naphtali my ancestor broke away from the dynasty of David,[b] and from Jerusalem, the city chosen out of all the tribes of Israel as the one place of sacrifice. It was there that God's dwelling-place, the temple, had been consecrated, built to last for 5 all generations. All my kinsmen, the whole house of Naphtali my ancestor, sacrificed on the mountains of Galilee to the calf which Jeroboam, king of 6 Israel, had made in Dan; at the festivals

I was the only one to make the frequent journey to Jerusalem prescribed for all Israel as an eternal commandment. I used to hurry off to Jerusalem with the firstfruits of crops and herds, the tithes of the cattle, and the first shearings of the sheep; and I gave them to the priests of Aaron's line for the altar, and the 7 tithe of wine, corn, olive oil, pomegranates and other fruits to the Levites ministering in Jerusalem. The second tithe for the six years I converted into money, and I went and distributed it in Jerusalem year by year among the 8 orphans and widows, and the converts who had attached themselves to Israel. Every third year when I brought it and gave it to them, we held a feast according to the rule laid down in the law of Moses and the instructions given by Deborah the mother of Hananiel our grandfather; for my father had died leaving me an orphan.

When I came of age I took a wife 9 from our kindred, and had a son by her whom I called Tobias. After the 10 deportation to Assyria when I was taken captive and came to Nineveh, everyone of my kindred and nation ate gentile food; but I myself scrupulously 11 avoided doing so. Since I was whole- 12

a Gk. Enemessaros.   b Gk. adds my ancestor.

1.1–3.17: Tobit's tale of his misfortunes. His zealous efforts to live the Law earn him the persecution of the pagans and the jeers of the other Jews.

1.1–2: Introduction. 1: *Tobit:* perhaps an abbreviated form of the Heb. *Tobiah* (Gk. *Tobias*, v. 9), meaning "the LORD is good." **2:** The tribe of *Naphtali* was deported to *Assyria*, not by *Shalmaneser* but by his predecessor, Tiglath-pileser III (745–727 B.C.); see 2 Kgs.15.29. *Thisbe* is located west-southwest of Lake Huleh in northern Palestine.

1.3–22: Tobit's virtuous life in exile. 3: *Nineveh:* capital of *Assyria*. **4:** The secession of the northern tribes from the *dynasty of David* (1 Kgs. ch. 12) took place about 922 B.C., 150 years before Tobit was born **5:** *Mountains . . . calf:* see 1 Kgs.12.28–31. **6–8:** *Firstfruits . . . tithes:* an idealized picture of Jewish piety; see Num.18.12–13; Deut.18.3–4. **10:** *Gentile food:* for-

53

13 heartedly mindful of my God, the Most High endowed me with a presence which won me the favour of Shalmaneser, and I became his buyer of supplies.

14 As long as he lived I used to travel to Media and buy for him there. I deposited bags of money to the value of ten talents of silver with my kinsman

15 Gabael son of Gabri in Media. When Shalmaneser died and was succeeded by his son Sennacherib, the roads to Media passed out of Assyrian control and I could no longer make the journey.

16 In the time of Shalmaneser, I did many acts of charity for my fellow-countrymen: I shared my food with the

17 hungry and provided clothes for the naked. If I saw the dead body of any man of my race lying outside the wall

18 of Nineveh, I buried it. I buried all those who fell victim to Sennacherib after his flight from Judaea, when the King of heaven executed judgement on him for all his blasphemies, and in his rage he killed many of the Israelites. I stole their bodies away and buried them, and Sennacherib looked for them but could

19 not find them. One of the Ninevites informed the king that I was giving burial to his victims; so I went into hiding. When I learnt that the king knew about me and that I was wanted for execution, I took fright and ran

20 away. All my property was seized and put into the royal treasury; I was left with nothing but Anna my wife and my

21 son Tobias. However, less than forty days afterwards, the king was murdered by two of his sons. They took refuge in the mountains of Ararat, and his son Esarhaddon succeeded him. He

appointed Ahikar son of my brother Anael to supervise all the finances of his kingdom; he had control of the entire administration. Then Ahikar 22 interceded on my behalf and I came back to Nineveh. For he had been chief cupbearer, keeper of the privy seal, comptroller, and treasurer when Sennacherib was king of Assyria; and Esarhaddon renewed the appointments. Ahikar was my nephew and so one of my kinsmen.

DURING THE REIGN OF ESARHADDON, I 2 returned to my house, and my wife Anna and my son Tobias were restored to me. At our festival of Pentecost, that is the Feast of Weeks, a good dinner was prepared for me and I sat down to eat. The table was laid and a 2 lavish meal was put before me. I said to my son Tobias: 'Go, my boy, and if you can find any poor man of our captive people in Nineveh who is wholeheartedly mindful of God, bring him and he shall share my dinner. I will wait for you until you return.' Tobias 3 went to look for a poor man of our people, but he came back and said, 'Father!' 'Yes, my son?' I replied. He answered, 'Father, one of our nation has been murdered and his body is lying in the market-place. He was strangled only a moment ago.' I 4 jumped up and left my dinner untasted. I took the body from the square and put it in one of the outbuildings until sunset when I could bury it; then I went home, duly 5 bathed myself, and ate my food in sorrow. I recalled the saying of the 6

bidden by the Law as unclean; see Deut.14.3–21. **13:** *Shalmaneser V:* the successor of Tiglath-pileser III in 727 B.C. **14:** *Ten talents of silver* would equal about $16,000. **15:** *Shalmaneser* V was followed by Sargon II (722–705 B.C.) and then only by *Sennacherib* (705–681 B.C.). Such historical inaccuracies suggest that the author intends, not history, but a story illustrative of Wisdom. **17:** A *dead body* left unburied was considered a curse, a punishment for an evil life, that somehow affected the peace of the deceased. See 2 Kgs.9.10; Jer.8.2; Ecclus.44.14. **18:** God *executed judgement* on Sennacherib at the siege of Jerusalem; a plague apparently struck his army, leaving many dead and forcing an unexpected retreat. See 2 Kgs.19.35–36; Isa.37.36–37. **21:** *Two of his sons:* see 2 Kgs.19.37. *Ahikar*, the hero of a popular ancient legend, was a wise and wealthy chancellor under several Assyrian kings. He raised and educated a nephew, Nadab, who betrayed him. Eventually he was vindicated and the nephew was punished. Perhaps the author brings Ahikar into the story of Tobit because they were both tested by misfortune and finally restored to a happy state. See also 2.10; 11.18; and 14.10, where their tribulations are further recorded.

2.1–14: Tobit's misfortunes. 1: The Jewish feast of *Pentecost* (Gr. "fifty [days]") was observed seven weeks after Passover (Lev.23.15–21) at the time of the grain harvest. **5:** Tobit *bathed himself* because contact with a corpse made him ritually unclean and unfit for public worship

prophet Amos in the passage about Bethel:

'Your feasts shall be turned into
        mourning,
and all your songs[c] into lamentation',

7 and I wept. After sunset I went and
8 dug a grave and buried the body. The neighbours jeered at me and said: 'Is he no longer afraid? He ran away last time, when they were hunting for him to put him to death for this very offence; and here he is burying the
9 dead again!' That night I bathed myself and went into my courtyard. I lay down to sleep by the courtyard wall, leaving my face uncovered be-
10 cause of the heat. I did not know that there were sparrows in the wall above me; and their droppings fell, still warm, right into my eyes and produced white patches. I went to the doctors to be cured, but the more they treated me with their ointments, the more my eyes were blinded by the white patches, until I lost my sight. For four years I was blind. All my kinsmen grieved for me, and Ahikar looked after me for two years until he moved to Elymais.
11   During that time my wife Anna used to earn money by women's work.
12 When she took what she had done to her employers they would pay her wages. One day, the seventh of Dystrus, when she had cut off the piece she had woven and delivered it, the owners not only paid her in full, but also gave her a kid from their herd of goats to take
13 home. When my wife came in to me the kid began to bleat. I called out to her: 'Where does that kid come from? I hope it was not stolen? Give it back to its owners; we have no right to eat
14 anything stolen.' She assured me: 'It was given me as a present, over and above my wages.' I did not believe her and insisted that she should give it back to its owners, and I blushed

with shame for what she had done. She retorted: 'So much for all your good works and acts of charity! Now we can see what you are!'

In deep distress I groaned and wept, **3** and as I groaned I prayed: 'Thou art **2** just, O Lord, and all thy acts are just; in all thy ways thou art merciful and true; thou art judge of the world. Remember me now, Lord, and look **3** upon me. Do not punish me for the sins and errors which I and my fathers have committed. We have sinned **4** against thee and disobeyed thy commandments, and thou hast given us up to plunder, captivity, and death, until we have become a byword, a proverb, and a taunt to all the nations among whom thou hast scattered us. I acknowledge the justice of thy many **5** judgements, the due penalty for my sins, for we have not obeyed thy commandments and have not lived in loyal obedience before thee. And now deal **6** with me at thy pleasure, and command that my life be taken away, so that I may be removed from the face of the earth and turned to earth. I should be better dead than alive, for I have had to hear undeserved reproaches and am in deep grief. Lord, command that I may be released from this misery; let me go to my long home; do not turn thy face from me, O Lord. It is better for me to die than to live in such misery and to hear such reproaches.'

On that same day it happened that **7** Sarah, the daughter of Raguel who lived at Ecbatana in Media, also had to listen to reproaches from one of her father's maidservants, because she had **8** been given in marriage to seven husbands, and before the marriage could be regularly consummated they had all been killed by the wicked demon Asmodaeus. The maidservant said to her: 'It is you who kill your husbands!

c So one Vs. (compare Amos 8. 10); Gk. ways.

(Num.19.11–13). **10:** *Elymais* is Elam, a region north of the Tigris on the Persian Gulf. **12:** *Dystrus:* the fifth month of the Macedonian (and Hellenistic) calendar (about February). **14:** *She retorted*, much as Job's wife did (Job 2.9), that Tobit suffered either because he was punished for secret sins or because virtue did not pay.

3.1–6: Tobit's prayer. 6: *Long home:* eternal abode. *Do not turn thy face:* do not remove your favor.

3.7–10: Sarah's plight. 7: *Ecbatana:* the capital of *Media*, present-day Iran. **8:** *Asmodaeus*

You have already been given in marriage to seven, and you have not borne the name of any one of them.

9 Why punish us because they are dead? Go and join your husbands! I hope we never see son or daughter of yours!'

10 She was sad at heart that day, and went in tears up to the attic in her father's house meaning to hang herself. But she had second thoughts and said to herself: 'Perhaps they will reproach my father and say to him, "You had one dear daughter and she hanged herself because of her troubles", and so I shall bring my aged father in sorrow to the grave. No, I will not hang myself; it would be better to beg the Lord to let me die and not live on

11 to hear such reproaches.' Then at once she spread out her hands towards the window in prayer and said: 'Praise to thee, merciful God, praise to thy name for ever; let all thy works praise thee

12 for evermore. Now I lift up my eyes

13 and look to thee. Command me to be removed from this earth so that I may

14 no longer hear such reproaches. Thou knowest, Lord, that I am a virgin, guiltless of intercourse with any man;

15 I have not disgraced my name nor my father's name in the land of my exile. I am my father's only child; he has no other to be his heir, nor has he any near kinsman or relative who might marry me, and for whom I should stay alive. Already seven husbands of mine have died. What have I to live for any longer? If it is not thy will, O Lord, to let me die, listen now to my complaint.'

16 At that very time the prayers of both of them were heard in the glorious presence of God. His angel Raphael 17 was sent to cure them both of their troubles: Tobit, by removing the white patches from his eyes so that he might see God's light again, and Sarah daughter of Raguel by giving her in marriage to Tobias son of Tobit and by setting her free from the wicked demon Asmodaeus; for it was the destiny of Tobias and not of any other suitor to possess her. At the moment when Tobit went back from the courtyard into his house, Sarah daughter of Raguel came down from the attic.

The adventures of Tobias

THAT SAME DAY TOBIT REMEMBERED THE 4 silver that he had deposited with Gabael at Rages in Media, and he said to him- 2 self, 'I have asked for death; before I die ought I not to send for my son Tobias and explain to him about this money?' So he sent for Tobias, and 3 when he came he said to him: 'Give me decent burial. Show proper respect to your mother, and do not leave her in the lurch as long as she lives; do what will please her, and never grieve her heart in any way. Remember, my son, 4 all the dangers she faced for your sake while you were in her womb. When she dies, bury her beside me in the same grave. And remember the Lord every 5 day of your life. Never deliberately do what is wrong or break his commandments. As long as you live do what is right. Do not fall into evil ways; for an 6 honest life leads to prosperity. To all who keep the law, the Lord gives good 19

---

means "destroyer" and the name occurs only here in the Bible. **10:** Sarah's concern lest she bring her *aged father in sorrow to the grave* reflects a theme repeatedly expressed in the Joseph novelette about the aged Jacob, e.g. in Gen.37.35; 42.38; 44.29. Premature death was deemed a curse.

3.11–15: Sarah's prayer. 15: This concern about a *near kinsman* reflects the clan law about marriage within the tribal group, a law with special significance in exile, where the maintenance of group identity was of great concern, lest the people disappear. Sarah here seems to be unware of the existence of Tobias.

3.16–17: God hears the prayers of Tobit and Sarah. 16: A phrase like *at that very time* suggests that the author is more interested in dramatic coincidence than historical probability. **17:** *Raphael* is a Heb. name meaning "God heals." An old tradition held that an angel was usually limited to a single errand. Here Raphael cures both at once.

4.1–9.6: Tobit sends for his son. Under the inspiration of the angel Raphael, Tobias himself is saved from danger and brings healing to others. His sage advice (4.3–20) reflects the morals of Judaism of the intertestamental age.

4.1–5.3: Tobias is sent to retrieve Tobit's money. 1: *Rages* was a city in *Media* situated near modern Teheran. **3:** *Decent burial:* see 1.17 n. **5–19:** Wise counseling as in Prov. and Ecclus.

guidance, and as he chooses he humbles men to the grave below.[d] Now, my son, remember these commands, let them never be effaced from your mind.

20 'Well now, my boy, let me tell you that I have ten talents of silver on deposit with Gabael son of Gabri, at 21 Rages in Media. Do not be anxious because we have become poor; there is great wealth waiting for you, if only you fear God and avoid all wickedness and do what is good in the sight of the Lord your God.'

5 Then Tobias said: 'I will do all that 2 you have told me, father. But how shall I be able to get this money from him, since he does not know me and I do not know him? What proof of identity shall I give him to make him believe me and give me this money? Also I do not know the roads to Media or how to get there.' 3 To this Tobit replied: 'He gave me his note of hand, and I gave him mine, which I divided in two. We took one part each, and I put mine with the money. It is twenty years since I made this deposit. And now, my boy, find someone reliable to go with you, and we will pay him up to the time of your return; then go and recover the money from Gabael.'

4 Tobias went out to find a man who knew the way and would accompany him to Media, and found himself face 5 to face with the angel Raphael. Not knowing he was an angel of God, he questioned him: 'Where do you come from, young man?' 'I am an Israelite,' he replied, 'one of your fellow-countrymen, and I have come here to find work.' Tobias asked, 'Do you know 6 the road to Media?' 'Yes,' he said, 'I have often been there; I am familiar with all the routes and know them well. I have often travelled into Media and used to lodge with Gabael our fellow-countryman who lives there in Rages.[e] It is two full days' journey from Ec-

batana to Rages; for Rages is in the hills, and Ecbatana is in the middle of the plain.' Tobias said: 'Wait for me, 7 young man, while I go in and tell my father. I need you to go with me and will pay you your wages.' 'All right, I will 8 wait,' he said; 'only do not be too long.'

Tobias went in and told his father. 'I have found a fellow-Israelite to accompany me', he said. His father replied, 'Call the man in, my son. I want to find out his family and tribe and make sure that he will be a trustworthy companion for you.'

Tobias went out and called him: 9 'Young man, my father is asking for you.' He went in, and Tobit greeted him first. To Raphael's reply, 'May all

d To all . . . below: *in place of these words some witnesses have* To all who keep the law (7) give alms from what you possess and never give with a grudging eye. Do not turn your face away from any poor man, and God will not turn away his face from you. (8) Let your almsgiving match your means. If you have little, do not be ashamed to give the little you can afford; (9) you will be laying up a sound insurance against the day of adversity. (10) Almsgiving saves the giver from death and keeps him from going down into darkness. (11) All who give alms are making an offering acceptable to the Most High.

(12) 'Beware, my son, of fornication; above all choose your wife from the race of your ancestors. Do not take a foreign wife who is not of your father's tribe, because we are descendants of the prophets. Remember, my son, that Noah, Abraham, Isaac, and Jacob, our ancestors, back to the earliest days, all chose wives from their kindred. They were blessed in their children, and their descendants shall possess the earth. (13) And you like them, my son, must love your kindred. Do not be too proud to take a wife from among the women of your own nation. Pride breeds ruin and anarchy, and the waster declines into poverty; waste is the mother of starvation.

(14) 'Pay your workmen their wages the same day; do not make any man wait for his money. If you serve God you will be repaid. Be circumspect, my son, in all that you do, and show yourself well-bred in all your behaviour. (15) Do not do to anyone what you yourself would hate. Do not drink to excess and so let drunkenness become a habit. (16) Give food to the hungry and clothes to the naked. Whatever you have beyond your own needs, give away to the poor, and do not give grudgingly. (17) Pour out your wine and offer your bread on the tombs of the righteous; but give nothing to sinners. (18) Ask any sensible man for his advice; do not despise any advice that may help you. (19) Praise the Lord God at all times and ask him to guide your course. Then all you do and all you plan will turn out well. The heathen all lack such guidance; it is the Lord himself who gives all good things, or humbles men at will, as he chooses.
e *Probable reading (compare 4. 1); Gk.* Ecbatana.

19: When Tobit urges his son to *remember these commands* he is voicing a constant theme of Jewish piety which viewed loyalty to God as an active remembrance of his favors. 20: *Ten talents*: see 1.14 n.

5.4–22: *Azarias (Raphael) is hired as Tobias' guide.* 6: The *journey from Ecbatana to Rages* cannot be made in *two full days* since it involves a distance of some 450 miles. Moreover, it is Ecbatana, not Rages, that is situated in mountainous terrain. Raphael's familiarity *with all the routes* seems to refer to the journey of his life rather than to the geography of Persia. 9: *I am a blind man*: Tobit speaks for Israel, symbolically blind to the ways of God's Providence. The

be well with you!', Tobit retorted: 'How can anything be well with me now? I am a blind man, I cannot see the light of heaven, but lie in darkness like the dead who cannot see the light. Though still alive, I am as good as dead. I hear men's voices, but the men I do not see.' Raphael answered: 'Take heart; in God's design your cure is at hand. Take heart.' Tobit went on: 'My son Tobias wishes to travel to Media. Can you go with him as his guide? I will pay you, my friend.' 'Yes,' he said, 'I can go with him; I know all the roads. I have often been to Media; I have travelled over all the plains and mountains there, and am familiar with 10 all its roads.' Tobit said to him, 'Tell me, my friend, what family and tribe 11 you belong to.' He asked, 'Why need you know my tribe?' Tobit said, 'I do indeed wish to know whose son you are, my friend, and what your name is.' 12 'I am Azarias,' he replied, 'son of the older Ananias, one of your kinsmen.' 13 Tobit said to him: 'Good luck and a safe journey to you! Do not be angry with me, my friend, because I wished to know the facts of your descent. It turns out that you are a kinsman, and a man of good family. I knew Ananias and Nathan the two sons of the older Semelias. They used to go with me to Jerusalem and worship with me there; they never went astray. Your kinsmen are worthy men; you come of a sound 14 stock. Good luck go with you.' Tobit added: 'I will pay you a drachma a day and allow you the same expenses as my 15 son. Keep him company on his travels, and I will add something to your wages.' 16 Raphael answered: 'I will go with him. Never fear; we shall travel there and back without mishap, because the road is safe.' Tobit replied, 'God bless you, my friend.' He called his son and said to him: 'My boy, get ready what you need for the journey, and set off with your kinsman. May God in heaven keep both of you safe on your journey there and restore you to me unharmed. May his angel safely escort you both.' Before setting out Tobias kissed his father and mother, and Tobit said to him, 'Goodbye, and a safe journey!'

Then his mother burst into tears. 17 'Why have you sent my boy away?' she said to Tobit. 'Is he not our prop and stay? Has he not always been at home with us? Why send money after 18 money? Write it off for the sake of our boy! Let us be content to live the life 19 the Lord has appointed for us.' Tobit 20 said to her: 'Do not worry; our son will go safely and come back safely, and you will see him with your own eyes on the day of his safe return. Do not worry or be anxious about them, my dear. A good angel will go with him, 21 and his journey will prosper, and he will come back safe and sound.' At that she 22 stopped crying.

THE BOY AND THE ANGEL LEFT THE 6 house together, and the dog came out with him and accompanied them. They travelled until night overtook them, and then camped by the river Tigris. Tobias went down to bathe his feet in 2 the river, and a huge fish leapt out of the water and tried to swallow the boy's foot. He cried out, and the angel said 3 to him, 'Seize the fish and hold it fast.' So Tobias seized it and hauled it on to the bank. The angel said to him: 'Split 4 the fish open and take out its gall, heart, and liver; keep them by you, but throw the guts away; the gall, heart, and liver can be used as medicine.' Tobias split 5 the fish open, and put together its gall, heart, and liver. He cooked and ate part of the fish; the rest he salted and kept.

They continued the journey together until they came near Media. Then the 6 boy asked the angel: 'Azarias, my friend, what medicine is there in the fish's heart, liver, and gall?' He said: 7

theme of the book is summed up in the appeal, *take heart*, directed to Israel. **12:** *Azarias* is the Gk. form of a Heb. name (Azariah) meaning "the Lord helps." **14:** A *drachma* was a normal day's wages, about sixteen cents.

6.1–17: Raphael guides Tobias to Ecbatana and they prepare to meet Sarah. 1: The *dog*, rarely noted in the Bible and even more rarely presented favorably, is introduced here to reinforce family atmosphere. See also 11.4 n. The *Tigris* river does not in fact cross the path of a journey from Nineveh to Ecbatana. **4:** Special medicinal qualities were often attributed to the internal

'You can use the heart and liver as a fumigation for any man or woman attacked by a demon or evil spirit; the attack will cease, and it will give no 8 further trouble. The gall is for anointing a man's eyes when white patches have spread over them, or for blowing on the white patches in the eyes; the eyes will then recover.'

9 When he had entered Media and was 10 now approaching Ecbatana, Raphael said to the boy, 'Tobias, my friend.' 'Yes?' he replied. Raphael said: 'We must stay the night with Raguel. He is your kinsman and he has a daughter named Sarah. Apart from Sarah he has 11 neither son nor daughter. You are her next of kin and have the right to marry her and inherit her father's property. 12 The girl is sensible, brave, and very beautiful, and her father is an honourable man.' He went on: 'It is right that you should marry her. Be guided by me, my friend; I will speak to her father about the girl this very night and ask for her hand as your bride, and on our return from Rages we will celebrate her marriage. I know that Raguel cannot withhold her from you or betroth her to another man without incurring the death penalty according to the ordinance in the book of Moses; and he is aware that his daughter belongs by right to you rather than to any other man. Now be guided by me, my friend; we will talk about the girl tonight and will betroth her to you, and when we return from Rages we shall take her back with us to your home.'

13 Then Tobias answered Raphael: 'Azarias, my friend, I have heard that she has already been given to seven husbands and they died the very night they went into the bridal chamber to 14 her. I have been told that it is a demon who kills them. And now it is my turn to be afraid; he does her no harm, but kills any man who tries to come near her. I am my father's only child; I am afraid that if I die I shall bring my father and mother to the grave with grief for me. They have no other son to bury them.' Raphael said to him: 15 'Have you forgotten the orders your father gave you? He told you to take a wife from your father's kindred. Now be guided by me, my friend: do not worry about the demon, but marry her. I am sure that this night she shall be given you as your wife. When you 16 enter the bridal chamber, take some of the fish's liver and its heart, and put them on the smoking incense. The 17 smell will spread, and when the demon smells it he will make off and never be seen near her any more. When you are about to go to bed with her, both of you must first stand up and pray, beseeching the Lord of heaven to grant you mercy and deliverance. Have no fear; she was destined for you before the world was made. You shall rescue her and she shall go with you. No doubt you will have children by her and they will be very dear to you.ᶠ So do not worry!' When Tobias heard what Raphael said, and learnt that she was his kinswoman and of his father's house, he was filled with love for her and set his heart on her.

WHEN THEY REACHED ECBATANA, 7 Tobias said, 'Azarias, my friend, take me straight to our kinsman Raguel.' So Azarias brought him to Raguel's house, and they found him sitting by the courtyard door. They greeted him first, and he replied, 'A hearty welcome to you, friends. I am glad to see you well after your journey.' He took them into his house and said to Edna his wife, 2 'Is not this young man like my kinsman Tobit?' Edna asked them, 'Where do 3 you come from, friends?' 'We belong to the tribe of Naphtali,' they answered, 'now in captivity at Nineveh.' 'Do you 4 know our kinsman Tobit?' she asked,

ᶠ Literally be like brothers to you.

---

organs of animals. **11:** Mosaic Law required a daughter who is heir to property to marry within her tribe (Num.36.8), so as to prevent the gradual loss of a tribe's property and support. **12:** There is no mention of the *death penalty* in Num.36.8. **14:** *To bury them:* the exiled Jew was continually preoccupied with the thought of burial because abandonment in death definitively confirmed God's abandonment of Israel in the Exile. **17:** *Stand up and pray:* the demon will be rendered powerless if passion is tempered by prayer.

7.1–15: Tobias and Sarah are married. Similar marriage arrangements are related in Gen.24.15; 29.9–12; Exod.2.16–21.

and they replied, 'Yes, we do.' 'Is he
5 well?' she said. 'He is alive and well',
they answered, and Tobias added, 'He
6 is my father.' Raguel jumped up and,
with tears in his eyes, he kissed him
7 and said, 'God bless you, my boy, son
of a good and noble father. But what
grievous news that so good and charitable a man has gone blind!' He embraced Tobias his kinsman and wept;
8 and Edna his wife and their daughter
Sarah also wept for Tobit. Then Raguel
slaughtered a ram from the flock and
made them warmly welcome.

After they had taken a bath and
washed their hands, and had sat down
to dinner, Tobias said to Raphael,
'Azarias, my friend, ask Raguel to
9 give me Sarah my kinswoman.' Raguel
overheard and said to the young man:
'Eat, drink, and be happy tonight.
10 There is no one but yourself who
should have my daughter Sarah; indeed
I have no right to give her to anyone
else, since you are my nearest kinsman.
But I must tell you the truth, my son:
11 I have given her in marriage to seven
of our kinsmen, and they all died on
their wedding night. My son, eat now
and drink, and may the Lord deal
kindly with you both.' Tobias answered,
'I will not eat or drink anything here
until you have disposed of this business
12 of mine.' Raguel said to him, 'I will
do so: I give her to you as the ordinance
in the book of Moses prescribes.
Heaven has ordained that she shall
be yours. Take your kinswoman. From
now on, you belong to her and she to
you; she is yours for ever from this day.
The Lord of heaven prosper you both
this night, my son, and grant you
mercy and peace.'
13 Raguel sent for his daughter Sarah,
and when she came he took her hand
and gave her to Tobias, saying: 'Take
her to be your wedded wife in accordance with the law and the ordinance

written in the book of Moses. Keep her
and take her home to your father; and
may the God of heaven keep you safe
and give you peace and prosperity.'
14 Then he sent for her mother and told
her to bring paper, and he wrote out a
marriage contract granting Sarah to
Tobias as his wife, as the law of Moses
ordains. After that they began to eat 15
and drink.

Raguel called his wife and said, 'My 16
dear, get the spare room ready and take
her in there.' Edna went and prepared 17
the room as he had told her, and took
Sarah into it. Edna cried over her, then
dried her tears and said: 'Courage, dear 18
daughter; the Lord of heaven give you
joy instead of sorrow. Courage,
daughter!' Then she went out.

When they had finished eating and 8
drinking and were ready for bed, they
escorted the young man to the bridal
chamber. Tobias recalled what Raphael 2
had told him; he took the fish's liver
and heart out of the bag in which he
kept them, and put them on the smoking incense. The smell from the fish 3
held the demon off, and he took flight
into Upper Egypt; and Raphael instantly followed him there and bound
him hand and foot.

When they were left alone and the 4
door was shut, Tobias rose from the
bed and said to Sarah, 'Get up, my love;
let us pray and beseech our Lord to
show us mercy and keep us safe.' She 5
got up and they began to pray that they
might be kept safe. Tobias said: 'We
praise thee, O God of our fathers, we
praise thy name for ever and ever. Let
the heavens and all thy creation praise
thee for ever. Thou madest Adam, and 6
Eve his wife to be his helper and support; and those two were the parents
of the human race. This was thy word:
"It is not good for the man to be alone;
let us make him a helper like him." I 7
now take this my beloved to wife, not

12: *The ordinance . . . :* Num.36.8. *Heaven has ordained:* the author strongly favors arranged
marriages (see also 6.17), probably because in a foreign society romantic marriages were likely to
involve non-Israelites or members of other tribes, thus weakening religious unity or tribal integrity.
7.16–8.21: The demon is cast out and the marriage is celebrated. 18: *Courage, daughter!* is an
exhortation that is also directed toward exiled Israel. **8.3:** *Upper Egypt* is a wilderness, the
traditional habitation of demons; see Lev.16.8–10 for the ritual of driving the goat bearing sins
into the wilderness. The demons are understood to be invaders of Israel from foreign parts.
Raphael and the demon represent respectively the forces of order and chaos which are at war
since the creation. **4:** *Let us pray:* see 6.17 n. **6:** *His helper:* see Gen.2.18; compare 1 Cor.11.8 9.

out of lust but in true marriage. Grant that she and I may find mercy and grow

8 old together.' They both said 'Amen',

9 and slept through the night.

Raguel got up and summoned his servants, and they went out and dug a

10 grave. For he said, 'He may have been killed, and then we shall have to face

11 scorn and disgrace.' When they had finished digging the grave, Raguel went

12 into the house and called his wife: 'Send one of the maidservants', he said, 'to go in and see if he is alive. If he is dead, let us bury him so that no one

13 may know.' They lit a lamp, opened the door, and sent a maidservant in; and she found them sound asleep together.

14 She came out and told them: 'He is alive and has come to no harm.'

15 Then they praised the God of heaven: 'We praise thee, O God, we praise thee with all our heart. Let men praise thee

16 throughout all ages. Praise to thee for the joy thou hast given me; the thing I feared has not happened, but thou hast

17 shown us thy great mercy. Praise to thee for the mercy thou hast shown to these two, these only children. Lord, show them mercy, keep them safe, and grant them a long life of happiness and affec-

18 tion.' Then he ordered his servants to fill in the grave before dawn came.

19 He told his wife to bake a great batch of bread; he went to the herd and brought two oxen and four rams and told his servants to get them ready; so

20 they set about the preparations. He then called Tobias and said: 'You shall not stir from here for two weeks. Stay with us; let us eat and drink together and cheer my daughter's heart after all her

21 suffering. Here and now take half of all I have, and go home to your father safe and sound; and the other half will come to you both when my wife and I die. Be reassured, my son, I am your father and Edna is your mother; we are as close to you as to your wife, now and always. You have nothing to fear, my son.'

Tobias called Raphael and said to 9 him: 'Azarias, my friend, take four 2 servants with you, and two camels, and make your way to Rages. Go to Gabael's house, give him the bond and collect the money, and bring him with you to the wedding-feast. You know 4 that my father will be counting the days and, if I am even one day late, it will distress him. You see what Raguel 3 has sworn, and I cannot go against his oath.' Raphael went with the four 5 servants and the two camels to Rages in Media and lodged there with Gabael. He gave him his bond and informed him that Tobit's son Tobias had taken a wife and was inviting him to the wedding-feast. At once Gabael counted out the bags to him with their seals intact, and they put them together. They 6 all made an early start and came to the wedding. When they entered Raguel's house and found Tobias at the feast, he jumped up and greeted Gabael. With tears in his eyes Gabael blessed him and said: 'Good sir, worthy son of a worthy father, that upright and charitable man, may the Lord give Heaven's blessing to you and your wife, your father and your mother-in-law. Praise be to God that I have seen my cousin Tobias, so like his father.'

Tobias's homecoming

NOW DAY BY DAY TOBIT WAS KEEPING 10 count of the time Tobias would take for his journey there and back. When the days had passed and his son had not returned, Tobit said: 'Perhaps he has 2 been detained there. Or perhaps Gabael is dead and there is no one to give him the money.' And he grew anxious. Anna 3,4 his wife said: 'My child has perished. He is no longer in the land of the living.' She began to weep and lament for her son: 'O my child, the light of my eyes, 5 why did I let you go?' Tobit said to her: 6

21: Tobias is asked to *take half* of Raguel's property now as a dowry; and the *other half* is to come to him as an inheritance.

9.1–6: Tobit's money is retrieved from Gabael. 5: The journey from Ecbatana to *Rages* would require about two weeks.

10.1–14.15: Tobias's homecoming. Sent to collect a debt of money for his father, the young Tobias brings him also a daughter (11.17) and healing for his eyes (11.14).

10.1–11.1: Tobias and Sarah leave Ecbatana. 5: When Sarah calls Tobias the *light of my eyes* she is expressing the symbolic sight–blindness motif: Israel is blind to the meaning of history

'Hush, do not worry, my dear; he is all right. Something has happened there to distract them. The man who went with him is one of our kinsmen and can be trusted. Do not grieve for him, my dear; 7 he will soon be back.' But she answered: 'Be quiet! Leave me alone! Do not try to deceive me. My boy is dead.' Each day she would rush out and look down the road her son had taken, and would listen to no one; and when she came indoors at sunset she could never sleep, but wept and lamented the whole night long.

The two weeks of wedding celebrations which Raguel had sworn to hold for his daughter came to an end, and Tobias went up to him and said: 'Let me be off on my journey; for I am sure that my parents are thinking they will never see me again. I beg you, father, let me go home now to my father Tobit. I have already told you how I left him.' 8 Raguel said to Tobias: 'Stay, my son. Stay with me, and I will send news of 9 you to your father.' But Tobias answered: 'No; please let me go home 10 to my father.' Then without further delay Raguel handed over to Tobias Sarah his bride and half of all that he possessed, male and female slaves, sheep and cattle, donkeys and camels, 11 clothes, money, and furniture. He saw them safely off and embraced Tobias, saying: 'Goodbye, my son; a safe journey to you! May the Lord of heaven give prosperity to you and Sarah your wife; and may I live to see your 12 children.' To his daughter Sarah he said: 'Go to your father-in-law's house; they are now your parents as much as if you were their own daughter. Go in peace, my child; I hope to hear good news of you as long as I live.' He bade them both goodbye and sent them on their way. Edna said to Tobias: 'Child and beloved cousin, may the Lord bring you safely home, you and my daughter Sarah, and may I live long enough to see your children. In the sight of the Lord I entrust my daughter to you; do

nothing to hurt her as long as you live. Go in peace, my son. From now on I am your mother and Sarah is your beloved wife. May we all be blessed with prosperity to the end of our days!' She kissed them both and saw them safely off. Tobias parted from Raguel in good **11** health and spirits, thankful to the Lord of heaven and earth, the king of all, for the success of his journey. Raguel's last words to him were: 'May the Lord give you the means to honour your parents all their lives.'

When they reached Caserin close to Nineveh, Raphael said: 'You know 2 how your father was when we left him; let us hurry on ahead of your wife and 3 see that the house is ready before the others arrive.' As the two of them went 4 on together Raphael said: 'Take the fish-gall in your hand.' The dog went with the angel and Tobias, following at their heels.

Anna sat watching the road by which 5 her son would return. She saw him 6 coming and exclaimed to his father, 'Here he comes, your son and the man who went with him!' Before Tobias 7 reached his father's house Raphael said: 'I know for certain that his eyes will be opened. Spread the fish-gall on 8 his eyes, and the medicine will make the white patches shrink and peel off. Your father will get his sight back and see the light of day.' Anna ran forward and 9 flung her arms round her son. 'Here you are, my boy; now I can die happy!' she cried out with tears in her eyes.

Tobit rose to his feet and came 10 stumbling out through the courtyard door. Tobias went up to him with 11 the fish-gall in his hand and blew it into his father's eyes, and took him by the arm and said: 'It will be all right, father.' Then when he had put the 12 medicine on and applied it, using both 13 hands he peeled off the patches from the corners of Tobit's eyes. Tobit flung his arms round him and burst into 14 tears. 'I can see you, my son, the light of my eyes!' he cried. 'Praise be to God,

---

but light will come at the end. See 11.14. **9**: Tobias's plea to be allowed to *go home* is meant to be a model for all exiled Israelites who should yearn constantly for home.

11.2–18: Tobias arrives at home and cures Tobit's blindness. 2: *Caserin:* unknown. **4:** *Dog:* see 6.1 n. Only those who had seen Tobit's blindness go ahead and are present at the cure; this would include the dog! **14:** See 10.5 n. **15:** God's *scourge* on Israel was the Exile, but salva-

and praise to his great name, and to all his holy angels. May his great name rest upon us. Praised be all the angels
15 for ever. He laid his scourge on me, and now, look, I see my son Tobias!'

Tobias went in, rejoicing and praising God with all his strength. He told his father about the success of his journey, how he had brought the money with him and had married Sarah daughter of Raguel. 'She is on her way,' he said, 'quite close to the city gate.'
16 Tobit went out joyfully to meet his daughter-in-law at the gate, praising God as he went. At the sight of him passing through the city in full vigour and walking without a guide, the people
17 of Nineveh were astonished; and Tobit gave thanks to God before them all for his mercy in opening his eyes. When he met Sarah, the wife of his son Tobias, he blessed her and said to her: 'Come in, my daughter, and welcome. Praise be to your God who has brought you to us, my daughter. Blessings on your father, and on my son Tobias, and blessings on you, my daughter. Come into your home and may health, blessings, and joy be yours; come in, my daughter.' It was a day of joy for all
18 the Jews in Nineveh; and Ahikar and Nadab, Tobit's cousins, came to share his happiness.

12 When the marriage-feast was over, Tobit called Tobias and said, 'My son, see that you pay the man who went with you, and give him something extra,
2 over and above his wages.' Tobias said: 'Father, how much shall I pay him? It would not hurt me to give him half the
3 money he and I brought back. He has kept me safe, cured my wife, helped me bring the money, and healed you. How
4 much extra shall I pay him?' Tobit replied, 'It is right, my son, for him to be given half of all that he has brought
5 with him.' So Tobias sent for him and said, 'Half of all that you have brought

with you is yours for your wages; take it, and fare you well.'

Then Raphael called them both 6 aside and said to them: 'Praise God and thank him before all men living for the good he has done you, so that they may sing hymns of praise to his name. Proclaim to all the world what God has done, and pay him honour; do not be slow to give him thanks. A 7 king's secret ought to be kept, but the works of God should be acknowledged publicly. Acknowledge them, therefore, and pay him honour. Do good, and evil shall not touch you. Better 8 prayer with sincerity, and almsgiving with righteousness, than wealth with wickedness. Better give alms than hoard up gold. Almsgiving preserves a man 9 from death and wipes out all sin. Givers of alms will enjoy long life; but sinners 10 and wrong-doers are their own worst enemies.

'I will tell you the whole truth; I will 11 hide nothing from you. Indeed I told you just now when I said, "A king's secret ought to be kept, but the works of God should be publicly honoured." When you and Sarah prayed, it was I 12 who brought your prayers into the glorious presence of the Lord; and so too whenever you buried the dead. That 13 day when you got up from your dinner without hesitation to go and bury the corpse, I was sent to test you; and 14 again God sent me to cure both you and Sarah your daughter-in-law at the same time. I am Raphael, one of the 15 seven angels who stand in attendance on the Lord and enter his glorious presence.'

The two men were shaken, and 16 prostrated themselves in awe. But he 17 said to them: 'Do not be afraid, all is well; praise God for ever. It is no thanks 18 to me that I have been with you; it was the will of God. Worship him all your life long, sing his praise. Take note 19

---

tion is promised. **16:** Israel's vindication at the end will astonish the nations, here represented by the people of Nineveh. **18:** *Ahikar* and *Nadab:* see 1.21 n.
  12.1–22: Raphael is thanked and identifies himself. 2: *Half the money* apparently refers to half the sum retrieved from Gabael, i.e. five talents of silver. **6–10:** Raphael's exhortation is typical of Wisdom literature. **11–14:** *The whole truth* is that God's Providence works through human misfortune to *test* man, a theme that pervades Wisdom literature; see Wis.3.6; Prov.17.3. **15:** *Seven angels:* nowhere do we find a complete list of these "chief" angels. Perhaps seven is a symbolic number, the full array of divine messengers.

that I ate no food; what appeared to
20 you was a vision. And now praise the
Lord, give thanks to God here on earth;
I am ascending to him who sent me.
Write down all these things that have
21 happened to you.' He then ascended,
and when they rose to their feet, he
22 was no longer to be seen. They sang
hymns of praise to God, giving him
thanks for these great deeds he had done
when his angel appeared to them.

13 TOBIT SAID:

'Praise to the ever-living God and to
his kingdom.
2 He punishes and he shows mercy;
he brings men down to the grave
below,
and up from the great destruction.
Nothing can escape his power.
3 Give him thanks, men of Israel, in
the presence of the nations,
for he has scattered you among them;
4 there he has shown you his greatness.
Exalt him in the sight of every living
creature,
for he is our Lord and God;
he is our Father and our God for
ever.
5 He will punish you for your
wickedness,
and he will show mercy to you all,
gathering you from among all the
nations
wherever you have been scattered.
6 When you turn to him with all your
heart and soul
and act in loyal obedience to him,
then he will turn to you
and hide his face from you no longer.
Consider now the deeds he has done
for you,
and give him thanks with full voice;
praise the righteous Lord
and exalt the King of ages.*g*

10 'Your sanctuary*h* shall be rebuilt for
you with rejoicing.
May he give happiness to all your
exiles

and cherish all who mourn and your
descendants for ever.
Your light shall shine brightly to all   11
the ends of the earth.
Many nations shall come to you from
afar,
from all the corners of the earth to
your holy name;
they shall bring gifts in their hands
for the King of heaven.
In you endless generations shall utter
their joy;
the name of the chosen city shall
endure for ever and ever.
There shall be a curse upon all who   12
speak harshly to you,
upon all who destroy you and pull
down your walls,
upon all who demolish your towers
and burn your houses;
but blessings shall be for evermore
upon those who hold you in
reverence.
Come then, be joyful for the   13
righteous,
for they shall all be gathered
together
and shall praise the eternal Lord.
How happy shall they be who love   14
you and rejoice in your
prosperity,
happy all who grieve for you in your
afflictions;
they shall rejoice over you and for
ever be witness of your joy.
My soul, praise the Lord, the great   15
king,
for Jerusalem shall be built as a city 16
for him to dwell in for ever.
How happy I shall be when the
remnant of my descendants
shall see your splendour

g Some witnesses add
In the land of my exile I give thanks to him
and declare his might and greatness to a sinful
nation.
Turn, you sinners, and do what is right in his eyes;
who knows whether he may not welcome you and
show you mercy?
I will exalt my God   7
and rejoice in the King of heaven.
Let all men tell of his majesty   8
and give him thanks in Jerusalem.
O Jerusalem, the holy city,   9
he will punish you for what your sons have done,
but he will again show mercy on the righteous.
Thank the good Lord and praise the King of ages. 10
h Or home.

13.1–18: Tobit praises God. 1–6: This is a prayer of thanksgiving in the hymnic style of
many psalms. The topic is God's kingdom which will ultimately be established in human history
through the homecoming of God's *scattered* people. **10:** The *sanctuary* is the Temple in
Jerusalem. **16–17:** See Rev.21.18–21.

and give thanks to the King of
heaven.
The gates of Jerusalem shall be built
of sapphire and emerald,
and all your walls of precious stones.
The towers of Jerusalem shall be
built of gold,
their battlements of the finest gold.

17 The streets of Jerusalem shall be
paved with garnets and jewels
of Ophir.

18 The gates of Jerusalem shall sing
hymns of joy
and all her houses shall say Alleluia,
praise to the God of Israel!
Blessed by him, they shall bless his
holy name for ever and ever.'

14 SO ENDED TOBIT'S THANKSGIVING. HE
died peacefully at the age of a hundred
and twelve, and was given honourable
2 burial in Nineveh. He was sixty-two
years old when his eyes were injured,
and after he recovered his sight he lived
in prosperity, doing his acts of charity
and never ceasing to praise God and
proclaim his majesty.

3 When he was dying he sent for his
son Tobias, and gave him these instructions: 'My son, you must take your
4 children and make your escape to
Media, for I believe God's word against
Nineveh spoken by Nahum. It will all
come true; everything will happen to
Asshur and Nineveh that was spoken by
the prophets of Israel whom God sent.
Not a word of it will fall short; everything will be fulfilled when the time
comes. It will be safer in Media than
in Assyria and Babylon; I know, I am
convinced, that all God's words will be
fulfilled. It will be so; not one of them
will fail. Our countrymen who live in
Israel will all be scattered and carried
off into captivity out of that good land,
and the whole territory of Israel laid
waste. Samaria and Jerusalem will lie
waste, and for a time the house of God
will be in mourning; it will be burnt to
the ground.
5 'Then God will have mercy on them
again and will bring them back to the

land of Israel. They will rebuild the
house of God, but not as it was before,
not until the time of fulfilment comes.
Then they will all return from their
captivity and rebuild Jerusalem glori-
ously; then indeed the house will be
built in her as the prophets of Israel
foretold. All the nations of the world 6
will be converted to the true worship of
God; they will abandon their idols
which led them astray into falsehood,
and praise the eternal God according 7
to his law. All the Israelites who survive
at that time and are firm in their loyalty
to God will be brought together; they
will come to Jerusalem to take possession of the land of Abraham, and live
there for ever in safety. Those who love
God in truth will rejoice; and sinners
and wrong-doers will disappear from
the earth. Now, my children, I give you 8
this command: serve God in truth and
do what pleases him. Train your chil- 9
dren to do what is right and give alms,
to keep God in mind at all times and
praise his name in sincerity with all
their strength.

'And now, my son, you must leave 10
Nineveh. Do not stay here; once you
have laid your mother in the grave
with me, do not spend another night
within the city boundaries. For I see
that the place is full of wickedness and
shameless dishonesty. My son, think
what Nadab did to Ahikar who brought
him up: he forced him to hide in a living
grave. Ahikar survived to see God requite the dishonour done to him; he
came out into the light of day, but
Nadab passed into eternal darkness for
his attempt to kill Ahikar. Because I
gave alms, Ahikar escaped from the
fatal trap Nadab set for him, and Nadab
fell into the trap himself and was de- 11
stroyed. So, my children, see what
comes of almsgiving, and see what
comes of wickedness—death. But now
my strength is failing.'
Then they laid him on his bed, and
he died; and they gave him honourable
burial. When his mother died, Tobias 12
buried her beside his father. He and his

14.1–15: **Tobit's final instructions to Tobias. 1:** Tobit's peaceful death at an advanced age
associates him with the patriarchs who, like him, kept the faith in a foreign environment.
4: The book of *Nahum* describes the destruction of *Nineveh*, the capital of *Asshur*, Assyria.
5: A second, and inferior, Temple was built about 515 B.C.; see Hag.1.1–15. **10:** *Ahikar* . . .

wife went away to Media and settled at Ecbatana with his father-in-law Raguel.
13 He honoured and cared for his wife's parents in their old age. He buried them at Ecbatana in Media, and he inherited the estate of Raguel as well as that of
14 his father Tobit. He died greatly respected at the age of one hundred and
15 seventeen. He lived long enough to hear of the destruction of Nineveh by

Ahasuerus king of Media and to see his prisoners of war brought from there into Media. So he praised God for all that he had done to the people of Nineveh and Asshur; and before he died he rejoiced over the fate of Nineveh and praised the Lord God who lives for ever and ever.

Amen.

Nadab: see 1.21 n. **15:** *Ahasuerus:* Xerxes I. *Nineveh* fell in 612 B.C. to an allied force of Medes under Cyaxares and of Babylonians, under Nabopolassar. The fall of Nineveh completes the vindication of Tobit's faith.

JUDITH

Judith is a good example of the Hebrew narrative art: vivid imagery; a paced combination of description and action; and resolute realism. The name Judith means "Jewess"; the heroine represents Israel's faith and spirit, strong and resourceful despite a weak and delicate appearance, which emerges triumphant from the drama of a confrontation between Israel, small and isolated, and all the great powers of the Near East.

There are historical contradictions in the story interpreted by some scholars as intended by the author to indicate unmistakably the fictional nature of the work, and thereby to point up the timeless quality of its contents.

Though set in earlier times, the narrative reflects conditions prevalent during the turmoil of the Hellenistic period described in 1 and 2 Maccabees: divine honors paid to kings (3.8); Jerusalem ruled by a high priest and a form of Sanhedrin (4.8; 15.8); and the like. This evidence of Hellenistic influence indicates a date of composition in the second century B.C. The original language was probably Hebrew, even though most ancient surviving texts are Greek. The author and place of composition are unknown.

The intention of the author seems to be to reassert, at a moment of historical disarray, the Jewish conviction of God's commitment to his people's survival and victory in the odyssey of human existence. Judith exercises the same power that worked through Moses to free Israel from Egyptian bondage. Conversely, the author affirms that the proper response to God's action is an avoidance of political and religious involvement with pagan nations, and an uncompromising observance of the Torah in true Jewish fidelity and piety.

The Assyrian invasion

1 IN THE TWELFTH YEAR OF THE REIGN of Nebuchadnezzar, who reigned over the Assyrians from his capital, Nineveh, Arphaxad was ruling the 2 Medes from Ecbatana. He it was who encircled Ecbatana with a wall built of hewn stones which were four and a half feet thick and nine feet long.[a] He made the wall a hundred and five feet high 3 and seventy-five feet thick, and at the city gates he set up towers a hundred and fifty feet high with foundations ninety 4 feet thick; and he made the gates a hundred and five feet high and sixty feet wide to allow his army to march out in full force with his infantry in forma- 5 tion. It was in those days, then, that King Nebuchadnezzar waged war against King Arphaxad in the great 6 plain on the borders of Ragau. Nebuchadnezzar was opposed by all the inhabitants of the hill-country, by all those who lived along the Euphrates, the Tigris, and the Hydaspes; and, on the plain, by Arioch king of Elam; and many tribes of the Chelodites joined forces with them.

Then Nebuchadnezzar king of As- 7 syria sent a summons to all the inhabitants of Persia, and to all who lived in the west: the inhabitants of Cilicia and Damascus, Lebanon and Antilebanon, all who lived near the coast, the peoples in Carmel and Gilead, 8 Upper Galilee, and the great plain of Esdraelon, all who were in Samaria 9 and its towns, and on the west of Jordan as far as Jerusalem, Betane, Chelus, Cadesh, and the frontier[b] of Egypt, those who lived in Tahpanhes, Rameses, and the whole land of Goshen as far as Tanis and Memphis, and all 10

a *In verses 2–4 the measurements are given in cubits in the Greek.*
b *Literally* river.

1.1–7.32: The Assyrian invasion. The other nations capitulate and Jewish resistance is gradually broken.

1.1–6: Nebuchadnezzar wages war on Arphaxad. 1: *Nebuchadnezzar:* king of the Babylonians from 605–561 B.C. He directed the destruction of Jerusalem in 587 B.C.; see 2 Kgs.25.1–9. His father had conquered the *Assyrians* and destroyed *Nineveh* in 612 B.C. The historically impossible combination here of Nebuchadnezzar and the Assyrians suggests that the author wished to combine Israel's traditional enemies to create a literary confrontation between faith and secular power. *Arphaxad* is unknown. **2–3:** *Ecbatana* was situated near present-day Hamadan in Iran. Its dimensions are exceedingly exaggerated, showing a high degree of fiction. **5:** *Ragau* is modern Rai, located near Teheran. **6:** The *Hydaspes* is a river near the eastern border of Persia. *Arioch* is unknown. The *Chelodites* are unknown.

1.7–12: Persia and the western nations arouse Nebuchadnezzar's anger. 7–10: The nations and towns listed represent the western portion of the Fertile Crescent—modern Syria, Lebanon,

the inhabitants of Egypt as far as the 11 borders of Ethiopia. But the entire region disregarded the summons of Nebuchadnezzar king of Assyria and did not join him in the war. They were not afraid of him, for he seemed to them to stand alone[c] and unsupported; and they treated his envoys with contempt and sent them back empty-handed. 12 This roused Nebuchadnezzar to fury against the whole region, and he swore by his throne and his kingdom that he would have his revenge on all the territories of Cilicia, Damascus, and Syria, and put their inhabitants to the sword, along with the Moabites, the Ammonites, and the people in all Judaea and in Egypt as far as the shores of the two seas. 13 In the seventeenth year of his reign he marshalled his forces against King Arphaxad and defeated him in battle, routing his entire army, cavalry, 14 chariots, and all. He occupied his towns; and when he reached Ecbatana he captured its towers, looted its bazaars, and turned its splendour to 15 abject ruin. He caught Arphaxad in the mountains of Ragau, speared him through, and so made an end of him. 16 Then he returned with his spoils to Nineveh, he and his combined forces, an immense host of warriors. There he rested and feasted with his army for four months.

2 In the eighteenth year, on the twenty-second day of the first month, a proposal was made in the palace of Nebuchadnezzar king of Assyria to carry out his threat of vengeance on the whole 2 region. Assembling all his officers and nobles, the king laid before them his personal decision about the region and declared his intention of putting an 3 end to its disaffection. They resolved that everyone who had not obeyed his summons should be put to death.

When his plans were completed,[d] 4 Nebuchadnezzar king of Assyria summoned Holophernes, his commander-in-chief, who was second only to himself, and said to him, 'This is the decree 5 of the Great King, lord of all the earth: Directly you leave my presence, you are to take under your command an army of seasoned troops, a hundred and twenty thousand infantry with a force of twelve thousand cavalry, and march 6 out against all the peoples of the west who have dared to disobey my command. Tell them to have ready their 7 offering of earth and water, for I am coming to vent my wrath on them. Their whole land will be smothered by my army, and I will give them up to be plundered by my troops. Their dead 8 will fill the valleys, and every stream and river will be choked with corpses; and I will send them into captivity to 9 the ends of the whole earth. Now go 10 and occupy all their territory for me. If they surrender to you, hold them for me until the time comes to punish them. But show no mercy to those who resist; 11 let them be slaughtered and plundered throughout the whole region. By my life 12 and my royal power I swear: I have spoken and I will be as good as my word. As for you, do not disobey a 13 single one of my orders, but see that you carry them out exactly as I your sovereign have commanded you. Do this without delay.'

After leaving his sovereign's presence, 14 Holophernes assembled all the marshals, generals, and officers of the Assyrian army, and mustered picked men, 15 as the king had commanded, a hundred and twenty thousand infantry and twelve thousand mounted archers, drawing them up in battle order. He 16,17 took an immense number of camels,

c *One witness reads* to be no more than their equal . . .
d *Or* When he had finished stating his purpose . . .

Palestine, and Egypt. *Betane* and *Chelus* are unknown. *Cadesh* may be in southern Palestine. **1.13–2.13:** Nebuchadnezzar defeats Arphaxad and declares war on the western nations. **14:** The Nebuchadnezzar of history did not capture *Ecbatana*. **2.1:** *The eighteenth year* of Nebuchadnezzar's reign is 587 B.C., the date when he ordered the destruction of Jerusalem. **4:** *Holophernes* is unknown as a famous Babylonian general; the name, indeed, is Persian and his presence adds the Persians to the artificial composite of Israel's enemies; see 1.1 n. **5:** Nebuchadnezzar's designation of himself as *lord* . . ., without reference to the rights of God, makes this a battle between the ungodly and the God-fearing. **7:** The *offering of earth and water* was a Persian expression for the provisioning of an invading and conquering army from the occupied country.

asses, and mules for their baggage, innumerable sheep, oxen, and goats for
18 provisions, and ample rations for every man, as well as a great quantity of gold
19 and silver from the royal palace. Then he set out with all his army to go ahead
of King Nebuchadnezzar and to overrun the entire region to the west with
chariots, cavalry, and picked infantry.
20 Along with them went a motley host like a swarm of locusts, countless as the
dust of the earth.
21 From Nineveh they marched for three days towards the plain of Bectileth, and encamped beside Bectileth near the mountain north of Upper
22 Cilicia. From there, Holophernes advanced into the hill-country with his
whole army, infantry, cavalry, and
23 chariots. He devastated Put and Lud, and plundered all the people of Rassis,
and the Ishmaelites on the edge of the desert south of the land of the Cheleans.
24 Then he followed^e the Euphrates and traversed Mesopotamia, destroying all
the fortified towns along the river
25 Abron as far as the sea. He occupied the territory of Cilicia and cut down all
who resisted him. Then he came south to the borders of Japheth fronting
26 Arabia. He surrounded the Midianites, burnt their encampments, and plun-
27 dered their sheepfolds. At the time of wheat harvest he went down to the
plain of Damascus, burnt their crops, exterminated their flocks and herds,
sacked their towns, laid waste their fields, and put all their young men to the
28 sword. Fear and dread of him fell on all the inhabitants of the coast at Tyre and
Sidon, of Sur and Okina, and of Jemnaan; the people of Azotus and Ascalon
were terrified of him.

3 They sent envoys to sue for peace,
who said: 'We are servants of the Great 2 King Nebuchadnezzar, we lie prostrate
before you; do with us as you please.
Our buildings, our territory, our wheat 3 fields, our flocks and herds and every
sheepfold in our encampments, all are yours to do with as you wish. Our 4
towns and their inhabitants are subject to you; come and deal with them as
you think fit.'

When the envoys came to Holo- 5 phernes with this message, he went 6
down to the coast with his army and garrisoned all the fortified towns,
taking from them picked men as auxiliaries. Both there and in all the sur- 7
rounding country he was welcomed with garlands, dancing, and tambourines. He demolished all their sanc- 8 tuaries^f and cut down their sacred
groves, for he had been commissioned to destroy all the gods of the land, so
that Nebuchadnezzar alone should be worshipped by every nation and invoked as a god by men of every tribe and tongue.

Holophernes then advanced towards 9 Esdraelon, near Dothan, which faces
the great ridge of Judaea, and en- 10 camped between Geba and Scythopolis,
where he remained for a whole month to collect supplies for his army.

WHEN THE ISRAELITES WHO LIVED IN 4 Judaea heard of all that had been done
to the nations by Holophernes, the commander-in-chief of Nebuchadnezzar king of Assyria, and how he had plundered and totally destroyed all
their temples, they were terrified at his 2 approach. They were in great alarm for
Jerusalem and for the temple of the Lord their God. For they had just 3

e Or crossed. f So one Vs.; Gk. borders.

2.14–3.10: Holophernes ravages the west as far as Palestine. 21: *Three days* to march from *Nineveh* to *Bectileth* (unknown city) in Upper Cilicia (southeastern Asia Minor) is impossible since the distance is about three hundred miles. 23: *Put* and *Lud* are perhaps in Asia Minor. *Rassis* is unknown. *Ishmaelites* usually means Arabs. The *Cheleans* are unknown. 24–28: The route of invasion is very erratic and most unlikely. Such an imposing list of victims is given for psychological and theological rather than historical purposes. 24: The *Abron* is unknown. 25: *Japheth* is unknown as a place name. 28: *Sur* and *Okina* are perhaps Dor and Acco in western Galilee. *Jemnaan* may be Jamnia, this one on the Lake of Galilee; *Azotus* (Ashdod) and *Ascalon* (Ashkelon) are Philistine cities. 3.8: The Babylonian rulers never claimed divine rights, but the Seleucid kings did (Dan.3.1–7). The persecution of the Jews by the Seleucids seems to be alluded to here. See 1.1 n.; 2.4 n.; 2 Macc.9.1–12. 9: *Esdraelon:* the great plain that lies between Galilee and Samaria. 10: *Geba:* a town in central Palestine. *Scythopolis:* Beth-shan, south of the Lake of Galilee.
4.1–15: The Israelites prepare to defend their land and Temple. 3: The Israelites could not

returned from captivity, and it was only recently that the people had been re united in Judaea, and the sacred vessels, the temple, and the altar sancti-
4 fied after their profanation. So they sent out a warning to the whole of Samaria, Cona, Beth-horon, Belmain and Jericho, Choba and Aesora and the
5 valley of Salem, and occupied the tops of all the high hills. They fortified the villages on them and laid up stores of food in preparation for war; for their
6 fields had just been harvested. Joakim, who was high priest in Jerusalem at the time, wrote to the people of Bethulia and Bethomesthaim, which is opposite Esdraelon facing the plain near Dothan.
7 He ordered them to occupy the passes into the hill-country, because they controlled access to Judaea, and it was easy to hold up an advancing army, for the approach was only wide enough for two
8 men. The Israelites obeyed the orders of the high priest Joakim and the senate
9 of all Israel in Jerusalem. Fervently they sent up a cry to God, every man of Israel, and fervently they humbled
10 themselves before him. They put on sackcloth—they themselves, their wives, their children, their livestock, and every resident foreigner, hired
11 labourer, and slave—and all the inhabitants of Jerusalem, men, women, and children, prostrated themselves in front of the sanctuary, and, with ashes on their heads, spread out their sackcloth before the Lord. They draped the
12 altar in sackcloth, and with one voice they earnestly implored the God of Israel not to allow their children to be captured, their wives carried off, their ancestral cities destroyed, and the

temple profaned and dishonoured, to the delight of the heathen. The Lord 13 heard their prayer and pitied their distress.
For many days the whole population of Judaea and Jerusalem fasted before the sanctuary of the Lord Almighty. Joakim the high priest and the priests 14 who stood in the presence of the Lord, and all who served in the temple, wore sackcloth when they offered the regular burnt-offering and the votive and free-will offerings of the people; and with 15 ashes on their turbans they cried aloud to the Lord to look favourably on the whole house of Israel.
When it was reported to Holo- 5 phernes, the Assyrian commander-in-chief, that the Israelites had prepared for war, and that they had closed the passes in the hill-country, fortified all the heights, and dug pitfalls in the plains, he was furious. He summoned 2 all the rulers of Moab, the Ammonite commanders, and all the governors of the coastal region, and said to them, 3 'Tell me, you Canaanites, what nation is this that lives in the hill-country? What towns do they inhabit? How big is their army? What gives them their power and strength? Who is the king that commands their forces? Why are 4 they the only people of the west who have refused to come and meet me?'
Then Achior, the leader of all the 5 Ammonites, said to him, 'My lord, if you will allow your servant to speak, I will tell you the truth about this nation that lives in the hill-country near here; and no lie shall pass my lips. They are 6 descended from the Chaldaeans; and 7 at one time they settled in Meso-

have *just returned from captivity* because the return took place under the Persians, many years after Nebuchadnezzar; compare Ezra 1.1–11. The sanctification of the *temple* and *altar* may refer to the rededication of the Temple under Judas Maccabeus in 164 B.C.; see 1 Macc.4.52–55. Israel's history is here telescoped. **4:** *Cona, Belmain, Choba,* and *Aesora* are unknown; the *valley of Salem* is an archaic name for Jerusalem (Gen.14.18). **6:** *Joakim* may refer to a high priest (named Joiakim) mentioned in Neh.12.10–12,26 but the circumstances there are quite different. *Bethulia*, mentioned frequently in Jdt., is not mentioned elsewhere in the Bible; this would be unthinkable if the story were historical. *Bethomesthaim* is unknown. **8:** There is no evidence of a *high priest* and a *senate* ruling in Jerusalem prior to Maccabean times (1 Macc.12.6; 2 Macc.11.27).

5.1–24: Achior, the Ammonite, briefs Holophernes on the history and religion of Israel. 3: Israel had generally controlled the *hill-country* where guerrilla tactics were effective; see Judg.1.19. **5:** *Achior* plays the role of the "objective witness" who allows the author to recall the historical basis for Israel's uniqueness. **6:** *Chaldaeans:* a reference to Abraham's origin (Gen.11.27–31). **7:** *Mesopotamia* here refers to the region around Harran where Abraham stopped on his way to Palestine (Gen.11.31). The Bible makes no mention of any religious

potamia, because they refused to worship the gods their fathers had wor-

6 shipped in Chaldaea. They abandoned the ways of their ancestors and worshipped the God of Heaven, the god whom they now acknowledged. When the Chaldaeans drove them out from the presence of their gods they fled to Mesopotamia, where they lived for a

9 long time. Then their god told them to leave their new home and go on to Canaan. They settled there and acquired great wealth in gold, silver, and livestock.

10 'Because of a famine which spread over the whole of Canaan, they went down to Egypt and lived there as long as they were supplied with food. While in Egypt, they multiplied so greatly that their numbers could not be

11 reckoned, and the king of Egypt turned against them. He exploited them by setting them to hard labour making bricks, and he reduced them

12 to abject slavery. They cried out to their god, and he inflicted incurable plagues on the whole of Egypt. So the Egyp-

13 tians turned them out; and their god

14 dried up the Red Sea for them and led them on to Sinai and Cadesh-barnea. Then they drove out all the inhabitants

15 of the wilderness and settled in the land of the Amorites, and they destroyed all the peoples of Heshbon by force of arms. After that they crossed the Jordan and occupied all the hill-

16 country, driving out the Canaanites, the Perizzites, the Jebusites, the Shechemites, and all the Girgashites. There they settled for a long time.

17 'As long as they did not sin against their god, they prospered; for theirs is a

18 god who hates wickedness. But when they left the path he had laid down for them, they suffered heavy losses in many wars and were carried captive to a foreign country; the temple of their god was razed to the ground, and their towns were occupied by their

19 enemies. But now that they have returned to their god, they have come back from the places where they had been

dispersed, and have taken possession of Jerusalem, where their sanctuary is, and have settled in the hill country, because it was uninhabited.

20 'Now, my lord and master, if these people are guilty of an error and are sinning against their god, and if we find out that they have committed this of-

21 fence, then we may go and make war on them. But if these people have committed no wickedness, leave them alone, my lord, for fear the god they serve should protect them and we become

22 the laughing-stock of the world.' When Achior stopped speaking there were protests from all those who stood round the tent. Holophernes' officers and all the people from the coastal region and from Moab demanded that Achior should be cut to pieces. 'We are

23 not going to be afraid of the Israelites,' they said, 'a people quite incapable of putting an effective army in the field. Let

24 us go ahead, Lord Holophernes; your great army will swallow them whole.'

6 When the hubbub among the men around the council had subsided, Holophernes, the Assyrian commander-in-chief, said to Achior and all the Ammonites, in the presence of the assembled foreigners: 'And who are

2 you, Achior, you and your Ammonite mercenaries, to play the prophet among us as you have done today, telling us not to make war against the people of Israel because their god will protect them? What god is there but Nebuchad-

3 nezzar? He will exert his power and wipe them off the face of the earth; and their god will not rescue them. We who serve Nebuchadnezzar will strike them all down as if they were only one man. They will not be able to stand up

4 to the weight of our cavalry; we shall overwhelm them. Their mountains will be drenched with blood, and their plains filled with their dead. They cannot stand their ground against us; they will be completely wiped out. This is the decree of King Nebuchadnezzar, lord of the whole earth. He has spoken; and what he has said will

---

problems in this context, but later Jewish tradition does. **14:** *Cadesh-barnea:* Num.20.1. **15:** *Heshbon:* Num.21.25–26.

    6.1–21: Holophernes condemns Achior. **2:** It is important for the author that the issue be

5 be made good. As for you, Achior, you Ammonite mercenary, the words you have spoken today are treason, so from today you shall not see my face again until I have taken vengeance on this 6 brood of runaways from Egypt. But when I come back, the warriors of my bodyguard will run you through and 7 add you to their victims. My men are going to take you away now to the hill-country and leave you in one of the 8 towns in the passes. You will not die 9 until you share their fate. If you are so confident that they will not fall into our hands, you need not look down-cast. I have spoken; and nothing that I have said will fail to come true.'

10 Then Holophernes ordered his men, who were standing by in his tent, to seize Achior, take him off to Bethulia, 11 and hand him over to the Israelites. So they seized him and took him outside the camp to the plain, and from there into the hill-country, until they arrived 12 at the springs below Bethulia. When the men of the town saw them, they picked up their weapons and came out of the town to the top of the hill; then all the slingers pelted the enemy with stones to prevent them from com-13 ing up. But they slipped through under cover of the hill, tied Achior up and left him lying at the foot of it, and went 14 back to their master. When the Israel-ites came down from the town and found him there, they untied him and took him into Bethulia, where they brought him before the town magis-15 trates then in office, Ozias son of Mica, of the tribe of Simeon, and Chabris son of Gothoniel, and Charmis son of 16 Melchiel. The magistrates summoned all the elders of the town; and all the young men and women came running to the assembly. When Achior had been brought before the people, Ozias 17 asked him what had happened. He answered by telling them all that had taken place in Holophernes' council,

what he himself had said in the presence of the Assyrian commanders, and how Holophernes had boasted of what he would do to Israel. Then the people 18 prostrated themselves in worship and cried out to God: 'O Lord, God of 19 heaven, mark their arrogance; pity our people in their humiliation; show favour this day to those who are thy own.' Then they reassured Achior and 20 commended him warmly. Ozias took 21 him from the assembly to his own house, and gave a feast for the elders; and all that night they invoked the help of the God of Israel.

THE NEXT DAY HOLOPHERNES ORDERED 7 his whole army and all his allies to strike camp and march on Bethulia, seize the passes into the hill-country, and make war on the Israelites. So the 2 whole force set out that day, an army of a hundred and seventy thousand infantry and twelve thousand cavalry, not counting the baggage train of the infantry, an immense host. They en-3 camped in the valley near Bethulia, be-side the spring; and their camp extended in breadth towards Dothan as far as Belbaim, and in length from Bethulia to Cyamon which faces Esdraelon. When the Israelites saw their numbers 4 they said to each other in great alarm, 'These men will strip the whole country bare; the high mountains, the valleys, and the hills will never be able to bear the burden of them.' Then each man 5 stood to arms; and they lit the beacons on the towers and remained on guard all that night.

On the following day Holophernes 6 led out all his cavalry in full view of the Israelites in Bethulia, and reconnoitred 7 the approaches to their town. He inspected the springs and seized them; and when he had stationed detachments of soldiers there, he returned to his army. Then all the rulers of the Edom-8 ites and all the leaders of Moab and

---

strictly religious, i.e. *what god is there?* **5:** *Egypt:* a derisive reference to the Exodus. **11:** *The springs below Bethulia:* this is of little help for identification, because most towns in Palestine were built on a hill for defense and near a water supply. **19:** The enemy represents the *arrogance* of any human attempt to displace God in history.

    7.1–18: Holophernes lays siege to Bethulia. 3: *Dothan:* a town in the plain of *Esdraelon;* see 3.9 n. *Belbaim . . . Cyamon:* unknown. **7:** Seizure of the *springs* was the first move in a siege, since the only other source of water was that collected in cisterns during the short rainy season; see v. 21. **8:** *Edomites:* descendants of Esau, traditional enemies of Israel, are also added

the commanders from the coastal region
9 came to him and said, 'Listen to our
advice, Lord Holophernes, and save
your army from a crushing defeat.
10 These Israelites do not trust in their
spears but in the height of the mountains where they live; for it is no easy
task to get up to the tops of these moun-
11 tains of theirs. Now, Lord Holophernes,
avoid fighting a pitched battle with
them, and you will not lose a single
12 man. Remain in your camp and keep
your men in their quarters; but let your
servants take possession of the spring
13 at the foot of the hill, for that is where
all the townspeople of Bethulia get their
water. When they are dying of thirst
they will surrender the town. Meanwhile, we and all our people will go up
to the tops of the neighbouring hills
and camp there to see that not a man
14 gets away from the town. They and their
wives and children will waste away with
famine; and before the sword reaches
them, their streets will be strewn with
15 their corpses. So you will make them
pay heavily for rebelling against you,
instead of receiving you peaceably.'
16 Holophernes and all his staff approved
this plan; and he gave orders that it
17 should be carried out. The Moabite
force moved forward in company with
five thousand Assyrians and encamped in the valley, where they seized
the springs which were the Israelites'
18 water-supply. Then the Edomites and
Ammonites went up and encamped in
the hill-country opposite Dothan, and
sent some of their number south-east*g*
in the direction of Egrebel, which is
near Chus on the Mochmur ravine.
The rest of the Assyrian army encamped on the plain. They filled the
entire country-side, their tents and baggage train forming an immense encampment, for they were a vast host.
19 Then the Israelites cried out to the
Lord their God. Their courage failed,
because all their enemies had surrounded them and there was no way of
20 escape. The whole Assyrian army, in-

fantry, cavalry, and chariots, kept them
blockaded for thirty-four days. The
citizens of Bethulia came to the end of
their household supplies of water. The 21
cisterns too were running dry; drinking-
water was so strictly rationed that there
was never a day when their needs were
satisfied. The children were lifeless, the 22
women and young men faint with thirst.
They collapsed in the streets and gateways from sheer exhaustion.
Then all the people, young men, 23
women, and children, gathered round
Ozias and the magistrates of the town,
shouting loudly. In the presence of the
elders they said: 'May God judge be- 24
tween us, for you have done us a great
wrong in not coming to terms with the
Assyrians. Now we have no one to help 25
us. God has sold us into their power;
they will find us dead of thirst, and the
ground strewn with our corpses. Sur- 26
render to them; let Holophernes' people
and his army sack the town. It is better 27
for us to be taken prisoner; for even as
slaves we shall still be alive, and shall
not have to watch our babies dying
before our eyes, and our wives and
children at their last gasp. We call 28
heaven and earth to witness, we call
our God, the Lord of our fathers, to
witness against you—the God who is
punishing us for our sins and for the
sins of our fathers. We pray that he may
not let our forebodings come true this
day.' Then the whole assembly broke 29
into loud lamentation and cried to the
Lord God. Ozias said to them, 30
'Courage, my friends! Let us hold out
for five more days; by that time the
Lord our God may show us his mercy
again. Surely he will not finally desert
us. But if by the end of that time no 31
help has reached us, then I will do what
you ask.' Then he dismissed the men 32
to their various posts; and they went
off to the walls and towers of the town.
The women and children he sent indoors. Throughout the town there was
deep dejection.

g Or south and east.

---

to the picture here; see 1.1 n. **18:** *Egrebel, Chus,* and *Mochmur* are located in the area southeast
of Shechem.
    7.19–32: The inhabitants of Bethulia contemplate surrender. 23–28: The complaints against
Ozias are reminiscent of the bitter murmuring of the Israelites against Moses in the desert;
see Num.14.2–3.

8 NEWS OF WHAT WAS HAPPENING reached Judith, daughter of Merari, son of Ox, son of Joseph, son of Oziel, son of Helkias, son of Elias, son of Chelkias, son of Eliab, son of Nathanael, son of Salamiel, son of Sarasadae, 2 son of Israel. Her husband Manasses, who belonged to her own tribe and clan, had died at the time of barley 3 harvest. While he was out in the fields supervising the binding of the sheaves, he got sunstroke, took to his bed, and died in Bethulia his native town; and they buried him beside his ancestors in the field between Dothan and Balamon. 4 For three years and four months Judith 5 had lived at home as a widow; she had a shelter erected on the roof of her house; she put on sackcloth and always 6 wore mourning. After she became a widow she fasted every day except sabbath eve, the sabbath itself, the eve of the new moon, the new moon, and the Israelite feasts and days of public re-7 joicing. She was a very beautiful and attractive woman. Her husband Manasses had left her gold and silver, male and female slaves, livestock and land, and 8 she lived on her estate. No one spoke ill of her, for she was a very devout woman.

9   When Judith heard of the shameful attack which the people had made upon Ozias the magistrate, because they were demoralized by the shortage of water, and how he had sworn to surrender the town to the Assyrians after five days, 10 she sent her maid who had charge of all her property to ask Ozias, Chabris, and Charmis, the elders of the town, to 11 come and see her. When they arrived she said to them: 'Listen to me, magistrates of Bethulia. You had no right to speak as you did to the people today,

and to bind yourselves by oath before God to surrender the town to our enemies if the Lord sends no relief within so many days. Who are you to test God 12 at a time like this, and openly set yourselves above him? You are putting the 13 Lord Almighty to the proof. You will never understand! You cannot plumb 14 the depths of the human heart or understand the way a man's mind works; how then can you fathom man's Maker? How can you know God's mind, and grasp his thought? No, my friends, do not rouse the anger of the Lord our God. For even if he does not 15 choose to help us within the five days, he is free to come to our rescue at any time he pleases, or equally to let us be destroyed by our enemies. It is not for 16 you to impose conditions on the Lord our God; God will not yield to threats or be bargained with like a mere man. So we must wait for him to deliver us, 17 and in the mean time appeal to him for help. If he sees fit he will hear us.

'There is not one of our tribes or 18 clans, districts or towns, that worships man-made gods today, or has done so within living memory. This did happen in days gone by, and that was why our 19 ancestors were abandoned to their enemies to be slaughtered and pillaged, and great was their downfall. But we ac- 20 knowledge no god but the Lord, and so we are confident that he will not spurn us or any of our race. For our capture 21 will mean the loss of all Judaea, and our temple will be looted; and God will hold us responsible for its desecration. The slaughter and deportation of our 22 fellow-countrymen, and the laying waste of the land we inherited, will bring his judgement upon us wherever we become slaves among the Gentiles. Our masters will regard us with disgust and contempt. There will be no happy 23

8.1–13.20: Judith and Holophernes. Risking honor and life, she combines great faith, grim courage, and scrupulous observance of the Law in liberating Israel.
8.1–8: Judith is introduced. 1: *Judith* is the feminine form of Judah. Perhaps the name, which occurs passingly in Gen.26.34, symbolizes the Jewish people. Judith's ancestors, aside from Israel (Jacob), cannot be identified. **3:** *Dothan:* 7.3 n. *Balamon:* unknown. **6:** The OT requires fasting only on the Day of Atonement. Rabbinic Judaism increased the number of fast days. Judith's fasting beyond the requirement implies an extraordinary piety.
8.9–36: Judith upbraids the magistrates and promises that God will deliver the city by her hand. 11–27: Judith's eloquent exhortation is an expression of what faith requires of Israel in the postexilic period of apparent abandonment by God. **12:** *To test God:* to lay down *conditions* (v. 16) for God's action, e.g. to hold out for five days more (7.30). **18:** This favorable judgment

ending to our servitude, no return to favour; the Lord our God will use it to dishonour us.

24 'So then, my friends, let us set an example to our fellow-countrymen; for their lives depend on us, and the fate of the sanctuary, the temple, and the

25 altar rests with us. We have every reason to give thanks to the Lord our God; he is putting us to the test as he did our

26 ancestors. Remember how he dealt with Abraham and how he tested Isaac, and what happened to Jacob in Syrian Mesopotamia when he was working as

27 a shepherd for his uncle Laban. He is not subjecting us to the fiery ordeal by which he tested their loyalty, or taking vengeance on us: it is for discipline that the Lord scourges his worshippers.'

28 Ozias replied, 'You are quite right; everything you say is true, and no one

29 can deny it. This is not the first time that you have given proof of your wisdom. Throughout your life we have all recognized your good sense and the

30 soundness of your judgement. But the people were desperate with thirst and compelled us to make this promise and to pledge ourselves by an oath we may

31 not break. Now, you are a devout woman; pray for us and ask the Lord to send rain to fill our cisterns, and then we shall no longer faint for lack of water.'

32 'Hear what I have to say', replied Judith. 'I am going to do a deed which will be remembered among our people

33 for all generations. Be at the gate to-night yourselves, and I will go out with my maid. Before the day on which you have promised to surrender the town to our enemies, the Lord will deliver

34 Israel by my hand. But do not try to find out my plan; I will not tell you until I have accomplished what I mean to

35 do.' Ozias and the magistrates said to

her, 'Go with our blessing, and may God be with you to take vengeance on our enemies.' So they left the roof- 36 shelter and returned to their posts.

Then Judith prostrated herself, put 9 ashes on her head, and uncovered the sackcloth she was wearing; and at the time when the evening incense was being offered in the temple in Jerusalem, she cried to the Lord: 'O Lord, the God of 2 my forefather Simeon! Thou didst put in his hand a sword to take vengeance on those foreigners who had stripped off a virgin's veil to defile her, uncovered her thighs to shame her, and polluted her womb to dishonour her. Thou didst say, "It shall not be done"; yet they did it. So thou didst give up 3 their rulers to be slain, and their bed, which blushed for their treachery, to be stained with blood; beneath thy stroke slaves fell dead upon the bodies of princes, and princes upon their thrones. Thou didst give up their wives as booty, 4 and their daughters as captives, and all their spoils to be divided among thy beloved sons, who, aflame with zeal for thy cause and aghast at the pollution of their blood, called on thee to help them. O God, thou art my God, hear now a widow's prayer. All that happened then, 5 and all that happened before and after, thou didst accomplish. The things that 6 are now, and are yet to be, thou hast designed; and what thou didst design has come to pass. The things thou hast foreordained present themselves and say, "We are here." Thy ways are prepared beforehand: foreknowledge determines thy judgement.

'Thou seest the Assyrians assembled 7 in their strength, proud of their horses and riders, boasting of the power of their infantry, and putting their faith in shield and javelin, bow and sling. They do not know that thou art the Lord

---

was generally accurate in the period after the Exile. **25:** God puts Israel to the *test* by awaiting a response of fidelity to himself in her difficulties. The argument is built on an antithesis: it is not that man tests God (v. 12) but, rather, God tests man. **27:** That suffering be viewed as *discipline* is a faith interpretation of history. **33:** The context and language are reminiscent of God's intervention to lead his people from Egypt by the *hand* of Moses (Exod. ch. 9). See also 13.14; 15.10.

9.1–14: Judith's prayer. 1: The time of the *evening* offering was considered a most propitious moment for prayer. See Exod.30.8; 1 Kgs.18.36. **2:** *Simeon* and Levi slaughtered the Shechemites for having violated their sister Dinah (Gen. ch. 34). But see also Gen.49.5–7 where their violence is condemned. **4:** The *widow's prayer* is the object of special divine attention and care in the OT. See Deut.10.18; Ecclus.35.14–15. **7:** A strong pacifist current developed in Israel beginning

8 who stamps out wars; the Lord is thy name. Shatter their strength by thy power and crush their might in thy anger. For they have planned to desecrate thy sanctuary, to pollute the dwelling-place of thy glorious name, and to strike down the horns of thy 9 altar with the sword. Mark their arrogance, pour thy wrath on their heads, and give to me, widow as I am, the 10 strength to achieve my end. Use the deceit upon my lips to strike them dead, the slave with the ruler, the ruler with the servant; shatter their pride 11 by a woman's hand. For thy might lies not in numbers nor thy sovereign power in strong men; but thou art the God of the humble, the help of the poor, the support of the weak, the protector of the desperate, the deliverer of the hope- 12 less. Hear, O hear, thou God of my forefather, God of Israel's heritage, ruler of heaven and earth, creator of the waters, king of all thy creation, hear 13 thou my prayer. Grant that my deceitful words may wound and bruise them; for they have cruel designs against thy covenant, thy sacred house, the summit of Zion, and thy children's home, their 14 own possession. Give thy whole nation and every tribe the knowledge that thou alone art God, God of all power and might, and that thou and thou alone art Israel's shield.'

10₁₋₂ When Judith had ended her prayer, prostrate before the God of Israel, she rose, called her maid, and went down into the house, where she was accustomed to spend her sabbaths and festi- 3 vals. She removed the sackcloth she was wearing and took off her widow's weeds; then she washed, and anointed herself with rich perfume. She did her hair, put on a headband, and dressed in her gayest clothes, which she used to wear when her husband Manasses was 4 alive. She put on sandals and anklets, bracelets and rings, her ear-rings and all her ornaments, and made herself very

attractive, so as to catch the eye of any man who might see her. She gave her 5 maid a skin of wine and a flask of oil; then she filled a bag with roasted grain, cakes of dried figs, and the finest bread, packed everything up, and gave it all to her maid to carry.

They went out towards the gate of 6 Bethulia and found Ozias standing there, with Chabris and Charmis the elders of the town. When they saw 7 Judith transformed in appearance and quite differently dressed, they were filled with admiration of her beauty, and said to her, 'The God of our fathers 8 grant you favour and fulfil your plans so that Israel may triumph and Jerusalem may be exalted!' Judith bowed to God in worship. Then she said to 9 them, 'Order the gate to be opened for me, and I will go out to accomplish all that you say.' They ordered the young men to open the gate as she had asked. When they had done so, Judith went 10 out, accompanied by her maid; and the men of the town watched her until she had gone down the hill-side and crossed the valley, and then they lost sight of her.

The women went straight across the 11 valley and were met by an Assyrian outpost; they seized Judith and ques- 12 tioned her: 'What is your nationality? Where have you come from? Where are you going?' 'I am a Hebrew,' she replied; 'but I am running away from my people, because they are going to fall into your hands and be devoured. I am on my way to Holophernes, your 13 commander-in-chief, with reliable information. I will show him a route by which he can gain command of the entire hill-country without losing a single man.'

As the men listened to her story they 14 looked at her face and were amazed at her beauty. 'You have saved your life', 15 they said, 'by coming down at once to see our master. Go to his tent straight away. Some of us will escort you and

---

with Isa.2.4. See also 16.3. **10:** The pious Judith prays for the success of her *deceit* because trickery was considered a very honorable weapon in war; see Josh.9.3–27.
10.1–17: Judith goes to Holophernes. 1–2: *Went down into the house:* from the tent on the roof where she spent most of her time. See 8.5. **5:** Judith *packed . . . up* her own food so that she would not be defiled by eating unclean food of the Gentiles; see 12.1–4. **12:** *Running away* from a city was not uncommon when a siege reached the decisive stage; see Jer.38.19; 39.9; 2 Chr.30.10.

16 hand you over to him. When you are in his presence, do not be afraid; just tell him what you have told us, and he
17 will treat you kindly.' They detailed a hundred of their number to accompany her and her maid, and they brought the two women to Holophernes' tent.

18 AS THE NEWS OF HER ARRIVAL SPREAD from tent to tent, men came running from all parts of the camp. They gathered round her as she stood outside Holophernes' tent waiting until he had
19 been told about her. Her wonderful beauty made them think that the Israelites must be a wonderful people. They said to each other, 'Who can despise a nation which has such women as this? We had better not leave a man of them alive, for if they get away they will be able to outwit the whole world.'
20 Then Holophernes' bodyguard and all his attendants came out and took her
21 into the tent. He was resting on his bed under a mosquito-net of purple interwoven with gold, emeralds, and
22 precious stones. When Judith was announced he came out into the front part of the tent, with silver lamps car-
23 ried before him. He and his attendants were all amazed at the beauty of her face as she stood before them. She prostrated herself and did obeisance to him; but his slaves raised her up.

11 'Take heart, madam,' said Holophernes; 'do not be afraid. I have never harmed anyone who chose to serve Nebuchadnezzar, king of all the earth.
2 I should never have raised my spear against your people in the hill-country if they had not insulted me; they brought
3 it on themselves. Now tell me why you have run away from them and joined us. By coming here you have saved your life. Take heart! You are in no danger tonight or in the future; no one will
4 harm you. You will enjoy the good

treatment which is given to the subjects of my master King Nebuchadnezzar.'
Judith replied, 'My lord, grant 5 your slave a hearing and listen to what I have to say to you. The information I am giving you tonight is the truth. If 6 you follow my advice, God will do some great thing through you, and my lord will not fail to attain his ends. By the 7 life of Nebuchadnezzar, king of all the earth, and by the living might of him who sent you to bring order to all creatures, I swear: not only do men serve him, thanks to you, but wild animals also, cattle and birds, will owe their lives to your power as long as Nebuchadnezzar and his dynasty reign.[h] We 8 have heard how wise and clever you are. You are known throughout the world as the man of ability unrivalled in the whole empire, of powerful intelligence and amazing skill in the art of war. We know about the speech 9 that Achior made in your council, because the men of Bethulia rescued him, and he told them what he had said to you. Do not disregard what he said, 10 my lord and master, but give full weight to his words. They are true. No punishment ever falls on our race and the sword does not subdue them, except when they sin against their God. But 11 now, my lord, you are not to be thwarted and cheated of success, for they are doomed to die. Sin has them in its power, and when they do wrong they will arouse their God's anger. Be- 12 cause they have run out of food and their water-supply is low, they have decided to lay hands on their cattle; they mean to consume everything that God by his laws has prohibited as food; and they have resolved to use up the 13

[h] *not only . . . reign: or* thanks to you and to your power, not only do men serve him, but wild animals also, cattle, and birds, will live at the disposal of Nebuchadnezzar and his household; *the text and meaning are uncertain.*

10.18–11.23: Judith is welcomed by Holophernes and explains her errand. 19: *Outwit the whole world:* superb irony. The Assyrians note that the trap into which they are falling would make a very good trap! **11.3–4:** Holophernes guarantees freedom from *danger* to his prospective executioner! The Bible delights in showing how God uses evil men to carry out his benevolent designs. **6:** *God will do some great thing through you* has an altogether different meaning for Judith than for Holophernes. Judith's conversation is full of such delightful ambiguities. **13:** *Firstfruits . . . tithes* were reserved for priests by Mosaic Law. See Exod.23.19; Lev.23.15–21; 27.30. The requirements of the Law (see Deut.26.1–15) seem to be extended here, possibly reflecting early quasi-Pharisaic interpretation and extension. Judith uses the same argument as Achior had done (5.17–21) but affirms Israel's guilt. It was commonly believed by the ancients

firstfruits of the grain and the tithes of wine and oil, although these are dedicated and reserved for the priests who stand in attendance before our God in Jerusalem, and no layman may 14 so much as handle them. They have sent men to Jerusalem to get permission from the senate, because even the 15 people there have done this. As soon as ever word reaches them and they act on it, on that very day they will be given up to you to be destroyed.

16 'So, my lord, when I learnt all this, I ran away from them; and God has sent me to do with you things that will be the wonder of the world, wherever 17 men hear about them. For I, your servant, am a religious woman: day and night I worship the God of heaven. I will stay with you now, my lord; and each night I shall go out into the valley and pray to God, and he will tell me when they have committed their 18 sins. Then, when I return and bring you word, you may lead out your whole army, and you will meet with no 19 resistance from any of them. I will guide you across Judaea until you reach Jerusalem, and I will set up your throne in the heart of the city. They will follow you like sheep that have lost their shepherd, and not a dog will so much as growl at you. I have been given fore-knowledge of this. It has been revealed to me, and I have been sent to announce it to you.'

20 Judith's words delighted Holophernes and all his attendants, and 21 they were amazed at her wisdom. 'In the whole wide world', they said, 'there is not a woman to compare with her for beauty of face or shrewdness of 22 speech.' Holophernes said to her, 'Thank God for sending you out from your people, to bring strength to us and destruction to those who have insulted 23 my lord! You are a beautiful woman and your words are good. If you do as

you have promised, your God shall be my God, and you shall live in King Nebuchadnezzar's palace and be re-nowned throughout the world.'

Holophernes then commanded them 12 to bring her in where his silver was set out, and he ordered a meal to be served for her from his own food and wine. But Judith said, 'I will not eat any of it, 2 in case I should be breaking our law. What I have brought with me will meet my needs.' Holophernes said to her, 3 'But if you use up all you have with you, where can we get you a fresh supply of the same kind? There is no one of your race here among us.' Judith replied, 4 'As sure as you live, my lord, I shall not finish what I have brought with me before the Lord accomplishes through me what he has planned.'

Holophernes' attendants brought her 5 into the tent; and she slept until mid-night. Shortly before the morning watch she got up and sent this message 6 to Holophernes: 'My lord, will you give orders for me to be allowed to go out and pray?' Holophernes ordered his 7 bodyguard to let her pass. She remained in the camp for three days, going out each night into the valley of Bethulia and bathing in the spring. When she 8 came up from the spring, she prayed the Lord, the God of Israel, to prosper her undertaking to restore her people. Then she returned to the camp purified, 9 and remained in the tent until she took her meal towards evening.

ON THE FOURTH DAY HOLOPHERNES 10 gave a banquet for his personal ser-vants only, and did not invite any of the army officers. He said to Bagoas, the 11 eunuch in charge of all his affairs: 'Go to the Hebrew woman who is in your care, and persuade her to join us and to eat and drink with us. It would be a 12 disgrace if we let such a woman go without enjoying her company. If

---

that ritual transgression was followed by punishment. **17:** By going out *each night*, Judith is establishing a pattern of conduct that will permit her later escape (13.10).

12.1–9: Judith prepares for the opportune moment. 2: Judith's scrupulous observance of the dietary laws reflects a norm of postexilic Jewish piety. **5–9:** That Holophernes is so easily manipulated is patently a literary device.

12.10–20: Holophernes invites Judith to a banquet. 11: *Bagoas* is a common Persian name (see 1.1 n.). A *eunuch* was usually in charge of the king's harem but in some cases he was also an important and influential person at court (Gen.37.36 n.; Dan.1.3).

we do not win her favours she will
13 laugh at us.' Bagoas left Holophernes'
presence, and went to Judith and said,
'Now, my beauty, do not be bashful;
come along to my master and give yourself the honour of his company. Drink
with us and enjoy yourself, and behave
today like one of the Assyrian women
in attendance at Nebuchadnezzar's
14 palace.' 'Who am I to refuse my
master?' said Judith. 'I am eager to do
whatever pleases him; and it will be
something to boast of till my dying
15 day.' She proceeded to dress herself
up and put on all her feminine finery.
Her maid went ahead of her, and
spread on the ground in front of
Holophernes the fleeces which she had
received from Bagoas for her daily use,
so that she might recline on them when
16 she ate. When Judith came in and took
her place, Holophernes was beside himself with desire for her. He shook with
passion and was filled with an ardent
longing to possess her; indeed he had
been looking for an opportunity to
17 seduce her ever since he first set eyes
on her. So he said to her, 'Drink and
18 enjoy yourself with us.' 'Indeed I will,
my lord,' said Judith; 'today is the
19 greatest day of my whole life.' Then
she took what her servant had prepared,
and ate and drank in his presence.
20 Holophernes was delighted with her,
and drank a great deal of wine, more,
indeed, than he had ever drunk on any
single day since he was born.

13 When it grew late, Holophernes'
servants quickly withdrew. Bagoas
closed the tent from outside, shutting
out all the attendants from his master's
presence, and they went to bed; the
banquet had lasted so long that they
2 were all worn out. Judith was left alone
in the tent, with Holophernes lying
sprawled on his bed, dead drunk.
3 Judith had told her maid to stand
outside the sleeping-apartment and
wait for her mistress to go out, as she
did every day; she had said that she
would be going out to pray, and had
4 explained this to Bagoas also. When

they had all gone and not a soul was
left, Judith stood beside Holophernes'
bed and prayed silently: 'O Lord, God
of all power, look favourably now on
what I am about to do to bring glory
to Jerusalem, for now is the time to 5
help thy heritage and to give success
to my plan for crushing the enemies
who have risen up against us.' She went 6
to the bed-rail beside Holophernes' head
and took down his sword, and stepping 7
close to the bed she grasped his hair.
'Now give me strength, O Lord, God
of Israel', she said; then she struck at 8
his neck twice with all her might, and
cut off his head. She rolled the body 9
off the bed and took the mosquito-net
from its posts; a moment later she went
out and gave Holophernes' head to the
maid, who put it in her food-bag. The 10
two of them went out together, as they
had usually done for prayer. Through
the camp they went, and round that
valley, and up the hill to Bethulia till
they reached the gates.

From a distance Judith called to the 11
sentries at the gates: 'Open! Open the
gate! God, our God is with us, still
showing his strength in Israel and his
might against our enemies. He has
shown it today!' When the citizens 12
heard her voice, they hurried down to
the gate and summoned the elders of
the town. Everyone high and low came 13
running, hardly able to believe that
Judith had returned. They opened the
gate and let the two women in; they lit
a fire to see by, and gathered round
them. Then Judith raised her voice and 14
cried, 'Praise God! O praise him! Praise
God, who has not withdrawn his mercy
from the house of Israel, but has
crushed our enemies by my hand this
very night!' Then she took the head from 15
the bag and showed it to them. 'Look!'
she said. 'The head of Holophernes,
the Assyrian commander-in-chief! And
here is the net under which he lay
drunk! The Lord has struck him down
by the hand of a woman! And I swear 16
by the Lord who has brought me safely
along the way I have travelled that,

13.1–20: Judith returns to Bethulia with the head of Holophernes. 6: *His sword:* a scimitar or
dagger. **9:** Judith *took the mosquito-net* as proof that she had been with Holophernes, since the
men of Bethulia could scarcely have recognized him (v. 15). **14:** *By my hand:* 8.33 n. **15:** To
be *struck down by the hand of a woman* was the ultimate disgrace for a warrior; see Judg.9.54.

though my face lured him to destruction, he committed no sin with me, and my honour is unblemished.'

17 The people were all astounded; and bowing down in worship to God, they said with one voice, 'Praise be to thee, O Lord our God, who hast humiliated the enemies of thy people this day.'

18 And Ozias said to Judith, 'My daughter, the blessing of God Most High is upon you, you more than all other women on earth; praise be to the Lord, the God who created heaven and earth, and guided you when you struck off the

19 head of the enemy commander. The sure hope which inspired you*i* will never fade from men's minds while they com-

20 memorate the power of God. May God make your deed redound to your honour for ever, and shower blessings upon you! You risked your life for our country when it was faced with humiliation. You went boldly to meet the disaster that threatened us, and held firmly to God's straight road.' All the people responded: 'Amen! Amen!'

The triumph of Israel

14 THEN JUDITH SAID TO THEM, 'LISTEN TO me, my friends; take this head and hang it out on the battlements of your wall.

2 As soon as dawn breaks and the sun rises, take up your weapons, every able-bodied man of you, and march out of the town. You must set a commander at your head, as if you were going down to the plain to attack the Assyrian out-

3 post; but do not go down. The Assyrians will take up their weapons and make for their camp, and rouse the commanders, who will run to Holophernes' tent but will not find him. They will all be seized with panic and

4 will flee from you; then pursue them, you and all who live within Israel's borders, and cut them down in their

5 tracks. But first of all summon Achior the Ammonite to me, so that he may

see and recognize the man who treated Israel with contempt and sent him to us as if to his death.'

They summoned Achior from Ozias's 6 house. When he came and saw Holophernes' head held by one of the men in the assembly of the people, he fainted and fell down. They lifted him up, and 7 he threw himself at Judith's feet and did obeisance to her, and said, 'Your praises will be sung in every camp in Judah and among all nations. They will tremble when they hear your name. Tell me now the whole story of what 8 you have done during these days.' Then Judith, in the hearing of the people, told him everything from the day she left until that very moment. As she 9 ended her story, the people raised a great shout and made the town ring with their cheers. And when Achior 10 realized all that the God of Israel had done, he came to full belief in God, and was circumcised, and admitted as a member of the community of Israel, as his descendants still are.

When dawn came they hung Holo- 11 phernes' head on the wall; then they all took their weapons and went out in companies into the approaches to the town. When the Assyrians saw them, 12 they sent word to their leaders, who then went to the generals, captains, and all the other officers. They came to 13 Holophernes' tent and said to his steward: 'Wake our master. These slaves have had the audacity to offer us battle; they are asking to be utterly wiped out.' Bagoas went in and knocked 14 at the screen of the inner tent, supposing that Holophernes was sleeping with Judith. When there was no reply, 15 he drew aside the screen, went into the sleeping-apartment, and found the dead body sprawling over a footstool, and the head gone. He gave a great cry, 16 wailing and groaning aloud, and tore his clothes. Then he went into the tent 17 which Judith had occupied; and not

i Or which you inspire.

18–20: Judith's victory is proof that power and violence can be conquered by faith and wisdom. The weak, oppressed, and demoralized postexilic Israel needs this reminder.

14.1–15.7: Judith directs the men of Bethulia in victory. 5: There is a double purpose in calling *Achior*: to *recognize*, i.e. identify the head of Holophernes and to *see* the defeat of the *man who treated Israel with contempt*, and thereby to have his witness to the vindication of Israel's God. **10:** Achior's conversion to Judaism represents a more lenient view than that in Deut.23.3. **13:** *These slaves:* this is a contemptuous reference to Israel's condition in Egypt.

finding her he rushed out to the people 10 shouting, 'The slaves have played us false. One Hebrew woman has brought shame on Nebuchadnezzar's kingdom. Look! Holophernes is lying on the 19 ground, and his head is gone!' His words filled the officers of the Assyrian army with dismay; they tore their clothes, and the camp rang with their shouts and cries.

15 When the news spread to the men in the camp, they were thrown into con- 2 sternation at what had happened. In terror and panic they all scattered at once, with no attempt to keep together, and fled by every path across the plain 3 and the hill-country. Those who were encamped in the hills round Bethulia also took to flight. Then all the Israel-ites of military age sallied out after 4 them. Ozias sent men to Bethomes-thaim, Choba, and Chola, and the whole territory of Israel, to give news of what had happened and to tell them to sally out against the enemy and 5 destroy them. When the news reached them, every man in Israel joined the attack and cut them down, going as far as Choba. The men from Jerusalem and all the hill-country also joined in, for they had been told what had hap-pened in the enemy camp. The men of Gilead and Galilee outflanked the As-syrians and inflicted heavy losses on them, continuing beyond Damascus 6 and the district round it. The rest of the inhabitants of Bethulia fell upon the camp and made themselves rich with 7 the spoils. When the Israelites returned from the slaughter, they took possession of what remained. The villages and hamlets in the hill-country and in the plain got masses of booty, for there was a huge quantity of it. 8 Joakim the high priest and the senate of Israel came from Jerusalem to see for themselves the great things the Lord had done for his people, and to meet 9 Judith and wish her well. When they arrived they praised her with one voice

and said, 'You are the glory of Jeru-salem, the heroine of Israel, the proud boast of our people! With your own 10 hand you have done all this, you have restored the fortunes of Israel, and God has shown his approval. Blessings on you from the Lord Almighty, for all time to come!' And all the people re-sponded, 'Amen!'

The looting of the camp went on for 11 thirty days. They gave Judith Holo-phernes' tent, with all his silver, and his couches, bowls, and furniture. She took them and loaded her mule, then got her wagons ready and piled the goods on them. All the Israelite women came 12 running to see her; they sang her praises, and some of them performed a dance in her honour. She took gar-landed wands in her hands and gave some also to the women who accom-panied her; and she and those who were 13 with her crowned themselves with olive leaves. Then, at the head of all the people, she led the women in the dance; and the men of Israel, in full armour and with garlands on their heads, fol-lowed them singing hymns.

IN THE PRESENCE OF ALL ISRAEL, JUDITH **16** struck up this hymn of praise and thanksgiving, in which all the people joined lustily:

'Strike up a song to my God with 2
    tambourines;
sing to the Lord with cymbals;
raise a psalm of praise*j* to him;
honour him and invoke his name.
The Lord is a God who stamps out 3
    wars;
he has brought me safe from my
    pursuers
into his camp among his people.
The Assyrian came from the 4
    mountains of the north;
his armies came in such myriads
that his troops choked the valleys,
his cavalry covered the hills.

j Some witnesses read a new psalm.

15.4: *Ozias:* a variant spelling of Uzziah. *Bethomesthaim, Choba,* and *Chola* have not been identified.
    15.8–13: The heroism of Judith is extolled. 10: *Your own hand:* see 8.33 n. **12–13:** The festive expressions described here are in keeping with Greek, not Jewish, custom. **13:** *She led the women in the dance,* much as Miriam led the dance after Israel's victory over Egypt (Exod.15.20). Many of the features of this triumph are borrowed from Israel's prototypal Exodus victory.
    16.1–17: Judith's hymn of thanksgiving. 3: *Stamps out wars:* see 9.7 n. **4:** Assyria lies mostly

5 He threatened to set fire to my land,
   put my young men to the sword,
   dash my infants to the ground,
   take my children as booty,
   and my maidens as spoil.

6 The Lord Almighty has thwarted
      them by a woman's hand.

7 It was no young man that brought
      their champion low;
   no Titan struck him down,
   no tall giant set upon him;
   but Judith daughter of Merari
      disarmed him by the beauty
      of her face.

8 She put off her widow's weeds
   to raise up the afflicted in Israel;
   she anointed her face with perfume,
   and bound her hair with a
      headband,
   and put on a linen gown to beguile
      him.

9 Her sandal entranced his eye,
   her beauty took his heart captive;
   and the sword cut through his neck.

10 The Persians shuddered at her
      daring,
   the Medes were daunted by her
      boldness.

11 Then my oppressed people shouted
      in triumph, and the enemy were
      afraid;
   my weak ones shouted, and the
      enemy cowered in fear;
   they raised their voices, and the
      enemy took to flight.

12 The sons of servant girls ran them
      through,
   wounding them like runaway slaves;
   they were destroyed by the army of
      my Lord.

13 'I will sing a new hymn to my God.
   O Lord, thou art great and glorious,
   thou art marvellous in thy strength,
      invincible.

14 Let thy whole creation serve thee;
   for thou didst speak and all things
      came to be;

thou didst send out thy spirit and it
      formed them.
No one can resist thy voice;
mountains and seas are stirred to 15
      their depths,
rocks melt like wax at thy presence;
but to those who revere thee
thou dost still show mercy.

For no sacrifice is sufficient to please 16
      thee with its fragrance,
and all the fat in the world is not
      enough for a burnt-offering,
but he who fears the Lord is always
      great.

Woe to the nations which rise up 17
      against my people!
The Lord Almighty will punish them
      on the day of judgement;
he will consign their bodies to fire
      and worms;
they will weep in pain for ever.'

When they arrived at Jerusalem they 18
worshipped God. As soon as the people
were purified, they offered their burnt-
offerings, freewill offerings, and gifts.
Judith dedicated to God all Holo- 19
phernes' possessions, which the people
had given to her; and the net, which
she had taken for herself from the
sleeping-apartment, she presented as a
votive offering. For three months the 20
people continued their celebrations in
Jerusalem in front of the sanctuary; and
Judith remained with them.

At the end of that time they all re- 21
turned to their own homes. Judith went
back to Bethulia and lived on her
estate. In her time she was famous
throughout the whole country. She had 22
many suitors; but she remained unmarried all her life after her husband
Manasses died and was gathered to his
fathers. Her fame continued to increase; 23
and she lived on in her husband's house
until she was a hundred and five years
old. She gave her maid her liberty.
She died in Bethulia and was buried

---

east of Palestine but the route of invasion was from the *north*. **7:** *Titan:* Greek influence.
10: *Persians . . . Medes:* see 1.1 n. **14:** Ps.33.6. **17:** The entire book is devoted to the theme of
the inviolability of God's *people* in a world of hostility on the part of the godless nations.
See 1.1 n.
   16.18–25: After a feast in Jerusalem, Judith returns to Bethulia. 19: *All Holophernes' possessions:* an example of detachment from worldly goods, perhaps to console the poverty-
stricken postexilic Jews. **23–24:** A long life, praise from one's people, and generosity toward
associates are all signs of a true Israelite.

in the same tomb as her husband
24 Manasses, and Israel observed mourning for her for seven days. Before her
death she divided her property among
all those who were most closely related
to her husband Manasses, and among
her own nearest relations.

No one dared to threaten the Israel- 25
ites again in Judith's lifetime, or for a
long time after her death.

THE REST OF THE CHAPTERS
OF THE BOOK OF
ESTHER

WHICH ARE FOUND NEITHER IN THE HEBREW
NOR IN THE SYRIAC

NOTE. *The portions of the Book of Esther commonly included in the Apocrypha are extracts from the Greek version of the book, which differs substantially from the Hebrew text (translated in* The New English Bible: Old Testament). *In order that they may be read in their original sequence, the whole of the Greek version is here translated, those portions which are not normally printed in the Apocrypha being enclosed in square brackets, with the chapter and verse numbers in italic figures. The order followed is that of the Greek text, but the chapter and verse numbers are made to conform to those of the Authorized Version. Proper names are given in the form in which they occur in the Greek version.*

To the book of Esther, as found in the Hebrew, six sections were added either by the Greek translator himself, or only a short time later by someone else. These additions may be dated as coming from about 114 B.C.

When Jerome prepared his Latin Vulgate translation of the Old Testament from the Hebrew, he also translated these Greek additions to Esther, but grouped them together at the end of the Hebrew story. In the text here (see "Note"), the whole Greek version is reconstructed, with the additions inserted into their proper place in the story. (Compare the Book of Esther in the Old Testament.) It should be noted that the chapter and verse numbers here conform to Stephen Langton's arrangement of 1214 A.D., which followed Jerome's order of the text.

The account in the Greek version is substantially identical with the Hebrew. However, the Greek additions are significant because they supply an explicit religious element strangely lacking in the original, e.g. God is never mentioned in the Hebrew. The Greek version also inserts, through Mardochaeus' dream (10.4–9), an apocalyptic and cosmic element into the story; thereby the episode of a Jewish deliverance from a Persian pogrom becomes a sign of God's dramatic eleventh-hour victory over all secular powers at the end of history. Thus, the Feast of Purim, to which the story of Esther purportedly gave rise, is made an occasion for expressing the Jewish hope of eventual deliverance from historical adversities.

11 2 IN THE SECOND YEAR OF THE REIGN OF Artaxerxes the Great King, on the first day of Nisan, Mardochaeus son of Jairus, son of Semeius, son of Kisaeus, of the tribe of Benjamin, had 3 a dream. Mardochaeus was a Jew living in the city of Susa, a man of high standing, who was in the royal 4 service; he came of those whom Nebuchadnezzar king of Babylon had taken into exile from Jerusalem with Jechonias king of Judah. This was his dream: din and tumult, peals of 5 thunder and an earthquake, confusion upon the earth. Then appeared two 6 great dragons, ready to grapple with each other, and the noise they made was terrible. Every nation was roused 7 by it to prepare for war, to fight against the righteous nation. It was a day of 8

11.2–12: Mardochaeus' dream. 2: *Artaxerxes* (Heb., Ahasuerus) is Xerxes I (485–464 B.C.). The *second year* of his reign is 484 B.C. The *first day of Nisan* is about March 15. *Mardochaeus* (Heb., Mordecai) is obviously a Jew but his name is probably Babylonian. **3:** *Susa:* a city in Mesopotamia. **4:** This deportation took place about 597 B.C., which would make Mardochaeus at least 113 years old at the time of his dream (v.2)! *Jechonias* is Jehoiachin (2 Kgs.24.12–13). **5–11:** The imagery of the dream is apocalyptic; the *dragons* (antagonists) are Mardochaeus and Haman, while the divinely decreed victory is effected through Esther (the *little spring*). See 10.6–9. **7:** *Righteous nation:* the Jews.

darkness and gloom, with distress and anguish oppression and great con-
9 fusion upon the earth. And the whole righteous nation was troubled, dreading the evils in store for them, and they
10 prepared for death. They cried aloud to God; and in answer to their cry there came as though from a little spring a great river brimming with
11 water. It grew light, and the sun rose; the humble were exalted and they
12 devoured the great. After he had had this dream and had seen what God had resolved to do, Mardochaeus woke; he kept it before his mind, seeking in every way to understand it, until nightfall.

12 Now when Mardochaeus was resting in the royal courtyard with Gabatha and Tharra, the two eunuchs who
2 guarded the courtyard, he heard them deep in discussion. He listened carefully to discover what was on their minds, and found that they were plotting violence against King Arta-xerxes. He denounced them to the king,
3 who had the two eunuchs interrogated. They confessed and were led away to
4 execution. Then the king wrote an account of the affair, to have it on record; Mardochaeus also wrote an
5 account of it. The king gave Mardo-chaeus an appointment at court, and
6 rewarded him for his services. But Haman, the son of Hamadathus, a Bugaean, who enjoyed the king's favour, sought to injure Mardochaeus and his people because of the two eunuchs.

A Jewess becomes queen in Persia

1 [THOSE EVENTS HAPPENED IN THE DAYS of Artaxerxes, the Artaxerxes who ruled

from India to Ethiopia, a hundred and
2 twenty-seven provinces. At this time he sat on his royal throne in the city of
3 Susa. Then in the third year of his reign he gave a banquet for the King's Friends and persons of various races, the Persian and Median nobles and the
4 leading provincial governors. And afterwards, after displaying to them the wealth of his empire and the splendour of his rich festivities for a hundred and
5 eighty days, when these days of feasting were over, the king gave a banquet for all the people of various races present in the city of Susa; it was held in the court of the king's palace and lasted six
6 days. The court was decorated with white curtains of linen and cotton stretched on cords of purple, and these were attached to blocks of gold and silver resting on stone and marble columns. There were couches of gold and silver set on a pavement of mala-chite, marble, and mother-of-pearl. There were mats of transparent weave
7 elaborately embroidered with roses arranged in a circle. The cups were of gold and silver, and there was displayed a miniature cup made of carbuncle worth thirty thousand talents. The wine was abundant and sweet, from the
8 king's own cellar. The drinking was not according to a fixed rule, but the king had laid it down that all the stewards of his palace should respect his will and
9 that of the guests. In addition, Queen Astin gave a banquet for the women in the same palace where King Artaxerxes was.

10 On the seventh day, when he was in high good humour, the king ordered Haman, Mazan, Tharra, Borazes, Zatholtha, Abataza, and Tharaba, the seven eunuchs who were in attendance
11 on the king's person, to bring the queen

12.1–6: Mardochaeus discovers a plot against the king and is rewarded. 5: The Hebrew story (6.3) knows nothing of this reward. **6:** *Haman* has the villain's role. He is here identified as *a Bugaean* but in Esther 3.1 he is an Agagite. In 16.10 he is identified as a Macedonian although his father's name is Persian. It may be significant that Mardochaeus, like Saul, was a Benjaminite (11.2) while Haman was apparently an Amalekite (1 Sam.15.8). Thus, there was a long previous historical basis for a blood feud between them.
1.1–9: Artaxerxes gives a lavish feast. 2: *Susa* was the winter residence of Persian kings; the official capital was Persepolis. **3:** *King's Friends:* see 1 Macc.2.18 n. **7:** *Thirty thousand talents:* the sum is astronomical. See Appendix, "Weights and Coins," p. 1035. The entire description seems to be greatly exaggerated. **9:** *Queen Astin* in the Hebrew account is called Vashti. She must have been a current favorite since Xerxes' official wife was Amestris.
1.10–22: Queen Astin disobeys Artaxerxes and is dethroned. 10: The Hebrew version attributes the king's *good humour* to drinking. *Eunuchs* were originally in charge of the king's harem but

before him, so that he might place the royal diadem on her head and let her display her beauty to the officers and people of various races; for she was 12 indeed a beautiful woman. But Queen Astin refused to obey him and come with the eunuchs. This offended the king and made him angry.

13 Then the king said to his courtiers, 'You hear what Astin said. Give your ruling and judgement in the matter.'
14 Then the nobles of Persia and Media who were closest to the king—Harkesaeus, Sarsathaeus, and Malesear, who sat next him in the chief seats—ap-15 proached him and declared what should be done according to the law to Queen Astin for disobeying the order which the king sent her by the eunuchs.
16 Then Muchaeus said to the king and the nobles: 'Queen Astin has done wrong, and not to the king alone, but to all his 17 nobles and officers as well.' (For he had repeated to them what the queen had said and how she had defied the king.)
18 'And just as she defied King Artaxerxes, so now the nobles of Persia and Media will find that all their ladies are bold enough to treat their husbands with contempt, when they hear what she 19 said to the king. If it please your majesty, let a royal decree go out from you, and let it be inscribed among the laws of the Medes and Persians, that Astin shall not again appear before the king; this is the only course. And let the king give her place as queen to another woman who is more worthy of 20 it than she. Let whatever law the king makes be proclaimed throughout his empire, and then all women will give due honour to their husbands, rich and 21 poor alike.' The advice pleased the king and the princes, and the king did as 22 Muchaeus had proposed. Letters were sent to all the provinces of the empire, to each province in its own language,

in order that every man might be respected in his own house.

Later, when the anger of King 2 Artaxerxes had died down, he remembered Astin and what she had done, and how he had given judgement against her. So the king's attendants said: 'Let 2 beautiful girls of unblemished virtue be sought out for your majesty. Let your 3 majesty appoint commissioners in all the provinces of the empire to select these beautiful virgins and bring them to the city of Susa, into the women's quarters. There let them be committed to the care of the king's eunuch in charge of the women, and let them be provided with cosmetics and everything else they need. Then the one who is 4 most acceptable to the king shall become queen in place of Astin.' The advice pleased the king, and he acted on it.

Now there was a Jew in the city of 5 Susa named Mardochaeus, son of Jairus, son of Semeius, son of Kisaeus, of the tribe of Benjamin; he had been 6 carried into exile from Jerusalem when it was taken by Nebuchadnezzar king of Babylon. He had a foster-child 7 named Esther, the daughter of his father's brother Aminadab. She had lost her parents, and he had brought her up to womanhood. She was a very beautiful girl. When the king's edict 8 was proclaimed, many girls were brought to Susa to be entrusted to Gai, who had charge of the women, and among them was Esther. She attracted 9 his notice and received his special favour: he readily provided her with her cosmetics and allowance of food, and also with seven maids assigned to her from the king's palace. He gave her and her maids honourable treatment in the women's quarters.

Esther had not disclosed her race or 10 country, because Mardochaeus had

---

later they acquired positions of great influence (Gen.37.36 n.; Dan.1.3). **12:** Perhaps *Astin refused* because the circumstances would have made her appearance degrading. **20:** Such naïvete may be due to the heavy drinking of these counselors!

2.1–14: Esther enters the competition to replace Queen Astin. 1–4: A beauty contest always makes for good storytelling. The scope of this contest serves to highlight the exceptional beauty of Esther. **3:** *Women's quarters:* the harem. **5:** Following the Hebrew version, the Greek text introduces *Mardochaeus* a second time; see 11.2–3. **7:** *Esther* is derived from the Babylonian goddess Ishtar, who was related to the god Marduk, from whom Mardochaeus derived his name. **10:** Concealment of Esther's background is important for the development of the story line; see 7.4.

11 forbidden her to do so. Every day Mardochaeus passed along by the fore court of the women's quarters to keep an eye on Esther and see what would happen to her.

12 The period after which a girl was to go to the king was twelve months. This was for the completion of the required treatment—six months with oil and myrrh and six months with perfumes

13 and cosmetics. Then the girl went to the king. She was handed to the person appointed, and accompanied him from the women's quarters to the king's

14 palace. She entered the palace in the evening and returned in the morning to Gai, the king's eunuch in charge of the women, in another part of the women's quarters. She did not go to the king again unless summoned by name.

15 When the time came for Esther, daughter of Aminadab the uncle of Mardochaeus, to go to the king, she neglected none of the instructions of Gai the king's eunuch in charge of the women; for Esther charmed all who

16 saw her. She was taken to King Artaxerxes in the twelfth month, that is, the month Adar, in the seventh year of his

17 reign. The king fell in love with her, finding her more acceptable than any of the other girls, and crowned her with

18 the queen's diadem. Then the king gave a banquet lasting seven days for all the King's Friends and the officers, to celebrate Esther's marriage. He also granted a remission of taxation to all subjects of his empire.

19 Mardochaeus was in attendance in
20 the courtyard. But Esther had not disclosed her country—such were the instructions of Mardochaeus; but she

was to fear God and keep his commandments just as she had done when she was with him. So Esther made no change in her way of life.

21 Two of the king's eunuchs, officers of the bodyguard, were offended at the advancement of Mardochaeus and

22 plotted to kill King Artaxerxes. This became known to Mardochaeus, who told Esther, and she revealed the plot

23 to the king. The king interrogated the two eunuchs and had them hanged, and he ordered that the service Mardochaeus had rendered should be recorded in the royal archives to his honour.

A plot against the Jews

3 AFTER THIS KING ARTAXERXES PROMOTED Haman son of Hamadathus the Bugaean, advancing him and giving him precedence above all the King's

2 Friends. So all who were at court did obeisance to Haman, for so the king had commanded; but Mardochaeus did

3 not do obeisance. Then the king's courtiers said to him, 'Mardochaeus, why do you flout the king's command?'

4 Day by day they challenged him, but he refused to listen to them. Then they informed Haman that Mardochaeus was resisting the king's command. Mardochaeus had told them that he

5 was a Jew. So when Haman learnt that Mardochaeus was not doing obeisance

6 to him, he was infuriated and plotted to exterminate all the Jews under Artaxerxes' rule.

7 In the twelfth year of King Artaxerxes he arrived at a decision by casting lots, taking the days and the months

---

2.15–20: **Esther wins the king's favor and is made queen. 16:** *Adar:* February–March. *The seventh year:* four years after Queen Astin's dismissal; see 1.3. **18:** *King's Friends:* see 1 Macc. 2.18 n. **20:** *Esther made no change in her way of life:* she maintained dietary laws and other such Jewish observances.

2.21–23: **Mardochaeus saves the king's life.** According to the Greek version (12.1–5), Mardochaeus was advanced only after he revealed the plot. The Heb. version (Esther 6.2–3), which is itself uncertain, makes a point of the fact that Mardochaeus was not rewarded for this service.

3.1–5.14: **A plot against the Jews.** Esther and Haman are pitted against each other as forces of good and evil.

3.1–6: **Mardochaeus refuses homage to Haman. 2:** The *obeisance* prescribed was certainly the normal deference required for the office of grand vizier or prime minister. But Mardochaeus, a Benjaminite, considers it irreligious to bow before an Agagite (see 12.6 n. above). Such defiance is presented as an ideal of Jewish attitudes toward Gentiles.

3.7–13: **Haman secures a royal edict to exterminate the Jews. 7:** *Twelfth year:* about 474 B.C. In common practice important decisions were made by the impartial method of *casting lots.*

one by one, to decide on one day for the destruction of the whole race of Mardochaeus. The lot fell on the thirteenth day of the month Adar.

8 Then Haman said to King Artaxerxes: 'There is a certain nation dispersed among the other nations of your empire. Their laws are different from those of every other nation; they do not keep your majesty's laws. It is not to your majesty's advantage to tolerate 9 them. If it please your majesty, let an order be made for their destruction; and I will contribute ten thousand talents of silver to the royal treasury.' 10 So the king took off his signet-ring and gave it to Haman to seal the decree 11 against the Jews. 'Keep the money, and deal with these people as you will', he said.

12 On the thirteenth day of the first month the king's secretaries were summoned, and in accordance with Haman's instructions, they wrote in the name of King Artaxerxes to his army commanders and governors in every province from India to Ethiopia. There were a hundred and twenty-seven provinces in all, and each was addressed 13 in its own language. Instructions were dispatched by courier to all the empire of Artaxerxes to exterminate the Jewish race, on a given day of the twelfth month, Adar, and to plunder their possessions.]

13 THIS IS A COPY OF THE LETTER:

Artaxerxes the Great King to the governors of the one hundred and twenty-seven provinces, from India to Ethiopia, and to the subordinate officials.

2 Ruler as I am over many nations and master of all the world, it is my will—not in the arrogance of power, but because my rule is mild and equitable—to ensure to my subjects a life permanently free from disturbance, to pacify my empire and make it safe for travel to its farthest limits, and to restore the peace that all men long for. I asked my counsellors how 3 this object might be achieved and received a reply from Haman. Haman is eminent among us for sound judgement, one whose worth is proved by his constant goodwill and steadfast loyalty, and who has gained the honour of the second place at our court. He represented 4 to us that scattered among all the races of the empire is a disaffected people, opposed in its laws to every nation, and continually ignoring the royal ordinances, so that our irreproachable plans for the unified administration of the empire cannot be made effective. We understand 5 that this nation stands alone in its continual opposition to all men, that it evades the laws by its strange manner of life, and in disloyalty to our government commits grievous offences, thus undermining the security of our empire. We therefore 6 order that those who are designated to you in the indictments drawn up by Haman, our vicegerent and second father, shall all, together with their wives and children, be utterly destroyed by the sword of their enemies, without mercy or pity, on the thirteenth[b] day of Adar, the twelfth month, of the present year. Those persons who have long been 7 disaffected shall meet a violent death in one day so that our government may henceforth be stable and untroubled.

a So some witnesses, and compare 8. 12 (page 93); other witnesses read fourteenth.
b Gk. fourteenth; *see note on 3. 7 (pages 87–88).*

The Akkadian word for "lot" is *pur* and this provides the name for the Feast of Purim to which this story was later attached; see 9.25–26. *Thirteenth day:* about March 1; see 2.16 n. **8:** The standard complaint against the pious Jews was that they were *different;* see Wis.2.15; 1 Macc. ch. 2. **9:** *Ten thousand talents:* an astronomical sum; see Appendix for "Weights and Coins," p. 1035. **12:** *First month:* Nisan (March–April). The Persian empire was divided into thirteen administrative districts called satrapies. These *provinces* may have been subdivisions. **13:** *Adar:* see 2.16 n.
   13.1–7; 3.14–15: Artaxerxes' edict to destroy the Jews. 4: *Disaffected people:* there is little doubt that the Jews, because of their adherence to distinctive customs ("strange manner of life"; v. 5), were viewed with a suspicion which lent credence to exaggerated and sometimes fantastic accusations. **6:** *Vicegerent:* an administrator in charge of royal affairs. *Adar:* see 2.16 n.

3 14   [Copies of the document were posted up in every province, and all nations of the empire were ordered to be ready 15 by that day. The matter was expedited also in Susa. While the king and Haman caroused together, the city of Susa was thrown into confusion.

4 WHEN MARDOCHAEUS LEARNT ALL THAT was being done, he tore his clothes, put on sackcloth and sprinkled himself with ashes; and he rushed through the city, crying loudly: 'An innocent nation 2 is being destroyed.' He went as far as the king's gate, and there he halted, because no one was allowed to enter the courtyard clothed with sackcloth and 3 ashes. In every province where the king's decree was posted up, there was a great cry of mourning and lamentation among the Jews, and they put on 4 sackcloth and ashes. When the queen's maids and eunuchs came and told her, she was distraught at the news, and sent clothes for Mardochaeus, urging him to take off his sackcloth; but he would 5 not consent. Then Esther summoned Hachrathaeus, the eunuch who waited upon her, and ordered him to obtain accurate information for her from 7 Mardochaeus.*c* So Mardochaeus told him all that had happened, and how Haman had promised to pay ten thousand talents into the royal treasury to bring about the destruction of the 8 Jews. He also gave him a copy of the written decree for their destruction which had been posted up in Susa, to show to Esther; and he gave him a message for her, that she should go to the king and plead for his favour and entreat him for her people. 'Remember', he said, 'those days when you were brought up in my humble home; for Haman, who stands next to the king, has spoken against us and demanded our death. Call upon the Lord, and

then speak for us to the king and save our lives.' Hachrathaeus returned and 9 told her what Mardochaeus had said. She sent him back with this message: 10 'All nations of the empire know that if 11 any person, man or woman, enters the king's presence in the inner court unbidden, there is no escape for him. Only one to whom the king stretches out the golden sceptre is safe; and it is now thirty days since I myself was called to go to the king.'

When Hachrathaeus delivered her 12 message, Mardochaeus told him to go 13 back and say: 'Do not imagine, Esther, that you alone of all the Jews in the empire will escape alive. For if you re- 14 main silent at such a time as this, the Jews will somewhere find relief and deliverance, but you and your father's family will perish. Who knows whether it is not for such a time as this that you have been made a queen?' Esther gave 15 the messenger this answer to take back to Mardochaeus: 'Go and assemble all 16 the Jews who are in Susa and fast for me; for three days take neither food nor drink, night or day, and I and my maids will also go without food. Then in defiance of the law I will enter the king's presence, even if it costs me my life.' So Mardochaeus went away and did as 17 Esther had bidden him.]

AND MARDOCHAEUS PRAYED TO THE 13 8 Lord, calling to mind all the works of the Lord. He said, 'O Lord, Lord and 9 King who rulest over all, because the whole world is under thy authority, and when it is thy will to save Israel there is no one who can stand against thee: thou didst make heaven and earth 10 and every wonderful thing under heaven; thou art Lord of all, and there 11

c Some witnesses add (6) So he went out to Mardochaeus in the street opposite the city gate.

3.15: *The King and Haman caroused together.* This was surely the height of Haman's triumph.
4.1–17: Esther is asked to plead for her kinsfolk. 1: *Tore his clothes:* sign of consternation; see 2 Kgs.5.7; Mt.26.65. *Sackcloth and ... ashes:* signs of grief. **4:** Not knowing the reason for his grief, Esther *sent clothes for Mardochaeus.* **11:** Entrance without being summoned was considered a hostile action; also compare 2.14. **14:** The author is certain that Esther's good fortune is for providential reasons. Mardochaeus' exhortation is directed to all the more fortunate Jews in exile who might forget their responsibility for less fortunate compatriots.
13.8–18: Mardochaeus' prayer. The Hebrew account never mentions the name of God. The Greek additions furnish a religious dimension. **9:** The universal *authority* of God was a primary tenet of Israelite faith in the postexilic period when history seemed beyond divine plan and

A plot against the Jews

is no one who can resist thee, the Lord.
12 Thou knowest all things; thou knowest,
Lord, that it was not from insolence or
arrogance or vainglory that I refused to
13 bow before proud Haman, for I could
gladly have kissed the soles of his feet
14 to save Israel; no, I did it so that I
might not hold a man in greater honour
than God; I will not bow before any
but thee, my Lord, and it is not from
arrogance that I refuse this homage.
15 And now Lord, God and King, God of
Abraham, spare thy people; for our
enemies are watching us to bring us to
ruin, and they have set their hearts upon
the destruction of thy chosen people,
16 thine from the beginning. Do not dis-
dain thy own possession which thou
didst ransom for thyself out of Egypt.
17 Hear my prayer, and have mercy on
thy heritage, and turn our mourning
into feasting, that we may live and sing
of thy name, Lord; do not put to silence
18 the lips that give thee praise.' And all
Israel cried aloud with all their might,
for death stared them in the face.

14 Then Queen Esther, caught up in
this deadly conflict,*d* took refuge in the
2 Lord. She stripped off her splendid
attire and put on the garb of mourning
and distress. Instead of proud perfumes
she strewed ashes and dung over her
head. She abased her body, and every
part that she had delightfully adorned
she covered with her dishevelled hair.
3 And so she prayed to the Lord God of
Israel:

'O my Lord, thou alone art our king;
help me who am alone, with no helper
4 but thee; for I am taking my life in my
5 hands. Ever since I was born I have
been taught by my father's family and
tribe that thou, O Lord, didst choose
Israel out of all the nations, and out of
all the founders of our race didst choose
our fathers for an everlasting possession, and that what thou didst promise
6 them, thou didst perform. But now we
have sinned against thee, and thou hast

handed us over to our enemies because 7
we honoured their gods; thou art just,
O Lord. But they are not content with 8
our bitter servitude; they have now
pledged themselves to their idols to 9
annul thy decree and to destroy thy
possession, silencing those who praise
thee, extinguishing the glory of thy
house, and casting down thy altar. They 10
would give the heathen cause to sing
the praises of their worthless gods, and
would have a mortal king held in everlasting honour.

'Yield not thy sceptre, O Lord, to 11
gods that are nothing; let not our
enemies mock at our ruin, but turn
their plot against themselves, and make
an example of the man who planned it.
Remember us, O Lord, make thy power 12
known in the time of our distress, and
give me courage, O King of gods, almighty Lord. Give me the apt word to 13
say when I enter the lion's den. Divert
his hatred to our enemy, so that there
may be an end of him and his confederates.

'Save us by thy power, and help me 14
who am alone and have no helper but
thee, Lord. Thou knowest all; thou 15
knowest that I hate the splendour of
the heathen, I abhor the bed of the
uncircumcised or of any Gentile. Thou 16
knowest in what straits I am: I loathe
that symbol of pride, the headdress that
I wear when I show myself abroad, I
loathe it as one loathes a filthy rag; in
private I refuse to wear it. I, thy servant, 17
have not eaten at Haman's table; I have
not graced a banquet of the king or
touched the wine of his drink-offerings;
I have not known festive joy from the 18
time that I was brought here until now
except in thee, Lord God of Abraham.
O God who dost prevail against all, 19
give heed to the cry of the despairing:
rescue us from the power of wicked
men, and rescue me from what I dread.'

---

d caught . . . conflict: *or* seized by mortal anxiety.

control. **12–14**: The story does not support such pure motivation on the part of Mardochaeus
(see 3.2 n.). **16**: The ultimate basis for Israel's confidence is God's free choice of her, as expressed
in the liberation from Egyptian bondage.
  14.1–19: Esther's prayer. 5: *Our fathers*: the sons of Jacob who established the twelve tribes
of Israel. **9**: Even if Israel deserves to be punished (v. 6), God cannot permit the foreign *idols*
to claim victory (see v. 11). **13**: *Lion's den*: the king's presence. **15–18**: *Hate the splendour*: an
exaggeration to underline her identification with the plight of Israel.

15 ON THE THIRD DAY ESTHER BROUGHT her prayers to an end. She took off the clothes she had worn while she worshipped and put on all her splendour.
2 When she was in her royal robes and had invoked the all-seeing God, her preserver, she took two maids with her;
3 on one she leaned for support, as be-
4 fitted a fine lady, while the other
5 followed, bearing her train. She was blushing and in the height of her beauty; her face was as cheerful as it was lovely, but her heart was in the grip
6 of fear. She passed through all the doors and reached the royal presence. The king was seated on his throne, in the full array of his majesty. He was all gold and precious stones, an awe-
7 inspiring figure. He looked up, his face glowing with regal dignity, and glanced at her in towering anger. The queen fell, changing colour in a faint, and swooning on the shoulder of the maid who went before her.
8 Then God changed the spirit of the king to gentleness, and in deep concern he leapt from his throne and took her in his arms until she came to herself. He soothed her with reassuring words:
9 'Esther, what is it? Have no fear of me,
10 your loving husband; you shall not die, for our order is only for our subjects.
11 Come to me.' And the king lifted his golden sceptre and laid it upon her
12 neck; then he kissed her and said, 'You
13 may speak to me.' She answered, 'I saw you, my lord, looking like an angel of God, and I was awestruck at your
14 glorious appearance; your countenance is so full of grace, my lord, that I look
15 on you in wonder.' But while she was
16 speaking she fell down in a faint; the king was distressed, and all his attendants comforted her.
5 3   [Then the king said, 'What is your wish, Queen Esther? What is your request? Up to half my empire, it shall be given you.' 'Today is a special day 4 for me', said Esther. 'If it please your majesty, will you come, and Haman with you, to a banquet which I shall give today?' The king ordered Haman 5 to be sent for in haste, so that Esther's wish might be fulfilled; and they both went to the banquet to which Esther had invited them. Over the wine the 6 king said to her, 'What is it, Queen Esther? Whatever you ask for shall be yours.' Esther said, 'This is my humble 7 request: if I have won your majesty's 8 favour, will your majesty and Haman come again tomorrow to the banquet which I shall give for you both, and tomorrow I will do as I have done today.'

So Haman went out from the royal 9 presence in good spirits and well pleased with himself. But when he saw Mardochaeus the Jew in the king's courtyard, he was filled with rage. He 10 went home, and called for his friends and his wife Zosara, and held forth to 11 them about his wealth and the honours with which the king had invested him, how he had made him first man in the empire. 'Queen Esther', he said, 'invited 12 no one but myself to accompany the king to her banquet; and I am invited again for tomorrow. Yet all this is no 13 pleasure to me so long as I see that Jew Mardochaeus in the courtyard.' Then 14 his wife Zosara and his friends said to him: 'Have a gallows put up, seventy-five feet*e* high, and in the morning speak to the king and have Mardochaeus hanged upon it. Then you can go with the king to the banquet and enjoy yourself.' Haman thought this an excellent plan, and the gallows was made ready.

e Gk. fifty cubits.

15.1–7: Esther dares to go to the king without being summoned. 3: Esther, knowing that her only chance before the powerful king was in a display of fear and weakness, *leaned for support.* **7:** *Towering anger:* this is explained in 4.11; it serves to heighten Esther's noble but risky intervention.

15.8–16: The king receives Esther graciously. 11: *Laid it upon her neck:* a sign of royal protection or forgiveness.

5.3–8: Esther's first banquet for the king and Haman. 4: A *banquet* is the special staging for Esther's request, serving the literary purpose of suspense. See v. 8.

5.9–14: Haman prepares a gallows for Mardochaeus. 9: *Haman* (like the Gentiles generally) was disturbed when he *saw* the "otherness" of *Mardochaeus* (the Jews). **14:** The completely unnecessary height of the *gallows* (*seventy-five feet*) is for literary effect and not meant to be taken literally.

6 THAT NIGHT THE LORD KEPT SLEEP from the king, so he ordered his private secretary to bring the court chronicle 2 and read it to him. He found written there the record about Mardochaeus, how he had given information about the two royal eunuchs who, while they were on guard, had plotted violence 3 against King Artaxerxes. Whereupon the king said, 'What honour or favour did we confer on Mardochaeus for this?' The king's courtiers who were in attendance replied, 'You have done 4 nothing for him.' While the king was inquiring about the service that Mardochaeus had rendered, Haman appeared in the courtyard. 'Who is that in the court?' asked the king. Now Haman had just come in to recommend to the king that Mardochaeus should be hanged on the gallows which he had 5 prepared; so the king's servants said, 'It is Haman standing in the court.' 6 'Call him', said the king. Then the king said to Haman, 'What shall I do for the man I wish to honour?' Haman said to himself, 'Whom would the king wish 7 to honour but me?' So he said to the king, 'For the man whom the king 8 wishes to honour, let the king's attendants bring a robe of fine linen from the king's own wardrobe and a horse 9 from the king's own stable. Let both be delivered to one of the king's most honourable Friends, and let him robe the man whom the king loves and mount him on the horse, and let him proclaim through the city: "This shall be the lot of any man whom the king 10 honours."' Then the king said to Haman, 'An excellent suggestion! Do all this for Mardochaeus the Jew who serves in the courtyard. Let nothing 11 that you have said be omitted.' So Haman took the robe and put it on Mardochaeus, and mounted him on the horse; then he went through the city, proclaiming: 'This shall be the lot

of any man whom the king wishes to honour.'

Then Mardochaeus returned to the 12 courtyard, and Haman hurried off home with head veiled in mourning. He told his wife Zosara and his friends 13 what had happened to him. They replied, 'If Mardochaeus is a Jew, and you have been humiliated before him, you are a lost man. You cannot get the better of him, because the living God is on his side.'

While they were still talking with 14 Haman, the king's eunuchs arrived and hurried him away to the banquet which Esther had prepared.

So the king and Haman went to the 7 queen's banquet. Again on that second 2 day, over the wine, the king said, 'What is it, Queen Esther? What is your request? What is your petition? You shall have it, up to half my empire.' Queen Esther answered: 'If I 3 have won your majesty's favour, my request is for my life, my petition is for my people. For it has come to my ears 4 that we have been sold, I and my people, to be destroyed, plundered, and enslaved, we and our children, male and female. Our adversary is a disgrace to the king's court.' The king said, 5 'Who is it that has dared to do such a thing?' 'Our enemy', said Esther, 'is this 6 wicked Haman.' Haman stood dumbfounded before the king and the queen. The king rose from the banquet and 7 went into the garden, and Haman began to plead with the queen, for he saw that things were going badly for him. When the king returned to the 8 banqueting hall from the garden, Haman in his entreaties had flung himself across the queen's couch. The king exclaimed, 'What! You assault the queen in my own house?' At those words Haman turned away in despair. Then Bugathan, one of the eunuchs, 9 said to the king, 'Look! Haman has even prepared a gallows for Mardochaeus, the man who reported the plot

---

6.1–11.1: **The intended fate of the Jews falls on their persecutors.**
6.1–14: **Mardochaeus is exalted and Haman is humiliated. 3:** *Nothing for him:* but see 12.5.
4: *Haman had just come in:* a coincidence dear to folklore. 13: *God . . . on his side:* recognition by Haman's friends that Providence has taken over.
7.1–10: **The second banquet results in Haman's death. 6:** Haman is *dumbfounded*, not knowing that Esther is a Jewess.

against the king, and there it stands, seventy five feet[f] high, in Haman's compound.' 'Have Haman hanged on
10 it', said the king. So Haman was hanged on the gallows that he himself had prepared for Mardochaeus. After that the king's rage died down.

8 That day King Artaxerxes gave Esther all that had belonged to Haman the persecutor; and Mardochaeus was called into the king's presence, for Esther had told him how he was related
2 to her. Then the king took off his signet-ring, which he had taken back from Haman, and gave it to Mardochaeus. And Esther put Mardochaeus in charge of Haman's estate.

3 Once again Esther spoke before the king, falling at his feet and pleading with him to avert the calamity planned by Haman and to frustrate his plot
4 against the Jews. The king stretched out the golden sceptre to Esther, and she rose and stood before the king.
5 'May it please your majesty,' she said; 'If I have won your favour, let an order be issued recalling the letters which Haman sent in pursuance of his plan to destroy the Jews in your empire.
6 How can I bear to see the downfall of my people? How escape myself when
7 my country is destroyed?' Then the king said to Esther: 'I have given Haman's property to you, and hanged him on the gallows because he threat-
8 ened the lives of the Jews. If you want anything further, you may draw up an order in my name, in whatever terms you think fit, and seal it with my signet. An order written at the king's direction and sealed with the royal signet cannot be contravened.'

9 And so, on the twenty-third day of the first month, Nisan, in the same year, the king's secretaries were summoned; and the Jews were informed in writing of the instructions given to the administrators and chief governors in the provinces, from India to Ethiopia, a hundred and twenty-seven provinces, to each province in its own language.
10 The orders were written as from the king and sealed with his signet, and
11 dispatched by courier. By these documents the king granted permission to the Jews in every city to observe their own laws and to defend themselves, and to deal as they would with their opponents and enemies, throughout
12 the empire of Artaxerxes, on a given day, the thirteenth of the twelfth month, Adar.]

THE FOLLOWING IS A COPY OF THIS **16** letter:

Artaxerxes the Great King to the governors of the one hundred and twenty-seven provinces, from India to Ethiopia, and to those who are of our allegiance, greeting.
2 Many who have been honoured only too often by the lavish generosity of their benefactors have
3 grown arrogant and not only attempt to ill-treat our subjects but, unable to carry the favours heaped upon themselves, even plot mischief
4 against those who grant them. Not content with destroying gratitude in men, they are carried away by the insolence of those who are strangers to good breeding; they even suppose that they will escape the justice of all-seeing God, who is no friend to
5 evil-doers. And often, when the king's business has been entrusted to those he counts his friends, they have, by their plausibility, made those in supreme authority partners in shedding innocent blood and involved them in irreparable mis-
6 fortunes, for their malevolence with its misleading sophistries has imposed upon the sincere goodwill of
7 their rulers. The evil brought about by those who wield power unworthily you can observe, not only in records of tradition and history but
8 also in your familiar experience, and apply the lesson to the future. Thus we shall peacefully free this realm

---

f Gk. fifty cubits.

8.1–12: Esther persuades the king to nullify his edict against the Jews. 2: With the *signet-ring* Mardochaeus receives the office of prime minister vacated by Haman's death. **12:** *The thirteenth of . . . Adar:* the date when the extermination of the Jews was to have taken place (3.7, 13).
    16.1–24; 8.13–17: The king's letter brings joy to the Jews. 5–6: The king attributes his mistake

from disturbance for the benefit of
9 all, making no changes but always
deciding matters which come under
our notice with firmness and equity.
10 Now Haman son of Hamadathus, a
Macedonian, an alien in fact with
no Persian blood, a man with nothing
of our kindly nature,*g* was accepted
11 by us and enjoyed*h* so fully the
benevolence with which we treat
every nation that he was proclaimed
our Father, and all along received
obeisance from everyone as second
12 only to our royal throne. But this
man in his unbridled arrogance
planned to deprive us of our empire
13 and our life by using fraud and
tortuous cunning to bring about the
destruction of Mardochaeus, our
constant benefactor who had saved
our life, and of Esther, our blameless
consort, together with their whole
14 nation. For he thought that by these
methods he would catch us defenceless and would transfer to the Macedonians the sovereignty now held by
15 the Persians. But we find that the
Jews, whom this triple-dyed villain
had consigned to extinction, are no
evil-doers; they order their lives by
16 the most just of laws, and are children
of the living God, most high, most
mighty, who maintains the empire
in most wonderful order, for us as
for our ancestors.
17 You will therefore disregard the
letters sent by Haman son of Hama-
18 dathus, because he, the contriver of
all this, has been hanged aloft at the
gate of Susa with his whole household, God who is Lord of all having
speedily brought upon him the
19 punishment that he deserved. Copies
of this letter are to be posted up in
all public places. Permit the Jews to
20 live under their own laws, and give
them every assistance so that on the
thirteenth day of Adar, the twelfth
month, on that very day, they may
avenge themselves on those who
were ranged against them*i* in the
21 time of their oppression. For God,

who has all things in his power, has
made this a day not of ruin, but of
joy, for his chosen people. Therefore 22
you also must keep it with all good
cheer, as a notable day among your
feasts of commemoration, so that 23
henceforth it may be a standing
symbol of deliverance to us and our
loyal Persians, but a reminder of
destruction to those who plot against
us. Any city or country whatsoever 24
which does not act upon these orders
shall incur our wrath and be wiped
out with fire and sword. No man shall
set foot in it and even the beasts and
birds shall shun it for all time.

[Let copies be posted up con- **8** *13*
spicuously throughout the empire,
so that the Jews may be prepared by
that day to fight against their enemies.

Mounted messengers set out with all *14*
speed to do what the king commanded;
and the decree was posted up also in
Susa.
Mardochaeus left the king's presence *15*
in royal robes, wearing a golden crown
and a turban of fine linen dyed purple,
and all in Susa rejoiced to see him. For *16*
the Jews there was light and gladness in *17*
every province and every city. Wherever
the decree was posted up there was joy
and gladness for the Jews, feasting and
merriment. And many of the Gentiles
were circumcised and professed Judaism, because they were afraid of the
Jews.

ON THE THIRTEENTH DAY OF THE **9**
twelfth month, Adar, the decree drawn
up by the king arrived. On that very
day the enemies of the Jews perished.
No one offered resistance, because they *2*
were afraid of them. The leading pro- *3*
vincial governors, the princes, and the
royal secretaries paid all respect to
the Jews, because fear of Mardochaeus
weighed upon them. For they had *4*
received the king's decree that his name
should be honoured throughout the

g Or a man fallen away greatly from our favour.
h Or won.
i Or may defend themselves against their assailants.

to *misleading* advice from *friends.* **10**: *Macedonian:* see 12.6 n. Haman is called a Macedonian,
a word synonymous with "enemy of the state." **12**: *Our empire:* an excessive charge not supported by the facts. **21**: The reversal of *ruin* into *joy* is an apocalyptic theme in late OT writings.
9.1–19: The Jews take vengeance on their enemies and establish a holiday. 1: *Thirteenth day:*

6 empire.*jk* In the city itself the Jews
7 slaughtered five hundred men, including
8 Pharsanestan, Delphon, Phasga, Phara-
9 datha, Barsa, Sarbacha, Marmasima,
Ruphaeus, Arsaeus, and Zabuthaeus,
10 the ten sons of Haman son of Hamadathus, the Bugaean, the Jews' great
enemy; and that day they took plunder.
11 When the number of those killed in
12 Susa was reported to the king, he said
to Esther, 'In the city of Susa the Jews
have killed five hundred men. What do
you suppose they have done in the
surrounding country? Whatever further
request you have will be granted.'
13 Esther answered him, 'Let the Jews be
allowed to do the same tomorrow, and
hang up the bodies of Haman's ten
14 sons.' The king consented; he handed
over the bodies of Haman's sons to the
15 Jews of the city to be hung up. The
Jews in Susa assembled on the fourteenth day of Adar also, and killed
three hundred, but they took no
plunder.
16–17 The rest of the Jews in the empire
rallied together in self-defence, and so
were quit of their enemies; for they
slaughtered fifteen thousand of them
on the thirteenth of Adar; but they
took no plunder. On the fourteenth
they rested, and made that day a day
of rest, with rejoicing and merriment.
18 The Jews in the city of Susa had assembled also on the fourteenth day of
the month; they did not rest on that
day, but they kept the fifteenth day with
19 rejoicing and merriment. That is why
Jews who are dispersed over the re-
moter parts keep the fourteenth day of
Adar as a holiday with rejoicing and
merriment, sending presents of food to
one another; but those who live in the
principal cities keep the fifteenth of
Adar as a holiday, sending presents
of food to one another.
20 Then Mardochaeus wrote down the
whole story in a book and sent it to all
the Jews in the empire of Artaxerxes,
21 far and near, ordering them to establish

these holidays, and to keep the fourteenth and fifteenth of Adar, because 22
these were the days on which the Jews
were quit of their enemies, and to
keep the whole month of Adar, in
which came the great change from
sorrow to joy and from mourning to
holiday, as a time for feasting and
merriment, days for sending presents of
food to friends and to the poor.
So the Jews formally accepted the 23
account which Mardochaeus wrote:
how Haman son of Hamadathus, the 24
Bugaean,*l* fought against them; how he
cast lots to decide the date of their
destruction; how he came before the 25
king with a proposal to hang Mardochaeus; and how all the evils which he
had plotted against the Jews recoiled
on his own head, and he and his sons
were hanged. This is why these days 26
were named 'Purim', which in the
Jews' language means 'lots'. Because
of all that was recorded in this letter—
all that they had experienced, all that
had happened—Mardochaeus directed
that this festival should be observed,
and the Jews undertook, on behalf of 27
themselves, their descendants, and all
who should join them, to do so without
fail. These were to be days of com- 28
memoration, duly celebrated age after
age in every town, family, and province.
These days of Purim were to be kept
for all time, and the commemoration
was never to cease throughout all ages.
Queen Esther daughter of Amina- 29
dab, and Mardochaeus the Jew, recorded in writing all that they had done,
and confirmed the regulations for
Purim. They made themselves respon- 30–31
sible for this decision and staked their
life upon the plan.*m* Esther established 32
it for all time by her decree, and it was
put on record.

j For they . . . empire: *probable reading; Gk. obscure.*
k Some witnesses add *from the Heb.* (5) So the Jews
put their enemies to the sword with great slaughter
and destruction; they worked their will on those who
hated them.
l Some witnesses read *the Macedonian.*
m They made . . . plan: *possible meaning; Gk. obscure.*

---

see 8.12 n. **11–15**: This is to explain why the urban Jews observed Purim for two days instead
of the usual one; see v. 19.
  9.20–10.3: Mardochaeus records the event; the Feast of Purim. 22: This feast celebrates the
Israelite conviction that the *sorrow* of oppression in all ages will be turned into *joy* through
God's fidelity to his promises. **26:** *Purim:* see 3.7 n. **32:** This insistence on authoritative establishment of the feast by Esther's *decree* suggests that its propriety was being questioned.

10 The king made decrees for the empire by land and sea. His strength and courage, his wealth and the splendour of his empire, are recorded in the annals of the kings of the Persians
3 and Medes. Mardochaeus acted for King Artaxerxes; he was a great man in the empire and honoured by the Jews. His way of life won him the affection of his whole nation.]

4 MARDOCHAEUS SAID, 'ALL THIS IS
5 God's doing. For I have been reminded of the dream I had about these things; not one of the visions I saw proved
6 meaningless. There was the little spring which became a river, and there was light and sun and water in abundance. The river is Esther, whom the king
7 married and made queen; the two
8 dragons are Haman and myself; the nations are those who gathered to wipe
9 out the Jews; my nation is Israel, which cried aloud to God and was delivered. The Lord has delivered his people, he has rescued us from all these evils. God performed great miracles and signs such as have not occurred among the nations. He made ready 10 two lots, one for the people of God and one for all the nations; then came the 11 hour and the time for these two lots to be cast, the day of decision by God before*ⁿ* all the nations; he remembered 12 his people and gave the verdict for his heritage.

'So they shall keep these days in the 13 month of Adar, the fourteenth and fifteenth of that month, by gathering with joy and gladness before God from one generation of his people to another, for ever.'

IN THE FOURTH YEAR OF THE REIGN OF 11 1 Ptolemy and Cleopatra, Dositheus, who said that he was a levitical priest, and Ptolemaeus his son, brought the foregoing letter about Purim, which they said was authentic and had been translated by Lysimachus son of Ptolemaeus, a resident in Jerusalem.

n Or the day of judgement by God upon . . .

10.4–13: Mardochaeus interprets his dream. 6–7: see 11.5–11 n. **10–12:** Another interpretation of Purim is that men seem to control history, but God casts the decisive *lots*.

11.1: The translation of the Book of Esther. 1: *Fourth year:* probably 114 B.C. *Letter:* the Book of Esther as a whole.

THE WISDOM OF
SOLOMON

The author of Wisdom purports to be King Solomon (9.8), but this ascription was regarded as a literary fiction by both Origen (182–251 A.D.) and Jerome (about 340–420). Rather, the author was an Alexandrian Jew, well read in his own tradition and in Greek thought, who wrote in Greek. He used the Septuagint translation of the Bible, completed in the second century B.C., but he was unacquainted with the ideas of Philo (20 B.C.–40 A.D.), possibly indicating that he wrote in the first century B.C. His hatred of the Egyptians suggests that he lived soon after the persecution of Egyptian Jewry by Ptolemy VII Physcon, about 100 B.C.

Biblical Wisdom literature is the source of many ideas in the book, and biblical poetry, with its parallel clauses, the model of its style (at least in the first sections). The review of Israel's history is embellished by expansions, many of which are found in late Jewish literature.

Under the impact of the cosmopolitan culture and a variety of philosophies and mystery religions of the Hellenistic world, the faith of many Jews was shaken. Moreover, as a result of the persecution, the perennial problem of the wicked prospering and the good suffering rose to a crisis level.

The author, denouncing the Jewish skeptics of his day who have forsaken inherited beliefs and practices, seeks to safeguard the faith of the rest of his coreligionists. He does so by proposing a religious philosophy of history (chs. 10–12; 16–19), by a clear affirmation of reward and punishment after death (chs. 1–5), and by identifying Wisdom with the traditional spirit of the Lord (1.4–7; 7.22–25); he is aided by the Platonic distinction of body from soul and the Greek ideas of providence (6.7; 14.3), conscience (17.11), and the cardinal virtues (8.7). He uses his synthesis to appeal also to the pagans to examine Judaism as a valid Wisdom and a way of life (1.1–2; 10.15–11.14).

The promise of immortality

1 LOVE JUSTICE, YOU RULERS OF THE earth; set your mind upon the Lord, as is your duty, and seek 2 him in simplicity of heart; for he is found by those who trust him without question, and makes himself known to 3 those who never doubt him. Dishonest thinking cuts men off from God, and if fools will take liberties with his power, he shows them up for what they are. 4 Wisdom will not enter a shifty soul, nor make her home in a body that is 5 mortgaged to sin. This holy spirit of discipline will have nothing to do with falsehood; she cannot stay in the presence of unreason, and will throw up her case at the approach of injustice.

Wisdom is a spirit devoted to man's 6 good, and she will not hold a blasphemer blameless for his words, because God is a witness of his inmost being, who sees clear into his heart and hears every word he says. For the spirit 7 of the Lord fills the whole earth, and that which holds all things together is well aware of what men say. Hence no 8 man can utter injustice and not be found out, nor will justice overlook him when she passes sentence. The devices 9 of a godless man will be brought to account, and a report of his words will come before the Lord as proof of his iniquity; no muttered syllable escapes 10 that vigilant ear. Beware, then, of futile 11 grumbling, and avoid all bitter words; for even a secret whisper will not go

1.1–5.23: God rewards the righteous and punishes the ungodly.
1.1–11: Wisdom, the key to immortality, is incompatible with deceit. 1: *Rulers of the earth:* lit. rulers in general; compare 6.1. But the real addressees were Alexandrian Jews. 4: Here and in subsequent passages (7.25–26), *Wisdom* attains the highest personification in the Bible. 5: *Discipline* in Wisdom Literature means religious instruction and correction. 6. *Inmost being:* lit. "kidneys," considered as the center of emotion and instinct. *Heart:* the center of intellect and will. Together they signify all man's inner forces. 7: The fact that God's spirit *fills the earth* guarantees the assertion in v. 6 that God knows and will punish all transgressions. Spirit is identified with Wisdom; compare Col.1.17; Heb.1.3.

unheeded, and a lying tongue is a man's 12 destruction. Do not stray from the path of life and so court death; do not draw disaster on yourselves by your 13 own actions. For God did not make death, and takes no pleasure in the 14 destruction of any living thing; he created all things that they might have being. The creative forces of the world make for life; there is no deadly poison in them. Death is not king on earth. 15,16 for justice is immortal; but godless men by their words and deeds have asked death for his company. Thinking him their friend, they have made a pact with him because they are fit members of his party; and so they have wasted away.

2 They said to themselves in their deluded way: 'Our life is short and full of trouble, and when a man comes to his end there is no remedy; no man was ever known to return from the grave. 2 By mere chance were we born, and afterwards we shall be as though we had never been, for the breath in our nostrils is but a wisp of smoke; our reason is a mere spark kept alive by the 3 beating of our hearts, and when that goes out, our body will turn to ashes and the breath of our life disperse like 4 empty air. Our names will be forgotten with the passing of time, and no one will remember anything we did. Our life will blow over like the last vestige of a cloud; and as a mist is chased away by the sun's rays and overborne by its 5 heat, so will it too be dispersed. A passing shadow—such is our life, and there is no postponement of our end; man's fate is sealed, and none returns. 6 Come then, let us enjoy the good things while we can, and make full use of the creation, with all the eagerness of 7 youth. Let us have costly wines and perfumes to our heart's content, and 8 let no flower of spring escape us. Let us

crown ourselves with rosebuds before they can wither. Let none of us miss 9 his share of the good things that are ours; who cares what traces our revelry leaves behind? This is the life for us; it is our birthright.

'Down with the poor and honest 10 man! Let us tread him under foot; let us show no mercy to the widow and no reverence to the grey hairs of old age. For us let might be right! Weak- 11 ness is proved to be good for nothing. Let us lay a trap for the just man; he 12 stands in our way, a check to us at every turn; he girds at us as law-breakers, and calls us traitors to our upbringing. He knows God, so he 13 says; he styles himself "the servant[a] of the Lord". He is a living condemna- 14 tion of all our ideas. The very sight of 15 him is an affliction to us, because his life is not like other people's, and his ways are different. He rejects us like 16 base coin, and avoids us and our ways as if we were filth; he says that the just die happy, and boasts that God is his father. Let us test the truth of his 17 words, let us see what will happen to him in the end; for if the just man is 18 God's son, God will stretch out a hand to him and save him from the clutches of his enemies. Outrage and torment 19 are the means to try him with, to measure his forbearance and learn how long his patience lasts. Let us 20 condemn him to a shameful death, for on his own showing he will have a protector.'

So they argued, and very wrong they 21 were; blinded by their own malev-olence, they did not understand God's 22 hidden plan; they never expected that holiness of life would have its recom-pense; they thought that innocence had no reward. But God created man 23 for immortality, and made him the
a Or child.

1.12–16: God made man immortal. 13: See 2.23–24 and Ezek.33.11. 16: *Godless men* are renegade Jews, the author's real opponents, for whom life is completely this-worldly, ended by *death*. See Isa.28.15 for the image of a "pact" with death.

2.1–20: Philosophy of the deluded sinners and its consequences. 2–3: The explanations of life are derived from the science of the author's day. 4: Since *no one will remember*, there is no difference whether one is good or evil. Compare Eccles.2.24; 3.12; 9.7–9. 10–12: The sinners' attitude toward the precepts of Judaism is slightly caricatured for the sake of emphasis. 15: The charge that the *ways* of the Jews were *different* was common in antiquity; compare Esther 3.8. 18: *God's son:* Ps.22.8–9 is the common source of this verse and of Mt.27.43.

2.21–24: Causes of the sinners' misconceptions. Wickedness leads to illogic. 23: See Gen.1.26.

image of his own eternal self; it was
24 the devil's spite that brought death
into the world, and the experience of
it is reserved for those who take his side.
3   But the souls of the just are in God's
hand, and torment shall not touch
2 them. In the eyes of foolish men they
seemed to be dead; their departure was
3 reckoned as defeat, and their going
from us disaster. But they are at peace,
4 for though in the sight of men they
may be punished, they have a sure
5 hope of immortality; and after a little
chastisement they will receive great
blessings, because God has tested them
6 and found them worthy to be his. Like
gold in a crucible he put them to the
proof, and found them acceptable
like an offering burnt whole upon the
7 altar. In the moment of God's coming
to them they will kindle into flame,
like sparks that sweep through stubble;
8 they will be judges and rulers over the
nations of the world, and the Lord
shall be their king for ever and ever.
9 Those who have put their trust in him
shall understand that he is true, and the
faithful shall attend upon him in love;
they are his chosen, and grace and
mercy shall be theirs.
10   But the godless shall meet with the
punishment their evil thoughts deserve,
because they took no account of
justice and rebelled against the Lord.
11 Wretched indeed is he who thinks
nothing of wisdom and discipline; such
men's hopes are void, their labours
12 unprofitable, their actions futile; their
wives are frivolous, their children
13 criminal, their parenthood is under a
curse. No, blessed is the childless
woman if she is innocent, if she has
never slept with a man in sin; at the

great assize of souls she shall find a
fruitfulness of her own. Blessed is the 14
eunuch, if he has never done anything
against the law and never harboured a
wicked thought against the Lord; he
shall receive special favour in return
for his faith, and a place in the Lord's
temple to delight his heart the more.
Honest work bears glorious fruit, and 15
wisdom grows from roots that are
imperishable. But the children of 16
adultery are like fruit that never ripens;
they have sprung from a lawless union,
and will come to nothing. Even if they 17
attain length of life, they will be of no
account, and at the end their old age
will be without honour. If they die 18
young, they will have no hope, no
consolation in the hour of judgement;
the unjust generation has a hard fate 19
in store for it.
    It is better to be childless, provided 4
one is virtuous; for virtue held in
remembrance is a kind of immortality,
because it wins recognition from God,
and from men too. They follow the 2
good man's example while it is with
them, and when it is gone they mourn
its loss; and through all time virtue
makes its triumphal progress, crowned
with victory in the contest for prizes
that nothing can tarnish. But the 3
swarming progeny of the wicked will
come to no good; none of their bastard
offshoots will strike deep root or take
firm hold. For a time their branches 4
may flourish, but as they have no sure
footing they will be shaken by the wind,
and by the violence of the winds uprooted. Their boughs will be snapped 5
off half-grown, and their fruit will be
worthless, unripe, uneatable, and good
for nothing. Children engendered in 6

24: *Devil's spite* alludes either to the fall of man (Gen. ch. 3) or to Cain and Abel (Gen. ch. 4).
    3.1–19: Rewards of the righteous and punishment of the ungodly. 4: The *immortality* reserved for
the righteous is of the soul (see v. 1); it is a Greek concept and supplants the Jewish resurrection
of the body (Dan.12.2). **5–6:** The righteous were only *tested* with *chastisement*, not punished;
compare Ps.66.10; 2 Macc.6.12–16. **7–8:** *God's coming* seems to allude to his definitive intervention in favor of the just, i.e. Israel, at the end of time. *Flame* and *sparks* in *stubble* are
images of victory; see Obad.18. **10:** The *punishment* will be appropriate to *their evil thoughts*
and not arbitrary. **13:** Traditional Jewish belief in large families (see Gen.30.23) is seemingly
abandoned. Perhaps the author means that sinful unions are so bad that even childlessness is
preferable; see 4.1. The *sin* may be the prohibited marriages of Jews to non-Jews. **14:** See Isa.
56.4–5. Whether the *Lord's temple* is in Jerusalem or heaven is unspecified. If the latter, it is one
of the first indications in the Bible of heaven as the dwelling of the godly.
    4.1–6: The true hierarchy of virtues. Compare Ecclus.16.3. **2:** *Virtue is crowned with victory*
like successful athletes at the Greek athletic games. **4–5:** Compare Pss.1.3–5; 92.13–15;
Ecclus.23.25.

unlawful union are living evidence of their parents' sin when God brings them to account.

7,8 But the good man, even if he dies an untimely death, will be at rest. For it is not length of life and number of years 9 which bring the honour due to age; if men have understanding, they have grey hairs enough, and an unspotted 10 life is the true ripeness of age. There was once such a man who pleased God, and God accepted him and took him while still living from among sinful 11 men. He was snatched away before his mind could be perverted by wickedness or his soul deceived by falsehood 12 (because evil is like witchcraft: it dims the radiance of good, and the waywardness of desire unsettles an innocent 13 mind); in a short time he came to the 14 perfection of a full span of years. His soul was pleasing to the Lord, who removed him early from a wicked 15 world. The mass of men see this and give it no thought; they do not lay to heart this truth, that those whom God has chosen enjoy his grace and mercy, and that he comes to the help of his 16 holy people. Even after his death the just man will shame the godless who are still alive; youth come quickly to perfection will shame the man grown 17 old in sin. Men will see the wise man's end, without understanding what the Lord had purposed for him and why 18 he took him into safe keeping; they will see it and make light of him, but it is they whom the Lord will laugh to scorn. In death their bodies will be dishonoured, and among the dead they will be an object of contempt for ever; 19 for he shall strike them speechless, fling them headlong, shake them from their foundations, and make an utter desert of them; they shall be full of anguish, and all memory of them shall 20 perish. So in the day of reckoning for their sins, they will come cringing, convicted to their face by their lawless doings.

5 Then the just man shall take his stand, full of assurance, to confront those who oppressed him and made 2 light of all his sufferings; at the sight of him there will be terror and confusion, and they will be beside themselves to see him so unexpectedly safe home. 3 Filled with remorse, groaning and gasping for breath, they will say among themselves: 'Was not this the man who was once our butt, a target for our con- 4 tempt? Fools that we were, we held his way of life to be madness and his end 5 dishonourable. To think that he is now counted one of the sons of God and assigned a place of his own among 6 God's people! How far we strayed from the road of truth! The lamp of justice never gave us light, the sun never rose 7 upon us. We roamed to our heart's content along the paths of wickedness and ruin, wandering through trackless deserts and ignoring the Lord's high- 8 way. What good has our pride done us? What can we show for all our 9 wealth and arrogance? All those things have passed by like a shadow, like a 10 messenger galloping by; like a ship that runs through the surging sea, and when she has passed, not a trace is to be found, no track of her keel among the 11 waves; or as when a bird flies through the air, there is no sign of her passing, but with the stroke of her pinions she lashes the insubstantial breeze and parts it with the whirr and the rush of her beating wings, and so she passes through it, and thereafter it bears no 12 mark of her assault; or as when an arrow is shot at a target, the air is parted and instantly closes up again and no one can tell where it passed 13 through. So we too ceased to be, as soon as we were born; we left no token of virtue behind, and in our wickedness 14 we frittered our lives away.' The hope of a godless man is like down flying on the wind, like spindrift swept before a storm and smoke which the wind whirls away, or like the memory of a guest who stayed for one day and passed on.

4.7–20: **The fate of the righteous and the ungodly contrasted. 10–11:** *Such a man:* Enoch *was snatched away* in this manner (Gen.5.21–24).

5.1–14: **Remorse of the ungodly.** This confession of the ungodly is in deliberate contrast with what they used to say; see 2.1–20. **5:** *Sons of God* is a poetic variant for *God's* own *people.* **9:** *Passed by like a shadow:* disappeared.

15 But the just live for ever; their reward is in the Lord's keeping, and the
16 Most High has them in his care. Therefore royal splendour shall be theirs, and a fair diadem from the Lord himself; he will protect them with his right hand
17 and shield them with his arm. He will put on from head to foot the armour of his wrath, and make all creation his
18 weapon against his enemies. With the cuirass of justice on his breast, and on his head the helmet of doom inflexible,
19 he will take holiness for his impene-
20 trable shield and sharpen his relentless anger for a sword; and his whole world shall join him in the fight against his
21 frenzied foes. The bolts of his lightning shall fly straight on the mark, they shall leap upon the target as if his bow in the
22 clouds were drawn in its full arc, and the artillery of his resentment shall let fly a fury of hail. The waters of the sea shall rage over them, and the rivers
23 wash them relentlessly away; a great tempest will arise against them, and blow them away like chaff before a whirlwind. So lawlessness will make the whole world desolate, and active wickedness will overturn the thrones of princes.

In praise of wisdom

6 HEAR THEN, YOU KINGS, TAKE THIS TO heart; learn your lesson, lords of the
2 wide world; lend your ears, you rulers of the multitude, whose pride is in the
3 myriads of your people. It is the Lord who gave you your authority; your power comes from the Most High. He will put your actions to the test and
4 scrutinize your intentions. Though you are viceroys of his kingly power, you have not been upright judges; you do not stand up for the law or guide your
5 steps by the will of God. Swiftly and terribly will he descend upon you, for

judgement falls relentlessly upon those in high place. The small man may find 6 pity and forgiveness, but the powerful will be called powerfully to account; for he who is all men's master is 7 obsequious to none, and is not overawed by greatness. Small and great alike are of his making, and all are under his providence equally, but it is 8 the powerful for whom he reserves the sternest inquisition. To you then who 9 have absolute power I speak, in hope that you may learn wisdom and not go astray; those who in holiness have kept 10 a holy course, will be accounted holy, and those who have learnt that lesson will be able to make their defence. Be 11 eager then to hear me, and long for my teaching; so you will learn.

Wisdom shines bright and never 12 fades; she is easily discerned by those who love her, and by those who seek her she is found. She is quick to make 13 herself known to those who desire knowledge of her; the man who rises 14 early in search of her will not grow weary in the quest, for he will find her seated at his door. To set all one's 15 thoughts on her is prudence in its perfect shape, and to lie wakeful in her cause is the short way to peace of mind. For she herself ranges in search 16 of those who are worthy of her; on their daily path she appears to them with kindly intent, and in all their purposes meets them half-way. The true 17 beginning of wisdom is the desire to learn, and a concern for learning means love towards her; the love of her means 18 the keeping of her laws; to keep her laws is a warrant of immortality; and 19 immortality brings a man near to God. Thus the desire of wisdom leads to 20 kingly stature. If, therefore, you value 21 your thrones and your sceptres, you rulers of the nations, you must honour wisdom, so that you may reign for ever.

5.15–23: Fate of the righteous and of the ungodly. 16: Compare Isa.62.3. **17–20:** Compare Ps.7.11–14; Isa.59.17. **21:** *Lightning* is a traditional representation of divine intervention; see Pss.18.14; 114.6.
6.1–9.18: The nature of Wisdom is explained.
6.1–11: Admonition to the rulers. 1: See 1.1 n. **4:** *Law:* compare 2.12. **6–8:** Not only is God *not overawed by greatness*, he is stricter in judging the mighty.
6.12–21: Wisdom desires to be found. Compare Prov.1.20–33; ch. 8. **17–21:** A chain argument called "sorites" of which the Stoics were fond, concludes that Wisdom is essential for rulers.

22 What wisdom is, and how she came into being, I will tell you; I will hide no secret from you. From her first beginnings I will trace out her course, and bring the knowledge of her into the light of day; I will not leave the truth 23 untold. Pale envy shall not travel in my company, for the spiteful man will have 24 no share in wisdom. Wise men in plenty are the world's salvation, and a prudent king is the sheet-anchor of his 25 people. Learn what I have to teach you, therefore, and it will be for your good.

7 I too am a mortal man like all the rest, descended from the first man, who 2 was made of dust, and in my mother's womb I was wrought into flesh during a ten-months space, compacted in blood from the seed of her husband and the pleasure that is joined with 3 sleep. When I was born, I breathed the common air and was laid on the earth that all men tread; and the first sound 4 I uttered, as all do, was a cry; they wrapped me up and nursed me and 5 cared for me. No king begins life in any 6 other way; for all come into life by a single path, and by a single path go out again.

7 Therefore I prayed, and prudence was given to me; I called for help, and 8 there came to me a spirit of wisdom. I valued her above sceptre and throne, and reckoned riches as nothing beside 9 her; I counted no precious stone her equal, because all the gold in the world compared with her is but a little sand, 10 and silver worth no more than clay. I loved her more than health and beauty; I preferred her to the light of day; for 11 her radiance is unsleeping. So all good things together came to me with her,

and in her hands was wealth past counting; and all was mine to enjoy, 12 for all follows where wisdom leads, and I was in ignorance before, that she is the beginning of it all. What I learnt 13 with pure intention I now share without grudging, nor do I hoard for myself the wealth that comes from her. She is 14 an inexhaustible treasure for mankind, and those who profit by it become God's friends, commended to him by the gifts they derive from her instruction.

God grant that I may speak accord- 15 ing to his will, and that my own thoughts may be worthy of his gifts; for even wisdom is under God's direc- tion and he corrects the wise; we and 16 our words, prudence and knowledge and craftsmanship, all are in his hand. He himself gave me true understanding 17 of things as they are: a knowledge of the structure of the world and the operation of the elements; the begin- 18 ning and end of epochs and their middle course; the alternating solstices and changing seasons; the cycles of the 19 years and the constellations; the nature 20 of living creatures and behaviour of wild beasts; the violent force of winds and the thoughts of men; the varieties of plants and the virtues of roots. I 21 learnt it all, hidden or manifest, for I 22 was taught by her whose skill made all things, wisdom.

For in wisdom there is a spirit intelli- gent and holy, unique in its kind yet made up of many parts, subtle, free- moving, lucid, spotless, clear, invul- nerable,[b] loving what is good, eager, unhindered, beneficent, kindly towards 23 men, steadfast, unerring, untouched by

b *invulnerable: or* working no harm.

6.22–25: **The true nature of Wisdom. 23:** Unlike the old philosophers or founders of mystery cults who hid their teachings out of *envy*, the author will reveal all.
7.1–6: **Wisdom is not inherited. 1:** Solomon, the wisest of men, was a *mortal* like the rest. **2:** *Ten* lunar *months* are nine calendar months. *Compacted in blood* alludes to the ancient view that the menstrual blood united with the sperm to form the fetus. **6:** *Single path* of entry and exit emphasizes the equality of all in the search for Wisdom; see Eccles.9.2.
7.7–14: **The values of Wisdom. 7:** Solomon *prayed* for Wisdom, a course open to all; see ch. 9. **11:** Solomon's *wealth* was as fabulous as his Wisdom; see 1 Kgs.3.13.
7.15–22a: **The extent of Wisdom.** The presentation is in scientific and philosophical terms; compare 1 Kgs.3.16–28; 5.7–12. **17:** *Things as they are:* metaphysics. *Structure of the world:* cosmology. *Elements:* the four elements of Greek science. **18–19:** *Beginning and end:* chronology. *Alternating . . . cycles:* astronomical knowledge. **20:** *Nature of living creatures:* zoology. *Thoughts of men:* psychology. *Varieties of plants:* botany. *Virtues of roots:* medicine and magic (compare Josephus, *Ant.* VIII.4.6).
7.22b–8.1: **Nature of Wisdom. 22b–23:** Wisdom has 3 × 7 (= 21, the most perfect number)

care, all-powerful, all-surveying, and permeating all intelligent, pure, and 21 delicate spirits. For wisdom moves more easily than motion itself, she pervades and permeates all things because 25 she is so pure. Like a fine mist she rises from the power of God, a pure effluence from the glory of the Almighty; so nothing defiled can enter into her by 26 stealth. She is the brightness that streams from[c] everlasting light, the flawless mirror of the active power of God and the image of his goodness. 27 She is but one, yet can do everything; herself unchanging, she makes all things new; age after age she enters into holy souls, and makes them God's 28 friends and prophets, for nothing is acceptable to God but the man who 29 makes his home with wisdom. She is more radiant than the sun, and surpasses every constellation; compared with the light of day, she is found to 30 excel; for day gives place to night, but against wisdom no evil can prevail. **8** She spans the world in power from end to end, and orders all things benignly.

2 Wisdom I loved; I sought her out when I was young and longed to win her for my bride, and I fell in love with 3 her beauty. She adds lustre to her noble birth, because it is given her to live with God, and the Lord of all things 4 has accepted her. She is initiated into the knowledge that belongs to God, and she decides for him what he shall 5 do. If riches are a prize to be desired in life, what is richer than wisdom, the 6 active cause of all things? If prudence shows itself in action, who more than 7 wisdom is the artificer of all that is? If virtue is the object of a man's affections, the fruits of wisdom's labours are the virtues; temperance and prudence, justice and fortitude, these are her

teaching, and in the life of men there is nothing of more value than these. If a 8 man longs, perhaps, for great experience, she knows the past, she can infer what is to come; she understands the subtleties of argument and the solving of problems, she can read signs and portents, and can foretell the outcome of events and periods. So I determined 9 to bring her home to live with me, knowing that she would be my counsellor in prosperity and my comfort in anxiety and grief. Through her, I 10 thought, I shall win fame in the eyes of the people and honour among older men, young though I am. When I sit in 11 judgement, I shall prove myself acute, and the great men will admire me; when I say nothing, they will wait for 12 me to speak; when I speak they will attend, and though I hold forth at length, they will lay a finger to their lips and listen. Through her I shall have 13 immortality, and shall leave an undying memory to those who come after me. I shall rule over many peoples, and 14 nations will become my subjects. Grim 15 tyrants will be frightened when they hear of me; among my own people I shall show myself a good king, and on the battlefield a brave one. When I 16 come home, I shall find rest with her; for there is no bitterness in her company, no pain in life with her, only gladness and joy.

I thought this over in my mind, and 17 I perceived that in kinship with wisdom lies immortality and in her friendship 18 is pure delight; that in doing her work is wealth that cannot fail, to be taught in her school gives understanding, and an honourable name is won by converse with her. So I went about in search of some way to win her for my own. As a 19

c *Or* She is the reflection of . . .

---

qualities, many of them Greek philosophical terms, some being divine attributes: *all-powerful, all-surveying*. **24:** Wisdom *pervades and permeates all things* like the spirit or world-soul of the Stoics. **26:** The relationship between Wisdom and God is described philosophically using the most immaterial images possible: *light, power, goodness*.

8.2–16: Solomon desires to take Wisdom as his bride. 3–4: The Lord himself *accepted* Wisdom as a bride; and she lives with him as his wife and *decides* the practicalities of life for him. **7:** The four virtues of Greek philosophy and the "cardinal virtues" of Christian morality—*temperance and prudence, justice and fortitude*—are founded on Wisdom. **8:** In the academic sphere Wisdom is central to *argument* (logic), *problems* (mathematics), *signs and portents* (religious insight), *events and periods* (history). **11:** See 1 Kgs.3.16–28. **12:** *Finger to lips:* a sign of silence in admiration of the speaker; see Job 29.9.

8.17–21: Solomon searches for Wisdom. 19–20: The preexistence of the soul is implied in *a*

20 child I was born to excellence, and a
noble soul fell to my lot; or rather, I
21 myself was noble, and I entered into an
unblemished body; but I saw that there
was no way to gain possession of her
except by gift of God—and it was a
mark of understanding to know from
whom that gift must come. So I pleaded
with the Lord, and from the depths of
my heart I prayed to him in these
words:

9 God of our fathers, merciful Lord,
who hast made all things by thy word,
2 and in thy wisdom hast fashioned man,
to be the master of thy whole creation,
3 and to be steward of the world in
holiness and righteousness, and to
administer justice with an upright
4 heart, give me wisdom, who sits beside
thy throne, and do not refuse me a
5 place among thy servants. I am thy
slave, thy slave-girl's son, a weak
ephemeral man, too feeble to under-
6 stand justice and law; for let a man be
ever so perfect in the eyes of his fellow-
men, if the wisdom that comes from
thee is wanting, he will be of no
7 account. Thou didst choose me to be
king of thy own people, and judge over
8 thy sons and daughters; thou didst tell
me to build a temple on thy sacred
mountain and an altar in the city
which is thy dwelling-place, a copy of
the sacred tabernacle prepared by thee
9 from the beginning. And with thee is
wisdom, who is familiar with thy works
and was present at the making of the
world by thee, who knows what is
acceptable to thee and in line with thy
10 commandments. Send her forth from
the holy heavens, and from thy glorious
throne bid her come down, so that she
may labour at my side and I may learn
11 what pleases thee. For she knows and
understands all things, and will guide

me prudently in all I do, and guard
me in her glory. So shall my life's work 12
be acceptable, and I shall judge thy
people justly, and be worthy of my
father's throne. For how can any man 13
learn what is God's plan? How can he
apprehend what the Lord's will is? The 14
reasoning of men is feeble, and our
plans are fallible; because a perishable 15
body weighs down the soul, and its
frame of clay burdens the mind so full
of thoughts. With difficulty we guess 16
even at things on earth, and laboriously
find out what lies before our feet; and
who has ever traced out what is in
heaven? Who ever learnt to know thy 17
purposes, unless thou hadst given
him wisdom and sent thy holy spirit
down from heaven on high? Thus it was 18
that those on earth were set upon the
right path, and men were taught what
pleases thee; thus were they preserved
by wisdom.

Divine wisdom in history

WISDOM IT WAS WHO KEPT GUARD OVER **10**
the first father of the human race, when
he alone had yet been made; she saved
him after his fall, and gave him the 2
strength to master all things. It was 3
because a wicked man forsook her in
his anger that he murdered his brother
in a fit of rage, and so destroyed himself. Through his fault the earth was 4
covered with a deluge, and again wisdom came to the rescue, and taught the
one good man to pilot his plain wooden
hulk. It was she, when heathen nations 5
leagued in wickedness were thrown into
confusion, who picked out one good
man and kept him blameless in the
sight of God, giving him strength to
resist his pity for his child. She saved a 6

---

noble soul fell to my lot; compare 9.15. The best that can be said for a body is that it is *un-blemished*. Both these doctrines are Platonic and foreign to the OT.
9.1–18: Solomon's prayer. Compare 1 Kgs.3.6–9. **4:** Compare Prov.8.30. **8:** The attribution of the book to Solomon is here clear in that the author claims to have built a *temple*; see 1 Kgs.6.1. The *sacred mountain* is Mount Zion, identified in Jewish tradition with Mount Moriah, the site of the Temple. The Temple was an earthly *copy* of the divine *tabernacle*, an idea derived from Exod.25.9,40. **15:** *Perishable body . . . of clay* alludes to the Platonic doctrine that the material world is less than real and is a prison of the spirit. **17:** *Holy spirit* is identified with Wisdom; compare 7.22.
10.1–21: From Adam to the Exodus. 1–2: Adam (Gen.1.26–5.5). **3:** Cain and Abel (Gen.4.1–16). **4:** Noah (Gen.5.28–9.29). For the flood as Cain's *fault* see Josephus, *Ant.* I.2.2. **5a:** The Tower of Babel (Gen.11.1–9). **5b:** Abraham (Gen.11.26–25.10). **6–9:** Lot (Gen. ch. 19). The *Five Cities* are Sodom and Gomorrah and their confederates (Gen.14.2; 19.20–33), located by

good man from the destruction of the godless, and he escaped the fire that came down on the Five Cities, cities whose wickedness is still attested by a smoking waste, by plants whose fruit can never ripen, and a pillar of salt standing there as a memorial of an unbelieving soul. Wisdom they ignored, and they suffered for it, losing the power to recognize what is good and leaving by their lives a monument of folly, such that their enormities can never be forgotten. But wisdom brought her servants safely out of their troubles. It was she, when a good man was a fugitive from his brother's anger, who guided him on the straight path; she showed him that God is king, and gave him knowledge of his holiness;[d] she prospered his labours and made his toil productive. When men in their rapacity tried to exploit him, she stood by him and made him rich. She kept him safe from his enemies, and preserved him from treacherous attacks; she gave him victory after a hard struggle, and taught him that godliness is the greatest power of all. It was she who refused to desert a good man when he was sold as a slave; she preserved him from sin and went down into the dungeon with him, nor did she leave him when he was in chains until she had brought him sceptre and kingdom and authority over his persecutors; she gave the lie to his accusers, and brought him undying fame. It was she who rescued a godfearing people, a blameless race, from a nation of oppressors; she inspired a servant of the Lord, and with his signs and wonders he defied

formidable kings. She rewarded the 17 labours of godfearing men, she guided them on a marvellous journey and became a covering for them by day and a blaze of stars by night. She 18 brought them over the Red Sea and guided them through its deep waters; but their enemies she engulfed, and 19 cast them up again out of the fathomless deep. So good men plundered the 20 ungodly; they sang the glories of thy holy name, O Lord, and praised with one accord thy power, their champion; for wisdom taught the dumb to speak, 21 and made the tongues of infants eloquent.

Wisdom, working through a holy **11** prophet, brought them success in all they did. They made their way across 2 an unpeopled desert and pitched camp in untrodden wastes; they resisted every 3 enemy, and beat off hostile assaults. When they were thirsty they called upon 4 thee, and water to slake their thirst was given them out of the hard stone of a rocky cliff. The self-same means by 5 which their oppressors had been punished were used to help them in their hour of need: those others found 6 their river no unfailing stream of water, but putrid and befouled with blood, in 7 punishment for their order that all the infants should be killed, while to these thou gavest abundant water unexpectedly. So from the thirst they then 8 endured, they learnt how thou hadst punished their enemies; when they 9 themselves were put to the test, though discipline was tempered with mercy,

d showed . . . holiness: or gave him a vision of God's realm, and knowledge of his holy angels.

Jewish tradition and some modern writers at the southern end of the Dead Sea. Natural phenomena embellished by legend account for *smoking waste* (heavy evaporation of Dead Sea); *fruit . . . never ripen* (apples of Sodom), and *pillar of salt* (salt deposit formation; Gen.19.26). See Philo, *De Abrahamo*, 137–141; Josephus, *B.J.* IV.8.4. **10–12:** Jacob (Gen.25.19–49.33, especially chs. 28–31). **13–14:** Joseph (Gen. chs. 37–50). **15–21:** The Exodus (Exod.1.1–15.21, especially chs. 12–15). **16:** *A servant:* Moses. *Formidable kings* are Pharaoh and others, as in Ps.135.9–10. **17:** The cloud of Exod.13.21 is thought of as a *covering;* see Num.10.34 and Ps.105.39. **20:** According to Josephus, *Ant.* II.16.6, the Egyptians were *plundered* at the Red Sea. **21:** *Dumb* who *speak* and *eloquent infants* refer to the Jewish tradition that even infants and embryos joined in the song of Israel at the Red Sea; see Exod.15.1–18.

11.1–14: The wandering in the desert (Exod.15.22–17.16). **4:** Events of Exod.17.1–7 are given according to an idealized version; compare Ps.107.4–6. **5–7:** Before the Exodus, water was turned into *blood* for the Egyptians by the first plague (Exod.7.19–25), a punishment, according to the author, for Pharaoh's decree that *all the infants* of the Israelites be *killed* by being drowned in the Nile. The Egyptians were thus punished by the sudden loss of drinking water but the Israelites were rewarded by finding it *unexpectedly* in the desert (Num.20.11). Exod. states that the Pharaoh ordered only the male children to be drowned (Exod.1.22) and the water was turned into blood not because of that decree, but because of Pharaoh's refusal to let Israel leave

they understood the tortures of the godless who were sentenced in anger.
10 Thy own people thou didst subject to an ordeal, warning them like a father; those others thou didst put to the torture, like a stern king passing sentence.
11 At home and abroad, they were equally
12 in distress, for a double misery had come upon them, and they groaned as
13 they recalled the past. When they heard that the means of their own punishment had been used to benefit thy people, they saw thy hand in it, O
14 Lord. The man who long ago had been abandoned and exposed, whom they had rejected with contumely, became in the event the object of their wonder and admiration; their thirst was such as the godly never knew.
15   In return for the insensate imagination of those wicked men, which deluded them into worshipping reptiles devoid of reason, and mere vermin, thou didst send upon them a swarm of creatures devoid of reason to chastise
16 them, and to teach them that the instruments of a man's sin are the
17 instruments of his punishment. For thy almighty hand, which created the world out of formless matter, was not without other resource: it could have let loose upon them a host of bears or
18 ravening lions or unknown ferocious monsters newly created, either breathing out blasts of fire, or roaring and belching smoke, or flashing terrible sparks like lightning from their eyes,
19 with power not only to exterminate them by the wounds they inflicted, but by their mere appearance to kill them
20 with fright. Even without these, a single breath would have sufficed to lay them low, with justice in pursuit and the breath of thy power to blow them

away; but thou hast ordered all things by measure and number and weight.
Great strength is thine to exert at 21 any moment, and the power of thy arm no man can resist, for in thy sight 22 the whole world is like a grain that just tips the scale or a drop of dew alighting on the ground at dawn. But thou art 23 merciful to all men because thou canst do all things; thou dost overlook the sins of men to bring them to repentance; for all existing things are dear to 24 thee and thou hatest nothing that thou hast created—why else wouldst thou have made it? How could anything 25 have continued in existence, had it not been thy will? How could it have endured unless called into being by thee? Thou sparest all things because they 26 are thine, our lord and master who lovest all that lives; for thy imperish- **12** able breath is in them all.
For this reason thou dost correct 2 offenders little by little, admonishing them and reminding them of their sins, in order that they may leave their evil ways and put their trust, O Lord, in thee. For example, the ancient in- 3 habitants of thy holy land were hateful 4 to thee for their loathsome practices, their sorcery and unholy rites, ruthless 5 murders of children, cannibal feasts of human flesh and blood; they were 6 initiates of a secret ritual in which parents slaughtered their defenceless children. Therefore it was thy will to destroy them at the hand of our forefathers, so that the land which is of all 7 lands most precious in thine eyes could receive in God's children settlers worthy of it. And yet thou didst spare 8 their lives because even they were men, sending hornets as the advance-guard of thy army to exterminate them

---

Egypt (Exod.7.16–17). **13:** Exod.32.12 also implies that the Egyptians could know what was occurring in the Wilderness, and that the *means of their own punishment had been used to benefit thy people.* **14:** Moses is the *man . . . abandoned,* both in his exposure at birth (Exod.2.1–10), and in his flight (Exod.2.11–22).
     11.15–20: The punishment of the Egyptians was appropriate. God could have chosen innumerable punishments. Instead, ironically, they were punished through the animals they worshiped. **15:** Exod. ch. 8 does not suggest that the Egyptians worshiped *reptiles* or *vermin.* Perhaps the author is exaggerating the practice of the temples of his day. See Philo, *De Vita Contemplativa,* 8–9. *Creatures devoid of reason* were the plagues of frogs, lice, and locusts, Exod. chs. 8 and 10. **17:** *Formless matter* may imply the Platonic philosophical concept of preexistent matter out of which the world was made, but compare Gen.1.2.
     11.21–12.1: God is merciful to all creatures. See Ps.145.9.
     12.2–11: God was merciful even to the Canaanites. 3–8: The charge of *cannibal feasts* is unattested in the Bible, but it was part of the Greek philosophical attack on Greek mythology.

9 gradually. It was well within thy power to let the godly overwhelm the godless in a pitched battle, or to wipe them out in an instant with cruel beasts or by 10 one stern word. But thou didst carry out their sentence gradually to give them space for repentance, knowing well enough that they came of evil stock, their wickedness ingrained, and that their way of thinking would not 11 change to the end of time, for there was a curse on their race from the beginning.

Nor was it out of deference to anyone else that thou gavest them an 12 amnesty for their misdeeds; for to thee no one can say 'What hast thou done?' or dispute thy verdict. Who shall bring a charge against thee for destroying nations which were of thy own making? Who shall appear against thee in court 13 to plead the cause of guilty men? For there is no other god but thee; all the world is thy concern, and there is none to whom thou must prove the justice of 14 thy sentence. There is no king or other ruler who can outface thee on behalf of 15 those whom thou hast punished. But thou art just and orderest all things justly, counting it alien to thy power to condemn a man who ought not to be 16 punished. For thy strength is the source of justice, and it is because thou art 17 master of all that thou sparest all. Thou showest thy strength when men doubt the perfection of thy power; it is when they know it and yet are insolent that 18 thou dost punish them. But thou, with strength at thy command, judgest in mercy and rulest us in great forbearance; for the power is thine to use when thou wilt.

19 By acts like these thou didst teach thy people that the just man must also be kind-hearted, and thou hast filled thy sons with hope by the offer of 20 repentance for their sins. If thou didst use such care and such indulgence even in punishing thy children's enemies, who deserved to die, granting them time and space to get free of their wickedness, with what discrimination 21 thou didst pass judgement on thy sons, to whose fathers thou hast given sworn covenants full of the promise of good!

So we are chastened by thee, but our 22 enemies thou dost scourge ten thousand times more, so that we may lay thy goodness to heart when we sit in judgement, and may hope for mercy when we ourselves are judged. This is why 23 the wicked who had lived their lives in heedless folly were tormented by thee with their own abominations. They 24 had strayed far down the paths of error, taking for gods the most contemptible and hideous creatures, deluded like thoughtless children. And so, as 25 though they were mere babes who have not learnt reason, thou didst visit on them a sentence that made them ridiculous; but those who do not take 26 warning from such derisive correction will experience the full weight of divine judgement. They were indignant at their 27 own sufferings, but finding themselves chastised through the very creatures they had taken to be gods, they recognized that the true God was he whom they had long ago refused to know. Thus the full rigour of condemnation descended on them.

The evils of idolatry

WHAT BORN FOOLS ALL MEN WERE WHO **13** lived in ignorance of God, who from the good things before their eyes could not learn to know him who really is, and failed to recognize the artificer though they observed his works! Fire, 2 wind, swift air, the circle of the starry signs, rushing water, or the great lights

---

On the gradual extermination of the *ancient inhabitants* of the holy land (Canaan) see Exod.23.28–30; Deut.7.20. **11:** Noah cursed *their race,* i.e. the Canaanites, Gen.9.25.

12.12–21: God's leniency is not due to weakness or fear. God's mercy is an example and warning to the Jews. The author avoids mentioning the sins of the Israelites.

12.22–27: Severe punishment for the Egyptians. 23–24: Compare 11.15–16.

13.1–15.19: Heathen worship is foolishness.

13.1–9: The folly of deifying nature. 1: The argument for God's existence from design was popular among the Stoics. God is described in philosophical terms as he *who really is*; see Sept. Exod.3.14. **2:** *Fire, wind,* etc. are aspects of nature worshiped by pagans and important to Greek philosophers; compare Deut.4.19.

in heaven that rule the world—these 3 they accounted gods. If it was through delight in the beauty of these things that men supposed them gods, they ought to have understood how much better is the Lord and Master of it all; for it was by the prime author of all 4 beauty that they were created. If it was through astonishment at their power and influence, men should have learnt from these how much more powerful is 5 he who made them. For the greatness and beauty of created things give us a corresponding idea of their Creator. 6 Yet these men are not greatly to be blamed, for when they go astray they may be seeking God and really wishing 7 to find him. Passing their lives among his works and making a close study of them, they are persuaded by appearances because what they see is so 8 beautiful. Yet even so they do not de-9 serve to be excused, for with enough understanding to speculate about the universe, why did they not sooner discover the Lord and Master of it all? 10 The really degraded ones are those whose hopes are set on dead things, who give the name of gods to the work of human hands, to gold and silver fashioned by art into images of living creatures, or to a useless stone carved 11 by a craftsman long ago. Suppose some skilled woodworker fells with his saw a convenient tree and deftly strips off all the bark, then works it up elegantly into some vessel suitable for everyday 12 use; and the pieces left over from his work he uses to cook his food, and 13 eats his fill. But among the waste there is one useless piece, crooked and full of knots, and this he takes and carves to occupy his idle moments, and shapes it with leisurely skill into the image of 14 a human being; or else he gives it the form of some contemptible creature, painting it with vermilion and raddling its surface with red paint, so that every 15 flaw in it is painted over. Then he makes a suitable shrine for it and fixes it on 16 the wall, securing it with iron nails. It

is he who has to take the precautions on its behalf to save it from falling, for he knows that it cannot fend for itself: it is only an image, and needs help. Yet he 17 prays to it about his possessions and his wife and children, and feels no shame in addressing this lifeless object; for health he appeals to a thing that is 18 feeble, for life he prays to a dead thing, for aid he implores something utterly incapable, for a prosperous journey something that has not even the use of its legs; in matters of earnings and 19 business and success in handicraft he asks effectual help from a thing whose hands are entirely ineffectual.

The man, again, who gets ready for **14** a voyage, and plans to set his course through the wild waves, cries to a piece of wood more fragile than the ship which carries him. Desire for gain 2 invented the ship, and the shipwright with his wisdom built it;*e* but it is thy 3 providence, O Father, that is its pilot, for thou hast given it a pathway through the sea and a safe course among the waves, showing that thou 4 canst save from every danger, so that even a man without skill can put to sea. It is thy will that the things made by 5 thy wisdom should not lie idle; and therefore men trust their lives even to the frailest spar, and passing through the billows on a mere raft come safe to land. Even in the beginning, when the 6 proud race of giants was being brought to an end, the hope of mankind escaped on a raft and, piloted by thy hand, bequeathed to the world a new breed of men. For a blessing is on the wooden 7 vessel through which right has prevailed; but the wooden idol made by 8 human hands is accursed, and so is its maker—he because he made it, and the perishable thing because it was called a god. Equally hateful to God are the 9 godless man and his ungodliness; the 10 doer and the deed shall both be punished.

e Other witnesses read and wisdom was the shipwright that built it.

13.10–19: The worship of idols is inexcusable. See Isa.44.9–20 and Let. Jer. This was a frequent theme in Jewish literature.
    14.1–10: Folly of the idolatrous navigator. 1: The *piece of wood more fragile* is the protective idol of the ship. 6: *Giants:* see Gen.6.1–4. *Hope of mankind:* Noah and his family; see Gen.5.28–9.29.

11 And so retribution shall fall upon the idols of the heathen, because though part of God's creation they have been made into an abomination, to make men stumble and to catch the 12 feet of fools. The invention of idols is the root of immorality; they are a contrivance which has blighted human 13 life. They did not exist from the beginning, nor will they be with us for ever; 14 superstition brought them into the world, and for good reason a short sharp end is in store for them.

15 Some father, overwhelmed with untimely grief for the child suddenly taken from him, made an image of the child and honoured thenceforth as a god what was once a dead human being, handing on to his household the ob-16 servance of rites and ceremonies. Then this impious custom, established by the passage of time, was observed as a law. Or again graven images came to be worshipped at the command of despotic 17 princes. When men could not do honour to such a prince before his face because he lived far away, they made a likeness of that distant face, and produced a visible image of the king they sought to honour, eager to pay court to the absent prince as though he were 18 present. Then the cult grows in fervour as those to whom the king is unknown are spurred on by ambitious craftsmen. 19 In his desire, it may be, to please the monarch, a craftsman skilfully distorts 20 the likeness into an ideal form, and the common people, beguiled by the beauty of the workmanship, take for an object of worship him whom lately they 21 honoured as a man. So this becomes a trap for living men: enslaved by mischance or misgovernment, men confer on stocks and stones the name that none may share.

22 Then, not content with gross error in their knowledge of God, men live in the constant warfare of ignorance and 23 call this monstrous evil peace. They

perform ritual murders of children and secret ceremonies and the frenzied 24 orgies of unnatural cults; the purity of life and marriage is abandoned; and a man treacherously murders his neighbour or corrupts his wife and breaks his 25 heart. All is in chaos—bloody murder, theft and fraud, corruption, treachery, 26 riot, perjury, honest men driven to distraction; ingratitude, moral corruption, sexual perversion, breakdown of marriage, adultery, debauchery. For the 27 worship of idols, whose names it is wrong even to mention, is the beginning, cause, and end of every evil. Men 28 either indulge themselves to the point of madness, or produce inspired utterance which is all lies, or live dishonest lives, or break their oath without 29 scruple. They perjure themselves and expect no harm because the idols they 30 trust in are lifeless. On two counts judgement will overtake them: because in their devotion to idols they have thought wrongly about God, and because, in their contempt for religion, they have deliberately perjured themselves. It is not any power in what they 31 swear by, but the nemesis of sin, that always pursues the transgression of the wicked.

But thou, our God, art kind and true **15** and patient, a merciful ruler of all that is. For even if we sin, we are thine; we 2 acknowledge thy power. But we will not sin, because we know that we are accounted thine. To know thee is the 3 whole of righteousness, and to acknowledge thy power is the root of immortality. We have not been led astray by 4 the perverted inventions of human skill or the barren labour of painters, by some gaudy painted shape, the sight of 5 which arouses in fools a passionate desire for a mere image without life or breath. They are in love with evil and 6 deserve to trust in nothing better, those who do these evil things or hanker after them or worship them.

14.11–31: Origin and evil results of idolatry. 13: Unnatural idols *did not exist from the beginning* but were invented. **17:** The worship of the *prince*, or ruler cult, was popular in the Hellenistic world, particularly in Egypt. See Rom.1.22–32 for similar licentious behavior in defiance of God and society.
15.1–6: Benefits of worshiping the true God. 1: See Exod.34.6 and Sept. Deut.32.4. **4:** Ancient statues were usually *painted.* **5:** Stories were told by Christian authors of the *passionate desire* aroused by a *mere image.*

7 For a potter kneading his clay laboriously moulds every vessel for our use, but out of the self-same clay he fashions without distinction the pots that are to serve for honourable uses and the opposite; and what the purpose of each one is to be, the moulder of the 8 clay decides. And then with ill-directed toil he makes a false god out of the same clay, this man who not long before was himself fashioned out of earth and soon returns to the place whence he was taken, when the living soul that 9 was lent to him must be repaid. His concern is not that he must one day fall sick or that his span of life is short; but he must vie with goldsmiths and silversmiths and copy the bronze-workers, and he thinks it does him credit to 10 make counterfeits. His heart is ashes, his hope worth less than common earth, and his life cheaper than his own clay, 11 because he did not recognize by whom he himself was moulded, or who it was that inspired him with an active soul and breathed into him the breath of 12 life. No, he reckons our life a game, and our existence a market where money can be made; 'one must get a living', he says, 'by fair means or foul'. 13 But this man knows better than anyone that he is doing wrong, this maker of fragile pots and idols from the same earthy stuff.

14 The greatest fools of all, and worse than infantile, were the enemies and 15 oppressors of thy people, for they supposed all their heathen idols to be gods, although they have eyes that cannot see, nostrils that cannot draw breath, ears that cannot hear, fingers that cannot feel, and feet that are use-16 less for walking. It was a man who made them; one who draws borrowed breath gave them their shape. But no human being has the power to shape a 17 god like himself: he is only mortal, but what he makes with his impious hands is dead; and so he is better than the

objects of his worship, for he is at least alive—they never can be.

Moreover, these men worship ani-10 mals, the most revolting animals. Compared with the rest of the brute creation, their divinities are the least intelligent. Even as animals they have 19 no beauty to make them desirable; when God approved and blessed his work, they were left out.

The pattern of divine justice

AND SO THE OPPRESSORS WERE FITTINGLY 16 chastised by creatures like these: they were tormented by swarms of vermin. But while they were punished, thou 2 didst make provision for thy people, sending quails for them to eat, an unwonted food to satisfy their hunger; for thy purpose was that whereas those 3 others, hungry as they were, should turn in loathing even from necessary food because the creatures sent upon them were so disgusting, thy people after a short spell of scarcity should enjoy unwonted delicacies. It was right 4 that the scarcity falling on the oppressors should be inexorable, and that thy people should learn by brief experience how their enemies were tormented. Even when fierce and furious snakes 5 attacked thy people and the bites of writhing serpents were spreading death, thy anger did not continue to the bitter end; their short trouble was sent them 6 as a lesson, and they were given a symbol*f* of salvation to remind them of the requirements of thy law. For 7 any man who turned towards it was saved, not by the thing he looked upon but by thee, the saviour of all. In this 8 way thou didst convince our enemies that thou art the deliverer from every evil. Those other men died from the 9 bite of locusts and flies, and no remedy was found to save their lives, because it

f Or pledge.

15.7–19: The manufacture of idols. 7: Compare Isa.45.9. **14–17:** *The greatest fools of all* in making *idols* were the Egyptians. **19:** Which *animals* worshiped by the Egyptians *were left out* of God's blessing is not clear, perhaps the unclean animals of 11.15 or the serpent cursed by God in Gen.3.14–15.
16.1–19.22: A theology of history is developed.
16.1–23: The punishment of the Egyptians and wicked Israelites. The theme is similar to that of chs. 10–12. **2:** *Quails:* Exod.16.13; Num.11.31; Ps.78.27. **5–6:** Num.21.4–9. **7:** This is based on Jewish exegesis of Num.21.9. **9:** Exod.10.17 may have suggested that the Egyptians *died*

was fitting for them to be chastised by
10 such creatures. But thy sons did not
succumb to the fangs of snakes, how
ever venomous, because thy mercy
11 came to their aid and healed them. It
was to remind them of thy utterances
that they were bitten and quickly recovered; it was for fear they might fall
into deep forgetfulness and become
12 unresponsive to thy kindness. For it
was neither herb nor poultice that
cured them, but thy all-healing word,
13 O Lord. Thou hast the power of life
and death, thou bringest a man down
to the gates of death and up again.
14 Man in his wickedness may kill, but he
cannot bring back the breath of life
that has gone forth nor release a soul
that death has arrested.
15 But from thy hand there is no
16 escape; for godless men who refused
to acknowledge thee were scourged by
thy mighty arm, pursued by extraordinary storms of rain and hail in
relentless torrents, and utterly destroyed
17 by fire. Strangest of all, in water, that
quenches everything, the fire burned
more fiercely; creation itself fights to
18 defend the godly. At one time the
flame was moderated, so that it should
not burn up the living creatures inflicted on the godless, who were to
learn from this that it was by God's
19 justice that they were pursued; at
another time it blazed even under water
with more than the natural power of
fire, to destroy the produce of a sinful
20 land. By contrast, thy own people were
given angels' food, and thou didst send
them from heaven, without labour of
their own, bread ready to eat, rich in
delight of every kind and suited to
21 every taste. The sustenance thou didst
supply showed thy sweetness towards
thy children, and the bread, serving the
desire of each man who ate it, was

changed into what he wished. Its snow 22
and ice resisted fire and did not melt,
to teach them that whereas their
enemies' crops had been destroyed by
fire that blazed in the hail and flashed
through the teeming rain, that same 23
fire had now forgotten its own power,
in order that the godly might be fed.
For creation, serving thee its maker, 24
exerts its power to punish the godless
and relaxes into benevolence towards
those who trust in thee. And so it was 25
at that time too: it adapted itself endlessly in the service of thy universal
bounty, according to the desire of thy
suppliants. So thy sons, O Lord, whom 26
thou hast chosen, were to learn that it
is not the growing of crops by which
mankind is nourished, but it is thy word
that sustains those who trust in thee.
That substance, which fire did not 27
destroy, simply melted away when
warmed by the sun's first rays, to 28
teach us that we must rise before the
sun to give thee thanks and pray to
thee as daylight dawns. The hope of an 29
ungrateful man will melt like the hoar-
frost of winter, and drain away like
water that runs to waste.
Great are thy judgements and hard **17**
to expound; and thus it was that uninstructed souls went astray. Thus 2
heathen men imagined that they could
lord it over thy holy people; but,
prisoners of darkness and captives of
unending night, they lay each immured
under his own roof, fugitives from
eternal providence. Thinking that their 3
secret sins might escape detection beneath a dark pall of oblivion, they lay
in disorder, dreadfully afraid, terrified
by apparitions. For the dark corner 4
that held them offered no refuge from
fear, but loud unnerving noises roared
around them, and phantoms with
downcast unsmiling faces passed before

---

from the bite of locusts and flies. See Josephus, *Ant.* II.14.3. **16:** See Exod.9.18–34. **17:** The strange quality of *fire* burning *in water* is derived from Jewish exegesis of Exod.9.24. **18:** The author assumes that the frogs and lice of the earlier plagues survived to be spared by the hail. This is contrary to Exod.8.13,31. **20:** *Angels' food:* the manna of Exod.16.4–21 ("bread from heaven") and Ps.78.25 ("bread of angels"). It was described by Jewish tradition as *suited to every taste.* **22:** *Snow and ice:* "the manna," according to Sept. Num.11.7–8.

16.24–29: Philosophical and moral lessons of the manna. 26: Compare Deut.8.3. **27:** Manna could be baked, and was seemingly indestructible by *fire*, but it was *melted away by the sun's first rays;* compare Exod.16.21. **28:** Jewish morning prayers may be recited only after *daylight dawns.*

17.1–18.4: The plague of darkness (Exod.10.21–23). **3:** *Secret sins* may allude to the mystery

111

5 their eyes. No fire, however great, had force enough to give them light, nor had the brilliant flaming stars strength to illuminate that hideous darkness.

6 There shone upon them only a blaze, of no man's making, that terrified them, and in their panic they thought the real world even worse than that

7 imaginary sight. The tricks of the sorcerers' art failed, and all their boasted wisdom was exposed and put to

8 shame; for the very men who profess to drive away fear and trouble from sick souls were themselves sick with

9 dread that made them ridiculous. Even if nothing frightful was there to terrify them, yet having once been scared by the advancing vermin and the hissing

10 serpents, they collapsed in terror, refusing even to look upon the air from

11 which there can be no escape.*g* For wickedness proves a cowardly thing when condemned by an inner witness, and in the grip of conscience gives way

12 to forebodings of disaster. Fear is nothing but an abandonment of the

13 aid that comes from reason; and hope, defeated by this inward weakness, capitulates before ignorance of the cause by which the torment comes.

14 So all that night, which really had no power against them because it came upon them from the powerless depths of hell, they slept the same haunted

15 sleep, now harried by portentous spectres, now paralysed by the treachery of their own souls; sudden and

16 unforeseen, fear came upon them. Thus a man would fall down where he stood and be held in durance, locked in a

17 prison that had no bars. Farmer or shepherd or labourer toiling in the wilds, he was caught, and awaited the inescapable doom; the same chain of

18 darkness bound all alike. The whispering breeze, the sweet melody of birds in spreading branches, the steady beat of

19 water that rushes by, the headlong crash of rocks falling, the racing of creatures as they bound along unseen, the roar

of fierce wild beasts, or echo reverberating from hollows in the hills—all these sounds paralysed them with fear.

20 The whole world was bathed in the bright light of day, and went about its

21 tasks unhindered; those men alone were overspread with heavy night, fit image of the darkness that awaited them; and heavier than the darkness was the burden each was to himself.

But for thy holy ones there shone a **18** great light. And so their enemies, hearing their voices but not seeing them, counted them happy because they had not suffered like themselves,

2 gave thanks for their forbearance under provocation, and begged as a favour that they should part company.

3 Accordingly, thy gift was a pillar of fire to be the guide of their uncharted journey, a sun that would not scorch

4 them on their glorious expedition. Their enemies did indeed deserve to lose the light of day and be kept prisoners in darkness, for they had kept in durance thy sons, through whom the imperishable light of the law was to be given to the world.

5 They planned to kill the infant children of thy holy people, but when one child had been exposed to death and rescued, thou didst deprive them of all their children in requital, and drown them all together in the swelling waves.

6 Of that night our forefathers were given warning in advance, so that, having sure knowledge, they might be heartened by

7 the promises which they trusted. Thy people were looking for the deliverance of the godly and the destruction of their

8 enemies; for thou didst use the same means to punish our enemies and to make us glorious when we heard thy

9 call. The devout children of a virtuous race were offering sacrifices in secret, and covenanted with one consent to keep the law of God and to share alike in the same blessings and the same dangers, and they were already singing

g Or there is no need to escape.

cults of the author's day which he attributes to the ancient Egyptians; compare 14.23. **5:** The details are derived from the Jewish exegesis of Exod.10.21. **7:** Compare Exod.7.11,22; 8.7,18; 9.11. **18.3:** See Exod.13.21; 14.24.
18.5–19: The Egyptians counsel death but are slain themselves. 5: *One child:* Moses; see Exod.1.15–2.10. **6:** The night of the first Passover was so well known as to be called *that night;* sec Exod.12.42. **9:** *Ancestral songs·* the author anachronistically pictures the first Passover in

their sacred ancestral songs of praise.
10 In discordant contrast there came an
outcry from their enemies, as piteous
lamentation for their children spread
11 abroad. Master and slave were punished together with the same penalty;
king and common man suffered the
12 same fate. All alike had their dead, past
counting, struck down by one common
form of death; there were not enough
living even to bury the dead; at one
stroke the most precious of their off-
13 spring had perished. Relying on their
magic arts, they had scouted all
warnings; but when they saw their first-
born dead, they confessed that thy
people have God as their father.
14 All things were lying in peace and
silence, and night in her swift course
15 was half spent, when thy almighty
Word leapt from thy royal throne in
heaven into the midst of that doomed
16 land like a relentless warrior, bearing
the sharp sword of thy inflexible decree,
and stood and filled it all with death,
his head touching the heavens, his feet
17 on earth. At once nightmare phantoms
appalled them, and unlooked-for fears
18 set upon them; and as they flung themselves to the ground half dead, one here,
one there, they confessed the reasons
19 for their deaths; for the dreams
that tormented them had taught them
before they died, so that they should
not die ignorant of the reason why they
suffered.
20 The godly also had a taste of death
when a multitude were struck down
in the wilderness; but the divine wrath
21 did not long continue. A blameless man
was quick to be their champion, bearing
the weapons of his priestly ministry,
prayer and the incense that propitiates;
he withstood the divine anger and set a
limit to the disaster, thus showing that
22 he was thy servant. He overcame the
avenging fury not by bodily strength or
force of arms; by words he subdued the
avenger, appealing to the sworn coven-

ants made with our forefathers. When 23
the dead had already fallen in heaps
one on another, he interposed himself
and beat back the divine wrath, barring
its line of attack upon the living. On 24
his long-skirted robe the whole world
was represented; the glories of the
fathers were engraved on his four rows
of precious stones; and thy majesty
was in the diadem upon his head. To 25
these the destroyer yielded, for these
made him afraid; only to taste his wrath
had been enough.
But the godless were pursued by **19**
pitiless anger to the bitter end, for
God knew their future also: how after 2
allowing thy people to depart, and even
urging their departure, they would
change their minds and set out in
pursuit. While they were still mourning, 3
still lamenting at the graves of their
dead, they rushed into another foolish
decision, and pursued as fugitives those
whom they had begged to leave. For 4
the fate they had merited was drawing
them on to this conclusion and made
them forget what had happened, so
that they might suffer the torments still
needed to complete their punishment,
and that thy people might achieve an 5
incredible journey, and that their
enemies might meet an outlandish
death.
The whole creation, with all its 6
elements, was refashioned in subservience to thy commands, so that
thy servants might be preserved unscathed. Men gazed at the cloud that 7
overshadowed the camp, at dry land
emerging where before was only water,
at an open road leading out of the Red
Sea, and a grassy plain in place of stormy
waves, across which the whole nation 8
passed, under the shelter of thy hand,
after all the marvels they had seen.
They were like horses at pasture, like 9
skipping lambs, as they praised thee,
O Lord, by whom they were rescued.
For they still remembered their life in 10

the format of his day at which Pss.113–118 were sung. **12:** *Not enough living:* exaggeration of
Num.33.3–4. **15:** *Word* of God is personified as the effective executor of his will. Compare
"God said" of Gen.1.2–29. **17–19:** The content has no foundation in the Exodus story but is
an embellishment of it. *Appalled them:* the firstborn who were to die. See Exod.12.28–30.
18.20–25: The Israelite plague of death was stayed by Aaron (Num.16.44–50).
19.1–21: God worked wonders at the time of the Exodus. The wicked Egyptians were grieved
by them and the Israelites liberated. **2:** See Exod.12.31–33; 14.23–28. **10:** Read Exod. ch. 8.

a foreign land: how instead of cattle the earth bred lice, and instead of fish the river spewed up swarms of frogs, 11 and how, after that, they had seen a new sort of bird when, driven by greed, they had begged for delicacies to eat, 12 and for their relief quails came up from the sea.

13 So punishment came upon those sinners, not unheralded by violent thunderbolts. They suffered justly for their own wickedness, for they had raised bitter hatred of strangers to a 14 new pitch. There had been others who refused to welcome strangers when they came to them, but these made slaves of guests who were their benefactors. 15 There is indeed a judgement awaiting those who treated foreigners as enemies; 16 but these, after a festal welcome, oppressed with hard labour men who had 17 earlier shared their rights. They were struck with blindness also, like the men at the door of the one good man, when yawning darkness fell upon them and each went groping for his own doorway.

For as the notes of a lute can make 18 various tunes with different names, though each retains its own pitch, so the elements combined among themselves in different ways, as can be accurately inferred from the observation of what happened. Land animals took 19 to the water and things that swim migrated to dry land; fire retained its 20 normal power even in water, and water forgot its quenching properties. Flames 21 on the other hand failed to consume the flesh of perishable creatures that walked in them, and the substance of heavenly food, like ice and prone to melt, no longer melted.

In everything, O Lord, thou hast 22 made thy people great and glorious, and hast not neglected in every time and place to be their helper.

12: As usual, the murmurings of the Israelites prior to the *quails* are omitted. See 16.2 n. **13:** There are no *thunderbolts* in Exod. ch. 14, but see Ps.77.16–19 and Josephus, *Ant.* II.16.3. **14:** *Others* are the Sodomites, Gen. ch. 19. **16:** The Israelites were given a *festal welcome* in Egypt at the time of Joseph (Gen.47.1–12) and were *oppressed with hard labour* by a later Pharaoh (Exod.1.8–11). **17:** Gen.19.11; Exod.10.21–23. **18–21:** God, dealing with the *elements* of nature as a musician with a *lute*, arranges and rearranges them to achieve the wonderful result. **19.22: The conclusion.** God directs Israel's history.

ECCLESIASTICUS

OR

THE WISDOM OF JESUS SON OF SIRACH

Ecclesiasticus, literally meaning a "church book," is so called either because it was used extensively in church worship or because the early Christian church rather than the synagogue received it into the canon. It is the work of a Jewish wisdom teacher of about 180 B.C. The book, also called the Wisdom of Sirach, or ben Sirach, or simply Sirach, after its author, Jesus the son of Sirach (see 50.27), stands in the wisdom tradition of Proverbs, which, attempting to discover the patterns at work in the circumstances of human life, concludes that wisdom is God's gift. But unlike the wise men of Proverbs, the author is also a close student of the Jewish Scriptures, especially the Torah (the Law). His work represents a fusion of wisdom and scribal piety.

Written in Hebrew, the original text was lost in early Christian times. About two-thirds of the book in Hebrew was rediscovered in Cairo around 1896. Since then other partial Hebrew manuscripts have been found, among them short fragments in the Judean desert at Qumran and Masada; these discoveries seem to indicate that the Hebrew text of Cairo, though not identical with the original, does derive from the original text, not from a retranslation from the Greek, as was once supposed. The present English translation is made from the Greek version prepared by the author's grandson (see Preface and notes) but is influenced by the recent Hebrew finds. At many points the books had been expanded by later additions, and the omission of these additions from this translation explains why the verse numbers are not always in consecutive order.

Preface

A LEGACY OF GREAT VALUE HAS come to us through the law, the prophets, and the writers who followed in their steps, and for this Israel's traditions of discipline and wisdom deserve recognition. It is the duty of those who study the scriptures not only to become expert themselves, but also to use their scholarship for the benefit of the outside world through both the spoken and the written word. So my grandfather Jesus, who had applied himself industriously to the study of the law, the prophets, and the other writings of our ancestors, and had gained a considerable proficiency in them, was moved to compile a book of his own on the themes of discipline and wisdom, so that, with this further help, scholars might make greater progress in their studies by living as the law directs.

You are asked then to read with sympathetic attention, and make allowances if, in spite of all the devoted work I have put into the translation, some of the expressions appear inadequate. For it is impossible for a translator to find precise equivalents for the original Hebrew in another language. Not only with this book, but with the law, the prophets, and the rest of the writings, it makes no small difference to read them in the original.

When I came to Egypt and settled there in the thirty-eighth year of[a] the reign of King Euergetes, I found great scope for education; and I thought it very necessary to spend some energy and labour on the translation of this book. Ever since then I have been

a Or there at the age of thirty-eight in . . .

Preface. The preface was written by the grandson of the author of Ecclesiasticus, when he translated the book into Gk. for the use of Egyptian Jews who did not know Heb. It mentions the three divisions of the Heb. Scriptures: *the law, the prophets, and the other writings;* this is the earliest reference to the third division of the canon, though the limits of the *writings* were not to be defined for another two centuries; see Lk.24.44. The translator, like the author, closely associates wisdom and study of Scripture. He asserts that a scholar should work not only for fellow specialists but for the *outside world;* the translator speaks of his grandfather but is also thinking of his own work. The *thirty-eighth year* of *King* Ptolemy *Euergetes* II Physcon of Egypt (one of the longest reigns in Egypt) was 132 B.C. This puts the original composition of Ecclus. about 180 B.C., shortly before the Maccabean uprising.

applying my skill night and day to complete it, and to publish it for the use of those who have made their home in a foreign land, and wish to become scholars by training themselves to live according to the law.

The ways of wisdom

1 ALL WISDOM IS FROM THE LORD;
   wisdom is with him for ever.

2 Who can count the sand of the sea,
   the drops of rain, or the days of
      unending time?

3 Who can measure the height of the
      sky,
   the breadth of the earth, or the
      depth of the abyss*b*?

4 Wisdom was first of all created
      things;
   intelligent purpose has been there
      from the beginning.*c*

6 Who has laid bare the root of
      wisdom?
   Who has understood her subtlety?*d*

8 One alone is wise, the Lord most
      terrible,
   seated upon his throne.

9 It is he who created her, surveyed
      and measured her,
   and infused her into all his works.

10 To all mankind he has given her in
      some measure,
   but in plenty to those who love him.

11 THE FEAR OF THE LORD BRINGS
      honour and pride,
   cheerfulness and a garland of joy.

12 The fear of the Lord gladdens the
      heart;
   it brings cheerfulness and joy and
      long life.

Whoever fears the Lord will be   13
   prosperous at the last;
blessings will be his on the day of
   his death.
The essence of wisdom is the fear of   14
   the Lord;
she is created with the faithful in
   their mother's womb,
she has built an everlasting home   15
   among men,
and will keep faith with their
   descendants.
Those who fear the Lord have their   16
   fill of wisdom;
she gives them deep draughts of her
   wine.
She stocks her home with all that   17
   the heart can desire
and her storehouses with her
   produce.
Wisdom's garland is the fear of the   18
   Lord,
flowering with peace and health.
She showers down knowledge and   19
   ability,
and bestows high honour on those
   who hold fast to her.
Wisdom is rooted in the fear of the   20
   Lord,
and long life grows on her branches.*e*

Unjust rage can never be excused;   22
when anger tips the scale it is a
   man's downfall.
Until the right time comes, a   23
   patient man restrains himself,
and afterwards cheerfulness breaks
   through again;

b Some witnesses add or wisdom.
c Some witnesses add (5) The fountain of wisdom is God's word on high, and her ways are the eternal commandments.
d Some witnesses add (7) Who has discovered all that wisdom knows, or understood her wealth of experience?
e Some witnesses add (21) The fear of the Lord drives away sins, and wherever it dwells it averts his anger.

1.1–10: The source of wisdom. The two major divisions of the book (chs. 1–23 and 24–51) are each introduced by a poem in praise of wisdom. See 24.1–22; Prov.8.1–31; Job 28.1–28. **1:** *Wisdom* includes the knowledge of man (both practical and ethical), nature, and God. **2–3:** The immeasurability of nature suggests the infinite depth of wisdom. **4:** *Wisdom* existed before the creation and informs it (see v. 9); it was later identified with the divine creative word; Jn.1.1–3. **6–10:** Against the tendency to make wisdom man's achievement, Ecclus. repeatedly (as here) affirms that it is God's gift. **10:** *Those who love him:* his people Israel; see 24.7–8.
   1.11–20: The definition of wisdom. Though much in Ecclus. is secular common sense, this poem equates the core of wisdom with the loyal and joyful reverence for the God of Israel. **11:** *The fear of the Lord:* reverent acceptance of God's lordship. **13:** Life's basic fairness to the wise man will be shown, if only *on the day of his death* (see 11.28). **15:** The *everlasting home* of wisdom is specifically Israel; see 24.7–8. **16–20:** The reward of wisdom is a full life in the present world; contrast such full life here with v. 13.
   1.22–30: Signs of wisdom. 22–23: Self-control (*restrains himself*) is such a sign (see 6.2–4).

24 until the right moment he keeps his
        thoughts to himself,
    and later his good sense is on
        everyone's lips.

25 In wisdom's store are wise proverbs,
    but godliness is detestable to a
        sinner.

26 If you long for wisdom, keep the
        commandments,
    and the Lord will give it you in
        plenty.

27 For the fear of the Lord is wisdom
        and discipline;
    fidelity and gentleness are his delight.

28 Do not disregard the fear of the Lord
    or approach him without sincerity.

29 Do not act a part before the eyes of
        the world;
    keep guard over your lips.

30 Never be arrogant, for fear you fall
    and bring disgrace on yourself;
    the Lord will reveal your secrets
    and humble you before the assembly,
    because it was not the fear of the
        Lord that prompted you,*f*
    but your heart was full of hypocrisy.

2   MY SON, IF YOU ASPIRE TO BE A
        servant of the Lord,
    prepare yourself for testing.

2   Set a straight course, be resolute,
    and do not lose your head in time
        of disaster.

3   Hold fast to him, never desert him,
    if you would end your days in
        prosperity.

4   Bear every hardship that is sent you;
    be patient under humiliation,
        whatever the cost.

5   For gold is assayed by fire,
    and the Lord proves men in the
        furnace of humiliation.

6   Trust him and he will help you;
    steer a straight course and set your
        hope on him.

7   You who fear the Lord, wait for
        his mercy;
    do not stray or you will fall.

8   You who fear the Lord, trust in him,
    and you shall not miss your reward.

9   You who fear the Lord, expect
        prosperity,
    lasting happiness and favour.

10 Consider the past generations and
        see:
    was anyone who trusted the Lord
        ever disappointed?
    was anyone who stood firm in the
        fear of him ever deserted?
    did he ever neglect anyone who
        prayed to him?

11 For the Lord is compassionate and
        merciful;
    he forgives sins and comes to the
        rescue in time of trouble.

12 Woe to faint hearts and nerveless
        hands
    and to the sinner who leads a
        double life!

13 Woe to the feeble-hearted! they
        have no faith,
    and therefore shall go unprotected.

14 Woe to you who have given up the
        struggle!
    What will you do when the Lord's
        reckoning comes?

15 Those who fear the Lord never
        disobey his words;
    and all who love him keep to his
        ways.

f Or because you had no concern for the fear of the Lord.

26–28: Here, as in the preceding poem (1.11–20), wisdom is identified with reverence. **29–30:** Public *disgrace* is a severe punishment; man's reputation is a frequent theme.

2.1–6: Testing and endurance. Testing of one's wholehearted devotion to God is here the central meaning of suffering (as in 4.17; 33.1; Job chs. 1–2), in contrast to discipline for past transgressions (Prov.3.11–12; Job 5.17–19). **1:** *My son:* the usual address of teacher to student (Prov.1.8). **3:** Though reward may be delayed, the righteous will be vindicated before they *end* their *days.* **5:** Man and *gold* alike show their wholeness through testing.

2.7–11: God's promise confirmed by experience. Three lines beginning *You who fear the Lord* are balanced by three with *Those who fear the Lord* (vv. 15–17); three *Woe*'s set in between complete the pattern (vv. 12–14). **10:** The history of *the past generations* is part of the evidence of experience; see Job 8.8–10.

2.12–14: Woe to the inconsistent. 12: The indecisiveness of *a double life* and of those who are *faint* and *feeble* of *heart* (v. 13) contrasts with the wholehearted decision of those who trust the Lord.

2.15–18: The character of the reverent. 15: From parallelism of the two poetic lines it is clear

16 Those who fear the Lord try to do
      his will;
   and all who love him steep
      themselves in the law.
17 Those who fear the Lord are always
      prepared;
   they humble themselves before him
      and say:
18 'We will fall into the hands of the
      Lord, not into the hands of
      men,
   for his majesty is equalled by his
      mercy.'

3 CHILDREN, LISTEN TO ME, FOR I AM
      your father;
   do what I tell you, if you wish to be
      safe.
2 It is the Lord's will that a father
      should be honoured by his
      children,
   and a mother's rights recognized by
      her sons.
3 Respect for a father atones for sins,
4 and to honour your mother is to
      lay up a fortune.
5 A son who respects his father will
      be made happy by his own
      children;
   when he prays, he will be heard.
6 He who honours his father will have
      a long life,
   and he who obeys the Lord comforts
      his mother;
7 he obeys his parents as though he
      were their slave.
8 My son, honour your father by word
      and deed,
   so that you may receive his blessing.
9 For a father's blessing strengthens
      his children's houses,
   but a mother's curse uproots their
      foundations.
10 Never seek honour at the cost of

discredit to your father;
how can his discredit bring honour
   to you?
A man is honoured if his father is   11
   honoured,
and neglect of a mother is a disgrace
   to children.
My son, look after your father in   12
   his old age;
do nothing to vex him as long as he
   lives.
Even if his mind fails, make   13
   allowances for him,
and do not despise him because you
   are in your prime.
If you support your father it will   14
   never be forgotten,
but be put to your credit against
   your sins;
when you are in trouble, it will be   15
   remembered in your favour,
and your sins will melt away like
   frost in the sunshine.
To leave your father in the lurch is   16
   like blasphemy,
and to provoke your mother's anger
   is to call down the Lord's
   curse.

My son, be unassuming in all you do, 17
and those the Lord approves will
   love you.
The greater you are, the humbler   18
   you must be,
and the Lord will show you favour.*g*
For his power is great,   20
and he is honoured by the humble.
Do not pry into things too hard for   21
   you
or examine what is beyond your
   reach.
Meditate on the commandments   22
   you have been given;

g Some witnesses add (19) Many are high and mighty;
but he reveals his secrets to the modest.

that *fear* and *love* of God are synonymous. **16:** The *law* of Israel is associated with wisdom
throughout Ecclus., in contrast to Prov. **18:** See 2 Sam.24.14; in contrast to Prov., Ecclus.
refers frequently to God's *mercy*.
   3.1–16: Respect for parents. The topic is drawn both from the wise men (Prov.10.1) and
especially from the Law (Exod.20.12; Deut.5.16). **1:** *Safe*, lit. "saved," means doing well in
this world. **2:** *The Lord's will* joins divine command to the teacher's mandate. The *mother's
rights* are asserted with the father's. **3:** Atoning *for sin* here and in v. 30 means that a good
deed cancels out a bad one; see vv. 14–15 and Dan.4.27. **16:** Deserting one's parents is
considered to be as serious as *blasphemy;* see Exod.21.17. *The Lord's curse* is an expression
of God's role in retribution. In closing, the poem returns to God's will, with which it began.
   3.17–24: Need for humility. Students of the wise men were often from wealthy and successful
families; see v. 18. **21–24:** The warning may be against Greek philosophy or against Jewish
apocalyptic speculation. The *commandments*—the Law—are sufficient study for the wise man.

what the Lord keeps secret is no
    concern of yours

23 Do not busy yourself with matters
    that are beyond you;
even what has been shown you is
    above man's grasp.

24 Many have been led astray by
    their speculations,
and false conjectures have impaired
    their judgement.[h]

26 Stubbornness will come to a bad end,
and the man who flirts with danger
    will lose his life.

27 Stubbornness brings a load of
    troubles;
the sinner piles sin on sin.

28 When calamity befalls the arrogant,
    there is no cure;
wickedness is too deeply rooted in
    him.

29 A sensible man will take a proverb
    to heart;
an attentive ear is the desire of the
    wise.

30 As water quenches a blazing fire,
so almsgiving atones for sin.

31 He who repays a good turn is
    mindful of the future;
when he falls he will find support.

4 My son, do not cheat a poor man of
    his livelihood
or keep him waiting with hungry
    eyes.

2 Do not tantalize a starving man
or drive him to desperation in his
    need.

3 If a man is desperate, do not add to
    his troubles
or keep him waiting for the charity
    he asks.

4 Do not reject the appeal of a man
    in distress

or turn your back on the poor;

5 when he begs for alms, do not look
    the other way
and so give him reason to curse you,

6 for if he curses you in his bitterness,
his Maker will listen to his prayer.

7 Make yourself popular in the
    assembly,
and show deference to the great.

8 When a poor man speaks to you,
    give him your attention
and answer his greeting politely.

9 Rescue the downtrodden from the
    oppressor,
and be firm when giving a verdict.

10 Be a father to orphans
and like a husband to their mother;
then the Most High will call you
    his son,
and his love for you will be greater
    than a mother's.

11 WISDOM RAISES HER SONS TO
    greatness
and cares for those who seek her.

12 To love her is to love life;
to rise early for her sake is to be
    filled with joy.

13 The man who attains her will win
    recognition;
the Lord's blessing rests upon
    every place she enters.

14 To serve her is to serve the Holy
    One,
and the Lord loves those who love
    her.

15 Her dutiful servant will give laws to
    the heathen,
and because he listens to her, his
    home will be secure.

16 If he trusts her, he will possess her
and bequeath her to his descendants.

h *Some witnesses add* (25) Without eyes you will be
deprived of light; if you have no knowledge, do not
lay claim to it.

3.26–31: The stubborn and the sensible man. The destructive consequences of not following
the warnings of vv. 17–24 are in contrast to the success of the teachable person. **28:** *Calamity*
will not work a *cure*, i.e. repentance in the *arrogant*.
    4.1–6: Responsibility to the poor. 1–2: Compare the proverb, "He who gives quickly gives
twice." **6:** The curse was a prayer of special potency; see Num.22.1–6.
    4.7–10: On being a leader. Leadership requires concern for, and courtesy to, rich and poor
alike. **10:** One becomes a *son* of God by acting as he does.
    4.11–19: Wisdom gives life. The rewards of *greatness* (v. 11), *recognition* (v. 13), and security
(v. 15) are summed up as *life* (v. 12). **11:** *Sons:* those who put *wisdom* into practice, i.e. her
disciples. **12:** The comparison of wisdom to an attractive woman was widespread (see
Prov. chs. 8–9), and the more striking since the danger of a woman's lure was also a standard
motif (9.2–9). **14:** Wisdom is not only common sense, it is also the worship of *the Holy One.*

17 At first she will lead him by devious
        ways,
filling him with craven fears.
Her discipline will be a torment to
        him,
and her decrees a hard test
until he trusts her with all his heart.*i*
18 Then she will come straight back
        to him again and gladden him,
and reveal her secrets to him.
19 But if he strays from her, she will
        desert him
and abandon him to his fate.

20 WATCH YOUR CHANCE AND DEFEND
        yourself against wrong,
and do not be over-modest in your
        own cause;
21 for there is a modesty that leads to
        sin,
as well as a modesty that brings
        honour and favour.
22 Do not be untrue to yourself in
        deference to another,
or so diffident that you fail in your
        duty.
23 Never remain silent when a word
        might put things right,
24 for wisdom shows itself by speech,
and a man's education must find
        expression in words.
25 Do not argue against the truth,
but have a proper sense of your
        own ignorance.
26 Never be ashamed to admit your
        mistakes,
nor try to swim against the current.
27 Do not let yourself be a doormat
        to a fool
or curry favour with the powerful.
28 Fight to the death for truth,
and the Lord God will fight on
        your side.

29 Do not be forward in your speech

but slack and neglectful in your
        work.
Do not play the lion in your home   30
or swagger*j* among your servants.
Do not keep your hand open to   31
        receive
and close it when it is your turn to
        give.

Do not rely upon your money   **5**
and say, 'I am independent.'
Do not yield to every impulse you   2
        can gratify
or follow the desires of your heart.
Do not say, 'I am my own master';   3
you may be sure the Lord will call
        you to account.
Do not say, 'I sinned, yet nothing   4
        happened to me';
it is only that the Lord is very
        patient.
Do not be so confident of pardon   5
that you sin again and again.
Do not say, 'His mercy is so great,   6
he will pardon my sins, however
        many.'
To him belong both mercy and
        wrath,
and sinners feel the weight of his
        retribution.
Come back to the Lord without   7
        delay;
do not put it off from one day to
        the next,
or suddenly the Lord's wrath will be
        upon you,
and you will perish at the time of
        reckoning.

Do not rely upon ill-gotten gains,   8
for they will not avail in time of
        calamity.
Do not winnow in every wind   9
or walk along every path.*k*

i Or until she can trust him.
j Possible meaning; Gk. obscure.
k Gk. adds this is the mark of duplicity (from 6. 1).

17: Nowhere else is the anguish of wisdom's *discipline* put so sharply; but see 6.18–21. **18:** Wisdom is not a public knowledge, but the *secret* of the few who earn it (39.7; Job 11.6).

4.20–31: False and inadequate humility. Just as true humility is praised (3.17–24), so both false humility, vv. 20–28, and its opposite, the fault of arrogance, vv. 29–31, are condemned. *Truth* (vv. 25, 28) is the balance. **26:** To try to justify one's *mistakes* is as useless as swimming against the *current*.

5.1–7: Reliance on God. Three sections (4.20–31; 5.1–7; 5.8–6.4) are held together by the frequent use of the negative command. In 5.1–6, six negatives show false bases of trust. **1:** *Do not rely:* this ties 5.1 to 5.8. **7:** Coming *back to the Lord* gives the true basis of trust. Though a delay of justice may be observed, nevertheless God will repay in this life.

5.8–6.4: Sincerity, integrity, and self-control. 9: To *winnow in every wind* means to be an

10 Stand firmly by what you know
   and be consistent in what you say.
11 Be quick to listen,
   but take time over your answer.
12 Answer a man if you know what to
   say,
   but if not, hold your tongue.
13 Honour or shame can come through
   speaking,
   and a man's tongue may be his
   downfall.
14 Do not get a name for being a gossip
   or lay traps with your tongue;
   for as there is shame in store for the
   thief,
   so there is harsh censure for
   duplicity.
15 Avoid the little faults as well as the
   great.
6 Do not change from a friend into
   an enemy,
   for a bad name brings shame and
   disgrace,
   and this is the mark of duplicity.

2 Never be roused by violent passions;
   they will tear you apart like a bull,[l]
3 they will eat up your leaves, destroy
   your fruit,
   and leave you a withered tree.
4 Evil passion ruins the man who
   harbours it,
   to the delight of his gloating enemies.
5 Pleasant words win many friends,
   and an affable manner makes
   acquaintance easy.
6 Accept a greeting from everyone,
   but advice from only one in a
   thousand.
7 When you make a friend, begin by
   testing him,
   and be in no hurry to trust him.
8 Some friends are loyal when it suits
   them
   but desert you in time of trouble.
9 Some friends turn into enemies
   and shame you by making the
   quarrel public.
10 Another sits at your table,

but is nowhere to be found in time
   of trouble;
when you are prosperous, he will   11
   be your second self
and make free with your servants,
but if you come down in the world,   12
   he will turn against you
and you will not see him again.
Hold your enemies at a distance,   13
and keep a wary eye on your
   friends.
A faithful friend is a secure shelter; 14
whoever finds one has found a
   treasure.
A faithful friend is beyond price;   15
his worth is more than money can
   buy.
A faithful friend is an elixir of life, 16
found only by those who fear the
   Lord.
The man who fears the Lord keeps   17
   his friendships in repair,
for he treats his neighbour as himself.

My son, seek wisdom's discipline   18
   while you are young,
and when your hair is white, you
   will find her still.
Come to her like a farmer ploughing   19
   and sowing;
then wait for her plentiful harvest.
If you cultivate her, you will labour
   for a little while,
but soon you will be eating her
   crops.
How harsh she seems to the   20
   undisciplined!
The fool cannot abide her;
like a stone she is a burden that   21
   tests his strength,
but he is quick to toss her aside.
Wisdom well deserves her name,   22
for she is not accessible to many.

Listen, my son, accept my   23
   judgement;

[l] *they . . . bull: probable meaning; Gk. and Heb. both
obscure.*

opportunist. **6.2–3:** Control of *passions* rather than their free expression is real vitality. **4:**
Gloating enemies: a form of punishment.
   6.5–17: Friendship. 5: *Pleasant words:* contrast with 5.10–14. **6–15:** *Friends,* false and true,
are nearly universal themes of secular wisdom. **16–17:** This common-sense section ends on the
religious note, *fear of the Lord.* On treating the *neighbour* as oneself, see 31.15.
   6.18–7.3: The struggle for, and choice of, wisdom. (Compare with 4.11–19.) **21:** *Stone . . . that
tests his strength:* perhaps a training exercise. **22:** An obscure Heb. pun may lie behind this
verse. **23–31:** Slavery to wisdom (*fetters, collar,* v. 24) becomes a princely status (vv. 29–31).

do not reject my advice.

24 Put your feet in wisdom's fetters
and your neck into her collar.

25 Stoop to carry her on your shoulders
and do not chafe at her bonds.

26 Come to her whole-heartedly,
and keep to her ways with all your
might.

27 Follow her track, and she will make
herself known to you;
once you have grasped her, never
let her go.

28 In the end you will find the relief
she offers;
she will transform herself into joy
for you.

29 Her fetters will become your strong
defence
and her collar a gorgeous robe.

30 Her yoke[m] is a golden ornament
and her bonds a purple cord.

31 You shall put her on like a gorgeous
robe
and wear her like a splendid crown.

32 If it is your wish, my son, you can
be trained;
if you give your mind to it, you can
become clever;

33 if you enjoy listening, you will learn;
if you are attentive, you will grow
wise.

34 When you stand among your elders,
decide who is wise and join him.

35 Listen gladly to every godly
argument
and see that no wise proverb
escapes you.

36 If you discover a wise man, rise
early to visit him;
let your feet wear out his doorstep.

37 Ponder the decrees of the Lord
and study his commandments at
all times.
He will strengthen your mind
and grant your desire for wisdom.

7 Do no evil, and evil will not come
upon you;

2 turn away from wrong, and it will
avoid you.

3 Do not sow in the furrows of
injustice,
for fear of reaping a sevenfold crop.

4 Do not ask the Lord for high office
or the king for preferment.

5 Do not pose as a righteous man
before the Lord
or play the sage in the king's presence.

6 Do not aspire to be a judge,
unless you have the strength to
put an end to injustice;
for you may be intimidated by a
man of rank
and so compromise your integrity.

7 Do not commit an offence against
the community
and so incur a public disgrace.

8 Do not pile sin upon sin,
for even one is enough to make you
guilty.

9 Do not say, 'My liberality will be
taken into account;
when I make an offering to God
Most High he will accept it.'

10 Do not grow weary of praying
or neglect the giving of charity.

11 Never laugh at a man in his bitter
humiliation,
for there is One who both humbles
and exalts.

12 Do not plot to deceive your
brother
or pay back a friend in his own coin.

13 Refuse ever to tell a lie;
it is a habit from which no good
comes.

14 Never be garrulous among your
elders
or repeat yourself when you pray.

15 Do not resent manual labour or
farm-work,
for it was ordained by the Most
High.

16 Do not enlist in the ranks of
sinners;
remember that retribution will not
delay.

m So Heb.; Gk. Upon her.

For *relief* (v. 28) and *yoke* (v. 30; compare 51.26), see Mt.11.28–30. **32–33:** The fourfold *if* emphasizes freedom of choice. **34–37:** To *listen* to the wise (vv. 34–36) and to *study* the Law (v. 37) bring the same wisdom.

    7.4–17: Warnings against pride. In this series of imperatives, the interplay of common sense and faith is noteworthy. **5:** Action *before the Lord* is paralleled to that *in the king's presence.* **14:** See Mt.6.7. **15:** *Farm-work* was widely praised as honorable (see Gen.2.15), but in 38.25

17 Humble yourself to the uttermost,
for the doom of the impious is fire
and worms.

18 Do not part with a friend for gain,[n]
or a true brother for all the gold of
Ophir.

19 Do not lose the chance of a wise
and good wife,
for her attractions are worth more
than gold.

20 Do not ill-treat a slave who works
honestly
or a hired servant whose heart is in
his work.

21 Love a good slave from the bottom
of your heart
and do not grudge him his freedom.

22 Have you cattle? Take care of them,
and if they bring you profit, keep them.

23 Have you sons? Discipline them
and break them in from their earliest
years.

24 Have you daughters? See that they
are chaste,
and do not be too lenient with them.

25 Marry your daughter, and a great
load will be off your hands;
but give her to a sensible husband.

26 If you have a wife after your own
heart, do not divorce her;
but do not trust yourself to one you
cannot love.

27 Honour your father with all your
heart
and do not forget your mother's
birth-pangs;

28 remember that your parents brought
you into the world;
how can you repay what they have
done for you?

29 Fear the Lord with all your heart
and reverence his priests.

30 Love your Maker with all your might
and do not leave his ministers
without support.

31 Fear the Lord and honour the priest
and give him his dues, as you have
been commanded,
the firstfruits, the guilt-offering, and
the shoulder of the victim,
the dedication sacrifice, and the
firstfruits of holy things.

32 Be open-handed also with the poor,
so that your own well-being may be
complete.

33 Every living man appreciates
generosity;
do not withhold your kindness
even when a man is dead.

34 Do not turn your back on those
who weep,
but mourn with those who mourn.

35 Do not hesitate to visit the sick,
for by such visits you will win their
affection.

36 Whatever you are doing, remember
the end that awaits you;
then all your life you will never go
wrong.

8 Do not pit yourself against a great
man,
for fear of falling into his power.

2 Do not quarrel with a rich man;
you may be sure he will outbid you.
For money has been the ruin of many
and has misled the minds of kings.

3 Do not argue with a long-winded
man,
and so add fuel to his fire.

4 Never make fun of an ill-mannered
man,
or you may hear your ancestors
insulted.

*n Probable reading (compare 27. 1), supported by Vss.;
Gk. for a trifle.*

---

it is seen as in conflict with study. **17:** *Fire and worms:* the underlying Gk. differs from the Heb., which speaks rather of death (worms) as the fate of all men, and not as punishment for the impious.

7.18–28: How to act in life's closest relationships. 18: *Ophir:* a well-known source for gold, perhaps in southwest Arabia; see 1 Kgs.9.28. **19:** *Do not lose the chance:* Heb. lit. "do not reject," alludes to divorce; see v. 26 and Deut.24.1. **22:** The only nonpersonal relationship in the list. **24–25:** Marriage was arranged by the father; until then the *daughter* was kept under close supervision. **27–28:** Here gratitude is the motive for honoring parents; contrast 3.1–16.

7.29–36: Religious duties. 29–31: In contrast to Prov., the priests and formal worship are important to the author; compare 50.1–21. **32–35:** Other religious duties are care for the *poor* and *sick. Kindness* to the *dead* means providing proper burial; see Tob.1.17. **36:** The same closing advice as in v. 17.

8.1–19: Behavior toward various people. This section deals with a wider circle than 7.18–28. **1–7:** Wisdom advises caution in difficult relationships; See also vv. 10–19. **3:** See Prov.26.21.

5 Do not rebuke a man who is
    already penitent;
remember that we are all guilty.
6 Despise no man for being old;
some of us are growing old as well.
7 Do not be smug over another man's
    death;
remember that we must all die.

8 Do not neglect the studies of the
    learned,
but apply yourself to their maxims;
from these you will learn discipline,
and how to be the servant of
    princes.
9 Do not ignore the discourse of your
    elders,
for they themselves learned from
    their fathers;
they can teach you to understand
and to have an answer ready in time
    of need.

10 Do not kindle a sinner's coals,
for fear of being burnt in the flames
    of his fire.
11 Do not let a man's insolence bring
    you to your feet;
he will only sit waiting to trap you
    with your own words.
12 Do not lend to a man with more
    influence than yourself,
or, if you do, write off the loan as a
    loss.
13 Do not stand surety beyond your
    means,
and, when you do stand surety, be
    prepared to pay.

14 Do not go to law with a judge,
for in deference to his position they
    will give him the verdict.
15 Do not go travelling with a reckless
    man:
you may find him a burden on you.
He will do as he fancies,

and his folly will bring death on you
    as well.
Do not fall out with a hot-tempered 16
    man
or walk with him in unfrequented
    places;
he thinks nothing of bloodshed,
and where no help is at hand he will
    set upon you.
Never discuss your plans with a fool, 17
for he cannot keep a secret.
Do nothing private in the presence 18
    of a stranger;
you do not know what use he will
    make of it.
Do not tell what is in your mind to 19
    all comers
or accept favours from them.

Do not be jealous over the wife you **9**
    cherish,
and so put into her head the idea of
    wronging you.
Do not surrender yourself to a woman 2
and let her trample down your
    strength.
Do not go near a loose woman, 3
for fear of falling into her snares.
Do not keep company with a 4
    dancing-girl,
or you may be caught by her tricks.
Do not let your mind dwell on a 5
    virgin,
or you may be trapped into paying
    damages for her.
Never surrender yourself to 6
    prostitutes,
for fear of losing all you possess,
nor gaze about you in the city streets 7
or saunter in deserted corners.
Do not let your eye linger on a 8
    woman's figure
or your thoughts dwell on beauty
    not yours to possess.
Many have been seduced by the
    beauty of a woman,

8–9: In contrast, toward the *learned* and the *elders*, one can be open. **8:** Training for the service of *princes*, i.e. government service, was an age-old function of wisdom teaching; here the maxim may be merely traditional, or it may apply to the defense of Jewish interests before Hellenistic rulers. **9:** The chain of tradition was important to the ancients. **15:** Caution in traveling comes from the author's own experience; see 39.4; 51.13. **19:** Here, as throughout the chapter, except in vv. 8–9, the clue to wisdom is withholding oneself.
   9.1–9: Behavior toward women. All that follows, aside from v. 1, urges holding oneself back from trouble. **1:** *Do not be jealous,* i.e. have confidence, is the only positive advice. **2:** *Do not surrender yourself:* probably alludes to one's wife; a warning against too much confidence. **5:** *Damages* would be paid to her father (Exod.22.16–17; Deut.22.29). Financial and social risks rather than personal loyalty in marriage are stressed.

which kindles passion like fire.

9 Never sit at table with another man's
      wife
or join her in a drinking party,
for fear of succumbing to her charms
and slipping into fatal disaster.

10 Do not desert an old friend;
a new one is not worth as much.
A new friend is like new wine;
you do not enjoy drinking it until
      it has matured.

11 Do not envy a bad man his success;
you do not know what fate is in
      store for him.

12 Take no pleasure in the pleasures
      of the wicked;
remember that they will not go
      scot-free all their lives.

13 Keep clear of a man who has power
      to kill,
and you will not be haunted by the
      fear of death.
If you do approach him, make no
      false step
or you will risk losing your life.
Tell yourself that you are making
      your way among pitfalls,
or walking on the battlements of
      the city.

14 Take the measure of your neighbours
      as best you can,
and accept advice from those who
      are wise.

15 Let your discussion be with intelligent
      men
and all your talk about the law of
      the Most High.

16 Choose the company of good men
      at table,
and take pride in fearing the Lord.

17 A craftsman is recognized by his
      skilful hand
and a councillor by his words of
      wisdom.

18 A gossip is the terror of his town,
detested for his unguarded talk.

A wise ruler trains his people,   10
and gives them sound and orderly
      government.
Like ruler, like ministers;   2
like sovereign, like subjects;
a king untutored is the people's ruin,   3
but wise rulers make a city fit to
      live in.

Man's life under divine providence

THE GOVERNMENT OF THE WORLD IS   4
      in the hand of the Lord;
at the right time he appoints the
      right man to rule it.
In the Lord's hand is all human   5
      success;
it is he who confers honour on the
      legislator.

Do not nurse a grievance against   6
      your neighbour for every
      offence,
and do not resort to acts of
      insolence.
Arrogance is hateful to God and   7
      man,
and injustice is offensive to both.
Empire passes from nation to nation   8
because of injustice, insolence, and
      greed.
What has man to be so proud of?   9
      He is only dust and ashes,
subject even in life to bodily decay.*o*
A long illness mocks the doctor's   10
      skill;
today's king is tomorrow's corpse.
When a man dies, he comes into an   11
      inheritance
of maggots and vermin and worms.
The origin of pride is to forsake the 12
      Lord,
man's heart revolting against his
      Maker;
as its origin is sin,   13

---

o subject . . . decay: *probable meaning, based on Heb.;*
Gk. obscure.

9.10–16: Social behavior. 11: God's justice and the uncertainty of life are held together in
this statement. **13:** *Walk on battlements:* expose oneself to deadly weapons.
   9.17–10.3: The skill of rulers. The language shifts from command to description. **17:** A leader
is like a *craftsman.* **10.2–3:** The ideal government is paternalistic. *King* was a traditional term
in wisdom, here equivalent to *ruler;* the Jews had no king at this time.
   10.4–11.28: Rulership and pride. A series of poems on pride repeatedly alludes to the ruler
as prince, a model of the man tempted to pride. 1 Sam.2.1–10 may have suggested many of
the themes in this section. **4–5:** Babylonian and Egyptian kings also claimed to be appointed
by God. **6–11:** Against pride which destroys both *man* (v. 9) and *nation* (v. 8), the poet points

so persistence in it brings on a deluge
   of depravity,
Therefore the Lord sends upon
   them signal punishments
and brings them to utter disaster.

14 The Lord overturns the thrones of
   princes
and enthrones the gentle in their
   place.
15 The Lord pulls up nations by the
   roots
and plants the humble instead.
16 The Lord lays waste the territory of
   nations,
destroying them to the very
   foundations of the earth.
17 Some he shrivels away to nothing,
so that all memory of them vanishes
   from the earth.
18 Pride was not the Creator's design
   for man
nor violent anger for those born of
   woman.

19 What creature is worthy of honour?
   Man.
What men? Those who fear the Lord.
What creature is worthy of contempt?
   Man.
What men? Those who break the
   commandments.
20 As the members of the family honour
   their head,
so the Lord honours those who fear
   him.*p*
22 The rich, the famous, and the
   poor—
their only boast is the fear of the
   Lord.
23 It is unjust to despise a poor man
   who is intelligent,
and wrong to honour a man who is
   a sinner.
24 The prince, the judges, and the ruler
   win high honours,
but none of them is as great as the
   godfearing man.
25 The wise slave will have free men to
   wait on him,
and a man of sense will not grumble
   at it.

26 DO NOT BE TOO CLEVER TO DO A
   day's work
or boast when you have nothing to
   live on.
27 It is better to work and have more
   than enough
than to boast and go hungry.
28 My son, in all modesty, keep your
   self-respect
and value yourself at your true
   worth.
29 Who will speak up for a man who
   is his own enemy,
or respect one who disparages
   himself?
30 A poor man may be honoured for
   his wisdom,
a rich man for his wealth;
31 if a man is honoured in poverty,
   how much more in wealth!
And if he is despised in wealth,
   how much more in poverty!
11 A poor man with wisdom can hold
   his head high
and take his seat among the great.

2 Do not overrate one man for his
   good looks
or be repelled by another man's
   appearance.
3 The bee is small among winged
   creatures,
yet her produce takes first place
   for sweetness.
4 Do not pride yourself on your fine
   clothes
or be haughty when honours come
   to you;
for the Lord can perform marvels
which are hidden from the eyes of
   men.
5 Many kings have been reduced to
   sitting on the ground
while a mere nobody has worn the
   crown.
6 Many rulers have been stripped of
   their honours,
and great men have found themselves
   at the mercy of others.

p Some witnesses add (21) Fear the Lord, and you will
be accepted; be obstinate and proud, and you will be
rejected.

---

to death which levels all, even the *king* (vv. 10–11). **14–18:** Compare Isa.40.15–17,23–24.
19: The same answer to opposite questions was a teaching device. **25:** There is no literal
implication here of freeing the slave; contrast 7.21. **30–31:** In themselves *poverty* and *wealth*
are neutral as true values but wealth does make a difference in the way a man is treated. **11.2–6:**

7 Do not find fault before examining
  the evidence;
think first, and criticize afterwards.

8 Do not answer without first listening,
and do not interrupt when another
  is speaking.

9 Never take sides in a quarrel not
  your own
or become involved in the disputes
  of rascals.

10 My son, do not engage in too many
  transactions;
if you attempt too much, you will
  come to grief.
When you are in pursuit, you will
  not overtake;
when you are in flight, you will not
  escape.

11 One man slaves and strains and
  hurries
and is all the farther behind.

12 Another is slow-witted and in need
  of help,
lacking in strength and abounding
  in poverty;
but the Lord turns a kindly eye
  upon him
and lifts him up out of his miserable
  plight.

13 He raises him to dignity
to the amazement of all.

14 Good fortune and bad, life and death,
poverty and wealth, all come from
  the Lord.*q*

17 His gifts to the devout are lasting;
his approval brings unending success.

18 A man may grow rich by stinting
  and sparing,
but what does he get for his pains?

19 When he says, 'I have earned my
  rest,
now I can live on my savings',
he does not know how long it will be
before he must die and leave his
  wealth to others.

20 Stand by your contract and give
  your mind to it;

grow old at your work.

21 Do not envy a rogue his success;
trust the Lord and stick to your job.
It is no difficult thing for the Lord
to make a poor man rich in a
  moment.

22 The Lord's blessing is the reward
  of piety,
which blossoms in one short hour.

23 Do not say, 'What use am I?
What good*r* can the future hold for
  me?'

24 And do not say, 'I am independent;
nothing can ever go wrong for me.'

25 Hardship is forgotten in time of
  success,
and success in time of hardship.

26 Even on the day a man dies it is
  easy for the Lord
to give him his deserts.

27 One hour's misery wipes out all
  memory of delight,
and a man's end reveals his true
  character.

28 Call no man happy before he dies,
for not until death is a man known
  for what he is.*s*

29 DO NOT INVITE ALL COMERS INTO YOUR
  home;
dishonesty has many disguises.

30 A proud man's mind is like a decoy-
  partridge in its cage,
or like a spy watching for a false
  step.

31 He waits for a chance to twist good
  into evil
or to cast blame on innocent actions.

32 A small spark kindles many coals,
and the insinuations of a bad man
  end in bloodshed.

33 Beware of a scoundrel and his evil
  plots,
or he may ruin your reputation for
  ever.

q Some witnesses add (15) From the Lord come wisdom, understanding, and love, knowledge of the law, and the doing of good works. (16) Error and darkness have been with sinners from their birth, and evil grows old along with those who take delight in it.
r Or 'What more do I need? What greater success . . .
s not . . . he is: *so Heb.; Gk.* a man is known by his children.

The unpredictability of life is a warning against pride. **7–9:** Discretion in judgment implies avoiding overinvolvement. **10–13:** Overreaching oneself is self-destructive; compare vv. 2–6. **14–19:** God's gifts are *lasting* (v. 17); one's own achievement may be snatched away (v. 19). **20–28:** This poem is a meditation on the popular proverb, *Call no man happy before he dies* (v. 28). The skeptical proverb is given religious meaning.
  11.29–13.13: Caution against being taken advantage of. God is mentioned only in 12.2,6 in

34 Admit a stranger to your home and
    he will stir up trouble for you
and make you a stranger to your
    own flesh and blood.

12 If you do a good deed, make sure
    to whom you are doing it;
then you will have credit for your
    kindness.

2 A good turn done to a godfearing
    man will be rewarded,
if not by him, then by the Most High.

3 No good comes to the persistent
    wrong-doer
or to the man who never gives alms;*t*

5 refuse him bread; give him nothing
    at all;
he will only use your gifts to get the
    better of you,
and you will suffer a double wrong
in return for the favours you have
    done him.

6 The Most High himself hates sinners
and sends bad men what they
    deserve.

7 Give to a good man, but never help
    a sinner;
keep your good works for the
    humble, not the insolent.*u*

8 Prosperity does not reveal your
    friends;
adversity does not conceal your
    enemies.

9 When all goes well a man's enemies
    are friendly,*v*
but in hard times even his friend
    will desert him.

10 Never trust your enemy;
he will turn vicious as sure as metal
    rusts.

11 If he appears humble and
    obsequious,
take care! Be on your guard against
    him!
Behave towards him like a man who
    polishes a mirror
to make sure that it does not corrode
    away.

12 Do not have him at your side,

or he will trip you up and supplant
    you.
Do not let him sit at your right
    hand,
or he will soon be wanting your own
    seat;
and in the end you will see the force
    of my words
and recall my warning with regret.

13 Who sympathizes with a snake-
    charmer when he is bitten,
or with a tamer of wild animals?

14 No more does anyone pity the man
    who keeps bad company
and involves himself in another's
    wickedness.

15 He may stand by you for a while,
but, if you falter, his friendship will
    not last.

16 An enemy has honey on his lips,
but in his heart he plans to trip you
    into the ditch.
He may have tears in his eyes,
but give him a chance and he will
    not stop at bloodshed.

17 If disaster overtakes you, you will
    find him there ahead of you,
ready, with a pretence of help, to
    pull your feet from under you.

18 Then he will nod his head and rub
    his hands
and spread gossip, showing his true
    colours.

13 Handle pitch and it will make you
    dirty;
keep company with an arrogant man
    and you will grow like him.

2 Do not lift a weight too heavy for
    you,
keeping company with a man greater
    and richer than yourself.
How can a jug be friends with a
    kettle?

*t The order of the following verses has been disturbed
in all versions; Gk. reads . . . gives alms; (4) give to
a godfearing man, but never help a sinner; (5) keep
your good works for the humble, not the insolent;
refuse him . . . (compare verse 7).
u keep . . . insolent: this is the beginning of verse 5 in Gk.
v So Heb.; Gk. grieve.*

---

this hardheaded, practical section. **12.1–7:** Reciprocity in good deeds is urged. God's hatred
of *sinners* is the motivation for the advice, *never help a sinner* (vv. 6–7); contrast Ezek.18.23.
11: The *mirror* was of metal and needed constant polishing; likewise, constant vigilance is the
only protection from the corrosion (v. 10) of the enemy's wiles. **12:** The reference to *my words*
is a threat of "I told you so" from the teacher. **18:** *Nod his head:* a gesture of triumphant
derision. **13.1:** The first line has become an English proverb. **2:** The *jug* of clay would be broken

If they knock together, the one will
　　be smashed.
3　A rich man does wrong, and adds
　　insult to injury;
　a poor man is wronged, and must
　　apologize into the bargain.
4　If you can serve his turn, a rich man
　　will exploit you,
　but if you are in need, he will leave
　　you alone.
5　If you are in funds, he will be your
　　constant companion,
　and drain you dry without a twinge
　　of remorse.
6　He may need you; and then he will
　　deceive you,
　and will be all smiles and
　　encouragement,
　paying you compliments and asking,
　　'What can I do for you?',
7　embarrassing you with his hospitality,
　until he has drained you two or
　　three times over;
　but in the end he will laugh at you.
　Afterwards, when he sees you, he
　　will pass you by,
　nodding his head over you.

8　Take care not to be led astray
　and humiliated when you are
　　enjoying yourself.
9　If a great man invites you, be slow
　　to accept,
　and he will be the more pressing in
　　his invitation.
10　Do not be forward, for fear of a
　　rebuff,
　but do not keep aloof, or you may
　　be forgotten.
11　Do not presume to converse with
　　him as an equal
　or be over-confident if he holds you
　　long in talk.
　The more he speaks, the more he is
　　testing you,
　examining you even while he smiles.
12　The man who cannot keep your
　　secrets is without compunction
　and will not spare you harm or
　　imprisonment;

so keep your secrets to yourself and　13
　be very careful,
for you are walking on the brink of
　ruin.*w*

Every animal loves its like,　15
and every man his neighbour.
All creatures flock together with　16
　their kind,
and men form attachments with
　their own sort.
What has a wolf in common with a　17
　lamb,
or a sinner with a man of piety?
What peace can there be between　18
　hyena and dog,
what peace between rich man and
　pauper?
As lions prey on the wild asses of　19
　the desert,
so the rich batten on the poor.
As humility disgusts the proud,　20
so is the rich man disgusted by the
　poor.

If a rich man staggers, he is held up　21
　by his friends;
a poor man falls, and his friends
　disown him as well.
When a rich man slips, many come　22
　to his rescue;
if he says something outrageous,
　they make excuses for him.
A poor man makes a slip, and they
　all criticize him;
even if he talks sense, he is not
　given a hearing.
A rich man speaks, and all are silent;　23
then they praise his speech to the
　skies.
A poor man speaks, and they say,
　'Who is this?',
and if he stumbles, they give him
　an extra push.

WEALTH IS GOOD, IF SIN HAS NOT　24
　tainted it;

w Some witnesses add When you hear this in your
sleep, wake up. (14) Love the Lord all your life and
appeal to him for salvation.

---

by the metal *kettle*. **3–7**: The tactics of the *rich* require constant guard. **9**: The *great man* is
the political authority who is trying to extract information; see vv. 12–13.
　13.15–23: The incompatibility of rich and poor. 21–23: Society readily supports the rich;
compare v. 3 and contrast 10.23–24.
　13.24–14.2: True contentment. The harsh facts of the preceding section are balanced by the
thought that true happiness comes from within.

poverty is a crime only to the
ungodly.

25 It is a man's heart that changes the
look on his face
either for better or worse.

26 The sign of a happy heart is a
cheerful face,
but the invention of proverbs
involves wearisome thought.

14 Happy the man who has never let
slip a careless word,
who has never felt the sting of
remorse!

2 Happy the man whose conscience
does not accuse him,
whose hope has never been
disappointed!

3 It is not proper for a mean man to
be rich:
what use is money to a miser?

4 He deprives himself only to hoard
for other men;
others will live in luxury on his riches.

5 How can a man be hard on himself
and kind to others?
His possessions bring him no
enjoyment.

6 No one is worse than the man who
is grudging to himself:
his niggardliness is its own
punishment.

7 If ever he does good, it is by mistake,
and then in the end he reveals his
meanness.

8 It is a hard man who has a grudging
eye;
he turns his back on need and looks
the other way.

9 A covetous man's eye is not satisfied
with his share;
greedy injustice shrivels the soul.

10 A miser grudges bread
and keeps an empty table.

11 My son, if you can afford it, do
yourself well,

always offering to the Lord the
sacrifice due to him.

Remember that death is not to be 12
postponed;
the hour of your appointment with
the grave is undisclosed.

Before you die, do good to your 13
friend;
reach out as far as you can to help
him.

Do not miss a day's enjoyment
or forgo your share of innocent 14
pleasure.

Are you to leave to others all you
have laboured for 15
and let them draw lots for your
hard-earned wealth?

Give and receive; indulge yourself; 16
you need not expect luxuries in the
grave.

Man's body wears out like a 17
garment;
for the ancient sentence stands:
You shall die.

In the thick foliage of a growing tree 18
one crop of leaves falls and another
grows instead;
so the generations of flesh and blood
pass
with the death of one and the birth
of another.

All man's works decay and vanish, 19
and the workman follows them into
oblivion.

HAPPY THE MAN WHO FIXES HIS 20
thoughts on wisdom
and uses his brains to think,
the man who contemplates her ways 21
and ponders her secrets.

Stalk her like a hunter 22
and lie in wait beside her path!

The man who peers in at her windows 23
and listens at her keyhole,
who camps beside her house, 24
driving his tent-peg into her wall,

14.3–19: Wrong and right uses of money. 3–10: Money is useless to a *mean man* or a *miser;*
it is a basic conviction of the author that if you cannot be good to yourself, you cannot be
good to others; see v. 5. **12:** The *grave:* lit. Hades, Heb. *Sheol,* the gloomy underworld. God
knows the *hour* of death, but it is unknown to man. **17:** The *ancient sentence:* see Gen.2.17.
18: Comparison of passing generations to falling *leaves* was widespread; compare Homer,
Iliad, VI 145–50. **19:** Contrast Rev.14.13.

14.20–15.10: The quest for wisdom. Compare with 4.11–19 and Prov.8.32–9.6. **20:** *Happy*
("blessed" in the earlier translations) introduces a set style of wisdom speech which declares
the way to the fullness of life. **23:** *Peers in:* is on familiar terms; contrast the etiquette of
21.23–24 ("a well-bred man stands outside"). **24:** The *tent peg:* a symbol of setting up a home.

25 who pitches his tent close by her,
where it is best for men to live—

26 he will put his children in her shade
and camp beneath her branches,

27 sheltered by her from the heat,
and dwelling in the light of her
presence.

15 The man who fears the Lord will do
all this,
and if he masters the law, wisdom
will be his.

2 She will come out to meet him like
a mother;
she will receive him like a young bride.

3 For food she will give him the bread
of understanding
and for drink the water of knowledge.

4 He will lean on her and not fall;
he will rely on her to save him from
disgrace.

5 She will promote him above his
neighbours,
and find words for him when he
speaks in the assembly.

6 He shall be crowned with joy and
exultation;
lasting honour shall be his heritage.

7 Fools shall never possess wisdom;
sinners shall catch no glimpse of her.

8 She holds aloof from arrogance,
far from the thoughts of liars.

9 Worship is out of place on the lips
of a sinner,
unprompted as he is by the Lord.

10 Worship is the outward expression
of wisdom,
and the Lord himself inspires it.

11 Do not say, 'The Lord is to blame
for my failure';
it is for you to avoid doing what he
hates.

12 Do not say, 'It was he who led me
astray';

he has no use for sinful men.
The Lord hates every kind of vice; 13
you cannot love it and still fear him.

When he made man in the beginning, 14
he left him free to take his own
decisions;
if you choose, you can keep the 15
commandments;
whether or not you keep faith is
yours to decide.

He has set before you fire and 16
water;
reach out and take which you choose;
before man lie life and death, 17
and whichever he prefers is his.

For in his great wisdom and mighty 18
power
the Lord sees everything.

He keeps watch over those who 19
fear him;
no human act escapes his notice.

But he has commanded no man to 20
be wicked,
nor has he given licence to commit
sin.

DO NOT SET YOUR HEART ON A LARGE **16**
family of ne'er-do-wells
or be content if your sons are godless.

However many they are, do not 2
think yourself happy,
unless the fear of the Lord is in them.

Do not count on their living to be 3
old
or rely on their numbers;
for one son can be better than a
thousand;
better indeed to die childless than
to have godless children.

Thanks to one man of good sense a 4
city may be populous,
while a tribe of lawless men becomes
a desert.

Many a time have I seen this with 5
my own eyes,

15.1: *All this* ties 15.1–8 to 14.20–27. *Law* and *wisdom* coincide here as throughout the book.
6: Compare this poetic glorification of the wise man with the pragmatic observation of wisdom's limits in 13.2–13. **9–10:** Wisdom is *worship;* compare 1.11–20. *Sinners:* probably Hellenized Jews careless about observation of the Law.
15.11–20: Freedom of choice. "Determinism" or "predestination" is strongly rejected, to make clear that God is not responsible for man's sin, which he *hates* (vv. 11,13). **14–15:** Man was created free and is still free; contrast Rom.1.18–3.20; 7.1–25. **16–17:** Compare Deut.30.19–20. **18–20:** Though God does not determine man's deeds, he *keeps watch* over the pious.
16.1–14: Retribution and reward. 1–3: A large family was held to be one of God's greatest gifts. **5:** *Seen this with my own eyes:* the teacher's personal experience gives weight to tradition.

and still weightier examples have come to my ears.

6 Where sinners gather, the fire breaks out;
retribution blazes up in a rebellious nation.

7 There was no pardon for the giants of old,
who revolted in all their strength.

8 There was no reprieve for Lot's adopted home,
abhorrent in its arrogance.

9 There was no mercy for the doomed nation,
exterminated for their sins—

10 those six hundred thousand warriors
marshalled in stubborn defiance.

11 Even if only one man were obstinate,
it would be a miracle for him to escape punishment.
For mercy and anger belong to the Lord;
he shows his power in forgiveness, or in the flood of his wrath.

12 His mercy is great, but great also is his condemnation;
he judges a man by what he has done.

13 He does not let the sinner escape with his loot
or try the patience of the godly too long.

14 He opens a way for every work of mercy,
and everyone is treated according to his own deserts.ˣ

17 Do not say, 'I am hidden from the Lord;
who is there in heaven to give a thought to me?
Among so many I shall not be noticed;

what is my life compared with the measureless creation?

18 Heaven itself, the highest heaven, the abyss and the earth are shaken at his coming;

19 the very mountains and the foundations of the world tremble when he looks upon them.

20 What human mind can grasp this, or comprehend his ways?

21 As a squall takes men unawares, so most of his works are done in secret.

22 Who is to declare his acts of justice or wait for his remote decree?'

23 These are the thoughts of a small mind,
the absurdities of a senseless and misguided man.

24 LISTEN TO ME, MY SON, AND LEARN sense;
pay close attention to what I say;

25 I will show you exact discipline and teach you accurate knowledge.

26 When the Lord created his works in the beginning,
and after making them definedʸ their boundaries,

27 he disposed them in an eternal order and fixed their influences for all time.
They do not grow hungry or weary, or abandon their tasks;

28 one does not jostle another; they never disobey his word.

29 The Lord then looked at the earth and filled it with his good things.

30 With every kind of living creature he covered the ground,
into which they must all return.

x *Some witnesses add* (15) The Lord made Pharaoh too stubborn to acknowledge him, so that his deeds might be published to the world. (16) He displays his mercy to the whole creation, and has separated light from darkness with a plumb-line.
y When . . . defined: *probable reading, based on Heb.; Gk.* The works of the Lord have been under his judgement from the beginning, . . . he defined . . .

7: The *giants:* see Gen.6.4; compare Bar.3.26–28; Wis.14.6. **8:** *Lot's adopted home:* Sodom; see Gen.19.23–25. **9:** *The doomed nation:* the Canaanites; see Deut.7.1–6 and Gen.15.16. **10:** *Six hundred thousand:* rebellious Israelites; see 46.8; Exod.12.37; Num.14.22–23. **11–14:** God's *mercy* and *anger* are in tension; the author is sure that mercy will not provide an easy out for sinners.

16.17–23: God's universal knowledge. Only the *absurdities* of a *small mind* (v. 23) will lead to the wrong view that man can escape God's notice because his *creation* is *measureless* (v. 17).

16.24–30: God the Creator. This section, extending vv. 17–23, is drawn especially from Gen. ch. 1. **26–28:** The orderly heavens are *his works* (compare Isa.40.26) which do not *grow hungry or weary.* **29–30:** In contrast to the eternal heavens, the living beings on earth, even though *good,* are temporary.

17 The Lord created man from the
earth
and sent him back to it again.
2 He set a fixed span of life for men
and granted them authority over
everything on earth.
3 He clothed them with strength like
his own,^z
forming them in his own image.
4 He put the fear of man into all
creatures
and gave him lordship over beasts
and birds.^a
6 He gave men tongue and eyes and
ears,
the power of choice and a mind for
thinking.
7 He filled them with discernment
and showed them good and evil.
8 He kept watch over their hearts,
to display to them the majesty of
his works.^b
10 They shall praise his holy name,
proclaiming the grandeur of his works.
11 He gave them knowledge as well
and endowed them with the life-giving
law.
12 He established a perpetual covenant
with them
and revealed to them his decrees.
13 Their eyes saw his glorious majesty,
and their ears heard the glory of his
voice.
14 He said to them, 'Guard against all
wrongdoing',
and taught each man his duty
towards his neighbour.

15 Their conduct always lies open
before him,
never hidden from his scrutiny.^c
17 For every nation he appointed a
ruler,

but chose Israel to be his own
possession.^d
So whatever they do is clear to him   19
as daylight;
he keeps constant watch over their
lives.
Their wrongdoing is not hidden   20
from the Lord;
he observes all their sins.^e
A man's good deeds he treasures   22
like a signet-ring,
and his kindness like the apple of
his eye.
In the end he will rise up and give   23
the wicked their deserts,
bringing down their recompense on
their own heads.
Yet he leaves a way open for the   24
penitent to return to him,
and gives the waverer strength to
endure.

Turn to the Lord and have done   25
with sin;
make your prayer in his presence,
and so lessen your offence.
Come back to the Most High,   26
renounce wrongdoing,
and hate intensely what he abhors.
Who will praise the Most High in   27
the grave

z *So one Vs.; Gk. their own.*
a *Some witnesses add* (5) The Lord gave them the use
of the five faculties; as a sixth gift he distributed to
them mind, and as a seventh, reason, the interpreter of those faculties.
b *Some witnesses add* (9) He has given them the right
to boast for ever of his marvels.
c *Some witnesses read* . . . scrutiny. (16) Every man
from his youth tended towards evil; they could not
make themselves hearts of flesh in place of their
hearts of stone. (17) When he distributed the nations
over all the earth, for every . . .
d *Some witnesses add* (18) He rears them with discipline
as his first-born, imparting to them the light of love
and never neglecting them.
e *Some witnesses add* (21) The Lord who is gracious
and knows what they are made of has neither rejected nor deserted them, but spared them.

17.1–14: God's creation of man. The recurring *He* (God) emphasizes that man is God's
creature. **1:** Man's transitory nature links this poem to 16.24–30. **2–4:** Compare Gen.1.26–28.
6: The *power of choice* is what makes man man; it links the universally human to the covenant
at Sinai (v. 12). **11:** The apex of creation is the *Law*, which enables man to be fully human.
13: *Glorious majesty:* theophany on Sinai; see Exod.19.16–19. **14:** *Duty towards* the *neighbour*
is the core of the Law.
17.15–24: God's watchful care of his people. This is the closing poem of the section beginning
in 16.17, the final answer to the absurdities of 16.17–23. **17:** A higher standard is set for *Israel*,
which stands directly under God, not under an earthly *ruler*. **23–24:** The familiar contrast
between the righteous and the *wicked* is modified by the introduction of the *penitent*, those who
pass from the wicked group to the righteous. *Strength to endure:* the phrase, from Isa.40.31,
ties the end of the section to its beginning, 16.17, which is drawn from Isa.40.27.
17.25–32: A call to repentance. This poem gives a practical application to what precedes. The
sharp contrast between man's insignificance and God's greatness makes the point that pride
is the basic sin. **27:** The *grave:* see 14.12 n.

in place of the living who give him
    thanks?

28 When a man is dead and ceases to
    be, his gratitude dies with him;
    it is when he is alive and well that
    he praises the Lord.

29 How great is the Lord's mercy
    and his pardon to those who turn
    to him!

30 Not everything is within man's
    reach,
    for the human race is not immortal.

31 Is anything brighter than the sun?
    Yet the sun suffers eclipse.
    So flesh and blood have evil thoughts.

32 The Lord marshals the armies of
    high heaven,
    but all men are dust and ashes.

18 He who lives for ever is the Creator
    of the whole universe;
2 right belongs to the Lord alone.*f*
4 To no man is it given to unfold the
    story of his works;
    who can trace his marvels to their
    source?
5 No one can measure his majestic
    power,
    still less, tell the full tale of all his
    mercies.
6 Man can neither increase nor diminish
    them,
    nor fathom the wonders of the Lord.
7 When a man comes to the end of
    them he is still at the beginning,
    and when he has finished he will still
    be perplexed.
8 What is man and what use is he?
    What do his good or evil deeds
    signify?
9 His span of life is at the most a
    hundred years;
10 compared with endless time, his few
    years
    are like one drop of sea-water or a
    single grain of sand.
11 This is why the Lord is patient with
    them,

lavishing his mercy upon them.
He sees and knows the harsh fate   12
    in store for them,
    and therefore gives full play to his
    forgiveness.
Man's compassion is only for his   13
    neighbour,
    but the Lord's compassion is for
    every living thing.
He corrects and trains and teaches
    and brings them back as a shepherd
    his flock.
He has compassion on those who   14
    accept discipline
    and are eager to obey his decrees.

My son, do good without scolding;   15
    do not spoil your generosity with
    hard words.
Does not the dew give respite from   16
    the sweltering heat?
So a word can do more than a gift.
A kind word counts for more than   17
    a rich present;
    with a gracious man you will find
    both.
A fool cannot refrain from tactless   18
    criticism,
    and a grudging giver makes no eyes
    sparkle.

Before you speak, learn;   19
    and before you fall sick, consult a
    doctor.
Before judgement comes, examine   20
    yourself,
    and you will find pardon in the hour
    of scrutiny.
Before you fall ill, humble yourself; 21
    show your penitence as soon as you
    sin.
Let nothing hinder the prompt   22
    discharge of your vows;
    do not wait till death to be absolved.
Before you make a vow, give it due   23
    thought;

f Some witnesses add and there is none beside him,
(3) who can steer the world with his little finger, so
that all things obey his will; as king of the universe,
he has power to fix the bounds between what is
holy and what is profane.

18.1–7: **The limits of man's knowledge.** This poem expands the thought of 17.30–32.
   18.8–14: **God's compassion. 8:** Contrast Ps.8. **9:** The *hundred years* of a life span extend the
seventy or eighty of Ps.90.10. **12:** The *harsh fate* is death. **13–14:** God is presented as a patient
teacher; it is not accidental that the author was a teacher himself.
   18.15–18: **The deed and the word.** The theme of doing *good* is suggested by 18.13.
   18.19–29: **Looking ahead.** Foresight is a central virtue of secular wisdom. **19:** The advice to
consult a doctor views illness in common-sense terms. **21:** Here illness is seen as punishment

do not be like those who try the
Lord's patience.

24 Think of the wrath you must face
in the hour of death,
when the time of reckoning comes,
and he turns away his face.

25 In time of plenty remember the
time of famine,
poverty and need in days of wealth.

26 Between dawn and dusk times may
alter;
all change comes quickly, when the
Lord wills it.

27 A wise man is always on his guard;
when sin is rife, he will beware of
negligence.

28 Every man of sense makes
acquaintance with wisdom,
and to him who finds her she gives
cause for thankfulness.

29 Skilled speakers display their special
wisdom
by a flow of apt proverbs.

Maxims of prudence and self-discipline

30 DO NOT LET YOUR PASSIONS BE YOUR
guide,
but restrain your desires.

31 If you indulge yourself with all that
passion fancies,
it will make you the butt of your
enemies.

32 Do not revel in great luxury,
or the expense of it may ruin you.

33 Do not beggar yourself by feasting
on borrowed money,
when there is nothing in your purse.

19 A drunken workman never grows
rich;
carelessness in small things leads
little by little to ruin.

2 Wine and women rob the wise of
their wits,
and a frequenter of prostitutes becomes
more and more reckless,

3 till sores*g* and worms take possession
of him,

and his recklessness becomes his
undoing.

4 To trust a man hastily shows a
shallow mind,
and to sin is to do an injury to
yourself.

5 To delight in wickedness is to
court condemnation,

6 but evil loses its hold on the man
who hates gossip.

7 Never repeat what you hear,
and you will never be the loser.

8 Tell no tales about friend or foe;
unless silence makes you an accomplice,
never betray a man's secret.

9 Suppose he has heard you and learnt
to distrust you,
he will seize the first chance to show
his hatred.

10 Have you heard a rumour? Let it
die with you.
Never fear, it will not make you
burst.

11 A fool with a secret goes through
agony
like a woman in childbirth.

12 As painful as an arrow through the
thigh
is a rumour in the heart of a fool.

13 Confront your friend with the gossip
about him; he may not have
done it;
or if he did it, he will know not to
do it again.

14 Confront your neighbour; he may
not have said it;
or if he did say it, he will know not
to say it again.

15 Confront your friend; it will often
turn out to be slander;
do not believe everything you hear.

16 A man may let slip more than he
intends;
whose tongue is always free from
guilt?

17 Confront your neighbour before
you threaten him,

g Or decay.

---

for sin. **24:** Since retribution, for Ecclus., is limited to this life, man will be repaid for his deeds
before the *hour of death*. When God *turns away his face* from a person, it is always a sign of
his wrath; see Pss.13.1; 44.24.
18.30–19.17: Self-control. 30: The poem of 18.30–19.3 is a commentary on this popular
proverb. **19.2:** *Wine and women* are frequently associated already in Egyptian wisdom. See
Prov.31.3–5. **4–17:** Self-control in speech is discussed in two sections: vv. 4–12 on not speaking
and vv.13–17 on proper speech, direct confrontation of rumor. **17:** God's *law* is mentioned in
closing, a typical pattern.

and let the law of the Most High
take its course.[h]

20 All wisdom is the fear of the Lord
and includes the fulfilling of the law.[i]
22 The knowledge of wickedness is not
wisdom,
nor is there good sense in the advice
of sinners.
23 There is a cleverness that is
loathsome,
and some fools are merely ignorant.
24 Better to be godfearing and lack
brains
than to have great intelligence and
break the law.
25 A meticulous cleverness may lead
to injustice,
and a man may make himself
offensive in order that right
may prevail.
26 There is a scoundrel who stoops
and wears mourning,
but who is a fraud at heart.
27 He covers his face and pretends to
be deaf,
but when nobody is looking, he
will steal a march on you;
28 and if lack of strength prevents
him from doing wrong,
he will still harm you at the first
opportunity.
29 Yet you can tell a man by his looks
and recognize good sense at first
sight.
30 A man's clothes, and the way he
laughs,
and his gait, reveal his character.

20 A reproof may be untimely,
and silence may show a man's good
sense.
2 Yet how much better it is to complain
than to nurse a grudge,
and confession saves a man from
disgrace.[j]
4 Like a eunuch longing to seduce a
girl

is the man who tries to do right by
violence.
One man is silent and is found to be   5
wise;
another is hated for his endless
chatter.
One man is silent, at a loss for an   6
answer;
another is silent, biding his time.
The wise man is silent until the right   7
moment,
but a swaggering fool is always
speaking out of turn.
A garrulous man makes himself   8
detested,
and one who abuses his position
arouses hatred.

A MAN SOMETIMES FINDS PROFIT IN   9
adversity,
and a windfall may result in loss.
Sometimes liberality does not benefit   10
the giver,
sometimes it brings a double return.
The quest for honour may lead to   11
disgrace,
but there are those who have risen
from obscurity to eminence.
A man may make a good bargain,   12
but pay for it seven times over.
A wise man endears himself when   13
he speaks,
but fools scatter compliments in vain.
A gift from a fool will bring you no   14
benefit;
it looks bigger to him than it does
to you.
He gives small gifts accompanied by   15
long lectures,

h *Some witnesses add* without giving way to anger.
(18) The fear of the Lord is the way towards acceptance, and wisdom wins love from him. (19) The
knowledge of the Lord's commandments is life-
giving discipline, and those who do what pleases him
eat from the tree of immortality.
i *Some witnesses add* and a knowledge of his omnip-
otence. (21) A servant who says, 'I will not do as you
wish', even if he does it later, angers the man who
feeds him.
j *Some witnesses add* (3) How good it is to respond
to reproof with repentance, and so escape deliberate
sin!

19.20–30: True wisdom and mere cleverness. This is the first of a series of observations; except
for 21.1–11, after the initial reference to God (v. 20), he is not mentioned again until 23.1.
Notice also the scarcity of imperatives. **22–28:** Clever knowledge (probably Hellenistic learning)
that disregards God's *law* (v. 24) destroys human trust. Covering the *face* (v. 27) was probably
a begging technique. **29–30:** Wisdom includes the ability to judge character.
    20.1–8: Qualities of silence and speaking. The poem searches for a middle way between the
wrong silence of nursing a *grudge* (v. 2) and the wrong self-expression of doing *right by violence*
(v. 4).
    20.9–17: Surprising outcomes. The wise man expects the unexpected. **12:** *Seven times:* many times.

and opens his mouth as wide as the
    town crier.
He gives a loan today and asks it
    back tomorrow,
obnoxious fellow that he is!

16 The fool says, 'I have no friends,
I get no thanks for my kindnesses;
though they eat my bread, they
    speak ill of me.'

17 How everyone will laugh at him—
    and how often!

18 Better a slip on the stone floor than
    a slip of the tongue;
and the fall of the wicked comes
    just as suddenly.

19 An ill-mannered man is like an
    unseasonable story,
continually on the lips of the
    ill-bred.

20 A proverb will fall flat when uttered
    by a fool,
for he will produce it at the wrong
    time.

21 Poverty may keep a man from doing
    wrong;
when the day's work is over,
    conscience will not trouble him.

22 A man's diffidence may be his
    undoing,
or the foolish figure he cuts in the
    eyes of the world.

23 A man may be shamed into making
    promises to a friend
and needlessly turn him into an
    enemy.

24 A lie is an ugly blot on a man's
    name,
and is continually on the lips of
    those who know no better.

25 It is better to be a thief than a
    habitual liar,
but both will come to the same bad
    end.

26 A lying disposition brings disgrace;
the shame of it can never be shaken
    off.

27 A wise man advances himself when
    he speaks,
and a man of sense makes himself
    pleasant to the great.

28 The man who tills his land heaps up
    a harvest,
and he who pleases the great reaps
    pardon for his wrongdoing.

29 Hospitality and presents make wise
    men blind;
like a gag in the mouth they silence
    criticism.

30 Hidden wisdom and buried treasure,
what use is there in either?

31 Better a man who hides his folly
than one who hides his wisdom!*k*

21 Have you done wrong, my son? Do
    it no more,
but ask pardon for your past
    wrongdoing.

2 Avoid wrong as you would a viper,
for if you go near, it will bite you;
its teeth are like a lion's teeth
and can destroy the lives of men.

3 Every breach of the law is like a
    two-edged sword;
it inflicts an incurable wound.

4 By intimidation and insolence a man
    forfeits his wealth;
thus a proud man will be stripped
    of his possessions.

5 The Lord listens to the poor man's
    appeal,
and his verdict follows without delay.

6 To hate reproof is to go the way of
    sinners,
but whoever fears the Lord will
    repent whole-heartedly.

7 A great talker is known far and wide,
but a sensible man is aware of his
    failings.

8 To build a house with borrowed
    money
is like collecting stones for your own
    tomb.*l*

---

k Some witnesses add (32) Better to seek the Lord with
unremitting patience than to be the masterless
charioteer of one's own life.
l Some witnesses read like harvesting stones against the
winter.

16–17: The *fool* is disappointed because he expects to be repaid for everything he does.
20.18–31: Wise and foolish speech. 18: A popular proverb, known also from the Greek
philosopher Zeno, recorded in Diogenes Laertius VII, 26. **21–23:** Improper shame (especially
of a debtor who is not candid to his creditor) will destroy a friendship. **30–31:** *Wisdom* must
not be hidden; contrast the wise man's silence, 20.1–8.
    21.1–11: Warnings against sin. This section differs from the shrewd observations of 19.20–
20.31 in its frequent reference to the Lord. **8:** *A house:* a symbol of one's whole existence.

9 A gathering of lawless men is like a
    bundle of tow,
  which ends by going up in flames.

10 The road of sinners is smoothly
    paved,
  but it leads straight down to the
    grave.

11 Whoever keeps the law keeps his
    thoughts under control;
  the fear of the Lord has its outcome
    in wisdom.

12 A MAN WHO IS NOT CLEVER CANNOT
    be taught,
  but there is a cleverness which only
    breeds bitterness.

13 A wise man's knowledge is like a
    river in full spate,
  and his advice is a life-giving
    spring.

14 A fool's mind is a leaky bucket:
  it cannot hold anything it learns.

15 If an instructed man hears a wise
    saying,
  he applauds it and improves on it.
  If a rake hears it, he is annoyed
  and throws it behind his back.

16 Listening to a fool is like travelling
    with a heavy pack,
  but there is delight to be found in
    intelligent conversation.

17 The assembly welcomes a word
    from the wise man,
  and thinks over what he says.

18 A fool's wisdom is like a tumbledown
    house;
  his knowledge is a string of ill-
    digested sayings.

19 To fools education is like fetters,
  like a handcuff on the wrist.

21 To the wise education is a golden
    ornament
  like a bracelet on the arm.

20 A fool laughs out loud;
  a clever man smiles quietly, if at all.

22 A fool rushes into a house,

while a man of experience hangs
    back politely.

23 A boor peers into the house from
    the doorstep,
  while a well-bred man stands outside.

24 It is bad manners to listen at doors;
  a man of sense would think it a
    crushing disgrace.

25 The glib only repeat what others
    have said,
  but the wise weigh every word.

26 Fools speak before they think;
  wise men think first and speak
    afterwards.

27 When a bad man curses his
    adversary,[m]
  he is cursing himself.

28 A tale-bearer blackens his own
    character
  and makes himself hated throughout
    the neighbourhood.

22 An idler is like a filthy stone;
  everyone jeers at his disgrace.

2 An idler is like a lump of dung;
  whoever picks it up shakes it off
    his hand.

3 There is shame in being father to a
    spoilt son,
  and the birth of a daughter means
    loss.

4 A sensible daughter wins a husband,
  but an immodest one is a grief to
    her father.

5 A brazen daughter disgraces both
    father and husband
  and is despised by both.

6 Unseasonable talk is like music in
    time of mourning,
  but the lash of wisdom's discipline
    is always in season.

7 Teaching a fool is like mending
    pottery with glue,
  or like rousing a sleeper from heavy
    sleep.

8 As well reason with a drowsy man
    as with a fool;

m Or curses Satan.

9: See 16.6. **10:** The smooth *road* leads quickly to one's destruction; see Prov.14.12; Mt.7.13.
    21.12–28: The wise man and the fool. 12: See 19.20–30 on *cleverness*. **13:** The *river* and
life-giving spring are contrasted to stagnant cistern water and even more to the *leaky bucket*
(v. 14). **22–28:** Etiquette was a major subject of ancient wisdom. **27:** *His adversary* is literally
"Satan" (see Tfn. *m*), but here the reference is to the human adversary.
    22.1–26: Bad experiences. 1–2: The *idler* is frequently rebuked in Prov. (Prov.10.4; 15.19;
24.30–34), but is a target of Ecclus. only here and in 33.24–28. **3–5:** The *daughter* meant *loss*
because she could not carry on the family name. **7:** Ancient *glue* was not strong enough to

when you have finished, he will say,
    'What was that?'[n]

11 Mourn over the dead for the eclipse
    of his light;
  mourn over the fool for the eclipse
    of his wits.
  Mourn less bitterly for the dead,
    for he is at rest;
  but the fool's life is worse than
    death.
12 Mourning for the dead lasts seven
    days,
  but for a godless fool it lasts all his
    life.
13 Do not talk long with a fool
  or visit a stupid man.
  Beware of him, or you may be in
    trouble
  and find yourself bespattered when
    he shakes himself.
  Avoid him, if you are looking for
    peace,
  and you will not be worn out by his
    folly.
14 What is heavier than lead?
  What is its name but 'Fool'?
15 Sand, salt, and a lump of iron
  are less of a burden than a stupid
    man.

16 A tie-beam fixed firmly into a
    building
  is not shaken loose by an
    earthquake;
  so a mind kept firm by intelligent
    advice
  will not be daunted in a crisis.
17 A mind solidly backed by intelligent
    thought
  is like the stucco that decorates a
    smooth wall.
18 As a fence set on a hill-top
  cannot stand against the wind,
  so a mind made timid by foolish
    fancies
  is not proof against any terror.

19 Hurt the eye and tears will flow;
  hurt the mind and you will find it
    sensitive.

Throw a stone at the birds and you   20
    scare them away;
abuse a friend and you break off
    your friendship.
If you have drawn your sword on a   21
    friend,
do not give up hope, there is still a
    way back.
If you have quarrelled with your   22
    friend,
never fear, there can still be a
    reconciliation.
But abuse, scorn, a secret betrayed,
    a stab in the back—
these will make any friend keep his
    distance.
Win your neighbour's confidence   23
    while he is poor,
and you will share the joy of his
    prosperity;
stand by him in time of trouble,
and you will be his partner when he
    comes into a fortune.
As furnace-fumes and smoke come   24
    before the flame,
so insults come before bloodshed.
I will not be afraid to protect my   25
    friend
nor will I turn my back on him.
If harm should befall me on his   26
    account,
everyone who hears of it will beware
    of him.

OH FOR A SENTRY TO GUARD MY   27
    mouth
and a seal of discretion to close my
    lips,
to keep them from being my
    downfall,
and to keep my tongue from
    causing my ruin!
Lord, Father, and Ruler of my life,   **23**
do not abandon me to the tongue's
    control
or allow me to fall on its account.

n Some witnesses add (9) Children well brought up
reveal no trace of any humble origin. (10) But those
who run riot, haughty and undisciplined, sully the
nobility of their parentage.

---

mend *pottery*. **11–13:** These imperatives are not the usual moral commands (as in 21.1) but
shrewd observation of life. The *seven days of mourning* (v. 12) were traditional (see Gen.50.10);
contrast 38.17. **19:** The *mind* is that of a friend who will be hurt. **23:** The pairing of opposites
(*prosperity, trouble*) was a favorite way of building proverbs.
    22.27–23.6: A prayer for self-control. 27: The *mouth* is viewed as a gate which needs a *sentry*.
See Ps.141.3 and compare Prov.21.23. **23.1:** God is *Father* also in the closing prayer of 51.10.

2 Oh for wisdom's lash to curb my
   thoughts
   and to discipline my mind,
   without overlooking my mistakes
   or condoning my sins!
3 Then my mistakes would not multiply
   nor my sins increase,
   humiliating me before my opponents
   and giving my enemy cause to gloat.
4 Lord, Father, and God of my life,
   do not let me have a supercilious
      eye.
5 Protect me from the onslaught of
      desire;
6 let neither gluttony nor lust take hold
      of me,
   nor give me over to the power of
      shameless passion.

7 Hear, my sons, how to discipline the
      mouth,
   take warning, and you will never be
      caught out.
8 It is by his own words that the sinner
      is ensnared;
   he is tripped up by his own scurrility
      and pride.
9 Do not inure your mouth to oaths
   or make a habit of naming the Holy
      One.
10 As a slave constantly under the lash
   is never free from weals,
   so the man who has oaths and the
      sacred name for ever on his lips
   will never be clear of guilt.
11 A man given to swearing is lawless
      to the core;
   the scourge will never be far from
      his house.
   If he goes back on his word, he must
      bear the blame;
   if he wilfully neglects it, he sins twice
      over;
   if his oath itself was insincere, he
      cannot be acquitted;
   his house will be filled with trouble.

12 There is a kind of speech that is the
      counterpart of death;

may it never be found among
   Jacob's descendants!
The pious keep clear of such conduct
   and do not wallow in sin.
Do not make a habit of coarse,   13
   vulgar talk,
or you will be bound to say
   something sinful.
Remember your father and mother   14
   when you take your seat among
      the great,
or you may forget yourself in their
      presence
and make a fool of yourself through
      bad habit;
then you will wish you had never
      been born,
and curse the day of your birth.
A man addicted to scurrilous talk   15
will never learn better as long as he
      lives.

TWO KINDS OF MEN ADD SIN TO SIN,   16
and a third brings retribution on
      himself.
Hot lust that blazes like a fire
can never be quenched till life is
      destroyed.
A man whose whole body is given
      to sensuality
never stops till the fire consumes
      him.
To a seducer every loaf is as sweet   17
      as the last,
and he does not weary until he dies.
The man who strays from his own   18
      bed
says to himself, 'Who can see me?
All around is dark and the walls
      hide me;
nobody can see me, why need I
      worry?
The Most High will not take note
      of my sins.'
The eyes of men are all he fears;   19
he forgets that the eyes of the Lord
are ten thousand times brighter than
      the sun,

4: The *supercilious eye* may mean the eye of desire (the "bold looks" of 26.9 represents the same word).

23.7–15: Control of the tongue. 9–11: *Oaths* carried a special weight of punishment if not fulfilled. The naming of the *Holy One* made an oath sacred, but such use of the holy name was to be avoided (see Exod.20.7). **12–15:** Here the subject is restraint from vulgar talk.

23.16–27: Sins of lust.

23.16–21: The adulterous man. 16: A sequence of numbers (*two . . . a third*) was a favorite way of shaping a proverb; compare 25.7; Prov.30.15–31. The three *kinds of men* are put in a

observing every step men take
and penetrating every secret.

20 Before the universe was created, it
was known to him,
and so it is since its completion.

21 This man will pay the penalty in the
public street,
caught where he least expected it.

22 So too with the woman who is
unfaithful to her husband,
presenting him with an heir by a
different father:

23 first, she disobeys the law of the
Most High;
secondly, she commits an offence
against her husband;
thirdly, she has prostituted herself
by bearing bastard children.

24 She shall be disgraced before the
assembly,
and the consequences will fall on
her children.

25 Her children will not take root,
nor will fruit grow on her branches.

26 A curse will rest on her memory,
and her shame will never be blotted
out.

27 All who survive her will learn
that nothing is better than the fear
of the Lord
or sweeter than obeying his
commandments.*o*

The praise of wisdom

24 HEAR THE PRAISE OF WISDOM FROM
her own mouth,
as she speaks with pride among her
people,

2 before the assembly of the Most High
and in the presence of the heavenly
host:

3 'I am the word which was spoken by
the Most High;

it was I who covered the earth like
a mist.

4 My dwelling-place was in high
heaven;
my throne was in a pillar of cloud.

5 Alone I made a circuit of the sky
and traversed the depth of the abyss.

6 The waves of the sea, the whole
earth,
every people and nation were under
my sway.

7 Among them all I looked for a home:
in whose territory was I to settle?

8 Then the Creator of the universe
laid a command upon me;
my Creator decreed where I should
dwell.
He said, "Make your home in
Jacob;
find your heritage in Israel."

9 Before time began he created me,
and I shall remain for ever.

10 In the sacred tent I ministered in
his presence,
and so I came to be established in
Zion.

11 Thus he settled me in the city he
loved
and gave me authority in Jerusalem.

12 I took root among the people
whom the Lord had honoured
by choosing them to be his special
possession.

13 'There I grew like a cedar of Lebanon,
like a cypress on the slopes of
Hermon,

14 like a date-palm at Engedi,
like roses at Jericho.
I grew like a fair olive-tree in the
vale,
or like a plane-tree planted beside
the water.

---

o Some witnesses add (28) To follow God brings great
honour; to win his approval means long life.

---

climactic order in vv. 16–18. **20:** God's knowledge *before the universe was created* is not in
conflict with freedom of choice (15.11–20) in the author's total view.
  23.22–27: The adulterous woman. The penalty for adultery was death (Deut.22.22). For the
suspicion of adultery on the part of a wife, and for the attendant consequences, see Num.5.11–31.
  24.1–22: Wisdom's praise. A hymn to wisdom introduces the second main part of the book;
compare 1.1–10. **1:** The *people* are Israel. **2:** The *assembly* is the heavenly council; see Ps.89.6–7.
3: Wisdom speaks, as in Prov.8.22–36 on which much of this section is modeled. The *mist*
represents the creative power of wisdom, parallel to the wind of Gen.1.2; compare Gen.2.6.
4: *High heaven:* God's throne above the reservoir of waters supported by the vault of the sky;
see Gen.1.6–8; Ps.29.10. **7:** Wisdom looked for a *home,* but found it only in Israel (v. 8), which
has God's law. **13–14:** The massiveness and majesty of the *cedar* and *cypress,* the fruitfulness
of the *date-palm,* the beauty of the *rose,* and the fairness of the *olive* are symbolic of wisdom.

15 Like cassia or camel-thorn I was
    redolent of spices,
 I spread my fragrance like choice
    myrrh,
 like galban, aromatic shell, and gum
    resin;
 I was like the smoke of incense in
    the sacred tent.

16 Like a terebinth I spread out my
    branches,
 laden with honour and grace.

17 I put forth lovely shoots like the vine,
 and my blossoms were a harvest of
    wealth and honour.*p*

19 'Come to me, you who desire me,
 and eat your fill of my fruit.

20 The memory of me is sweeter than
    syrup,
 the possession of me sweeter than
    honey dripping from the comb.

21 Whoever feeds on me will be hungry
    for more,
 and whoever drinks from me will
    thirst for more.

22 To obey me is to be safe from
    disgrace;
 those who work in wisdom will not
    go astray.'

23 All this is the covenant-book of
    God Most High,
 the law which Moses enacted to be
    the heritage of the assemblies
    of Jacob.*q*

25 He sends out wisdom in full flood
    like the river Pishon
 or like the Tigris at the time of
    firstfruits;

26 he overflows with understanding like
    the Euphrates
 or like Jordan at the time of
    harvest.

27 He pours forth instruction like the
    Nile,*r*

like the Gihon at the time of vintage.
28 No man has ever fully known
    wisdom;
 from first to last no one has fathomed
    her;
29 for her thoughts are vaster than the
    ocean
 and her purpose deeper than the
    great abyss.

30 As for me, I was like a canal leading
    from a river,
 a watercourse into a pleasure-garden.
31 I said, 'I will water my garden,
 drenching its flower-beds';
 and at once my canal became a river
 and my river a sea.
32 I will again make discipline shine
    like the dawn,
 so that its light may be seen from
    afar.
33 I will again pour out doctrine like
    prophecy
 and bequeath it to future generations.
34 Truly, my labour has not been for
    myself alone
 but for all seekers of wisdom.

25

THERE ARE THREE SIGHTS WHICH
    warm my heart*s*
 and are beautiful in the eyes of the
    Lord and of men:
 concord among brothers, friendship
    among neighbours,
 and a man and wife who are
    inseparable.
2 There are three kinds of men who
    arouse my hatred,

p Some witnesses add (18) I give birth to noble love,
reverence, knowledge, and holy hope; and I give all
these my eternal progeny to God's elect (*probable
meaning; Gk. obscure*).
q Some witnesses add (24) Never fail to be strong in
the Lord; hold fast to him, so that he may strengthen
you; the Lord Almighty is God alone; beside him
there is no saviour.
r So one Vs.; Gk. He makes instruction shine like light.
s So Vss.; Gk. which make me beautiful.

15: These were prized aromatic substances used in worship. **19–22:** Wisdom's call is paralleled
in 51.23–30, where a wisdom teacher speaks; see also Prov.9.1–6 and Mt.11.28–30. **21:** Unlike
food for the stomach which satiates, the use of wisdom creates *more hunger* for it and so brings
continual enjoyment; contrast Jn.6.35.
    24.23–29: Wisdom and Law. This is the author's interpretation of wisdom's speech above.
25–27: The productiveness of *wisdom* is compared to the *Jordan* and the four rivers of
Gen.2.10–14. The *Gihon* was identified with the *Nile* (but see Tfn. *r*), which is at its height
in the time of vintage.
    24.30–34: The author's encounter with wisdom. The life-giving symbolism of water is carried
forward from wisdom (24.23–29) to the author himself.
    25.1–2: A numerical saying. The main theme is marriage which is the final element in each
series of three.

who disgust me by their manner of
life.
a poor man who boasts, a rich man
who lies,
and an old fool who commits
adultery.

3 If you have not gathered wisdom in
your youth,
how will you find it when you are
old?
4 Sound judgement sits well on grey
hairs
and wise advice comes well from
older men.
5 Wisdom is fitting in the aged,
and ripe counsel in men of
eminence.
6 Long experience is the old man's
crown,
and his pride is the fear of the Lord.

7 I can think of nine men I count
happy,
and I can tell you of a tenth:
a man who can take delight in his
children,
and one who lives to see his enemy's
downfall;
8 happy the husband of a sensible
wife,
the farmer who does not plough
with ox and ass together,*t*
the man whose tongue never betrays
him,
and the servant who has never
worked for an inferior!
9 Happy the man who has found a
friend,*u*
and the speaker who has an attentive
audience!
10 How great is the man who finds
wisdom!
But no greater than he who fears
the Lord.
11 The fear of the Lord excels all
other gifts;
to what can we compare the man
who has it?*v*

Counsels upon social behaviour

ANY WOUND BUT A WOUND IN THE 13
heart!
Any spite but a woman's!
Any disaster but one caused by hate! 14
Any vengeance but the vengeance
of an enemy!
There is no venom*w* worse than a 15
snake's,
and no anger worse than an enemy's.

I would sooner share a home with 16
a lion or a snake
than keep house with a spiteful wife.
Her spite changes her expression, 17
making her look as surly as a bear.
Her husband goes to a neighbour 18
for his meals
and cannot repress a bitter sigh.

There is nothing so bad as a bad 19
wife;
may the fate of the wicked overtake
her!*x*
It is as easy for an old man to climb 20
a sand-dune
as for a quiet husband to live with
a nagging wife.
Do not be enticed by a woman's 21
beauty
or set your heart on possessing her.
If a man is supported by his wife 22
he must expect tantrums,
shamelessness, and outrage.
A bad wife brings humiliation, 23
downcast looks, and a wounded
heart.
Slack of hand and weak of knee
is the man whose wife fails to make
him happy.
Woman is the origin of sin, 24
and it is through her that we all die.
Do not leave a leaky cistern to drip 25

t the farmer . . . together: so Heb.; Gk. omits.
u So Vss.; Gk. found good sense.
*v Some witnesses add (12) The fear of the Lord is the
source of love for him, and faith is the source of
loyalty to him.*
w Probable meaning, based on one Vs.; Gk. head.
x Or may it fall to her lot to marry a scoundrel!

25.3–6: Wisdom is the crown of old age. 6: *Experience* in a stable environment makes the
old man's advice valuable.
25.7–11: A numerical saying. The speaker is the wisdom teacher. **10:** *Wisdom* is here
distinguished as a lower stage than *fear of the Lord*, a distinction not usually made in this book.
11: *Fear of the Lord* is the climactic happiness.
25.13–26.18: The good and bad wife. Ecclesiasticus is not affirmative about women; his view
is not merely personal, but draws on an old wisdom tradition. **24:** The *woman:* Eve (Gen.3.1–24);
apparently the earliest interpretation of Gen. as teaching that *woman* was the *origin of sin.*

or allow a bad wife to say what she
likes.

26 If she does not accept your control,
divorce her and send her away.

26 A good wife makes a happy
husband;
she doubles the length of his life.

2 A staunch wife is her husband's joy;
he will live out his days in peace.

3 A good wife means a good life;
she is one of the Lord's gifts to
those who fear him.

4 Rich or poor, they are light-hearted,
and always have a smile on their faces.

5 Three things there are that alarm
me,
and a fourth I am afraid to face:
the scandal of the town, the gathering
of a mob,
and calumny—all harder to bear
than death;

6 but it is heart-ache and grief when
a wife is jealous of a rival,
and everyone alike feels the lash of
her tongue.

7 A bad wife is a chafing yoke;
controlling her is like clutching a
scorpion.

8 A drunken wife is a great
provocation;
she cannot keep her excesses secret.

9 A loose woman betrays herself by
her bold looks;
you can tell her by her glance.

10 Keep close watch over a headstrong
daughter;
if she finds you off your guard, she
will take her chance.

11 Beware of her impudent looks
and do not be surprised if she
disobeys you.

12 As a parched traveller with his
tongue hanging out
drinks from any spring that offers,
she will open her arms to every
embrace,
and her quiver to the arrow.

A wife's charm is the delight of her 13
husband,
and her womanly skill puts flesh on
his bones.

A silent wife is a gift from the Lord; 14
her restraint is more than money
can buy.

A modest wife has charm upon 15
charm;
no scales can weigh the worth of her
chastity.

As beautiful as the sunrise in the 16
Lord's heaven
is a good wife in a well-ordered
home.

As bright as the light on the sacred 17
lamp-stand
is a beautiful face in the settled
prime of life.

Like a golden pillar on a silver 18
base
is a shapely leg with a firm foot.*y z*

TWO THINGS GRIEVE MY HEART, 28
and a third excites my anger:
a soldier in distress through poverty,
wise men treated with contempt,
and a man deserting right conduct
for wrong—
the Lord will bring him to the
scaffold.

y is . . . foot: probable meaning; Gk. obscure.
z Some witnesses add
My son, guard your health in the bloom of your 19
youth,
and do not waste your vigour on what belongs to
others.
Search the whole plain for a fertile plot; 20
sow your own seed, trusting in your pedigree.
Then the children you leave behind 21
will prosper, confident in their parentage.
A woman of the streets counts as mere spittle, 22
a married woman as a mortuary for her lovers.
A godless woman is a good match for a lawless 23
husband,
a pious one for a man who fears the Lord.
A brazen woman courts disgrace, 24
but a virtuous one is modest even before her
husband.
A wilful woman is a shameless bitch, 25
but a modest one fears the Lord.
A woman who honours her husband is accounted 26
wise by all,
but if she despises him, all know her as proud and
godless.
A good wife makes a happy husband;
she doubles the length of his life.
A strident, garrulous wife is like a trumpet 27
sounding the charge;
in a home like hers a man lives in the tumult of war.

26: *Divorce* was permitted in Deut.24.1. 26.1–3: The long *life* of the husband is the direct
result of his marriage to a good wife. 4: Inner harmony is important to marital relationships.
6: The *rival* presupposes polygamy; see Lev.18.18; Deut.21.15–17; 1 Sam.1.1–7. 9–12: The
disloyal wife is the theme of the poem, despite the word *daughter* (v. 10), which means wife.
13–18: Meditation on the good wife climaxes in appreciation of her physical beauty.
     26.28–28.26: Types of sin. 26.29–27.3: Dishonesty destroys the merchant just as the *peg*

29 How hard it is for a merchant to
  keep clear of wrong
or for a shopkeeper to be innocent
  of dishonesty!

27 Many have cheated for gain;[a]
a money-grubber will always turn
  a blind eye.

2 As a peg is held fast in the joint
  between stones,
so dishonesty squeezes in between
  selling and buying.

3 Unless a man holds resolutely to the
  fear of the Lord,
his house will soon be in ruins.

4 Shake a sieve, and the rubbish
  remains;
start an argument and discover a
  man's faults.

5 As the work of a potter is tested in
  the furnace,
so a man is tried in debate.

6 As the fruit of the tree reveals the
  skill of its grower,
so the expression of a man's thought
  reveals his character.

7 Do not praise a man till you hear
  him in discussion,
for this is the test.

8 If justice is what you seek, you will
  succeed,
and wear it like a splendid robe.

9 Birds of a feather roost together,
and honesty comes home to those
  who practise it.

10 A lion lies in wait for its prey,
and so do sins for those who do
  wrong.

11 The conversation of the pious is
  constantly wise,
but a fool is as changeable as the
  moon.

12 Grudge every minute spent among
  fools,
but linger among the thoughtful.

13 The conversation of fools is
  repulsive;
they make a joke of unbridled vice.

14 Their cursing and swearing make
  the hair stand on end;

when such men quarrel, others stop
  their ears.

15 The quarrels of the proud lead to
  bloodshed;
their abuse offends the ear.

16 The betrayer of secrets loses his
  credit
and can never find an intimate friend.

17 Love your friend and keep faith with
  him,
but if you betray his secrets, keep
  out of his way;

18 as a man kills his enemy,
so you have killed your neighbour's
  friendship.

19 As a bird that is allowed to escape
  your hand,
your neighbour, once lost, will not
  be caught again.

20 He has gone too far for you to
  pursue him,
and escaped like a gazelle from a
  trap.

21 A wound may be bandaged, an
  insult pardoned,
but the betrayer of secrets has
  nothing to hope for.

22 A man who winks is plotting
  mischief;
those who know him will keep their
  distance.

23 He speaks sweetly enough to your
  face
and admires whatever you say,
but later he will change his tune
and use your own words to trip you.

24 There are many things I hate, but
  him above all;
The Lord will hate him too.

25 Whoever throws a stone up in the air
  is throwing it at his own head,
and a treacherous blow means
  wounds all round.

26 Dig a pit and you will fall into it;
set a trap and you will be caught
  by it.

27 The wrong a man does recoils on
  him,

a Some witnesses read for a trifle.

(27.2) driven between the *stones* is the first step in tearing down the house. **27.16–21:** Betraying *secrets* has irreversible results; but contrast 22.21–22 which says that broken friendships can be restored. **22:** Winking was a frequent symbol for deception; compare Prov.6.12–13. **25:** The *stone* describes any deception which is self-destructive. **26:** One digs *a pit* to trap another.

and he does not know where it has come from.

28 An arrogant man deals in mockery and insults,
but retribution lies in wait for him like a lion.

29 Those who rejoice at the downfall of good men will be trapped
and consumed with pain before they die.

30 Rage and anger, these also I abhor,
but a sinner has them ready at hand.

28 The vengeful man will face the vengeance of the Lord,
who keeps strict account of his sins.

2 Forgive your neighbour his wrongdoing;
then, when you pray, your sins will be forgiven.

3 If a man harbours a grudge against another,
is he to expect healing from the Lord?

4 If he has no mercy on his fellow-man,
is he still to ask forgiveness for his own sins?

5 If a mere mortal cherishes rage,
where is he to look for pardon?

6 Think of the end that awaits you, and have done with hate;
think of mortality and death, and be true to the commandments;

7 think of the commandments, and do not be enraged at your neighbour;
think of the covenant of the Most High, and overlook faults.

8 To avoid a quarrel is a setback for sin,
for it is a hot temper that kindles quarrels.

9 A sinner sows trouble between friends
and spreads scandal where before there was peace.

10 A fire is kept hot by stoking and a quarrel by persistence.
A man's rage is in proportion to his strength,

and his anger in proportion to his wealth.

11 A hasty argument kindles a fire,
and a hasty quarrel leads to bloodshed.

12 Blow on a spark to make it glow,
or spit on it to put it out;
both results come from the one mouth.

13 Curses on the gossip and the tale-bearer!
For they have been the ruin of many peaceable men.

14 The talk of a third party has wrecked the lives of many
and driven them from country to country;
it has destroyed fortified towns
and demolished the houses of the great.

15 The talk of a third party has brought divorce on staunch wives
and deprived them of all they have laboured for.

16 Whoever pays heed to it will never again find rest
or live in peace of mind.

17 The lash of a whip raises weals,
but the lash of a tongue breaks bones.

18 Many have been killed by the sword,
but not so many as by the tongue.

19 Happy the man who is sheltered from its onslaught,
who has not been exposed to its fury,
who has not borne its yoke,
or been chained with its fetters!

20 For its yoke is of iron,
its fetters of bronze.

21 The death it brings is an evil death;
better the grave than the tongue!

22 But it has no power over the godfearing;
they cannot be burned in its flames.

23 Those who desert the Lord fall victim to it;
among them it will burn like fire and not be quenched.

28.2–5: Man's forgiveness is prerequisite to receiving God's forgiveness; compare Lev.19.18; Mt.5.7,23–24; Mk.11.25. **3:** *Healing* means forgiveness. **13–26:** This poem on slander is noteworthy for the tension between the shrewd observation that the righteous do suffer (the *staunch wives*, v. 15) and the assertion of faith that the *godfearing* (v. 22) are protected from the power of slander.

It will launch itself against them
　　like a lion
and tear them like a leopard.

24 As you enclose your garden with
　　a thorn hedge,
and lock up your silver and gold,

25 so weigh your words and measure
　　them,
and make a door and a bolt for
　　your mouth.

26 Beware of being tripped by your
　　tongue
and falling into the power of a
　　lurking enemy.

29 A DEVOUT MAN LENDS TO HIS
　　neighbour;
by supporting him he keeps the
　　commandments.

2 Lend to your neighbour in his time
　　of need;
repay your neighbour punctually.

3 Be as good as your word and keep
　　faith with him,
and your needs will always be met.

4 Many treat a loan as a windfall
and bring trouble on those who
　　helped them.

5 Until he gets a loan, a man kisses
　　his neighbour's hand
and talks with bated breath about
　　his money;
but when it is time to repay, he
　　postpones it,
pays back only perfunctory promises,
and alleges that the time is too
　　short.[b]

6 If he can pay, his creditor will
　　scarcely get back half,
and will count himself lucky at
　　that;
if he cannot pay, he has defrauded
　　the other of his money,
and gratuitously made an enemy
　　of him;[c]
he will pay him back in curses and
　　insults
and with shame instead of honour.

7 Because of such dishonesty many
　　refuse to lend,
for fear of being needlessly defrauded.

Nevertheless be patient with the　8
　　penniless,
and do not keep him waiting for
　　your charity;
for the commandment's sake help　9
　　the poor,
and in his need do not send him
　　away empty-handed.

Be ready to lose money for a　10
　　brother or a friend;
do not leave it to rust away under
　　a stone.

Store up for yourself the treasure　11
　　which the Most High has
　　commanded,
and it will benefit you more than
　　gold.

Let almsgiving be the treasure in　12
　　your strong-room,
and it will rescue you from every
　　misfortune.

It will arm you against the enemy　13
better than stout shield or strong
　　spear.

A good man will stand surety for　14
　　his neighbour;
only a man who has lost all sense
　　of shame will fail him.

If a man stands surety for you, do　15
　　not forget his kindness,
for he has staked his very self for
　　you.

A sinner wastes the property of his　16
　　surety,
and an ungrateful man fails his　17
　　rescuer.

Suretyship has ruined the prosperity　18
　　of many
and wrecked them like a storm at sea;
it has driven men of influence into
　　exile,
and set them wandering in foreign
　　countries.

When a sinner commits himself to　19
　　suretyship,
his pursuit of gain will involve him
　　in lawsuits.

Help your neighbour to the best　20
　　of your ability,

b *Or* that times are hard.
c *and . . . him: some witnesses read* and the other has
won himself an enemy at his own expense.

29.1–28: Borrowing and lending. 1–7: Lending is encouraged in accord with the *commandment* (see Deut.15.7–11), though the risks are clearly stated. **14–20:** Becoming *surety* for another is here favored within common-sense limits, in contrast to Prov., which warns against suretyship (Prov.6.1–5; 11.15). In other words, Ecclus. advocates surety, but not to the extent of

but beware of becoming too deeply
involved.

21 The necessities of life are water,
bread, and clothes,
and a home with its decent privacy;

22 better the life of a poor man in his
own hut
than a sumptuous banquet in
another man's house.

23 Be content with whatever you have,
and do not get a name for living
on hospitality.*d*

24 It is a poor life going from house
to house,
keeping your mouth shut because
you are a visitor.

25 You receive the guests and hand
the drinks without being
thanked for it,
and into the bargain must listen
to words that rankle:

26 'Come here, stranger, and lay the
table;
whatever you have there, hand it
to me.'

27 'Be off, stranger! Make way for a
more important guest;
my brother has come to stay, and
I need the guest-room.'

28 How hard it is for a sensible man
to bear
criticism from the household or
abuse from his creditor!

30 A MAN WHO LOVES HIS SON WILL
whip him often
so that when he grows up he may
be a joy to him.

2 He who disciplines his son will find
profit in him
and take pride in him among his
aquaintances.

3 He who gives his son a good education
will make his enemy jealous
and will boast of him among his
friends.

When the father dies, it is as if he   4
were still alive,
for he has left a copy of himself
behind him.

While he lived he saw and rejoiced,   5
and when he died he had no regrets.

He has left an heir to take   6
vengeance on his enemies
and to repay the kindness of his
friends.

A man who spoils his son will   7
bandage every wound
and will be on tenterhooks at every
cry.

An unbroken horse turns out   8
stubborn,
and an unchecked son turns out
headstrong.

Pamper a boy and he will shock you;   9
play with him and he will grieve you.

Do not share his laughter, for fear   10
of sharing his pain;
you will only end by grinding your
teeth.

Do not give him freedom while he   11
is young
or overlook his errors.

Break him in while he is young,   12
beat him soundly while he is still a
child,
or he may grow stubborn and
disobey you
and cause you vexation.

Discipline your son and take pains   13
with him
or he may offend you by some
disgraceful act.

BETTER A POOR MAN WHO IS HEALTHY   14
and fit
than a rich man racked by disease.

Health and fitness are better than   15
any gold,
and bodily vigour than boundless
prosperity.

d Reading based on one Vs.; Gk. and do not hear re-
proaches from your family.

---

deprivation. **21–28:** This praise of simplicity and warning against a life of imposition on the
hospitality of others was directed to the teacher's upper-class clientele. **23:** The theme of being
content is quite usual in both Jewish and Christian counsel. (Phil.4.11; 1 Tim.6.8; Heb. 13.5).
    30.1–13: Raising children. 1–6: Discipline and *education* (v. 3) will enable a son to carry on
his father's tradition, even to avenging him against his *enemies* (v. 6); the motive for discipline
is the benefit to the parent. **7:** The author is making fun of the oversolicitous parent. **8–13:**
Lack of discipline will produce a rebellious son.
    30.14–20: Health better than wealth. 18: Food *offerings . . . placed on a tomb* were forbidden

16 There is no wealth to compare with
 health of body,
 no festivity to equal a joyful heart.

17 Better death than a life of misery,
 eternal rest than a long illness.

18 Good things spread before a man
 without appetite
 are like offerings of food placed on
 a tomb.

19 What use is a sacrifice to an idol
 which can neither taste nor smell?
 So it is with the man afflicted by
 the Lord.

20 He gazes at the food before him
 and sighs
 as a eunuch sighs when he embraces
 a girl.

21 Do not give yourself over to sorrow
 or distress yourself deliberately.

22 A merry heart keeps a man alive,
 and joy lengthens his span of days.

23 Indulge yourself, take comfort,
 and banish sorrow;
 for sorrow has been the death of
 many,
 and no advantage ever came of it.

24 Envy and anger shorten a man's
 life,
 and anxiety brings premature old
 age.

25 A man with a gay heart has a good
 appetite
 and relishes the food he eats.

31 A rich man loses weight by wakeful
 nights,
 when the cares of wealth drive sleep
 away;

2 sleepless worry keeps him wide
 awake,
 just as serious illness banishes[e] sleep.

3 A rich man toils to amass a fortune,
 and when he relaxes he enjoys every
 luxury.

4 A poor man toils to make a slender
 living,

and when he relaxes he finds himself
 in need.

5 Passion for gold can never be right;
 the pursuit of money leads a man
 astray.[f]

6 Many a man has come to ruin for
 the sake of gold
 and found disaster staring him in
 the face.

7 Gold is a pitfall to those who are
 infatuated with it,
 and every fool is caught by it.

8 Happy the rich man who has
 remained free of its taint
 and has not made gold his aim!

9 Show us that man, and we will
 congratulate him;
 he has performed a miracle among
 his people.

10 Has anyone ever come through this
 test unscathed?
 Then he has good cause to be proud.
 Has anyone ever had it in his power
 to sin and refrained,
 or to do wrong and has not done it?

11 Then he shall be confirmed in his
 prosperity,
 and the whole people will hail him
 as a benefactor.

12 IF YOU ARE SITTING AT A GRAND
 table,
 do not lick your lips and exclaim,
 'What a spread!'

13 Remember, it is a vice to have a
 greedy eye.
 There is no greater evil in creation
 than the eye;
 that is why it must shed tears at
 every turn.

14 Do not reach for everything you
 see,

e banishes: *probable meaning, based on Heb.; Gk.
 obscure.*
f the pursuit . . . astray: *so Heb.; Gk.* the man who
 pursues destruction shall have his fill of it.

Jews; see Deut.26.14, but compare Tob.4.17. **19:** Compare Ps.115.4–6. Sickness is heavy to
bear because it is an affliction from the *Lord.*
 30.21–31.4: Enjoyment of the present. 21–25: In contrast to the frequent advice to restrain
the emotions in the face of insecurity (as in 11.29–13.13), here a relaxed self-expression in
security is the ideal; compare 14.11–19. **31.1–4:** Indicatives (rather than the imperatives of
30.21–25) offer a sober comment on the difficulty of enjoying the present.
 31.5–11: Good and bad uses of money. The ambiguity of wealth is a problem in Ecclus. The
temptations are clearly stated. **10:** The rhetorical question seems to expect the answer "no."
11: Yet financial security is the proper reward for righteousness; compare v. 8.
 31.12–21: Etiquette. Table manners was a subject of wisdom teaching through the centuries.

or jostle your fellow-guest at the
   dish;

15 judge his feelings by your own
   and always behave considerately.

16 Eat what is set before you like a
   gentleman;
do not munch and make yourself
   objectionable.

17 Be the first to stop for good manners
   sake
and do not be insatiable, or you will
   give offence.

18 If you are dining in a large company,
do not reach out your hand before
   others.

19 A man of good upbringing is content
   with little,
and he is not short of breath when
   he goes to bed.

20 The moderate eater enjoys healthy
   sleep;
he rises early, feeling refreshed.
But sleeplessness, indigestion, and
   colic
are the lot of the glutton.

21 If you cannot avoid overeating at
   a feast,
leave the table and find relief by
   vomiting.

22 Listen to me, my son; do not
   disregard me,
and in the end my words will come
   home to you.
Whatever you do, do it shrewdly,
and no illness will come your
   way.

23 Everyone has a good word for a
   liberal host,
and the evidence of his generosity
   is convincing.

24 The whole town grumbles at a mean
   host,
and there is precise evidence of his
   meanness.

25 Do not try to prove your manhood
   by drinking,

for wine has been the ruin of many.

26 As the furnace tests iron when it is
   being tempered,
so wine tests character when
   boastful men are wrangling.

27 Wine puts life into a man,
if he drinks it in moderation.
What is life to a man deprived of
   wine?
Was it not created to warm men's
   hearts?

28 Wine brings gaiety and high spirits,
if a man knows when to drink and
   when to stop;

29 but wine in excess makes for bitter
   feelings
and leads to offence and retaliation.

30 Drunkenness inflames a fool's anger
   to his own hurt;
it saps his strength and exposes him
   to injury.

31 At a banquet do not rebuke your
   fellow-guest
or make him feel small while he is
   enjoying himself.
This is no time to take up a quarrel
   with him
or pester him to pay his debts.

32 If they choose you to preside at a
   feast, do not put on airs;
behave to them as one of themselves.
Look after the others before you
   sit down;

2 do not take your place until you
   have discharged all your duties.
Let their enjoyment be your pleasure,
and you will win the prize for good
   manners.

3 Speak, if you are old—it is your
   privilege—
but come to the point and do not
   interrupt the music.

4 Where entertainment is provided, do
   not keep up a stream of talk;
it is the wrong time to show off
   your wisdom.

Moderation is the key. **15:** This is a form of the "Golden Rule"; compare 6.17; Tob.4.15;
Mt.7.12. **18:** The *before* is temporal.
   31.22–24: How to entertain. 23: The *liberal host* is the ideal.
   31.25–31: Moderation in drinking. 26: *Wine*, which *tests character*, is not to be avoided but
rightly used; for Ecclesiasticus life was full of such tests. **27–28:** The good effects of *wine* point
up the motif of enjoying the moment; compare 30.21–25.
   32.1–13: Behavior at banquets. 1 2: Presiding *at a feast* was a great honor. **3:** The right of
the *old* to *speak* first was widely recognized. **4:** Incessant talkers disturb a concert and bore

5 Like a signet of ruby in a gold ring
is a concert of music at a banquet.
6 Like a signet of emerald in a gold
setting
is tuneful music with good wine.

7 Speak, if you are young, when the
need arises,
but twice at the most, and only
when asked.
8 Be brief, say much in few words,
like a man who knows and can still
hold his tongue.
9 Among the great do not act as their
equal
or go on chattering when another is
speaking.
10 As lightning travels ahead of
thunder,
so popularity goes before a modest
man.
11 Leave in good time and do not be
the last to go;
go straight home without lingering.
12 There you may amuse yourself to
your heart's content,
and run no risk of arrogant talk.
13 And one thing more: give praise to
your Maker,
who has filled your cup with his
blessings.

14 THE MAN WHO FEARS THE LORD WILL
accept his discipline,
and the diligent will receive his
approval.
15 The genuine student will find
satisfaction in the law,
but it will prove a stumbling-block
to the insincere.
16 Those who fear the Lord will
discover what is right,
and will make his decrees*g* shine out
like a lamp.
17 A sinner will not accept criticism;
he will find precedents to justify
his choice.

18 A sensible man can always take a
hint;
but an arrogant heathen does not
know the meaning of diffidence.
19 Never do anything without
deliberation,
and afterwards you will have no
regrets.*h*
20 Do not travel by a road full of
obstacles
and stumble along through its
boulders.
21 Do not be careless on a clear road
22 but watch where you are going.*i*
23 Whatever you are doing, rely on
yourself,
for this too is a way of keeping the
commandments.
24 To rely on the law is to heed its
commandments,
and to trust the Lord is to want for
nothing.

33 Disaster never comes the way of
the man who fears the Lord:
in times of trial he will be rescued
again and again.
2 A wise man never hates the law,
but the man who is insincere about
it is like a boat in a squall.
3 A sensible man trusts the law
and finds it as reliable as the divine
oracle.

4 Prepare what you have to say, if you
want a hearing.
marshall your learning and then give
your answer.
5 The feelings of a fool turn like a
cart-wheel,
and his thoughts spin like an axle.
6 A sarcastic friend is like a stallion
which neighs no matter who is on
its back.

g Or their good conduct.
h you . . . regrets: or do not change your mind.
i but . . . going: so Heb.; Gk. and keep an eye on your
children.

and annoy. **7:** The *young* are to speak *only when asked.* **13:** The poem closes on a religious
note, as frequently, with *praise to your Maker.*
32.14–33.6: Contrasts between the reverent man and the fool. 15: The receptiveness of the wise
man enables him to find *satisfaction in the law.* **17:** By contrast, the *sinner* is not receptive and
cannot *accept criticism.* **18–24:** Foresight and self-reliance mark the wise. **33.1–2:** The staying
power of the reverent man derives from his trust in the Law. **3:** The *divine oracle:* the Urim
and Thummim (see Exod.28.15 n.), which were no longer in use. Ecclesiasticus holds that such
oracles are no longer necessary since the *law* fully discloses God's will. **6:** The *stallion* has no
fixed loyalty to anyone.

7 why is one day more important than
   another,
   when every day in the year has its
   light from the sun?
8 It was by the Lord's decision that
   they were distinguished;
   he appointed the various seasons and
   festivals:
9 some days he made high and holy,
   and others he assigned to the
   common run of days.
10 All men alike come from the
   ground;
   Adam was created out of earth.
11 Yet in his great wisdom the Lord
   distinguished them
   and made them go various ways:
12 some he blessed and lifted high,
   some he hallowed and brought near
   to himself,
   some he cursed and humbled
   and removed from their place.
13 As clay is in the potter's hands,
   to be moulded just as he chooses,
   so are men in the hands of their
   Maker,
   to be dealt with as he decides.
14 Good is the opposite of evil, and
   life of death;
   yes, and the sinner is the opposite
   of the godly.
15 Look at all the works of the Most
   High:
   they go in pairs, one the opposite
   of the other.

16 I was the last to wake up,
   I was like a gleaner following the
   grape-pickers;
   by the Lord's blessing I arrived
   in time
   to fill my winepress as full as any
   of them.
17 Remember that I did not toil for
   myself alone,

but for all who seek learning.
18 Listen to me, you dignitaries;
   leaders of the assembly, give me
   your attention.

19 As long as you live, give no one
   power over yourself—
   son or wife, brother or friend.
   Do not give your property to
   another,
   in case you change your mind and
   want it back.
20 As long as you have life and breath,
   never change places with anyone.
21 It is better for your children to ask
   from you
   than for you to be dependent on
   them.
22 Whatever you are doing, keep the
   upper hand,
   and allow no blot on your
   reputation.
23 Let your life run its full course,
   and then, at the hour of death,
   distribute your estate.

24 Fodder, and stick, and burdens for
   the donkey;
   bread, and discipline, and work for
   the servant!
25 Make your slave work, if you want
   rest for yourself;
   if you leave him idle, he will be
   looking for his liberty.
26 The ox is tamed by yoke and
   harness,
   the bad servant by racks and tortures.
27 Put him to work to keep him from
   being idle,
   for idleness is a great teacher of
   mischief.
28 Set him to work, for that is what he
   is for,
   and if he disobeys you, load him
   with fetters.

33.7–15: God and the opposites. Classing things in pairs and opposites was a favorite way of finding order in the world. **8:** Pairs and distinctions exist by *the Lord's decision*. **13:** The varied vessels made of *clay* correspond to the various stations of men; compare Jer.18.1–12; Rom.9.19–23. **14–15:** The *sinner* is paired against the *godly* among the *works of the Most High;* yet sin remains man's responsibility; compare 15.11–20.

33.16–18: The author's task. In the light of vv. 11–13, the author now sets forth the mission given him by God. Ancient writers tended to glorify the old (compare chs. 44–50); here Ecclesiasticus boldly states that his teaching is as good as the old.

33.19–23: The father as property holder. 20: Do not *change places* of authority. **21:** *Children* were dependent on their fathers until the latter's death.

33.24–31: Relations with slaves. 24 28: Bad and lazy slaves require stern treatment. The slave is made parallel to the domestic animal. **29–31:** The stern verses (24–28) are balanced

29 Do not be too exacting towards anyone
or do anything contrary to justice.

30 If you have a servant, treat him as an equal,
because you bought him with blood.

31 If you have a servant, treat him like a brother;
you will need him as much as you need yourself.
If you ill-treat him and he takes to his heels,
where will you go to look for him?

34 Vain hopes delude the senseless,
and dreams give wings to a fool's fancy.

2 It is like clutching a shadow, or chasing the wind,
to take notice of dreams.

3 What you see in a dream is nothing but a reflection,
like the image of a face in a mirror.

4 Purity cannot come out of filth;
how then can truth issue from falsehood?

5 Divination, omens, and dreams are all futile,
mere fantasies, like those of a woman in labour.

6 Unless they are sent by intervention from the Most High,
pay no attention to them.

7 Dreams have led many astray
and ruined those who built their hopes on them.

8 Such delusions can add nothing to the completeness of the law;
the wisdom spoken by the faithful is complete in itself.

9 An educated man knows many things,
and a man of experience understands what he is talking about.

10 An inexperienced man knows little,
but a man who travels grows in ability.

11 I have seen many things in the course of my travels,
and understand more than I can tell.

12 I have often been in deadly danger
and escaped, thanks to the experience I had gained.

True piety and the mercy of God

13 THOSE WHO FEAR THE LORD SHALL live,
for their trust is in one who can keep them safe.

14 The man who fears the Lord will have nothing else to fear;
he will never be a coward, because his trust is in the Lord.

15 How blest is the man who fears the Lord!
He knows where to look for support.

16 The Lord keeps watch over those who love him,
their strong shield and firm support,
a shelter from scorching wind and midday heat,
a safeguard against stumbles and falls.

17 He raises the spirits and makes the eyes sparkle,
giving health, and life, and blessing.

18 A sacrifice derived from ill-gotten gains is contaminated,
a lawless mockery that cannot win approval.

19 The Most High is not pleased with the offering of the godless,
nor do endless sacrifices win his forgiveness.

20 To offer a sacrifice from the possessions of the poor

---

by advice about equable relations with good servants. **30:** *Blood* refers to the hard labor by which the slave was bought.

34.1–12: The unsubstantiality of dreams. 1: Empty *hopes delude* because they are an escape from reality. **5:** The objection here stems from such practices by pagan peoples. **6:** Nonetheless, "true" dreams may be *sent* by the *Most High*. **8:** Normally, however, the *wisdom* provided in the *law* is sufficient. **9:** Empirical experience, rather than dreams, provides real knowledge. **11–12:** *Travels* were a practical source of experience (compare 51.13); the author's opposition to paganism does not prevent him from gaining knowledge of the world outside Judea. **34.13–36.17: True piety and the mercy of God** are united only in good conduct. **34.13–17: A psalm of deliverance from fear.** It is God who gives what the dream seekers (34.1–8) were after. **34.18–26: Empty observances. 18:** *A sacrifice:* this cannot substitute for moral obedience.

is like killing a son before his
father's eyes.

21 Bread is life to the destitute,
and it is murder to deprive them of it.

22 To rob your neighbour of his
livelihood is to kill him,
and the man who cheats a worker
of his wages sheds blood.

23 When one builds and another pulls
down,
what have they gained except hard
work?

24 When one prays and another curses,
which is the Lord to listen to?

25 Wash after touching a corpse and
then touch it again,
and what have you gained by your
washing?

26 So it is with the man who fasts for
his sins
and goes and does the same again;
who will listen to his prayer?
what has he gained by his penance?

35 Keeping the law is worth many
offerings;
to heed the commandments is to
sacrifice a thank-offering.

2 A kindness repaid is an offering of
flour,
and to give alms is a praise-offering.

3 The way to please the Lord is to
renounce evil;
and to renounce wrongdoing is to
make atonement.

4 Yet do not appear before the Lord
empty-handed;

5 perform these sacrifices because
they are commanded.

6 When the just man brings his
offering of fat to the altar,
its fragrance rises to the presence
of the Most High.

7 The just man's sacrifice is acceptable;
it will never be forgotten.

8 Be generous in your worship of the
Lord
and present the firstfruits of your
labour in full measure.

9 Give all your gifts cheerfully
and be glad to dedicate your tithe.

10 Give to the Most High as he has
given to you,
as generously as you can afford.

11 For the Lord always repays;
you will be repaid seven times over.

12 Do not offer him a bribe, for he will
not accept it,
and do not rely on a dishonest
sacrifice;
for the Lord is a judge
who knows no partiality.

13 He has no favourites at the poor
man's expense,
but listens to his prayer when he is
wronged.

14 He never ignores the appeal of the
orphan
or the widow when she pours out
her complaint.

15 How the tears run down the widow's
cheeks,
and her cries accuse the man who
caused them!

16 To be accepted a man must serve
the Lord as he requires,
and then his prayer will reach the
clouds.

17 The prayer of the humble pierces
the clouds,
but he is not consoled until it
reaches its destination.
He does not desist until the Most
High intervenes,
gives the just their rights, and sees
justice done.

18 The Lord will not be slow,
neither will he be patient with the
wicked,

21–22: Withholding *wages* was forbidden in Lev.19.13. **24–26:** When the poor *curses* the rich, he will cancel out the latter's prayers; compare 35.17. Likewise, *penance*, in the form of ritual washing or fasting, is nullified by the repetition of the act which necessitated it. God, who *listens* to the *prayer* of the penitent, will not heed the prayer of the insincere.

    35.1–11: Right sacrifice. 1: The moral commands come first in *keeping the law*. **4–5:** Nevertheless, the ceremonial acts are not to be neglected. **9–11:** The view here draws on the motivation of self-interest.

    35.12–20: God's justice and mercy. 12: The *bribe* refers to the false sacrifices of 34.18–20. God shows no *partiality* to the rich; compare Deut.10.17–18. **13–17:** Delay of justice means that the *prayer* of *orphan* and *widow* may have to be very persistent; but God will see *justice done*. **18–20:** Perhaps by the metaphor of Israel as a widow (v. 14; Lam.1.1), the justice of God toward Israel becomes the subject.

until he crushes the sinews of the
merciless
and sends retribution on the
heathen;
until he blots out the insolent, one
and all,
and breaks the power of the unjust;

19 until he gives all men their deserts,
judging their actions by their
intentions;
until he gives his people their rights
and gladdens them with his mercy.

20 His mercy is as timely in days of
trouble
as rain-clouds in days of drought.

36 HAVE PITY ON US, O LORD, THOU
God of all; look down,

2 and send thy terror upon all
nations.

3 Raise thy hand against the heathen,
and let them see thy power.

4 As they have seen thy holiness
displayed among us,
so let us see thy greatness displayed
among them.

5 Let them learn, as we also have
learned,
that there is no God but only thou,
O Lord.

6 Renew thy signs, repeat thy miracles,
win glory for thy hand, for thy right
arm.

7 Rouse thy wrath, pour out thy fury,
destroy the adversary, wipe out the
enemy.

8 Remember the day thou hast
appointed and hasten it,*j*
and give men cause to recount thy
wonders.

9 Let fiery anger devour the survivors,
and let the oppressors of thy people
meet their doom.

10 Crush the heads of hostile princes,
who say, 'There is no one to match us.'

11 Gather all the tribes of Jacob,

and grant them their inheritance,*k*
as thou didst long ago.

12 Have pity, O Lord, on the people
called by thy name,
Israel, whom thou hast named thy
first-born.

13 Show mercy to the city of thy
sanctuary,
Jerusalem, the city of thy rest.

14 Fill Zion with the praise of thy
triumph;
fill thy people with thy glory.

15 Thou didst create them at the
beginning; acknowledge them
now
and fulfil the prophecies spoken
in thy name.

16 Reward those who wait for thee;
prove thy prophets trustworthy.

17 Listen, O Lord, to the prayer of
thy servants,
who claim Aaron's blessing upon
thy people.
Let all who live on earth
acknowledge
that thou art the Lord, the eternal
God.

Man in society

18 ALL IS FOOD FOR THE STOMACH,
but one food is better than another.

19 As the palate identifies game by its
taste,
so the discerning mind detects lies.

20 A warped mind makes trouble,
but a man of experience can pay it
back.

21 A woman will take any man for
husband,
but a man may prefer one girl to
another.

22 A woman's beauty makes a man
happy,

j Remember . . . it: *some witnesses read* Hasten the day
and remember thy oath.
k Or and take them to be thy own.

36.1–17: A prayer for Israel. In language of appeal to God this section takes up the theme
of 35.18–20. 1: *God of all:* compare 50.22. 4: God's *holiness* was shown in his punishing Israel
by exile. 6: The *signs* and *miracles* are those of Exod.7.14–11.10; 12.29–32; 14.1–15.21.
8: The *day* of the Lord was both a popular and prophetic hope; see Amos 5.18–20. 9–11: Some
of the elements of the "day" were to *crush* the *oppressors* of Israel and to *gather* the dispersed
tribes of Jacob. Inheritance: land of Palestine. 12: *Called by thy name:* belonging to you. 17:
Along with the prophecies, the writer invokes the priestly blessing of *Aaron;* see Num.6.23–26.
36.18–20: Discernment. Three proverbs introduce a collection of poems (36.18–39.11) about
judgment and discrimination.
36.21–26: The married life. 21: The *woman* had no choice; marriage was arranged by the

and there is nothing he desires more.

23 If she has a kind and gentle tongue,
   then her husband is luckier than
      most men.

24 The man who wins a wife has the
      beginnings of a fortune,
   a helper to match his needs and a
      pillar to support him.

25 Where there is no hedge, property
      is plundered;
   and where there is no wife, the
      wanderer sighs for a home.

26 Does anyone trust a roving bandit
   who swoops on town after town?
   No more will they trust a homeless
      man
   who lodges wherever night overtakes
      him.

37 Every friend says, 'I too am your
      friend';
   but some are friends in name only.

2 What a mortal grief it is
   when a dear friend turns into an
      enemy!

3 Oh this propensity to evil, how did it
      creep in
   to cover the earth with treachery?

4 A friend may be all smiles when you
      are happy,
   but turn against you when trouble
      comes.

5 Another shares your toil for the sake
      of a meal,
   and yet may protect you against an
      enemy.

6 Never forget a friend
   or neglect him when prosperity comes
      your way.

7 Every counsellor says his own advice
      is best
   but some have their own advantage
      in view.

8 Beware of the man who offers
      advice,
   and find out beforehand where his
      interest lies.

His advice will be weighted in his
   own favour
and may tip the scales against you.

He may say, 'Your road is clear',   9
and stand aside to see what happens.

Do not consult a man who is   10
   suspicious of you
or reveal your intentions to those
   who envy you.

Never consult a woman about her   11
   rival
or a coward about war,
a merchant about a bargain
or a buyer about a sale,
a skinflint about gratitude
or a hard-hearted man about a kind
   action,
an idler about work of any sort,
a casual labourer about finishing
   the job,
or a lazy servant about an exacting
   task—
do not turn to them for any advice.

Rely rather on a godfearing man   12
whom you know to be a keeper of
   the commandments,
whose interests are like your own,
who will sympathize if you have a
   setback.

But also trust your own judgement,   13
for it is your most reliable counsellor.

A man's own mind has sometimes   14
   a way of telling him more
than seven watchmen posted high on
   a tower.

But above all pray to the Most High   15
to keep you on the straight road of
   truth.

Every undertaking begins in   16
   discussion,
and consultation precedes every
   action.

Here you can trace the mind's   17
   variety.

Four kinds of destiny are offered to   18
   men,
good and evil, life and death;

---

father. **24–26:** Despite negative remarks about women, Ecclesiasticus strongly disapproves of
men who avoid marriage.
   37.1–6: Choosing a friend. Compare 6.5–17. **1–4:** A true friend is hard to discern. **6:** The
section ends with an imperative which sets the qualifications aside.
   37.7–15: Choosing a counselor. As in 37.1–6, the main theme is watchfulness against the
other's interest. **11:** Lists were a typical way of collecting wisdom; compare 25.7–10. *Rival:*
see 26.6 n. **13–14:** Factors that warp others' insight do not apply in the same way to your own.
15: The shrewd, practical section closes on a religious note; see also v. 12.
   37.16–26: Productive and unproductive wisdom. 22: Success in managing one's own life is a

and always it is the tongue that
decides the issue.

19 A man may be clever enough to
teach others
and yet be useless to himself.

20 A brilliant speaker may make
enemies
and end by dying of hunger,

21 if the Lord has withheld the gift of
popular appeal,
because he is devoid of wisdom.

22 If a man is wise in the conduct of
his own life,
his good sense can be trusted when
he speaks.

23 If a man is wise and instructs his
people,
then his good sense can be trusted.

24 A wise man will have praise heaped
on him,
and all who see him will count him
happy.

25 The days of a man's life can be
numbered,
but the days of Israel are countless.

26 A wise man will possess the
confidence of his people,
and his name will live for ever.

27 MY SON, TEST YOURSELF ALL YOUR
life long;
take note of what is bad for you and
do not indulge in it.

28 For not everything is good for
everyone;
we do not all enjoy the same things.

29 Do not be greedy for every delicacy
or eat without restraint.

30 For illness is a sure result of
overeating,
and gluttony is next door to colic.

31 Gluttony has been the death of
many;
be on your guard and prolong your
life.

38 Honour the doctor for his services,
for the Lord created him.

His skill comes from the Most High, 2
and he is rewarded by kings.

The doctor's knowledge gives him 3
high standing
and wins him the admiration of the
great.

The Lord has created medicines from 4
the earth,
and a sensible man will not disparage
them.

Was it not a tree that sweetened 5
water
and so disclosed its properties^l?

The Lord has imparted knowledge 6
to men,
that by their use of his marvels he
may win praise;

by using them the doctor^m relieves 7
pain
and from them the pharmacist makes 8
up his mixture.

There is no end to the works of the
Lord,
who spreads health over the whole
world.

My son, if you have an illness, do 9
not neglect it,
but pray to the Lord, and he will
heal you.

Renounce your faults, amend your 10
ways,
and cleanse your heart from all sin.

Bring a savoury offering and bring 11
flour for a token
and pour oil on the sacrifice; be as
generous as you can.^{n}

Then call in the doctor, for the Lord 12
created him;
do not let him leave you, for you
need him.

There may come a time when your 13
recovery is in their hands;
then they too will pray to the Lord 14
to give them success in relieving pain
and finding a cure to save their
patient's life.

l Or and revealed the power of the Lord.
m the doctor: so Heb.; Gk. he heals and . . .
n be . . . can: so Heb.; Gk. obscure.

---

mark of productive wisdom. **24:** Public reputation is another mark. **26:** Lasting fame is a third
criterion.
   37.27–31: Know your own limits. These verses make the generalized proverbs of 36.18–19
into literal rules for finding one's own dietary style.
   38.1–15: The doctor. 3: Social *standing* is cited as proof of the validity of the doctor's work.
4: Apparently some did *disparage medicines*, because they believed that faith alone should
heal. Ecclus. advocates both faith (compare vv. 9–11) and the doctor. **5:** For the *sweetened
water*, see Exod.15.23–25.

15 When a man has sinned against his
Maker,
let him put himself in the doctor's
hands.

16 My son, shed tears for the dead;
raise a lament for your grievous loss.
Shroud his body with proper
ceremony,
and do not neglect his burial.
17 With bitter weeping and passionate
lament
make your mourning worthy of him.
Mourn for a few days as propriety
demands,
and then take comfort for your
grief.
18 For grief may lead to death,
and a sorrowful heart saps the
strength.
19 When a man is taken away, suffering
is over,
but to live on in poverty goes against
the grain.
20 Do not abandon yourself to grief;
put it from you and think of your
own end.
21 Never forget! there is no return;
you cannot help him and can only
injure yourself.
22 Remember that his fate will also be
yours:
'Mine today and yours tomorrow.'
23 When the dead is at rest, let his
memory rest too;
take comfort as soon as he has
breathed his last.

24 A SCHOLAR'S WISDOM COMES OF
ample leisure;
if a man is to be wise he must be
relieved of other tasks.
25 How can a man become wise who
guides the plough,
whose pride is in wielding his goad,
who is absorbed in the task of
driving oxen,
and talks only about cattle?

26 He concentrates on ploughing his
furrows,
and works late to give the heifers
their fodder.
27 So it is with every craftsman or
designer
who works by night as well as by day,
such as those who make engravings
on signets,
and patiently vary the design;
they concentrate on making an
exact representation,
and sit up late to finish their task.
28 So it is with the smith, sitting by
his anvil,
intent on his iron-work.
The smoke of the fire shrivels his
flesh,
as he wrestles in the heat of the
furnace.
The hammer rings again and again
in his ears,
and his eyes are on the pattern he is
copying.
He concentrates on completing the
task,
and stays up late to give it a perfect
finish.
29 So it is with the potter, sitting at his
work,
turning the wheel with his feet,
always engrossed in the task
of making up his tally;
30 he moulds the clay with his arm,
crouching forward to apply his
strength.
He concentrates on finishing the
glazing,
and stays awake to clean out the
furnace.

31 All these rely on their hands,
and each is skilful at his own craft.
32 Without them a city would have
no inhabitants;
no settlers or travellers would
come to it.
33 Yet they are not in demand at
public discussions

38.16–23: **Mourning for the dead.** 16–17: _Proper ceremony_ is important, partly because it makes possible the psychological break with the dead which is so important; see vv. 20–23. Mourning _as propriety demands_ involves a sensitivity to public opinion on which the author constantly kept his eye. 18–23: The finality of _your own end_ (v. 20) can help you to accept another's. 22: The dead man speaks a proverb.

38.24–39.11: **Ordinary work and the work of the wise.** 24: _Leisure_ is to be used acquiring _wisdom._ 25–34: Farming (honored in 7.15,22) and crafts allow no leisure for study. Yet later

or prominent in the assembly,
They do not sit on the judge's bench
or understand the decisions of the
courts.
They cannot expound moral or
legal principles
and are not ready with maxims.
34 But they maintain the fabric of this
world,
and their prayers are about their
daily work.*o*

39 How different it is with the man
who devotes himself
to studying the law of the Most High,
who investigates all the wisdom of
the past,
and spends his time studying the
prophecies!
2 He preserves the sayings of famous
men
and penetrates the intricacies of
parables.
3 He investigates the hidden meaning
of proverbs
and knows his way among riddles.
4 The great avail themselves of his
services,
and he is seen in the presence of
rulers.
He travels in foreign countries
and learns at first hand the good or
evil of man's lot.
5 He makes a point of rising early
to pray to the Lord, his Maker,
and prays aloud to the Most High,
asking pardon for his sins.
6 If it is the will of the great Lord,
he will be filled with a spirit of
intelligence;
then he will pour forth wise sayings
of his own
and give thanks to the Lord in prayer.
7 He will have sound advice and
knowledge to offer,
and his thoughts will dwell on the
mysteries he has studied.

He will disclose what he has learnt 8
from his own education,
and will take pride in the law of the
Lord's covenant.
Many will praise his intelligence; 9
it will never sink into oblivion.
The memory of him will not die
but will live on from generation to
generation;
the nations will talk of his wisdom, 10
and his praises will be sung in the
assembly.
If he lives long, he will leave a name 11
in a thousand,
and if he goes to his rest, his
reputation is secure.*p*

I HAVE STILL MORE IN MY MIND TO 12
express;
I am full like the moon at mid-month.
Listen to me, my devout sons, and 13
blossom
like a rose planted by a stream.
Spread your fragrance like incense, 14
and bloom like a lily.
Scatter your fragrance; lift your
voices in song,
praising the Lord for all his works.
Ascribe majesty to his name 15
and give thanks to him with praise,
with songs on your lips, and with
harps;
let these be your words of
thanksgiving:
'All that the Lord has made is very 16
good;
all that he commands will happen
in due time.'
No one should ask, 'What is this?' 17
or 'Why is that?'
At the proper time all such questions
will be answered.
When he spoke the water stood
up like a heap,
and his word created reservoirs for it.

o Or and their daily work is their prayer.
p his reputation is secure: possible reading; Gk. obscure.

---

on Jewish scholars regularly practiced a craft; compare Acts 18.3. **39.1:** The wise man is a
scholar of the Scriptures. In the threefold division of the Bible, the order is usually Law,
Prophecy, and the Writings, the latter equivalent to Wisdom. Here the author, because of his
own interest, puts *wisdom* before *prophecies*. **4:** He is also a shrewd, practical advisor in public
affairs. *Travels:* see 34.11–12 n. **9–11:** Enduring *memory* is an important test to Ecclus.; compare
44.10–15.
    39.12–35: God's works. 16–31: A psalm opposes skeptics with the argument that everything
is good in its time. The skeptics (vv. 17,21,34) represent the pessimistic facet in the wisdom
tradition (compare the interpretation of "times" in Eccles.3.1–11). **17:** The *water stood up* in

18 When he commands, his purpose is fulfilled,
and no one can thwart his saving power.

19 He sees the deeds of all mankind;
there is no hiding from his gaze.

20 From the beginning to the end of time he keeps watch,
and nothing is too marvellous for him.

21 No one should ask, 'What is this?' or 'Why is that?'
Everything has been created for its own purpose.

22 His blessing is like a river in flood
which inundates the parched ground.

23 But the doom he assigns the heathen is his wrath,
as when he turned a watered plain into a salt desert.

24 For the devout his paths are straight,
but full of pitfalls for the wicked.

25 From the beginning good things were created for the good,
and evils for sinners.

26 The chief necessities of human life are water, fire, iron, and salt,
flour, honey, and milk,
the juice of the grape, oil, and clothing.

27 All these are good for the godfearing,
but turn to evil for sinners.

28 There are winds created to be agents of retribution,
with great whips to give play to their fury;
on the day of reckoning, they exert their force
and give full vent to the anger of their Maker.

29 Fire and hail, famine and deadly disease,
all these were created for retribution;

30 beasts of prey, scorpions and vipers,
and the avenging sword that destroys the wicked.

31 They delight in carrying out his orders,
always standing ready for his service on the earth;
and when their time comes, they never disobey.

32 I have been convinced of all this from the beginning;
I have thought it over and left it in writing:

33 all the works of the Lord are good,
and he supplies every need as it occurs.

34 No one should say, 'This is less good than that',
for all things prove good at their proper time.

35 Come then, sing with heart and voice,
and praise the name of the Lord.

40 HARD WORK IS THE LOT OF EVERY man,
and a heavy yoke is laid on the sons of Adam,
from the day when they come from their mother's womb
until the day of their return to the mother of all;

2 troubled thoughts and fears are theirs,
and anxious expectation of the day of their death.

3 Whether a man sits in royal splendour on a throne
or grovels in dust and ashes,

4 whether he wears the purple and a crown
or is clothed in sackcloth,

5 his life is nothing but anger and jealousy, worry and perplexity,
fear of death, and guilt, and rivalry.
Even when he goes to bed at night,
sleep only brings to mind the same things in a new form.

6 His rest is little or nothing;
he begins to struggle as hard in his sleep as in the day.[q]
Disturbed by nightmares,

---

q he begins . . . . day: *possible meaning; Gk. obscure.*

---

being separated from the land, Gen.1.9–10. **23:** The *watered plain* is that of Sodom and Gomorrah, Gen.19.25; compare Ps.107.34. **26:** This list of ten necessities drawn from secular wisdom (compare 29.21) is used to show that God made all things good, though they can be turned to evil by the sinner.

40.1–11: Suffering as the lot of man. In striking contrast to the previous psalm, Ecclus. here recognizes the universality of suffering, even for the righteous. **5–7:** Ecclus. avoids a religious

he fancies himself a fugitive from the
battlefield;

7 and at the moment when he reaches
safety, he wakes up,
astonished to find his fears groundless.

8 To all living creatures, man and
beast—
and seven times over to sinners—
9 come death and bloodshed, quarrel
and sword,
disaster, famine, ruin, and plague.
10 All these were created for the wicked,
and on their account the flood
happened.
11 All that is of earth returns to earth
again,
and all that is of water finds its way
back to the sea.

12 Bribery and injustice will all vanish,
but good faith will last for ever.
13 The wealth of the wicked will dry
up like a torrent
and die away like a great roll of
thunder in a storm.
14 As a generous man will have cause
for rejoicing,
so law-breakers will come to utter
ruin.
15 The shoots of an impious stock put
out few branches;
their tainted roots are planted on
sheer rock.
16 The rush that grows on every
river-bank
is pulled up before any other grass,
17 but kindness is like a luxuriant
garden,
and almsgiving lasts for ever.

18 To be employed and to be one's own
master, both are sweet,
but it is better still to find a treasure.
19 Offspring and the founding of a city
perpetuate a man's name,
but better still is a perfect wife.

Wine and music gladden the heart, 20
but better still is the love of wisdom.
Flute and harp make pleasant 21
melody,
but better still is a pleasant voice.
A man likes to see grace and beauty, 22
but better still the green shoots in a
cornfield.
A friend or companion is always 23
welcome,
but better still to be man and wife.
Brothers and helpers are a standby 24
in time of trouble,
but better still is almsgiving.
Gold and silver make a man stand 25
firm,
but better still is good advice.
Wealth and strength make for 26
confidence,
but better still is the fear of the Lord.
To fear the Lord is to lack nothing
and never to be in need of support.
The fear of the Lord is like a 27
luxuriant garden;
it shelters a man better than any
riches.

My son, do not live the life of a 28
beggar;
it is better to die than to beg.
When a man starts looking to 29
another man's table,
his existence is not worth calling life.
It is demoralizing to live on another
man's food,
and a wise, well-disciplined man will
guard against it. 30
When a man has lost all shame, he
speaks as if begging were sweet,
but inside him there is a blazing fire.

Death, how bitter is the thought **41**
of you
to a man living at ease among his
possessions,
free from anxiety, prosperous in
all things,

---

interpretation of dreams (compare 34.1–8); they are part of man's burden. **8–11:** At least the
burden of suffering is greater for *sinners*.
  40.12–17: The victory of the good. To counteract the previous pessimistic observations,
Ecclesiasticus here affirms the transience of *bribery* and *injustice* and all evil, and the permanence
of *good faith* and all good.
  40.18–30: Good and bad things. 18–27: Eighteen good things are listed in a complex parallel
pattern. **26–27:** *The fear of the Lord* is the best. **28–30:** A beggar's life is the opposite of a good
thing. **30:** The inner conflict is the worst feature of begging.
  41.1–4: Acceptance of death. Regardless of one's emotional response, one must accept
the inevitable.

and still vigorous enough to enjoy
    a good meal!

2 Death, how welcome is your
    sentence
to a destitute man whose strength
    is failing,
worn down by age and endless
    anxiety,
resentful and at the end of his
    patience!

3 Do not be afraid of death's summons;
remember those who have gone
    before you, and those who will
    come after.

4 This is the Lord's decree for all
    living men;
why try to argue with the will of the
    Most High?
Whether life lasts ten years, or a
    hundred, or a thousand,
there will be no questions asked in
    the grave.

5 What a loathsome brood are the
    children of sinners,
brought up in haunts of vice!

6 Their inheritance dwindles away,
and their descendants suffer a lasting
    disgrace.

7 A godless father is blamed by his
    children
for the disgrace they endure on his
    account.

8 Woe to you, godless men
who have abandoned the law of
    God Most High!

9 When you are born, you are born to
    a curse,
and when you die, a curse is your
    lot.

10 Whatever comes from earth returns
    to earth;
so too the godless go from curse
    to ruin.

11 Men grieve over the death of the
    body,
but sinners have no good name to
    survive them.

12 Take thought for your name, for it
    will outlive you
longer than a thousand hoards of
    gold.

13 The days of a good life are
    numbered,
but a good name lasts for ever.

14 MY CHILDREN, BE TRUE TO YOUR
    training and live in peace.
Wisdom concealed and treasure
    hidden—
what is the use of either?

15 Better a man who hides his folly
than one who hides his wisdom!

16 Show deference then to my
    teaching:
shame is not always to be
    encouraged,
or given unqualified approval in all
    circumstances.

17 Be ashamed to be found guilty of
    fornication by your parents,
or of lies by a ruler or prince;

18 of crime by a judge or magistrate,
or of a breach of the law by the
    assembly and people;
of dishonesty by a partner or
    friend,

19 or of theft by the neighbourhood;
be ashamed before the truth of God
    and his covenant.
Be ashamed of bad manners at
    table,
of giving or receiving with a sneer,

20 of refusing to return a greeting,
or of ogling a prostitute.

21 Be ashamed of turning away a
    relative,
of robbing someone of his rightful
    share,
or of eyeing another man's wife.

22 Be ashamed of meddling with his
    slave-girl,
and keep away from her bed.
Be ashamed of reproaching your
    friends,
or following up your charity with
    a lecture.

23 Be ashamed of repeating what you
    have heard
and of betraying a secret.

24 Then you will be showing a proper
    shame
and will be popular with everyone.

41.5–13: Consequences that outlast death. 5–10: *Children* bear the consequences of their
godless father's life. **11–13:** A *good name* is the most lasting memorial; compare Prov.22.1;
Eccles.7.1.
    41.14–42.8: Proper and improper shame. 17–23: Proper bases of shame are listed. **24:** The

42 But at other times you must not
     be ashamed,
or you will do wrong out of
     deference to others.

2 Do not be ashamed of the law and
     covenant of the Most High,
or of justice, for fear you acquit the
     guilty;

3 of settling accounts with a partner
     or a travelling-companion,
or of sharing an inheritance with the
     other heirs;

4 of using accurate weights and measures,
or of business dealings, large or small,

5 and making a profit out of trade;
of frequent disciplining of children,
or of drawing blood from the back
     of a worthless servant.

6 If your wife is untrustworthy, or
     where many hands are at work,
it is well to keep things under lock
     and key.

7 When you make a deposit, see that
     it is counted and weighed,
and when you give or receive, have
     it all in writing.

8 Do not be ashamed to correct the
     ignorant and foolish,
or a greybeard guilty of fornication.
Then you will be showing your
     sound upbringing
and will win everyone's approval.

9 A daughter is a secret anxiety to her
     father,
and the worry of her keeps him
     awake at night;
when she is young, for fear she may
     grow too old to marry,
and when she is married, for fear she
     may lose her husband's love;

10 when she is a virgin, for fear she
     may be seduced
and become pregnant in her father's
     house,
when she has a husband, for fear

she may misbehave,
and after marriage, for fear she may   11
     be barren.
Keep close watch over a headstrong
     daughter,
or she may give your enemies cause
     to gloat,
making you the talk of the town and
     a byword[r] among the people,
and shaming you in the eyes of the
     world.
Do not let her display her beauty to   12
     any man,
or gossip in the women's quarters.[s]
For out of clothes comes the moth,   13
and out of woman comes woman's
     wickedness.
Better a man's wickedness than a   14
     woman's goodness;
it is woman who brings shame and
     disgrace.

The wonders of creation

NOW I WILL CALL TO MIND THE   15
     works of the Lord
and describe what I have seen;
by the words of the Lord his works
     are made.
As the sun in its brilliance looks   16
     down on everything,
so the glory of the Lord fills his
     creation.
Even to his angels the Lord has not   17
     given the power
to tell the full story of his marvels,
which the Lord Almighty has
     established
so that the universe may stand firm
     in his glory.
He fathoms the abyss and the heart   18
     of man,
he is versed in their intricate secrets;
for the Lord possesses all knowledge

---

r a byword: *so Heb.; Gk. obscure.*
s Do not . . . quarters: *so Heb.; Gk. obscure.*

---

conclusion is a secular rather than a religious one; but compare v. 19. **42.2–7:** Things not to be ashamed of are listed in contrast to 41.17–23. **8:** The conclusion parallels 41.24.
    42.9–14: Problems with women. 9–12: *Anxiety* for a *daughter* is sketched through the stages of her life. **13–14:** The generalizing conclusion is probably a popular proverb.
    42.15–43.33: The wonders of creation. This poem on the wonders of creation introduces 44.1–50.21, on the heroes of Israel's past; Pss.104 (creation) and 105–106 (Israel's past) exhibit a similar pattern. These concluding chapters make clear that the practical human wisdom of the earlier part of the book is to be seen in the framework of God's all-embracing, benign influence in all of nature, but especially in Israel's history and in the lives of those who made it.
    42.15–25: God's lordship in the creation. 15: The *works of the Lord* make up the whole visible universe. **18:** Man's *heart* (i.e. his mind) is considered to be as inscrutable as the *abyss,* the

and observes the signs of all time.

19 He discloses the past and the future,
and uncovers the traces of the
world's mysteries.

20 No thought escapes his notice,
and not a word is hidden from him.

21 He has set in order the masterpieces
of his wisdom,
he who is from eternity to eternity;
nothing can be added, nothing taken
away,
and he needs no one to give him advice.

22 How beautiful is all that he has made,
down to the smallest spark that can
be seen!

23 His works endure, all of them active
for ever
and all responsive to their various
purposes.

24 All things go in pairs, one the
opposite of the other;
he has made nothing incomplete.

25 One thing supplements the virtues
of another.
Who could ever contemplate his
glory enough?

43 What a masterpiece is the clear
vault of the sky!
How glorious is the spectacle of the
heavens!

2 The sun comes into view proclaiming
as it rises
how marvellous a thing it is, made
by the Most High.

3 At noon it parches the earth,
and no one can endure its blazing heat.

4 The stoker of a furnace works in
the heat,
but three times as hot is the sun
scorching the hills.
It breathes out fiery vapours,
and its glare blinds the eyes.

5 Great is the Lord who made it,
whose word speeds it on its course.

6 He made the moon also to serve
in its turn,
a perpetual sign to mark the divisions
of time.

7 From the moon, feast-days are
reckoned;

it is a light that wanes as it completes
its course.

8 The moon gives its name to the
month;
it waxes marvellously as its phases
change,
a beacon to the armies of heaven,
shining in the vault of the sky.

9 The brilliant stars are the beauty of
the sky,
a glittering array in the heights of
the Lord.

10 At the command of the Holy One
they stand in their appointed
place;
they never default at their post.

11 Look at the rainbow and praise its
Maker;
it shines with a supreme beauty,
12 rounding the sky with its gleaming
arc,
a bow bent by the hands of the
Most High.

13 His command speeds the snow-storm
and sends the swift lightning to
execute his sentence.
14 To that end the storehouses are
opened,
and the clouds fly out like birds.
15 By his almighty power the clouds are
piled up
and the hailstones broken small.
16–17 The crash of his thunder makes
the earth writhe,
and, when he appears, an earthquake
shakes the hills.
At his will the south wind blows,
the squall from the north and the
hurricane.
He scatters the snow-flakes like birds
alighting;
they settle like a swarm of locusts.
18 The eye is dazzled by their beautiful
whiteness,
and as they fall the mind is entranced.
19 He spreads frost on the earth like
salt,
and icicles form like pointed stakes.
20 A cold blast from the north,

subterranean reservoir of water. **24–25:** The appearance of *pairs* helps explain the apparent contradictions in life; compare 33.15.
   43.1–26: Examples of God's work. Astonishment at the rapid yet controlled changes of the natural environment is the leading theme.

and ice grows hard on the water,
settling on every pool,
as though the water were putting
on a breastplate.

21 He consumes the hills, scorches the
wilderness,
and withers the grass like fire.

22 Cloudy weather quickly puts all to
rights,
and dew brings welcome relief after
heat.

23 By the power of his thought he
tamed the deep
and planted it with islands.

24 Those who sail the sea tell stories
of its dangers,
which astonish all who hear them;

25 in it are strange and wonderful
creatures,
all kinds of living things and huge
sea-monsters.

26 By his own action he achieves his
end,
and by his word all things are held
together.

27 However much we say, we cannot
exhaust our theme;
to put it in a word: he is all.

28 Where can we find the skill to sing
his praises?
For he is greater than all his works.

29 The Lord is terrible and very great,
and marvellous is his power.

30 Honour the Lord to the best of
your ability,
and he will still be high above all
praise.
Summon all your strength to declare
his greatness,
and be untiring, for the most you
can do will fall short.

31 Has anyone ever seen him, to be
able to describe him?
Can anyone praise him as he truly
is?

32 We have seen but a small part of
his works,

and there remain many mysteries
greater still.
The Lord has made everything   33
and has given wisdom to the godly.

Heroes of Israel's past

LET US NOW SING THE PRAISES OF   **44**
famous men,
the heroes of our nation's history,
through whom the Lord established   2
his renown,
and revealed his majesty in each
succeeding age.
Some held sway over kingdoms   3
and made themselves a name by
their exploits.
Others were sage counsellors,
who spoke out with prophetic power.
Some led the people by their   4
counsels
and by their knowledge of the
nation's law;
out of their fund of wisdom they
gave instruction.
Some were composers of music or   5
writers of poetry.
Others were endowed with wealth   6
and strength,
living peacefully in their homes.
All these won fame in their own   7
generation
and were the pride of their times.
Some there are who have left a name   8
behind them
to be commemorated in story.
There are others who are   9
unremembered;
they are dead, and it is as though
they had never existed,
as though they had never been born
or left children to succeed them.
Not so our forefathers; they were   10
men of loyalty,
whose good deeds have never been
forgotten.
Their prosperity is handed on to   11
their descendants,

43.27–33: God's power. This is the conclusion of 42.15–43.33. **27:** To say that God *is all* is a poetic exaggeration, for he is not the things he has created; compare Wis.1.7. **32:** What we have *seen* (nature) points beyond itself, to the *mysteries* of the invisible worlds and of God himself.

44.1–15: Introduction to the praises of famous men. 1–2: *Famous men* are remembered not for themselves, but because they reveal God's *majesty*. **3–7:** The prominence of *sage counsellors* here contrasts with the actual functions of the men named later. **9:** The *unremembered*, according to Ecclus., are men of power who were disloyal to God.

and their inheritance to future
generations.[t]

12 Thanks to them their children are
within the covenants—
the whole race of their descendants.

13 Their line will endure for all time,
and their fame will never be blotted
out.

14 Their bodies are buried in peace,
but their name lives for ever.

15 Nations will recount their wisdom,
and God's people will sing their
praises.

16 Enoch pleased the Lord and was
carried off to heaven,
an example of repentance to future
generations.

17 Noah was found perfect and
righteous,
and thus he made amends in the
time of retribution;
therefore a remnant survived on
the earth,
when the flood came.

18 A perpetual covenant was established
with him,
that never again should all life be
swept away by a flood.

19 Great Abraham was the father of
many nations;
no one has ever been found to equal
him in fame.

20 He kept the law of the Most High;
he entered into covenant with
him,
setting upon his body the mark of
the covenant;
and, when he was tested, he proved
faithful.

21 Therefore the Lord swore an oath
to him,
that nations should find blessing
through his descendants,
that his family should be countless
as the dust of the earth
and be raised as high as the stars,

and that their possessions should
reach from sea to sea,
from the Great River to the ends of
the earth.

22 To Isaac he made the same promise
for the sake of his father Abraham,
a blessing for all mankind and a
covenant;

23 and so he transmitted them to
Jacob.
He confirmed him in the blessings
he had received
and gave him the land he was to
inherit,
dividing it into portions,
which he allotted to the twelve tribes.

45 From Jacob's stock the Lord
raised up a loyal servant,
who won the approval of all mankind,
beloved by God and men,
Moses of blessed memory.

2 The Lord made him equal in glory
to the angels
and gave him power to strike terror
into his enemies.

3 At his request he put an end to the
portents,
and enhanced his reputation with
kings.
He gave him commandments for his
people
and showed him a vision of his own
glory.

4 For his loyalty and humility he
consecrated him,
choosing him out of all mankind.

5 He let him hear his voice
and led him into the dark cloud.
Face to face, he gave him the
commandments,
a law that brings life and knowledge,
so that he might teach Jacob the
covenant
and Israel his decrees.

*t Their prosperity . . . generations: probable meaning,
based on other Vss.; Gk. obscure.*

44.16–18: Enoch and Noah. 16: *Enoch* also appears at 49.14 and may be a copyist's addition
here. **17–18:** On the *covenant* with *Noah*, see Gen.8.20–22; 9.8–17.
    44.19–23: Abraham, Isaac, and Jacob. 20: Ecclus. remembers *Abraham* because he *kept the
law* (Gen.26.5); contrast Rom.4.1–25. The *mark of the covenant* was circumcision; see
Gen.17.10–14,23–27.
    45.1–5: Moses. 2: The *angels* represent a weakened Gk. translation of Exod.4.16; 7.1, where
Moses is like a "god" to Aaron and Pharaoh; the same Heb. word *elohim* is translated by
"god" and "angels." **3:** The *portents* were the plagues of Egypt; see Exod.7.14–11.10; 12.29–32.
The *vision* was that of Exod.33.18–34.8. **4:** For Moses' *humility*, see Num.12.3.

6 He raised to a like holy office
Moses' brother Aaron from the
tribe of Levi.

7 He made a perpetual covenant with
him,
conferring on him the priesthood of
the nation.
He honoured him with splendid
ornaments
and clothed him in gorgeous
vestments.

8 He robed him in perfect splendour
and armed him with the emblems
of power,
the breeches, the mantle, and the
tunic.

9 Round his robe he placed
pomegranates
and a circle of many golden bells,
to make music as he walked,
ringing aloud throughout the temple
as a reminder to his people.

10 He gave him the sacred vestment
adorned by an embroiderer
with gold and violet and purple;
the oracle of judgement with the
tokens of truth;*u*

11 the scarlet thread spun with a
craftsman's art;
the precious stones, engraved like
seals,
and placed by the jeweller in a gold
setting
with inscriptions to serve as
reminders,
one for each of the tribes of Israel;

12 the gold crown upon his turban,
engraved like a seal with 'Holy to
the Lord'.*v*
What rich adornments to feast the
eyes!
What a miracle of art! What a
proud honour!

13 Before him no such splendour
existed,
and no one outside his family has
ever put them on,
no one except his sons
and his descendants in perpetuity.

14 Twice every day without fail
they present his sacrifice of a whole-
offering.

15 It was Moses who ordained him
and anointed him with sacred oil,
in token of the perpetual covenant
made with him
and with his descendants as long
as the heavens endure,
that he should be the Lord's minister
in the priestly office
and bless his people in his name.

16 He chose him out of all mankind
to bring offerings to the Lord,
incense and the fragrance of
memorial sacrifice,
to make atonement for the people.

17 He entrusted to him his
commandments,
with authority to pronounce legal
decisions,
to teach Jacob his decrees
and enlighten Israel about his law.

18 Upstarts grew jealous of him
and conspired against him in the
desert,
Dathan and Abiram with their
supporters
and Korah's band in their violent
anger.

19 The Lord saw and refused his
sanction;
he destroyed them in the heat of
his wrath,
and worked a miracle against them
by consuming them in a blazing
fire.

20 But he added fresh honours to
Aaron
and gave him a special privilege,
allotting to the priests the choicest
firstfruits,
to ensure that they above all should
have bread in plenty.

21 For they eat the sacrifices of the
Lord,
which he gave to Aaron and his
descendants.

22 But he was to have no inheritance
in the land of his people,
no portion allotted to him among
them;

*u the oracle . . . truth: or the breast-piece of judgement
with the Urim and Thummim (Exodus 28. 30).*
v Compare Exodus 28. 36; literally a seal of holiness.

45.6–26: Aaron and Phinehas. As founder of the priestly line, Aaron receives far more
attention than Moses; compare the long treatment of Simon (50.1–21). **7–13:** For the *splendid
ornaments*, see Exod.28.1–43; they symbolize the glory of God's service. **15:** For Aaron's
anointing with *sacred oil*, see Lev.8.10–13. **18–22:** For *Dathan, Abiram,* and *Korah,* see

for the Lord himself is his portion,
his inheritance.

23 Phinehas son of Eleazar ranks third
in renown
for being zealous in his reverence
for the Lord,
and for standing firm with noble
courage,
when the people were in revolt;
by so doing he made atonement
for Israel.

24 Therefore a covenant was established
with him,
assuring him command of the
sanctuary and of the nation,
conferring on him and his
descendants
the high-priesthood for ever.

25 Just as a covenant was made with
David son of Jesse of the tribe
of Judah,
that the royal succession should
always pass from father to son,
so the succession was to pass from
Aaron to his descendants.

26 May the Lord grant you a wise mind
to judge his people with justice,
so that their prosperity may never
vanish
and their glory may be handed on
to future generations!

46 Joshua son of Nun was a mighty
warrior,
who succeeded Moses in the prophetic
office.
He lived up to his name
as a great liberator of the Lord's
chosen people,
able to take reprisals on the
enemies who attacked them,
and to put Israel in possession of
their territory.

2 How glorious he was when he raised
his hand
and brandished his sword against
cities!

3 Never before had a man made such
a stand,
for he was fighting the Lord's battles.

Was it not through him that the sun 4
stood still
and made one day as long as two?
He called on the Most High, the 5
Mighty One,
when the enemy was pressing him
on every side,
and the great Lord answered his
prayer
with violent storm of hail. 6
He overwhelmed that nation in battle
and crushed his assailants as they
fled down the pass,
to make the nations recognize his
strength in arms
and teach them that he fought under
the very eyes of the Lord,
for he followed the lead of the
Mighty One.

In the time of Moses he had proved 7
his loyalty,
he and Caleb son of Jephunneh:
they stood their ground against the
whole assembly,
restrained the people from sin,
and silenced their wicked grumbling.
Out of six hundred thousand warriors 8
these two alone escaped with their
lives
to enter the land and take possession
of it,
the land flowing with milk and honey.
The Lord gave Caleb strength, 9
which still remained with him in his
old age,
so that he was able to invade the
hill-country
and win possession of it for his
descendants.
So all Israel could see 10
how good it is to be a loyal follower
of the Lord.

Then there are the judges, name 11
after famous name,
all of them men who rejected idolatry
and never rebelled against the Lord:
blessings be on their memory!
May their bones send forth new life 12
from the ground where they lie!

Num.16.1–33. **23–26:** The defense of *Phinehas* (see Num.25.1–13) may reflect a challenge to
the priestly line in the time of the author.
   46.1–10: Joshua and Caleb. **1:** For *Joshua's* succession to the *prophetic office*, see Deut.34.9.
7: The *loyalty* of Joshua and Caleb (see Num.14.5–10) makes them exemplary.
   46.11–12: The judges.

May the fame of the honoured dead
 be matched by their sons!

13 Samuel was beloved by his Lord;
 as prophet of the Lord he established
  the monarchy
 and anointed rulers over his people.
14 As long as he dispensed justice
 according to the law of the
  Lord,
 the Lord kept watch over Jacob.
15 Because of his fidelity he proved to
  be an accurate prophet;
 the truth of his vision was shown
  by his utterances.
16 He called on the Mighty Lord,
 when enemies were pressing him on
  every side,
 and offered a sucking-lamb in
  sacrifice;
17 then the Lord thundered from
  heaven,
 making his voice heard in a mighty
  crash,
18 and routed the leaders of the
  enemy,[w]
 all the rulers of the Philistines.
19 Before the time came for his eternal
  sleep,
 Samuel called the Lord and his
  anointed to witness:
 'I never took any man's property,
 not so much as a pair of shoes';
 and no man accused him.
20 Even after he had gone to his rest
  he prophesied
 and foretold to the king his death,
 lifting up his voice in prophecy
  from the ground
 to wipe out the people's guilt.

47 After him Nathan came forward
 to be prophet in the reign of David.
2 As the fat is separated from the
  sacrifice,
 so David was chosen out of all
  Israel.
3 He played with lions as though they
  were kids,

with bears as though they were
 lambs.
In his youth did he not kill a giant 4
and restore the honour of his
  people,
when he whirled his sling with its
  stone
and brought down boastful
  Goliath?
For he called on the Lord Most 5
 High,
who gave strength to his right arm
to strike down that mighty warrior
and win victory for his people.
So they hailed him as conqueror of 6
 tens of thousands,
they sang his praises for the blessings
 bestowed by the Lord,
when he was offered the royal
 diadem.
For he subdued their enemies on 7
 every side
and crushed the resistance of the
 Philistines,
whose power remains broken to
 this day.
In all he did he gave thanks, 8
ascribing glory to the Holy One, the
 Most High.
With his whole heart he sang hymns
 of praise,
to show his love for his Maker.
He appointed musicians to stand 9
 before the altar
and sing sweet music to the harp.
So he gave splendour to the 10
 festivals
and fixed for all time the round of
 sacred seasons,
when men praise the holy name of
 the Lord
and the sanctuary resounds from
 morning to night.
The Lord pardoned his sins 11
and endowed him with great power
 for ever:
he gave him a covenant of kingship
and the glorious throne of Israel.

w the enemy: so Heb.; Gk. Tyre.

46.13–20: Samuel. 15: Samuel's *accurate* prophecy (see 1 Sam.3.19–21; 9.6) is based on his *fidelity* which all can emulate. **20:** Despite his opposition to divination (compare 34.5), Ecclus. includes the incident of the necromancer of En-dor among Samuel's achievements (see 1 Sam.28.3–20).
 47.1–11: Nathan and David. 1: Nathan (2 Sam.7.1–17; 12.1–14) links the prophetic line of Samuel to Elijah. **8–11:** David's sponsorship of ceremonial worship (1 Chr.23.1–6,24–32) is mentioned in line with the author's interest in cult.

12 He was succeeded by a wise son,
      Solomon,
   who, thanks to his father David,
      lived in spacious days.
13 He reigned in an age of peace,
   because God made all his frontiers
      quiet,
   and so he was able to build a house
      in God's honour,
   a sanctuary founded to last for ever.
14 How wise you were, Solomon, in
      your youth!
   Your mind was like a brimming river;
15 your influence spread throughout
      the world,
   which you filled with your proverbs
      and riddles.
16 Your fame reached to distant islands,
   and you were beloved for your
      peaceful reign.
17 Your songs, your proverbs, your
      parables,
   and the answers you gave were the
      admiration of the world.
18 In the name of the Lord God,
   who is known as the God of Israel,
   you amassed gold and silver
   as though they were tin and lead.
19 But you took women to lie at your
      side
   and gave yourself up to their control.
20 You stained your reputation
   and tainted your line.
   You brought retribution on your
      children
   and made them grieve over your
      folly,
21 because it divided the sovereignty
   and produced out of Ephraim a rebel
      kingdom.
22 But the Lord never ceases to be
      merciful;
   he does not destroy what he himself
      has made;
   he will not wipe out the children of
      his chosen servant
   or cut short the line of the man who
      has loved him.
   So he granted a remnant to Jacob
   and let one scion of David survive.

23 So Solomon died like his forefathers
   and left one of his sons to succeed
      him,
   a man of weak intelligence, the fool
      of the nation,
   Rehoboam, whose policy drove the
      people to revolt.
   Then Jeroboam son of Nebat led
      Israel into sin
   and started Ephraim on its wicked
      course.
24 Their sins increased beyond measure,
   until they were driven into exile
      from their native land;
25 for they had explored every kind of
      wickedness,
   until retribution came upon them.

48 Then Elijah appeared, a prophet
      like fire,
   whose word flamed like a torch.
2 He brought famine upon them,
   and his zeal made their numbers
      small.
3 By the word of the Lord he shut up
      the sky
   and three times called down fire.
4 How glorious you were, Elijah, in
      your miracles!
   Who else can boast such deeds?
5 You raised a corpse from death
   and from the grave, by the word of
      the Most High.
6 You sent kings and famous men
   from their sick-beds down to their
      deaths.
7 You heard a denunciation at Sinai,
   a sentence of doom at Horeb.
8 So you anointed kings for vengeance,
   and prophets to succeed you.
9 You were taken up to heaven in a
      fiery whirlwind,
   in a chariot drawn by horses of fire.
10 It is written that you are to come
      at the appointed time with
      warnings,
   to allay the divine wrath before its
      final fury,
   to reconcile father and son,
   and to restore the tribes of Jacob.

47.12–22: Solomon. 14–17: Solomon was a model *wise* man; see 1 Kgs.3.6–12; 4.29–34.
19–20: *Women* were Solomon's downfall; compare 9.2; 1 Kgs.11.1–13. **21:** Solomon's greed
and *folly* were the root of the *rebel kingdom;* 1 Kgs.12.1–5.
   47.23–25: Rehoboam and Jeroboam. See 1 Kgs.12.1–20. **23:** Jeroboam *led Israel into sin* by
initiating illicit worship; 1 Kgs.12.28 31.
   48.1–16: Elijah and Elisha. See 1 Kgs.17.1–19.21; 21.1–29; 2 Kgs.1.1–9.3. **10:** *It is written*

11 Happy are those who saw you
and were honoured with your love!*

12 When Elijah had vanished in a
whirlwind,
Elisha was filled with his spirit.
Throughout his life no ruler made
him tremble;
no one could make him subservient.

13 Nothing was too difficult for him;
even in the grave his body kept its
prophetic power.

14 In life he worked miracles,
and in death his deeds were marvellous.

15 In spite of all this the people did not
repent
or renounce their sins,
until they were carried off as plunder
from their land
and scattered over the whole earth.
Only a tiny nation was left,
with a ruler from the house of
David;

16 and of these some did what was
pleasing to the Lord,
but others heaped sin upon sin.

17 Hezekiah fortified his city,
bringing water within its walls;
he drilled through the rock with
tools of iron
and made cisterns for the water.

18 In his reign Sennacherib invaded
the country.
He sent Rab-shakeh from Lachish,*
who made threats against Zion
and grew arrogant in his boasting.

19 Then they were unnerved in heart
and hand;
they suffered the anguish of a
woman in labour.

20 So they called on the merciful
Lord,
spreading out their hands in
supplication to him.
The Holy One quickly answered
their prayer from heaven
by sending Isaiah to the rescue;

21 he struck down the Assyrian camp,
and his angel wiped them out.

22 For Hezekiah did what was pleasing
to the Lord,
and kept firmly to the ways of his
ancestor David,
as he was instructed by Isaiah,
the great prophet whose vision could
be trusted.

23 In his time the sun went back,
and he added many years to the
king's life.

24 With inspired power he saw the
future
and comforted the mourners in Zion.

25 He revealed things to come before
they happened,
the secrets of the future to the end
of time.

49 The memory of Josiah is fragrant
as incense
blended by the skill of the perfumer,
sweet as honey to every palate
or as music at a banquet.

2 He did what was right: he reformed
the nation
and rooted out their loathsome and
lawless practices.

3 He was whole-heartedly loyal to the
Lord
and in lawless times made godliness
prevail.

4 Except David, Hezekiah, and Josiah,
all were guilty of wrongdoing,
for they deserted the law of the Most
High;
and so the royal line of Judah came
to an end.

5 They surrendered their power to
others
and their glory to a foreign nation,

6 who set fire to the chosen city, the
city of the sanctuary,
and left its streets deserted, as
Jeremiah prophesied;

7 for they had ill-treated him,
a prophet consecrated even before
his birth

x honoured . . . love: *probable meaning; Gk. adds* for
we also shall certainly live.
y from Lachish: *other witnesses read* and went away.

---

refers to Mal.4.5–6; compare 2 Esd.6.26; Mt.17.10–13. **15:** *Scattered:* see 2 Kgs.17.6.
  48.17–25: Hezekiah and Isaiah. See 2 Kgs. chs. 18–20. **24:** See Isa.40.1–2. **25:** The view that
prophecy *revealed . . . secrets* for later times was widespread; compare Isa.41.22–23; 44.7.
  49.1–7: Josiah and Jeremiah. 1–3: See 2 Kgs.22.1–23.30. **7:** *Ill-treated:* see Jer.37.15–38.
Uproot . . . plant: see Jer.1.10.

to uproot, to destroy, and to
    demolish,
but also to build and to plant.

8 Ezekiel had a vision of the Glory,
    which was revealed enthroned on
        the chariot of the cherubim.
9 The Lord remembered his enemies
        and sent a storm,
    but he did good to those who kept
        to the straight path.
10 May the bones of the twelve prophets
        also
    send forth new life from the ground
        where they lie!
    For they put new heart into
        Jacob,
    and rescued the people by their
        confident hope.

11 How can we tell the greatness of
        Zerubbabel,
    who was like a signet-ring on the
        Lord's right hand?
12 With him was Joshua son of
        Jehozadak;
    in their days they built the house,
    raising a holy temple to the Lord,
    destined for eternal glory.
13 Great is the memory of Nehemiah,
    who raised our fallen walls,
    constructed gates and bars,
    and rebuilt our ruined homes.

14 No one on earth has been created
        to equal Enoch,
    for he was taken up from the earth.
15 No man has been born to be
        Joseph's peer,
    the ruler of his brothers and the
        strength of his people;
    and the Lord kept watch over his
        body.
16 Shem and Seth were given distinction
        among men,
    but Adam holds pre-eminence over
        all creation.

It was the high priest Simon son of   **50**
    Onias.
in whose lifetime the house was
    repaired,
in whose days the temple was fortified.
He laid the foundation for the high   2
    double wall,
the high retaining wall of the temple
    precinct.
In his day they dug[z] the reservoir,   3
    a cistern broad as the sea.
He applied his mind to protecting   4
        his people from ruin
and strengthened the city against
    siege.
How glorious he was, surrounded   5
        by the people,
when he came from behind the
    temple curtain!
He was like the morning star   6
        appearing through the clouds
or the moon at the full;
like the sun shining on the temple   7
        of the Most High
or the light of the rainbow on the
    gleaming clouds;
like a rose in spring   8
or lilies by a fountain of water;
like a green shoot upon Lebanon
        on a summer's day
or burning incense in the censer;   9
like a cup of beaten gold,
decorated with every kind of
    precious stone;
like an olive-tree laden with fruit   10
or a cypress with its top in the
    clouds.
When he put on his gorgeous   11
        vestments,
robed himself in perfect splendour,
and went up to the holy altar,
he added lustre to the court of the
    sanctuary.
When the priests were handing him   12
        the portions of the sacrifice,
as he stood by the altar hearth

z they dug: *so Heb.; Gk. obscure.*

49.8–10: Ezekiel and the twelve prophets. 8: See Ezek.1.1–28. **10:** The *twelve* minor *prophets*
are regarded as a single book. Some of the twelve lived after the return from captivity and
encouraged the captives to rebuild: see Zech.1.16; Hag.1.8; 2.3–9.
    49.11–13: Zerubbabel, Joshua, and Nehemiah. Hag.1.1; 2.2–4; Zech. chs. 3–4; Neh.7.1. Note
that Ezra is not specifically named.
    49.14–16: Ancient heroes. Rather oddly these early heroes are inserted at this point; see 44.16.
    50.1–21: Simon the son of Onias. He was high priest about 225–200 B.C.; although there may
have been an earlier Simon, it is the consensus that this one, actually known to the author, is
meant. **5 21:** These verses describe the service on the Day of Atonement. On this day only,
in connection with the blessing, the high priest pronounced the sacred *name* of Yahweh (v. 20).

with his brothers round him like
a garland,
he was like a young cedar of
Lebanon
in the midst of a circle of palms.

13 All the sons of Aaron in their
magnificence
stood with the Lord's offering in
their hands
before the whole congregation of
Israel.

14 To complete the ceremonies at the
altar
and adorn the offering of the Most
High, the Almighty,

15 he held out his hand for the libation
cup
and poured out the blood of the
grape,
poured its fragrance at the foot of
the altar
to the Most High, the King of all.

16 Then the sons of Aaron shouted
and blew their trumpets of beaten
silver;
they sounded a mighty fanfare
as a reminder before the Lord.

17 Instantly the people as one man fell
on their faces
to worship the Lord their God, the
Almighty, the Most High.

18 Then the choir broke into praise,
in the full sweet strains of resounding
song,

19 while the people of the Most High
were making their petitions to the
merciful Lord,
until the liturgy of the Lord was
finished
and the ritual complete.

20 Then Simon came down and raised
his hands
over the whole congregation of
Israel,
to pronounce the Lord's blessing,
proud to take his name on his lips:

21 and a second time they bowed in
worship
to receive the blessing from the
Most High.

22 COME THEN, PRAISE THE GOD OF THE
universe,
who everywhere works great
wonders,
who from our birth ennobles our
life[a]
and deals with us in mercy.

23 May he grant us a joyful heart,
and in our time send Israel lasting
peace.

24 May he confirm his mercy towards
us,
and in his own good time grant us
deliverance.

25 Two nations I detest,
and a third is no nation at all:

26 the inhabitants of Mount Seir,[b] the
Philistines,
and the senseless folk that live at
Shechem.

27 In this book I have written
lessons of good sense and
understanding,
I, Jesus son of Sirach,[c] of Jerusalem,
whose mind was a fountain of
wisdom.

28 Happy the man who occupies
himself with these lessons,
who lays them to heart and grows
wise!

29 If he lives by them, he will be equal
to anything,
with the light of the Lord shining on
his path.

Epilogue

51 I THANK THEE, MY LORD AND KING,
I praise thee, my God and Saviour,
I give thee thanks,

2 because thou hast been my protector
and helper,
rescuing me from death,
from the trap laid by a slanderous
tongue

a ennobles our life: *or* brings us up.
b Mount Seir: *so Heb.; Gk.* the mountain of Samaria.
c Sirach: *some witnesses read* Sirach Eleazar.

50.22–24: Conclusion to the praise of famous men. 23: The language shows uneasiness about
lasting peace.
50.25–26: A fragment. It is directed against the Idumeans, the Philistines, and the Samaritans.
50.27–29: The author's conclusion. Unlike other writers in the Apocrypha, he gives his own
name.
51.1–30: Epilogue; two psalms. 1–12: This psalm is modeled after the psalms of deliverance;

and from lips that utter lies.
In the face of my assailants thou
    didst come to my help;
3 in the fullness of thy mercy and
    glory thou didst rescue me
from grinding teeth which waited
    to devour me,
from hands that threatened my
    life,
from the many troubles I endured,
4 from the choking fire around me,
from the flames I had not kindled,
5 from the deep recesses of the
    grave,
from the foul tongue and its lies—
6 a wicked slander spoken in the
    king's presence.
I came near to death;
I was on the brink of the grave.
7 They surrounded me on every
    side,
and there was no one to help me.
I looked for human aid and there
    was none.
8 Then I remembered thy mercy,
    Lord,
thy deeds in bygone days;
thou dost deliver those who patiently
    trust thee
and free them from the power of
    their enemies.
9 So I sent up a prayer from the
    earth
and begged for rescue from death.
10 I cried, 'Lord, thou art my Father;*d*
do not desert me in time of trouble,
when I am helpless in the face of
    arrogance.
11 I will praise thee continually,
I will sing hymns of thanksgiving.'
And my prayer was granted;
12 for thou didst save me from death
and rescue me from my desperate
    plight.
Therefore I will thank thee and
    praise thee
and bless thee, O Lord.

13 When I was still young, before I set
    out on my travels,
I asked openly for wisdom in my
    prayers.

In the forecourt of the sanctuary   14
    I laid claim to her,
and I shall seek her out to the end.
From the first blossom to the   15
    ripening of the grape
she has been the delight of my
    heart.
From my youth my steps have
    followed her without swerving.
I had hardly begun to listen when   16
    I was rewarded,
and I gained for myself much
    instruction.
I made progress in my studies;   17
all honour to him who gives me
    wisdom!
I determined to practise what I had   18
    learnt;
I pursued goodness, and shall never
    regret it.
I strove for wisdom with all my   19
    might,
and was scrupulous in whatever
    I did.
I spread out my hands to heaven
    above,
deploring my ignorance;
I set my heart on possessing wisdom,   20
and by keeping myself pure I found
    her.
With her I gained understanding
    from the first;
therefore I shall never be at a
    loss.
Because I passionately yearned to   21
    discover her,
I won a noble prize.
The Lord gave me eloquence as my   22
    reward,
and with it I will praise him.

Come to me, you who need   23
    instruction,
and lodge in my house of learning.
Why do you admit to a lack of   24
    these things,
yet leave your great thirst
    unslaked?
I have made my proclamation: 25
'Buy for yourself without money,

---

d thou . . . Father: *so Heb.; Gk.* Father of my lord.

---

compare Ps.18.1–19,49. **13–30:** An acrostic (alphabetical) psalm. **13–22:** A young man searches for wisdom, which is personified as a beautiful woman; see 4.12 n. **23–30:** A wisdom teacher invites pupils in language very similar to the appeal of wisdom; see 4.11–19; 24.19–22. **23:** The *house of learning* was later the regular term for rabbinical schools.

26 bend your neck to the yoke,
   be ready to accept discipline;
   you need not go far to find it.'
27 See for yourselves how little were
   my labours
   compared with the great peace I
   have found.
28 Your share of instruction may cost
   you a large sum of silver,

but it will bring you a large return
in gold.
May you take delight in the Lord's 29
mercy
and never be ashamed of praising
him.
Do your duty in good time, 30
and in his own time he will reward
you.

BARUCH

This book carries the name of Baruch, Jeremiah's close friend and secretary (Jer. chs. 32 and 45).
If that Baruch were indeed the author, the book would have come from the sixth pre-Christian
century, but a later date and different authorship seem involved. The book was probably
written in Hebrew, but the original writing has not survived. It shows little or no unity respecting
authorship, style, age, and even Greek translator or translators. The divergent viewpoints
(compare 1.11 and 2.22 with 4.15,25) and the book's dependence on later writings (i.e. 1.15–3.8
on Neh. ch. 9 and Dan.9.4–19) suggest a date between 200 and 150 B.C., although a date as
late as the first century B.C. is possible.

This anthology of prayers and hymns provides a rare glimpse of religion in the synagogues
outside Palestine, reflecting devotion to the Temple and the religious authority at Jerusalem,
resistance to foreign idolatry, and continuous meditation on the Law and other sacred writings
like Jeremiah, Isaiah (chs. 40–55, 60–62), Daniel, Proverbs, and Job.

After a narrative introduction (1.1–14), there follow a group confession of sins and lamentation in prose (1.15–3.8), then in poetic meter a hymnic praise of Wisdom (3.9–4.4) and a medley
of prophetic poems of hope or tender lament about Jerusalem (4.5–5.9).

A message to a conquered people

1 THIS IS THE BOOK OF BARUCH, SON
of Neriah, son of Mahseiah, son
of Zedekiah, son of Hasadiah, son
2 of Hilkiah, written in Babylon, on the
seventh day of the month, in the fifth
year after the Chaldaeans had captured
and burnt Jerusalem.
3 Baruch read the book aloud to
Jeconiah son of Jehoiakim, king of
Judah, and to all the people who had
4 assembled to hear it: the nobles, the
princes of the royal blood, the elders,
and the whole community, high and
low—in short, all who lived in Babylon,
5 by the river Soud. Then they prayed to
6 the Lord with tears and fasting; and
each of them collected as much money
7 as he could, and they sent it to Jerusalem, to Jehoiakim the high priest, son
of Hilkiah, son of Shallum, and to the
priests and all the people who were
8 with him. This was the time when he
took the vessels belonging to the house
of the Lord which had been looted from
the temple, and returned them to the
land of Judah, on the tenth of the month
Sivan. These were the silver vessels
made by Zedekiah son of Josiah, king
of Judah, after Nebuchadnezzar king 9
of Babylon had deported Jeconiah, the
rulers, the captives, the nobles, and the
common people from Jerusalem and
taken them to Babylon.

They said: We are sending you 10
money to buy whole-offerings, sin-
offerings, and incense; provide a grain-
offering, and offer them all upon the
altar of the Lord our God; and pray 11
for Nebuchadnezzar king of Babylon,
and for his son Belshazzar, that their
life on earth may last as long as the
heavens. So the Lord will give us 12
strength, and light to walk by, and we
shall live under the protection of
Nebuchadnezzar king of Babylon, and
of Belshazzar his son; we shall give
them long service and gain their favour.
Pray also for us to the Lord our God, 13
because we have sinned against him,
and to this day the Lord's anger and

1.1–14: Introduction. By means of a pseudohistorical setting this section unites the liturgical
prayers and pilgrimages of the Jews in the Diaspora with those of their forefathers in the Babylonian Exile (587–539 B.C.). Historical difficulties are many, such as the *month* intended in v. 2.
Too, *Jehoiakim the high priest* (v. 7) is unknown to us except in the historical romance of Jdt.4.6
(see n. there), where the spelling is "Joakim." The Temple is presumed to be destroyed in v. 2
and to be already rebuilt by its devastator in v. 10. *Belshazzar* (v. 11) was actually the son of
Nabonidus, not of *Nebuchadnezzar;* see Dan.1.1 n.,5.2,13,18,22. (Nabonidus, the last king of
Babylon, reigned from 555–539 B.C.). **2:** *Jerusalem* fell in July 587 B.C. and was burned to the
ground by order of Nebuchadnezzar a month later (2 Kgs.25.3,8–9). **3:** *Jeconiah:* King Jehoiachin, considered the legitimate king by fellow exiles (see Ezek.1.2). **4:** *The river Soud* was undoubtedly one of the many irrigation canals carrying water from the Euphrates. **5:** *Fasting*
became more frequent in postexilic times (Dan.9.3; Zech.7.1–5). **8:** *Sivan:* third month (May–
June). **11:** This request to pray for the foreigner *Nebuchadnezzar* reveals a broad-minded spirit
of prayer reaching beyond national prejudice as well as a monotheistic faith in one God for

176

wrath have not been averted from us.
14 You are to read this book that we are sending you, and make your confession in the house of the Lord on the feast day and during the festal season, 15 and say: The Lord our God is in the right; but on us the shame rests to this very day—on the men of Judah, the 16 citizens of Jerusalem, on our kings and rulers, on our priests and prophets, and 17 on our fathers. We have sinned against 18 the Lord and disobeyed him; we did not listen to the Lord our God or follow 19 the precepts he gave us. From the day when the Lord brought our fathers out of Egypt until now, we have been disobedient to the Lord our God and have 20 heedlessly disregarded his voice. So here we are today in the grip of adversity, suffering under the curse which the Lord commanded his servant Moses to pronounce, when he led our fathers out of Egypt to give us a land flowing 21 with milk and honey. Moreover we refused to hear the Lord our God speaking in all the words of the proph-22 ets he sent us; we went our own way, each following the promptings of his own wicked heart, serving other gods, doing what was evil in the sight of the Lord our God.

2 So the Lord made good the warning he had given to us, to our magistrates in Israel, our kings and our rulers, and 2 the men of Israel and Judah. Nowhere under heaven have such deeds been done as were done in Jerusalem, thus fulfilling what was foretold in the law 3 of Moses, that we should eat the flesh of our children, one his own son and 4 another his own daughter. The Lord made our nation subject to all the kingdoms round us, our land a waste, our name a byword to all the nations among 5 whom he had scattered our people. Instead of rising to the top, they sank to

the bottom, because we sinned against the Lord our God and did not listen 6 to his voice. The Lord our God is in the right; but on us and our fathers the 7 shame rests to this very day. All these evils of which the Lord warned us have 8 come about. Yet we did not entreat the Lord that we might all turn away from 9 the thoughts of our wicked hearts. The Lord kept strict watch and brought these evils on our heads, because he is just; he laid all these commandments upon us, but we did not listen to his 10 voice or follow the precepts which he gave us.

And now, Lord God of Israel, who 11 didst bring thy people out of Egypt with a mighty hand, with signs and portents, with great power and arm uplifted, winning for thyself a renown that lives on to this day: by our sin, 12 our godlessness, and our injustice we have broken all thy commandments, O Lord our God. Be angry with us no 13 longer, for we are left a mere handful among the heathen where thou hast scattered us. Listen, O Lord, to our 14 prayer and our entreaty, deliver us for thy own sake, and grant us favour with those who have taken us into exile, so 15 that the whole earth may know that thou art the Lord our God, who hast named Israel and his posterity as thy own.

O Lord, look down from thy holy 16 dwelling and think of us. Turn thy ear to us, Lord, and hear us; open thine 17 eyes and see. The dead are in their graves, the breath is gone from their bodies; it is not they who can sing the Lord's praises or applaud his justice; it is living men, mourning their fall 18 from greatness, walking the earth bent and feeble, blind and famished—it is these who will sing thy praises, O Lord, and applaud thy justice.

Not for any just deeds of our fathers 19

---

all men; see Rom.13.1–7. **14:** The Jews fortunate to be living in Jerusalem are directed to *make* their humble *confession* of sin in the name of the exiles *on the feast day* of Tabernacles, the final harvest festival and victory celebration of the Lord's kingship (Lev.23.33–43; Zech.14.16–21).
　1.15–3.8: Penitential prayer of the exiles. From an original Heb. text, this prose lament recasts a popular prayer, preserved even more carefully in Dan.9.4–19; see Ezra 9.6–15; Neh. ch. 9. Because of 2.17, this lament is to be dated around 180 B.C., the period of Ecclus., since both books are silent about the resurrection (Ecclus.17.27–28; Ps.6.5), which is explicitly stated in Dan.12.1–3 and 2 Macc. ch. 7. The principal theme is that of God's justice, his merciful fidelity in fulfilling his promises to Israel; see 1.15; 2.6. **20:** *Curse of Moses:* Deut.28.15–37. **2.3:** *Eat the flesh of our children:* see 2 Kgs.6.28; Lam.2.20. **11:** Transition from the lament to Israel's petition. **17–18:** For the pious Jew the impossibility of praising God in Sheol is the

and our kings do we lay before thee our plea for pity, O Lord our God.
20 Thou hast vented upon us that wrath and anger of which thou didst warn us through thy servants the prophets who
21 said: 'These are the words of the Lord: Bow your shoulders and serve the king of Babylon and you shall remain in the
22 land that I gave to your fathers; but if you do not listen to the Lord and serve
23 the king of Babylon, then I will banish from Jerusalem and the cities of Judah all sounds of joy and merriment, the voice of bride and bridegroom; the whole land shall lie waste and un-
24 inhabited.' But we did not obey thy command to serve the king of Babylon. And so thou didst make good the warning given through thy servants the prophets: the bones of our kings and of our fathers have been taken
25 from their resting-place; and there they lie, exposed to the heat by day and the frost by night. They died a painful death by famine, sword, and disease.*a*
26 And because of the wickedness of Israel and Judah the house that was named as thine has become what it is today.
27 Yet thou hast shown us, O Lord our God, all thy wonted forbearance and
28 great mercy. For this is what thou didst promise through thy servant Moses, on the day thou didst command him to write thy law in the presence of the
29 Israelites: 'If you will not listen to my voice, this great swarming multitude will be reduced to a tiny remnant among
30 the heathen where I will scatter them. I know they will not hear me, this stubborn people, but in the land of their
31 exile they will come to their senses and know that I am the Lord their God. I will give them a mind to understand
32 and ears to hear. Then they will praise

me in the land of their exile and will turn their thoughts to me; they will 33 repent of their stubbornness and their wicked deeds, for they will recall how their fathers sinned against the Lord. Then I will restore them to the land that 34 I swore to give to their forefathers, Abraham, Isaac, and Jacob, and they shall rule over it. And I will increase their number: they shall never dwindle away. I will enter into an eternal cov- 35 enant with them, that I will become their God and they shall become my people. Never again will I remove my people Israel from the land that I have given them.'

O Lord Almighty, God of Israel, the 3 soul in anguish and the fainting spirit cry out to thee. Listen, Lord, and have 2 mercy, for we have sinned against thee. Thou art enthroned for ever; we are 3 for ever passing away. Now, Almighty 4 Lord, God of Israel, hear the prayer of Israel's dead and of the sons of those who sinned against thee. They did not heed the voice of their God, and so we are in the grip of adversity. Do not re- 5 call the misdeeds of our fathers, but remember now thy power and thy name, for thou art the Lord our God, 6 and we will praise thee, O Lord. It is 7 for this that thou hast put the fear of thee in our hearts, to make us call upon thy name. And we will praise thee in our exile, for we have put away from us all the wrongdoing of our fathers who sinned against thee. Today we are in 8 exile; thou hast scattered us and made us a byword and a curse, to be punished for all the sins of our fathers, who rebelled against the Lord our God.

LISTEN, ISRAEL, TO THE COMMANDMENTS 9

a disease: *probable meaning (compare Jeremiah 32. 36); Gk. obscure.*

greatest tragedy of death. Here it is given as a motive in asking God for deliverance. See Ps. 115.17–18. **21–24:** Jer.7.34 and 27.12 are merged; to have rejected Jeremiah was to have disobeyed God. Jeremiah advised surrender to the Babylonians while the city was under siege, and was considered a traitor; see Jer.26.16–19; 38.1–13. **35:** *Eternal covenant:* see Jer.31.31; Ezek.37.26. This expression of hope reverts to a more primitive stage of "messianism," for it is silent about David and Jerusalem (2 Sam.7.12–16; 1 Chr. chs. 28–29) and the glorious rule (Amos 9.11–15) over all nations (Isa.2.1–4). **3.4:** *Israel's dead:* those still in exile; see Ezek.37.11–13. **5–8:** Here reappears the old theology which held that social and religious solidarity implied collective guilt and demanded collective punishment (Josh. ch. 7) so that children were *punished for all the sins of the fathers.* This view was condemned in its excessive form by Jeremiah (31.29) and Ezekiel (ch. 18). Compare Jn.9.2.

3.9 4.1: In praise of Wisdom. This passage is in verse form like other Wisdom writings. Composed originally in Heb. during a peaceful period like that of Ecclus. (200–180 B.C.), it

10 of life; hear, and learn wisdom. Why is it, Israel, that you are in your enemies' country, that you have grown old in an alien land? Why have you shared the 11 defilement of the dead and been numbered with those that lie in the grave? 12 It is because you have forsaken the 13 fountain of wisdom. If you had walked in the way of God, you would have 14 lived in peace for ever. Where is understanding, where is strength, where is intelligence? Learn that, and then you will know where to find life and light to 15 walk by, long life and peace. Has any man discovered the dwelling-place of wisdom or entered her storehouse? 16 Where are the rulers of the nations now? Where are those who have hunted 17 wild beasts or the birds of the air for sport? Where are those who have hoarded the silver and gold men trust in, never satisfied with their gains? 18 Where are the silversmiths with their patient skill and the secrets of their 19 craft? They have all vanished and gone down to the grave, and others have 20 risen to take their place. A younger generation saw the light of day and dwelt in the land. But they did not learn 21 the way of knowledge, or discover its paths; they did not lay hold of it; their 22 sons went far astray. Wisdom was not heard of in Canaan, nor seen in Teman. 23 The sons of Hagar who sought for understanding on earth, the merchants of Merran and Teman, the myth-makers, the seekers after knowledge, none of them discovered the way of wisdom, or remembered her paths. 24 How great, O Israel, is God's dwelling-place, how vast the extent of 25 his domain! Great it is, and boundless, 26 lofty, and immeasurable. There in ancient time the giants were born, a famous race, great in stature, skilled in war. But these men were not chosen by 27 God, nor shown the way of knowledge. So their race died out because they had 28 no understanding; they lacked the wit to survive. Has any man gone up to 29 heaven to gain wisdom and brought her down from the clouds? Has any 30 man crossed the sea to find her or bought her for fine gold? No one can 31 know the path or conceive the way that will lead to her. Only the One who 32 knows all things knows her: his understanding discovered her. He who established the earth for all time filled it with four-footed beasts. He sends forth the 33 light, and it goes on its way; he called it, it feared him and obeyed. The stars 34 shone at their appointed stations and rejoiced; he called them and they answered, 'We are here!' Joyfully they shone for their Maker. This is our God; 35 there is none to compare with him. The 36 whole way of knowledge he found out and gave to Jacob his servant, and to Israel, whom he loved. Thereupon 37 wisdom appeared on earth and lived among men. She is the book of the 4 commandments of God, the law that stands for ever. All who hold fast to her shall live, but those who forsake her shall die. Return, Jacob, and lay 2 hold of her; set your course towards her radiance, and face her beacon light. Do not give up your glory to another 3 or your privileges to an alien people. Happy are we, Israel, because we know 4 what is pleasing to God!

Take heart, my people, you who keep 5 Israel's name alive. You were sold to the 6 heathen, but not to be destroyed; it was because you roused God's anger that you were handed over to your enemies. You provoked your Maker by sacrific- 7

---

is related thematically to texts like Prov. ch. 1–9, Job 28.12–28, and Ecclus. ch. 24. Addressing Israel, the writer celebrates God's supreme gift of the Law as the source of all life (see Deut.4.1–40; Ecclus.24.19–34)—the extent of Baruch's "messianic" expectations. **10:** *Defilement of the dead:* contact with the Babylonians who do not know the Lord or the Law, the source of life; see Deut.4.4; Ezek.4.13; 7.21–22; Ps.119.93. **22–23:** Israel's God-given *wisdom* excelled that of places famous for knowledge, like *Canaan,* from whom the invading Israelites learned city culture and its vices, or like *Teman* to the southeast (Job 4.1; Jer.49.7), or the bedouin *sons of Hagar* (Gen. ch. 16), or *Merran* (perhaps, Midian, renowned merchants, Gen.37.28). **24:** *God's dwelling-place* is not the Jerusalem Temple but the cosmos (Ezek. ch. 1; Isa.40.21–28). **26:** *Giants* (Gen.6.4) destroyed at the flood of Noah were popular figures in later Jewish literature.
　　4.5–5.9: Songs of encouragement and lament. These lyrics, composed originally in Gk. and showing the influence of Deut., Isa. chs. 40–66, and Jer., are unified by the recurring theme of God's eternity. **5:** *Keep Israel's name alive:* physically by new generations of children and

ing to demons and to that which is not
8 God. You forgot the Everlasting God
who nurtured you, and you grieved
9 Jerusalem who fostered you, for she
saw how God's anger had come upon
you, and she said: Listen, you neighbours of Zion, God has brought great
10 grief upon me. I have seen the captivity
of my sons and daughters which the
11 Everlasting has inflicted upon them; I
nursed them in delight, but with tears
12 and mourning I saw them go. Let no
one exult over me in my widowhood,
bereaved of so many. I have been left
desolate through the sins of my children, through their turning away from
13 the law of God. They would not learn
his statutes, or follow his commandments, or let God guide and train them
in his righteousness.
14 Come then, neighbours of Zion,
remember the captivity of my sons
and daughters which the Everlasting
15 has inflicted upon them. For he brought
down on them a nation from far away,
a ruthless nation speaking a strange
language and without reverence for age
16 or pity for children. They carried off
the widow's beloved sons, and left her
in loneliness, deprived of her daughters.
17,18 But I, how can I help you? Only the
One who brought these evils upon you
19 can deliver you from your enemies. Go
your way, my children, go, for I am left
20 desolate. I have put off the robes of
peaceful days, and put on the sackcloth
of a supplicant. I will cry out to the
Everlasting as long as I live.
21 Take heart, my children! Cry out to
God, and he will rescue you from
tyranny and from the power of your
22 enemies. For I have set my hope of your
deliverance on the Everlasting; the Holy
One, your everlasting saviour, has filled
me with joy over the mercy soon to be
23 granted you. I saw you go with mourning and tears, but God will give you
back to me with joy and gladness for
24 ever. For as the neighbours of Zion have

now seen your captivity, so they will
soon see your deliverance coming upon
you from your God with the great glory
25 and splendour of the Everlasting. My
children, endure in patience the wrath
God has brought upon you; your
enemy has hunted you down, but soon
you will see him destroyed, and will
put your foot upon his neck. My pam-
26 pered children have trodden rough
paths; they have been carried off like a
flock seized by raiders.
27 Take heart, my children! Cry out to
God, for he who afflicted you will not
28 forget you. You once resolved to go
astray from God; now with tenfold zeal
you must turn about and seek him.
29 He who brought these calamities upon
you will bring you everlasting joy when
he delivers you.
30 Take heart, Jerusalem! He who
called you by name will comfort you.
31 Wretched shall they be who despoiled
you and gloated over your fall;
32 wretched the cities where your children
were slaves; wretched the city that re-
33 ceived your sons! The same city that
rejoiced at your downfall and made
merry over your ruin shall grieve over
34 her own desolation. I will strip her of
the multitudes that were her boast, and
35 turn her pride to mourning. Fire from
the Everlasting shall be her doom for
many a day, and long shall she be a
haunt of demons.
36 Jerusalem, look eastwards and see
the joy that is coming to you from God.
37 They come, the sons from whom you
parted, they come, gathered together
at the word of the Holy One from east
to west, rejoicing in the glory of God.
5 Jerusalem, strip off the garment of
your sorrow and affliction, and put on
for ever the glorious majesty that is the
2 gift of God. Wrap about you his robe
of righteousness; set on your head for
diadem the splendour of the Everlast-
3 ing; for God will show your radiance
4 to every land under heaven. You shall

---

spiritually by obedience to God. **8:** *Everlasting God:* a recurring expression found only in the
poetic section 3.8–5.9. In contrast, the word "Lord" is found only in the first section. **12:**
Jerusalem's *widowhood,* as in Isa. ch. 54 or Lam.1.1–2, symbolizes her seeming rejection by God,
her spouse. **24:** *Glory and splendour* indicate an extraordinary manifestation of God's wonder
from within Zion or Jerusalem (Isa.60.2). **30:** *Called you by name* probably refers to God's own
name (see 3.5), just as Jerusalem is to be clothed in God's robes (5.1–4), because she reveals his
redemptive action in her midst. **35:** Jerusalem's persecutors will be a desert, the traditional

receive from God for ever the name Righteous Peace, Godly Splendour.

Jerusalem, arise and stand upon the height; look eastwards and see from west to east your children gathered together at the word of the Holy One, rejoicing that God has remembered them.

6 They went away from you on foot, led off by their enemies, but God is bringing them home to you borne aloft in

7 glory, like a king on his throne. For God has commanded every high mountain and the everlasting hills to be made low, and the valleys to be filled and levelled, so that Israel may walk safely in the glory of God. And woods and 8 every fragrant tree shall give Israel shade by God's command. For God 9 shall lead Israel with joy in the light of his glory, granting them his mercy and his righteousness.

---

haunt of *demons* (Tob.8.3; Lk.11.24). **5.5–9:** These lines, reflecting Isa.40.3–5 and 60.1–2, are quoted almost verbatim in the nonbiblical Psalms of Solomon 11.2–7, dated around 50 B.C. Again the messianic prospects of Baruch are limited to the ingathering of the exiles (see Jer.31.7–14; Isa.43.1–7).

A LETTER OF
JEREMIAH

This harangue against idolatry is repetitious, sarcastic, and impassioned. Possibly it originated as a synagogal sermon. Following a tradition known from 2 Macc.2.1–4, the author attributed it to Jeremiah, who actually did write a letter to the exiles in Babylon (Jer. ch. 29). The writer drew upon Jer.10.1–16 and other sources, mainly Isa.44.9–20.

The period in which he wrote, according to v. 3, was seven generations after the beginning of the Babylonian Exile; that date could be about 317 B.C. Some scholars, however, tend to date the book in the Maccabean period, between 165 and 110 B.C.

If "Babylon" is taken as a cryptic name for the area outside Judea, the letter could have been intended for the Jews in the Greek dispersion.

The language of the original seems to have been Hebrew (v. 72 n.); since there are no extant Hebrew manuscripts, some scholars think it could have been Aramaic or Greek. A fragment in the Greek (vv. 43–44) turned up in one of the caves where the Dead Sea Scrolls were found; scholars date the writing around 100 B.C.

The Latin Vulgate and the Authorized Version consider A Letter of Jeremiah to be ch. 6 of Baruch.

Two series of refrains divide the letter into paragraphs; vv. 16,23,29,65,69; and vv. 40,44,52,56.

The folly of idolatry

6ᵃ A COPY OF A LETTER SENT BY Jeremiah to the captives who were to be taken to Babylon by the king of Babylon, conveying a message entrusted to him by God.

2 The sins you have committed in the sight of God are the cause of your being led away captive to Babylon by Nebuchadnezzar king of Babylon. 3 Once you are in Babylon, your stay there will be long; it will last for many years, up to seven generations; but afterwards I will lead you out in peace and prosperity.

4 Now in Babylon you will see carried on men's shoulders gods made of silver, gold, and wood, which fill the heathen 5 with awe. Be careful, then, never to imitate these Gentiles; do not be over-awed by their gods when you see them in the midst of a procession of wor- 6 shippers. But say in your hearts, 'To thee alone, Lord, is worship due.' 7 For my angel is with you; your lives are in his care.

8 The idols are plated with gold and silver, they have tongues fashioned by a craftsman, but they are a fraud and cannot speak. And the people take gold 9 and make crowns for the heads of their gods, as one might for a girl fond of finery. Sometimes also the priests filch 10 gold and silver from their gods and spend it on themselves; they will even 11 give some of it to the prostitutes in the inner chamber. They dress up the idols in clothes like human beings, these gods of silver, gold, and wood. But the gods, 12 decked in purple though they are, cannot protect themselves against rust and moth. The dust in the temple, too, 13 lies thick upon them, so that their faces have to be wiped clean. Like a human 14 judge the god holds a sceptre, yet he cannot put to death anyone who offends him. In his right hand he has a dagger 15 and an axe, yet he cannot deliver himself from war and pillage. This shows 16 they are not gods, so have no fear of them.

Their gods are no more use than a 17 broken tool, sitting there in their tem-

ᵃ The chapter and verse numbering is that of the Authorized Version, in which this forms chapter 6 of Baruch.

6.1–73: The folly of idolatry. 1: Major Gk. MSS. do not include this opening inscription as v. 1 and therefore differ in the numbering of the verses, being one digit lower than the numbers that appear here. 3: Seven generations may be symbolic of perfection or fullness, rounding out the Exile. But since this phrase differs from the phrase "seventy years" in Jer.25.12, some scholars take it literally, and reckoning a generation as forty years (Num.32.13), relate the 280 years to the fall of Jerusalem, either in 597 B.C. or in 587 B.C. (2 Kgs.24.10–17; 25.1–12). Hence, a Let. Jer. would then have been written in 317 or 307 B.C. See Introduction. 7: My angel: an indirect reference to God's continuing protection (Ex.23.20–23). 11: Sacred prostitutes accommodated

182

ples. Their eyes get filled with dust from the feet of those who come in. And 18 just as the palace-court is barricaded to secure a traitor awaiting execution, so the priests secure their temples with doors and bolts and bars to guard 19 against plundering by robbers. They light lamps, more than they need for themselves—yet the idols can see none 20–21 of them. They are like one of the beams of the temple; their hearts are eaten out, as the saying is, for creatures crawl out of the ground and devour them and their clothing. When their faces are blackened by the smoke of the temple they are quite unaware of it. 22 Bats and swallows and birds of all kinds perch on their heads and bodies, 23 and cats do the same. From all this you may be sure that they are not gods, so have no fear of them.

24 Though plated with gold for ornament, the idols will not shine, unless someone rubs off the tarnish. Even when they were being cast they did not 25 feel it. They were bought at great cost, 26 but there is no breath in them. As they have no real feet they are carried on men's shoulders, which shows how 27 worthless they are. Even those who serve them are ashamed, because if ever an idol falls on the ground, it does not get up by itself; nor, if anyone sets it up again, can it move by its own effort, and if it is tilted it cannot straighten itself. To set offerings before them is like setting them before the 28 dead. The sacrifices made to gods are sold by the priests, who spend the proceeds on themselves. Their wives are no better; they take portions of these sacrifices and cure the meat, and give 29 no share to the poor or helpless. Their offerings are touched by women who are menstruating or by mothers fresh from childbed. Be assured by all this that they are not gods, and have no fear of them.

30 Why should they be called gods? These gods of silver, gold, and wood have food served to them by women. 31 In their temples the priests sit shaven and shorn, with their clothes rent, and their heads uncovered. They shout and 32 howl before these gods of theirs, like mourners at a funeral feast. The priests 33 strip vestments from the gods to clothe their own wives and children. Should 34 anyone do these gods either injury or service they will not be able to repay it. They cannot set up or depose a king. So also they are incapable of bestowing 35 wealth or money; if someone makes a vow to them and does not honour it, they will never exact payment. They 36 will never save any man from death, never rescue the weak from the strong. They cannot restore the blind man's 37 sight or give relief to the needy. They 38 do not pity the widow or befriend the orphan. They are like blocks from the 39 quarry, these wooden things plated with gold and silver, and their worshippers will be humiliated. How then can any- 40 one suppose them to be gods or call them so?

Besides, even the Chaldaeans themselves bring these idols of theirs into disrepute; for, when they see a dumb 41 man without the power of articulate speech, they bring him into the temple and make him call upon Bel, as if Bel could understand him. They cannot 42 see the folly of it and abandon the idols, because they themselves have no understanding. The women too sit in 43 the street with cords round them, burning bran for incense. And when a passer-by has pulled one of them to him and she has lain with him, she taunts her neighbour, because she has not been thought as attractive as herself and her cord has not been broken. Everything to do with these idols is 44 fraud and delusion. How then can anyone suppose them to be gods or call them so?

They are things manufactured by 45 carpenters and goldsmiths; they can be nothing but what the craftsmen

male devotees for fertility rites in the *inner chamber* of their temples. **28:** The *poor* were to be helped (Deut.14.28–29). **29–32:** These actions at the pagan *temples* were forbidden to the Jews and indeed were repellent to the Jews (Lev.12.1–4; 15.19–20; 21.5,11). **36–38:** These statue-gods do not possess the kindly power of the Lord (Ps.146.7–9; Isa.35.4–6). **40:** *Chaldaeans:* Babylonians. **41:** *Bel:* the same as Marduk, the main god of Babylon (see Dan. & Bel) **43:** The Greek writer, Herodotus, verifies this practice, demanded of all Babylonian women, to ask the gods

46 wish them to be. Even their makers'
   lives cannot be prolonged; what, then,
47 can the things they make expect? It is
   simply a scandalous fraud that they have
48 bequeathed to posterity. When war and
   disasters befall the gods, it is the priests
   who discuss amongst themselves where
49 they and their gods can hide. How then
   can men fail to see that these are not
   gods, when they cannot save themselves
50 from war and disaster? Since they are
   nothing but wood plated with gold
   and silver, they will in time be rec-
51 ognized for the frauds they are. All the
   heathen and their kings will plainly
   see that they are not gods but the work
   of men's hands, with no divine power
52 in them at all. Can there still be anyone
   who does not realize that they are not
   gods?
53   They cannot set up a king over a
   country, and they cannot give men
54 rain. They cannot decide a case or
   redress a wrong.*b* They are as helpless
55 as crows tossed about in mid air. When
   fire breaks out in a temple belonging to
   those wooden gods all gilded and
   silvered, their priests will run away to
   safety, but the gods will be burnt up
56 in the flames like timbers. They cannot
   resist king or enemy. How then can
   anyone allow or believe that they are
   gods?
57   They cannot save themselves from
   thieves and robbers, these wooden gods,
58 plated with silver and gold. Anyone
   who can will strip away their gold and
   silver and make off with the clothing
   they wear, and the gods can do nothing
59 to help themselves. It is better to be
   a king who proves his courage than such
   a sham god, better a household vessel
   that serves its owner's purpose, better
   even the door of a house that keeps
   the contents safe, or a wooden pillar
60 in a palace. Sun and moon and the

stars that shine so brightly are sent to
serve a purpose, and they obey. So 61
too, when the lightning flashes, it is
seen far and wide. It is the same with
the wind; it blows in every land. And 62
when God orders the clouds to travel
over all the world they carry out their
task, and so does fire when it is sent 63
down from above to consume mountains and forests. But idols are not to
be compared with any of these, in
appearance or in power. It follows that 64
they are not to be considered gods or
called by that name, seeing that they
are incapable of pronouncing judgement or of conferring benefits on
mankind. Recognize, therefore, that 65
they are not gods, and have no fear of
them.
   They wield no power over kings, 66
either to curse them or to bless them;
and they cannot provide heavenly 67
signs for the nations, either by shining
like the sun or by giving light like the
moon. They are more helpless than 68
wild beasts, which can at least save
themselves by taking cover. There is no 69
evidence at all that they are gods,
so have no fear of them.
   These wooden gods of theirs, plated 70
with gold and silver, give no better
protection than a scarecrow in a plot of
cucumbers. They are like a thorn-bush 71
in a garden, a perch for every bird,
like a corpse cast out in the dark. Such
are their wooden gods, with their plating of gold and silver. The purple and 72
fine linen*c* rotting on them proves that
they are not gods; in the end they will
themselves be eaten away, held in
contempt throughout the land.
   Better, then, is an upright man who 73
has no idols; he will be in no danger of
contempt.

*b Some witnesses read cannot judge in their own cause
  or redress a wrong done them.*
c fine linen: probable meaning; Gk. marble.

for fertility in their marriage. **67:** Even God cannot use the idols as *signs* (portents of his presence
and activity) as he can do with natural phenomena; see Joel 2.30; Lk.21.11,25. **72:** The Gk.
text (see Tfn. *c*) apparently mistranslated a Heb. word meaning "linen."

THE SONG OF
THE THREE

AN ADDITION IN THE GREEK VERSION
OF DANIEL BETWEEN 3. 23 AND 3. 24

The three most substantial of many additions to the Hebrew-Aramaic text of Daniel are: The Song of the Three; Daniel and Susanna; and Daniel, Bel, and the Snake. Whether these materials were first written in Hebrew, Aramaic, or Greek is debated, but puns on two Greek words in Daniel and Susanna favor Greek as the original language of at least that addition. These additions were probably written during the second or first century B.C.

The Song of the Three has two parts: a prayer of Azariah (Abed-nego), vv. 1–22, and a hymn to God sung by the three companions of Daniel: Shadrach, Meshach, and Abed-nego, vv. 23–68. The addition echoes major biblical themes, reflecting especially the thought of Ps. 148 and the form of Ps. 136. The prayer and the hymn were used extensively in worship by churches in later centuries.

1 THEY WALKED IN THE HEART OF the fire, praising God and blessing 2 the Lord. Azariah stood still among the flames and began to pray 3 aloud: 'Blessed art thou, O Lord, the God of our fathers, thy name is worthy of praise and glorious for ever: 4 thou art just in all thy deeds and true in all thy works; straight are thy paths, and all thy judgements just. 5 Just sentence hast thou passed in all that thou hast brought upon us and upon Jerusalem the holy city of our fathers: yes, just sentence thou hast 6 passed upon our sins. For indeed we sinned and broke thy law in 7 rebellion against thee, in all we did we sinned; we did not heed thy commandments, we did not keep them, we did not do what thou hadst commanded 8 us for our good. In all the punishments thou hast sent upon us thy 9 judgements have been just. Thou hast handed us over to our bitterest enemies, rebels against thy law, and to a wicked king, the vilest in the world. 10 And so now we are speechless for shame: contempt has fallen on thy servants and thy worshippers. For thy 11 honour's sake do not abandon us for ever; do not annul thy covenant. Do 12 not withdraw thy mercy from us, for the sake of Abraham, thy beloved, for the sake of Isaac, thy servant, and Israel, thy holy one. Thou didst 13 promise to multiply their descendants as the stars in the sky and the sand on the sea-shore. But now, Lord, we 14 have been made the smallest of all nations; for our sins we are today the most abject in the world. We have no 15 ruler, no prophet, no leader now; there is no burnt-offering, no sacrifice, no oblation, no incense, no place to make an offering before thee and find mercy. But because we come with 16 contrite heart and humbled spirit, accept us. As though we came with 17 burnt-offerings of rams and bullocks and with thousands of fat lambs, so let our sacrifice be made before thee this day. Accept our pledge of loyalty to thee,[a] for no shame shall come to those who put their trust in thee. Now we will 18 follow thee with our whole heart

a Accept our . . . thee: *possible meaning; Gk. obscure.*

1–27: **Azariah prays. 1:** *They:* Daniel's friends; see Dan.3.23. **2:** *Azariah:* Abed-nego's Heb. name; see Dan.1.7. **3:** Many OT passages declare that God was *just* in punishing Israel by the Babylonian Exile; see Neh.9.33; Lam.1.18. **9:** The *wicked king* in Dan. is Nebuchadnezzar (Dan.3.19); in the writer's day, however, Antiochus IV Epiphanes was *the vilest* because he sacked Jerusalem and profaned the Temple; see 1 Macc.1.41–60. **11:** *For thy honour's sake:* compare Ezek.36.22. **13:** *Thou didst promise:* see Gen.15.5; 22.17. **14–15:** Judah, deprived of its *ruler*, was *the most abject* because God's covenant with the Davidic dynasty seemed to be broken. See 2 Sam.7.13–16; Lam.2.9; Hos.3.4. **16–18:** *Accept:* a technical cult term applied to sacrifices pleasing to God. Qualities of the spirit are seen as the cultic equivalents of animal

and fear thee. We seek thy presence;
19 do not put us to shame, but deal
with us in thy forbearance and in the
20 greatness of thy mercy. Grant us again
thy marvellous deliverance, and win
glory for thy name, O Lord. Let all
who do thy servants harm be humbled;
21 may they be put to shame and stripped
of all their power, and may their
22 strength be crushed; let them know
that thou alone art the Lord God, and
glorious over all the world.'
23 The servants of the king who threw
them in kept on feeding the furnace
with naphtha, pitch, tow, and faggots,
24 and the flames poured out above it to
25 a height of seventy-five feet.*b* They
spread out and burnt those Chaldaeans
who were caught near the furnace.
26 But the angel of the Lord came down
into the furnace to join Azariah and
his companions; he scattered the flames
27 out of the furnace and made the heart
of it as if a moist wind were whistling
through. The fire did not touch them
at all and neither hurt nor distressed
them.

The praises of creation

28 THEN THE THREE WITH ONE VOICE
praised and glorified and blessed God
in the furnace:

29 'Blessed art thou, O Lord, the God
of our fathers;
worthy of praise, highly exalted for
ever.
30 Blessed is thy holy and glorious
name;
highly to be praised, highly exalted
for ever.
31 Blessed art thou in thy holy and
glorious temple;

most worthy to be hymned and
glorified for ever.
Blessed art thou who dost behold   32
the depths from thy seat upon
the cherubim;
worthy of praise, highly exalted for
ever.
Blessed art thou on thy royal throne; 33
most worthy to be hymned, highly
exalted for ever.
Blessed art thou in the dome of   34
heaven;
worthy to be hymned and glorified
for ever.

'Let the whole creation bless the Lord, 35
sing his praise and exalt him for
ever.
Bless the Lord, you heavens;   36
sing his praise and exalt him for
ever.
Bless the Lord, you angels of the   37
Lord;
sing his praise and exalt him for
ever.
Bless the Lord, all you waters above 38
the heavens;
sing his praise and exalt him for
ever.
Bless the Lord, all you his hosts;   39
sing his praise and exalt him for
ever.
Bless the Lord, sun and moon;   40
sing his praise and exalt him for
ever.
Bless the Lord, stars of heaven;   41
sing his praise and exalt him for
ever.
Bless the Lord, all rain and dew;   42
sing his praise and exalt him for
ever.
Bless the Lord, all winds that blow; 43
sing his praise and exalt him for
ever.

b Gk. forty-nine cubits.

sacrifices; compare 1 Sam.15.22; Ps.51.16–17; Hos.6.6. **20–21:** God would *win glory* for his *name* by ending the power of Babylon and granting Israel *deliverance* from captivity as he did at the time of the Exodus from Egypt. **24:** *Naphtha:* a natural petroleum substance. *Faggots:* bundles of sticks. **25:** See Dan.3.22. **26:** *The angel of the Lord* in the OT is often the Lord himself in angelic form; see Gen.16.7–14. **27:** In Palestine, when a *moist wind* blows from the Mediterranean it brings refreshing coolness, in contrast to the hot wind which blows from the eastern desert.

28–68: A song of exaltation. The constant refrain recalls Ps. 136. **32:** *Thy seat* is the mercy seat atop the Ark of the Covenant which was conceived as God's throne; see Exod.25.20–22. **35:** *Let . . . creation bless:* after addressing the Lord (vv. 29–34; see Ps.104), the song exhorts the whole creation, part by part (vv. 35–59), person by person (vv. 60–68), to *bless the Lord,* i.e. to *praise* God (compare Ps.148). **38:** *Waters . . . heavens:* see Gen. 1.7; Ps.148.4. **39:** *Hosts:*

44 Bless the Lord, fire and heat;
 sing his praise and exalt him for
 ever.

45 Bless the Lord, scorching blast and
 bitter cold;
 sing his praise and exalt him for
 ever.

46 Bless the Lord, dews and falling
 snow;
 sing his praise and exalt him for
 ever.

47 Bless the Lord, nights and days;
 sing his praise and exalt him for
 ever.

48 Bless the Lord, light and darkness;
 sing his praise and exalt him for
 ever.

49 Bless the Lord, frost and cold;
 sing his praise and exalt him for
 ever.

50 Bless the Lord, rime and snow;
 sing his praise and exalt him for
 ever.

51 Bless the Lord, lightnings and clouds;
 sing his praise and exalt him for
 ever.

52 'O earth, bless the Lord;
 sing his praise and exalt him for
 ever.

53 Bless the Lord, mountains and hills;
 sing his praise and exalt him for
 ever.

54 Bless the Lord, all that grows in the
 ground;
 sing his praise and exalt him for
 ever.

56 Bless the Lord, seas and rivers;
 sing his praise and exalt him for
 ever.

55 Bless the Lord, you springs;
 sing his praise and exalt him for
 ever.

57 Bless the Lord, you whales and all
 that swim in the waters;
 sing his praise and exalt him for
 ever.

58 Bless the Lord, all birds of the air;
 sing his praise and exalt him for
 ever.

59 Bless the Lord, you cattle and wild
 beasts;
 sing his praise and exalt him for
 ever.

60 'All men on earth, bless the Lord;
 sing his praise and exalt him for
 ever.

61 Bless the Lord. O Israel;
 sing his praise and exalt him for
 ever.

62 Bless the Lord, you priests of the
 Lord;
 sing his praise and exalt him for
 ever.

63 Bless the Lord, you servants of the
 Lord;
 sing his praise and exalt him for
 ever.

64 Bless the Lord, all men of upright
 spirit;
 sing his praise and exalt him for
 ever.

65 Bless the Lord, you that are holy
 and humble in heart;
 sing his praise and exalt him for
 ever.

66 Bless the Lord, Hananiah, Azariah,
 and Mishael;
 sing his praise and exalt him for
 ever.

For he has rescued us from the grave
 and from the power of death:
he has saved us from the furnace
 of burning flame;
he has rescued us from the heart of
 the fire.

67 Give thanks to the Lord, for he is
 good;
for his mercy endures for ever.

68 All who worship the Lord, bless the
 God of gods;
sing his praise and give him thanks,
for his mercy endures for ever.'

---

compare Ps.148.2–3. **44–51**: See Ps.148.8. **50**: *Rime:* a type of frost. **53**: See Ps.148.9. **58–65**:
Compare Ps.148.10–12.

DANIEL AND SUSANNA

The story of Susanna is a "detective story" from the second or first pre-Christian centuries. It is about Daniel, and is an addition to that book.

A masterpiece of the storyteller's art, the tale combines effective characterization with suspenseful plot development to proclaim its moral that God does not desert the innocent who trust and pray.

Some interpreters see the story as a criticism of the judicial system, especially the need to examine witnesses more carefully (vv. 48–49) and to insure against perjury by inflicting adequate punishment (v. 62).

This addition to Daniel appears in different places in the versions. In the Septuagint and Vulgate a slightly variant form of the story follows the end as ch. 13. The story comes first in the Greek text of Theodotion and in other versions, perhaps because Daniel is described (v. 45) as a "young man." On original language and the date, see Introduction to the Song of the Three.

Innocence vindicated

1 THERE ONCE LIVED IN BABYLON A
2 man named Joakim. He married
Susanna daughter of Hilkiah, a
3 very beautiful and devout woman. Her
parents, religious people, had brought
up their daughter according to the law
4 of Moses. Joakim was very rich and his
house had a fine garden adjoining it,
which was a regular meeting-place for
the Jews, because he was the man of
greatest distinction among them.
5 Now two elders of the community
were appointed that year as judges. It
was of them that the Lord had said,
'Wickedness came forth from Babylon
from elders who were judges and were
6 supposed to govern my people.' These
men were constantly at Joakim's house,
and everyone who had a case to be tried
came to them there.
7 When the people went away at noon,
Susanna used to go and walk in her
8 husband's garden. Every day the two
elders saw her entering the garden and
taking her walk, and they were obsessed
9 with lust for her. They no longer prayed
to God, but let their thoughts stray
from him and forgot the claims of
10 morality. They were both infatuated
with her; but they did not tell each
11 other what pangs they suffered, because
they were ashamed to confess that they

wanted to seduce her. Day after day 12
they watched eagerly to see her.
One day they said, 'Let us go home; 13
it is time for lunch.' So they went off in 14
different directions, but soon retraced
their steps and found themselves face
to face. When they questioned one
another, each confessed his passion.
Then they agreed on a time when they
might find her alone.
And while they were watching for an 15
opportune day, she went into the
garden as usual with only her two
maids; it was very hot, and she wished
to bathe there. No one else was in the 16
garden except the two elders, who had
hidden and were spying on her. She said 17
to her maids, 'Bring me soap and olive
oil, and shut the garden doors so that I
can bathe.' They did as she told them: 18
they closed the garden doors and went
out by the side door to fetch the things
they had been ordered to bring; they
did not see the elders because they were
hiding. As soon as the maids had gone, 19
the two elders started up and ran to
Susanna. 'Look!' they said, 'the garden 20
doors are shut, and no one can see us.
We are burning with desire for you, so
consent and yield to us. If you refuse, 21
we shall give evidence against you that
there was a young man with you and
that was why you sent your maids
away.' Susanna groaned and said: 'I 22

1–64: God's direct intervention fills a youth with wisdom to confound the craftiness of old age, thus vindicating innocence.

1–14: Wicked elders lust after Susanna. **2:** *Susanna* means "lily." **4:** Jewish names recorded on clay tablets in Babylonian archives show that some Jews became *rich* and rose to positions of *distinction* in their captivity in Babylon. **5:** *The Lord had said* may allude to Jer.29.21–23.

15–27: Seduction attempted. 22: For an unfaithful wife *the penalty* was *death* by stoning; see

see no way out. If I do this thing, the penalty is death; if I do not, you will have me at your mercy. My choice is made: I will not do it. It is better to be at your mercy than to sin against the Lord.'

24 With that Susanna gave a loud shout, but the two elders shouted her down.
25 One of them ran and opened the garden
26 door. The household, hearing the uproar in the garden, rushed in through the side door to see what had happened
27 to her. And when the elders had told their story, the servants were deeply shocked, for no such allegation had ever been made against Susanna.

28 Next day, when the people gathered at her husband Joakim's house, the two elders came, full of their criminal design
29 to put Susanna to death. In the presence of the people they said, 'Send for Susanna daughter of Hilkiah, Joakim's
30 wife.' So they sent for her, and she came with her parents and children and
31 all her relatives. Now Susanna was a woman of great beauty and delicate
32 feeling. She was closely veiled, but those scoundrels ordered her to be unveiled so that they might feast their eyes on
33 her beauty. Her family and all who saw
34 her were in tears. Then the two elders stood up before the people and put their
35 hands on her head. She looked up to heaven through her tears, for she
36 trusted in the Lord. The elders said: 'As we were walking alone in the garden, this woman came in with two maids. She shut the garden doors and
37 dismissed her maids. Then a young man, who had been in hiding, came and
38 lay down with her. We were in a corner of the garden, and when we saw this
39 wickedness we ran up to them. Though we saw them in the act, we could not hold the man; he was too strong for us, and he opened the door and forced his
40 way out. We seized the woman and asked who the young man was, but she

would not tell us. That is our evidence.'

As they were elders of the people and 41 judges, the assembly believed them and condemned her to death. Then Susanna 42 cried out loudly: 'Eternal God, who dost know all secrets and foresee all things, thou knowest that their evidence 43 against me was false. And now I am to die, guiltless though I am of all the wicked things these men have said against me.'

The Lord heard her cry. Just as she 44,45 was being led off to execution, God inspired a devout young man named Daniel to protest, and he shouted out, 46 'I will not have this woman's blood on my head.' All the people turned and 47 asked him, 'What do you mean by that?' He came forward and said: 'Are 48 you such fools, you Israelites, as to condemn a woman of Israel, without making careful inquiry and finding out the truth? Re-open the trial; the 49 evidence these men have brought against her is false.'

So the people all hurried back, and 50 the rest of the elders said to him, 'Come, take your place among us and state your case, for God has given you the standing of an elder.' Daniel said to 51 them, 'Separate these men and keep them at a distance from each other, and I will examine them.' When they 52 had been separated Daniel summoned one of them. 'You hardened sinner,' he said, 'the sins of your past have now come home to you. You gave unjust 53 decisions, condemning the innocent, and acquitting the guilty, although the Lord has said, "You shall not put to death an innocent and guiltless man." Now then, if you saw this woman, tell 54 us, under what tree did you see them together?' He answered, 'Under a clove-tree.'[a] Then Daniel retorted, 55 'Very good: this lie has cost you your life, for already God's angel has

a clove: *literally* mastic.

Lev.20.10; Deut.22.21–22. **23:** *Sin against the Lord:* see Gen.39.9; Ps.51.4. All sin is against God.

28–43: Susanna condemned through perjury. 34: To identify her as accused and themselves as witnesses of the crime and accusers, the elders *put their hands on her head;* see Lev.24.14.

44–49: Daniel intervenes. 46: According to Jewish tradition a herald preceded one being led to execution and appealed for possible evidence of his innocence. The entire community shared responsibility for *blood* shed in executions.

50–64: Susanna is acquitted; her accusers, the two elders, are put to death. 50: The invitation to Daniel to take his place as an *elder* is undoubtedly said in sarcasm. **53:** See Exod.23.7.

received your sentence from God, and
56 he will cleave[b] you in two.' And he told
him to stand aside, and ordered them
to bring in the other.

He said to him: 'Spawn of Canaan,
no son of Judah, beauty has been your
undoing, and lust has corrupted your
57 heart! Now we know how you have
been treating the women of Israel,
frightening them into consorting with
you; but here is a woman of Judah who
would not submit to your villainy.
58 Now then, tell me, under what tree did
you surprise them together?' 'Under a
59 yew-tree',[c] he replied. Daniel said to
him, 'Very good: this lie has cost you
your life, for the angel of God is waiting
with his sword to hew[d] you down and
destroy you both.'
60   Then the whole assembly gave a

great shout and praised God, the
saviour of those who trust in him. They 61
turned on the two elders, for out of
their own mouths Daniel had convicted
them of giving false evidence; they   62
dealt with them according to the law of
Moses, and put them to death, as they
in their wickedness had tried to do to
their neighbour. And so an innocent
life was saved that day. Then Hilkiah   63
and his wife gave praise for their
daughter Susanna, because she was
found innocent of a shameful deed, and
so did her husband Joakim and all her
relatives. And from that day forward   64
Daniel was a great man among his
people.

b clove . . . cleave: *there is a play on words in the Gk.*
c yew: *literally* oak.
d yew . . . hew: *there is a play on words in the Gk.*

56: *Spawn of Canaan* may be an allusion to the notorious sexual laxity of the Canaanites.
62: Deut.19.16–21 requires that a false witness receive the treatment he intended for the accused.
During Alexander Jannaeus' reign (105–79 B.C.) the Sadducees sought to apply this law only in
cases where the falsely accused was executed, but the Pharisees demanded stricter interpretation.

DANIEL, BEL, AND THE SNAKE

The third major addition to the Book of Daniel consists of two related tales designed to ridicule heathen idolatry. In the first story (vv. 1–22), Daniel is again presented (see Daniel and Susanna) as a clever detective who exposes the deception practiced by the priests of Bel. Daniel thus exposes the Bel statue as lifeless, no god at all. In the second story (vv. 23–42), Daniel demonstrates that a serpent worshiped by the Babylonians, while a living being, is surely not divine.

The wisdom and courage of the faithful Daniel and the truth that God delivers his faithful people are significant themes in both stories.

On date and original language, see Introduction to the Song of the Three.

The destruction of Bel

1 WHEN KING ASTYAGES WAS gathered to his fathers he was succeeded on the throne 2 by Cyrus the Persian. Daniel was a confidant of the king, the most honoured of all the King's Friends.

3 Now the Babylonians had an idol called Bel, for which they provided every day twelve bushels of fine flour, forty sheep, and fifty gallons of wine. 4 The king held it to be divine and went daily to worship it, but Daniel worshipped his God. So the king said to him, 'Why do you not worship Bel?' 5 He replied, 'Because I do not believe in man-made idols, but in the living God who created heaven and earth and is sovereign over all mankind.' 6 The king said, 'Do you think that Bel is not a living god? Do you not see how much he eats and drinks each day?' 7 Daniel laughed and said, 'Do not be deceived, your majesty; this Bel of yours is only clay inside and bronze outside, and has never eaten anything.' 8 Then the king was angry, and summoned the priests of Bel and said to them, 'If you cannot tell me who it is that eats up all these provisions, 9 you shall die; but if you can show that it is Bel that eats them, then Daniel shall die for blasphemy against Bel.' Daniel said to the king, 'Let it be as 10 you command.' (There were seventy priests of Bel, not counting their wives and children.) Then the king went with Daniel into the temple of Bel. The 11 priests said, 'We are now going outside; set out the food yourself, your majesty, and mix the wine; then shut the door and seal it with your signet. When you come back in the morning, 12 if you do not find that Bel has eaten it all, let us be put to death; but if Daniel's charges against us turn out to be false, then he shall die.' They treated 13 the whole affair with contempt, because they had made a hidden entrance under the table, and they regularly went in by it and ate everything up.

So when the priests had gone, the 14 king set out the food for Bel; and Daniel ordered his servants to bring ashes and sift them over the whole temple in the presence of the king alone. Then they left the temple, closed the door, sealed it with the king's signet, and went away. During the night the 15 priests, with their wives and children, came as usual and ate and drank everything. Early in the morning the king 16 came, and Daniel with him. The king 17 said, 'Are the seals intact, Daniel?' He answered, 'They are intact, your majesty.' As soon as he opened the 18 door, the king looked at the table and cried aloud, 'Great art thou, O Bel! In thee there is no deceit at all.' But 19 Daniel laughed and held back the king from going in. 'Just look at the floor,' he said, 'and judge whose footprints these are.' The king said, 'I see the 20

1–22: Daniel destroys an idol. 1: *King Astyages* was the last king of the Medes, defeated by *Cyrus the Persian* about 550 B.C. **2:** *King's Friends:* a technical term; see 1 Macc.2.18 n. **3:** Cyrus became the king of the *Babylonians* by defeating Nabonidus, the last king of Babylon, in 539 B.C. *Bel:* the chief Babylonian god, also known as Marduk; see Jer.51.44. **6:** Represented by a colossal image, Bel was believed a voracious eater. Historical sources confirm the huge

191

footprints of men, women, and children.' In a rage he put the priests under arrest, with their wives and children. Then they showed him the secret doors through which they used to go in and consume what was on the table. ²² So the king put them to death, and handed Bel over to Daniel, who destroyed the idol and its temple.

The destruction of the snake

²³ NOW THERE WAS A HUGE SNAKE, which the Babylonians held to be divine. ²⁴ The king said to Daniel, 'You cannot say that this is not a living god; so ²⁵ worship him.' Daniel answered, 'I will worship the Lord my God, for he ²⁶ is the living God. But give me authority, your majesty, and without sword or staff I will kill the snake.' 'I give it ²⁷ you', said the king. So Daniel took pitch and fat and hair, boiled them together, and made them into cakes, which he put into the mouth of the snake. When the snake ate them, it burst. Then Daniel said, 'See what ²⁸ things you worship!' When the Babylonians heard of this they gathered in an angry crowd to oppose the king. 'The king has turned Jew!' they cried. 'He has pulled down Bel, killed the snake, and put the priests to the ²⁹ sword.' So they went to the king and said, 'Hand Daniel over to us, or else we will kill you and your family.' ³⁰ The king, finding himself hard pressed, was compelled to give Daniel up to them. They threw him into the lion-³¹ pit, and he was there for six days. There were seven lions in the pit, and ³² every day two men and two sheep were fed to them; but now they were given nothing, to make sure that they would devour Daniel.

Now the prophet Habakkuk was in ³³ Judaea; he had made a stew and crumbled bread into the bowl, and he was on the way to his field, carrying it to the reapers, when an angel of the LORD ³⁴ said, 'Habakkuk, carry the meal you have with you to Babylon, for Daniel, who is in the lion-pit.' Habakkuk said, ³⁵ 'My lord, I have never been to Babylon. I do not know where the lion-pit is.' Then the angel took the prophet ³⁶ by the crown of his head, and carrying him by his hair, he swept him to Babylon with the blast of his breath and put him down above the pit. Habakkuk called out, 'Daniel, Daniel, ³⁷ take the meal that God has sent you!' Daniel said, 'O God, thou dost indeed ³⁸ remember me; thou dost never forsake those who love thee.' Then he got up ³⁹ and ate; and God's angel returned Habakkuk at once to his home. On the ⁴⁰ seventh day the king went to mourn for Daniel, but when he arrived at the pit and looked in, there sat Daniel! Then the king cried aloud, 'Great art ⁴¹ thou, O Lord, the God of Daniel, and there is no God but thou alone.' So the king drew Daniel up; and ⁴² the men who had planned to destroy him he flung into the pit, and then and there they were eaten up before his eyes.

---

food offerings (v. 3). **22:** *Put them to death:* see Dan.2.12; 6.24. Ancient historians record that the Persian King Xerxes (485–464 B.C.) *destroyed the idol and its temple* in 479 B.C.

23–42: The destruction of the snake. The serpent was often regarded in the Ancient Near East as a religious symbol; see Num.21.8; 2 Kgs.18.4. There is no evidence that the Babylonians worshiped a live *snake*. Earlier English translations speak of "dragon," rather than snake.

28–42: Daniel rescued. 31: *The lion-pit:* see Dan.6.16–24. **33:** *Habakkuk* lived a century earlier and hence could not have so served. **34:** *The meal:* see 1 Kgs.17.4–6. **36:** For a precedent of a prophet carried *by his hair* see Ezek.8.3. **38:** That God does not *forsake those who love* him is the point of all three additions to the Hebrew Daniel; it was an assurance needed by the Jews during the Maccabean struggle against King Antiochus IV Epiphanes (175–164 B.C.).

THE PRAYER OF MANASSEH

This brief devotional piece conveys sincere repentance and deep religious feeling.

Manasseh, son of the good king Hezekiah, appears in 2 Kgs.21.1–18 as a most wicked ruler who led Judah into gross idolatry, including human sacrifice, and perpetrated extensive violence. The Chronicler adds, however, that this evil king, after a very, very long reign, repented of his evil and called upon God for deliverance. Restored to his kingdom after being carried off to Babylon, he instituted partial reforms (2 Chr.33.1–20).

Mention is made in 2 Chr.33.19 of a prayer of Manasseh, but no prayer is given there. To fill this gap, some pious Jew composed a prayer such as Manasseh might have voiced.

The date and origin of the prayer are uncertain, but many place the composition in the last pre-Christian centuries and consider it originally written in Greek instead of Hebrew or Aramaic.

In Roman Catholic tradition, wherein the Apocrypha are regarded as canonical, this book is not so regarded.

Repentance

1 LORD ALMIGHTY,
God of our fathers,
of Abraham, Isaac, and Jacob,
and of their righteous offspring;
2 who hast made heaven and earth in
their manifold array;
3 who hast confined the ocean by thy
word of command,
who hast shut up the abyss and sealed
it with thy fearful and glorious
name;
4 all things tremble and quake in the
face of thy power.
5 For the majesty of thy glory is more
than man can bear,
and none can endure thy menacing
wrath against sinners;
6 the mercy in thy promise is beyond
measure: none can fathom it.
7 For thou art Lord Most High,
compassionate, patient, and of great
mercy,
relenting when men suffer for their
sins.
For out of thy great goodness thou,
O God,
hast promised repentance and
remission to those who sin
against thee,
and in thy boundless mercy thou hast
appointed repentance for sinners
as the way to salvation.[a]
8 So thou, Lord God of the righteous,
didst not appoint repentance for
Abraham, Isaac, and Jacob,
who were righteous and did not sin
against thee,
but for me, a sinner,
9 whose sins are more in number than
the sands of the sea.
My transgressions abound, O Lord,
my transgressions abound,
and I am not worthy to look up and
gaze at the height of heaven
because of the number of my
wrongdoings.
10 Bowed down with a heavy chain of
iron,
I grieve over my sins and find no relief,
because I have provoked thy anger
and done what is evil in thine eyes,
setting up idols and so piling sin on
sin.
11 Now I humble my heart, imploring
thy great goodness.
12 I have sinned, O Lord, I have sinned,
and I acknowledge my transgressions.
13 I pray and beseech thee,
spare me, O Lord, spare me,

a *Some witnesses omit* For out of . . . salvation.

1–8: God is praised as mighty Creator (1–4) who offers forgiveness to the penitent (5–8). **1:** *Righteous offspring:* faithful Israelites, descendants of the patriarchs. **2–3:** *Word of command:* the creative "God said" of Gen.1.6,10. Compare Job 38.8–11. **5:** God's majesty was considered so awesome that no man could experience it and live. Compare Isa.6.5; Ezek. 1.28–2.2. **7:** Since *men suffer for their sins* the possibility for *repentance* is a *mercy* from God.

9–13a: Repentance. 9: *My wrongdoings:* Manasseh's sins; see 2 Kgs.21.1–8. **10:** *Chain of iron:* Manasseh's captivity in Babylon (2 Chr.33.11).

destroy me not with my transgressions
on my head,
do not be angry with me for ever, nor
store up evil for me.
Do not condemn me to the grave,
for thou, Lord, art the God of the
penitent.
14 Thou wilt show thy goodness towards
me,

for unworthy as I am thou wilt save
me in thy great mercy;
and so I shall praise thee continually   15
all the days of my life.
For all the host of heaven sings thy
praise,
and thy glory is for ever and ever.
Amen.

13b–15: Confidence in divine mercy followed by a doxology closes the prayer. **13b:** God stored up *evil* by being *angry* and not giving a person repentance. **15:** To *praise* God *continually* with the lips as well as with a repentant and upright life was considered the object and fulfillment of human life and Israel's call; see Ps.51.13–17.

THE FIRST BOOK OF THE

MACCABEES

The word Maccabee, possibly meaning "hammer," was a popular epithet for Judas (1 Macc.2.4), the third son of the priest Mattathias. The plural Maccabees came to allude to the Jewish guerrillas who, under Mattathias, revolted against the Seleucid kings of Syria then ruling Palestine. The revolt began in 167 B.C. This and three other books bear the name Maccabees; 1 and 2 Maccabees and the nonbiblical 4 Maccabees are about the revolt, but 3 Maccabees is not.

Written originally in Hebrew (only a Greek translation survived antiquity), 1 Maccabees summarizes the events (1.1–64) which spurred the revolt of Mattathias (2.1–70) and follows the course of the resistance as it was carried on by his sons, especially Judas (3.1–9.22), Jonathan (9.23–12.53), and Simon (13.1–16.24). The latter was named King of Judea about 150 B.C.

1 Maccabees is a simple history written in the manner of the day by an unknown adherent of the Hasmonean kings descended from Simon. It is also meant to teach the author's Palestinian contemporaries that by fidelity to the Law of God the Jewish people may expect continued divine support, for God is still active in Israel's history. The book was probably written about 100 B.C.

Antiochus and the Jewish revolt

1 ALEXANDER OF MACEDON, THE SON of Philip, marched from the land of Kittim, defeated Darius, king of Persia and Media, and seized his throne, being already king of 2 Greece.*a* In the course of many campaigns he captured fortified towns, 3 slaughtered kings, traversed the earth to its remotest bounds, and plundered innumerable nations. When at last the world lay quiet under his rule, his 4 pride knew no limits; he built up an extremely powerful army, and ruled over countries, nations, and dominions; all paid him tribute.

5 The time came when he fell ill, and, 6 knowing that he was dying, he summoned his generals, nobles who had been brought up with him from childhood, and divided his empire among 7 them while he was still alive. Alexander had reigned twelve years when he died. 8 His generals took over the government, 9 each in his own province. On his death

they were all crowned as kings, and their descendants succeeded them for many years. They brought untold miseries upon the world.

A scion of this stock was that 10 wicked man, Antiochus Epiphanes, son of King Antiochus. He had been a hostage in Rome before he succeeded to the throne in the year 137 of the Greek era.*b*

At that time there appeared in Israel 11 a group of renegade Jews, who incited the people. 'Let us enter into a covenant with the Gentiles round about,' they said, 'because disaster upon disaster has overtaken us since we segregated ourselves from them.' The people thought this a good argu- 12 ment, and some of them in their en- 13 thusiasm went to the king and received authority to introduce non-Jewish laws and customs. They built a sports- 14 stadium in the gentile style in Jerusalem.

a being . . . Greece: *probable meaning; Gk. obscure.*
b *That is* 175 B.C.

1.1–64: Background to the Maccabean revolt. The author notes the spread of Greek power from Alexander the Great (356–323 B.C.) through his successors, down to Antiochus IV Epiphanes. This Seleucid king's harsh treatment of the Jews and brutal imposition of Hellenic culture upon them led Mattathias to revolt. **1:** *Kittim:* Macedonia. **3:** Alexander's army reached the *remotest bounds* of the author's Mediterranean world, the Beas river of the Punjab in northern India. In *his pride,* Alexander accepted divine honors. **7:** *Alexander* died at Babylon in June, 323 B.C., at the age of thirty-two. **8–9:** After *his death,* Alexander's *generals* fought over his empire. Three powers emerged, the Antigonids of Macedonia, the Ptolemies of Egypt, and the Seleucids of Syria. **10:** *Antiochus* IV, surnamed *Epiphanes,* i.e. "[God] manifest" but nicknamed "madman" (Gk. *epimanes*), was the son of Antiochus III, "the Great." On the father's defeat by the Romans at the battle of Magnesia (190 B.C.), the son was sent as a hostage to Rome to insure fidelity to the treaty of Apamea (188 B.C.). See 8.6–8. **11:** The *renegade Jews* were led by

They removed their marks of circumcision and repudiated the holy covenant.
15 They intermarried with Gentiles, and abandoned themselves to evil ways.

16 When he was firmly established on his throne, Antiochus made up his mind to become king of Egypt and so
17 to rule over both kingdoms. He assembled a powerful force of chariots, elephants, and cavalry, and a great fleet,
18 and invaded Egypt. When battle was joined, Ptolemy king of Egypt was seized with panic and took to flight,
19 leaving many dead. The fortified towns were captured and the land pillaged.

20 On his return from the conquest of Egypt, in the year 143,[c] Antiochus marched with a strong force against
21 Israel and Jerusalem. In his arrogance he entered the temple and carried off the golden altar, the lamp-stand with
22 all its equipment, the table for the Bread of the Presence, the sacred cups and bowls, the golden censers, the curtain, and the crowns. He stripped off all the
23 gold plating from the temple front. He seized the silver, gold, and precious vessels, and whatever secret treasures
24 he found, and took them all with him when he left for his own country. He had caused much bloodshed, and he gloated over all he had done.

25 Great was the lamentation
　　throughout Israel;
26 rulers and elders groaned in bitter
　　grief.
Girls and young men languished;
the beauty of our women was
　　disfigured.
27 Every bridegroom took up the
　　lament,
and every bride sat grieving in her
　　chamber.
28 The land trembled for its inhabitants,

and all the house of Jacob was
　　wrapped in shame.

29 Two years later, the king sent to the towns of Judaea a high revenue official, who arrived at Jerusalem
30 with a powerful force. His language was friendly, but full of guile. For, once he had gained the city's confidence, he suddenly attacked it. He dealt it a heavy blow, and killed many Israelites,
31 plundering the city and setting it ablaze. He pulled down houses and walls on
32 every side; women and children were made prisoners, and the cattle seized.
33 The city of David was turned into a citadel, enclosed by a high, stout wall
34 with strong towers, and garrisoned by impious foreigners and renegades.
35 Having made themselves secure, they accumulated arms and provisions, and deposited there the massed plunder of Jerusalem. There they lay in ambush,
36 a lurking threat to the temple and a perpetual menace to Israel.

37 They shed the blood of the innocent
　　round the temple;
they defiled the holy place.
38 The citizens of Jerusalem fled for
　　fear of them;
she became the abode of aliens,
and alien herself to her offspring:
her children deserted her.
39 Her temple lay desolate as a
　　wilderness;
her feasts were turned to mourning,
her sabbaths to a reproach,
her honour to contempt.
40 The shame of her fall matched the
　　greatness of her renown,
and her pride was bowed low in grief.

41 The king then issued a decree throughout his empire: his subjects
42 were all to become one people and

c That is 169 B.C.

Jason (Joshua), the brother of the Jewish high priest Onias III; see 2 Macc.4.7–20. **18:** *Ptolemy* VI Philometor (180–145 B.C.). **20–24:** *Antiochus* robbed the *temple* to replenish the royal treasury depleted by war. **29–32:** Antiochus invaded Egypt again in 168 B.C. Forced to retire by the Roman emissary Popilius Laenas, who threatened war with Rome, Antiochus vented his wrath on Judea, which he thought to be in revolt. See 2 Macc.5.1–14. *Two years later* than Antiochus' first Egyptian campaign, i.e. in 167 B.C., Apollonius, chief of the Mysian mercenaries, was sent to put down the unruly city again; see 2 Macc.5.23b–26. **33–34:** *Impious foreigners* (Seleucid troops) *and renegades* (Hellenizing Jews) now fortified the westernmost hill of Jerusalem. This citadel remained in their hands until 141 B.C., when Simon drove them out (1 Macc.13.49–50). **37–40:** A lament similar to that of Ps.79. **41–50:** Hoping to weld into a political unity the

abandon their own laws and religion. The nations everywhere complied with
43 the royal command, and many in Israel accepted the foreign worship, sacrificing to idols and profaning the sabbath.
44 Moreover, the king sent agents with written orders to Jerusalem and the towns of Judaea. Ways and customs foreign to the country were to be
45 introduced. Burnt-offerings, sacrifices, and libations in the temple were forbidden; sabbaths and feast-days were
46 to be profaned; the temple and its
47 ministers to be defiled. Altars, idols, and sacred precincts were to be established; swine and other unclean beasts
48 to be offered in sacrifice. They must leave their sons uncircumcised; they must make themselves in every way abominable, unclean, and profane,
49 and so forget the law and change all
50 their statutes. The penalty for disobedience was death.
51   Such was the decree which the king issued to all his subjects. He appointed superintendents over all the people, and instructed the towns of Judaea to
52 offer sacrifice, town by town. People thronged to their side in large numbers, every one of them a traitor to the law. Their wicked conduct throughout the
53 land drove Israel into hiding in every possible place of refuge.
54   On the fifteenth day of the month Kislev in the year 145,*d* 'the abomination of desolation' was set up on the altar. Pagan altars were built through-
55 out the towns of Judaea; incense was offered at the doors of houses and in
56 the streets. All scrolls of the law which were found were torn up and burnt.
57 Anyone discovered in possession of a Book of the Covenant, or conforming to the law, was put to death by the

king's sentence. Thus month after 58 month these wicked men used their power against the Israelites whom they found in their towns,
    On the twenty-fifth day of the 59 month they offered sacrifice on the pagan altar which was on top of the altar of the Lord. In accordance with 60 the royal decree, they put to death women who had had their children circumcised. Their babies, their families, 61 and those who had circumcised them, they hanged by the neck. Yet many in 62 Israel found strength to resist, taking a determined stand against eating any unclean food. They welcomed death 63 rather than defile themselves and profane the holy covenant, and so they died. The divine wrath raged against Israel.*e* 64

AT THIS TIME A CERTAIN MATTATHIAS, 2 son of John, son of Symeon, appeared on the scene. He was a priest of the Joarib family from Jerusalem, who had settled at Modin. Mattathias 2 had five sons, John called Gaddis, Simon called Thassis, Judas called 3,4 Maccabaeus, Eleazar called Avaran, 5 and Jonathan called Apphus.
    When Mattathias saw the sacri- 6 legious acts committed in Judaea and Jerusalem, he said: 7

'Oh! Why was I born to see this,
    the crushing of my people, the ruin
        of the holy city?
They sat idly by when it was
        surrendered,
when the holy place was given up
        to the alien.
Her temple is like a man robbed of   8
        honour;

d That is 167 B.C.
e The divine . . . Israel: or Israel lived under a reign of terror.

---

many ethnic and linguistic groupings over which he ruled, Antiochus IV decreed a common culture (Hellenism) and religion (the worship of Zeus Olympios) for all of his subjects. For Jews, conformity to the decree meant abandonment of the Mosaic Law and apostasy from the God of Israel. **54:** On December 7, 167 B.C., Antiochus built an altar to Zeus Olympios on the Temple's altar of holocausts (see v. 59). This *abomination* replaced the Holy of Holies as the center of worship in the Temple, and the worship of Zeus replaced that of Israel's God. **55:** Apparently, Jews adopted Grecian shrines for their streets and houses. **57:** *Book of the Covenant:* the Law of Moses. **59:** December 17, 167 B.C. **62–63:** See 2 Macc.6.18–7.42 for examples.
    2.1–70: Mattathias begins active resistance. What began under Mattathias' direction as armed resistance to the Hellenizing program eventually escalated into a war for autonomy led by his sons. **1:** *Joarib* headed one priestly division of twenty-four appointed for alternate duty in the Temple. See 1 Chr.24.1–19 (especially v. 7). *Modin* is modern el-Midyah, seven miles east of Lod. **2:** The surnames of Mattathias' sons have been explained as meaning "fortunate," "burning," "designated by Yahweh" (or "the hammerer," or "hammer-headed"), "awake,"

9 its glorious vessels are carried off as
spoil,
Her infants are slain in the street,
her young men by the sword of the
foe.
10 Is there a nation that has not
usurped her sovereignty,*f*
a people that has not plundered her?
11 She has been stripped of all her
adornment,
no longer free, but a slave.

12 Now that we have seen our temple
with all its beauty and splendour
laid waste and profaned by the
13 Gentiles, why should we live any
14 longer?' So Mattathias and his sons
tore their garments, put on sackcloth,
and mourned bitterly.
15 The king's officers who were en-
forcing apostasy came to the town of
Modin to see that sacrifice was offered,
16 and many Israelites went over to them.
Mattathias and his sons stood in a
17 group. The king's officers spoke to
Mattathias: 'You are a leader here,'
they said, 'a man of mark and influence
in this town, with your sons and
18 brothers at your back. You be the first
now to come forward and carry out
the king's order. All the nations have
done so, as well as the leading men in
Judaea and the people left in Jerusalem.
Then you and your sons will be enrolled
among the King's Friends; you will all
receive high honours, rich rewards of
silver and gold, and many further
benefits.'
19 To this Mattathias replied in a
ringing voice: 'Though all the nations
within the king's dominions obey him
and forsake their ancestral worship,
though they have chosen to submit to
20 his commands, yet I and my sons and
brothers will follow the covenant of
21 our fathers. Heaven forbid we should
ever abandon the law and its statutes.
22 We will not obey the command of the
king, nor will we deviate one step from
our forms of worship.'
23 As soon as he had finished, a Jew

stepped forward in full view of all to
offer sacrifice on the pagan altar at
Modin, in obedience to the royal
command. The sight stirred Mattathias 24
to indignation; he shook with passion,
and in a fury of righteous anger rushed
forward and slaughtered the traitor on
the very altar. At the same time he 25
killed the officer sent by the king to
enforce sacrifice, and pulled the pagan
altar down. Thus Mattathias showed 26
his fervent zeal for the law, just as
Phinehas had done by killing Zimri
son of Salu. 'Follow me,' he shouted 27
through the town, 'every one of you
who is zealous for the law and strives
to maintain the covenant.' He and his 28
sons took to the hills, leaving all their
belongings behind in the town.
At that time many who wanted to 29
maintain their religion and law went
down to the wilds to live there. They 30
took their sons, their wives, and their
cattle with them, for their miseries
were more than they could bear. Word 31
soon reached the king's officers and the
forces in Jerusalem, the city of David,
that men who had defied the king's
order had gone down into hiding-
places in the wilds. A large body of 32
men went quickly after them, came
up with them, and occupied positions
opposite. They prepared to attack them
on the sabbath. 'There is still time,' 33
they shouted; 'come out, obey the
king's command, and your lives will
be spared.' 'We will not come out,' 34
the Jews replied; 'we will not obey the
king's command or profane the sabbath.' Without more ado the attack 35
was launched; but the Israelites did 36
nothing in reply; they neither hurled
stones, nor barricaded their caves.
'Let us all meet death with a clear 37
conscience,' they said; 'we call heaven
and earth to testify that there is no
justice in this slaughter.' So they were 38
attacked and massacred on the sabbath,
men, women, and children, up to a thousand in all, and their cattle with them.

f Or occupied her palaces.

---

and "favorite." **18:** Mattathias was offered the lowest of four honorary ranks of *the King's Friends* (friends, honored friends, first, and preferred friends). See 10.65; 11.27; 2 Macc.8.9. **24:** Mattathias obeyed God's law. See Deut.13.6–11. **26:** See Num.25.6–15. **29–38:** Josephus (*Ant.* XII.6.2) records that Jews who had met secretly in a cave to observe the Sabbath were suffocated by setting fire to brush that had been piled at the mouth of the cave; see also 2

39 Great was the grief of Mattathias and his friends when they heard the 40 news. They said to one another, 'If we all do as our brothers have done, if we refuse to fight the Gentiles for our lives as well as for our laws and customs, then they will soon wipe us off 41 the face of the earth.' That day they decided that, if anyone came to fight against them on the sabbath, they would fight back, rather than all die as their brothers in the caves had done.

42 It was then that they were joined by a company of Hasidaeans, stalwarts of Israel, every one of them a volunteer 43 in the cause of the law; and all who were refugees from the troubles came to swell their numbers, and so add to their 44 strength. Now that they had an organized force, they turned their wrath on the guilty men and renegades. Those who escaped their fierce attacks took refuge with the Gentiles.

45 Mattathias and his friends then swept through the country, pulling 46 down the pagan altars, and forcibly circumcising all the uncircumcised boys found within the frontiers of Israel. 47 They hunted down their arrogant enemies, and the cause prospered in 48 their hands. Thus they saved the law from the Gentiles and their kings, and broke the power of the tyrant.

49 The time came for Mattathias to die, and he said to his sons: 'Arrogance now stands secure and gives judgement against us; it is a time of calamity and 50 raging fury. But now, my sons, be zealous for the law, and give your lives for the covenant of your fathers. 51 Remember the deeds they did in their generations, and great glory and eternal 52 fame shall be yours. Did not Abraham prove steadfast under trial, and so 53 gain credit as a righteous man? Joseph kept the commandments, hard-pressed though he was, and became lord of Egypt. Phinehas, our father, never 54 flagged in his zeal, and his was the covenant of an everlasting priesthood. Joshua kept the law, and he became a 55 judge in Israel. Caleb bore witness 56 before the congregation, and a share in the land was his reward. David was 57 a man of loyalty, and he was granted the throne of an everlasting kingdom. Elijah never flagged in his zeal for 58 the law, and he was taken up to heaven. Hananiah, Azariah, and Mishael had 59 faith, and they were saved from the blazing furnace. Daniel was a man of 60 integrity, and he was rescued from the lions' jaws. As generation succeeds 61 generation, follow their example; for no one who trusts in Heaven shall ever lack strength. Do not fear a wicked 62 man's words; all his success will end in filth and worms. Today he may be 63 high in honour, but tomorrow there will be no trace of him, because he will have returned to the dust and all his schemes come to nothing. But you, 64 my sons, draw your courage and strength from the law, for by it you will win great glory.

'Now here is Symeon, your brother; 65 I know him to be wise in counsel: always listen to him, for he shall be a father to you. Judas Maccabaeus has 66 been strong and brave from boyhood; he shall be your commander in the field, and fight his people's battles. Gather to your side all who observe the 67 law, and avenge your people's wrongs. Repay the Gentiles in their own coin, 68 and always heed the law's commands.'

Then Mattathias blessed them, and 69 was gathered to his fathers. He died in 70 the year 146,*g* and was buried by his

g *That is* 166 B.C.

Macc.6.11. **42:** The *Hasidaeans* ("Pious" or "Faithful") were the forerunners of both the Pharisees and the Essenes. **44:** 2 Macc.8.1 estimates this *organized force* as numbering about 6,000. *Guilty men:* pagans. *Renegades:* apostate Jews. **48:** *They saved the law* by preventing the absorption of Judaism into a mixture of pagan and Jewish worship. **49–70:** Mattathias' deathbed scene recalls that of Jacob (Gen. ch. 49) and Moses (Deut. ch. 33). Mattathias urges imitation of those who remained faithful to God's word despite difficult circumstances: Abraham (Gen. ch. 22), Joseph (Gen. ch. 39), Phinehas (Num. ch. 25), Joshua (Josh. ch. 1), Caleb (Num. chs. 13–14), David (2 Sam. ch. 7.), Elijah (1 Kgs. ch. 18; 2 Kgs. ch. 2), Hananiah, Azariah, Mishael (Dan. ch. 1), and Daniel (Dan. ch. 6). See similar praises in Ecclus. chs. 44–50. **62:** *Filth and worms* were the final lot of Antiochus (2 Macc.9.5–10). **65:** Although *Symeon* was older, he became the leader of the people only after his brothers Judas and Jonathan had died. **70:** *Family tomb at Modin:* see 13.25–30.

sons in the family tomb at Modin. All Israel raised a loud lament for him.

The war under Judas and Jonathan

3 THEN JUDAS MACCABAEUS CAME FOR-
2 ward in his father's place. He had the support of all his brothers and his father's followers, and they carried on the fight for Israel with zest.

3 He enhanced his people's glory.
  He put on his breastplate like a
      giant,
  and girt himself with weapons of war.
  He fought battle on battle;
  he guarded his army with his sword.
4 He was like a lion in his exploits,
  like a lion's whelp roaring for prey.
5 He hunted and tracked down the
      lawless;
  he blasted the troublers of his people.
6 The lawless cowered in fear of him;
  all evil-doers were confounded.
  The cause of freedom prospered in
      his hands;
7 he provoked many kings to anger.
  But he made Jacob glad by his deeds;
  he is remembered for ever in blessing.
8 He passed through the towns of
      Judaea;
  he destroyed the godless there.
  He turned wrath away from Israel;
9 his fame spread to the ends of the
      earth,
  and he rallied a people near to
      destruction.

10 Apollonius now collected a gentile force and a large contingent from
11 Samaria, to fight against Israel. When Judas heard of it, he marched out to meet him, and defeated and killed him. Many of the Gentiles fell, and the rest took to flight. From the arms they 12 captured, Judas took the sword of Apollonius, and used it in his campaigns for the rest of his life.

When Seron, who commanded the 13 army in Syria, heard that Judas had mustered a large force, consisting of all his loyal followers of military age, he 14 said to himself, 'I will win a glorious reputation in the empire by making war on Judas and his followers, who defy the royal edict.' Seron was re- 15 inforced by a strong contingent of renegade Jews, who marched up to help him take vengeance on Israel. When 16 he reached the pass of Beth-horon, Judas advanced to meet him with a handful of men. When his followers 17 saw the host coming against them, they said to Judas, 'How can so few of us fight against so many? Besides, we have had nothing to eat all day, and we are exhausted.'

Judas replied: 'Many can easily 18 be overpowered by a few; it makes no difference to Heaven to save by many or by few. Victory does not depend on 19 numbers; strength comes from Heaven alone. Our enemies come filled with 20 insolence and lawlessness to plunder and to kill us and our wives and children. But we are fighting for our 21 lives and our religion. Heaven will crush 22 them before our eyes. You need not be afraid of them.'

When he had finished speaking, he 23 launched a sudden attack, and Seron and his army broke before him. They 24 pursued them down the pass of Beth-horon as far as the plain; some eight hundred of the enemy fell, and the rest fled to Philistia.

3.1–9.73: The Jews regain religious freedom. Under Judas, the Jews defeat the forces of Antiochus and his son, purify the Temple, punish persecutors and regain religious freedom. When persecution is renewed, Judas resumes the struggle. Jonathan continues the war with success.
    3.1–9: A poetic preface praises Judas. 5: *Blasted:* burned; see 5.5,35,44. **7:** *Kings:* Antiochus IV Epiphanes (3.27), Antiochus V Eupator (6.28, but not mentioned by name; see 3.33 n.) and Demetrius I Soter (9.1). **8:** By purging the land, Judas mollified the divine *wrath.* See 2 Macc. 6.12–16. **9:** *Ends of the earth:* Rome; see 8.17–32.
    3.10–24: Judas' early victories. 10: *Apollonius,* who had earlier sacked Jerusalem (1.29–35), now led a contingent including his Mysian mercenaries (2 Macc.5.24) against Judea. **16:** Two towns, two miles apart ,"Upper" and "Lower" *Beth-horon,* were connected by a pass which led from the coastal plains to the highlands north of Jerusalem. Judas ambushed Seron in the pass and defeated him with fewer men. **18–19:** 1 Macc. never uses "God" or "Lord," but prefers *Heaven.* **24:** *Philistia:* the seacoast, once home of the Philistines.

25 Thus Judas and his brothers began to be feared, and alarm spread to the
26 Gentiles all round. His fame reached the ears of the king, and the story of his battles was told in every nation.
27 When King Antiochus heard this news, he flew into a rage and ordered all the forces of his empire to be assembled, an
28 immensely powerful army. He opened his treasury and gave a year's pay to his troops, ordering them to be prepared
29 for any duty. But he found that his resources were running low; his tribute, too, had dwindled as a result of the disaffection and violence he had brought upon the world by abolishing
30 traditional laws and customs. He now saw with alarm that he might be short of money, as had happened once or twice before, both for his normal expenses and for the gifts he had been accustomed to distribute with an even more lavish hand than any of his predecessors on the throne.
31 For a time he was much perplexed; then he decided to go to Persia, collect the tribute due from the provinces, and raise a large sum of ready money.
32 He left Lysias, a distinguished member of the royal family, as viceroy of the territories between the Euphrates and
33 the Egyptian frontier. He also appointed him guardian of his son Antiochus
34 until his return. He transferred to Lysias half the armed forces, together with the elephants, and told him all that he wanted done, especially to the population of Judaea and Jerusalem.
35 Against these Lysias was to send a force, and break and destroy the strength of Israel and those who were

left in Jerusalem, to blot out all memory of them from the place. He was to settle 36 foreigners in all their territory, and allot the land to the settlers. The other 37 half of the forces the king took with him, and set out from Antioch, his capital, in the year 147.[h] He crossed the Euphrates and marched through the upper provinces.

Lysias chose Ptolemaeus son of 38 Dorymenes, with Nicanor and Gorgias, all three powerful members of the order of King's Friends, and sent with 39 them forty thousand infantry and seven thousand cavalry to invade Judaea and devastate the country as the king had commanded. They set out 40 with all their forces and encamped near Emmaus in the lowlands. The 41 merchants of the region, impressed by what they heard of the army, took a large quantity of silver and gold, with a supply of fetters, and came into the camp to buy the Israelites for slaves. The army was also reinforced by troops from Syria and Philistia.

Judas and his brothers saw that their 42 plight had become grave, with the enemy encamped inside their frontiers. They learnt, too, of the commands which the king had given for the complete destruction of the nation. So they 43 said to one another, 'Let us restore the shattered fortunes of our nation; let us fight for our nation and for the holy place.' They gathered in full 44 assembly to prepare for battle, and to pray and seek divine mercy and compassion.

h That is 165 B.C.

3.25–37: Antiochus goes to Persia. He makes provision for settling the "Jewish question" in his absence. That the king gathered a powerful army in response to the exploits of Judas is an exaggeration. A more likely reason was to quell a rebellion in the east, indicated by overdue tribute (v. 31), to secure the eastern frontier against the Parthians and to replenish his depleted treasury (vv. 29–30) by conquest. 29: Antiochus' problems largely resulted from his imposition of Hellenic religion and customs on native populations. 31: Persia in 1 and 2 Macc. is all the area east of the Tigris. 32: Lysias belonged to the highest court order of the realm, "the king's kinsmen." 33: The son is Antiochus V Eupator (164–161 B.C.), who was then only seven. 37: Antioch is modern Antakya in eastern Turkey. The upper provinces included the valleys of the Tigris and Euphrates.

3.38–4.27: Judas defeats the Seleucid generals. See 2 Macc.8.8–29. 38: Ptolemaeus: in 2 Macc. 8.8, he is governor of Coele-syria and Phoenicia. His region included Palestine. Nicanor: see 1 Macc.7.26–50; 2 Macc.8.9; 14.15. Gorgias: see 5.59; 2 Macc.8.9; 10.14; 12.32–35. King's Friends: see 2:18 n. 40: Emmaus is about twenty miles northwest of Jerusalem. 41: Jews were to be sold as slaves to raise money for tribute (2 Macc.8.10–11). The Greek translator probably misread Aram (= Syria) for Edom, the Heb. words being easily confused. The main body of troops was already from Syria. 43–46: Because the holy place, the Temple, was defiled by the pagans and apostates (v. 45), the Jews assembled for prayer at Mizpah, an ancient Israelite

45 Jerusalem lay deserted like a
wilderness;
none of her children went in or out.
Her holy place was trampled down;
aliens and heathen lodged in her
citadel.
Joy had been banished from Jacob;
and flute and harp were dumb.

46 They assembled at Mizpah, opposite
Jerusalem, for in former times Israel
had a place of worship at Mizpah.
47 That day they fasted, put on sackcloth,
sprinkled ashes on their heads, and tore
48 their garments. They unrolled the scroll
of the law, seeking the guidance
which Gentiles seek from the images
49 of their gods. They brought the priestly
vestments, the firstfruits, and the tithes;
they presented Nazirites who had
50 completed their vows, and they cried
to Heaven: 'What shall we do with
these Nazirites, and where shall we
51 take them? Thy holy place is trodden
down and defiled, and sorrow and
humiliation have come upon thy priests.
52 And see, the Gentiles have gathered
against us to destroy us. Thou knowest
53 the fate they plan for us; how can we
withstand them unless thou help us?'
54 Then the trumpets sounded, and a
great shout went up.
55 Judas then appointed leaders of the
people, officers over thousands, hun-
56 dreds, fifties, and tens. As the law
commands, he ordered back to their
homes those who were building their
houses or were newly wed or who were
planting vineyards, or who were faint-
57 hearted. Thereupon the army moved
and took up their positions to the south
58 of Emmaus, where Judas thus addressed them: 'Prepare for action and
show yourselves men. Be ready at
dawn to fight these Gentiles who are
massed against us to destroy us and
59 our holy place. Better die fighting than
look on while calamity overwhelms

our people and the holy place. But it 60
will be as Heaven wills.'

Gorgias, taking a detachment of 4
five thousand men and a thousand
picked cavalry, set out by night to attack 2
the Jewish army and fall upon them
unawares; his guides were men from
the citadel. But Judas had word of this, 3
and he and his soldiers moved out to
attack the king's army in Emmaus,
while its forces were still divided. 4
Gorgias reached the camp of Judas 5
during the night, but found no one
there. He set out to search for them
in the hills, thinking, 'These Jews are
running away from us.'

At daybreak, there was Judas in the 6
plain with three thousand men, though
they had not all the armour and the
swords they wanted. They saw the 7
Gentiles' camp strongly fortified with
breastworks, while mounted guards,
seasoned troops, patrolled round it.

Judas said to his men: 'Do not be 8
afraid of their great numbers or panic
when they charge. Remember how our 9
fathers were saved at the Red Sea,
when Pharaoh and his army were
pursuing them. Let us cry now to 10
Heaven to favour our cause, to remember the covenant made with our fathers,
and to crush this army before us today.
Then all the Gentiles will know that 11
there is One who saves and liberates
Israel.'

When the foreigners looked up and 12
saw them advancing to the attack,
they marched out of their camp to give 13
battle. Judas and his men sounded their
trumpets and closed with them. The 14
Gentiles broke, and fled to the plain.
All the rearmost fell by the sword. 15
The pursuit was pressed as far as Gazara
and the lowlands of Idumaea, Azotus
and Jamnia; about three thousand of
the enemy were killed.

Judas and his force then broke off 16
the pursuit and returned. He said to 17

---

sanctuary eight miles north of Jerusalem. See Judg.20.1; 1 Sam.7.5; 10.17; Jer.40.6. **48:** Unable
to cast lots (the Urim and Thummim of 1 Sam.14.41), after the Exile (Ezra 2.63; Neh.7.65),
Israel sought guidance from the Lord by reading *the scroll of the law*. **49–51:** The *Nazirites*
could not complete *their vows* (see Num.6.1–21), because the *holy place* (Temple) was defiled.
55: The *leaders* included Judas' brothers (2 Macc.8.22–23). **56:** See Deut.20.5–8. 2 Macc.8.13
cites only cowardice. **4.2:** *Men from the citadel:* renegade Jews probably; see 1.33–34 n. **6:**
2 Macc.8.16 doubles Judas' army. **8–11:** See 2 Macc.8.16–20, where the incidents cited in Judas'
speech as motives for confidence are different. Ancient authors reported what a speaker should
have said rather than exact words. **15:** The defeated enemy fled to the cities of the coastal

the people: 'Curb your greed for spoil; there is more fighting before us:
18 Gorgias and his force are in the hills near by. Stand firm now against our enemies and fight; after that, plunder as you please.'

19 Before Judas had finished speaking, an enemy patrol appeared, recon-
20 noitring from the hills. They saw that their army was in flight, and that their camp was being set on fire; the smoke that met their gaze showed what had
21 happened. They were filled with panic as they took in the scene, and when they saw the army of Judas in the
22 plain, ready for battle, they all fled to Philistia.

23 Then Judas turned back to plunder the camp, and there they got much gold and silver, violet and purple stuffs,
24 and great riches. On their return they sang songs of thanksgiving and praised Heaven, 'for it is right, because his
25 mercy endures for ever'. That day saw a great deliverance for Israel.

26 Those of the Gentiles who escaped with their lives went and reported to
27 Lysias all that had happened. On hearing the news he was overwhelmed with disappointment, because Israel had not suffered the disaster he had hoped for, and the issue was not what the king had ordered.

28 In the following year he gathered sixty thousand picked infantry and five thousand cavalry to make war on
29 the Jews. They marched into Idumaea, and encamped at Bethsura, where Judas met them with ten thousand men.
30 When he saw the strength of the enemy's army, he prayed: 'All praise to thee, the Saviour of Israel, who didst break the attack of the giant by thy servant David. Thou didst deliver the army of the Philistines into the power of Saul's son, Jonathan, and of his armour-
31 bearer. In like manner put this army into the power of thy people Israel.

Humble their pride in their forces and
32 their mounted men. Strike them with panic, turn their insolent strength to water, make them reel under a crushing
33 defeat. Overthrow them by the sword of those who love thee, and let all who know thy name praise thee with songs of thanksgiving.'

34 So they joined battle, and Lysias lost about five thousand men in the
35 close fighting. When he saw his own army routed and Judas's army full of daring, ready to live or die nobly, he departed for Antioch, and there col-lected a force of mercenaries, in order to return to Judaea with a much larger army than before.[i]

36 But Judas and his brothers said: 'Now that our enemies have been crushed, let us go up to Jerusalem to cleanse the temple and rededicate it.'
37 So the whole army was assembled and
38 went up to Mount Zion. There they found the temple laid waste, the altar profaned, the gates burnt down, the courts overgrown like a thicket or wooded hill-side, and the priests' rooms
39 in ruin. They tore their garments, wailed
40 loudly, put ashes on their heads, and fell on their faces to the ground. They sounded the ceremonial trumpets, and cried aloud to Heaven.

41 Then Judas detailed troops to en-gage the garrison of the citadel while
42 he cleansed the temple. He selected priests without blemish, devoted to
43 the law, and they purified the temple,

i in order . . . before: *probable meaning; Gk. obscure.*

---

lowlands: *Gazara* (Gezer), *Azotus* (Ashdod), and *Jamnia* (Jabneh). **23:** The *gold and silver* of the slave traders now fell to their intended victims (2 Macc.8.25). **24:** See the refrain of Ps.136. **26:** The survivors included Nicanor (2 Macc.8.34–36).

4.28–35: Judas defeats Lysias at Bethsura. See 2 Macc.11.1–12. **28–29:** *In the following year,* 164 B.C., Lysias besieged *Bethsura* (Beth-zur), which was friendly toward Judas (2 Macc.11.6–7). **30:** Judas encouraged his men by recalling how, against all odds, David overcame Goliath (1 Sam. ch. 17) and Jonathan slew the Philistine outpost (1 Sam. ch. 14). **35:** 2 Macc.11.13–15 notes that Lysias came to terms with the Jews some time after his devastating defeat in this battle.

4.36–61: The purification and dedication of the Temple. See 2 Macc.10.1–8. The death of Antiochus IV Epiphanes (6.1–16), and the accession of his son Antiochus V Eupator (6.17) preceded the Temple's purification (4.36–51) and dedication (4.52–59) in December 164 B.C. (2 Macc.9.1–29). 10.10–11 retains the correct historical sequence. **41:** *The citadel:* see 1.33–34 n. **42:** For earlier purifications of the Temple see 2 Kgs. 23.4–25; 2 Chr. ch. 29. **43:** *The stones which defiled* the Temple, those of the altar to Zeus Olympios (1.54,59), were taken *to an unclean*

44 removing to an unclean place the stones which defiled it. They discussed what to do with the altar of burnt-offering, 45 which was profaned, and rightly decided to demolish it, for fear it might become a standing reproach to them because it had been defiled by the Gentiles. They therefore pulled down 46 the altar, and stored away the stones in a fitting place on the temple hill, until a prophet should arise who could be 47 consulted about them. They took unhewn stones, as the law commands, and built a new altar on the model of 48 the previous one. They rebuilt the temple and restored its interior, and 49 consecrated the temple courts. They renewed the sacred vessels and the lamp-stand, and brought the altar of incense and the table into the temple. 50 They burnt incense on the altar and lit the lamps on the lamp-stand to shine 51 within the temple. When they had put the Bread of the Presence on the table and hung the curtains, all their work was completed.

52 Then, early on the twenty-fifth day of the ninth month, the month Kislev, 53 in the year 148,*j* sacrifice was offered as the law commands on the newly 54 made altar of burnt-offering. On the anniversary of the day when the Gentiles had profaned it, on that very day, it was rededicated, with hymns of thanksgiving, to the music of harps and 55 lutes and cymbals. All the people prostrated themselves, worshipping and praising Heaven that their cause had prospered.

56 They celebrated the rededication of the altar for eight days; there was great rejoicing as they brought burnt-offerings and sacrificed peace-offerings 57 and thank-offerings. They decorated the front of the temple with golden wreaths and ornamental shields. They renewed the gates and the priests' rooms, and fitted them with doors. There was great 58 merry-making among the people, and the disgrace brought on them by the Gentiles was removed.

59 Then Judas, his brothers, and the whole congregation of Israel decreed that the rededication of the altar should be observed with joy and gladness at the same season each year, for eight days, beginning on the twenty-fifth of Kislev.

60 At that time they encircled Mount Zion with high walls and strong towers to prevent the Gentiles from coming and trampling it down as they 61 had done before. Judas set a garrison there; he also fortified Bethsura, so that the people should have a fortress facing Idumaea.

5 WHEN THE GENTILES ROUND ABOUT heard that the altar had been rebuilt and the temple rededicated, they were 2 furious, and determined to wipe out all those of the race of Jacob who lived among them. Thus began the work of massacre and extermination among the people.

3 Judas then made war on the descendants of Esau in Idumaea and attacked Acrabattene, because they had hemmed Israel in. There he inflicted on them a

j That is 164 B.C.

---

place, i.e. a place for refuse (possibly the Kidron valley, see 2 Kgs.23.4,6,12). **44:** The *altar of burnt-offering* had been *profaned* by the altar to Zeus built upon it, but because it had been devoted to the worship of the Lord, the stones were sacred and could not be put to a secular use. **46:** Only a *prophet* could declare what should be done with *the stones*, but lack of a prophet is noted; see also 9.27; 14.41. **47:** The *law:* Exod.20.25; Deut.27.5–6. **53–54:** For the pertinent laws on *sacrifice*, see Exod.29.38–41; Num. 7.10–88. **56–59:** The Jewish feast which commemorates the Temple's *rededication* in December 164 B.C., takes its present name from the Heb. word "Hanukkah," meaning "dedication." **60–61:** Judas took precautions against further efforts of Lysias (v. 35).

5.1–68: Judas rescues his persecuted countrymen. The dedication of the Temple and the Jewish exemption from the edict of Antiochus (2 Macc.11.27–33) which followed Judas' victory over Lysias (1 Macc.4.28–35) aroused the envy and hostility of neighboring peoples. Soon after Antiochus' death, a series of anti-Jewish incidents led Judas to undertake reprisals and to rescue and relocate those Jews in danger. **1:** *The Gentiles round about* are those of Idumea (vv. 3–5; 2 Macc.10.14–23), Ammon (vv. 6–8; possibly 2 Macc.8.30–33), Gilead (vv. 9–13,24–54; 2 Macc. 12.10–31), Galilee (vv. 14–23), and the land of the Philistines (vv. 66–68; 2 Macc.12.3–9). **2:** The *race of Jacob* and similar archaic expressions in this chapter (e.g. *the descendants of Esau*, v. 3) are meant to evoke the memory of Israel's earlier conquest of the land, which the Jews still regarded as their own. **3:** The location of *Acrabattene* is unknown. **4:** *The Baeanites*

severe and humiliating defeat, and took
4 spoils from them. He remembered also
the wrong done by the Baeanites, who
with their traps and road-blocks were
5 continually ambushing the Israelites. He
first confined them to their forts and
took up positions against them; then
he solemnly committed them to destruction and set the forts ablaze with
6 all their occupants. He crossed over to
the Ammonites, and came upon a
strong and numerous force under the
7 command of a certain Timotheus. He
fought many battles with them, and they
broke before him and were crushed.
8 After capturing Jazer and its dependent
villages, he returned to Judaea.

9 Then the Gentiles in Gilead gathered
against the Israelites within their
territory, intending to destroy them;
but they took refuge in the fortress of
10 Dathema, and sent this letter to Judas
and his brothers:

The Gentiles round us have
11 gathered to wipe us out. They are
preparing to come and seize the
fortress where we have taken refuge;
Timotheus is in command of their
12 army. So come at once and rescue
us from their clutches, for many of
our number have already fallen.
13 All our fellow-Jews in the region of
Tubias have been massacred, their
wives and their children taken captive, and their property carried off.
About a thousand men there have
lost their lives.

14 While the letter was being read,
other messengers with their garments
15 torn arrived from Galilee. 'Ptolemais,
Tyre and Sidon,' they said, 'and all
heathen Galilee have mustered their
forces to make an end of us.'
16 When Judas and the people heard

this, a full assembly was called to
decide what they should do for their
fellow-countrymen in distress and
under enemy attack. Judas said to 17
Simon his brother, 'Choose your men,
and go and rescue your countrymen
in Galilee while I and my brother
Jonathan march into Gilead.' The rest 18
of his forces he left for the defences of
Judaea, with Josephus son of Zacharias,
and Azarias, leading citizens, and gave 19
them this order: 'Take charge of the
people of Jerusalem, but on no account
join battle with the Gentiles until we
return.' Simon was allotted three 20
thousand men for the march on Galilee,
and Judas eight thousand for the march
on Gilead.

Simon invaded Galilee and, after 21
many battles, broke the resistance of
the Gentiles. He pursued them as far as 22
the gate of Ptolemais, killed nearly
three thousand of them, and stripped
their corpses. He took back with him 23
the Jews from Galilee and Arbatta,
their wives and children, and all their
property, and brought them to Judaea
with great jubilation.

Meanwhile Judas Maccabaeus and 24
his brother Jonathan crossed the Jordan
and made a three days' march through
the desert. They came upon some 25
Nabataeans, who met them peacefully, and gave them an account of all
that had happened to their fellow-
Jews in Gilead: many of them were 26
held prisoner in Bozrah and Bezer, in
Alema, Casphor, Maked, and Carnaim
—all large fortified towns; some in the 27
other towns of Gilead. 'Your enemies',
they told them, 'are marshalling their
forces to storm your fortresses tomorrow so as to capture them and
destroy all the Jews in them in a single
day.'

Then Judas and his army suddenly 28

are difficult to identify; perhaps they were nomads and the mercenaries of 2 Macc.10.14.
6: *Ammonites:* people in the region near modern Amman, Jordan. **8:** Ancient *Jazer* was west
and slightly north of Amman. **9:** *Gilead*, the area immediately east of the Jordan and to the
north of the Jabbok river, extended north of the Yarmuk river in Hellenistic times. *Dathema:*
location unknown. **11–13:** The letter exaggerates. Not all the Jews in *the region of Tubias*, i.e.
Gilead, were massacred; see vv. 26–27. **14–15:** *Heathen Galilee:* the coastal region of Galilee,
as the cities named indicate. **22:** *Ptolemais* is modern Acre, a coastal town north of Haifa.
23: For their own protection against reprisals, the *Jews from Galilee and Arbatta* (i.e. Narbata,
the coastal region just south of Galilee) resettled in Judea. **25:** The *Nabataeans*, an Arab
people, grew rich as caravan traders. **26–36:** These towns were all located east of the Sea of
Galilee and just north of the Yarmuk river, but the precise location is not known in every

turned aside to Bozrah by way of the desert, captured the town, and put all the males to the sword. He plundered all their property and set fire to the 29 town. From there he made a night-march and came within reach of the 30 fortress of Dathema. When dawn broke they saw in front of them an innumerable host, bringing up scaling-ladders and siege-engines and engaging the defenders, to capture the fortress. 31 Judas saw that battle was already joined, and a cry went up to heaven from the town, with trumpeting and loud 32 shouting. Judas said to his men: 'Now is the time to fight for our brothers.'

33   They marched out in three columns to take the enemy in the rear. Then they sounded the trumpets and cried 34 aloud in prayer, and the army of Timotheus recognized that it was Maccabaeus and took to flight before him. He inflicted a severe defeat on them, and nearly eight thousand of the enemy fell that day.

35   Judas then turned aside to Alema,[k] attacked and captured it, and killed all the males. He plundered the town and 36 set it on fire. From there he moved on and occupied Casphor, Maked, Bezer, and the other towns of Gilead.

37   After these events, Timotheus gathered another army, and took up position opposite Raphon, on the other 38 side of the ravine. Judas sent spies to their camp, and they reported that all the Gentiles in the neighbourhood had rallied in very great strength to Timo-39 theus, who had also hired Arab mercenaries to help them; they were encamped on the far side of the ravine, ready to engage him in battle. So Judas marched to meet them.

40   As Judas and his army were approaching the flooded ravine, Timotheus said to his officers: 'If Judas crosses over to our side first, we shall not be able to stand up to him; he will certainly get the better of us. If, however, 41 his courage fails him and he takes up

a position on the other side of the river, then we will cross over and get the better of him.' When Judas reached the 42 ravine, he stationed the officers of the muster on its banks, with instructions that no one should be allowed to take up a fixed position, but that all should advance to battle. Thus Judas fore-43 stalled the enemy by crossing to attack them, with all his people following. The Gentiles broke before him; they all threw away their arms and took refuge in the temple at Carnaim. Judas 44 captured the town and burnt the temple together with all its occupants: Carnaim was completely subdued and could no longer withstand him.

Then Judas gathered together all 45 the Israelites in Gilead to escort them to Judaea. They amounted to an immense host, small and great, women and children, with their property. They 46 came as far as Ephron, a large and strongly fortified town on the road: it was impossible to pass by it on either side; the only route was through the town. But the townsmen kept them 47 out, barricading their gates with boulders. Judas sent them a conciliatory 48 message: 'We have to pass through your territory to reach our own. No one shall do you any harm: we shall only march through.' But they refused to open their gates to him.

Judas issued orders to the whole 49 host for everyone to halt where he was. Then the fighting men took up battle 50 positions and attacked the town all that day and all the night, until it fell into their hands. They put every male to the 51 sword, razed the town to the ground and plundered it, and then marched through it over the bodies of the dead. They crossed the Jordan to the great 52 plain opposite Bethshan, while Judas 53 brought up the stragglers and encouraged the people all along the road till he arrived in Judaea. They went up 54 to Mount Zion with gladness and

k Some witnesses read Maapha.

---

instance. **37:** *Raphon* lay on a northern tributary of the Yarmuk. **39:** Perhaps these *mercenaries* were the Arabs of 2 Macc.12.10–12. **42:** *The officers of the muster* were scribes, who could easily make notes of the laggards. **43:** The *temple* was that of Atargatis (the horned Astarte) *at Carnaim*, another city in the same region; see 2 Macc.12.26. **46:** *Ephron* lay to the south of the Yarmuk, close to the Jordan. **52:** *Bethshan* is the Scythopolis of 2 Macc.12.29–30, about four miles west of the Jordan and eighteen south of the Sea of Galilee. **54:** The victors arrived

jubilation, and offered burnt-offerings, because they had returned in safety without the loss of a single man.

55 Now while Judas and Jonathan were in Gilead, and Simon their brother in 56 Galilee was besieging Ptolemais, the two commanders, Josephus son of Zacharias, and Azarias, heard of their 57 exploits in battle. 'We too', they said, 'must make a name for ourselves: let us go and fight the Gentiles in our neigh- 58 bourhood.' So they gave orders to their forces and marched against Jamnia. 59 Gorgias came out of the town with his 60 men to meet them in battle; and Josephus and Azarias were routed and pursued to the frontier of Judaea. Some two thousand of the people fell that 61 day. So the Israelites suffered a heavy defeat, because their commanders, thinking to play the hero themselves, had not obeyed Judas and his brothers. 62 They were not, however, of that family to whom it was granted to bring deliverance to Israel.

63 Judas and his brothers won a great reputation in all Israel and among the Gentiles, wherever their fame was 64 heard, and crowds flocked to acclaim them.

65 After this, Judas marched out with his brothers and made war on the descendants of Esau to the south. He struck at Hebron and its villages, de- molished its fortifications, and burnt 66 down its forts on all sides. He then set out to invade Philistine territory, march- 67 ing through Marisa. On that day several priests, who had ill-advisedly gone into action wishing to distinguish them- 68 selves, fell in battle. Then Judas turned aside to Azotus in Philistia. He pulled down their altars, burnt the images of their gods, carried off the spoil from their towns, and returned to Judaea.

As King Antiochus marched through 6 the upper provinces he heard that there was a city in Persia called Elymais, famous for its wealth in silver and gold. Its temple was very rich, full of 2 gold shields, coats of mail, and arms, left there by Alexander son of Philip, king of Macedon and the first to be king over the Greeks. Antiochus came 3 and tried to capture and plunder the city, but failed because his plan had become known to the citizens. They 4 gave battle and put him to flight, and he withdrew to Babylon in bitter disappointment.

A messenger met him in Persia with 5 the news that the armies which had invaded Judaea were in full retreat. Lysias had marched up with an 6 exceptionally strong force, only to be flung back before the enemy, and the strength of the Jews had grown by the capture of arms, equipment, and spoils from the Syrian armies they had defeated. They had pulled down the 7 abomination he had built on the altar in Jerusalem, and surrounded their temple with high walls as before, and had even fortified Bethsura.

When the king heard this news, 8 he was thrown into such deep dismay that he took to his bed, ill with grief at the miscarriage of his plans. There 9 he lay for many days, his bitter grief breaking out again and again, and he realized that he was dying. So he 10 summoned all his Friends and said to them: 'Sleep has deserted me; the weight of care has broken my heart. At first I said to myself, "Why am I 11 overwhelmed by this flood of trouble, I who was kind and well-loved in the day of my power?" But now I re- 12 member the wrong I did in Jerusalem, when I took all her vessels of silver and gold, and when I made an unjustified

---

in time to celebrate the Feast of Weeks (Pentecost); 2 Macc.12.31. **55–64:** The punitive raids of 2 Macc.12.3–9 preceded this incident. The defeat is here attributed to disobedience of orders, but 2 Macc.12.40 notes a different reason for the casualties. **62:** The *family* is that of Mattathias and his sons. **65:** The *descendants of Esau:* Edomites. *Hebron* is twenty miles south of Jerusalem. **66:** *Marisa* lay west of Hebron. **67:** See vv. 55–64.
   6.1–17: The death of Antiochus IV. See 2 Macc.9.1–29. The author continues the story begun in 3.37. **1:** The *upper provinces* were in Mesopotamia and the Iranian plateau. *Elymais* is not a city but the country Elam, the area around Susa, particularly north and east of that city. **2:** Possibly the *temple* was that of Nanaea at Susa (see 2 Macc.1.13). *Alexander:* the Great. **5–7:** Antiochus died after Lysias' defeat but before Judas purified the Temple. The author merely summarizes 4.28–61 here. **10:** *Friends:* see 2.18 n. **12–13:** Obviously, these are the

13 attempt to wipe out the inhabitants of Judaea. It is for this, I know, that these misfortunes have come upon me; and here I am, dying of grief in a foreign land.'

14 He summoned Philip, one of his Friends, and appointed him regent

15 over his whole empire, giving him the crown, the royal robe, and the signet-ring, with authority to take his son Antiochus and bring him up to be king.

16 King Antiochus died there in the year 149.[l]

17 When Lysias learnt that the king was dead, he placed the young Antiochus, whom he had brought up from boyhood, on the throne in succession to his father, and gave him the name of Eupator.

18 MEANWHILE THE GARRISON OF THE citadel were confining the Israelites to the neighbourhood of the temple, and giving continual support to the Gentiles

19 by their harassing tactics. Judas therefore determined to make an end of them. He gathered all the people together to

20 lay siege to the citadel in the year 150,[m] erecting emplacements and siege-engines against the enemy.

21 Now some of the besieged garrison escaped and were joined by a number

22 of renegade Israelites. They went to the king and said: 'How long must we wait for you to do justice and avenge

23 our comrades? We were willing to serve your father, to follow his instructions

24 and to obey his decrees, and what was the result? Our own countrymen became our enemies. They actually killed as many of us as they could find, and

25 robbed us of our property. Nor are we the only ones to suffer at their hands. They have attacked all their neigh-

26 bours as well. At this very moment they are besieging the citadel in Jeru-

salem and mean to capture it; and they have fortified both the temple and

27 Bethsura. Unless your majesty quickly overpowers them they will go to yet greater lengths, and you will not be able to keep them in check.'

28 When the king heard this he was furious. He assembled all his Friends, the commanders of his army, and his

29 cavalry officers. He was joined by mercenary troops from other kingdoms

30 and from the islands. His forces numbered one hundred thousand infantry, twenty thousand cavalry, and

31 thirty-two war-elephants. They passed through Idumaea and laid siege to Bethsura. They kept up the attack for a long time and erected siege-engines, but the defenders made a sortie and set fire to them, and fought back manfully.

32 Judas now withdrew from the citadel and encamped at Bethzacharia, oppo-

33 site the camp of the king. Early next morning the king broke camp and rushed his army along the road to Bethzacharia; there his forces were drawn up for battle and the trumpets

34 were sounded. The elephants were roused for battle with the juice of grapes

35 and of mulberries. The great beasts were distributed among the phalanxes; by each were stationed a thousand men, equipped with coats of chain-mail and bronze helmets. Five hundred picked horsemen were also assigned

36 to each animal. These had been stationed beforehand where the beast was; and wherever it went, they went with it,

37 never leaving it. Each animal had a strong wooden turret fastened on its back with a special harness, by way of protection, and carried four[n] fighting

38 men as well as an Indian driver. The rest of the cavalry Lysias stationed on

l That is 163 B.C.
m That is 162 B.C.
n Probable reading; Gk. thirty-two (compare verse 30).

---

sentiments of the author and not those of Antiochus. **14-15:** Earlier, Antiochus had entrusted his son to Lysias (3.33), who faithfully declared the young Antiochus V Eupator king (v. 17). Philip soon proved to be ambitious (vv. 55-56). **17:** *Eupator* means "of a good father."

6.18-63: Lysias' second Judean campaign. 18-27: To neutralize the citadel (1.33-34 n.), Judas besieged it. *King* Antiochus V Eupator (v. 21) was reminded of the garrison's loyalty to his *father*, Antiochus IV Epiphanes (v. 23), and of Judas' attacks on *all their neighbours* (v. 25; 5.1-68). Actually, Lysias, the regent, was in charge, since the king was then only ten years old (1.33 n.). **28-63:** See 2 Macc.13.1-26. **28:** *Friends:* see 2.18 n. **29:** These *mercenary troops* were Greek-speaking (2 Macc.13.2). **30:** The exaggerated numbers soften Judas' defeat. **31:** Because of his elephants and cavalry, Lysias kept to the coastal plain until he reached Bethsura, which Judas had garrisoned (4.61); then Lysias swung in from the south through Idumea. **34:** *Roused:*

either flank of the army, to harass the enemy while themselves protected by the

39 phalanxes. When the sun shone on the gold and bronze shields, they lit up the hills, which flashed like torches.

40 Part of the king's army was deployed over the heights, and part over the low ground. They advanced con-

41 fidently and in good order. All who heard the din of this marching multitude and its clashing arms shook with fear. It was a very great and powerful array indeed.

42 Judas advanced with his army and gave battle, and six hundred of the

43 king's men were killed. Eleazar Avaran, seeing that one of the elephants wore royal armour and stood out above all the rest, thought that the king was

44 riding on it. So he gave his life to save his people and win everlasting renown

45 for himself. He ran boldly towards it, into the middle of the phalanx, dealing death right and left, while they fell

46 back on either side before him. He got in underneath the elephant, and thrust at it from below and killed it. It fell to the ground on top of him, and there he died.

47 When the Jews saw the strength and impetus of the imperial forces, they fell

48 back before them. Part of the king's army marched up to Jerusalem to renew the engagement, and the king put Judaea and Mount Zion into a state of

49 siege. He made peace with the people of Bethsura, who abandoned the town, having no more food there to withstand a siege, as it was a sabbatical year when the land was left fallow.

50 Thus the king occupied Bethsura and detailed a garrison to hold it.

51 He then attacked the temple and subjected it to a long siege; he set up emplacements and siege-engines, with flame-throwers, catapults for discharging stones and barbed missiles,

52 and slings. But the defenders too constructed engines to counter his engines, and put up a prolonged resistance.

There was no food, however, in the 53 stores[o] because of the sabbatical year; those who from time to time had arrived in Judaea as refugees from the Gentiles had eaten up all that remained of the provisions. There were 54 only a few men left in the temple, because the famine had been too severe for them, and they had scattered to their own homes.

Lysias heard that Philip, whom 55 King Antiochus had appointed before he died to educate his son Antiochus for the kingship, had returned from 56 Persia and Media with the late king's expeditionary force, and that he was seeking to take over the government. So he hastily gave orders for depar- 57 ture, saying to the king, his commanders, and his troops: 'Every day we are growing weaker, provisions are low, the place we are besieging is strong, and the affairs of the empire are pressing. So let us offer these men 58 terms and make peace with them and their whole nation. Let us guarantee 59 their right to follow their laws and customs as they used to do, for it was our abolition of these very customs and laws that roused their resentment, and produced all these consequences.'

The proposal met with the approval 60 of the king and the commanders, and an offer of peace was sent and accepted. The king and his commanders bound 61 themselves by oath, and on the agreed terms the besieged emerged from their stronghold. But when the king en- 62 tered Mount Zion and saw how strongly the place was fortified, he went back on the oath he had sworn, and gave orders for the surrounding wall to be demolished. He then set off at 63 top speed for Antioch, where he found Philip in possession; a battle ensued, and the city was taken by storm.

IN THE YEAR 151,[p] DEMETRIUS SON OF 7 Seleucus left Rome, landed with a

o *Some witnesses read* in the temple.   p *That is* 161 B.C.

---

intoxicated. **43:** *Eleazar* was Judas' brother (2.5). **47:** On lower ground (v. 40), Judas' guerillas were no match for the superior armament and professionalism of the king's soldiers. **49:** On the *sabbatical year*, see Exod.23.10–11; Lev.25.3–7. **55:** *King Antiochus:* IV Epiphanes. **60:** *The king*, i.e. Lysias (see vv. 18–27 n.), granted religious but not civil liberty. 2 Macc.11.22–26,27–33 describe the peace terms. **63:** Josephus says Antiochus captured and killed *Philip* (*Ant.* XII.9.7).
   7.1–25: The expedition of Bacchides and Alcimus. 1: *Demetrius* I Soter (161–150 B.C.), whose

handful of men at a town on the coast, and there made himself king. 2 While he was travelling to the royal seat of his ancestors, the army seized Antiochus and Lysias, intending to 3 hand them over to him. When this was reported to him, he said, 'Do not let 4 me set eyes on them.' The soldiers accordingly put them to death, and Demetrius ascended the throne.

5 All the godless renegades from Israel, led by Alcimus, who aspired 6 to be high priest, came to the king and brought charges against their people. They said to him: 'Judas and his brothers have killed all your supporters, and have driven us from our country. 7 Be pleased now to send a man whom you trust, to go and see what devastation they have brought upon us and upon the king's territory, and to punish 8 them and all their supporters.' The king chose Bacchides, one of the royal Friends, who was governor beyond the Euphrates, a man of high standing in the empire and loyal to the 9 king. He sent him and the godless Alcimus, on whom he had conferred the high-priesthood, with orders to take vengeance on Israel.

10 They set out with a large army and entered Judaea. Bacchides sent envoys to Judas and his brothers to make 11 false offers of friendship; but when they saw what a large force he had brought with him, they took no notice of these offers.

12 A deputation of doctors of the law came before Alcimus and Bacchides, 13 asking for justice. The Hasidaeans were in fact the first group in Israel to 14 make overtures to them; for they said to themselves, 'A priest of the family of Aaron has come with their forces, and he will do us no harm.' The lan- 15 guage of Alcimus was conciliatory; he assured them on oath that no harm was intended to them or their friends. But once he had gained their con- 16 fidence, he arrested sixty of them and put them to death in a single day; as Scripture says:

'The bodies of thy saints were 17
    scattered,
their blood was shed round
    Jerusalem,
and there was none to bury them.'

This put all the people in fear and 18 terror of them, and they said to each other, 'There is neither truth nor justice among them; they have broken their pledge and the oath they swore.' Then Bacchides left Jerusalem and 19 camped in Bethzaith; and he ordered the arrest of many of those who had deserted to him, together with some of the people, and had them slaughtered and thrown into a great pit. He 20 assigned the whole district to Alcimus, detailed some troops to assist him, and returned to the king.

Alcimus fought hard for his high- 21 priesthood. All the trouble-makers 22 rallied to him; they gained control over Judaea, and did terrible damage in Israel. When Judas saw all the mis- 23 chief which Alcimus and his followers had brought upon the Israelites, far worse than anything the Gentiles had done, he marched through all the 24 territory of Judaea and its environs, punishing deserters and debarring

hopes to succeed his uncle Epiphanes (175–164 B.C.) were frustrated earlier when the Romans instead recognized the young Eupator (164–161 B.C.), escaped from Rome, where he had been held hostage, and moved to claim the kingdom once ruled by his father *Seleucus* IV (187–175 B.C.). The coastal *town* was Tripolis (2 Macc.14.1). **2:** As Demetrius marched on Antioch, his ancestral *seat*, the citizens there and the army switched allegiance to him. **5–7:** The Jewish historian Josephus says (*Ant.* XII.9.7) that *Alcimus* (also called Jakeimos) succeeded Menelaus (2 Macc.13.4–8) as high priest. Perhaps Judas was forced by his treaty with Lysias to accept the defiled Alcimus for a time (2 Macc.14.3). The change of government may have seemed to Judas the opportunity for driving out Alcimus. **8:** *Bacchides, one of the royal Friends* (see 2.18 n.), governed the area between the *Euphrates* and Egypt (Lysias had the same territory; 3.32). The king planned to go east—as Epiphanes had (3.27–37)—to subdue the eastern provinces. **12–13:** Some of Judas' *Hasidaeans* (2.42; 2 Macc.14.6) now left him, recognized Alcimus, and asked for *justice*, i.e. terms for reconciliation. **16–17:** See Ps.79.2–3. **19:** *Bethzaith* is about three and a half miles north of Bethsura. Bacchides thus fulfilled his commission (v. 9). **20–25:** Pushed from the cities by Alcimus' superior numbers, Judas denied him the countryside by guerrilla warfare.

25 them from access to the country districts. When Alcimus saw that Judas and his band had grown powerful, and recognized that he was unable to withstand them, he returned to the king and accused them of atrocities.

26 Then the king sent Nicanor, one of his distinguished commanders and a bitter enemy of Israel, with orders to

27 wipe them out. Nicanor arrived at Jerusalem with a large force, and sent envoys to Judas and his brothers to

28 make false offers of friendship: 'Let there be no quarrel between us,' he said; 'I propose to come with a few men for a friendly personal meeting.'

29 He came to Judas and they greeted one another as friends, yet the enemy were preparing to kidnap Judas.

30 When Judas discovered that Nicanor's visit was a trick, he took alarm and

31 refused to meet him again. Nicanor, realizing that his plan had been detected, marched out to engage Judas

32 near Capharsalama. About five hundred of Nicanor's army were killed, and the rest escaped to the city of David.

33 After these events, Nicanor went up to Mount Zion, and some of the priests and members of the senate came out from the temple to give him a friendly welcome, and to show him the burnt-offering which was being sacrificed for

34 the king. But he mocked them, jeered at them, and spat on them,*q* boasting

35 and swearing angrily: 'Unless Judas and his army are surrendered to me at once, when I return victorious I will burn down this house.' And he went off

36 in a rage. Thereupon the priests went in, and stood facing the altar and the

37 temple. They wept and said: 'Thou didst choose this house to bear thy name, to be a house of prayer and

38 supplication for thy people; take vengeance on this man and his army, and

make them fall by the sword. Remember all their blasphemy, and grant them no reprieve.'

39 Nicanor moved from Jerusalem and

40 encamped at Beth-horon, where he was joined by an army from Syria. Judas encamped at Adasa with three thousand

41 men; there he prayed in these words: 'There was a king whose followers blasphemed, and thy angel came forth and struck down one hundred and

42 eighty-five thousand of them. So do thou crush this army before us today, and let all men know that Nicanor has reviled thy holy place; judge him as his wickedness deserves.'

43 The armies joined battle on the thirteenth of the month Adar, and the army of Nicanor suffered a crushing defeat, he himself being the first to fall

44 in the battle. When his army saw that Nicanor had fallen, they threw away

45 their arms and took to flight. The Jews, sounding the signal trumpets in the enemy's rear, pursued them as far as Gazara, a day's journey from

46 Adasa. From all the villages of Judaea round about, the inhabitants came out and attacked their flanks, forcing them back upon their pursuers. They all fell by the sword; there were no sur-

47 vivors. The Jews seized spoil and booty; they cut off Nicanor's head and that right hand which he had stretched out so arrogantly, and brought them to

48 be displayed at Jerusalem. There was great public rejoicing and that day was

49 kept as a special day of jubilation. It was ordained that the day should be observed annually, on the thirteenth of

50 Adar. Thus Judaea entered upon a short period of peace.

8 Now JUDAS HAD HEARD ABOUT THE Romans: they were renowned for their

q Literally and polluted them.

7.26–50: **Nicanor's defeat.** See 2 Macc.14.11–15.37. **26:** *Nicanor* had ample reason (3.38–4.25) to be Israel's *bitter enemy*. Formerly in charge of the king's elephants, he was now made governor of Judea (2 Macc.14.12). **27–30:** 2 Macc.14.18–30 records a brief period of peace and friendship between *Judas* and *Nicanor* which is omitted here. **31:** *Capharsalama* is about seven miles from Jerusalem. **32:** *City of David:* Jerusalem. **33:** The sacrifice offered for the king was proof of basic loyalty to the empire. **34–38:** Contrast Nicanor's attitude with that expressed in Isa.56.6–8. **41:** Judas refers to the angelic slaughter (plague may be meant) of Sennacherib's army besieging Jerusalem (2 Kgs.19.35; 2 Macc.15.22). **43:** *Adar:* March, 160 B.C. **49:** The feast of Nicanor was dropped from the Jewish calendar after the destruction of the Temple in 70 A.D.

8.1–32: **Judas' treaty with the Romans.** Hoping to curb the Seleucids, Judas allied himself

military power and for the welcome they gave to those who became their allies; any who joined them could ² be sure of their firm friendship. He was told about the wars they had fought, and the valour they had shown in their conquest of the Gauls, whom they had ³ laid under tribute. He heard of their successes in Spain, where they had seized silver-mines and gold-mines, ⁴ maintaining their hold on the entire country—distant as it was from their own land—by their patience and good judgement. There were kings from far and near who had marched against them, but they had been beaten off after crushing defeats; others paid them annual tribute. ⁵ They had crushed in battle and conquered Philip, and Perseus king of Kittim, and all who had attacked them. ⁶ Antiochus the Great, king of Asia, had marched against them with one hundred and twenty elephants, with cavalry and chariots and an immense force, but they had totally defeated ⁷ him. They had taken the king alive, and had required that he and his successors should pay them a large ⁸ annual tribute, give hostages, and cede the territories of India, Media, and Lydia, together with some of their finest provinces. These they had taken from him and given to King Eumenes. ⁹ When the Greeks planned to attack ¹⁰ and destroy them, they heard of it and sent a single general against them. Battle was joined, and many of the Greeks fell; the Romans took their women and children prisoner, plundered their territory and annexed it, razed their fortifications, and made

them slaves, as they are to this day. The remaining kingdoms, the islands, ¹¹ and all who had ever opposed them, they destroyed or reduced to slavery. With their friends, however, and all ¹² who put themselves under their protection, they maintained firm friendship. They thus conquered kings near and far, and all who heard their fame went in fear of them. Those whom ¹³ they wished to help and to appoint as kings, became kings, and those they wished to depose, they deposed; and thus they rose to great heights of power. For all this, not one of them made any ¹⁴ personal claim to greatness by wearing the crown or donning the purple. They ¹⁵ had established a senate where three hundred and twenty senators met daily to deliberate, giving constant thought to the proper ordering of the affairs of the common people. They ¹⁶ entrusted their government and the ruling of all their territory to one of their number every year, all obeying this one man without envy or jealousy among themselves.

Judas accordingly chose Eupolemus ¹⁷ son of John son of Accos, and Jason son of Eleazar, and sent them to Rome to conclude a treaty of friendship and alliance, so that the Romans might rid ¹⁸ them of tyranny, for it was clear that the Greek empire was reducing Israel to slavery. They made the long journey ¹⁹ to Rome and entered the Senate, where they spoke as follows: 'Judas, known ²⁰ as Maccabaeus, his brothers, and the Jewish people have sent us to you to conclude a treaty of friendly alliance with you, so that we may be enrolled as your allies and friends.' The Romans ²¹

with the Romans, who seized the opportunity to befriend an enemy of Demetrius while extending their own influence. **2**: The Cisalpine *Gauls* were conquered very easily in the second century B.C. **5**: *Philip* V of Macedon (*Kittim*) was defeated in 197 B.C.; *Perseus*, Philip's son, was defeated in 168 B.C. **6–8**: *Antiochus* (III) *the Great, king of Asia*, i.e. the lands at the eastern end of the Mediterranean, lost to Lucius Scipio at Magnesia (now western Turkey) in 190 B.C. The author uses an exaggerated report; *Antiochus* had only fifty-four *elephants* and was not captured. Under the treaty of Apamea (188 B.C.), Antiochus and his successors had to pay tribute (see 2 Macc.8.10) and give hostages; see 1.10 n. **8**: Ionia (here by scribal error, *India*), Mysia (here, *Media*), and *Lydia*, territories in Asia Minor, were ceded to *Eumenes* II of Pergamum (in western Turkey), an ally of Rome at Magnesia. **9–10**: The Roman consul Lucius Mummius defeated the Achaean League of Greek city-states in 146 B.C. The author gets ahead of himself here; in 160 B.C., Judas would not have heard of this. **13**: Among the *kings* appointed by the Romans was Alexander Balas (10.1). **15–16**: It was three hundred (not *three hundred and twenty*) Roman senators, who did not meet *daily*, nor did they elect *one man*, but two consuls, who ruled jointly. While very pro-Roman in his report, the author has an imperfect knowledge of Rome's government. **17**: *John*, the father of *Eupolemus*, had earlier won concessions for the

22 found the proposal acceptable, and the following is a copy of the reply which they inscribed on tablets of bronze and sent to Jerusalem, so that the Jews there might have a record of the treaty of alliance:

23 Success to the Romans and the Jewish nation by sea and land for ever! May sword and foe be far
24 from them! But if war breaks out first against Rome or any of her allies throughout her dominion,
25 then the Jewish nation shall support them whole-heartedly as occasion
26 may require. To the enemies of Rome or of her allies the Jews shall neither give nor supply provisions, arms, money, or ships; so Rome has decided; and they shall observe their commitments, without compensation.
27 Similarly, if war breaks out first against the Jewish nation, then the Romans shall give them hearty support as occasion may require.
28 To their enemies there shall be given neither provisions, arms, money, nor ships; so Rome has decided. These commitments shall be kept without breach of faith.
29 These are the terms of the agreement which the Romans have made
30 with the Jewish people. But if, hereafter, both parties shall agree to add or to rescind anything, then they shall do as they decide; any such addition or rescindment shall be valid.

31 To this the Romans added: As for the misdeeds which King Demetrius is perpetrating against the Jews, we have written to him as follows: 'Why have you oppressed our friends and allies
32 the Jews so harshly? If they make any further complaint against you, then we will see that justice is done them, and will make war upon you by sea and by land.'

When Demetrius heard that Nicanor 9 and his forces had fallen in battle, he sent Bacchides and Alcimus a second time into Judaea, with the right wing of his army. They marched along the 2 Gilgal road, laid siege to Messaloth in Arbela, and captured it, inflicting heavy loss of life.

In the first month of the year 152,[r] 3 they moved camp to Jerusalem. From 4 there they marched to Berea with twenty thousand infantry and two thousand cavalry. Now Judas was in 5 camp at Alasa, with three thousand picked men. But when they saw the size 6 of the enemy forces, their courage failed, and many deserted, leaving a mere eight hundred men in the field.

When Judas saw that with the 7 campaign going against him his army had melted away, his heart sank, for there was no time to rally them. Though much discouraged, he said to 8 those who were left, 'Let us move to the attack and see if we can defeat them.' But his men tried to dissuade 9 him: 'Impossible!' they said. 'No; let us save our lives now and come back later with our comrades to fight them. Now we are too few.' But Judas replied: 10 'Heaven forbid that I should do such a thing as run away! If our time is come, let us die bravely for our fellow-countrymen, and leave no stain on our honour.'

The Syrian army left its camp and 11 took up position to meet the Jews. The cavalry[s] was divided into two detachments; the slingers and the archers went ahead of the main force, and the picked troops were in the front line. Bacchides was on the right. 12 The phalanx came on in two divisions with trumpets sounding; Judas's men 13 also sounded their trumpets. The earth shook at the din of the armies as

r That is 160 B.C.
s The Syrian army . . . cavalry: *or* The Jewish army left its camp and stood to meet the enemy. The Syrian cavalry . . .

Jews from Antiochus III (2 Macc.4.11). **22:** Josephus says that the *tablets of bronze* were kept in Rome's capitol (*Ant.* XII.10.6); a copy was sent in a letter to Judas. **23–30:** The treaty follows the standard Roman form for a treaty between equals. **31:** This addition came separately; it is not part of the treaty.

9.1–22: The defeat and death of Judas. 1: As before (7.8–10), the king sent an army too large for Judas to defeat in open battle. **2:** *Messaloth in Arbela:* about three miles west of Lake Gennesaret. **4–5:** *Berea* is located ten miles north of Jerusalem; *Alasa* is less than a mile away.

battle was joined, and they fought from dawn until evening.

14 When Judas saw that Bacchides and the main strength of his army was on the right flank, all his stout-hearted 15 men rallied to him, and they broke the Syrian right; then he pursued them as 16 far as Mount Azotus. When the Syrians on the left wing saw that their right had been broken, they turned about and followed on the heels of Judas and his men, attacking them in the 17 rear. The fighting became very heavy, 18 and many fell on both sides. Judas himself fell, and the rest of the Jews 19 took to flight. Jonathan and Simon carried off Judas their brother; they buried him in the family tomb at 20 Modin, and wept over him. Great was the grief in Israel, and they mourned for many days, saying,

21   'How is our champion fallen,
     the saviour of Israel!'

22 The rest of the history of Judas, his wars, exploits, and achievements— all these were so numerous that they have not been written down.

23 AFTER THE DEATH OF JUDAS THE renegades raised their heads in every part of Israel, and all the evil-doers 24 reappeared. In those days a terrible famine broke out, and the country went 25 over to their side. Bacchides chose apostates to be in control of the country. 26 These men set inquiries on foot, and tracked down the friends of Judas and brought them before Bacchides, who

took vengeance on them, loading them with indignities. It was a time of 27 great affliction for Israel, worse than any since the day when prophets ceased to appear among them. Then all the 28 friends of Judas assembled and said to Jonathan: 'Since your brother Judas 29 died, there has not been a man like him to take the lead against our enemies, Bacchides and those of our own nation who are hostile to us. Today, 30 therefore, we choose you to succeed him as our ruler and leader and to fight our battles.' So Jonathan took over the 31 leadership at that time in place of his brother Judas.

The news reached Bacchides, and he 32 set himself to kill Jonathan. When 33 Jonathan and his brother Simon and all their men learnt of this, they took refuge in the desert of Tekoa, en- camping by the pool of Asphar. Bac- 34 chides discovered this on the sabbath, and crossed the Jordan with his whole army. So Jonathan sent his brother 35 John to take the camp followers and appeal to his friends the Nabataeans to look after their baggage train, which was of some size. But the Jambrites 36 appeared from Medaba and kidnapped John; they seized the baggage and made off with it. Some time afterwards, news 37 was brought to Jonathan and his brother Simon that the Jambrites were celebrating an important wedding, and bringing the bride, the daughter of one of the great nobles of Canaan, from Nadabath with a large retinue. Remembering how their brother John 38 had been killed, Jonathan and his men

---

15: *Mount Azotus* is a scribal error for Mount Hazor, some six miles from Berea; see 2 Sam.13.23; Neh.11.33. **19:** Later, Simon turned *the family tomb at Modin* into a monument; see 13.25–30. **22:** This verse echoes the stock phrase used of the kings (1 Kgs.11.41).

9.23–73: Jonathan continues the struggle. Jonathan improves the Jewish position through political and military activity and fortifies Judea.

9.23–31: Jonathan replaces Judas. Passing over Simon, the elder brother, for reasons un- known to us, the Jews chose Jonathan to lead them. **24:** Since the king's men controlled food supplies, the *famine* brought about desertions to their side. **27:** Malachi is the last of the uni- versally recognized *prophets* in the Bible (about 500–450 B.C.), but scholars discern the presence of later prophetic material in other books, as in Zech. chs. 9–14, which speak of the Greeks and describe conditions during the Greek period of the fourth and third centuries B.C. The author also notes the lack of a prophet in 4.46; 14.41.

9.32–49: Jonathan escapes Bacchides. 33: The mountainous and deserted region about *Tekoa* enabled Jonathan to evade pursuit and to assemble his forces. **34:** This verse is a mis- placed repetition of the substance of v. 43. **35:** *Nabataeans:* see 5.25 n. **36:** The *Jambrites*, probably an Arab tribe, were based at *Medaba*, a city some fifteen miles southeast of the Jordan's entrance into the Dead Sea. They not only *kidnapped John*, they killed him (vv. 38,42). **37:** The Greek translator misread the original Heb. *kenaani*, "trader," as the ancient name for the Holy Land, Canaan. This was a great merchant's daughter. *Nadabath* (= Nabatha =

set out and hid themselves under cover of a hill. They looked out and there they saw the bridegroom, in the middle of a bustling crowd and a train of baggage, coming to meet the bridal party, escorted by his friends and kinsmen fully armed, to the sound of drums and instruments of music. 40 Emerging from ambush, Jonathan attacked and cut them down; many fell, while others made off into the hills and the Jews took all their goods as 41 spoil. So the wedding was turned into mourning, and the sound of music to 42 lamentation. The blood of their brother was fully avenged, and Jonathan returned to the marshes of Jordan.

43 Bacchides heard this and came to the banks of Jordan on the sabbath 44 with a powerful force. Jonathan said to his men: 'Now is the time to fight for our lives; we are today in worse 45 plight than ever: the enemy in front, the water of Jordan behind, to right and left marsh and thicket; there is 46 no escape. Cry to Heaven to save you 47 from the hands of the enemy.' Battle was joined, and Jonathan had raised his hand to strike down Bacchides, when he fell back and evaded him. 48 Then Jonathan and his men leapt into the Jordan and swam over to the other side; but the enemy did not cross the 49 river in pursuit. The army of Bacchides lost about a thousand men that day.

50 Bacchides returned to Jerusalem and fortified with high walls, gates, and bars a number of places in Judaea: the fortress at Jericho, Emmaus and Beth-horon, Bethel, Timnath-phara-51 thon, and Tephon; in all of these he placed garrisons to harass Israel. He 52 fortified the towns of Bethsura and Gazara and the citadel, placing forces and stores of provisions there. He took 53 the sons of the leading men of the country as hostages and put them under guard in the citadel at Jerusalem.

In the second month of the year 54 153,[t] Alcimus gave orders for the wall of the inner court of the temple to be demolished, thereby destroying the work of the prophets. But at the 55 moment when he began demolition, Alcimus had a stroke, which put a stop to his activities. Paralysed and with his speech impaired, he could not utter a word or give final instructions about his property. Thus he died in 56 great torment. On learning that Al-57 cimus was dead, Bacchides returned to the king, and for two years Judaea had peace.

Then the renegades put their heads 58 together: 'Look!' they said, 'Jonathan and his people are living in peace and security. Let us bring Bacchides here; he will capture them all in a single night.' They went and conferred with 59 Bacchides, and he set out with a large 60 force, sending letters secretly to all his supporters in Judaea, with instructions to seize Jonathan and his men. But they were unable to do so, because their plan leaked out. About 61 fifty of the ringleaders of this villainy in Judaea were seized and put to death. Jonathan, Simon, and their men then 62 made their way out to Bethbasi in the desert, built up its ruined fortifications, and strengthened it. When Bacchides 63

t That is 159 B.C.

Nebo) was a little town on Mount Nebo not far from Medaba. **42:** *Blood* vengeance was considered a duty by ancient Semitic peoples. In desert regions, it was a deterrent to the type of crime committed against John. **43:** *Bacchides* thought ambush *on the sabbath* would add to the surprise. **44–48:** When the trap was sprung, in one of the many loops of the Jordan where it enters the Dead Sea, Jonathan had to abandon his spoils and save his men. Bacchides blocked his way; Jambrites probably pursued. Fighting his way through, Jonathan crossed to the west bank and the safety of his camp. Bacchides did not follow, perhaps pausing to pick up the spoils. **49:** A *thousand* casualties, the report of the partisan, seems exaggerated.

9.50–53: Bacchides fortifies Judea. Bacchides assured Seleucid control of Judea by fortifying strategic sites. *Timnath-pharathon, and Tephon* were in Samaria and governed the northern approaches to Judea. The *hostages* guaranteed the cooperation of their fathers.

9.54–57: Alcimus dies. The author views the death of *Alcimus* as punishment for his ordering the destruction of the *wall* separating the *inner court*, to which the Israelites had access, from the outer court, where Gentiles were permitted. **54:** The *prophets* whose work Alcimus destroyed were Haggai and Zechariah, who had brought about reconstruction of the Temple (520–516 B.C.), after the Babylonian Exile. **57:** *Judaea had peace*, because Bacchides had effectively curbed Jewish resistance for a time.

9.58–73: Jonathan escapes and defeats Bacchides. 62: *Bethbasi* lay between Bethlehem and

learnt of this, he gathered together all his army and sent word to those in
64 Judaea. He came and took up position against Bethbasi, and attacked it for a
65 long time, erecting siege-engines. Jonathan left his brother Simon in the town and slipped out into the country
66 with a few men. He attacked Odomera and his people and the Phasirites in
67 their encampment; he began to get the better of them and to advance towards Bethbasi with his forces.

Simon and his men made a sally out of the town and set fire to the siege-
68 engines. They fought Bacchides and defeated him. They kept up heavy pressure upon him, and so his plan and his expedition proved fruitless.
69 There was great anger against the renegades at whose instance he had invaded the land, and many of them were put to death. Bacchides then decided to return to his own country.
70 When Jonathan learnt of this, he sent envoys to Bacchides to arrange terms of peace with him and a return of the
71 Jewish prisoners. Bacchides agreed and did as Jonathan proposed, swearing to do him no harm for the rest of his
72 life. He sent him back the prisoners he had taken previously from Judaea, and returned to his own country; never
73 again did he enter their territory. So the war came to an end in Israel. Jonathan took up residence in Michmash and began to govern the people, rooting the godless out of Israel.

Jonathan rules the nation

10 IN THE YEAR 160,[u] ALEXANDER EPIPHanes son of Antiochus came and took possession of Ptolemais, where he was welcomed and proclaimed king. When 2
King Demetrius heard of this, he raised a huge army and marched out to meet him in battle. At the same 3
time Demetrius sent Jonathan a letter in friendly and flattering terms; for he 4
said to himself, 'Let us forestall Alexander by making peace with the Jews before Jonathan comes to terms with him against us, for he will remember all 5
the harm we have done him by our treatment of his brothers and of his nation.' He gave Jonathan authority to 6
collect and equip an army, conferred on him the title of ally, and ordered the hostages in the citadel to be handed over to him. Jonathan came to Jeru- 7
salem and read the letter aloud before all the people and the garrison of the citadel, who were filled with appre- 8
hension when they heard that the king had given Jonathan authority to raise an army. They surrendered the hos- 9
tages to him, and he restored them to their parents.

Jonathan took up his quarters in 10
Jerusalem and began to repair and rebuild the city. He gave orders to 11
those engaged on the work to build the walls and surround Mount Zion with a fortification of squared stones, and this was done. The foreigners in the 12
strongholds which Bacchides had built made their escape, each man leaving his 13
post and returning to his own country; however, in Bethsura there were still 14
left some of those who had abandoned the law and ordinances, and had found asylum there.

King Alexander heard of the prom- 15
ises which Demetrius had sent to

u *That is* 152 B.C.

Tekoa, about three miles north and slightly east of the latter. **66:** *Odomera* and *the Phasirites* were presumably allies of Bacchides whom Jonathan surprised at night before they could join the siege at Bethbasi. **68–69:** Conditions elsewhere in the empire must have brought about the recall of Bacchides and forced him to make a treaty with the unruly Jonathan. See, similarly, 6.55–61. **70:** The *return of the Jewish prisoners* did not include the hostages in the citadel (9.53; 10.6). **73:** From *Michmash*, eight miles northeast of Jerusalem, the emboldened Jonathan continued the purge of his enemies.

10.1–12.53: Jonathan is appointed high priest and wields both political and religious authority. Demetrius makes overtures.

10.1–21: Jonathan is courted by rival kings. 1: *Alexander* Balas (150–145 B.C.) also called *Epiphanes* (because he claimed Antiochus IV was his father) *took possession of Ptolemais* by treason, according to Josephus (*Ant.* XIII.2.1). **2:** Alexander lost this first battle. **6–14:** Jonathan took full advantage of Demetrius' situation and promises, even though he was going over to Alexander. **9:** *The hostages:* see 9.50–53 n. **10:** *Rebuild the city:* see 1.31; 4.60. **12:** *The foreigners* may have gone to help Demetrius. **14:** *Bethsura*, Gazara (11.41; 13.43) and the citadel at

Jonathan, and was told of the battles and heroic deeds of Jonathan and his brothers, and the hardships they had 16 endured. 'Where shall we ever find another man like this?' he exclaimed. 'Let us make him our friend and 17 ally.' He therefore wrote a letter to Jonathan to this effect:

18   King Alexander to his brother Jonathan, greeting.

19   We have heard about you, what a valiant man you are and how fit 20 to be our friend. Now therefore we do appoint you this day to be High Priest of your nation with the title of King's Friend, to support our cause and to keep friendship with us.

He sent him a purple robe and a gold crown.

21   Jonathan assumed the vestments of the high priest in the seventh month of the year 160[v] at the Feast of Tabernacles, and he gathered an army together and prepared a large supply of arms.

22   When this news reached Deme-
23 trius he was mortified. 'How did we come to let Alexander forestall us', he asked, 'in gaining the friendship and 24 support of the Jews? I too will send them cordial messages and offer honours and gifts to keep them on my 25 side.' So he sent a message to the Jews to this effect:

    King Demetrius to the Jewish nation, greeting.

26   We have heard with great pleasure that you have kept your agreements and remained in friendship with us and have not gone over to our 27 enemies. Continue, then, to keep faith with us, and we shall reward you well for all that you do in our cause, 28 both by granting you numerous

exemptions and making you gifts.

29   I hereby release and exempt you and all Jews whatsoever from tribute, from the tax on salt, and from the 30 crown-money. From today and hereafter I release you from the one-third of the grain-harvest and the half of the fruit-harvest due to me. From today and for all time, I will no longer exact them from Judaea or from the three administrative districts, formerly part of Samaria and Galilee, which I now attach to 31 Judaea. Jerusalem and its environs, with its tithes and tolls, shall be sacred and tax free. I also surrender 32 authority over the citadel in Jerusalem and grant the High Priest the right to garrison it with men of his own choice. All Jewish prisoners of 33 war taken from Judaea into any part of my kingdom, I set at liberty without ransom. No man shall exact any levy whatsoever on the cattle of the Jews. All their festivals, 34 sabbaths, new moons, and appointed days, and three days preceding and following each festival, shall be days of exemption and release for all the Jews in my kingdom; no one 35 shall have authority to impose any exaction or burden on a Jew in any respect.

36   Jews shall be enlisted in the forces of the King to the number of thirty thousand men; they shall receive the usual army pay. Some of 37 them shall be stationed in the great royal fortresses, others put in positions of trust in the kingdom. Their commanders and officers shall be of their own race, and they shall follow their own customs, just as the King has ordered for Judaea.

38   The three districts added to Judaea from the territory of Samaria shall be attached to Judaea so as to be

v That is 152 B.C.

Jerusalem (*Ant.* XIII.21.1) received the renegade Jews. **20:** Jonathan already belonged to a priestly family (2.1). The *purple robe* and *gold crown* symbolized the high priesthood. The purple robe also identified Jonathan as a *King's Friend* (see 2.18 n.). **21:** For the *Feast of Tabernacles*, see Lev.23.33–36. By officiating, Jonathan implicitly declared himself for Alexander.
    10.22–50: Demetrius appeals to the Jewish nation as a whole. 30: *The three . . . districts* (11.34) are Apherema (= Ephraim; Jn.11.54), Lydda, and Ramathaim (= Aramathea, Mk.15.43). **31:** Being *sacred*, Jerusalem could pay its taxes to God (via the Temple) instead of to the king. **32:** Demetrius recognized the status of *High Priest* conferred on Jonathan by Alexander! **36:** Jewish soldiers would be paid as *usual*, but at the king's expense and not, as

under one authority, and subject to the High Priest alone.

39 Ptolemais and the lands belonging to it I make over to the temple in Jerusalem, to meet the expenses proper to it. 40 I give fifteen thousand silver shekels annually, charged on my own royal accounts, to be drawn from such places as may prove convenient. 41 And the arrears of the subsidy, in so far as it has not been paid by the revenue officials, as it formerly was, shall henceforth be paid in for the needs of the temple. 42 In addition, the five thousand silver shekels which used to be taken from the annual income of the temple are also released, because they belong to the ministering priests. 43 Whoever shall take sanctuary in the temple of Jerusalem, or in any part of its precincts, because of a debt to the crown or any other debt, shall be free from distraint on his person or on his property within my kingdom. 44 The cost of the rebuilding and repair of the temple shall be borne by the royal revenue; 45 also the repair of the walls of Jerusalem and its surrounding fortification, as well as of the fortresses in Judaea, shall be at the expense of the royal revenue.

46 When Jonathan and the people heard these proposals, they did not believe or accept them, for they recalled the terrible calamity the king had brought upon Israel, and his harsh 47 oppression. They favoured Alexander, because it was he who had been the initiator of peaceful overtures; so they remained his allies to the end. 48 King Alexander mustered powerful forces and took up position against 49 Demetrius, and the two kings joined battle. The army of Alexander took to flight, and Demetrius pursued him and 50 got the better of them. He fought hard till sunset, but on that day Demetrius fell.

51 Thereupon Alexander sent ambassadors to Ptolemy king of Egypt, with a message to this effect: 'I have 52 returned to my kingdom and sit on the throne of my ancestors. I have assumed the government, defeated Demetrius, and made myself master of our country; 53 for I gave him battle, and he and his army were crushed by us, and we sit on the throne of his kingdom. 54 Let us now form an alliance; make me your son-in-law by giving me your daughter in marriage, and I will give presents to you and her worthy of your royal state.'

55 King Ptolemy replied: 'It was a happy day when you returned to the land of your ancestors and ascended the throne of their realm. 56 I will now do as you ask; only come to Ptolemais so that we may meet, and I will become your father-in-law as you propose.'

57 In the year 162,[w] Ptolemy set out from Egypt, with his daughter Cleopatra, and arrived at Ptolemais, where 58 King Alexander met him, and Ptolemy gave him his daughter in marriage. The wedding was celebrated in royal style, with great pomp.

59 King Alexander wrote to Jonathan to come and meet him. 60 Jonathan went in state to Ptolemais, where he met the two kings; he gave them silver and gold, and also made many gifts to their Friends; and so he won their favour.

61 There were some scoundrelly Jewish renegades who conspired to lodge complaints against Jonathan. The king, however, paid no attention to them, 62 but gave orders for Jonathan to be divested of the garment he wore and robed in purple, and this was done. 63 The king made him sit at his side, and told his officers to go with Jonathan into the centre of the city and proclaim that no one should bring any complaint against him or make trouble for him for any reason whatsoever. 64 When this proclamation was made and those who planned to lodge complaints saw Jonathan's splendour, and the purple robe he wore, they all made off. 65 Thus the king honoured him, enrolling him in the first class of the order of King's

[w] *That is* 150 B.C.

was customary, at Judea's. **39:** Demetrius gave away *Ptolemais*, which Alexander held (10.1).
    10.51–66: Jonathan at Alexander's wedding. Alexander married Cleopatra Thea, daughter of Ptolemy VI Philometor (180–145 B.C.). **65:** *First ... King's Friends:* see 2.18 n. *Governor:* presumably of Judea.

Friends, and making him a general and
66 a provincial governor. Jonathan returned to Jerusalem well pleased with
his success.

67 IN THE YEAR 165,ˣ DEMETRIUS, THE SON
of King Demetrius, arrived in the land
68 of his fathers from Crete. King Alexander was greatly upset by this news,
69 and returned to Antioch. Demetrius
appointed as his commander Apollonius the governor of Coele-syria, who
raised a powerful force and encamped
at Jamnia. From there he sent this
message to Jonathan the high priest:
70 'You are all alone in resisting us, and
you are making me look ridiculous
and absurd. Why do you defy us up
71 there in the hills? If you have confidence in your forces, come down to
meet us on the plain, and let us try
conclusions with each other there, for
I have the power of cities behind me.
72 Make inquiries; find out who I am and
who are our allies; you will be told that
you cannot stand your ground against
us, for your predecessors have twice
73 been routed in their own territory, and
now you will not be able to resist my
cavalry, and such a force as mine, on
the plain, where there is not so much as
a stone or a pebble to give you cover,
or any place to which you can escape.'
74 Jonathan was provoked by this
message from Apollonius. He took
ten thousand men and marched out
from Jerusalem, and was joined by his
brother Simon with reinforcements.
75 He laid siege to Joppa, whose gates the
citizens had closed against him because
76 Apollonius had a garrison there. But
when fighting started, the citizens took
fright and opened the gates; thus Jon-
77 athan became master of Joppa. When
Apollonius heard of it he took three
thousand cavalry and a large force of
infantry, and marched to Azotus as if to
pass through it, but at the same time,

relying on his numerous cavalry, he
advanced into the plain. Jonathan went 78
in pursuit as far as Azotus, where the
armies joined battle. But Apollonius 79
had left a thousand cavalry in hiding in
their rear, and Jonathan discovered 80
that there was an ambush behind him.
The enemy surrounded his army,
showering arrows on our people from
dawn till dusk. But they stood fast as 81
Jonathan had ordered them, and the
enemy cavalry grew weary. At that point 82
Simon led out his troops and joined
battle with the enemy phalanx, now that
the cavalry was exhausted. They were
routed by him and took to flight.

The horsemen scattered across the 83
plain and took refuge in Azotus, where
they sought asylum in the temple of
Dagon their idol. But Jonathan set fire 84
to Azotus and its surrounding villages,
and plundered them; the temple of
Dagon, and those who had taken refuge
there, he destroyed with fire. The 85
numbers of those who fell by the sword,
together with those who lost their
lives in the fire, reached eight thousand.
Jonathan marched away from Azotus, 86
and encamped at Ascalon, where the
citizens came out to meet him with
great pomp. Then he and his men re- 87
turned to Jerusalem loaded with spoil.

When King Alexander heard of all 88
this, he did Jonathan still greater
honour, sending him the gold clasp 89
which it is the custom to give to the
King's Kinsmen. He also presented
him with Accaron and all its districts.

The king of Egypt collected a huge 11
army, countless as the sand on the
sea-shore, and a great fleet of ships,
meaning to make himself master of
Alexander's kingdom by treachery and
add it to his own. He set out for Syria 2
with professions of peace, and the
people of the towns proceeded to open
their gates to him and went to meet

ˣ *That is* 147 B.C.

10.67–89: Jonathan defeats Apollonius. *Demetrius* II (145–139 and 129–125 B.C.), son of
Demetrius I (161–150 B.C.), arrived in Cilicia to claim the Seleucid throne. **69:** This *Apollonius*
had helped Demetrius I to escape from Rome. **71–73:** On the plains, the Jews often proved to
be no match for the superior armaments—chariots, cavalry, elephants—of their enemies.
74–76: Jonathan's capture of *Joppa* cut Apollonius' line of communications. **77–87:** Pretending
to retreat even further southward, Apollonius lured Jonathan into the plain. Trapped, Jonathan
won anyway, with the help of Simon's fresh reserves. **89:** *The gold clasp* signifying Jonathan's
new promotion fastened the recipient's purple cloak at the shoulder.
  11.1–19: Alexander and Ptolemy fall out. 3: The garrisons indicate Ptolemy's treacherous

him; King Alexander had ordered them to do this, because Ptolemy was his father-in-law.

3 As he went on his progress from town to town, Ptolemy left a detachment of troops in each of them as a
4 garrison. When he reached Azotus, he was shown the burnt-out temple of Dagon, the city itself and its ruined suburbs strewn with corpses, and, piled up along his way, the bodies of those who had been burned in the course
5 of the fighting. They told the king that it was Jonathan's doing, hoping that he would reprimand him; but the king
6 said nothing. Jonathan met him in state at Joppa, where they exchanged greet-
7 ings and passed the night. Jonathan accompanied the king as far as the river Eleutherus and then returned to
8 Jerusalem. King Ptolemy made himself master of the coast towns as far as Seleucia-by-the-sea. He was harbouring malicious designs against Alexander.

9 He sent ambassadors to King Demetrius with the following message: 'I propose that you and I should make a pact: I will give you my daughter, now Alexander's wife, and you shall reign
10 over the kingdom of your father. I now regret having given my daughter to him, for he has tried to kill me.'
11 He maligned Alexander in this way
12 because he coveted his kingdom, and he took his daughter away and gave her to Demetrius. This led to a breach between him and Alexander, and to open enmity.
13 Ptolemy now entered Antioch, where he assumed the crown of Asia; thus he wore two crowns, that of Egypt and that of Asia.
14 King Alexander was at this time in Cilicia, because the inhabitants of that
15 region were in revolt. But when he heard the news he marched against Ptolemy, who came to meet him with a powerful
16 army and routed him. Alexander fled to Arabia for protection, and King

Ptolemy was triumphant. Zabdiel the 17 Arab chieftain cut off Alexander's head and sent it to Ptolemy. But two 18 days later King Ptolemy died, and his garrisons in the fortresses were killed by the inhabitants. So in the year 167^y 19 Demetrius became king.

At this time Jonathan gathered 20 together the Judaeans to assault the citadel in Jerusalem, and they brought up many siege-engines against it. But 21 a number of renegades, enemies of their own people, went to the king and reported that Jonathan was besieging the citadel. The king was furious at the 22 news and immediately moved his quarters to Ptolemais. He wrote to Jonathan ordering him to raise the siege, and to meet him for conference at Ptolemais with all speed.

When Jonathan received this letter, 23 he gave orders for the siege to be continued. Then, selecting elders of Israel and priests to accompany him, he set out on his dangerous mission. He took with him silver and gold, 24 and robes, and many other gifts, and went to meet the king at Ptolemais.

He won the favour of Demetrius, although some renegade Jews tried to lodge 25 complaints against him. But the king 26 treated him just as his predecessors had done, honouring him in the presence of all his Friends. He confirmed him in the 27 high-priesthood and in all his former dignities, and appointed him head of the first class of the King's Friends.

Jonathan requested the king to 28 exempt Judaea and the three Samaritan districts^z from tribute, promising him in return three hundred talents. King 29 Demetrius consented, writing to Jonathan on all these affairs as follows:

King Demetrius to his brother 30 Jonathan, and to the Jewish nation, greeting.

y *That is* 145 B.C.
z three . . . districts: *probable reading; Gk.* three districts and Samaria.

intent. **6–7:** Apparently, Ptolemy deceived Jonathan. The *Eleutherus* river is the Nahr el-Kebir, nineteen miles north of Tripolis. **13:** Ptolemy did not want all of Asia (i.e. the Seleucid empire; see 8.6) but only Palestine. He left the rest for Demetrius. **18:** Ptolemy died of wounds received in battle with Alexander at the Oenoparas river near Antioch. **19:** The sixteen-year-old *Demetrius* now began to call himself Nicator, "Conquerer," because of his success over Alexander.
   11.20–53: Jonathan serves Demetrius. 20–27: Jonathan wins over the new king as he had Alexander (10.59–66). **30:** *Jonathan was brother* or kinsman to Demetrius as he had once been

31 This is a copy of our letter written to our kinsman Lasthenes about you, which we have had made for your information:

32 'King Demetrius to his respected kinsman Lasthenes, greeting.

33 'Because our friends the Jewish nation show us goodwill, and observe their obligations to us, we are resolved 34 to become their benefactor. We have therefore settled on them the lands of Judaea and the three districts, Apherema, Lydda, and Ramathaim, which are now transferred from Samaria to Judaea, together with all the lands adjacent thereto, for the benefit of the priesthood at Jerusalem. This is a transfer of the annual dues which the King formerly received from these territories, from the produce of the soil and of the 35 orchards. Other of our revenues, the tithes and tolls now pertaining to us, the salt-pans, and the crown-money, all these we shall cede to 36 them. These provisions are irrevocable from now for all future time. 37 See to it then that you make a copy of them to be given to Jonathan and set by him in a conspicuous position on the holy mountain.'

38 When King Demetrius saw that the country was quiet under his rule and resistance was at an end, he disbanded all his forces, sending every man home, with the exception of the foreign mercenaries he had hired from the islands of the Gentiles. Then all the troops enlisted under his predecessors turned 39 against the king. A certain Trypho, formerly of the party of Alexander, aware of the disaffection of all the forces towards Demetrius, went to Imalcue, the Arab chieftain, who had charge of the child Antiochus, Alexander's son, and kept pressing him to 40 hand the boy over to him to be made king in succession to his father. He also informed Imalcue of all the measures Demetrius was taking and of his unpopularity with his troops. There he remained for some time.

Meanwhile Jonathan sent to King 41 Demetrius requesting him to withdraw from the citadel in Jerusalem and from the fortresses, the garrisons which were constantly harassing Israel. Demetrius sent Jonathan this reply: 'I will not 42 only meet your request, but when opportunity arises I will do you and your people the highest honour. And now be so good as to send men to support me, for all my troops are in revolt.'

Jonathan dispatched three thousand 44 fighting men to Antioch, and the king was much relieved at their arrival. The 45 citizens poured into the centre of the city, a hundred and twenty thousand strong, bent on killing the king. He took 46 refuge in the palace, while the citizens seized control of the streets and fighting broke out. King Demetrius called the 47 Jews to his assistance, and they rallied to him at once. They then dispersed all over the city and slaughtered that day as many as a hundred thousand, setting 48 the city on fire and taking much booty. And thus they saved the king's life.

When the citizens saw that the Jews 49 had the city completely at their mercy, their courage failed them and they clamoured to the king to accept their 50 surrender and to stop the Jews fighting against them and the city. They threw 51 down their arms and made peace; and the Jews, now in high repute with the king and all his subjects, returned to Jerusalem loaded with booty. But when 52 King Demetrius was secure upon his throne, with the country quiet under him, he went back on all his promises 53

---

to Alexander (10.89). **31:** *Lasthenes* was leader of the Cretan mercenaries (10.67) and chief minister to the king. **32–37:** Many of the privileges promised by Demetrius I (10.25–45) were confirmed by his son, but nothing is said of the citadel. Demetrius also confirmed Jonathan in the dignities conferred by Alexander (10.20,65). **38:** The *King* kept his Cretan *mercenaries* (see 10.67), but he dismissed his regular army without its normal peacetime pay. **39:** Diodotus *Trypho* changed sides frequently, having served Demetrius I, Alexander, Ptolemy, Demetrius II, and now Antiochus. **41:** Demetrius I had not kept his promise (10.32) to give *the citadel* to the high priest. The other *garrisons* are Bethsura (10.14) and Gazara (13.43). **43:** Trypho had sparked a *revolt*. **44–50:** Actually, the Cretan mercenaries put down the revolt, according to the ancient historians Diodorus and Josephus, but Jewish aid turned the tide in the king's favor. **53:** *Severe pressure:* the demand for tribute (according to Josephus, *Ant.* XIII.5.3).

and broke off relations with Jonathan; instead of repaying the benefits he had received, he put severe pressure upon him,

54 After this, Trypho returned, and with him Antiochus, a mere lad.
55 Antiochus was crowned, and all the forces Demetrius had so contemptuously discharged rallied to the king. These fought against Demetrius, and
56 he was utterly routed. Trypho brought up his elephants and made himself
57 master of Antioch. The young Antiochus wrote to Jonathan confirming him in the high-priesthood, with authority over the four districts, and making him
58 one of the King's Friends. He also sent him a service of gold plate, and gave him the right to drink from a gold cup, to be robed in purple, and to wear the
59 gold clasp. He appointed Jonathan's brother Simon as officer commanding the area from the Ladder of Tyre to the borders of Egypt.
60 Jonathan made a tour through the country on the far side of the river and the towns there; and all the forces of Syria gathered to his support.

He went to Ascalon, where he was received with great honour by the citi-
61 zens. From there he went on to Gaza, but the inhabitants closed the gates against him; so he blockaded the city, set fire to its suburbs, and plundered
62 them. The citizens of Gaza then sought peace, and he made terms with them, taking the sons of their magistrates as hostages and sending them off to Jerusalem; he himself continued his progress through the country in the direction of Damascus.
63 Jonathan heard that Demetrius's officers had arrived at Kedesh-in-Galilee with a large force to prevent
64 him from reaching his objective. He went to meet them, leaving his brother
65 Simon in Judaea. Simon took up position against Bethsura and, after

prolonged fighting, blockaded it. Fin- 66 ally the citizens sued for terms of peace and Simon consented; he evicted them, took over the town, and installed a garrison there.

Jonathan, who had encamped with 67 his army by the Lake of Gennesaret, marched out early in the morning into the plain of Asor. There in the plain 68 the gentile army was advancing to meet him; they had set an ambush for him in the hills, while they themselves confronted him. When the men from 69 the ambush emerged and joined in the fighting, all Jonathan's men took to flight; not one remained except Matta- 70 thias son of Absalom, and Judas son of Chalphi, officers in the army. Jonathan tore his clothes, put dust upon 71 his head, and prayed. Then he turned 72 upon the enemy and routed them in headlong flight. When the fugitives of 73 Jonathan's army saw this, they rallied to him and joined in the pursuit as far as the enemy base at Kedesh; there they encamped. That day about three 74 thousand of the Gentiles fell. Jonathan then returned to Jerusalem.

JONATHAN NOW SAW HIS OPPORTUNITY 12 and sent picked men on a mission to Rome to confirm and renew the treaty of friendship with that city. He sent 2 letters to the same effect to Sparta and to other places. The envoys travelled 3 to Rome and went to the Senate House to deliver their message: 'Jonathan the High Priest and the Jewish people have sent us to renew their former pact of friendship and alliance.' The Romans 4 gave them letters requiring the authorities in each place to give them safe conduct to Judaea.

Here follows a transcript of the letter 5 which Jonathan wrote to the Spartans:

Jonathan the High Priest, the 6 Senate of the Jews, the priests, and

---

11.54–74: **Jonathan goes over to Antiochus. 54:** *Antiochus* VI Epiphanes Dionysius was a *mere lad* dominated by his minister *Trypho.* **57:** *The four districts* probably included those of 10.30 n.,38; 11.34. **59:** *The Ladder of Tyre,* a series of mountainous ascents, lies north of Ptolemais. **61:** *Gaza* and other coastal cities were still in Demetrius' control. **63:** *Kedesh* was only twenty-two miles southeast of Tyre. **67:** *The plain of Asor* (Hazor) is just west of the Jordan above the Sea of Galilee. **68:** Demetrius' generals Sarpedon and Palamedes set the *ambush.* **70:** Josephus says about fifty remained with *Mattathias* and *Judas* (*Ant.* XIII.5.7). **71:** *Tore his clothes . . . dust:* signs of distress.
12.1–23: **The treaties with Sparta and Rome. 2:** The defeat of the Achaean League by the

the rest of the Jewish people, to our brothers of Sparta, greeting.

7 On a previous occasion a letter was sent to Onias the High Priest from Arius your king, acknowledging our kinship; a copy is given below.

8 Onias welcomed your envoy with full honours and received the letter in which the terms of the alliance and

9 friendship were set forth. We do not regard ourselves as needing such alliances, since our support is the

10 holy books in our possession. Nevertheless, we now venture to send and renew our pact of brotherhood and friendship with you, so that we may not become estranged, for it is many

11 years since you wrote to us. We never lose any opportunity, on festal and other appropriate days, of remembering you at our sacrifices and in our prayers, as it is right and proper to

12 remember kinsmen; and we rejoice

13 at your fame. We ourselves have been under the pressure of hostile attacks on every side; all the surrounding kings have made war upon

14 us. In the course of these wars we had no wish to trouble you or the

15 rest of our allies and friends: we have the aid of Heaven to support us, and so we have been saved from our enemies, and they have been hum-

16 bled. Accordingly, we chose Numenius son of Antiochus, and Antipater son of Jason, and have sent them to the Romans to renew our former friendship and alliance with them.

17 We instructed them to go to you also with our greetings, and to deliver this letter about the renewal of our

18 pact of brotherhood. And now we pray you to send us a reply to this letter.

19 This is a copy of the letter sent by the Spartans to Onias:

20 Arius, King of Sparta, to Onias the High Priest, greeting.

21 A document has come to light which shows that Spartans and Jews are kinsmen, descended alike from Abraham. Now that we have

22 learnt this, we beg you to write and tell us how your affairs prosper. The message we return to you is,

23 'What is yours, your cattle and every kind of property, is ours, and what is ours is yours', and we have therefore instructed our envoys to report to you in these terms.

24 Jonathan heard that Demetrius's generals had returned to attack him

25 with larger forces than before. He marched from Jerusalem and met them in the region of Hamath, giving them no chance to set foot in his territory.

26 He sent spies to their camp, who on their return reported that preparations were being made for a night attack. At

27 sunset Jonathan gave orders to his men to stay awake and stand to arms all night, ready for battle; and he stationed outposts all round the camp.

28 When the enemy heard that Jonathan and his men were ready for battle, they were alarmed; their courage failed, and they withdrew, first lighting watch-fires in their camp. Jonathan

29 and his men, seeing the watch-fires burning, did not realize what had happened until morning. Then Jonathan

30 set out in pursuit, but failed to overtake them, for they had crossed the river Eleutherus. So Jonathan turned aside

31 against the Arabs called Zabadaeans, and he dealt them a severe blow and plundered them. He struck camp and

32 came to Damascus, and then made a march through the whole country.

33-34 Simon set out and marched as far as Ascalon and the neighbouring fortresses. He then turned towards Joppa; he had heard that the citizens intended to hand it over to the supporters of Demetrius, but before they could do so, he occupied the town and placed a garrison there to defend it.

Romans in 146 B.C. brought *Sparta* to new prominence in Greece. **6:** The *Senate (gerousia)* was the forerunner of the Sanhedrin. **7:** *Onias* I (about 300 B.C.) received the letter of *Arius* I (309–265 B.C.). **10:** A *pact of brotherhood* in the ancient world often resulted in the diplomatic fiction of a common ancestry (see v. 21). **16:** Possibly the *Jason* of 8.17.

12.24–38: Further military activity. 25: *The region of* the "entrance to *Hamath*" lay between the Lebanon and Anti-Lebanon ranges. **30:** *Eleutherus:* see 11.6–7 n. **36:** The defenses razed

35 When Jonathan returned he convened the senate. With their agreement he decided to build fortresses in 36 Judaea, to heighten the walls of Jerusalem, and to erect a high barrier to separate the citadel from the city and so to isolate it that the garrison could 37 not buy or sell. They assembled to rebuild the city, for the wall along the ravine to the east had partly collapsed, and he repaired the section of the wall 38 called Chaphenatha. Simon also rebuilt and fortified Adida in the Shephelah, erecting gates and bars.

39 Trypho now aspired to be king of Asia; he meant to rebel against King Antiochus and assume the crown 40 himself. But he was afraid that Jonathan would fight to prevent this, so he cast about for some means of capturing and killing him. He set off and reached 41 Bethshan. Jonathan marched out to meet him with forty thousand picked troops, and he also reached Bethshan. 42 Trypho, seeing that Jonathan had a large force with him, was afraid to 43 attack. So he received him honourably and commended him to all his Friends, gave him presents, and ordered his Friends and his troops to obey Jonathan as they would himself. 44 He said to Jonathan: 'Why have you put all these men to so much trouble, 45 when we are not at war? Send them home now and choose a few to accompany you, and come with me to Ptolemais. I will hand it over to you with all the other fortresses, the rest of the troops, and all the officials, and then I will leave the country. This is the only 46 purpose of my coming.' Jonathan took him at his word and did as he said: he dismissed his forces and they re- 47 turned to Judaea. He kept back three thousand men, of whom he left two thousand in Galilee, while a thousand

accompanied him. But when Jonathan 48 entered Ptolemais, the citizens closed the gates, seized him, and put to the sword all who had entered with him.

Trypho sent a force of infantry and 49 cavalry into Galilee to the great plain, to wipe out all Jonathan's men. They 50 now learnt that Jonathan had been seized and was lost, along with his escort, but they put heart into one another and marched in close formation, ready for battle. When their pur- 51 suers saw that they would fight to the death, they turned back. So all came 52 safely home to Judaea, mourning for Jonathan and his followers, and filled with alarm. All Israel was plunged in grief. The surrounding Gentiles were 53 now bent on destroying them root and branch, saying to themselves, 'The Jews have no leader or champion, so now is the time to attack, and we shall blot out all memory of them among men.'

The high-priesthood of Simon

THE NEWS REACHED SIMON THAT TRYPHO 13 had mustered a large force for the invasion and destruction of Judaea, and it threw the people into a state of 2 panic. When Simon saw this, he went up to Jerusalem, called an assembly, and encouraged them in these words: 3 'I need not remind you of all that my brothers and I and my father's house have done for the laws and the holy place, what battles we have fought, what hardships we have endured. My 4 brothers have all fallen in this cause, fighting for Israel, and I am the only one left. Now Heaven forbid that I 5 should grudge my own life in any moment of danger, for I am not worth more than my brothers. No! I will take 6

---

by Antiochus IV (1.31) and Antiochus V (6.62) were only partially rebuilt (10.10). *The citadel* was to be starved out. **37**: *Chaphenatha* is thought to have been in the new or "second quarter" of Jerusalem, northwest of the Temple. **38**: *Adida*, northeast of Lydda, lay *in the Shephelah*, the foothills east of the coastal plain.

12.39–53: Jonathan is captured by Trypho. 41: Trypho's armed presence must have made *Jonathan* wary enough to bring *troops*. **43**: *Friends*: see 2.18 n. **49**: *The great plain*: Esdraelon. **52**: Their *mourning* was premature; Jonathan died later (13.23).

13.1–16.24: The high-priesthood of Simon. Simon's victories and relatively peaceful reign led the people to make his rule hereditary.

13.1–30: Simon becomes leader and frustrates Trypho. 3: *The holy place*: the Temple. **4**: Eventually, all five *brothers* died violently (6.46; 9.18,36–38; 13.23; 16.16). **11**: The *inhabitants*

up the cause of my nation and the holy place, of your wives and children, since all the Gentiles in their hatred have
7 gathered to destroy us.' At these words
8 the people plucked up courage, and they shouted in answer: 'You shall be our leader in place of Judas and your
9 brother Jonathan. Fight our battles, and
10 we will do whatever you tell us.' So Simon mustered all the fighting men and hurried on the completion of the walls of Jerusalem until it was fortified
11 on all sides. He sent Jonathan son of Absalom with a considerable force to Joppa; he expelled its inhabitants and remained in possession of the town.
12 Trypho marched out from Ptolemais with a large force to invade Judaea, taking Jonathan with him as a prisoner.
13 Simon encamped at Adida on the edge
14 of the plain. When Trypho learnt that Simon had come forward to take the place of his brother Jonathan, and that he was about to join battle with him, he sent envoys to Simon with the
15 following message: 'We are detaining your brother Jonathan because of certain monies which he owed to the royal treasury in connection with the
16 offices he held. To ensure that he will not again revolt if we release him, send one hundred talents of silver and two of his sons as hostages, and we will
17 let him go.' Simon himself realized that this was a trick, but he had the money and the children brought to him, fearing that otherwise he might arouse deep
18 animosity among the people, who would say, 'It was because you did not send the money and the children
19 that Jonathan lost his life.' So he sent the children and the hundred talents, but Trypho broke his word and did not release Jonathan.
20 After this, Trypho set out to invade the country and ravage it, taking a roundabout way through Adora. Simon and his army marched parallel with him
21 everywhere he went. Meanwhile the

garrison of the citadel were sending emissaries to Trypho, urging him to come to them by way of the desert, and
22 to send them provisions. Trypho prepared to send all his cavalry, but that night there was a severe snow-storm, which prevented their arrival; so he
23 withdrew into Gilead. When he reached Bascama, he had Jonathan put to death,
24 and there he was buried. Trypho then turned and went back to his own country.
25 Simon had the body of his brother
26 Jonathan brought to Modin, and buried in the town of their fathers; and all Israel made a great lamentation and
27 mourned him for many days. Simon built a high monument over the tomb of his father and his brothers, visible at a great distance, faced back and
28 front with polished stone. He erected seven pyramids, those for his father and mother and his four brothers arranged
29 in pairs. For the pyramids he contrived an elaborate setting: he surrounded them with great columns surmounted with trophies of armour for a perpetual memorial, and between the trophies carved ships, plainly visible
30 to all at sea. This mausoleum which he made at Modin stands to this day.
31 Trypho now plotted against the young King Antiochus and murdered
32 him. He usurped his throne and assumed the crown of Asia. This was a disaster for the country.
33 Simon rebuilt the fortresses of Judaea, furnishing them with high towers and great walls with gates and bars; he also provisioned the for-
34 tresses. He sent representatives to King Demetrius to negotiate a remission of taxes for the country, on the ground that all Trypho's exactions had
35 been exorbitant. Demetrius replied favourably to this request and wrote him a letter in the following terms:

36 King Demetrius to Simon the High Priest and friend of kings, and

---

of *Joppa* were politically unreliable (12.33–34); see, similarly, 11.66. **16:** The (ransom) money was in payment for the alleged debts, and the *hostages* were to assure Jonathan's compliance. **20:** *Adora* (Dura): five miles southwest of Hebron. **21:** The *garrison* needed *provisions* because of the siege (12.36). *By way of the desert* may have been via the Transjordan. **23:** *Bascama* was located northeast of the Sea of Galilee. "Gilead" in v. 22 is the Greek text's error for "Galilee." **13.31–42: Simon supports Demetrius II again. 31:** Actually, *Trypho* arranged for *Antiochus* VI's doctors to kill him during an operation in 139 B.C., some four years after he had deposed him. *The crown of Asia* was that of the Seleucid empire (8.6). **36:** The letter repeats much of

to the Senate and nation of the Jews, greeting.

37 We have received the golden crown and the palm branch which you sent, and we are ready to make a lasting peace with you and to instruct the revenue officers to grant you im-
38 munities. All our agreements with you stand, and the strongholds which you built shall remain yours.
39 We give a free pardon for any errors of omission or commission, to take effect from the date of this letter. We remit the crown-money which you owed us, and every other tax formerly exacted in Jerusalem is
40 henceforth cancelled. All those of you who are suitable for enrolment in our retinue shall be so enrolled. Let there be peace between us.

41 In the year 170,^a Israel was released
42 from the gentile yoke. The people began to write on their contracts and agreements, 'In the first year of Simon, the great high priest, general and leader of the Jews'.
43 Then Simon invested Gazara,^b and surrounded it with his forces. He constructed a siege-engine and brought it up to the town, made a breach in
44 one of the towers and captured it. The men on the siege-engine leapt out of it into the town, and there was a great
45 commotion. The townspeople and their wives and children climbed up on to the city wall with their garments torn, clamouring to Simon to offer
46 them terms. 'Do not treat us as our wickedness deserves,' they cried, 'but
47 as your mercy prompts you.' Simon came to terms with them, and brought the war to an end. But he expelled them

from the town, and after purifying the houses in which the idols stood, he made his entry with songs of thanks-giving and praise. He removed every 48 pollution from it and settled men in it who would keep the law. He strength-ened its fortifications and built a residence there for himself.

The men in the citadel in Jerusalem 49 were prevented from going in and out to buy and sell in the country; famine set in and many of them died of star-vation. They clamoured to Simon to 50 accept their surrender, and he agreed: he expelled them from the citadel and cleansed it from its pollutions. It was 51 on the twenty-third day of the second month in the year 171^c that he made his entry, with a chorus of praise and the waving of palm branches, with lutes, cymbals, and zithers, with hymns and songs, to celebrate Israel's final riddance of a formidable enemy. Simon decreed that this day should be 52 observed as an annual festival. He fortified the temple hill opposite the citadel, and he and his men took up residence there. When Simon saw that 53 his son John had become a man, he made him commander of all the forces, with Gazara as his headquarters.

In the year 172,^d King Demetrius **14** mustered his army and went into Media to recruit additional forces for his war against Trypho. When Arsakes 2 king of Persia and Media heard that Demetrius had entered his territories, he sent one of his generals to capture him alive. The general marched out and 3

a *That is* 142 B.C.
b *Probable reading; Gk.* Gaza.
c *That is* 141 B.C.
d *That is* 140 B.C.

11.33–37 (see 10.25–45). **37:** *The golden crown and the palm branch* signify homage and allegiance. **39:** These *errors* included support of Trypho. Remission of the *crown-money* (tribute), in effect, meant liberation (see v. 41). **40:** Demetrius thought well of Jewish soldiers (11.41–51). **42:** This *first year* was that of Simon's high priesthood and not the beginning of a new era, as the author thought.

13.43–53: Simon takes Gazara and the citadel. While Demetrius and Trypho were occupied with each other, Simon decided to remove the last hostile strongholds in Judea: Gazara (vv. 43–48) and the citadel (vv. 49–53). **44:** The *siege-engine* was a tower as high as the city walls. **49:** The siege may have lasted three years; see 12.36; 13.21. **50:** The *pollutions* were pagan shrines; see 1.54. **51:** This *enemy* had plagued Israel for over twenty-five years (1.33–36). **53:** *John* Hyrcanus (134–104 B.C.) succeeded Simon as high priest.

14.1–3: The Parthian capture of Demetrius. Demetrius II (reigned 145–139 B.C. and 129–125 B.C.) went east to dislodge the Parthian King Mithridates I (also known dynastically as Arsakes VI, 171–138 B.C.) from captured Seleucid territories, as well as to gain troops. Captured by treachery, Demetrius was a Parthian prisoner until released in 129 B.C. He was murdered in 125 B.C.

defeated Demetrius, captured him and brought him to Arsakes who put him in prison.

4 As long as Simon lived, Judaea was at peace. He promoted his people's welfare, and they lived happily all through the glorious days of his reign.
5 Among other notable achievements he captured the port of Joppa to secure
6 his communications overseas. He extended his nation's territories and made himself master of the whole land.
7 He repatriated a large number of prisoners of war. Without meeting any resistance he gained control over Gazara and Bethsura and over the citadel, and removed their pollution.
8 They farmed their land in peace, and the land produced its crops, and
9 the trees in the plains their fruit. Old men sat in the streets, talking together of their blessings; and the young men dressed themselves in splendid military
10 style. Simon supplied the towns with food in plenty and equipped them with weapons for defence. His renown
11 reached the ends of the earth. He restored peace to the land, and there were great rejoicings throughout Israel.
12 Each man sat under his own vine and fig-tree, and they had no one to fear.
13 Those were days when every enemy vanished from the land and every
14 hostile king was crushed. Simon gave his protection to the poor among the people; he paid close attention to the law and rid the country of lawless
15 and wicked men. He gave new splendour to the temple and furnished it with a wealth of sacred vessels.

16 THE REPORT OF JONATHAN'S DEATH reached Rome, and Sparta too, and
17 they were deeply grieved. When they heard, however, that his brother Simon had become high priest in his place,

and was in firm control of the country and the towns in it, they inscribed on 18 bronze tablets a renewal of the treaty of friendship and alliance which they had established with his brothers Judas and Jonathan. This was read before the 19 assembly in Jerusalem. The following 20 is a copy of the letter from Sparta:

The rulers and city of Sparta to the High Priest Simon, to the Senate, the priests, and the rest of the Jewish people, our brothers, greeting.
The envoys you sent to our people 21 have told us about your fame and honour; their visit has given us great pleasure. We have entered a tran- 22 script of the message they brought in the minutes of the public assembly: 'Numenius son of Antiochus, and Antipater son of Jason, envoys of the Jews, visited us to renew their treaty of friendship with us. It was resolved 23 by the public assembly to receive these men with honour and to place a copy of their address in the public archives, so that the Spartans might have it on permanent record. A copy of this document has been made for Simon the High Priest.'

After this, Simon sent Numenius to 24 Rome with a large gold shield, worth a thousand minas, to confirm the alliance with the Romans.
When the people heard of these 25 events they asked themselves how they could show their gratitude to Simon and his sons. For he, with his brothers 26 and his father's family, had stood firm, fought off the enemies of Israel, and ensured his nation's freedom. So an 27 inscription was engraved on tablets of bronze and placed on a monument on Mount Zion. A copy of the inscription follows:

14.4–15: **Simon's achievements. 6:** Simon *extended the nation's territories* by the addition of Joppa, Gazara, and Bethsura. Josephus adds Jamnia (*Ant.* XIII.6.7). **7:** Simon *repatriated* Galilean Jews (5.23). **8–15:** Simon's reign has the *blessings* promised for observance of the Law. See Lev.26.3–4; Zech.3.10; 8.4. **12:** That *each man* enjoy *his own vine and fig-tree* is an ancient expression for universal peace and contentment; see 1 Kgs.4.25; Isa.36.16; Mic.4.4.
14.16–24: **Renewal of alliances with Rome and Sparta.** In antiquity, when leadership changed, treaties were renewable. **17–19:** The more important treaty with the Romans is placed first and summarized. **22:** These were also Jonathan's envoys (12.16). **24:** *After this* visit to Sparta, the envoys continued on to Rome.
14.25–49: **The edict honoring Simon.** The decree honors Simon in the way that Greek cities honored their benefactors. **27:** *Tablets of bronze* preserved important documents (8.22 n.;

On the eighteenth day of the month Elul, in the year 172,[e] the third year of Simon's high-priest-
28 hood, at Asaramel, in a large assembly of priests, people, rulers of the nation, and elders of the land, the following facts were placed on rec-
29 ord. Whereas our land had been subject to frequent wars, Simon son of Mattathias, a priest of the Joarib family, and his brothers, risked their lives in resisting the enemies of their people, in order that the temple and law might be preserved, and they brought great glory to their nation.
30 Jonathan rallied the nation, became their high priest, and then was
31 gathered to his fathers. Their enemies resolved to invade their land and destroy it, and to attack the temple.
32 Then Simon came forward and fought for his nation. He spent large sums of his own money to arm the soldiers of his nation and to
33 provide their pay. He fortified the towns of Judaea, and Bethsura on the boundaries of Judaea, formerly an enemy arsenal, and stationed a garri-
34 son of Jews there. He fortified Joppa by the sea, and Gazara near Azotus, formerly occupied by the enemy. There he settled Jews, and provided these towns with everything needful
35 for their welfare. When the people saw Simon's patriotism and his resolution to win fame for his nation, they made him their leader and high priest, in recognition of all that he had done, of his just conduct, his loyalty to his nation, and his constant efforts to enhance its renown.
36 His leadership was crowned with success, and the Gentiles were expelled from the land, as were also the troops in Jerusalem who had built themselves a citadel in the city of David, from which they sallied forth to bring defilement upon the whole precinct of the temple and do
37 violence to its purity. He settled Jews in it and fortified it for the security of the land and of the city, and he raised the height of the walls of Jerusalem. King Demetrius con- 38 firmed him in the office of high priest, made him one of his Friends, 39 and granted him the highest honours; for he had heard that the 40 Romans were naming the Jews friends, allies, and brothers, and had gone in state to meet Simon's envoys.

The Jews and their priests con- 41 firmed Simon as their leader and high priest in perpetuity until a true prophet should appear. He was to 42 be their general, and to have full charge of the temple; and in addition to this the supervision of their labour, of the country, and of the arms and fortifications was to be entrusted to him. He was to be 43 obeyed by all; all contracts in the country were to be drawn up in his name. He was to wear the purple robe and the gold clasp.

None of the people or the priests 44 shall have authority to abrogate any of these decrees, to oppose commands issued by Simon or convene any assembly in the land without his consent, to be robed in purple, or to wear the gold clasp. Whoever shall contravene these 45 provisions or neglect any of them shall be liable to punishment. It is 46 the unanimous decision of the people that Simon shall officiate in the ways here laid down. Simon has 47 agreed and consented to be high priest, general and ethnarch of the Jews and the priests, and to be the protector of them all.

This inscription, it was declared, 48 should be engraved on bronze tablets and set up within the precincts of the temple in a conspicuous position, and 49 copies should be placed in the treasury, in the keeping of Simon and his sons.

[e] *That is* 140 B.C.

14.18). **28:** The Heb. phrase for *at Asaramel* means "as prince of the people of God." **32:** Simon's payment of soldiers with *his own money* indicated his princely status, since it followed royal custom. **41:** The titles of *leader* and *high priest* were now made hereditary in Simon's family. For lack of prophecy see also 4.46; 9.27 n. **49:** As successors of Simon, *his sons* received copies of the decree.

15 Antiochus son of King Demetrius sent a letter from overseas to Simon the high priest and ethnarch of the 2 Jews, and to the whole nation. The contents were as follows:

> King Antiochus to Simon, High Priest and Ethnarch, and to the Jewish nation, greeting.

3 Whereas certain traitors have seized my ancestral kingdom, I have now decided to assert my claim to it, so that I may restore it to its former condition. I have raised a large body of mercenaries and fitted out ships of 4 war. I intend to land in my country and to attack those who have ravaged my kingdom and destroyed many of 5 its cities. Now therefore I confirm all the tax remissions which my royal predecessors granted you, and all their other remissions of 6 tribute. I permit you to mint your own coinage as currency for your 7 country. Jerusalem and the temple shall be free. All the arms you have prepared, and the fortifications which you have built and now hold, shall 8 remain yours. All debts now owing to the royal treasury and all future liabilities thereto shall be cancelled 9 from this time on for ever. When we have re-established our kingdom, we shall confer the highest honours upon you, your nation and temple, to make your country's greatness apparent to the whole world.

10 In the year 174,*f* Antiochus marched into his ancestral domain, and all the armed forces came over to him, leaving 11 very few with Trypho. Antiochus pursued him, and Trypho came as a 12 fugitive to Dor by the sea. He knew that his position was desperate now that all his troops had deserted. Anti- 13 ochus, at the head of a hundred and twenty thousand trained soldiers and eight thousand horsemen, laid siege to Dor. He encircled the town, and his 14 ships joined in the blockade from the sea. He thus exerted heavy pressure on it from both land and sea, and prevented anyone from leaving or entering.

NUMENIUS AND HIS PARTY ARRIVED 15 from Rome with a letter to the various kings and countries, which read as follows:

> Lucius, Consul of the Romans, to 16 King Ptolemy, greeting.
> Envoys have come to us from our 17 friends and allies the Jews, sent by Simon the High Priest and the Jewish people, to renew their original treaty of friendship and alliance. They brought a gold shield worth a 18 thousand minas. We have decided, 19 therefore, to write to the kings and countries, requiring them to do no harm to the Jews, nor make war on them or their cities or their country, nor ally themselves with those who so make war. And we have decided 20 to accept the shield from them. If 21 therefore any traitors have escaped from their country to you, hand them over to Simon the High Priest to be punished by him according to the law of the Jews.

The same message was sent to King 22 Demetrius, to Attalus, Ariarathes, Arsakes, Sampsakes, and the Spartans, 23 and also to the following places: Delos, Myndos, Sicyon, Caria, Samos, Pamphylia, Lycia, Halicarnassus, Rhodes, Phaselis, Cos, Sidé, Aradus, Gortyna,

f That is 138 B.C.

15.1–14: Antiochus VII seeks Simon's support in his struggles with Trypho for the throne of Demetrius II. **1:** *Antiochus* VII Sidetes (138–129 B.C.) was the son of *Demetrius* I (161–150 B.C.) and brother of the captured Demetrius II (145–139, 129–125 B.C.). **6:** Although Antiochus added to previous fiscal concessions the right to coin money (see 10.26–35; 13.37–39), Simon seems never to have used it. The right was soon revoked (15.27). **10–14:** Antiochus married Cleopatra, the wife of his brother Demetrius. Trypho's troops deserted to her, and she transferred them to Antiochus' command. *Dor* lay fifteen miles south of Mount Carmel.
15.15–24: Return of the envoys. 16: *Lucius* Caecilius Metullus Calvus, who was *Consul* in 142 B.C., wrote (v. 16) to *Ptolemy* VIII (Euergetes II Physcon) of Egypt (145–116 B.C.). **22:** Copies of the *message* went to *Demetrius* II of Asia (145–139 and 129–125 B.C.), *Attalus* II of Pergamum (159–138 B.C.), *Ariarathes* V of Cappadocia (162–131 B.C.), *Arsakes* VI (Mithridates I, 171–138 B.C.) of Parthia, and to various free city-states.

24 Cnidus, Cyprus, and Cyrene. A copy was sent to Simon the high priest.

25 KING ANTIOCHUS LAID SIEGE TO DOR for the second time,*g* and launched repeated attacks against it; he had siege-engines constructed, and blockaded Trypho, preventing all movement in or out of the town.

26 Simon sent Antiochus two thousand picked men to assist him, with silver 27 and gold and much equipment; but he refused the offer. He repudiated all his previous agreements with Simon and 28 broke off relations. He sent Athenobius, one of the Friends, to parley with him. This was his message: 'You are occupying Joppa and Gazara and the citadel in Jerusalem, cities that belong to my 29 kingdom. You have laid waste their territories, and done great damage to the country, and have made yourselves masters of many places in my kingdom. 30 I demand the return of the cities you have captured and the surrender of the tribute exacted from places beyond the frontiers of Judaea over which you 31 have assumed control. Otherwise, you must pay five hundred talents of silver on their account, and another five hundred as compensation for the destruction you have caused and for the loss of tribute from the cities. Failing this, we shall go to war with you.'

32 Athenobius, the King's Friend, came to Jerusalem, and when he saw the splendour of Simon's establishment, the gold and silver vessels on his sideboard, and his display of wealth, he was amazed. He delivered the king's 33 message, to which Simon replied: 'We have not occupied other people's land or taken other people's property, but only the inheritance of our ancestors, unjustly seized for a time by 34 our enemies. We have grasped our opportunity and have claimed our 35 patrimony. With regard to Joppa and Gazara, which you demand, these

towns were doing a great deal of damage among our people and in our land. For these we offer one hundred talents.'

36 Athenobius answered not a word, but went off in a rage to the king; he reported what Simon had said, and described Simon's splendour and all the things he had seen. The king was furious.

37 Meanwhile Trypho boarded a ship and made good his escape to Orthosia. 38 The king appointed Kendebaeus as commander-in-chief of the coastal zone, and gave him infantry and cavalry. 39 He instructed him to blockade Judaea, to rebuild Kedron and strengthen its gates, and to make war on our people, while he himself continued the pursuit of Trypho. Kendebaeus arrived 40 in Jamnia and began to harass our people by invading Judaea, and by capturing and killing the inhabitants. 41 He rebuilt Kedron, stationing cavalry and troops there to sally out and patrol the roads of Judaea, in accordance with the king's instructions.

16 John came from Gazara and reported to his father Simon the results 2 of Kendebaeus's campaign. Simon summoned his two eldest sons Judas and John, and said to them: 'My brothers and I and my father's family have fought Israel's battles from our youth until this day, and many a time we have been successful in rescuing Israel. Now I am old, but mercifully 3 you are in the prime of life. Take my place and my brother's and go out and fight for our nation. And may help from on high be with you.'

4 He then levied from the country twenty thousand picked warriors and cavalry, and they marched against Kendebaeus. After passing the night at 5 Modin they rose early and proceeded to the plain, where a large force of infantry and cavalry stood ready to meet them on the far side of a gully. 6 When his army had taken up a position

g Some witnesses read on the second day.

15.25–36: Antiochus VII alienates Simon. 26–27: Josephus says the king accepted this aid (*Ant.* XIII.7.2). **30:** The *places beyond the frontiers* probably include those of 11.34. **32:** *King's Friends:* see 2.18 n.
15.37–16.10: John Hyrcanus defeats Kendebaeus. 37: From *Orthosia*, north of Tripolis, Trypho went to Apamea where Antiochus captured and killed him. **38:** Simon held this post under Antiochus VI (11.59). **39:** *Kedron* lay three miles southeast of Jamnia. **16.3:** Simon was about sixty years *old.* **4:** This is the first mention of Maccabean *cavalry.* **6:** John's crossing recalls Judas's (5.40,43).

opposite. John saw that his men were afraid to cross the gully. So he crossed first himself; his men saw him and 7 followed. John drew up his army with the cavalry in the centre of the infantry, for the enemy cavalry were very nu-8 merous. The trumpets were sounded, and Kendebaeus and his army were routed; many of them fell, and the remainder 9 took refuge in the fortress. It was in this engagement that John's brother Judas was wounded. John kept up the pursuit until Kendebaeus reached 10 Kedron, which he had rebuilt. The enemy took refuge in the towers in the open country round Azotus, whereupon John set fire to Azotus. Some two thousand of the enemy fell in the fighting, and John returned to Judaea in safety.

11 Now Ptolemaeus son of Abubus had been appointed commander for the plain of Jericho. He had great wealth, 12 for he was the high priest's son-in-law. 13 But he became over-ambitious; he proposed to make himself master of the country and plotted to put Simon and 14 his sons out of the way. In the course of a tour to inspect the towns in that region and to attend to their needs, Simon came to Jericho with his sons Mattathias and Judas in the year 177,*h* in the eleventh month, the month of 15 Shebat. The son of Abubus, with treachery in his heart, received them at the small fort called Dok which he had built, and entertained them lavish-

ly. But he had men in concealment there, and when Simon and his sons 16 had drunk freely, Ptolemaeus and his accomplices jumped up, seized their weapons, and rushed in to the banquet. They attacked Simon and killed him, along with his two sons and some of his servants. It was an act of base 17 treachery in which evil was returned for good.

Ptolemaeus sent news of this in a 18 dispatch to the king, asking him to send troops to his assistance and to give him authority over the country and its towns. He sent some of his men 19 to Gazara to kill John, and wrote to the army officers urging them to join him, and offering them silver and gold and presents. Other troops he sent to 20 take Jerusalem and the temple hill. But 21 someone ran ahead and reported to John at Gazara that his father and brothers had been murdered, and that Ptolemaeus had sent men to kill him as well. When John heard this he was 22 beside himself; he arrested the men who came to kill him, and put them to death, because he had discovered their plot against his life.

The rest of the story of John, his 23 wars and the deeds of valour he performed, the walls he built, and his exploits, are written in the annals of his 24 high-priesthood from the time when he succeeded his father.

h That is 134 B.C.

16.11–24: John Hyrcanus succeeds his murdered father. 15: The hill fortress of *Dok* lay five miles northwest of Jericho. 16: Josephus says the sons were killed later (*Ant.* XIII.8.1). 18: *Ptolemaeus* appealed to Antiochus VII. 22: Eventually, Ptolemaeus fled to Philadelphia (Amman). 23–24: The wording recalls that used of the kings of Israel (1 Kgs.14.19,29). The *annals* have been lost.

THE SECOND BOOK OF THE
MACCABEES

2 Maccabees is a shortened version of a five-volume historical work, now lost, by Jason of Cyrene (2 Macc.2.19–32). To this shortened version the "abbreviator" prefixed two letters (1.1–10a; 1.10b–2.18) which Palestinian Jews addressed to their Egyptian brethren, urging them to observe the feast celebrating the Temple's rededication in 164 B.C. The abridgment of Jason's work exemplifies "pathetic history," a genre of writing which seeks not only to tell the story, but to arouse the reader's sympathetic emotions and give him pleasure. With invented dialogue, exaggerated numbers, apparitions and miracles, the "abbreviator," or Epitomist, as he is technically called, traces the decline of the high priesthood (3.1–4.50), Antiochus Epiphanes' attempt to impose Hellenism upon the Jews (5.1–7.42), and Judas Maccabeus' successful resistance, culminating in his triumphal cleansing of the Temple (8.1–10.8), and his subsequent struggles (10.9–15.39).

2 Maccabees was written in Greek in Egypt about 124 B.C. It covers the period approximately 180–160 B.C., and parallels the events narrated in 1 Macc.1.10–7.50.

Foreword: letters to the Jews in Egypt

1 To THEIR JEWISH KINSMEN IN EGYPT, the Jews who are in Jerusalem and those in the country of Judaea send brotherly greeting.
2 May God give you peace and prosperity and remember his covenant with Abraham, Isaac, and Jacob, his faithful
3 servants. May he give to you all a will to worship him, to fulfil his purposes
4 eagerly with heart and soul. May he give you a mind open to his law and
5 precepts. May he make peace and answer your prayers, and be reconciled to you and not forsake you in an evil
6 hour. Here and now we are praying for you.
7 In the reign of Demetrius, in the year 169,*a* we the Jews wrote to you during the persecution and the crisis that came upon us in those years since the time

when Jason and his partisans revolted from the holy land and the kingdom. They set the porch of the temple on fire 8 and shed innocent blood. Then we prayed to the Lord and were answered. We offered a sacrifice and fine flour, we lit the lamps, and set out the Bread of the Presence. And now, you are to 9 observe the celebration of a Feast of Tabernacles in the month Kislev.
Written in the year 188.*b* 10

FROM THE PEOPLE OF JERUSALEM AND Judaea, from the Senate, and from Judas, to Aristobulus, the teacher of King Ptolemy and a member of the high-priestly family, and to the Jews in Egypt, greeting and good health.
We have been saved by God from 11 great dangers, and give him all thanks, as men standing ready to resist the king.

a That is 143 B.C.
b That is 124 B.C.

1.1–10a: The first letter. The Palestinian Jews urge those in Egypt to observe the feast (v. 9) which celebrates the rededication of the Temple. This letter, written in 124 B.C. (= 188 in the Seleucid calendar) refers to an earlier letter of 143 B.C. (= 169 in the Seleucid calendar), which described the events from Jason's apostasy (4.7–5.10) to the Temple's dedication (10.1–8; 1 Macc.4.36–61) and probably informed the Egyptian Jews of Jonathan's death (1 Macc.12.39–53; 13.23). **1–2:** The two-fold salutation includes the Hellenistic *greeting* and the Hebraic *peace*. **7–8a:** Jason slaughtered his own people (5.5–7) in the *holy land* (Zech.2.12), thus also revolting against the Seleucid *kingdom*. **8b:** After purifying the Temple, Judas and his men *offered a sacrifice* there (10.3; 1 Macc.4.50–51). **9:** A feast is now to take place in *Kislev* (December); it came to be called Hanukkah. The biblical *Feast of Tabernacles*, which Hanukkah resembles at least in length (eight days), was in Tishri (September–October).
1.10b–2.18: The second letter. Written earlier, in 164 B.C., this letter urges Egyptian Jews to celebrate the dedication of the newly purified Temple (10.1–8; 1 Macc.4.36–59) even though not prescribed in the Pentateuch, since Judas' victory was God's salvation for all Jews (2.17). **10:** *Aristobulus* was a Jewish "philosopher" of Alexandria, who "taught" Ptolemy VI Philometor (180–145 B.C.) by dedicating a book to him which "proved" that the Greeks derived their wisdom and philosophy from the Law and the Prophets. **11:** *The king* is Antiochus IV Epiphanes

232

12 It was God who drove out the enemy force in the holy city.

13 For when the king went into Persia with an army that seemed invincible, they were cut to pieces in the temple of Nanaea through a stratagem employed

14 by Nanaea's priests. Antiochus, along with his Companions, arrived at the temple to marry the goddess, in order to secure the considerable treasure by

15 way of dowry. After this had been laid out by the priests, he went into the temple precinct with a small retinue. When Antiochus entered, the priests

16 shut the sanctuary, opened a secret door in the panelling, and hurled stones at them. The king fell, as if struck by a thunderbolt. They hacked off limbs and heads and threw them to those outside.

17 Blessed in all things be our God, who handed over the evil-doers to death!

18 We are about to celebrate the purification of the temple on the twenty-fifth of Kislev, and think it right to inform you, so that you also for your part may celebrate a Feast of Tabernacles, in honour of the fire which appeared when Nehemiah offered sac-rifices, after he had built the temple and

19 the altar. When our fathers were carried off to Persia, the pious priests of those days secretly took fire from the altar and concealed it in a dry well. It proved a safe hiding-place and re-

20 mained undiscovered. After many years had passed, in God's good time, Nehemiah was sent back by the king of Persia. He then dispatched the descendants of the priests who had hidden it to get the fire, and they informed our people that they found, not fire, but a

21 thick liquid. Nehemiah ordered them to draw some out and bring it to him. When the materials of the sacrifice had been presented, he ordered the priests to sprinkle this liquid over the wood

and the things laid upon it, and this was 22 done. Some time passed; then the sun, which earlier had been hidden by clouds, shone out and the altar burst into a great blaze, so that everyone marvelled. As the sacrifice was burn- 23 ing, the priests offered prayer, they and all those present: Jonathan began and the rest responded, led by Nehemiah.

The prayer was in this style: 'O Lord 24 God, creator of all things, thou the terrible, the mighty, the just, and the merciful, the only King, the only gracious one, the only giver, the only 25 just, omnipotent, and everlasting one, who dost deliver Israel from every evil, who didst choose the patriarchs and set them apart: accept this sacrifice on 26 behalf of thy whole people Israel; they are thy own, watch over them and sanctify them. Gather the dispersed, 27 free those who are in slavery among the heathen, look favourably on the despised and detested; let the heathen know that thou art our God. Punish 28 our oppressors for their insolent brutality and make them suffer torment; but plant thy people in thy holy 29 place, as Moses said.'

Then the priests chanted the hymns. 30 After the materials of the sacrifice had 31 been consumed, Nehemiah further ordered what remained of the liquid to be poured over some great stones.[c] At 32 this a flame shot up, but burnt itself out as soon as the fire on the altar outshone it.[d]

These events became widely known. 33 The king of Persia was told that, in the place where the priests who were deported had hidden the fire, a liquid had appeared, and that Nehemiah and

---

[c] what remained . . . stones: *so some witnesses; others read* that great stones should enclose what remained of the liquid.

[d] *Or* but hardly had the light been reflected from the altar, when it burnt itself out.

(175–164 B.C.). **13:** The Elamite goddess *Nanaea* (Anaitis) was identified with the Greek goddess Artemis in Hellenistic times. **16–17:** Actually, Antiochus was driven off, not killed (9.2). The letter writer's sources may have confused the king's representative with the *king* himself. **18:** Lighting candles, *fire*, is a special feature of the present feast of Hanukkah. The *temple* was *built* long before Nehemiah's time; see Ezra 3.1–2; 6.6–16. The fire at the time of Nehemiah's sacrifices is not found in the Book of Nehemiah but apparently comes from the apocryphal memoirs of Nehemiah (2.13), now lost. The purpose of the allusion is to emphasize the privileges of the Temple and the continuity and orthodoxy of its worship. The many difficulties in the story that follows show its fictional character. **19:** The Exile (587 B.C.; see 2 Kgs.25.11–12) was to Babylon, which later became part of the Persian empire. **20:** *The king* who sent Nehemiah to govern Palestine was Artaxerxes I Longimanus (464–424 B.C.). The *thick liquid* was naphtha,

his companions had used it to burn up
34 the materials of the sacrifice. When he
had verified the fact, the king enclosed
35 the site and made it sacred. The
custodians he appointed received a
share of the very substantial revenue
36 that the king derived from it. Nehemiah
and his companions called the liquid
'nephthar', which means 'purification';
but most people call it 'naphtha'.

2 The records show that it was the
prophet Jeremiah who ordered the
exiles to hide the fire, as has been
2 mentioned; also that, having given
them the law, he charged them not to
neglect the ordinances of the Lord, or
be led astray by the sight of images of
3 gold and silver with all their finery. In
similar words he appealed to them not
to abandon the law.
4 Further, this document records that,
prompted by a divine message, the
prophet gave orders that the Tent of
Meeting and the ark should go with
him. Then he went away to the mountain from the top of which Moses saw
5 God's promised land. When he reached
the mountain, Jeremiah found a cave-
dwelling; he carried the tent, the ark,
and the incense-altar into it, then
6 blocked up the entrance. Some of his
companions came to mark out the way,
7 but were unable to find it. When
Jeremiah learnt of this he reprimanded
them. 'The place shall remain unknown', he said, 'until God finally
gathers his people together and shows
8 mercy to them. Then the Lord will
bring these things to light again, and
the glory of the Lord will appear with
the cloud, as it was seen both in the
time of Moses and when Solomon
prayed that the shrine might be
worthily consecrated.'
9 It was also related that Solomon,
having the gift of wisdom, offered the

dedication sacrifice at the completion
of the temple; and that, just as Moses 10
prayed to the Lord and fire came down
from heaven and burnt up the sacrificial offerings, so Solomon prayed and
the fire came down and consumed the
whole-offerings. (Moses said: 'The sin- 11
offering was burnt up in the same way
because it was not eaten.') Solomon 12
celebrated the feast for eight days.
These same facts are set out in the 13
official records and in the memoirs of
Nehemiah. Just as Nehemiah collected
the chronicles of the kings, the writings
of prophets, the works of David, and
royal letters about sacred offerings, to
found his library, so Judas also has 14
collected all the books that had been
scattered as a result of our recent
conflict. These are in our possession,
and if you need any of them, send 15
messengers for them.
As, then, we are about to celebrate 16
the purification of the temple, we are
writing to impress upon you the duty
of celebrating this festival. God has 17
saved his whole people and granted to
all of us the holy land, the kingship, the
priesthood, and the consecration, as 18
he promised by the law; and in him we
have confidence that he will soon be
merciful to us and gather us from every
part of the world to the holy temple.
For he has delivered us from great evils
and purified the temple.

Preface to this abridgement

IN FIVE BOOKS JASON OF CYRENE HAS 19
set out the history of Judas Maccabeus
and his brothers, the purification of the
great temple, and the dedication of the
altar. He has described the battles with 20
Antiochus Epiphanes and with his son
Eupator, and the apparitions from 21

---

or petroleum (v. 36). **36:** The Persian word for the *liquid* is *neft*. *Nephthar* involves a play on
this word and on the Heb. root *thr*, "purify." **2.4–8:** This story is improbable, too; see Jer.3.16.
Moses' *mountain* was Nebo (Deut.32.49). **9–10:** On the theme of *fire ... from heaven*, see
Lev.9.24; Judg.6.21; 1 Kgs.18.38; 2 Chr.7.1. **11:** The meaning of this verse is not clear but
see Lev.10.16–20. **13:** The inclusion of the *royal letters* of Persian kings shows this collection
was not limited to sacred books. For Nehemiah's *memoirs* see 1.18 n.
    2.19–32: A summary of the five books. The abbreviator leaves responsibility for accuracy to
Jason, while attempting to make one readable, memorable, pleasurable, and profitable book
out of Jason's five. **19:** *Jason* is otherwise unknown. *Cyrene* (now in Libya) was culturally one
with Egypt. **21:** This is the first appearance of the term *Judaism* (see also 8.1; 14.38; Gal.1.14)
to describe a way of life; it is contrasted to Hellenism (4.13).

heaven which appeared to those who vied with one another in fighting manfully for Judaism. Few though they were, they ravaged the whole country 22 and routed the foreign hordes; they restored the world-renowned temple, freed the city of Jerusalem, and reaffirmed the laws which were in danger of being abolished. All this they achieved because the Lord was merciful and gracious to them.

23 These five books of Jason I shall try 24 to summarize in a single work; for I was struck by the mass of statistics and the difficulty which the bulk of the material causes to those wishing to 25 grasp the narratives of this history. I have tried to provide for the entertainment of those who read for pleasure, the convenience of students who must commit the facts to memory, and the 26 profit of even the casual reader. The task which I have taken upon myself in making this summary is no easy one. 27 It means toil and late nights, just as it is no light task for the man who plans a dinner-party and aims to satisfy his guests. Nevertheless, I will gladly undergo this hard labour for the 28 benefit of^e readers in general. I shall leave to the original author the minute discussion of every detail, and concentrate on the main points of my 29 outline. As the architect of a new house must concern himself with the whole of the structure, while the man who paints in encaustic on the walls needs to discover only what is necessary for the ornamentation, so, I judge, it is 30 with me also. It is the province of the original author of a history to take possession of the field, to spread himself in discussion, and to inquire closely 31 into particular questions. The man who makes a paraphrase must be allowed to aim at conciseness of

expression and to omit a full treatment of the subject-matter.

Here, then, without adding anything 32 further, I begin my narrative. It would be absurd to make a lengthy introduction to the history and cut short the history itself.

Syrian oppression of the Jews

DURING THE RULE OF THE HIGH PRIEST 3 Onias, the holy city enjoyed complete peace and prosperity, and the laws were still observed most scrupulously, because he was a pious man and hated wickedness. The kings themselves held 2 the sanctuary in honour and used to embellish the temple with the most splendid gifts; even Seleucus, king of 3 Asia, bore all the expenses of the sacrificial worship from his own revenues.

But a certain Simon, of the clan 4 Bilgah,^f who had been appointed administrator of the temple, quarrelled with the high priest about the regulation of the city market. Unable to get 5 the better of Onias, he went to Apollonius son of Thrasaeus, then governor of Coele-syria and Phoenicia, and 6 alleged that the treasury at Jerusalem was full of untold riches—indeed the total of the accumulated balances was incalculable and did not correspond with the account for the sacrifices; he suggested that these balances might be brought under the control of the king. When Apollonius met the king, he 7 reported what he had been told about the riches. The king selected Heliodorus, his chief minister, and sent him with orders to remove these treasures.

e for . . . of: *so some witnesses; others read* to win the gratitude of . . .
f *So some witnesses (compare Nehemiah 12.5, 18); others read* Benjamin.

3.1–4.50: The decline of the priesthood. After the defeat of Magnesia (190 B.C.) and the consequent loss of most of Asia Minor, the Seleucid kings needed money badly to pay the indemnities forced on them by the treaty of Apamea (188 B.C.). Seleucus saw a chance to rob the rich treasury of Jerusalem's Temple. The priesthood moves from Onias (3.1), to the usurper Jason (4.7), and then to Menelaus (4.23).
3.1–4.6: The story of Heliodorus and its aftermath. 1: *Onias* III, son of Simon II (Ecclus.50.1–21), was a descendant, through Jedaiah (Ezra 2.36), of Joshua, the high priest of the postexilic community (Hag.1.1). **3:** *Seleucus* IV Philopator (187–175 B.C.) was *king of Asia*, i.e. of lands bordering the eastern Mediterranean. **4:** *Bilgah* is one of the twenty-four divisions for priestly service listed in 1 Chr.24.1–19. **5:** *Apollonius* was son of Menestheus (4.4,21). *Coele-syria:* southern Syria including Palestine. **7:** *Heliodorus*, chancellor to Seleucus, later murdered the

8 Heliodorus set off at once, ostensibly to make a tour of inspection of the cities of Coele-syria and Phoenicia, but in fact to carry out the purpose of the 9 king. When he arrived at Jerusalem and had been courteously received by the high priest and the citizens, he explained why he had come: he told them about the allegations and asked 10 if they were in fact true. The high priest intimated that the deposits were held 11 in trust for widows and orphans, apart from what belonged to Hyrcanus son of Tobias, a man of very high standing; the matter was being misrepresented by the impious Simon. In all there were four hundred talents of silver and two 12 hundred of gold. It was unthinkable, he said, that wrong should be done to those who had relied on the sanctity of the place, on the dignity and inviolability of the world-famous tem- 13 ple. But Heliodorus, in virtue of the king's orders, replied that these deposits must without question be handed over to the royal treasury.

14 He fixed a day and went into the temple to make an inventory. At this there was great distress throughout the 15 whole city. The priests, prostrating themselves in their vestments before the altar, prayed to Heaven, to the Lawgiver who had made deposits sacred, to keep them intact for their 16 rightful owners. The high priest's looks pierced every beholder to the heart, for his face and its changing colour be- 17 trayed the anguish of his soul. Alarm and shuddering gripped him, and the pain he felt was clearly apparent to the 18 onlookers. The people rushed pell-mell from their houses to join together in supplication because of the dishonour which threatened the holy place. 19 Women in sackcloth, their breasts bare, filled the streets; unmarried girls who were kept in seclusion ran to the gates or walls of their houses, while others 20 leaned out from the windows; all with outstretched hands made solemn en- 21 treaty to Heaven. It was pitiful to see the crowd all lying prostrate in utter confusion, and the high priest in an agony of apprehension.

22 While the people were calling upon the Lord Almighty to keep the deposits intact and safe for those who had 23 deposited them, Heliodorus proceeded to carry out his decision. But at the very 24 moment when he arrived with his bodyguard at the treasury, the Ruler of spirits and of all powers produced a mighty apparition, so that all who had the audacity to accompany Heliodorus were faint with terror, stricken with panic at the power of God. They saw a 25 horse, splendidly caparisoned, with a rider of terrible aspect; it rushed fiercely at Heliodorus and, rearing up, attacked him with its hooves. The rider was wearing golden armour. There also 26 appeared to Heliodorus two young men of surpassing strength and glorious beauty, splendidly dressed. They stood on either side of him and scourged him, raining ceaseless blows upon him. He 27 fell suddenly to the ground, over- whelmed by a great darkness, and his men snatched him up and put him on a litter. This man, who so recently had 28 entered the treasury with a great throng and his whole bodyguard, was now borne off by them quite helpless, publicly compelled to acknowledge the sovereignty of God.*g*

29 While he lay speechless, deprived by this divine act of all hope of recovery, the Jews were praising the Lord for the 30 miracle he had performed in his own house. The temple, which a short time before was full of alarm and confusion, now overflowed with joy and festiv- ity, because the Lord Almighty had appeared.

31 Some of Heliodorus's companions hastily begged Onias to pray to the Most High, and so to spare the life of their master now lying at his very last gasp. The high priest, fearing that the 32 king might suspect that Heliodorus had

g *was now . . . of God: so some witnesses; others read* they, recognizing the sovereignty of God, now bore off quite helpless.

king in an unsuccessful bid to assume the regency. **11:** The Temple's treasure was today's equivalent of several million dollars. **12:** Onias pleads a form of "sanctuary" or *inviolability* for the money (see, similarly, 1 Macc.10.43). **22–36:** Miraculous apparitions are a feature of "pathetic" history. Some suggest Onias saved the treasure by conspiring with Heliodorus against Seleucus (see 4.2). **26:** *Two young men:* angels.

met with foul play at the hands of the Jews, brought a sacrifice for the man's 33 recovery. As the high priest was making the expiation, the same young men, dressed as before, again appeared to Heliodorus. They stood over him and said: 'Be very grateful to Onias the high priest; for his sake the Lord has spared 34 your life. You have been scourged by God; now tell all men of his mighty power.' When they had said this, they vanished.

35 Heliodorus offered a sacrifice and made lavish vows to the Lord who had spared his life; then, after taking friendly leave of Onias, he led his troops 36 back to the king. He bore witness to everyone of the miracles of the supreme God which he had seen with his own eyes.

37 When the king asked him what sort of man would be suitable to send to Jerusalem another time, Heliodorus 38 replied: 'If you have an enemy or someone plotting against your government, that is the place to send him; you will receive him back soundly flogged, if he survives at all, for beyond doubt there is a divine power surrounding the 39 temple. He whose habitation is in heaven watches over it himself and gives it his aid; those who approach the place with evil intent he strikes and destroys.'

40 So runs the story of Heliodorus and the preservation of the treasury.

4 BUT THE SIMON MENTIONED EARLIER, the man who had made allegations against his country about the money, slandered Onias, alleging that he had attacked Heliodorus and had been the 2 author of these troubles. He had the effrontery to accuse him of conspiracy against the government—this benefactor of the holy city, this protector of his fellow-Jews, this zealot for the laws. 3 The enmity grew so great that one of Simon's trusted followers even resorted 4 to murder. Onias, realizing that Simon's

rivalry was dangerous and that Apollonius son of Menestheus, governor of Coele-syria and Phoenicia, was encouraging his evil ways, paid a visit to 5 the king. He did not appear as an accuser of his fellow-citizens, but as concerned for the interests of all the Jews, both as a nation and as individuals. For he saw that unless the 6 king intervened there could not possibly be peace in public affairs, nor could Simon be stopped in his mad course.

But when Seleucus was dead and 7 had been succeeded by Antiochus, known as Epiphanes, Jason, Onias's brother, obtained the high-priesthood by corrupt means. He petitioned the 8 king and promised him three hundred and sixty talents in silver coin immediately, and eighty talents from future revenue. In addition he under- 9 took to pay another hundred and fifty talents for the authority to institute a sports-stadium, to arrange for the education of young men there, and to enrol in Jerusalem a group to be known as the 'Antiochenes'.[h] The king agreed, 10 and, as soon as he had seized the high-priesthood, Jason made the Jews conform to the Greek way of life.

He set aside the royal privileges 11 established for the Jews through the agency of John, the father of that Eupolemus who negotiated a treaty of friendship and alliance with the Romans. He abolished the lawful way of life and introduced practices which were against the law. He lost no time 12 in establishing a sports-stadium at the foot of the citadel itself, and he made the most outstanding of the young men assume the Greek athlete's hat. So 13 Hellenism reached a high point with the introduction of foreign customs through the boundless wickedness of the impious Jason, no true high priest. As a result, the priests no longer had 14 any enthusiasm for their duties at the

h *Or* enrol the inhabitants of Jerusalem as citizens of Antioch.

4.7–22: Jason as high priest introduces Hellenism. Antiochus IV Epiphanes (175–164 B.C.) sought to unify his disparate subjects by imposing Hellenistic culture and religion on them. **7:** *Seleucus was dead*, assassinated by Heliodorus. **9:** The *sports-stadium* gave youth an *education* in cultural, physical, and premilitary affairs. The *Antiochenes*, honorary citizens of Antioch, the Seleucid capital, were a corporation of Hellenized Jews who had certain political and commercial privileges. **11:** See 1 Macc.8.17. **12:** *Athlete's hat:* the traditional wide-brimmed hat

altar, but despised the temple and neglected the sacrifices; and in defiance of the law they eagerly contributed to the expenses of the wrestling-school whenever the opening gong called 15 them. They placed no value on their hereditary dignities, but cared above 16 everything for Hellenic honours. Because of this, grievous misfortunes beset them, and the very men whose way of life they strove after, and tried so hard to imitate, turned out to be 17 their vindictive enemies. To act profanely against God's laws is no light matter, as will become clear in due time.

18 When the quinquennial games were being held at Tyre in the presence of 19 the king, the blackguard Jason sent, as envoys to represent Jerusalem, Antiochenes carrying three hundred drachmas in cash for the sacrifice to Hercules. Even the bearers thought it improper that this money should be used for a sacrifice, and considered that 20 it should be spent otherwise. So, thanks to the bearers, the money designed by the sender for the sacrifice to Hercules went to fit out the triremes.

21 When Apollonius son of Menestheus was sent to Egypt for the enthronement of King Philometor, Antiochus learnt that Philometor was now hostile to his state, and became anxious for his own security. So he went to Joppa, and 22 then on to Jerusalem, where he was lavishly welcomed by Jason and the city and received with torch-light and ovations. After this, he quartered his army in Phoenicia.

23 Three years later, Jason sent Menelaus, brother of the Simon mentioned above, to convey money to the king and to carry out his directions about 24 urgent business. But Menelaus established his position with the king by acting as if he were a person of great authority, outbid Jason by three hundred talents in silver, and so diverted the high-priesthood to himself. He 25 arrived back with the royal mandate, but with nothing else to make him worthy of the high-priesthood; he still had the temper of a cruel tyrant and the fury of a savage beast. Jason, who had 26 supplanted his own brother, was now supplanted in his turn and forced to flee to Ammonite territory. As for 27 Menelaus, he continued to hold the high-priesthood but without ever paying any of the money he had promised the king, although it was demanded by Sostratus, the commander of the citadel, who was responsible for col- 28 lecting the revenues. In consequence they were both summoned by the king. As their deputies, Menelaus left his 29 brother Lysimachus, and Sostratus left Crates, the commander of the Cypriots.

It was at this point that the inhabitants 30 of Tarsus and Mallus revolted, because their cities had been handed over as a gift to the king's concubine Antiochis. The king hastened off to restore order, 31 leaving as regent Andronicus, one of his ministers. Menelaus, thinking he 32 had obtained a favourable opportunity, made a present to Andronicus of some of the gold plate belonging to the temple which he had appropriated. He had already sold some of it to Tyre and to the neighbouring cities. When Onias 33 heard this on good authority, he withdrew to sanctuary at Daphne near Antioch and denounced him. As a 34 result, Menelaus approached Andronicus privately and urged him to kill Onias. The regent went to Onias bent on treachery; he greeted him, gave him assurances on oath, and persuaded him, though still suspicious, to leave the sanctuary. Then at once, with no respect for justice, he made away with him.

His murder filled not only Jews, but 35 many from other nations as well, with alarm and anger. So when the king 36 returned from Cilicia, the Jews of

of Hermes, god of gymnastic skill. **19:** The Tyrian god Melqart was, in Hellenistic fashion, assimilated to Heracles, the Roman *Hercules*. **20:** *Triremes* were warships with three banks of oars. **21–22:** Ptolemy VI *Philometor* (180–145 B.C.) planned to regain Palestine for Egypt; Epiphanes prepared for the invasion by stationing troops in *Joppa* and other Phoenician ports.
   4.23–50: Menelaus as high priest. Corruption marks the reign of Menelaus, who succeeded in driving out his rivals. **23:** *Three years later*; 171 B.C. *Simon*: see 3.4 n. **26:** *Jason* fled east of the Jordan. **30:** *Tarsus and Mallus*, which lay in Cilicia (on the southeast coast of Turkey), objected for reasons of revenue, not morality. **33:** *Onias* took refuge in the temple of Apollo(!)

Antioch sent him a petition about the senseless killing of Onias, the Gentiles sharing in their detestation of the 37 crime. Antiochus was deeply grieved, and was moved to pity and tears as he thought of the prudence and disci- 38 plined habits of the dead man. In a burning fury, he immediately stripped Andronicus of the purple, tore off his clothes, led him round the whole city to that very place where he had committed sacrilege against Onias, and there disposed of the murderer. Thus the Lord repaid him with the retribution he deserved.

39 Lysimachus committed many acts of sacrilegious plunder in Jerusalem with the connivance of Menelaus. When the news of them became public and the people heard that much of the gold plate had been disposed of, they banded together against Lysimachus. 40 Since the crowds were seething with rage and getting out of hand, Lysimachus armed some three thousand men and began to launch a vicious attack, led by a certain Auranus, a man advanced in years and no less in folly. 41 Realizing that the attack came from Lysimachus, some of the crowd seized stones and others blocks of wood, while others again took handfuls of the ashes that were lying round, and there was complete confusion as they all hurled 42 them at Lysimachus and his men. As a result, they wounded many, killed some, and routed them all; the sacrilegious man himself they dispatched near the treasury.

43 An action was brought against Menelaus in connection with this 44 incident. When the king came to Tyre, the three men sent by the Jewish senate pleaded the case before him. 45 Menelaus's cause was as good as lost; but he promised a large sum of money to Ptolemaeus son of Dorymenes to 46 win over the king. So Ptolemaeus led the king aside into a colonnade, as if to take the air, and persuaded him to change his mind. The king acquitted 47 Menelaus, the cause of all the mischief, dismissed the charges brought against him, and condemned his unfortunate accusers to death, men who would have been discharged as entirely innocent had they appeared even before Scythians. Without more ado those who 48 had pleaded for their city, their people, and their sacred vessels, suffered the unjust penalty. At this, even some of 49 the Tyrians showed their detestation of the crime by providing a splendid funeral for the victims. Menelaus, 50 thanks to the greed of those in power, remained in office. He went from bad to worse, this arch-plotter against his own fellow-citizens.

About this time Antiochus under- 5 took his second invasion of Egypt. Apparitions were seen in the sky all 2 over Jerusalem for nearly forty days: galloping horsemen in golden armour, companies of spearmen standing to arms, swords unsheathed, cavalry divi- 3 sions in battle order. Charges and countercharges were made on each side, shields were shaken, spears massed and javelins hurled; breastplates and golden ornaments of every kind shone brightly. All men prayed that this 4 apparition might portend good.

Upon a false report of Antiochus's 5 death, Jason collected no less than a thousand men and made a surprise attack on Jerusalem. The defenders on the wall were driven back and the city was finally taken; Menelaus took refuge in the citadel, and Jason continued to 6 massacre his fellow-citizens without pity. He little knew that success against one's own kindred is the greatest of failures, and he imagined that the trophies he raised marked the defeat of enemies, not of fellow-countrymen. He did not, however, gain 7 control of the government; he gained only dishonour as the result of his plot, and returned again as a fugitive to Ammonite territory. His career came 8

at Daphne, five miles southwest of Antioch. **45:** *Ptolemaeus*, the governor of the region, later opposed the Maccabean resistance (8.8; 1 Macc.3.38). **47:** The *Scythians*, who lived just north of the Black Sea, were notorious for their cruelty.
  5.1–14: Jason's attack upon Jerusalem and its aftermath. 1: 168 B.C. **2–4:** The Jewish historian Josephus describes similar celestial portents preceding the destruction of the Temple in 70 A.D. (*B.J.* VI.5.3). **8:** The charge brought before *Aretas* (Harith I, king of the Nabataeans), Jason's

to a miserable end; for, after being imprisoned by Aretas the ruler of the Arabs, he fled from city to city, hunted by all, hated as a rebel against the laws, and detested as the executioner of his country and his fellow-citizens, and finally was driven to take refuge in 9 Egypt. In the end the man who had banished so many from their native land himself died in exile after setting sail for Sparta, where he had hoped to obtain shelter because of the Spartans' 10 kinship with the Jews. He who had cast out many to lie unburied was himself unmourned; he had no funeral of any kind, no resting-place in the grave of his ancestors.

11 When news of this reached the king, it became clear to him that Judaea was in a state of rebellion. So he set out from Egypt in savage mood, took 12 Jerusalem by storm, and ordered his troops to cut down without mercy everyone they met and to slaughter those who took refuge in the houses. 13 Young and old were murdered, women and children massacred, girls and 14 infants butchered. At the end of three days their losses had amounted to eighty thousand: forty thousand killed in action, and as many sold into slavery.

15 Not satisfied with this, the king had the audacity to enter the holiest temple on earth, guided by Menelaus, who had turned traitor both to his religion 16 and his country. He laid impious hands on the sacred vessels; his desecrating hands swept together the votive offerings which other kings had set up to enhance the splendour and fame of the shrine.

17 The pride of Antiochus passed all bounds. He did not understand that the sins of the people of Jerusalem had angered the Lord for a short time, and that this was why he left the temple to 18 its fate. If they had not already been guilty of many sinful acts, Antiochus would have fared like Heliodorus who was sent by King Seleucus to inspect the treasury; like him he would have been scourged and his insolent plan foiled at once. But the Lord did not 19 choose the nation for the sake of the sanctuary; he chose the sanctuary for the sake of the nation. Therefore even 20 the sanctuary itself first had its part in the misfortunes that overtook the nation, and afterwards shared its good fortune. It was abandoned when the Lord Almighty was angry, but restored again in all its splendour when he became reconciled.

Antiochus, then, carried off eighteen 21 hundred talents from the temple and hastened back to Antioch. In his arrogance he was rash enough to think that he could make ships sail on dry land and men walk over the sea. He 22 left commissioners behind to oppress the Hebrews: in Jerusalem Philip, by race a Phrygian, by disposition more barbarous than his master, and in 23 Mount Gerizim, Andronicus, to say nothing of Menelaus, who was more brutally overbearing to the citizens than the others. Such was the king's hostility towards the Jews that he sent 24 Apollonius, the general of the Mysian mercenaries, with an army of twenty-two thousand men, and ordered him to kill all the adult males and to sell the women and boys into slavery. When Apollonius arrived at Jerusalem, 25 he posed as a man of peace; he waited until the holy sabbath day and, finding the Jews abstaining from work, he ordered a review of his troops. All who 26 came out to see the parade he put to the sword; then, charging into the city with his soldiers, he killed a great number of people.

BUT JUDAS, ALSO CALLED MACCABAEUS, 27 with about nine others, escaped into

---

former protector, is not known. **9:** For this fictional *kinship*, see 1 Macc.12.1–23, especially v. 10 n. **11:** Forced out of Egypt by the Romans, Antiochus was already in a *savage mood*.
5.15–23a: Antiochus robs the Temple. This misplaced incident belongs after Antiochus' *first* Egyptian campaign in 169 B.C. (1 Macc.1.20–24). **16:** *Other kings* included Seleucus IV (3.3). **21:** The amount seems excessive. **22:** *Philip* appears in 6.11; 8.8. He is not the Philip of 9.29; 1 Macc.6.14,55–63. **23a:** *Andronicus* is not the murderer of 4.31–38.
5.23b–27: Apollonius attacks Jerusalem; Judas flees. Epiphanes punished the revolt led by Jason and fortified Jerusalem. See 1 Macc.1.29–36. Later, Judas defeated and killed Apollonius (1 Macc.3.10–12). **27:** The story of Mattathias is omitted (1 Macc. ch. 2; especially v. 28).

the desert, where he and his companions lived in the mountains, fending for themselves like the wild animals. They remained there living on what vegetation they found, so as to have no share in the pollution.

6 Shortly afterwards King Antiochus sent an elderly Athenian to force the Jews to abandon their ancestral customs and no longer regulate their lives 2 according to the laws of God. He was also commissioned to pollute the temple at Jerusalem and dedicate it to Olympian Zeus, and to dedicate the sanctuary on Mount Gerizim to Zeus God of Hospitality, following the practice of the local inhabitants.

3 This evil hit them hard and was a 4 severe trial. The Gentiles filled the temple with licentious revelry: they took their pleasure with prostitutes and had intercourse with women in the sacred precincts. They also brought forbidden 5 things inside, and heaped the altar with impure offerings prohibited by the law. 6 It was forbidden either to observe the sabbath or to keep the traditional festivals, or to admit to being a Jew 7 at all. On the monthly celebration of the king's birthday, the Jews were driven by brute force to eat the entrails of the sacrificial victims; and on the feast of Dionysus they were forced to wear ivy-wreaths and join the procession in 8 his honour. At the instigation of the inhabitants of Ptolemais*ⁱ* an order was published in the neighbouring Greek cities to the effect that they should adopt the same policy of compelling 9 the Jews to eat the entrails and should kill those who refused to change over to Greek ways.

Their miserable fate was there for 10 all to see. For instance, two women were brought to trial for having had their children circumcised. They were paraded through the city, with their babies hanging at their breasts, and

then flung down from the fortifications. Other Jews had assembled in 11 caves near Jerusalem to keep the sabbath in secret; they were denounced to Philip and were burnt alive, since they scrupled to defend themselves out of regard for the holiness of the day.

Now I beg my readers not to be 12 disheartened by these calamities, but to reflect that such penalties were inflicted for the discipline of our race and not for its destruction. It is a sign of great 13 kindness that acts of impiety should not be let alone for long but meet their due recompense at once. The Lord did 14 not see fit to deal with us as he does with the other nations: with them he patiently holds his hand until they have reached the full extent of their sins, but 15 upon us he inflicted retribution before our sins reached their height. So he 16 never withdraws his mercy from us; though he disciplines his people by calamity, he never deserts them. Let it 17 be enough for me to have recalled this truth; after this short digression, I must continue with my story.

There was Eleazar, one of the leading 18 teachers of the law, a man of great age and distinguished bearing. He was being forced to open his mouth and eat pork, but preferring an honourable 19 death to an unclean life, he spat it out and voluntarily submitted to the flogging, as indeed men should act who 20 have the courage to refuse to eat forbidden food even for love of life. For 21 old acquaintance' sake, the officials in charge of this sacrilegious feast had a word with Eleazar in private; they urged him to bring meat which he was permitted to eat and had himself prepared, and only pretend to be eating the sacrificial meat as the king had ordered. In that way he would escape 22 death and take advantage of the clemency which their long-standing

i Some witnesses read At the instigation of Ptolemaeus ...

6.1–17: The imposition of Hellenism. The author describes the religious persecution. See 1 Macc.1.41–64. **2:** The Syrian deity, *ba'al šamēm*, "Lord of Heaven," was identified with the supreme Greek divinity, *Zeus*. Erection of an altar to him on the Temple's altar of holocausts constituted the "abomination" of 1 Macc.1.54; Dan.11.31. Josephus says the rival Samaritan temple *on Mount Gerizim* was dedicated to Zeus Hellenios (*Ant.* XII.5.5). **5:** The *impure offerings* included swine; see v. 18; 7.1; Lev.11.7; 1 Macc.1.47. **7:** *Dionysus:* god of revelry, identified with Roman Bacchus; *ivy* was his symbol. **11:** See 1 Macc.2.29–41.

6.18–7.42: Examples of martyrdom. Old men, women, and children willingly die for the *law*. The stories are typical "Acts of Martyrs," a literary form to encourage others under persecution.

23 friendship merited. But Eleazar made an honourable decision, one worthy of his years and the authority of old age, worthy of the grey hairs he had attained to and wore with such distinction, worthy of his perfect conduct from childhood up, but above all, worthy of the holy and God-given law. So he answered at once: 'Send me quickly to 24 my grave. If I went through with this pretence at my time of life, many of the young might believe that at the age of ninety Eleazar had turned apostate. 25 If I practised deceit for the sake of a brief moment of life, I should lead them astray and bring stain and pollu- 26 tion on my old age. I might for the present avoid man's punishment, but, alive or dead, I shall never escape from 27 the hand of the Almighty. So if I now die bravely, I shall show that I have 28 deserved my long life and leave the young a fine example, to teach them how to die a good death, gladly and nobly, for our revered and holy laws.'

When he had finished speaking, he was immediately dragged away to be 29 flogged. Those who a little while before had shown him friendship now became his enemies because, in their view, what 30 he had said was madness. When he was almost dead from the blows, Eleazar sighed deeply and said: 'To the Lord belongs all holy knowledge. He knows what terrible agony I endure in my body from this flogging, though I could have escaped death; yet he knows also that in my soul I suffer gladly, because I stand in awe of him.'

31 So he died; and by his death he left a heroic example and a glorious memory, not only for the young but also for the great body of the nation.

7 Again, seven brothers with their mother had been arrested, and were being tortured by the king with whips and thongs to force them to eat pork, 2 when one of them, speaking for all, said: 'What do you expect to learn by interrogating us? We are ready to die rather than break the laws of our 3 fathers.' The king was enraged and

ordered great pans and cauldrons to be heated up, and this was done at once. 4 Then he gave orders that the spokesman's tongue should be cut out and that he should be scalped and mutilated before the eyes of his mother and his six brothers. This wreck of a man the 5 king ordered to be taken, still breathing, to the fire and roasted in one of the pans. As the smoke from it streamed out far and wide, the mother and her sons encouraged each other to die nobly. 'The Lord God is watching', 6 they said, 'and without doubt has compassion on us. Did not Moses tell Israel to their faces in the song denouncing apostasy: "He will have compassion on his servants"?'

After the first brother had died in 7 this way, the second was subjected to the same brutality. The skin and hair of his head were torn off, and he was asked: 'Will you eat, before we tear you limb from limb?' He replied in his 8 native language, 'Never!', and so he in turn underwent the torture. With his 9 last breath, he said: 'Fiend though you are, you are setting us free from this present life, and, since we die for his laws, the King of the universe will raise us up to a life everlastingly made new.'

After him the third was tortured. 10 When the question was put to him, he at once showed his tongue, boldly held out his hands, and said courageously: 11 'The God of heaven gave me these. His laws mean far more to me than they do, and it is from him that I trust to receive them back.' When they heard 12 this, the king and his followers were amazed at the young man's spirit and his utter disregard for suffering.

When he too was dead, they tortured 13 the fourth in the same cruel way. At 14 the point of death, he said to the king: 'Better to be killed by men and cherish God's promise to raise us again. There will be no resurrection to life for you!'

Then the fifth was dragged forward 15 for torture. Looking at the king, he 16 said: 'You have authority over men, mortal as you are, and can do as you

---

26: This verse hints at the sinner's punishment after death, an advance on earlier OT ideas (see also Dan.12.2). 7.1: In this contrived story, the chief persecutor, *king* Antiochus, appears himself. 6: See Deut.32.36. 8: The martyrs refuse to speak Greek (vv. 21,27; 12.37; 15.29). 9–14: The *resurrection* of the just appears throughout this story (see Dan.12.1–3); universal

please. But do not imagine that God
11 has abandoned our race. Wait and see
how his great power will torment you
and your descendants.'

18 Next the sixth was brought and said
with his dying breath: 'Do not delude
yourself. It is our own fault that we
suffer these things; we have sinned
against our God and brought these
appalling disasters upon ourselves.
19 But do not suppose you will escape the
consequences of trying to fight against
God.'

20 The mother was the most remarkable
of all, and deserves to be remembered
with special honour. She watched her
seven sons all die in the space of a
single day, yet she bore it bravely
because she put her trust in the Lord.
21 She encouraged each in turn in her
native language. Filled with noble
resolution, her woman's thoughts fired
by a manly spirit, she said to them:
22 'You appeared in my womb, I know
not how; it was not I who gave you life
and breath and set in order your bodily
23 frames. It is the Creator of the universe
who moulds man at his birth and plans
the origin of all things. Therefore he,
in his mercy, will give you back life and
breath again, since now you put his
laws above all thought of self.'
24 Antiochus felt that he was being
treated with contempt and suspected
an insult in her words. The youngest
brother was still left, and the king, not
content with appealing to him, even
assured him on oath that the moment
he abandoned his ancestral customs he
would make him rich and prosperous,
by enrolling him as a King's Friend and
25 entrusting him with high office. Since
the young man paid no attention to
him, the king summoned the mother
and urged her to advise the lad to save
26 his life. After much urging from the
king, she agreed to persuade her son.
27 She leaned towards him, and flouting
the cruel tyrant, she said in their native
language: 'My son, take pity on me.
I carried you nine months in the
womb, suckled you three years, reared
you and brought you up to your

present age. I beg you, child, look at 28
the sky and the earth; see all that is in
them and realize that God made them
out of nothing, and that man comes
into being in the same way. Do not be 29
afraid of this butcher; accept death
and prove yourself worthy of your
brothers, so that by God's mercy I may
receive you back again along with
them.'
She had barely finished when the 30
young man spoke out: 'What are you
all waiting for? I will not submit to the
king's command; I obey the command
of the law given by Moses to our
ancestors. And you, King Antiochus, 31
who have devised all kinds of harm for
the Hebrews, you will not escape God's
hand. We are suffering for our own 32
sins, and though to correct and 33
discipline us our living Lord is angry
for a short time, yet he will again be
reconciled to his servants. But you, 34
impious man, foulest of the human
race, do not indulge vain hopes or be
carried away by delusions of greatness,
you who lay hands on God's servants.
You are not yet safe from the judge- 35
ment of the almighty all-seeing God.
My brothers have now fallen in loyalty 36
to God's covenant, after brief pain
leading to eternal life;ʲ but you will pay
the just penalty of your insolence by
the verdict of God. I, like my brothers, 37
surrender my body and my life for the
laws of our fathers. I appeal to God to
show mercy speedily to his people and
by whips and scourges to bring you to
admit that he alone is God. With me 38
and my brothers may the Almighty's
anger, which has justly fallen on all
our race, be ended!'
The king, exasperated by these 39
scornful words, was beside himself
with rage. So he treated him worse than
the others, and the young man died, 40
putting his whole trust in the Lord,
without having incurred defilement.
Then finally, after her sons, the mother 41
died.

ʲ in loyalty . . . life: *or* after a brief time of pain, in
loyalty to God's covenant of everlasting life.

resurrection is not explicitly taught. **17:** The *descendants* are the king's successors. **24:** *Friend:*
see 1 Macc.2.18 n. **28:** This is the first biblical mention of creation from nothingness; see
Gen.1.1 n. **33:** See 5.17. **38:** See vicarious suffering also in Isa.52.13–53.12.

42 This, then, must conclude our account of the eating of the entrails and the monstrous outrages that accompanied it.

The revolt of Judas Maccabaeus

8 MEANWHILE JUDAS, ALSO CALLED MAC-cabaeus, and his companions were making their way into the villages unobserved. They summoned their kinsmen and enlisted others who had remained faithful to Judaism, until they had collected about six thousand 2 men. They invoked the Lord to look down and help his people, whom all were trampling under foot, to take pity on the temple profaned by impious 3 men, and to have mercy on Jerusalem, which was being destroyed and would soon be levelled to the ground. They prayed him also to give ear to the blood that cried to him for vengeance, 4 to remember the infamous massacre of innocent children and the deeds of blasphemy against his name, and to show his hatred of wickedness. 5 Once his band of partisans was organized, Maccabaeus proved invincible to the Gentiles, for the Lord's 6 anger had changed to mercy. He came on towns and villages without warning and burnt them; he occupied the key positions, and inflicted many severe 7 reverses on the enemy, choosing the night-time as being especially favourable for these attacks. His heroism[k] 8 was talked about everywhere. When Philip realized that the small gains made by Judas were occurring with growing frequency, he wrote to Ptolemaeus, the governor of Coele-syria and Phoenicia, asking for his help in pro-

tecting the royal interests. Ptolemaeus 9 immediately selected Nicanor, son of Patroclus, a member of the highest order of King's Friends, and sent him at the head of at least twenty thousand troops of various nationalities to exterminate the entire Jewish race. With him Ptolemaeus associated Gorgias, a general of wide experience. Nicanor determined to pay off the two 10 thousand talents due from the king as tribute to the Romans, by the sale of the Jews he would take prisoner; and 11 he at once made an offer of Jewish slaves to the coastal towns, undertaking to deliver them at the price of ninety to the talent. But he did not expect the vengeance of the Almighty, which was soon to be at his heels.

Word of Nicanor's advance reached 12 Judas, and he informed his men that the enemy was at hand. The cowards 13 who doubted God's justice took themselves off and fled. But the rest disposed 14 of their remaining possessions, and they prayed together to the Lord to save them from the impious Nicanor, who had sold them even before they met in battle; and if they could not ask this 15 for their own merits, they did so on the ground of the covenants God had made with their ancestors, and of his holy and majestic Name which they bore. Maccabaeus assembled his fol- 16 lowers, six thousand in number, and appealed to them not to flee in panic before the enemy nor to be afraid of the great host which was attacking them without just cause. Rather they should fight nobly, having before their 17 eyes the wicked crimes of the Gentiles against the temple, their callous outrage upon Jerusalem, and, further, their

k Or His numerous force.

8.1–10.8: Judas Maccabaeus succeeds in purifying the Temple. The Lord's anger (6.12–17) is appeased and turns to mercy (8.5), enabling Judas and his guerrillas to rededicate the Temple.
    8.1–36: Judas' initial successes. See 1 Macc.2.42–48. **2–3:** The guerrillas pray, then fight. 2 Macc. emphasizes the role of prayer in the victories. For similar descriptions of the evils faced, see 1 Macc.1.24–28,36–40; 2.7–12; 3.45,50–53. **8–29,34–36:** See 1 Macc.3.38–4.27. **8:** *Philip:* see 5.22; 6.11. *Ptolemaeus:* see 4.45; 1 Macc.3.38. In Hellenistic times, *Coele-syria* designated first the region between the Lebanon and Anti-Lebanon mountains, then also Palestine generally. **9:** Victory for *Nicanor* (vv. 14–15; 1 Macc.3.38; 7.26–50), one of the *King's Friends* (see 1 Macc.2.18 n.), would *exterminate the entire Jewish race* by destroying defenders of its distinctiveness and assimilating the survivors to Hellenism. **10:** The *tribute* may be arrears from the money owed by the treaty of Apamea (188 B.C.). **11:** Nicanor's offer was half the average price per slave in Greece. **13:** 1 Macc.3.56 gives the reasons of Deut.20.5–8 for their departure. **14:** They *disposed of their . . . possessions* lest Nicanor confiscate them anyway.

suppression of the traditional Jewish
18 way of life. They rely on their weapons
and their audacity,' he said, 'but we
rely on God Almighty, who is able to
overthrow with a nod our present
assailants and, if need be, the whole
19 world.' He went on to recount to them
the occasions when God had helped
their ancestors: how, in Sennacherib's
time, one hundred and eighty-five thou-
20 sand of the enemy had perished, and
also how, on the occasion of the battle
against the Galatians in Babylonia, all
the Jews engaged in the combat had
numbered no more than eight thousand, with four thousand Macedonians, yet, when the Macedonians were
hard pressed, the eight thousand
through heaven's aid had destroyed
one hundred and twenty thousand and
taken much booty.

21   His words put them in good heart
and made them ready to die for their
laws and for their country. He then
22 divided the army into four and gave
each of his brothers, Simon, Josephus,
and Jonathan, command of a division
23 of fifteen hundred men. Besides this, he
appointed Eleazar to read the holy
book aloud[l], and giving the signal for
battle with the cry 'God is our help',
and taking command of the leading
division in person, he engaged Nicanor.
24 The Almighty fought on their side, and
they slaughtered over nine thousand
of the enemy, wounded and disabled
the greater part of Nicanor's forces,
25 and routed them completely. They
seized the money of those who had
come to buy them as slaves. After
chasing the enemy a considerable
distance, they were forced to break off
26 because it was late; for it was the day
before the sabbath, and for that reason
27 they called off the pursuit. When they
had collected the enemy's weapons and
stripped the dead, they turned to keep
the sabbath. They offered thanks and
praises loud and long to the Lord who
had kept the first drops of his mercy to
28 shed on them that day.[m] After the

sabbath was over, they distributed
some of the spoils among the victims
of persecution and the widows and
orphans; the remainder they divided
among themselves. This done, all 29
together made supplication to the
merciful Lord, praying him to be fully
reconciled with his servants.

The Jews now engaged the forces of 30
Timotheus and Bacchides and killed
over twenty thousand of them. They
gained complete control of some high
strongholds, and divided the immense
booty, giving shares equal to their own
to the victims of persecution, to the
widows and orphans, and to the old
men as well. They carefully collected 31
all the enemy's weapons and stored
them at strategic points; the remainder
of the spoils they brought into Jerusalem. They killed the officer command- 32
ing the forces of Timotheus, an utterly
godless man who had caused the Jews
great suffering. During the victory 33
celebrations in their capital, they
burnt alive the men who had set fire to
the sacred gates, including Callisthenes,
who had taken refuge in a small house;
he thus received the due reward of his
impiety.

Thus, by the Lord's help, Nicanor, 34–35
that double-dyed villain who had
brought the thousand merchants to
buy the Jewish captives, was humiliated
by the very people whom he despised
above all others. He threw off his
magnificent uniform, and all alone like
a runaway slave made his escape
through the interior, and was, indeed,
very lucky to reach Antioch after losing
his whole army. So the man who had 36
undertaken to secure tribute for the
Romans by taking prisoner the inhabitants of Jerusalem showed the
world that the Jews had a champion
and were therefore invulnerable, because they kept the laws he had given
them.

l Besides . . . aloud: *probable reading; Gk. obscure.*
m kept . . . day: *so some witnesses; others read* brought
them safely to that day and had appointed it as the
beginning of mercy for them.

19: *Sennacherib's time:* see 2 Kgs.19.35. **20:** This incident is otherwise unknown. **30–33:**
See 1 Macc.5.6–13,24–54. **30:** For *Timotheus* see 1 Macc.5.6–8,37–44; 2 Macc.12.10–25, and
for *Bacchides*, see 1 Macc.7.8–20. **33:** *Callisthenes* is otherwise unknown. The fire may be that
of 1 Macc.1.31. **36:** *Champion:* God.

9 It so happened that, about this time, Antiochus had returned in disorder from Persia. He had entered the city of Persepolis and attempted to plunder its temples and assume control. But the populace rose and rushed to arms in their defence, with the result that Antiochus was routed by civilians and forced to beat a humiliating retreat. ³ When he was near Ecbatana, news reached him of what had happened to Nicanor and the forces of Timotheus. ⁴ Transported with fury, he conceived the idea of making the Jews pay for the injury inflicted by those who had put him to flight, and so he ordered his charioteer to drive without stopping until the journey was finished.

But riding with him was the divine judgement! For in his arrogance he said: 'When I reach Jerusalem, I will make it a common graveyard for the ⁵ Jews.' But the all-seeing Lord, the God of Israel, struck him a fatal and invisible blow. As soon as he had said the words, he was seized with incurable pain in his bowels and with sharp ⁶ internal torments—a punishment entirely fitting for one who had inflicted many unheard-of torments on the ⁷ bowels of others. Still he did not in the least abate his insolence; more arrogant than ever, he breathed fiery threats against the Jews. After he had given orders to speed up the journey, it happened that he fell out of his chariot as it hurtled along, and so violent was his fall that every joint in his body was ⁸ dislocated. He, who in his pretension to be more than man had just been thinking that he could command the waves of the sea and weigh high mountains on the scales, was brought to the ground and had to be carried in a litter, thus making God's power[n] ⁹ manifest to all. Worms swarmed even from the eyes of this godless man and, while he was still alive and in agony, his flesh rotted off, and the whole army was disgusted by the stench of

his decay. It was so unbearably ¹⁰ offensive that nobody could escort the man who only a short time before had seemed to touch the stars in the sky.

In this broken state, Antiochus began ¹¹ to abate his great arrogance. Under God's lash, and racked with continual pain, he began to see things in their true light. He could not endure his own ¹² stench and said, 'It is right to submit oneself to God and, being mortal, not to think oneself equal to him.' Then ¹³ the villain made a solemn promise to the Lord, who had no intention of sparing him any longer, and it was to this effect: Jerusalem the holy city, ¹⁴ which he had been hurrying to level to the ground and to transform into a graveyard, he would now declare a free city; to all the Jews, whom he had not ¹⁵ considered worthy of burial but only fit to be thrown out with their children as prey for birds and beasts, he would give privileges equal to those enjoyed by the citizens of Athens. The holy ¹⁶ temple which he had earlier plundered he would adorn with the most splendid gifts; he would replace all the sacred utensils on a much more lavish scale; he would meet the cost of the sacrifices from his own revenues. In addition to ¹⁷ all this, he would even turn Jew and visit every inhabited place to proclaim God's might.

When his pains in no way abated, ¹⁸ because the just judgement of God had fallen on him, he was in despair and, as a kind of olive branch, wrote to the Jews the letter here copied:

To my worthy citizens, the Jews, ¹⁹ warm greetings and good wishes for their health and prosperity from Antiochus, King and Chief Magistrate.

May you and your children flourish ²⁰ and your affairs go as you wish. Having my hope in heaven, I keep an ²¹

---

n *Some witnesses read* litter. God made his power . . .

9.1–29: The death of the persecutor. The false god Epiphanes, "(Zeus) manifest," falls by the manifest power of the true God. See 1 Macc.6.1–17. **8:** See v. 12; 5.21. **9–17:** Theology, rather than history, seems to be the object of the description of the king's last illness. The allusions are to Isa.14.11; 66.24; Ecclus.7.17; 19.3. For similar descriptions of the deaths of the impious, see Josephus on Herod the Great (*Ant.* XVII.6.5) and Acts 12.23 on Herod Agrippa. **18–27:** The letter is sent to Hellenized Jews or Antiochenes. Jews faithful to the Law would not re-

affectionate remembrance of your regards and goodwill.

As I was returning from Persia, I suffered a tiresome illness, and so I have judged it necessary to provide 22 for the general safety of you all. Not that I despair of my condition—on the contrary I have good hopes of 23 recovery—but I observed that my father, whenever he made an expedition east of the Euphrates, 24 appointed a successor, so that, if anything unexpected should happen or if some tiresome report should spread, his subjects would not be disturbed, since they would know to whom the empire had been left. 25 Further, I know well that the neighbouring princes on the frontiers of my kingdom are watching for an opportunity and waiting on events. So I have designated as king my son Antiochus, whom I frequently entrusted and recommended to most of you during my regular visits to the satrapies beyond the Euphrates. I have written to him what is here 26 copied. Wherefore I pray and entreat each one of you to maintain your existing goodwill towards myself and my son, remembering the services I have rendered to you both as a 27 community and as individuals. For I am sure my son will follow my own policy of moderation and benevolence and will accommodate himself to your wishes.

28 Thus this murderer and blasphemer, suffering the worst of agonies, such as he had made others suffer, met a pitiable end in the mountains of a foreign 29 land. His body was brought back by Philip, his intimate friend; but he was afraid of Antiochus's son and went

over to Ptolemy Philometor in Egypt.

Maccabaeus with his men, led by 10 the Lord, recovered the temple and city of Jerusalem. He demolished the altars 2 erected by the heathen in the public square, and their sacred precincts as well. When they had purified the 3 sanctuary, they constructed another altar; then, striking fire from flints, they offered a sacrifice for the first time for two whole years, and restored the incense, the lights, and the Bread of the Presence. This done, they prostrated 4 themselves and prayed the Lord not to let them fall any more into such disasters, but, should they ever happen to sin, to discipline them himself with clemency and not hand them over to blasphemous and barbarous Gentiles. The sanctuary was purified on the 5 twenty-fifth of Kislev, the same day of the same month as that on which foreigners had profaned it. The joyful 6 celebration lasted for eight days; it was like the Feast of Tabernacles, for they recalled how, only a short time before, they had kept that feast while they were living like wild animals in the mountains and caves; and so they 7 carried garlanded wands and branches with their fruits, as well as palm-fronds, and they chanted hymns to the One who had so triumphantly achieved the purification of his own temple. A 8 measure was passed by the public assembly to the effect that the entire Jewish race should keep these days every year.

The campaign against Eupator

WE HAVE ALREADY RECOUNTED THE 9 end of Antiochus called Epiphanes. Now we will describe what happened 10

---

member Antiochus' *services* (v. 26) kindly. **23:** Antiochus III had appointed Seleucus IV to succeed him. **29:** *Philip:* see 1 Macc.6.14–15.

10.1–8: Judas purifies the Temple. See 1 Macc.4.36–61. **2:** See 1 Macc.1.47. **3:** The interval of *two years* is three in 1 Macc.1.54; 4.52. For the *incense, lights,* and *Bread,* see Exod.30.7–8; 25.30. **5:** December 17, 164 B.C. **6:** Unable to celebrate the *Feast of Tabernacles* properly while on the run (5.27; 6.6), Judas and his men now celebrate the Temple's purification and rededication as a Feast of Tabernacles in Kislev (1.9 n.). **7:** *Palm-fronds:* symbols of independence found on Jewish coins of the period and later; see 1 Macc.13.51. **8:** This explains the letters of 1.1–10a; 1.10b–2.18.

10.9–13.26: The defeat of Lysias and others. Since Antiochus V Eupator was only about seven years old when his father died, the main actors are Lysias and various generals.

10.9–12.1: Battles with Seleucid generals. The events leading up to the treaty with Lysias are

under that godless man's son, Antiochus Eupator, in a brief summary of the principal evils brought about by
11 his wars. At his accession, Eupator appointed as vicegerent a man called Lysias who had succeeded Ptolemaeus Macron as governor-general of Coele-
12 syria and Phoenicia. For Ptolemaeus had taken the lead in reversing the former unjust treatment of the Jews and had attempted to maintain peaceful
13 relations with them, and as a result he was denounced by the King's Friends to Eupator. On every side he was called traitor, because he had already abandoned Cyprus, entrusted to him by Philometor, and had gone over to Antiochus Epiphanes. He still enjoyed power, but no longer respect, and in despair he ended his life by poison.
14 When Gorgias became governor, he engaged mercenaries and took every
15 opportunity of attacking the Jews. At the same time the Idumaeans, who were in control of strategic fortresses, were also harassing them; they harboured the fugitives from Jerusalem and tried
16 to carry on the war. Maccabaeus and his men made public supplication and prayed God to fight on their side. They made an assault on the Idumaean
17 fortresses, pressed the attack vigorously, and captured them; they drove off all who were manning the walls, and killed all they met, to the number of at least twenty thousand.
18 Nine thousand or more of the enemy took refuge in two towers, very strongly fortified and fully equipped
19 against a siege. Maccabaeus himself set out for the places which were being hard pressed, but left Simon and Josephus behind, with Zacchaeus and his men, enough to prosecute the siege.
20 But Simon's men were too fond of money, and when they were bribed with seventy thousand drachmas by

some of those in the towers, they let
21 them slip through their lines. When Maccabaeus was informed of this, he assembled the leaders of the army and denounced these men for having sold their brothers for money by letting their enemies escape. Then he executed the
22 men who had turned traitor, and immediately the two towers fell to him.
23 His military operations were completely successful; in the two fortresses he destroyed over twenty thousand of the enemy.
24 After his previous defeat by the Jews, Timotheus collected a huge force of mercenaries and Asian cavalry, and advanced to take Judaea by storm.
25 As he approached, Maccabaeus and his men made their prayer to God. They sprinkled dust on their heads and
26 put sackcloth round their waists; they prostrated themselves on the altar-step and begged God to favour them, 'to be an enemy of their enemies and an opponent of their opponents', as the law clearly states.
27 When they had finished their prayer, they took up their weapons, advanced a good distance from Jerusalem, and halted near the enemy. At first light the
28 two armies joined battle. For the Jews, success and victory were guaranteed not only because of their bravery but even more because the Lord was their refuge, whereas the Gentiles had only their own fury to lead them into battle.
29 As the fighting grew hot, the enemy saw in the sky five magnificent figures riding horses with golden bridles, who placed themselves at the head of the Jews, formed a circle round Mac-
30 cabaeus, and kept him invulnerable under the protection of their armour. They launched arrows and thunderbolts at the enemy, who, confused and blinded, broke up in complete disorder.
31 Twenty thousand five hundred of the

---

described. **11:** Although *Lysias* was regent and guardian of Antiochus V Eupator (164–161 B.C.), he had to struggle with Philip to maintain this post (1 Macc.3.33; 6.14,55–63). **12–13:** *Ptolemaeus* had governed *Cyprus* for the Egyptian king Ptolemy VI *Philometor* (180–145 B.C.), but deserted to *Epiphanes* when that Seleucid king's fleet approached Cyprus. **14–23:** See 1 Macc.5.3–5. **14:** *Gorgias* was *governor* of Idumea (12.32). **17:** The *twenty thousand* here, "nine thousand" in v. 18, and "seventy thousand" in v. 20 all seem excessive. The author tends to inflate numbers. **22:** Once the evil is removed, God, who fights with Judas (v. 16), *immediately* allows success. The author never loses sight of the source of victory. **24–38:** This incident, unparalleled in 1 Macc., belongs chronologically after 12.10–31; 1 Macc.5.9 13,24–54. **26:** See Exod.23.22. **29–31:** Fighting for the Law, Judas gets help from heaven, i.e., he receives supernatural

infantry, as well as six hundred cavalry, were slaughtered.

32 Timotheus himself fled to a fortress called Gazara, commanded by Chac- 33 reas and strongly garrisoned. Maccabaeus and his men welcomed this, and for four days they laid siege to the 34 place. The garrison, confident in the strength of their position, hurled horrible and impious blasphemies at them, 35 until, at dawn on the fifth day, twenty young men from the force of Maccabaeus, burning with rage at the blasphemy, courageously stormed the wall and in savage anger cut down all 36 they met. Under cover of this distraction others got up the same way, attacked the defenders, set light to the towers, and started fires on which they burnt the blasphemers alive. Others broke down the gates and let in the rest of the army, and thus the city was 37 occupied. Timotheus had hidden himself in a cistern, but he was killed along with his brother Chaereas and Apol- 38 lophanes. To celebrate their achievement, the Jews praised with hymns and thanksgivings the Lord who showers blessings on Israel and gives them the victory.

11 Very shortly afterwards, Lysias the vicegerent, the king's guardian and 2 relative, angered by these events, collected about eighty thousand troops, in addition to his entire cavalry, and advanced on the Jews. He reckoned on making Jerusalem a settlement for 3 Gentiles, subjecting the temple to taxation like all gentile shrines, and putting up the high-priesthood for sale 4 annually. He reckoned not at all with the might of God, but was elated with his myriads of infantry, his thousands 5 of cavalry, his eighty elephants. Penetrating into Judaea, he approached Bethsura, a fortified place about twenty miles from Jerusalem, and closely invested it.

6 When Maccabaeus and his men learnt that Lysias was besieging their fortresses, they and all the people, wailing and weeping, prayed the Lord

to send a good angel to deliver Israel. Maccabaeus was the first to arm him- 7 self, and he urged the rest to share his danger and come to the help of their brothers. One and all, they set out eagerly. They were still in the neigh- 8 bourhood of Jerusalem when there appeared at their head a horseman arrayed in white, brandishing his golden weapons. Then with one voice 9 they praised their merciful God and felt so strong in spirit that they could have attacked not only men but also the most savage animals, and even walls of iron. They came on fully armed, 10 with their heavenly ally, under the mercy of the Lord. They hurled them- 11 selves like lions against the enemy, cut down eleven thousand of them, as well as sixteen hundred cavalry, and put all the rest to flight. Most of those who 12 escaped lost their weapons and were wounded, and Lysias saved his life only by running away.

Lysias was no fool, and as he took 13 stock of the defeat he had suffered he realized that the Hebrews were invincible, because the mighty God fought on their side. So he proposed a 14 settlement on terms entirely acceptable, promising also to win the king over by putting pressure on him to show friendship to the Jews. Maccabaeus 15 agreed to all the proposals of Lysias out of regard for the general welfare, for the king had accepted all the proposals from the Jewish side which Maccabaeus had forwarded to Lysias in writing.

The letter of Lysias to the Jews ran 16 as follows:

Lysias to the Jewish community, greeting.

Your representatives John and 17 Absalom have handed to me the document here copied and have asked me to ratify what is contained in it. Whatever needed to be brought 18 to the king's knowledge, I have communicated to him, and what was within my own competence, I have

protection and truly miraculous military assistance. **11.1–15:** See 1 Macc.4.28–35. This event preceded the death of Antiochus IV Epiphanes. **11:** 1 Macc.4.34 gives much lower numbers. **13:** The reason is the author's, not that of Lysias. **16–38:** The letters, except for vv. 22–26, belong to the peace negotiations. **17:** *John* may be Mattathias' son (1 Macc.2.2). **18:** The king

19 granted. If, therefore, you maintain your goodwill towards the empire, I for my part will endeavour to promote your welfare for the future.

20 I have ordered your representatives and mine to confer with you about

21 the details. Farewell.

The twenty-fourth of Dioscorus in the year 148.*°*

22 The king's letter ran as follows:

King Antiochus to his brother Lysias, greeting.

23 Now that our royal father has gone to join the gods, we desire that our subjects be undisturbed in the

24 conduct of their own affairs. We have learnt that the Jews do not consent to adopt Greek ways, as our father wished, but prefer their own mode of life and request that they be allowed to observe their own laws.

25 We choose, therefore, that this nation like the rest should be left undisturbed, and decree that their temple be restored to them and that they shall regulate their lives in accordance with their ancestral cus-

26 toms. Have the goodness, therefore, to inform them of this and ratify it, so that, knowing what our intentions are, they may settle down confidently and quietly to manage their own affairs.

27 To the people the king's letter ran thus:

King Antiochus to the Jewish Senate and people, greeting.

28 We hope that you prosper. We too

29 are in good health. Menelaus has informed us of your desire to return

30 to your own homes. Therefore we declare an amnesty for all who return before the thirtieth of Xanthi

31 cus. The Jews may follow their own food laws as heretofore, and none of them shall be charged with any previous infringement. I am

32 sending Menelaus to reassure you. Farewell.

33 The fifteenth of Xanthicus in the year 148.*°*

34 The Romans also sent the Jews the following letter:

Quintus Memmius and Titus Manius, Roman legates, to the Jewish people, greeting.

35 We give our assent to all that Lysias, the king's relative, has

36 granted you. But examine carefully the questions which he reserved for reference to the king; then send someone immediately, so that we may make suitable proposals, for we are proceeding to Antioch. Send

37 messengers therefore without delay, so that we also may know what your opinion is. Farewell.

38 The fifteenth of Xanthicus in the year 148.*°*

12 When these agreements had been concluded, Lysias went off to the king, and the Jews returned to their farming.

2 But some of the governors in the region, Timotheus and Apollonius son of Gennaeus and also Hieronymus and Demophon, and in addition Nicanor, chief of the Cypriot mercenaries, would not allow them to enjoy security and live in quiet.

3 I MUST NOW DESCRIBE AN ATROCITY committed by the inhabitants of Joppa.

o That is 164 B.C.

---

here is Epiphanes, not Eupator. **21:** This is March 164 B.C. **22–26:** This misplaced letter belongs to the peace negotiations following Lysias' second campaign against Judas (13.1–26; 1 Macc. 6.28–63). It confirms religious freedom for the Jews. Here the *king* is *Antiochus V* Eupator. The terms were forced on Lysias by political necessity (1 Macc.6.55–63). **23:** The dynasty was considered to draw its origin from the gods; its rulers were given divine honors during their lifetime and so went to *join the gods* after death. **27–33:** *Antiochus* retracts the hated edicts regarding food (6.7–8). *Xanthicus:* March–April. **34–38:** The *questions* referred *to the king* (see v. 18) are not known. *Quintus Memmius* is otherwise unknown. *Titus Manius* is actually two men, *Titus* Manilius and *Manius* Sergius, both well-known Roman diplomats active in the east at this time.

12.2–45: Battles with neighboring peoples. See 1 Macc.5.1–68. Harassment by neighboring peoples led to a series of Jewish punitive raids. **2:** For *Timotheus,* see 8.30–33; 10.24–38;

They invited the Jews living in the town to embark with their wives and children in boats which they provided, with no indication of any ill will towards them.
4 As it was a public decision by the whole town, and because they wished to live in peace and suspected nothing, they accepted; but when they were out at sea, the people of Joppa sank the boats, drowning no fewer than two
5 hundred of them. When Judas learnt of this brutal treatment of his fellow-countrymen, he alerted his troops,
6 invoked God, the just judge, and fell upon their murderers. He set the harbour of Joppa on fire by night, burnt the shipping, and put to the sword those who had taken refuge
7 there. But finding the town gates closed, he withdrew, meaning however to return and root out the entire
8 community. When he learnt that the people of Jamnia intended to do the same to the Jews who lived among
9 them, he attacked Jamnia by night and set fire to its harbour and fleet; the light of the flames was visible in Jerusalem thirty miles away.
10 When they had marched more than a mile further in their advance against Timotheus, they were set upon by not less than five thousand Arabs, with
11 five hundred cavalry. A violent combat ensued, in which by divine help Judas and his men were victorious. The defeated nomads begged Judas to make an alliance with them, and promised to supply him with cattle and to give the
12 Jews every other kind of help. Judas realized that they could indeed be useful in many ways; so he agreed to make peace with them, and, after receiving assurances from him, they went back to their tents.
13 Judas also attacked Caspin, a walled town, strongly fortified and inhabited
14 by a motley crew of Gentiles. Confident in the strength of their walls and in their store of provisions, the defenders behaved provocatively towards Judas and his men, abusing them and also uttering the most wicked
15 blasphemies. But they invoked the world's great Sovereign who in the days of Joshua threw down the walls of Jericho without battering-rams or siege-engines. They attacked the wall
16 fiercely and, by the will of God, captured the town. The carnage was indescribable; the adjacent lake, a quarter of a mile wide, appeared to be overflowing with blood.
17 Advancing about ninety-five miles from there, they reached Charax, which is inhabited by the Tubian Jews, as they
18 are called. They did not find Timotheus there; he had by that time left the district, having had no success, but in one place he had left behind an
19 extremely strong garrison. Dositheus and Sosipater, Maccabaeus's generals, set out and destroyed the garrison, which consisted of over ten thousand
20 men. Maccabaeus for his part grouped his army in several divisions, appointed commanders for them,*p* and hurried after Timotheus, whose forces numbered a hundred and twenty thousand infantry and two thousand five hundred
21 cavalry. When he learnt of Judas's approach, Timotheus sent off the women and children with all the baggage to a town called Carnaim, this being an inaccessible place, hard to storm because all the approaches to it
22 were narrow. But when Judas's first division appeared, terror and panic seized the enemy at the manifestation of the all-seeing One. In their flight they rushed headlong in every direction, so that frequently they were injured by their comrades and were run through by the points of their swords.
23 Judas pressed the pursuit vigorously and put thirty thousand of these criminals to the sword. Timotheus him-
24

p Probable meaning, based on one Vs.; Gk. appointed them to command the divisions.

12.10–31; 1 Macc.5.24–54. The other *governors* are otherwise unknown. **10:** This *mile further* is not measured from Joppa or Jamnia but from some unspecified point in Gilead. The verse abruptly introduces a sizeable fragment (vv. 10–31) from a narrative of Judas' battles with Timotheus (see v. 2) which seems to have become disarranged at some point in its transmission. **13:** *Caspin* is the Casphor of 1 Macc.5.26,36. **15:** *Walls of Jericho*: see Josh.6.1–21. **17:** *Charax* is literally a fortified camp. These *Tubian Jews* lived in the region of Tubias, i.e. in Gilead (1 Macc.5.13). **21–26:** For the battle near, and at, *Carnaim*, see 1 Macc.5.37–44. *Atargatis* was

self was taken prisoner by the troops of Dositheus and Oosipater. With much cunning, he begged them to let him go in safety, pointing out that most of them had parents, and some of them brothers, who were in his hands, and

25 might never be heard of again. He pledged himself over and over again to restore these hostages safe and sound; and so they let him go in order to save their relatives.

26 Judas moved on Carnaim and the sanctuary of Atargatis, and killed twenty-five thousand people there.

27 After this victory and destruction he next marched on Ephron, a fortified town inhabited by a mixed population.*q* Stalwart young men took up their position in front of the walls and fought vigorously, while inside there was a great supply of engines of war

28 and ammunition. But the Jews invoked the Sovereign whose might shatters all the strength of the enemy. They made themselves masters of the town and killed twenty-five thousand of the

29 defenders. Leaving that place, they advanced to Scythopolis, some seventy-

30 five miles from Jerusalem. The Jews who lived there testified to the goodwill shown them by the people of Scythopolis and the kindness with which they had treated them in their bad

31 times; so Judas and his men thanked them, and charged them to be equally friendly to the Jewish race for the future. They returned to Jerusalem in time for the Feast of Weeks.

32 After celebrating Pentecost, as it is called, they advanced to attack Gorgias,

33 the general in charge of Idumaea, who met them with three thousand infantry

34 and four hundred cavalry. When the ranks joined battle, a small number of

35 the Jews fell. But a cavalryman of great strength called Dositheus, one of the Tubian Jews, had hold of Gorgias by his cloak and was dragging the villain

off by main force, with the object of taking him alive, when a Thracian horseman bore down on him and chopped off his arm; so Gorgias escaped to Marisa.

36 Esdrias and his men had been fighting for a long time and were exhausted. But Judas invoked the Lord to show himself their ally and leader in battle.

37 Striking up hymns in his native language as a battle-cry, he put the forces of Gorgias to flight by a surprise attack.

38 Regrouping his forces, he led them to the town of Adullam. The seventh day was coming on, so they purified themselves, as custom dictated, and kept the sabbath there. Next day they

39 went, as had by now become necessary, to collect the bodies of the fallen in order to bury them with their relatives in the ancestral graves. But on every

40 one of the dead, they found, under the tunic, amulets sacred to the idols of Jamnia, objects which the law forbids to Jews. It was evident to all that here was the reason why these men had

41 fallen. Therefore they praised the work of the Lord, the just judge, who reveals what is hidden; and, turning to prayer,

42 they asked that this sin might be entirely blotted out. The noble Judas called on the people to keep themselves free from sin, for they had seen with their own eyes what had happened to the fallen because of their sin. He

43 levied a contribution from each man, and sent the total of two thousand silver drachmas to Jerusalem for a sin-offering—a fit and proper act in which he took due account of the resurrection.

44 For if he had not been expecting the fallen to rise again, it would have been foolish and superfluous to pray for the

45 dead. But since he had in view the wonderful reward reserved for those who die a godly death, his purpose

q Some witnesses add where Lysias had his headquarters.

the famed Syrian goddess. **27–28:** Judas took *Ephron* because it refused him passage (1 Macc. 5.46–51). **29:** *Scythopolis* is the Bethshan of 1 Macc.5.52. **31:** For the *Feast of Weeks*, or Pentecost, see Exod.34.22; Deut.16.9–12. **32–45:** See 1 Macc.5.55–62, according to which Judas went to the relief of the defeated Josephus and Azarias (*Esdrias*, v. 36). **40:** 1 Macc.5.61 gives a different reason for the defeat. Deut.7.25–26 forbade taking these idol *amulets*. **42–44:** Judas, by *prayer* and *sin-offering*, hoped to avoid guilt by association (Josh. ch. 7) for the living. The author sees this as Judas' prayer for the dead. Thus, those who had died piously in battling for God's Law (v 45) needed to be cleansed of this sin before the resurrection of the just (vv. 43–44). Later, Christian theologians would see here the essence of their doctrine of Purgatory.

was a holy and pious one. And this was why he offered an atoning sacrifice to free the dead from their sin.

13 In the year 149,[r] information reached Judas and his men that Antiochus Eupator was advancing on Judaea 2 with a large army; he was accompanied by Lysias, his guardian and vicegerent, bringing in addition a Greek force, consisting of one hundred and ten thousand infantry, five thousand three hundred cavalry, twenty-two elephants, and three hundred chariots armed with scythes. 3 Menelaus also joined them and urged Antiochus on; this he did most disingenuously, not for his country's good, but because he believed he 4 would be maintained in office. However, the King of kings aroused the rage of Antiochus against Menelaus: Lysias produced evidence that this criminal was responsible for all Antiochus's troubles, and so the king ordered him to be taken to Beroea and there to be executed in the manner 5 customary at that place. Now in Beroea there is a tower some seventy-five feet[s] high, filled with ashes; it has a circular device sloping sheer on all 6 sides into the ashes. This is where the citizens take anyone guilty of sacrilege or any other notorious crime, and 7 thrust him to his doom; and such was the fate of the law-breaker Menelaus, who was not even allowed burial—a 8 fate he richly deserved. Many a time he had desecrated the hallowed ashes of the altar-fire, and by ashes he met his death. 9 So the king came on with the barbarous intention of inflicting on the Jews suffering far worse than his 10 father had inflicted. When Judas heard this he ordered the people to invoke the Lord day and night and pray that now more than ever he would come

to their aid, since they were on the point of losing law, country, and temple; and that he would not allow 11 them, just when they had begun to breathe again, to fall into the hands of blaspheming Gentiles. They all obeyed 12 his orders: for three days without respite they prayed to their merciful Lord, they wailed, they fasted, they prostrated themselves. Then Judas urged them to action and called upon them to stand by him.

After holding a council of war with 13 the elders, he decided not to wait until the royal army invaded Judaea and took Jerusalem, but to march out and with God's help to bring things to a decision. He entrusted the outcome to 14 the Creator of the world; his troops he charged to fight bravely to the death for the law, for the temple and for Jerusalem, for their country and their way of life. He pitched camp near Modin, and giving his men the signal 15 for battle with the cry 'God's victory!', he made a night attack on the royal pavilion with a picked force of the bravest young men. He killed as many as two thousand in the enemy camp, and his men stabbed to death[t] the leading elephant and its driver. In the 16 end they reduced the whole camp to panic and confusion, and withdrew victorious. It was all over by daybreak, 17 through the help and protection which Judas had received from the Lord.

Now that he had had a taste of 18 Jewish daring, the king tried stratagems in attacking their strong-points. He 19 advanced on Bethsura, one of their powerful forts; he was repulsed; he attacked, he was beaten. Judas sent in 20 supplies to the garrison, but a soldier 21 in the Jewish ranks, Rhodocus by name, betrayed their secrets to the

[r] *That is* 163 B.C.
[s] some . . . feet: *Gk.* fifty cubits.
[t] stabbed to death: *probable reading, based on one Vs.*

13.1–26: Lysias' second campaign against Judas. See 1 Macc.6.28–63. While 2 Macc. speaks of victories and notes the eventual success of Judas, 1 Macc. points out more realistically how close to disaster the Jews came. Only the threat of Philip's coup at Antioch (v. 23; 1 Macc.6.55–63) brought Lysias to the terms of the letter in 2 Macc.11.22–26. **2:** The figures here and in 1 Macc.6.30 are inflated. **3:** *Antiochus* V Eupator was a minor; Lysias as regent made the decisions. **4:** *Beroea* is the name given to Aleppo by Seleucus 1 Nicator (305–281 B.C.). *Menelaus'* execution may have resulted from Lysias' frustration over Judas' subsequent victory, or it may have been due to Menelaus' failure to pay what he promised (4.27–28). **5–8:** The method of execution was Persian. **15:** See 8.23. Judas' brother Eleazar killed the *elephant* (1 Macc.6.43–46). **18–23:** See 1 Macc.6.31,49–50, 55–63.

enemy. However, he was tracked down,
11 arrested, and put away. The king
parleyed for the second time with the
inhabitants of Bethsura, and, when he
had given and received guarantees, he
withdrew; he then attacked Judas and
23 his men, but had the worst of it. He
now received news that Philip, whom
he had left in charge of state affairs in
Antioch, had gone out of his mind. In
dismay he summoned the Jews, agreed
to their terms, took an oath to respect
all their rights, and, after this settlement, offered a sacrifice, paid honour
24 to the sanctuary and its precincts, and
received Maccabaeus graciously. He
left behind Hegemonides as governor
of the region from Ptolemais to Gerra,
25 and went himself to Ptolemais. Its
inhabitants were furious at the treaty
he had made, and in their alarm wanted
26 to repudiate it. Lysias mounted the
rostrum, made the best defence he
could, won the people over, calmed
them down, and, having thus gained
their support, left for Antioch.

Such was the course of the king's
offensive and retreat.

The victory of Maccabaeus over Nicanor

14 AFTER AN INTERVAL OF THREE YEARS,
information reached Judas and his
men that Demetrius son of Seleucus
had sailed into the harbour of Tripolis
2 with a powerful army and fleet, and,
after disposing of Antiochus and his
guardian Lysias, had taken possession
of the country.
3 There was a man called Alcimus,
who had formerly been high priest but
had submitted voluntarily to pollutions
at the time of the secession. This man,
realizing that there was not now the
slightest guarantee of his safety, or any
possibility of access to the holy altar,
4 came to King Demetrius, about the
year 151,*ᵘ* and presented him with a

gold crown and palm, and also some
of the customary olive branches from
the temple. On that particular occasion
he kept quiet; but he found a chance 5
of forwarding his own mad scheme
when Demetrius summoned him to his
council and questioned him about the
attitude and plans of the Jews. He
replied: 'Those of the Jews who are 6
called Hasidaeans and are led by Judas
Maccabaeus are keeping the war alive
and fomenting sedition, refusing to
leave the kingdom in peace. Thus, 7
although I have been deprived of my
hereditary dignity—I mean the high-
priesthood—I am here today from two
motives: first, a genuine concern for 8
the king's rights; and secondly, a regard
for my fellow-citizens, since our whole
race is suffering considerable hardship
as a result of the folly of the people I
have just mentioned. I would advise 9
your majesty to acquaint yourself with
every one of these matters and then
make provision for our country and
our beleaguered nation, as befits your
universal kindness and goodwill. For 10
the empire will enjoy no peace so long
as Judas remains alive.'

When he had spoken to this effect, 11
the other Friends, who were hostile to
Judas, immediately inflamed Demetrius
still more. The king at once selected 12
Nicanor, commander of the elephant
corps, gave him command of Judaea,
and sent him off with a commission to 13
dispose of Judas himself and disperse
his forces, and to install Alcimus as
high priest of the great temple. The 14
gentile population of Judaea, refugees
from the attacks of Judas, now flocked
to Nicanor, thinking that defeat and
misfortune for the Jews would mean
prosperity for themselves.

When they learnt of Nicanor's 15
offensive and the gentile attack, the
Jews sprinkled dust over themselves
and prayed to the One who established

ᵘ That is 161 B.C.

14.1–15.37: The victory of Maccabaeus over Nicanor. 2 Macc. details the final major victory
of Judas. See 1 Macc. ch. 7. **1:** *Demetrius* I Soter (161–150 B.C.) was the oldest surviving *son
of Seleucus* IV (187–175 B.C.) and considered *Antiochus* IV Epiphanes (175–164 B.C.) and his
son Antiochus V Eupator (164–161 B.C.) as usurpers. **3:** The author barely alludes to Bacchides'
earlier expedition and its resultant establishment of *Alcimus* as *high priest* (1 Macc.7.8–25).
The *secession* or separation is probably the persecution of Epiphanes, which divided the Jews.
6: The *Hasidaeans* (1 Macc.2.42 43; 7.12–18) were forerunners of the parties of the Pharisees
and the Essenes. **11:** *Friends:* See 1 Macc. 2.18 n. **12:** *Nicanor:* see 8.8–29; 1 Macc.3.38–4.25;

his people for ever, who never fails to manifest himself when his chosen are 16 in need of help. At their leader's command, they immediately struck camp and joined battle with the enemy 17 at the village of Adasa.[v] Simon, the brother of Judas, had fought an engagement with Nicanor, but, because the enemy came up[w] unexpectedly, he 18 had suffered a slight reverse. In spite of this, when Nicanor learnt how brave Judas and his troops were and how courageously they fought for their country, he shrank from deciding the 19 issue in battle. So he sent Posidonius, Theodotus, and Mattathias to negotiate a settlement.

20　　After a lengthy consideration of the proposals, Judas informed his men of them; they were unanimous in agreeing 21 to make peace. A day was fixed for a private meeting of the leaders. A chariot advanced from each of the two lines, and seats were placed for them; 22 but Judas posted armed men at strategic points ready to deal with any unforeseen treachery on the enemy's part. The discussion between the two 23 leaders was harmonious. Nicanor stayed some time in Jerusalem and behaved correctly; he dismissed the crowds that had flocked round him, 24 and kept Judas always close to himself. He had acquired a real affection for 25 him, and urged him to marry and start a family. So Judas married and settled down to the quiet life of an ordinary citizen.

26　　Alcimus noticed their friendliness and got hold of a copy of the agreement they had concluded. He went to Demetrius and said that Nicanor was pursuing a policy detrimental to the interests of the empire, by appointing that traitor Judas King's Friend desig- 27 nate. The king was furious and was provoked by these villainous slanders to write to Nicanor expressing his dissatisfaction with the agreement and ordering him to arrest Maccabaeus 28 and send him at once to Antioch. This message filled Nicanor with dismay; he took it hard that he should have to

break his agreement although the man had committed no offence, but 29 since there was no going against the king, he watched for a favourable opportunity of carrying out the order by means of some stratagem. Mac- 30 cabaeus, however, observed that Nicanor had become less friendly towards him and no longer showed him the same civility. He realized that this unfriendliness boded no good, so he collected a large number of his followers and went into hiding from Nicanor.

When Nicanor recognized that he 31 had been outmanoeuvred by the resolute action of Judas, he went to the great and holy temple at the time when the priests were offering the regular sacrifices, and ordered them to surrender Judas to him. The priests declared 32 on oath that they did not know the whereabouts of the wanted man. But 33 Nicanor stretched out his right hand towards the shrine and swore this oath: 'Unless you surrender Judas into my custody, I will raze God's sanctuary to the ground, I will destroy the altar, and on this spot I will build a temple to Dionysus for all the world to see.' With these words he left; but the 34 priests with outstretched hands prayed to Heaven, the constant champion of our race: 'Lord, thou hast no need of 35 anything in the world, yet it was thy pleasure that among us there should be a shrine for thy dwelling-place. Now, 36 Lord, who alone art holy, keep this house, so newly purified, for ever free from defilement.'

A man called Razis, a member of 37 the Jerusalem senate, was denounced to Nicanor. He was very highly spoken of, a patriot who for his loyalty was known as 'Father of the Jews'. In the 38 early days of the secession he had stood his trial for practising Judaism, and with the utmost eagerness had risked life and limb for that cause. Nicanor 39 wished to give clear proof of his hostility towards the Jews, and sent

v Adasa: probable reading; compare 1 Macc. 7. 40.
w came up: probable reading, based on one Vs.

7.26–50. **16–30:** The preliminary skirmishes (vv. 15–19) and the friendship of Nicanor for Judas are summarized in 1 Macc.7.27–30. **31–36:** See 1 Macc.7.33–38. **38:** *Secession:* see v. 3 n.

more than five hundred soldiers to
40 arrest Razis; he reckoned that his
arrest would be a severe blow to the
41 Jews. The troops were on the point of
capturing the tower where Razis was,
and were trying to force the outer door.
Then an order was given to set the door
on fire, and Razis, hemmed in on all
42 sides, turned his sword on himself. He
preferred to die nobly rather than fall
into the hands of criminals and be
43 subjected to gross humiliation. In his
haste and anxiety he misjudged the
blow, and with the troops pouring
through the doors he ran without
hesitation on to the wall and heroically
threw himself down into the crowd.
44 The crowd hurriedly gave way and he
45 fell in the space they left. He was still
breathing, still on fire with courage;
so, streaming with blood and severely
wounded, he picked himself up and
dashed through the crowd. Finally,
46 standing on a sheer rock, and now
completely drained of blood, he took
his entrails in both hands and flung
them at the crowd. And thus, invoking
the Lord of life and breath to give
these entrails back to him again, he
died.

15 Nicanor received information that
Judas and his men were in the region
of Samaria, and he determined to
attack them on their day of rest, when
it could be done without any danger.
2 Those Jews who were forced to
accompany his army said, 'Do not
carry out such a savage and barbarous
massacre, but respect the day singled
out and made holy by the all-seeing
3 One.' The double-dyed villain retorted,
'Is there a ruler in the sky who has
ordered the sabbath day to be ob-
4 served?' The Jews declared, 'The living
Lord himself is ruler in the sky, and he
ordered the seventh day to be kept
5 holy.' 'But I', replied Nicanor, 'am a
ruler on earth, and I order you to take
your arms and do your duty to the
king.' However, he did not succeed in
carrying out his cruel plan.

Now Nicanor, in his pretentious 6
and extravagant conceit, had resolved
upon erecting a public trophy from the
spoils of Judas's forces. But Mac- 7
cabaeus's confidence never wavered,
and he had not the least doubt that he
would obtain help from the Lord. He 8
urged his men not to be afraid of the
gentile attack, but to bear in mind the
aid they had received from heaven in
the past and so look to the Almighty
for the victory which he would send
this time also. He drew encouragement 9
for them from the law and the prophets
and, by reminding them of the struggles
they had already come through, filled
them with a fresh enthusiasm. When 10
he had roused their courage, he gave
them their orders, reminding them at
the same time of the Gentiles' broken
faith and perjury. He armed each one 11
of them, not so much with the security
of shield and spear, as with the
encouragement that brave words bring;
and he also told them of a trustworthy
dream he had had, a sort of waking
vision, which put them all in good
heart.

What he had seen was this: the 12
former high priest Onias appeared to
him, that great gentleman of modest
bearing and mild disposition, apt
speaker, and exponent from childhood
of the good life. With outstretched
hands he was praying earnestly for
the whole Jewish community. Next 13
there appeared in the same attitude a
figure of great age and dignity, whose
wonderful air of authority marked him
as a man of the utmost distinction.
Then Onias said, 'This is God's prophet 14
Jeremiah, who loves his fellow-Jews
and offers many prayers for our people
and for the holy city.' Jeremiah ex- 15
tended his right hand and delivered to
Judas a golden sword, saying as he did
so, 'Take this holy sword, the gift of 16
God, and with it crush your enemies.'

The eloquent words of Judas had the 17
power of stimulating everyone to
bravery and making men out of boys.

46: Razis, too, believes in the resurrection of the just. **15.1–5:** Despite Nicanor's plan, Judas
would fight on the Sabbath if attacked (1 Macc.2.41). **10:** The Gentiles had perjured themselves
with the Hasidaeans (1 Macc.7.12–18). Judas warned his men what to expect if they surrendered.
12–16: The vision of *Onias* III (3.1; 4.34) and *Jeremiah* represented the support of the Law
(through the Temple's priesthood) and the Prophets for Judas' cause. The author notes the

Encouraged by them, the Jews made up their minds not to remain in camp, but to take the offensive manfully and fight hand to hand with all their strength until the issue was decided. This they did because Jerusalem, their religion, and their temple were in 18 danger. Their fear was not chiefly for their wives and children, not to mention brothers and relatives, but first and 19 foremost for the sacred shrine. The distress of those shut up in Jerusalem was no less, for they were anxious at the prospect of a battle on open ground. 20 All were waiting for the decisive struggle which lay ahead. The enemy had already concentrated his forces; his army was drawn up in order of battle, the elephants stationed in a favourable position and the cavalry 21 ranged on the flank. When Maccabaeus observed the deployment of the troops, the variety of their equipment, and the ferocity of the elephants, with hands upraised he invoked the Lord, the worker of miracles, for he knew that God grants victory to those who deserve it, not because of their military strength but as he himself 22 decides. This was his prayer: 'Master, thou didst send thy angel in the days of Hezekiah king of Judah, and he killed as many as a hundred and eighty-five thousand men in Sennacherib's camp. 23 Now, Ruler of heaven, send once again a good angel to go in front of us 24 spreading fear and panic. May they be struck down by thy strong arm, these blasphemers who are coming to attack thy holy people!' Thus he ended.

25 Nicanor and his forces advanced 26 with trumpets and war-songs, but Judas and his men joined battle with in-27 vocations and prayers. Fighting with their hands and praying to God in their hearts, they killed no fewer than thirty-five thousand men, and were greatly cheered by the divine intervention.

28 The action was over, and they were joyfully disbanding, when they recog-nized Nicanor lying dead in his armour. Then with tumultuous shouts they 29 praised their Master in their native language. Judas their leader, who had 30 always fought body and soul on behalf of his fellow-Jews, never losing his youthful patriotism, now ordered Nicanor's head to be cut off, also his hand and arm, and taken to Jerusalem. On 31 arrival there he summoned all the people and stationed the priests before the altar. Then he sent for the men in the citadel, and showed them the head 32 of the blackguardly Nicanor and the hand which this bragging blasphemer had extended against the Almighty's holy temple. He cut out the tongue of 33 the impious Nicanor, and said he would give it to the birds bit by bit; and he gave orders that the evidence of what Nicanor's folly had brought upon him should be hung up opposite the shrine. They all made the sky ring with 34 the praises of the Lord who had shown his power: 'Praise to him who has preserved his own sanctuary from defilement!' Judas hung Nicanor's 35 head from the citadel, a clear proof of the Lord's help, for all to see. It was 36 unanimously decreed that this day should never pass unnoticed but be regularly celebrated. It is the thirteenth of the twelfth month, called Adar in Aramaic, the day before Mordecai's Day. Such, then, was the fate of 37 Nicanor, and from that time Jerusalem has remained in the possession of the Hebrews.

AT THIS POINT I WILL BRING MY WORK to an end. If it is found well written 38 and aptly composed, that is what I myself hoped for; if cheap and medi-ocre, I could only do my best. For, just 39 as it is disagreeable to drink wine alone or water alone, whereas the mixing of the two gives a pleasant and delightful taste, so too variety of style in a literary work charms the ear of the reader. Let this then be my final word.

---

intercessory prayer of the saints (vv. 12,14). **22:** Judas refers to the angelic slaughter (probably by plague) of *Sennacherib's* army as it besieged Jerusalem (2 Kgs.19.35; Isa.37.36; 1 Macc.7.41). **33:** Instead of having a public trophy or monument to Judas' defeat (v. 6), *Nicanor* became one to his own. **36:** The feast of Nicanor was struck from the Jewish calendar after the destruction of the Temple in 70 A.D. For *Mordecai's Day*, see Esther 3.7; 9.20–23.
    15.38–39: The Epitomist ends his version before the story of Judas's death (1 Macc.9.1–22).

THE NEW
ENGLISH BIBLE

THE NEW TESTAMENT
OXFORD STUDY EDITION

CONTENTS

INTRODUCTION
TO THE NEW TESTAMENT

This translation of the New Testament was undertaken with the object of providing English readers, whether familiar with the Bible or not, with a faithful rendering of the best available Greek text into the current speech of our own time, and a rendering which should harvest the gains of recent biblical scholarship.

It is now some three centuries and a half since King James's men put out what we have come to know as the Authorized Version. Two hundred and seventy years later the New Testament was revised. The Revised Version of the New Testament, which appeared in 1881, marked a new departure especially in that it abandoned the so-called Received Text, which had reigned ever since printed editions of the New Testament began, but which the advance of textual criticism had antiquated. The Revisers no longer followed (as their predecessors had done) the text of the majority of manuscripts, which, being for the most part of late date, had been exposed not only to the accidental corruptions of long-continued copying, but also in part to deliberate correction and 'improvement'. Instead, they followed a very small group of manuscripts, the earliest, and in their judgement the best, of those which had survived. During the years which have passed since their time, textual criticism has not stood still. Manuscripts have been discovered of substantially earlier date than any which the Revisers knew. Other important sources of evidence have been either freshly discovered or made more fully available. Meanwhile the methods of textual criticism have themselves been refined and estimates of the value of particular manuscripts have sometimes been reconsidered. The problem of restoring a form of text as near as possible to the vanished autographs now appears less simple than it did to our predecessors. There is not at the present time any critical text which would command the same degree of general acceptance as the Revisers' text did in its day. Nor has the time come, in the judgement of most scholars, to construct such a text, since new material constantly comes to light, and the debate continues. The present translators therefore could do no other than consider variant readings on their merits, and, having weighed the evidence for themselves, select for translation in each passage the reading which to the best of their judgement seemed most likely to represent what the author wrote. Where other readings seemed to deserve serious consideration they have been recorded in footnotes. In assessing the evidence, the translators have taken into account (*a*) ancient manuscripts of the New Testament in Greek, (*b*) manuscripts of early translations into other languages, and (*c*) quotations from the New Testament by early Christian writers. These three sources of evidence are collectively referred to as 'witnesses'. A large number of variants, however, are such as could make no appreciable difference to the meaning so far as it could be represented in translation, and these have been passed over in silence. The translators are well aware that their judgement is at best provisional, but they believe the text they have followed to be an improvement on that underlying the earlier translations. This text can now be read in *The Greek New Testament*, edited by R. V. G. Tasker (Oxford and Cambridge University Presses, 1964).

So much for the text. The next step was the effort to understand the original as accurately as possible, as a preliminary to turning it into English. The Revisers of 1881 believed that a better knowledge of the Greek language made it possible to correct a number of mistranslations in the older version, though in doing so they were somewhat limited by the instruction 'to introduce as few alterations as possible . . . consistently with faithfulness'. Since their time the study of the Greek language has no more stood still than has textual criticism. In particular, our knowledge of the kind of Greek used by most of the New Testament writers has been greatly enriched since 1881 by the discovery of many thousands of papyrus documents in popular or non-literary Greek of about the same period as the New Testament. It would be wrong to suggest that they lead to any far-reaching change in our understanding of the Greek of the New Testament period, but they have often made possible a better appreciation of the finer shades of idiom, which sometimes clarifies the meaning of passages in the New Testament. Its language is indeed in many respects more flexible and easy-going than the Revisers were ready to allow, and invites the translator to use a larger freedom.

Our task, however, differed in an important respect from that of the Revisers of 1881. They were instructed not only to introduce as few alterations as possible, but also 'to limit, as far as possible, the expression of such alterations to the language of the Authorised and earlier English Versions'. The present translators were subject to no such limitation. In accordance with the original decision of the Joint Committee they were to make the attempt to use consistently the idiom of contemporary English to convey the meaning of the Greek.

The older translators, on the whole, considered that fidelity to the original demanded that they should reproduce, as far as possible, characteristic features of the language in which it was written, such as the syntactical order of words, the structure and division of sentences, and even such irregularities of grammar as were indeed natural enough to authors writing in the easy idiom of popular Hellenistic Greek, but less natural when turned into English. The present translators were enjoined to replace Greek constructions and idioms by those of contemporary English.

This meant a different theory and practice of translation, and one which laid a heavier burden on the translators. Fidelity in translation was not to mean keeping the general framework of the original intact while replacing Greek words by English words more or less equivalent. A word, indeed, in one language is seldom the exact equivalent of a word in a different language. Each word is the centre of a whole cluster of meanings and associations, and in different languages these clusters overlap but do not often coincide. The place of a word in the clause or sentence, or even in a larger unit of thought, will determine what aspect of its total meaning is in the foreground. The translator can hardly hope to convey in another language every shade of meaning that attaches to the word in the original, but if he is free to exploit a wide range of English words covering a similar area of meaning and association he may hope to carry over the meaning of the sentence as a whole. Thus we have not felt obliged (as did the Revisers of 1881) to make an effort to render the same Greek word everywhere by the same English word. We have in this respect returned to the wholesome practice of King James's men, who (as they expressly state in their preface) recognized no such obligation.

We have conceived our task to be that of understanding the original as precisely as we could (using all available aids), and then saying again in our own native idiom what we believed the author to be saying in his. We have found that in practice this frequently compelled us to make decisions where the older method of translation allowed a comfortable ambiguity. In such places we have been aware that we take a risk, but we have thought it our duty to take the risk rather than remain on the fence.

In doing our work, we have constantly striven to follow our instructions and render the Greek, as we understood it, into the English of the present day, that is, into the natural vocabulary, constructions, and rhythms of contemporary speech. We have sought to avoid archaism, jargon, and all that is either stilted or slipshod.

It should be said that our intention has been to offer a translation in the strict sense, and not a paraphrase, and we have not wished to encroach on the field of the commentator. But if the best commentary is a good translation, it is also true that every intelligent translation is in a sense a paraphrase. The line between translation and paraphrase is a fine one. But we have had recourse to deliberate paraphrase with great caution, and only in a few passages where without it we could see no way to attain our aim of making the meaning as clear as it could be made. Taken as a whole, our version claims to be a translation, free, it may be, rather than literal, but a faithful translation nevertheless, so far as we could compass it.

For this edition, the translation of the New Testament has been given a careful revision, in which account has been taken of numerous criticisms and suggestions which have come in from various quarters. It is hoped that the modifications introduced, mostly in minor details and seldom reflecting any substantial change of view about the meaning of a passage, will be found to be in the direction of improvement.

In the course of revision, consideration has been given to passages from the Old Testament quoted in the New. These have now been harmonized with the present version of the Old Testament, where this seemed desirable, and practicable. But the quotations are in Greek, and the Greek is by no means always an exact equivalent of the Hebrew. Where it is not, we have deemed it our duty to render the Greek as it lay before us, and not to attempt to reproduce the underlying Hebrew. On this point there has been consultation between representatives of the Old and the New Testament panels.

The translators are as conscious as anyone can be of the limitations and imperfections of their work. No one who has not tried it can know how impossible an art translation is. Only those who have meditated long upon the Greek original are aware of the richness and subtlety of meaning that may lie even within the most apparently simple sentence, or know the despair that attends all efforts to bring it out through the medium of a different language. Yet we may hope that we have been able to convey to our readers something at least of what the New Testament has said to us during these years of work, and trust that under the providence of Almighty God this translation may open the truth of the Scriptures to many who have been hindered in their approach to it by barriers of language.

C. H. D.

Marginal Numbers

The conventional verse divisions in the New Testament date only from 1551 and have no basis in the manuscripts. Any system of division into numbered verses is foreign to the spirit of this translation, which is intended to convey the meaning in continuous natural English rather than to correspond sentence by sentence with the Greek.

For purposes of reference, and of comparison with other translations, verse numbers are placed in the margin opposite the line in which the first word belonging to the verse in question appears. Sometimes, however, successive verses are combined in a continuous English sentence, so that the precise point where a new verse begins cannot be fixed; occasionally in the interests of clarity the order of successive verses is reversed (e.g. at John 4.7,8).

THE GOSPEL

THE GOSPEL

THE GOSPEL ACCORDING TO
MATTHEW

The Gospel of Matthew has long been regarded as the most Jewish of the Gospels: the author's preference for the term kingdom of Heaven (see 3.2 n.), his description of Peter's commission in scribal categories (16.19 n.), and his interest in the Law (5.17–19 nn.) are traits which point in this direction. Yet, he shows an anti-Pharisaic bias (e.g. ch. 23), probably intends 23.37–24.2 to imply the repudiation of Israel, and concludes his book with a scene which directs the disciples out into the Gentile mission (28.16–20). With good reason (see 16.18 n.; 18.1–19.1 nn.), this has also been called an "ecclesiastical" Gospel; on almost every page the author's concern for the life of the Church may be detected.

The feature of the book which attracts immediate attention is the organization of the teaching tradition into five great discourses (chs. 5–7; 10; 13; 18; 24–25). A narrative section precedes each discourse. This scheme is prefaced by chs. 1–2, which introduce the Messiah-Son of David, and is climaxed by the concluding report of the crucifixion and resurrection in chs. 26–28.

The book was probably written about 90 A.D.

The coming of Christ

1 A TABLE OF THE DESCENT OF JESUS Christ, son of David, son of Abraham.

2 Abraham was the father of Isaac, Isaac of Jacob, Jacob of Judah and his 3 brothers, Judah of Perez and Zarah (their mother was Tamar), Perez of 4 Hezron, Hezron of Ram, Ram of Amminadab, Amminadab of Nahshon, 5 Nahshon of Salma, Salma of Boaz (his mother was Rahab), Boaz of Obed (his 6 mother was Ruth), Obed of Jesse; and Jesse was the father of King David.

David was the father of Solomon (his mother had been the wife of 7 Uriah), Solomon of Rehoboam, Reho- 8 boam of Abijah, Abijah of Asa, Asa of Jehoshaphat, Jehoshaphat of Joram, 9 Joram of Azariah, Azariah of Jotham, Jotham of Ahaz, Ahaz of Hezekiah, 10 Hezekiah of Manasseh, Manasseh of 11 Amon, Amon of Josiah; and Josiah was the father of Jeconiah and his brothers at the time of the deportation to Babylon.

12 After the deportation Jeconiah was the father of Shealtiel, Shealtiel of 13 Zerubbabel, Zerubbabel of Abiud,

Abiud of Eliakim, Eliakim of Azor, Azor of Zadok, Zadok of Achim, Achim 14 of Eliud, Eliud of Eleazar, Eleazar of 15 Matthan, Matthan of Jacob, Jacob of Joseph, the husband of Mary, who gave 16 birth to[a] Jesus called Messiah.

There were thus fourteen generations 17 in all from Abraham to David, fourteen from David until the deportation to Babylon, and fourteen from the deportation until the Messiah.

THIS IS THE STORY OF THE BIRTH OF 18 the Messiah. Mary his mother was betrothed to Joseph; before their marriage she found that she was with child by the Holy Spirit. Being a man 19 of principle, and at the same time wanting to save her from exposure, Joseph desired to have the marriage contract set aside quietly. He had 20 resolved on this, when an angel of the Lord appeared to him in a dream. 'Joseph son of David,' said the angel, 'do not be afraid to take Mary home with you as your wife. It is by the Holy Spirit that she has conceived this child.

a *Some witnesses read* betrothed to, whom was betrothed Mary, a virgin, who gave birth to . . .; *one witness has* Joseph, and Joseph, to whom Mary, a virgin, was betrothed, was the father of . . .

1.1–17: **Genealogy of the Messiah** (compare Lk.3.23–38). **1:** Lit. *Christ* (or *Messiah*, v. 17) means "anointed one" and was frequently used of the royal figure whose rule would bring about the final age of righteousness and justice. The genealogy presents Jesus as this ruler, descended from *King David* (vv. 1,6) through the royal line (vv. 6–11). **2–11:** These names are drawn from Ruth 4.18–22; 1 Chr.2.1–3.19. **17:** *Fourteen generations:* perhaps reflecting the numerical value of *David* in Heb.; $d(4) + v(6) + d(4) = 14$. *Messiah:* see v. 1 n.

1.18–25: **The birth of Jesus** (compare Lk.1.26–38; 2.1–7). The theme of the miraculous birth pervades the passage (vv. 18,20,23,25). **20:** Both the *angel* ("messenger") and the *dream* are

3

21 She will bear a son; and you shall give him the name Jesus (Saviour), for he will save his people from their sins.'

22 All this happened in order to fulfil what the Lord declared through the

23 prophet: 'The virgin will conceive and bear a son, and he shall be called Emmanuel', a name which means 'God

24 is with us'. Rising from sleep Joseph did as the angel had directed him; he

25 took Mary home to be his wife, but had no intercourse with her until her son was born. And he named the child Jesus.

2 JESUS WAS BORN AT BETHLEHEM IN Judaea during the reign of Herod. After his birth astrologers from the

2 east arrived in Jerusalem, asking, 'Where is the child who is born to be king of the Jews?*b* We observed the rising of his star, and we have come to

3 pay him homage.' King Herod was greatly perturbed when he heard this;

4 and so was the whole of Jerusalem. He called a meeting of the chief priests and lawyers of the Jewish people, and put before them the question: 'Where is it

5 that the Messiah is to be born?' 'At Bethlehem in Judaea', they replied; and they referred him to the prophecy

6 which reads: 'Bethlehem in the land of Judah, you are far from least in the eyes of*c* the rulers of Judah; for out of you shall come a leader to be the shepherd of my people Israel.'

7 Herod next called the astrologers to meet him in private, and ascertained from them the time when the star had

8 appeared. He then sent them on to Bethlehem, and said, 'Go and make a careful inquiry for the child. When you have found him, report to me, so that I may go myself and pay him homage.'

9 They set out at the king's bidding; and the star which they had seen at its rising went ahead of them until it stopped above the place where the child lay. At the sight of the star they 10 were overjoyed. Entering the house, 11 they saw the child with Mary his mother, and bowed to the ground in homage to him; then they opened their treasures and offered him gifts: gold, frankincense, and myrrh. And 12 being warned in a dream not to go back to Herod, they returned home another way.

After they had gone, an angel of the 13 Lord appeared to Joseph in a dream, and said to him, 'Rise up, take the child and his mother and escape with them to Egypt, and stay there until I tell you; for Herod is going to search for the child to do away with him.' So 14 Joseph rose from sleep, and taking mother and child by night he went away with them to Egypt, and there he 15 stayed till Herod's death. This was to fulfil what the Lord had declared through the prophet: 'I called my son out of Egypt.'

When Herod saw how the astrologers 16 had tricked him he fell into a passion, and gave orders for the massacre of all children in Bethlehem and its neighbourhood, of the age of two years or less, corresponding with the time he had ascertained from the astrologers. So the words spoken through Jeremiah 17 the prophet were fulfilled: 'A voice was 18 heard in Rama, wailing and loud laments; it was Rachel weeping for her children, and refusing all consolation, because they were no more.'

The time came that Herod died; and 19 an angel of the Lord appeared in a dream to Joseph in Egypt and said to 20 him, 'Rise up, take the child and his mother, and go with them to the land of Israel, for the men who threatened

b Or Where is the king of the Jews who has just been born?
c Or least among.

---

customary devices for reporting revelations (see 2.12–13,22). **21,23:** The chief significance of the account for Mt. lies in the pointedly explained names, *Jesus* and *Emmanuel*. **22–23:** See Isa.7.14 n. Mt. frequently introduces OT quotations with a phrase like *to fulfil what the Lord declared through the prophets* (e.g. 2.15; 8.17; 27.9–10).

2.1–12: The infant Jesus in Bethlehem. 1: *Bethlehem*, the city of David, was the expected birthplace of the Messiah (vv. 4–6). *Reign of Herod:* 37 B.C.–4 B.C. **4:** *Lawyers:* interpreters of Scripture, especially of the Law of Moses. **6:** Mic.5.2. In the OT *shepherd* frequently means "ruler."

2.13–23: Escape and return. The story of the flight to Egypt is told only by Mt. **15:** Hos.11.1. **16:** The *massacre* is not reported elsewhere, but Herod's barbarity was notorious. **18:** Jer.31.15.

4

21 the child's life are dead.' So he rose, took mother and child with him, and
22 came to the land of Israel. Hearing, however, that Archelaus had succeeded his father Herod as king of Judaea, he was afraid to go there. And being warned by a dream, he withdrew to the
23 region of Galilee; there he settled in a town called Nazareth. This was to fulfil the words spoken through the prophets: 'He shall be called a Nazarene.'

3 ABOUT THAT TIME JOHN THE BAPTIST appeared as a preacher in the Judaean
2 wilderness; his theme was: 'Repent; for the kingdom of Heaven is upon
3 you!' It is of him that the prophet Isaiah spoke when he said, 'A voice crying aloud in the wilderness, "Prepare a way for the Lord; clear a straight path for him."'
4 John's clothing was a rough coat of camel's hair, with a leather belt round his waist, and his food was locusts and
5 wild honey. They flocked to him from Jerusalem, from all Judaea, and the
6 whole Jordan valley, and were baptized by him in the River Jordan, confessing their sins.
7 When he saw many of the Pharisees and Sadducees coming for baptism he said to them: 'You vipers' brood! Who warned you to escape from the
8 coming retribution? Then prove your

repentance by the fruit it bears; and 9 do not presume to say to yourselves, "We have Abraham for our father." I tell you that God can make children for Abraham out of these stones here. Already the axe is laid to the roots of 10 the trees; and every tree that fails to produce good fruit is cut down and thrown on the fire. I baptize you with 11 water, for repentance; but the one who comes after me is mightier than I. I am not fit to take off his shoes. He will baptize you with the Holy Spirit and with fire. His shovel is ready in his 12 hand and he will winnow his threshing-floor; the wheat he will gather into his granary, but he will burn the chaff on a fire that can never go out.'

Then Jesus arrived at the Jordan 13 from Galilee, and came to John to be baptized by him. John tried to dissuade 14 him. 'Do you come to me?' he said; 'I need rather to be baptized by you.' Jesus replied, 'Let it be so for the 15 present; we do well to conform in this way with all that God requires.' John then allowed him to come. After 16 baptism Jesus came up out of the water at once, and at that moment heaven opened; he saw the Spirit of God descending like a dove to alight upon him; and a voice from heaven 17 was heard saying, 'This is my Son, my Beloved,[d] on whom my favour rests.'

d *Or* This is my only Son.

22: *Archelaus* ruled from 4 B.C. to 6 A.D. **23:** Probably Isa.11.1 (which contains a Heb. word, *nezer*, translated "branch," similar to *Nazareth*) is the intended reference.
   3.1–12: The work of the Baptist (Mk.1.1–8; Lk.3.1–18; Jn.1.6,15,19–28). **1:** *Wilderness:* the arid Judean territory southeast of Jerusalem, including the lower *Jordan* valley (v. 6). **2:** *Repent:* to change one's mind (Gk.), to return, to turn around (Heb.). *Kingdom:* see Mk.1.15 n. In Jewish piety, *Heaven* was an ordinary manner of referring to God. **3:** Isa.40.3. **4:** 2 Kgs.1.8 attributes similar clothing to Elijah. **7:** *Baptism,* dipping in water, was an important ritual in the Dead Sea community and was also administered to Gentile converts to Judaism. The *Pharisees* were a predominantly Jewish movement marked by an elastic interpretation of the Law, though in terms of a special, inherited tradition; they accepted as authoritative not only the "books of Moses," but also other literature including the prophets and other writings; they believed in such "new" doctrines as the resurrection; after the fall of Jerusalem (70 A.D.), they were the dominant force in Judaism. The *Sadducees,* who interpreted Scripture literally, were a priestly-oriented party who enjoyed considerable civil power in Roman times and were theologically conservative (e.g. they did not believe in the resurrection). There were other distinctive Jewish groups, including the Essenes (of whose literature and practices the Dead Sea Scrolls provide rich information); about these, the NT is silent. **9:** *Abraham for our father:* see Lk.3.8n. **11:** *Holy Spirit* and *fire:* see Lk.3.16 n.
   3.13–17: The baptism of Jesus (Mk.1.9–11 n.; Lk.3.21–22; Jn.1.32–34). **14–15:** Jesus' baptism by John presented several problems to the early church. These verses show, first, that John was subordinate to Jesus (v. 14) and second, that Jesus' submission to baptism was not evidence of his sinfulness (vv. 6,15). **16:** The origin of the *Spirit-dove* imagery is unknown; the Spirit's "hovering" over the deep in Gen.1.2 is a frequently conjectured source. The descent of the *Spirit* appears to have marked Jesus' installation as Son in the primitive tradition. **17:** On *Son, Beloved,* see Mk.1.11 n.

4 JESUS WAS THEN LED AWAY BY THE Spirit into the wilderness, to be tempted by the devil.

2 For forty days and nights he fasted, and at the end of them he was famished.

3 The tempter approached him and said, 'If you are the Son of God, tell

4 these stones to become bread.' Jesus answered, 'Scripture says, "Man cannot live on bread alone; he lives on every word that God utters."'

5 The devil then took him to the Holy City and set him on the parapet of the

6 temple. 'If you are the Son of God,' he said, 'throw yourself down; for Scripture says, "He will put his angels in charge of you, and they will support you in their arms, for fear you should strike your foot against a stone."'

7 Jesus answered him, 'Scripture says again, "You are not to put the Lord your God to the test."'

8 Once again, the devil took him to a very high mountain, and showed him all the kingdoms of the world in their

9 glory. 'All these', he said, 'I will give you, if you will only fall down and do

10 me homage.' But Jesus said, 'Begone, Satan! Scripture says, "You shall do homage to the Lord your God and worship him alone."'

11 Then the devil left him; and angels appeared and waited on him.

12 When he heard that John had been arrested, Jesus withdrew to Galilee;

13 and leaving Nazareth he went and settled at Capernaum on the Sea of Galilee, in the district of Zebulun and

14 Naphtali. This was to fulfil the passage

15 in the prophet Isaiah which tells of 'the land of Zebulun, the land of Naphtali, the Way of the Sea, the land beyond Jordan, heathen Galilee', and says:

'The people that lived in darkness 16
   saw a great light;
light dawned on the dwellers in the
   land of death's dark shadow.'

From that day Jesus began to proclaim 17 the message: 'Repent; for[e] the kingdom of Heaven is upon you.'

JESUS WAS WALKING BY THE SEA OF 18 Galilee when he saw two brothers, Simon called Peter and his brother Andrew, casting a net into the lake; for they were fishermen. Jesus said to 19 them, 'Come with me, and I will make you fishers of men.' And at once they 20 left their nets and followed him.

He went on, and saw another pair of 21 brothers, James son of Zebedee and his brother John; they were in the boat with their father Zebedee, overhauling their nets. He called them, and at once 22 they left the boat and their father, and followed him.

He went round the whole of Galilee, 23 teaching in the synagogues, preaching the gospel of the Kingdom, and curing whatever illness or infirmity there was among the people. His fame reached 24 the whole of Syria; and sufferers from every kind of illness, racked with pain, possessed by devils, epileptic, or paralysed, were all brought to him, and he cured them. Great crowds also 25 followed him, from Galilee and the Ten Towns,[f] from Jerusalem and Judaea, and from Transjordan.

The Sermon on the Mount

WHEN HE SAW THE CROWDS HE WENT **5**

e *Some witnesses omit* Repent; for.   f *Greek* Decapolis.

4.1–11: The temptation (Mk.1.12–13; Lk.4.1–13). **1**: The *devil*, or *Satan*, (v. 10) is properly defined as the *tempter* in v. 3; he is a personification of the evil force which opposes God. **2**: *Forty days and nights* is reminiscent of fasts of Moses (Exod.34.28; Deut.9.9,18) and Elijah (1 Kgs.19.8). **3,6**: The issue at stake in the incident is: *if you are the Son of God*, what is the meaning of true sonship? **4**: Deut.8.3. **5**: *Holy City*: Jerusalem. **6**: Ps.91.11–12. **7**: Deut.6.16. **8–9**: The world is conceived as under Satan's power until God's kingdom is realized (v. 17). **10**: Deut.6.13.

    4.12–25: The beginning of Jesus' ministry (Mk.1.14–20; Lk.4.14–15; 5.1–11; Jn.1.35–51). **15–16**: Isa.9.1–2. **17**: On *kingdom of Heaven*, see 3.2 n. and Mk.1.15 n. **18–22**: See Mk.1.16–20 n. **18**: *Simon called Peter*: compare 16.18; Jn.1.42. **24**: *Devils*: demons, spirits acting as agents of Satan to work evil. **25**: *Ten Towns*: Decapolis, in Gk.; a confederation of ten independent cities, most of which were southeast of the Sea of Galilee.

    5.1–7.29: The Sermon on the Mount is the first of five great discourses in Mt. (see Introduction). Mt. has organized traditions from various sources to develop the theme of the "higher righteousness" (v. 20 n.). **1**: *Hill*: mountains are frequently associated with revelation (compare

*Salt & Light = we have
a responsibility to fulfill.
if we don't do it, we're useless.*

up the hill. There he took his seat, and when his disciples had gathered round him he began to address them. And 2 this is the teaching he gave:

3 'How blest are these who know their need of God; *i.e. poor in spirit* the kingdom of Heaven is theirs.

4 How blest are the sorrowful; they shall find consolation.

5 How blest are those of a gentle spirit; they shall have the earth for their possession.

6 How blest are those who hunger and thirst to see right prevail;[g] *to do what is right.* they shall be satisfied.

7 How blest are those who show mercy; mercy shall be shown to them.

8 How blest are those whose hearts are pure; *purity of intention* they shall see God.

9 How blest are the peacemakers; God shall call them his sons.

10 How blest are those who have suffered persecution for the cause of right; the kingdom of Heaven is theirs.

11 'How blest you are, when you suffer insults and persecution and every kind 12 of calumny for my sake. Accept it with gladness and exultation, for you have a rich reward in heaven; in the same way they persecuted the prophets before you.

'You are salt to the world. And if 13 salt becomes tasteless, how is its saltness to be restored? It is now good for nothing but to be thrown away and trodden underfoot.

'You are light for all the world. A 14 town that stands on a hill cannot be hidden. When a lamp is lit, it is not 15 put under the meal-tub, but on the lamp-stand, where it gives light to everyone in the house. And you, like 16 the lamp, must shed light among your fellows, so that, when they see the good you do, they may give praise to your Father in heaven.

'DO NOT SUPPOSE THAT I HAVE COME 17 to abolish the Law and the prophets; I did not come to abolish, but to complete. I tell you this: so long as 18 heaven and earth endure, not a letter, not a stroke, will disappear from the Law until all that must happen has happened.[h] If any man therefore sets 19 aside even the least of the Law's demands, and teaches others to do the same, he will have the lowest place in the kingdom of Heaven, whereas anyone who keeps the Law, and teaches others so, will stand high in the kingdom of Heaven. I tell you, 20 unless you show yourselves far better men than the Pharisees and the

g Or to do what is right.
h Or before all that it stands for is achieved.

17.1; 28.16); contrast Lk.6.17. The Jewish teacher customarily sat when delivering instruction. **2:** *His disciples* seems to limit the audience (but see 7.28).

5.3–10: The Beatitudes (Lk.6.20–23). **3:** *How blest* (or "blessed") introduces a form, popularly called a beatitude, which in the OT and Apoc. commends a type of behavior or attitude for which this worldly happiness is the promised reward (Ps.1.1–2; Prov.8.32–34; Ecclus.25.7–10). In vv. 3–10 (compare Rev.1.3) the promise is eschatological; i.e. the rewards are related to God's coming kingdom and the beatitudes become conditions for admission to the kingdom. *Know their need of God* (for the familiar "poor in spirit") catches the religious dimension of a form of Jewish piety for which "poverty" and "utter dependence on God" were synonymous. **6:** The text, *to see right prevail*, implies "to witness the final vindication of right"; Tln. *g*, *to do what is right*, reflects the meaning the Gk. word *dikaiosyne* usually has for Mt.

5.11–16: The task of the disciples. 11–12: The disciples are to expect suffering, which is their lot as *prophets;* compare Lk.6.22–23. **13–14:** Both *salt* and *light* are metaphors for the learning of the wise and should perhaps be regarded as "names" (see 16.18 n.); see Mk.4.21; 9.50; Lk.8.16; 11.33; 14.34–35. **13:** The word translated *becomes tasteless* can also mean "becomes foolish."

5.17–20: The permanence of the Law. 17: The *Law* (the "Five Books of Moses") and the writings of the *prophets* are regarded as one body of Scripture (compare 11.13). The section strongly affirms the abiding validity of the Law. **18:** *Stroke:* Lk.16.17 n. **19:** A scribe who *sets aside* (interprets too freely) the *demands* may, in effect, nullify both letter and spirit of the Law. **20:** *Show yourselves far better men* calls for a "higher righteousness" which the remainder of the Sermon describes. *Pharisees:* see 3.7 n. *Doctors of the law* (scribes): interpreters of the Law; although there must have been Sadducean and other interpreters, Mt. probably refers here to legal specialists among the Pharisees. *Enter the kingdom:* participate in the salvation accompanying God's rule (see Mk.1.15 n.).

doctors of the law, you can never enter the kingdom of Heaven.

31 'You have learned that our fore-fathers were told, "Do not commit murder; anyone who commits murder 22 must be brought to judgement." But what I tell you is this: Anyone who nurses anger against his brother[i] must be brought to judgement. If he abuses his brother he must answer for it to the court; if he sneers at him he will have to answer for it in the fires of hell.

23 'If, when you are bringing your gift to the altar, you suddenly remember that your brother has a grievance 24 against you, leave your gift where it is before the altar. First go and make your peace with your brother, and only then come back and offer your gift.

25 'If someone sues you, come to terms with him promptly while you are both on your way to court; otherwise he may hand you over to the judge, and the judge to the constable, and you 26 will be put in jail. I tell you, once you are there you will not be let out till you have paid the last farthing.

27 'You have learned that they were 28 told, "Do not commit adultery." But what I tell you is this: If a man looks on a woman with a lustful eye, he has already committed adultery with her in his heart.

29 'If your right eye is your undoing, tear it out and fling it away; it is better for you to lose one part of your body than for the whole of it to be 30 thrown into hell. And if your right hand is your undoing, cut it off and fling it away; it is better for you to lose one part of your body than for the whole of it to go to hell.

'They were told, "A man who 31 divorces his wife must give her a note of dismissal." But what I tell you is 32 this: If a man divorces his wife for any cause other than unchastity he involves her in adultery; and anyone who marries a divorced woman commits adultery.

'Again, you have learned that our 33 forefathers were told, "Do not break your oath", and, "Oaths sworn to the Lord must be kept." But what I tell 34 you is this: You are not to swear at all—not by heaven, for it is God's throne, nor by earth, for it is his 35 footstool, nor by Jerusalem, for it is the city of the great King, nor by your 36 own head, because you cannot turn one hair of it white or black. Plain 37 "Yes" or "No" is all you need to say; anything beyond that comes from the devil.

'You have learned that they were 38 told, "Eye for eye, tooth for tooth." But what I tell you is this: Do not set 39 yourself against the man who wrongs you. If someone slaps you on the right cheek, turn and offer him your left. If 40 a man wants to sue you for your shirt, let him have your coat as well. If a 41 man in authority makes you go one mile, go with him two. Give when you 42 are asked to give; and do not turn your back on a man who wants to borrow.

'You have learned that they were 43 told, "Love your neighbour, hate your enemy." But what I tell you is this: 44 Love your enemies[j] and pray for your

---

i Some witnesses insert without good cause.
j Some witnesses insert bless those who curse you, do good to those who hate you.

5.21–48: The meaning of the Law. A series of six statements characterized by the formula, *You have learned...but what I tell you,* gives the Law a more radical (usually, an inward) dimension **21–26: On murder and anger. 21:** Exod.20.13; Deut.5.17, with some addition from the Jewish interpretative tradition. **23–24:** A restored relationship with God (through *altar* sacrifice in the Jerusalem Temple) requires prior reconciliation with the *brother* (compare 6.14–15). **27–30: On adultery and lust. 27:** Exod.20.14; Deut.5.18. **29–30:** Compare 18.7–9 n.; Mk.9.43–48. **31–32: On divorce.** Deut.24.1–4; first-century legal interpretation sometimes allowed men to divorce their wives for trivial reasons (see Mk.10.12 n.). **32:** *Other than unchastity* (see also 19.9): omitted in Mk.10.11; Lk.16.18; 1 Cor.7.10–11. Matthew's form agrees with a strict type of Pharisaic interpretation. **33–37: On oath taking. 33:** Lev.19.12; Num.30.2 **34–36:** Compare 23.16–22. **35:** *The great King:* God. **37:** This radical rule on oaths is carefully stated in Jas.5.12. **38–42: On retaliation** (Lk.6.29–30). **38:** Exod.21.23–24, Lev.24.19–20; Deut.19.21. **43–48: On enemies** (Lk.6.27–28,32–36). **43:** *Love your neighbour* (Lev.19.18) was central to Jewish, as well as Christian, ethical concern in the first century. *Hate your enemy* is not found in the OT or Pharisaic, Rabbinic Judaism; some other source must be assumed. The positive teaching radicalizes the obligation to love, not only by including

43 persecutors;[k] only so can you be children of your heavenly Father, who makes his sun rise on good and bad alike, and sends the rain on the honest 46 and the dishonest. If you love only those who love you, what reward can you expect? Surely the tax-gatherers 47 do as much as that. And if you greet only your brothers, what is there extraordinary about that? Even the heathen 48 do as much. There must be no limit to your goodness, as your heavenly Father's goodness knows no bounds.

6 'BE CAREFUL NOT TO MAKE A SHOW OF your religion before men; if you do, no reward awaits you in your Father's house in heaven.

2   'Thus, when you do some act of charity, do not announce it with a flourish of trumpets, as the hypocrites do in synagogue and in the streets to win admiration from men. I tell you this: they have their reward already. 3 No; when you do some act of charity, do not let your left hand know what 4 your right is doing; your good deed must be secret, and your Father who sees what is done in secret will reward you.[l]

5   'Again, when you pray, do not be like the hypocrites; they love to say their prayers standing up in synagogue and at the street-corners, for everyone to see them. I tell you this: they have 6 their reward already. But when you pray, go into a room by yourself, shut the door, and pray to your Father who is there in the secret place; and your Father who sees what is secret will reward you.[l]

7   'In your prayers do not go babbling on like the heathen, who imagine that the more they say the more likely they 8 are to be heard. Do not imitate them.

Your Father knows what your needs are before you ask him.

'This is how you should pray: 9

"Our Father in heaven,
thy name be hallowed;
thy kingdom come,   10
thy will be done,
on earth as in heaven.
Give us today our daily bread.[m]   11
Forgive us the wrong we have done, 12
as we have forgiven those who have
        wronged us.
And do not bring us to the test,   13
but save us from the evil one."[n] [o]

For if you forgive others the wrongs 14 they have done, your heavenly Father will also forgive you; but if you do not 15 forgive others, then the wrongs you have done will not be forgiven by your Father.

'So too when you fast, do not look 16 gloomy like the hypocrites: they make their faces unsightly so that other people may see that they are fasting. I tell you this: they have their reward already. But when you fast, anoint 17 your head and wash your face, so that 18 men may not see that you are fasting, but only your Father who is in the secret place; and your Father who sees what is secret will give you your reward.

'DO NOT STORE UP FOR YOURSELVES 19 treasure on earth, where it grows rusty and moth-eaten, and thieves break in to steal it. Store up treasure in heaven, 20 where there is no moth and no rust to spoil it, no thieves to break in and

k *Some witnesses insert* and those who treat you spitefully.
l *Some witnesses add* openly.
m *Or* our bread for the morrow.
n *Or* from evil.
o *Some witnesses add* For thine is the kingdom and the power and the glory, for ever. Amen.

---

enemies (v. 44), but by appealing to God's impartial dealing with all men (v. 45). **45:** *Sons:* see Lk.6.35 n. **46–47:** See 5.20. **48:** See Lev.19.2. The verse summarizes vv. 21–48; only an unrestricted obedience, which measures itself by God's goodness, is true righteousness.

6.1–18: Sincere piety seeks to serve God unostentatiously, without the fanfare of the *hypocrites* (lit. "playactors," vv. 2,5,16). **2:** Almsgiving (*act of charity*) was a special virtue in Judaism. *Synagogue:* see Lk.4.16 n. **9–13:** The Lord's Prayer (compare the shorter form in Lk.11.2–4) centers in the hope for the *kingdom* of God (Mk.1.15 n.). **9:** Rom.8.15 is an example of the importance early Christians attached to addressing God as *Father*. **11:** The Gk. word translated *daily* (Tfn. *m: for the morrow*) does not appear elsewhere and its meaning is uncertain; in context, the petition must be a statement of trust in the One whose rule is coming. **12,14–15:** On forgiveness of others, see 18.21–35.

6.19–34: Trust in God and material possessions compared (Lk.11.34–36; 12.22–31,33–34).

21 steal. For where your treasure is, there will your heart be also.

22 'The lamp of the body is the eye. If your eyes are sound, you will have
23 light for your whole body; if the eyes are bad, your whole body will be in darkness. If then the only light you have is darkness, the darkness is doubly dark.

24 'No servant can be the slave of two masters; for either he will hate the first and love the second, or he will be devoted to the first and think nothing of the second. You cannot serve God and Money.

25 'Therefore I bid you put away anxious thoughts about food and drink to keep you alive, and clothes to cover your body. Surely life is more than food, the body more than clothes.
26 Look at the birds of the air; they do not sow and reap and store in barns, yet your heavenly Father feeds them.
27 You are worth more than the birds! Is there a man of you who by anxious thought can add a foot to his height*p*?
28 And why be anxious about clothes? Consider how the lilies grow in the fields; they do not work, they do not
29 spin;*q* and yet, I tell you, even Solomon in all his splendour was not attired
30 like one of these. But if that is how God clothes the grass in the fields, which is there today, and tomorrow is thrown on the stove, will he not all the more clothe you? How little faith you have!
31 No, do not ask anxiously, "What are we to eat? What are we to drink?
32 What shall we wear?" All these are things for the heathen to run after, not for you, because your heavenly Father
33 knows that you need them all. Set your mind on God's kingdom and his justice before everything else, and all
34 the rest will come to you as well. So do not be anxious about tomorrow; tomorrow will look after itself. Each day has troubles enough of its own.

'PASS NO JUDGEMENT, AND YOU WILL 7
not be judged. For as you judge others, 2 so you will yourselves be judged, and whatever measure you deal out to others will be dealt back to you. Why 3 do you look at the speck of sawdust in your brother's eye, with never a thought for the great plank in your own? Or how can you say to your 4 brother, "Let me take the speck out of your eye", when all the time there is that plank in your own? You hypocrite! 5 First take the plank out of your own eye, and then you will see clearly to take the speck out of your brother's.

'Do not give dogs what is holy; do 6 not throw your pearls to the pigs: they will only trample on them, and turn and tear you to pieces.

'Ask, and you will receive; seek, and 7 you will find; knock, and the door will be opened. For everyone who 8 asks receives, he who seeks finds, and to him who knocks, the door will be opened.

'Is there a man among you who will 9 offer his son a stone when he asks for bread, or a snake when he asks for 10 fish? If you, then, bad as you are, 11 know how to give your children what is good for them, how much more will your heavenly Father give good things to those who ask him!

'Always treat others as you would 12 like them to treat you: that is the Law and the prophets.

'Enter by the narrow gate. The gate 13 is wide that leads to perdition, there is plenty of room on the road,*r* and many go that way; but the gate that leads to 14 life is small and the road is narrow,*s* and those who find it are few.

'Beware of false prophets, men who 15

p Or a day to his life.
q One witness reads Consider the lilies: they neither card nor spin, nor labour.
r Some witnesses read The road that leads to perdition is wide with plenty of room.
s Some witnesses read but the road that leads to life is small and narrow.

22: *Sound* and *bad* eyes probably contrast "generosity" and "stinginess." Generosity in acts of charity (v. 2 n.) is a way of storing *up treasure in heaven* (v. 20). **24:** Lk.16.13. **25–34:** God can be trusted from day to day (vv. 26,30,32); the man of faith (v. 30) is free to put *God's kingdom* first (v. 33).
    7.1–14: General instructions. 1–5: Lk.6.37–38,41–42. **2:** Mk.4.24. **7–11:** Lk.11.9–13. **12:** The Golden Rule (Lk.6.31) is a widespread principle in ancient ethical literature, including that of Judaism. A related summary of *the Law and the prophets* is found in 22.34–40 (compare Mk.12.28–34; Lk.10.25–28 n.). **13–14:** Lk.13.23–24.
    7.15–23: Warnings against false leaders (Lk.6.43–46). Since the *false prophets* appear as

come to you dressed up as sheep while underneath they are savage wolves.
16 You will recognize them by the fruits they bear. Can grapes be picked from
17 briars, or figs from thistles? In the same way, a good tree always yields good fruit, and a poor tree bad fruit.
18 A good tree cannot bear bad fruit, or a
19 poor tree good fruit. And when a tree does not yield good fruit it is cut down
20 and burnt. That is why I say you will recognize them by their fruits.
21 'Not everyone who calls me "Lord, Lord" will enter the kingdom of Heaven, but only those who do the will
22 of my heavenly Father. When that day comes, many will say to me, "Lord, Lord, did we not prophesy in your name, cast out devils in your name, and in your name perform many
23 miracles?" Then I will tell them to their face, "I never knew you; out of my sight, you and your wicked ways!"
24 'What then of the man who hears these words of mine and acts upon them? He is like a man who had the
25 sense to build his house on rock. The rain came down, the floods rose, the wind blew, and beat upon that house; but it did not fall, because its founda-
26 tions were on rock. But what of the man who hears these words of mine and does not act upon them? He is like a man who was foolish enough to build
27 his house on sand. The rain came down, the floods rose, the wind blew, and beat upon that house; down it fell with a great crash.'
28 When Jesus had finished this dis-course the people were astounded at
29 his teaching; unlike their own teachers he taught with a note of authority.

Teaching and healing

AFTER HE HAD COME DOWN FROM THE **8** hill he was followed by a great crowd. And now a leper[t] approached him, 2 bowed low, and said, 'Sir, if only you will, you can cleanse me.' Jesus 3 stretched out his hand, touched him, and said, 'Indeed I will; be clean again.' And his leprosy was cured immediately. Then Jesus said to him, 4 'Be sure you tell nobody; but go and show yourself to the priest, and make the offering laid down by Moses for your cleansing; that will certify the cure.'

When he had entered Capernaum a 5 centurion came up to ask his help. 'Sir,' he said, 'a boy of mine lies at 6 home paralysed and racked with pain.' Jesus said, 'I will come and cure him.'[u] 7 But the centurion replied, 'Sir, who am 8 I to have you under my roof? You need only say the word and the boy will be cured. I know, for I am myself 9 under orders, with soldiers under me. I say to one, "Go", and he goes; to another, "Come here", and he comes; and to my servant, "Do this", and he does it.' Jesus heard him with astonish- 10 ment, and said to the people who were following him, 'I tell you this: nowhere, even in Israel, have I found such faith.

'Many, I tell you, will come from east 11 and west to feast with Abraham, Isaac, and Jacob in the kingdom of Heaven. But those who were born to the king- 12 dom will be driven out into the dark, the place of wailing and grinding of teeth.' Then Jesus said to the centurion, 13 'Go home now; because of your faith,

---

t The words leper, leprosy, *as used in this translation, refer to some disfiguring skin disease which entailed ceremo-nial defilement. It is different from what is now called* leprosy.
u Or Am I to come and cure him?

---

sheep (although in disguise, v. 15) and confess Jesus as *Lord* (vv. 21–22), they represent a danger within the Church. **17–18:** 12.33–35. **19:** Compare 3.10; Lk.3.9. **23:** Lk.13.27; Ps.6.8.

7.24–29: The wise and foolish builders (Lk.6.47–49) concludes the Sermon, warning the faithful to hear and act on Jesus' words. Of the five discourses in Mt. (see Introduction), only that in ch. 10 fails to close with a parable. **28:** A phrase like *when Jesus had finished this discourse* marks the end of the four other collections in the book (11.1; 13.53; 19.1; 26.1).

8.1–9.38: Jesus' teaching and healing. While teaching is interspersed between narratives, this section is comprised primarily of a collection of ten miracles. **1–4: A leper healed** (Mk.1.40–45; Lk.5.12–16). **2:** A *leper* was the victim of a skin ailment (not Hansen's disease) which required his isolation from society; the rules are given in Lev. ch. 13. *Cleanse:* the leper asks to be rendered ritually pure as well as healed. **5–13: The centurion's servant** (Lk.7.1–10; compare Jn.4.46–53). **5:** *Centurion:* a commander of a unit of about one hundred infantry in the Roman army. *Boy:* the Gk. may mean "son" or "servant." **11–12:** In Jewish thought, an eschatological banquet (*feast*) is a theme frequently connected with God's final rule; Lk.13.28–30. **11:** Compare Ps.107.2–3. **13:** A phrase like *because of your faith* is frequently associated with healing in the

so let it be.' At that moment the boy recovered.

14 Jesus then went to Peter's house and found Peter's mother-in-law in bed 15 with fever. So he took her by the hand; the fever left her, and she got up and waited on him.

16 When evening fell, they brought to him many who were possessed by devils; and he drove the spirits out with a word and healed all who were 17 sick, to fulfil the prophecy of Isaiah: 'He took away our illnesses and lifted our diseases from us.'*v*

18 AT THE SIGHT OF THE CROWDS SURrounding him Jesus gave word to 19 cross to the other shore. A doctor of the law came up, and said, 'Master, I will follow you wherever you go.' 20 Jesus replied, 'Foxes have their holes, the birds their roosts; but the Son of Man has nowhere to lay his head.' 21 Another man, one of his disciples, said to him, 'Lord, let me go and bury my 22 father first.' Jesus replied, 'Follow me, and leave the dead to bury their dead.' 23 Jesus then got into the boat, and his 24 disciples followed. All at once a great storm arose on the lake, till the waves were breaking right over the boat; but 25 he went on sleeping. So they came and woke him up, crying: 'Save us, Lord; 26 we are sinking!' 'Why are you such cowards?' he said; 'how little faith you have!' Then he stood up and rebuked the wind and the sea, and there was a 27 dead calm. The men were astonished at what had happened, and exclaimed, 'What sort of man is this? Even the wind and the sea obey him.'

28 When he reached the other side, in the country of the Gadarenes, he was met by two men who came out from the tombs; they were possessed by devils, and so violent that no one 29 dared pass that way. 'You son of God,' they shouted, 'what do you want with us? Have you come here to

torment us before our time?' In the 30 distance a large herd of pigs was feeding, and the devils begged him: 31 'If you drive us out, send us into that herd of pigs.' 'Begone!' he said. Then 32 they came out and went into the pigs; the whole herd rushed over the edge into the lake, and perished in the water.

The men in charge of them took to 33 their heels, and made for the town, where they told the whole story, and what had happened to the madmen. Thereupon all the town came out to 34 meet Jesus; and when they saw him they begged him to leave the district and go. So he got into the boat and 9 crossed over, and came to his own town.

And now some men brought him a 2 paralysed man lying on a bed. Seeing their faith Jesus said to the man, 'Take heart, my son; your sins are forgiven.' At this some of the lawyers said to 3 themselves, 'This is blasphemous talk.' Jesus knew what they were thinking, 4 and said, 'Why do you harbour these evil thoughts? Is it easier to say, 5 "Your sins are forgiven", or to say, "Stand up and walk"? But to convince 6 you that the Son of Man has the right on earth to forgive sins'—he turned to the paralysed man—'stand up, take your bed, and go home.' Thereupon 7 the man got up, and went off home. The people were filled with awe at the 8 sight, and praised God for granting such authority to men.

AS HE PASSED ON FROM THERE JESUS 9 saw a man named Matthew at his seat in the custom-house, and said to him, 'Follow me'; and Matthew rose and followed him.

When Jesus was at table in the house, 10 many bad characters—tax-gatherers and others—were seated with him and his disciples. The Pharisees noticed this, 11 and said to his disciples, 'Why is it that

v Or and bore the burden of our diseases.

Gospels; usually, this *faith* seems to be simple confidence in Jesus' power to cure. **14–17: Peter's mother-in-law** (Mk.1.29–34; Lk.4.38–41). **17:** Isa.53.4. **18:** Mk.4.35. **19–22:** Lk.9.57–60. **20:** *Son of Man:* see Mk.2.10 n. **23–27: Rebuke of a storm** (Mk.4.35–41; Lk.8.22–25). **28–34: The Gadarene demoniacs** (Mk.5.1–20; Lk.8.26–39). **28–29:** The *devils* (see Mk.1.23 n.) recognize the *son of God* (see 16.16 n.; Mk.1.24 n.). **28:** *Gadarene:* see Mk.5.1 n. *Two men:* Mk. and Lk. have one man. **30:** *Pigs* are unclean animals in Mosaic law (Lev.11.7; Deut.14.8). **9.1–8: A paralytic;** see Mk.2.1–12 nn.; Lk.5.17–20. **9:** *Matthew:* called Levi in Mk.2.14; Lk.5.27. **10–13:** Tax-gatherers and sinners. Mk.2.15–17; Lk.5.29–32. **10:** *Tax-gatherers:* see Lk.3.12 n.

your master eats with tax-gatherers and
12 sinners?' Jesus heard it and said, 'It is
not the healthy that need a doctor, but
13 the sick. Go and learn what that text
means, "I require mercy, not sacrifice."
I did not come to invite virtuous
people, but sinners.'

14 Then John's disciples came to him
with the question: 'Why do we and
the Pharisees fast, but your disciples
15 do not?' Jesus replied, 'Can you
expect the bridegroom's friends to go
mourning while the bridegroom is with
them? The time will come when the
bridegroom will be taken away from
them; that will be the time for them
to fast.

16 'No one sews a patch of unshrunk
cloth on to an old coat; for then the
patch tears away from the coat, and
17 leaves a bigger hole. Neither do you
put new wine into old wineskins; if
you do, the skins burst, and then the
wine runs out and the skins are spoilt.
No, you put new wine into fresh skins;
then both are preserved.'

18 EVEN AS HE SPOKE, THERE CAME A
president of the synagogue, who bowed
low before him and said, 'My daughter
has just died; but come and lay your
19 hand on her, and she will live.' Jesus
rose and went with him, and so did his
disciples.

20 Then a woman who had suffered
from haemorrhages for twelve years
came up from behind, and touched the
21 edge of his cloak; for she said to
herself, 'If I can only touch his cloak,
22 I shall be cured.' But Jesus turned and
saw her, and said, 'Take heart, my
daughter; your faith has cured you.'
And from that moment she recovered.

23 When Jesus arrived at the president's
house and saw the flute-players and
24 the general commotion, he said, 'Be
off! The girl is not dead: she is asleep';

and they only laughed at him. But, 25
when everyone had been turned out,
he went into the room and took the
girl by the hand, and she got up. This 26
story became the talk of all the country
round.

As he passed on Jesus was followed 27
by two blind men, who cried out, 'Son
of David, have pity on us!' And when 28
he had gone indoors they came to
him. Jesus asked, 'Do you believe that
I have the power to do what you
want?' 'Yes, sir', they said. Then he 29
touched their eyes, and said, 'As you
have believed, so let it be'; and their 30
sight was restored. Jesus said to them
sternly, 'See that no one hears about
this.' But as soon as they had gone 31
out they talked about him all over the
country-side.

They were on their way out when a 32
man was brought to him, who was
dumb and possessed by a devil; the 33
devil was cast out and the patient
recovered his speech. Filled with
amazement the onlookers said,
'Nothing like this has ever been seen
in Israel.'*w*

SO JESUS WENT ROUND ALL THE TOWNS 35
and villages teaching in their synagogues, announcing the good news of
the Kingdom, and curing every kind
of ailment and disease. The sight of the 36
people moved him to pity: they were
like sheep without a shepherd, harassed
and helpless; and he said to his 37
disciples, 'The crop is heavy, but
labourers are scarce; you must there- 38
fore beg the owner to send labourers
to harvest his crop.'

Then he called his twelve disciples **10**
to him and gave them authority to
cast out unclean spirits and to cure
every kind of ailment and disease.

w Some witnesses add (34) But the Pharisees said, 'He
casts out devils by the prince of devils.'

13: Hos.6.6; quoted again in 12.7. **14–17**: Fasting (Mk.2.18–22; Lk.5.33–39). **14**: *John's
disciples:* see Mk.2.18 n. **16–17**: See Mk. 2.21–22 n. **18–26: Jairus' daughter and a woman with
a chronic ailment** (Mk.5.21–43; Lk.8.40–56). See Mk.5.21–43 n. **18**: *A president of the synagogue:*
by name, Jairus in Mk.5.22; Lk.8.41. **22**: *Cured:* see Lk.7.50 n. **23**: *Flute-players* provided
accompaniment to the customary wailing of mourners. **27–31: Two blind men** (20.29–34;
Mk.10.46–52; Lk.18.35–43). **32–33: A dumb man.** Tfn. *w* may be borrowed from the story in
12.22–24.
  9.35–38: A transition from the miracles of chs. 8–9 to the "missionary discourse" of ch. 10;
compare 4.23–25. **36**: Mk.6.34; Num.27.17; 1 Kgs.22.17.
  10.1–11.1: The (second) missionary discourse. 1: Mk.3.14–15; 6.7; Lk.9.1. **2–4**: Mk.3.16–19;

2 These are the names of the twelve apostles: first Simon, also called Peter, and his brother Andrew; James son of Zebedee, and his brother John; Philip and Bartholomew, Thomas and Matthew the tax-gatherer, James son of 4 Alphaeus, Lebbaeus,[x] Simon, a member of the Zealot party, and Judas Iscariot, the man who betrayed him.

5 These twelve Jesus sent out with the following instructions: 'Do not take the road to gentile lands, and do not 6 enter any Samaritan town; but go rather to the lost sheep of the house of 7 Israel. And as you go proclaim the message: "The kingdom of Heaven is 8 upon you." Heal the sick, raise the dead, cleanse lepers, cast out devils. You received without cost; give without charge.

9 'Provide no gold, silver, or copper 10 to fill your purse, no pack for the road, no second coat, no shoes, no stick; the worker earns his keep.

11 'When you come to any town or village, look for some worthy person in it, and make your home there until 12 you leave. Wish the house peace as you 13 enter it, so that, if it is worthy, your peace may descend on it; if it is not worthy, your peace can come back to 14 you. If anyone will not receive you or listen to what you say, then as you leave that house or that town shake the 15 dust of it off your feet. I tell you this: on the day of judgement it will be more bearable for the land of Sodom and Gomorrah than for that town.

16 'Look, I send you out like sheep among wolves; be wary as serpents, innocent as doves.

17 'And be on your guard, for men will hand you over to their courts, they will flog you in the synagogues, 18 and you will be brought before governors and kings, for my sake, to testify before them and the heathen. But when you are arrested, do not 19 worry about what you are to say; when the time comes, the words you need will be given you; for it is not 20 you who will be speaking: it will be the Spirit of your Father speaking in you.

'Brother will betray brother to death, 21 and the father his child; children will turn against their parents and send them to their death. All will hate you 22 for your allegiance to me; but the man who holds out to the end will be saved. When you are persecuted in one 23 town, take refuge in another; I tell you this: before you have gone through all the towns of Israel the Son of Man will have come.

'A pupil does not rank above his 24 teacher, or a servant above his master. The pupil should be content to share 25 his teacher's lot, the servant to share his master's. If the master has been called Beelzebub, how much more his household!

'So do not be afraid of them. There 26 is nothing covered up that will not be uncovered, nothing hidden that will not be made known. What I say to you 27 in the dark you must repeat in broad daylight; what you hear whispered you must shout from the house-tops. Do 28 not fear those who kill the body, but cannot kill the soul. Fear him rather who is able to destroy both soul and body in hell.

'Are not sparrows two a penny? Yet 29 without your Father's leave not one of them can fall to the ground. As for you, 30 even the hairs of your head have all been counted. So have no fear; you 31 are worth more than any number of sparrows.

'Whoever then will acknowledge me 32 before men, I will acknowledge him

x *Some witnesses read* Thaddaeus.

Lk.6.14–16. **2:** *Apostles:* commissioned representatives; this designation appears in Mt. only in this verse. **3:** *Lebbaeus:* Mk.3.18, as well as many MSS. of Mt., has "Thaddaeus"; Lk.6.16 and Acts 1.13 have "Judas the son of James." **4:** *Zealot:* see Mk.3.18 n. **5–6:** Contrast the instruction in 28.19. **7–15:** Mk.6.8–11; Lk.9.2–5; 10.3–12. **7:** Compare the Baptist's (3.2) and Jesus' (4.17) messages. **8:** On the close relation of healing and the kingdom, consider 12.28; Lk.10.9; 11.20; the Gospels present the career of Jesus as the proclamation of the kingdom joined with healing activity. **15:** *Sodom and Gomorrah* (Gen. ch. 29) were the epitome of evil. **17–25:** 24.9–13; Mk.13.9–13; Lk.12.11–12; 21.12–17,19. Persecution in both Jewish (v. 17) and Roman (v. 18) settings is assumed. **21:** See vv. 35–36. **24–25:** Lk.6.40; Jn.13.16. **25:** *Beelzebub:* Satan (see 9.34; 12.22; Mk.3.22; Lk.11.15). **26–33:** Lk.12.2 9. **26 27:** Compare Mk.4.22, 24–25 n.; Lk.8.17; 12.2–3 n. **28:** See Lk.12.4–5 n. **29–32:** *God's providence:* 6.26–33; Lk.12.6–8.

33 before my Father in heaven; and whoever disowns me before men, I will disown him before my Father in heaven.

34 'You must not think that I have come to bring peace to the earth; I have not come to bring peace, but a

35 sword. I have come to set a man against his father, a daughter against her mother, a son's wife against her

36 mother-in-law; and a man will find his enemies under his own roof.

37 'No man is worthy of me who cares more for father or mother than for me; no man is worthy of me who cares for

38 son or daughter; no man is worthy of me who does not take up his cross and

39 walk in my footsteps. By gaining his life a man will lose it; by losing his life for my sake, he will gain it.

40 'To receive you is to receive me, and to receive me is to receive the One who

41 sent me. Whoever receives a prophet as a prophet will be given a prophet's reward, and whoever receives a good man because he is a good man will be

42 given a good man's reward. And if anyone gives so much as a cup of cold water to one of these little ones, because he is a disciple of mine, I tell you this: that man will assuredly not go unrewarded.'

11 When Jesus had finished giving his twelve disciples their instructions, he left that place and went to teach and preach in the neighbouring towns.

2 JOHN, WHO WAS IN PRISON, HEARD what Christ was doing, and sent his

3 own disciples to him with this message: 'Are you the one who is to come, or

4 are we to expect some other?' Jesus answered, 'Go and tell John what you

5 hear and see: the blind recover their sight, the lame walk, the lepers are made clean, the deaf hear, the dead are raised to life, the poor are hearing the

6 good news—and happy is the man who does not find me a stumbling-block.'

When the messengers were on their 7 way back, Jesus began to speak to the people about John: 'What was the spectacle that drew you to the wilderness? A reed-bed swept by the wind? No? Then what did you go out to see? 8 A man dressed in silks and satins? Surely you must look in palaces for that. But why did you go out? To see a 9 prophet? Yes indeed, and far more than a prophet. He is the man of whom 10 Scripture says,

"Here is my herald, whom I send on
　　ahead of you,
and he will prepare your way before
　　you."

I tell you this: never has there appeared on earth a mother's son greater 11 than John the Baptist, and yet the least in the kingdom of Heaven is greater than he.

'Ever since the coming of John the 12 Baptist the kingdom of Heaven has been subjected to violence and violent men*y* are seizing it. For all the prophets 13 and the Law foretold things to come until John appeared, and John is the 14 destined Elijah, if you will but accept it. If you have ears, then hear. 15

'How can I describe this generation? 16 They are like children sitting in the market-place and shouting at each other,

"We piped for you and you would 17
　　not dance."
"We wept and wailed, and you would
　　not mourn."

For John came, neither eating nor 18 drinking, and they say, "He is possessed." The Son of Man came eating 19 and drinking, and they say, "Look at him! a glutton and a drinker, a friend

y Or has been forcing its way forward, and men of force . . .

34–36: Lk.12.51,53; the proclamation of the kingdom calls for a decision which draws lines of separation. 37–39: Compare Lk.14.26–27. 38–39: *Cross* and *losing life* sayings are also connected in 16.24–25; Mk.8.34–35; Lk.9.23–24; *life* and *follow me* sayings, in Jn.12.25–26. The associated ideas would be particularly meaningful in situations involving mission or persecution. 39: Lk.17.33. 40–42: Jesus affirms his identification with his disciples. 11.1: See 7.28 n.
　11.2–12.50: **Claims and conflict. 11.2–19: Jesus and John the Baptist:** see Lk.7.18–35 nn. **2:** *In prison:* 14.3–4; Mk.6.17–18. **5:** Isa.29.18–19; 35.5–6; 61.1. **10:** Mal.3.1. **12–15:** John's career marks the beginning of the fulfillment of God's promises; compare Lk.16.16 n. **14:** *John* fulfills the prophecy on *Elijah;* Mal.4.5; see Lk.1.17. **19:** *Its results:* lit. "her deeds"; compare Lk.7.25 n.

of tax-gatherers and sinners!" And yet God's wisdom is proved right by its results.'

20 THEN HE SPOKE OF THE TOWNS IN which most of his miracles had been performed, and denounced them for 21 their impenitence. 'Alas for you, Chorazin!' he said; 'alas for you, Bethsaida! If the miracles that were performed in you had been performed in Tyre and Sidon, they would have repented long ago in sackcloth and 22 ashes. But it will be more bearable, I tell you, for Tyre and Sidon on the day of judgement than for you. And as for you, Capernaum, will you be exalted to the skies? No, brought down to the depths! For if the miracles had been performed in Sodom which were performed in you, Sodom would be 24 standing to this day. But it will be more bearable, I tell you, for the land of Sodom on the day of judgement than for you.'

25   At that time Jesus spoke these words: 'I thank thee, Father, Lord of heaven and earth, for hiding these things from the learned and wise, and 26 revealing them to the simple. Yes, 27 Father, such*z* was thy choice. Everything is entrusted to me by my Father; and no one knows the Son but the Father, and no one knows the Father but the Son and those to whom the Son may choose to reveal him.

28   'Come to me, all whose work is hard, whose load is heavy; and I will give 29 you relief. Bend your necks to my yoke, and learn from me, for I am gentle and humble-hearted; and your 30 souls will find relief. For my yoke is good to bear, my load is light.'

Controversy

12 ONCE ABOUT THAT TIME JESUS WENT through the cornfields on the Sabbath;

and his disciples, feeling hungry, began to pluck some ears of corn and eat them. The Pharisees noticed this, and 2 said to him, 'Look, your disciples are doing something which is forbidden on the Sabbath.' He answered, 'Have you 3 not read what David did when he and his men were hungry? He went into the 4 House of God and ate the sacred bread, though neither he nor his men had a right to eat it, but only the priests. Or 5 have you not read in the Law that on the Sabbath the priests in the temple break the Sabbath and it is not held against them? I tell you, there is 6 something greater than the temple here. If you had known what that text 7 means, "I require mercy, not sacrifice", you would not have condemned the innocent. For the Son of Man is 8 sovereign over the Sabbath.'

He went on to another place, and 9 entered their synagogue. A man was 10 there with a withered arm, and they asked Jesus, 'Is it permitted to heal on the Sabbath?' (They wanted to frame a charge against him.) But he said to 11 them, 'Suppose you had one sheep, which fell into a ditch on the Sabbath; is there one of you who would not catch hold of it and lift it out? And 12 surely a man is worth far more than a sheep! It is therefore permitted to do good on the Sabbath.' Turning to the 13 man he said, 'Stretch out your arm.' He stretched it out, and it was made sound again like the other. But the 14 Pharisees, on leaving the synagogue, laid a plot to do away with him.

Jesus was aware of it and withdrew. 15 Many followed, and he cured all who were ill; and he gave strict injunctions 16 that they were not to make him known. This was to fulfil Isaiah's 17 prophecy:

'Here is my servant, whom I have   18
    chosen,

z Or Yes, I thank thee, Father, that such . . .

20–24: Judgment of Galilean cities (Lk.10.13–15). **21:** *Tyre* and *Sidon:* Gentile (Phoenician) cities condemned by the prophets (Jer.47.4). *Sackcloth and ashes:* symbols of mourning. *Sodom:* see 10.15 n. **25–27: Thanksgiving for revelation.** See Lk.10.21–22 n. **28–30:** An invitation modeled on those extended by the heavenly Wisdom (Lk.7.35 n.); see Prov.8.1–21 and Ecclus. 6.18–31. **12.1–14: Sabbath controversy** (Mk.2.23–3.6 nn.; Lk.6.1–11). **1:** Deut.23.25. **2:** Exod. 20.10; Deut.5.14. **3:** 1 Sam.21.1. **7:** Lev.24.7–9. **5:** Num.28.9–10. **7:** Hos.6.6; compare 9.13. **9–14:** See Mk.3.1–6 n. **11:** Lk.14.5. **15–21: Healing the sick. 18–21:** Isa.42.1–4. **22–29: Jesus and**

my beloved, on whom my favour
rests;
I will put my Spirit upon him,
and he will proclaim judgement
among the nations.

19 He will not strive, he will not shout,
nor will his voice be heard in the
streets.

20 He will not snap off the broken reed,
nor snuff out the smouldering wick,
until he leads justice on to victory.

21 In him the nations shall place their
hope.'

22 THEN THEY BROUGHT HIM A MAN WHO
was possessed; he was blind and dumb;
and Jesus cured him, restoring both
23 speech and sight. The bystanders were
all amazed, and the word went round:
24 'Can this be the Son of David?' But
when the Pharisees heard it they said,
'It is only by Beelzebub prince of
devils that this man drives the devils
out.'

25 He knew what was in their minds;
so he said to them, 'Every kingdom
divided against itself goes to ruin; and
no town, no household, that is divided
26 against itself can stand. And if it is
Satan who casts out Satan, Satan is
divided against himself; how then can
27 his kingdom stand? And if it is by
Beelzebub that I cast out devils, by
whom do your own people drive them
out? If this is your argument, they
28 themselves will refute you. But if it is
by the Spirit of God that I drive out
the devils, then be sure the kingdom of
God has already come upon you.

29 'Or again, how can anyone break
into a strong man's house and make
off with his goods, unless he has first
tied the strong man up before ran-
sacking the house?

30 'He who is not with me is against me,
and he who does not gather with me
scatters.

31 'And so I tell you this: no sin, no
slander, is beyond forgiveness for men,
except slander spoken against the
Spirit, and that will not be forgiven.
32 Any man who speaks a word against
the Son of Man will be forgiven; but
if anyone speaks against the Holy
Spirit, for him there is no forgiveness,
either in this age or in the age to come.

33 'Either make the tree good and its
fruit good, or make the tree bad and
its fruit bad; you can tell a tree by its
34 fruit. You vipers' brood! How can
your words be good when you yourselves are evil? For the words that the
mouth utters come from the over-
35 flowing of the heart. A good man
produces good from the store of good
within himself; and an evil man from
evil within produces evil.

36 'I tell you this: there is not a
thoughtless word that comes from
men's lips but they will have to
account for it on the day of judgement.
37 For out of your own mouth you will
be acquitted; out of your own mouth
you will be condemned.'

38 At this some of the doctors of the
law and the Pharisees said, 'Master,
we should like you to show us a sign.'
39 He answered: 'It is a wicked, godless
generation that asks for a sign; and
the only sign that will be given it is the
40 sign of the prophet Jonah. Jonah was
in the sea-monster's belly for three
days and three nights, and in the same
way the Son of Man will be three days
and three nights in the bowels of the
41 earth. At the Judgement, when this
generation is on trial, the men of
Nineveh will appear against it[a] and
ensure its condemnation, for they
repented at the preaching of Jonah;
and what is here is greater than Jonah.
42 The Queen of the South will appear at
the Judgement when this generation is
on trial,[b] and ensure its condemnation,
for she came from the ends of the
earth to hear the wisdom of Solomon;

a Or will rise again together with it.
b Or At the Judgement the Queen of the South will be
raised to life together with this generation.

Satan (Mk.3.22–27; Lk.11.14–22). 23: Son of David: the Messiah (1.1 n.). 24–28: Beelzebub:
Satan (v. 26). 27: Your own people (lit. "your sons") ascribes the effective practice of exorcism
to others. 30: Lk.11.23; contrast Mk.9.39–40 n. 31–32: See Mk.3. 29n.; Lk.12.10. Mt. may intend
the saying to distinguish between slander of the earthly Jesus and slander of the risen Lord.
33–37: 7.16–20; Lk.6.43–45. 38–42: The request for a sign (Lk.11.29–32) is perhaps regarded
as evil because its intent is to "test" (compare 4.7). 39–41: Jonah 1.17; 3.5. The sign of the
prophet Jonah for Mt. is interpreted by v. 40; compare Lk.11.29 n. Queen of the South:

and what is here is greater than Solomon.

43 'When an unclean spirit comes out of a man it wanders over the deserts seeking a resting-place, and finds none.
44 Then it says, "I will go back to the home I left." So it returns and finds the house unoccupied, swept clean, and
45 tidy. Off it goes and collects seven other spirits more wicked than itself, and they all come in and settle down; and in the end the man's plight is worse than before. That is how it will be with this wicked generation.'

46 He was still speaking to the crowd when his mother and brothers appeared; they stood outside, wanting to
47 speak to him. Someone said, 'Your mother and your brothers are here outside; they want to speak to you.'
48 Jesus turned to the man who brought the message, and said, 'Who is my
49 mother? Who are my brothers?'; and pointing to the disciples, he said, 'Here are my mother and my brothers.
50 Whoever does the will of my heavenly Father is my brother, my sister, my mother.'

13 THAT SAME DAY JESUS WENT OUT AND
2 sat by the lake-side, where so many people gathered round him that he had to get into a boat. He sat there, and
3 all the people stood on the shore. He spoke to them in parables, at some length.

4 He said: 'A sower went out to sow. And as he sowed, some seed fell along the footpath; and the birds came and
5 ate it up. Some seed fell on rocky ground, where it had little soil, and it sprouted quickly because it had no
6 depth of earth; but when the sun rose the young corn was scorched, and as
7 it had no root it withered away. Some seed fell among thistles; and the thistles shot up, and choked the corn.
8 And some of the seed fell into good soil, where it bore fruit, yielding a hundredfold or, it might be, sixtyfold or thirtyfold. If you have ears, then 9 hear.'

10 The disciples went up to him and asked, 'Why do you speak to them in parables?' He replied, 'It has been 11 granted to you to know the secrets of the kingdom of Heaven; but to those others it has not been granted. For the 12 man who has will be given more, till he has enough and to spare; and the man who has not will forfeit even what he has. That is why I speak to them in 13 parables; for they look without seeing, and listen without hearing or understanding. There is a prophecy of Isaiah 14 which is being fulfilled for them: "You may hear and hear, but you will never understand; you may look and look, but you will never see. For this people's 15 mind has become gross; their ears are dulled, and their eyes are closed. Otherwise, their eyes might see, their ears hear, and their mind understand, and then they might turn again, and I would heal them."

'But happy are your eyes because 16 they see, and your ears because they hear! Many prophets and saints, I tell 17 you, desired to see what you now see, yet never saw it; to hear what you hear, yet never heard it.

'You, then, may hear the parable of 18 the sower. When a man hears the word 19 that tells of the Kingdom but fails to understand it, the evil one comes and carries off what has been sown in his heart. There you have the seed sown along the footpath. The seed sown on 20 rocky ground stands for the man who, on hearing the word, accepts it at once with joy; but as it strikes no root in 21 him he has no staying-power, and when there is trouble or persecution on account of the word he falls away at once. The seed sown among thistles 22 represents the man who hears the word,

---

1 Kgs.10.1–10. **43–45**: Lk.11.24–26. **43**: *Deserts* were often associated with demons. **46–50**: Mk.3.31–35; Lk.8.19–21.

    13.1–53a: **The third discourse** (see Introduction) is comprised of parables of the kingdom (Mk. ch. 4; Lk.8.4–18; 10.23–24; 13.18–21). **2**: On *parables*, see Mk.4.2 n. **3–9**: **The sower** (Mk.4.1–9; Lk.8.4–8). **3–8**: See Mk.4.3–8 n. **8**: See Mk.4.8 n. **10–17**: **The use of parables** (Mk.4.10–12; Lk.8.9–10; 10.23–24). See Mk.4.11 n., 13–20 n. **13**: In Mt. the use of parables is a consequence of the failure to "see" or "hear"; contrast Mk.4.12 n. **14–16**: Isa.6.9–10. **16–17**: Lk.10.23–24. **18–23**: An interpretation of the sower. See Mk.4.13–20 n. **19**: The term *understand* here and in v. 23 is used to serve the view of Mt. that the disciples are men of insight

but worldly cares and the false glamour of wealth choke it, and it proves 23 barren. But the seed that fell into good soil is the man who hears the word and understands it, who accordingly bears fruit, and yields a hundredfold or, it may be, sixtyfold or thirtyfold.'

24 Here is another parable that he put before them: 'The kingdom of Heaven is like this. A man sowed his field with 25 good seed; but while everyone was asleep his enemy came, sowed darnel 26 among the wheat, and made off. When the corn sprouted and began to fill out, 27 the darnel could be seen among it. The farmer's men went to their master and said, "Sir, was it not good seed that you sowed in your field? Then where 28 has the darnel come from?" "This is an enemy's doing", he replied. "Well then," they said, "shall we go and 29 gather the darnel?" "No," he answered; "in gathering it you might pull up the 30 wheat at the same time. Let them both grow together till harvest; and at harvest-time I will tell the reapers, 'Gather the darnel first, and tie it in bundles for burning; then collect the wheat into my barn.' " '

31 And this is another parable that he put before them: 'The kingdom of Heaven is like a mustard-seed, which a 32 man took and sowed in his field. As a seed, mustard is smaller than any other; but when it has grown it is bigger than any garden-plant; it becomes a tree, big enough for the birds to come and roost among its branches.'

33 He told them also this parable: 'The kingdom of Heaven is like yeast, which a woman took and mixed with half a hundredweight of flour till it was all leavened.'

34 In all this teaching to the crowds Jesus spoke in parables; in fact he never 35 spoke to them without a parable. This was to fulfil the prophecy of Isaiah:[c]

'I will open my mouth in parables; I will utter things kept secret since the world was made.'

36 He then dismissed the people, and went into the house, where his disciples came to him and said, 'Explain to us the parable of the darnel in the field.' 37 And this was his answer: 'The sower of the good seed is the Son of Man. 38 The field is the world; the good seed stands for the children of the Kingdom, the darnel for the children of the evil one. 39 The enemy who sowed the darnel is the devil. The harvest is the end of time. The reapers are angels. As 40 the darnel, then, is gathered up and burnt, so at the end of time the Son 41 of Man will send out his angels, who will gather out of his kingdom whatever makes men stumble, and all whose deeds are evil, and these will be 42 thrown into the blazing furnace, the place of wailing and grinding of teeth. And then the righteous will shine as 43 brightly as the sun in the kingdom of their Father. If you have ears, then hear.

44 'The kingdom of Heaven is like treasure lying buried in a field. The man who found it, buried it again; and for sheer joy went and sold everything he had, and bought that field.

45 'Here is another picture of the kingdom of Heaven. A merchant 46 looking out for fine pearls found one of very special value; so he went and sold everything he had, and bought it.

47 'Again the kingdom of Heaven is like a net let down into the sea, where fish of every kind were caught in it. 48 When it was full, it was dragged ashore. Then the men sat down and collected the good fish into pails and 49 threw the worthless away. That is how it will be at the end of time. The angels will go forth, and they will

c Some witnesses omit of Isaiah.

(contrast the tone of Mk.4.13). **24–30: The weeds in the field. 25:** *Darnel:* a weed similar in appearance to wheat. **31–32: The mustard seed** (see Mk.4.26–32 nn.; Lk.13.18–19). **33:** *Yeast* (Lk.13.20–21). Although a fermenting agent (yeast) is regularly a symbol for evil influence elsewhere (e.g. 16.6,11; Gal.5.8–9); here the metaphor suggests the idea of the irreversible power of the kingdom. *Half a hundredweight:* fifty pounds. **35:** Ps.78.2 is quoted; therefore, Isa. is not mentioned in some MSS. (Tfn. *c*). **36–43: An interpretation of the parable** of the weeds. **38:** The *evil one:* the devil. **43:** Dan.12.3. **44–46: The treasure and the pearls** parables speak either (a) of the cost of the kingdom or (b) of its value which makes even that cost a joy. **47–50: The net.** The proclamation of the kingdom attracts both good and bad; their separation must

separate the wicked from the good,
10 and throw them into the blazing
furnace, the place of wailing and
grinding of teeth.
51 'Have you understood all this?' he
52 asked; and they answered, 'Yes.' He
said to them, 'When, therefore, a
teacher of the law has become a
learner in the kingdom of Heaven, he
is like a householder who can produce
from his store both the new and the
old.'

53 WHEN HE HAD FINISHED THESE PARABLES
54 Jesus left that place, and came to his
home town, where he taught the people
in their synagogue. In amazement they
asked, 'Where does he get this wisdom
from, and these miraculous powers? Is
55 he not the carpenter's son? Is not his
mother called Mary, his brothers
James, Joseph, Simon, and Judas?
56 And are not all his sisters here with
us? Where then has he got all this
57 from?' So they fell foul of him, and
this led him to say, 'A prophet will
always be held in honour, except in
his home town, and in his own family.'
58 And he did not work many miracles
there: such was their want of faith.

14   It was at that time that reports about
Jesus reached the ears of Prince
2 Herod. 'This is John the Baptist,' he
said to his attendants; 'John has been
raised to life, and that is why these
miraculous powers are at work in him.'

3 NOW HEROD HAD ARRESTED JOHN, PUT
him in chains, and thrown him into
prison, on account of Herodias, his
4 brother Philip's wife; for John had
told him: 'You have no right to her.'
5 Herod would have liked to put him to
death, but he was afraid of the people,
in whose eyes John was a prophet.
6 But at his birthday celebrations the
daughter of Herodias danced before
the guests, and Herod was so delighted
7 that he took an oath to give her

anything she cared to ask. Prompted 8
by her mother, she said, 'Give me here
on a dish the head of John the Baptist.'
The king was distressed when he heard 9
it; but out of regard for his oath and
for his guests, he ordered the request to
be granted, and had John beheaded in 10
prison. The head was brought in on a 11
dish and given to the girl; and she
carried it to her mother. Then John's 12
disciples came and took away the body,
and buried it; and they went and told
Jesus.

WHEN HE HEARD WHAT HAD HAPPENED 13
Jesus withdrew privately by boat to a
lonely place; but people heard of it,
and came after him in crowds by land
from the towns. When he came ashore, 14
he saw a great crowd; his heart went
out to them, and he cured those of
them who were sick. When it grew late 15
the disciples came up to him and said,
'This is a lonely place, and the day has
gone; send the people off to the
villages to buy themselves food.' He 16
answered, 'There is no need for them
to go; give them something to eat
yourselves.' 'All we have here', they 17
said, 'is five loaves and two fishes.'
'Let me have them', he replied. So he 18,19
told the people to sit down on the
grass; then, taking the five loaves and
the two fishes, he looked up to heaven,
said the blessing, broke the loaves,
and gave them to the disciples; and the
disciples gave them to the people. They 20
all ate to their hearts' content; and the
scraps left over, which they picked up,
were enough to fill twelve great baskets.
Some five thousand men shared in this 21
meal, to say nothing of women and
children.

Then he made the disciples embark 22
and go on ahead to the other side,
while he sent the people away; after 23
doing that, he went up the hill-side to
pray alone. It grew late, and he was
there by himself. The boat was already 24

wait for the final judgment. **51–52:** The disciple's resources now include both the *new* message
of the kingdom and the *old* tradition based on the law and the prophets. See 7.24–29 n. **53a:**
See 7.28 n.
    13.53b–58: Jesus in Nazareth (Mk.6.1–6; compare Lk.4.16–30). **54:** *Home town:* Nazareth.
57: *Fell foul:* were offended.
    14.1–12: Herod and John (Mk.6.14–29; Lk.3.19–20; 9.7–9). **1:** *Herod:* Antipas (Lk.3.1 n.).
14.13–21: Feeding of five thousand (Mk.6.30–44; Lk.9.10–17; Jn.6.1–13). See Mk.6.30–44 nn.
14.22–36: Walking on the sea (Mk.6.45–56 and note; Jn.6.16–21). The attempt of *Peter* to walk

some furlongs from the shore,[d] battling with a head-wind and a rough sea. 25 Between three and six in the morning he came to them, walking over the 26 lake. When the disciples saw him walking on the lake they were so shaken that they cried out in terror: 27 'It is a ghost!' But at once he spoke to them: 'Take heart! It is I; do not be afraid.' 28 Peter called to him: 'Lord, if it is you, tell me to come to you over 29 the water.' 'Come', said Jesus. Peter stepped down from the boat, and walked over the water towards Jesus. 30 But when he saw the strength of the gale he was seized with fear; and beginning to sink, he cried, 'Save me, 31 Lord.' Jesus at once reached out and caught hold of him, and said, 'Why did you hesitate? How little faith you 32 have!' They then climbed into the boat; 33 and the wind dropped. And the men in the boat fell at his feet, exclaiming, 'Truly you are the Son of God.'

34 So they finished the crossing and 35 came to land at Gennesaret. There Jesus was recognized by the people of the place, who sent out word to all the country round. And all who were ill 36 were brought to him, and he was begged to allow them simply to touch the edge of his cloak. And everyone who touched it was completely cured.

15 THEN JESUS WAS APPROACHED BY A group of Pharisees and lawyers from 2 Jerusalem, with the question: 'Why do your disciples break the ancient tradition? They do not wash their hands 3 before meals.' He answered them: 'And what of you? Why do you break God's commandment in the interest of your 4 tradition? For God said, "Honour your father and mother", and, "The man who curses his father or mother 5 must suffer death." But you say, "If a man says to his father or mother, 'Anything of mine which might have

been used for your benefit is set apart for God', then he must not honour his 6 father or his mother." You have made God's law null and void out of respect for your tradition. What hypocrisy! 7 Isaiah was right when he prophesied about you: "This people pays me 8 lip-service, but their heart is far from me; their worship of me is in vain, for 9 they teach as doctrines the commandments of men."'

He called the crowd and said to 10 them, 'Listen to me, and understand this: a man is not defiled by what goes 11 into his mouth, but by what comes out of it.'

Then the disciples came to him and 12 said, 'Do you know that the Pharisees have taken great offence at what you have been saying?' His answer was: 13 'Any plant that is not of my heavenly Father's planting will be rooted up. Leave them alone; they are blind 14 guides,[e] and if one blind man guides another they will both fall into the ditch.'

Then Peter said, 'Tell us what that 15 parable means.' Jesus answered, 'Are 16 you still as dull as the rest? Do you 17 not see that whatever goes in by the mouth passes into the stomach and so is discharged into the drain? But what 18 comes out of the mouth has its origins in the heart; and that is what defiles a man. Wicked thoughts, murder, adul- 19 tery, fornication, theft, perjury, slander —these all proceed from the heart; and 20 these are the things that defile a man; but to eat without first washing his hands, that cannot defile him.'

Jesus and his disciples

JESUS THEN LEFT THAT PLACE AND 21 withdrew to the region of Tyre and Sidon. And a Canaanite woman from 22

---

d *Some witnesses read* already well out on the water.
e *Some witnesses insert* of blind men.

---

on the water, told only in Mt., illustrates both the power of faith and the way fear threatens faith. **33:** Unlike the report in Mk.6.52 (see n.), the event awakens a confession of faith in its observers. For Mt., understanding is characteristic of the disciples (see 16.12 n.). A confession (16.16; Mk.8.29) also follows the second account of a feeding and sea crossing in Mt. and Mk. (see Mk.6.30–44 nn.); compare Jn.6.16–21,66–71.
  15.1–20: The ancient traditions (Mk.7.1–23). **2:** See Mk.7.5 n. **4a:** Exod.20.12; Deut.5.16. **4b:** Exod.21.17; Lev.20.9. **8–9:** Isa.29.13. **11:** *Defiled:* made ritually impure.
  15.21–31: Healings (Mk.7.24–31,36–37). See Mk.7.24–37 n. **22:** The story revolves around a

those parts came crying out, 'Sir! have pity on me, Son of David; my daughter

23 is tormented by a devil.' But he said not a word in reply. His disciples came and urged him: 'Send her away; see how

24 she comes shouting after us.' Jesus replied, 'I was sent to the lost sheep of the house of Israel, and to them alone.'

25 But the woman came and fell at his

26 feet and cried, 'Help me, sir.' To this Jesus replied, 'It is not right to take the children's bread and throw it to

27 the dogs.' 'True, sir,' she answered; 'and yet the dogs eat the scraps that

28 fall from their masters' table.' Hearing this Jesus replied, 'Woman, what faith you have! Be it as you wish!' And from that moment her daughter was restored to health.

29 After leaving that region Jesus took the road by the Sea of Galilee and went up to the hills. When he was

30 seated there, crowds flocked to him, bringing with them the lame, blind, dumb, and crippled, and many other sufferers; they threw them down at his

31 feet, and he healed them. Great was the amazement of the people when they saw the dumb speaking, the crippled strong, the lame walking, and sight restored to the blind; and they gave praise to the God of Israel.

32 Jesus called his disciples and said to them, 'I feel sorry for all these people; they have been with me now for three days and have nothing to eat. I do not want to send them away unfed; they

33 might turn faint on the way.' The disciples replied, 'Where in this lonely place can we find bread enough to feed

34 such a crowd?' 'How many loaves have you?' Jesus asked. 'Seven,' they replied;

35 'and there are a few small fishes.' So he ordered the people to sit down on the

36 ground; then he took the seven loaves and the fishes, and after giving thanks to God he broke them and gave to the disciples, and the disciples gave to the

people. They all ate to their hearts' 37 content, and the scraps left over, which they picked up, were enough to fill seven baskets. Four thousand men 38 shared in this meal, to say nothing of women and children. He then dismissed 39 the crowds, got into a boat, and went to the neighbourhood of Magadan.

The Pharisees and Sadducees came, **16** and to test him they asked him to show them a sign from heaven. His answer 2 was:*f* 'It is a wicked generation that 4 asks for a sign; and the only sign that will be given it is the sign of Jonah.' So he went off and left them.

In crossing to the other side the 5 disciples had forgotten to take bread with them. So, when Jesus said to 6 them, 'Beware, be on your guard against the leaven of the Pharisees and Sadducees', they began to say among 7 themselves, 'It is because we have brought no bread!' Knowing what was 8 in their minds, Jesus said to them: 'Why do you talk about bringing no bread? Where is your faith? Do you 9 not understand even yet? Do you not remember the five loaves for the five thousand, and how many basketfuls you picked up? Or the seven loaves 10 for the four thousand, and how many basketfuls you picked up? How can 11 you fail to see that I was not speaking about bread? Be on your guard, I said, against the leaven of the Pharisees and Sadducees.' Then they understood: 12 they were to be on their guard, not against baker's leaven, but against the teaching of the Pharisees and Sadducees.

WHEN HE CAME TO THE TERRITORY OF 13 Caesarea Philippi, Jesus asked his disciples, 'Who do men say that the

f Some witnesses here insert 'In the evening you say, "It will be fine weather, for the sky is red"; (3) and in the morning you say, "It will be stormy today; the sky is red and lowering." You know how to interpret the appearance of the sky; can you not interpret the signs of the times?'

---

non-Jewish (*Canaanite*) woman and the question of Jesus' mission (v. 24). Mt. thinks of a mission limited to Israel during Jesus' human career (see 10.5–6) but ultimately intended to reach out to all (see 28.19).

15.32–39: Feeding of four thousand (Mk.8.1–10). See Mk.6.30–44 nn. **36:** See Mk.8.6.

16.1–12: Sea crossing and discussions (Mk.8.11–21; Lk.11.29; 12.1,54–56). **1:** After a boat trip (15.39), the question of a *sign* is again raised. **2–3:** (Tfn. *f*). See Lk.12.54–56 n. **4:** See 12.38–42 n., 39–41 n. **6:** *Leaven:* see Mk.8.15 n. **12:** Understanding is characteristic of the disciples in this Gospel; contrast Mk 8.17–18,21 n.

16.13–23: Peter's confession and Jesus' prediction of his suffering (Mk.8.27–33; Lk.9.18–22).

14 Son of Man is?' They answered, 'Some say John the Baptist, others Elijah, others Jeremiah, or one of the proph-
15 ets.' 'And you,' he asked, 'who do
16 you say I am?' Simon Peter answered: 'You are the Messiah, the Son of the
17 living God.' Then Jesus said: 'Simon son of Jonah, you are favoured indeed! You did not learn that from mortal man; it was revealed to you by my
18 heavenly Father. And I say this to you: You are Peter, the Rock; and on this rock I will build my church, and the powers of death shall never conquer
19 it.ʰ I will give you the keys of the kingdom of Heaven; what you forbid on earth shall be forbidden in heaven, and what you allow on earth shall be
20 allowed in heaven.' He then gave his disciples strict orders not to tell anyone that he was the Messiah.

21   From that time Jesus began to make it clear to his disciples that he had to go to Jerusalem, and there to suffer much from the elders, chief priests, and doctors of the law; to be put to death and to be raised again on the
22 third day. At this Peter took him by the arm and began to rebuke him: 'Heaven forbid!' he said. 'No, Lord,
23 this shall never happen to you.' Then Jesus turned and said to Peter, 'Away with you, Satan; you are a stumbling-block to me. You think as men think, not as God thinks.'

24   Jesus then said to his disciples, 'If anyone wishes to be a follower of mine, he must leave self behind; he must take up his cross and come with me.
25 Whoever cares for his own safety is lost; but if a man will let himself be

lost for my sake, he will find his true self. What will a man gain by winning 26 the whole world, at the cost of his true self? Or what can he give that will buy that self back? For the Son of 27 Man is to come in the glory of his Father with his angels, and then he will give each man the due reward for what he has done. I tell you this: there 28 are some of those standing here who will not taste death before they have seen the Son of Man coming in his kingdom.'

SIX DAYS LATER JESUS TOOK PETER, **17** James, and John the brother of James, and led them up a high mountain where they were alone; and in their 2 presence he was transfigured; his face shone like the sun, and his clothes became white as the light. And they 3 saw Moses and Elijah appear, con-versing with him. Then Peter spoke: 4 'Lord,' he said, 'how good it is that we are here! If you wish it, I will make three shelters here, one for you, one for Moses, and one for Elijah.' While 5 he was still speaking, a bright cloud suddenly overshadowed them, and a voice called from the cloud: 'This is my Son, my Beloved,ⁱ on whom my favour rests; listen to him.' At the 6 sound of the voice the disciples fell on their faces in terror. Jesus then came 7 up to them, touched them, and said, 'Stand up; do not be afraid.' And when 8 they raised their eyes they saw no one, but only Jesus.

g *Some witnesses read* that I, the Son of Man, am.
h *Or* the gates of death shall never close upon it.
i *Or* This is my only Son.

13: *Son of Man:* see Mk.2.10 n. 14: See Mk.8.28 n. 16: *Messiah:* see 1.1 n. *Son of (the living) God* is a title with a wide range of meanings—from "a person who lives according to God's will" (see Lk.6.35 n.) to "a preexistent being of divine nature" (see Jn.1.14). Although *Son of God* apparently was not a pre-Christian title for the *Messiah*, the OT contains evidence of a "divine kingship" motif which might correspond to the synonymous use of the two terms (see Mk.1.1 n.). 18: Simon is given a new name, *Rock*, and the name is explained (compare Gen.32.28; also Mt.5.13–14 n.). In both Gk. and Aram. the name (*Peter*, "*Rock*") is a play on a common noun meaning "rock." In the Gospels the word *church* appears only here and in 18.17. 19: The *keys* may signify the office of doctor of the law (compare 23.13; Lk.11.52); to *forbid* and to *allow* are functions of legal authorities (2.4 n.; 5.20 n.). 21: *Jesus* must *suffer:* see Mk.8.31 n.; compare 17.22–23; 20.18–19. 23: *Satan:* tempter. *Stumbling-block* may be "stumbling stone" in contrast to v. 18.
   16.24–28: **Following Jesus** (Mk.8.34–9.1; Lk.9.23–27). See 10.38–39 n.; Mk.8.34 n.
   17.1–8: **The transfiguration** (Mk.9.2–8; Lk.9.28–36). The story is marked by a number of features characteristic of revelation scenes: the mountain (v. 1; see 5.1 n.), the cloud (v. 5; see, e.g. Exod.24.15–18), the heavenly voice (v. 5). 2: *Transfigured:* "changed in appearance," as the following words indicate (compare Lk.9.29). *His face shone:* see Exod.34.29–35. 3: *Moses and Elijah:* see Mk.8.28 n. 5: *This is my Son:* see Mk.1.11 n.

9 On their way down the mountain, Jesus enjoined them not to tell anyone of the vision until the Son of Man had
10 been raised from the dead. The disciples put a question to him: 'Why then do our teachers say that Elijah
11 must come first?' He replied, 'Yes, Elijah will come and set everything
12 right. But I tell you that Elijah has already come, and they failed to recognize him, and worked their will upon him; and in the same way the Son of Man is to suffer at their hands.'
13 Then the disciples understood that he meant John the Baptist.
14 When they returned to the crowd, a man came up to Jesus, fell on his knees
15 before him, and said, 'Have pity, sir, on my son: he is an epileptic and has bad fits, and he keeps falling about,
16 often into the fire, often into water. I brought him to your disciples, but
17 they could not cure him.' Jesus answered, 'What an unbelieving and perverse generation! How long shall I be with you? How long must I endure
18 you? Bring him here to me.' Jesus then spoke sternly to the boy; the devil left him, and from that moment he was cured.
19 Afterwards the disciples came to Jesus and asked him privately, 'Why
20 could not we cast it out?' He answered, 'Your faith is too small. I tell you this: if you have faith no bigger even than a mustard-seed, you will say to this mountain, "Move from here to there!", and it will move; nothing will prove impossible for you.'*j*

22 THEY WERE GOING ABOUT TOGETHER IN Galilee when Jesus said to them, 'The Son of Man is to be given up into the
23 power of men, and they will kill him; then on the third day he will be raised

again.' And they were filled with grief.

24 On their arrival at Capernaum the collectors of the temple tax came up to
Peter and asked, 'Does your master not pay temple-tax?' 'He does', said Peter.
25 When he went indoors Jesus forestalled him by asking, 'What do you think about this, Simon? From whom do earthly monarchs collect tax or toll? From their own people, or from
26 aliens?' 'From aliens', said Peter.' Why then,' said Jesus, 'their own people are
27 exempt! But as we do not want to cause offence, go and cast a line in the lake; take the first fish that comes to the hook, open its mouth, and you will find a silver coin; take that and pay it in; it will meet the tax for us both.'

18 At that time the disciples came to Jesus and asked, 'Who is the greatest
2 in the kingdom of Heaven?' He called
3 a child, set him in front of them, and said, 'I tell you this: unless you turn round and become like children, you will never enter the kingdom of
4 Heaven. Let a man humble himself till he is like this child, and he will be the greatest in the kingdom of Heaven.
5 Whoever receives one such child in my name receives me. But if a man is a
6 cause of stumbling to one of these little ones who have faith in me, it would be better for him to have a millstone hung round his neck and be
7 drowned in the depths of the sea. Alas for the world that such causes of stumbling arise! Come they must, but woe betide the man through whom they come!
8 'If your hand or your foot is your undoing, cut it off and fling it away; it is better for you to enter into life

j Some witnesses add (21) But there is no means of casting out this sort but prayer and fasting.

17.9–13: Elijah has come. Verse 13 identifies *Elijah* as *John the Baptist.* See also Mk.9.9–13 nn.
17.14–20: An epileptic boy (Mk.9.14–29; Lk.9.37–43a). **20:** The importance of *faith* (see Mk.9.23 n.), central to the narrative, is further heightened by the hyperbole of a minute faith which achieves the impossible (compare Lk.17.6).
17.22–23: The second prediction (see 16.21) **of suffering** (Mk.9.30–32; Lk.9.43b–45) which in Mk.9.32 meets with bewilderment, arouses *grief* in Mt. (v. 23).
17.24–27: The temple-tax was required of every male Jew.
18.1–19.2: The fourth discourse (see Introduction) is sometimes described as a "book of church discipline." **1–14:** The pastoral responsibility of Christian leaders is the subject of this section, in which *children* (vv. 2–5) and *little ones* (vv. 6,10,14) are terms for simple Christian believers. **1–5:** Mk.9.33–37; 10.15; Lk.9.46–48; 18.17. The *greatest* is the one who can accept a position of humility. **6:** Mk.9.42; Lk.17.1–2. To cause a *little one* to *stumble* (compare 5.19) is a heinous wrong. **7–9:** Mk.9.43–48. The seriousness of causing sin is expressed in a series

maimed or lame, than to keep two hands or two feet and be thrown into 9 the eternal fire. If it is your eye that is your undoing, tear it out and fling it away; it is better to enter into life with one eye than to keep both eyes and be thrown into the fires of hell.

10 'Never despise one of these little ones; I tell you, they have their guardian angels in heaven, who look continually on the face of my heavenly Father.*k*

12 'What do you think? Suppose a man has a hundred sheep. If one of them strays, does he not leave the other ninety-nine on the hill-side and go in 13 search of the one that strayed? And if he should find it, I tell you this: he is more delighted over that sheep than over the ninety-nine that never strayed. 14 In the same way, it is not your heavenly Father's will that one of these little ones should be lost.

15 'If your brother commits a sin,*l* go and take the matter up with him, strictly between yourselves, and if he listens to you, you have won your 16 brother over. If he will not listen, take one or two others with you, so that all facts may be duly established on the 17 evidence of two or three witnesses. If he refuses to listen to them, report the matter to the congregation; and if he will not listen even to the congregation, you must then treat him as you would a pagan or a tax-gatherer. 18 'I tell you this: whatever you forbid on earth shall be forbidden in heaven, and whatever you allow on earth shall be allowed in heaven.

19 'Again I tell you this: if two of you agree on earth about any request you have to make, that request will be 20 granted by my heavenly Father. For where two or three have met together in my name, I am there among them.'

21 Then Peter came up and asked him, 'Lord, how often am I to forgive my brother if he goes on wronging me? As many as seven times?' Jesus replied, 'I 22 do not say seven times; I say seventy times seven.*m*

'The kingdom of Heaven, therefore, 23 should be thought of in this way: There was once a king who decided to settle accounts with the men who served him. At the outset there appeared before 24 him a man whose debt ran into millions.*n* Since he had no means of 25 paying, his master ordered him to be sold to meet the debt, with his wife, his children, and everything he had. The 26 man fell prostrate at his master's feet. "Be patient with me," he said, "and I will pay in full"; and the master was 27 so moved with pity that he let the man go and remitted the debt. But no 28 sooner had the man gone out than he met a fellow-servant who owed him a few pounds;*o* and catching hold of him he gripped him by the throat and said, "Pay me what you owe." The man fell 29 at his fellow-servant's feet, and begged him, "Be patient with me, and I will pay you"; but he refused, and had him 30 jailed until he should pay the debt. The 31 other servants were deeply distressed when they saw what had happened, and they went to their master and told him the whole story. He accordingly sent 32 for the man. "You scoundrel!" he said to him; "I remitted the whole of your debt when you appealed to me; were 33 you not bound to show your fellow-servant the same pity as I showed you?" And so angry was the master 34 that he condemned the man to torture until he should pay the debt in full. And that is how my heavenly Father 35 will deal with you, unless you each forgive your brother from your hearts.'

k Some witnesses add (11) For the Son of Man came to save the lost.
l Some witnesses insert against you.
m Or seventy-seven times.
n Literally who owed 10,000 talents.
o Literally owed him 100 denarii.

---

of effective hyperboles; such exaggerations as *millstones* around the neck (v. 6), amputated *hands* and *feet*, torn out *eyes* are meant seriously, but not literally. **10–14:** The parable of the lost sheep illustrates the unrelenting love the church leader is to show for the *little ones* in his flock (contrast Lk.15.3–7 n.). **15–17:** This rule regulates relations between fellow Christians; a similar rule was followed in the Dead Sea community. Compare Lk.17.3–4 n. **17:** *Congregation:* or, "church"; see 16.18 n. **18:** See 16.19 n. **21–22:** Lk.17.4. **23–35:** See 5.24–29 n. **23:** In light of the magnitude of the debt (v. 24) *the men who served* the king would be officials of high rank. **24,28:** The contrast between the *millions* of v. 24 and the insignificant amount of v. 28 (*a few pounds*) makes the first man's action in vv. 28–30 intolerable. **35:** As in v. 15, the *brother* is

19 WHEN JESUS HAD FINISHED THIS DIS-
course he left Galilee and came into the
2 region of Judaea across Jordan. Great
crowds followed him, and he healed
them there.

3 Some Pharisees came and tested him
by asking, 'Is it lawful for a man to
divorce his wife on any and every
4 ground?'*p* He asked in return, 'Have
you never read that the Creator made
them from the beginning male and
5 female?'; and he added, 'For this
reason a man shall leave his father and
mother, and be made one with his
wife; and the two shall become one
6 flesh. It follows that they are no longer
two individuals: they are one flesh.
What God has joined together, man
7 must not separate.' 'Why then', they
objected, 'did Moses lay it down that a
man might divorce his wife by note of
8 dismissal?' He answered, 'It was
because your minds were closed that
Moses gave you permission to divorce
your wives; but it was not like that
9 when all began. I tell you, if a man
divorces his wife for any cause other
than unchastity, and marries another,
he commits adultery.'*q*

10 The disciples said to him, 'If that is
the position with husband and wife, it
11 is better not to marry.' To this he
replied, 'That is something which not
everyone can accept, but only those
12 for whom God has appointed it. For
while some are incapable of marriage
because they were born so, or were
made so by men, there are others who
have themselves renounced marriage
for the sake of the kingdom of Heaven.
Let those accept it who can.'

13 They brought children for him to lay
his hands on them with prayer. The
disciples rebuked them, but Jesus said 14
to them, 'Let the children come to me;
do not try to stop them; for the
kingdom of Heaven belongs to such
as these.' And he laid his hands on the 15
children, and went his way.

And now a man came up and asked 16
him, 'Master, what good must I do to
gain eternal life?' 'Good?' said Jesus. 17
'Why do you ask me about that? One
alone is good. But if you wish to enter
into life, keep the commandments.'
'Which commandments?' he asked. 18
Jesus answered, 'Do not murder; do
not commit adultery; do not steal; do
not give false evidence; honour your 19
father and mother; and love your
neighbour as yourself.' The young man 20
answered, 'I have kept all these.
Where do I still fall short?' Jesus said 21
to him, 'If you wish to go the whole
way, go, sell your possessions, and give
to the poor, and then you will have
riches in heaven; and come, follow me.'
When the young man heard this, he 22
went away with a heavy heart; for he
was a man of great wealth.

Jesus said to his disciples, 'I tell you 23
this: a rich man will find it hard to
enter the kingdom of Heaven. I repeat, 24
it is easier for a camel to pass through
the eye of a needle than for a rich man
to enter the kingdom of God.' The 25
disciples were amazed to hear this.
'Then who can be saved?' they asked.
Jesus looked at them, and said, 'For 26
men this is impossible; but everything
is possible for God.'

p Or Is there any ground on which it is lawful for a man
to divorce his wife?
q Some witnesses add And the man who marries a
woman so divorced commits adultery.

for Mt. a fellow Christian. **19.1:** This is the conclusion to ch. 18, the third discourse. See 7.28 n.
19.3–12: Marriage and divorce (see 5.31–32 n.; Mk.10.2–12; Lk.16.18; 1 Cor.7.10–11).
3: For *Pharisees* divorce was *lawful* but they disagreed about the *grounds* on which it may
be allowed; see Mk.10.3 n. **4–6:** See Mk.10.6,7–8 nn. **7–8:** See Mk.10.4–5 n. **9:** See 5.32 n.
10–12: *Marriage* and celibacy both fall within God's purpose; compare 1 Cor.7.25–28.
19.13–15: Children and the kingdom (Mk.10.13–16; Lk.18.15–17). Compare 18.2–4.
19.16–30: Possessions and the kingdom (Mk.10.17–31; Lk.18.18–30). **16–17:** In Mk.10.17–18
and Lk.18.18–19 the opening exchange between Jesus and the young man could be interpreted
as implying that Jesus disclaimed being good; Mt., then, might be thought to correct this
implication by reformulating these verses. Yet the point is the same in the three Gospels: for
life, a man must look to the *One* (God) who *alone is good* and who gives the *commandments*
with which the quest for life begins (Lev.18.5). **18–19:** Exod.20.12–16; Lev.19.18; Deut.5.16–20;
compare 22.39; Rom.13.8–9. **19:** Mt. has a special interest in the *love* commandment, which
the parallel accounts omit in this narrative. **21:** *To go the whole way:* lit. to be perfect. The
remainder of the challenge (*go, sell, give*) makes the general counsel on almsgiving elsewhere
(e.g. 6.22 n.) thoroughgoing. **22:** Only Mt. calls him a *young* man. **24:** *Camel ... eye of a*

[handwritten: Jews + Gentiles called at different times]

27 At this Peter said, 'We here have left everything to become your followers. 28 What will there be for us?' Jesus replied, 'I tell you this: in the world that is to be, when the Son of Man is seated on his throne in heavenly splendour, you my followers will have thrones of your own, where you will sit as judges of the twelve tribes of 29 Israel. And anyone who has left brothers or sisters, father, mother, or children, land or houses for the sake of my name will be repaid many times 30 over, and gain eternal life. But many who are first will be last, and the last first.

20 'The kingdom of Heaven is like this. There was once a landowner who went out early one morning to hire labourers 2 for his vineyard; and after agreeing to pay them the usual day's wage[r] he sent 3 them off to work. Going out three hours later he saw some more men 4 standing idle in the market-place. "Go and join the others in the vineyard," he said, "and I will pay you a fair wage"; 5 so off they went. At midday he went out again, and at three in the afternoon, and made the same arrangement as 6 before. An hour before sunset he went out and found another group standing there; so he said to them, "Why are you standing about like this all day 7 with nothing to do?" "Because no one has hired us", they replied; so he told them, "Go and join the others in the 8 vineyard." When evening fell, the owner of the vineyard said to his steward, "Call the labourers and give them their pay, beginning with those who came last and ending with the 9 first." Those who had started work an hour before sunset came forward, and 10 were paid the full day's wage.[s] When it was the turn of the men who had come first, they expected something extra, but were paid the same amount

as the others. As they took it, they 11 grumbled at their employer: "These 12 late-comers have done only one hour's work, yet you have put them on a level with us, who have sweated the whole day long in the blazing sun!" The owner turned to one of them and 13 said, "My friend, I am not being unfair to you. You agreed on the usual wage for the day,[t] did you not? Take your 14 pay and go home. I choose to pay the last man the same as you. Surely I am 15 free to do what I like with my own money. Why be jealous because I am kind?" Thus will the last be first, and 16 the first last.' *[handwritten: One lesson! Envy at another's good fortune.]*

Challenge to Jerusalem

JESUS WAS JOURNEYING TOWARDS JERU- 17 salem, and on the way he took the Twelve aside, and said to them, 'We 18 are now going to Jerusalem, and the Son of Man will be given up to the chief priests and the doctors of the law; they will condemn him to death and hand him over to the foreign 19 power, to be mocked and flogged and crucified, and on the third day he will be raised to life again.'

The mother of Zebedee's sons then 20 came before him, with her sons. She bowed low and begged a favour. 'What 21 is it you wish?' asked Jesus. 'I want you', she said, 'to give orders that in your kingdom my two sons here may sit next to you, one at your right, and the other at your left.' Jesus turned to 22 the brothers and said, 'You do not understand what you are asking. Can you drink the cup that I am to drink?' 'We can', they replied. Then he said 23 to them, 'You shall indeed share my cup; but to sit at my right or left is not

r Literally one denarius for the day.
s Literally one denarius each.
t Literally You agreed on a denarius.

---

needle is a hyperbole which prepares for v. 26. **27,29:** In contrast to the rich man, the disciples *have left everything* and *will . . . gain eternal life*. **28:** Lk.22.30. **30:** 20.16; Mk.10.31; Lk.13.30.
  20.1–16: The laborers in the vineyard. The laborers are hired around 6 a.m. (v. 2), 9 a.m. (v. 3), noon (v. 5), 3 p.m. (v. 5), and 5 p.m. (v. 6). Only those hired in v. 2 are promised a specific amount (*the usual day's wage*). The surprise comes in vv. 9–10 when all receive the same sum, regardless of their working hours.
  20.17–19: The third prediction of suffering (16.21; 17.22–23; Mk.10.32–34 n.; Lk.18.31–34).
  20.20–28: Position in the kingdom (Mk.10.35–45; Lk.22.24–27). **20:** The *mother* initiates the request in Mt., the *sons* in Mk.10.35. **21:** *Right . . . left:* see Mk.10.37 n. **22:** *Cup:* see Mk.10.38 n. **23:** See Mk.10.40 n. Some scholars interpret *Kingdom* here to mean the church, rather than the

for me to grant; it is for those to whom it has already been assigned by my Father.'

24 When the other ten heard this, they were indignant with the two brothers. 25 So Jesus called them to him and said, 'You know that in the world, rulers lord it over their subjects, and their great men make them feel the weight 26 of authority; but it shall not be so with you. Among you, whoever wants 27 to be great must be your servant, and whoever wants to be first must be the 28 willing slave of all—like the Son of Man; he did not come to be served, but to serve, and to give up his life as a ransom for many.'

29 As they were leaving Jericho he was followed by a great crowd of people. 30 At the roadside sat two blind men. When they heard it said that Jesus was passing they shouted, 'Have pity on us, 31 Son of David.' The people told them sharply to be quiet. But they shouted all the more, 'Sir, have pity on us; 32 have pity on us, Son of David.' Jesus stopped and called the men. 'What do you want me to do for you?' he asked. 33 'Sir,' they answered, 'we want our 34 sight.' Jesus was deeply moved, and touched their eyes. At once their sight came back, and they followed him.

21 THEY WERE NOW NEARING JERUSALEM; and when they reached Bethphage at the Mount of Olives, Jesus sent two 2 disciples with these instructions: 'Go to the village opposite, where you will at once find a donkey tethered with her foal beside her; untie them, and 3 bring them to me. If anyone speaks to

you, say, "Our Master needs them"; and he will let you take them at once.'*u* 4 This was to fulfil the prophecy which 5 says, 'Tell the daughter of Zion, "Here is your king, who comes to you in gentleness, riding on an ass, riding on the foal of a beast of burden."'

6 The disciples went and did as Jesus 7 had directed, and brought the donkey and her foal; they laid their cloaks on 8 them and Jesus mounted. Crowds of people carpeted the road with their cloaks, and some cut branches from 9 the trees to spread in his path. Then the crowd that went ahead and the others that came behind raised the shout: 'Hosanna to the Son of David! Blessings on him who comes in the name of the Lord! Hosanna in the heavens!'

10 When he entered Jerusalem the whole city went wild with excitement. 11 'Who is this?' people asked, and the crowd replied, 'This is the prophet Jesus, from Nazareth in Galilee.'

12 Jesus then went into the temple and drove out all who were buying and selling in the temple precincts; he upset the tables of the money-changers and the seats of the dealers in pigeons; 13 and said to them, 'Scripture says, "My house shall be called a house of prayer"; but you are making it a robbers' cave.'

14 In the temple blind men and cripples 15 came to him, and he healed them. The chief priests and doctors of the law saw the wonderful things he did, and heard the boys in the temple shouting,

u Or "Our Master needs them and will send them back straight away."

world as destined to be reigned over by God. **28:** *Ransom for many:* see Mk.10.45 n.; see also 2 Macc.7.37–38.
20.29–34: Two blind men healed (Mk.10.46–52; Lk.18.35–43). **30:** *Two blind men:* contrast Mk.10.46; Lk.18.35. **31:** *Son of David:* see 1.1 n. **34:** *Followed:* see Mk.10.52 n.
21.1–25.46: Jesus in Jerusalem (Mk.11.1–13.37 n.; Lk.19.28–21.38).
21.1–9: The entry into Jerusalem (Mk.11.1–11; Lk.19.28–38; Jn.12.12–19). **1:** The *Mount of Olives:* associated with the appearance of the Messiah. The Gospel writers understand the entry as a messianic claim, and the account has been influenced by the picture of the humble king in Zech.9.9 (see v. 5 n.). **2:** Mt. speaks of two animals, presumably because of his interpretation of the prophecy he records in v. 5. **5:** Isa.62.11 and Zech.9.9 are combined; Jn.12.15 also quotes Zech. **9:** Ps.118.25–26. *Hosanna,* lit. means "O, save!" In Jesus' day, it could be simply a shout of praise. *Son of David:* see 1.1 n.
21.10–17: Cleansing of the Temple (Mk.11.15–19; Lk.19.45–48). **11:** *Prophet:* see 21.26,46; Mk.8.28 n. **12:** The *temple* area involved would be the so-called Court of the Gentiles, to which even non-Jews were admitted. *Money-changers* converted ordinary money into the Tyrian half-shekels required at the Temple. *Pigeons:* for inexpensive animal sacrifices. See Mk.11.15–16 n. **13:** See Mk.11.17 n.; Isa.56.7; Jer.7.11. **14:** Mt. apparently sees this as the Temple's true function. **16:** Ps.8.2.

16 'Hosanna to the Son of David!', and they asked him indignantly, 'Do you hear what they are saying?' Jesus answered, 'I do; have you never read that text, "Thou hast made children and babes at the breast sound aloud 17 thy praise"?' Then he left them and went out of the city to Bethany, where he spent the night.

18 Next morning on his way to the city 19 he felt hungry; and seeing a fig-tree at the roadside he went up to it, but found nothing on it but leaves. He said to the tree, 'You shall never bear fruit any more!'; and the tree withered away 20 at once. The disciples were amazed at the sight. 'How is it', they asked, 'that the tree has withered so suddenly?' 21 Jesus answered them, 'I tell you this: if only you have faith and have no doubts, you will do what has been done to the fig-tree; and more than that, you need only say to this mountain, "Be lifted from your place and hurled into the sea", and what you say 22 will be done. And whatever you pray for in faith you will receive.'

23 He entered the temple, and the chief priests and elders of the nation came to him with the question: 'By what authority are you acting like this? Who 24 gave you this authority?' Jesus replied, 'I have a question to ask you too; answer it, and I will tell you by what 25 authority I act. The baptism of John: was it from God, or from men?' This set them arguing among themselves: 'If we say, "from God", he will say, "Then why did you not believe him?" 26 But if we say, "from men", we are afraid of the people, for they all take 27 John for a prophet.' So they answered, 'We do not know.' And Jesus said:

'Then neither will I tell you by what authority I act.

'But what do you think about this? 28 A man had two sons. He went to the first, and said, "My boy, go and work today in the vineyard." "I will, sir", 29 the boy replied; but he never went. The father came to the second and 30 said the same. "I will not", he replied, but afterwards he changed his mind and went. Which of these two did as 31 his father wished?' 'The second', they said. Then Jesus answered, 'I tell you this: tax-gatherers and prostitutes are entering the kingdom of God ahead of you. For when John came to show 32 you the right way to live, you did not believe him, but the tax-gatherers and prostitutes did; and even when you had seen that, you did not change your minds and believe him.

'Listen to another parable. There was 33 a landowner who planted a vineyard: he put a wall round it, hewed out a winepress, and built a watch-tower; then he let it out to vine-growers and went abroad. When the vintage season 34 approached, he sent his servants to the tenants to collect the produce due to him. But they took his servants and 35 thrashed one, killed another, and stoned a third. Again, he sent other 36 servants, this time a larger number; and they did the same to them. At 37 last he sent to them his son. "They will respect my son", he said. But 38 when they saw the son the tenants said to one another, "This is the heir; come on, let us kill him, and get his inheritance." And they took him, 39 flung him out of the vineyard, and killed him. When the owner of the 40 vineyard comes, how do you think he

---

21.18–22: The cursing of the fig tree (Mk.11.12–14,20–25). **19:** The narrative is frequently taken as an "acted parable or allegory" of the rejection of Israel or as a development of the parable in Lk.13.6–9. **20–22:** The story has attracted sayings about the power of *faith* and *prayer* which are also found elsewhere (17.20; Lk.17.6).
21.23–27: Jesus' authority challenged (Mk.11.27–33; Lk.20.1–8). **25:** *From God:* lit. "from heaven" (a typical Jewish circumlocution to avoid the careless use of "God"; compare 3.2 n.). **26:** *Prophet:* see Mk.8.28 n.
21.28–32: The parable of the two sons. 31: That religious outcasts (*tax-gatherers* and *prostitutes*) should have priority over religious leaders is not a popular notion even in modern times. **32:** In this context, to *believe him* (*John* the Baptist) appears to assure entrance into the kingdom.
21.33–46: The evil tenants (Mk.12.1–12; Lk.20.9–19). **33:** If originally a *parable*, the story as now told has the marks of an allegory; see Mk.4.2 n. The *vineyard* is a conventional symbol for Israel as the chosen people; compare Isa.5.1–7. **34:** Early Christian readers would identify the *servants* as the prophets and the *tenants* as the Jewish leaders of the day. **37:** *Son:* Jesus.

41 will deal with those tenants?' 'He will bring those bad men to a bad end', they answered, 'and hand the vineyard over to other tenants, who will let him have his share of the crop when the 42 season comes.' Then Jesus said to them, 'Have you never read in the scriptures: "The stone which the builders rejected has become the main corner-stone. This is the Lord's doing, 43 and it is wonderful in our eyes"? Therefore, I tell you, the kingdom of God will be taken away from you, and given to a nation that yields the proper fruit.'*v*

45 When the chief priests and Pharisees heard his parables, they saw that he 46 was referring to them; they wanted to arrest him, but they were afraid of the people, who looked on Jesus as a prophet.

22 THEN JESUS SPOKE TO THEM AGAIN IN 2 parables: 'The kingdom of Heaven is like this. There was a king who prepared a feast for his son's wedding; 3 but when he sent his servants to summon the guests he had invited, 4 they would not come. He sent others again, telling them to say to the guests, "See now! I have prepared this feast for you. I have had my bullocks and fatted beasts slaughtered; everything is ready; come to the 5 wedding at once." But they took no notice; one went off to his farm, 6 another to his business, and the others seized the servants, attacked them 7 brutally, and killed them. The king was furious; he sent troops to kill those murderers and set their town on fire. 8 Then he said to his servants, "The wedding-feast is ready; but the guests I invited did not deserve the honour. 9 Go out to the main thoroughfares, and invite everyone you can find to the 10 wedding." The servants went out into

the streets, and collected all they could find, good and bad alike. So the hall was packed with guests.

'When the king came in to see the 11 company at table, he observed one man who was not dressed for a wedding. "My friend," said the king, "how do 12 you come to be here without your wedding clothes?" He had nothing to say. The king then said to his atten- 13 dants, "Bind him hand and foot; turn him out into the dark, the place of wailing and grinding of teeth." For 14 though many are invited, few are chosen.'

THEN THE PHARISEES WENT AWAY AND 15 agreed on a plan to trap him in his own words. Some of their followers were 16 sent to him in company with men of Herod's party. They said, 'Master, you are an honest man, we know; you teach in all honesty the way of life that God requires, truckling to no man, whoever he may be. Give us your ruling 17 on this: are we or are we not permitted to pay taxes to the Roman Emperor?' Jesus was aware of their malicious 18 intention and said to them, 'You hypocrites! Why are you trying to catch me out? Show me the money in 19 which the tax is paid.' They handed him a silver piece. Jesus asked, 'Whose 20 head is this, and whose inscription?' 'Caesar's', they replied. He said to 21 them, 'Then pay Caesar what is due to Caesar, and pay God what is due to God.' This answer took them by 22 surprise, and they went away and left him alone.

The same day Sadducees came to 23 him, maintaining that there is no resurrection. Their question was this:

---

v Some witnesses add (44) *Any man who falls on this stone will be dashed to pieces; and if it falls on a man he will be crushed by it.*

42: *The stone...is wonderful:* Ps.118.22–23; see Mk.12.10–11 n.; Acts 4.11; 1 Pet.2.4,7.
   22.1–14: The wedding feast (Lk.14.16–24). **2**: *Feast:* see Lk.14.15 n. **3**: *To summon the guests:* see Lk.14.17 n. **5–6**: The feature of the *servants* being *attacked* is peculiar to Mt. (see Lk.14.18–20); the rejection of John and Jesus probably suggested this embellishment. **7**: Here the tradition may reflect the destruction of Jerusalem in 70 A.D. **11–14**: In light of v. 10, the expectation of "correct dress" may indicate that these verses are from a second "feast parable" which Mt. has appended to vv. 2–10.
   22.15–22: Caesar's tax (Mk.12.13–17; Lk.20.20–26). **17**: Advice against paying such *taxes* would amount to treason; advice in favor of paying would be unpopular with Jewish nationalists.
   22.23 33: A resurrection puzzle (Mk.12.18–27; Lk.20.27–40). **23**: On differences between

24 'Master, Moses said, "If a man should die childless, his brother shall marry the widow and carry on his brother's
25 family." Now we knew of seven brothers. The first married and died, and as he was without issue his wife was
26 left to his brother. The same thing happened with the second, and the
27 third, and so on with all seven. Last of
28 all the woman died. At the resurrection, then, whose wife will she be, for they
29 had all married her?' Jesus answered: 'You are mistaken, because you know neither the scriptures nor the power of
30 God. At the resurrection men and women do not marry; they are like angels in heaven.
31 'But about the resurrection of the dead, have you never read what God
32 himself said to you: "I am the God of Abraham, the God of Isaac, and the God of Jacob"? He is not God of the
33 dead but of the living.' The people heard what he said, and were astounded at his teaching.
34 Hearing that he had silenced the Sadducees, the Pharisees met together;
35 and one of their number*w* tested him
36 with this question: 'Master, which is the greatest commandment in the
37 Law?' He answered, ' "Love the Lord your God with all your heart, with all
38 your soul, with all your mind." That is the greatest commandment. It comes
39 first. The second is like it: "Love your
40 neighbour as yourself." Everything in the Law and the prophets hangs on these two commandments.'

Turning to the assembled Pharisees 41 Jesus asked them, 'What is your 42 opinion about the Messiah? Whose son is he?' 'The son of David', they replied. 'How then is it', he asked, 43 'that David by inspiration calls him "Lord"? For he says, "The Lord said 44 to my Lord, 'Sit at my right hand until I put your enemies under your feet.' " If David calls him "Lord", 45 how can he be David's son?' Not a 46 man could say a word in reply; and from that day forward no one dared ask him another question.

JESUS THEN ADDRESSED THE PEOPLE AND 23 his disciples in these words: 'The 2 doctors of the law and the Pharisees sit in the chair of Moses; therefore do 3 what they tell you; pay attention to their words. But do not follow their practice; for they say one thing and do another. They make up heavy packs 4 and pile them on men's shoulders, but will not raise a finger to lift the load themselves. Whatever they do is done 5 for show. They go about with broad phylacteries*x* and with large tassels on their robes; they like to have places of 6 honour at feasts and the chief seats in synagogues, to be greeted respectfully 7 in the street, and to be addressed as "rabbi".

'But you must not be called "rabbi"; 8 for you have one Rabbi, and you are all brothers. Do not call any man on 9

w Some witnesses insert a lawyer.
x See Deuteronomy 6. 8–9 and Exodus 13. 9.

Sadducees and *Pharisees* (v. 15), see 3.7 n. **24**: Deut.25.5–10. **30**: *The scriptures:* apparently Exod.3.6, which is quoted in v. 32 as proof of the resurrection.
　　22.34–40: The double commandment of love (Mk.12.28–34; compare Lk.10.25–28). **35**: Mt. attributes the motive of testing to the inquirers; compare Mk.12.28; Lk.10.27 n. **37**: Deut.6.5. **39**: Lev.19.18. **40**: Compare 7.12.
　　22.41–46: Messiah, son of David (Mk.12.35–37; Lk.20.41–44). **42**: *Messiah . . . the son of David:* see 1.1 n. **44**: Ps.110.1 is interpreted to mean "God (*the Lord*) said to the Messiah (*my Lord*)"; compare Acts 2.34–36. **45**: While the story may represent a stratum of tradition which rejected a son of David Christology, that cannot have been the intention of the evangelist, in light e.g. of chs. 1–2.
　　23.1–39: Alas for lawyers and Pharisees (compare Lk.11.42–54). **1**: It is difficult to decide whether ch. 23 is the climax of the reported controversy of the preceding chs. or the beginning of the final discourse in Mt. The fact that the Pharisees appear as Jesus' chief opponents in the synoptic Gospels—and especially in Mt.—probably reflects the situation after 70 A.D., when Pharisaism was the form of Judaism which the Church normally confronted. In the very old traditions of the passion (beginning with ch. 26 and its parallels), not the Pharisees, but the politically important priestly and Sadducaic elements seem to be most prominent in the fateful final conflict. **3**: On *doctors of the law* (*lawyers*, vv. 13,15,23,25,27,29; *teachers*, v. 34!), see 2.4 n.; 5.20 n. *The chair of Moses:* at one time, a place provided in the synagogue for authoritative teaching. **5**: *Phylacteries* were small leather containers holding certain passages of Scripture; compare Exod.13.9. **8–10**: *Rabbi, father, teacher:* titles for teachers of the Law.

earth "father"; for you have one
10 Father, and he is in heaven. Nor must
you be called "teacher"; you have one
11 Teacher, the Messiah. The greatest
12 among you must be your servant. For
whoever exalts himself will be humbled;
and whoever humbles himself will be
exalted.

13 'Alas, alas for you, lawyers and
Pharisees, hypocrites that you are!
You shut the door of the kingdom of
Heaven in men's faces; you do not
enter yourselves, and when others are
entering, you stop them.*y*

15 'Alas for you, lawyers and Pharisees,
hypocrites! You travel over sea and
land to win one convert; and when you
have won him you make him twice as
fit for hell as you are yourselves.

16 'Alas for you, blind guides! You say,
"If a man swears by the sanctuary,
that is nothing; but if he swears by the
gold in the sanctuary, he is bound by
17 his oath." Blind fools! Which is the
more important, the gold, or the
sanctuary which sanctifies the gold?
18 Or you say, "If a man swears by the
altar, that is nothing; but if he swears
by the offering that lies on the altar, he
19 is bound by his oath." What blindness!
Which is the more important, the
offering, or the altar which sanctifies
20 it? To swear by the altar, then, is to
swear both by the altar and by what-
21 ever lies on it; to swear by the sanctuary
is to swear both by the sanctuary and
22 by him who dwells there; and to swear
by heaven is to swear both by the
throne of God and by him who sits
upon it.

23 'Alas for you, lawyers and Pharisees,
hypocrites! You pay tithes of mint and
dill and cummin; but you have
overlooked the weightier demands of
the Law, justice, mercy, and good
faith. It is these you should have
practised, without neglecting the others.
24 Blind guides! You strain off a midge,
yet gulp down a camel!

'Alas for you, lawyers and Pharisees, 25
hypocrites! You clean the outside of
cup and dish, which you have filled
inside by robbery and self-indulgence!
Blind Pharisee! Clean the inside of the 26
cup first; then the outside will be clean
also.

'Alas for you, lawyers and Pharisees, 27
hypocrites! You are like tombs covered
with whitewash; they look well from
outside, but inside they are full of dead
men's bones and all kinds of filth. So 28
it is with you: outside you look like
honest men, but inside you are brim-
full of hypocrisy and crime.

'Alas for you, lawyers and Pharisees, 29
hypocrites! You build up the tombs
of the prophets and embellish the
monuments of the saints, and you say, 30
"If we had been alive in our fathers'
time, we should never have taken part
with them in the murder of the
prophets." So you acknowledge that 31
you are the sons of the men who killed
the prophets. Go on then, finish off 32
what your fathers began!*z*

'You snakes, you vipers' brood, how 33
can you escape being condemned to
hell? I send you therefore prophets, 34
sages, and teachers; some of them you
will kill and crucify, others you will
flog in your synagogues and hound
from city to city. And so, on you will 35
fall the guilt of all the innocent blood
spilt on the ground, from innocent
Abel to Zechariah son of Berachiah,
whom you murdered between the
sanctuary and the altar. Believe me, 36
this generation will bear the guilt of it
all.

'O Jerusalem, Jerusalem, the city that 37
murders the prophets and stones the
messengers sent to her! How often have
I longed to gather your children, as a
hen gathers her brood under her wings;
but you would not let me. Look, look! 38

y Some witnesses add (14) Alas for you, lawyers and
Pharisees, hypocrites! You eat up the property of
widows, while you say long prayers for appearance'
sake. You will receive the severest sentence.
z Or You too must come up to your fathers' standards.

13: *Alas for:* see Lk.6.24–26 n. *Shut the door:* compare 16.19 n.; Lk.11.52. **16–22:** The purpose
of oaths of the type described was to guard against the profaning of the holy sanctuary or altar
(and, ultimately, the name of God) by broken oaths; compare 5.33–37. **23:** *Tithes* of such
produce probably exceed the actual requirements of Deut.14.22–23. *The weightier demands:* see
Mic.6.8. **24:** *Midge:* or, gnat. **27–32:** Compare Lk.11.44–48. **33:** 3.7; Lk.3.7. **34–36:** See
Lk.11.49–51 n. **34:** *Teachers:* see 23.3 n. **35:** *Abel:* Gen.4.8. *Son of Berachiah* (2 Chr.24.20–22;
Zech.1.1) is not found in Lk.11.51 (see n.); probably the identification is mistaken. **37–38:** See

there is your temple, forsaken by 39 God.[a][b] And I tell you, you shall never see me until the time when you say, "Blessings on him who comes in the name of the Lord."'

Prophecies and warnings

24 JESUS WAS LEAVING THE TEMPLE WHEN his disciples came and pointed to the 2 temple buildings. He answered, 'Yes, look at it all. I tell you this: not one stone will be left upon another; all will be thrown down.'

3 When he was sitting on the Mount of Olives the disciples came to speak to him privately. 'Tell us,' they said, 'when will this happen? And what will be the signal for your coming and the end of the age?'

4 Jesus replied: 'Take care that no one 5 misleads you. For many will come claiming my name and saying, "I am the Messiah"; and many will be misled 6 by them. The time is coming when you will hear the noise of battle near at hand and the news of battles far away; see that you are not alarmed. Such things are bound to happen; but the 7 end is still to come. For nation will make war upon nation, kingdom upon kingdom; there will be famines and 8 earthquakes in many places. With all these things the birth-pangs of the new age begin.

9 'You will then be handed over for punishment and execution; and men of all nations will hate you for your 10 allegiance to me. Many will fall from their faith; they will betray one 11 another and hate one another. Many

false prophets will arise, and will mislead many; and as lawlessness 12 spreads, men's love for one another will grow cold. But the man who holds 13 out to the end will be saved. And this 14 gospel of the Kingdom will be proclaimed throughout the earth as a testimony to all nations; and then the end will come.

'So when you see "the abomination 15 of desolation", of which the prophet Daniel spoke, standing in the holy place (let the reader understand), then 16 those who are in Judaea must take to the hills. If a man is on the roof, he 17 must not come down to fetch his goods from the house; if in the field, he must 18 not turn back for his coat. Alas for 19 women with child in those days, and for those who have children at the breast! Pray that it may not be winter 20 when you have to make your escape, or Sabbath. It will be a time of great 21 distress; there has never been such a time from the beginning of the world until now, and will never be again. If 22 that time of troubles were not cut short, no living thing could survive; but for the sake of God's chosen it will be cut short.

'Then, if anyone says to you, "Look, 23 here is the Messiah", or, "There he is", do not believe it. Impostors will come 24 claiming to be messiahs or prophets, and they will produce great signs and wonders to mislead even God's chosen, if such a thing were possible. See, I 25 have forewarned you. If they tell you, 26 "He is there in the wilderness", do not go out; or if they say, "He is there in

a Or Look, your home is desolate.
b Some witnesses add and laid waste.

Lk.13.34–35 n. **39:** For Mt., *until the time* looks forward to the end time; contrast Lk.13.35 n. *Blessings . . . Lord:* Ps.118.26.

24.1–26.1a: The (fifth) eschatological discourse. See 23.1 n.; 7.28 n. Compare Mk.13.1–37 n. **24.1–2: Temple's destruction predicted** (Mk.13.1–4; Lk.21.5–7). Herod the Great instituted the building of a magnificent temple about 20 B.C.; although it was substantially complete, work on it still continued in Jesus' day (see Jn.2.20). Several traditions suggest that Jesus foretold the Temple's destruction (compare Jn.2.19); another form of the prediction had it that Jesus himself would destroy the Temple (compare 26.61; Mk.14.58; 15.29; Acts 6.14). The destruction occurred in 70 A.D. as a consequence of the revolt against Rome. **24.3–41: Signs, false signs, and warnings** (Mk.13.3–37; Lk.21.8–36). **3:** *Mount of Olives:* see 21.1 n. **4–5:** Compare vv. 23–24; Acts 8.9–11. **8:** *Birth-pangs:* conventional imagery for suffering associated with the dawn of the *new age* (e.g. 1 Thess.5.3). **13:** 10.22. **14:** See 28.18–20; Mk.13.10. **15:** "*The abomination of desolation*" (see Dan.9.27; 11.31; 12.11): a symbol of pagan profanation of the holy place. The comment *let the reader understand* calls attention to the cryptic character of this material. **18:** Lk.17.31. **20:** Mt. alone shows concern about violating the rule limiting *Sabbath* travel; compare Mk.13.18. **21:** Dan.12.1. **24:** Deut.13.1–2. **26–28:**

27 the inner room", do not believe it. Like lightning from the east, flashing as far as the west, will be the coming of the Son of Man.

28 Wherever the corpse is, there the vultures will gather.

29 'As soon as the distress of those days has passed, the sun will be darkened, the moon will not give her light, the stars will fall from the sky, the celestial powers will be shaken.

30 Then will appear in heaven the sign that heralds the Son of Man. All the peoples of the world will make lamentation, and they will see the Son of Man coming on the clouds of heaven

31 with great power and glory. With a trumpet blast he will send out his angels, and they will gather his chosen from the four winds, from the farthest bounds of heaven on every side.

32 'Learn a lesson from the fig-tree. When its tender shoots appear and are breaking into leaf, you know that

33 summer is near. In the same way, when you see all these things, you may know that the end is near,ᶜ at the very

34 door. I tell you this: the present generation will live to see it all.

35 Heaven and earth will pass away; my words will never pass away.

36 'But about that day and hour no one knows, not even the angels in heaven, not even the Son; only the Father.

37 'As things were in Noah's days, so will they be when the Son of Man

38 comes. In the days before the flood they ate and drank and married, until the day that Noah went into the ark,

39 and they knew nothing until the flood came and swept them all away. That is how it will be when the Son of Man

40 comes. Then there will be two men in the field; one will be taken, the other

41 left; two women grinding at the mill; one will be taken, the other left.

42 'Keep awake, then; for you do not know on what day your Lord is to

43 come. Remember, if the householder had known at what time of night the burglar was coming, he would have kept awake and not have let his house be broken into. Hold yourselves ready,

44 therefore, because the Son of Man will come at the time you least expect him.

45 'Who is the trusty servant, the sensible man charged by his master to manage his household staff and issue their rations at the proper time?

46 Happy that servant who is found at

47 his task when his master comes! I tell you this: he will be put in charge of

48 all his master's property. But if he is a bad servant and says to himself, "The

49 master is a long time coming", and begins to bully the other servants and to eat and drink with his drunken

50 friends, then the master will arrive on a day that servant does not expect, at a

51 time he does not know, and will cut him in pieces. Thus he will find his place among the hypocrites, where there is wailing and grinding of teeth.

25 'When that day comes, the kingdom of Heaven will be like this. There were ten girls, who took their lamps and

2 went out to meet the bridegroom. Five of them were foolish, and five prudent;

3 when the foolish ones took their lamps,

4 they took no oil with them, but the others took flasks of oil with their

5 lamps. As the bridegroom was late in

6 coming they all dozed off to sleep. But at midnight a cry was heard: "Here is the bridegroom! Come out to meet

7 him." With that the girls all got up

8 and trimmed their lamps. The foolish said to the prudent, "Our lamps are going out; give us some of your oil."

9 "No," they said; "there will never be enough for all of us. You had better go to the shop and buy some for

c Or that he is near.

Lk.17.23–24,37. **29**: The portents described here have OT roots; e.g. Isa.13.10. **30**: Dan.7.13. **31**: Isa.27.13; 1 Cor.15.52; Deut.30.4. **34**: Compare 10.23; 16.28. A late first-century Christian could have understood the saying literally only of the destruction of the Temple, not of the end of the age; see v. 36. **35**: 5.18; Lk.16.17. **37–41**: Lk.17.26–27,34–35; Gen. chs. 6–7.

24.42–26.1a: Parables of judgment.

24.43–44: The wakeful householder (Lk.12.39–40). The "thief" motif was widespread; e.g. 1 Thess.5.2; Rev.3.3.

24.45–51: The trusty servant (Lk.12.42–46).

25.1–13: The girls at the wedding celebration. The parable uses the wedding customs of the time to urge preparedness for the kingdom. **1**: No doubt the early Church thought of Jesus as the

10 yourselves." While they were away the bridegroom arrived; those who were ready went in with him to the wedding, 11 and the door was shut. And then the other five came back. "Sir, sir," they 12 cried, "open the door for us." But he answered, "I declare, I do not know 13 you." Keep awake then; for you never know the day or the hour.

14 'It is like a man going abroad, who called his servants and put his capital 15 in their hands; to one he gave five bags of gold, to another two, to another one, each according to his capacity. Then he left the country. 16 The man who had the five bags went at once and employed them in business, 17 and made a profit of five bags, and the man who had the two bags made two. 18 But the man who had been given one bag of gold went off and dug a hole in the ground, and hid his master's 19 money. A long time afterwards their master returned, and proceeded to 20 settle accounts with them. The man who had been given the five bags of gold came and produced the five he had made: "Master," he said, "you left five bags with me; look, I have 21 made five more." "Well done, my good and trusty servant!" said the master. "You have proved trustworthy in a small way; I will now put you in charge of something big. Come and 22 share your master's delight." The man with the two bags then came and said, "Master, you left two bags with me; 23 look, I have made two more." "Well done, my good and trusty servant!" said the master. "You have proved trustworthy in a small way; I will now put you in charge of something big. Come and share your master's delight." 24 Then the man who had been given one bag came and said, "Master, I knew you to be a hard man: you reap where you have not sown, you gather where 25 you have not scattered; so I was

afraid, and I went and hid your gold in the ground. Here it is—you have what belongs to you." "You lazy 26 rascal!" said the master. "You knew that I reap where I have not sown, and gather where I have not scattered? Then you ought to have put my 27 money on deposit, and on my return I should have got it back with interest. Take the bag of gold from him, and 28 give it to the one with the ten bags. For the man who has will always be 29 given more, till he has enough and to spare; and the man who has not will forfeit even what he has. Fling the 30 useless servant out into the dark, the place of wailing and grinding of teeth!"

'When the Son of Man comes in his 31 glory and all the angels with him, he will sit in state on his throne, with all 32 the nations gathered before him. He will separate men into two groups, as a shepherd separates the sheep from the goats, and he will place the sheep on 33 his right hand and the goats on his left. Then the king will say to those on his 34 right hand, "You have my Father's blessing; come, enter and possess the kingdom that has been ready for you since the world was made. For when I 35 was hungry, you gave me food; when thirsty, you gave me drink; when I was a stranger you took me into your home, when naked you clothed me; when I 36 was ill you came to my help, when in prison you visited me." Then the 37 righteous will reply, "Lord, when was it that we saw you hungry and fed you, or thirsty and gave you drink, a 38 stranger and took you home, or naked and clothed you? When did we see 39 you ill or in prison, and come to visit you?" And the king will answer, 40 "I tell you this: anything you did for one of my brothers here, however humble, you did for me." Then he will 41 say to those on his left hand, "The curse is upon you; go from my sight

---

bridegroom. **13:** Mt. interprets the parable in this way to carry forward the theme of 24.42–44.

25.14–30: The parable of the talents. In contrast to the similar parable in Lk.19.12–27 (see nn. there), immense sums are left in the hands of the servants. (In other, more literal, translations, "talents" appears rather than *bags of gold:* a talent was an ancient measure of money).

25.31–46: The sheep and the goats. See 7.24–29 n. The parable begins with familiar images: *the Son of man . . . in his glory* (v. 1; Dan.7.13–15); the assembling of the *nations*—i.e. even Gentiles (v. 2; e.g. Isa.2.2–4); the judging of the flocks (Ezek.34.17). **40:** *Brothers* may be a technical term for "Christians"; see 18.35 n. **40,45:** 10.42; Mk.9.41. **26.1a:** See 7.28 n.

to the eternal fire that is ready for the 42 devil and his angels. For when I was hungry you gave me nothing to eat, 43 when thirsty nothing to drink; when I was a stranger you gave me no home, when naked you did not clothe me; when I was ill and in prison you did 44 not come to my help." And they too will reply, "Lord, when was it that we saw you hungry or thirsty or a stranger or naked or ill or in prison, and did 45 nothing for you?" And he will answer, "I tell you this: anything you did not do for one of these, however humble, 46 you did not do for me." And they will go away to eternal punishment, but the righteous will enter eternal life.'

The final conflict

26 WHEN JESUS HAD FINISHED THIS DIS-
2 course he said to his disciples, 'You know that in two days' time it will be Passover, and the Son of Man is to be handed over for crucifixion.'
3   Then the chief priests and the elders of the nation met in the palace of the 4 High Priest, Caiaphas; and there they conferred together on a scheme to have Jesus arrested by some trick and put to 5 death. 'It must not be during the festival,' they said, 'or there may be rioting among the people.'

6 JESUS WAS AT BETHANY IN THE HOUSE 7 of Simon the leper, when a woman came to him with a small bottle of fragrant oil, very costly; and as he sat at table he began to pour it over his 8 head. The disciples were indignant when they saw it. 'Why this waste?' 9 they said; 'it could have been sold for a good sum and the money given to the

poor.' Jesus was aware of this, and said 10 to them, 'Why must you make trouble for the woman? It is a fine thing she has done for me. You have the poor 11 among you always; but you will not always have me. When she poured 12 this oil on my body it was her way of preparing me for burial. I tell you 13 this: wherever in all the world this gospel is proclaimed, what she has done will be told as her memorial.'

THEN ONE OF THE TWELVE, THE MAN 14 called Judas Iscariot, went to the chief priests and said, 'What will you give 15 me to betray him to you?' They weighed him out*d* thirty silver pieces. From that moment he began to look 16 out for an opportunity to betray him.

On the first day of Unleavened 17 Bread the disciples came to ask Jesus, 'Where would you like us to prepare for your Passover supper?' He answered, 'Go to a certain man in 18 the city, and tell him, "The Master says, 'My appointed time is near; I am to keep Passover with my disciples at your house.'"' The disciples did as 19 Jesus directed them and prepared for Passover.

In the evening he sat down with the 20 twelve disciples; and during supper he 21 said, 'I tell you this: one of you will betray me.' In great distress they 22 exclaimed one after the other, 'Can you mean me, Lord?' He answered, 'One 23 who has dipped his hand into this bowl with me will betray me. The Son of 24 Man is going the way appointed for him in the scriptures; but alas for that man by whom the Son of Man is betrayed! It would be better for that

d Or agreed to pay him . . .

26.1b–27.66: The final conflict (Mk.14.1–15.47; Lk.22.1–23.56; Jn. chs. 12–19). See Lk.22.1–23.56 n. **2:** See Mk.14.1 n. **6–13:** Mk.14.3–9 (similar stories in Lk.7.36–50; Jn.12.1–8). **7:** *Pour:* an act of social courtesy (compare Lk.7.44–46 n.). **12:** The courtesy (v. 7) is given a significance that reaches beyond the woman's intention. **14–16:** Mk.14.10–11; Lk.22.3–6. **15:** *Thirty silver pieces:* compare Zech.11.12–13.
26.17–19: Preparation for the Passover (Mk.14.12–16; Lk.22.7–13). In Roman fashion Mt. (and Mk.; Lk.) describes the preparation (Thursday during the day) and the meal (Thursday evening) as taking place within the one day. However, by Jewish reckoning (in which a new day began at sunset), the preparation (vv. 17–19) fell on Nisan 14; *evening* (v. 20) was viewed as a new day, Nisan 15 (*Passover*). The crucifixion is thus also dated on Nisan 15 in the synoptic Gospels. Jn. dates the final meal and the crucifixion on Nisan 14 (e.g. Jn.18.28). **18:** Jerusalem residents customarily provided visitors to the city with space for observing the Passover meal.
26.20–29: The Last Supper (Mk.14.17–25; Lk.22.14–38). **20:** *Sat down:* lit. "reclined," as was the custom at Passover meals. **21 25:** See also Jn.13.21–30. **24:** The motif of Jesus' death as

25 man if he had never been born.' Then Judas spoke, the one who was to betray him. 'Rabbi, can you mean me?' Jesus replied, 'The words are yours.'[e]

26 During supper Jesus took bread, and having said the blessing he broke it and gave it to the disciples with the words: 'Take this and eat; this is my body.'

27 Then he took a cup, and having offered thanks to God he gave it to them with the words: 'Drink from it,

28 all of you. For this is my blood, the blood of the covenant, shed for many

29 for the forgiveness of sins. I tell you, never again shall I drink from the fruit of the vine until that day when I drink it new with you in the kingdom of my Father.'

30 After singing the Passover Hymn, they went out to the Mount of Olives.

31 Then Jesus said to them, 'Tonight you will all fall from your faith on my account; for it stands written: "I will strike the shepherd down and the sheep of his flock will be scattered."

32 But after I am raised again, I will go on

33 before you into Galilee.' Peter replied, 'Everyone else may fall away on your

34 account, but I never will.' Jesus said to him, 'I tell you, tonight before the cock crows you will disown me three times.'

35 Peter said, 'Even if I must die with you, I will never disown you.' And all the disciples said the same.

36 JESUS THEN CAME WITH HIS DISCIPLES to a place called Gethsemane. He said to them, 'Sit here while I go over there

37 to pray.' He took with him Peter and the two sons of Zebedee. Anguish and

38 dismay came over him, and he said to them, 'My heart is ready to break with grief. Stop here, and stay awake with

39 me.' He went on a little, fell on his face in prayer, and said, 'My Father, if it is possible, let this cup pass me by. Yet not as I will, but as thou wilt.'

40 He came to the disciples and found them asleep; and he said to Peter, 'What! Could none of you stay awake

41 with me one hour? Stay awake, and pray that you may be spared the test. The spirit is willing, but the flesh is weak.'

42 He went away a second time, and prayed: 'My Father, if it is not possible for this cup to pass me by without my

43 drinking it, thy will be done.' He came again and found them asleep, for their

44 eyes were heavy. So he left them and went away again; and he prayed the third time, using the same words as before.

45 Then he came to the disciples and said to them, 'Still sleeping? Still taking your ease? The hour has come!

46 The Son of Man is betrayed to sinful men. Up, let us go forward; the traitor is upon us.'

47 While he was still speaking, Judas, one of the Twelve, appeared; with him was a great crowd armed with swords and cudgels, sent by the chief priests

48 and the elders of the nation. The traitor gave them this sign: 'The one I

49 kiss is your man; seize him'; and stepping forward at once, he said,

50 'Hail, Rabbi!', and kissed him. Jesus replied, 'Friend, do what you are here to do.'[f] They then came forward, seized Jesus, and held him fast.

51 At that moment one of those with Jesus reached for his sword and drew it, and he struck at the High Priest's

52 servant and cut off his ear. But Jesus said to him, 'Put up your sword. All who take the sword die by the sword.

e Or It is as you say.
f Or Friend, what are you here for?

---

the fulfillment of the *scriptures* is prominent in the passion narrative of each Gospel. It is to be recognized particularly in the way several OT passages (e.g. Ps.22) are introduced as part of the account (e.g. Mt.27.46). **26–29:** See also 1 Cor.11.23–26. **28:** The idea of sacrificial *blood* as the seal of a *covenant* relies on Exod.24.8 (Zech.9.11); see Lk.22.17–19 n. *Many:* see Mk.10.45 n.

26.30–46: Gethsemane (Mk.14.26–42; Lk.22.39–46). **30:** Jn.18.1. *Passover Hymn:* the concluding half of the "Hallel," Pss.115–118. **31:** Zech.13.7. **32:** 28.7–10,16. **33–35:** Lk.22.31–34; Jn.13.36–38 place this prediction prior to the departure from the supper. **36–46:** See Lk.22.40–46 n. **38–39:** Compare Jn.12.27–28. **38:** Ps.42.6. **39:** *Cup:* see Mk.10.38 n.; Jn.18.11. **42:** 6.10.

26.47–56: The arrest (Mk.14.43–52; Lk.22.47–53; Jn.18.2–11). **48:** The *kiss* was a disciple's usual greeting of his teacher. **51:** Jn.18.10 identifies the *one* as Peter. **52:** Jer.15.2; Rev.13.10.

53 Do you suppose that I cannot appeal to my Father, who would at once send to my aid more than twelve legions of
54 angels? But how then could the scriptures be fulfilled, which say that this must be?'

55   At the same time Jesus spoke to the crowd: 'Do you take me for a bandit, that you have come out with swords and cudgels to arrest me? Day after day I sat teaching in the temple, and
56 you did not lay hands on me. But this has all happened to fulfil what the prophets wrote.'

    Then the disciples all deserted him and ran away.

57 JESUS WAS LED OFF UNDER ARREST TO the house of Caiaphas the High Priest, where the lawyers and elders were
58 assembled. Peter followed him at a distance till he came to the High Priest's courtyard, and going in he sat down there among the attendants, meaning to see the end of it all.

59   The chief priests and the whole Council tried to find some allegation against Jesus on which a death-
60 sentence could be based; but they failed to find one, though many came forward with false evidence. Finally
61 two men alleged that he had said, 'I can pull down the temple of God, and
62 rebuild it in three days.' At this the High Priest rose and said to him, 'Have you no answer to the charge that these witnesses bring against you?'
63 But Jesus kept silence. The High Priest then said, 'By the living God I charge you to tell us: Are you the Messiah,
64 the Son of God?' Jesus replied, 'The words are yours.*g* But I tell you this: from now on, you will see the Son of Man seated at the right hand of God*h* and coming on the clouds of heaven.'
65 At these words the High Priest tore his

robes and exclaimed, 'Blasphemy! Need we call further witnesses? You have heard the blasphemy. What is 66 your opinion?' 'He is guilty,' they answered; 'he should die.'

Then they spat in his face and struck 67 him with their fists; and others said, as they beat him, 'Now, Messiah, if you 68 are a prophet, tell us who hit you.'

Meanwhile Peter was sitting outside 69 in the courtyard when a serving-maid accosted him and said, 'You were there too with Jesus the Galilean.' Peter denied it in face of them all. 'I do 70 not know what you mean', he said. He then went out to the gateway, 71 where another girl, seeing him, said to the people there, 'This fellow was with Jesus of Nazareth.' Once again he 72 denied it, saying with an oath, 'I do not know the man.' Shortly afterwards 73 the bystanders came up and said to Peter, 'Surely you are another of them; your accent gives you away!' At this 74 he broke into curses and declared with an oath: 'I do not know the man.' At that moment a cock crew; and Peter 75 remembered how Jesus had said, 'Before the cock crows you will disown me three times.' He went outside, and wept bitterly.

WHEN MORNING CAME, THE CHIEF **27** priests and the elders of the nation met in conference to plan the death of Jesus. They then put him in chains and 2 led him away, to hand him over to Pilate, the Roman Governor.

When Judas the traitor saw that 3 Jesus had been condemned, he was seized with remorse, and returned the thirty silver pieces to the chief priests and elders. 'I have sinned,' he said; 'I 4 have brought an innocent man to his death.' But they said, 'What is that to

g Or It is as you say.   *h* Literally of the Power.

53: *Twelve legions:* a legion was an infantry brigade numbering about five thousand men.
  26.57–75: Before the Jewish authorities (Mk.14.53–72; Lk.22.54–71; Jn.18.12–27). The Gospel accounts of Jesus' appearance before Jewish officials are not entirely harmonious. Whatever proceedings took place before the native Council (v. 59 n.), the crucial outcome was the charge as transmitted for the Roman trial. **57:** *Caiaphas:* see Lk.3.2 n. **59:** The *Council* (or *Sanhedrin*) of Jerusalem was Judea's highest native judicial tribunal. **61:** See 24.1–3 n. *Two men:* see Num.35.30; Deut.19.15. **63:** *Messiah, the Son of God:* see 16.16 n. **64:** Dan.7.13; Ps.110.1. **65–66:** The claim to be the *Messiah* would not, in itself, be *blasphemy;* the penalty for *blasphemy* was death by stoning (Lev.24.13–16). **75:** Compare v. 34.
  27.1–31: Before Roman authority (Mk.15.1–20; Lk.23.1–25; Jn.18.28–19.16). **2:** *Pilate:* see Lk.3.1 n. **3–10:** Compare Acts 1.18–19. **9–10:** Jer.32.6–13; Zech.11.12–13. **11:** *King:* see

5 us? See to that yourself.' So he threw the money down in the temple and left them, and went and hanged himself.

6 Taking up the money, the chief priests argued: 'This cannot be put into the temple fund; it is blood-money.' 7 So after conferring they used it to buy the Potter's Field, as a 8 burial-place for foreigners. This explains the name 'Blood Acre', by which that field has been known ever since; 9 and in this way fulfilment was given to the prophetic utterance of Jeremiah: 'They took[i] the thirty silver pieces, the price set on a man's head (for that was 10 his price among the Israelites), and gave the money for the potter's field, as the Lord directed me.'

11 Jesus was now brought before the Governor; and as he stood there the Governor asked him, 'Are you the king of the Jews?' 'The words are 12 yours',[j] said Jesus; and to the charges laid against him by the chief priests 13 and elders he made no reply. Then Pilate said to him, 'Do you not hear all this evidence that is brought against 14 you?'; but he still refused to answer one word, to the Governor's great astonishment.

15 At the festival season it was the Governor's custom to release one 16 prisoner chosen by the people. There was then in custody a man of some notoriety, called Jesus[k] Bar-Abbas. 17 When they were assembled Pilate said to them, 'Which would you like me to release to you—Jesus[k] Bar-Abbas, or 18 Jesus called Messiah?' For he knew that it was out of malice that they had brought Jesus before him.

19 While Pilate was sitting in court a message came to him from his wife: 'Have nothing to do with that innocent man; I was much troubled on his account in my dreams last night.'

20 Meanwhile the chief priests and elders had persuaded the crowd to ask for the release of Bar-Abbas and to 21 have Jesus put to death. So when the Governor asked, 'Which of the two do you wish me to release to you?', they said, 'Bar-Abbas.' 'Then what am I to 22 do with Jesus called Messiah?' asked Pilate; and with one voice they answered, 'Crucify him!' 'Why, what 23 harm has he done?' Pilate asked; but they shouted all the louder, 'Crucify him!'

Pilate could see that nothing was 24 being gained, and a riot was starting; so he took water and washed his hands in full view of the people, saying, 'My hands are clean of this man's blood; see to that yourselves.' And with one 25 voice the people cried, 'His blood be on us, and on our children.' He then 26 released Bar-Abbas to them; but he had Jesus flogged, and handed him over to be crucified.

PILATE'S SOLDIERS THEN TOOK JESUS 27 into the Governor's headquarters, where they collected the whole company round him. They stripped him 28 and dressed him in a scarlet mantle; and plaiting a crown of thorns they 29 placed it on his head, with a cane in his right hand. Falling on their knees before him they jeered at him: 'Hail, King of the Jews!' They spat on him, 30 and used the cane to beat him about the head. When they had finished 31 their mockery, they took off the mantle and dressed him in his own clothes.

Then they led him away to be 32 crucified. On their way out they met a man from Cyrene, Simon by name, and pressed him into service to carry his cross.

So they came to a place called 33 Golgotha (which means 'Place of a skull') and there he was offered a 34 draught of wine mixed with gall; but when he had tasted it he would not drink.

After fastening him to the cross they 35 divided his clothes among them by casting lots, and then sat down there 36 to keep watch. Over his head was 37 placed the inscription giving the charge: 'This is Jesus the king of the Jews.'

i Or I took.
j Or It is as you say.
k Some witnesses omit Jesus.

Lk.23.2 n. **15:** The *custom* is known only from the Gospels. **16:** *Bar-Abbas:* probably, "son of the father." The man was a revolutionary (Mk.15.7; Lk.23.25). **24:** Deut.21.6–9.
27.32–66: The crucifixion (Mk.15.21–47; Lk.23.26–54; Jn.19.17–42). **32:** *Simon:* see Mk.15.21 n.; contrast Jn.19.17. **34:** Ps.69.21; see Lk.23.36 n. **35:** Ps.22.18; see Lk.23.32 n.

38 Two bandits were crucified with him, one on his right and the other on his left.

39 The passers-by hurled abuse at him:
40 they wagged their heads and cried, 'You would pull the temple down, would you, and build it in three days? Come down from the cross and save yourself, if you are indeed the Son of
41 God.' So too the chief priests with the
42 lawyers and elders mocked at him: 'He saved others,' they said, 'but he cannot save himself. King of Israel, indeed! Let him come down now from the cross, and then we will believe him.
43 Did he trust in God? Let God rescue him, if he wants him—for he said he
44 was God's Son.' Even the bandits who were crucified with him taunted him in the same way.

45 From midday a darkness fell over the whole land, which lasted until
46 three in the afternoon; and about three Jesus cried aloud, '*Eli, Eli, lema sabachthani?*', which means, 'My God, my God, why hast thou forsaken me?'
47 Some of the bystanders, on hearing
48 this, said, 'He is calling Elijah.' One of them ran at once and fetched a sponge, which he soaked in sour wine, and held it to his lips on the end of a cane.
49 But the others said, 'Let us see if Elijah will come to save him.'
50 Jesus again gave a loud cry, and
51 breathed his last. At that moment the curtain of the temple was torn in two from top to bottom. There was an
52 earthquake, the rocks split and the graves opened, and many of God's
53 saints were raised from sleep; and coming out of their graves after his resurrection they entered the Holy City,
54 where many saw them. And when the centurion and his men who were keeping watch over Jesus saw the earthquake and all that was happening, they were filled with awe, and they said, 'Truly this man was a son of God.'[l]

55 A NUMBER OF WOMEN WERE ALSO present, watching from a distance; they had followed Jesus from Galilee
56 and waited on him. Among them were Mary of Magdala, Mary the mother of James and Joseph, and the mother of the sons of Zebedee.

57 When evening fell, there came a man of Arimathaea, Joseph by name, who was a man of means, and had himself become a disciple of Jesus. He ap-
58 proached Pilate, and asked for the body of Jesus; and Pilate gave orders that he should have it. Joseph took the
59 body, wrapped it in a clean linen sheet, and laid it in his own unused
60 tomb, which he had cut out of the rock; he then rolled a large stone against the entrance, and went away.
61 Mary of Magdala was there, and the other Mary, sitting opposite the grave.

62 Next day, the morning after that Friday, the chief priests and the Pharisees came in a body to Pilate.
63 'Your Excellency,' they said, 'we recall how that impostor said while he was still alive, "I am to be raised again after three days." So will you give
64 orders for the grave to be made secure until the third day? Otherwise his disciples may come, steal the body, and then tell the people that he has been raised from the dead; and the final deception will be worse than the
65 first.' 'You may have your guard,' said Pilate; 'go and make it secure as best
66 you can.' So they went and made the grave secure; they sealed the stone, and left the guard in charge.

28 THE SABBATH WAS OVER, AND IT WAS about daybreak on Sunday, when Mary

l Or the Son of God.

38: Isa.53.12. **39:** Ps.22.7. **40:** 24.1–3 n. **43:** Ps.22.8. **44:** Compare Lk.23.39–43. **46:** This is the first verse of Ps.22, the remembrance of which has influenced the crucifixion narrative at several points (e.g. vv. 35,43). **47:** The anticipation of *Elijah's* return (see Mk.6.15 n.) lies behind this apparent misunderstanding of the cry. **48:** Ps.69.21. **51:** The rending of the *curtain* before the Holy of Holies may have signified to early Christians God's accessibility to all men at all times; see Exod.26.31–33; Lev.16.1–2. **54:** Whatever a Roman soldier might mean by *a son of God* (perhaps, "divine hero"; see Mk.1.1 n.), the Gospel writer probably understood the words as a Christian confession (see Tfn.*l*). **59:** Deut.21.22–23. **60:** The *tomb* was a chamber cut into rock, with the entrance sealed by a wheel-like *stone*. **62–66:** Only Mt. has this tradition, which seems intended to counteract claims like that in 28.13.
   28.1–15: The empty tomb (Mk.16.1–8; Lk.24.1–11; Jn.20.1–18). **1:** See Mk.16.1 n.;

of Magdala and the other Mary came
2 to look at the grave. Suddenly there
was a violent earthquake; an angel of
the Lord descended from heaven; he
came to the stone and rolled it away,
3 and sat himself down on it. His face
shone like lightning; his garments were
4 white as snow. At the sight of him the
guards shook with fear and lay like the
dead.
5 The angel then addressed the women:
'You', he said, 'have nothing to fear. I
know you are looking for Jesus who
6 was crucified. He is not here; he has
been raised again, as he said he would
be. Come and see the place where he
7 was laid, and then go quickly and tell
his disciples: "He has been raised
from the dead and is going on before
you into Galilee; there you will see
him." That is what I had to tell you.'
8 They hurried away from the tomb
in awe and great joy, and ran to tell
9 the disciples. Suddenly Jesus was
there in their path. He gave them his
greeting, and they came up and
clasped his feet, falling prostrate
10 before him. Then Jesus said to them,
'Do not be afraid. Go and take word
to my brothers that they are to leave
for Galilee. They will see me there.'

The women had started on their way 11
when some of the guard went into the
city and reported to the chief priests
everything that had happened. After 12
meeting with the elders and conferring
together, the chief priests offered the
soldiers a substantial bribe and told 13
them to say, 'His disciples came by
night and stole the body while we were
asleep.' They added, 'If this should 14
reach the Governor's ears, we will put
matters right with him and see that
you do not suffer.' So they took the 15
money and did as they were told. This
story became widely known, and is
current in Jewish circles to this day.

The eleven disciples made their way 16
to Galilee, to the mountain where
Jesus had told them to meet him. When 17
they saw him, they fell prostrate before
him, though some were doubtful.
Jesus then came up and spoke to them. 18
He said: 'Full authority in heaven and
on earth has been committed to me.
Go forth therefore and make all 19
nations my disciples; baptize men
everywhere in the name of the Father
and the Son and the Holy Spirit, and 20
teach them to observe all that I have
commanded you. And be assured, I am
with you always, to the end of time.'

Lk.23.55–56 n. **2:** *Stone:* 27.60 n. **4:** *Guards:* see 27.62–66. **7-10:** 26.32. **8:** Contrast Mk.16.8.
11–15: 27.62–66; 28.4. **15:** *This day:* i.e. in Mt.'s time the charge of the stolen body was used
to counter the proclamation of Jesus' resurrection.
    28.16–20: Appearance and commissioning in Galilee. 16: *Mountain:* see 5.1 n. **17:** *Fell
prostrate:* worshiped. **19:** The command to go to *all nations* directs the Church into the Gentile
mission, beyond the limits of 10.5–6. **20:** *All that I have commanded:* compare chs. 5–7 (the
Sermon on the Mount). *I am with you:* compare 1.23; 18.20.

THE GOSPEL ACCORDING TO
MARK

Probably the oldest of the Gospels, Mark is a collection of traditions about Jesus brought together around 70 A.D. The import of the term "collection" should not mislead one to suppose that the material is presented haphazardly. On the contrary, the author depicts Jesus' early ministry as centered in Galilee, where he proclaims the kingdom of God and performs wonders; at its climax comes Peter's confession of faith and the first announcement of the passion (8.27–33). From that crucial point, the story moves relentlessly toward the cross and resurrection (chs. 14–16). Within this general framework, other "turning points" may also be found: e.g. 1.14; 3.6; 10.1.

Moreover, certain motifs which are of special concern to the evangelist are repeated. Perhaps the most important of these, at least in the Galilean section, is the kingdom's victory over demonic forces through Jesus' healing activity. Other Markan themes include the "secret of the Messiahship" (e.g. 1.34 n.) and the obtuseness even of the disciples (e.g. 8.17; 9.32).

The book's purpose is succinctly expressed: to proclaim the good news of Jesus Christ, the Son of God (1.1; 15.39).

The coming of Christ

1 HERE BEGINS THE GOSPEL OF JESUS Christ the Son of God.*a*
2 In the prophet Isaiah it stands written: 'Here is my herald whom I send on ahead of you, and he 3 will prepare your way. A voice crying aloud in the wilderness, "Prepare a way for the Lord; clear a straight path 4 for him."' And so it was that John the Baptist appeared in the wilderness proclaiming a baptism in token of repentance, for the forgiveness of sins; 5 and they flocked to him from the whole Judaean country-side and the city of Jerusalem, and were baptized by him in the River Jordan, confessing their sins.

6 John was dressed in a rough coat of camel's hair, with a leather belt round his waist, and he fed on locusts and wild honey. His proclamation ran: 7 'After me comes one who is mightier than I. I am not fit to unfasten his shoes. I have baptized you with water; 8 he will baptize you with the Holy Spirit.'

It happened at this time that Jesus 9 came from Nazareth in Galilee and was baptized in the Jordan by John. At the 10 moment when he came up out of the water, he saw the heavens torn open and the Spirit, like a dove, descending upon him. And a voice spoke from 11 heaven: 'Thou art my Son, my Beloved;*b* on thee my favour rests.'

Thereupon the Spirit sent him away 12 into the wilderness, and there he 13 remained for forty days tempted by

a Some witnesses omit the Son of God.
b Or Thou art my only Son.

1.1–8: **The work of the Baptist** (Mt.3.1–12; Lk.3.1–20; Jn.1.6,15,19–28). **1:** By *gospel* (i.e. the good news) the author means not the book, but the proclamation of *Jesus Christ;* it begins with the ministry of John the Baptist (compare Acts 1.22). Behind the use of the *Son of God* title in the Markan community are influences as diverse as the Jewish expectation of a royal Messiah (see Mt.1.1 n.) and Hellenistic ideas about wonder-working "divine heroes" and persons of divine nature. **2:** Mal.3.1. **3:** Isa.40.3. **4:** *Wilderness:* Mt.3.1 n. *Baptism:* see Mt.3.7 n. *Repentance:* see Mt.3.2 n. **6:** Elijah is clothed similarly in 2 Kgs.1.8. **7:** The Baptist's role in the Gospel is as the forerunner of Christ; hence, he is sometimes identified with Elijah (see 6.15 n.; 9.11–12; Mt.11.14; 17.10–13). **8:** *Holy Spirit:* see Lk.3.16 n.

1.9–11: **The baptism of Jesus** (Mt.3.13–17; Lk.3.21–22; Jn.1.32–34). In early Christian tradition, the striking account of Jesus' baptism by John serves at least three significant purposes: it narrates his becoming the Son (see Mt.3.16 n.); it explains the origin of the Church's initiatory rite; and it locates in the history of his people the beginning of Jesus' activity. **10–11:** *Spirit, dove:* see Mt.3.16 n. **11:** Ps.2.7 (*Son*) and Isa.42.1 (*Beloved*, meaning "chosen one") are combined.

1.12–13: **The temptation** (Mt.4.1–11; Lk.4.1–13). This brief account introduces a major concern of Mk.—the conflict of the *Spirit*-led Son with *Satan*, the evil one (3.22–30). **13:** *Forty*

[handwritten: v.15 In Greek "keep on repenting, keep on believing". Action words.]

[handwritten, left margin: Not a place but The rule of God in us, over us]

Satan. He was among the wild beasts; and the angels waited on him.

In Galilee: success and opposition

14 AFTER JOHN HAD BEEN ARRESTED, JESUS came into Galilee proclaiming the 15 Gospel of God: 'The time has come; the kingdom of God is upon you; repent, and believe the Gospel.'

16 Jesus was walking by the Sea of Galilee when he saw Simon and his brother Andrew on the lake at work with a casting-net; for they were 17 fishermen. Jesus said to them, 'Come with me, and I will make you fishers 18 of men.' And at once they left their nets and followed him.

19 When he had gone a little further he saw James son of Zebedee and his brother John, who were in the boat 20 overhauling their nets. He called them; and, leaving their father Zebedee in the boat with the hired men, they went off to follow him.

21 They came to Capernaum, and on the Sabbath he went to synagogue and 22 began to teach. The people were astounded at his teaching, for, unlike the doctors of the law, he taught with 23 a note of authority. Now there was a man in the synagogue possessed by an 24 unclean spirit. He shrieked: 'What do you want with us, Jesus of Nazareth? Have you[c] come to destroy us? I know who you are—the Holy One of God.' 25 Jesus rebuked him: 'Be silent', he said, 26 'and come out of him.' And the unclean spirit threw the man into convulsions 27 and with a loud cry left him. They were all dumbfounded and began to ask one another, 'What is this? A new kind of teaching! He speaks with authority.

When he gives orders, even the unclean spirits submit.' The news spread 28 rapidly, and he was soon spoken of all over the district of Galilee.

On leaving the synagogue they went 29 straight to the house of Simon and Andrew; and James and John went with them. Simon's mother-in-law was 30 ill in bed with fever. They told him about her at once. He came forward, 31 took her by the hand, and helped her to her feet. The fever left her and she waited upon them.

That evening after sunset they 32 brought to him all who were ill or possessed by devils; and the whole 33 town was there, gathered at the door. He healed many who suffered from 34 various diseases, and drove out many devils. He would not let the devils speak, because they knew who he was.

Very early next morning he got up 35 and went out. He went away to a lonely spot and remained there in prayer. But 36 Simon and his companions searched him out, found him, and said, 'They 37 are all looking for you.' He answered, 38 'Let us move on to the country towns in the neighbourhood; I have to proclaim my message there also; that is what I came out to do.' So all through 39 Galilee he went, preaching in the synagogues and casting out the devils.

Once he was approached by a leper, 40 who knelt before him begging his help. 'If only you will,' said the man, 'you can cleanse me.' In warm indignation 41 Jesus stretched out his hand,[d] touched him, and said, 'Indeed I will; be clean again.' The leprosy left him im- 42

c *Or* You have.
d *Some witnesses read* Jesus was sorry for him and stretched out his hand; *one witness has simply* He stretched out his hand.

days: see Mt.4.2 n. Satan: see Mt.4.1 n. Whether Mk. meant the beasts to represent the dangers of the wilderness or the restoration of creation's harmony is not clear.
1.14–20: The beginning of Jesus' ministry (Mt.4.12–22; Lk.4.14–15; 5.1–11; Jn.1.35–51). **15:** The *time* is the long-anticipated dawning of the kingdom of God. The *kingdom of God* signifies God's final victory over evil, when his rule is fully established, as well as the sphere of salvation thus inaugurated. *Repent:* change your ways. **16–20:** The first disciples are called without any indication of prior acquaintance with Jesus. **16:** *Simon:* Peter (compare Mt.4.18). **18:** *Followed:* became his disciples.
1.21–38: Jesus in Capernaum (Mt.8.14–17; Lk.4.31–43). **23:** *Unclean spirit:* a demon, believed to have power to cause illness; see v. 32. Such demons are allied with Satan (see 3.22–23) in opposition to God's will for men. **24:** The demon has knowledge not possessed by men. **32:** *Sunset:* see Lk.4.40 n. **34:** In Mk., Jesus repeatedly imposes silence about his identity, not only on demons (e.g. 3.12), but also on friends (e.g. 8.30).
1.40–45: A leper healed (Mt.8.1–4; Lk.5.12–16). **40:** *Leper . . . cleanse me:* see Mt.8.2 n.

In Galilee: success and opposition

43 mediately, and he was clean. Then he dismissed him with this stern warning: 44 'Be sure you say nothing to anybody. Go and show yourself to the priest, and make the offering laid down by Moses for your cleansing; that will certify the 45 cure.' But the man went out and made the whole story public; he spread it far and wide, until Jesus could no longer show himself in any town, but stayed outside in the open country. Even so, people kept coming to him from all quarters.

2 When after some days he returned to Capernaum, the news went round that 2 he was at home; and such a crowd collected that the space in front of the door was not big enough to hold them. And while he was proclaiming the 3 message to them, a man was brought who was paralysed. Four men were 4 carrying him, but because of the crowd they could not get him near. So they opened up the roof over the place where Jesus was, and when they had broken through they lowered the stretcher on which the paralysed man 5 was lying. When Jesus saw their faith, he said to the paralysed man, 'My son, your sins are forgiven.'

6 Now there were some lawyers sitting there and they thought to themselves, 7 'Why does the fellow talk like that? This is blasphemy! Who but God 8 alone can forgive sins?' Jesus knew in his own mind that this was what they were thinking, and said to them: 'Why do you harbour thoughts like these? 9 Is it easier to say to this paralysed man, "Your sins are forgiven", or to say, "Stand up, take your bed, and walk"? 10 But to convince you that the Son of Man has the right on earth to forgive sins'—he turned to the paralysed man—'I say to you, stand up, take 11 your bed, and go home.' And he got 12 up, and at once took his stretcher and went out in full view of them all, so that they were astounded and praised God. 'Never before', they said, 'have we seen the like.'

Once more he went away to the lake- 13 side. All the crowd came to him, and he taught them there. As he went along, 14 he saw Levi son of Alphaeus at his seat in the custom-house, and said to him, 'Follow me'; and Levi rose and followed him.

When Jesus was at table in his house, 15 many bad characters—tax-gatherers and others—were seated with him and his disciples; for there were many who followed him. Some doctors of the law 16 who were Pharisees noticed him eating in this bad company, and said to his disciples, 'He eats with tax-gatherers and sinners!' Jesus heard it and said to 17 them, 'It is not the healthy that need a doctor, but the sick; I did not come to invite virtuous people, but sinners.'

Once, when John's disciples and the 18 Pharisees were keeping a fast, some people came to him and said, 'Why is it that John's disciples and the disciples of the Pharisees are fasting, but yours are not?' Jesus said to them, 'Can you 19 expect the bridegroom's friends to fast while the bridegroom is with them? As long as they have the bridegroom with them, there can be no fasting. But 20 the time will come when the bridegroom will be taken away from them, and on that day they will fast.

'No one sews a patch of unshrunk 21

43: See v. 34 n. 44: See Lev.14.1–32. 45: Mt. has no parallel to this verse, while Lk. recasts it, omitting the suggestion that *Jesus could no longer show himself in any town.*

2.1–3.6: Healing and conflict.

2.1–12: A paralytic (Mt.9.1–8; Lk.5.17–26). 4: A *roof* of mud and branches is meant (contrast Lk.5.19). 5: The account assumes a connection between illness and sin; compare Jn.9.2. *Faith:* see Mt.8.13 n. 6: *Lawyers:* see Mt.2.4 n. 10: *Son of Man* in some NT contexts may be only the equivalent of a Semitic phrase meaning "man." In most places, however, *Son of Man* is a title for an exalted figure who will serve as judge at the end of history (see Dan.7.13–14). The expression is found almost exclusively in sayings attributed to Jesus. In some occurrences, the *Son of Man* is clearly identified with Jesus, even in his earthly humility and suffering.

2.13–17: Jesus, friend of outcasts (Mt.9.9–13; Lk.5.27–32). 15: Eating with *tax-gatherers* (see Lk.3.12 n.) and other outcasts was a practice of Jesus' of which his opponents strongly disapproved.

2.18–22: Fasting (Mt.9.14–17; Lk.5.33–39). 18: *John's disciples* developed into a continuing religious movement; see Acts 19.1–6. 21–22: Such a radical distinction between the *new* and the *old* shows the seriousness of the reported conflict.

cloth on to an old coat; if he does, the patch tears away from it, the new from
22 the old, and leaves a bigger hole. No one puts new wine into old wine-skins; if he does, the wine will burst the skins, and then wine and skins are both lost. Fresh skins for new wine!'

23 One Sabbath he was going through the cornfields; and his disciples, as they went, began to pluck ears of corn.
24 The Pharisees said to him, 'Look, why are they doing what is forbidden on the
25 Sabbath?' He answered, 'Have you never read what David did when he and his men were hungry and had nothing
26 to eat? He went into the House of God, in the time of Abiathar the High Priest, and ate the sacred bread, though no one but a priest is allowed to eat it, and even gave it to his men.'

27 He also said to them, 'The Sabbath was made for the sake of man and not
28 man for the Sabbath: therefore the Son of Man is sovereign even over the Sabbath.'

3 On another occasion when he went to synagogue, there was a man in the congregation who had a withered arm;
2 and they were watching to see whether Jesus would cure him on the Sabbath, so that they could bring a charge
3 against him. He said to the man with the withered arm, 'Come and stand out
4 here.' Then he turned to them: 'Is it permitted to do good or to do evil on the Sabbath, to save life or to kill?'
5 They had nothing to say; and, looking round at them with anger and sorrow at their obstinate stupidity, he said to the man, 'Stretch out your arm.' He stretched it out and his arm was
6 restored. But the Pharisees, on leaving the synagogue, began plotting against him with the partisans of Herod to see how they could make away with him.

7 JESUS WENT AWAY TO THE LAKE-SIDE with his disciples. Great numbers from
8 Galilee, Judaea and Jerusalem, Idumaea and Transjordan, and the neighbourhood of Tyre and Sidon, heard what he was doing and came to
9 see him. So he told his disciples to have a boat ready for him, to save him from
10 being crushed by the crowd. For he cured so many that sick people of all kinds came crowding in upon
11 him to touch him. The unclean spirits too, when they saw him, would fall at his feet and cry aloud, 'You are the
12 Son of God'; but he insisted that they should not make him known.

13 He then went up into the hill-country and called the men he wanted; and they
14 went and joined him. He appointed twelve as his companions, whom he would send out to proclaim the
15 Gospel, with a commission to drive
16 out devils. So he appointed the Twelve:
17 to Simon he gave the name Peter; then came the sons of Zebedee, James and his brother John, to whom he gave the name Boanerges, Sons of Thunder;
18 then Andrew and Philip and Bartholomew and Matthew and Thomas and James the son of Alphaeus and Thaddaeus and Simon, a member of the Zealot party, and Judas Iscariot, the
19 man who betrayed him.

20 He entered a house; and once more such a crowd collected round them that
21 they had no chance to eat. When his family heard of this, they set out to take charge of him; for people were saying that he was out of his mind.[e]

22 The doctors of the law, too, who had come down from Jerusalem, said, 'He is possessed by Beelzebub', and, 'He drives out devils by the prince of devils.'
23 So he called them to come forward,

e Or of him. 'He is out of his mind', they said.

2.23–3.6: **Sabbath controversy** (Mt.12.1–14; Lk.6.1–11). Strict Sabbath observance required refraining from all work and was of prime importance for first-century Jewish piety. **23:** Deut.23.25. **24:** Exod.20.10; Deut.5.14. **26:** *Abiathar* is a slip of the memory; Abiathar's father, Ahimelech, was the priest in this instance (1 Sam.21.1–6). On the rule involved, see Lev.24.7–9. **27:** Deut.5.12–14. **28:** *Son of Man:* see 2.10 n. **3.1–6:** While healing in general was prohibited on the Sabbath, Pharisaic interpretation permitted treatment when a life was at stake.

3.7–12: **Summary of activity** and Jesus' rapport with the common people (Mt.4.24–25; 12.15–16; Lk.6.17–19).

3.13–19: **The Twelve appointed** (Mt.10.1–4; Lk.6.12–16). **18:** The *Zealot party* was a group of violent revolutionaries.

3.20–30: **Suspicion and accusation** (Mt.12.22–37; Lk.11.14–23; 12.10). **22:** *Beelzebub:* Satan.

and spoke to them in parables: 'How
24 can Satan drive out Satan? If a kingdom
is divided against itself, that kingdom
25 cannot stand; if a household is divided
against itself, that house will never
26 stand; and if Satan is in rebellion
against himself, he is divided and cannot stand; and that is the end of him.
27 'On the other hand, no one can
break into a strong man's house and
make off with his goods unless he has
first tied the strong man up; then he
can ransack the house.
28 'I tell you this: no sin, no slander, is
29 beyond forgiveness for men; but whoever slanders the Holy Spirit can never
be forgiven; he is guilty of eternal sin.'
30 He said this because they had declared
that he was possessed by an unclean
spirit.
31 Then his mother and his brothers
arrived, and remaining outside sent in
a message asking him to come out to
32 them. A crowd was sitting round and
word was brought to him: 'Your
mother and your brothers are outside
33 asking for you.' He replied, 'Who is my
34 mother? Who are my brothers?' And
looking round at those who were
sitting in the circle about him he said,
'Here are my mother and my brothers.
35 Whoever does the will of God is my
brother, my sister, my mother.'

4 ON ANOTHER OCCASION HE BEGAN TO
teach by the lake-side. The crowd that
gathered round him was so large that
he had to get into a boat on the lake,
and there he sat, with the whole crowd
on the beach right down to the water's
2 edge. And he taught them many things
by parables.

As he taught he said:
'Listen! A sower went out to sow. 3
And it happened that as he sowed, some 4
seed fell along the footpath; and the
birds came and ate it up. Some seed 5
fell on rocky ground, where it had little
soil, and it sprouted quickly because it
had no depth of earth; but when the 6
sun rose the young corn was scorched,
and as it had no root it withered away.
Some seed fell among thistles; and the 7
thistles shot up and choked the corn,
and it yielded no crop. And some of the 8
seed fell into good soil, where it came
up and grew, and bore fruit; and the
yield was thirtyfold, sixtyfold, even a
hundredfold.' He added, 'If you have 9
ears to hear, then hear.'

When he was alone, the Twelve and 10
others who were round him questioned
him about the parables. He replied, 11
'To you the secret of the kingdom of
God has been given; but to those who
are outside everything comes by way of
parables, so that (as Scripture says) 12
they may look and look, but see
nothing; they may hear and hear, but
understand nothing; otherwise they
might turn to God and be forgiven.'

So he said, 'You do not understand 13
this parable? How then are you to
understand any parable? The sower 14
sows the word. Those along the foot- 15
path are people in whom the word is
sown, but no sooner have they heard it
than Satan comes and carries off the
word which has been sown in them.
It is the same with those who receive 16
the seed on rocky ground; as soon as
they hear the word, they accept it with
joy, but it strikes no root in them; they 17
have no staying-power; then, when

29: A difficult saying (compare Mt.12.31–32 n.; Lk.12.10), which appears in several forms in early Christian literature, is interpreted by Mk. to prohibit *slander* against the power at work in Jesus (v. 30).

3.31–35: Jesus' true family (Mt.12.46–50; Lk.8.19–21). **31:** *Arrived:* see v. 21.

4.1–34: The use of parables (Mt. ch. 13; Lk.8.4–18; 13.18–21). **2:** A *parable* is a realistic story or true-to-experience observation which points beyond the everyday situation it describes. The parable is to be contrasted with the allegory, which is a puzzle whose meaning is discovered by unlocking the symbolic significance of each detail in the story. The parable's message is found by letting the metaphor stimulate the imagination to see things (God's kingdom, human relations, life) in a new way. **3–8:** The procedure in farming was to sow the seed first and then to plow. Inevitably, some seed would fall on ground with an abundance of subsurface rock. **8:** The *yield* exceeds normal expectations. **11:** The *secret* probably is that God's kingdom is manifesting itself. Here, *parables* appears to mean "puzzles" and may mistranslate a Semitic word; if so, the translation had fateful consequences (vv. 13–20 n.). **12:** See Isa.6.9–10; in Mk. (but see Mt.13.13 n.), the parables are a cause of that hardening of men's hearts which occurs within God's purpose (compare Jn.12.40). **13–20:** In line with v. 11 (see n.), the parable is

there is trouble or persecution on account of the word, they fall away at
18 once. Others again receive the seed
19 among thistles; they hear the word, but worldly cares and the false glamour of wealth and all kinds of evil desire come in and choke the word, and it proves
20 barren. And there are those who receive the seed in good soil; they hear the word and welcome it; and they bear fruit thirtyfold, sixtyfold, or a hundred-fold.'

21   He said to them, 'Do you bring in the lamp to put it under the meal-tub, or under the bed? Surely it is brought
22 to be set on the lamp-stand. For nothing is hidden unless it is to be disclosed, and nothing put under cover
23 unless it is to come into the open. If you have ears to hear, then hear.'

24   He also said, 'Take note of what you hear; the measure you give is the measure you will receive, with some-
25 thing more besides. For the man who has will be given more, and the man who has not will forfeit even what he has.'

26   He said, 'The kingdom of God is like this. A man scatters seed on the land;
27 he goes to bed at night and gets up in the morning, and the seed sprouts and
28 grows—how, he does not know. The ground produces a crop by itself, first the blade, then the ear, then full-grown
29 corn in the ear; but as soon as the crop is ripe, he plies the sickle, because harvest-time has come.'

30   He said also, 'How shall we picture the kingdom of God, or by what
31 parable shall we describe it? It is like the mustard-seed, which is smaller than any seed in the ground at its sowing.
32 But once sown, it springs up and grows taller than any other plant, and forms branches so large that the birds can settle in its shade.'

With many such parables he would 33 give them his message, so far as they were able to receive it. He never spoke 34 to them except in parables; but privately to his disciples he explained everything.

Miracles of Christ

THAT DAY, IN THE EVENING, HE SAID TO 35 them, 'Let us cross over to the other side of the lake.' So they left the crowd 36 and took him with them in the boat where he had been sitting; and there were other boats accompanying him. A heavy squall came on and the waves 37 broke over the boat until it was all but swamped. Now he was in the stern 38 asleep on a cushion; they roused him and said, 'Master, we are sinking! Do you not care?' He awoke, rebuked the 39 wind, and said to the sea, 'Hush! Be still!' The wind dropped and there was a dead calm. He said to them, 'Why 40 are you such cowards? Have you no faith even now?' They were awestruck 41 and said to one another, 'Who can this be? Even the wind and the sea obey him.'

So they came to the other side of the 5 lake, into the country of the Gerasenes. As he stepped ashore, a man possessed 2 by an unclean spirit came up to him from among the tombs where he had 3 his dwelling. He could no longer be controlled; even chains were useless; he had often been fettered and chained 4 up, but he had snapped his chains and broken the fetters. No one was strong enough to master him. And so, 5 unceasingly, night and day, he would cry aloud among the tombs and on the hill-sides and cut himself with stones. When he saw Jesus in the distance, he 6 ran and flung himself down before him,

---

interpreted as an allegory. **21**: Mt.5.15; Lk.8.16. **22**: Mt.10.26; Lk.8.17; 12.2. **24–25**: Compare Mt.7.2; 13.12; Lk.6.38; 8.18; the use of these sayings at this place (vv. 10–12,33–34) underlines the privileged knowledge of the chosen ones, the secret truth which they will one day make public (v. 22). **26–32**: The kingdom is all but invisible, but its consummation is certain. **30**: The *mustard seed* (Mt.13.31–32; Lk.13.18–19) is proverbially, although not literally, the smallest seed. **32**: Compare Dan.4.12. **34**: See vv. 24–25 n.
 4.35–41: Rebuke of a storm (Mt.8.23–27; Lk.8.22–25).
 5.1–20: The Gerasene demoniac (Mt.8.28–34; Lk.8.26–39). **1**: *Country of the Gerasenes* would mean Gerasa (Jerash), a city of the Decapolis (Mt.4.25 n.). Mt.8.28 (Gadarene), Lk.8.26 (Gergesene), and manuscripts of all three synoptics show confusion about the location. A place on the southeast side of the Sea of Galilee is apparently meant. **2**: See 1.23. **6**: See Mt.8.28–29 n.

7 shouting loudly, 'What do you want with me, Jesus, son of the Most High God? In God's name do not torment

8 me.' (For Jesus was already saying to him, 'Out unclean spirit, come out of

9 this man!') Jesus asked him, 'What is your name?' 'My name is Legion,' he

10 said, 'there are so many of us.' And he begged hard that Jesus would not send them out of the country.

11 Now there happened to be a large herd of pigs feeding on the hill-side,

12 and the spirits begged him, 'Send us among the pigs and let us go into them.'

13 He gave them leave; and the unclean spirits came out and went into the pigs; and the herd, of about two thousand, rushed over the edge into the lake and were drowned.

14 The men in charge of them took to their heels and carried the news to the town and country-side; and the people came out to see what had happened.

15 They came to Jesus and saw the madman who had been possessed by the legion of devils, sitting there clothed and in his right mind; and they were

16 afraid. The spectators told them how the madman had been cured and what

17 had happened to the pigs. Then they begged Jesus to leave the district.

18 As he was stepping into the boat, the man who had been possessed begged to

19 go with him. Jesus would not allow it, but said to him, 'Go home to your own folk and tell them what the Lord in his

20 mercy has done for you.' The man went off and spread the news in the Ten Towns*f* of all that Jesus had done for him; and they were all amazed.

21 As soon as Jesus had returned by boat to the other shore, a great crowd once more gathered round him. While

22 he was by the lake-side, the president of one of the synagogues came up, Jairus by name, and, when he saw him, threw himself down at his feet

23 and pleaded with him. 'My little daughter', he said, 'is at death's door. I beg you to come and lay your hands on her to cure her and save her life.'

24 So Jesus went with him, accompanied by a great crowd which pressed upon him.

25 Among them was a woman who had

26 suffered from haemorrhages for twelve years; and in spite of long treatment by many doctors, on which she had spent all she had, there had been no improvement; on the contrary, she had

27 grown worse. She had heard what people were saying about Jesus, so she came up from behind in the crowd and

28 touched his cloak; for she said to herself, 'If I touch even his clothes, I shall

29 be cured.' And there and then the source of her haemorrhages dried up and she knew in herself that she was

30 cured of her trouble. At the same time Jesus, aware that power had gone out of him, turned round in the crowd and

31 asked, 'Who touched my clothes?' His disciples said to him, 'You see the crowd pressing upon you and yet you *r*

32 ask, "Who touched me?"' Meanwhile he was looking round to see who had

33 done it. And the woman, trembling with fear when she grasped what had happened to her, came and fell at his

34 feet and told him the whole truth. He said to her, 'My daughter, your faith has cured you. Go in peace, free for ever from this trouble.'

35 While he was still speaking, a message came from the president's house, 'Your daughter is dead; why

36 trouble the Rabbi further?' But Jesus, overhearing the message as it was delivered, said to the president of the synagogue, 'Do not be afraid; only

37 have faith.' After this he allowed no one to accompany him except Peter and James and James's brother John.

38 They came to the president's house, where he found a great commotion,

39 with loud crying and wailing. So he went in and said to them, 'Why this crying and commotion? The child is

40 not dead: she is asleep'; and they only laughed at him. But after turning all the others out, he took the child's father

f Greek Decapolis.

9: Power over a person was believed to be gained by knowing his *name*. *Legion:* a Roman army unit of about five thousand men. **11:** *Pigs:* see Mt.8.30 n. **20:** *Ten Towns:* see Mt.4.25 n.
    5.21–43: Jairus' daughter and a woman with a chronic ailment (Mt.9.18–26; Lk.8.40–56). Both narratives display the elements common to ancient miracle stories: description, cure, proof of cure (compare 5.1–16). **34:** On *cured*, see Lk.7.50 n. **38:** The customary noisy mourning practices.

[handwritten margin note: We can hold people "prisoner" to their pas. or to what we think they are a should be.]

and mother and his own companions and went in where the child was
41 lying. Then, taking hold of her hand, he said to her, '*Talitha cum*', which
42 means, 'Get up, my child.' Immediately the girl got up and walked about—she was twelve years old. At that they were
43 beside themselves with amazement. He gave them strict orders to let no one hear about it, and told them to give her something to eat.

6 He left that place and went to his home town accompanied by his dis-
2 ciples. When the Sabbath came he began to teach in the synagogue; and the large congregation who heard him were amazed and said, 'Where does he get it from?', and, 'What wisdom is this that has been given him?', and, 'How
3 does he work such miracles? Is not this the carpenter, the son of Mary,*g* the brother of James and Joseph and Judas and Simon? And are not his sisters here with us?' So they fell foul of him.
4 Jesus said to them, 'A prophet will always be held in honour except in his home town, and among his kinsmen
5 and family.' He could work no miracle there, except that he put his hands on
6 a few sick people and healed them; and he was taken aback by their want of faith. *[handwritten: We can somehow block God's power to heal]*

ON ONE OF HIS TEACHING JOURNEYS
7 round the villages he summoned the Twelve and sent them out in pairs on a mission. He gave them authority over
8 unclean spirits, and instructed them to take nothing for the journey beyond a stick: no bread, no pack, no money in
9 their belts. They might wear sandals,
10 but not a second coat. 'When you are admitted to a house', he added, 'stay
11 there until you leave those parts. At any place where they will not receive you or listen to you, shake the dust off your feet as you leave, as a warning to
12 them.' So they set out and called
13 publicly for repentance. They drove

out many devils, and many sick people they anointed with oil and cured.
14 Now King Herod heard of it, for the fame of Jesus had spread; and people were saying,*h* 'John the Baptist has been raised to life, and that is why these miraculous powers are at work in him.'
15 Others said, 'It is Elijah.' Others again, 'He is a prophet like one of the old
16 prophets.' But Herod, when he heard of it, said, 'This is John, whom I beheaded, raised from the dead.'
17 For this same Herod had sent and arrested John and put him in prison on account of his brother Philip's wife,
18 Herodias, whom he had married. John had told Herod, 'You have no right to
19 your brother's wife.' Thus Herodias nursed a grudge against him and would willingly have killed him, but
20 she could not; for Herod went in awe of John, knowing him to be a good and holy man; so he kept him in custody. He liked to listen to him, although the listening left him greatly perplexed.
21 Herodias found her opportunity when Herod on his birthday gave a banquet to his chief officials and commanders and the leading men of
22 Galilee. Her daughter came in*i* and danced, and so delighted Herod and his guests that the king said to the girl, 'Ask what you like and I will give it
23 you.' And he swore an oath to her: 'Whatever you ask I will give you, up
24 to half my kingdom.' She went out and said to her mother, 'What shall I ask for?' She replied, 'The head of John the
25 Baptist.' The girl hastened back at once to the king with her request: 'I want you to give me here and now, on a dish,
26 the head of John the Baptist.' The king was greatly distressed, but out of regard for his oath and for his guests he could not bring himself to refuse her.

g Some witnesses read Is not this the son of the carpenter and Mary ...
h Some witnesses read and he said ...
i Or A festive occasion came when Herod on his birthday gave ... of Galilee. The daughter of Herodias came in ...

41: *Talitha cum* is Aram.; the command is preserved in transliteration, perhaps in the belief that the strange-sounding phrase has special power.
6.1–6: Jesus in Nazareth (Mt.13.53b–58; compare Lk.4.16–30). **1**: *Home town*: Nazareth.
3: *Fell foul*: were offended.
6.7–13: Mission of the Twelve (Mt.9.35; 10.1,9–11,14; Lk.9.1–6). **7**: See Mt.10.8 n.
6.14–29: Herod and John (Mt.14.1–12; Lk.3.19–20; 9.7–9). **14**: The *Herod* meant is Antipas (see Lk.3.1 n.); he was actually a client prince, not a *king*. **15**: *Elijah* was expected to return to introduce the age of salvation (Mal.4.5–6; Ecclus.48.10).

27 So the king sent a soldier of the guard with orders to bring John's head. The soldier went off and beheaded him in the prison, brought the head on a dish, and gave it to the girl; and she gave it to her mother.

29   When John's disciples heard the news, they came and took his body away and laid it in a tomb.

30   The apostles now rejoined Jesus and reported to him all that they had done 31 and taught. He said to them, 'Come with me, by yourselves, to some lonely place where you can rest quietly.' (For they had no leisure even to eat, so many 32 were coming and going.) Accordingly, they set off privately by boat for a lonely 33 place. But many saw them leave and recognized them, and came round by land, hurrying from all the towns towards the place, and arrived there first. 34 When he came ashore, he saw a great crowd; and his heart went out to them, because they were like sheep without a shepherd; and he had much to 35 teach them. As the day wore on, his disciples came up to him and said, 'This is a lonely place and it is getting very 36 late; send the people off to the farms and villages round about, to buy them- 37 selves something to eat.' 'Give them something to eat yourselves', he answered. They replied, 'Are we to go and spend twenty pounds*j* on bread to 38 give them a meal?' 'How many loaves have you?' he asked; 'go and see.' They found out and told him, 'Five, and two 39 fishes also.' He ordered them to make the people sit down in groups on the 40 green grass, and they sat down in rows, 41 a hundred rows of fifty each. Then, taking the five loaves and the two fishes, he looked up to heaven, said the blessing, broke the loaves, and gave them to the disciples to distribute. He also divided the two fishes among them. 42 They all ate to their hearts' content; 43 and twelve great basketfuls of scraps were picked up, with what was left of

the fish. Those who ate the loaves 44 numbered five thousand men.

As soon as it was over he made his 45 disciples embark and cross to Bethsaida ahead of him, while he himself sent the people away. After taking leave of 46 them, he went up the hill-side to pray. It grew late and the boat was already 47 well out on the water, while he was alone on the land. Somewhere between 48 three and six in the morning, seeing them labouring at the oars against a head-wind, he came towards them, walking on the lake. He was going to pass them by; but when they saw him 49 walking on the lake, they thought it was a ghost and cried out; for they all 50 saw him and were terrified. But at once he spoke to them: 'Take heart! It is I; do not be afraid.' Then he climbed into 51 the boat beside them, and the wind dropped. At this they were completely dumbfounded, for they had not under- 52 stood the incident of the loaves; their minds were closed.

So they finished the crossing and 53 came to land at Gennesaret, where they made fast. When they came ashore, he 54 was immediately recognized; and the 55 people scoured that whole country-side and brought the sick on stretchers to any place where he was reported to be. Wherever he went, to farmsteads, 56 villages, or towns, they laid out the sick in the market-places and begged him to let them simply touch the edge of his cloak; and all who touched him were cured.

Growing tension

A GROUP OF PHARISEES, WITH SOME 7 doctors of the law who had come from Jerusalem, met him and noticed that 2 some of his disciples were eating their food with 'defiled' hands—in other words, without washing them. (For the 3

j Literally 200 denarii.

6.30–44: Feeding of five thousand (Mt.14.13–21; Lk.9.10–17; Jn.6.1–13). Mt.5.32–39 and Mk.8.1–10 both have a second account of the feeding of a multitude (followed by a sea crossing); some believe the two accounts are variant forms of the same report. **30:** *Apostles:* see Mt.10.2 n. **37:** *Twenty pounds* (Tfn. *j, 200 denarii*): one denarius was about a day's wage. **41:** See 8.6 n.
    6.45–56: Walking on the sea (Mt.14.22–36; Jn.6.15–21). **52:** The obtuseness of the disciples here contrasts sharply with the ending of the episode in Mt.14.33 (see n.); in 8.14–21 the obtuseness theme is expanded.
    7.1–23: The ancient traditions (Mt.15.1–20). **3:** *Washing the hands* was an act of ritual

Pharisees and the Jews in general never eat without washing the hands,[k] in obedience to an old-established tradi-
4 tion; and on coming from the market-place they never eat without first washing. And there are many other points on which they have a traditional rule to maintain, for example, washing
5 of cups and jugs and copper bowls.) Accordingly, these Pharisees and the lawyers asked him, 'Why do your disciples not conform to the ancient tradition, but eat their food with
6 defiled hands?' He answered, 'Isaiah was right when he prophesied about you hypocrites in these words: "This people pays me lip-service, but their
7 heart is far from me: their worship of me is in vain, for they teach as doctrines
8 the commandments of men." You neglect the commandment of God, in order to maintain the tradition of men.'
9 He also said to them, 'How well you set aside the commandment of God in order to maintain[l] your tradition!
10 Moses said, "Honour your father and your mother", and, "The man who curses his father or mother must suffer
11 death." But you hold that if a man says to his father or mother, "Anything of mine which might have been used for your benefit is Corban"' (meaning, set
12 apart for God), 'he is no longer permitted to do anything for his father or
13 mother. Thus by your own tradition, handed down among you, you make God's word null and void. And many other things that you do are just like that.'
14 On another occasion he called the people and said to them, 'Listen to me,
15 all of you, and understand this: nothing that goes into a man from outside can defile him; no, it is the things that come out of him that defile a man.'[m]
17 When he had left the people and gone indoors, his disciples questioned him
18 about the parable. He said to them, 'Are you as dull as the rest? Do you

not see that nothing that goes from outside into a man can defile him,
because it does not enter into his heart 19 but into his stomach, and so passes out into the drain?' Thus he declared all foods clean. He went on, 'It is what 20 comes out of a man that defiles him. For from inside, out of a man's heart, 21 come evil thoughts, acts of fornication, of theft, murder, adultery, ruthless 22 greed, and malice; fraud, indecency, envy, slander, arrogance, and folly; these evil things all come from inside, 23 and they defile the man.'

Then he left that place and went away 24 into the territory of Tyre. He found a house to stay in, and he would have liked to remain unrecognized, but this was impossible. Almost at once a 25 woman whose young daughter was possessed by an unclean spirit heard of him, came in, and fell at his feet. (She was a Gentile, a Phoenician of 26 Syria by nationality.) She begged him to drive the spirit out of her daughter. He said to her, 'Let the children be 27 satisfied first; it is not fair to take the children's bread and throw it to the dogs.' 'Sir,' she answered, 'even the 28 dogs under the table eat the children's scraps.' He said to her, 'For saying 29 that, you may go home content; the unclean spirit has gone out of your daughter.' And when she returned 30 home, she found the child lying in bed; the spirit had left her.

On his return journey from Tyrian 31 territory he went by way of Sidon to the Sea of Galilee through the territory of the Ten Towns.[n] They brought to 32 him a man who was deaf and had an impediment in his speech, with the request that he would lay his hand on him. He took the man aside, away from 33 the crowd, put his fingers into his ears,

k *Some witnesses insert* with the fist; *others insert* frequently, *or* thoroughly.
l *Some witnesses read* establish.
m *Some witnesses here add* (16) If you have ears to hear, then hear.
n *Greek* Decapolis.

purification. **5:** The *ancient tradition* (also, v. 13) was not only the OT but also the oral expansion of the Law accepted by the Pharisees (see Mt.3.7 n.). **6–7:** Isa.29.13. **10a:** Exod.20.12; Deut.5.16. **10b:** Exod.21.17; Lev.20.9. **11:** The technicalities of the *Corban* oath are unclear. **15:** *Defile:* render ritually impure.
7.24–37: Healings (Mt.15.21–28). Jesus now appears in territory that is predominantly Gentile. **24–30:** See Mt.15.22 n. **26:** *Phoenician:* or, as in Mt.15.22, Canaanite. **31:** The itinerary

34 spat, and touched his tongue. Then, looking up to heaven, he sighed, and said to him, '*Ephphatha*', which means
33 'Be opened.' With that his ears were opened, and at the same time the impediment was removed and he spoke
36 plainly. Jesus forbade them to tell anyone; but the more he forbade them, the more they published it. Their astonish-
37 ment knew no bounds: 'All that he does, he does well,' they said; 'he even makes the deaf hear and the dumb speak.'

8 THERE WAS ANOTHER OCCASION ABOUT this time when a huge crowd had collected, and, as they had no food, Jesus called his disciples and said to them,
2 'I feel sorry for all these people; they have been with me now for three days
3 and have nothing to eat. If I send them home unfed, they will turn faint on the way; some of them have come from a
4 distance.' The disciples answered, 'How can anyone provide all these people
5 with bread in this lonely place?' 'How many loaves have you?' he asked; and
6 they answered, 'Seven.' So he ordered the people to sit down on the ground; then he took the seven loaves, and, after giving thanks to God, he broke the bread and gave it to his disciples to distribute; and they served it out to
7 the people. They had also a few small fishes, which he blessed and ordered
8 them to distribute. They all ate to their hearts' content, and seven baskets were
9 filled with the scraps that were left. The people numbered about four thousand.
10 Then he dismissed them; and, without delay, got into the boat with his disciples and went to the district of Dalmanutha.⁰
11 Then the Pharisees came out and engaged him in discussion. To test him they asked him for a sign from heaven.

He sighed deeply to himself and said, 12 'Why does this generation ask for a sign? I tell you this: no sign shall be given to this generation.' With that 13 he left them, re-embarked, and went off to the other side of the lake.

Now they had forgotten to take bread 14 with them; they had no more than one loaf in the boat. He began to warn 15 them: 'Beware,' he said, 'be on your guard against the leaven of the Pharisees and the leaven of Herod.' They said among themselves, 'It is 16 because we have no bread.' Knowing 17 what was in their minds, he asked them, 'Why do you talk about having no bread? Have you no inkling yet? Do you still not understand? Are your minds closed? You have eyes: can you 18 not see? You have ears: can you not hear? Have you forgotten? When I 19 broke the five loaves among five thousand, how many basketfuls of scraps did you pick up?' 'Twelve', they said. 'And how many when I broke 20 the seven loaves among four thousand?' They answered, 'Seven.' He said, 'Do 21 you still not understand?'

They arrived at Bethsaida. There the 22 people brought a blind man to Jesus and begged him to touch him. He took 23 the blind man by the hand and led him away out of the village. Then he spat on his eyes, laid his hands upon him, and asked whether he could see anything. The man's sight began to come 24 back, and he said, 'I see men; they look like trees, but they are walking about.' Jesus laid his hands on his eyes 25 again; he looked hard, and now he was cured so that he saw everything clearly. Then Jesus sent him home, saying, 26 'Do not tell anyone in the village.'ᵖ

o Some witnesses give Magedan; *others give* Magdala.
p Some witnesses read Do not go into the village.

---

described is strange. *Ten Towns:* see Mt.4.25 n. **34:** *Ephphatha* is transliterated Aram., compare 5.41 (see n.). **36:** See 1.34 n.
  8.1–10a: Feeding of four thousand. (Mt.15.32–39; compare 6.30–44). **6:** The words used are rather reminiscent of eucharistic language; see, e.g. Lk.22.19, but also Acts 27.35.
  8.10b–21: Sea crossing and discussions (Mt.16.1–12; Lk.11.29; 12.1). **12:** *No sign* is stronger than Mt.12.38–42 (see nn.); 16.4; Lk.11.29. **15:** *Leaven* is a conventional symbol for an evil influence; compare Mt.13.33 n. **17–18,21:** As in 6.52, the disciples are unable to understand. V. 18 brings to mind the outsiders who could not grasp the parables in 4.11–12 (compare Jer.5.21; Ezek.12.2; Isa.6.9–10; contrast Mt.16.12).
  8.22–26: Healing of a blind man. Mk. probably intended this to be understood symbolically: the disciples' eyes (v. 18) are also gradually opened, as the following narrative shows (vv. 27–29).

27 JESUS AND HIS DISCIPLES SET OUT FOR the villages of Caesarea Philippi. On the way he asked his disciples, 'Who 28 do men say I am?' They answered, 'Some say John the Baptist, others Elijah, others one of the prophets.' 29 'And you,' he asked, 'who do you say I am?' Peter replied: 'You are the 30 Messiah.' Then he gave them strict orders not to tell anyone about him; 31 and he began to teach them that the Son of Man had to undergo great sufferings, and to be rejected by the elders, chief priests, and doctors of the law; to be put to death, and to rise again 32 three days afterwards. He spoke about it plainly. At this Peter took him by 33 the arm and began to rebuke him. But Jesus turned round, and, looking at his disciples, rebuked Peter. 'Away with you, Satan,' he said; 'you think as men think, not as God thinks.'

34   Then he called the people to him, as well as his disciples, and said to them, 'Anyone who wishes to be a follower of mine must leave self behind; he must take up his cross, and come with 35 me. Whoever cares for his own safety is lost; but if a man will let himself be lost for my sake and for the Gospel, 36 that man is safe. What does a man gain by winning the whole world at the cost 37 of his true self? What can he give to 38 buy that self back? If anyone is ashamed of me and mine*q* in this wicked and godless age, the Son of Man will be ashamed of him, when he comes in the glory of his Father and of the holy angels.'*r*

9   He also said, 'I tell you this: there are some of those standing here who will not taste death before they have seen the kingdom of God already come in power.'

2   Six days later Jesus took Peter, James, and John with him and led them up a high mountain where they were alone; and in their presence he was 3 transfigured; his clothes became dazzling white, with a whiteness no bleacher 4 on earth could equal. They saw Elijah appear, and Moses with him, and there 5 they were, conversing with Jesus. Then Peter spoke: 'Rabbi,' he said, 'how good it is that we are here! Shall we make three shelters, one for you, one for Moses, and one for Elijah?' (For 6 he did not know what to say; they 7 were so terrified.) Then a cloud appeared, casting its shadow over them, and out of the cloud came a voice: 'This is my Son, my Beloved;*s* listen to him.' And now suddenly, when they 8 looked around, there was nobody to be seen but Jesus alone with themselves.

9   On their way down the mountain, he enjoined them not to tell anyone what they had seen until the Son of Man had risen from the dead. They seized 10 upon those words, and discussed among themselves what this 'rising from the dead' could mean. And they put a 11 question to him: 'Why do our teachers say that Elijah must come first?' He 12 replied, 'Yes, Elijah does come first to set everything right. Yet how is it*t* that the scriptures say of the Son of Man that he is to endure great sufferings and to be treated with contempt? How- 13

q Some witnesses read me and my words.
r Some witnesses read Father with the holy angels.
s Or This is my only Son.
t Or Elijah, you say, comes first to set everything right: then how is it . . .

8.27–33: Peter's confession and Jesus' prediction of his suffering (Mt.16.13–23; Lk.9.18–22). **27:** *Caesarea Philippi* locates the event on the edge of Gentile territory. **28:** The return of an ancient prophet (see 6.15 n.) or the coming of a prophet like Moses (Deut.18.15) or the appearance of a true prophet (1 Macc.4.46) in connection with the messianic age were popular expectations. **30:** *Messiah:* see Mt.1.1 n. **31:** This is the first of three (see 9.31–32; 10.33–34) predictions of the suffering of the *Son of Man* (see 2.10 n.). These predictions probably reflect the way in which the cross and resurrection were preached by early missionaries, so that their present form may have been influenced by that preaching. From this point the story of Mk. moves forward with the cross clearly in view. **32:** Suffering and death were not a part of the popular program for the Messiah. **33:** *Satan:* see Mt.4.1 n.
     8.34–9.1: Following Jesus (Mt.16.24–28; Lk.9.23–27). See Mt.10.38–39 n. **34:** The expression, *take up his cross*, is more than a metaphor for burden-bearing or even "sacrificial living"; the possibility of actually dying must be among the terms of discipleship.
     9.2–8: The transfiguration (Mt.17.1–8; Lk.9.28–36). See notes on Mt.17.1–8.
     9.9–13: Elijah has come (Mt.17.9–13). **9–10:** Since death did not fit the conception held of the *Son of Man* (8.32), it seemed impossible to think of his resurrection. **11–13:** On *Elijah* and his identification with the Baptist, see 6.15 n.; 8.28 n.; Lk.1.17 n.

ever, I tell you, Elijah has already come and they have worked their will upon him, as the scriptures say of him.'

14 When they came back to the disciples they saw a large crowd surrounding them and lawyers arguing with them. 15 As soon as they saw Jesus the whole crowd were overcome with awe, and they ran forward to welcome him. 16 He asked them, 'What is this argument 17 about?' A man in the crowd spoke up: 'Master, I brought my son to you. He is possessed by a spirit which makes 18 him speechless. Whenever it attacks him, it dashes him to the ground, and he foams at the mouth, grinds his teeth, and goes rigid. I asked your disciples to cast it out, but they 19 failed.' Jesus answered: 'What an unbelieving and perverse generation! How long shall I be with you? How long must I endure you? Bring him to 20 me.' So they brought the boy to him; and as soon as the spirit saw him it threw the boy into convulsions, and he fell on the ground and rolled about 21 foaming at the mouth. Jesus asked his father, 'How long has he been like this?' 'From childhood,' he replied; 22 'often it has tried to make an end of him by throwing him into the fire or into water. But if it is at all possible for you, take pity upon us and help us.' 23 'If it is possible!' said Jesus. 'Everything is possible to one who has faith.' 24 'I have faith,' cried the boy's father; 25 'help me where faith falls short.' Jesus saw then that the crowd was closing in upon them, so he rebuked the unclean spirit. 'Deaf and dumb spirit,' he said, 'I command you, come out of him 26 and never go back!' After crying aloud and racking him fiercely, it came out; and the boy looked like a corpse; in 27 fact, many said, 'He is dead.' But Jesus

took his hand and raised him to his feet, and he stood up.

Then Jesus went indoors, and his 28 disciples asked him privately, 'Why could not we cast it out?' He said, 29 'There is no means of casting out this sort but prayer.'[u]

THEY NOW LEFT THAT DISTRICT AND 30 made a journey through Galilee. Jesus wished it to be kept secret; for he was 31 teaching his disciples, and telling them, 'The Son of Man is now to be given up into the power of men, and they will kill him, and three days after being killed, he will rise again.' But they 32 did not understand what he said, and were afraid to ask.

So they came to Capernaum; and 33 when he was indoors, he asked them, 'What were you arguing about on the way?' They were silent, because on the 34 way they had been discussing who was the greatest. He sat down, called the 35 Twelve, and said to them, 'If anyone wants to be first, he must make himself last of all and servant of all.' Then he 36 took a child, set him in front of them, and put his arm round him. 'Whoever 37 receives one of these children in my name', he said, 'receives me; and whoever receives me, receives not me but the One who sent me.'

John said to him, 'Master, we saw a 38 man driving out devils in your name, and as he was not one of us, we tried to stop him.' Jesus said, 'Do not stop 39 him; no one who does a work of divine power in my name will be able the next moment to speak evil of me. For he who 40 is not against us is on our side. I tell 41 you this: if anyone gives you a cup of water to drink because you are followers

u *Some witnesses add* and fasting.

9.14–29: An epileptic boy (Mt.17.14–20; Lk.9.37–43a). 23: *Faith*, an important element in early Christian miracle stories, receives special stress in this account; the father's response (v. 24) is that of every man who knows his faith is incomplete. 29: Only *prayer* succeeds in the difficult situation because only God's power is adequate.
9.30–32: The second prediction (see 8.31 n.) of suffering (Mt.17.22–23; Lk.9.43b–45) is given; as often in Mk., the disciples still do not understand (see 8.17–18,21 n.).
9.33–37: Greatness and servanthood (Mt.18.1–5; Lk.9.46–48). 35: 10.43–44; Mt.20.26–27; 23.11; Lk.22.26. 37: Mt.10.40.
9.38–41: An exorcist who is not a disciple (Lk.9.49–50). 39–40: The saying assumes that the unnamed exorcist is friendly, as v. 41 perhaps shows. Mt.12.30 and Lk.11.23 preserve a similar saying which assumes the opposite, i.e. the one not clearly "with us" is "against us." 41: See Mt.10.42 for a somewhat different version of this verse.

of the Messiah, that man assuredly will not go unrewarded.

42 'As for the man who is a cause of stumbling to one of these little ones who have faith, it would be better for him to be thrown into the sea with a 43 millstone round his neck. If your hand is your undoing, cut it off; it is better for you to enter into life maimed than to keep both hands and go to hell and 45 the unquenchable fire.*v* And if your foot is your undoing, cut it off; it is better to enter into life a cripple than to keep both your feet and be thrown 47 into hell.*w* And if it is your eye, tear it out; it is better to enter into the kingdom of God with one eye than to keep both eyes and be thrown into hell, 48 where the devouring worm never dies and the fire is not quenched.

49 'For everyone will be salted with fire.
50 'Salt is a good thing; but if the salt loses its saltness, what will you season it with?

'Have salt in yourselves; and be*x* at peace with one another.'

10 ON LEAVING THOSE PARTS HE CAME into the regions of Judaea and Transjordan; and when a crowd gathered round him once again, he followed his usual practice and taught them. 2 The question was put to him:*y* 'Is it lawful for a man to divorce his wife?' 3 This was to test him. He asked in return, 'What did Moses command 4 you?' They answered, 'Moses permitted a man to divorce his wife by note 5 of dismissal.' Jesus said to them, 'It was because your minds were closed 6 that he made this rule for you; but in the beginning, at the creation, God 7 made them male and female. For this reason a man shall leave his father and

mother, and be made one with his wife;*z* and the two shall become one 8 flesh. It follows that they are no longer two individuals: they are one flesh. What God has joined together, man 9 must not separate.'

When they were indoors again the 10 disciples questioned him about this matter; he said to them, 'Whoever 11 divorces his wife and marries another commits adultery against her: so too, 12 if she divorces her husband and marries another, she commits adultery.'

They brought children for him to 13 touch. The disciples rebuked them, but when Jesus saw this he was in- 14 dignant, and said to them, 'Let the children come to me; do not try to stop them; for the kingdom of God belongs to such as these. I tell you, 15 whoever does not accept the kingdom of God like a child will never enter it.' And he put his arms round them, laid 16 his hands upon them, and blessed them.

As he was starting out on a journey, 17 a stranger ran up, and, kneeling before him, asked, 'Good Master, what must I do to win eternal life?' Jesus said to 18 him, 'Why do you call me good? No one is good except God alone. You 19 know the commandments: "Do not murder; do not commit adultery; do not steal; do not give false evidence; do not defraud; honour your father and mother."' 'But, Master,' he replied, 20 'I have kept all these since I was a boy.' Jesus looked straight at him; his heart 21 warmed to him, and he said, 'One thing

v Some witnesses add (44) *where the devouring worm never dies and the fire is not quenched.*
w Some witnesses add (46) *where the devouring worm never dies and the fire is not quenched.*
x Or Have the salt of fellowship and be . . .; *or* You have the salt of fellowship between you; then be . . .
y Some witnesses read The Pharisees came forward and asked him the question . . .
z Some witnesses omit and be made . . . wife.

9.42–50: On being an example (Mt.18.6–9; Lk.17.1–2). Mk. uses the negative illustration of the *cause of stumbling* (v. 42) and the positive metaphor of *salt* which *seasons* (v. 50) to encourage exemplary living. **42–48:** See Mt.18.7–9 n. **50:** Compare Mt.5.13; Lk.14.34–35.

10.1–12: Marriage and divorce (Mt.19.1–12; compare Mt.5.31–32 n.; Lk.16.18; 1 Cor.7.10–11). **1:** *Judaea and Transjordan* anticipates v. 32. **3:** The question is only a *test*, since the Law clearly allows divorce. **4–5:** The divorce provisions of Deut.24.1–4 were provided to guide men whose *minds were closed* to the intention of the Creator. **6:** Gen.1.27. **7–8:** From Gen.2.(21–)24 Jesus argues that in God's purpose marriage establishes an indissoluble unity. **12:** Since Jewish women could not divorce their husbands, this verse has been added to meet the needs of a Gentile environment.

10.13–16: Children and the kingdom (Mt.19.13–15; Lk.18.15–17). **15:** *Like a child:* with simple trust; see Mt.18.3.

10.17–31: Possessions and the kingdom (Mt.19.16–30; Lk.18.18–30). **17–19a:** *No one is good except God:* see Mt.19.16–17 n. **19:** Exod.20.12–16; Deut.5.16–20. **21:** See Mt.19.21 n.

you lack: go, sell everything you have, and give to the poor, and you will have riches in heaven; and come, follow me.' At these words his face fell and he went away with a heavy heart; for he was a man of great wealth.

23 Jesus looked round at his disciples and said to them, 'How hard it will be for the wealthy to enter the kingdom 24 of God!' They were amazed that he should say this, but Jesus insisted, 'Children, how hard it is*a* to enter the 25 kingdom of God! It is easier for a camel to pass through the eye of a needle than for a rich man to enter the kingdom of 26 God.' They were more astonished than ever, and said to one another, 'Then 27 who can be saved?' Jesus looked at them and said, 'For men it is impossible, but not for God; everything is possible for God.'

28 At this Peter spoke. 'We here', he said, 'have left everything to become 29 your followers.' Jesus said, 'I tell you this: there is no one who has given up home, brothers or sisters, mother, father or children, or land, for my sake 30 and for the Gospel, who will not receive in this age a hundred times as much— houses, brothers and sisters, mothers and children, and land—and persecutions besides; and in the age to come 31 eternal life. But many who are first will be last and the last first.'

Challenge to Jerusalem

32 THEY WERE ON THE ROAD, GOING UP TO Jerusalem, Jesus leading the way; and the disciples were filled with awe, while those who followed behind were afraid. He took the Twelve aside and began to tell them what was to happen to him. 'We are now going to Jerusalem,' he 33 said; 'and the Son of Man will be given up to the chief priests and the doctors of the law; they will condemn him to death and hand him over to the foreign power. He will be mocked and spat 34 upon, flogged and killed; and three days afterwards, he will rise again.'

James and John, the sons of Zebedee, 35 approached him and said, 'Master, we should like you to do us a favour.' 'What is it you want me to do?' he 36 asked. They answered, 'Grant us the 37 right to sit in state with you, one at your right and the other at your left.' Jesus 38 said to them, 'You do not understand what you are asking. Can you drink the cup that I drink, or be baptized with the baptism I am baptized with?' 'We can', they answered. Jesus said, 39 'The cup that I drink you shall drink, and the baptism I am baptized with shall be your baptism; but to sit at my 40 right or left is not for me to grant; it is for those to whom it has already been assigned.'*b*

When the other ten heard this, they 41 were indignant with James and John. Jesus called them to him and said, 42 'You know that in the world the recognized rulers lord it over their subjects, and their great men make them feel the weight of authority. That is not 43 the way with you; among you, whoever wants to be great must be your servant, and whoever wants to be first must be 44 the willing slave of all. For even the 45 Son of Man did not come to be served but to serve, and to give up his life as a ransom for many.'

a *Some witnesses insert* for those who trust in riches.
b *Some witnesses add* by my Father.

25–27: *Eye of a needle:* see Mt.19.24 n. 28–30: See Mt.19.27,29 n. 31: Mt.19.30; 20.16; Lk.13.30.
  10.32–34: **The third prediction** (see 8.31 n.) **of suffering** (Mt.20.17–19; Lk.18.31–34). The story must end in *Jerusalem* (v. 32) and Mk. has had the end in mind from the beginning. Yet, the geographical notice takes on increased importance through its connection with the third passion prediction (vv. 33–34) and by the subsequent attention to itinerary (v. 46; 11.1). The tension and drama mount as the account moves toward its climax.
  10.35–45: **Position in the kingdom** (Mt.20.20–28; Lk.22.24–27). 35: *James and John*, along with Peter, are given unusual prominence in the Gospels (e.g. 1.16–20; 9.2). 37: Seats on the *right* and *left* hands are reserved for men of great authority. 38: The *cup* immediately suggests 14.36; but as a metaphor for experiencing trouble, "drinking of a *cup*" was a familiar manner of speaking (e.g. Ps.75.8; compare Jn.18.11). Unless the phrase about *baptism* has been added as a way of referring specifically to Christian martyrdom, the saying alludes to the ancient picture of the sufferer as a victim of overwhelming "waves" of tribulation; compare Lk.12.50. 40: Tfn. *b* correctly interprets the verse; see Mt.20.23. 45: Lit. *ransom* is the sum paid to win freedom for slaves or captives; it is one of several metaphors employed to express the idea

46 They came to Jericho; and as he was leaving the town, with his disciples and a large crowd, Bartimaeus son of Timaeus, a blind beggar, was seated at 47 the roadside. Hearing that it was Jesus of Nazareth, he began to shout, 'Son of 48 David, Jesus, have pity on me!' Many of the people told him to hold his tongue; but he shouted all the more, 49 'Son of David, have pity on me.' Jesus stopped and said, 'Call him'; so they called the blind man and said, 'Take 50 heart; stand up; he is calling you.' At that he threw off his cloak, sprang up, 51 and came to Jesus. Jesus said to him, 'What do you want me to do for you?' 'Master,' the blind man answered, 'I 52 want my sight back.' Jesus said to him, 'Go; your faith has cured you.' And at once he recovered his sight and followed him on the road.

11 THEY WERE NOW APPROACHING JERU-salem, and when they reached Beth-phage and Bethany, at the Mount of 2 Olives, he sent two of his disciples with these instructions: 'Go to the village opposite, and, just as you enter, you will find tethered there a colt which no one has yet ridden. Untie it and bring 3 it here. If anyone asks, "Why are you doing that?", say, "Our Master*c* needs it, and will send it back here without 4 delay."' So they went off, and found the colt tethered at a door outside in 5 the street. They were untying it when some of the bystanders asked, 'What 6 are you doing, untying that colt?' They

answered as Jesus had told them, and were then allowed to take it. So they 7 brought the colt to Jesus and spread their cloaks on it, and he mounted. And people carpeted the road with 8 their cloaks, while others spread brush-wood which they had cut in the fields; and those who went ahead and the 9 others who came behind shouted, 'Hosanna! Blessings on him who comes in the name of the Lord! Blessings on 10 the coming kingdom of our father David! Hosanna in the heavens!'

He entered Jerusalem and went into 11 the temple, where he looked at the whole scene; but, as it was now late, he went out to Bethany with the Twelve.

On the following day, after they had 12 left Bethany, he felt hungry, and, 13 noticing in the distance a fig-tree in leaf, he went to see if he could find any-thing on it. But when he came there he found nothing but leaves; for it was not the season for figs. He said to the 14 tree, 'May no one ever again eat fruit from you!' And his disciples were listening.

So they came to Jerusalem, and he 15 went into the temple and began driving out those who bought and sold in the temple. He upset the tables of the money-changers and the seats of the dealers in pigeons; and he would not 16 allow anyone to use the temple court as a thoroughfare for carrying goods.

c Or Its owner.

---

that Jesus' death effects mankind's salvation. The Heb. term for *many* is equivalent to "all" in some contexts.

10.46–52: Blind Bartimaeus healed (Mt.20.29–34; Lk.18.35–43). **46:** *Son of Timaeus* simply translates the Aram. name, *Bartimaeus*. **47:** *Son of David:* see Mt.1.1 n. **52:** *Cured:* see Lk.7.50 n. With Jerusalem and the cross so near, *followed him on the way* implies courageous discipleship.

11.1–13.37: Jesus in Jerusalem (Mt.21.1–25.46; Lk.19.28–21.38). From this point, the Gospel narrative becomes increasingly circumstantial with respect to sequence of events, locations (four place names in 11.1!), and time (especially in Mk. where the material is organized carefully, using the scheme of the "days of the last week"). Such attention to detail and the dramatic character of the reported events and controversies signal the approaching climax of the story.

11.1–11: The entry into Jerusalem (Mt.21.1–9; Lk.19.28–38; Jn.12.12–19). **1:** See Mt.21.1 n. **9–10:** Ps.118.25–26. *Hosanna:* see Mt.21.9 n. **11:** Nearby *Bethany* seems to have served as Jesus' base for Jerusalem activities; only Mk. delays the cleansing of the Temple to the next day (see Mt.21.12; Lk.19.45).

11.12–14: The cursing of the fig tree (Mt.21.18–19). The story is in two parts, with the end in vv. 20–25. In Mt. the two parts are presented as a single unit following the cleansing of the Temple. **14:** See Mt.21.19 n.

11.15–19: Cleansing of the Temple (Mt.21.10–17; Lk.19.45–48). **15–16:** Jesus' objections to the misuse of the Temple agree with Jewish regulations of the time. On *temple, money-changers,*

17 Then he began to teach them, and said, 'Does not Scripture say, "My house shall be called a house of prayer for all the nations"? But you have made it a 18 robbers' cave.' The chief priests and the doctors of the law heard of this and sought some means of making away with him; for they were afraid of him, because the whole crowd was spell- 19 bound by his teaching. And when evening came he went out of the city.

20 Early next morning, as they passed by, they saw that the fig-tree had 21 withered from the roots up; and Peter, recalling what had happened, said to him, 'Rabbi, look, the fig-tree which 22 you cursed has withered.' Jesus an- 23 swered them, 'Have faith in God. I tell you this: if anyone says to this mountain, "Be lifted from your place and hurled into the sea", and has no inward doubts, but believes that what he says is happening, it will be done 24 for him. I tell you, then, whatever you ask for in prayer, believe that you have received it and it will be yours.

25 'And when you stand praying, if you have a grievance against anyone, for- give him, so that your Father in heaven may forgive you the wrongs you have done.'d

[margin handwritten: They stood w/ hands in "orans" position]

[margin handwritten: → means "anything"!]

27 THEY CAME ONCE MORE TO JERUSALEM. And as he was walking in the temple court the chief priests, lawyers, and 28 elders came to him and said, 'By what authority are you acting like this? Who gave you authority to act in this way?' 29 Jesus said to them, 'I have a question to ask you too; and if you give me an answer, I will tell you by what authority 30 I act. The baptism of John: was it from 31 God, or from men? Answer me.' This set them arguing among themselves: 'What shall we say? If we say, "from God", he will say, "Then why did you 32 not believe him?" Shall we say, "from men"?'—but they were afraid of the people, for all held that John was in fact a prophet. So they answered, 'We 33 do not know.' And Jesus said to them, 'Then neither will I tell you by what authority I act.'

He went on to speak to them in 12 parables: 'A man planted a vineyard and put a wall round it, hewed out a winepress, and built a watch-tower; then he let it out to vine-growers and went abroad. When the season came, 2 he sent a servant to the tenants to collect from them his share of the produce. But they took him, thrashed him, and 3 sent him away empty-handed. Again, 4 he sent them another servant, whom they beat about the head and treated outrageously. So he sent another, and 5 that one they killed; and many more besides, of whom they beat some, and killed others. He had now only one 6 left to send, his own dear son.e In the end he sent him. "They will respect my son", he said. But the tenants said to 7 one another, "This is the heir; come on, let us kill him, and the property will be ours." So they seized him and 8 killed him, and flung his body out of the vineyard. What will the owner of 9 the vineyard do? He will come and put the tenants to death and give the vineyard to others.

'Can it be that you have never read 10 this text: "The stone which the builders rejected has become the main corner- stone. This is the Lord's doing, and it is 11 wonderful in our eyes"?'

Then they began to look for a way to 12 arrest him, for they saw that the parable was aimed at them; but they were afraid of the people, so they left him alone and went away.

A NUMBER OF PHARISEES AND MEN OF 13 Herod's party were sent to trap him with a question. They came and said, 14

d *Some witnesses add* (26) But if you do not forgive others, then the wrongs you have done will not be for- given by your Father in heaven. e *Or* his only son.

---

pigeons, see Mt.21.12 n. **17**: *For all nations* probably indicates a concern for Gentile worship; see Mt.21.12 n.; Isa.56.7; Jer.7.11; compare Mt.21.13; Lk.19.46.
11.20–25: The lesson of the fig tree. See Mt.21.20–22 n.
11.27–33: Jesus' authority challenged (Mt.21.23–27; Lk.20.1–8). **30**: *From God:* see Mt.21.25 n. **32**: *Prophet:* see 8.28 n.
12.1–12: The evil tenants (Mt.21.33–46; Lk.20.9–19). **1**: On *parables, vineyard,* see Mt.21.33 n. **2**: On *servant, tenants,* see Mt.21.34 n. **6**: *Son:* Jesus. **10–11**: Ps.118.22–23. Early Christians applied this and other OT "stone sayings" to Jesus; compare 1 Pet.2.6–8.
12.13–17: Caesar's tax (Mt.22.15–22; Lk.20.20–26). **14**: *Taxes:* see Mt.22.17 n.

'Master, you are an honest man, we know, and truckle to no one, whoever he may be; you teach in all honesty the way of life that God requires. Are we or are we not permitted to pay taxes to 15 the Roman Emperor? Shall we pay or not?' He saw how crafty their question was, and said, 'Why are you trying to catch me out? Fetch me a silver piece, 16 and let me look at it.' They brought one, and he said to them, 'Whose head is this, and whose inscription?' 'Caesar's', 17 they replied. Then Jesus said, 'Pay Caesar what is due to Caesar, and pay God what is due to God.' And they heard him with astonishment.

18 Next Sadducees came to him. (It is they who say that there is no resurrec-19 tion.) Their question was this: 'Master, Moses laid it down for us that if there are brothers, and one dies leaving a wife but no child, then the next should marry the widow and carry on his 20 brother's family. Now there were seven brothers. The first took a wife and died without issue. Then the second married 21 her, and he too died without issue. So 22 did the third. Eventually the seven of them died, all without issue. Finally 23 the woman died. At the resurrection, when they come back to life, whose wife will she be, since all seven had married 24 her?' Jesus said to them, 'You are mistaken, and surely this is the reason: you do not know either the scriptures 25 or the power of God. When they rise from the dead, men and women do not marry; they are like angels in heaven.

26 'But about the resurrection of the dead, have you never read in the Book of Moses, in the story of the burning bush, how God spoke to him and said, "I am the God of Abraham, the God 27 of Isaac, and the God of Jacob"? God is not God of the dead but of the living. You are greatly mistaken.'

28 Then one of the lawyers, who had been listening to these discussions and had noted how well he answered, came forward and asked him, 'Which commandment is first of all?' Jesus an-29 swered, 'The first is, "Hear, O Israel: the Lord our God is the only Lord; love the Lord your God with all your 30 heart, with all your soul, with all your mind, and with all your strength." The second is this: "Love your neigh-31 bour as yourself." There is no other commandment greater than these.' The lawyer said to him, 'Well said, 32 Master. You are right in saying that God is one and beside him there is no other. And to love him with all your 33 heart, all your understanding, and all your strength, and to love your neighbour as yourself—that is far more than any burnt offerings or sacrifices.' When 34 Jesus saw how sensibly he answered, he said to him, 'You are not far from the kingdom of God.'

After that nobody ventured to put any more questions to him; and Jesus 35 went on to say, as he taught in the temple, 'How can the teachers of the law maintain that the Messiah is "Son of David"? David himself said, when 36 inspired by the Holy Spirit, "The Lord said to my Lord, 'Sit at my right hand until I put your enemies under your feet.'" David himself calls him "Lord"; 37 how can he also be David's son?'

There was a great crowd and they listened eagerly.*f* He said as he taught 38 them, 'Beware of the doctors of the law, who love to walk up and down in long robes, receiving respectful greetings in the street; and to have the chief 39 seats in synagogues, and places of honour at feasts. These are the men 40 who eat up the property of widows, while they say long prayers for appearance' sake, and they will receive the severest sentence.'*g*

Once he was standing opposite the 41

f Or The mass of the people listened eagerly.
g Or As for those who eat up the property of widows, while they say long prayers for appearance' sake, they will have an even sterner judgement to face.

12.18–27: A resurrection puzzle (Mt.22.23–33; Lk.20.27–40). **18:** On differences between *Sadducees* and *Pharisees* (v. 13), see Mt.3.7 n. **19:** Deut.25.5–10. **24:** *Scriptures:* v. 26; see Mt.22.30 n. **26:** Exod.3.6.

12.28–34: The double commandment of love (Mt.22.34–40; compare Lk.10.25–28). **30:** Deut.6.4–5; the verses comprise the "Jewish creed." **31:** Lev.19.18. **32–34:** Compare Lk.10.27 n. **12.35–37: Messiah, son of David** (Mt.22.41–46; Lk.20.41–44). **35:** *Messiah . . . son of David:* see Mt.1.1 n. **36:** Ps.110.1; see Mt.22.44 n. **37:** See Mt.22.45 n.

12.38–40: Warning against pride (see Mt.23.6; Lk.11.43; 20.45–47).

temple treasury, watching as people dropped their money into the chest. Many rich people were giving large 42 sums. Presently there came a poor widow who dropped in two tiny coins, 43 together worth a farthing. He called his disciples to him. 'I tell you this,' he said: 'this poor widow has given 44 more than any of the others; for those others who have given had more than enough, but she, with less than enough, has given all that she had to live on.'

13 AS HE WAS LEAVING THE TEMPLE, ONE of his disciples exclaimed, 'Look, Master, what huge stones! What fine 2 buildings!' Jesus said to him, 'You see these great buildings? Not one stone will be left upon another; all will be thrown down.'

3 When he was sitting on the Mount of Olives facing the temple he was questioned privately by Peter, James, John, 4 and Andrew. 'Tell us,' they said, 'when will this happen? What will be the sign when the fulfilment of all this is at hand?'

5 Jesus began: 'Take care that no one 6 misleads you. Many will come claiming my name, and saying, "I am he"; and many will be misled by them.

7 'When you hear the noise of battle near at hand and the news of battles far away, do not be alarmed. Such things are bound to happen; but the end 8 is still to come. For nation will make war upon nation, kingdom upon kingdom; there will be earthquakes in many places; there will be famines. With these things the birth-pangs of the new age begin.

9 'As for you, be on your guard. You will be handed over to the courts. You will be flogged in synagogues. You will be summoned to appear before governors and kings on my account to testify in their presence. But before 10 the end the Gospel must be proclaimed to all nations. So when you are 11 arrested and taken away, do not worry beforehand about what you will say, but when the time comes say whatever is given you to say; for it is not you who will be speaking, but the Holy Spirit. Brother will betray brother to 12 death, and the father his child; children will turn against their parents and send them to their death. All will hate you 13 for your allegiance to me; but the man who holds out to the end will be saved.

'But when you see "the abomination 14 of desolation" usurping a place which is not his (let the reader understand), then those who are in Judaea must take to the hills. If a man is on the roof, he 15 must not come down into the house to fetch anything out; if in the field, he 16 must not turn back for his coat. Alas 17 for women with child in those days, and for those who have children at the breast! Pray that it may not come in 18 winter. For those days will bring 19 distress such as never has been until now since the beginning of the world which God created—and will never be again. If the Lord had not cut short 20 that time of troubles, no living thing could survive. However, for the sake of his own, whom he has chosen, he has cut short the time.

'Then, if anyone says to you, "Look, 21 here is the Messiah", or, "Look, there he is", do not believe it. Impostors will 22 come claiming to be messiahs or prophets, and they will produce signs and wonders to mislead God's chosen, if such a thing were possible. But you 23 be on your guard; I have forewarned you of it all.

'But in those days, after that distress, 24

12.41–44: The widow's gift (Lk.21.1–4). **41:** *Chest:* see Lk.21.1 n. **42:** *Coins:* see Lk.21.2 n.
13.1–37: The eschatological discourse. All three synoptic Gospels introduce at this point (Mt.24.1; Lk.21.5) a collection of sayings, some of which relate to the destruction of Jerusalem, some to the end of history. Standing immediately before the passion narrative (chs. 14–15), this chapter, built out of diverse traditions, serves as a solemn final message of judgment and warning.
13.1–2: Temple's destruction predicted (Mt.24.1–3 n.; Lk.21.5–7).
13.3–37: Signs, false signs, and warnings (Mt.24.4–44; Lk.21.8–36). **3:** *Mount of Olives:* Mt.21.1 n. The limiting of the audience to *Peter, James, John,* and *Andrew* makes the discourse in Mk. secret teaching. **5–6:** See vv. 21–23. **8:** *Birth-pangs:* see Mt.24.8 n. **9–13:** Mt.10.17–21. **11:** Mt.10.20; Lk.12.11–12. **13:** Mt.10.22. **14:** *"The abomination of desolation":* see Mt.24.15 n. **16:** Lk.17.31. **19:** Dan.12.1. **22:** Deut.13.1–2. **23:** *Forewarned:* see vv. 5–6. **24–26:** See Mt.24.29 n.

the sun will be darkened, the moon will
25 not give her light; the stars will come
falling from the sky, the celestial powers
26 will be shaken. Then they will see the
Son of Man coming in the clouds with
27 great power and glory, and he will send
out the angels and gather his chosen
from the four winds, from the farthest
bounds of earth to the farthest bounds
of heaven.
28   'Learn a lesson from the fig-tree.
When its tender shoots appear and are
breaking into leaf, you know that
29 summer is near. In the same way,
when you see all this happening, you
may know that the end is near,*h* at the
30 very door. I tell you this: the present
31 generation will live to see it all. Heaven
and earth will pass away; my words
will never pass away.
32   'But about that day or that hour no one
knows, not even the angels in heaven,
not even the Son; only the Father.
33   'Be alert, be wakeful.*i* You do not
34 know when the moment comes. It is
like a man away from home: he has
left his house and put his servants in
charge, each with his own work to do,
and he has ordered the door-keeper to
35 stay awake. Keep awake, then, for you
do not know when the master of the
house is coming. Evening or midnight,
36 cock-crow or early dawn—if he comes
suddenly, he must not find you asleep.
37 And what I say to you, I say to everyone: Keep awake.'

The final conflict

14 NOW THE FESTIVAL OF PASSOVER AND
Unleavened Bread was only two days
off; and the chief priests and the doctors
of the law were trying to devise some
cunning plan to seize him and put him
2 to death. 'It must not be during the
festival,' they said, 'or we should have
rioting among the people.'

Jesus was at Bethany, in the house of 3
Simon the leper. As he sat at table, a
woman came in carrying a small bottle
of very costly perfume, pure oil of nard.
She broke it open and poured the oil
over his head. Some of those present 4
said to one another angrily, 'Why this
waste? The perfume might have been 5
sold for thirty pounds*j* and the money
given to the poor'; and they turned
upon her with fury. But Jesus said, 6
'Let her alone. Why must you make
trouble for her? It is a fine thing she has
done for me. You have the poor among 7
you always, and you can help them
whenever you like; but you will not
always have me. She has done what lay 8
in her power; she is beforehand with
anointing my body for burial. I tell 9
you this: wherever in all the world the
Gospel is proclaimed, what she has
done will be told as her memorial.'
    Then Judas Iscariot, one of the 10
Twelve, went to the chief priests to
betray him to them. When they heard 11
what he had come for, they were
greatly pleased, and promised him
money; and he began to look for a
good opportunity to betray him.

NOW ON THE FIRST DAY OF UNLEAVENED 12
Bread, when the Passover lambs were
being slaughtered, his disciples said to
him, 'Where would you like us to go
and prepare for your Passover supper?'
So he sent out two of his disciples with 13
these instructions: 'Go into the city,
and a man will meet you carrying a jar
of water. Follow him, and when he 14
enters a house give this message to the
householder: "The Master says, 'Where
is the room reserved for me to eat the
Passover with my disciples?'" He will 15
show you a large room upstairs, set out
in readiness. Make the preparations
for us there.' Then the disciples went 16

h Or that he is near.   i Some witnesses add and pray.
j Literally 300 denarii; some witnesses read more than
300 denarii.

26: Dan.7.13. 27: Deut.30.4; Isa.60.4–5. 30: 9.1; see Mt.24.34 n. Compare v. 32. 31: Compare
Mt.5.17; Lk.16.17.
    14.1–15.47: The final conflict (Mt.26.1–27.66; Lk.22.1–23.56; Jn. chs.12–19). See Lk.22.1–
23.56 n. 1: *Passover* and *Unleavened Bread* were originally two festivals (see Lev.23.5–6) which
had coalesced as a celebration of the deliverance from Egypt (Exod.12.1–20). 3–9: Mt.26.6–13
(similar stories in Lk.7.36–50; Jn.12.1–8). 3: *Poured:* see Mt.26.7 n. 8: See Mt.26.12 n. 10–11:
Mt.26.14–16; Lk.22.3–6.
    14.12–16: Preparation for the Passover (Mt.26.17–19; Lk.22.7–13). 12: See Mt.26.17 n.
14–15: See Mt.26.18 n.

off, and when they came into the city they found everything just as he had told them. So they prepared for Passover.

17 In the evening he came to the house 18 with the Twelve. As they sat at supper Jesus said, 'I tell you this: one of you will betray me—one who is eating with 19 me.' At this they were dismayed; and one by one they said to him, 'Not I, 20 surely?' 'It is one of the Twelve', he said, 'who is dipping into the same 21 bowl with me. The Son of Man is going the way appointed for him in the scriptures; but alas for that man by whom the Son of Man is betrayed! It would be better for that man if he had never been born.'

22 During supper he took bread, and having said the blessing he broke it and gave it to them, with the words: 'Take 23 this; this is my body.' Then he took a cup, and having offered thanks to God he gave it to them; and they all drank 24 from it. And he said, 'This is my blood, the blood of the covenant, shed for 25 many. I tell you this: never again shall I drink from the fruit of the vine until that day when I drink it new in the kingdom of God.'

26 After singing the Passover Hymn, they went out to the Mount of Olives. 27 And Jesus said, 'You will all fall from your faith; for it stands written: "I will strike the shepherd down and the 28 sheep will be scattered." Nevertheless, after I am raised again I will go on 29 before you into Galilee.' Peter answered, 'Everyone else may fall away, 30 but I will not.' Jesus said, 'I tell you this: today, this very night, before the cock crows twice, you yourself will 31 disown me three times.' But he insisted and repeated: 'Even if I must die with you, I will never disown you.' And they all said the same.

32 WHEN THEY REACHED A PLACE CALLED Gethsemane, he said to his disciples,

'Sit here while I pray.' And he took 33 Peter and James and John with him. Horror and dismay came over him, and he said to them, 'My heart is ready 34 to break with grief; stop here, and stay awake.' Then he went forward a little, 35 threw himself on the ground, and prayed that, if it were possible, this hour might pass him by. 'Abba, Father,' 36 he said, 'all things are possible to thee; take this cup away from me. Yet not what I will, but what thou wilt.'

He came back and found them 37 asleep; and he said to Peter, 'Asleep, Simon? Were you not able to stay awake for one hour? Stay awake, all 38 of you; and pray that you may be spared the test. The spirit is willing, but the flesh is weak.' Once more he 39 went away and prayed.[k] On his return 40 he found them asleep again, for their eyes were heavy; and they did not know how to answer him.

The third time he came and said to 41 them, 'Still sleeping? Still taking your ease? Enough![l] The hour has come. The Son of Man is betrayed to sinful men. Up, let us go forward! My 42 betrayer is upon us.'

Suddenly, while he was still speaking, 43 Judas, one of the Twelve, appeared, and with him was a crowd armed with swords and cudgels, sent by the chief priests, lawyers, and elders. Now the 44 traitor had agreed with them upon a signal: 'The one I kiss is your man; seize him and get him safely away.' When he reached the spot, he stepped 45 forward at once and said to Jesus, 'Rabbi', and kissed him. Then they 46 seized him and held him fast.

One of the party[m] drew his sword, 47 and struck at the High Priest's servant, cutting off his ear. Then Jesus spoke: 48 'Do you take me for a bandit, that you have come out with swords and cudgels

k Some witnesses add using the same words.
l The Greek is obscure; a possible meaning is 'The money has been paid', 'The account is settled.'
m Or of the bystanders.

14.17–25: The Last Supper (Mt.26.20–29; Lk.22.14–23). **17–21:** See also Jn.13.21–30. **18:** Ps.41.9. *Sat:* see Mt.26.20 n. **21:** *Scriptures:* see Mt.26.24 n. **22–25:** See also 1 Cor.11.23–26. **24:** *Blood of the covenant:* Mt.26.28 n.; Lk.22.17–19 n. *Many:* see Mk.10.45 n.
14.26–42: Gethsemane (Mt.26.30–46; Lk.22.39–46). **26:** Jn.18.1. *Hymn:* see Mt.26.30 n. **27:** Zech.13.7. **28:** See 16.7. **32–42:** See Lk.22.40–46 n. **34–36:** Compare Jn.12.27–28. **34:** Ps.42.6. **36:** *Abba:* Aram. for "Father"; see Rom.8.15; Gal.4.6. *Cup:* see Mk.10.38 n.; Jn.18.11.
14.43–52: The arrest (Mt.26.47–56; Lk.22.47–53; Jn.18.2–12). **44:** *Kiss:* see Mt.26.48 n.

49 to arrest me? Day after day I was within your reach as I taught in the temple, and you did not lay hands on me. But let the scriptures be fulfilled.'
50 Then the disciples all deserted him and ran away.

51 Among those following was a young man with nothing on but a linen cloth.
52 They tried to seize him; but he slipped out of the linen cloth and ran away naked.

53 THEN THEY LED JESUS AWAY TO THE High Priest's house, where the chief priests, elders, and doctors of the law
54 were all assembling. Peter followed him at a distance right into the High Priest's courtyard; and there he remained, sitting among the attendants, warming himself at the fire.
55 The chief priests and the whole Council tried to find some evidence against Jesus to warrant a death-
56 sentence, but failed to find any. Many gave false evidence against him, but
57 their statements did not tally. Some stood up and gave false evidence
58 against him to this effect: 'We heard him say, "I will pull down this temple, made with human hands, and in three days I will build another, not made
59 with hands."' But even on this point their evidence did not agree.
60 Then the High Priest stood up in his place and questioned Jesus: 'Have you no answer to the charges that these
61 witnesses bring against you?' But he kept silence; he made no reply.
Again the High Priest questioned him: 'Are you the Messiah, the Son of
62 the Blessed One?' Jesus said, 'I am; and you will see the Son of Man seated at the right hand of God[n] and coming
63 with the clouds of heaven.' Then the High Priest tore his robes and said,
64 'Need we call further witnesses? You have heard the blasphemy. What is your opinion?' Their judgement was unanimous: that he was guilty and should be put to death.

65 Some began to spit on him, blindfolded him, and struck him with their fists, crying out, 'Prophesy!'[o] And the High Priest's men set upon him with blows.
66 Meanwhile Peter was still below in the courtyard. One of the High Priest's
67 serving-maids came by and saw him there warming himself. She looked into his face and said, 'You were there too, with this man from Nazareth, this Jesus.' But he denied it: 'I know noth-
68 ing,' he said; 'I do not understand what you mean.' Then he went outside into the porch;[p] and the maid saw him there
69 again and began to say to the by-
70 standers, 'He is one of them'; and again he denied it.
Again, a little later, the bystanders said to Peter, 'Surely you are one of them. You must be; you are a Galilean.'
71 At this he broke out into curses, and with an oath he said, 'I do not know
72 this man you speak of.' Then the cock crew a second time; and Peter remembered how Jesus had said to him, 'Before the cock crows twice you will disown me three times.' And he burst into tears.

15 AS SOON AS MORNING CAME, THE CHIEF priests, having made their plan with the elders and lawyers in full council, put Jesus in chains; then they led him away
2 and handed him over to Pilate. Pilate asked him, 'Are you the king of the Jews?' He replied, 'The words are
3 yours.'[q] And the chief priests brought
4 many charges against him. Pilate questioned him again: 'Have you nothing to say in your defence? You see how many charges they are bringing
5 against you.' But, to Pilate's astonishment, Jesus made no further reply.
6 At the festival season the Governor used to release one prisoner at the
7 people's request. As it happened, the

n *Literally* of the Power.
o *Some witnesses add* Who hit you? *as in Matthew and Luke.*
p *Some witnesses insert* and a cock crew.
q *Or* It is as you say.

47: *One:* see Mt.26.51 n. 51: The *young man* appears only in Mk. and his identity is unknown.
14.53–72: **Before the Jewish authorities** (Mt.26.57–75 n.; Lk.22.54–71; Jn.18.13–27). 55: *Council:* See Mt.26.59 n. 57–58: 13.2; 15.29; see Mt.24.1–3 n. 61: *Messiah . . . Son:* see Mt.16.16 n. 62: Dan.7.13; Ps.110.1. 63–64: *Blasphemy:* see Mt.26.65–66 n. 72: Compare v. 30.
15.1–20: **Before Roman authority** (Mt.27.1–31; Lk.23.1–25; Jn.18.28–19.16). 1: *Pilate:* see Lk.3.1 n. 2: *King:* see Lk.23.2 n. 6: Mt.27.15 n. 7: *Barabbas:* Mt.27.16 n.

man known as Barabbas was then in custody with the rebels who had committed murder in the rising. When the 8 crowd appeared[r] asking for the usual 9 favour, Pilate replied, 'Do you wish me to release for you the king of the 10 Jews?' For he knew it was out of malice that they had brought Jesus 11 before him. But the chief priests incited the crowd to ask him to release Barab-12 bas rather than Jesus. Pilate spoke to them again: 'Then what shall I do with the man you call king of the Jews?' 13 They shouted back, 'Crucify him!' 14 'Why, what harm has he done?' Pilate asked; but they shouted all the louder, 15 'Crucify him!' So Pilate, in his desire to satisfy the mob, released Barabbas to them; and he had Jesus flogged and handed him over to be crucified.

16 Then the soldiers took him inside the courtyard (the Governor's headquarters[s]) and called together the whole 17 company. They dressed him in purple, and plaiting a crown of thorns, placed 18 it on his head. Then they began to salute him with, 'Hail, King of the Jews!' 19 They beat him about the head with a cane and spat upon him, and then knelt 20 and paid mock homage to him. When they had finished their mockery, they stripped him of the purple and dressed him in his own clothes.

THEN THEY TOOK HIM OUT TO CRUCIFY 21 him. A man called Simon, from Cyrene, the father of Alexander and Rufus, was passing by on his way in from the country, and they pressed him into service to carry his cross. 22 They brought him to the place called Golgotha, which means 'Place of a 23 skull'. He was offered drugged wine, 24 but he would not take it. Then they fastened him to the cross. They divided his clothes among them, casting lots to decide what each should have. 25 The hour of the crucifixion was nine 26 in the morning, and the inscription

giving the charge against him read, 'The king of the Jews.' Two bandits 27 were crucified with him, one on his right and the other on his left,[t]

The passers-by hurled abuse at him: 29 'Aha!' they cried, wagging their heads, 'you would pull the temple down, would you, and build it in three days? Come 30 down from the cross and save yourself!' So too the chief priests and lawyers 31 jested with one another: 'He saved others,' they said, 'but he cannot save himself. Let the Messiah, the king of 32 Israel, come down now from the cross. If we see that, we shall believe.' Even those who were crucified with him taunted him.

At midday a darkness fell over the 33 whole land, which lasted till three in the afternoon; and at three Jesus cried 34 aloud, *'Eli, Eli, lema sabachthani?'*, which means, 'My God, my God, why hast thou forsaken me?'[u] Some of the bystanders, on hearing this, said, 'Hark, 35 he is calling Elijah.' A man ran and 36 soaked a sponge in sour wine and held it to his lips on the end of a cane. 'Let us see', he said, 'if Elijah will come to take him down.' Then Jesus gave a 37 loud cry and died. And the curtain of 38 the temple was torn in two from top to bottom. And when the centurion who 39 was standing opposite him saw how he died,[v] he said, 'Truly this man was a son of God.'[w]

A NUMBER OF WOMEN WERE ALSO 40 present, watching from a distance. Among them were Mary of Magdala, Mary the mother of James the younger and of Joseph, and Salome, who had all 41 followed him and waited on him when he was in Galilee, and there were several

r Some witnesses read shouted.
s Greek praetorium.
t Some witnesses add (28) That that text of Scripture came true which says, 'He was reckoned among criminals.'
u Some witnesses read My God, my God, why hast thou shamed me?
v Some witnesses read saw that he died with a cry.
w Or the Son of God.

15.21–47: The crucifixion (Mt.27.32–66; Lk.23.26–54; Jn.19.17–42). **21:** *Simon* was probably a Jew from *Cyrene*. The mention of *Alexander* and *Rufus* suggests that they may have been known in the church of Mk. Contrast Jn.19.17. **23:** Ps.69.21; on *wine*, see Lk.23.36 n. **24:** Ps.22.18. On crucifixion, see Lk.23.32 n. **25:** *Nine in the morning:* contrast Jn.19.14. **29:** See 14.57–58 n. **32b:** Contrast Lk.23.39–43. **34:** See Mt.27.46 n. **35:** *Elijah:* see Mt.27.47 n. **36:** Ps.69.21. **38:** *Curtain:* see Mt.27.51 n. **39:** *Son of God:* see Mt.27.54 n. **43:** *Council:* see Mt.26.59 n. **46:** Deut.21.22–23.

others who had come up to Jerusalem with him.

42 By this time evening had come; and as it was Preparation-day (that is, the 43 day before the Sabbath), Joseph of Arimathaea, a respected member of the Council, a man who looked forward to the kingdom of God, bravely went in to Pilate and asked for the body 44 of Jesus. Pilate was surprised to hear that he was already dead; so he sent for the centurion and asked him 45 whether it was long since he died. And when he heard the centurion's report, he gave Joseph leave to take the dead 46 body. So Joseph bought a linen sheet, took him down from the cross, and wrapped him in the sheet. Then he laid him in a tomb cut out of the rock, and rolled a stone against the entrance. 47 And Mary of Magdala and Mary the mother of Joseph were watching and saw where he was laid.

16 When the Sabbath was over, Mary of Magdala, Mary the mother of James, and Salome bought[x] aromatic oils in- 2 tending to go and anoint him; and very early on the Sunday morning, just after 3 sunrise, they came to the tomb. They were wondering among themselves who would roll away the stone for them from the entrance to the tomb, 4 when they looked up and saw that the stone, huge as it was, had been rolled 5 back already. They went into the tomb, where they saw a youth sitting on the right-hand side, wearing a white robe; 6 and they were dumbfounded. But he said to them, 'Fear nothing; you are looking for Jesus of Nazareth, who was crucified. He has been raised again; he is not here; look, there is the place 7 where they laid him. But go and give this message to his disciples and Peter: "He is going on before you into Galilee; there you will see him, as he told you."' 8 Then they went out and ran away from the tomb, beside themselves with terror.

They said nothing to anybody, for they were afraid.[y]

9 When he had risen from the dead early on Sunday morning he appeared first to Mary of Magdala, from whom he had formerly cast out seven devils. 10 She went and carried the news to his 11 mourning and sorrowful followers, but when they were told that he was alive and that she had seen him they did not believe it.

12 Later he appeared in a different guise to two of them as they were walking, 13 on their way into the country. These also went and took the news to the others, but again no one believed them.

14 Afterwards while the Eleven were at table he appeared to them and reproached them for their incredulity and dullness, because they had not believed those who had seen him after he was raised from the dead. Then he 15 said to them: 'Go forth to every part of the world, and proclaim the Good News to the whole creation. Those who 16 believe it and receive baptism will find salvation; those who do not believe will be condemned. Faith will bring 17 with it these miracles: believers will cast out devils in my name and speak in strange tongues; if they handle 18 ✓ snakes or drink any deadly poison, they will come to no harm; and the sick on whom they lay their hands will recover.'

19 So after talking with them the Lord Jesus was taken up into heaven, and he took his seat at the right hand of God; but they went out to make their proc- 20 lamation everywhere, and the Lord

---

x Some witnesses omit When the Sabbath ... Salome, *reading* And they went and bought ...
y At this point some of the most ancient witnesses bring the book to a close; others continue with verses 9–20, as printed here, or in some cases expanded with additional matter; yet others insert here the paragraph And they delivered ... eternal salvation (*here printed below verse 20*), *and in one of them this is the conclusion of the book; in the remainder, verses 9–20 follow it.*

16.1–20: The empty tomb (Mt.28.1–8; Lk.24.1–9; Jn.20.1–3). **1:** The *Sabbath* ended at sunset on Saturday; compare Lk.23.55–56 n. **3–4:** *Stone:* Mt.27.60 n. **7:** See 14.28. Perhaps the verse originally prepared for an account (now lost) of a Galilean appearance; compare Mt.28.16–20; Jn. ch. 21. **8:** Textual evidence seems to favor the view that the Gospel ended here (Tfn. *y*). However, the phrase *for they were afraid* is more abrupt in Greek than in English, and many scholars believe that there must have been additional material. Vv. 9–20 are found in numerous witnesses. **9–11:** Jn.20.11–18; Mt.28.9–10. **12–13:** Lk.24.13–35. **14–16:** Mt.28.16–20. **19:** Lk.24.50–51. **20:** However the book may have originally ended (Tfn. *y*), the Church in which

worked with them and confirmed their words by the miracles that followed.

And they delivered all these instructions briefly to Peter and his companions. Afterwards Jesus himself sent out by them from east to west the sacred and imperishable message of eternal salvation.[z]

z See note y on page 65.

---

it was cherished was not left in fear (v. 8), but *went out to make their proclamation everywhere.* If Mk. indeed ended at v. 8, the felt need which prompted additions was the absence of a resurrection appearance (found in Mt.28.18, Lk.24.15–27, and Jn.20.14–17) which is foreshadowed in 14.28, but not thereafter directly narrated. The addition, or additions, provide both a resurrection appearance and also (v. 19) the ascension of the risen Christ to heaven (compare Acts 1.9–11).

THE GOSPEL ACCORDING TO
LUKE

The Gospel of Luke was written about 90 A.D. by a Gentile Christian, one of the first Church writers with a real awareness of himself as a literary figure (see 1.1–4 n). Basic to the design of his work is the place that Luke assigns the career of Jesus in a more comprehensive view of the course of God's dealings with men. Jesus' ministry is the period in terms of which the previous and subsequent history of salvation is given meaning: it is the culmination of ancient Israel's promise and the ground of the Church's hope and life.

After a lengthy introduction (1.1–4.13), Luke describes Jesus' career as a procession that begins in Galilee (4.14–9.50) and moves on the way to Jerusalem (9.51–19.27) where the nature of divine Sonship is fully revealed (19.28–24.53).

But the story of salvation does not end here. It is taken up again in a second volume (Acts of the Apostles) where, in the experience of the Church, the way that once led to Jerusalem now extends to "the ends of the earth" (Acts 1.8).

---

1 THE AUTHOR TO THEOPHILUS: MANY writers have undertaken to draw up an account of the events that ² have happened among us, following the traditions handed down to us by the original eyewitnesses and servants ³ of the Gospel. And so I in my turn, your Excellency, as one who has gone over the whole course of these events in detail, have decided to write a ⁴ connected narrative for you, so as to give you authentic knowledge about the matters of which you have been informed.

The coming of Christ

⁵ IN THE DAYS OF HEROD KING OF JUDAEA there was a priest named Zechariah, of the division of the priesthood called after Abijah. His wife also was of priestly descent; her name was Eliza ⁶ beth. Both of them were upright and devout, blamelessly observing all the commandments and ordinances of the ⁷ Lord. But they had no children, for Elizabeth was barren, and both were well on in years.

Once, when it was the turn of his ⁸ division and he was there to take part in divine service, it fell to his lot, by ⁹ priestly custom, to enter the sanctuary of the Lord and offer the incense; and ¹⁰ the whole congregation was at prayer outside. It was the hour of the incense-offering. There appeared to him an ¹¹ angel of the Lord standing on the right of the altar of incense. At this ¹² sight Zechariah was startled, and fear overcame him. But the angel said to ¹³ him, 'Do not be afraid, Zechariah; your prayer has been heard: your wife Elizabeth will bear you a son, and you shall name him John. Your heart will ¹⁴ thrill with joy and many will be glad that he was born; for he will be great ¹⁵ in the eyes of the Lord. He shall never touch wine or strong drink. From his very birth he will be filled with the Holy Spirit; and he will bring back ¹⁶ many Israelites to the Lord their God. He will go before him as forerunner,[a] ¹⁷ possessed by the spirit and power of Elijah, to reconcile father and child, to convert the rebellious to the ways of

---

a *Or* In his sight he will go forth.

1.1–4: The preface follows the form customary in the literature of the period (compare Acts 1.1–5). **1:** Both this Gospel and Acts are dedicated to an unknown *Theophilus* (lit. "friend of God"), perhaps a Roman official (v. 3, *your Excellency;* see Acts 23.26). *Many* perhaps should be understood as "several" writers. **3:** *A connected narrative* may imply logical, rather than strictly chronological, arrangement.
1.5–80: Preparation for Jesus' birth.
1.5–25: The birth of John the Baptist is promised. 5: There were twenty-four *divisions of the priesthood,* to whom the privilege of temple service fell by rotation (v. 8). **7:** Compare Gen.17.15–18.15. **9:** To *offer the* (morning or evening) *incense* was a highly cherished honor. **13:** *John:* see vv. 60,63 n. **15:** There are OT provisions against *wine and strong drink* for priests (Lev.10.8–11) and Nazirites (Num.6.1–21). **17:** The words *spirit and power of Elijah* and allusions

the righteous, to prepare a people that shall be fit for the Lord.'

18 Zechariah said to the angel, 'How can I be sure of this? I am an old man and my wife is well on in years.'

19 The angel replied, 'I am Gabriel; I stand in attendance upon God, and I have been sent to speak to you and 20 bring you this good news. But now listen: you will lose your power of speech, and remain silent until the day when these things happen to you, because you have not believed me, though at their proper time my words will be proved true.'

21 Meanwhile the people were waiting for Zechariah, surprised that he was 22 staying so long inside. When he did come out he could not speak to them, and they realized that he had had a vision in the sanctuary. He stood there making signs to them, and remained dumb.

23 When his period of duty was completed Zechariah returned home. 24 After this his wife Elizabeth conceived, and for five months she lived in 25 seclusion, thinking, 'This is the Lord's doing; now at last he has deigned to take away my reproach among men.'

26 In the sixth month the angel Gabriel was sent from God to a town in 27 Galilee called Nazareth, with a message for a girl betrothed to a man named Joseph, a descendant of David; the 28 girl's name was Mary. The angel went in and said to her, 'Greetings, most favoured one! The Lord is with you.' 29 But she was deeply troubled by what he said and wondered what this 30 greeting might mean. Then the angel said to her, 'Do not be afraid, Mary, 31 for God has been gracious to you; you shall conceive and bear a son, and you 32 shall give him the name Jesus. He will be great; he will bear the title "Son of

the Most High"; the Lord God will give him the throne of his ancestor David, and he will be king over 33 Israel[b] for ever; his reign shall never end.' 'How can this be?' said Mary; 'I 34 am still a virgin.' The angel answered, 35 'The Holy Spirit will come upon you, and the power of the Most High will overshadow you; and for that reason the holy child to be born will be called "Son of God".[c] Moreover your kins- 36 woman Elizabeth has herself conceived a son in her old age; and she who is reputed barren is now in her sixth month, for God's promises can never fail.'[d] 37 'Here am I,' said Mary; 'I am the 38 Lord's servant; as you have spoken, so be it.' Then the angel left her.

About this time Mary set out and 39 went straight to a town in the uplands of Judah. She went into Zechariah's 40 house and greeted Elizabeth. And 41 when Elizabeth heard Mary's greeting, the baby stirred in her womb. Then Elizabeth was filled with the Holy Spirit and cried aloud, 'God's blessing 42 is on you above all women, and his blessing is on the fruit of your womb. Who am I, that the mother of my Lord 43 should visit me? I tell you, when your 44 greeting sounded in my ears, the baby in my womb leapt for joy. How happy 45 is she who has had faith that the Lord's promise would be fulfilled!'

And Mary[e] said: 46

'Tell out, my soul, the greatness of
        the Lord,
rejoice, rejoice, my spirit, in God my   47
        saviour;

b *Literally* the house of Jacob.
c *Or* the child to be born will be called holy, "Son of God".
d *Some witnesses read* for with God nothing will prove impossible.
e *So the majority of witnesses; some read* Elizabeth; *the original may have had no name.*

---

to Mal.3.1; 4.5–6 suggest a near identification of the Baptist and Elijah (see Mt.11.14; 17.10–13) not characteristic of Lk. outside this chapter. **19:** *Gabriel* (Dan.8.16–17; 9.21–22) was regarded as the angel of highest rank, especially in the noncanonical book of Enoch. **25:** *My reproach:* the shame associated with barrenness; see 1 Sam.1.1–20; Ps.113.9.

1.26–38: Jesus' birth promised (see Mt.1.18–25). As in Mt., the story speaks of a miraculous birth (vv. 34–35), stresses Joseph's Davidic descent (vv. 27,32), and emphasizes the child's names or titles (vv. 31,32,35). **32:** *Son of the Most High:* a title for the royal Messiah (see Mt.1.1 n.) as is shown by the words, *throne of his ancestor David* (1 Chr.17.7–14; Isa.11.1–10). **34:** Not physical impregnation by a divine being, but a miraculous generation of life through the Spirit is meant.

1.39–56: Mary visits Elizabeth. 43: Lk., as here, frequently uses the title *Lord* for Jesus, but in

48 so tenderly has he looked upon his
     servant,
       humble as she is.
     For, from this day forth,
     all generations will count me blessed,
49 so wonderfully has he dealt with me,
       the Lord, the Mighty One.

       His name is Holy;
50 his mercy sure from generation to
     generation
       toward those who fear him;
51 the deeds his own right arm has done
     disclose his might:
     the arrogant of heart and mind he
       has put to rout,
52 he has brought down monarchs from
     their thrones,
     but the humble have been lifted
       high.
53 The hungry he has satisfied with
     good things,
     the rich sent empty away.

54 He has ranged himself at the side of
     Israel his servant;
55   firm in his promise to our
     forefathers,
     he has not forgotten to show mercy
       to Abraham
       and his children's children, for
       ever.'

56   Mary stayed with her about three
months and then returned home.

57 NOW THE TIME CAME FOR ELIZABETH'S
child to be born, and she gave birth
58 to a son. When her neighbours and
relatives heard what great favour the
Lord had shown her, they were as
59 delighted as she was. Then on the
eighth day they came to circumcise the
child; and they were going to name
60 him Zechariah after his father. But his
mother spoke up and said, 'No! he is
61 to be called John.' 'But', they said,
'there is nobody in your family who

has that name.' They inquired of his 62
father by signs what he would like him
to be called. He asked for a writing- 63
tablet and to the astonishment of all
wrote down, 'His name is John.'
Immediately his lips and tongue were 64
freed and he began to speak, praising
God. All the neighbours were struck 65
with awe, and everywhere in the
uplands of Judaea the whole story
became common talk. All who heard 66
it were deeply impressed and said,
'What will this child become?' For
indeed the hand of the Lord was upon
him.*f*

     And Zechariah his father was filled 67
with the Holy Spirit and uttered this
prophecy:

       'Praise to the God of Israel! 68
For he has turned to his people, saved
       them and set them free,
and has raised up a deliverer of 69
       victorious power
     from the house of his servant
       David.

So he promised: age after age he 70
     proclaimed
     by the lips of his holy prophets,
that he would deliver us from our 71
       enemies,
     out of the hands of all who
       hate us;
that he would deal mercifully with 72
       our fathers,
     calling to mind his solemn
       covenant.

Such was the oath he swore to our 73
     father Abraham,
     to rescue us from enemy hands, 74
and grant us, free from fear, to
       worship him
     with a holy worship, with 75
       uprightness of heart,
     in his presence our whole life long.

f Some witnesses read 'What will this child become, for
indeed the hand of the Lord is upon him?'

---

vv. 45–46 it refers to God. **46–55:** The "Magnificat" reads like a very old hymn celebrating
God's goodness to Israel (vv. 54–55); compare 1 Sam.2.1–10. **59:** Circumcision on the *eighth
day* was prescribed in the Law (Lev.12.3; Lk.2.21). **60,63:** The emphasis shows that the meaning
of the name *John* ("God is gracious") is important.
     1.67–79: The "Benedictus" celebrates the coming of the royal Messiah (v. 69), the fulfillment
of the promise to Abraham (vv. 73–75), and John's Elijah-like commission (vv. 76–77; Mal.3.1;
Isa.40.3; see v. 17 n.).

76 And you, my child, you shall be
     called Prophet of the Highest,
   for you will be the Lord's forerunner
     to prepare his way
77   and lead his people to salvation
       through knowledge of him,
     by the forgiveness of their sins:
78 for in the tender compassion of our
     God
   the morning sun from heaven
     will rise*g* upon us,
79 to shine on those who live in darkness,
     under the cloud of death,
   and to guide our feet into the
     way of peace.'

80 As the child grew up he became
strong in spirit; he lived out in the
wilds until the day when he appeared
publicly before Israel.

2 IN THOSE DAYS A DECREE WAS ISSUED BY
the Emperor Augustus for a registration to be made throughout the
2 Roman world. This was the first
registration of its kind; it took place
when Quirinius*h* was governor of
3 Syria. For this purpose everyone made
4 his way to his own town; and so
Joseph went up to Judaea from the
5 town of Nazareth in Galilee, to
register at the city of David, called
Bethlehem, because he was of the
house of David by descent; and with
him went Mary who was betrothed to
6 him. She was expecting a child, and
while they were there the time came
7 for her baby to be born, and she gave
birth to a son, her first-born. She
wrapped him in his swaddling clothes,
and laid him in a manger, because
there was no room for them to lodge
in the house.
8 Now in this same district there were
shepherds out in the fields, keeping
watch through the night over their
9 flock, when suddenly there stood before
them an angel of the Lord, and the
splendour of the Lord shone round

them. They were terror-stricken, but 10
the angel said, 'Do not be afraid; I
have good news for you: there is great
joy coming to the whole people.
Today in the city of David a deliverer 11
has been born to you—the Messiah,
the Lord.*i* And this is your sign: you 12
will find a baby lying wrapped in his
swaddling clothes, in a manger.' All at 13
once there was with the angel a great
company of the heavenly host, singing
the praises of God:

   'Glory to God in highest heaven,   14
   and on earth his peace for men on
     whom his favour rests.'*j*

After the angels had left them and 15
gone into heaven the shepherds said to
one another, 'Come, we must go
straight to Bethlehem and see this
thing that has happened, which the
Lord has made known to us.' So they 16
went with all speed and found their
way to Mary and Joseph; and the
baby was lying in the manger. When 17
they saw him, they recounted what they
had been told about this child; and all 18
who heard were astonished at what the
shepherds said. But Mary treasured up 19
all these things and pondered over
them. Meanwhile the shepherds re- 20
turned glorifying and praising God for
what they had heard and seen; it had
all happened as they had been told.
Eight days later the time came to 21
circumcise him, and he was given the
name Jesus, the name given by the
angel before he was conceived.
Then, after their purification had 22
been completed in accordance with the
Law of Moses, they brought him up
to Jerusalem to present him to the
Lord (as prescribed in the law of the 23

g Some witnesses read has risen.
*h Or This was the first registration carried out while
    Quirinius . . .*
i Some witnesses read to you—the Lord's Messiah.
*j Some witnesses read and on earth his peace, his favour
    towards men.*

2.1–40: The birth of Jesus. 1: *Augustus* reigned from 30 B.C. to 14 A.D. **2:** The *registration*
under *Quirinius* is dated in 6 or 7 A.D. by the first-century Jewish historian Josephus. **7:** The
first-born belong to God and must be redeemed (Exod.13.1–2,12–13); see vv. 22–24. *Swaddling
clothes:* the cloth strips with which infants were wrapped. A *manger* (or small feed trough)
would serve well as a crib. **11:** *Deliverer* (or, "Savior") may be a play on the name Jesus;
compare Mt.1.21. *Lord:* see 1.43 n. **13:** The *angel* who brings the message is joined by a *great
company* (compare Dan.7.10). **21:** *Eight days:* see 1.59 n. On *Jesus*, see v. 11 n. **22–24:**See v. 7 n.;

Lord: 'Every first-born male shall be
24 deemed to belong to the Lord'), and
also to make the offering as stated in
the law: 'A pair of turtle doves or two
young pigeons.'

25 There was at that time in Jerusalem
a man called Simeon. This man was
upright and devout, one who watched
and waited for the restoration of
Israel, and the Holy Spirit was upon
26 him. It had been disclosed to him by
the Holy Spirit that he would not see
death until he had seen the Lord's
27 Messiah. Guided by the Spirit he came
into the temple; and when the parents
brought in the child Jesus to do for
him what was customary under the
28 Law, he took him in his arms, praised
God, and said:

29 'This day, Master, thou givest thy
        servant his discharge in peace;
        now thy promise is fulfilled.
30 For I have seen with my own eyes
31 the deliverance which thou hast made
        ready in full view of all the
        nations:
32 a light that will be a revelation to
        the heathen,
        and glory to thy people Israel.'

33 The child's father and mother were
full of wonder at what was being said
34 about him. Simeon blessed them and
said to Mary his mother, 'This child is
destined to be a sign which men reject;
35 and you too shall be pierced to the
heart. Many in Israel will stand or
fall[k] because of him, and thus the
secret thoughts of many will be laid
bare.'
36 There was also a prophetess, Anna
the daughter of Phanuel, of the tribe
of Asher. She was a very old woman,
who had lived seven years with her
husband after she was first married,
37 and then alone as a widow to the age
of eighty-four.[l] She never left the
temple, but worshipped day and night,

fasting and praying. Coming up at that 38
very moment, she returned thanks to
God; and she talked about the child
to all who were looking for the
liberation of Jerusalem.

When they had done everything 39
prescribed in the law of the Lord, they
returned to Galilee to their own town
of Nazareth. The child grew big and 40
strong and full of wisdom; and God's
favour was upon him.

Now it was the practice of his parents 41
to go to Jerusalem every year for the
Passover festival; and when he was 42
twelve, they made the pilgrimage as
usual. When the festive season was 43
over and they started for home, the
boy Jesus stayed behind in Jerusalem.
His parents did not know of this; but 44
thinking that he was with the party
they journeyed on for a whole day, and
only then did they begin looking for
him among their friends and relations.
As they could not find him they 45
returned to Jerusalem to look for him;
and after three days they found him 46
sitting in the temple surrounded by the
teachers, listening to them and putting
questions; and all who heard him were 47
amazed at his intelligence and the
answers he gave. His parents were 48
astonished to see him there, and his
mother said to him, 'My son, why have
you treated us like this? Your father
and I have been searching for you
in great anxiety.' 'What made you 49
search?' he said. 'Did you not know
that I was bound to be in my Father's
house?' But they did not understand 50
what he meant. Then he went back 51
with them to Nazareth, and continued
to be under their authority; his
mother treasured up all these things in
her heart. As Jesus grew up he 52
advanced in wisdom and in favour
with God and men.

---

k Or Many in Israel will fall and rise again . . .
l Or widow for another eighty-four years.

Lev.12.1–8. 25–26: *The restoration of Israel* was expected of the Messiah (see Acts 1.6).
29: *Discharge* suggests "liberation." 31–32: The Messiah's function beyond Israel is stated in
terms of Isa.52.10; 42.6; 49.6. 38: *Liberation of Jerusalem:* see vv. 25–26 n.
    2.41–52: Jesus in the Temple as a boy. 41: Deut.16.16 required Jewish men to be in Jerusalem
every year for the Passover festival, which celebrated Israel's escape from Egypt (Exod. ch. 12).
52: *Wisdom* (also v. 40) is a complex term which includes such meanings as "practical
knowledge about life," "knowledge of the Law," and "revealed knowledge."

3 IN THE FIFTEENTH YEAR OF THE EMPEROR Tiberius, when Pontius Pilate was governor of Judaea, when Herod was prince of Galilee, his brother Philip prince of Ituraea and Trachonitis, and 2 Lysanias prince of Abilene, during the high-priesthood of Annas and Caiaphas, the word of God came to John son of Zechariah in the wilderness. 3 And he went all over the Jordan valley proclaiming a baptism in token of repentance for the forgiveness of 4 sins, as it is written in the book of the prophecies of Isaiah:

'A voice crying aloud in the wilderness,
"Prepare a way for the Lord;
clear a straight path for him.
5 Every ravine shall be filled in,
and every mountain and hill levelled;
the corners shall be straightened,
and the rugged ways made smooth;
6 and all mankind shall see God's
deliverance."'

7 Crowds of people came out to be baptized by him, and he said to them: 'You vipers' brood! Who warned you to escape from the coming retribution? 8 Then prove your repentance by the fruit it bears; and do not begin saying to yourselves, "We have Abraham for our father." I tell you that God can make children for Abraham out of 9 these stones here. Already the axe is laid to the roots of the trees; and every tree that fails to produce good fruit is cut down and thrown on the fire.'

10 The people asked him, 'Then what 11 are we to do?' He replied, 'The man with two shirts must share with him who has none, and anyone who has food must do the same.' Among those 12 who came to be baptized were tax-gatherers, and they said to him, 'Master, what are we to do?' He told 13 them, 'Exact no more than the assessment.' Soldiers on service also asked 14 him, 'And what of us?' To them he said, 'No bullying; no blackmail; make do with your pay!'

The people were on the tiptoe of 15 expectation, all wondering about John, whether perhaps he was the Messiah, but he spoke out and said to them all: 16 'I baptize you with water; but there is one to come who is mightier than I. I am not fit to unfasten his shoes. He will baptize you with the Holy Spirit and with fire. His shovel is ready in his 17 hand, to winnow his threshing-floor and gather the wheat into his granary; but he will burn the chaff on a fire that can never go out.'

In this and many other ways he made 18 his appeal to the people and announced the good news. But Prince Herod, when 19 he was rebuked by him over the affair of his brother's wife Herodias and for his other misdeeds, crowned them all 20 by shutting John up in prison.

DURING A GENERAL BAPTISM OF THE 21 people, when Jesus too had been baptized and was praying, heaven opened and the Holy Spirit descended 22 on him in bodily form like a dove; and there came a voice from heaven, 'Thou art my Son, my Beloved;*m* on thee my favour rests.'*n*

When Jesus began his work he was 23

m Or Thou art my only Son.
n Some witnesses read My Son art thou; this day I have begotten thee.

3.1–20: **The work of the Baptist.** (Mt.3.1–12; Mk.1.1–8; Jn.1.6,15,19–28). **1:** *Tiberius' fifteenth year:* 27 A.D. Roman governors ruled Judea after 6 A.D.; *Pilate*'s tenure covered 26–36. *Herod* Antipas (a son of Herod the Great), who ruled Galilee and Perea, is meant. **2:** *Annas* was an influential former high priest; *Caiaphas*, his son-in-law, was high priest during Pilate's governorship. *Wilderness:* see Mt.3.1 n. **3:** *Baptism:* see Mt.3.7 n. **4–6:** Isa.40.3–5. **8:** Descendants of *Abraham* share the promise made to him (Gen.17.4–8; 22.18). **12:** *Tax-gatherers* were private citizens who contracted with the Roman authorities to collect duties in a specific area; Jews who engaged in this "business" were regarded as traitors. **15–16:** See Mk.1.7 n. **16:** *With the Holy Spirit and with fire* probably originally meant "with divine power and judgment"; for Lk., *fire* is symbolically identified with *Spirit* (see Acts 1.5; 2.1–5). **19:** See Mk.6.17–20.
3.21–22: **The baptism of Jesus** (Mt.3.13–17; Mk.1.9–11 n.; Jn.1.32–34). **21:** Jesus' *praying* is frequently mentioned by Lk. (e.g. 5.16; 9.18). **22:** *Spirit, dove:* see Mt.3.16 n. *Beloved:* see Mk.1.11 n.
3.23–38: **Genealogy of Jesus** (compare Mt.1.1–17). V. 20 formally closes the career of the Baptist; with v. 21 attention turns exclusively to Jesus whose genealogy is given. **23:** *Thirty*

about thirty years old, the son, as people thought, of Joseph, son of Heli,
24 son of Matthat, son of Levi, son of Melchi, son of Jannai, son of Joseph,
25 son of Mattathiah, son of Amos, son of Nahum, son of Esli, son of Naggai,
26 son of Maath, son of Mattathiah, son of Semein, son of Josech, son of Joda,
27 son of Johanan, son of Rhesa, son of Zerubbabel, son of Shealtiel, son of
28 Neri, son of Melchi, son of Addi, son of Cosam, son of Elmadam, son of Er,
29 son of Joshua, son of Eliezer, son of Jorim, son of Matthat, son of Levi,
30 son of Symeon, son of Judah, son of Joseph, son of Jonam, son of Eliakim,
31 son of Melea, son of Menna, son of Mattatha, son of Nathan, son of
32 David, son of Jesse, son of Obed, son of Boaz, son of Salmon, son of
33 Nahshon, son of Amminadab,*o* son of Arni,*p* son of Hezron, son of Perez,
34 son of Judah, son of Jacob, son of Isaac, son of Abraham, son of Terah,
35 son of Nahor, son of Serug, son of Reu, son of Peleg, son of Eber, son of
36 Shelah, son of Cainan, son of Arpachshad, son of Shem, son of Noah, son
37 of Lamech, son of Methuselah, son of Enoch, son of Jared, son of Mahalaleel,
38 son of Cainan, son of Enosh, son of Seth, son of Adam, son of God.

4 Full of the Holy Spirit, Jesus
2 returned from the Jordan, and for forty days was led by the Spirit up and down the wilderness and tempted by the devil.

All that time he had nothing to eat, and at the end of it he was famished.
3 The devil said to him, 'If you are the Son of God, tell this stone to become
4 bread.' Jesus answered, 'Scripture says, "Man cannot live on bread alone." '
5 Next the devil led him up and

showed him in a flash all the kingdoms of the world. 'All this dominion will I 6 give to you,' he said, 'and the glory that goes with it; for it has been put
7 in my hands and I can give it to anyone I choose. You have only to do
7 homage to me and it shall all be yours.' Jesus answered him, 'Scripture 8 says, "You shall do homage to the Lord your God and worship him alone." '

The devil took him to Jerusalem and 9 set him on the parapet of the temple. 'If you are the Son of God,' he said, 'throw yourself down; for Scripture 10 says, "He will give his angels orders to take care of you", and again, "They 11 will support you in their arms for fear you should strike your foot against a stone." ' Jesus answered him, 'It has 12 been said, "You are not to put the Lord your God to the test." '

So, having come to the end of all his 13 temptations, the devil departed, biding his time.

In Galilee: success and opposition

THEN JESUS, ARMED WITH THE POWER 14 of the Spirit, returned to Galilee; and reports about him spread through the whole country-side. He taught in their 15 synagogues and all men sang his praises.

So he came to Nazareth, where he 16 had been brought up, and went to synagogue on the Sabbath day as he regularly did. He stood up to read the lesson and was handed the scroll of the 17 prophet Isaiah. He opened the scroll and found the passage which says,

o Some witnesses add son of Admin.
p Some witnesses read Aram; *Ruth 4. 19 and 1 Chronicles 2. 9 have Ram.*

---

years old would mean shortly after 25 A.D., reckoning from Herod's death in 4 B.C. (Mt.2.1–20.)
31: While descent from *David* is still important for the Messiah (Mt.1.1 n.), vv. 23–31 do not trace Jesus' ancestry through David's royal progeny (as does Mt.1.6–11). **38:** The genealogy extends beyond *Abraham* (i.e. beyond the Jewish limits of Mt.1.1–17) to *Adam, son of God,* perhaps to affirm Jesus' kinship with all mankind.
4.1–13: The temptation (Mt.4.1–11; Mk.1.12–13). Except for a different sequence of temptations, the account closely parallels Mt. 4.1–11 (see notes there). **13:** *Biding his time* implies the later renewal of the contest (see 22.3,28,31).
4.14–15: Jesus appears in Galilee (Mt.4.12–17; Mk.1.14–15). **14:** In Jesus' ministry, the *Spirit* is uniquely operative (3.22; 4.1,18–21). The phrase *returned to Galilee,* i.e. home (see 2.39), prepares for the scene in vv. 16–30. **15:** *Taught in their synagogues:* see Mt.9.35.
4.16–30: Jesus in Nazareth (compare Mt.13.54–58; Mk.6.1–6). **16:** Only Lk. places the *Nazareth* visit at the beginning of Jesus' ministry. The *synagogue* was a place for instruction

18 'The spirit of the Lord is upon me
     because he has anointed me;
   he has sent me to announce good
     news to the poor,
   to proclaim release for prisoners and
     recovery of sight for the blind;
   to let the broken victims go free,
19 to proclaim the year of the Lord's
     favour.'

20 He rolled up the scroll, gave it back to
   the attendant, and sat down; and all
   eyes in the synagogue were fixed on
   him.
21   He began to speak: 'Today', he said,
   'in your very hearing this text has come
22 true.'*q* There was a general stir of
   admiration; they were surprised that
   words of such grace should fall from
   his lips. 'Is not this Joseph's son?' they
23 asked. Then Jesus said, 'No doubt
   you will quote the proverb to me,
   "Physician, heal yourself!", and say,
   "We have heard of all your doings at
   Capernaum; do the same here in your
24 own home town." I tell you this,' he
   went on: 'no prophet is recognized in
25 his own country. There were many
   widows in Israel, you may be sure, in
   Elijah's time, when for three years and
   six months the skies never opened, and
   famine lay hard over the whole country;
26 yet it was to none of those that Elijah
   was sent, but to a widow at Sarepta in
27 the territory of Sidon. Again, in the
   time of the prophet Elisha there were
   many lepers in Israel, and not one of
   them was healed, but only Naaman,
28 the Syrian.' At these words the whole
29 congregation were infuriated. They
   leapt up, threw him out of the town,
   and took him to the brow of the hill
   on which it was built, meaning to hurl
30 him over the edge. But he walked
   straight through them all, and went
   away.
31   Coming down to Capernaum, a
   town in Galilee, he taught the people on
32 the Sabbath, and they were astounded

at his teaching, for what he said had
the note of authority. Now there was a 33
man in the synagogue possessed by a
devil, an unclean spirit. He shrieked at
the top of his voice, 'What do you 34
want with us, Jesus of Nazareth? Have
you*r* come to destroy us? I know who
you are—the Holy One of God.'
Jesus rebuked him: 'Be silent', he said, 35
'and come out of him.' Then the devil,
after throwing the man down in front
of the people, left him without doing
him any injury. Amazement fell on 36
them all and they said to one another:
'What is there in this man's words? He
gives orders to the unclean spirits with
authority and power, and out they go.'
So the news spread, and he was the 37
talk of the whole district.

   On leaving the synagogue he went to 38
Simon's house. Simon's mother-in-law
was in the grip of a high fever; and they
asked him to help her. He came and 39
stood over her and rebuked the fever.
It left her, and she got up at once and
waited on them.

   At sunset all who had friends 40
suffering from one disease or another
brought them to him; and he laid his
hands on them one by one and cured
them. Devils also came out of many of 41
them, shouting, 'You are the Son of
God.' But he rebuked them and
forbade them to speak, because they
knew that he was the Messiah.

   When day broke he went out and 42
made his way to a lonely spot. But the
people went in search of him, and
when they came to where he was they
pressed him not to leave them. But he 43
said, 'I must give the good news of the
kingdom of God to the other towns
also, for that is what I was sent to do.'
So he proclaimed the Gospel in the 44
synagogues of Judaea.*s*

q Or 'Today', he said, 'this text which you have just
heard has come true.'
r Or You have.
s Or the Jewish synagogues: *some witnesses read* the
synagogues of Galilee.

---

in the Law and for nonsacrificial worship. *Sabbath* begins at sunset on Friday. **18–19:** Isa.61.1–2;
58.6. **18:** *Spirit:* see 4.14 n. **20:** *Sat:* see Mt.5.1 n. **25–27:** Two OT examples of God's goodness
to non-Israelites are cited (1 Kgs. ch. 17; 2 Kgs.5.1–19), thus emphasizing the universal reach
of Jesus' mission.
   4.31–44: Jesus in Capernaum (Mt.8.14–17; Mk.1.21–38). **33:** *Devil:* see Mk.1.23 n. **38:**
Simon: Peter (see Mt.4.18). **40:** *Sunset* on Saturday marks the end of Sabbath; see v. 16 n.
44: For Lk., *Judaea* sometimes means the entire "Holy Land" (including Galilee).

5 One day as he stood by the Lake of Gennesaret, and the people crowded upon him to listen to the word of God, 2 he noticed two boats lying at the water's edge; the fishermen had come ashore and were washing their nets. 3 He got into one of the boats, which belonged to Simon, and asked him to put out a little way from the shore; then he went on teaching the crowds 4 from his seat in the boat. When he had finished speaking, he said to Simon, 'Put out into deep water and let down 5 your nets for a catch.' Simon answered, 'Master, we were hard at work all night and caught nothing at all; but if you say so, I will let down the nets.' 6 They did so and made a big haul of 7 fish; and their nets began to split. So they signalled to their partners in the other boat to come and help them. This they did, and loaded both boats 8 to the point of sinking. When Simon saw what had happened he fell at Jesus's knees and said, 'Go, Lord, 9 leave me, sinner that I am!' For he and all his companions were amazed at 10 the catch they had made; so too were his partners James and John, Zebedee's sons. 'Do not be afraid,' said Jesus to Simon; 'from now on you will be 11 catching men.' As soon as they had brought the boats to land, they left everything and followed him.

12 He was once in a certain town where there happened to be a man covered with leprosy; seeing Jesus, he bowed to the ground and begged his help. 'Sir,' he said, 'if only you will, you can 13 cleanse me.' Jesus stretched out his hand, touched him, and said, 'Indeed I will; be clean again.' The leprosy left 14 him immediately. Jesus then ordered him not to tell anybody. 'But go,' he said, 'show yourself to the priest, and make the offering laid down by Moses for your cleansing; that will certify the 15 cure.' But the talk about him spread all the more; great crowds gathered to hear him and to be cured of their ailments. And from time to time he 16 would withdraw to lonely places for prayer.

One day he was teaching, and 17 Pharisees and teachers of the law were sitting round. People had come from every village of Galilee and from Judaea and Jerusalem,[t] and the power of the Lord was with him to heal the sick. Some men appeared carrying a 18 paralysed man on a bed. They tried to bring him in and set him down in front of Jesus, but finding no way to 19 do so because of the crowd, they went up on to the roof and let him down through the tiling, bed and all, into the middle of the company in front of Jesus. When Jesus saw their faith, he 20 said, 'Man, your sins are forgiven you.'

The lawyers and the Pharisees began 21 saying to themselves, 'Who is this fellow with his blasphemous talk? Who but God alone can forgive sins?' But 22 Jesus knew what they were thinking and answered them: 'Why do you harbour thoughts like these? Is it 23 easier to say, "Your sins are forgiven you", or to say, "Stand up and walk"? But to convince you that the Son of 24 Man has the right on earth to forgive sins'—he turned to the paralysed man —'I say to you, stand up, take your bed, and go home.' And at once he 25 rose to his feet before their eyes, took up the bed he had been lying on, and went home praising God. They were 26 all lost in amazement and praised God; filled with awe they said, 'You would never believe the things we have seen today.'

Later, when he went out, he saw a 27 tax-gatherer, Levi by name, at his seat in the custom-house, and said to him, 'Follow me'; and he rose to his feet, 28 left everything behind, and followed him.

t Some witnesses read and Pharisees and teachers of the law, who had come from every village of Galilee and from Judaea and Jerusalem, were sitting round.

5.1–11: The first disciples called (compare Mt.4.18–22; Mk.1.16–20; Jn.1.35–51; 21.1–8). **1:** *Lake of Gennesaret:* Sea of Galilee.
5.12–16: A leper healed (Mt.8.1–4; Mk.1.40–45). **12:** *Leprosy, cleanse:* see Mt.8.2 n. **14:** See Lev.14.1–32. **16:** *Prayer:* see 3.21 n.
5.17–6.11: Healing and conflict.
5.17–26: A paralytic (Mt.9.1–8; Mk.2.1–12). **17:** *Power* may mean "Spirit"; see 4.14 n. **19:** *Tiling:* compare Mk.2.4 n. **21:** *Lawyers:* see Mt.2.4 n. **24:** *Son of Man:* see Mk.2.10 n.
5.27–32: Friend of outcasts (Mt.9.9–13; Mk.2.13–17). **27:** *A tax-gatherer* was despised; see 3.12 n.

29 Afterwards Levi held a big reception in his house for Jesus; among the guests was a large party of tax-
30 gatherers and others. The Pharisees and the lawyers of their sect complained to his disciples: 'Why do you eat and drink', they said, 'with tax-
31 gatherers and sinners?' Jesus answered them: 'It is not the healthy that need a
32 doctor, but the sick; I have not come to invite virtuous people, but to call sinners to repentance.'
33 Then they said to him, 'John's disciples are much given to fasting and the practice of prayer, and so are the disciples of the Pharisees; but yours
34 eat and drink.' Jesus replied, 'Can you make the bridegroom's friends fast while the bridegroom is with them?
35 But a time will come: the bridegroom will be taken away from them, and that will be the time for them to fast.'
36 He told them this parable also: 'No one tears a piece from a new cloak to patch an old one: if he does, he will have made a hole in the new cloak, and the patch from the new will not match
37 the old. Nor does anyone put new wine into old wine-skins; if he does, the new wine will burst the skins, the wine will be wasted, and the skins
38, 39 ruined. Fresh skins for new wine! And no one after drinking old wine wants new; for he says, "The old wine is good."'

6 One Sabbath he was going through the cornfields, and his disciples were plucking the ears of corn, rubbing them
2 in their hands, and eating them. Some of the Pharisees said, 'Why are you doing what is forbidden on the
3 Sabbath?' Jesus answered, 'So you have not read what David did when he
4 and his men were hungry? He went into the House of God and took the

sacred bread to eat and gave it to his men, though priests alone are allowed to eat it, and no one else.' He also 5 said, 'The Son of Man is sovereign even over the Sabbath.'

On another Sabbath he had gone to 6 synagogue and was teaching. There happened to be a man in the congregation whose right arm was withered; and 7 the lawyers and the Pharisees were on the watch to see whether Jesus would cure him on the Sabbath, so that they could find a charge to bring against him. But he knew what was in their 8 minds and said to the man with the withered arm, 'Get up and stand out here.' So he got up and stood there. Then Jesus said to them, 'I put the 9 question to you: is it permitted to do good or to do evil on the Sabbath, to save life or to destroy it?' He looked 10 round at them all and then said to the man, 'Stretch out your arm.' He did so, and his arm was restored. But they 11 were beside themselves with anger, and began to discuss among themselves what they could do to Jesus.

During this time he went out one 12 day into the hills to pray, and spent the night in prayer to God. When day 13 broke he called his disciples to him, and from among them he chose twelve and named them Apostles: Simon, to 14 whom he gave the name of Peter, and Andrew his brother, James and John, Philip and Bartholomew, Matthew and 15 Thomas, James son of Alphaeus, and Simon who was called the Zealot, Judas son of James, and Judas Iscariot 16 who turned traitor.

He came down the hill with them 17 and took his stand on level ground. There was a large concourse of his disciples and great numbers of people from Jerusalem and Judaea and from

---

29: *Reception*: only Lk. clearly places the dinner in *Levi*'s house (compare Mt.9.10; Mk.2.15).
5.33–39: **Fasting and prayer** (Mt.9.14–17; Mk.2.18–22). 33: *John's disciples:* see Mk.2.18 n.
36–38: See Mk.2.21–22 n. 39: This may have been intended as sarcastic comment about the preference of Jesus' opponents for the old ways.
6.1–11: **Sabbath controversy** (Mt.12.1–14; Mk.2.23–3.6). See Mk.2.23–3.6 n. 1: Deut.23.25.
2: Exod.20.10; Deut.5.14. 3: 1 Sam.21.1–7. 4: Lev.24.7–9. 7–11: See Mk.3.1–6 n.
6.12–16: **The Twelve chosen** (Mt.10.1–4; Mk.3.13–19). The choosing of the Twelve is a prelude to the sermon which follows; notice again the reference to *prayer* (3.21 n.). 13: *Apostles:* see Mt.10.2 n. 15: *Zealot:* Mk.3.18 n.
6.17–49: **Sermon on the Plain.** The Sermon in Lk. includes sayings also found in the Sermon on the Mount in Mt. chs. 5–7.
6.17–19: **The setting.** See Mt.4.25;12.15–21; Mk.3.7–12. 17: Contrast Mt.5.1. Lk. thinks of mountains for settings requiring privacy; public teaching tends to take place on *level ground*.

the seaboard of Tyre and Sidon, who had come to listen to him, and to be 18 cured of their diseases. Those who were troubled with unclean spirits were 19 cured; and everyone in the crowd was trying to touch him, because power went out from him and cured them all.

20 THEN TURNING TO HIS DISCIPLES HE began to speak:

'How blest are you who are in need; the kingdom of God is yours.

21 'How blest are you who now go hungry; your hunger shall be satisfied.

'How blest are you who weep now; you shall laugh.

22 'How blest you are when men hate you, when they outlaw you and insult you, and ban your very name as infamous, because of the Son of Man.

23 On that day be glad and dance for joy; for assuredly you have a rich reward in heaven; in just the same way did their fathers treat the prophets.

24 'But alas for you who are rich; you have had your time of happiness.

25 'Alas for you who are well-fed now; you shall go hungry.

'Alas for you who laugh now; you shall mourn and weep.

26 'Alas for you when all speak well of you; just so did their fathers treat the false prophets.

27 'But to you who hear me I say:

'Love your enemies; do good to 28 those who hate you; bless those who curse you; pray for those who treat 29 you spitefully. When a man hits you on the cheek, offer him the other cheek too; when a man takes your coat, let 30 him have your shirt as well. Give to everyone who asks you; when a man takes what is yours, do not demand it 31 back. Treat others as you would like them to treat you.

32 'If you love only those who love you,

what credit is that to you? Even sinners love those who love them. Again, if 33 you do good only to those who do good to you, what credit is that to you? Even sinners do as much. And 34 if you lend only where you expect to be repaid, what credit is that to you? Even sinners lend to each other to be repaid in full. But you must love your 35 enemies and do good; and lend without expecting any return;*u* and you will have a rich reward: you will be sons of the Most High, because he himself is kind to the ungrateful and wicked. Be compassionate as your 36 Father is compassionate.

'Pass no judgement, and you will 37 not be judged; do not condemn, and you will not be condemned; acquit, and you will be acquitted; give, and 38 gifts will be given you. Good measure, pressed down, shaken together, and running over, will be poured into your lap; for whatever measure you deal out to others will be dealt to you in return.'

He also offered them a parable: 'Can 39 one blind man be guide to another? Will they not both fall into the ditch? A pupil is not superior to his teacher; 40 but everyone, when his training is complete, will reach his teacher's level.

'Why do you look at the speck of 41 sawdust in your brother's eye, with never a thought for the great plank in your own? How can you say to your 42 brother, "My dear brother, let me take the speck out of your eye", when you are blind to the plank in your own? You hypocrite! First take the plank out of your own eye, and then you will see clearly to take the speck out of your brother's.

'There is no such thing as a good 43

u Or without ever giving up hope; some witnesses read without giving up hope of anyone.

6.20–23: The Beatitudes (Mt.5.3–12). On form, see Mt.5.3 n. Unlike Mt., Lk. reports all these Beatitudes in the second person. Also, Lk. does not "spiritualize" the conditions described as "blest"; see vv. 24–26 n.

6.24–26: The Woes (*Alas for you . . .*) represent a form which warns against qualities of life or types of behavior that have bad consequences; here, the warning has been heightened to eschatological threat. As vv. 20,21,24,25 show, *in need* and *hungry* are understood literally by Lk.; contrast Mt.5.3 n., 6 n.

6.27–36: Love of enemies (Mt.5.39–42,44–48). **31:** The Golden Rule; see Mt.7.12 n. **35:** Sonship is shown in behavior that conforms to God's dealing with men.

6.37–46: Judging others (Mt.7.1–5). **39:** Mt.15.14. **40:** Mt.10.24–25; Jn.13.16. **43–46:** Proof of goodness (Mt.7.16–21; 12.33–35).

tree producing worthless fruit, nor yet a worthless tree producing good fruit. 44 For each tree is known by its own fruit; you do not gather figs from thistles, and you do not pick grapes 45 from brambles. A good man produces good from the store of good within himself; and an evil man from evil within produces evil. For the words that the mouth utters come from the overflowing of the heart.

46 'Why do you keep calling me "Lord, Lord"—and never do what I tell you? 47 Everyone who comes to me and hears what I say, and acts upon it—I will 48 show you what he is like. He is like a man who, in building his house, dug deep and laid the foundations on rock. When the flood came, the river burst upon that house, but could not shift it, 49 because it had been soundly built. But he who hears and does not act is like a man who built his house on the soil without foundations. As soon as the river burst upon it, the house collapsed, and fell with a great crash.'

7 WHEN HE HAD FINISHED ADDRESSING 2 the people, he went to Capernaum. A centurion there had a servant whom he valued highly; this servant was ill and 3 near to death. Hearing about Jesus, he sent some Jewish elders with the request that he would come and save 4 his servant's life. They approached Jesus and pressed their petition earnestly: 'He deserves this favour 5 from you,' they said, 'for he is a friend of our nation and it is he who built us 6 our synagogue.' Jesus went with them; but when he was not far from the house, the centurion sent friends with this message: 'Do not trouble further, sir; it is not for me to have you under 7 my roof, and that is why I did not presume to approach you in person. But say the word and my servant will 8 be cured. I know, for in my position I am myself under orders, with soldiers

under me. I say to one, "Go", and he goes; to another, "Come here", and he comes; and to my servant, "Do 9 this", and he does it.' When Jesus heard this, he admired the man, and, turning to the crowd that was following him, he said, 'I tell you, nowhere, even in Israel, have I found faith like this.' 10 And the messengers returned to the house and found the servant in good health.

11 Afterwards*v* Jesus went to a town called Nain, accompanied by his 12 disciples and a large crowd. As he approached the gate of the town he met a funeral. The dead man was the only son of his widowed mother; and many of the townspeople were there with her. When the Lord saw her his 13 heart went out to her, and he said, 'Weep no more.' With that he stepped 14 forward and laid his hand on the bier; and the bearers halted. Then he spoke: 'Young man, rise up!' The dead man 15 sat up and began to speak; and Jesus gave him back to his mother. Deep 16 awe fell upon them all, and they praised God. 'A great prophet has arisen among us', they said, and again, 'God has shown his care for his people.' The story of what he had 17 done ran through all parts of Judaea and the whole neighbourhood.

18 John too was informed of all this by his disciples. Summoning two of their 19 number he sent them to the Lord with this message: 'Are you the one who is to come, or are we to expect some other?' The messengers made their 20 way to Jesus and said, 'John the Baptist has sent us to you: he asks, "Are you the one who is to come, or are we to expect some other?"' There 21 and then he cured many sufferers from diseases, plagues, and evil spirits; and on many blind people he bestowed sight. Then he gave them his answer: 22 'Go', he said, 'and tell John what you

v Some witnesses read On the next day.

6.47–49: **The wise and foolish builders** (Mt.7.24–27).

7.1–10: **The centurion's servant** (Mt.8.5–13). 2: *Centurion:* see Mt.8.5 n. In Lk., the sick person is clearly a *servant;* compare Mt.8.5 n.

7.11–17: **The widow's son.** Compare 1 Kgs.17.17–24; 2 Kgs.4.32–37.

7.18–35: **Jesus and John the Baptist** (Mt.11.2–19). The passage advances high claims for both Jesus and the Baptist. John's question (v. 19) elicits not only Jesus' testimony about his own works (vv. 22–23), but also his commendation of the Baptist (vv. 24–28). Vv. 22–23 are based on

have seen and heard: how the blind recover their sight, the lame walk, the lepers are made clean, the deaf hear, the dead are raised to life, the poor are
23 hearing the good news and happy is the man who does not find me a stumbling-block.'

24 After John's messengers had left, Jesus began to speak about him to the crowds: 'What was the spectacle that drew you to the wilderness? A reed-bed
25 swept by the wind? No? Then what did you go out to see? A man dressed in silks and satins? Surely you must look in palaces for grand clothes and
26 luxury. But what did you go out to see? A prophet? Yes indeed, and far
27 more than a prophet. He is the man of whom Scripture says,

"Here is my herald, whom I send on
    ahead of you,
and he will prepare your way before
    you."

28 I tell you, there is not a mother's son greater than John, and yet the least in the kingdom of God is greater than he.'
29 When they heard him, all the people, including the tax-gatherers, praised God, for they had accepted John's
30 baptism; but the Pharisees and lawyers, who refused his baptism, had rejected[w] God's purpose for themselves.
31 'How can I describe the people of this generation? What are they like?
32 They are like children sitting in the market-place and shouting at each other,

"We piped for you and you would
    not dance."
"We wept and wailed, and you would
    not mourn."

33 For John the Baptist came neither eating bread nor drinking wine, and
34 you say, "He is possessed." The Son of Man came eating and drinking, and you say, "Look at him! a glutton and

a drinker, a friend of tax-gatherers and sinners!" And yet God's wisdom is 35 proved right by all who are her children.'

One of the Pharisees invited him to 36 eat with him; he went to the Pharisee's house and took his place at table. A 37 woman who was living an immoral life in the town had learned that Jesus was at table in the Pharisee's house and had brought oil of myrrh in a small flask. She took her place behind him, by his 38 feet, weeping. His feet were wetted with her tears and she wiped them with her hair, kissing them and anointing them with the myrrh. When his host 39 the Pharisee saw this he said to himself, 'If this fellow were a real prophet, he would know who this woman is that touches him, and what sort of woman she is, a sinner.' Jesus 40 took him up and said, 'Simon, I have something to say to you.' 'Speak on, Master', said he. 'Two men were in 41 debt to a money-lender: one owed him five hundred silver pieces, the other fifty. As neither had anything to pay 42 with he let them both off. Now, which will love him most?' Simon replied, 'I 43 should think the one that was let off most.' 'You are right', said Jesus. Then turning to the woman, he said to 44 Simon, 'You see this woman? I came to your house: you provided no water for my feet; but this woman has made my feet wet with her tears and wiped them with her hair. You gave me no 45 kiss; but she has been kissing my feet ever since I came in. You did not 46 anoint my head with oil; but she has anointed my feet with myrrh. And so, 47 I tell you, her great love proves that her many sins have been forgiven; where little has been forgiven, little love is shown.' Then he said to her, 48 'Your sins are forgiven.' The other 49 guests began to ask themselves, 'Who

w Or '. . . greater than he. And all the people, including the tax-gatherers, when they heard him, accepted John's baptism and acknowledged the righteous dealing of God; but the Pharisees and lawyers, by refusing his baptism, rejected . . .'

Isa.29.18–19; 35.5–6; 61.1. **27:** Mal.3.1. **33:** *Possessed*, i.e. by a demon, out of his mind. **34:** Tax-gatherers: see Lk.3.12 n. **35:** *Wisdom* is the personified source of revelation as in Prov.1.20–33; Ecclus.24.1–23.
7.36–50: Dinner with a Pharisee (compare Mt.26.6–13; Mk.14.3–9; Jn.12.1–8). **37:** Custom permitted such intrusions on private parties. *Myrrh:* a fragrant substance. **40:** *Simon* was a name in common use. **44–46:** Special courtesies which the host might have provided are

50 is this, that he can forgive sins?' But he said to the woman, 'Your faith has saved you; go in peace.'

8 AFTER THIS HE WENT JOURNEYING FROM town to town and village to village, proclaiming the good news of the kingdom of God. With him were the 2 Twelve and a number of women who had been set free from evil spirits and infirmities: Mary, known as Mary of Magdala, from whom seven devils had 3 come out, Joanna, the wife of Chuza a steward of Herod's, Susanna, and many others. These women provided for them out of their own resources.

4   People were now gathering in large numbers, and as they made their way to him from one town after another, he 5 said in a parable: 'A sower went out to sow his seed. And as he sowed, some seed fell along the footpath, where it was trampled on, and the birds ate it 6 up. Some seed fell on rock and, after coming up, withered for lack of 7 moisture. Some seed fell in among thistles, and the thistles grew up with 8 it and choked it. And some of the seed fell into good soil, and grew, and yielded a hundredfold.' As he said this he called out, 'If you have ears to hear, then hear.'

9   His disciples asked him what this 10 parable meant, and he said, 'It has been granted to you to know the secrets of the kingdom of God; but the others have only parables, so that they may look but see nothing, hear but understand nothing.

11   'This is what the parable means. 12 The seed is the word of God. Those along the footpath are the men who hear it, and then the devil comes and carries off the word from their hearts for fear they should believe and be 13 saved. The seed sown on rock stands for those who receive the word with joy when they hear it, but have no root; they are believers for a while, but in the time of testing they desert. That which fell among thistles repre- 14 sents those who hear, but their further growth is choked by cares and wealth and the pleasures of life, and they bring nothing to maturity. But the seed in 15 good soil represents those who bring a good and honest heart to the hearing of the word, hold it fast, and by their perseverance yield a harvest.

'Nobody lights a lamp and then 16 covers it with a basin or puts it under the bed. On the contrary, he puts it on a lamp-stand so that those who come in may see the light. For there is 17 nothing hidden that will not become public, nothing under cover that will not be made known and brought into the open.

'Take care, then, how you listen; for 18 the man who has will be given more, and the man who has not will forfeit even what he thinks he has.'

His mother and his brothers arrived 19 but could not get to him for the crowd. He was told, 'Your mother and 20 brothers are standing outside, and they want to see you.' He replied, 'My 21 mother and my brothers—they are those who hear the word of God and act upon it.'

One day he got into a boat with his 22 disciples and said to them, 'Let us cross over to the other side of the lake.' So they put out; and as they 23 sailed along he went to sleep. Then a heavy squall struck the lake; they began to ship water and were in grave danger. They went to him, and roused 24 him, crying, 'Master, Master, we are sinking!' He awoke, and rebuked the wind and the turbulent waters. The storm subsided and all was calm. 'Where is your faith?' he asked. In fear and 25 astonishment they said to one another, 'Who can this be? He gives his orders to wind and waves, and they obey him.'

performed instead by the woman. **50:** In miracle stories the Gk. words here translated *saved you* mean "cured you" (e.g. 8.48).
   8.1–3: Women disciples serve.
   8.4–15: The parable of the sower and its meaning (Mt.13.1–23; Mk.4.1–20). **4:** On *parables*, see Mk.4.2 n. **6:** See Mk.4.3–8 n. **8:** See Mk.4.8 n. **9–10:** *Look, hear:* see Mk.4.12 n.; Mt.13.13 n. **11–15:** See Mk.4.13–20 n.
   8.16–21: Miscellaneous sayings. 16–18: See Mk.4.24–25 n. **16:** Mt.5.15; Mk.4.21. **17:** Mt.10.26; Mk.4.22. **18:** 19.26; Mt.13.12; 25.29; Mk.4.25. **19–21:** Mt.12.46–50; Mk.3.31–35.
   8.22–25: Rebuke of a storm (Mt.8.23–27; Mk.4.35–41).

80

26 So they landed in the country of the Gergesenes,[x] which is opposite Galilee. 27 As he stepped ashore he was met by a man from the town who was possessed by devils. For a long time he had neither worn clothes nor lived in a house, but stayed among the tombs. 28 When he saw Jesus he cried out, and fell at his feet shouting, 'What do you want with me, Jesus, son of the Most High God? I implore you, do not torment me.' 29 For Jesus was already ordering the unclean spirit to come out of the man. Many a time it had seized him, and then, for safety's sake, they would secure him with chains and fetters; but each time he broke loose, and with the devil in charge made off to the solitary places. 30 Jesus asked him, 'What is your name?' 'Legion', he replied. This was because so many devils had taken possession of him. 31 And they begged him not to banish them to the Abyss. 32 There happened to be a large herd of pigs nearby, feeding on the hill; and the spirits begged him to let them go into these pigs. He gave them leave; 33 the devils came out of the man and went into the pigs, and the herd rushed over the edge into the lake and were drowned. 34 The men in charge of them saw what had happened, and, taking to their heels, they carried the news to 35 the town and country-side; and the people came out to see for themselves. When they came to Jesus, and found the man from whom the devils had gone out sitting at his feet clothed and in his right mind, they were afraid. 36 The spectators told them how the 37 madman had been cured. Then the whole population of the Gergesene[y] district asked him to go, for they were in the grip of a great fear. So he got 38 into the boat and returned. The man from whom the devils had gone out begged leave to go with him; but 39 Jesus sent him away: 'Go back home,'

he said, 'and tell them everything that God has done for you.' The man went all over the town spreading the news of what Jesus had done for him.

When Jesus returned, the people 40 welcomed him, for they were all expecting him. Then a man appeared— 41 Jairus was his name and he was president of the synagogue. Throwing himself down at Jesus's feet he begged him to come to his house, because he 42 had an only daughter, about twelve years old, who was dying. And while Jesus was on his way he could hardly breathe for the crowds.

Among them was a woman who had 43 suffered from haemorrhages for twelve years; and[z] nobody had been able to cure her. She came up from behind and 44 touched the edge of[a] his cloak, and at once her haemorrhage stopped. Jesus 45 said, 'Who was it that touched me?' All disclaimed it, and Peter and his companions said, 'Master, the crowds are hemming you in and pressing upon you!' But Jesus said, 'Someone did 46 touch me, for I felt that power had gone out from me.' Then the woman, 47 seeing that she was detected, came trembling and fell at his feet. Before all the people she explained why she had touched him and how she had been instantly cured. He said to her, 'My 48 daughter, your faith has cured you. Go in peace.'

While he was still speaking, a man 49 came from the president's house with the message, 'Your daughter is dead; trouble the Rabbi no further.' But Jesus 50 heard, and interposed. 'Do not be afraid,' he said; 'only show faith and she will be well again.' On arrival at 51 the house he allowed no one to go in with him except Peter, John, and James, and the child's father and mother. And all were weeping and 52 lamenting for her. He said, 'Weep no more; she is not dead: she is asleep';

x *Some witnesses read* Gerasenes; *others read* Gadarenes.
y *Some witnesses read* Gerasene; *others read* Gadarene.
z *Some witnesses add* though she had spent all she had on doctors.
a *Some witnesses omit* the edge of.

8.26–39: The Gergesene demoniac (Mt.8.28–34; Mk.5.1–20). **26**: *Gergesenes:* see Mk.5.1 n. **28**: *Son:* see Mt.8.28–29 n. **30**: On *name, Legion,* see Mk.5.9 n. **32**: *Pigs:* see Mt.8.30 n.
8.40–56: Jairus' daughter and a woman with a chronic ailment (Mt.9.18–26; Mk.5.21–43). See Mk.5.21–43 n. **48**: *Cured:* see 7.50 n. **50**: *Rabbi:* lit. "my teacher," a respectful form of address to a teacher of the Law.

53 and they only laughed at him, well
54 knowing that she was dead. But Jesus
took hold of her hand and called her:
55 'Get up, my child.' Her spirit returned,
she stood up immediately, and he told
56 them to give her something to eat. Her
parents were astounded; but he forbade
them to tell anyone what had happened.

9 HE NOW CALLED THE TWELVE TOGETHER
and gave them power and authority to
overcome all the devils and to cure
2 diseases, and sent them to proclaim the
3 kingdom of God and to heal. 'Take
nothing for the journey,' he told them,
'neither stick nor pack, neither bread
nor money; nor are you each to have a
4 second coat. When you are admitted
to a house, stay there, and go on from
5 there. As for those who will not receive
you, when you leave their town shake
the dust off your feet as a warning to
6 them.' So they set out and travelled
from village to village, and everywhere
they told the good news and healed
the sick.
7   Now Prince Herod heard of all that
was happening, and did not know
what to make of it; for some were
saying that John had been raised from
8 the dead, others that Elijah had
appeared, others again that one of the
old prophets had come back to life.
9 Herod said, 'As for John, I beheaded
him myself; but who is this I hear such
talk about?' And he was anxious to
see him.
10   On their return the apostles told
Jesus all they had done; and he took
them with him and withdrew privately
11 to a town called Bethsaida. But the
crowds found out and followed him.
He welcomed them, and spoke to them
about the kingdom of God, and cured
those who were in need of healing.

When evening was drawing on, the 12
Twelve came up to him and said, 'Send
these people away; then they can go
into the villages and farms round about
to find food and lodging; for we are
in a lonely place here.' 'Give them 13
something to eat yourselves', he replied.
But they said, 'All we have is five loaves
and two fishes, nothing more—unless
perhaps we ourselves are to go and buy
provisions for all this company.' (There 14
were about five thousand men.) He said
to his disciples, 'Make them sit down
in groups of fifty or so.' They did so 15
and got them all seated. Then, taking 16
the five loaves and the two fishes, he
looked up to heaven, said the blessing
over them, broke them, and gave them
to the disciples to distribute to the
people. They all ate to their hearts' 17
content; and when the scraps they left
were picked up, they filled twelve great
baskets.
One day when he was praying alone 18
in the presence of his disciples, he
asked them, 'Who do the people say I
am?' They answered, 'Some say John 19
the Baptist, others Elijah, others that
one of the old prophets has come back
to life.' 'And you,' he said, 'who do 20
you say I am?' Peter answered, 'God's
Messiah.' Then he gave them strict 21
orders not to tell this to anyone. And 22
he said, 'The Son of Man has to
undergo great sufferings, and to be
rejected by the elders, chief priests, and
doctors of the law, to be put to death
and to be raised again on the third day.'
And to all he said, 'If anyone wishes 23
to be a follower of mine, he must leave
self behind; day after day he must take
up his cross, and come with me.
Whoever cares for his own safety is 24
lost; but if a man will let himself be
lost for my sake, that man is safe.

9.1–6: **Mission of the Twelve** (see 10.1 n.; Mt.9.35; 10.1,9–11,14; Mk.6.7–13). 1–2: *Cure, proclaim:* see Mt.10.8 n.
9.7–9: **Herod and Jesus** (Mt.14.1–2; Mk.6.14–16). 7: *Herod:* Antipas (see 3.1 n.). *John:* the Baptist. 8: *Elijah:* see Mk.6.15 n.
9.10–17: **Feeding of five thousand** (Mt.14.13–21; Mk.6.30–44; Jn.6.1–13). See Mk.6.30–44 n.; Lk. has only one account of such a feeding.
9.18–22: **Peter's confession and Jesus' prediction of his suffering** (Mt.16.13–23; Mk.8.27–33; Jn.6.66–71). 18: *Praying alone:* see 3.21 n. 19: *John, Elijah:* see Mk.8.28 n. 20: *Messiah:* see Mt.1.1 n. 22: 9.44; 18.31–33; see Mk.8.31 n.
9.23–27: **Following Jesus** (Mt.16.24–28; Mk.8.34–9.1). 23: *Cross:* see Mt.10.38–39 n. The addition of *day after day* in Lk. (compare Mt.16.24; Mk.8.34 n.) spiritualizes the meaning of *take up his cross.*

25 What will a man gain by winning the whole world, at the cost of his true 26 self? For whoever is ashamed of me and mine,[b] the Son of Man will be ashamed of him, when he comes in his glory and the glory of the Father and 27 the holy angels. And I tell you this: there are some of those standing here who will not taste death before they have seen the kingdom of God.'

28 About eight days after this conversation he took Peter, John, and James with him and went up into the hills to 29 pray. And while he was praying the appearance of his face changed and his 30 clothes became dazzling white. Suddenly there were two men talking with 31 him; these were Moses and Elijah, who appeared in glory and spoke of his departure, the destiny he was to fulfil 32 in Jerusalem. Meanwhile Peter and his companions had been in a deep sleep; but when they awoke, they saw his glory and the two men who stood 33 beside him. And as these were moving away from Jesus, Peter said to him, 'Master, how good it is that we are here! Shall we make three shelters, one for you, one for Moses, and one for Elijah?'; but he spoke without knowing 34 what he was saying. The words were still on his lips, when there came a cloud which cast a shadow over them; they were afraid as they entered the 35 cloud, and from it came a voice: 'This is my Son, my Chosen; listen to him.' 36 When the voice had spoken, Jesus was seen to be alone. The disciples kept silence and at that time told nobody anything of what they had seen.

37 Next day when they came down from the hills he was met by a large crowd. 38 All at once there was a shout from a man in the crowd: 'Master, look at my son, I implore you, my only child. 39 From time to time a spirit seizes him, gives a sudden scream, and throws him into convulsions with foaming at the mouth, and it keeps on mauling him and will hardly let him go. I asked 40 your disciples to cast it out, but they could not.' Jesus answered, 'What an 41 unbelieving and perverse generation! How long shall I be with you and endure you all? Bring your son here.' But before the boy could reach him the 42 devil dashed him to the ground and threw him into convulsions. Jesus rebuked the unclean spirit, cured the boy, and gave him back to his father. And they were all struck with awe at 43 the majesty of God.

Amid the general wonder and admiration at all he was doing, Jesus said to his disciples, 'What I now say is for 44 you: ponder my words. The Son of Man is to be given up into the power of men.' But they did not understand 45 this saying; it had been hidden from them, so that they should not[c] grasp its meaning, and they were afraid to ask him about it.

A dispute arose among them: which 46 of them was the greatest? Jesus knew 47 what was passing in their minds, so he took a child by the hand and stood him at his side, and said, 'Whoever receives 48 this child in my name receives me; and whoever receives me receives the One who sent me. For the least among you all—he is the greatest.'

'Master,' said John, 'we saw a man 49 driving out devils in your name, but as he is not one of us we tried to stop him.' Jesus said to him, 'Do not stop 50 him, for he who is not against you is on your side.'

Journeys and encounters

AS THE TIME APPROACHED WHEN HE 51 was to be taken up to heaven, he set his face resolutely towards Jerusalem,

b *Some witnesses read* me and my words.
c *Or* it was so obscure to them that they could not . . .

9.28–36: The transfiguration (Mt.17.1–8; Mk.9.2–8). See Mt.17.1–8 nn. **28:** *To pray:* see 3.21 n. **31:** *Departure* may refer to death or to Jesus' death, resurrection, and ascension.
9.37–43a: An epileptic boy (Mt.17.14–20; Mk.9.14–29). Lk. has greatly abbreviated the story.
9.43b–45: The second prediction (see 9.19) **of suffering** (Mt.17.22–23; Mk.9.30–32).
9.46–50: The true disciple (Mt.18.1–5; Mk.9.33–41). The true disciple is not embroiled in arguments about rank (v. 46) or privilege (vv. 49–50); rather he knows the joy of humble service (v. 48). **49–50:** See Mk.9.39–40 n.
9.51–19.27: The Lukan travel narrative. Perhaps taking his clue from brief but dramatic

52 and sent messengers ahead. They set out and went into a Samaritan village 53 to make arrangements for him; but the villagers would not have him because 54 he was making for Jerusalem. When the disciples James and John saw this they said, 'Lord, may we call down fire 55 from heaven to burn them up[d]?' But 56 he turned and rebuked them,[e] and they went on to another village.

57   As they were going along the road a man said to him, 'I will follow you 58 wherever you go.' Jesus answered, 'Foxes have their holes, the birds their roosts; but the Son of Man has 59 nowhere to lay his head.' To another he said, 'Follow me', but the man replied, 'Let me go and bury my father first.' 60 Jesus said, 'Leave the dead to bury their dead; you must go and announce the kingdom of God.' 61   Yet another said, 'I will follow you, sir; but let me first say good-bye to my 62 people at home.' To him Jesus said, 'No one who sets his hand to the plough and then keeps looking back[f] is fit for the kingdom of God.'

10   After this the Lord appointed a further seventy-two[g] and sent them on ahead in pairs to every town and place 2 he was going to visit himself. He said to them: 'The crop is heavy, but labourers are scarce; you must therefore beg the owner to send labourers to 3 harvest his crop. Be on your way. And look, I am sending you like lambs 4 among wolves. Carry no purse or pack, and travel barefoot. Exchange no 5 greetings on the road. When you go into a house, let your first words be, 6 "Peace to this house." If there is a man of peace there, your peace will rest upon him; if not, it will return and 7 rest upon you. Stay in that one house,

sharing their food and drink; for the worker earns his pay. Do not move from house to house. When you come 8 into a town and they make you welcome, eat the food provided for you; heal the sick there, and say, "The 9 kingdom of God has come close to you." When you enter a town and they 10 do not make you welcome, go out into its streets and say, "The very dust of 11 your town that clings to our feet we wipe off to your shame. Only take note of this: the kingdom of God has come close." I tell you, it will be more 12 bearable for Sodom on the great Day than for that town.

'Alas for you, Chorazin! Alas for 13 you, Bethsaida! If the miracles that were performed in you had been performed in Tyre and Sidon, they would have repented long ago, sitting in sackcloth and ashes. But it will be 14 more bearable for Tyre and Sidon at the Judgement than for you. And as 15 for you, Capernaum, will you be exalted to the skies? No, brought down to the depths!

'Whoever listens to you listens to 16 me; whoever rejects you rejects me. And whoever rejects me rejects the One who sent me.'

The seventy-two[g] came back jubilant. 17 'In your name, Lord,' they said, 'even the devils submit to us.' He replied, 'I 18 watched how Satan fell, like lightning, out of the sky. And now you see that I 19 have given you the power to tread underfoot snakes and scorpions and all the forces of the enemy, and

d *Some witnesses add* as Elijah did.
e *Some witnesses insert* 'You do not know', he said, 'to what spirit you belong; (56) for the Son of Man did not come to destroy men's lives but to save them.'
f *Some witnesses read* No one who looks back as he sets hand to the plough . . .
g *Some witnesses read* seventy.

notices in Mk.10.1,32, Lk. has developed the journey to Jerusalem into a narrative which prepares, not only for the death and resurrection in the Holy City (see, e.g. 13.33), but also for the subsequent journey of the church to the "ends of the earth" (Acts 1.8; see, e.g. 9.51–10.24 with notes). For most of this section (see 18.15–17 n.) Lk. does not follow the order of Mk.
    9.51–10.24: The mission of the seventy-two. 51: *Taken up:* see Acts 1.11. **52:** The enmity between Jews and *Samaritans* was ancient and deep, of the sort possible only where there are rival claims to being the true guardians of a common tradition (the Law of Moses). **57–62:** Three candidates who wish to *follow* in Jesus' way are introduced; in each case, the heavy demands of discipleship are presented (compare Mt.8.19–22). **10.1:** Lk. has two missions: of the Twelve (9.1–6; perhaps a symbolic mission to Israel) and of the *seventy-two* (perhaps, symbolically, to the Gentile nations). **2–12:** Compare Mt.9.37–38; 10.7–16; Mk.6.7–11. **8–9:** *Heal, kingdom:* see Mt.10.8 n. **12:** *Sodom:* see Mt.10.15 n. **13–15:** *Tyre, Sidon:* see Mt.11.21 n. **16:** See Mt.10.40–42 n.; Jn.13.20. **18:** *I watched how Satan fell* may report a vision of God's

20 nothing will ever harm you.*h* Nevertheless, what you should rejoice over is not that the spirits submit to you, but that your names are enrolled in heaven.'

21 At that moment Jesus exulted in the Holy*i* Spirit and said, 'I thank thee, Father, Lord of heaven and earth, for hiding these things from the learned and wise, and revealing them to the simple. Yes, Father, such*j* was thy 22 choice.' Then turning to his disciples he said,*k* 'Everything is entrusted to me by my Father; and no one knows who the Son is but the Father, or who the Father is but the Son, and those to whom the Son may choose to reveal him.'

23 Turning to his disciples in private he said, 'Happy the eyes that see what 24 you are seeing! I tell you, many prophets and kings wished to see what you now see, yet never saw it; to hear what you hear, yet never heard it.'

25 ON ONE OCCASION A LAWYER CAME forward to put this test question to him: 'Master, what must I do to inherit 26 eternal life?' Jesus said, 'What is written in the Law? What is your 27 reading of it?' He replied, 'Love the Lord your God with all your heart, with all your soul, with all your strength, and with all your mind; and 28 your neighbour as yourself.' 'That is the right answer,' said Jesus; 'do that and you will live.'

29 But he wanted to vindicate himself, so he said to Jesus, 'And who is my 30 neighbour?' Jesus replied, 'A man was on his way from Jerusalem down to

Jericho when he fell in with robbers, who stripped him, beat him, and went off leaving him half dead. It so 31 happened that a priest was going down by the same road; but when he saw him, he went past on the other side. So 32 too a Levite came to the place, and when he saw him went past on the other side. But a Samaritan who was 33 making the journey came upon him, and when he saw him was moved to pity. He went up and bandaged his 34 wounds, bathing them with oil and wine. Then he lifted him on to his own beast, brought him to an inn, and looked after him there. Next day he 35 produced two silver pieces and gave them to the innkeeper, and said, "Look after him; and if you spend any more, I will repay you on my way back." Which of these three do you think was 36 neighbour to the man who fell into the hands of the robbers?' He answered, 37 'The one who showed him kindness.' Jesus said, 'Go and do as he did.'

While they were on their way Jesus 38 came to a village where a woman named Martha made him welcome in her home. She had a sister, Mary, who 39 seated herself at the Lord's feet and stayed there listening to his words. Now Martha was distracted by her 40 many tasks, so she came to him and said, 'Lord, do you not care that my sister has left me to get on with the work by myself? Tell her to come and lend a hand.' But the Lord answered, 41 'Martha, Martha, you are fretting and

h Or and he will have no way at all to harm you.
i Some witnesses omit Holy.
j Or Yes, I thank thee, Father, that such . . .
k Some witnesses omit Then . . . he said.

---

final victory or interpret the success of the disciples as a sign of that victory. **21–22:** Revelation to the humble (*simple*), rather than to the *"wise* of the world" was a familiar theme, common in NT times, but with ancient roots; see, e.g. Isa.29.14; Prov.26.12; 1 Cor.1.19–20. **23–24:** Mt.13.16–17.

10.25–28: The double commandment of love (Mt.22.34–40; Mk.12.28–31). **27:** The commandments are taken from Deut.6.5; Lev.19.18. It is significant that, even though Lk. regards the question as a *test*, he can credit the lawyer with providing this summary of the Law; similar summaries can be found in Jewish sources of the period, as well as in Paul (Rom.13.9–10; Gal.5.14) and Jas.2.8. **28b:** *Do . . . live:* Lev.18.5; the implication is that v. 27 comprehends the whole Law (compare Mt.22.40; Rom.10.5; 13.10).

10.29–37: The good Samaritan. The *priest* (v. 31) and the *Levite* (v. 32), as Temple officials, represent highly visible members of the religious establishment. While their failure to act as neighbors would attract the attention of the hearers of the parable, the hearers would also know that contact with the body beside the road—if it was dead—would render them unfit for Temple service. **33:** Among Jews nothing good would be expected of a *Samaritan* (see 9.52 n.), which makes his action all the more notable.

10.38–42: Mary and Martha. 38: The words *on their way* pick up the theme of the journey;

42 fussing about so many things; but one thing is necessary.[l] The part that Mary has chosen is best; and it shall not be taken away from her.'

11 Once, in a certain place, Jesus was at prayer. When he ceased, one of his disciples said, 'Lord, teach us to pray, 2 as John taught his disciples.' He answered, 'When you pray, say,

"Father,[m] thy name be hallowed;
thy kingdom come.[n]
3 Give us each day our daily bread.[o]
4 And forgive us our sins,
for we too forgive all who have done us wrong.
And do not bring us to the test."'[p]

5 Then he said to them, 'Suppose one of you has a friend who comes to him in the middle of the night and says, 6 "My friend, lend me three loaves, for a friend of mine on a journey has turned up at my house, and I have 7 nothing to offer him"; and he replies from inside, "Do not bother me. The door is shut for the night; my children and I have gone to bed; and I cannot get up and give you what you want." 8 I tell you that even if he will not provide for him out of friendship, the very shamelessness of the request will make him get up and give him all he 9 needs. And so I say to you, ask, and you will receive; seek, and you will find; knock, and the door will be 10 opened. For everyone who asks receives, he who seeks finds, and to him who knocks, the door will be opened.

11 'Is there a father among you who will offer his son[q] a snake when he 12 asks for fish, or a scorpion when he 13 asks for an egg? If you, then, bad as you are, know how to give your children what is good for them, how much more will the heavenly Father give the Holy Spirit[r] to those who ask him!'

HE WAS DRIVING OUT A DEVIL WHICH 14 was dumb; and when the devil had come out, the dumb man began to speak. The people were astonished, but some of them said, 'It is by 15 Beelzebub prince of devils that he drives the devils out.' Others, by way 16 of a test, demanded of him a sign from heaven. But he knew what was in 17 their minds, and said, 'Every kingdom divided against itself goes to ruin, and a divided household falls. Equally if 18 Satan is divided against himself, how can his kingdom stand?—since, as you would have it, I drive out the devils by Beelzebub. If it is by Beelzebub that I 19 cast out devils, by whom do your own people drive them out? If this is your argument, they themselves will refute you. But if it is by the finger of God 20 that I drive out the devils, then be sure the kingdom of God has already come upon you.

'When a strong man fully armed is 21 on guard over his castle his possessions are safe. But when someone stronger 22 comes upon him and overpowers him, he carries off the arms and armour on which the man had relied and divides the plunder.

'He who is not with me is against me, 23 and he who does not gather with me scatters.[s]

'When an unclean spirit comes out 24 of a man it wanders over the deserts seeking a resting-place; and if it finds none, it says, "I will go back to the

l Some witnesses read but few things are necessary, or rather, one alone; *others omit* you are fretting . . . necessary.
m Some witnesses read Our Father in heaven.
n One witness reads thy kingdom come upon us; *some others have* thy Holy Spirit come upon us and cleanse us; *some insert* thy will be done, on earth as in heaven.
o Or our bread for the morrow.
p Some witnesses add but save us from the evil one (or from evil).
q Some witnesses insert a stone when he asks for bread, or . . .
r Some witnesses read a good gift; *some others read* good things.
s Some witness add me.

see 9.51–19.27 n. *Martha* and *Mary* (vv. 38–39) are presumably the sisters mentioned in Jn. ch. 11.
11.1–13: On prayer. 1: The occasion for the Lord's Prayer is reported in this way only by Lk. **2–4:** See Mt.6.9–13 n. **2:** *Father:* see Mt.6.9 n. **3:** *Daily:* see Mt.6.11 n. **9–13:** Mt.7.7–11. **13:** Emphasis on the *Holy Spirit* is a characteristic of Lk.; Mt.7.11 has "give good things."
11.14–36: Signs, Beelzebub, Jonah. 14–23: Mt.12.22–30; Mk.3.22–27. **15:** *Beelzebub:* Satan. **16:** The demand for a *sign* (see Mt.12.38–42 n.) could not be satisfied by exorcism, since there were other exorcists (v. 19); the observers are challenged to see the *kingdom of God* (v. 20) bursting upon them in the activity of Jesus. **20:** *Finger of God* is a lively metaphor which calls to mind Exod.8.19; Mt.12.28 reads instead "Spirit of God." **23:** See Mk.9.39–40 n. **24–26:**

25 home I left." So it returns and finds
26 the house*t* swept clean, and tidy. Off it goes and collects seven other spirits more wicked than itself, and they all come in and settle down, and in the end the man's plight is worse than before.'

27 While he was speaking thus, a woman in the crowd called out, 'Happy the womb that carried you and the
28 breasts that suckled you!' He rejoined, 'No, happy are those who hear the word of God and keep it.'

29 With the crowds swarming round him he went on to say: 'This is a wicked generation. It demands a sign, and the only sign that will be given it
30 is the sign of Jonah. For just as Jonah was a sign to the Ninevites, so will the Son of Man be to this gener-
31 ation. At the Judgement, when the men of this generation are on trial, the Queen of the South will appear against*u* them and ensure their condemnation, for she came from the ends of the earth to hear the wisdom of Solomon; and what is here is greater
32 than Solomon. The men of Nineveh will appear at the Judgement when this generation is on trial, and ensure*v* its condemnation, for they repented at the preaching of Jonah; and what is here is greater than Jonah.

33 'No one lights a lamp and puts it in a cellar,*w* but rather on the lamp-stand so that those who enter may see the
34 light. The lamp of your body is the eye. When your eyes are sound, you have light for your whole body; but when the eyes are bad, you are in darkness.
35 See to it then that the light you have is
36 not darkness. If you have light for your whole body with no trace of darkness, it will all be as bright as when a lamp flashes its rays upon you.'

37 WHEN HE HAD FINISHED SPEAKING, A Pharisee invited him to a meal. He came in and sat down. The Pharisee
38 noticed with surprise that he had not begun by washing before the meal. But
39 the Lord said to him, 'You Pharisees! You clean the outside of cup and plate; but inside you there is nothing but greed and wickedness. You fools!
40 Did not he who made the outside make the inside too? But let what is in the
41 cup*x* be given in charity, and all is clean.

42 'Alas for you Pharisees! You pay tithes of mint and rue and every garden-herb, but have no care for justice and the love of God. It is these you should have practised, without neglecting the others.*y*

43 'Alas for you Pharisees! You love the seats of honour in synagogues, and salutations in the market-places.

44 'Alas, alas, you are like unmarked graves over which men may walk without knowing it.'

45 In reply to this one of the lawyers said, 'Master, when you say things like
46 this you are insulting us too.' Jesus rejoined: 'Yes, you lawyers, it is no better with you! For you load men with intolerable burdens, and will not put a single finger to the load.

47 'Alas, you build the tombs of the prophets whom your fathers murdered,
48 and so testify that you approve of the deeds your fathers did; they committed the murders and you provide the tombs.

49 'This is why the Wisdom of God said, "I will send them prophets and messengers; and some of these they will persecute and kill"; so that this
50 generation will have to answer for the blood of all the prophets shed since the

t Some witnesses insert unoccupied.
u Or will be raised to life together with . . .
v Or At the Judgement the men of Nineveh will rise again together with this generation and will ensure . . .
w Some witnesses insert or under the meal-tub.
x Or what you can afford.
y Some witnesses omit It is . . . others.

Mt.12.43–45. **24:** *Deserts:* see Mt.12.43 n. **29–32:** Mt.12.38–42. **29:** *Sign:* see Mt.12.38–42 n. Lk. has nothing like Mt.12.40 and interprets the *sign of Jonah* as the prophet's preaching (v. 32). **33:** Mt.5.15. **34–36:** *Eyes . . . sound . . . eyes . . . bad:* see Mt.6.22 n. For Lk. the sayings speak of the *light* by which Jesus is seen; sound eyes are organs of spiritual perception.
    11.37–54: Alas for Pharisees and lawyers (compare Mt. ch. 23). **38:** *Washing:* see Mk.7.3 n. **42:** Mic.6.8. **43:** 20.46; Mk.12.38–39. **44:** *Graves* were believed to make a man ritually unclean (see Num.19.16). **49–51:** The introductory formula reads as if a document authored by the *Wisdom of God* is being quoted (compare Mk.7.10; 12.36). *Wisdom* (see Lk.7.35 n.) was thought of as sending *prophets* in every generation (vv. 49–50; e.g. Wis.7.27 and chs. 10–11). Mt.23.34

51 foundation of the world; from the blood of Abel to the blood of Zechariah who perished between the altar and the sanctuary. I tell you, this generation will have to answer for it all.

52 'Alas for you lawyers! You have taken away the key of knowledge. You did not go in yourselves, and those who were on their way in, you stopped.'

53 After he had left the house, the lawyers and Pharisees began to assail him fiercely and to ply him with a host 54 of questions, laying snares to catch him with his own words.

12 MEANWHILE, WHEN A CROWD OF MANY thousands had gathered, packed so close that they were treading on one another, he began to speak first to his disciples: 'Beware of the leaven of the Pharisees; I mean their hypocrisy.

2 There is nothing covered up that will not be uncovered, nothing hidden that 3 will not be made known. You may take it, then, that everything you have said in the dark will be heard in broad daylight, and what you have whispered behind closed doors will be shouted from the house-tops.

4 'To you who are my friends I say: Do not fear those who kill the body and after that have nothing more they 5 can do. I will warn you whom to fear: fear him who, after he has killed, has authority to cast into hell. Believe me, he is the one to fear.

6 'Are not sparrows five for twopence? And yet not one of them is overlooked 7 by God. More than that, even the hairs of your head have all been counted. Have no fear; you are worth more than any number of sparrows.

8 'I tell you this: everyone who acknowledges me before men, the Son of Man will acknowledge before the 9 angels of God; but he who disowns me before men will be disowned before the angels of God.

'Anyone who speaks a word against 10 the Son of Man will receive forgiveness; but for him who slanders the Holy Spirit there will be no forgiveness.

'When you are brought before 11 synagogues and state authorities, do not begin worrying about how you will conduct your defence or what you will say. For when the time comes the Holy 12 Spirit will instruct you what to say.'

A man in the crowd said to him, 13 'Master, tell my brother to divide the family property with me.' He replied, 14 'My good man, who set me over you to judge or arbitrate?'[z] Then he said 15 to the people, 'Beware! Be on your guard against greed of every kind, for even when a man has more than enough, his wealth does not give him life.' And he told them this parable: 16 'There was a rich man whose land yielded heavy crops. He debated with 17 himself: "What am I to do? I have not the space to store my produce. This is what I will do," said he: "I will 18 pull down my storehouses and build them bigger. I will collect in them all my corn and other goods, and then say 19 to myself, 'Man, you have plenty of good things laid by, enough for many years: take life easy, eat, drink, and enjoy yourself.'" But God said to him, 20 "You fool, this very night you must surrender your life; you have made your money—who will get it now?" That is how it is with the man who 21 amasses wealth for himself and remains a pauper in the sight of God.[a]

'Therefore', he said to his disciples, 22 'I bid you put away anxious thoughts about food to keep you alive and clothes to cover your body. Life is 23 more than food, the body more than clothes. Think of the ravens: they 24 neither sow nor reap; they have no

z *Some witnesses omit* or arbitrate.
a *Some witnesses omit* That . . . God; *others add at the end* When he said this he cried out, 'If you have ears to hear, then hear.'

attributes the saying to Jesus. **51:** *Abel to . . . Zechariah:* from the first prophet to the last. **52:** *Key of knowledge:* see Mt.16.19 n.; 23.13.
   12.1–59: Encouragement and warning. **1–12:** Mt.10.26–33. **1:** *Leaven:* see Mk.8.15 n. **2–3:** 8.17; see Mt.10.26–27; Mk.4.22,24–25 n. Here, the saying promises that *hypocrisy* (v. 1) will be exposed. **5:** *Him who...has authority:* propably Satan is intended; but see Heb.10.30–31. **8:** The saying is ambiguous about the relation of Jesus (*me*) and the *Son of Man* (see Mk.2.10 n.). **10:** See Mt.12.31–32 n.; Mk.3.29 n. **11–12:** 21.14–15; Mt.10.19–20; Mk.13.11. **13–14:** The title *Master* probably indicates identification of Jesus as a rabbi, who as an expert on the Law would be expected *to judge*. **18:** *Corn:* grain. **20:** Jer.17.11 has a similar saying about a man

storehouse or barn; yet God feeds them. You are worth far more than the
25 birds! Is there a man among you who by anxious thought can add a foot to
26 his height*b*? If, then, you cannot do even a very little thing, why are you anxious about the rest?

27 'Think of the lilies: they neither spin nor weave;*c* yet I tell you, even Solomon in all his splendour was not
28 attired like one of these. But if that is how God clothes the grass, which is growing in the field today, and tomorrow is thrown on the stove, how much more will he clothe you! How
29 little faith you have! And so you are not to set your mind on food and drink;
30 you are not to worry. For all these are things for the heathen to run after; but you have a Father who knows that you
31 need them. No, set your mind upon his kingdom, and all the rest will come to you as well.

32 'Have no fear, little flock; for your Father has chosen to give you the
33 Kingdom. Sell your possessions and give in charity. Provide for yourselves purses that do not wear out, and never-failing treasure in heaven, where no thief can get near it, no moth
34 destroy it. For where your treasure is, there will your heart be also.

35 'Be ready for action, with belts
36 fastened and lamps alight. Be like men who wait for their master's return from a wedding-party, ready to let him in the moment he arrives and knocks.
37 Happy are those servants whom the master finds on the alert when he comes. I tell you this: he will fasten his belt, seat them at table, and come
38 and wait on them. Even if it is the middle of the night or before dawn when he comes, happy they if he finds
39 them alert. And remember, if the householder had known what time the burglar was coming he would not have
40 let his house be broken into. Hold yourselves ready, then, because the

Son of Man will come at the time you least expect him.'

41 Peter said, 'Lord, do you intend this parable specially for us or is it for
42 everyone?' The Lord said, 'Well, who is the trusty and sensible man whom his master will appoint as his steward, to manage his servants and issue their rations at the proper time? Happy that
43 servant who is found at his task when
44 his master comes! I tell you this: he will be put in charge of all his master's
45 property. But if that servant says to himself, "The master is a long time coming", and begins to bully the menservants and maids, and eat and drink and get drunk; then the master
46 will arrive on a day that servant does not expect, at a time he does not know, and will cut him in pieces. Thus he will find his place among the faithless.

47 'The servant who knew his master's wishes, yet made no attempt to carry
48 them out, will be flogged severely. But one who did not know them and earned a beating will be flogged less severely. Where a man has been given much, much will be expected of him; and the more a man has had entrusted to him the more he will be required to repay.

49 'I have come to set fire to the earth, and how I wish it were already kindled!
50 I have a baptism to undergo, and what constraint I am under until the ordeal
51 is over! Do you suppose I came to establish peace on earth? No indeed, I
52 have come to bring division. For from now on, five members of a family will be divided, three against two and two
53 against three; father against son and son against father, mother against daughter and daughter against mother, mother against son's wife and son's wife against her mother-in-law.'

54 He also said to the people, 'When you see cloud banking up in the west,

b Or a day to his life.
c Some witnesses read they grow, they do not toil or spin.

---

who gets his wealth unjustly. **22–31:** See Mt.6.25–34 n. **32:** *Little flock:* the community of the Messiah. **33–34:** Mt.6.19–21. **35:** *With belts fastened:* i.e. with the robe gathered securely at the waist so as to *be ready for action.* **39–46:** Mt.24.43–51. **48:** The privilege of special knowledge (compare 8.18) carries the burden of special responsibility. **49–53:** Mt.10.34–36. **49:** *Fire* is a symbol of judgment (compare 3.16 n.). **50:** *Baptism* is a metaphor for martyrdom (compare Mk.10.38). **51:** *Peace,* though promised in 2.14, is not to be hoped for apart from decisions which produce *division.* **52–53:** See Mic.7.6. **54–56:** The *cloud* blows in from the Mediterranean;

you say at once, "It is going to rain", and rain it does. And when the wind is from the south, you say, "There will 56 be a heat-wave", and there is. What hypocrites you are! You know how to interpret the appearance of earth and sky; how is it you cannot interpret this fateful hour?

57 'And why can you not judge for yourselves what is the right course? 58 When you are going with your opponent to court, make an effort to settle with him while you are still on the way; otherwise he may drag you before the judge, and the judge hand you over to the constable, and the constable put 59 you in jail. I tell you, you will not come out till you have paid the last farthing.'

13 AT THAT VERY TIME THERE WERE SOME people present who told him about the Galileans whose blood Pilate had 2 mixed with their sacrifices. He answered them: 'Do you imagine that, because these Galileans suffered this fate, they must have been greater sinners than 3 anyone else in Galilee? I tell you they were not; but unless you repent, you will all of you come to the same end. 4 Or the eighteen people who were killed when the tower fell on them at Siloam—do you imagine they were more guilty than all the other people 5 living in Jerusalem? I tell you they were not; but unless you repent, you will all of you come to the same end.' 6 He told them this parable: 'A man had a fig-tree growing in his vineyard; and he came looking for fruit on it, but 7 found none. So he said to the vine-dresser, "Look here! For the last three years I have come looking for fruit on this fig-tree without finding any. Cut it down. Why should it go on using up 8 the soil?" But he replied, "Leave it, sir, this one year while I dig round it

and manure it. And if it bears next 9 season, well and good; if not, you shall have it down."'

One Sabbath he was teaching in a 10 synagogue, and there was a woman 11 there possessed by a spirit that had crippled her for eighteen years. She was bent double and quite unable to stand up straight. When Jesus saw her 12 he called her and said, 'You are rid of your trouble.' Then he laid his hands 13 on her, and at once she straightened up and began to praise God. But the 14 president of the synagogue, indignant with Jesus for healing on the Sabbath, intervened and said to the congregation, 'There are six working-days: come and be cured on one of them, and not on the Sabbath.' The Lord gave 15 him his answer: 'What hypocrites you are!' he said. 'Is there a single one of you who does not loose his ox or his donkey from the manger and take it out to water on the Sabbath? And 16 here is this woman, a daughter of Abraham, who has been kept prisoner by Satan for eighteen long years: was it wrong for her to be freed from her bonds on the Sabbath?' At these words 17 all his opponents were covered with confusion, while the mass of the people were delighted at all the wonderful things he was doing.

'What is the kingdom of God like?' 18 he continued. 'What shall I compare it with? It is like a mustard-seed which a 19 man took and sowed in his garden; and it grew to be a tree and the birds came to roost among its branches.'

Again he said, 'The kingdom of God, 20 what shall I compare it with? It is like 21 yeast which a woman took and mixed with half a hundredweight of flour till it was all leavened.'

HE CONTINUED HIS JOURNEY THROUGH 22

---

the scorching *heat* comes across the desert. Men who know so much about the weather should be able to see the imminence of the kingdom in Jesus' ministry. **57–59**: Mt.5.25–26.

13.1–9: The necessity of repentance. 1: *Pilate:* see 3.1 n. The allusion is to an uprising of *Galileans* in Jerusalem which is not reported in other sources. **2:** Those who *suffered this fate* might have been regarded as *greater sinners* since such a tragedy could be understood as God's judgment; see v. 4. **3,5:** Jesus does not allow the view of v. 2 n. to become the basis for complacency; all are called to *repent*.

13.10–17: A Sabbath story. 13: *Laid his hands on her:* compare 4.40; 5.13. **14–15:** Exod.20.9; Deut.5.13. See 14.5 n.; Jn.5.10–12.

13.18–21: The kingdom of God. See notes on Mk.4.26–32,30,32 and Mt.13.33.

13.22–35: Continuing in the way. These verses are an interlude, during which the reader is

towns and villages, teaching as he made his way towards Jerusalem

23 Someone asked him, 'Sir, are only a few to be saved?' His answer was:

24 'Struggle to get in through the narrow door; for I tell you that many will try to enter and not be able.

25 'When once the master of the house has got up and locked the door, you may stand outside and knock, and say, "Sir, let us in!", but he will only answer, "I do not know where you

26 come from." Then you will begin to say, "We sat at table with you and you

27 taught in our streets." But he will repeat, "I tell you, I do not know where you come from. Out of my sight, all of you, you and your wicked

28 ways!" There will be wailing and grinding of teeth there, when you see Abraham, Isaac, and Jacob, and all the prophets, in the kingdom of God,

29 and yourselves thrown out. From east and west people will come, from north and south, for the feast in the kingdom

30 of God. Yes, and some who are now last will be first, and some who are first will be last.'

31 At that time a number of Pharisees came to him and said, 'You should leave this place and go on your way;

32 Herod is out to kill you.' He replied, 'Go and tell that fox, "Listen: today and tomorrow I shall be casting out devils and working cures; on the third

33 day I reach my goal." However, I must be on my way today and tomorrow and the next day, because it is unthinkable for a prophet to meet his death anywhere but in Jerusalem.

34 'O Jerusalem, Jerusalem, the city that murders the prophets and stones the messengers sent to her! How often have I longed to gather your children, as a hen gathers her brood under her

35 wings; but you would not let me. Look, look! there is your temple, forsaken by God. And I tell you, you shall never see me until the time comes when you

say, "Blessings on him who comes in the name of the Lord!"'

14 ONE SABBATH HE WENT TO HAVE A MEAL
2 in the house of a leading Pharisee; and they were watching him closely. There,
in front of him, was a man suffering from dropsy. Jesus asked the lawyers 3
and the Pharisees: 'Is it permitted to cure people on the Sabbath or not?' They said nothing. So he took the man, 4 cured him, and sent him away. Then 5 he turned to them and said, 'If one of you has a donkey[d] or an ox and it falls into a well, will he hesitate to haul it up on the Sabbath day?' To this they 6 could find no reply.

When he noticed how the guests were 7 trying to secure the places of honour, he spoke to them in a parable: 'When 8 you are asked by someone to a wedding-feast, do not sit down in the place of honour. It may be that some person more distinguished than yourself has been invited; and the host will 9 come and say to you, "Give this man your seat." Then you will look foolish as you begin to take the lowest place. No, when you receive an invitation, go 10 and sit down in the lowest place, so that when your host comes he will say, "Come up higher, my friend." Then all your fellow-guests will see the respect in which you are held. For 11 everyone who exalts himself will be humbled; and whoever humbles himself will be exalted.'

Then he said to his host, 'When you 12 are having a party for lunch or supper, do not invite your friends, your brothers or other relations, or your rich neighbours; they will only ask you back again and so you will be repaid. But when you give a party, ask the 13 poor, the crippled, the lame, and the blind; and so find happiness. For they 14 have no means of repaying you; but

d Some witnesses read son.

---

reminded of the theme of the journey (vv. 22,33); see 9.51–19.27 n. **23–24:** Mt.7.13–14. **25–30:** Mt.7.22–23; 8.11–12; 19.30; 25.10–12. **27:** Ps.6.8. **29:** Ps.107.3. On the *feast,* see 14.15 n. **31:** *Herod:* Antipas (see 3.1 n.). **32–33:** *Today . . . tomorrow . . . the third day* is a conventional manner of speaking of a short period of time. **34–35:** This saying is a dirge which may be quoted as a lament of Wisdom (see 7.35 n.). **35:** For Lk., *until the time comes* appears to point to the entry into Jerusalem (see 19.38); compare Mt.23.39 n. *Blessings . . . Lord:* Ps.118.26.
　14.1–14: Jesus, a guest of a Pharisee. See Mk.3.1–6 n. **5:** The Dead Sea community prohibited such activity on the Sabbath. **8–10:** Compare Prov.25.6–7. **11:** See 18.14; Mt.23.12.

you will be repaid on the day when good men rise from the dead.'

15 One of the company, after hearing all this, said to him, 'Happy the man who shall sit at the feast in the kingdom
16 of God!' Jesus answered, 'A man was giving a big dinner party and had sent
17 out many invitations. At dinner-time he sent his servant with a message for his guests, "Please come, everything is
18 now ready." They began one and all to excuse themselves. The first said, "I have bought a piece of land and I must go and look over it; please accept
19 my apologies." The second said, "I have bought five yoke of oxen, and I am on my way to try them out; please
20 accept my apologies." The next said, "I have just got married and for that
21 reason I cannot come." When the servant came back he reported this to his master. The master of the house was angry and said to him, "Go out quickly into the streets and alleys of the town, and bring me in the poor, the crippled, the blind, and the lame."
22 The servant said, "Sir, your orders have been carried out and there is still
23 room." The master replied, "Go out on to the highways and along the hedgerows and make them come in; I
24 want my house to be full. I tell you that not one of those who were invited shall taste my banquet."'
25 Once when great crowds were accompanying him, he turned to them and
26 said: 'If anyone comes to me and does not hate his father and mother, wife and children, brothers and sisters, even his own life, he cannot be a disciple of
27 mine. No one who does not carry his cross and come with me can be a
28 disciple of mine. Would any of you think of building a tower without first sitting down and calculating the cost, to see whether he could afford to finish
29 it? Otherwise, if he has laid its founda-

tion and then is not able to complete it, all the onlookers will laugh at him.
30 "There is the man", they will say, "who started to build and could not finish."
31 Or what king will march to battle against another king, without first sitting down to consider whether with ten thousand men he can face an enemy coming to meet him with twenty
32 thousand? If he cannot, then, long before the enemy approaches, he sends
33 envoys, and asks for terms. So also none of you can be a disciple of mine without parting with all his possessions.
34 'Salt is a good thing; but if salt itself becomes tasteless, what will you use to
35 season it? It is useless either on the land or on the dung-heap; it can only be thrown away. If you have ears to hear, then hear.'

15 ANOTHER TIME, THE TAX-GATHERERS and other bad characters were all
2 crowding in to listen to him; and the Pharisees and the doctors of the law began grumbling among themselves: 'This fellow', they said, 'welcomes sinners and eats with them.' He
3 answered them with this parable: 'If
4 one of you has a hundred sheep and loses one of them, does he not leave the ninety-nine in the open pasture and go after the missing one until he has
5 found it? How delighted he is then!
6 He lifts it on to his shoulders, and home he goes to call his friends and neighbours together. "Rejoice with me!" he cries. "I have found my lost sheep."
7 In the same way, I tell you, there will be greater joy in heaven over one sinner who repents than over ninety-nine righteous people who do not need to repent.
8 'Or again, if a woman has ten silver pieces and loses one of them, does she not light the lamp, sweep out the house, and look in every corner till she has

14.15–24: **The Great Supper** (Mt.22.1–10). **15:** The *feast* was a frequently used symbol of the joy of the *kingdom;* see 13.28–29. **17:** The *message* is a customary courtesy reminder to guests who have been invited previously. **18:** The excuses which follow are not frivolous, but the master's anger (v. 21) is understandable since the guests had had a prior notice. **21,23:** Lk. probably means for the two groups to represent (a) sinners among the Jews and (b) Gentiles.
14.25–35: **The cost of discipleship. 26:** *Hate* probably means "love less"; see Mt.10.37. **27:** *Carry his cross:* see 9.23 n.; Mk.8.34 n.; Mt.10.38; 16.24. **34–35:** Compare Mt.5.13; Mk.9.50.
15.1–32: **Joy over repentant sinners. 1–2:** *Tax-gatherers:* see Mk.2.15 n. **3–7:** Lk. doubtless preserves the parable's original concern for outcasts; Mt.18.10–14 (and n.) applies it differently.

9 found it? And when she has, she calls her friends and neighbours together, and says, "Rejoice with me! I have
10 found the piece that I lost." In the same way, I tell you, there is joy among the angels of God over one sinner who repents.'
11 Again he said: 'There was once a man
12 who had two sons; and the younger said to his father, "Father, give me my share of the property." So he divided
13 his estate between them. A few days later the younger son turned the whole of his share into cash and left home for a distant country, where he squandered
14 it in reckless living. He had spent it all, when a severe famine fell upon that country and he began to feel the pinch.
15 So he went and attached himself to one of the local landowners, who sent him
16 on to his farm to mind the pigs. He would have been glad to fill his belly with*e* the pods that the pigs were eating; and no one gave him anything.
17 Then he came to his senses and said, "How many of my father's paid servants have more food than they can eat, and here am I, starving to death!
18 I will set off and go to my father, and say to him, 'Father, I have sinned,
19 against God and against you; I am no longer fit to be called your son; treat me as one of your paid servants.'"
20 So he set out for his father's house. But while he was still a long way off his father saw him, and his heart went out to him. He ran to meet him, flung his
21 arms round him, and kissed him. The son said, "Father, I have sinned, against God and against you; I am no longer
22 fit to be called your son."*f* But the father said to his servants, "Quick! fetch a robe, my best one, and put it on him; put a ring on his finger and shoes
23 on his feet. Bring the fatted calf and kill it, and let us have a feast to cele-
24 brate the day. For this son of mine was dead and has come back to life; he was

lost and is found." And the festivities began.
25 'Now the elder son was out on the farm; and on his way back, as he approached the house, he heard music
26 and dancing. He called one of the ser-
27 vants and asked what it meant. The servant told him, "Your brother has come home, and your father has killed the fatted calf because he has him back
28 safe and sound." But he was angry and refused to go in. His father came out and pleaded with him; but he retorted,
29 "You know how I have slaved for you all these years; I never once disobeyed your orders; and you never gave me so much as a kid, for a feast with my
30 friends. But now that this son of yours turns up, after running through your money with his women, you kill the
31 fatted calf for him." "My boy," said the father, "you are always with me,
32 and everything I have is yours. How could we help celebrating this happy day? Your brother here was dead and has come back to life, was lost and is found."'

He said to his disciples, 'There was a **16** rich man who had a steward, and he received complaints that this man was squandering the property. So he sent 2 for him, and said, "What is this that I hear? Produce your accounts, for you cannot be manager here any longer." The steward said to himself, "What 3 am I to do now that my employer is dismissing me? I am not strong enough to dig, and too proud to beg. I know 4 what I must do, to make sure that, when I have to leave, there will be people to give me house and home." He sum- 5 moned his master's debtors one by one. To the first he said, "How much do you owe my master?" He replied, "A 6 thousand gallons of olive oil." He said, "Here is your account. Sit down and

e Some witnesses read to have his fill of ...
f Some witnesses add treat me as one of your paid servants.

12: The *younger* son's *share* would be one-third; see Deut.21.17. 13: The rate of emigration of Palestinian Jews to the urban centers of the Gentile world was very high. 15–16: Since *pigs* are unclean animals, everything about the job would have been repugnant. 20–23: *Kiss, robe, ring,* and *fatted calf* show that the son is not only forgiven, but received with honor. 31: The elder son is still accepted.

16.1–31: **The uses of wealth.** Except for vv. 16–18, the traditional units in ch. 16 seem to have been assembled around the theme of wealth. 1–8: This very difficult parable about a *dishonest steward* (v. 8) commends a scoundrel for having the good sense to act decisively in a

make it five hundred; and be quick
7 about it." Then he said to another,
"And you, how much do you owe?"
He said, "A thousand bushels of
wheat", and was told, "Take your
account and make it eight hundred."
8 And the master applauded the dishonest steward for acting so astutely.
For the worldly are more astute than
the other-worldly in dealing with their
own kind.

9 'So I say to you, use your worldly
wealth to win friends for yourselves, so
that when money is a thing of the past
you may be received into an eternal
home.

10 'The man who can be trusted in little
things can be trusted also in great; and
the man who is dishonest in little things
11 is dishonest also in great things. If,
then, you have not proved trustworthy
with the wealth of this world, who will
trust you with the wealth that is real?
12 And if you have proved untrustworthy
with what belongs to another, who will
give you what is your own?

13 'No servant can be the slave of two
masters; for either he will hate the first
and love the second, or he will be
devoted to the first and think nothing of
the second. You cannot serve God and
Money.'

14 The Pharisees, who loved money,
15 heard all this and scoffed at him. He
said to them, 'You are the people who
impress your fellow-men with your
righteousness; but God sees through
you; for what sets itself up to be admired by men is detestable in the sight
of God.

16 'Until John, it was the Law and the
prophets: since then, there is the good
news of the kingdom of God, and
everyone forces his way in.

17 'It is easier for heaven and earth to

come to an end than for one dot or
stroke of the Law to lose its force.
'A man who divorces his wife and 18
marries another commits adultery; and
anyone who marries a woman divorced
from her husband commits adultery.

'There was once a rich man, who 19
dressed in purple and the finest linen,
and feasted in great magnificence every
day. At his gate, covered with sores, 20
lay a poor man named Lazarus, who 21
would have been glad to satisfy his
hunger with the scraps from the rich
man's table. Even the dogs used to
come and lick his sores. One day the 22
poor man died and was carried away
by the angels to be with Abraham. The
rich man also died and was buried, and 23
in Hades, where he was in torment, he
looked up; and there, far away, was
Abraham with Lazarus close beside
him. "Abraham, my father," he called 24
out, "take pity on me! Send Lazarus to
dip the tip of his finger in water, to cool
my tongue, for I am in agony in this
fire." But Abraham said, "Remember, 25
my child, that all the good things fell
to you while you were alive, and all the
bad to Lazarus; now he has his consolation here and it is you who are in agony.
But that is not all: there is a great 26
chasm fixed between us; no one from
our side who wants to reach you can
cross it, and none may pass from your
side to us." "Then, father," he replied, 27
"will you send him to my father's
house, where I have five brothers, to 28
warn them, so that they too may not
come to this place of torment?" But 29
Abraham said, "They have Moses and
the prophets; let them listen to them."
"No, father Abraham," he replied, 30
"but if someone from the dead visits
them, they will repent." Abraham 31
answered, "If they do not listen to

time of crisis. **8:** *Master* (lit. "lord") may refer either to the rich man who discharged his
steward or to Jesus. The *other-worldly* are, lit. "the sons of light" (Jn.12.36; 1 Th.5.5; Eph.5.8);
the Dead Sea sect used "children of light" as a designation of itself as the community of the
elect. **9:** The saying perhaps commends dispensing *wealth* in acts of charity. **13:** Mt.6.24.
16: *John* (the Baptist) marks the dividing line between the age of anticipation and the age of
salvation. It is not clear on which side of the line John himself stands for Lk.; compare
Mt.11.12–15 n. **17:** *Stroke:* the allusion is to a small mark made in writing Heb. letters. **18:**
On *divorce*, see notes on Mt.5.31–32. **19–31:** The "rich man-poor man" motif is found in
similar stories from other sources. The primary theme is the reversal of fortunes in the world
to come for the poor (righteous) and the rich (unrighteous). Their fates are seen as a motive
for repentance. **29,31:** The two ages of v. 16 are suggested by the appeal, on the one hand,
to *Moses and the prophets*, and the hint, on the other hand, of one who will *rise from the dead.*

Moses and the prophets they will pay no heed even if someone should rise from the dead.'"

17 HE SAID TO HIS DISCIPLES, 'CAUSES of stumbling are bound to arise; but woe betide the man through whom they 2 come. It would be better for him to be thrown into the sea with a millstone round his neck than to cause one of 3 these little ones to stumble. Keep watch on yourselves.

'If your brother wrongs you, reprove him; and if he repents, forgive him. 4 Even if he wrongs you seven times in a day and comes back to you seven times saying, "I am sorry", you are to forgive him.'

5 The apostles said to the Lord, 'In-6 crease our faith'; and the Lord replied, 'If you had faith no bigger even than a mustard-seed, you could say to this mulberry-tree, "Be rooted up and re-planted in the sea"; and it would at once obey you.

7 'Suppose one of you has a servant ploughing or minding sheep. When he comes back from the fields, will the master say, "Come along at once and 8 sit down"? Will he not rather say, "Prepare my supper, fasten your belt, and then wait on me while I have my meal; you can have yours afterwards"? 9 Is he grateful to the servant for carry-10 ing out his orders? So with you: when you have carried out all your orders, you should say, "We are servants and deserve no credit; we have only done our duty."'

11 In the course of his journey to Jerusalem he was travelling through the borderlands of Samaria and Galilee. 12 As he was entering a village he was met by ten men with leprosy. They stood some way off and called out to him, 13 'Jesus, Master, take pity on us.' When 14 he saw them he said, 'Go and show yourselves to the priests'; and while they were on their way, they were made clean. One of them, finding himself 15 cured, turned back praising God aloud. He threw himself down at Jesus's feet 16 and thanked him. And he was a Samaritan. At this Jesus said: 'Were 17 not all ten cleansed? The other nine, where are they? Could none be found 18 to come back and give praise to God except this foreigner?' And he said to 19 the man, 'Stand up and go on your way; your faith has cured you.'

THE PHARISEES ASKED HIM, 'WHEN WILL 20 the kingdom of God come?' He said, 'You cannot tell by observation when the kingdom of God comes. There will 21 be no saying, "Look, here it is!" or "there it is!"; for in fact the kingdom of God is among you.'*g*

He said to the disciples, 'The time 22 will come when you will long to see one of the days of the Son of Man, but you will not see it. They will say to you, 23 "Look! There!" and "Look! Here!" Do not go running off in pursuit. For 24 like the lightning-flash that lights up the earth from end to end, will the Son of Man be when his day comes. But 25 first he must endure much suffering and be repudiated by this generation.

'As things were in Noah's days, so 26 will they be in the days of the Son of Man. They ate and drank and married, 27

g Or for in fact the kingdom of God is within you, *or* for in fact the kingdom of God is within your grasp, *or* for suddenly the kingdom of God will be among you.

17.1–10: Faithful discipleship. 1–2: See Mt.18.6 n.,7–9 n.; Mk.9.42. **3–4:** Compare Mt.18.15, 21–22. The responsibility for righting a wrong between brothers lies with the one who is wronged (v. 3) and has no limits (v. 4). Lk. does not have the Church discipline provisions of Mt.18.16–17. **5–6:** Compare Mt.17.20. The hyperbole of a *faith* which uproots trees corresponds to the hyperbolic challenges of vv. 2,4.

17.11–19: Ten lepers on the way. 11: *Journey to Jerusalem:* see 13.22–35 n. *Through the border lands of Samaria and Galilee* is an attempt to translate a Gk. phrase which is grammatically and geographically difficult; Lk. is more interested in the journey than in its precise itinerary. **12:** *Leprosy:* see Mt.8.2 n. **16:** That a *Samaritan* should be the one to show gratitude is a surprise; see 9.52 n.; 10.33 n.

17.20–37: The coming of the kingdom. 21: The verse is sufficiently ambiguous to invite alternative translations (see Tfn. *g*; Mt.24.23). The *when* of the Pharisee's question (v. 20) provides the unifying thread for vv. 20–37, so that Lk. appears to understand v. 21 in a manner consistent with the futuristic thrust of the remaining verses. **23–24:** Compare Mt.24.26–27; Mk.13.21. **24:** The coming of the *Son of Man* (see Mk.2.10 n.) will leave no room for guesses

until the day that Noah went into the ark and the flood came and made an
28 end of them all. As things were in Lot's days, also: they ate and drank; they bought and sold; they planted and
29 built; but the day that Lot went out from Sodom, it rained fire and sulphur from the sky and made an end of them
30 all—it will be like that on the day when the Son of Man is revealed.
31 'On that day the man who is on the roof and his belongings in the house must not come down to pick them up; he, too, who is in the fields must not go
32,33 back. Remember Lot's wife. Whoever seeks to save his life will lose it; and whoever loses it will save it, and live.
34 'I tell you, on that night there will be two men in one bed: one will be taken,
35 the other left. There will be two women together grinding corn: one will be
37 taken, the other left.'[h] When they heard this they asked, 'Where, Lord?' He said, 'Where the corpse is, there the vultures will gather.'

18 HE SPOKE TO THEM IN A PARABLE TO show that they should keep on praying
2 and never lose heart: 'There was once a judge who cared nothing for God or
3 man, and in the same town there was a widow who constantly came before him demanding justice against her
4 opponent. For a long time he refused; but in the end he said to himself, "True,
5 I care nothing for God or man: but this widow is so great a nuisance that I will see her righted before she wears me
6 out with her persistence."' The Lord said, 'You hear what the unjust judge
7 says; and will not God vindicate his chosen, who cry out to him day and
8 night, while he listens patiently to

them[i]? I tell you, he will vindicate them soon enough. But when the Son of Man comes, will he find faith on earth?'

And here is another parable that he 9 told. It was aimed at those who were sure of their own goodness and looked down on everyone else. 'Two men 10 went up to the temple to pray, one a Pharisee and the other a tax-gatherer. The Pharisee stood up and prayed 11 thus:[j] "I thank thee, O God, that I am not like the rest of men, greedy, dishonest, adulterous; or, for that matter, like this tax-gatherer. I fast twice a 12 week; I pay tithes on all that I get." But the other kept his distance and 13 would not even raise his eyes to heaven, but beat upon his breast, saying, "O God, have mercy on me, sinner that I am." It was this man, I tell you, and 14 not the other, who went home acquitted of his sins. For everyone who exalts himself will be humbled; and whoever humbles himself will be exalted.'

They even brought babies for him to 15 touch. When the disciples saw them they rebuked them, but Jesus called for 16 the children and said, 'Let the little ones come to me; do not try to stop them; for the kingdom of God belongs to such as these. I tell you that whoever 17 does not accept the kingdom of God like a child will never enter it.'

A man of the ruling class put this 18 question to him: 'Good Master, what must I do to win eternal life?' Jesus 19 said to him, 'Why do you call me good? No one is good except God alone. You 20 know the commandments: "Do not commit adultery; do not murder; do

h Some witnesses add (36) two men in the fields: one will be taken, the other left.
i Or delays to help them.
j Some witnesses read stood up by himself and prayed thus; *others read* stood up and prayed thus privately.

(v. 23), but will be self-illuminating. **27:** Mt.24.37–39. *Noah:* Gen. chs. 6–7. **28–32:** *The days of Lot:* Gen.19.1–29. **31:** Mt.24.17–18; Mk.13.15–16. **33:** The reference to *Lot's wife* (v. 32) gives the saying about saving and losing life an unusual setting; see Mt.10.38–39 n. **34–35:** Mt.24.40–41. **37:** Mt.24.28.

18.1–17: Preparation for the kingdom. 1: To *keep on praying* is a familiar theme (3.21 n.); *never* to *lose heart* may indicate that this parable is meant for a time of trouble (perhaps of persecution, vv. 6–7). **6–7:** The point is not that God must be worn down like the unjust judge, but rather that the prayers of the *chosen* will surely be heard by the Righteous Judge. Compare 11.11–13. **9:** *Pharisee:* Mt.3.7 n. *Tax-gatherer:* Lk.3.12 n. **11–12:** For the original hearers, the Pharisee would be a genuinely good man, fasting far beyond the Law's requirements, tithing above the literal commandment (Deut.14.22–29). **14:** The *tax-gatherer* is *acquitted* because he knows his sin and repents; see 15.7,10. **15–17:** Mt.19.13–15; 18.3; Mk.10.13–16. For the first time since 9.51, Lk. again takes up the content and order of Mk.

18.18–30: Possessions and the kingdom (Mt.19.16–30; Mk.10.17–31). **18–20a:** See Mt.19.16–17 n. **18:** Only Lk. places the man in the *ruling class.* **20:** Exod.20.12–16; Deut.5.16–20.

not steal; do not give false evidence;
21 honour your father and mother."' The
man answered, 'I have kept all these
22 since I was a boy.' On hearing this
Jesus said, 'There is still one thing
lacking: sell everything you have and
distribute to the poor, and you will have
riches in heaven; and come, follow
23 me.' At these words his heart sank; for
24 he was a very rich man. When Jesus
saw it he said, 'How hard it is for the
wealthy to enter the kingdom of God!
25 It is easier for a camel to go through
the eye of a needle than for a rich man
26 to enter the kingdom of God.' Those
who heard asked, 'Then who can be
27 saved?' He answered, 'What is impossible for men is possible for God.'
28 Peter said, 'We here have left our
belongings to become your followers.'
29 Jesus said, 'I tell you this: there is no
one who has given up home, or wife,
brothers, parents, or children, for the
30 sake of the kingdom of God, who will
not be repaid many times over in this
age, and in the age to come have eternal
life.'

Challenge to Jerusalem

31 HE TOOK THE TWELVE ASIDE AND SAID,
'We are now going up to Jerusalem;
and all that was written by the prophets
32 will come true for the Son of Man. He
will be handed over to the foreign
power. He will be mocked, maltreated,
33 and spat upon. They will flog him and
kill him. And on the third day he will
34 rise again.' But they understood nothing of all this; they did not grasp what
he was talking about; its meaning was
concealed from them.
35 As he approached Jericho a blind
man sat at the roadside begging.
36 Hearing a crowd going past, he asked
37 what was happening. They told him,

'Jesus of Nazareth is passing by.' Then 38
he shouted out, 'Jesus, Son of David,
have pity on me.' The people in front 39
told him to hold his tongue; but he
called out all the more, 'Son of David,
have pity on me.' Jesus stopped and 40
ordered the man to be brought to him.
When he came up he asked him, 'What 41
do you want me to do for you?' 'Sir, I
want my sight back', he answered.
Jesus said to him, 'Have back your 42
sight; your faith has cured you.' He 43
recovered his sight instantly; and he
followed Jesus, praising God. And all
the people gave praise to God for what
they had seen.

Entering Jericho he made his way **19**
through the city. There was a man 2
there named Zacchaeus; he was
superintendent of taxes and very rich.
He was eager to see what Jesus looked 3
like; but, being a little man, he could
not see him for the crowd. So he ran on 4
ahead and climbed a sycomore-tree in
order to see him, for he was to pass that
way. When Jesus came to the place, he 5
looked up and said, 'Zacchaeus, be
quick and come down; I must come
and stay with you today.' He climbed 6
down as fast as he could and welcomed
him gladly. At this there was a general 7
murmur of disapproval. 'He has gone
in', they said, 'to be the guest of a
sinner.' But Zacchaeus stood there and 8
said to the Lord, 'Here and now, sir,
I give half my possessions to charity;
and if I have cheated anyone, I am
ready to repay him four times over.'
Jesus said to him, 'Salvation has come 9
to this house today!—for this man too
is a son of Abraham, and the Son of 10
Man has come to seek and save what
is lost.'

While they were listening to this, he 11
went on to tell them a parable, because
he was now close to Jerusalem and
they thought the reign of God might

22: See Mt.19.21 n. **25,27:** On *camel, needle,* see Mt.19.24 n. **28–30:** See Mt.19.27,29 n.
   18.31–34: The third prediction of suffering. See 9.22,44–45; Mt.20.17–19; Mk.10.32–34 n.
   18.35–43: A blind man healed (Mt.20.29–34; Mk.10.46–52). **38:** *Son of David:* see Mt.1.1 n.
42: *Cured:* see 7.50 n. **43:** *Followed:* see Mk.10.52 n.
   19.1–10: Zacchaeus. 2: *Superintendent of taxes:* see 3.12 n. **7:** *Guest of a sinner:* see Mk.2.15 n.
On the restitution of illegal gain, see Lev.6.1–7.
   19.11–27: The parable of the pounds (compare Mt.25.14–30). **11:** *Close to Jerusalem* is the
last of several notices which serve the "journey theme"; with v. 27 Luke's special section comes
to a close (see 9.51–19.27 n.). Lk. employs the parabolic tradition to prepare for (apparent)
defeat rather than (immediate) victory in Jerusalem and to encourage patient and trustworthy

12 dawn at any moment. He said, 'A man of noble birth went on a long journey abroad, to be appointed king and then 13 return. But first he called ten of his servants and gave them a pound each, saying, "Trade with this while I am 14 away." His fellow-citizens hated him, and they sent a delegation on his heels to say, "We do not want this man as 15 our king." However, back he came as king, and sent for the servants to whom he had given the money, to see what 16 profit each had made. The first came and said, "Your pound, sir, has made 17 ten more." "Well done," he replied; "you are a good servant. You have shown yourself trustworthy in a very small matter, and you shall have 18 charge of ten cities." The second came and said, "Your pound, sir, has made 19 five more"; and he also was told, "You 20 too, take charge of five cities." The third came and said, "Here is your pound, sir; I kept it put away in a handker- 21 chief. I was afraid of you, because you are a hard man: you draw out what you never put in and reap what you did 22 not sow." "You rascal!" he replied; "I will judge you by your own words. You knew, did you, that I am a hard man, that I draw out what I never put 23 in, and reap what I did not sow? Then why did you not put my money on deposit, and I could have claimed it with interest when I came back?" 24 Turning to his attendants he said, "Take the pound from him and give it 25 to the man with ten." "But, sir," they 26 replied, "he has ten already." "I tell you," he went on, "the man who has will always be given more; but the man who has not will forfeit even what he 27 has. But as for those enemies of mine

who did not want me for their king, bring them here and slaughter them in my presence.'

WITH THAT JESUS WENT FORWARD AND 28 began the ascent to Jerusalem. As he 29 approached Bethphage and Bethany at the hill called Olivet, he sent two of the disciples with these instructions: 'Go to 30 the village opposite; as you enter it you will find tethered there a colt which no one has yet ridden. Untie it and bring it here. If anyone asks why you are 31 untying it, say, "Our Master needs it." ' The two went on their errand and 32 found it as he had told them; and while 33 they were untying the colt, its owners asked, 'Why are you untying that colt?' They answered, 'Our Master needs it.' 34 So they brought the colt to Jesus. 35

Then they threw their cloaks on the colt, for Jesus to mount, and they 36 carpeted the road with them as he went on his way. And now, as he approached 37 the descent from the Mount of Olives, the whole company of his disciples in their joy began to sing aloud the praises of God for all the great things they had seen:

'Blessings on him who comes as king 38
        in the name of the Lord!
Peace in heaven, glory in highest
        heaven!'

Some Pharisees who were in the 39 crowd said to him, 'Master, reprimand your disciples.' He answered, 'I tell you, 40 if my disciples keep silence the stones will shout aloud.'

When he came in sight of the city, he 41 wept over it and said, 'If only you had 42 known, on this great day, the way that

---

service while waiting for the kingdom. **12** (also **15,27**): The matter of a man who *journeys abroad, to be appointed king* may be an allusion to some historical incident involving Rome and a member of the Herodian dynasty. However, the rejected *king* (vv. 15,27) of Lk. is intended allegorically as a reference to the Messiah. **13:** The *ten servants* introduced here dwindle to three in vv. 16,18,20; Mt.25.14–15 also has only three. *Pound* translates "mina," a modest sum (in contrast to the sizable responsibilities of Mt.25.14–30). **27:** See v. 11 n.

19.28–21.38: Jesus in Jerusalem (Mt.21.1–25.46; Mk.11.1–13.37). See Mk.11.1–13.37 n.

19.28–40: The entry into Jerusalem (Mt.21.1–9; Mk.11.1–11; Jn.12.12–15). **28:** The *ascent to Jerusalem* marks the end of the "travel narrative" (see 9.51–19.27 n.) and the beginning of the final stage of Jesus' ministry. In Jerusalem, the Holy City, Jesus' Sonship is fully revealed and the stage is set for the new beginning which Acts reports (see Introduction). **29:** *Olivet:* see Mt.21.1 n. **38:** Ps.118.26; Lk. has Jesus acclaimed as *king* without mention of David (compare Mt.21.9; Mk.11.10), perhaps to emphasize that Jesus is more than a Davidic ruler (see 20.41–44). *Peace, glory* recall the angelic hymn in 2.14.

19.41–44: Prediction of Jerusalem's destruction. Lk. writes after the fall of Jerusalem (70 A.D.),

leads to peace! But no; it is hidden
43 from your sight. For a time will come
upon you, when your enemies will set
up siege-works against you; they will
encircle you and hem you in at every
44 point; they will bring you to the
ground, you and your children within
your walls, and not leave you one
stone standing on another, because you
did not recognize God's moment when
it came.'

45 Then he went into the temple and
46 began driving out the traders, with
these words: 'Scripture says, "My
house shall be a house of prayer"; but
you have made it a robbers' cave.'

47 Day by day he taught in the temple.
And the chief priests and lawyers were
bent on making an end of him, with the
48 support of the leading citizens, but
found they were helpless, because the
people all hung upon his words.

20 ONE DAY, AS HE WAS TEACHING THE
people in the temple and telling them
the good news, the priests and lawyers,
and the elders with them, came upon
2 him and accosted him. 'Tell us', they
said, 'by what authority you are acting
like this; who gave you this authority?'
3 He answered them, 'I have a question
4 to ask you too: tell me, was the
baptism of John from God or from
5 men?' This set them arguing among
themselves: 'If we say, "from God", he
will say, "Why did you not believe
6 him?" And if we say, "from men", the
people will all stone us, for they are
convinced that John was a prophet.'
7 So they replied that they could not tell.
8 And Jesus said to them, 'Then neither
will I tell you by what authority I act.'

9 He went on to tell the people this
parable: 'A man planted a vineyard,
let it out to vine-growers, and went
10 abroad for a long time. When the
season came, he sent a servant to the
tenants to collect from them his share
of the produce; but the tenants thrashed
him and sent him away empty-handed.
He tried again and sent a second ser- 11
vant; but he also was thrashed,
outrageously treated, and sent away
empty-handed. He tried once more with 12
a third; this one too they wounded and
flung out. Then the owner of the vineyard said, "What am I to do? I will 13
send my own dear son;ᵏ perhaps they
will respect him." But when the tenants 14
saw him they talked it over together.
"This is the heir," they said; "let us
kill him so that the property may come
to us." So they flung him out of the 15
vineyard and killed him. What then will
the owner of the vineyard do to them?
He will come and put these tenants to 16
death and let the vineyard to others.'

When they heard this, they said,
'God forbid!' But he looked straight 17
at them and said, 'Then what does this
text of Scripture mean: "The stone
which the builders rejected has become
the main corner-stone"? Any man who 18
falls on that stone will be dashed to
pieces; and if it falls on a man he will
be crushed by it.'

The lawyers and chief priests wanted 19
to lay hands on him there and then,
for they saw that this parable was aimed
at them; but they were afraid of the
people. So they watched their oppor- 20
tunity and sent secret agents in the
guise of honest men, to seize upon
some word of his as a pretext for handing him over to the authority and
jurisdiction of the Governor. They put 21
a question to him: 'Master,' they said,
'we know that what you speak and
teach is sound; you pay deference to
no one, but teach in all honesty the
way of life that God requires. Are we or 22

k Or my only son.

but the language of this oracle is natural to the threatened destruction (compare Ps.137.9; Isa.29.3–4; Jer.6.6–8).

19.45–48: Cleansing of the Temple (Mt.21.10–17; Mk.11.15–19; compare Jn.2.12–22). See notes at parallel passages. **47–48:** Although Lk. relates the cleansing episode very briefly, he depicts Jesus as "in control" of the Temple.

20.1–8: Jesus' authority challenged (Mt.21.23–27; Mk.11.27–33). **4:** *From God:* see Mt.21.25 n. **6:** *Prophet:* see Mk.8.28 n.

20.9–18: The evil tenants (Mt.21.33–43; Mk.12.1–11). **9:** On *parable, vineyard,* see Mt.21.33 n. **10:** On *servant, tenants,* see Mt.21.34 n. **13:** *Son:* Jesus. **17:** Ps.118.22; see Mk.12.10–11 n. **18:** Isa.8.14–15.

20.19–26: Caesar's tax (Mt.22.15–22; Mk.12.13–17). **22:** *Taxes:* see Mt.22.17 n.

are we not permitted to pay taxes to the
23 Roman Emperor?' He saw through
24 their trick and said, 'Show me a silver
piece. Whose head does it bear, and
whose inscription?' 'Caesar's', they
25 replied. 'Very well then,' he said, 'pay
Caesar what is due to Caesar, and pay
26 God what is due to God.' Thus their
attempt to catch him out in public
failed, and, astonished by his reply,
they fell silent.

27   Then some Sadducees came forward.
They are the people who deny that
there is a resurrection. Their question
28 was this: 'Master, Moses laid it down
for us that if there are brothers, and one
dies leaving a wife but no child, then
the next should marry the widow and
29 carry on his brother's family. Now,
there were seven brothers: the first
30 took a wife and died childless; then the
31 second married her, then the third. In
this way the seven of them died leaving
32 no children. Afterwards the woman
33 also died. At the resurrection whose
wife is she to be, since all seven had
34 married her?' Jesus said to them, 'The
men and women of this world marry;
35 but those who have been judged worthy
of a place in the other world and of the
resurrection from the dead, do not
36 marry, for they are not subject to death
any longer. They are like angels; they
are sons of God, because they share in
37 the resurrection. That the dead are
raised to life again is shown by Moses
himself in the story of the burning
bush, when he calls the Lord, "the God
38 of Abraham, Isaac, and Jacob". God is
not God of the dead but of the living;
for him all are*l* alive.'

39   At this some of the lawyers said,
40 'Well spoken, Master.' For there was
no further question that they ventured
to put to him.

He said to them, 'How can they say 41
that the Messiah is son of David? For 42
David himself says in the Book of
Psalms: "The Lord said to my Lord,
'Sit at my right hand until I make your 43
enemies your footstool.'" Thus David 44
calls him "Lord"; how then can he be
David's son?'

In the hearing of all the people Jesus 45
said to his disciples: 'Beware of the 46
doctors of the law who love to walk up
and down in long robes, and have a
great liking for respectful greetings in
the street, the chief seats in our
synagogues, and places of honour at
feasts. These are the men who eat up 47
the property of widows, while they say
long prayers for appearance' sake; and
they will receive the severest sentence.'

He looked up and saw the rich **21**
people dropping their gifts into the
chest of the temple treasury; and he 2
noticed a poor widow putting in two
tiny coins. 'I tell you this,' he said: 3
'this poor widow has given more than
any of them; for those others who have 4
given had more than enough, but she,
with less than enough, has given all she
had to live on.'

SOME PEOPLE WERE TALKING ABOUT THE 5
temple and the fine stones and votive
offerings with which it was adorned.
He said, 'These things which you are 6
gazing at—the time will come when
not one stone of them will be left upon
another; all will be thrown down.'
'Master,' they asked, 'when will it all 7
come about? What will be the sign
when it is due to happen?'

He said, 'Take care that you are not 8
misled. For many will come claiming
my name and saying, "I am he", and,
"The Day is upon us." Do not follow

l Or they are all.

20.27–40: A resurrection puzzle (Mt.22.23–33; Mk.12.18–27). **27:** *Sadducees:* see Mt.3.7 n.
28: Deut.25.5–10. **35–36:** The mode of existence in the new age will be completely different
than in this age. **36:** *Angels* are sometimes called *sons of God* in the OT. **37:** Exod.3.6.
   20.41–44: Messiah, son of David (Mt.22.41–46; Mk.12.35–37). **41:** *Messiah . . . son of David:*
see Mt.1.1 n. **42–43:** Ps.110.1; see Mt.22.44 n. **44:** See Mt.22.45 n.
   20.45–47: Warning against pride. 46: 11.43; Mt.23.6; Mk.12.38–40.
   21.1–4: The widow's gift (Mk.12.41–44). **1:** Several *chests* were located in the section of the
Temple open to Jewish women. **2:** The value of the *coins* was too small to be meaningfully
defined in terms of modern currency.
   21.5–38: The eschatological discourse. See Mk.13.1–37 n. **5–7:** The Temple's destruction: see
Mt.24.1–3 n.; Mk.13.1–4.
   21.8–36: Signs, false signs, and warnings (Mt.24.4–44; Mk.13.5–7). **8:** 17.23; see Mt.24.4–5 n.

9 them. And when you hear of wars and insurrections, do not fall into a panic These things are bound to happen first; but the end does not follow im- 10 mediately.' Then he added, 'Nation will make war upon nation, kingdom 11 upon kingdom; there will be great earthquakes, and famines and plagues in many places; in the sky terrors and great portents.

12 'But before all this happens they will set upon you and persecute you. You will be brought before synagogues and put in prison; you will be haled before kings and governors for your allegiance 13 to me. This will be your opportunity to 14 testify; so make up your minds not to 15 prepare your defence beforehand, because I myself will give you power of utterance and a wisdom which no opponent will be able to resist or refute. 16 Even your parents and brothers, your relations and friends, will betray you. 17 Some of you will be put to death; and all will hate you for your allegiance to 18 me. But not a hair of your head shall be 19 lost. By standing firm you will win true life for yourselves.

20 'But when you see Jerusalem encircled by armies, then you may be 21 sure that her destruction is near. Then those who are in Judaea must take to the hills; those who are in the city itself must leave it, and those who are out in 22 the country must not enter; because this is the time of retribution, when all that stands written is to be fulfilled. 23 Alas for women who are with child in those days, or have children at the breast! For there will be great distress in the land and a terrible judgement 24 upon this people. They will fall at the sword's point; they will be carried captive into all countries; and Jerusalem will be trampled down by foreigners until their day has run its course. 25 'Portents will appear in sun, moon,

and stars. On earth nations will stand helpless, not knowing which way to turn from the roar and surge of the sea; men will faint with terror at the 26 thought of all that is coming upon the world; for the celestial powers will be shaken. And then they will see the Son 27 of Man coming on a cloud with great power and glory. When all this begins 28 to happen, stand upright and hold your heads high, because your liberation is near.'

He told them this parable: 'Look at 29 the fig-tree, or any other tree. As soon 30 as it buds, you can see for yourselves that summer is near. In the same way, 31 when you see all this happening, you may know that the kingdom of God is near. 'I tell you this: the present genera- 32 tion will live to see it all. Heaven and 33 earth will pass away; my words will never pass away.

'Keep a watch on yourselves; do not 34 let your minds be dulled by dissipation and drunkenness and worldly cares so that the great Day closes upon you suddenly like a trap; for that day will 35 come on all men, wherever they are, the whole world over. Be on the alert, 36 praying at all times for strength to pass safely through all these imminent troubles and to stand in the presence of the Son of Man.'

His days were given to teaching in 37 the temple; and then he would leave the city and spend the night on the hill called Olivet. And in the early morning 38 the people flocked to listen to him in the temple.*m*

The final conflict

Now the festival of unleavened **22** Bread, known as Passover, was ap-

m Some witnesses here insert the passage printed on p. 138.

12–17: Mt.10.17–22. 14–15: 12.11–12; Acts 6.10. 16: 12.52–53. 17: Mt.10.22. 18: 12.7; Mt.10.30; Acts 27.34. 20: Lk. speaks, not of a cryptic "abomination of desolation" (Mt.24.15 n.), but directly of the siege of Jerusalem in 70 A.D. 22: Deut.32.35. 24: Isa.63.18; Zech.12.3 (Sept.). 25–26: See Mt.24.29 n. 27: Dan.7.13. 32: 9.27; see Mt.24.34 n. 33: 16.17.
    21.37–38: Summary. Lk. apparently thinks of the final period in Jerusalem as longer than the "week" of Mk. (see Mk.11.1–13.37 n.).
    22.1–23.56: The final conflict (Mt.26.1–27.66; Mk.14.1–15.47; Jn. chs. 12–19). While individual episodes (e.g. 23.27–31) can be removed from the narrative leading up to the crucifixion, the outline of the passion story appears to have been fixed quite early and is carried by all four Gospels in much the same form. However, Lk. and Jn., when compared with Mt.-Mk.,

2 proaching, and the chief priests and the doctors of the law were trying to devise some means of doing away with him; for they were afraid of the people.

3 Then Satan entered into Judas Iscariot, who was one of the Twelve;
4 and Judas went to the chief priests and officers of the temple police to discuss ways and means of putting Jesus into
5 their power. They were greatly pleased and undertook to pay him a sum of
6 money. He agreed, and began to look out for an opportunity to betray him to them without collecting a crowd.

7 Then came the day of Unleavened Bread, on which the Passover victim
8 had to be slaughtered, and Jesus sent Peter and John with these instructions: 'Go and prepare for our Passover
9 supper.' 'Where would you like us to make the preparations?' they asked.
10 He replied, 'As soon as you set foot in the city a man will meet you carrying a jar of water. Follow him into the house
11 that he enters and give this message to the householder: "The Master says, 'Where is the room in which I may eat
12 the Passover with my disciples?'" He will show you a large room upstairs all set out: make the preparations there.'
13 They went and found everything as he had said. So they prepared for Passover.

14 When the time came he took his place at table, and the apostles with
15 him; and he said to them, 'How I have longed[n] to eat this Passover with you
16 before my death! For I tell you, never again shall I[o] eat it until the time when it finds its fulfilment in the kingdom of God.'

17 Then he took a cup, and after giving thanks he said, 'Take this and share it
18 among yourselves; for I tell you, from this moment I shall drink from the fruit of the vine no more until the time when
19 the kingdom of God comes.' And he took bread, gave thanks, and broke it; and he gave it to them, with the words: 'This is my body.'[p]

'But mark this—my betrayer is here, 21 his hand with mine on the table. For the 22 Son of Man is going his appointed way; but alas for that man by whom he is betrayed!' At this they began to ask 23 among themselves which of them it could possibly be who was to do this thing.

Then a jealous dispute broke out: 24 who among them should rank highest? But he said, 'In the world, kings lord it 25 over their subjects; and those in authority are called their country's "Benefactors". Not so with you: on the 26 contrary, the highest among you must bear himself like the youngest, the chief of you like a servant. For who is greater 27 —the one who sits at table or the servant who waits on him? Surely the one who sits at table. Yet here am I among you like a servant. "Deacon"

'You are the men who have stood 28 firmly by me in my times of trial; and 29 now I vest in you the kingship which my Father vested in me; you shall eat 30 and drink at my table in my kingdom and sit[q] on thrones as judges of the twelve tribes of Israel.

'Simon, Simon, take heed: Satan has 31 been given leave to sift all of you like wheat; but for you I have prayed that 32 your faith may not fail; and when you have come to yourself, you must lend strength to your brothers.' 'Lord,' he 33 replied, 'I am ready to go with you to prison and death.' Jesus said, 'I tell you, 34

n *Or said to them, 'I longed . . .'*
o *Some witnesses read For I tell you, I shall not . . .*
p *Some witnesses add, in whole or in part, and with various arrangements, the following:* 'which is given for you; do this as a memorial of me.' (20) In the same way he took the cup after supper, and said, "This cup, poured out for you, is the new covenant sealed by my blood.'
q *Or* trial; and as my Father gave me the right to reign, so I give you the right to eat and to drink . . . and to sit . . .

---

show sufficient dissimilarity in detail as to suggest the existence of more than one passion tradition. **1:** See Mk.14.1 n. **3–6:** Mt.26.14–16; Mk.14.10–11. **3:** See 4.13 n.; *Satan* is not mentioned as the agent in Mt. or Mk.; compare Jn.6.70–71; 13.2,27.
    22.7–13: Preparation for the Passover (Mt.26.17–19; Mk.14.12–16). **7–8:** See Mt.26.17 n. **10–12:** See Mt.26.18 n.
    22.14–38: The Last Supper (Mt.26.20–29; Mk.14.17–21). **14:** See Mt.26.20 n. **15–20:** See also 1 Cor.11.23–26. **17–19:** Lk. apparently follows a special tradition which places the cup ahead of the loaf. If Tfn. *p* represents the original text, the *new covenant* (v. 20) refers to Jer.31.31; see Mt.26.28 n. **21–23:** See also Jn.13.21–30. **24–26:** Mt.20.25–28; Mk.10.42–45. **29:** Compare Acts 1.6–8. **30:** Mt.19.28. **31–34:** Mt.26.30–35 (see 33–35 n.); Mk.14.26–31; Jn.13.36–38. **31:** 4.13 n. **35:** 10.4. **37:** Isa.53.12.

Peter, the cock will not crow tonight until you have three times over denied that you know me.'

35 He said to them, 'When I sent you out barefoot without purse or pack, were you ever short of anything?'

36 'No,' they answered. 'It is different now,' he said; 'whoever has a purse had better take it with him, and his pack too; and if he has no sword, let him

37 sell his cloak to buy one. For Scripture says, "And he was counted among the outlaws", and these words, I tell you, must find fulfilment in me; indeed, all that is written of me is being fulfilled.'

38 'Look, Lord,' they said, 'we have two swords here.' 'Enough, enough!' he replied.

39 THEN HE WENT OUT AND MADE HIS WAY as usual to the Mount of Olives, accom-

40 panied by the disciples. When he reached the place he said to them, 'Pray that you may be spared the hour

41 of testing.' He himself withdrew from them about a stone's throw, knelt

42 down, and began to pray: 'Father, if it be thy will, take this cup away from me. Yet not my will but thine be done.'

43 And now there appeared to him an angel from heaven bringing him

44 strength, and in anguish of spirit he prayed the more urgently; and his sweat was like clots of blood falling to the ground.*r*

45 When he rose from prayer and came to the disciples he found them asleep,

46 worn out by grief. 'Why are you sleeping?' he said. 'Rise and pray that you may be spared the test.'

47 WHILE HE WAS STILL SPEAKING A CROWD appeared with the man called Judas, one of the Twelve, at their head. He

48 came up to Jesus to kiss him; but Jesus said, 'Judas, would you betray the Son of Man with a kiss?'

49 When his followers saw what was coming, they said, 'Lord, shall we use

50 our swords?' And one of them struck

at the High Priest's servant, cutting off

51 his right ear. But Jesus answered, 'Let them have their way.' Then he touched the man's ear and healed him.*s*

52 Turning to the chief priests, the officers of the temple police, and the elders, who had come to seize him, he said, 'Do you take me for a bandit, that you have come out with swords and cudgels to arrest me? Day after day, when

53 I was in the temple with you, you kept your hands off me. But this is your moment—the hour when darkness reigns.'

54 Then they arrested him and led him away. They brought him to the High Priest's house, and Peter followed at a

55 distance. They lit a fire in the middle of the courtyard and sat round it, and

56 Peter sat among them. A serving-maid who saw him sitting in the firelight stared at him and said, 'This man was with him too.' But he denied it:

57 'Woman,' he said, 'I do not know

58 him.' A little later someone else noticed him and said, 'You also are one of them.' But Peter said to him, 'No, I

59 am not.' About an hour passed and another spoke more strongly still: 'Of course this fellow was with him. He must have been; he is a Galilean.'

60 But Peter said, 'Man, I do not know what you are talking about.' At that moment, while he was still speaking, a

61 cock crew; and the Lord turned and looked at Peter. And Peter remembered the Lord's words, 'Tonight before the cock crows you will disown me three times.'*t*

63 The men who were guarding Jesus

64 mocked at him. They beat him, they blindfolded him, and they kept asking him, 'Now, prophet, who hit you?

65 Tell us that.' And so they went on heaping insults upon him.

66 WHEN DAY BROKE, THE ELDERS OF THE

r Some witnesses omit And now ... ground.
s Or 'Let me do as much as this', and touching the man's ear, he healed him.
t Some witnesses add (62) He went outside, and wept bitterly, *as in Matthew 26. 75.*

22.39–46: Gethsemane (Mt.26.30–46; Mk.14.26–42). **39:** Jn.18.1. **40–46:** Several elements in this scene are reminiscent of the Lord's Prayer (e.g. vv. 40,42,46). **42:** *Cup:* see Mk.10.38 n.
22.47–53: The arrest (Mt.26.47–56; Mk.14.43–52; Jn.18.2–11). **47:** *Kiss:* see Mt.26.48 n. **50:** *One:* see Mt.26.51 n.
22.54–71: Before the Jewish authorities (Mt.26.57–75; Mk.14.53–72; Jn.18.12–27). See Mt.26.57–75 n. **61:** Compare v. 34. **63–65:** See Mt.26.67–68; Mk.14.65. **66:** *Council:* see

nation, chief priests, and doctors of
the law assembled, and he was brought
67 before their Council. 'Tell us,' they
said, 'are you the Messiah?' 'If I tell
you,' he replied, 'you will not believe
68 me; and if I ask questions, you will not
69 answer. But from now on, the Son of
Man will be seated at the right hand
70 of Almighty God.'*u* 'You are the Son
of God, then?' they all said, and he re-
71 plied, 'It is you who say I am.'*v* They
said, 'Need we call further witnesses?
We have heard it ourselves from his
own lips.'

23 With that the whole assembly rose,
and they brought him before Pilate.
2 They opened the case against him by
saying, 'We found this man subverting
our nation, opposing the payment of
taxes to Caesar, and claiming to be
3 Messiah, a king.'*w* Pilate asked him,
'Are you the king of the Jews?' He
4 replied, 'The words are yours.'*x* Pilate
then said to the chief priests and the
crowd, 'I find no case for this man to
5 answer.' But they insisted: 'His teaching is causing disaffection among the
people all through Judaea. It started
from Galilee and has spread as far as
this city.'
6 When Pilate heard this, he asked if
7 the man was a Galilean, and on learning that he belonged to Herod's jurisdiction he remitted the case to him, for
Herod was also in Jerusalem at that
8 time. When Herod saw Jesus he was
greatly pleased; having heard about
him, he had long been wanting to see
him, and had been hoping to see some
9 miracle performed by him. He
questioned him at some length without
10 getting any reply; but the chief priests
and lawyers appeared and pressed the
11 case against him vigorously. Then
Herod and his troops treated him with
contempt and ridicule, and sent him
back to Pilate dressed in a gorgeous
12 robe. That same day Herod and Pilate

became friends; till then there had
been a standing feud between them.
Pilate now called together the chief 13
priests, councillors, and people, and 14
said to them, 'You brought this man
before me on a charge of subversion.
But, as you see, I have myself examined
him in your presence and found nothing
in him to support your charges. No 15
more did Herod, for he has referred
him back to us. Clearly he has done
nothing to deserve death. I therefore 16
propose to let him off with a flogging.'
But*y* there was a general outcry. 'Away 18
with him! Give us Barabbas.' (This 19
man had been put in prison for a rising
that had taken place in the city, and for
murder.) Pilate addressed them again, 20
in his desire to release Jesus, but they 21
shouted back, 'Crucify him, crucify
him!' For the third time he spoke to 22
them: 'Why, what wrong has he done?
I have not found him guilty of any
capital offence. I will therefore let him
off with a flogging.' But they insisted 23
on their demand, shouting that Jesus
should be crucified. Their shouts prevailed and Pilate decided that they 24
should have their way. He released the 25
man they asked for, the man who had
been put in prison for insurrection and
murder, and gave Jesus up to their will.

As THEY LED HIM AWAY TO EXECUTION 26
they seized upon a man called Simon,
from Cyrene, on his way in from the
country, put the cross on his back, and
made him walk behind Jesus carrying it.
Great numbers of people followed, 27
many women among them, who
mourned and lamented over him. Jesus 28
turned to them and said, 'Daughters of
Jerusalem, do not weep for me; no,

u Literally of the Power of God.
v Or You are right, for I am.
w Or to be an anointed king.
x Or It is as you say.
y Some witnesses read (17) At festival time he was
obliged to release one person for them; (18) and
now . . .

Mt.26.59 n. **67,70:** *Messiah, Son:* see Mt.1.1 n.; 16.16 n. **69:** Dan.7.13; Ps.110.1. *Son of Man:*
see Mk.2.10 n.
    23.1–25: Before Roman authority (Mt.27.1–31; Mk.15.1–20; Jn.18.28–19.16). **1:** *Pilate:* see
3.1 n. **2:** *Opposing the payment of* Roman *taxes* and claiming to be *king* are obviously seditious;
Lk. has made the charge quite clear (see v. 14). **4:** In Lk., Pilate pronounces Jesus innocent
three times in the course of the hearing (vv. 4,14,22); see Acts 3.13–14. **7:** *Herod:* Antipas (see
3.1 n.). The appearance before Antipas is found only in Lk.; see Acts 4.27–28. **8:** 9.9. **11:**
Compare Mt.27.27–31; Mk.15.16–20; Jn.19.2–3. **18:** *Barabbas:* Mt.27.16 n.
    23.26–56: The crucifixion (Mt.27.32–66; Mk.15.21–47; Jn.19.17–42). **26:** *Simon:* see

weep for yourselves and your children.
29 For the days are surely coming when they will say, "Happy are the barren, the wombs that never bore a child, the
30 breasts that never fed one." Then they will start saying to the mountains, "Fall on us", and to the hills, "Cover
31 us." For if these things are done when the wood is green, what will happen when it is dry?'

32 There were two others with him, criminals who were being led away to
33 execution; and when they reached the place called The Skull, they crucified him there, and the criminals with him, one on his right and the other on his
34 left. Jesus said, 'Father, forgive them; they do not know what they are doing.'[z]

They divided his clothes among them
35 by casting lots. The people stood looking on, and their rulers jeered at him: 'He saved others: now let him save himself, if this is God's Messiah, his
36 Chosen.' The soldiers joined in the mockery and came forward offering
37 him their sour wine. 'If you are the king of the Jews,' they said, 'save your-
38 self.' There was an inscription above his head which ran: 'This is the king of the Jews.'

39 One of the criminals who hung there with him taunted him: 'Are not you the
40 Messiah? Save yourself, and us.' But the other rebuked him: 'Have you no fear of God? You are under the same
41 sentence as he. For us it is plain justice; we are paying the price for our misdeeds; but this man has done nothing
42 wrong.' And he said, 'Jesus, remember me when you come to your throne.'[a]
43 He answered, 'I tell you this: today you shall be with me in Paradise.'

44 By now it was about midday and a darkness fell over the whole land, which lasted until three in the after-
45 noon; the sun's light failed. And the curtain of the temple was torn in two.
46 Then Jesus gave a loud cry and said, 'Father, into thy hands I commit my spirit'; and with these words he died.
The centurion saw it all, and gave 47 praise to God. 'Beyond all doubt', he said, 'this man was innocent.'

The crowd who had assembled for 48 the spectacle, when they saw what had happened, went home beating their breasts.

HIS FRIENDS HAD ALL BEEN STANDING AT 49 a distance; the women who had accompanied him from Galilee stood with them and watched it all.

Now there was a man called Joseph, 50 a member of the Council, a good, upright man, who had dissented from 51 their policy and the action they had taken. He came from the Judaean town of Arimathaea, and he was one who looked forward to the kingdom of God. This man now approached Pilate and 52 asked for the body of Jesus. Taking it 53 down from the cross, he wrapped it in a linen sheet, and laid it in a tomb cut out of the rock, in which no one had been laid before. It was Friday, and the 54 Sabbath was about to begin. The women who had accompanied 55 him from Galilee followed; they took note of the tomb and observed how his body was laid. Then they went home 56 and prepared spices and perfumes: and on the Sabbath they rested in obedience to the commandment. But **24** on the Sunday morning very early they came to the tomb bringing the spices they had prepared. Finding that the 2 stone had been rolled away from the tomb, they went inside; but the body 3 was not to be found. While they stood 4 utterly at a loss, all of a sudden two men in dazzling garments were at their side. They were terrified, and stood 5 with eyes cast down, but the men said, 'Why search among the dead for one

z *Some witnesses omit* Jesus said, 'Father . . . doing.'
a *Some witnesses read* come in royal power.

Mk.15.21 n.; contrast Jn.19.17. **29:** Compare 21.23. **30:** Hos.10.8. **32:** Crucifixion was a form of Roman punishment reserved for dangerous criminals; further, Judaism regarded anyone who was crucified as cursed (Deut.21.23). **33:** Isa.53.12. **34:** *Forgive them:* compare Acts 7.60. **35:** Ps.22.18. **36:** The *wine* was probably offered as a sedative. **43:** *Paradise*, in Jewish thought, was the garden in which the righteous lived after death; compare Rev.2.7. **45:** *Curtain:* see Mt.27.51 n. **46:** Ps.31.5. **49:** Ps.38.11. **50:** *Council:* see Mt.26.59 n. **53:** Deut.21.22–23. **55–56:** The women delay the burial anointing because the Sabbath has begun and work must be postponed (Deut.5.12–14).
24.1–11: The empty tomb (Mt.28.1–10; Mk.16.1–8; Jn.20.1–18). **2:** *Stone:* see Mt.27.60 n.

6 who lives?[b] Remember what he told
7 you while he was still in Galilee, about
the Son of Man: how he must be given
up into the power of sinful men and be
crucified, and must rise again on the
8 third day.' Then they recalled his words
9 and, returning from the tomb, they
reported all this to the Eleven and all
the others.
10   The women were Mary of Magdala,
Joanna, and Mary the mother[c] of
James, and they, with the other women,
11 told the apostles. But the story appeared to them to be nonsense, and they
would not believe them.[d]

13 THAT SAME DAY TWO OF THEM WERE ON
their way to a village called Emmaus,
which lay about seven miles from
14 Jerusalem, and they were talking
together about all these happenings.
15 As they talked and discussed it with one
another, Jesus himself came up and
16 walked along with them; but something kept them from seeing who it was.
17 He asked them, 'What is it you are
debating as you walk?' They halted,
18 their faces full of gloom, and one,
called Cleopas, answered, 'Are you the
only person staying in Jerusalem not to
know[e] what has happened there in the
19 last few days?' 'What do you mean?'
he said. 'All this about Jesus of
Nazareth,' they replied, 'a prophet
powerful in speech and action before
20 God and the whole people; how our
chief priests and rulers handed him over
to be sentenced to death, and crucified
21 him. But we had been hoping that he
was the man to liberate Israel. What is
more, this is the third day since it
22 happened, and now some women of
our company have astounded us: they
23 went early to the tomb, but failed to
find his body, and returned with a story
that they had seen a vision of angels
24 who told them he was alive. So some
of our people went to the tomb and
found things just as the women had
said; but him they did not see.'
25   'How dull you are!' he answered.
'How slow to believe all that the proph-

ets said! Was the Messiah not bound to 26
suffer thus before entering upon his
glory?' Then he began with Moses and 27
all the prophets, and explained to them
the passages which referred to himself
in every part of the scriptures.
    By this time they had reached the 28
village to which they were going, and
he made as if to continue his journey,
but they pressed him: 'Stay with us, 29
for evening draws on, and the day is
almost over.' So he went in to stay with
them. And when he had sat down with 30
them at table, he took bread and said
the blessing; he broke the bread, and
offered it to them. Then their eyes were 31
opened, and they recognized him; and
he vanished from their sight. They said 32
to one another, 'Did we not feel our
hearts on fire as he talked with us on the
road and explained the scriptures to us?'
    Without a moment's delay they set 33
out and returned to Jerusalem. There
they found that the Eleven and the rest
of the company had assembled, and 34
were saying, 'It is true: the Lord has
risen; he has appeared to Simon.' Then 35
they gave their account of the events of
their journey and told how he had been
recognized by them at the breaking of
the bread.
    As they were talking about all this, 36
there he was, standing among them.[f]
Startled and terrified, they thought 37
they were seeing a ghost. But he said 38
'Why are you so perturbed? Why do
questionings arise in your minds?
Look at my hands and feet. It is I my- 39
self. Touch me and see; no ghost has
flesh and bones as you can see that I
have.'[g] They were still unconvinced, 41
still wondering, for it seemed too good
to be true. So he asked them, 'Have
you anything here to eat?' They offered 42

b *Some witnesses insert* He is not here: he has been
  raised.
c *Or* wife, *or* daughter.
d *Some witnesses add* (12) Peter, however, got up and
  ran to the tomb, and, peering in, saw the wrappings
  and nothing more; and he went home amazed at what
  had happened.
e *Or* Have you been staying by yourself in Jerusalem,
  that you do not know . . .
f *Some witnesses insert* And he said to them, 'Peace be
  with you!'
g *Some witnesses insert* (40) After saying this he showed
  them his hands and feet.

6: Contrast Mt.28.7; Mk.16.7; in Lk. the resurrection appearances are restricted to the vicinity
of Jerusalem.
    24.13–53: Appearances and commissioning. 27: *Moses and all the prophets:* v. 44; see Mt.5.17 n.
30: The scene obviously suggests a eucharistic setting. 34: 1 Cor.15.5. 36–43: Jn.20.19–29.

him a piece of fish they had cooked,
43 which he took and ate before their eyes.
44 And he said to them, 'This is what I
meant by saying, while I was still with
you, that everything written about me
in the Law of Moses and in the prophets and psalms was bound to be ful-
45 filled.' Then he opened their minds
46 to understand the scriptures. 'This', he
said, 'is what is written: that the
Messiah is to suffer death and to rise
47 from the dead on the third day, and
that in his name repentance bringing
the forgiveness of sins is to be proclaimed to all nations. Begin from

Jerusalem; it is you who are the wit- 48
nesses to it all. And mark this: I am 19
sending upon you my Father's promised
gift; so stay here in this city until you
are armed with the power from above.'
Then he led them out as far as 50
Bethany, and blessed them with uplifted hands; and in the act of blessing 51
he parted from them.*h* And they*i* re- 52
turned to Jerusalem with great joy, and 53
spent all their time in the temple
praising God.

h Some witnesses add and was carried up into heaven.
i Some witnesses insert worshipped him and . . .

44: V. 27; Mt.5.17 n. **46:** Hos.6.2. **47–49:** Compare Mt.28.18–20; Acts 1.4–8. **47:** *From Jerusalem:* v. 52 n. **49:** *Power from above:* compare Acts 1.8; 2.1–4. **50–51:** Acts 1.9–12. **52:** As the Gospel concludes, the disciples are in *Jerusalem* (compare Acts 1.12–14), but the reader is assured (v. 47) that what began in Galilee and culminated in the Holy City would now move out "to the ends of the earth" (Acts 1.8).

THE GOSPEL ACCORDING TO
JOHN

While the Gospel According to John stands in contrast to Matthew, Mark, and Luke in matters of theological perspective, arrangement of its contents, and its distinctive use of imagery and symbols, it nevertheless clearly belongs to the same form of literature as do the other three. Its author, whose identity is unknown, displays exact knowledge both of Palestinian topography and of the Judaism of the first Christian century. This Gospel seems to record a tradition independent of that reflected in Matthew, Mark, and Luke, a tradition which may well go back to John, the son of Zebedee (see 21.2 n.), to whom the book was ascribed in the late second century. In Christian tradition John has often been called the "spiritual" Gospel, because of its attention to the spiritual import of the incidents it reports.

The Gospel is frequently analyzed into "The Book of Signs" (1.19–12.50) and "The Book of Glory" (13.1–20.31), with 1.1–18 as a Prologue and ch. 21 as an Epilogue. A "sign" is an act of power by Jesus, which points to a truth inaccessible to sight and touch, but apprehensible by faith. Paradoxically, "glory," an Old Testament term signifying God's presence, is for the evangelist publicly manifest in the earthly career of Jesus—who, to eyes of faith, reveals himself as the Son of God in certain significant events and through his death and resurrection. The writer's aim is "that you may hold the faith that Jesus is the Christ, the Son of God, and that through this faith you may possess life by his name" (20.31).

The Gospel probably originated in Asia Minor, possibly at Ephesus, shortly before the end of the first century.

The coming of Christ

1 WHEN ALL THINGS BEGAN, THE Word already was.[a] The Word dwelt with God, and what God 2 was, the Word was. The Word, then, 3 was with God at the beginning, and through him all things came to be; no single thing was created without him. 4 All that came to be was alive with his life,[b] and that life was the light of men. 5 The light shines on in the dark, and the darkness has never mastered it.

6 There appeared a man named John, 7 sent from God; he came as a witness to testify to the light, that all might 8 become believers through him. He was not himself the light; he came to bear 9 witness to the light. The real light which enlightens every man was even then coming into the world.[c]

10 He was in the world;[d] but the world, though it owed its being to him, did not recognize him. He entered his own 11 realm, and his own would not receive him. But to all who did receive him, to 12 those who have yielded him their allegiance, he gave the right to become children of God, not born of any 13 human stock, or by the fleshly desire of a human father, but the offspring of God himself. So the Word became 14 flesh; he came to dwell among us, and we saw his glory, such glory as befits the Father's only Son, full of grace and truth.

Here is John's testimony to him: he 15 cried aloud, 'This is the man I meant when I said, "He comes after me, but takes rank before me"; for before I was born, he already was.'

a Or The Word was at the creation.
b Or no single created thing came into being without him. There was life in him . . .
c Or The light was in being, light absolute, enlightening every man born into the world.
d Or The Word, then, was in the world.

1.1–18: The prologue. 1: The *Word* (Gk. *logos*) as the title of Jesus Christ (v. 17) appears only here in Jn.; compare 1 Jn.1.1; Rev.19.13. *Word* and related terms in earlier Jewish tradition (see Wis.9.1–4,9,17–18; Ecclus.24.1–12) prepared the way for its use here to denote Jesus as revealer of the unseen God. **4:** *Life* in Jn. always means eternal (not merely natural) life (see 3.15). This *life* becomes *the light of men* in that it reveals the Father to them. **5:** The *darkness* symbolizes those death-dealing forces in history irreconcilably opposed to God. **6:** *John* (in Mt., Mk., Lk., "the Baptist") is in Jn. a *witness* (see 1.19–51 n.) to Jesus, but in every way less important than he (1.19–27; 3.25–30). **11:** *His own realm:* the Holy Land. *His own:* the people of Israel. Jn. may think of the earlier appearance of the Word in the Mosaic Law (see v. 17; compare Ecclus.24.1–3,8,23). **14:** *Flesh:* human. *Came to dwell* (lit. pitched his tent): perhaps an echo of the glory of God which filled the Tent of the Presence (Exod.40.34–38). *Glory.*

108

16 Out of his full store we have all re-
17 ceived grace upon grace; for while the Law was given through Moses, grace and truth came through Jesus Christ.
18 No one has ever seen God; but God's only Son, he who is nearest to the Father's heart, he has made him known.*e*

19 THIS IS THE TESTIMONY WHICH JOHN gave when the Jews of Jerusalem sent a deputation of priests and Levites to ask
20 him who he was. He confessed without reserve and avowed, 'I am not the
21 Messiah.' 'What then? Are you Elijah?' 'No', he replied. 'Are you the prophet
22 we await?' He answered 'No.' 'Then who are you?' they asked. 'We must give an answer to those who sent us. What account do you give of yourself?'
23 He answered in the words of the prophet Isaiah: 'I am a voice crying aloud in the wilderness, "Make the Lord's highway straight."'
24 Some Pharisees who were in the
25 deputation asked him, 'If you are not the Messiah, nor Elijah, nor the proph-
26 et, why then are you baptizing?' 'I baptize in water,' John replied, 'but among you, though you do not know
27 him, stands the one who is to come after me. I am not good enough to
28 unfasten his shoes.' This took place at Bethany beyond Jordan, where John was baptizing.
29 The next day he saw Jesus coming towards him. 'Look,' he said, 'there is the Lamb of God; it is he who takes
30 away the sin of the world. This is he of whom I spoke when I said, "After me a man is coming who takes rank before me"; for before I was born, he already
31 was. I myself did not know who he was; but the very reason why I came, baptizing in water, was that he might be revealed to Israel.'
32 John testified further: 'I saw the Spirit coming down from heaven like a
33 dove and resting upon him. I did not know him, but he who sent me to baptize in water had told me, "When you see the Spirit coming down upon someone and resting upon him, you will know that this is he who is to baptize in Holy Spirit." I saw it myself, and I
34 have borne witness. This is God's Chosen One.'*f*

35 The next day again John was stand-
36 ing with two of his disciples when Jesus passed by. John looked towards him and said, 'There is the Lamb of God.' The two disciples heard him say
37 this, and followed Jesus. When he
38 turned and saw them following him, he asked, 'What are you looking for?' They said, 'Rabbi', (which means a teacher), 'where are you staying?' 'Come and see', he replied. So they
39 went and saw where he was staying, and spent the rest of the day with him. It was then about four in the afternoon.
40 One of the two who followed Jesus after hearing what John said was Andrew, Simon Peter's brother. The
41 first thing he did was to find*g* his brother Simon. He said to him, 'We

e Some witnesses read but the only one, the one nearest to the Father's heart, has made him known; *others read* but the only one, himself God, the nearest to the Father's heart, has made him known.
f Some witnesses read This is the Son of God.
g Some witnesses read In the morning he found ...

radiance; therefore, the presence of God. **16:** *Grace upon grace:* God's gift to mankind in Jesus Christ is added to that of the Mosaic Law. **18:** The generalization that *no one has ever seen God* is modified in 14.9; there, to have seen Jesus is equivalent to having seen God.

1.19–51: Testimonies to Jesus. The language of the courtroom, frequent in biblical literature (e.g. Isa.43.10–13), is particularly important to the description of Jesus' public life in Jn. Thus *testimony* (v. 19 and elsewhere) has a quasi-juridical meaning and seems to point to the climax at 12.31–32 ("judgement for this world"). **19:** *The Jews* is the evangelist's generalized name for the religious authorities who oppose Jesus (such as the chief priests, scribes, etc., of the Synoptics), not literally meant to include all Jews. The term probably also reflects tensions between the Johannine church and the synagogue late in the first century. **20–21:** *The Messiah:* see Mt.1.1 n. *Elijah:* see Mt.17.10–13; Mk.6.15 n. *Prophet:* see 6.14 n.; Mk.8.28 n. **23:** See Isa.40.3. **24:** *Pharisees:* see Mt.3.7 n. **27:** *To unfasten his shoes:* the task of the slave who washed the master's feet. **28:** The exact location of this *Bethany* is unknown. **29:** *The Lamb of God* derives from Isa.53.7–12, especially Isa.53.7. See also 1 Cor.5.7 where Jesus is identified with the paschal lamb of Exod.12.3–10. Compare 19.14 n. **30:** Although Jesus appears in history after John, in reality *he already was,* i.e. already existed before John's time. In Jn., Jesus has always existed (1.1; 8.56–57). **32:** Jn. does not narrate the baptism of Jesus as do Mt., Mk., Lk., but only the *coming down* of the Spirit which accompanied it; see Mk.1.9–11 n. **34:** *Chosen One:* see Isa.42.1. **35:** *Two disciples:* see v. 40. **40:** *Andrew* appears more prominently in Jn.

have found the Messiah' (which is the
42 Hebrew for 'Christ'). He brought
Simon to Jesus, who looked at him and
said, 'You are Simon son of John.
You shall be called Cephas' (that is,
Peter, the Rock).
43   The next day Jesus decided to leave
44 for Galilee. He met Philip, who, like
Andrew and Peter, came from Bethsaida, and said to him, 'Follow me.'
45 Philip went to find Nathanael, and
told him, 'We have met the man spoken
of by Moses in the Law, and by the
prophets: it is Jesus son of Joseph,
46 from Nazareth.' 'Nazareth!' Nathanael
exclaimed; 'can anything good come
from Nazareth?' Philip said, 'Come
47 and see.' When Jesus saw Nathanael
coming, he said, 'Here is an Israelite
worthy of the name; there is nothing
48 false in him.' Nathanael asked him,
'How do you come to know me?' Jesus
replied, 'I saw you under the fig-tree
49 before Philip spoke to you.' 'Rabbi,'
said Nathanael, 'you are the Son of
50 God; you are king of Israel.' Jesus
answered, 'Is this the ground of your
faith, that I told you I saw you under
the fig-tree? You shall see greater
51 things than that.' Then he added, 'In
truth, in very truth I tell you all, you
shall see heaven wide open, and God's
angels ascending and descending upon
the Son of Man.'

Christ the giver of life

2 ON THE THIRD DAY THERE WAS A
wedding at Cana-in-Galilee. The
2 mother of Jesus was there, and Jesus
3 and his disciples were guests also. The

wine gave out, so Jesus's mother said
to him, 'They have no wine left.' He 4
answered, 'Your concern, mother, is
not mine. My hour has not yet come.'
His mother said to the servants, 'Do 5
whatever he tells you.' There were six 6
stone water-jars standing near, of the
kind used for Jewish rites of purification; each held from twenty to thirty
gallons. Jesus said to the servants, 7
'Fill the jars with water', and they filled
them to the brim. 'Now draw some 8
off', he ordered, 'and take it to the
steward of the feast'; and they did so.
The steward tasted the water now 9
turned into wine, not knowing its
source; though the servants who had
drawn the water knew. He hailed the
bridegroom and said, 'Everyone serves 10
the best wine first, and waits until the
guests have drunk freely before serving
the poorer sort; but you have kept the
best wine till now.'
    This deed at Cana-in-Galilee is the 11
first of the signs by which Jesus revealed
his glory and led his disciples to believe
in him.

AFTER THIS HE WENT DOWN TO CAPER- 12
naum in company with his mother, his
brothers, and his disciples, but they
did not stay there long. As it was near 13
the time of the Jewish Passover, Jesus
went up to Jerusalem. There he found 14
in the temple the dealers in cattle, sheep,
and pigeons, and the money-changers
seated at their tables. Jesus made a 15
whip of cords and drove them out of
the temple, sheep, cattle, and all. He
upset the tables of the money-changers,
scattering their coins. Then he turned 16
on the dealers in pigeons: 'Take them

(6.8; 12.22) than in the Synoptics. **44:** *Bethsaida* lay north of the Lake of Galilee and east of the
Jordan. **45:** Although *Nathanael* is sometimes identified with Bartholomew (Mk.3.18), this
identification is not justified by NT evidence. **49:** *King:* the Messiah (see Mt.1.1 n.). **51:** Jacob's
vision of *God's angels* mediating between heaven and earth (Gen.28.12) provides this image
about the *Son of Man* (see Mk.2.10 n.).
    2.1–12: First sign at Cana. 1: Jn. envisages the events of 1.19–2.12 as encompassing a week.
He has previously (1.19–28,29–34,35–42,43–51) indicated the first four days of Jesus' ministry;
hence *the third day* here marks the conclusion of this week. *Cana* is nine miles north of Nazareth.
The mother of Jesus appears again in 19.25–27. **4:** *Mother:* lit. woman. *Hour* in Jn. denotes the
climactic moment of Jesus' passion and glorification (see also 12.27). **11:** *Signs:* see Introduction.
His glory: see 12.23; 17.24. **12:** *Capernaum* (Mk.1.21–28) is on the Lake of Galilee.
    2.13–25: The cleansing of the Temple. 13: Jn. understands Jesus' ministry to have spanned
three *Passovers* (see also 6.4; 11.55) of which this is the first. Contrast the Synoptics where only
a single Passover is involved. On Passover, see Mk.14.1 n. **14:** The *temple* here includes the
entire area of which the sanctuary proper is the center; see v. 19 n. *Money-changers:* see
Mt.21.12 n. **15:** This action is symbolic; there are a good many "acted" prophecies in the OT

17 out,' he said; 'you must not turn my Father's house into a market.' His disciples recalled the words of Scripture, 'Zeal for thy house will destroy
18 me.' The Jews challenged Jesus: 'What sign', they asked, 'can you show as
19 authority for your action?' 'Destroy this temple,' Jesus replied, 'and in three
20 days I will raise it again.' They said, 'It has taken forty-six years to build this temple. Are you going to raise it
21 again in three days?' But the temple he
22 was speaking of was his body. After his resurrection his disciples recalled what he had said, and they believed the Scripture and the words that Jesus had spoken.

23 WHILE HE WAS IN JERUSALEM FOR Passover many gave their allegiance to him when they saw the signs that he
24 performed. But Jesus for his part would not trust himself to them. He knew men
25 so well, all of them, that he needed no evidence from others about a man, for he himself could tell what was in a man.

3 THERE WAS ONE OF THE PHARISEES named Nicodemus, a member of the
2 Jewish Council, who came to Jesus by night. 'Rabbi,' he said, 'we know that you are a teacher sent by God; no one could perform these signs of yours un-
3 less God were with him.' Jesus answered, 'In truth, in very truth I tell you, unless a man has been born over again he cannot see the kingdom of
4 God.' 'But how is it possible', said Nicodemus, 'for a man to be born

when he is old? Can he enter his mother's womb a second time and be
5 born?' Jesus answered, 'In truth I tell you, no one can enter the kingdom of God without being born from water
6 and spirit. Flesh can give birth only to flesh; it is spirit that gives birth to
7 spirit. You ought not to be astonished, then, when I tell you that you must be
8 born over again. The wind[h] blows where it wills; you hear the sound of it, but you do not know where it comes from, or where it is going. So with everyone who is born from spirit[h].'

9 Nicodemus replied, 'How is this
10 possible?' 'What!' said Jesus. 'Is this famous teacher of Israel ignorant of such things? In very truth I tell you, we
11 speak of what we know, and testify to what we have seen, and yet you all reject our testimony. If you disbelieve me
12 when I talk to you about things on earth, how are you to believe if I should talk about the things of heaven?

13 'No one ever went up into heaven except the one who came down from heaven, the Son of Man whose home is in heaven.[i] This Son of Man must be
14 lifted up as the serpent was lifted up by Moses in the wilderness, so that every-
15 one who has faith in him may in him possess eternal life.

16 'God loved the world so much that he gave his only Son, that everyone who has faith in him may not die but
17 have eternal life. It was not to judge

h wind and spirit are translations of the same Greek word, which has both meanings.
i Some witnesses omit whose home is in heaven.

(see, e.g. Jer.13.1–11). **16:** *Market:* see Zech.14.21. **17:** In Jn. the term *recalled* usually points to something associated with Jesus which was understood only in Christian reflection after his time (see v. 22; 12.16; 14.26). See Ps.69.9 and Tfn. *q* there. **19:** *Temple* here indicates the sanctuary itself; contrast v. 14. **20:** *Forty-six years:* see Mt.24.1–3 n. The date would appear to be 27 A.D. **21:** *His body:* Jesus' risen body was to supersede the sanctuary; see Mt.24.1–3 n. **23:** See 4.48 n.

3.1–21: Jesus with Nicodemus. 1: *Pharisees:* Mt.3.7 n. *Jewish Council:* Judea's highest native court, called the Sanhedrin in other translations. *Nicodemus* reappears at 7.50; 19.39. *Rabbi:* see Mt.23.8–10 n. **3:** The Gk. for *over again* can also mean "from above." The expression *kingdom of God,* frequent in the Synoptics (see Mk.1.15 n.), is found in Jn. only here and in v. 5. **5:** *Water and spirit:* baptism; see 1 Cor.6.11. **6:** *Flesh* describes man in his creaturely limitations, while *spirit* can reflect divine action on man. The contrast between flesh and spirit, frequent in the Hellenistic world, is given a strongly religious turn here and in 6.63; 7.79. In 4.24, God is described as spirit. **8:** *Wind, spirit:* Tfn. *h.* **13:** *Went up:* writing after the resurrection, Jn. refers to the ascension as a past event. **14:** *Lifted up* is a term with a paradoxical double meaning which includes both Jesus' crucifixion and his glorification (see 8.28; 12.32,34). On *Moses* and the *serpent,* see Num.21.4–9; Wis.16.5–6. **16:** God's giving *his only Son* in love may allude to Abraham's near sacrifice of Isaac (Gen.22.1–12); see Rom.8.32. In Jn. *the world* may denote mankind in a good sense (as here) but also in a pejorative sense as in 12.31. **17:** Although Jesus' purpose is to save rather than to condemn, Jn. is aware of Jesus' role as *judge* (5.22; 9.39).

the world that God sent his Son into the world, but that through him the world might be saved.

18 'The man who puts his faith in him does not come under judgement; but the unbeliever has already been judged in that he has not given his allegiance 19 to God's only Son. Here lies the test: the light has come into the world, but men preferred darkness to light because 20 their deeds were evil. Bad men all hate the light and avoid it, for fear their 21 practices should be shown up. The honest man comes to the light so that it may be clearly seen that God is in all he does.'

22 AFTER THIS, JESUS WENT INTO JUDAEA with his disciples, stayed there with 23 them, and baptized. John too was baptizing at Aenon, near to Salim, because water was plentiful in that region; and people were constantly 24 coming for baptism. This was before John's imprisonment.

25 Some of John's disciples had fallen into a dispute with Jews about purifica-26 tion; so they came to him and said, 'Rabbi, there was a man with you on the other side of the Jordan, to whom you bore your witness. Here he is, baptizing, and crowds are flocking to 27 him.' John's answer was: 'A man can 28 have only what God gives him. You yourselves can testify that I said, "I am not the Messiah; I have been sent as his 29 forerunner." It is the bridegroom to whom the bride belongs. The bride-groom's friend, who stands by and listens to him, is overjoyed at hearing the bridegroom's voice. This joy, this 30 perfect joy, is now mine. As he grows greater, I must grow less.'

31 He who comes from above is above all others; he who is from the earth belongs to the earth and uses earthly speech. He who comes from heaven[j]

bears witness to what he has seen and 32 heard, yet no one accepts his witness. To accept his witness is to attest that 33 God speaks the truth; for he whom 34 God sent utters the words of God, so measureless is God's gift of the Spirit. The Father loves the Son and has en-35 trusted him with all authority. He who 36 puts his faith in the Son has hold of eternal life, but he who disobeys the Son shall not see that life; God's wrath rests upon him.

A REPORT NOW REACHED THE PHARISEES: 4 'Jesus is winning and baptizing more disciples than John'; although, in fact, 2 it was only the disciples who were baptizing, and not Jesus himself. When Jesus learned this, he left Judaea and 3 set out once more for Galilee. He had 4 to pass through Samaria, and on his 5 way came to a Samaritan town called Sychar, near the plot of ground which Jacob gave to his son Joseph and the 6 spring called Jacob's well. It was about noon, and Jesus, tired after his journey, sat down by the well.

The disciples had gone away to the 8 town to buy food. Meanwhile a 7 Samaritan woman came to draw water. Jesus said to her, 'Give me a drink.' The Samaritan woman said, 'What! 9 You, a Jew, ask a drink of me, a Samaritan woman?' (Jews and Samari-tans, it should be noted, do not use vessels in common.[k]) Jesus answered 10 her, 'If only you knew what God gives, and who it is that is asking you for a drink, you would have asked him and he would have given you living water.' 'Sir,' the woman said, 'you have no 11 bucket and this well is deep. How can you give me "living water"? Are you a 12 greater man than Jacob our ancestor, who gave us the well, and drank from it

j *Some witnesses insert* is above all and . . .
k *Or* Jews, it should be noted, are not on familiar terms with Samaritans; *some witnesses omit these words.*

3.22–36: Jesus and John. 22: The statement that Jesus *baptized* is qualified in 4.2. **23:** *Aenon* (Aram. "springs"): like *Salim*, probably a Samaritan village. **24:** Mk.1.14, however, states that Jesus began his ministry after John's arrest. **29:** *The bridegroom* imagery recalls the OT theme of God's marriage with Israel (Hos. chs. 1–2). For Jesus' self-designation as the bride-groom see Mk.2.19–20; compare Mt.25.1–13. The imagery appears also in Rev.19.7; 21.2.

4.1–42: Jesus and the Samaritans. 5: *Sychar* is probably Shechem, connected with *Jacob* in Gen.33.18–19. **9:** After the fall of the kingdom of Israel (721 B.C.) the population was mixed, though largely Gentile. The descendants are the *Samaritans*. Rebuffed by the Jews returning from the Babylonian Exile (Neh.3.20), the Samaritans built their own temple on Mount Gerizim (v. 20). **10:** *Living water*, from a spring (contrasted in Jer.2.13 with cistern water), here sym-

himself, he and his sons, and his cattle
13 too?' Jesus said, 'Everyone who drinks
14 this water will be thirsty again, but
whoever drinks the water that I shall
give him will never suffer thirst any
more. The water that I shall give him
will be an inner spring always welling
15 up for eternal life.' 'Sir,' said the
woman, 'give me that water, and then I
shall not be thirsty, nor have to come
all this way to draw.'

16   Jesus replied, 'Go home, call your
17 husband and come back.' She answered, 'I have no husband.' 'You are
right', said Jesus, 'in saying that you
18 have no husband, for, although you
have had five husbands, the man with
whom you are now living is not your
husband; you told me the truth there.'
19 'Sir,' she replied, 'I can see that you are
20 a prophet. Our fathers worshipped on
this mountain, but you Jews say that the
temple where God should be wor-
21 shipped is in Jerusalem.' 'Believe me,'
said Jesus, 'the time is coming when
you will worship the Father neither on
22 this mountain, nor in Jerusalem. You
Samaritans worship without knowing
what you worship, while we worship
what we know. It is from the Jews that
23 salvation comes. But the time approaches, indeed it is already here,
when those who are real worshippers
will worship the Father in spirit and in
truth. Such are the worshippers whom
24 the Father wants. God is spirit, and
those who worship him must worship
25 in spirit and in truth.' The woman
answered, 'I know that Messiah' (that
is Christ) 'is coming. When he comes
26 he will tell us everything.' Jesus said,
'I am he, I who am speaking to you
now.'

27   At that moment his disciples returned, and were astonished to find him
talking with a woman; but none of
them said, 'What do you want?' or,
28 'Why are you talking with her?' The
woman put down her water-jar and
went away to the town, where she said
29 to the people, 'Come and see a man

who has told me everything I ever did.
Could this be the Messiah?' They came 30
out of the town and made their way
towards him.

Meanwhile the disciples were urging 31
him, 'Rabbi, have something to eat.'
But he said, 'I have food to eat of which 32
you know nothing.' At this the disciples 33
said to one another, 'Can someone
have brought him food?' But Jesus 34
said, 'It is meat and drink for me to do
the will of him who sent me until I have
finished his work.

'Do you not say, "Four months more 35
and then comes harvest"? But look, I
tell you, look round on the fields; they
are already white, ripe for harvest. The 36
reaper is drawing his pay and gathering
a crop for eternal life, so that sower and
reaper may rejoice together. That is 37
how the saying comes true: "One sows,
and another reaps." I sent you to reap 38
a crop for which you have not toiled.
Others toiled and you have come in for
the harvest of their toil.'

Many Samaritans of that town came 39
to believe in him because of the
woman's testimony: 'He told me
everything I ever did.' So when these 40
Samaritans had come to him they
pressed him to stay with them; and he
stayed there two days. Many more 41
became believers because of what they
heard from his own lips. They told the 42
woman, 'It is no longer because of
what you said that we believe, for we
have heard him ourselves; and we know
that this is in truth the Saviour of the
world.'

WHEN THE TWO DAYS WERE OVER HE 43
set out for Galilee; for Jesus himself 44
declared that a prophet is without
honour in his own country. On his 45
arrival in Galilee the Galileans gave
him a welcome, because they had seen
all that he did at the festival in Jerusalem; they had been at the festival
themselves.

Once again he visited Cana-in- 46
Galilee, where he had turned the water

---

bolizes the Holy Spirit. **16:** *Husband:* a play on words is involved, since the same Gk. word
means both "husband" and "man." **23:** God is to be worshiped in *spirit* and *truth*, rather than
by visits to cultic holy places. **24:** That *God is spirit* does not mean for Jn. that God is remote
from history; rather, it affirms his involvement in history. **35:** Compare Mt.9.37–38.
    4.43–54: Second sign at Cana. See 2.1–11. **44:** See Mk.6.4. **45:** *In Jerusalem:* see 2.23. **46:** This

into wine. An officer in the royal service was there, whose son was lying ill at 47 Capernaum. When he heard that Jesus had come from Judaea into Galilee, he came to him and begged him to go down and cure his son, who was at the 48 point of death. Jesus said to him, 'Will none of you ever believe without 49 seeing signs and portents?' The officer pleaded with him, 'Sir, come down 50 before my boy dies.' Then Jesus said, 'Return home; your son will live.' The man believed what Jesus said and 51 started for home. When he was on his way down his servants met him with the 52 news, 'Your boy is going to live.' So he asked them what time it was when he began to recover. They said, 'Yesterday at one in the afternoon the 53 fever left him.' The father noted that this was the exact time when Jesus had said to him, 'Your son will live', and he and all his household became believers.

54 This was now the second sign which Jesus performed after coming down from Judaea into Galilee.

5 LATER ON JESUS WENT UP TO JERU- salem for one of the Jewish festivals.[l] 2 Now at the Sheep-Pool in Jerusalem there is a place with five colonnades. Its name in the language of the Jews is 3 Bethesda. In these colonnades there lay a crowd of sick people, blind, lame, 5 and paralysed.[m] Among them was a man who had been crippled for thirty- 6 eight years. When Jesus saw him lying there and was aware that he had been ill a long time, he asked him, 'Do you want 7 to recover?' 'Sir,' he replied, 'I have no one to put me in the pool when the water is disturbed, but while I am moving, someone else is in the pool 8 before me.' Jesus answered, 'Rise to

your feet, take up your bed and walk.' The man recovered instantly, took up 9 his stretcher, and began to walk.

That day was a Sabbath. So the 10 Jews said to the man who had been cured, 'It is the Sabbath. You are not allowed to carry your bed on the Sabbath.' He answered, 'The man who 11 cured me said, "Take up your bed and walk."' They asked him, 'Who is the 12 man who told you to take up your bed and walk?' But the cripple who had 13 been cured did not know; for the place was crowded and Jesus had slipped away. A little later Jesus found him in 14 the temple and said to him. 'Now that you are well again, leave your sinful ways, or you may suffer something worse.' The man went away and told 15 the Jews that it was Jesus who had cured him.

It was works of this kind done on the 16 Sabbath that stirred the Jews to per- secute Jesus. He defended himself by 17 saying, 'My Father has never yet ceased his work, and I am working too.' This made the Jews still more 18 determined to kill him, because he was not only breaking the Sabbath, but, by calling God his own Father, he claimed equality with God.

To this charge Jesus replied, 'In 19 truth, in very truth I tell you, the Son can do nothing by himself; he does only what he sees the Father doing: what the Father does, the Son does. For the Father loves the Son and shows 20 him all his works, and will show greater yet, to fill you with wonder. As 21 the Father raises the dead and gives them life, so the Son gives life to men,

l Some witnesses read for the Jewish festival.
m Some witnesses add waiting for the disturbance of the water; *some further insert* (4) for from time to time an angel came down into the pool and stirred up the water. The first to plunge in after this disturbance recovered from whatever disease had afflicted him.

officer was probably in the employ of Herod Antipas (see Lk.3.1 n.). **48:** Jn. exhibits an ambiv- alence with respect to *signs*, which provide the substance of 1.19–12.50 (the Book of Signs; see Introduction). Here, Jn. attempts to establish limits to their significance; *signs and portents* cannot produce real faith, for Jesus is no mere wonder-worker.

5.1–15: Cure of a cripple on the Sabbath. 1: *One of the Jewish festivals:* possibly Pentecost. **2:** In addition to the four *colonnades* which surrounded the pool, a fifth divided it in half. **14:** Since Jesus' admonition, *leave your sinful ways,* comes after the healing, it is not intended to connect the man's disability with sin (see 9.3). Rather, it teaches that the purpose of the healing is to lead to a new life.

5.16–30: Jesus' divine Sonship. For Jn., Jesus is the Son of God in that he exercises uniquely divine prerogatives which show he is one with the Father (10.30; 17.11,22). **17:** God continues *his work* even on the Sabbath in sustaining the world. **19–30:** That the *Son . . . does only what he sees the Father doing* (v. 19) is explained in the following verses. First (vv. 21,24–26), as the

22 as he determines. And again, the Father does not judge anyone, but has 23 given full jurisdiction to the Son, it is his will that all should pay the same honour to the Son as to the Father. To deny honour to the Son is to deny it to the Father who sent him.

24 'In very truth, anyone who gives heed to what I say and puts his trust in him who sent me has hold of eternal life, and does not come up for judgement, but has already passed from death to life. 25 In truth, in very truth I tell you, a time is coming, indeed it is already here, when the dead shall hear the voice of the Son of God, and all who hear shall 26 come to life. For as the Father has life-giving power in himself, so has the Son, by the Father's gift.

27 'As Son of Man, he has also been 28 given the right to pass judgement. Do not wonder at this, because the time is coming when all who are in the grave 29 shall hear his voice and come out: those who have done right will rise to life; those who have done wrong will 30 rise to hear their doom. I cannot act by myself; I judge as I am bidden, and my sentence is just, because my aim is not my own will, but the will of him who sent me.

31 'If I testify on my own behalf, that 32 testimony does not hold good. There is another who bears witness for me, and 33 I know that his testimony holds. Your messengers have been to John; you 34 have his testimony to the truth. Not that I rely on human testimony, but I remind you of it for your own salvation. 35 John was a lamp, burning brightly, and for a time you were ready to exult in his 36 light. But I rely on a testimony higher than John's. There is enough to testify that the Father has sent me, in the works my Father gave me to do and to finish—the very works I have in hand.

This testimony to me was given by the 37 Father who sent me, although you never heard his voice, or saw his form. But his word has found no home in 38 you, for you do not believe the one whom he sent. You study the scriptures 39 diligently, supposing that in having them you have eternal life; yet, although their testimony points to me, you refuse to come to me for that life. 40 'I do not look to men for honour. 41 But with you it is different, as I know 42 well, for you have no love for God in you. I have come accredited by my 43 Father, and you have no welcome for me; if another comes self-accredited you will welcome him. How can you 44 have faith so long as you receive honour from one another, and care nothing for the honour that comes from him who alone is God? Do not 45 imagine that I shall be your accuser at the Father's tribunal. Your accuser is Moses, the very Moses on whom you have set your hope. If you believed 46 Moses you would believe what I tell you, for it was about me that he wrote. But if you do not believe what he wrote, 47 how are you to believe what I say?'

SOME TIME LATER JESUS WITHDREW TO **6** the farther shore of the Sea of Galilee (or Tiberias), and a large crowd of 2 people followed who had seen the signs he performed in healing the sick. Then 3 Jesus went up the hill-side and sat down with his disciples. It was near the time 4 of Passover, the great Jewish festival. Raising his eyes and seeing a large 5 crowd coming towards him, Jesus said to Philip, 'Where are we to buy bread to feed these people?' This he said to 6 test him; Jesus himself knew what he meant to do. Philip replied, 'Twenty 7 pounds[n] would not buy enough bread

n *Literally* 200 denarii.

Son, he *gives life to men* (v. 21). Second (vv. 22,27–30), as *Son of Man* (see Mk.2.10 n.), he is the judge of mankind at the final resurrection (vv. 28–29).
5.31–47: Further testimonies to Jesus. See 1.19–51 and n. The preceding material seems to be regarded as Jesus' testimony to himself; now other witnesses are evoked. **32:** *Another:* God; see 8.18. **33–35:** *John:* see 1.35–39. **36–37:** Jesus' *works:* for example, 2.1–11. **39–40:** The *scriptures:* see, for example, 6.45. The passage may reflect debate with opponents over the proper interpretation of OT passages. **46:** The appeal to *Moses* refers specifically to Deut.18.15, or possibly to the Pentateuch as a whole.
6.1–15: The sign of the bread. 3: *Hill-side:* a frequent motif; see Mt.5.1 n. Jn. may wish to contrast Jesus, who takes his disciples onto the mountain with him, with Moses, who ascended alone according to Exod.19.10–24. **7:** The sum of money was the equivalent of two hundred

for every one of them to have a little.'
8 One of his disciples, Andrew, the brother of Simon Peter, said to him, 9 'There is a boy here who has five barley loaves and two fishes; but what is that among so many?' Jesus said, 'Make the 10 people sit down.' There was plenty of grass there, so the men sat down, about 11 five thousand of them. Then Jesus took the loaves, gave thanks, and distributed them to the people as they sat there. He did the same with the fishes, and they 12 had as much as they wanted. When everyone had had enough, he said to his disciples, 'Collect the pieces left over, so that nothing may be lost.' 13 This they did, and filled twelve baskets with the pieces left uneaten of the five barley loaves.

14   When the people saw the sign Jesus had performed, the word went round, 'Surely this must be the prophet that 15 was to come into the world.' Jesus, aware that they meant to come and seize him to proclaim him king, withdrew again to the hills by himself.

16   At nightfall his disciples went down 17 to the sea, got into their boat, and pushed off to cross the water to Capernaum. Darkness had already fallen, and Jesus had not yet joined 18 them. By now a strong wind was blow-19 ing and the sea grew rough. When they had rowed about three or four miles they saw Jesus walking on the sea and approaching the boat. They were 20 terrified, but he called out, 'It is I; do 21 not be afraid.' Then they were ready to take him aboard, and immediately the boat reached the land they were making for.

22 NEXT MORNING THE CROWD WAS STANDING on the opposite shore. They had seen only one boat there, and Jesus, they knew, had not embarked with his disciples, who had gone away without

him. Boats from Tiberias, however, 23 came ashore*o* near the place where the people had eaten the bread over which the Lord gave thanks.*p* When the 24 people saw that neither Jesus nor his disciples were any longer there, they themselves went aboard these boats and made for Capernaum in search of Jesus. They found him on the other 25 side. 'Rabbi,' they said, 'when did you come here?' Jesus replied, 'In very truth 26 I know that you have not come looking for me because you saw signs, but because you ate the bread and your hunger was satisfied. You must work, 27 not for this perishable food, but for the food that lasts, the food of eternal life.

'This food the Son of Man will give you, for he it is upon whom God the Father has set the seal of his authority.' 'Then what must we do', they asked 28 him, 'if we are to work as God would have us work?' Jesus replied, 'This is 29 the work that God requires: believe in the one whom he has sent.'

They said, 'What sign can you give 30 us to see, so that we may believe you? What is the work you do? Our 31 ancestors had manna to eat in the desert; as Scripture says, "He gave them bread from heaven to eat."' Jesus answered, 'I tell you this; the 32 truth is, not that Moses gave you the bread from heaven, but that my Father gives you the real bread from heaven. The bread that God gives comes down*q* 33 from heaven and brings life to the world.' They said to him, 'Sir, give us 34 this bread now and always.' Jesus said 35 to them, 'I am the bread of life. Whoever comes to me shall never be hungry, and whoever believes in me shall never be thirsty. But you, as I 36

---

o Some witnesses read Other boats from Tiberias came ashore . . .
p Some witnesses omit over which . . . thanks.
q Or is he who comes down . . .

---

days' wages. **14:** The *prophet* here, as in 1.21,25, is the one like Moses (see Deut.18.15). **15:** The avoidance of being proclaimed *king* probably is intended to clarify for the reader that Jesus was not a political figure; see 18.33–37.

   6.16–21. Jesus walks on the Sea of Galilee. 18: The incident of the storm is described tersely compared with Mk.6.47–51. **20:** The scene focuses on Jesus' words, "*It is I*" (lit. 'I am'); *do not be afraid*" (see 8.24 n.).

   6.22–71: The bread of life. 26–28: The crowd fails to see beyond the material "sign" of the miraculous feeding to the *food of eternal life* which *the Son of Man will give*. **31:** On *manna*, see Exod.16.14. The quotation is from Ps.78.24. **32–33:** Jesus, sent by the Father (3.31), is *the real bread from heaven*. **32:** *Moses:* compare v.14 n. **35:** *Never . . . be thirsty:* see 4.14–15.

said, do not believe although you have
37 seen.[r] All that the Father gives me will
come to me, and the man who comes
38 to me I will never turn away. I have
come down from heaven, not to do my
own will, but the will of him who sent
39 me. It is his will that I should not lose
even one of all that he has given me,
but raise them all up on the last day.
40 For it is my Father's will that everyone
who looks upon the Son and puts his
faith in him shall possess eternal life;
and I will raise him up on the last
day.'
41 At this the Jews began to murmur
disapprovingly because he said, 'I am
the bread which came down from
42 heaven.' They said, 'Surely this is Jesus
son of Joseph; we know his father and
mother. How can he now say, "I have
43 come down from heaven"?' Jesus
answered, 'Stop murmuring among
44 yourselves. No man can come to me
unless he is drawn by the Father who
sent me; and I will raise him up on the
45 last day. It is written in the prophets:
"And they shall all be taught by God."
Everyone who has listened to the
Father and learned from him comes
to me.
46 'I do not mean that anyone has seen
the Father. He who has come from
God has seen the Father, and he alone.
47 In truth, in very truth I tell you, the
48 believer possesses eternal life. I am the
49 bread of life. Your forefathers ate the
manna in the desert and they are dead.
50 I am speaking of the bread that comes
down from heaven, which a man may
51 eat, and never die. I am that living
bread which has come down from
heaven; if anyone eats this bread he
shall live for ever. Moreover, the bread
which I will give is my own flesh; I give
it for the life of the world.'
52 This led to a fierce dispute among
the Jews. 'How can this man give us his
53 flesh to eat?' they said. Jesus replied,
'In truth, in very truth I tell you, unless
you eat the flesh of the Son of Man and
drink his blood you can have no life in
you. Whoever eats my flesh and drinks
54 my blood possesses eternal life, and I
55 will raise him up on the last day. My
flesh is real food; my blood is real
56 drink. Whoever eats my flesh and
drinks my blood dwells continually in
57 me and I dwell in him. As the living
Father sent me, and I live because of
the Father, so he who eats me shall live
58 because of me. This is the bread which
came down from heaven; and it is not
like the bread which our fathers ate:
they are dead, but whoever eats this
bread shall live for ever.'

59 THIS WAS SPOKEN IN SYNAGOGUE WHEN
Jesus was teaching in Capernaum.
60 Many of his disciples on hearing it
exclaimed, 'This is more than we can
stomach! Why listen to such talk?'
61 Jesus was aware that his disciples were
murmuring about it and asked them,
62 'Does this shock you? What if you see
the Son of Man ascending to the place
63 where he was before? The spirit alone
gives life; the flesh is of no avail; the
words which I have spoken to you are
64 both spirit and life. And yet there are
some of you who have no faith.' For
Jesus knew all along who were without
faith and who was to betray him. So
65 he said, 'This is why I told you that no
one can come to me unless it has been
granted to him by the Father.'
66 From that time on, many of his
disciples withdrew and no longer went
67 about with him. So Jesus asked the
Twelve, 'Do you also want to leave
68 me?' Simon Peter answered him, 'Lord,
to whom shall we go? Your words are
69 words of eternal life. We have faith,
and we know that you are the Holy
70 One of God.' Jesus answered, 'Have I
not chosen you, all twelve? Yet one of
71 you is a devil.' He meant Judas, son of
Simon Iscariot. He it was who would
betray him, and he was one of the
Twelve.

r Some witnesses add me.

37b: See 17.2,7,24. **45:** See Isa.54.13; Jer.31.33–34 for the experiential, inner knowledge of
God. **51–54:** Notice the allusion to Jesus' words over the bread and wine at the Last Supper
(see 1 Cor.11.24). **63:** Until Jesus' glorification (v. 62; 7.39), his words are not known as *spirit
and life* (see 2.22; 12.16). **68–69:** Peter's profession of faith; see Mt.16.13–16 where no mention
is made of disciples who have withdrawn from Jesus. **70–71:** In Mt.16.23, Jesus addresses
Peter as "Satan"; here, Judas is identified as *a devil*.

→ Jesus does not correct them as if they misunderstood.
(Verses 52, 60, 66) He meant it LITERALLY.

The great controversy

7 AFTERWARDS JESUS WENT ABOUT IN Galilee. He wished to avoid Judaea because the Jews were looking for a 2 chance to kill him. As the Jewish Feast 3 of Tabernacles was close at hand, his brothers said to him, 'You should leave this district and go into Judaea, so that your disciples there may see the great 4 things you are doing. Surely no one can hope to be in the public eye if he works in seclusion. If you really are doing such things as these, show yourself to 5 the world.' For even his brothers had 6 no faith in him. Jesus said to them, 'The right time for me has not yet come, but any time is right for you. 7 The world cannot hate you; but it hates me for exposing the wickedness of its 8 ways. Go to the festival yourselves. I am not[s] going up to this festival because the right time for me has not yet come.' 9 With this answer he stayed behind in Galilee.

10   Later, when his brothers had gone to the festival, he went up himself, not 11 publicly, but almost in secret. The Jews were looking for him at the festival and 12 asking, 'Where is he?', and there was much whispering about him in the crowds. 'He is a good man', said some. 'No,' said others, 'he is leading the 13 people astray.' However, no one talked about him openly, for fear of the Jews.

14 WHEN THE FESTIVAL WAS ALREADY HALF over, Jesus went up to the temple and 15 began to teach. The Jews were astonished: 'How is it', they said, 'that this untrained man has such learning?' 16 Jesus replied, 'The teaching that I give is not my own; it is the teaching of 17 him who sent me. Whoever has the will to do the will of God shall know whether my teaching comes from him 18 or is merely my own. Anyone whose teaching is merely his own, aims at honour for himself. But if a man aims at the honour of him who sent him he is sincere, and there is nothing false in him.

'Did not Moses give you the Law? 19 Yet you all break it. Why are you trying to kill me?' The crowd answered, 20 'You are possessed! Who wants to kill you?' Jesus replied, 'Once only have I 21 done work on the Sabbath, and you are all taken aback. But consider: Moses 22 gave you the law of circumcision (not that it originated with Moses but with the patriarchs) and you circumcise on the Sabbath. Well then, if a child is 23 circumcised on the Sabbath to avoid breaking the Law of Moses, why are you indignant with me for giving health on the Sabbath to the whole of a man's body? Do not judge superficially, but 24 be just in your judgements.'

At this some of the people of 25 Jerusalem began to say, 'Is not this the man they want to put to death? And 26 here he is, speaking openly, and they have not a word to say to him. Can it be that our rulers have actually decided that this is the Messiah? And 27 yet we know where this man comes from, but when the Messiah appears no one is to know where he comes from.' Thereupon Jesus cried aloud as 28 he taught in the temple, 'No doubt you know me; no doubt you know where I come from.[t] Yet I have not come of my own accord. I was sent by the One who truly is, and him you do not know. I know him because I come 29 from him and he it is who sent me.' At this they tried to seize him, but no 30 one laid a hand on him because his appointed hour had not yet come. Yet 31 among the people many believed in him. 'When the Messiah comes,' they

s *Some witnesses read* not yet.
t *Or* Do you know me? And do you know where I come from?

7.1–36: The Feast of Tabernacles. 2: *Tabernacles* was a thanksgiving festival, associated with Israel's wandering in the desert, held for seven days in September–October (Lev.23.39–43; Deut.16.13–15). In Jn. chs. 7–8, it provides the background in terms of which Jesus' self-revelation is interpreted (see v. 37 n.; 8.12 n.). **6:** *The right time:* the moment determined by God's will. Jn. consistently conceives of a preordained schedule of events in the career of Jesus. **8:** *I am not going up* involves a play on words in that it can also refer to Jesus' ascension (20.17). **15:** Jesus apparently lacks formal schooling in Scripture and, therefore, is regarded as *untrained.* **19:** The polemic against the *Law* is heightened as the Gospel proceeds; see 8.17 n.; 10.34. **21:** See 5.1–9. **26:** *Our rulers:* that is, leaders. **27:** The hidden character of the Messiah was a motif, too, in ancient Jewish Enoch literature; it is possibly alluded to in Mk.8.28; Mt.24.23–27,

said, 'is it likely that he will perform more signs than this man?'

32 The Pharisees overheard these mutterings of the people about him, so the chief priests and the Pharisees sent temple police to arrest him. Then Jesus
33 said, 'For a little longer I shall be with you; then I am going away to him who
34 sent me. You will look for me, but you will not find me. Where I am, you
35 cannot come.' So the Jews said to one another, 'Where does he intend to go, that we should not be able to find him? Will he go to the Dispersion among the Greeks, and teach the Greeks?
36 What did he mean by saying, "You will look for me, but you will not find me. Where I am, you cannot come"?'*u*

37 ON THE LAST AND GREATEST DAY OF THE festival Jesus stood and cried aloud, 'If anyone is thirsty let him come to
38 me; whoever believes in me, let him drink.' As Scripture says, 'Streams of living water shall flow out from within
39 him.'*v* He was speaking of the Spirit which believers in him would receive later; for the Spirit had not yet been given, because Jesus had not yet been glorified.
40 On hearing this some of the people said, 'This must certainly be the
41 expected prophet.' Others said, 'This is the Messiah.' Others again, 'Surely the Messiah is not to come from
42 Galilee? Does not Scripture say that the Messiah is to be of the family of David, from David's village of Bethlehem?'
43 Thus he caused a split among the
44 people. Some were for seizing him, but no one laid hands on him.
45 The temple police came back to the chief priests and Pharisees, who asked, 'Why have you not brought him?'
46 'No man', they answered, 'ever spoke

as this man speaks.' The Pharisees 47 retorted, 'Have you too been misled?
48 Is there a single one of our rulers who has believed in him, or of the Pharisees?
49 As for this rabble, which cares nothing for the Law, a curse is on them.' Then
50 one of their number, Nicodemus (the man who had once visited Jesus), intervened. 'Does our law', he asked 51 them, 'permit us to pass judgement on a man unless we have first given him a hearing and learned the facts?' 'Are 52 you a Galilean too?' they retorted. 'Study the scriptures and you will find that prophets do not come from Galilee.'*w*

8 12 ONCE AGAIN JESUS ADDRESSED THE people: 'I am the light of the world. No follower of mine shall wander in the dark; he shall have the light of life.'
13 The Pharisees said to him, 'You are witness in your own cause; your testimony is not valid.' Jesus replied, 14 'My testimony is valid, even though I do bear witness about myself; because I know where I come from, and where I am going. You do not know either where I come from or where I am going. You judge by worldly stan- 15 dards. I pass judgement on no man, but 16 if I do judge, my judgement is valid because it is not I alone who judge, but I and he who sent me. In your own law 17 it is written that the testimony of two witnesses is valid. Here am I, a witness 18 in my own cause, and my other witness is the Father who sent me.' They 19 asked, 'Where is your father?' Jesus replied, 'You know neither me nor my

u Some witnesses here insert the passage printed on p. 138.
v Or 'If any man is thirsty let him come to me and drink.
He who believes in me, as Scripture says, streams of living water shall flow out from within him.'
w Some witnesses here insert the passage 7. 53–8. 11, which is printed on p. 138.

as well. **33–36**: The theme of *going away*, with the significant overtone of Jesus' ascension, recurs in 8.21; 13.33.
7.37–52: Jesus, the source of living water. 37: At Tabernacles (see 7.2 n.), water was carried in a gold pitcher from the spring of Siloam and was poured out as a petition for rain. **38:** *Scripture:* see Isa.12.3; Pss.78.15–16; 105.41. The text presents Jesus, not the believer (see Tfn. *v*), as the source of *living water*, a symbol of the Spirit. **39:** See Jn.14.15–16. The giving of the *Spirit* is the result of Jesus' death and glorification. **42:** 2 Sam.7.12–14; Mic.5.2. That Jesus was descended from King David was a significant motif in early Christology (see Mt.1.1 n.; Rom.1.3; 2 Tim.2.8). **52:** See Tfn. *w*.
8.12–30: Jesus, the light of the world. 12: At Tabernacles (see 7.2 n.) the Temple court was brightly illuminated; Jesus is described as the *light* (see 1.4 n.,9; 3.19; 9.5; 12.46) who brings *life* to men (1.4). **14:** See 5.31. **17:** By referring to the *law* as *your own*, Jn. has Jesus dissociate himself from the Mosaic institutions (see 7.19) or from Judaism (see 1.19 n.). **19:** See 14.7; 16.3.

Father; if you knew me you would know my Father as well.'

20 These words were spoken by Jesus in the treasury as he taught in the temple. Yet no one arrested him, because his hour had not yet come.

21 Again he said to them, 'I am going away. You will look for me, but you will die in your sin; where I am going

22 you cannot come.' The Jews then said, 'Perhaps he will kill himself: is that what he means when he says, "Where

23 I am going you cannot come"?' So Jesus continued, 'You belong to this world below, I to the world above. Your home is in this world, mine is not.

24 That is why I told you that you would die in your sins. If you do not believe that I am what I am, you will die in

25 your sins.' They asked him, 'Who are you?' Jesus answered, 'Why should I

26 speak to you at all?*x* I have much to say about you—and in judgement. But he who sent me speaks the truth, and what I heard from him I report to the world.'

27 They did not understand that he was

28 speaking to them about the Father. So Jesus said to them, 'When you have lifted up the Son of Man you will know that I am what I am. I do nothing on my own authority, but in all that I say,

29 I have been taught by my Father. He who sent me is present with me, and has not left me alone; for I always do

30 what is acceptable to him.' As he said this, many put their faith in him.

31 Turning to the Jews who had believed him, Jesus said, 'If you dwell within the revelation I have brought,

32 you are indeed my disciples; you shall know the truth, and the truth will set

33 you free.' They replied, 'We are Abraham's descendants; we have never been in slavery to any man. What do you mean by saying, "You will become

34 free men"?' 'In very truth I tell you', said Jesus, 'that everyone who commits

35 sin is a slave. The slave has no permanent standing in the household, but

36 the son belongs to it for ever. If then the Son sets you free, you will indeed be free.

37 'I know that you are descended from Abraham, but you are bent on killing me because my teaching makes no

38 headway with you. I am revealing in words what I saw in my Father's presence; and you are revealing in action what you learned from your

39 father.' They retorted, 'Abraham is our father.' 'If you were Abraham's chil-

40 dren', Jesus replied, 'you would do as Abraham did.*y* As it is, you are bent on killing me, a man who told you the truth, as I heard it from God. That is

41 not how Abraham acted. You are doing your own father's work.'

They said, 'We are not base-born; God is our father, and God alone.'

42 Jesus said, 'If God were your father, you would love me, for God is the source of my being, and from him I come. I have not come of my own

43 accord; he sent me. Why do you not understand my language? It is because my revelation is beyond your grasp.

44 'Your father is the devil and you choose to carry out your father's desires. He was a murderer from the beginning, and is not rooted in the truth; there is no truth in him. When he tells a lie he is speaking his own language, for he is a liar and the

45 father of lies. But I speak the truth and therefore you do not believe me.

46 Which of you can prove me in the wrong?*z* If what I say is true, why do

47 you not believe me? He who has God for his father listens to the words of God. You are not God's children; that is why you do not listen.'

48 The Jews answered, 'Are we not right

x Or What I have told you all along.
y Some witnesses read 'If you are Abraham's children', Jesus replied, 'do as Abraham did.'
z Or Which of you convicts me of sin?

20: *In the treasury:* see Lk.21.1 n. 21: See 7.33–36 and n. *Your sin:* the refusal to believe in Jesus as the Son of God (see also v. 24). 24: *I am what I am* (lit. "I am"): perhaps this is an echo of Exod.3.14 used to indicate Jesus' divine nature (see vv. 28,58; 13.19). 25: The meaning of Jesus' reply is not sufficiently clear for any translation to be regarded as secure (see Tfn. *x*). 28: *Lifted up* is another term with extended meaning. Jesus is lifted up on the cross, but this is also his exaltation or glorification (12.32).

8.31–59: **Further controversies.** 32: *Set you free:* from sin. The saving *truth* is not abstract but rather that found in the gospel and apprehended by faith. 35: This seems to be a paren- thetical remark by Jn., not a word of Jesus; compare Heb.3.3–6. 48: *Samaritan:* a term of abuse;

49 in saying that you are a Samaritan, and that you are possessed?' 'I am not possessed,' said Jesus; 'I am honouring
50 my Father, but you dishonour me. I do not care about my own glory; there is
51 one who does care, and he is judge. In very truth I tell you, if anyone obeys my teaching he shall never know what it is to die.'
52   The Jews said, 'Now we are certain that you are possessed. Abraham is dead; the prophets are dead; and yet you say, "If anyone obeys my teaching he shall not know what it is to die."
53 Are you greater than our father Abraham, who is dead? The prophets are dead too. What do you claim to be?'
54   Jesus replied, 'If I glorify myself, that glory of mine is worthless. It is the Father who glorifies me, he of whom
55 you say, "He is our God", though you do not know him. But I know him; if I said that I did not know him I should be a liar like you. But in truth I know him and obey his word.
56   'Your father Abraham was overjoyed to see my day; he saw it and
57 was glad.' The Jews protested, 'You are not yet fifty years old. How can
58 you have seen Abraham?'[a] Jesus said, 'In very truth I tell you, before Abraham was born, I am.'
59   They picked up stones to throw at him, but Jesus was not to be seen; and he left the temple.[b]

9 AS HE WENT ON HIS WAY JESUS SAW A
2 man blind from his birth. His disciples put the question, 'Rabbi, who sinned, this man or his parents? Why was he
3 born blind?' 'It is not that this man or his parents sinned,' Jesus answered; 'he was born blind so that God's power
4 might be displayed in curing him. While daylight lasts we[c] must carry on the work of him who sent me; night comes,
5 when no one can work. While I am in the world I am the light of the world.'
6   With these words he spat on the ground and made a paste with the spittle, he spread it on the man's eyes,
7 and said to him, 'Go and wash in the pool of Siloam.' (The name means 'sent'.) The man went away and washed, and when he returned he could see.
8   His neighbours and those who were accustomed to see him begging said, 'Is not this the man who used to sit and
9 beg?' Others said, 'Yes, this is the man.' Others again said, 'No, but it is someone like him.' The man himself said,
10 'I am the man.' They asked him, 'How
11 were your eyes opened?' He replied, 'The man called Jesus made a paste and smeared my eyes with it, and told me to go to Siloam and wash. I went and washed, and gained my sight.' 'Where
12 is he?' they asked. He answered, 'I do not know.'

13 THE MAN WHO HAD BEEN BLIND WAS
14 brought before the Pharisees. As it was a Sabbath day when Jesus made the
15 paste and opened his eyes, the Pharisees now asked him by what means he had gained his sight. The man told them, 'He spread a paste on my eyes; then I
16 washed, and now I can see.' Some of the Pharisees said, 'This fellow is no man of God: he does not keep the Sabbath.' Others said, 'How could such signs come from a sinful man?' So they
17 took different sides. Then they continued to question him: 'What have you to say about him? It was your eyes he opened.' He answered, 'He is a prophet.'
18   The Jews would not believe that the man had been blind and had gained his
19 sight, until they had summoned his parents and questioned them: 'Is this man your son? Do you say that he was born blind? How is it that he can see
20 now?' The parents replied, 'We know that he is our son and that he was born

a *Some witnesses read* How can Abraham have seen you?
b *Or the division may be made after the words* was not to be seen; *the paragraph following would then begin* Then Jesus left the temple, and as he went ...
c *Some witnesses read* I.

see 4.9 n. **56:** *He saw it:* similarly 12.41 with respect to Isaiah. Since the Christ was preexistent, he already existed in Abraham's time and Isaiah's. Later Jewish tradition (based on Gen. 15.13–17) portrays Abraham as having had the entire future history of his descendants revealed to him. **58:** *I am:* see 8.24 n. The preexistent Christ preceded Abraham.
   9.1–41: Cure of a blind man on the Sabbath. This "sign" reveals Jesus as the light of men, who not only restores physical sight, but confers spiritual sight through faith and baptism. **2–3:** Compare Lk.13.1–5. **6:** A ritual "anointing." **7:** *Siloam:* Heb. *shiloah*, lit. "sent," but denoting "conduit." Jn. wishes to associate Jesus and the pool, both *sent* by God; Jn. sees

21 blind. But how it is that he can now see, or who opened his eyes, we do not know. Ask him; he is of age; he will 22 speak for himself.' His parents gave this answer because they were afraid of the Jews; for the Jewish authorities had already agreed that anyone who acknowledged Jesus as Messiah should 23 be banned from the synagogue. That is why the parents said, 'He is of age; ask him.'

24 So for the second time they summoned the man who had been blind, and said, 'Speak the truth before God. We know that this fellow is a sinner.' 25 'Whether or not he is a sinner, I do not know', the man replied. 'All I know is this: once I was blind, now I can see.' 26 'What did he do to you?' they asked. 27 'How did he open your eyes?' 'I have told you already,' he retorted, 'but you took no notice. Why do you want to hear it again? Do you also want to 28 become his disciples?' Then they became abusive. 'You are that man's disciple,' they said, 'but we are disciples 29 of Moses. We know that God spoke to Moses, but as for this fellow, we do not know where he comes from.' 30 The man replied, 'What an extraordinary thing! Here is a man who has opened my eyes, yet you do not know 31 where he comes from! It is common knowledge that God does not listen to sinners; he listens to anyone who is 32 devout and obeys his will. To open the eyes of a man born blind—it is unheard 33 of since time began. If that man had not come from God he could have done 34 nothing.' 'Who are you to give us lessons,' they retorted, 'born and bred in sin as you are?' Then they expelled him from the synagogue.

35 Jesus heard that they had expelled him. When he found him he asked, 'Have you faith in the Son of Man*d*?' 36 The man answered, 'Tell me who he is, sir, that I should put my faith in him.'

37 'You have seen him,' said Jesus; 'indeed, it is he who is speaking to you.' 38 'Lord, I believe', he said, and bowed before him.

39 Jesus said, 'It is for judgement that I have come into this world—to give sight to the sightless and to make blind those who see.' Some Pharisees in his 40 company asked, 'Do you mean that we are blind?' 'If you were blind,' said 41 Jesus, 'you would not be guilty, but because you say "We see", your guilt remains.

'IN TRUTH I TELL YOU, IN VERY TRUTH, **10** the man who does not enter the sheepfold by the door, but climbs in some other way, is nothing but a thief or a robber. The man who enters by the 2 door is the shepherd in charge of the sheep. The door-keeper admits him, 3 and the sheep hear his voice; he calls his own sheep by name, and leads them out. When he has brought them all out, 4 he goes ahead and the sheep follow, because they know his voice. They will 5 not follow a stranger; they will run away from him, because they do not recognize the voice of strangers.'

This was a parable that Jesus told 6 them, but they did not understand what he meant by it.

So Jesus spoke again: 'In truth, in 7 very truth I tell you, I am the door of the sheepfold. The sheep paid no heed 8 to any who came before me, for these were all thieves and robbers. I am the 9 door; anyone who comes into the fold through me shall be safe. He shall go in and out and shall find pasturage.

'The thief comes only to steal, to 10 kill, to destroy; I have come that men may have life, and may have it in all its fullness. I am the good shepherd; the 11 good shepherd lays down his life for the sheep. The hireling, when he sees the 12 wolf coming, abandons the sheep and

d Some witnesses read Son of God.

baptismal symbolism in the incident. **22:** *Banned from the synagogue:* the practice of expelling Jewish Christians apparently arose near the end of the first century. See also v. 34. **29:** The issue of *where he* (Jesus) *comes from* is raised in different, "earthly" ways by Jesus' opponents (see also 7.27,41–42); Jn. intends the question to elicit the response: "From God" (v. 33; 8.42). **35–38:** The dialogue is often viewed as reflecting the late first-century baptismal interrogation of the neophyte.

10.1–21: Jesus, the Good Shepherd. 3: God is spoken of often as the shepherd; see Isa.40.11; Jer.23.3; Ps.23.1. **11:** The ancient ideal of a *good shepherd* (as in Ezek.34.23) is regarded as

runs away, because he is no shepherd and the sheep are not his. Then the wolf harries the flock and scatters the 13 sheep. The man runs away because he is a hireling and cares nothing for the sheep.

14 'I am the good shepherd; I know my own sheep and my sheep know me— 15 as the Father knows me and I know the Father—and I lay down my life for the 16 sheep. But there are other sheep of mine, not belonging to this fold, whom I must bring in; and they too will listen to my voice. There will then be one 17 flock, one shepherd. The Father loves me because I lay down my life, to re- 18 ceive it back again. No one has robbed me of it; I am laying it down of my own free will. I have the right to lay it down, and I have the right to receive it back again; this charge I have received from my Father.'

19 These words once again caused a 20 split among the Jews. Many of them said, 'He is possessed, he is raving. Why 21 listen to him?' Others said, 'No one possessed by an evil spirit could speak like this. Could an evil spirit open blind men's eyes?'

22 IT WAS WINTER, AND THE FESTIVAL OF the Dedication was being held in 23 Jerusalem. Jesus was walking in the temple precincts, in Solomon's Portico. 24 The Jews gathered round him and asked: 'How long must you keep us in suspense? If you are the Messiah say so 25 plainly.' 'I have told you,' said Jesus, 'but you do not believe. My deeds done in my Father's name are my credentials, 26 but because you are not sheep of my 27 flock you do not believe. My own sheep listen to my voice; I know them 28 and they follow me. I give them eternal life and they shall never perish; no one 29 shall snatch them from my care. My Father who has given them to me is

greater than all, and no one can snatch them out of the Father's care. My 30 Father and I are one.'

Once again the Jews picked up stones 31 to stone him. At this Jesus said to 32 them, 'I have set before you many good deeds, done by my Father's power; for which of these would you stone me?' The Jews replied, 'We are 33 not going to stone you for any good deed, but for your blasphemy. You, a mere man, claim to be a god.'f Jesus 34 answered, 'Is it not written in your own Law, "I said: You are gods"? Those 35 are called gods to whom the word of God was delivered—and Scripture cannot be set aside. Then why do you 36 charge me with blasphemy because I, consecrated and sent into the world by the Father, said, "I am God's son"? 'If I am not acting as my Father 37 would, do not believe me. But if I am, 38 accept the evidence of my deeds, even if you do not believe me, so that you may recognize and know that the Father is in me, and I in the Father.'

This provoked them to one more 39 attempt to seize him. But he escaped from their clutches.

Victory over death

JESUS WITHDREW AGAIN ACROSS THE 40 Jordan, to the place where John had been baptizing earlier. There he stayed, while crowds came to him. They said, 41 'John gave us no miraculous sign, but all that he said about this man was true.' Many came to believe in him there. 42

There was a man named Lazarus 11 who had fallen ill. His home was at Bethany, the village of Mary and her

e *Some witnesses read* My Father is greater than all, and that which he has given me no one can snatch . . .; *others read* That which my Father has given me is greater than all, and no one can snatch it . . .
f *Or* claim to be God.

fulfilled in Jesus. **16:** *Other sheep:* Gentiles. **17–18:** A series of key expressions—*lay down*, *receive it back*, and *right*—reflect a major motif that the anticipated crucifixion and vindication of Jesus are not imposed by human decision, but result from Jesus' *free* decision in obedience to the Father's will. **21:** An allusion to the incident in ch. 9.

10.22–39: Further controversy. 22: *Dedication*, Hanukkah, a Jewish feast held in December, commemorated the reconsecration of the Temple (164 B.C.) after its profanation by Antiochus Epiphanes (167 B.C.). **24–38:** This exchange can call to mind the trial scene before the Sanhedrin (see Lk.22.66–71). Here, too, the issue is raised whether Jesus claims to be Messiah (vv. 24–31) or the Son of God (vv. 33–38). **34:** *You are gods:* an allusion to Ps.82.6.

10.40–11.54: The supreme sign: Lazarus' resurrection. 40: See 1.28. **11.1:** This *Bethany*

2 sister Martha. (This Mary, whose brother Lazarus had fallen ill, was the woman who anointed the Lord with ointment and wiped his feet with her 3 hair.) The sisters sent a message to him: 'Sir, you should know that your friend 4 lies ill.' When Jesus heard this he said, 'This illness will not end in death; it has come for the glory of God, to bring 5 glory to the Son of God.' And therefore, though he loved Martha and her sister 6 and Lazarus, after hearing of his illness Jesus waited for two days in the place where he was.

7 After this, he said to his disciples, 8 'Let us go back to Judaea.' 'Rabbi,' his disciples said, 'it is not long since the Jews there were wanting to stone you. 9 Are you going there again?' Jesus replied, 'Are there not twelve hours of daylight? Anyone can walk in daytime without stumbling, because he sees the 10 light of this world. But if he walks after nightfall he stumbles, because the light fails him.'

11 After saying this he added, 'Our friend Lazarus has fallen asleep, but I 12 shall go and wake him.' The disciples said, 'Master, if he has fallen asleep he 13 will recover.' Jesus, however, had been speaking of his death, but they thought 14 that he meant natural sleep. Then Jesus 15 spoke out plainly: 'Lazarus is dead. I am glad not to have been there; it will be for your good and for the good of your faith. But let us go to him.' 16 Thomas, called 'the Twin', said to his fellow-disciples, 'Let us also go, that we may die with him.'

17 ON HIS ARRIVAL JESUS FOUND THAT Lazarus had already been four days in 18 the tomb. Bethany was just under two 19 miles from Jerusalem, and many of the people had come from the city to Martha and Mary to condole with them 20 on their brother's death. As soon as she heard that Jesus was on his way,

Martha went to meet him, while Mary stayed at home.

Martha said to Jesus, 'If you had 21 been here, sir, my brother would not have died. Even now I know that what- 22 ever you ask of God, God will grant you.' Jesus said, 'Your brother will rise 23 again.' 'I know that he will rise again', 24 said Martha, 'at the resurrection on the last day.' Jesus said, 'I am the resurrec- 25 tion and I am life.*g* If a man has faith in me, even though he die, he shall come to life; and no one who is alive and has 26 faith shall ever die. Do you believe this?' 'Lord, I do,' she answered; 'I 27 now believe that you are the Messiah, the Son of God who was to come into the world.'

With these words she went to call her 28 sister Mary, and taking her aside, she said, 'The Master is here; he is asking for you.' When Mary heard this she 29 rose up quickly and went to him. Jesus 30 had not yet reached the village, but was still at the place where Martha had met him. The Jews who were in the house 31 condoling with Mary, when they saw her start up and leave the house, went after her, for they supposed that she was going to the tomb to weep there.

So Mary came to the place where 32 Jesus was. As soon as she caught sight of him she fell at his feet and said, 'O sir, if you had only been here my brother would not have died.' When 33 Jesus saw her weeping and the Jews her companions weeping, he sighed heavily and was deeply moved. 'Where have 34 you laid him?' he asked. They replied, 'Come and see, sir.' Jesus wept. The 35,36 Jews said, 'How dearly he must have loved him!' But some of them said, 37 'Could not this man, who opened the blind man's eyes, have done something to keep Lazarus from dying?'

Jesus again sighed deeply; then he 38 went over to the tomb. It was a cave,

g Some witnesses omit and I am life.

(contrast 1.28) was a town near Jerusalem (see v. 18). *Mary and her sister Martha* appear in Lk.10.38–42. On Mary's anointing of Jesus, see 12.1–8 and nn. **2:** *Lord:* a title rare in Jn. before the postresurrection narratives (see 6.23, and probably 4.1); it is frequent in Lk.–Acts, and in Paul's letters. **4:** *Son of God:* see 5.16–30 n. **9:** *The light of this world:* the sun, but with the overtone that even daylight is a sign through which Jesus reveals himself as the true light. **17:** It was popularly held that corruption of the body began the third day after death; hence, the point of *four days* is to assert that Lazarus was truly dead and his resurrection real. **25:** *I am the resurrection and I am life:* This, like other sayings in Jn. (e.g., 3.13; 5.25; 17.10 n.; perhaps

39 with a stone placed against it. Jesus said, 'Take away the stone.' Martha, the dead man's sister, said to him, 'Sir, by now there will be a stench; he has
40 been there four days.' Jesus said, 'Did I not tell you that if you have faith you
41 will see the glory of God?' So they removed the stone.

Then Jesus looked upwards and said, 'Father, I thank thee; thou hast heard
42 me. I knew already that thou always hearest me, but I spoke for the sake of the people standing round, that they might believe that thou didst send me.'
43 Then he raised his voice in a great
44 cry: 'Lazarus, come forth.' The dead man came out, his hands and feet swathed in linen bands, his face wrapped in a cloth. Jesus said, 'Loose him; let him go.'

45 NOW MANY OF THE JEWS WHO HAD come to visit Mary and had seen what
46 Jesus did, put their faith in him. But some of them went off to the Pharisees and reported what he had done.
47 Thereupon the chief priests and the Pharisees convened a meeting of the Council. 'What action are we taking?' they said. 'This man is performing
48 many signs. If we leave him alone like this the whole populace will believe in him. Then the Romans will come and sweep away our temple and our nation.'
49 But one of them, Caiaphas, who was High Priest that year, said, 'You know
50 nothing whatever; you do not use your judgement; it is more to your interest that one man should die for the people, than that the whole nation should be destroyed.' He did not say this of his
51 own accord, but as the High Priest in office that year, he was prophesying that Jesus would die for the nation—would
52 die not for the nation alone but to gather together the scattered children

of God. So from that day on they 53 plotted his death.

Accordingly Jesus no longer went 54 about publicly in Judaea, but left that region for the country bordering on the desert, and came to a town called Ephraim, where he stayed with his disciples.

THE JEWISH PASSOVER WAS NOW AT 55 hand, and many people went up from the country to Jerusalem to purify themselves before the festival. They 56 looked out for Jesus, and as they stood in the temple they asked one another, 'What do you think? Perhaps he is not coming to the festival.' Now the chief 57 priests and the Pharisees had given orders that anyone who knew where he was should give information, so that they might arrest him.

SIX DAYS BEFORE THE PASSOVER FESTIVAL 12 Jesus came to Bethany, where Lazarus lived whom he had raised from the dead. There a supper was given in his 2 honour, at which Martha served, and Lazarus sat among the guests with Jesus. Then Mary brought a pound of 3 very costly perfume, pure oil of nard, and anointed the feet of Jesus and wiped them with her hair, till the house was filled with the fragrance. At this, 4 Judas Iscariot, a disciple of his—the one who was to betray him—said, 'Why 5 was this perfume not sold for thirty pounds[h] and given to the poor?' He 6 said this, not out of any care for the poor, but because he was a thief; he used to pilfer the money put into the common purse, which was in his charge. 'Leave her alone', said Jesus. 7 'Let her keep it till the day when she prepares for my burial; for you have 8

h Literally for 300 denarii.

4.38), is best understood if the speaker is viewed as the risen Christ. **40:** This remark reflects Jesus' previous statements to the disciples (v. 4) and Martha (vv. 25–26). *Glory of God:* see Introduction. **45–48:** Jn. views the raising of Lazarus as the chief basis of the hostility which caused Jesus' death (but, on the other hand, see 10.17–18 n.). **47:** Jn. alone ascribes to the *Pharisees* a role in the ordeal of Jesus (see 18.3), probably reflecting the tension between Christianity and Pharisaic Judaism when this Gospel was written about 90 A.D. **49:** *Caiaphas* was high priest from 18 to 36 A.D. **52:** *The scattered children of God* probably denotes the Gentiles. **54:** *Ephraim:* not the well-known region, but a town which cannot now be located.
11.55–12.50: Conclusion of Jesus' public ministry. 55: This is the third *Passover* in Jesus' public life (see 2.13 n.; 6.4). **12.1:** See Mk.14.3–9 for a different account of Jesus' anointing. **3:** That Mary anointed *the feet* (rather than the head) *of Jesus* is strange; compare Lk.7.37–38,

Victory over death

the poor among you always, but you will not always have me.[i]

9 A great number of the Jews heard that he was there, and came not only to see Jesus but also Lazarus whom he had
10 raised from the dead. The chief priests then resolved to do away with Lazarus
11 as well, since on his account many Jews were going over to Jesus and putting their faith in him.

12 THE NEXT DAY THE GREAT BODY OF pilgrims who had come to the festival, hearing that Jesus was on the way to
13 Jerusalem, took palm branches and went out to meet him, shouting, 'Hosanna! Blessings on him who comes in the name of the Lord! God bless the
14 king of Israel!' Jesus found a donkey and mounted it, in accordance with the
15 text of Scripture: 'Fear no more, daughter of Zion; see, your king is coming, mounted on an ass's colt.'
16 At the time his disciples did not understand this, but after Jesus had been glorified they remembered that this had been written about him, and
17 that this had happened to him. The people who were present when he called Lazarus out of the tomb and raised him from the dead told what they had seen
18 and heard. That is why the crowd went to meet him; they had heard of this sign
19 that he had performed. The Pharisees said to one another, 'You see you are doing no good at all; why, all the world has gone after him!'

20 AMONG THOSE WHO WENT UP TO worship at the festival were some
21 Greeks. They came to Philip, who was from Bethsaida in Galilee, and said to him, 'Sir, we should like to see Jesus.'
22 So Philip went and told Andrew, and
23 the two of them went to tell Jesus. Then Jesus replied: 'The hour has come for
24 the Son of Man to be glorified. In truth,

in very truth I tell you, a grain of wheat remains a solitary grain unless it falls into the ground and dies; but if it dies,
25 it bears a rich harvest. The man who loves himself is lost, but he who hates himself in this world will be kept safe
26 for eternal life. If anyone serves me, he must follow me; where I am, my servant will be. Whoever serves me will be honoured by my Father.
27 'Now my soul is in turmoil, and what am I to say? Father, save me from this hour.[j] No, it was for this that I came
28 to this hour. Father, glorify thy name.' A voice sounded from heaven: 'I have glorified it, and I will glorify it again.'
29 The crowd standing by said it was thunder, while others said, 'An angel
30 has spoken to him.' Jesus replied, 'This voice spoke for your sake, not mine.
31 Now is the hour of judgement for this world; now shall the Prince of this
32 world be driven out. And I shall draw all men to myself, when I am lifted up
33 from the earth.' This he said to indicate the kind of death he was to die.
34 The people answered, 'Our Law teaches us that the Messiah continues for ever. What do you mean by saying that the Son of Man must be lifted up?
35 What Son of Man is this?' Jesus answered them: 'The light is among you still, but not for long. Go on your way while you have the light, so that darkness may not overtake you. He who journeys in the dark does not know
36 where he is going. While you have the light, trust to the light, so that you may become men of light.' After these words Jesus went away from them into hiding.

37 IN SPITE OF THE MANY SIGNS WHICH Jesus had performed in their presence
38 they would not believe in him, for the prophet Isaiah's utterance had to be

i *Some witnesses omit* for you have ... have me.
j *Or* ... turmoil. Shall I say, "Father, save me from this hour"?

perhaps a related tradition. **9–11:** The raising of Lazarus is linked by these verses to the messianic entry in vv. **12–19;** in Jewish tradition, the advent of the Messiah was related to the resurrection of the dead. **12–19:** Jesus' entry into the city is interpreted as messianic by citing Zech.9.9. **13:** *Hosanna:* see Mt.21.9 n. **16:** *Remembered:* see 2.17 n. **20:** *Some Greeks:* possibly Gentiles who acknowledged the God of Israel; see Acts 10.2 n. **23:** *Hour:* see 2.4 n. **27:** *My soul is in turmoil* is reminiscent of the Synoptic narrative of Jesus' suffering in Gethsemane (see Mk.14.32–42). **31–32:** *Judgement for this world:* see 1.19–51 n. **35–36:** The theme of judgment and salvation is restated in terms of *light* and *darkness* (see 1.5; 3.19–21). **37–43:** Jn. concludes the Book of Signs (see Introduction) by noting that Jesus' own people did not respond to him. **38–41:** Jesus' lack of success with fellow Jews is explained by two citations fulfilled: 'Lord, who has believed what we reported, and to whom has the Lord's power been revealed?' So it was 39 that they could not believe, for there is another saying of Isaiah's: 'He has 40 blinded their eyes and dulled their minds, lest they should see with their eyes, and perceive with their minds, and turn to me to heal them.' Isaiah said 41 this because[k] he saw his glory and spoke about him.

For all that, even among those in 42 authority a number believed in him, but would not acknowledge him on account of the Pharisees, for fear of being banned from the synagogue. For 43 they valued their reputation with men rather than the honour which comes from God.

So Jesus cried aloud: 'when a man 44 believes in me, he believes in him who sent me rather than in me; seeing me, 45 he sees him who sent me. I have come 46 into the world as light, so that no one who has faith in me should remain in darkness. But if anyone hears my 47 words and pays no regard to them, I am not his judge; I have not come to judge the world, but to save the world. There is a judge for the man who rejects 48 me and does not accept my words; the word that I spoke will be his judge on the last day. I do not speak on my own 49 authority, but the Father who sent me has himself commanded me what to say and how to speak. I know that his 50 commands are eternal life. What the Father has said to me, therefore—that is what I speak.'

Farewell discourses

13 It was before the Passover festival. Jesus knew that his hour had come and he must leave this world and go to the Father. He had always loved his own who were in the world, and now he was to show them the full extent of his love.

The devil had already put it into the 2 mind of Judas son of Simon Iscariot to betray him. During supper, Jesus, well 3 aware that the Father had entrusted everything to him, and that he had come from God and was going back to God, rose from table, laid aside his 4 garments, and taking a towel, tied it round him. Then he poured water into 5 a basin, and began to wash his disciples' feet and to wipe them with the towel.

When it was Simon Peter's turn, 6 Peter said to him, 'You, Lord, washing my feet?' Jesus replied, 'You do not 7 understand now what I am doing, but one day you will.' Peter said, 'I will 8 never let you wash my feet.' 'If I do not wash you,' Jesus replied, 'you are not in fellowship with me.' 'Then, Lord,' 9 said Simon Peter, 'not my feet only; wash my hands and head as well!'

Jesus said, 'A man who has bathed 10 needs no further washing;[l] he is altogether clean; and you are clean, though not every one of you.' He added 11 the words 'not every one of you' because he knew who was going to betray him.

After washing their feet and taking 12 his garments again, he sat down. 'Do you understand what I have done for you?' he asked. 'You call me "Master" 13 and "Lord", and rightly so, for that is what I am. Then if I, your Lord and 14 Master, have washed your feet, you also ought to wash one another's feet. I have set you an example: you are to 15 do as I have done for you. In very truth 16 I tell you, a servant is not greater than his master, nor a messenger than the one who sent him. If you know this, 17 happy are you if you act upon it. 'I am not speaking about all of you; 18 I know whom I have chosen. But there

k *Some witnesses read* when.
l *Some witnesses read* needs only to wash his feet.

from the prophet Isaiah (53.1; 6.10). Moreover, Jn. interprets Isa.6.1–13 as a preview of Christ's glorification. **44–50:** The message of the Book of Signs (see Introduction) is recapitulated in these verses.
    13.1–30: The Last Supper. 1: *His hour had come:* an important theme of the Johannine passion narrative is that Jesus *knew* in advance all that was to happen to him (see 16.28; 18.4; 19.28). **3–5:** Jesus washes his disciples' feet to symbolize the humiliation of his death, which is the sole source of forgiveness of sins and of fellowship with him (v. 8). **7:** The contrast between the disciples' limited understanding before Jesus' death and their future understanding, to take place *one day* is frequent; see 2.22; 12.16; 16.12. **11:** *Betray him:* 6.64. **18:** See Ps.41.9.

is a text of Scripture to be fulfilled: "He who eats bread with me has turned

19 against me."*m* I tell you this now, before the event, so that when it happens you

20 may believe that I am what I am. In very truth I tell you, he who receives any messenger of mine receives me; receiving me, he receives the One who sent me.'

21   After saying this, Jesus exclaimed in deep agitation of spirit, 'In truth, in very truth I tell you, one of you is going

22 to betray me.' The disciples looked at one another in bewilderment: whom

23 could he be speaking of? One of them, the disciple he loved, was reclining close

24 beside Jesus. So Simon Peter nodded to him and said, 'Ask who it is he

25 means.' That disciple, as he reclined, leaned back close to Jesus and asked,

26 'Lord, who is it?' Jesus replied, 'It is the man to whom I give this piece of bread when I have dipped it in the dish.' Then, after dipping it in the dish, he took it out and gave it to Judas son of

27 Simon Iscariot. As soon as Judas had received it Satan entered him. Jesus said to him, 'Do quickly what you have

28 to do.' No one at the table understood

29 what he meant by this. Some supposed that, as Judas was in charge of the common purse, Jesus was telling him to buy what was needed for the festival, or to make some gift to the poor. As

30 soon as Judas had received the bread he went out. It was night.

31 WHEN HE HAD GONE OUT JESUS SAID, 'Now the Son of Man is glorified, and

32 in him God is glorified. If God is glorified in him,*n* God will also glorify him in himself; and he will glorify him

33 now. My children, for a little longer I am with you; then you will look for me, and, as I told the Jews, I tell you now,

34 where I am going you cannot come. I give you a new commandment: love one another; as I have loved you, so

35 you are to love one another. If there is this love among you, then all will know that you are my disciples.'

Simon Peter said to him, 'Lord, 36 where are you going?' Jesus replied, 'Where I am going you cannot follow me now, but one day you will.' Peter 37 said, 'Lord, why cannot I follow you now? I will lay down my life for you.' Jesus answered, 'Will you indeed lay 38 down your life for me? I tell you in very truth, before the cock crows you will have denied me three times.

'Set your troubled hearts at rest. **14** Trust in God always; trust also in me. There are many dwelling-places in my 2 Father's house; if it were not so I should have told you; for I am going there on purpose to prepare a place for you.*o* And if I go and prepare a place 3 for you, I shall come again and receive you to myself, so that where I am you may be also; and my way there is 4 known to you.'*p* Thomas said, 'Lord, 5 we do not know where you are going, so how can we know the way?' Jesus 6 replied, 'I am the way; I am the truth and I am life; no one comes to the Father except by me.

'If you knew me you would know my 7 Father too.*q* From now on you do know him; you have seen him.' Philip 8 said to him, 'Lord, show us the Father and we ask no more.' Jesus answered, 9 'Have I been all this time with you, Philip, and you still do not know me? Anyone who has seen me has seen the Father. Then how can you say, "Show us the Father"? Do you not believe 10 that I am in the Father, and the Father in me? I am not myself the source of the words I speak to you: it is the Father who dwells in me doing his own work. Believe me when I say that I am 11 in the Father and the Father in me; or else accept the evidence of the deeds themselves. In truth, in very truth I tell 12 you, he who has faith in me will do what

m Literally has lifted his heel against me.
n Some witnesses omit If God . . . in him.
o Or if it were not so, should I have told you that I am going to prepare a place for you?
p Some witnesses read also. You know where I am going and you know the way.
q Some witnesses read If you know me you will know my Father too.

19: *I am:* see 8.24 n. **23:** *The disciple he loved:* see 18.15 n. **27:** The words *Satan entered him* prepare the reader to see that Jesus' confrontation in 18.2–6 is really with Satan. See also Lk.22.3.
   13.31–14.31: Jesus' farewell discourse. This final message is partly repeated later in chs. 15–16. **33:** See 7.34; 8.21. **34:** Jesus' death for his friends (15.13) makes the observance of the *new commandment* of fraternal love possible. **14.1:** The words *set your troubled hearts at rest* (repeated

I am doing; and he will do greater things still because I am going to the 13 Father. Indeed anything you ask in my name I will do, so that the Father 14 may be glorified in the Son. If you ask[r] anything in my name I will do it.

15 16 'If you love me you will obey my commands; and I will ask the Father, and he will give you another to be your Advocate, who will be with you for 17 ever—the Spirit of truth. The world cannot receive him, because the world neither sees nor knows him; but you know him, because he dwells with you 18 and is[s] in you. I will not leave you 19 bereft; I am coming back to you. In a little while the world will see me no longer, but you will see me; because I 20 live, you too will live; then you will know that I am in my Father, and you 21 in me and I in you. The man who has received my commands and obeys them—he it is who loves me; and he who loves me will be loved by my Father; and I will love him and disclose myself to him.'

22 Judas asked him—the other Judas, not Iscariot—'Lord, what can have happened, that you mean to disclose yourself to us alone and not to the 23 world?' Jesus replied, 'Anyone who loves me will heed what I say; then my Father will love him, and we will come to him and make our dwelling with 24 him; but he who does not love me does not heed what I say. And the word you hear is not mine: it is the word of the 25 Father who sent me. I have told you all 26 this while I am still here with you; but your Advocate, the Holy Spirit whom the Father will send in my name, will teach you everything, and will call to mind all that I have told you.

27 'Peace is my parting gift to you, my own peace, such as the world cannot give. Set your troubled hearts at rest, 28 and banish your fears. You heard me say, "I am going away, and coming back to you." If you loved me you would have been glad to hear that I was going to the Father; for the Father is greater than I. I have told you now, 29 beforehand, so that when it happens you may have faith.

'I shall not talk much longer with 30 you, for the Prince of this world approaches. He has no rights over me; but the world must be shown that I love 31 the Father, and do exactly as he commands; so up, let us go forward![t]

'I AM THE REAL VINE, AND MY FATHER IS 15 the gardener. Every barren branch of 2 mine he cuts away; and every fruiting branch he cleans, to make it more fruitful still. You have already been 3 cleansed by the word that I spoke to you. Dwell in me, as I in you. No 4 branch can bear fruit by itself, but only if it remains united with the vine; no more can you bear fruit, unless you remain united with me.

'I am the vine, and you the branches. 5 He who dwells in me, as I dwell in him, bears much fruit; for apart from me you can do nothing. He who does not 6 dwell in me is thrown away like a withered branch. The withered branches are heaped together, thrown on the fire, and burnt.

'If you dwell in me, and my words 7 dwell in you, ask what you will, and you shall have it. This is my Father's 8 glory, that you may bear fruit in plenty and so be my disciples.[u] As the Father 9 has loved me, so I have loved you. Dwell in my love. If you heed my 10 commands, you will dwell in my love, as I have heeded my Father's commands, and dwell in his love.

r *Some witnesses insert* me.
s *Some witnesses read* shall be.
t *Or* for the Prince of this world is coming, though he has nothing in common with me. But he is coming so that the world may recognize that I love the Father, and do exactly as he commands. Up, and let us go forward to meet him!
u *Some witnesses read* that you may bear fruit in plenty. Thus you will be my disciples.

at v. 27) state the theme of the discourse; i.e. Jesus' departure is to make possible the mutual indwelling of Father, Son, and disciples (see vv. 2,20,23). **13–14:** The phrases *in my name* and *I will do* indicate the belief that Jesus and the Father are so related (vv. 9–10) that petitionary prayer may be directed to the Son. See 15.16 n.; 16.23–26 n. **26:** *Your Advocate* is identified as *the Holy Spirit* sent in Jesus' name by the Father (compare v. 16). Compare 1 Jn.2.1 n. **28:** *The Father is greater than I:* see v. 10; 5.19 n.

15.1–17: The abiding of Christians in Jesus and in one another. 1: Jesus, *the real vine*, fulfills the prophetic images of Israel as vineyard (Isa.5.1–7) and vine (Jer.2.21; Ezek.19.10–14). **4:** The invitation to *dwell in me* implies obedience to Jesus' commands (v. 10), especially that

[Handwritten margin notes:]
To have the sun + heart attitude as
Christ's peace is stable + interior; world's is transient & unpredictable

[Handwritten note at bottom:]
Advocate = PARAKLETOS = DEFENDER, COUNSELOR, (Greek) LAWYER, INTERCESSOR

11 'I have spoken thus to you, so that my joy may be in you, and your joy complete.*v* This is my commandment: love one another, as I have loved you. 13 There is no greater love than this, that a man should lay down his life for his 14 friends. You are my friends, if you 15 do what I command you. I call you servants no longer; a servant does not know what his master is about. I have called you friends, because I have disclosed to you everything that I heard 16 from my Father. You did not choose me: I chose you. I appointed you to go on and bear fruit, fruit that shall last; so that the Father may give you all that 17 you ask in my name. This is my commandment to you: love one another.

18 'If the world hates you, it hated me 19 first, as you know well.*w* If you belonged to the world, the world would love its own; but because you do not belong to the world, because I have chosen you out of the world, for that 20 reason the world hates you. Remember what I said: "A servant is not greater than his master." As they persecuted me, they will persecute you; they will follow your teaching as little as they 21 have followed mine. It is on my account that they will treat you thus, because they do not know the One who sent me.

22 'If I had not come and spoken to them, they would not be guilty of sin; but now they have no excuse for their 23 sin: he who hates me, hates my Father. 24 If I had not worked among them and accomplished what no other man has done, they would not be guilty of sin; but now they have both seen and hated 25 both me and my Father.*x* However, this text in their Law had to come true:*y* "They hated me without reason." 26 'But when your Advocate has come,

whom I will send you from the Father—the Spirit of truth that issues from the Father—he will bear witness to me. And you also are my witnesses, 27 because you have been with me from the first.

'I have told you all this to guard you 16 against the breakdown of your faith. They will ban you from the synagogue; 2 indeed, the time is coming when anyone who kills you will suppose that he is performing a religious duty. They will 3 do these things because they do not know either the Father or me. I have 4 told you all this so that when the time comes for it to happen you may remember my warning. I did not tell you this at first, because then I was with you; but now I am going away to him 5 who sent me. None of you asks me "Where are you going?" Yet you are 6 plunged into grief because of what I have told you. Nevertheless I tell you 7 the truth: it is for your good that I am leaving you. If I do not go, your Advocate will not come, whereas if I go, I will send him to you. When he 8 comes, he will confute the world, and show where wrong and right and judgement lie. He will convict them of 9 wrong, by their refusal to believe in me; he will convince them that right is on 10 my side, by showing that I go to the Father when I pass from your sight; and he will convince them of divine 11 judgement, by showing that the Prince of this world stands condemned.

'There is still much that I could say 12 to you, but the burden would be too great for you now. However, when he 13

v Or so that I may have joy in you and your joy may be complete.
w Or bear in mind that it hated me first.
x Or but now they have indeed seen my work and yet hated both me and my Father.
y Or let this text in their Law come true.

parakletos/paraclete

of fraternal love (v. 17). **14:** The title *friend* denotes great intimacy; it was bestowed on Abraham (Isa.41.8; Jas.2.23). **16:** In this passage (see 16.23–26 n.), the efficacy of prayer *in my name* is presented as a product of the close union with Jesus (see v. 4 n.) to which the disciples have been called.

15.18–27: The Christian is separated from the world. 18: *The world:* a term often ambivalent, here indicates Jesus' enemies, as in 12.31; 14.17; 16.33; 17.9; see 3.16 n. **20:** The *servant, master* saying occurs several times with varying interpretations; see 13.16 (compare 12.26); Mt.10.24; Lk.6.40. **25:** See Pss.35.19; 69.4.

16.1–15: Jesus' departure; the sending of the Advocate. 4: *Remember:* 2.17 n. **7–11:** As the one who represents the risen Christ, the *Advocate* is here assigned a three-fold task: to pass judgment on the sin of the world, to testify to Jesus' presence with the Father, and to attest to God's condemnation of the powers of evil. See also v. 13; 14.26.

comes who is the Spirit of truth, he will guide you into all the truth; for he will not speak on his own authority, but will tell only what he hears; and he will make known to you the things that are
14 coming. He will glorify me, for everything that he makes known to you he
15 will draw from what is mine. All that the Father has is mine, and that is why I said, "Everything that he makes known to you he will draw from what is mine."

16 'A LITTLE WHILE, AND YOU SEE ME NO more; again a little while, and you will
17 see me.' Some of his disciples said to one another, 'What does he mean by this: "A little while, and you will not see me, and again a little while, and you will see me", and by this: "Because I
18 am going to my Father"?' So they asked, 'What is this "little while" that he speaks of? We do not know what he means.'
19 Jesus knew that they were wanting to question him, and said, 'Are you discussing what I said: "A little while, and you will not see me, and again a
20 little while, and you will see me"? In very truth I tell you, you will weep and mourn, but the world will be glad. But though you will be plunged in grief,
21 your grief will be turned to joy. A woman in labour is in pain because her time has come; but when the child is born she forgets the anguish in her joy that a man has been born into the
22 world. So it is with you; for the moment you are sad at heart; but I shall see you again, and then you will be joyful, and no one shall rob you of
23 your joy. When that day comes you will ask nothing of me. In very truth I tell you, if you ask the Father for anything
24 in my name, he will give it you.^z So far you have asked nothing in my name. Ask and you will receive, that your joy may be complete.

'Till now I have been using figures 25 of speech; a time is coming when I shall no longer use figures, but tell you of the Father in plain words. When 26 that day comes you will make your request in my name, and I do not say that I shall pray to the Father for you, for the Father loves you himself, be- 27 cause you have loved me and believed that I came from God. I came from the 28 Father and have come into the world. Now I am leaving the world again and going to the Father.' His disciples said, 29 'Why, this is plain speaking; this is no figure of speech. We are certain now 30 that you know everything, and do not need to be questioned; because of this we believe that you have come from God.'

Jesus answered, 'Do you now be- 31 lieve? Look,^a the hour is coming, has 32 indeed already come, when you are all to be scattered, each to his home, leaving me alone. Yet I am not alone, because the Father is with me. I have 33 told you all this so that in me you may find peace. In the world you will have trouble. But courage! The victory is mine; I have conquered the world.'

AFTER THESE WORDS JESUS LOOKED UP **17** to heaven and said:

'Father, the hour has come. Glorify thy Son, that the Son may glorify thee. For thou hast made him sovereign over 2 all mankind, to give eternal life to all whom thou hast given him. This is 3 eternal life: to know thee who alone art truly God, and Jesus Christ whom thou hast sent.

'I have glorified thee on earth by 4 completing the work which thou gavest me to do; and now, Father, glorify me 5 in thy own presence with the glory which I had with thee before the world began.

^z *Some witnesses read* if you ask the Father for anything, he will give it you in my name.
^a *Or* At the moment you believe; but look . . .

16.16–33: Jesus' return to the disciples. 16: *You will see me* is a promise which includes Christ's postresurrection appearances, his presence through the Spirit, and his second (final) coming. **23–26:** Jn. now completes his teaching on prayer *in my name* (see 14.13–14 n.; 15.16 n.): it is a form of prayer which arises from Jesus' glorification and the gift of the Spirit (vv. 13–14); it is heard because of the intimacy between the Father and the believer. **32:** Mk.14.27 and Mt.26.31 connect this prophecy with the Gethsemane scene; see Zech. 13.7.
    17.1–8: Jesus prays for the revelation of God's glory. 1: Jesus' intercession has a high-priestly character reminiscent of Rom.8.34 and Heb. He does not pray for himself, except perhaps in v. 5, but for the completion of his mission, to reveal the unseen God, who can be seen in the Son.

Unity is a sign of Christ (handwritten)

6 'I have made thy name known to the men whom thou didst give me out of the world. They were thine, thou gavest them to me, and they have obeyed thy 7 command. Now they know that all thy 8 gifts have come to me from thee; for I have taught them all that I learned from thee, and they have received it: they know with certainty that I came from thee; they have had faith to believe that thou didst send me.

9 'I pray for them; I am not praying for the world but for those whom thou hast given me, because they belong to 10 thee. All that is mine is thine, and what is thine is mine; and through them has my glory shone.

11 'I am to stay no longer in the world, but they are still in the world, and I am on my way to thee. Holy Father, protect by the power of thy name those whom thou hast given me,[b] that they may be 12 one, as we are one. When I was with them, I protected by the power of thy name those whom thou hast given me,[c] and kept them safe. Not one of them is lost except the man who must be lost, for Scripture has to be fulfilled.

13 'And now I am coming to thee; but while I am still in the world I speak these words, so that they may have my 14 joy within them in full measure. I have delivered thy word to them, and the world hates them because they are 15 strangers in the world, as I am. I pray thee, not to take them out of the world, but to keep them from the evil one. 16 They are strangers in the world, as I 17 am. Consecrate them by the truth;[d] 18 thy word is truth. As thou hast sent me into the world, I have sent them 19 into the world, and for their sake I now consecrate myself, that they too may be consecrated by the truth.[d]

20 'But it is not for these alone that I pray, but for those also who through their words put their faith in me; may 21 they all be one; as thou, Father, art in me, and I in thee, so also may they be in us, that the world may believe that thou didst send me. The glory which 22 thou gavest me I have given to them, that they may be one, as we are one; I in them and thou in me, may they be 23 perfectly one. Then the world will learn that thou didst send me, that thou didst love them as thou didst me.

'Father, I desire that these men, who 24 are thy gift to me, may be with me where I am, so that they may look upon my glory, which thou hast given me because thou didst love me before the world began. O righteous Father, 25 although the world does not know thee, I know thee, and these men know that thou didst send me. I made thy 26 name known to them, and will make it known, so that the love thou hadst for me may be in them, and I may be in them.'

The final conflict

AFTER THESE WORDS, JESUS WENT OUT **18** with his disciples, and crossed the Kedron ravine. There was a garden there, and he and his disciples went into it. The place was known to Judas, 2 his betrayer, because Jesus had often met there with his disciples. So Judas 3 took a detachment of soldiers, and police provided by the chief priests and the Pharisees, equipped with lanterns, torches, and weapons, and made his way to the garden. Jesus, knowing all 4 that was coming upon him, went out to them and asked, 'Who is it you want?'

b *Or* keep in loyalty to thee those whom thou hast given me; *some witnesses read* protect them by the power of thy name which thou hast given me.
c *Or* kept in loyalty to thee those whom thou hast given me; *some witnesses read* protected them by the power of thy name which thou hast given me.
d *Or* in truth.

17.9–19: Jesus' intercession for the disciples. 10: *Through them has my glory shone* refers to the disciple's postresurrection faith, which grasps Jesus' identity as the Son of God. **12:** *The man who must be lost* is Judas (see 6.70–71). **19:** *I now consecrate myself* expresses Jesus' self-offering to God through his death.
17.20–26: Jesus' intercession for future Christians. 20: *Through their words:* i.e. the gospel handed down by the first disciples, which provides the occasion for the gift of faith to future Christians (see Rom.10.10–17). **23:** *The world will learn:* the complete unity of the believers will challenge the world to recognize Jesus' mission from the Father.
18.1–11: The garden. 1: *The Kedron ravine* lay between Mount Moriah to the west, and the Mount of Olives to the east. Jn. lacks the place name Gethsemane (Mk.14.32) and Jesus' prayer and struggle (Mk.14.33–42); but see 12.27 n. **3:** See 11.47 n. **4:** *Knowing all:* compare 10.17–18 n.

5 'Jesus of Nazareth', they answered. Jesus said, 'I am he.' And there stood 6 Judas the traitor with them. When he said, 'I am he', they drew back and fell 7 to the ground. Again Jesus asked, 'Who is it you want?' 'Jesus of Nazareth', 8 they answered. Then Jesus said, 'I have told you that I am he. If I am the man 9 you want, let these others go.' (This was to make good his words, 'I have not lost one of those whom thou gavest 10 me.') Thereupon Simon Peter drew the sword he was wearing and struck at the High Priest's servant, cutting off his right ear. (The servant's name was 11 Malchus.) Jesus said to Peter, 'Sheathe your sword. This is the cup the Father has given me; shall I not drink it?'

12 THE TROOPS WITH THEIR COMMANDER, and the Jewish police, now arrested 13 Jesus and secured him. They took him first to Annas.*e* Annas was father-in-law of Caiaphas, the High Priest for that 14 year*e*—the same Caiaphas who had advised the Jews that it would be to their interest if one man died for the 15 whole people. Jesus was followed by Simon Peter and another disciple. This disciple, who was acquainted with the High Priest, went with Jesus into the 16 High Priest's courtyard, but Peter halted at the door outside. So the other disciple, the High Priest's acquaintance, went out again and spoke to the woman at the door, and brought Peter 17 in. The maid on duty at the door said to Peter, 'Are you another of this man's 18 disciples?' 'I am not', he said. The servants and the police had made a charcoal fire, because it was cold, and were standing round it warming themselves. And Peter too was standing with them, sharing the warmth.

The High Priest questioned Jesus 19 about his disciples and about what he taught. Jesus replied, 'I have spoken 20 openly to all the world; I have always taught in synagogue and in the temple, where all Jews congregate; I have said nothing in secret. Why question me? 21 Ask my hearers what I told them; they know what I said.' When he said this, 22 one of the police who was standing next to him struck him on the face, exclaiming, 'Is that the way to answer the High Priest?' Jesus replied, 'If I 23 spoke amiss, state it in evidence; if I spoke well, why strike me?'

So Annas sent him bound to 24 Caiaphas the High Priest.*f*

Meanwhile Simon Peter stood warm- 25 ing himself. The others asked, 'Are you another of his disciples?' But he denied it: 'I am not', he said. One of the High 26 Priest's servants, a relation of the man whose ear Peter had cut off, insisted, 'Did I not see you with him in the garden?' Peter denied again; and just 27 then a cock crew.

FROM CAIAPHAS JESUS WAS LED INTO 28 the Governor's headquarters. It was now early morning, and the Jews themselves stayed outside the headquarters to avoid defilement, so that they could eat the Passover meal.*g* So Pilate went out to them and asked, 29 'What charge do you bring against this man?' 'If he were not a criminal,' they 30 replied, 'we should not have brought him before you.' Pilate said, 'Take him 31 away and try him by your own law.' The Jews answered, 'We are not

e See note on verse 24.
f Some witnesses give this verse after first to Annas in verse 13; others at the end of verse 13.
g Or could share in the offerings of the Passover season.

9: *His words:* see 6.39; 17.12. **11:** The words seem to echo Jesus' prayer in Mk.14.36; Mt.26.39, 42; Lk.22.42.

18.12–27: Interrogation by Annas. 12: The Gk. term for *troops* (lit. "cohort") may imply Roman intervention. **13:** *Annas* had been high priest from 6–15 A.D. **14:** *The same Caiaphas:* see 11.49 (and n.)–51. **15:** *Another* is plausibly the same *disciple* as in 20.2–10, the friend of Peter (13.23–25; 21.7,20–24), possibly John, the son of Zebedee. **20:** The tradition consistently records the claim that Jesus taught openly in the Temple; see Mt.26.55; Mk.14.49; Lk.22.53. **24:** Jn. apparently omits an official Jewish trial, substituting for it an informal hearing; but see 10.24–38 n.

18.28–19.16: Jesus and Pilate. 28: The site of the trial was either the Fortress Antonia, which was connected with the Temple area, or the palace which had been built by Herod and was sometimes used as the *Governor's headquarters.* In Jn. the *Passover* meal was celebrated in the evening following Jesus' crucifixion, in apparent contradiction to the other Gospels (see Mt.26.17 n.). **31:** *We are not allowed:* under Roman rule, the Sanhedrin lacked the authority

32 allowed to put any man to death.' Thus they ensured the fulfilment of the words by which Jesus had indicated the manner of his death,

33 Pilate then went back into his headquarters and summoned Jesus. 'Are you the king of the Jews?' he asked.[h]

34 Jesus said, 'Is that your own idea, or have others suggested it to you?'

35 'What! am I a Jew?' said Pilate. 'Your own nation and their chief priests have brought you before me. What have you

36 done?' Jesus replied, 'My kingdom does not belong to this world. If it did, my followers would be fighting to save me from arrest by the Jews. My kingly

37 authority comes from elsewhere.' 'You are a king, then?' said Pilate. Jesus answered, ' "King" is your word. My task is to bear witness to the truth. For this was I born; for this I came into the world, and all who are not deaf to

38 truth listen to my voice.' Pilate said, 'What is truth?', and with those words went out again to the Jews. 'For my part,' he said, 'I find no case against

39 him. But you have a custom that I release one prisoner for you at Passover. Would you like me to release the king

40 of the Jews?' Again the clamour rose: 'Not him; we want Barabbas!' (Barabbas was a bandit.)

19 Pilate now took Jesus and had him
2 flogged; and the soldiers plaited a crown of thorns and placed it on his head, and robed him in a purple cloak.

3 Then time after time they came up to him, crying, 'Hail, King of the Jews!', and struck him on the face,

4 Once more Pilate came out and said to the Jews, 'Here he is; I am bringing him out to let you know that I find no

5 case against him'; and Jesus came out, wearing the crown of thorns and the purple cloak. 'Behold the Man!' said

Pilate. The chief priests and their 6 henchmen saw him and shouted, 'Crucify! crucify!' 'Take him and crucify him yourselves,' said Pilate; 'for my part I find no case against him.' The Jews answered, 'We have a law; 7 and by that law he ought to die, because he has claimed to be Son of God.'

When Pilate heard that, he was more 8 afraid than ever, and going back into 9 his headquarters he asked Jesus, 'Where have you come from?' But Jesus gave him no answer. 'Do you refuse to 10 speak to me?' said Pilate. 'Surely you know that I have authority to release you, and I have authority to crucify you?' 'You would have no authority 11 at all over me', Jesus replied, 'if it had not been granted you from above; and therefore the deeper guilt lies with the man who handed me over to you.'

From that moment Pilate tried hard 12 to release him; but the Jews kept shouting, 'If you let this man go, you are no friend to Caesar; any man who claims to be a king is defying Caesar.' When Pilate heard what they were 13 saying, he brought Jesus out and took his seat on the tribunal at the place known as 'The Pavement' ('Gabbatha' in the language of the Jews). It was the 14 eve of Passover,[i] about noon. Pilate said to the Jews, 'Here is your king.' They shouted, 'Away with him! Away 15 with him! Crucify him!' 'Crucify your king?' said Pilate. 'We have no king but Caesar', the Jews replied. Then at 16 last, to satisfy them, he handed Jesus over to be crucified.

JESUS WAS NOW TAKEN IN CHARGE AND, 17 carrying his own cross, went out to the Place of the Skull, as it is called (or, in

h Or 'You are king of the Jews, I take it', he said.
i Or It was Friday in Passover.

---

to execute criminals, though some commentators have raised questions about the full accuracy of the statement. **32:** See 3.14; 8.28; 12.32. **33:** The implication of *king of the Jews* is ambiguous. Either it might be a purely religious title ("king of Israel," see 1.49) or, on the contrary, it could carry the political connotation of opposition to Rome. **40:** *Bandit:* probably, a revolutionary. **19.1–5:** Jn. highlights Jesus' royalty by locating his mockery as king in the center of his trial by Romans. **11:** Jn. views Pilate as the appointed instrument of the divine will in these predetermined events. *Who handed me over:* either the high priest (18.28,35) or, perhaps, Judas (13.2). **13:** *Took his seat:* the Gk. is ambiguous; it could mean that Pilate seated Jesus *on the tribunal.* **14:** *About noon:* the time when the paschal lamb was slaughtered by the priests; Jesus is the "paschal lamb"; see also 1.29 n.

19.17–37: Events on Calvary. 17: Unlike the Synoptics, Jn. does not mention Simon of Cyrene (Mk.15.21 n.). His account also omits the mockery at the cross, the darkness, the tearing

18 the Jews' language, 'Golgotha'), where they crucified him, and with him two others, one on the right, one on the left, and Jesus between them.

19 And Pilate wrote an inscription to be fastened to the cross; it read, 'Jesus
20 of Nazareth King of the Jews.' This inscription was read by many Jews, because the place where Jesus was crucified was not far from the city, and the inscription was in Hebrew, Latin,
21 and Greek. Then the Jewish chief priests said to Pilate, 'You should not write "King of the Jews"; write, "He claimed
22 to be king of the Jews."' Pilate replied, 'What I have written, I have written.'

23 The soldiers, having crucified Jesus, took possession of his clothes, and divided them into four parts, one for each soldier, leaving out the tunic. The tunic was seamless, woven in one piece
24 throughout; so they said to one another, 'We must not tear this; let us toss for it'; and thus the text of Scripture came true: 'They shared my garments among them, and cast lots for my clothing.'
25 That is what the soldiers did. But meanwhile near the cross where Jesus hung stood his mother, with her sister, Mary wife of Clopas, and Mary of
26 Magdala. Jesus saw his mother, with the disciple whom he loved standing beside her. He said to her, 'Mother,
27 there is your son'; and to the disciple, 'There is your mother'; and from that moment the disciple took her into his home.
28 After that, Jesus, aware that all had now come to its appointed end, said in
29 fulfilment of Scripture, 'I thirst.' A jar stood there full of sour wine; so they soaked a sponge with the wine, fixed it on a javelin,[j] and held it up to his lips.
30 Having received the wine, he said, 'It is accomplished!' He bowed his head and gave up his spirit.[k]

Because it was the eve of Passover,[l] 31 the Jews were anxious that the bodies should not remain on the cross for the coming Sabbath, since that Sabbath was a day of great solemnity; so they requested Pilate to have the legs broken and the bodies taken down. The soldiers accordingly came to the 32 first of his fellow-victims and to the second, and broke their legs; but when 33 they came to Jesus, they found that he was already dead, so they did not break his legs. But one of the soldiers 34 stabbed his side with a lance, and at once there was a flow of blood and water. This is vouched for by an 35 eyewitness, whose evidence is to be trusted. He knows that he speaks the truth, so that you too may believe; for 36 this happened in fulfilment of the text of Scripture: 'No bone of his shall be broken.' And another text says, 'They 37 shall look on him whom they pierced.'

AFTER THAT, PILATE WAS APPROACHED 38 by Joseph of Arimathaea, a disciple of Jesus, but a secret disciple for fear of the Jews, who[m] asked to be allowed to remove the body of Jesus. Pilate gave the permission; so Joseph came and took the body away. He was joined by 39 Nicodemus (the man who had first visited Jesus by night), who brought with him a mixture of myrrh and aloes, more than half a hundredweight. They 40 took the body of Jesus and wrapped it, with the spices, in strips of linen cloth according to Jewish burial-customs. Now at the place where he had been 41 crucified there was a garden, and in the garden a new tomb, not yet used for burial. There, because the tomb was 42 near at hand and it was the eve of the Jewish Sabbath, they laid Jesus.

j *So one witness; the others read* on marjoram.
k *Or* breathed out his life.
l *Or* Because it was Friday in Passover . . .
m *Or* of Arimathaea. He was a disciple of Jesus, but had gone into hiding for fear of the Jews. He now . . .

---

of the Temple curtain, and the centurion's remark (see Mk.15.29–39). **19:** Jn. ascribes to the Romans a bitter irony in this scornful *inscription* about Jesus' kingship; see Mt.27.37; Mk.15.26; Lk.23.38. **23:** *His clothes:* see Ps.22.18. **25–27:** Jn. alone mentions the presence of Jesus' *mother* and her relationship to the beloved disciple. **34:** In the *blood and water* Jn. perceives a deep theological significance (see 7.38–39; 1 Jn.5.6,8); he intends this as a symbol of the gift of the Spirit or, possibly, of baptism. **35:** This *eyewitness* is the beloved disciple of v. 26. **36:** Compare Exod.12.46. **37:** See Zech.12.10.

19.38–42: Jesus' burial. 39: *Nicodemus:* see 3.1. Jn. omits the presence of the women (compare Mt.27.61; Mk.15.47; Lk.23.55–56). **40:** In accordance with *Jewish burial-customs* the corpse was not eviscerated, as in Egyptian mummification; thus, Jesus' body would remain intact.

20 EARLY ON THE SUNDAY MORNING, WHILE it was still dark, Mary of Magdala came to the tomb. She saw that the stone had been moved away from the
2 entrance, and ran to Simon Peter and the other disciple, the one whom Jesus loved. 'They have taken the Lord out of his tomb,' she cried, 'and we do not
3 know where they have laid him.' So Peter and the other set out and made
4 their way to the tomb. They were running side by side, but the other disciple outran Peter and reached the
5 tomb first. He peered in and saw the linen wrappings lying there, but did
6 not enter. Then Simon Peter came up, following him, and he went into the tomb. He saw the linen wrappings lying,
7 and the napkin which had been over his head, not lying with the wrappings but rolled together in a place by itself.
8 Then the disciple who had reached the tomb first went in too, and he saw and
9 believed; until then they had not understood the scriptures, which showed that he must rise from the dead.
10 So the disciples went home again;
11 but Mary stood at the tomb outside, weeping. As she wept, she peered into
12 the tomb; and she saw two angels in white sitting there, one at the head, and one at the feet, where the body of
13 Jesus had lain. They said to her, 'Why are you weeping?' She answered, 'They have taken my Lord away, and I do not
14 know where they have laid him.' With these words she turned round and saw Jesus standing there, but did not
15 recognize him. Jesus said to her, 'Why are you weeping? Who is it you are looking for?' Thinking it was the gardener, she said, 'If it is you, sir, who removed him, tell me where you have laid him, and I will take him away.'
16 Jesus said, 'Mary!' She turned to him and said, 'Rabbuni!' (which is Hebrew for 'My Master'). Jesus said, 'Do not 17 cling to me,[n] for I have not yet ascended to the Father. But go to my brothers, and tell them that I am now ascending[o] to my Father and your Father, my God and your God.' Mary 18 of Magdala went to the disciples with her news: 'I have seen the Lord!' she said, and gave them his message.

Late that Sunday evening, when the 19 disciples were together behind locked doors, for fear of the Jews, Jesus came and stood among them. 'Peace be with you!' he said, and then showed them 20 his hands and his side. So when the disciples saw the Lord, they were filled with joy. Jesus repeated, 'Peace be 21 with you!', and said, 'As the Father sent me, so I send you.' Then he 22 breathed on them, saying, 'Receive the Holy Spirit! If you forgive any man's 23 sins, they stand forgiven; if you pronounce them unforgiven, unforgiven they remain.'

One of the Twelve, Thomas, that is 24 'the Twin', was not with the rest when Jesus came. So the disciples told him, 25 'We have seen the Lord.' He said, 'Unless I see the mark of the nails on his hands, unless I put my finger into the place where the nails were, and my hand into his side, I will not believe it.'

A week later his disciples were again 26 in the room, and Thomas was with them. Although the doors were locked, Jesus came and stood among them, saying, 'Peace be with you!' Then he 27 said to Thomas, 'Reach your finger here; see my hands. Reach your hand here and put it into my side. Be unbelieving no longer, but believe.' Thomas said, 'My Lord and my God!' 28

n Or Touch me no more.
o Or I am going to ascend ...

20.1–23: The first Easter. 1: *Sunday* became the Christian day of worship rather than Saturday. **2:** *Lord:* see 11.2 n. *The other disciple:* see 18.15 n. **6–8:** Peter's reaction shows that inspection of the empty tomb did not in itself cause faith in Jesus' resurrection; however, the *disciple* (v. 2) whom Jn. favors above Peter *saw and believed*. **9:** That without Christian faith the disciples *had not understood the scriptures* is crucial, since it shows that the OT in itself had not led them to anticipate Jesus' resurrection. **14:** Mary *did not recognize him* because she did not yet have faith in the risen Jesus. **17:** Jesus' prohibition, *do not cling to me,* shows that Mary's gesture of adoration is premature, because his glorification is incomplete. **22:** *Breathed on them* recalls God's creative action in Gen.2.7. **23:** The risen Lord bestows the power to forgive sins on the Church.

20.24–29: Thomas. This account of Thomas' doubt and ensuing faith invites belief which is not dependent on physical evidence.

29 Jesus said, 'Because you have seen me you have found faith. Happy are they who never saw me and yet have found faith.'

30 There were indeed many other signs that Jesus performed in the presence of his disciples, which are not recorded 31 in this book. Those here written have been recorded in order that you may hold the faith[p] that Jesus is the Christ, the Son of God, and that through this faith you may possess life by his name.

21 SOME TIME LATER, JESUS SHOWED HIM-self to his disciples once again, by the 2 Sea of Tiberias; and in this way. Simon Peter and Thomas 'the Twin' were together with Nathanael of Cana-in-Galilee. The sons of Zebedee and two 3 other disciples were also there. Simon Peter said, 'I am going out fishing.' 'We will go with you', said the others. So they started and got into the boat. But that night they caught nothing.

4 Morning came, and there stood Jesus on the beach, but the disciples did not 5 know that it was Jesus. He called out to them, 'Friends, have you caught 6 anything?' They answered 'No.' He said, 'Shoot the net to starboard, and you will make a catch.' They did so, and found they could not haul the net aboard, there were so many fish in it. 7 Then the disciple whom Jesus loved said to Peter, 'It is the Lord!' When Simon Peter heard that, he wrapped his coat about him (for he had stripped) and plunged into the sea. 8 The rest of them came on in the boat, towing the net full of fish; for they were not far from land, only about a hundred yards. 9 When they came ashore, they saw a charcoal fire there, with fish laid on it, 10 and some bread. Jesus said, 'Bring 11 some of your catch.' Simon Peter went aboard and dragged the net to land,

full of big fish, a hundred and fifty-three of them; and yet, many as they were, the net was not torn. Jesus said, 12 'Come and have breakfast.' None of the disciples dared to ask 'Who are you?' They knew it was the Lord. Jesus now came up, took the bread, 13 and gave it to them, and the fish in the same way.

This makes the third time that Jesus 14 appeared to his disciples after his resurrection from the dead.

After breakfast, Jesus said to Simon 15 Peter, 'Simon son of John, do you love me more than all else[q]?' 'Yes, Lord,' he answered, 'you know that I love you.'[r] 'Then feed my lambs', he said. A second time he asked, 'Simon son of 16 John, do you love me?' 'Yes, Lord, you know I love you.'[r] 'Then tend my 17 sheep.' A third time he said, 'Simon son of John, do you love me[s]?' Peter was hurt that he asked him a third time. 'Do you love me?'[t] 'Lord,' he said, 'you know everything; you know I love you.'[r] Jesus said, 'Feed my sheep.

'And further, I tell you this in very 18 truth: when you were young you fastened your belt about you and walked where you chose; but when you are old you will stretch out your arms, and a stranger will bind you fast, and carry you where you have no wish to go.' He said this to indicate the manner 19 of death by which Peter was to glorify God. Then he added, 'Follow me.'

Peter looked round, and saw the 20 disciple whom Jesus loved following—the one who at supper had leaned back close to him to ask the question, 'Lord, who is it that will betray you?' When 21 he caught sight of him, Peter asked, 'Lord, what will happen to him?' Jesus said, 'If it should be my will that 22

p Some witnesses read that you may come to believe . . .
q Or more than they do.
r Or that I am your friend.   s Or are you my friend.
t Or that at the third asking he should have said, 'Are you my friend?'

20.30–31: The first conclusion of the Gospel. See 21.1–25 n. **30:** Although Jn. is aware of *many other signs*, he has recounted only seven. **31:** The purpose of the Gospel is expressly stated here.

21.1–25: The epilogue. This chapter is sometimes regarded as a later appendix. **2:** *The sons of Zebedee*, prominent in Mt., Mk., Lk., are now mentioned for the first time in Jn.; some scholars think this points to John, the son of Zebedee, as the source of this Gospel's tradition. **7:** Note this Gospel's apparent preference for the beloved *disciple* over *Peter*. **12:** Hesitation or doubt appears in all accounts of the disciples' postresurrection experiences (see Mt.28.17; Lk.24.37–38; Jn.20.25). **15–17:** Peter is given a unique task among the disciples (see Mt.16.18; Lk.22.31–32). **20:** See 13.23–25. **22:** *Until I come* probably has more than one meaning: see

he wait until I come, what is it to you? Follow me.'

23 That saying of Jesus became current in the brotherhood, and was taken to mean that that disciple would not die. But in fact Jesus did not say that he would not die; he only said, 'If it should be my will that he wait until I come, what is it to you?'

24 It is this same disciple who attests what has here been written. It is in fact he who wrote it, and we know that his testimony is true.[u]

25 There is much else that Jesus did. If it were all to be recorded in detail, I suppose the whole world could not hold the books that would be written.

An incident in the temple*

53* AND THEY WENT EACH TO HIS HOME, 1,2 and Jesus to the Mount of Olives. At daybreak he appeared again in the temple, and all the people gathered round him. He had taken his seat and 3 was engaged in teaching them when the doctors of the law and the Pharisees brought in a woman caught committing adultery. Making her stand out in the middle they said to him, 4 'Master, this woman was caught in the very act of adultery. In the Law Moses 5 has laid down that such women are to be stoned. What do you say about it?' They put the question as a test, hoping 6 to frame a charge against him. Jesus bent down and wrote with his finger on the ground. When they continued to 7 press their question he sat up straight and said, 'That one of you who is faultless shall throw the first stone.' Then once again he bent down and 8 wrote on the ground. When they heard 9 what he said, one by one they went away,[v] the eldest first; and Jesus was left alone, with the woman still standing there. Jesus again sat up and[w] said to 10 the woman, 'Where are they? Has no one condemned you?' She answered, 11 'No one, sir.' Jesus said, 'Nor do I condemn you. You may go; do not sin again.'

u *Some witnesses here insert the passage printed below.*
* *This passage, which in the most widely received editions of the New Testament is printed in the text of John, 7. 53–8. 11, has no fixed place in our witnesses. Some of them do not contain it at all. Some place it after Luke 21. 28, others after John 7. 36, or 7. 52, or 21. 24.*
v *Some witnesses insert* convicted by their conscience.
w *Some witnesses insert* seeing no one but the woman.

16.16 n. **24:** *This same disciple* refers to the one on whose authority the Gospel of John rests.
   7.53–8.11: The woman accused of adultery. 1: The terms *Mount of Olives, daybreak* (v. 2), *the doctors of the law and the Pharisees* (v. 3) are expressions more typical of the Synoptics, than of Jn. **5:** See Lev.20.10; Deut.22.20–21. **6:** The *question* was a *test* in that it posed a dilemma for Jesus: whether to show mercy or to advocate the death penalty. What, if anything, Jesus *wrote on the ground* is unimportant in the story. **11:** *Do not sin again:* see 5.14.

ACTS OF THE
APOSTLES

ACTS OF THE APOSTLES

With this book the author of the third Gospel continues his story of the birth of the Christian Church. Acts shows a wide acquaintance with the Hellenistic world, its customs and political organizations; and its good, if not artistic, Greek betrays the hand of a cosmopolitan author, whom tradition has identified as Luke, a physician (Col.4.14; 2 Tim.4.11). Written to show how God continues to fulfill his plan for the salvation of mankind, a plan which our author understands to have begun with Israel, Acts follows the Church from its origin at Pentecost (ch. 2) through the geographical progression which Jesus himself had announced (1.8). Led by God's Spirit, the Church moved from a small Jewish group centered in Jerusalem to a worldwide movement embracing Rome, the capital of the world (ch. 28). This shift from Jewish to Gentile mission was a primary interest of the author, and he details how admission of the first Gentiles (ch. 10) led to a council (ch. 15) whose decision opened Christian fellowship to all men. Following ancient custom, Luke has composed summaries (e.g. 2.42–43; 5.12–16; 9.31–32) and speeches (e.g. 2.14–36; 3.12–26; 5.35–39; 7.2–53; 10.34–43; 15.13–21; 17.22–31; 28.25–28) as a method of informing the reader about the meaning of the events which he narrates. Our author may have had some sources at his disposal (e.g. the "we" sections: 16.10–18; 20.5–15; 21.1–18; 27.1–28.16; collections of local traditions from Palestine and Antioch), but he has worked them so skillfully into his narrative that their reconstruction is very difficult. That his sources were incomplete, however, is indicated by the inexact chronological references throughout the narrative, and by the fact that information contained in Paul's letters seems not to have been available to him. Despite that fact, Acts stands as a mighty witness to the conviction that God is at work within human history to accomplish his saving purpose for mankind.

The beginnings of the church

1 IN THE FIRST PART OF MY WORK, Theophilus, I wrote of all that Jesus did and taught from the beginning 2 until the day when, after giving instructions through the Holy Spirit to the apostles whom he had chosen, he was 3 taken up to heaven. He showed himself to these men after his death, and gave ample proof that he was alive: over a period of forty days he appeared to them and taught them about the 4 kingdom of God. While he was in their company he told them not to leave Jerusalem. 'You must wait', he said, 'for the promise made by my Father, about which you have heard me speak: 5 John, as you know, baptized with water, but you will be baptized with the Holy Spirit, and within the next few days.'

6 So, when they were all together, they asked him, 'Lord, is this the time when you are to establish once again the sovereignty of Israel?' He answered, 7 'It is not for you to know about dates or times, which the Father has set within his own control. But you will 8 receive power when the Holy Spirit comes upon you; and you will bear witness for me in Jerusalem, and all over Judaea and Samaria, and away to the ends of the earth.'

9 When he had said this, as they watched, he was lifted up, and a cloud removed him from their sight. As he 10 was going, and as they were gazing intently into the sky, all at once there stood beside them two men in white 11 who said, 'Men of Galilee, why stand there looking up into the sky? This Jesus, who has been taken away from you up to heaven, will come in the same way as you have seen him go.'

12 Then they returned to Jerusalem

1.1–5: Preface. 1: *Theophilus* (lit. lover of—or loved by—God) was probably a patron who would sponsor the distribution of this book. 2: These instructions are summarized in Lk.24.44–49. 3: *Forty days* is a general number; see Lk.4.1–2. 4: On the *promise* concerning baptism, see Lk.3.16; Isa.44.2–5; Ezek.39.28–29; Joel 2.28–29. 5: In Lk.3.16 this saying is attributed to John the Baptist.

1.6–14: Jesus' ascension. 6: *All together* may imply table-fellowship; compare 10.41. On the problem of when and how the Kingdom comes, see Lk.7.20–23; 19.11; 21.5–36. 7: *Dates or times:* see 1 Th.5.1. 8: Compare 28.14 n. 12: *Sabbath day's journey:* the travel permitted Jews,

141

from the hill called Olivet, which is near Jerusalem, no farther than a 13 Sabbath day's journey. Entering the city they went to the room upstairs where they were lodging: Peter and John and James and Andrew, Philip and Thomas, Bartholomew and Matthew, James son of Alphaeus and Simon the Zealot, and Judas son of 14 James. All these were constantly at prayer together, and with them a group of women, including Mary the mother of Jesus, and his brothers.

15 It was during this time that Peter stood up before the assembled brotherhood, about one hundred and twenty 16 in all, and said: 'My friends, the prophecy in Scripture was bound to come true, which the Holy Spirit, through the mouth of David, uttered about Judas who acted as guide to those who 17 arrested Jesus. For he was one of our number and had his place in this 18 ministry.' (This Judas, be it noted, after buying a plot of land with the price of his villainy, fell forward on the ground, and burst open, so that his 19 entrails poured out. This became known to everyone in Jerusalem, and they named the property in their own language Akeldama, which means 20 'Blood Acre'.) 'The text I have in mind', Peter continued, 'is in the Book of Psalms: "Let his homestead fall desolate; let there be none to inhabit it"; and again, "Let another take over his 21 charge." Therefore one of those who bore us company all the while we had the Lord Jesus with us, coming and 22 going, from John's ministry of baptism until the day when he was taken up from us—one of those must now join us as a witness to his resurrection.'

23 Two names were put forward: Joseph, who was known as Barsabbas, and bore the added name of Justus; and Matthias. Then they prayed and 24 said, 'Thou, Lord, who knowest the hearts of all men, declare which of these two thou hast chosen to receive 25 this office of ministry and apostleship which Judas abandoned to go where he belonged.' They drew lots and the lot 26 fell on Matthias, who was then assigned a place among the twelve apostles.[a]

WHILE THE DAY OF PENTECOST WAS **2** running its course they were all together in one place, when suddenly there 2 came from the sky a noise like that of a strong driving wind, which filled the whole house where they were sitting. And there appeared to them tongues 3 like flames of fire, dispersed among them and resting on each one. And they 4 were all filled with the Holy Spirit and began to talk in other tongues, as the Spirit gave them power of utterance.

Now there were living in Jerusalem 5 devout Jews[b] drawn from every nation under heaven; and at this sound the 6 crowd gathered, all bewildered because each one heard his own language spoken. They were amazed and in their 7 astonishment exclaimed, 'Why, they are all Galileans, are they not, these men who are speaking? How is it then 8 that we hear them, each of us in his own native language? Parthians, Medes, 9 Elamites; inhabitants of Mesopotamia, of Judaea and Cappadocia, of Pontus and Asia, of Phrygia and Pamphylia, of 10 Egypt and the districts of Libya around Cyrene; visitors from Rome, both Jews and proselytes, Cretans and 11 Arabs, we hear them telling in our own tongues the great things God has done.' And they were all amazed and 12

a *Some witnesses read* was then appointed a colleague of the eleven apostles.
b *Some witnesses read* devout men.

about a thousand paces. **13:** *Room upstairs*, or upper room, was a normal meeting place (see 20.8), not necessarily to be identified with the locus of the Last Supper. **14:** Jesus' *brothers* are named in Mk.6.3. Hitherto they had not been his followers; compare Mk.3.21. *Group of women:* compare Lk.8.1–3; 23.49.

1.15–26: Replacement of Judas. 16: *Bound to come true:* see 2.23 n. **17:** *One of our number:* see Lk.6.12–16. **18:** The meaning of *fell forward* is uncertain; Papias (an early second-century Christian) took it to mean "became swollen." According to Mt.27.5 Judas hanged himself. **20:** The *text* is Pss.69.25; 109.8. **23:** Many Jews bore two names, one Jewish (*Joseph*), the other Latin or Greek (*Justus*).

2.1–47: Pentecost. 1: *Pentecost,* fifty days following Passover, was a harvest festival which at this time celebrated the covenant (Lev.23.15–21). **2–3:** *Wind* and *fire* are meant to be understood symbolically, not literally. **4:** It is not clear whether *other tongues* means languages (vv. 6,8,11) or ecstatic speaking (v. 13.) **9–11:** Examples are given illustrating the universality expressed in

perplexed, saying to one another,
13 'What can this mean?' Others said
contemptuously, 'They have been
drinking!'
14   But Peter stood up with the Eleven,
raised his voice, and addressed them:
'Fellow Jews, and all you who live in
Jerusalem, mark this and give me a
15 hearing. These men are not drunk, as
you imagine; for it is only nine in the
16 morning. No, this is what the prophet
17 spoke of: "God says, 'This will happen
in the last days: I will pour out upon
everyone a portion of my spirit; and
your sons and daughters shall prophesy; your young men shall see visions,
and your old men shall dream dreams.
18 Yes, I will endue even my slaves,
both men and women, with a portion
of my spirit, and they shall prophesy.
19 And I will show portents in the sky
above, and signs on the earth below—
blood and fire and drifting smoke.
20 The sun shall be turned to darkness,
and the moon to blood, before that
great, resplendent day, the day of the
21 Lord, shall come. And then, everyone
who invokes the name of the Lord
shall be saved.'"
22   'Men of Israel, listen to me: I speak
of Jesus of Nazareth, a man singled out
by God and made known to you
through miracles, portents, and signs,
which God worked among you through
23 him, as you well know. When he had
been given up to you, by the deliberate
will and plan of God, you used heathen
24 men to crucify and kill him. But God
raised him to life again, setting him
free from the pangs of death, because
it could not be that death should keep
him in its grip.
25   'For David says of him:

"I foresaw that the presence of the
    Lord would be with me always,
for he is at my right hand so that I
    may not be shaken;

therefore my heart was glad and my   26
    tongue spoke my joy;
moreover, my flesh shall dwell in
    hope,
for thou wilt not abandon my soul   27
    to death,
nor let thy loyal servant suffer
    corruption.
Thou hast shown me the ways of life,   28
thou wilt fill me with gladness by
    thy presence."

'Let me tell you plainly, my friends,   29
that the patriarch David died and was
buried, and his tomb is here to this very
day. It is clear therefore that he spoke   30
as a prophet, who knew that God had
sworn to him that one of his own direct
descendants should sit on his throne;
and when he said he was not abandoned   31
to death, and his flesh never suffered
corruption, he spoke with foreknowledge of the resurrection of the Messiah. The Jesus we speak of has been   32
raised by God, as we can all bear witness. Exalted thus with*c* God's right   33
hand, he received the Holy Spirit from
the Father, as was promised, and all
that you now see and hear flows from
him. For it was not David who went   34
up to heaven; his own words are:
"The Lord said to my Lord, 'Sit at my
right hand until I make your enemies   35
your footstool.'" Let all Israel then   36
accept as certain that God has made
this Jesus, whom you crucified, both
Lord and Messiah.'
   When they heard this they were cut   37
to the heart, and said to Peter and the
apostles,*d* 'Friends, what are we to do?'
'Repent,' said Peter, 'repent and be   38
baptized, every one of you, in the name
of Jesus the Messiah for the forgiveness
of your sins; and you will receive the
gift of the Holy Spirit. For the promise   39
is to you, and to your children, and to

c Or at.
d Some witnesses read the rest of the apostles.

---

v. 5. **14–36: Peter's sermon. 14:** *Addressed* is the same word as "utterance" (v. 4); the Spirit
also empowers Peter's words. **17–21:** Joel 2.28–32a. **22:** Proof of Jesus' divine mission by
miracles is a regular part of Lukan theology; compare 10.38; Lk.4.16–27. **23:** *Plan of God* is a
regular motif of Lukan theology; compare Lk.22.22. **25–28:** Ps.16.8–11a. **30:** The language
reflects Ps.132.11. **32:** *Bear witness:* to qualify as an apostle one had to have seen the risen Jesus;
see 1 Cor.9.1; 15.3–8. **36:** This verse says nothing about the time at which *Jesus* became *Messiah;*
for Luke, Jesus was Messiah already during his lifetime, see 10.38; Lk.4.18. **37–41: Response
to the sermon. 38:** Baptism and reception of the *Holy Spirit* are usually simultaneous; when

all who are far away, everyone whom the Lord our God may call.'

40 In these and many other words he pressed his case and pleaded with them: 'Save yourselves', he said, 'from this
41 crooked age.' Then those who accepted his word were baptized, and some three thousand were added to their number that day.
42 They met constantly to hear the apostles teach, and to share the common life, to break bread, and to pray.
43 A sense of awe was everywhere, and many marvels and signs were brought
44 about through the apostles. All whose faith had drawn them together held
45 everything in common:*e* they would sell their property and possessions and make a general distribution as the need
46 of each required. With one mind they kept up their daily attendance at the temple, and, breaking bread in private houses, shared their meals with un-
47 affected joy, as they praised God and enjoyed the favour of the whole people. And day by day the Lord added to their number those whom he was saving.

3 ONE DAY AT THREE IN THE AFTERNOON, the hour of prayer, Peter and John were on their way up to the temple.
2 Now a man who had been a cripple from birth used to be carried there and laid every day by the gate of the temple called 'Beautiful Gate', to beg
3 from people as they went in. When he saw Peter and John on their way into
4 the temple he asked for charity. But Peter fixed his eyes on him, as John did also, and said, 'Look at us.'
5 Expecting a gift from them, the man
6 was all attention. And Peter said, 'I

have no silver or gold; but what I have I give you: in the name of Jesus Christ of Nazareth, walk.' Then he grasped 7 him by the right hand and pulled him up; and at once his feet and ankles grew strong; he sprang up, stood on 8 his feet, and started to walk. He entered the temple with them, leaping and praising God as he went. Everyone 9 saw him walking and praising God, and when they recognized him as the 10 man who used to sit begging at Beautiful Gate, they were filled with wonder and amazement at what had happened to him.

And as he was clutching Peter and 11 John all the people came running in astonishment towards them in Solomon's Portico, as it is called. Peter saw 12 them coming and met them with these words: 'Men of Israel, why be surprised at this? Why stare at us as if we had made this man walk by some power or godliness of our own? The God of 13 Abraham, Isaac, and Jacob, the God of our fathers, has given the highest honour to his servant Jesus, whom you committed for trial and repudiated in Pilate's court—repudiated the one who 14 was holy and righteous when Pilate had decided to release him. You begged as a favour the release of a murderer, and 15 killed him who has led the way to life. But God raised him from the dead; of that we are witnesses. And the name of 16 Jesus, by awakening faith, has strengthened this man, whom you see and know, and this faith has made him completely well, as you can all see for yourselves.

e Or All who had become believers held everything together in common.

---

they are not, it is due to special reasons; see 8.16–17; 10.47; 19.1–6. **42–47: Summary of early Christian life. 42:** *Break bread* refers to common meals which included the Eucharist. **44–45:** It was a usual practice in religious communities, including Qumran, to hold everything in common. Such common ownership (Gk., *koina*) was an expression of community (Gk., *koinonia*).

3.1–4.31: Apostolic activity and Jewish persecution.

3.1–10: Peter heals a cripple. 1: Herod's *temple*, an entire complex of courtyards and buildings, was still under construction. **2:** The exact location of the *Beautiful Gate* is unknown. **6:** Typically for Acts, *the name of Jesus Christ* implies acting in his full power and authority; see 4.10,18,30. **8:** Jesus' word in Mt.10.8 begins to receive its fulfillment.

3.11–26: Peter's second sermon. 11: *Solomon's Portico* was a colonnade on the east side of the great court of the Temple, the "Court of the Gentiles." **13:** *Servant* as a title for Jesus is taken from Isa.52.13–53.11, and is used only three other times in the NT, all in Acts (v. 26; 4.27,30). *The God of Abraham:* see Exod.3.6,15. The reference shows that the church is the continuation of Israel. **14:** On *Pilate's* decision, see Lk.23.4a,13–25. **15:** *Witnesses* to resurrec-

17 'And now, my friends, I know quite well that you acted in ignorance, and so
18 did your rulers; but this is how God fulfilled what he had foretold in the utterances of all the prophets: that his
19 Messiah should suffer. Repent then and turn to God, so that your sins may be wiped out. Then the Lord may grant
20 you a time of recovery and send you the Messiah he has already appointed, that
21 is, Jesus. He must be received into heaven until the time of universal restoration comes, of which God spoke by
22 his holy prophets.*f* Moses said, "The Lord God will raise up a prophet for you from among yourselves as he raised me;*g* you shall listen to every-
23 thing he says to you, and anyone who refuses to listen to that prophet must
24 be extirpated from Israel." And so said all the prophets, from Samuel onwards; with one voice they all predicted this present time.
25 'You are the heirs of the prophets; you are within the covenant which God made with your fathers, when he said to Abraham, "And in your offspring all the families on earth shall find bless-
26 ing." When God raised up his Servant, he sent him to you first, to bring you blessing by turning every one of you from your wicked ways.'

4 They were still addressing the people when the chief*h* priests came upon them, together with the Controller of
2 the Temple and the Sadducees, exasperated at their teaching the people and proclaiming the resurrection from the
3 dead—the resurrection of Jesus. They were arrested and put in prison for the
4 night, as it was already evening. But many of those who had heard the message became believers. The number of men now reached about five thousand.
5 Next day the Jewish rulers, elders,

and doctors of the law met in Jeru-
6 salem. There were present Annas the High Priest, Caiaphas, Jonathan,*l* Alexander, and all who were of the
7 high-priestly family. They brought the apostles before the court and began the examination. 'By what power', they asked, 'or by what name have such
8 men as you done this?' Then Peter, filled with the Holy Spirit, answered,
9 'Rulers of the people and elders, if the question put to us today is about help given to a sick man, and we are asked
10 by what means he was cured, here is the answer, for all of you and for all the people of Israel: it was by the name of Jesus Christ of Nazareth, whom you crucified, whom God raised from the dead; it is by his name*j* that this man stands here before you fit and well.
11 This Jesus is the stone rejected by the builders which has become the keystone—and you are the builders.
12 There is no salvation in anyone else at all,*k* for there is no other name under heaven granted to men, by which we may receive salvation.'
13 Now as they observed the boldness of Peter and John, and noted that they were untrained laymen, they began to wonder, then recognized them as for-
14 mer companions of Jesus. And when they saw the man who had been cured standing with them, they had nothing
15 to say in reply. So they ordered them to leave the court, and then discussed
16 the matter among themselves. 'What are we to do with these men?' they said; 'for it is common knowledge in Jerusalem that a notable miracle has come about through them; and we

f Some witnesses add from the beginning of the world.
g Or like me.
h Some witnesses omit chief.
i Some witnesses read John.
j Some witnesses insert and no other.
k Some witnesses omit There is no . . . at all.

---

tion: see 2.32 n. **17:** *You acted in ignorance:* compare Lk.23.34. **18:** See 2.23 n. **20:** *Send you the Messiah:* Peter implies Jesus will return when the Jews turn to Jesus; compare Rom.11.25–31. **22:** Compare Deut.18.15–19; Lev.23.29. **25:** Compare Gen.22.18. *Offspring* here refers to Jesus, as in Gal.3.16. **26:** That the Jews were the first to whom God *sent* his Son is a common theme in Acts; see Mk.7.27; Rom.1.16; 2.9.
4.1–31: Peter and John arrested, then freed. 1: *The Controller of the Temple* headed the Levitical guard which kept order in the Temple precincts. *Sadducees:* See Mt.3.7 n. **2:** See 23.6–8; Lk.20.27. **5–22:** Hearing before *Jewish* authorities. **5:** Members of these groups constituted the Sanhedrin, the ruling council of the Jews. **6:** The office of *High Priest* was no longer of lifetime tenure; because of its political prestige, it was granted and removed by Rome. The author may mean *Annas* (Lk.3.2 n.) or Ananias (23.2 n.). Neither was in office at this time, although the former still had great influence. **7:** See 12.11–12. **11:** Ps.118.22; compare 1 Pet.2.7–8.

145

17 cannot deny it. But to stop this from spreading further among the people, we had better caution them never again 18 to speak to anyone in this name.' They then called them in and ordered them to refrain from all public speaking and teaching in the name of Jesus.

19   But Peter and John said to them in reply: 'Is it right in God's eyes for us to obey you rather than God? Judge 20 for yourselves. We cannot possibly give up speaking of things we have seen and heard.'

21   The court repeated the caution and discharged them. They could not see how they were to punish them, because the people were all giving glory to God 22 for what had happened. The man upon whom this miracle of healing had been performed was over forty years old.

23   As soon as they were discharged they went back to their friends and told them everything that the chief priests 24 and elders had said. When they heard it, they raised their voices as one man and called upon God:

'Sovereign Lord, maker of heaven and earth and sea and of everything in 25 them, who by the Holy Spirit,*l* through the mouth of David thy servant, didst say,

"Why did the Gentiles rage and the
     peoples lay their plots in vain?
26 The kings of the earth took their
     stand and the rulers made
     common cause
against the Lord and against his
     Messiah."

27 They did indeed make common cause in this very city against thy holy servant Jesus whom thou didst anoint as Messiah. Herod and Pontius Pilate conspired with the Gentiles and peoples 28 of Israel to do all the things which, under thy hand and by thy decree,

were foreordained. And now, O Lord, 29 mark their threats, and enable thy servants to speak thy word with all boldness. Stretch out thy hand to heal 30 and cause signs and wonders to be done through the name of thy holy servant Jesus.'

When they had ended their prayer, 31 the building where they were assembled rocked, and all were filled with the Holy Spirit and spoke the word of God with boldness.

THE WHOLE BODY OF BELIEVERS WAS 32 united in heart and soul. Not a man of them claimed any of his possessions as his own, but everything was held in common, while the apostles bore wit- 33 ness with great power to the resurrection of the Lord Jesus. They were all held in high esteem; for they had never 34 a needy person among them, because all who had property in land or houses sold it, brought the proceeds of the sale, and laid the money at the feet of 35 the apostles; it was then distributed to any who stood in need.

For instance, Joseph, surnamed by 36 the apostles Barnabas (which means 'Son of Exhortation'), a Levite, by birth a Cypriot, owned an estate, which 37 he sold; he brought the money, and laid it at the apostles' feet.

But there was another man, called **5** Ananias, with his wife Sapphira, who sold a property. With the full knowl- 2 edge of his wife he kept back part of the purchase-money, and part he brought and laid at the apostles' feet. But Peter said, 'Ananias, how was it 3 that Satan so possessed your mind that you lied to the Holy Spirit, and kept back part of the price of the land? While it remained, did it not remain 4 yours? When it was turned into money, was it not still at your own disposal?

l Some witnesses omit by the Holy Spirit.

23–31: Return of Peter and John. 24: *Sovereign Lord* (Gk., *despota*), used also in Lk.2.29, is a Hellenistic prayer formula. **25:** Compare Ps.2.1–2. **27:** *Herod* Antipas: see Mk.6.14 n. *Herod and Pontius Pilate:* see Lk.23.6–12. **30:** *Cause signs and wonders:* the further narrative of Acts shows the author felt this prayer was granted. **31:** See 2.1–4.

4.32–5.12: Communal life. 32–37: All property was held in common. **32:** See 2.44–45 n. **34:** As 5.4 makes clear, such disposal of personal property was not mandatory, but was done at the prompting of the Spirit. **36:** *Joseph . . . Barnabas:* see 11.22–26; 13.2–3.

5.1–12: Ananias and Sapphira. This story is intended to show the powerful and immediate presence of the Spirit with the early church, represented in the person of the apostles: compare vv. 15–16. **4:** See 4.34. **5:** The sin is that they *lied*, rather than any refusal to turn property over

What made you think of doing this thing? You have lied not to men but to
3 God.' When Ananias heard these words he dropped dead; and all the others
6 who heard were awestruck. The younger men rose and covered his body, then carried him out and buried him.

7 About three hours passed, and then his wife came in, unaware of what had
8 happened. Peter turned to her and said, 'Tell me, were you paid such and such a price for the land?' 'Yes,' she
9 said, 'that was the price.' Then Peter said, 'Why did you both conspire to put the Spirit of the Lord to the test? Hark! there at the door are the footsteps of those who buried your husband; and they will carry you away.'
10 And suddenly she dropped dead at his feet. When the young men came in, they found her dead; and they carried her out and buried her beside her husband.
11 And a great awe fell upon the whole church, and upon all who heard of
12 these events; and many remarkable and wonderful things took place among the people at the hands of the apostles.

THEY USED TO MEET BY COMMON
13 consent in Solomon's Portico, no one from outside their number venturing to join with them. But people in general
14 spoke highly of them,*m* and more than that, numbers of men and women were added to their ranks as believers in the
15 Lord.*n* In the end the sick were actually carried out into the streets and laid there on beds and stretchers, so that even the shadow of Peter might fall on
16 one or another as he passed by; and the people from the towns round Jerusalem flocked in, bringing those who were ill or harassed by unclean spirits, and all of them were cured.
17 Then the High Priest and his colleagues, the Sadducean party as it then was, were goaded into action by jealousy. They proceeded to arrest the
18 apostles, and put them in official custody. But an angel of the Lord
19 opened the prison doors during the night, brought them out, and said, 'Go,
20 take your place in the temple and speak to the people, and tell them about this new life and all it means.' Accordingly
21 they entered the temple at daybreak and went on with their teaching.

When the High Priest arrived with his colleagues they summoned the 'Sanhedrin', that is, the full senate of the Israelite nation, and sent to the
22 jail to fetch the prisoners. But the police who went to the prison failed to find them there, so they returned
23 and reported, 'We found the jail securely locked at every point, with the warders at their posts by the doors, but when we opened them we found no
24 one inside.' When they heard this, the Controller of the Temple and the chief priests were wondering what could have become of them,*o* and then a man
25 arrived with the report, 'Look! the men you put in prison are there in the temple teaching the people.' At that
26 the Controller went off with the police and fetched them, but without using force for fear of being stoned by the people.
27 So they brought them and stood them before the Council; and the High
28 Priest began his examination. 'We expressly ordered you', he said, 'to desist from teaching in that name; and what has happened? You have filled Jerusalem with your teaching, and you are trying to make us responsible for
29 that man's death.' Peter replied for himself and the apostles: 'We must obey God rather than men. The God
30 of our fathers raised up Jesus whom you had done to death*p* by hanging him on a gibbet. He it is whom God has
31 exalted with his own right hand*q* as

m Or ... Portico. Although others did not venture to join them, the common people spoke highly of them.
n Or and an ever-increasing number of believers, both men and women, were added to the Lord.
o Or wondering about them, what this could possibly mean.
p Or ... Jesus, and you did him to death ...
q Or at his right hand.

---

to the apostles. **12:** Along with vv. 15–16, this shows that the prayer in 4.30 was answered.
13: *Solomon's Portico:* see 3.11 n.
  5.13–42: Further Jewish persecution. 17: Despite such opposition by Jewish authorities, especially the priestly party, the masses of Jews remained sympathetic; see vv. 14,26. **19:** *Angel:* compare 12.6–10. **27–32: Peter before the Sanhedrin. 29:** What *Peter* says is a summary of the whole apostolic tradition. **30:** *Hanging on a gibbet* (regarded as equivalent to crucifixion):

leader and saviour, to grant Israel repentance and forgiveness of sins.
32 And we are witnesses to all this, and so is the Holy Spirit given by God to those who are obedient to him.'

33 This touched them on the raw, and
34 they wanted to put them to death. But a member of the Council rose to his feet, a Pharisee called Gamaliel, a teacher of the law held in high regard by all the people. He moved that the men be put
35 outside for a while. Then he said, 'Men of Israel, be cautious in deciding what
36 to do with these men. Some time ago Theudas came forward, claiming to be somebody, and a number of men, about four hundred, joined him. But he was killed and his whole following was
37 broken up and disappeared. After him came Judas the Galilean at the time of the census; he induced some people to revolt under his leadership, but he too perished and his whole following was
38 scattered. And so now: keep clear of these men, I tell you; leave them alone. For if this idea of theirs or its execution is of human origin, it will collapse;
39 but if it is from God, you will never be able to put them down, and you risk finding yourselves at war with God.'
40 They took his advice. They sent for the apostles and had them flogged; then they ordered them to give up speaking in the name of Jesus, and dis-
41 charged them. So the apostles went out from the Council rejoicing that they had been found worthy to suffer in-
42 dignity for the sake of the Name. And every day they went steadily on with their teaching in the temple and in private houses, telling the good news of Jesus the Messiah.[r]

The church moves outwards

6 During this period, while disciples were growing in number, there was disagreement between those of them who spoke Greek[s] and those who spoke the language of the Jews.[t] The former party complained that their widows were being overlooked in the daily distribu-
2 tion. So the Twelve called the whole body of disciples together and said, 'It would be a grave mistake for us to neglect the word of God in order to wait at table. Therefore, friends, look
3 out seven men of good reputation from your number, men full of the Spirit and of wisdom, and we will appoint them to deal with these matters, while we devote
4 ourselves to prayer and to the ministry
5 of the Word.' This proposal proved acceptable to the whole body. They elected Stephen, a man full of faith and of the Holy Spirit, Philip, Prochorus, Nicanor, Timon, Parmenas, and Nicolas of Antioch, a former convert to
6 Judaism. These they presented to the apostles, who prayed and laid their hands on them.

7 The word of God now spread more and more widely; the number of disciples in Jerusalem went on increasing rapidly, and very many of the priests adhered to the Faith.

8 Stephen, who was full of grace and power, began to work great miracles
9 and signs among the people. But some members of the synagogue called the Synagogue of Freedmen, comprising Cyrenians and Alexandrians and people from Cilicia and Asia, came forward

r *Or* the good news that the Messiah was Jesus.
s *Literally* the Hellenists.
t *Literally* the Hebrews.

---

compare Deut.21.22–23; Gal.3.13. **33–39: Gamaliel's advice. 33:** There is some question as to whether the Romans permitted the Jews to exercise such punishment at that time; see Jn.18.31. **34:** As a *Pharisee* (see Mt.23.7 n.), *Gamaliel* (see 22.3 n.) belonged to a movement which opposed both the theology and politics of the Sadducees. **36–37:** *Theudas's* rebellion occurred some years after Gamaliel is reported to have made this speech, and long after *Judas* led his uprising about 6 A.D. **40:** *Flogged:* see Deut.25.1–3. Rabbinic law sets thirty-nine lashes as the maximum (see 2 Cor.11.24), although sentences of fewer were usual. **41:** Compare Lk.6.22; 9.23; 1 Pet.4.14–18.
  6.1–7.60: The Hellenists and Stephen.
  6.1–7: Choosing the Seven. 1: Luke uses the word *disciples* as equivalent to Christians. *Widows:* see 1 Tim.5.3 n., 9 n. **3:** *Your number* is addressed to the Hellenists, not all believers. **6:** It is evident from the following verses that they were ordained as evangelists, rather than table overseers; compare 21.8. Paul and Barnabas were set apart for mission in the same way (13.3). This passage has nothing to do with the later "deaconate" as a church order.
  6.8–15: Stephen is brought before the council. 8: By performing *miracles and signs, Stephen* functioned as an evangelist, rather than as a table waiter; see v. 2; see also 2.43; 14.3. **11:** Jesus

10 and argued with Stephen, but could not hold their own against the inspired

11 wisdom with which he spoke. They then put up men who alleged that they had heard him make blasphemous statements against Moses and against

12 God. They stirred up the people and the elders and doctors of the law, set upon him and seized him, and brought

13 him before the Council. They produced false witnesses who said, 'This man is for ever saying things against this holy

14 place and against the Law. For we have heard him say that Jesus of Nazareth will destroy this place and alter the customs handed down to us by Moses.'

15 And all who were sitting in the Council fixed their eyes on him, and his face appeared to them like the face of an angel.

7 Then the High Priest asked, 'Is this

2 so?' And he said, 'My brothers, fathers of this nation, listen to me. The God of glory appeared to Abraham our ancestor while he was in Mesopotamia,

3 before he had settled in Harran, and said: "Leave your country and your kinsfolk and come away to a land that

4 I will show you." Thereupon he left the land of the Chaldaeans and settled in Harran. From there, after his father's death, God led him to migrate to this

5 land where you now live. He gave him nothing in it to call his own, not one yard; but promised to give it in possession to him and his descendants after him, though he was then childless.

6 God spoke in these terms: "Abraham's descendants shall live as aliens in a foreign land, held in slavery and oppression for four hundred years.

7 And I will pass judgement", said God, "on the nation whose slaves they are; and after that they shall come out free,

8 and worship me in this place." He then gave him the covenant of circumcision, and so, after Isaac was born, he circumcised him on the eighth day; and

Isaac begot Jacob, and Jacob the twelve patriarchs.

'The patriarchs out of jealousy sold 9 Joseph into slavery in Egypt, but God was with him and rescued him from all 10 his troubles. He also gave him a presence and powers of mind which so commended him to Pharaoh king of Egypt, that he appointed him chief administrator for Egypt and the whole of the royal household.

'But famine struck all Egypt and 11 Canaan, and caused great hardship; and our ancestors could find nothing to eat. But Jacob heard that there was 12 food in Egypt and sent our fathers there. This was their first visit. On the 13 second visit Joseph was recognized by his brothers, and his family connections were disclosed to Pharaoh. So 14 Joseph sent an invitation to his father Jacob and all his relatives, seventy-five persons altogether; and Jacob went 15 down into Egypt. There he ended his days, as also our forefathers did. Their 16 remains were later removed to Shechem and buried in the tomb which Abraham had bought and paid for from the clan of Emmor at Shechem.

'Now as the time approached for 17 God to fulfil the promise he had made to Abraham, our nation in Egypt grew and increased in numbers. At length 18 another king, who knew nothing of Joseph, ascended the throne of Egypt. He made a crafty attack on our race, 19 and cruelly forced our ancestors to expose their children so that they should not survive. At this time Moses 20 was born. He was a fine child, and pleasing to God. For three months he was nursed in his father's house, and when he was exposed, Pharaoh's 21 daughter herself adopted him and brought him up as her own son. So 22 Moses was trained in all the wisdom of the Egyptians, a powerful speaker and a man of action.

---

also was charged with blasphemy; see Mk.14.64. **12:** The people here oppose Stephen; compare 5.26. **14:** *Destroy this place:* see Mt.24.1–3 n. A similar charge of trying to *alter the customs* was leveled against Paul (21.21).

   7.1–53: Stephen's speech. 3: Gen.12.1. **5:** See Gen.12.7; 17.8; for other discussions of Abraham, see Rom. ch. 4; Gal. ch. 3. **6:** *Four hundred years:* Gen.15.13; but according to Exod. 12.40, it was 430 years. **14:** *Seventy-five persons* are reported in Gen.46.27 Sept. **16:** This is at variance with the OT, according to which *Abraham* bought the cave of Machpelah (Gen.23) at Hebron. The purchase from *Emmor* (Hamor) was made by Jacob (Gen.33.19) and provided Joseph's burial place at *Shechem* (Josh.24.32). **22:** *Powerful speaker:* the opposite is reported in

23 'He was approaching the age of forty, when it occurred to him to look into the conditions of his fellow country
24 men the Israelites. He saw one of them being ill-treated, so he went to his aid, and avenged the victim by striking
25 down the Egyptian. He thought his fellow-countrymen would understand that God was offering them deliverance through him, but they did not under-
26 stand. The next day he came upon two of them fighting, and tried to bring them to make up their quarrel. "My men," he said, "you are brothers; why
27 are you ill-treating one another?" But the man who was at fault pushed him away. "Who set you up as a ruler and
28 judge over us?" he said. "Are you going to kill me as you killed the
29 Egyptian yesterday?" At this Moses fled the country and settled in Midianite territory. There two sons were born to him.
30 'After forty years had passed, an angel appeared to him in the flame of a burning bush in the desert near Mount
31 Sinai. Moses was amazed at the sight. But as he approached to look closely,
32 the voice of the Lord was heard: "I am the God of your fathers, the God of Abraham, Isaac, and Jacob." Moses
33 was terrified and dared not look. Then the Lord said to him, "Take off your shoes; the place where you are standing
34 is holy ground. I have indeed seen how my people are oppressed in Egypt and have heard their groans; and I have come down to rescue them. Up, then; let me send you to Egypt."
35 'This Moses, whom they had rejected with the words, "Who made you ruler and judge?"—this very man was commissioned as ruler and liberator by God himself, speaking through the angel who appeared to him in the bush.
36 It was Moses who led them out, working miracles and signs in Egypt, at the Red Sea, and for forty years in the
37 desert. It was he again who said to the Israelites, "God will raise up a prophet for you from among yourselves as he

raised me."[u] He it was who, when they 38 were assembled there in the desert, conversed with the angel who spoke to him on Mount Sinai, and with our forefathers; he received the living utterances of God, to pass on to us.
'But our forefathers would not ac- 39 cept his leadership. They thrust him aside. They wished themselves back in Egypt, and said to Aaron, "Make us 40 gods to go before us. As for that Moses, who brought us out of Egypt, we do not know what has become of him." That was when they made the 41 bull-calf, and offered sacrifice to the idol, and held a feast in honour of the thing their hands had made. But God 42 turned away from them and gave them over to the worship of the host of heaven, as it stands written in the book of the prophets: "Did you bring me victims and offerings those forty years in the desert, you house of Israel? No, 43 you carried aloft the shrine of Moloch and the star of the god Rephan, the images which you had made for your adoration. I will banish you beyond Babylon."
'Our forefathers had the Tent of the 44 Testimony in the desert, as God commanded when he told Moses to make it after the pattern which he had seen. Our fathers of the next generation, with 45 Joshua, brought it with them when they dispossessed the nations whom God drove out before them, and there it was until the time of David. David found 46 favour with God and asked to be allowed to provide a dwelling-place for the God of Jacob;[v] but it was Solomon 47 who built him a house. However, the 48 Most High does not live in houses made by men: as the prophet says, "Heaven is my throne and earth my 49 footstool. What kind of house will you build for me, says the Lord; where is my resting-place? Are not all these 50 things of my own making?"
'How stubborn you are, heathen still 51

u Or like me.
v Some witnesses read for the house of Jacob.

Exod.4.10. In accordance with Hellenistic-Jewish practice, Moses is described in terms of the Hellenistic "divine man"; see 14.11 n.; 28.6 n. 23: Later Jewish tradition divided Moses' life into three periods of forty years each. 32: Exod.3.6. 33: Exod.3.5. 34: Exod.3.7. 37: Deut.18.15. 40: Exod.32.1–6. 42: See Amos 5.25–27. 48: For Stephen, building the Temple dishonored God. 49: Isa.66.1–2; compare 1 Kgs.8.29. 51: For a similar attack, see Jesus' words in Mt.23.13–36.

at heart and deaf to the truth! You always fight against the Holy Spirit. Like
52 fathers, like sons. Was there ever a prophet whom your fathers did not persecute? They killed those who foretold the coming of the Righteous One; and now you have betrayed him and
53 murdered him, you who received the Law as God's angels gave it to you, and yet have not kept it.'
54   This touched them on the raw and
55 they ground their teeth with fury. But Stephen, filled with the Holy Spirit, and gazing intently up to heaven, saw the glory of God, and Jesus standing
56 at God's right hand. 'Look,' he said, 'there is a rift in the sky; I can see the Son of Man standing at God's right
57 hand!' At this they gave a great shout and stopped their ears. Then they made
58 one rush at him and, flinging him out of the city, set about stoning him. The witnesses laid their coats at the feet of
59 a young man named Saul. So they stoned Stephen, and as they did so, he called out, 'Lord Jesus, receive my
60 spirit.' Then he fell on his knees and cried aloud, 'Lord, do not hold this sin against them', and with that he died.
8 And Saul was among those who approved of his murder.

THIS WAS THE BEGINNING OF A TIME OF violent persecution for the church in Jerusalem; and all except the apostles were scattered over the country districts
2 of Judaea and Samaria. Stephen was given burial by certain devout men, who made a great lamentation for him.
3 Saul, meanwhile, was harrying the church; he entered house after house,

seizing men and women, and sending them to prison.
     As for those who had been scattered, 4 they went through the country preaching the Word. Philip came down to a 5 city in Samaria and began proclaiming the Messiah to them. The crowds, to a 6 man, listened eagerly to what Philip said, when they heard him and saw the miracles that he performed. For in 7 many cases of possession the unclean spirits came out with a loud cry; and many paralysed and crippled folk were cured; and there was great joy in that 8 city.
     A man named Simon had been in the 9 city for some time, and had swept the Samaritans off their feet with his magical arts, claiming to be someone great. All of them, high and low, listened 10 eagerly to him. 'This man', they said, 'is that power of God which is called "The Great Power".' They listened 11 because they had for so long been carried away by his magic. But when 12 they came to believe Philip with his good news about the kingdom of God and the name of Jesus Christ, they were baptized, men and women alike. Even Simon himself believed, and was 13 baptized, and thereupon was constantly in Philip's company. He was carried away when he saw the powerful signs and miracles that were taking place.
     The apostles in Jerusalem now heard 14 that Samaria had accepted the word of God. They sent off Peter and John, who went down there and prayed for 15 the converts, asking that they might receive the Holy Spirit. For until then 16 the Spirit had not come upon any of

---

53: *The Law as God's angels gave it to you:* contrast Gal.3.19, where the intention seems to be to reduce the Law's importance.
     7.54–60: The stoning of Stephen. 56: *Son of Man:* see Lk.12.8 n.; 22.69; Mk.2.10 n. **58:** *Saul* (Paul) appears here for the first time in the Acts account. *Stoning* was the punishment for blasphemy; see Lev.24.10–16. **59:** *Receive my spirit:* compare Lk.23.46. **60:** *Do not hold this sin:* compare Lk.23.34. The account here seems intended to stress the similarity of Stephen's death to that of Jesus'.
     8.1–40: The mission spreads beyond Jerusalem. 1: The *violent persecution* was apparently directed only against the Hellenistic Jews who shared Stephen's views. **3:** See 9.1,21; 22.4; 26.10–11; 1 Cor.15.9; Gal.1.13,23; Phil.3.6. **5:** *Samaria* is the area of the former Northern Kingdom of Israel, settled by non-Jews when it fell to Assyria (see 2 Kgs.17.24–41). **6:** Like Stephen, *Philip*, one of the Seven, performed *miracles* and preached, thus doing the apostolic work; compare 4.30; 6.8 n. **8:** *Great joy:* the Samaritans had a lively expectation of the coming of a redeemer; compare Jn.4.25. **9–24:** *Simon* the magician. **9:** His *magical arts* put *Simon* in competition with the wonder-working disciples of Jesus; compare Mk.13.22. Such competition was common, and recognized as valid, in the Hellenistic world. **15:** Acts pictures Jerusalem as the continuing center of the church, overseeing all its operations. **16:** *Spirit had not yet come:*

them. They had been baptized into the name of the Lord Jesus, that and 17 nothing more. So Peter and John laid their hands on them and they received the Holy Spirit.

18 When Simon saw that the Spirit was bestowed through the laying on of the apostles' hands, he offered them money 19 and said, 'Give me the same power too, so that when I lay my hands on anyone, he will receive the Holy Spirit.' 20 Peter replied, 'Your money go with you to damnation, because you thought 21 God's gift was for sale! You have no part nor lot in this, for you are dis-22 honest with God. Repent of this wickedness and pray the Lord to forgive you for imagining such a thing. 23 I can see that you are doomed to taste the bitter fruit and wear the fetters of 24 sin.'*w* Simon answered, 'Pray to the Lord for me yourselves and ask that none of the things you have spoken of may fall upon me.'

25 So, after giving their testimony and speaking the word of the Lord, they took the road back to Jerusalem, bringing the good news to many Samaritan villages on the way.

26 Then the angel of the Lord said to Philip, 'Start out and go south to the road that leads down from Jerusalem 27 to Gaza.' (This is the desert road.) So he set out and was on his way when he caught sight of an Ethiopian. This man was a eunuch, a high official of the Kandake, or Queen, of Ethiopia, in charge of all her treasure. He had been 28 to Jerusalem on a pilgrimage and was now on his way home, sitting in his carriage and reading aloud the prophet 29 Isaiah. The Spirit said to Philip, 'Go 30 and join the carriage.' When Philip ran up he heard him reading the prophet Isaiah and said, 'Do you understand 31 what you are reading?' He said, 'How can I understand unless someone will

give me the clue?' So he asked Philip to get in and sit beside him.

32 The passage he was reading was this. 'He was led like a sheep to be slaughtered; and like a lamb that is dumb before the shearer, he does not open his mouth. He has been humiliated and 33 has no redress. Who will be able to speak of his posterity? For he is cut off from the world of living men.'

34 'Now', said the eunuch to Philip, 'tell me, please, who it is that the prophet is speaking about here: himself or someone else?' Then Philip began. 35 Starting from this passage, he told him the good news of Jesus. As they were 36 going along the road, they came to some water. 'Look,' said the eunuch, 'here is water: what is there to prevent my being baptized?';*x* and he ordered 38 the carriage to stop. Then they both went down into the water, Philip and the eunuch; and he baptized him. When they came up out of the water 39 the Spirit snatched Philip away, and the eunuch saw no more of him, but went happily on his way. Philip ap-40 peared at Azotus, and toured the country, preaching in all the towns till he reached Caesarea.

9 MEANWHILE SAUL WAS STILL BREATHING murderous threats against the disciples of the Lord. He went to the High Priest and applied for letters to the syna-2 gogues at Damascus authorizing him to arrest anyone he found, men or women, who followed the new way, and bring them to Jerusalem. While he 3 was still on the road and nearing Damascus, suddenly a light flashed from the sky all around him. He fell 4 to the ground and heard a voice saying, 'Saul, Saul, why do you persecute me?'

w Literally you are for gall of bitterness and a fetter of unrighteousness.
x Some witnesses insert (37) Philip said, 'If you wholeheartedly believe, it is permitted.' He replied, 'I believe that Jesus Christ is the Son of God.'

---

see 2.38 n. **17:** *Received the Holy Spirit:* compare 10.44 n. **26–40:** *Philip* and the *Ethiopian eunuch.* **27:** In ancient times, Ethiopia, peopled by the Nubians, centered in what is now the Sudan; compare Ps.68.31. *Eunuch:* compare Isa.56.3–5. **28:** *Reading aloud* was the common practice, even when reading alone. **32:** Isa.53.7–8. Isa. ch. 53 was a key passage in the earliest Christian proclamation (compare Mt.8.17; Jn.12.38; 1 Pet.2.22–25). **38:** *They both went down into the water:* baptism of adults was by immersion, as Rom.6.3–4 ("By baptism we were buried with him...") indicates.
9.1–30: Saul converted. **1:** For other accounts of this conversion, see chs. 22; 26. **3:** There is no hint in Acts that Paul at this time suffered inner turmoil; Phil.3.6 indicates he felt no guilt while pursuing the law. **4:** *Persecute me:* Jesus identifies himself with the Church Paul is

5 'Tell me, Lord,' he said, 'who you are.' The voice answered, 'I am Jesus, whom
6 you are persecuting. But get up and go into the city, and you will be told what
7 you have to do.' Meanwhile the men who were travelling with him stood speechless; they heard the voice but
8 could see no one. Saul got up from the ground, but when he opened his eyes he could not see; so they led him by the hand and brought him into Damascus.
9 He was blind for three days, and took no food or drink.

10 There was a disciple in Damascus named Ananias. He had a vision in which he heard the voice of the Lord: 'Ananias!' 'Here I am, Lord', he
11 answered. The Lord said to him, 'Go at once to Straight Street, to the house of Judas, and ask for a man from Tarsus named Saul. You will find him at
12 prayer; he has had a vision of a man named Ananias coming in and laying his hands on him to restore his sight.'
13 Ananias answered, 'Lord, I have often heard about this man and all the harm he has done to thy people in Jeru-
14 salem. And he is here with authority from the chief priests to arrest all who
15 invoke thy name.' But the Lord said to him, 'You must go, for this man is my chosen instrument to bring my name before the nations and their kings, and
16 before the people of Israel. I myself will show him all that he must go through for my name's sake.'
17 So Ananias went. He entered the house, laid his hands on him and said, 'Saul, my brother, the Lord Jesus, who appeared to you on your way here, has sent me to you so that you may recover your sight, and be filled with the Holy
18 Spirit.' And immediately it seemed that scales fell from his eyes, and he regained his sight. Thereupon he was
19 baptized, and afterwards he took food and his strength returned.

He stayed some time with the dis-

ciples in Damascus. Soon he was pro- 20 claiming Jesus publicly in the synagogues: 'This', he said, is the Son of God.' All who heard were astounded. 21 'Is not this the man', they said, 'who was in Jerusalem trying to destroy those who invoke this name? Did he not come here for the sole purpose of arresting them and taking them to the chief priests?' But Saul grew more and 22 more forceful, and silenced the Jews of Damascus with his cogent proofs that Jesus was the Messiah.

As the days mounted up, the Jews 23 hatched a plot against his life; but 24 their plans became known to Saul. They kept watch on the city gates day and night so that they might murder him; but his converts took him one 25 night and let him down by the wall, lowering him in a basket.

When he reached Jerusalem he tried 26 to join the body of disciples there; but they were all afraid of him, because they did not believe that he was really a convert. Barnabas, however, took him 27 by the hand and introduced him to the apostles. He described to them how Saul had seen the Lord on his journey, and heard his voice, and how he had spoken out boldly in the name of Jesus at Damascus. Saul now stayed 28 with them, moving about freely in Jerusalem. He spoke out boldly and 29 openly in the name of the Lord, talking and debating with the Greek-speaking Jews.*y* But they planned to murder him, and when the brethren learned of 30 this they escorted him to Caesarea and saw him off to Tarsus.

MEANWHILE THE CHURCH, THROUGHOUT 31 Judaea, Galilee, and Samaria, was left in peace to build up its strength. In the fear of the Lord, upheld by the Holy Spirit, it held on its way and grew in numbers.

y Literally the Hellenists.

---

tormenting; compare Lk.10.16. **7:** The details of who *heard* and who saw are reversed in 22.9.
12: Mutually confirming visions or dreams also appear in Hellenistic religious literature.
15: *The people of Israel:* Acts reports that Paul regularly preached to the Jews (13.15; 14.1; 17.1–2); his own letters give a different impression (Gal.1.16; 2.8). **17:** Compare 22.12–16.
20: At this point, the account in Acts begins to diverge significantly from Paul's account of these events in Gal.1.13–2.10. **23–25:** Plot against Saul. **23:** With *a plot against his life,* the prediction in v. 16 begins its fulfillment. **25:** Compare 2 Cor.11.32–33. **26–30: Saul in Jerusalem.**
27: Paul gives a different account of these events in Gal.1.16–20.
9.31–43: Peter performs two miracles. Mighty deeds were understood to accredit authorita-

32 Peter was making a general tour, in the course of which he went down to visit God's people at Lydda. There he found a man named Aeneas who had been bed-ridden with paralysis for 34 eight years. Peter said to him, 'Aeneas, Jesus Christ cures you; get up and make your bed', and immediately he stood 35 up. All who lived in Lydda and Sharon saw him; and they turned to the Lord.

36 In Joppa there was a disciple named Tabitha (in Greek, Dorcas, meaning a gazelle), who filled her days with acts of 37 kindness and charity. At that time she fell ill and died; and they washed her 38 body and laid it in a room upstairs. As Lydda was near Joppa, the disciples, who had heard that Peter was there, sent two men to him with the urgent request, 'Please come over to us with- 39 out delay.' Peter thereupon went off with them. When he arrived they took him upstairs to the room, where all the widows came and stood round him in tears, showing him the shirts and coats that Dorcas used to make while she 40 was with them. Peter sent them all outside, and knelt down and prayed. Then, turning towards the body, he said, 'Get up, Tabitha.' She opened her 41 eyes, saw Peter, and sat up. He gave her his hand and helped her to her feet. Then he called the members of the congregation and the widows and 42 showed her to them alive. The news spread all over Joppa, and many came 43 to believe in the Lord. Peter stayed on in Joppa for some time with one Simon, a tanner.

10 At Caesarea there was a man named Cornelius, a centurion in the Italian 2 Cohort, as it was called. He was a religious man, and he and his whole family joined in the worship of God. He gave generously to help the Jewish people, and was regular in his prayers 3 to God. One day about three in the afternoon he had a vision in which he clearly saw an angel of God, who came into his room and said, 'Cornelius!' He stared at him in terror. 'What is it, 4 my lord?' he asked. The angel said, 'Your prayers and acts of charity have gone up to heaven to speak for you before God. And now send to Joppa 5 for a man named Simon, also called Peter: he is lodging with another Simon, 6 a tanner, whose house is by the sea.' So when the angel who was speaking 7 to him had gone, he summoned two of his servants and a military orderly who 8 was a religious man, told them the whole story, and sent them to Joppa. Next day, while they were still on 9 their way and approaching the city, about noon Peter went up on the roof to pray. He grew hungry and wanted 10 something to eat. While they were getting it ready, he fell into a trance. He saw a rift in the sky, and a thing 11 coming down that looked like a great sheet of sail-cloth. It was slung by the four corners, and was being lowered to the ground. In it he saw creatures of 12 every kind, whatever walks or crawls or flies. Then there was a voice which 13 said to him, 'Up, Peter, kill and eat.' But Peter said, 'No, Lord, no: I have 14 never eaten anything profane or unclean.' The voice came again a second 15 time: 'It is not for you to call profane what God counts clean.' This hap- 16 pened three times; and then the thing was taken up again into the sky.

While Peter was still puzzling over 17 the meaning of the vision he had seen, the messengers of Cornelius had been asking the way to Simon's house, and now arrived at the entrance. They 18 called out and asked if Simon Peter was lodging there. But Peter was think- 19 ing over the vision, when the Spirit said to him, 'Some*z* men are here look-

z One witness reads Two; *others read* Three.

---

tive persons; see 14.11 n. **35:** In Acts, miracles validly lead to faith; but compare Jn.20.29; Mk.8.12; Mt.16.4. **36:** For similarities between this account and a miracle of Jesus, see Mk.5.37-42. **39:** On *widows,* compare 1 Tim.5.3 n., 9 n.

10.1-48: Peter and Cornelius. 1: *Caesarea,* the Roman capital of the provinces of Judea and Samaria, was the official residence of the procurators who ruled them. A *centurion* commanded one hundred men. A *cohort* was a military unit, part of a legion. **2:** *Worship of God,* lit. he was a God-fearer: a term applied to Gentiles who observed Jewish rites without becoming converts; compare 13.50; 16.14. **14:** *Profane or unclean:* see Lev. ch. 11. **15:** The voice annuls Jewish food laws, and thus the distinction between Jew and Gentile; see also v. 28; Mk.7.1-23. **17:** *Cornelius:* see v. 3. **19-22:** This is another case of mutually confirming visions; see 9.12 n.

20 ing for you; make haste and go down-stairs. You may go with them without any misgiving, for it was I who sent
21 them.' Peter came down to the men and said, 'You are looking for me? Here I am. What brings you here?'
22 'We are from the centurion Cornelius,' they replied, 'a good and religious man, acknowledged as such by the whole Jewish nation. He was directed by a holy angel to send for you to his house and to listen to what
23 you have to say.' So Peter asked them in and gave them a night's lodging. Next day he set out with them, accompanied by some members of the congregation at Joppa.
24 The day after that, he arrived at Caesarea. Cornelius was expecting them and had called together his rela-
25 tives and close friends. When Peter arrived, Cornelius came to meet him, and bowed to the ground in deep rever-
26 ence. But Peter raised him to his feet and said, 'Stand up; I am a man like
27 anyone else.' Still talking with him he went in and found a large gathering.
28 He said to them, 'I need not tell you that a Jew is forbidden by his religion to visit or associate with a man of another race; yet God has shown me clearly that I must not call any man
29 profane or unclean. That is why I came here without demur when you sent for me. May I ask what was your reason for sending?'
30 Cornelius said, 'Four days ago, just about this time, I was in the house here saying the afternoon prayers, when suddenly a man in shining robes stood
31 before me. He said: "Cornelius, your prayer has been heard and your acts of
32 charity remembered before God. Send to Joppa, then, to Simon Peter, and ask him to come. He is lodging in the house
33 of Simon the tanner, by the sea." So I sent to you there and then; it was kind of you to come. And now we are all met here before God, to hear all

that the Lord has ordered you to say.'
34 Peter began: 'I now see how true it
35 is that God has no favourites, but that in every nation the man who is god-fearing and does what is right is ac-
36 ceptable to him. He sent his word to the Israelites and gave the good news of peace through Jesus Christ, who is Lord of all. I need not tell you what
37 happened lately all over the land of the Jews, starting from Galilee after the baptism proclaimed by John. You
38 know about Jesus of Nazareth, how God anointed him with the Holy Spirit and with power. He went about doing good and healing all who were oppressed by the devil, for God was with him. And we can bear witness to all
39 that he did in the Jewish country-side and in Jerusalem. He was put to death
40 by hanging on a gibbet; but God raised him to life on the third day, and al-
41 lowed him to appear, not to the whole people, but to witnesses whom God had chosen in advance—to us, who ate and drank with him after he rose from the dead. He commanded us to pro-
42 claim him to the people, and affirm that he is the one who has been designated by God as judge of the living and the dead. It is to him that all the
43 prophets testify, declaring that everyone who trusts in him receives forgiveness of sins through his name.'
44 Peter was still speaking when the Holy Spirit came upon all who were
45 listening to the message. The believers who had come with Peter, men of Jewish birth, were astonished that the gift of the Holy Spirit should have been
46 poured out even on Gentiles. For they could hear them speaking in tongues of ecstasy and acclaiming the greatness of
47 God. Then Peter spoke: 'Is anyone prepared to withhold the water for baptism from these persons, who have received the Holy Spirit just as we did ourselves?' Then he ordered them to
48 be baptized in the name of Jesus Christ.

23: *Some members:* in 11.12 there are six who function as witnesses at this turning point in the life of the church. **30:** *Four days ago:* the Gr. is obscure for this. **34–35:** These verses justify the Gentile mission which now begins. **36–38:** *Lord of all*, as well as *doing good* and *healing*, were claims commonly made for deities and rulers in the Hellenistic world. **41:** *Who ate and drank:* compare 1.6; Lk.24.30,42. **42:** *As judge:* compare 17.31. **43:** *All the prophets:* see 3.24. *Everyone:* compare 13.39. **44–46:** The coming of the *Holy Spirit* is here identified with *speaking in tongues of ecstasy:* see 8.15–17 where the same may be implied. **48:** *Baptized:* see 2.38 n.

After that they asked him to stay on with them for a time.

11 News came to the apostles and the members of the church in Judaea that Gentiles too had accepted the word of God; and when Peter came up to Jeru-2 salem those who were of Jewish birth 3 raised the question with him. 'You have been visiting men who are un-circumcised,' they said, 'and sitting at 4 table with them!' Peter began by laying before them the facts as they had happened.

5 'I was in the city of Joppa', he said, 'at prayer; and while in a trance I had a vision: a thing was coming down that looked like a great sheet of sail-cloth, slung by the four corners and lowered 6 from the sky till it reached me. I looked intently to make out what was in it and I saw four-footed creatures of the earth, wild beasts, and things that crawl or 7 fly. Then I heard a voice saying to me, 8 "Up, Peter, kill and eat." But I said, "No, Lord, no: nothing profane or un-9 clean has ever entered my mouth." A voice from heaven answered a second time, "It is not for you to call profane 10 what God counts clean." This hap-pened three times, and then they were 11 all drawn up again into the sky. At that moment three men, who had been sent to me from Caesarea, arrived at the 12 house where I was*a* staying; and the Spirit told me to go with them.*b* My six companions here came with me and 13 we went into the man's house. He told us how he had seen an angel standing in his house who said, "Send to Joppa 14 for Simon also called Peter. He will speak words that will bring salvation 15 to you and all your household." Hardly had I begun speaking, when the Holy Spirit came upon them, just as upon 16 us at the beginning. Then I recalled what the Lord had said: "John bap-tized with water, but you will be bap-tized with the Holy Spirit." God gave 17 them no less a gift than he gave us when we put our trust in the Lord Jesus Christ, then how could I pos-sibly stand in God's way?'

When they heard this their doubts 18 were silenced. They gave praise to God and said, 'This means that God has granted life-giving repentance to the Gentiles also.'

MEANWHILE THOSE WHO HAD BEEN 19 scattered after the persecution that arose over Stephen made their way to Phoenicia, Cyprus, and Antioch, bring-ing the message to Jews only and to no others. But there were some natives of 20 Cyprus and Cyrene among them, and these, when they arrived at Antioch, began to speak to Gentiles as well, tell-ing them the good news of the Lord Jesus. The power of the Lord was with 21 them, and a great many became be-lievers, and turned to the Lord.

The news reached the ears of the 22 church in Jerusalem; and they sent Barnabas to Antioch. When he arrived 23 and saw the divine grace at work, he rejoiced, and encouraged them all to hold fast to the Lord with resolute hearts; for he was a good man, full of 24 the Holy Spirit and of faith. And large numbers were won over to the Lord.

He then went off to Tarsus to look 25 for Saul; and when he had found him, 26 he brought him to Antioch. For a whole year the two of them lived in fellow-ship with the congregation there, and gave instruction to large numbers. It was in Antioch that the disciples first got the name of Christians.

During this period some prophets 27 came down from Jerusalem to Antioch.

a Some witnesses read we were.
b Some witnesses add making no distinctions; *others add* without any misgiving, *as in 10. 20.*

11.1–18: Peter in Jerusalem. 2: Of *Jewish birth* (or, of the circumcision party): compare Gal.2.12. **12:** These *companions* are apparently to help Peter in his presentation. **15:** *At the beginning:* i.e. Pentecost; compare 2.1–4 (and nn.); 10.44–46 (and n.). **16:** See 1.5 n. **18:** *Repentance* is also used as a synonym for faith in 5.31.

11.19–30: Expanding missionary activity among Gentiles. 19: *Antioch,* the third largest city in the Roman Empire, was the official residence of the Roman administrator of the province of Syria. Here, it now becomes the center of the Gentile mission. **20:** For the first time, *Gentiles* are evangelized as a general practice. Vv. 19–20 reflect Acts' missionary scheme: first to *Jews,* then to *Gentiles.* **22:** *They sent Barnabas,* apparently because the Gentile mission was still regarded with suspicion; compare 15.1; Gal.2.11–14. **26:** *The name of Christians,* coined by outsiders, was not necessarily derisive in intent, as some interpreters assert. **27:** *Prophets:* compare 13.1;

28 One of them, Agabus by name, was inspired to stand up and predict a severe and world-wide famine, which in fact
29 occurred in the reign of Claudius. So the disciples agreed to make a contribution, each according to his means, for the relief of their fellow-Christians in
30 Judaea. This they did, and sent it off to the elders, in the charge of Barnabas and Saul.

12 IT WAS ABOUT THIS TIME THAT KING Herod attacked certain members of the
2 church. He beheaded James, the brother
3 of John, and then, when he saw that the Jews approved, proceeded to arrest Peter also. This happened during the
4 festival of Unleavened Bread. Having secured him, he put him in prison under a military guard, four squads of four men each, meaning to produce him in
5 public after Passover. So Peter was kept in prison under constant watch, while the church kept praying fervently for him to God.
6 On the very night before Herod had planned to bring him forward, Peter was asleep between two soldiers, secured by two chains, while outside the doors sentries kept guard over the
7 prison. All at once an angel of the Lord stood there, and the cell was ablaze with light. He tapped Peter on the shoulder and woke him. 'Quick! Get up', he said, and the chains fell
8 away from his wrists. The angel then said to him, 'Do up your belt and put your sandals on.' He did so. 'Now wrap your cloak round you and follow
9 me.' He followed him out, with no idea that the angel's intervention was real:
10 he thought it was just a vision. But they passed the first guard-post, then the second, and reached the iron gate leading out into the city, which opened for them of its own accord. And so they came out and walked the length of one street; and the angel left him.

Then Peter came to himself. 'Now I 11 know it is true,' he said; 'the Lord has sent his angel and rescued me from Herod's clutches and from all that the Jewish people were expecting.' When 12 he realized how things stood, he made for the house of Mary, the mother of John Mark, where a large company was at prayer. He knocked at the outer 13 door and a maid called Rhoda came to answer it. She recognized Peter's voice 14 and was so overjoyed that instead of opening the door she ran in and announced that Peter was standing outside. 'You are crazy', they told her; 15 but she insisted that it was so. Then they said, 'It must be his guardian angel.'

Meanwhile Peter went on knocking, 16 and when they opened the door and saw him, they were astounded. With a 17 movement of the hand he signed to them to keep quiet, and told them how the Lord had brought him out of prison. 'Report this to James and the members of the church', he said. Then he left the house and went off elsewhere.

When morning came, there was con- 18 sternation among the soldiers: what could have become of Peter? Herod 19 made close search, but failed to find him, so he interrogated the guards and ordered their execution.

Afterwards he left Judaea to reside 20 for a time at Caesarea. He had for some time been furiously angry with the people of Tyre and Sidon, who now by common agreement presented themselves at his court. There they won over Blastus the royal chamberlain, and sued

---

15.32; 21.9. **28:** *Agabus:* see 21.10–12. *Claudius* was emperor of Rome in 41–54 A.D. Although there was a famine in Palestine about 46-48, there is no record of a *world-wide famine.* **29:** There is some confusion as to when the *contribution* was sent. According to this account, it was sent prior to the Apostolic Council (ch. 15). According to Gal.2.10, it occurred after the Council, as is implied in Acts 24.17; compare Rom.15.25–29. The reference to Claudius (v. 28) makes either time possible.

   12.1–25: Herod's persecution. 1: *Herod* Agrippa I ruled as *king* of Judea 41–44 A.D., by the appointment of the Emperor Claudius. **2:** *James, John:* see Mk.1.19. On the fate of *John,* the NT is silent. **10:** The wondrous opening of locked doors is a widespread theme in Hellenistic stories. **12:** *John Mark:* 12.25; 13.5,13; Col.4.10; Philem.24; 2 Tim.4.11. **15:** In popular thought, each person had a *guardian angel* who was identical in appearance to the person. **17:** From this point on, *James,* Jesus' brother, emerges as the leader of the church in Jerusalem (compare Gal.1.19; 2.12), and there is no further mention of the Twelve. Peter reappears only at 15.7. **20:** Since the time of Solomon, Phoenicia *drew its supplies* from Judea; see 1 Kgs.5.9–11;

for peace, because their country drew its supplies from the king's territory. 21 So, on an appointed day, attired in his royal robes and seated on the rostrum, 22 Herod harangued them; and the populace shouted back, 'It is a god speak- 23 ing, not a man!' Instantly an angel of the Lord struck him down, because he had usurped the honour due to God; he was eaten up with worms and died. 24 Meanwhile the word of God continued to grow and spread.

25 Barnabas and Saul, their task fulfilled, returned from Jerusalem,*c* taking John Mark with them.

The church breaks barriers

13 THERE WERE AT ANTIOCH, IN THE congregation there, certain prophets and teachers: Barnabas, Simeon called Niger, Lucius of Cyrene, Manaen, who had been at the court of Prince 2 Herod, and Saul. While they were keeping a fast and offering worship to the Lord, the Holy Spirit said, 'Set Barnabas and Saul apart for me, to do the work to which I have called them.' 3 Then, after further fasting and prayer, they laid their hands on them and let them go.

4 So these two, sent out on their mission by the Holy Spirit, came down to Seleucia, and from there sailed to 5 Cyprus. Arriving at Salamis, they declared the word of God in the Jewish synagogues. They had John with them 6 as their assistant. They went through the whole island as far as Paphos, and there they came upon a sorcerer, a Jew who posed as a prophet, Bar-Jesus by 7 name. He was in the retinue of the Governor, Sergius Paulus, an intelligent man, who had sent for Barnabas and Saul and wanted to hear the word of God. This Elymas the sorcerer (so *a* his name may be translated) opposed them, trying to turn the Governor away from the Faith. But Saul, also 9 known as Paul, filled with the Holy Spirit, fixed his eyes on him and said, 10 'You swindler, you rascal, son of the devil and enemy of all goodness, will you never stop falsifying the straight ways of the Lord? Look now, the hand 11 of the Lord strikes: you shall be blind, and for a time you shall not see the sunlight.' Instantly mist and darkness came over him and he groped about for someone to lead him by the hand. When the Governor saw what had 12 happened he became a believer, deeply impressed by what he learned about the Lord.

Leaving Paphos, Paul and his com- 13 panions went by sea to Perga in Pamphylia; John, however, left them and returned to Jerusalem. From Perga they 14 continued their journey as far as Pisidian Antioch. On the Sabbath they went to synagogue and took their seats; and after the readings from the 15 Law and the prophets, the officials of the synagogue sent this message to them: 'Friends, if you have anything to say to the people by way of exhortation, let us hear it.' Paul rose, made a 16 gesture with his hand, and began:

'Men of Israel and you who worship our God, listen to me! The God of this 17 people of Israel chose our fathers. When they were still living as aliens in Egypt he made them into a nation and

c Some witnesses read their task fulfilled, returned to Jerusalem; *or, as it might be rendered,* their task at Jerusalem fulfilled, returned.

Ezek.27.17. **23:** Josephus (a first-century Jewish historian) confirms Herod's sudden death (*Ant.* xix, 8.2) and the detail that he was acclaimed as divine. After the death of Herod Agrippa I, Judea reverted to an imperial province, ruled by governors; see 23.24.

13.1–14.28: Paul's missionary travels (first journey). 1–3: Barnabas and Saul set apart. 1: *Niger* means black. *Prince Herod* is Herod Antipas, the Tetrarch, not the Herod of 12.1. **2:** Acts' conviction that the *Holy Spirit* guided the Church is again evident here. **3:** The laying on of *hands* commissioned persons for special tasks; compare 6.6. **4–12: Elymas confounded. 4:** Travelers at that time *sailed* on any available boat; passenger ships plying regular routes were unknown. **6:** *Paphos* was the capital of Cyprus. **8:** The meaning of *Elymas* is unknown. **9:** *Paul* a Latin name, would be appropriate for a Roman citizen (22.25–29); but see 1.23 n. **11:** Acts' opposition to magic is clear here; compare also 8.9–11; 19.13–20. **13–15: To Pisidian Antioch. 13:** There was some altercation accompanying *John*'s leaving, as 15.38 makes clear. **14:** *Pisidian Antioch*, a remotely situated Roman colony (see 16.12 n.), was in the southern part of the province of Galatia, as were the other cities visited on this "journey." **16–41: Paul's sermon. 17:** As did Peter (13.25) and Stephen (7.2–50), Paul recounts the origins of the Jewish people as

brought them out of that country with
18 arm outstretched. For some forty years
he bore with their conduct[d] in the
19 desert. Then in the Canaanite country
he overthrew seven nations, whose
lands he gave them to be their heritage
20 for some four hundred and fifty years,
and afterwards appointed judges for
them until the time of the prophet
Samuel.
21 'Then they asked for a king and God
gave them Saul the son of Kish, a man
of the tribe of Benjamin, who reigned
22 for forty years. Then he removed him
and set up David as their king, giving
him his approval in these words: "I
have found David son of Jesse to be a
man after my own heart, who will carry
23 out all my purposes." This is the man
from whose posterity God, as he promised, has brought Israel a saviour,
24 Jesus. John made ready for his coming
by proclaiming baptism as a token of
repentance to the whole people of
25 Israel. And when John was nearing the
end of his course, he said, "I am not
what you think I am. No, after me
comes one whose shoes I am not fit to
unfasten."
26 'My brothers, you who come of the
stock of Abraham, and others among
you who revere our God, we are the
people to whom the message of this
27 salvation has been sent. The people of
Jerusalem and their rulers did not
recognize him, or understand the
words of the prophets which are read
Sabbath by Sabbath; indeed they fulfilled them by condemning him.
28 Though they failed to find grounds for
the sentence of death, they asked Pilate
29 to have him executed. And when they
had carried out all that the scriptures
said about him, they took him down
from the gibbet and laid him in a tomb.
30 But God raised him from the dead;
31 and there was a period of many days
during which he appeared to those who
had come up with him from Galilee to
Jerusalem.

'They are now his witnesses before
our nation, and we are here to give you 32
the good news that God, who made the
promise to the fathers, has fulfilled it 33
for the children[e] by raising Jesus from
the dead, as indeed it stands written, in
the second[f] Psalm: "You are my son;
this day I have begotten you." Again, 34
that he raised him from the dead, never
again to revert to corruption, he declares in these words: "I will give you
the blessings promised to David, holy
and sure." This is borne out by another 35
passage: "Thou wilt not let thy loyal
servant suffer corruption." As for 36
David, when he had served the purpose
of God in his own generation, he died,
and was gathered to his fathers, and
suffered corruption; but the one whom 37
God raised up did not suffer corruption; and you must understand, my 38
brothers, that it is through him that
forgiveness of sins is now being proclaimed to you. It is through him that 39
everyone who has faith is acquitted of
everything for which there was no
acquittal under the Law of Moses.
Beware, then, lest you bring down 40
upon yourselves the doom proclaimed
by the prophets: "See this, you scoffers, 41
wonder, and begone; for I am doing a
deed in your days, a deed which you
will never believe when you are told of
it."'

As they were leaving the synagogue 42
they were asked to come again and
speak on these subjects next Sabbath;
and after the congregation had dis- 43
persed, many Jews and gentile worshippers went along with Paul and
Barnabas, who spoke to them and urged
them to hold fast to the grace of God.
On the following Sabbath almost the 44
whole city gathered to hear the word
of God. When the Jews saw the crowds, 45
they were filled with jealous resentment, and contradicted what Paul said,
with violent abuse. But Paul and Bar- 46

d *Some witnesses read* he sustained them.
e *Some witnesses read* our children; *others read* us their
children.   f *Some witnesses read* first.

---

the necessary presupposition of understanding the Christian faith. **18b–19a:** Compare Deut.7.1.
20: *Afterwards* refers to the occupation of Canaan (v. 19), not the 450 years; the Greek text is
not entirely clear. **22:** Compare 1 Sam.13.14; Ps.89.21. **25:** Compare Mk.1.7; Lk.3.16. **33:**
Ps.2.7. **35–37:** Compare 2.25–31. **35:** Ps.16.10. **41:** Hab.1.5. Paul's more sophisticated Christology, and his eschatological concerns, characteristic of his letters, are absent from this sermon.
42–52: Paul and Barnabas turn to Gentiles. 46: This point is repeated in 18.6 and 28.28; compare

nabas were outspoken in their reply. 'It was necessary', they said, 'that the word of God should be declared to you first. But since you reject it and thus condemn yourselves as unworthy of eternal life, we now turn to the Gen-

47 tiles. For these are our instructions from the Lord: "I have appointed you to be a light for the Gentiles, and a means of salvation to earth's farthest

48 bounds."' When the Gentiles heard this, they were overjoyed and thankfully acclaimed the word of the Lord, and those who were marked out for

49 eternal life became believers. So the word of the Lord spread far and wide

50 through the region. But the Jews stirred up feeling among the women of standing who were worshippers, and among the leading men of the city; a persecution was started against Paul and Barnabas, and they were expelled

51 from the district. So they shook the dust off their feet in protest against them

52 and went to Iconium. And the converts were filled with joy and with the Holy Spirit.

14 At Iconium similarly they went[g] into the Jewish synagogue and spoke to such purpose that a large body both of Jews and Gentiles became believers.

2 But the unconverted Jews stirred up the Gentiles and poisoned their minds

3 against the Christians. For some time Paul and Barnabas stayed on and spoke boldly and openly in reliance on the Lord; and he confirmed the message of his grace by causing signs and miracles

4 to be worked at their hands. The mass of the townspeople were divided, some siding with the Jews, others with the

5 apostles. But when a move was made by Gentiles and Jews together, with the connivance of the city authorities,

6 to maltreat them and stone them, they got wind of it and made their escape to the Lycaonian cities of Lystra and

Derbe and the surrounding country, where they continued to spread the 7 good news.

At Lystra sat a crippled man, lame 8 from birth, who had never walked in his life. This man listened while Paul 9 was speaking. Paul fixed his eyes on him and saw that he had the faith to be cured, so he said to him in a loud voice, 10 'Stand up straight on your feet'; and he sprang up and started to walk. When 11 the crowds saw what Paul had done, they shouted, in their native Lycaonian, 'The gods have come down to us in human form.' And they called Barna- 12 bas Jupiter, and Paul they called Mercury, because he was the spokesman. And the priest of Jupiter, whose temple 13 was just outside the city, brought oxen and garlands to the gates, and he and all the people were about to offer sacrifice.

But when the apostles Barnabas and 14 Paul heard of it, they tore their clothes and rushed into the crowd shouting, 'Men, what is this that you are doing? 15 We are only human beings, no less mortal than you. The good news we bring tells you to turn from these follies to the living God, who made heaven and earth and sea and everything in them. In past ages he allowed all 16 nations to go their own way; and yet he 17 has not left you without some clue to his nature, in the kindness he shows: he sends you rain from heaven and crops in their seasons, and gives you food and good cheer in plenty.'

With these words they barely man- 18 aged to prevent the crowd from offering sacrifice to them.

Then Jews from Antioch and Icon- 19 ium came on the scene and won over the crowds. They stoned Paul, and dragged him out of the city, thinking him dead. The converts formed a ring 20

g *Or* At Iconium they went together . . .

also 19.8–9. **50:** The risen Jesus had foretold such persecution of Paul; see 9.16. **51:** They thus follow a command of Jesus: Lk.9.5; compare 10.10–11. **14.1–7: On to Iconium. 1:** *Iconium,* like Antioch a Roman colony, was a commercial center for its area (see 13.14 n.). **4:** Paul and Barnabas are called *apostles* only here and in v. 14; the term is normally reserved in Acts for the leaders in Jerusalem (compare 15.2), although Paul himself claimed to be an apostle: see 1 Cor.9.1; Gal.1.1. **8–20: Paul and Barnabas at Lystra. 8:** *Lystra* was also a Roman colony. **11:** The idea of "divine men" was common in the Hellenistic world; great deeds were attributed to divine power in such persons; compare 28.6 n. **12:** *Jupiter:* lit. Zeus. *Mercury:* lit. Hermes, the god who, in Greek mythology, brought men messages from the gods. **15:** Ps.146.6; compare Acts 4.24. Peter also rejected any attribute of divinity (10.26). **19:** See

round him, and he got to his feet and went into the city. Next day he left with Barnabas for Derbe.

21 After bringing the good news to that town, where they gained many converts, they returned to Lystra, then to 22 Iconium, and then to Antioch, heartening the converts and encouraging them to be true to their religion. They warned them that to enter the kingdom of God we must pass through many hardships. 23 They also appointed elders for them in each congregation, and with prayer and fasting committed them to the Lord in whom they had put their faith.

24 Then they passed through Pisidia and 25 came into Pamphylia. When they had given the message at Perga, they went 26 down to Attalia, and from there set sail for Antioch, where they had originally been commended to the grace of God for the task which they had now com-27 pleted. When they arrived and had called the congregation together, they reported all that God had done through them, and how he had thrown open the gates of faith to the Gentiles. 28 And they stayed for some time with the disciples there.

15 NOW CERTAIN PERSONS WHO HAD COME down from Judaea began to teach the brotherhood that those who were not circumcised in accordance with Mosaic 2 practice could not be saved. That brought them into fierce dissension and controversy with Paul and Barnabas. And so it was arranged that these two and some others from Antioch should go up to Jerusalem to see the apostles and elders about this question.

3 They were sent on their way by the congregation, and travelled through Phoenicia and Samaria, telling the full story of the conversion of the Gentiles. The news caused great rejoicing among all the Christians there.

When they reached Jerusalem they 4 were welcomed by the church and the apostles and elders, and reported all that God had done through them. Then 5 some of the Pharisaic party who had become believers came forward and said, 'They must be circumcised and told to keep the Law of Moses.'

The apostles and elders held a meet- 6 ing to look into this matter; and, after 7 a long debate, Peter rose and addressed them. 'My friends,' he said, 'in the early days, as you yourselves know, God made his choice among you and ordained that from my lips the Gentiles should hear and believe the message of the Gospel. And God, who can read 8 men's minds, showed his approval of them by giving the Holy Spirit to them, as he did to us. He made no difference be- 9 tween them and us; for he purified their hearts by faith. Then why do you now 10 provoke God by laying on the shoulders of these converts a yoke which neither we nor our fathers were able to bear? No, we believe that it is by the 11 grace of the Lord Jesus that we are saved, and so are they.'

At that the whole company fell silent 12 and listened to Barnabas and Paul as they told of all the signs and miracles that God had worked among the Gentiles through them.

When they had finished speaking, 13 James summed up: 'My friends,' he said, 'listen to me. Simeon has told 14 how it first happened that God took notice of the Gentiles, to choose from among them a people to bear his name; and this agrees with the words of the 15 prophets, as Scripture has it:

"Thereafter I will return and rebuild 16
   the fallen house of David;
even from its ruins I will rebuild it,
   and set it up again,
that they may seek the Lord—all the 17
   rest of mankind,

---

2 Cor.11.25. **21–28**: *Return to Antioch.* **23**: *Prayer and fasting:* compare 13.3. **28**: Such inexact time references are typical of Acts, and make the construction of historical chronology impossible.

15.1–35: The Apostolic Council. 2: This is the *controversy* with which Paul's letter to the Galatians deals, although in that letter, it occurs much later in Paul's career (see Gal.2.1). **7**: According to Gal.2.7–8, Peter was sent to the Jews. **8**: Compare 10.44–45; 11.15. The conversion of Cornelius is the classic example in Acts. **10**: That the law was not universally regarded as a burdensome yoke is clear from Ps.19.7–11. **13**: *James* is at this time clearly the head of the mother church in Jerusalem; see 12.17 n. **14**: Although a *Simeon* is mentioned in

and the Gentiles, whom I have claimed for my own.

Thus says the Lord, whose work it is,
18 made known long ago.'

19 'My judgement therefore is that we should impose no irksome restrictions on those of the Gentiles who are turn-
20 ing to God, but instruct them by letter to abstain from things polluted by contact with idols, from fornication, from anything that has been strangled, and
21 from blood.[h] Moses, after all, has never lacked spokesmen in every town for generations past; he is read in the synagogues Sabbath by Sabbath.'

22 Then the apostles and elders, with the agreement of the whole church, resolved to choose representatives and send them to Antioch with Paul and Barnabas. They chose two leading men in the community, Judas Barsabbas
23 and Silas, and gave them this letter to deliver:

'We, the apostles and elders, send greetings as brothers to our brothers of gentile origin in Antioch, Syria, and
24 Cilicia. Forasmuch as we have heard that some of our number, without any instructions from us, have[i] disturbed you with their talk and unsettled your
25 minds, we have resolved unanimously to send to you our chosen representatives with our well-beloved Barnabas
26 and Paul, who have devoted themselves to the cause of our Lord Jesus
27 Christ. We are therefore sending Judas and Silas, who will themselves confirm
28 this by word of mouth. It is the decision of the Holy Spirit, and our decision, to lay no further burden
29 upon you beyond these essentials: you are to abstain from meat that has been offered to idols, from blood, from anything that has been strangled,[j] and from fornication.[k] If you keep yourselves free from these things you will be doing right. Farewell.'

So they were sent off on their jour- 30
ney and travelled down to Antioch, where they called the congregation together, and delivered the letter. When 31 it was read, they all rejoiced at the encouragement it brought. Judas and 32 Silas, who were prophets themselves, said much to encourage and strengthen the members, and, after spending some 33 time there, were dismissed with the good wishes of the brethren, to return to those who had sent them.[l] But Paul 35 and Barnabas stayed on at Antioch, and there, along with many others, they taught and preached the word of the Lord.

Paul leads the advance

AFTER A WHILE PAUL SAID TO BARNABAS, 36
'Ought we not to go back now to see how our brothers are faring in the various towns where we proclaimed the word of the Lord?' Barnabas want- 37 ed to take John Mark with them; but 38 Paul judged that the man who had deserted them in Pamphylia and had not gone on to share in their work was not the man to take with them now. The dispute was so sharp that they 39 parted company. Barnabas took Mark with him and sailed for Cyprus, while 40 Paul chose Silas. He started on his journey, commended by the brothers to the grace of the Lord, and travelled 41 through Syria and Cilicia bringing new strength to the congregations.

He went on to Derbe and to Lystra, 16 and there he found a disciple named Timothy, the son of a Jewish Christian

h *Some witnesses omit* from fornication; *others omit* from anything that has been strangled; *some add (after* blood) and to refrain from doing to others what they would not like done to themselves.
i *Some witnesses read* have gone out and . . .
j *Some witnesses omit* from anything that has been strangled.
k *Some witnesses omit* and from fornication; *and some add* and refrain from doing to others what you would not like done to yourselves.
l *Some witnesses add* (34) But Silas decided to remain there.

13.1 in connection with Antioch, a center for the Gentile mission, Luke clearly refers here to Peter. 20: Paul does not mention any such compromise (see Gal.2.6,9–10); he seems to contradict it in 1 Cor.8.8; 10.27. 24–29: The apostolic letter. 24: *Without any instructions:* a different impression is given in Gal.2.12 ("from James"). 29: Observance of these rules would make possible table-fellowship with law-observing Jewish-Christians; see Lev. chs. 17–18.

15.36–18.22: Paul's further missionary travels (second journey). 36–41: Paul and Barnabas separate. 36: See 14.28 n. **38:** See 13.13. **39:** In Gal.2.13, Paul's dispute with *Barnabas* turned on the more basic issue of table-fellowship between Jewish and Gentile Christians. **16.1–5: Timothy chosen. 1:** *Timothy* was a trusted associate (2 Cor.1.19; Rom.16.21), whom Paul

2 mother and a Gentile father. He was well spoken of by the Christians at
3 Lystra and Iconium, and Paul wanted to have him in his company when he left the place. So he took him and circumcised him, out of consideration for the Jews who lived in those parts; for they all knew that his father was a
4 Gentile. As they made their way from town to town they handed on the decisions taken by the apostles and elders in Jerusalem and enjoined their ob-
5 servance. And so, day by day, the congregations grew stronger in faith and increased in numbers.
6 They travelled through the Phrygian and Galatian region,[m] because they were prevented by the Holy Spirit from delivering the message in the province
7 of Asia; and when they approached the Mysian border they tried to enter Bithynia; but the Spirit of Jesus would
8 not allow them, so they skirted[n] Mysia
9 and reached the coast at Troas. During the night a vision came to Paul: a Macedonian stood there appealing to him and saying, 'Come across to Mace-
10 donia and help us.' After he had seen this vision we at once set about getting a passage to Macedonia, concluding that God had called us to bring them the good news.
11 So we sailed from Troas and made a straight run to Samothrace, the next
12 day to Neapolis, and from there to Philippi, a city of the first rank in that district of Macedonia, and a Roman colony. Here we stayed for some days,
13 and on the Sabbath day we went outside the city gate by the river-side, where we thought there would be a place of prayer,[o] and sat down and talked to the women who had gathered
14 there. One of them named Lydia, a dealer in purple fabric from the city of Thyatira, who was a worshipper of God, was listening, and the Lord

opened her heart to respond to what Paul said. She was baptized, and her 15 household with her, and then she said to us, 'If you have judged me to be a believer in the Lord, I beg you to come and stay in my house.' And she insisted on our going.
Once, when we were on our way to 16 the place of prayer, we met a slave-girl who was possessed by an oracular spirit and brought large profits to her owners by telling fortunes. She fol- 17 lowed Paul and the rest of us, shouting, 'These men are servants of the Supreme God, and are declaring to you a way of salvation.' She did this day after day, 18 until Paul could bear it no longer. Rounding on the spirit he said, 'I command you in the name of Jesus Christ to come out of her', and it went out there and then.
When the girl's owners saw that their 19 hope of gain had gone, they seized Paul and Silas and dragged them to the city authorities in the main square; and 20 bringing them before the magistrates, they said, 'These men are causing a disturbance in our city; they are Jews; they are advocating customs which it 21 is illegal for us Romans to adopt and follow.' The mob joined in the attack; 22 and the magistrates tore off the prisoners' clothes and ordered them to be flogged. After giving them a severe 23 beating they flung them into prison and ordered the jailer to keep them under close guard. In view of these 24 orders, he put them in the inner prison and secured their feet in the stocks.
About midnight Paul and Silas, at 25 their prayers, were singing praises to God, and the other prisoners listening, when suddenly there was such 26 a violent earthquake that the founda-

m *Or* through Phrygia and the Galatian region.
n *Possibly* traversed.
o *Some witnesses read* where there was a recognized place of prayer.

---

often sent on important errands; see 1 Cor.4.17; 16.10. **3:** Paul did not think circumcision necessary for Christians; see Gal.2.3; 5.11; 6.15. **6–10: Paul's vision. 7:** *Bithynia* was the northernmost province in Asia Minor. **9:** Paul continues his westward movement; this seems to have been his overall strategy (see Rom.15.19 n.). *Macedonia* was a Roman province in northern Greece. **11–15: Lydia converted. 11:** *Samothrace* is an island about halfway between *Troas* and *Neapolis*. **12:** As a *Roman colony, Philippi* was a military outpost and had a civil government modeled after Rome. **14:** *Worshipper of God:* see 10.2 n. **16–40: Trouble in Philippi.** In using the *name of Jesus Christ*, Paul literally fulfills the prayer of 4.30. **19:** Paul may refer to this episode in 1 Th.2.2. **22:** Paul suffered three such floggings at the hands of the Romans, who used rods (see 2 Cor.11.25). **25–26:** *A violent earthquake...all the doors burst open;*

tions of the jail were shaken; all the doors burst open and all the prisoners
27 found their fetters unfastened. The jailer woke up to see the prison doors wide open, and assuming that the prisoners had escaped, drew his sword
28 intending to kill himself. But Paul shouted, 'Do yourself no harm; we are
29 all here.' The jailer called for lights, rushed in and threw himself down before Paul and Silas, trembling with
30 fear. He then escorted them out and said, 'Masters, what must I do to be
31 saved?' They said, 'Put your trust in the Lord Jesus, and you will be saved,
32 you and your household.' Then they spoke the word of the Lord*p* to him and
33 to everyone in his house. At that late hour of the night he took them and washed their wounds; and immediately afterwards he and his whole family
34 were baptized. He brought them into his house, set out a meal, and rejoiced with his whole household in his new-found faith in God.
35 When daylight came the magistrates sent their officers with instructions to
36 release the men. The jailer reported the message to Paul: 'The magistrates have sent word that you are to be released. So now you may go free, and blessings
37 on your journey.'*q* But Paul said to the officers: 'They gave us a public flogging, though we are Roman citizens and have not been found guilty; they threw us into prison, and are they now to smuggle us out privately? No indeed! Let them come in person and escort us
38 out.' The officers reported his words. The magistrates were alarmed to hear
39 that they were Roman citizens, and came and apologized to them. Then they escorted them out and requested
40 them to go away from the city. On leaving the prison, they went to Lydia's house, where they met their fellow-Christians, and spoke words of encouragement to them; then they departed.

17 THEY NOW TRAVELLED BY WAY OF Amphipolis and Apollonia and came to Thessalonica, where there was a

Jewish synagogue. Following his usual 2 practice Paul went to their meetings; and for the next three Sabbaths he argued with them, quoting texts of Scripture which he expounded and 3 applied to show that the Messiah had to suffer and rise from the dead. 'And this Jesus,' he said, 'whom I am proclaiming to you, is the Messiah.' Some 4 of them were convinced and joined Paul and Silas; so did a great number of godfearing Gentiles and a good many influential women.*r*

But the Jews in their jealousy re- 5 cruited some low fellows from the dregs of the populace, roused the rabble, and had the city in an uproar. They mobbed Jason's house, with the intention of bringing Paul and Silas before the town assembly. Failing to find them, 6 they dragged Jason himself and some members of the congregation before the magistrates, shouting, 'The men who have made trouble all over the world have now come here; and Jason 7 has harboured them. They all flout the Emperor's laws, and assert that there is a rival king, Jesus.' These words caused 8 a great commotion in the mob, which affected the magistrates also. They 9 bound over Jason and the others, and let them go.

As soon as darkness fell, the mem- 10 bers of the congregation sent Paul and Silas off to Beroea. On arrival, they made their way to the synagogue. The 11 Jews here were more civil than those at Thessalonica; they received the message with great eagerness, studying the scriptures every day to see whether it was as they said. Many of them there- 12 fore became believers, and so did a fair number of Gentiles, women of standing as well as men. But when the Thessalon- 13 ian Jews learned that the word of God had now been proclaimed by Paul in Beroea, they came on there to stir up trouble and rouse the rabble. There- 14 upon the members of the congregation

p Some witnesses read of God.
q Some witnesses read . . . free and take your journey.
r Some witnesses read a good many wives of leading men.

see 12.10 n. **37:** Paul's letters do not mention his *Roman* citizenship. **38:** Flogging Roman citizens was forbidden; hence, *the magistrates were alarmed . . . and came and apologized to them.* See 22.24 n. **17.1–9: Paul in Thessalonica:** this city, the capital of the province of Macedonia, became an important Christian center (1 Th.1.8). **10–14: Trouble in Beroea. 13:** Similar

sent Paul off at once to go down to the coast, while Silas and Timothy both
15 stayed behind. Paul's escort brought him as far as Athens, and came away with instructions for Silas and Timothy to rejoin him with all speed.

16 Now while Paul was waiting for them at Athens he was exasperated to see
17 how the city was full of idols. So he argued in the synagogue with the Jews and gentile worshippers, and also in the city square every day with casual
18 passers-by. And some of the Epicurean and Stoic philosophers joined issue with him. Some said, 'What can this charlatan be trying to say?'; others, 'He would appear to be a propagandist for foreign deities'—this because he was preaching about Jesus and Resur-
19 rection. So they took him and brought him before the Court of Areopagus*s* and said, 'May we know what this new
20 doctrine is that you propound? You are introducing ideas that sound strange to us, and we should like to
21 know what they mean.' (Now the Athenians in general and the foreigners there had no time for anything but talking or hearing about the latest novelty.)

22 Then Paul stood up before the Court of Areopagus*t* and said: 'Men of Athens, I see that in everything that concerns religion you are uncommonly
23 scrupulous. For as I was going round looking at the objects of your worship, I noticed among other things an altar bearing the inscription "To an Unknown God". What you worship but do not know—this is what I now proclaim.
24 'The God who created the world and everything in it, and who is Lord of

heaven and earth, does not live in shrines made by men. It is not because 25 he lacks anything that he accepts service at men's hands, for he is himself the universal giver of life and breath and all else. He created every race of 26 men of one stock, to inhabit the whole earth's surface. He fixed the epochs of their history*u* and the limits of their territory. They were to seek God, and, 27 it might be, touch and find him; though indeed he is not far from each one of us, for in him we live and move, 28 in him we exist; as some of your own poets*v* have said, "We are also his offspring." As God's offspring, then, we 29 ought not to suppose that the deity is like an image in gold or silver or stone, shaped by human craftsmanship and design. As for the times of ignorance, 30 God has overlooked them; but now he commands mankind, all men everywhere, to repent, because he has fixed 31 the day on which he will have the world judged, and justly judged, by a man of his choosing; of this he has given assurance to all by raising him from the dead.'

When they heard about the raising of 32 the dead, some scoffed; and others said, 'We will hear you on this subject some other time.' And so Paul left the as-33 sembly. However, some men joined 34 him and became believers, including Dionysius, a member of the Court of Areopagus; also a woman named Damaris, and others besides.

After this he left Athens and went to **18** Corinth. There he fell in with a Jew 2 named Aquila, a native of Pontus, and

s *Or* brought him to Mars' Hill.
t *Or* in the middle of Mars' Hill.
u *Or* fixed the ordered seasons . . .
v *Some witnesses read* some among you.

events are reported in 13.50; 14.19. **15–34: Paul in Athens. 16:** *Athens*, although less important commercially and politically at this time than Corinth, remained the intellectual center of the western world, and an important city for ancient tourists. **17:** *The city square* lay north of the Acropolis. **18:** Many ancient deities had descriptive names, e.g. Fate, Victory, Wisdom; some of Paul's listeners apparently assumed that *Resurrection* also referred to a specific goddess. **19:** The *Areopagus*, or Mars Hill, lies south of the market and west of the Acropolis. There is no hint of any formal legal trial, although *the Court of Areopagus* was the highest court in Athens. **22–34:** Paul's witness in *Athens*. **23:** No *altar* with this specific wording has been found. **24:** Compare 7.48; this was a regular point made by Jewish preachers as well as Stoic philosophers. **25:** That the gods need nothing was a commonplace belief among Greek philosophers and religious thinkers. **28:** The quotation is from Aratus' (a fourth-century B.C. poet) *Phaenomena* 5. **31:** That Jesus would come at the end as judge was a common early Christian theme; see 10.42; Mt.13.41; 16.27; 2 Cor.5.10. **18.1–17: Paul in Corinth. 1:** *Corinth*, the capital of the province of Achaia and a major port for east-west trade, had a wide reputation for low morals. **2:** On *Aquila* and *Priscilla* (or Prisca), see Rom.16.3; 1 Cor.16.19. *Claudius' . . . edict* is reported

[handwritten marginal note: V. 28 Paul quotes from hymn to Zeus that can be found in many places]

his wife Priscilla; he had recently arrived from Italy because Claudius had issued an edict that all Jews should leave Rome. Paul approached them 3 and, because he was of the same trade, he made his home with them, and they carried on business together; they were 4 tent-makers. He also held discussions in the synagogue Sabbath by Sabbath, trying to convince both Jews and Gentiles.

5 Then Silas and Timothy came down from Macedonia, and Paul devoted himself entirely to preaching, affirming before the Jews that the Messiah was 6 Jesus. But when they opposed him and resorted to abuse, he shook out the skirts of his cloak and said to them, 'Your blood be on your own heads! My conscience is clear; now I shall go 7 to the Gentiles.' With that he left, and went to the house of a worshipper of God named Titius Justus, who lived 8 next door to the synagogue. Crispus, who held office in the synagogue, now became a believer in the Lord, with all his household; and a number of Corinthians listened and believed, and were 9 baptized. One night in a vision the Lord said to Paul, 'Have no fear: go on with your preaching and do not be silenced, 10 for I am with you and no one shall attempt to do you harm;*w* and there are many in this city who are my 11 people.' So he settled down for eighteen months, teaching the word of God among them.

12 But when Gallio was proconsul of Achaia, the Jews set upon Paul in a body and brought him into court. 13 'This man', they said, 'is inducing people to worship God in ways that 14 are against the law.' Paul was just about to speak when Gallio said to them, 'If it had been a question of crime or grave misdemeanour, I should, of course, have

given you Jews a patient hearing, but if 15 it is some bickering about words and names and your Jewish law, you may see to it yourselves; I have no mind to be a judge of these matters.' And he had 16 them ejected from the court. Then 17 there was a general attack on Sosthenes, who held office in the synagogue, and they gave him a beating in full view of the bench. But all this left Gallio quite unconcerned.

Paul stayed on for some time, and 18 then took leave of the brotherhood and set sail for Syria, accompanied by Priscilla and Aquila. At Cenchreae he had his hair cut off, because he was under a vow. When they reached 19 Ephesus he parted from them and went himself into the synagogue, where he held a discussion with the Jews. He was 20 asked to stay longer, but declined and 21 set out from Ephesus, saying, as he took leave of them, 'I shall come back to you if it is God's will.' On landing 22 at Caesarea, he went up and paid his respects to the church, and then went down to Antioch. After spending some 23 time there, he set out again and made a journey through the Galatian country and on through Phrygia, bringing new strength to all the converts.

NOW THERE ARRIVED AT EPHESUS A JEW 24 named Apollos, an Alexandrian by birth, an eloquent man,*x* powerful in his use of the scriptures. He had been 25 instructed in the way of the Lord and was full of spiritual fervour; and in his discourses he taught accurately the facts about Jesus,*y* though he knew only John's baptism. He now began to 26 speak boldly in the synagogue, where Priscilla and Aquila heard him; they took him in hand and expounded the

w Or and you will not be harmed by anyone's attacks.
x Or a learned man.
y Some witnesses read about the Lord.

to have been issued about 49 A.D. **3:** Paul regularly earned his own living; see 20.33–34; 1 Cor.4.12; 1 Th.2.9; compare 2 Cor.11.7–10. **6:** See 13.46; 28.28. **9:** Such a *vision* was not uncommon for Paul; see 2 Cor.12.1–5. For another such *vision*, see 22.17–21. **12:** *Gallio*, the older brother of the philosopher Seneca, *was proconsul* (governor) *of Achaia* about 51–53 A.D. **18–22: Return to Antioch. 18:** *Cenchreae* was the port on the east side of the Isthmus of Corinth. **19:** *Ephesus* was the chief city of the province of Asia. **22:** The Greek for *went up* (taken with the landing at Caesarea) implies Paul visited *the church* in Jerusalem, rather than going directly to Antioch, although there is no hint as to why such a visit should be made.

18.23–21.17: Paul's final missionary travels (third journey). 24–28: Apollos the Alexandrian. 24: *Apollos·* see 1 Cor.1.12; 3.4–6,22; 4.6; 16.12. **25:** Apparently disciples of John the Baptist continued an active mission (compare 19.3); this is all we hear of it directly in the NT.

new way[z] to him in greater detail.
27 Finding that he wished to go across to
Achaia, the brotherhood gave him their
support, and wrote to the congregation
there to make him welcome. From the
time of his arrival, he was very helpful
to those who had by God's grace be-
28 come believers; for he strenuously
confuted the Jews, demonstrating publicly from the scriptures that the Messiah is Jesus.

19 While Apollos was at Corinth, Paul
travelled through the inland regions
till he came to Ephesus. There he found
a number of converts, to whom he said,
2 'Did you receive the Holy Spirit when
you became believers?' 'No,' they replied, 'we have not even heard that
3 there is a Holy Spirit.' He said, 'Then
what baptism were you given?' 'John's
4 baptism', they answered. Paul then
said, 'The baptism that John gave was
a baptism in token of repentance, and
he told the people to put their trust in
one who was to come after him, that is,
5 in Jesus.' On hearing this they were
baptized into the name of the Lord
6 Jesus; and when Paul had laid his
hands on them, the Holy Spirit came
upon them and they spoke in tongues of
7 ecstasy and prophesied. Altogether they
were about a dozen men.
8 During the next three months he
attended the synagogue and, using
argument and persuasion, spoke boldly
and freely about the kingdom of God.
9 But when some proved obdurate and
would not believe, speaking evil of the
new way before the whole congregation, he left them, withdrew his converts,
and continued to hold discussions
daily in the lecture-hall of Tyran-
10 nus. This went on for two years, with
the result that the whole population of
the province of Asia, both Jews and
Gentiles, heard the word of the Lord.
11 And through Paul God worked singular

miracles: when handkerchiefs and 12
scarves which had been in contact with
his skin were carried to the sick, they
were rid of their diseases and the evil
spirits came out of them.
But some strolling Jewish exorcists 13
tried their hand at using the name of
the Lord Jesus on those possessed by
evil spirits; they would say, 'I adjure
you by Jesus whom Paul proclaims.'
There were seven sons of Sceva, a 14
Jewish chief priest, who were using this
method, when the evil spirit answered 15
back and said, 'Jesus I acknowledge,
and I know about Paul, but who are
you?' And the man with the evil spirit 16
flew at them, overpowered them all,
and handled them with such violence
that they ran out of the house stripped
and battered. This became known to 17
everybody in Ephesus, whether Jew or
Gentile; they were all awestruck, and
the name of the Lord Jesus gained in
honour. Moreover many of those who 18
had become believers came and openly
confessed that they had been using
magical spells. And a good many of 19
those who formerly practised magic
collected their books and burnt them
publicly. The total value was reckoned
up and it came to fifty thousand pieces
of silver. In such ways the word of the 20
Lord showed its power, spreading more
and more widely and effectively.
When things had reached this stage, 21
Paul made up his mind[a] to visit Macedonia and Achaia and then go on to
Jerusalem; and he said, 'After I have
been there, I must see Rome also.' So 22
he sent two of his assistants, Timothy
and Erastus, to Macedonia, while he
himself stayed some time longer in the
province of Asia.
Now about that time, the Christian 23
movement gave rise to a serious dis-

z *Some witnesses read* the way of God.
a *Or* Paul, led by the Spirit, resolved . . .

27: Writing letters of introduction was one way of guarding against false or unauthorized
missionaries; Paul refers to this practice in 2 Cor.3.1. **19.1–41: Paul's mission in Ephesus. 2:** This
is a key question, since the presence of the *Holy Spirit* is the sign of true Christian faith; compare
11.15–18. **3:** See 18.25 n. **4:** Compare 13.24; Mk.1.4,7; Lk.3.3–16. **6:** The presence of *tongues*
and prophecy is a sign of the presence of the *Spirit;* compare 2.4–11; 10.46. **8:** *Kingdom of God:*
see 20.25; 28.23,31; the phrase also occurs in Paul's letters (e.g. 1 Cor.4.20; Gal.5.21);
it was central in Jesus' preaching (see Mk.1.15 n.). **9:** Compare 13.46; 18.6. **14:** There is no
other record of a *Sceva* having been chief priest. **19:** *Books* of *magic* from Ephesus enjoyed a
worldwide reputation, and were eagerly sought and highly prized. **20:** Luke refers on other
occasions as well to the Christian faith overcoming the practice of magic: 8.9–13; 13.8–11.

24 turbance. There was a man named Demetrius, a silversmith who made silver shrines of Diana and provided a great deal of employment for the crafts-

25 men. He called a meeting of these men and the workers in allied trades, and addressed them. 'Men,' he said, 'you know that our high standard of living

26 depends on this industry. And you see and hear how this fellow Paul with his propaganda has perverted crowds of people, not only at Ephesus but also in practically the whole of the province of Asia. He is telling them that gods made by human hands are not gods at

27 all. There is danger for us here; it is not only that our line of business will be discredited, but also that the sanctuary of the great goddess Diana will cease to command respect; and then it will not be long before she who is worshipped by all Asia and the civilized world is brought down from her divine pre-eminence.'

28 When they heard this they were roused to fury and shouted, 'Great is

29 Diana of the Ephesians!' The whole city was in confusion; they seized Paul's travelling-companions, the Macedonians Gaius and Aristarchus,

30 and made a concerted rush with them into the theatre. Paul wanted to appear before the assembly but the other

31 Christians would not let him. Even some of the dignitaries of the province, who were friendly towards him, sent and urged him not to venture into the

32 theatre. Meanwhile some were shouting one thing, some another; for the assembly was in confusion and most of them did not know what they had all

33 come for. But some of the crowd explained the trouble to Alexander, whom the Jews had pushed to the front, and he, motioning for silence, attempted to make a defence before the as-

34 sembly. But when they recognized that he was a Jew, a single cry arose from them all: for about two hours they kept on shouting, 'Great is Diana of the Ephesians!'

The town clerk, however, quieted the 35 crowd. 'Men of Ephesus,' he said, 'all the world knows that our city of Ephesus is temple-warden of the great Diana and of that symbol of her which fell from heaven. Since these facts are 36 beyond dispute, your proper course is to keep quiet and do nothing rash. These men whom you have brought 37 here as culprits have committed no sacrilege and uttered no blasphemy against our goddess. If therefore 38 Demetrius and his craftsmen have a case against anyone, assizes are held and there are such people as proconsuls; let the parties bring their charges and countercharges. If, on the other 39 hand, you have some further question to raise, it will be dealt with in the statutory assembly. We certainly run 40 the risk of being charged with riot for this day's work. There is no justification for it, and if the issue is raised we shall be unable to give any explanation of this uproar.' With that he dismissed 41 the assembly.

WHEN THE DISTURBANCE HAD CEASED, **20** Paul sent for the disciples and, after encouraging them, said good-bye and set out on his journey to Macedonia. He travelled through those parts of the 2 country, often speaking words of encouragement to the Christians there, and so came into Greece. When he had 3 spent three months there and was on the point of embarking for Syria, a plot was laid against him by the Jews, so he decided to return by way of Macedonia. He was accompanied by Sopater son of 4 Pyrrhus, from Beroea, the Thessalonians Aristarchus and Secundus, Gaius the Doberian[b] and Timothy, and the Asians Tychicus and Trophimus. These 5 went ahead and waited for us at Troas; we ourselves set sail from Philippi 6

b *Some witnesses read* the Derbaean.

24: *Diana* (Artemis) was a fertility goddess whose temple was one of the seven wonders of the ancient world and a major tourist attraction. 26: Demetrius seems to identify the images of Artemis with the goddess herself; compare 17.24–25. 29: The *theatre*, recovered through excavation, had places for about 29,000 people. 34: This is an indication of the anti-Semitism prevalent in many parts of the ancient world; compare 16.20–21. **20.1–6: Return to Greece. 2–4;** This journey, with its change of plans, appears to be reflected in 1 Cor.16.5–9; 2 Cor.1.15–2.13; 7.5–7. 4: The many traveling companions imply Paul is bringing the collection to Jerusalem;

after the Passover season,*c* and in five days reached them at Troas, where we spent a week.

7 On the Saturday night, in our assembly for the breaking of bread, Paul, who was to leave next day, addressed them, and went on speaking until mid- 8 night. Now there were many lamps in the upper room where we were as- 9 sembled; and a youth named Eutychus, who was sitting on the window-ledge, grew more and more sleepy as Paul went on talking. At last he was completely overcome by sleep, fell from the third storey to the ground, and was 10 picked up for dead. Paul went down, threw himself upon him, seizing him in his arms, and said to them, 'Stop this commotion; there is still life in him.' 11 He then went upstairs, broke bread and ate, and after much conversation, which lasted until dawn, he departed. 12 And they took the boy away alive and were immensely comforted.

13 We went ahead to the ship and sailed for Assos, where we were to take Paul aboard. He had made this arrangement, 14 as he was going to travel by road. When he met us at Assos, we took him aboard 15 and went on to Mitylene. Next day we sailed from there and arrived opposite Chios, and on the second day we made Samos. On the following day*d* we 16 reached Miletus. For Paul had decided to pass by Ephesus and so avoid having to spend time in the province of Asia; he was eager to be in Jerusalem, if he possibly could, on the day of Pente- 17 cost. He did, however, send from Miletus to Ephesus and summon the 18 elders of the congregation; and when they joined him, he spoke as follows:

'You know how, from the day that I first set foot in the province of Asia, for the whole time that I was with you, 19 I served the Lord in all humility amid the sorrows and trials that came upon

me through the machinations of the Jews. You know that I kept back 20 nothing that was for your good: I delivered the message to you; I taught you, in public and in your homes; with 21 Jews and Gentiles alike I insisted on repentance before God and trust in our Lord Jesus. And now, as you see, I am 22 on my way to Jerusalem, under the constraint of the Spirit.*e* Of what will befall me there I know nothing, except 23 that in city after city the Holy Spirit assures me that imprisonment and hardships await me. For myself, I set 24 no store by life; I only want to finish the race, and complete the task which the Lord Jesus assigned to me, of bearing my testimony to the gospel of God's grace.

'One word more: I have gone about 25 among you proclaiming the Kingdom, but now I know that none of you will see my face again. That being so, I here 26 and now declare that no man's fate can be laid at my door; for I have kept 27 back nothing; I have disclosed to you the whole purpose of God. Keep watch 28 over yourselves and over all the flock of which the Holy Spirit has given you charge, as shepherds of the church of the Lord,*f* which he won for himself by his own blood.*g* I know that when I am 29 gone, savage wolves will come in among you and will not spare the flock. Even from your own body there will 30 be men coming forward who will distort the truth to induce the disciples to break away and follow them. So be on 31 the alert; remember how for three years, night and day, I never ceased to counsel each of you, and how I wept over you.

c Literally after the days of Unleavened Bread.
d Some witnesses read . . . Samos, and, after stopping at Trogyllium, on the following day . . .
e Or under an inner compulsion.
f Some witnesses read of God.
g Or, according to some witnesses, by the blood of his Own.

---

compare 24.17. **7–12: Eutychus survives. 7:** *Saturday night* may also be translated "Sunday," when Christian gatherings were usually held; see 1 Cor.16.2. The *breaking of bread* was a regular Christian act (see 2.42), and probably included the Eucharist. **10:** The Greek implies Paul restored him to life; compare 1 Kgs.17.21–22. **13–16: On to Miletus. 14–15:** *Mitylene, Chios* and *Samos* are located on offshore islands. **17–38: Paul's farewell to the Ephesian elders. 19:** Paul's Corinthian correspondence refers to his *sorrows* (2 Cor.1.5–10) and *trials* (1 Cor.15.32) in Ephesus. **20:** See 2 Cor.4.2. **23:** See 9.16; for one form of such a warning, see 21.10–11. **25:** *Proclaiming the Kingdom:* see 19.8 n. The latter part of this verse anticipates Paul's imprisonment and death. **27:** That everything happens according to the *purpose of God*, compare 2.23 (and n.); 4.28; 13.48. **29:** Similar trouble at Ephesus is described in Rev.2.1–7. *Wolves:*

32 'And now I commend you to God and to his gracious word, which has power to build you up and give you your heritage among all who are dedi-33 cated to him. I have not wanted any-34 one's money or clothes for myself; you all know that these hands of mine earned enough for the needs of myself 35 and my companions. I showed you that it is our duty to help the weak in this way, by hard work, and that we should keep in mind the words of the Lord Jesus, who himself said, "Happiness lies more in giving than in receiving." '

36 As he finished speaking, he knelt 37 down with them all and prayed. Then there were loud cries of sorrow from them all, as they folded Paul in their 38 arms and kissed him. What distressed them most was his saying that they would never see his face again. So they escorted him to his ship.

21 When we had parted from them and set sail, we made a straight run and came to Cos; next day to Rhodes, and 2 thence to Patara.*h* There we found a ship bound for Phoenicia, so we went 3 aboard and sailed in her. We came in sight of Cyprus, and leaving it to port, we continued our voyage to Syria, and put in at Tyre, for there the ship was to 4 unload her cargo. We went and found the disciples and stayed there a week; and they, warned by the Spirit, urged Paul to abandon his visit to Jerusalem. 5 But when our time ashore was ended, we left and continued our journey; and they and their wives and children all escorted us out of the city. We knelt 6 down on the beach and prayed, then bade each other good-bye; we went aboard, and they returned home.

7 We made the passage from Tyre and reached Ptolemais, where we greeted the brotherhood and spent one day 8 with them. Next day we left and came to Caesarea. We went to the home of Philip the evangelist, who was one of

the Seven, and stayed with him. He had 9 four unmarried daughters, who possessed the gift of prophecy. When we 10 had been there several days, a prophet named Agabus arrived from Judaea. He came to us, took Paul's belt, 11 bound his own feet and hands with it, and said, 'These are the words of the Holy Spirit: Thus will the Jews in Jerusalem bind the man to whom this belt belongs, and hand him over to the Gentiles.' When we heard this, we and 12 the local people begged and implored Paul to abandon his visit to Jerusalem. Then Paul gave his answer: 'Why all 13 these tears? Why are you trying to weaken my resolution? For my part I am ready not merely to be bound but even to die at Jerusalem for the name of the Lord Jesus.' So, as he would 14 not be persuaded, we gave up and said, 'The Lord's will be done.'

At the end of our stay we packed our 15 baggage and took the road up to Jerusalem. Some of the disciples from 16 Caesarea came along with us, bringing a certain Mnason of Cyprus, a Christian from the early days, with whom we were to lodge. So we reached Jeru-17 salem, where the brotherhood welcomed us gladly.

Next day Paul paid a visit to James; 18 we were with him, and all the elders attended. He greeted them, and then 19 described in detail all that God had done among the Gentiles through his ministry. When they heard this, they 20 gave praise to God. Then they said to Paul: 'You see, brother, how many thousands of converts we have among the Jews, all of them staunch upholders of the Law. Now they have been given 21 certain information about you: it is said that you teach all the Jews in the gentile world to turn their backs on Moses, telling them to give up circumcising their children and following our way of life. What is the position, then? 22

h Some witnesses add and Myra.

---

see Mt.7.15 (and n.). **35:** This saying of Jesus does not appear in any of the Gospels. **21.1–17: To Jerusalem via Caesarea. 8:** Compare 8.40. *Evangelist:* compare Eph.4.11; 2 Tim.4.5 n. *The Seven:* see 6.5. **10:** *Agabus* acts out his message as did the OT prophets; see Jer. chs.27–28; Ezek. ch. 4; Isa. ch. 20.

21.18–22.29: Paul arrested in Jerusalem. 18–26: Paul undergoes ritual purification. 20–25: These verses are written as though the events surrounding the Apostolic Council had not happened, and as if Paul had not known of the letter sent to the Gentile churches; see ch. 15. **21: As** far as Paul's conduct in Acts is concerned, these charges are false, as v. 26 and 16.3 affirm.

They are sure to hear that you have 23 arrived. You must therefore do as we tell you. We have four men here who 24 are under a vow; take them with you and go through the ritual of purification with them, paying their expenses, after which they may shave their heads. Then everyone will know that there is nothing in the stories they were told about you, but that you are a practising Jew and 25 keep the Law yourself. As for the gentile converts, we sent them our decision that they must abstain from meat that has been offered to idols, from blood, from anything that has been strangled,*i* 26 and from fornication.' So Paul took the four men, and next day, after going through the ritual of purification with them, he went into the temple to give notice of the date when the period of purification would end and the offering be made for each one of them.

From Jerusalem to Rome

27 BUT JUST BEFORE THE SEVEN DAYS WERE up, the Jews from the province of Asia saw him in the temple. They stirred up the whole crowd, and seized him, 28 shouting, 'Men of Israel, help, help! This is the fellow who spreads his doctrine all over the world, attacking our people, our law, and this sanctuary. On top of all this he has brought Gentiles into the temple and profaned this 29 holy place.' For they had previously seen Trophimus the Ephesian with him in the city, and assumed that Paul had brought him into the temple. 30 The whole city was in a turmoil, and people came running from all directions. They seized Paul and dragged him out of the temple; and at once the 31 doors were shut. While they were clamouring for his death, a report

reached the officer commanding the cohort, that all Jerusalem was in an uproar. He immediately took a force 32 of soldiers with their centurions and came down on the rioters at the double As soon as they saw the commandant and his troops, they stopped beating Paul. The commandant stepped for- 33 ward, arrested him, and ordered him to be shackled with two chains: he then asked who the man was and what he had been doing. Some in the crowd 34 shouted one thing, some another. As he could not get at the truth because of the hubbub, he ordered him to be taken into barracks. When Paul reached 35 the steps, he had to be carried by the soldiers because of the violence of the mob. For the whole crowd were at their 36 heels yelling, 'Kill him!'

Just before Paul was taken into the 37 barracks he said to the commandant, 'May I have a word with you?' The commandant said, 'So you speak Greek, do you? Then you are not the 38 Egyptian who started a revolt some time ago and led a force of four thousand terrorists out into the wilds?' Paul replied, 'I am a Jew, a Tarsian 39 from Cilicia, a citizen of no mean city. I ask your permission to speak to the people.' When permission had been 40 given, Paul stood on the steps and with a gesture called for the attention of the people. As soon as quiet was restored, he addressed them in the Jewish language:

'Brothers and fathers, give me a 22 hearing while I make my defence before you.' When they heard him speaking 2 to them in their own language, they listened the more quietly. 'I am a true- 3 born Jew,' he said, 'a native of Tarsus in Cilicia. I was brought up in this city,

i Some witnesses omit from anything that has been strangled.

23: *A vow:* perhaps the Nazirite; see 18.18; Num.6.1–21. **26:** Compare Num.6.13–21. **27–40: Paul arrested in the Temple. 28:** Compare the charges against Stephen: 6.13–14. *Into the temple:* into the Court of the Israelites. Gentiles were permitted only in the outer court. **30:** *The doors* separated the Court of the Israelites from the Court of the Gentiles, into which Paul was now dragged. **32:** The Roman *soldiers* charged with keeping order in the Temple were stationed in the Tower of Antonia, a fortress adjoining the Temple at the northwest corner. **35:** The *steps* led up into the Tower of Antonia; there were two flights. **38:** The Jewish historian Josephus puts the original army of this *Egyptian* at thirty thousand, but his attempt to conquer Jerusalem was defeated by the procurator Felix (23.24), and only a portion of the revolutionaries escaped. **22.1–21: Paul's speech in Jerusalem. 3:** *Gamaliel* (see 5.34) enjoyed some fame as a rabbi, but is not mentioned in any of Paul's letters nor by the contemporary Jewish writers, Philo and

and as a pupil of Gamaliel I was thoroughly trained in every point of our ancestral law. I have always been ardent in God's service, as you all are
4 today. And so I began to persecute this movement to the death, arresting its followers, men and women alike, and
5 putting them in chains. For this I have as witnesses the High Priest and the whole Council of Elders. I was given letters from them to our fellow-Jews at Damascus, and had started out to bring the Christians there to Jerusalem
6 as prisoners for punishment; and this is what happened. I was on the road and nearing Damascus, when suddenly about midday a great light flashed from
7 the sky all around me, and I fell to the ground. Then I heard a voice saying to me, "Saul, Saul, why do you per-
8 secute me?" I answered, "Tell me, Lord, who you are." "I am Jesus of Nazareth," he said, "whom you are
9 persecuting." My companions saw the light, but did not hear the voice that
10 spoke to me. "What shall I do, Lord?" I said, and the Lord replied, "Get up and continue your journey to Damascus; there you will be told of all the
11 tasks that are laid upon you." As I had been blinded by the brilliance of that light, my companions led me by the hand, and so I came to Damascus.
12 'There, a man called Ananias, a devout observer of the Law and well spoken of by all the Jews of that place,
13 came and stood before me and said, "Saul, my brother, recover your sight." Instantly I recovered my sight and saw
14 him. He went on: "The God of our fathers appointed you to know his will and to see the Righteous One and to
15 hear his very voice, because you are to be his witness before the world, and testify to what you have seen and

heard. And now why delay? Be bap- 16 tized at once, with invocation of his name, and wash away your sins."
'After my return to Jerusalem, I was 17 praying in the temple when I fell into a trance and saw him there, speaking to 18 me. "Make haste", he said, "and leave Jerusalem without delay, for they will not accept your testimony about me." "Lord," I said, "they know that I im- 19 prisoned those who believe in thee, and flogged them in every synagogue; and when the blood of Stephen thy 20 witness was shed I stood by, approving, and I looked after the clothes of those who killed him." But he said to me, 21 "Go, for I am sending you far away to the Gentiles."'
Up to this point they had given him a 22 hearing; but now they began shouting, 'Down with him! A scoundrel like that is better dead!' And as they were yelling 23 and waving their cloaks and flinging dust in the air, the commandant ordered 24 him to be brought into the barracks and gave instructions to examine him by flogging, and find out what reason there was for such an outcry against him. But when they tied him up for the 25 lash,[j] Paul said to the centurion who was standing there, 'Can you legally flog a man who is a Roman citizen, and moreover has not been found guilty?' When the centurion heard this, he went 26 and reported it to the commandant. 'What do you mean to do?' he said. 'This man is a Roman citizen.' The 27 commandant came to Paul. 'Tell me, are you a Roman citizen?' he asked. 'Yes', said he. The commandant re- 28 joined, 'It cost me a large sum to acquire this citizenship.' Paul said, 'But it was mine by birth.' Then those 29 who were about to examine him with-

_j Or_ tied him up with thongs.

Josephus. **5:** The _Council of Elders_ is the Sanhedrin; see Mt.26.59 n. **6–11:** Compare 9.3–9; 26.13–16. **7:** _Persecute me:_ see 9.4 n. **12:** _Ananias:_ compare 9.10–16, although his attitude to the _Law_ is not mentioned there. **14:** _Appointed you:_ Paul expressly denied he received his commission from any man (Gal.1.1). **18:** _Leave Jerusalem without delay_, implying Paul did not preach in Jerusalem, agrees with Gal.1.16–20; but see 9.28–29. **19–20:** In a situation like this, the testimony of a Jewish convert to the Christian faith could be expected to carry considerable weight. **21:** The immediate occasion of Paul's arrest was temple profanation (21.28); here the point at issue seems to be Paul's association with _Gentiles_ and the resulting dissolution of the Law. Later the charge will concern resurrection (23.6). **22–29: Reaction to Paul's speech. 24:** It was Roman practice to obtain testimony from slaves and noncitizens by torture (_flogging_), on the assumption that lying in such circumstances was not likely. **27:** The penalty for falsely claiming citizenship was death.

drew hastily, and the commandant himself was alarmed when he realized that Paul was a Roman citizen and that he had put him in irons.

30 THE FOLLOWING DAY, WISHING TO BE quite sure what charge the Jews were bringing against Paul, he released him and ordered the chief priests and the entire Council to assemble. He then took Paul down and stood him before them.

23 Paul fixed his eyes on the Council and said, 'My brothers, I have lived all my life, and still live today, with a per-2 fectly clear conscience before God.' At this the High Priest Ananias ordered his attendants to strike him on the 3 mouth. Paul retorted, 'God will strike you, you whitewashed wall! You sit there to judge me in accordance with the Law; and then in defiance of the 4 Law you order me to be struck!' The attendants said, 'Would you insult 5 God's High Priest?' 'My brothers,' said Paul, 'I had no idea that he was High Priest; Scripture, I know, says: "You must not abuse the ruler of your people."'

6 Now Paul was well aware that one section of them were Sadducees and the other Pharisees, so he called out in the Council, 'My brothers, I am a Pharisee, a Pharisee born and bred; and the true issue in this trial is our hope of the 7 resurrection of the dead.' At these words the Pharisees and Sadducees fell out among themselves, and the as-8 sembly was divided. (The Sadducees deny that there is any resurrection, or angel, or spirit, but the Pharisees ac-9 cept them.) So a great uproar broke out; and some of the doctors of the law belonging to the Pharisaic party openly took sides and declared, 'We can find no fault with this man; perhaps an

angel or spirit has spoken to him.' The 10 dissension was mounting, and the commandant was afraid that Paul would be torn to pieces, so he ordered the troops to go down, pull him out of the crowd, and bring him into the barracks.

The following night the Lord ap-11 peared to him and said, 'Keep up your courage; you have affirmed the truth about me in Jerusalem, and you must do the same in Rome.'

When day broke, the Jews banded 12 together and took an oath not to eat or drink until they had killed Paul. There 13 were more than forty in this con-spiracy. They came to the chief priests 14 and elders and said, 'We have bound ourselves by a solemn oath not to taste food until we have killed Paul. It 15 is now for you, acting with the Council, to apply to the commandant to bring him down to you, on the pretext of a closer investigation of his case; and we have arranged to do away with him before he arrives.'

But the son of Paul's sister heard of 16 the ambush; he went to the barracks, obtained entry, and reported it to Paul. Paul called one of the centurions and 17 said, 'Take this young man to the commandant; he has something to report.' The centurion took him and 18 brought him to the commandant. 'The prisoner Paul', he said, 'sent for me and asked me to bring this young man to you; he has something to tell you.' The 19 commandant took him by the arm, drew him aside, and asked him, 'What is it you have to report?' He said, 'The 20 Jews have made a plan among them-selves and will request you to bring Paul down to the Council tomorrow, on the pretext of obtaining more pre-cise information about him. Do not 21 listen to them; for a party more than

---

22.30–24.27: Paul and Felix. 23.1–10: Paul before the Council. 1: The *clear conscience* mentioned here apparently is meant to include the events recited in 22:19–20; Paul refers to his persecution of Christians in his letters, but does not relate it to a *clear conscience*. **2:** The *High Priest Ananias* entered that office about 48 A.D., was deposed during the rule of Felix, and was murdered in 66 A.D.; see 4.6 n. **5:** Exod.22.28. This continues Acts' picture of Paul as a true follower of the Law; compare 16.3; 22.26; 24.14; Lk.24.44. For Luke, the Christian faith is the true fulfillment of Judaism. **6:** See 22.21 n. **8:** On *Sadducees* and *resurrection*, see 4.2; Mt.3.7 n.; Lk.20.27–38. **11:** Key events in Paul's life were revealed to him by the *Lord*, or by the Holy Spirit; see 18.9–10; 20.23; 22.17–21. **12–22: A plot against Paul. 13:** Such a *conspiracy* is repeated in 25.3 (compare 9.23); it was possible under Jewish law to be released from such an *oath*. **16:** That Paul's nephew was able to *obtain entry* was not unusual; see Mt.11.2; 25.36.

forty strong are lying in wait for him. They have sworn not to eat or drink until they have done away with him, they are now ready, and wait only for

22 your consent.' So the commandant dismissed the young man, with orders not to let anyone know that he had given him this information.

23 Then he called a couple of his centurions and issued these orders: 'Get ready two hundred infantry to proceed to Caesarea, together with seventy cavalrymen and two hundred light-armed troops;*k* parade three hours after

24 sunset. Provide also mounts for Paul so that he may ride through under safe

25 escort to Felix the Governor.' And he wrote a letter to this effect:

26 'Claudius Lysias to His Excellency the Governor Felix. Your Excellency:

27 This man was seized by the Jews and was on the point of being murdered when I intervened with the troops and removed him, because I discovered that

28 he was a Roman citizen. As I wished to ascertain the charge on which they were accusing him, I took him down

29 to their Council. I found that the accusation had to do with controversial matters in their law, but there was no charge against him meriting death or

30 imprisonment. However, I have now been informed of an attempt to be made on the man's life, so I am sending him to you at once, and have also instructed his accusers to state their case against him before you.'*l*

31 Acting on their orders, the infantry took Paul and brought him by night

32 to Antipatris. Next day they returned to their barracks, leaving the cavalry

33 to escort him the rest of the way. The cavalry entered Caesarea, delivered the letter to the Governor, and handed

34 Paul over to him. He read the letter, asked him what province he was from, and learned that he was from Cilicia.

35 'I will hear your case', he said, 'when your accusers arrive.' He then ordered

him to be held in custody at his headquarters in Herod's palace.

FIVE DAYS LATE THE HIGH PRIEST 24 Ananias came down, accompanied by some of the elders and an advocate named Tertullus, and they laid an information against Paul before the Governor. When the prisoner was 2 called, Tertullus opened the case.

'Your Excellency,' he said, 'we owe it to you that we enjoy unbroken peace. It is due to your provident care that, in all kinds of ways and in all sorts of places, improvements are being made for the good of this province. We wel- 3 come this, sir, most gratefully. And 4 now, not to take up too much of your time, I crave your indulgence for a brief statement of our case. We have 5 found this man to be a perfect pest, a fomenter of discord among the Jews all over the world, a ringleader of the sect of the Nazarenes. He even made an 6 attempt to profane the temple; and then we arrested him.*m* If you will 8 examine him yourself you can ascertain from him the truth of all the charges we bring.' The Jews supported the 9 attack, alleging that the facts were as he stated.

Then the Governor motioned to 10 Paul to speak, and he began his reply: 'Knowing as I do that for many years you have administered justice in this province, I make my defence with confidence. You can ascertain the facts for 11 yourself. It is not more than twelve days since I went up to Jerusalem on a pilgrimage. They did not find me argu- 12 ing with anyone, or collecting a crowd, either in the temple or in the synagogues or up and down the city; and 13 they cannot make good the charges

k *Or* two hundred spearmen (*the meaning of the Greek word is uncertain*).
l *Some witnesses read* '. . . before you. Farewell.'
m *Some witnesses insert* It was our intention to try him under our law; (7) but Lysias the commandant intervened and took him by force out of our hands, (8) ordering his accusers to come before you.

23–35: Paul is taken to Felix. 23: *Caesarea:* see 10.1 n. **24:** Antonius *Felix*, probably a freed slave of the mother of Emperor Claudius, was procurator about 52–55 A.D.; his reputation as procurator was not a good one. **35:** The exact location of *Herod's palace* is unknown. **24.1–9: Jewish charges against Paul. 1:** Compare 23.30. *Ananias:* see 23.2 n. **2:** Historically, Palestine at this time was wracked with murder and revolt. Such praise is, however, rhetorical convention. **4:** This is a further example of Hellenistic rhetorical convention. **6:** The *attempt to profane the temple* was a baseless charge; see 21.26,29. **10–21: Paul's defense. 10:** *For many years:* Felix was procurator for about three years in this province, but, again, this is rhetorical con-

14 they bring against me. But this much I will admit: I am a follower of the new way (the "sect" they speak of), and it is in that manner that I worship the God of our fathers; for I believe all that is written in the Law and the 15 prophets, and in reliance on God I hold the hope, which my accusers too accept, that there is to be a resurrection of 16 good and wicked alike. Accordingly I, no less than they, train myself to keep at all times a clear conscience before God and man.

17 'After an absence of several years I came to bring charitable gifts to my 18 nation and to offer sacrifices. They found me in the temple ritually purified and engaged in this service. I had no crowd with me, and there was no disturbance. But some Jews from the prov- 19 ince of Asia were there, and if they had any charge against me it is they who ought to have been in court to 20 state it. Failing that, it is for these persons here present to say what crime they discovered when I was brought 21 before the Council, apart from this one open assertion which I made as I stood there: "The true issue in my trial before you today is the resurrection of the dead."'

22 Then Felix, who happened to be well informed about the Christian movement, adjourned the hearing. 'When Lysias the commanding officer comes down', he said, 'I will go into your 23 case.' He gave orders to the centurion to keep Paul under open arrest and not to prevent any of his friends from making themselves useful to him.

24 Some days later Felix came with his wife Drusilla, who was a Jewess, and sending for Paul he let him talk to him 25 about faith in Christ Jesus. But when the discourse turned to questions of morals, self-control, and the coming judgement, Felix became alarmed and exclaimed, 'That will do for the present; when I find it convenient I will send for you again.' At the same time 26 he had hopes of a bribe from Paul; and for this reason he sent for him very often and talked with him. When two 27 years had passed, Felix was succeeded by Porcius Festus. Wishing to curry favour with the Jews, Felix left Paul in custody.

THREE DAYS AFTER TAKING UP HIS **25** appointment Festus went up from Caesarea to Jerusalem, where the chief 2 priests and the Jewish leaders brought before him the case against Paul. They 3 asked Festus to favour them against him, and pressed for him to be brought up to Jerusalem, for they were planning an ambush to kill him on the way. Festus, however, replied, 'Paul is in 4 safe custody at Caesarea, and I shall be leaving Jerusalem shortly myself; so let your leading men come down 5 with me, and if there is anything wrong, let them prosecute him.'

After spending eight or ten days at 6 most in Jerusalem, he went down to Caesarea, and next day he took his seat in court and ordered Paul to be brought up. When he appeared, the 7 Jews who had come down from Jerusalem stood round bringing many grave charges, which they were unable to prove. Paul's plea was: 'I have com- 8 mitted no offence, either against the Jewish law, or against the temple, or against the Emperor.' Festus, anxious 9 to ingratiate himself with the Jews, turned to Paul and asked, 'Are you willing to go up to Jerusalem and stand trial on these charges before me there?' But Paul said, 'I am now stand- 10

---

vention. **15:** Only the Pharisees among his *accusers* accepted the *resurrection:* see 23.8. **17:** Compare Rom.15.25–27. While this may be historically true, the bringing of charitable gifts was not given as the reason for this trip to Jerusalem in 19.21; see 11.29 n. **21:** See 22.21 n. **22–27: Discussion between Paul and Felix. 24:** *Drusilla,* the daughter of Herod Agrippa (see 12.1(and n.)–23), was one of three noble ladies Felix married, this one having deserted her husband, King Azizus of Emesa, for him. **26:** This accords with the way Felix is described by ancient historians. This also informs us why Paul, though innocent, was not released. There was no legal way he could compel a decision to be rendered.

25.1–26.32: Paul and Festus. 1–5: Festus goes to Jerusalem. 1: Little is known of Porcius *Festus:* he probably assumed office about 55 A.D. **3:** *Planning an ambush:* see 23.12–15. **6–12: Paul appeals to Caesar. 6:** This is Paul's second hearing in *Caesarea;* see 24.1–21. **9:** *Paul* was a similar pawn to Felix (24.24–26); this verse again explains why Paul, though innocent, was

ing before the Emperor's tribunal, and that is where I must be tried. Against the Jews I have committed no offence, 11 as you very well know. If I am guilty of any capital crime, I do not ask to escape the death penalty; but if there is no substance in the charges which these men bring against me, it is not open to anyone to hand me over as a 12 sop to them. I appeal to Caesar!' Then Festus, after conferring with his advisers, replied, 'You have appealed to Caesar: to Caesar you shall go.'

13   After an interval of some days King Agrippa and Bernice arrived at Caesa- 14 rea on a courtesy visit to Festus. They spent several days there, and during this time Festus laid Paul's case before the king. 'We have a man', he said, 'left 15 in custody by Felix; and when I was in Jerusalem the chief priests and elders of the Jews laid an information against 16 him, demanding his condemnation. I answered them, "It is not Roman practice to hand over any accused man before he is confronted with his accusers and given an opportunity of 17 answering the charge." So when they had come here with me I lost no time; the very next day I took my seat in court and ordered the man to be 18 brought up. But when his accusers rose to speak, they brought none of the 19 charges I was expecting; they merely had certain points of disagreement with him about their peculiar religion, and about someone called Jesus, a dead man whom Paul alleged to be alive. 20 Finding myself out of my depth in such discussions, I asked if he was willing to go to Jerusalem and stand his trial there 21 on these issues. But Paul appealed to be remanded in custody for His Imperial Majesty's decision, and I ordered him to be detained until I could send him

to the Emperor.' Agrippa said to 22 Festus, 'I should rather like to hear the man myself.' 'Tomorrow', he answered, 'you shall hear him.'

So next day Agrippa and Bernice 23 came in full state and entered the audience-chamber accompanied by high-ranking officers and prominent citizens; and on the orders of Festus Paul was brought up. Then Festus said, 24 'King Agrippa, and all you gentlemen here present with us, you see this man: the whole body of the Jews approached me both in Jerusalem and here, loudly insisting that he had no right to remain alive. But it was clear to me that he had 25 committed no capital crime, and when he himself appealed to His Imperial Majesty, I decided to send him. But I 26 have nothing definite about him to put in writing for our Sovereign. Accordingly I have brought him up before you all and particularly before you, King Agrippa, so that as a result of this preliminary inquiry I may have something to report. There is no sense, it seems to 27 me, in sending on a prisoner without indicating the charges against him.'

Agrippa said to Paul, 'You have our **26** permission to speak for yourself.' Then Paul stretched out his hand and began his defence:

'I consider myself fortunate, King 2 Agrippa, that it is before you that I am to make my defence today upon all the charges brought against me by the Jews, particularly as you are expert in 3 all Jewish matters, both our customs and our disputes. And therefore I beg you to give me a patient hearing.

'My life from my youth up, the life 4 I led from the beginning among my people and in Jerusalem, is familiar to all Jews. Indeed they have known me 5 long enough and could testify, if they

---

not released. **11:** In this way, the words of the Lord to Paul (23.11) began their fulfillment. Little is known, apart from this verse, about the circumstances surrounding an *appeal to Caesar* in the time of the Roman Empire. **13–22: Agrippa and Festus. 13:** *King* Marcus Julius *Agrippa* II, king of some territories in northern Palestine, was the son of Herod Agrippa I (12.1–5, 20–23), and a brother of Drusilla (24.24). *Bernice*, a widow at this time, was another of Agrippa's sisters; their constant companionship was an ancient scandal. **16:** Festus himself did not hold to this *practice* in Paul's case, nor did Felix; see 24.18–19. **23–27: Preliminary inquiry instituted. 25:** The commandant in Jerusalem had come to the same decision (23.29); the Pharisees, too, had declared him innocent (23.9). **26.1–32: Paul makes his defense.** This speech sums up Paul's career as portrayed in Acts. **1:** When Paul spoke to King *Agrippa*, the prophecy of Jesus about Paul's career (9.15) was fulfilled; compare Lk.21.12. **2–3:** Such an introduction was a Hellenistic rhetorical convention; see 24.2–3,10. **4:** See 22.3. **5:** See 23.6; Phil.3.5. **7:** *Twelve tribes hope:*

only would, that I belonged to the strictest group in our religion: I lived
6 as a Pharisee. And it is for a hope kindled by God's promise to our fore-fathers that I stand in the dock today.
7 Our twelve tribes hope to see the fulfil-ment of that promise, worshipping with intense devotion day and night; and for this very hope I am impeached, and impeached by Jews, Your Majesty.
8 Why is it considered incredible among you that God should raise dead men to life?
9 'I myself once thought it my duty to work actively against the name of Jesus
10 of Nazareth; and I did so in Jerusalem. It was I who imprisoned many of God's people by authority obtained from the chief priests; and when they were con-demned to death, my vote was cast
11 against them. In all the synagogues I tried by repeated punishment to make them renounce their faith; indeed my fury rose to such a pitch that I extended my persecution to foreign cities.
12 'On one such occasion I was travel-ling to Damascus with authority and
13 commission from the chief priests; and as I was on my way, Your Majesty, in the middle of the day I saw a light from the sky, more brilliant than the sun, shining all around me and my travel-
14 ling-companions. We all fell to the ground, and then I heard a voice saying to me in the Jewish language, "Saul, Saul, why do you persecute me? It is hard for you, this kicking against the
15 goad." I said, "Tell me, Lord, who you are"; and the Lord replied, "I am
16 Jesus, whom you are persecuting. But now, rise to your feet and stand upright. I have appeared to you for a purpose: to appoint you my servant and witness, to testify both to what you have seen
17 and to what you shall yet see of me. I will rescue you from this people and from the Gentiles to whom I am send-
18 ing you. I send you to open their eyes and turn them from darkness to light,

from the dominion of Satan to God, so that, by trust in me, they may obtain forgiveness of sins and a place with those whom God has made his own."
'And so, King Agrippa, I did not 19 disobey the heavenly vision. I turned 20 first to the inhabitants of Damascus, and then to Jerusalem and all the coun-try of Judaea, and to the Gentiles, and sounded the call to repent and turn to God, and to prove their repentance by deeds. That is why the Jews seized me 21 in the temple and tried to do away with me. But I had God's help, and so to this 22 very day I stand and testify to great and small alike. I assert nothing beyond what was foretold by the prophets and by Moses: that the Messiah must suffer, 23 and that he, the first to rise from the dead, would announce the dawn to Israel and to the Gentiles.'
While Paul was thus making his 24 defence, Festus shouted at the top of his voice, 'Paul, you are raving; too much study is driving you mad.' 'I am 25 not mad, Your Excellency,' said Paul, 'what I am saying is sober truth. The 26 king is well versed in these matters, and to him I can speak freely. I do not believe that he can be unaware of any of these facts, for this has been no hole-and-corner business. King Agrippa, do 27 you believe the prophets? I know you do.' Agrippa said to Paul, 'You think 28 it will not take much to win me over and make a Christian of me.' 'Much or little,' said Paul, 'I wish to God that not 29 only you, but all those also who are listening to me today, might become what I am, apart from these chains.'
With that the king rose, and with 30 him the Governor, Bernice, and the rest of the company, and after they 31 had withdrawn they talked it over. 'This man', they said, 'is doing nothing that deserves death or imprisonment.' Agrippa said to Festus, 'The fellow 32 could have been discharged, if he had not appealed to the Emperor.'

---

see 24.14–15. **8:** See 22.21 n. **9–11:** See 8.3 n. **12–15:** See 9.3–6; 22.4–10. **14:** *Kicking against the goad* comes from a Greek proverb. **16–18:** According to 22.14–15, Paul received his com-mission from Ananias (see 9.6); the present account conforms more closely to Paul's own account (Gal.1.1,15–17). **21:** *Do away with me:* see 21.30–32. **22:** The *prophets* and *Moses:* see 23.5 n. **23:** See Mk.8.31 for parallels; Lk.24.44–47. *First to rise:* see 1 Cor.15.20–23. **28:** *Christian:* see 11.26 n. **30–32: Paul's innocence recognized. 31:** This is the third time Paul's innocence has been implied (see 23.9; 25.25; also 23.29; compare Lk.23.4 n.). **32:** Not enough is known of

27 WHEN IT WAS DECIDED THAT WE SHOULD sail for Italy, Paul and some other prisoners were handed over to a centurion named Julius, of the Augustan 2 Cohort. We embarked in a ship of Adramyttium, bound for ports in the province of Asia, and put out to sea. In our party was Aristarchus, a Mace- 3 donian from Thessalonica. Next day we landed at Sidon; and Julius very considerately allowed Paul to go to his 4 friends to be cared for. Leaving Sidon we sailed under the lee of Cyprus be- 5 cause of the head-winds, then across the open sea off the coast of Cilicia and Pamphylia, and so reached Myra in Lycia.

6   There the centurion found an Alex- andrian vessel bound for Italy and put 7 us aboard. For a good many days we made little headway, and we were hard put to it to reach Cnidus. Then, as the wind continued against us, off Salmone we began to sail under the lee of Crete, 8 and, hugging the coast, struggled on to a place called Fair Havens, not far from the town of Lasea.

9   By now much time had been lost, the Fast was already over, and it was risky to go on with the voyage. Paul there- 10 fore gave them this advice: 'I can see, gentlemen," he said, 'that this voyage will be disastrous: it will mean grave loss, loss not only of ship and cargo 11 but also of life.' But the centurion paid more attention to the captain and to the owner of the ship than to what Paul 12 said; and as the harbour was unsuitable for wintering, the majority were in favour of putting out to sea, hoping, if they could get so far, to winter at Phoenix, a Cretan harbour exposed 13 south-west and north-west. So when a southerly breeze sprang up, they thought that their purpose was as good as achieved, and, weighing anchor, they sailed along the coast of Crete

hugging the land. But before very long 14 a fierce wind, the 'North-easter' as they call it, tore down from the landward side. It caught the ship and, as it was 15 impossible to keep head to wind, we had to give way and run before it. We 16 ran under the lee of a small island called Cauda, and with a struggle man- aged to get the ship's boat under con- trol. When they had hoisted it aboard, 17 they made use of tackle and under- girded the ship. Then, because they were afraid of running on to the shal- lows of Syrtis, they lowered the main- sail and let her drive. Next day, as we 18 were making very heavy weather, they began to lighten the ship; and on the 19 third day they jettisoned the ship's gear with their own hands. For days on end 20 there was no sign of either sun or stars, a great storm was raging, and our last hopes of coming through alive began to fade.

When they had gone for a long time 21 without food, Paul stood up among them and said, 'You should have taken my advice, gentlemen, not to sail from Crete; then you would have avoided this damage and loss. But now I urge 22 you not to lose heart; not a single life will be lost, only the ship. For last 23 night there stood by me an angel of the God whose I am and whom I worship. "Do not be afraid, Paul," he said; "it 24 is ordained that you shall appear before the Emperor; and, be assured, God has granted you the lives of all who are sailing with you." So keep up your 25 courage: I trust in God that it will turn out as I have been told; though we 26 have to be cast ashore on some island.'

The fourteenth night came and we 27 were still drifting in the Sea of Adria. In the middle of the night the sailors felt that land was getting nearer. They 28 sounded and found twenty fathoms. Sounding again after a short interval

---

Roman law to determine whether a prisoner who had *appealed to the Emperor* could be released by some other judicial officer. This verse implies he could not.
 27.1–28.31: Paul taken to Rome. 5–6: *Myra in Lycia* was an important way station for grain ships that regularly brought wheat from Egypt to Rome. *Alexandria* was the chief city of Egypt. **8:** The exact locations of *Fair Havens* and *Lasea* are unknown. **9:** *The Fast* probably refers to the Jewish Day of Atonement, which comes in early fall, a risky time for sailing. By November, all sailing ceased due to winter storms. **15:** Ancient ships had severely limited capabilities of beating into the wind. **17:** The meaning of *tackle* is unsure. How such a *ship* was *undergirded* is also unclear. *Lowered the mainsail* may also mean raise a (storm) sail, or rig a sea-anchor. **23–24:** See 23.11 n. **24:** Divine rescue from danger at sea was attributed to

29 they found fifteen fathoms; and fearing that we might be cast ashore on a rugged coast they dropped four anchors from the stern and prayed for daylight 30 to come. The sailors tried to abandon ship; they had already lowered the ship's boat, pretending they were going to lay out anchors from the bows, 31 when Paul said to the centurion and the soldiers, 'Unless these men stay on board you can none of you come off 32 safely.' So the soldiers cut the ropes of the boat and let her drop away.

33 Shortly before daybreak Paul urged them all to take some food. 'For the last fourteen days', he said, 'you have lived in suspense and gone hungry; you have 34 eaten nothing whatever. So I beg you to have something to eat; your lives depend on it. Remember, not a hair of 35 your heads will be lost.' With these words, he took bread, gave thanks to God in front of them all, broke it, and 36 began eating. Then they all plucked up courage, and took food themselves. 37 There were on board two hundred and 38 seventy-six of us in all. When they had eaten as much as they wanted they lightened the ship by dumping the corn in the sea.

39 When day broke they could not recognize the land, but they noticed a bay with a sandy beach, on which they planned, if possible, to run the ship 40 ashore. So they slipped the anchors and let them go; at the same time they loosened the lashings of the steering-paddles, set the foresail to the wind, 41 and let her drive to the beach. But they found themselves caught between cross-currents and ran the ship aground, so that the bow stuck fast and remained immovable, while the stern was being 42 pounded to pieces by the breakers. The soldiers thought they had better kill the prisoners for fear that any should swim 43 away and escape; but the centurion wanted to bring Paul safely through

and prevented them from carrying out their plan. He gave orders that those who could swim should jump over-board first and get to land; the rest 44 were to follow, some on planks, some on parts of the ship. And thus it was that all came safely to land.

Once we had made our way to safety 28 we identified the island as Malta. The 2 rough islanders treated us with un-common kindness; because it was cold and had started to rain, they lit a bon-fire and made us all welcome. Paul had 3 got together an armful of sticks and put them on the fire, when a viper, driven out by the heat, fastened on his hand. The islanders, seeing the snake 4 hanging on to his hand, said to one another, 'The man must be a murderer; he may have escaped from the sea, but divine justice has not let him live.' Paul, 5 however, shook off the snake into the fire and was none the worse. They still 6 expected that any moment he would swell up or drop down dead, but after waiting a long time without seeing any-thing extraordinary happen to him, they changed their minds and now said, 'He is a god.'

In the neighbourhood of that place 7 there were lands belonging to the chief magistrate of the island, whose name was Publius. He took us in and enter-tained us hospitably for three days. It 8 so happened that this man's father was in bed suffering from recurrent bouts of fever and dysentery. Paul visited him and, after prayer, laid his hands upon him and healed him; whereupon the 9 other sick people on the island came also and were cured. They honoured us 10 with many marks of respect, and when we were leaving they put on board pro-vision for our needs.

Three months had passed when we 11 set sail in a ship which had wintered in the island; she was the *Castor and Pollux* of Alexandria. We put in at 12

---

many Hellenistic deities. **37:** The number is well within the capacity of such a ship. **39–44:** Paul reports suffering three earlier shipwrecks and drifting once twenty-four hours at sea (2 Cor.11.25), but Acts gives no report of these incidents.

28.1–10: Paul at Malta. 1: Sometime after leaving Cauda, the wind must have shifted to the east; a continuing northeast wind would have landed them on the coast of Africa (27.17), not *Malta*. **6:** Much of what Paul did and said in 27.9–28.10 would make him appear to be a Hellenistic divine man, or even a god.

28.11–15: On to Rome. 11: *Three months:* probably between November and February.

Syracuse and spent three days there; then we sailed round and arrived at Rhegium. After one day a south wind sprang up and we reached Puteoli in two days. There we found fellow-Christians and were invited to stay a week with them. And so to Rome. The Christians there had had news of us and came out to meet us as far as Appii Forum and Tres Tabernae, and when Paul saw them, he gave thanks to God and took courage.

16 WHEN WE ENTERED ROME PAUL WAS allowed to lodge by himself with a soldier in charge of him. Three days later he called together the local Jewish leaders; and when they were assembled, he said to them: 'My brothers, I, who never did anything against our people or the customs of our forefathers, am here as a prisoner; I was handed over to the Romans at Jerusalem. They examined me and would have liked to release me because there was no capital charge against me; but the Jews objected, and I had no option but to appeal to the Emperor; not that I had any accusation to bring against my own people. That is why I have asked to see you and talk to you, because it is for the sake of the hope of Israel that I am in chains, as you see.' They replied, 'We have had no communication from Judaea, nor has any countryman of ours arrived with any report or gossip to your discredit. We should like to hear from you what your views are; all we know about this sect is that no one has a good word to say for it.'

So they fixed a day, and came in large numbers as his guests. He dealt at length with the whole matter; he spoke urgently of the kingdom of God and sought to convince them about Jesus by appealing to the Law of Moses and the prophets. This went on from dawn to dusk. Some were won over by his arguments; others remained sceptical. Without reaching any agreement among themselves they began to disperse, but not before Paul had said one thing more: 'How well the Holy Spirit spoke to your fathers through the prophet Isaiah when he said, "Go to this people and say: You may hear and hear, but you will never understand; you may look and look, but you will never see. For this people's mind has become gross; their ears are dulled, and their eyes are closed. Otherwise, their eyes might see, their ears hear, and their mind understand, and then they might turn again, and I would heal them." Therefore take notice that this salvation of God has been sent to the Gentiles; the Gentiles will listen.'[n]

He stayed there two full years at his own expense, with a welcome for all who came to him, proclaiming the kingdom of God and teaching the facts about the Lord Jesus Christ quite openly and without hindrance.

n *Some witnesses add* (29) After he had spoken, the Jews went away, arguing vigorously among themselves.

Sailing resumed in late February or early March. **13**: Grain ships from Egypt unloaded at *Puteoli*, the major Roman harbor for foreign trade. **14**: When Paul reached *Rome*, the prophecy of 23.11 was fulfilled, as well as the program outlined in 1.8; see also Rom.15.22–24,28. **15**: Though Paul had never been to Rome, he and the *Christians there* knew about each other; see Rom.1.8; 15.14–16. The NT tells us nothing about the origin of the Christian congregation in Rome.

28.16–31: Paul in Rome. 17: This was the original accusation by the Jews from Asia; see 21.28. **18**: *No capital charge;* see 23.29; 25.25; 26.31. **23**: *Kingdom of God:* see 19.8 n. **26**: Isa.6.9–10 Sept.; compare Mk.4.12 and parallels. This is similar to Stephen's condemnation of the Jews (7.51–53). **28**: As the whole narrative has shown, this is a major theme of Acts; see 13.46 n. **31**: The story which began with Jesus in Galilee (the Gospel of Luke) has now moved through Jerusalem to Rome, and, in the author's view, will continue to the ends of the earth (1.8). Although we would like to know the outcome of Paul's imprisonment, that information is not essential for the author's purpose. He has had in mind a story that remains incomplete until the fulfillment of God's plan in the remote future. Meanwhile, men will be *proclaiming the kingdom of God and teaching the facts about the Lord Jesus Christ.*

LETTERS

THE LETTER OF PAUL TO THE
ROMANS

The longest of Paul's letters (and first in the New Testament sequence) contains the fullest and most balanced statement of his theology. For a year or two Paul had been collecting relief money for the Christian poor in Jerusalem (15.16; 1 Cor.16.1; 2 Cor.8.4; 9.1). Now, perhaps because of Judaizers (see Introduction to Galatians), he has decided that he can no longer work in his old territory (from Syria to Illyricum; 15.19,23). He proposes to visit Rome, after he has delivered this collection (15.25), in order to open a new mission farther west ("Spain"; 15.24,28). To introduce himself to the Romans, a church he has never visited, he fills this impressive letter with insights derived from past crises in his eventful ministry. Perhaps he also intends to scotch any rumors that labeled him as antinomian (3.8,31; 7.12; chs. 13–14) or anti-Jewish (3.1–3; chs. 9–11).

As to the date: the collection project implies the chronological sequence—1 Corinthians, 2 Corinthians, chs. 1–9, Romans—over a period of perhaps two years. The Judaizing crisis suggests that Galatians immediately preceded Romans. Opinions about the year vary from 48 A.D. to 58 A.D.

The Gospel according to Paul

1 FROM PAUL, SERVANT OF CHRIST Jesus, apostle by God's call, set apart for the service of the Gospel. 2 This Gospel God announced beforehand in sacred scriptures through his prophets. 3 It is about his Son: on the human level he was born of David's 4 stock, but on the level of the spirit—the Holy Spirit—he was declared Son of God by a mighty act in that he rose from the dead:[a] it is about Jesus Christ 5 our Lord. Through him I received the privilege of a commission in his name to lead to faith and obedience men in 6 all nations, yourselves among them, you who have heard the call and belong to Jesus Christ.

7 I send greetings to all of you in Rome whom God loves and has called to be his dedicated people. Grace and peace to you from God our Father and the Lord Jesus Christ.

8 Let me begin by thanking my God, through Jesus Christ, for you all, because all over the world they are telling 9 the story of your faith. God is my witness, the God to whom I offer the humble service of my spirit by preaching the gospel of his Son: God knows how continually I make mention of you in my prayers, and am always asking 10 that by his will I may, somehow or other, succeed at long last in coming to visit you. 11 For I long to see you; I want to bring you some spiritual gift 12 to make you strong; or rather, I want to be among you to be myself encouraged by your faith as well as you by mine.

13 But I should like you to know,[b] my brothers, that I have often planned to come, though so far without success, in the hope of achieving something among you, as I have in other parts of the 14 world. I am under obligation to Greek and non-Greek, to learned and simple; 15 hence my eagerness to declare the Gospel to you in Rome as well as to 16 others. For I am not ashamed of the Gospel. It is the saving power of God for everyone who has faith—the Jew

---

a Or declared Son of God with full powers from the time when he rose from the dead.
b Some witnesses read I believe you know.

1.1–7: Salutation. Greek letters began with the names of the sender and the recipient. **1:** Apostle: see 1 Cor.9.1 n. **5:** Paul here affirms his apostleship to the nations, i.e. Gentiles. **7:** The word grace (i.e. God's favor) replaces the usual and similar-sounding Greek salutation; peace is the Jewish salutation (e.g. Mt.10.13).

1.8–15: Opening thanksgiving. Next in an ancient Greek letter there was usually a prayer for the recipient's health. Similarly, Paul begins all his letters, except the angry Gal. (and 2 Cor. chs. 10–13 if that is indeed a separate letter; see annotation there), by thanking God for the addressees, mentioning in the process the major themes of the letter.

1.16–17: The thesis of the letter is that God's way of righting wrong gives unmerited acceptance to (i.e. justifies) the believer on the basis of his faith (i.e. trust). **16:** Jew first: see 2.9–10 n.

183

17 first, but the Greek also—because here is revealed God's way of righting wrong, a way that starts from faith and ends in faith;*c* as Scripture says, 'he shall gain life who is justified through faith'.

God's attitude towards sin a ka wrath

18 FOR WE SEE DIVINE RETRIBUTION revealed from heaven and falling upon all the godless wickedness of men. In their wickedness they are stifling the

19 truth. For all that may be known of God by men lies plain before their eyes; indeed God himself has disclosed

20 it to them. His invisible attributes, that is to say his everlasting power and deity, have been visible, ever since the world began, to the eye of reason, in the things he has made. There is therefore no possible defence for their con-

21 duct; knowing God, they have refused to honour him as God, or to render him thanks. Hence all their thinking has ended in futility, and their misguided minds are plunged in darkness.

22 They boast of their wisdom, but they

23 have made fools of themselves, exchanging the splendour of immortal God for an image shaped like mortal man, even for images like birds, beasts, and creeping things.

24 For this reason God has given them up to the vileness of their own desires, and the consequent degradation of their

25 bodies, because they have bartered away the true God for a false one,*d* and have offered reverence and worship to created things instead of to the Creator, who is blessed for ever; amen.

26 In consequence, I say God has given them up to shameful passions. Their women have exchanged natural inter-

27 course for unnatural, and their men in turn, giving up natural relations with women, burn with lust for one another; males behave indecently with males, and are paid in their own persons the fitting wage of such perversion.

28 Thus, because they have not seen fit to acknowledge God, he has given them up to their own depraved reason. This leads them to break all rules of conduct. They are filled with every kind 29 of injustice, mischief, rapacity, and malice; they are one mass of envy, murder, rivalry, treachery, and malevolence; whisperers and scandal-mongers, 30 hateful to God, insolent, arrogant, and boastful; they invent new kinds of mischief, they show no loyalty to parents, no conscience, no fidelity to their 31 plighted word; they are without natural affection and without pity. They know 32 well enough the just decree of God, that those who behave like this deserve to die, and yet they do it; not only so, they actually applaud such practices.

You therefore have no defence—you 2 who sit in judgement, whoever you may be—for in judging your fellow-man you condemn yourself, since you, the judge, are equally guilty. It is admitted that God's judgement is rightly 2 passed upon all who commit such crimes as these; and do you imagine— 3 you who pass judgement on the guilty while committing the same crimes yourself—do you imagine that you, any more than they, will escape the judgement of God? Or do you think lightly 4 of his wealth of kindness, of tolerance, and of patience, without recognizing that God's kindness is meant to lead you to a change of heart? In the rigid 5 obstinacy of your heart you are laying up for yourself a store of retribution for the day of retribution, when God's just judgement will be revealed, and he 6 will pay every man for what he has done. To those who pursue glory, 7 honour, and immortality by steady persistence in well-doing, he will give eternal life; but for those who are 8 governed by selfish ambition, who refuse obedience to the truth and take the wrong for their guide, there will be

c Or ... wrong. It is based on faith and addressed to faith.
d Or the truth of God for the lie.

17: *God's way ... ends in faith:* the book's theme; see 3.22. *Scripture:* Hab.2.4 (Gal.3.11).
   1.18–32: The depravity of the Gentiles. "The heavens tell out the glory of God" (Ps.19.1), but men have *refused to honour him* (v. 21). **19:** *All that may be known,* i.e. except God's special revelation to Jews and Christians. **23:** For the Jewish scorn of idols see Isa.44.13–20; Wis. chs. 13–15. **24–28:** Therefore *God has given them up* (vv. 24,26,28) to increasing wickedness that leads to death. **29–31:** See Gal.5.19–21.
   2.1–16: The Jews will be judged also, although they presume to *sit in* moral *judgement* over the Gentiles. **5:** God's wrath, already evident (1.18), will culminate in *the day of retribution*

Like wine, true blessedness.

9 the fury of retribution. There will be trouble and distress for every human being who 13 an evil-doer, for the Jew first and for the Greek also; and for

10 every well-doer there will be glory, honour, and peace, for the Jew first and also for the Greek.

11,12 For God has no favourites: those who have sinned outside the pale of the Law of Moses will perish outside its pale, and all who have sinned under

13 that law will be judged by the law. It is not by hearing the law, but by doing it, that men will be justified before God.

14 When Gentiles who do not possess the law carry out its precepts by the light of nature, then, although they have no

15 law, they are their own law, for they display the effect of the law inscribed on their hearts. Their conscience is called as witness, and their own thoughts argue the case on either side,

16 against them or even for them, on the day when God judges the secrets of human hearts through Christ Jesus. So my gospel declares.

17 But as for you—you may bear the name of Jew; you rely upon the law and

18 are proud of your God; you know his will; instructed by the law, you know

19 right from wrong; you are confident that you are the one to guide the blind,

20 to enlighten the benighted, to train the stupid, and to teach the immature, because in the law you see the very shape

21 of knowledge and truth. You, then, who teach your fellow-man, do you fail to teach yourself? You proclaim, 'Do not steal'; but are you yourself a

22 thief? You say, 'Do not commit adultery'; but are you an adulterer? You abominate false gods; but do you rob

23 their shrines? While you take pride in the law, you dishonour God by break-

24 ing it. For, as Scripture says, 'Because of you the name of God is dishonoured among the Gentiles.'

25 Circumcision has value, provided you keep the law; but if you break the law, then your circumcision is as if it

26 had never been. Equally, if an uncircumcised man keeps the precepts of the law, will he not count as circumcised?

27 He may be uncircumcised in his natural state, but by fulfilling the law he will pass judgement on you who break it, for all your written code and

28 your circumcision. The true Jew is not he who is such in externals, neither is the true circumcision the external mark

29 in the flesh. The true Jew is he who is such inwardly, and the true circumcision is of the heart, directed not by written precepts but by the Spirit; such a man receives his commendation not from men but from God.

3 Then what advantage has the Jew? What is the value of circumcision?

2 Great, in every way. In the first place, the Jews were entrusted with the oracles of God. What if some of them

3 were unfaithful? Will their faithlessness cancel the faithfulness of God?

4 Certainly not! God must be true though every man living were a liar; for we read in Scripture, 'When thou speakest thou shalt be vindicated, and win the verdict when thou art on trial.'

5 Another question: if our injustice serves to bring out God's justice, what are we to say? Is it unjust of God (I speak of him in human terms) to bring

6 retribution upon us? Certainly not! If God were unjust, how could he judge the world?

7 Again, if the truth of God brings him all the greater honour because of my falsehood, why should I any longer

8 be condemned as a sinner? Why not indeed 'do evil that good may come', as some libellously report me as saying? To condemn such men as these is surely no injustice.

(see 1 Cor.1.8 n.). **9–10**: Since the *Jew* has special knowledge of God (3.2; 9.4–5), he is *first*. **11–16**: But Jews and Gentiles equally are *judged* by their actions (v. 13; see Mt.7.20–21; Gal.3.21; Jas.1.22–25), the Jews under the *Law of Moses* (v. 12) as found in Scripture, the Gentiles by the same standard as *inscribed on their hearts* (v. 15; see v. 29; 2 Cor.3.2–3 n.). **16**: *Day*: see v. 5 n.

2.17–29: The immorality of the adherents of the Law. 21–22: Exod.20.3–6,14–15. **24**: Isa.52.5; Ezek.36.20. **25**: *Circumcision* is the symbol of God's covenant with Judaism (Gen.17.11). **26**: See 1 Cor.7.19; Gal.5.6. **29**: *Circumcision . . . of the heart*: see Deut.10.16; Jer.4.4.

3.1–8: Jews have the advantage of God's *oracles*, i.e. the Scriptures, and the unalterable promises they contain. **4**: Ps.51.4. **8**: *Libellously*: see 6.1 n.

9 What then? Are we Jews any better off?[e] No, not at all![f] For we have already drawn up the accusation that Jews and Greeks alike are all under the 10 power of sin. This has scriptural warrant:

'There is no just man, not one;
11 no one who understands, no one
        who seeks God.
12 All have swerved aside, all alike have
        become debased;
    there is no one to show kindness; no,
        not one.

13 Their throat is an open grave,
    they use their tongues for treachery,
    adders' venom is on their lips,
14 and their mouth is full of bitter
        curses.

15 Their feet hasten to shed blood,
16 ruin and misery lie along their paths,
17 they are strangers to the high-road of
        peace,
18 and reverence for God does not
        enter their thoughts.'

19 Now all the words of the law are addressed, as we know, to those who are within the pale of the law, so that no one may have anything to say in self-defence, but the whole world may be exposed to the judgement of God. 20 For (again from Scripture) 'no human being can be justified in the sight of God' for having kept the law: law brings only the consciousness of sin.

21 BUT NOW, QUITE INDEPENDENTLY OF law, God's justice has been brought to light. The Law and the prophets both 22 bear witness to it: it is God's way of righting wrong, effective through faith in Christ for all who have such faith—

all, without distinction. For all alike 23 have sinned, and are deprived of the divine splendour, and all are justified 24 by God's free grace alone, through his act of liberation in the person of Christ Jesus. For God designed him to be the 25 means of expiating sin by his sacrificial death, effective through faith. God meant by this to demonstrate his justice, because in his forbearance he had overlooked the sins of the past— to demonstrate his justice now in the 26 present, showing that he is himself just and also justifies any man who puts his faith in Jesus.

What room then is left for human 27 pride? It is excluded. And on what principle? The keeping of the law would not exclude it, but faith does. For our argument is that a man is 28 justified by faith quite apart from success in keeping the law.

Do you suppose God is the God of 29 the Jews alone? Is he not the God of Gentiles also? Certainly, of Gentiles also, if it be true that God is one. And 30 he will therefore justify both the circumcised in virtue of their faith, and the uncircumcised through their faith. Does this mean that we are using faith 31 to undermine law? By no means: we are placing law itself on a firmer footing.

WHAT, THEN, ARE WE TO SAY ABOUT 4 Abraham, our ancestor in the natural line? If Abraham was justified by any- 2 thing he had done, then he has a ground for pride. But he has no such ground before God; for what does 3 Scripture say? 'Abraham put his faith in God, and that faith was counted to him as righteousness.' Now if a man 4

e Or Are we Jews any worse off?
f Or Not in all respects.

3.9–20: **But all are equally guilty,** for the law itself condemns its followers (5.13; 7.7–11; Gal.3.10). **10–18:** Pss.14.1–3; 5.9; 140.3; 10.7; Isa.59.7–8; Ps.36.1. **19:** *Words of the law:* here Scripture as a whole (contrast v. 21). **20:** Ps.143.2 (Gal.2.16); *sin:* see 7.7–13 n.
    3.21–31: **God's gracious acceptance** (i.e. justifying, vv. 24,26,28,30; see Gal.2.16 n.) of the believer is now revealed **21:** *Law and the prophets:* Scripture, which later included a third part, Writings. **22:** God's way of dealing with sin (i.e. *righting wrong*) depends on the believer's trust (i.e. *faith*) in Christ. *All:* both Jews and Gentiles (see vv. 29–30). **24:** *Act of liberation* (from sin) applies the metaphor of freeing from slavery to God's deed in Christ. **25–26:** The *past sins* of the believer are not ignored, since God is *just*. Instead, now using the language of sacrifice, Christ's death is God's way of cleansing the believer's sins (4.25; 5.9). **27–28:** *The keeping of the law* could be an achievement leading to *pride*. However, salvation is a gift resting on *faith:* thus pride is *excluded*. **31:** God's basic intention in the *law* is accomplished by *faith*.
    4.1–12: **Abraham was justified by his faith** and not by *anything he had done*. **3:** Paul finds his

does a piece of work, his wages are not 'counted' as a favour; they are paid as debt. But if without any work to his credit he simply puts his faith in him who acquits the guilty, then his faith is [5] indeed 'counted as righteousness'. In [6] the same sense David speaks of the happiness of the man whom God 'counts' as just, apart from any specific acts of justice: 'Happy are they', he [7] says, 'whose lawless deeds are forgiven, whose sins are buried away; happy is [8] the man whose sins the Lord does not count against him.' Is this happiness [9] confined to the circumcised, or is it for the uncircumcised also? Consider: we say, 'Abraham's faith was counted as righteousness'; in what circumstances [10] was it so counted? Was he circumcised at the time, or not? He was not yet circumcised, but uncircumcised; and [11] he later received the symbolic rite of circumcision as the hall-mark of the righteousness which faith had given him when he was still uncircumcised. Consequently, he is the father of all who have faith when uncircumcised, so that righteousness is 'counted' to them; and at the same time he is the [12] father of such of the circumcised as do not rely upon their circumcision alone, but also walk in the footprints of the faith which our father Abraham had while he was yet uncircumcised.

For it was not through law that [13] Abraham, or his posterity, was given the promise that the world should be his inheritance, but through the right-eousness that came from faith. For if [14] those who hold by the law, and they alone, are heirs, then faith is empty and the promise goes for nothing, because [15] law can bring only retribution; but where there is no law there can be no breach of law. The promise was made [16] on the ground of faith, in order that it might be a matter of sheer grace, and that it might be valid for all Abraham's

posterity, not only for those who hold by the law, but for those also who have the faith of Abraham. For he [13] is the father of us all, as Scripture says: 'I [17] have appointed you to be the father of many nations.' This promise, then, was valid before God, the God in whom he put his faith, the God who makes the dead live and summons things that are not yet in existence as if they already were. When hope [18] seemed hopeless, his faith was such that he became 'father of many na-tions', in agreement with the words which had been spoken to him: 'Thus shall your descendants be.' Without [19] any weakening of faith he contem-plated his own body, as good as dead (for he was about a hundred years old), and the deadness of Sarah's womb, and [20] never doubted God's promise in un-belief, but, strong in faith, gave honour to God, in the firm conviction of his [21] power to do what he had promised. And that is why Abraham's faith was [22] 'counted to him as righteousness'.

Those words were written, not for [23] Abraham's sake alone, but for our [24] sake too: it is to be 'counted' in the same way to us who have faith in the God who raised Jesus our Lord from the dead; for he was given up to death [25] for our misdeeds, and raised to life to justify us.*g*

THEREFORE, NOW THAT WE HAVE BEEN [5] justified through faith, let us continue at peace*h* with God through our Lord Jesus Christ, through whom we have [2] been allowed to enter the sphere of God's grace, where we now stand. Let us exult*i* in the hope of the divine splendour that is to be ours. More than [3] this: let us even exult*j* in our present sufferings, because we know that

g Or raised to life because we were now justified.
h Some witnesses read we are at peace.
i Or We exult.
j Or we even exult.

understanding of *faith* confirmed by Gen.15.6 (Sept.; Gal.3.6). **6**: *David:* the traditional author of the Psalter. **7–8**: Ps.32.1–2. **10–11**: He was not circumcised until Gen.17.11,24.
4.13–25: Faith and not law was the basis of God's *promise* to *Abraham* and to his *posterity* (compare Gal.3.16–18). **15**: *Retribution, breach of law:* see 3.10–20; 5.13,20; 7.7–11. **17**: Gen.17.5. *Nations:* see 1.5 n. **18**: Gen.15.5. **19**: Gen.17.17; 18.11. **22–23**: See v. 3. **24**: *For our sake:* see 15.4 n.; Gal.3.29. **25**: See 3.25–26 n.; 5.9.
5.1–11: Peace and reconciliation. *God* accepts us on the basis of our *faith* (v. 1). His *love* (v. 5) expressed in *Christ's* death (vv. 6–10) and communicated by the *Spirit* (v. 5), gives assurance to our *hope* (vv. 2,4,5) of salvation (see 1 Cor.12.4–6 n. and 13.13 n.). **3**: *Sufferings:*

[Handwritten margin notes, left: "The true 'Jew' so to speak (Faith) yet is made such by Trust (Faith) not by circumcision."]
[Handwritten margin note, right: "FAITH = TRUST"]

4 suffering trains us to endure, and endurance brings proof that we have stood the test, and this proof is the 5 ground of hope. Such a hope is no mockery, because God's love has flooded our inmost heart through the Holy Spirit he has given us.

6 For at the very time when we were still powerless, then Christ died for the 7 wicked. Even for a just man one of us would hardly die, though perhaps for a good man one might actually brave 8 death; but Christ died for us while we were yet sinners, and that is God's own 9 proof of his love towards us. And so, since we have now been justified by Christ's sacrificial death, we shall all the more certainly be saved through 10 him from final retribution. For if, when we were God's enemies, we were reconciled to him through the death of his Son, how much more, now that we are reconciled, shall we be saved by his 11 life! But that is not all: we also exult in God through our Lord Jesus, through whom we have now been granted reconciliation. (atonement)

12 Mark what follows. It was through one man that sin entered the world, and through sin death, and thus death pervaded the whole human race, inas-13 much as all men have sinned. For sin was already in the world before there was law, though in the absence of law 14 no reckoning is kept of sin. But death held sway from Adam to Moses, even over those who had not sinned as Adam did, by disobeying a direct command—and Adam foreshadows the Man who was to come.

15 But God's act of grace is out of all proportion to Adam's wrongdoing. For if the wrongdoing of that one man brought death upon so many, its effect is vastly exceeded by the grace of God and the gift that came to so many by the grace of the one man, Jesus Christ. 16 And again, the gift of God is not to be compared in its effect with that one man's sin; for the judicial action, following upon the one offence, issued in a verdict of condemnation, but the act of grace, following upon so many misdeeds, issued in a verdict of acquittal. 17 For if by the wrongdoing of that one man death established its reign, through a single sinner, much more shall those who receive in far greater measure God's grace, and his gift of righteousness, live and reign through the one man, Jesus Christ.

18 It follows, then, that as the issue of one misdeed was condemnation for all men, so the issue of one just act is acquittal and life for all men. For as 19 through the disobedience of the one man the many were made sinners, so through the obedience of the one man the many will be made righteous.

20 Law intruded into this process to multiply law-breaking. But where sin was thus multiplied, grace immeasurably exceeded it, in order that, as sin 21 established its reign by way of death, so God's grace might establish its reign in righteousness, and issue in eternal life through Jesus Christ our Lord.

6 What are we to say, then? Shall we persist in sin, so that there may be all 2 the more grace? No, no! We died to sin: how can we live in it any longer? 3 Have you forgotten that when we were baptized into union with Christ Jesus we were baptized into his death? 4 By baptism we were buried with him, and lay dead, in order that, as Christ was raised from the dead in the splendour of the Father, so also we might set our feet upon the new path of life.

5 For if we have become incorporate with him in a death like his, we shall also be one with him in a resurrection

---

see 2 Cor.4.8–11; 11.23–30; 12.10. **5**: *Spirit:* see ch. 8; 2 Cor.5.5 n. **8–10**: As *sinners* we were God's *enemies* (v. 10), but by his unique *love* (see Jn.15.13) we are now *reconciled*, and we shall surely be acquitted in the Last Judgment. **9**: See 3.25–26 n.

5.12–21: Adam and Christ, *disobedience* (Gen.2.17; 3.6) and *obedience* (v. 19), *sin* and *righteousness*, *condemnation* (Gen.3.19) and *acquittal*, *death* for *all men* and *life* for *all men*— these are Paul's contrasts (compare 1 Cor.15.21–23,45–49). **13**: See v. 20. **14**: *Adam, Man:* see 1 Cor.15.45–49 n. **20**: The *law* of Moses *intruded* (Gal.3.17–20) and, by specifying sin (v. 13; 3.20), made it more flagrant (see 7.7–13 n.).

6.1–14: Dying and rising with Christ. 1: *Sin* to obtain *more grace* (also v. 15; 3.8)? The idea is ludicrous and probably represents one of several ways Paul's gospel was twisted by his opponents (see Introduction). **3–4**: *Baptism* means dying to *sin* and rising to life *into union with*

[handwritten margin notes:] at -one-ment (unity)

[handwritten circled 12 with arrow]

[handwritten bottom notes:] Rom 5:12-21 1) Linked to Adam we inherit sin and fallen human nature because we come from him. 2) Joined to Christ we inherit grace and justification. We are spiritually descended / linked to him by Baptism.

6 like his. We know that the man we once were has been crucified with Christ, for the destruction of the sinful self, so that we may no longer be the
7 slaves of sin, since a dead man is no
8 longer answerable for his sin. But if we thus died with Christ, we believe that we shall also come to life with him.
9 We know that Christ, once raised from the dead, is never to die again: he is no longer under the dominion of death.
10 For in dying as he died, he died to sin, once for all, and in living as he lives,
11 he lives to God. In the same way you must regard yourselves as dead to sin and alive to God, in union with Christ Jesus.
12 So sin must no longer reign in your mortal body, exacting obedience to the
13 body's desires. You must no longer put its several parts at sin's disposal, as implements for doing wrong. No: put yourselves at the disposal of God, as dead men raised to life; yield your bodies to him as implements for doing
14 right; for sin shall no longer be your master, because you are no longer under law, but under the grace of God.
15 What then? Are we to sin, because we are not under law but under grace?
16 Of course not. You know well enough that if you put yourselves at the disposal of a master, to obey him, you are slaves of the master whom you obey; and this is true whether you serve sin, with death as its result; or obedience,
17 with righteousness as its result. But God be thanked, you, who once were slaves of sin, have yielded whole-hearted obedience to the pattern of teaching to which you were made sub-
18 ject,[k] and, emancipated from sin, have
19 become slaves of righteousness (to use words that suit your human weakness) —I mean, as you once yielded your bodies to the service of impurity and lawlessness, making for moral anarchy,

so now you must yield them to the service of righteousness, making for a holy life.
20 When you were slaves of sin, you were free from the control of righteous-
21 ness; and what was the gain? Nothing but what now makes you ashamed, for the end of that is death. But now, freed
22 from the commands of sin, and bound to the service of God, your gains are such as make for holiness, and the end is eternal life. For sin pays a wage, and
23 the wage is death, but God gives freely, and his gift is eternal life, in union with Christ Jesus our Lord.
7 You cannot be unaware, my friends —I am speaking to those who have some knowledge of law—that a person is subject to the law so long as he is alive,
2 and no longer. For example, a married woman is by law bound to her husband while he lives; but if her husband dies, she is discharged from the obligations of the marriage-law. If, therefore, in
3 her husband's lifetime she consorts with another man, she will incur the charge of adultery; but if her husband dies she is free of the law, and she does not commit adultery by consorting with another man. So you, my friends,
4 have died to the law by becoming identified with the body of Christ, and accordingly you have found another husband in him who rose from the dead, so that we may bear fruit for God. While we lived on the level of our
5 lower nature, the sinful passions evoked by the law worked in our bodies, to bear fruit for death. But now, having
6 died to that which held us bound, we are discharged from the law, to serve God in a new way, the way of the spirit, in contrast to the old way, the way of a written code.
7 What follows? Is the law identical

k Or which was handed on to you.

Christ. **6:** *Crucified:* see Gal.5.24; 6.14. **12–14:** The basis of Paul's ethic is expressed here. That God has freed us from sin's power (v. 7) is the meaning of Christ's death; therefore we must live as if we are indeed free. *Obedience* to sin is unthinkable. See 8.5–13; Gal.5.16–25.
  6.15–23: No slave can serve two masters, and by God's mercy the *slaves of sin* (v. 17) have become the *slaves of righteousness* (v. 18). Once again, obedience to sin is out of the question. **15:** See v. 1 n. **22:** *Holiness:* a consecrated life (as in v. 19).
  7.1–6: The marriage law as an analogy. How is it that the Christian is not "under law, but under . . . grace" (6.14–15)? **4–6:** In the same way we have *died* to *the* law and thus are free of the *law. Fruit* is a conventional metaphor for "the product of a manner of life."
  7.7–13: The Law and Sin contrasted. Paul often speaks (especially in Gal.; see Gal.3.19–20 n.)

v. 14-25 classic → human powerlessness "Step 1"

with sin? Of course not. But except through law I should never have become acquainted with sin. For example, I should never have known what it was to covet, if the law had not said, 'Thou 8 shalt not covet.' Through that commandment sin found its opportunity, and produced in me all kinds of wrong desires. In the absence of law, sin is a 9 dead thing. There was a time when, in the absence of law, I was fully alive; but when the commandment came, 10 sin sprang to life and I died. The commandment which should have led to life proved in my experience to lead to 11 death, because sin found its opportunity in the commandment, seduced me, and through the commandment killed me.

12 Therefore the law is in itself holy, and the commandment is holy and 13 just and good. Are we to say then that this good thing was the death of me? By no means. It was sin that killed me, and thereby sin exposed its true character: it used a good thing to bring about my death, and so, through the commandment, sin became more sinful than ever.

14 We know that the law is spiritual; but I am not: I am unspiritual, the pur- 15 chased slave of sin. I do not even acknowledge my own actions as mine, for what I do is not what I want to do, but 16 what I detest. But if what I do is against my will, it means that I agree with the 17 law and hold it to be admirable. But as

things are, it is no longer I who perform the action, but sin that lodges in me. For I know that nothing good lodges 18 in me—in my unspiritual nature. I mean—for though the will to do good is there, the deed is not. The good which 19 I want to do, I fail to do; but what I do is the wrong which is against my will; and if what I do is against my will, 20 clearly it is no longer I who am the agent, but sin that has its lodging in me.

I discover this principle, then: that 21 when I want to do the right, only the wrong is within my reach. In my in- 22 most self I delight in the law of God, but I perceive that there is in my bodily 23 members a different law, fighting against the law that my reason approves and making me a prisoner under the law*l* that is in my members, the law of sin. Miserable creature that I am, who 24 is there to rescue me out of this body doomed to death*m*? God alone, 25 through Jesus Christ our Lord! Thanks be to God! In a word then, I myself, subject to God's law as a rational being, am yet,*n* in my unspiritual nature, a slave to the law of sin.

The conclusion of the matter is this: 8 there is no condemnation for those who are united with Christ Jesus, be- 2 cause in Christ Jesus the life-giving law of the Spirit has set you free from the law of sin and death. What the law 3

v. 24 - steps 2 + 3

l Or by means of the law.
m Or out of the body doomed to this death.
n Or Thus, left to myself, while subject ... rational being, I am yet ...

---

as if he thought of *the law* as *identical with sin* (compare "died to sin" in Rom.6.10 with "died to the law" in v. 4). Here, however, he makes his most positive assessment of the Law: it is *holy and just and good*, since it reflects God's intentions. But in practice the Law is powerless against *sin* and even encourages it (v. 8; compare 5.13,20; Gal.3.21–22). 7–8: *"Thou shalt not covet"* (Exod.20.17; Deut.5.21) is the only commandment in the Decalogue which restricts a man's thoughts; here *sin* finds *its opportunity.* 9–11: Paul speaks of leaving childhood and assuming responsibility under the Law in terms reminiscent of the Eden story (Gen.3.1–19; 2 Cor.11.3). 11: *Seduced:* tricked (Gen.3.13).

7.14–25: The divided man. In his *inmost self* (v. 22) Paul knows that the Law is *spiritual* (v. 14), *admirable* (v. 16), and a *delight* (v. 22). But sin enslaves his body so that it acts *against* his *will* (vv.15–17,20). 14: *Unspiritual:* lit. "fleshly." Here and in ch. 8 Paul contrasts "flesh" and "spirit"; compare 8.4,5–8,9–10 nn.; Gal.5.16–17; 2 Cor.4.7–5.5; 1 Cor.15.39–53. 17,20: Paul thinks of *sin* as a power and occasionally personifies it: *no longer I* but *sin* acts. But as chs. 1–3 show, man is still responsible for his actions. 23,25: *A different law, the law of sin:* a foreign principle, sin's command. 24–25: Paul expresses both ultimate despair at being *doomed to death* and simultaneously his profoundest *thanks* for God's *rescue* (see 8.1–4).

8.1–4: God's act of rescue has turned the tables. Divided by sin we could only expect *condemnation* and *death*. But Christ, by sharing our *sinful nature* and dying *as a sacrifice for sin* (see 3.25–26 n.), has diverted the expected condemnation to *sin* itself and given us new life instead. 1: Paul's language is fluid. The believer is *united with Christ* (lit. "in Christ") because he has the *Spirit* "dwelling within" him (v. 9). Paul also speaks of Christ "dwelling within" the believer (v 10 and Gal.2.20; Eph.3.17). 3: *Sending his own son:* see v. 32 and 5.8. The phrase,

190

could never do, because our lower nature robbed it of all potency, God has done: by sending his own Son in a form like that of our own sinful nature, and as a sacrifice for sin,[o] he has passed judgement against sin within that very 4 nature, so that the commandment of the law may find fulfilment in us, whose conduct, no longer under the control of our lower nature, is directed by the Spirit.

5 Those who live on the level of our lower nature have their outlook formed 6 by it, and that spells death; but those who live on the level of the spirit have the spiritual outlook, and that is life 7 and peace. For the outlook of the lower nature is enmity with God; it is not subject to the law of God; indeed 8 it cannot be: those who live on such a level cannot possibly please God.

9 But that is not how you live. You are on the spiritual level, if only God's Spirit dwells within you; and if a man does not possess the Spirit of Christ, he 10 is no Christian. But if Christ is dwelling within you, then although the body is a dead thing because you sinned, yet the spirit is life itself because you have been 11 justified.[p] Moreover, if the Spirit of him who raised Jesus from the dead dwells within you, then the God who raised Christ Jesus from the dead will also give new life to your mortal bodies through his indwelling Spirit.

12 It follows, my friends, that our lower nature has no claim upon us; we are not 13 obliged to live on that level. If you do so, you must die. But if by the Spirit you put to death all the base pursuits of the body, then you will live.

14 For all who are moved by the Spirit 15 of God are sons of God. The Spirit you have received is not a spirit of slavery leading you back into a life of fear, but a Spirit that makes us sons, enabling us 16 to cry 'Abba! Father!' In that cry the Spirit of God joins with our spirit in testifying that we are God's children; 17 and if children, then heirs. We are God's heirs and Christ's fellow-heirs, if we share his sufferings now in order to share his splendour hereafter.

18 For I reckon that the sufferings we now endure bear no comparison with the splendour, as yet unrevealed, which 19 is in store for us. For the created universe waits with eager expectation for 20 God's sons to be revealed. It was made the victim of frustration, not by its own choice, but because of him who made 21 it so;[q] yet always there was hope, because[r] the universe itself is to be freed from the shackles of mortality and enter upon the liberty and splendour 22 of the children of God. Up to the present, we know, the whole created universe groans in all its parts as if in the 23 pangs of childbirth. Not only so, but even we, to whom the Spirit is given as firstfruits of the harvest to come, are groaning inwardly while we wait for God to make us his sons and[s] set our 24 whole body free. For we have been saved, though only in hope. Now to see

o *Or* and to deal with sin.
p *Or* so that you may live rightly.
q *Or* because God subjected it.
r *Or* with the hope that . . .
s *Some witnesses omit* make us his sons and.

---

a form like that of our own sinful nature (compare Phil.2.7), does not mean that Paul doubted Jesus' full humanity. On the contrary, his argument requires it. **4:** Now *directed by the Spirit*, our *conduct* can fulfill the Law's basic requirement: love (see 13.8–10; Gal.5.14,22). *Lower nature:* lit. "flesh" (see 7.14 n.).

8.5–11: The old life and the new. 5–8: Those whose lives are directed by their *lower nature* (see Gal.5.19–21) live in *enmity* with God (see 5.10) and can only expect *death*. **9–10:** But those who live on the *spiritual level* (see 7.14 n.) have *life itself. Dwelling:* see v. 1 n. *The body* is *dead*, i.e. mortal, because of *sin* (see 5.12). **11:** The *indwelling Spirit* is our promise (see 2 Cor.1.22; 5.5) of a resurrection like Christ's.

8.12–17: God's adopted sons. Compare Gal.4.5–7. **12–13:** See 6.12–14 n. **14–15:** Paul's previous use of slavery motifs (3.24; 6.15–23; 7.14) makes his new language dramatic. Sin made us slaves; the Spirit *makes us* God's *sons.* Thus we can call God *"Father"* (notably in the Lord's Prayer) with the Aram. word that Jesus used, *"Abba."* **16:** See vv. 26–27. **17:** Christ is *heir* to all God's promises (Gal.3.16), and we also, as we are found in him (Gal.3.29) and share his suffering (Phil.3.10–11). In v. 29 Paul even calls us Christ's brothers.

8.18–25: The liberation of the whole creation. Just as we share in Christ's sufferings (v. 17), so all of nature suffers with us (v. 22). And the whole *universe*, ourselves included, now waits eagerly to be *freed* from *mortality* and to *enter* upon the *liberty and splendour* (v. 21) which is our heritage (v. 17). **20:** God *made it so:* see Gen.3.17. **23:** *Firstfruits:* see 1 Cor.15.20 n. and 2 Cor.5.5. *Groaning:* see 2 Cor.5.2. **24–25:** See 2 Cor.5.6–7.

is no longer to hope: why should a man endure and wait[t] for what he already sees? But if we hope for something we do not yet see, then, in waiting for it, we show our endurance. ²⁵

In the same way the Spirit comes to the aid of our weakness. We do not even know how we ought to pray,[u] but through our inarticulate groans the Spirit himself is pleading for us, and God who searches our inmost being knows what the Spirit means, because he pleads for God's people in God's own way; and in everything, as we know, he co-operates for good with those who love God[v] and are called according to his purpose. For God knew his own before ever they were, and also ordained that they should be shaped to the likeness of his Son, that he might be the eldest among a large family of brothers; and it is these, so fore-ordained, whom he has also called. And those whom he called he has justified, and to those whom he justified he has also given his splendour. ²⁶ ²⁷ ²⁸ ²⁹ ³⁰

With all this in mind, what are we to say? If God is on our side, who is against us? He did not spare his own Son, but gave him up for us all; and with this gift how can he fail to lavish upon us all he has to give? Who will be the accuser of God's chosen ones? It is God who pronounces acquittal; then who can condemn? It is Christ—Christ who died, and, more than that, was raised from the dead—who is at God's right hand, and indeed pleads our cause.[w] Then what can separate us from the love of Christ? Can affliction or hardship? Can persecution, hunger, nakedness, peril, or the sword? 'We ³¹ ³²(*No one!*) ³³ ³⁴ ³⁵ ³⁶

are being done to death for thy sake all day long,' as Scripture says; 'we have been treated like sheep for slaughter'— and yet, in spite of all, overwhelming victory is ours through him who loved us. For I am convinced that there is nothing in death or life, in the realm of spirits or superhuman powers, in the world as it is or the world as it shall be, in the forces of the universe, in heights or depths—nothing in all creation that can separate us from the love of God in Christ Jesus our Lord. *Amen! Alleluia!* ³⁷ ³⁸ ³⁹

The purpose of God in history

I AM SPEAKING THE TRUTH AS A Christian, and my own conscience, enlightened by the Holy Spirit, assures me it is no lie: in my heart there is great grief and unceasing sorrow. For I could even pray to be outcast from Christ myself for the sake of my brothers, my natural kinsfolk. They are Israelites: they were made God's sons; theirs is the splendour of the divine presence, theirs the covenants, the law, the temple worship, and the promises. Theirs are the patriarchs, and from them, in natural descent, sprang the Messiah.[x] May God, supreme above all, be blessed for ever![y] Amen. **9** ² ³ ⁴ ⁵

t *Some witnesses read* why should a man hope . . .
u *Or* what it is right to pray for.
v *Or* and, as we know, all things work together for good for those who love God; *some witnesses read* and we know God himself co-operates for good with those who love God.
w *Or* Who will be the accuser of God's chosen ones? Will it be God himself? No, he it is who pronounces acquittal. Who will be the judge to condemn? Will it be Christ—he who died, and, more than that, . . . right hand? No, he it is who pleads our cause.
x *Greek* Christ.
y *Or* sprang the Messiah, supreme above all, God blessed for ever; *or* sprang the Messiah, who is supreme above all. Blessed be God for ever!

8.26–30: God's loving care supports us in *our weakness* (i.e. suffering) by the Spirit's intercession (vv. 26–28) and by the revelation of his plans for us (vv. 29–30). **26:** *We do not . . . know how . . . to pray* until the Spirit teaches us to say "Father" (v. 15; compare Lk.11.1–2) and gives us ecstatic speech (see 1 Cor. chs. 12–14). **28–29:** The final goal of God's purpose for us is *likeness* to *his Son* (see 2 Cor.3.18; Eph.4.13). **30:** For Paul's own experience see Gal.1.15–16.

8.31–39: Our ultimate trust in God's love. Terms like *against us* (v. 31) and *accuser* (v. 33) suggest the heavenly court at the Last Judgment. **31:** Ps. 118.6. **35:** Paul's *hardships* (2 Cor. 11.23–28) were, of course, not unique to him. **36:** Ps.44.22. **38–39:** *Death* is but one of the forces which attempt to separate us from God (see 1 Cor.2.6–8 n.).

9.1–5: Paul's anguish at Israel's unbelief. 3: *Outcast:* see 1 Cor.16.22 n.; Exod.32.32. **4:** *Israelites:* descendants of Jacob, renamed Israel (Gen.32.28). The name emphasizes God's special choice. *Sons:* see, e.g. Exod.4.22; Jer.31.9. *Splendour:* see Exod.16.10; 24.16; 40.34. *Covenants:* see, e.g. Gen.6.18; 9.9; 17.7; Exod.19.5; 34.10. *Law:* notably Exod.20.1–17; Deut.5.1–21. *Promises:* see 4.13–21.

6   It is impossible that the word of God should have proved false. For not all descendants of Israel are truly Israel, 7 nor, because they are Abraham's offspring, are they all his true children;[z] but, in the words of Scripture, 'Through the line of Isaac your descendants shall 8 be traced.'[a] That is to say, it is not those born in the course of nature who are children of God; it is the children born through God's promise who are reckoned as Abraham's descendants. 9 For the promise runs: 'At the time fixed I will come, and Sarah shall have a son.'

10   But that is not all, for Rebekah's children had one and the same father, 11 our ancestor Isaac; and yet, in order that God's selective purpose might stand, based not upon men's deeds but 12 upon the call of God, she was told, even before they were born, when they had as yet done nothing, good or ill, 'The elder shall be servant to the 13 younger'; and that accords with the text of Scripture, 'Jacob I loved and Esau I hated.'

14   What shall we say to that? Is God to be charged with injustice? By no means. 15 For he says to Moses, 'Where I show mercy, I will show mercy, and where I 16 pity, I will pity.' Thus it does not depend on man's will or effort, but on 17 God's mercy. For Scripture says to Pharaoh, 'I have raised you up for this very purpose, to exhibit my power in my dealings with you, and to spread 18 my fame over all the world.' Thus he not only shows mercy as he chooses, but also makes men stubborn as he chooses.

19   You will say, 'Then why does God blame a man? For who can resist his 20 will?' Who are you, sir, to answer God back? Can the pot speak to the potter and say, 'Why did you make me like 21 this?'? Surely the potter can do what he likes with the clay. Is he not free to make out of the same lump two vessels, one to be treasured, the other for common use?

22   But what if God, desiring to exhibit[b] his retribution at work and to make his power known, tolerated very patiently those vessels which were objects of retribution due for destruction, and did 23 so in order to make known the full wealth of his splendour upon vessels which were objects of mercy, and which from the first had been prepared for this splendour?

24   Such vessels are we, whom he has called from among Gentiles as well as 25 Jews, as it says in the Book of Hosea: 'Those who were not my people I will call My People, and the unloved nation I will call My Beloved. For in the very 26 place where they were told "you are no people of mine", they shall be called Sons of the living God.' But Isaiah 27 makes this proclamation about Israel: 'Though the Israelites be countless as the sands of the sea, only a remnant shall be saved; for the Lord's sentence 28 on the land will be summary and final'; as also he said previously, 'If the Lord 29 of Hosts had not left us the mere germ of a nation, we should have become like Sodom, and no better than Gomorrah.'

30   Then what are we to say? That Gentiles, who made no effort after righteousness, nevertheless achieved it, a righteousness based on faith; whereas 31 Israel made great efforts after a law of righteousness, but never attained to it. Why was this? Because their efforts 32 were not based on faith, but (as they supposed) on deeds. They fell over the 'stone' mentioned in Scripture: 'Here 33 I lay in Zion a stone to trip over, a rock

z *Or* all children of God.
a *Or* God's call shall be for your descendants in the line of Isaac.
b *Or* although he had the will to exhibit . . .

9.6–29: God never intended that his promises should descend to more than a *remnant* (v. 27) of *Abraham's offspring*, for of Abraham's sons only Isaac was chosen (compare Gal.4.21–5.1) and of Isaac's sons, only *Jacob*. 7: Gen.21.12. 9: Gen.18.10. 12: Gen.25.23. 13: Mal.1.2–3. 14–23: Not injustice but mercy lies behind God's choices, for men have no claims against his supreme sovereignty. 15: Exod.33.19. 17: Exod.9.16. 20: Isa.29.16; 45.9. 21: Jer.18.6. 24–26: Now, as the church's mission shows, Gentiles are also *called*. Paul finds the promise in Hos.1.10; 2.23. 27–28: Isa.10.22–23. *Remnant*, germ (v. 29) prepare for 11.1–12. 29: Isa.1.9. *Sodom* and *Gomorrah*: Gen.19.24–25.

9.30–10.10: God's righteousness comes by faith. 30: See 3.22; 10.20; Gal.2.16; Phil.3.9. 33: Paul equates Christ with "the *stone* which the builders rejected" (Ps.118.22), which he relates

to stumble against; but he who has faith in him will not be put to shame.'

10 Brothers, my deepest desire and my prayer to God is for their salvation. 2 To their zeal for God I can testify; but 3 it is an ill-informed zeal. For they ignore God's way of righteousness, and try to set up their own, and therefore they have not submitted themselves to 4 God's righteousness. For Christ ends the law and brings righteousness for everyone who has faith.*c*

5 Of legal righteousness Moses writes, 'The man who does this shall gain life 6 by it.' But the righteousness that comes by faith says, 'Do not say to yourself, "Who can go up to heaven?"' (that is 7 to bring Christ down), 'or, '"Who can go down to the abyss?"' (to bring 8 Christ up from the dead). But what does it say? 'The word is near you: it is upon your lips and in your heart.' This means the word of faith which we pro-9 claim. If on your lips is the confession, 'Jesus is Lord', and in your heart the faith that God raised him from the 10 dead, then you will find salvation. For the faith that leads to righteousness is in the heart, and the confession that leads to salvation is upon the lips.

11 Scripture says, 'Everyone who has faith in him will be saved from shame' 12 —everyone: there is no distinction between Jew and Greek, because the same Lord is Lord of all, and is rich enough for the need of all who invoke him. 13 For everyone, as it says again—'everyone who invokes the name of the Lord 14 will be saved'. How could they invoke one in whom they had no faith? And how could they have faith in one they had never heard of? And how hear without someone to spread the news? 15 And how could anyone spread the news

without a commission to do so? And that is what Scripture affirms: 'How welcome are the feet of the messengers of good news!'

But not all have responded to the 16 good news. For Isaiah says, 'Lord, who has believed our message?' We 17 conclude that faith is awakened by the message, and the message that awakens it comes through the word of Christ. But, I ask, can it be that they never 18 heard it? Of course they did: 'Their voice has sounded all over the earth, and their words to the bounds of the inhabited world.' But, I ask again, can 19 it be that Israel failed to recognize the message? In reply, I first cite Moses, who says, 'I will use a nation that is no nation to stir your envy, and a foolish nation to rouse your anger.' But Isaiah 20 is still more daring: 'I was found', he says, 'by those who were not looking for me; I was clearly shown to those who never asked about me'; while to 21 Israel he says, 'All day long I have stretched out my hands to an unruly and defiant people.'

I ask then, has God rejected his **11** people? I cannot believe it! I am an Israelite myself, of the stock of Abra-ham, of the tribe of Benjamin. No! 2 God has not rejected the people which he acknowledged of old as his own. You know (do you not?) what Scrip-ture says in the story of Elijah—how Elijah pleads with God against Israel: 'Lord, they have killed thy prophets, 3 they have torn down thine altars, and I alone am left, and they are seeking my life.' But what does the divine voice 4 say to him? 'I have left myself seven thousand men who have not knelt to

c Or Christ is the end of the law as a way to righteous-ness for everyone who has faith.

---

to Isa.8.14–15; 28.16. Compare 1 Pet.2.4(and n.)–8. **10.4:** See 3.21–26; Gal.3.19,24. **5:** Although *the man who does* the Law will indeed be saved (Lev.18.5; Gal.3.12), the task is beyond our strength (3.9–20; 7.7–25). **6–10:** Deut.9.4 and 30.12–14 are interpreted to mean that the *faith* which *leads to righteousness* and *the confession* of Christ that *leads to salvation* (v. 10) are now available. **9:** Compare Phil.2.11.

10.11–21: Israel has been deaf to the *good news* of Christ. **11:** See 9.33; Isa.28.16. **12:** See 3.29; Gal.3.28. **13:** Joel 2.32 (*Lord* is taken to mean Christ). **15:** Isa.52.7. **16:** Isa.53.1. **17:** *Word of Christ:* the preaching about Christ. **18:** Ps.19.4. **19–21:** *The message* is so simple that (*foolish*) Gentiles understand it; Israel, however, has failed to respond because they are *an unruly* and *defiant* people (v. 21). **19:** Deut.32.21. *Envy:* see 11.11,14. **20–21:** Isa.65.1–2.

11.1–12: Israel's rejection is not complete as long as a *"remnant"* (v. 5) exists, i.e. the church. **1:** *Israelite myself:* see 9.4 n.; 2 Cor.11.22; Phil.3.5. **2–4:** *Elijah* mistakenly believed that Israel's

5 Baal.' In just the same way at the present time a 'remnant' has come into being, selected by the grace of God.
6 But if it is by grace, then it does not rest on deeds done, or grace would cease to be grace.
7 What follows? What Israel sought, Israel has not achieved, but the selected few have achieved it. The rest were
8 made blind to the truth, exactly as it stands written: 'God brought upon them a numbness of spirit; he gave them blind eyes and deaf ears, and so
9 it is still.' Similarly David says:

'May their table be a snare and a trap,
both stumbling-block and retribution!
10 May their eyes become so dim that they lose their sight!
Bow down their backs unceasingly!'

11 I now ask, did their failure mean complete downfall? Far from it! Because they offended, salvation has come to the Gentiles, to stir Israel to emula-
12 tion. But if their offence means the enrichment of the world, and if their falling-off means the enrichment of the Gentiles, how much more their coming to full strength!
13 But I have something to say to you Gentiles. I am a missionary to the Gentiles, and as such I give all honour
14 to that ministry when I try to stir emulation in the men of my own race,
15 and so to save some of them. For if their rejection has meant the reconciliation of the world, what will their acceptance mean? Nothing less than
16 life from the dead! If the first portion of dough is consecrated, so is the whole lump. If the root is consecrated, so are
17 the branches. But if some of the branches have been lopped off, and

you, a wild olive, have been grafted in among them, and have come to share the same root and sap as the olive, do 18 not make yourself superior to the branches. If you do so, remember that it is not you who sustain the root: the root sustains you.
You will say, 'Branches were lopped 19 off so that I might be grafted in.' Very 20 well: they were lopped off for lack of faith, and by faith you hold your place. Put away your pride, and be on your guard; for if God did not spare the 21 native branches, no more will he spare you. Observe the kindness and the 22 severity of God—severity to those who fell away, divine kindness to you, if only you remain within its scope; otherwise you too will be cut off, whereas 23 they, if they do not continue faithless, will be grafted in; for it is in God's power to graft them in again. For if 24 you were cut from your native wild olive and against all nature grafted into the cultivated olive, how much more readily will they, the natural olive-branches, be grafted into their native stock!
For there is a deep truth here, my 25 brothers, of which I want you to take account, so that you may not be complacent about your own discernment: this partial blindness has come upon Israel only until the Gentiles have been admitted in full strength; when 26 that has happened, the whole of Israel will be saved, in agreement with the text of Scripture:

'From Zion shall come the Deliverer;
he shall remove wickedness from Jacob.
And this is the covenant I will grant 27 them,
when I take away their sins.'

rebellion was complete (1 Kgs.19.10,14,18). **2**: Ps.94.14. **6**: See 4.4–5; Gal.3.18. **7–12**: At present God gives Israel *a numbness of spirit* (vv. 7–10,25), but only to allow time to call the *Gentiles*, who will in turn *stir Israel to emulation* (v. 11; 10.19). **8**: Isa.29.10; Deut.29.4 (compare Mk.4.10–12). **9–10**: Ps.69.22–23. *David:* see 4.6 n.
  11.13–24: Israel is God's olive tree (Jer.11.16; Hos.14.6). **13**: See 1.5; 15.16; Gal.1.16; 2.9. **14**: See 1 Cor.9.22. **15**: Without Israel God has achieved the *reconciliation of the world* (5.10–11), but when Israel receives God's *acceptance*, what a glorious consummation! **16**: *First portion* (Num.15.20–21) and *root* probably mean the patriarchs (v. 28; 9.5). **17**: *The branches . . . lopped off* are the Jews, who lack faith (v. 20); the Gentiles are shoots from a *wild olive grafted in* "against all nature" (v. 24). **21–22**: Compare 1 Cor.10.12. **24**: The restoration of Israel will be swifter than the mission to the Gentiles.
  11.25–36: The salvation of all mankind, both Gentiles and Jews, will be accomplished by God's *mercy* (v. 32). **25–27**: *Blindness:* see vv. 8,10. *Gentiles . . . in full strength* and *the whole*

28 In the spreading of the Gospel they are treated as God's enemies for your sake, but God's choice stands, and they are his friends for the sake of the patri-29 archs. For the gracious gifts of God and 30 his calling are irrevocable. Just as formerly you were disobedient to God, but now have received mercy in the 31 time of their disobedience, so now, when you receive mercy, they have proved disobedient, but only in order 32 that they too may receive mercy. For in making all mankind prisoners to disobedience, God's purpose was to show mercy to all mankind.

33 O depth of wealth, wisdom, and knowledge in God! How unsearchable his judgements, how untraceable his 34 ways! Who knows the mind of the Lord? Who has been his counsellor? 35 Who has ever made a gift to him, to 36 receive a gift in return? Source, Guide, and Goal of all that is—to him be glory for ever! Amen.

Christian behaviour

12 THEREFORE, MY BROTHERS, I IMPLORE you by God's mercy to offer your very selves to him: a living sacrifice, dedicated and fit for his acceptance, the worship offered by mind and heart.[d] 2 Adapt yourselves no longer to the pattern of this present world, but let your minds be remade and your whole nature thus transformed. Then you will be able to discern the will of God, and to know what is good, acceptable, and perfect.

3 In virtue of the gift that God in his grace has given me I say to everyone among you: do not be conceited or think too highly of yourself; but think your way to a sober estimate based on the measure of faith that God has dealt 4 to each of you. For just as in a single

human body there are many limbs and organs, all with different functions, so 5 all of us, united with Christ, form one body, serving individually as limbs and organs to one another.

The gifts we possess differ as they are 6 allotted to us by God's grace, and must be exercised accordingly: the gift of inspired utterance, for example, in proportion to a man's faith; or the gift of 7 administration, in administration. A teacher should employ his gift in teaching, and one who has the gift of stirring 8 speech should use it to stir his hearers. If you give to charity, give with all your heart; if you are a leader, exert yourself to lead; if you are helping others in distress, do it cheerfully.

Love in all sincerity, loathing evil 9 and clinging to the good. Let love for 10 our brotherhood breed warmth of mutual affection. Give pride of place to one another in esteem.

With unflagging energy, in ardour of 11 spirit, serve the Lord.[e]

Let hope keep you joyful; in trouble 12 stand firm; persist in prayer.

Contribute to the needs of God's 13 people, and practise hospitality.

Call down blessings on your per- 14 secutors—blessings, not curses.

With the joyful be joyful, and mourn 15 with the mourners.

Care as much about each other as 16 about yourselves. Do not be haughty, but go about with humble folk. Do not keep thinking how wise you are.

Never pay back evil for evil. Let your 17 aims be such as all men count honourable. If possible, so far as it lies with 18 you, live at peace with all men. My 19 dear friends, do not seek revenge, but leave a place for divine retribution; for there is a text which reads, 'Justice is mine, says the Lord, I will repay.' But 20

d Or . . . acceptance, for such is the worship which you, as rational creatures, should offer.
e Some witnesses read meet the demands of the hour.

of Israel: corporately but not necessarily every individual. *Scripture:* Isa.59.20–21; 27.9. **34:** Isa.40.13 (1 Cor.2.16). **35:** Job 41.11. **36:** See 1 Cor.8.6; Col.1.16.
  12.1–8: The dedicated life. 1: See 6.13,16,19. *A living sacrifice:* in contrast to the offering of a dead animal. **2:** See 8.5–13. **3:** *Gift:* Paul's apostleship (see 1.5). *Measure of faith:* the amount and nature of the spiritual gifts (v. 6) received by faith. **4–8:** The passage is a reworking of 1 Cor.12.4–31. **6:** *In proportion to a man's faith:* see v. 3 n.
  12.9–21: The greatness of love (see 1 Cor. ch. 13). **13:** *Hospitality:* see 16.2 n. **14:** See Mt.5.44. **16:** Prov.3.7. **17a:** Prov.20.22; 1 Th.5.15. **17b:** Prov.3.4 (Sept.); 2 Cor.8.21. **19:** Men must not *seek revenge* (Lev.19.18; Mt.5.39). *Leave a place for:* leave it to. *A text:* Deut.32.35. **20:** Prov.25.21–22 (Mt.5.44); *coals of fire:* deep shame and remorse.

there is another text: 'If your enemy is hungry, feed him, if he is thirsty, give him a drink; by doing this you will 21 heap live coals on his head.' Do not let evil conquer you, but use good to defeat evil.

13 Every person must submit to the supreme authorities. There is no authority but by act of God, and the existing authorities are instituted by 2 him; consequently anyone who rebels against authority is resisting a divine institution, and those who so resist have themselves to thank for the 3 punishment they will receive. For government, a terror to crime, has no terrors for good behaviour. You wish to have no fear of the authorities? Then continue to do right and you will 4 have their approval, for they are God's agents working for your good. But if you are doing wrong, then you will have cause to fear them; it is not for nothing that they hold the power of the sword, for they are God's agents of punishment, for retribution on the 5 offender. That is why you are obliged to submit. It is an obligation imposed not merely by fear of retribution but by 6 conscience. That is also why you pay taxes. The authorities are in God's service and to these duties they devote their energies.

7 Discharge your obligations to all men; pay tax and toll, reverence and respect, to those to whom they are due. 8 Leave no claim outstanding against you, except that of mutual love. He who loves his neighbour has satisfied 9 every claim of the law. For the commandments, 'Thou shalt not commit adultery, thou shalt not kill, thou shalt not steal, thou shalt not covet', and any other commandment there may be, are 10 all summed up in the one rule, 'Love

your neighbour as yourself.' Love cannot wrong a neighbour; therefore the whole law is summed up in love.*f*

In all this, remember how critical the 11 moment is. It is time for you to wake out of sleep, for deliverance is nearer to us now than it was when first we believed. It is far on in the night; day is 12 near. Let us therefore throw off the deeds of darkness and put on our armour as soldiers of the light. Let us be-13 have with decency as befits the day: no revelling or drunkenness, no debauchery or vice, no quarrels or jealousies! Let Christ Jesus himself be the armour 14 that you wear; give no more thought to satisfying the bodily appetites.

IF A MAN IS WEAK IN HIS FAITH YOU MUST 14 accept him without attempting to settle doubtful points. For instance, one man 2 will have faith enough to eat all kinds of food, while a weaker man eats only vegetables. The man who eats must not 3 hold in contempt the man who does not, and he who does not eat must not pass judgement on the one who does; for God has accepted him. Who are 4 you to pass judgement on someone else's servant? Whether he stands or falls is his own Master's business; and stand he will, because his Master has power to enable him to stand.

Again, this man regards one day 5 more highly than another, while that man regards all days alike. On such a point everyone should have reached conviction in his own mind. He who 6 respects the day has the Lord in mind in doing so, and he who eats meat has the Lord in mind when he eats, since he gives thanks to God; and he who abstains has the Lord in mind no less, since he too gives thanks to God.

f Or the whole law is fulfilled by love.

13.1–7: The Christian's duty to the state is to be an obedient subject (compare Wis.6.1–5; 1 Pet.2.13–17; 3.13). Paul had experienced both the benefits of the Roman government and its *punishment* (v. 2; see 2 Cor.11.25 n.), but since he believed that the government's *authority* came *by act of God*, he counseled obedience. **6–7:** See Mk.12.17.

13.8–10: Love sums up the law. 9: *The commandments:* Exod.20.13–15,17; Deut.5.17–19,21 (see Rom.7.7). *One rule:* Lev.19.18 (compare Mk.12.31; Mt.19.18; Gal.5.14).

13.11–14: The end of the age approaches. 11: We must *wake* and put the obligation of love into action. The passage is a reworking of 1 Th.5.1–8. **12:** *Armour:* see 1 Th.5.8; Eph.6.14–17. **14:** See 6.12–14 n.; Gal.3.27 n.

14.1–23: Love respects the scruples of others. Those who remain in bondage to laws about *meat* (vv. 6,21), *wine* (v. 21), and Sabbath observance (vv. 5–6) are *weak in faith.* Paul regards these scruples as unnecessary (v. 14), but counsels tolerance based on *love* (v. 15). Paul here adapts 1 Cor.8.7–13 and 10.27–11.1 for the benefit of the Romans. **5:** Compare Gal.4.10.

7 For no one of us lives, and equally
8 no one of us dies, for himself alone. If
we live, we live for the Lord; and if
we die, we die for the Lord. Whether
therefore we live or die, we belong to
9 the Lord. This is why Christ died and
came to life again, to establish his
10 lordship over dead and living. You, sir,
why do you pass judgement on your
brother? And you, sir, why do you
hold your brother in contempt? We
shall all stand before God's tribunal.
11 For Scripture says, 'As I live, says the
Lord, to me every knee shall bow and
12 every tongue acknowledge God.' So,
you see, each of us will have to answer
for himself.
13 Let us therefore cease judging one
another, but rather make this simple
judgement: that no obstacle or stumbling-block be placed in a brother's way.
14 I am absolutely convinced, as a Christian,*g* that nothing is impure in itself;
only, if a man considers a particular
thing impure, then to him it is impure.
15 If your brother is outraged by what
you eat, then your conduct is no longer
guided by love. Do not by your eating
bring disaster to a man for whom
16 Christ died! What for you is a good
thing must not become an occasion for
17 slanderous talk; for the kingdom of
God is not eating and drinking, but
justice, peace, and joy, inspired by the
18 Holy Spirit. He who thus shows himself a servant of Christ is acceptable to
God and approved by men.
19 Let us then pursue the things that
make for peace and build up the com-
20 mon life. Do not ruin the work of God
for the sake of food. Everything is pure
in itself, but anything is bad for the
man who by his eating causes another
21 to fall. It is a fine thing to abstain from
eating meat or drinking wine, or doing
anything which causes your brother's
22 downfall. If you have a clear conviction, apply it to yourself in the sight of
God. Happy is the man who can make

his decision with a clear conscience!*h*
But a man who has doubts is guilty if 23
he eats, because his action does not
arise from his conviction, and anything
which does not arise from conviction is
sin.*i* Those of us who have a robust **15**
conscience must accept as our own
burden the tender scruples of weaker
men, and not consider ourselves. Each 2
of us must consider his neighbour and
think what is for his good and will build
up the common life. For Christ too did 3
not consider himself, but might have
said, in the words of Scripture, 'The
reproaches of those who reproached
thee fell upon me.' For all the ancient 4
scriptures were written for our own
instruction, in order that through the
encouragement they give us we may
maintain our hope with fortitude. And 5
may God, the source of all fortitude
and all encouragement, grant that you
may agree with one another after the
manner of Christ Jesus, so that with 6
one mind and one voice you may praise
the God and Father of our Lord Jesus
Christ.

In a word, accept one another as 7
Christ accepted us, to the glory of God.
I mean that Christ became a servant of 8
the Jewish people to maintain the truth
of God by making good his promises
to the patriarchs, and at the same time 9
to give the Gentiles cause to glorify
God for his mercy. As Scripture says,
'Therefore I will praise thee among the
Gentiles and sing hymns to thy name';
and again, 'Gentiles, make merry to- 10
gether with his own people'; and yet 11
again, 'All Gentiles, praise the Lord;
let all peoples praise him.' Once again, 12
Isaiah says, 'There shall be the Scion
of Jesse, the one raised up to govern
the Gentiles; on him the Gentiles shall
set their hope.' And may the God of 13
hope fill you with all joy and peace by

g Or on the authority of the Lord Jesus.
h Or who does not bring judgement upon himself by what he approves!
i See p. 200, note r.

7: See Gal.2.20; 2 Cor.5.15. **8:** *Live . . . die:* see Phil.1.20. **10:** *Tribunal:* final judgment (see 2.5,16; 2 Cor.5.10). **11:** Isa.45.23 (Phil.2.10–11). **14:** See Mk.7.18–19.
15:1–13: To put others first is to imitate Christ. 3: See Phil.2.5–8; 2 Cor.8.9. *Scripture:* Ps.69.9. **4:** See 4.23–24; 1 Cor.9.10; 10.11. **8:** Christ was born a Jew, obedient to the Law (Gal.4.4–5), so as to *maintain the truth* of God's *promises to the patriarchs* (see 4.13–21; 9.4–13). 9 **12:** As a result the *Gentiles* share in God's promises: Ps.18.49; Deut.32.43; Ps.117.1; Isa.11.10. **12:** *Scion of Jesse:* Messiah; see Mt.1.1 n.

your faith in him until, by the power of the Holy Spirit, you overflow with hope.

14 MY FRIENDS, I HAVE NO DOUBT IN MY own mind that you yourselves are quite full of goodness and equipped with knowledge of every kind, well able to 15 give advice to one another; nevertheless I have written to refresh your memory, and written somewhat boldly at times, in virtue of the gift I have 16 from God. His grace has made me a minister of Christ Jesus to the Gentiles; my priestly service is the preaching of the gospel of God, and it falls to me to offer the Gentiles to him as*j* an acceptable sacrifice, consecrated by the Holy Spirit.

17 Thus in the fellowship of Christ Jesus I have ground for pride in the service of 18 God. I will venture to speak of those things alone in which I have been Christ's instrument to bring the Gentiles into his allegiance, by word and 19 deed, by the force of miraculous signs and by the power of the Holy Spirit. As a result I have completed the preaching of the gospel of Christ from Jeru-20 salem as far round as Illyricum. It is my ambition to bring the Gospel to places where the very name of Christ has not been heard, for I do not want to build on another man's foundation; 21 but, as Scripture says,

'They who had no news of him shall see,
and they who never heard of him shall understand.'

22 That is why I have been prevented all 23 this time from coming to you. But now I have no further scope in these parts, and I have been longing for many years

to visit you on my way to Spain; for I 24 hope to see you as I travel through, and to be sent there with your support after having enjoyed your company for a while. But at the moment I am on my 25 way to Jerusalem, on an errand to God's people there. For Macedonia 26 and Achaia have resolved to raise a common fund for the benefit of the poor among God's people at Jerusalem. They have resolved to do so, 27 and indeed they are under an obligation to them. For if the Jewish Christians shared their spiritual treasures with the Gentiles, the Gentiles have a clear duty to contribute to their material needs. So when I have finished 28 this business and delivered the proceeds under my own seal, I shall set out for Spain by way of your city, and I am 29 sure that when I arrive I shall come to you with a full measure of the blessing of Christ.

I implore you by our Lord Jesus 30 Christ and by the love that the Spirit inspires, be my allies in the fight; pray to God for me that I may be saved 31 from unbelievers in Judaea and that my errand to Jerusalem may find acceptance with God's people, so that by his 32 will I may come to you in a happy frame of mind and enjoy a time of rest with you. The God of peace be with you 33 all. Amen.*k*

I COMMEND TO YOU PHOEBE, A FELLOW- **16** Christian who holds office in the congregation at Cenchreae. Give her, in 2 the fellowship of the Lord, a welcome worthy of God's people, and stand by her in any business in which she may need your help, for she has herself been

j Or ... of God, so that the worship which the Gentiles offer may be ...
k See page, 200 note r.

15.14–21: A polite postscript lest the Romans consider him presumptuous (see Introduction; 1.12). **14:** *One another:* perhaps an indication that they have no apostolic leader. **19:** *Miraculous signs:* see 2 Cor.12.12; Gal.3.5. *Jerusalem ... Illyricum:* Paul has been moving round the Mediterranean Sea systematically. He hopes that this program will carry him to Rome and Spain (v. 24). **20:** Paul makes it a principle not to work where other missionaries have preceded him (see 1 Cor.3.10–15; 2 Cor.10.15–16). **21:** Isa.52.15.

15.22–33: Paul plans to visit Rome on his way to Spain. **22–23:** See 1.10–13. *No further scope:* see Introduction and v. 19 n. **25:** Paul's *errand* is the collection (see Introduction). **26:** Galatia is not mentioned. Paul's angry letter to them may have resulted in their abandoning the project (contrast 2 Cor.8.1–9.15 n.; 8.10–11 n.). **30–32:** Presumably Paul's fears were justified and this visit to *Jerusalem* resulted in his arrest (Acts 21.17–24.27).

16.1–23: The closing greetings are unusually numerous. Paul lists people known by the Romans who could vouch for him. Nothing is known about most of these persons. **2:** *Welcome:*

a good friend to many, including myself.

3 Give my greetings to Prisca and Aquila, my fellow-workers in Christ 4 Jesus. They risked their necks to save my life, and not I alone but all the gentile congregations are grateful to 5 them. Greet also the congregation at their house.

Give my greetings to my dear friend Epaenetus, the first convert to Christ 6 in Asia, and to Mary, who toiled hard 7 for you. Greet Andronicus and Junias*l* my fellow-countrymen and comrades in captivity. They are eminent among the apostles, and they were Christians before I was.

8 Greetings to Ampliatus, my dear friend in the fellowship of the Lord, 9 to Urban my comrade in Christ, and to 10 my dear Stachys. My greetings to Apelles, well proved in Christ's service, 11 to the household of Aristobulus, and my countryman Herodion, and to those of the household of Narcissus 12 who are in the Lord's fellowship. Greet Tryphaena and Tryphosa, who toil in the Lord's service, and dear Persis who 13 has toiled in his service so long. Give my greetings to Rufus, an outstanding follower of the Lord, and to his 14 mother, whom I call mother too. Greet Asyncritus, Phlegon, Hermes, Patrobas, Hermas, and all friends in their 15 company. Greet Philologus and Julia,*m* Nereus and his sister, and Olympas, and all God's people associated with them.

16 Greet one another with the kiss of peace. All Christ's congregations send you their greetings.

17 I implore you, my friends, keep your eye on those who stir up quarrels and lead others astray, contrary to the teaching you received. Avoid them, for 18 such people are servants not of Christ our Lord but of their own appetites, and they seduce the minds of innocent people with smooth and specious words. The fame of your obedience has 19 spread everywhere. This makes me happy about you; yet I should wish you to be experts in goodness but simpletons in evil; and the God of 20 peace will soon crush Satan beneath your feet. The grace of our Lord Jesus be with you!*n*

Greetings to you from my colleague 21 Timothy, and from Lucius, Jason, and Sosipater my fellow-countrymen. (I 22 Tertius, who took this letter down, add my Christian greetings.) Greetings also 23 from Gaius, my host and host of the whole congregation, and from Erastus, treasurer of this city, and our brother Quartus.*o*

To HIM WHO HAS POWER TO MAKE YOUR 25 standing sure, according to the Gospel I brought you and the proclamation of Jesus Christ, according to the revelation of that divine secret kept in silence for long ages but now disclosed, and 26 through prophetic scriptures by eternal God's command made known to all nations, to bring them to faith and obedience—to God who alone is wise, 27 through Jesus Christ,*p* be glory for endless ages! Amen.*q r*

l Or Junia; *some witnesses read* Julia, *or* Julias.
m Or Julias; *some witnesses read* Junia, *or* Junias.
n The words The grace . . . with you *are omitted at this point in some witnesses; in some, these or similar words are given as verse 24, and in some others after verse 27 (see note on verse 23).*
o Some witnesses add (24) The grace of our Lord Jesus Christ be with you all! Amen.
p Some witnesses insert to whom.
q Here some witnesses add The grace of our Lord Jesus Christ be with you!
r Some witnesses place verses 25–27 at the end of chapter 14, one other places them at the end of chapter 15, and others omit them altogether.

Christian travelers depended on the hospitality of their fellows (see 12.13). **3–5:** *Prisca and Aquila* were in Ephesus (1 Cor.16.19); now they are back (Acts 18.2) at Rome. *House:* see v. 23 n. **7:** *Apostles:* see 1 Cor.9.1 n. **16:** The Christian *kiss* of ceremonial greeting (1 Cor.16.20; 2 Cor.13.12; 1 Th.5.26; 1 Pet.5.14) became a part of the church's liturgy (see 1 Cor.16.22 n.). **17–18:** See Gal.1.6–9; 6.12–13; 2 Cor.11.12–15; Phil.3.2–3,18–19. **19:** *Experts, simpletons:* see 1 Cor.14.20; Mt.10.16; Jer.4.22. **20:** *Satan,* the serpent, will be crushed (Gen.3.15); see 1 Cor. 15.25. *Grace . . . :* see 2 Cor.13.14 n. **21:** *Timothy:* see 1 Cor.16.10 n. **22:** Paul dictated (compare 1 Cor.1.16 n.) this letter to the scribe *Tertius.* **23:** *Gaius:* the Christian of 1 Cor.1.14? *Host:* early Christians worshiped in houses (v. 5), not yet in churches.
   16.25–27: The Benediction echoes some of the major themes of the letter (compare 1.2–6). **25:** *Gospel:* see 2.16; Gal.1.6–9. *Secret:* see 1 Cor.2.6–7; Col.1.26–27. **26:** *All nations:* see 1.5 n.

THE FIRST LETTER OF PAUL TO THE
CORINTHIANS

This letter gives a uniquely comprehensive picture of an early Christian congregation and of its founder (3.6,10), Paul. It contains the earliest written tradition of Jesus' resurrection (15.3–8) and of the Lord's Supper (11.23–26), as well as the moving "hymn" on Christian love (ch. 13). This is apparently the second letter Paul wrote to the Corinthians. The previous letter, mentioned in 5.9, is lost (unless 2 Cor.6.14–7.1 is a surviving fragment), but the Corinthians' reply to that letter provides the subject matter for chs. 7–16 of the present letter: marriage (7.1–24), celibacy (7.25–40), food offered to idols (8.1–11.1), worship (11.2–34), spiritual gifts (especially glossolalia, the gift of tongues; chs. 12–14), bodily resurrection (ch. 15), the "collection" of money for the Jerusalem Christians (16.1–11), and Apollos (16.12). But first Paul reasserts his authority at Corinth by dealing with three disciplinary lapses which have occurred there: congregational factions (chs. 1–4), a case of immorality (ch. 5), and lawsuits among Christians (ch. 6).

The letter was written from Ephesus (16.8). Paul's directions about the "collection" date the letter a year or so before 2 Cor. chs. 1–9 (see 2 Cor.8.10; 9.2 and Introduction to Rom.).

Unity and order in the church

1 FROM PAUL, APOSTLE OF JESUS CHRIST at God's call and by God's will, together with our colleague Sos- 2 thenes, to the congregation of God's people at Corinth, dedicated to him in Christ Jesus, claimed by him as his own, along with all men everywhere who invoke the name of our Lord Jesus Christ—their Lord as well as ours. 3 Grace and peace to you from God our Father and the Lord Jesus Christ.

4 I am always thanking God for you. I thank him for his grace given to you in 5 Christ Jesus. I thank him for all the enrichment that has come to you in Christ. You possess full knowledge and 6 you can give full expression to it, because in you the evidence for the truth of Christ has found confirmation. 7 There is indeed no single gift you lack, while you wait expectantly for our 8 Lord Jesus Christ to reveal himself. He will keep you firm to the end, without reproach on the Day of our Lord Jesus. It is God himself who called you to 9 share in the life of his Son Jesus Christ our Lord; and God keeps faith.

I appeal to you, my brothers, in the 10 name of our Lord Jesus Christ: agree among yourselves, and avoid divisions; be firmly joined in unity of mind and thought. I have been told, my brothers, 11 by Chloe's people that there are quarrels among you. What I mean is this: 12 each of you is saying, 'I am Paul's man', or 'I am for Apollos'; 'I follow Cephas', or 'I am Christ's.' Surely 13 Christ has not been divided among you! Was it Paul who was crucified for you? Was it in the name of Paul that you were baptized? Thank God, I 14 never baptized one of you—except Crispus and Gaius. So no one can say 15 you were baptized in my name.—Yes, 16 I did baptize the household of Stephanas: I cannot think of anyone else. Christ did not send me to baptize, but 17 to proclaim the Gospel; and to do it

---

1.1–3: **Salutation:** see Rom.1.1–7 nn. **1:** *Sosthenes* is unknown (but see Acts 18.17).

1.4–9: **Opening thanksgiving:** see Rom.1.8–15 n. **8:** The *Day* refers to Christ's impending (7.29,31) return to end the present age (2 Th.1.7–2.12) and to establish his kingdom (15.23–26,50) in a time of severe testing (3.13–15; 4.5; 5.5).

1.10–4.21: **Paul's apostolic authority.** In the face of divided loyalties Paul asserts his authority as founder (3.5–15), teacher (2.6–7; 3.1–2), and father (4.14–15) of the congregation.

1.10–17: **Factiousness in Corinth. 11:** *Chloe's people* are slaves or employees of this unknown lady. **12:** *Apollos:* the principal missionary at Corinth after Paul (3.4–6; 4.6; 16.12; see Acts 18.24–19.1). *Cephas:* the Aram. equivalent of "Peter" (meaning "rock"; see Mt.16.18). **14–17:** Baptism was not unimportant to Paul (see 6.11; Rom.6.3–4), but the actual rite he usually left to his assistants. **14:** *Crispus:* see Acts 18.8. *Gaius:* see Rom.16.23 n. **16:** Paul dictated his letters (see 16.21–24 n. and Rom.16.22 n.). Here he corrects himself. *Stephanas:* see 16.15–17 n.

without relying on the language of worldly wisdom, so that the fact of Christ on his cross might have its full weight.

18 This doctrine of the cross is sheer folly to those on their way to ruin, but to us who are on the way to salvation it 19 is the power of God. Scripture says, 'I will destroy the wisdom of the wise, and bring to nothing the cleverness of 20 the clever.' Where is your wise man now, your man of learning, or your subtle debater—limited, all of them, to this passing age? God has made the 21 wisdom of this world look foolish. As God in his wisdom ordained, the world failed to find him by its wisdom, and he chose to save those who have faith 22 by the folly of the Gospel. Jews call for 23 miracles, Greeks look for wisdom; but we proclaim Christ—yes, Christ nailed to the cross; and though this is a stumbling-block to Jews and folly to Greeks, 24 yet to those who have heard his call, Jews and Greeks alike, he is the power of God and the wisdom of God.

25 Divine folly is wiser than the wisdom of man, and divine weakness stronger 26 than man's strength. My brothers, think what sort of people you are, whom God has called. Few of you are men of wisdom, by any human standard; few are powerful or highly born. 27 Yet, to shame the wise, God has chosen what the world counts folly, and to shame what is strong, God has chosen 28 what the world counts weakness. He has chosen things low and contemptible, mere nothings, to overthrow the 29 existing order. And so there is no place for human pride in the presence of God. 30 You are in Christ Jesus by God's act, for God has made him our wisdom; he is our righteousness; in him we are 31 consecrated and set free. And so (in the words of Scripture), 'If a man must boast, let him boast of the Lord.'

2 As for me, brothers, when I came to you, I declared the attested truth of God[a] without display of fine words or wisdom. I resolved that while I was with 2 you I would think of nothing but Jesus Christ—Christ nailed to the cross. I 3 came before you weak, nervous, and shaking with fear. The word I spoke, 4 the gospel I proclaimed, did not sway you with subtle arguments; it carried conviction by spiritual power, so that 5 your faith might be built not upon human wisdom but upon the power of God.

And yet I do speak words of wisdom 6 to those who are ripe for it, not a wisdom belonging to this passing age, nor to any of its governing powers, which are declining to their end; I speak 7 God's hidden wisdom, his secret purpose framed from the very beginning to bring us to our full glory. The 8 powers that rule the world have never known it; if they had, they would not have crucified the Lord of glory. But, 9 in the words of Scripture, 'Things beyond our seeing, things beyond our hearing, things beyond our imagining, all prepared by God for those who love him', these it is that God has re- 10 vealed to us through the Spirit.

For the Spirit explores everything, even the depths of God's own nature. Among men, who knows what a man is 11 but the man's own spirit within him? In the same way, only the Spirit of God knows what God is. This is the Spirit 12 that we have received from God, and not the spirit of the world, so that we may know all that God of his own grace has given us; and, because we are 13 interpreting spiritual truths to those who have the Spirit, we speak of these gifts of God in words found for us not by our human wisdom but by the Spirit. A man who is unspiritual refuses 14 what belongs to the Spirit of God; it is folly to him: he cannot grasp it, because it needs to be judged in the light of the Spirit. A man gifted with the 15

a *Some witnesses read* I declared God's secret purpose . . .

1.18–2.5: The paradox of the cross: God saves through weakness and in spite of folly, revealing in *Christ nailed to the cross* his true *power* and *wisdom*. **19:** Isa.29.14. **22:** *Miracles* or "signs": see Mk.8.11–12; *wisdom:* see 2.4–8. **31:** Jer.9.24 (2 Cor.10.17). **2.3–4:** See 2 Cor.10.10.
2.6–16: The true wisdom of God is given by his Spirit. **6–8:** *This passing age* (in contrast to the coming age or kingdom): see 1.8 n. The *governing powers* (or "elemental spirits" or "authorities") are demonic astral or planetary beings that *rule the world* (Gal.4.3,9; Rom.8.38–39; Col.1.16). By crucifying Christ they have brought their own coming destruction upon themselves (15.24; Col.2.14–15). **9:** Perhaps Isa.64.4. **13:** See chs. 12–14. **15:** See 4.3–5. **16:** Isa.40.13.

Spirit can judge the worth of everything, but is not himself subject to
16 judgement by his fellow-men. For (in the words of Scripture) 'who knows the mind of the Lord? Who can advise him?' We, however, possess the mind of Christ.

3 FOR MY PART, MY BROTHERS, I COULD not speak to you as I should speak to people who have the Spirit. I had to deal with you on the merely natural
2 plane, as infants in Christ. And so I gave you milk to drink, instead of solid food, for which you were not yet ready. Indeed, you are still not ready for it,
3 for you are still on the merely natural plane. Can you not see that while there is jealousy and strife among you, you are living on the purely human level
4 of your lower nature? When one says, 'I am Paul's man', and another, 'I am for Apollos', are you not all too human?
5 After all, what is Apollos? What is Paul? We are simply God's agents in bringing you to the faith. Each of us performed the task which the Lord
6 allotted to him: I planted the seed, and Apollos watered it; but God made it
7 grow. Thus it is not the gardeners with their planting and watering who count,
8 but God, who makes it grow. Whether they plant or water, they work as a team,[b] though each will get his own
9 pay for his own labour. We are God's fellow-workers;[c] and you are God's garden.
10 Or again, you are God's building. I am like a skilled master-builder who by God's grace laid the foundation, and someone else is putting up the building.
11 Let each take care how he builds. There can be no other foundation beyond that which is already laid; I mean Jesus
12 Christ himself. If anyone builds on that foundation with gold, silver, and fine stone, or with wood, hay, and straw,
13 the work that each man does will at last be brought to light; the day of judge-ment will expose it. For that day dawns in fire, and the fire will test the worth of each man's work. If a man's build-
14 ing stands, he will be rewarded; if it
15 burns, he will have to bear the loss; and yet he will escape with his life, as one might from a fire. Surely you know
16 that you are God's temple, where the Spirit of God dwells. Anyone who de-
17 stroys God's temple will himself be destroyed[d] by God, because the temple of God is holy; and that temple you are.

Make no mistake about this: if there
18 is anyone among you who fancies himself wise—wise, I mean, by the standards of this passing age—he must become a fool to gain true wisdom. For the
19 wisdom of this world is folly in God's sight. Scripture says, 'He traps the wise in their own cunning', and again,
20 'The Lord knows that the arguments of the wise are futile.' So never make
21 mere men a cause for pride. For though everything belongs to you—Paul,
22 Apollos, and Cephas, the world, life, and death, the present and the future, all of them belong to you—yet you
23 belong to Christ, and Christ to God.

We must be regarded as Christ's 4 subordinates and as stewards of the secrets of God. Well then, stewards are 2 expected to show themselves trust-worthy. For my part, if I am called to 3 account by you or by any human court of judgement, it does not matter to me in the least. Why, I do not even pass judgement on myself, for I have no- 4 thing on my conscience; but that does not mean I stand acquitted. My judge is the Lord. So pass no premature 5 judgement; wait until the Lord comes. For he will bring to light what dark-ness hides, and disclose men's inward motives; then will be the time for each to receive from God such praise as he deserves.

Into this general picture, my friends, 6 I have brought Apollos and myself on

b *Or* Whether they plant or water, it is all the same.
c *Or* We are fellow-workers in God's service.
d *Some witnesses read* is himself destroyed.

3.1–23: Teachers and pupils. 1–2: *Infants:* see 13.11; 14.20. **3–4:** See 1.12. **8:** *Pay:* see vv. 14–15 n. **10:** See Rom. 15.20 n. **13:** *The day:* see 1.8 n. **14–15:** *Good workmanship will be rewarded,* but even a bad workman *will escape,* i.e. be saved. **16:** *Surely you know:* Paul had instructed them (possibly in his previous letter; see Introduction and 2 Cor.6.16). **19:** Job 5.13. **20:** Ps.94.11. **22:** See 1.12.
4.1–13: The humility of the apostles. 5: See 1.8 n.; 5.12–13 n.; Mt.13.24–30,36–43. **6:** Builders

your account, so that you may take our case as an example, and learn to 'keep within the rules', as they say, and may not be inflated with pride as you patronize one and flout the other. Who makes you, my friend, so important? What do you possess that was not given you? If then you really received it all as a gift, why take the credit to yourself? All of you, no doubt, have everything you could desire. You have come into your fortune already. You have come into your kingdom—and left us out. How I wish you had indeed won your kingdom; then you might share it with us! For it seems to me God has made us apostles the most abject of mankind. We are like men condemned to death in the arena, a spectacle to the whole universe—angels as well as men. We are fools for Christ's sake, while you are such sensible Christians. We are weak; you are so powerful. We are in disgrace; you are honoured. To this day we go hungry and thirsty and in rags; we are roughly handled; we wander from place to place; we wear ourselves out working with our own hands. They curse us, and we bless; they persecute us, and we submit to it; they slander us, and we humbly make our appeal. We are treated as the scum of the earth, the dregs of humanity, to this very day.

I am not writing thus to shame you, but to bring you to reason; for you are my dear children. You may have ten thousand tutors in Christ, but you have only one father. For in Christ Jesus you are my offspring, and mine alone, through the preaching of the Gospel.

I appeal to you therefore to follow my example. That is the very reason why I have sent Timothy, who is a dear son to me and a most trustworthy Christian; he will remind you of the way of life in Christ which I follow, and which I teach everywhere in all our congregations. There are certain persons who are filled with self-importance because they think I am not coming to Corinth. I shall come very soon, if the Lord will; and then I shall take the measure of these self-important people, not by what they say, but by what power is in them. The kingdom of God is not a matter of talk, but of power. Choose, then: am I to come to you with a rod in my hand, or in love and a gentle spirit?

I ACTUALLY HEAR REPORTS OF SEXUAL immorality among you, immorality such as even pagans do not tolerate: the union of a man with his father's wife. And you can still be proud of yourselves! You ought to have gone into mourning; a man who has done such a deed should have been rooted out of your company. For my part, though I am absent in body, I am present in spirit, and my judgement upon the man who did this thing is already given, as if I were indeed present: you all being assembled in the name of our Lord Jesus, and I with you in spirit, with the power of our Lord Jesus over us, this man is to be consigned to Satan for the destruction of the body, so that his spirit may be saved on the Day of the Lord.

Your self-satisfaction ill becomes

(see 5.10–11) besides Paul and *Apollos* should fear judgment. 8–13: With biting irony Paul contrasts his humiliating hardships with their complacency. 9: *Arena:* compare 15.32. *Angels:* see 6.2–3 n. 12: *Working with our own hands* (see Acts 18.3) is an especially bitter complaint (see 2 Cor.11.7–10 n.).
4.14–21: Paul's fatherly authority extends itself to the Corinthians by means of *Timothy's* mission and Paul's impending visit. 15: *Tutors* were normally slaves who supervised a boy's conduct outside of school; their temporary (Gal.3.24) authority derived from the boy's *father*. 17: *Timothy:* see 16.10 n. 18–19: Sternly Paul speaks of his visit as *very soon;* his actual plans are more elaborate (16.5–9). 20: *Power,* i.e. of the Spirit (2.4).
5.1–13: A case of sexual immorality. 1: Paul has received *reports* (possibly from Chloe's people; see 1.11) about a Christian who is living with his stepmother, who may have been widowed. Neither Roman nor Jewish law (Lev.18.8; 20.11) permitted such a *union*. 2: The Corinthians' pride (also v. 6) is worse than the sin itself. Perhaps the experiments in sexual asceticism discussed in ch. 7 (see 7.36–38 n.) have created the problem here. 3–5: Paul orders a formal assembly to expel the offender (see 2 Cor.2.5–11 n.). Excluded from the table-fellowship he becomes Satan's prey. His death (11.30 n.) will end his sin, but, like all Christians, he has been marked for salvation *on the Day* (1.8 n.). 6: *Leaven,* i.e. yeast, was both useful (Mt.13.33)

you. Have you never heard the saying, 'A little leaven leavens all the dough'? 7 The old leaven of corruption is working among you. Purge it out, and then you will be bread of a new baking. As Christians you are unleavened Passover bread; for indeed our Passover has begun; the sacrifice is offered—Christ 8 himself. So we who observe the festival must not use the old leaven, the leaven of corruption and wickedness, but only the unleavened bread which is sincerity and truth.

9 In my letter I wrote that you must 10 have nothing to do with loose livers. I was not, of course, referring to pagans who lead loose lives or are grabbers and swindlers or idolaters. To avoid them you would have to get out of the 11 world altogether. I now write that you must have nothing to do with any so-called Christian who leads a loose life, or is grasping, or idolatrous, a slanderer, a drunkard, or a swindler. You should not even eat with any such 12 person. What business of mine is it to 13 judge outsiders? God is their judge. You are judges within the fellowship. Root out the evil-doer from your community.

6 IF ONE OF YOUR NUMBER HAS A DISPUTE with another, has he the face to take it to pagan law-courts instead of to the 2 community of God's people? It is God's people who are to judge the world; surely you know that. And if the world is to come before you for judgement, are you incompetent to deal 3 with these trifling cases? Are you not aware that we are to judge angels? How much more, mere matters of

business! If therefore you have such 4 business disputes, how can you entrust jurisdiction to outsiders, men who count for nothing in our community? I write this to shame you. Can it be that 5 there is not a single wise man among you able to give a decision in a brother-Christian cause? Must brother 6 go to law with brother—and before unbelievers? Indeed, you already fall 7 below your standard in going to law with one another at all. Why not rather suffer injury? Why not rather let yourself be robbed? So far from this, you 8 actually injure and rob—injure and rob your brothers! Surely you know 9 that the unjust will never come into possession of the kingdom of God. Make no mistake: no fornicator or idolater, none who are guilty either of adultery or of homosexual perversion, no thieves or grabbers or drunkards or 10 slanderers or swindlers, will possess the kingdom of God. Such were some of 11 you. But you have been through the purifying waters; you have been dedicated to God and justified through the name of the Lord Jesus and the Spirit of our God.

'I am free to do anything', you say. 12 Yes, but not everything is for my good. No doubt I am free to do anything, but I for one will not let anything make free with me. 'Food is for the belly and 13 the belly for food', you say. True; and one day God will put an end to both. But it is not true that the body is for lust; it is for the Lord—and the Lord for the body. God not only raised our 14 Lord from the dead; he will also raise us by his power. Do you not know that 15 your bodies are limbs and organs of

---

and, like mold, corrupting. **7–8:** Writing perhaps near Passover (16.8 n.), Paul compares the expulsion of the immoral man to the Jewish custom of discarding all household leaven before baking the *unleavened Passover bread* (Deut.16.1,3–4). This leads him to speak of Christ as the lamb sacrificed at Passover (v. 7; Deut.16.2; Exod.12.21; Jn.1.29). **9:** *Letter:* see Introduction. **12–13:** Church discipline applies only to church members. Judgment in these matters is an exception to Paul's rule that Christians should not judge others until they judge the world in the new age (4.5; 6.2). *Root out:* v. 2; Deut.22.21,24.

6.1–11: Lawsuits among Christians. It is shameful that quarrelling believers should seek justice from *pagan law-courts.* **2–3:** In the age to come Christians will *judge the world* and *judge angels.* For Paul, *angels,* i.e. "messengers," are fearsome embodiments of supernatural power. They may be good (2 Cor.11.14) or from Satan (2 Cor.12.7). **9–11:** *The unjust* of the world (this list of vices is stereotyped; see Gal.5.19–24) will have no part in *the kingdom* (1.8 n.), but believers have been washed (in baptism) and made holy.

6.12–20: Conclusion (to chs. 1–6) **and preface** (to chs. 7–15). **12:** *"I am free . . ."* is a slogan of the Corinthians (10.23). **13:** *"Food is for the belly . . ."* is another of their slogans (see chs. 8–10). *Body* not *for lust:* ch. 7. **14:** See ch. 15. **15:** *Limbs and organs of Christ:* see 12.12–13 n.

Christ? Shall I then take from Christ his bodily parts and make them over to a
16 harlot? Never! You surely know that anyone who links himself with a harlot becomes physically one with her (for Scripture says, 'The pair shall become
17 one flesh'); but he who links himself with Christ is one with him, spiritually.
18 Shun fornication. Every other sin that a man can commit is outside the body; but the fornicator sins against his own
19 body. Do you not know that your body is a shrine of the indwelling Holy Spirit, and the Spirit is God's gift to you?
20 You do not belong to yourselves; you were bought at a price. Then honour God in your body.

The Christian in a pagan society

7 AND NOW FOR THE MATTERS YOU WROTE about.

It is a good thing for a man to have
2 nothing to do with women;[e] but because there is so much immorality, let each man have his own wife and each
3 woman her own husband. The husband must give the wife what is due to her, and the wife equally must give the husband his due. The wife cannot claim
4 her body as her own; it is her husband's. Equally, the husband cannot claim his body as his own; it is his
5 wife's. Do not deny yourselves to one another, except when you agree upon a temporary abstinence in order to devote yourselves to prayer; afterwards you may come together again; otherwise, for lack of self-control, you may be tempted by Satan.
6 All this I say by way of concession,
7 not command. I should like you all to be as I am myself; but everyone has the gift God has granted him, one this gift and another that.

To the unmarried and to widows I 8 say this: it is a good thing if they stay as I am myself; but if they cannot con- 9 trol themselves, they should marry Better be married than burn with vain desire.

To the married I give this ruling, 10 which is not mine but the Lord's: a wife must not separate herself from her husband; if she does, she must either 11 remain unmarried or be reconciled to her husband; and the husband must not divorce his wife.

To the rest I say this, as my own 12 word, not as the Lord's: if a Christian has a heathen wife, and she is willing to live with him, he must not divorce her; and a woman who has a heathen 13 husband willing to live with her must not divorce her husband. For the 14 heathen husband now belongs to God through his Christian wife, and the heathen wife through her Christian husband. Otherwise your children would not belong to God, whereas in fact they do. If on the other hand the 15 heathen partner wishes for a separation, let him have it. In such cases the Christian husband or wife is under no compulsion; but God's call is a call to live in peace. Think of it: as a wife you 16 may be your husband's salvation; as a husband you may be your wife's salvation.

However that may be, each one must 17 order his life according to the gift the Lord has granted him and his condition when God called him. That is what I teach in all our congregations. Was a 18 man called with the marks of circumcision on him? Let him not remove them. Was he uncircumcised when he was called? Let him not be circumcised. Circumcision or uncircumcision 19 is neither here nor there; what matters

e *Or* You say, 'It is a good thing ... women'; ...

16: Gen.2.24 (1 Cor. ch. 7; Mk.10.6–8; Eph.5.31). **19:** The *gift* of the *Spirit:* see chs. 12–14. **20:** *Bought at a price:* like slaves set free (see 7.23; Rom.3.24 n.).
    7.1–16: "Should we not avoid sex and marriage?" Some such question probably stood in the Corinthians' letter to Paul (see Introduction). **1:** *It is a good thing . . . :* probably a Corinthian slogan; see Tfn. *e.* **2–5:** Paul urges full conjugal rights, permitting only temporary asceticism. **6–9:** Paul is unmarried and because of the nearness of the Day (1.8 n.; 7.29,31) considers this preferable. But it is a *gift*, not a rule. The distractions of married life (7.32–34) are infinitely preferable to moral lapses. **10:** *The Lord's:* Jesus' (see Mk.10.2–12); contrast vv. 12,25. **12–16:** The *divorce* even of unbelieving partners is not encouraged.
    7.17–24: Stay as you are. The end of this age is near (vv. 29,31). Therefore believers should not try to change their outward condition. **19:** See Rom.2.25–29.

20 is to keep God's commands. Every man should remain in the condition in
21 which he was called. Were you a slave when you were called? Do not let that trouble you; but if a chance of liberty
22 should come, take it.*f* For the man who as a slave received the call to be a Christian is the Lord's freedman, and, equally, the free man who received the call is a slave in the service of Christ.
23 You were bought at a price; do not
24 become slaves of men. Thus each one, my friends, is to remain before God in the condition in which he received his call.
25 On the question of celibacy, I have no instructions from the Lord, but I give my judgement as one who by God's mercy is fit to be trusted.
26 It is my opinion, then, that in a time of stress like the present this is the best way for a man to live—it is best for a
27 man to be as he is. Are you bound in marriage? Do not seek a dissolution. Has your marriage been dissolved?
28 Do not seek a wife. If, however, you do marry, there is nothing wrong in it; and if a virgin marries, she has done no wrong. But those who marry will have pain and grief in this bodily life, and my aim is to spare you.
29 What I mean, my friends, is this. The time we live in will not last long. While it lasts, married men should be
30 as if they had no wives; mourners should be as if they had nothing to grieve them, the joyful as if they did not rejoice; buyers must not count on
31 keeping what they buy, nor those who use the world's wealth on using it to the full. For the whole frame of this world is passing away.
32 I want you to be free from anxious care. The unmarried man cares for the Lord's business; his aim is to please
33 the Lord. But the married man cares for worldly things; his aim is to please
34 his wife; and he has a divided mind.

The unmarried or celibate woman cares*g* for the Lord's business; her aim is to be dedicated to him in body as in spirit; but the married woman cares for worldly things; her aim is to please her husband.
35 In saying this I have no wish to keep you on a tight rein. I am thinking simply of your own good, of what is seemly, and of your freedom to wait upon the Lord without distraction.
36 But if a man has a partner in celibacy*h* and feels that he is not behaving properly towards her, if, that is, his instincts are too strong for him,*i* and something must be done, he may do as he pleases; there is nothing wrong in it; let them marry.*j* But if a man is stead-
37 fast in his purpose, being under no compulsion, and has complete control of his own choice; and if he has decided in his own mind to preserve his partner*k* in her virginity, he will do well.
38 Thus, he who marries his partner*l* does well, and he who does not will do better.
39 A wife is bound to her husband as long as he lives. But if the husband die, she is free to marry whom she will, provided the marriage is within the Lord's fellowship. But she is better off as she
40 is; that is my opinion, and I believe that I too have the Spirit of God.

NOW ABOUT FOOD CONSECRATED TO **8** heathen deities.
Of course we all 'have knowledge', as you say. This 'knowledge' breeds conceit; it is love that builds. If any-
2 one fancies that he knows, he knows nothing yet, in the true sense of know-

f Or but even if a chance of liberty should come, choose rather to make good use of your servitude.
g Some witnesses read ... his wife. And there is a difference between the wife and the virgin. The unmarried woman cares ...
h Or a virgin daughter (*or* ward).
i Or if she is ripe for marriage.
j Or let the girl and her lover marry.
k Or his daughter.
l Or gives his daughter in marriage.

7.25–38: "Should our celibate couples abandon their vows?" (See 7.1–16 n.). **25:** *Celibacy:* lit. "virgins" (referring to both sexes); see vv. 36–38 n. **26–34:** Paul reiterates the argument of vv. 17–24. **36–38:** Apparently some Corinthians had chosen *partners in celibacy* by undertaking some sort of mutual vow, either like the marital ascetics of v. 5 or like engaged couples.
7.39–40: An afterthought to vv. 1–16.
8.1–11.1: "Surely there is no harm in eating meat consecrated to a heathen deity?" (See 7.1–16 n.). The extent of consecration varied from full temple sacrifice to the merest slaughterhouse gesture.
8.1–13: Love is superior to knowledge (also ch. 13). **1–4:** The Corinthians' slogans (see also

3 ing. But if a man loves,[m] he is acknowledged by God.[n]

4 Well then, about eating this consecrated food; of course, as you say, 'a false god has no existence in the real 5 world. There is no god but one.' For indeed, if there be so-called gods, whether in heaven or on earth—as indeed there are many 'gods' and many 'lords' 6 —yet for us there is one God, the Father, from whom all being comes, towards whom we move; and there is one Lord, Jesus Christ, through whom all things came to be, and we through him.

7 But not everyone knows this. There are some who have been so accustomed to idolatry[o] that even now they eat this food with a sense of its heathen consecration, and their conscience, being 8 weak, is polluted by the eating. Certainly food will not bring us into God's presence: if we do not eat, we are none the worse, and if we eat, we are none 9 the better. But be careful that this liberty of yours does not become a pit-10 fall for the weak. If a weak character sees you sitting down to a meal in a heathen temple—you, who 'have knowledge'—will not his conscience be em-11 boldened to eat food consecrated to the heathen deity? This 'knowledge' of yours is utter disaster to the weak, the 12 brother for whom Christ died. In thus sinning against your brothers and wounding their conscience,[p] you sin 13 against Christ. And therefore, if food be the downfall of my brother, I will never eat meat any more, for I will not be the cause of my brother's downfall.

9 AM I NOT A FREE MAN? AM I NOT AN apostle? Did I not see Jesus our Lord? Are not you my own handiwork, in the 2 Lord? If others do not accept me as an apostle, you at least are bound to do so, for you are yourselves the very seal of my apostolate, in the Lord,

To those who put me in the dock 3 this is my answer: Have I no right to 4 eat and drink? Have I no right to take 5 a Christian wife about with me, like the rest of the apostles and the Lord's brothers, and Cephas? Or are Barnabas 6 and I alone bound to work for our living? Did you ever hear of a man 7 serving in the army at his own expense? or planting a vineyard without eating the fruit of it? or tending a flock without using its milk? Do not suppose I 8 rely on these human analogies, for the law says the same; in the Law of Moses 9 we read, 'You shall not muzzle a threshing ox.' Do you suppose God's concern is with oxen? Or is the reference clearly 10 to ourselves? Of course it refers to us, in the sense that the ploughman should plough and the thresher thresh in the hope of getting some of the produce. If 11 we have sown a spiritual crop for you, is it too much to expect from you a material harvest? If you allow others 12 these rights, have not we a stronger claim?

But I have availed myself of no such right. On the contrary, I put up with all that comes my way rather than offer any hindrance to the gospel of Christ. You know (do you not?) that those 13 who perform the temple service eat the temple offerings, and those who wait upon the altar claim their share of the sacrifice. In the same way the Lord gave 14 instructions that those who preach the Gospel should earn their living by the Gospel. But I have never taken ad-15 vantage of any such right, nor do I intend to claim it in this letter. I had rather die! No one shall make my boast

m *Some witnesses read* loves God.
n *Or* he is recognized.
o *Some witnesses read* in whom the consciousness of the false god is so persistent . . .
p *Some witnesses insert* weak as it is.

10.23) defend their freedom. **6**: Mal.2.10; Eph.4.6; Col.1.16; Jn.1.3. **7–13**: Out of loving concern for the *weak* the mature Christian should limit his own *liberty*. **10**: Men often entertained their friends with a *meal* at some *temple*, using meat previously sacrificed. The affair was largely social; thus Christians might attend (see 10.27).

9.1–27: Paul's own self-restraint extends to other matters as well. **1**: An *apostle* has both *seen* the resurrected *Jesus* (15.5–9) and received from him a missionary task (see Gal.1.16).

9.3–12a: Paul's right to financial support. 5: *The Lord's brothers:* see Mk.6.3; Gal.1.19. **6**: *Barnabas:* see Acts 4.36; Gal.2.1. *Work:* tent-making (Acts 18.3). **9**: Deut.25.4. **10**: The promises of Scripture apply to the new Israel (see 10.11; Rom.15.4).

9.12b–18: The Gospel free of charge. 13: Deut.18.1–4 and in pagan cults. **14**: Mt.10.10. **15–18**: *Boast, satisfaction:* see 2 Th.3.7–9; 2 Cor.11.7–10 n.

16 an empty boast. Even if I preach the Gospel, I can claim no credit for it; I cannot help myself; it would be misery
17 to me not to preach. If I did it of my own choice, I should be earning my pay; but since I do it apart from my own choice, I am simply discharging a
18 trust.*q* Then what is my pay? The satisfaction of preaching the Gospel without expense to anyone; in other words, of waiving the rights which my preaching gives me.
19 I am a free man and own no master; but I have made myself every man's servant, to win over as many as pos-
20 sible. To Jews I became like a Jew, to win Jews; as they are subject to the Law of Moses, I put myself under that law to win them, although I am not
21 myself subject to it. To win Gentiles, who are outside the Law, I made myself like one of them, although I am not in truth outside God's law, being
22 under the law of Christ. To the weak I became weak, to win the weak. Indeed, I have become everything in turn to men of every sort, so that in one way or
23 another I may save some. All this I do for the sake of the Gospel, to bear my part in proclaiming it.
24 You know (do you not?) that at the sports all the runners run the race, though only one wins the prize. Like
25 them, run to win! But every athlete goes into strict training. They do it to win a fading wreath; we, a wreath that
26 never fades. For my part, I run with a clear goal before me; I am like a boxer
27 who does not beat the air; I bruise my own body and make it know its master, for fear that after preaching to others I should find myself rejected.

10 You should understand, my brothers, that our ancestors were all under the pillar of cloud, and all of them
2 passed through the Red Sea; and so

they all received baptism into the fellowship of Moses in cloud and sea.
3 They all ate the same supernatural
4 food, and all drank the same supernatural drink; I mean, they all drank from the supernatural rock that accompanied their travels—and that
5 rock was Christ. And yet, most of them were not accepted by God, for the desert was strewn with their corpses.
6 These events happened as symbols to warn us not to set our desires on
7 evil things, as they did. Do not be idolaters, like some of them; as Scripture has it, 'the people sat down to
8 feast and rose up to revel'. Let us not commit fornication, as some of them did—and twenty-three thousand died
9 in one day. Let us not put the power of the Lord*r* to the test, as some of them did—and were destroyed by ser-
10 pents. Do not grumble against God, as some of them did—and were destroyed by the Destroyer.
11 All these things that happened to them were symbolic, and were recorded for our benefit as a warning. For upon us the fulfilment of the ages has come.
12 If you feel sure that you are standing
13 firm, beware! You may fall. So far you have faced no trial beyond what man can bear. God keeps faith, and he will not allow you to be tested above your powers, but when the test comes he will at the same time provide a way out, by enabling you to sustain it.

14 SO THEN, DEAR FRIENDS, SHUN IDOLATRY.
15 I speak to you as men of sense. Form your own judgement on what I say.
16 When we bless 'the cup of blessing', is it not a means of sharing in the blood of Christ? When we break the bread, is it not a means of sharing in the body of

q Or If I do it willingly I am earning my pay; if I did it unwillingly I should still have a trust laid upon me.
r Some witnesses read of Christ.

9.19–27: The highest goal requires self-sacrifice. 19–23: In his behavior Paul has a higher purpose than consistency: to *win* men for Christ. **27:** The *body* is not an enemy; Paul is speaking figuratively of his disciplined life. *Rejected:* see 10.5–13.
10.1–13: It is possible to provoke God and perish; baptism and the Lord's Supper do not prevent sin or excuse from judgment. **1–2:** *Cloud:* sea: see Exod.14.22. **3:** *Food:* manna (Exod.16.4–35). **4:** *Drink:* water from the *rock* (Exod.17.6; Num. 20.11). Legend had it that the *rock* followed the Israelites in their *travels*. Paul identifies the source of this life-giving water with *Christ* (compare Jn.4.14). **5:** Num.14.29–30. **7:** Exod.32.4,6. **8–10:** Num.25.1–18; 21.5–6; 16.41,49. **11:** *Fulfillment:* end; compare 1.8 n.
10.14–22: Danger from demons. *Idols* indeed are nothing (8.4), but *demons* use them as camouflage (Deut.32.17). Thus eating food consecrated to heathen gods is defiance of God

17 Christ? Because there is one loaf, we, many as we are, are one body;[s] for it is one loaf of which we all partake.

18 Look at the Jewish people. Are not those who partake in the sacrificial meal 19 sharers in the altar? What do I imply by this? that an idol is anything but an idol? or food offered to it anything 20 more than food? No; but the sacrifices the heathen offer are offered (in the words of Scripture) 'to demons and to that which is not God'; and I will not have you become partners with demons. You cannot drink the cup of the 21 Lord and the cup of demons. You cannot partake of the Lord's table and the 22 table of demons. Can we defy the Lord? Are we stronger than he?

23 'We are free to do anything', you say. Yes, but is everything good for us? 'We are free to do anything', but does everything help the building of the com- 24 munity? Each of you must regard, not his own interests, but the other man's.

25 You may eat anything sold in the meat-market without raising questions 26 of conscience; for the earth is the Lord's and everything in it.

27 If an unbeliever invites you to a meal and you care to go, eat whatever is put before you, without raising questions 28 of conscience. But if somebody says to you, 'This food has been offered in sacrifice', then, out of consideration for him, and for conscience' sake, do 29 not eat it—not your conscience, I mean, but the other man's.

'What?' you say, 'is my freedom to be called in question by another man's 30 conscience? If I partake with thankfulness, why am I blamed for eating food 31 over which I have said grace?' Well, whether you eat or drink, or whatever you are doing, do all for the honour of 32 God: give no offence to Jews, or 33 Greeks, or to the church of God. For my part I always try to meet everyone half-way, regarding not my own good

but the good of the many, so that they may be saved. Follow my example as I **11** follow Christ's.

I COMMEND YOU FOR ALWAYS KEEPING 2 me in mind, and maintaining the tradition I handed on to you. But I wish 3 you to understand that, while every man has Christ for his Head, woman's head is man,[t] as Christ's Head is God. A man who keeps his head covered 4 when he prays or prophesies brings shame on his head; a woman, on the 5 contrary, brings shame on her head if she prays or prophesies bare-headed; it is as bad as if her head were shaved. If a woman is not to wear a veil she 6 might as well have her hair cut off; but if it is a disgrace for her to be cropped and shaved, then she should wear a veil. A man has no need to cover 7 his head, because man is the image of God, and the mirror of his glory, whereas woman reflects the glory of man.[u] For man did not originally spring from 8 woman, but woman was made out of man; and man was not created for 9 woman's sake, but woman for the sake of man; and therefore it is woman's 10 duty to have a sign of authority[v] on her head, out of regard for the angels.[w] And yet, in Christ's fellowship woman 11 is as essential to man as man to woman. If woman was made out of man, it is 12 through woman that man now comes to be; and God is the source of all.

Judge for yourselves: is it fitting for 13 a woman to pray to God bare-headed? Does not Nature herself teach you that 14 while flowing locks disgrace a man, they are a woman's glory? For her 15 locks were given for covering.

However, if you insist on arguing, 16 let me tell you, there is no such custom

s *Or* For we, many as we are, one loaf, one body.
t *Or* a woman's head is her husband.
u *Or* a woman reflects her husband's glory.
v *Some witnesses read* to have a veil.
w *Or* and therefore a woman should keep her dignity on her head, for fear of the angels.

(Deut.32.21). **16–17:** See 11.23–26; Mk.14.22–25. **20:** Deut.32.17. **21:** See 2 Cor.6.15–16.
10.23–11.1: Paul closes the section on idol meat (8.1–11.1) with directions which allow freedom, if it is restrained by love. **23:** Another Corinthian slogan (compare 8.1–4 n.). **26:** Pss.24.1; 50.12. **27:** See 8.10 n. **10.28–11.1:** See 8.7–13.
11.2–16: "Is it necessary for women to worship with their heads covered?" (See 7.1–16 n.). Christian women enjoyed considerable freedom, including the right to preach (prophesy), but worship without *veils* may have reminded Paul of pagan cults. **7:** *Image:* Gen.1.26. **8–12:** See Gen.2.18,21–24. **10:** Women must wear veils as a *sign of authority* or power. These *angels* (see 6.2–3 n.) are perhaps the lustful spirits of a legend based on Gen.6.1–4. **16:** See 14.36–38 n.

among us, or in any of the congregations of God's people.

17 In giving you these injunctions I must mention a practice which I cannot commend: your meetings tend to 18 do more harm than good. To begin with, I am told that when you meet as a congregation you fall into sharply divided groups; and I believe there is 19 some truth in it (for dissensions are necessary if only to show which of 20 your members are sound). The result is that when you meet as a congregation, it is impossible for you to eat the 21 Lord's Supper, because each of you is in such a hurry to eat his own, and while one goes hungry another has too 22 much to drink. Have you no homes of your own to eat and drink in? Or are you so contemptuous of the church of God that you shame its poorer members? What am I to say? Can I commend you? On this point, certainly not! 23 For the tradition which I handed on to you came to me from the Lord himself: that the Lord Jesus, on the night 24 of his arrest, took bread and, after giving thanks to God, broke it and said: 'This is my body, which is for you; do 25 this as a memorial of me.' In the same way, he took the cup after supper, and said: 'This cup is the new covenant sealed by my blood. Whenever you drink it, do this as a memorial of me.' 26 For every time you eat this bread and drink the cup, you proclaim the death of the Lord, until he comes.

27 It follows that anyone who eats the bread or drinks the cup of the Lord unworthily will be guilty of desecrating 28 the body and blood of the Lord. A man must test himself before eating his share of the bread and drinking from the cup. 29 For he who eats and drinks eats and drinks judgement on himself if he does not discern the Body. That is why many 30 of you are feeble and sick, and a number have died. But if we examined our- 31 selves, we should not thus fall under judgement. When, however, we do fall 32 under the Lord's judgement, he is disciplining us, to save us from being condemned with the rest of the world.

Therefore, my brothers, when you 33 meet for a meal, wait for one another. If you are hungry, eat at home, so that 34 in meeting together you may not fall under judgement. The other matters I will arrange when I come.

Spiritual gifts

ABOUT GIFTS OF THE SPIRIT, THERE ARE 12 some things of which I do not wish you to remain ignorant.

You know how, in the days when 2 you were still pagan, you were swept off to those dumb heathen gods, however you happened to be led.ˣ For this rea- 3 son I must impress upon you that no one who says 'A curse on Jesus!' can be speaking under the influence of the Spirit of God. And no one can say 'Jesus is Lord!' except under the influence of the Holy Spirit.

There are varieties of gifts, but the 4 same Spirit. There are varieties of ser- 5 vice, but the same Lord. There are 6 many forms of work, but all of them, in all men, are the work of the same God. In each of us the Spirit is manifested in 7 one particular way, for some useful purpose. One man, through the Spirit, 8 has the gift of wise speech, while another, by the power of the same Spirit, can put the deepest knowledge into words. Another, by the same 9

x Or . . . pagan, you would be seized by some power which drove you to those dumb heathen gods.

11.17–34: The Lord's Supper properly observed. Paul has more news (v. 18) of their *dissensions* (compare 1.11–12). The Lord's Supper was then a full meal; the Corinthians' greed shattered the "one body" (10.16–17) with dire consequences (v. 30). **17**: Contrast v. 2. **23–25**: This is the earliest written account of the Lord's Supper (compare Mk.14.22–25; Lk.22.14–20). **23**: *Handed on:* see 15.3 n. **25**: *Covenant, blood:* Exod.24.8. **30**: They had expected to live until Christ's return (v. 26; 15.51); Paul explains why some had died (see 5.3–5 n.).

12.1–14.40: "Ecstatic utterance in worship is the gift of the Spirit, is it not?" (See 7.1–16 n.) Paul's long response occupies chs. 12–14.

12.1–31: Other and better gifts. *Ecstatic utterance* (v. 10) is indeed a *gift*, but it is not the only gift. Of all the Spirit's *gifts* it ranks last (vv. 10,28,30). **2–3**: Not all ecstatic speech is from the Spirit; some is pagan. **4–6**: *Spirit . . . Lord . . . God:* the triad foreshadows the later doctrine of the Trinity. **7**: *Useful:* the test is utility (compare Mt.7.16–20). **9**: *Faith* here (and in 13.2) is a

[Handwritten marginal notes: "Earliest account of Last Supper Eucharist"]

[Handwritten notes at bottom: "Holy Communion requires: 1) Faith in Real Presence 2) Clean conscience"]

Spirit, is granted faith; another, by the 10 one Spirit, gifts of healing, and another miraculous powers; another has the gift of prophecy, and another ability to distinguish true spirits from false; yet another has the gift of ecstatic utterance of different kinds, and another the 11 ability to interpret it. But all these gifts are the work of one and the same Spirit, distributing them separately to each individual at will.

12 For Christ is like a single body with its many limbs and organs, which, many as they are, together make up 13 one body. For indeed we were all brought into one body by baptism, in the one Spirit, whether we are Jews or Greeks, whether slaves or free men, and that one Holy Spirit was poured out for all of us to drink.

14 A body is not one single organ, but 15 many. Suppose the foot should say, 'Because I am not a hand, I do not belong to the body', it does belong to the 16 body none the less. Suppose the ear were to say, 'Because I am not an eye, I do not belong to the body', it does 17 still belong to the body. If the body were all eye, how could it hear? If the body were all ear, how could it smell? 18 But, in fact, God appointed each limb and organ to its own place in the body, 19 as he chose. If the whole were one single organ, there would not be a 20 body at all; in fact, however, there are many different organs, but one body. 21 The eye cannot say to the hand, 'I do not need you'; nor the head to the feet, 22 'I do not need you.' Quite the contrary: those organs of the body which seem to be more frail than others are in-23 dispensable, and those parts of the body which we regard as less honourable are treated with special honour. To our unseemly parts is given a more 24 than ordinary seemliness, whereas our

seemly parts need no adorning. But God has combined the various parts of the body, giving special honour to the humbler parts, so that there might be 25 no sense of division in the body, but that all its organs might feel the same concern for one another. If one organ 26 suffers, they all suffer together. If one flourishes, they all rejoice together.

Now you are Christ's body, and each 27 of you a limb or organ of it. Within 28 our community God has appointed, in the first place apostles, in the second place prophets, thirdly teachers; then miracle-workers, then those who have gifts of healing, or ability to help others or power to guide them, or the gift of ecstatic utterance of various kinds. Are 29 all apostles? all prophets? all teachers? Do all work miracles? Have all gifts of 30 healing? Do all speak in tongues of ecstasy? Can all interpret them? The 31 higher gifts are those you should aim at.

And now I will show you the best way of all.

I may speak in tongues of men or of **13** angels, but if I am without love, I am a sounding gong or a clanging cymbal. I 2 may have the gift of prophecy, and know every hidden truth; I may have faith strong enough to move mountains; but if I have no love, I am nothing. I may dole out all I possess, or 3 even give my body to be burnt,*y* but if I have no love, I am none the better.

Love is patient; love is kind and 4 envies no one. Love is never boastful, nor conceited, nor rude; never selfish, 5 not quick to take offence. Love keeps no score of wrongs; does not gloat over 6 other men's sins, but delights in the truth. There is nothing love cannot 7 face; there is no limit to its faith, its hope, and its endurance.

Love will never come to an end. Are 8

y Some witnesses read even seek glory by self-sacrifice.

special gift, rather than the characteristic of every believer (as in 1.21; 2.5; 3.5). **10:** *Prophecy:* preaching (14.1–5). *Distinguish . . . spirits:* see vv. 2–3. **12–13:** Christians are "in Christ" (Rom. 8.1 n.), not separately but "corporately." Paul speaks of the church as the *body* of Christ (v. 27) and of Christians as its differing but mutually dependent "members." **14–26:** Paul argues that a church whose members exhibit but one spiritual gift is like a body composed solely of an *eye* or an *ear*. **27:** See Rom.12.4–5; Eph.1.22–23; Col.1.18–24. **28–30:** Roughly parallel to vv. 8–10.
   13.1–13: Love, the best gift of all. This famous chapter is closely linked to chs. 12 and 14. **1:** *Tongues . . . of angels:* ecstatic speech. *Angels:* see 6.2–3 n. *Gong . . . cymbal:* mere noise-makers used in pagan cults. **2:** *Prophecy:* see 12.10 n. *Faith:* see 12.9 n.; Mk.11.22–23. **3:** *Burnt:* perhaps as a martyr (Dan.3.19–23; 2 Macc.7.2–6). **4–6,11:** Paul betrays his opinion of the

This describes Jesus and is thus a description of a Christian

there prophets? their work will be over. Are there tongues of ecstasy? they will cease. Is there knowledge? it will van-
9 ish away; for our knowledge and our
10 prophecy alike are partial, and the par-tial vanishes when wholeness comes.
11 When I was a child, my speech, my outlook, and my thoughts were all childish. When I grew up, I had finished
12 with childish things. Now we see only puzzling reflections in a mirror, but then we shall see face to face. My knowl-edge now is partial; then it will be
13 whole, like God's knowledge of me. In a word, there are three things that last for ever: faith, hope, and love; but the greatest of them all is love.

14 o Put love first; but there are other gifts of the Spirit at which you should aim also, and above all prophecy.
2 When a man is using the language of ecstasy he is talking with God, not with men, for no man understands him; he is no doubt inspired, but he
3 speaks mysteries. On the other hand, when a man prophesies, he is talking to men, and his words have power to build; they stimulate and they encour-
4 age. The language of ecstasy is good for the speaker himself, but it is proph-ecy that builds up a Christian com-
5 munity. I should be pleased for you all to use the tongues of ecstasy, but better pleased for you to prophesy. The prophet is worth more than the man of ecstatic speech—unless indeed he can explain its meaning, and so help to
6 build up the community. Suppose, my friends, that when I come to you I use ecstatic language: what good shall I do you, unless what I say contains some-thing by way of revelation, or enlighten-ment, or prophecy, or instruction?
7 Even with inanimate things that pro-duce sounds—a flute, say, or a lyre—unless their notes mark definite inter-vals, how can you tell what tune is being
8 played? Or again, if the trumpet-call is not clear, who will prepare for battle?

In the same way if your ecstatic utter- 9 ance yields no precise meaning, how can anyone tell what you are saying? You will be talking into the air. How 10 many different kinds of sound there are, or may be, in the world! Nothing is altogether soundless. Well then, if I do 11 not know the meaning of the sound the speaker makes, his words will be gib-berish to me, and mine to him. You 12 are, I know, eager for gifts of the Spirit; then aspire above all to excel in those which build up the church.

I say, then, that the man who falls 13 into ecstatic utterance should pray for the ability to interpret. If I use such 14 language in my prayer, the Spirit in me prays, but my intellect lies fallow. What then? I will pray as I am inspired 15 to pray, but I will also pray intelligent-ly. I will sing hymns as I am inspired to sing, but I will sing intelligently too. Suppose you are praising God in the 16 language of inspiration: how will the plain man who is present be able to say 'Amen' to your thanksgiving, when he does not know what you are saying? Your prayer of thanksgiving may be all 17 that could be desired, but it is no help to the other man. Thank God, I am 18 more gifted in ecstatic utterance than any of you,[z] but in the congregation I 19 would rather speak five intelligible words, for the benefit of others as well as myself, than thousands of words in the language of ecstasy.

Do not be childish, my friends. Be as 20 innocent of evil as babes, but at least be grown-up in your thinking. We read 21 in the Law: 'I will speak to this nation through men of strange tongues, and by the lips of foreigners; and even so they will not heed me, says the Lord.' Clearly then these 'strange tongues' are 22 not intended as a sign for believers, but for unbelievers, whereas prophecy is designed not for unbelievers but for

z *Or* . . . man. I say the thanksgiving; I use ecstatic speech more than any of you.

Corinthians' pride in their special gifts. **12:** *Mirror:* ancient metal mirrors gave distorted *reflections*. **13:** *Faith, hope,* and *love:* a favorite triad for Paul (1 Th.1.3; 5.8; Rom.5.1–5; Col.1.4–5).
   14.1–40: Rational preaching is of far more value than ecstatic utterance. 1: *Love:* for love's sake they ought to make themselves understood when they *pray* (vv. 13–17). **16:** Christians adopted *"Amen"* (lit. "so be it"), the Jewish reponse to prayer (e.g. Neh.8.6; Ps.106.48). **18:** Probably the Corinthians had learned *ecstatic utterance* from Paul (see also 2 Cor.12.1–4 n.). **20:** See 2.6; 3.1–2; 13.11. **21:** Isa.28.11–12 is cited as *Law*, rather than Prophet; see Rom.3.19 n.

23 those who hold the faith. So if the whole congregation is assembled and all are using the 'strange tongues' of ecstasy, and some uninstructed persons or unbelievers should enter, will they 24 not think you are mad? But if all are uttering prophecies, the visitor, when he enters, hears from everyone something that searches his conscience and 25 brings conviction, and the secrets of his heart are laid bare. So he will fall down and worship God, crying, 'God is certainly among you!'

26 To sum up, my friends: when you meet for worship, each of you contributes a hymn, some instruction, a revelation, an ecstatic utterance, or the interpretation of such an utterance. All of these must aim at one thing: to 27 build up the church. If it is a matter of ecstatic utterance, only two should speak, or at most three, one at a time, 28 and someone must interpret. If there is no interpreter, the speaker had better not address the meeting at all, but speak 29 to himself and to God. Of the prophets, two or three may speak, while the rest exercise their judgement upon what is 30 said. If someone else, sitting in his place, receives a revelation, let the first 31 speaker stop. You can all prophesy, one at a time, so that the whole congregation may receive instruction and 32 encouragement. It is for prophets to 33 control prophetic inspiration, for the God who inspires them is not a God of disorder but of peace.

As in all congregations of God's 34 people, women[a] should not address the meeting. They have no licence to speak, but should keep their place as the law 35 directs. If there is something they want to know, they can ask their own husbands at home. It is a shocking thing that a woman should address the congregation.

Did the word of God originate with 36 you? Or are you the only people to whom it came? If anyone claims to be 37 inspired or a prophet, let him recognize that what I write has the Lord's authority. If he does not acknowledge 38 this, God does not acknowledge him.[b]

In short, my friends, be eager to 39 prophesy; do not forbid ecstatic utterance; but let all be done decently and 40 in order.

Life after death

AND NOW, MY BROTHERS, I MUST REMIND 15 you of the gospel that I preached to you; the gospel which you received, on which you have taken your stand, and 2 which is now bringing you salvation. Do you still hold fast the Gospel as I preached it to you? If not, your conversion was in vain.[c]

First and foremost, I handed on to 3 you the facts which had been imparted to me: that Christ died for our sins, in accordance with the scriptures; that he 4 was buried; that he was raised to life on the third day, according to the scriptures; and that he appeared to Cephas, 5 and afterwards to the Twelve. Then he 6 appeared to over five hundred of our brothers at once, most of whom are still alive, though some have died. Then 7 he appeared to James, and afterwards to all the apostles.

In the end he appeared even to me. 8 It was like an abnormal birth; I had 9 persecuted the church of God and am therefore inferior to all other apostles —indeed not fit to be called an apostle.

a *Or* of peace, as in all communities of God's people. Women . . .
b *Some witnesses read* If he refuses to recognize this, let him refuse!
c *Or* Do you remember the terms in which I preached the Gospel to you?—for I assume you did not accept it thoughtlessly.

23–25: This form of worship was not closed to *visitors,* as the Lord's Supper (11.23–32) presumably was. **34–35:** In view of 11.5 many consider these verses not by Paul, but a later insertion (compare 1 Tim.2.11–12). **36–38:** For another abrupt closing of a difficult discussion see 11.16.
    15.1–58: "Are Christians resurrected in bodily form?" (See 7.1–16 n.). **1–11:** An early Christian creed (vv. 3–5) serves to *remind* them that Christ's resurrection is basic to the *gospel* message. **3:** *Handed on, imparted:* Paul uses a traditional Jewish formula (also at 11.23) to emphasize that he is transmitting traditions which antedate his own ministry. *Scriptures* (here and in v. 4) probably means the OT in general. Later tradition cited Isa.52.13–53.12 for Jesus' death and Ps.16.10 (Acts 2.31) for his resurrection. **7:** *James:* Jesus' brother (Gal.1.19; Mk.6.3). **8:** *Appeared . . . to me:* see 9.1; Gal.1.16; Acts 9.3–6. *Abnormal birth* is obscure; Paul may have been ridiculed for his appearance (2 Cor.10.10; Gal.4.13–14). **9:** *Persecuted:* see Gal.1,13–14.

10 However, by God's grace I am what I am, nor has his grace been given to me in vain; on the contrary, in my labours I have outdone them all—not I, indeed, but the grace of God working with me.
11 But what matter, I or they? This is what we all proclaim, and this is what you believed.
12 Now if this is what we proclaim, that Christ was raised from the dead, how can some of you say there is no resurrec-
13 tion of the dead? If there be no resurrection, then Christ was not raised;
14 and if Christ was not raised, then our gospel is null and void, and so is your
15 faith; and we turn out to be lying witnesses for God, because we bore witness that he raised Christ to life, whereas, if the dead are not raised, he did not
16 raise him. For if the dead are not raised, it follows that Christ was not
17 raised; and if Christ was not raised, your faith has nothing in it and you are
18 still in your old state of sin. It follows also that those who have died within
19 Christ's fellowship are utterly lost. If it is for this life only that Christ has given us hope,[d] we of all men are most to be pitied.
20 But the truth is, Christ was raised to life—the firstfruits of the harvest of the
21 dead. For since it was a man who brought death into the world, a man also brought resurrection of the dead.
22 As in Adam all men die, so in Christ
23 all will be brought to life; but each in his own proper place: Christ the firstfruits, and afterwards, at his coming,
24 those who belong to Christ. Then comes the end, when he delivers up the kingdom to God the Father, after abolishing every kind of domination,
25 authority, and power. For he is destined to reign until God has put all
26 enemies under his feet; and the last enemy to be abolished is death.[e] Scrip-
27 ture says, 'He has put all things in subjection under his feet.' But in saying 'all things', it clearly means to exclude
28 God who subordinates them; and when all things are thus subject to him, then the Son himself will also be made subordinate to God who made all things subject to him, and thus God will be all in all.
29 Again, there are those who receive baptism on behalf of the dead. Why should they do this? If the dead are not raised to life at all, what do they mean by being baptized on their behalf?
30 And we ourselves—why do we face
31 these dangers hour by hour? Every day I die: I swear it by my pride in you, my brothers—for in Christ Jesus our Lord I am proud of you. If, as the saying is,
32 I 'fought wild beasts' at Ephesus, what have I gained by it?[f] If the dead are never raised to life, 'let us eat and drink, for tomorrow we die'.
33 Make no mistake: 'Bad company is
34 the ruin of a good character.' Come back to a sober and upright life and leave your sinful ways. There are some who know nothing of God; to your shame I say it.
35 But, you may ask, how are the dead
36 raised? In what kind of body? How foolish! The seed you sow does not come to life unless it has first died;
37 and what you sow is not the body that shall be, but a naked grain, perhaps of wheat, or of some other kind; and God
38 clothes it with the body of his choice, each seed with its own particular body.

d Or If it is only an uncertain hope that our life in Christ has given us . . .
e Or Then at the end, when . . . power (for he . . . feet), the last enemy, death, will be abolished.
f Or If, as men do, I had fought wild beasts at Ephesus, what good would it be to me? or If I had been in no better case than one fighting beasts in the arena at Ephesus, what good would it be to me?

10: *Grace:* God's graciousness. 11: Paul asserts the unity of the proclamation, despite differences among proclaimers.
15.12–34: Believing the Gospel means believing in resurrection. Paul is discussing only those few (11.30) who have died since becoming Christians (vv. 18,23,51–53 n.; 1 Th.4.13–18). **20:** As the *firstfruits* ritually symbolized the whole *harvest* (Lev.23.10), so Christ's resurrection pledges the resurrection of Christians. 21–22: See vv. 45–49 n.; Gen.2.17. **23:** *Coming:* see 1.8 n.; 1 Th.2.19 n. **24–28:** Paul summarizes briefly the events of Christ's *kingdom.* **24–25:** *Domination . . . enemies:* see 2.6–8 n. **26:** Perhaps at this point those from past ages held prisoner by *death* are released for judgment (see 6.2–3 n.). **27:** Ps.8.6. **29:** Apparently Christians were *baptized* vicariously for previously deceased loved ones to insure their resurrection. **31:** *Die:* risk death. **32:** Paul does not explain what or who the *beasts* were (compare 4.9). *Let us eat:* Isa.22.13. **33:** Doubters are *bad company,* quoting the Greek poet Menander.
15.35–58: "How are the dead raised?" The immortality of the soul freed of its bodily prison

39 All flesh is not the same flesh: there is flesh of men, flesh of beasts, of birds,
40 and of fishes—all different. There are heavenly bodies and earthly bodies; and the splendour of the heavenly bodies is one thing, the splendour of
41 the earthly, another. The sun has a splendour of its own, the moon another splendour, and the stars another, for
42 star differs from star in brightness. So it is with the resurrection of the dead. What is sown in the earth as a perish-
43 able thing is raised imperishable. Sown in humiliation, it is raised in glory; sown in weakness, it is raised in power;
44 sown as an animal body, it is raised as a spiritual body.

If there is such a thing as an animal
45 body, there is also a spiritual body. It is in this sense that Scripture says, 'The first man, Adam, became an animate being', whereas the last Adam has
46 become a life-giving spirit. Observe, the spiritual does not come first; the animal body comes first, and then the
47 spiritual. The first man was made 'of the dust of the earth': the second man
48 is from heaven. The man made of dust is the pattern of all men of dust, and the heavenly man is the pattern of all
49 the heavenly. As we have worn the likeness of the man made of dust, so we shall wear the likeness of the heavenly man.
50 What I mean, my brothers, is this: flesh and blood can never possess the kingdom of God, and the perishable
51 cannot possess immortality. Listen! I will unfold a mystery: we shall not all
52 die, but we shall all be changed in a flash, in the twinkling of an eye, at the last trumpet-call. For the trumpet will sound, and the dead will rise immortal,
53 and we shall be changed. This perishable being must be clothed with the

imperishable, and what is mortal must be clothed with immortality. And 54 when[g] our mortality has been clothed with immortality, then the saying of Scripture will come true: 'Death is swallowed up; victory is won!' 'O 55 Death, where is your victory? O Death, where is your sting?' The sting of death 56 is sin, and sin gains its power from the law; but, God be praised, he gives us 57 the victory through our Lord Jesus Christ.

Therefore, my beloved brothers, 58 stand firm and immovable, and work for the Lord always, work without limit, since you know that in the Lord your labour cannot be lost.

Christian giving

AND NOW ABOUT THE COLLECTION IN **16** aid of God's people: you should follow my directions to our congregations in Galatia. Every Sunday each of you is 2 to put aside and keep by him a sum in proportion to his gains, so that there may be no collecting when I come. When I arrive, I will give letters of 3 introduction to persons approved by you, and send them to carry your gift to Jerusalem. If it should seem worth 4 while for me to go as well, they shall go with me.

I shall come to Corinth after passing 5 through Macedonia—for I am travelling by way of Macedonia—and I may 6 stay with you, perhaps even for the whole winter, and then you can help me on my way wherever I go next. I 7 do not want this to be a flying visit; I hope to spend some time with you, if the Lord permits. But I shall remain at 8

g *Some witnesses insert* our perishable nature has been clothed with the imperishable, and . . .

---

was an idea natural to Greeks. The Corinthians seem to have balked at the idea of bodily resurrection. Paul agrees that the *flesh* has no part in the *kingdom* (v. 50), arguing that there are many kinds of bodies and that Christians will receive bodies made not of flesh, but of spirit. **45–49:** Speculation based on Gen. chs. 1–2 featured an ideal Man (Heb., "Adam") who would initiate the Age to Come. Thus Paul contrasts Christ as the *last Adam* (v. 45) or *second Man* (v. 47) with the sinful and mortal *first man* (see vv. 21–22; Rom. 5.12–19; compare Phil. 2.6–11). *Dust:* Gen.2.7. **51–53:** Most Christians (Paul included) will survive until Christ's return (see 1.8 n.), but *all*, whether living or dead, must receive spirit bodies. **52:** See 1 Th.4.15–17. **54–55:** Isa.25.8; Hos.13.14. **56:** *Law:* see Rom.5.13; 7.7–8; Gal.3.21–22.

16.1–11: "How is the offering for Jerusalem to be collected?" (See 7.1–16 n.). **1:** *Collection:* see Introduction to Rom. *Galatia:* see Rom.15.26 n. and Introduction to Gal. **2:** *No collecting:* each Christian will have a sum ready. **3–4:** Compare with the men in Acts 20.4. **5:** *Macedonia:* see 2 Cor.1.8–2.13 n. **8:** *Whitsuntide:* Pentecost (the "fiftieth" day after Passover); it fell in

9 Ephesus until Whitsuntide, for a great opportunity has opened for effective work, and there is much opposition.

10 If Timothy comes, see that you put him at his ease; for it is the Lord's work that he is engaged upon, as I am myself; so no one must slight him.

11 Send him happily on his way to join me, since I am waiting for him with our friends. As for our friend Apollos,

12 I urged him strongly to go to Corinth with the others, but he was quite determined not to go[h] at present; he will go when opportunity offers.

13 Be alert; stand firm in the faith; be valiant and strong. Let all you do be

14 done in love.

15 I have a request to make of you, my brothers. You know that the Stephanas family were the first converts in Achaia, and have laid themselves out

16 to serve God's people. I wish you to give their due position to such persons, and indeed to everyone who labours

17 hard at our common task. It is a great pleasure to me that Stephanas, Fortunatus, and Achaicus have arrived, be-

18 cause they have done what you had no chance to do; they have relieved my mind—and no doubt yours too. Such men deserve recognition.

19 Greetings from the congregations in Asia. Many greetings in the Lord from Aquila and Prisca and the congregation at their house. Greetings from all

20 the brothers. Greet one another with the kiss of peace.

21 This greeting is in my own hand— PAUL.

22 If anyone does not love the Lord, let him be outcast.

Marana tha—Come, O Lord!

23 The grace of the Lord Jesus Christ be with you.

24 My love to you all in Christ Jesus. Amen.

h *Or* but it was by no means the will of God that he should go . . .

May–June. **10:** *Timothy:* a trusted assistant of Paul's (4.17; 2 Th.1.1; 1 Th.1.1; 3.2,6; Phil.1.1; 2.19; 2 Cor.1.1,19; Rom.16.21; Col.1.1; Philem.1). **11:** *Our friends* (the others, v. 12): Timothy is one of a group of traveling church workers.

16.12: "When can Apollos return to us?" This is the final item from the Corinthians' letter (see Introduction). *Apollos:* see 1.12 n.

16.13–24: Final directions. 15–17: *Stephanas* (1.16), with *Fortunatus* and *Achaicus* (otherwise unknown), probably brought the Corinthians' letter to Paul (see Introduction). **19:** *Aquila, Prisca:* see Rom.16.3–5 n. **20:** *Kiss:* see v. 22 n.; Rom.16.16 n. **21–24:** Having finished dictating (see 1.16 n.), Paul "signs" the letter with a short paragraph (see 2 Th.3.17; Gal.6.11; Col.4.18). **22:** *Outcast:* lit. anathema, i.e. cursed. *Marana tha* is Aram. for *Come, O Lord.* The kiss of peace (v. 20), the anathema, and this invocation (compare Rev.22.20) perhaps echo an early Lord's Supper liturgy.

THE SECOND LETTER OF PAUL TO THE
CORINTHIANS

In the interval between 1 and 2 Corinthians Paul experienced two crises: (a) A visit to Corinth to deal with a sudden disciplinary problem was a painful failure (2.1). Retreating to Ephesus he wrote the Corinthians a severe letter (2.3–4; 7.8), now lost (see 10.1–13.14 n.), and sent it by Titus, one of his assistants. (b) Then Paul apparently underwent a crisis that caused him to despair of his life (1.8–10). When he was again able to travel, he went to Troas (2.12) and then to Macedonia (2.13; 7.5–6) before meeting Titus again. Titus had good news: the Corinthians had had a change of heart (7.7–12). Gratefully Paul wrote 2 Cor. chs. 1–9, urging forgiveness for the one who had caused the first crisis (2.5–11) and painting a joyful picture of the Christian life enjoyed despite sufferings like his second crisis (2.14–7.4). His remarks on the "collection" (chs. 8–9) date chs. 1–9 between 1 Corinthians and Romans.

Chapters 10–13, which contain valuable autobiographical material, are so angry and "boastful" that many believe Paul wrote them on quite another occasion. In any case, these chapters respond to news of Jewish-Christian interlopers in Corinth, a topic not mentioned in chs. 1–9.

Personal religion and the ministry

1 FROM PAUL, APOSTLE OF CHRIST JESUS by God's will, and our colleague Timothy, to the congregation of God's people at Corinth, together with all who are dedicated to him throughout the whole of Achaia.

2 Grace and peace to you from God our Father and the Lord Jesus Christ.

3 Praise be to the God and the Father of our Lord Jesus Christ, the all-merciful Father, the God whose consolation never fails us! He comforts us 4 in all our troubles, so that we in turn may be able to comfort others in any trouble of theirs and to share with them the consolation we ourselves receive 5 from God. As Christ's cup of suffering overflows, and we suffer with him, so also through Christ our consolation 6 overflows. If distress be our lot, it is the price we pay for your consolation, for your salvation; if our lot be consolation, it is to help us to bring you comfort, and strength to face with fortitude the same sufferings we now endure.

7 And our hope for you is firmly grounded;[a] for we know that if you have part in the suffering, you have part also in the divine consolation.

8 In saying this, we should like you to know, dear friends, how serious was the trouble that came upon us in the province of Asia. The burden of it was far too heavy for us to bear, so heavy that we even despaired of life. Indeed, 9 we felt in our hearts that we had received a death-sentence. This was meant to teach us not to place reliance on ourselves, but on God who raises the dead. From such mortal peril God 10 delivered us; and he will deliver us again,[b] he on whom our hope is fixed. Yes, he will continue to deliver us, if 11 you will co-operate by praying for us. Then, with so many people praying for our deliverance, there will be many to give thanks on our behalf for the gracious favour God has shown towards us.

There is one thing we are proud of: 12 our conscience assures us that in our dealings with our fellow-men, and above all in our dealings with you, our conduct has been governed by a devout and godly sincerity,[c] by the grace of God and not by worldly wisdom.

a *Some witnesses give these clauses* If distress ... firmly grounded *in different sequence.*
b *Some witnesses read* and he still delivers us.
c *Some witnesses read* by sincere and godly singleness of mind.

1.1–7: Salutation and thanksgiving: see Rom.1.1–7 nn. and 1.8–15 n. Paul *praises* God for his escape from danger and for Titus' good news (see Introduction). **1:** *Timothy:* see 1 Cor.16.10 n.

1.8–2.13: Explanation for a change in travel plans. Apparently in his "severe" *letter* (see Introduction) Paul had threatened an immediate return visit. He later decided to wait for Titus' firsthand report, which he finally obtained in Macedonia (2.13; 7.6). **8–10:** *Trouble:* see

13 There is nothing in our letters to you but what you can read for yourselves, 14 and understand too. Partial as your present knowledge of us is, you will I hope come to understand fully that you have as much reason to be proud of us, as we of you, on the Day of our Lord Jesus.

15 It was because I felt so confident about all this that I had intended to come first of all to you[d] and give you 16 the benefit of a double visit: I meant to visit you on my way to Macedonia, and after leaving Macedonia, to return to you, and you would then send me on 17 my way to Judaea. That was my intention; did I lightly change my mind?[e] Or do I, when I frame my plans, frame them as a worldly man might, so that it should rest with me to say 'yes' 18 and 'yes', or 'no' and 'no'? As God is true, the language in which we address you is not an ambiguous blend of Yes 19 and No. The Son of God, Christ Jesus, proclaimed among you by us (by Silvanus and Timothy, I mean, as well as myself), was never a blend of Yes and No. With him it was, and is, Yes. 20 He is the Yes pronounced upon God's promises, every one of them. That is why, when we give glory to God, it is through Christ Jesus that we say 21 'Amen'. And if you and we belong to Christ, guaranteed as his and anointed, 22 it is all God's doing; it is God also who has set his seal upon us, and as a pledge of what is to come has given the Spirit to dwell in our hearts.

23 I appeal to God to witness what I am going to say; I stake my life upon it: it was out of consideration for you that I 24 did not after all come to Corinth. Do not think we are dictating the terms of your faith; your hold on the faith is secure enough. We are working with you 2 for your own happiness. So I made up my mind that my next visit to you must 2 not be another painful one. If I cause pain to you, who is left to cheer me up,

except you, whom I have offended? This is precisely the point I made in my 3 letter: I did not want, I said, to come and be made miserable by the very people who ought to have made me happy; and I had sufficient confidence in you all to know that for me to be happy is for all of you to be happy. That letter I sent you came out of great 4 distress and anxiety; how many tears I shed as I wrote it! But I never meant to cause you pain; I wanted you rather to know the love, the more than ordinary love, that I have for you.

Any injury that has been done, has 5 not been done to me; to some extent, not to labour the point, it has been done to you all. The penalty on which 6 the general meeting has agreed has met the offence well enough. Something 7 very different is called for now: you must forgive the offender and put heart into him; the man's sorrow must not be made so severe as to overwhelm him. I urge you therefore to assure him of 8 your love for him by a formal act. I 9 wrote, I may say, to see how you stood the test, whether you fully accepted my authority. But anyone who has your 10 forgiveness has mine too; and when I speak of forgiving (so far as there is anything for me to forgive), I mean that as the representative of Christ I have forgiven him for your sake.[f] For Satan 11 must not be allowed to get the better of us; we know his wiles all too well.

Then when I came to Troas, where I 12 was to preach the gospel of Christ, and where an opening awaited me for the Lord's work, I still found no relief of 13 mind, for my colleague Titus was not there to meet me; so I took leave of the people there and went off to Macedonia. But thanks be to God, who 14 continually leads us about, captives in Christ's triumphal procession, and

d *Or* had originally intended to come to you . . .
e *Or* In forming this intention, did I act irresponsibly?
f *Or* that I have forgiven him for your sake, in the presence of Christ.

Introduction. *Us, we, ourselves:* see 10.11 n. **13:** See 10.10; 2 Pet.3.16. **14:** *Day:* see 1 Cor.1.8 n. **17–20:** *Amen* (see 1 Cor.14.16 n.) can mean *yes* or *true*. **19:** *Silvanus:* an assistant of Paul's (see 1 Th.1.1; 2 Th.1.1; as "Silas," Acts 15.22–18.5). **21–22:** *Christ . . . God . . . Spirit:* see 1 Cor.12.4–6 n. **22:** *Pledge:* see 5.5 n. **2.1–4:** *Visit, letter:* see Introduction. **5–11:** The offending Corinthian has been disciplined (for a possible comparison see 1 Cor.5.1–5) and he is now in need of *forgiveness.* **12–13:** The narrative of Paul's movements resumes in 7.5.
 2.14–7.4: The apostle's ministry of suffering occupies the main section of the letter. **14:** See

everywhere uses us to reveal and spread abroad the fragrance of the
15 knowledge of himself! We are indeed the incense offered by Christ to God, both for those who are on the way to salvation, and for those who are on the
16 way to perdition: to the latter it is a deadly fume that kills, to the former a vital fragrance that brings life. Who is
17 equal to such a calling? At least we do not go hawking the word of God about, as so many do; when we declare the word we do it in sincerity, as from God and in God's sight, as members of Christ.

3 ARE WE BEGINNING ALL OVER AGAIN TO produce our credentials? Do we, like some people, need letters of introduc-
2 tion to you, or from you? No, you are all the letter we need, a letter written on our heart; any man can see it for
3 what it is and read it for himself. And as for you, it is plain that you are a letter that has come from Christ, given to us to deliver: a letter written not with ink but with the Spirit of the living God, written not on stone tablets but on the pages of the human heart.
4 It is in full reliance upon God, through Christ, that we make such
5 claims. There is no question of our being qualified in ourselves: we cannot claim anything as our own. The qualification we have comes from God;
6 it is he who has qualified us to dispense his new covenant—a covenant expressed not in a written document, but in a spiritual bond; for the written law condemns to death, but the Spirit gives life.
7 The law, then, engraved letter by letter upon stone, dispensed death, and yet it was inaugurated with divine splendour. That splendour, though it was soon to fade, made the face of Moses so bright that the Israelites

could not gaze steadily at him. But if 8 so, must not even greater splendour rest upon the divine dispensation of the Spirit? If splendour accompanied the 9 dispensation under which we are condemned, how much richer in splendour must that one be under which we are acquitted! Indeed, the splendour that 10 once was is now no splendour at all; it is outshone by a splendour greater still. For if that which was soon to fade 11 had its moment of splendour, how much greater is the splendour of that which endures!

With such a hope as this we speak 12 out boldly; it is not for us to do as 13 Moses did: he put a veil over his face to keep the Israelites from gazing on that fading splendour until it was gone. But in any case their minds had been 14 made insensitive, for that same veil is there to this very day when the lesson is read from the old covenant; and it is never lifted, because only in Christ is the old covenant abrogated.*g* But to 15 this very day, every time the Law of Moses is read, a veil lies over the minds of the hearers. However, as Scripture 16 says of Moses, 'whenever he turns to the Lord the veil is removed'.*h* Now the 17 Lord of whom this passage speaks is the Spirit; and where the Spirit of the Lord is, there is liberty. And because 18 for us there is no veil over the face, we all reflect as in a mirror the splendour of the Lord; thus we are transfigured into his likeness, from splendour to splendour; such is the influence of the Lord who is Spirit.

SEEING THEN THAT WE HAVE BEEN 4 entrusted with this commission, which we owe entirely to God's mercy, we never lose heart. We have renounced 2 the deeds that men hide for very shame;

g Or in Christ is it abolished.
h Or as Scripture says, when one turns to the Lord the veil is removed.

---

1 Cor.4.9. **15:** For Paul as a sacrifice compare Phil.2.17. **17:** *Hawking:* peddling or huckstering.
3.1–18: **The power of the new covenant;** the impotence of the old. **1:** *All over again* implies some previous self-defense and criticism of it. Paul has his rivals in mind (see 10.1–13.14 n.), who carry *letters* of accreditation. **2–3:** The idea of the Corinthians as Paul's living credentials suggests Jer.31.33, the law written on men's *hearts* rather than on *stone tablets* (Exod.34.1,4). **6:** The *written law* both *condemns to death* (Rom.3.9–20) and is powerless to *give life* (Gal.3.21–22). **7–18:** See Exod.34.29–35. Moses' veil symbolically prevents Judaism from seeing that the Law's original *splendour* has *gone*. **16:** Exod.34.34. **18:** *Are transfigured:* are now at the present time being transfigured. *From splendour to splendour:* by increasing degrees.
4.1–15: **The apostle's faithfulness** shown by his sufferings. **3:** *Veiled:* Paul's critics may have

we neither practise cunning nor distort the word of God; only by declaring the truth openly do we recommend ourselves, and then it is to the common conscience of our fellow-men and in the 3 sight of God. And if indeed our gospel be found veiled, the only people who find it so are those on the way to 4 perdition. Their unbelieving minds are so blinded by the god of this passing age, that the gospel of the glory of Christ, who is the very image of God, cannot dawn upon them and bring 5 them light. It is not ourselves that we proclaim; we proclaim Christ Jesus as Lord, and ourselves as your servants, 6 for Jesus' sake. For the same God who said, 'Out of darkness let light shine', has caused his light to shine within us, to give the light of revelation—the revelation of the glory of God in the face of Jesus Christ.

7 We are no better than pots of earthenware to contain this treasure, and this proves that such transcendent power does not come from us, but is 8 God's alone. Hard-pressed on every side, we are never hemmed in; bewildered, we are never at our wits' end; 9 hunted, we are never abandoned to our fate; struck down, we are not left to die. 10 Wherever we go we carrry death with us in our body, the death that Jesus died, that in this body also life may reveal 11 itself, the life that Jesus lives. For continually, while still alive, we are being surrendered into the hands of death, for Jesus' sake, so that the life of Jesus also may be revealed in this 12 mortal body of ours. Thus death is at work in us, and life in you.

13 But Scripture says, 'I believed, and therefore I spoke out', and we too, in the same spirit of faith, believe and therefore speak out; for we know that 11 he who raised the Lord Jesus to life will with Jesus raise us too, and bring us to his presence, and you with us. 15 Indeed, it is for your sake that all things are ordered, so that, as the abounding grace of God is shared by more and more, the greater may be the chorus of thanksgiving that ascends to the glory of God.

16 No wonder we do not lose heart! Though our outward humanity is in decay, yet day by day we are inwardly renewed. Our troubles are slight and 17 short-lived; and their outcome an eternal glory which outweighs them far. Meanwhile our eyes are fixed, not on 18 the things that are seen, but on the things that are unseen: for what is seen passes away; what is unseen is eternal. For we know that if the earthly frame 5 that houses us today should be demolished, we possess a building which God has provided—a house not made by human hands, eternal, and in heaven. In this present body we do 2 indeed groan; we yearn to have our heavenly habitation put on over this one—in the hope that, being thus 3 clothed, we shall not find ourselves naked. We groan indeed, we who are 4 enclosed within this earthly frame; we are oppressed because we do not want to have the old body stripped off. Rather our desire is to have the new body put on over it, so that our mortal part may be absorbed into life immortal. God himself has shaped us 5 for this very end; and as a pledge of it he has given us the Spirit.

Therefore we never cease to be con- 6 fident. We know that so long as we are

---

called him obscure. *Perdition:* see 2.15–16. **4:** *The god of this passing age,* i.e. Satan (see 1 Cor.1.8 n.). *Image of God* recalls Adam (see Gen.1.27; 1 Cor.15.45–49 n.; Phil.2.6). **6:** Gen.1.3. Paul associates *light* and *glory* (or "splendour," 3.18) with possession of the Spirit (5.5). **8–11:** Daily hardships (see Mk.8.34) produce likeness to Christ (see Phil.3.10–11); Paul's *mortal body* is becoming like his Lord's (see 3.18). **12:** Paul accepts more than his proper share of suffering so as to provide them with *life* (see 1.6). **13:** Ps.116.10.

4.16–5.10: Our changing bodies. *Day by day* our suffering is eroding our *outward humanity* (i.e. our flesh bodies), but simultaneously we are *inwardly renewed* by spirit. (By contrast, in 1 Cor.15.42–57 this change of bodies is considered to occur instantly at Christ's return). **18:** *Things . . . seen:* the external body; *things . . . unseen:* the interior possession of the Spirit. **5.1–4:** Figuratively, the body is our home, or alternatively, our clothing. **1:** Our spirit body is *eternal* and destined for life *in heaven.* **2–4:** Paul *yearns* for the change to be completed and suffering ended (see Rom.8.23). Unbelievers, since they do not receive spirit bodies, are *naked* at death. **5:** The *pledge* is the down payment which puts a contract in force and implies further payments (in this case, of *the Spirit;* so also 1.22). **6–8:** Phil.1.21–24.

at home in the body we are exiles from
7 the Lord; faith is our guide, we do not
8 see him.[l] We are confident, I repeat,
and would rather leave our home in the
9 body and go to live with the Lord. We
therefore make it our ambition, wherever we are, here or there, to be accept-
10 able to him. For we must all have our
lives laid open before the tribunal of
Christ, where each must receive what
is due to him for his conduct in the
body, good or bad.

11 WITH THIS FEAR OF THE LORD BEFORE
our eyes we address our appeal to men.
To God our lives lie open, as I hope
they also lie open to you in your heart
12 of hearts. This is not another attempt
to recommend ourselves to you: we
are rather giving you a chance to show
yourselves proud of us; then you will
have something to say to those whose
pride is all in outward show and not in
13 inward worth. It may be we are beside
ourselves, but it is for God; if we are in
14 our right mind, it is for you. For the
love of Christ leaves us no choice, when
once we have reached the conclusion
that one man died for all and therefore
15 all mankind has died. His purpose in
dying for all was that men, while still
in life, should cease to live for themselves, and should live for him who for
their sake died and was raised to life.
16 With us therefore worldly standards
have ceased to count in our estimate of
any man; even if once they counted in
our understanding of Christ, they do so
17 now no longer. When anyone is united
to Christ, there is a new world;[j] the old
order has gone, and a new order has
already begun.[k]
18 From first to last this has been the
work of God. He has reconciled us men
to himself through Christ, and he has
enlisted us in this service of reconcilia-

tion. What I mean is, that God was in 19
Christ reconciling the world to himself,[l] no longer holding men's misdeeds
against them, and that he has entrusted
us with the message of reconciliation.
We come therefore as Christ's am- 20
bassadors. It is as if God were appealing
to you through us: in Christ's name, we
implore you, be reconciled to God!
Christ was innocent of sin, and yet for 21
our sake God made him one with the
sinfulness of men,[m] so that in him we
might be made one with the goodness
of God himself. Sharing in God's work, 6
we urge this appeal upon you: you have
received the grace of God; do not let
it go for nothing. God's own words are: 2

'In the hour of my favour I gave
    heed to you;
on the day of deliverance I came to
    your aid.'

The hour of favour has now come;
now I say, has the day of deliverance
dawned.

In order that our service may not be 3
brought into discredit, we avoid giving
offence in anything. As God's servants, 4
we try to recommend ourselves in all
circumstances by our steadfast endurance: in distress, hardships, and dire
straits; flogged, imprisoned, mobbed; 5
overworked, sleepless, starving. We
recommend ourselves by the inno- 6
cence of our behaviour, our grasp of
truth, our patience and kindliness; by
gifts of the Holy Spirit, by sincere love,
by declaring the truth, by the power of 7
God. We wield the weapons of

i Or faith is our guide and not the things we see.
j Or a new act of creation.
k Or When anyone is united to Christ he is a new
  creature: his old life is over; a new life has already
  begun.
l Or God was reconciling the world to himself by Christ.
m Or and yet God made him a sin-offering for us.

5.11–6.10: The reconciling ministry of Christ and his apostles. **12:** *Another attempt:* see 3.1 n.
13: *Beside ourselves:* in ecstasy (see 12.1–4 n.). **14:** *Love of Christ:* Christ's love for us. *One
man:* Christ, the second Adam (see 1 Cor.15.45–49 n.), represents *all mankind.* In principle the
old humanity has ended. **15:** See Mk.8.35. **16:** *Once,* before his conversion, Paul thought of
Jesus as a crucified criminal. **17:** For Christians the new life *has already begun* (see 4.16–5.10 n.).
18–20: By extension the apostle shares Christ's *reconciling* ministry. **19–21:** *In Christ* (v. 19):
through Christ as his agent. Christ accepted mankind's *sinfulness* that men *in Christ* might *no
longer* have their *misdeeds* held *against them* (v. 19; Rom.3.21–26). **6.2:** Isa.49.8. *Now:* see
5.17 n. **3:** *Discredit:* see 3.1 n. **4–5:** See 11.23–29. *In all circumstances:* see 1 Cor.9.19–23.
6: Paul here emphasizes his *patience and kindliness* by alluding to the abundance of personal
sufferings he has undergone, all specified in v. 5. **7:** *Weapons:* see Eph.6.14–17; 1 Th.5.8.

righteousness in right hand and left.
8 Honour and dishonour, praise and
blame, are alike our lot: we are the
9 impostors who speak the truth, the
unknown men whom all men know;
dying we still live on; disciplined by
10 suffering, we are not done to death; in
our sorrows we have always cause for
joy; poor ourselves, we bring wealth to
many; penniless, we own the world.
11 Men of Corinth, we have spoken
very frankly to you; we have opened
12 our heart wide to you all. On our part
there is no constraint; any constraint
13 there may be is in yourselves. In fair
exchange then (may a father speak so
to his children?) open wide your hearts
to us.

Problems of church life and discipline

14 DO NOT UNITE YOURSELVES WITH UN-
believers; they are no fit mates for you.
What has righteousness to do with
wickedness? Can light consort with
15 darkness? Can Christ agree with Belial,
or a believer join hands with an un-
16 believer? Can there be a compact
between the temple of God and the
idols of the heathen? And the temple of
the living God is what we are. God's
own words are: 'I will live and move
about among them; I will be their God,
17 and they shall be my people.' And
therefore, 'come away and leave them,
separate yourselves, says the Lord;
touch nothing unclean. Then I will
18 accept you, says the Lord, the Ruler of
all being; I will be a father to you, and
you shall be my sons and daughters.'
7 Such are the promises that have been
made to us, dear friends. Let us therefore cleanse ourselves from all that can
defile flesh or spirit, and in the fear of
God complete our consecration.

DO MAKE A PLACE FOR US IN YOUR 2
hearts! We have wronged no one,
ruined no one, taken advantage of no
one. I do not want to blame you. Why, 3
as I have told you before, the place you
have in our heart is such that, come
death, come life, we meet it together.
I am perfectly frank with you. I have 4
great pride in you. In all our many
troubles my cup is full of consolation,
and overflows with joy.

Even when we reached Macedonia 5
there was still no relief for this poor
body of ours; instead, there was trouble
at every turn, quarrels all round us,
forebodings in our heart. But God, 6
who brings comfort to the downcast,
has comforted us by the arrival of Titus,
and not merely by his arrival, but by 7
his being so greatly comforted about
you. He has told us how you long for
me, how sorry you are, and how eager
to take my side; and that has made me
happier still.

Even if I did wound you by the letter 8
I sent, I do not now regret it. I may
have been sorry for it when I saw that
the letter had caused you pain, even if
only for a time; but now I am happy, 9
not that your feelings were wounded
but that the wound led to a change of
heart. You bore the smart as God
would have you bear it, and so you are
no losers by what we did. For the 10
wound which is borne in God's way
brings a change of heart too salutary
to regret; but the hurt which is borne
in the world's way brings death. You 11
bore your hurt in God's way, and see
what its results have been! It made you
take the matter seriously and vindicate
yourselves. How angered you were,
how apprehensive! How your longing
for me awoke, yes, and your devotion
and your eagerness to see justice done!
At every point you have cleared your-

8–10: The apostle's ministry (like Jesus') is full of paradoxes (see 4.8–12; 1 Cor.4.9–13).
   6.11–13: Paul appeals with open heart to the Corinthians for complete reconciliation free of
constraint. (For their past disagreements see Introduction.) Paul here reaches the climax of
2.14–7.4.
   6.14–7.1: Avoid unbelievers. The section is very probably misplaced (see 7.2–4 n. and
Introduction to 1 Cor.). **15:** *Belial:* Satan. **16–18:** Paul links together a chain of texts: Lev.26.12;
Ezek.37.27; Isa.52.11; 2 Sam.7.14. **7.1:** *Complete our consecration*, i.e. our dedication to
holiness.
   7.2–4: Paul continues his plea. These verses would follow on 6.13, if 6.14–7.1 are misplaced
(see Introduction to 1 Cor.).
   7.5–16: Paul's narrative resumes from 2.13. (For the sequence of events see Introduction).
8: Although Paul was sorry that he had sent the "severe" letter, the effect in the end was healthful.

12 selves of blame in this trouble. And so, although I did send you that letter, it was not the offender or his victim that most concerned me. My aim in writing was to help to make plain to you, in the sight of God, how truly you are de-13 voted to us. That is why we have been so encouraged.

But besides being encouraged ourselves we have also been delighted beyond everything by seeing how happy Titus is: you have all helped to set his 14 mind completely at rest. Anything I may have said to him to show my pride in you has been justified. Every word we ever addressed to you bore the mark of truth; and the same holds of the proud boast we made in the presence of Titus: that also has proved true. 15 His heart warms all the more to you as he recalls how ready you all were to do what he asked, meeting him as you did 16 in fear and trembling. How happy I am now to have complete confidence in you!

8 WE MUST TELL YOU, FRIENDS, ABOUT the grace of generosity which God has imparted to[n] our congregations in 2 Macedonia. The troubles they have been through have tried them hard, yet in all this they have been so exuberantly happy that from the depths of their poverty they have shown themselves 3 lavishly open-handed. Going to the limit of their resources, as I can testify, 4 and even beyond that limit, they begged us most insistently, and on their own initiative, to be allowed to share in this generous service to their fellow-5 Christians. And their giving surpassed our expectations; for they gave their very selves, offering them in the first instance to the Lord, but also, under 6 God, to us. The upshot is that we have asked Titus, who began it all, to visit you and bring this work of generosity

also to completion. You are so rich in 7 everything—in faith, speech, knowledge, and zeal of every kind, as well as in the loving regard you have for us[o] —surely you should show yourselves equally lavish in this generous service! This is not meant as an order; by telling 8 you how keen others are I am putting your love to the test. For you know 9 how generous our Lord Jesus Christ has been: he was rich, yet for your sake he became poor, so that through his poverty you might become rich.

Here is my considered opinion on 10 the matter. What I ask you to do is in your own interests. You made a good beginning last year both in the work you did and in your willingness to undertake it. Now I want you to go on 11 and finish it: be as eager to complete the scheme as you were to adopt it, and give according to your means. Pro-12 vided there is an eager desire to give, God accepts what a man has; he does not ask for what he has not. There is 13 no question of relieving others at the cost of hardship to yourselves; it is a 14 question of equality. At the moment your surplus meets their need, but one day your need may be met from their surplus. The aim is equality; as 15 Scripture has it, 'The man who got much had no more than enough, and the man who got little did not go short.'

I thank God that he has made Titus 16 as keen on your behalf as we are! For 17 Titus not only welcomed our request; he is so eager that by his own desire he is now leaving to come to you. With 18 him we are sending one of our company whose reputation is high among our congregations everywhere for his services to the Gospel. Moreover they 19 have duly appointed him to travel with us and help in this beneficent work, by

n *Or* how gracious God has been to . . .
o *Some witnesses read* the love we have for you *or the* love which we have kindled in your hearts.

12: *The offender:* see 2.5–11 n. *His victim:* probably Paul. **14:** What Paul wrote to the Corinthians was angry; what he *said* to Titus expressed *pride*. **15–16:** Paul prepares for 8.6–8,16–17.
  8.1–9.15: The offering for the poor of the Jerusalem church (see Introduction to Rom.). Reconciliation assumed, Paul now turns to the collection. **1–5:** Paul describes the *generosity* of the Macedonians (see Phil.4.15–18) to spur the Corinthians on (contrast 9.2). **6:** See vv. 16–17 n. **7:** See 1 Cor.12.8–10. **9:** *Became poor:* see Phil.2.5–11. **10–11:** *Finish, complete* suggests that the dispute between Paul and the Corinthians interrupted the collection project. **14:** *Surplus:* contrast v. 2. **15:** Exod.16.18. **16–17:** Titus will precede Paul (see 9.4–5 n.). **18–24:** *One of our company:* lit. "the brother." This unidentified missionary has been *appointed* (probably by Jerusalem) to help with the collection (*this beneficent work*). He and the other "brother" of

which we do honour to the Lord himself and show our own eagerness to
20 serve. We want to guard against any criticism of our handling of this
21 generous gift; for our aims are entirely honourable, not only in the Lord's eyes, but also in the eyes of men.

22 With these men we are sending another of our company whose enthusiasm we have had many opportunities of testing, and who is now all the more earnest because of the great
23 confidence he has in you. If there is any question about Titus, he is my partner and my associate in dealings with you; as for the others, they are delegates of our congregations, an hon-
24 our to Christ.*p* Then give them clear expression of your love and justify our pride in you; justify it to them, and through them to the congregations.

9 About the provision of aid for God's people, it is superfluous for me to write
2 to you. I know how eager you are to help; I speak of it with pride to the Macedonians: I tell them that Achaia had everything ready last year; and most of them have been fired by your
3 zeal. My purpose in sending these friends is to ensure that what we have said about you in this matter should not prove to be an empty boast. By that I mean, I want you to be prepared, as
4 I told them you were; for if I bring with me men from Macedonia and they find you are not prepared, what a disgrace it will be to us, let alone to you, after all the confidence we have
5 shown! I have accordingly thought it necessary to ask these friends to go on ahead to Corinth, to see that your promised bounty is in order before I come; it will then be awaiting me as a bounty indeed, and not as an extortion.
6 Remember: sparse sowing, sparse

reaping; sow bountifully, and you will reap bountifully. Each person should 7 give as he has decided for himself; there should be no reluctance, no sense of compulsion; God loves a cheerful giver. And it is in God's power to 8 provide you richly with every good gift; thus you will have ample means in yourselves to meet each and every situation, with enough and to spare for every good cause. Scripture says of such 9 a man: 'He has lavished his gifts on the needy, his benevolence stands fast for ever.' Now he who provides seed 10 for sowing and bread for food will provide the seed for you to sow; he will multiply it and swell the harvest of your benevolence, and you will always 11 be rich enough to be generous. Through our action such generosity will issue in thanksgiving to God, for as a piece of 12 willing service this is not only a contribution towards the needs of God's people; more than that, it overflows in a flood of thanksgiving to God. For 13 through the proof which this affords, many will give honour to God when they see how humbly you obey him and how faithfully you confess the gospel of Christ; and will thank him for your liberal contribution to their need and to the general good. And as they join 14 in prayer on your behalf, their hearts will go out to you because of the richness of the grace which God has imparted to you. Thanks be to God 15 for his gift beyond words!

Trials of a Christian missionary

BUT I, PAUL, APPEAL TO YOU BY THE 10 gentleness and magnanimity of Christ— I, so feeble (you say) when I am face to

p Or they are . . . congregations; they reflect Christ.

---

v. 22 are called "apostles" (*delegates*) in v. 23. **20:** On the Corinthians' suspicions about Paul and money see 12.16–18; 11.7–10 n. **21:** Prov.3.4 (Sept.). **9.2:** See 8.1–5 n. **4–5:** Paul will come with representatives *from Macedonia*. From *Corinth* they will sail to Jerusalem (1 Cor.16.3–4). **7:** Prov.22.8 (Sept.). **9:** Ps.112.9. **15:** God's *gift beyond words:* his son (see Rom.8.32).

10.1–13.14: Paul's boast against false apostles. Because of the tone of chs. 10–13, some have taken them to be part of the "severe" letter which preceded 2 Cor. chs. 1–9 (see Introduction). However, the problem of traveling Jewish "apostles" in chs. 10–13 is more probably subsequent to chs. 1–9. On the lack of an opening thanksgiving see Rom.1.8–15 n. Note the accusations against Paul: unethical (v. 2), weak (v. 3), boastful (v. 8), brave from a distance but ineffectual in person (vv. 1,10–11), an amateur "apostle" (11.7–11), a man without pedigree (11.22–23), a nobody (12.11).

10.1–18: Paul's bold counterattack. 1: On Christ's humility see Phil.2.5–8, especially v. 8.

face with you, so brave when I am
2 away. Spare me, I beg you, the necessity
of such bravery when I come, for I
reckon I could put on as bold a face
as you please against those who charge
3 us with moral weakness. Weak men we
may be, but it is not as such that we
4 fight our battles. The weapons we wield
are not merely human,*q* but divinely
5 potent to demolish strongholds; we
demolish sophistries and all that rears
its proud head against the knowledge
of God; we compel every human
thought to surrender in obedience to
6 Christ; and we are prepared to punish
all rebellion when once you have put
yourselves in our hands.

7   Look facts in the face.*r* Someone is
convinced, is he, that he belongs to
Christ? Let him think again, and reflect
that we belong to Christ as much as he
8 does. Indeed, if I am somewhat over-
boastful about our authority—an authority given by the Lord to build you
up, not pull you down—I shall make
9 my boast good. So you must not think
of me as one who scares you by the
10 letters he writes. 'His letters', so it is
said, 'are weighty and powerful; but
when he appears he has no presence,
and as a speaker he is beneath con-
11 tempt.' People who talk in that way
should reckon with this: when I come,
my actions will show the same man as
my letters showed in my absence.

12   We should not dare to class ourselves
or compare ourselves with any of those
who put forward their own claims.
What fools they are to measure themselves by themselves, to find in themselves their own standard of com-
13 parison!*s* With us there will be no
attempt to boast beyond our proper
sphere; and our sphere is determined
by the limit God laid down for us,
which permitted us to come as far as
14 Corinth. We are not overstretching our

commission, as we should be if it did
not extend to you, for we were the first
to reach Corinth in preaching the
gospel of Christ. And we do not boast 15
of work done where others have
laboured, work beyond our proper
sphere. Our hope is rather that, as your
faith grows, we may attain a position
among you greater than ever before,
but still within the limits of our sphere.
Then we can carry the Gospel to lands 16
that lie beyond you, never priding ourselves on work already done in another
man's sphere. If a man must boast, let 17
him boast of the Lord. Not the man 18
who recommends himself, but the man
whom the Lord recommends—he and
he alone is to be accepted.

I wish you would bear with me in a **11**
little of my folly; please do bear with
me. I am jealous for you, with a divine 2
jealousy; for I betrothed you to Christ,
thinking to present you as a chaste
virgin to her true and only husband.
But as the serpent in his cunning 3
seduced Eve, I am afraid that your
thoughts may be corrupted and you
may lose your*t* single-hearted devotion
to Christ. For if someone comes who 4
proclaims another Jesus, not the Jesus
whom we proclaimed, or if you then
receive a spirit different from the Spirit
already given to you, or a gospel different from the gospel you have already
accepted, you manage to put up with
that well enough. Have I in any way 5
come   short   of   those   superlative
apostles? I think not. I may be no 6
speaker, but knowledge I have; at all
times we have made known to you the
full truth.

Or was this my offence, that I made 7

q Or charge us with worldly standards. We live, no
doubt, in the world; but it is not on that level that we
fight our battles. The weapons we wield are not those
of the world . . .
r Or You are looking only at what catches the eye.
s Some witnesses read On the contrary we measure
ourselves by ourselves, by our own standard of
comparison. *t Some witnesses insert* purity and . . .

2: *Moral weakness:* unethical action. **3–4:** Paul adopts phrases by which his opponents have
disparaged him: *weak men, merely human. Weapons:* see 6.7; Eph.6.14–17; 1 Th.5.8. **8:** Words
meaning *boast* or *boastful* appear nineteen times in 10.8–12.9. **9–10:** See 2.3–4; 11.6 n. **11:** *I, my:*
lit. "we," "our." Here, as often, the plural stands primarily for Paul. **15–16:** *Our . . . sphere:*
see Rom.15.20 n. *Lands that lie beyond you,* i.e. to the west, perhaps Spain (Rom.15.23–28).
17: Jer.9.24 (1 Cor.1.31).
    11.1–15: Satan's apostles. **1:** *Folly:* see v. 16. **2:** See Hos.2.19–20; Eph.5.26–27. **3:** Paul
compares his opponents to the serpent of Gen.3.4; see vv. 13–15 n. **5:** The *superlative apostles*
are paid (vv. 7–10) preachers (v. 6), Jewish–Christians (vv. 22–23) probably from Jerusalem.
6: See 10.10; 1 Cor.2.3. **7–10:** Apparently Paul's practice was to accept money for himself but

no charge for preaching the gospel of God, lowering myself to help in raising 8 you? It is true that I took toll of other congregations, accepting*u* support from 9 them to serve you. Then, while I was with you, if I ran short I sponged on no one; anything I needed was fully met by our friends who came from Macedonia; I made it a rule, as I always 10 shall, never to be a burden to you. As surely as the truth of Christ is in me, I will preserve my pride in this matter throughout Achaia, and nothing shall 11 stop me. Why? Is it that I do not love you? God knows I do.

12 And I shall go on doing as I am doing now, to cut the ground from under those who would seize any chance to put their vaunted apostleship on the 13 same level as ours. Such men are sham-apostles, crooked in all their practices, masquerading as apostles of Christ. 14 There is nothing surprising about that; Satan himself masquerades as an angel 15 of light. It is therefore a simple thing for his agents to masquerade as agents of good. But they will meet the end their deeds deserve.

16 I repeat: let no one take me for a fool; but if you must, then give me the privilege of a fool, and let me have my 17 little boast like others. I am not speaking here as a Christian, but like a fool, 18 if it comes to bragging. So many people brag of their earthly distinctions that I 19 shall do so too. How gladly you bear with fools, being yourselves so wise! 20 If a man tyrannizes over you, exploits you, gets you in his clutches, puts on airs, and hits you in the face, you put 21 up with it. And we, you say, have been weak! I admit the reproach.

But if there is to be bravado (and here I speak as a fool), I can indulge in 22 it too. Are they Hebrews? So am I. Israelites? So am I. Abraham's de-23 scendants? So am I. Are they servants

of Christ? I am mad to speak like this, but I can outdo them. More over-worked than they, scourged more severely, more often imprisoned, many a time face to face with death. Five times 24 the Jews have given me the thirty-nine strokes; three times I have been beaten 25 with rods; once I was stoned; three times I have been shipwrecked, and for twenty-four hours I was adrift on the open sea. I have been constantly on the 26 road; I have met dangers from rivers, dangers from robbers, dangers from my fellow-countrymen, dangers from foreigners, dangers in towns, dangers in the country, dangers at sea, dangers from false friends. I have toiled and 27 drudged, I have often gone without sleep; hungry and thirsty, I have often gone fasting; and I have suffered from cold and exposure.

Apart from these external things,*v* 28 there is the responsibility that weighs on me every day, my anxious concern for all our congregations. If anyone is 29 weak, do I not share his weakness? If anyone is made to stumble, does my heart not blaze with indignation? If 30 boasting there must be, I will boast of the things that show up my weakness. The God and Father of the Lord Jesus 31 (blessed be his name for ever!) knows that what I say is true. When I was in 32 Damascus, the commissioner of King Aretas kept the city under observation so as to have me arrested; and I was 33 let down in a basket, through a window in the wall, and so escaped his clutches.

I AM OBLIGED TO BOAST. IT DOES NO **12** good; but I shall go on to tell of visions and revelations granted by the Lord. I know a Christian man who fourteen 2 years ago (whether in the body or out

u Or Did I take toll of other congregations by accepting . . .?
v Or Apart from things which I omit.

---

never to ask for it (see 1 Cor.9.12b–18). The Corinthians, unlike the *Macedonians* (Phil.4.14–18), had not offered to support him. Ironically, he is now criticized for not receiving support as a "true" apostle should. **13–15:** See also Gal.5.12, a passage only slightly more intemperate.

11.16–33: Paul's credentials are his hardships. 21–23: *Hebrews:* Aram. speaking. *Israelites:* Jews by birth (see Rom.9.4 n.). Compare Phil.3.4–6. So well did Paul adapt himself to his environment (1 Cor.9.19–23) that at times he had to assert his Jewish pedigree. **24:** *Thirty-nine strokes:* see Acts 5.40 n. **25:** *Rods:* a Roman punishment (see Acts 16.22). *Stoned:* see Acts 14.19. **32–33:** See Acts 9.23–25. Aretas IV was king of Nabataea.

12.1–10: Paul's visions and "thorn in the flesh." **1–4:** Paul was given to *visions and revelations* (see v. 7; 5.13)); he could also speak in tongues (see 1 Cor.14.18). **2:** *Christian man:* Paul (v.7).

of it, I do not know—God knows) was caught up as far as the third heaven.
3 And I know that this same man (whether in the body or out of it, I do
4 not know—God knows) was caught up into paradise, and heard words so secret that human lips may not repeat
5 them. About such a man as that I am ready to boast; but I will not boast on my own account, except of my weak-
6 nesses. If I should choose to boast, it would not be the boast of a fool, for I should be speaking the truth. But I refrain, because I should not like anyone to form an estimate of me which goes beyond the evidence of his own eyes
7 and ears. And so, to keep me from being unduly elated by the magnificence of such revelations, I was given[w] a sharp physical pain[x] which came as Satan's messenger to bruise me; this was to save me from being unduly
8 elated. Three times I begged the Lord
9 to rid me of it, but his answer was: 'My grace is all you need; power comes to its full strength in weakness.' I shall therefore prefer to find my joy and pride in the very things that are my weakness; and then the power of Christ will come and rest upon me.
10 Hence I am well content, for Christ's sake, with weakness, contempt, persecution, hardship, and frustration; for when I am weak, then I am strong.

11 I AM BEING VERY FOOLISH, BUT IT WAS you who drove me to it; my credentials should have come from you. In no respect did I fall short of these superlative apostles, even if I am a nobody.
12 The marks of a true apostle were there, in the work I did among you, which called for such constant fortitude, and was attended by signs, marvels, and
13 miracles. Is there anything in which

you were treated worse than the other congregations—except this, that I never sponged upon you? How unfair of me! I crave forgiveness.
14 Here am I preparing to pay you a third visit; and I am not going to sponge upon you. It is you I want, not your money; parents should make provision for their children, not children for their parents. As for me, I will
15 gladly spend what I have for you—yes, and spend myself to the limit. If I love you overmuch, am I to be loved the less? But, granted that I did not prove
16 a burden to you, still I was unscrupulous enough, you say, to use a trick to
17 catch you. Who, of the men I have sent to you, was used by me to defraud you?
18 I begged Titus to visit you, and I sent our friend with him. Did Titus defraud you? Have we not both been guided by the same Spirit, and followed the same course?
19 Perhaps you think that all this time we have been addressing our defence to you. No; we are speaking in God's sight, and as Christian men. Our whole aim, my own dear people, is to build you up. I fear that when I come I may
20 perhaps find you different from what I wish you to be, and that you may find me also different from what you wish. I fear I may find quarrelling and jealousy, angry tempers and personal rivalries, backbiting and gossip, arrogance and general disorder. I am afraid
21 that, when I come again, my God may humiliate me in your presence, that I may have tears to shed over many of those who have sinned in the past and have not repented of their unclean lives, their fornication and sensuality.

w *Some witnesses read* ... ears, and because of the magnificence of the revelations themselves. Therefore to keep me from being unduly elated I was given ...
x *Or* a painful wound to my pride (*literally* a stake, *or* thorn, for the flesh).

The third heaven may mean the highest; or else the third of seven, as the Jews viewed heaven.
4: *Paradise:* the heavenly Eden. 7: *Sharp physical pain:* traditionally, "thorn in the flesh." Some suggest a recurrent illness (compare Gal.4.13–14); others, a human adversary (*Satan's messenger*). 9: Just as the *power of Christ* was expressed in weakness, Paul understands that his own *weakness* is transformed into strength by means of *grace*. (Compare Phil.2.5–11; 3.7–11).
10: See 11.23–30; 4.7–12; 1 Cor.4.11–13; Rom.8.35.
12.11–21: Paul's fatherly concern for his congregation. 11: *Superlative apostles:* see 11.5 n.
12: *Signs, marvels,* and *miracles:* see Rom.15.19; Gal.3.5. 13–15: See 11.7–10 n. 14: *Third visit:* see 13.1–2 n. *Parents, children:* compare 1 Cor.4.14–15. 18: *Begged Titus:* see 8.6,16–17 n. *Our friend:* see 8.22; 18–24 n. 20–21: All the old difficulties spring to Paul's mind (see 1 Cor.1.11; 5.1; 6.12–20), but the lists are partly stereotyped (see 1 Cor.6.9–11 n.; Rom.1.29–31; Gal.5.19–21). *Humiliate,* perhaps an echo of 2.1.

13 This will be my third visit to you; and all facts must be established by the

2 evidence of two or three witnesses. To those who have sinned in the past, and to everyone else, I repeat the warning I gave before; I gave it in person on my second visit, and I give it now in absence. It is that when I come this

3 time, I will show no leniency. Then you will have the proof you seek of the Christ who speaks through me, the Christ who, far from being weak with you, makes his power felt among you.

4 True, he died on the cross in weakness, but he lives by the power of God; and we who share his weakness shall by the power of God live with him in your service.

5 Examine yourselves: are you living the life of faith? Put yourselves to the test. Surely you recognize that Jesus Christ is among you?—unless of course

6 you prove unequal to the test. I hope you will come to see that we are not

7 unequal to it. Our prayer to God is that you may do no wrong; we are not concerned to be vindicated ourselves; we want you to do what is right, even if we should seem to be discredited.

8 For we have no power to act against the truth, but only for it. We are well

9 content to be weak at any time if only you are strong. Indeed, my whole prayer is that all may be put right with you. My purpose in writing this letter

10 before I come, is to spare myself, when I come, any sharp exercise of authority —authority which the Lord gave me for building up and not for pulling down.

And now, my friends, farewell. Mend

11 your ways; take our appeal to heart; agree with one another; live in peace; and the God of love and peace will be with you. Greet one another with the

12 kiss of peace. All God's people send

13 you greetings.

The grace of the Lord Jesus Christ,

14 and the love of God, and fellowship in the Holy Spirit, be with you all.

13.1–14: Final warnings, greetings and blessing. 1–2: Paul's approaching visit (see 9.4–5 n). will be his *third*. The first was the founding visit (see 10.14); his *second visit* was "painful" (see Introduction). The *three witnesses* (Deut.19.15) may be the three visits: the Corinthians have one chance left. **12:** *Kiss:* see Rom.16.16 n. **14:** This is the fullest form of Paul's usual benediction (see 1 Cor.12.4–6 n.).

THE LETTER OF PAUL TO THE
GALATIANS

Freedom is the message of this extremely important letter. The immediate issue is whether Christians should observe Jewish law. Paul's churches in Galatia (perhaps at Iconium, Lystra, and Derbe; Acts ch. 14) had been visited by Christian Jews who preached at least a partial observance of Mosaic Law. Paul cites circumcision (5.2; 6.12) and the ritual calendar (4.10). Apparently they presented both themselves and Paul as subject to the authority of the Jerusalem Church. Paul asserts his divine commission and complete freedom from Jerusalem, giving us valuable autobiographical information (1.10–2.14). He attacks "legalism" as a denial in principle of the divine acceptance ("justification") which can depend only on utter trust ("faith") in Christ (2.15–3.29). The Mosaic Law is for "slaves," whereas Christians are God's adopted children (ch. 4); their brotherly love supersedes the law (5.13–6.10). Sarcastically, Paul accuses the Judaizers of seeking to give Christianity the appearance of a Jewish sect only to avoid persecution (6.12).

The date of the letter is a problem. Many of the same issues (and phrases) appear in Romans, suggesting that the interval between the two was not great. Because these issues are more urgent here in Galatians, this letter is the earlier.

Faith and freedom

1 FROM PAUL, AN APOSTLE, NOT BY human appointment or human commission, but by commission from Jesus Christ and from God the 2 Father who raised him from the dead. I and the group of friends now with me send greetings to the Christian congregations of Galatia.

3 Grace and peace to you from God the Father and our Lord Jesus Christ,[a] 4 who sacrificed himself for our sins, to rescue us out of this present age of wickedness, as our God and Father 5 willed; to whom be glory for ever and ever. Amen.

6 I am astonished to find you turning so quickly away from him who called you by grace,[b] and following a different 7 gospel. Not that it is in fact another gospel; only there are persons who unsettle your minds by trying to distort 8 the gospel of Christ. But if anyone, if we ourselves or an angel from heaven, should preach a gospel at variance with the gospel we preached to you, he shall 9 be held outcast. I now repeat what I have said before: if anyone preaches a gospel at variance with the gospel which you received, let him be outcast!

10 Does my language now sound as if I were canvassing for men's support? Whose support do I want but God's alone? Do you think I am currying favour with men? If I still sought men's favour, I should be no servant of Christ.

11 I must make it clear to you, my friends, that the gospel you heard me preach is no human invention. I did not 12 take it over from any man; no man taught it me; I received it through a revelation of Jesus Christ.

13 You have heard what my manner of life was when I was still a practising Jew: how savagely I persecuted the church of God, and tried to destroy it; 14 and how in the practice of our national religion I was outstripping many of my Jewish contemporaries in my boundless devotion to the traditions of my an- 15 cestors. But then in his good pleasure God, who had set me apart from birth and called me through his grace, chose 16 to reveal his Son to me and through

a *Some witnesses read* God our Father and the Lord Jesus Christ.
b *Some witnesses read* from Christ who called you by grace, *or* from him who called you by grace of Christ.

1.1–5: **Salutation.** See Rom.1.1–7 nn. **1:** From the first line Paul emphasizes again and again that he is an *apostle* independent of human authority. **3–5:** See Rom.1.7 n. and 1.8–15 n. **4:** See 2.20; 1 Cor.15.3. *Age:* see 1 Cor.2.6–8n.
1.6–10: **The Galatian apostasy** from God. **8–9:** *Angel:* see 2 Cor.11.14. *Outcast:* compare 1 Cor.16.22 n.; 5.2–5. **10:** 1 Th.2.4; 1 Cor.9.19–23.
1.11–17: **Paul's gospel is from God** not man. **12:** Compare 1 Cor.15.8 and 2 Cor.12.1–4 n. with 1 Cor.15.3 n. **13–14:** See Phil.3.4–6 and compare Acts 8.3; 22.3–5; 26.4–11. **15–16:** *From*

me, in order that I might proclaim him among the Gentiles. When that happened, without consulting any human being, without going up to Jerusalem to see those who were apostles before me, I went off at once to Arabia, and afterwards returned to Damascus.

18 Three years later I did go up to Jerusalem to get to know Cephas. I

19 stayed with him for a fortnight, without seeing any other of the apostles, except[c] James the Lord's brother.

20 What I write is plain truth; before God I am not lying.

21 Next I went to the regions of Syria

22 and Cilicia, and remained unknown by sight[d] to Christ's congregations in

23 Judaea. They only heard it said, 'Our former persecutor is preaching the good news of the faith which once he tried to

24 destroy'; and they praised God for me.

2 Next, fourteen years later, I went again[e] to Jerusalem with Barnabas, tak-

2 ing Titus with us. I went up because it had been revealed by God that I should do so. I laid before them—but at a private interview with the men of repute —the gospel which I am accustomed to preach to the Gentiles, to make sure that the race I had run, and was run-

3 ning, should not be run in vain. Yet even my companion Titus, Greek though he is, was not compelled to be

4 circumcised. That course was urged only as a concession to certain[f] sham-Christians, interlopers who had stolen in to spy upon the liberty we enjoy in the fellowship of Christ Jesus. These men wanted to bring us into bondage,

5 but not for one moment did I yield to their dictation; I was determined that the full truth of the Gospel should be maintained for you.[g]

6 But as for the men of high reputation (not that their importance matters to

me: God does not recognize these personal distinctions)—these men of repute, I say, did not prolong the con-

7 sultation,[h] but on the contrary acknowledged that I had been entrusted with the Gospel for Gentiles as surely as Peter had been entrusted with the Gospel for Jews. For God whose action

8 made Peter an apostle to the Jews, also made me an apostle to the Gentiles.

9 Recognizing, then, the favour thus bestowed upon me, those reputed pillars of our society, James, Cephas, and John, accepted Barnabas and myself as partners, and shook hands upon it, agreeing that we should go to the Gentiles while they went to the Jews.

10 All they asked was that we should keep their poor in mind, which was the very thing I made[i] it my business to do.

11 But when Cephas came to Antioch, I opposed him to his face, because he was clearly in the wrong. For until certain

12 persons[j] came from James he was taking his meals with gentile Christians; but when they[k] came he drew back and began to hold aloof, because he was afraid of the advocates of circumcision.

13 The other Jewish Christians showed the same lack of principle; even Barnabas was carried away and played false

14 like the rest. But when I saw that their conduct did not square with[l] the truth of the Gospel, I said to Cephas, before the whole congregation, 'If you, a Jew

c *Or* but only. d *Or* unknown personally.
e *Some witnesses omit* again.
f *Or* The question was later raised because of certain . . .
g *Or, following the reading of some witnesses,* Yet even . . . is, was under no absolute compulsion to be circumcised, but for the sake of certain . . . of Christ Jesus, with the intention of bringing us into bondage, I yielded to their demand for the moment, to ensure that gospel truth should not be prevented from reaching you.
h *Or* gave me no further instructions.
i *Or* had made, *or* have made.
j *Some witnesses read* a certain person.
k *Some witnesses read* he.
l *Or* I saw that they were not making progress towards . . .

birth: see Jer.1.5. *To me and through me:* lit. "in me" (see v. 12 n.). **17:** Paul denies that he is a *Jerusalem* apostle.
 1.18–24: Paul's first visit to Jerusalem. 18: *Cephas:* see 1 Cor.1.12 n. **19:** *James:* see Mk.6.3; Acts 15.13.
 2.1–10: Paul's second visit to Jerusalem confirms his apostolic freedom (compare Acts 15.2–29). **1:** *Barnabas:* see Acts 4.36. *Titus:* see Introduction to 2 Cor. **2:** *Men of repute:* see v. 9. **3–9:** Conservative Jewish-Christians demanded that *Titus* be circumcised, but the Jerusalem apostles did not make circumcision a requirement for *Gentiles.* **9:** *John:* see Mk.1.19. **10:** This request probably inaugurated the "collection" for the *poor* (see Introduction to Rom.).
 2.11–21: Paul argues with Peter over table-fellowship between Jewish and Gentile Christians, asserting that God's acceptance comes through trust (*faith*) and not by legal observances. **12:** *James:* see 1.19 n. *Circumcision:* see vv. 3–5. **13:** *Other Jewish Christians:* those at Antioch.

born and bred, live like a Gentile, and not like a Jew, how can you insist that Gentiles must live like Jews?

15 We ourselves are Jews by birth, not 16 Gentiles and sinners. But we know that no man is ever justified by doing what the law demands, but only through faith in Christ Jesus; so we too have put our faith in Jesus Christ, in order that we might be justified through this faith, and not through deeds dictated by law; for by such deeds, Scripture says, no mortal man shall be justified. 17 If now, in seeking to be justified in Christ, we ourselves no less than the Gentiles turn out to be sinners against the law,*m* does that mean that Christ 18 is an abettor of sin? No, never! No, if I start building up again a system which I have pulled down, then it is that I show myself up as a transgressor of the 19 law. For through the law I died to law 20 —to live for God. I have been crucified with Christ: the life I now live is not my life, but the life which Christ lives in me; and my present bodily life is lived by faith in the Son of God, who loved me and gave himself up for me. 21 I will not nullify the grace of God; if righteousness comes by law, then Christ died for nothing.

3 YOU STUPID GALATIANS! YOU MUST HAVE been bewitched—you before whose eyes Jesus Christ was openly displayed upon 2 his cross! Answer me one question: did you receive the Spirit by keeping the law or by believing the gospel mes-3 sage*n*? Can it be that you are so stupid? You started with the spiritual; do you now look to the material to make you 4 perfect? Have all your great experiences been in vain—if vain indeed they should 5 be? I ask then: when God gives you the Spirit and works miracles among you, why is this? Is it because you keep the law, or is it because you have faith in the

gospel message? Look at Abraham: he 6 put his faith in God, and that faith was counted to him as righteousness.

You may take it, then, that it is the 7 men of faith who are Abraham's sons. And Scripture, foreseeing that God 8 would justify the Gentiles through faith, declared the Gospel to Abraham beforehand: 'In you all nations shall find blessing.' Thus it is the men of faith 9 who share the blessing with faithful Abraham.

On the other hand those who rely on 10 obedience to the law are under a curse; for Scripture says, 'A curse is on all who do not persevere in doing everything that is written in the Book of the Law.' It is evident that no one is ever justified 11 before God in terms of law; because we read, 'he shall gain life who is justified through faith'. Now law is not at 12 all a matter of having faith: we read, 'he who does this shall gain life by what he does'.

Christ bought us freedom from the 13 curse of the law by becoming for our sake an accursed thing; for Scripture says, 'A curse is on everyone who is hanged on a gibbet.' And the purpose 14 of it all was that the blessing of Abraham should in Jesus Christ be extended to the Gentiles, so that we might receive the promised Spirit through faith.

My brothers, let me give you an 15 illustration. Even in ordinary life, when a man's will and testament has been duly executed, no one else can set it aside or add a codicil. Now the promises 16 were pronounced to Abraham and to his 'issue'. It does not say 'issues' in the plural, but in the singular, 'and to your issue'; and the 'issue' intended is Christ. What I am saying is this: a testament, 17 or covenant, had already been validated

m Or no less than the Gentiles have accepted the position of sinners against the law.
n Or or by the message of faith, *or* or by hearing and believing.

15–21: This section summarizes Paul's basic argument (compare Rom.3.9–26). **16:** See 3.6–14. *Justified:* accepted by God as righteous (see Rom.1.16–17 n.; 3.20). *Scripture:* Ps.143.2. **17–18:** Paul and Cephas indeed break the *law* (e.g. by eating with Gentiles); the real *transgressor*, however, is the adherent of the Law (see 3.10). **20:** Compare 6.14,17.
　　3.1–18: Abraham's faith foreshadows the Christian's trust in Christ (Rom. ch. 4.). **1:** *Openly displayed,* i.e. in Paul's preaching (see 1 Cor.1.18–24). **2:** *Receive the Spirit:* see 2 Cor.5.5 n. **3:** *The material:* keeping the law. **5:** *Miracles:* see 1 Cor.12.10; 2 Cor.12.12. **6:** Gen.15.6. **8:** Gen.12.3; 18.18. **10:** See Rom.3.9–20. *Scripture:* Deut.27.26. **11:** Hab.2.4 (Rom.1.17). **12:** Lev.18.5 (Rom.10.5). **13:** Deut.21.23 (compare 2 Cor.5.21). **16:** *Issue:* see e.g. Gen.17.1–8. **17:** *Testament* and *covenant* translate a single Gk. word, which in the Sept. (e.g. Gen.9.9; 17.7)

by God; it cannot be invalidated, and its promises rendered ineffective, by a law made four hundred and thirty years 18 later. If the inheritance is by legal right, then it is not by promise; but it was by promise that God bestowed it as a free gift on Abraham.

19 Then what of the law? It was added to make wrongdoing a legal offence.[o] It was a temporary measure pending the arrival of the 'issue' to whom the promise was made. It was promulgated through angels, and there was an inter-20 mediary; but an intermediary is not needed for one party acting alone, and God is one.

21 Does the law, then, contradict the promises? No, never! If a law had been given which had power to bestow life, then indeed righteousness would have 22 come from keeping the law. But Scripture has declared the whole world to be prisoners in subjection to sin, so that faith in Jesus Christ may be the ground on which the promised blessing is given, and given to those who have such faith.

23 Before this faith came, we were close prisoners in the custody of law, pending 24 the revelation of faith. Thus the law was a kind of tutor in charge of us until Christ should come,[p] when we should 25 be justified through faith; and now that faith has come, the tutor's charge is at an end.

26 For through faith you are all sons of 27 God in union with Christ Jesus. Baptized into union with him, you have all 28 put on Christ as a garment. There is no such thing as Jew and Greek, slave and freeman, male and female; for you are 29 all one person in Christ Jesus. But if you thus belong to Christ, you are the 'issue' of Abraham, and so heirs by promise.

This is what I mean: so long as the 4 heir is a minor, he is no better off than a slave, even though the whole estate is his; he is under guardians and trustees 2 until the date fixed by his father. And 3 so it was with us. During our minority we were slaves to the elemental spirits of the universe,[q] but when the term was 4 completed, God sent his own Son, born of a woman, born under the law, to 5 purchase freedom for the subjects of the law, in order that we might attain the status of sons.

To prove that you are sons, God has 6 sent into our hearts the Spirit of his Son, crying 'Abba! Father!' You are 7 therefore no longer a slave but a son, and if a son, then also by God's own act an heir.

Formerly, when you did not acknowl-8 edge God, you were the slaves of beings which in their nature are no gods.[r] But 9 now that you do acknowledge God—or rather, now that he has acknowledged you—how can you turn back to the mean and beggarly spirits of the elements?[s] Why do you propose to enter their service all over again? You 10 keep special days and months and seasons and years. You make me fear 11 that all the pains I spent on you may prove to be labour lost.

PUT YOURSELVES IN MY PLACE, MY 12 brothers, I beg you, for I have put myself in yours. It is not that you did me any wrong. As you know, it was bodily 13 illness that originally[t] led to my bringing you the Gospel, and you resisted 14

o Or added because of offences.
p Or a kind of tutor to conduct us to Christ.
q Or the elements of the natural world, or elementary ideas belong to this world.
r Or were slaves to 'gods' which in reality do not exist.
s See note on 4. 3.
t Or formerly, or on the first of my two visits.

frequently refers to God's irrevocable *promises* (vv. 16–18,21) offered with certain conditions (v. 22), and in common Greek to a will by which *heirs* (v. 29) receive their *inheritance* (v. 18). Exod.12.40 (Sept.) gives *four hundred and thirty years* as the interval between Abraham and Moses.
3.19–4.7: The Law as temporary guardian of God's children. **19–20:** See Rom.3.20; 5.13; 7.7–8. Here, by contrast with Rom.7.12,22, Paul suggests that God is not directly responsible for the *law*. Instead, the *law* came from the *angels* (Deut.33.2 Sept.; see 1 Cor.6.2–3 n.) with Moses as their *intermediary*. **22:** *Scripture:* see v. 10 n. **24–25:** *Tutor:* see 1 Cor.4.15 n. **27:** *Put on Christ:* see Rom.13.14; Col.3.10–12. **28:** See 1 Cor.7.18–22; Col.3.11. **29:** *Christ* stands corporately for the new Israel, the church (see 6.16 n.). *Promise:* see vv. 17–18. **4.1–2:** See 3.24–25 n. **3:** *Elemental spirits:* see 1 Cor.2.6–8 n. **6–7:** See Rom.8.14–17.
   4.8–20: A reminder of the Galatians' conversion. **8–10:** At the instigation of the Judaizers (see Introduction) they *keep* the Jewish ritual calendar, which Paul connects with astrology and the worship of demonic *spirits* (v. 3). **13:** Paul appears to attribute his original visit in Galatia

any temptation to show scorn or disgust at the state of my poor body;[u] you welcomed me as if I were an angel of God, as you might have welcomed 15 Christ Jesus himself. Have you forgotten how happy you thought yourselves in having me with you? I can say this for you: you would have torn out your very eyes, and given them to me, had 16 that been possible! And have I now made myself your enemy by being frank with you?

17 The persons I have referred to are envious of you, but not with an honest envy:[v] what they really want is to bar the door to you so that you may come 18 to envy[w] them. It is always a fine thing to deserve an honest envy[x]—always, and not only when I am present with 19 you, dear children. For my children you are, and I am in travail with you over again until you take the shape of 20 Christ. I wish I could be with you now; then I could modify my tone;[y] as it is, I am at my wits' end about you.

21 TELL ME NOW, YOU WHO ARE SO anxious to be under law, will you not 22 listen to what the Law says? It is written there that Abraham had two sons, one by his slave and the other by his free-23 born wife. The slave-woman's son was born in the course of nature, the free 24 woman's through God's promise. This is an allegory. The two women stand for two covenants. The one bearing children into slavery is the covenant that comes from Mount Sinai: that is 25 Hagar. Sinai is a mountain in Arabia and it represents the Jerusalem of to-day, for she and her children are in 26 slavery. But the heavenly Jerusalem is 27 the free woman; she is our mother. For Scripture says, 'Rejoice, O barren woman who never bore child; break into a shout of joy, you who never knew a mother's pangs; for the deserted wife shall have more children than she who lives with the husband.'

28 And you, my brothers, like Isaac, are 29 children of God's promise. But just as in those days the natural-born son persecuted the spiritual son, so it is today. 30 But what does Scripture say? 'Drive out the slave-woman and her son, for the son of the slave shall not share the inheritance with the free woman's son.' 31 You see, then, my brothers, we are no slave-woman's children; our mother is the free woman. Christ set us free, to be 5 free men.[z] Stand firm, then, and refuse to be tied to the yoke of slavery again.

2 Mark my words: I, Paul, say to you that if you receive circumcision Christ 3 will do you no good at all. Once again, you can take it from me that every man who receives circumcision is under 4 obligation to keep the entire law. When you seek to be justified by way of law, your relation with Christ is completely severed: you have fallen out of the do-5 main of God's grace. For to us, our hope of attaining that righteousness which we eagerly await is the work of 6 the Spirit through faith. If we are in union with Christ Jesus circumcision makes no difference at all, nor does the want of it; the only thing that counts is faith active in love.[a]

7 You were running well; who was it hindered you from following the truth? 8 Whatever persuasion he used, it did not 9 come from God who is calling you; 'a little leaven', remember, 'leavens all the 10 dough'. United with you in the Lord, I am confident that you will not take the wrong view; but the man who is unsettling your minds, whoever he may 11 be, must bear God's judgement. And

u *Or* you showed neither scorn nor disgust at the trial my poor body was enduring.
v *Or* paying court to you, but not with honest intentions.
w *Or* pay court to.   x *Or* to be honourably wooed.
y *Or* now, and could exchange words with you.
z *Or* What Christ has done is to set us free.
a *Or* inspired by love.

to physical weakness rather than to design. *Illness:* see 2 Cor.12.7 n. **15:** Possibly Paul had eye trouble (see 6.11, "these big letters"). **19:** *Travail:* a metaphor depicting Paul as an expectant "mother" awaiting the rebirth of the Galatians.
   4.21–5.1: The allegory of Sarah and Hagar (compare Rom.9.6–13). **22:** *Slave:* Hagar, mother of Ishmael (Gen.16.15). *Free-born:* Sarah, mother of Isaac (Gen.21.2–3). **23:** *Promise:* see Gen.17.15–21. **25–28:** Paradoxically the Jews (who count Isaac as their ancestor) are called *children of Hagar;* the church is the promised heir *like Isaac.* **27:** Isa.54.1. **29:** *Persecuted:* see Gen.16.12; 21.9-10. *Today:* see 5.11; 1 Th.2.14–16. **30:** Gen.21.10.
   5.2–12: The Judaizers' message is slavery. 3: The Judaizers apparently preached *circumcision* but not the *entire law* (see 6.12–13). **9:** *Leaven:* see 1 Cor.5.6 n. **11:** Paul's own troubles

I, my friends, if I am still advocating circumcision, why is it I am still persecuted? In that case my preaching of the cross is a stumbling-block no more.

12 As for these agitators, they had better go the whole way and make eunuchs of themselves!

13 YOU, MY FRIENDS, WERE CALLED TO BE free men, only do not turn your freedom into licence for your lower nature, but be servants to one another in love.

14 For the whole law can be summed up in a single commandment: 'Love your

15 neighbour as yourself.' But if you go on fighting one another, tooth and nail, all you can expect is mutual destruction.

16 I mean this: if you are guided by the Spirit you will not fulfil the desires of

17 your lower nature. That nature sets its desires against the Spirit, while the Spirit fights against it. They are in conflict with one another so that what you

18 will to do you cannot do. But if you are led by the Spirit, you are not under law.

19 Anyone can see the kind of behaviour that belongs to the lower nature: fornication, impurity, and indecency;

20 idolatry and sorcery; quarrels, a contentious temper, envy, fits of rage, selfish ambitions, dissensions, party

21 intrigues, and jealousies; drinking bouts, orgies, and the like. I warn you, as I warned you before, that those who behave in such ways will never inherit the kingdom of God.

22 But the harvest of the Spirit is love, joy, peace, patience, kindness, good-

23 ness, fidelity, gentleness, and self-control. There is no law dealing with

24 such things as these. And those who belong to Christ Jesus have crucified the lower nature with its passions and

25 desires. If the Spirit is the source of our life, let the Spirit also direct our course.

26 We must not be conceited, challeng-

ing one another to rivalry, jealous of one another. If a man should do something 6 wrong, my brothers, on a sudden impulse,[b] you who are endowed with the Spirit must set him right again very gently. Look to yourself, each one of you: you may be tempted too. Help 2 one another to carry these heavy loads and in this way you will fulfil the law of Christ.

For if a man imagines himself to be 3 somebody, when he is nothing, he is deluding himself. Each man should 4 examine his own conduct for himself; then he can measure his achievement by comparing himself with himself and not with anyone else. For everyone has 5 his own proper burden to bear.

When anyone is under instruction in 6 the faith, he should give his teacher a share of all good things he has.

Make no mistake about this: God is 7 not to be fooled; a man reaps what he sows. If he sows seed in the field of his 8 lower nature, he will reap from it a harvest of corruption, but if he sows in the field of the Spirit, the Spirit will bring him a harvest of eternal life. So let us 9 never tire of doing good, for if we do not slacken our efforts we shall in due time reap our harvest. Therefore, as 10 opportunity offers, let us work for the good of all, especially members of the household of the faith.

YOU SEE THESE BIG LETTERS? I AM NOW 11 writing to you in my own hand. It is all 12 those who want to make a fair outward and bodily show who are trying to force circumcision upon you; their sole object is to escape persecution for the cross of Christ. For even those who do receive 13 circumcision are not thoroughgoing observers of the law; they only want

b Or If a man is caught doing something wrong, my brothers, . . .

(see 4.29; 6.14,17 n.) refute the Judaizers' allegation that *circumcision* was actually part of his gospel also (see 6.12 n.). *Cross:* see 1 Cor.1.18–2.5.
  5.13–25: The ethics of freedom is not *licence* but *love.* **13:** Mk.10.43. **14:** Lev.19.18 (see Rom.13.8–10; Mk.12.31). **16–17:** *Lower nature:* lit. "flesh" (compare 1 Cor.15.35–53; Rom.7.14–25; 7.14 n.). **19–24:** The lists are stereotyped (see Col.3.1–15; compare Col. 3.18–4.1 n.). **24:** *Crucified:* see Rom.6.6.
  5.26–6.10: Appeal for love and generosity. 6.2: *The law of Christ* is love (see 5.14 n.). **6:** A *teacher* should be paid (see 1 Cor.9.4–14). **7–10:** *Sow* and *reap* echo 2 Cor.9.6–10 on the collection project (see Rom.15.25–26 nn.).
  6.11–18: Conclusion. 11: See 1 Cor.16.21–24 n. **12:** *Circumcision* would prevent *persecution* by bringing Christians under the legal protection enjoyed by Judaism (see 5.11 n.). **13:** See 5.3 n.

you to be circumcised in order to boast of your having submitted to that out-
14 ward rite. But God forbid that I should boast of anything but the cross of our Lord Jesus Christ, through which[c] the world is crucified to me and I to the
15 world! Circumcision is nothing; uncircumcision is nothing; the only thing
16 that counts is new creation! Whoever they are who take this principle for their guide, peace and mercy be upon them, and upon the whole Israel of God!

In future let no one make trouble for 17 me, for I bear the marks of Jesus branded on my body.

The grace of our Lord Jesus Christ 18 be with your spirit, my brothers. Amen.

_c Or_ whom.

14: _Cross:_ see 3.1; 5.24; Phil.3.10. 16: _Israel of God:_ the church (see 4.25–28 n.). 17: _Marks:_ scars received in Jesus' service (see 2 Cor.4.10–11; 11.23–28). 18: See 2 Cor.13.14 n.

THE LETTER OF PAUL TO THE
EPHESIANS

The main theme of the letter to the Ephesians is the church, the body of Christ, in which Jew and Gentile have been united and made "a single new humanity" (2.15). The letter presents itself as written by Paul during a time of imprisonment (3.1), and its close relationship to Colossians has led many to suppose a common situation for both: Paul's captivity in Rome (61–63 A.D.).

The best and earliest manuscripts lack the words "at Ephesus" in 1.1. Therefore, some scholars have offered the suggestion that it was originally intended for many churches, not just the one at Ephesus.

Moreover, there is some basis on which doubts have arisen that the letter was written by Paul himself. Thus, though there are points of contact in thought and wording with every Pauline letter (except perhaps 2 Thessalonians) and especially with Colossians, yet in many instances these points of contact also reflect differences. For example, Eph.2.8–10 is closely related to the thought of Romans, but does not mention justification, which is central to that epistle. Again, the "revealed secret" is conceived differently in Colossians and in Ephesians; in Colossians, it is the union of Christ and his people (Col.1.27); in the latter, it is the union of Jew and Gentile in the one church (Eph.3.6). Accordingly, many (perhaps most) modern scholars regard Ephesians as the work of a member of the Pauline "school" and date it around 100 A.D.

The glory of Christ in the church

1 FROM PAUL, APOSTLE OF CHRIST JESUS, commissioned by the will of God, to God's people at Ephesus,[a] believers incorporate in Christ Jesus.

2 Grace to you and peace from God our Father and the Lord Jesus Christ.

3 Praise be to the God and Father of our Lord Jesus Christ, who has bestowed on us in Christ every spiritual blessing in the heavenly realms. In 4 Christ he chose us before the world was founded, to be dedicated, to be without blemish in his sight, to be full of love; 5 and he[b] destined us—such was his will and pleasure—to be accepted as his 6 sons through Jesus Christ, in order that the glory of his gracious gift, so graciously bestowed on us in his Beloved, 7 might redound to his praise. For in Christ our release is secured and our sins are forgiven through the shedding of his blood. Therein lies the richness of God's free grace lavished upon us, 8 imparting full wisdom and insight. He 9 has made known to us his hidden purpose—such was his will and pleasure determined beforehand in Christ—to 10 be put into effect when the time was ripe: namely, that the universe, all in heaven and on earth, might be brought into a unity in Christ.

11 In Christ indeed we have been given our share in the heritage, as was decreed in his design whose purpose is everywhere at work. For it was his will that 12 we, who were the first to set our hope on Christ,[c] should cause his glory to be praised. And you too, when you had 13 heard the message of the truth, the good

a *Some witnesses omit* at Ephesus.
b *Or . . . sight. In his love he . . .*
c *Or who already enjoyed the hope of Christ, or whose expectation and hope are in Christ.*

1.3–14: Praise of God. The greeting (vv. 1–2) is followed not by the usual thanksgiving, but by a long prayer of praise to God for what he has done in Christ. Such praise is frequent in the OT and in Jewish prayer; compare 2 Cor.1.3–4. **3:** In the NT, the phrase *in the heavenly realms* (or a variation of it) occurs only in this letter (1.20; 2.6; 3.10; 6.12). Apocalyptic literature speaks of a series of heavens (frequently seven) extending above and beyond the earth, with the throne of God in the highest heaven. At times, the *heavenly realms* were thought of as accessible to men only in the future age to come, but at other times as immediately available to the dead. Here the faithful, through union with Christ (2.6), share his exaltation *in the heavenly realms* (see v. 14 n.). **4:** God's choosing of his people (the church) is traced back beyond creation. *Without blemish*: see Col.1.22 n. **10:** Although the main theme of the letter is the church, here the universe is viewed as intended for the *unity* destined to be achieved *in Christ*. **11–13:** In the preceding verses "we" includes all Christians. This passage, however, suggests a contrast between *we* (v. 11) and *you* (v. 13), with *we* here meaning Jewish Christians (*first . . . Christ*) and *you*, later Gentile

237

news of your salvation, and had believed it, became incorporate in Christ and received the seal of the promised 14 Holy Spirit; and that Spirit is the pledge that we shall enter upon our heritage, when God has redeemed what is his own, to his praise and glory.

15 Because of all this, now that I have heard of the faith you have in the Lord Jesus and of the love you bear towards 16 all God's people, I never cease to give thanks for you when I mention you in 17 my prayers. I pray that the God of our Lord Jesus Christ, the all-glorious Father, may give you the spiritual powers of wisdom and vision, by which 18 there comes the knowledge of him. I pray that your inward eyes may be illumined, so that you may know what is the hope to which he calls you, what the wealth and glory of the share he offers you among his people in their 19 heritage, and how vast the resources of his power open to us who trust in him. They are measured by his strength and 20 the might which he exerted in Christ when he raised him from the dead, when he enthroned him at his right hand in 21 the heavenly realms, far above all government and authority, all power and dominion, and any title of sovereignty that can be named, not only in 22 this age but in the age to come. He put everything in subjection beneath his feet, and appointed him as supreme 23 head to the church, which is his body and as such holds within it the fullness of him who himself receives the entire fullness of God.[d]

2 TIME WAS WHEN YOU WERE DEAD IN

your sins and wickedness, when you 2 followed the evil ways of this present age, when you obeyed the commander of the spiritual powers of the air, the spirit now at work among God's rebel subjects. We too were once of their 3 number: we all lived our lives in sensuality, and obeyed the promptings of our own instincts and notions. In our natural condition we, like the rest, lay under the dreadful judgement of God. But God, rich in mercy, for the great 4 love he bore us, brought us to life with 5 Christ even when we were dead in our sins; it is by his grace you are saved. And in union with Christ Jesus he 6 raised us up and enthroned us with him in the heavenly realms, so that he might 7 display in the ages to come how immense are the resources of his grace, and how great his kindness to us in Christ Jesus. For it is by his grace you 8 are saved, through trusting him; it is not your own doing. It is God's gift, not a reward for work done. There is 9 nothing for anyone to boast of. For 10 we are God's handiwork, created in Christ Jesus to devote ourselves to the good deeds for which God has designed us.

Remember then your former condition: you, Gentiles as you are out- 11 wardly,[e] you, 'the uncircumcised' so called by those who are called 'the circumcised' (but only with reference to an outward rite)—you were at that 12 time separate from Christ, strangers

d *Or* as supreme head to the church, which is his body and as such holds within it the fullness of him who fills the universe in all its parts; *or* as supreme head to the church which is his body, and to be all that he himself is who fills the universe in all its parts.
e *Or* by birth.

---

converts (*became . . . Christ*). *Seal . . . Holy Spirit* means baptism. **14:** *The pledge:* see 2 Cor. 5.5 n. The present possession of the Spirit is the guarantee of the coming full possession of their *heritage.* Then the redemption of God's people will be complete.

1.15–23: Thanksgiving and prayer. 20: *Enthroned at his right hand:* see Ps.110.1; the NT frequently applies this OT verse to the ascended Christ (e.g. Acts 2.33–34). **21:** *Government . . . authority . . . title:* see 1 Cor.2.6–8 n.; Col.1.16. **22–23:** *Head, body:* see Col.1.18 n. The *subjection* of all to Christ is expressed by a paraphrase of Ps.8.6, one of the favorite proof texts of the early church; compare 1 Cor.15.27. On Christ as the *fullness* of God, see Col.1.19 n. Here the church is conceived of as the fullness of Christ.

2.1–10: The passage from "death" to "life." 2: Compare 1 Cor.2.12; 2 Cor.4.4; Gal.1.4. The *commander* is Satan. An extrabiblical book (see 2 Enoch 29.5) regarded the *air* as Satan's dwelling place. **8–10:** The emphasis on *grace* is in conformity with Paul's teaching. But the view here (and in v. 5) that salvation is already accomplished diverges from normal Pauline thought in which salvation belongs to the future (Rom.5.10) or is at most only in process (see 1 Cor.1.18). Such differences may support the opinion that Ephesians is a late product of a Pauline "school" (see Introduction).

2.11–22: The unity of all mankind in Christ. 14–15: The Mosaic Law had been a *dividing wall*

to the community of Israel, outside God's covenants and the promise that goes with them. Your world was a world 13 without hope and without God. But now in union with Christ Jesus you who once were far off have been brought near through the shedding of Christ's 14 blood. For he is himself our peace. Gentiles and Jews, he has made the two one, and in his own body of flesh and blood has broken down the enmity which stood like a dividing wall be- 15 tween them; for he annulled the law with its rules and regulations, so as to create out of the two a single new humanity in himself, thereby making 16 peace. This was his purpose, to reconcile the two in a single body to God through the cross, on which he killed the enmity.*f*

17 So he came and proclaimed the good news: peace to you who were far off, and peace to those who were near by; 18 for through him we both alike have access to the Father in the one Spirit. 19 Thus you are no longer aliens in a foreign land, but fellow-citizens with God's people, members of God's house- 20 hold. You are built upon the foundation laid by the apostles and prophets, and Christ Jesus himself is the founda- 21 tion-stone.*g* In him the whole building*h* is bonded together and grows into a 22 holy temple in the Lord. In him you too are being built with all the rest into a spiritual dwelling for God.

3 WITH THIS IN MIND I MAKE MY PRAYER, I, Paul, who in the cause of you Gentiles am now the prisoner of Christ Jesus— 2 for surely you have heard how God has assigned the gift of his grace to me 3 for your benefit. It was by a revelation that his secret was made known to me.

I have already written a brief account of this, and by reading it you may per- 1 ceive that I understand the secret of Christ. In former generations this was 5 not disclosed to the human race; but now it has been revealed by inspiration to his dedicated apostles and prophets, that through the Gospel the Gentiles 6 are joint heirs with the Jews, part of the same body, sharers together in the promise made in Christ Jesus. Such is 7 the gospel of which I was made a minister, by God's gift, bestowed unmerited on me in the working of his power. To me, who am less than the 8 least of all God's people, he has granted of his grace the privilege of proclaiming to the Gentiles the good news of the unfathomable riches of Christ, and of 9 bringing to light how this hidden purpose was to be put into effect. It was hidden for long ages in God the creator of the universe, in order that now, 10 through the church, the wisdom of God in all its varied forms might be made known to the rulers and authorities in the realms of heaven. This is in accord 11 with his age-long purpose, which he achieved in Christ Jesus our Lord. In 12 him we have access to God with freedom, in the confidence born of trust in him. I beg you, then, not to lose heart 13 over my sufferings for you; indeed, they are your glory.

With this in mind, then, I kneel in 14 prayer to the Father, from whom every 15 family*i* in heaven and on earth takes its name, that out of the treasures of his 16 glory he may grant you strength and power through his Spirit in your inner

f Or . . . cross. Thus in his own person he put the enmity to death.
g Or built upon the foundation of the apostles and prophets, and Christ Jesus himself is the keystone.
h Or every structure.
i Or his whole family.

---

between Jew and Gentile. *A single new humanity:* lit. one new man. **17:** See Isa.57.19. **20:** The symbolism changes abruptly from that of a body (v. 16; 1.22–23) to that of a building (vv. 20–22). *Foundation-stone:* see Isa.28.16; Ps.118.22; compare Mt.21.42 and parallels.

    3.1–13: Paul's apostolate. 1: *Prisoner:* see Introduction. **3:** *Revelation:* see Gal.1.15–16. The *brief account* probably refers not to an earlier letter, but to 2.11–22. **5–6:** *Revealed . . . apostles:* some take this passage as an indication that Paul did not write the letter (see Introdution), because in Gal.2.8–9 he distinguishes between his commission to preach to the Gentiles and that of the Jerusalem apostles to preach to the Jews (compare Rom.11.13). *Prophets:* see 1 Cor.12.28; Rom.12.6. The secret, *now . . . revealed,* is that the Gentiles are one with the Jews in the *body* of Christ, the church. **10:** The secret is not only to be made known on earth but also among the angelic powers (see Col.1.16 n.); this is to be done by *the church,* which has a heavenward dimension. See 6.12.

    3.14–21: Prayer and doxology. 14–15: A play on the Gk. words for *father* (*pater*) and *family* (*patria*) stresses the relationship of God to all his creation. The families *in heaven* are the angels.

17 being, that through faith Christ may dwell in your hearts in love. With deep
18 roots and firm foundations, may you be strong to grasp, with all God's people, what is the breadth and length
19 and height and depth of the love of Christ, and to know it, though it is beyond knowledge. So may you attain to fullness of being, the fullness of God himself.*j*
20 Now to him who is able to do immeasurably more than all we can ask or conceive, by the power which is at
21 work among us, to him be glory in the church and in Christ Jesus from generation to generation evermore! Amen.

4 I ENTREAT YOU, THEN—I, A PRISONER for the Lord's sake: as God has called
2 you, live up to your calling. Be humble always and gentle, and patient too. Be forbearing with one another and
3 charitable. Spare no effort to make fast with bonds of peace the unity which
4 the Spirit gives. There is one body and one Spirit, as there is also one hope held
5 out in God's call to you; one Lord, one
6 faith, one baptism; one God and Father of all, who is over all and through all and in all.
7 But each of us has been given his gift, his due portion of Christ's bounty.
8 Therefore Scripture says:

'He ascended into the heights
  with captives in his train;
  he gave gifts to men.'

9 Now, the word 'ascended' implies that he also descended to the lowest
10 level, down to the very earth.*k* He who descended is no other than he who ascended far above all heavens, so that
11 he might fill the universe. And these were his gifts: some to be apostles, some prophets, some evangelists, some

pastors and teachers, to equip God's 12 people for work in his service, to the building up of the body of Christ. So 13 shall we all at last attain to the unity inherent in our faith and our knowledge of the Son of God—to mature manhood, measured by nothing less than the full stature of Christ. We are 14 no longer to be children, tossed by the waves and whirled about by every fresh gust of teaching, dupes of crafty rogues and their deceitful schemes. No, let us 15 speak the truth in love; so shall we fully grow up into Christ. He is the head, and on him the whole body depends. 16 Bonded and knit together by every constituent joint, the whole frame grows through the due activity of each part, and builds itself up in love.

This then is my word to you, and I 17 urge it upon you in the Lord's name. Give up living like pagans with their good-for-nothing notions. Their wits 18 are beclouded, they are strangers to the life that is in God, because ignorance prevails among them and their minds have grown hard as stone. Dead to all 19 feeling, they have abandoned themselves to vice, and stop at nothing to satisfy their foul desires. But that is not 20 how you learned Christ. For were you 21 not told of him, were you not as Christians taught the truth as it is in Jesus? —that, leaving your former way of life, 22 you must lay aside that old human nature which, deluded by its lusts, is sinking towards death. You must be 23 made new in mind and spirit, and put 24 on the new nature of God's creating, which shows itself in the just and devout life called for by the truth.

Then throw off falsehood; speak the 25 truth to each other, for all of us are the parts of one body.

If you are angry, do not let anger 26

j Or the fullness which God requires.
k Or descended to the regions beneath the earth.

21: This juxtaposition of *the church* and *Christ Jesus* is unique in the NT; yet, it flows naturally from the image of the *church* as the body of *Christ*.
  4.1–16: Christian unity. 1: *Prisoner:* see Introduction. **7:** The rich variety of individual gifts contributes to the unity of the church. **8–9:** *Captives in his train:* the author means the angelic powers; see Col.2.15. In the manner of rabbinic exegesis, the wording of Ps.68.18 is altered to accommodate it to its new interpretation; the "ascent" is applied to Christ and is understood as implying a prior "descent" in the incarnation. Less probably, even the translation of Tfn. *k* might be adopted, in which case a "descent into hell" would be implied; compare 1 Pet. 3.19–20 n. **11–13:** His *gifts* are the ministries of the church. *Evangelists:* missionary preachers.
  4.17–5.20: Exhortation to the Christian life. 21: *The truth* may refer to the inherited teachings

lead you into sin; do not let sunset find
27 you still nursing it; leave no loop hole
for the devil.

28 The thief must give up stealing, and
instead work hard and honestly with
his own hands, so that he may have
something to share with the needy.

29 No bad language must pass your lips,
but only what is good and helpful to the
occasion, so that it brings a blessing to
30 those who hear it. And do not grieve
the Holy Spirit of God, for that Spirit
is the seal with which you were marked
31 for the day of our final liberation. Have
done with spite and passion, all angry
shouting and cursing, and bad feeling
of every kind.

32 Be generous to one another, tender-
hearted, forgiving one another as God
in Christ forgave you.

5 In a word, as God's dear children,
2 try to be like him, and live in love as
Christ loved you, and gave himself up
on your behalf as an offering and
sacrifice whose fragrance is pleasing to
God.

3 Fornication and indecency of any
kind, or ruthless greed, must not be so
much as mentioned among you, as befits
4 the people of God. No coarse, stupid,
or flippant talk; these things are out of
place; you should rather be thanking
5 God. For be very sure of this: no one
given to fornication or indecency, or
the greed which makes an idol of gain,
has any share in the kingdom of Christ
and of God.

6 Let no one deceive you with shallow
arguments; it is for all these things that
God's dreadful judgement is coming
7 upon his rebel subjects. Have no part
8 or lot with them. For though you were
once all darkness, now as Christians
you are light. Live like men who are at
9 home in daylight, for where light is,
there all goodness springs up, all justice
10 and truth. Try to find out what would
11 please the Lord; take no part in the
barren deeds of darkness, but show

them up for what they are. The things 12
they do in secret it would be shameful
even to mention. But everything, when 13
once the light has shown it up, is illumined, and everything thus illumined
is all light. And so the hymn says: 14

'Awake, sleeper,
rise from the dead,
and Christ will shine upon you.'

Be most careful then how you con- 15
duct yourselves: like sensible men, not
like simpletons. Use the present op- 16
portunity to the full, for these are evil
days. So do not be fools, but try to 17
understand what the will of the Lord is.
Do not give way to drunkenness and 18
the dissipation that goes with it, but
let the Holy Spirit fill you: speak to 19
one another in psalms, hymns, and*l*
songs; sing and make music in your
hearts to the Lord; and in the name 20
of our Lord Jesus Christ give thanks
every day for everything to our God
and Father.

Be subject to one another out of 21
reverence for Christ.
Wives, be subject to your husbands 22
as to the Lord; for the man is the head 23
of the woman, just as Christ also is the
head of the church. Christ is, indeed, the
Saviour of the body; but just as the 24
church is subject to Christ, so must women be to their husbands in everything.
Husbands, love your wives, as Christ 25
also loved the church and gave himself
up for it, to consecrate it, cleansing it 26
by water and word, so that he might 27
present the church to himself all
glorious, with no stain or wrinkle or
anything of the sort, but holy and without blemish. In the same way men also 28
are bound to love their wives, as they
love their own bodies. In loving his
wife a man loves himself. For no one 29
ever hated his own body: on the contrary, he provides and cares for it; and

l Some witnesses insert spiritual, *as in Colossians 3. 16.*

of the historical *Jesus.* **5.1–2:** *Like him:* lit. imitators of God. *Fragrance . . . pleasing to God:*
see Lev.2.9. **8:** *Darkness . . . light:* see 1 Th.5.4–7 n. **14:** These lines (compare Isa.60.1) may
have been drawn from an early Christian baptismal hymn; see v. 19.
    5.21–6.9: Christian domestic life. The Christianizing of the lists of household virtues (see
Col.3.18–4.1 n.) is especially clear here in the treatment of marriage. **26:** Baptism is seen as the
nuptial bath preparing the bride for her husband. The *word* may refer to the liturgical formula,
including the invocation of the name of Jesus, pronounced over the candidate at baptism;

that is how Christ treats the church, because it is his body, of which we are
31 living parts. Thus it is that (in the words of Scripture) 'a man shall leave his father and mother and shall be joined to his wife, and the two shall become
32 one flesh'. It is a great truth that is hidden here. I for my part refer it to Christ
33 and to the church, but it applies also individually: each of you must love his wife as his very self; and the woman must see to it that she pays her husband all respect.

6 Children, obey your parents, for it is
2 right that you should. 'Honour your father and mother' is the first command-
3 ment with a promise attached, in the words: 'that it may be well with you and that you may live long in the land'.
4 You fathers, again, must not goad your children to resentment, but give them the instruction, and the correction, which belong to a Christian upbringing.
5 Slaves, obey your earthly masters with fear and trembling, single-mind-
6 edly, as serving Christ. Do not offer merely the outward show of service, to curry favour with men, but, as slaves of Christ, do whole-heartedly the will
7 of God. Give the cheerful service of those who serve the Lord, not men.
8 For you know that whatever good each man may do, slave or free, will be repaid him by the Lord.
9 You masters, also, must do the same by them. Give up using threats; remember you both have the same Master in heaven, and he has no favourites.
10 Finally then, find your strength in the
11 Lord, in his mighty power. Put on all the armour which God provides, so that you may be able to stand firm against
12 the devices of the devil. For our fight

is not against human foes, but against cosmic powers, against the authorities and potentates of this dark world, against the superhuman forces of evil in the heavens. Therefore, take up 13 God's armour; then you will be able to stand your ground when things are at their worst, to complete every task and still to stand. Stand firm, I say. Fasten 14 on the belt of truth; for coat of mail put on integrity; let the shoes on your 15 feet be the gospel of peace, to give you firm footing; and, with all these, take 16 up the great shield of faith, with which you will be able to quench all the flaming arrows of the evil one. Take salva- 17 tion for helmet; for sword, take that which the Spirit gives you—the words that come from God. Give yourselves 18 wholly to prayer and entreaty; pray on every occasion in the power of the Spirit. To this end keep watch and persevere, always interceding for all God's people; and pray for me, that I 19 may be granted the right words when I open my mouth, and may boldly and freely make known his hidden purpose, for which I am an ambassador—in 20 chains. Pray that I may speak of it boldly, as it is my duty to speak.

You will want to know about my 21 affairs, and how I am; Tychicus will give you all the news. He is our dear brother and trustworthy helper in the Lord's work. I am sending him to you 22 on purpose to let you know all about us, and to put fresh heart into you.

Peace to the brotherhood and love, 23 with faith, from God the Father and the Lord Jesus Christ. God's grace be 24 with all who love our Lord Jesus Christ, grace and immortality.*m*

m Or who love . . . Christ with love imperishable.

---

see 1 Cor.6.11. **31:** See Gen.2.24. **32–33:** The *great truth . . . hidden* is that Gen.2.24 can be taken to allude to the union of Christ and the church in one body; but the verse *applies also individually*, that is, it also speaks directly to the duty of a husband to love his wife as himself.
   6.10–20: The Christian battle. 11,13–17: *Armour:* see 1 Th.5.8 n. **12:** *Cosmic powers:* see 1 Cor.2.6–8 n.; Col.1.6 n. **20:** *In chains:* a prisoner; see Introduction.
   6.21–24: Final greetings and blessing. 21: *Tychicus:* a companion of Paul; see Col.4.7–8.

THE LETTER OF PAUL TO THE
PHILIPPIANS

The church of Philippi was the first Paul founded on the continent of Europe (Acts 16.11–40; 1 Th.2.2). His cordial relations with it can be seen from the unusual warmth of this letter and from the fact that it was the only one of his churches from which he accepted support (Phil.4.15–16).

The letter was written from prison (1.7,13,17) and together with Colossians, Ephesians, and Philemon makes up the group known as the Captivity Letters. Two major imprisonments of Paul are recorded in Acts, one at Caesarea (23.33–26.32), the other at Rome (28.16–31), and Rome has traditionally been identified as the place from which Philippians was written.

However, the differences in thought between Colossians (also usually assigned to the Roman imprisonment) and Philippians make it difficult to ascribe both of these letters to the same period. Moreover, Philippians speaks of four journeys made by friends between the place of Paul's imprisonment and Philippi and of a fifth which is about to take place (2.25–26)—an unlikely number considering the great distance between Rome and Philippi. On the other hand, if one of Paul's many imprisonments (2 Cor.11.23) occurred during his three-year stay at Ephesus (Acts 20.31), so many trips are easier to understand; Ephesus and Philippi were only about ten days apart. Inscriptions discovered at Ephesus show that members of the Praetorian Guard and of the imperial establishment were stationed in the Roman province of Asia; consequently, the references in 1.13 and 4.22 are as consistent with an origin in Ephesus as in Rome.

If composition at Ephesus is accepted, Philippians belongs to the period of Paul's "third missionary journey," and may be dated around 56 A.D.

It is not certain that the present document was always a unit; it may have been assembled from as many as three originally distinct letters: a note of thanks for the gift sent through Epaphroditus (4.10–20); a letter motivated by Paul's concern for the church in the face of potentially disruptive persons whose position is not clearly defined (1.1–3.1a; 4.2–9, 21–23); and a letter warning against false teachers about whose doctrines the apostle has become better informed (3.1b–4.1).

The apostle and his friends

1 FROM PAUL AND TIMOTHY, SERVANTS of Christ Jesus, to all those of God's people, incorporate in Christ Jesus, who live at Philippi, including their bishops and deacons.

2 Grace to you and peace from God our Father and the Lord Jesus Christ.

3 I thank my God whenever I think of 4 you; and when I pray for you all, my 5 prayers are always joyful, because of the part you have taken in the work of the Gospel from the first day until now. 6 Of one thing I am certain: the One who started the good work in you will bring it to completion by the Day of Christ 7 Jesus. It is indeed only right that I should feel like this about you all, be-cause you hold me in such affection, and because, when I lie in prison or appear in the dock to vouch for the truth of the Gospel, you all share in the privilege that is mine.[a] God knows how 8 I long for you all, with the deep yearning of Christ Jesus himself. And this 9 is my prayer, that your love may grow ever richer and richer in knowledge and insight of every kind, and may thus 10 bring you the gift of true discrimination.[b] Then on the Day of Christ you will be flawless and without blame, reaping the full harvest of righteousness 11

a Or I am justified in taking this view about you all, because I hold you in closest union, as those who, when I lie . . . of the Gospel, all share in the privilege that is mine.

b Or may teach you by experience what things are most worth while.

1.1–2: Greeting. 1: *Bishops and deacons* are mentioned only here in the certainly authentic letters of Paul. (The Pastoral Epistles are sometimes regarded as not by Paul; see Introduction to 1 Tim.). Later ecclesiastical developments should not be read into the terms here. Bishops (lit. "overseers") are those who exercise supervision; deacons are probably their assistants.
1.3–11: Thanksgiving and prayer. 3: *The part you have taken:* their support of Paul; see 2.25; 4.15–16. **6:** *The Day of Christ Jesus:* the Parousia; see 1 Th.2.19 n. **7:** *Prison:* see Introduction. **11:** The *harvest* does not consist in *righteousness* but is produced by it, and Jesus is its source.

243

that comes through Jesus Christ, to the glory and praise of God.

12 Friends, I want you to understand that the work of the Gospel has been helped on, rather than hindered, by this 13 business of mine. My imprisonment in Christ's cause has become common knowledge to all at headquarters*c* here, and indeed among the public at large; 14 and it has given confidence to most of our fellow-Christians to speak the word of God fearlessly and with extra-ordinary courage.

15 Some, indeed, proclaim Christ in a jealous and quarrelsome spirit; others 16 proclaim him in true goodwill, and these are moved by love for me; they know that it is to defend the Gospel 17 that I am where I am. But the others, moved by personal rivalry, present Christ from mixed motives, meaning to stir up fresh trouble for me as I lie in 18 prison.*d* What does it matter? One way or another, in pretence or sincerity, Christ is set forth, and for that I rejoice. 19 Yes, and rejoice I will, knowing well that the issue of it all will be my de-liverance, because you are praying for me and the Spirit of Jesus Christ is given 20 me for support.*e* For, as I passionately hope, I shall have no cause to be ashamed, but shall speak so boldly that now as always the greatness of Christ will shine out clearly in my person, whether through my life or through my 21 death. For to me life is Christ, and death 22 gain; but what if my living on in the body may serve some good purpose? Which then am I to choose? I cannot 23 tell. I am torn two ways: what I should like is to depart and be with 24 Christ; that is better by far; but for your sake there is greater need for me to stay

25 on in the body. This indeed I know for certain: I shall stay, and stand by you all to help you forward and to add joy 26 to your faith, so that when I am with you again, your pride in me may be unbounded in Christ Jesus.

27 Only, let your conduct be worthy of the gospel of Christ, so that whether I come and see you for myself or hear about you from a distance, I may know that you are standing firm, one in spirit, one in mind, contending as one man for 28 the gospel faith, meeting your oppo-nents without so much as a tremor. This is a sure sign to them that their doom is sealed, but a sign of your salvation, and one afforded by God 29 himself; for you have been granted the privilege not only of believing in Christ 30 but also of suffering for him. You and I are engaged in the same contest; you saw me in it once, and, as you hear, I am in it still.

2 IF THEN OUR COMMON LIFE IN CHRIST yields anything to stir the heart, any loving consolation, any sharing of the Spirit, any warmth of affection or com-passion, fill up my cup of happiness by 2 thinking and feeling alike, with the same love for one another, the same turn of mind, and a common care for unity. 3 There must be no room for rivalry and personal vanity among you, but you must humbly reckon others better than 4 yourselves. Look to each other's interest and not merely to your own.

5 Let your bearing towards one an-other arise out of your life in Christ

c Or to all the imperial guard, *or* to all at the Residency (*Greek* Praetorium).
d Or meaning to make use of my imprisonment to stir up fresh trouble.
e Or supplies me with all I need.

1.12–30: **Paul's situation and prospects. 13:** *Headquarters* may mean the residence of the provincial governor (see Acts 23.25) or the headquarters of the Praetorian Guard in Rome; see Tfn. *c.* 15–18: In contrast to the situation in Corinth, where doctrinal differences occasioned factionalism, here the *rivalry* of those who *proclaim Christ in a jealous . . . spirit* seems to be personal. 19: Whether *deliverance* here means ultimate salvation or only release from prison is uncertain; as vv. 20,25–26 show, Paul views both freedom and execution as possible outcomes of his situation. 21: See Gal.2.20. 22: *Death* is *gain* for it will make Paul's union with Christ even closer (v. 23). Here Paul views the state of the Christian between his death and the Parousia as superior to life in the world. This view does not contradict, but rather complements the futuristic resurrection hope expressed in 3.21. 28: *Opponents:* in 3.1–11 they are "Judaizers," that is, Christians who advocated the observance of Jewish Law by Christians; here they are outsiders, pagans who denied the religious hopes and contentions of Christians, or scorned Christians for their way of life.

2.1–11: **Call to unity and humility.** Except for what appears to be a minor disagreement mentioned in 4.2, the church of Philippi seems to have been an unusually harmonious con-

6 Jesus.*f* For the divine nature was his from the first; yet he did not think to
7 snatch at equality with God,*g* but made himself nothing, assuming the nature of a slave. Bearing the human likeness,
8 revealed in human shape, he humbled himself, and in obedience accepted
9 even death—death on a cross. Therefore God raised him to the heights and bestowed on him the name above all
10 names, that at the name of Jesus every knee should bow—in heaven, on earth,
11 and in the depths—and every tongue confess, 'Jesus Christ is Lord', to the glory of God the Father.

12 So you too, my friends, must be obedient, as always; even more, now that I am away, than when I was with you. You must work out your own
13 salvation in fear and trembling; for it is God who works in you, inspiring both the will and the deed, for his own chosen purpose.

14 Do all you have to do without com-
15 plaint or wrangling. Show yourselves guileless and above reproach, faultless children of God in a warped and crooked generation, in which you
16 shine*h* like stars in a dark world*i* and proffer the world of life.*j* Thus you will be my pride on the Day of Christ, proof that I did not run my race in vain, or
17 work in vain. But if my life-blood is to crown that sacrifice which is the offering up of your faith, I am glad of it, and I share my gladness with you all.

Rejoice, you no less than I, and let us 18 share our joy.

I HOPE (UNDER THE LORD JESUS) TO SEND 19 Timothy to you soon; it will cheer me to hear news of you. There is no one else 20 here who sees things as I do, and takes*k* a genuine interest in your concerns; they are all bent on their own ends, not 21 on the cause of Christ Jesus. But 22 Timothy's record is known to you: you know that he has been at my side in the service of the Gospel like a son working under his father. Timothy, then, I 23 hope to send as soon as ever I can see how things are going with me; and I 24 am confident, under the Lord, that I shall myself be coming before long.

I feel also I must send our brother 25 Epaphroditus, my fellow-worker and comrade, whom you commissioned to minister to my needs. He has been miss- 26 ing all of you sadly, and has been distressed that you heard he was ill. (He was indeed dangerously ill, but 27 God was merciful to him, and merciful no less to me, to spare me sorrow upon sorrow.) For this reason I am all the 28 more eager to send him, to give you the happiness of seeing him again, and to relieve my sorrow. Welcome him then 29

f Or Have that bearing towards one another which was also found in Christ Jesus.
g Or yet he did not prize his equality with God.
h Or ... generation. Shine out among them ...
i Or in the firmament.
j Or as the very principle of its life.
k Or no one else here like him, who takes ...

gregation. The tone here suggests not the presence of factions, but the apostle's encouragement of a healthy community spirit. **6–11:** In the view of most scholars, Paul has here incorporated into his letter an ancient Christian hymn. The hymn exalts the saving work of Christ. But because it speaks of a Christ who *made himself nothing* (v. 7) and *humbled himself* (v. 8), Paul quotes it to set forth Christ as the primary example of the humility which he here urges upon the Philippians. The hymn consists of two strophes, vv. 6–8 and 9–11; the words *death on a cross* (v. 8) were probably added by Paul. The first strophe presents a downward movement, from heavenly preexistence to human life; the second describes the exaltation of the obedient Jesus. **6:** The alternative translation, *yet he did not prize his equality with God* (see Tfn. *g*), fits the first part of the verse best. **7:** *Made himself nothing* (lit. emptied himself): instead of clinging to a divine state of existence he assumed that of a *slave* in the incarnation. **8:** The phrases *bearing the human likeness* and *revealed in human shape* are probably intended to suggest that, while truly a man, he was something more, i.e. the preexistent being who possessed "the divine nature ... from the first" (v. 6). **9:** *Raised him to the heights:* a contrast to the "he humbled himself" of v. 8. *The name above all names:* the title "Lord." **10–11:** *Heaven, earth, the depths* probably reflect a view of a three-tiered universe ruled by angelic spirits who join in confessing Jesus' lordship.

2.12–18: The work of salvation. 12–13: *Fear and trembling:* a reverential attitude, since the work of *salvation* with which they must cooperate is actually the work of God. **17:** Paul again speaks of the possibility of his execution. In relation to the Philippians' *faith*, which is spoken of as a sacrificial gift (see Rom.12.1), his own blood, shed in execution, would be like the drink-offering poured out *to crown that sacrifice*, as in Exod.29.40; Num.28.7. Through it all Paul hopes he will live to see the Day of Christ, i.e. the Second Coming (v. 16).

2.19–3.1a: Timothy and Epaphroditus. 19: *Timothy:* see 1 Cor.16.10 n. **29:** See 1 Cor.16.18.

in the fellowship of the Lord with whole-hearted delight. You should honour 30 men like him; in Christ's cause he came near to death, risking his life to render me the service you could not give.

3 And now, friends, farewell; I wish you joy in the Lord.

TO REPEAT WHAT I HAVE WRITTEN TO you before is no trouble to me, and it 2 is a safeguard for you. Beware of those dogs and their malpractices. Beware of those who insist on mutilation—'cir- 3 cumcision' I will not call it; we are the circumcised, we whose worship is spiritual,*l* whose pride is in Christ Jesus, and who put no confidence in anything 4 external. Not that I am without grounds myself even for confidence of that kind. If anyone thinks to base his claims on externals, I could make a 5 stronger case for myself: circumcised on my eighth day, Israelite by race, of the tribe of Benjamin, a Hebrew born and bred;*m* in my attitude to the law, 6 a Pharisee; in pious zeal, a persecutor of the church; in legal rectitude, fault- 7 less. But all such assets I have written 8 off because of Christ. I would say more: I count everything sheer loss, because all is far outweighed by the gain of knowing Christ Jesus my Lord, for whose sake I did in fact lose everything. I count it so much garbage,*n* for the 9 sake of gaining Christ and finding my-self incorporate in him, with no right-eousness of my own, no legal rectitude,

but the righteousness which comes*o* from faith in Christ, given by God in response to faith. All I care for is to 10 know Christ, to experience the power of his resurrection, and to share his sufferings, in growing conformity with his death, if only I may finally arrive 11 at the resurrection from the dead.

It is not to be thought that I have al- 12 ready achieved all this. I have not yet reached perfection, but I press on, hop-ing to take hold of that for which Christ once took hold of me. My 13 friends, I do not reckon myself to have got hold of it yet. All I can say is this: forgetting what is behind me, and reach-ing out for that which lies ahead, I 14 press towards the goal to win the prize which is God's call to the life above, in Christ Jesus.

Let us then keep to this way of think- 15 ing, those of us who are mature. If there is any point on which you think dif-ferently, this also God will make plain to you. Only let our conduct be con- 16 sistent with the level we have already reached.

Agree together, my friends, to follow 17 my example. You have us for a model; watch those whose way of life conforms to it. For, as I have often told you, and 18 now tell you with tears in my eyes, there

l Some witnesses read who worship God in the spirit; others read who worship by the Spirit of God.
m Or a Hebrew-speaking Jew of a Hebrew-speaking family.
n Or dung.
o Or and in him finding that, though I have no righteous-ness of my own, no legal rectitude, I have the righteousness which comes . . .

30: Epaphroditus' *risking his life* may refer to the illness which he contracted while on his mission to Paul. **3.1a:** The *farewell* here, taken with the quite different tone of the ensuing section, suggests that one letter breaks off here and the following is a fragment of another letter.

3.1b–4.1: Warning against false teachers. See note on 3.1a. Here Paul's tone is sharp, as he speaks of opponents who threaten the faith of the Philippians. **2:** *Dogs* was a Jewish term of contempt for pagans, applied here to those who disturb the peace of the church. These may be Jewish Christian missionaries, as their insistence on *circumcision* suggests. Paul contends that physical circumcision is only *mutilation.* **3:** See Jer.4.4; Rom.2.28–29. **4–8:** Paul could cite *grounds . . . for confidence* similar to his opponents', but he regards it all as worthless. **5:** *Pharisee:* see Mt.3.7 n. **6:** *Persecutor:* see Acts 8.3; 9.1; Gal.1.13; 2.23. **9:** If in *legal rectitude* he could claim to have been *faultless* (v. 6), Paul's conversion did not arise merely from despair at fulfilling the law as is sometimes supposed. But he now believes that *righteousness,* far from being earned, can only be the gift which God gives to all who believe in Christ. **10:** *To know Christ* is to have not merely intellectual knowledge but to *experience* his *power* and to be united with him by sharing his *sufferings.* **12–13:** Paul's statement that he has not *already achieved all this* or *yet reached perfection* may indicate that the false teachers he is opposing have claimed such achievement for themselves. If so, their errors may have included not only Judaizing practices but Gnostic views such as that expressed in 2 Tim.2.18. "Judaizing" alludes to a tendency on the part of Christians to imitate a legalistic Judaism. Gnostics believed themselves to be in posses-sion of a supernatural revelation by which they escaped the bondage of evil, material existence. **15–16:** Probably these verses are ironic, directed against those who thought they had already achieved perfection. **17:** *My example:* see 1 Cor.11.1. **18–19:** *Enemies of the cross:* Paul's

are many whose way of life makes them
19 enemies of the cross of Christ. They are
heading for destruction, appetite is their
god, and they glory in their shame.
Their minds are set on earthly things.
20 We, by contrast, are citizens of heaven,
and from heaven we expect our deliverer to come, the Lord Jesus Christ.
21 He will transfigure the body belonging
to our humble state, and give it a form
like that of his own resplendent body,
by the very power which enables him
to make all things subject to himself.
4 Therefore, my friends, beloved friends
whom I long for, my joy, my crown,
stand thus firm in the Lord, my
beloved!

2   I beg Euodia, and I beg Syntyche, to
agree together in the Lord's fellowship.
3 Yes, and you too, my loyal comrade,
I ask you to help these women, who
shared my struggles in the cause of the
Gospel, with Clement and my other
fellow-workers, whose*p* names are in
the roll of the living.

4   Farewell; I wish you all joy in the
Lord. I will say it again: all joy be yours.

5   Let your magnanimity be manifest
to all.

6   The Lord is near; have no anxiety,
but in everything make your requests
known to God in prayer and petition
7 with thanksgiving. Then the peace of
God, which is beyond our utmost
understanding,*q* will keep guard over
your hearts and your thoughts, in
Christ Jesus.

8   And now, my friends, all that is true,
all that is noble, all that is just and pure,
all that is lovable and gracious,*r* whatever is excellent and admirable—fill all
your thoughts with these things.

The lessons I taught you, the tradi- 9
tion I have passed on, all that you
heard me say or saw me do, put into
practice; and the God of peace will be
with you.

IT IS A GREAT JOY TO ME, IN THE LORD, 10
that after so long your care for me has
now blossomed afresh. You did care
about me before for that matter; it was
opportunity that you lacked. Not that 11
I am alluding to want, for I have learned
to find resources in myself whatever my
circumstances. I know what it is to be 12
brought low, and I know what it is to
have plenty. I have been very thoroughly initiated into the human lot
with all its ups and downs—fullness
and hunger, plenty and want. I have 13
strength for anything through him who
gives me power. But it was kind of you 14
to share the burden of my troubles.

As you know yourselves, Philippians, 15
in the early days of my mission, when I
set out from Macedonia, you alone of
all our congregations were my partners
in payments and receipts; for even at 16
Thessalonica you contributed to my
needs, not once but twice over. Do not 17
think I set my heart upon the gift; all
I care for is the profit accruing to you.
However, here I give you my receipt 18
for everything—for more than everything; I am paid in full, now that I have
received from Epaphroditus what you
sent. It is a fragrant offering, an acceptable sacrifice, pleasing to God. And 19
my God will supply all your wants out
of the magnificence of his riches in

p Some witnesses read my fellow-workers, and the
others whose . . .
q Or of far more worth than human reasoning.
r Or of good repute.

invective is too general (*appetite . . . shame*) for one to deduce what practices are being attacked.
   4.2–9: Final exhortations. 3: *Comrade:* this translates the Gk. word *syzygos*, which can serve
as, and may here be, a proper name. The OT concept of a *roll of the living* from which names
were struck out at the time of death (see Exod.32.32; Ps.69.28) is transformed; the roll becomes
a list of those who are destined to everlasting life (see Rev.3.5; 13.8). **6:** *The Lord is near:* an
allusion to the Parousia; see 1 Th.2.19 n.
   4.10–20: Thanks for the Philippians' gift; see Introduction. **10–14:** The main reason for
Paul's *joy* about the gift is its evidence of the Philippians' devotion to him. Without being
ungracious, he states that he is indifferent to material wants. **11–13:** *To find resources in myself:*
lit. to be self-sufficient. This ideal of Greek philosophy is realized by Paul, not by his own
efforts, but *through* God *who gives* him *power* (v. 13). **15:** Through commercial terms, Paul
tells the Philippians that their support of him is payment for the spiritual goods they received
through his ministry. *You alone:* only from the Philippians did he accept financial aid. **18:** By
receipt for everything, Paul acknowledges that he has been *paid in full*—possibly a delicate
indication that he does not expect to receive anything more from them. The gift, now described
in terms of OT sacrifice, *is a fragrant offering* (see Lev.1.9), *an acceptable sacrifice* (see Lev.1.3).

The apostle and his friends

20 Christ Jesus. To our God and Father be glory for endless ages! Amen.

21 Give my greetings, in the fellowship of Christ Jesus, to each one of God's people. The brothers who are now with

22 me send their greetings to you, and so do all God's people here, particularly those who belong to the imperial establishment.

The grace of our Lord Jesus Christ 23 be with your spirit.

4.21–23: Final greetings. 22: *The imperial establishment:* lit. Caesar's household; see Introduction.

THE LETTER OF PAUL TO THE
COLOSSIANS

Colossae was a city of the Roman province of Asia, east of Ephesus and near Laodicea and Hierapolis. It had been evangelized by Epaphras (see 1.7). The unity, stability, and survival of the church were threatened by doctrinal diversity, especially by a faction which had blended together with the Christian gospel some pagan and marginal Jewish elements. This amalgam detracted from the uniqueness and supremacy of Christ through the worship of heavenly beings. The principal aim of Colossians is to assert the preeminence of Christ.

Paul's authorship of Colossians is sometimes questioned because of the differences in style, vocabulary, and doctrine between it and his undisputed letters. Those who uphold its authenticity explain these differences as due to the new situation to which he addresses himself and to the maturing of his thought. If authentic, Colossians probably dates from the Roman imprisonment of Paul (61–63 A.D.). The certainly genuine Letter to Philemon has several points of contact with Colossians (see Introduction to Philemon).

The centre of Christian belief

1 FROM PAUL, APOSTLE OF CHRIST JESUS commissioned by the will of God, 2 and our colleague Timothy, to God's people at Colossae, brothers in the faith, incorporate in Christ.

Grace to you and peace from God our Father.

3 In all our prayers to God, the Father of our Lord Jesus Christ, we thank him 4 for you, because we have heard of the faith you hold in Christ Jesus, and the love you bear towards all God's people. 5 Both spring from the hope stored up for you in heaven—that hope of which you learned when the message of the 6 true Gospel first came to you. In the same way it is coming to men the whole world over; everywhere it is growing and bearing fruit as it does among you, and has done since the day when you heard of the graciousness of God and 7 recognized it for what in truth it is. You were taught this by Epaphras, our dear fellow-servant, a trusted worker for 8 Christ on our[a] behalf, and it is he who has brought us the news of your God-given love.[b]

9 For this reason, ever since the day we heard of it, we have not ceased to pray for you. We ask God that you may receive from him all wisdom and spiritual understanding for full insight into his will, so that your manner of life 10 may be worthy of the Lord and entirely pleasing to him. We pray that you may bear fruit in active goodness of every kind, and grow in the knowledge of God. May he strengthen you, in his 11 glorious might, with ample power to meet whatever comes with fortitude, patience, and joy; and to give thanks[c] 12 to the Father who has made you fit to share the heritage of God's people in the realm of light,

13 He rescued us from the domain of darkness and brought us away into the kingdom of his dear Son, in whom our 14 release is secured and our sins forgiven. He is the image of the invisible God; 15

a Some witnesses read your.
b Or your love within the fellowship of the Spirit.
c Or with fortitude and patience, and to give joyful thanks . . .

1.3–14: Thanksgiving and prayer. 9–10: True *wisdom* and *understanding* produce a *worthy manner of life.* Probably there is an implied contrast with the false wisdom which involved the worship of spiritual powers (see 1.16 n.). **12–14:** In the OT *the heritage of God's people* was Palestine. Here the *heritage* is *in the realm of light,* i.e. a share in Christ's *kingdom.* As Israel was delivered in the Exodus from Egypt, so too the Christians have been rescued. The words *release* (lit. redemption), *heritage,* and *rescued* draw upon the Exodus tradition to interpret Christian experience as release from the *domain of darkness,* i.e. of evil and evil powers.

1.15–20: A hymn to Christ. Most scholars agree that these verses are taken over and modified by Paul from an earlier hymn. Hence, many currents of thought, even pagan, are suggested as lying behind the hymn. The dominant source of its themes, however, is probably the OT and noncanonical Jewish Wisdom literature. Israel's developed portrait of divine Wisdom (see Prov.8.22–31; Ecclus.24.1–22) is the forerunner of the portrayal of Christ as creator and redeemer. **15:** *The image of the invisible God:* see Wis.7.26. *His is the primacy over all created*

his is the primacy over[d] all created 16 things. In him everything in heaven and on earth was created, not only things visible but also the invisible orders of thrones, sovereignties, authorities, and powers: the whole universe has been 17 created through him and for him. And he exists before everything, and all 18 things are held together in him. He is, moreover, the head of the body, the church. He is its origin, the first to return from the dead, to be in all things 19 alone supreme. For in him the complete being of God, by God's own 20 choice, came to dwell. Through him God chose to reconcile the whole universe to himself, making peace through the shedding of his blood upon the cross—to reconcile all things, whether on earth or in heaven, through him alone.

21 Formerly you were yourselves estranged from God; you were his enemies in heart and mind, and your 22 deeds were evil. But now by Christ's death in his body of flesh and blood God has reconciled you to himself, so that he may present you before himself as dedicated men, without blemish and 23 innocent in his sight. Only you must continue in your faith, firm on your foundations, never to be dislodged from the hope offered in the gospel which you heard. This is the gospel which has been proclaimed in the whole

creation under heaven; and I, Paul, have become its minister.

It is now my happiness to suffer for 24 you. This is my way of helping to complete, in my poor human flesh, the full tale of Christ's afflictions still to be endured, for the sake of his body which is the church. I became its servant by 25 virtue of the task assigned to me by God for your benefit: to deliver his message in full; to announce the secret hid- 26 den for long ages and through many generations, but now disclosed to God's people, to whom it was his will to make 27 it known—to make known how rich and glorious it is among all nations. The secret is this: Christ in[e] you, the hope of a glory to come.

He it is whom we proclaim. We ad- 28 monish everyone without distinction, we instruct everyone in all the ways of wisdom, so as to present each one of you as a mature member of Christ's body. To this end I am toiling stren- 29 uously with all the energy and power of Christ at work in me. For I want you **2** to know how strenuous are my exertions for you and the Laodiceans and 2 all who have never set eyes on me. I want them to continue in good heart and in the unity of love, and to come to the full wealth of conviction which understanding brings, and grasp God's

d _Or image of the invisible God, born before ..._
e _Or among._

---

things: see Prov.8.22. **16:** Since all else was _created through him_ (see Wis.7.22) _and for him_, he is superior to all, as the source and end of their being. _Invisible orders:_ in the religious currents of the time, it was believed that many divine beings (_thrones, sovereignties, authorities, and powers_) existed; in some thought, these were represented as angelic beings (compare 1 Cor. 2.6–8 n.). The passage subordinates such spiritual beings to Christ, for they too are created things (v. 15). **18:** In the earlier Pauline letters Christ and Christians form one body (see 1 Cor.12.12); in Col. and Eph. a distinction is made between the _body_ (the church) and its _head_ (Christ). Also distinctive is the fact that here _church_ means the entire Christian community, not simply a local church as in the earlier Pauline usage. _The first to return from the dead:_ lit. the firstborn from the dead. **19:** _The complete being of God:_ lit. the entire fullness. This has been interpreted by some scholars as a rebuttal of the notion that God's attributes were distributed among many angelic beings who mediate between God and man. Others doubt that that concept was current so early as to have called forth a rebuttal from Paul. **20:** The _whole universe_ is understood as having been estranged from God, and rebellious; this estrangement has been overcome by the reconciliation effected by the death of Christ (_the shedding of his blood upon the cross_).
1.21–23: The reconciled community. The universal reconciliation (1.20) is here applied to the local church. **22:** _Without blemish:_ the phrase draws on OT sacrificial requirements (Exod.12.5; Lev.9.3; and often).
1.24–2.5: The apostle's suffering and dedication. 24: The expression _Christ's afflictions still to be endured_ does not imply a lack in sufferings of the historical Jesus; rather, these afflictions are to be borne by the apostle and are "Christ's" because they will be endured _for the sake of his body_, i.e. the church. The passage also reflects the apocalyptic notion that God's victory over evil would be preceded by a period of trial and suffering; see Rev.6.11; 1 Th.3.3 n. **2.1:** _Laodiceans:_ neighbors of the Colossians. **3:** The notion that these _treasures lie hidden_ in Christ is possibly derived from Prov.2.3–5, which likens wisdom to buried treasure; see also Isa.45.3.

3 secret. That secret is Christ himself; in him lie hidden all God's treasures of
4 wisdom and knowledge. I tell you this to save you from being talked*f* into error
5 by specious arguments. For though absent in body, I am with you in spirit, and rejoice to see your orderly array and the firm front which your faith in Christ presents.

6 THEREFORE, SINCE JESUS WAS DELIVERED to you as Christ and Lord, live your
7 lives in union with him. Be rooted in him; be built in him; be consolidated in the faith you were taught;*g* let your
8 hearts overflow with thankfulness. Be on your guard; do not let your minds be captured by hollow and delusive speculations, based on traditions of man-made teaching and centred on the elemental spirits of the universe*h* and not on Christ.
9 For it is in Christ that the complete being of the Godhead dwells embodied,*i*
10 and in him you have been brought to completion. Every power and authority in the universe is subject to him as
11 Head. In him also you were circumcised, not in a physical sense, but by being divested of the lower nature; this is Christ's way of circumcision.
12 For in baptism*j* you were buried with him, in baptism also you were raised to life with him through your faith in the active power of God who raised him
13 from the dead. And although you were dead because of your sins and because you were morally uncircumcised, he has made you alive with Christ. For
14 he has forgiven us all our sins; he has cancelled the bond which pledged us to the decrees of the law. It stood against us, but he has set it aside, nail-
15 ing it to the cross. On that cross he discarded the cosmic powers and authorities like a garment; he made a public spectacle of them and led them*k* as captives in his triumphal procession.

ALLOW NO ONE THEREFORE TO TAKE YOU 16 to task about what you eat or drink, or over the observance of festival, new moon, or sabbath. These are no more 17 than a shadow of what was to come; the solid reality is Christ's. You are not 18 to be disqualified by the decision of people who go in for self-mortification and angel-worship, and try to enter into some vision of their own. Such people, bursting with the futile conceit of worldly minds, lose hold upon the 19 Head; yet it is from the Head that the whole body, with all its joints and ligaments, receives its supplies, and thus knit together grows according to God's design.

Did you not die with Christ and pass 20 beyond reach of the elemental spirits of the universe*l*? Then why behave as though you were still living the life of the world? Why let people dictate to you: 'Do not handle this, do not taste 21 that, do not touch the other'—all of 22 them things that must perish as soon as they are used? That is to follow merely human injunctions and teaching. True, it has an air of wisdom, with its 23 forced piety, its self-mortification, and its severity to the body; but it is of no use at all in combating sensuality.

Were you not raised to life with 3 Christ? Then aspire to the realm above, where Christ is, seated at the right hand of God, and let your thoughts dwell on 2 that higher realm, not on this earthly life. I repeat, you died; and now your 3 life lies hidden with Christ in God.

f Or What I mean is this: no one must talk you ...
g Or by your faith, as you were taught.
h Or the elements of the natural world, *or* elementary ideas belonging to this world.
i Or corporately.
j Or ... nature, in the very circumcision of Christ himself; for in baptism ...
k Or he stripped himself of his physical body, and thereby boldly made a spectacle of the cosmic powers and authorities, and led them ...; *or* he despoiled the cosmic powers and authorities, and boldly made a spectacle of them, leading them ...
l Or the elements of the natural world, *or* elementary ideas belonging to this world.

2.6–23: Warning against false teaching. 8: *The elemental spirits of the universe:* see v. 20; 1 Cor.2.6–8 n.; Gal.4.3,9. **11–12:** Beyond the partial stripping off of flesh in *circumcision, baptism* causes one to be totally divested of *the lower nature* (lit. the body of flesh). **15:** Since the angelic powers were thought to be the guardians of the Law (compare Gal.3.19), its nullification means the end of their dominion. *Captives* were paraded in a public victory celebration; compare Eph.4.8. **16–18:** The false teaching specified in these verses includes both Jewish and pagan religious practices. *To enter into some vision* probably refers to the experience claimed in some pagan mystery cults.
3.1–17: The demands of life in Christ. 3: *Died:* abandoned your former life; compare

Handwritten at top: But I will not see it in this life. This is the Little way of darkness (Fr. Gaitley book)

Handwritten in left margin: Put on the Lord Jesus Christ. Rom. 13:14

4 When Christ, who is our life, is manifested, then you too will be manifested with him in glory.

5 Then put to death those parts of you which belong to the earth—fornication, indecency, lust, foul cravings, and the ruthless greed which is nothing less than 6 idolatry. Because of these, God's dread- 7 ful judgement is impending; and in the life you once lived these are the ways 8 you yourselves followed. But now you must yourselves lay aside all anger, passion, malice, cursing, filthy talk— 9 have done with them! Stop lying to one another, now that you have discarded 10 the old nature with its deeds and have put on the new nature, which is being constantly renewed in the image of its Creator and brought to know God. 11 There is no question here of Greek and Jew, circumcised and uncircumcised, barbarian, Scythian, slave and freeman; but Christ is all, and is in all.

12 Then put on the garments that suit God's chosen people, his own, his beloved: compassion, kindness, humility, 13 gentleness, patience. Be forbearing with one another, and forgiving, where any of you has cause for complaint: you must forgive as the Lord forgave you. 14 To crown all, there must be love, to bind all together and complete the 15 whole. Let Christ's peace be arbiter in your hearts; to this peace you were called as members of a single body. 16 And be filled with gratitude. Let the message of Christ dwell among you in all its richness. Instruct and admonish each other with the utmost wisdom. Sing thankfully in your hearts to God,[m] with psalms and hymns and spiritual 17 songs. Whatever you are doing, whether you speak or act, do everything in the name of the Lord Jesus, giving thanks to God the Father through him.

18 WIVES, BE SUBJECT TO YOUR HUSBANDS;

that is your Christian duty. Husbands, 19 love your wives and do not be harsh with them. Children, obey your parents 20 in everything, for that is pleasing to God and is the Christian way. Fathers, do 21 not exasperate your children, for fear they grow disheartened. Slaves, give 22 entire obedience to your earthly masters, not merely with an outward show of service, to curry favour with men, but with single-mindedness, out of reverence for the Lord. Whatever 23 you are doing, put your whole heart into it, as if you were doing it for the Lord and not for men, knowing that 24 there is a Master who will give you your heritage as a reward for your service. Christ is the Master whose slaves you must be. Dishonesty will 25 be requited, and he has no favourites. Masters, be just and fair to your slaves, **4** knowing that you too have a Master in heaven.

Persevere in prayer, with mind awake 2 and thankful heart; and include a 3 prayer for us, that God may give us an opening for preaching, to tell the secret of Christ; that indeed is why I am now in prison. Pray that I may make the 4 secret plain, as it is my duty to do.

Behave wisely towards those outside 5 your own number; use the present opportunity to the full. Let your con- 6 versation be always gracious, and never insipid; study how best to talk with each person you meet.

YOU WILL HEAR ALL ABOUT MY AFFAIRS 7 from Tychicus, our dear brother and trustworthy helper and fellow-servant in the Lord's work. I am sending him 8 to you on purpose to let you know all about us and to put fresh heart into you. With him comes Onesimus, our trust- 9 worthy and dear brother, who is one of

m Some witnesses read the Lord.

Rom.6.1–11. **4:** Although Paul emphasizes the present sharing in Christ's risen life, he nevertheless continues to look forward to the Parousia (see 1 Th.2.19 n.). **5:** Paradoxically, those who are in Christ have died (v. 3) but they must *put to death* (give up completely) what is earthly in them. **10:** *In the image:* see Gen.1.26–27. **11:** *Barbarian:* non-Greek and hence—like a *Scythian*—uncivilized.

    3.18–4.1: Christian domestic ethics. These counsels are paralleled by the lists of household virtues found in both pagan and Jewish literature. Paul gives them a Christian tone by his additions, such as *out of reverence for the Lord* (v. 22).

    4.2–18: Final admonition, greetings, and blessing. Among those greeted, note especially *Tychicus* (v. 7), *Onesimus* (v. 9), and *Archippus* (v. 17); see Philem.1 and Introduction to Philem.

yourselves. They will tell you all the news here.

10 Aristarchus, Christ's captive like myself, sends his greetings; so does Mark, the cousin of Barnabas (you have had instructions about him; if he comes, 11 make him welcome), and Jesus Justus. Of the Jewish Christians, these are the only ones who work with me for the kingdom of God, and they have been 12 a great comfort to me. Greetings from Epaphras, servant of Christ, who is one of yourselves. He prays hard for you all the time, that you may stand fast, ripe in conviction[n] and wholly devoted to 13 doing God's will. For I can vouch for him, that he works tirelessly for you and the people at Laodicea and Hiera-

polis. Greetings to you from our dear 14 friend Luke, the doctor, and from Demas. Give our greetings to the 15 brothers at Laodicea, and Nympha and the congregation at her house.[o] And 16 when this letter is read among you, see that it is also read to the congregation at Laodicea, and that you in return read the one from Laodicea. This 17 special word to Archippus: 'Attend to the duty entrusted to you in the Lord's service, and discharge it to the full.'

This greeting is in my own hand— 18 PAUL. Remember I am in prison. God's grace be with you.

n Or stand fast, mature and complete ...
o Some witnesses read Nymphas and the congregation at his house.

THE FIRST LETTER OF PAUL TO THE
THESSALONIANS

According to Acts 17.1–18.5, Paul came to Thessalonica (modern Salonica) with Silas and Timothy during his second missionary journey, after leaving Philippi. His stay of three weeks was spent in preaching the messiahship of Jesus in the local synagogue. Some Jews and many "God-fearing" Gentiles were converted. Jews precipitated a riot, and charged the missionaries with acting against the laws of the emperor. Consequently, the Christians sent Paul and Silas by night to the neighboring town of Beroea. Success in preaching there prompted the Jews of Thessalonica to come and create a disturbance similar to that made in their own city, and for safety's sake Paul was constrained to leave alone for Athens. He next went to Corinth where he was joined by Silas and Timothy.

This picture does not correspond with the one found in the letter itself. The letter presupposes a much longer stay at Thessalonica (2.7–9; see Phil.4.16) and a church predominantly composed of converts from paganism (1.9); the letter does not speak of any persecution suffered by Paul in the city; it states that it was from Athens that Paul sent Timothy back to Thessalonica (3.1). The letter was probably written from Corinth just after Timothy's completion of his mission (3.6). While at Corinth (Acts 18.12) Paul was brought before the tribunal of the Roman Gallio, whose term as proconsul was around 51–52 A.D.; if that information is reliable 1 Thessalonians, written around 51 A.D., is the first of the Pauline epistles.

The letter deals primarily with questions concerning the Parousia (the future coming of Christ): its time (e.g. 5.1–2), the suffering of Christians in relation to it (e.g. 3.3), and the destiny of those who die in advance of its arrival (e.g. 4.13–14).

Hope and discipline

1 FROM PAUL, SILVANUS, AND TIMOTHY to the congregation of Thessalonians who belong to God the Father and the Lord Jesus Christ. Grace to you and peace.

2 We always thank God for you all, and mention you in our prayers continually. 3 We call to mind, before our God and Father, how your faith has shown itself in action, your love in labour, and your hope of our Lord Jesus Christ in fortitude. 4 We are certain, brothers beloved by God, that he has chosen you and that[a] 5 when we brought you the Gospel, we brought it not in mere words but in the power of the Holy Spirit, and with strong conviction, as you know well. That is the kind of men we were at Thessalonica, and it was for your sake.

6 And you, in your turn, followed the example set by us and by the Lord; the welcome you gave the message meant grave suffering for you, yet you rejoiced in the Holy Spirit; 7 thus you have become a model for all believers in Macedonia and in Achaia. 8 From Thessalonica the word of the Lord rang out; and not in Macedonia and Achaia alone, but everywhere your faith in God has reached men's ears. No words of ours are needed, for they themselves 9 spread the news of our visit to you and its effect: how you turned from idols, to be servants of the living and true God, and to wait expectantly for the 10 appearance from heaven of his Son Jesus, whom he raised from the dead, Jesus our deliverer from the terrors of judgement to come.

a Or . . . chosen you, because . . .

1.1: Greeting. *Silvanus* is the Latinized form of the name "Silas" used in Acts, for example, Acts 15.39. *Timothy:* see 1 Cor.16.10 n., Acts 16.1–3. Of all his coworkers Timothy is the one most frequently mentioned by Paul. The letter is written in the name of all three, yet *Paul* is clearly the principal writer; see 3.5; 5.27. *Grace . . . peace:* see Rom.1.7 n.
1.2–10: Thanksgiving for a fruitful ministry. 5: *The power of the Holy Spirit* may refer not only to the force inherent in the apostolic preaching, but also to certain miracles accompanying it; see Rom.15.19. **6:** Paul comforts the Thessalonians in their *grave suffering* by the *example set* by Paul and Jesus. **7:** *Macedonia:* the Roman province in northern Greece of which Thessalonica was the capital. *Achaia:* the province in southern Greece from which Paul writes. **10:** The expectation of the early return of the resurrected Jesus is a dominant motif in the letter. Jesus' resurrection gives assurance of his *appearance from heaven.*

2 You know for yourselves, brothers, that our visit to you was not fruitless. **2** Far from it; after all the injury and outrage which to your knowledge we had suffered at Philippi, we declared the gospel of God to you frankly and fearlessly, by the help of our God. A hard **3** struggle it was. Indeed, the appeal we make never springs from error or base motive; there is no attempt to deceive; **4** but God has approved us as fit to be entrusted with the Gospel, and on those terms we speak. We do not curry favour with men; we seek only the favour of God, who is continually testing our **5** hearts. Our words have never been flattering words, as you have cause to know; nor, as God is our witness, have **6** they ever been a cloak for greed. We have never sought honour from men, from you or from anyone else, although as Christ's own envoys we might have **7** made our weight felt; but we were as gentle with you as a nurse caring fondly **8** for her children. With such yearning love we chose to impart to you not only the gospel of God but our very selves, **9** so dear had you become to us. Remember, brothers, how we toiled and drudged. We worked for a living night and day, rather than be a burden to anyone, while we proclaimed before you the good news of God.

10 We call you to witness, yes and God himself, how devout and just and blameless was our behaviour towards **11** you who are believers. As you well know, we dealt with you one by one, as a father deals with his children, appealing to you by encouragement, as well as by solemn injunctions, to live **12** lives worthy of the God who calls you into his kingdom and glory

This is why we thank God con- **13** tinually, because when we handed on God's message, you received it, not as the word of men, but as what it truly is, the very word of God at[b] work in you who hold the faith. You have fared **14** like the congregations in Judaea, God's people in Christ Jesus. You have been treated by your countrymen as they are treated by the Jews, who killed the Lord **15** Jesus and the prophets[c] and drove us out, the Jews who are heedless of God's will and enemies of their fellow-men, hindering us from speaking to the **16** Gentiles to lead them to salvation. All this time they have been making up the full measure of their guilt, and now retribution has overtaken them for good and all.[d]

MY FRIENDS, WHEN FOR A SHORT SPELL **17** you were lost to us—lost to sight, not to our hearts—we were exceedingly anxious to see you again. So we did **18** propose to come to Thessalonica—I, Paul, more than once—but Satan thwarted us. For after all, what hope **19** or joy or crown of pride is there for us, what indeed but you, when we stand before our Lord Jesus at his coming? It is you who are indeed our glory and **20** our joy.

So when we could bear it no longer, **3**

b *Or* word of God who is at . . .
c *Some witnesses read* their own prophets.
d *Or* now at last retribution has overtaken them.

2.1–12: Defense of the missionaries' conduct. 2: *We suffered at Philippi:* see Acts 16.19–24. **3–6:** Paul and his companions were not like the itinerant pagan preachers; the latter were frequently mercenary charlatans who traded on flattery and deceit. **9:** Unlike the charlatans (vv. 3–6 n.), it was Paul's practice not to accept support from the churches which he founded (see 1 Cor.9.3–18). Philippi was the exception (see Phil.4.15–16); Paul accepted their freely offered gifts, abstaining from any demand of support.
2.13–16: Consequences of accepting the Gospel. The persecution of the Thessalonian church is compared to that of the churches of Judea by the Jews. **14–16:** Some scholars regard these verses as an addition from a much later time, containing a reference to the Roman destruction of the Temple in 70 A.D. **16:** *Full measure of their guilt:* the concept is that divine punishment is deferred until the sins which call it forth have reached their climax. Swift chastisement was a sign of mercy; see 2 Macc.6.14–15. The *retribution* which *has overtaken* the Jews is probably their obduracy in unbelief. For a similar view of moral evil as the punishment for previous sin, see Rom.1.18,24,26,28.
2.17–3.13: Paul's concern for the church. 17–18: Paul's mention of his repeated desire to return to Thessalonica is probably a response to a charge that he had not done so because he feared being caught in the persecution there (2.13–16). *Satan:* see Mt.4.1 n. The precise circumstances (illness, opposition?) in which Paul sees Satan's activity are not known. **19:** *His coming:* Gk., *parousia*, ordinarily used of the "coming" of a king on a visit. This is the earliest instance in the NT of the use of Parousia for the coming of the resurrected Jesus in glory. Frequent in

we decided to remain alone at Athens,
2 and sent Timothy, our brother and
God's fellow-worker[e] in the service of
the gospel of Christ, to encourage you
3 to stand firm for the faith and, under
all these hardships, not to be shaken;[f]
for you know that this is our appointed
4 lot. When we were with you we warned
you that we were bound to suffer hardship; and so it has turned out, as you
5 know. And thus it was that when I
could bear it no longer, I sent to find
out about your faith, fearing that the
tempter might have tempted you and
my labour might be lost.

6 But now Timothy has just arrived
from Thessalonica, bringing good news
of your faith and love. He tells us that
you always think kindly of us, and are
as anxious to see us as we are to see you.
7 And so in all our difficulties and hardships your faith reassures us about you.
8 It is the breath of life to us that you
stand firm in the Lord. What thanks
9 can we return to God for you? What
thanks for all the joy you have brought
us, making us rejoice before our God
10 while we pray most earnestly night and
day to be allowed to see you again and
to mend your faith where it falls short?
11 May our God and Father himself,
and our Lord Jesus, bring us direct to
12 you; and may the Lord make your love
mount and overflow towards one another and towards all, as our love does
13 towards you. May he make your hearts
firm, so that you may stand before our
God and Father holy and faultless when
our Lord Jesus comes with all those
who are his own.

4 AND NOW, MY FRIENDS, WE HAVE ONE
thing to beg and pray of you, by our
fellowship with the Lord Jesus. We
passed on to you the tradition of the
way we must live to please God; you

are indeed already following it, but we
beg you to do so yet more thoroughly.
For you know what orders we gave 2
you, in the name of the Lord Jesus.
This is the will of God, that you should 3
be holy: you must abstain from fornication; each one of you must learn to 4
gain mastery over his body, to hallow
and honour it, not giving way to lust 5
like the pagans who are ignorant of
God; and no man must do his brother 6
wrong in this matter,[g] or invade his
rights, because, as we told you before
with all emphasis, the Lord punishes
all such offences. For God called us to 7
holiness, not to impurity. Anyone 8
therefore who flouts these rules is flouting, not man, but God who bestows
upon you his Holy Spirit.

About love for our brotherhood you 9
need no words of mine, for you are
yourselves taught by God to love one
another, and you are in fact practising 10
this rule of love towards all your fellow-
Christians throughout Macedonia. Yet
we appeal to you, brothers, to do better
still. Let it be your ambition to keep 11
calm and look after your own business,
and to work with your hands, as we
ordered you, so that you may command 12
the respect of those outside your own
number, and at the same time may
never be in want.

WE WISH YOU NOT TO REMAIN IN 13
ignorance, brothers, about those who
sleep in death; you should not grieve
like the rest of men, who have no hope.
We believe that Jesus died and rose 14
again; and so it will be for those who
died as Christians; God will bring them
to life with Jesus.[h]

e *Or* and fellow-worker for God; *one witness has simply*
and fellow-worker.
f *Or* beguiled away.
g *Or* must overreach his brother in his business (*or in*
lawsuits).
h *Or* will bring them in company with Jesus.

later NT literature, Paul's use of it in the sense here intended is confined to 1 and 2 Th. and
1 Cor. 15.23. **3.3:** The *hardships* are not only necessary to Christian life, but are the inevitable
accompaniments of the near approach of the end of time and, thus, constitute *our appointed
lot*. A similar view of pre-Messianic tribulations is found in the Judaism of the time. **5:** *Tempter:*
Satan; compare 2.18. **13:** *All those who are his own:* lit. all his holy ones, probably meaning
the "angels"; see also Zech.14.5.
 4.1–12: An exhortation to Christian living. 4: *Body:* the Gk. word can also mean "wife."
9: *Taught by God:* see Jer.31.33–34. **11–12:** These injunctions were probably motivated by
irresponsibility similar to that described in 2 Th.3.6–11.
 4.13–18: The destiny of the Christian dead. 13–14: Possibly Timothy had brought a report
about a concern over the fate of those who had died before the Parousia (see 2.19 n.); this

15 For this we tell you as the Lord's word. We who are left alive until the Lord comes shall not forestall those 16 who have died; because at the word of command, at the sound of the archangel's voice and God's trumpet-call, the Lord himself will descend from heaven; first the Christian dead will 17 rise, then we who are left alive shall join them, caught up in clouds to meet the Lord in the air. Thus we shall always 18 be with the Lord. Console one another, then, with these words.

5 About dates and times, my friends, 2 we need not write to you, for you know perfectly well that the Day of the Lord 3 comes like a thief in the night. While they are talking of peace and security, all at once calamity is upon them, sudden as the pangs that come upon a woman with child; and there will be no 4 escape. But you, my friends, are not in the dark, that the day should overtake 5 you like a thief.[i] You are all children of light, children of day. We do not belong 6 to night or darkness, and we must not sleep like the rest, but keep awake and 7 sober. Sleepers sleep at night, and 8 drunkards are drunk at night, but we, who belong to daylight, must keep sober, armed with faith and love for coat of mail, and the hope of salvation 9 for helmet. For God has not destined us to the terrors of judgement, but to the full attainment of salvation through 10 our Lord Jesus Christ. He died for us so that we, awake or asleep, might 11 live in company with him. Therefore hearten one another, fortify one another—as indeed you do.

WE BEG YOU, BROTHERS, TO ACKNOWL- 12 edge those who are working so hard among you, and in the Lord's fellowship are your leaders and counsellors. Hold 13 them in the highest possible esteem and affection for the work they do.

You must live at peace among yourselves. And we would urge you, 14 brothers, to admonish the careless, encourage the faint-hearted, support the weak, and to be very patient with them all.

See to it that no one pays back wrong 15 for wrong, but always aim at doing the best you can for each other and for all men.

Be always joyful; pray continually; 16,17 give thanks whatever happens; for this 18 is what God in Christ wills for you.

Do not stifle inspiration, and do not 19,20 despise prophetic utterances, but bring 21 them all to the test and then keep what is good in them and avoid the bad of 22 whatever kind.[j]

May God himself, the God of peace, 23 make you holy in every part, and keep you sound in spirit, soul, and body, without fault when our Lord Jesus Christ comes. He who calls you is to be 24 trusted; he will do it.

Brothers, pray for us also. 25

Greet all our brothers with the kiss 26 of peace.

I adjure you by the Lord to have this 27 letter read to the whole brotherhood.

The grace of our Lord Jesus Christ 28 be with you!

---

i Some witnesses read thieves.
j Or . . . utterances. Put everything to the test; keep hold of what is good and avoid every kind of evil.

---

passage answers that concern. **15:** *The Lord's word* probably means that Paul believes he speaks here with the authority of the Lord; compare 1 Cor.14.37. **16:** An archangel is a chief angel. *God's trumpet-call:* see Exod.19.16,19. That a trumpet call would usher in the final salvation is derived from Isa.27.13; see also Mt.24.31; 1 Cor.15.52. At the Parousia of the monarch (see 2.19 n.), the townsmen went out of the city to receive him. Since the Lord *will descend from heaven*, the Christians will meet him *in the air*.

5.1–11: Uncertainty about the time of the Parousia: 1–2: The precise time of the final saving intervention of God was a characteristic concern of apocalyptic thought; see Dan.9.24–27. Paul considers such preoccupation useless. In the OT, *the Day of the Lord* is God's future judgment day (see Amos 5.18; Joel 2.14–15 n.). Here, since the judgment comes with the Parousia, the Lord is Jesus. *Like a thief in the night:* the point of the comparison is its unexpectedness; compare Mt.24.43–44; Lk.12.39–40. **3:** *Pangs . . . a woman with child:* compare Isa.13.8; Jer.6.24. **4–7:** A similar contrast between men of *light* and those of *darkness*, appears in the Dead Sea Scrolls. **8:** Aspects of God's judgment are described as pieces of divine armor (Isa.59.17; Wis.5.17–20). Here and in Eph.6.13–17 the Christians' preparedness for salvation is similarly described. **10:** *Awake or asleep:* alive or dead.

5.12–28: Final admonitions and blessing. 12: *Leaders and counsellors:* see Rom.12.6–8. **23:** *Spirit, soul,* and *body:* the complete man, not three separate aspects of him.

THE SECOND LETTER OF PAUL TO THE
THESSALONIANS

Paul's authorship of 2 Thessalonians has been disputed on several grounds. First, the literary similarities with 1 Thessalonians have suggested to some that an anonymous author, writing in Paul's name, copied from the authentic letter. If, however, one supposes that Paul wrote the second letter very shortly after the first, that hypothesis loses much of its force.

A second and more substantial argument is that in 1 Thessalonians Paul, while emphasizing that the Parousia (see 1 Th.2.19 n.) will come unexpectedly, speaks as if it were near; 2 Thessalonians, on the other hand, indicates that there will be a considerable delay between his letter and the Parousia, and he gives detailed signs which must occur first. However, these signs are not incompatible with the view that the Parousia will take place within the lifetime of those to whom the apostle writes, or that it will occur unexpectedly even though preceded by such signs.

Third, the strongest argument for inauthenticity is that this letter speaks against the teaching that "the Day of the Lord is already here" (2.2). It is difficult to suppose that this latter view, which treats the Parousia as a present spiritual experience, would flourish in Thessalonica at the same time as the opposite, the fervent expectation of the Lord's coming as a future event, found in 1 Thessalonians. Nevertheless, it is possible that Paul responded to a new problem which arose after the writing of the earlier letter.

Hope and discipline

1 FROM PAUL, SILVANUS, AND TIMOTHY to the congregation of Thessalonians who belong to God our Father and the Lord Jesus Christ.

2 Grace to you and peace from God the Father and the Lord Jesus Christ.

3 Our thanks are always due to God for you, brothers. It is right that we should thank him, because your faith increases mightily, and the love you have, each for all and all for each, 4 grows ever greater. Indeed we boast about you ourselves among the congregations of God's people, because your faith remains so steadfast under all your persecutions, and all the 5 troubles you endure. See how this brings out the justice of God's judgement. It will prove you worthy of the kingdom of God, for which indeed you are suffering.

6 It is surely just that God should balance the account by sending trouble 7 to those who trouble you, and relief to you who are troubled, and to us as well, when our Lord Jesus Christ is revealed from heaven with his mighty angels in 8 blazing fire. Then he will do justice upon those who refuse to acknowledge God and upon those who will not obey[a] the gospel of our Lord Jesus. They will suffer the punishment of eter- 9 nal ruin, cut off from the presence of the Lord and the splendour of his might, when on that great Day he comes to be 10 glorified among his own and adored among all believers; for you did indeed believe the testimony we brought you.

With this in mind we pray for you 11 always, that our God may count you worthy of his calling, and mightily bring to fulfilment every good purpose and every act inspired by faith, so that the 12 name of our Lord Jesus may be glorified in you, and you in him, according to the grace of our God and the Lord Jesus Christ.

AND NOW, BROTHERS, ABOUT THE 2 coming of our Lord Jesus Christ and his gathering of us to himself: I beg

a Or justice upon those who refuse ... and will not obey ...

1.3–12: Thanksgiving and encouragement. 4: *Persecutions:* see 1 Th.2.13–16. **7:** The imagery of *blazing fire* in connection with Jesus being *revealed from heaven* is related to OT statements about God coming in judgment; see Ps.97.3; Isa.66.15. The association of the *angels* with the fire may be derived from a Jewish tradition arising from Deut.33.2–3 (Sept.). See also the extra-biblical 2 Enoch 29.3.

2.1–12: The delay of the Parousia. The portrayal of the events to precede the Parousia has points of contact with Mk. ch. 13 and parallels, and with some OT descriptions of the evils

2 you, do not suddenly lose your heads or alarm yourselves, whether at some oracular utterance, or pronouncement, or some letter purporting to come from us, alleging that the Day of the Lord 3 is already here. Let no one deceive you in any way whatever. That day cannot come before the final rebellion against God, when wickedness will be revealed in human form, the man doomed to 4 perdition. He is the Enemy. He rises in his pride against every god, so called, every object of men's worship, and even takes his seat in the temple of God claiming to be a god himself.

5 You cannot but remember that I told 6 you this while I was still with you; you must now be aware of the restraining hand which ensures that he shall be 7 revealed only at the proper time. For already the secret power of wickedness is at work, secret only for the present until the Restrainer disappears from 8 the scene. And then he will be revealed, that wicked man whom the Lord Jesus will destroy with the breath of his mouth, and annihilate by the radiance 9 of his coming. But the coming of that wicked man is the work of Satan. It will be attended by all the powerful signs 10 and miracles of the Lie, and all the deception that sinfulness can impose on those doomed to destruction. Destroyed they shall be, because they did not open their minds to love of the 11 truth, so as to find salvation. Therefore God puts them under a delusion, which 12 works upon them to believe the lie, so that they may all be brought to judgement, all who do not believe the truth

but make sinfulness their deliberate choice.

BUT WE ARE BOUND TO THANK GOD 13 always for you, brothers beloved by the Lord, because from the beginning of time God chose you[b] to find salvation in the Spirit that consecrates you, and in the truth that you believe. It was for 14 this that he called you through the gospel we brought, so that you might possess for your own the splendour of our Lord Jesus Christ.

Stand firm, then, brothers, and hold 15 fast to the traditions which you have learned from us by word or by letter. And may our Lord Jesus Christ himself 16 and God our Father, who has shown us such love, and in his grace has given us such unfailing encouragement and such bright hopes, still encourage and fortify 17 you in every good deed and word!

And now, brothers, pray for us, that **3** the word of the Lord may have everywhere the swift and glorious course that it has had among you, and that 2 we may be rescued from wrong-headed and wicked men; for it is not all who have faith. But the Lord is to be trusted, 3 and he will fortify you and guard you from the evil one. We feel perfect con- 4 fidence about you, in the Lord, that you are doing and will continue to do what we order. May the Lord direct your 5 hearts towards God's love and the steadfastness of Christ!

These are our orders to you, brothers, 6 in the name of our Lord Jesus Christ:

b *Some witnesses read* because God chose you as his firstfruits . . .

---

which will come before the arrival of God's kingdom. **2:** *Oracular utterance* (lit. a spirit): the word of one who claims to be speaking under the influence of the Spirit; see 1 Th.5.19–21. *Purporting to come from us:* possibly a forged *letter. The Day . . . is already here:* see Introduction and 2 Tim.2.18 n. **3:** *The final rebellion against God* (lit. the apostasy): a falling away from the faith; see Mt.24.10. Similarly, during the persecution by Antiochus IV Epiphanes (175–164 B.C.) many Jews abandoned the God of Israel; see 1 Macc.2.15. The figure of Antiochus has influenced Paul's description of *the man doomed to perdition;* this "man" is an evil imitation of Jesus, and his coming is described in terms similar to that of Jesus; see v. 9 and 1.7. **4:** See the descriptions of Antiochus in Dan.11.36–37 and of the prince of Tyre in Ezek.28.2. The search for "the" historical person or institution fitting Paul's prediction has been fruitless. **6–7:** Some force, specified only as *the restraining hand* or *the Restrainer* is holding back the revelation of the wicked person. **8:** *With the breath of his mouth* is a figure for the destroying word of judgment; see Isa.11.4. **9–10:** The author's dismay at the wicked one's likeness to Jesus continues. On *signs and miracles* at the *coming*, see Mk.13.22. **11–12:** The *delusion* under which the sinners fall is seen as God's punishment for their refusal to accept the truth.

2.13–3.5: Exhortation to steadfastness. 15: Although the Thessalonian letters were written early in Christian experience (see Introduction to 1 Th.), the church already had a body of material which could be referred to as *traditions*.

3.6–18: Treatment of the idlers. 6: Some in the community are refusing to work and becoming

hold aloof from every Christian brother who falls into idle habits, and does not follow the tradition you received from 7 us. You know yourselves how you ought to copy our example: we were no 8 idlers among you; we did not accept board and lodging from anyone without paying for it; we toiled and drudged, we worked for a living night and day, rather than be a burden to 9 any of you—not because we have not the right to maintenance, but to set an 10 example for you to imitate. For even during our stay with you we laid down the rule: the man who will not work 11 shall not eat. We mention this because we hear that some of your number are idling their time away, minding every-12 body's business but their own. To all such we give these orders, and we

appeal to them in the name of the Lord Jesus Christ to work quietly for their living.

But you, my friends, must never tire 13 of doing right. If anyone disobeys our 14 instructions given by letter, mark him well, and have no dealings with him until he is ashamed of himself. I do not 15 mean treat him as an enemy, but give him friendly advice, as one of the family. May the Lord of peace himself 16 give you peace at all times and in all ways.*c* The Lord be with you all.

The greeting is in my own hand, 17 signed with my name, PAUL; this authenticates all my letters; this is how I write. The grace*d* of our Lord Jesus 18 Christ be with you all.

c Some witnesses read at all times, wherever you may be.
d Or . . . letters. My message is this: the grace . . .

---

public charges, regarding themselves as released from ordinary obligations since this age is to endure only briefly. **17:** *My own hand:* see 1 Cor.16.21–24 n.

THE FIRST LETTER OF PAUL TO
TIMOTHY

The letters to Timothy and Titus, commonly called the "Pastoral Epistles" because they contain much material related to the pastoral oversight of churches, form a distinct grouping within the collection of Pauline correspondence. Closely similar to one another in content, diction, and theology, they differ enough from the other Pauline letters to raise a question about their true authorship. Lacking many of the typical Pauline theological motifs, such as justification by faith and redemption through the death of Christ on the cross, they use other terms in a way foreign to Paul. Faith, for example, does not define a relationship to Christ, but signifies a body of doctrine which must be kept free of perversion. Problems of church order also emerge, and are discussed in a detail absent from Paul's other letters. The travels presumed in the Pastoral Epistles cannot be fitted into the framework of Paul's journeys as detailed in Acts, but that is also true of some genuine letters (e.g. Rom.15.19), and is not a telling argument for non-Pauline authorship. Most persuasive against Paul's authorship, however, are the language and style of these three letters. Bearing clear marks of typical Hellenistic diction, they do not contain stylistic traits displayed by the epistles to the Romans, Galatians, or Corinthians (traits such as the frequent use of rhetorical questions and complex sentence structure). Similar differences are to be noted in the vocabulary of Paul and the Pastorals. Containing a plea to believers to live quiet lives of moral and doctrinal purity, the Pastorals are probably best understood as compositions of a group who looked to Paul for leadership in religious matters, and who, after his death, sought to meet new problems in a way Paul, as they thought, would have met them.

Timothy, to whom the first of the Pastorals is addressed, was the child of a Jewish mother and a Gentile father (Acts 16.1), and a trusted friend of Paul; see 1 Cor.16.10 n. He shared in the task of Christian proclamation (2 Cor.1.19) and, on at least one occasion, was sent by Paul to clear up some problems within a Christian congregation (1 Cor.4.17). This letter also contains the earliest evidence we have of the emergence of formal leadership within the church, concentrated in the offices of bishop and elder.

Church order

1 FROM PAUL, APOSTLE OF CHRIST JESUS by command of God our Saviour and Christ Jesus our hope, to **2** Timothy his true-born son in the faith.

Grace, mercy, and peace to you from God the Father and Christ Jesus our Lord.

3 When I was starting for Macedonia, I urged you to stay on at Ephesus. You were to command certain persons to give up teaching erroneous doctrines **4** and studying those interminable myths and genealogies, which issue in mere speculation and cannot make known God's plan for us, which works through faith.[a]

The aim and object of this command **5** is the love which springs from a clean heart, from a good conscience, and from faith that is genuine. Through **6** falling short of these, some people have gone astray into a wilderness of words. They set out to be teachers of the moral **7** law, without understanding either the words they use or the subjects about which they are so dogmatic.

We all know that the law is an **8** excellent thing, provided we treat it as

a *Or* cannot promote the faithful discharge of God's stewardship.

1.1–2: Salutation. 1: On *Timothy*, see the Introduction. *God our Saviour* is typical of the Pastorals (e.g. 1 Tim.2.3; Ti.1.3; 3.4), and reflects OT usage more than Paul's, for whom Christ is savior (Phil.3.20).
1.3–20: The struggle for faith. 3: *Starting for Macedonia:* such a journey cannot be fitted into what we know of Paul's journeys from Acts. On *Ephesus*, see Acts 18.19 n.; 19.23–41. **4:** The presence of teachers of *erroneous doctrines* is a major concern of the author. The nature of the false teaching cannot be simply stated, but included: myths and genealogies (as here), asceticism (e.g. 4.2–3), and a dangerous mysticism (2 Tim.2.18). *Myths:* see 2 Tim.4.4; Ti.1.14. *Genealogies* may refer to Gnostic or Jewish speculations; the meaning is not sure. *God's plan:* see Eph.1.10; 3.9. **5:** *Good conscience*, along with clear conscience, is a characteristic virtue in

261

9 law, recognizing that it is not aimed at good citizens, but at the lawless and unruly, the impious and sinful, the irreligious and worldly; at parricides 10 and matricides, murderers and fornicators, perverts, kidnappers, liars, perjurers—in fact all whose behaviour 11 flouts the wholesome teaching which conforms with the gospel entrusted to me, the gospel which tells of the glory of God in his eternal felicity.

12 I thank him who has made me equal to the task, Christ Jesus our Lord; I thank him for judging me worthy of this trust and appointing me to his service— 13 although in the past I had met him with abuse and persecution and outrage. But because I acted ignorantly in unbelief I was dealt with mercifully; 14 the grace of our Lord was lavished upon me, with the faith and love which are ours in Christ Jesus.

15 Here are words you may trust, words that merit full acceptance: 'Christ Jesus came into the world to save sinners'; 16 and among them I stand first. But I was mercifully dealt with for this very purpose, that Jesus Christ might find in me the first occasion for displaying all his patience, and that I might be typical of all who were in future to have faith in 17 him and gain eternal life. Now to the King of all worlds, immortal, invisible, the only God, be honour and glory for ever and ever! Amen.

18 This charge, son Timothy, I lay upon you, following that prophetic utterance which first pointed you out to me. So 19 fight gallantly, armed with faith and a good conscience. It was through spurning conscience that certain persons made shipwreck of their faith, among 20 them Hymenaeus and Alexander, whom I consigned to Satan, in the hope that through this discipline they might learn not to be blasphemous.

FIRST OF ALL, THEN, I URGE THAT 2 petitions, prayers, intercessions, and thanksgivings be offered for all men; for sovereigns and all in high office, 2 that we may lead a tranquil and quiet life in full observance of religion and high standards of morality. Such prayer 3 is right, and approved by God our Saviour, whose will it is that all men 4 should find salvation and come to know the truth. For there is one God, and 5 also one mediator between God and men, Christ Jesus, himself man, who 6 sacrificed himself to win freedom for all mankind, so providing, at the fitting time, proof of the divine purpose; of 7 this I was appointed herald and apostle (this is no lie, but the truth), to instruct the nations in the true faith.

It is my desire, therefore, that every- 8 where prayers be said by the men of the congregation, who shall lift up their hands with a pure intention, excluding angry or quarrelsome thoughts. Wo- 9 men again must dress in becoming manner, modestly and soberly, not with elaborate hair-styles, not decked out with gold or pearls, or expensive clothes, but with good deeds, as befits 10 women who claim to be religious. A 11 woman must be a learner, listening quietly and with due submission. I do 12 not permit a woman to be a teacher, nor must woman domineer over man; she should be quiet. For Adam was 13

the Pastorals. **10:** Such lists of vices were common in the Hellenistic world; for other NT examples see 6.4–5; 2 Tim.3.2–5; Ti.3.3; Rom.1.29–31; Gal.5.19–21. *Wholesome teaching*, a characteristic phrase in the Pastorals, occurs nowhere else in the NT, but frequently in other contemporary authors. **13:** *I had met him:* Christ and his Church are identified in similar language in Acts 9.4–5. *Persecution:* see Acts 26.11; 1 Cor.15.9; Gal.1.13. **15:** *Words you may trust* is a formula that probably introduces traditional material. *I stand first:* see 1 Cor.15.9. **17:** *Of all worlds*, or, of the ages; this language is typical of Hellenistic descriptions of god(s), as well as Jewish ascriptions of praise. **20:** *I consigned to Satan:* the meaning is unclear; see 1 Cor.5.5; compare Job 2.6–8.
2.1–15: Advice on prayer. 1: This is not an exhaustive list of kinds of prayer; see Phil.4.6. **4:** *Come to know the truth:* see 2 Tim.3.7 n. *All men* points to the universality of the Christian community grounded in God's saving will; see vv. 1,6; 4.10. **5:** *One God:* see Deut.6.4–9, a passage repeated daily by pious Jews. *One mediator* intends to validate Jesus among the many mediators proclaimed in the Hellenistic world. **8:** *Everywhere* may refer to regular liturgical services. **9:** This verse (and v. 8) probably refers to dress and conduct in worship; compare 1 Pet.3.3–5. **11–15:** These verses, dealing with liturgical services, reflect the position of women in some areas of the Hellenistic religious world; they are hardly to be taken as legislative. **13:** See 1 Cor.11.3–16. **14:** See Gen.3.6; also 2 Cor.11.3. That for Paul himself *Adam* also sinned

14 created first, and Eve afterwards; and it was not Adam who was deceived; it was the woman who, yielding to de-
15 ception, fell into sin. Yet she will be saved through motherhood[b]—if only women continue in faith,[c] love, and holiness, with a sober mind.

3 There is a popular saying:[d] 'To aspire to leadership is an honourable
2 ambition.' Our leader, therefore, or bishop, must be above reproach, faithful to his one wife,[e] sober, temperate, courteous, hospitable, and a good
3 teacher; he must not be given to drink, or a brawler, but of a forbearing disposition, avoiding quarrels, and no
4 lover of money. He must be one who manages his own household well and wins obedience from his children, and
5 a man of the highest principles. If a man does not know how to control his own family, how can he look after a
6 congregation of God's people? He must not be a convert newly baptized, for fear the sin of conceit should bring upon him a judgement contrived by the
7 devil.[f] He must moreover have a good reputation with the non-Christian public, so that he may not be exposed to scandal and get caught in the devil's snare.
8 Deacons, likewise, must be men of high principle, not indulging in double talk, given neither to excessive drinking
9 nor to money-grubbing. They must be men who combine a clear conscience with a firm hold on the deep truths of
10 our faith. No less than bishops, they must first undergo a scrutiny, and if there is no mark against them, they may
11 serve. Their wives,[g] equally, must be women of high principle, who will not talk scandal, sober and trustworthy in

every way. A deacon must be faithful 12 to his one wife,[g] and good at managing his children and his own household. For deacons with a good record of ser- 13 vice may claim a high standing and the right to speak openly on matters of the Christian faith.

I am hoping to come to you before 14 long, but I write this in case I am de- 15 layed, to let you know how men ought to conduct themselves in God's household, that is, the church of the living God, the pillar and bulwark of the truth. And great beyond all question is 16 the mystery of our religion:

'He who was manifested in the body,
    vindicated in the spirit,
        seen by angels;
who was proclaimed among the
        nations,
believed in throughout the world,
    glorified in high heaven.'

THE SPIRIT SAYS EXPRESSLY THAT IN 4 after times some will desert from the faith and give their minds to subversive doctrines inspired by devils, through the 2 specious falsehoods of men whose own conscience is branded with the devil's sign. They forbid marriage and incul- 3 cate abstinence from certain foods, though God created them to be enjoyed with thanksgiving by believers who have inward knowledge of the truth. For everything that God created is 4

b *Or* saved through the Birth of the Child, *or* brought safely through childbirth.
c *Or* if only husband and wife continue in mutual fidelity . . .
d *Some witnesses read* Here are words you may trust, *which some interpreters attach to the end of the preceding paragraph.*
e *Or* married to one wife, *or* married only once.
f *Or* the judgement once passed on the devil.
g *Or* . . . serve. Deaconesses . . .

is clear from Rom.5.12–14. **15:** The meaning of the first half of this verse is unclear (see Tfn. *b*).
3.1–16: Leadership in the church. 2: *Bishop* is not used in a technical sense; see Ti.1.5–9, where bishop and elder are identified. The virtues are common ideals in the Hellenistic world. **8:** We cannot tell from the NT what different duties were given to bishops, elders, and *deacons*. Paul could describe his apostleship as a diaconate ("commission" in 2 Cor.4.1) and thus deacons may have had responsibility for preaching; see also v. 9; 4.6; Acts 6.4 ("ministry"); also Acts 6.2 ("to wait"), 6 n. **9:** *Deep truths* refer to the content of the Christian faith as revealing God's plan for mankind; see v. 16, where the content is Christ, as in Col.1.27. **16:** This verse is probably an early Christian hymn, or confession of faith. The rhythm of the Greek points to three couplets, rather than two stanzas.
4.1–16: True service to Christ. 1: See 2 Tim.3.1–9; 4.3–4; the point is made throughout the NT. **2:** In the Hellenistic world, slaves were sometimes *branded* to indicate ownership. **3:** *God created them to be enjoyed:* see Acts 10.15. Some contemporary sects thought that anything material was evil; only the spiritual was good. Jewish ritual purity may also be involved; compare Ti.1.14; **4:** *Everything that God created is good:* see Rom.14.14; 1 Cor.10.25–26.

good, and nothing is to be rejected when it is taken with thanksgiving, 5 since it is hallowed by God's own word and by prayer.

6 By offering such advice as this to the brotherhood you will prove a good servant of Christ Jesus, bred in the precepts of our faith and of the sound instruction which you have followed. 7 Have nothing to do with those godless myths, fit only for old women. Keep yourself in training for the practice of 8 religion. The training of the body does bring limited benefit, but the benefits of religion are without limit, since it holds promise not only for this life but 9 for the life to come. Here are words you may trust, words that merit full 10 acceptance: 'With this before us we labour and struggle,*h* because*i* we have set our hope on the living God, who is the Saviour of all men'—the Saviour, above all, of believers.

11 Pass on these orders and these 12 teachings. Let no one slight you because you are young, but make yourself an example to believers in speech and behaviour, in love, fidelity, and purity. 13 Until I arrive devote your attention to the public reading of the scriptures, to 14 exhortation, and to teaching. Do not neglect the spiritual endowment you possess, which was given you, under the guidance of prophecy, through the laying on of the hands of the elders as a body.*j*

15 Make these matters your business and your absorbing interest, so that your progress may be plain to all. 16 Persevere in them, keeping close watch on yourself and your teaching; by doing so you will further the salvation of yourself and your hearers.

5 Never be harsh with an elder; appeal to him as if he were your father. Treat 2 the younger men as brothers, the older women as mothers, and the younger as your sisters, in all purity.

3 The status of widow is to be granted only to widows who are such in the full sense. But if a widow has children or 4 grandchildren, then they should learn as their first duty to show loyalty to the family and to repay what they owe to their parents and grandparents; for this God approves. A widow, however, in 5 the full sense, one who is alone in the world, has all her hope set on God, and regularly attends the meetings for prayer and worship night and day. But 6 a widow given over to self-indulgence is as good as dead. Add these orders to 7 the rest, so that the widows may be above reproach. But if anyone does not 8 make provision for his relations, and especially for members of his own household, he has denied the faith and is worse than an unbeliever.

A widow should not be put on the 9 roll under sixty years of age. She must have been faithful in marriage to one man, and must produce evidence of 10 good deeds performed, showing whether she has had the care of children, or given hospitality, or washed the feet of God's people, or supported those in distress—in short, whether she has taken every opportunity of doing good.

Younger widows may not be placed 11 on the roll. For when their passions draw them away from Christ, they hanker after marriage and stand con- 12 demned for breaking their troth with him. Moreover, in going round from 13 house to house they learn to be idle, and worse than idle, gossips and busy-bodies, speaking of things better left unspoken. It is my wish, therefore, that 14 young widows shall marry again, have

h Some witnesses read suffer reproach.
i Or since 'It holds promise . . . to come.' These are words . . . acceptance. For this is the aim of all our labour and struggle, since . . .
j Or through your ordination as an elder.

6: *Sound instruction:* see 1.10 n. **7:** *Godless myths:* see 1.4. **9:** *Here are words you may trust* may refer to v. 8. **10:** *Of all men:* see 2.4 n. **12:** *You are young* could, in that time, be applied to anyone under forty. **14:** *Laying on of the hands* conferred a task; see e.g. Acts 6.6; 13.3.

5.1–16: General admonitions. 1–2: On personal relations. This kind of advice was popular in the Hellenistic world. **3–16:** On *widows.* **3:** There were no governmental provisions for the care of the destitute in the Hellenistic world, though care of widows was an obligation for Jews (Exod.22.22; Deut.24.17–22). The church early assumed this reponsibility (Acts 6.1). **9:** This is our earliest evidence of an ecclesiastical order of *widows,* an order well known by the third century; see Acts 9.39. **12:** *Breaking their troth* may imply a promise by a widow not to remarry. **13:** *Going round from house to house* was apparently one of a widow's duties, perhaps as a Christian visitor.

children, and preside over a home;
then they will give no opponent
15 occasion for slander. For there have in
fact been some who have taken the
wrong turning and gone to the devil.

16 If a Christian man or woman has
widows in the family, he must support
them himself;*k* the congregation must
be relieved of the burden, so that it may
be free to support those who are
widows in the full sense of the term.

17 Elders who do well as leaders should
be reckoned worthy of a double stipend,
in particular those who labour at
18 preaching and teaching. For Scripture
says, 'You shall not muzzle a threshing
ox'; and besides, 'the worker earns his
pay.'

19 Do not entertain a charge against an
elder unless it is supported by two or
20 three witnesses. Those who commit
sins you must expose publicly, to put
21 fear into the others. Before God and
Christ Jesus and the angels who are his
chosen, I solemnly charge you, maintain these rules, and never pre-judge
the issue, but act with strict impartiality.
22 Do not be over-hasty in laying on
hands in ordination,*l* or you may find
yourself responsible for other people's
misdeeds; keep your own hands clean.
23 Stop drinking nothing but water;
take a little wine for your digestion, for
your frequent ailments.

24 While there are people whose offences
are so obvious that they run before
them into court, there are others whose
offences have not yet overtaken them.
25 Similarly, good deeds are obvious, or
even if they are not, they cannot be
concealed for ever.

6 All who wear the yoke of slavery
must count their own masters worthy
of all respect, so that the name of God
and the Christian teaching are not
2 brought into disrepute. If the masters
are believers, the slaves must not
respect them any less for being their

Christian brothers. Quite the contrary;
they must be all the better servants
because those who receive the benefit
of their service are one with them in
faith and love.

THIS IS WHAT YOU ARE TO TEACH AND
preach. If anyone is teaching otherwise, 3
and will not give his mind to wholesome
precepts—I mean those of our Lord
Jesus Christ—and to good religious
teaching, I call him a pompous ignora- 4
mus. He is morbidly keen on mere
verbal questions and quibbles, which
give rise to jealousy, quarrelling, slander, base suspicions, and endless wran- 5
gles: all typical of men who have let
their reasoning powers become atro-
phied and have lost grip of the truth.
They think religion should yield dividends; and of course religion does 6
yield high dividends, but only to the
man whose resources are within him.
We brought nothing into the world; 7
for that matter we cannot take anything with us when we leave, but if we 8
have food and covering we may rest
content. Those who want to be rich fall 9
into temptations and snares and many
foolish harmful desires which plunge
men into ruin and perdition. The love 10
of money is the root of all evil things,
and there are some who in reaching for
it have wandered from the faith and
spiked themselves on many thorny
griefs.

But you, man of God, must shun all 11
this, and pursue justice, piety, fidelity,
love, fortitude, and gentleness. Run the 12
great race of faith and take hold of
eternal life. For to this you were called;
and you confessed your faith nobly
before many witnesses. Now in the 13
presence of God, who gives life to all
things, and of Jesus Christ, who himself made the same noble confession

k Some witnesses read If a Christian woman has widows
in her family, she must support them herself.
l Or in restoring an offender by the laying on of hands.

5.17–6.21: Advice on proper conduct. 17: *Elders* shared *teaching* duties with bishops; see
3.2 (and n.); Ti.1.5,7 nn. **18:** Deut.25.4; see 1 Cor.9.9; Lk.10.7. **19:** *Two or three witnesses:*
see Deut.19.15; Mt.18.16; 2 Cor.13.1. **23:** Timothy may have drunk *nothing but water* as an
ascetic practice; the validity of such a practice is here denied; compare 4.3. **6.1:** For mention
of *slavery* in the NT, see Ti.2.9–10; 1 Cor.7.21–22; Eph.6.5–8; Col. 3.22–25; Philem.15–16;
1 Pet.2.18–25. **4:** See 1.10 n. **5:** The following teachings reflect Hellenistic moral maxims and
teachings. **7:** See Job 1.21; Eccles.5.15. **8:** To *rest content* with little was a popular Stoic ideal.
10: This proverb about *love of money* was widely known and popular in the Hellenistic world;
but it is not to be construed that money in itself is *evil*; see vv. 17–19 n. **13:** See Jn.18.36–37.

and gave his testimony to it before

14 Pontius Pilate, I charge you to obey your orders irreproachably and without fault until our Lord Jesus Christ ap-

15 pears. That appearance God will bring to pass in his own good time—God who in eternal felicity alone holds sway. He is King of kings and Lord of

16 lords; he alone possesses immortality, dwelling in unapproachable light. No man has ever seen or ever can see him. To him be honour and might for ever! Amen.

17 Instruct those who are rich in this world's goods not to be proud, and not to fix their hopes on so uncertain a thing as money, but upon God, who endows us richly with all things to enjoy. Tell them to do good and to 18 grow rich in noble actions, to be ready to give away and to share, and so 19 acquire a treasure which will form a good foundation for the future. Thus they will grasp the life which is life indeed.

Timothy, keep safe that which has 20 been entrusted to you. Turn a deaf ear to empty and worldly chatter, and the contradictions of so-called 'knowledge', for many who lay claim to it have shot 21 far wide of the faith.

Grace be with you all!

15–16: This may be a fragment of an early Christian hymn. *King of kings and Lord of lords:* see Deut.10.17. **17–19:** As in v. 10, it is not wealth, but attachment to it, that is condemned. Compare Mt.6.19–21 (and 22 n.). **20:** *That which has been entrusted to you* refers to sound Christian doctrine in its totality. *Contradictions* (lit. antitheses) were a favorite construction of Hellenistic philosophers, occasionally used to test another's skill in thinking.

THE SECOND LETTER OF PAUL TO
TIMOTHY

Of the three Pastorals, this one is the closest to Pauline style and thought, and has the best claim to authenticity. It is sometimes suggested that the letter has incorporated fragments of genuine Pauline correspondence. However, attempts to isolate such fragments have not proved generally convincing. For more detailed information on this letter, see the Introduction to 1 Timothy.

Character of a Christian minister

1 FROM PAUL, APOSTLE OF JESUS CHRIST by the will of God, whose promise of life is fulfilled in Christ Jesus, 2 to Timothy his dear son.

Grace, mercy, and peace to you from God the Father and our Lord Jesus Christ.

3 I thank God—whom I, like my forefathers, worship with a pure intention—when I mention you in my prayers; 4 this I do constantly night and day. And when I remember the tears you shed, I long to see you again to make my 5 happiness complete. I am reminded of the sincerity of your faith, a faith which was alive in Lois your grandmother and Eunice your mother before you, and which, I am confident, lives in you also.

6 That is why I now remind you to stir into flame the gift of God which is within you through the laying on of my 7 hands. For the spirit that God gave us is no craven spirit, but one to inspire 8 strength, love, and self-discipline. So never be ashamed of your testimony to our Lord, nor of me his prisoner, but take your share of suffering for the sake of the Gospel, in the strength that 9 comes from God. It is he who brought us salvation and called us to a dedicated life, not for any merit of ours but of his own purpose and his own grace, which was granted to us in Christ Jesus from all eternity, but has now at length been 10 brought fully into view by the appearance on earth of our Saviour Jesus Christ. For he has broken the power of death and brought life and immortality to light through the Gospel.

Of this Gospel I, by his appointment, 11 am herald, apostle, and teacher. That 12 is the reason for my present plight; but I am not ashamed of it, because I know who it is in whom[a] I have trusted, and am confident of his power to keep safe what he has put into my charge,[b] until the great Day. Keep 13 before you an outline of the sound teaching which[c] you heard from me, living by the faith and love which are ours in Christ Jesus. Guard the treasure 14 put into our charge, with the help of the Holy Spirit dwelling within us.

As you know, everyone in the prov- 15 ince of Asia deserted me, including Phygelus and Hermogenes. But may 16 the Lord's mercy rest on the house of Onesiphorus! He has often relieved me in my troubles. He was not ashamed to visit a prisoner, but took pains to 17 search me out when he came to Rome, and found me. I pray that the Lord may 18 grant him to find mercy from the Lord on the great Day. The many services he rendered at Ephesus you know better than I could tell you.

a Or I know the one whom . . .
b Or what I have put into his charge.
c Or Keep before you as a model of sound teaching that which . . .

1.1–2: Salutation. On Timothy, see Introduction to 1 Tim. Compare 1 Tim.1.1 n.
1.3–18: Timothy's gifts and responsibilities. 3–5: It was Hellenistic custom to include an opening prayer in a private letter, a custom followed in all Pauline and sub-Pauline letters except Gal., 1 Tim., and Ti. **5:** On Timothy's *mother*, see Acts 16.1. **6:** See 1 Tim.4.14 (n.). **10:** *Saviour*, a title widely applied to deities and rulers in the Hellenistic world, is used both for Christ (Ti.2.13; 3.6) and for God (see 1 Tim.1.1 n.) in the Pastorals. **12:** *What he has put in my charge:* see 1 Tim.6.20 n. **13:** *Sound* (or wholesome) *teaching:* see 1 Tim.1.10 n. **15:** *Asia* was the Roman *province* of which Ephesus was the chief city. **18:** *That the Lord,* i.e. Jesus; *from the Lord,* i.e. the Father; see Mt.25.34,36.

2 Now therefore, my son, take strength from the grace of God which is ours in
2 Christ Jesus. You heard my teaching in the presence of many witnesses; put that teaching into the charge of men you can trust, such men as will be competent to teach others.

3 Take your share of hardship, like a
4 good soldier of Christ Jesus. A soldier on active service will not let himself be involved in civilian affairs; he must be wholly at his commanding officer's
5 disposal. Again, no athlete can win a
6 prize unless he has kept the rules. The farmer who gives his labour has first
7 claim on the crop. Reflect on what I say, for the Lord will help you to full understanding.

8 Remember Jesus Christ, risen from the dead, born of David's line. This is
9 the theme of my gospel, in whose service I am exposed to hardship, even to the point of being shut up like a common criminal; but the word of
10 God is not shut up. And I endure it all for the sake of God's chosen ones, with this end in view, that they too may attain the glorious and eternal salvation which is in Christ Jesus.

11 Here are the words you may trust:

'If we died with him, we shall live
    with him;
12 if we endure, we shall reign with him. If we deny him, he will deny us.
13 If we are faithless, he keeps faith, for he cannot deny himself.'

14 GO ON REMINDING PEOPLE OF THIS, AND charge them solemnly before God to stop disputing about mere words; it does no good, and is the ruin of those
15 who listen. Try hard to show yourself worthy of God's approval, as a labourer who need not be ashamed; be straightforward in your proclamation of the
16 truth. Avoid empty and worldly chatter; those who indulge in it will stray further and further into godless courses, and the infection of their teaching will 17 spread like a gangrene. Such are Hymenaeus and Philetus; they have 18 shot wide of the truth in saying that our resurrection has already taken place, and are upsetting people's faith. But God has laid a foundation, and it 19 stands firm, with this inscription: 'The Lord knows his own', and, 'Everyone who takes the Lord's name upon his lips must forsake wickedness.' Now in 20 any great house there are not only utensils of gold and silver, but also others of wood or earthenware; the former are valued, the latter held cheap. To be among those which are valued 21 and dedicated, a thing of use to the Master of the house, a man must cleanse himself from all those evil things;[d] then he will be fit for any honourable purpose.

Turn from the wayward impulses of 22 youth, and pursue justice, integrity, love, and peace with all who invoke the Lord in singleness of mind. Have 23 nothing to do with foolish and ignorant speculations. You know they breed quarrels, and the servant of the Lord 24 must not be quarrelsome, but kindly towards all. He should be a good teacher, tolerant, and gentle when 25 discipline is needed for the refractory. The Lord may grant them a change of heart and show them the truth, and 26 thus they may come to their senses and escape from the devil's snare, in which they have been caught and held at his will.[e]

You must face the fact: the final age **3** of this world is to be a time of troubles. Men will love nothing but money and 2 self; they will be arrogant, boastful, and abusive; with no respect for parents, no

d *Or* must separate himself from these persons.
e *Or* escape from the devil's snare, caught now by God and made subject to his will.

2.1–26: **The way to wholehearted Christian service. 2:** Apostolic tradition was transmitted in the manner described in this verse; see 1.14. **11–13:** These verses appear to be a fragment of an early Christian hymn. **11:** *Words you may trust:* see 1 Tim.1.15 n. *If we died with him:* see Rom.6.8. **12:** *If we deny him:* see Mt.10.33. **13:** *He keeps faith:* see Rom.3.3–4. **18:** Some apparently thought that *the resurrection has already taken place* in some spiritual or mystical experience, perhaps at baptism; contrast 1 Cor.15.50–55. **19:** The first quotation reflects Num.16.5 Sept.; the second a variety of OT verses, e.g. Isa.26.13; Ps.6.8–9. **22:** *Impulses of youth:* see 1 Tim.4.12 n. **23:** See 1 Tim.1.4; Ti.3.9. **25:** The *truth:* see 3.7 n.
3.1–17: **Admonitions to stand fast amid error and persecution. 1:** Christians believed *the final age* had already begun; compare Acts 2.16–21. **2–4:** See 1 Tim.1.10 n. **7:** The *truth* here

[handwritten margin note: Jesus keeps his Word; His promises endure, even if we don't.]

3 gratitude, no piety, no natural affection, they will be implacable in their hatreds, scandal-mongers, intemperate and fierce, strangers to all goodness, 4 traitors, adventurers, swollen with self-importance. They will be men who put 5 pleasure in the place of God, men who preserve the outward form of religion, but are a standing denial of its reality. 6 Keep clear of men like these. They are the sort that insinuate themselves into private houses and there get miserable women into their clutches, women burdened with a sinful past, and led on 7 by all kinds of desires, who are always wanting to be taught, but are incapable of reaching a knowledge of the truth. 8 As Jannes and Jambres defied Moses, so these men defy the truth; they have lost the power to reason, and they 9 cannot pass the tests of faith. But their successes will be short-lived, for, like those opponents of Moses, they will come to be recognized by everyone for the fools they are.

10 But you, my son, have followed, step by step, my teaching and my manner of life, my resolution, my faith, patience, and spirit of love, and my 11 fortitude under persecutions and sufferings—all that I went through at Antioch, at Iconium, at Lystra, all the persecutions I endured; and the Lord 12 rescued me out of them all. Yes, persecution will come to all who want to 13 live a godly life as Christians, whereas wicked men and charlatans will make progress from bad to worse, deceiving 14 and deceived. But for your part, stand by the truths you have learned and are assured of. Remember from whom you 15 learned them; remember that from early childhood you have been familiar with the sacred writings which have power to make you wise and lead you

to salvation through faith in Christ Jesus. Every inspired scripture has its 16 use for teaching the truth and refuting error, or for reformation of manners and discipline in right living, so that the 17 man who belongs to God may be efficient and equipped for good work of every kind.

Before God, and before Christ Jesus **4** who is to judge men living and dead, I charge you solemnly by his coming appearance and his reign, proclaim the 2 message, press it home on all occasions,*f* convenient or inconvenient, use argument, reproof, and appeal, with all the patience that the work of teaching requires. For the time will come when 3 they will not stand wholesome teaching, but will follow their own fancy and gather a crowd of teachers to tickle their ears. They will stop their ears to 4 the truth and turn to mythology. But 5 you yourself must keep calm and sane at all times; face hardship, work to spread the Gospel, and do all the duties of your calling.

AS FOR ME, ALREADY MY LIFE IS BEING 6 poured out on the altar, and the hour for my departure is upon me. I have run 7 the great race, I have finished the course, I have kept faith. And now 8 the prize awaits me, the garland of righteousness which the Lord, the all-just Judge, will award me on that great Day; and it is not for me alone, but for all who have set their hearts on his coming appearance.

Do your best to join me soon; for 9,10 Demas has deserted me because his heart was set on this world; he has gone to Thessalonica, Crescens to Galatia,*g* Titus to Dalmatia; I have no one with 11

f Or be on duty at all times.
g Or Gaul; some witnesses read Gallia.

---

means the Christian gospel, as in 2.25; 1 Tim.2.4; Ti.1.1. **8:** *Jannes and Jambres* are the names ancient Jewish tradition gave to the Egyptian magicians of Pharaoh's court who opposed Moses; see Exod.7.11; 9.11. **10:** On Paul as a model for faith, see also Acts 20.18–21. **11:** *All that I went through:* see 2 Cor.11.23–27. *At Antioch:* see Acts 13.50–51. *At Iconium:* see Acts 14.2–7. *At Lystra:* see Acts 14.19–20. **13:** The Gk. word translated *charlatans* can also mean magicians; see v. 8 n. **15:** *Sacred writings:* see v. 16 n. **16:** *Scripture* refers to the OT; the NT had not yet been assembled.

4.1–5: Charge to Timothy. 1: *Jesus who is to judge:* see Acts 10.42. **3:** *Wholesome teaching:* see 1 Tim.1.10 n. **4:** *Mythology:* see 1 Tim.1.4; 4.7; Ti.1.14. **5:** *Work to spread the Gospel* (or, Do the work of an evangelist); see Acts 21.8; Eph.4.11, where such an office is mentioned.

4.6–22: Concluding personal remarks. 7: Compare Phil.2.16–17. **8:** *The garland* was the prize given the winner of a race or other Greek athletic contest. **10:** On *Titus*, see the Introduction

me but Luke. Pick up Mark and bring him with you, for I find him a useful
12 assistant. Tychicus I have sent to
13 Ephesus. When you come, bring the cloak I left with Carpus at Troas, and the books, above all my notebooks.
14   Alexander the copper-smith did me a great deal of harm. Retribution will
15 fall upon him from the Lord. You had better be on your guard against him too, for he violently opposed everything
16 I said. At the first hearing of my case no one came into court to support me; they all left me in the lurch; I pray that
17 it may not be held against them. But the Lord stood by me and lent me strength, so that I might be his instrument in making the full proclamation of the Gospel for the whole pagan world to

hear; and thus I was rescued out of the lion's jaws. And the Lord will rescue 18 me from every attempt to do me harm, and keep me safe until his heavenly reign begins.[h] Glory to him for ever and ever! Amen.
    Greetings to Prisca and Aquila, and 19 the household of Onesiphorus.
    Erastus stayed behind at Corinth, 20 and I left Trophimus ill at Miletus. Do 21 try to get here before winter.
    Greetings from Eubulus, Pudens, Linus, and Claudia, and from all the brotherhood here.
    The Lord be with your spirit. Grace 22 be with you all!

h *Or* from all that evil can do, and bring me safely into his heavenly kingdom.

to 1 Ti. **13:** On *Troas*, see Acts 16.8; 20.6; 2 Cor.2.12. **14:** *Retribution* (lit. payment): see Ps.28.4; Rom.2.6. **17:** *Rescued out of the lion's jaws* may be used figuratively here, as it is in Ps.22.21. **19:** *Prisca and Aquila:* see Acts 18.2 n. **21:** During the *winter*, travel by sea was hazardous; see Acts 27.9(and n.)–44; 28.11 n.

THE LETTER OF PAUL TO
TITUS

Titus, like Timothy, was a trusted friend and companion of Paul. Born of Gentile parents (Gal.2.3), he accompanied Paul to the Apostolic Council in Jerusalem (Gal.2.1; see also Acts 15), and played a significant role in collecting money from the Corinthians (2 Cor.8.6, 16–23) for the poor in Jerusalem (see Gal.2.10). This document is the earliest evidence we have for the presence of the Christian faith on the island of Crete. For more information on this letter, see the Introduction to 1 Timothy.

Training for the Christian life

1 FROM PAUL, SERVANT OF GOD AND apostle of Jesus Christ, marked as such by faith and knowledge and hope—the faith of God's chosen people, knowledge of the truth as our 2 religion has it, and the hope of eternal life.ᵃ Yes, it is eternal life that God, who cannot lie, promised long ages ago, 3 and now in his own good time he has openly declared himself in the proclamation which was entrusted to me by ordinance of God our Saviour.

4 To Titus, my true-born son in the faith which we share, grace and peace from God our Father and Christ Jesus our Saviour.

5 My intention in leaving you behind in Crete was that you should set in order what was left over, and in particular should institute elders in each town. In doing so, observe the tests I 6 prescribed: is he a man of unimpeachable character, faithful to his one wife,ᵇ the father of children who are believers, who are under no imputation of loose 7 living, and are not out of control? For as God's steward a bishop must be a man of unimpeachable character. He must not be overbearing or short-tempered; he must be no drinker, no 8 brawler, no money-grubber, but hos-

pitable, right-minded, temperate, just, devout, and self-controlled. He must 9 adhere to the true doctrine, so that he may be well able both to move his hearers with wholesome teaching and to confute objectors.

There are all too many, especially 10 among Jewish converts, who are out of all control; they talk wildly and lead men's minds astray. Such men must be 11 curbed, because they are ruining whole families by teaching things they should not, and all for sordid gain. It was a 12 Cretan prophet, one of their own countrymen, who said, 'Cretans were always liars, vicious brutes, lazy gluttons'—and he told the truth! All the 13 more reason why you should pull them up sharply, so that they may come to a sane belief, instead of lending their ears 14 to Jewish myths and commandments of merely human origin, the work of men who turn their backs upon the truth.

To the pure all things are pure; but 15 nothing is pure to the tainted minds of disbelievers, tainted alike in reason and conscience. They profess to acknowl- 16 edge God, but deny him by their actions. Their detestable obstinacy disqualifies them for any good work.

ᵃ Or apostle of Jesus Christ, to bring God's chosen people to faith and to a knowledge of the truth as our religion has it, with its hope for eternal life.
ᵇ See note on 1 Timothy 3. 2.

1.1–4: Salutation. 1: *Knowledge of the truth:* see 2 Tim.3.7 n. **3:** *His own good time* (or, at the appropriate time): the early Christians saw in the history of Israel and the coming of Jesus the unfolding of God's plan for the salvation of mankind. In accordance with this plan, God had sent Jesus at the time he (God) found appropriate; see Rom.5.6; Gal.4.4; Eph.1.10. **4:** On *Titus,* see Introduction to 1 Tim.
1.5–16: The need for Christian discipline. 5: *Elders:* in 1 Tim.3.1–7, a similar list describes the qualifications of a bishop; see 1 Tim.3.2 n. **7:** *Bishop* seems identical here to "elder" in v. 5. **9:** *Wholesome teaching:* see 1 Tim.1.10 n. **10–11:** The problems here are similar to those discussed in 1 Tim.1.3–4; 6.4–5; 2 Tim.2.14,16; 3.6–7. **12:** *Cretan prophet:* probably Epimenides (sixth century B.C.). **14:** *Jewish myths and commandments:* see 1 Tim.4.3 n. **15:** *To the pure:* probably meant here in the sense that a man's inner quality determines whether what he perceives and expresses will be good or evil; see Mt.7:16–18. Compare Rom.14.14, where it refers to dietary practices.

2 For your own part, what you say must be in keeping with wholesome doctrine. **2** Let the older men know that they should be sober, high-principled, and temperate, sound in faith, in love, and in endurance. **3** The older women, similarly, should be reverent in their bearing, not scandal-mongers or slaves to strong drink; they must set a high standard, and **4** school the younger women to be loving wives and mothers, **5** temperate, chaste, and kind, busy at home, respecting the authority of their own husbands. Thus the Gospel will not be brought into disrepute.

6 Urge the younger men, similarly, to be temperate in all things, and **7** set them a good example yourself. In your teaching, you must show integrity and high principle, and **8** use wholesome speech to which none can take exception. This will shame any opponent, when he finds not a word to say to our discredit.

9 Tell slaves to respect their masters' authority in everything, and to comply with their demands without answering **10** back; not to pilfer, but to show themselves strictly honest and trustworthy; for in all such ways they will add lustre to the doctrine of God our Saviour.

11 For the grace of God has dawned upon the world with healing for all **12** mankind; and by it we are disciplined to renounce godless ways and worldly desires, and to live a life of temperance, honesty, and godliness in the present **13** age, looking forward to the happy fulfilment of our hope when the splendour of our great God and Saviour[c] Christ **14** Jesus will appear. He it is who sacrificed himself for us, to set us free from all wickedness and to make us a pure people marked out for his own, eager to do good.

These, then, are your themes; urge **15** them and argue them. And speak with authority: let no one slight you.

3 Remind them to be submissive to the government and the authorities, to obey them, and to be ready for any honourable form of work;[d] to slander **2** no one, not to pick quarrels, to show forbearance and a consistently gentle disposition towards all men.

For at one time we ourselves in our **3** folly and obstinacy were all astray. We were slaves to passions and pleasures of every kind. Our days were passed in malice and envy; we were odious ourselves and we hated one another. But **4** when the kindness and generosity of God our Saviour dawned upon the world, then, not for any good deeds of **5** our own, but because he was merciful, he saved us through the water of rebirth and the renewing power of[e] the Holy Spirit. For he sent down the **6** Spirit upon us plentifully through Jesus Christ our Saviour, so that, justified by **7** his grace, we might in hope become heirs to eternal life. These are words **8** you may trust.

Such are the points I should wish you to insist on. Those who have come to believe in God should see that they engage in honourable occupations, which are not only honourable in themselves, but also useful to their fellow-men.[f] But steer clear of foolish **9** speculations, genealogies, quarrels, and controversies over the Law; they are unprofitable and pointless.

A heretic should be warned once, **10** and once again; after that, have done

c Or of the great God and our Saviour . . .
d Or ready always to do good.
e Or the water of rebirth and of renewal by . . .
f Or should make it their business to practise virtue. These precepts are good in themselves and useful to society.

2.1–3.2: All Christians must lead disciplined lives. 1: *Wholesome doctrine:* see 1 Tim.1.10 n. **5:** *Respecting the authority of their own husbands:* see 1 Tim.2.11–14. **9:** *Slaves:* see 1 Tim.6.1 n. **10:** *God our Saviour:* see 1 Tim.1.1 n. **11:** *For all mankind:* see 1 Tim.2.4 n. **12:** These ideals also characterized the doctrine of much Hellenistic philosophy, although it did not speak of doing them *by* God's *grace.* **13:** *God* and *Saviour* were titles regularly applied in the Hellenistic world to gods and emperors. **14:** *A pure people marked out for his own:* see Exod.19.5; Deut.7.6; 14.2. **3.1:** See Rom.13.1–7; 1 Tim.2.2. Cretans had a reputation as a turbulent people.

3.3–8a: God is generous in mercy. 4: *God our Saviour:* see 1 Tim.1.1 n. Hellenistic rulers frequently claimed *generosity* as a characteristic of their acts. **5:** *Water of rebirth* means baptism; see Eph.5.26; 1 Pet.1.3. **8:** *Words . . . trust:* see 1 Tim.1.15 n. The phrase refers here to vv. 4–7.

3.8b–15: Concluding exhortations. 8b–11: These verses serve as a summary of the author's counsel; we do not possess sufficient information to specify exactly what he meant by his references to *foolish speculations, genealogies, quarrels, and controversies over the Law* (see 1 Tim.1.4 n.). **10:** See Mt.18.15–17; 2 Th.3.14–15. The word *heretic* appears only here in the

11 with him, recognizing that a man of that sort has a distorted mind and stands self-condemned in his sin.

12 When I send Artemas to you, or Tychicus, make haste to join me at Nicopolis, for that is where I have 13 determined to spend the winter. Do your utmost to help Zenas the lawyer and Apollos on their travels, and see that they are not short of anything.

And our own people must be taught to 14 engage in honest employment to produce the necessities of life; they must not be unproductive.

All who are with me send you 15 greetings. My greetings to those who are our friends in truth.*g* Grace be with you all!

g Or our friends in the faith.

NT; it is probably not meant in the formal sense it later acquired, but simply designates one whose views the author finds unacceptable. **12:** It is uncertain to which of several cities named *Nicopolis* this refers. **13:** *Apollos:* see Acts 18.24–19.1; he is also mentioned frequently in 1 Cor. chs. 1–4.

THE LETTER OF PAUL TO

PHILEMON

This most personal of all the Pauline letters—his plea for a runaway slave—was written during an imprisonment of the apostle, probably his house arrest at Rome (61–63 A.D.). Philemon was a leading member of his community, at whose house the Christians met for worship. That he was a resident of Colossae is indicated by Col.4.7–9. It tells that Paul's companion Tychicus would carry his letter to the Colossians, and "with him comes Onesimus," the slave mentioned in Philem.11–16.

Onesimus has run away; the penalty for this on recapture was severe. Paul is sending him back and appeals to Philemon to receive Onesimus without punishment. He does not speak against the institution of slavery, but reminds Philemon that since Onesimus has become a Christian their relations have changed—they are now brothers in Christ.

A runaway slave

1 FROM PAUL, A PRISONER OF CHRIST Jesus, and our colleague Timothy, to Philemon our dear friend and 2 fellow-worker, and Apphia our sister, and Archippus our comrade-in-arms, and the congregation at your house.

3 Grace to you and peace from God our Father and the Lord Jesus Christ.

4 I thank my God always when I 5 mention you in my prayers, for I hear of your love and faith towards the Lord Jesus and towards all God's people. 6 My prayer is that your fellowship with us in our common faith may deepen the understanding of all the blessings that 7 our union with Christ brings us.[a] For I am delighted and encouraged by your love; through you, my brother, God's people have been much refreshed.

8 Accordingly, although in Christ I might make bold to point out your 9 duty, yet, because of that same love, I would rather appeal to you. Yes, I, Paul, ambassador as I am of Christ 10 Jesus—and now his prisoner—appeal to you about my child, whose father I have become in this prison.

11 I mean Onesimus, once so little use to you, but now useful indeed, both to you and to me. I am sending him back to you, and in doing so I am sending a 12 part of myself. I should have liked to 13 keep him with me, to look after me as you would wish, here in prison for the Gospel. But I would rather do nothing 14 without your consent, so that your kindness may be a matter not of compulsion, but of your own free will. For 15 perhaps this is why you lost him for a time, that you might have him back for good, no longer as a slave, but as 16 more than a slave—as a dear brother, very dear indeed to me and how much dearer to you, both as man and as Christian.

If, then, you count me partner in the 17 faith, welcome him as you would welcome me. And if he has done you any 18 wrong or is in your debt, put that down to my account. Here is my signature, 19 PAUL; I undertake to repay—not to mention that you owe your very self to me as well. Now brother, as a Christian, 20 be generous with me, and relieve my anxiety; we are both in Christ!

I write to you confident that you will 21 meet my wishes; I know that you will in fact do better than I ask. And one 22 thing more: have a room ready for me,

a Or that bring us to Christ.

1–3: **Salutation.** The form is usual in ancient letters. **2:** *Congregation at your house:* as yet no church edifices existed.

4–7: **Prayer of thanksgiving.** Such prayers are usual in Paul's letters; see Rom.1.8–15, where he begins with "thanking my God."

8–21: **The plea for Onesimus. 10:** *Child . . . father:* see 1 Cor.4.15. **11:** *Little use . . . useful indeed:* the name Onesimus means "the useful one"; the verse puns on the name. **13–14:** Perhaps Paul is here hinting that Philemon should send the slave back to continue his service to the apostle. **15–16:** Paul acknowledges Philemon's right to have Onesimus *back for good,* although the apostle's own hope is expressed in v. 14. In any case, Philemon will henceforth know Onesimus as a *brother,* rather than merely as a *slave.* **19:** The *signature* is this verse and

for I hope that, in answer to your prayers, God will grant me to you.

23, 24 Epaphras, Christ's captive like myself, sends you greetings. So do Mark, Aristarchus, Demas, and Luke, my fellow-workers.

25 The grace of the Lord Jesus Christ be with your spirit!

perhaps the following ones: see 1 Cor.16.21–24 n. *Owe . . . to me:* an allusion to Paul's conversion of Philemon. **23–24:** These companions of Paul are mentioned also in Col.4.10,11,14.

A LETTER TO
HEBREWS

While the final paragraphs (see 13.18–25 n.) imply that Hebrews is a letter, in style and content it is a sermonic tract, an "exhortation" (13.22). The readers have endured great suffering because of their faith (10.32–34) and are now admonished to continue firm in their hope of salvation (e.g. 7.19), although apathy or even apostasy may seem the easier way. For backsliders into sin there is no second chance for salvation (6.4–8; 10.26–31).

The basis and content of hope is God's gift of his Son (ch. 1), and the first chs. (1.1–10.18) expound the significance of Christ's faithfulness (e.g. 2.18; 5.8–10) and death. The thesis is that Christ is the great high priest (8.1–2), the mediator of a new covenant (e.g. 8.6–13) who offers the one truly effective sacrifice (e.g. 9.11–14,25–28). The last chs. (10.19–13.17) urge Christians to follow in "the new, living way" provided by Christ (10.20), as God's pilgrim people, "seekers after the city which is to come" (13.14).

There have been many attempts to name the author of this tract (some early Christians even assigned it to Paul), but he remains anonymous. In spite of the traditional title the addressees were probably Gentile Christians. Earliest evidence of its use comes from Rome at the end of the first century, one possible clue as to its date and origin.

Christ divine and human

1 WHEN IN FORMER TIMES GOD spoke to our forefathers, he spoke in fragmentary and varied fashion through the prophets.
2 But in this the final age he has spoken to us in the Son whom he has made heir to the whole universe, and through whom he created all orders of existence:
3 the Son who is the effulgence of God's splendour and the stamp of God's very being, and sustains[a] the universe by his word of power. When he had brought about the purgation of sins, he took his seat at the right hand of
4 Majesty on high, raised as far above the angels, as the title he has inherited is superior to theirs.
5 For God never said to any angel, 'Thou art my Son; today I have begotten thee', or again, 'I will be father
6 to him, and he shall be my son.' Again, when he presents the first-born to the world, he says, 'Let all the angels of
7 God pay him homage.' Of the angels he says,

'He who makes his angels winds,
and his ministers a fiery flame';

but of the Son,

8 'Thy throne, O God, is for ever and ever,
and the sceptre[b] of justice is the sceptre of his kingdom.
9 Thou hast loved right and hated wrong;
therefore, O God, thy God[c] has set thee above thy fellows,
by anointing with the oil of exultation.'

10 And again,

'By thee, Lord, were earth's foundations laid of old,
and the heavens are the work of thy hands.
11 They shall pass away, but thou endurest;
like clothes they shall all grow old;
12 thou shalt fold them up like a cloak;
yes, they shall be changed like any garment.
But thou art the same, and thy years shall have no end.'

a Or bears along.
b Or God is thy throne for ever and ever, and thy sceptre . . .
c Or therefore God who is thy God . . .

1.1–3.6a: The supremacy of Christ and the significance of his suffering.
1.1–14: Christ's supremacy over the angels. 2–3a: See Jn.1.1–3; Wis.7.25. 3: The idea of Christ's exaltation to a position of supreme authority (*right hand*) in the heavenly "court" is derived from Ps.110.1 which is quoted in v. 13; 5.6; 7.21 where it is applied to Christ. 4: Jesus' *title* Is "Son"; see vv. 2–3,5. 5: Ps.2.7 (see Mt.3.17); 2 Sam.7.14. 6: Deut.32.43 Sept. (see Ps.97.7). 7: Ps.104.4. 8–9: Ps.45.6–7. 10–12: Ps.102.25–27. 13: Ps.110.1.

13 To which of the angels has he ever
said, 'Sit at my right hand until I make
14 thy enemies thy footstool'? What are
they all but ministrant spirits, sent out
to serve, for the sake of those who are
to inherit salvation?

2 Thus we are bound to pay all the
more heed to what we have been told,
for fear of drifting from our course.
2 For if the word spoken through angels
had such force that any transgression
or disobedience met with due retribu-
3 tion, what escape can there be for us if
we ignore a deliverance so great? For
this deliverance was first announced
through the lips of the Lord himself;
those who heard him confirmed it to us,
4 and God added his testimony by signs,
by miracles, by manifold works of
power, and by distributing the gifts of
the Holy Spirit at his own will.
5 For it is not to angels that he has
subjected the world to come, which is
6 our theme. But there is somewhere a
solemn assurance which runs:

'What is man, that thou rememberest
　　him,
or the son of man, that thou hast
　　regard to him?
7 Thou didst make him for a short
　　while lower than the angels;
thou didst crown him with glory and
　　honour;
8 thou didst put all things in subjection
　　beneath his feet.'

For in subjecting all things to him, he
left nothing that is not subject. But in
fact we do not yet see all things in
9 subjection to man. In Jesus, however,
we do see one who[d] for a short while
was made lower than the angels,
crowned now with glory and honour
because he suffered death, so that, by
God's gracious will, in tasting death he
should stand[e] for us all.

It was clearly fitting that God for 10
whom and through whom all things
exist should, in bringing many sons to
glory, make the leader who delivers
them perfect through sufferings. For a 11
consecrating priest and those whom he
consecrates are all of one stock; and
that is why the Son does not shrink
from calling men his brothers, when he 12
says, 'I will proclaim thy name to my
brothers; in full assembly I will sing thy
praise'; and again, 'I will keep my trust 13
fixed on him'; and again, 'Here am I,
and the children whom God has given
me.' The children of a family share the 14
same flesh and blood; and so he too
shared ours, so that through death he
might break the power of him who had
death at his command, that is, the
devil; and might liberate those who, 15
through fear of death, had all their
lifetime been in servitude. It is not 16
angels, mark you, that he takes to
himself, but the sons of Abraham.
And therefore he had to be made like 17
these brothers of his in every way, so
that he might be merciful and faithful
as their high priest before God, to
expiate the sins of the people. For since 18
he himself has passed through the test
of suffering, he is able to help those
who are meeting their test now.

Therefore, brothers in the family of 3
God, who share a heavenly calling,
think of the Apostle and High Priest
of the religion we profess,[f] who was 2
faithful to God who appointed him.
Moses also was faithful in God's
household; and Jesus, of whom I speak, 3
has been deemed worthy of greater
honour than Moses, as the founder of
a house enjoys more honour than his
household. For every house has its 4
founder; and the founder of all is God.

d *Or* in subjection to him. But we see Jesus, who . . .
e *Some witnesses read* so that apart from God he should
　taste death . . .
f *Or* of him whom we confess as God's Envoy and
　High Priest.

2.1–18: **The significance of Christ's suffering. 2:** See, e.g. Acts 7.53. **3–4:** There is a triple
witness to salvation: Christ, the apostles, and God himself, whose power is manifest in many
wondrous deeds and in diverse spiritual gifts. **6–8:** Ps.8.4–6 Sept. **10:** See 5.8–10. **11:** Christ,
the *priest*, and *those whom he consecrates* are all sons of God. **12:** Ps.22.22. **13:** Isa.8.17–18.
17: See 4.14–5.10. **18:** Christ's sacrifice is effective for salvation because he, through the trials
of temptation and persecution, is able to identify fully with human suffering. See 4.15.
3.1–6a: **Christ's supremacy over Moses. 1:** Christ is God's *Apostle* to men, and as *High
Priest* he is the mediator between God and men. **2–6:** The author supports Christ's supremacy
by arguing that, while Moses was a servant in *God's . . . household* (Num.12.7), Jesus is the
master's *son.*

5 Moses, then, was faithful as a servitor in God's whole household; his task was to bear witness to the words that God 6 would speak; but Christ is faithful as a son, set over his household. And we are that household of his, if only we are fearless and keep our hope high.

7 'TODAY', THEREFORE, AS THE HOLY Spirit says—

'Today if you hear his voice,
8   do not grow stubborn as in those days of rebellion,
  at that time of testing in the desert,
9   where your forefathers tried me and tested me,
  and saw*g* the things I did for forty years.
10   And so, I was indignant with that generation
  and I said, Their hearts are for ever astray;
  they would not discern my ways;
11   as I vowed in my anger, they shall never enter my rest.'

12   See to it, brothers, that no one among you has the wicked, faithless heart of a deserter from the living God; 13 but day by day, while that word 'Today' still sounds in your ears, encourage one another, so that no one of you is made stubborn by the wiles 14 of sin. For we have become Christ's partners*h* if only we keep our original confidence firm to the end. 15 When Scripture says, 'Today if you hear his voice, do not grow stubborn as 16 in those days of rebellion', who, I ask, were those who heard and rebelled? All those, surely, whom Moses had led 17 out of Egypt. And with whom was God indignant for forty years? With those, surely, who had sinned, whose bodies lay where they fell in the desert.

And to whom did he vow that they 18 should not enter his rest, if not to those who had refused to believe? We per- 19 ceive that it was unbelief which prevented their entering.

Therefore we must have before us the 4 fear that while the promise of entering his rest remains open, one or another among you should be found to have missed his chance. For indeed we have 2 heard the good news, as they did. But in them the message they heard did no good, because it met with no faith in those who heard it. It is we, we who 3 have become believers, who enter the rest referred to in the words, 'As I vowed in my anger, they shall never enter my rest.' Yet God's work has been finished ever since the world was created; for does not Scripture some- 4 where speak thus of the seventh day: 'God rested from all his work on the seventh day'?—and once again in the 5 passage above we read, 'They shall never enter my rest.' The fact remains 6 that someone must enter it, and since those who first heard the good news failed to enter through unbelief, God 7 fixes another day. Speaking through the lips of David after many long years, he uses the words already quoted: 'Today if you hear his voice, do not grow stubborn.' If Joshua had given 8 them rest, God would not thus have spoken of another day after that. Therefore, a sabbath rest still awaits 9 the people of God; for anyone who 10 enters God's rest, rests from his own work as God did from his. Let us then 11 make every effort to enter that rest, so that no one may fall by following this evil example of unbelief.

For the word of God is alive and 12 active. It cuts more keenly than any

g Or though they saw ...
h Or have been given a share in Christ.

3.6b–4.13: The danger of unbelief. Characteristically, this author turns from theological exposition (1.1–3.6a) to ethical exhortation. He begins with a lengthy exposition of Scripture (3.7–11) which is applied to the readers' present needs. **6b:** God's people must keep their *hope high* lest they fall into unbelief (see vv.14,18–19; 4.11). **7–11:** Ps.95.7-11. **12–13:** Israel's misadventures in the wilderness should serve as warning to Christians who may be faced with the temptation to apathy or apostasy. **14:** Christians are *Christ's partners* if they remain loyal sons in God's household; see v. 1; 2.11–17. **15:** See vv. 7–8. **17:** Num.14.29. **18:** The *rest* which awaited those who were obedient (v. 11; Num.14.22–23) was the promised land of Canaan. **4.1–2:** God's *rest* (3.18) is interpreted as the final promised salvation which Christians, like Israel, can attain only by faithfulness. **3:** Ps.95.11. **4:** Gen.2.2. **5:** See v. 3. **6:** Israel disobeyed, but the promise was renewed. **7:** Ps.95.7-8 (see 3.7–11). **8:** Joshua's settlement of Canaan

two-edged sword, piercing as far as the place where life and spirit, joints and marrow, divide. It sifts the purposes 13 and thoughts of the heart. There is nothing in creation that can hide from him; everything lies naked and exposed to the eyes of the One with whom we have to reckon.

14　Since therefore we have a great high priest who has passed through the heavens, Jesus the Son of God, let us hold fast to the religion we profess. 15 For ours is not a high priest unable to sympathize with our weaknesses, but one who, because of his likeness to us, has been tested every way,*i* only 16 without sin. Let us therefore boldly approach the throne of our gracious God, where we may receive mercy and in his grace find timely help.

The shadow and the real

5 FOR EVERY HIGH PRIEST IS TAKEN FROM among men and appointed their representative before God, to offer gifts 2 and sacrifices for sins. He is able to bear patiently with the ignorant and erring, since he too is beset by weak- 3 ness; and because of this he is bound to make sin-offerings for himself no less 4 than for the people. And nobody arrogates the honour to himself: he is called by God, as indeed Aaron was. 5 So it is with Christ: he did not confer upon himself the glory of becoming high priest; it was granted by God, who said to him, 'Thou art my Son; 6 today I have begotten thee'; as also in another place he says, 'Thou art a priest for ever, in the succession of Mel-

chizedek.' In the days of his earthly 7 life he offered up prayers and petitions, with loud cries and tears, to God who was able to deliver him from the grave. Because of his humble submission his prayer was heard: son though he was, 8 he learned obedience in the school of suffering, and, once perfected, became 9 the source of eternal salvation for all who obey him, named by God high 10 priest in the succession of Melchizedek.

About Melchizedek we have much to 11 say, much that is difficult to explain, now that you have grown so dull of hearing. For indeed, though by this 12 time you ought to be teachers, you need someone to teach you the ABC of God's oracles over again; it has come to this, that you need milk instead of solid food. Anyone who lives on milk, 13 being an infant, does not know*j* what is right. But grown men can take solid 14 food; their perceptions are trained by long use to discriminate between good and evil.

Let us then stop discussing the rudi- 6 ments of Christianity. We ought not to be laying over again the foundations of faith in God and of repentance from the deadness of our former ways, by 2 instruction*k* about cleansing rites and the laying-on-of-hands, about the resurrection of the dead and eternal judgement. Instead, let us advance towards maturity; and so we shall, if 3 God permits.

For when men have once been en- 4 lightened, when they have had a taste of the heavenly gift and a share in the

i Or who has been tested every way, as we are.
j Or is incompetent to speak of . . .
k Or, according to some witnesses, laying the foundations over again: repentance from the deadness of our former ways and faith in God, instruction . . .

(Deut.31.7; Josh. ch. 22) did not fulfill the promise, for it had to be issued again "through . . . David" (v. 7); see Ps.95.7–8. **12–13:** The *word of God* probes and judges all *creation*.
　　4.14–5.10: Christ, the great high priest. This is the author's most important way of interpreting the meaning of Christ's redemptive work. The development of the idea is interrupted temporarily by exhortations (5.11–6.12; see 3.6b–4.13 n.), but then resumed at 6.13. **14–16:** God's *mercy* and *grace* are sure because Christ himself withstood the trials of *our weaknesses . . . without sin*, and thereby serves as the effective mediator between men and God. See 2.17–18. **5.1–4:** See Ex.28.1; Lev.9.7; 16.6. **5:** See 1.5 n. **6:** Ps.110.4. See 7.1–10 n. **7–8:** See the stories of Jesus' passion, e.g. Mt.26.36–46. **9–10:** See 9.24–28.
　　5.11–6.12: Warning against backsliding. 11–14: The explanation of Melchizedek's priesthood is deferred (see ch. 7). First, the readers need to be nurtured by the *milk* of some basic instruction about discerning *good and evil*. **6.1–3:** Certain *rudiments of Christianity*, like *faith, repentance, resurrection* and *judgement*, ought to be self-evident. (It is not clear what *cleansing rites and the laying-on-of-hands* refer to.) Once the basic Christian doctrines have been understood, it is essential that one *advance towards maturity*, i.e. give himself over to that perfect consecration to God's service which Christ's sacrifice has made possible (10.12–14). **4–8:** For sins committed after

5 Holy Spirit, when they have experienced the goodness of God's word and the spiritual energies of the age to 6 come, and after all this have fallen away, it is impossible to bring them again to repentance; for with their own hands they are crucifying[l] the Son of God and making mock of his death. 7 When the earth drinks in the rain that falls upon it from time to time, and yields a useful crop to those for whom it is cultivated, it is receiving its share of 8 blessing from God; but if it bears thorns and thistles, it is worthless and God's curse hangs over it; the end of 9 that is burning. But although we speak as we do, we are convinced that you, my friends, are in the better case, and 10 this makes for your salvation. For God would not be so unjust as to forget all that you did for love of his name, when you rendered service to his people, as 11 you still do. But we long for every one of you to show the same eager concern, 12 until your hope is finally realized. We want you not to become lazy, but to imitate those who, through faith and patience, are inheriting the promises. 13 When God made his promise to Abraham, he swore by himself, because 14 he had no one greater to swear by: 'I vow that I will bless you abundantly 15 and multiply your descendants.' Thus it was that Abraham, after patient 16 waiting, attained the promise. Men swear by a greater than themselves, and the oath provides a confirmation to 17 end all dispute; and so God, desiring to show even more clearly to the heirs of his promise how unchanging was his 18 purpose, guaranteed it by oath. Here, then, are two irrevocable acts in which

God could not possibly play us false, to give powerful encouragement to us, who have claimed his protection by grasping[m] the hope set before us. That 19 hope we hold. It is like an anchor for our lives, an anchor safe and sure. It enters in through the veil, where Jesus 20 has entered on our behalf as forerunner, having become a high priest for ever in the succession of Melchizedek.

THIS MELCHIZEDEK, KING OF SALEM, 7 priest of God Most High, met Abraham returning from the rout of the kings and blessed him; and Abraham gave 2 him a tithe of everything as his portion. His name, in the first place, means 'king of righteousness'; next he is king of Salem, that is, 'king of peace'. He 3 has no father, no mother, no lineage; his years have no beginning, his life no end. He is like the Son of God: he remains a priest for all time.

Consider now how great he must be 4 for Abraham the patriarch to give him a tithe of the finest of the spoil. The 5 descendants of Levi who take the priestly office are commanded by the Law to tithe the people, that is, their kinsmen, although they too are descendants of Abraham. But Melchizedek, 6 though he does not trace his descent from them, has tithed Abraham himself, and given his blessing to the man who received the promises; and beyond 7 all dispute the lesser is always blessed by the greater. Again, in the one 8 instance tithes are received by men who must die; but in the other, by one whom Scripture affirms to be alive. It 9

l Or crucifying again.
m Or to give to us, who have claimed his protection, a powerful incentive to grasp . . .

---

baptism no amount of repentance will suffice; backsliders have no second chance (see 10.26–31; 2 Pet.2.20–22). They remain under a curse like Adam (vv. 7–8; see Gen.1.11–12; 3.17–18). **9–12:** Here the writer addresses those who, however, still show *faith*, *hope* and *love* and for whom *salvation* is still in prospect if they remain true to their baptismal vows.

6.13–10.18: The new covenant. The writer now returns (see 4.14–5.10) to his theological discussion. His aim in what follows is to demonstrate that Christ mediates, and by his death effectively seals, a new covenant for forgiveness of sins (10.16–18). This point is made by contrasting the redemptive character of Jesus' life, death, and exaltation with the inferior rites of the Jewish sacrificial system.

6.13–8.13: Christ is a new high priest. 13–18: *Two irrevocable acts* show God's faithfulness to Abraham, his promise and his oath; see Gen.22.16–17. **19–20:** *The veil* of the Temple in Jerusalem guarded its innermost sanctuary which was entered only once a year and only by the high priest; see 9.1–5. This priestly function of opening an approach to God for the people is now served by Jesus; see 4.14–5.10. **7.1–10:** *Melchizedek* (see Gen.14.17–20) is called *a priest for all time* (v. 3) because Scripture happens to say nothing about either his birth or his death. He is thus the prototype of Christ, the eternal high priest (see vv. 23–25). **8:** The Levitical priests

might even be said that Levi, who receives tithes, has himself been tithed 10 through Abraham; for he was still in his ancestor's loins when Melchizedek met him.

11 Now if perfection had been attainable through the Levitical priesthood (for it is on this basis that the people were given the Law), what further need would there have been to speak of another priest arising, in the succession of Melchizedek, instead of the succession 12 of Aaron? For a change of priesthood 13 must mean a change of law. And the one here spoken of belongs to a different tribe, no member of which has ever had 14 anything to do with the altar. For it is very evident that our Lord is sprung from Judah, a tribe to which Moses made no reference in speaking of priests.

15 The argument becomes still clearer, if the new priest who arises is one like 16 Melchizedek, owing his priesthood not to a system of earth-bound rules but to the power of a life that cannot be 17 destroyed. For here is the testimony: 'Thou art a priest for ever, in the suc-18 cession of Melchizedek.' The earlier rules are cancelled as impotent and 19 useless, since the Law brought nothing to perfection; and a better hope is introduced, through which we draw near to God.

20 How great a difference it makes that 21 an oath was sworn! There was no oath sworn when those others were made priests; but for this priest an oath was sworn, as Scripture says of him: 'The Lord has sworn and will not go back on his word, "Thou art a priest for ever."' 22 How far superior must the covenant also be of which Jesus is the guarantor! 23 Those other priests are appointed in numerous succession, because they are prevented by death from continuing in office; but the priesthood which Jesus 24 holds is perpetual, because he remains for ever. That is why he is also able to 25 save absolutely those who approach God through him; he is always living to plead on their behalf.

Such a high priest does indeed fit our 26 condition—devout, guileless, undefiled, separated from sinners, raised high above the heavens. He has no need to 27 offer sacrifices daily, as the high priests do, first for his own sins and then for those of the people; for this he did once and for all when he offered up himself. The high priests made by the 28 Law are men in all their frailty; but the priest appointed by the words of the oath which supersedes the Law is the Son, made perfect now for ever.

NOW THIS IS MY MAIN POINT: JUST SUCH 8 a high priest we have, and he has taken his seat at the right hand of the throne of Majesty in the heavens, a ministrant 2 in the real sanctuary, the tent pitched by the Lord and not by man. Every high 3 priest is appointed to offer gifts and sacrifices; hence, this one too must have[n] something to offer. Now if he 4 had been on earth, he could not even have been a priest, since there are already priests who offer the gifts which the Law prescribes, though they minis- 5 ter in a sanctuary which is only a copy and shadow of the heavenly. This is implied when Moses, about to erect the tent, is instructed by God: 'See to it that you make everything according to the pattern shown you on the mountain.' But in fact the ministry 6 which has fallen to Jesus is as far superior to theirs as are the covenant he mediates and the promises upon which it is legally secured.

n Or must have had.

are mortal, Melchizedek is not. **11–14:** The inferiority of the old priesthood required the institution of a new order of priests which, in turn, involved *a change of law.* Under the old law priests were chosen only from the tribe of Levi (see Num.18.21–24), but Jesus was from the tribe of Judah. **15–19:** Christ's priesthood depends on no legal statute of the Pentateuch, but rather on the uniqueness of his own person as God's eternal Son (see 1.1–4; 13.8). Therefore he secures for the people *a better hope* (v. 19). **17:** Ps.110.4. **20–25:** The author resumes his argument that Jesus' priestly office was conferred by a divine oath (Ps.110.4; see 6.13–18). Because death does not terminate his service he is *able to save absolutely.* **26–28:** The preceding argument is summarized: Christ's priestly mediation is alone redemptive because he is God's *Son,* himself without sin, *appointed* to his office *by . . . the oath,* not *the Law,* and because he offers the *once and for all* sacrifice of his own life and subsequently is *raised high above the heavens* to be with God. See 9.11–12.

8.1–13: Christ exercises his priesthood in the Lord's sanctuary, not in man's. This intensifies

7 Had that first covenant been faultless, there would have been no need to look
8 for a second in its place. But God, finding fault with them, says, 'The days are coming, says the Lord, when I will conclude a new covenant with the house of Israel and the house of Judah.
9 It will not be like the covenant I made with their forefathers when I took them by the hand to lead them out of Egypt; because they did not abide by the terms of that covenant, and I abandoned
10 them, says the Lord. For the covenant I will make with the house of Israel after those days, says the Lord, is this: I will set my laws in their understanding and write them on their hearts; and I will be their God, and they shall be
11 my people. And they shall not teach one another, saying to brother and fellow-citizen,⁰ "Know the Lord!" For all of them, high and low, shall know
12 me; I will be merciful to their wicked deeds, and I will remember their sins
13 no more.' By speaking of a new covenant, he has pronounced the first one old; and anything that is growing old and ageing will shortly disappear.

9 THE FIRST COVENANT INDEED HAD ITS ordinances of divine service and its sanctuary, but a material sanctuary.
2 For a tent was prepared—the first tent—in which was the lamp-stand, and the table with the bread of the Presence; this is called the Holy Place.
3 Beyond the second curtain was the
4 tent called the Most Holy Place. Here was a golden altar of incense, and the ark of the covenant plated all over with gold, in which were a golden jar containing the manna, and Aaron's staff which once budded, and the tablets of
5 the covenant; and above it the cherubim of God's glory, overshadowing the place of expiation. On these we cannot now enlarge.

Under this arrangement, the priests 6 are always entering the first tent in the discharge of their duties; but the 7 second is entered only once a year, and by the high priest alone, and even then he must take with him the blood which he offers on his own behalf and for the people's sins of ignorance. By this the 8 Holy Spirit signifies that so long as the earlier tent still stands, the way into the sanctuary remains unrevealed. All 9 this is symbolic, pointing to the present time. The offerings and sacrifices there prescribed cannot give the worshipper inward perfection. It is only a matter 10 of food and drink and various rites of cleansing—outward ordinances in force until the time of reformation.

But now Christ has come, high priest 11 of good things already in being.ᵖ The tent of his priesthood is a greater and more perfect one, not made by men's hands, that is, not belonging to this created world; the blood of his sacrifice 12 is his own blood, not the blood of goats and calves; and thus he has entered the sanctuary once and for all and secured an eternal deliverance. For if the blood 13 of goats and bulls and the sprinkled ashes of a heifer have power to hallow those who have been defiled and restore their external purity, how much greater 14 is the power of the blood of Christ; he offered himself without blemish to God, a spiritual and eternal sacrifice; and his blood will cleanse our conscience from the deadness of our former ways and fit us for the service of the living God.

And therefore he is the mediator of 15 a new covenant, or testament, under which, now that there has been a death to bring deliverance from sins committed under the former covenant, those whom God has called may

o *Some witnesses read* brother and neighbour.
p *Some witnesses read* good things which were (*or* are) to be.

---

the author's view that there is a new covenant by which the old cultus has been rendered obsolete, a theme developed in several ways in the tract. **8–12**: Jer.31.31–34.
   9.1–10.18: A new and better sacrifice is offered by Christ. 1–10: These verses provide an idealized picture of the earthly place of sacrifice. **1–5**: See Ex. chs. 25–26. **6–9**: Under the old system only the *high priest* is permitted into the inmost *sanctuary* (beyond the second curtain), and he must first atone for his own and his family's sins (v. 7; Lev. ch. 16). **10–12**: The new covenant brings a *time of reformation* (v. 10), for with *Christ* as *high priest* (v. 11) the annual rites are replaced by one perfect sacrifice effective for *eternal deliverance* (v. 12). **13–14**: This priest's sacrificial offering is *without blemish* (see 4.15; 5.9) and it therefore achieves an inward cleansing for God's people. **15–22**: God's *new covenant* with his people is compared to a human *testament* which *is*

282

16 receive the promise of the eternal inheritance. For where there is a testament it is necessary for the death of the
17 testator to be established. A testament is operative only after a death: it cannot possibly have force while the testator is
18 alive. Thus we find that the former covenant itself was not inaugurated
19 without blood. For when, as the Law directed, Moses had recited all the commandments to the people, he took the blood of the calves, with water, scarlet wool, and marjoram, and sprinkled the law-book itself and all
20 the people, saying, 'This is the blood of the covenant which God has enjoined
21 upon you.' In the same way he also sprinkled the tent and all the vessels of
22 divine service with blood. Indeed, according to the Law, it might almost be said, everything is cleansed by blood and without the shedding of blood there is no forgiveness.
23 If, then, these sacrifices cleanse the copies of heavenly things, those heavenly things themselves require better
24 sacrifices to cleanse them. For Christ has entered, not that sanctuary made by men's hands which is only a symbol of the reality, but heaven itself, to appear now before God on our behalf.
25 Nor is he there to offer himself again and again, as the high priest enters the sanctuary year by year with blood not
26 his own. If that were so, he would have had to suffer many times since the world was made. But as it is, he has appeared once and for all at the climax of history to abolish sin by the sacrifice
27 of himself. And as it is the lot of men to die once, and after death comes judge-
28 ment, so Christ was offered once to bear the burden of men's sins,*q* and will appear a second time, sin done away, to bring salvation to those who are watching for him.

10 FOR THE LAW CONTAINS BUT A SHADOW, and no true image,*r* of the good things

which were to come; it provides for the same sacrifices year after year, and with these it can never bring the worshippers
2 to perfection for all time.*s* If it could, these sacrifices would surely have ceased to be offered, because the worshippers, cleansed once for all, would
3 no longer have any sense of sin. But instead, in these sacrifices year after
4 year sins are brought to mind, because sins can never be removed by the blood of bulls and goats.
5 That is why, at his coming into the world, he says:

'Sacrifice and offering thou didst not desire,
but thou hast prepared a body for me.
6 Whole-offerings and sin-offerings thou didst not delight in.
7 Then I said, "Here am I: as it is written of me in the scroll,
I have come, O God, to do thy will."'

8 First he says, 'Sacrifices and offerings, whole-offerings and sin-offerings, thou didst not desire nor delight in'— although the Law prescribes them—
9 and then he says, 'I have come to do thy will.' He thus annuls the former to
10 establish the latter. And it is by the will of God that we have been consecrated, through the offering of the body of Jesus Christ once and for all.
11 Every priest stands performing his service daily and offering time after time the same sacrifices, which can
12 never remove sins. But Christ offered for all time one sacrifice for sins, and took his seat at the right hand of God,
13 where he waits henceforth until his
14 enemies are made his footstool. For by one offering he has perfected for all time those who are thus consecrated.
15 Here we have also the testimony of the
16 Holy Spirit: he first says, 'This is the

q Or to remove men's sins.
r One witness reads a shadow and likeness . . .
s Or bring to perfection the worshippers who come continually.

operative only after the testator's *death*. Similarly, the *new covenant* is inaugurated by Christ's death. **18–22:** Ex.24.3–8. **23–28:** The main points of the discussion are again summarized (see vv. 26–28), and attention is directed to the salvation which awaits believers (v. 28). **10.1–18:** The *Law* does not lead to salvation. It betrays its own inferiority in dealing with sin by providing for repeated sacrifices. In contrast, Christ's sacrifice is *once and for all* (v. 10), therefore, self-validating. **5–7:** Ps.40.6–8 Sept., cited as Jesus' own words. **8–10:** In Christ's sacrifice the old system is annulled and God's people are now *consecrated* for true obedience. **12–13:** Ps.110.1. **16–17:** Jer.31.33–34. **18:** See vv. 11–12.

covenant which I will make with them after those days, says the Lord: I will set my laws in their hearts and write them on their understanding'; then he
17 adds, 'and their sins and wicked deeds
18 I will remember no more at all.' And where these have been forgiven, there are offerings for sin no longer.

19 SO NOW, MY FRIENDS, THE BLOOD OF Jesus makes us free to enter boldly into
20 the sanctuary by the new, living way which he has opened for us through
21 the curtain, the way of his flesh.*t* We have, moreover, a great priest set over
22 the household of God; so let us make our approach in sincerity of heart and full assurance of faith, our guilty hearts sprinkled clean, our bodies
23 washed with pure water. Let us be firm and unswerving in the confession of our hope, for the Giver of the
24 promise may be trusted. We ought to see how each of us may best arouse
25 others to love and active goodness, not staying away from our meetings, as some do, but rather encouraging one another, all the more because you see the Day drawing near.
26   For if we wilfully persist in sin after receiving the knowledge of the truth,
27 no sacrifice for sins remains: only a terrifying expectation of judgement and a fierce fire which will consume God's
28 enemies. If a man disregards the Law of Moses, he is put to death without pity on the evidence of two or three wit-
29 nesses. Think how much more severe a penalty that man will deserve who has trampled under foot the Son of God, profaned the blood of the covenant by which he was consecrated, and affront-
30 ed God's gracious Spirit! For we know who it is that has said, 'Justice is mine: I will repay'; and again, 'The Lord will
31 judge his people.' It is a terrible thing to fall into the hands of the living God.

Remember the days gone by, when, 32 newly enlightened, you met the challenge of great sufferings and held firm. Some of you were abused and tor- 33 mented to make a public show, while others stood loyally by those who were so treated. For indeed you shared the 34 sufferings of the prisoners, and you cheerfully accepted the seizure of your possessions, knowing that you possessed something better and more lasting. Do not then throw away your 35 confidence, for it carries a great reward. You need endurance, if you are 36 to do God's will and win what he has promised. For 'soon, very soon' (in the 37 words of Scripture), 'he who is to come will come; he will not delay; and by 38 faith my righteous servant shall find life; but if a man shrinks back, I take no pleasure in him.' But we are not 39 among those who shrink back and are lost; we have the faith to make life our own.

A call to faith

AND WHAT IS FAITH? FAITH GIVES **11** substance*u* to our hopes, and makes us certain of realities we do not see.

It is for their faith that the men of 2 old stand on record.

By faith we perceive that the universe 3 was fashioned by the word of God, so that the visible came forth from the invisible.

By faith, Abel offered a sacrifice 4 greater than Cain's, and through faith his goodness was attested, for his offerings had God's approval; and through faith he continued to speak after his death.

By faith Enoch was carried away to 5 another life without passing through

t Or through the curtain of his flesh.
u Or assurance.

10.19–13.17: Exhortations to live as God's pilgrim people. The theological discussion now gives way entirely to practical appeals. The hope enshrined in the new covenant and sealed by Christ's sacrifice should sustain and shape the life of God's people in this world. **19–39:** The author renews his plea that Christians remain *firm* and *unswerving* in the face of their difficulties. The exalted Christ is their *new, living way* to God (compare Jn.14.6). **26–31:** See 6.4–8 n. **28:** See, e.g. Deut.17.6. **30:** See Deut.32.35–36; Ps.135.14. **31:** See 12.29. **32–39:** Earlier post-conversion zeal should not be abandoned. **37–38:** Hab.2.3–4.

11.1–40: Examples of faith from Scripture are rehearsed to support the preceding exhortations. **1:** *Faith*, in this writer's view, means primarily holding fast to hope. See, e.g. vv.22–23; 6.11–12,19; 7.18–19. **3:** Gen. ch. 1. **4:** Gen.4.3–10. **5:** Gen.5.21–24. **7:** Gen.6.13–22. **8–9:** Gen.12.1–8.

death; he was not to be found, because God had taken him. For it is the testimony of Scripture that before he was 6 taken he had pleased God, and without faith it is impossible to please him; for anyone who comes to God must believe that he exists and that he rewards those who search for him.

7 By faith Noah, divinely warned about the unseen future, took good heed and built an ark to save his household. Through his faith he put the whole world in the wrong, and made good his own claim to the righteousness which comes of faith.

8 By faith Abraham obeyed the call to go out to a land destined for himself and his heirs, and left home without 9 knowing where he was to go. By faith he settled as an alien in the land promised him, living in tents, as did Isaac and Jacob, who were heirs to the same 10 promise. For he was looking forward to the city with firm foundations, whose architect and builder is God.

11 By faith even Sarah herself received strength to conceive, though she was past the age, because she judged that he who had promised would keep faith; 12 and therefore from one man, and one as good as dead, there sprang descendants numerous as the stars or as the countless grains of sand on the sea-shore.

13 All these persons died in faith. They were not yet in possession of the things promised, but had seen them far ahead and hailed them, and confessed themselves no more than strangers or passing 14 travellers on earth. Those who use such language show plainly that they are 15 looking for a country of their own. If their hearts had been in the country they had left, they could have found 16 opportunity to return. Instead, we find them longing for a better country— I mean, the heavenly one. That is why God is not ashamed to be called their God; for he has a city ready for them.

17 By faith Abraham, when the test came, offered up Isaac: he had received the promises, and yet he was on the point of offering his only son, of whom 18 he had been told, 'Through the line of Isaac your descendants shall be traced.'*v* For he reckoned that God 19 had power even to raise from the dead—and from the dead, he did, in a sense, receive him back.

By faith Isaac blessed Jacob and Esau 20 and spoke of things to come. By faith 21 Jacob, as he was dying, blessed each of Joseph's sons, and worshipped God, leaning on the top of his staff. By faith 22 Joseph, at the end of his life, spoke of the departure of Israel from Egypt, and instructed them what to do with his bones.

By faith, when Moses was born, his 23 parents hid him for three months, because they saw what a fine child he was; they were not afraid of the king's edict. By faith Moses, when he grew 24 up, refused to be called the son of Pharaoh's daughter, preferring to suffer 25 hardship with the people of God rather than enjoy the transient pleasures of sin. He considered the stigma that rests 26 on God's Anointed greater wealth than the treasures of Egypt, for his eyes were fixed upon the coming day of recompense. By faith he left Egypt, and not 27 because he feared the king's anger; for he was resolute, as one who saw the invisible God.

By faith he celebrated the Passover 28 and sprinkled the blood, so that the destroying angel might not touch the first-born of Israel. By faith they 29 crossed the Red Sea as though it were dry land, whereas the Egyptians, when they attempted the crossing, were drowned.

By faith the walls of Jericho fell down 30 after they had been encircled on seven successive days. By faith the prostitute 31 Rahab escaped the doom of the un-

v Or God's call shall be for your descendants in the line of Isaac.

10: The *city* is the new, spiritual Jerusalem; see, e.g. Rev. ch. 21. 11: Gen.18.9–15; 21.2. 12: Gen.15.5; 22.17–18. 13–16: Faith is hopeful pilgrimage toward the city of God, i.e. into God's presence; see 13.14. 17: Gen. ch. 22. 18: Gen.21.12. 19: Isaac was offered but did not die (Gen.22.13). 20: Gen.27.27–29,39–40. 21: Gen. ch. 48; 47.31 Sept. 22: Gen.50.24–25. 23: Ex.2.2; 1.22. 24–26: Moses' suffering is regarded as obedience to the example of Jesus, *God's Anointed*, who also shared the lot of *the people of God* (see Rom.15.3; Ex.2.10–15). 27: Ex.12.40–51. 28: Ex.12.21–30. 29: Ex.14.5–31. 30: Josh. ch. 6. 31: The basis is Josh.2.1–21; 6.22–25.

believers, because she had given the spies a kindly welcome.

32 Need I say more? Time is too short for me to tell the stories of Gideon, Barak, Samson, and Jephthah, of David and Samuel and the prophets.
33 Through faith they overthrew kingdoms, established justice, saw God's promises fulfilled. They muzzled raven-
34 ing lions, quenched the fury of fire, escaped death by the sword. Their weakness was turned to strength, they grew powerful in war, they put foreign
35 armies to rout. Women received back their dead raised to life. Others were tortured to death, disdaining release,
36 to win a better resurrection. Others, again, had to face jeers and flogging,
37 even fetters and prison bars. They were stoned,*w* they were sawn in two, they were put to the sword, they went about dressed in skins of sheep or goats, in
38 poverty, distress, and misery. They were too good for a world like this. They were refugees in deserts and on the hills, hiding in caves and holes in the
39 ground. These also, one and all, are commemorated for their faith; and yet they did not enter upon the promised
40 inheritance, because, with us in mind, God had made a better plan, that only in company with us should they reach their perfection.

12 AND WHAT OF OURSELVES? WITH ALL these witnesses to faith around us like a cloud, we must throw off every encumbrance, every sin to which we cling,*x* and run with resolution the race
2 for which we are entered, our eyes fixed on Jesus, on whom faith depends from start to finish: Jesus who, for the sake of the joy that lay ahead of him,*y* endured the cross, making light of its disgrace, and has taken his seat at the right hand of the throne of God.

3 Think of him who submitted to such opposition from sinners, that will help you not to lose heart and grow faint.
4 In your struggle against sin, you have not yet resisted to the point of shedding
5 your blood. You have forgotten the the text of Scripture which addresses you as sons and appeals to you in these words:

'My son, do not think lightly of the
    Lord's discipline,
nor lose heart when he corrects you;
6 for the Lord disciplines those whom
    he loves;
he lays the rod on every son whom
    he acknowledges.'

7 You must endure it as discipline: God is treating you as sons. Can anyone be a son, who is not disciplined by his
8 father? If you escape the discipline in which all sons share, you must be
9 bastards and no true sons. Again, we paid due respect to the earthly fathers who disciplined us; should we not submit even more readily to our spiritual Father, and so attain life?
10 They disciplined us for this short life according to their lights; but he does so for our true welfare, so that we may
11 share his holiness. Discipline, no doubt, is never pleasant; at the time it seems painful, but in the end it yields for those who have been trained by it the peace-
12 ful harvest of an honest life. Come, then, stiffen your drooping arms and
13 shaking knees, and keep your steps from wavering. Then the disabled limb will not be put out of joint, but regain its former powers.
14 Aim at peace with all men, and a holy life, for without that no one will

w Some witnesses insert they were put to the question.
x Or every clinging sin; *one witness reads* the sin which all too readily distracts us.
y Or who, in place of the joy that was open to him, . . .

32: *Gideon:* Judg. chs. 6–8. *Barak:* Judg. chs. 4–5. *Samson:* Judg. chs. 13–16. *Jephthah:* Judg. chs. 11–12. *David:* 1 Sam. chs. 16–30; 2 Sam. chs. 1–24; 3 1 Kgs.1.1–2.12. *Samuel:* 1 Sam. chs. 1–12; 15.1–16.13. **33–34:** *Lions . . . fire:* see Dan. chs. 6; 3. **35:** 1 Kgs.17.17–24; 2 Kgs.4.25–37; 2 Macc.6.18–7.42. **36:** Jer.20.2; 37.15; 38.6–13. **37:** 2 Chr.24.20–21; 1 Kgs.19.10; Jer.26.23; 2 Macc.5.27. **38:** 2 Macc.6.11; 10.6. **39–40:** The *better plan* was for a new covenant mediated by Christ (9.15–28).
    12.1–17: The discipline of faith. 1: The readers, like the *witnesses to faith* just recalled (ch. 11), should *run . . . the race* for salvation with disciplined *resolution;* see 10.39. **2:** Jesus' *joy* was to be seated at God's *right hand.* See 1.3 n. **5–6:** Prov. 3.11–12. **11–13:** After dealing with *discipline* in a familial context (vv. 7–10), the author returns to the analogy of the athletic contest (see vv. 1–2). **12:** Isa.35.3. **15:** Deut.29.18 Sept. **16–17:** Gen.25.29–34; 27.30–40.

15 see the Lord. Look to it that there is no one among you who forfeits the grace of God, no bitter, noxious weed 16 growing up to poison the whole, no immoral person, no one worldly-minded like Esau. He sold his birthright for 17 a single meal, and you know that although he wanted afterwards to claim the blessing, he was rejected; though he begged for it to the point of tears, he found no way open for second thoughts.

18 REMEMBER WHERE YOU STAND: NOT before the palpable, blazing fire of Sinai, with the darkness, gloom, and 19 whirlwind, the trumpet-blast and the oracular voice, which they heard, and 20 begged to hear no more; for they could not bear the command, 'If even an animal touches the mountain, it must 21 be stoned.' So appalling was the sight, that Moses said, 'I shudder with fear.' 22 No, you stand before Mount Zion and the city of the living God, heavenly 23 Jerusalem, before myriads of angels, the full concourse and assembly of the first-born citizens of heaven, and God the judge of all, and the spirits of good men 24 made perfect, and Jesus the mediator of a new covenant, whose sprinkled blood has better things to tell than the 25 blood of Abel. See that you do not refuse to hear the voice that speaks. Those who refused to hear the oracle speaking on earth found no escape; still less shall we escape if we refuse to hear the One who speaks from heaven. 26 Then indeed his voice shook the earth, but now he has promised, 'Yet once again I will shake not earth alone, but 27 the heavens also.' The words 'once again'—and only once—imply that the shaking of these created things means their removal, and then what is not shaken will remain. The kingdom we 28 are given is unshakable; let us therefore give thanks to God, and so worship him as he would be worshipped, with reverence and awe; for our God is a de- 29 vouring fire.

NEVER CEASE TO LOVE YOUR FELLOW- **13** Christians.

Remember to show hospitality. There 2 are some who, by so doing, have entertained angels without knowing it.

Remember those in prison as if you 3 were there with them; and those who are being maltreated, for you like them are still in the world.

Marriage is honourable; let us all keep 4 it so, and the marriage-bond inviolate; for God's judgement will fall on fornicators and adulterers.

Do not live for money; be content 5 with what you have; for God himself has said, 'I will never leave you or desert you'; and so we can take courage 6 and say, 'The Lord is my helper, I will not fear; what can man do to me?'

Remember your leaders, those who 7 first spoke God's message to you; and reflecting upon the outcome of their life and work, follow the example of their faith.

Jesus Christ is the same yesterday, 8 today, and for ever. So do not be swept 9 off your course by all sorts of outlandish teachings; it is good that our souls should gain their strength from the grace of God, and not from scruples about what we eat, which have never done any good to those who were governed by them.

Our altar is one from which[z] the 10 priests of the sacred tent have no right to eat. As you know, those animals 11 whose blood is brought as a sin-offering

z *Or* one like that from which . . .

12.18–29: The true worship of God is enabled by the new covenant, not by the old. **18–21:** The old covenant produces fear; see Ex.19.12–22; 20.18–20. **22–29:** Glorious as the new covenant is (vv. 22–24,28), there is all the more reason for the disobedient to fear. **22:** See 11.10 n. **24:** Christ's blood means forgiveness, not revenge; see Gen.4.10. **26:** Hag.2.6. **29:** Deut.4.24.
 13.1–17: Concluding admonitions. 1: See 10.24. **2:** Itinerant Christian teachers should be accommodated; see 3 Jn.5–8. The mention of *angels* recalls Gen. chs. 18–19. **3:** See Mt.25.31–46. The Christians' pilgrimage toward heaven (see, e.g. v. 14) does not exempt them from being actively concerned about the welfare of those in distress, for during the time of their pilgrimage they *are still in the world.* **5:** Josh.1.5. **6:** Ps.118.6. **7:** The *leaders* mentioned here are probably not the heroes and heroines of faith cataloged in ch. 11, but Christian preachers and teachers, perhaps including both the original apostles (2.3) and those who now exercise leadership in the church (v. 17). **8:** See 1.12. **9:** See Col.2.16–23. **11:** *Sin-offering . . . outside:* see Lev.16.27.

by the high priest into the sanctuary, have their bodies burnt outside the
12 camp, and therefore Jesus also suffered outside the gate, to consecrate the
13 people by his own blood. Let us then go to him outside the camp, bearing
14 the stigma that he bore. For here we have no permanent home, but we are seekers after the city which is to come.
15 Through Jesus, then, let us continually offer up to God the sacrifice of praise, that is, the tribute of lips which ac-
16 knowledge his name, and never forget to show kindness and to share what you have with others; for such are the sacrifices which God approves.
17 Obey your leaders and defer to them; for they are tireless in their concern for you, as men who must render an account. Let it be a happy task for them, and not pain and grief, for that would bring you no advantage.
18 Pray for us; for we are convinced that our conscience is clear; our one

desire is always to do what is right. All 19 the more earnestly I ask for your prayers, that I may be restored to you the sooner.

May the God of peace, who brought 20 up from the dead our Lord Jesus, the great Shepherd of the sheep, by the blood of the eternal covenant, make 21 you perfect in all goodness so that you may do his will; and may he make of us what he would have us be through Jesus Christ, to whom be glory for ever and ever! Amen.

I beg you, brothers, bear with this 22 exhortation; for it is after all a short letter. I have news for you: our friend 23 Timothy has been released; and if he comes in time he will be with me when I see you.

Greet all your leaders and all God's 24 people. Greetings to you from our Italian friends.

God's grace be with you all!   25

12–14: Christians are a pilgrim people consecrated by Christ, *seekers after* the new Jerusalem (see 11.10). **15–16:** The true *sacrifice of praise* (see Lev.7.12) is offered by Christians and is manifest in their conduct. See Jas.1.27.

13.18–25: Epistolary conclusion. Some or all of these last paragraphs may have been added by a later editor, for the writing overall has more characteristics of a homily than of a letter. **23:** *Timothy:* see Acts 16.1 n.

A LETTER OF
JAMES

This writer is concerned to rescue sinners from their "crooked ways" (5.20) by providing a manual for Christian conduct. Many topics are handled in fairly miscellaneous fashion, although four points receive more sustained attention: the evil of showing partiality (2.1–12), the need for works along with faith (2.14–26), the danger of loose talk (3.1–12), and the sins of the rich (4.13–5.6). This manual has been sent out to the church as a whole, and its purpose is completely practical. Doctrinal matters are not taken up, and the content of the moral advice does not reveal much about the author's own theological point of view. Most of his teaching is common to other Hellenistic Wisdom literature of his day.

If the writing is indeed from James, the Lord's brother (see 1.1 n.), a date no later than about 60 A.D. is required. However, because the ritual and cultic concerns attributed to James elsewhere (see Gal.2.12) are absent and because the overall cast is so Hellenistic, many scholars question the traditional view of authorship. Some have held that the tract is of Jewish origin, subsequently lightly Christianized. More often, it is ascribed to a Christian writer of the late first or early second century. There is no consensus as to the place of writing.

Practical religion

1 FROM JAMES, A SERVANT OF GOD AND the Lord Jesus Christ.

Greetings to the Twelve Tribes dispersed throughout the world.

2 My brothers, whenever you have to face trials of many kinds, count your- 3 selves supremely happy, in the knowledge that such testing of your faith 4 breeds fortitude, and if you give fortitude full play you will go on to complete a balanced character that 5 will fall short in nothing. If any of you falls short in wisdom, he should ask God for it and it will be given him, for God is a generous giver who neither 6 refuses nor reproaches anyone. But he must ask in faith, without a doubt in his mind; for the doubter is like a heav- 7 ing sea ruffled by the wind. A man of that kind must not expect the Lord to 8 give him anything; he is double-minded, and never can keep[a] a steady course.

9 The brother in humble circumstances may well be proud that God 10 lifts him up; and the wealthy brother must find his pride in being brought low. For the rich man will disappear like the flower of the field; once the sun 11 is up with its scorching heat the flower withers, its petals fall, and what was lovely to look at is lost for ever. So shall the rich man wither away as he goes about his business.

Happy the man who remains stead- 12 fast under trial, for having passed that test he will receive for his prize the gift of life promised to those who love God. No one under trial or temptation should 13 say, 'I am being tempted by God'; for God is untouched by evil,[b] and does not himself tempt anyone. Temptation 14 arises when a man is enticed and lured 15 away by his own lust; then lust conceives, and gives birth to sin; and sin full-grown breeds death.

Make no mistake, my friends. All 16,17 good giving, every perfect gift, comes[c] from above, from the Father of lights of heaven. With him there is no variation, no play of passing shadows.[d] Of his set purpose, by declaring the 18 truth, he gave us birth to be a kind of firstfruits of his creatures.

a *Or* anything; a double-minded man never keeps ...
b *Or* God cannot be tempted by evil.
c *Or* All giving is good, and every perfect gift comes ...
d *Some witnesses read* no variation, or shadow caused by change.

1.1: Salutation. *James:* probably the brother of Jesus (Mt.13.55; see Jude 1), although this is not specified. The church is in the world like the *Twelve Tribes* of Israel. **1.2–27: Miscellaneous topics:** *fortitude* (vv. 2–4), *wisdom* (vv. 5–8), *wealth* (vv. 9–11), *trial* (v. 12), *temptation* (vv. 13–15), God's beneficence (vv. 16–18), *anger* (vv. 19–21), true religion (vv. 22–27). **2–4:** *Fortitude:* see 5.7–11; Prov.3.11–12. **5–8:** *Wisdom* is understood by James as moral purity; see 3.13–17. *Faith* is belief in God; see 2.19. **9–11:** The theme of the *wealthy* and the *humble* is important in this tract; see 2.1–7; 4.13–5.6. **10–11:** Isa.40.6–7. **12:** Outward trials: see Dan.12.12 Sept.; Rev.2.10; 1 Pet.5.4. **18:** As *firstfruits* Christians are heralds of a new age;

19 Of that you may be certain, my friends. But each of you must be quick to listen, slow to speak, and slow to be 20 angry. For a man's anger cannot pro- 21 mote the justice of God. Away then with all that is sordid, and the malice that hurries to excess, and quietly accept the message planted in your hearts, which can bring you salvation.

22 Only be sure that you act on the message and do not merely listen; for that 23 would be to mislead yourselves. A man who listens to the message but never acts upon it is like one who looks in a 24 mirror at the face nature gave him. He glances at himself and goes away, and at once forgets what he looked like. 25 But the man who looks closely into the perfect law, the law that makes us free, and who lives in its company, does not forget what he hears, but acts upon it, and that is the man who by acting will find happiness.

26 A man may think he is religious, but if he has no control over his tongue, he is deceiving himself; that man's religion 27 is futile. The kind of religion which is without stain or fault in the sight of God our Father is this: to go to the help of orphans and widows in their distress and keep oneself untarnished by the world.

2 MY BROTHERS, BELIEVING AS YOU DO IN our Lord Jesus Christ, who reigns in glory, you must never show snobbery. 2 For instance, two visitors may enter your place of worship, one a well-dressed man with gold rings, and the other a poor man in shabby clothes. 3 Suppose you pay special attention to the well-dressed man and say to him, 'Please take this seat', while to the poor man you say, 'You can stand; or you may sit here*e* on the floor by my foot- 4 stool', do you not see that you are in-

consistent and judge by false standards?

Listen, my friends. Has not God 5 chosen those who are poor in the eyes of the world to be rich in faith and to inherit the kingdom he has promised to those who love him? And yet you 6 have insulted the poor man. Moreover, are not the rich your oppressors? Is it not they who drag you into court and 7 pour contempt on the honoured name by which God has claimed you?

If, however, you are observing the 8 sovereign law laid down in Scripture, 'Love your neighbour as yourself', that is excellent. But if you show snobbery, 9 you are committing a sin and you stand convicted by that law as transgressors. For if a man keeps the whole law apart 10 from one single point, he is guilty of breaking all of it. For the One who said, 11 'Thou shalt not commit adultery', said also, 'Thou shalt not commit murder.' You may not be an adulterer, but if you commit murder you are a law-breaker all the same. Always speak and act as 12 men who are to be judged under a law of freedom. In that judgement there 13 will be no mercy for the man who has shown no mercy. Mercy triumphs over judgement.

MY BROTHERS, WHAT USE IS IT FOR A MAN 14 to say he has faith when he does nothing to show it? Can that faith save him? Suppose a brother or a sister is in 15 rags with not enough food for the day, and one of you says, 'Good luck to you, 16 keep yourselves warm, and have plenty to eat', but does nothing to supply their bodily needs, what is the good of that? So with faith; if it does not lead to ac- 17 tion, it is in itself a lifeless thing.

But someone may object: 'Here is 18 one who claims to have faith and an-

---

e Some witnesses read Stand where you are or sit here . . .; *others read* Stand where you are or sit . . .

---

see Rom.8.23; 11.16. **19–21**: On *anger*, see 3.1–12. **21**: The *message* is the gospel. **22–25**: On moral *action*, see 2.14–26. **25**: The gospel is *the perfect law . . . that makes us free*, and demands studied attention and obedience. **26**: On false speech, see 3.1–12. **27**: True religion is defined here, not as doctrine or knowledge or ritual, but as moral action. *World:* see 2.5; 3.6; 4.4.

2.1–13: On partiality and privilege. No favors should be accorded the rich. **5:** See 1 Cor. 1.26–31. **6–7:** Christians are reminded of the social and economic exploitation for which rich nonbelievers are responsible; see 5.4–6. *The honoured name* is "Christ." **8:** The *sovereign law:* either *Scripture* as a whole or the love commandment in particular (Lev.19.18). **11:** Ex.20.13–14. **12:** *Freedom:* see 1.25 n. **13:** See, e.g. Mt.5.7.

2.14–26: On faith and works. 14 17: If *faith* only means belief in God (see v. 19) it is as meaningless as if one were to wish the needy well without lending a hand. **18:** *Someone:* a

other who points to his deeds.' To which I reply: 'Prove to me that this faith you speak of is real though not accompanied by deeds, and by my deeds 19 I will prove to you my faith.' You have faith enough to believe that there is one God. Excellent! The devils have faith like that, and it makes them tremble. 20 But can you not see, you quibbler, that faith divorced from deeds is barren? 21 Was it not by his action, in offering his son Isaac upon the altar, that our father 22 Abraham was justified? Surely you can see that faith was at work in his actions, and that by these actions the integrity 23 of his faith was fully proved. Here was fulfilment of the words of Scripture: 'Abraham put his faith in God, and that faith was counted to him as righteousness'; and elsewhere he is 24 called 'God's friend'. You see then that a man is justified by deeds and not by 25 faith in itself. The same is true of the prostitute Rahab also. Was not she justified by her action in welcoming the messengers into her house and sending 26 them away by a different route? As the body is dead when there is no breath left in it, so faith divorced from deeds is lifeless as a corpse.

3 My BROTHERS, NOT MANY OF YOU should become teachers, for you may be certain that we who teach shall ourselves be judged with greater strictness. 2 All of us often go wrong; the man who never says a wrong thing is a perfect character, able to bridle his whole being. 3 If we put bits into horses' mouths to make them obey our will, we can direct 4 their whole body. Or think of ships: large they may be, yet even when driven by strong gales they can be directed by a tiny rudder on whatever course the 5 helmsman chooses. So with the tongue.

It is a small member but it can make huge claims.*f*

What an immense stack of timber*g* can be set ablaze by the tiniest spark! And the tongue is in effect a fire. It rep- 6 resents among our members the world with all its wickedness; it pollutes our whole being; it keeps the wheel of our existence red-hot, and its flames are fed by hell. Beasts and birds of every kind, 7 creatures that crawl on the ground or swim in the sea, can be subdued and have been subdued by mankind; but no 8 man can subdue the tongue. It is an intractable evil, charged with deadly venom. We use it to sing the praises of 9 our Lord and Father, and we use it to invoke curses upon our fellow-men who are made in God's likeness. Out 10 of the same mouth come praises and curses. My brothers, this should not be so. Does a fountain gush with both 11 fresh and brackish water from the same opening? Can a fig-tree, my brothers, 12 yield olives, or a vine figs? No more does salt water yield fresh.

WHO AMONG YOU IS WISE OR CLEVER? 13 Let his right conduct give practical proof of it, with the modesty that comes of wisdom. But if you are harbouring 14 bitter jealousy and selfish ambition in your hearts, consider whether your claims are not false, and a defiance of the truth. This is not the wisdom that 15 comes from above; it is earth-bound, sensual, demonic. For with jealousy 16 and ambition come disorder and evil of every kind. But the wisdom from 17 above is in the first place pure; and then peace-loving, considerate, and open to reason; it is straightforward and sincere, rich in mercy and in the kindly deeds that are its fruit. True 18

f Or it is a great boaster. *g Or* What a huge forest . . .

---

hypothetical inquirer who misunderstands the point that the same person must give evidence of both faith and action (v. 17). **21:** See Gen.22.9–19; Heb.11.17–19. **23:** Jewish teaching (see 1 Macc.2.52) associated Gen. ch. 22 with the commendation of Abraham's *righteousness* in Gen.15.6. Whereas Paul interpreted *counted* (Gen.15.6) to mean God's free gift of acquittal (Rom.4.3–5), here it is interpreted as God's acceptance of Abraham's works. *Friend:* a common description of Abraham; see 2 Chr.20.7; Isa.41.8. **25:** *Rahab:* see Josh. ch. 2; 6.17; Heb.11.31.

3.1–12: On the evils of the tongue. 6: See 1.27. *Wheel of our existence:* a phrase borrowed from the Hellenistic mystery religions, used here to describe the orderly design of man's life. **7:** See Gen.9.2–3. Elsewhere it is presumed one's tongue can be controlled (vv. 2–4; 1.26). **9:** *In God's likeness:* see Gen. 1.26–27.

3.13–5.20: Miscellaneous topics.

3.13–18: On true wisdom. The essence of wisdom is moral uprightness. **17:** See Paul's description of love, 1 Cor. ch. 13. **18:** See Prov.11.30; 13.2; Phil.1.11.

justice is the harvest reaped by peace-makers from seeds sown in a spirit of peace.

4 What causes conflicts and quarrels among you? Do they not spring from the aggressiveness of your bodily 2 desires? You want something which you cannot have, and so you are bent on murder; you are envious, and cannot attain your ambition, and so you quarrel and fight. You do not get what you want, because you do not pray for 3 it. Or, if you do, your requests are not granted because you pray from wrong motives, to spend what you get on 4 your pleasures. You false, unfaithful creatures! Have you never learned that love of the world is enmity to God? Whoever chooses to be the world's 5 friend makes himself God's enemy. Or do you suppose that Scripture has no meaning when it says that the spirit which God implanted in man turns 6 towards envious desires? And yet the grace he gives is stronger. Thus Scripture says, 'God opposes the arrogant 7 and gives grace to the humble.' Be sub-missive then to God. Stand up to the 8 devil and he will turn and run. Come close to God, and he will come close to you. Sinners, make your hands clean; you who are double-minded, see that 9 your motives are pure. Be sorrowful, mourn and weep. Turn your laughter into mourning and your gaiety into 10 gloom. Humble yourselves before God and he will lift you high.

11 Brothers, you must never disparage one another. He who disparages a brother or passes judgement on his brother disparages the law and judges the law. But if you judge the law, you are not keeping it but sitting in judge-12 ment upon it. There is only one law-giver and judge, the One who is able to save life and destroy it. So who are you to judge your neighbour?

A WORD WITH YOU, YOU WHO SAY, 13 'Today or tomorrow we will go off to such and such a town and spend a year there trading and making money.' Yet 14 you have no idea what tomorrow will bring. Your life, what is it? You are no more than a mist, seen for a little while and then dispersing. What you ought 15 to say is: 'If it be the Lord's will, we shall live to do this or that.' But instead, 16 you boast and brag, and all such boast-ing is wrong. Well then, the man who 17 knows the good he ought to do and does not do it is a sinner.

Next a word to you who have great 5 possessions. Weep and wail over the miserable fate descending on you. Your 2 riches have rotted; your fine clothes are moth-eaten; your silver and gold have 3 rusted away, and their very rust will be evidence against you and consume your flesh like fire. You have piled up wealth in an age that is near its close. The 4 wages you never paid to the men who mowed your fields are loud against you, and the outcry of the reapers has reached the ears of the Lord of Hosts. You have lived on earth in wanton 5 luxury, fattening yourselves like cattle —and the day for slaughter has come. You have condemned the innocent and 6 murdered him; he offers no resistance.

Be patient, my brothers, until the 7 Lord comes. The farmer looking for the precious crop his land may yield can only wait in patience, until the autumn and spring rains have fallen. You too must be patient and stout-8 hearted, for the coming of the Lord is near. My brothers, do not blame your 9 troubles on one another, or you will fall under judgement; and there stands the Judge, at the door. If you want a 10 pattern of patience under ill-treatment, take the prophets who spoke in the name of the Lord; remember: 'We 11 count those happy who stood firm.'

4.1–5: **On friendship with the world. 3:** See Mt.17.20. **4:** See 1.27; 2.23. **5:** It is unclear what *Scripture* reference is meant.
4.6–10: **On drawing near to God. 6:** Prov.3.34; see 1 Pet.5.5. **7–8:** See 1 Pet.5.8–9; Heb.10.22. **9–10:** The penitent sinner receives God's forgiveness.
4.11–12: **On judging a neighbor.** The *law* demands love, not judgment (Lev.19.18; see 2.9–13).
4.13–5.6: **On the sins of the rich. 13–17:** Traveling merchants are criticized for their worldliness. 5.1–6: Wealthy landholders are criticized for their greed and indifference to social justice. Compare Ecclus.29.10–13. **6:** See Wis.2.10–20.
5.7–11: **On patience. 7:** *The Lord:* perhaps a reference to God (v. 4; 3.9), but probably a reference to Christ's return. **9:** See 4.11–12. **10:** See Heb.11.32–38. **11:** See Job ch. 1; 42.10–16.

You have all heard how Job stood firm, and you have seen how the Lord treated him in the end. For the Lord is full of pity and compassion.

12 ABOVE ALL THINGS, MY BROTHERS, DO not use oaths, whether 'by heaven' or 'by earth' or by anything else. When you say yes or no, let it be plain 'Yes' or 'No', for fear that you expose yourselves to judgement.

13 Is anyone among you in trouble? He should turn to prayer. Is anyone in good
14 heart? He should sing praises. Is one of you ill? He should send for the elders of the congregation to pray over him and anoint him with oil in the name
15 of the Lord. The prayer offered in faith will save the sick man, the Lord will raise him from his bed, and any sins he

may have committed will be forgiven.
16 Therefore confess your sins to one another, and pray for one another, and then you will be healed. A good man's prayer is powerful and effective. Elijah
17 was a man with human frailties like our own; and when he prayed earnestly that there should be no rain, not a drop fell on the land for three years and a
18 half; then he prayed again, and down came the rain and the land bore crops once more.

19 My brothers, if one of your number should stray from the truth and another
20 succeed in bringing him back, be sure of this: any man who brings a sinner back from his crooked ways will be rescuing his soul from death and cancelling innumerable sins.

5.12: On oaths. See Mt.5.34–37.
5.13–18: On prayer. 14: See Mk.6.13. **15:** See 1 Cor.13.2. **17–18:** 1 Kgs. chs. 17–18 says nothing about Elijah's prayers; the reference is to noncanonical Jewish traditions.
5.19–20: On restoring sinners. 19: The *truth:* the gospel; see 1.18. **20:** See 1 Pet.4.8 n.

THE FIRST LETTER OF
PETER

This letter is directed to congregations of predominantly Gentile Christians scattered throughout several Roman provinces in Asia Minor. It is an appeal to Christians to "stand fast" in the gospel (5.12) and to rejoice in whatever sufferings they are called upon to endure for their faith (4.12–16).

Following the salutation (1.1–2) a prefatory section focuses on the reality and responsibilities of the new life in Christ (1.3–2.10). Subsequently, a number of specific exhortations are issued which deal with the Christian's conduct in his daily affairs (2.11–4.6) and with his relationship to others in the church itself (4.7–11). Finally, the writer summarizes the meaning of suffering as a Christian (4.12–19) and concludes with some specific matters (5.1–14).

If Peter himself wrote this letter, or caused it to be written by Silvanus (5.12), it perhaps reflects Nero's persecution of Christians about 64 A.D. Some scholars, however, believe the good Greek style and the theological point of view preclude Petrine authorship or sponsorship. In this case the author would be an anonymous Christian concerned for the church's tribulations during the reign either of Domitian (81–96 A.D.) or of Trajan (98–117 A.D.), and would perhaps be using some traditional liturgical and catechetical materials (1.3–4.11).

The calling of a Christian

1 FROM PETER, APOSTLE OF JESUS Christ, to those of God's scattered people who lodge for a while in Pontus, Galatia, Cappadocia, Asia, 2 and Bithynia—chosen of old in the purpose of God the Father, hallowed to his service by the Spirit, and consecrated with the sprinkled blood of Jesus Christ.

Grace and peace to you in fullest measure.

3 Praise be to the God and Father of our Lord Jesus Christ, who in his great mercy gave us new birth into a living hope by the resurrection of Jesus Christ 4 from the dead! The inheritance to which we are born is one that nothing can destroy or spoil or wither. It is kept 5 for you in heaven, and you, because you put your faith in God, are under the protection of his power until salvation comes—the salvation which is even now in readiness and will be revealed at the end of time.

6 This is cause for great joy, even though now you smart for a little while, if need be, under trials of many kinds.
7 Even gold passes through the assayer's fire, and more precious than perishable gold is faith which has stood the test. These trials come so that your faith may prove itself worthy of all praise, glory, and honour when Jesus Christ is revealed.

8 You have not seen him, yet you love him; and trusting in him now without seeing him, you are transported with a joy too great for words, while you reap 9 the harvest of your faith, that is, salvation for your souls. This salvation was 10 the theme which the prophets pondered and explored, those who prophesied about the grace of God awaiting you. They tried to find out what was the 11 time,*a* and what the circumstances, to which the spirit of Christ in them pointed, foretelling the sufferings in store for Christ and the splendours to follow; and it was disclosed to them 12 that the matter they treated of was not for their time but for yours. And now it has been openly announced to you through preachers who brought you the Gospel in the power of the Holy Spirit sent from heaven. These are things that angels long to see into.

a Or who was the person . . .

1.1–2: Salutation. Christians are temporary residents of this world, for they belong to God; see 2.9–10. *Sprinkled blood* refers to baptism into Christ's death; see Heb.9.13–14.

1.3–9: The new birth. 4: Our *inheritance* is God's continuing love, accepted through baptism. **5:** *Salvation* is sure, but comes fully only in the future. **6:** The *trials* faced by Christians could include even persecution; see Introduction.

1.10–12: The testimony of the prophets. Salvation has always been God's purpose; even the prophets preached the gospel; see 1.23–25.

13 You must therefore be mentally stripped for action, perfectly self-controlled. Fix your hopes on the gift of grace which is to be yours when Jesus
14 Christ is revealed. As obedient children, do not let your characters be shaped any longer by the desires you cherished
15 in your days of ignorance. The One who called you is holy; like him, be
16 holy in all your behaviour, because Scripture says, 'You shall be holy, for I am holy.'
17 If you say 'our Father' to the One who judges every man impartially on the record of his deeds, you must stand in awe of him while you live out your
18 time on earth. Well you know that it was no perishable stuff, like gold or silver, that bought your freedom from the empty folly of your traditional
19 ways. The price was paid in precious blood, as it were of a lamb without mark or blemish—the blood of Christ.
20 Predestined before the foundation of the world, he was made manifest in this last period of time for your sake.
21 Through him you have come to trust in God who raised him from the dead and gave him glory, and so your faith and hope are fixed on God.
22 Now that by obedience to the truth you have purified your souls until you feel sincere affection towards your brother Christians, love one another whole-heartedly with all your strength.
23 You have been born anew, not of mortal parentage but of immortal, through the living and enduring word
24 of God.*b* For (as Scripture says)

'All mortals are like grass;
all their splendour like the flower of the field;
the grass withers, the flower falls;
25 but the word of the Lord endures for evermore.'

And this 'word' is the word of the Gospel preached to you.

2 Then away with all malice and deceit, away with all pretence and jealousy and recrimination of every kind! Like the
2 new-born infants you are, you must crave for pure milk (spiritual milk, I mean), so that you may thrive upon it
3 to your souls' health. Surely you have tasted that the Lord is good.
4 So come to him, our living Stone — the stone rejected by men but choice and precious in the sight of God. Come,
5 and let yourselves be built, as living stones, into a spiritual temple; become a holy priesthood,*c* to offer spiritual sacrifices acceptable to God through Jesus Christ. For it stands written:
6

'I lay in Zion a choice corner-stone of great worth.
The man who has faith in it will not be put to shame.'

7 The great worth of which it speaks is for you who have faith. For those who have no faith, the stone which the builders rejected has become not only the corner-stone,*d* but also 'a stone to
8 trip over, a rock to stumble against'. They fall when they disbelieve the Word. Such was their appointed lot!
9 But you are a chosen race, a royal priesthood, a dedicated nation, and a people claimed by God for his own, to proclaim the triumphs of him who has called you out of darkness into his marvellous light. You are now the
10 people of God, who once were not his people; outside his mercy once, you have now received his mercy.

11 DEAR FRIENDS, I BEG YOU, AS ALIENS IN a foreign land, to abstain from the lusts

b Or through the word of the living and enduring God.
c Or a spiritual temple for the holy work of priesthood.
d Or the apex of the building.

1.13–2.10: **The responsibilities of obedient children. 13–16:** Hope should conform one's life to the holiness of God himself; see Lev.11.44–45; Eph.2.1–3. **17:** *Our Father:* the Lord's Prayer. **20:** See 1.10–12 n. **21:** See 1.2–3. **22:** *Now . . . purified:* in baptism; see vv. 1–2 n., 4 n. **25:** The *Gospel* is that God remains active for salvation (Isa.40.6–9); see 1.10–12. **2.2:** *Pure milk:* the Lord's goodness (2.3); see Ps.34.8. **4:** *Our living Stone:* the risen Christ; see Ps.118.22; Isa. 8.14; 28.16, passages frequently applied to Christ in the early church. **5:** Since Christ is a new *temple,* replacing the one in Jerusalem (see Jn.2.19–22), Christians are its *living stones,* and are a new *priesthood,* replacing the Jerusalem priests. *Spiritual sacrifices:* Christian obedience (see Rom.12.1). **6:** Isa.28.16. **7:** Ps.118.22. **8:** Unbelievers will be judged; see Isa.8.14–15. **9–10:** See the images in Isa.43.20–21; Ex.19.6; Hos. chs. 1–2. God's people are not passive. **2.11–4.6: Christian conduct in the world. 11–12:** *As aliens:* see 1.1–2 n.; Rom.12.2.

of the flesh which are at war with the
12 soul. Let all your behaviour be such as
even pagans can recognize as good, and
then, whereas they malign you as
criminals now, they will come to see
for themselves that you live good lives,
and will give glory to God on the day
when he comes to hold assize.

13 Submit yourselves to every human
institution for the sake of the Lord,
whether to the sovereign as supreme,
14 or to the governor as his deputy for the
punishment of criminals and the com-
15 mendation of those who do right. For
it is the will of God that by your good
conduct you should put ignorance and
stupidity to silence.

16 Live as free men; not however as
though your freedom were there to
provide a screen for wrongdoing, but as
17 slaves in God's service. Give due
honour to everyone: love to the
brotherhood, reverence to God, honour
to the sovereign.

18 Servants, accept the authority of
your masters with all due submission,
not only when they are kind and considerate, but even when they are
19 perverse. For it is a fine*e* thing if a man
endure the pain of undeserved suffering
20 because God is in his thoughts. What
credit is there in fortitude when you
have done wrong and are beaten for it?
But when you have behaved well and
suffer for it, your fortitude is a fine
21 thing*f* in the sight of God. To that you
were called, because Christ suffered*g*
on your behalf, and thereby left you an
example; it is for you to follow in his
22 steps. He committed no sin, he was
23 convicted of no falsehood; when he
was abused he did not retort with
abuse, when he suffered he uttered no
threats, but committed his cause to the
24 One who judges justly. In his own person he carried our sins to*h* the gibbet,
so that we might cease to live for sin
and begin to live for righteousness. By
25 his wounds you have been healed. You
were straying like sheep, but now you

have turned towards the Shepherd and
Guardian of your souls.

3 In the same way you women must
accept the authority of your husbands,
so that if there are any of them who disbelieve the Gospel they may be won
2 over, without a word being said, by
observing the chaste and reverent behaviour of their wives. Your beauty 3
should reside, not in outward adornment—the braiding of the hair, or
jewellery, or dress—but in the inmost 4
centre of your being, with its imperishable ornament, a gentle, quiet spirit,
which is of high value in the sight of
God. Thus it was among God's people 5
in days of old: the women who fixed
their hopes on him adorned themselves
by submission to their husbands. Such 6
was Sarah, who obeyed Abraham and
called him 'my master'. Her children
you have now become, if you do good
and show no fear.

In the same way, you husbands must 7
conduct your married life with understanding: pay honour to the woman's
body, not only because it is weaker,
but also because you share together in
the grace of God which gives you life.
Then your prayers will not be hindered.

To sum up: be one in thought and 8
feeling, all of you; be full of brotherly
affection, kindly and humble-minded.
Do not repay wrong with wrong, or 9
abuse with abuse; on the contrary,
retaliate with blessing, for a blessing is
the inheritance to which you yourselves
have been called.

'Whoever loves life and would see   10
    good days
must restrain his tongue from evil
and his lips from deceit;
must turn from wrong and do good,   11
seek peace and pursue it.
For the Lord's eyes are turned   12
    towards the righteous,

e Or creditable.
f Or is creditable.
g Some witnesses read died.
h Or on.

13–15: *Human institution:* the political order, which deserves support when it functions for the public good. See also Rom.13.1–7. **16–17:** See Rom.6.15–23. **18–25:** The death of Christ, identified here with that of the "suffering servant" of Isa.53.5–12, is first advanced as an *example* of trust (see Eph.6.5–8; Col.3.22–25). **24–25:** Christ's death is also redemptive (see 3.18; Rom.5.6–11; Col.2.14). **3.1–7:** See Eph.5.21–33; Col.3.18–19. **6:** Gen.18.12. **8–12:** *Brotherly affection* is the sign of the new birth; see 1.22. **9:** Lk.6.27–28; Rom.12.17. **10:** Ps.34.12–16.

his ears are open to their prayers;
but the Lord's face is set against
wrong-doers.'

13 WHO IS GOING TO DO YOU WRONG IF
14 you are devoted to what is good? And
yet if you should suffer for your virtues,
you may count yourselves happy. Have
no fear of them:*i* do not be perturbed,
15 but hold the Lord Christ in reverence
in your hearts.*j* Be always ready with
your defence whenever you are called
to account for the hope that is in you,
but make that defence with modesty
16 and respect. Keep your conscience
clear, so that when you are abused,
those who malign your Christian con-
17 duct may be put to shame. It is better
to suffer for well-doing, if such should
be the will of God, than for doing
18 wrong. For Christ also died*k* for our
sins*l* once and for all. He, the just,
suffered for the unjust, to bring us to
God.

In the body he was put to death, in
19 the spirit he was brought to life. And
in the spirit he went and made his proclamation to the imprisoned spirits.
20 They had refused obedience long ago,
while God waited patiently in the days
of Noah and the building of the ark,
and in the ark a few persons, eight in
all, were brought to safety through the
21 water. This water prefigured the water
of baptism through which you are now
brought to safety. Baptism is not the
washing away of bodily pollution, but
the appeal made to God by a good
conscience; and it brings salvation
through the resurrection of Jesus
22 Christ, who entered heaven after receiving the submission of angelic authorities and powers, and is now at the
right hand of God.

4 Remembering that Christ endured
bodily suffering, you must arm yourselves with a temper of mind like his.

When a man has thus endured bodily
suffering he has finished with sin, and 2
for the rest of his days on earth he may
live, not for the things that men desire,
but for what God wills. You had time 3
enough in the past to do all the things
that men want to do in the pagan world.
Then you lived in licence and debauchery, drunkenness, revelry, and
tippling, and the forbidden worship
of idols. Now, when you no longer 4
plunge with them into all this reckless
dissipation, they cannot understand it,
and they vilify you accordingly; but 5
they shall answer for it to him who
stands ready to pass judgement on the
living and the dead. Why was the 6
Gospel preached to those who are
dead? In order that, although in the
body they received the sentence common to men, they might in the spirit
be alive with the life of God.

The end of all things is upon us, so 7
you must lead an ordered and sober life,
given to prayer. Above all, keep your 8
love for one another at full strength,
because love cancels innumerable sins.
Be hospitable to one another without 9
complaining. Whatever gift each of you 10
may have received, use it in service to
one another, like good stewards dispensing the grace of God in its varied
forms. Are you a speaker? Speak as if 11
you uttered oracles of God. Do you
give service? Give it as in the strength
which God supplies. In all things so act
that the glory may be God's through
Jesus Christ; to him belong glory and
power for ever and ever. Amen.

MY DEAR FRIENDS, DO NOT BE BEWIL- 12
dered by the fiery ordeal that is upon
you, as though it were something

i Or Do not fear what they fear.
j Or hold Christ in reverence in your hearts, as Lord.
k Some witnesses read suffered.
*l Some witnesses read for sins; others read for sins on
our behalf.*

13–17: See 2.11–12. **18:** See 2.24–25 n. **19–20:** *Imprisoned spirits:* either Noah's disobedient
contemporaries (Gen. chs. 6–9), or specifically the disobedient *Nephilim* (see Gen.6.1–4 n.);
perhaps both. The idea is that the gospel is withheld from no one; but the exact meaning remains
problematic. **21–22:** As *water* was decisive in Noah's career, so it is in saving the Christian, the
latter through *baptism.* **4.3:** The *past:* before conversion to Christ. **5:** For Christ as judge, see
Acts10.42; 2 Tim.4.1. **6:** See 3.19–20 n.
 4.7–11: Christian conduct in the church. 7: *The end:* the day of judgment and salvation;
see 1.5,7,13. **8:** Where love is active sin subsides. See Prov.10.12; Ecclus.3.30; Jas.5.19–20.
9: *Be hospitable:* to Christian travelers; see Heb.13.2 n.
 4.12–19: The meaning of suffering as a Christian. 12: *Ordeal:* persecution; *fiery* implies "bitter."

13 extraordinary. It gives you a share in Christ's sufferings, and that is cause for joy; and when his glory is revealed,
14 your joy will be triumphant. If Christ's name is flung in your teeth as an insult, count yourselves happy, because then that glorious Spirit which is the Spirit
15 of God is resting upon you. If you suffer, it must not be for murder, theft, or sorcery,[m] nor for infringing the
16 rights of others. But if anyone suffers as a Christian, he should feel it no disgrace, but confess that name to the honour of God.
17 The time has come for the judgement to begin; it is beginning with God's own household. And if it is starting with you, how will it end for those who
18 refuse to obey the gospel of God? It is hard enough for the righteous to be saved; what then will become of the
19 impious and sinful? So even those who suffer, if it be according to God's will, should commit their souls to him—by doing good; their Maker will not fail them.
5 And now I appeal to the elders of your community, as a fellow-elder and a witness of Christ's sufferings, and also a partaker in the splendour that is to be
2 revealed. Tend that flock of God whose shepherds you are, and do it, not under compulsion, but of your own free will, as God would have it; not for gain but
3 out of sheer devotion; not tyrannizing over those who are allotted to your care,
4 but setting an example to the flock. And

then, when the Head Shepherd appears, you will receive for your own the unfading garland of glory.
5 In the same way you younger men must be subordinate to your elders. Indeed, all of you should wrap yourselves in the garment of humility towards each other, because God sets his face against the arrogant but favours the humble. Humble yourselves then
6 under God's mighty hand, and he will lift you up in due time. Cast all your
7 cares on him, for you are his charge.
8 Awake! be on the alert! Your enemy the devil, like a roaring lion, prowls round looking for someone to devour. Stand up to him, firm in faith, and
9 remember that your brother Christians are going through the same kinds of suffering while they are in the world. And the God of all grace, who called
10 you into his eternal glory in Christ, will himself, after your brief suffering, restore, establish, and strengthen you on a firm foundation. He holds do-
11 minion for ever and ever. Amen.
12 I write you this brief appeal through Silvanus, our trusty brother as I hold him, adding my testimony that this is the true grace of God. In this stand fast.
13 Greetings from her who dwells in Babylon, chosen by God like you, and
14 from my son Mark. Greet one another with the kiss of love.
Peace to you all who belong to Christ!

m Or other crime.

13–19: Joyful acceptance of undeserved suffering demonstrates trust in God's ultimate faithfulness; see 2.18–25 n. **14:** Isa.11.2. **16:** *Christian:* see Acts 11.26 n. **18:** Prov.11.31.
5.1–14: Concluding matters. 1–7: Harmony should prevail as the church awaits in hope the coming of Christ, *the Head Shepherd* (see also 2.25). **5:** Prov.3.34. **7:** Ps.55.22. **8–11:** The church under persecution must stand united against unbelief (*the devil;* see Job.1.7). **12:** *Silvanus,* the stenographer, is probably "Silas" (Acts 15.22). **13:** *From her . . . in Babylon:* the church in Rome; see Rev.17.1–5,15. In early Christian tradition *Mark* was regarded as Peter's spiritual heir; see Acts 12.12. **14:** *Kiss of love:* a liturgical gesture, the "holy kiss" (e.g. Rom.16.16).

THE SECOND LETTER OF
PETER

In form, this writing is Peter's "last will and testament," a passionate attempt to support orthodox Christian doctrines, especially beliefs in the glorious return of Christ. The purpose, style, and point of view sharply distinguish this testament from 1 Peter, and most scholars have concluded that it was written in Peter's name by a later churchman interested in representing its teaching as well-established apostolic tradition. The salutation (1.1–2) is followed by a preface which stresses the writer's authority (1.3–15). In 1.16 3.10 there are various arguments assembled to show that the hope of the Lord's coming is sure, and the readers are admonished in conclusion to be ready for that day (3.11–18).

Virtually all the arguments in 2 Peter duplicate those in Jude 3–18. The majority of interpreters believe that the author of 2 Peter has drawn on Jude in formulating his own appeal. That 2 Peter used Jude (not Jude, 2 Peter) is suggested by the absence from 2 Peter of a passage in Jude 9 which alludes to a legend about Moses' body; that 2 Peter omitted this seems to scholars more likely than that Jude added it. Dependence on Jude and the association of Paul's letters with Scripture (3.16) suggest a date for 2 Peter well into the second century, perhaps about 150 A.D.

The remedy for doubt

1 FROM SIMEON PETER, SERVANT AND apostle of Jesus Christ, to those who through the justice of our God and Saviour Jesus Christ share our faith and enjoy equal privilege with ourselves.

2 Grace and peace be yours in fullest measure, through the knowledge of God and Jesus our Lord.

3 His divine power has bestowed on us everything that makes for life and true religion, enabling us to know the One who called us by his own splendour 4 and might. Through this might and splendour he has given us his promises, great beyond all price, and through them you may escape the corruption with which lust has infected the world, and come to share in the very being of God.

5 With all this in view, you should try your hardest to supplement your faith with virtue, virtue with knowledge, 6 knowledge with self-control, self-control with fortitude, fortitude with 7 piety, piety with brotherly kindness, and brotherly kindness with love. 8 These are gifts which, if you possess and foster them, will keep you from being either useless or barren in the knowledge of our Lord Jesus Christ. The man who lacks them is short- 9 sighted and blind; he has forgotten how he was cleansed from his former sins. All the more then, my friends, 10 exert yourselves to clinch God's choice and calling of you. If you behave so, you will never come to grief. Thus you 11 will be afforded full and free admission into the eternal kingdom of our Lord and Saviour Jesus Christ.

And so I will not hesitate to remind 12 you of this again and again, although you know it and are well grounded in the truth that has already reached you. Yet I think it right to keep refreshing 13 your memory so long as I still lodge in this body. I know that very soon I must 14 leave it; indeed our Lord Jesus Christ has told me so.[a] But I will see to it that 15 after I am gone you will have means of remembering these things at all times.

It was not on tales artfully spun that 16 we relied when we told you of the power of our Lord Jesus Christ and his coming; we saw him with our own eyes in majesty, when at the hands of God 17 the Father he was invested with honour and glory, and there came to

[a] Or I must leave it, as our Lord Jesus Christ told me.

1.1–2: Salutation.
1.3–15: The writer's purpose and authority. 5: See Jude 3. 9: *Sins* are *cleansed* at baptism. 12: *The truth*: Christian doctrine; see Jude 5. 13–14: Perhaps a reference to the prediction of Jn.21.18–19. 15: The view that Mark's Gospel is derived from Peter may be reflected here. 1.16–3.10: The hope of the Lord's coming is no myth. 16–18: Peter was one of those present

him from the sublime Presence a voice which said: 'This is my Son, my Beloved,[b] on whom my favour rests.'
18 This voice from heaven we ourselves heard; when it came, we were with him on the sacred mountain.
19 All this only confirms for us the message of the prophets,[c] to which you will do well to attend, because it is like a lamp shining in a murky place, until the day breaks and the morning star rises to illuminate your minds.

20 BUT FIRST NOTE THIS: NO ONE CAN interpret any prophecy of Scripture by
21 himself. For it was not through any human will that men prophesied of old; men they were, but, impelled by the Holy Spirit, they spoke the words of God.

2 But Israel had false prophets as well as true; and you likewise will have false teachers among you. They will import disastrous heresies, disowning the very Master who bought them, and bringing
2 swift disaster on their own heads. They will gain many adherents to their dissolute practices, through whom the true way will be brought into disrepute.
3 In their greed for money they will trade on your credulity with sheer fabrications.
But the judgement long decreed for them has not been idle; perdition waits
4 for them with unsleeping eyes. God did not spare the angels who sinned, but consigned them to the dark pits of hell,[d] where they are reserved for judgement.
5 He did not spare the world of old (except for Noah, preacher of righteousness, whom he preserved with seven others), but brought the deluge upon
6 that world of godless men. The cities of Sodom and Gomorrah God burned to ashes, and condemned them to total destruction, making them an object-lesson for godless men in future
7 days. But he rescued Lot, who was a good man, shocked by the dissolute
8 habits of the lawless society in which he lived; day after day every sight, every

sound, of their evil courses tortured that good man's heart. Thus the Lord 9 is well able to rescue the godly out of trials, and to reserve the wicked under punishment until the day of judgement.
Above all he will punish those who 10 follow their abominable lusts. They flout authority; reckless and headstrong, they are not afraid to insult celestial beings, whereas angels, for all 11 their superior strength and might, employ no insults in seeking judgement against them before the Lord.
These men are like brute beasts, 12 born in the course of nature to be caught and killed. They pour abuse upon things they do not understand; like the beasts they will perish, suffering 13 hurt for the hurt they have inflicted. To carouse in broad daylight is their idea of pleasure; while they sit with you at table they are an ugly blot on your company, because they revel in their own deceptions.[e]
They have eyes for nothing but 14 women, eyes never at rest from sin. They lure the unstable to their ruin; past masters in mercenary greed, God's curse is on them! They have abandoned 15 the straight road and lost their way. They have followed in the steps of Balaam son of Beor, who consented to take pay for doing wrong, but had 16 his offence brought home to him when the dumb beast spoke with a human voice and put a stop to the prophet's madness.
These men are springs that give no 17 water, mists driven by a storm; the place reserved for them is blackest darkness. They utter big, empty words, 18 and make of sensual lusts and debauchery a bait to catch those who have barely begun to escape from their heathen environment. They promise 19 them freedom, but are themselves

b *Or* This is my only Son.
c *Or* And in the message of the prophets we have something still more certain.
d *Some witnesses read* consigned them to darkness and chains in hell.
e *Some witnesses read* in their love-feasts.

at the transfiguration, Mt.17.1–8. **19**: Christ will dawn as the *morning star* on *the day* of his return. **20–21**: See 3.16 n.
2.1–22: False teachers will be punished. See Jude 4,5–16 nn. **7–8**: See Gen.19.4–29. **11**: In Jude 9 the angel Michael is named, but here the reference is more general (see Introduction). **18–22**: New converts are especially vulnerable to false teaching. Backsliders are worse off than

slaves of corruption; for a man is the slave of whatever has mastered him.
20 They had once escaped the world's defilements through the knowledge of our Lord and Saviour Jesus Christ; yet if they have entangled themselves in these all over again, and are mastered by them, their plight in the end is
21 worse than before. How much better never to have known the right way, than, having known it, to turn back and abandon the sacred command-
22 ments delivered to them! For them the proverb has proved true: 'The dog returns to its own vomit', and, 'The sow after a wash rolls in the mud again.'

3 THIS IS NOW MY SECOND LETTER TO YOU, my friends. In both of them I have been recalling to you what you already know, to rouse you to honest thought.
2 Remember the predictions made by God's own prophets, and the commands given by the Lord and Saviour through your apostles.
3 Note this first: in the last days there will come men who scoff at religion
4 and live self-indulgent lives, and they will say: 'Where now is the promise of his coming? Our fathers have been laid to their rest, but still everything continues exactly as it has always been since the world began.'
5 In taking this view they lose sight of the fact *f* that there were heavens and earth long ago, created by God's word
6 out of water and with water; and by water that first world was destroyed,
7 the water of the deluge. And the present heavens and earth, again by God's word, have been kept in store for burning; they are being reserved until the day of judgement when the godless will be destroyed.
8 And here is one point, my friends, which you must not lose sight of: with the Lord one day is like a thousand years and a thousand years like one

day. It is not that the Lord is slow in 9 fulfilling his promise, as some suppose, but that he is very patient with you, because it is not his will for any to be lost, but for all to come to repentance.

But the Day of the Lord will come; 10 it will come, unexpected as a thief. On that day the heavens will disappear with a great rushing sound, the elements will disintegrate in flames, and the earth with all that is in it will be laid bare.*g*

Since the whole universe is to break 11 up in this way, think what sort of people you ought to be, what devout and dedicated lives you should live! Look eagerly for the coming of the 12 Day of God and work to hasten it on; that day will set the heavens ablaze until they fall apart, and will melt the elements in flames. But we have his 13 promise, and look forward to new heavens and a new earth, the home of justice.

With this to look forward to, do your 14 utmost to be found at peace with him, unblemished and above reproach in his sight. Bear in mind that our Lord's 15 patience with us is our salvation, as Paul, our friend and brother, said when he wrote to you with his inspired wisdom. And so he does in all his other 16 letters, wherever he speaks of this subject, though they contain some obscure passages, which the ignorant and unstable misinterpret to their own ruin, as they do the other scriptures.*h*

But you, my friends, are forewarned. 17 Take care, then, not to let these unprincipled men seduce you with their errors; do not lose your own safe foothold. But grow in the grace and in the 18 knowledge of our Lord and Saviour Jesus Christ.*i* To him be glory now and for all eternity!

f Or They choose to overlook the fact . . .
g Some witnesses read will be burnt up.
h Or his other writings.
i Or But grow up, by the grace of our Lord and Saviour Jesus Christ, and by knowing him.

---

are the unconverted. See also Heb.6.4–6; 10.26–31. **22:** *Dog returns to its own vomit:* see Prov.26.11.

3.1–10: Predicted events have occurred. See Acts 20.29–30. **1:** *Second letter:* the first is presumed to be 1 Pet. **3–4:** See 2.1–3. **5–7:** See Gen.1.1–10; chs. 7–8. **8:** Ps.90.4. **10:** Compare, e.g. Mt.24.43–44; Zeph.1.18; 3.8.

3.11–18: Exhortations to prepare for the end. 12: See Isa.34.4. **13:** See, e.g. Isa.65.17; Rev.21.1ff. **14:** See Jude 24. **15:** See v. 9. Perhaps Paul's letters to the Thessalonians are in mind, or passages like 1 Cor.1.7–9. **16:** Heretics are false interpreters of the *scriptures* (see 1.19–21), within which Paul's letters are included (see Introduction).

THE FIRST LETTER OF

JOHN

Unlike 2 and 3 John, this book is not a letter but a tract, occasioned by the denial of the reality of the incarnation (2.22; 4.2–3,15) by some heretical Christians (2.19). These claim to be superior in knowing God (2.3–4), in love for God (4.20), and in communion with God (1.6).

The treatise may well be from the same hand that wrote 2 and 3 John. Its style and themes also recall those of the Fourth Gospel: centrality of the incarnation, the mission of the only Son, the Word (1.1). Still, no mention is made of the Holy Spirit as personal (Jesus is the "Advocate" in 2.1), or of "glory," or of "judging," all important in the Gospel. This may indicate that the tract had an earlier origin than the Gospel, or that it was written by a different author from the same school of thought. Tradition has associated the tract with Asia Minor and the name of John.

The main body of the book is enclosed between a prologue (1.1–4) and an epilogue (5.13–21). Three aspects of God are developed in concentric circles: God is "Light" (1.5–2.27), the "Holy One" (2.28–4.6), "Love" (4.7–5.12).

Recall to fundamentals

1 IT WAS THERE FROM THE BEGINNING; we have heard it; we have seen it with our own eyes; we looked upon it, and felt it with our own hands; and it is of this we tell. Our theme is the 2 word of life. This life was made visible; we have seen it and bear our testimony; we here declare to you the eternal life which dwelt with the Father and was 3 made visible to us. What we have seen and heard we declare to you, so that you and we together may share in a common life, that life which we share with the Father and his Son Jesus 4 Christ. And we write this in order that the joy of us all may be complete.

5 Here is the message we heard from him and pass on to you: that God is light, and in him there is no darkness 6 at all. If we claim to be sharing in his life while we walk in the dark, our 7 words and our lives are a lie; but if we walk in the light as he himself is in the light, then we share together a common life, and we are being cleansed from every sin by the blood of Jesus his Son.

If we claim to be sinless, we are self- 8 deceived and strangers to the truth. If 9 we confess our sins, he is just, and may be trusted to forgive our sins and cleanse us from every kind of wrong; but if we say we have committed no sin, 10 we make him out to be a liar, and then his word has no place in us.

My children, in writing thus to you 2 my purpose is that you should not commit sin. But should anyone commit a sin, we have one to plead our cause^a with the Father, Jesus Christ, and he is just. He is himself the remedy for the 2 defilement of our sins, not our sins only but the sins of all the world.

Here is the test by which we can 3 make sure that we know him: do we keep his commands? The man who 4 says, 'I know him', while he disobeys his commands, is a liar and a stranger

_a *Literally* we have an advocate . . .

1.1–4: The prologue. 1: The impersonal *it* refers to *the word of life*, which may denote the gospel, since *word* is not as clearly a title for Jesus Christ as in Jn. (see Jn.1.1, 14 nn.). However, *from the beginning* (the creation) suggests the preexistence of Christ (see 2.13–14). As in Jn.1.14, the pronoun *we* indicates the apostolic witnesses, who attest their personal experience of Jesus' earthly life. The *theme* is that announced in Jn.1.1–18. **2:** *This life*, described as *eternal, which dwelt with the Father* (see Jn.1.1–2), has become *visible* through the incarnation (see Jn.1.14). **3:** The key Gk. term behind the phrase, *share in a common life*, is found only here and in vv. 6–7 in Johannine literature, but is characteristic of Paul (e.g. 1 Cor.1.9). However, the idea of *life which we share with the Father and his Son* is very Johannine (see Jn.5.26; 14.6). **4:** The *joy* communicated by Christ is mentioned in Jn.15.11; 16.22; 17.13.

1.5–2.27: God is Light. 5: *Light* and *darkness,* a frequent antithesis in Jn., signify truth and error and reflect a moral dualism (see Jn.1.5; 3.19). **7:** The *common life* is not created by man's goodwill, but by Christ's redemptive act (see Rev.1.5). **9:** Jas.5.16 also urges the confession of *sins.* **2.1:** The Gospel of Jn. (e.g. 14.16) calls the Holy Spirit the Advocate (see Tfn. *a*). **2:** Only here and at 4.10 in Johannine literature is Jesus called *the remedy for the defilement of our sins.*

302

5 to the truth; but in the man who is obedient to his word, the divine love has indeed come to its perfection.

Here is the test by which we can 6 make sure that we are in him: whoever claims to be dwelling in him, binds himself to live as Christ himself lived. 7 Dear friends, I give you no new command. It is the old command which you always had before you; the old command is the message which you 8 heard at the beginning. And yet again it is a new command that I am giving you—new in the sense that the darkness is passing and the real light already shines. Christ has made this true, and it is true in your own experience.

9 A man may say, 'I am in the light'; but if he hates his brother, he is still in 10 the dark. Only the man who loves his brother dwells in light: there is nothing 11 to make him stumble. But one who hates his brother is in darkness; he walks in the dark and has no idea where he is going, because the darkness has made him blind.

12 I write to you, my children, because
 your sins have been forgiven
 for his sake.[b]
13 I write to you, fathers, because you
 know him who is and has been
 from the beginning.[c]
 I write to you, young men, because
 you have mastered the evil one.

 To you, children, I have written
 because you know the Father.
14 To you, fathers, I have written
 because you know him who is
 and has been from the
 beginning.[c]
 To you, young men, I have written
 because you are strong; God's
 word remains in you, and you
 have mastered the evil one.

15 Do not set your hearts on the godless world or anything in it. Anyone who loves the world is a stranger to the Father's love. Everything the world 16 affords, all that panders to the appetites or entices the eyes, all the glamour of its life, springs not from the Father but from the godless world. And that world 17 is passing away with all its allurements, but he who does God's will stands for evermore.

MY CHILDREN, THIS IS THE LAST HOUR! 18 You were told that Antichrist was to come, and now many antichrists have appeared; which proves to us that this is indeed the last hour. They went out 19 from our company, but never really belonged to us; if they had, they would have stayed with us. They went out, so that it might be clear that not all in our company truly belong to it.[d]

You, no less than they, are among 20 the initiated;[e] this is the gift of the Holy One, and by it you all have knowledge.[f] It is not because you are ignorant of 21 the truth that I have written to you, but because you know it, and because lies, one and all, are alien to the truth.

Who is the liar? Who but he that 22 denies that Jesus is the Christ? He is Antichrist, for he denies both the Father and the Son: to deny the Son is 23 to be without the Father; to acknowledge the Son is to have the Father too. You therefore must keep in your hearts 24 that which you heard at the beginning; if what you heard then still dwells in you, you will yourselves dwell in the Son and also in the Father. And this is 25 the promise that he himself gave us, the promise of eternal life.

So much for those who would mis- 26 lead you. But as for you, the initiation[g] 27 which you received from him stays with

b Or forgiven, since you bear his name.
c Or him whom we have known from the beginning.
d Or that none of them truly belong to us.
e Literally have an anointing (*Greek* chrism).
f Some witnesses read you have all knowledge.
g Literally the anointing.

The meaning is that by Jesus' death (see 1.7) God has revealed his gracious, loving forgiveness of man. The atoning power of Christ's death is limitless. **5**: Jn.14.15 and 15.10 assert that Christian love implies obedience. **7–8**: The *old* yet *new command*: see Jn.13.34. **16**: *The world* here is opposed to God (see Jn.3.16 n.) and is exemplified by three common evil tendencies in man: lust, avarice, arrogant self-sufficiency. **18**: *Antichrist*, found only in 1 and 2 Jn., is a personification of "enmity to Christ." **20–21**: The presence of the Spirit in the Christian brings *knowledge* of divine *truth* (see Jn.14.26; 16.13–15). **22–23**: The denial of the incarnation is the basic heresy attacked by the author. **27**: Jer.31.33–34 promises a new covenant when men will be divinely taught and *need no other teacher*.

you; you need no other teacher, but learn all you need to know from his initiation, which is real and no illusion. As he taught you, then, dwell in him.

28 Even now, my children, dwell in him, so that when he appears we may be confident and unashamed before him 29 at his coming. If you know that he is righteous, you must recognize that every man who does right is his child. 3 How great is the love that the Father has shown to us! We were called God's children, and such we are;[h] and the reason why the godless world does not recognize us is that it has not known 2 him. Here and now, dear friends, we are God's children; what we shall be has not yet been disclosed, but we know that when it is disclosed[i] we shall be like him,[j] because we shall see 3 him as he is. Everyone who has this hope before him purifies himself, as Christ is pure.

4 To commit sin is to break God's law: 5 sin, in fact, is lawlessness. Christ appeared, as you know, to do away with 6 sins, and there is no sin in him. No man therefore who dwells in him is a sinner; the sinner has not seen him and does not know him.

7 My children, do not be misled: it is the man who does right who is righteous, 8 as God is righteous; the man who sins is a child of the devil, for the devil has been a sinner from the first; and the Son of God appeared for the very purpose of undoing the devil's work.

9 A child of God does not commit sin, because the divine seed remains in him; he cannot be a sinner, because he is 10 God's child. That is the distinction between the children of God and the children of the devil: no one who does not do right is God's child, nor is anyone who does not love his brother. 11 For the message you have heard from the beginning is this: that we should 12 love one another; unlike Cain, who was a child of the evil one and murdered his brother. And why did he murder him? Because his own actions were wrong, and his brother's were right.

13 My brothers, do not be surprised if 14 the world hates you. We for our part have crossed over from death to life; this we know, because we love our brothers. The man who does not love 15 is still in the realm of death, for everyone who hates his brother is a murderer, and no murderer, as you know, has eternal life dwelling within him. It 16 is by this that we know what love is: that Christ laid down his life for us. And we in our turn are bound to lay down our lives for our brothers. But if 17 a man has enough to live on, and yet when he sees his brother in need shuts up his heart against him, how can it be said that the divine love[k] dwells in him?

18 My children, love must not be a matter of words or talk; it must be 19 genuine, and show itself in action. This is how we may know that we belong to the realm of truth, and convince ourselves in his sight that even if our con- 20 science condemns us, God is greater than our conscience[l] and knows all.

21 Dear friends, if our conscience does not condemn us, then we can approach 22 God with confidence, and obtain from him whatever we ask, because we are keeping his commands and doing what he approves. This is his command: to 23 give our allegiance to his Son Jesus Christ and love one another as he commanded. When we keep his commands 24 we dwell in him and he dwells in us. And this is how we can make sure that he dwells within us: we know it from the Spirit he has given us.

h *Or* We are called children of God! Not only called, we really are his children.
i *Or* when he appears.
j *Or* we are God's children, though he has not yet appeared; what we shall be we know, for when he does appear we shall be like him.
k *Or* that love for God . . .
l *Or* and reassure ourselves in his sight in matters where our conscience condemns us, because God is greater than our conscience . . . ; *or* and yet we shall do well to convince ourselves that if even our own conscience condemns us, still more will God who is greater than conscience . . .

2.28–4.6: God is the Holy One. 28: This is the only place in the Johannine writings which speaks unambiguously of Christ's (future) coming; but see Jn.16.16 n. **3.1–3:** *The love that the Father has shown* by Jesus' redemptive mission has made the Christian one of God's children; yet this sonship remains a mystery and a *hope* until Christ appears. **9:** *The divine seed* is probably the Spirit of v. 24 and 4.13. The Christian *cannot be a sinner* in the fundamental sense that he must remain united to God (v. 6); that, in fact, he commits sin is affirmed in 1.8–10. **12:** *Cain:* Gen.4.3–8. **19–20:** A life spent in loving service for others proves our union with God, whose

4 BUT DO NOT TRUST ANY AND EVERY spirit, my friends; test the spirits, to see whether they are from God, for among those who have gone out into the world there are many prophets 2 falsely inspired. This is how we may recognize the Spirit of God: every spirit which acknowledges that Jesus Christ has come in the flesh is from 3 God, and every spirit which does not thus acknowledge Jesus is not from God. This is what is meant by 'Antichrist';*m* you have been told that he was to come, and here he is, in the world already!

4 But you, my children, are of God's family, and you have the mastery over these false prophets, because he who 5 inspires you is greater than he who inspires the godless world. They are of that world, and so therefore is their teaching; that is why the world listens 6 to them. But we belong to God, and a man who knows God listens to us, while he who does not belong to God refuses us a hearing. That is how we distinguish the spirit of truth from the spirit of error.

7 Dear friends, let us love one another, because love is from God. Everyone who loves is a child of God and knows 8 God, but the unloving know nothing 9 of God. For God is love; and his love was disclosed to us in this, that he sent his only Son into the world to bring us 10 life. The love I speak of is not our love for God, but the love he showed to us in sending his Son as the remedy for 11 the defilement of our sins. If God thus loved us, dear friends, we in turn are 12 bound to love one another. Though God has never been seen by any man, God himself dwells in us if we love one another; his love is brought to perfection within us.

Here is the proof that we dwell in 13 him and he dwells in us. he has imparted his Spirit to us. Moreover, we 14 have seen for ourselves, and we attest, that the Father sent the Son to be the saviour of the world, and if a man 15 acknowledges that Jesus is the Son of God, God dwells in him and he dwells in God. Thus we have come to know 16 and believe the love which God has for us.

God is love; he who dwells in love is dwelling in God, and God in him. This 17 is for us the perfection of love, to have confidence on the day of judgement, and this we can have, because even in this world we are as he is. There is no 18 room for fear in love; perfect love banishes fear. For fear brings with it the pains of judgement, and anyone who is afraid has not attained to love in its perfection. We love because he 19 loved us first. But if a man says, 'I love 20 God', while hating his brother, he is a liar. If he does not love the brother whom he has seen, it cannot be that he loves God whom he has not seen. And 21 indeed this command comes to us from Christ himself: that he who loves God must also love his brother.

Everyone who believes that Jesus is **5** the Christ is a child of God, and to love the parent means to love his child; it 2 follows that when we love God and obey his commands we love his children too. For to love God is to keep 3 his commands; and they are not burdensome, because every child of God is 4 victor over the godless world. The victory that defeats the world is our faith, for who is victor over the world 5 but he who believes that Jesus is the Son of God?

m Or This is the spirit of Antichrist.

---

love and mercy keeps us from despair, *even if our conscience condemns us.* **4.1–6:** The author's admonition to *test the spirits* is an example of the church's distinction between types of "spiritual phenomena" (see 1 Cor.12.3; 1 Th.5.19–22).
4.7–5.21: God is Love. While 1 Jn. in many respects displays a less sophisticated theology than the Fourth Gospel, this cannot be said of its understanding of Christian love. **9–10:** The statement that *God is love* is not a definition of God, but a description of his redemptive action in Christ. **11–12:** The way to "see" the invisible God (compare Jn.1.14,18) in this life is to *love one another.* **14–16:** The authenticity of our love is derived from our grasp of the reality of the incarnation and our redemption by Christian faith. The theme of the mutual indwelling of God and the believer is characteristically Johannine (see 3.24; Jn.15.5). **5.1:** Faith in the incarnate Son as *the Christ* enables us to recognize others as God's *children* and leads to true Christian love. **4:** The acknowledgment by *our faith* of Jesus' true character (v. 5) is what

6   This is he who came with water and blood: Jesus Christ. He came, not by water alone, but by water and blood; and there is the Spirit to bear witness, 7,8 because the Spirit is truth. For there are three witnesses, the Spirit, the water, and the blood, and these three are in 9 agreement. We accept human testimony, but surely divine testimony is stronger, and this threefold testimony is indeed that of God himself, the 10 witness he has borne to his Son. He who believes in the Son of God has this testimony in his own heart, but he who disbelieves God, makes him out to be a liar, by refusing to accept God's 11 own witness to his Son. The witness is this: that God has given us eternal life, and that this life is found in his 12 Son. He who possesses the Son has life indeed; he who does not possess the Son of God has not that life.

13   THIS LETTER IS TO ASSURE YOU THAT YOU have eternal life. It is addressed to those who give their allegiance to the Son of God.
14   We can approach God with con-

fidence for this reason: if we make requests which accord with his will he listens to us; and if we know that our 15 requests are heard, we know also that the things we ask for are ours.

If a man sees his brother committing 16 a sin which is not a deadly sin, he should pray to God for him, and he will grant him life—that is, when men are not guilty of deadly sin. There is such a thing as deadly sin, and I do not suggest that he should pray about that; but although all wrongdoing is sin, 17 not all sin is deadly sin.

We know that no child of God is a 18 sinner; it is the Son of God who keeps him safe, and the evil one cannot touch him.

We know that we are of God's 19 family, while the whole godless world lies in the power of the evil one.

We know that the Son of God has 20 come and given us understanding to know him who is real; indeed we are in him who is real, since we are in his Son Jesus Christ. This is the true God, this is eternal life. My children, be on the 21 watch against false gods.

---

defeats the world, which opposes God. **6:** Jesus was proclaimed *the Son of God* after his baptism with water (Mt.3.17); but Jn.19.34–35 attests that *by water and blood* Jesus was revealed as Savior of men. **7–8:** An ancient trinitarian formula (which identifies "Father, Word, and Spirit" as "heavenly witnesses") was a gloss inserted into this passage in some Latin versions. **13:** This statement of purpose recalls Jn.20.31. **14–15:** Christian *confidence* in being heard is an important element of petitionary prayer. **16:** The *deadly sin*, not specified by the author, is of such a nature as to defy forgiveness, possibly that cited in 2.18–29. **20:** By *him who is real*, the author means God.

THE SECOND LETTER OF

JOHN

This is a real letter, written to a specific Christian community by "the Elder." A man of authority in his own church, the author feels a certain responsibility for the faith of another community. It is all but impossible to discover the date, place of origin, or destination of this note. Its purpose is to alert the church addressed to the dangers of the heretical denial of the incarnation. To counter these dangers, it urges fidelity to the traditional commandment of fraternal love, which involves obedience to apostolic authority. Stylistic similarities suggest that this writer also composed 3 John; he may be the author of 1 John also.

Truth and love

1 THE ELDER TO THE LADY CHOSEN BY God, and her children, whom I love in truth—and not I alone 2 but all who know the truth—for the sake of the truth that dwells among us and will be with us for ever.

3 Grace, mercy, and peace shall be with us from God the Father and from Jesus Christ the Son of the Father, in truth and love.

4 I was delighted to find that some of your children are living by the truth, as we were commanded by the Father. 5 And now I have a request to make of you. Do not think I am giving a new command; I am recalling the one we have had before us from the beginning: 6 let us love one another. And love means following the commands of God. This is the command which was given you from the beginning, to be your rule of life.

7 Many deceivers have gone out into the world, who do not acknowledge Jesus Christ as coming in the flesh. These are the persons described as the Antichrist, the arch-deceiver. Beware 8 of them, so that you may not lose all that we worked for, but receive your reward in full.

9 Anyone who runs ahead too far, and does not stand by the doctrine of the Christ, is without God; he who stands by that doctrine possesses both the Father and the Son. If anyone comes 10 to you who does not bring this doctrine, do not welcome him into your house or give him a greeting; for anyone 11 who gives him a greeting is an accomplice in his wicked deeds.

12 I have much to write to you, but I do not care to put it down in black and white. But I hope to visit you and talk with you face to face, so that our joy may be complete. The children of your 13 Sister, chosen by God, send their greetings.

1–3: Address and wish. 1: *Elder*: a term used elsewhere to designate the leader(s) of a local church (see Acts 14.23; 20.17; 1 Tim.5.17; Ti.1.5). The community addressed is called *the Lady*, which in Gk. is the feminine equivalent of "Lord." The title may be related to the familiar imagery of the church as the "bride of Christ" (see 2 Cor.11.2; Eph.5.26–27; Rev.19.7). The phrase *chosen by God* (used here of the church) indicates Jesus in Jn.1.34. **2:** The *truth* is the divine presence; its possession is assured by fidelity to the *doctrine of the Christ* (v. 9).
4–12: The body of the letter. 4: Since only *some* are *living by the truth*, the heresy has made serious inroads into the community. **5:** The writer's remedy is faithfulness to the *command* of fraternal love (see 1 Jn.2.7–10; Jn.13.34). **6:** This association of *love* with *the commands of God* is characteristic of Johannine thought (see Jn.14.23). **7:** See 1 Jn.2.22. *Antichrist:* see 1 Jn.2.18 n. **9:** The heretic *runs ahead too far* by minimizing the reality of the incarnation.
13: Final greeting. *The children of your Sister:* the members of the Elder's church.

THE THIRD LETTER OF
JOHN

This genuine letter is addressed to an individual member of a Christian church, whose leader, Diotrephes, has refused to receive the emissaries of the Elder led by Demetrius. Gaius, the addressee, a man of probity, is asked to provide hospitality for Demetrius and his companions. The author is the same Elder who wrote 2 John, as the vocabulary and style indicate; also, the two letters are of equal length.

Trouble in the church

1 THE ELDER TO DEAR GAIUS, WHOM I love in truth.

2 My dear Gaius, I pray that you may enjoy good health, and that all may go well with you, as I know 3 it goes well with your soul. I was delighted when friends came and told me how true you have been; indeed 4 you are true in your whole life. Nothing gives me greater joy than to hear that my children are living by the truth.

5 My dear friend, you show a fine loyalty in everything that you do for these our fellow-Christians, strangers 6 though they are to you. They have spoken of your kindness before the congregation here. Please help them on their journey in a manner worthy of 7 the God we serve. It was on Christ's work that they went out; and they would accept nothing from pagans. 8 We are bound to support such men, and so play our part in spreading the truth.

I sent a letter to the congregation, 9 but Diotrephes, their would-be leader,*a* will have nothing to do with us. If I 10 come, I will bring up the things he is doing. He lays baseless and spiteful charges against us; not satisfied with that, he refuses to receive our friends, and he interferes with those who would do so, and tries to expel them from the congregation.

My dear friend, do not imitate bad 11 examples, but good ones. The well-doer is a child of God; the evil-doer has never seen God.

Demetrius gets a good testimonial 12 from everybody—yes, and from the truth itself. I add my testimony, and you know that my testimony is true.

I have much to write to you, but I 13 do not care to set it down with pen and ink. I hope to see you very soon, and 14 we will talk face to face. Peace be with you. Our friends send their greetings. Greet our friends one by one.

a Or who enjoys being their leader.

1–2: Address and prayer. 1: *Gaius*, an exemplary Christian, has already aided itinerant preachers (v. 6). To *love in truth* is to love as a Christian.
3–14: The body of the letter. 4: In 2 Jn.4 the phrase *living by the truth* means obedience to the Father. **5:** The writer recommends Demetrius (v. 12) and his associates to Gaius' care as *our fellow-Christians*. **9:** *Diotrephes* is not heretical but he is a foe of the Elder, overambitious, unjust, and uncharitable. **11:** The Christian *well-doer* is called *a child of God* in 1 Jn.3.9. **13–14:** See 2 Jn.12–13. The note ends with a wish of *peace*, the sum total of all Christ's blessings.

A LETTER OF

JUDE

Most New Testament letters are addressed to one or more specific congregations. This author, however, writes to all Christians. Following the salutation (vv. 1–2) he gives his reasons for writing: to urge Christians everywhere to defend the faith against false teaching (v. 3) and to oppose "the enemies of religion" (v. 4). In vv. 5–16 the effectiveness of God's judgment of evil is stressed, while in vv. 17–23 the readers are urged to take action to prevent themselves and others from falling into error. An impressive doxology (vv. 24–25) gives assurance of God's aid in holding fast to the faith.

Although this author is concerned to safeguard right doctrine, he offers no systematic refutation of false teaching, but rather condemns the immorality of those who espouse it. A similar tactic and some of the same points are present in 2 Peter (see Introduction there). The author calls himself "Jude" the "brother of James," and probably means for the readers to infer that he is therefore one of the brothers of Jesus himself (see Mt.13.55; Mk.6.3). Most scholars, however, believe that the style, content, and probable date of this tract (late first or early second century) require the conclusion that Jude's name has been used by a later writer to lend authority to his urgent appeal.

The danger of false belief

1 FROM JUDE, SERVANT OF JESUS CHRIST and brother of James, to those whom God has called, who live in the love of God the Father and in the safe keeping of Jesus Christ.

2 Mercy, peace, and love be yours in fullest measure.

3 My friends, I was fully engaged in writing to you about our salvation—which is yours no less than ours—when it became urgently necessary to write at once and appeal to you to join the struggle in defence of the faith, the faith which God entrusted to his people 4 once and for all. It is in danger from certain persons who have wormed their way in, the very men whom Scripture long ago marked down for the doom they have incurred. They are the enemies of religion; they pervert the free favour of our God into licentiousness, disowning Jesus Christ, our only Master and Lord.[a]

5 You already know it all, but let me remind you how the Lord,[b] having once delivered the people of Israel out of Egypt, next time destroyed those who were guilty of unbelief. Remember too 6 the angels, how some of them were not content to keep the dominion given to them but abandoned their proper home; and God has reserved them for judgement on the great Day, bound beneath the darkness in everlasting chains. Remember Sodom and Go- 7 morrah and the neighbouring towns; like the angels, they committed fornication and followed unnatural lusts; and they paid the penalty in eternal fire, an example for all to see.

So too with these men today. Their 8 dreams lead them to defile the body, to flout authority, and to insult celestial beings. In contrast, when the archangel 9 Michael was in debate with the devil, disputing the possession of Moses's body, he did not presume to condemn him in insulting words,[c] but said, 'May the Lord rebuke you!'

But these men pour abuse upon 10 things they do not understand; the things they do understand, by instinct like brute beasts, prove their undoing.

a Or disowning our one and only Master, and Jesus Christ our Lord.
b Some witnesses read Jesus (which might be understood as Joshua).
c Or to charge him with blasphemy.

1–2: Salutation. See Introduction.
3–4: Preface. 3: The faith is the Christian doctrinal tradition entrusted to God's people (perhaps a specific reference to the apostles). 4. A warning against certain false teachers who, in particular, deny that Jesus is Master and Lord: see 2 Jn.7. Scripture: see vv. 14–15 n., 17–18 n.
5–16: The judgment of God. 5: See Num.14.11–35. 6: See Gen.6.1–4; Deut.32.8; 1 Enoch (an ancient noncanonical book) chs. 6–10; 18.14–16; 21.2. 7: See Gen.19.23–25; Deut.29.23; Wis.10.6. 8: Angelic powers, in this writer's view, deserve respect; contrast Eph.1.21–22; Col.2.15–19. 9: The literary source of the legend referred to is now lost, but perhaps stood in

11 Alas for them! They have gone the way of Cain; they have plunged into Balaam's error for pay; they have rebelled like Korah, and they share his doom.

12 These men are a blot on your love-feasts, where they eat and drink without reverence. They are shepherds who take care only of themselves. They are clouds carried away by the wind without giving rain, trees that in season bear no fruit, dead twice over and

13 pulled up by the roots. They are fierce waves of the sea, foaming shameful deeds; they are stars that have wandered from their course, and the place for ever reserved for them is blackest darkness.

14 It was to them that Enoch, the seventh in descent from Adam, directed his prophecy when he said: 'I saw the Lord come with his myriads of angels,

15 to bring all men to judgement and to convict all the godless of all the godless deeds they had committed, and of all the defiant words which godless sinners had spoken against him.'

16 They are a set of grumblers and malcontents. They follow their lusts. Big words come rolling from their lips, and they court favour to gain their ends.

17 But you, my friends, should remember the predictions made by the apostles of our Lord Jesus Christ. This was the 18 warning they gave you: 'In the final age there will be men who pour scorn on religion, and follow their own godless lusts.'

These men draw a line between 19 spiritual and unspiritual persons, although they are themselves[d] wholly unspiritual. But you, my friends, must 20 fortify yourselves in your most sacred faith. Continue to pray in the power of the Holy Spirit. Keep yourselves in the 21 love of God, and look forward to the day when our Lord Jesus Christ in his mercy will give eternal life.

There are some doubting souls who 22 need your pity;[e] snatch them from the 23 flames and save them.[f] There are others for whom your pity must be mixed with fear; hate the very clothing that is contaminated with sensuality.

Now to the One who can keep you 24 from falling and set you in the presence of his glory, jubilant and above reproach, to the only God our Saviour, 25 be glory and majesty, might and authority, through Jesus Christ our Lord, before all time, now, and for evermore. Amen.

d *Or* These men create divisions; they are ...
e *Some witnesses read* There are some who raise disputes; these you should refute.
f *So one witness; the rest read* some you should snatch from the flames and save.

---

the incompletely preserved writing, "Assumption of Moses." **11:** *Cain* symbolizes lust and self-indulgence (e.g. Wis.10.3). *Balaam's error* was covetousness (Num. chs. 22–24); *Korah* led a rebellion against Moses and Aaron (Num. ch. 16). **12–13:** *Love-feasts* were church meals probably separate from the "Lord's Supper." *Dead twice over:* see Rev.20.14; 21.8. For other images used here, see Prov.25.14; Isa.14.12–15; 57.20; the nonbiblical book 1 Enoch 18.12–16; 21.3ff. **14–15:** See the nonbiblical book 1 Enoch 1.1–9; 5.4; 27.2; 60.8; 93.2.

17–23: The need for right doctrine. 17–18: See, e.g. Paul in Acts 20.29–30. **20.** *Sacred faith:* see v. 3 n. **21–22:** *The day* of Christ's return will bring both mercy and judgment. **23:** Fleshly lusts should be despised; see Zech.3.2–7.

24–25: Doxology. See Rom.16.25–27.

THE REVELATION
OF JOIIN

THE REVELATION
OF JOHN

The Revelation of John encourages Christians to keep faith in the face of trial and persecution. The author is a Christian prophet, John, who is persecuted himself and writes from exile on the island of Patmos in the Aegean Sea to churches in what is now western Turkey. He often employs the visionary and symbolic language characteristic of apocalyptic ("unveiling," revelatory) literature to give his readers confidence that God, not Satan or the Roman emperor, is the Lord of history. Though there are symbolic images that seem to refer to Nero (54–68 A.D.) and parts may have been written before the fall of Jerusalem in 70 A.D., the book in its present form probably was written during the reign of Domitian (81–96 A.D.), a period when emperor worship was geographically extensive and coercive.

Among New Testament writings, Revelation is unique as a thoroughly apocalyptic document; it has forerunners in parts of such Old Testament books as Daniel, Isaiah, and Zechariah. Its very structure and language seem strongly influenced by Ezekiel. Like other apocalyptic writings composed in times of crisis and danger and portraying a struggle between God and his adversaries, Revelation veils its message to hide it from pagan foes. Yet, the purpose of the symbols is to unveil or reveal to believers God's ultimate victory and to encourage their loyalty to him. Steeped in Old Testament references, many of the seemingly cryptic statements are clarified when the reader consults these Scriptures.

The structure of Revelation is dominated by series of sevens, the biblical number of fullness or completeness. In powerful imagery and sometimes moving liturgical language, history is portrayed as unfolding toward that ultimate fullness of God's triumph in his new heaven and new earth. God and the Lamb (Jesus Christ) are "the first and the last." To them belong "praise and honor, glory and might forever." Such a message, though rooted in the first century, has been spiritually uplifting to poets, musicians, artists, and ordinary Christians through the ages.

---

1 THIS IS THE REVELATION GIVEN BY God to Jesus Christ. It was given to him so that he might show his servants what must shortly happen. He made it known by sending his angel 2 to his servant John, who, in telling all that he saw, has borne witness to the word of God and to the testimony of Jesus Christ.[a]

3 Happy is the man who reads, and happy those who listen to the words of this prophecy and heed what is written in it. For the hour of fulfilment is near.

A message from Christ to the churches

JOHN TO THE SEVEN CHURCHES IN THE 4 province of Asia.

Grace be to you and peace, from him who is and who was and who is to come, from the seven spirits before his throne, and from Jesus Christ, the faith- 5 ful witness, the first-born from the dead and ruler of the kings of the earth.

To him who loves us and freed us from our sins with his life's blood, who 6

a Or has borne his testimony to the word of God and to Jesus Christ.

1.1–3: The foreword. The opening declares the ultimate source of the revelation, its purpose (*to show . . . what must shortly happen*), and the manner of its mediation to John (see 22.6,16). **1:** *Servants* (lit. slaves) is a recurrent way of speaking of God's agents (compare Amos 3.7). The delivery of the revelation by an *angel* reflects the motif in postexilic prophecy that God's distant majesty required mediating messengers (see Zech.1.19). **2:** Here *the word of God* means God's message; in 19.13 (see Jn.1.1) Jesus is the Word of God. **3:** *Happy* (or, blessed) introduces one of seven blessings in Rev.; here (as in 22.7) it blesses those who read and hear the revelation in public worship.

1.4–8: Greeting, confession, and doxology. The traditional greeting of *grace* and *peace* (see Rom.1.7 n.) is expanded into a confession of God's past, present, and future reign, as well as of the lordship of Jesus Christ; they, not Satan or Caesar, are the true rulers of history. **5:** The *seven spirits* (see 3.1; 4.5; 5.6) point to the fullness of God's reigning power (*throne*). *Faithful witness* (or, martyr) implies Jesus' faithfulness unto death. *First-born from the dead:* see Rom. 8.29; Col.1.15,18; compare Ps.89.27. *Ruler of the kings:* see 11.15–18; 19.16. **6:** *Royal house* and *priests* apply OT political and cultic designations of Israel to Christians; see Exod.19.6;

made of us a royal house, to serve as the priests of his God and Father—to him be glory and dominion for ever and ever! Amen.

7 Behold, he is coming with the clouds! Every eye shall see him, and among them those who pierced him; and all the peoples of the world shall lament in remorse. So it shall be. Amen.

8 'I am the Alpha and the Omega', says the Lord God, who is and who was and who is to come, the sovereign Lord of all.

9 I, John, your brother, who share with you in the suffering and the sovereignty and the endurance which is ours in Jesus—I was on the island called Patmos because I had preached God's word and borne my testimony to Jesus.

10 It was on the Lord's day, and I was caught up by the Spirit; and behind me I heard a loud voice, like the sound

11 of a trumpet, which said to me, 'Write down what you see on a scroll and send it to the seven churches: to Ephesus, Smyrna, Pergamum, Thyatira, Sardis,

12 Philadelphia, and Laodicea.' I turned to see whose voice it was that spoke to me; and when I turned I saw seven standing

13 lamps of gold, and among the lamps one like a son of man, robed down to his feet, with a golden girdle round his

14 breast. The hair of his head was white as snow-white wool, and his eyes flamed

15 like fire; his feet gleamed like burnished brass refined in a furnace, and his voice

was like the sound of rushing waters. In his right hand he held seven stars, 16 and out of his mouth came a sharp two-edged sword; and his face shone like the sun in full strength.

When I saw him, I fell at his feet as 17 though dead. But he laid his right hand upon me and said, 'Do not be afraid. I am the first and the last, and I am the 18 living one; for I was dead and now I am alive for evermore, and I hold the keys of Death and Death's domain. Write down therefore what you have 19 seen, what is now, and what will be hereafter.

'Here is the secret meaning of the 20 seven stars which you saw in my right hand, and of the seven lamps of gold: the seven stars are the angels of the seven churches, and the seven lamps are the seven churches.

'TO THE ANGEL OF THE CHURCH AT **2** Ephesus write:

'"These are the words of the One who holds the seven stars in his right hand and walks among the seven lamps of gold: I know all your ways, your toil 2 and your fortitude. I know you cannot endure evil men; you have put to the proof those who claim to be apostles but are not, and have found them false. Fortitude you have; you have borne 3 up in my cause and never flagged. But I have this against you: you 4 have lost your early love. Think from 5

Isa.61.6; compare Rev.5.10; 1 Pet.2.9. **7:** *Coming with the clouds:* see Dan.7.13; Mt.24.30. *Pierced, lament:* Zech.12.10; compare Jn.19.37. *So it shall be* translates the Heb. *Amen.* **8:** *Alpha* and *Omega* (applied again to God in 21.6 and to Jesus in 22.13) are the first and last letters of the Gk. alphabet; compare "first" and "last" in 1.17; Isa.44.6; 48.12.

1.9–20: John's vision and commission. 10: *The Lord's day:* Sunday. *Caught up by the Spirit* reflects ecstatic experience; see Ezek.3.12. **11:** *Trumpet:* compare Exod.19.16,19; as related to the end-time see Mt.24.37; 1 Cor.15.52; 1 Th.4.16. *Write down:* compare Isa.30.8. **12:** *Seven . . . lamps* (see Exod.25.37; Zech.4.2) are identified in v. 20 as the seven churches. These churches, named in v. 11, stood on a great road that circumscribed the west-central region of the province of Asia. **13–15:** *Son of man* (see 14.14), a figure in Dan.7.13, here and especially in the Gospels is applied to Jesus; the description of him (see Dan.7.9–10,12–13; 10.5–6; Ezek.1.24–8; 43.2) expresses priesthood, kingship, eternity, omniscience, strength. **16:** *Right hand* is a symbol of power; Christ, not Caesar, holds the *seven stars* (identified in v. 20 as the angels, perhaps guardian angels, of the churches); the stars are perhaps contrasted with the seven stars which appear on Roman coins as a symbol of imperial power. *Sword* suggests the power of his word; see Isa.11.4; 49.2; Eph.6.17; Heb.4.12. *Shining face:* compare Dan.10.6; Mt.13.43; 17.2. **17:** *Fell at his feet:* compare Dan.10.9; Ezek.1.28; Mt.17.6; Lk.5.8. **18:** The affirmation that Christ is *first* and *last* (see v. 8 n.) here includes his victory over death.

2.1–3.22: The seven letters. Each contains initial descriptions of Christ, followed by encouragement, admonition, and promise.

2.1–7: Ephesus: Roman Asia's chief city. **1:** *Angel:* see 1.20. *One:* the risen Christ; see 1.17–18. *Stars:* see 1.16 n., 1.20. *Lamps:* see 1.12 n., 1.20. **2:** *Apostles:* missionaries; on *false* apostles, compare 2 Cor.11.12–15. **4:** *Early love:* initial, waning enthusiasm; see Jer.2.2; Hos.2.14–16.

314

what a height you have fallen; repent, and do as you once did. Otherwise, if you do not repent, I shall come to you and remove your lamp from its place. 6 Yet you have this in your favour: you hate the practices of the Nicolaitans, as 7 I do. Hear, you who have ears to hear, what the Spirit says to the churches! To him who is victorious I will give the right to eat from the tree of life that stands in the Garden of God."

8 'To the angel of the church at Smyrna write:
'"These are the words of the First and the Last, who was dead and came 9 to life again: I know how hard pressed you are, and poor—and yet you are rich; I know how you are slandered by those who claim to be Jews but are 10 not—they are Satan's synagogue. Do not be afraid of the suffering to come. The Devil will throw some of you into prison, to put you to the test; and for ten days you will suffer cruelly. Only be faithful till death, and I will give you 11 the crown of life. Hear, you who have ears to hear, what the Spirit says to the churches! He who is victorious cannot be harmed by the second death."

12 'To the angel of the church at Pergamum write:
'"These are the words of the One who has the sharp two-edged sword: 13 I know where you live; it is the place where Satan has his throne. And yet you are holding fast to my cause. You did not deny your faith in me even at the time when Antipas, my faithful witness, was killed in your city, the home 14 of Satan. But I have a few matters to

bring against you: you have in Pergamum some that hold to the teaching of Balaam, who taught Balak to put temptation in the way of the Israelites. He encouraged them to eat food sacrificed to idols and to commit fornication, and in the same way you also 15 have some who hold the doctrine of the Nicolaitans. So repent! If you do not, 16 I shall come to you soon and make war upon them with the sword that comes out of my mouth. Hear, you who have 17 ears to hear, what the Spirit says to the churches! To him who is victorious I will give some of the hidden manna; I will give him also a white stone, and on the stone will be written a new name, known to none but him that receives it."

'To the angel of the church at 18 Thyatira write:
'"These are the words of the Son of God, whose eyes flame like fire and whose feet gleam like burnished brass: I know all your ways, your love and 19 faithfulness, your good service and your fortitude; and of late you have done even better than at first. Yet I 20 have this against you: you tolerate that Jezebel, the woman who claims to be a prophetess, who by her teaching lures my servants into fornication and into eating food sacrificed to idols. I have 21 given her time to repent, but she refuses to repent of her fornication. So I will 22 throw her on to a bed of pain,[b] and plunge her lovers into terrible suffering, unless they forswear what she is doing;

b *One witness reads* into a furnace.

6: The *Nicolaitans* apparently taught that Christians were free to eat meat offered to idols and to practice immorality; see vv. 14–15. **7:** *The tree of life* (Gen.2.9; 3.22) suggests paradise restored; see 22.14.

2.8–11: Smyrna. Modern Izmir. **8:** *The First . . . Last:* see 1.8,18 nn. *Poor—and yet you are rich:* see the opposite in 3.17. **9:** *Satan's synagogue* refers to false Jews who spurred the authorities to persecute those who refused to worship at Smyrna's emperor cult shrine. **10:** *Ten days:* a short period; see Dan.1.12. **11:** *Second death:* final condemnation; see 20.14; 21.8. *Crown of life:* an athletic symbol of ultimate victory; see 3.11; Jas.1.12 (translated "gift of life").

2.12–17: Pergamum. That it was the first center of emperor worship in Asia Minor may explain *where Satan has his throne* (v. 12). **12:** The *two-edged sword:* see 1.16 n. **14–15:** *Balaam* (see Num. chs. 22–24; 31.16), here related to the *Nicolaitans* (vv. 6 n., 15), was regarded in NT times as the forerunner of all corrupt teachers. **17:** *Manna:* bread from heaven (see Exod. ch. 16). Jews believed that the gift of manna would be repeated in the messianic age; see 2 Baruch 29.8 (noncanonical); compare Jn.6.47–51. *White* (like "light" and "brightness") is a frequent symbol for good in Rev.; see 1.14; 3.5; 7.9; 19.14; 20.11. The *white stone* may be related to the lot-casting Urim and Thummim; see Exod.28.15 n. Is it here for those who "cast their lot" with God? *A new name:* compare Isa.62.2; see 3.12 n.

2.18–29: Thyatira. A city renowned for its trade guilds and idolatrous feasts (see Acts 16.14). **18:** *Fire . . . bronze:* see Dan.10.6. **20:** *Jezebel:* name of Ahab's wicked, idolatrous queen

23 and her children I will strike dead. This will teach all the churches that I am the searcher of men's hearts and thoughts, and that I will reward each 24 one of you according to his deeds. And now I speak to you others in Thyatira, who do not accept this teaching and have had no experience of what they like to call the deep secrets of Satan; on you I will impose no further burden. 25 Only hold fast to what you have, until 26 I come. To him who is victorious, to him who perseveres in doing my will to the end, I will give authority over 27 the nations—that same authority which I received from my Father—and he shall rule them with an iron rod, smash-28 ing them to bits like earthenware; and I will give him also the star of dawn. 29 Hear, you who have ears to hear, what the Spirit says to the churches!"

3 'To the angel of the church at Sardis write:

'"These are the words of the One who holds the seven spirits of God, the seven stars: I know all your ways; that though you have a name for being alive, 2 you are dead. Wake up, and put some strength into what is left, which must otherwise die! For I have not found any work of yours completed in the 3 eyes of my God. So remember the teaching you received; observe it, and repent. If you do not wake up, I shall come upon you like a thief, and you will not know the moment of my coming. 4 Yet you have a few persons in Sardis who have not polluted their clothing. They shall walk with me in white, for 5 so they deserve. He who is victorious shall thus be robed all in white; his name I will never strike off the roll of the living, for in the presence of my

Father and his angels I will acknowl-edge him as mine. Hear, you who have 6 ears to hear, what the Spirit says to the churches!"

'To the angel of the church at 7 Philadelphia write:

'"These are the words of the holy one, the true one, who holds the key of David; when he opens none may shut, when he shuts none may open: I know 8 all your ways; and look, I have set be-fore you an open door, which no one can shut. Your strength, I know, is small, yet you have observed my commands and have not disowned my name. So 9 this is what I will do: I will make those of Satan's synagogue, who claim to be Jews but are lying frauds, come and fall down at your feet; and they shall know that you are my beloved people. Because you have kept my command 10 and stood fast, I will also keep you from the ordeal that is to fall upon the whole world and test its inhabitants. I am coming soon; hold fast what you 11 have, and let no one rob you of your crown. He who is victorious—I will 12 make him a pillar in the temple of my God; he shall never leave it. And I will write the name of my God upon him, and the name of the city of my God, that new Jerusalem which is coming down out of heaven from my God, and my own new name. Hear, you who have 13 ears to hear, what the Spirit says to the churches!"

'To the angel of the church at 14 Laodicea write:

'"These are the words of the Amen, the faithful and true witness, the prime source of all God's creation: I know 15 all your ways; you are neither hot nor cold. How I wish you were either hot

(1 Kgs.16.31; 18.1–5; 19.1–3; 21.5–24). **23**: *Her children*: those who follow her teaching. *Searcher . . . deeds*: compare Jer.17.10. **24**: *Deep secrets of Satan*: heretical teachings (see v. 20). **27**: See Ps.2.9. **28**: *Star of dawn*: Christ himself (see 22.16).

   3.1–6: Sardis. A city known as carefree, wealthy, immoral. **1**: *Alive . . . dead*: nominal, not true, Christians. **3**: *Like a thief*: 1 Th.5.1–2 n.; Mt.24.42–44. **4**: *Polluted their clothing* is an image of unfaithfulness; the faithful are *in white* (see 2.17 n.). **5**: *The roll of the living*: a register of the faithful (see 13.8; 17.8; 20.12,15; compare Exod.32.32; Ps.69.28; Dan.12.1; Mal.3.16; Lk.10.20); see Phil.4.3 n. *Acknowledge him*: compare Mt.10.32.

   3.7–13: Philadelphia. A small city (compare v. 8). **7**: *Key of David*: symbol of authority; see Isa.22.22. **9**: *Satan's synagogue*: see 2.9 n. *Fall down at your feet*: compare Isa.49.23; 60.14. **10**: *Ordeal*: see 7.14; Dan.12.1; Mk.13.19–20. It refers to the three and a half years of the beast's rule; see 13.5–10. **12**: *New Jerusalem*: see 21.2. *New name*: see 2.17; 19.12; 22.4 n.; compare Ezek.48.35.

   3.14–22: Laodicea. A proud and wealthy city near Colossae (Col.4.13–16). **14**: Here, as in 2 Cor.1.20, Jesus is the *Amen*, God's "Yes" to man's hope (see Isa.65.16; compare 1.7 n.).

16 or cold! But because you are lukewarm, neither hot nor cold, I will spit you out
17 of my mouth. You say, 'How rich I am! And how well I have done! I have everything I want.' In fact, though you do not know it, you are the most pitiful
18 wretch, poor, blind, and naked. So I advise you to buy from me gold refined in the fire, to make you truly rich, and white clothes to put on to hide the shame of your nakedness, and ointment
19 for your eyes so that you may see. All whom I love I reprove and discipline. Be on your mettle therefore and repent.
20 Here I stand knocking at the door; if anyone hears my voice and opens the door, I will come in and sit down to
21 supper with him and he with me. To him who is victorious I will grant a place on my throne, as I myself was victorious and sat down with my Father
22 on his throne. Hear, you who have ears to hear, what the Spirit says to the churches!"'

The opening of the sealed book

4 AFTER THIS I LOOKED, AND THERE BEFORE my eyes was a door opened in heaven; and the voice that I had first heard speaking to me like a trumpet said, 'Come up here, and I will show you
2 what must happen hereafter.' At once I was caught up by the Spirit. There in heaven stood a throne, and on the
3 throne sat one whose appearance was like the gleam of jasper and cornelian; and round the throne was a rainbow,
4 bright as an emerald. In a circle about

this throne were twenty-four other thrones, and on them sat twenty-four elders, robed in white and wearing crowns of gold. From the throne went 5 out flashes of lightning and peals of thunder. Burning before the throne were seven flaming torches, the seven spirits of God, and in front of it 6 stretched what seemed a sea of glass, like a sheet of ice.

In the centre, round the throne itself, were four living creatures, covered with eyes, in front and behind. The first crea- 7 ture was like a lion, the second like an ox, the third had a human face, the fourth was like an eagle in flight. The 8 four living creatures, each of them with six wings, had eyes all over, inside and out; and by day and by night without a pause they sang:

'Holy, holy, holy is God the sovereign Lord of all, who was, and is, and is to come!'

As often as the living creatures give 9 glory and honour and thanks to the One who sits on the throne, who lives for ever and ever, the twenty-four 10 elders fall down before the One who sits on the throne and worship him who lives for ever and ever; and as they lay their crowns before the throne they cry:

'Thou art worthy, O Lord our God, 11 to receive glory and honour and power, because thou didst create all things; by thy will they were created, and have their being!'

The prime source: compare Jn.1.3; Col.1.15–18; Heb.1.2. **17:** *Rich . . . poor:* contrast with 2.9; compare Hos.12.8. **18:** Famous for its wealth, wool, and medical school, Laodicea is now to receive true *gold . . . white clothes . . . ointment* from Christ. **19:** *Reprove:* see Prov.3.11–12; Heb.12.5–6. **20:** The *supper* can refer both to the Lord's Supper (see Mt.26.26–29) and to the future messianic banquet. **21:** The faithful will share Christ's *throne* and power; compare 2.26–27; Lk.22.30.
  4.1–5.14: A vision of the heavenly worship (see Isa.6.1–3).
  4.1–11: The praise of God the Creator. 1: *Voice:* compare 1.10. *Trumpet:* see 1.11 n. *Come up here:* the writer is transplanted to heaven, a conventional motif in ancient apocalyptic literature. **2:** *Throne:* a symbol of sovereignty occurring more than forty times in Rev.; compare Ezek.1.26–28; Jer.17.12. **4:** *Twenty-four elders* may refer to the twelve tribes and twelve apostles, symbolizing the unity of old and new covenant peoples: see 21.13-14. **5:** *Lightning . . . thunder:* compare Exod.19.16. *Seven spirits:* see 1.5 n. **6:** *Sea of glass:* probably conceived as before the "throne" in the heavenly temple; see 1 Kgs.7.23–26. *Four living creatures* (see Ezek.1.5) symbolize the created world. *Covered with eyes* (see Ezek.1.18) symbolizes all-seeing watchfulness. **7:** *Lion . . . ox . . . face of a man . . . eagle* (see Ezek.1.10): in later Christian tradition, related respectively to Mk., Lk., Mt., and Jn. **8:** *Holy, holy, holy:* see Isa.6.3. **10:** *The One:* see vv. 2,9. *Throne:* see v. 2 n.

5 Then I saw in the right hand of the One who sat on the throne a scroll, with writing inside and out, and it was sealed up with seven seals. And I saw a mighty angel proclaiming in a loud voice, 'Who is worthy to open the scroll 3 and to break its seals?' There was no one in heaven or on earth or under the earth able to open the scroll or to look 4 inside it. I was in tears because no one was found who was worthy to open the 5 scroll or to look inside it. But one of the elders said to me: 'Do not weep; for the Lion from the tribe of Judah, the Scion of David, has won the right to open the scroll and break its seven seals.'

6 Then I saw standing in the very middle of the throne, inside the circle of living creatures and the circle of elders,*c* a Lamb with the marks of slaughter upon him. He had seven horns and seven eyes, the eyes which are the seven spirits of God sent out over all the 7 world. And the Lamb went up and took the scroll from the right hand of 8 the One who sat on the throne. When he took it, the four living creatures and the twenty-four elders fell down before the Lamb. Each of the elders had a harp, and they held golden bowls full of incense, the prayers of God's people, 9 and they were singing a new song:

'Thou art worthy to take the scroll and to break its seals, for thou wast slain and by thy blood didst purchase for God men of every tribe and 10 language, people and nation; thou hast made of them a royal house, to serve our God as priests; and they shall reign upon earth.'

11 Then as I looked I heard the voices of countless angels. These were all round the throne and the living creatures and the elders. Myriads upon myriads there were, thousands upon thousands, and they cried aloud: 12

'Worthy is the Lamb, the Lamb that was slain, to receive all power and wealth, wisdom and might, honour and glory and praise!'

Then I heard every created thing in 13 heaven and on earth and under the earth and in the sea, all that is in them, crying:

'Praise and honour, glory and might, to him who sits on the throne and to the Lamb for ever and ever!'

And the four living creatures said, 14 'Amen', and the elders fell down and worshipped.

THEN I WATCHED AS THE LAMB BROKE 6 the first of the seven seals; and I heard one of the four living creatures say in a voice like thunder, 'Come!' And there 2 before my eyes was a white horse, and its rider held a bow. He was given a crown, and he rode forth, conquering and to conquer.

When the Lamb broke the second 3 seal, I heard the second creature say, 'Come!' And out came another horse, 4 all red. To its rider was given power to take peace from the earth and make men slaughter one another; and he was given a great sword.

When he broke the third seal, I heard 5 the third creature say, 'Come!' And there, as I looked, was a black horse;

c Or standing between the throne, with the four living creatures, and the elders ...

5.1–14: The praise of the Lamb the Redeemer. 1: *A scroll . . . sealed:* see Isa.29.11; Ezek.2.9–10. The *seven seals* are to be opened to reveal the secrets of the future. **5:** *Lion from the tribe of Judah* (see Gen.49.9), *the Scion* (descendant) *of David* (see Isa.11.1) are messianic titles. **6:** *Lamb with the marks of slaughter* refers to Jesus' death, though now he is at the *throne;* see 3.21. The title *Lamb* appears nearly thirty times in Rev.; compare Isa.53.7; Jn.1.29,36 (though a different Gk. word is used). *Seven horns* and *seven eyes* portray authority and omniscience; see Zech.4.10; Dan.7.7–8,20. **8:** *Incense . . . and prayers:* see Ps.141.2. **9:** *By thy blood didst purchase:* redemption was won at the cost of Christ's life; see 1.5; 12.11; 1 Cor.6.19–20. **10:** *A royal house . . . as priests:* see 1.6 n. **12:** *Worthy is the Lamb:* the Redeemer is offered the same kind of worship as the Creator. The Lamb, not the caesar (emperor), shares the divine sovereignty.

6.1–17: The opening of the first six seals. As the first four seals are opened, horsemen (compare Zech.1.7–17; 6.1–8) appear, portraying coming disasters; all six correspond to the scheme of Mk.13.7–8, 24–25 (compare Lev.26.21–39). **2:** *A white horse, and its rider* (in 19.11 the rider is Jesus) symbolize victory. **4:** *Another horse, all red* promotes war. **5–6:** *A black horse* brings a

and its rider held in his hand a pair of
6 scales. And I heard what sounded like
a voice from the midst of the living
creatures, which said, 'A whole day's
wage for a quart of flour, a whole day's
wage for three quarts of barley-meal!
But spare the olive and the vine.'

7 When he broke the fourth seal, I
heard the voice of the fourth creature
8 say, 'Come!' And there, as I looked,
was another horse, sickly pale; and its
rider's name was Death, and Hades
came close behind. To him was given
power over a quarter of the earth, with
the right to kill by sword and by
famine, by pestilence and wild beasts.

9 When he broke the fifth seal, I saw
underneath[d] the altar the souls of those
who had been slaughtered for God's
word and for the testimony they bore.
10 They gave a great cry: 'How long,
sovereign Lord, holy and true, must it
be before thou wilt vindicate us and
avenge our blood on the inhabitants
11 of the earth?' Each of them was given a
white robe; and they were told to rest a
little while longer, until the tally should
be complete of all their brothers in
Christ's service who were to be killed
as they had been.

12 Then I watched as he broke the sixth
seal. And there was a violent earthquake; the sun turned black as a funeral
pall and the moon all red as blood;
13 the stars in the sky fell to the earth, like
14 figs shaken down by a gale; the sky
vanished, as a scroll is rolled up, and
every mountain and island was moved
15 from its place. Then the kings of the
earth, magnates and marshals, the rich
and the powerful, and all men, slave or
free, hid themselves in caves and
16 mountain crags; and they called out to
the mountains and the crags, 'Fall on
us and hide us from the face of the One

who sits on the throne and from the
vengeance of the Lamb.' For the great 17
day of their vengeance has come, and
who will be able to stand?

After this I saw four angels stationed 7
at the four corners of the earth, holding
back the four winds so that no wind
should blow on sea or land or on any
tree. Then I saw another angel rising 2
out of the east, carrying the seal of the
living God; and he called aloud to
the four angels who had been given the
power to ravage land and sea: 'Do no 3
damage to sea or land or trees until we
have set the seal of our God upon the
foreheads of his servants.' And I heard 4
the number of those who had received
the seal. From all the tribes of Israel
there were a hundred and forty-four
thousand: twelve thousand from the 5
tribe of Judah, twelve thousand from
the tribe of Reuben, twelve thousand
from the tribe of Gad, twelve thousand 6
from the tribe of Asher, twelve thousand from the tribe of Naphtali, twelve
thousand from the tribe of Manasseh,
twelve thousand from the tribe of 7
Simeon, twelve thousand from the tribe
of Levi, twelve thousand from the tribe
of Issachar, twelve thousand from the 8
tribe of Zebulun, twelve thousand from
the tribe of Joseph, and twelve thousand from the tribe of Benjamin.

After this I looked and saw a vast 9
throng, which no one could count,
from every nation, of all tribes, peoples,
and languages, standing in front of the
throne and before the Lamb. They were
robed in white and had palms in their
hands, and they shouted together: 10

'Victory to our God who sits on the
throne, and to the Lamb!'

d Or at the foot of . . .

---

famine of grain. **7–8:** *Another horse, sickly pale* bears *Death, and Hades* (in 1.18 *Hades* is
translated as "Death's domain"; compare Ezek.5.12). **9–11:** Breaking the fifth seal discloses
the souls of the martyred dead crying out for vengeance; see Ps.79.5–10; contrast Lk.23.34;
Acts 7.60. *Underneath the altar* may reflect a Jewish saying: "The souls of the righteous are
kept safely under the throne of glory." *Until the tally should be complete:* compare 2 Esd.4.35–37.
12–17: Breaking the sixth seal brings cosmic catastrophe. **12:** See Joel 2.31; Acts 2.20. **14:**
Isa.34.4. **15:** Isa.2.10. **16:** Hos.10.8. **17:** Joel 2.11; Mal.3.2.

7.1–17: The marking of God's servants falls between the sixth and seventh seals, securing the
faithful from destruction. **1:** *The four winds:* see Zech.6.5. **3:** *Set the seal . . . upon the foreheads:*
see Ezek.9.4. **4:** *A hundred and forty-four thousand* is a "perfect" number ($12 \times 12 \times 1000$);
it may symbolize Israel's future full participation in Christ (compare Rom.9.25–27) or the return of the ten "lost" tribes; see 2 Esd.13.40–48). **9:** With *throng, every nation* the seer points

319

11 And all the angels stood round the throne and the elders and the four living creatures, and they fell on their faces before the throne and worshipped 12 God, crying:

'Amen! Praise and glory and wisdom, thanksgiving and honour, power and might, be to our God for ever and ever! Amen.'

13 Then one of the elders turned to me and said, 'These men that are robed in white—who are they and from where 14 do they come?' But I answered, 'My lord, you know, not I.' Then he said to me, 'These are the men who have passed through the great ordeal; they have washed their robes and made them 15 white in the blood of the Lamb. That is why they stand before the throne of God and minister to him day and night in his temple; and he who sits on the 16 throne will dwell with them. They shall never again feel hunger or thirst, the sun shall not beat on them nor any 17 scorching heat, because the Lamb who is at the heart of the throne will be their shepherd and will guide them to the springs of the water of life; and God will wipe all tears from their eyes.'

8 Now when the Lamb broke the seventh seal, there was silence in heaven for what seemed half an hour. 2 Then I looked, and the seven angels that stand in the presence of God were given seven trumpets. 3 Then another angel came and stood at the altar, holding a golden censer; and he was given a great quantity of incense to offer with the prayers of all God's people upon the golden altar in 4 front of the throne. And from the angel's hand the smoke of the incense went up before God with the prayers of his people. Then the angel took the 5 censer, filled it from the altar fire, and threw it down upon the earth; and there were peals of thunder, lightning, and an earthquake.

The powers of darkness conquered

THEN THE SEVEN ANGELS THAT HELD THE 6 seven trumpets prepared to blow them.

The first blew his trumpet; and there 7 came hail and fire mingled with blood, and this was hurled upon the earth. A third of the earth was burnt, a third of the trees were burnt, all the green grass was burnt.

The second angel blew his trumpet; 8 and what looked like a great blazing mountain was hurled into the sea. A third of the sea was turned to blood, a 9 third of the living creatures in it died, and a third of the ships on it foundered.

The third angel blew his trumpet; 10 and a great star shot from the sky, flaming like a torch; and it fell on a third of the rivers and springs. The 11 name of the star was Wormwood; and a third of the water turned to wormwood, and men in great numbers died of the water because it had been poisoned.

The fourth angel blew his trumpet; 12 and a third part of the sun was struck, a third of the moon, and a third of the stars, so that the third part went dark and a third of the light of the day failed, and of the night.

Then I looked, and I heard an eagle 13 calling with a loud cry as it flew in mid-heaven: 'Woe, woe, woe to the inhabitants of the earth when the trumpets sound which the three last angels must now blow!'

beyond Israel (vv. 4–8) to the Gentile world (see Dan.7.14). **12:** Note the seven-fold ascription; compare 5.12. **14:** *The great ordeal:* see 3.10 n. *The blood of the Lamb:* see 5.9 n.; 1 Jn.1.7. **15:** Compare 21.3. **16:** 21.4; Ps.121.6; Isa.25.8; 49.10. **17:** *Shepherd:* see Ps.23.1–2; Ezek.34.23. *Springs of the water of life:* see 21.6; 22.1,17; compare Jn.4.10; 7.37–38.

8.1–5: The opening of the seventh seal introduces the *seven trumpets* (v. 2). **1:** *Silence in heaven:* the calm before the storm. **2:** *Seven angels:* probably the seven archangels; compare Tob.12.15. **3:** *Incense:* see Ps.141.2. *Golden altar:* see Exod.30.1–3. **5:** *Took the censer ... and threw it:* compare Ezek.10.2.

8.6–9.21: The first six trumpets proclaim catastrophes in nature as judgment on the wicked. **6–13:** Compare the plagues in Egypt, as in Exod.7.17–21; 9.23,25; 10.21–23. **6–7:** In connection with several trumpet blasts, a *third* of creation is affected. **8–9:** The volcanic island of Thera, visible from Patmos, may have suggested a *blazing mountain ... hurled into the sea.* **10:** *Great star:* shooting star or meteor. **11:** *Wormwood:* a bitter drug; see Jer.9.15; 23.15. **13:** The three

9 Then the fifth angel blew his trumpet; and I saw a star that had fallen from heaven to earth, and the star was given the key of the shaft of the abyss. 2 With this he opened the shaft of the abyss; and from the shaft smoke rose like smoke from a great furnace, and the sun and the air were darkened by 3 the smoke from the shaft. Then over the earth, out of the smoke, came locusts, and they were given the powers that 4 earthly scorpions have. They were told to do no injury to the grass or to any plant or tree, but only to those men who had not received the seal of God 5 on their foreheads. These they were allowed to torment for five months, with torment like a scorpion's sting; 6 but they were not to kill them. During that time these men will seek death, but they will not find it; they will long to die, but death will elude them.

7 In appearance the locusts were like horses equipped for battle. On their heads were what looked like golden crowns; their faces were like human 8 faces and their hair like women's hair; 9 they had teeth like lions' teeth, and wore breastplates like iron; the sound of their wings was like the noise of horses and chariots rushing to battle; 10 they had tails like scorpions, with stings in them, and in their tails lay their power to plague mankind for five 11 months. They had for their king the angel of the abyss, whose name, in Hebrew, is Abaddon, and in Greek, Apollyon, or the Destroyer.

12 The first woe has now passed. But there are still two more to come.

13 The sixth angel then blew his trumpet; and I heard a voice coming from between the horns of the golden altar that stood in the presence of God. 14 It said to the sixth angel, who held the trumpet: 'Release the four angels held

bound at the great river Euphrates!' So the four angels were let loose, to kill 15 a third of mankind. They had been held ready for this moment, for this very year and month, day and hour. And 16 their squadrons of cavalry, whose count I heard, numbered two hundred million.

This was how I saw the horses and 17 their riders in my vision: They wore breastplates, fiery red, blue, and sulphur-yellow; the horses had heads like lions' heads, and out of their mouths came fire, smoke, and sulphur. By 18 these three plagues, that is, by the fire, the smoke, and the sulphur that came from their mouths, a third of mankind was killed. The power of the horses lay 19 in their mouths, and in their tails also; for their tails were like snakes, with heads, and with them too they dealt injuries.

The rest of mankind who survived 20 these plagues still did not abjure the gods their hands had fashioned, nor cease their worship of devils and of idols made from gold, silver, bronze, stone, and wood, which cannot see or hear or walk. Nor did they repent of 21 their murders, their sorcery, their fornication, or their robberies.

THEN I SAW ANOTHER MIGHTY ANGEL **10** coming down from heaven. He was wrapped in cloud, with the rainbow round his head; his face shone like the sun and his legs were like pillars of fire. In his hand he held a little scroll un- 2 rolled. His right foot he planted on the sea, and his left on the land. Then he 3 gave a great shout, like the roar of a lion; and when he shouted, the seven thunders spoke. I was about to write 4 down what the seven thunders had said; but I heard a voice from heaven saying, 'Seal up what the seven thunders have said; do not write it down.' Then the 5

---

woes correspond to the last three trumpet blasts. **9.1:** Since stars were identified as angels (1.20), *a star that had fallen* may refer to Satan as a fallen angel; see v. 11; Isa.14.12–16; Lk.10.18. **2–5:** *Locusts:* compare Exod.10.12–15; Joel 1.4; 2.10. **4:** *The seal . . . on their foreheads:* see 7.3 n. **7:** *Like horses:* see Joel 2.4. **8:** *Teeth like lions':* Joel 1.6. **9:** *Chariots:* Joel 2.5. **11:** *Abaddon* (or, Destruction) in the OT is equivalent to Sheol or Hades; see Job 26.6; 28.22; Prov.15.11. **13:** *Golden altar:* see Exod.30.1–3. **14:** *The four angels* (not those in 7.2) are here at the Euphrates, whence Rome feared a Parthian invasion; compare "the kings from the east" in 16.12. **20:** Compare the view of idolatry here with Ps.115.4–7; 135.15–17; Dan.5.23. As frequently in the Bible, idolatry leads (v. 21) to further sin.
    10.1–11.14: The little scroll and the two witnesses. This section falls between the sixth and seventh trumpets. **4:** *Seal up . . . do not write:* see Dan.12.4,9. **5–6:** *The angel . . . swore:* Dan.12.7.

angel that I saw standing on the sea and the land raised his right hand to heaven
6 and swore by him who lives for ever and ever, who created heaven and earth and the sea and everything in them: 'There shall be no more delay;
7 but when the time comes for the seventh angel to sound his trumpet, the hidden purpose of God will have been fulfilled, as he promised to his servants the prophets.'
8   Then the voice which I heard from heaven was speaking to me again, and it said, 'Go and take the open scroll in the hand of the angel that stands on
9 the sea and the land.' So I went to the angel and asked him to give me the little scroll. He said to me, 'Take it, and eat it. It will turn your stomach sour, although in your mouth it will
10 taste sweet as honey.' So I took the little scroll from the angel's hand and ate it, and in my mouth it did taste sweet as honey; but when I swallowed it my stomach turned sour.
11   Then they said to me, 'Once again you must utter prophecies over peoples and nations and languages and many kings.'

11   I was given a long cane, a kind of measuring-rod, and told: 'Now go and measure the temple of God, the altar, and the number of the worshippers.
2 But have nothing to do with the outer court of the temple; do not measure that; for it has been given over to the Gentiles, and they will trample the Holy City underfoot for forty-two
3 months. And I have two witnesses, whom I will appoint to prophesy, dressed in sackcloth, all through those
4 twelve hundred and sixty days.' These

are the two olive-trees and the two lamps that stand in the presence of the Lord of the earth. If anyone seeks to 5 do them harm, fire pours from their mouths and consumes their enemies; and thus shall the man die who seeks to do them harm. These two have the 6 power to shut up the sky, so that no rain may fall during the time of their prophesying; and they have the power to turn water to blood and to strike the earth at will with every kind of plague. But when they have completed 7 their testimony, the beast that comes up from the abyss will wage war upon them and will defeat and kill them. Their corpses will lie in the street of the 8 great city, whose name in allegory is Sodom, or Egypt, where also their Lord was crucified. For three days and a half 9 men from every people and tribe, of every language and nation, gaze upon their corpses and refuse them burial. All men on earth gloat over them, make 10 merry, and exchange presents; for these two prophets were a torment to the whole earth. But at the end of the 11 three days and a half the breath of life from God came into them; and they stood up on their feet to the terror of all who saw it. Then a loud voice was 12 heard speaking to them from heaven, which said, 'Come up here!' And they went up to heaven in a cloud, in full view of their enemies. At that same 13 moment there was a violent earthquake, and a tenth of the city fell. Seven thousand people were killed in the earthquake; the rest in terror did homage to the God of heaven.

The second woe has now passed. 14 But the third is soon to come.

8–10: On the eating of the scroll compare Ezek.2.8–3.3. **11:** The writer's sweet-sour (vv. 8–10; sweet for the faithful, sour for the faithless) *prophecies* (see Jer.1.10) unfolds in chs. 12–22. **11.1–14:** The scene seems to reflect material from the time of the Jewish War (66–70 A.D.) prior to the destruction of the Jerusalem Temple in 70 A.D. **1:** *Measure the temple:* see Ezek.40.3–42.20; Zech.2.1–5. **2:** *Forty-two months* is equivalent to 1,260 days, or three and a half years, or "a time and times and half a time"; see Dan.7.25 n.; 9.27 n.; 12.7. Dan. divides seven years in half, with three and a half years of acute persecution prior to 168 B.C. (when Antiochus IV set up an image of Zeus in the Temple), and three and a half years of deliverance after. These events came to be regarded as foreshadowing the time of the Antichrist. **3–6:** *Two witnesses:* probably Elijah (see 1 Kgs.17.1; Mal.4.5–6) and Moses (see Exod.7.17–21; Deut. 18.15–18); compare Mk.9.11–13. It was a Jewish expectation that Elijah and Moses would return before the end of the age. In v. 4 Elijah and Moses are the *olive trees* and *lamps* (though in Zech. ch. 4 these symbols represent Zerubbabel and Joshua). **7:** *The beast . . . from the abyss:* see 17.7–8 n. **8:** *The great city . . . Sodom, or Egypt,* is here Jerusalem; see Isa.1.9 10; Ezek.23.27. **11:** *The breath of life . . . came upon them:* see Ezek.37.5,10. **12:** See 2 Kgs.2.11. **14:** *Second woe:* see 8.13 for the prediction of three woes, associated with the last trumpet blasts.

15 Then the seventh angel blew his trumpet; and voices were heard in heaven shouting:

'The sovereignty of the world has passed to our Lord and his Christ, and he shall reign for ever and ever!'

16 And the twenty-four elders, seated on their thrones before God, fell on their 17 faces and worshipped God, saying:

'We give thee thanks, O Lord God, sovereign over all, who art and who wast, because thou hast taken thy great power into thy hands and 18 entered upon thy reign. The nations raged, but thy day of retribution has come. Now is the time for the dead to be judged; now is the time for recompense to thy servants the prophets, to thy dedicated people, and all who honour thy name, both great and small, the time to destroy those who destroy the earth.'

19 Then God's temple in heaven was laid open, and within the temple was seen the ark of his covenant. There came flashes of lightning and peals of thunder, an earthquake, and a storm of hail.

12 NEXT APPEARED A GREAT PORTENT IN heaven, a woman robed with the sun, beneath her feet the moon, and on her 2 head a crown of twelve stars. She was pregnant, and in the anguish of her labour she cried out to be delivered. 3 Then a second portent appeared in heaven: a great red dragon with seven heads and ten horns; on his heads were 4 seven diadems, and with his tail he swept

down a third of the stars in the sky and flung them to the earth. The dragon stood in front of the woman who was about to give birth, so that when her child was born he might devour it. She 5 gave birth to a male child, who is destined to rule all nations with an iron rod. But her child was snatched up to God and his throne; and the woman 6 herself fled into the wilds, where she had a place prepared for her by God, there to be sustained for twelve hundred and sixty days.

Then war broke out in heaven. 7 Michael and his angels waged war upon the dragon. The dragon and his angels fought, but they had not the 8 strength to win, and no foothold was left them in heaven. So the great dragon 9 was thrown down, that serpent of old that led the whole world astray, whose name is Satan, or the Devil—thrown down to the earth, and his angels with him.

Then I heard a voice in heaven 10 proclaiming aloud: 'This is the hour of victory for our God, the hour of his sovereignty and power, when his Christ comes to his rightful rule! For the accuser of our brothers is overthrown, who day and night accused them before our God. By the sacrifice of the Lamb 11 they have conquered him, and by the testimony which they uttered;[e] for they did not hold their lives too dear to lay them down. Rejoice then, you heavens 12 and you that dwell in them! But woe to you, earth and sea, for the Devil has come down to you in great fury, knowing that his time is short!'

When the dragon found that he had 13 been thrown down to the earth, he went

e Or the word of God to which they bore witness.

11.15–19: **The seventh trumpet** brings the heavenly proclamation of God's sovereignty, indirectly introducing the final woe of chs. 12–19. **15:** *Our Lord and his Christ:* note v. 18, and compare Ps.2.1–2. **19:** *Ark of his covenant:* see 1 Kgs.8.1–6.
12.1–17: **The woman, child, and dragon.** The struggle between Satan and God's people is described in imagery possibly drawn from a widespread ancient myth. **1:** Here, the *woman* represents Israel from whom Jesus sprang (v. 5). *Twelve stars:* the twelve tribes. **2:** *The anguish of her labour:* see Isa.66.7; Mic.4.9–10. **3:** *A great red dragon:* Satan (see v. 9; compare descriptions of the beast in 13.1). *Ten horns:* see Dan.7.7. **5:** *A male child:* Jesus, *destined to rule all nations* (see 2.27; 19.15; Ps.2.9); reference is made only to his birth and ascension! **6:** The *woman*, now probably seen as Jewish Christians, is to be safe during the three and a half years of Satan's persecution (see v. 14; 11.2 n.; compare Mk.13.14–20). **7–17:** The dragon's defeat is portrayed (see Lk.10.18; Jn.12.31), though he still is active for a short time (vv. 12,14). **7:** The archangel *Michael* is Israel's champion (see Dan.10.13,21; 12.1). **9:** *That serpent of old:* an allusion to Gen.3.1,14–15. **10:** *The accuser:* Satan; see Job 1.6–12; Zech.3.1. **11:** *Sacrifice of the lamb:* lit. blood; see 5.9 n. **12:** *Rejoice then, you heavens:* compare Isa.44.23; 49.13.

in pursuit of the woman who had given 14 birth to the male child. But the woman was given two great eagle's wings, to fly to the place in the wilds where for three years and a half she was to be sustained, out of reach of the serpent. 15 From his mouth the serpent spewed a flood of water after the woman to 16 sweep her away with its spate. But the earth came to her rescue and opened its mouth and swallowed the river which the dragon spewed from his mouth. 17 At this the dragon grew furious with the woman, and went off to wage war on the rest of her offspring, that is, on those who keep God's commandments and maintain their testimony to Jesus.

13 He took his stand on the sea-shore.

Then*f* out of the sea I saw a beast rising. It had ten horns and seven heads. On its horns were ten diadems, and on 2 each head a blasphemous name. The beast I saw was like a leopard, but its feet were like a bear's and its mouth like a lion's mouth. The dragon conferred upon it his power and rule, and 3 great authority. One of its heads appeared to have received a death-blow; but the mortal wound was healed. The whole world went after the 4 beast in wondering admiration. Men worshipped the dragon because he had conferred his authority upon the beast; they worshipped the beast also, and chanted, 'Who is like the Beast? Who can fight against it?'

5 The beast was allowed to mouth bombast and blasphemy, and was given the right to reign for forty-two months. 6 It opened its mouth in blasphemy against God, reviling his name and his 7 heavenly dwelling.*g* It was also allowed to wage war on God's people and to defeat them, and was granted*h* authority over every tribe and people, language and nation. All on earth will 8 worship it, except those whose names the Lamb that was slain keeps in his roll of the living, written there since the world was made.

Hear, you who have ears to hear! 9 Whoever is to be made prisoner, a 10 prisoner he shall be. Whoever takes the sword to kill, by the sword he is bound to be killed. This is where the fortitude and faithfulness of God's people have their place.

Then I saw another beast, which 11 came up out of the earth; it had two horns like a lamb's, but spoke like a dragon. It wielded all the authority of 12 the first beast in its presence, and made the earth and its inhabitants worship this first beast, whose mortal wound had been healed. It worked great 13 miracles, even making fire come down from heaven to earth before men's eyes. By the miracles it was allowed to 14 perform in the presence of the beast it deluded the inhabitants of the earth, and made them erect an image in honour of the beast that had been wounded by the sword and yet lived. It was allowed to give breath to the 15 image of the beast, so that it could speak, and could cause all who would not worship the image to be put to death. Moreover, it caused everyone, 16 great and small, rich and poor, slave and free, to be branded with a mark on

f Some witnesses read . . . testimony to Jesus. Then I stood by the sea-shore and . . .
g Some witnesses read reviling his name and his dwelling-place, that is, those that live in heaven.
h Some witness read It was granted . . . (omitting the words was also . . . them, and).

14: *Eagle's wings:* see Exod.19.4. **17:** *The rest of her offspring* (probably Gentile Christians): Jewish Christians are "sealed" but others must bear "the great ordeal" (compare ch. 7).

13.1–18: The two beasts. Chs. 4–5 portrayed God and the Lamb; chs. 12–13 portray their evil counterparts, the dragon and the beast (Satan and Rome). **1:** The *beast* is Rome. The empire is identified with the emperor Nero whose return was popularly expected; his persecution of Christians made him a dreaded figure (see ch. 17; compare Dan.7.1–6). *Ten horns:* (Parthian) kings who conspire with Nero; compare 17.12; Dan.7.7. *Seven heads:* seven hills of Rome or seven kings (see 17.9–10). *A blasphemous name:* the divine title claimed by the emperor. **2:** On the animals, see Dan.7.4–6. *The dragon . . . conferred his power:* i.e. Satan works through the beast. **3:** *Death-blow . . . wound was healed* (see vv. 12,14) points to Nero's rumored survival of suicide and return (see 17.8; compare with Jesus in 1.18; 5.6). **5:** *Bombast:* boastful words (see Dan.7.8). *Forty-two months:* see 11.2 n. **7:** Compare 5.9; Dan.7.21. **8:** *Roll of the living:* see 3.5 n. **9–10:** This may indicate that Christians are not to strike a blow in their own defense; compare Mt.26.52; Jer.15.2. **11–18:** The second *beast* (called "the false prophet" in 19.20) may refer to the priesthood that supported emperor worship (see v. 12); compare Dan.3.1–7; 2 Th.2.9–10. **16:** *Branded with a mark:* compare the marking of the faithful (see 7.3; 14.1).

17 his right hand or forehead, and no one was allowed to buy or sell unless he bore this beast's mark, either name 18 or number. (Here is the key; and anyone who has intelligence may work out the number of the beast. The number represents a man's name, and the numerical value of its letters is six hundred and sixty-six.)

Visions of the end

14 THEN I LOOKED, AND ON MOUNT ZION stood the Lamb, and with him were a hundred and forty-four thousand who had his name and the name of his 2 Father written on their foreheads. I heard a sound from heaven like the noise of rushing water and the deep roar of thunder; it was the sound of 3 harpers playing on their harps. There before the throne, and the four living creatures and the elders, they were singing a new song. That song no one could learn except the hundred and forty-four thousand, who alone from the whole world had been ransomed. 4 These are men who did not defile themselves with women, for they have kept themselves chaste, and they follow the Lamb wherever he goes. They have been ransomed as the firstfruits of 5 humanity for God and the Lamb. No lie was found in their lips; they are faultless.

6 Then I saw an angel flying in midheaven, with an eternal gospel to proclaim to those on earth, to every nation 7 and tribe, language and people. He cried in a loud voice, 'Fear God and pay him homage; for the hour of his judgement has come! Worship him who made heaven and earth, the sea and the water-springs!'

Then another angel, a second, 8 followed, and he cried, 'Fallen, fallen is Babylon the great, she who has made all nations drink the fierce wine of[i] her fornication!'

Yet a third angel followed, crying 9 out loud, 'Whoever worships the beast and its image and receives its mark on his forehead or hand, he shall drink the 10 wine of God's wrath, poured undiluted into the cup of his vengeance. He shall be tormented in sulphurous flames before the holy angels and before the Lamb. The smoke of their torment 11 will rise for ever and ever, and there will be no respite day or night for those who worship the beast and its image or receive the mark of its name.' This is 12 where the fortitude of God's people has its place—in keeping God's commands and remaining loyal to Jesus.

Moreover, I heard a voice from 13 heaven, saying, 'Write this: "Happy are the dead who die in the faith of Christ! Henceforth",[j] says the Spirit,[k] "they may rest from their labours; for they take with them the record of their deeds."'

Then as I looked there appeared a 14 white cloud, and on the cloud sat one like a son of man. He had on his head a crown of gold and in his hand a sharp sickle. Another angel came out 15 of the temple and called in a loud voice to him who sat on the cloud: 'Stretch out your sickle and reap; for harvesttime has come, and earth's crop is overripe.' So he who sat on the cloud put 16 his sickle to the earth and its harvest was reaped.

Then another angel came out of the 17 heavenly temple, and he also had a

i *Or* drink the wine of God's wrath upon . . .
j *Or* Assuredly.
k *Some witnesses read* ". . . the dead who henceforth die in the faith of Christ!" "Yes," says the Spirit . . .

18: In Heb., the letters of the name "Nero Caesar" have numerical values which total *six hundred and sixty-six.*

14.1–20: Three visions of reassurance, admonition, and the harvest. 1–5: The *ransomed.* **1:** *Mount Zion:* the heavenly Jerusalem; see Heb.12.22. *A hundred and forty-four thousand:* here, not Israel (as in 7.4–8), but those *who alone from the whole world had been ransomed* (v. 3). **3:** *A new song:* see 5.8–10. **4:** *Chaste:* lit. virgins. It may mean celibacy, either literally or symbolically (see 2.20–22; compare 2 Cor.11.2; Mt.19.12); it could refer to abstinence from such pollutions as are prohibited in Deut.27.20–30. *Firstfruits:* see Exod.23.19; Jas.1.18. They are here the first part of the ransomed, with the whole to come later. **6–13:** Judgment and warning. **8:** *Babylon the great* (see Isa.21.9): here, Rome is meant (see ch.18). **10:** *Wine of God's wrath:* see Jer.25.15–16. *Sulphurous flames:* see 19.20; 20.10. *Smoke of their torment:* compare Isa.34.10. **14–20:** The *harvest:* a familiar symbol of judgment (see Joel 3.13; Mt.13.30). **14:** *One like a son of man:* see 1.13–15 n. **17–20:** *Grape-harvest:* see 19.15; Isa.63.1–6.

18 sharp sickle. Then from the altar came yet another, the angel who has authority over fire, and he shouted to the one with the sharp sickle: 'Stretch out your sickle, and gather in earth's grape-
19 harvest, for its clusters are ripe.' So the angel put his sickle to the earth and gathered in its grapes, and threw them into the great winepress of God's
20 wrath. The winepress was trodden outside the city, and for two hundred miles around blood flowed from the press to the height of the horses' bridles.

15 Then I saw another great and astonishing portent in heaven: seven angels with seven plagues, the last plagues of all, for with them the wrath of God is consummated.
2 I saw what seemed a sea of glass shot with fire, and beside the sea of glass, holding the harps which God had given them, were those who had won the victory over the beast and its image and the number of its name.
3 They were singing the song of Moses, the servant of God, and the song of the Lamb, as they chanted:

'Great and marvellous are thy deeds, O Lord God, sovereign over all; just and true are thy ways, thou king of
4 the ages.[1] Who shall not revere thee, Lord, and do homage to thy name? For thou alone art holy. All nations shall come and worship in thy presence, for thy just dealings stand revealed.'

5 After this, as I looked, the sanctuary of the heavenly Tent of Testimony was
6 thrown open, and out of it came the seven angels with the seven plagues. They were robed in fine linen, clean and shining, and had golden girdles
7 round their breasts. Then one of the four living creatures gave the seven angels seven golden bowls full of the wrath of God who lives for ever and ever;
8 and the sanctuary was filled with smoke from the glory of God and his power, so that no one could enter it until the seven plagues of the seven angels were completed.

16 Then from the sanctuary I heard a loud voice, and it said to the seven angels, 'Go and pour out the seven bowls of God's wrath on the earth.'
2 So the first angel went and poured his bowl on the earth; and foul malignant sores appeared on those men that wore the mark of the beast and worshipped its image.
3 The second angel poured his bowl on the sea, and it turned to blood like the blood from a corpse; and every living thing in the sea died.
4 The third angel poured his bowl on the rivers and springs, and they turned to blood.
5 Then I heard the angel of the waters say, 'Just art thou in these thy judge-
6 ments, thou Holy One who art and wast; for they shed the blood of thy people and of thy prophets, and thou hast given them blood to drink. They
7 have their deserts!' And I heard the altar cry, 'Yes, Lord God, sovereign over all, true and just are thy judgements!'
8 The fourth angel poured his bowl on the sun; and it was allowed to burn men with its flames. They were fearfully
9 burned; but they only cursed the name of God who had the power to inflict such plagues, and they refused to repent or do him homage.
10 The fifth angel poured his bowl on the throne of the beast; and its kingdom was plunged in darkness. Men gnawed their tongues in agony, but they only

1 Some witnesses read king of the nations.

15.1–8: Introduction to the seven plagues of the seven bowls. 2: *The sea of glass:* see 4.6 n. *Those who* (like Jesus) *had won the victory:* the martyred faithful (compare Jn.16.31–33). **3:** *Song of Moses . . . song of the Lamb* combines the first deliverer, Moses (see Exod.15.1–18; Ps.145.17), with the second, Jesus (the new exodus, a central NT theme): Moses' victory over Pharaoh foreshadows victory over the beast; compare Ps.145.17. **4:** Compare Ps.86.9–10; Jer.10.7. **5:** *Tent of Testimony:* forerunner of the Temple (see Exod.40.34). **8:** *Filled with smoke:* see Isa.6.4.

16.1–21: The seven bowls of God's wrath (similar to the ten plagues of Exod. chs. 7–11). **1:** *From the sanctuary . . . loud voice . . . pour:* compare Isa.66.6; Ps.69.24. **2:** *Sores:* see Exod. 9.10–11; Deut.28.27. **3–4:** *Sea . . . springs . . . turned to blood:* see Exod.7.17–21. **5:** *Just art thou:* see Ps.119.137. **7:** *I heard the altar cry:* see 6.9–10. **8 12:** While the plagues here are not fully parallel to those in Exod., on the fifth (v. 10, *darkness*), compare Exod.10.21–23. **10:** *The throne*

cursed the God of heaven for their sores and pains, and would not repent of what they had done.

12 The sixth angel poured his bowl on the great river Euphrates; and its water was dried up, to prepare the way for the kings from the east.

13 Then I saw coming from the mouth of the dragon, the mouth of the beast, and the mouth of the false prophet,

14 three foul spirits like frogs. These spirits were devils, with power to work miracles. They were sent out to muster all the kings of the world for the great day of battle of God the sovereign

15 Lord. ('That is the day when I come like a thief! Happy the man who stays awake and keeps on his clothes, so that he will not have to go naked and

16 ashamed for all to see!') So they assembled the kings at the place called in Hebrew Armageddon.

17 Then the seventh angel poured his bowl on the air; and out of the sanctuary came a loud voice from the

18 throne, which said, 'It is over!' And there followed flashes of lightning and peals of thunder, and a violent earthquake, like none before it in human

19 history, so violent it was. The great city was split in three; the cities of the world fell in ruin; and God did not forget Babylon the great, but made her drink the cup which was filled with the

20 fierce wine of his vengeance. Every island vanished; there was not a

21 mountain to be seen. Huge hailstones, weighing perhaps a hundredweight, fell on men from the sky; and they cursed God for the plague of hail, because that plague was so severe.

17 THEN ONE OF THE SEVEN ANGELS THAT held the seven bowls came and spoke to me and said, 'Come, and I will show you the judgement on the great whore,

2 enthroned above the ocean. The kings of the earth have committed fornication with her, and on the wine of her fornication men all over the world

3 have made themselves drunk.' In the Spirit he carried me away into the wilds, and there I saw a woman mounted on a scarlet beast which was covered with blasphemous names and

4 had seven heads and ten horns. The woman was clothed in purple and scarlet and bedizened with gold and jewels and pearls. In her hand she held a gold cup, full of obscenities and the foulness of her fornication;

5 and written on her forehead was a name with a secret meaning: 'Babylon the great, the mother of whores and of every obscenity on earth.' The woman,

6 I saw, was drunk with the blood of God's people and with the blood of those who had borne their testimony to Jesus.

As I looked at her I was greatly astonished. But the angel said to me,

7 'Why are you so astonished? I will tell you the secret of the woman and of the beast she rides, with the seven heads and the ten horns. The beast you have

8 seen is he who once was alive, and is alive no longer, but has yet to ascend out of the abyss before going to perdition. Those on earth whose names have not been inscribed in the roll of the living ever since the world was made will all be astonished to see the beast; for he once was alive, and is

of the beast: Rome. **12:** *Dried up:* compare Exod.14.21; Isa.11.15–16. Perhaps the drying up of the *Euphrates* alludes to opening the way for the expected return of Nero with the *kings from the east.* See 13.1,3 nn.; 17.15–18. **13:** *Dragon . . . beast . . . false prophet:* a trinity of evil over against God, the Lamb and the Spirit (the inspirer of true prophets). **14:** *All the kings of the world* (not the kings from the east; compare 17.15–18; 19.19–21): see Ps.2; Joel 3.2; Zech.14.1–3. **15:** *Like a thief:* 1 Th.5.1–2 n. **16:** *Armageddon* ("Hill of Megiddo," a strategic military post in antiquity; see Judg.5.19; 2 Kgs.23.29–30; 2 Chr.35.22); in apocalyptic literature, the scene of the final battle between good and evil (compare 19.17–21). **17–21:** The seventh bowl pours out judgments similar to the seven trumpets (chs. 8–11). **19:** *Babylon:* Rome. *Fierce wine:* 14.10 n. **21:** *Hail:* Exod.9.23.

   17.1–18: The future fall of Babylon/Rome. 1: The description of a great, sinful city as a *whore* goes back to the prophets (compare Isa.23.16; Ezek.16.15; Nah.3.4); here, the city is Rome, destroyed by the beast (Nero) in v. 16; contrast the bride (New Jerusalem) in 19.7; 21.2,9. *Enthroned above the ocean* echoes Jer.51.13. **2:** *Fornication:* here, emperor worship, not just idolatry in general. **3:** *A woman . . . on a scarlet beast:* the city, Rome, and its imperial power. *Blasphemous names:* see 13.1 n. *Seven heads . . . ten horns:* defined in vv. 9–12. **4:** *A gold cup:* see Jer.51.7. **6:** *Drunk with the blood* may once have referred to the Jewish War (see 11.1–14 n.); here it is applied to later persecution. **7–18:** The *beast* destroys the *whore.* **7–8:** This perhaps

alive no longer, and has still to appear. 'But here is the clue for those who can interpret it. The seven heads are seven hills on which the woman sits. 10 They represent also seven kings,[m] of whom five have already fallen, one is now reigning, and the other has yet to come; and when he does come he is 11 only to last for a little while. As for the beast that once was alive and is alive no longer, he is an eighth—and yet he is one of the seven, and he is going to 12 perdition. The ten horns you saw are ten kings who have not yet begun to reign, but who for one hour are to share with the beast the exercise of royal 13 authority; for they have but a single purpose among them and will confer their power and authority upon the 14 beast. They will wage war upon the Lamb, but the Lamb will defeat them, for he is Lord of lords and King of kings, and his victory will be shared by his followers, called and chosen and faithful.'[n] 15 Then he said to me, 'The ocean you saw, where the great whore sat, is an ocean of peoples and populations, 16 nations and languages. As for the ten horns you saw, they together with the beast will come to hate the whore; they will strip her naked and leave her desolate, they will batten on her flesh 17 and burn her to ashes. For God has put it into their heads to carry out his purpose, by making common cause and conferring their sovereignty upon the beast until all that God has spoken is 18 fulfilled. The woman you saw is the great city that holds sway over the kings of the earth.'

18 After this I saw another angel coming down from heaven; he came with great authority and the earth was lit up with 2 his splendour. Then in a mighty voice

he proclaimed, 'Fallen, fallen is Babylon the great! She has become a dwelling for demons, a haunt for every unclean spirit, for every vile and loathsome bird. For all nations have drunk 3 deep of[o] the fierce wine of her fornication; the kings of the earth have committed fornication with her, and merchants the world over have grown rich on her bloated wealth.'

Then I heard another voice from 4 heaven that said: 'Come out of her, my people, lest you take part in her sins and share in her plagues. For her sins are 5 piled high as heaven, and God has not forgotten her crimes. Pay her back in 6 her own coin, repay her twice over for her deeds! Double for her the strength of the potion she mixed! Mete out 7 grief and torment to match her voluptuous pomp! She says in her heart, "I am a queen on my throne! No mourning for me, no widow's weeds!" Because 8 of this her plagues shall strike her in a single day—pestilence, bereavement, famine, and burning—for mighty is the Lord God who has pronounced her doom!'

The kings of the earth who com- 9 mitted fornication with her and wallowed in her luxury will weep and wail over her, as they see the smoke of her conflagration. They will stand at a 10 distance, for horror at her torment, and will say, 'Alas, alas for the great city, the mighty city of Babylon! In a single hour your doom has struck!'

The merchants of the earth also will 11 weep and mourn for her, because no one any longer buys their cargoes, cargoes of gold and silver, jewels and 12 pearls, cloths of purple and scarlet,

m Or emperors.
n Or ... kings, and his followers are faithful men, called and selected for service.
o Other witnesses read have been ruined by ...

identifies Domitian as the "returned Nero"; see 13.1,3 nn. **9:** Rome was built on *seven hills*. **10:** *Seven kings:* This is difficult to decipher; probably Domitian (81–96 A.D.) is seen as the *one ... now reigning.* **11:** *An eighth—and yet he is one of the seven:* Nero. **12:** The *ten kings* are Nero's companions from the east; see 16.12 n. **14:** *Will wage war on the Lamb:* i.e. in the future (see 19.19–21), but before that they will destroy Rome (vv. 16–18). *Lord of lords:* Deut.10.17; Dan.2.47. **16:** *Batten:* feed gluttonously. *Burn her to ashes:* see 18.16; Nero was suspected of starting the destructive fire in Rome in 64 A.D.

18.1–24: The fall of and lament over Babylon (compare the dirge over Tyre in Ezek. chs. 26–27). Elements of several OT prophecies against Babylon are woven into a condemnation of Rome. **2:** *Fallen, fallen:* see Isa.13.19–22; 21.9. **4:** *Come out of her:* compare Jer.50.8; 51.45. **7–8:** Compare the boast with Isa.47.7 9. **9 10:** See Ezek.26.16–18. **11:** Ezek.27.31. **12–16:** Ezek.27.15–16. Rome's power as a world trade center is vividly depicted in the list of rich goods.

silks and fine linens; all kinds of scented woods, ivories, and every sort of thing made of costly woods, bronze, iron, or 13 marble; cinnamon and spice, incense, perfumes and frankincense; wine, oil, flour and wheat, sheep and cattle, horses, chariots, slaves, and the lives of 14 men. 'The fruit you longed for', they will say, 'is gone from you; all the glitter and the glamour are lost, never 15 to be yours again!' The traders in all these wares, who gained their wealth from her, will stand at a distance for horror at her torment, weeping and 16 mourning and saying, 'Alas, alas for the great city, that was clothed in fine linen and purple and scarlet, bedizened with 17 gold and jewels and pearls! Alas that in one hour so much wealth should be laid waste!'

Then all the sea-captains and voyagers, the sailors and those who traded 18 by sea, stood at a distance and cried out as they saw the smoke of her conflagration: 'Was there ever a city like 19 the great city?' They threw dust on their heads, weeping and mourning and saying, 'Alas, alas for the great city, where all who had ships at sea grew rich on her wealth! Alas that in a single hour she should be laid waste!'

20 But let heaven exult over her; exult, apostles and prophets and people of God; for in the judgement against her he has vindicated your cause!

21 Then a mighty angel took up a stone like a great millstone and hurled it into the sea and said, 'Thus shall Babylon, the great city, be sent hurtling down, 22 never to be seen again! No more shall the sound of harpers and minstrels, of flute-players and trumpeters, be heard in you; no more shall craftsmen of any trade be found in you; no more shall the sound of the mill be heard in you; 23 no more shall the light of the lamp be seen in you; no more shall the voice of the bride and bridegroom be heard in you! Your traders were once the merchant princes of the world, and

with your sorcery you deceived all the nations.'

For the blood of the prophets and of 24 God's people was found in her, the blood of all who had been done to death on earth.

After this I heard what sounded like 19 the roar of a vast throng in heaven; and they were shouting:

'Alleluia! Victory and glory and power belong to our God, for true 2 and just are his judgements! He has condemned the great whore who corrupted the earth with her fornication, and has avenged upon her the blood of his servants.'

Then once more they shouted: 3

'Alleluia! The smoke goes up from her for ever and ever!'

And the twenty-four elders and the 4 four living creatures fell down and worshipped God as he sat on the throne, and they too cried:

'Amen! Alleluia!'

Then a voice came from the throne 5 which said: 'Praise our God, all you his servants, you that fear him, both great and small!'

Again I heard what sounded like a 6 vast crowd, like the noise of rushing water and deep roars of thunder, and they cried:

'Alleluia! The Lord our God, sovereign over all, has entered on his reign! Exult and shout for joy and do 7 him homage, for the wedding-day of the Lamb has come! His bride has made herself ready, and for her dress 8 she has been given fine linen, clean and shining.'

(Now the fine linen signifies the righteous deeds of God's people.)

17–20: Contrast vv. 17–19 with v. 20. **18:** *Was there ever a city:* see Ezek.27.32. **19:** *Dust on their heads:* see Ezek.27.30. **21:** *A great millstone:* compare Jer.51.63–64. **22–24:** See Jer.25.10.
19.1–5: Rejoicing over Rome's destruction. 2: *Alleluia:* the Gk. transliteration of Heb. *hallelujah,* "Praise God," found only in this ch. in the NT.
19.6–10: The marriage of the Lamb. 7–8: The OT sometimes sees Israel as God's *bride* (e.g. Jer.2.2); here the *bride* of the Lamb is the church (compare 2 Cor.11.2; Eph.5.25–33).

9 Then the angel said to me, 'Write this. "Happy are those who are invited to the wedding-supper of the Lamb!"'
And he added, 'These are the very
10 words of God.' At this I fell at his feet to worship him. But he said to me, 'No, not that! I am but a fellow-servant with you and your brothers who bear their testimony to Jesus. It is God you must worship. Those who bear testimony to Jesus are inspired like the prophets.'*p*

11 THEN I SAW HEAVEN WIDE OPEN, AND there before me was a white horse; and its rider's name was Faithful and True, for he is just in judgement and just in
12 war. His eyes flamed like fire, and on his head were many diadems. Written upon him was a name known to none but
13 himself, and he was robed in a garment drenched in blood.*q* He was called the
14 Word of God, and the armies of heaven followed him on white horses, clothed in fine linen, clean and shining.
15 From his mouth there went a sharp sword with which to smite the nations; for he it is who shall rule them with an iron rod, and tread the winepress of the wrath and retribution of God the
16 sovereign Lord. And on his robe and on his thigh there was written the name: 'King of kings and Lord of lords.'
17 Then I saw an angel standing in the sun, and he cried aloud to all the birds flying in mid-heaven: 'Come and gather
18 for God's great supper, to eat the flesh of kings and commanders and fighting men, the flesh of horses and their riders, the flesh of all men, slave and free,
19 great and small!' Then I saw the beast and the kings of the earth and their armies mustered to do battle with the
20 Rider and his army. The beast was taken prisoner, and so was the false

prophet who had worked miracles in its presence and deluded those that had received the mark of the beast and worshipped its image. The two of them were thrown alive into the lake of fire with its sulphurous flames. The rest 21 were killed by the sword which went out of the Rider's mouth; and all the birds gorged themselves on their flesh.
Then I saw an angel coming down **20** from heaven with the key of the abyss and a great chain in his hands. He 2 seized the dragon, that serpent of old, the Devil or Satan, and chained him up for a thousand years; he threw him 3 into the abyss, shutting and sealing it over him, so that he might seduce the nations no more till the thousand years were over. After that he must be let loose for a short while.
Then I saw thrones, and upon them 4 sat those to whom judgement was committed. I could see the souls of those who had been beheaded for the sake of God's word and their testimony to Jesus, those who had not worshipped the beast and its image or received its mark on forehead or hand. These came to life again and reigned with Christ for a thousand years, though the rest of 5 the dead did not come to life until the thousand years were over. This is the first resurrection. Happy indeed, and 6 one of God's own people, is the man who shares in this first resurrection! Upon such the second death has no claim; but they shall be priests of God and of Christ, and shall reign with him for the thousand years.
When the thousand years are over, 7 Satan will be let loose from his dungeon; and he will come out to seduce 8 the nations in the four quarters of the

p Or ... worship. For testimony to Jesus is the spirit that inspires prophets.
q Some witnesses read spattered with blood.

10: *God you must worship:* there is to be no worship of angelic beings; see 22.8–9; Col.2.18.
19.11–21: Christ's victory over the beast. 11: *A white horse:* see 6.2. **12:** *Eyes ... like fire:* see 2.18. **13:** *A garment drenched in blood:* see Isa.63.1–6. *The Word of God:* see 1.2 n. **15:** *A sharp sword:* see 1.16 n.; 2.12. *An iron rod:* Ps.2.9. *Winepress:* see 14.10 n.,17–20. **16:** *Lord of lords:* Deut.10.17; Dan.2.47. **17–21:** Compare Ezek.39.17–20. **19:** The final battle anticipated in 16.14–16. **20:** *The lake of fire:* see 14.10; 20.10.
20.1–15: The events of the last Judgment. 2–4: With *Satan* bound (v. 2), the martyred dead (others later; see v. 5) are to rise and reign with Christ (following a Jewish messianic expectation). **2:** *Thousand years:* the millennium (from Latin *mille*, thousand, and *annus*, year). **4:** *Thrones ... judgement:* see Dan.7.9,22,27; Mt.19.28; Lk.22.30. **6:** *The second death:* defined in v. 14; see 2.11. **7:** The short release of Satan (see v. 3) may follow the Babylonian legend of Tiamat, the sea monster of chaos who is to be released at the end of history to be defeated again by Marduk, the god of light. **8:** *The hosts of Gog and Magog* (see Ezek. chs. 38–39) are identified

earth and to muster them for battle, yes, the hosts of Gog and Magog, 9 countless as the sands of the sea. So they marched over the breadth of the land and laid siege to the camp of God's people and the city that he loves. But fire came down on them from 10 heaven and consumed them; and the Devil, their seducer, was flung into the lake of fire and sulphur, where the beast and the false prophet had been flung, there to be tormented day and night for ever.

11 Then I saw a great white throne, and the One who sat upon it; from his presence earth and heaven vanished away, and no place was left for them. 12 I could see the dead, great and small, standing before the throne; and books were opened. Then another book was opened, the roll of the living. From what was written in these books the dead were judged upon the record of 13 their deeds. The sea gave up its dead, and Death and Hades gave up the dead in their keeping; they were judged each 14 man on the record of his deeds. Then Death and Hades were flung into the lake of fire. This lake of fire is the 15 second death; and into it were flung any whose names were not to be found in the roll of the living.

21 THEN I SAW A NEW HEAVEN AND A NEW earth, for the first heaven and the first earth had vanished, and there was no 2 longer any sea. I saw the holy city, new Jerusalem, coming down out of heaven from God, made ready like a bride 3 adorned for her husband. I heard a loud voice proclaiming from the throne: 'Now at last God has his dwelling among men! He will dwell

among them and they shall be his people, and God himself will be with them.[r] He will wipe every tear from 4 their eyes; there shall be an end to death, and to mourning and crying and pain; for the old order has passed away!'

Then he who sat on the throne said, 5 'Behold! I am making all things new!' (And he said to me, 'Write this down; for these words are trustworthy and true. Indeed they are already fulfilled.') 6 'I am the Alpha and the Omega, the beginning and the end. A draught from the water-springs of life will be my free gift to the thirsty. All this is the victor's 7 heritage; and I will be his God and he shall be my son. But as for the cow- 8 ardly, the faithless, and the vile, murderers, fornicators, sorcerers, idolaters, and liars of every kind, their lot will be the second death, in the lake that burns with sulphurous flames.'

Then one of the seven angels that 9 held the seven bowls full of the seven last plagues came and spoke to me and said, 'Come, and I will show you the bride, the wife of the Lamb.' So in the 10 Spirit he carried me away to a great high mountain, and showed me the holy city of Jerusalem coming down out of heaven from God. It shone with 11 the glory of God; it had the radiance of some priceless jewel, like a jasper, clear as crystal. It had a great high wall, with 12 twelve gates, at which were twelve angels; and on the gates were inscribed the names of the twelve tribes of Israel. There were three gates to the east, three 13 to the north, three to the south, and three to the west. The city wall had 14

[r] *Some witnesses read* God-with-them shall himself be their God (*see Isaiah 7. 14; 8. 8*).

with *the nations* who gather for the final battle against God's people; this also provides an opportunity to depict a final siege of *the city*, i.e. Jerusalem (v. 9); see Zech. ch. 14. **9:** *Fire came down:* compare 2 Kgs.1.10–12. **10:** The *Devil, beast,* and *false prophet* are defeated forever. **11–15:** Here is the last judgment by the *books* (see 3.5 n.; compare Dan.7.9–10; Mt.16.27; 25.31–46; Rom.2.6) in connection with the "second resurrection" (see v. 5); and *Death* and *Hades* (Death's domain; see 1.18) are vanquished (see 21.4).

21.1–21: The new heaven and earth and the new Jerusalem. 1: The future holds promise of a transformation so complete that there will be *a new heaven and . . . earth;* see Isa.65.17; 66.22; Rom. 8.19–21. *No longer any sea:* perhaps, as in Babylonian legend, the sea is regarded as hostile. **2:** The *new Jerusalem* is not in heaven but comes down from it (see v. 10; 3.12). *Bride:* see 19.7–8 n. **3:** *God has his dwelling among men:* compare Ezek.37.27. **4:** *Wipe away every tear:* see 7.17; Isa.25.8; 35.10. **5:** Only here and in 1.8 does God himself speak. *All things new:* Isa.43.19. **6:** *Alpha* and *Omega:* see 1.8 n. *To the thirsty . . . water:* see 7.17 n.; 22.1; Isa.55.1. **7:** *His God . . . my son:* Pss. 2.7; 89.27–28. **10:** *Showed me the holy city:* compare Ezek.40.2. **12–14:** The juxtaposition of *twelve tribes* (v. 12) and *twelve apostles* (v. 14) points to old and

twelve foundation-stones, and on them were the names of the twelve apostles of the Lamb.

15 The angel who spoke with me carried a gold measuring-rod, to measure the 16 the city, its wall, and its gates. The city was built as a square, and was as wide as it was long. It measured by his rod twelve thousand furlongs, its length and 17 breadth and height being equal. Its wall was one hundred and forty-four cubits high, that is, by human measurements, 18 which the angel was using. The wall was built of jasper. while the city itself was of pure gold, bright as clear glass. 19 The foundations of the city wall were adorned with jewels of every kind, the first of the foundation-stones being jasper, the second lapis lazuli, the third 20 chalcedony, the fourth emerald, the fifth sardonyx, the sixth cornelian, the seventh chrysolite, the eighth beryl, the ninth topaz, the tenth chrysoprase, the eleventh turquoise, and the twelfth 21 amethyst. The twelve gates were twelve pearls, each gate being made from a single pearl. The streets of the city were of pure gold, like translucent glass.

22 I saw no temple in the city; for its temple was the sovereign Lord God 23 and the Lamb. And the city had no need of sun or moon to shine upon it; for the glory of God gave it light, and 24 its lamp was the Lamb. By its light shall the nations walk, and the kings of the earth shall bring into it all their 25 splendour. The gates of the city shall never be shut by day—and there will 26 be no night. The wealth and splendour of the nations shall be brought into it; 27 but nothing unclean shall enter, nor anyone whose ways are false or foul,

but only those who are inscribed in the Lamb's roll of the living.

22 Then he showed me the river of the water of life, sparkling like crystal, flowing from the throne of God and of 2 the Lamb down the middle of the city's street. On either side of the river stood a tree of life, which yields twelve crops of fruit, one for each month of the year; the leaves of the trees serve for the 3 healing of the nations. Every accursed thing shall disappear. The throne of God and of the Lamb will be there, and 4 his servants shall worship him; they shall see him face to face, and bear his 5 name on their foreheads. There shall be no more night, nor will they need the light of lamp or sun, for the Lord God will give them light; and they shall reign for evermore.

6 THEN HE SAID TO ME, 'THESE WORDS ARE trustworthy and true. The Lord God who inspires the prophets has sent his angel to show his servants what must 7 shortly happen. And, remember, I am coming soon!'

Happy is the man who heeds the words of prophecy contained in this 8 book! It is I, John, who heard and saw these things. And when I had heard and seen them, I fell in worship at the feet of the angel who had shown them 9 to me. But he said to me, 'No, not that! I am but a fellow-servant with you and your brothers the prophets and those who heed the words of this book. It is 10 God you must worship.' Then he told me, 'Do not seal up the words of prophecy in this book, for the hour of fulfilment is near. Meanwhile, let the 11 evil-doer go on doing evil and the filthy-

---

new covenant peoples; see 4.4 n. **15:** *A gold measuring rod:* see Ezek.40.5. **16:** The dimensions correspond to the Temple's Holy of Holies, but there is no longer to be a temple (see 21.22) and all (as priests; see 1.6 n.; Isa.61.6), not only the high priest, have access to God. **18–20:** Exod.28.15–21; Isa.54.11–12.

21.22–22.5: A city of light and life. 23: *No need of sun:* see Isa.60.19. **24:** Isa.60.3,5. **25:** Isa.60.11. **26:** Isa.60.3–9. **27:** *Nothing unclean:* see Isa.52.1. **22.1:** *The river of the water of life:* compare Ezek.47.1–12, where it flows from the Temple; here it flows from the *throne* (see Zech.14.7–8). **2:** *A tree of life:* see 2.7 n.; Ezek.47.7. *Healing of the nations:* compare Ezek.47.12, Sept.; also Isa.49.6. **3:** *Every accursed thing shall disappear:* in Gen.3.17–18 it is man who is accursed; now he is redeemed in a new paradise with access to the tree of life. **4:** *They shall see him face to face:* Ps.17.15; 1 Cor.13.12. *Bear his name . . .:* see 3.12 n.; in Exod.28.36–38 the high priest has "Holy to the Lord" on his forehead, but now all are priests and bear his name.

22.6–21: Final admonitions and promises. 6: *Sent his angel:* see 1.1; 22.16. **7:** *I am coming soon:* see 16.15. **8:** *I, John:* see Introduction; 1.1,4,9. **9:** *No, not that:* see 19.10 n. **10:** *Do not seal up . . . the hour . . . is near:* the command to conceal in Dan.8.26; 12.4,9 is reversed because of the anticipation of the imminent end. **11:** There is no time for change; compare Dan.12.10.

minded wallow in his filth, but let the good man persevere in his goodness and the dedicated man be true to his dedication.'

12 'Yes, I am coming soon, and bringing my recompense with me, to requite
13 everyone according to his deeds! I am the Alpha and the Omega, the first and the last, the beginning and the end.'

14 Happy are those who wash their robes clean! They will have the right to the tree of life and will enter by the
15 gates of the city. Outside are dogs, sorcerers and fornicators, murderers and idolaters, and all who love and practise deceit.

16 'I, Jesus, have sent my angel to you with this testimony for the churches. I am the scion and offspring of David, the bright star of dawn.'

17 'Come!' say the Spirit and the bride.

'Come!' let each hearer reply

Come forward, you who are thirsty; accept the water of life, a free gift to all who desire it.

For my part, I give this warning to 18 everyone who is listening to the words of prophecy in this book: should anyone add to them, God will add to him the plagues described in this book; should anyone take away from the 19 words in this book of prophecy, God will take away from him his share in the tree of life and the Holy City, described in this book.

He who gives this testimony speaks: 20 'Yes, I am coming soon!'

Amen. Come, Lord Jesus!

The grace of the Lord Jesus be with 21 you all.[s]

s Some witnesses read with all; *others read* with all God's people; *others read* with God's people; *some add* Amen.

12: *Requite everyone:* see 20.11–15 n.; compare Isa.40.10; Jer.17.10. **14:** *Who wash their robes:* see 7.14. **15:** *Outside:* compare Mt.8.12. *Dogs:* impure persons; compare Phil.3.2. *Sorcerers:* lit. *poisoners;* see 21.8. **16:** *I, Jesus:* see 1.1 2. *Scion and offspring* of *David:* see 5.5 n. *Morning star:* see 2.28; compare Num.24.17. **17:** *The bride:* see 19.7–8 n. **18–19:** *Should anyone add . . . should anyone take away:* compare Deut.4.2; 12.32. **20:** *Come, Lord Jesus:* compare 1 Cor.16.22 n.

SPECIAL ARTICLES

READING THE BIBLE

The passing of centuries has both hallowed the words of the Bible and created gaps of time and space between Scripture and the modern reader. Only as these gaps narrow, and hopefully close, can the fullness of the meaning and feeling of this repository of exalted literature permeate his being. Surely the heart of man has not changed from ancient times; man's ability to think, despite countless historic shifts in the modes and manner of thought, remains constant. But can today's reader overcome hundreds, indeed thousands of years, and the distance of thousands of miles, and make the words, the sentences, the books of so long ago his very own? Not without tools.

He needs tools of different kinds, some perhaps ready at hand and as tangible as a carpenter's ruler, others available only in whatever native gifts a person chances to possess, perhaps the chief of which is imagination—a fertile mind figuratively to cross over space and time.

The Bible emerged from the hearts and minds of living human beings. An Isaiah spoke to *people* gathered at the Temple; a Jesus preached to *people* assembled on a mount; the Psalmist was a *man* who burst into rapture as he saw the beauties of nature; and in Proverbs a concerned *father* wished to convey to his *son* the ripeness of the wisdom distilled from human experience. A harassed Jeremiah wrote a letter of sound counsel to his fellow Jews spiritually adrift in alien Babylon, and a Paul ended an epistle to a church divided by factions with personal regards to specific friends and acquaintances. Imagination is the ability to recognize that the recorded words come from flesh and blood people and to transport one's self to that time and place when the ancient words were first spoken or written. Imagination, in this sense, is a gift purely within the reader, and much as he can benefit from help that may come from outside him, only his own creative mind will cultivate and foster his readings.

It is important to apply imagination to all literature and especially so to Scripture. Unlike some other worthy writings of the ancient past, Scripture remains constant in our learning and in our everyday way of living and speaking. Even more profoundly, Scripture touches on, or deals penetratingly with, man's experiences. There are first his natural, personal experiences—when he is born, as he grows in strength, when he passes his prime, and when he becomes aware that his span of life is limited. Then Scripture is concerned with the community, the corporate body, called the Israel of God (Gal.6.16). That Scripture deals so centrally with God's people—individually and collectively—gives the Bible its eminence over all other literatures.

It is natural for Scripture to be spoken of as "inspired," a word often used in two related but different senses. In the first sense, inspiration signifies some super-human, even divine, quality. Many religious communities regard Scripture as inspired in this specific sense. From this standpoint, however, much as these sacred writings may be regarded as the product of men, it was God acting behind

3

these men, or through them, that gives Scripture its special quality and special authority.

A second sense of "inspired" is somewhat different. If a painting is flat, dull, unable to reach out to us or move us, we would not call it "inspired." We use the word, rather, in awe of genius. That a Beethoven could have written a Ninth Symphony, or that a da Vinci could have painted a Last Supper, or that man could have conquered space, is awesome. So we restrict the word "inspired" in this sense to just such extraordinary creations and feats because we marvel at such rare and unexpected peaks of attainment. It is no exaggeration to say that much, indeed very much, of Scripture represents an artistry and power in its architectonic quality that richly merits the accolade "inspired." Yet only as we cultivate our imagination can we attune to the aesthetic beauty of Scripture.

Just as the carpenter's ruler is a most useful tool in building, so also is some basic knowledge useful in reading Scripture. To begin with, a reader must know that Scripture is not simply one book, but that it is an assembly of books, indeed, an assembly of assemblies, a veritable library. The Bible can be read without this information, but how easily it can also be misread! The books of Scripture were written over a span of at least a thousand years. They not only reflect the very moments of the times when they were written; they also speak to men in all ages. We can, therefore, share in the misery and despair which moved the author of Lamentations to record his sense of calamity at the destruction of Jerusalem in the year 587 B.C., but his poetry awakens within us too a misery and despair transcending the tragedy itself. It is possible to read Lamentations without knowing anything about the history of Israel, but to know about the event that prompted the dirge increases its power and beauty.

Similarly, to know why one speaks of "up from Jericho into the hill-country" (Josh.16.1) alerts us to a very ancient city in the Jordan valley, below the hills of Judah, in which Jerusalem nestled. It helps to know that the coast of Palestine was flat, bounded on the east by low-lying hills; that the southern area of the Holy Land was better suited for raising sheep than for farming, but that in the north, where the fertile great Plain of Esdraelon was located, agriculture flourished. A minimum of knowledge about the history and geography of the Bible, and about when the individual books were written and why, is an inescapable necessity. But the richer our store of knowledge, the richer our appreciation. The annotations in this edition, although restricted in scope because of space limitations, provide a good measure of such knowledge and enrichment.

The information contained in the annotations, useful as it is, is a matter of the relevant externals. The internal matter is the content of Scripture. However exalted sacred writing is as writing, it is the idea *behind* the writing that is the crux. The biblical mode of thought differs from the Greek and Latin modes so influential on us, in that the biblical manner is concrete rather than abstract; biblical authors expressed their thoughts through stories and poems, through striking incidents and memorable characters, and not through philosophical ideas. These writers viewed definitions as unnecessary, and differentiation through precise formulation as needed only in matters of law. Books as diverse as Genesis, Samuel, the Gospel According to Matthew, and Acts of the Apostles all convey their content by narration. Their stories, however, were always more than merely stories, and their poems far more than wondrous lyrical outbursts. Their subjects were God and man, and sin and righteousness, and the purpose and mystery of living.

The Bible puts forth no philosophical inquiry about God. His existence is presumed without any effort to prove it. He is not directly defined, but in repudiating idolatry and polytheism, the Bible does define him. Affirmatively, Scripture speaks of what it regards as his actions in history, of his control of history, of its conviction that the march of history has revealed him. Its objective was not to *define* revelation, but rather to assert that in specific given events, God partly, or fully, revealed to men his power, or his uniqueness, or his very essence. Where the Greeks sought for ultimates through analyzing the physical nature of a static world, or a world revolving in great circles of time, the biblical authors sought such quintessence in the events of history, in the one-way flow of time toward a purpose and goal. God was at work—in the biblical view in the call of Abraham, in the Exodus, in Sinai, in the entry into Canaan, in the rise and fall of monarchy, in Jesus, and in Paul (and, for the ancient Jewish sages, in the oral revelation which inspired the rabbis). In the Bible, history is never only a record of an event in itself; it also is the meaning of that human event in relationship to God. And so we find that biblical modes of thought are no less profound than those found in the formalities of Greek or Latin philosophy.

So long a span of time is represented in the Bible that a phenomenon needs to be observed: Chronicles was written on the basis, and made use, of Samuel and Kings. Conversely, Samuel–Kings influenced Chronicles. Similarly, Genesis–Exodus influenced some psalms. More significantly, the Old Testament influenced the Apocrypha and the New Testament. In a sense, the New Testament is a commentary on, and an extension of, the Old Testament.

This matter of influence, at points extending to derivation, has two meanings. First, the phenomenon lends some sense of unity to books of disparate ages and content. Second, the later books, in exhibiting the influence on them of earlier books, provide a continuity with them.

The ancient mode of commentary-explanation was not that of bare factual definition. Rather, in early Christian times, both Jews and Christians appear to have addressed themselves to the question, What does this Old Testament passage *signify* (predict)? rather than, What does this passage *mean* (at present)? Jews and Christians readily understood that Abraham left Ur; but they wanted to know what his departure from the land *signified*. Both Jews and Christians of two thousand years ago saw in Abraham's departure the decisive step by means of which the patriarch abandoned idolatry for the worship of the true God; both traditions viewed Abraham as the father of all true believers. Much of the thought in the Gospels and in the Epistles acquires specific substance from the Old Testament literature from which it is directly derived, and without which the later writings would be unintelligible. With the Old Testament, we know that when John the Baptist declares that God can raise true sons of Abraham from stones (Lk.3.7–8), or that when Paul speaks of Christ as the Passover sacrifice (1 Cor.5.7), or that when rabbis in the Mishnah (a legal commentary on Scripture) specify what activities are inadmissible on the Sabbath, they are extending the thoughts they inherited, and merging them with their own perceptions.

For today's student, not only the glory, but also the "problem" in Scripture is, on the one hand, its antiquity, which would seem to allocate it to the past; and is on the other hand its unending relevance for all generations, including his own. Translation became a necessity more than twenty centuries ago, when Jews moved to Greek-speaking lands where they continued to cherish Scripture, yet had forgotten the ancestral Hebrew tongue. Translation is a vehicle for understanding, and understanding is the first step toward applying the insights of the ancient writings to a later age and milieu.

Many Bibles have been translated into English, some so long ago that even though they are in our own tongue, we have trouble understanding these old renderings. Hence, the continual need for new translations expedient to new times. There is an essential difference between the New English Bible and other modern versions. In their determination to avoid the pitfall of simply converting a Hebrew or Greek word into an English equivalent, the translating panels boldly chose to translate the *ideas* behind the words. As a result, they have achieved a remarkably high approximation of the tone and feeling and thought of the Hebrew and Greek originals.

One reads to be entertained, or to learn, or to be lifted to some high level of aspiration and dedication. The Bible, like no other literature, offers just such an extensive range of rewards; and in it the reader may hear the echo of, or indeed, the very voice of God himself.

LITERARY FORMS
OF THE BIBLE

The Bible can be read from many perspectives. From a historical view, one can read it to learn about the past; from the standpoint of religion, one can read it to clarify or strengthen faith; from a literary angle, one can appreciate its poetry, its narrative style, and its use of imagery. Another kind of concern is developed here—an attempt to acquaint the reader with the many literary forms which the Bible represents.

Awareness of literary form is fundamental to understanding. In reading poetry we do not look for the same thing that we look for in reading novels; legal contracts use language different from that which is used in short stories. Moreover, because in a typical biblical book various kinds of material stand side by side, the reader must know what the natural unit is. Furthermore, later use frequently obscured the original shape of the material; but awareness of the form can help the student distinguish earlier from later layers. The Bible is such a rich and diverse book that only a general sketch, with a few examples, can be undertaken here, with the hope that the reader will be encouraged to pursue the study of literary form on his own.

In terms of literary form, the Bible as a whole ought not to be taken for granted. We shall therefore begin by noting its structure and history. From there we shall look at the kinds of books in the Bible, then to the kinds of literary forms within the individual books. Finally, we shall reflect on the value of pursuing this kind of analysis.

THE BIBLE AS A WHOLE

WHAT IS THE BIBLE? From a literary point of view the Bible is an anthology, or a collection of literature, containing narratives, poetry, prophetic books, letters, and apocalypses. It is not organized according to types of literature; rather, different kinds of literature (called "books") stand side by side. Furthermore, many individual books themselves juxtapose narratives, poetry, and legal codes. Understanding the Bible from a literary point of view requires us to see the character of the anthology as a whole, and how it came to be what it now is.

In the first place, the contents of the collection depend on whose Bible we are talking about. What Jews call "the Bible," Christians call "the Old Testament"; moreover, because of the Apocrypha, Christians have not always agreed among themselves, nor with the Jews, on what constitutes the Old Testament. Roman Catholics have always included the Apocrypha in the Old Testament, but Protestants sometimes printed the books between the Old and New Testaments, or omitted them entirely. (They are now part of The New English Bible, placed between the two Testaments.) The reasons for this are complex, but the facts are simple enough: the Protestant Old Testament is the Bible of the Palestinian synagogue as determined by the rabbis after the fall of Jerusalem in 70 A.D. The Apocrypha, on the other hand, was part of the Bible of the Greek synagogues. This Bible in turn became the Scripture of the Greek-speaking church; later it was translated into Latin. However, in the sixteenth century, Reformation Protestants reverted to the Palestinian canon for their Old Testament, and relegated the Apocrypha to the status of books "good and useful to read," while denying them full authority as Scripture, but at the Council of Trent Catholics determined to continue to include them in the Old Testament.

Nor did Christians always agree about the content of the New Testament. The earliest list of books which agrees with our present New Testament comes from 367 A.D., yet it was not until many centuries later that all Christians— Protestant, Catholic, and Orthodox—agreed on what constituted the New Testament. From this rudimentary sketch, it is clear that what the word "Bible" refers to depends on the particular religious community one has in view, and on the history of these communities with their Scriptures.

In the second place, the way in which the anthology called the Bible is organized also depends on whether one has in mind the Jewish or the Christian Bible. The Hebrew Bible, quite apart from the placement of the Apocrypha, is structured differently from the Christian Old Testament. It has three divisions: the Torah ("the Law"), the Prophets (subdivided into "the former prophets" and "the latter prophets"), and the Writings. When Christians adopted the Greek Bible, they also accepted a different order, which today is preserved in Catholic editions. For example, in the Christian Old Testament, the literary prophets (called "latter prophets" in the Hebrew Bible) come at the very end.

In the third place, the present order of books in the New Testament results from historical factors, especially the rejection of Marcion, a second-century heretic. Marcion demanded that Christians discard the Synagogue Bible altogether and rely solely on a Christian Bible consisting of the Gospel of Luke and the Letters of Paul (from both of which he had deleted passages favorable to Judaism and the God of the Old Testament). In rejecting Marcion, the church retained the Old Testament; it also insisted that the New Testament should have four gospels and the letters of more than one apostle. Eventually the Book of Revelation was included as well. These factors, succinctly stated here, explain why "the Bible" refers to several anthologies, and why the tables of contents vary as they do.

It is difficult to classify a piece of literature precisely if it was edited subsequently, or if it is itself a compilation of several writings. But this is exactly what we have in most books of the Bible. On the one hand, some works came to be divided into several books. For example, what we now know as 1 and 2 Chronicles, Ezra, and Nehemiah were originally a single work. The long work became divided and the divided parts acquired individual names. On the other hand, books which are essentially compilations are common. In the Hebrew Bible the twelve (minor) prophets are a single "book" which compiled the individual works into one scroll. 2 Corinthians combines parts of at least five letters, none of which is preserved entirely.

Broadly speaking, nonetheless, we may classify the books of the Bible into

8

five kinds of literature: 1. Narrative books (e.g. Genesis, Samuel, Kings, Maccabees, the Gospels, the Acts of the Apostles), 2. Poetry (e.g. Psalms, Song of Songs, Proverbs); 3. Prophetic books; 4. Epistles (e.g. the Letters of Paul); 5. Apocalypses (Daniel, Revelation, 2 Esdras [4 Ezra]) Each of these will be discussed below. First, however, several considerations merit attention.

To begin with, the distribution is of interest. Narrative and apocalypse are found throughout the Old and New Testaments, and the Apocrypha. On the other hand, except for the Letter of Jeremiah in some manuscripts, epistles as separate writings are found only in the New Testament, while only the Old Testament has books of poetry and collections of proverbs. Second, many types of literature do not appear in the Bible at all: drama, satire, autobiography, myth (an extended narrative about the gods), commentaries. Third, none of the literary types found in the Bible is peculiarly biblical. Therefore, the study of types or genres of literature in general, and especially those of antiquity, illumines the particular biblical literature. Fourth, most of the books contain several literary forms. For example, Exodus contains narrative, laws, and poetry; Jeremiah contains narrative, poetry, and letters; some of the epistles, such as 1 Corinthians ch. 13, contain poetic passages.

There are various reasons for the existence of multiple literary forms within a given book. The book may be a compilation (e.g. Daniel begins with narratives about pious Jews in Babylon, and then adds reports of visions). Or, the book may use diverse kinds of materials, including earlier documents. For example, the Deuteronomic history (Deuteronomy, Joshua, Judges, 1 and 2 Samuel, 1 and 2 Kings) used earlier documents, such as annals and previous histories.

AUTHORSHIP. Finally, the above observations affect the questions of "authorship." In belles-lettres, an author chooses the form in which he wants to express himself, moving from various poetic to prose forms as content requires, or as he wishes to experiment. There is no reason to consider the biblical writers in this light, for they were not self-conscious literary figures writing for a public, nor were they writing to express their personal views. They were either writing for religious communities which they sought to address as effectively as possible, or else they were recording fixed traditions. They were not professional authors who earned their livelihood by writing. Indeed, to what extent the writers were self-conscious "authors" is highly uncertain. We know few of their names. The vast majority of the books are anonymous; "authors" were assigned to them at a later date by the communities as acts of piety. Thus, the Pentateuch was attributed to Moses, the Psalms to David, Proverbs to Solomon, the Gospels to apostles or their associates. Furthermore, some of the literature was actually written in the name of well-known figures. All apocalypses, except the Revelation of John, claim to be written by persons long dead. Certain letters of Paul (Ephesians, Timothy, Titus), and probably the letters of James, Jude, Peter, and John were written in the name of these apostles. More important, the identity of none of the compilers is known, nor are the names of the writers whose works have been incorporated in books which we now have. In many instances it is not at all clear whether the compilation was done by an individual or by a group. For example, it is customary to speak of "the Yahwist" or "the Priestly writer" of certain strata of the Pentateuch, or of the "author" of the Fourth Gospel. But no one knows whether these works represent the efforts of a single mind or of a group. Similarly, the Gospels are end products of a process of development to which several persons or groups made their contribution. For example, Matthew appropriated most of Mark, some of which he rewrote, and supplemented it with a collection (itself restructured) of Jesus' teachings and with other material. Most of the individuals who wrote the literature of the Bible drew on materials already known. The creativity of the writer usually lay in how he used his material. Thus, biblical literature is much less the product of creative writing than the product of creative editing done within the context of communities of faith.

TYPES OF BOOKS

NARRATIVE WORKS. Many of the books are essentially narratives. As such, they include at least the rudiments of a plot, an indication of where the events transpired, and some greater or lesser portrayal of the characters. Ordinarily the larger narratives have a chronological order. The various narrative genres may be distinguished from one another on the basis of plot, setting, and characterization, and on the basis of specific purposes. Was a work composed in order to entertain, to edify, or to transmit factual information?

A great many different narrative genres appear in the Bible. A number of the books and literary works may be classified as histories, though not in the modern scholarly sense. A history is a written narrative of past events which is governed by facts, as far as the writer could ascertain and interpret them, and not by thematic or aesthetic organization. It will, then, in most cases be chronological in sequence. Most of the biblical histories are popular histories; that is, the writer's determination of the facts was not based on critically assessed and reliable sources (such as eye-witness testimony or accurate records), but on traditional material (such as stories and legends). Much of the popular history of the Bible could also be called salvation history, since it aims at showing how the sequence of events was directed by God. A major example of history in these senses is the Deuteronomic sequence (see above), which includes many diverse literary types, but viewed as a whole comprises a single interpretative account of the history of Israel from the Exodus to the Exile. The Tetrateuch ("four books": Genesis, Exodus, Leviticus, Numbers) likewise is such a history, though its sequence is not so neatly ordered because of its history of composition; furthermore, it includes within its historical framework a considerable amount of legal material. Critical analysis of the Tetrateuch has shown that it is composed of two or more originally separate but complete histories of salvation, the works of the Yahwist and Priestly writer. Other major examples of salvation histories are the Chronicler's work (1 and 2 Chronicles, Ezra, and Nehemiah), 1 and 2 Maccabees, 1 Esdras, and Acts.

Some narrative books are essentially stories, that is, their structure is determined primarily by plot. Stories create interest by arousing tension (suspense) and releasing it. In addition to stories, such as the Joseph narrative, employed in larger works, a number of separate books belong to this category. Many of these owe their content or shape to popular tradition, and thus may be called tales. The Book of Ruth is a short story which probably rests on a folktale; Jonah is a didactic (teaching) story developed from legend. In terms of content, the Book of Esther could be called a historical novel, or in terms of purpose, a festival legend, since it seems to have been written to explain the meaning and significance of the Feast of Purim. In the Apocrypha the books of Tobit; Judith; Daniel and Susanna; and Daniel, Bel, and the Snake are imaginative didactic stories—works of fiction, novelistic in character, and written in order to convey lessons.

Generally speaking, gospels are narratives about Jesus. Their literary form is basically similar to ancient biographies of popular teachers. The title "gospel" was attached to a rather diverse body of narratives about Jesus, only four of which were included in the New Testament. The canonical Gospels generally narrate the public ministry of Jesus; each of them has its own structure, though they all culminate in the story of Jesus' death and resurrection. The apocryphal gospels (those never included in the canon), on the other hand, vary considerably in content. Some, such as the infancy Gospel of Thomas or the Gospel of Peter, fill in "gaps," that is, give information not provided by the canonical Gospels. Others claim to furnish secret traditions; one newly-found gospel, that of Thomas, is a collection of sayings but without any real narrative at all.

The canonical Gospels are the results of the transmission and use of traditions about Jesus, including his teachings. The so-called "Synoptics" (the first three Gospels) are interdependent, since Matthew and Luke used Mark; John apparently did not use the Synoptics but did have access to some materials found also in the others. Essentially, however, John's traditions were independent of the Synoptics, and were developed in distinctive ways. The canonical Gospels were written forty to seventy years after the events which they report. All of the Gospels were probably developed for various uses in the Christian congregations, whose problems are reflected both in the selection of the individual traditions and in the emphases of the individual Gospels.

POETIC BOOKS. Many books of the Bible are poetic works, but this category is not adequate as a generic classification because there are several very distinct types. Moreover, though the prophetic books contain a considerable amount of poetry, they are sufficiently distinctive to merit a separate classification. Divided broadly, there are two kinds of poetic books: cultic poetry and Wisdom literature. The primary example of the former is the Book of Psalms, which is not simply a collection of poems but is the hymn and prayer book of the Temple in late Old Testament times. For the most part the psalms and cultic poems are lyrical, that is, meant to be sung (see below). The only other book of cultic poetry in the Old Testament is Lamentations, a collection of dirges and mourning liturgies concerning national disaster. In the Apocrypha, books of liturgical poetry are represented by the Prayer of Manasseh, a short devotional piece, and the Prayer of Azariah in the Song of the Three, added to the Book of Daniel on its translation into Greek.

The other poetic books are more difficult to classify. They generally are considered Wisdom literature, itself a wide range of types. The Song of Songs, for example, is lyrical poetry. Though sometimes interpreted as the liturgy of a sacred marriage ceremony, it is in reality a collection of secular love poetry, perhaps assembled for use at weddings. Other Wisdom poetry ranges from the collection of sayings and poems in the Book of Proverbs (see below) through the lengthy instructions in the apocryphal Book of Ecclesiasticus, to the carefully constructed poem of Job. Still other examples of this literature are Ecclesiastes and the apocryphal Wisdom of Solomon. All of these works have in common a certain literary self-consciousness seldom found in other biblical literature. Behind these works often stand poets in the sense of creative individuals.

In The New English Bible, as in most modern translations, poetry can be recognized by its verse (metrical) form. This procedure enables the reader to see that the basic principle of Hebrew poetry is the parallelism of members, or the "thought rhyme" of two (or sometimes three) successive lines. For example, in Ps.29.8 we have

> The voice of the LORD makes the wilderness writhe in travail;
> the LORD makes the wilderness of Kadesh writhe.

The second line introduces no new thought, but parallels the first. Scholars have recognized different types of parallelism. In the example cited, the two lines are synonymous. Others are antithetical, that is, the second line verbalizes the opposite of the first, or states negatively what the first had presented positively. Still others have been called synthetic or formal parallelism, for the second line may develop the thought of the first. Other poetic features more familiar to us, such as meter, rhyme, alliteration, assonance, and the like appear, but they are not as basic as parallelism. There is usually some regularity of meter in the sense of balanced numbers of accented syllables, but this feature seems to be derived from the balancing of parallel lines.

PROPHETIC BOOKS. While prophets were found elsewhere in antiquity, no other culture, before or since, has developed prophetic literature as did ancient Israel. Prophets were known in ancient Mesopotamia, but not prophetic books. Books called prophecies were written in Egypt, but they are quite different from the Old Testament prophetic books. Neither are there prophetic books in the Apocrypha nor in the New Testament, though the Book of Revelation has some affinities with prophetic literature.

The prophetic books receive their distinctive stamp from the prophets' self-understanding as spokesmen for God. The prophets were men who, on the basis of a particular call and special revelations, announced God's word concerning his people, and other nations as well. They were preoccupied with declaring God's actions in the immediate future.

We must distinguish the prophetic words themselves from the prophetic books. Study of the prophets in recent generations has emphasized that they were not authors who wrote books, but speakers. It was usually their followers or other listeners who committed their words to writing. Occasionally we catch a glimpse of the way the spoken words were written down, eventually to form books or parts of books, as in Jeremiah ch. 36. Isaiah, when he was not heeded, gave instructions to "Fasten up the message, seal the oracle with my teaching"

(Isa.8.16). It seems clear from such texts and other indications that something new and significant had occurred when the words were written down. At least two factors were involved. First, writing the speeches preserved the revelation and kept it from being stifled when the prophet was either prevented from speaking, or ignored. Second, there arose a concern that future generations should know that what they were experiencing had already been set into motion by God's word once spoken through his prophets.

The first prophetic "books" doubtless were collections of the sayings of individual prophets. As we shall see, those sayings were of many different types, but for the most part they were short, poetic units. But the prophetic books contain other classes of literature as well, such as narratives. Most of these are reports of prophetic activities, either in autobiographical or biographical style. They range from short accounts, setting the occasions for particular speeches, to lengthy tales; from reports of the prophet's call to accounts of symbolic actions performed as messages. The third genre found in the prophetic books is prayer, such as the so-called complaints of Jeremiah in the Book of Jeremiah, or the hymnic fragments in the Book of Amos.

From the jotting down of the first prophetic utterance to the books we read today was a long journey. The details of that journey elude us, but some of the landmarks can be reconstructed from the evidence in the books themselves. In most cases, the first stage was the recording of individual speeches and small collections of sayings. Often we can recognize some of these earlier collections within the present books; Isa.2.1, for instance, appears to be the heading for such a unit. Then other materials were added, sometimes organized loosely on the basis of similar content or type, or on the basis of chronology. Most of these emerging books continued to be expanded by later additions which claimed the authority of the original man of God. As a result, most of the books now reflect the experience and the thought of several generations. At least two centuries after the death of Isaiah, for example, prophetic writings still were being added to the book which bears his name.

The prophetic books were read and expounded in the Israelite communities which developed and preserved them long before they were canonized as sacred Scriptures. When the Babylonian exiles in the sixth pre-Christian century heard the voice of Amos of the eighth century announcing punishment, they understood their experience as arising from God's activity, and they could turn to the future which they believed lay in his hands. Again, Jeremiah's pronouncements against Judah were used as texts for sermons exhorting obedience. And Deutero-Isaiah (Isaiah chs. 40–55) argued that Israel's Lord was the only God of history and human affairs, for he had announced beforehand through his prophets what was to come.

LETTERS. The New Testament is dominated by letters. Of the twenty-seven books, twenty-one are called epistles (the Greek word for letters), most of which are linked to Paul. The letter form became the most important genre in early Christianity. This development is best appreciated when it is seen in light of the Hellenistic letter-writing conventions. Hebrew or Aramaic letters do not appear to have been as influential as the Greek.

Even before the emergence of Christianity, the Greek letter had already become a remarkably stable literary form, despite the diverse kinds of letters which were written. It is useful to distinguish private letters (correspondence between friends or business letters) from public letters. A considerable quantity of private correspondence, mostly on papyrus, has been preserved; much of it has been published since the late nineteenth century. The public letter could be an official correspondence between a public official and a city council, or a series of discussions of moral or political topics cast in letter form, a letter-essay, or a body of magical information made available as a letter. Almost any kind of material could be presented in the form of a public letter, for it was intended for publication and sale.

Both the private and the public letters followed established conventions, with considerable flexibility in detail. The Hellenistic letter had three main parts: the introduction, the body, and the conclusion. The introduction normally named the writer and the recipient, stated a greeting, and may have included the writer's thanksgiving for deliverance from illness and/or a wish for the reader's health. The body could be short and to the point in private correspondence, or lengthy in essays cast as letters. The conclusion expressed greetings and wishes for the persons known to both the writer and the reader, a final greeting, and sometimes the date. Christian letters followed these conventions and modified them at the same time.

A rigid distinction between public and private letters will not work for Paul's correspondence because of the nature of his writing. Paul responded to particular issues by means of letters only because he could not deal with the issues face to face. His letters stand somewhere between private correspondence and public letters; they were not designed to be published and sold in the book stalls, but rather to be read to his congregations and then exchanged (in some cases at least) with other congregations.

Paul follows the convention of naming the writer and the readers (X to Y); but he modifies this by frequently naming his associates, by characterizing the receiving congregation, and by changing the greeting from "Greetings" (Greek *charein*) to "Grace" (*charis*) and by adding "peace" (from the Hebrew shalom). In Romans, possibly the last letter genuinely from Paul, the opening becomes more complex, for in it Paul summarized the Gospel in six verses before proceeding to write "to all of you in Rome whom God loves and has called to be his dedicated people." Generally, Paul also modified the thanksgiving; instead of expressing thanks for his own safety and health, he wrote his thanks for the life of the congregation, and did so in a way as to subtly indicate the theme of the body of the letter which followed. The body of the letter was developed according to the needs of the occasion, but regularly included exhortations and a section in which he spoke of his travel plans, expressing a desire to visit the congregation personally. The closing not only amplified the greeting pattern, but frequently included a personal word in his own hand (e.g. 1 Cor.16.21 ff.; Gal.6.11 ff.; Philem.19 ff.) in accord with the practice of official letters in Hellenistic times.

The post-Pauline generation not only imitated Paul's letter writing but developed the catholic (general) epistle to the church at large (e.g. 1 John) or to the churches of a region (1 Peter). The post-Pauline letters tended to become letter-treatises, from which the personal touches are generally absent (e.g. Ephesians, Hebrews, 1 John, 2 Peter); 2 John and 3 John are exceptions. In the second century, the letter-writing tradition continued to flourish but did not enter the canon.

In the New Testament, the epistles stand in a clear order: first, those associated with Paul, with Hebrews standing at the end because it was once thought to be from Paul, and then the Catholic Epistles. Of the Pauline Epistles, those addressed to churches stand first, then come four letters addressed to individuals. The Catholic Epistles begin with James, traditionally thought to be Jesus' brother and head of the Jerusalem church, followed by letters attributed to Peter, John, and Jude. Thus the sequence of letters in the epistle section of the New Testament disregards chronological order.

APOCALYPSES. That there is a type of literature called "apocalypse" is inferred from the fact that there is a body of literature, mostly noncanonical, which is generally similar to one book in the Bible which calls itself an apocalypse—the Revelation of John (the word apocalypse means revelation). Although the word apocalyptic is used also to characterize certain theological ideas, we shall restrict ourselves here to a sketch of the chief features of that literature called apocalypses.

There are few pure examples of the genre. Even the apocalypse of John begins with seven letters to seven churches in Asia Minor; the oldest apocalypse, Daniel (165 B.C.), begins with stories about Daniel and his friends; the truly apocalyptic material begins at chapter six. Fourth Ezra is an apocalypse only in chapters three to fourteen. Moreover, modern scholars often list with apocalyptic literature books which contain only sections regarded as apocalyptic because of their content (e.g. the Testament of the XII Patriarchs, Jubilees, the life of Adam and Eve [also called the Apocalypse of Moses]). Indeed, if the presence of a block of apocalyptic material justifies classifying whole books among apocalyptic literature, the list could include Isaiah, Ezekiel, Zechariah, the Synoptic Gospels, 1 and 2 Thessalonians, and 2 Peter. From the observation of this diversity three conclusions can be drawn: 1. There is no clear definition of what constitutes an apocalypse. 2. The diversity results largely from the fact that these texts are either compilations or the result of drawing on diverse sources (oral and/or written). 3. Classifying a text as "apocalyptic" often reflects the theological content and tenor of a writing as much as the literary form.

Given this intriguing diversity, all attempts to draw up a list of features which make a book (or a section of a book) apocalyptic have only a rough preliminary value. Though it is easy to name exceptions, a general characterization will include the following items: 1. Apocalyptic literature is generally pseudonymous —it claims to be written by an ancient figure, such as Enoch, Moses, Ezra, Daniel, Baruch (Jeremiah's associate); however, the New Testament apocalypse openly identifies the author as John, a contemporary of the readers (and hence is known as the Revelation of John). The "War of the Sons of Light and the Sons of Darkness," one of the Dead Sea Scrolls, is anonymous. The hidden identity of the author reflects the view that contemporary events were disclosed long ago, thereby attesting to the belief that everything is happening according to the plan of God. 2. Apocalyptic literature contains visions which portray the history of God's people, especially their experiences of suffering; these visions usually culminate in the overturning of the malign present and the impending vindication of faithfulness by the intervention of God. 3. Using an abundance of symbols, apocalypses generally express the view that "this age" is to be contrasted with the glorious "age to come." The language of apocalyptic literature expresses this contrast and discontinuity in dramatic and violent images: the return of primeval chaos (e.g. the stars will fall and the moon will turn to blood); unprecedented war, especially against the saints (e.g. Armageddon in the Revelation of John, or the war of the sons of light in the Dead Sea book), or the "birth pangs" of the messianic age. 4. What lies either at the end of history or even beyond the end, is sometimes portrayed in terms of the divine promise to Israel (the time of the Messiah), or sometimes in terms of a rejuvenated earth, or, as in Revelation, both "a new heaven and new earth." The obverse is the punishment of the wicked, sometimes portrayed in lurid images, as is the case in noncanonical writings, the Apocalypse of Peter and the Book of Enoch.

The core conviction, however, which spurred this florid imagery, is that the sovereign God is faithful despite his people's experiences of suffering and persecution. Apocalyptic literature flourished in times of suppression and insurrection. The theological tradition had asserted earlier that calamity was God's punishment for infidelity; now, it appeared that fidelity brought calamity. To interpret this, apocalyptists saw the historical experience of the faithful as part of a cosmic struggle of good and evil, traced either to Adam (as in 4 Ezra) or to the "fallen angels" (as in the Book of Enoch). Thus, the whole of mankind's history was involved; that is to say, a radical view of history brought with it a radical view about God and his ancient revelation of history's character and destiny. Thus, the literary form and its magnificent and dramatic imagery express a radical and daring theology, with form and content compatible throughout.

GENRES WITHIN BOOKS

We have already noted that a given book may contain diverse types of materials either because it is a compilation or because the author used and reproduced diverse sources (documents); moreover, the utilized sources themselves contain various forms. Our task now is to suggest the range of diverse materials, and to account, in a sketchy way, for their inclusion in the biblical documents.

The diversity of genres is so rich and the problem of distinguishing one from the other sometimes so complex, that only a general sampling can be undertaken here. Nonetheless, it may show both the disparity in the Bible's forms, and the importance of paying attention to them for understanding the text itself. One fundamental factor must be borne in mind—that much of the content of the Bible was handed down by word of mouth (technically called 'oral tradition') before it was written.

NARRATIVES. It is important to recognize that there are different narrative genres within the biblical books, for they arose in different social settings and served different purposes. Histories, because they attempt to reconstruct the past on the basis of the best information available, are more reliable documents for the modern historian than, for example, fables. And impersonal records or reports are more reliable still.

The Old Testament document which most closely approximates history in the modern sense is not the longer popular or salvation histories mentioned above, but the court history of David (2 Sam. chs. 9–20; 1 Kgs. chs. 1–2). Its writer had access to excellent sources, he reconstructed a segment of the past into a meaningful account, and he interpreted the events in terms of cause and effect. The sense of divine providence and activity is here implicit rather than explicit, as it is in the Book of Judges.

A great many of the individual narratives in the Bible are stories; as noted earlier, they generate interest by arousing tension and releasing it. Most stories in the Old Testament—such as those of the patriarchs in Genesis—are folktales; that is, they use motifs, patterns, and techniques supplied by the oral tradition. Stories serve many different purposes: to amuse, to teach, to enlighten, or to present the most profound theological affirmations. If a story is primarily concerned with the wonderful and aimed at edification, it is a legend (though a legend need not take the form of a story; it may be a simple report). Legends ordinarily deal with holy men, holy places, or religious ceremonies. They speak of the miraculous and the awesome. But the legends of Elisha, for example, do not mean to boast of the prophet's power as such, but to bear witness to the power of Israel's God made visible through him. Very often legends or other stories of sacred places or religious ceremonies are etiological, that is, they explain the sacredness of the place or the importance of the ritual by an account of its origin. For example, the story of Jacob's dream at Bethel (Gen.28.10 ff.) is told—in part—to explain how the place was known to be holy, and how it got its name.

In the New Testament, and especially in the Gospels, many different traditional narrative genres are employed. Often the shape and content of these types are clues to their use in the oral tradition handed down by the earliest Christian communities. One genre is the pronouncement story or paradigm, a short, concise narrative which focuses upon a memorable saying of Jesus. The story provides the framework, the occasion, for the saying. Thus the story of the disciples eating grain on the Sabbath (Mk.2.23–28) is the framework for the saying, "The Sabbath was made for the sake of man, and not man for the Sabbath." Another kind is the miracle story, which concentrates either on Jesus himself (instead of on his sayings) or else on the other characters. Most of these stories tersely report the malady, the healing, and the onlookers' response of wonder. The Christian miracle stories are similar to those in Hellenistic culture generally, but unlike the latter, they seldom report the techniques of the miracle worker. The New Testament also contains narratives which are classed as legends because they express the church's esteem for the hero, such as the story of Peter's release from prison (Acts ch. 12) or the accounts of Jesus' temptations.

PROPHETIC GENRES. In understanding prophetic literature, the reader's first step, as noted above, must be an effort to distinguish the individual units from one another. The meaning of individual lines depends in large measure on the context to which they belong, including the limits of the unit of which they are a part. (The chapter and verse divisions are misleading as often as they are helpful; anyway they date from medieval times.) In distinguishing one unit from another, the reader should be aware of the formulas and genres of prophetic literature, their typical structures, and intentions. Certain formulas, for example, indicate quite clearly the beginning of speeches. Among these are the call to attention, "Listen to these words . . . ," and the expression, "The word of the Lord came to me . . . ."

We have noted that generally speaking the prophetic books contain speeches, narratives, and a few prayers, but in order to recognize the units and interpret them we must be more specific. The range of types of speech found in prophetic utterance is wide; the prophets employed virtually every possible form of verbal communication known in their culture. While the freedom with which they borrowed and adapted from all spheres of life has led some to doubt that there is a distinctively prophetic form of speech, it is preferable to recognize that there are some genres which are particularly and intimately related to the prophetic role. The frequent recurrence of the messenger formula, "thus says the LORD," and the fact that the prophets speak for the LORD, often quoting him directly, have led many scholars in recent years to characterize prophetic address as messenger speech. Whether "messenger speech" or simply "prophecy" is the most apt description of the prophetic addresses, it is clear that these men regarded themselves as the LORD's spokesmen, both revealing and setting into motion his future activities.

One of the genres most frequently encountered in the preexilic prophets is the prophecy of punishment (or prophetic "*judgment* speech"). This type has two main elements, a statement of reasons for punishment (or accusation) and the announcement of punishment (or *judgment*), bound together by a transition which emphasizes that the latter is the result of the former. Such speeches were addressed to individuals, to groups, or to the nation as a whole. On the other hand, in later prophets such as Deutero-Isaiah and in the additions to the preexilic books, prophecies of salvation predominate. In these addresses the prophets announce the LORD's intervention on behalf of Israel, usually without giving reasons.

Other genres closely related to the prophetic office itself are reports of visions, reports of God's call of the prophet, and reports of symbolic actions. Vision reports range from the brief accounts in Amos to the lengthy and detailed descriptions in Ezekiel which often approach the imagery of apocalyptic literature, but they ordinarily include an account of what was seen and an interpretation of its meaning. The "call reports" are not presented in order to give autobiographical information, but rather to authenticate the prophet and his message. So, too, the symbolic action stories are not biographical or autobiographical, but means of communicating the prophetic word.

The prophet's freedom to employ forms of speech from all spheres of Israelite life seems unlimited, but when such genres were used they usually were modified. When Amos sings a dirge, for example, it has become an announcement of punishment: "She has fallen to rise no more, the virgin Israel, prostrate on her own soil, with no one to lift her up" (Amos 5.2). Proverbs, parables, and other forms of speech associated with Wisdom literature are employed freely. And though the prophets should not be viewed primarily as preachers of repentance, but as proclaimers of God's future, they often instruct, admonish, exhort, and warn their hearers. Further, the image of the prophets as consistent opponents of the cult is tempered when we recognize their frequent use of cultic genres. Second Isaiah (chs. 40–55), for example, often speaks in the words of the "salvation oracle," a genre similar to the Old Testament priestly absolutions. Often, of course, the prophets employ cultic expressions to criticize the cult, as when Amos (4.4) uses a call to worship ironically. And frequently we recognize that the prophets are speaking in juridical terms, either in allusions to Israel's laws or in using expressions and motifs from the legal procedure.

LEGAL GENRES. Since the time of the Apostle Paul, Christians often have thought of the Old Testament, in whole or in part, as "the law." This impression stems in large measure from the Greek title of the first part of the Jewish canon, the Torah, which Greek Jews translated "law." But to characterize the Torah (the Pentateuch) as "law" obscures as much as it reveals. We have already observed that the first five books of the Bible are narratives, not law books. But a considerable body of legal material is presented within that narrative framework, either as the report of what was revealed at Sinai or—in Deuteronomy—as part of the report of the last will and testament of Moses.

In fact, none of the books of the Bible can be accurately described as a law book. What we do find, however, are legal codes of different kinds. It seems clear that most of these codes had been organized and handed down in the context of juridical and cultic activity long before they were placed in their present literary contexts. Some of these codes are quite short; they are the collections of ten or twelve laws found in Exodus chs. 20 and 34, and Deuteronomy ch. 5. Other codes are "the book of the covenant" (Exodus chs. 21–23), containing laws mainly concerned with what we would call civil and criminal matters; the Holiness Code (Leviticus chs. 17–26), which is not so much a code as sermons on law. (In view of its expansive literary character it is doubtful that we should call the large body of instructions in the Priestly document—Exodus ch. 25–Numbers ch. 10—a law code.) The old Testament law codes are similar in many ways to their Ancient Near Eastern predecessors: all are collections which tend to organize laws loosely on the basis of content and form; all are the results of many centuries of growth; and there are some distinct similarities of form and content.

In recent scholarship the individual laws in the Old Testament have been classified into two categories. The first is casuistic or case law. These laws closely parallel those in the Ancient Near Eastern codes both in form and content. Each has two main parts, a conditional clause describing a case and a conclusion specifying the penalty: "When [or if] a man steals an ox or a sheep and slaughters or sells it, he shall repay five beasts for the ox and four sheep for the sheep" (Exod.22.1). Such laws must have been related to the everyday practice of law. The second genre has been called apodictic, absolute commands or prohibitions which require no accompanying argumentation since they are taken to be expressions of the will of God. As the Ten Commandments reveal, their content is not limited to specifically religious or cultic affairs, but include social relationships. Whatever the origin of these different genres may have been, eventually all of Israel's laws were associated with Moses and the covenant at Sinai.

In addition to laws, the Old Testament contains a considerable body of material from the judicial process itself. This material is in the form of reports of legal proceedings, allusions to the practice of law in court and cult, and judicial genres and formulas employed in different contexts, such as prophetic speeches. Viewing this data as a whole gives us a picture of the formalities of the trial, of the way contracts were formalized, of the way priests instructed the laity concerning the interpretation or application of cultic laws, and of how law was related to the life of Israel.

WISDOM AND INSTRUCTION. The proverb is one of the most widely known forms of expression and its original oral character is beyond dispute. Proverbs are found in many parts of the Bible apart from the book bearing the name. Proverbs are folk wisdom distilled into pithy, memorable sayings. In isolation, a proverb expresses a general insight (e.g. "haste makes waste"); inevitably one can think of exceptions or of other proverbs which express an apparently conflicting insight. Thus, proverbs must not be treated as first principles but rather as practical wisdom gained from experience. In contrast with divine oracles and apocalyptic visions, proverbs themselves do not claim to be revealed knowledge but distilled human insight. Their specific meaning depends almost entirely on the context in which they are used.

Biblical proverbs or wisdom sayings have many forms. Some are simple declarative statements, such as, "Where the corpse is, there the vultures will gather" (Lk.17.37). More common is the doublet in which the second half contrasts with the first, as in, "A simple man believes every word he hears; a clever man understands the need for proof" (Prov.14.15). Others are structured according to the principle of synonymous parallelism, as in, "Experience uses few words; discernment keeps a cool head" (Prov.17.27). Sometimes a proverb is put in the form of a comparison, as, "Better sit humbly with those in need than divide the spoil with the proud" (Prov.16.19).

Because proverbs express wisdom, it is natural that in the Book of Proverbs wisdom itself is extolled, and even spoken of as if she (the word "wisdom" is feminine) were a person. Furthermore, the proverbs are then regarded as the counsel of wisdom: "My son, keep my words, store up my commands in your mind" (Prov.7.1). Wisdom can also tell a story (in poetic form), as occurs in Proverbs ch. 7 and especially in Ecclesiasticus. In the Wisdom of Solomon wisdom guides the history of Israel. Wisdom materials were originally secular; however, there developed the view that human wisdom is derived from divine Wisdom. Indeed, divine Wisdom—especially when personified—came to be regarded as the self-manifestation of God; inevitably, the sages came to regard both the Wisdom tradition and the Torah as revealed.

Wisdom materials are found in various biblical literature, especially in the Synoptic Gospels. Often proverbs have been expanded to make the meaning explicit, as in the case of "No servant can be the slave of two masters," to which has been added, "for either he will hate the first and love the second, or he will be devoted to the first and think nothing of the second. You cannot serve God and Money" (Mt.6.24). On the other hand, proverbs have also been added to teachings to provide a broader application. Thus, some form of "By gaining his life a man will lose it; by losing his life for my sake, he will gain it" (Mt.10.39), is added to various sayings of Jesus (Mt.16.25; Lk.17.33). Wisdom materials need to be read on two levels: the inherent meaning of the original material (usually discerned by noting the balanced structure of the phrases and ideas), and the specific meaning which the material receives from its present context.

The most famous genre associated with Jesus is the parable. He did not invent the parable form, of course, but developed it from the parabolic tradition of Judaism in the Old Testament. What we normally call a parable is distinguished from a metaphor and a simile in that it has a rudimentary plot. "You vipers' brood" is a metaphor; "becoming like a child" is a simile. The parable, on the other hand, is a brief narrative whose plot implies an analogy between the story and another situation or dimension of reality. Because the point is not on the surface, so to speak, the parable demands insight and appropriation, and its point can be missed. What the New Testament calls "parable" translates a Hebrew term (*mashal*) which can refer to a variety of forms, such as the riddle and epigram. Thus Jesus' saying, "Nothing that goes into a man from outside can defile him; no, it is the things that come out of him that defile a man" (Mk.7.15), is called a "parable" because like the word *mashal*, it means "epigram."

It is customary to distinguish parables from allegories, though a *mashal* can also be an allegory. In an allegory, each item in the story stands for something else, so that one can "decode" the story into its true religious or theological meaning. For example, in the noncanonical Book of Enoch, the story of Israel is told as the history of sheep who endure all sorts of bad experiences from wolves, bears, etc. The reader quickly translates the story by equating Israel with the sheep and the series of enemies with the marauding animals. It is generally believed that Jesus himself used parables but not allegories, but that the parables were later allegorized by the church. Thus, the parable of the abundant harvest (Mk.4.3–8) was allegorized into the story of various kinds of soils (Mk.4.14–20). This is a clear case where sensitivity to literary forms enables the reader to distinguish layers of tradition.

There are sermons in the Bible, but we must not confuse the New Testament "sermon" with what comes to mind when we use the term today. Rather, the biblical sermon generally was an extended religious discourse. Also, largely because the preaching of both Jesus and the earliest church was anchored in synagogue preaching, which was as much instruction as it was proclamation, it is difficult to distinguish New Testament preaching from teaching. That synagogue preaching in turn doubtless was rooted in Old Testament instructional preaching, is best represented by the addresses exhorting obedience in Deuteronomy and the prose speeches in the Book of Jeremiah. In any case, even though Christianity spread by preaching, and even though Jesus is reported to have preached in the synagogue, the New Testament contains no transcripts of any sermon. It does, however, include a number of discourses which have been called "sermons." On the one hand, the sermons of Jesus, including the Sermon on the Mount, are not real discourses but collections of sayings, clustered around certain themes. On the other hand, the speeches in Acts are not real sermons either but discourses composed by the author and placed at key points in the narrative in accord with the Hellenistic practice of having key figures say what the writer believed was important to have said at that point. This does not rule out the likelihood that the author used old traditions in composing these speeches. Interestingly, the New Testament possibly contains parts of sermons elsewhere; for example, it has sometimes been suggested that 1 Peter is basically a baptismal sermon, or a part of one, which has been given the appearance of a letter.

PRAYERS, HYMNS, AND RITUALS. Many biblical passages are prayers—words addressed to God. However, it is sometimes difficult to distinguish a prayer from a hymn because frequently both appear as poetry and are addressed to God. Hymns were presumably sung or chanted, probably by choirs, whereas prayers were spoken. While the Old Testament Psalms enshrine the hymns of the Temple at various stages of its life, there is no comparable Christian collection in the New Testament.

The rich cultic life of ancient Israel gave rise to a great many different types of song and prayer, preserved for the most part in the Book of Psalms (see above, "Poetic books"). These types usually reflect use in various liturgies, though the festival occasions themselves are not named. Approximately one third of the psalms are songs of individual complaints (frequently called "Laments"), in which the sufferer petitions God for relief and deliverance. On the basis of the structure of such songs—in particular, changes in speaker—and allusions to worship, it has been suggested recently that the individual complaints were used in prayer services for persons in distress. Similar are songs of communal complaint (see Introduction to the Psalms). Closely related to these types are the songs of individual and communal thanksgiving, which were employed in celebrations of deliverance from particular difficulties. We also recognize a great many hymns of praise, which were associated primarily with the regularly scheduled services of worship. The hymns characteristically call to praise, expound the reasons for praising God in terms of his acts or his nature, and conclude with the renewed summons to praise (see Psalm 113). The so-called "Enthronement Psalms" (e.g. Psalms 29–47, 93, 95–99) may have been developed for a New Year's festival when God's kingship was celebrated; these songs are characterized by the acclamation, "The LORD reigns!" There are also "Royal Psalms" which celebrate the king as the regent of God (e.g. Psalms 2, 20, 21, 45).

The variety of hymns and prayerlike poetry collected in the psalter is found in many other places in the Old Testament as well. For example, in Exodus ch. 15 we have two celebrations of the deliverance at the sea, a very old couplet in v. 21 (the Song of Miriam), and a more elaborate younger one in vv. 1–18. 2 Samuel 1.19–27 is the lament of David over the death of Saul and Jonathan, while 2 Samuel ch. 22 (virtually identical with Psalm 18) contains a victory song.

In the New Testament, hymnic materials are of three kinds: the messianic hymns, the christological hymns, and hymns of the eschatological victory. In Luke chs. 1 and 2 the evangelist used messianic hymns inherited from certain Jewish circles to express the hope for the coming redemption. There are three passages which appear to be christological hymns. Embedded in the prologue of John (1.1 18) is an earlier hymn to the Word, the Creator; Phil.2.5–11 celebrates the humiliation of the preexistent Christ and his subsequent exaltation; Col.1,15–20 celebrates the relation of the preexistent Christ to the cosmos. Fragments of hymns (or possibly confessional pieces) appear also in Eph.5.14 and 1 Tim.3.16. At key points in the Book of Revelation, the reader is apprised of hymns of deliverance being sung in heaven; these are usually considered to reflect the hymnody of the churches of Asia Minor.

In addition to poetic pieces used in ritual and liturgy, the Bible also contains narratives which were used in worship before they were included in the biblical text. By means of these narrative materials, the community recited fundamental events of its history and thereby celebrated its relation to God. Many scholars have seen in Joshua ch. 24 and other Old Testament texts the outlines of a covenant renewal ceremony by which the Israelite tribes recalled the Exodus and pledged their common fealty to God. These texts are for the most part narratives, but they mention either directly or indirectly the liturgical acts involved. Many of the steps in the liturgy of covenant renewal closely paralleled the points in Ancient Near Eastern treaties.

In the New Testament, the accounts of the Lord's Supper (Mt.26.17–29; Mk.14.12–24; Lk.22.7–38; 1 Cor.11.23–25) differ from one another because they reflect the actual usages of the churches; but they all center in the words of Jesus concerning the bread and the wine. None of these accounts is as liturgically complete as the account of the first Passover in Exodus ch. 12. Although the Book of Esther is traditionally associated with the Festival of Purim, the story itself does not refer explicitly to the festival. The books of Maccabees report the events that led up to the rededication of the Temple, celebrated as Hanukkah, but there are no clear Hanukkah observance materials in the Bible, just as there are no observances linked with Pentecost. Centuries later, Christians associated both the stories of Jesus' wine miracle at Cana and the coming of the Magi with January 6 (Epiphany), but, of course, this belongs to the history of the interpretation of the Bible. These stories did not originate in connection with Epiphany.

This introduction to the literary types of the Bible has, of necessity, been more illustrative than exhaustive. Many important forms of literary and oral expression have not been mentioned. But this basically literary approach, in addition to providing a description of some of the types of biblical literature, serves the serious reader of the Bible in several ways. In the first place, it opens up the historical depth of the biblical material. The Bible is a historical book not merely because it is preoccupied with history, but because its contents also have a history. This literary history of the materials has been recovered in large part because scholars have analyzed the individual literary genres and related these to the life of the communities in which they were used. In many cases we are able to reconstruct the history of the transmission of sayings and stories up to the way the text now reads. What emerges from such careful exploratory work is a keen appreciation of the fact that the Bible is the literary deposit of living tradition which reflects the beliefs and practices of real Israelite, Jewish, and Christian communities. So instead of reading the text in a "flat" way, simply for plot or for bare content, we can now recognize the texture of the matter, perceive its layers, and know how the material functioned in various stages. Second, the concern with genres of literary and oral expression enables the reader to relate the stages of a text to the life of the communities which originated, used, and preserved it. Often particular genres can be located within certain social contexts, such as the worship in the Temple, the practice of law, or the missionary activity of the early church. In the process we see that behind each text stand not primarily creative writers—though there were such—but communities of faith, for which certain genres and particular texts served very important purposes. Finally, this kind of study can facilitate fruitful dialogues with the texts themselves. Posing these literary questions—What kind of text is it? Where did it come from? How was it used?—enables the texts to speak to us, and not simply to reflect our own expectations of them. By looking at the Bible in this way our appreciation and understanding of it should be both broadened and deepened.

A SKETCH OF THE HISTORY
AND GEOGRAPHY
OF THE LANDS OF THE BIBLE

In the centuries before and after Abraham, the mountains and hills and the valleys and plains of the Ancient Near East have remained relatively constant, as have the climate and the weather patterns. A few modifications have taken place: the soil of Sumer has become saline; modern Israel has planted palm trees in the Negeb around Beersheba; and Israeli engineers have dried up the swamps of Lake Huleh. Nevertheless, through all the convulsions of the last five thousand years in the countries of the Ancient East, the lands of the Bible have stood firm.

The Near Eastern centers of civilization in the period before Abraham were Egypt and Mesopotamia; the cities of Memphis and Babylon were the London and New York of the Ancient Near East. The backbone of these two lands was their rivers, along which cities grew up and nations were engendered. The river Nile made Egypt; the Tigris and Euphrates rivers produced Sumer, Babylonia, and Assyria. Without the rivers, and the flat plains sheathing them, these nations could not have been born. Long before Israel had been even conceived, civilizations of enduring accomplishments had flourished and fallen. To these cultural centers of Egypt and Mesopotamia we owe the invention of writing and the beginnings of many of the literary, political, military, engineering, and astronomical arts we take for granted today.

In the third millennium B.C.E. (before the common era) while the Nile land and the land between the Tigris and Euphrates were prospering, Canaan was hardly more than a "place in the road" between the big cities. It was a narrow strip of land along the eastern end of the Mediterranean Sea which joined Egypt with the land of Mitanni, later Syria. Prior to the second millennium this land, dotted with settlements called city-states, was not yet called Canaan; it was not unified, and it was not under the rule of any one country, although Egypt considered it in her sphere of influence.

The southern part of Canaan, later called Palestine, also had a river, the Jordan, for its spine. However, the very deep riverbed of the Jordan, with lofty plateaus to the east and high mountains to the west, made it of little use for agricultural purposes. The Jordan did not annually inundate broad alluvial plains as did the Nile, but large annual rainfall in Canaan, west of the mountains and north of Jerusalem, did make it a land flowing with milk and honey, especially for its neighbors who dwelt in the southern deserts of Negeb and Sinai and in the deserts east of Edom, Moab, and Ammon. Since Canaan was the connecting link between Mesopotamia and Egypt, it became a well-traveled country. A fertile land of hills and valleys, Canaan was destined to be coveted by the homeless, the hungry, and the ambitious conqueror.

ABRAHAM AND THE PATRIARCHS

In the latter part of the E.B. (Early Bronze Age) and through the M.B. (Middle Bronze Age) migrations of people were not uncommon in the Near East. At the end of the E.B. period a group of "westerners," the Amorites, took over the city-states of Mesopotamia as well as the city-states of Canaan. These Bedouin-type peoples may have come originally from the Syrian desert. Archaeological excavations and literary sources indicate that their penetration into the Canaanite cities was not always peaceful. Others besides the Amorites were probably moving into Canaan at this time also. It is easy to understand how Abraham could have migrated to Palestine from Mesopotamia, for history establishes such migrations as the order of the day in the late E.B. and throughout the M.B. periods.

The Bible connects Abraham with Ur and Charran (or Haran), two cultural and economic centers of Mesopotamia in the M.B. Both cities were under the patronage of the moon god, Sin. It has been shown repeatedly that Abraham's story and the other patriarchal narratives in Genesis reflect well the life and times of the M.B. in Palestine. The journey of Abraham from Ur to Palestine has been interpreted as the case of a man following a dream—the dream of a cult and culture free of capricious gods and stifling materialism (e.g. Speiser in *AB Genesis*). The biblical author with his simple faith says, "So Abram set out as the LORD had bidden him" (Gen.12.4). The wanderings of Abram led him down the length of Palestine from Shechem to the Negeb, into Egypt and back to Hebron where he settled at Mamre. The other patriarchal narratives are played out on a stage similar but wider. The stories of Isaac and Jacob require the addition of Transjordan to the stage.

In the last half of the M.B. (1900–1550 B.C.) new waves of people poured into Palestine. From the North came groups of diverse background—Hurrian, Semitic, Indo-Aryan—who flooded into many of the cities of Palestine, moved on, and left behind destroyed towns. Known to the Egyptians as "rulers of foreign countries" (called the Hyksos), this heterogeneous crowd poured into Egypt after their destruction of Canaanite cities. Part of the Hyksos success was due to their use of a new strategic weapon, the lightweight horse-drawn chariot. This weapon, of only limited value in mountainous country, was on the flat lands of Canaan and Egypt, a most formidable military tool in the first half of the second millennium. Between 1750–1550 B.C. the Hyksos played a dominant role in Egyptian affairs. They succeeded in setting up the ruling Fifteenth Dynasty and established as their capital, Avaris (which is possibly Zoan–Tanis). The entrance of Joseph and his brothers into Egypt is frequently associated with this south-westerly sweep of Semites, Hurrians, and Indo-Aryans who composed the Hyksos multitude. In Egypt the ancestors of the Israelites increased and multiplied and filled the land of Goshen until Pharaoh was frightened by the population explosion of the Hebrews. Accordingly, the Pharaohs made slaves of these fertile Semites. With their labor, building projects were undertaken and cities constructed. Some of the Semite slaves undoubtedly belonged to a class of people called *Hap/biru*, which name has recurrently been considered to be related etymologically to the word "Hebrew."

THE EXODUS

From slavery in Egypt the Hebrews were liberated, probably in the reign of Ramesses II (1290–1224 B.C.). The Bible gives the belief of ancient Israel that this liberation was accomplished by the power of God who used Moses and Aaron as his spokesmen, and nature as his instrument. To tell what actually happened at the Exodus through the Reed Sea (not Red Sea as is found in the Greek text), is impossible for the historian, just as it is impossible for the geographer to locate with certainty the Reed Sea. The usual localizations of the sea are at the southern tip of Lake Menzaleh or in the vicinity of the Bitter Lakes. The data in the Old Testament on the route of the Exodus presents difficulties and irreconcilable conflicts. This much is certain, that by 1220 B.C. there was a people called "Israel" that had either escaped or had been expelled from Egypt. Lending credence to this conviction are these words on the Merneptah Stele (line 55): "Israel is laid waste; his seed is not."

These fugitives from Egypt, ancestors of the Israelites, had certain experiences in the desert of Sinai which determined all later history of Israel. At Mount Sinai (the exact location is uncertain) God revealed himself to this group and made known his will for them through Moses. Historians cannot determine what events were acts of God; they can, however, determine what a people believed about certain events. Israel believed, and her historians asserted, that God had made a "treaty" with them at Mount Sinai and that, like all treaties, it bound Israel to definite obligations toward God and neighbor. This treaty (in biblical language, covenant) was associated with Sinai in Israelite tradition. Whether the "treaty format" can be found in Exodus chs. 19–24; or whether the conceptualization of God's relationship to Israel as a covenant partner in the twelfth century B.C. is reliable or anachronistic; or, just when the notion of covenant became widespread in Israel, are matters of warm scholarly debate. Regardless of the answers to these questions, however, this can be said: some of the oldest records of Israel (e.g. Judges ch. 5 and Exodus ch. 15) do speak of one God, the LORD, Yahweh, as active in the nation's history.

After a generation of roaming in the desert the Israelite rebels entered the land of Canaan. The biblical narrative speaks of the entrance into Canaan as coming from Transjordan because Moses and his followers had been unsuccessful in their attempted entry from the South. Detoured from this southern penetration at Arad the Israelites traveled either the highlands of Edom and Moab, or else the deserts east of Edom and Moab, to arrive at the plains of Moab, just east of Jericho. According to biblical tradition Moses died at Mount Nebo at this time, and was succeeded by Joshua who led the children of Israel into the land of promise.

OCCUPATION OF THE LAND

The Book of Joshua gives the clear impression that the Israelites captured Canaan by quick military conquest. Careful historical study suggests, rather, that the sons of Israel first moved, more or less peacefully, into the mountainous regions in central Palestine and then gradually spread throughout the land. The slow infiltration led to a gradual assimilation of Canaanite culture, and a consequent transformation of the religious and political practices of the Canaanites to conform with their own faith. Rather than a war of conquest, there were limited battles, local engagements, incidental to the slow settlement of the Israelites in the land.

Moreover, insights gained from archaeological excavations (especially at Jericho, Gibeon, and Shechem) have helped us understand the biblical narrative of the conquest as a kind of epic. Some of the pre-Israelite inhabitants of Canaan may have been ethnically related to the incoming Hebrews. It is possible that a flight from slavery in Egypt to freedom in Canaan had been made by many Semite serfs even before the time of Moses. Perhaps the Hebrews who entered Canaan under Joshua received a welcome on reunion with relatives already in the land; the peaceful occupation of Shechem by the forces of Joshua seems to hint that such was the case (compare Josh.8.30–35).

Particular sections within Canaan resisted Hebrew capture; these were the five principal Philistine cities: Gaza, Gath, Ashkelon, Ashdod, Ekron. At the beginning of the Iron Age (1200 B.C.) the Philistines had settled on the Canaanite coast around Gaza. This people is part of a larger group referred to as "the Sea Peoples" whose place of origin is unknown, though Crete is often suggested. The introduction of iron into the Canaanite economy was due to these Philistines and because of their greater technology in weaponry and toolmaking they were a perennial threat to the Israelites until their power was broken by David. They gave their name to the land, Philistia–Palestine.

From the death of Joshua to the time of the first king, Saul, was a period of about 200 years (1200–1020 B.C.). During this time of Israelite consolidation in Canaan the tribes of Israel were ruled by "judges." Such judges were charismatic leaders, designated to command the people in time of military need. The political organization of Israel in this period was based on a religious unity expressed both by the maintenance of a commonly recognized shrine (e.g. Shiloh), and by a sociological unity expressed by acknowledged membership in a tribe. The historical antecedents of the twelve tribes are clouded in uncertainty, but whatever be their origins, they formed the federation of Israel and the tribal organization persisted until replaced by a new form of government, monarchy. The land claims of the twelve tribes of Israel are extremely complex; modern interpretations of both their historical and geographic values are disparate.

RISE OF THE MONARCHY

The Book of Judges closes with the complaint, "In those days there was no king in Israel and every man did what was right in his own eyes." Hebrews, like the author of this verse, wanted a monarchy; others passionately resisted kingship in Israel. Nevertheless, with the designation of Saul as king by the popular Samuel, as commanded by God (see 1 Sam.9.15–16), a monarchy came to Israel.

Kingship is an old institution in the Near East where it originated at the beginning of the third millennium from the need for a war leader. To the Hebrews of the eleventh century the charismatic "judges" did not seem adequate for maintaining security; a permanent leader was needed. In the face of hostile pressure from the Philistines and a need for law and order, Israel adopted a monarchical form of government. Even after the adoption of a monarchy, however, the king, in Israel, needed divine approval mediated by a prophet.

The greatest of the kings in Israelite history and tradition was David. Widespread tales depicted his rise from shepherd to warrior and giant-killer, from musician and poet to king. Included in David's biography are his attempted assassination by Saul, his leadership of guerrillas in the Judean desert, his recognition first by two southern tribes as king, and then by the northern tribes, thus becoming king of all Israel.

David extended the boundaries of Israel farther than did Saul or subsequent kings. Longitudinally the boundaries were thought of as from Dan in the North to Beersheba in the South, 150 miles as the crow flies; David's territory exceeded this. Also, by subjugating all of Transjordan from Aram to Edom he more than doubled the width of his kingdom. (From the Sea of Galilee to the coast is 30 miles, from the northern tip of the Dead Sea to the coast is 50.)

Acceptance as king by both the North and the South required David to exhibit fairness to both. As a sign of belonging to both, yet owned by neither, David chose as his capital a non-Israelite town, Jerusalem, on the common border. It then became the chief political city of Judah, David's city, and after the Temple was built by David's son, Solomon, it became also the religious center of the united kingdom of all Israel.

Solomon reorganized the nation so that the remnants of the tribal federation were repressed. Through his successful political machinations and economic adventures peace and prosperity prevailed under him. Yet his was a despotic rule. High taxation and the limitation of individual liberty through forced labor were so characteristic of Solomon's reign that the division of the nation into two kingdoms after his death came readily. Despite the influence of the new Temple in Jerusalem, it could not counterbalance the revulsion away from the tyrannical ways of foreign kings.

THE DIVIDED KINGDOM

Solomon was succeeded by Rehoboam, against whom the northern tribes rebelled, with the leader, Jeroboam, becoming their king. The border tribe Benjamin joined Judah in loyalty to Rehoboam, while the other tribes and the Transjordan lands were loyal to the North. Judah was, accordingly, much smaller and more homogeneous than the Northern Kingdom; perhaps that is why throughout the history of Judah only one dynasty, David's, ruled, while in Israel to the North no dynasty survived longer than three generations. Assassination ended the lives of numerous kings of the North, for coups d'etat were sporadic.

As the Arameans (Syrians), led especially by Damascus, became strong, Israel had to concern herself with defense against attacks from her northern neighbors. This particular threat to Israel was removed by the rising power of the neo-Assyrian Empire which became the master of satellite states in the neighborhood of Palestine after the battle of Qarqar in 853 B.C.

The most prestigious royal line in Israel was that of Omri. For this reason the nation Israel in contemporary extrabiblical documents is called "the house of Omri." This dynasty (878-858 B.C.) selected Samaria as its capital. Religious centers were erected, at Dan in the northern edge, and Bethel in the southern extreme. The leaders of the North hoped that these two shrines would satisfy the religious needs of the Israelites, and obviate pilgrimage to Jerusalem, the capital of the South, and a reminder of the earlier national unity.

A number of charismatic individuals, known as prophets, appeared in Palestine. At times ecstatic, frequently antimonarchical, sometimes living in communities but more often loners, occasionally employed at a temple but most often anticultic, the prophets spoke the word of Yahweh to their contemporaries, often in judgment and condemnation.

From the early ninth century, Assyrian domination spread in the Near East. At the battle of Qarqar the Assyrians defeated a coalition of Syrian and Palestinian armies. Thereafter, Assyria was a constant bridle on the independence of Israel, Judah, and the Arameans. For the next century city-states of the region attempted to free themselves from the Mesopotamian net. When, about 734 B.C., Damascus and Israel failed to persuade Judah to unite with them in a revolt against Assyrian rule, the two allied states resorted to pressure on the South for its participation. King Ahaz of Judah, frightened by these forceful neighbors, called for help to Tiglath-pileser III of Assyria. This monarch, named Pul in the Bible, marched westward in response, and this campaign was the beginning of the end for Israel (732 B.C.). Pul divided Syria into five provinces, each subject to an Assyrian governor, while the upper part of Israel became the Assyrian provinces of Dor, Megiddo, and Gilead. After the disasters of 732 B.C., Israel suicidally continued to seek liberation by political as well as by military means. Such machinations, however, so provoked Assyria that Shalmaneser V besieged Samaria in 724 B.C. Two years later Shalmaneser's general and successor, Sargon II, devastated stubborn Samaria. Thousands of Israel's citizens were deported to the east, and Israel ceased to exist as an independent state. After 722 B.C. biblical history is the story of Judah.

From Qarqar (853 B.C.) to the battle of Carchemish (605 B.C.), Assyria dominated the Near East. In the year 612, the Babylonians and the Medes leveled Nineveh, the Assyrian capital.

From Samaria's collapse in 722 B.C. to the destruction of Jerusalem in 587 B.C., 135 years later, religious infidelity was, according to the Hebrew prophets, a constant phenomenon. The cultural assimilation of Yahwism to Canaanite fertility cults, the bending of Hebrew values to Mesopotamian and Canaanite ways of life, and the imitation of Egyptian and Assyrian methods of power politics were the grounds for the prophetic indictment of the nation. Occasional religious reformations, such as those under Hezekiah (about 705 B.C.) and Josiah (621 B.C.), did not last long, and the just punishment of God, said the prophets, must certainly come. When Nebuchadnezzar, king of Babylonia, subjected Judah to his rule, and his general Nebuzaradan burned Jerusalem and dismantled her walls in 587 B.C., the oracles of doom spoken by the prophets were considered fulfilled. For many Judahites the razing of the Holy City occasioned the end of hope in their kings, their nation, and their God. The

Babylonian victors exiled 4,600 Jews to the area around Nippur, with many in Jerusalem believing that finis had been written on the history of Israel.

EXILE AND RESTORATION

In war-torn Judah, sparsely populated and neglected, the rule by David's line ceased when the royal family was exiled to Babylon with the other deportees. Dwelling along the Chebar Canal in Babylonia, the transplanted Jews adapted to their new situation. A religion without Temple worship was developed; a rethinking of sacred and localized traditions, occasioned by enforced separation from Jerusalem, fostered a new understanding of old laws and produced insightful understanding of remembered prophetic sayings. Secretaries began to record old laws and new interpretations, oracles of deceased prophets, and sermons of living preachers. Out of the successively collected records of Israel's past and the writings of the scribes, the book we now know as the Bible began to take shape.

The Exile ended in 538 B.C. by decree of Cyrus the Great, king of the Persians, conqueror of Babylonia, and liberator of the Jews. Among the returnees to Judah (after 538 B.C.) were the prophets Haggai and Zechariah and the prince Sheshbazzar. They urged the Jewish community to rebuild the Temple, contending that renewed prosperity in the land depended on it. Yet the completion of the Temple in 515 B.C. did not fully satisfy, for the rebuilt structure seemed puny in comparison to Solomon's original.

Governor Nehemiah and Ezra, priest-scribe, came to Jerusalem from Babylon about the middle of the fifth century (but see Introduction to Ezra). In the religious chaos of that period both labored heroically to keep Jews faithful to God. Such efforts included a ban on mixed marriages. Nehemiah rebuilt the walls of Jerusalem, in spite of strong opposition from neighboring peoples like the Samaritans. The repatriated lived in the villages and cities located near Jerusalem. The settlement farthest from Jerusalem was less than thirty miles away. This clustering around Jerusalem reflects the insecurity of the Jews who had returned from Exile.

Palestinian sources from the time of Ezra–Nehemiah (450–390 B.C.) until the time of the Maccabees (168 B.C.) are so scarce that the fourth century in Judah is a dark age to us. From Greek sources much is known about the battles of Persians against Greeks at this time, and about the subsequent ascension to power of Alexander the Great, who subjected the entire Near East; many Hellenistic cities were developed in Palestine after Alexander crushed Gaza and Samaria in 332 B.C.

The motto of Alexander was "harmony"; hence, religious toleration and a modicum of political liberty were allowed in the conquered satrapies. When Alexander died at Babylon in 323 B.C., however, his generals began immediately to divide the empire which Alexander had formed. After the bickering and quibbling, one general, Seleucus, received Syria and Mesopotamia, while Egypt went to another, Ptolemy, son of Lagos. Palestine, in between the two, was disputed territory.

Though after the battle of Ipsus (301 B.C.) the Seleucidians were awarded

Palestine, the Ptolemies of Egypt actually controlled the land until 198 B.C. when Antiochus III, after a victory at the battle of Paneas, drove the Egyptians from Palestine. Under the Ptolemies the Jews had enjoyed religious autonomy. Given the right to emigrate, a colony had settled in Alexandria and prospered there. To this Greek-speaking Jewish community we owe the Septuagint, the Greek Old Testament, the first part of which translation is often dated in 250 B.C.

In Judea, however, conditions under the Seleucids were disquieting. The monarchs had a chronic need for money, because of large indemnities due to lost wars. The extortion of money from subjects marked the reigns of Seleucus IV (187–175 B.C.) and Antiochus IV Epiphanes (175–163 B.C.). Much of this income the Seleucids paid to Rome, which had newly become a force in the Near East. Rome, unhurriedly but firmly, annexed Seleucid possessions from the time of her first victory over the Greeks in Asia (Magnesia) in 190 B.C.; in 64 B.C. Pompey occupied Damascus and established the Roman province of Syria.

THE MACCABEES

From the Judean standpoint, the worst of the Seleucids was Antiochus IV Epiphanes. Not only a robber of temples, he was also a tyrant who encouraged religious persecution and fostered cultural domination by Hellenism. Proclaiming himself a manifestation of Zeus, he erected an altar to his patron deity in the Jerusalem Temple. Revolt erupted, led by the zealous Mattathias and his five sons. The Maccabees attracted the zealous faithful to their guerrilla army. Three years of resistance under the leadership of Judas, the son of Mattathias, climaxed when the Maccabees liberated Jerusalem. The Temple was then repaired and purified (in December 164 B.C.) and its reopening thereafter observed as the Feast of Hanukkah (rededication). The Maccabeans had founded a dynasty.

The struggle for freedom, first under Judas, next under his brother Jonathan, then under another brother, Simon, occupied the following three decades for the Jews. Accounts of alliances, intrigues, raids, and negotiations are recorded in 1 and 2 Maccabees. Not all Judeans agreed with the Maccabees' viewpoint. Some, for example, hospitable to Hellenistic culture, actively pursued it. At the other extreme the Hasidim (pious) neither wanted nor tolerated contact with Hellenism. The strict observance of the Law marked the Pharisees, a separatist group growing at this time, while the aristocratic and priestly Sadducees were receptive to the worldliness of the Greeks. On the fringes of Judean society, the Zealots wanted independence at any price; the Essenes chose to withdraw from normal living to the Qumran area of the wilderness. The multiplicity and diversity of socioeconomic, political, and religious viewpoints found in post-Maccabean Judaism urge that one be wary of facile, and hence false, simplifications of Judaism in the age of Jesus.

Rome, though present in the Near East after 198 B.C., did not frequently interject herself into Palestinian affairs during the reigns of the Maccabean monarchs. Busy with more dangerous enemies, and striving for richer spoils, Rome was not to be distracted by hinterland squabbles.

But irreconcilable conflicts among Jerusalem Jews occasioned the loss of Judean independence to the Romans. In 69 B.C., when the Jewish queen-mother,

Salome Alexandra, died, her two sons vied for the throne. Civil war resulted. One son, Hyrcanus II, accepted the support of, or machinations by, the Herodian family; the other had the backing of the Sadducees and of "nationalists." Pompey, wanting the civil strife in Jerusalem stopped, dispatched a peace mission to Jerusalem. When it failed, Pompey himself came to the Holy City, stopped the fighting by force, installed Hyrcanus as high priest of the Temple, and annexed Palestine to the province of Syria. The Roman legate at Syria became the (official) ruler of Judea.

Upheavals in Rome such as those during the Catiline conspiracies, the assassination of Julius Caesar in 44 B.C., the rise of Augustus Caesar, and the love affair of Marc Antony with Cleopatra of Egypt all impinged on the Judean throne. Yet through all these tumultuous events, the family of Herod managed to retain the favor of those in power in Rome. This family, of Idumean extraction, was one of the most devious political families of antiquity. Accordingly, Herod the Great was named king of Judea by Augustus Caesar in 40 B.C., but actually began to reign three years later, and reigned until 4 B.C. A vassal of Rome, Herod was subject directly to the Emperor, rather than indirectly through the provincial governor of Syria. Herod used his direct access to Caesar with cunning, for Roman power and favor were the pillars of his kingdom. After his death, Caesar divided the territories, by now vastly increased, among Herod's three sons.

CHRISTIAN BEGINNINGS

Christianity began within Judaism. And, although a significant part of the Christian movement was oriented to the Gentile world by the mid-first century, its history is intricately related to the experience of Judaism for most of the first century. Jesus of Nazareth was, of course, a Palestinian Jew. Born shortly before the demise of Herod the Great in 4 B.C., Jesus died during the period when Pontius Pilate was the Roman governor of Judea (26–36 A.D.). Our knowledge of Jesus' career is almost wholly dependent on the canonical Gospels. From a modern perspective, the traditions about Jesus preserved in the Gospels are both too meager and insufficiently circumstantial to permit the writing of a biography; nothing is known of his childhood that contributes to the understanding of his "development"; a sequence which would allow us to trace the unfolding of his career cannot be wrested from the sources. The Gospels were composed completely from the viewpoint of faith and reflect that faith in every line. Nevertheless, behind the figure to whom faith testifies, there is a recognizable human subject: Jesus' career was that of an itinerant teacher; the center of his message was the dawning of the Kingdom of God; his career was marked by fraternal association with sinners, whom many righteous people considered beyond the pale but to whom he proclaimed God's forgiveness; he performed mighty works; he was apparently somewhat lax about Sabbath observance; his death by crucifixion can only mean that he was condemned as an enemy of the state by Roman authorities.

Shortly after his death some of his disciples had experiences which convinced them that Jesus had been raised from the dead and began to proclaim him as the

Christ (Messiah). At first the movement remained within Judaism, distinguished by the belief that he was the Messiah, and by rites which included initiation by baptism and the sharing of a sacred meal. The impulse to share what these early disciples called the "good news" soon led to a mission beyond Palestine among non-Jews which resulted in the dramatic establishment of predominantly Gentile churches. By the middle of the first century the Gentile question (whether non-Jews could become Christian without submitting to circumcision and Jewish laws of purity) required a "Council" in Jerusalem, at which time Paul (himself a former Pharisee) was recognized as leader of the Gentile mission. The decision to admit Gentiles without requiring full compliance with Jewish legal requirements was adopted as a compromise but was in effect a victory of the Gentile mission. Nevertheless, the church continued to maintain its (doubtless strained) ties with Judaism, whose Scriptures (the Old Testament) it has shared over the centuries.

Through most of the first century, the story of the land of Palestine was one of restive Jewish submission to Roman domination. Living in a land covenanted to them by a God who intended their freedom, Palestinian Jews found foreign domination unnatural and eventually intolerable. In 66 A.D. the province revolted. The rebellion was suppressed in 70 A.D., when Jerusalem was taken by the Roman general Titus and the Temple was destroyed. A handful of Jews held on at the desert fortress, Masada, until it also fell in 73 A.D. During the conflict there was an exodus of Jews and Jewish Christians from Jerusalem.

The destruction of the Temple is a critical date for both Judaism and Christianity. After 70 A.D. the synagogue became the sole center of Jewish culture, as pharisaism-rabbinism attained full ascendancy in Jewish affairs. Before the end of the century, a normative list of sacred books (the Old Testament) was developed. Oral materials used in synagogue teaching began to be collected and recorded, eventuating in rabbinic literature.

In Christianity also, the period following 70 A.D. was a time of new development. The tension between synagogue and church increased and finally became a gap which separated the two, as the church became predominantly Gentile. There was a fresh outbreak of Christian literary activity—including the writing of the Gospels according to Matthew, Mark, Luke, and John. Paul's letters (originally written around 50 A.D.) were collected, copied, and circulated. Out of the literary activity of the last quarter of the first century, the New Testament began to emerge.

The tragedy of Judea was still not at an end. In 132 A.D. the Emperor Hadrian's order that a new city, *Aelia Capitolina*, be built on the ruins of Jerusalem brought on the so-called second revolt. The leader of the Jewish insurgents was popularly known as Bar-Cochba (Son of a Star), a nickname which apparently was related to the expectation that he might be the Messiah and deliverer of Israel. After three bloody years, the Roman legions again subdued the land and Jerusalem was rebuilt as a monument to Hadrian. Jews were no longer allowed in the city.

But beyond the city and the land, both Jews and Christians lived out their chosen lives and planted in the Mediterranean world a seed that was integral to the flowering of subsequent Western civilization.

RECKONING TIME

CHRONOLOGY

The ancient world produced no universal system of chronology. Rather, the method by which the time of an event's occurrence was recorded varied from culture to culture. In Babylon and Assyria, for example, each year was named after a different public official, and the events of the year were identified with the eponym (i.e. the name of the person associated with that year). Lists of the sequence of such eponyms were preserved and used as a basis for reckoning the length of time between events in those countries.

Frequently, events were dated by reference to the reigning monarch's accession to the throne; for example, "In the fourth year of Solomon's reign" (1 Kgs.6.37); "in the fifteenth year of the Emperor Tiberius" (Lk.3.1). This was true in Babylon, Egypt, Assyria, and Palestine.

Only relatively late did the "era" come into use. In an era, time is reckoned from an important event or a given point. Thus, for a while the Exodus served as the point from which time was calculated by the Israelites (Exod.16.1; Num.9.1; 1 Kgs.6.1).

A non-Jewish era used for reckoning time in Jewish history was the so-called Seleucid, which began in 312 B.C. (1 Macc.1.10; 2 Macc.1.7; 11.21). It was named for Seleucus Nicator who founded the Seleucid Kingdom in Syria after the death of Alexander the Great and the division of his empire, the major part of which was acquired by Seleucus.

It was usual for Roman historians to date events *ab urbe condita* ("from the founding of the city" of Rome), this indicated by the letters A.U.C. That date is generally fixed in terms of the Christian era at 753 B.C. The Greeks reckoned time by Olympiads, which were the four-year periods between Olympic contests in athletics, poetry, and music; the first Olympiad began in 776 B.C.

The Christian era is now generally used to construct a universal chronology. It is measured from the birth of Christ and indicated by the letters B.C. (before Christ) and A.D. (anno Domini—in the year of our Lord—after Christ). Its use dates back to the sixth century A.D. when "Dennis the Short," a Roman monk, computed the birth of Christ to have occurred in 754 of the Roman era (A.U.C.). Dennis' computations, however, have been proved partly in error, so that the birth of Jesus is given by modern scholars about 6 B.C.

Today we can usually establish the dates of the reigns of kings of the Ancient Near East rather accurately in terms of the Christian era (that is, B.C. and A.D.) by correlating data concerning regnal years left by Babylon and Egypt, and by translating the results in terms of the chronology of Greece and Rome.

After the fifteenth century A.D., the Jewish community has normally used an older, sporadic chronology based on an era beginning with (the supposed date of) creation, which in Christian chronology would have been 3,761–3,760 B.C. This number was arrived at by computing such elements as the ages of the patriarchs and the length of the reigns of kings as given in the Bible. In both Jewish and some non-Jewish usage, B.C.E. (before the common era) supplants B.C. and A.C.E. (after the common era) supplants A.D.

Certain Hebrew dates differ among scholars; for example, the destruction of the Temple by the Babylonians is sometimes 587 B.C. and sometimes 586 B.C. The explanation for the disagreement is as follows: A year, e.g. 1925, in terms of the Western calendar, runs from January through December. Since the Hebrew calendar runs from fall to fall, the Hebrew equivalent of 1925 would in part be 5265 and in part 5266. Because of the lack of direct equivalence, some scholars have treated a Hebrew date so as to yield the year 586, while others have arrived at 587 for the same occasion. Either of these would be "correct," for there does not exist a uniform opinion among scholars. Indeed, some have sought to get around the lack of equivalence by a double date, e.g. 722/21 or 587/86.

THE HEBREW YEAR

The basic Hebrew year had twelve months, each determined by the moon. Since a moon's cycle consists of approximately twenty-nine and a half days, a Hebrew year would contain approximately three hundred and fifty-four days. A solar year, i.e. one determined by the annual revolution of the sun, consists of approximately three hundred and sixty-five and one quarter days. Since it is the solar year which determines the seasons with their agricultural activities (with which the Hebrew festivals of firstfruits and harvest were inseparably bound), periodically another month had to be added to take care of the difference between three hundred and fifty-four and three hundred and sixty-five days. At first the addition of this extra "leap year" month was done for practical reasons, i.e. when it was determined that in a given year the barley would not be ripe for harvest if Nisan, the first month, directly followed the previous twelfth month, Adar. The insertion of the additional month created a leap year of three hundred and eighty-three days. Later a more fixed calendar resulted in a cycle of nineteen years respecting leap years, with every third, sixth, eighth, fourteenth, seventeenth, and nineteenth being leap years.

There is evidence of varying Hebrew calendars; in general, however, the Hebrew *religious* year began in the spring with the month of Nisan, also called Abib (March–April; Exod.12.2, 18), while the *civil* year began with the seventh month, Tishri (September–October; Exod.23.16; 34.22; Lev.25.4).

THE MONTH

The Hebrew month began with the appearance of the new moon as determined by visual observation rather than by astronomical calculation. As mentioned above, the period of the moon's revolution requires twenty-nine and a half days; hence the length of the Hebrew lunar months could be either twenty-nine or thirty days.

The months could be indicated either by number or by name. Ancient Canaanite names for four months occur in the Bible: Abib, the first month (Exod.13.4; 23.15; 34.18; Deut.16.1); Ziv, the second (1 Kgs.6.1, 37); Ethanim, the seventh (1 Kgs.8.2); Bul, the eighth (1 Kgs.6.38). After the Exile, Babylonian names as well as numbers were given to the lunar months; seven of the twelve names occur in the Bible: Nisan (alternate of Abib), the first month (Neh.2.1; Esther 3.7); Sivan, the third (Esther 8.9); Elul, the sixth (Neh.6.15); Kislev, the ninth (Neh.1.1; Zech.7.1); Tebeth, the tenth (Esther 2.16); Shebat, the eleventh (Zech.1.7); Adar, the twelfth (Ezra 6.15; Esther 3.7, 13; 8.12; 9.1, 15, 17, 19, 21).

Since the new moon marked the beginning of a natural division of time, it was observed as a holy day with joy and feasting (1 Sam.20.5); trumpets were blown (Ps.81.3); ordinary work was prohibited (Amos 8.5); additional sacrifices were offered (Num.28.11–14).

THE WEEK

The Hebrew week consisted of seven days, the only one called by a name being the Sabbath (Mt.28.1); the others were indicated by numbers, e.g. first day. Nothing similar to the institution of the Sabbath existed in Babylon or Egypt. The Sabbath was probably observed even before Sinai (Exod.16.23). Thereafter its observance came to be considered a sign of God's covenant with Israel (Exod.31.12–13).

THE DAY

Presumably because of the lunar orientation of the calendar, the Hebrews reckoned a day as beginning at sunset and lasting until the following sunset (Gen.1.5; Exod.12.18). Originally the night was divided into three watches (Judg.7.19: "middle watch") and the daylight into three equal parts: morning, noon, and evening (Ps.55.17; Dan.6.10), these sometimes indicated by such terms as "sunrise," "heat of the day" (2 Sam.4.5) or "sunset." Later, the Roman division of the day and night into four parts was used (Mt.14.25 mentions a fourth watch), as was also the division of daylight into twelve hours (Mt.20.1–6; Jn.11.9).

SELECT INDEX TO PEOPLE, PLACES, AND THEMES IN THE BIBLE

This index is designed to enable the reader to locate *persons*, *places*, and *ideas* in the Bible. Biblical books (such as Job, Micah, Isaiah) do not appear, but references are listed to passages of primary significance concerning the men: Job in Ezekiel and James; Micah in Jeremiah; and Isaiah in Kings, Chronicles, and in some of the books of the Apocrypha and the New Testament. Passing mention of principal characters such as even Abraham in Gen.50.24, for example, is not included. Therefore, since the index is necessarily selective, it is suggested that a complete concordance to the Bible be consulted.

40

41

43

15.11; 20.32; Rom.1.7; 3.21–24; 4.1–5; 5.1–2,13–17,20–21; 6.1,12–15; 11.5–6; 12.3,6; 1 Cor.1.3; 15.10; 2 Cor.1.2,12–13; 6.1–2; 12.8–9; Gal.1.3, 6–9,15–17; 2.9; 5.2–4; Eph.1.4–7; 2.4–7; 3.8; 6.24; 2 Tim.1.9; Ti.2.11; 3.7; Heb.4.16; 10.29; Jas.4.5–7; 1 Pet.1.8–10

Holiness of: Lev.11.44–45; 19.2; 20.26; 21.8; 22.2; Josh.24.19; Pss.23.3; 99.3,5,9; Isa.5.16; 6.1–3; 40.25.26; 57.15; Ezek.36.20–23; Hos.11.9; Mt.6.9

Image of: Gen.1.26–27; 5.1–3; 9.3–6; Wis.2.23–24; Ecclus.17.3; 1 Cor.11.7; Jas.3.9

Names for: Gen.2.5; 4.26; 14.18; 16.13; 17.1; 21.33; 22.14; 31.42; Exod.3.6,12–15; 6.3; Deut.32.30; 1 Sam.1.3; 2.10; Dan.2.20; 4.34; 6.26; 7.7,13,22

Gog and Magog: Ezek. chs.38–39; Rev.20.8

Golden Rule, The: Lev.19.19; Ecclus.31.15; Tob.4.15; Mt.7.12; Lk.6.31

Golgotha (Calvary): Mt.27.33; Mk.15.22; Lk.23.33; Jn.19.17–18

Goliath: 1 Sam.17.4–54; 2 Sam.21.19; 1 Chr.20.5

Gomer: Hos.1.3–11

Gomorrah: *See* Sodom and Gomorrah

Goshen: Gen.45.10; 46.28–47.27

Grasshopper: *See* Locust

Greatest Commandment: Lev.19.17–18; Deut.6.4–5; Mt.22.34–40

Greece/Greek (Gentile): Dan.8.21; 10.20–11.2; Joel 3.6; 1 Macc.1.1–10,16–31,41–50; 3.10–41; 4.1–34; 6.1–17,28–31,48–63; 7.1–4,8–11,19–20, 26–50; 9.1–4,11–15,43–53,57,63–64; 10.1–6,15–20,22–58,67–77,88–89; 11.1–19,28–53,54–59,60–66; 12.39–43,49; 13.12–24,31–32,34–42; 14.1–3; ch. 15; 16.11–22; 2 Macc.2.19–23; 4.7–22; 5.1–27; 6.1–6; 8.8–9.29; 10.10–13; 11.1–38; 12.32–36; 13.1–2,9,18–26; 14.1–26,37–46; 15.1–36; Mk.7.26; Jn.7.35; 12.20–22; Acts 6.1; 9.29; 13.44–14.7; 16.1–2; 18.4; 19.10–11; 20.2,20–21; 21.28; Rom.1.14–16; 10.11–12; 1 Cor.1.22–24; Gal. 2.1–3; 3.28; Col.3.11; *see also* Hellinists; Javan

Guilt-offering: Lev.5.14–6.7; 7.1–7; 14.12–13; 19.21; Ezra 10.19

Hadadezer: *See* Aram

Hadassah: Esther 2.7

Hades: Lk.16.23; Rev.20.13–15; *see also* Benhinnom, Valley of; Hell; Sheol

Hagar: Gen.16.1–16; 21.8–21; Gal.4.21–31

Hail: Exod.9.18–23; 10.5; Josh.10.11; Job 38.22; Pss.18.12–13; 78.47–48; 105.32; 148.8; Isa.28.2, 17; 30.30; Ezek.13.11–13; Hag.2.17; Rev.8.7; 11.19; 16.21

Ham: Gen.5.32; 7.13; 8.18–22; 10.1,6–20; Pss.78.50–51; 105.23–27; 106.22; *see also* Shem, Ham, and Japheth

Haman: Esther 3.1–15; 5.4–14; 6.6,12–13; 7.6–10; 8.1; 9.10; Rest of Est.11.2–12

Hamath/Lebo-hamath: Num.13.21; 34.8; 2 Sam.9.8; 2 Kgs.14.28; 17.24–30; 18.34; 19.13; Isa.10.9; 11.11; Jer.39.5; 49.23; Ezek.47.16–17,20; Zech. 9.2

Hamor: Gen.33.19; 34.2–26; Judg.9.28

Hannah: 1 Sam.1.2–2.21

Harran: Gen.11.31–32; 12.4–5; 27.43; 28.10; 29.4; 2 Kgs.19.12

Hazael: 1 Kgs.19.15–17; 2 Kgs.8.8–9,13–15; 28–29; 10.32–33; 12.17–18; 13.1–3,7,22–24; Amos 1.4

Heathens: *See* Nations

Heaven: Gen.1.1,8,14–15,20; 7.11; 8.2; 14.19; 22.11;

28.17; Exod.24.10; Deut.4.26,32,36; 10.14; 1 Kgs.8.27; Job 11.8; 20.27; 22.14; 26.11; Pss.19.6; 69.34; Isa.40.12; 66.1; Ezek.8.3; Dan.7.13; 2 Esd.8.52; Mt.3.2,17; 5.3,12,19,45; 6.9–10; 8.11; 13.24; 18.23; 21.25; 23.22; 24.30–35; Mk.1.10; 11.30; 13.27,31; 14.62; Lk.3.21; 10.18; 11.2; 20.4; 21.26,33; Jn.1.32,51; 3.13,31; 6.38; Acts 1.11; 2.25; 9.3; 11.5,9; Rom.1.18; 1 Cor.15.47; Gal.1.8; 1 Th.4.16; 2 Th.1.7; Rev.3.12; 4.1–2; 5.3; 6.14; 8.1,10,13; 9.1; 10.4,6; 11.6,19; 12.7–10; 13.13; 16.17,21; 20.9,11; 21.1,10

Hebrew (the name): Gen.14.13; 39.14,17; 40.15; 41.12; Exod.1.15–19; 2.6–7,11–13; 3.18; 5.3; 9.1,13; Deut.15.12; 1 Sam.4.6,9; 13.3,19; 14.11, 21; 29.3; Jer.34.9,14; Jonah 1.9; Acts 6.1; 2 Cor. 11.22; Phil.3.5

Hebron/Kiriath-arba: Gen.23.2–17; 37.14; Num. 13.22; Josh.10.39; 14.15; 20.7; Judg.1.10; 2 Sam. 2.1,11,32; 3.2,32; 5.3,13; 15.7,10

Hell: 2 Esd.7.[36],[70]; Mt.5.22,29–30; 10.28; 18.9; 23.15,33; Mk.9.43–48; Lk.12.5; Jas.3.6; 2 Pet.2.4; Rev.1.18; *see also* Ben-hinnom, Valley of; Hades; Sheol

Hellenists: Acts 6.1; *see also* Greece/Greek; Javan

Hephzi-bah: Isa.62.4

Hermon: Deut.4.48; Josh.13.11; Pss.89.12; 133.3; S. of S.4.8

Herod Antipas: Mt.14.1–6; Mk.6.14–22; Lk.3.1,19; 9.7,9; 23.7–15; Acts 4.27

Herod the Great: Mt.2.1–16; Lk.1.5

Hezekiah: 2 Kgs.18.1–20.21; 2 Chr. chs. 29–32; Prov.25.1; Isa. chs 36–39; Jer 26.18–19; Ecclus.48.17–25; 2 Esd.7.40[110]

Hill-shrines/High Places: Lev.26.30; Num.21.28; 22.41; 33.52; Deut.33.29; 1 Sam.9.12–14,19–25; 1 Kgs.3.1–4; 11.7; 12.31–32; 13.2,32–33; 14.23; 15.14; 22.43; 2 Kgs.18.4; 21.3; 23.4–14; Ps.78.58; Isa.36.7; Ezek.6.1–14; 16.16; Hos.10.8

Hiram/Huram: 2 Sam.5.11; 1 Kgs.5.1,10–12; 7.13,40; 9.12,27; 10.11,22; 1 Chr.14.1

Hittites: Gen.25.9; 26.34; 36.2; Josh.9.1; 11.3; 1 Sam.26.6; 2 Sam.11.6,21; 12.9–10; Ezek.16.3

Hivites: Exod.3.8,17; 13.5; 23.23,28; Deut.7.1; 20.17; Josh.3.10; 9.1; Judg.3.5

Hobab: *See* Jethro

Holophernes: Jdt.2.4–14.13

Holy of Holies/Most Holy Place: Exod.26.33; 1 Kgs.6.16; 7.50; 8.6; Ezek.41.4; 43.12; 45.3; Dan.9.24

Holy Spirit: Num.11.24–29; 2 Kgs.2.9; Pss.51.11; 139.7; 143.10; Isa.11.2; 48.16; 63.10–14; Joel 2.28–29; Zech.4.6; Mt.1.18,20; 3.16; 12.32; 28.19; Mk.1.8,10; 3.29; 13.11; Lk.1.15,35,41,67; 3.22; 4.14–15,18; 11.13; Jn.1.33; 4.24; 14.26; 20.22; Rom.5.5; Eph.1.13; Heb.2.4

Hope: Ezra 10.2; Job 4.6; 5.16; 11.18; 14.19; Pss.71.5,14; 119.116; 146.5; Prov.10.28; 13.12; Eccles.9.4; Hos.2.15; Zech.9.12; Acts 2.26; 23.6; 26.6–7; 28.20; Rom. 4.18; 5.1–5; 8.20–25; 15.4,13; 1 Cor.9.10; 13.7,13; 15.19; 2 Cor.3.12; 10.15; Eph.2.12; Col.1.5,27; Ti.1.2; 2.13; Heb.11.1; 1 Pet.1.3,21

Hor, Mount: Num.20.22; 21.4; 33.37; Deut.32.50

Horeb: Exod.3.1; 17.6; 33.6; Deut.1.2,6,19; 4.10,15; 5.2; 9.8; 18.16; 29.1; 2 Chr.5.10; Ps.106.19; Mal.4.4; *see also* Sinai

Horites: Gen.14.6; 36.2; Deut.2.12,22

Hormah: Num.14.45; 21.3; Deut.1.44; Josh.15.30; 19.4

49

INDEX TO MAPS

W

MAP 9

North & Central Palestine in the Time of Jesus

– – – Political boundaries
JUDEA Political units
● Places mentioned in the New Testament
▲ Cities of the Decapolis
▲ " " mentioned in the New Testament
■ Fortresses

0   5   10 Miles
0   5   10 Kilometres

X

Tyre

35°

35° 30'

Daphne • • Caesarea Philippi (Paneas)

Ladder of Tyre

R. Litani

• Cadasa
Capar Ganaeoi •

TETRARCH'

L. Semechonitis (Lake Huleh)
• Thella

• Ecdippa (Achzib)

PHOENICIA

PROVINCE of SYRIA

• Gischala
• Jamneith

Seleucia •

OF

• Baca
• Meroth
• Sepph

GALILEE

• Bersabe
• Acchabare
Sogane •

GAULANITIS

Ptolemais

• Chorazin

• Saab
Chabulon • Selame
• Sogane

Capernaum (Gennesaret)
• Ginnesar

• Bethsaida-Julias

PHILIP

Jotapata •
• Cana

Arbela •
Taricheae (Magadan. Dalmanutha)

Gergesa ? •
• Gamala

Sycaminum •

Mt. Carmel

• Asochis
• Rumah

Bethmaus •

Dion

Sepphoris •

• Garis

Ammathus
Tiberias

Sea of Galilee

Hippos • Susitha)

3

Bucolon Polis •

Gabae (Hippcum)
• Besara
Simonias •

• Nazareth
Japha •

• Sigoph
Dabaritta (Dabira) •
• Itabyrium (Tabor)

Sennabris •
Beth-yerah (Philoteria)

Yarmuk

Emmatha •

Abila

Gadara

• Gabata

The Great Plain

R. Kishon

• Exaloth

• Nain

D

Wadi

• Capitolias

Dora (Dor)

The Great Plain (Esdraelon)

• Agrippina

E

• Arbela

Crocodilon Polis •

V. of Jezreel

Mt. Gilboa

C

2° 30'

Caesarea

• Narbata

• Ginae

Scythopolis

Pella

32°

A

• Gitta

Salim •
Aenon •

Brook Cherith

P

Plain of Sharon

• Bemesilis

O

• Yishub

SAMARIA

Sebaste (Samaria)

Mt. Ebal •
• Sychar
Tirathana •

(Wadi Farah)

Herod

L

Gerasa

4

pollonia zusa
• Capharsaba

administration

Neapolis
Mt. Gerizim •
• Pharaton

• Mahnayim

• Amathus

R. Jabbok

I

4

Brook of Kanah

• Arus

• Acrabbein

S

Antipatris (Pegai) •
Tower of Aphek •

Tephon •
• Anathu Borcaeus

• Coreae

■ Alexandrium

• Zia

oppa

D

Roman

• Selo (Shiloh)

• Phasaelis

Antipas)

• Gadara

Rathamin (Arimathea?) •

32°

Lydda

• Thamna (Timnath)

Archelais •

U

• Adida
• Modein

• Ilon

• Berzetho
• Gophna
Ephraim (Aphairema) •

Philadelphia (Rabbah)

(under

• Sappho

• Bethel
• Berea   Aialon? •

Michmash •

P

Jericho

• Gazara
Emmaus (Nicopolis) •

Lower Beth-horon •
Upper Beth-horon •

Adasa •
Gabaon • Capharsalama •

Taurus •
• Cyprus

• Betharamphtha (Livias-Julias)

E

R

Cariathiaiem •

Colonia Amasa (Emmaus?) •

Gabath Saul •
• Anathoth
Mt. Scopus •

• Esbus

Belus •

(Kedron)

• Bethphage

(Kh. Qumran: settlement of Dead Sea 'sect')

E

A

• Accaron (Ekron)

Jerusalem
• Bethany

J   U   D   E   A

© Oxford University Press

5

X

35°

35° 30'

Y

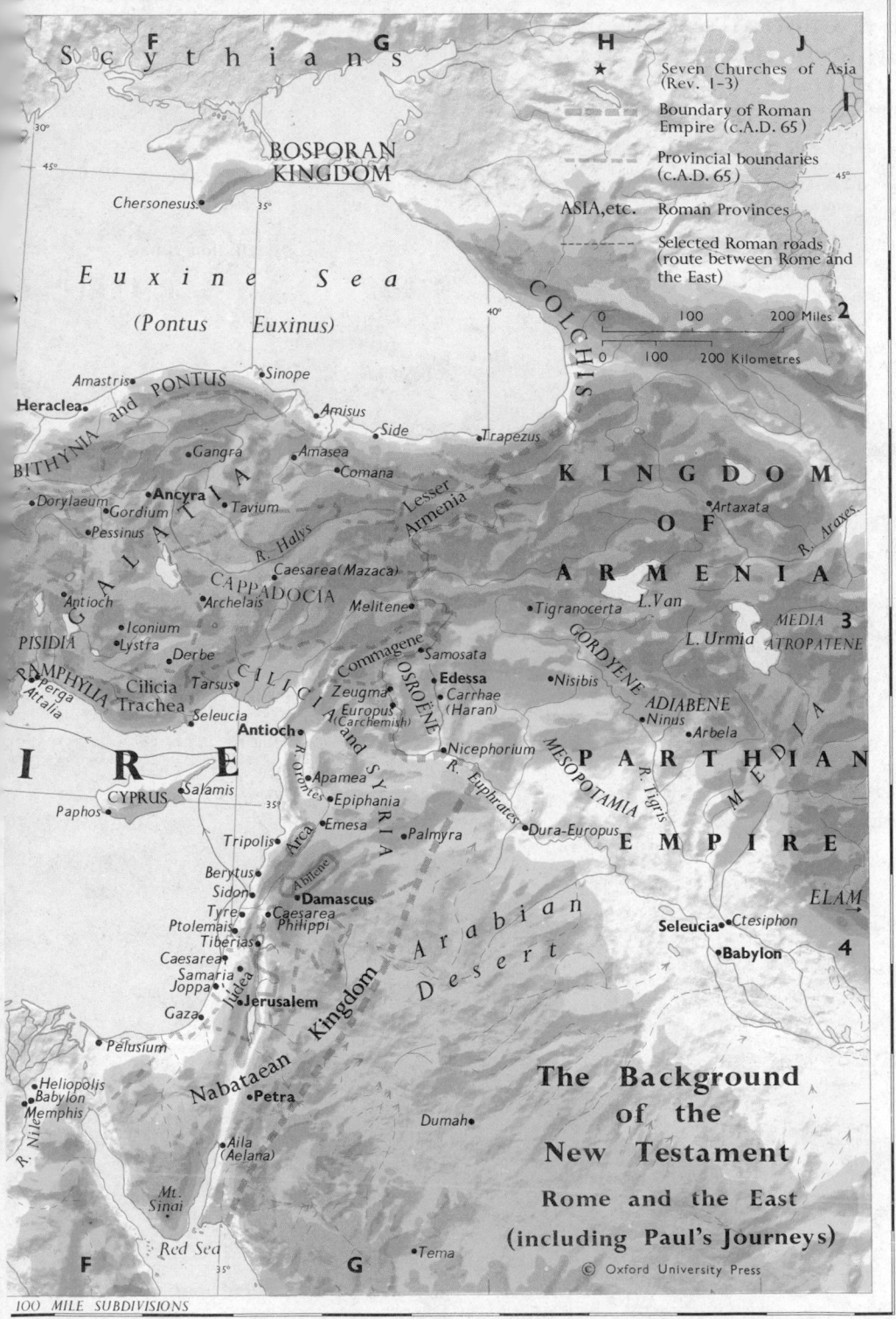

**The Background
of the
New Testament**

Rome and the East

(including Paul's Journeys)

© Oxford University Press

*Seven Churches of Asia
(Rev. 1–3)*

*Boundary of Roman
Empire (c.A.D. 65)*

*Provincial boundaries
(c.A.D. 65)*

ASIA, etc.   *Roman Provinces*

*Selected Roman roads
(route between Rome and
the East)*

0   100   200 Miles

0   100   200 Kilometres

100 MILE SUBDIVISIONS

S c y t h i a n s

BOSPORAN
KINGDOM

Chersonesus

E u x i n e   S e a

(Pontus   Euxinus)

COLCHIS

Amastris   •Sinope

Heraclea•

BITHYNIA and PONTUS

Amisus

Side

Trapezus

Gangra

Amasea

Comana

Dorylaeum

Gordium   •Tavium

Ancyra

Pessinus

G A L A T I A

Lesser
Armenia

K I N G D O M

O F

A R M E N I A

•Artaxata

R. Araxes

R. Halys

Caesarea (Mazaca)

CAPPADOCIA

Archelais

Melitene

Tigranocerta

L. Van

L. Urmia

MEDIA
ATROPATENE

Antioch

Iconium

Lystra   Derbe

PISIDIA

PAMPHYLIA

Perga

Attalia

Cilicia
Trachea

Tarsus

Seleucia

C I L I C I A

Commagene

Samosata

OSROENE

Zeugma

Europus
(Carchemish)

Edessa

Carrhae
(Haran)

GORDYENE

Nisibis

ADIABENE

Ninus

•Arbela

Antioch

R. Orontes

a n d   S Y R I A

Apamea

Epiphania

Nicephorium

R. Euphrates

M E S O P O T A M I A

R. Tigris

P A R T H I A N

M E D I A

CYPRUS

Salamis

Paphos•

I R E

Emesa

Palmyra

Dura-Europus

E M P I R E

Tripolis

Arca

Abilene

Berytus•

Sidon

Tyre•

Ptolemais

Tiberias

Caesarea•

Samaria

Joppa•

Gaza•

Damascus

Caesarea
Philippi

Judaea

Jerusalem

K i n g d o m

A r a b i a n

D e s e r t

ELAM

Seleucia•   Ctesiphon

•Babylon

Pelusium•

Heliopolis

Babylon

Memphis

Aila
(Aelana)

N a b a t a e a n

•Petra

Dumah•

R. Nile

Mt.
Sinai

Red Sea

•Tema

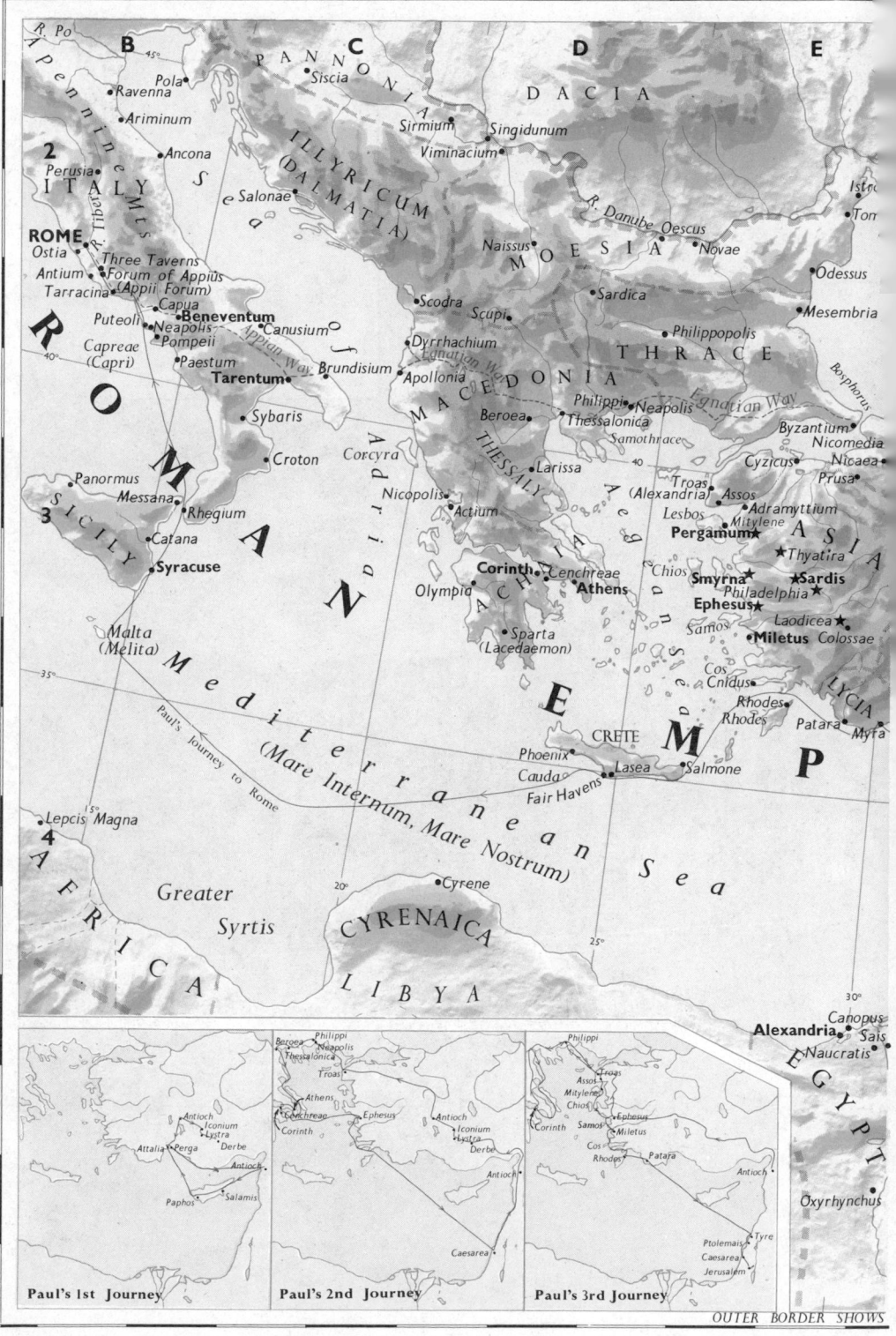

MAP 8

B   C   D   E

R. Po
Apennine Mts   P A N N O N I A   D A C I A
Pola
Ravenna   Siscia
Ariminum   Sirmium   Singidunum
Perusia   Ancona   Viminacium
2   ITALY   ILLYRICUM
(DALMATIA)   Salonae   R. Danube Oescus   Istr
ROME   MOESIA   Novae   Ton
Ostia   Three Taverns   Naissus
Antium   Forum of Appius   Odessus
Tarracina   (Appii Forum)   Scodra   Scupi   Sardica
Capua   Beneventum   Dyrrhachium   Philippopolis   Mesembria
Puteoli   Canusium   Apollonia   THRACE
Neapolis   Egnatian Way
Pompeii   Appian Way   Brundisium   M A C E D O N I A   Byzantium
Capreae   Paestum   Beroea   Philippi Neapolis   Egnatian Way   Nicomedia
(Capri)   TARENTUM   Thessalonica   Samothrace   Cyzicus   Nicaea
R O M A N   Sybaris   T H E S S A L Y   Prusa
40°   Larissa   Troas   Assos
Croton   Nicopolis   (Alexandria)   Adramyttium   A S I A
Panormus   Corcyra   Actium   Lesbos   Mitylene
Messana   Pergamum   Thyatira
SICILY   Rhegium   A C H A I A   Chios   Smyrna   Sardis
Catana   Corinth   Cenchreae   Philadelphia
Syracuse   Olympia   Athens   Ephesus   Laodicea
Samos   Miletus   Colossae
Malta   Sparta   Cos   Cnidus
(Melita)   (Lacedaemon)   Rhodes   LYCIA
M e d i t e r r a n e a n   Rhodes   Patara
35°   Paul's Journey to Rome   Cos   Myra
E M P
Lepcis Magna   CRETE   Salmone
Phoenix   Lasea
4   Cauda   Fair Havens
A F R I C A   (Mare Internum, Mare Nostrum)   S e a
Greater   Cyrene
Syrtis   CYRENAICA
LIBYA   Canopus
Alexandria   Sais
E G Y P T   Naucratis
Oxyrhynchus

Paul's 1st Journey   Paul's 2nd Journey   Paul's 3rd Journey

OUTER BORDER SHOWS

MAP 7

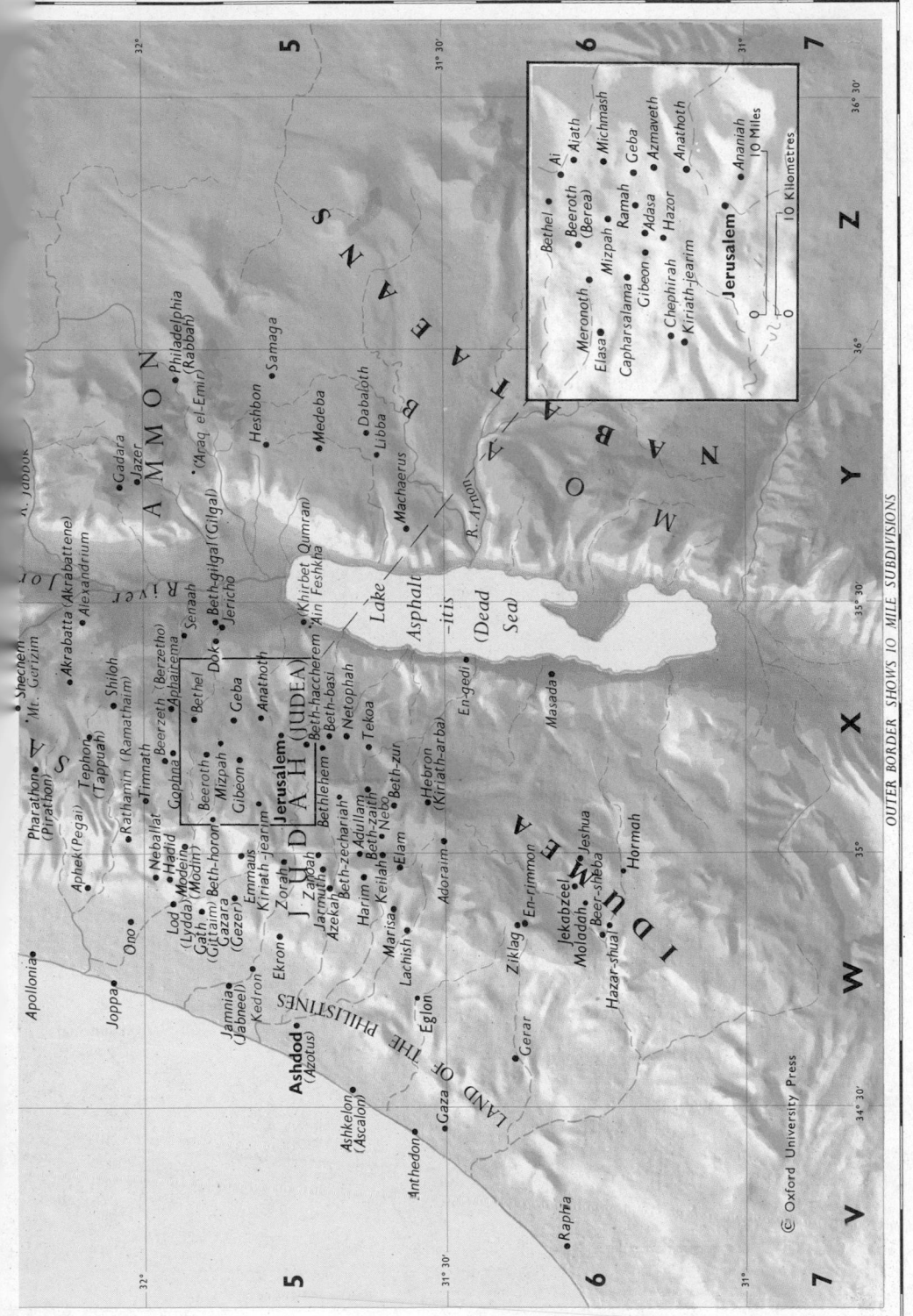

OUTER BORDER SHOWS 10 MILE SUBDIVISIONS

© Oxford University Press

MAP 7

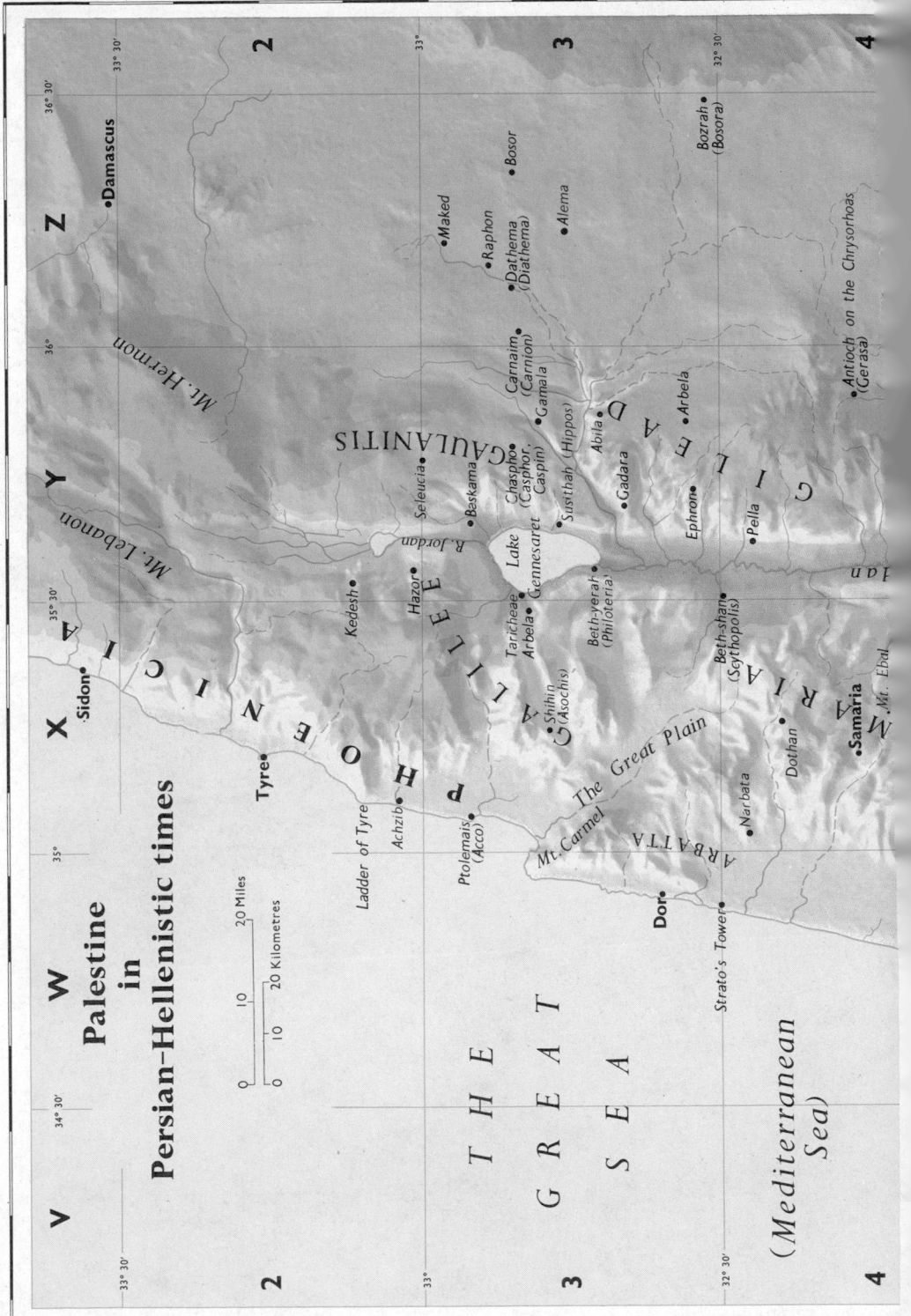

Palestine
in
Persian–Hellenistic times

20 Miles

20 Kilometres

MAP 6

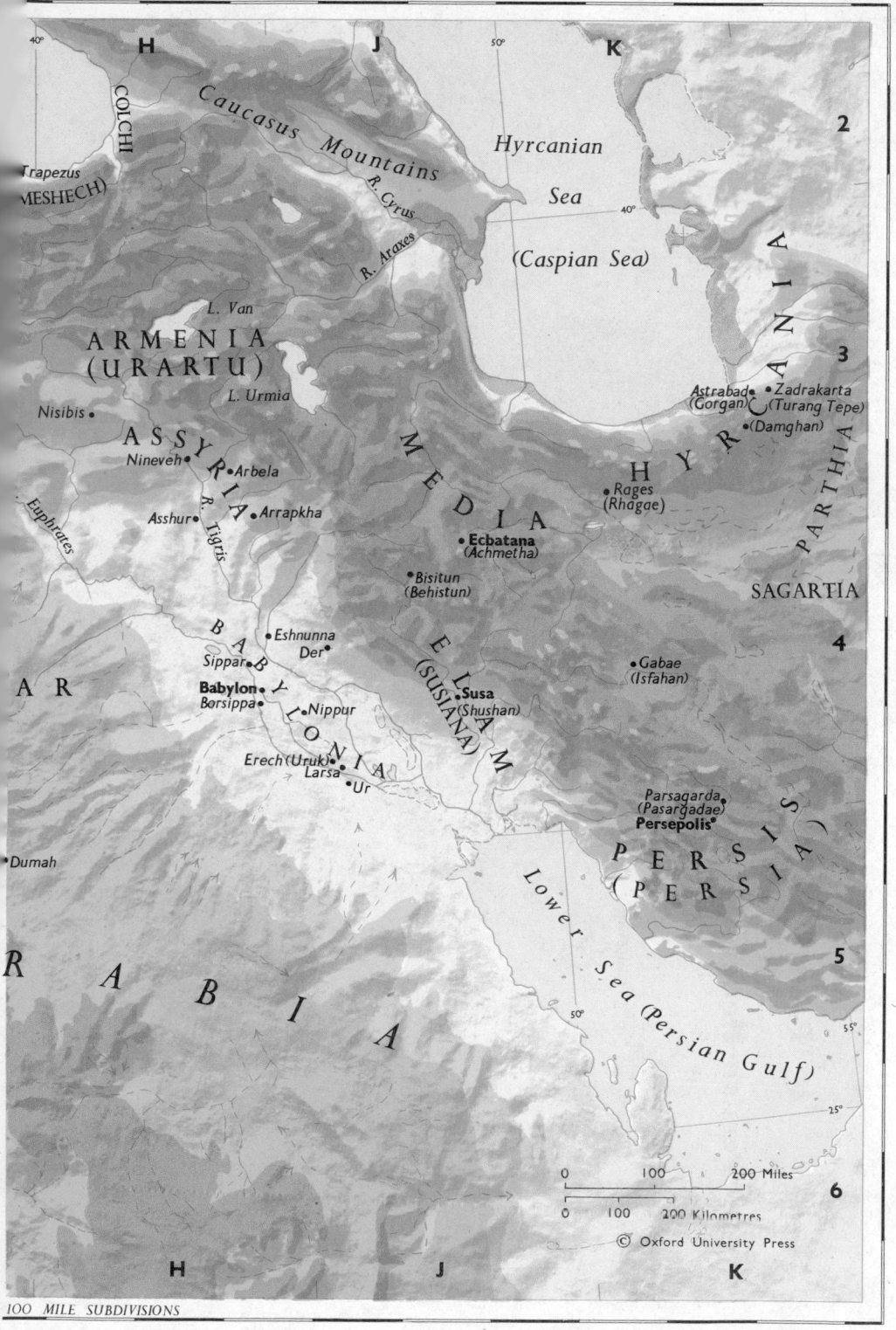

H   J   50°   K

40°

COLCHI

Trapezus
(MESHECH)

Caucasus Mountains

R. Cyrus

R. Araxes

Hyrcanian
Sea

(Caspian Sea)

40°

2

HYRCANIA

PARTHIA

L. Van

ARMENIA
(URARTU)

L. Urmia

Nisibis

ASSYRIA

Nineveh   Arbela

Asshur   Arrapkha

MEDIA

Astrabad   Zadrakarta
(Gorgan)   (Turang Tepe)

Damghan

Rages
(Rhagae)

Ecbatana
(Achmetha)

3

SAGARTIA

Euphrates

R. Tigris

Bisitun
(Behistun)

4

BABYLONIA

Eshnunna
Der

Sippar

AR

Babylon

Borsippa   Nippur

Erech (Uruk)
Larsa
Ur

Dumah

ELAM
(SUSIANA)

Susa
(Shushan)

Gabae
(Isfahan)

Parsagarda
(Pasargadae)
Persepolis

PERSIS
(PERSIA)

5

RABIA

Lower Sea (Persian Gulf)

50°

55°

25°

6

0   100   200 Miles

0   100   200 Kilometres

© Oxford University Press

H   J   K

100 MILE SUBDIVISIONS

MAP 6

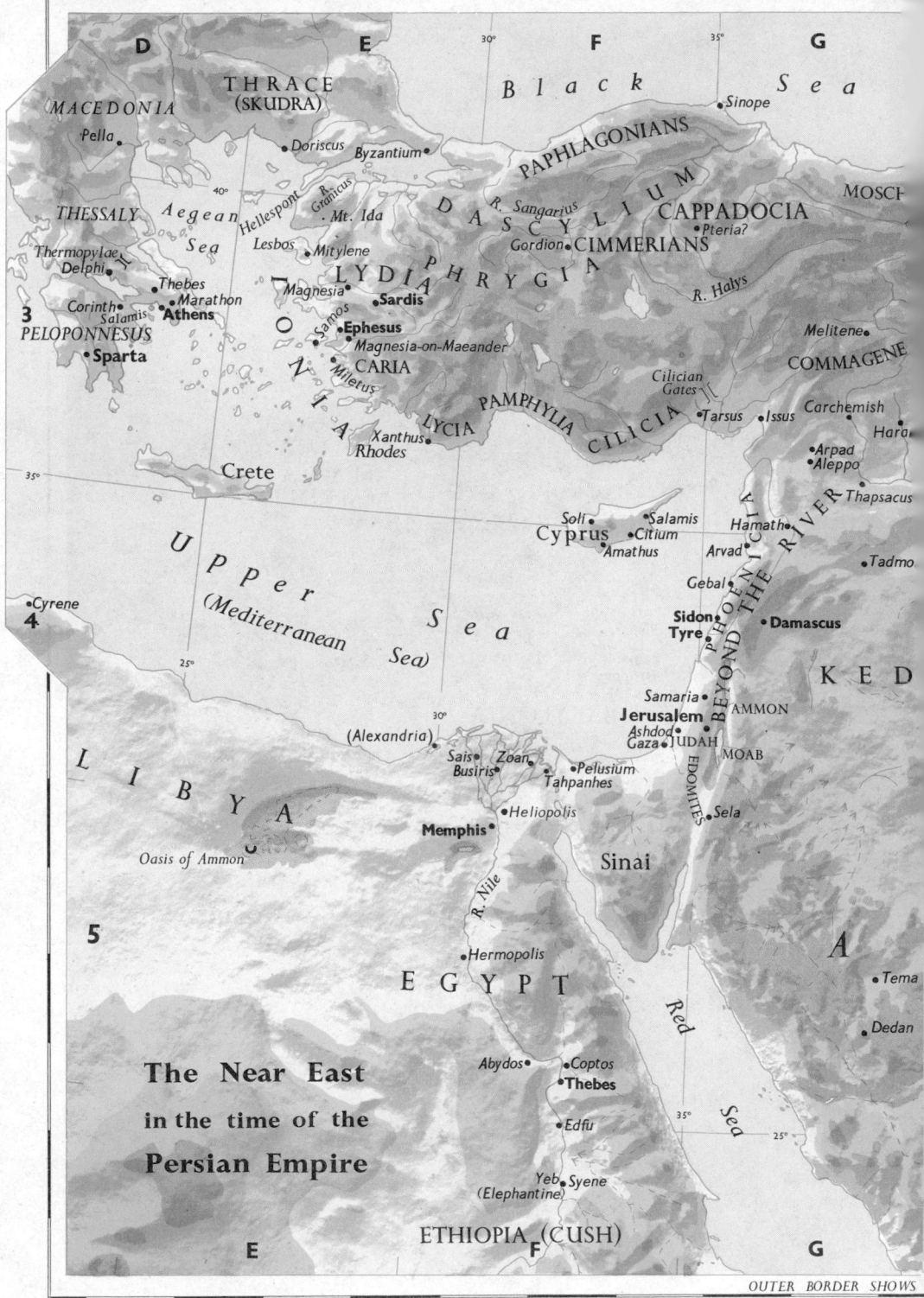

The Near East

in the time of the

Persian Empire

MACEDONIA
Pella

THRACE
(SKUDRA)

Doriscus

Byzantium

Black   Sea

Sinope

PAPHLAGONIANS

THESSALY

Aegean
Sea

Hellespont

R. Granicus

Mt. Ida

Lesbos

Mitylene

DASCYLIUM

CAPPADOCIA

MOSCH

R. Sangarius

Gordion

CIMMERIANS

Pteria?

R. Halys

MELITENE
Melitene

COMMAGENE

Thermopylae
Delphi

Thebes
Corinth   Marathon
Salamis
Athens

Magnesia

LYDIA

Sardis

PHRYGIA

3

PELOPONNESUS

Sparta

Samos

Ephesus

Magnesia-on-Maeander

CARIA

Miletus

IONIA

Xanthus
Rhodes

LYCIA

PAMPHYLIA

CILICIA

Cilician
Gates

Tarsus

Issus

Carchemish

Hara

Arpad
Aleppo

Thapsacus

Crete

Soli

Cyprus

Salamis
Citium

Amathus

Hamath

Arvad

Gebal

BEYOND THE RIVER

Tadmo

35°

U   p   p   e   r

Sea

(Mediterranean

Sea)

Sidon
Tyre

PHOENICIA

Damascus

KED

Cyrene

25°

4

LIBYA

(Alexandria)

Sais   Zoan
Busiris

Pelusium

Tahpanhes

Heliopolis

Samaria

Jerusalem
Ashdod
Gaza   JUDAH

AMMON

MOAB

EDOMITES

Sela

A

Memphis

Oasis of Ammon

Sinai

5

Hermopolis

E   G   Y   P   T

R. Nile

Red

Sea

Tema

Dedan

Abydos

Coptos
Thebes

Edfu

Yeb
(Elephantine)   Syene

ETHIOPIA (CUSH)

MAP 5

The Near East

in the time of the

Assyrian Empire

Approximate extent of Assyrian domination
in the latter part of the 8th. century.

(Later, under Esarhaddon (681-669), Assyria conquered Egypt.)

0   100   200 Miles

0   100   200 Kilometres

© Oxford University Press

100 MILE SUBDIVISIONS

MAP 5

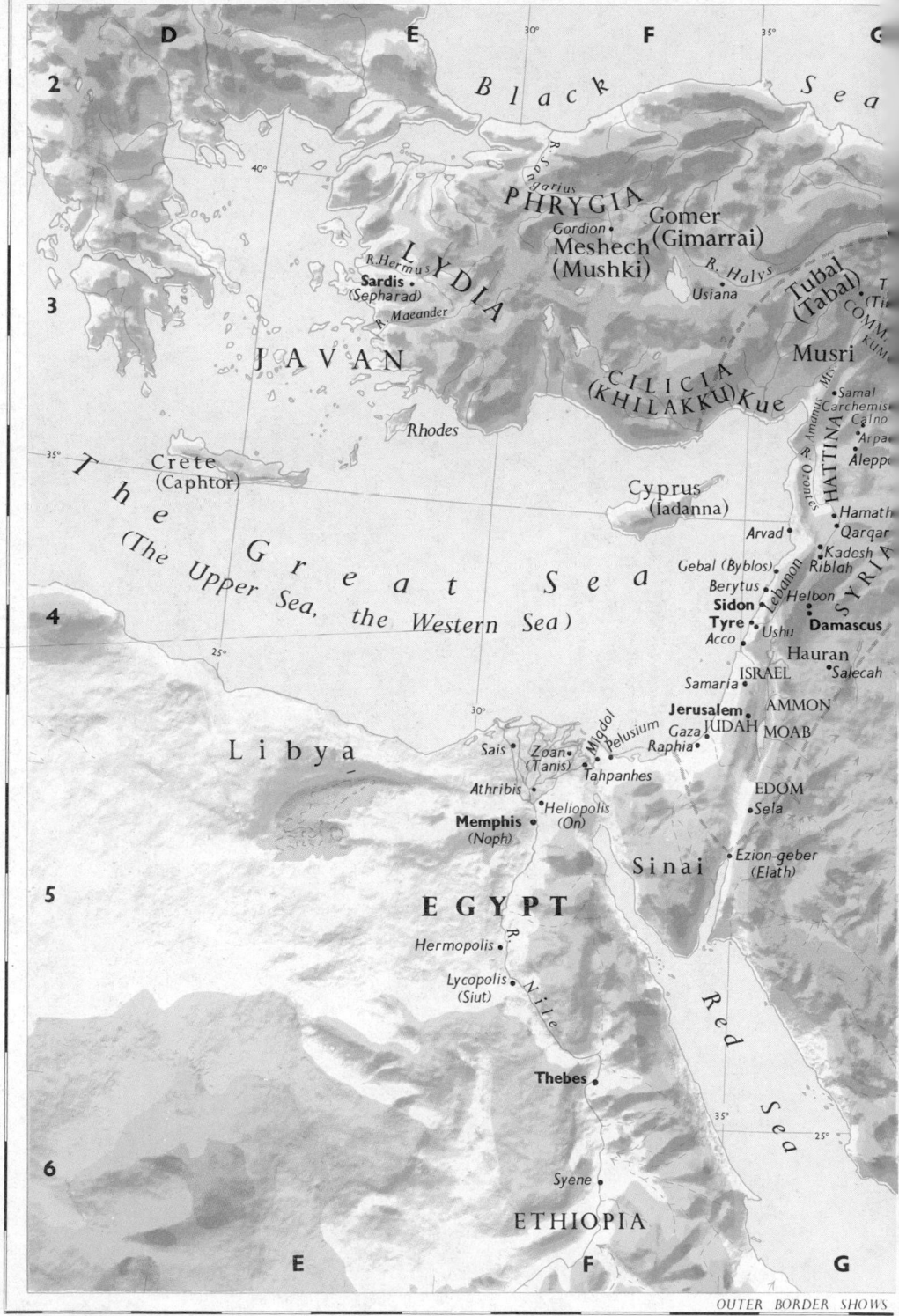

D   E   30°   F   35°   G

B l a c k   *S e a*

2

40°

R. Sangarius

PHRYGIA

Gordion •

Gomer
(Gimarrai)

Meshech
(Mushki)

R. Hermus

3

Sardis •
(Sepharad)

R. Maeander

LYDIA

R. Halys

Usiana •

Tubal
(Tabal)

T

COMM
KUM

Musri

J A V A N

CILICIA
(KHILAKKU) Kue

Samal •
Carchemis
Calno •
Arpa

HATTINA

Rhodes •

35°

T h e

Crete
(Caphtor)

Cyprus
(Iadanna)

Aleppo

Hamath

Arvad •

Qarqar

R. Orontes

SYRIA

(T h e   *G r e a t*   *S e a*

Kadesh

Gebal (Byblos) •

Riblah

25°

U p p e r   *S e a,*   *t h e*   *W e s t e r n*   *S e a)*

Berytus •

Helbon •

Lebanon

Sidon •

4

Tyre •

Ushu •

Damascus

Acco •

Hauran

Samaria •

ISRAEL

Salecah •

25°

Libya

30°

Jerusalem •

AMMON

Sais •

Zoan
(Tanis)

Pelusium

Gaza •

JUDAH **MOAB**

Raphia •

Migdol

Athribis •

Tahpanhes •

EDOM

Sela •

Heliopolis
(On)

Memphis •
(Noph)

Sinai

Ezion-geber
(Elath)

5

E G Y P T

Hermopolis •

R. Nile

Lycopolis
(Siut)

Red

6

Thebes •

35°

Sea

25°

Syene •

ETHIOPIA

E   F   G

MAP 4

5

6

7

32°

31° 30'

31°

36° 30'

36°

35° 30'

35°

© Oxford University Press

OUTER BORDER SHOWS 10 MILE SUBDIVISIONS

M
M
A
•Mahanaim
Penuel• •Succoth
River
The Jabbok
Jabbok
Shechem
Mt. Gerizim
Pirathon•
Baal-shalishah•
Tappuah•
•Shiloh
Jeshanah•
Baal-hazor•

Rabbah
(Rabbath-ammon)
G
•Jazer
Heshbon•
•Nebo
Medeba•
Baal-peor•
R. Nimrim
Gilgal•
Jericho•

Bezer (Bozrah?)
•Beth-meon (Baal-meon)
•Beth-diblathaim
Jahaz•
B
O
Nebo•
Ataroth•
Kiriathaim•
Dibon•
Aroer•
R. Arnon
A
M
O
Kir-hareseth
W
Brook Zered
E D O M
Y
Z

City of Salt
Jericho•
Jeshanah•
Ephron•
Ai•
•Upper
Beth-horon
Lower Beth-horon
Bethel• Mizpah•
Ramah•
Geba•
Gibeah •Anathoth
Jerusalem
Zemaraim•

Waters of
Nimrim
Zoar•

Salt Sea
(Sea of the Arabah)

Tekoa•
Etam•
Beth-zur•
•Ziph
•Carmel
Great Arad
Zair•
Hebron•
Ascent of Ziz
En-gedi•

J U D A H
Wilderness
of
Judah
Br. Kidron
Secacah•
Nibshan•
Middin•
V. of Achor
Netophah•
Giloh•
Bethlehem•
Beth-zur•

Joppa•
Gath-rimmon•
Plain
Gimzo•
Gezer•
Shaalbim•
Gibbethon•
Shikkeron•
Makaz•
Ekron•
Timnah•
Beth-shemesh
Zorah•
Kirjath-jearim
Soco•
Adullam•
Azekah•
Socoh•
Mareshah•
Lachish•
Gath (Gittaim)•
Jabneel (Jabneh)•
Mount Baalah•
Baalath•
Ashdod•
Libnah•
V. of Zephathah
A

P H I L I S T I A
Ashkelon•
Gaza•
Gath?•
Gerar•
Sharuhen•
Raphia•
Brook Besor

The Shephelah (Lowland)
Adoraim•
Debir•
Ziklag•
Kabzeel?•
Beer-sheba•
Gurbaal•
Valley of Salt
Arad of Beth-yeroham?

The Negeb
A M A L E K

X
Tamar
(30° 48'N)

MAP 4

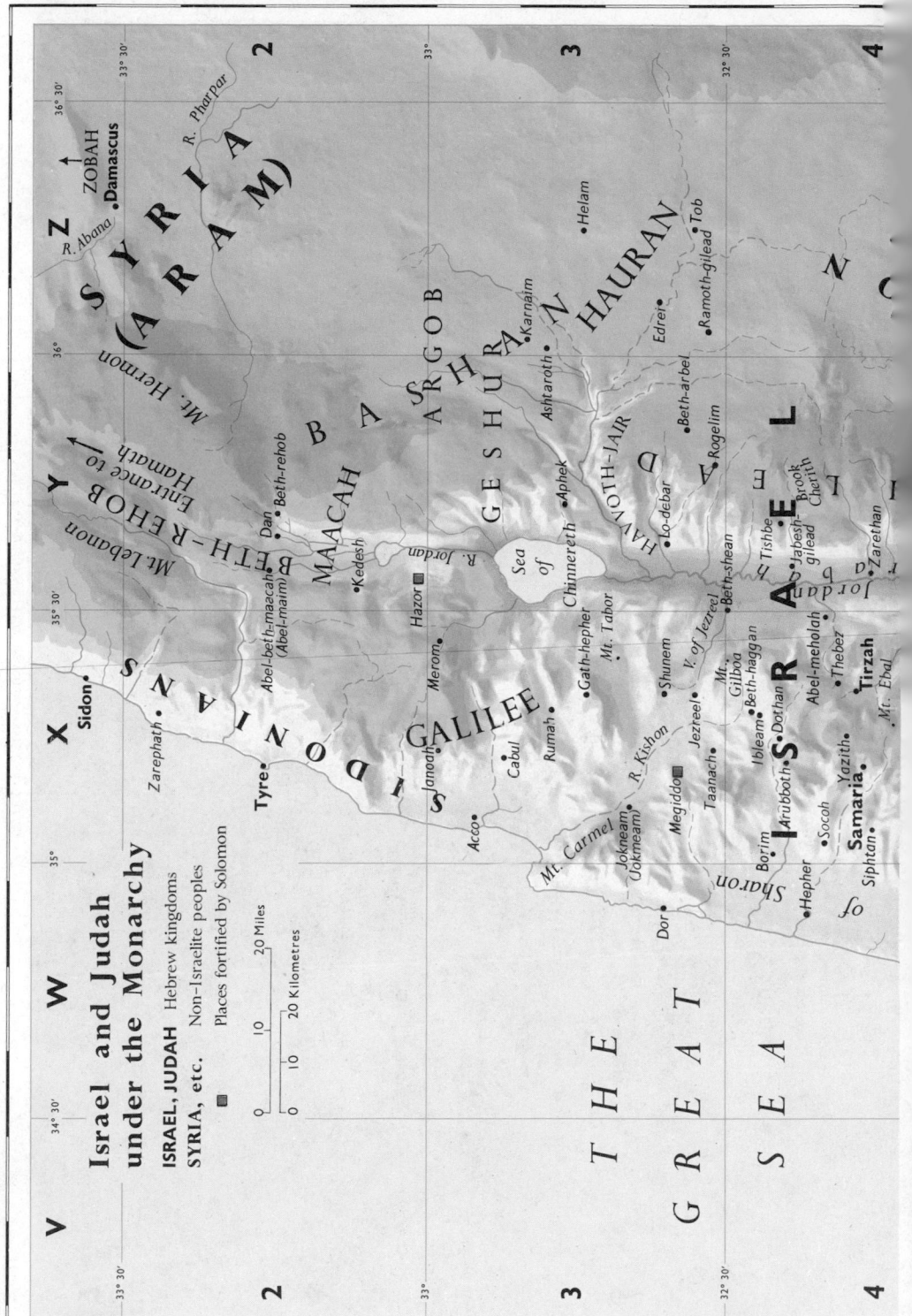

Israel and Judah under the Monarchy

ISRAEL, JUDAH Hebrew kingdoms
SYRIA, etc. Non-Israelite peoples
▣ Places fortified by Solomon

20 Miles
10   20 Kilometres
0   10
0

SYRIA (ARAM)
ZOBAH
•Damascus
R. Abana
R. PharPar
Mt. Hermon
Mt. Lebanon
Entrance to Hamath
BETH-REHOB
Y
Z
X
Sidon•
Zarephath•
Tyre•
SIDONIANS
Acco•
Dor•
THE GREAT SEA
Mt. Carmel
R. Kishon
GALILEE
Cabul
Janoah•
Rumah•
Merom•
Abel-beth-maacah
(Abel-maim)
•Kedesh
MAACAH
Dan•
•Beth-rehob
Hazor ▣
R. Jordan
Sea of Chinnereth
Gath-hepher•
Mt. Tabor
Shunem•
V. of Jezreel
Jezreel•
Jokneam•
Jokmeam•
Taanach•
Megiddo ▣
Ibleam•
Dothan•
Mt. Gilboa
Beth-haggan•
Arubboth•
Borim•
Hepher•
Sharon
Socoh•
Siphtan•
Yazith•
Samaria ▣
Tirzah
Mt. Ebal
Thebez•
Abel-meholah•
Beth-shean•
Tishbe•
Jabesh-gilead•
Zarethan•
Jordan
Brook Cherith
Rogelim•
•Beth-arbel
Lo-debar•
•Aphek
GESHUR
HAVOTH-JAIR
BASHAN
ARGOB
Ashtaroth•
Karnaim•
Edrei•
HAURAN
•Helam
•Tob
Ramoth-gilead•
ISRAEL
GILEAD
AMMON

33° 30' 34° 30' 35° 35° 30' 36° 36° 30' 33° 30' 33°

V W X Y Z
2 3 4
2 3 4
33° 32° 30'

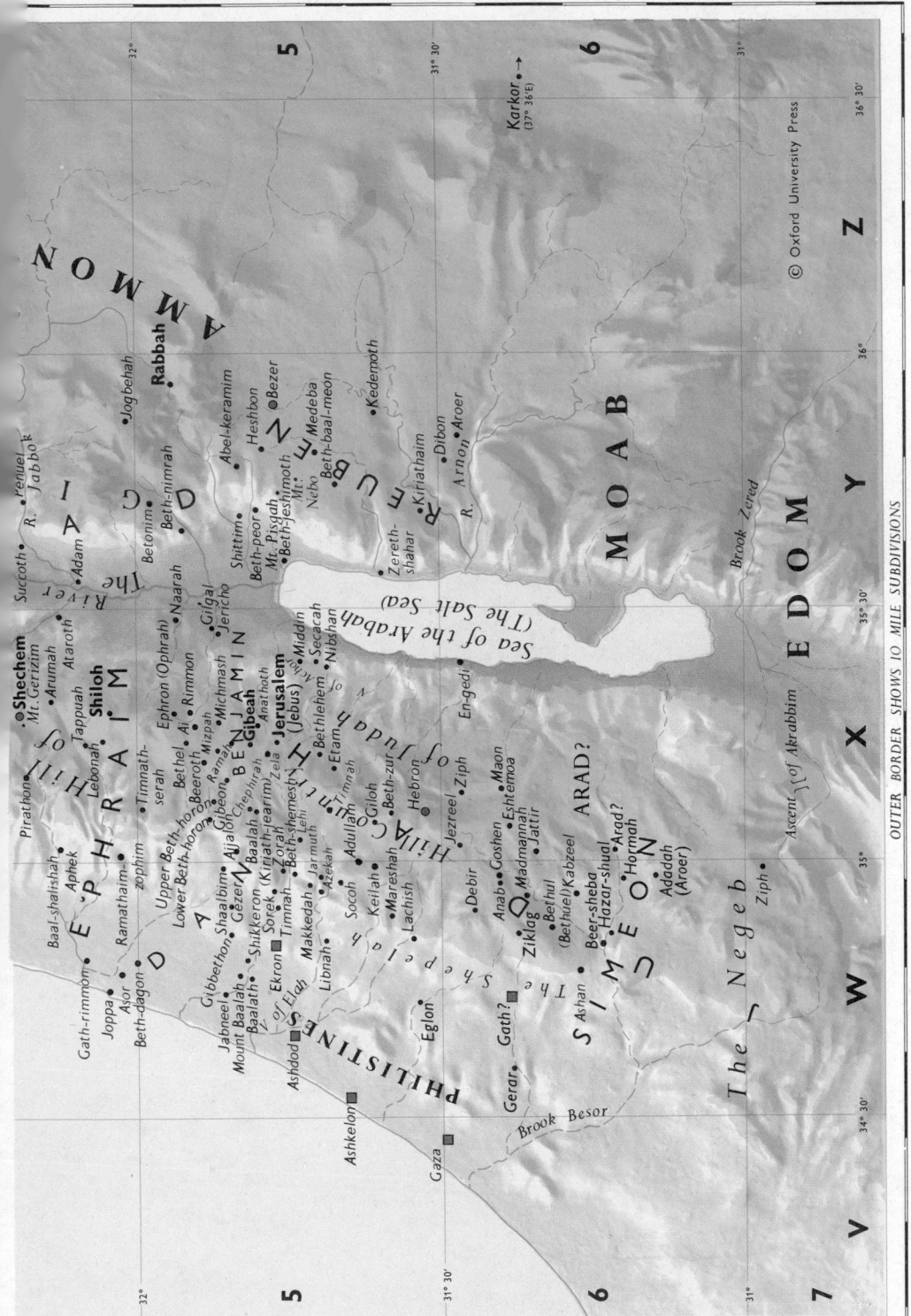

MAP 3

MAP 3

Karkor
(37° 36'E)

5

6

Z

© Oxford University Press

AMMON

Rabbah

Jogbehah

Penuel

R. Jabbok

Succoth

Adam

The River

GILEAD

REUBEN

MOAB

Betonim

Beth-nimrah

Abel-keramim

Heshbon

Bezer

Medeba

Beth-baal-meon

Kedemoth

Naarah

Shittim

Beth-peor

Mt. Pisgah
Nebo
Beth-jeshimoth

Kiriathaim

Dibon

Arnon

Aroer

R.

Zereth-shahar

Gilgal

Jericho

Mt: Mt.

Middin

Secacah

Nibshan

Brook Zered

EDOM

Y

Sea of the Arabah
(The Salt Sea)

Shechem
Mt. Gerizim

Arumah

Ataroth

Tappuah

Shiloh

Lebonah

Timnath-serah

Ephron (Ophrah)

Rimmon

Ai

Bethel

Beeroth

Mizpah

Ramah

Michmash

Anathoth

EPHRAIM

BENJAMIN

Gibeah

Jerusalem

(Jebus)

Bethlehem

Etam

Beth-zur

Engedi

Pirathon

Baal-shalishah

Aphek

Asor

Ramathaim

Zophim

Beth-dagon

Hill Country of Ephraim

Upper Beth-horon

Lower Beth-horon

Gibeon

Chephirah

Kiriath-jearim

Zela

Lehi

DAN

Shaalbim

Gezer

Baalah

Beth-shemesh

Trimnah

Gath-rimmon

Joppa

Jabneel

Baalath

Mount Baalah

Shikkeron

Gibbethon

Sorek

Zorah

Jarmuth

Azekah

Hill Country of Judah

Jezreel

Ziph

Hebron

Ashdod

V. of Ekron

Timnah

Libnah

Makkedah

Socoh

Keilah

Adullam

Mareshah

Lachish

Debir

Anab

Goshen

Eshtemoa

Maon

Jattir

ARAD?

PHILISTINE

Ashkelon

Gaza

Gerar

Gath?

Eglon

The Shephelah

Ziklag

Madmannah

(Bethul) Kabzeel

Bethul

Beer-sheba

Hazar-shual

Hormah

Arad?

Adadah
(Aroer)

SIMEON

Ashan

The Negeb

Ziph

Ascent of Akrabbim

X

W

V

Brook Besor

5

6

7

MAP 3

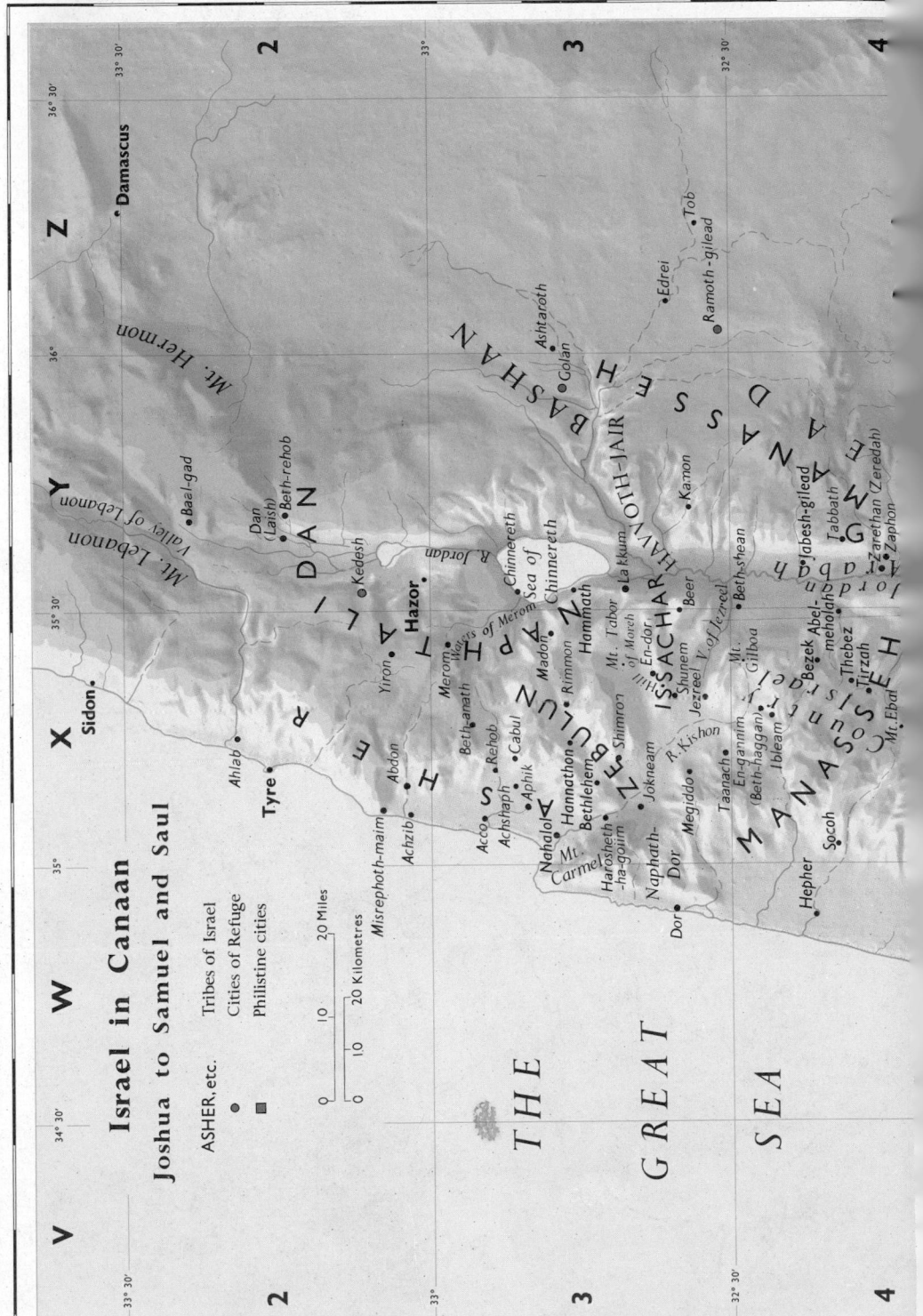

Israel in Canaan
Joshua to Samuel and Saul

ASHER, etc.   Tribes of Israel
●   Cities of Refuge
■   Philistine cities

20 Miles
20 Kilometres

THE
GREAT
SEA

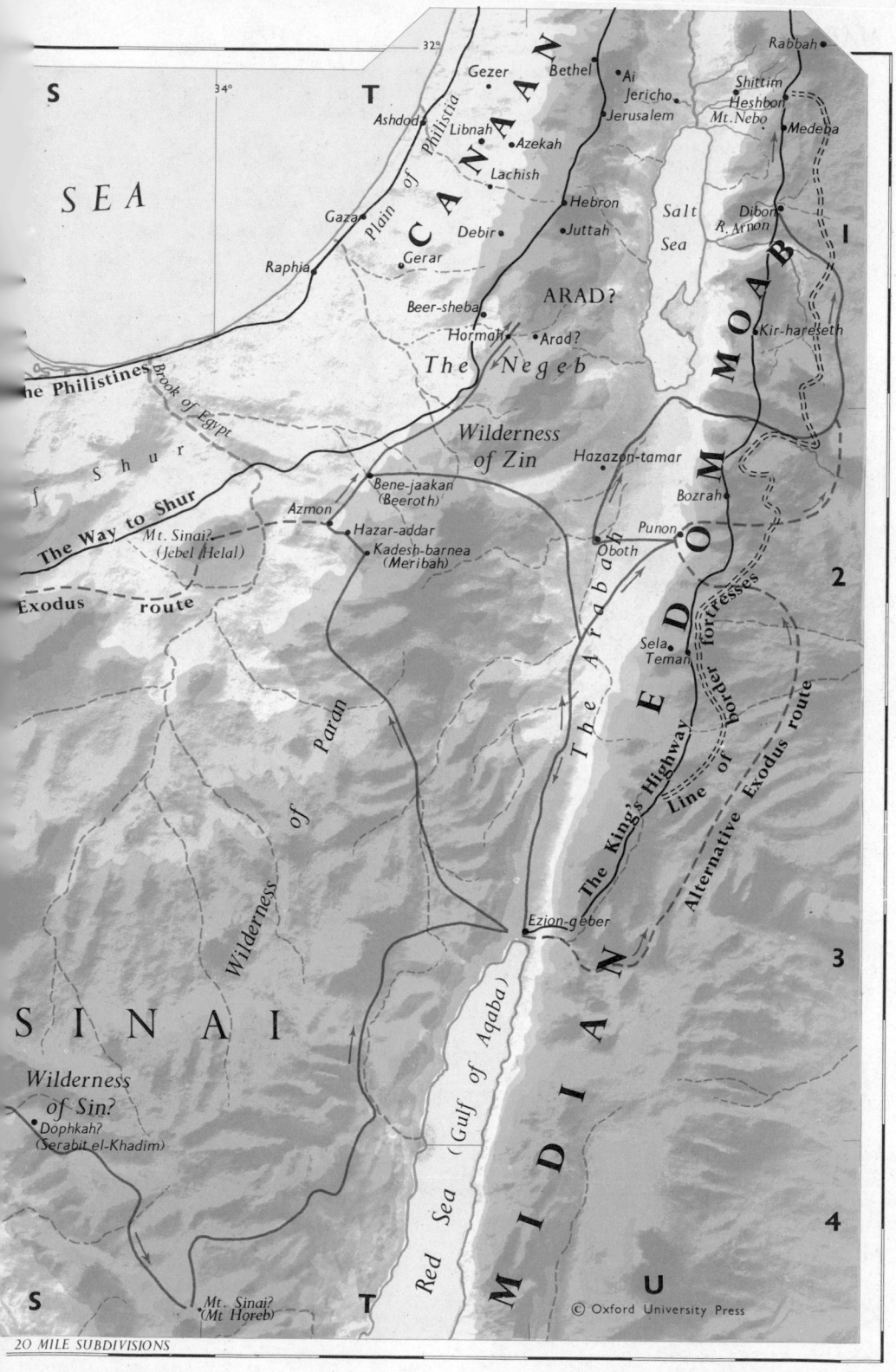

S   32°
                34°
                                    T   Rabbah
    S   Gezer   Bethel   Ai   Shittim
                                                    Jericho   Heshbon
                            Ashdod   Libnah   Jerusalem   Mt.Nebo   Medeba
    SEA   Plain of Philistia   Azekah
                                    Lachish
                                                                Dibon
                            Gaza   Hebron   Salt   R. Arnon
                                    Debir   Juttah   Sea
                Raphia   Gerar   Kir-hareseth
                                C A N A A N   M O A B
                                    Beer-sheba   ARAD?
                                    Hormah   Arad?
    The Philistines Brook of Egypt   The   Negeb
                        Shur   E
                                        Wilderness
                            Azmon   of Zin   Hazazon-tamar   D
                        Bene-jaakan   Bozrah   O
    The Way to Shur Mt. Sinai? (Beeroth)   Punon   M   2
                (Jebel Helal) Hazar-addar   Oboth
    Exodus   route   Kadesh-barnea
                            (Meribah)   Sela
                                                Teman
                                        Wilderness
                                        of
                                        Paran
                                                The Arabah

    S I N A I

    Wilderness
    of Sin?
    Dophkah?
    (Serabit el-Khadim)   Ezion-geber   3

                                    M I D I A N

                        S   Red Sea (Gulf of Aqaba)   T   U   4

                            Mt. Sinai?   © Oxford University Press
                            (Mt Horeb)

20 MILE SUBDIVISIONS

MAP 2

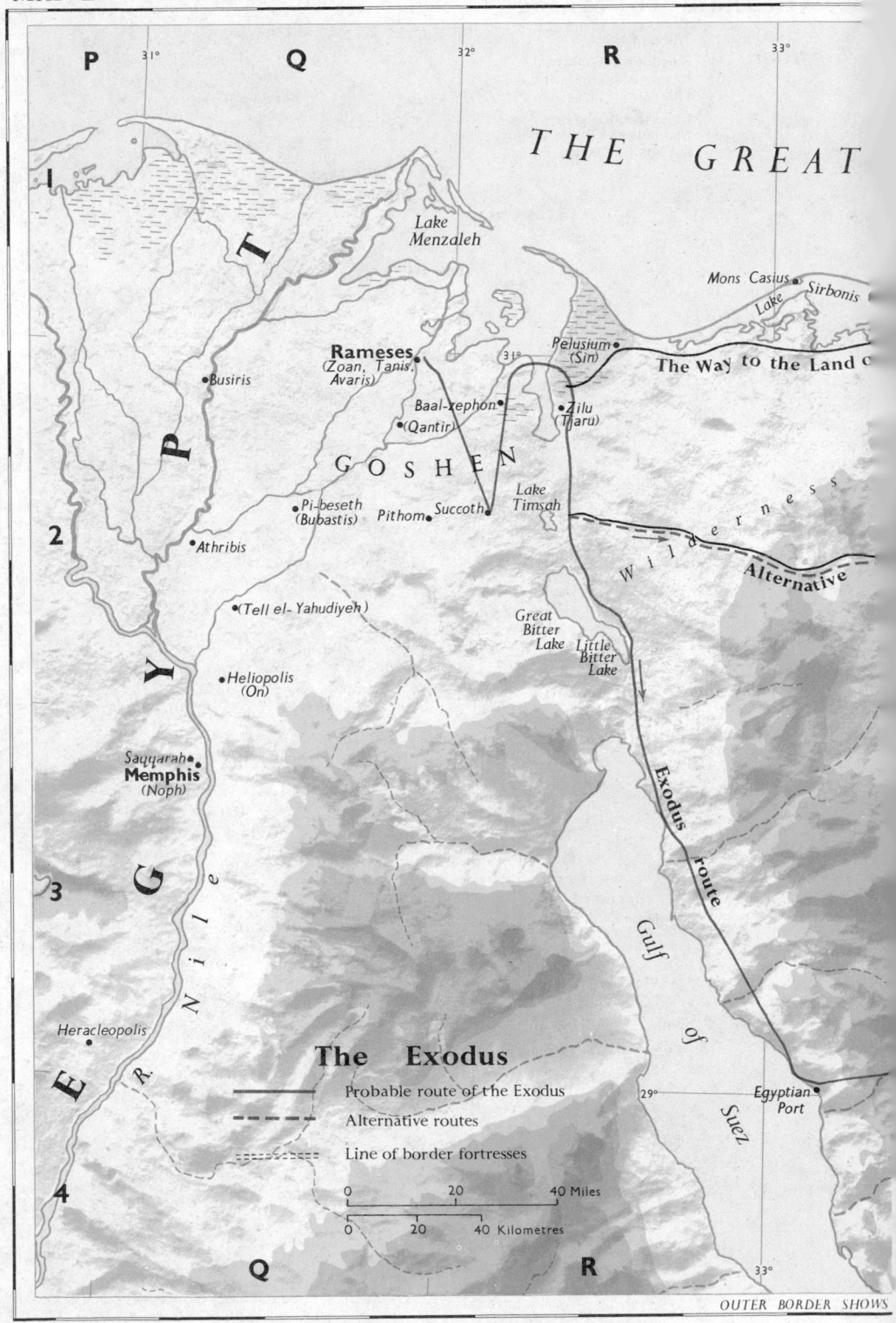

P   31°   Q   32°   R   33°

I

THE GREAT

P

T

Lake
Menzaleh

Mons Casius
Lake Sirbonis

Pelusium
(Sin)

Rameses
(Zoan, Tanis,
Avaris)

The Way to the Land of

Busiris

31°

Zilu
(Tjaru)

Baal-zephon
(Qantir)

G O S H E N

2

Pi-beseth
(Bubastis)

Pithom

Succoth

Lake
Timsah

Wilderness

Alternative

Athribis

(Tell el-Yahudiyeh)

Great
Bitter
Lake

Little
Bitter
Lake

Heliopolis
(On)

Y

Saqqarah
Memphis
(Noph)

G

R. Nile

3

Exodus route

Gulf

of

Heracleopolis

The Exodus

——————— Probable route of the Exodus

– – – – – Alternative routes

▪▪▪▪▪▪ Line of border fortresses

E

Suez

29°

Egyptian
Port

0   20   40 Miles

0   20   40 Kilometres

Q   R   33°

4

The Land of Canaan
Abraham to Moses

MAP 1

GAD, etc. Tribes of Israel

EDOM, etc Kingdoms encountered by the Israelites in the 13th century, B.C.

• Cities mentioned in Numbers and Deuteronomy, but not in Genesis.

0 — 10 — 20 Miles
0 — 10 — 20 Kilometres

THE GREAT SEA

(The Western Sea)

Sidon
Damascus
Mt. Hermon (Sirion, Senir)
Tyre
Uzu
Ijon
Abel
Laish (Dan)
MAACAH
Kanah
Kedesh
Achzib
Janoah
Hazor
Merom
Aduru
GESHUR
ARGOB
Acco
Beth-anath
BASHAN
Achshaph
Chinnereth
Sea of Chinnereth
Karnaim
Hannathon
Madon
Golan
Ashtaroth
Mt. Carmel
Shimron
Beth-yerah (Philoteria)
Yanoam
HAVVOTH-JAIR
Jokneam
Japhia
Edrei
Dor
Anaharath
Shunem
Ramoth-gilead
Megiddo
Aruna
Taanach
Beth-shean
Ham
Beth-haggan (En-gannim)
Rehob
Pehel (Pella)
Plain of Sharon
Migdal
Ibleam
Dothan
Gath of Sharon
Arubboth
Yehem
Socoh
Tirzah
GILEAD
MANASSEH
Mt. Ebal
Shechem
Succoth
Mahanaim
Mt. Gerizim
Jabbok
Penuel
Aphek
R. Jabbok
Joppa
Ono
Jazer
Jogbehah
AMMON
Beth-dagon
Lod
Rabbah
Bethel (Luz)
Ai
Beth-nimrah
Gezer
Jericho
Gilgal
Plains of Abel-shittim (Shittim)
Beth-horon
Aijalon
Moab
Ekron
Gibeon
Elealeh
Beth-shemesh
Jerusalem (Salem?)
Mt. Pisgah
Heshbon
Bezer
Ashdod
Timnah
Bethlehem (Ephrath)
Beth-jeshimoth
Mt. Nebo
Medeba
Socoh
Chezib
Adullam
Baal-meon (Beon)
Ashkelon
Keilah
REUBEN
Kedemoth
Eglon
Lachish
Mamre
Mattanah
Gaza
Beth-tappuah
Hebron (Kiriath-arba)
R. Nahaliel
Kiriathaim
Beth-eglaim (Eglaim)
Debir
Ataroth
Dibon
Yurza
Gath?
Aroer
Gerar
City of Moab
Sharuhen
R. Arnon
Moladah
ARAD?
Ar
Beer-sheba
Hormah
Arad?
MOAB
Aroer
Rehoboth
Ziph
THE Negeb
Zoar
Brook Zered
Ascent of Akrabbim
Hazazon-tamar (30° 48'N)
EDOM

THE Shephelah
Hill Country of Judah
Hill Country of Israel
Salt Sea (Sea of the Arabah)
River Jordan
The Arabah

Possible location of Valley of Siddim, and the cities of Sodom, Gomorrah, Admah, Zeboiim, now covered by shallow waters.

NOBM 13
Maps printed in Great Britain
© Oxford University Press